Forensic and Legal Medicine

Clinical and Pathological Aspects

A comprehensive and accessible resource covering all aspects of forensic and legal medicine. The text provides a foundation for those working in both the clinical and forensic aspects of care and will also be an asset to those involved in the police or judicial systems. Including clear guidelines with practical applications, and further enhanced by its many illustrations and case examples, this text is a valuable resource in an increasingly complex field. The authoritative work is written by those who have extensive experience for a wide audience including, but not limited to, forensic pathologists, general pathologists, pediatric pathologists, forensic physicians, forensic scientists, coroners, emergency department physicians, judges and legal practitioners.

Forensic and Legal Medicine

Clinical and Pathological Aspects

Editors

Jason Payne-James
LLM MSc FFFLM FRCS FRCP FCSFS
FFCFM(RCPA) RCPathME DFM
LBIPP Dip MOD
Specialist in Forensic & Legal Medicine & Consultant Forensic Physician
Lead Medical Examiner, Norfolk & Norwich University Hospital, Norwich, United Kingdom
Honorary Clinical Professor
William Harvey Research Institute, Queen Mary University of London, United Kingdom
Chair, UK Scientific Advisory Committee on the Medical Implications of Less-Lethal Weapons
Executive Board Member – European Council of Legal Medicine

Roger Byard
AO PSM DSc FAHMS (BMedSci MBBS MMedSci-Paed PhD
MD FCAP FRCPC FRCPath FRCPA FFFLM FFSc FRSN FFPMI
Emeritus Professor of Pathology at The University of Adelaide
Senior Specialist Forensic Pathologist
Forensic Science SA in Adelaide
Australia

CRC Press
Taylor & Francis Group
Boca Raton London New York

CRC Press is an imprint of the
Taylor & Francis Group, an **informa** business

Cover Image Shutterstock ID 583943026

First edition published 2024
by CRC Press
2385 NW Executive Center Drive, Suite 320, Boca Raton, FL 33431

and by CRC Press
4 Park Square, Milton Park, Abingdon, Oxon, OX14 4RN

CRC Press is an imprint of Taylor & Francis Group, LLC

Library of Congress Cataloging in Publication Data
Names: Payne-James, Jason, editor. | Byard, Roger W, editor.
Title: Forensic and legal medicine : clinical and pathological aspects / edited by Jason Payne-James and Roger Byard.
Description: First edition. | Boca Raton : CRC Press, 2023. | Includes bibliographical references and index. | Summary: "This edited, multi-authored text provides state-of-the-art information about the forensic and legal aspects of medicine. Chapters ranging from Human Rights Law to Forensic Odontology make this book a valuable source for those working in or alongside any aspect of forensic medicine. With the input of a wide range of acknowledged specialists, this text showcases expertise in a contemporary context to broaden the scope of information and understanding and offer a more complete overview of the fields of clinical, pathological and legal forensic medicine. This amalgamation of knowledge results in a comprehensive book that will prove to be an asset to those working in both the clinical and pathological forensic elements of care, assessment investigation and diagnosis of victims. It will also provide a foundation for those involved in police or judicial systems. This book includes clear guidelines for practical applications, further enhanced by its many illustrations and case examples which offer up-to-date and authoritative references, making this text a valuable resource in an increasingly complex field"— Provided by publisher.
Identifiers: LCCN 2022061383 (print) | LCCN 2022061384 (ebook) | ISBN 9780367672454 (hardback) | ISBN 9781003138754 (ebook)
Subjects: MESH: Forensic Medicine—methods
Classification: LCC RA1063.4 (print) | LCC RA1063.4 (ebook) | NLM W 700 | DDC 614/.1—dc23/eng/20230901
LC record available at https://lccn.loc.gov/2022061383
LC ebook record available at https://lccn.loc.gov/2022061384

ISBN: 978-0-367-67245-4 (hbk)
ISBN: 978-1-003-13875-4 (ebk)

DOI: 10.1201/9781003138754

Typeset in Sabon
by Apex CoVantage, LLC

The Open Access version of chapter 62 is funded by Open Government License, Crown Copyright.

To Lucy without whose unwavering support this text would not have been possible

Roger Byard, Adelaide, Australia

With thanks to my family for their support and to the many friends and colleagues with whom I have collaborated over the years.

Jason Payne-James, Southminster, UK

Contents

Section 3: Clinical Forensic Medicine

Section 4: Forensic Science and Related Specialties

Editor Biographies

Jason Payne-James LLM, MSc, FFFLM, FRCS, FRCP, FCSFS, FRFCFM(RCPA), RCPathME, DFM, LBIPP, Dip MOD is a Specialist in Forensic and Legal Medicine and is based in the UK. He has been a forensic physician for 30 years. Previously he worked in hospital medicine, predominantly in surgical, trauma and gastroenterological specialties.

He has published on a wide range of subjects including injury, wound and scar documentation and interpretation, imaging of injury and scars, clinical and ethical aspects of healthcare in custody, complaints against healthcare professionals, forensic evidence collection, restraint and less-lethal systems, miscarriages of justice, harm and death in custody and torture.

He is Honorary Clinical Professor, William Harvey Research Institute, Queen Mary University of London; Lead Medical Examiner Norfolk, Norwich University Hospital NHS Trust; external Consultant to the UK National Crime Agency; former Editor-in-Chief - Journal of Forensic & Legal Medicine; Member of the Executive Committee, European Council of Legal Medicine; Visiting Professor at the University of Belgrade, Serbia; member of the UK Scientific Advisory Committee on the Medical Implications of Less-Lethal Weapons; member of the International Forensic Expert Group of the International Rehabilitation Council for Torture Victims. He was President of the Faculty of Forensic & Legal Medicine of the Royal College of Physicians, London (2015-2017); President of the World Police Medical Officers (2011-2014). He has co-authored and co-edited a variety of publications including the Encyclopaedia of Forensic & Legal Medicine with Roger Byard (1st & 2nd editions); Symptoms and Signs of Substance Misuse (3 editions); he is lead author of the 13th and 14th editions of Simpson's Forensic Medicine; he co-authored the Oxford Handbook of Forensic Medicine.

He co-edited Age Estimation in the Living Current Practice in Forensic Medicine (1st & 2nd volumes); Monitoring Detention, Custody, Torture and Ill-treatment. He designed the ForensiGraph® and the ForensiDoc® App. He was lead editor on the 1st edition of Forensic Medicine: Clinical & Pathological Aspects.

Roger Byard AO PSM, DSc, FAHMS (BMedSci, MB, BS, MMedSci-Paed, PhD, MD, FCAP, FRCPC, FRCPath, FRCPA, FFFLM, FFSc, FRSN, FFPMI is an Emertius Professor of Pathology at The University of Adelaide and is a Senior Specialist Forensic Pathologist at Forensic Science SA in Adelaide, Australia.

In November 2021, in the Australian National Research Awards Professor Byard was named a world leader in forensic science among Australia's top lifetime achievers, and in 2022 was ranked as the top-rated expert of 83 821 published authors internationally in the Forensic Sciences 2012–2022 (https://expertscape.com/ex/forensic+science).

In 2004, he was awarded the Australian Public Service Medal (PSM) for outstanding service to paediatric pathology, and in 2013 became an Officer in the Order of Australia (AO) for distinguished service to medicine in the field of forensic pathology. He was registered as an Expert with the International Criminal Court (ICC) in the Hague in 2009. In 2016, he was elected a Fellow of the Australian Academy of Health and Medical Sciences (FAHMS) for distinguished professional achievements and outstanding leadership in a field related to health and medicine.

In 2016, he was also the recipient of the Distinguished Researcher Award from the International Society for the Study and Prevention of Perinatal and Infant Death (ISPID). He has received 18 awards for published papers and book chapters from the National Institute of Forensic Science, Australia. In 2018, he received the John Harbor Phillips Award from ANZPAA/NIFS (National Institute of Forensic Science) for outstanding achievement and excellence in the advancement of the forensic sciences in Australia and New Zealand.

He is an alumnus of six universities: the University of Tasmania (Distinguished Alumnus 2016), The University of Adelaide (Distinguished Alumnus 2013), the University of South Australia (Australia), McMaster University, the University of Toronto and the University of Ottawa (Canada).

He has a specific interest in sudden infant and childhood death, and general forensic research, and has published over 1 000 chapters and peer-reviewed papers (>550 first authorships) and a number of textbooks.

He was the Editor-in-Chief/Managing Editor of *Forensic Science Medicine and Pathology* (Springer Publishers, New York) from 2008 to 2021.

He was awarded the Humanitarian Overseas Service Medal (HOSM – Indian Ocean clasp – for "humanitarian service overseas in hazardous circumstances"), the RCPA medal and the Australian Federal Police (AFP) Operations Medal (Cawdor and Alliance clasps) for disaster victim identification work in Bali after the bombings in 2002 and in Thailand after the tsunami in 2004.

He has been invited to give educational forensic workshops/presentations in a number of countries including Argentina, Austria, Canada, China, Croatia, Denmark, Finland, France, Germany, Hong Kong, Iceland, India, Indonesia, Israel, Italy, Japan, Kazakhstan, Malaysia, Myanmar, New Guinea, New Zealand, Norway, Portugal, Saudi Arabia, Serbia, Singapore, South Africa, Spain, Sri Lanka, Switzerland, the Netherlands, the United Kingdom, the United States and Uruguay.

He was made a Distinguished Fellow of the Royal College of Pathologists of Australasia in 2018 in recognition of outstanding contributions to pathology and to the medical and wider community. In addition to his basic medical and other post graduate qualifications Professor Byard has three higher doctorates: a Doctor of Philosophy (PhD), a Doctor of Medicine (MD) and a Doctor of Science (DSc).

Contributors

Anil Aggrawal MBBS MD (Forensic Med)
Former Director, Professor of Forensic Medicine
Maulana Azad Medical College, India

George D. Annas MD MPH
Forensic Psychiatry Consulting, LLC
Diplomate of the American Board of Psychiatry and Neurology
Adult and Forensic Psychiatry
Syracuse, USA

Melanie Archer BSc (Hons) PhD MBBS FRCPA FFPMI (FRCPA)
Forensic Pathologist/Entomologist
Victorian Institute of Forensic Medicine
Monash University, Australia

Marianne Arnestad MD PhD
Dept of Forensic Sciences
Oslo University Hospital
Oslo, Norway

Alok Atreya MD
Associate Professor
Dept of Forensic Medicine and Toxicology
Lumbini Medical College
Palpa, Nepal

Liliana Bachs MD PhD
Dept of Forensic Sciences
Oslo University Hospital
Oslo, Norway

Philip S.L. Beh MBBS (HK) DMJ (Clin & Path) (Lond) FHKCPath FHKAM
Professor
Principal Clinical Practitioner
Dept of Pathology
The University of Hong Kong, Hong Kong

Peter G. Blain CBE BMedSCI MBBS PhD (Neurotoxicology) FBTS FRBS FFOM FRCP(Lon) FRCP(Edin)
Emeritus Professor
Translational and Clinical Research Institute
Faculty of Medical Sciences, Newcastle University
Honorary Consultant (Acute Medicine)
Newcastle Hospitals NHS Foundation Trust
Emergency Response Medicine at the UK Health Security Agency, UK

Soren Blau BA (Hons) MSc Ph, FFSc (RCPA)
Manager, Identification Services/Snr Forensic Anthropologist
Victorian Institute of Forensic Medicine
Dept of Forensic Medicine
Monash University, Australia

James Bloomer
Barrister
London, UK

Jan Bollen LLM MD PhD
Anesthesiologist and Lawyer
KNMG, The Netherlands

Stephen Boos MD FAAP
Professor of Pediatrics, UMass Chan Medical School – Baystate
Baystate Medical Center
Springfield, MA, USA

William P. Bozeman MD FACEP
Professor, Director of Prehospital Research
Wake Forest University
Dept of Emergency Medicine
Winston-Salem, NC, USA

Marie Brasholt MD
Snr Medical Advisor
Danish Institute Against Torture, Denmark
Member of SPT – UN Subcommittee on Prevention of Torture

Bruce Budowle PhD
Professor
Dept of Forensic Medicine
University of Helsinki, Finland
Visiting Scientist, Forensic Science Institute
Radford University, VA, USA

Julian L. Burton MB ChB(Hons) Med FHEA
Lead Coronial Pathologist
The Medicolegal Centre, UK

Roger W. Byard
AO PSM DSc FAHMS BMedSci MBBS MMedSci-Paed PhD
MD FCAP FRCPC FRCPath FRCPA FFFLM FFSc FRSN FFPMI
Emeritus Professor of Pathology
The University of Adelaide
Senior Specialist Forensic Pathologist
Forensic Science SA in Adelaide
Adelaide, Australia

Mark Byers OBE MBBS FRCGP FIMC FFSEM MRCEM
Consultant in Pre-Hospital Emergency Medicine
Great North Air Ambulance Service
Clinical and Northern Specialist Emergency Care Hospital
Northumberland, UK

Katherine Callahan MD
Forensic Pathologist
Hill Country Forensics
Georgetown, TX, USA

Sue Carney-Gannon MPhil BSc (Hons) MCSFS ChFP (Biology)
Consultant Forensic Scientist
and Chartered Forensic Practitioner
Ethos Forensics
Southport, UK

Sean Carruthers FFLM (MFC) UKAFN
Registered Nurse
Forensic Nurse Practitioner
University of Brighton
& University of Northumbria, UK
Queen Alexandra's Royal Naval Nursing Service
– Royal Navy/Royal Naval Reserves, UK

Rossana Cecchi MD
Institute of Legal Medicine
Dept of Medicine and Surgery
University of Parma
Parma, Italy

Juliet Cohen MA MBBS DipRACOG MRCGP FFFLM
Independent Forensic Physician

Marta C. Cohen OBE MD FRCPath DMJ (Pathol) Dip Med Ed
Consultant Paediatric and Perinatal Histopathologist
Sheffield Children's NHS Foundation Trust
Honorary Professor
Dept and Oncology and Metabolism
University of Sheffield
Sheffield, UK

Isobel Colclough MSc BEng FHEA MCSFS
Independent Forensic Investigation Consultant and Trainer
ILC Forensics Ltd, Weston-Super-Mare, UK
Independent Technical Assessor: IEC/ISO
Teacher, Cranfield Defence and Security and Cranfield Forensic Institute
Cranfield University, Bedfordshire, UK

Gary L. Collins MD
Board Certified in Pathology and Forensic Pathology
Chief Medical Examiner
Delaware Division of Forensic Science
Wilmington, DE, USA

Kim A. Collins MC FCAP FNAME
Forensic Pathologist
Newberry Pathology Group
Newberry, SC, USA
Director for SharingHope SC
Organ and Tissue Donation Services
Charleston, SC, USA

John E. Cooper DTVM FRCPath FRSB Hon FFFLM FRCVS
Professor
RCVS Specialist in Veterinary Pathology
Diplomate, European College of Veterinary Pathologists
Diplomate, European College of Zoological Medicine
Wildlife Health, Forensic and Comparative Pathology Services, UK

Margaret E. Cooper LLB FLS Hon FFFLM Hon FRCPath
Solicitor
Wildlife Health, Forensic and Comparative Pathology Services, UK

Neil Corney
Research Associate, Omega Research Foundation, UK

Sondra S. Crosby MD
Professor of Medicine and Public Health
Center for Health Law, Ethics, and Human Rights
Boston University
Boston, MA, USA

Denis A. Cusack FRCPI FFFLM FCLMM FCIArb Barrister-at-Law
Professor Emeritus
Forensic & Legal Medicine,
University College Dublin, Ireland
Snr Coroner for the District of Kildare, Ireland
President, European Council of Legal Medicine
Vice-President, International Academy of Legal Medicine

Christopher Day BA App Sci (Med Sci) MBBS
Forensic Pathologist
Forensic and Scientific Services
Prevention Division
Queensland Health
Queensland, Australia

Hans H. de Boer MD PhD DipPMCT FRCPA
Forensic Pathologist
Victorian Institute of Forensic Medicine
Dept of Forensic Medicine
Monash University, Australia

Gisela de Heus
Dept of Forensic Medicine
Netherlands Forensic Institute
The Hague, The Netherlands

Russell J. Delaney MB ChB MRCS FRCPath
Home Office Registered Forensic Pathologist
South West Forensic Pathology Group Practice
Bristol, UK

Michael Devlin LLM MBA FRCP FRCGP FFFLM
Head of Professional Standards and Liaison
Medical Defence Union, UK

Matthew Di Rago BA App Sci
Snr Scientist (Analytical Specialist) Toxicology
Victorian Institute of Forensic Medicine
Southbank, Victoria
Dept of Forensic Medicine
Monash University
Clayton, Victoria, Australia

Elke Doberentz
Professor of Forensic Medicine
Medical University of Innsbruck
Innsbruck, Austria

Olaf H. Drummer AO FRCPA FFSC FACBS Hon FFFLM Dr.h.c.(Antwerp) PhD(Melb) BA App Sci(RMIT) CChem
Emeritus Professor
Antwerp, Belgium
Victorian Institute of Forensic Medicine and Dept of Forensic Medicine
School of Public Health and Preventive Medicine
Faculty of Medicine, Nursing and Health Sciences
Monash University
Clayton, Victoria, Australia

Lorraine du Toit-Prinsloo
NSW Health Pathology
Forensic & Analytical Science Service
Forensic Medicine
Newcastle, Australia

Wilma L.J.M. Duijst MD LLM PhD (Law)
Professor in Forensic Medicine and Health and Criminal Law
Maastricht University
Maastricht, The Netherlands

Inga Duval
Institute of Forensic Medicine
University of Bonn
Bonn, Germany

Stevan R. Emmett, BSc, MB ChB DPhil (Oxon) DoHNS FRSB FFPM
Chief Medical Officer
Defence Science and Technology Laboratories
Consultant Pharmaceutical Physician
Snr Clinical Fellow Emergency Medicine
Royal United Hospitals NHS Bath
Snr Research Fellow, Medical School
University of Bristol
Bristol, UK

Sam Evans PhD
Chief Clinical Photographer
Dental Photography
School of Dentistry
College of Biomedical and Life Sciences
Cardiff University
Cardiff, UK

Liliane Field
Assistant Deputy Coroner, Inner South London, UK
Formerly Consultant in Anaesthesia and Intensive Care and Snr Medicolegal Adviser Medical Protection

Vittorio Fineschi
Dept of Anatomical, Histological, Forensic and Orthopedic Sciences
University of Rome
Rome, Italy

Thomas Ka-Chung Foo MBBS(HK) FHKCPath FHKAM
Senior Forensic Pathologist
Forensic Pathology Service, Dept of Health
The Hong Kong Special Administrative Region
Hong Kong

Victoria Francis
Forensic Pathologist
Victorian Institute of Forensic Medicine
Southbank, VA, Australia

Ian Freckelton AO KC
Judge, Supreme Court of the Republic of Nauru
Professor of Law and Professorial Fellow in Psychiatry
University of Melbourne, Australia
Honorary Professor of Forensic Medicine
Monash University,
Clayton, VA, Australia

Judith Fronczek MD PhD FRCPA
Victorian Institute of Forensic Medicine
Forensic Pathologist
Dept of Forensic Science
Monash University
Clayton, VA, Australia

John A.M. Gall BSc (Hons) MB BS PhD FFFLM FFCFM (RCPA) DMJ (Clin & Path)
Clinical Associate Professor
Dept of Paediatrics, The University of Melbourne
Victorian Forensic Paediatric Medical Service
The Royal Children's Hospital and Monash Medial Centre, Melbourne
Era Health, Melbourne, Australia

Patrick J. Gallagher MD PhD FRCPath
Medical Education
Bristol Medical School
Bristol, UK

Peter Attila Gergely MD
Faculty of Medicine
Dept of Forensic Medicine
University of Debrecen
Debrecen, Hungary

Dimitri Gerostamoulos PhD(Med)(Monash) BSc(Hons) FFCP
Victorian Institute of Forensic Medicine & Dept of Forensic Medicine
Monash University
Clayton, VA, Australia

Jan M. Gorniak DO MHSA
Clark County Office of the Coroner/Medical Examiner
Las Vegas, NV, USA

Alex J. Gorton MB BCh MRCS LLM DLM FFLM RCPathME
Consultant Forensic Physician
Medical Examiner
NHS Wales Shared Services Partnership
Speciality Doctor in Emergency Medicine
Princess of Wales Hospital, Bridgend
Less Lethal Weapons Lead
Faculty of Forensic and Legal Medicine
Cardiff, UK

Peter Green MBBS CKJ FFFLM
Consultant Forensic Physician
Cameron Forensic Medical Sciences
Barts and the London School of Medicine and Dentistry
London, UK

Rohini J. Haar MD MPH
Emergency Medicine Physician
Oakland California
Adjunct Professor, Dept of Epidemiology
School of Public Health
University of California
Berkeley, CA, USA

Christine A. Hall MD MSc (Clin Epidemiol) FRCPC (Emerg Med)
University of British Columbia
Vancouver, Canada

Joey C.A. Hardy
Dept of Medical Imaging
Maastricht University Medical Center
Maastricht, The Netherlands

Denice Higgins BDS GDipForOdont PhD
Associate Professor
Forensic Odontology Unit
Faculty of Health and Medical Sciences
University of Adelaide
Adelaide, Australia

Judith A. Hinchliffe BDS
Independent Forensic Odontologist
Darwin, Australia

Deborah Hodes MBBS BSc DRCOG FRCPCH
Consultant Paediatrician
Dept of Paediatrics
University College London Hospitals
London, UK

Paul A.M. Hofman MD PhD
Professor of Forensic and Post-Mortem Radiology
Dept of Medical Imaging
Maastricht University Medical Center
Maastricht, The Netherlands

John Holden MB BS MPhil MRCGP DCH DRCOG FFFLM
Chief Medical Officer
The Medical and Dental Defence Union of Scotland
Glasgow, Scotland

Julie Howe MBA RHIA D-ABMDI
Associate Professor
Clinical Health Sciences
Saint Louis University
St. Louis, MO, USA

Sarah Hull BM BCh MA(Oxon) FFFLM LLM
Professor/Consultant Forensic Physician
Clinical Director
The Rowan SARC Northern Ireland
Medical Protection Society
Visiting Professor, Ulster University
Belfast, UK

Rebecca A. Irvine MD
Forensic Pathologist
NSW Health Pathology
Forensic & Analytical Science Service
Forensic Medicine Sydney
Sydney, Australia

Megan Jenkins BM BS BMedSci
Forensic Pathology Unit
Royal Liverpool University Hospital, UK

Nikolas P. Johnston BMedBiotech (Hons) PhD
Research Fellow
School of Life Sciences
University of Technology Sydney
Sydney, Australia

Marie Louise Jørkov
Dept of Forensic Medicine
University of Copenhagen
Copenhagen, Denmark

Tanuj Kanchan MD MAMS FIAMLE
Professor and Head
Dept of Forensic Medicine and Toxicology
All India Institute of Medical Sciences
Jodhpur, India

Navpreet Kaur PhD
Advocate
Punjab & Haryana High Court
Chandigarh, India

Eva Keller MD PhD
Faculty of Medicine
Dept of Forensic Medicine
University of Debrecen
Debrecen, Hungary

Kevin Kinch MB ChB FRCPath
Consultant Neuropathologist and Honorary Clinical Snr Lecturer
Academic Dept of Neuropathology
Centre for Clinical Brain Sciences
University of Edinburgh
Edinburgh, UK

Emrys Kirkman OBE PhD
Principal Scientist
Physiology, Defence Science and Technology Laboratory
Dstl Porton Down
Salisbury, UK

Panagiota Kitsanta PhD
Consultant Histopathologist
Head of School of Pathology in Yorkshire and Humber
Snr Lecturer (Hons), University of Sheffield
Dept of Histopathology, Royal Hallamshire Hospital
Sheffield, UK

Laura D. Knight MD
Chief Medical Examiner & Coroner
Washoe County Regional Medical Examiner's Office
Associate Professor, Pathology and Pediatrics Depts
University of Nevada–Reno School of Medicine
Reno, NV, USA

Peter Juel Thiis Knudsen MD
Associate Professor (USA)/ Snr Lecturer (UK)
Deputy Chief Forensic Pathologist
Institute of Forensic Medicine
University of Southern Denmark
Odense, Denmark

Kewal Krishan PhD, FRAI
Professor and Former Chair
Dept of Anthropology, Panjab University
Chandigarh, India

Mark W. Kroll PhD FACC FHRS FAIMBE
Adjunct Professor of Biomedical Engineering
University of Minnesota
Minneapolis, MN, USA

Matt N. Krosch BA App Sci (Hons) PhD FRES
Principal Research Officer
Queensland Police Service
Brisbane, Australia

Sara Tangmose Larsen MD
Dept of Forensic Medicine
University of Copenhagen
Copenhagen, Denmark

Bartholomeus G.H. Latten MD
Dept of Forensic Pathology
Netherlands Forensic Institute
The Hague, The Netherlands

Hazel I. Learner BM MRCOG MFSRH
Consultant in Paediatric and Adolescent Gynaecology
Dept of Women's Health
University College London Hospitals
London, UK

Joannah Lee
Northern Territory Police
Fire and Emergency Services
Darwin, Australia

Kirsty L. Lloyd MB ChB BSc (Hons)
Consultant Histopathologist
Sheffield Teaching Hospitals NHS Foundation Trust
Sheffield, UK

Larissa Lohner MD BEng
Institute of Legal Medicine
University Medical Center
Hamburg-Eppendorf, Germany

Bertrand Ludes MD PhD
Université de Paris CNRS Babel
Institut Médico-légal de Paris
Paris, France

Matthew Lynch MBBS LLB (Hons) FRCPA
Forensic Pathologist
Victorian Institute of Forensic Medicine
Southbank, VIC, Australia

Niels Lynnerup MD PhD
Dept of Forensic Medicine
University of Copenhagen
Copenhagen, Denmark

Burkhard Madea MD
Professor
Institute of Forensic Medicine
University of Bonn
Bonn, Germany

Gordon McDavid MB ChB LLM MRCP
Snr Medicolegal Adviser, MDDUS
Glasgow, Scotland

Katie McDonald MD
Honorary Snr Clinical Lecturer
University of Sheffield
Consultant Histopathologist
Sheffield Teaching Hospitals
Sheffield, UK

Matthew McEvoy
Research Associate
Omega Research Foundation, UK

Aniello Maiese MD PhD
Dept of Surgical Pathology
Medical, Molecular and Critical Area
Institute of Legal Medicine
University of Pisa
Pisa, Italy

Xanthé Mallett PhD MPhil (CANTAB) BSc
Associate Professor of Criminology
Newcastle Law School
University of Newcastle
Newcastle, UK

Alice Chiara Manetti MD
Dept of Surgical Pathology
Medical, Molecular and Critical Area
Institute of Legal Medicine
University of Pisa
Pisa, Italy

Paul Marks BA LLM MD FRCS FFFLM RCPath ME
HM Snr Coroner for Hull & East Yorkshire
President of the Faculty of Forensic & Legal Medicine
Honorary Professor of Medical Jurisprudence
Hull York Medical School
Hull, UK

Rudo Masanzu MBChB (Hons) MMed(Urol) MSc LLM FFFLM DFMS DFCASA LBIPP
Professor/Consultant Forensic Physician
Visiting Professor Ulster University
The Havens Sexual Assault Referral Centres London
University of Ulster
Belfast, Ireland

Vittoria Masotti MD
Institute of Legal Medicine
Dept of Medicine and Surgery
University of Parma
Parma, Italy

Jakob Matschke MD
Assistant Professor
Forensic Neuropathology Unit
Institute of Neuropathology
University Hospital Hamburg-Eppendorf
Hamburg, Germany

Mikko I. Mäyränpää
Clinical Lecturer
Dept of Pathology
University of Helsinki
Helsinki University Hospital
Helsinki, Finland

Ritesh George Menezes MBBS MD DNB
Forensic Medicine Division
Dept of Pathology, College of Medicine
King Fahd Hospital of the University
Imam Abdulrahman Bin Faisal University
Dammam, KSA

Vikas Meshram MD
Associate Professor
Dept of Forensic Medicine and Toxicology
All India Institute of Medical Sciences
Jodhpur, India

Nathan Milne MD FRCPA MFFLM MACLM
Snr Forensic Pathologist
Forensic and Scientific Services
Prevention Division, Queensland Health
Snr Lecturer
Faculty of Medicine
The University of Queensland
Honorary Adjunct Asst Professor
Faculty of Health Sciences and Medicine
Bond University
Gold Coast, QLD, Australia

Christopher M. Milroy MB ChB MD LLB LLM FRCPath FRCPC FFFLM DMJ
Forensic Pathologist
Eastern Ontario Regional Forensic Pathology Unit
Full Professor, University of Ottawa
The Ottawa Hospital
Ottawa, Canada

Jens Modvig MD PhD
Danish Institute Against Torture
Former Member of and Chair of the UN Committee Against Torture
København, Denmark

Slobodan Nikolić MD PhD
Professor
University of Belgrade
School of Medicine, Institute of Forensic Medicine
Beograd, Serbia

Maria Nittis MB BS FFCFM RCPA FFFLM FACLM FACBS
Adjunct Clinical Associate Professor
Head of Clinical Forensic Medicine Service for the Victorian Institute of Forensic Medicine
Adjunct Clinical Associate Professor
Monash University
Melbourne, VIC, Australia

Curtis E. Offiah BSc MB CHB FRCS FRCR
Consultant Clinical and Forensic Radiologist
Royal London Hospital, Barts Health NHS Trust
Honorary Snr Lecturer in Forensic Medical Sciences
William Harvey Research Institute
Barts and the London School of Medicine and Dentistry
Queen Mary University
London, UK

Beng Beng Ong MD
Snr Forensic Pathologist
Forensic and Scientific Services
Prevention Division, Queensland Health
Snr Lecturer
Faculty of Medicine
University of Queensland
Queensland, VIC, Australia

Matthew M. Orde MB ChB FRCPath FRCPA DMJ(Path) DipForMed(SA) MFFLM LLDip PgDLS
Barrister-at-Law
Forensic Pathologist
Canadian Forensic Medical Consulting, Vancouver, British Columbia
Clinical Associate Professor, Faculty of Medicine, University of British Columbia
Associate Professor, College of Medicine, University of Saskatchewan, Canada

Roger D. Palmer BSc(Hons) PhD LLM FRCPCH FRCP Edin
Medicolegal Consultant Team Leader
Medical Protection Society (MPS)
Edinburgh, UK

Utsav Parekh MD
Assistant Professor
Dept of Forensic Medicine and Toxicology
All India Institute of Medical Sciences
Rajkot, Gujarat, India

Vanita Parekh MB ChB FAChSHM (RACP) FFCFM (RCPA) M Forensic M Dip Med Tox DFRSH Dip Ven Grad Cert HE
Unit Director, Clinical Forensic Medical Services, The Canberra Hospital
Associate Professor, The Australian National University
Adjunct Associate Professor, The University of Canberra
Canberra, Australia

Jason Payne-James LLM MSc FFFLM FRCS FRCP FCSFS FFCFM(RCPA) RCPathME DFM LBIPP Dip MOD
Specialist in Forensic & Legal Medicine & Consultant Forensic Physician
Lead Medical Examiner
Norfolk & Norwich University Hospital
Honorary Clinical Professor
William Harvey Research Institute
Queen Mary University of London
London, UK

Matthew Peel RN (Adult) MSc BSc DipHe V300 ASET
UK Association of Forensic Nurses and Paramedics, UK
Advanced Clinical Practitioner (General Forensic Medicine)
Leeds Community Healthcare NHS Trust
Leeds, UK

Clifford Perera MBBS DLM MD MA LLB DMJ(Lond) MFFLM(UK)
Snr Lecturer in Forensic Medicine & Consultant Forensic Pathologist
Dept of Forensic Medicine
Faculty of Medicine
University of Ruhuna
Matara, Sri Lanka

Harry Perkins BDS
Forensic Odontology Unit
Faculty of Health and Medical Sciences
University of Adelaide
Adelaide, SA, Australia

Michael J. Pickup MSc MD FRCPC
Forensic Pathologist and Medical Manager of Postmortem Imaging
Ontario Forensic Pathology Service
Assistant Professor
Dept of Laboratory Medicine and Pathobiology
University of Toronto
Toronto, Canada

Henrietta Poon MB ChB PhD FRCSEd (Vasc Surg)
UK Ministry of Defence
University of Birmingham
Birmingham, UK

Karen E. Rogstad MB BS (Hons) FRCP MBA PG Cert MedEd
Associate Director of Student Affairs and Academic Director
Academic Unit of Medical Education, University of Sheffield
Consultant Physician, Dept of Infectious Diseases
Sheffield Teaching Hospitals NHS Foundation Trust
Sheffield, UK

Gert Saayman MB ChB(Pret) MBChB MMed(MedForens)(Pret) FCForPath(SA)
(Retired) Clinical Head: Forensic Pathology Service, Pretoria
(Retired) Professor and Head: Dept of Forensic Medicine
Faculty of Health Sciences
University of Pretoria
Pretoria, South Africa

Antti Sajantila MD PhD
Professor
Dept of Forensic Medicine
University of Helsinki
Chief Medical Examiner, Forensic Medicine Unit
Finnish Institute of Health and Welfare
Helsinki, Finland

Matilde Sassani MD
Institute of Metabolism and Systems Research
College of Medical and Dental Sciences
University of Birmingham
Birmingham, UK

Irene Scheimberg
Former Consultant Paediatric and Perinatal Pathologist
Barts and the Royal London Hospital, UK

Carol A. Seymour-Richards MA(Oxon) MA(Cantab) MSc PhD FRCP FRCPath PgDipLaw PgDLS FFFLM
Emeritus Professor
Chair of Special Advisory Committee in Forensic and Legal Medicine
Joint Royal Colleges of Physicians Training Board, UK

Colin Smith MD FRCPath
Professor of Neuropathology
Academic Dept of Neuropathology
Centre for Clinical Brain Sciences
University of Edinburgh
Edinburgh, UK

Jennie Smith RGN MSc PG Cert ASET V300 UCPPD
Clinical Lead, Care and Custody Health Ltd
President, UK Association of Forensic Nurses and Paramedic, UK

Jan-Peter Sperhake MD
Professor
Institute of Legal Medicine
University Medical Center Hamburg-Eppendorf
Hamburg, Germany

Margaret Stark MB BS LLM MSc (Med Ed) FFLM FACBS FHEA FACLM FRCP FFCFM (RCPA) RCPathME DGM DMJ DAB
Honorary Professor, Teesside University
Immediate Past President
Faculty of Forensic & Legal Medicine
Royal College of Physicians
London, UK

Lilli Stephenson BA Hlth Sci
Adelaide School of Medicine
The University of Adelaide
Adelaide, Australia

Sebastian O. Sterling PhD MD
The Adelaide Medical School
University of Adelaide
Central Adelaide Local Health Network
The Royal Adelaide Hospital
Adelaide, Australia

Jennifer Anne Sutherland Smith, MBBS FRACP MForensMed FFCFM(RCPA) AFRACMA MPH MHLM
Director, Victorian Forensic Paediatric Medical Service
Royal Children's Hospital, Melbourne
Clinical Associate Professor, University of Melbourne
Snr Lecturer, Monash University
Clayton, Australia

S. Kim Suvarna MBBS BSc FRCP FRCPath
Honorary Professor
University of Sheffield
Consultant Pathologist
Sheffield Teaching Hospitals
Sheffield, UK

Denise Syndercombe Court MRSB CBiol FIBMS CSci DMedT MCFS PhD Dip Forensic Statistics
Professor of Forensic Genetics
King's Forensics
Dept of Analytical, Environmental and Forensic Sciences
King's College
London, UK

Sam Thompson
Snr Lecturer
St George's
University of London
London, UK

Marianne Tiemensma FRCPA
Forensic Pathology Unit
Royal Darwin Hospital and Northern Territory Medical Program
College of Medicine and Public Health
Flinders University
Adelaide, Australia

Eu-Wing Toh FRCPath
Consultant Histopathologist
Sheffield Teaching Hospitals NHS Foundation Trust
Sheffield, UK

Evi Untoro Sp FM
Forensic Pathologist
Lecturer at Faculty of Medicine
University of Trisakti
Jakarta, Indonesia

Rick R. Van Rijn PhD
Professor
Dept of Forensic Medicine, Section on Forensic Paediatrics
Netherlands Forensic Institute, The Hague
Amsterdam Center for Forensic Science and Medicine
Amsterdam UMC, Dept of Radiology and Nuclear Medicine
Emma Children's Hospital
University of Amsterdam
Amsterdam, The Netherlands

Gary M. Vilke MD FACEP FAAEM
Professor of Clinical Emergency Medicine
University of California
San Diego School of Medicine
La Jolla, CA, USA

Chiara Villa
Dept of Forensic Medicine
University of Copenhagen
Copenhagen, Denmark

Alfredo E. Walker HBM FRCPath DMJ (Path) MBBS MFFLM MCSFS
Vice Chair and Director of Education
Dept of Pathology and Laboratory Medicine
Faculty of Medicine
University of Ottawa
Ottawa, Canada

Ian Francis Wall FRCP FRCGP FFFLM FACLM FFCFM(RCPA) SFFMLM DMJ(Clin)
Consultant Forensic Physician and Specialist in Forensic & Legal Medicine
Visiting Professor, Teeside University
Consultant in SARC Services
Northamptonshire Healthcare NHS Foundation Trust
Kettering, UK

James F. Wallman BSc (Hons) PhD FFSc(RCPA) FRES FRSN
Dean, Faculty of Science
University of Technology Sydney
Sydney, Australia

Sarah A. Watts PhD BVETMED MRCVS
Snr Principal Scientist
CBR Division
Dstl Porton Down
Salisbury, UK

Putut T. Widodo
Retired Police Officer and Former Head of DNA Laboratory of INP (Indonesian National Police)
Jakarta, Indonesia

Angela Williams MBBS MForensMed MBA GAICD MPH MHM. FFFLM(UK) FFCFM(RCPA) AFRACMA PRI NMAS LLB GDLP
Consultant Clinical Forensic Physician
Victorian Institute of Forensic Medicine
Senior Lecturer
Dept of Forensic Medicine
Monash University
Clayton, VIC, Australia

Heather Williams MD
SAFEchild Advocacy Center
WakeMed Children's Hospital
Raleigh, NC, USA

Linzi Wilson-Wilde OAM PhD
Director Forensic Science South Australia
Professor of Forensic Science
Forensic Science SA
Adelaide, SA, Australia

Vladimir Živković, MD PhD
Professor
School of Medicine
Institute of Forensic Medicine
University of Belgrade
Beograd, Serbia

Preface

> "Convictions are more dangerous enemies of truths than lies".
>
> Friedrich Nietzsche (1844–1900)

Increasingly the field of forensic and legal medicine has become more complex in many areas that include not only the recording, investigation and processing of cases, but also in dealing with the increasing sophistication of laboratory analyses and in navigating the sometimes byzantine world of court interrogations and processes. Media scrutiny, often with criticism, is ever present in high profile cases.

Practitioners in all medicolegal areas are now required to keep abreast of the literature which entails not only reading current research and opinion papers but also being able to correctly identify bogus reports propagated by so-called predatory journals. The adversarial system encourages debate which unfortunately may be based on convictions rather than on a careful and dispassionate analysis of the facts; Nietzsche clearly pointed out his concerns about the dangers of convictions.

For this reason, the era of the solo practitioner is coming to an end. Peer review with more collaborative case analyses in the workplace is becoming the norm in an attempt to circumvent idiosyncratic practices with erroneous conclusions that did occur in the past when practitioners were isolated. The same is occurring with textbooks, with considerable strength and credibility being achieved by multi-author content. While this has occurred in the following chapters, it is not imagined that there is going to be agreement on all of the topics discussed. However, it is hoped that clear analysis of the literature with well-founded and defensible opinions by individual authors or groups of authors may be useful to the reader. It is felt that the text will act as a substantial foundation for further reading on specific topics.

The text is, therefore, an attempt to provide an up-to-date general treatise on forensic and legal medicine covering both clinical and pathologic aspects with a multitude of high-quality images and practical tables. It has been broadly divided into four sections dealing firstly with general principles of forensic and legal medicine. In this section, topics include the history and development of forensic and legal medicine, international ethical principles and human rights law, issues around euthanasia and professional conduct for not only medical practitioners but also for nurses and paramedics. Overviews of the roles of medical defense organizations, coroners and medical examiners and the United Nations and non-governmental organizations are provided. The principles of death investigations are outlined, with pointers on how to give evidence in court.

The second section deals with traditional pathologic issues such as the differences between hospital and medicolegal autopsies and the analysis of sharp and blunt force trauma to various bodily regions. Natural deaths (including those related to COVID-19), suicides and homicides are described, along with infant and childhood, maternal and perioperative deaths. Ballistic and blast trauma are evaluated, with an assessment of custody and restraint deaths. Problems with the timing of death and post-mortem identifications and age assessments are listed. Environmental issues such as thunderstorm asthma are investigated with chapters on heat deaths, drowning, burns and electrocution. Forensic post-mortem imaging and associated technologies are summarized with comments on the Minnesota Protocol.

The third section covers all aspects of clinical forensic medicine ranging from the role of the forensic physician and sexual offense examiner to healthcare in detention and determination of fitness to detain and interview, as well as issues with the use of herbal medicines and the features of female genital mutilation. Novel psychoactive substances are described with sections on substance misuse in detention and acute behavioral disturbances. The interpretation of injuries and those pertaining to sexual assault are reviewed in addition to the role of the Istanbul Protocol in monitoring ill treatment and abuse in custody. Restraint and control techniques, including the use of conducted energy devices are analysed.

The fourth and final section provides information on a range of forensic science and related specialities including chapters on misinterpretation and fallacies in forensic evidence and the principles of crime scene management and blood pattern analysis. In addition, there is information on forensic photography, odontology, toxicology, DNA analysis, microbiology, anthropology and entomology. Other topics covered include disaster victim identification, veterinary forensic pathology and working with the media. The full listing of topics may be found in the Table of Contents.

Thus, this text provides over 100 chapters written by contemporary experts in their fields from all over the globe, on a full range of medicolegal topics. The editors also have considerable experience in forensic medicine and pathology and have published extensively in the peer-reviewed literature on a wide range of subjects. For this reason, the book stands alone as an example of international multidisciplinary collaboration that has produced a definitive new multi-layered text on medicolegal matters that will be essential reading for forensic clinical practitioners, pathologists, medical examiners, coroners, lawyers and any individual involved in forensic case work and the courts. In addition, it will be a necessary text for university and college libraries to provide access for students of law, medicine, nursing, forensic science and ancillary disciplines.

It has been a great privilege to work with contributors of such high caliber and to see the text evolve into such an impressive tome. We look forward to seeing it extensively utilized over the years and hope that it will assist in the guidance, development and practice of this most complex of disciplines.

Jason Payne-James
Roger Byard

SECTION 1

Principles of Forensic & Legal Medicine

CHAPTER 1

History and Current Status of Forensic and Legal Medicine

Jason Payne-James

INTRODUCTION

Forensic medicine, legal medicine, and forensic pathology are terms that have been used interchangeably around the world. The term "forensic & legal medicine" embraces these and brings them together to indicate all branches of medicine and related specialties that interact with legal processes, either directly or indirectly. Forensic & legal medicine is recognized as a specialty area of medicine in some countries, but not all. Although not a monospecialty, the Union Européenne des Médecine Spécialistes (European Union of Medical Specialists [UEMS]) recognizes "legal & forensic medicine" as a thematic federation (1). Forensic & legal medicine embraces forensic pathology, which investigates unnatural, unexpected, or violent death, or when the cause of death is unknown, and clinical forensic medicine, which is used to refer to that branch of medicine which involves interaction between the living person, medicine and legal or judicial processes (2).

A forensic pathologist does not usually (in general) deal with living individuals, whereas a forensic physician does not usually deal with the deceased. There are, however, many medical practitioners in some jurisdictions whose workloads embrace both clinical and pathological aspects of forensic & legal medicine. Many practitioners have qualifications or training in medicine, law, and science. There are many areas where both clinical and pathological aspects of forensic & legal medicine overlap, and this is reflected in the history and development of the field and its contribution to part of the wide field of forensic sciences. The term "forensic pathologist" is used generally to describe those who undertake autopsies performed on the instructions and request of legal bodies responsible for the investigation of sudden, suspicious, obscure, unnatural, litigious, or criminal deaths. A forensic pathologist undertakes the examinations to assist and advise the state or other investigating agencies in the interpretation of the findings and to suggest further relevant investigation. The legal bodies that may make these requests may be agents of the state, the judiciary, the police, lawyers representing those arrested for murder, those involved in legal action, health and safety organisations, and many other possible sources.

"Clinical forensic medicine" refers to medical practice whose scope involves interaction between the law, the judiciary and the police involving (generally) living persons. Clinical forensic medicine is a term that has become generally recognized in the last four decades or so, although the phrase has been used at least since 1951 in the UK, when the Association of Police Surgeons (which became the Association of Forensic Physicians in 2003 until it in turn was replaced by the Faculty of Forensic & Legal Medicine of the Royal College of Physicians) was first established. Previously, terms such as police surgeon, divisional surgeon, forensic medical officer (FMO) and forensic medical examiner (FME) have been used and persist in some jurisdictions. Table 1.1 gives examples of the range of roles which may be applicable to forensic physicians and Table 1.2 illustrates themes that may have relevance to all practitioners of forensic & legal medicine. Some forensic practitioners work in all these areas, while others (such as sexual offense examiners) focus on one aspect. A forensic pathologist and forensic physician need to have a good knowledge of "medical jurisprudence" – the application of medical science and related specialties to the law. The function and role of forensic pathologists and forensic physicians can differ widely or overlap, depending on local judicial systems or statute and, in many cases, result in the need for a special understanding of medical law and medical ethics.

ORIGINS AND DEVELOPMENT

The origins of forensic and legal medicine go back many centuries although the terms forensic medicine and medical jurisprudence date back to the earliest part of the nineteenth century. In 1840, Thomas Stuart Traill emphasized the range of terminology used, stating "*...it is known in Germany, the country in which it took its rise, by the name of State Medicine, in Italy and France it is termed Legal Medicine; and with us it is usually denominated Medical Jurisprudence or Forensic Medicine*" (3).

Pharmacology and pharmacognosy (the branch of knowledge concerned with medicinal drugs obtained from plants or other natural sources) were subjects of writings in China from around 3000 BCE. In 1975, Chinese

DOI: 10.1201/9781003138754-2

TABLE 1.1 Examples of some current functions of forensic physicians (roles and functions vary in different jurisdictions)
Medical care of prisoners in police custody
Forensic assessment of prisoners in police custody
Assessment of those arrested for traffic offenses
Forensic assessment of complainants (including biological sample taking and wound documentation)
Medical care of complainants
Mental health assessment of complainants
Assessment of complainants of sexual assault
Assessment of complainants or suspects in hospitals/police custody/prison custody
Child protection/safeguarding
Adult safeguarding
Assessment of intimate partner violence
Medical assessment of police or prison personnel
Forensic assessment of police or prison personnel
Refugee and asylum seeker assessment
Assessment of detainees in Immigration Removal Centers
Assessment of torture and CIDT claims
Written evidence to courts, tribunals, coroners and others
Live evidence to courts, tribunals, coroners and others

TABLE 1.2 Contemporary themes in forensic and legal medicine
Abusive head trauma in children
Causes of death in custody
Disclosure of evidence in sexual assault cases
DNA: current developments and perspectives
Fitness to plead and stand trial
Forensic radiology in evaluation of soft-tissue injury
Medical and toxicological aspects of chemical warfare
Needs and problems of the older person in prison
Non-fatal strangulation
Non-lethal physical abuse in the elderly
Post-mortem radiological autopsy
Sudden death
Weapons used to police public assemblies around the world
Who makes false allegations and why?
Working with torture victims

archeologists discovered a number of bamboo pieces that had information on the rules and regulations for examining injuries – these dated from approximately 220 BCE. The Hammurabi Code (named after the king of Babylon – now in modern Iraq) dated back to approximately 2200 BCE and dealt specifically with the rights and duties of physicians, including medical malpractice. Penalties for such malpractice ranged from cutting off the hands of the offending physician to financial compensation.

The Law of Manu (India) dates back to approximately 10 BCE and dealt with issues still particularly relevant today, including the competence of witnesses in courts. In Egypt, laws regulated the medical profession and physicians had to strictly follow the methods used by ancient physicians. Stab wounds were categorized and closed head injuries with skull fractures described. Papyri related to Roman Egypt dating from the latter part of the first to the latter part of the fourth century AD contain information about forensic medical examination or investigation. In Persia (now Iran), there was an official scale of medical fees and a restriction of medical practices to certain castes and classes of the community, and penalties were meted out for medical malpractice. Injuries were subdivided into several groups; abortion was a serious crime.

Amundsen and Ferngren reviewed the role of physicians as expert witnesses in classical Greece and concluded that forensic medicine was used by Athenian courts and other public bodies and that the testimony of physicians in matters of a medical nature was given particular credence (4,5). In the Roman Republic, the Lex Duodecim Tabularum (449 BCE) made minor reference to medicolegal matters including length of gestation (to determine legitimacy), disposal of the dead, punishments dependent on the degree of injury caused by an assailant, and poisoning (6). The Lex Aquilia of 572 BCE dealt with the lethality of wounds. The "novus actus interveniens" in relation to deaths from wounds was brought into play and declared as a break in causation. Sulla's "Lex Cornelia" (138–78 BCE) declared that a physician should be exiled or executed if it was established that he had caused the death of his patient. The body of Julius Caesar (100–44 BCE) after his murder in the forum was examined by the physician Antistius who declared that there were 23 stab wounds, only one of which was a fatal wound. The Emperor Justinian (AD 483–565) in his "Digest", recorded that "*physicians are not ordinary witnesses, but give judgment rather than testimony*" which is also an early indicator of the role of opinion rather than factual evidence.

Between the fifth and the tenth centuries, the "Dark Ages", the "Leges Barbarorum" of the Goths, Visigoths and Vandals laid down clearly when medical experts were called for. "Wergeld" (blood money) was payable to the victim or on death to relatives of the decedent by the perpetrator – and these principles apply in certain cultures today. The first Holy Roman Emperor, Charlemagne (742–814) had his bishops produce the "Capitularies" in which the need for expert medical testimony was required in wounding, abortion, rape, incest, infanticide and suicide. In 1209, the influence of the Church was formalized by Pope Innocent III with the appointment of physicians to the courts. In 1234, Gregory IX in his "Compilatio Decretalium" collected all decisions and edicts in relation to medicolegal matters and these held sway in France until 1677.

Many forensic and legal medicine texts were produced from a wide variety of centers in the sixteenth to eighteenth centuries, and these and earlier key dates are identified by Madea (7) summarizing data from Payne-James (8), Bonte (9) and Smith (10).

Traill (3) stated that "*Medical Jurisprudence as a science cannot date farther back than the 16th century*" and identified George, Bishop of Bamberg who proclaimed a penal code in 1507, as the originator of the first examples of codes where medical evidence was a necessity in certain cases. However, it was the Constitutio Criminalis Carolina – the code of law published and proclaimed in 1553 in Germany by Emperor Charles V – that has a reasonable claim to have originated legal medicine as a specialty. Within these codes of 1553, expert medical testimony became a requirement rather than an option to give opinions in cases of murder, wounding, poisoning, hanging, drowning, infanticide and abortion. In 1575, the military surgeon Ambrose Paré produced his book on medicolegal reports and also wrote about deaths from lightning, antemortem versus post-mortem injuries, and poisoning by carbon monoxide and corrosives.

In 1595, the text "Methods Testificandi" was published by Codronchius, a physician from Imola and, in the following year, Fortunatus Fidelis published "De Relationibus Medicorum" from Palermo. The French physician, Séverin Pineau wrote his book on defloration and virginity, and he discussed at some length the existence of the hymen. Paulo Zacchia (1584–1659) was the principal physician to Pope Innocent X and Alexander VII and between 1621 and 1635 published "Quaestiones Medico Legales", a huge and authoritative work in several volumes including subjects such as age, legitimacy, insanity poisoning, virginity, rape and wounds. Paolo Zacchia has been referred to as "*the father of forensic medicine*" (7). Figure 1.1 shows the frontispiece of one of the original volumes and a facsimile version of that is still available (Figure 1.2). Beck & Darwell also referred to the "Pandects of Valentini" published in Germany in 1702 which they describe as "*an extensive retrospect of the opinions and decisions of preceding writers on legal medicine*" (11). In France in 1796, Fodere published the first edition in three octavo volumes of his work "Les lois éclairées par les sciences physiques, ou traité de médecine-légale et d'hygiène publique".

Autopsies for medicolegal purposes were well documented in parts of Italy and Germany five centuries

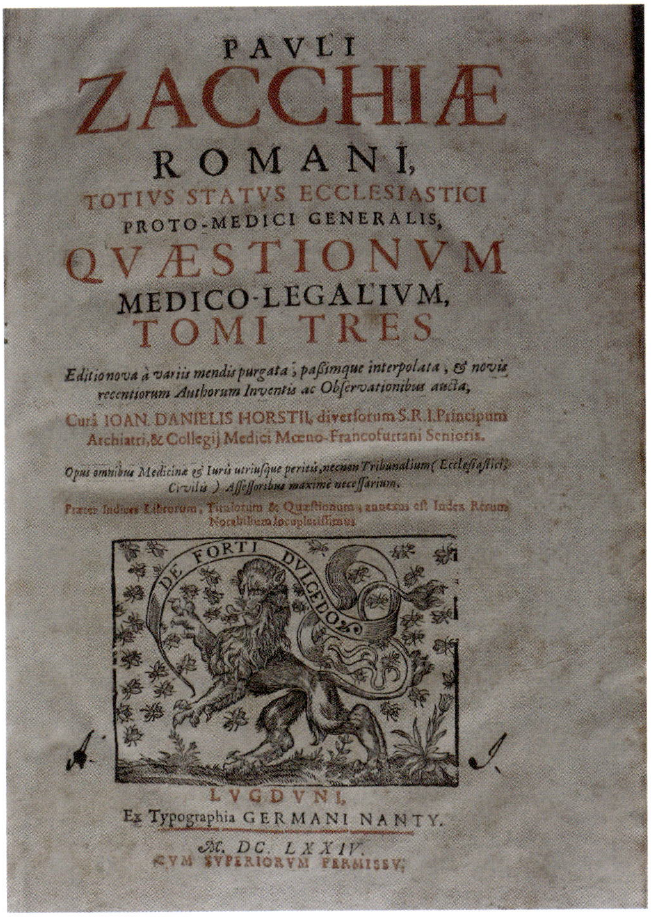
PAVLI
ZACCHIÆ
ROMANI,
TOTIVS STATVS ECCLESIASTICI
PROTO-MEDICI GENERALIS,
QVÆSTIONVM
MEDICO-LEGALIVM,
TOMI TRES

LVGDVNI,
Ex Typographia GERMANI NANTY.
M. DC. LXXIV.
CVM SVPERIORVM PERMISSV.

1.1 Frontispiece of one of the original volumes of Paulo Zacchia's *Quaestiones Medico Legales*. This one dates from 1674.

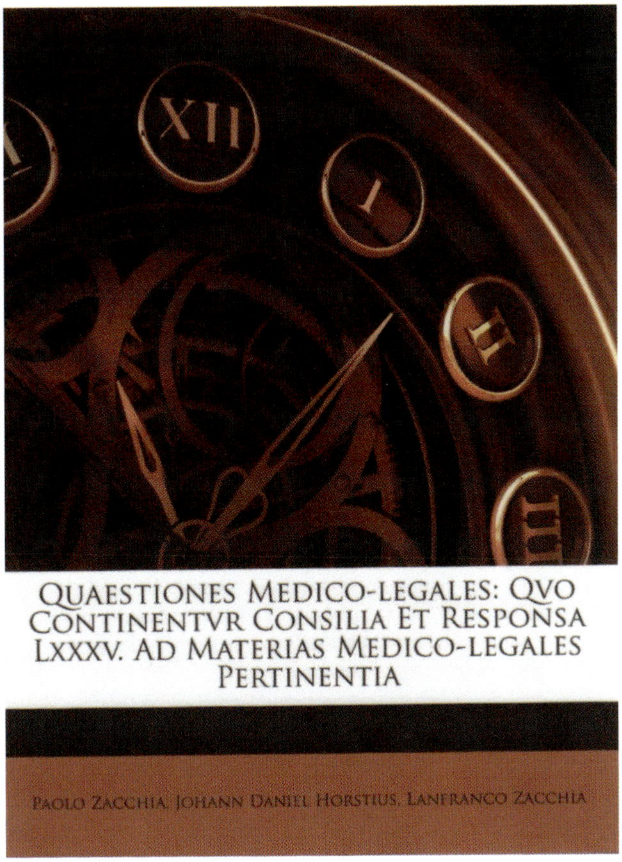

1.2 A facsmile version of Paulo Zacchia's *Quaestiones Medico Legales*.

before the use of such procedures within the English coronial setting. The use of such expertise was not limited to deaths or to Europe. Cassar describes an early example of such expertise reviewing a recorded medicolegal report of the sixteenth century from Malta from 1542, which refers to the depositions of two medical experts, Dr Joseph Callus and Dr Rainerio de Bonellis in which it was established that the male partner was incapable of sexual intercourse, and this resulted in a marriage annulment (12).

These historical references of medical expertise being used in the context of law prior to the eighteenth and nineteenth centuries confirm the longstanding recognition of the need for, and the status of, forensic and legal medicine in many jurisdictions.

PUBLISHED WORKS FROM THE EIGHTEENTH CENTURY ONWARD

Multiple books and treatises concerning forensic medicine and medical jurisprudence were published in the English language (or translated into English) in the eighteenth century. What is notable is that the issues addressed by many of the authors are ones that would not be out of place in a contemporary setting, although many of these principles are restated today as though they are new. Table 1.3 provides examples of questions addressed in such texts that have direct relevance today (13–15). During the course of the next two centuries, numerous medicolegal texts appeared in Germany and France; chairs of medical jurisprudence were installed in Paris, Strasbourg, and Montpellier with such major authorities as Mahon, and later Orfila and Tardieu in Paris, Chaussier in Dijon, Foderé in Strasbourg, Johann Ludwig Casper in Berlin, and Eduard Ritter von Hofmann in Vienna.

In 1783, William Hunter (16) published essays related to the findings in the murder of bastard children, and this may be the earliest "forensic medicine" publication from England. The first larger work ("Elements of Medical Jurisprudence") was published in 1788 by Samuel Farr, itself translated from 1767 Fazelius of Geneva's publication "Elementa Medicinae Forensis". Davis refers to these and to "Remarks on Medical Jurisprudence" by William Dease of Dublin, and OW Bartley of Bristol's "Treatise on Forensic Medicine or Medical Jurisprudence" (17). Davis considers both of these of poor quality and makes the statement that the "first original and satisfactory work" was George Male's "Epitome of Juridical or Forensic Medicine", published in 1816. A second edition was published in 1821. Male was a physician at Birmingham General Hospital and is sometimes considered to be the father of English medical jurisprudence. However, the first course of lectures to medical students on legal medicine were given in Britain by Andrew Duncan (senior), then Professor of Physiology in Edinburgh, in 1789. These were published in 1792 as the Heads of Lectures on Medical Jurisprudence or the Institutiones Medicinae Legalis. Duncan's eldest son occupied the first chair of medical jurisprudence and medical police created by central government as a Regius Chair with royal patronage in 1807. Chairs were later established in Glasgow (1839) – Robert Cowan, and in Aberdeen (1857) – Francis Ogston. In England, the first professor was John Gordon Smith (1773–1832) and later George Edward Male (1779–1845). Others followed later in the London medical schools. In 1856, a course in medical jurisprudence was an essential prerequisite for admission to the Faculty of Advocates in Edinburgh (18, 19).

Benjamin Rush (1745–1813) in New York (yet another Edinburgh medical graduate) and a signatory of the Declaration of Independence, wrote on medical jurisprudence. In 1804, an Edinburgh-trained physician, JA Stringham (1775–1813), was appointed as a lecturer in medical jurisprudence at the College of Physicians and Surgeons of New York and was appointed to a Chair in 1813.

Texts on forensic medicine began to appear more rapidly with much broader content. John Gordon Smith (17) in his book "The Principles of Forensic Medicine Systematically Arranged and Applied to British Practice", published in 1821, stated that "*Forensic Medicine – Legal, Judiciary, or Juridical Medicine – and Medical Jurisprudence are synonymous terms.*"

Figure 1.3(a) and (b) shows the frontispiece of this book and reproduces the forms from it used to document information about neonatal deaths and stillborn babies. Smith refers in his Preface to the earlier books and notes: "*It is but justice to mention that the American schools have outstripped us in attention to Forensic Medicine*" – and he may have been referring to the work of Theodore Romeyn Beck and others. TR Beck and his brother JB Beck (both pupils of Stringham) became leaders in their field by their publications and lecturing.

TR Beck published the first American textbook two years later. The 3rd edition of "Elements of Medical Jurisprudence" was published (with John Darwall) in 1829 and this edition helpfully provides (for medical historians at least) a "*catalogue of books referred to*" extracts of which are reproduced in Figure 1.4 (20). He had provided his first lectures on medical jurisprudence in 1815 at Western Medical College, New York.

TABLE 1.3 Examples of questions (and their sources) raised in historical texts relevant today
How far can medical jurists, from the external inspection of a body, form an opinion as to the length of time that a person has been dead? (13)
What weapon was used? Was the injury inflicted during life or after death? Was the injury the result of accident, or self-inflicted or inflicted by another? (14)
Was death due to drowning or to some other cause operating before immersion? (14)
Was the drowning accidental, suicidal or homicidal? (14)
Can a female during sleep be violated without her knowledge? (14)
Of whom is this body? (13)
Is ecchymosis a necessary result of violence? (20)

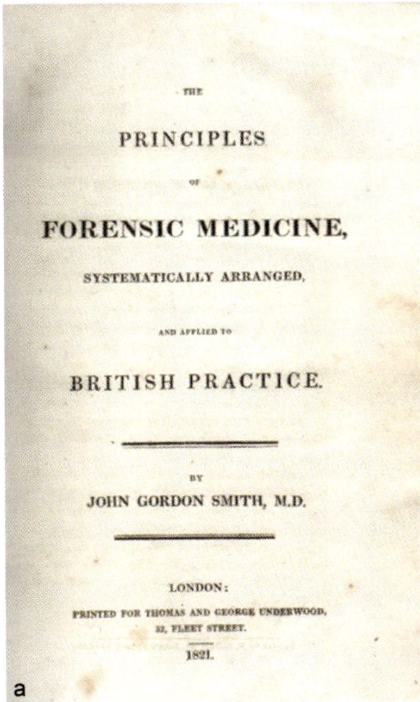

THE

PRINCIPLES

OF

FORENSIC MEDICINE,

SYSTEMATICALLY ARRANGED,

AND APPLIED TO

BRITISH PRACTICE.

BY

JOHN GORDON SMITH, M.D.

LONDON:

PRINTED FOR THOMAS AND GEORGE UNDERWOOD,

32, FLEET STREET.

1821.

a

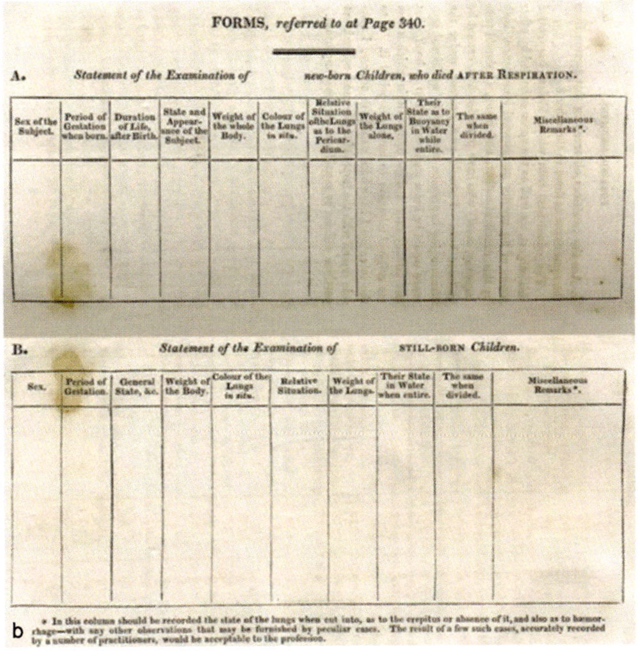

FORMS, *referred to at Page 340.*

A. *Statement of the Examination of new-born Children, who died* AFTER RESPIRATION.

Sex of the Subject.	Period of Gestation when born.	Duration of Life, after Birth.	State and Appearance of the Subject.	Weight of the whole Body.	Colour of the Lungs in situ.	Relative Situation of the Lungs as to the Pericardium.	Weight of the Lungs alone.	Their State as to Buoyancy in Water while entire.	The same when divided.	Miscellaneous Remarks*.

B. *Statement of the Examination of* STILL-BORN *Children.*

Sex.	Period of Gestation.	General State, &c.	Weight of the Body.	Colour of the Lungs in situ.	Relative Situation.	Weight of the Lungs.	Their State in Water when entire.	The same when divided.	Miscellaneous Remarks*.

* In this column should be recorded the state of the lungs when cut into, as to the crepitus or absence of it, and also as to hemorrhage—with any other observations that may be furnished by peculiar cases. The result of a few such cases, accurately recorded by a number of practitioners, would be acceptable to the profession.

b

1.3 John Gordon Smith's 1821 *The principles of forensic medicine systematically arranged and applied to British practice.* **(a)** and **(b)** show the frontispiece of this book and reproduce the forms from it used to document information about neonatal deaths and stillborn babies.

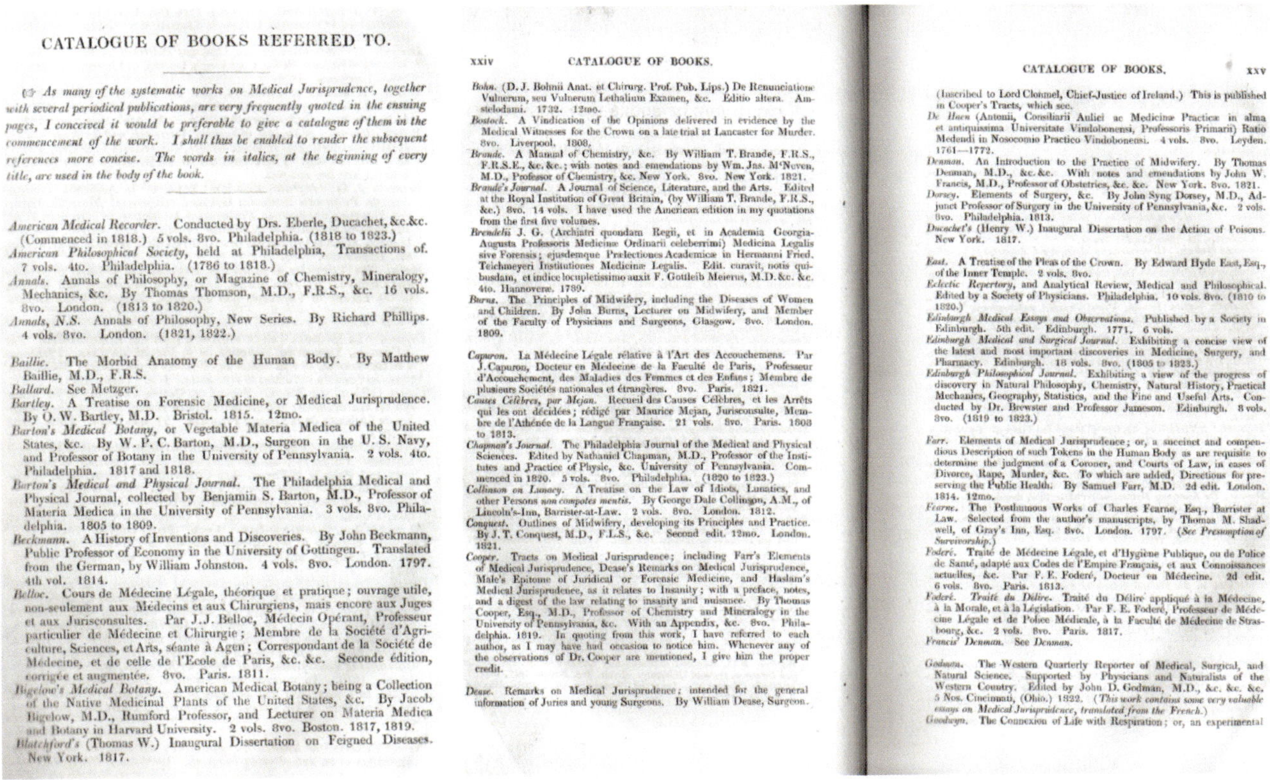

CATALOGUE OF BOOKS REFERRED TO.

☞ *As many of the systematic works on Medical Jurisprudence, together with several periodical publications, are very frequently quoted in the ensuing pages, I conceived it would be preferable to give a catalogue of them in the commencement of the work. I shall thus be enabled to render the subsequent references more concise. The words in italics, at the beginning of every title, are used in the body of the book.*

American Medical Recorder. Conducted by Drs. Eberle, Ducachet, &c.&c. (Commenced in 1818.) 5 vols. 8vo. Philadelphia. (1818 to 1823.)

American Philosophical Society, held at Philadelphia, Transactions of. 7 vols. 4to. Philadelphia. (1786 to 1818.)

Annals. Annals of Philosophy, or Magazine of Chemistry, Mineralogy, Mechanics, &c. By Thomas Thomson, M.D., F.R.S., &c. 16 vols. 8vo. London. (1813 to 1820.)

Annals, N.S. Annals of Philosophy, New Series. By Richard Phillips. 4 vols. 8vo. London. (1821, 1822.)

Baillie. The Morbid Anatomy of the Human Body. By Matthew Baillie, M.D., F.R.S.

Ballard. See Metzger.

Bartley. A Treatise on Forensic Medicine, or Medical Jurisprudence. By O. W. Bartley, M.D. Bristol. 1815. 12mo.

Barton's Medical Botany, or Vegetable Materia Medica of the United States, &c. By W. P. C. Barton, M.D., Surgeon in the U. S. Navy, and Professor of Botany in the University of Pennsylvania. 2 vols. 4to. Philadelphia. 1817 and 1818.

Barton's Medical and Physical Journal. The Philadelphia Medical and Physical Journal, collected by Benjamin S. Barton, M.D., Professor of Materia Medica in the University of Pennsylvania. 3 vols. 8vo. Philadelphia. 1805 to 1809.

Beckmann. A History of Inventions and Discoveries. By John Beckmann, Public Professor of Economy in the University of Gottingen. Translated from the German, by William Johnston. 4 vols. 8vo. London. 1797. 4th vol. 1814.

Belloc. Cours de Médecine Légale, théorique et pratique; ouvrage utile, non-seulement aux Médecins et aux Chirurgiens, mais encore aux Juges et aux Jurisconsultes. Par J.J. Belloc, Médecin Opérant, Professeur particulier de Médecine et Chirurgie; Membre de la Société d'Agriculture, Sciences, et Arts, séante à Agen; Correspondant de la Société de Médecine, et de celle de l'Ecole de Paris, &c. &c. Seconde édition, corrigée et augmentée. 8vo. Paris. 1811.

Bigelow's Medical Botany. American Medical Botany; being a Collection of the Native Medicinal Plants of the United States, &c. By Jacob Bigelow, M.D., Rumford Professor, and Lecturer on Materia Medica and Botany in Harvard University. 2 vols. 8vo. Boston. 1817, 1819.

Blatchford's (Thomas W.) Inaugural Dissertation on Feigned Diseases. New York. 1817.

xxiv CATALOGUE OF BOOKS.

Bohn. (D. J. Bohnii Anat. et Chirurg. Prof. Pub. Lips.) De Renunciatione Vulnerum, seu Vulnerum Lethalium Examen, &c. Editio altera. Amstelodami. 1732. 12mo.

Bostock. A Vindication of the Opinions delivered in evidence by the Medical Witnesses for the Crown on a late trial at Lancaster for Murder. 8vo. Liverpool. 1808.

Brande. A Manual of Chemistry, &c. By William T. Brande, F.R.S., F.R.S.E., &c. &c.; with notes and emendations by Wm. Jas. M'Neven, M.D., Professor of Chemistry, &c. New York. 8vo. New York. 1821.

Brande's Journal. A Journal of Science, Literature, and the Arts. Edited at the Royal Institution of Great Britain, (by William T. Brande, F.R.S., &c.) 8vo. 14 vols. I have used the American edition in my quotations from the first five volumes.

Brendelii J. G. (Archiatri quondam Regii, et in Academia Georgia-Augusta Professoris Medicinæ Ordinarii celeberrimi) Medicina Legalis sive Forensis; ejusdemque Prælectiones Academicæ in Hermanni Fried. Teichmeyeri Institutiones Medicinæ Legalis. Edit. curavit, notis quibusdam, et indice locupletissimo auxit F. Gottleib Meierus, M.D. &c. &c. 4to. Hannoveræ. 1789.

Burns. The Principles of Midwifery, including the Diseases of Women and Children. By John Burns, Lecturer on Midwifery, and Member of the Faculty of Physicians and Surgeons, Glasgow. 8vo. London. 1809.

Capuron. La Médecine Légale rélative à l'Art des Accouchemens. Par J. Capuron, Docteur en Médecine de la Faculté de Paris, Professeur d'Accouchement, des Maladies des Femmes et des Enfans; Membre de plusieurs Sociétés nationales et étrangères. 8vo. Paris. 1821.

Causes Célèbres, par Mejan. Recueil des Causes Célèbres, et les Arrêts qui les ont décidées; rédigé par Maurice Mejan, Jurisconsulte, Membre de l'Athénée de la Langue Française. 21 vols. 8vo. Paris. 1808 to 1813.

Chapman's Journal. The Philadelphia Journal of the Medical and Physical Sciences. Edited by Nathaniel Chapman, M.D., Professor of the Institutes and Practice of Physic, &c. University of Pennsylvania. Commenced in 1820. 5 vols. 8vo. Philadelphia. (1820 to 1823.)

Collinson on Lunacy. A Treatise on the Law of Idiots, Lunatics, and other Persons *non compotes mentis.* By George Dale Collinson, A.M., of Lincoln's-Inn, Barrister-at-Law. 2 vols. 8vo. London. 1812.

Conquest. Outlines of Midwifery, developing its Principles and Practice. By J. T. Conquest, M.D., F.L.S., &c. Second edit. 12mo. London. 1821.

Cooper. Tracts on Medical Jurisprudence; including Farr's Elements of Medical Jurisprudence, Dease's Remarks on Medical Jurisprudence, Male's Epitome of Juridical or Forensic Medicine, and Haslam's Medical Jurisprudence, as it relates to Insanity; with a preface, notes, and a digest of the law relating to insanity and nuisance. By Thomas Cooper, Esq., M.D., Professor of Chemistry and Mineralogy in the University of Pennsylvania, &c. With an Appendix, &c. 8vo. Philadelphia. 1819. In quoting from this work, I have referred to each author, as I may have had occasion to notice him. Whenever any of the observations of Dr. Cooper are mentioned, I give him the proper credit.

Dease. Remarks on Medical Jurisprudence; intended for the general information of Juries and young Surgeons. By William Dease, Surgeon.

CATALOGUE OF BOOKS. xxv

(Inscribed to Lord Clonmel, Chief-Justice of Ireland.) This is published in Cooper's Tracts, which see.

De Haen (Antonii, Consiliarii Aulici ac Medicinæ Practicæ in alma et antiquissima Universitate Vindobonensi, Professoris Primarii) Ratio Medendi in Nosocomio Practico Vindobonensi. 4 vols. 8vo. Leyden. 1761—1772.

Denman. An Introduction to the Practice of Midwifery. By Thomas Denman, M.D., &c. &c. With notes and emendations by John W. Francis, M.D., Professor of Obstetrics, &c. &c. New York. 8vo. 1821.

Dorsey. Elements of Surgery, &c. By John Syng Dorsey, M.D., Adjunct Professor of Surgery in the University of Pennsylvania, &c. 2 vols. 8vo. Philadelphia. 1813.

Ducachet's (Henry W.) Inaugural Dissertation on the Action of Poisons. New York. 1817.

East. A Treatise of the Pleas of the Crown. By Edward Hyde East, Esq., of the Inner Temple. 2 vols. 8vo.

Eclectic Repertory, and Analytical Review, Medical and Philosophical. Edited by a Society of Physicians. Philadelphia. 10 vols. 8vo. (1810 to 1820.)

Edinburgh Medical Essays and Observations. Published by a Society in Edinburgh. 5th edit. Edinburgh. 1771. 6 vols.

Edinburgh Medical and Surgical Journal. Exhibiting a concise view of the latest and most important discoveries in Medicine, Surgery, and Pharmacy. Edinburgh. 18 vols. 8vo. (1805 to 1823.)

Edinburgh Philosophical Journal. Exhibiting a view of the progress of discovery in Natural Philosophy, Chemistry, Natural History, Practical Mechanics, Geography, Statistics, and the Fine and Useful Arts. Conducted by Dr. Brewster and Professor Jameson. Edinburgh. 8 vols. 8vo. (1819 to 1823.)

Farr. Elements of Medical Jurisprudence; or, a succinct and compendious Description of such Tokens in the Human Body as are requisite to determine the judgment of a Coroner, and Courts of Law, in cases of Divorce, Rape, Murder, &c. To which are added, Directions for preserving the Public Health. By Samuel Farr, M.D. 2d edit. London. 1814. 12mo.

Fearne. The Posthumous Works of Charles Fearne, Esq., Barrister at Law. Selected from the author's manuscripts, by Thomas M. Shadwell, of Gray's Inn, Esq. 8vo. London. 1797. (*See Presumption of Survivorship.*)

Foderé. Traité de Médecine Légale, et d'Hygiène Publique, ou de Police de Santé, adapté aux Codes de l'Empire Français, et aux Connoissances actuelles, &c. Par F. E. Foderé, Docteur en Médecine. 2d edit. 6 vols. 8vo. Paris. 1813.

Foderé. Traité du Délire. Traité du Délire appliqué à la Médecine, à la Morale, et à la Législation. Par F. E. Foderé, Professeur de Médecine Légale et de Police Médicale, à la Faculté de Médecine de Strasbourg, &c. 2 vols. 8vo. Paris. 1817.

Francis' Denman. See *Denman.*

Godman. The Western Quarterly Reporter of Medical, Surgical, and Natural Science. Supported by Physicians and Naturalists of the Western Country. Edited by John D. Godman, M.D., &c. &c. &c. 5 Nos. Cincinnati, (Ohio.) 1822. (*This work contains some very valuable essays on Medical Jurisprudence, translated from the French.*)

Goodwyn. The Connexion of Life with Respiration; or, an experimental

1.4 "Catalogue of books referred to" from Theodore Romeyn Beck's 3rd Edition of *Elements of jurisprudence*, published in 1824.

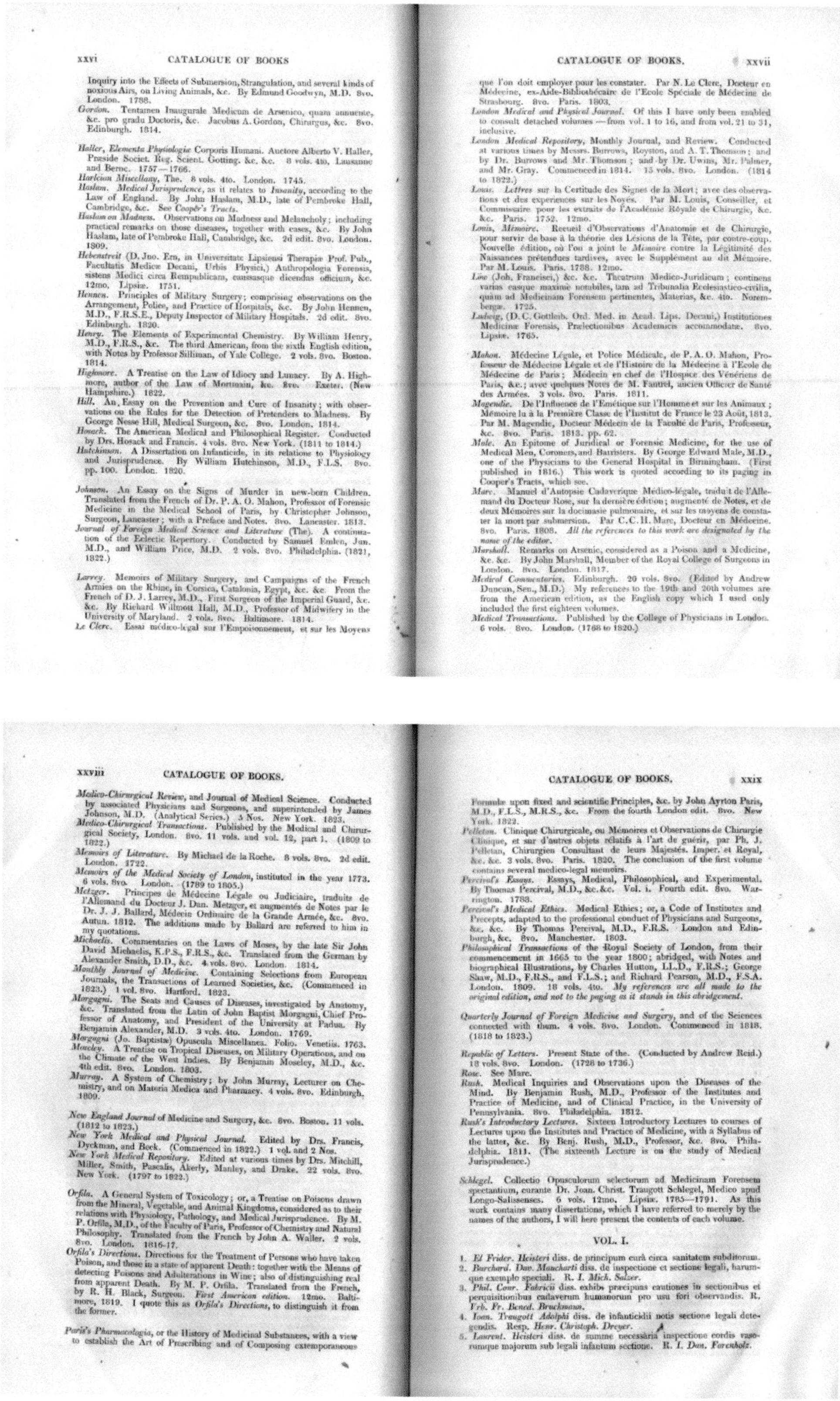

xxvi CATALOGUE OF BOOKS

Inquiry into the Effects of Submersion, Strangulation, and several kinds of noxious Airs, on Living Animals, &c. By Edmund Goodwyn, M.D. 8vo. London. 1788.

Gordon. Tentamen Inaugurale Medicum de Arsenico, quam annuente, &c. pro gradu Doctoris, &c. Jacobus A. Gordon, Chirurgus, &c. 8vo. Edinburgh. 1814.

Haller, Elementa Physiologiæ Corporis Humani. Auctore Alberto V. Haller, Præside Societ. Reg. Scient. Gotting. &c. &c. 8 vols. 4to. Lausanne and Berne. 1757—1766.

Harleian Miscellany, The. 8 vols. 4to. London. 1745.

Haslam. Medical Jurisprudence, as it relates to *Insanity,* according to the Law of England. By John Haslam, M.D., late of Pembroke Hall, Cambridge, &c. See *Cooper's Tracts.*

Haslam on Madness. Observations on Madness and Melancholy; including practical remarks on those diseases, together with cases, &c. By John Haslam, late of Pembroke Hall, Cambridge, &c. 2d edit. 8vo. London. 1809.

Hebenstreit (D. Jno. Ern, in Universitate Lipsiensi Therapiæ Prof. Pub., Facultatis Medicæ Decani, Urbis Physici,) Anthropologia Forensis, sistens Medici circa Rempublicam, caussasque dicendas officium, &c. 12mo. Lipsiæ. 1751.

Hennen. Principles of Military Surgery; comprising observations on the Arrangement, Police, and Practice of Hospitals, &c. By John Hennen, M.D., F.R.S.E., Deputy Inspector of Military Hospitals. 2d edit. 8vo. Edinburgh. 1820.

Henry. The Elements of Experimental Chemistry. By William Henry, M.D., F.R.S., &c. The third American, from the sixth English edition, with Notes by Professor Silliman, of Yale College. 2 vols. 8vo. Boston. 1814.

Highmore. A Treatise on the Law of Idiocy and Lunacy. By A. Highmore, author of the Law of Mortmain, &c. 8vo. Exeter. (New Hampshire.) 1822.

Hill. An Essay on the Prevention and Cure of Insanity; with observations on the Rules for the Detection of Pretenders to Madness. By George Nesse Hill, Medical Surgeon, &c. 8vo. London. 1814.

Hosack. The American Medical and Philosophical Register. Conducted by Drs. Hosack and Francis. 4 vols. 8vo. New York. (1811 to 1814.)

Hutchinson. A Dissertation on Infanticide, in its relations to Physiology and Jurisprudence. By William Hutchinson, M.D., F.L.S. 8vo. pp. 100. London. 1820.

Johnson. An Essay on the Signs of Murder in new-born Children. Translated from the French of Dr. P. A. O. Mahon, Professor of Forensic Medicine in the Medical School of Paris, by Christopher Johnson, Surgeon, Lancaster; with a Preface and Notes. 8vo. Lancaster. 1813.

Journal of Foreign Medical Science and Literature (The). A continuation of the Eclectic Repertory. Conducted by Samuel Emlen, Jun. M.D., and William Price, M.D. 2 vols. 8vo. Philadelphia. (1821, 1822.)

Larrey. Memoirs of Military Surgery, and Campaigns of the French Armies on the Rhine, in Corsica, Catalonia, Egypt, &c. &c. From the French of D. J. Larrey, M.D., First Surgeon of the Imperial Guard, &c. &c. By Richard Willmott Hall, M.D., Professor of Midwifery in the University of Maryland. 2 vols. 8vo. Baltimore. 1814.

Le Clerc. Essai médico-légal sur l'Empoisonnement, et sur les Moyens

CATALOGUE OF BOOKS. xxvii

que l'on doit employer pour les constater. Par N. Le Clerc, Docteur en Médecine, ex-Aide-Bibliothécaire de l'Ecole Spéciale de Médecine de Strasbourg. 8vo. Paris. 1803.

London Medical and Physical Journal. Of this I have only been enabled to consult detached volumes—from vol. 1 to 16, and from vol. 21 to 31, inclusive.

London Medical Repository, Monthly Journal, and Review. Conducted at various times by Messrs. Burrows, Royston, and A. T. Thomson; and by Dr. Burrows and Mr. Thomson; and by Dr. Uwins, Mr. Palmer, and Mr. Gray. Commenced in 1814. 15 vols. 8vo. London. (1814 to 1822.)

Louis. Lettres sur la Certitude des Signes de la Mort; avec des observations et des experiences sur les Noyés. Par M. Louis, Conseiller, et Commissaire pour les extraits de l'Académie Royale de Chirurgie, &c. &c. Paris. 1752. 12mo.

Louis, Mémoire. Recueil d'Observations d'Anatomie et de Chirurgie, pour servir de base à la théorie des Lésions de la Tête, par contre-coup. Nouvelle édition, où l'on a joint le *Mémoire* contre la Légitimité des Naissances prétendues tardives, avec le Supplément au dit Mémoire. Par M. Louis. Paris. 1788. 12mo.

Löw (Joh. Francisci,) &c. &c. Theatrum Medico-Juridicum; continens varias easque maximè notabiles, tam ad Tribunalia Ecclesiastico-civilia, quàm ad Medicinam Forensem pertinentes, Materias, &c. 4to. Norembergæ. 1725.

Ludwig, (D. C. Gottleib. Ord. Med. in Acad. Lips. Decani,) Institutiones Medicinæ Forensis, Prælectionibus Academicis accommodatæ. 8vo. Lipsiæ. 1765.

Mahon. Médecine Légale, et Police Médicale, de P. A. O. Mahon, Professeur de Médecine Légale et de l'Histoire de la Médecine à l'Ecole de Médecine de Paris; Médecin en chef de l'Hospice des Vénériens de Paris, &c.; avec quelques Notes de M. Fautrel, ancien Officier de Santé des Armées. 3 vols. 8vo. Paris. 1811.

Magendie. De l'Influence de l'Emétique sur l'Homme et sur les Animaux; Mémoire lu à la Première Classe de l'Institut de France le 23 Août, 1813. Par M. Magendie, Docteur Médecin de la Faculté de Paris, Professeur, &c. 8vo. Paris. 1813. pp. 62.

Male. An Epitome of Juridical or Forensic Medicine, for the use of Medical Men, Coroners, and Barristers. By George Edward Male, M.D., one of the Physicians to the General Hospital in Birmingham. (First published in 1816.) This work is quoted according to its paging in Cooper's Tracts, which see.

Marc. Manuel d'Autopsie Cadavérique Médico-légale, traduit de l'Allemand du Docteur Rose, sur la dernière édition; augmenté de Notes, et de deux Mémoires sur la docimasie pulmonaire, et sur les moyens de constater la mort par submersion. Par C. C. H. Marc, Docteur en Médecine. 8vo. Paris. 1808. *All the references to this work are designated by the name of the editor.*

Marshall. Remarks on Arsenic, considered as a Poison and a Medicine, &c. &c. By John Marshall, Member of the Royal College of Surgeons in London. 8vo. London. 1817.

Medical Commentaries. Edinburgh. 20 vols. 8vo. (Edited by Andrew Duncan, Sen., M.D.) My references to the 19th and 20th volumes are from the American edition, as the English copy which I used only included the first eighteen volumes.

Medical Transactions. Published by the College of Physicians in London. 6 vols. 8vo. London. (1768 to 1820.)

xxviii CATALOGUE OF BOOKS.

Medico-Chirurgical Review, and Journal of Medical Science. Conducted by associated Physicians and Surgeons, and superintended by James Johnson, M.D. (Analytical Series.) 5 Nos. New York. 1823.

Medico-Chirurgical Transactions. Published by the Medical and Chirurgical Society, London. 8vo. 11 vols. and vol. 12, part 1. (1809 to 1822.)

Memoirs of Literature. By Michael de la Roche. 8 vols. 8vo. 2d edit. London. 1722.

Memoirs of the Medical Society of London, instituted in the year 1773. 6 vols. 8vo. London. (1789 to 1805.)

Metzger. Principes de Médecine Légale ou Judiciaire, traduits de l'Allemand du Docteur J. Dan. Metzger, et augmentés de Notes par le Dr. J. J. Ballard, Médecin Ordinaire de la Grande Armée, &c. 8vo. Autun. 1812. The additions made by Ballard are referred to him in my quotations.

Michaelis. Commentaries on the Laws of Moses, by the late Sir John David Michaelis, K.P.S., F.R.S., &c. Translated from the German by Alexander Smith, D.D., &c. 4 vols. 8vo. London. 1814.

Monthly Journal of Medicine. Containing Selections from European Journals, the Transactions of Learned Societies, &c. (Commenced in 1823.) 1 vol. 8vo. Hartford. 1823.

Morgagni. The Seats and Causes of Diseases, investigated by Anatomy, &c. Translated from the Latin of John Baptist Morgagni, Chief Professor of Anatomy, and President of the University at Padua. By Benjamin Alexander, M.D. 3 vols. 4to. London. 1769.

Morgagni (Jo. Baptistæ) Opuscula Miscellanea. Folio. Venetiis. 1763.

Moseley. A Treatise on Tropical Diseases, on Military Operations, and on the Climate of the West Indies. By Benjamin Moseley, M.D., &c. 4th edit. 8vo. London. 1803.

Murray. A System of Chemistry; by John Murray, Lecturer on Chemistry, and on Materia Medica and Pharmacy. 4 vols. 8vo. Edinburgh. 1809.

New England Journal of Medicine and Surgery, &c. 8vo. Boston. 11 vols. (1812 to 1823.)

New York Medical and Physical Journal. Edited by Drs. Francis, Dyckman, and Beck. (Commenced in 1822.) 1 vol. and 2 Nos.

New York Medical Repository. Edited at various times by Drs. Mitchill, Miller, Smith, Pascalis, Akerly, Manley, and Drake. 22 vols. 8vo. New York. (1797 to 1822.)

Orfila. A General System of Toxicology; or, a Treatise on Poisons drawn from the Mineral, Vegetable, and Animal Kingdoms, considered as to their relations with Physiology, Pathology, and Medical Jurisprudence. By M. P. Orfila, M.D., of the Faculty of Paris, Professor of Chemistry and Natural Philosophy. Translated from the French by John A. Waller. 2 vols. 8vo. London. 1816-17.

Orfila's Directions. Directions for the Treatment of Persons who have taken Poison, and those in a state of apparent Death: together with the Means of detecting Poisons and Adulterations in Wine; also of distinguishing real from apparent Death. By M. P. Orfila. Translated from the French, by R. H. Black, Surgeon. *First American edition.* 12mo. Baltimore, 1819. I quote this as *Orfila's Directions,* to distinguish it from the former.

Paris's Pharmacologia, or the History of Medicinal Substances, with a view to establish the Art of Prescribing and of Composing extemporaneous

CATALOGUE OF BOOKS. xxix

Formulæ upon fixed and scientific Principles, &c. by John Ayrton Paris, M.D., F.L.S., M.R.S., &c. From the fourth London edit. 8vo. New York. 1822.

Pelletan. Clinique Chirurgicale, ou Mémoires et Observations de Chirurgie Clinique, et sur d'autres objets rélatifs à l'art de guérir, par Ph. J. Pelletan, Chirurgien Consultant de leurs Majestés. Imper. et Royal, &c. &c. 3 vols. 8vo. Paris. 1820. The conclusion of the first volume contains several medico-legal memoirs.

Percival's Essays. Essays, Medical, Philosophical, and Experimental. By Thomas Percival, M.D., &c. &c. Vol. i. Fourth edit. 8vo. Warrington. 1788.

Percival's Medical Ethics. Medical Ethics; or, a Code of Institutes and Precepts, adapted to the professional conduct of Physicians and Surgeons, &c. &c. By Thomas Percival, M.D., F.R.S. London and Edinburgh, &c. 8vo. Manchester. 1803.

Philosophical Transactions of the Royal Society of London, from their commencement in 1665 to the year 1800; abridged, with Notes and biographical Illustrations, by Charles Hutton, LL.D., F.R.S.; George Shaw, M.D., F.R.S., and F.L.S.; and Richard Pearson, M.D., F.S.A. London. 1809. 18 vols. 4to. *My references are all made to the original edition, and not to the paging as it stands in this abridgement.*

Quarterly Journal of Foreign Medicine and Surgery, and of the Sciences connected with them. 4 vols. 8vo. London. Commenced in 1818. (1818 to 1823.)

Republic of Letters. Present State of the. (Conducted by Andrew Reid.) 18 vols. 8vo. London. (1728 to 1736.)

Rose. See Marc.

Rush. Medical Inquiries and Observations upon the Diseases of the Mind. By Benjamin Rush, M.D., Professor of the Institutes and Practice of Medicine, and of Clinical Practice, in the University of Pennsylvania. 8vo. Philadelphia. 1812.

Rush's Introductory Lectures. Sixteen Introductory Lectures to courses of Lectures upon the Institutes and Practice of Medicine, with a Syllabus of the latter, &c. By Benj. Rush, M.D., Professor, &c. 8vo. Philadelphia. 1811. (The sixteenth Lecture is on the study of Medical Jurisprudence.)

Schlegel. Collectio Opusculorum selectorum ad Medicinam Forensem spectantium, curante Dr. Joan. Christ. Traugott Schlegel, Medico apud Longo-Salissenses. 6 vols. 12mo. Lipsiæ. 1785—1791. As this work contains many dissertations, which I have referred to merely by the names of the authors, I will here present the contents of each volume.

VOL. I.

1. *El Frider. Heisteri* diss. de principum curâ circa sanitatem subditorum.
2. *Burchard. Dav. Mauchartí* diss. de inspectione et sectione legali, harumque exemplo speciali. R. *I. Mich. Salzer.*
3. *Phil. Conr. Fabricii* diss. exhibs præcipuas cautiones in sectionibus et perquisitionibus cadaverum humanorum pro usu fori observandis. R. *Frh. Fr. Bened. Bruckmann.*
4. *Ioan. Traugott Adolphi* diss. de infanticidii notis sectione legali detegendis. Resp. *Henr. Christoph. Dreyer.*
5. *Laurent. Heisteri* diss. de summe necessària inspectione cordis vasorumque majorum sub legali infantum sectione. R. *I. Dan. Forenholz.*

1.4 (Continued)

Alfred Swaine Taylor (Lecturer on Medical Jurisprudence at Guy's Hospital) in his book "A Manual of Medical Jurisprudence" defined medical jurisprudence as "*that science, which teaches the application of every branch of medical knowledge to the purpose of the law*" (21). In his preface to the 5th edition in 1854 he notes that "*. . . there have been issues from the press, since the first publication of this work in November 1843, ten thousand seven hundred and fifty copies*" – a number which must have delighted the publishers (22).

There was a clear demand for such books and for repeat editions, and "Traill's Outlines of a Course of Lectures on Medical Jurisprudence" (3) (published in 1840 when he was Regius Professor of Jurisprudence and Medical Police at Edinburgh) was the second edition of a book initially published in 1834 (3). It was in Edinburgh in 1807 where the first Chair of Forensic Medicine was established in the UK, with subsequent non-professorial academic forensic medicine posts at Guy's Hospital and Charing Cross Hospital, London. In 1839 and 1875, respectively, academic chairs of medical jurisprudence were created in Glasgow and Aberdeen (23).

This demand for publications was not limited to the USA and Europe. IB Lyon – Brigade Surgeon to Bombay Medical Services and Professor of Chemistry and Medical Jurisprudence at Grant Medical College, Bombay makes reference to the availability of other works from India in his 1889 "A Textbook of Medical Jurisprudence for India" stating in the Preface "*. . . my object has been to supply a want which I have often felt while lecturing on Medical Jurisprudence in an Indian college, viz, that of a concise manual specially adapted for use in India. In doing so I have made the freest use of the numerous standard treatises on Medical Jurisprudence and subject allied to it and of the admirable Bengal Medico-legal Reports of my friends Surgeons-Major K McLeod and R Harvey*" (14).

A common theme of most of these texts could not be said to be brevity. It is of note, and possibly reflecting the verbosity and length of some texts, that William McCallin in his 1901 "Introduction to Medical Jurisprudence" stated "*...In this book an attempt has been made to state the essentials of Medical Jurisprudence and, at the same time, as briefly as possible...The points of law most likely to arise are set forth without comment, since in this form the reader can find out what the law ....more satisfactorily than when it is stated together with confusing opinions with regard to what it ought to be*" (24). Sentiments with which it is hard to disagree.

Illustrations were initially quite limited, often simple line drawings, or simple concepts such as the series of heart tracings taken after judicial hanging (25) (Figure 1.5). However, by the end of the nineteenth century, new techniques meant that images could be reproduced providing striking examples of conditions described. Figure 1.6 shows examples from the 1898 "Atlas of Legal Medicine" produced by Dr E Von Hofmann, Professor of Legal Medicine and Director of the Medical Institute in Vienna. In the Preface to the English translation of the Atlas, Frederick Peterson states "*There is perhaps no field*

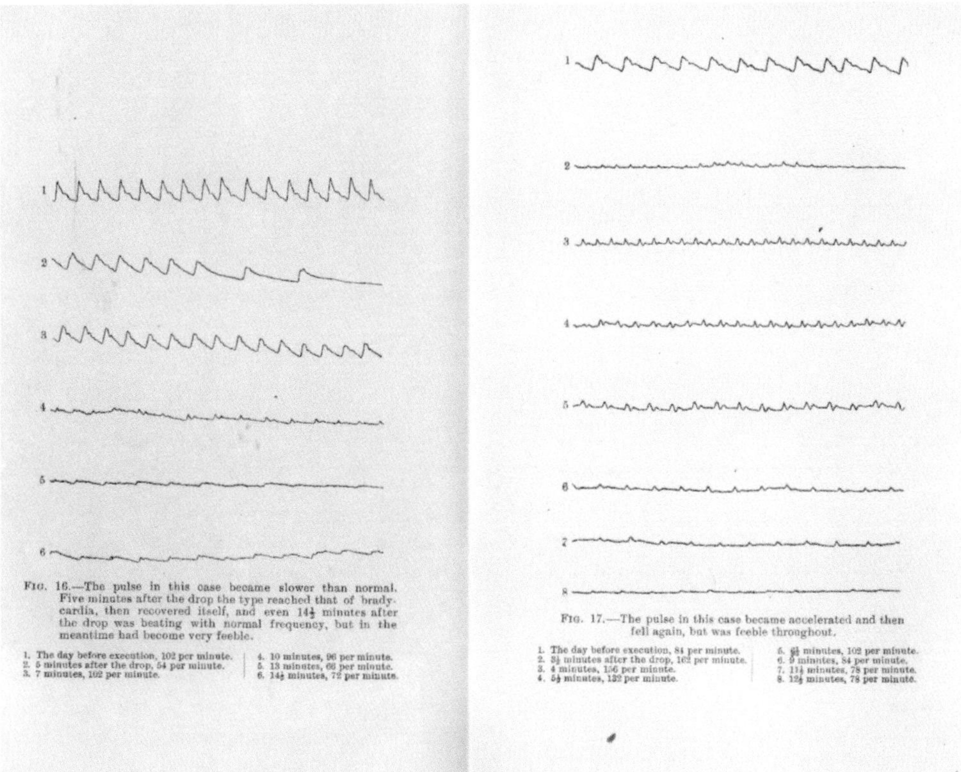

1.5 A series of heart tracings taken after judicial hanging taken from RJM Buchanan (25) Dr Buchanan writes: "The heart may, however, continue to beat for a varying period after death – in some cases as long as 14 and a half minutes. The following interesting series of pulse tracings were taken by Dr Llewellyn Morgan of Liverpool and kindly placed at my disposal."

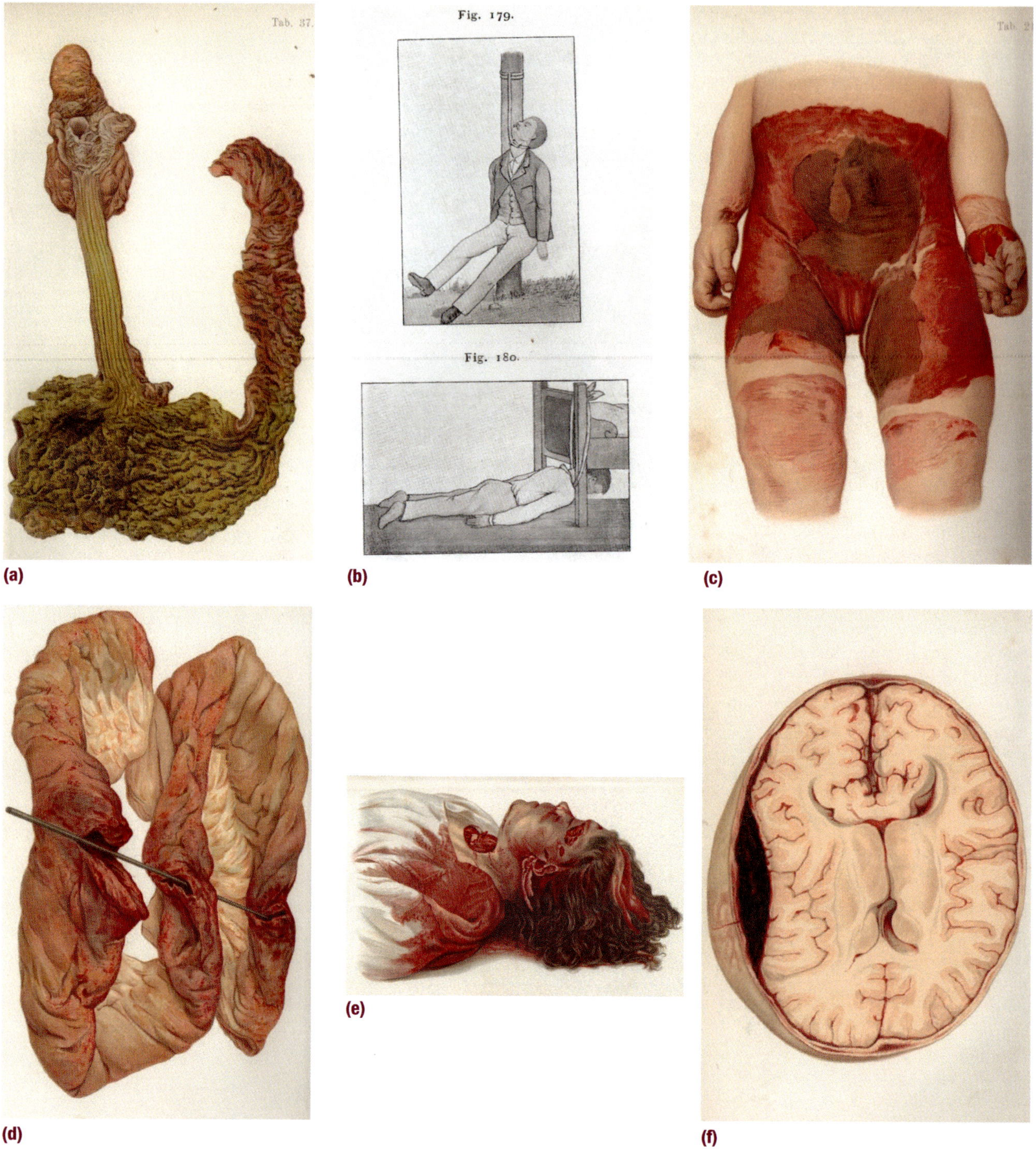

1.6 Images from E. Von Hofmann *Atlas of Legal Medicine*. WB Saunders. Philadelphia. 1898 (26). **(a)** Poisoning with concentrated nitric acid. **(b)** Suicide by hanging in the semi-sitting posture and suicide by hanging in the prone posture. **(c)** Burns produced by flames. **(d)** Triple injury to the small intestine produced by a stab. Peritonitis. **(e)** Murder as the result of various blows inflicted with different instruments. **(f)** Fracture of the base of the skull with extradural hemorrhage.

in science in which the value of illustration is greater than in forensic medicine" (26). A point well made.

The relevant areas of interest to forensic medicine and medical jurisprudence were gradually becoming better defined. Table 1.4 summarizes the chapter contents of Smith's (1821) text (17). It will be noted that almost two centuries ago much of the content is recognizable and relevant to contemporary forensic physicians and forensic pathologists. So, by the end of the nineteenth century, in Europe, India, the UK, and USA and those related jurisdictions a framework of forensic and legal medicine was established that persists today.

TABLE 1.4 Example chapter contents of Smith's (1821) text *The principles of forensic medicine systematically arranged and applied to British practice* (17)

Of sudden death in the healthy state:
• The phenomena of death
• States of the living body resembling death
• Tests of the reality of death
• Sudden death without cause of crimination
• Sudden death from intrinsic or morbid causes
• Death by personal agency or homicide
• Mineral poisons
• Vegetable poisons
• Occult poisoning
• Suffocation
• Drowning
• Hanging
• Smothering
• Death by spontaneous agency or suicide
• Infanticide
Questions arising from injuries done to the person not leading to the extinction of life
• Mutilation
• Rape
Disqualifications for the discharge of social or civil functions
• Mental disqualification
• Mania sexual identity
Personal identity

CONTEMPORARY FORENSIC PATHOLOGY

The forensic pathologist's work is directed to assisting in predominantly judicial or legal processes by establishing manner, time and cause of death. Forensic pathology is a recognized part of the specialty of pathology. Forensic pathology is generally practiced by those with a background in histopathology or anatomic pathology. Their pathologic skills must be supported by an ability to integrate the medical aspects of the workload with toxicologic, scientific and legal issues. Forensic pathologists are assigned a variety of names around the world, for example, legal medicine specialists, medical examiners (the latter with the exception of England & Wales) – but all are primarily involved in the investigation of death – by the use of autopsy and associated techniques including histopathology, toxicology, radiology and genetics. Forensic pathologists may work in academic departments, state or government institutions, or independently. It is to be expected that their work and the reporting of their work is and is seen to be independent of any body or organization, whether police or governmental, and free from political interference. A forensic pathologist is expected to have special knowledge in the following areas: anatomy, cytopathology, hematology, microbiology, immunology, chemical pathology and toxicology. Many forensic pathologists around the world will also have special relationships with public health, occupational health and community health issues, reflecting for some, the historic origins of the workload. Many will be employed by the state or official bodies. Many forensic pathologists will also have workloads relating to the clinical aspects of forensic medicine.

CONTEMPORARY CLINICAL FORENSIC MEDICINE

One definition of clinical forensic medicine is: ". . . Clinical forensic medicine includes all medical (healthcare) fields which may relate to legal, judicial, and police systems" (2). It is only in the last two decades that research and academic interest in clinical forensic medicine has become an area of much more focused interest and research, although doctors have worked with the police in London, UK for more than a century. Figure 1.7 shows the frontispiece of two books written by a police surgeon working in the East End of London in the late 1800s/early 1900s. The nature of the cases is not far removed from those seen today. In part, this increased relevance relates to much wider awareness of human rights abuses and civil liberties which, in turn, have directed much attention to the conditions of detention of prisoners, and to the application of justice to both victim and suspect. The differing and potentially conflicting roles that a forensic physician may have when attending a prisoner or other person detained by the state or other body have been recognized by identifying three possible facets of medical care: (1) the role of medicolegal expert for a law enforcement agency, (2) the role of a treating doctor and (3) the examination and treatment of detainees who allege that they have been mistreated by the police during their arrest, during interrogation, or during the various stages of police custody. This conflict is well recognized by forensic physicians (27). Some jurisdictions recognize clinical forensic medicine as a distinct medical specialty. The European Council of Legal Medicine continues to make progress to have Legal and Forensic Medicine (which includes both forensic pathology and clinical forensic medicine) as a recognized monospecialty. As yet, this has still to be achieved although the UEMS has now created a thematic federation in the subject. In both the UK and Australasia, applications to create specialties of respectively forensic and legal medicine and clinical forensic medicine are in progress. These applications and the processes attached to them may take some years to complete. Some countries (e.g. France) have developed a group of regional centers (Urgences Medico-Judiciaires) which are medicolegal units sitting alongside hospital emergency departments and having access to their facilities. There are no international standards of practice or training – international standards are still lacking, but more countries appear to be developing national standards. The Faculty of Forensic and Legal Medicine of the Royal College of Physicians (www.fflm.ac.uk) has pioneered the

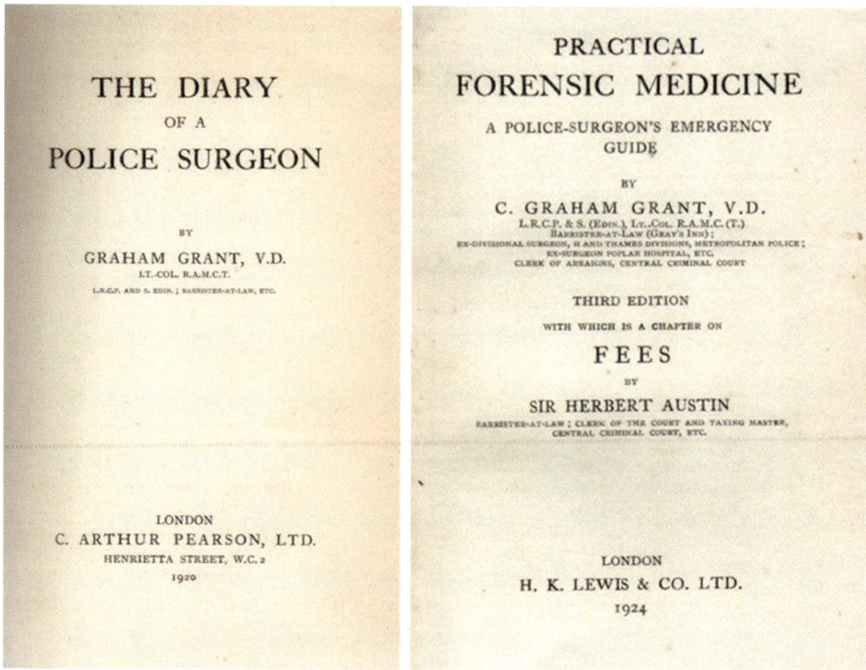
THE DIARY
OF A
POLICE SURGEON
BY
GRAHAM GRANT, V.D.
LT.-COL. R.A.M.C.T.
L.R.C.P. AND S. EDIN.; BARRISTER-AT-LAW; ETC.
LONDON
C. ARTHUR PEARSON, LTD.
HENRIETTA STREET, W.C. 2
1920

PRACTICAL
FORENSIC MEDICINE
A POLICE-SURGEON'S EMERGENCY GUIDE
BY
C. GRAHAM GRANT, V.D.
L.R.C.P. & S. (EDIN.), LT.-COL. R.A.M.C. (T.)
BARRISTER-AT-LAW (GRAY'S INN);
EX-DIVISIONAL SURGEON, H AND THAMES DIVISIONS, METROPOLITAN POLICE;
EX-SURGEON POPLAR HOSPITAL, ETC.
CLERK OF ARRAIGNS, CENTRAL CRIMINAL COURT
THIRD EDITION
WITH WHICH IS A CHAPTER ON
FEES
BY
SIR HERBERT AUSTIN
BARRISTER-AT-LAW; CLERK OF THE COURT AND TAXING MASTER, CENTRAL CRIMINAL COURT, ETC.
LONDON
H. K. LEWIS & CO. LTD.
1924

1.7 Frontispiece of two books written by a police surgeon (forensic physician) working in the East End of London around the turn of the twentieth century.

development of quality standards for healthcare professionals working in custodial and sexual offense settings but also produces consensus guidelines on other matters, such as standards for those working with victims of torture.

CONCLUSION

Forensic and legal medicine arises from a long tradition of links between the law and medicine and now includes a wide variety of complementary needs and skills intertwining medicine, pathology, science, the law and ethics. Forensic and legal medicine in its various forms may represent the oldest true medical specialty with its current functions capable of being traced back in academic writings globally for five centuries and beyond. Various individuals have been proposed as the "father of" the discipline and many texts "the first." All are open to challenge as it is clear that it is possible to find in all cultures and jurisdictions the essence of forensic and legal medicine in some form or another. This also confirms that forensic and legal medicine is crucial to the proper administration of justice in all its formats and origins. Every forensic practitioner, whether clinical, pathologic, or both, should be aware of their responsibilities, not only to their patient or the deceased, but to society as whole, and be able to utilize their skills and competences to provide robust evidence and opinions to ensure that their contribution to the justice process is unimpeachable.

REFERENCES

1. Union Européenne Des Médecine Spécialistes. Available from: https://www.uems.eu/about-us/medical-specialties (Accessed 23 March 2023).
2. Payne-James JJ. Clinical forensic medicine. *J Clin Forensic Med* 1994; **1**: 1.
3. Traill TS. *Outlines of a Course of Lectures on Medical Jurisprudence*, 2nd ed. Madrid: Hardpress Publishing; 2012.
4. Amundsen DW, Ferngren GB. The physician as an expert witness in Athenian Law. *Bull Hist Med* 1977; **51**(2): 202–13.
5. Amundsen DW, Ferngren GB. Forensic role of physicians in Roman law. *Bull Hist Med* 1977; 53: 39–56.
6. Brittain RP. Origins of legal medicine. Roman law: Lex Duodecim Tabularum. *Med Leg J* 1967; 35: 71–72.
7. Madea B. *History of Forensic Medicine*. Berlin: Lehmanns Media; 2017.
8. Payne-James JJ. History of Forensic Medicine. In: Payne-James JJ, Byard R, Corey T, Henderson C (eds), *Encyclopedia of Forensic & Legal Medicine*. Amsterdam: Elsevier; 2005, pp. 539–67.
9. Bonte W. History: Forensic Medicine. In: Siegel JA, Saukko P, Knupfer G (eds), *Encyclopedia of Forensic Sciences*. San Diego: Academic Press; 2000, pp. 1064–70.
10. Smith S. The history and development of forensic medicine. *BMJ* 1951; **1**: 599–607.
11. Beck TR, Darwall J. *Elements of Medical Jurisprudence*, 3rd ed. London: Longman; 1829.
12. Cassar P. A Medico-Legal Report of the 16th Century from Malta. *Med Hist* 1974; 18(4): 354–9.
13. Meymott Tidy C. *Legal Medicine. Part 1*. London: Smith, Elder and Co; 1882.
14. Lyon IB. *A Textbook of Medical Jurisprudence for India*. Bombay: Thacker, Spink & Co; 1889.
15. Taylor AS. *The Principles and Practice of Medical Jurisprudence*, 4th ed. London: John Churchill & Sons; 1894.
16. Hunter W. *On the Uncertainty of the Signs of Murder in the Case of Bastard Children*. London; 1783.
17. Smith JG. *The Principles of Forensic Medicine Systematically Arranged and Applied to British Practice*. London: Thomas & George Underwood; 1821.
18. Clark M, Crawford C. (eds). *Legal Medicine in History*. New York: Cambridge University Press, 1994.
19. Chaiullé SE, Origin and Progress of Medical Jurisprudence 1776–1876 *J Crim Law Criminol* 1949; 40(4) 397–444.
20. Beck TR. *Elements of Medical Jurisprudence*, 3rd ed. London: Longman, Reese, Orme, Brown and Green; 1829.
21. Taylor AS. *A Manual of Medical Jurisprudence*. London: John Churchill & Sons; 1844.
22. Taylor AA. *Medical Jurisprudence*, 5th ed. London: John Churchill; 1854.
23. Forbes TR. *Surgeons at the Bailey. English Forensic Medicine to 1878*. New Haven, London: Yale University Press; 1985.
24. McCallin W. *Medical Jurisprudence*. London: Baillière, Tindall and Cox; 1901.
25. Buchanan RJM. *Text-book of Forensic Medicine and Toxicology*, 8th ed. Edinburgh: E & S Livingstone; 1919.
26. Von Hofmann E. *Atlas of Legal Medicine*. Philadelphia: WB Saunders; 1898.
27. Editorial. Three-faced practice: doctors and police custody. *Lancet* 1993; **341**: 1245–7.

CHAPTER

2

Ethical Principles Involved in International Forensic Medical Examinations

Sondra S. Crosby and George David Annas

INTRODUCTION

In this chapter, we discuss the medical ethics principles which embody the obligations of health professionals to individuals and to society. These obligations are universal and are incorporated in statements by international, national and local health organizations and professional societies. International ethics guidelines are articulated in "The World Medical Association's (WMA) International Code of Medical Ethics", first adopted by the 3rd General Assembly of the WMA in 1949 (Table 2.1) (1). The central tenet of all health professional ethics is to respect human dignity and always act in the patient's best interest. A knowledge of human rights and their relevant instruments is increasingly important in a globalized world where health professionals are faced with issues such as care of migrants who are forcibly displaced, allocation of scarce resources (such as in pandemics), and healthcare inequities, all of which may require the ethical principle of societal justice to be weighed more heavily than the needs of the individual patient. Principles common to all codes of medical ethics include beneficence, non-maleficence, confidentiality, respect for patient autonomy, and justice (1). Specific situations can be complex and create exceptions to this framework, and these exceptions will be discussed in detail later in this chapter.

TABLE 2.1 WMA international code of medical ethics

Duties of physicians in general	
A physician shall	always exercise his/her independent professional judgment and maintain the highest standards of professional conduct.
A physician shall	respect a competent patient's right to accept or refuse treatment.
A physician shall	not allow his/her judgment to be influenced by personal profit or unfair discrimination.
A physician shall	be dedicated to providing component medical service in full professional and moral independence, with compassion and respect for human dignity.
A physician shall	deal honestly with patients and colleagues, and report to the appropriate authorities those physicians who practice unethically or incompetently or who engage in fraud or deception.
A physician shall	not receive any financial benefits or other incentives solely for referring patients or prescribing specific products.
A physician shall	respect the rights and preferences of patients, colleagues, and other health professionals.
A physician shall	recognize his/her important role in educating the public but should use due caution in divulging discoveries or new techniques or treatment through non-professional channels.
A physician shall	certify only that which he/she has personally verified.
A physician shall	strive to use healthcare resources in the best way to benefit patients and their community.
A physician shall	seek appropriate care and attention if he/she suffers from mental or physical illness.
A physician shall	respect the local and national code of ethics.

(*Continued*)

DOI: 10.1201/9781003138754-3

TABLE 2.1 (Continued) WMA international code of medical ethics

Duties of physicians to patients	
A physician shall	always bear in mind the obligation to respect human life.
A physician shall	act in the patient's best interest when providing medical care.
A physician shall	owe his/her patients, complete loyalty and all the scientific resources available to him/her. Whenever an examination or treatment is beyond the physician's capacity, he/she should consult with or refer to another physician who has the necessary ability.
A physician shall	respect a patient's right to confidentiality. It is ethical to disclose confidential information when the patient consents to it or when there is a real and imminent threat of harm to the patient or to others and this threat can only be removed by a breach of confidentiality.
A physician shall	give emergency care as a humanitarian duty unless he/she is assured that others are willing and able to give such care.
A physician shall	In situations when he/she is acting for a third party, ensure that the patient has full knowledge of that situation.
A physician shall	not enter into a sexual relationship with his/her current patient or into any other abusive or exploitative relationship.
Duties of physicians to patients	
A physician shall	behave toward colleagues as he/she would have them behave toward him/her.
A physician shall	NOT undermine the patient-physician relationship of colleagues in order to attract patients.
A physician shall	when medically necessary, communicate with colleagues who are involved in the care of the same patient. This communication should respect patient confidentiality and be confined to necessary information.

Source: Adopted by the 3rd General Assembly of the WMA, London, England, October 1949 and amended by the 12th WMA, Sydney, Australia, August 1968 and the 35th WMA, Venice, Italy, October 1983 and the 57th WMA General Assembly, Pilanesberg, South Africa, October 2006.

It is essential to emphasize that there are certain ethical obligations of health professionals which apply to all encounters with individuals wherein professional knowledge or skills are used for any purpose, including forensic medical examinations conducted outside of the typical doctor-patient relationship. Health professionals conducting forensic evaluations are bound by ethical principles, however, there are unique circumstances faced by health professionals in a forensic, compared to a treatment, context. The nature of the forensic encounter is distinct from that between a patient and a treating clinician. Typically, there is no therapeutic relationship between the forensic examiner and the individual, and the usual expectation of confidentiality is limited. For example, in cases of a state-ordered forensic examination, or for the purposes of litigation, personal information may be widely disseminated as part of the discovery process. These vulnerabilities obligate the forensic medical examiner to take extreme precautions to avoid acting in a manner to cause direct harm to the person while addressing the forensic question as objectively as possible. In this chapter, we use the term "examinee," "individual" or other similar term in the place of "patient," to differentiate the relationship of the forensic examiner compared to a clinical evaluation in a treatment setting.

INFORMED CONSENT

Informed consent is an established core ethics principle of all professional practice that derived from the Nuremberg Code (2). Informed consent is imperative for evaluation and treatment of all mentally competent patients, including for forensic examinations. The basic elements of informed consent include the following: The health professionals should provide their names and explain their role in conducting the examination. They should explain who appointed them to perform the evaluation and briefly summarize their qualifying credentials. The purpose of and the process of the evaluation (including photographs, psychological instruments, physical examination), the limits of confidentiality, and the risks and benefits of the examination, all should be fully understood by the individual. The individual may consent to a partial or limited forensic evaluation. For example, the examinee can decline to answer certain questions, or decline a full physical examination. Health professionals should make every effort to honor preference for gender of the clinician. For example, a female rape victim may strongly oppose being examined by a male health professional.

During the informed consent process, the examinee must be told how the information will be stored and protected, who will have access to it and how the information will be used, including if it could be used against the individual, for example, in legal proceedings. The risks/benefits of participating in the evaluation must be fully understood by the examinee before they consent to participate.

There are special considerations for obtaining informed consent of prisoners who are especially vulnerable to harm or coercion. In persons who are being held in the custody of abusive jailers, it is crucial to consider that the prisoner may be at risk of retaliation for participating in a forensic evaluation. Prison officials often attempt to conceal prisoner abuse and may threaten prisoners explicitly or implicitly if they reveal information about abusive practices to anyone (including forensic evaluators). Retaliation for participation in the interview could include physical harm to the prisoner or worsening of conditions of confinement (solitary confinement, withholding of food or medical treatment, threats). The possibility of secret surveillance must be considered in some carceral settings; for example, recording devices disguised as smoke detectors were discovered at Guantanamo Bay prison in places where attorneys had met with their clients under assumed privacy (3). It is important to discuss the potential for retaliation against family members.

In addition to the risks, the benefits of participation in the evaluation must be explained and understood, including explicit statements if there is no benefit to the examinee. For example, in the case of prisoners, the examinee may expect or infer that participation in the examination will result in intervention with prison officials to improve conditions of confinement or simply as a venue to obtain access to the outside world, including arranging for family contact. When in a vulnerable and desperate state, the prisoner may consent to the examination in the false hope that the interviewers will improve their conditions or allow access to their family. Alternatively, they may believe that refusal to participate in the examination could result in further punishment or worse treatment. It is important for the examiner to be mindful of the fact that power dynamics, structural racism and classism may interfere with the informed consent process and make it coercive (see Case Study 2.1).

The potential mental health sequelae arising from traumatic experiences or torture (post-traumatic stress disorder, depression, anxiety, cognitive disorders) could interfere with the examinee's ability to provide voluntary informed consent and must be assessed when obtaining informed consent. The individual may feel coerced or "helpless" to decline participation, stop the examination, or rescind consent for participation. Mental health disorders do not preclude the ability to provide consent, but a careful assessment is required to determine if the individual has the specific decision-making capacity to consent to participate in the examination. It may be necessary to postpone the evaluation until the examinee has full decision-making capacity and can fully consent. The health professional should consider the risks of re-traumatization and exacerbation of traumatic symptoms during the examination and discuss this risk with the examinee as part of the informed consent process. It is also important to identify a treatment source should re-traumatization occur or if the person requires medical or mental healthcare for injuries discovered during the evaluation (*see* Case Study 2.2).

CASE STUDY 2.1

A forensic medical examination was requested by attorneys representing a man who had been held in the United States custody at "black sites" for approximately 5 years and was subsequently released without charges to his home country. He alleged extreme psychological and physical torture during his detainment and was seeking damages in a civil lawsuit.

A medical evaluator traveled to the person's home country with the individual's legal team to perform the evaluation. The examiner was specifically asked to perform a diagnostic examination of the client and document all diagnoses with a reasonable degree of medical certainty. Written informed consent was obtained for the evaluation, a private space was secured, and a comprehensive evaluation based on the Istanbul Protocol guidelines was performed.

During an evaluation, it was discovered that the examinee was suffering from severe, complex post-traumatic stress disorder, depression, and from a range of physical injuries, which in totality resulted in ongoing suffering and significantly impaired his ability to function in day-to-day life.

There were no available mental health resources to refer the individual to, in his home country.

What are the ethical obligations of the evaluating health professional when he/she uncovers clinical conditions during a forensic examination?

The forensic evaluator is not in the role of a treating clinician, however, is still bound by the core medical ethics value of non-maleficence and must not act in a way that would likely cause direct harm to the individual. During the informed consent process, the forensic evaluator has a duty to disclose to the individual the possibility that the evaluation itself could cause re-traumatization and exacerbation of symptoms. The forensic evaluating clinician is obligated to properly document and report back to the point of contact (such as the attorney) the conditions found.

Discussion/additional considerations

If a condition requiring treatment is discovered during the forensic evaluation, then general recommendations for appropriate follow-up care should also be provided in the report. As a practical matter, in such situations it is recommended that referral sources are identified in advance of the evaluation in case follow-up care is necessary.

In this situation, referral to local treatment was not possible, but with the assistance of NGOs and the UN, an emergency grant was obtained for a clinician in a neighboring country to travel and provide treatment on a short-term basis.

CASE STUDY 2.2

The examinee was a female asylum seeker in her mid thirties referred by her immigration lawyer for a forensic examination to diagnose and document her medical conditions.

After obtaining written informed consent, the examinee agreed to have the report released to her lawyer as part of her asylum application. The examination was performed in a private clinic room and the documentation was stored on an encrypted hard drive.

Her medical history was significant for cerebral palsy, and she required a walker to ambulate at the time of the examination. When discussing her history, she alleged having sustained multiple injuries including rape, cutting wounds with a knife, and burns from an iron while arrested and interrogated in her country because of her support for an opposition political group. In addition, she reported blunt trauma to her right ankle with a stick resulting in a traumatic fracture that required surgical repair. Physical examination was notable for multiple healed scars that were consistent/highly consistent with healed lacerations, burns and cutting wounds. There was a well-healed linear scar on the right anterior ankle, highly consistent with a healed surgical incision, as well as decreased range of motion. Radiograph revealed a right ankle fusion, a procedure commonly done to treat foot drop. The radiographic findings were not consistent with a traumatic fracture.

What are the ethical issues raised in this case?

The health professional has the duty for truthful reporting and honest communication with the examinee. She had physical evidence consistent with traumatic experiences, but not all of evidence was consistent with her reporting of events. When questioned about the discrepancy, the patient admitted that she did not know why she had the surgery, but she had assumed it was for the trauma.

The preponderance of the evidence supported her allegations of trauma, however, there were some discrepancies which could bring credibility into question, and potentially harm her chances at being granted asylum.

Discussion/additional considerations

It is possible that the examinee did not know the reason for her surgery, or that memories were distorted due to trauma. It is also possible that the patient embellished her story to include the ankle fracture to make her case "more compelling". Asylum seekers may be pressured by individuals in their community to "bolster" their cases to supposedly increase their chances of being granted asylum. This possibility must be honestly addressed with the patient.

Regarding the report, you may offer to defer continuing working on the case, and not write a report, should the attorney feel that such an option would be more beneficial to the client. However, if you decide to write the report, you would be obligated to include the evidence for the discrepancies noted. Additionally, while your duty in this situation is not to treat the examinee yourself, should you find conditions that require treatment, it would be most ethically sound of you to report them back to the attorney or point of contact and provide general recommendations of the type of follow-up care that she would require.

In situations where there is a judicially ordered evaluation with the purpose of answering a specific question related to mental health (for example, competence to stand trial), it is considered acceptable to proceed even if the capability of the person being examined to give informed consent is in question. However, in such circumstances, all reasonable attempts should be made to explain the purpose of the evaluation, the role of the examiners as well as the potential outcomes of the examination in question. Additionally, such examinations should only be done if the attorney for the defendant has been informed. In the USA, information gathered in a competence to stand trial evaluation cannot be used as evidence in a subsequent criminal trial, without the consent of the defendant. For example, in some insanity defense cases, the defense counsel may find the forensic evaluation to contain evidence that is favorable to the defense and agree to release the report.

Children are a special vulnerable group, and informed consent for children generally requires approval of the legal representative of the child, however, this is not always possible. It is not uncommon for children to be separated from their guardians in environments of conflict or in other situations where a forensic medical examination might be performed. Assent can be obtained in this situation; the child actively agrees to participate after being provided with information that is developmentally appropriate. For example, there are record numbers of unaccompanied youth from the Northern Triangle countries crossing the US southwest border seeking protection from persecution. The benefits of the forensic evaluation, which may include asylum and referral to resources and treatment, are generally regarded to be in their best interest.

Written consent is usually preferable; however oral consent may be necessary in certain circumstances to preserve confidentiality or in cases where the examinee does not wish to sign a document (some prisoners have been forced to sign confessions and may be reluctant to sign any document). The examiner should provide adequate time to the examinee to consider his or her decision to consent to the evaluation. The examinee should also have an opportunity to ask any questions. The health professional should carefully document the entire consent process.

If the above conditions cannot be adequately addressed and mitigated, and voluntary informed consent cannot be obtained, the examination should not proceed. In such situations where the examination is court-ordered and appropriate protections are in place (such as counsel being assigned and informed), such examinations may proceed. However, the lack of capacity to consent to the process should be documented in the examination report.

CONFIDENTIALITY

The duty of confidentiality is a fundamental ethics principle and generally must be respected unless the individual provides informed consent to share information. Confidentiality is not absolute and may be breached in exceptional circumstances where, without disclosure, harm to an individual may result, or there is an imminent threat to public safety. These risks of harm to a third party or to the public must be weighed as greater than the potential harm of breaching the examinee's privacy. An example is the case of an individual's disclosure that prison staff are abusing multiple prisoners, and the person does not agree to the reporting of this information. In such cases, if it is decided that the benefit of reporting the abuse outweighs the risks of breaking confidentiality, only the minimal necessary amount of information should be disclosed to the necessary party, the examinee should be informed of the disclosure and reasonable steps should be taken to mitigate any potential resulting harm.

In cases where health professionals act for another party, such as a judge or prosecutor, which is often the case for forensic medical examinations, the examinee must be told who will have access to the information, both presently and in the future. Health professionals may be pressured by outside parties such as States or other officials to share confidential information obtained during the evaluation. Complying with such a request would violate confidentiality and could result in harm to the examinee. In this circumstance, clinicians are bound by their professional obligations to not breach confidentiality and should receive any necessary support from professional organizations when exercising this ethical duty.

Forensic medical evaluations often occur in environments where data safety cannot be assured and risks to breaches of confidentiality exist. Health professionals must make every effort to protect patient records and information. Novel methods of safeguarding information have been developed for use in conflict zones, or other environments where protection of data is at risk. An example is Physician's for Human Rights mobile app MediCapt, which utilizes a digital platform for forensic documentation that includes sophisticated encryption and cloud data storage which can be securely transmitted (4).

Health professionals also have obligations when utilizing interpreters. It is optimal when the health professional and examinee share a common language. If the health professional is not fluent in the examinee's language and an interpreter is utilized, the interpreter should be professionally trained and understand their obligation to maintain confidentiality. The health professional must confirm that the examinee and interpreter understand each other, as there are often multiple dialects in the same language. The interpreter should be neutral, that is, not part of the examinee's family or local community, and not from an opposing political faction. For example, it has happened with one of the authors that a Somalian interpreter from a tribe that persecuted the person being examined was unknowingly employed.

CONFLICTS OF INTEREST

Health professionals may have conflicts of interest, that is, to third parties or to society. It is generally accepted that physicians may, in exceptional situations, place the interests of others above the patient (that is, reporting of child abuse outweighing obligation to confidentiality). However, even in these circumstances, the health professional must always do their best to protect the person and inform them of the disclosure. In an increasingly complicated healthcare industrial complex, these conflicts of interest are vast and comprise a range of situations, some of which do not have easy solutions. For example, during the global COVID-19 pandemic, some hospitals developed "Crisis Standards of Care" guidelines for use when faced with potential shortages of intensive care beds and ventilators. Patients were prioritized to receive scarce resources based on protocols utilizing scoring systems designed to "save the most life-years," raising ethical questions about equity, autonomy, and informed consent (5). Conflict of interest situations are especially acute for health professionals working in a treatment capacity in carceral settings.

In 2020, the United Nations specifically addressed the ethical obligations of doctors and other health professionals working with prisoners and detainees. These obligations make clear that health professionals have a moral duty to protect detainees" physical and mental health. In particular, it is a gross violation of health professional ethics to participate, actively or passively, in torture, cruel, inhuman and degrading treatment or condone it in any way. Like all other persons working in prison systems, health professionals must observe the UN Standard Minimum Rules for the Treatment of Prisoners, revised in 2015, and known as the Nelson Mandela Rules or "Mandela Rules" (6).

Mandela Rule 34 requires healthcare professionals who "become aware of any signs of torture or other cruel, inhuman or degrading treatment or punishment..." to "...document and report such cases to the competent medical, administrative or judicial authority. Proper procedural safeguards shall be followed in order not to expose the prisoner or associated persons to a foreseeable risk of harm" (see also, Istanbul Protocols, United Nations 2004) (7).

In addition, the WMA Resolution on the Responsibility of Physicians in the Documentation and Denunciation of Acts of Torture or Cruel or Inhuman or Degrading Treatment summarizes the duty of physicians to document and denounce acts of torture and ill-treatment and that a failure to do so constitutes complicity in such abuse (8).

This duty represents an effort to prevent the passive complicity of health professionals in these abuses and to facilitate the effective reporting of torture and ill-treatment to independent monitoring and prevention bodies. This duty applies to **all physicians** – governmental and non-governmental, forensic, and non-forensic – whether they encounter alleged or suspected victims of torture in medicolegal or any other setting. A dilemma may occur when the health professional reasonably believes that abuse has occurred, and the prisoner refuses to report the harm to authorities. In this situation, as previously discussed, the health professional must weigh the risks and benefits to the patient and to the other prisoners. State-employed health professionals (such as in prisons) may face significant challenges in their duties when patients refuse to engage or decline care due to a lack of trust because the health professional is viewed to be complicit with an oppressive system, and not to be independent. In this case, the health professional has the duty to inform the patient of their right to be examined by an independent health professional.

PSYCHIATRIC EXAMINATIONS

In some forensic psychiatric evaluations, a conflict may arise between the duty to serve the best interest of the individual being examined and the pursuit of truth-to-serve justice, that is, when forensic examinations are ordered by the courts to determine a person's competency to stand trial. The stakes may be high, and harm from the evaluation in the form of life imprisonment or even capital punishment in some countries, may be the result. It is important to keep in mind, however, that a conviction is based on the evidence at hand in regard to the defendant's guilt or innocence, not based on the decision regarding the person's competence to stand trial. Therefore, the examiner would not explain the "risks" of being found competent to stand trial, as this is the purpose of the evaluation at hand, and there are few situations where a truly competent individual would be better off wrongfully being declared unfit. As in all situations, the mental health professional has an obligation to be open about the purpose of the evaluation, and the person's option to refuse the evaluation. If such an evaluation is court-ordered, the individual may not have a right to refuse to be examined. However, the consequences for refusal would be unlikely to be enforced harshly, other than situations where it appears the defendant is intentionally delaying the proceedings by deliberately refusing to speak with the examiners. In situations such as these, the health professional also has the duty for objective truth telling, which makes the exclusive use of principlism inadequate. The core ethical value of beneficence to the individual patient may be outweighed by justice, truth telling and respect for persons in this context (9). Therefore, the adoption of additional ethical principles and guidelines is necessary to help avoid harm when clinicians delve into roles outside of treatment.

One such organization that has aided this adoption is the American Academy of Psychiatry and the Law (AAPL) whose guidelines, state the following: "...the practice of forensic psychiatry entails inherent potentials for complications, conflicts, misunderstandings and abuses." Therefore, the forensic psychiatrist needs to be mindful to work in a way that honors the principles of "... respect for persons, honesty, justice, and social responsibility." Additionally, they comment on four basic guidelines that a forensic psychiatrist should follow: 1. Consent (obtaining consent for the evaluation when possible), 2. Confidentiality (disclosing the limits to- and staying within the bounds of- confidentiality, outside of mandated release of information), 3. Striving for Objectivity (putting all efforts into giving an unbiased opinion, while recognizing that no one is immune from personal biases) and 4. Qualifications (only proffering an opinion on matters in which you are qualified to do so) (10). Thus, one in this role is reminded that "absolving" oneself of a duty to take into account the beneficence of the person being evaluated, brings with it a new set of obligations.

COMPETENCE AND SECONDARY TRAUMA

Health professionals have the duty to be competent in their field of work, and this includes not only

BOX 2.1 Rational Ethical Decision-Making

1. Determine whether the issue at hand is an ethical one.
2. Consult authoritative sources such as the Medical Association Codes of Ethics and Policies and respected colleagues to see how physicians generally deal with such issues.
3. Consider alternative solutions in light of the principles and values they uphold and their likely consequences.
4. Discuss your proposed solution with those whom it will affect.
5. Make your decision and act on it, with sensitivity to others affected.
6. Evaluate your decision and be prepared to act differently in future.

technical skills, but ethical knowledge and attitudes as new situations arise with changing environments. Health professionals are at risk of experiencing burnout and secondary trauma, which not only impacts them, but can negatively affect their objectivity and harm patients. Health professionals have the duty to recognize the risks of secondary trauma, to care for themselves and protect their health, and to seek help when necessary.

CONCLUSION

The current complicated global healthcare environment creates medical ethical dilemmas which are complex and difficult for individual healthcare professionals to navigate. The WMA, in addition to some other professional organizations, have provided a useful framework and general approach to sound ethical decision-making for health professionals when faced with these dilemmas (*see* Box 2.1).

REFERENCES

1. World Medical Association. WMA international code of medical ethics, 2022. Available from: https://www.wma.net/what-we-do/education/medical-ethics-manual/ (Accessed: 27th July 2023).
2. Grodin MA. Historical Origins of the Nuremberg Code. In: Annas GJ, Grodin MA (eds), *The Nazi Doctors and the Nuremberg Code*. Oxford: Oxford University Press; 1992, pp. 121–44.
3. Savage C. Guantánamo lawyers challenge government's explanation for hidden microphone, 2018. Available from: https://www.nytimes.com/2018/03/12/us/politics/guantanamo-hidden-microphone.html (Accessed 23 March 2023).
4. Physicians for Human Rights. PHR works to end impunity for sexual violence and to bring justice to survivors of these terrible crimes, 2022. Available from: https://phr.org/issues/sexual-violence/medicapt-innovation-2/ (Accessed 23 March 2023).
5. National Academies of Science, Engineering, and Medicine. Rapid expert consultation on crisis standards of care for the COVID-19 pandemic, 2021. Available from: https://nap.nationalacademies.org/catalog/25765/rapid-expert-consultation-on-crisis-standards-of-care-for-the-covid-19-pandemic-march-28–2020 (Accessed 23 March 2023).
6. United Nations Office on Drugs and Crime. The United Nations standard minimum rules for the treatment of prisoners (the Nelson Mandela rules). Available from: https://www.unodc.org/documents/justice-and-prison-reform/Nelson_Mandela_Rules-E-ebook.pdf (Accessed 27 April 2023).
7. United Nations. Istanbul protocol: Manual on the effective investigation and documentation of torture and other cruel, inhuman or degrading treatment or punishment, 2004. Available from: https://www.ohchr.org/en/publications/policy-and-methodological-publications/istanbul-protocol-manual-effective-0. (Accessed 23 March 2023).
8. World Medical Association. WMA resolution on the responsibility of physicians in the documentation and denunciation of acts of torture or cruel or inhuman or degrading treatment, 2022. Available from: https://www.wma.net/policies-post/wma-resolution-on-the-responsibility-of-physicians-in-the-documentation-and-denunciation-of-acts-of-torture-or-cruel-or-inhuman-or-degrading-treatment/ (Accessed 23 August 2023).
9. Appelbaum PS. A theory of ethics for forensic psychiatry. *J Am Acad Psychiatry Law* 1997; **25**: 233–47.
10. American Academy of Psychiatry and the Law. Ethics guidelines for the practice of forensic psychiatry, 2005. Available from: https://www.aapl.org/ethics.htm (Accessed 23 March 2023).

CHAPTER

3

Human Rights Law

Ian Freckelton

INTRODUCTION

The content of what were recognized as human rights changed fundamentally as a result of exposure of the atrocities and unethical war practices of both the Nazi and Japanese regimes during the Second World War. This is not to say that unethical practices in medicine started with the Berlin and Tokyo regimes or that serious efforts toward formulation of both bioethical principles (1,2) (and the ethics of war (3–6) did not have a lengthy and honorable history before the 1940s. However, the post-war determination to learn and change was given a fillip by revelations about the human subject experimentation in Germany (7–10) and Japan (11–13) and also from the bombardments of London, Rotterdam, Dresden, Hamburg, Pearl Harbor, Hiroshima and Nagasaki as tactics for securing military advantage from infliction of death and destruction indiscriminately, including on civilians (14). Also, after the Second World War, civilian populations have routinely taken on a strategic importance as a target for ethnic cleansing, as a shield for attacks, as a means for leveraging morale-sapping pressure on regimes and as a focus for reprisal actions (15–18). This includes the infliction of intimidatory sexual violence (19–21). With such tactics has come the need for proof of such conduct to enable harnessing the denunciation of the international community and the taking of deterrent action against States that have sanctioned such conduct. Part of this has involved the use of international law which, in turn, has required the contribution of legal medicine and forensic medicine.

The phenomenon of unethical practices rationalized as justified by imminent or actual wartime exigencies has contributed to the evolving fabric of both contemporary bioethics (22,23) and "international humanitarian law", the law relating to the conduct of individuals and nations during wartime (24,25). Its initiator was the International Committee of the Red Cross (25,26). The basis of humanitarian law is the principle of humanity which requires respect for human beings in their full diversity and entails belligerents not inflicting on their adversaries, harm out of proportion to the object of warfare – destroying or weakening the military strength of the enemy (25,27). It also requires that those who are hors-de-combat and those who do not participate directly in hostilities are respected, protected and treated humanely (28,29).

Leaning (30) has observed that such law does not furnish detailed road maps for negotiating the complex terrain of war and preparation for war but, along with established principles of medical ethics, has contributed to the rules and standards by which the international community has determined that medicine, science and government must all be held accountable. An important role for international humanitarian law is the exposure and clarification of illegal acts against civilians (24,31–33) so that breaches can be identified and so that human rights and humanitarian norms can be asserted and enforced as standards to which all countries are required to subscribe (34) or at least a means of amending strategic expectations (35). The ethical practice of medicine during war, including on, and in the vicinity of, a battlefield, is fundamental to protection of the wounded and sick during armed conflict under international humanitarian law (36).

In turn, legal medicine and forensic medicine have a crucial role to play in assisting international criminal courts and domestic criminal courts in determining whether allegations of genocide, crimes against humanity, war crimes and crimes of aggression are substantiated according to proper curial processes and standards of proof. In 1986, the International Court of Justice defined "humanitarian action" as activities carried out by organizations and individuals "to prevent and alleviate human suffering wherever it may be found" and "to protect life and health and to ensure respect for the human being" (alive or dead) (*Nicaragua v United States of America*, 1986: para 242 [37]) Tidball-Binz and Cordner (38) (see also Tidball-Binz, [39]) have promoted recognition of "humanitarian forensic action", an emerging field of forensic medicine and science, as a form of humanitarian response to armed conflicts. A role for both forensic pathology and forensic science is to help ensure the dignified management of persons who have died during conflict and to document torture, ill-treatment and, more broadly, the causes and circumstances of death (40–42).

This chapter discusses human rights in the context of deaths in declared and undeclared wars, mechanisms for proof of such conduct, based upon expert evidence from forensic physicians and scientists and, also, the responsibilities of the state to ensure prompt, efficient and rigorous investigation of deaths with which a state is associated.

DOI: 10.1201/9781003138754-4

THE INITIATIVES OF NUREMBERG

An important concomitant of the Nuremberg trials (see *United States v Brandt,* 1946 (43), especially those focusing on the Nazi doctors, was the "Nuremberg Code" (1947) (44) which addressed permissible medical experiments. The Code emphasized the need for experimentation on human subjects "to be kept within reasonably well-defined bounds" and to "conform to the ethics of the medical profession generally." It identified as fundamental the giving of voluntary consent by patients and the need for medical experiments to be such as to "yield fruitful results for the good of society, unprocurable by other methods or means of study, and not random and unnecessary in nature", as well as the need for experiments to be conducted so as to "avoid all unnecessary physical and mental suffering and injury". The Nuremberg Code continues to influence contemporary values about experimentation on human subjects (45–47).

In 2005, the General Conference of UNESCO adopted by declaration, the Universal Declaration on Bioethics and Human Rights (2005) (48) which committed Member States and the international community to respect and apply the fundamental principles of bioethics, expanding upon the earlier provisions in the Nuremberg Code. The Universal Declaration constitutes an important formalitation on the basis of international consensus about the fundamental attributes of bioethical work undertaken by medical practitioners and scientists. Its distinguishing features are its extension into broader determinants of health, including the environment, the biosphere and biodiversity, and its identification of the importance of cultural diversity, non-discrimination and internationalism. However, many challenges lie ahead to ensure its effective implementation (49).

THE UNIVERSAL DECLARATION OF HUMAN RIGHTS

In 1948, the General Assembly of the United Nations proclaimed the Universal Declaration of Human Rights (50). In its preamble, the Declaration was overtly responsive to the fact that "disregard and contempt for human rights have resulted in barbarous acts which have outraged the conscience of mankind". The Declaration was predicated upon the proposition that "All human beings are born free and equal in dignity and rights" (Art 1) and entitled to rights and freedoms as set out in the Declaration. These included the rights to life, liberty and security of the person (Art 3) and not to be "subjected to torture or to cruel, inhuman or degrading treatment or punishment" (Art 5). It also provided for "freedom from arbitrary interference with privacy, family, home, and correspondence" (Art 12), as well as stipulating a right to "freedom of movement" (Art 13) and to "freedom of thought, conscience and religion" (Art 18) and "freedom of peaceful assembly and association" (Art 20). It identified a "right to work, to free choice of employment and to equal pay for equal work without discrimination" (Art 23). Article 25 stated that everyone has the right to "a standard of living adequate for the health and well-being of himself and of his family, including food, clothing, housing and medical care and necessary social services" (Art 25).

THE CONVENTION ON THE PREVENTION AND PUNISHMENT OF THE CRIME OF GENOCIDE

The 1948 Convention on the Prevention and Punishment of the Crime of Genocide came into force in 1951 (51). It implemented the declaration made by the General Assembly of the United Nations in its resolution 96(I) on 11 December 1946 that genocide is a crime under international law "contrary to the spirit and aims of the United Nations and condemned by the civilized world" (52) (Pinch, 1949). It defined genocide as the following acts when committed with intent to destroy, in whole or in part, a national, ethnical, racial, or religious group:

(a) Killing members of the group
(b) Causing serious bodily or mental harm to members of the group
(c) Deliberately inflicting on the group conditions of life calculated to bring about its physical destruction in whole or in part
(d) Imposing measures intended to prevent births within the group
(e) Forcibly transferring children of the group to another group (Art 2)

Article 4 provided that persons who commit genocide "shall be punished, whether they are constitutionally responsible rulers, public officials or private individuals" and Article 7 stated that genocide is not to be considered a political crime for the purposes of extradition.

However, given the number of cases of genocide since the Convention, pessimism has been expressed about its efficacy as an instrument for the protection of human rights (53) and prosecution for the crime of genocide has proved challenging (54,55). Questions have also been raised about cultural issues that underlie the rationales for the creation of genocide as a crime (56).

THE GENEVA CONVENTIONS

Another development in the immediate aftermath of the Second World War was a series of Geneva Conventions that built substantially on the Hague Conventions of 1899 and 1927 (57) and the first of the Geneva Conventions in 1864 (25,58):

- The Convention for the Amelioration of the Condition of the Wounded and Sick in Armed Forces in the Field (1949)
- The Convention for the Amelioration of the Condition of the Wounded, Sick and Shipwrecked Members of Armed Forces at Sea (1949)

- Convention Relative to the Treatment of Prisoners of War (1949)
- Convention Relative to the Protection of Civilian Persons in Time of War (1949).

The Conventions were a product of complex political tensions among their drafters (59) but maintain considerable contemporary relevance (60). They have attained nearly universal recognition, having been ratified by more States than any other convention with the exception of the (less contentious) Convention on the Rights of the Child (1989) and, although they have often been violated, have secured the protection of great numbers of prisoners of war and detainees and made possible extensive relief operations for victims of war (61).

THE INTERNATIONAL COVENANTS ON CIVIL AND POLITICAL RIGHTS AND ECONOMIC, SOCIAL AND CULTURAL RIGHTS

A pair of international covenants, the International Covenant on Civil and Political Rights (ICCPR) (62) and the International Covenant on Economic, Social and Cultural Rights (ICESCR) (63) were adopted in 1966 and came into force in 1976. Arguably, they are the two most significant contemporary human rights instruments. However, their division of rights into two categories by two different instruments has been blamed for creating a distinction that has "hovered like an albatross over the development of human rights protection" (64).

Article 3 of the ICCPR binds States to undertake to ensure the equal rights of men and women to the enjoyment of civil and political rights set out in the Covenant. ICCPR provides for the "inherent right to life" (Art 6); it precludes torture and cruel, inhuman or degrading treatment or punishment and provides that no one should be subjected without free consent to medical or scientific experimentation (Art 7). It precludes slavery (Art 8), provides for a right to liberty and security of the person (Art 9) and requires that persons deprived of their liberty must be treated "with humanity and with respect for the inherent dignity of the human person" (Art 10). It provides for persons lawfully within a State to have the right of liberty of movement and freedom to choose their residence, as well as to leave (Art 12) and for persons to have the right to freedom of thought, conscience and religion (Art 18), as well as to hold opinions without interference (Art 19). Propaganda for war must be prohibited by law (Art 20) and the right of peaceful assembly is recognized (Art 21). In those States in which ethnic, religious, or linguistic minorities exist, persons belonging to such minorities are not to be denied the right, in community with the other members of their group, to enjoy their own culture, to profess and practise their own religion, or to use their own language (Art 27).

The ICESCR provides protection for the right to self-determination (Art 1); equal rights for men and women (Art 3); the right to work and just and favorable conditions of work (Arts 6 & 7); the right to social security and collective bargaining (Art 8); the right to social security and insurance (Art 10); the right to an adequate standard of living, including adequate food, clothing and housing (Art 11); the right to freedom from hunger (Art 11); the right to the highest attainable standard of physical and mental health (Art 12); the right to education (13) and the right to culture and to benefit from scientific progress (Art 15).

The ICCPR and the ICESCR remain the international community's most influential rights conventions (65,66). However, a number of States have either declined to ratify the two Conventions or persist in flagrantly disregarding their provisions. For instance, Russia ratified both Conventions in 1973 but has consistently breached their provisions. China has not ratified the ICCPR, although it signed it in 1988, and ratified the ICESCR in 2001 but regularly breaches it. The United States ratified the ICCPR in 1992, 15 years after President Carter signed it, but attached an unprecedented number of reservations, understandings and declarations that derogated from its effectiveness (67).

INTERNATIONAL CRIMINAL CONDUCT

In turn, these various conventions influenced the terms of the evolving concept of core crimes which are recognized by international criminal law. Einarson (68) categorized these as conduct manifestly violating universal values or interests; conduct universally regarded as punishable due to its inherent gravity; conduct recognized as a matter of serious international concern; where the proscriptive norm is anchored in the law – creating sources of international law; and where criminal liability and prosecution is not dependent on the consent of a concerned State. In turn, these considerations influenced the terms of the Rome Statute of the International Criminal Court (ICC) which by Article 5 builds upon the Convention on the Prevention and Punishment of the Crime of Genocide by giving the ICC jurisdiction over the crime of genocide, crimes against humanity, war crimes and the crime of aggression. "Genocide" is defined by Article 6:

> "...any of the following acts committed with intent to destroy, in whole or in part, a national, ethnical, racial or religious group, as such:

(a) Killing members of the group
(b) Causing serious bodily or mental harm to members of the group
(c) Deliberately inflicting on the group conditions of life calculated to bring about its physical destruction in whole or in part
(d) Imposing measures intended to prevent births within the group
(e) Forcibly transferring children of the group to another group

Article 7 defines "crimes against humanity as any of the following acts when committed as part of a widespread or systematic attack directed against any civilian population, with knowledge of the attack:

(a) Murder
(b) Extermination
(c) Enslavement
(d) Deportation or forcible transfer of population
(e) Imprisonment or other severe deprivation of physical liberty in violation of fundamental rules of international law
(f) Torture
(g) Rape, sexual slavery, enforced prostitution, forced pregnancy, enforced sterilization, or any other form of sexual violence of comparable gravity
(h) Persecution against any identifiable group or collectivity on political, racial, national, ethnic, cultural, religious, gender as defined in paragraph 3, or other grounds that are universally recognized as impermissible under international law, in connection with any act referred to in this paragraph or any crime within the jurisdiction of the Court
(i) Enforced disappearance of persons
(j) The crime of apartheid
(k) Other inhumane acts of a similar character intentionally causing great suffering, or serious injury to body or to mental or physical health

"War crimes" are defined by Article 8(2) as:

(a) Grave breaches of the Geneva Conventions of 12 August 1949, namely, any of the following acts against persons or property protected under the provisions of the relevant Geneva Convention:

    (i) Wilful killing
    (ii) Torture or inhuman treatment, including biological experiments
    (iii) Wilfully causing great suffering, or serious injury to body or health
    (iv) Extensive destruction and appropriation of property, not justified by military necessity and carried out unlawfully and wantonly
    (v) Compelling a prisoner of war or other protected person to serve in the forces of a hostile Power
    (vi) Wilfully depriving a prisoner of war or other protected person of the rights of fair and regular trial
    (vii) Unlawful deportation or transfer or unlawful confinement
    (viii) Taking of hostages.

(b) Other serious violations of the laws and customs applicable in international armed conflict, within the established framework of international law, namely, any of the following acts:

    (i) Intentionally directing attacks against the civilian population as such or against individual civilians not taking direct part in hostilities
    (ii) Intentionally directing attacks against civilian objects, that is, objects which are not military objectives
    (iii) Intentionally directing attacks against personnel, installations, material, units or vehicles involved in a humanitarian assistance or peacekeeping mission in accordance with the Charter of the United Nations, as long as they are entitled to the protection given to civilians or civilian objects under the international law of armed conflict
    (iv) Intentionally launching an attack in the knowledge that such attack will cause incidental loss of life or injury to civilians or damage to civilian objects or widespread, long-term and severe damage to the natural environment which would be clearly excessive in relation to the concrete and direct overall military advantage anticipated
    (v) Attacking or bombarding, by whatever means, towns, villages, dwellings or buildings which are undefended, and which are not military objectives
    (vi) Killing or wounding a combatant who, having laid down his arms or having no longer means of defence, has surrendered at discretion
    (vii) Making improper use of a flag of truce, of the flag or of the military insignia and uniform of the enemy or of the United Nations, as well as of the distinctive emblems of the Geneva Conventions, resulting in death or serious personal injury
    (viii) The transfer, directly or indirectly, by the Occupying Power of parts of its own civilian population into the territory it occupies, or the deportation or transfer of all or parts of the population of the occupied territory within or outside this territory
    (ix) Intentionally directing attacks against buildings dedicated to religion, education, art, science or charitable purposes, historic monuments, hospitals and places where the sick and wounded are collected, provided they are not military objectives
    (x) Subjecting persons who are in the power of an adverse party to physical mutilation or to medical or scientific experiments of any kind which are neither justified by the medical, dental or hospital treatment of the person concerned nor carried out in his or her interest, and which cause death to or seriously endanger the health of such person or persons
    (xi) Killing or wounding treacherously individuals belonging to the hostile nation or army
    (xii) Declaring that no quarter will be given
    (xiii) Destroying or seizing the enemy's property unless such destruction or seizure be imperatively demanded by the necessities of war
    (xiv) Declaring abolished, suspended or inadmissible in a court of law the rights and actions of the nationals of the hostile party
    (xv) Compelling the nationals of the hostile party to take part in the operations of war directed against their own country, even if they were in the belligerent's service before the commencement of the war
    (xvi) Pillaging a town or place, even when taken by assault

(xvii) Employing poison or poisoned weapons
(xviii) Employing asphyxiating, poisonous or other gases, and all analogous liquids, materials or devices
(xix) Employing bullets which expand or flatten easily in the human body, such as bullets with a hard envelope which does not entirely cover the core or is pierced with incisions
(xx) Employing weapons, projectiles and material and methods of warfare which are of a nature to cause superfluous injury or unnecessary suffering or which are inherently indiscriminate in violation of the international law of armed conflict, provided that such weapons, projectiles and material and methods of warfare are the subject of a comprehensive prohibition and are included in an annex to this Statute, by an amendment in accordance with the relevant provisions set forth in articles 121 and 123
(xxi) Committing outrages upon personal dignity, in particular humiliating and degrading treatment
(xxii) Committing rape, sexual slavery, enforced prostitution, forced pregnancy, as defined in article 7, paragraph 2 (f), enforced sterilization, or any other form of sexual violence also constituting a grave breach of the Geneva Conventions
(xxiii) Utilizing the presence of a civilian or other protected person to render certain points, areas or military forces immune from military operations
(xxiv) Intentionally directing attacks against buildings, material, medical units and transport, and personnel using the distinctive emblems of the Geneva Conventions in conformity with international law
(xxv) Intentionally using starvation of civilians as a method of warfare by depriving them of objects indispensable to their survival, including wilfully impeding relief supplies as provided for under the Geneva Conventions
(xxvi) Conscripting or enlisting children under the age of fifteen years into the national armed forces or using them to participate actively in hostilities.

States Parties to the Geneva Conventions (and Additional Protocol 1) are obliged to criminalize grave breaches at a national level and to either prosecute or, relevantly, extradite suspects of such crimes (69). The final category of crimes over which the ICC has jurisdiction is the "crime of aggression" which is defined by Article 8 (inserted in 2010) as: "the planning, preparation, initiation or execution, by a person in a position effectively to exercise control over or to direct the political or military action of a State, of an act of aggression which, by its character, gravity and scale, constitutes a manifest violation of the Charter of the United Nations." For this purpose, Article 8 states that "act of aggression" means "the use of armed force by a State against the sovereignty, territorial integrity or political independence of another State, or in any other manner inconsistent with the Charter of the United Nations", including:

(a) The invasion or attack by the armed forces of a State of the territory of another State, or any military occupation, however temporary, resulting from such invasion or attack, or any annexation by the use of force of the territory of another State or part thereof
(b) Bombardment by the armed forces of a State against the territory of another State or the use of any weapons by a State against the territory of another State
(c) The blockade of the ports or coasts of a State by the armed forces of another State
(d) An attack by the armed forces of a State on the land, sea or air forces, or marine and air fleets of another State
(e) The use of armed forces of one State which are within the territory of another State with the agreement of the receiving State, in contravention of the conditions provided for in the agreement or any extension of their presence in such territory beyond the termination of the agreement
(f) The action of a State in allowing its territory, which it has placed at the disposal of another State, to be used by that other State for perpetrating an act of aggression against a third State
(g) The sending by or on behalf of a State of armed bands, groups, irregulars or mercenaries, which carry out acts of armed force against another State of such gravity as to amount to the acts listed above, or its substantial involvement therein.

TRIALS BEFORE THE INTERNATIONAL CRIMINAL COURT

There are limitations to the jurisdiction and effectiveness of the ICC. Trials in absentia are not permitted; the accused must be present during the trial (Art 63). This means that for a person to be brought within the jurisdiction of the ICC, they must be arrested, detained and surrendered to the ICC but the ICC does not have any powers to ensure arrest and surrender suspects. The limitation on the powers of the ICC has been paralleled by comparable limitations for comparable ad hoc criminal tribunals, such as the International Criminal Tribunal for the Former Yugoslavia (ICTY), the International Criminal Tribunal for Rwanda (ICTR), the Extraordinary Chambers in the Courts of Cambodia (ECCC) and the Special Court for Sierra Leone (SCSL). This limitation on powers led Antonio Cassese (70) to describe the ICTY as a "giant without arms and legs – it needs artificial limbs to walk and work." His point was that the international criminal tribunals are wholly dependent on the preparedness of State authorities to co-operate with them. This constitutes a significant impediment, for instance, to the capacity of the ICC to take action against senior officials in Kenya (71) and against senior Russian personnel for war crimes that have been committed in Ukraine by Russia (72).

A wide variety of trials have taken place before the ICC. Some have resulted in findings of not guilty, others in findings of guilty. Three prominent examples of such cases are summarized below to illustrate both the limitations and strengths of the ICC jurisdiction in respect of egregious breaches of human rights.

In March 2016, the Trial Chamber of the ICC convicted Jean-Pierre Bemba Gombo, a person effectively acting as a military commander in the Democratic Republic of the Congo, of the crimes of murder as a crime against humanity; murder as a war crime; rape as a crime against humanity; rape as a war crime; and pillaging as a war crime (73) (*Prosecutor v Gombo*, March 2016). In June 2016, Gombo was sentenced to 18 years of imprisonment (*Prosecutor v Gombo*, June 2016) (74). However, in June 2018, the Appeals Chamber decided by majority (*Gombo v Prosecutor*, June 2018) (75) that Gombo had been wrongly convicted for criminal acts that were outside the scope of the charges brought against him; and in its assessment of whether Gombo had taken all necessary and reasonable measures to prevent, repress or punish the commission by his subordinates of the other crimes within the scope of the case, the Trial Chamber had made serious errors. Furthermore, in the view of the Appeals Chamber majority, there was an apparent discrepancy between the limited number of crimes within the case's scope for which Gombo was held responsible and the Trial Chamber's assessment of which measures Gombo should have taken. The appellate outcome constituted a significant setback for ICC prosecutions.

In January 2019, the Trial Chamber of the ICC by majority found former Côte d'Ivoire President Laurent Gbagbo and youth leader Charles Blé Goudé not guilty of all charges of four counts of crimes against humanity, including murder, rape and other inhumane acts or—in the alternative—attempted murder and persecution. This was the first occasion on which a head of state had appeared before the ICC. The crimes in question were alleged to have been committed in Côte d'Ivoire's capital Abidjan during a march against supporters of rival Allasane Ouattara after Gbagbo lost the country's presidential election. In its July 2019 reasons the majority found that the Prosecutor:

- Had failed to demonstrate that there was a "common plan" to keep Gbagbo in power, which included the commission of crimes against civilians
- Had failed to demonstrate the existence of the alleged policy to attack a civilian population on the basis of the alleged patterns of violence and other circumstantial evidence cited in support
- Had failed to demonstrate that the crimes as alleged in the charges were committed pursuant to or in furtherance of a State or organizational policy to attack the civilian population
- Had failed to demonstrate that public speeches by Gbagbo or Blé Goudé constituted ordering, soliciting, or inducing the alleged crimes or that either of the accused otherwise knowingly or intentionally contributed to the commission of such crimes (76) (*Prosecutor v Gbagbo*, 16 July 2019)

In March 2021, the Appeals Chamber confirmed by majority the acquittal decision. Again, this was a high-profile failure of a prosecution.

However, in an important decision in February 2021, the Trial Chamber of the ICC (77) (*Prosecutor v Ongwen*, 4 February 2021) found the head of the Lord's Resistance Army in Uganda, Dominic Ongwen, guilty of 61 counts of crimes against humanity and war crimes committed in Northern Uganda between July 2002 and December 2005. In particular, it found him guilty of:

- attacks against the civilian population in the form of murder, attempted murder, torture, enslavement, outrages upon personal dignity, pillaging, destruction of property and persecution, committed in the context of attacks on internally displaced persons camps
- sexual and gender-based crimes: forced marriage, torture, rape, sexual slavery, enslavement, forced pregnancy and outrages upon personal dignity he committed against seven women (whose names and individual stories are specified in the judgment) who were abducted and placed into his household
- A number of further sexual and gender-based crimes he committed against girls and women: namely forced marriage, torture, rape, sexual slavery and enslavement
- The crime of conscripting children under the age of 15 and using them to participate actively in hostilities

The decision by the Trial Chamber emphatically rejected the quality of mental health expert evidence adduced on behalf of Ongwen in an effort to show him not to have been criminally responsible for his conduct by reason of insanity, finding the defense witnesses to be unduly accepting of Ongwen's accounts, inadequately rigorous, confusing the tests for fitness to stand trial and insanity, implausible, and inconsistent with available lay evidence. It sentenced him to imprisonment for 25 years (78) (*Prosecutor v Ongwen*, 6 May 2021). At the time of writing, the Appeals Chamber had not delivered its findings.

EXPERT EVIDENCE IN INTERNATIONAL CRIMINAL LAW TRIALS

The ICC and the ad hoc criminal law tribunals rely heavily upon expert medical and scientific evidence on a wide variety of matters in their hearings (79,80). The evidence of forensic pathologists about cause and circumstances of death is particularly important. It is expected that experts who are called in ICC and ad hoc tribunal proceedings have acknowledged expertise in their field and have a level of impartiality (*Prosecutor v Milutinovic* (2006) (81). In the *Sesay* judgment Judge Thompson of the Special Court for Sierra Leone took note of the admissibility criteria in common law countries.

With specific reference to the admissibility of expert evidence, the law may be compendiously stated thus:

(a) The subject matter of the proposed testimony must be a proper topic for expert evidence and not a matter within the knowledge and experience of the Court. For instance, where experts draw conclusions about the role of the accused, or fail to assist the Trial Chamber

(b) Where the subject matter is a proper one for expert evidence, it must be relevant in the sense of assisting the Court to determine an issue in dispute
(c) The expert must possess the necessary qualifications and credentials in the professed field of expertise
(d) The reasoning or methodology underlying the testimony must be valid and properly applicable to the facts in issue
(e) The expert must be independent (*Prosecutor v Sesay*, 25 February 2009, para 27) (82)

Should the expert be shown to have engaged in inadequately discerning evaluative processes their testimony, if admitted, will be given little probative value (*Prosecutor v Ongwen*, 4 February 2021) (77).

CONCLUSION

For human rights to be addressed adequately in both domestic law and international criminal law cases, it is necessary that expert medical and scientific evidence be placed before decision makers to shed accurate, technically informed light on the circumstances and causes of deaths. In addition, English and European jurisprudence has determined that the right to life requires that investigations into deaths involving the State impose demanding systems, operational and investigative obligations on the State (*R (MG) v Secretary of State for the Home Department*, 2022) (83), be thorough, effective (*R (Middleton) v HM Coroner for West Somerset*, 2004 (84); (*Jordan v United Kingdom*, 2003) (85), where possible prompt (*Al Skeini v United Kingdom*, 2011) (86), and be conducted with significant levels of independence (*R (Amin) v Secretary of State for Home Department*, 2004) (87). This has become a requirement for coronial inquests convened in the United Kingdom in respect of deaths that have occurred in the context of State action.

In both domestic and international contexts, an important objective of death investigations is the public clarification by proper process of what has brought about a death or cohort of deaths and the breaches of human rights that these may have involved. International humanitarian law, as well as criminal processes before the ICC and the ad hoc tribunals, enable two levels of response. The first is exposure of acts that may have constituted breaches of ethical and legal obligations, determined by reference to international instruments, so that denunciation and other deterrent measures can be adopted. The second is the institution of criminal proceedings against those responsible for conduct that constitutes offenses such as genocide, crimes against humanity, war crimes and acts of aggression. It is only by such determinations by international bodies instituted to undertake such investigations and make such determinations that victims can receive the solace of justice.

Since the Second World War, significant advances in relation to the recognition of human rights and bioethics have been made internationally. Inevitably, though, the instruments that have been published are substantially declaratory. There are limited mechanisms for enforcement of rights and obligations in individual cases, although in a small number of cases, the International Criminal Court has found charges proved and imposed significant penalties. However, the ongoing endorsement of such instruments by most countries increasingly marginalizes States that do not subscribe to the instruments or that breach rights. This is likely to be an ongoing trend with pressures escalating for compliance with key tenets of international humanitarian law.

REFERENCES

1. Nicosia FR, Huener J, (eds). *Medicine and Medical Ethics in Nazi Germany: Origins, Practices, Legacies*. Oxford, New York: Berghahn Books; 2002.
2. Baker RB, McCullough LB, (eds). *The Cambridge World History of Medical Ethics*. Cambridge: Cambridge University Press; 2009.
3. Coates AJ. *The Ethics of War*. Manchester: Manchester University Press; 1997.
4. Dower N. *The Ethics of War and Peace*. Cambridge: Polity Press; 2009.
5. Allhoff F, Evans NG, Henschke A, (eds). *Routledge Handbook of Ethics and War: Just War Theory in the Twenty-First Century*. Abingdon-on-Thames: Routledge; 2013.
6. Frowe H. *The Ethics of War and Peace: An Introduction*. Abingdon-on-Thames: Routledge; 2015.
7. Lifton RJ. *The Nazi Doctors: Medical Killing and the Psychology of Genocide*. Stuttgart: Macmillan; 1987.
8. Annas GJ, Grodin MA. *The Nazi Doctors and the Nuremberg Code: Human Rights in Human Experimentation*. Oxford: Oxford University Press; 1992.
9. Caplan AL, (ed). *When Medicine Went Bad: Bioethics and the Holocaust*. New York: Springer; 2012.
10. Weindling P. *Victims and Survivors of Nazi Human Experiments: Science and Suffering in the Holocaust*. London: Bloomsbury; 2014.
11. Harris SA. *Factories of Death: Japanese Biological Warfare, 1932–1945, and the American Cover-up*. Abingdon-on-Thames: Routledge; 1994.
12. Gold H. *Japan's Infamous Unit 731: Firsthand Accounts of Japan's Wartime Human Experimentation Regime*. Clarendon: Tuttle Publishing; 2019.
13. Chan J. *Marutas of Unit 731: Human Experimentation of the Forgotten Asian Auschwitz*. San Francisco: Pacific Atrocities Education; 2020.
14. Dinstein Y. Distinction and loss of civilian protection in international armed conflicts. *Int Law Stud* 2008; 84: 183–98.
15. Shaw M. *What is Genocide?* 2nd ed. Cambridge: Polity Press; 2015.
16. Pegorier C. *Ethnic Cleansing: A legal Qualification*. Abingdon-on-Thames: Routledge; 2013.
17. Downes AB. *Targeting Civilians in War*. Ithaca: Cornell University Press; 2008.
18. Rothbart D, Korostelina KV. *Why They Die: Civilian Devastation in Violent Conflict*. Ann Arbor: University of Michigan Press; 2011.
19. Wells D. Sexual violence interventions: Considerations for humanitarian settings. *Forensic Sci Int* 2017; **276**: 1–4.
20. Zalewski K, Majewski MS. The History of Sexual Violence in War. In: Zaleski K (ed), *Understanding and Treating Military Sexual Trauma*. New York: Springer; 2015, pp. 1–14.
21. Katz LS, (ed). *Treating Military Sexual Trauma*. New York: Springer; 2016.
22. Ferber S. *Bioethics in Historical Perspective*. London: Bloomsbury; 2013.
23. Gallin S, Bedzow I, (eds). *Bioethics and the Holocaust: A Comprehensive Study in How the Holocaust Continues to

Shape the Ethics of Health, Medicine and Human Rights. New York: Springer; 2022.

24. Crawford E, Pert A. *International Humanitarian Law*. Cambridge: Cambridge University Press; 2020.
25. Pictet J. The medical profession and international humanitarian law. *Int Rev Red Cross* 1995; **247**: 191–209.
26. Melzer N. *International humanitarian llaw*. Switzerland: ICRC; 2016.
27. Goodman R. The power to kill or capture enemy combatants. *Eur J Int Law* 2013; **24**(**3**): 819–53.
28. Borelli S, Laufer H. Protection of Individuals Hors de Combat. In: Rogers D (ed), *Human Rights in War*. New York: Springer; 2022, pp. 309–43.
29. Nwotite A. No longer foes but friends: Hors de combat in humanitarian law. *IJOCLLEP*. 2021; **3**(**1**): 199–205.
30. Leaning J. Medicine and international humanitarian law. *BMJ* 1999; **319** (**7207**): 393–4.
31. Bruderlein C, Leaning J. New challenges for humanitarian protection. *BMJ* 1999; **319**: 422–52.
32. Sassoli M. *International Humanitarian Law: Rules, Controversies, and Solutions to Problems Arising in Warfare*. Cheltenham: Edward Elgar Publishing; 2019.
33. Saul B, Akande D. *The Oxford Guide to International Humanitarian Law*. Oxford: Oxford University Press; 2020.
34. Meron T. *The Humanization of International Law*, Vol. 3. Leiden: Martinus Nijhoff Publishers; 2006.
35. Morrow JD. *Order Within Anarchy: The Laws of War as an International Institution*. Cambridge: Cambridge University Press; 2014.
36. Gunn MJ, McCoubrey H. Medical ethics and the laws of armed conflict. *J Confl Secur Law* 1998; **3**(**2**): 133–61.
37. *Nicaragua v United States* [1986] ICJ 1; [1986] ICJ Rep 14. Available from: http://www.worldlii.org/int/cases/ICJ/1986/1.html (Accessed 25 March 2023).
38. Tidball-Binz MV, Cordner S. Humanitarian forensic action: A new forensic discipline helping to implement international law and construct peace. *WIREs Forensic Sci* 2021; **4**(**1**): e1438.
39. Tidball-Binz M, Extraordinary Deathwork: New Developments in, and the Social Significance of, Forensic Humanitarian Action. In: Parra RC, Zapico SC and Ubelaker DH (eds). *Forensic Science and Humanitarian Action: Interacting with the Dead and the Living*. 2020, Wiley.
40. Pollanen MS. The pathology of torture. *Forensic Sci Int* 2018; **284**: 85–96.
41. Thomsen JL. The role of the pathologist in human rights abuses. *J Clin Pathol* 2000; **53**(**8**): 569–72.
42. Thomsen JL, Voigt J. Forensic medicine and human rights. *Forensic Sci Int* 1988; **36**: 147–51.
43. Annas GJ, Grodin MA, *The Nazi Doctors and the Nuremberg Code: Human Rights in Human Experimentation*. 1992. Oxford University Press.
44. Nuremberg Code. *BMJ* 1966; **313**: 1448.
45. Moreno JD, Schmidt U, Joffe S. 2017. The Nuremberg code 70 years later. *JAMA* 2017; **318**(**9**): 795–6.
46. Thieren M, Mauron A. Nuremberg code turns 60. *Bull World Health Organ* 2007; **85**(**8**): 573.
47. Shuster E. Fifty years later: The significance of the Nuremberg code. *N Engl J Med* 1997; **337**: 1436–40.
48. Universal Declaration on Bioethics and Human Rights, 2005. Available from: https://unesdoc.unesco.org/ark:/48223/pf0000146180 (Accessed 25 March 2023).
49. Freckelton I. The Universal Declaration on Bioethics and Human Rights. *J Law Med* 2008; **16**(**2**): 187–92.
50. Universal Declaration of Human Rights, 1948. Available from: https://www.un.org/en/about-us/universal-declaration-of-human-rights (Accessed 25 March 2023).
51. Convention on the Prevention and Punishment of the Crime of Genocide, 1948. Available from: https://www.un.org/en/genocideprevention/documents/atrocity-crimes/Doc.1_Convention%20on%20the%20Prevention%20and%20Punishment%20of%20the%20Crime%2020Genocide.pdf (Accessed 25 March 2023).
52. Pinch GA. The genocide convention. *AJIL* 1949; **43**(**4**): 732–8.
53. Ratner SR. The genocide convention after fifty years. *Proc Annu Meet Am Soc Int Law* 1998; **92**: 1–19.
54. Safferling CJM, Conze E-A. *The Genocide Convention Sixty Years After its Adoption*. New York: Springer; 2010.
55. Adanan A. Reflecting on the genocide convention in its eighth decade: How universal jurisdiction developed over genocide. *J Int Crim Justice* 2021; **19**(**5**): 1039–65.
56. Murndorff K. *A Cultural Interpretation of the Genocide Convention*. Abingdon-on-Thames: Routledge; 2021.
57. Bouchet-Saulnier F. *The Practical Guide to Humanitarian Law*, 3rd English ed. Trans: Brav L, Michel C. Lanham: Rowman & Littlefield; 2014.
58. Dunant H. *A Memory of Solferino*. Ravenio Books; 2013.
59. Van Dijk B. *Preparing for War: The Making of the Geneva Conventions*. Oxford: Oxford University Press; 2022.
60. Evangelista M. How the Geneva Conventions Matter. In: Evangelista M, Tannenwald N (eds), *Do the Geneva Conventions Matter?* Oxford: Oxford University Press; 2017.
61. Schindler D. Significance of the Geneva conventions for the contemporary world. *RICR* 1999; **81**(**836**): 715–29.
62. United Nations. International Covenant on Civil and Political Rights, 1966. Available from: https://www.ohchr.org/en/instruments-mechanisms/instruments/international-covenant-civil-and-political-rights (Accessed 25 March 2023).
63. United Nations. International Covenant on Economic, Social and Cultural Rights, 1966. Available from: https://www.ohchr.org/en/instruments-mechanisms/instruments/international-covenant-economic-social-and-cultural-rights (Accessed 25 March 2023).
64. Scott C. Canada's international human rights obligations and disadvantaged members of Society: Finally into the spotlight? *Constit Forum* 1999; **10**: 97–102.
65. Ssenyonjo M. The influence of the international covenant on economic, social and cultural rights in Africa. *NILR*; 2017; **64**: 259–89.
66. Moeckli D, Keller H, Heri C. *The Human Rights Covenants at 50: Their Past, Present, and Future*. Oxford: Oxford University Press; 2018.
67. Ash K. US reservations to the international covenant on civil and political rights: Credibility maximisation and global influence, 2005. Available from: https://scholarlycommons.law.northwestern.edu/cgi/viewcontent.cgi?referer=&httpsredir=1&article=1018&context=njihr (Accessed 25 March 2023).
68. Einarsen T. *The Concept of Universal Crimes in International Law*. Brussels: Torkel Opsahl Academic Epublisher; 2012.
69. Mehring S. *First Do No Harm: Medical Ethics in International Humanitarian Law*. Leiden: Brill Martinus Nijhoff Publishers; 2015.
70. Cassese A. The statute of the international criminal court: Some preliminary reflections. *Eur J Int Law* 1999; **10**: 144–71.
71. Dancy, G, Dutton YM, Alleblas T, et al. What determines perceptions of bias toward the international criminal court? Evidence from Kenya. *J Conflict Resolut* 2019; **64**: 1443–69.
72. Einarsen T, Rikhof K. Prosecuting the Russian leadership for the crime of aggression at the International Criminal Court, 2022. Available from: https://www.toaep.org/pbs-pdf/129-einarsen-rikhof/ (Accessed 25 March 2023).
73. *Prosecutor v Gombo*, ICC Trial Chamber III, 2016. Available from: https://www.legal-tools.org/doc/edb0cf/pdf (Accessed 25 March 2023).
74. *Prosecutor v Gombo*, ICC Trial Chamber III, 2016. Available from: https://www.icc-cpi.int/sites/default/files/CourtRecords/CR2016_04476.PDF (Accessed 25 March 2023).
75. *Gombo v Prosecutor*, ICC Appeals Chamber, 2018. Available from: https://www.icc-cpi.int/sites/default/files/CourtRecords/CR2018_02984.PDF (Accessed 25 March 2023).
76. *Prosecutor v Gbagbo and Goude*, ICC Trial Chamber I, 2019. Available from: https://www.icc-cpi.int/court-record/icc-02/11-01/15-1263 (Accessed 25 March 2023).
77. *Prosecutor v Ongwen*, ICC Trial Chamber IX, 2021. Available from: https://www.icc-cpi.int/court-record/icc-02/04-01/15-1762-red (Accessed 25 March 2023).
78. *Prosecutor v Ongwen*, ICC Trial Chamber IX, 2021. Available from: https://www.icc-cpi.int/sites/default/files/itemsDocuments/210506-ongwen-sentence-summary-eng.pdf (Accessed 25 March 2023).
79. Appazov A. *Expert Evidence and International Criminal Justice*. New York: Springer; 2016.
80. Freckelton I, *Expert Evidence: Law, Practice, Procedure and Advocacy*, 7th ed. Sydney: Lawbook Company Thomson Reuters; 2023.
81. *Prosecutor v Milutinovic*, Case IT-05-87-T, Transcript, 2006, pp. 840–44.
82. *The Prosecutor v Issa Hassan Sesay, Morris Kallon and Augustine Gbao*, Special Court for Sierra Leone (trial Chamber 1), 25 February 2009: https://internationalcrimesdatabase.org/Case/793/Sesay-et-al/ *Prosecutor v Sesay* 2009

83. *R (MG) v Secretary of State for the Home Department* [2022] EWHC 1847 (Admin).
84. *R (Middleton) v West Somerset Coroner* [2004] 2 AC 182.
85. *Jordan v United Kingdom* [2003] 37 EHRR 2.
86. *Al Skeini v United Kingdom* [2011] 53 EHRR 18.
87. *R (Amin) v Secretary of State for the Home Department* [2004] 1 AC 653.

CHAPTER

4

Euthanasia

Wilma L.J.M. Duijst and Jan Bollen

INTRODUCTION

One cause of non-acceptance of euthanasia may be the fact that the term was first used during the Nazi regime under Hitler. Because of this connection with the Third Reich, perhaps euthanasia will keep its negative connotations (1). All over the world, there are ongoing discussions about euthanasia and about the fear for "the slippery slope" and dark numbers (2,3).

The term euthanasia is used differently in countries around the world. In the Netherlands, the term euthanasia is used to actively describe ending the life of a person and assisted suicide by a medical doctor. In other countries, the term euthanasia is used for end-of-life decisions (passive euthanasia) and the active ending of life (active euthanasia) (4). In this chapter, the term euthanasia is reserved for actively ending life and assisted suicide by a medical doctor. Assisted suicide by an individual who is not a medical doctor will not be discussed.

HUMAN RIGHTS AND PROFESSIONAL OBLIGATIONS

In recent years, euthanasia and assisted suicide have led to a lot of discussion in European countries. Some of the conflicts that emerged were presented to the European Court of Human Rights (ECHR). The rulings of the ECHR on euthanasia focus on two human rights: the right to life (art. 2 Convention) and the right to self-determination (included in the right to privacy, art. 8 Convention). In recent years, the ECHR has occasionally discussed euthanasia and the right to assisted suicide in relation to the right to life, but more often, the court has given rulings on the subject of the right to self-determination (5). The question of whether legalization of euthanasia and/or assisted suicide is a breach of the right to life has never been presented to the court.

The question of whether the right to live implies the right to take one's own life has been answered negatively in *Pretty v. UK* (6). In *Jehovah's witnesses v. Russia*, the court ruled that the right to self-determination includes the right to make medical decisions, even if this means the person involved will die because of this decision. In *Koch v. Switzerland* (7) and *Lambert v. France*, (8) the court stated that there was no consensus among the Member States of the Council of Europe as to the question of whether or not to allow any form of assisted suicide or euthanasia. The decision is within the margin of appreciation of the States. In *Haas v. Switzerland*, the court emphasizes that a government does not have the obligation to allow euthanasia but needs to be clear whether euthanasia is permitted (9).

Within the medical world, euthanasia is still a major ethical issue. In 2002 the World Medical Association (WMA) adopted the Declaration on Euthanasia and Physician-Assisted Suicide, stating that with a commitment to the principles of medical ethics the utmost respect must be maintained for human life. The WMA is firmly opposed to euthanasia and physician-assisted suicide. This statement was reiterated and reaffirmed in 2013 and 2019.[i] Although the WMA opposes euthanasia, the public debate about euthanasia is open worldwide among medical and judicial professionals and among different cultures.

THE NETHERLANDS

As the Netherlands was the first country in the world to legalize euthanasia and other countries have more or less adopted the Dutch system, the Dutch system will be described extensively. The debate in Dutch society and parliament took over 25 years. It took several rulings of Dutch courts to determine a system of checks and balances. The checks are important before euthanasia is performed and after the procedure has ended. At the end of every procedure, the public prosecutor is informed and reserves the right to have a criminal investigation whenever this is regarded necessary. The public prosecutor wants to retain the right to prosecute in order to "set the judicial norm". The public prosecutor is the gate keeper of keeping the balance between what is medically perceived as just and what is legally right.

In the Netherlands, the term euthanasia is used for active termination of life and for assisted suicide. The

i Adopted by the 53rd WMA General Assembly, Washington, DC, USA, October 2002, reaffirmed with minor revision by the 194th WMA Council Session, Bali, Indonesia, April 2013 and rescinded and archived by the 70th WMA General Assembly, Tbilisi, October 2019.

DOI: 10.1201/9781003138754-5

judicial rules are laid down in the Penal Code and in the Act on terminating life and assisted suicide. In article 293 (active termination of life) and 294 (assisted suicide) of the Dutch Penal Code, euthanasia and assisted suicide are formulated as criminal offenses with criminal immunity (in the Penal Code) for medical doctors who have met the criteria for due care for euthanasia and reported the euthanasia as is required by law. The same rules for criminal immunity apply for both active termination of life and assisted suicide.

The criteria for due care are the following:

1. The treating physician must be convinced that the patient has made the request on his/her own account and is persistent in his/her will. A request must be made by a person who is competent. Persistent means that the request has to be done more than once in order to be sure that it is the patient's wish to die. A written request is not necessary. A written request can replace a verbally uttered wish.
2. The suffering of the patient needs to be unbearable and with no prospect of improvement. The suffering has to have a medical ground and can be both somatic and psychological. What is experienced as unbearable is ultimately the decision of the patient.
3. The patient has to be informed about his/her situation and his/her prospects. The doctor has to inform the patient about the prospects of his/her illness and about the possibilities to ease the suffering. The patient has to understand the information given by the doctor.
4. There has to be no other reasonable solution. The patient is to decide whether another solution is reasonable.
5. At least one other medical doctor has to give his/her opinion on whether the criteria of due care are met. The second doctor needs to be a medical doctor, not a nurse or a psychologist. When there is psychological suffering an extra consultation by a psychiatrist needs to be done.
6. Euthanasia has to be performed following the rules of the profession. The rules of the profession prescribe that the act of euthanasia is performed with Thiopental and Rocuronium by intravenous infusion. The doctor needs to bring a spare set of drugs. In assisted suicide the drug of choice is thiopental as a drink. The doctor has to stay with his/her patients until death has occurred.

After the procedure has been followed, the medical doctor has to report the euthanasia to a forensic physician and hand over a written report for the Euthanasia Review Committee. The forensic physician checks whether there was a request, whether the report is complete, whether a second doctor was consulted and whether the right medication was used. After this check, the forensic physician calls the public prosecutor to release the body.

The Euthanasia Review Committee is formed by a medical doctor, a lawyer and an ethicist. The three members of the committee decide whether the report gives rise to questions. If the answer is "no", the decision of the commission is that the euthanasia was diligent. When one of the members of the committee has questions, the report will be discussed in a review panel, consisting of an extra doctor, ethicist and lawyer. If necessary, the review panel can ask the medical doctor who performed the euthanasia for extra information. The decision of the Euthanasia Review Committee can either be "diligent" or "not diligent". When the decision is "diligent" the MD will receive a letter and the case is closed. When the decision is "not diligent" the case is reported to the Medical Inspectorate and to the public prosecutor. Both the Inspectorate and the public prosecutor will decide on the follow up of the case. The Inspectorate can choose to submit the case to the Medical Disciplinary Board. The public prosecutor can decide to start a criminal investigation. The reports handed to the Euthanasia Review Committee will be used in the criminal investigation. After the investigation, the public prosecutor will decide on whether or not to start a criminal prosecution.

Euthanasia has become more and more accepted in the Netherlands. In 2002, the physician needed to be the medical doctor who had given medical aid to the patient. For several years, the Expertise Center for Euthanasia has been active in the field of euthanasia (10). This organization helps people in more difficult situations, for example, when the reason to ask for euthanasia involves mental problems, problems of old age and/or dementia. The number of cases of euthanasia is increasing nearly every year. In 2022, approximately 8720 individuals have elected euthanasia. In more than 99 percent of these cases, the euthanasia was diligent. In only a few cases was a criminal prosecution started.

PROBLEMATIC SITUATIONS

Although euthanasia is legalized and accepted by the community in several countries around the world, legal and ethical discussions have not stopped. In every country where euthanasia is legalized, the discussion concentrates on psychiatric disorders, old age and dementia, and children (11). The common factor in these "problematic areas" is the mental competence of the patient. The question is not only whether the patient is competent at the moment he/she is uttering his/her request but also whether the patient is, or needs to be, competent when the euthanasia is performed.

Psychiatric disorders

In psychiatric disorders, the discussion about competence is an ongoing problem. Should the request be regarded as caused by the mental disorder or should the request be regarded as an existential need? In the first case, help for the mental disorder should be given as an alternative to euthanasia. In the second case, euthanasia can be a solution to the experienced problem. In most countries, it is necessary to consult a psychiatrist in a request from psychiatric patients. When the patient is competent to make this particular medical decision, he/she should be asked for consent before the euthanasia is actually performed.

Dementia

In dementia, the problems are also in the field of competence but in a quite different manner than for psychiatric disorders. In dementia, the request has to be uttered when the patient is still competent, preferably verbally and in writing. In the written request, the patient should describe the situation in which euthanasia is desired. The second problem occurs in the moment the euthanasia is performed. The question is whether the patient should be able to consent and perhaps even more importantly, is it possible to revise a former consent? This problem was addressed in the Netherlands in a ruling by the Supreme Court on 21st April 2020 (12). In this case, an attending doctor had performed euthanasia on a woman suffering from dementia. The patient had a written consent for euthanasia, stating that she wanted her life to be ended were she to be diagnosed with dementia. The doctor and the family decided that the situation which the woman had described in her written consent had occurred. When the moment was there to end the woman's life, the doctor did not ask for a renewed consent at the start of the procedure. The patient showed signs of resistance and needed to be sedated in order to be able to perform the euthanasia. In this case, the decision of the committee was "not diligent". The Inspectorate reported the case to the Medical Disciplinary Board. The Board disciplined the medical doctor. The public prosecutor started a criminal procedure, and the doctor was sentenced. The medical doctor appealed to the Dutch Supreme Court and the court decided that there was no criminal liability and also overruled the decision of the Medical Disciplinary Board. The Supreme Court ruled that a medical doctor had no legal obligation to check whether a patient, who is not incapable of making legal decisions, has an active wish to die at the moment euthanasia is performed.

The Supreme Court appeared to state that a person can suffer from dementia to such a degree that the person is no longer able to say that he/she does not want to die. This ruling led to a change in the rules for euthanasia for those suffering from dementia. The discussion in the literature about this ruling of the Supreme Court is still ongoing (13).

Children

Euthanasia in children is special and delicate for several reasons. Children are protected by the Convention on the Rights of the Child (CRC). All decisions have to be made in the best interest of the child. The child has the right to give his/her opinion on every matter of his/her concern. This right is not limited by age. Children need to be protected from threatening of their life and from inhuman treatment. When a child is ill, there may come a moment when the medical treatment is no longer helpful and there may come a time when the child no longer wants to hold on to his/her life and even asks to end his/her life. The question is if a child is capable of making the decision to request euthanasia and, if so, if this capability is limited by (young) age. In countries in which euthanasia is permitted, the discussion about children has led to very different outcomes. Recently, in The Netherlands, it has been decided that in future, euthanasia for children should be possible. Also, for example, in Belgium, children can be granted the right to euthanasia but in Canada they cannot. In most countries, there are age limitations for euthanasia in combination with the consent from the parents or the obligation to inform the parents. An overview is given in the next paragraph.

THE STATE OF LEGALIZATION OF EUTHANASIA WORLDWIDE

After the Netherlands legalized euthanasia in 2002, Belgium followed in the same year. In 2021, there were seven countries in which a form of euthanasia was permitted. Due to the different legal systems in the world the legal arrangements have different appearances (Table 4.1). The grounds for euthanasia are mostly a form of severe medically (somatic and/or psychiatric) based suffering. In some countries, the patient has to be terminally ill. In other countries, a patient can have euthanasia without being in the last stages of life. In some countries, there are age limitations for euthanasia. In other countries, there are no

TABLE 4.1 An overview of the rules for euthanasia globally

Country and year of legalization	Legal framework	Age limitation	Ground
The Netherlands, 2002 (14)	Arts. 293 and 294 Penal Code Criminal immunity for doctors performing the euthanasia Wet toetsing levensbeëindiging op verzoek en hulp bij zelfdoding (WTL) The death is regarded as non-natural	<12 years: no request is possible 12–16 years: with permission of the parents 16–18 years: the parents must be informed	Unbearable suffering Medical based
Belgium 2002 with adjustments in 2021 (15)	Legal Euthanasiewet The death is regarded as natural death	No limitations in age	Medically incurable condition with unbearable mental or physical suffering
Luxembourg 2008 (16)	Loi du 16 Mars 2009 sur l'Euthanasie et l'Assistance au Suicide Civil and criminal immunity for doctors	16–18 years: with consent of the parents	Incurable condition with constant unbearable suffering and no prospect of improvement

(Continued)

TABLE 4.1 (Continued) An overview of the rules for euthanasia globally

Country and year of legalization	Legal framework	Age limitation	Ground
Colombia 2015, with adjustments in 2018 (17)	Legal The Constitutional Court of Colombia legalized euthanasia, but its government has not yet legislated or regulated the practice	7–14 years, with permission of the parents >14 years no consent of the parents needed	Terminal phase of a disease
Australia (Victoria and Western Australia) 2019	Legal Voluntary Assisted Dying Act 2017	No limitation in age	Illness leading to suffering and death expected within 6 months
Canada, medical assistance in dying (MAID) 2016 with adjustments in 2021 (18)	Legal Loi modifiant le Code criminel et apportant des modifications connexes à d'autres lois (aide médicale à mourir) Criminal immunity for doctors performing the euthanasia	>18 years	Grievous and irremediable medical condition with enduring and unbearable physical or psychological suffering
Spain 2021 (19)	Legal Law for the regulation of euthanasia Death will be regarded as natural death	No limitations in age	Serious and incurable disease or suffering from a serious, chronic and disabling disease

age limitations, but the patient needs to be competent to request euthanasia.

The number of cases of euthanasia show an almost constant rise in the Netherlands, with nearly 8720 cases in 2022 (in nearly 18 million inhabitants) (20). In Belgium, the number of cases has been approximately 2500 persons (in 11.5 million inhabitants) for several years. In Luxembourg, 25 cases occurred in 2020 (in 600 000 inhabitants) (21).

EUTHANASIA IN COMBINATION WITH ORGAN DONATION

It is possible to donate organs following euthanasia (22). This combined procedure is being performed in Belgium, the Netherlands and Canada (where euthanasia is called "medical assistance in dying" [MAID]). Between 2012 and 2021, organ donation after euthanasia in the Netherlands was performed 74 times, resulting in 223 transplants. The process is essentially the same as donation of organs after circulatory death (DCD) by patients in the intensive care unit (ICU), following withdrawal of life-sustaining therapy, also referred to as "Maastricht Category III." The main advantage of this combined procedure is that the patient can give first-person consent, compared with a comatose patient in the ICU, whose wish to donate has to be verified in a donor registry or by his relatives.

Both euthanasia and the DCD procedure need to be strictly separated, to prevent a patient choosing euthanasia *because* they can then donate organs. The performing physician, most often the general practitioner, has to establish whether the patient meets all due diligence criteria before organ donation is discussed. It is preferred that the patient requests organ donation him or herself, to avoid any pressure from the physician.

If the patient is willing to be an organ donor, their medical records, as well as a blood and urine sample, are investigated for any contraindications. Not all patients who undergo euthanasia are eligible for donation. The majority suffer from malignancy, which is a contraindication for donation. Previous research of Belgian euthanasia data demonstrated that 10 percent of all patients who underwent euthanasia might have been medically eligible for donation. These patients suffered from a neurodegenerative disease (e.g. multiple sclerosis, amyotrophic lateral sclerosis, or Huntington chorea) or psychiatric illness.

To be able to transport the patient immediately to the operating room following death, it is necessary to perform euthanasia in a hospital. However, the majority of euthanasia procedures are performed at home, which is why occasionally patients do not continue the combined procedure. If the patient appears suitable for donation, the patient, together with the performing physician and the organ donation co-ordinator from the hospital, will choose a date for the combined procedure. The patient is often admitted to the ICU since its staff are familiar with organ donation. Additional medical imaging is required to initiate the process of organ allocation, which is often performed on the day of the procedure. In the Netherlands, euthanasia is a non-natural death, thus the public prosecutor and municipal coroner need to be informed beforehand.

The patient's relatives need to be prepared for the mental impact the procedure may have on them. They are allowed to be present in the ICU while the performing physician first induces coma, followed by a muscle relaxant. Depending on local protocols, it is possible to have an arterial line in place, to immediately determine the time of cardiac arrest. Following five minutes of "no touch time," to respect the dead-donor rule, the patient is transported immediately to the operating room where the organs are procured. The patient's lungs, kidneys, liver and pancreas may be donated, and the first procedures have been performed where the heart was also donated. Preliminary data show that the organs function adequately following transplantation.

A Euthanasia Review Committee determines whether all due diligence criteria were fulfilled. If this is not the case, the performing physician could still be prosecuted. After several weeks, the patient's relatives receive anonymized information about whether the transplantation procedure was successful. Organs are distributed in accordance with the local transplant waiting lists. Eurotransplant, the organization managing the waiting lists for eight European countries, requires that organs donated following euthanasia can only be transplanted in countries where euthanasia is also lawful.

REFERENCES

1. Herbots P. *A Plea for Euthanasia Without Borders*. Antwerp: Maklu; 2021.
2. Fontalis A. Euthanasia and assisted dying: What is the current position and what are the key arguments informing the debate? *J R Soc Med* 2018; **111(11)**: 407–13.
3. Sprung C. Physician-assisted suicide and euthanasia: Emerging issues from a global perspective. *J Palliat Care* 2018; **33(4)**: 197–203.
4. Annadurai K. Euthanasia: Right to die with dignity. *J Family Med Prim Care* 2014; **3(4)**: 477–8.
5. European Court of Human Rights. Factsheet. End of life and the European convention on human rights, 2022. Available from: https://www.echr.coe.int/documents/fs_euthanasia_eng.pdf (Accessed 26 March 2023).
6. *Pretty v. the United Kingdom* ECHR 29 April 2002 (Chamber judgment), no. 2346/02.
7. *Koch v. Germany* 19 July 2012 (Chamber judgment), no 497/09.
8. *Lambert and Others v. France* 5 June 2015 (Grand Chamber), no 46043/14.
9. *Haas v. Switzerland* ECHR 20 January 2011 (Chamber judgment), *no.* 31322/07.
10. Euthanasia in the Netherlands. Available from: https://expertisecentrumeuthanasie.nl/en/ (Accessed 26 March 2023).
11. Hendriks A. Right to life and right to a self-chosen death: An assessment of the Dutch Euthanasia Act against the ECHR. *NTM-NJCM Bull* 2014/13.
12. ECLI:NL:HR:2020:712 (Accessed 26 March 2023).
13. Rozemond K. The human rights deficit of Dutch euthanasia law. *NJCM Bull* 2020; **29**: 365–76.
14. Text and Commentary Criminal Law/Health Law. Alphen aan den Rijn, Netherlands: Wolters Kluwer, 2021.
15. Herbots P. *Euthanasia Without Borders*. Antwerp: Maklu; 2021.
16. *No authors listed*. Euthanasia in Belgium, the Netherlands and Luxembourg. *Prescribe Int* 2013; **22(143)**: 274–8.
17. Emanuel EJ, Onwuteaka-Philipsen BD, Urwin JW, Cohen J. Attitudes and practices of euthanasia and physician-assisted suicide in the United States, Canada, and Europe. *JAMA* 2016; **316(1)**: 79–90.
18. Villeneuve M. Medical assistance in dying: A review of Canadian regulatory documents. *Policy Polit Nurs Pract* 2020; **21(2)**: 56–9.
19. Rada A. Spain will become the sixth country worldwide to allow euthanasia and assisted suicide. *BMJ* 2021; **372**: n147.
20. Regional Euthanasia Review Committees. Euthanasia and assisted suicide: Number of reports, 2021. Available from: https://www.staatvenz.nl/kern-cijfers/euthanasie-aantal-meldingen (Accessed 26 March 2023).
21. One of Us Study. Euthanasia deaths increase 56% in Luxembourg in 2020, 2020. Available from: https://oneofus.eu/euthanasia-deaths-increase-56-in-luxembourg-in-2020/ (Accessed 26 March 2023).
22. Bollen J. *Organ Donation After Euthanasia; Medical, Legal and Ethical Considerations*. Maastricht: Gildeprint and Maastricht University Press; 2019.

CHAPTER

5

Professional Conduct – Medical Practitioners

Liliane Field and Gordon McDavid

ACCOUNTABILITY

Doctors are accountable for their professional conduct to their patients, the public, their peers and, alongside their contractual accountability, to their employers. Those practising medicine are accountable to all those who have placed their trust in them to perform their duties to the standard expected of their profession.

A doctor may become answerable for their professional conduct in a variety of fora including local disciplinary procedures, civil and criminal legal processes, inquests and inquiries and, increasingly, the media. Ultimately, however, all doctors' professional accountability is managed through compulsory registration with a regulator. In the United Kingdom (UK), the regulator for doctors is the General Medical Council (GMC) and for illustrative purposes, the remainder of this chapter will focus on medical professional conduct in the UK and the role of the GMC.

The GMC's powers are statutory arising from the Medical Act 1983. The GMC's overarching objective is the protection of the public which involves protecting, promoting and maintaining *"the health, safety and well-being of the public"*, promoting and maintaining *"public confidence in the medical profession"* and promoting and maintaining *"proper professional standards and conduct for members of that profession"* (1).

THE DUTIES OF A DOCTOR

Standards of medical professional conduct are set and measured against the key concepts of modern medical ethics and professionalism which are self-determination or autonomy, honesty or integrity, confidentiality, fairness and equity, and harm and benefit (2). These concepts are always consistent with and often more restrictive than the law.

In its 2007 report *Doctors in Society: Medical professionalism in a changing world* (3), the Royal College of Physicians defines medical professionalism as *"a set of values, behaviours and relationships that underpins the trust that the public has in doctors"*, the values being integrity, compassion, altruism, continuous improvement, excellence and *"working in partnership with members of the wider healthcare team."* It goes on to state *"Medicine is a vocation in which a doctor's knowledge, clinical skills and judgement are put in the service of protecting and restoring human well-being. This purpose is realised through a partnership between patient and doctor, one based on mutual respect, individual responsibility, and appropriate accountability."* Modern medical professionalism has been further described as a dynamic concept, one that must be able to adapt to societal and governmental expectations as well as those of the profession (4).

First published in 1995 the current, fifth edition of *Good Medical Practice* (*GMP*) came into effect in April 2013, albeit this is under review at the time of writing (5). *GMP* provides a framework which *"sets out the professional values, knowledge, skills and behaviours expected of all doctors working in the UK"* (6). This is a binding code which distinguishes overriding duties or principles that *must* be complied with, from those which, to only a marginally lower level of expectation *should* be complied with (7).

These duties are identified as existing across four domains: knowledge, skills and performance; safety and quality; communication, partnership and teamwork; and maintaining trust (8). The duties have evolved, underscoring the dynamic nature of medical professionalism, and reflecting the developing professional and societal expectations of the doctor-patient relationship including, most importantly, the move away from a paternalistic (medical decision-making) approach to patient care, to a doctor–patient partnership model (2). This was first tentatively referenced in the 2001 edition of *GMP*, developed in subsequent editions and culminated in an assured statement of principle in the current edition (9).

The duties are unambiguous but discharging those obligations to a particular situation will require professional judgement. To assist doctors in deciding how to act, *GMP* is supplemented by explanatory guidance covering the broad range of a doctor's responsibilities including confidentiality, maintaining professionalism,

DOI: 10.1201/9781003138754-6

considerations for treating children and young people, prescribing, consent, care at the end of life, leadership and management, raising concerns and research. The relevance of some may depend on a doctor's area of work. *Confidentiality: good practice in handling patient information* (10) and *Decision making and consent* (11) deal with the fundamental ethical principles of confidentiality and self-determination (or autonomy) that are pivotal to every doctor's routine daily practice.

The general principles of *GMP* apply to all registered medical practitioners in all professional settings, including detention establishments (2), where the traditional therapeutic partnership model does not fully describe the relationship between forensic physician (FP) and detainee. There are therapeutic responsibilities but also competing forensic responsibilities such as assessment of fitness for custody and interview, forensic examination and sampling (2). Furthermore, when giving witness evidence, FPs have a separate overriding duty to the court (12). FPs are frequently called upon to balance the seemingly incompatible duties to individual patients with duties to the court and in the wider public interest (13), while often having to factor in the extreme vulnerability of a detainee. Their duties and consequentially decisions are therefore often finely balanced and case dependent. Further explanatory guidance which a forensic practitioner may find useful to help them navigate the role include *Confidentiality: reporting gunshot and knife wounds* (14), *Raising and acting on concerns about patient safety* (15), *Acting as a witness in legal proceedings* (12) and *Personal beliefs and medical practice* (16).

There is a stated obligation on all registered medical practitioners to be familiar with the GMC's guidance, to apply it and be able to justify decisions and actions by reference to it (17). To use the legal analogy, lack of knowledge of the guidance is no defense.

FITNESS TO PRACTISE

Departures from the standards of *GMP may* give rise to a concern that a doctor's fitness to practise is impaired such that: "*Serious or persistent failure to follow the guidance, which poses a risk to patients and/or the public or undermines confidence in doctors will put a doctor's registration at risk*" (18). However, it is important to point out that *GMP* "*sets out the principles of good practice, not the thresholds at which a doctor is unsafe to work*" (18). It is "*the benchmark that doctors are expected to meet subject to any mitigating or aggravating factors*" (18). This is a recognition that every doctor can make mistakes. It is usually the seriousness and persistence of an issue that will raise a concern.

The circumstances that may lead to impairment are defined by statute (19). As well as performance, misconduct (including criminal convictions or cautions in the UK or abroad), adverse findings by another regulator and lack of necessary knowledge of the English language, they include the concern that fitness to practise may be impaired by health. As a matter of professional conduct, doctors are under an obligation to recognise risks posed by their own health, seek help and follow advice (20). Though cautious to step in, the regulator may intervene when a doctor fails to meet that obligation.

The assessment of impairment across these categories is explained in *The meaning of fitness to practise* (21). It is mostly patient centered, focusing on the harm or potential harm caused to patients; however, maintaining public trust in doctors is also important. There may be times when a doctor's personal conduct diminishes them in the eyes of the public to such an extent that it becomes a matter of both individual and professional credibility.

POLICING STANDARDS

In 2019, the GMC received 7398 complaints relating to doctors fitness to practise (22), predominantly from the public (5001). However, many (657) came from other doctors. This is not surprising given a doctor's duty to raise concerns about patient safety (23). Some (615) were self-referred: in certain situations, a doctor is obliged to self-refer to the GMC. For example if, anywhere in the world, they accepted a caution or have been criticized by an official inquiry (e.g. by a coroner or a judge), been charged or found guilty of a criminal offense, or if another professional body has made a finding against them as a result of fitness to practise procedures (24). In 302 of the complaints received, the GMC acted on its own initiative such as in response to media reports. Referrals were also received from employers (266) and the police (106). Complaints from miscellaneous sources (451) might include referrals from public bodies such as the Care Quality Commission and other healthcare regulators.

The GMC can only investigate the concerns that meet the statutory definition of impairment and is bound by the "5 year rule" which excludes allegations where, unless the issue is in the public interest, the most recent events are more than 5 years old (25).

The Investigation

Upon receipt of concerns about a doctor, the GMC may assess that no further investigation is required by them, may undertake a Provisional Enquiry (PE) or decide to open an investigation. For concerns that *may* suggest impairment of the doctor's fitness to practise, a PE enables the GMC to gather information to assess if an investigation is needed or not.

Once a decision to investigate has been made (in 2019, almost 1500 referrals progressed to investigation [26]), the doctor is notified and given the opportunity to provide comments. The doctor does not have to, so should seek advice before doing so; however, doctors are obliged to provide details of their employer(s) to the GMC, who request this using standardized proformas (27). Doctors working in certain positions, such as in general practice, will have an obligation to inform their employing or commissioning body of the investigation.

The GMC then gathers evidence. In addition to any comments provided by the doctor, this might include documentary evidence from employers and the police, transcripts from court proceedings, medical records, expert reports and witness statements. Depending on the nature of the concerns, the doctor may be directed to undergo one or more assessments of health, performance (28) and/or English language (29). A failure to do so may trigger a non-compliance hearing (30) and a potential sanction of conditions or suspension (31).

Once the requisite information has been obtained by the GMC, the doctor is given a further opportunity to comment on the evidence and allegations derived from it and, again, should seek advice before doing so.

Convictions resulting in a custodial sentence are referred directly to the Medical Practitioners Tribunal Service (MPTS) for a hearing before a Medical Practitioners Tribunal (MPT) (32). Otherwise, the file is reviewed by a medical and a lay case examiner who, in deciding how to conclude a case must have in mind the GMC's over-arching objective and *"whether there is a realistic prospect of establishing that a doctor's fitness to practise is impaired to a degree justifying action on their registration* " (32). The options available to the case examiners are no action, referral to an MPT, offer undertakings, issue a warning or give advice.

Of 1279 case examiner decisions in 2019, 719 investigations were concluded with no action, 347 were referred to an MPT, undertakings were agreed in 76, a warning was issued in 85 and 52 concluded with advice (33).

Referral to an MPT occurs when there is a realistic prospect that the doctor's fitness to practise will be found to be impaired (34). In serious cases, such as sexual assault or indecency, sexual or improper emotional relationship with a patient or someone close to them, violence, dishonesty, discrimination, knowingly practising without a licence, gross negligence or recklessness, impairment is presumed (35). Absent a presumption, the nature of the allegations, their seriousness, whether they are easily remediable and have been remediated (35) and the likelihood of any repetition must be assessed (35).

Undertakings may be agreed, avoiding a referral to a MPT, if considered sufficient to protect the public (36). They are suitable in cases relating to health, of deficient performance or knowledge of English. They tend not to be appropriate for misconduct cases unless contributed to by health. Undertakings must be *"workable, measurable, attainable and proportionate"* (37). If the doctor were to subsequently breach the undertakings, this may result in referral to an MPT.

Warnings are issued when there has been a significant departure from the principles of *GMP* or a performance assessment has identified a significant cause for concern but not to an extent that the doctor's fitness to practise is impaired. Repetition of the behavior warned of would warrant referral to an MPT and a finding of impairment of fitness to practise. A doctor may challenge the decision to issue a warning by requesting a hearing before the GMC's Investigation Committee.

Issuing a letter of advice provides guidance for future practice and may be given when there has been a minor departure from the principles of *GMP* (38). It is not an adverse finding against a doctor's registration.

Interim orders

When patients may be at risk if a doctor under investigation continues practising without restriction or when it is otherwise in the public or doctor's interest to do so, the matter will be referred to an Interim Orders Tribunal (IOT) (38). Of the 358 IOTs held in 2019, conditions were imposed on 225 occasions and registration was suspended in 52 cases (39). A decision to suspend is not taken lightly. An interim order can be made for up to 18 months with provision for extension. A doctor may therefore be prevented from practising for an extended period, even though this is termed an interim measure, to enable the investigation to proceed safely.

Medical Practitioner Tribunal Service

The MPTS is a statutory committee of the GMC and is accountable to the GMC Council and the UK Parliament. However, it is independent from the GMC in its decision making (40) because its functions are adjudicatory (41), whereas the GMC investigates and presents the case against the doctor at a hearing.

The MPT hearing progresses through three stages: findings of fact, findings on impairment and sanction. The GMC presents and must prove its case. The standard of proof is the balance of probabilities.

In making a determination on impairment, the tribunal must apply the same principles as applied by the GMC at the end of the investigation stage. The tribunal will apply particular value to the extent of any remediation undertaken and evidence of genuine insight; however, these do not easily displace a presumption of impairment in serious cases.

The sanction must be sufficient to protect the public. It must not be intended to be punitive, although it may well be (42). It must be *"appropriate and proportionate"* but *"the reputation of the profession as a whole is more important than the interests of any individual doctor"* (42).

Sanctions available are conditions, suspension for up to 12 months or erasure (42). In 2019, conditions were imposed in 14 cases, suspension in 120 cases, erasure in 55. In 17 of the 61 cases where no impairment was found, a warning was given (43).

Appeals

At the time of writing, both the practitioner and the GMC may appeal the outcome of a tribunal hearing (44) in the High Court. In the GMC's case, this can only be done if there are grounds for believing the decision did not sufficiently protect the public (45). The GMC's right of appeal may be removed (46).

An MPT decision can also be challenged by the Professional Standards Authority (PSA). The PSA has oversight of the regulation and registration of healthcare professionals, one aspect of which involves reviewing outcomes of fitness to practise proceedings. If the PSA considers that an MPT decision does not offer sufficient public protection, it may refer the decision to the High Court (47).

MEDICAL PROFESSIONAL CONDUCT IN CONTEXT

This chapter offers a general overview of medical professional conduct, and its policing. Given the extensive guidance, standard setting and regulation, the reader may be forgiven for thinking that doctors are considered a hazard to the public which must be contained. However, doctors remain near the top of the most trusted (48) and respected (49) professions in the UK, reflecting the vocational nature of their work, public perception and the investment they have made in building and continuously developing their professionalism. Medicine is a highly regulated profession with scrutiny at a local level and by the GMC. Doctors, like many professions, have also become accountable for their professional conduct in an increasingly wide range of unregulated fora, such as social media, which can be brutal and unforgiving in their adjudication.

The GMC sets the expected standards of medical practice through *GMP* and its guidance. The GMC's guidance is intended to assist and support doctors to make sound and justifiable professional judgements. However, the guidelines are also used to assess a doctor's fitness to practise when concerns are raised. The GMC guidance, and the benchmarks they set, have evolved and been refined over time. Each iteration of the guidance documents undergoes considerable consultation. For example, the planned review of *GMP* intends to consult with professionals, organizations and the public, and the review is anticipated to take two years.

Policing professional conduct can feel punitive, not only in terms of any adverse outcome but also, and perhaps more so, in respect of the process followed which can be onerous and protracted even in those cases when no further action is taken. However, it is not intended to be. By law, the over-arching objective is to protect the public, not punish doctors, such that at all times the GMC and MPTS decision-makers must apply the principle of proportionality. It is these authors' experience that, ultimately, the majority of doctors are their own harshest critics if they do not meet the standards expected of them and which they expect of themselves.

REFERENCES

1. Medical Act 1983s 1(1A).
2. British Medical Association. *Medical Ethics Today*, 3rd ed. Chichester: Wiley-Blackwell; 2012.
3. Royal College of Physicians. *Doctors in society: Medical professionalism in a changing world*, 2005. Available from: https://cdn.shopify.com/s/files/1/0924/4392/files/doctors_in_society_reportweb.pdf?15745311214883953343 (Accessed 5 July 2023).
4. Rosen R, Dewar S. *On Being a Doctor: Redefining medical professionalism for better patient care*, 2004. Available from: https://www.kingsfund.org.uk/sites/default/files/field/field_publication_file/on-being-a-doctor-redefining-medical-professionalism-better-patient-care-rebecca-rosen-steve-dewar-kings-fund-1-november-2004.pdf (Accessed 5 July 2023).
5. General Medical Council. Good medical practice review. Available from: https://www.gmc-uk.org/ethical-guidance/good-medical-practice-review (Accessed 29 March 2023).
6. General Medical Council. Ethical guidance for doctors. Available from: https://www.gmc-uk.org/ethical-guidance/ethical-guidance-for-doctors#good-medical-practice (Accessed 29 March 2023).
7. General Medical Council. Good medical practice, paragraph 5, 2013. Available from: https://www.gmc-uk.org/ethical-guidance/ethical-guidance-for-doctors/good-medical-practice/professionalism-in-action (Accessed 29 March 2023).
8. General Medical Council. Good medical practice, paragraph 8, 2013. Available from: https://www.gmc-uk.org/ethical-guidance/ethical-guidance-for-doctors/good-medical-practice/duties-of-a-doctor (Accessed 29 March 2023).
9. General Medical Council. Good medical practice, paragraph 46–52, 2013. Available from: https://www.gmc-uk.org/ethical-guidance/ethical-guidance-for-doctors/good-medical-practice/domain-3---communication-partnership-and-teamwork#paragraph-46 (Accessed 29 March 2023).
10. General Medical Council. Confidentiality: Good practice in handling patient information, 2017. Available from: https://www.gmc-uk.org/ethical-guidance/ethical-guidance-for-doctors/confidentiality (Accessed 29 March 2023).
11. General Medical Council. Decision making and consent, 2020. Available from: https://www.gmc-uk.org/ethical-guidance/ethical-guidance-for-doctors/decision-making-and-consent (Accessed 29 March 2023).
12. General Medical Council. Acting as a witness in legal proceedings, paragraph 4, 2013. Available from: https://www.gmc-uk.org/ethical-guidance/ethical-guidance-for-doctors/acting-as-a-witness (Accessed 29 March 2023).
13. General Medical Council. Confidentiality: Good practice in handling patient information, paragraph 9(e) and 22–23, 2017. Available from: https://www.gmc-uk.org/ethical-guidance/ethical-guidance-for-doctors/confidentiality/disclosing-patients-personal-information-a-framework (Accessed 29 March 2023).
14. General Medical Council. Confidentiality: Reporting gunshot and knife wounds, 2017. Available from: https://www.gmc-uk.org/ethical-guidance/ethical-guidance-for-doctors/confidentiality---reporting-gunshot-and-knife-wounds (Accessed 29 March 2023).
15. General Medical Council. Raising and acting on concerns about patient safety, 2012. Available from: https://www.gmc-uk.org/ethical-guidance/ethical-guidance-for-doctors/raising-and-acting-on-concerns (Accessed 29 March 2023).
16. General Medical Council. Personal beliefs and medical practice, 2013. Available from: https://www.gmc-uk.org/ethical-guidance/ethical-guidance-for-doctors/personal-beliefs-and-medical-practice (Accessed 29 March 2023).
17. General Medical Council and Medical Practitioners Tribunal Service. Sanctions guidance for members of Medical Practitioners Tribunals and for the General Medical Council's decision makers, 2020. Available from: https://www.mpts-uk.org/doctors-and-representatives/sanctions-guidance (Accessed 29 March 2023).
18. *Ibid., paragraph 12.*
19. Medical Act 1983 s35C(2).
20. General Medical Council. Good medical practice, paragraph 28, 2013. Available from: https://www.gmc-uk.org/ethical-guidance/ethical-guidance-for-doctors/good-medical-practice/domain-2----safety-and-quality#paragraph-28 (Accessed 29 March 2023).
21. General Medical Council. The meaning of fitness to practise, 2021. Available from: https://www.gmc-uk.org/-/media/documents/DC4591_The_meaning_of_fitness_to_practise_25416562.pdf (Accessed 29 March 2023).
22. General Medical Council. The state of medical education and practice in the UK: Fitness to practise data tables, 2020. Available from: https://www.gmc-uk.org/about/what-we-do-and-why/data-and-research/the-state-of-medical-education-and-practice-in-the-uk (Accessed 29 March 2023).
23. General Medical Council. Good medical practice, paragraph 25, 2013. Available from: https://www.gmc-uk.org/ethical-guidance/ethical-guidance-for-doctors/good-medical-practice/domain-2----safety-and-quality#paragraph-24 and Raising and acting on concerns, 2012. Available from: https://www.gmc-uk.org/ethical-guidance/ethical-guidance-for-doctors/raising-and-acting-on-concerns (Accessed 29 March 2023).
24. General Medical Council. Good medical practice, paragraph 75, 2013. Available

from: https://www.gmc-uk.org/ethical-guidance/ethical-guidance-for-doctors/good-medical-practice/domain-4---maintaining-trust#paragraph-72 (Accessed 29 March 2023).
25. Fitness to Practise Rules 2004 rule 4(5).
26. General Medical Council. The state of medical education and practice in the UK: fitness to practise data tables, 2020. Available from: https://www.gmc-uk.org/about/what-we-do-and-why/data-and-research/the-state-of-medical-education-and-practice-in-the-uk (Accessed 29 March 2023).
27. Medical Act 1983 s35A.
28. Fitness to Practise Rules 2004 rule 7(3).
29. Fitness to Practise Rules 2004 rule 7(3A).
30. Fitness to Practise Rules 2004 rule 17ZA.
31. Medical Act 1983 Schedule 4 Paragraph 5A(3D) and 5C(4).
32. General Medical Council. Making decisions on cases at the end of the investigation stage: Guidance for the Investigation Committee and case examiners, 2021. Available from: https://www.gmc-uk.org/-/media/documents/DC4599_CE_Decision_Guidance___Making_decisions_on_cases_at_the_end_of_the_investigation_stage.pdf_58070536.pdf (Accessed 29 March 2023).
33. General Medical Council. Fitness to practise statistics, 2019. Available from: https://www.gmc-uk.org/-/media/documents/fitness-to-practise-statistics-report-2019_pdf-84848269.pdf (Accessed 29 March 2023).
34. General Medical Council. The realistic prospect test. Available from: https://www.gmc-uk.org/-/media/documents/dc4592-ce-decision-guidance---annex b---realistic-prospect-test_pdf-25416411.pdf (Accessed 29 March 2023).
35. General Medical Council. Making decisions on cases at the end of the investigation stage: Guidance for the Investigation Committee and case examiners, 2021. Available from: https://www.gmc-uk.org/-/media/documents/DC4599_CE_Decision_Guidance___Making_decisions_on_cases_at_the_end_of_the_investigation_stage.pdf_58070536.pdf (Accessed 29 March 2023).
36. General Medical Council. Guidance to the GMC's fitness to practise rules 2004 (as amended), 2019. Available from: https://www.gmc-uk.org/-/media/documents/dc4483-guidance-to-the-ftp-rules-28626691.pdf (Accessed 29 March 2023).
37. General Medical Council. Guidance for decision makers on agreeing, varying and revoking undertakings. Available from: https://www.gmc-uk.org/-/media/documents/dc4595-undertakings---agreeing-varying-and-revoking-them---ce-guidance-57741459.pdf (Accessed 29 March 2023).
38. General Medical Council. Guidance to the GMC's fitness to practise rules 2004 (as amended), 2019. Available from: https://www.gmc-uk.org/-/media/documents/dc4483-guidance-to-the-ftp-rules-28626691.pdf (Accessed 29 March 2023).
39. General Medical Council. Fitness to practise statistics, 2019. Available from: https://www.gmc-uk.org/-/media/documents/fitness-to-practise-statistics-report-2019_pdf-84848269.pdf (Accessed 29 March 2023).
40. Medical Practitioners Tribunal Service. Our role. Available from: https://www.mpts-uk.org/about/our-role (Accessed 29 March 2023).
41. Medical Act 1983 ss35D, 35E and 38.
42. General Medical Council and Medical Practitioners Tribunal Service. Sanctions guidance for members of Medical Practitioners Tribunals and for the General Medical Council's decision makers, 2020. Available from: https://www.mpts-uk.org/-/media/mpts-documents/dc4198-sanctions-guidance---16th-november-2020_pdf-84606971.pdf (Accessed 29 March 2023).
43. General Medical Council. Fitness to practise statistics, 2019. Available from: https://www.gmc-uk.org/-/media/documents/fitness-to-practise-statistics-report-2019_pdf-84848269.pdf (Accessed 29 March 2023).
44. Medical Act1983 ss40 and 40A.
45. Medical Act 1983 ss40A(3) and 40A(4).
46. Department of Health and Social Care. Promoting professionalism, reforming regulation: Government response to the consultation, 2019. Available from: https://www.gov.uk/government/consultations/promoting-professionalism-reforming-regulation (Accessed 29 March 2023).
47. National Health Service Reform and Health Care Professions Act 2002 s29.
48. Ipsos MORI. 2020. Ipsos MORI veracity index, 2020. Available from: https://www.ipsos.com/ipsos-mori/en-uk/ipsos-mori-veracity-index-2020-trust-in-professions (Accessed 29 March 2023).
49. YouGov. Profession perceptions (international), 2021. Available from: https://docs.cdn.yougov.com/etz2olm0pn/YouGov%20-%20Profession%20perceptions%20(international).pdf (Accessed 29 March 2023).

CHAPTER

6

Professional Conduct – Nurses

Jennie Smith and Matthew Peel

INTRODUCTION

This chapter aims to discuss professional conduct and what it means to nursing and the nursing profession. To explore this fully, it is necessary to visit the history of nursing regulation and registration and delve into the definitions of professional conduct, their significance and how nursing has embraced the fundamental elements of these definitions in its practice. Finally, it will discuss how the nursing profession is a successful one, which engenders trust through its ability to reflect, learn and importantly, police its members through a code of conduct, which sits at the heart of the profession.

NURSING REGULATION

A brief history of nursing

The word "*nurse*" comes from the Latin word "*nutrire*", meaning to nourish, referring to the ancient Roman wet-nurses, women who breastfed and cared for another's child (1). However, it was not until the late sixteenth century when nursing acquired its modern meaning of a person who cares for the ill. It was during the Crimean War (1853–1856) when Florence Nightingale laid the foundations for the modern-day nursing profession in her book "*Notes on Nursing: What it is and What it is not*" which was published in 1859 (2). Nightingale is credited with saving lives and reducing mortality by introducing infection prevention and control methods, including cleaning hospitals, ordering supplies and introducing handwashing practices (2). In addition, Nightingale founded a nurse training school at St Thomas" Hospital London in 1860, laying down the foundation for professional nursing (3).

It was not until the 1880s that the "Hospitals Association" and the "Royal British Nurses" Association' (RBNA) introduced the first voluntary nursing registers (4,5). However, the "Hospital Association" was merely an administration list of nurses (5). In contrast, the RBNA was concerned with standards and training and had the power to discipline nurses who violated these standards (4). Nursing was an unregulated profession before 1919, when the Nurses Regulation Act was passed by Parliament (6). Something which perturbed prominent trained nurses of the day, including Dame Sarah Swift, the founder of the College of Nursing, who felt standardized training and the examination of knowledge was imperative for the profession (6).

It was the work of Ethel Fenwick, the former Matron of St Bartholomew's Hospital, with her steadfast determination, that ensured that the Act was passed on 23rd December 1919, watched closely by Fenwick herself from the public gallery in the House of Commons. Fenwick went on to become the first State Registered Nurse (7). She worked tirelessly, seeking better protection for nurses and their professional status, and ensuring that patients were sure that anyone calling themselves a nurse had met consistent training standards (7). Fenwick even extended the length of nurse training from 2 to 3 years during her tenure as Matron (even though this approach was not popular with her peers, including Florence Nightingale, who feared that this would create barriers for women from poorer and less educated backgrounds from joining the nursing community) (7).

However, despite the 1919 "Nurses Registration Act" and the establishment of the General Nursing Council, it was not until the Nurses Act 1943 that registration was made a legal requirement for all nurses (5). The General Nursing Council was replaced by the United Kingdom Central Council for Nursing, Midwifery and Health Visiting (UKCC) in 1983, which was subsequently replaced by The Nursing and Midwifery Council in 2002 and remains the regulatory body for all nurses and midwives to date (5,8).

THE NURSING AND MIDWIFERY COUNCIL

Currently, there are 688495 nurses registered with the Nursing and Midwifery Council (NMC) in the United Kingdom (9). The NMC's overarching objective is the protection of the public by (9):

- Maintaining a register of nurses, midwives and nurse associates

DOI: 10.1201/9781003138754-7

- Setting the requirements for professional education
- Developing and promoting standards
- Investigating complaints or concerns and acting if needed

The standards expected of a nurse by the regulator and the public are set out in "The Code: Professional Standards of Practice and Behaviour for Nurses, Midwives and Nursing Associates," hereafter referred to as "The Code" (Figure 6.1). Nurses must uphold these standards and act in line with "The Code" when providing direct care to individuals, groups, or communities and whenever bringing their professional knowledge to other roles such as leadership, education and research (10). "The Code" applies to all nurses, in all settings, at all times and is not negotiable or discretionary. "The Code" comprises 25 standards across four themes; prioritize people, practice effectively, preserve safety, and promote professionalism and trust (Table 6.1) (10). Deviation from "The Code" may result in complaints and regulatory action.

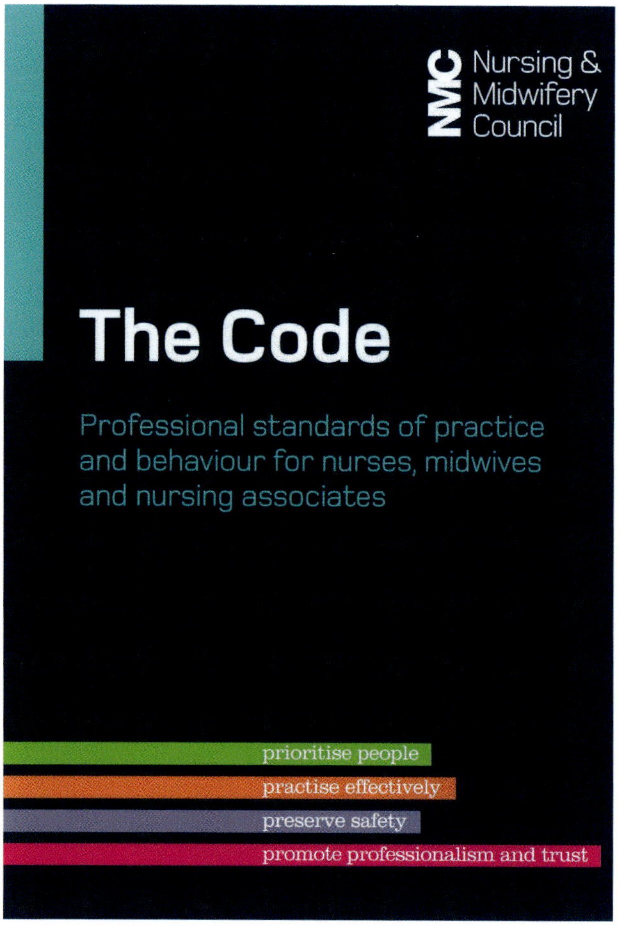

6.1 The Code. (Reprinted with permission from the Nursing and Midwifery Council, UK).

PROFESSIONS AND PROFESSIONAL CONDUCT

Berhauser (11) stated that nursing is a profession, not a vocation for which short-term technical training will suffice, and believes it needs highly knowledgeable and competent individuals. A profession is defined as one which involves special training and is respected due to the high level of education required (12). Professional status is believed to be characterized by a body of knowledge and skills, according to Downie as cited in Beach (13). An important feature of a profession is that its individuals benefit from respect and trust in their expertise from their community, but it is also believed that professions have a vital role providing trusted expertise, underpinned by standards that not only "police" the profession but also ensure the expectations of good practice are achieved (14). In addition, professions create and maintain distinct professional values or moral obligations, for example, codes of conduct. Professionals enhance their reputations and skills by adhering to their professional bodies" standards and requirements (15).

This is in keeping with the definitions of professional conduct. The crudest internet search, using a popular search engine and the term "professional conduct" will garner 617 million options from which to choose, covering all manner of professions, yet there is no one specific definition pertaining solely to nursing. Given this lack of specific nursing definition, it is incumbent to look to other professions and their approach and definition.

The Collins English Dictionary does not define the term "professional conduct'; however, it does provide single explanations of the individual words (12). Professional is described as relating to or belonging to a profession, especially roles that require specialist training, which we have already established would apply to nursing. However, while acquiring academic recognition and qualifications is an important way to gauge knowledge, there is a train of thought that believes one needs more than professional qualifications to be a professional (16).

This leads us to conduct, defined as how a person behaves, especially in a particular place or situation (12). According to Fuller (17), in its simplest form, professional behavior or conduct is a form of etiquette in the workplace linked primarily to respectful and courteous behavior. If we look to our colleagues in the legal field, who bring the words together, they define professional conduct as the accepted manner in which an individual will act (17).

So, professionalism is having the correct skills, judgements and behaviors (18). The saying goes, "Professionalism is not the job you do, it's how you do the job" (18). The same goes for nurses' professional conduct: it is how nurses present themselves and their behavior while undertaking their role. All individuals can and should expect to be cared for compassionately, professionally and with dignity, which leads us to a key central factor associated with professional conduct in nursing: the nurse-patient relationship (19).

TABLE 6.1 The Code summary

Prioritize people	1. Treat people as individuals and uphold their dignity 2. Listen to people and respond to their preferences and concerns 3. Make sure that people's physical, social and psychological needs are assessed and responded to 4. Act in the best interests of people at all times 5. Respect people's right to privacy and confidentiality
Practice effectively	6. Always practice in line with the best available evidence 7. Communicate clearly 8. Work cooperatively 9. Share your skills, knowledge and experience for the benefit of people receiving care and your colleagues 10. Keep clear and accurate records relevant to your practice 11. Be accountable for your decisions to delegate takes and duties to other people 12. Have in place an indemnity arrangement that provides appropriate cover for any practice you take on as a nurse in the United Kingdom
Preserve safety	13. Recognize and work within the limits of your competence 14. Be open and candid with all service users about all aspects of care and treatment, including when any mistakes or harm have taken place 15. Always offer help if an emergency arises in your practice setting or anywhere else 16. Act without delay if you believe that there is a risk to patient safety or public protection 17. Raise concerns immediately if you believe a person is vulnerable or at risk and needs extra support and protection 18. Advise on, prescribe, supply, dispense or administer medicines within the limits of your training and competence, the law, NMC guidance and other relevant policies, guidance and regulation 19. Be aware of, and reduce as far as possible, any potential for harm associated with your practice
Promote professionalism and trust	20. Uphold the reputation of your profession at all times 21. Uphold your position as a registered nurse 22. Fulfill all registration requirements 23. Cooperate with all investigations and audits 24. Provide leadership to make sure people's wellbeing is protected and to improve their experiences of the health and care system

Source: Nursing and Midwifery Council (10).

THE NURSE–PATIENT RELATIONSHIP

According to Ipsos MORI's annual poll, nurses are the most trusted profession, with 93 percent of the British public trusting them to tell the truth (20). Closely followed are doctors at 91 percent, with police officers appearing further down the list with only 71 percent of Britons considering them to be truthful (20). Reasons for this high degree of trust are likely multifactorial but includes how nurses conduct themselves professionally. The public expects nurses to be "good" people in addition to being kind and caring (21). This overwhelming trust of nurses by the public is both essential and necessary (22). It is necessary as nurses make intimate and sensitive inquiries and deliver intimate and sensitive care (23). By the nature of the role, nurses frequently encounter individuals when they are at their most vulnerable, putting nurses in a position of power.

So, professional conduct must be maintained, both for the individual nurse and as a professional group. Individual failures of professional conduct can lead to a breakdown in trust between an individual nurse and a patient, local disciplinary proceedings, or referral to the regulator. As a professional group, failures in professional conduct can lead to a general lack of trust in the profession.

Furthermore, the relationship between nurses and patients is therapeutic. This therapeutic relationship is essential for trust, respect and dignity (24). A therapeutic relationship exists in every nurse-patient contact for the sole benefit of the patient (25,26). This therapeutic relationship sets boundaries, or limits, on what is considered acceptable and unacceptable behavior (27). The relationship is a professional one governed by different

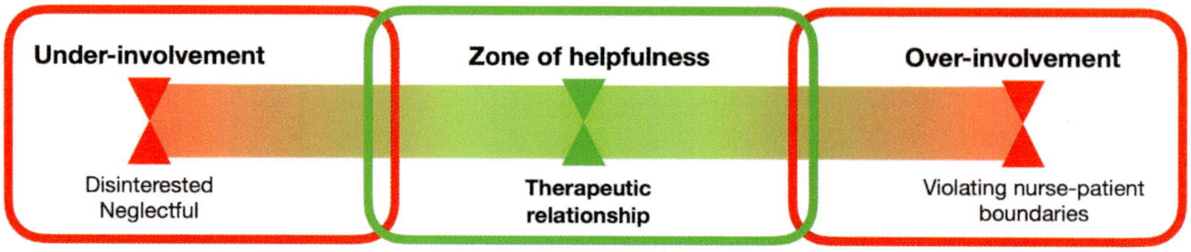

6.2 Nurse-patient relationship boundaries.

TABLE 6.2 Behaviors breaching the zone of helpfulness
• Sharing intimate or personal issues with a patient
• Flirting
• Keeping secrets (with a patient or for a patient)
• Super nurse behavior (believing only you understand or can help a patient)
• Spending more time than is needed with a specific patient
• Speaking poorly about your employer or colleagues with the patient or their family
• Exhibiting favoritism
• Meeting patients outside of work settings

Source: National Council for State Boards of Nursing (28).

rules, expectations and behaviors than would be appropriate for a personal relationship (28). For the nurse-patient relationship to remain therapeutic, the nurse must remain within the "zone of helpfulness". The nurse-patient relationship is best viewed as a continuum (Figure 6.2). While working within this zone, the nurse's professional conduct remains in line with the relevant standards and codes. As well as maintaining a therapeutic relationship, it also protects the patient's vulnerability from the nurse's power (29). As we can see in Figure 6.2, there is some overlap between the boundary groups.

Where nurses briefly cross a boundary for the patient's benefit, it is referred to as a "boundary crossing". An example of an intentional boundary crossing is a nurse sharing their experience of how they felt when diagnosed with diabetes to a newly diagnosed patient. Boundary-crossing is intended to bring some comfort to the patient. In contrast, "boundary violations" tend to put the needs of the nurse above those of the patients. Nurses violating these boundaries either become over- or under-involved (27). Nurses violating boundaries may not be malicious in intent. Sometimes to be liked, nurses overstep boundaries from being friendly to overly familiar (28). However, boundary violations can lead to confusion between the needs of the nurse and the patient, which can lead to harm or distress (28). For examples of how nurses can breach these boundaries, see Table 6.2.

REFLECTION AND REFLEXIVITY

Reflection has become a cornerstone to nursing professionalism and a key concept to the development of nursing expertise in theory; the use of reflective practice in nursing is widely recognized (30,31). Continuous reflection is a core aspect of nursing because professional practice is not simply applying theory to practice (32,33). Instead, it is much more complex and involves intuition, experience and knowledge (34). The varied explanations of reflection include mulling over and evaluating an experience, an active process of exploration and discovery, allowing corrections in our beliefs and errors in our problem solving (35,36). In addition, reflection on patient interactions, boundary crossings and boundary violations enhance the nurse's awareness of self, attitudes, values, beliefs and behaviors (27,28,37). Finally, reflection involves drawing out new knowledge by working out what is known and unknown, leading to greater understanding and new meanings (37).

Reflexivity is an additional broader, deeper and advanced dimension of reflection rather than a replacement (38). It is complex to understand, compounded by a lack of direction, like reflection a generation ago (38,39). Reflexivity is described as the turning back of experience of the individual upon themself, or the individual directing awareness towards itself (40,41). Reflexivity is helpful as it provides a more profound and overall understanding of an event (42). Successful reflexivity requires self-awareness during clinical practice (42).

A reflexive capacity allows the individual to understand, adjust and modify future behavior (40). To become reflexive, nurses must develop strategies to question their attitudes, values, thought processes, assumptions, habits and prejudices (43). Reflexivity involves interrogating professional knowledge, its construction and acceptance (44). Being reflexive involves an awareness of how practice may marginalize or even exclude others and understanding of how one's interaction with others shapes the surroundings (43). It is a continuous consciousness of one's self-awareness (45). To be self-aware involves an understanding of one's values and beliefs (46). Where nurses are honest and open, their practice, values and assumptions can be challenged (42).

FITNESS TO PRACTICE

Where concerns are raised to the regulator regarding a nurse, the process involves "Fitness to Practice." Being fit to practice relies on the nurse having the necessary skills, knowledge, health and character to deliver safe, high-quality care (9). There are, on average, 5500 concerns raised to the NMC per year, and 95 percent of these relate to nurses (9). This is not unexpected as nurses form the largest group of registrants, 94 percent (9). The NMC will consider any concern raised relating to a nurse. Typically, this will include alleged misconduct, lack of competence, criminal convictions, serious ill health, missing the necessary knowledge of the English language and fraudulent or incorrect register entries (9). Numerous sources may raise concerns, including service users, the public, employers, police, self-referral and other health and care regulators (i.e. General Medical Council, Health and Care Professions Council). However, the majority of referrals are from a patient/public or employer (9). The top three categories where most allegations are proven has remained the same since publication started in 2018–2019, although their positionings have changed slightly (9). The most common reason for allegations being found proven is "Prescribing and medicines management," accounting for 25 percent of all proved allegations (9). This is followed by "patient care" with 18 percent and "record keeping" with 12 percent (9).

Approximately 9 out of 10 referrals made to the NMC result in no regulatory action (9). Where a referral or concern is raised, the NMC will follow a stepped process. The first stage involves a complaint being screened to ensure a documented concern is serious enough to warrant regulatory action to protect the public (48). Furthermore, does the nurse currently remain fit for practice with or without an interim order? For example, serious allegations or concerns may lead to an interim order where a registrant is temporarily suspended from the register, or restrictions are placed on their practice while the concern is investigated (49). Additionally, concerns or allegations that may be considered not to amount to a serious concern, such as a parking offense, are screened out at an early stage (48)

The second stage involves an investigation of the concerns carried out by the investigation team (50). An investigation typically involves gathering evidence such as documents, witness statements and information from employers, which can take more than six months. At this stage, the registrant is offered the opportunity to respond to the concern raised.

Once the investigation is completed, it progresses to the third stage, where it is passed to a pair of case examiners whose role is to review all the information gathered by the investigation team, including the nurse's response and consider whether there is a case to answer (51). At this stage, the case officers typically take no further action or refer nurses to the "Fitness to Practice Committee" (Table 6.3). Alternatively, the case officer can provide "Advice" to the nurse, which remains private and is not visible on their registration. They may also consider a "Warning," which is visible on the register for 12 months. Finally, if considered suitable, the case officers and nurse can agree on measures to be put in place to address the concerns, known as an "Undertaking".

At this final stage, stage four, the "Fitness to Practice Committee" decides on a case with either a meeting or a hearing (52). At a meeting, the panel considers all the evidence submitted and decides without the registrant or any witnesses attending. Alternatively, the nurse and witnesses may attend a hearing providing live evidence. To find fitness to practice impaired, the committee must decide that the nurse either presents a risk to patients, was responsible for their conduct or failings, or breached a fundamental tenet of the profession (53). Regardless of meeting or hearing, where the panel finds fitness to practice impaired, it decides a sanction to impose (Table 6.4). The imposing of sanctions are not intended to be punitive but to reflect the need for public protection. The most frequent sanction imposed by the committee is suspension followed by a striking-off order (47) (Table 6.5). However, these reflect less than 4 percent of all concerns raised to the regulator (47).

Support for nurses during fitness to practice

It is recognized that nurses undergoing the fitness to practice process can find it distressing, see Table 6.6 for sources or support. In 2019, the NMC's new chief executive, Andrea Sutcliffe, outlined how she wanted registrants to be treated with kindness, dignity and empathy (58). The chief executive wanted to distinguish between those cases referred to the regulator where a nurse was at fault and those where the nurse was faced with unreasonable pressure due to system failures (58).

In August 2020, the NMC developed a "Risk of suicide and self-harm" protocol to be followed where such concerns are raised involving a nurse undergoing fitness to practice (47). Since 2018 when the NMC started

TABLE 6.3 Case officer outcomes for nurses

	2020–2021	2019–2020	2018–2019
Refer to "Fitness to Practice Committee"	410 (40%)	514 (39%)	490 (32%)
Advice	9 (<1%)	5 (<1%)	12 (1%)
Warning	35 (4%)	6 (<1%)	94 (6%)
Undertaking	25 (2%)	41 (3%)	37 (2%)
No further action	546 (53%)	757 (57%)	919 (59%)
Total	**1025**	**1323**	**1552**

Source: Nursing and Midwifery Council (9).

TABLE 6.4 Sanctions available to the "Fitness to Practice Committee"

No sanction	The panel can decide to impose no sanction and take no further action, the least severe sanction. However, this is used only in rare cases where a nurse's fitness to practice is impaired (53).
Caution order	A caution order does not affect a nurse's right to practice, but it is recorded on the register and published on the NMC website for between one and five years (54). It is the least restrictive and therefore appropriate where there is no risk to the public, but the panel want to mark the behavior as unacceptable (54).
Conditions of practice	Conditions of practice allow nurses to continue to practice, but with conditions in place for up to three years and reviewed before it expires (55). The specific conditions will depend on the nature of the cause but are intended to protect the public and be relevant, proportionate workable and measurable (55). Examples of conditions include limits to practice, supervision or training (55).
Suspension	This order suspends the nurse's registration for up to one year and is reviewed before it expires (56). The committee may provide expectations or actions, which the nurse must complete for the committee to review the order.
Strike off	A strike-off order removes the nurse from the register permanently. They cannot practice as a nurse and may only apply to re-join the register after five years (57). It is the most severe sanction open to the committee.

TABLE 6.5 "Fitness to Practice Committee" outcomes for nurses

	2020–2021	2019–2020	2018–2019
Strike off	55 (28%)	123 (29%)	155 (25%)
Suspension	80 (41%)	132 (31%)	224 (35%)
Conditions of practice	25 (13%)	62 (15%)	92 (15%)
Undertaking	14 (7%)	39 (9%)	57 (9%)
Proved sub-total	**174 (89%)**	**356 (84%)**	**528 (84%)**
Facts not proved	6 (3%)	4 (<1%)	16 (2%)
FtP not impaired	15 (8%)	64 (15%)	88 (14%)
Not proved sub-total	**21 (11%)**	**68 (16%)**	**104 (16%)**
Totals	**195**	**424**	**632**

Source: Nursing and Midwifery Council (9).

TABLE 6.6 Where is help available?

- NMC fitness to practice careline; 0800 587 7396 (24 hours, 365 days)
- Well Online; www.well-online.co.uk (a free resource for immediate emotional support and confidential online chat with a therapist. **Username:** ftpcareline **Password:** wellbeing)
- Samaritans; 116 123
- Your union organisation
- Your General Practitioner

publishing data, there have been five suicides among registrants involved in fitness to practice (47).

CONCLUSION

This chapter has looked at professional conduct in nursing, from the beginning of nurse regulation and registration over one hundred years ago with the Nursing Regulation Act 1919 and the subsequent formation of the General Nurses Council in 1920, whose responsibility it was to maintain a register of all working nurses, to the modern-day Nursing and Midwifery Council and how they approach their responsibilities around fitness to practice (47,59).

The definition of professional conduct is behaving in a certain way, using learned skills and knowledge, but it has also shown professional conduct is inextricably linked to professional standards, codes of conduct and self-regulation (12,17,60). Since the beginning of the twentieth century, nursing has continually grown to embody the very definition of professional conduct and its elements through its expectations around knowledge and experience and the structures in place to safeguard nurses and patients alike because of its code.

It is these attributes which we find at the heart of nursing and it is these characteristics which will take nursing and its professional status far into the future for generations of nurses to come.

REFERENCES

1. Borsay A, Hunter B, (eds). *Nursing and Midwifery in Britain since 1700*. Basingstoke: Palgrave Macmillan; 2012.
2. Newsom SWB. The history of infection control: Florence Nightingale part 1: 1820–1856. *J Inf Prev* 2016; **4(2)**: 22–25.
3. Agha R, Agha M. A history of Guy's, King's and St. Thomas" hospitals from 1649 to 2009: 360 Years of innovation in science and surgery. *Int J Surg* 2021; **9**: 414–27.
4. Royal British Nurses' Association. *The Lancet*. 1893; **142(3664)**: 1266.
5. Hallet C, Cooke H. *Historical Investigations into the Professional Self-Regulation of Nursing and Midwifery 1860–1998*, Vol. 1. London: Nursing and Midiwfery Council; 2011.
6. Royal College of Nursing. *The Voice of Nursing*. London: Royal College of Nursing; 2017.
7. Nursing and Midwifery Council. Ethel Fenwick: Always caring, always nursing, 2019. Available from: https://www.nmc.org.uk/always-caring-always-nursing/ethel-fenwicks-story (Accessed 27 March 2023).
8. Shepherd J. Ethel Gordon Fenwick and the campaign to make nursing a registered profession. *Nursing Times* 2011; **115(12)**: 8–9.
9. Nursing & Midwifery Council. Annual report and accounts 2020–2021 and strategic plan 2021–2022, 2021. Available from: https://www.nmc.org.uk/globalassets/sitedocuments/annual_reports_and_accounts/2021-annual-reports/annual-report-2020-21 (Accessed 27 March 2023).
10. Nursing and Midwifery Council. *The Code. Professional Standards of Practice and Behaviours for Nurses, Midwives and Nursing Associates*. London: Nursing and Midwifery Council; 2018.
11. Bernhauser S. Degrees will equip nurses to meet future challenges in healthcare. *Nursing Times* 2010; **106(21)**: 8.
12. Collins English Dictionary. Professional, 2021. Available from: https://www.collinsdictionary.com/dictionary/english/professional (Accessed 27 March 2023).
13. Beach D. Professional knowledge and its impact on nursing practice. *Nurse Educ Pract*, 2002; **2**: 80–86.
14. Evetts J. The sociological analysis of professionalism. *Int Sociol* 2003; **18(2)**: 395–415.
15. Professional Standards Councils. The benefits of professions, 2021. Available from: https://www.psc.gov.au/what-is-a-profession/the-benefits-of-professions (Accessed 27 March 2023).
16. Khera, S. One needs more than professional qualifications to be a professional, 2020. Available from: https://shivkhera.com/2020/10/28/one-needs-more-than-professional-qualifications-to-be-a-professional (Accessed 27 March 2023).
17. Fuller B. 12 Professional behaviour tips, 2021. Available from: https://www.katieroberts.com.au/career-advice-blog/12-professional-behaviour-tips (Accessed 27 March 2023).
18. Ichikawa N, Yamamoto-Mitani N, Takai Y, et al. Understanding and measuring nurses' professionalism: Development and validation of the Nurses' Professionalism Inventory. *J Nurs Manag* 2020; **28(7)**: 1607–18.
19. Snelling PC. The metaethics of nursing codes of ethics and conduct. *Nurs Philos* 2016; **17(4)**: 229–49.
20. Ipsos MORI. Ipsos MORI Veracity Index, 2020. Available from: https://www.ipsos.com/ipsos-mori/en-uk/ipsos-mori-veracity-index-2020-trust-in-professions (Accessed 27 March 2023).
21. Day-Calder M. Advice and developement; Professional conduct, 2016. Available from: https://rcni.com/nursing-standard/students/advice-and-development/professional-conduct-48101 (Accessed 27 March 2023).
22. Leslie JL, Lonneman W. Promoting trust in the registered nurse-patient relationship. *Home Health Now* 2016; **34(1)**: 38–42.
23. Ozaras G, Abaan S. Investigation of the trust status of the nurse-patient relationship. *Nurs Ethics* 2018; **25(5)**: 628–39.
24. Zou P, Luo Y, Krolak K, et al. Student's experiences on learning therapeutic relationship: A narrative inquiry. *Can J Nurs Res* 2021; **53(1)**: 78–87.
25. Strandas M, Bondas T. The nurse-patient relationship as a story of health enhancement in community care: A meta-ethnography. *J Adv Nurs* 2018; **74(1)**: 11–22.
26. Ashton K. Teaching nursing students about terminating professional relationships, boundaries, and social media. *Nurse Educ Today* 2016; **37**: 170–2.
27. Nursing and Midwifery Board of Australia. A nurse's guide to professional boundaries. Melbourne: Nursing and Midwifery Board of Austration, 2010. Available from: https://www.google.com/url?sa=t&rct=j&q=&esrc=s&source=web&cd=&ved=2ahUKEwi0lY_-48TyAhXQSsAKHdqDDKkQFnoECAIQAQ&url=https%3A%2F%2Fwww.nursingmidwiferyboard.gov.au%2Fdocuments%2Fdefault.aspx%3Frecord%3DWD10%252F1347%26dbid%3DAP%26chksum%3Dbes7sYtZAWnmggO%252FzV0uBQ%253D%253D&usg=AOvVaw0OFK_yq_K8VGY-1zo188t4O (Accessed 27 March 2023).
28. National Council for State Boards of Nursing. A nurse's guide to professional boundaries. Chicago: National Council of State Boards of Nursing, 2018. Available from: https://www.ncsbn.org/brochures-and-posters/a-nurses-guide-to-professional-boundaries (Accessed 27 March 2023).
29. Hechinger M, Mayer H, Fringer A. Kenneth Gergen's concept of multi-being: an application to the nurse-patient relationship. *Med Health Care Philos* 2019; **22(4)**: 599–611.
30. Newell R. Anxiety, accuracy and reflection: The limits of professional development. *J Adv Nurs* 1992; **17**: 1326–33.
31. Rich A, Parker DL. Reflection and critical incident analysis: Ethical and moral implications of their use within nursing and midwifery education. *J Adv Nurs* 1995; **22**: 1050–7.
32. Choperena A, Oroviogoicoechea C, Zaragoza Salcedo A, et al. Nursing narratives and reflective practice: A theoretical review. *J Adv Nurs* 2019; **75(8)**: 1637–47.
33. Nursing & Midwifery Council. Written reflective accounts, 2021. Available from: https://www.nmc.org.uk/revalidation/requirements/written-reflective-accounts/ (Accessed 27 March 2023).
34. Schön DA. *The Reflective Practitioner: How Professionals Think in Action*. New York: Basic Books; 1983.
35. Boud D, Keogh R, Walker D. *Reflection: Turning Experience into Learning*. Oxon: Routledge; 1985.
36. Mezirow J and Associates. *Fostering Critical Reflection in Adulthood*. San Francisco: Jossey-Bass Inc; 1990.
37. Paterson C, Chapman J. Enhancing skills of critical reflection to evidence learning in professional practice. *Phys Ther Sport* 2013; **14(3)**: 133–8.
38. Tremblay MC, Richard L, Brousselle A, Beaudet N. Learning reflexively from a health promotion professional development program in Canada. *Health Promot Int* 2014; **29(3)**: 538–48.
39. Shaw R. A model of the transformative journey into reflexivity: An exploration into students' experiences of critical reflection. *Reflective Pract* 2013; **14(3)**: 319–35.
40. Mead GH, Morris CW, (eds). *Mind, Self and Society*. Chicago: University of Chicago Press; 1962.
41. Adams M. *Self and Social Change*. London: Sage Publications Ltd; 2007.
42. Timmins F. Critical practice in nursing care: Analysis, action and reflexivity. *Nurs Stand* 2006; **20(39)**: 49–54.
43. Bolton G, Delderfield R. *Reflective Practice: Writing and Professional Development*, 5th ed. London: SAGE Publications Ltd; 2018.
44. Phelvin A. Getting the message: Intuition and reflexivity in professional interpretations of non-verbal behaviours in people with profound learning disabilities. *BJLD* 2013; **41(1)**: 31–37.
45. Wilson CB. The value of reflexivity in resolving ethical dilemmas research in care homes. *J Adv Nurs* 2011; **67(9)**: 2068–77.

46. Devenny B, Duffy K. Person-centred reflective practice. *Nurs Stand* 2014; **28(28)**: 37–43.
47. Nursing and Midwifery Council. Annual fitness to practice report 2020–2021. London: Nursing and Midwifery Council, 2021. Available from: https://www.nmc.org.uk/globalassets/sitedocuments/annual_reports_and_accounts/2021-annual-reports/annual-ftp-report-2020-21 (Accessed 27 March 2023).
48. Nursing & Midwifery Council. The three stages of our screening decision, 2021. Available from: https://www.nmc.org.uk/ftp-library/screening/our-overall-approach/the-three-stages-of-our-screening-decision/ (Accessed 4 May 2023).
49. Nursing & Midwifery Council. How we deterimine seriousness, 2021. Available from: https://www.nmc.org.uk/ftp-library/understanding-fitness-to-practise/how-we-determine-seriousness/ (Accessed 27 March 2023).
50. Nursing & Midwifery Council. Investigations, 2017. Available from: https://www.nmc.org.uk/ftp-library/investigations/ (Accessed 27 March 2023).
51. Nursing & Midwifery Council. Examining cases, 2018. Available from: https://www.nmc.org.uk/ftp-library/understanding-fitness-to-practise/examining-cases/ (Accessed 27 March 2023).
52. Nursing & Midwifery Council. Meetings and hearings, 2018. Available from: https://www.nmc.org.uk/ftp-library/understanding-fitness-to-practise/about-ftp-meetings-and-hearings/ (Accessed 27 March 2023).
53. Nursing & Midwifery Council. Taking no further action, 2018. Available from: https://www.nmc.org.uk/ftp-library/sanctions/the-sanctions/no-further-action/ (Accessed 27 March 2023).
54. Nursing & Midwifery Council. Caution order, 2018. Available from: https://www.nmc.org.uk/ftp-library/sanctions/the-sanctions/caution-order/ (Accessed 27 March 2023).
55. Nursing & Midwifery Council. Conditions of pracrice order, 2020. Available from: https://www.nmc.org.uk/ftp-library/sanctions/the-sanctions/conditions-of-practice-order/ (Accessed 27 March 2023).
56. Nursing & Midwifery Council. Suspension order, 2018. Available from: https://www.nmc.org.uk/ftp-library/sanctions/the-sanctions/suspension-order/ (Accessed 27 March 2023).
57. Nursing & Midwifery Council. Striking-off order, 2020. Available from: https://www.nmc.org.uk/ftp-library/sanctions/the-sanctions/striking-off-order/ (Accessed 27 March 2023).
58. Agnew T. The NMC isn't all about striking people off – there's so much we can do to support care. *Nurs Stand* 2019; **34(5)**: 8–10.
59. The Health Foundation. The nurses registration act, 2021. Available from: https://navigator.health.org.uk/theme/nurses-registration-act (Accessed 27 March 2023).
60. Thomas BG. Memories of nursing, 2016. Available from: https://memoriesofnursing.uk/articles/a-brief-history-of-nursing-in-the-uk (Accessed 27 March 2023).

CHAPTER

7

Professional Conduct – Paramedics

Sam Thompson

INTRODUCTION

The role of the forensic physician is to secure the provision of safe care for all those who become involved in the criminal justice system, be they complainants, detainees or otherwise (1–5), This has long been recognized by the Faculty of Forensic and Legal Medicine (FFLM), however in recent years, changes to the provision of healthcare in the forensic setting have seen paramedics joining the multidisciplinary team providing and initiating this care.

FFLM guidance exists to help define the role of the Forensic Health Professional (1) and although this has recently been adopted by the College of Paramedics, there is currently a paucity in academic writing while paramedics become established within the role. This can result in paramedics entering the profession dependant on generic information to inform their professional conduct and practice.

In September 2021, the College of Paramedics defined Paramedics as:

> "...a registered healthcare professional who works autonomously, often in uncontrolled environments, drawing on critical and dynamic decision making to assess and manage an undifferentiated and unpredictable caseload safely and effectively." (6)

By this definition, the paramedic would appear to be ably equipped to fulfill the role of the Forensic Health Professional, and the FFLM has introduced "Quality Standards for nurses and paramedics," to support and give guidance to both nurses and paramedics working in this role (7). However, while both FFLM documents support the development of a generic understanding of healthcare professionals in the forensic setting, neither address the nuances or challenges which are unique to paramedics in this role.

It is well documented that healthcare professionals working in custody have a variety of conflicting roles (8, 9). In addition to being aware of their responsibilities to detained persons, the police and the Criminal Justice System, paramedics face additional dilemmas, both practical and ethical.

One key area of concern for paramedics is practising with a reduced scope of practice (10) and the impact this may have on their professional registration. When, for example, a paramedic is working in a custody suite, they must of course work within the parameters included within their job description and therefore level of indemnity for their role. Commonly in the forensic setting, the skill set may be narrower in some areas than those that they would undertake in a frontline role in an ambulance. The range of equipment available to them is also likely to be limited; for example, a custody suite is unlikely to have equipment to obtain an electrocardiogram (ECG). Paramedics may feel frustration, particularly if the consequence is that an ambulance must be called to undertake assessments which would normally be performed by the paramedic themselves.

On the face of it, these may appear minor frustrations, but the paramedic may also be concerned that working within this reduced skill set for protracted periods without maintaining other core skills may ultimately result in them being unable to continue to meet their professional standards for Health and Care Professions Council (HCPC) registration.

In the following cases, we will explore this and other ethical challenges that may present themselves to the forensic paramedic in practice.

CASE STUDY 1

Consider the hypothetical case of Philippe, who is a paramedic with 3 years frontline experience, and who has recently started working in a custody suite. He has read and understood his employers' Scope of Practice, has signed their Patient Group Directives (PGDs) and has noted that, for some of the drugs available to him while working in custody, the indications, inclusion and exclusion criteria vary from his frontline work.

As an autonomous evidence-based practitioner, Philippe expressed concern about this in his training, and was informed he must remain within the scope of practice for his role in custody and not step outside this.

DOI: 10.1201/9781003138754-8

One Sunday morning, Philippe is beginning a 12-hour shift in custody and, on handover, is informed there a detained person with a history of heart failure who has been in police custody for 36 hours having been denied bail.

The detained person has received all their normal medication, but when Philippe goes to introduce himself, he notices him/her to be tachypnoeic, unable to speak in complete sentences with a tripod posture. Following a rapid assessment, Philippe quickly diagnoses acute cardiogenic pulmonary edema.

Having sent for an ambulance, and initiated appropriate oxygen therapy, Philippe reaches for the GTN spray he would always deliver in this situation, and suddenly checks himself, remembering that the PGD he signed to work in custody does not include acute cardiogenic pulmonary edema as an indicator for the administration of GTN.

His frontline clinical practice in this situation is somewhat different, as illustrated below:

Custody Patient Group Directive	JRCALC (2021) Patient Group Directive
Glyceryl Trinitrate (GTN) 400 mcg/metered dose	**Glyceryl Trinitrate (GTN)** 400 mcg/metered dose
Indications • Cardiac chest pain due to angina or myocardial infarction when systolic blood pressure is greater than 90 mmHg. • Patients with suspected cocaine toxicity presenting with chest pain.	**Indications** • Cardiac chest pain due to angina or myocardial infarction when systolic blood pressure is greater than 90 mmHg. • **Breathlessness due to pulmonary edema in acute heart failure when systolic blood pressure is greater than 110 mmHg.** • Patients with suspected cocaine toxicity presenting with chest pain.

Adapted from Brown et al. (2022) (11).

Philippe feels compromised; as an autonomous evidence-based practitioner he is aware optimal care for his patient includes the administration of 400µg of GTN, but the scope of practice laid down by his employer clearly precludes it. He is equally aware, by withholding this medication, he could be deemed clinically negligent under his HCPC professional standards.

What can Philippe use to inform his clinical decision making?

CASE STUDY 2

Consider also the case of Ameerah, who is a very experienced paramedic on the road for many years. As part of their role, they work as a Paramedic Community Responder mobilized from home by the ambulance service Emergency Operations Control room and, as a result of this, have a fully stocked resuscitation bag in the boot of their car. They also work bank shifts as a forensic paramedic in a custody suite.

While working a custody shift, one of the detained persons becomes acutely unwell and then goes into cardiac arrest. In the custody suite, Ameerah is limited to using the Immediate Life Support (ILS) bag provided by their employer to manage the resuscitation. Ameerah is acutely aware that less than 2 minutes away in their car is a full paramedic resuscitation bag with cardiac arrest drugs, intra-osseous access kit and everything they will need to secure this patient's airway definitively, monitor end tidal CO_2 and undertake full Advanced Life Support (ALS). They are also aware that early ALS will maximize this patient's chances of a good outcome (12).

Ameerah feels compromised; do they send someone to the car for their paramedic bag, or do they work within the limits of the kit available to them?

THE DILEMMA

The FFLM Quality Standards for nurses and paramedics establishes a clear criterion that multidisciplinary health teams providing care for detained persons should have the ultimate goal of ensuring there is:

> "… care of a high quality and equivalence to that offered in other settings such as the National Health Service (NHS)." (7)

On the face of it, this guidance appears to compound the dilemma, as in both case studies, if the paramedics were working in their role in the NHS, they would be able to provide the "*high quality and equivalence*" the level of their training permits and ensure the parity of care the FFLM describe. Working to their limited scope of practice and with limited equipment immediately restricts their capability to work at the level of their training and competence.

It appears to demonstrate an intractable paradigm.

PARAMEDIC SCOPE OF PRACTICE

Paramedics are professionally registered under the HCPC which sets out their standards for professional education, training and practice (13).

As part of their professional standards, HCPC registrants are required to work within their profession's Scope of Practice, which they identify as:

> "The limit of knowledge, skills and experience which individuals possess in relation to their professional role, and the enactment of these lawfully, safely and effectively." (6)

The HCPC are, however, clear in that they do not define the registrant's scope of practice, and no set list of tasks are identified that their professions can and cannot perform, as not only does this vary from profession to profession but, within the professions, it varies from registrant to registrant.

The standards of proficiency act as a guide on initial registration, but entry to a specialism, such as a Forensic Health Professional, as well as developing a registrant's practice, may narrow their scope (14). This is reinforced by the dictum that the registrant's ongoing scope of practice may also depend on limitations imposed by their job role; on this matter the HCPC suggest that registrants refer to their professional body for further guidance.

The College of Paramedics recognized that, alongside the developing role of the paramedic into a variety of multidisciplinary areas, came the need to provide definitive information on the fundamental principles, standards and guidelines underpinning their scope of practice. This was particularly undertaken to meet the concerns of specialist paramedics moving into a wide-range of disciplines, who, while developing their skills and knowledge in their chosen specialism, may be moving away from their "classic paramedic skills" and be concerned they no longer meet the standards required of them by the HCPC.

PROFESSION-WIDE SCOPE OF PRACTICE

In September 2021, the College of Paramedics Education Advisory Group met this challenge by updating the paramedic scope of practice document to include a: "Profession Wide" as well as an: "Individual" scope of practice (15).

The profession-wide scope of practice establishes the broad parameters of the profession, including all those areas practiced and recognized as a part of paramedic practice.

In essence, the College of Paramedics identified four core characteristics which epitomized the professional identity and uniqueness of the paramedic and together, distinguished them from other health professions.

The four core characteristics were identified as:

1. **Managing uncertainty**
   Paramedic training and education prepares them for making decisions in complex, high-pressure situations, often in challenging, unpredictable settings. Their autonomy and clinical skills and judgement permit them to manage this uncertainty and take responsibility for their clinical decision-making. Managing uncertainty is therefore at the core of the paramedic role and was recognized as a unique identifier when compared with other healthcare professionals.

   Reflecting on this for the role of the Forensic Health Professional, there can be no doubt that specialist paramedics undertaking this role manage uncertainty on a day-to-day basis.
2. **Broad capabilities**
   Paramedics are essentially generalists, able to manage patients requiring physical or psychological care, from treating the most minor ailment, to independently and autonomously managing a scene with multiple traumatic injuries or team-leading advanced life support across the entire lifespan. This is unique to paramedic practice and not only identifies them, but also permits them to move into a diverse range of specialisms.

   Once more, paramedics working as Forensic Health Professionals would reasonably be expected to fulfil this criterion.
3. **Gatekeeping clinicians**
   The consultation undertaken by paramedics is normally time-limited, with little if any supervision, or right of consultation or advice. The care paramedics deliver to patients is dynamic, undertaking constant risk-benefit analysis before referring on to the most appropriate specialism. In essence, they are the gatekeeper of the patient's care.

   Although the Forensic Health Professional may refer to their colleagues or the forensic physician on occasion, generally they work as autonomous clinicians and certainly fulfil the gatekeeping role described.
4. **Integrated working**
   Although they are autonomous practitioners, paramedics are also part of a multidisciplinary integrated team working with a broad spectrum of disciplines and extending education, leadership and research roles.

   Forensic Health Professionals undoubtedly work as part of a multidisciplinary integrated team not only within healthcare but also within the wider criminal justice system.

The College of Paramedics identified this range of characteristics to be unique to paramedics and to form a core part of their professional standards (13). The specialist paramedic working in the role of the Forensic Health Professional, appears therefore to be able to be reassured that, as a profession, they still meet the profession-wide scope of practice and therefore the criteria to call themselves a paramedic.

The College of Paramedics took this one step further. Having described a profession-wide scope of practice, they then directly related this revised Scope of Practice, to the Standards of Proficiency for Paramedics (13). This recognized that the journey from student to experienced paramedic – and indeed specialist paramedic (including Forensic Health Professional), brings with it a change and development in the skills, knowledge and experience the registrant has, so that the professional scope of practice they are following in their chosen field will differ from (for example) the scope of practice for a newly qualified paramedic.

They identified this as the paramedic's "Individual Scope of Practice".

INDIVIDUAL SCOPE OF PRACTICE

We have seen that the HCPC support the notion that throughout a paramedic's career, their individual scope of practice may vary and, alongside this, the application of the standards of proficiency may likewise change. Acknowledging this, the College of Paramedics recognized that although individuals may be unable to demonstrate that they meet all of the standards that apply for their profession, providing they may continue to practice lawfully, safely and effectively they may continue to be deemed to meet the standard.

Some fundamental principles are described which will always apply to an individual scope of practice, and these include to:

- be able to practice safely and effectively within their scope of practice
- be able to practice within the legal and ethical boundaries of the profession
- be able to maintain fitness to practice
- be able to practice in a non-discriminatory manner
- be aware of the impact of culture, equality and diversity on practice
- understand the importance of and be able to maintain confidentiality
- be able to communicate effectively
- be able to work appropriately with others
- be able to reflect on and review practice

Reflecting on this list, the Forensic Paramedic may be reassured that they also fulfill the criteria for the individual scope of practice.

Importantly for the Forensic Paramedic, the College of Paramedic guidance specifically notes that:

> "..... an individual's ability to practice to the full extent of their individual scope of practice may be curtailed by terms of employment, specific job description, and range of equipment provided by the employer. An individual's range of skills to be deployed within a particular job role must be agreed with their employer, particularly in relation to arrangements for vicarious liability." (15)

The above statement may reassure the Forensic Paramedic who has concerns that the limitations in their scope of practice or available equipment exposes them to liability in the event that harm befalls a patient as a result of their inaction or inability to take action due to these restrictions.

The HCPC underpin this in their guidance on biennial renewal of registration. At renewal, paramedics are asked to sign a declaration that they continue to meet the standards of proficiency applicable to their scope of practice. The HCPC note:

> "Your particular scope of practice may mean that you are unable to continue to demonstrate that you meet all of the standards that apply for the whole of your profession.
>
> As long as you make sure that you are practising safely and effectively within your given scope of practice and do not practise in the areas where you are not proficient to do so, this will not be a problem." (13)

This guidance releases the Forensic Paramedic in the forensic health setting from responsibility for harm that befalls a patient as a result of limitations in either scope of practice or available equipment.

Furthermore, in the case studies to hand, both Philippe and Ameerah will satisfy the obligations of their professional registration if they limit the care they give to their employers' scope of practice.

ETHICAL ISSUES

The freedom for a Forensic Paramedic to withhold care in order to remain within their scope of practice without fear of litigation, does not release the Forensic Paramedic from the ethical dilemmas our case studies present.

Where legal and ethical issues conflict, it has already been demonstrated that healthcare professionals must adhere to clearly identified standards of conduct, performance and ethics (13). So, can the decision to withhold care that they are qualified to give be tested against those ethical principles?

Medical ethics arose from the Hippocratic oath, requiring physicians to "*insert wisdom in medicine*" (16) and broadly divide it into deontological and teleological theories. Deontological theories are absolutist; it would be intrinsically correct to deliver the care, regardless of any potential ramifications to the clinician. Teleological theories, on the other hand, consider the outcome alone as the key determinant of the ethical nature of an action (17).

This creates a complex double bind for the forensic paramedic where the needs of the patient and themselves are in conflict.

Modern ethical theories consider that four key tenets determine the ethical nature of an action: beneficence, non-maleficence, autonomy and justice (18).

Beneficence and non-maleficence are inextricably intertwined. However, being morally forbidden to cause harm and morally required to do good may be counterintuitive. Kagan (1991) idealistically proposes beneficence to be both limitless and obligatory (19) however Gert (2004) theorizes that moral ideals distinct from obligations require that we only reduce harm rather than specifically promote good (20).

Beneficence mandates urgent medical care for the patient with time-critical or life-threatening conditions as seen in our case study, and although the tenet of non-maleficence could be challenged by a paramedic working outside their scope of practice, in both our case studies, the Forensic Paramedic is clearly competent to deliver the care and has the necessary drugs and equipment available to do so. In this situation, does the paramedic fail in their ethical responsibility in deliberately withholding life-saving care?

Examining the ethical tenet of justice, it is necessary for the Forensic Paramedic to weigh up whether their actions are ethical or not. In determining this, they are required to consider whether their actions will be lawful as well as being balanced, fair, and meeting the rights of the patient. This includes the right that the patient is not unfairly disadvantaged when it comes to access to healthcare (18). For the Forensic Paramedic in this situation, it is easy to argue that the patient is being disadvantaged if they are being precluded from being provided with the care they would receive if they were treated by the same professional outside of the forensic setting. Does the decision therefore to remain within the Forensic Paramedic's scope of practice as identified by their employer breach this ethical tenet?

Regardless of whether they are in the forensic setting or not, patients have the right to autonomy as the final ethical tenet. Essentially, this means that unless a patient is deemed unable to make autonomous decisions, they have ultimate decision-making responsibility for their own treatment and medical practitioners cannot impose treatment on them. In the case studies to hand, the patient cannot force the Forensic Paramedic to deliver particular levels of care, but the failure to do so would certainly represent an ethical dilemma.

VICARIOUS LIABILITY

Reviewing the College of Paramedic guidance again regarding the protection proffered to paramedics by remaining within their employer's scope of practice, particular reference was made to arrangements for vicarious liability (15). To resolve the dilemmas of our case studies, it is helpful to examine this further.

In the United Kingdom in common law, if an employee undertakes an act in the course of their employment, and that act turns out to be a wrongful act or an infringement of a right (other than under contract) which leads to legal liability, that liability will be transferred from the employee to the employer because of the legally recognized relationship between them. This is called vicarious liability (21).

In healthcare, this can be illustrated by the hypothetical example of a paramedic, who, in the course of their work, inadvertently delivers to a patient an overdose of a drug that sits within their scope of practice and clinical guidelines. The paramedic would not be liable for damages unless it could be shown that they had undertaken this deliberately or with criminal intent. The employer would be what is called: "vicariously" liable for the loss.

While undoubtedly this vicarious relationship would protect the Forensic Paramedic from litigation arising as a result of them remaining within their scope of practice and withholding care they were qualified to deliver, it clearly does not protect them in the event that they deliver the care which is outside their scope of practice, and something goes awry which leads to litigation.

Of course, none of this necessarily helps the Forensic Paramedic with the ethical dilemmas arising in the two case studies to hand.

In both cases, the Forensic Paramedics were in a position where they were considering working outside their employer's scope of practice, but well within both their professional and their individual scope of practice by dint of their profession. They also had the means available to them to do so.

The HCPC appear to address this by noting:

> "If you want to move outside of your scope of practice, you should be certain that you are capable of working lawfully, safely and effectively. This means that you need to exercise personal judgement by undertaking any necessary training or gaining experience, before moving into a new area of practice" (13).

In and of itself, this does not protect the paramedic from working outside their employer's scope of practice because, in both scenarios, the events occur during the period they are actively working for and on behalf of that employer, rather than undertaking the care as part of the development of their practice.

Significantly for the Forensic Paramedic, the tenet of vicarious liability will also not protect them if they work outside their employer's scope of practice, as if they harm the patient as a result, they will not be vicariously covered by their employer for that action. In this situation, they may be personally liable for the harm (21).

NEGLIGENCE

Could a Forensic Paramedic be deemed negligent because they withhold the care, or negligent if they deliver care by stepping outside their professional standards? Negligence is commonly addressed in law using the Bolam Test (or Bolam Standard) (22).

The Bolam Test is applied to establish the standard of care a professional was obliged to deliver to a patient where clinical negligence is claimed. It relates to a precedent arising from: *Bolam v Friern* Hospital Management Committee (1957) 1 WLR 583 which established:

> *"if a doctor acts in accordance with a responsible body of medical opinion, he or she will not be negligent."*

This "Standard of Care" test was amended by the Bolitho amendment to include the requirement that:

> *"the doctor should also have behaved in a way that 'withstands logical analysis' regardless of the body of medical opinion."*

The decision surrounding the application of the Bolitho amendment falls to the court (22).

Using the Bolam Standard of Care test as a benchmark, in the first case study, where Philippe has the GTN spray available to him and delivers it for acute cardiogenic pulmonary oedema, although he is not working within his scope of practice he is clearly "*acting in accordance with a responsible body of medical opinion*," and therefore appears to meet the standard of care test established by Bolam. It may also be reasonably argued however that another responsible body of medical opinion may well take the decision to remain within the parameters of their scope of practice and withhold the drug.

It may also be argued that Philippe is behaving in a way that withstands logical analysis, also meeting the Bolitho amendment, although again some healthcare professionals may find acting outside their scope of practice to be entirely illogical and not withstanding logical analysis.

On the balance of probability, however, it may reasonably be assumed that delivering a drug known to be beneficial in the circumstances presenting would be unlikely to be deemed negligent, regardless of the limitations of his employer's scope of practice, and the potential consequences of acting outside of it to the Forensic Paramedic.

In contrast, in withholding the drug, the argument could be presented that he is not acting in accordance with a responsible body of medical opinion. He has failed to meet the standard of care test established by Bolam, and he does not appear to be behaving in a way that withstands logical analysis when the ethical tenets of beneficence, non-maleficence and justice are clearly not met.

In the second scenario, which is included specifically because it typifies the profile of many Forensic Paramedics and represents a position a Forensic Paramedic could very easily find themselves in, the dilemma is extended because they are choosing to send for and use equipment and extended skills that are not included on any level in their employer's scope of practice. Similarly, failure to use them when they are available, in life-saving situations, could also be argued to fail the ethical tenets of beneficence, non-maleficence and justice.

CLINICAL DECISION MAKING

Under their Professional Standards, Paramedics are required to be able to make: "reasoned decisions" in the initiation, continuation, modification or ceasing of care and use appropriate techniques and procedures to do so.

This process is known as "clinical decision making," where such decisions are based on the balance of knowledge, experience, awareness, information gathering and evidence available to them at the time.

Furthermore, they should be able to exercise personal initiative and recognize their personal responsibility for any decisions they make including being able to justify them after the fact (13).

The Forensic Paramedic, like every other paramedic is, by definition, an autonomous practitioner, working in uncontroled environments, drawing on critical and dynamic decision making to assess and manage an undifferentiated and unpredictable caseload safely and effectively.

No two cases will be the same, no two sets of circumstances will be the same, and no two practitioners will be the same and, for this reason, no conclusions are drawn or offered in the management of the dilemmas presented for consideration.

Instead, each case will need to be managed, and clinical decisions made, based on the case to hand, the presenting circumstances and the individual clinician making the decision, mindful of their own ability to balance their professional standards, ethical tenets and underlying legal framework presented herein.

REFERENCES

1. Faculty of Forensic & Legal Medicine. The role of the healthcare professional: GFM and SOM January, 2019. Available from: The-Role-of-the-Healthcare-Professional-S-Fewkes-J-Smith-and-Dr-M-Stark-Jan-2021.pdf (Accessed 26 March 2023).
2. Department of Health and Social Care. Darzi, Lord. High quality care for all: NHS next stage review final report. Summary, 2008. Available from: https://navigator.health.org.uk/theme/high-quality-care-all-nhs-next-stage-review-final-report? (Accessed 23 March 2023).
3. Department of Health and Social Care. Department of health NHS next stage review. A high quality workforce, 2008. Available from: https://webarchive.nationalarchives.gov.uk/ukgwa/20130105061318mp_/http://www.dh.gov.uk/prod_consum_dh/groups/dh_digitalassets/@dh/@en/documents/digitalasset/dh_085841.pdf (Accessed 5 July 2023).
4. Department of Health. Improving health, supporting justice. The national delivery plan of the health and criminal justice programme board, 2009. Available from: https://www.choiceforum.org/docs/justicebd.pdf (Accessed 26 March 2023).
5. European Committee for the Prevention of Torture and Inhuman and Degrading Treatment or Punishment (CPT), 2009. Available from: www.cpt.coe.int (Accessed 23 March 2023).
6. College of Paramedics. Scope of practice. Available from: https://collegeofparamedics.co.uk/COP/ProfessionalDevelopment/Scope_of_Practice.aspx (Accessed 23 March 2023).
7. Faculty of Forensics & Legal Medicine. Quality Standards for Nurses and Paramedics – General Forensic Medicine (GFM). Available from: https://fflm.ac.uk/resources/publications/fflm-quality-standards-for-nurses-and-paramedics-general-forensic-medicine-gfm/ (Accessed 23 March 2023).
8. No authors listed. Three-faced practice: Doctors and police custody. *Lancet* 1993; **341**: 1245–7.
9. Payne-James JJ. Healthcare and forensic medical services in police custody – to degrade or to improve? *Clin Med* 2017; **17(1)**: 6–7.
10. College of Paramedics. Practising with a reduced scope of practice. Available from: collegeofparamedics.co.uk (Accessed 23 March 2023).
11. Brown SN, Walker A, James C, Wrigley, F. (eds). *JRCALC Clinical Guidelines*. Bridgewater, Somerset, UK: Class Professional Publishing; 2022.
12. Kurz MC, Schmickerr RH, Leroux B, et al. Advanced vs. basic life support in the treatment of out-of-hospital cardiopulmonary arrest in the resuscitation outcomes consortium. *Resuscitation* 2018; **128**: 132–7.
13. Health and Care Professions Council. Standards of conduct, performance and ethics. Available from: https://www.hcpc-uk.org/standards/standards-of-conduct-performance-and-ethics/ (Accessed 23 March 2023).
14. Health and Care Professions Council. Identifying your current scope of practice. Available from: https://www.hcpc-uk.org/standards/meeting-our-standards/scope-of-practice/what-is-your-scope-of-practice/identifying-your-current-scope-of-practice/ (Accessed 23 March 2023).
15. Collen A. Scope of Practice and Clinical Standards Policy. South East Coast Ambulance Service NHS Foundation Trust, 2015. Available from: https://www.whatdotheyknow.com/request/444296/response/1092684/attach/7/Scope%20of%20Practice%20and%20Clinical%20Stds%20Policy%201.pdf?cookie_passthrough=1 (Accessed 23 March 2023).
16. Antoniou SA, Antoniou GA, Granderath FA, et al. Reflections of the Hippocratic Oath in modern medicine. *World J Surg* 2010; **34(12)**: 3075–9.
17. Kamm FM. Toward the Essence of Nonconsequentialist Constraints on Harming. In: *Intricate Ethics: Rights, Responsibilities, and Permissible Harm*. Oxford: Oxford University Press; 2007, pp. 130–89.
18. Beauchamp TL, Childress JF. *Principles of Biomedical Ethics*, 7th ed. Oxford: Oxford University Press; 2012.
19. Kagan S. *Oxford Ethics Series: The Limits of Morality*. Oxford: Clarendon Press; 1991.
20. Gert B. *Common Morality*. Oxford: Oxford University Press; 2004.
21. Lewis J. Vicarious liability. Available from: https://uk.practicallaw.thomsonreuters.com/3-521-4527?transitionType=Default&contextData=(sc.Default)&firstPage=true (Accessed 23 March 2023).
22. Law J, Martin E, (eds). Bolam and Bolitho tests. In: *Concise Medical Dictionary*. Oxford: OUP; 2020.

CHAPTER

8

The Role of Medical Defense Organizations

Michael Devlin, John S.F. Holden, Roger D. Palmer and Carol A. Seymour-Richards

INTRODUCTION

Medical practitioners ("doctors'/"practitioners') have long had a professional obligation to ensure adequate indemnity or insurance is in place to cover their clinical work but, since July 2014, this became a legal requirement. The General Medical Council (GMC) were given new legal powers to check that any doctor practising in the UK had adequate and appropriate insurance or indemnity to cover their clinical work and the GMC could remove the doctor's licence to practise or refuse to grant a licence if that indemnity was not in place. However, the GMC requirement only refers to an indemnity for claims in clinical negligence ("claims'). Medical Defense Organizations (MDOs) are mutual organisations and offer much more than a defense to claims, covering advice for a wide range of non-claims matters.[i]

HISTORY OF MEDICAL DEFENSE ORGANIZATIONS

The latter half of the nineteenth century was of profound medicolegal significance. The Medical Act 1858 introduced the General Council of Medical Education and Registration of the United Kingdom (now the GMC), with the aim of establishing a single register of medical practitioners, standardising medical education and publishing a pharmacopeia.[ii] While registration brought many benefits in terms of the protection of the public, it also generated jeopardies for practitioners. The fear of criticism was well summarized by Dr Robert W Forrest, Convener of the Medical and Dental Defence Union of Scotland (MDDUS), 1902–1910, who stated:

> *"No member of the profession, however he may have enjoyed immunity from attack and however confident he may be of the care with which he discharges his duties, can claim to be free from charges and claims made against him. Such claims are made when they are least expected and deserved."*

Indeed, the *British Medical Journal* (BMJ), in 1883, reported the experience of Dr Bower and Dr Keates, who were vexatiously accused of the manslaughter of a child, leading to the creation of a committee of eminent practitioners to collect subscriptions to assist with the accused practitioners' legal costs. Around that time, Dr David Bradley spent eight months in prison following a conviction for allegedly assaulting a female patient in his surgery, before receiving a full pardon. He also benefited from the same fund. In recognition of the need for a more permanent solution to the needs of practitioners facing criticism, the Medical Defence Union (MDU) was formed in 1885. Some members later resigned from the MDU and formed the London and Counties Medical Protection Society (now known as the Medical Protection Society; MPS) in 1896. Later, a clinical negligence claim arising from the management by an Edinburgh doctor of an infected finger led, in 1902, to the formation of the MDDUS (1).

These three institutions are today regarded as the UK's leading MDOs (Figure 8.1) and continue to operate as not-for-profit mutuals. They all operate across the UK; only the MPS currently operates outside the British Isles. The organizations include within their membership both doctors and dentists (regulated by the General Dental Council; GDC) as well as a range of other regulated healthcare professionals.

ROLE OF MDOs

Medical practitioners, and indeed all health professionals, are vulnerable to a range of jeopardies resulting from criticism of their care of patients. These jeopardies may be multiple, arising either in parallel or serially following a single incident.

As well as a predominant role in advising and supporting doctors in claims of alleged clinical negligence, the MDOs also have unique and multiple roles in

[i] https://www.bma.org.uk/advice-and-support/medical-indemnity/medical-indemnity/nhs-medical-indemnity

[ii] https://www.gmc-uk.org/about/who-we-are/our-history

DOI: 10.1201/9781003138754-9

8.1 The 3 principal UK MDOs. (a) The Medical Defence Union (MDU), https://www.themdu.com/; (b) The Medical Protection Society (MPS), https://www.medicalprotection.org/; (c) The Medical and Dental Defence Union of Scotland (MDDUS), https://www.mddus.com/.

providing advice and support to health professionals with a range of non-claims issues such as responding to complaints in general practice or an NHS trust or with the response to investigation by the Parliamentary and Health Service Ombudsman (PHSO) or for regulatory Council or disciplinary inquiries arising from matters of health, performance and professional conduct.

The MDOs also advise and support in relation to inquests and public inquiries, for example, to assist in preparing a report for the coroner and providing advice on how to conduct themselves at an inquest or Fatal Accident Inquiry (FAI) and, where appropriate, arrange for legal representation.

The MDOs can also assist if a member becomes the subject of criminal investigations that arises directly from the clinical care they have provided to patients. This might include investigation or prosecution for gross negligence manslaughter (GNM) or if they face an allegation of indecent or sexual assault where that arises from their clinical practice. Another aspect of the non-claims role is that the advisers can provide experienced and expert advice on the handling of all aspects of unwanted media attention, including speaking with journalists on a member's behalf and preparing statements for the press, normally in association with the member's NHS Trust, where that applies.

MDOs ensure an absolute commitment to giving members the highest quality service 24 hours a day throughout the year. The organizational cultures in each MDO are established to put members' needs first, doing the utmost to help the member in the best and most appropriate way. The medicolegal advisers/consultants are available to members whether that is today or in the future.

Thus, an MDO can provide assistance for a range of professional work that may take the form of:

- Advisory work – by telephone or by written/direct communication
- Complaints, regulatory and disciplinary processes
- Claims in clinical negligence
- Criminal investigations, Coronial Inquests, Inquiries and Public Inquiries
- Education – learning from non-claims matters, guidance, publications and lectures to health professionals at all levels of clinical practice
- Policy work – liaison with government departments, political changes affecting clinical practice

Advisory role

A common reason for health professionals to request guidance from their MDO is to obtain general medicolegal advice or to seek clarification on professional issues that arise from the practice of medicine. This encompasses practitioners in all specialties and healthcare systems, whether in primary or secondary care, state delivered or privately provided. One example is to clarify the current guidance on the minimum retention periods for medical records, another being the steps to consider following a patient's request for a copy of their medical records (a subject access request). However, the practitioner may seek guidance on a challenging ethical dilemma or following an unexpected or a rarely encountered clinical or workplace situation, such as managing a request for a child's medical records following an acrimonious parental separation or concerns where a colleague is performing poorly.

Alternatively, the contact may follow a specific incident being investigated, such as the receipt of a patient complaint or a letter from a solicitor indicating that a "claim" is to be pursued. Typically, the dilemma or incident is initially addressed on the telephone, the health professional contacting their MDO to describe the predicament faced, so this may be analysed and discussed with reference to the relevant regulatory guidance or legal principles and processes. MDOs receive tens of thousands of requests for advice on the telephone annually; for the majority of telephone contacts, the ensuing discussion equips the health professional to address the dilemma and reflect on the situation further, and often leads to resolution of the matter.

More complex requests, such as those detailed in the following sections will require written advice, which may be quickly resolved in the case of a simple complaint or extend over many months or even years particularly with regulatory and disciplinary matters. It is not uncommon for two or more processes to run concurrently.

Healthcare delivery and its medicolegal consequences are not restricted to office hours. While most, telephone advice is available from trained advisers 24 hours a day. While most interactions occur during the working day, an out-of-hours service is available for emergencies where health professionals require urgent advice or immediate assistance from medicolegal and dentolegal advisers.

Complaints

Almost certainly during their professional career, most practitioners will be the subject of a complaint. Complaints may vary across a wide spectrum from minor expressions of dissatisfaction to more serious concerns that have the potential to extend to regulatory or disciplinary investigations.

Complaints arising from care within the National Health Service (NHS) in England are subject to the Local Authority Social Services and National Health Service Complaint (England) Regulations 2009 (the 2009 Regulations).[iii] The complaint may be made in the first instance to the NHS provider directly (such as a GP surgery, hospital or trust) or the body that commissions the service. The onus is on the organisation to whom the complaint is addressed to liaise with other organizations, where relevant, and to coordinate a response.[iv] Similar processes are in place in Scotland, Wales and Northern Ireland. If the complainant is unsatisfied once the local resolution stage is complete, they may seek an independent review by the PHSO (England), or equivalent across the UK jurisdictions.[v]

Medical practitioners are required to co-operate with NHS complaints processes. They also have ethical duties in this respect, as stated by the GMC, and are required to *"respond promptly, fully and honestly to complaints and apologise when appropriate."*[vi] The 2009 Regulations allow a claim and complaint to run in parallel, which can generate further anxiety for doctors. However, Section 2 of the Compensation Act 2006 states that *"An apology, an offer of treatment or other redress, shall not of itself amount to an admission of negligence or breach of statutory duty."* Accordingly, a well-constructed, empathic, genuine account and explanation and, where appropriate, an apology, is a powerful aid to restoring relationships between practitioner and patient and may be very effective in resolving a complaint. The process also provides an opportunity for the practitioner to reflect carefully and objectively on their actions. This is now a required action in the mandatory appraisal system with which every practitioner with a licence to practise has to accord (2).

It is well known that when a patient has cause to complain, significant stress may be caused to the patient and their family. Stress and anxiety may also arise in those complained about. Indeed, a survey in 2021 by the MDU and Healthcare Leadership Academy found that, of the 741 doctors surveyed, 70 percent perceived the complaint had an impact on their professional life while 65 percent said it had also impacted their personal lives (3).

The MDOs are well placed to provide support and assistance to their members who need to respond to a complaint, including advice on the wording of a draft response, steering a practitioner through the process and providing the supportive ear of a fellow medical professional.

iii https://www.legislation.gov.uk/uksi/2009/309/contents/made

iv https://www.nhs.uk/using-the-nhs/about-the-nhs/how-to-complain-to-the-nhs/

v the Scottish Public Service Ombudsman, the Public Services Ombudsman for Wales, & the Northern Ireland Public Services Ombudsman's Office.

vi Good medical practice 2013, at paragraph 61

GENERAL MEDICAL COUNCIL

An investigation by the GMC is perhaps the jeopardy most feared by practitioners, as a practitioner's licence to practise is fundamental to their ability to work and earn a living.

The GMC has five statutory functions:

- Maintaining a medical register of practitioners
- Setting standards for doctors
- Overseeing medical education and training
- Overseeing revalidation of doctors holding a licence to practise
- Investigating and acting on concerns about doctors that put patients, or public confidence in doctors, at risk

The GMC assesses a concern by considering whether it meets the threshold for investigation. Where it is not clear whether an investigation is needed, a provisional enquiry may be undertaken.

In 2020, the GMC considered 8468 cases at initial triage of which only 1043 were investigated, 415 were submitted to a provisional enquiry, 310 referred back to the practitioner's employer or contracting body and the overwhelming majority (6700) were closed. In addition, over 75 percent of the complaints that underwent provisional enquiry were also closed. Overall, 83 percent of enquiries in 2020 were closed at the triage stage.

Once the GMC's investigation is concluded, two case examiners (one medical and one lay) review the allegations in each case. The options are to:

- Close the case with no further action
- Close the case with advice to the doctor
- Issue a warning to the doctor
- Agree undertakings with the doctor
- Refer the case to a medical practitioner tribunal

The Medical Practitioners Tribunal Service (MPTS) is a statutory committee of the GMC. It is accountable to the GMC Council and the UK Parliament. However, the MPTS operates separately from the investigatory role of the GMC and makes decisions independently of the GMC.

The MPTS undertakes Interim Order Tribunals (IOTs) as well as substantive tribunals. An IOT is a hearing with power to suspend or restrict a doctor's practice (impose conditions) while an investigation about the practitioner is underway. A practitioner may be referred to an IOT at any stage of the investigation.

Even though the majority of GMC referrals are closed at the triage stage, any referral to the regulator is enormously stressful for the practitioner. Where an investigation takes place, the process is often drawn out, particularly if the matter is referred to a tribunal (Table 8.1). Even if no ultimate sanction is imposed, a practitioner may be unable to work in the meantime, especially when an interim order is imposed. This may be for up to 18 months or longer if extended by the High Court. The importance of membership of an MDO cannot be overstated, as the benefits will

TABLE 8.1 The GMC's published outcomes of medical practitioner tribunals for 2016–2020

	2016	2017	2018	2019	2020
Erasure	70	62	65	55	43
Suspension	93	76	101	120	52
Conditions	17	13	25	14	14
Undertakings	0	0	0	0	0
No impairment – Warning	11	13	10	17	17
Impairment – No further action	2	4	2	4	0
No impairment	34	27	41	44	16
Voluntary Erasure	2	0	3	3	2
Total	**229**	**195**	**247**	**257**	**144**

Source: The decrease of 44% from 2019 to 2020 was stated to be due to the COVID-19 pandemic. Full detail is available in the GMC's annual report.

normally include the expert support of a medically qualified medicolegal adviser and the provision and funding of specialist legal assistance.

Discipline

Disciplinary procedures frequently run in parallel with complaints and regulatory processes and may arise from concerns about professional conduct, performance or health.

In England, the regulatory framework for managing performance concerns of medical, dental and general ophthalmic practitioners who provide primary care services is the National Health Service (Performers Lists) (England) Regulations 2013.[vii] NHS England, in its capacity as commissioner of primary care services, manages matters such as the admission (or not) to performers lists according to its framework for managing performer concerns.[viii] The framework also addresses NHS England's powers in terms of suspension or removal from the performers lists and the imposition of conditions. These functions are supported by the creation, within local teams of NHS England, of Performance Advisory Groups and Performers List Decision Panels.

The conduct, performance and health of medical and dental practitioners who are employed by NHS organizations in England are subject to the national framework *"Maintaining High Professional Standards in the Modern NHS"* (MHPS).[ix] NHS Trusts have been required, since 2005, to have local processes consistent with this framework to address and investigate concerns. The guidance was issued to NHS Foundation Trusts as advice and, although such Trusts are not legally required to adopt the process, in practice they normally do so.

Impartial advice, assessment and intervention, training courses and other expert services are available to NHS organizations from "Practitioner, Performance Advice" (PPA; formerly the "National Clinical Assessment Service"). This is a service delivered by NHS Resolution with the purpose of providing *"expertise to the NHS on resolving concerns fairly, share learning for improvement and preserve resources for patient care."*[x]

MDOs can guide and support their members with these processes by advising on the drafting of comments and how to undertake reflections effectively. Not all hearings will require legal representation, but if NHS England's concerns proceed as far as an oral hearing against the practitioner, legal representation may be instructed by the MDO should it be necessary. In hospital Trust hearings, the wording of MHPS has historically generated dispute regarding legal representation. Following the case of *Kulkarni* (4), it is accepted that formal legal representation is permitted where that is provided by an MDO.

Clinical negligence claims

MDOs have provided indemnity for clinical negligence claims as a benefit of membership for over a century. Further information is included on the websites of each MDO (*see* Figure 8.1). MDO members may seek assistance with a range of medicolegal matters, including claims, typically on an "occurrence" basis. Occurrence-based indemnity means that so long as the practitioner was an MDO member at the time of the incident they may seek assistance, even if the matter was not reported until many years later. Prior to the introduction of NHS indemnity[xi] for hospital

[vii] https://www.legislation.gov.uk/uksi/2013/335/contents

[viii] https://www.england.nhs.uk/publication/framework-for-managing-performer-concerns/

[ix] https://webarchive.nationalarchives.gov.uk/ukgwa/20130123204228/http://www.dh.gov.uk/en/Publicationsandstatistics/Publications/PublicationsPolicyAndGuidance/DH_4103586

[x] https://resolution.nhs.uk/services/practitioner-performance-advice/

[xi] NHS indemnity for hospital doctors was introduced in January 1990.

practitioners, the risk was borne by the individual, rather than by their employer, for their NHS work by virtue of a 1954 Health Circular (5). By the late 1980s, the cost to the individual practitioner of obtaining indemnity was becoming unaffordable. Although there are many medicolegal jeopardies that practitioners face, claims, particularly the claimant damages element, are by far the most expensive. It is the cost of indemnifying claims that has the most significant impact on determining the cost of the MDO subscriptions.

The problems did not end with the introduction of NHS indemnity: claims inflation has historically run at a much higher rate than other comparable measures, such as wages, house price or consumer price inflation. The high rate of claims inflation persisted into the early decades of the twenty-first century, leading to annual NHS claims payments in England quadrupling to £2.2 billion in the 15 years to 2020–2021 (6). General practitioners who, as independent contractors within the NHS, remained liable for clinical negligence claims brought against them, also found their indemnity subscriptions becoming increasingly unaffordable over this period. For a second time, a new form of NHS indemnity was necessary, currently for NHS work undertaken by GPs in England and Wales which has been in force since April 2019 (7,8).

The drivers of claims inflation remain unchecked and practitioners who practise outside the NHS, for example in independent practice, must still obtain adequate and appropriate indemnity or insurance for their claims liabilities. Typically, this is provided by MDOs. In some specialities where there is a significant risk of high-value claims, such as obstetric care or spinal surgery, some practitioners may consider it less economically viable to continue the full spectrum of their private work. Patients who would otherwise have been seen in the independent sector may increasingly be reviewed within the NHS. This risks those high-value claims being passed to the NHS indemnity schemes and, ultimately, the taxpayer. Independent practice continues to be underwritten by MDOs, including through corporate insurance products which are increasingly available. MDOs also campaign for a more affordable solution to clinical negligence claims, to avoid practitioners facing increasingly expensive indemnity for any part of their clinical practice not covered by the NHS schemes.

CRIMINAL INQUIRY

There are numerous situations that may place a practitioner at risk of criminal prosecution. Many are unrelated to the practice of medicine, such as motoring convictions. However, health practitioners also face additional risk from their professional interactions and may approach their MDO for assistance with these. The prospect of support and representation is important and essential given the potential consequences of criminal prosecution arising from the delivery of patient care.

Situations in which criminal allegations might arise include the absence of patient consent, as patient autonomy is enshrined in the ethical standards and legal principles that apply. For example, to perform an examination, investigation or procedure without suitably informed or valid consent from the patient may result in a successful claim, in battery or in negligence, and can result in criminal investigation for assault.[xii] Irrespective of consent, certain acts would constitute a criminal act, such as female genital mutilation (FGM).[xiii] However, criminal investigation into GNM following the death of a patient is a relatively rare situation. Furthermore, the importance of a chaperone, for clinical examination, is paramount given the potential for intimate examinations to result in a complaint that alleges a sexual component or motivation.[xiv]

The first prosecution of a practitioner in the UK for FGM occurred in 2015, following an accusation that the suture placed into a laceration post-delivery amounted to a re-infibulation, and resulted in acquittal (9). In GNM, it is the seriousness of the breach of duty, whether an act or an omission, that defines it as a crime (10). While the prosecution of GNM remains rare, the incidence (11) and the conviction rates (12) are increasing. MDOs are increasingly approached for assistance in cases where gross negligence manslaughter is being investigated or charged (13). Of course, all health professionals should be accountable for their actions. Disciplinary and regulatory investigation and sanction(s) ensure that, but the fear of criminal prosecution should not be an occupational norm. As described later, MDOs have made representations to support change in how GNM is applied in healthcare settings and the GMC responds in such situations.

CORONIAL INQUIRY

A request for MDO assistance with preparation when invited to attend an inquest (in England, Wales and Northern Ireland) or an FAI (in Scotland) is common and follows an unexpected or inexplicable patient death, one that was violent or unnatural or a death that occurred while in detention (prison, police custody or under the Mental Health Act). An inquest or FAI is an inquisitorial, fact-finding investigation rather than an adversarial process, to determine who was the deceased, where and when they died, and in what circumstances. Health professionals may be called to provide a statement and to give oral evidence as a witness of fact or as an "interested person". The latter designation places the health professional on notice that there is consideration that their involvement may have caused or contributed to the death. However, irrespective of the rationale, it

---

[xii] Offences against the Person Act 1861

[xiii] Female Genital Mutilation Act 2003 (England, Wales, Northern Ireland), Prohibition of Female Genital Mutilation (Scotland) Act 2005

[xiv] Sexual Offences Act 2003

entitles the practitioner to disclosure of the evidence, to attend with legal representation, and to ask questions of other witnesses. Preparation and knowing what to expect is key (14). An MDO will support its members in preparing for attendance and, where appropriate, represent the member at the hearing.

A 2020 Supreme Court judgment clarified that the standard of proof for suicide and unlawful killing in an inquest is the civil standard of the balance of probabilities and not the criminal standard of beyond reasonable doubt (15).

The most common conclusions a coroner may reach are:

- Natural causes (including fatal medical conditions)
- Accident or misadventure
- Industrial disease
- Dependence on drugs/non-dependent abuse of drugs
- Attempted/self-induced abortion
- Disasters subject to public inquiry
- Lawful killing (such as deaths caused during acts of war, or self-defense)
- Unlawful killing
- Suicide
- Open verdict (where there is insufficient evidence for any other verdict)
- Alcohol/drug related death
- Road traffic collision

The outcome will not apportion fault or blame to individuals but, if unlawful killing is more likely to be concluded, it raises the possibility of further GNM investigations. Notwithstanding the possibility of criminal proceedings, the coroner (or sheriff in Scotland) may make recommendations that might have prevented the death. Such recommendations, including a prevention of future deaths (PFD) report in England and Wales, and Northern Ireland, requires the individuals and organizations, to whom it is sent, to respond to the issues within 56 days.[xv] MDOs can assist members throughout the course of the inquest or FAI, to reflect on the coroner's conclusion(s) and respond to any recommendations. This extends to advising on the duty to inform the regulator if charged or found guilty of a criminal offense and where the health professional is criticized by an official inquiry (which would include a coroner's inquest/FAI).

INQUIRIES

Healthcare inquiries are reserved for the most important or concerning events that have occurred in healthcare. These focus on learning from the events and result in a number of recommendations to improve safe delivery of healthcare. Currently, a number of external investigations are conducted within, or impact on practitioners within, the NHS, such as through the Healthcare Safety Investigation Branch (HSIB),[xvi] NHS Improvement (NHSI) and safeguarding reviews. Health practitioners are required to co-operate with formal inquiries and can approach their MDO for assistance and guidance with these.

PUBLIC INQUIRIES

Public inquiries are government commissioned independent reviews.[xvii] These are more wide-ranging reviews, often taking many years to conclude, which address matters of public concern and can single out individuals and services for criticism. Examples include The Victoria Climbié inquiry chaired by Lord Laming[xviii] following the tragic death of an 8 year old in 2000, providing learning on information sharing; the Mid Staffordshire NHS Foundation Trust public inquiry chaired by Sir Robert Francis QC[xix] following failings at the Trust, providing recommendations on openness and candor, and the current Infected Blood Inquiry chaired by Sir Brian Langstaff[xx] that aims to understand how infected blood products were given in the NHS. Witnesses can be compelled to give evidence. Inquiries reviewing specific policy areas can also be undertaken by Parliamentary Select Committees and may seek evidence from health professionals. Advice, guidance and support is available from MDOs to their members before, during and following the conclusion of an inquiry.

EDUCATION

An important, but lesser-recognized function of the MDOs is the provision of educational and risk-management material, training and continuous professional development (CPD) on medicolegal issues. This may be through online or electronic learning platforms (both live and recorded), in-person presentations, seminars and workshops. MDOs provide a wealth of learning resources to support both individual and team learning, as well as to reduce medicolegal risk.

While it is recognized that MDOs have considerable experience in medicolegal issues, they also use the information and data available to provide guidance to the profession based on that knowledge with the aim of reducing practitioner risk and improving patient

xv https://www.cps.gov.uk/legal-guidance/coroners

xvi https://www.hsib.org.uk/organisational-transformation/. As of April 2023 a new statutory non-departmental public body, the Health Services Safety Investigations Body (HSSIB) will operate as an independent healthcare investigation body for the NHS and independent sector (Health and Care Bill at Part 4) and a separate Maternity and Newborn Safety Investigations (MNSI) special health authority will replace HSIB.

xvii Inquiries Act 2005

xviii https://www.gov.uk/government/publications/the-victoria-climbie-inquiry-report-of-an-inquiry-by-lord-laming

xix https://www.gov.uk/government/publications/report-of-the-mid-staffordshire-nhs-foundation-trust-public-inquiry

xx www.infectedbloodinquiry.org.uk

outcomes (16). Further educational material is provided by MDOs to regularly inform health practitioners of up-to-date medicolegal issues through access to their publications and updates. In addition, research, conducted to inform and educate, is published by the MDOs, including in the peer reviewed medical literature (17).

In addition to the direct dissemination of learning and educational material, MDOs will sponsor and support educational forums, including events that recognize and celebrate innovative improvements in the delivery of care, extend team inclusivity and forge improvements in the provision of safe healthcare.

Furthermore, as part of an ongoing commitment to support improvements in patient safety and health professional well-being, MDOs are now funding medical and dental research projects which have these aims. This includes the award of research grants for peer-reviewed research applications and commissioned research topics.[xxi]

POLICY AND EXTERNAL RELATIONS WORK

Another lesser-recognized function of MDOs is to represent their members' interests in a variety of ways, such as the policy and external relations exercises evidenced in the paragraphs above describing the relationship between claims and indemnity costs, where the MDOs have been key voices calling for a raft of legal measures to make compensating patients both fairer and affordable.

Further examples of MDOs working on behalf of their membership as a whole (rather than their traditional function of assisting individual members) are in relation to GNM in England and Wales. Two seminal cases deeply troubled the medical profession. In the first, an experienced and respected colorectal surgeon, Mr David Sellu, was convicted of the GNM of a patient under his care in 2010. His conviction was eventually found by the Criminal Court of Appeal in 2016 to be unsafe and was quashed (18). The Appeal Court judges found the judge's direction to the jury to be inadequate: for a person to be found guilty of GNM, the breach of their duty of care and skill would need to be "so truly exceptionally bad" to turn the negligent act into a crime (19).

The second case was that of a pediatrician in training, Dr Hadiza Bawa-Garba. In 2015, she was found guilty of GNM for a child under her care who died from septic shock. Following her conviction, for which she received a suspended sentence, Dr Bawa-Garba was suspended from the GMC's medical register after an MPTS[xxii] hearing. The GMC appealed this MPTS sanction and the High Court substituted a sanction of erasure for suspension. This in turn was successfully appealed in 2018 by Dr Bawa-Garba in the Court of Appeal (20), and the suspension was reinstated.

These two cases brought into sharp focus the anxieties and risks practitioners face when working in often difficult and under-resourced conditions. The then Secretary of State, Jeremy Hunt MP, ordered a rapid review into GNM in healthcare settings. The review was led by Professor Sir Norman Williams and resulted in a number of constructive recommendations to help ensure that prosecution decisions were appropriate and proportionate (21). A separate review commissioned by the GMC and chaired by cardiac surgeon, Mr Leslie Hamilton, into the way Dr Bawa-Garba's case was handled also resulted in several positive recommendations. This included agreement with the Williams Review that the GMC should lose its right to appeal decisions made by the MPTS (22). In both cases, MDOs provided key evidence to the inquiries, based on many decades' experience assisting practitioners who had faced criminal investigations arising from their clinical practice. This was in addition to the advisory and legal support for the individual members.

The work of the MDOs in policy areas is dynamic. There is always a need to engage with interested parties to ensure the systems that hold practitioners to account are fair and proportionate. Although it may be an area of activity that many practitioners would not necessarily associate with MDOs, it is nevertheless an important MDO role that potentially has profound implications on their professional practice.

CONCLUSION

Being a practising clinician is not easy and presents constant clinical and other challenges. A broad clinical knowledge and ability to apply this under difficult, pressurized clinical circumstances is vital. Practitioners must work ever in the public eye and in the public interest and, occasionally, with anxious, possibly unco-operative, patients and relatives in less-than-ideal circumstances, both in primary and secondary care, whether state delivered or privately provided. They must have the courage to make decisions that may be unpopular with patients, relatives, clients and hospital staff while recognizing the autonomy in respect of consent and confidentiality which applies to these individuals.

Thus, MDOs can advise and assist with many of the challenges to clinical practice. They have roles in supporting, advising and directing health professional members in relation to a range of medical and legal processes as outlined in this chapter, which evidences their unique role and responsibilities, and that they provide much more than a defense, that the name implies.

[xxi] https://www.thempsfoundation.org/

[xxii] MPTS is the Medical Practitioners Tribunal Service, which operates as an independent, statutory committee of the GMC that makes decisions about doctors' impairment of their fitness to practise and sanctions in relation to such impairment.

REFERENCES

1. Muir NC, Bell JD. *A Century of Care: A History of the Medical and Dental Defence Union of Scotland*. Glasgow: MDDUS; 2002.
2. General Medical Council. The good medical practice framework for appraisal and revalidation, 2013. Available from: https://www.gmc-uk.org/-/media/documents/the-good-medical-practice-framework-for-appraisal-and-revalidation---dc5707_pdf-56235089.pdf (Accessed 26 March 2023).
3. MDU. Nearly all GPs have faced a complaint during their career according to an MDU survey, 2021. Available from: https://www.themdu.com/press-centre/press-releases/nearly-all-gps-have-faced-a-complaint-during-their-career-mdu-member-survey (Accessed 26 March 2023).
4. *Kunal Kulkarni v Milton Keynes Hospital NHS Foundation Trust* [2009] EWCA Civ 789.
5. Dingwall R, Fenn P. Is NHS Indemnity working and is there a better way? *BJA* 1994; 73: 69–77.
6. Department of Health and Social Care. UK parliament. Health & social care committee. NHS litigation reform inquiry: Written evidence, 2021. Available from: https://committees.parliament.uk/writtenevidence/42609/pdf/ (Accessed 25 March 2023).
7. NHS Resolution. Clinical negligence scheme for general practice, 2021. Available from: https://resolution.nhs.uk/services/claims-management/clinical-schemes/general-practice-indemnity/clinical-negligence-scheme-for-general-practice/ (Accessed 25 March 2023).
8. NHS Wales. Scheme for general medical practice indemnity (GMPI) guidelines, 2020. Available from: https://nwssp.nhs.wales/ourservices/legal-risk-services/legal-risk-services-documents/general-medical-practice-indemnity-gmpi-docs/gmpi-guidelines/ (Accessed 24 March 2023).
9. Dyer C. Surgeon acquitted of carrying out female genital mutilation in a prosecution criticised by obstetricians. *BMJ* 2015; **350**: h703.
10. *R v Adomako* [1995] 1 AC 171.
11. Ferner RE, McDowell SE. Doctors charged with manslaughter in the course of medical practice, 1795–2005: a literature review. *J R Soc Med* 2006; **99(6)**: 309–14.
12. White P. More doctors charged with manslaughter are being convicted, shows analysis. *BMJ* 2015; **10**: 351:h4402.
13. Dyer C. Medical Defence Union questions value of prosecuting doctors for manslaughter. *BMJ* 2010; **341**: c6892.
14. Van Dellen A, Harris A, Merryweather J, et al. What the psychiatrist needs to know about the coroner's court in England and Wales. *B J Psych Adv* 2021; **28(3)**: 1–8.
15. R (on the application of Maughan) v. HM Senior Coroner for Oxfordshire UKSC, 2020. Available from: https://www.supremecourt.uk/cases/uksc-2019-0137.html (Accessed 26 March 2023).
16. Bhan A, Dave D, Vernon SA, et al. Risk management strategies following analysis of cataract negligence claims. *Eye (Lond)* 2005; **19(3)**: 264–8.
17. Baylis D, Price J, Bowie P. Content analysis of 50 clinical negligence claims involving test results management systems in general practice. *BMJ Open Qual* 2018; **7(4)**: e000463.
18. Sellu v R [2016] EWCA Crim 1716. Available from: https://medicalnegligencenow.com/sellu-v-the-crown-2016-ewca-crim-1716–15-november-2016–3/ (Accessed 23 March 2023).
19. *Ibid.* See judgement in *Sellu*, paragraph 152.
20. Bawa-Garba v General Medical Council [2018] EWCA Civ 1879. Available from: https://www.judiciary.uk/wp-content/uploads/2018/08/bawa-garba-v-gmc-final-judgment.pdf (Accessed 23 March 2023).
21. Department of Health. *Gross negligence manslaughter in healthcare: the report of a rapid policy review*. London: HMSO; 2018.
22. General Medical Council. *Fitness to Practise Statistics*. London: General Medical Council; 2020.

CHAPTER

9

Principles of Forensic and Medicolegal Death Investigation

Denis A. Cusack

INTRODUCTION

In considering the general principles to be applied to forensic and medicolegal death investigation, three core questions arise. The first is when is a death investigation needed, the second is why it is needed, and the third is by whom it should be undertaken. These questions must also be framed within the various legal and criminal systems in the different classes of jurisdictions worldwide. Certain categories of death simply need a legal certification by the attending physician as to the cause of death. Other categories such as unexplained, unnatural, violent, or suspicious deaths involving a third party require a forensic investigation in a framework of judicial and/or police oversight and possible judicial inquiry and criminal prosecution prior to being certified and closed in the records of the State.

Basics of investigation

Regardless of the legal system in which the death is investigated, there are common facts to be established by the inquiry: the identification of the deceased; when the death occurred; where it occurred; how it occurred and in what circumstances. It must also make inquiry to exclude the involvement of a third party in bringing about the death of the deceased. If there are any questions of involvement of the State in the circumstances of the death, there will also be an added dimension in the national and international laws to be applied. Where there are multiple deaths through criminal or terrorist actions, or where there are mass disasters, then further specialist investigative considerations will be added as appropriate.

Who investigates?

The forensic investigation is overseen by a judicial or State authority such as an investigating magistrate, coroner or medical examiner independent of (although usually in co-operation with) the State and of the police authority. The judicial officer typically utilizes the services of the police and also of a forensic specialist. The forensic specialists usually include, primarily, a medically qualified person (most often a pathologist but sometimes a physician) but will also include forensic scientists, anthropologists, entomologists, odontologists and others as required and appropriate.

The investigation must include an examination of the site of the death; a full autopsy examination of the deceased with appropriate specialist tests (including toxicology, histology, biochemistry, microbiology and radiology and other imaging techniques such as computed tomography (CT) and magnetic resonance imaging (MRI) where available); and a comprehensive and structured report on the death for the relevant authority.

Outcome of investigation

The death investigation may lead to death certification and registration; or to a public non-criminal inquiry; or to a criminal prosecution in the State. In special circumstances, such as mass disasters or crimes against humanity, the outcome may be an inquiry or prosecution in an international forum. If the death has been deemed to be natural, then the certification will be by the attending physician or judicial officer and will form an intrinsic part of the health information system of the State for healthcare planning (including prevention of infectious diseases and other illnesses). If the death is deemed to be unnatural or violent, then the certification will only be completed at the conclusion of the relevant judicial officer's investigation.

THE LEGAL FRAMEWORK OF DEATH INVESTIGATION

There is a forensic continuum within the legal framework of all jurisdictions consisting of: Parliamentary Laws; Judicial investigation; Police enforcement and investigation; Forensic Medicine and Science (with Pathology and Laboratory analyses); Judicial Public Inquiry and Prosecution; and Investigation outcome with Inquiry and possibly Criminal Verdict through which the death investigation process is structured.

There are various categories of forensic and medicolegal death investigation systems throughout the world.

DOI: 10.1201/9781003138754-10

These can be broadly classified into the Investigating Magistrate (Civil Law Jurisdictions), the Coroner (Common Law or Anglo-Saxon law based Jurisdictions), Mixed Systems (e.g. Japan and Scotland), the Medical Examiner (parts of the United States) and Police and State Authority Systems (parts of the Middle East and Asia and some of the Nordic countries). However, all systems share common goals to confirm the death and examine the scene, to establish the medical cause of death, to investigate the surrounding circumstances and to assist the criminal justice system, the civil law courts, public health medicine and epidemiology and healthcare planning.

The purpose of forensic death investigation must be based in human rights and recognition of the right to life and thus an obligation on the State to certify and investigate all deaths to ensure proper accountability. A number of important human rights codes underpin this obligation (1,2).

THE FORENSIC MEDICAL AND OTHER COGNATE SPECIALISTS

Forensic experts play a core role in the death investigation process. They help determine in an evidence-based medical and scientific way the causes and manner of the unexpected or unnatural death. Their expertise must meet international standards and be independent, impartial, effective and prompt in their methods. Forensic Specialists should be appropriately trained and certified by a recognized competent professional body. In addition, standards of professional performance within the forensic services must be met using valid, established and acceptable criteria. Accreditation and certification criteria should be available to assess this expertise. The Minnesota Protocol of 2016, the European Council of Legal Medicine (ECLM), the National Association of Medical Examiners (USA), the Faculty of Forensic and Legal Medicine and Faculty of Pathologists (England and Scotland) are examples of bodies who have set out policies and procedures for reliable and recognized forensic professionals and services and harmonized autopsy rules to which reference must be made (3–14).

Forensic investigations should be conducted by professionally certified experts in the field of forensic medicine, pathology and science without a hierarchical relationship with the prosecuting authorities and with access to appropriate standard forensic facilities and services (8). The Forensic Specialists must be ready to present their expert findings to courts and other judicial bodies in a competent and professional manner and be prepared to assist in such fora where their evidence will be scrutinized. Clarity in explanation of forensic findings and terminology to a non-medical audience is in itself a highly skilled task. The professional conduct of Forensic Specialists may also be subject to review by regulatory authorities in their country of practice.

The ECLM checklist for accreditation or certification of a forensic service includes standards under a number of headings: General requirements; Investigation procedures; Morgue operations; Histology facilities and practice; Toxicology; Reports and records; Professional staffing; and other Forensic Specialists (8). These main areas are further subdivided into categories which prioritize standards that are absolutely essential requirements and those which are not absolutely essential with accreditation being granted if found to have no essential requirement deficiencies and no more than one-third non-essential deficiencies (Table 9.1).

TABLE 9.1 Accreditation of forensic services

A. General requirements
• *Facilities*
• *Security of premises*
• *Administrative space*
• *Safety and maintenance of service*
• *Mass disaster plan*
• *Quality assurance procedure*
• *Annual report*
B. Investigation Procedures
• *Scene*
• *Body identification*
C. Morgue Operations
• *Body handling*
• *Autopsy room specifications*
• *Radiologic facilities*
• *Evidence and specimen collection*
• *Chain of custody policy*
D. Histology Facilities and Practices
E. Toxicology Requirements
• *Laboratory*
• *Practices*
• *Toxicologists*
• *Specimen information and collection*
F. Reports and Records
• *Keeping of records*
• *Information release*
• *Scene investigation report*
• *Post-mortem examination reports*
• *Photographic records*
G. Personnel and Staffing
• *Forensic Pathologists*
• *Forensic Technical Staff*
• *Administrative Staff*
H. Availability of Other Specialist Consultants

Source: Adapted from (8) with permission.

THE SCENE OF DEATH AND COLLECTION OF INFORMATION

The application of standards and principles at the scene of death by recognized forensic experts will ensure that forensic evidence at the scene is observed, assessed, gathered and preserved by the relevant specialists for presentation to the judicial authority. A physician with basic competent forensic knowledge and training must, first of all, confirm the death (pronounce life extinct) (9). In some jurisdictions, this may also be performed by a competently trained nurse or paramedical professional. The scene of death must be preserved intact and undisturbed by a police officer and, if appropriate, by a trained scenes of crime police officer until the initial assessment of the circumstances of the death is completed. The scene preservation must be continued in full if the circumstances of the death appear unnatural or suspicious.

An on-site inspection of the scene and corpse then follows and is an essential part of the forensic and medicolegal examination prior to autopsy, particularly in the circumstances of an unnatural, violent or suspicious death but also in the circumstances of any sudden or unexpected death (9,13).

The scene and body inspection must be performed within a framework of co-ordination between the forensic experts, the police and the judicial authority with clear definition and separation of these roles in the overall investigation. The procedures for such an inspection include the requirements set out in Table 9.2.

A detailed and comprehensive menu of on-site inspection forms under six sections for Forensic Pathology, Anthropology, Odontology, Genetics, Entomology and Toxicology for forensic and medicolegal scene and corpse investigation has been agreed by the 33 Member Countries of the ECLM in the context of the agreed ECLM standards for forensic services. The aim of these agreed template forms is to facilitate an operational method for harmonization and common standards across the various legal jurisdictions of the member countries and may form a guiding reference for other non-ECLM jurisdictions but also acknowledging that this is only one of a number of internationally available guides to which reference has already been made (14).

These principles should be considered as a set of general guidelines to be adapted to the particular and unique situation of the death and interpreted using medical and scientific knowledge of the relevant procedures as applied to the facts of the individual case. They must also be read in the context of the jurisprudence and laws of the jurisdiction and incorporate the role of the police in that jurisdiction with applicable national, regional or local laws but without compromising forensic medical principles and the independence of the forensic expert.

THE FORENSIC AUTOPSY

The harmonization of forensic and medicolegal autopsy principles and procedures across jurisdictions is an invaluable tool for consistency and peer review of autopsy (5).

The autopsy follows the examination of the scene and, where applicable, of the body at the scene (13). Such examinations may be required in cases of apparent natural death where the death is sudden, unexpected or unexplained. This is necessary for an accurate death certification system to inform public health and healthcare planning in society. The autopsy is also necessary in all obvious or suspected unnatural deaths, of which there is a recognized extensive list of such categories (Table 9.3).

A summary of the principles of the autopsy includes provisions for identification of the body and external and internal examinations of the body (Table 9.4).

The autopsy report is a critical part of the procedure and must be clear and comprehensible as it will be read and relied upon by non-medical persons including

TABLE 9.2 On-site forensic and medicolegal scene and corpse investigation
Initial assessment on arrival at the scene of a death
Viewing and examining the body and site
Possessing the necessary materials and equipment
Collecting and preserving the relevant evidence
Obtaining relevant collateral information
Preservation of digital and telephonic evidence concerning deceased
Liaison with other forensic specialists
Recording of all the findings on a standardized protocol form
Preparing a report of the scene examination

Source: Adapted from (13) with permission.

TABLE 9.3 Categories of deaths requiring autopsy
Homicide or suspected homicide
Violation of human rights including torture or ill-treatment contributing to the death
Suicide or suspected suicide
Suspected medical malpractice
Accidents in the home, at work or in transport
Occupational diseases and hazards
Technologic or environmental disasters
Terrorist incidents
Deaths in custody or involving state authorities
Unidentified or skeletonized remains

Source: Adapted from (8) with permission.

TABLE 9.4 Autopsy procedure

Identification of the body
• *Visual*
• *Personal effects*
• *Physical characteristics*
• *Dental examination*
• *Anthropological features*
• *Fingerprints*
• *Genetic*
External examination of the body
• *Clothing*
• *Description of the body characteristics*
• *Post-mortem changes including rigor mortis, hypostasis and decomposition*
• *Findings on primary external inspection*
• *Detailed description of injuries including abrasions, bruises, lacerations and other marks*
Internal examination of the body
• *Three cavities examination of head, thorax and abdomen*
• *Dissection of soft tissues and musculature*
• *Dissection of internal organs following guidelines of pathologic anatomy*
• *Detailed description of all internal injuries and lesions*
• *Radiologic imaging as relevant*
• *Sampling of blood for toxicology, biochemistry and DNA profiling*
• *Additional body samples as required from urine, gastric contents, vitreous humor, bile and hair*

Source: Adapted from (8) with permission.

TABLE 9.5 Minimum requirements for the autopsy report contents

Legal authority basing the forensic examination
Details and qualifications of the forensic specialist
Details of the deceased
Date, place and time of death
Date, place and time of autopsy
Assistants and others present at the autopsy
Confirmation of identification of the deceased
Summary of the history and circumstances of the death as provided to the forensic specialist
Description of the scene of death
Details of the external and internal examination of the body
List of samples taken from the body for examination and the results of the tests performed
Results of all ancillary examinations
Evaluation of the significance of the accumulated information, findings and results
Final interpretation of the cause of death using the International Classification of Disease
Ranking of probable causes of death if no single cause identified or certified as unascertained if none identified
Date and signature on all provisional, interim and final reports

Source: Adapted from (8) and (13) with permission.

judicial, legal and family members. The minimum content is set out in Table 9.5.

The further development of the imaging autopsy through post-mortem computed tomography (PMCT) and magnetic resonance imaging (MRI) as complementary or adjuvant to the traditional external examination and physical dissection will also change the methodology and procedures of forensic pathology and other forensic specialties such as anthropology in death investigation in the future (15,16).

Specific procedures may be required for certain types of death as set out in Table 9.6 (8,10,11). Certain international forensic and criminal investigations of deaths may be guided by International Forensic Scientific Expert Advisory Boards, for example the Scientific Advisory Board to the Office of the Prosecutor of the International Criminal Court (12).

LIAISON WITH FAMILIES OF DECEASED PERSONS

As part of the death investigation process, a family liaison officer (FLO) should be appointed by the relevant authority to liaise with the family of the deceased to ensure that the procedure is explained to them and that appropriate communication and support services are put in place for them.

This liaison must ensure that appropriate information is given to the family and this includes an explanation that certain information of a sensitive criminal nature may have to be withheld from them pending the completion of any decision concerning criminal prosecution.

The family should be provided with an explanation of the autopsy process and how the dignity of the deceased will be preserved and sensitivity shown to the family throughout the process. They should be informed of the timescale for release of the body to them for their chosen method of burial, cremation etc. and a full explanation must be given if any organs or tissues need to be retained as part of the investigation and the arrangements for ultimate disposal of those organs or tissues in consultation with them.

TABLE 9.6 Special categories for death autopsy
Constriction of the neck in hanging and manual and ligature strangulation
Drowning and immersion
Sexual violence
Child abuse and neglect
Infanticide
Stillbirths and neonatal period
Shooting
Explosive devices
Blunt and sharp force
Fires
Intoxication

Source: Adapted from (8) with permission.

DEATH CERTIFICATION

Death investigation of natural deaths as part of a forensic and medicolegal framework is also critical to societies by way of healthcare planning based on disease patterns and morbidity on clinical inquiry following the death, and on the findings of the autopsy in sudden, unexplained or unexpected deaths. It also contributes to public health measures in prevention or reduction of mortalities from avoidable or treatable diseases if recognized. Death certification also plays a role in modern society in life insurance procedures and inquiries for families of the deceased person. Therefore, competent and full investigation of deaths and accurate certification are both a medical and legal obligation for general and forensic physicians and pathologists and for other forensic specialists alike (5,9). In some jurisdictions, there may be an overall medical oversight system to ensure accuracy of death certification (17,18). The recently established Medical Examiner system in England (doctors appointed to oversee medical cause of death certification) should not be confused with the system of the same name in the United States (US) (referring to appointed pathologists who carry out autopsy examinations in certain areas of the US). A Medical Reviewer system (similar to the English one) has also been established in Scotland (19).

Certain causes of death may be categorized as being due to natural causes but, because of the circumstances of the death or because of proper and legitimate questions raised by families and other interested persons, they may require further investigation prior to any decision being made to close the death inquiry by simple certification. Such deaths may include natural causes but due to occupational disease (e.g. mesothelioma as a consequence of workplace exposure to asbestos or secondary domestic exposure to asbestos through the working clothes of a family member working with asbestos). They may also include deaths due to natural causes but where questions arise in relation to the healthcare provided or, in some jurisdictions, other classes of natural death, for example maternal deaths. These categories of deaths may require autopsy and some may require a public hearing to address issues of public health or more general concern. In these situations, the cause of death may be certified in conjunction with certification from the relevant judicial investigating authority or judicial officer (such as Investigating Magistrate or Judge or a Coroner). A recent example of mandatory inquiry into deaths due to natural causes is COVID-19 SARS-CoV-2 deaths which required further investigation prior to death certification in some jurisdictions (20). The concept of excess mortality is defined as the number of deaths from all causes relative to what would normally have been expected for a given period, and its measurement plays an important part of the clinical epidemiology and public health medicine into which death investigation feeds.

The international form of the medical certificate of cause of death uses the international classification of diseases system and is adapted to each individual jurisdiction. The accepted standard template includes a statement of the immediate medical cause leading directly to the death and any antecedent medical conditions giving rise to that direct cause, together with any significant conditions contributing to the death (but not related to the disease or condition causing it). The medical conditions certified should follow the World Health Organization's International Statistical Classification of Diseases and Related Health Problems, currently ICD 11. Death certification is a medical skill which requires training of physicians to ensure accuracy and requires oversight by a Medical Examiner (as recently introduced in England) or by a trained public official in the death registration service (17–21).

In the event of mass deaths due to natural causes such as pandemic infection, the collation and accurate recording of the direct and contributing causes of death, combined with details of the demographics of the deceased persons, will play a core role in the public health epidemiology and prevention of spread of such infectious diseases (20). This has become a critical tool in the SARS-CoV-2 global pandemic.

Internationally, there is a generally agreed standardized template form of the certificate for registration and collation of medical cause of death (Table 9.7) (22). This may be completed by a medical practitioner or by a judicial officer (e.g. Coroner) or Medical Examiner (US system). This standardized certification facilitates comparative international epidemiologic studies of morbidity and mortality. The World Health Organization published new guidance on death certification in 2023 (23).

CONCLUSION

Forensic death investigation may lead to death certification and registration or it may also, of necessity, involve a public non-criminal inquiry or a criminal prosecution in the State. In special circumstances, such as mass disasters or crimes against humanity, the outcome may be an inquiry or prosecution in an international forum. If the death has been deemed to be natural, then the certification will be by the attending physician or

TABLE 9.7 Model standard template for medical cause of death certification by a medical practitioner or equivalent certification by the investigating judicial officer

Part I. The immediate cause of death*
The disease, injury or condition causing death is stated here with any underlying cause(s) listed sequentially ("due to or as a consequence of") with the initiating cause listed last
Disease or condition directly leading to death
I (a) ....
Antecedent causes
I (b) due to (or as a consequence of) ....
I (c) due to (or as a consequence of) ....
Part II. Other significant conditions contributing to death but not related to or resulting in the underlying cause stated in Part I
II Other Significant conditions ....
The approximate interval between onset of the disease or condition and the death should also be stated by the certifying medical practitioner or judicial officer

* Cause of death does not mean the manner of dying or mode of death (cardiac arrest, respiratory arrest, cardiac failure, etc.).

judicial officer and will form an intrinsic part of the health information system of the State for healthcare planning (including prevention of infectious diseases). If the death is deemed to be unnatural or violent or unexplained then the certification will only be completed at the conclusion of the relevant judicial officer's investigation.

International and national guidelines and protocols form an invaluable reference source for underpinning the harmonization and standardization of forensic death investigation across different jurisdictions to the highest professional standards through the practice of accredited forensic medicine and pathology in the pursuit of justice for the deceased and the bereaved.

REFERENCES

1. European Convention on Human Rights, Article 2, 1953. Available from: https://www.echr.coe.int/Documents/Guide_Art_2_ENG.pdf (Accessed 28 March 2023).
2. United Nations Declaration of Human Rights, Article 3, 1948. Available from: https://www.un.org/en/about-us/universal-declaration-of-human-rights (Accessed 29 March 2023).
3. Office of the United Nations High Commissioner for Human Rights. The Minnesota protocol on the investigation of potentially unlawful death, 2017. Available from: https://www.ohchr.org/sites/default/files/Documents/Publications/MinnesotaProtocol.pdf (Accessed 28 March 2023).
4. Brinkmann B. Harmonisation of medico-legal autopsy rules. *Int J Legal Med* 1999; **113:** 1–14.
5. European Council of Legal Medicine. ECLM principles and rules relating to medico-legal autopsy procedures (Harmonisation of medico-legal autopsy rules), 2014. Available from: http://www.eclm.eu/en/documents/harmonization-of-medico-legal-autopsy-protocol/ (Accessed 29 March 2023).
6. National Association of Medical Examiners. Inspection and accreditation policies and procedures manual, 2014. Available from: https://name.memberclicks.net/assets/docs/IA%20POLICY%204%202021.pdf (Accessed 26 March 2023).

7. National Association of Medical Examiners. Inspection and accreditation checklist for autopsy services, 2014. Available from: https://www.thename.org/assets/docs/NAME%20Accreditation%20Checklist%202019%20-%202024.pdf (Accessed 23 March 2023).
8. Mangin P, Bonbled F, Väli M, et al. European Council of Legal Medicine (ECLM) accreditation of forensic pathology services in Europe. *Int J Legal Med* 2015; **129**: 395–403.
9. Faculty of Forensic and Legal Medicine, Royal College of Physicians. Sudden death – forensic notes, 2021. Available from: https://fflm.ac.uk/wp-content/uploads/2021/05/Sudden-Death-pro-forma-Dr-B-Butler-and-Prof-M-Stark-April-2021.pdf (Accessed 28 March 2023).
10. Home Office, The Forensic Science Regulator, Department of Justice and The Royal College of Pathologists. Code of practice and performance standards for forensic pathology in England, Wales and Northern Ireland, 2018. Available from: https://www.google.com/search?q=Code+of+practice+and+performance+standards+for+forensic+pathology+in+England%2C+Wales+and+Northern+Ireland&oq=Code+of+practice+and+performance+standards+for+forensic+pathology+in+England%2C+Wales+and+Northern+Ireland&aqs=chrome..69i57.524j0j15&sourceid=chrome&ie=UTF-8 (Accessed 29 March 2023).
11. The Royal College of Pathologists and Crown Office and Procurator Fiscal Service (Scotland). Code of practice and performance standards for forensic pathologists dealing with suspicious deaths in Scotland, 2016. Available from: https://www.rcpath.org/uploads/assets/02e0662c-9a13-4063-a0b1c404a74f5a28/g066_copforforensicpathscotland_jan16.pdf (Accessed 29 March 2023).
12. International Criminal Court: The Scientific Advisory Board of the Office of the Prosecutor 7th Annual Meeting, 2020. Available from: https://www.icc-cpi.int/Pages/item.aspx?name=pr1557 (Accessed 29 March 2023).
13. Cusack D, Ferrara SD, Keller E, et al. European Council of Legal Medicine (ECLM) principles for on-site forensic and medico-legal scene and corpse investigation. *Int J Legal Med* 2017; **131**: 1119–22.
14. Cecchi R, Cusack D, Ludes B, et al. European Council of Legal Medicine (ECLM) on-site inspection forms for Forensic Pathology, Anthropology, Genetics, Entomology and Toxicology for forensic and medico-legal scene and corpse investigation. *Int J Legal Med* 2022; **136(4)**: 1037–49.
15. Bolliger SA, Thali MJ. Imaging and virtual autopsy: looking back and forward. *Philos Trans R Soc Lond B Biol Sci* 2015; **370(1674)**: 20140253.
16. Biggs MJP, Morgan B, Rutty GN. Using freely-available 3D software to reconstruct traumatic bone injuries detected with post mortem computed tomography. *Forensic Sci Med Pathol* 2019; **16(1)**: 113–8.
17. NHS. National Medical Examiner System. Available from: https://www.england.nhs.uk/establishing-medical-examiner-system-nhs/ (Accessed 29 March 2023).
18. Royal College of Pathologists. Become a medical examiner. Available from: https://www.rcpath.org/profession/medical-examiners/become-a-medical-examiner.html#:~:text=Medical%20examiners%20should%20have%20at,examiner%20after%20completing%20the%20training. (Accessed 29 March 2023).
19. NHS Education for Scotland. The Scottish MCCD review process. Available from: http://www.sad.scot.nhs.uk/atafterdeath/the-scottish-mccd-review-process/roles-and-responsibilities/ (Accessed 29 March 2023).
20. Cusack DA. COVID-19 pandemic: Coroner's database of death inquiries with clinical epidemiology and total and excess mortality analyses in the District of Kildare March to June. *J Forensic Leg Med* 2020; **76**: 102072.
21. Adeyinka A, Bailey K. Death certification, 2021. https://www.ncbi.nlm.nih.gov/books/NBK526015/ (Accessed 29 March 2023).
22. World Health Organisation. International Statistical Classification of Diseases and Related Health Problems (ICD). Available from: https://www.who.int/standards/classifications/classification-of-diseases#:~:text=International%20Statistical%20Classification%20of%20Diseases%20and%20Related%20Health%20Problems%20(ICD)&text=ICD%20serves%20a%20broad%20range,and%20coded%20with%20the%20ICD. (Accessed 29 March 2023).
23. World Health Organization. WHO Recommendations for conducting an external inspection of a body and filling in the Medical Certificate of Cause of Death. 2023 https://cdn.who.int/media/docs/default-source/classification/icd/cause-of-death/who-recommendations-for-conducting-an-external-inspection-of-a-body-and-filling-in-the-medical-certificate-of-cause-of-death-_vf_published.pdf?sfvrsn=edaa1998_13&download=true (accessed September 2023).

CHAPTER

10

Role of the Coroner in England & Wales

Paul Marks

HISTORICAL DEVELOPMENT OF THE CORONER SYSTEM

The ancient office of Coroner dates from the time of Richard I and was established through the Articles of Eyre in 1194. This provided for three knights and one clerk to "keep the pleas of the crown"[i] in each county. The duties of the mediaeval Coroner were more extensive and varied than those of his modern counterpart, but essentially involved activities that raised revenue for the Crown. Coroners were known as *Crowners,* from which it is obviously how the current term derived.

Some of the more unusual and recherche duties of the medieval Coroner are shown in Box 10.1, but it should be noted that while most have long since disappeared, Coroners still have jurisdiction over *treasure* and operate under the provisions of the Treasure Act 1996. This defines what constitutes treasure, formerly referred to as *treasure trove,* and this Act provides a basic framework, which includes making it a criminal offense for failing to report the finding of treasure, as well as providing a detailed description of what constitutes treasure, in terms of precious metal content and age.

Until recently, coroners operated under the Coroners Act 1988, which was essentially a consolidation of the Coroners Act 1887, basically Victorian legislation. At least two attempts had been made to reform the coronial jurisdiction in the twentieth century. The Wright Committee of 1936 recommended merging small coronial jurisdictions and the Broderick Committee of 1965 suggested some quite radical reforms, but both reports were largely disregarded.

BOX 10.1 Medieval Coroner's duties

- Tax collector – "amercements"
- Investigation of sudden death
- Jurisdiction over felons
- The right of sanctuary
- Abduration of the Realm
- Trial by Ordeal
- Treasure trove

Two apparently unrelated events provided a stimulus for reform at the turn of the century.

Firstly, Tom Luce, a senior civil servant, was tasked by the Home Office with chairing a *fundamental review of the coroner and death certification systems,* and this reported in June 2003. It concluded that neither the certification nor the investigation system was fit for purpose in modern society, and that substantial reform was needed.

Secondly, the criminal activity of serial killer, Harold Shipman, a general practitioner who was found guilty of 15 counts of murder at Preston Crown Court[ii], provided the unexpected drive to reform the coroners' service. It would ensure that *all* deaths, whether suspicious or otherwise would be the subject of scrutiny.

Dame Janet Smith, a High Court Judge, chaired the Shipman Inquiry and reported her phase 1 findings in June 2002 which addressed the number of patients who were killed, and her phase 2 findings, which looked at death certification, cremation and the coroner, reported in July 2003. Her findings were similar, but not identical with those of Tom Luce. He took the differences into consideration and published a position paper in 2004.

The Fundamental Review and the Shipman Inquiry provided the necessary impetus for reform which culminated in the Coroners & Justice Act 2009, but it took until 25th July 2013 for the legislation to come into force and its form was diluted in comparison with its original provisions. Importantly, one of Dame Janet Smith's recommendations was to establish a *Medical Examiner System* to provide independent statutory scrutiny of *all* deaths. Indeed, sections 18–21 of the Coroners and Justice Act 2009 lay down the framework for such a service, which also provides for the appointment of a *National Medical Examiner,* a post currently held by Dr Alan Fletcher.

CORONERS & JUSTICE ACT 2009

The Coroners and Justice Act 2009 (the Act) is the law under which coroners now operate. It received Royal

[i] In Latin this was termed "custos placitorum coronae" corrupted to "crowner' and then coroner.

[ii] There is evidence that Shipman probably killed somewhere in the region of 250 of his patients.

DOI: 10.1201/9781003138754-11

Assent on 12th November 2009, but it took until 25th July 2013 for it to come into force.

Initially, it appeared that the Act would not come into force at all, and the Office of Chief Coroner would not be filled. However, in September 2012, His Honor Judge Peter Thornton, QC, became the first Chief Coroner of England and Wales and has been responsible for the implementation of the Act and its accompanying Rules and Regulations[iii]. Since then, HHJ Mark Lucraft has held office as Chief Coroner until his preferment as Recorder of London, and since 24th December 2020, the office is held by HHJ Thomas Teague, QC. There are two Deputy Chief Coroners, one a judge and the other a senior coroner.

Several provisions that were in the original legislation have not been implemented such as the appeal of conclusions to the Chief Coroner.

One of the most significant changes introduced by the Act is the concept of the *investigation* which is distinguished from the *inquest*.

The new Act also brought with it a change in terminology: Coroners' Districts are now referred to as Coroners' Areas; the Coroner in an area now becomes a **Senior Coroner.** In the transitional arrangements between the old and new Acts, all Deputy Coroners and all Assistant Deputy Coroners become **Assistant Coroners** but in the new hierarchy, the new post of **Area Coroner** has been created.

The Inquisition Form is now termed the *Record of Inquest* and the term verdict has been replaced by *conclusion as to the death.*

THE WORK AND ORGANIZATION OF THE CORONIAL SERVICE

The Coroner's Court is an inferior court of record and is one of the few examples in English law of an *inquisitorial* system, as opposed to an *adversarial* system.

A coroner is an independent judicial officer who is appointed and paid by the relevant Local Authority, but the appointment must be approved by the Lord Chancellor and Chief Coroner. Once appointed, a coroner can only be removed from office by the Lord Chancellor with agreement of the Lord Chief Justice.

There are currently 88 coroner areas in England and Wales and leadership and direction is provided by the Chief Coroner who is a judge appointed by the Lord Chief Justice, following consultation with the Lord Chancellor. The Chief Coroner is based at the Royal Courts of Justice and is supported by his own team and office.

To be appointed to coronial office, a prospective applicant must satisfy the *judicial eligibility criteria,* be under the age of 70 years and receive approval for appointment from the Lord Chancellor and Chief Coroner. Legally qualified medical practitioners cannot be appointed to office unless they are also solicitors, barristers or Fellows of the Chartered Institute of Legal Executives, thereby fulfilling the judicial eligibility criteria. A popular misconception is that coroners are forensic pathologists.

The situation in Northern Ireland is slightly different as there is a unified coroners' service governed by the Department of Justice and headed by a High Court Judge.

INVESTIGATION

One of the most significant changes that occurred with the 2009 Act is the concept of an *Investigation* and this is described in section 1 of the Act. A consequence of the investigation is that a coroner will no longer need to open an inquest to release a body for funeral purposes.

The duty to investigate pursuant to section 1 involves:

(1) A senior coroner who is made aware of the deceased person in that coroner's area must, as soon as practicable, conduct an investigation into the person's death if subsection (2) applies
(2) This subsection applies if the coroner has reason to suspect that:
   (a) the deceased died a violent or unnatural death
   (b) the cause of death is unknown, or
   (c) the deceased died while in custody or otherwise in state detention

Interestingly, a coroner is able to conduct preliminary inquiries under the authority of section 1(7) of the Act and this seeks to determine whether section 1(1) is engaged. Such inquiries would typically comprise a post-mortem Examination[iv].

If a natural cause of death is found by post-mortem examination, the Coroner is obliged to discontinue the investigation and inform the next of kin or personal representatives of this in writing.

However, if the cause of death is natural, but has occurred in state detention or custody, the coroner must, in these circumstances, continue to investigate and proceed to inquest.

REFERRAL OF DEATHS TO THE CORONER

Deaths are referred to the coroners in the circumstances shown below.

- No doctor saw the deceased during his or her last illness.
- While a doctor may have attended the deceased during the last illness, the doctor is not able or available, for any reason, to certify the death.
- The cause of death is unknown.
- The death occurred during an operation or before recovery from the effects of an anesthetic

[iii] Rules & Regulations Coroners (Investigations) Regulations 2013, Coroners (Inquests) Rules 2013 & Coroners Allowances, Fees and Expenses Regulations 2013

[iv] The Act does not define post-mortem examination, and this was deliberate, to permit alternatives to invasive autopsy such as CT or MRI scanning to be employed.

- The death occurred at work or was due to industrial disease or poisoning.
- The death was sudden and unexplained.
- The death was unnatural.
- The death was due to violence or neglect.
- The death was in other suspicious circumstances, e.g. suspected suicide.
- The death may be due to an abortion.
- The death occurred in prison, police custody or another type of state detention.
- All deaths of children and young people under 18, even if due to natural causes. This is for safeguarding purposes.
- The death may be linked to an accident, *however long ago it happened.*

A statutory requirement for such reporting falls to the Registrar of Births and Deaths[v] but in practice, coroners will take referrals from many sources including medical practitioners, medical examiners, family members, police and funeral directors.

Following referral, the Coroner will decide whether to investigate the case further. It may be that following discussion with the relevant doctor, sufficient information is available to permit a natural cause of death to be recorded and subsequently registered. In these circumstances, the Coroner can issue a certificate known as *Form 100A* that enables the Registrar of Births, Deaths & Marriages to register the death without an autopsy or inquest. This form supports the certificate of the medical cause of death issued by the doctor.

If, however, the cause of death is unknown, the Coroner will order an autopsy and if the cause is *natural,* he can issue *Form 100B,* which permits the death to be registered following the autopsy but without recourse to inquest.

There is little doubt that the routine work of a coroner's office, culminating in the disposal of cases by issuing Form 100A & 100B will represent, at least in numerical terms, most of the caseload. However, the high-profile work, which in terms of cases is far less, are inquests; generally, for every ten referrals that are made, only one inquest will need to be opened and concluded.

THE LEGAL BASIS FOR ORDERING A POST-MORTEM EXAMINATION

The Coroner's power to order a post-mortem examination and to remove a body is set out in Sections 14 and 15 of the Act. Readers are referred to these sections of the Act as well as to the Chief Coroner's Guidance No 32 which covers post-mortem examinations, including second post-mortem examinations.

The important points raised in this guidance are:

> While a coroner has legal control over the body of a deceased person, it is for the coroner to decide whether to commission a first or subsequent post-mortem examination and it is for the coroner to decide whether to permit a second examination of the body on the instruction of an interested party. Despite there being a widespread misconception (particularly in homicide cases), there is no automatic right to a second post-mortem examination and requests should be scrutinized rigorosly by the coroner on a case to case basis.

[v] Regulation 41 of Registration of Births and Deaths Regulations 1987

WHAT IS A POST-MORTEM EXAMINATION?

The Act does not define what constitutes a post-mortem examination; this is not an omission but is deliberate, so that methods other than invasive autopsy, where appropriate can be employed to determine the cause of death. These would include, CT or MRI scanning, limited post-mortem examination, toxicology alone, external examination only, to name but a few.

ADJOURNMENT

After receiving evidence of identification of the deceased, the coroner will open and adjourn the inquest to a date and time to be set down pending further investigation. In homicide cases, the inquest will typically not be resumed, as the matters a coroner needs to address will inevitably be ventilated in the Crown Court. An exception to this would be if there was a murder/suicide, in which case, both inquests would need to be resumed and concluded.

INQUESTS

In the above section, the distinction between an investigation and an inquest has been made, but in what circumstances will an inquest need to be held?

Section 1(2) and Section 4(2) of the Act requires that an inquest is held where a coroner is made aware that the body of a person is within his or her area and that there is reason to suspect that:

- The deceased has died a violent or unnatural death
- The cause of death is unknown
- The deceased died while in custody or otherwise in state detention

The remit of an inquest is limited and set out in Section 5 of the Act but, on occasions, a coroner may have to sensitively but firmly manage expectations. An inquest is required to address two limited but factual questions which are:

(a) Who the deceased was;
(b) How, when and where the deceased came by his or her death;

The particulars (if any) are required by the 1953 Act to be registered concerning the death.

Section 5(3) of the Act prohibits the Senior Coroner or the jury from expressing any opinion on any other matter and section 10(2) prohibits any *determination* being framed in such a way as to appear to determine any question of:

(a) Criminal liability on the part of a named person, or
(b) Civil liability

In the majority of cases in which an inquest is held, the Coroner will sit alone. Indeed section 7(1) of the Act requires a coroner to sit alone unless the requirements in section 7(2) are fulfilled. Under these particular circumstances, it is incumbent on him to sit with a jury, but section 7(3) provides a discretionary power to sit with a jury empaneled.

Approximately 3 percent of inquests are heard with a jury which comprises between 7 and 11 jurors who are randomly selected from the electoral role.

Section 7(2) of the Act provides that:

An inquest into a death must be held with a jury if the senior coroner has reason to suspect:

(a) That the deceased died while in custody or otherwise in state detention, and that either:
   (i) The death was a violent or unnatural one
   (ii) The cause of death is unknown
(b) That the death resulted from an act or omission of:
   (i) a police officer
   (ii) a member of a service police force
   in the purported execution of the officer's or member's duty as such, or
(c) That the death was caused by a notifiable accident, poisoning or disease.

As a point of procedure, during jury cases, if advocates address the Coroner on points of law or make submissions, these are heard in the absence of the jury. The task of the jury is more exacting in coronial cases than in criminal cases, where it is a matter of deciding guilt or otherwise.

After all the evidence is adduced in a jury case, the Coroner must sum up the case and direct the jury as to the relevant law and leave them with conclusions to consider. He must draw the jury's attention to sections 5(1) and 5(3) of the Act as well as the prohibitions in respect of civil and criminal liability as stated in section 10(2).

TYPES OF INQUEST

Most inquests will be "common law", ordinary or Jamieson inquests. However, the European Convention on Human Rights, as enshrined in our domestic law by the Human Rights Act 1998, in particular Article 2, provides that *everyone's life shall be protected by law*. This has important ramifications and consequences for inquests in which Article 2 is engaged where deaths might have involved *agents of the state*.

Article 2 provides for two substantive duties and an implied obligation. The State has a negative duty to refrain from taking life and a positive duty to protect life by setting up an appropriate infrastructure of laws and practices to ensure this. It also means that there is an implied procedural obligation to investigate deaths by an effective and independent public body in which it might be arguable that the State has breached its negative or positive obligations. In these circumstances an "enhanced" or Middleton inquest will occur. Instances where such a hearing would be set down might include prison deaths, police shootings and deaths involving detained psychiatric patients. In physically ill patients who die in hospital, in certain circumstances, Article 2 might be engaged but this would be determined on a case-to-case basis.

An enhanced inquest will permit the Coroner or jury to go into further detail and, in practical terms, this means that the question *how* the deceased came by his or her death is expanded to include *by what means and in what circumstances* the deceased met his or her death.

It should be noted that at present, legal aid is generally not available for most inquests but can be made available for inquests in which Article 2 is engaged.

Standard of proof

The standard of proof required in a coroner's court is the *civil* standard of proof. On the balance of probabilities, whether an event is more likely to have occurred than not, or if expressed mathematically, a 51/49 percent split in the evidence. This now applies to *all* coroner's conclusions, formerly known as verdicts. Prior to the United Kingdom (UK) Supreme Court handing down judgement in the case of *R (Maughan) v HM Senior Coroner for Oxfordshire* [2020] UKSC46, suicide and unlawful killing were determined to the criminal standard of proof, *beyond reasonable doubt*.

Evidence

The rules of evidence are not as strict in the coronial jurisdiction as in other jurisdictions. For example, *hearsay* evidence is admissible. Evidence in a coroner's court comes in two basic forms, evidence heard on oath in the witness stand pursuant to rule 20 (1) of the Coroners (Inquests) Rules 2013 and documentary evidence. Rule 23 of the Coroners (Inquests) Rules 2013 permits written evidence to be admitted in the absence of the person who has made the statement. There are, however, a number of conditions and safeguards that must be addressed before such evidence can be used.

The coroner must be satisfied that:

(a) it is not possible for the maker of the written evidence to give evidence at the inquest hearing at all, or within a reasonable time
(b) there is good and sufficient reason why the maker of the written evidence should not attend the inquest hearing
(c) there is good and sufficient reason to believe that the maker of the written evidence will not attend the inquest hearing
(d) the written evidence (including evidence in admission form) is unlikely to be disputed.

It is important to note that *before* such evidence is admitted under this authority, the Coroner must announce in open court the nature of the evidence, the full name of the author, and that interested persons may object to such admission and their entitlement to seeing a copy of the evidence.

BEFORE THE INQUEST

In particularly complex or contentious inquests, a *pre-inquest review hearing* (PIR) may be held. Prior to the 2009 Act, PIRs were held and acknowledged to be good practice for case management but rule 6 of the Coroners (Inquests) Rules 2013 has put them on a formal basis. An agenda should be provided to all interested persons and a PIR will address matters such as the scope of the inquest, whether Article 2 ECHR is engaged, whether a jury is required, the need for independent expert evidence, what evidence will be heard and what will be dealt with under rule 23, who are designated as *interested persons,* together with other matters such as the date and duration of the final hearing.

Disclosure

The 2009 Act brought with it a far wider duty to disclose reports and documents. The presumption now is for *full* disclosure to take place to *interested persons* (see below), but there is limited discretion under rule 15 of *Coroners (Inquest) Rules 2013* to refuse a request for disclosure, if that request is unreasonable.

Interested persons

An *interested person* is not someone who has mere idle curiosity about the case, but someone defined as such within section 47 (2) of the Act. Such persons would include relatives, personal representatives of the deceased, a beneficiary under a policy of insurance or insurance company, a trade union representative, a person who may have by his actions or omissions caused or contributed to the death, a person appointed by, or representative of, an enforcing authority, a Chief Constable etc. The coroner has discretion to accord interested person status, if he thinks that individual has a sufficient interest.

The significance of being an interested person is essentially two-fold. Firstly, it entitles the interested person to disclosure and secondly, it allows the interested person to examine a witness either directly or through an advocate.

Witnesses at inquests are generally compellable and refusal to attend without proper reason is a contempt of court. Coroners are familiar with attempts by witnesses not to attend court by presenting "a sick note", but inability to attend work needs to be carefully distinguished from being unfit to attend court.

A statutory protection exists for witnesses against *self-incrimination* under rule 22 of the Coroners (Inquests) rules 2013. This means that a witness is not obliged to answer if he or she has been asked an incriminating question. In such circumstances, the Coroner must inform the witness that he is not obliged to answer. Of course, a witness may choose to waive this right and answer, if he wishes. As the term *incriminate* would suggest, the privilege only extends to criminal proceedings and not to civil or disciplinary proceedings.

CONCLUSION

In general, conclusions are of two types; *short-form* and *narrative.* The Chief Coroner will issue guidance about short-form and narrative conclusions. The outcome of an inquest is set out in the *Record of Inquest* and will show the medical cause of death and the conclusion, short-form or narrative.

The Chief Coroner advises that wherever possible, short-form conclusions should be returned. These might include accidental death, misadventure, suicide, drugs/alcohol, natural causes, unlawful killing, lawful killing, open, road traffic collision, industrial disease, and so on.

Narrative conclusions are becoming increasingly common and this, some argue, may be due to the widening of circumstances in which they can be employed due to Article 2 of ECHR. The case law relating to this is highly specialized, but interested readers are directed to the *further reading* section for guidance on this.

A narrative conclusion must not offend against Section 5(1) or Section 10 (2) of the Act, but acts or omissions may be recorded. However, expressions suggestive of civil liability such as "carelessness" or "neglect" should be avoided.

An example of a narrative conclusion that does not identify an individual or offend against Section 5(1) and Section 10(2) might be:

"The deceased was admitted for a radical cystectomy and fashioning of an ileal conduit for advance carcinoma of the bladder. In the post-operative period, he developed an anastomotic leak which was not recognised for 5 days, during which time appropriate investigations and treatment were not undertaken. He subsequently died from peritonitis and multi-organ failure. An opportunity existed to diagnose and treat this anastomotic leak and if taken, the deceased would not have died on 12th April 2022".

In short-form conclusions, if the facts support a conclusion that an opportunity to treat a patient was missed and that such treatment, on the balance of probabilities, if administered, would have resulted in survival, then the Coroner can add the rider of *neglect.* For example, a surgical operation may have gone wrong, and the postoperative management was woefully inadequate. If the evidence adduced shows that the deceased's condition was known, or should have been known as such, for action to have been taken, and that this omission amounted to gross failure and that there was a clear and causal relationship with the death, then a conclusion of *misadventure to which neglect contributed* may be recorded. The test as set out in Lord Bingham's judgment in *R v HM Coroner for North Humberside ex parte Jamieson* is stringent and a high bar to jump.

Aftermath

On concluding an inquest, a number of administrative matters need attention, notably, issuing the *Record of Inquest* and supplying the Registrar of Deaths a Form 99 (certificate after inquest).

Although the Act initially made provision for appeals to be made to the Chief Coroner in respect of inquest conclusions, this had not occurred, and the relevant legislation was repealed during debates on the Public Bodies Bill 2011.

There are two remedies whereby the conclusion of a coroner's court can be examined by the High Court. The first is by *judicial review* and the second is by the statutory remedy pursuant to Section 13 of the 1988 Coroners Act, which remains in force.

Judicial review is a complex area of law and is quite distinct from an appeal where there is a rehearing of the case by a superior court. With judicial review, consideration is given to process and, for example, whether the procedure was unreasonable, unfair or failed to take into consideration relevant evidence. The process is time limited to 3 months for the submission of an application.

A Section 13 fiat brought under the 1988 Act is *not time limited* however, and confers upon the High Court certain powers, but these can only be exercised with the authority of the Attorney General.

Typical reasons for an application include refusal to hold an inquest, the inquest is unsatisfactory due to insufficiency of inquiry, rejection of relevant evidence, fraud or irregularity of proceedings or importantly, if new facts or evidence have emerged.

The High Court can order that an inquest is held or quash the original Record of Inquest and a new hearing occurs.

Prevention of future deaths

Under the1988 Coroners Act and the Coroners Rules 1984, there was provision for a coroner to make a report under the authority of rule 43 to prevent future deaths and this represented an important public health and safety measure. Although the rule was "strengthened" in 2008, it still lacked "teeth".

Coroners now have a *duty* to report under regulation 28 of the Coroners (Investigations) Regulations 2013.

Such *reports to prevent future deaths* can now be made at an early stage without needing to await the conclusion of the inquest. However, the Coroner is required to have considered all the documents, evidence and information that are relevant before making the report. This regulation imposes a duty upon the Coroner to report the matter to a person whom the Coroner believes may have power to take action.

A *response* pursuant to *Regulation 28* must contain details of any action taken or that is proposed to be taken or an explanation as to why no action is proposed. The response must be provided within 56 days.

FURTHER READING

Coroners and Justice Act, 2009. Available from: https://www.legislation.gov.uk/ukpga/2009/25/contents (Accessed 23 March 2023).

Dorries C. *Coroners' Courts: A Guide to Law and Practice*, 3rd ed. Oxford: Oxford University Press, 2014.

Hunnisett RF. *The Medieval Coroner*. Cambridge: Cambridge University Press; 1961.

Matthews P. *Jervis On Coroners*, 14th ed. Edinburgh: Sweet & Maxwell; 2019.

CHAPTER

11

Role of the Medical Examiner in England & Wales

Jason Payne-James

INTRODUCTION

In any textbook of Forensic & Legal Medicine which embraces a wide range of jurisdictions, definitions of terminology are essential. When discussing the Medical Examiner (ME) system in England and Wales, it is important to understand that the term is not used to describe forensic pathologists (as it is in many countries) and MEs in England and Wales do not undertake post mortems but come from a wide variety of clinical backgrounds.

The ME system was introduced in England and Wales in April 2019 (1). In this system, an ME in England and Wales is an independent, senior doctor who reviews (scrutinizes) deaths that are not investigated by the England and Wales coronial system (see Chapter 10). The ME system works very closely with coronial services. The overall numbers of deaths have been distorted upward by the coronavirus pandemic. In England and Wales in 2022, there were 540 338 deaths registered, which was a decreased from the pandemic high of 607 922 deaths in 2020. In 2021, there were more male deaths registered than female deaths (297 989 male deaths and 288 345 female deaths (2). 195 200 deaths (33%) were reported to coroners in 2021, the lowest level since 1995 which was down 5 percent (10 300) compared to 2020. Post-mortem examinations were carried out on 43 percent of all deaths reported in 2021. There were 84 600 post-mortem examinations ordered by coroners in 2021, a 7 percent rise compared to 2020. Thirty-two thousand eight hundred inquests were opened in 2021, up 2 percent compared to 2020. In 2021, 32 300 inquest conclusions were recorded in total, up 4 percent on 2020 (3). Those deaths not reported to HM Coroners will all, in the near future, be reviewed by the ME system.

It has taken more than two decades to establish the Medical Examiner system since it was first recommended following an Inquiry by the UK House of Commons Constitutional Affairs Committee which stated: "*This Inquiry was set up to investigate the systems of death certification and investigation in England and Wales against a background of continued inaction by the Government in response to two reports published in 2003: Death Certification and the Investigation of Deaths by Coroners, the 3rd Report of the Shipman Inquiry under Dame Janet Smith (the 'Shipman Inquiry'); and Death Certification and Investigation in England, Wales and Northern Ireland: The Report of a Fundamental Review 2003 under Tom Luce (the 'Luce Review'). Both reports found the systems for the certification and investigation of deaths in England and Wales to be unfit for modern* society" (4).

REASONS FOR THE INTRODUCTION OF THE MEDICAL EXAMINER SYSTEM

Harold Shipman was a general practitioner (primary care physician) from Hyde in Greater Manchester, UK, who in January 2000 was found guilty of murdering 15 patients and sentenced to life imprisonment. He died by suicide in prison on 13 January 2004. It was considered likely that over a period of 20 or more years, he was responsible for the murder of around 250 of his patients. The Shipman Inquiry was initiated to investigate how he had been able to do this and it established that he was able to kill his patients because the systems in place permitted him to avoid questions being asked as he was the one writing his patients' Medical Certificates of Cause of Death (MCCDs) without any other scrutiny or oversight.

The Shipman Inquiry was set up in January 2001 and in a series of reports published between 2001 and 2003, the Inquiry made a number of recommendations for the reform of various British systems related to medical practice (5). The Inquiry also established that there were flaws in the system for reviewing cremations where doctors appointed as medical referees whose role was to independently review the cause of death prior to cremation. For those patients undergoing burials, the causes of death proposed by D Shipman were accepted and registered without question. The system was dependent on the integrity and honesty of the doctor writing the MCCD. The system, as it was, provided inadequate safeguards against possible criminal activity.

DOI: 10.1201/9781003138754-12

TABLE 11.1 Extracts from the 2009 Coroners and Justice Act introducing the Medical Examiner into Legislation

19	Medical Examiners
(1)	[Local authorities] (in England) and Local Health Boards (in Wales) must appoint persons as Medical Examiners to discharge the functions conferred on Medical Examiners by or under this Chapter.
(3)	A person may be appointed as a medical examiner only if, at the time of the appointment, he or she—
(c)	is a registered medical practitioner and has been throughout the previous 5 years, and
(b)	practises as such or has done within the previous 5 years.

The Shipman Inquiry recommended that a new national coroners' service under a Chief Coroner should be established. This service would be responsible for the final certification of death and for deciding whether further investigation was necessary in all deaths. The new system would include both medical coroners, who would be responsible for establishing the medical cause of death, and judicial coroners, who would carry out further investigations where necessary (e.g. in the case of suspicious deaths). It was this proposed role of "medical coroner" that evolved into the present ME, with the role of ME formally included in the England and Wales jurisdiction by the Coroners and Justice Act 2009 (see Table 11.1) (6).

The Department of Health had proposed in a consultation: "*While a series of checks is made before a body can be released for cremation, a single certificate is required for burial. The Government …is proposing to introduce a single system for death certification for both cremations and burials. The proposed arrangements are intended to provide a common level of assurance to all bereaved families that there were no suspicious circumstances surrounding the death, while simplifying the administrative process. They will also improve public health surveillance of cause of death. The new arrangements will be overseen by a Medical Examiner attached to a local Primary Care Trust (or an equivalent organisation in Wales)*" (7).

It took almost two decades after Harold Shipman was convicted and 10 years after the Coroners and Justice Act before a national rollout of MEs was begun, and in the interim, other hospital-based scandals were the subject of major inquiries.

Perhaps the most significant additional driver for the (at that time non-existent apart from some pilot sites) ME system was the 2013 Report of the Mid-Staffordshire NHS Foundation Trust Public Inquiry, chaired by Robert Francis, QC (8). The Francis Report made 290 recommendations, of which a number made specific reference to the need for an independent ME system. Table 11.2 shows its recommendations regarding MEs.

Multiple hospital-based scandals since then have highlighted poor care or deaths that may have been prevented had an effective system of independent scrutiny been in place.

In 2015, the Morecambe Bay Investigation concluded: "*It is our view that the possibility of outlying behavior such as this requires a failsafe system that would provide early warning of such problems by scrutinizing the pattern of deaths of both mothers and babies… a mechanism already in use in other countries has been put forward to scrutinize all deaths in this way that would, by its nature, pick up maternal and neonatal deaths. This is the appointment of medical examiners, initially proposed by Dame Janet Smith as a recommendation of the Shipman Inquiry, subsequently endorsed by the Luce review, put into enabling legislation in 2009 but not yet implemented. It is our view that implementing these proposals should be reactivated as the best means to provide the necessary scrutiny, not just of maternity-related deaths, but of all deaths*" (9).

Seemingly spurred on by this, the Department of Health published a Consultation which outlined the intended benefits of a new ME system to the public, health service and local authorities (*see* Table 11.3) (7).

Following that consultation, another inquiry into the Gosport War Memorial Hospital found 450 patients had their lives shortened while in the hospital, despite concerns being raised by families about care and by nurses about prescribing practices of opiate medicine (10).

In June 2018, Jeremy Hunt (then Secretary of State for Health) announced the rollout of MEs (11).

Thus, from April 2019, a national system of MEs was introduced to acute National Health Service (NHS) trusts (and some specialist trusts) in England, and by NHS Wales Shared Services Partnership (NWSSP) in Wales.

It will be noted that the new ME system was being established in 2019/2020 and, barely nine months into this development, health services were suddenly facing unprecedented pressures caused by the coronavirus pandemic. In response to the pandemic, the Coronavirus Act 2020 provided easements to facilitate the certification of deaths and reduce the administrative burden on overstretched doctors (6). Guidance was issued by NHS England and NHS Improvement about the Coronavirus Act easements, which simplified and streamlined many death certification functions and enabled ME offices to continue to develop and, if anything, the coronavirus pandemic made the need for the development of the ME system even more relevant (12).

That development continues and, at present, the ME system is non-statutory, although it is expected that the ME system will be statutory by 2024.

TABLE 11.2 Recommendations relevant to the Medical Examiner role from the 2013 Report of the Mid-Staffordshire NHS Foundation Trust Public Inquiry

Number	Recommendation
275	It is of considerable importance that independent medical examiners are independent of the organization whose patients' deaths are being scrutinized.
276	Sufficient numbers of independent medical examiners need to be appointed and resourced to ensure that they can give proper attention to the workload.
277	National guidance should set out standard methodologies for approaching the certification of the cause of death to ensure, so far as possible, that similar approaches are universal
278	It should be a routine part of an independent medical examiners' role to seek out and consider any serious untoward incidents or adverse incident reports relating to the deceased, to ensure that all circumstances are taken into account whether or not referred to in the medical records.
279	So far as is practicable, the responsibility for certifying the cause of death should be undertaken and fulfilled by the consultant, or another senior and fully qualified clinician in charge of a patient's case or treatment.
280	Appropriate and sensitive contact with bereaved families. Both the bereaved family and the certifying doctor should be asked whether they have any concerns about the death or the circumstances surrounding it, and guidance should be given to hospital staff encouraging them to raise any concerns they may have with the independent medical examiner.
281	It is important that independent medical examiners and any others having to approach families for this purpose have careful training in how to undertake this sensitive task in a manner least likely to cause additional and unnecessary distress.

TABLE 11.3 Perceived benefits of the introduction of the Medical Examiner System to England and Wales*

- It will be fair – all deaths will be scrutinized in a robust, and proportionate way regardless of whether they are followed by burial or cremation;
- It will be independent – a medical examiner will scrutinize all medical certificates of cause of death (MCCDs) prepared by the attending doctor;
- It will be transparent – families will have the cause of death explained to them, including clarification of medical terms, and be able to ask questions or raise concerns;
- It will be robust – there will be a protocol that recognizes different levels of risk depending on the circumstances and stated cause of death;
- It will be accurate – the medical examiner will be an experienced doctor, capable of ensuring that the MCCD is completed fully and accurately, providing the NHS, the Office for National Statistics, local authorities and wide range of other users with better quality cause of death statistics to inform health policy, the planning and evaluation of health services and international comparisons;
- It will be efficient – it will help to make sure that the right cases are reported to coroners; and
- It will improve safety – the new system will allow easier identification of trends, unusual patterns and local clinical governance issues and make malpractice easier to detect.

* Adapted from (15).

FUNCTION AND STRUCTURE OF MEDICAL EXAMINER SERVICES

The ME system is intended to:

- provide bereaved families with greater transparency and opportunities to raise concerns
- improve the quality/accuracy of MCCDs
- ensure referrals to HM Coroner are appropriate
- support local learning/improvement by identifying matters in need of clinical governance and related processes
- provide the public with greater safeguards through improved and consistent scrutiny of all non-coronial deaths, and support healthcare providers to improve care through better learning
- align with related systems such as the NHS National Learning from Deaths Framework and Universal Mortality Reviews

MEs are supported by Medical Examiner Officers (MEOs), and scrutinize (review) all deaths that do not fall under HM Coroner's jurisdiction across a local area. MEs are trained, independent, senior doctors. The UK Royal College of Pathologists is the lead medical Royal

College for MEs and is currently responsible for training MEs and MEOs. MEs and MEOs are employed in the NHS but have an additional, separate professional line of accountability to regional and national ME teams. Independence from treating clinical teams is overseen by the National Medical Examiner (NME), supported by seven regional teams of Regional Medical Examiners and Regional Medical Examiner Officers (13).

The role of the NME is to provide professional and strategic leadership to the Regional Medical Examiner teams (in England) and Lead Medical Examiner for Wales. For practical reasons, Medical Examiner Services (MESs) have been located in acute NHS hospitals. Most trusts have a Lead ME and a number of other MEs who may come from a range of different medical specialties. The ME system commenced by reviewing all in-hospital deaths and is expected to be rolled out to all deaths (including those in the community) by 2024. The ME system will thus provide oversight to ~400 000 deaths per annum.

Current guidance suggests that, in order to provide adequate cover to scrutinize 100 percent of deaths, one whole-time equivalent ME and three whole-time MEOs will be required for every 3000 deaths (13).

MEs are trained in the legal and clinical elements of death certification processes. In all cases not investigated by HM Coroner, the ME addresses the following issues (14):

- What did the person die from? (ensuring accuracy of cause of death on the MCCD)
- Does this case need to be reported to a coroner? (ensuring timely, accurate referral)
- Are there any clinical governance concerns? (ensuring the relevant authority is notified)

In order to achieve this, MEs complete the following steps to arrive at their decision:

- speak to the doctor who was treating the patient on their final illness (the qualified attending practitioner – QAP) to discuss the proposed MCCD and enquire about any concerns of care
- review the medical records and any supporting diagnostic information
- agree the proposed cause of death and the overall accuracy of the MCCD with the QAP (and may offer suggestions as to how the MCCD can be improved)
- discuss the cause of death with the next of kin/informant and establish if they have any concerns with care

The MEs and MEOs also work closely with other services involved in the management of the deceased and bereaved by:

- acting as a medical advice resource for HM Coroner
- acting as a medical advice resource for registration services
- acting as a medical advice resource for organ donation teams
- initiating escalations for deaths where learning might be gained utilizing clinical and mortality governance systems
- ensuring that patterns or concerns about care by clinicians and others are raised appropriately
- feeding back praise or compliments to individuals and teams.

MEOs provide the bedrock of the MEService. They provide the continuity between (mostly part-time) MEs and all other parties involved in the care of the deceased and bereaved. Their relationship to MEs can be equated to that of coroners' officers and coroners. They perform many of the functions of the ME, via delegated authority. MEOs manage the ME Service under the guidance of the MEs (15).

MEOs cannot perform the final scrutiny of the medical records of deceased patients but may undertake a preliminary screening of those records, support and assist MEs, and make contact with QAPs and bereaved families. MEOs come from a wide range of backgrounds, including nursing, bereavement and mortuary. The broader the range of backgrounds of all the ME Service team, the better the ME Service can meet the needs of other stakeholders. Those appointed to MEO roles should include those who:

- have previously had experience in a patient- or customer-facing role and of working in either current death certification systems, or a clinical or NHS setting
- have an understanding of medical records and disease pathology
- are able to provide advice on terminology and causes of death, and to explain these and the ME's thoughts and rationale to coroner's officers, doctors and those with no medical or healthcare background
- have strong interpersonal skills and be comfortable working with people following a bereavement
- are able to build and maintain effective relationships with other stakeholders such as faith groups, funeral directors and legal services

MEOs undergo core training and face-to-face training in the same way as MEs. This training is delivered by the Royal College of Pathologists (16).

HOW DOES A MEDICAL EXAMINER SERVICE WORK?

As the ME system has been developing across England & Wales, each ME Service will adapt to different local processes and protocols to best service the needs of their population.

As the ME Service is undertaking contact with clinicians and others, such as families, it is essential that there is documentary evidence of any contact, to enable review of decision-making and assist in further investigations. Two main documents are common to ME offices, the ME-1A and ME-1B forms which may be locally adapted and, in most cases, are now in electronic form. Form ME-1A (not always used) predominantly contains basic administrative data. This form may not always be used in hospitals but may be more useful for remote working, and for assisting with community deaths. Form ME-1B (see Figure 11.1) provides information about the scrutiny undertaken by the ME Service including the date and time of the deceased's death, the ME review of notes, the sources of information used, any discussions with the QAP, HM Coroner and the family, and any record of escalation. It also records the outcomes of these discussions, including any modification to the MCCD. It is an important record that summarizes the entire scrutiny process and may be discoverable in any litigation.

When an ME Service is made aware of a death, the MEO (under delegated authority) may undertake a pre-review of the deceased's medical records and contact the QAP to determine what is proposed for the

ME Advice and Scrutiny Form ME-1 (Part B)

All parts of the ME-1 are confidential and are only available for authorised use by, or on behalf of, the Medical Examiner Service & HM Coroner Service.

Name: Given name Family Name	Date & Time of death: Date Time

Information Scrutinised: ☐ MCCD ☐ Medical records ☐ Summary Medical Record ☐ Other (noted below)

Documented cause of death available before scrutiny? ☐ Yes - on ME-1A ☐ Yes - on MCCD ☐ Yes - Cremation 4 ☐ No

Notes made by medical examiner during scrutiny:

Burial ☐ Yes Cremation ☐ Yes

Under 18 ☐ Yes

Community Death ☐ Yes

Escallation or Referral of Cases

Case to be referred to HM Coroner ☐ Yes ☐ No ☐ Already referred
Reason for referral:

Potential learning Identified ☐ Yes ☐ No
Refer to ☐ Local Governance ☐ DATIX ☐ Other please specify
Reason for review:

Structured Judgement Review case ☐ **Yes** ☐ **No**
Criteria:
☐ Deaths where the bereaved or staff raise significant concerns about the care
☐ Deaths of those with learning disabilities or severe mental illness
☐ Deaths in a specialty, diagnosis or treatment group where an alarm has been raised (for example, an elevated mortality rate, concerns from audit, CQC concerns)
☐ Deaths where the patient was not expected to die - for example, in elective procedures
☐ Deaths where learning will inform the providers quality improvement work
☐ Homeless
☐ Maternal or neonatal deaths

Death: ☐ Unexpected ☐ Sudden but not unexpected ☐ Expected ☐ After care on recognised end-of-life pathway

☐ Proposed / certified causes of death documented on Farm ME-1A before scrutiny accepted without change
☐ Cause(s) of death established during Medical Examiner scrutiny (and documented below)

1a) ....

1b) ....

1c) ....

2) ....

11.1 The ME-1B Form: The basic form, often adapted locally to include more detailed information.

ME-1A Completed ☐ ME-1A Partially Completed (give reason below) ☐ ME-1A Not Completed (give reason below) ☐

Reason:

ME-1A Doctor discussed with:

☐ Medical examiner

☐ MEO

Name:

Date: ____________

Time: ____________

Summary of discussion with ME-1A completing doctor after scrutiny *(if required)*::

☐ Proposed / certified causes of death documented before scrutiny (or noted above) accepted without change

☐ Causes established by the medical examiner during scrutiny (given in section B5) accepted by ME-1A doctor

☐ ME-1A doctor and medical examiner have agreed alternative causes of death as documented below

1a) ____________

1b) ____________

1c) ____________

2) ____________

Outcome of scrutiny

☐ No concerns identified by MES, healthcare professional or bereaved - MCCD not changed from ME-1A

☐ Coroner has agreed to open an investigation and a MCCD is not required HM Coroner Reference Number: CR ____________

☐ Attending doctor has certified (or will certify) the death using causes agreed / revised during scrutiny

Discussion with HM Coroner / HM Coroner's office (if required during or after scrutiny):

☐ Coroner does not need to investigate the death and has issued an HMC-1

Cause of death discussed with Family Member/Next of Kin/Other: *(name & contact details)* ____________ *(status)*

Cause of death discussed by Medical Examiner/Medical Examiner Officer /Other: *(date)* ____________ **at** *(time)* ____________

Please record time(s) and date(s) of any failed contact with NaK: ____________

Condolences offered: ☐

Concerns about care: ____________

____

MCCD Content discussed: ____________

Other matters arising (separate sheet if required): ____________

____

Outcome (eg referral to SJR, LG, HM Coroner), praise to individual or team) ____________

I confirm the Medical Examiner Services has carried out an independent and proportionate scrutiny of this death as required. It required the following time for each element *(minutes)* - 1 Review of notes: ______ 2 Discussion with MCCD doctor: ______ 3 Contacting and discussion with Next of Kin: ______ 4 Completion of Cremation Form 5 & Viewing of Deceased: ______

Name of Medical Examiner *(Print)* ____________ Signature: Date: ____________

11.1 (Continued) The ME-1B Form: The basic form, often adapted locally to include more detailed information.

MCCD and identify any concerns. These will then be discussed with the ME, who may make their own further enquiries having fully scrutinized the deceased's last medical admission. Sometimes (e.g. if there is lack of clarity about previous employment and the patient has died with a possible employment-related condition such as pulmonary fibrosis) further review will be required. Scrutiny should always be proportionate. It is not expected to be a detailed forensic analysis and it must be emphasized that MEs flag issues; their role is not to investigate.

Once the MCCD wording is agreed with the QAP (suggestions on the wording or formulation of the MCCD are only advisory, but rarely ignored), then the bereaved family can be contacted for their comments. The ME Service offers condolences; asks whether there were any concerns about their relative's care; and explains the wording on the MCCD.

The wording on the MCCD is also subject to review by the local registration team (part of the General Register Office). When an informant (normally a relative) registers a death, the registrar will review the MCCD. The Royal College of Pathologists publishes the Cause of Death List (17), a document that is intended not to reflect every possible cause of death but to address those conditions that often result in discussion between the MCCD-writing doctor, registrar and HM Coroner. The Notification of Deaths Regulations 2019 (18), the Cause of Death List and a further publication, *Guidance for Doctors Completing Medical Certificates of Cause of Death in England and Wales* (19) are documents with which MEs and MEOs must be familiar to undertake their functions, and to appropriately advise others. These are sometimes modified (the latter were modified for the emergency period of the coronavirus pandemic) and so the ME Service needs to monitor any changes in guidance closely.

If concerns about care are raised, either by the bereaved or the QAP, it is for the ME Service to identify and escalate or, on some occasions, direct the family to a body, person or organization most appropriate for their concerns. All of this should be documented in detail on the ME-1B. Under delegated authority, the MEOs can carry out many of the functions of the ME with the exception of the full review of the medical records and signing off the whole process (scrutiny) as complete.

WORKLOADS

As an example of workload, the Norfolk and Norwich University Hospital (NNUH) is a 1200-bed teaching hospital providing care for a population of one million people in the East of England. There are approximately 2800 deaths per annum. The NNUH established its ME Service in May 2019, initially staffed by MEs, until MEOs were recruited in June 2020.

Data show that around 97 percent of deaths were scrutinized in that time period. Figure 11.2 shows the workload and outcome of the NNUH ME Service from June 2020 to June 2021 (20). This period covered a time when the coronavirus pandemic had commenced. These data are used to provide an example of the nature and extent of the possible workload at a large acute hospital. The NNUH ME Service during this time had two full-time equivalent MEOs and eight part-time MEs (a total of one full equivalent), of whom one was Lead ME. The MEOs were from nursing and bereavement backgrounds, while the MEs were from a range of specialties, including general practice, vascular surgery, palliative care and forensic and legal medicine. The rollout to include local community deaths will create a caseload of 6000 deaths per annum.

GOOD PRACTICE FOR MEDICAL EXAMINER SERVICES

The NME has been developing a Good Practice series focusing on specific aspects of the ME role. These embrace a wide range of relevant topics and are summarized in Table 11.4. Examples of the first two Good Practice publications include the first in the series, "*How Medical Examiners can support people of Black, Asian and minority ethnic heritage and their relatives*,"

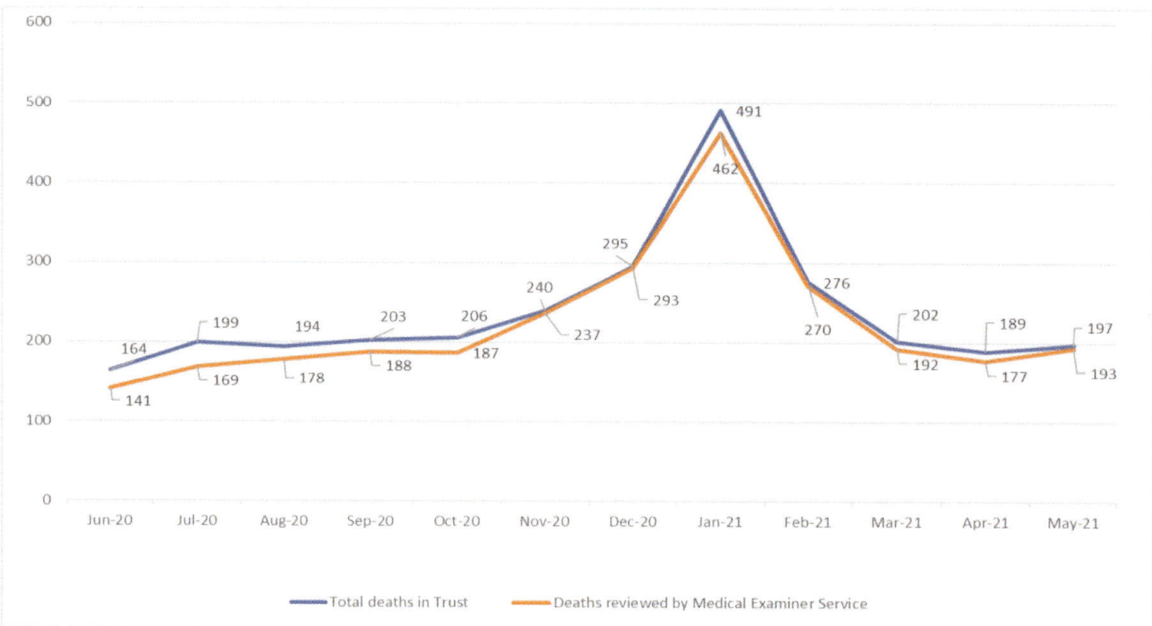

11.2 The number of deaths for each month (June 2020–May 2021) compared with the number of patients scrutinized by the NNUH ME Service (20).

TABLE 11.4 The England & Wales Medical Examiner Good Practice series topics

Guide Number	Title
1	Good Practice Series: Supporting people of Black, Asian and minority ethnic heritage
2	Good Practice Series: Urgent release of a body
3	Learning disability and autism
4	Organ and tissue donation
5	Post-mortem examinations
6	Child deaths
7	Mental health and eating disorders
8	Out-of-hours arrangements

Taken from https://www.rcpath.org/profession/medical-examiners/good-practice-series.html.

which provides recommendations that include: "*Medical Examiners should actively monitor trends and patterns for further action/health planning response, including whether outcomes for patients and relatives of those from Black, Asian and minority ethnic communities differ from those of other communities*"; and that "*Medical Examiners should be sensitive to the cultural and religious expectations and needs of all those who have suffered loss…*" (21).

Good Practice Series Number 2 provides guidance on "*How Medical Examiners can facilitate urgent release of a body*." This advises on identifying which communities may have particular needs or wishes regarding timely release of a body and recommends working closely with other departments such as bereavement or the mortuary to undertake this. This may be used and adapted for those where death is anticipated and may be assisted by discussing the proposed cause of death in advance (22).

These guidance documents address questions and matters of concern that arise on a frequent basis within the ME setting but are of use to anyone working in the management or care of the deceased and bereaved. On a global level guidance for completion of MCCDs has been published by the World Health Organization and identifies broad principles applicable worldwide (23).

CONCLUSION

It is likely that, by 2024, all non-coronial deaths in England and Wales (~400 000 per annum) will be subject to ME scrutiny. The ME system represents a new process in the medicolegal investigation of death in England and Wales. It has three main aims – to provide bereaved families with greater transparency and opportunities to raise concerns; to improve the quality/accuracy of medical certification of cause of death; and to ensure referrals to coroners are appropriate. Currently, these aims appear to be being achieved. The national rollout of a new system in April 2019 could have been thwarted by the coronavirus pandemic, but instead appears to have been given added impetus. Training and recruitment of MEs and MEOs, and the establishment of local ME services working closely with bereavement, mortuary, coronial and registration services has been achieved in 3 years. Although the ME system is in the adolescent stage of its development, it is on course to achieve the aim of scrutinizing all non-coronial deaths by independent MEs, supported by trained MEOs, by 2024. It is hoped that this will improve patient safety, reduce the risk of further healthcare scandals, and improve the quality of MCCDs while providing a voice for the bereaved and for whistleblowers.

REFERENCES

1. Payne-James JJ, Lishman S. *The Medical Examiner Service. A Practical Guide for England & Wales*. Abingdon: CRC Press; 2022.
2. Office for National Statistics. Deaths registered in England and Wales 2021, 2022. Available from: https://www.ons.gov.uk/peoplepopulationandcommunity/birthsdeathsandmarriages/deaths/bulletins/deathsregistrationsummarytables/2021 (Accessed 23 March 2023).
3. Ministry of Justice. Coroners' statistics 2021: England and Wales, 2022. Available from: https://www.gov.uk/government/statistics/coroners-statistics-2021/coroners-statistics-2021-england-and-wales (Accessed 22 March 2023).
4. House of Commons Constitutional Affairs Committee. Reform of the coroners' system and death certification: Eighth report of session 2005–2006. Available from: https://publications.parliament.uk/pa/cm200506/cmselect/cmconst/902/902i.pdf (Accessed 20 March 2023).
5. Home Office/Department of Health. The Shipman Enquiry. Third report. Death certification and investigation of deaths by coroners, 2003. Available from: https://assets.publishing.service.gov.uk/government/uploads/system/uploads/attachment_data/file/273227/5854.pdf (Accessed 20 March 2023).
6. Coroners and Justice Act, 2009. Available from: https://www.legislation.gov.uk/ukpga/2009/25/data.pdf (Accessed 10 March 2023).
7. DoH. Introduction of medical examiners and reforms to death certification in England and Wales: Policy and draft regulations, 2016. Available from: https://assets.publishing.service.gov.uk/government/uploads/system/uploads/attachment_data/file/517184/DCR_Consultion_Document.pdf (Accessed 17 March 2023).
8. Francis R. Report of the Mid Staffordshire NHS Foundation Trust public inquiry, 2013. Available from: https://www.gov.uk/government/publications/report-of-the-mid-staffordshire-nhs-foundation-trust-public-inquiry (Accessed 28 March 2023).
9. Kirkup B. The report of the Morecambe Bay Investigation, 2015. Available from: https://assets.publishing.service.gov.uk/government/uploads/system/uploads/attachment_data/

file/408480/47487_MBI_Accessible_v0.1.pdf (Accessed 17 March 2023).

10. Gosport War Memorial Hospital. The report of the gosport independent panel, 2018. Available from: https://www.gosportpanel.independent.gov.uk/panel-report (Accessed 28 March 2023).
11. Laville S. NHS patient deaths to be investigated by medical examiners, 2018. Available from: https://www.theguardian.com/society/2018/jun/11/nhs-patient-deaths-investigated-medical-examiners-jeremy-hunt (Accessed 28 March 2023).
12. NHS England and NHS Improvement. Coronavirus Act – Excess death provisions: Information and guidance for medical practitioners, 2020. Available from: https://www.england.nhs.uk/coronavirus/wp-content/uploads/sites/52/2020/03/COVID-19-Act-excess-death-provisions-info-and-guidance-31-03-20.pdf (Accessed 28 March 2023).
13. Payne-James JJ, Lishman S. The Medical Examiner Service in England & Wales: Structure. In: Payne-James JJ, Lishman S (eds), *The Medical Examiner Service. A Practical Guide for England & Wales*. Abingdon: CRC Press; 2022.
14. Shelley-Fraser G. The Role of the Medical Examiner. In: Payne-James JJ, Lishman S (eds), *The Medical Examiner Service. A Practical Guide for England & Wales*. Abingdon: CRC Press; 2022.
15. Shale D, Parapanos L. The Role of the Medical Examiner Officer. In: Payne-James JJ, Lishman S (eds), *The Medical Examiner Service. A Practical Guide for England & Wales*. Abingdon: CRC Press; 2022.
16. Royal College of Pathologists. Medical examiner officers. Available from: https://www.rcpath.org/profession/medical-examiners/medical-examiner-officers.html (Accessed 25 March 2023).
17. Royal College of Pathologists. Cause of death list, 2020. Available from: https://www.rcpath.org/uploads/assets/c16ae453-6c63-47ff-8c45fd2c56521ab9/G199-Cause-of-death-list.pdf (Accessed 25 March 2023).
18. Ministry of Justice. Notification of deaths regulations 2019 guidance, 2019. Available from: https://www.gov.uk/government/publications/notification-of-deaths-regulations-2019-guidance (Accessed 25 March 2023).
19. Office of National Statistics. Guidance for doctors completing medical certificates of cause of death in England and Wales, 2020. Available from: https://assets.publishing.service.gov.uk/government/uploads/system/uploads/attachment_data/file/877302/guidance-for-doctors-completing-medical-certificates-of-cause-of-death-covid-19.pdf (Accessed 25 March 2023).
20. Payne-James JJ, Parapanos L, Carpenter K, Lopez B. The workload of a Medical Examiner Service at an acute National Health Service hospital during the COVID-19 pandemic: The Norfolk & Norwich University Hospital Experience. *Med Sci Law* 2023; 63(1): 6–13.
21. National Medical Examiner. National Medical Examiner's Good Practice Series No. 1. How medical examiners can support people of Black, Asian and minority ethnic heritage and their relatives, 2021. Available from: https://www.rcpath.org/uploads/assets/72675084-5ed3-43a1-b518c61395dd1194/Good-Practice-Series-BAME-paper.pdf (Accessed 20 March 2023).
22 National Medical Examiner. National Medical Examiner's Good Practice Series No. 2. How medical examiners can facilitate urgent release of a body, 2021. Available from: https://www.rcpath.org/uploads/assets/3590bf7f-a43e-4248-980640c5c12354c4/Good-Practice-Series-Urgent-release-of-a-bodyFor-Publication.pdf (Accessed 25 March 2023).
23. World Health Organization. WHO Recommendations for conducting an external inspection of a body and filling in the Medical Certificate of Cause of Death. 2023 Available from: https://cdn.who.int/media/docs/default-source/classification/icd/cause-of-death/who-recommendations-for-conducting-an-external-inspection-of-a-body-and-filling-in-the-medical-certificate-of-cause-of-death-_vf_published.pdf?sfvrsn=edaa1998_13&download=true (Accessed 22 September 2023).

CHAPTER

12

Principles of Investigation of War Crimes and Torture & Cruel, Inhuman and Degrading Treatment & Other Matters

Jason Payne-James

INTRODUCTION

War crimes are those acts committed during armed conflict which violate the international humanitarian laws and instruments intended to protect civilians. After the Second World War, the war crime trials established the Nuremberg principles of law, including that international criminal law defines what is a war crime (*see* Table 12.1). In 1949, the Geneva Conventions legally defined new war crimes and established that States could exercise universal jurisdiction over war criminals (1). These laws are codified in a range of treaties such as the Hague Conventions of 1899 (2) and 1907 (3) and the 1949 Geneva Convention (4). The Rome Statute drafted on 17 July 1998, which came into force on 1 July 2002, established the International Criminal Court (ICC) as the primary body that holds individuals accountable for war crimes (5). The Rome Statute identifies those actions and crimes that lie within the jurisdiction of the ICC which includes war crimes, genocide, crimes against humanity and crimes of aggression, each of which may require evidence provided by forensic medical practitioners.

The right to freedom from torture and cruel and inhuman and degrading treatment is also an essential part of humanitarian laws and instruments and is intended to protect individuals from being intentionally subjected to severe physical or psychological distress by, or with the approval or acquiescence of, government agents acting for a specific purpose, including to inflict punishment or to obtain information. Under international humanitarian law, which applies in the context of armed conflict, the consent, action or acquiescence of a State agent is not necessary for the abuse to constitute torture. Cruel, inhuman, or degrading treatment or punishment is generally prohibited in the same international instruments but involves a lower level of suffering and need not be inflicted for a specific purpose.

In the forensic and legal medicine setting, forensic practitioners (whether for the deceased or living) may be the primary source of evidence used by the relevant bodies to make a determination as to whether or not the specific crimes or actions or maltreatment have taken place. The forensic practitioner may encounter such cases in the course of their routine work and need to escalate to investigating bodies or be referred specific casework by investigating bodies to capture evidence of breaches of law. The definitions of these crimes are discussed and the nature of investigation required, along with examples of such prosecutions. It has been suggested recently that forensic pathologists, and forensic experts in general, are the only professional figures specialized in providing scientific evidence of crimes compatible with war crimes (6).

DEFINITIONS

Part 2 of the Rome Statute in Articles 5–8 outlines the jurisdiction of the court and further defines the specific elements which constitute the particular crimes (5). Table 12.2 shows these Articles in detail and identifies those elements which may be of particular relevance to forensic medical practitioners.

As an example of a national approach to prosecution in England and Wales, the Metropolitan Police Services states "*War crimes are crimes that come under the collective name of 'core international crimes'. Core international crimes are some of the gravest crimes in international law, examples of them can include; the crime of genocide, crimes against humanity, war crimes and torture.*" It further states through international treaties that the UK has a responsibility to investigate and prosecute those who have committed core international crimes. If a UK resident has been responsible for core international crimes anywhere in the world, they may be investigated and prosecuted in England and Wales (7). Table 12.3 gives examples of how the Metropolitan Police Service defines the core international crimes which can fall under the four different categories.

DOI: 10.1201/9781003138754-13

TABLE 12.1 Principles of International Law recognized in the Charter of the Nuremberg Tribunal and in the Judgment of the Tribunal

Principle I

- Any person who commits an act which constitutes a crime under international law is responsible therefore and liable to punishment.

Principle II

- The fact that internal law does not impose a penalty for an act which constitutes a crime under international law does not relieve the person who committed the act from responsibility under international law.

Principle III

- The fact that a person who committed an act which constitutes a crime under international law acted as Head of State or responsible Government official does not relieve him from responsibility under international law.

Principle IV

- The fact that a person acted pursuant to order of his Government or of a superior does not relieve him from responsibility under international law, provided a moral choice was in fact possible to him.

Principle V

- Any person charged with a crime under international law has the right to a fair trial on the facts and law.

Principle VI

- The crimes hereinafter set out are punishable as crimes under international law:

  (a) Crimes against peace:

    (i) Planning, preparation, initiation or waging of a war of aggression or a war in violation of international treaties, agreements or assurances;

    (ii) Participation in a common plan or conspiracy for the accomplishment of any of the acts mentioned under (i).

  (b) War crimes:

  Violations of the laws or customs of war which include, but are not limited to, murder, ill-treatment or deportation to slave-labor or for any other purpose of civilian population of or in occupied territory, murder or ill-treatment of prisoners of war, of persons on the seas, killing of hostages, plunder of public or private property, wanton destruction of cities, towns, or villages, or devastation not justified by military necessity.

  (c) Crimes against humanity:

  Murder, extermination, enslavement, deportation and other inhuman acts done against any civilian population, or persecutions on political, racial or religious grounds, when such acts are done, or such persecutions are carried on in execution of or in connection with any crime against peace or any war crime.

Principle VII

- Complicity in the commission of a crime against peace, a war crime, or a crime against humanity as set forth in Principle VI is a crime under international law.

TABLE 12.2 The Rome Statute Articles defining crimes falling under the jurisdiction of the ICC. Those most relevant to forensic practitioners are italicized

Article 6 Genocide

For the purpose of this Statute, "genocide" means any of the following acts committed with intent to destroy, in whole or in part, a national, ethnical, racial or religious group, as such:

(a) *Killing members of the group;*

(b) *Causing serious bodily or mental harm to members of the group;*

(c) Deliberately inflicting on the group conditions of life calculated to bring about its physical destruction in whole or in part;

(d) *Imposing measures intended to prevent births within the group;*

(e) Forcibly transferring children of the group to another group.

TABLE 12.2 (Continued) The Rome Statue Articles defining crimes falling under the jurisdiction of the ICC. Those most relevant to forensic practioners are italicized.

Article 7
Crimes against humanity
1. For the purpose of this Statute, "crime against humanity" means any of the following acts when committed as part of a widespread or systematic attack directed against any civilian population, with knowledge of the attack:
(a) *Murder;*
(b) *Extermination;*
(c) *Enslavement;*
(d) *Deportation or forcible transfer of population;*
(e) *Imprisonment or other severe deprivation of physical liberty in violation of fundamental rules of international law;*
(f) *Torture;*
(g) *Rape, sexual slavery, enforced prostitution, forced pregnancy, enforced sterilization, or any other form of sexual violence of comparable gravity;*
(h) Persecution against any identifiable group or collectivity on political, racial, national, ethnic, cultural, religious, gender as defined in paragraph 3, or other grounds that are universally recognized as impermissible under international law, in connection with any act referred to in this paragraph or any crime within the jurisdiction of the Court;
(i) Enforced disappearance of persons;
(j) The crime of apartheid;
(k) *Other inhumane acts of a similar character intentionally causing great suffering, or serious injury to body or to mental or physical health.*
2. For the purpose of paragraph 1:
(a) "Attack directed against any civilian population" means a course of conduct involving the multiple commission of acts referred to in paragraph 1 against any civilian population, pursuant to or in furtherance of a State or organizational policy to commit such attack;
(b) *"Extermination" includes the intentional infliction of conditions of life, inter alia the deprivation of access to food and medicine, calculated to bring about the destruction of part of a population;*
(c) "Enslavement" means the exercise of any or all of the powers attaching to the right of ownership over a person and includes the exercise of such power in the course of trafficking in persons, in particular women and children;
(d) "Deportation or forcible transfer of population" means forced displacement of the persons concerned by expulsion or other coercive acts from the area in which they are lawfully present, without grounds permitted under international law;
(e) *"Torture" means the intentional infliction of severe pain or suffering, whether physical or mental, upon a person in the custody or under the control of the accused; except that torture shall not include pain or suffering arising only from, inherent in or incidental to, lawful sanctions;*
(f) *"Forced pregnancy" means the unlawful confinement of a woman forcibly made pregnant, with the intent of affecting the ethnic composition of any population or carrying out other grave violations of international law. This definition shall not in any way be interpreted as affecting national laws relating to pregnancy;*
(g) "Persecution" means the intentional and severe deprivation of fundamental rights contrary to international law by reason of the identity of the group or collectivity;
(h) "The crime of apartheid" means inhumane acts of a character similar to those referred to in paragraph 1, committed in the context of an institutionalized regime of systematic oppression and domination by one racial group over any other racial group or groups and committed with the intention of maintaining that regime;
(i) "Enforced disappearance of persons" means the arrest, detention or abduction of persons by, or with the authorization, support or acquiescence of, a State or a political organization, followed by a refusal to acknowledge that deprivation of freedom or to give information on the fate or whereabouts of those persons, with the intention of removing them from the protection of the law for a prolonged period of time.
3. For the purpose of this Statute, it is understood that the term "gender" refers to the two sexes, male and female, within the context of society. The term "gender" does not indicate any meaning different from the above.
Article 8
War crimes
1. The Court shall have jurisdiction in respect of war crimes in particular when committed as part of a plan or policy or as part of a large-scale commission of such crimes.

TABLE 12.2 (Continued) The Rome Statue Articles defining crimes falling under the jurisdiction of the ICC. Those most relevant to forensic practioners are italicized.

2. For the purpose of this Statute, "war crimes" means:		
(a) Grave breaches of the Geneva Conventions of 12 August 1949, namely, any of the following acts against persons or property protected under the provisions of the relevant Geneva Convention:		
	(i)	*Wilful killing;*
	(ii)	*Torture or inhuman treatment, including biological experiments;*
	(iii)	*Wilfully causing great suffering, or serious injury to body or health;*
	(iv)	Extensive destruction and appropriation of property, not justified by military necessity and carried out unlawfully and wantonly;
	(v)	Compelling a prisoner of war or other protected person to serve in the forces of a hostile Power;
	(vi)	Wilfully depriving a prisoner of war or other protected person of the rights of fair and regular trial;
	(vii)	*Unlawful deportation or transfer or unlawful confinement;*
	(viii)	Taking of hostages.
(b) Other serious violations of the laws and customs applicable in international armed conflict, within the established framework of international law, namely, any of the following acts:		
	(i)	*Intentionally directing attacks against the civilian population as such or against individual civilians not taking direct part in hostilities;*
	(ii)	Intentionally directing attacks against civilian objects, that is, objects which are not military objectives;
	(iii)	*Intentionally directing attacks against personnel, installations, material, units or vehicles involved in a humanitarian assistance or peacekeeping mission in accordance with the Charter of the United Nations, as long as they are entitled to the protection given to civilians or civilian objects under the international law of armed conflict;*
	(iv)	*Intentionally launching an attack in the knowledge that such attack will cause incidental loss of life or injury to civilians or damage to civilian objects or widespread, long-term and severe damage to the natural environment which would be clearly excessive in relation to the concrete and direct overall military advantage anticipated;*
	(v)	Attacking or bombarding, by whatever means, towns, villages, dwellings or buildings which are undefended and which are not military objectives;
	(vi)	*Killing or wounding a combatant who, having laid down his arms or having no longer means of defence, has surrendered at discretion;*
	(vii)	Making improper use of a flag of truce, of the flag or of the military insignia and uniform of the enemy or of the United Nations, as well as of the distinctive emblems of the Geneva Conventions, resulting in death or serious personal injury;
	(viii)	The transfer, directly or indirectly, by the Occupying Power of parts of its own civilian population into the territory it occupies, or the deportation or transfer of all or parts of the population of the occupied territory within or outside this territory;
	(ix)	Intentionally directing attacks against buildings dedicated to religion, education, art, science or charitable purposes, historic monuments, hospitals and places where the sick and wounded are collected, provided they are not military objectives;
	(x)	*Subjecting persons who are in the power of an adverse party to physical mutilation or to medical or scientific experiments of any kind which are neither justified by the medical, dental or hospital treatment of the person concerned nor carried out in his or her interest, and which cause death to or seriously endanger the health of such person or persons;*
	(xi)	*Killing or wounding treacherously individuals belonging to the hostile nation or army;*
	(xii)	Declaring that no quarter will be given;
	(xiii)	Destroying or seizing the enemy's property unless such destruction or seizure be imperatively demanded by the necessities of war;
	(xiv)	Declaring abolished, suspended or inadmissible in a court of law the rights and actions of the nationals of the hostile party;
	(xv)	Compelling the nationals of the hostile party to take part in the operations of war directed against their own country, even if they were in the belligerent's service before the commencement of the war;
	(xvi)	Pillaging a town or place, even when taken by assault;
	(xvii)	*Employing poison or poisoned weapons;*
	(xviii)	*Employing asphyxiating, poisonous or other gases, and all analogous liquids, materials or devices;*

TABLE 12.2 (Continued) The Rome Statue Articles defining crimes falling under the jurisdiction of the ICC. Those most relevant to forensic practioners are italicized.

(xix) *Employing bullets which expand or flatten easily in the human body, such as bullets with a hard envelope which does not entirely cover the core or is pierced with incisions;*

(xx) *Employing weapons, projectiles and material and methods of warfare which are of a nature to cause superfluous injury or unnecessary suffering or which are inherently indiscriminate in violation of the international law of armed conflict, provided that such weapons, projectiles and material and methods of warfare are the subject of a comprehensive prohibition and are included in an annex to this Statute, by an amendment in accordance with the relevant provisions set forth in articles 121 and 123;*

(xxi) *Committing outrages upon personal dignity, in particular humiliating and degrading treatment;*

(xxii) *Committing rape, sexual slavery, enforced prostitution, forced pregnancy, as defined in article 7, paragraph 2 (f), enforced sterilization, or any other form of sexual violence also constituting a grave breach of the Geneva Conventions;*

(xxiii) Utilizing the presence of a civilian or other protected person to render certain points, areas or military forces immune from military operations;

(xxiv) Intentionally directing attacks against buildings, material, medical units and transport, and personnel using the distinctive emblems of the Geneva Conventions in conformity with international law;

(xxv) *Intentionally using starvation of civilians as a method of warfare by depriving them of objects indispensable to their survival, including wilfully impeding relief supplies as provided for under the Geneva Conventions;*

(xxvi) *Conscripting or enlisting children under the age of fifteen years into the national armed forces or using them to participate actively in hostilities.*

(c) In the case of an armed conflict not of an international character, serious violations of article 3 common to the four Geneva Conventions of 12 August 1949, namely, any of the following acts committed against persons taking no active part in the hostilities, including members of armed forces who have laid down their arms and those placed hors de combat by sickness, wounds, detention or any other cause:

(i) *Violence to life and person, in particular murder of all kinds, mutilation, cruel treatment and torture;*

(ii) *Committing outrages upon personal dignity, in particular humiliating and degrading treatment;*

(iii) Taking of hostages;

(iv) The passing of sentences and the carrying out of executions without previous judgement pronounced by a regularly constituted court, affording all judicial guarantees which are generally recognized as indispensable.

(d) Paragraph 2 (c) applies to armed conflicts not of an international character and thus does not apply to situations of internal disturbances and tensions, such as riots, isolated and sporadic acts of violence or other acts of a similar nature.

(e) Other serious violations of the laws and customs applicable in armed conflicts not of an international character, within the established framework of international law, namely, any of the following acts:

(i) *Intentionally directing attacks against the civilian population as such or against individual civilians not taking direct part in hostilities;*

(ii) Intentionally directing attacks against buildings, material, medical units and transport, and personnel using the distinctive emblems of the Geneva Conventions in conformity with international law;

(iii) *Intentionally directing attacks against personnel, installations, material, units or vehicles involved in a humanitarian assistance or peacekeeping mission in accordance with the Charter of the United Nations, as long as they are entitled to the protection given to civilians or civilian objects under the international law of armed conflict;*

(iv) Intentionally directing attacks against buildings dedicated to religion, education, art, science or charitable purposes, historic monuments, hospitals and places where the sick and wounded are collected, provided they are not military objectives;

(v) Pillaging a town or place, even when taken by assault;

(vi) *Committing rape, sexual slavery, enforced prostitution, forced pregnancy, as defined in article 7, paragraph 2 (f), enforced sterilization, and any other form of sexual violence also constituting a serious violation of article 3 common to the four Geneva Conventions;*

(vii) *Conscripting or enlisting children under the age of fifteen years into armed forces or groups or using them to participate actively in hostilities;*

(viii) Ordering the displacement of the civilian population for reasons related to the conflict, unless the security of the civilians involved or imperative military reasons so demand;

(ix) *Killing or wounding treacherously a combatant adversary;*

(x) Declaring that no quarter will be given;

(xi) *Subjecting persons who are in the power of another party to the conflict to physical mutilation or to medical or scientific experiments of any kind which are neither justified by the medical, dental or hospital treatment of the person concerned nor carried out in his or her interest, and which cause death to or seriously endanger the health of such person or persons;*

(xii) Destroying or seizing the property of an adversary unless such destruction or seizure be imperatively demanded by the necessities of the conflict;

TABLE 12.2 (Continued) The Rome Statue Articles defining crimes falling under the jurisdiction of the ICC. Those most relevant to forensic practioners are italicized.

(xiii) *Employing poison or poisoned weapons;*
(xiv) *Employing asphyxiating, poisonous or other gases, and all analogous liquids, materials or devices;*
(xv) *Employing bullets which expand or flatten easily in the human body, such as bullets with a hard envelope which does not entirely cover the core or is pierced with incisions.*
(f) Paragraph 2 (e) applies to armed conflicts not of an international character and thus does not apply to situations of internal disturbances and tensions, such as riots, isolated and sporadic acts of violence or other acts of a similar nature. It applies to armed conflicts that take place in the territory of a State when there is protracted armed conflict between governmental authorities and organized armed groups or between such groups.
3. Nothing in paragraph 2 (c) and (e) shall affect the responsibility of a Government to maintain or re-establish law and order in the State or to defend the unity and territorial integrity of the State, by all legitimate means.
Article 8 (supplementary and inserted by resolution RC/Res.6 of 11 June 2010)
Crime of aggression
1. For the purpose of this Statute, "crime of aggression" means the planning, preparation, initiation or execution, by a person in a position effectively to exercise control over or to direct the political or military action of a State, of an act of aggression which, by its character, gravity and scale, constitutes a manifest violation of the Charter of the United Nations.
2. For the purpose of paragraph 1, "act of aggression" means the use of armed force by a State against the sovereignty, territorial integrity or political independence of another State, or in any other manner inconsistent with the Charter of the United Nations. Any of the following acts, regardless of a declaration of war, shall, in accordance with United Nations General Assembly resolution 3314 (XXIX) of 14 December 1974, qualify as an act of aggression:
(a) The invasion or attack by the armed forces of a State of the territory of another State, or any military occupation, however temporary, resulting from such invasion or attack, or any annexation by the use of force of the territory of another State or part thereof;
(b) Bombardment by the armed forces of a State against the territory of another State or the use of any weapons by a State against the territory of another State;
(c) The blockade of the ports or coasts of a State by the armed forces of another State;
(d) An attack by the armed forces of a State on the land, sea or air forces, or marine
(e) The use of armed forces of one State which are within the territory of another State with the agreement of the receiving State, in contravention of the conditions provided for in the agreement or any extension of their presence in such territory beyond the termination of the agreement;
(f) The action of a State in allowing its territory, which it has placed at the disposal of another State, to be used by that other State for perpetrating an act of aggression against a third State;
(g) The sending by or on behalf of a State of armed bands, groups, irregulars or mercenaries, which carry out acts of armed force against another State of such gravity as to amount to the acts listed above, or its substantial involvement therein.

Those most relevant to forensic practitioners are italicized.

LEGAL ASPECTS OF WAR CRIMES

The International Law Commission (ILC) was created in 1947 and is a body of experts elected by the United Nations General Assembly (UNGA) every five years to help develop and codify international law (8). In 1950, the ILC published the Principles of International Law Recognized in the Charter of the Nürnberg Tribunal and in the Judgment of the Tribunal – generally referred to as the Nuremberg Principles (see Table 12.1) (9). The Commission has continued to work extensively in the field of international criminal law including in 1994 creating a draft Statute for an International Criminal Court (10) at its 46th session and in 1996 (48th session) the draft Code of Crimes against the Peace and Security of Mankind (11).

The ICC investigates and, where warranted, tries individuals charged with the gravest crimes of concern to the international community: genocide, war crimes, crimes against humanity and the crime of aggression. The Assembly of States Parties is the Court's management oversight and legislative body and is composed of representatives of the States which have ratified or acceded to the Rome Statute. One hundred and twenty-three countries are parties to the Rome Statute. Out of them, 33 are African States, 19 are Asia-Pacific States, 18 are from Eastern Europe, 28 are from Latin American and Caribbean States, and 25 are from Western European and other States. The United States of America has not ratified the Rome Statute. China and India are two of the States that oppose the ICC. Pursuant to article 12(3) of the Rome Statute, a State that is not a party to the Statute may "*by declaration lodged with the Registrar, accept the exercise of jurisdiction by the Court with respect to the crime in question.*" Examples of such States include Ukraine and Palestine. There is no statute of limitations. However, investigations can be prolonged, in part because of the challenges of collecting the evidence while a conflict is ongoing especially against senior political or military leaders. War crimes are no different from other crimes and the same processes for investigation will be followed such as through interviewing witnesses, reviewing photos or videos and collecting forensic evidence, including ballistics analysis, autopsies or DNA testing. Prosecutors need to prove, beyond a reasonable doubt, that individuals knowingly committed the crimes. The ICC only obtained jurisdiction over the crime of aggression in 2018 (12). Only 43 of the 123 member states have ratified that additional crime. The ICC investigates and prosecutes international crimes committed by individuals and should be distinguished from the International Court of Justice which resolves disputes between States (13).

TABLE 12.3 Examples of Core International Crimes (as summarized from the Metropolitan Police Service, London, UK)
War Crimes
Violations of the laws or customs of war, including:
• atrocities or offences against persons or property, constituting violations of the laws or customs of war
• murder, ill treatment or deportation to slave labor or for any other purpose of the civilian population in occupied territory
• murder or ill treatment of prisoners of war or persons on the seas
• killing of hostages
• torture or inhuman treatment, including biological experiments
• breaches of the Geneva Conventions
• plunder of public or private property
• wanton destruction of cities, towns or villages
• devastation not justified by military necessity
• destruction of property that is of particular cultural significance
Torture
• It is an offence for a public official or person acting in an official capacity to intentionally inflict severe pain or suffering on another in the performance or purported performance of their official duties, without lawful authority.
Genocide
Genocide is a crime under international law even if it is not a crime in the country where it takes place, and incitement to commit genocide is also a crime.
Genocide means any of the following acts committed with intent to destroy, in whole or in part, a national, ethnic, racial or religious group:
• killing members of the group
• causing serious bodily or mental harm to members of the group
• deliberately inflicting on the group conditions of life calculated to bring about its physical destruction in whole or in part
• imposing measures intended to prevent births within the group
• forcibly transferring children of the group to another group
Crimes against humanity
Atrocities and offences committed against any civilian population, as part of a widespread attack, including:
• murder
• extermination
• enslavement
• deportation
• mass systematic rape and sexual enslavement in a time of war
• other inhumane acts
• persecutions on political, racial or religious grounds in execution of or in connection with any other crime against humanity

INVESTIGATION AND PROSECUTION OF WAR CRIMES AND OTHER MATTERS

The Office of the Prosecutor (OTP) is an independent organ of the ICC and examines situations under the jurisdiction of the ICC where genocide, crimes against humanity, war crimes and aggression appear to have been committed. It investigates and prosecutes those individuals alleged to be responsible for those crimes (14).

Article 12 of the Rome Statute provides three ways that the Court's jurisdiction can be triggered where crimes under the Court's jurisdiction appear to have been committed:

1) Any State Party to the Rome Statute may request the Prosecutor to carry out an investigation.
2) The United Nations Security Council (UNSC) may also refer a situation to the Prosecutor.
3) The Prosecutor may open an investigation on their own initiative after the authorization of the judges. The Prosecutor cannot initiate investigations with respect to States not Party to the Rome Statute unless the matter involves nationals of States Parties allegedly involved in committing Rome Statute crimes on the territory of the non-State Party in question.

Any individual, group or State can send information to the OTP regarding alleged crimes falling under the jurisdiction of the Court. By late 2022, the OTP had received more than 12 000 communications of this nature, which may be the initial basis of the Office's preliminary examinations.

Exceptionally, States may accept the jurisdiction on an ad hoc basis, by submitting a declaration pursuant to article 12(3) of the Rome Statute. Examples of this include Ukraine, which is not a State Party to the Rome Statute but has twice exercised its prerogatives to accept the Court's jurisdiction over alleged crimes under the Rome Statute occurring on its territory, via article 12(3). The first declaration lodged by the Government of Ukraine accepted ICC jurisdiction with respect to alleged crimes committed on Ukrainian territory from 21 November 2013 to 22 February 2014. The second declaration extended this time period on an open-ended basis to encompass ongoing alleged crimes committed throughout the territory of Ukraine from 20 February 2014 onwards. More recently, on 28 February 2022, the ICC Prosecutor announced they would seek authorization to open an investigation into the situation in Ukraine, on the basis of the Office's earlier conclusions arising from its preliminary examination and encompassing any new alleged crimes falling within the jurisdiction of the Court (15). In that statement, the ICC Prosecutor also indicated that active investigations by the OPC would be significantly expedited if a State Party to the Rome Statute (the "Statute") were to refer the situation to my Office, as provided in article 14 of the Statute. On 2 March 2022, the following co-ordinated group of 39 States Parties submitted a joint referral (16): Republic of Albania, Commonwealth of Australia, Republic of Austria, Kingdom of Belgium, Republic of Bulgaria, Canada, Republic of Colombia, Republic of Costa Rica, Republic of Croatia, Republic of Cyprus, Czech Republic, Kingdom of Denmark, Republic of Estonia, Republic of Finland, Republic of France, Georgia, Federal Republic of Germany, Hellenic Republic, Hungary, Republic of Iceland, Ireland, Republic of Italy, Republic of Latvia, Principality of Liechtenstein, Grand Duchy of Luxembourg, Republic of Malta, New Zealand, Kingdom of Norway, Kingdom of the Netherlands, Republic of Poland, Republic of Portugal, Romania, Slovak Republic, Republic of Slovenia, Kingdom of Spain, Kingdom of Sweden, Swiss Confederation, and United Kingdom of Great Britain and Northern Ireland.

The OTP conducts a preliminary examination to decide whether there is a reasonable basis to initiate an investigation but is required to assess and verify a number of legal criteria. These include: whether the crimes were committed after 1 July 2002 (the date the Rome Statute came into force); whether the crimes took place in the territory of a State Party or were committed by a national of a State Party (unless the situation was referred by the UNSC); whether they amount to war crimes, crimes against humanity or genocide; the gravity of these crimes; and if there are no genuine investigations or prosecutions for the same crimes at the national level.

It is important to recognize that national authorities have the primary responsibility to investigate and prosecute those most responsible for the commission of mass crimes. The ICC will investigate only when the national authorities have failed to uphold their primary responsibility and in the absence of national proceedings.

Taking into account the facts and circumstances of each situation, the Prosecutor has the options to: (i) decline to initiate an investigation; (ii) continue to collect information on crimes and relevant national proceedings in order to make a determination; or (iii) initiate the investigation, subject to judicial authorization as appropriate.

Preliminary examinations may make national authorities aware of their duty to fulfil their primary responsibility to carry out investigations and prosecutions themselves. By utilizing the Rome Statute criteria, the OTP determines whether it needs to open an investigation.

To conduct its investigations, generally, the OTP sends missions – made up of investigators, co-operation advisers, and if necessary, prosecutors – to concerned countries, collects and examines different forms of evidence, and questions a range of persons, from those being investigated to victims and witnesses. To undertake these activities, the OTP is heavily reliant on the co-operation of States Parties, international and regional organisations, as well as civil society.

When gathering evidence, the OTP identifies the gravest incidents and those most responsible for these crimes. The OTP has an obligation to gather both incriminating and exonerating evidence. Any exonerating information will be disclosed to the Defence teams as part of the proceedings.

Once the OTP considers that it has sufficient evidence to prove before the judges that an individual is responsible for a crime in the Court's jurisdiction, the Office will request the judges to issue a warrant of arrest or a summons to appear. Based on the evidence it gathers during an investigation, the OTP can submit a request to the ICC judges, asking them to issue arrest warrants or summonses to appear.

Once the judges determine that there are reasonable grounds to believe that a person has committed a crime within the Court's jurisdiction, the judges will only issue an arrest warrant to ensure the person's appearance at trial, to ensure the person does not obstruct or endanger the investigation or Court proceedings, or to prevent the person from continuing to commit the crime in question.

Once the person for whom an arrest warrant or a summons to appear has been issued is in the Court's custody or decides to come voluntarily to the Court, the OTP will first have to convince the judges, at the Pre-Trial phase, that it has sufficient evidence to commit the case to trial. At this stage, the judges will have to decide whether to confirm, decline, or review the charges presented by the OTP against the defendant.

If the judges confirm the charges, the case goes to trial. Once at trial, the OTP is first to present its case, and bears the burden of proof that the accused person is guilty beyond reasonable doubt. The OTP can present evidence in the form of documents, other tangible objects, or witness statements; the OTP's witnesses are also questioned by the Defence, and vice versa.

As part of the proceedings, the OTP discloses both incriminating and exonerating information to the Defence. The OTP is obligated to gather both during its investigations, in order to establish the truth about a given situation.

Once the OTP has presented all its evidence, it is the turn of the accused, with the assistance of his or her counsel, to present his or her Defence.

DECIDED CASES

The ICC publishes information on its current cases including current cases, defendants and preliminary investigations on its website (17).

Examples of successful prosecutions include that of Germain Katanga, alleged commander of the Force de résistance patriotique en Ituri (FRPI). He was found guilty, on 7 March 2014, as an accessory to one count of a crime against humanity (murder) and four counts of war crimes (murder, attacking a civilian population, destruction of property and pillaging) committed on 24 February 2003 during the attack on the village of Bogoro, in the Ituri district of the Democratic Republic of Congo. He was sentenced to a total of 12 years' imprisonment (18). Thomas Lubanga Dylio, former President of the Union des Patriotes Congolais/Forces Patriotiques pour la Libération du Congo (UPC/FPLC) was found guilty, on 14 March 2012, of the war crimes of enlisting and conscripting children under the age of 15 years and using them to participate actively in hostilities (child soldiers). He was sentenced, on 10 July 2012, to a total of 14 years' imprisonment (19).

DEFINITIONS OF TORTURE AND CRUEL INHUMAN AND DEGRADING TREATMENTS

Although definitions may sometimes vary, the most widely used definition of torture under international law is that provided by the United Nations Convention Against Torture and Other Cruel, Inhuman or Degrading Treatment or Punishment (CAT) which was adopted on 10 December 1984 by General Assembly resolution 39/46 (20). This Convention defines torture as:

> *"any act by which severe pain or suffering, whether physical or mental, is intentionally inflicted on a person for such purposes as obtaining from him or a third person information or a confession, punishing him for an act he or a third person has committed or is suspected of having committed, or intimidating or coercing him or a third person, or for any reason based on discrimination of any kind, when such pain or suffering is inflicted by or at the instigation of or with the consent or acquiescence of a public official or other person acting in an official capacity. It does not include pain or suffering arising only from, inherent in or incidental to lawful sanctions."*

Therefore, three elements combine constitute torture under this definition:

1) intentional infliction of severe pain or suffering;
2) for a specific purpose, such as to obtain information, as punishment, or to intimidate, or for any reason based on discrimination;
3) by or at the instigation of or with the consent or acquiescence of State authorities.

It will be recognized that each of these elements allows some freedom of interpretation and have been further refined via case law. If the nature of the degree of harm does reach the definition of torture, the victim may still be able to show the infliction of cruel, inhuman, or degrading treatment or punishment, which does not require specific intent on the part of those involved but must still reach a minimum level of severity.

INVESTIGATION OF TORTURE AND CRUEL INHUMAN AND DEGRADING TREATMENTS

The Istanbul Protocol is the United Nations Manual on the Effective Investigation and Documentation of Torture and Other Cruel, Inhuman or Degrading Treatment and provides "*international guidelines for the assessment of persons who allege torture or ill-treatment, for investigating cases of alleged torture and for reporting findings to the judiciary or any other investigative body*" (21). The "Istanbul Principles" in Annexe I of the document outline the minimum standards for States to follow in order to ensure the effective documentation of torture. The updated edition includes revised information on international law and the diagnostic reference criteria. Additionally, there are sections on investigation and documentation of torture of children and of LGBTI persons, on the role of healthcare professionals in documentation of torture in different contexts and on the required conditions for States' implementation of the Istanbul Protocol. It is further discussed in Chapter 82: – "Sexually Transmitted Infections Following Sexual Assault".

CONCLUSION

The ubiquity of war crimes, torture and other crimes proscribed by national and international laws and instruments raises the need for the highest quality evidence to support prosecutions. For many of these crimes, forensic & legal medicine practitioners will be providing the basic medical evidence to support (or exonerate) such allegations. It is, therefore, crucial that such practitioners have the appropriate skills and expertise to provide independent, unbiased evidence to the relevant courts of law and tribunals, and that they understand how broad that role can be.

REFERENCES

1. United Nations Human Rights. Office of the High Commissioner. Geneva convention relative to the treatment of prisoners of war, 1949. Available from: https://www.ohchr.org/en/instruments-mechanisms/instruments/geneva-convention-relative-treatment-prisoners-war#:~:text=Prisoners%20of%20war%20must%20at,breach%20of%20the%20present%20Convention (Accessed 23 March 2023).
2. ICRC. Final act of the International Peace Conference, 1899. Available from: https://ihl-databases.icrc.org/en/ihl-treaties/hague-finact-1899?activeTab=historical (Accessed 23 March 2023).
3. ICRC. Final act of the Hague Peace Conference, 1907. Available from: https://ihl-databases.icrc.org/en/ihl-treaties/hague-finact-1907?activeTab=historical (Accessed 23 March 2023).
4. ICRC. The Geneva Conventions of 1949 and their additional protocols. Available from: https://www.icrc.org/en/doc/war-and-law/treaties-customary-law/geneva-conventions/overview-geneva-conventions.htm (Accessed 23 March 2023).
5. United Nations Human Rights. Office of the High Commissioner. Rome statute of the International Criminal Court, 1998. Available from: https://www.ohchr.org/en/instruments-mechanisms/instruments/rome-statute-international-criminal-court (Accessed 20 March 2023).
6. Cioffi Ai, Cecannecchia C. Role of forensic medicine in addressing the war crimes: Perspective from Russia-Ukraine conflict during the COVID-19 pandemic. *Med Sci Law* 2023; **63(2)**: 168–73.
7. Metropolitan Police Service. What is a war crime? 2022. Available from: https://www.met.police.uk/advice/advice-and-information/war-crimes/what-is-a-war-crime/ (Accessed 23 March 2023).
8. International Law Commission. Available from: https://legal.un.org/ilc/ (Accessed 20 March 2023).
9. International Law Commission. Principles of international law recognized in the charter of the Nürnberg tribunal and in the judgment of the tribunal, 1950. Available from: https://legal.un.org/ilc/texts/instruments/english/draft_articles/7_1_1950.pdf (Accessed 20 March 2023).
10. International Law Commission. Draft statute for an international criminal court, 1994. Available from: https://legal.un.org/ilc/texts/instruments/english/draft_articles/7_4_1994.pdf (Accessed 20 March 2023).
11. International Law Commission. Draft code of crimes against the peace and security of mankind, 1996. Available from: https://legal.un.org/ilc/texts/instruments/english/draft_articles/7_4_1996.pdf (Accessed 20 March 2023).
12. International Criminal Court. Crime of aggression: Amendments ratification, 2019. Available from: https://asp.icc-cpi.int/crime-of-aggression (Accessed 20 March 2023).
13. International Court of Justice. Available from: https://www.icj-cij.org/en (Accessed 20 March 2023).
14. International Criminal Court. Office of the prosecutor. Available from: https://www.icc-cpi.int/about/otp (Accessed 20 March 2023).
15. Office of the Prosecutor. International criminal court. Statement of ICC prosecutor, Karim A.A. Khan QC, on the situation in Ukraine: Referrals from Japan and North Macedonia; Contact portal launched for provision of information, 2022. Available from: https://www.icc-cpi.int/news/statement-icc-prosecutor-karim-aa-khan-qc-situation-ukraine-i-have-decided-proceed-opening (Accessed 20 March 2023).
16. Office of the Prosecutor. International criminal court. Statement of ICC prosecutor, Karim A.A. Khan QC, on the situation in Ukraine: Receipt of referrals from 39 states parties and the opening of an investigation, 2022. Available from: https://www.icc-cpi.int/news/statement-icc-prosecutor-karim-aa-khan-qc-situation-ukraine-receipt-referrals-39-states (Accessed 20 March 2023).
17. International Criminal Court. 31 cases. Available from: https://www.icc-cpi.int/cases (Accessed 20 March 2023).
18. International Criminal Court. The Prosecutor v Germain Katanga. ICC-01/04–01/07, 2007. Available from: https://www.icc-cpi.int/drc/katanga (Accessed 20 March 2023).
19. International Criminal Court. The Prosecutor v Thomas Lubanga Dyilo. ICC-01/04–01/06, 2006. Available from: https://www.icc-cpi.int/drc/lubanga (Accessed 20 March 2023).
20. United Nations, Office of the High Commissioner on Human Rights. Convention against torture and other cruel, inhuman or degrading treatment or punishment, 1984. Available from: https://www.ohchr.org/en/instruments-mechanisms/instruments/convention-against-torture-and-other-cruel-inhuman-or-degrading (Accessed 20 March 2023).
21. United Nations Human Rights, Office of the High Commissioner. Istanbul Protocol. Professional training series No.8 Revision 2. Manual on the effective investigation and documentation of torture and other cruel, inhuman or degrading treatment or punishment, 2022. Available from: https://www.ohchr.org/sites/default/files/documents/publications/2022-06-29/Istanbul-Protocol_Rev2_EN.pdf (Accessed 20 March 2023).

CHAPTER 13

The Role of the United Nations and NGOs in the Scrutiny of and Prevention of Torture and Other CIDT

Jens Modvig and Marie Brasholt

INTRODUCTION

Prevention of torture

Prevention of torture may be divided into primary prevention, which prevents cases of torture from occurring, and secondary prevention, which reduces the impact of torture that has already taken place.

An example of primary prevention is preventive monitoring of places of detention, which may stop torture from occurring. The preventive monitoring team during its visit identifies conditions or practices which amount to, or may develop into, torture or ill-treatment and makes recommendations for change to increase the protection of detainees against torture and ill-treatment (1). The changing of legal frameworks is another example. For instance, granting all people deprived of their liberty a legal right to have a lawyer present from the moment of arrest, is, when effectively implemented, likely to contribute to prevention of torture (2).

An example of secondary prevention is the provision of redress (3,4) to victims, including compensation and rehabilitation as well as having perpetrators brought to justice (satisfaction). If effectively implemented, such measures may contribute to reducing the impact of torture for individual victims (5). However, the pursuit of redress is not always successful and may be an arduous and lengthy process ending up having a negative impact on the victim (6).

When impunity prevails, when torturers are not prosecuted, and victims are not provided with redress; this sends a signal from the State that torture will not be sanctioned and can continue unpunished. Conversely, initiatives to provide redress to victims and to have perpetrators brought to justice send a different signal, that is, that torture is not acceptable and will be punished. Thus, access to justice – while being an example of secondary prevention – may have an indirect primary prevention impact: preventing future cases of torture from occurring by means of a deterrent effect.

Scrutiny of torture

Scrutiny may be undertaken by many different bodies that may all have the opportunity to critically observe or examine how the State organizes its criminal justice system to protect citizens against human rights violations. They may also look for manifest violations such as torture and ill-treatment. So, scrutiny may focus on the way the criminal justice system operates, looking for improvements to increase protection (primary prevention), or on manifestations of failure, that is, victims of human rights violations, where the protective measures were not successful (secondary prevention).

Examples of bodies scrutinizing the criminal justice system are:

- Local and national civil society organizations
- Police and prison inspectorates
- Parliamentary committees
- National preventive mechanism bodies
- International NGOs
- Regional monitoring bodies
- UN treaty bodies
- UN special procedures

When the focus is on how the system works, one example of an area of interest could be the fundamental legal safeguards that should be in place during arrest and detention (the right to a lawyer, the right to inform relatives, and the right to request and receive a medical examination). In this case, scrutiny might give rise to concerns and recommendations, such as ensuring that the legal framework explicitly grants these rights to people deprived of their liberty, and that the rights are enjoyed in practice. Improved access to legal safeguards prevents torture from occurring (primary prevention).

When the focus is on violations of human rights, for example cases of torture and ill-treatment, this is when the system has failed. While attending to securing the rights and needs of victims (secondary prevention), the case would

DOI: 10.1201/9781003138754-14

still allow for an analysis of why the protection system failed and what should be done to remedy this.

This chapter will elaborate upon the systems of primary and secondary torture preventive measures at the national, regional and international levels, including non-governmental as well as intergovernmental agencies and mechanisms.

SCRUTINY BY THE UNITED NATIONS

The UN human rights system may be divided into the treaty-based system and the special procedures system. The main difference is that the treaty-based system is founded on ten legally binding human rights treaties (or conventions or covenants), each ratified by a number of States, whereas the special procedures are mechanisms politically agreed to by the Human Rights Council (HRC). These mechanisms do not involve legal obligations of States.

Within the fight against torture, the main treaties are the UN Convention against Torture and Other Cruel, Inhuman or Degrading Treatment of Punishment (UNCAT) and its Optional Protocol on the Prevention of Torture (OPCAT), and the International Covenant on Civil and Political Rights (ICCPR). The most relevant bodies are the UN Special Rapporteur on Torture (UNSRT) and perhaps the Universal Periodic Review (UPR).

Treaty-based system

A treaty is ratified on a voluntary basis by States that then become *States Parties* to the treaty. This entails an obligation to implement the provisions of the treaty. Each treaty has a treaty body – a group of independent experts, elected by all the States Parties to the treaty, with the mandate of examining whether the States have implemented the provisions of the treaty.

For UNCAT (7) and ICCPR (8), their treaty bodies (the Committee against Torture and the Human Rights Committee, respectively) exercise their monitoring function by receiving a report from each State Party every 4–8 years. This report is used for scrutinizing the state's system and the occurrence of torture, ending with a 2-day dialogue with a delegation from the government, reflected in *concluding observations* issued by the treaty body. The concluding observations are the results of the scrutiny and contain concerns and recommendations to the State Party on how better to implement the provisions of the convention/covenant in question. When the State Party submits its next report to the Committee, obviously the Committee will keep a focus on whether the recommendations given earlier were implemented or not.

OPCAT (9) is slightly different. While there is a treaty body (Subcommittee for the Prevention of Torture – SPT), States Parties to OPCAT do not have to submit reports. Rather, SPT may undertake monitoring visits to the States parties and visit places of detention with a view to evaluating the way the system functions, and also any occurrence of torture and ill-treatment. SPT provides recommendations to the State and issues a report on its findings, but it is up to the State Party to decide whether the report will be made public or not. Following a visit, a written follow-up may take place as well as a follow-up visit if urgent issues have been identified. Obviously, in subsequent visits, the SPT will also aim to assess how recommendations have been followed up by the State.

Special procedures

The HRC (10) comprises 47 States, elected by the UN General Assembly, and has as its mandate to strengthen the promotion and protection of human rights around the globe and address situations of human rights violations and make recommendations on them. The HRC has thus established a great number of so-called special procedures, such as special rapporteurs, inquiry commissions, fact-finding missions and working groups. These special procedures are typically established as a response to a critical human rights situation – some of a lasting nature, others more temporary. The special procedures have in common that there is no legal basis for their mandates, which means that States are not legally obliged to interact with the procedures and can choose not to.

The UNSRT is the most prominent torture-related special procedure. The UNSRT is elected by the HRC for a term of office of three years. The UNSRT (11) sends urgent appeals to States regarding individuals reported to be at risk of torture, undertakes fact-finding country visits, and submits annual reports to the HRC and the General Assembly. While the special procedures lack a legally binding mandate, they are not – as treaty bodies – limited to interact with a certain group of States but can address torture in any country. However, fact-finding missions require an invitation by the State in question.

Regional mechanisms

Certain areas of the world have regional human rights mechanisms, which include an anti-torture component (Table 13.1). Most prominently, the Council of Europe's Convention for the Prevention of Torture (12) establishes the Committee for the Prevention of Torture (CPT) (13), which undertakes preventive monitoring visits to places of detention in the 47 member States of Council of Europe. The Convention entered into force in 1989, and the regional convention and the CPT have been the model on which the global OPCAT and SPT were built more than a decade later.

Also, the African system founded with the African Charter on Human and Peoples' Rights (14) has a specific system for the prevention of torture – the Committee for the Prevention of Torture in Africa (CPTA) (15). While the CPTA does not undertake preventive monitoring visits in the same sense as the CPT, the CPTA proposes and facilitates the implementation of the Robben Island Guidelines (the Guidelines and Measures for the Prohibition and Prevention of Torture, Cruel, Inhuman or Degrading Treatment or Punishment in Africa) (16).

Similarly, in the Inter-American system, a convention is directed toward the fight against torture: the Inter-American Convention to Prevent and Punish Torture (17). While it has similarities with UNCAT, it does not establish any pro-active visiting mechanism like the European Convention for the Prevention of Torture.

TABLE 13.1 Comparing the three main UN anti-torture bodies

	UNCAT and CAT	OPCAT and SPT	Special Rapporteur on Torture
States covered by the mechanism	173 States Parties	91 States Parties	All States
Body elected by	States Parties	States Parties	HRC
Number of persons in body	10	25	1
States legally obliged by mechanism	Yes	Yes	No
Mechanisms addressing States	Periodic review of States Parties' compliance Confidential inquiry of indications of systematic torture	Periodic visit to States Parties' places of detention Establishment of National Preventive Mechanism	Reports to the HRC Fact-finding missions Public statements
Mechanisms addressing individuals	Individual communications (Legal basis in Convention)	-	Individual communications (No legal basis)

Scrutiny by civil society organizations

Civil society organizations (CSOs), particularly non-governmental organizations (NGOs) (18) play an important role in holding governments accountable. States are scrutinized by NGOs that monitor States' performances, document violations of human rights and other international standards, publish the results, and undertake advocacy to evoke changes. In principle, CSOs can look into the same aspects as the international bodies and in some contexts, CSOs have relatively easy access to places of deprivation of liberty and can build their recommendations, advocacy activities, and so on, on direct observations. The Robben Island Guidelines mentioned above even specify that States should encourage and facilitate visits by NGOs to places of detention. However, in repressive regimes, it is more usual for NGOs to have only limited, if any, access at all.

National NGOs may be vulnerable in repressive regimes, and their scrutiny of States met with legal and administrative measures (prohibition of receiving foreign funding, administrative searches, arrest and detention under the pretext of terrorism or tax evasion, etc.). As a counter against national isolation, many national human rights NGOs are collaborating with or are even members of international coalitions. International collaboration may also allow for national NGOs to publish their findings anonymously within international NGOs' reports.

NGOs may use the international mechanisms for communicating their observations, thereby adding weight and credibility to the scrutiny by the UN and regional bodies. In particular, NGOs may submit so-called shadow reports or alternative reports to the UN, including the treaty bodies and the UPR by the HRC.

In the subsequent boxes, we provide two examples of NGO scrutiny. In both cases, several hundred NGOs presented poor human rights records to all UN member states (for the Universal Periodic Review) and to the United Nations Human Rights Council respectively (for a special session to establish an independent UN reporting mechanism). In this way, scrutiny by NGOs may lead to scrutiny by the international community, including the United Nations.

BOX 13.1 NGO scrutiny of Australia's human rights record (19)

Leading up to the UPR of Australia in 2021, the Human Rights Law Centre, an Australian NGO, published the following on their webpage:

"At the Universal Periodic Review (UPR), other countries will question Australia about its human rights record and recommend improvements. Australia can make voluntary commitments to improve its human rights performance and can agree to implement other countries" recommendations.

The Human Rights Law Centre's Executive Director, Hugh de Kretser, said Australia can expect a number of rights issues to face intense scrutiny. "As a wealthy, stable democracy, Australia could lead the world on human rights yet too often Australian governments fail to respect people's human rights in critical areas. Australia's treatment of Aboriginal and Torres Strait Islander people and refugees and people seeking asylum in particular are likely to be in the spotlight at the review."

The Human Rights Law Centre, Kingsford Legal Centre and Caxton Legal Centre co-ordinated an NGO coalition which prepared a detailed report to inform the review and briefed UN member States ahead of the review. The NGO report has been endorsed by over 200 Australian NGOs. "The NGO report outlines 88 recommendations for Australian governments to lead on human rights, such as raising the age of criminal responsibility so that children as young as 10 cannot be locked up, implementing the Uluru Statement from the Heart, and stronger commitments to address climate change."

"At Australia's last review in 2015, 104 countries made 290 recommendations to Australia to improve rights. Despite Australia agreeing to many of those recommendations, only 17% have been fully implemented. "The Australian governments must do better. If Australian governments uphold the human rights of all people, we will have stronger, healthier communities across the country," added Mr de Kretser."

BOX 13.2 NGO scrutiny of China's human rights record (20)

In 2020, a global coalition called for a special session of the HRC to explore human rights violations in China. Voice of America reported:

"A global coalition of 321 civil society groups from 60 countries is calling for China to face greater scrutiny for its alleged systemic and serious human rights violations. The coalition plans to demand an end to China's impunity at the UN Human Rights Council, during the council's upcoming session next week. The group sent an open letter to the UN Secretary General and UN High Commissioner for Human Rights raising its concerns about China's human rights record. The signatories stress the need to address what they call rampant human rights violations across China, including in Hong Kong, Tibet, and the northwestern province of Xinjiang.

China Director at Human Rights Watch, Sophie Richardson, says the sheer magnitude of the violations committed inside China and outside the country warrant a fundamental different response from the UN Human Rights Council. "It is high time the Chinese government actually has some sense that it would face consequences for doing things like continuing to arbitrarily detain a million people simply on the basis of their ethnic identity and for a slew of other serious violations," said Richardson.

One million mainly Muslim Uighurs reportedly are incarcerated in so-called re-education camps in Xinjiang. In its statement, the coalition highlights China's efforts to distort the mandate of the UN Human Rights Council. It says China persecutes activists who seek redress from repression. It says the government in Beijing opposes initiatives to shine a light on its alleged serious rights violations and international crimes committed in countries around the world. The Chinese government rejects the UN's assessment of its human rights record as "gross interference."

Geneva Director at Human Rights Watch, John Fisher, says the UN needs to act on the growing chorus of voices calling for China to be held accountable for its rights abuses. "I think what has been striking around this appeal has been to say that so many NGO's from so many different countries, not just expressing concern at China's suppression of rights within its own borders, which are serious enough and warrant scrutiny on their own terms, but also the global impact of China's contempt for human rights," Fisher said.

The global coalition is calling for a special session of the Human Rights Council to explore the range of violations by China's government. "It urges the council to establish an impartial and independent UN mechanism to closely monitor and report on China's human rights situation annually. It says the UN must insist that the government comply with its international human rights obligations."

THE ROLE OF HEALTH PROFESSIONALS IN THE PREVENTION AND SCRUTINY OF TORTURE

Health professionals, mainly medical doctors, may play important roles in connection with torture and ill-treatment. As addressed elsewhere in this book, this is particularly so for doctors working in the criminal justice system, positively or negatively.

A negative role would imply medical complicity in torture. This may entail *active* complicity such as taking part in torture, either by perpetrating torture or by supporting the perpetrators, for instance, through the use of medical knowledge. Assessing fitness for torture would be one example. Medical complicity in torture may also, however, be *passive*, for instance, by not describing facts of an injury or not asking a detainee about the circumstances under which the injury occurred. Also, certifying death by unknown causes, when death due to torture or related violence is likely, falls under passive complicity in torture. Measures to prevent medical complicity are mentioned below.

A positive role in connection with torture would involve, for example, the early identification of victims of torture, documentation of medical sequelae of torture, reporting of cases of alleged torture to competent authorities for investigation, and referring to, or being actively involved in, treatment and rehabilitation of victims of torture.

In addition to the positive roles mentioned above, medical doctors are also key staff in monitoring teams and fact-finding missions undertaken by national or international bodies (21). The goals of such teams and missions are either to document cases of torture or to address areas for prevention of torture.

Prevention of medical complicity in torture

The problem of dual loyalty of medical doctors employed by law enforcement agencies (police, prisons, military) is well described elsewhere (22). Often, there are dilemmas between security and health concerns. Such dilemmas may be resolved if the doctor is guaranteed clinical independence, that is, absence of interference from law enforcement staff or managers in decisions made by the doctor for the individual patient. Also, treating health professionals should not be given any role in security matters.

Clinical independence of prison health staff is an internationally agreed upon standard (23). Whether such independence applies in practice depends on the structure and functioning of the prison health system, including reporting lines of the prison doctor. Medical associations may play an important role in ensuring such independence for its members (24).

A different, norm-setting, approach to prevent medical complicity is undertaken by the World Medical Association (WMA). The WMA has adopted numerous international declarations for medical doctors to promote compliance with international ethical and human rights standards, notably in relation to torture (25). Starting with the Helsinki Declaration of 1948, the WMA is the main contributor to the development of guidelines and standards for medical ethics and the role of medical doctors in combating torture.

An important way of preventing health professionals' involvement in torture is to ensure that they have received proper education and information regarding the prohibition of torture. This has been recognized in the UNCAT that obliges States' Parties to ensure such education and information and fully include it in the training of medical personnel and others who may be involved in the custody, interrogation or treatment of any individual subjected to any form of arrest, detention or imprisonment, as well as to include the prohibition of torture in the rules and instructions issued in regard to the duties and functions of such persons (UNCAT Article 10).

Prevention by medical doctors in the criminal justice system

Prison doctors, and other medical doctors employed in the criminal justice system, may often have a role in the Initial Medical Assessment (IMA), which is an international standard described in the Mandela Rules as well as in the European Prison Rules. The rules state that a medical doctor or other health professional should examine any newly arrived prisoner or detainee as soon as possible in order to identify urgent medical needs including suicide risk, ensure continuation of medical treatment, and to identify any cases of torture or ill-treatment. If such cases are identified, the doctor should document the medical sequelae and report the case to competent authorities for further investigation and possible prosecution of perpetrators.

Further, any doctor, including prison doctors, should at all times be alert to possible cases of torture and offer to document and report such cases. Obviously, every such case requires a thorough assessment of security risks and a procedure of informed consent. Nevertheless, medical doctors have a special position and opportunity to identify and document cases of torture. Lack of responsible reaction to such cases may amount to medical complicity in torture. As mentioned earlier, organizational and institutional support to doctors in exercising this responsibility is important and is often the responsibility of the Medical Association.

Doctors' role in treatment and rehabilitation

Another obviously important role for health professionals to play in relation to victims of torture is in the treatment and rehabilitation of the often severe physical, psychological and social consequences that may follow torture. Specialized rehabilitation centers exist in many countries in the world. Many of these are CSOs that collaborate via the International Rehabilitation Council for Torture Victims (IRCT) (26), the world's largest membership-based CSO specializing in the field of torture rehabilitation.

Doctors' role in scrutiny

Health professionals also play important roles in the abovementioned bodies and organizations which scrutinise States for their practices in relation to torture. Since its beginning, health professionals have been members of the Committee Against Torture, and even chairs of the Committee. Of the 25 experts who currently serve as members of the SPT, six are medical doctors, and two are clinical psychologists. In these committees, the health professionals play an important role in providing expertise in the scrutiny and monitoring of those aspects that are specifically related to health, healthcare and health systems, but their functions are not limited to the health-related aspects, and they also play more general roles alongside the other members of the committees. At the national level, many National Preventive Mechanisms – monitoring mechanisms in the States' Parties to the OPCAT that carry out functions very similar to the SPT – have doctors as part of their team.

Many health professionals are also active in CSOs. In some instances, they provide clinical services to victims of torture and ill-treatment, but they may also – as with the international committees – provide their expertise during scrutiny and monitoring of health-related aspects, and they may use their often-privileged positions in society when advocating for change.

REFERENCES

1. Carver R, Handley L. *Does Torture Prevention Work?* Liverpool: Liverpool University Press; 2016, pp. 93–98.
2. Carver R, Handley L. *Does Torture Prevention Work?* Liverpool: Liverpool University Press; 2016, pp. 68–69.
3. Refworld. Convention against torture and other Cruel, Inhuman or degrading Treatment or punishment: implementation of article 14 by States parties. General comment 3, 2012. Available from: https://www2.ohchr.org/english/bodies/cat/docs/gc/cat-c-gc-3_en.pdf (Accessed 20 March 2023).
4. UNHR. UNGA 2005 resolution: Basic principles and guidelines on the right to a remedy and reparation for victims of Gross violations of international human Rights Law and Serious Violations of International Humanitarian Law. Adopted and proclaimed by General Assembly resolution 60/147 of 16 December 2005. Available from: https://www.ohchr.org/en/instruments-mechanisms/instruments/basic-principles-and-guidelines-right-remedy-and-reparation (Accessed 20 March 2023).
5. Rauchfuss K, Schmolze B. Justice heals: The impact of impunity and the fight against it on the recovery of severe human rights violations' survivors. *Torture* 2008; **18**(**1**): 38–50.
6. REDRESS. Torture survivors' perceptions of reparation, 2001. Available from: https://redress.org/wp-content/uploads/2018/01/E.-June-2001-Torture-Survivors-Perceptions-of-Reparation.pdf (Accessed 20 March 2023).
7. United Nations. Convention against Torture and other cruel, inhuman or degrading treatment or punishment, 1987. Available from: https://legal.un.org/avl/ha/catcidtp/catcidtp.htm (Accessed 20 March 2023).

8. OHCHR. International covenant on civil and political rights, 1966. Available from: https://www.ohchr.org/en/instruments-mechanisms/instruments/international-covenant-civil-and-political-rights (Accessed 20 March 2023).
9. United Nations. Optional protocol to the convention against torture and other cruel, inhuman or degrading treatment or punishment, 2006. Available from: https://www.ohchr.org/en/instruments-mechanisms/instruments/optional-protocol-convention-against-torture-and-other-cruel (Accessed 20 March 2023).
10. UNHRC. Available from: https://www.ohchr.org/EN/HRBodies/HRC/Pages/Home.aspx (Accessed on 20 March 2023).
11. UNHR. Special rapporteur on torture, 2020. Available from: https://www.ohchr.org/en/issues/torture/srtorture/pages/srtortureindex.aspx (Accessed 18 March 2023).
12. Council of Europe. European convention for the prevention of torture and inhuman or degrading treatment or punishment: Text of the convention and explanatory report, 2002. Available from: https://rm.coe.int/16806dbaa3 (Accessed 20 March 2023).
13. Council of Europe. European convention for the prevention of torture and inhuman or degrading treatment or punishment, 2002. Available from: https://rm.coe.int/16806dbaa3 (Accessed 29 March 2023).
14. Organization of African Unity. African charter on human and peoples' Rights, 1981. Available from: https://au.int/sites/default/files/treaties/36390-treaty-0011_-_african_charter_on_human_and_peoples_rights_e.pdf (Accessed 1 May 2023).
15. International Justice Resource Center. Committee for the prevention of torture in Africa (CPTA). Available from: https://ijrcenter.org/regional/african/committee-for-the-prevention-of-torture-in-africa/ (Accessed 1 May 2023).
16. APT. The Robben Island guidelines, 2002. Available from: https://www.apt.ch/en/resources/publications/robben-island-guidelines-2002 (Accessed 20 March 2023).
17. Refworld. Inter-American convention to prevent and punish torture, 1987. Available from: https://www.refworld.org/docid/3ae6b3620.html (Accessed 20 March 2023).
18. UNDP. Working with civil society in foreign aid, 2013. Available from: https://www.cn.undp.org/content/china/en/home/library/south-south-cooperation/working-with-civil-society-in-foreign-aid.html (Accessed 12 March 2023).
19. HRLC. Australia's human rights record under scrutiny at major UN human rights review. Available from: https://www.hrlc.org.au/news/2021/1/20/united-nations-aust-govt-upr-review (Accessed 12 March 2023).
20. VOA. Global coalition calls for greater scrutiny of China on rights, 2020. Available from: https://www.voanews.com/a/east-asia-pacific_global-coalition-calls-greater-scrutiny-china-rights/6195659.html (Accessed 20 March 2023).
21. Dignity. Monitoring health in places of detention. An overview for health professionals, 2021. Available from: https://www.dignity.dk/en/nyheder/dignity-launches-a-manual-on-monitoring-health-in-places-of-detention/ (Accessed 23 March 2023).
22. Physicians for human rights. Dual loyalty and human rights in health professional practice: Proposed guidelines & instutional mechanism. Available from: https://phr.org/our-work/resources/dual-loyalty-and-human-rights-in-health-professional-practice/ (Accessed 20 March 2023).
23. UNODC. Mandela rule 25.2. Available at: https://www.unodc.org/unodc/justice-and-prison-reform/nelsonmandelarules.html (Accessed 20 March 2023).
24. Polatin P, Modvig J, Rytter T. Helping to stop doctors becoming complicit in torture. *BMJ* 2010; **340**: c973.
25. Nathanson V. Torture and International Medical Standards. In: Evans MD, Modvig J (eds), *Research Handbook on torture: Legal and Medical Perspectives on Prohibition and Prevention.* Cornwall: Elgar Publishing; 2020, pp. 393–409.
26. International Rehabilitation Council for Torture Victims. Available from: www.irct.org (Accessed 12 March 2023).

CHAPTER 14

Providing Evidence for Courts

James Bloomer

INITIAL INSTRUCTION

What will be received and what is to be assessed

When asked to prepare a quote for an expert report, you should be provided with a considerable body of material, sufficient for you to assess three vital things:

- What precisely am I being asked to report on?
- Is this within my specific area of expertise?
- How long will this take me, so that I can assess what to quote?

Important considerations when quoting for a report

It is critical that you are clear on the three questions set out above before quoting, because if you are not, you will be faced with having to seek additional funding having begun the report preparation exercise. The follow-on effect of this will be that the solicitor who has instructed you, inevitably under very substantial time pressure, will be forced to go back to the Legal Aid Agency (LAA) for this funding in the majority of criminal cases (these being publicly funded). They will be very likely to have to explain this delay to an increasingly irate Judge. This may even lead to your report not being heard at the trial concerned. It is not difficult to understand that the solicitor concerned will be relatively unlikely to seek to instruct you again in these circumstances.

PREPARING THE REPORT ITSELF

Information to insist upon

The easiest criticism of any expert report when evidence is given in court is that it has been prepared without access to vital background information, or in ignorance of this. An authoritative report, which commands the respect of the Court, will both ensure that it has all of the relevant information in the case before it in coming to its conclusion, and, as we will see later, is in fact required by the Criminal Procedure Rules to list, within the body of the report, the information upon which it is based.

In a criminal case, it is all too common for solicitors to provide less than the whole of the prosecution case evidence to the expert from whom the report is being asked. Even if they do achieve this, there can often be key pieces of information missing which the expert requires for the report. Examples might include medical or psychiatric records of the defendant, not relied upon by the Crown to seek to prove his guilt, but wholly critical to, say, a defense of diminished responsibility in a murder allegation; or detailed plans and photographs of a location at which an alleged offense occurred which exist but are not relied upon by the Crown to prove guilt.

Do not be afraid to ask the solicitor or CPS unit instructing you, in writing, for specific material. In fact, it is part of your duty as an expert witness to seek all relevant information before reporting.

Understanding precisely what is being asked of you

It is very common to see expert reports that provide a general overview of a particular individual or a particular aspect of a case susceptible to expertise, which do not answer any question of use to the party instructing the expert. These reports either end up not being used, with the expert concerned unlikely to be used again, or the expert will have the inconvenience of being approached as a matter of extreme urgency for answers to specific questions.

There are simple steps that can be taken to avoid this pitfall. Ensure that you have the barrister's formal advice for funding your report within your papers. The barrister will have had to specify the issues requiring answers from the expert witness within the report in this document, and it is thus a useful starting point for your report.

Many of us provide very specific questions to be answered within the report by the writer. Please understand that, in many cases, those are very carefully worded indeed, and the writer may not wish other issues outside the questions to be dealt with. If you are in any doubt either what you are being asked to report upon, or whether the questions you are being asked are sufficient to do justice to the case, please just ask the solicitor or CPS unit (whichever is instructing you). Far better that than to proceed under a misconception.

DOI: 10.1201/9781003138754-15

Timeliness

The legal system, and the participants therein, have never been as overstretched and time-pressured as they now are.

You will be asked for a time estimate for your report. If you are not asked for such an estimate, you would be well advised to volunteer one unasked. The estimate should at all costs be a realistic one. If it is not, the barrister or solicitor concerned will once again be left explaining to an irate Judge why a trial should be delayed by the lateness of your report. Should the Judge, as they are increasingly under pressure to do, wish the trial to proceed at all costs, the Judge concerned has a power worth remembering. It is to witness summons you to come to Court, report in hand, whatever your commitment, often at less than 24 hours' notice. It would once have been unheard of for a Judge to treat an expert in this way. It no longer is.

More than that, the barrister and solicitor placed in the position of having their client's case prejudiced by your report not arriving when planned are simply not going to contemplate instructing you again.

We all understand that, in a COVID and time-pressured era, life can get in the way of deadlines. That is to say, we understand, if and only if you let us know, as soon as you know, that there is to be a delay. Far easier to go to a Judge cap in hand well before a deadline has expired, for obvious reasons.

CONTENT

Legal requirements

The requirements of the Criminal Procedure Rules (CPR) and Criminal Practice Direction (CPD) govern the minimum content required of an expert evidence report in criminal proceedings. Similar, but not identical, provisions apply in civil proceedings and are set out in the Civil Procedure Rules (confusingly often also referred to as the CPR).

The specifics are set out at Rule 19 of the CPR. Without reciting them in full herein (and all expert witnesses would be well advised to read them in full) the essentials are:

(a) "objective and unbiased" reporting[i]
(b) "within the expert's ... expertise"[ii]
(c) the above duty "overrides any obligation to the person...by whom the expert is paid"[iii]
(d) to "define the expert's areas of expertise" in the report and in court and to inform all parties if the expert's opinion changes[iv]
(e) inform parties of anything that might reasonably be thought capable of undermining the reliability of the expert's opinion[v]
(f) provide copies of or allow inspection of notes and records lying behind the report[vi]

[i] CPR 2020 Rule 19.1.a.i
[ii] CPR 2020 Rule 19.1.a.ii
[iii] CPR 2020 Rule 19.2.2
[iv] CPR 2020 Rule 19.2.3
[v] CPR 2020 Rule 19.3.c.ii
[vi] CPR 2020 Rule 19.3.d

It is important to understand that (e) and (f) above are duties on your instructing client (be that a defence solicitor or CPS unit), not directly on you. On that basis, informing your instructing client of any material falling into this category (in writing) would seem likely to fulfil your duty as an expert witness. As to (e), to assist, a helpful list of examples of such material is provided in the CPD.[vii]

Further important and mandatory requirements are set out in the CPR as to the content of the report.[viii] Such is the importance of these provisions; they are reproduced in full herein below:

"*...an expert's report must—*

(a) *give details of the expert's qualifications, relevant experience and accreditation;*
(b) *give details of any literature or other information which the expert has relied on in making the report;*
(c) *contain a statement setting out the substance of all facts given to the expert which are material to the opinions expressed in the report, or upon which those opinions are based;*
(d) *make clear which of the facts stated in the report are within the expert's own knowledge;*
(e) *where the expert has based an opinion or inference on a representation of fact or opinion made by another person for the purposes of criminal proceedings (for example, as to the outcome of an examination, measurement, test or experiment)—*
    (i) *identify the person who made that representation to the expert,*
    (ii) *give the qualifications, relevant experience, and any accreditation of that person,*
    (iii) *and certify that that person had personal knowledge of the matters stated in that representation;*
(f) *where there is a range of opinion on the matters dealt with in the report—*
    summarise the range of opinion, and
    give reasons for the expert's own opinion;
(g) *if the expert is not able to give an opinion without qualification, state the qualification;*
(h) *include such information as the court may need to decide whether the expert's opinion is sufficiently reliable to be admissible as evidence;*
(i) *contain a summary of the conclusions reached;*
(j) *contain a statement that the expert understands an expert's duty to the court, and has complied and will continue to comply with that duty; and*
(k) *contain the same declaration of truth as a witness statement.*"

As to (k) above, a model example of "a declaration of truth" is in the CPD.[ix] I would recommend simply using it in full."

Style

Many expert witnesses tend to forget that the primary audience for their report is a jury of ordinary people,

[vii] CPD 19A.7.a-l and 19A.8
[viii] CPR 2020 Rule 19.4
[ix] CPD 19B.1

and (if a defence-instructed report) the client on trial on a criminal allegation, not the lawyers or judge involved. This is not a lecture or academic paper of any kind. The style and language used, while of course appropriately formal to a certain extent, would do well to reflect that.

Beyond this, clarity is everything. There is very little more likely to prevent your future instruction than a report that appears to give one view on the issue in the case, which then crumbles to uncertainty, or an opposite opinion in Court when probed. If you are not sure or are unable to express an opinion within your expertise, be clear about that.

CONFERENCE WITH THE INSTRUCTING LEGAL TEAM

It is relatively likely that the party instructing you may want a conference with you to discuss your report before Court. This is more likely the more serious the allegation involved. This can range from a short and informal telephone conversation to a formal meeting in person at a CPS office or solicitor's firm.

The reason for this is always the same. Many barristers recognize that the better they understand the limits of the expert evidence they are contemplating deploying, the more effective evidence they can deploy on their client's behalf, and the more able they are to avoid unpleasant surprises within the evidence in Court.

If you asked to have such a conference, please have all relevant material available to you. Here, again, clarity is all. If the barrister cannot understand the evidence, help him or her to do so. This will make them more, not less likely to think of you when asked to recommend an expert on the next occasion.

PRE-COURT

Conferences with experts instructed for the other party (be that prosecution or defence)

The specific rules governing such discussions, sometimes called experts' meetings, are set out in the CPR[x]. Beyond the provisions set out therein, it is essential that experts keep accurate notes of the discussions of such meetings, lest there be any dispute about the content of the discussion at a later stage. These need be no more than an accurate and complete summary. Such content cannot be referred to without the Court's permission.[xi] Before giving such permission, in the event of a dispute, the Court will wish to see such a note, or hear the expert's evidence on oath about it (perhaps assisted by the note).

Practicalities

Court timetabling of trials has never been more haphazard, or slower. To help yourselves with this, make sure you provide with your report, a full set of "dates to avoid" going at least a year into the future. Make sure, if these are materially changed, this is passed on to those instructing you.

Do not assume you will, as you should be, be provided with the trial date in a timely way. Ask proactively, and regularly. This is especially true when instructed by the CPS. Be clear on the dates you cannot do but seek to offer what availability you have. Courts will do what they can, sometimes including video links from one court centre to another to assist you when busy.

When attending, take with you all reports, and notes relating to those reports. You do not want to be embarrassed by being asked for a document you do not have access to, still less asked about the content of it.

GIVING CONTESTED ORAL EVIDENCE IN A CROWN OR MAGISTRATE'S COURT

When attending, you should make clear who you are, what case you are attending for, and ask to be directed to the Witness Service. It may be that you are required to fill out a form there to claim your fee for attending.

Come prepared to wait. Courts run unpredictably, and their administration is often less than efficient. If you have a deadline by which you must be away, tell both the Witness Service and those who instruct you when you arrive. If you wait until the deadline is close, there will (not may) be a problem.

In court itself

When called to give evidence you will be taken to where you should stand by an usher and asked to swear an oath or affirm to tell the truth. Please don't assume, unasked, that you may sit down. Some Judges are still likely to be offended by this and say so. If you ask, all will gladly say you may.

Standing or sitting, please make an effort to speak just a little more loudly than normal. Courts have notoriously bad acoustics and there is little point in being there if you are not heard. Do not be fooled by the microphone in front of you. In the vast majority of courts, these record for the audio record of proceedings. They do not amplify your voice. If the barrister asking you questions, or the Judge seems to want you to speak very slowly, notes are being taken all around the courtroom.

You will be asked questions first by the barrister for the party instructing you. These will refer you to your report or reports, and ought to be very straightforward. Then you will be asked questions by the other side of the criminal case, be that the prosecution barrister if you are defence-instructed, or one or more defence barristers if prosecution-instructed. These will inevitably be more challenging. You can be clear that the Judge will intervene if the question is inappropriate. Otherwise, assume you are to answer. If that answer is to say that you do not

[x] CPR 2020 Rule 19.6
[xi] CPR 2020 Rule 19.6.3

understand the question, or cannot answer within your expertise, there is no difficulty at all with that. There may be clarifying questions then asked by the party instructing you or the Judge.

Two important points of emphasis:

(a) If you are clear about something, say so, and remain so, notwithstanding the challenge. Nothing is worse than to instruct an expert whose opinion changes under challenge. If you have genuinely changed your mind, tell the party instructing you **before** you set foot in the witness box.

(b) Please remember that this is a conversation with a jury of non-expert people, however formal the setting may be. It is not a lecture or treatise of any kind. There is no benefit, and often great disadvantage to an expert who talks to, or worse still, at a jury. The most helpful expert evidence resembles someone talking with a jury, avoiding any unnecessary complication or use of technical language or jargon.

CHAPTER

15

Pathophysiology of Wound Healing

Michael J. Pickup

INTRODUCTION

Forensic examinations typically start at an endpoint and aim to work backward in time with the goal of determining how everything came to be. A chapter on wound healing in a forensic pathology textbook is the basis for an in-depth discussion about how forensic pathologists estimate the age of a given wound with respect to the time of death. In the context of the law, opinions regarding timing of injury can, on occasion, form the crux of a case for either the prosecution or defense by speaking to the legal concept of exclusive opportunity. Forensic pathologists are very comfortable speaking about causation as well as describing injuries and their physiologic impact. Opinions regarding timing of injury that serve to support exclusive opportunity represent a rare instance where the forensic pathologist may assist the court in determining who was responsible for an injury or death, the legal significance of which must not be taken lightly. The practice of forensic pathology, and in particular, timing of injuries lies squarely in the middle of a pervasive battle between medicine and the law. Timelines in wound healing are blurred and occur along a continuum with overlapping processes and occasionally unpredictable external and internal influences whereas the law strives to achieve clarity in expert evidence.

For immediately (or nearly immediately) lethal injuries, timing of injury is simple. In the absence of a physiologic capacity for survival, the injury clearly occurred at or close to the time of death. The introduction of a period of survival can add a layer of complexity, and a clear understanding of the stepwise processes of wound healing and factors that influence them is invaluable for the forensic pathologist. From a practical perspective, as the survival interval increases, determination of wound age is typically less legally relevant, which is helpful as precision with respect to wound age determination diminishes as the survival interval increases.

The phases of wound healing are discussed along with the important cell types and their functions and other influential factors.

PHASES OF WOUND HEALING

Full-thickness cutaneous trauma leads to bleeding and a potential portal of entry for bacteria and foreign material. Following injury, wounds undergo stepwise healing processes involving multiple cell types and mediators which attempt to achieve hemostasis, decontamination, and recreation of a barrier with eventual restoration of skin integrity. These distinct but overlapping phases include hemostasis, inflammation, proliferation (new tissue formation) and maturation (remodeling).

Hemostasis

Damage to cutaneous blood vessels exposes circulating platelets to a thrombogenic subendothelial matrix resulting in integrin activation and platelet aggregation. This and subsequent activation of coagulation pathways result in the formation of a platelet plug followed by deposition of stabilizing fibrin matrix along with complement components. The resultant matrix acts as a scaffold for early inflammatory cells recruited to the area via complement activation, platelet degranulation and bacterial degradation. Hemostasis also results in the release/formation of numerous substances such as histamine, serotonin, thromboxane, prostaglandin, platelet activating factor (PAF), platelet-derived growth factor (PDGF), and cytokines such as transforming growth factor-1β (TGF-1β), interleukin-1 (IL-1) and tumour necrosis factor (TNF) (1,2). Histamine and thromboxane facilitate vascular permeability leading to tissue edema and vasoconstriction, further assisting with hemostasis. These myriad liberated compounds are also involved in the initiation of the inflammatory phase of wound healing (3,4).

Hemostasis begins over the first seconds to minutes after an injury is sustained. Histologically, this phase is visible as a blood clot, chiefly composed of platelets, fibrin and entrapped erythrocytes (*see* Figure 15.1). Inflammatory cells are infrequent and are at the typical concentration seen in peripheral blood. At this phase, their presence is passive in nature, and should not be interpreted as active inflammation.

DOI: 10.1201/9781003138754-16

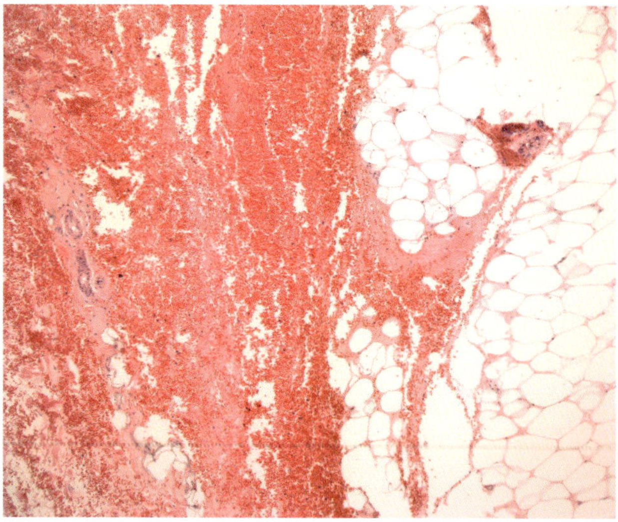

15.1 Acute subcutaneous hemorrhage with fibrin.

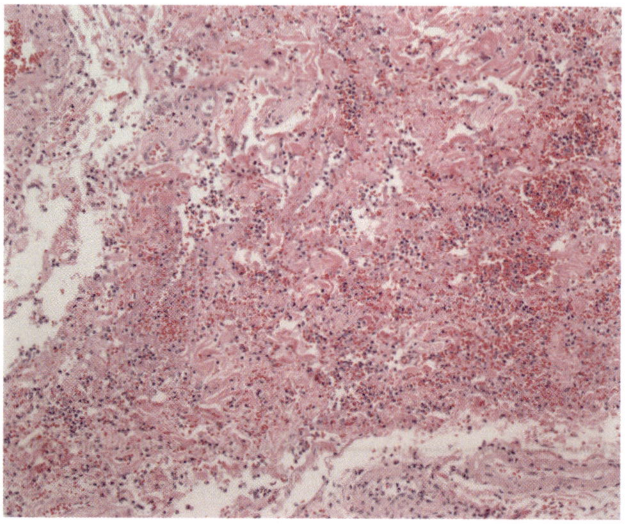

15.2 Acute inflammatory infiltrates with residual acute hemorrhage.

Grossly, these wounds appear fresh/hemorrhagic. As a result of bleeding/clotting, the wound appears red. There is no hyperemic border. Post-mortem drying at this stage may impart a dark red (dried blood) or yellow appearance to the wound.

Inflammatory phase

Forming part of the innate immune response, neutrophils attracted to the injury site by liberated chemotactic agents first marginate and then permeate the vessel wall. These processes are mediated by cytokines that stimulate endothelial cell expression of E-selectin on the luminal surface resulting in rolling adhesion. Subsequent activation of integrin receptors on the neutrophil mediate firm adhesion to the endothelial cells at the site of injury followed by transendothelial migration facilitating access to the interstitium.

Neutrophils have several functions in wound healing. Their primary function is to eradicate sites of tissue damage from bacteria and other microorganisms. This is typically done by engulfing the offending organisms in phagosomes and exposing them to neutrophil-derived reactive oxygen species (ROS) such as superoxide and hydrogen peroxide as well as proteolytic and hydrolytic enzymes (5). Neutrophils produce an array of ROSs through the actions of nicotinamide adenine dinucleotide phosphate (NADPH), oxidase type 2 (NOX2) and myeloperoxidase (MPO) (6). Spent apoptotic neutrophils are eventually cleared from the site of injury along with the scab or phagocytosed by macrophages. Neutrophils also produce cytokines such as TNF-α, IL-1β and IL-6, to amplify the inflammatory response.

Neutrophils can start to become visible in the interstitium at wound margins (outside the areas of hemorrhage) as early as 20–30 minutes after injury and are present in virtually all wounds greater than 15 hours old (7). In general, however, they represent the initial infiltrate in wounds between 2–6 hours where they persist as the predominant infiltrate for at least 20 hours with variability in the predominant cell type between 2 and 11 days (*see* Figure 15.2).

Neutrophil cell numbers then tend to decline, and macrophages take over as the predominant cell type in the inflammatory response. Neutrophils may still be present in wounds in much lower numbers more than 1 month after injury.

Grossly, due to the cellular infiltrates and leaky vessels, wounds in this phase appear erythematous and edematous. Depending on the size and depth of the wound, a scab may start to become visible progressing from red to a darker color. In larger, broader wounds, or those with ongoing trauma or infection, dried scab formation occurs later during the proliferative phase after granulation tissue has formed.

At the same time as neutrophils, circulating monocytes are recruited to the area in a similar fashion by TGF-1β and monocyte chemoattractant protein 1 (MCP1). Due to their slower mobility, they tend to arrive later than neutrophils. They also remain at the site longer. Once in the interstitium, along with resident macrophages, they become activated following exposure to pro-inflammatory cytokines, and pathogen- or damage-associated molecular patterns (PAMPs or DAMPs). Upon activation, they first acquire a pro-inflammatory phenotype (M1-type) and contribute to microbicidal activity through production of ROS as well as being principally involved in phagocytosis of cellular debris and breakdown products from hemorrhage. At this phase, macrophages are also involved in debridement of the wound through release of collagenases and elastases. Macrophage polarization from pro-inflammatory forms to an anti-inflammatory phenotype (M2-Type) occurs as the microenvironment of the wound changes, particularly as pathogen numbers decline and numbers of apoptotic neutrophils increase (8,9). M2-type macrophages switch from releasing IL-12 to IL-10 and these anti-inflammatory macrophages play a crucial role in the transition from the inflammatory phase of wound healing to the proliferation phase. M2-Type macrophages release growth factors such as TGF-1β, vascular endothelial growth factor (VEGF) and various forms of platelet derived growth factor (PDGF) to promote the formation of granulation tissue, the histologic hallmark of the proliferative phase (10,11).

Macrophages can be seen in wounds as early as 3 hours after infliction and are regularly visible within 15 hours. Macrophages tend to become the predominant cell type within 2–3 days, but this is variable, and they may not predominate for up to 12 days (7). Macrophages can persist for many months so their presence cannot be used to determine a maximum survival interval.

Based on the substance or cellular debris being cleared, the histologic appearance of the macrophage changes following phagocytosis. The appearance of these forms can also assist with aging of injuries with siderophages largely regarded as being the most reliable. So-called hemosiderin-laden macrophages are frequently easily identifiable on routine hematoxylin and eosin-stained slides as they contain typical brown pigmented material. It is prudent, however, to highlight hemosiderin using the Perls' Prussian blue reaction in order to differentiate iron-containing hemosiderin from other brown or black pigments in the wound (7,12). This analysis can also assist with estimating the quantity of hemosiderin deposits in a wound. The detection of considerable amounts (>20%) indicates a minimum survival interval of about one week (13). Lipophages and erythrophages containing fat and red cells respectively also tend to become visible starting at 3 days, however their presence can be delayed, and they can be more difficult to find, making their appearance as a marker of wound age less reliable than hemosiderin.

Hematoidin, the crystalized breakdown product of bilirubin, can be seen in wounds as early as 8 days after injury, but this is highly variable from being entirely absent to appearing much later (weeks to months). Nevertheless, hematoidin, when present, can be a helpful marker indicating wound age greater than a week or so.

Proliferation phase (new tissue formation)

Following macrophage polarization to the M2-type phenotype with subsequent release of chemokines, TNF, PDGF, TGF-1β and fibroblast growth factor (FGF), fibroblasts migrate to the site of damage and proliferate. Migration of fibroblasts through extracellular matrix (ECM) and cross-linked fibrin requires proteolysis, principally via the action of macrophage and fibroblast-derived matrix metalloproteinases (MMPs). Macrophages also release growth factors such as VEGF to stimulate angiogenesis. Capillary buds sprout from blood vessels adjacent to the site of injury in response to growth factors and other features of the microenvironment such as low oxygen tension. The appearance of increased numbers of fibroblasts and proliferation of small, immature blood vessels are features of granulation tissue, which commonly starts to become visible at the base of a broad abrasion or a wound healing

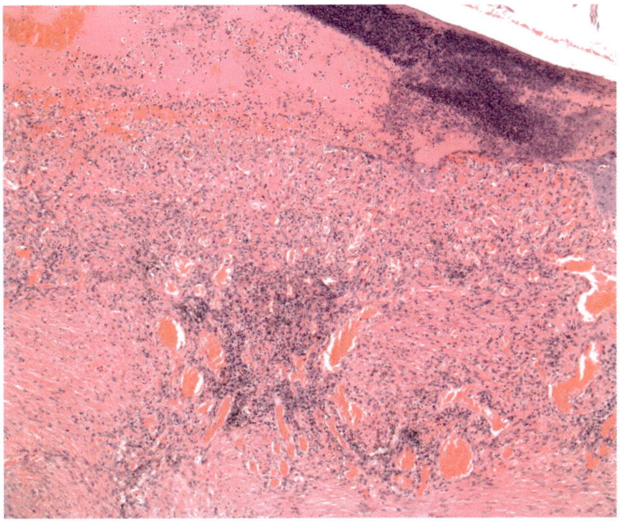

15.3 Granulation tissue with abundant fibroblasts and immature blood vessels.

by secondary intention at approximately 3 days (see Figure 15.3). Narrow or mechanically closed wounds undergo re-epithelialization more quickly as the epithelial gap is smaller. As a result, granulation tissue formation is far less exuberant and is typically not grossly visible in wounds healing by primary intention.

Along with immature blood vessels, granulation tissue contains abundant ECM composed of fibrous and glycoprotein components (collagens, elastins, fibronectin, proteoglycans and laminins) (14,15). At first, type III collagen is laid down in a random fashion creating a provisional matrix along with fibrin and fibronectin. This is later re-oriented and replaced with collagen I during the late proliferation and into the remodeling phase to increase mechanical strength and elasticity of the healing wound. Activated fibroblasts also synthesize proteoglycans with varying concentrations of glycosaminoglycans, first hyaluronic acid followed by increasing amounts of chondroitin sulfate and dermatan sulfate (16). These constituents of the ECM also have regulatory functions, supporting capillary growth as well as fibronectin and collagen formation (17,18).

In addition to the formation of granulation tissue with ECM synthesis, the process of re-epithelialization will start to occur during the proliferation phase. This is visible as keratinocyte migration followed by proliferation to restore the normal thickness and architecture of the skin surface with keratinization. Macrophages stimulate fibroblasts to produce keratinocyte growth factor 7 (KGF-7) and IL-6 (19). In turn, keratinocytes migrate from wound edges and hair follicles to fill the basal cell layer gap formed by the wound. Migration requires keratinocytes to loosen their desmosomal interactions with neighboring keratinocytes and with the ECM in the dermis below. Once free, they then migrate through newly synthesized ECM created by recruited fibroblasts. Migration through the ECM is facilitated by specialized MMPs and regulated by tissue inhibitors of metalloproteinases (TIMPs) (20). MMPs and TIMPs also play integral roles in the subsequent maturation/

remodeling phase of wound healing. The time it takes for re-epithelialization to complete is dependent on the wound size. Complete closure can occur as early as 5 days after infliction but is more routinely seen at 2–3 weeks.

In concert with re-epithelialization, wound contraction is an important step in the healing of large surface wounds, particularly those healing by secondary intention. Fibroblasts at the wound edges differentiate into myofibroblasts through the actions of growth factors (PDGF, TGF-1β and FGF-2) released by macrophages in the granulation tissue. Myofibroblasts express alpha-actin and create a network of cells with contractile properties that work to bring the wound edges closer together, making the task of re-epithelialization less onerous. The appearance of myofibroblasts within granulation tissue can be seen with immunohistochemical staining as early as 5 days into the healing process with most healing wounds containing a population of myofibroblasts between 5 days and 1 month after injury. Myofibroblasts can persist at the site of a healing wound for up to 2 months (21).

Once the wound base is closed through keratinocyte migration, the basal keratinocytes proliferate and undergo stratification and differentiation to restore the skin barrier with its typical architecture. This regulated process is mediated by several growth factors including HB-EGF, EGF, TGF-α and KGF.

At the conclusion of the proliferation phase, the scab has generally fallen off and progression to the next phase is grossly marked by a hypopigmented scar. The loss of scab is dependent on host factors and at least partially dependent on mechanical factors during normal activity. As a result, scabs may persist for many weeks in individuals who are comatose/immobile (22). The loss of the scab is therefore not a reliable marker of wound age.

At the earliest, starting at approximately the end of the second week, scar tissue can be visible with collagen and ECM filling the healing dermal defect. Vascular channels eventually regress, and the wound is converted into an area of dense collagen with fragments of elastin and other components of the ECM. The region is left permanently devoid of adnexal structures and evidence of the inflammatory response fades over subsequent weeks to months (23). At this phase, tissue staining with Masson's trichrome shows dense collagen matrix (staining blue).

Maturation (remodeling) phase

The final phase of wound healing is maturation and remodeling. This phase starts approximately 2–4 weeks after injury and evidence of maturation and remodeling can be seen for many months to years. It involves changes to the connective tissue to gradually re-approximate the pre-injury tensile strength of the skin.

Akin to the remodeling of human bone through the actions of osteoblasts and osteoclasts, remodeling of the ECM in healing skin wounds occurs through an orchestrated balance of synthesis and degradation of ECM components. Degradation occurs via the actions of numerous specific MMPs and serine proteases. MMPs are synthesized by keratinocytes, fibroblasts, macrophages and endothelial cells (24). Once produced, their action is quickly reversed by TIMPs produced by mesenchymal cells in order to keep degradation in check (25). A net increase in fibrillar type I collagen is responsible for initial recovery of tensile strength of the skin following injury. This process gradually increases the strength of the healing wound over the first few months after injury (26). Subsequent tensile strength is gained through structural modification of collagen fibers. Properly healed wounds reach a maximal tensile strength of approximately 80 percent that of unwounded skin and can take many months to years to reach this strength plateau.

FACTORS AFFECTING WOUND HEALING

Adding to the complexity of forensic aging of wounds, there are numerous factors affecting wound healing that can retard progression through this complex stepwise process. Factors affecting wound healing can be thought of in terms of local/wound factors and systemic factors. Many of the local factors can be mitigated by appropriate treatment of the wound such as debridement, mechanical closure, decontamination and the application of appropriate dressings. Systemic factors negatively affecting wound healing are sometimes more challenging to counteract.

While not directly related to wound-healing processes, it is important to note that adequate histologic sampling of wounds at autopsy is necessary to reduce errors in opinions regarding timing. The most robust responses to injury occur at sites of direct tissue damage (27). Typically sampling errors can be mitigated by oversampling.

Local/wound factors

Wound size and type influence the processes of wound healing, typically with larger, deeper wounds taking longer to heal than smaller ones. Wounds with significant tissue damage related to crush injury such as is seen with lacerations or when large regions are devascularized by trauma may stall in the inflammatory phase due to required additional debridement and digestion of dead/dying tissue. Similarly, foreign bodies left in wounds can prolong the inflammatory phase as the body tries to expel or wall off the offending matter.

Other local factors include infection and mechanical re-injury. Ongoing wound infection results in continued tissue injury and inflammation leading to delays in healing and the development of non-healing, chronic wounds (28). Mechanical re-injury can be a function of wound location with some areas of the body at higher risk of re-injury or mechanical stress from movement. Re-injury can show overlapping morphologies with acute features superimposed upon evidence of older wound healing phases.

To some degree, even the orientation of the wound may affect wound healing as wounds perpendicular to Langer's lines of skin tension tend to naturally gape and in the absence of mechanical closure, will require more lengthy healing by secondary intention.

Systemic factors

Blood supply with adequate oxygenation and venous drainage of the wound is required for all phases of healing to support the metabolic and proliferative activities of the various cell types involved in repair. To a small degree, blood supply is dependent on the body region as some areas of the body are naturally more vascular. More commonly and significantly however, blood supply to a wound site is dependent on circulatory status with atherosclerosis and systemic diseases such as diabetes mellitus being the most common reason for poor oxygenation of a particular body region. Localized venous insufficiency also impairs healing by impairing blood flow.

In addition to contributing to impaired oxygenation, diabetes has negative effects on angiogenesis during the proliferative phase. Hyperglycemia can increase oxidative stress at the wound site. In addition, studies on non-healing diabetic foot ulcers show elevated MMP levels, which tip the balance toward net degradation of ECM (29).

Elevated levels of glucocorticoids, whether administered or endogenously produced during times of stress, can blunt inflammation. Circulating cortisol modulates immune responses and stress also reduces the levels of pro-inflammatory cytokines that are important during the inflammatory phase of wound healing (30).

Nutritional status can have dramatic effects on wound healing. Nutritional components including protein, fatty acids, vitamin C, zinc and iron are important for inflammatory processes, biosynthesis of proteins, enzymes and nucleic acids, and oxygenation of wounds (31–33).

Advanced age has been shown to have effects on every phase of wound healing with blunted inflammatory responses, slower synthesis of matrix proteins and reduced capacity for cellular proliferation. As a result, wound healing takes longer in older individuals (34,35).

REFERENCES

1. Witte M, Barbul A. General principles of wound healing. *Surg Clin North Am* 1997; 77: 509.
2. Pool JG. Normal hemostatic mechanisms: A review. *Am J Med Technol* 1977; **43**: 776–80.
3. Golebiewska EM, Poole AW. Platelet secretion: From haemostasis to wound healing and beyond. *Blood Rev* 2015; **29**: 153–62.
4. Rodrigues M, Kosaric N, Bonham CA, et al. Wound healing: A cellular perspective. *Physiol Rev* 2019; **99(1)**: 665–706.
5. Hurst JK. What really happens in the neutrophil phagosome? *Free Radic Biol Med* 2012; 53: 508–20.
6. Winterbourn CC, Kettle AJ, Hampton MB. Reactive oxygen species and neutrophil function. *Annu Rev Biochem* 2016; 85: 765–92.
7. Betz P. Histological and enzyme histochemical parameters for the age estimation of human skin wounds. *Int J Legal Med* 1994; **107(2)**: 60–68.
8. Mosser DM, Edwards JP. Exploring the full spectrum of macrophage activation. *Nat Rev Immunol* 2008; **8**: 958–69.
9. Meszaros AJ, Reichner JS, Albina JE. Macrophage-induced neutrophil apoptosis. *J Immunol* 2000; **165**: 435–41.
10. Heldin C-H, Westermark B. Role of Platelet-Derived Growth Factor in Vivo. In: Clark RAF (ed), *The Molecular and Cellular Biology of Wound Repair*, 2nd ed. New York: Plenum Press; 1996, pp. 249–73.
11. Das A, Sinha M, Datta S, et al. Monocyte and macrophage plasticity in tissue repair and regeneration. *Am J Pathol* 2015; **185(10)**: 2596–606.
12. Vanezi P. Interpreting bruises at necropsy. *J Clin Pathol* 2001; **54**: 348–55.
13. Betz P, Eisenmenger W. Morphometrical analysis of hemosiderin deposits in relation to wound age. *Int J Legal Med* 1996; **108(5)**: 262–4.
14. Mouw JK, Ou G, Weaver VM. Extracellular matrix assembly: A multiscale deconstruction. *Nat Rev Mol Cell Biol* 2014; **15**: 771–85.
15. Frantz C, Stewart KM, Weaver VM. The extracellular matrix at a glane. *J Cell Sci* 2010; **123**: 4195.
16. Clark RAF. Overview and General Considerations of Wound Repair. In: Clark RAF, Henson PM (eds), *The Molecular and Cellular Biology of Wound Repair*. Boston: Springer; 1998, pp. 3–33.
17. Ortéga N, L'Faqihi FE, Plouët J. Control of vascular endothelial growth factor angiogenic activity by the extracellular matrix. *Biol Cell* 1998; **90(5)**: 381–90.
18. Grinnell F. Fibronectin and wound healing. *J Cell Biochem* 1984; **26(2)**: 107–16.
19. Tang A, Gilchrest BA. Regulation of keratinocyte growth factor gene expression in human skin fibroblasts. *J Dermatol Sci* 1996; **11**: 41.
20. Ravanti L, Kahari VM. Matrix metalloproteinases in wound repair (review). *Int J Mol Med* 2000; **6**: 391.
21. Betz P, Nerlich A, Wilske J, et al. Time-dependent appearance of myofibroblasts in granulation tissue of human skin wounds. *Int J Legal Med* 1992; **105(2)**: 99–103.
22. Javaregowda V, Sathyanarayana H, Gouri SRM, et al. A study on postmortem wound dating by gross and histopathological examination of abrasions. *Am J Forensic Med Pathol* 2017; **38(2)**: 167–73.
23. Profyris C, Tziotzios C, Do Vale I. Cutaneous scarring: Pathophysiology, molecular mechanisms, and scar reduction therapeutics Part I. The molecular basis of scar formation. *J Am Acad Dermatol* 2012; **66**: 1–10.
24. Parks WC. Matrix metalloproteinases in repair. *Wound Repair Regen* 1999; **7**: 423–32.
25. Madlener M, Parks WC, Werner S. Matrix metalloproteinases (MMPs) and their physiological inhibitors (TIMPs) are differentially expressed during excisional skin wound repair. *Exp Cell Res* 1998; **242**: 201–10.
26. Mignatti P, Rifkin DB, Welgus HG, et al. Proteinases and Tissue Remodeling. In: Clark RAF (ed), *The Molecular and Cellular Biology of Wound Repair*, 2nd ed. New York: Plenum Press; 1996, pp. 427–74.
27. Ross C, Langlois NEI, Heath K, Byard RW. Further evidence for the lack of reliability in the histologic aging of bruises: An autopsy study. *Aust J Forensic Sci* 2015; **47**: 224–9.
28. Edwards R, Harding KG. Bacteria and wound healing. *Curr Opin Infect Dis* 2004; **17**: 91–96.
29. Woo K, Ayello EA, Sibbald RG. The edge effect: Current therapeutic options to advance the wound edge. *Adv Skin Wound Care* 2007; **20**: 99–117.
30. Godbout JP, Glaser R. Stress-induced immune dysregulation: Implications for wound healing, infectious disease and cancer. *J Neuroimmune Pharmacol* 2006; **1**: 421–7.
31. McDaniel JC, Belury M, Ahijevych K, Blakely W. Omega-3 fatty acids effect on wound healing. *Wound Repair Regen* 2008; **16**: 337–45.
32. Ross V. Micronutrient recommendations for wound healing. *Support Line* 2002; **24(4)**: 3–9.
33. Fuhrman MP. Wound healing and nutrition. *Top Clin Nutr* 2003; **18**: 100–10.
34. Swift ME, Burns AL, Gray KL, DiPietro LA. Age-related alterations in the inflammatory response to dermal injury. *J Invest Dermatol* 2001; **117**: 1027–35.
35. Gosain A, DiPietro LA. Aging and wound healing. *World J Surg* 2004; **28**: 321–6.

CHAPTER

16

Aging of Injuries in the Living and Deceased

Burkhard Madea, Inga Duval and Elke Doberentz

CLASSIFICATION OF VIOLENCE

In the area of forensic medicine, several types of wounds are differentiated according to their origin: blunt force injury, sharp force injury, gunshot wounds, strangulation, injuries due to heat and coldness (Figure 16.1) (1–10).

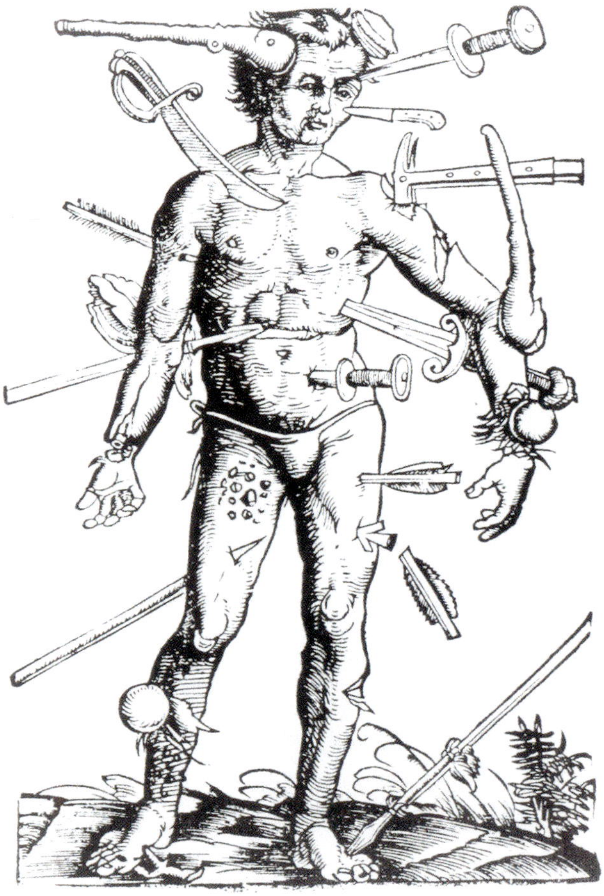

16.1 Different types of injuries (blunt force injury, stab wounds, shot wounds, arrow wounds) from an early sixteenth century book of surgery by Hans von Gersdorf (Feldbuch der Wundartzeney, Straßburg 1528) (4).

Different kinds of trauma cause characteristic patterns of injury and it is often the task of the forensic pathologist to reconstruct the causal mechanism of the injury based on the wound pattern. A detailed description of wounds include: size and exact localization of injuries (not just on the skull, but where on the skull: above or below the hat brim line, at the vertex, at the front or at the occiput etc.), and of course a precise description of the single injuries concerning, for example:

- Size; length and diameter
- Wound morphology (wound surface, wound edges, wound angle, wound edges apposable or tissue defects) (Figure 16.2)
- Discoloration (hematomas: color, demarcation from the surrounding tissue) (4)

Furthermore, wound morphology has to be compared and associated with the case history to determine whether injury findings and described causes of events are consistent. This is a task especially in, for example, cases of child abuse (5,9–11).

Primary causes of death due to mechanical violence are the following (4):

- Destruction of vital organs (brain, spinal cord, lungs, heart)
- Mechanical impairment of the functionality of vital organs
- Bleeding to death
- Embolism (air embolism, fat embolism)
- Suffocation

Mechanical destruction of vital organs occurs for example in cases of multiple trauma caused by traffic accidents, falls from height or railway accidents. Mechanical impairments of the functionality of vital organs include intracranial hematomas (epidural, subdural hematoma), bilateral pneumothorax (e.g. multiple rib fractures with collapse of the lungs), thoracic compression (Perthes thoracic compression) and pericardiac tamponade.

DOI: 10.1201/9781003138754-17

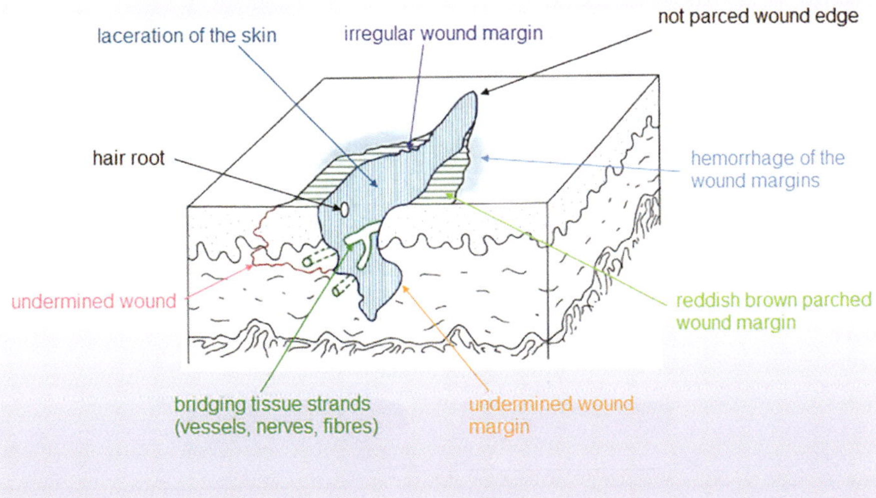

16.2 Morphologic criteria of skin lacerations due to blunt force injury. (According to R. Dirnhofer, Bern with kind permission.)

In case of surviving the primary trauma typical secondary causes of death may be:

- Infections (wound infections, sepsis)
- Embolism
- Circulatory shock (hemorrhagic or traumatic shock) or
- Burns

If the trauma is at least survived for some time, an estimation of the wound age may be necessary. However, even in skin wounds, this may be very difficult due to the following factors (4,5,12,13):

- Different types of trauma
- Different intensity of injury
- Different locations/sites of trauma (for instance with varying vascularization)
- Varying degree of tissue destruction
- Repeated trauma with fresh and older wound response to tissue trauma
- Age, disturbed wound healing

There are different types of skin injuries: for instance, skin injuries due to mechanical trauma, skin injuries due to thermal trauma and skin injuries due to chemical trauma, corrosive poison (14).

Skin injuries due to mechanical trauma include (4,5,14):

- Bruising
- Incised wound
- Stab wound
- Lacerations due to different mechanisms
- Abrasions/excoriation
- Avulsions
- Shot wounds
- Wounds from biting

Skin injuries due to thermal trauma may be (4,15–19):

- Wounds due to hypothermia: erythema, stadium bullosum, necrosis
- Burning wounds } erythema, stadium bullosum,
- Scalding wounds } necrosis, burning charring
- Tissue damages due to electricity

In skin injuries due to chemical trauma/corrosive poisons, the skin is discolored and corroded (14).

WOUND AGE ESTIMATION

Vitality and wound healing or wound age estimation are phenomena which are closely related to each other, in particular with regard to skin lesions. According to Oehmichen (20), one of the pioneers of wound age estimation, there is overlapping in the early phase of repair processes following trauma: alterations within the first 30 minutes can be regarded as both vital reactions and signs of wound healing. Both phenomena (vitality of wounds and estimation of the age of wounds) are central issues in daily forensic casework. They have been major research areas worldwide over the last 50 years. According to the scientific development the fields of interest changed from enzyme histochemistry over immunohistochemistry to molecular pathology (20–24).

In the assessment of corpses, wound age describes the time interval between the infliction of an injury and the time of death. It can also be considered the survival time of the individual following a physical injury. The most difficult question is to differentiate between wounds inflicted shortly before and shortly after death as in the supravital period, especially during resuscitation, local vital reactions may develop even after the death of the individual (25–30).

Generally, various influencing factors must be considered in the time course of wound healing which is comparable with inflammatory processes (Table 16.1).

TABLE 16.1 Factors influencing the time course of inflammation or wound healing

Local factors
• Type and intensity of trauma
• Severity and extension of damage
• Type of tissue
• Temperature
• Circulation
Systemic factors
• Hereditary factors
• Age
• Sex
• Nutritional state
• Diseases
• Endocrinopathy
• Metabolic disturbances
Exogenous factors
• Drugs

Modified according to Helpap (12)

The main questions to be answered are:

- Was an injury inflicted during lifetime and not in the supravital or post-mortem period (vitality)? (27)
- Is it possible to differentiate between vital and (early) post-mortem infliction? (30)
- How long was the survival time after the infliction of an injury (wound age estimation)?

After tissue trauma, there are different time dependent phases of wound repair (Figure 16.3, Table 16.2) (4,13,14,31)

- Blood clotting
- Inflammation
- Tissue formation
- Tissue remodeling

Schematic drawings of wound healing are shown in Figures 16.4–16.6.

After disruption of vessels due to tissue injury, there is extravasation of blood with its constituents with blood clot hemostasis; the blood clot then provides a provisional extracellular matrix for cell migration (Figure 16.5).

Several cytokines affect wound healing (Table 16.3). For instance, platelets do not only facilitate the formation of a hemostatic plug but also secrete several mediators of wound healing. Several cells are attracted by mediators, at first neutrophil granulocytes than macrophages, lymphocytes, fibrocytes. Afterwards neovascularization commences (Figure 16.7) (14,31).

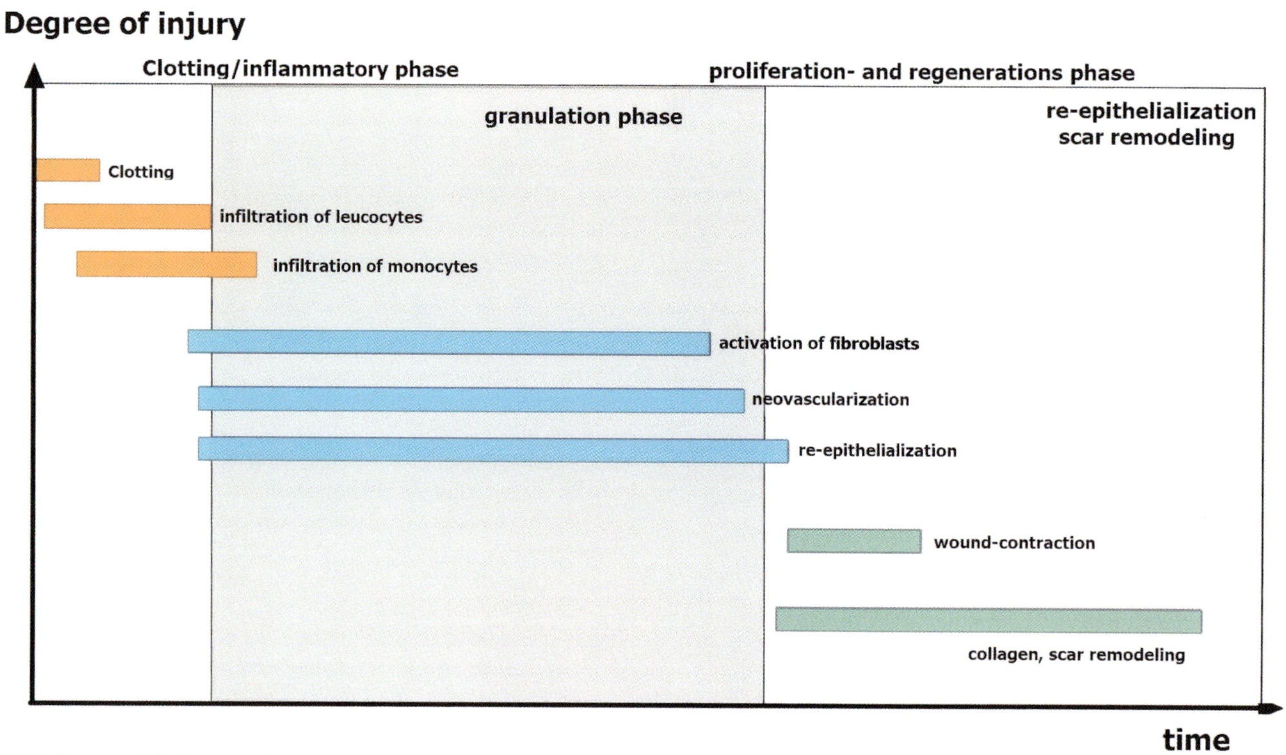

16.3 Sequential phases of wound healing (4).

TABLE 16.2 Phases of wound repair in different tissues (13)

Phase	Mechanism	Interval	Main factors (cellular or molecular mediators)
1	Clotting	Minutes	Fibrin, thrombocytes
2	Formation of a provisional extracellular matrix Wound edema increased enzyme activity	Hours	Fibronectin, fibrin, collagen, Molecules which are released from thrombocytes and neutrophil granulocytes
3	An Inflammatory reaction	Hours	
3.1	Chemokines from neutrophil granulocytes		Some components of the complement system and tissue fibronectin, plasma fibronectin, neutrophils, macrophages
3.2	Migration of cells into the wound		Fibroblasts and endothelial cells
3.3	Fibrinolysis and proteolysis		Macrophages and neutrophils
3.4	Resorption of fibrin degradation products, damaged cells and componence of the ECM[1] by phagocytosis Hemosiderin		Macrophages and neutrophils, siderophages
4	Operative phase Fiber formation	Days	
4.1	Development of a temporary ECM, Granulation tissue Beginning of re-epithelization, neovascularization		Fibroblasts, myofibroblasts, endothelial cells, macrophages
4.2	Formation of a scar (collagen-Type III)	Weeks	Fibroblasts
4.3	Formation of mature scar (collagen-Type I)	Months	Fibroblasts

[1] ECM: extracellular matrix.

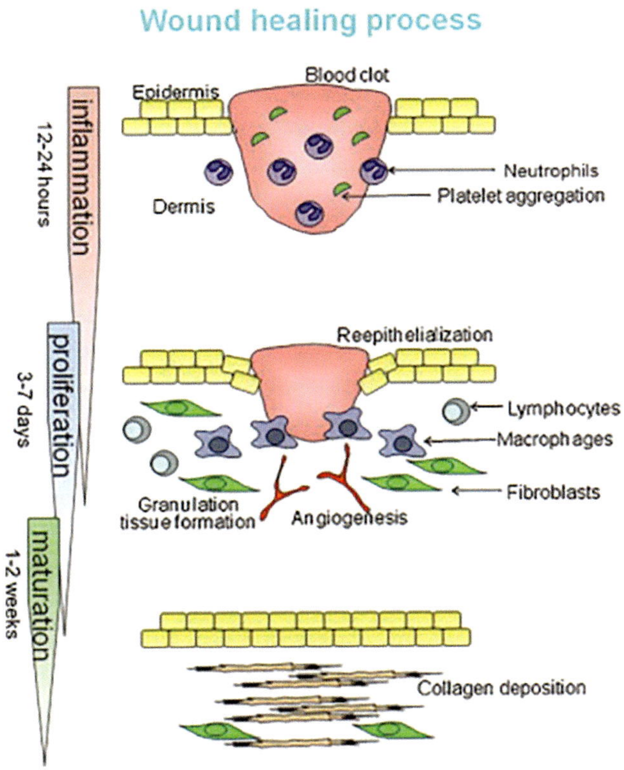

16.4 Schema of skin-wound healing. (Used with kind permission of T. Kondo.)

The biochemistry and immunology of cutaneous wound healing is quite well understood and comprises the following phases (31):

- Hemostasis
- Inflammation
- Epithelialization
- Formation of granulation tissue, proliferation
- Neovascularization, remodeling
- Wound contraction and extracellular matrix reorganization

Healing of skin wounds depends on the kind of skin injury, the origin (type of injury) and of course of the intensity of the skin injury. In clinical medicine, three types of wound healing are distinguished (14):

- Healing by primary intention
- Healing under the hemostatic plug
- Healing by secondary intention

METHODS OF WOUND AGE ESTIMATION

The main methods to address the above-mentioned questions are (Table 16.4):

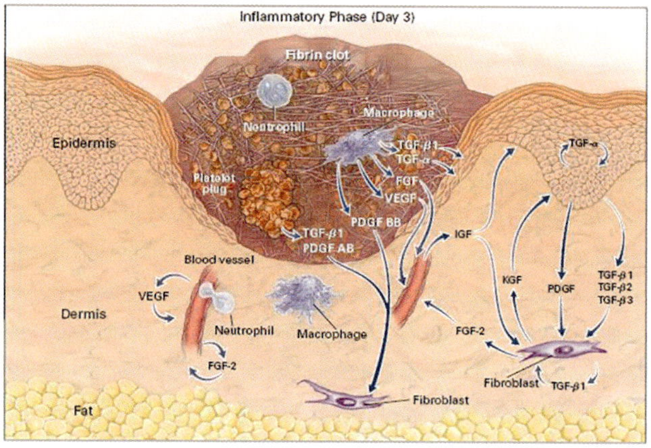

16.5 A cutaneous wound three days after injury. Growth factors thought to be necessary for cell movement into the wound are shown. In chapter 15 it was TGF-1β, TGF-β2, and TGF-β3 denote transforming growth factor β1, β2, and β3, respectively; TGF-α transforming growth factor α; FGF fibroblast growth factor, VEGF vascular endothelial growth factor, PDGF, PDGF AB, and PDGF BB platelet-derived growth factor, platelet-derived growth factor AB, and platelet-derived growth factor BB, respectively; IGF insulin-like growth factor; and KGF keratinocyte growth factor (31).

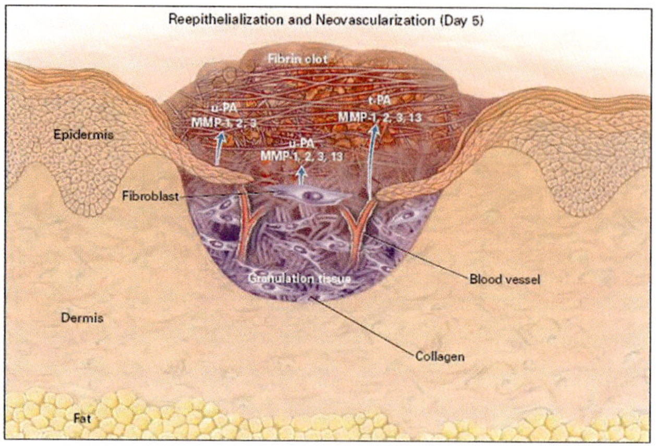

16.6 A cutaneous wound five days after injury. Blood vessels are seen sprouting into the fibrin clot as epidermal cells resurface the wound. Proteinases thought to be necessary for cell movement are shown. The abbreviation u-PA denotes urokinase-type plasminogen activator; MMP-1, 2, 3, and 13 matrix metalloproteinase 1, 2, 3 (collagenase 1, gelatinase A, stromelysin 1, and collagenase 3, respectively); and t-PA tissue plasminogen activator (31).

TABLE 16.3 Cytokines that affect wound healing (31)

Cytokine	Major source	Target cells and major effects
Epidermal growth factor family	Platelets	Epidermal and mesenchymal regeneration
Epidermal growth factor	Macrophages, epidermal cells	Pleiotropic-cell motility and proliferation
Transforming growth factor α Heparin-binding epidermal growth factor	Macrophages	Pleiotropic-cell motility and proliferation
Fibroblast growth factor family	Macrophages, endothelial cells	Wound vascularization
Basic fibroblast growth factor	Macrophages, endothelial cells	Angiogenesis and fibroblast proliferation
Acidic fibroblast growth factor	Fibroblast	Angiogenesis and fibroblast proliferation
Keratinocyte growth factor	Platelets, macrophages	Epidermal-cell motility and proliferation
Transforming growth factor β family	Macrophages	Fibrosis and increased tensile strength
Transforming growth factor β1 and β2	Platelets, macrophages	Epidermal-cell motility, chemotaxis of macrophages and fibroblast, extracellular-matrix synthesis and remodeling
Transforming growth factor β3	epidermal cells	Antiscarring
Other	Epidermal cells, macrophages	Fibroblast proliferation and chemoattraction, macrophage chemoattraction and activation
Platelet-derived growth factor	Neutrophils	Angiogenesis and increased vascular permeability
Vascular endothelial growth factor	Neutrophils	Pleiotropic expression of growth factors
Tumor necrosis factor α	Fibroblasts, epidermal cells	Re-epithelialization and granulation-tissue formation
Interleukin-1	Multiple cells	Macrophage activation and granulation-tissue formation
Insulin-like growth factor I		
Colony-stimulation factor I		

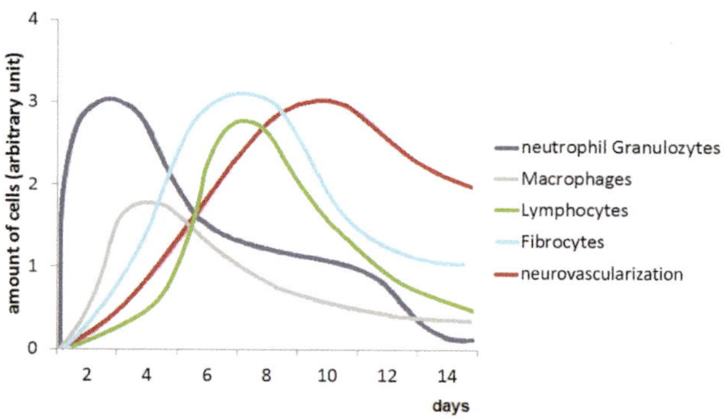

16.7 Time-dependent appearance of the different cells during the granulation phase.

TABLE 16.4 Methodology for studying vitality and wound age estimation (4,27)

Level	Method
Cellular structures	Routine histology Special staining methods
Protein/antigen	Immunohistochemistry Quantitative biochemical methods
mRNA	*In situ* hybridization Rt-PCR

- Routine histology with paraffin embedding of tissue samples and staining with hematoxylin-eosin (HE). For a special differentiation of substructures (e.g. connective tissue, hemosiderophages), there exists a variety of further staining methods (e.g. elastic-van Gieson stain, E.v.G. and Prussian blue stains) (Table 16.5) (13,20–22,24).

By means of the relatively simple routine histology (H&E and additional standard staining) the following basic phenomena can be assessed:

- Hemorrhage
- Detection of (initial) neutrophil granulocytes (ca. 20–30 min) (Figure 16.8)
- Increase of granulocytes and macrophages (hours) (Figure 16.9a)
- Detection of hemosiderophages (3 days) (Figure 16.10a–c)

It is a characteristic feature of wound age estimation that in comparison to data from experimental studies – only a minimum wound age can be determined (the earliest detection of a marker with a special method). It is generally not possible to give time intervals or maximum time spans. Furthermore, it must be kept in mind that many results in the literature are based on cell culture or animal experiments. A critical evaluation of such data is necessary. The highest reliability can be usually expected from studies with human autopsy material.

Furthermore, many investigations on skin wounds were carried out on surgical incisions during operations with informed consent of patients.

Enzyme histochemical methods are not further used in routine casework. Much of the basic experimental research was not reproduced. These methods were more and more replaced by:

- Immunohistochemistry, which is the method of choice in investigations of vitality and wound age. In the last 30 years, numerous parameters have been

TABLE 16.5 Earliest, routine and latest appearance of routine histologically detectable parameters for the age estimation of human skin wounds (22)

Parameter	Earliest appearance	Routine appearance	Latest appearance
Neutrophils (PMN)	15–30 min	>15 h	Months
Macrophages	2–3 h	> 3 days	Months
Macrophages > PMN	20 h	>11 days	Months
Migrating keratinocytes	2 days	>9 days	-
Lipophages	3 days	-	Months
Erythrophages	3 days	-	Months
Siderophages/ hemosiderin	3 days	-	Months
Granulation tissue	3 days	-	Months
Re-epithelialization complete	5 days	–21 days	-
Hematoidin	8 days	-	Months
Lymphocytes-infiltrates	8 days	-	Months

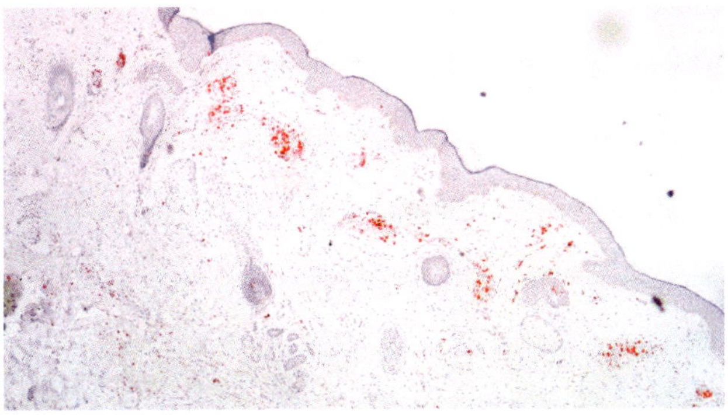

16.8 Leucocytes in human skin wound. Accumulation of LCA positive cells. LCA x 200.

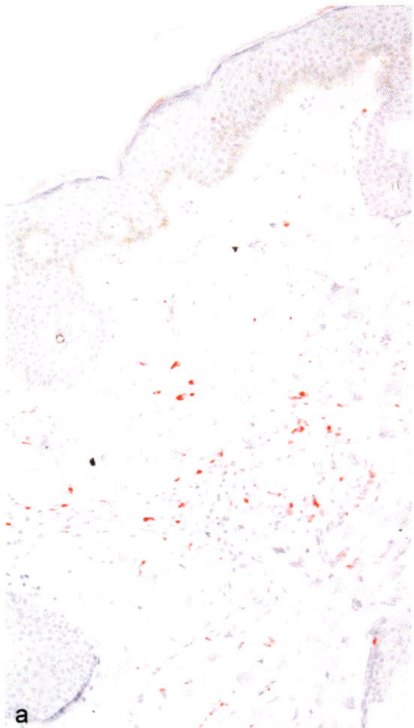

a

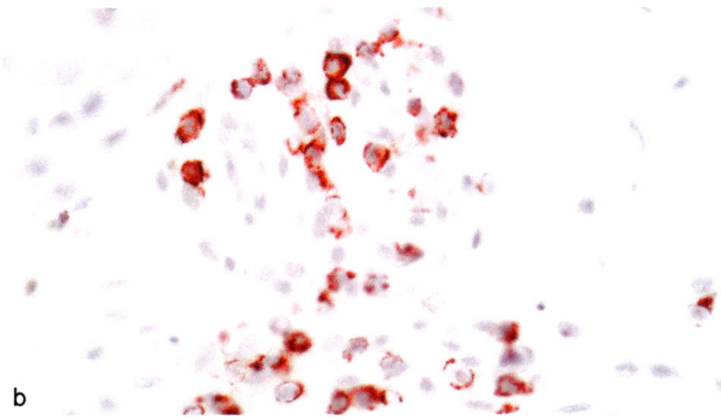

b

16.9 Accumulation of macrophages in incised wound. CD68 x 200 **(a)**; CD68 x 400 **(b).**

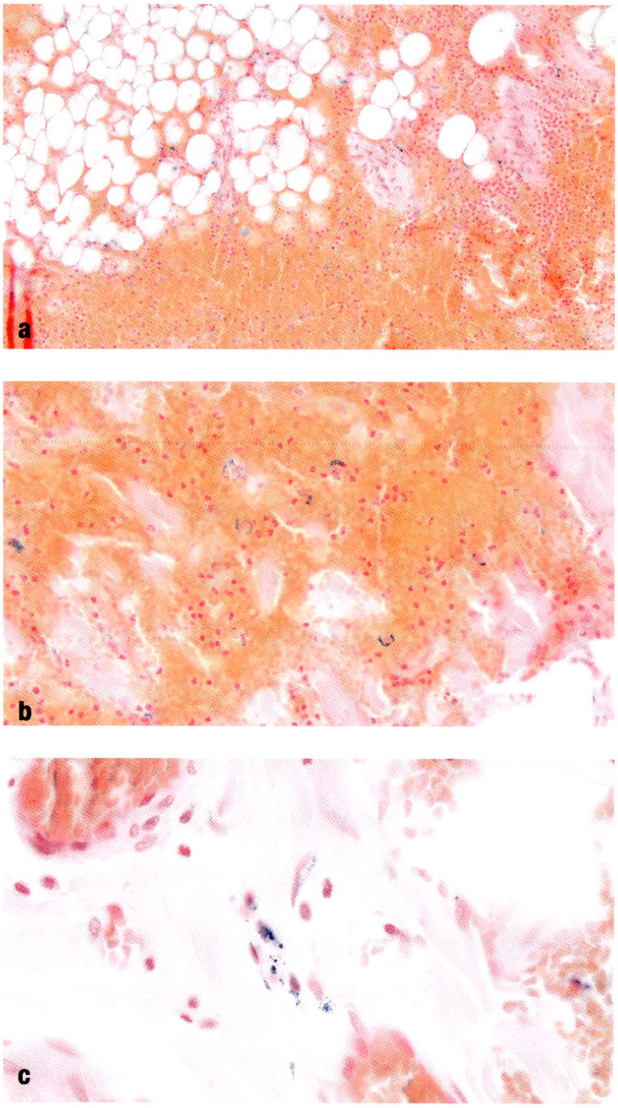

16.10 Siderophages in subcutaneous hemorrhage. Prussian blue x 200 (a,b); x 400 (c).

tested with respect to their time-dependent appearance in wound repair (some examples are given in Table 16.6) (22,23,32–34,55). Besides the parameters given in Table 16.6 further markers such as adhesion molecules (Table 16.7), cytokines and chemokines, growth factor and stress proteins (Table 16.8) have been studied.

Routine histologically detectable parameters for the age estimation of human skin wounds have been investigated for several decades.

However, there are always limitations. Byard et al. (56) have investigated the histologic dating of bruises in moribund infants and young children and came to the following conclusions:

1. Bruises in some young children with severe craniocerebral trauma may be present for up to 79 hours without a leukocyte infiltrate.
2. Lack of neutrophils in a bruise may, therefore, not necessarily imply that the injury is recent (i.e. less than 4–12 h of age).

TABLE 16.6 Examples for wound age estimation by immunohistochemical methods in human skin lesions (4)

Antigen/Marker	Earliest detection	Regular detection or marked reaction	Longest detection
TGF-β1	Minutes	30–60 min	
TGF-α	Ca. 10 min	30–60 min	
Fibronectin	Ca. 10–20 min	> 4 h	Months
IL-1β	15 min	30–60 min	
IL-6	20 min	60–90 min	
TNF-α	15 min	60–90 min	
ICAM-1	50 min	> 2 h	
VCAM-1	30 min	> 1.5 h	
E-selectin	30 min	> 1–1.5 h	
L-selectin	30 min	> 1.5 h	
Tenascin	2–3 days	From 5 days	Months
Collagen III	2–3 days	From 6 days	Months
Collagen V	3 days	From 6–7 days	Months
Collagen VI	3 days	From 6–7 days	Months
Collagen I	4–6 days	From 7 days	Months
Myofibroblasts:			
Laminin	Ca. 1.5 days		Months
HSPG	Ca. 1.5 days		Months
Collagen IV	4 days		Months
SMC-actin	5 days		Months
Marker of macrophages:			
RM 3/1	7 days		Months
25 F 9	11 days		Months
G 16/1	12 days		Months
Epithelial basal membrane:			
Fragments (Lm, HSPG, K IV, K VII)	4 days	From 13 days	Ca. 21 days
Complete restitution	8 days	From 21 days	
Keratin 5:			
Complete staining of basal layer	13 days	From 23 days	

TABLE 16.7 Adhesion molecules (4, 23)

Markers	Earliest	Latest
P-selectin	A few min	7 h
E-selectin	1 h	17 days
ICAM-1	1.5 h	3.5 days
VCAM-1	3 h	3.5 days

TABLE 16.8 Cytokines, growth factors and stress protein (4)

Markers	Positive ratio	Wound age
IL-1α	>30%	4 h–1 day
IL-8	>50%	1–4 days
MCP-1	>30%	1–7 days
MIP-1α	>40%	1–9 days
VEGF	>50%	7–14 days
Ubiquitin	>30%	7–21 days
ORP-150	>40%	7–21 days
COX-2	>50%	8 h–2 days

3. Caution should be exercised in assigning too rigid a time course to bruising in infants and young children.
4. Whether severe craniocerebral trauma plays a role in delaying cellular response in injury is unclear.

Animal experiments with subcutaneous injection of blood had also interesting results (56):

1. Injection of blood under the skin results in a focal inflammatory reaction that is maximal at the site of injection.
2. The local inflammatory reaction, with subsequent formation of hemosiderin following injection of blood under the skin, appears identical to the reaction following local blunt trauma combined with injection of blood.
3. Blood that diffuses from the site of injection produces only a low-grade inflammatory reaction.
4. The intensity of hemosiderin staining has a gradient, from maximal at the site of injection to lowest at the outer limit of blood diffusion from the injection site.
5. Histologic changes observed in a bruise may depend on where the sample was taken from with respect to the site trauma. This has potential implication for estimation the age of bruises.

FURTHER PARAMETERS

Aquaporins

Aquaporins are membrane water channels that are part of the control of the water content of cells (42,51,54,58,59). They are expressed in many epithelial and endothelial cells. Studies showed that aquaporin 3 (AQ3) is considered as a marker of ante-mortem neck compression. In the authors' study, they investigated if AQ3 can be used as a vitality marker for all kinds of ante-mortem skin injuries. The authors were able to show that there is a high expression rate of AQ3 in epithelial cells in all kinds of skin injuries, not only strangulation marks (Figure 16.11a–d). There is no significant difference between the ligature group on the one hand and other forms of external violence to the skin on the other. As already shown by Sakamoto et al. in 2015, although AQ3 is a valuable marker for the diagnosis of vital neck compression and skin injury, it might be a very useful vitality marker of all kinds of ante-mortem skin injuries (42).

HEAT SHOCK PROTEIN

Heat shock proteins (HSPs) are a group of proteins that belong to molecular chaperones (25,43,60–66). HSPs were first described in 1962. They have a cytoprotective function and support cells to survive in (sub)lethal conditions. HSPs control protein biosynthesis by supporting accurate protein synthesis, preventing aggregation of newly folded proteins, and stabilizing various cell structures. HPs are expressed in cells when there is exposure to variable stressful stimuli. HP expression is stimulated by hypo- or hyperthermia, as well as by every other external and internal physiological stress. These stresses include a lack of energy (ATP), oxidative stress, heavy metals, ischemia, UV light, chemicals, injuries, mechanical stress, chemotherapeutic substances and cytokines, which increase the number of these proteins in the cellular cytoplasm. HSPs are also expressed in erythrocytes, macrophages and leukocytes.

As a direct result of hypo- and hyperthermia, metabolism is increased with a consecutive higher requirement of oxygen. This results in metabolic acidosis with destruction of cellular structures.

Important HSPs are HP27 and HSP70, named according to their molecular weight (Table 16.9, Figure 16.12). HP70 is an established marker for cellular stress in heat and fire deaths in the tissue of the upper respiratory tract (Figure 16.11). Whether other organ systems (heart and kidney) express HP in cases of ante-mortem hyperthermic stress is a research area of interest. Identifying a valid vitality marker, which could complete the well-known markers for soot aspiration and ingestion, as well as elevated carbon monoxide blood levels, could be important.

Expression of HPs has been extensively studied in renal and pulmonary tissue (Figure 16.13a,b), especially in cases of hypo- and hyperthermia. HPs are expressed in renal tissue in cases of lethal hypothermia. In a study group of 100 cases of death due to hypothermia, renal glomerular HP 70 expression was observed in 80 percent of cases and renal tubular expression was found in 89 percent of cases compared with a control group (n = 50). Additionally, in this control group, there were short and long agonal periods where no renal glomerular expression was found in 84 percent of cases and no renal tubular expression in 66 percent of all cases.

Extensive investigations on the expression of HSPs have been carried out in fire-related fatalities, in hypothermia, in amphetamine-related deaths and in sudden infant death syndrome (SIDS). In fire-related fatalities, an extensive and different expression pattern of HSP27 and

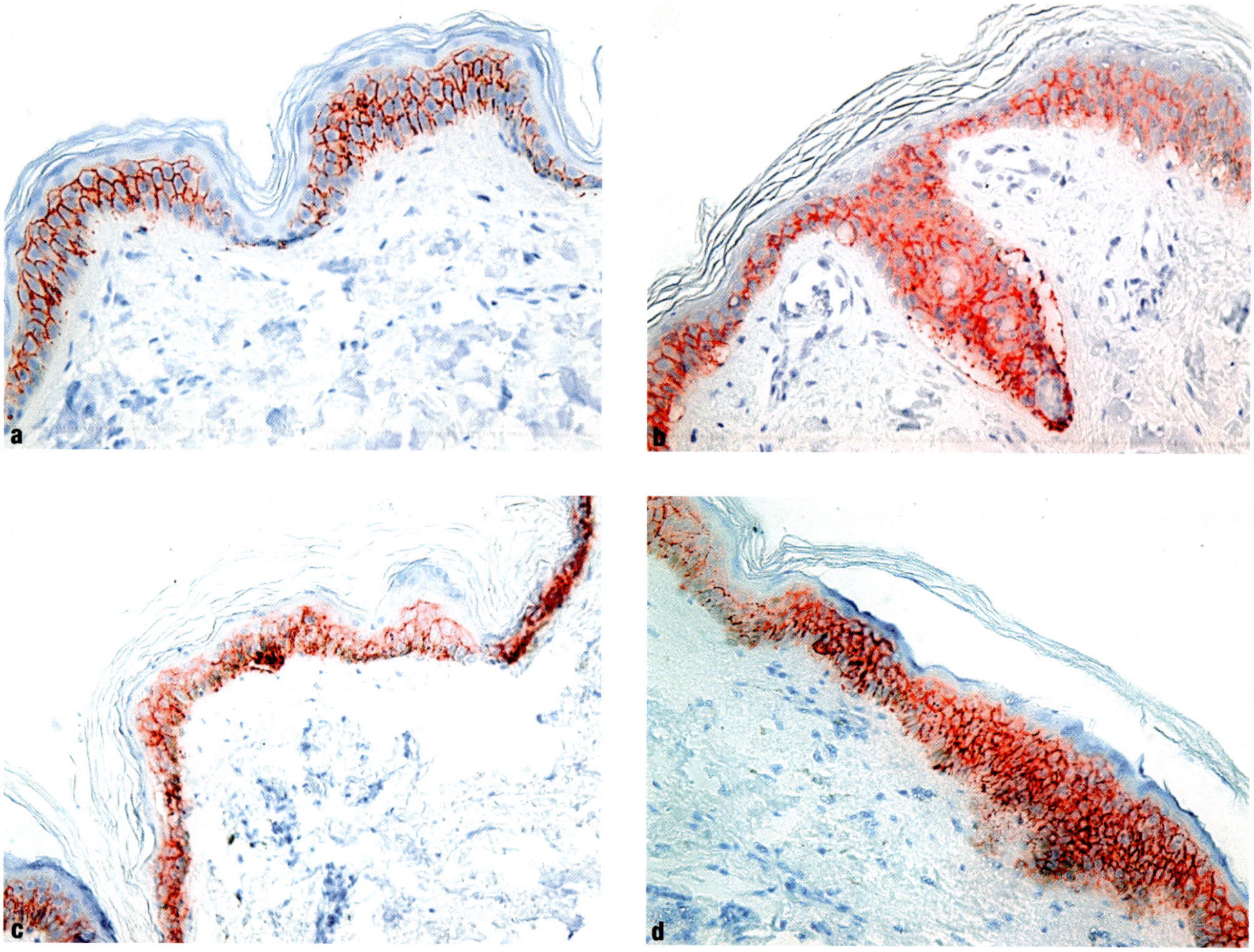

16.11 **(a)** Aquaporine 3 staining, gunshot entrance wound, 100% positive, x 400. **(b)** Aquaporine 3 staining, frost erythma, 100% positive, x 400. **(c)** Aquaporine 3 staining, excoriation 100% positive staining of the epidermis, x 400. **(d)** Aquaporine 3 staining, incised wound, 100% positive staining of epidermis, x 400.

TABLE 16.9 The main HSPs, their localization and main function (1–63)

HSP family	Localization	Main function
HSP27	Cytosol and nucleus	Stabilization of microfilaments
HSP60	Mitochondria	Protection of proteins and repair of proteins
HSP70	Cytosol and nucleus	Protein folding and cytoprotection
HSP72	Cytosol and nucleus	Protein folding and cytoprotection
HSP73	Cytosol and nucleus	Protein translocation
HSP75	Mitochondria	Protein translocation
HSP78	Endoplasmatic reticulum	Cytoprotection and protein translocation
HSP90	Cytosol, nucleus, endoplasmic reculum	Protein translocation and regulation of receptors
HSP100–104	Cytosol	Protein folding

HSP70 according to the survival time can be observed. HSP27 is rapidly expressed in short-term survivors, and HSP70 is higher in long-term survivors. In fire-related fatalities in particular, a very rapid HSP27 expression can be found in the pulmonary tissues, but also in renal tissues. With increasing survival time, HSP70 expression greatly increased, and the long-term survivors had the highest expression levels in all cases. Similar results for the bronchial tubes were found in the pulmonary vessels.

Regarding mechanical and thermal skin injuries, investigations on the expression of HSP are missing. Therefore, we started the investigation of the expression of HSPs 27, 60 and 70 in mechanical and thermal skin injuries in comparison to uninjured skin. Our study

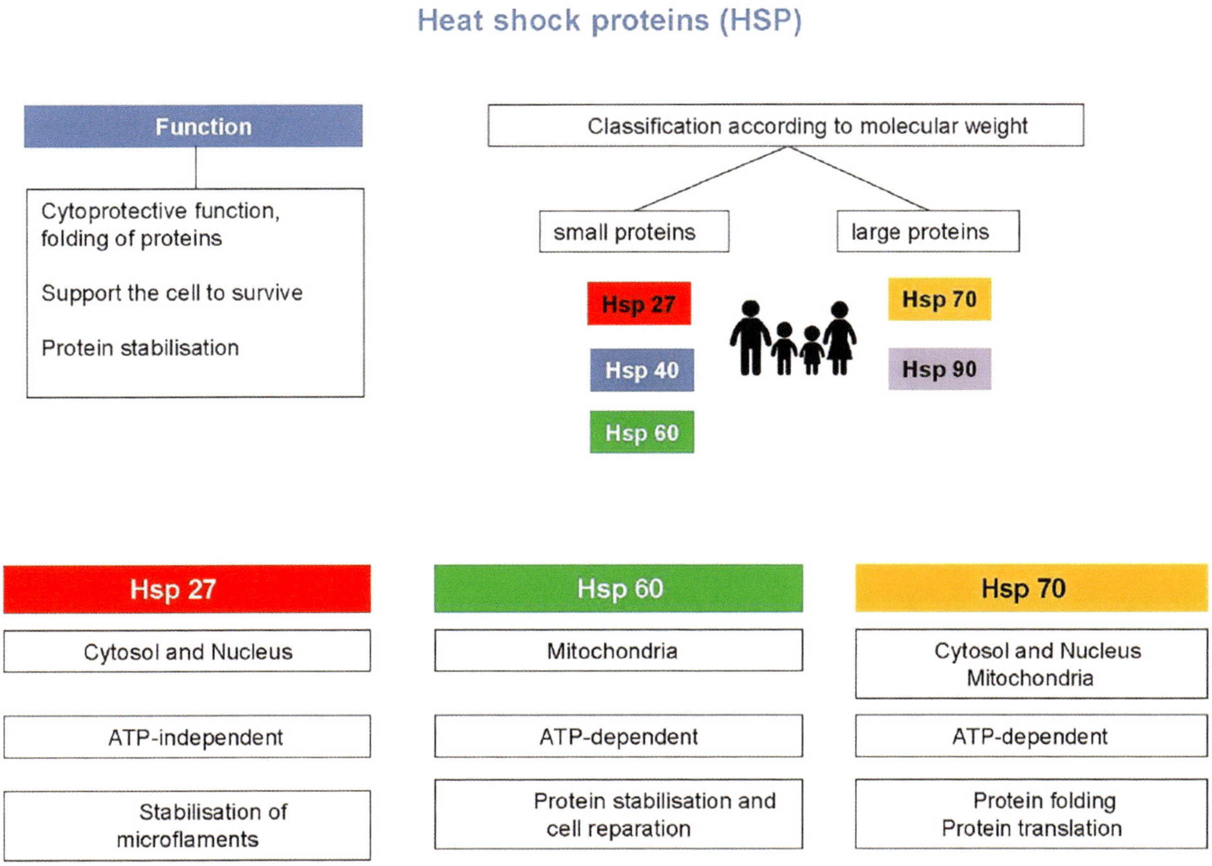

16.12 Heat shock proteins. Classification, function and localization.

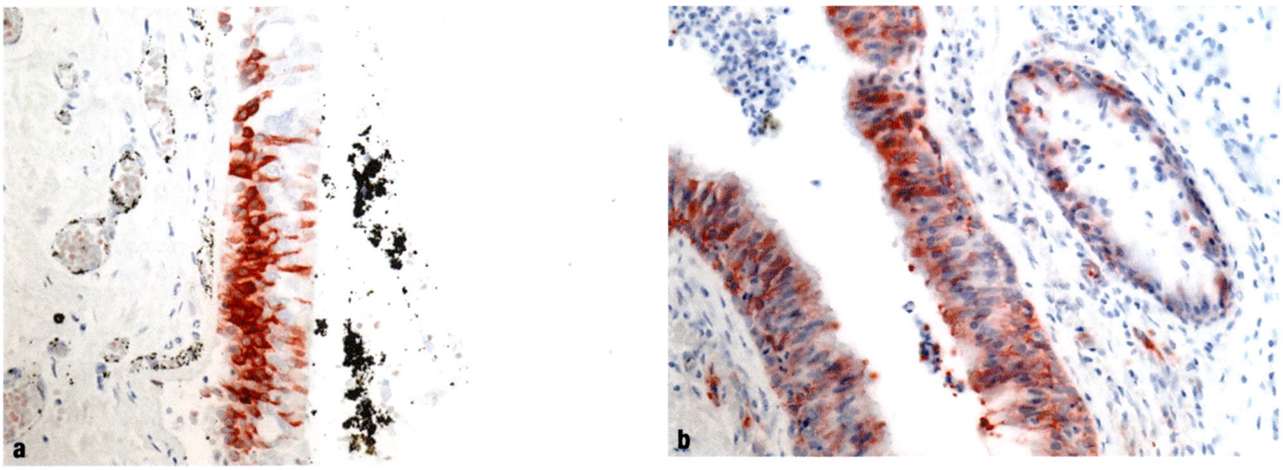

16.13 Heat shock proteins in fire death. Positive expressions of the trachea and soot aspiration **(a)**, and positive expression of intrapulmonary tissue **(b)**.

collective comprises between 30 and 35 cases with an age range of the deceased between 19 and 95 years. The skin injury comprises different kinds of blunt force, sharp force, strangulation marks, thermal injury, gunshot wounds and frost erythema. In all kinds of mechanical and thermal injury, there was a slightly increased expression of HSP 27 than in uninjured skin. HSP 70 showed a marginally higher expression in uninjured skin and regarding HSP 60 only a negligible expression could be observed in both injured and uninjured skin. In conclusion, there were no significant differences in HSP expression between injured and uninjured skin. Therefore, HSP does not appear to be suitable as local vitality markers in mechanical and thermal skin injuries (43).

Whereas the methods mentioned so far serve for the detection of vitality and wound markers on a protein level, it is also possible to analyze the earlier stages of a reaction on the mRNA level (4,23,52). Rt-PCR analysis

TABLE 16.10 Time cause of earlier and routine appearance of different immunohistochemical parameters in closed head injury (67)

Parameter	Earliest appearance	Routine appearance
Cellular reaction		
CD15	10 min	14 h – 1,6 d
LCA	1,1 d	9–21 d
CD3	2d	13,3–19 d
UCHL-1	3,7 d	10–19 d
Reactive gliosis		
α1-ACT	3,1 h	-
Vimentin	22 h	5,5 d – 4 w
GFAP	1 d	1–4 w
MIB-1	3,1 d	7–11 d
Tenascin	7 d	-
Neovascularization		
F VIII	3 h	6 d – 4 w
Tenascin	1,6 d	1–4 w
Thrombomodulin	6,8 d	1–2 w
MIB-1	1 w	1–2 w

could detect mRNA of certain molecules in forensic autopsy samples with early post-mortem intervals. After incision in mice, the local IL-6 mRNA level peaked at 6 h, while the peak levels of mRNA for IL-1α, IL-1β and TNF-α occurred between 48 and 72 h. On the contrary, IL-10 is one of the anti-inflammatory cytokines, IL-10 mRNA started to increase at 15 min, indicating that IL-10 was the most sensitive cytokine. In daily forensic casework, it depends on the aims and the experience of the investigator to select the appropriate method and to achieve the best results for his/her purpose (Table 16.4).

In the past, many investigations on skin wounds were carried out on surgical incisions removed during operations with informed consent of the patients. Furthermore, quite exactly dated skin wounds were investigated. However, systematic investigations of other types of skin injuries are missing, specifically those for internal organs.

Comparable to skin, some systematic investigations have been carried out on the timing of cortical contusions (Table 16.10).

AGE ESTIMATION OF INJURIES OF INTERNAL ORGANS

Beneke (1) addressed the age determination of injuries of internal organs and summarized his experiments and experiences as follows:

> *"Age-determination of injuries of internal organs is of great practical importance in forensic medicine. In most instances, these investigations are performed on cadaver material. Environmental conditions for the cadavers and the post-mortem interval are different from one case to another. The use of modern morphologic methods, such as histochemical enzyme methods or autoradiography are therefore impossible for the determination of age of a tissue injury. Light microscopy must consequently be used for age-determination of injuries. The various stages of the reparative process must be recognized for this method of evaluation. Three general reactions are significant in this process: 1. the degenerative changes of the injured cells, 2. the local reaction of the blood circulation and 3. the reaction on non-injured parenchyma and connective tissue cells in proximity of the injury. The time relationship of these reactions can only be studied in experimental animals. The result of such experiments indicates that time relationship of cellular reactions varies with many conditions. For instance, delay of cellular repair is observed in animals which are injured before or during starvation or hemorrhagic shock. The cellular reaction is also diminished in older animals. Results obtained from animal experiments may only be applied to humans with extreme caution. The histologic parameter of injury to adipose tissue, liver and kidney is demonstrated. The following parameters are of importance. The presence of necrosis or fatty degeneration of the damaged cells, the appearance of polymorphnucleated leucocytes, the appearance of iron-pigment, changes in the size of nuclei and mitoses in the parenchymatous and connective tissue cells in proximity of the injury indicating proliferation, the appearance of new-formed mucopolysaccharides, collagen and elastic fibers. Cellular repair reaction is especially dependent on the extent of the injury. It is impossible to use only one of these histologic criteria. As many as possible of these criteria must be compared and correlated with the conditions under which the injury was inflicted."*

AGING OF BRUISES IN THE LIVING

The aging of bruises is of special importance in child abuse, elder abuse and domestic violence. Typical types of blunt violence and their consequences are shown in Figure 16.14.

Inflicted bruises show a number of different patterns. Hand marks (arms, trunk, cheeks) are common. While accidental injuries may often involve unprotected parts of the body such as the shins, knees or elbows, injuries of "protected" areas (buttocks, thighs and chest) should raise suspicions of physical harm (Figure 16.15) (10,68). Hand marks may be seen as grab marks or fingertip bruises, for example, on the limbs, face and chest wall (Figure 16.16). Another form of appearance is a hand print or linear finger mark (e.g. on the cheek) (Figure 16.17). Slap marks – often two or three finger-sized linear marks – are observed with a stripe effect. Rings may leave a tell-tale mark. Bruising around the limbs (wrist, forearm, upper arm, thigh) are due to gripping

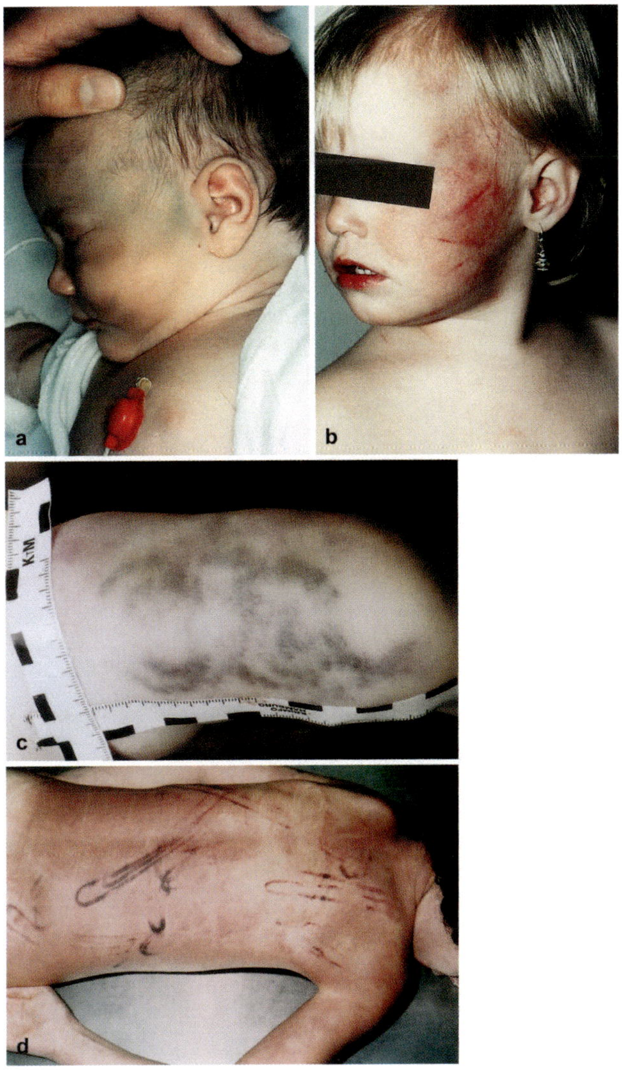

16.14 **(a)** Four-month-old child with a hematoma of left cheek and forehead, taken to hospital by the parents after a "fall from table" immediately prior to hospitalization. The child died 4 weeks later due to hypoxic brain damage. Bruises on cheek and forehead were not recent and there is a typical hand mark on the left cheek caused by hitting with the right hand. **(b)** Two-year-old girl, hit by her father obviously using an object. **(c)** One-year-old girl. Cause of death: craniocerebral trauma. Patterns of subcutaneous hematoma obviously due to hitting with an object on the left thigh. **(d)** Eleven-year-old girl. Cause of death: suicidal hanging. Suicide as immediate reaction after being hit by the mother. Many tram-like hemorrhages of the back, the buttock and the arms.

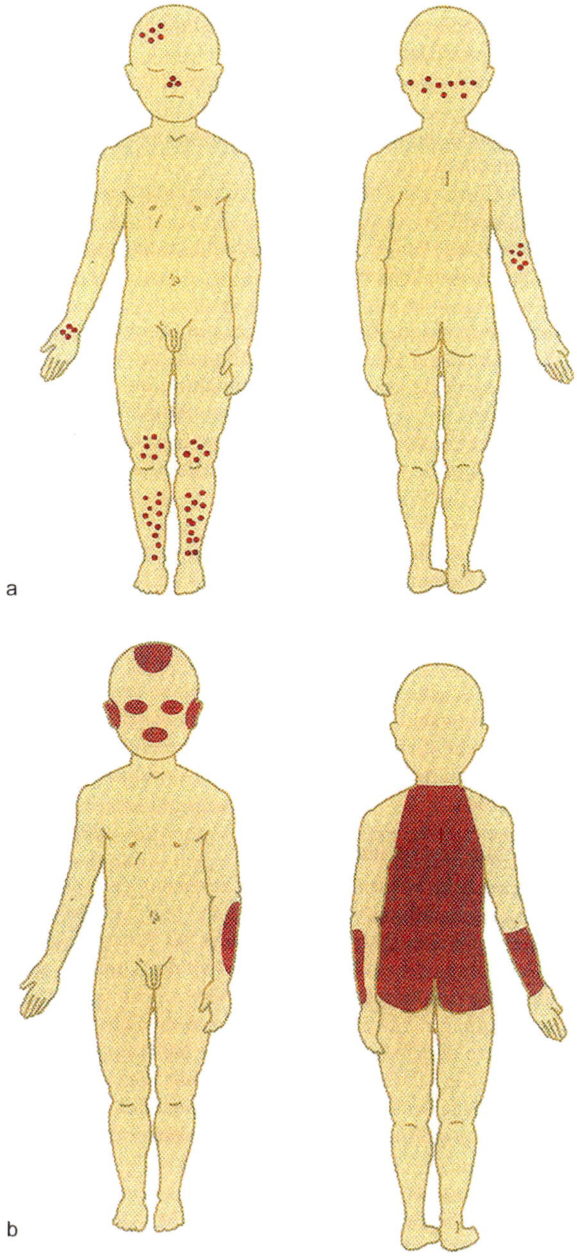

16.15 **(a)** Accidental injuries in unprotected areas like chin, knee, elbow, forehead. **(b)** Inflicted injuries in "protected" areas like back, buttocks, chest, furthermore cheek and top of the scalp (4).

of a child. Bruising on the buttocks and back are often due to being beaten with a hand or a strap. Bruising of the face originates from beating with a hand, with the cheek, mouth, ear and forehead commonly involved. The lips may be swollen, the inner lips lacerated and the lip frenulum damaged. Bruises on the chest and back originate usually from punctate finger pressure. Deep visceral injuries with liver lacerations or rupture of the pancreas and duodenum may occur without visible external signs of violence over the abdomen (3–5).

Tsokos summarized the diagnostic criteria for cutaneous injuries in child abuse as follows (9):

1. The diagnostic criteria for cutaneous injuries in child abuse are localization, patterned bruising, repeated injuries (juxtaposition of injuries of different ages) and clustered injuries (three or more individual injuries in the same body region).
2. Thermal injuries and bite injuries in children are always suspicious of an abusive origin.

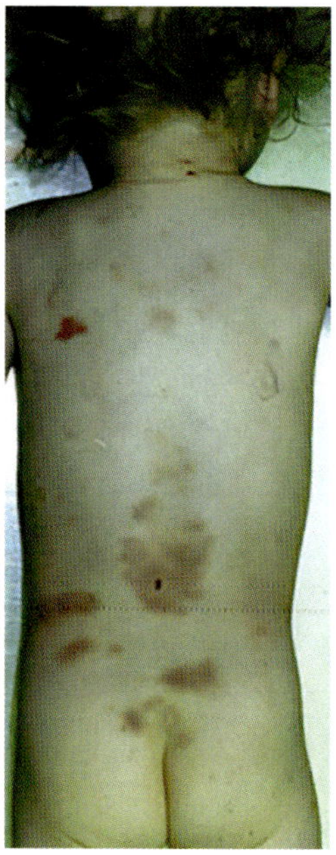

16.16 Bruises on the back showing typical fingertip bruises.

TABLE 16.11 Aging of bruises according to different authors (68)

One scheme (Schmitt 1987)	Age	Color
	0–2 d	Swollen, tender
	0–5 d	Red, blue, purple
	5–7 d	Green
	7–10 d	Yellow
	10–14 d (or more)	Brown
	2–4 wks	Cleared
Other scheme		
	Recent (24–48 h)	Reddish, purple, swollen, tender
	2–3 d	Brownish purple
	4–7 d	Brownish green
	7 d +	Yellow

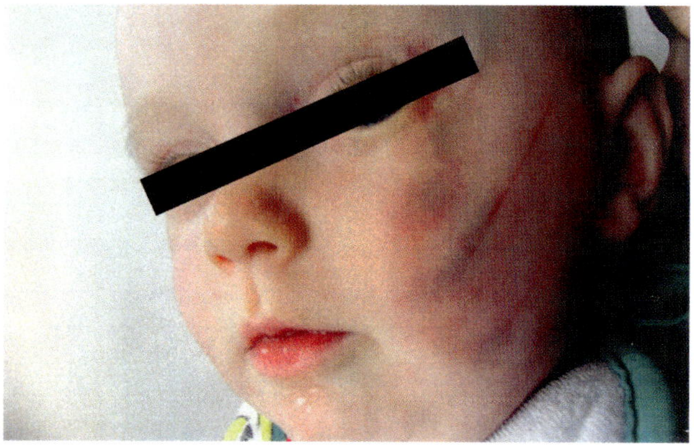

16.17 Typical hand mark on the left cheek with a handprint.

3. Detailed documentation of findings (i.e. photographic documentation with visual scale), among other things, is absolutely essential for any subsequent criminal proceedings.
4. A thorough examination of the whole body of the affected child in a calm and neutral atmosphere, as well as competent and advanced diagnostics as needed (for instance, imaging techniques, laboratory analyses, and consultation by medical specialists), is essential to the well-being of the child – also with a view to exoneration of wrongly suspected parents or caregivers.
5. Possible differential diagnoses of cutaneous lesions in children must be taken into account (if necessary, including consultation by a dermatologic specialist).

Of special importance is the aging of bruises (11, 69–74). The observed age may be at odds with the history given by the parents, and bruises of different ages may indicate injuries happening at different times. Table 16.11 and Figure 16.18 give some clues for aging bruises. There is, of course, a great interindividual variability of color changes and it is impossible to give an exact age of bruises from their color alone. Therefore, it is of utmost importance to document the color and the demarcation of bruises instead of giving a too-precise estimation of their age (10,68,76).

Langlois and Gresham (71) have summarized the opinion of different authors on the time sequence of color changes in bruises in Table 16.12.

Their conclusion is as follows: The appearance of a yellow coloration is a highly significant color change in a bruise ($P < 0.001$). No bruises in the time intervals 0–6 and 7–18 hours showed a yellow color. Thus, if a bruise has a yellow color it is very likely to be more than 18 hours old; unfortunately, it is not possible to assign a probability value to a study of this kind. Older subjects showed a slower development of a yellow color ($P < 0.001$). The colors red, blue and purple/black could occur anytime from within 1 hour of bruising to resolution (up to 21 days in this study). The appearance of red coloration has no bearing on the age as there is no significant change. Although blue and purple/black colorations may show a significant decrease in appearance with time, their small overall change and variability render them unlikely to be useful for aging. It must also be noted that bruises of identical age and etiology on a subject may not show the same color or undergo changes at an equal rate. Therefore, we conclude that a bruise which shows a yellow color must be more than 18 hours old, but the converse (that a bruise without a yellow color is less than 18 hours old) is not necessarily true. However, it must be noted that bruises may not develop a visible yellow color until much later than after 18 hours.

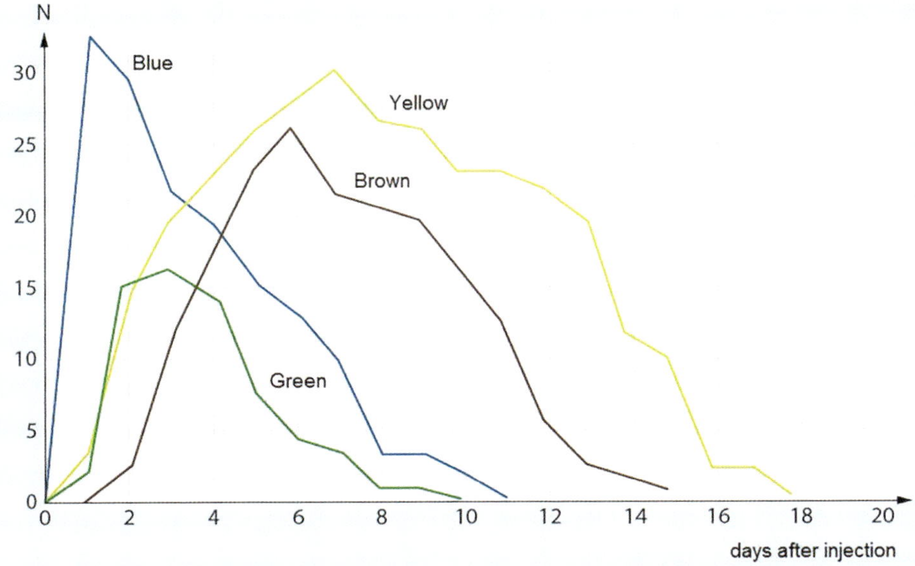

16.18 Aging of bruises after subcutaneous injection of the patient's own blood. Fresh bruises are reddish-purple in color, but already after 24 hours the color has begun to turn to yellow as well (4).

TABLE 16.12 Different authors´ opinions on the time sequence of color changes in bruises (71)

Source	Color(s) in bruises	
Camps	Red Dusty purple/black Green Yellow Resolution	Immediate Soon after Days 4–5 Days 7–10 Days 14–15
Glaister	Violet Blue Green Yellow Resolution	Immediate Day 3 Days 5–7 Days 8–10 Days 13–18
Polson and Gee	Red/dark red/black Greenish tinge Yellowing Resolution	<24 h Around day 7 Around day 14 Up to 30 days
Smith and Fiddes	Red Purple/Black Green Yellow Resolution	Immediate Soon after Days 4–5 Days 7–10, but small and superficial day 3 Days 15

The conclusion on the yellow color is in accordance with a subcutaneous self-injcction experiment of blood (Figure 16.18) (77).

Stephenson and Bialas (75) investigated 50 accidental bruises of known age in 23 children. These bruises were photographed by a medical photographer using the same equipment throughout. The photographs were reviewed by a single observer, blind to the true age of the injury, who described the colors present in the bruise (Table 16.13).

Red coloration was seen in 15 out of 37 bruises, which were less than one week old. Yellow coloration was seen in 10 out of 42 bruises over one day old. Aging in bruises from photographs was much less precise than textbooks imply. The colors which were identified yellow-brown are shown in Figure 16.19.

In Table 16.14, an estimation of the age of bruises from photographs is presented. "Fresh" <= 48 hours; "Intermediate" > 48 hours, <=7 days; "Old" >= 7 days; 24 estimations were correct, 20 wrong.

The authors concluded that aging of injuries from photographs is imprecise, even in a controled research setting.

THERMAL INJURIES

For thermal injuries, there are some rules of thumb as to how long wound healing will take. However, there is a great interindividual difference and only approximate estimations are possible (Table 16.15).

Conditions which may impair wound healing are listed in Table 16.16 (78).

TABLE 16.13 Schemes for the aging of bruises (75)

	Adelson	Rentoule and Smith	Camps	Polson and Gee	Spitz and Fisher
Initial	Red/Blue	Violet	Red	Red/Black	Blue/Red
1–3 Days	Blue/Brown	Dark blue	Purple/Black	Purple/Black	Dark purple
1 Week	Yellow/Green	Green	Green	Green	Green/Yellow
8–10 Days		Yellow	Yellow		Brown
2 Weeks		Normal	Normal	Yellow	Normal

TABLE 16.14 Estimation of the age of bruises from photographs (74)

	Estimated fresh	Estimated intermediate	Estimated old
True fresh	7	5	3
True intermediate	0	10	7
True old	0	5	7

Fresh <= 48 hours
Intermediate < 48 hours <=7 days
Old >= 7 days

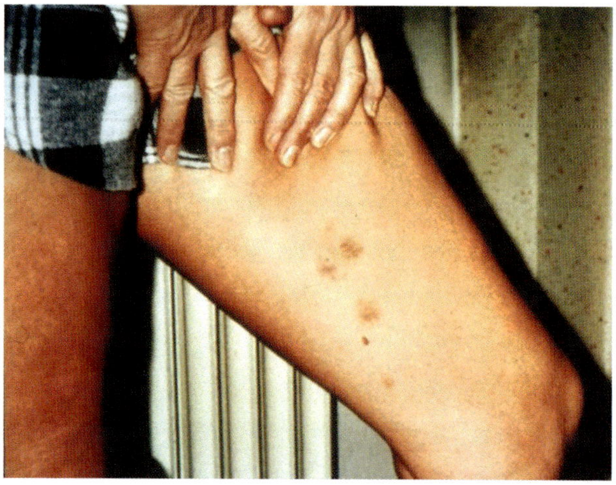

16.19 Woman claimed to have been raped by her friend. She had brown-yellow-colored hematomas of the inner part of the left thigh.

TABLE 16.15 Leading symptoms of burns (4)

Degree	Depth	Color, appearance	Tissue structure	Capillary filling	Sense of pain	Healing
1°	Superficially epidermal	Red	Normal	+	+	5–10 d
2° a)	Superficially dermal	Red, blisters	Edematous	+	+	12–20 d, few scars
b)	Deeply dermal	Pink or white, blisters	Thickened	+/–	+/–	20–60 d, scarring
3°	Transdermal	White, brown	Leathery	-	-	No spontaneous healing
4°	Subcutaneous	Charred	Skin is missing	-	-	No spontaneous healing

TABLE 16.16 Conditions which impair wound healing

Incomplete excised necrotic tissue from initial injury or subsequent rough handling
Delay or incomplete eschar separation
Foreign material – residual nidus of inflammation/infection
Shock–poor perfusion
Septicemia
Abnormal metabolic/electrolytic milieu
Acidosis with or without hypoxia
Hepatic failure – leading to abnormal protein synthesis, etc.
Renal failure – uremia
Prolonged steroid administration – associated with nitrogen and potassium depletion
Immune suppression – renders the immune system ineffective against bacteria, viruses, fungi
Excessive mobilization – damages wound bed, tears off grafts
Starvation – lack of adequate caloric, protein, mineral and vitamin intake

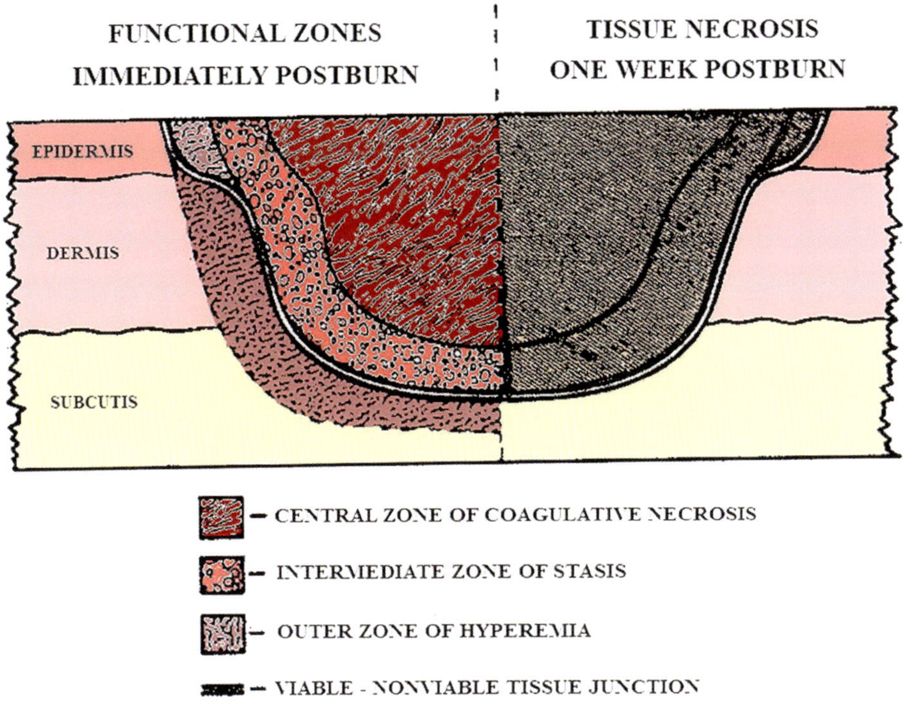

16.20 Functional zones in the immediate postburn period.

FUNCTIONAL ZONES OF THE BURN WOUND

There are three separate "functional" zones in the immediate postburn period (77):

- A zone of immediate coagulation
- A surrounding rim of capillary stasis
- A further surrounding region of hyperemia

The zone of hyperemia is characterized by an almost complete loss of epidermis but not apparent changes in the dermis. The intermediate zone of vascular stasis is in the early postburn period similarly erythematous as the zone of hyperemia but undergoes progressive vascular occlusion during the first 24 hours postburn and terminates in necrosis of tissue in this intermediate area.

The central zone of coagulated tissue appears pale white. Due to the progressive development of necrosis in the intermediate zone within the first 24 hours the apparent development of a third-degree burn is explained.

Full thickness (third degree) burns yield a white- to black, hard, "leathery," inelastic eschar. Coagulative necrosis affects the entire thickness of the epidermis and dermis and usually extends into subcutaneous fat. Deep dermal and subcutaneous blood vessels often contain thrombi. The polymorphonuclear leukocytic response seen at the base of full thickness burns is variable and may not appear for 8–10 days. With wound infection or other stresses, deep partial thickness burns may progress to full thickness through a reduction of patent blood vessels.

CONCLUSION

Although there is considerable research output on the dating of injuries, especially in the dead, the dating of injuries in both the deceased and living remains difficult. Precise estimations are not possible since there is a great interindividual variability of wound healing and numerous factors that influence the determination of the time course of healing and repair.

Furthermore, when considering wound age estimation in the dead, no forensic laboratory will have all of the stains that have been recommended in the literature. More important than precision is the reliability of wound age estimation to avoid a miscarriage of justice.

In practice, this interindividual variability must always to be taken into account and the best we can achieve is a reasoned estimate of the age of a wound.

REFERENCES

1. Beneke G. Age determination of injuries to internal organs. *Z Rechtsmed* 1972; **71**: 1–16.
2. Hagemeier L, Schyma C, Zillhardt H, et al. Gardner-Diamond-Syndrome: A rare differential diagnosis of child abuse. *BJD* 2011; **164**(**3**): 672–3.
3. Kirschner RH, Wilson H. Fatal Child Abuse: The Pathologists Perspective. In: Reece RM, Ludwig S (eds), *Child Abuse: Medical Diagnosis and Management*, 2nd ed. Baltimore: Lippincott Williams and Wilkins; 2001, pp. 467–90.
4. Madea B, (ed). *Handbook of Forensic Medicine*. Chichester: Wiley Blackwell; 2014.
5. Madea B, Noeker M, Franke I. Child abuse: Some Aspects for Neurosurgeons. In: Pickard JD (ed), *Advances and Technical Standards in Neurosurgery*, Vol. 36. New York: Springer Wien; 2011, pp. 80–135.
6. Madea B, Saukko P, Oliva A, Musshoff F. Molecular pathology in forensic medicine: Introduction. *Sci Int Lahore* 2010; 203: 3–14.

7. Reece RM, Christian CW, (ed). *Child Abuse: Medical Diagnosis and Management*, 3rd ed. Itasca: American Academy of Pediatrics; 2008.
8. Smarty S. Battered Child Syndrome. In: Jamieson A, Moenssens A (eds), *Wiley Encyclopaedia of Forensic Science*. Chichester: John Wiley & Sons; 2009, pp. 263–9.
9. Tsokos M. Diagnostic criteria for cutaneous injuries in child abuse: Classification, findings, and interpretation. *Forensic Sci Med Pathol* 2015; **11**: 235–42.
10. Wynne J. Child Physical and Emotional Abuse. In: Payne-James J, Busuttil A, Smock W (eds), *Forensic Medicine: Clinical and Pathological Aspects*. London: Greenwich Medical Media; 2003, pp. 469–85.
11. Banaschak S, Madea B. Child Abuse. In: Madea B (ed), *Forensice Medicine: Findings, Reconstruction, Assessment*, 3rd ed. Berlin, Heidelberg, New York: Springer; 2015, pp. 487–505.
12. Helpap B. *Guide to the General Theory of Inflammation*. Berlin, Heidelberg, New York: Springer; 1987.
13. Oberholzer M. *Understand Pathology. Molecular Foundations of General Pathology*. Stuttgart: Thieme; 2001.
14. Sandritter W, Beneke G. *General Pathology*. Stuttgart, New York: F. K. Schattauer; 1981.
15. Allgöwer M, Sigrist J. *Verbrennungen. Pathophysiologie, Pathologie, Klinik, Therapie*. Berlin, Göttingen, Heidelberg: Springer; 1957.
16. Madea B. Injuries Due to Heat. In: Madea B (ed), *Handbook of Forensic Medicine*, 2nd ed. Chichester: John Wiley & Sons; 2014, pp. 451–67.
17. Madea B, Schmidt PH. In: Brinkmann B, Madea B (eds), *Manual of forensic medicine*, Vol. 1. Berlin, Heidelberg: Springer-Verlag; 2003, pp. 839–74.
18. Moritz AR. Studies of thermal injury III: The pathology and pathogenesis of cutaneous burns in experimental study. *Am J Pathol* **23**: 915–41.
19. Moritz AR, Henriques FC. Studies of thermal injury II: The relative importance of time and surface temperature in the causation of cutaneous burns. *Am J Pathol* 1947; **23**: 695–720.
20. Oehmichen M. *The Health of Wounds: The Theory and Practice of Chrono-Morphoology of Injuries in Forensic Pathology*. Berlin, Heidelberg, New York: Springer; 1990.
21. Berg S. Vital Reactions and Time Estimates. In: Mueller B (ed), *Forensic Medicine*, Vol. 2. Berlin, Heidelberg, New York: Springer; 1975, pp. 326–40.
22. Betz P. *New Methods for Histological Age Determination of Human Skin Wounds: Working Methods of Medical and Scientific Criminalistics*, Vol. 20. Lübeck: Schmidt-Römhild; 1996.
23. Kondo T, Ishida Y. Molecular pathology of wound healing. *Forensic Sci Int* 2010: 203(1–3): 93–98.
24. Oehmichen M, Kirchner H. *The Wound Healing Process: Forensic Pathological Aspects*. Lübeck: Schmidt-Römhild; 1996.
25. Doberentz E, Madea B. Supravital expression of heat shock proteins. *Forensic Sci Int* 2019; **294**: 10–14.
26. Dotzauer G. Idiomuscular bulge and postmortem hemorrhage. *Dtsch Z Gerichtl Med* 1958; **46**: 761–71.
27. Madea B, Doberentz E, Jackowski C. Vital reactions: An updated review. *Forensic Sci Int* 2019; **305**: 110029.
28. Madea B, Grellner W. Vital Reactions. Part 1. *Forensic Med* 2002; **12**: 378–94.
29. Madea B, Grellner W. Vital Reactions. Part 2. *Forensic Med* 2002; **13**: 32–48.
30. Madea B, Grellner W. Vitality and Supravitality in Forensic Medicine. In: Oehmichen M, Kirchner H (ed), *The Wound Healing Process: Forensic Pathological Aspects*. Lübeck: Schmidt-Römhild; 1996, pp. 259–82.
31. Singer AJ, Clark RA. Cutaneous Wound healing. *NEJM* 1999; **341**: 738–46.
32. Betz P. Histological and enzyme histochemical parameters for the age estimation of human skin wounds. *Int J Legal Med* 1994; **107**: 60–68.
33. Betz P. Immunohistochemical parameters for the age estimation of human skin wounds. *Am J Forensic Med Pathol* 1995; **16**: 203–9.
34. Betz P, Nerlich A, Wilske J, et al. Immunohistochemical localization of collagen types I and VI in human skin wounds. *Int J Legal Med* 1993; **106**: 31–34.
35. Betz P, Nerlich A, Wilske J, et al. Analysis of the immunohistochemical localization of collagen type III and V for the time-estimation of human skin wounds. *Int J Legal Med* 1993; **105**: 329–32.
36. Betz P, Nerlich A, Wilske J, et al. The time-dependent rearrangement of the epithelial basement membrane in human skin wounds-immunohistochemical localization of collagen IV and VII. *Int J Legal Med* 1992; **105**: 93–97.
37. Betz P, Nerlich A, Wilske J, et al. Time-dependent pericellular expression of collagen type IV, laminin, and heparan sulfate proteoglycan in myofibroblasts. *Int J Legal Med* 1992; **105**: 169–72.
38. Betz P, Nerlich A, Wilske J, et al. Immunohistochemical localization of fibronectin as a tool for the age determination of human skin wounds. *Int J Legal Med* 1992; **105**: 21–26.
39. Dreßler J, Bachmann L, Kasper M, et al. Time dependence of the expression of ICAM-1 (C54) in human skin wounds. *Int J Legal Med* 1997; **110**: 299–304.
40. Dreßler J, Bachmann L, Koch R, et al. Enhanced expression of selectins in human skin wounds. *Int J Legal Med* 1999; **112**: 39–44.
41. Dreßler J, Bachmann L, Koch R, et al. Estimation of wound age and VCAM-1 in human skin. *Int J Legal Med* 1999; **112**: 159–62.
42. Prangenberg J, Doberentz E, Witte AL, et al. Aquaporin 1 and 3 as vitality markers in mechanical and thermal skin injuries. *Int J Legal Med* 2021; **135**(5): 1837–42.
43. Geile J, Doberentz E, Witte AL, et al. Heat shock protein 27, 60 and 70 as local vitality markers in mechanical and thermal skin injuries. *RJLM* 2022. submitted.
44. Grellner W. Time-dependent immunohistochemical detection of proinflammatory cytokines (IL-1β, IL-6, TNF-α) in human skin wounds. *Forensic Sci Int* 2002; **130**: 90–96.
45. Grellner W. *Cytokine and Adhesion Molecules in Forensic Medicine Vitality and Wound Age Determination*. Aachen: Shaker Verlag; 2004.
46. Grellner W, Dimmeler S, Madea B. Immunohistochemical detection of fibronectin in postmortem incised wounds of porcine skin. *Forensic Sci Int* 1998; **97**(2–3): 109–16.
47. Grellner W, Madea B, Kruppenbacher JP, et al. Interleukin-1α (IL-1α) and N-formyl-methionyl-leucyl-phenylalanine (FMLP) as potential inducers of supravital chemotaxis. *Int J Legal Med* 1996; **109**: 130–3.
48. Grellner W, Georg T, Wilske J. Quantitative analysis of proinflammatory cytokines (IL-1β, IL-6, TNF-α) in human skin wounds. *Forensic Sci Int* 2000; **113**: 251–64.
49. Grellner W, Vieler S, Madea B. Transforming growth factors (TGF-a und TGF-b1) in the determination of vitality and wound age: Immunohistochemical study on human skin wounds. *Forensic Sci Int* 2005; **153**: 174–180.
50. Hayashi T, Ishida Y, Kimura A, et al. Forensic application of VEGF expression to skin wound age determination. *Int J Legal Med* 2004; **118**: 320–25.
51. Ishida Y, Nosaka M, Shimada E, et al. Forensic application of epidermal AQP3 expression to determination of wound vitality in human compressed neck skin. *Int J Legal Med* 2018; **132**(5): 1375–80.
52. Ishikawa T, Kondo T, Maeda H. Innovative concepts and technology for medico-legal consultation and postmortem investigation support center (MLCPI). Available from: http://www.med.osaka-cu.ac.jp/legalmed/eng/index_hojin.html (Accessed 23 March 2023).
53. Kondo T, Tanaka J, Ishida Y, et al. Ubiquitin expression in skin wounds and its application to forensic wound age determination. *Int J Legal Med* 2002; **116**: 267–72.
54. Sakamoto S, Ishida Y, Kimura A, et al. *Forensic diagnosis of compression based on expression of aquaporin-3 but not aquaporin-1 in human neck skin*. Lecture, 94th Annual Meeting of the German Society of Legal Medicine, 2015, Leipzig.
55. Turillazzi E, Vacchiano G, Luna-Maldonado A, et al. Tryptase, CD15 and IL-15 as reliable markers for the determination of soft and hard ligature marks vitality. *Histol Histopathol* 2010; **25**: 1539–46.
56. Byard RW, Wick R, Gilbert JD, et al. Histologic dating of bruises in moribund infants and young children. *Forensic Sci Med Pathol* 2008; **4**: 187–92.
57. Ross C, Byard RW, Langlois N. Does the intensity of the inflammatory reaction in a bruise depend on its proximity to the site of trauma. *Forensic Sci Med Pathol* 2013; **9**: 358–62.
58. Ishida Y, Nosaka M, Shimada E, et al. Immunohistochemical analysis on aquaporin-1 and aquaporin-3 in skin wounds from the aspects of wound age determination. *Int J Legal Med* 2018; **132**(1): 237–42.
59. Sebastian R, Chau E, Fillmore P, et al. Epidermal aquaporin-3 is increased in the cutaneous burn wound. *Burns* 2015; **41**: 843–7.
60. Doberentz E, Genneper L, Böker D, et al. Expression of heat shock proteins (Hsp) 27 and 70 in various organ systems in cases of death Due to fire. *Int J Legal Med* 2014; **128**: 967–78.

61. Doberentz E, Genneper L, Wagner R, et al. Expression times for Hsp27 and Hsp70 as an indicator of thermal stress during death due to fire. *Int J Legal Med* 2017; **131**(**6**): 1707–18.
62. Doberentz E, Madea B. Heat shock protein expression in various tissues in thermal stress. In: Asea A, Kaur P (ed), Regulation of Heat Shock Protein Responses, Vol. 14. Berlin, Heidelberg, New York: Springer; 2018, pp. 429–61.
63. Doberentz E, Madea B. Heat shock proteins: Forensically and clinically important stress markers, Part 1. *CME Contrib Forensic Med* 2019; **29**: 219–31.
64. Doberentz E, Madea B. Heat shock proteins: Forensically and clinically important stress markers, Part 2. *CME Contrib Forensic Med* 2019; **29**: 303–19.
65. Madea B, Wagner R, Markwcrth P, ct al. Heat shock protein expression in cardiac tissue in amphetamine related deaths. *Rom J Leg Med* 2017; **25**: 8–13.
66. Preuss J, Dettmeyer R, Poster S, et al. The expression of heat shock protein 70 in kidneys in cases of death due to hypothermia. *Forensic Sci Int* 2008; **176**: 248–52.
67. Hausmann R. *The Age Determination of Brain Contusions in Closed Craniocerebral Trauma.* Lübeck: Schmidt-Römhild; 2002.
68. Hobbs CJ, Hanks HGI, Wynne JM. *Child Abuse and Neglect: A Clinician's Handbook*, 2nd ed. Edinburgh: Churchill Livingstone; 1993.
69. Grossmann SE, Johnson A, Vanezis P, et al. Can we assess the age of bruises? An attempt to develop an objective technique. *Med Sci Law* 2011; **51**: 170–6.
70. King BR. Aging bruises an inexact science. *Emerg Med News* 2004; **26**: 10.
71. Langlois N, Gresham GA. The ageing of bruises: A review and study of the colour changes with time. *Forensic Sci Int* 1991; **50**: 227–38.
72. Langlois NEI. The Science behind the quest to determine the age of bruises: A review of the English language literature. *Forensic Sci Med Pathol* 2007; **3**(**4**): 241–51.
73. Nash KR, Sheridan DJ. Can one accurately date a bruise? State of the science. *J Forensic Nurs* 2009; **5**: 31–37.
74. Stephenson T, Bialas Y. Estimation of the age of bruising. *ADC* 1996; **74**: 53–55.
75. Schwartz AJ, Ricci LR. How accurately can bruises be aged in abused children? Literature review and synthesis. *Pediatrics* 1996; **97**: 254–57.
76. Tutsch-Bauer E, Baur C, Tröger HD, et al. Investigations to determine the age of artificially placed hematomas. *Beitr Gericht Med* 1981; **39**: 83–86.
77. Panke TW, Mc Leod CG. *Pathology of Thermal Injury: A Practical Approach.* Orlando: Grune and Stratton; 1985.

SECTION

2

Forensic Pathology

CHAPTER

17

Identification of the Deceased

Marianne Tiemensma, Judith Hinchliffe and Joannah Lee

APPROACH TO IDENTIFICATION

Identification of human remains fulfils the legal, ethical and moral obligations to the deceased and their next of kin; it forms an integral part of death investigation. Identification must comply with legal requirements specific to the jurisdiction in which the death investigation is carried out or where the remains have been found. A multidisciplinary team (MDT) is needed for identification and those to be considered for inclusion may comprise forensic odontologists, radiologists, fingerprint experts, DNA experts, police investigators and anthropologists.

The primary identification methods such as fingerprints, DNA, forensic odontology and medical characteristics such as prostheses (especially those having serial numbers) are the most scientifically reliable (1). Secondary identifying features such as general personal descriptions, medical findings, tattoos and personal effects (especially in combination) may provide sufficient information to allow for formal identification where primary identification methods have failed. It is well known that visual identification is inherently unreliable and may be highly erroneous in advanced states of decomposition. Distortion, damage to tissues and the emotional state of the identifier compromise accuracy. Visual identification, however, may be of use when the body is fresh, intact and well known to the identifier.

The approach to the identification of human remains is dictated by the number of bodies involved. Single, or a few unidentified bodies, mass fatality incidents (open, closed or mixed), missing persons or human rights investigations and mass exhumations, each have different requirements. The condition of the remains (intact, decomposed, incinerated, fragmented, commingled or mutilated beyond recognition), the specific setting, and the facilities available also modify the approach.

Categories of identification comprise (a) tentative, (b) presumptive, and (c) positive. Each category is characterized by particular attributes that correspond with the level of certainty (see Table 17.1) (2). Admissibility criteria varies among jurisdictions and countries (3). Exclusion can be as important as positive identification.

TABLE 17.1 Categories of identification

Category of identification	Description
Tentative	Implies suspected identity based on circumstantial materials, for example, procurement of a driver's licence from the decedent's wallet.
Presumptive	Includes additional identification attributes such as those characterizing the decedent or the place of death.
Positive	Requires the successful demonstration of individualization or expert confirmation of a particular set of characteristics unique to the decedent.

IDENTIFICATION OF HUMAN REMAINS OUTSIDE THE SETTINGS OF MASS DISASTER OR EXHUMATION

Identification of the deceased starts at the scene with investigators collecting items of interest that may assist with identification. These items include various forms of documentation (identification material such as bank cards, drivers' licenses, passports and other items that may contain personal details). This type of identification is tentative and will have to be confirmed by visual (if appropriate) or, preferably, scientific means.

Pathologic examination of the remains

The forensic pathologist plays an important role that includes carefully recording general and specific morphologic features/characteristics and collecting samples for DNA analysis. The array of post-mortem characteristics is then matched with antemortem parameters of a named individual. The specific feature, or combination of features, will add weight to the conclusions.

DOI: 10.1201/9781003138754-19

General characteristics to record, preferably on a standardized template, include:

- Height and weight of the body
- General body build
- Sex
- Color, modifications, length and style of head hair
- Body hair: distribution, and any particular features, such as hirsutism
- Skin pigmentation (however, it is advisable to reserve opinion in a decomposed body)
- Identifying racial and ethnic features, such as tribal scarification, epicanthic folds
- Eye color where possible (only reliable in a non-decomposed body) and the presence of contact lenses
- Estimated age:
    - One should resist the temptation to be too dogmatic when estimating age, especially in persons over the age of 25 years where ossification centers and dental development stages are completed.
    - In fetuses, the general appearances, weight, crown-to-heel length, crown-to-rump length, foot length, head circumference, and ossification centers are all deployed to determine the gestational age. Foot length is generally considered to be a reliable parameter particularly when other parameters (such as short-limb dysplasia, hydrocephalus or anencephaly) may not accurately predict gestational age (4).
    - In children, teenagers and young adults, physical maturation, together with the growth stages of the skeleton and dentition assist with determining age. However, this is not without difficulty, notably in the context of migrant and mixed populations and the unavailability of updated population-specific charts to compare anthropometric measurements (5).

Specific characteristics should be described carefully and ideally documented photographically with the description of the site and appearance of any identifying features. These include:

- Physical deformities
- Scars – surgical, tribal, self-harm, or mutilating scars
- Evidence of any medical or surgical intervention, such as implantable cardiac devices, joint replacements, or breast implants, many of which display a manufacturer's symbol and the unique serial number permitting a link to the specific individual (Figure 17.1)
- Tattoos
- Body piercings and jewellery
- Teeth (any evidence of dental work should be referred to a forensic odontologist for specialist opinion)
- Occupational stigmata
- Personal effects and clothing (including brands, sizes, fabric designs, and contents of pockets).

These sets of characteristics can be compared with available antemortem records and information obtained by other investigating agencies.

When one, or a few, intact bodies are discovered at a location where the person or persons were known to frequent or reside, then circumstantial visual identification by a close relative or friend, together with matching of ante- and post-mortem features, may satisfy the legal requirements without the need for further confirmatory investigations. However, where any doubt exists, it is recommended that identification is confirmed by means of fingerprint examination, forensic dental examination or DNA analysis.

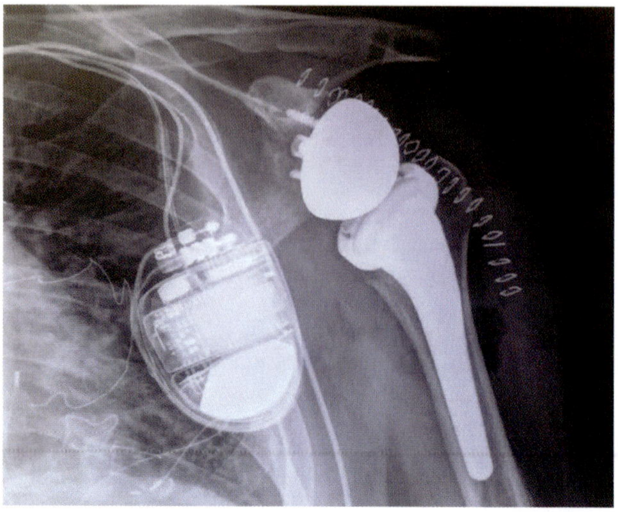

17.1 Evidence of a unique combination of medical (implanted cardiac device) and surgical (shoulder joint prostheses) interventions on radiographic examination that may assist with identification.

In dealing with mutilated (including fragmented or decomposed) remains, surviving characteristics and distinguishing features should be documented. Additionally, the body should undergo post-mortem radiologic examination (whole body X-ray or computerized tomography [CT] scanning) where facilities are available (6). Samples should be collected for DNA analysis. Forensic dental examination and fingerprinting can be arranged at this stage.

Fingerprint examination

Fingerprint comparison remains one of the most commonly used and cost-efficient identification techniques. Antemortem fingerprints may be available from national fingerprint database(s), or in the event that the person has never provided fingerprints for criminal or employment purposes, comparison to prints located at the individual's home or on a personal effect can provide a robust sample for comparison.

It can still be possible to obtain full or partial fingerprints from mutilated, mummified or decomposed bodies even when there is skin slippage (7,8). Special care should be taken when handling fragile skin.

Post-mortem radiology

Post-mortem radiology (whole body X-ray and/or CT scan) is a valuable and increasingly available tool for medicolegal death investigation. This can supplement the traditional autopsy external examination (where an autopsy may be difficult or has been declined).

Post-mortem radiologic examination is advised in all cases where identity has to be confirmed, as this can provide highly valuable information, and it is a permanent record of characteristics of the remains. Comparative radiography by imaging experts may be utilized where antemortem radiographs are available. Typically, post-mortem radiographs that simulate the antemortem radiographs in scope and projection should be performed where possible. Point-by-point comparison should be made for consistencies and inconsistencies including bone morphology, deformity, or pathology, the presence of foreign materials, and skull and dental features.

DNA analysis

As one of the primary identifiers, the selection of a suitable sample for DNA analysis may be crucial for identification. Table 17.2 details the sampling types and quantities of tissue required. It is recommended that the local DNA laboratory be contacted as legislative requirements and workflow considerations may affect the sample preference of the analyst.

For critical or complex cases, it is recommended that a forensic biologist be in attendance or be available by telephone in order to provide sampling guidance. It is recommended that at least two samples be collected from each body or body fragment.

TABLE 17.2 Preferred subsample types for DNA-based identification of unknown human remains*

Circumstances of remains	Preferred subsample
Intact/ non-decomposed	Blood (i.e. FTA® Card, swab)
	Toenail
	Tissue (deep-seated red muscle preferred) including any internal organs
Decomposed	Toenail
	Bone – protected and intact
	Invertebral disk
Skeletonized (whole)	Petrous temporal bone (pyramid shaped bone at the base of the skull between the sphenoid and occipital bones)
	Intact femur
	Intact other long bone
	Intact tooth (molar preferred)
Partial skeleton	Intact/undamaged bone is preferred
	Refer to general rule above, if available
Incinerated	Bladder swab (i.e. internal lining)
	Intact vertebra
	Intact bone
Water-immersed	Bone – protected and intact
	Toenail

* Developed by Forensic Biology Team of the Northern Territory Police, Australia.

DNA technology is rapidly evolving, and a number of different techniques and database types exist. The most common DNA analysis technique in use today for both criminal cases and missing persons'/unknown Human Remains (UHR) is STR (short tandem repeat) analysis. There are a range of kits on the market in use in different countries and laboratories varying from around 10 to 20 autosomal STR loci. A sex marker providing an indicator of the sex of the donor is also included and at times other loci such as Y chromosome STR or indels are also included. The majority of the Criminal DNA databases currently in use are based on STR loci and the focus of these databases is to locate a match between an "unknown" and a "known" sample. In some jurisdictions, these databases are also used for the identification of missing persons. Alternatively, there may be a separate DNA database for this purpose. More recently, the ability of some databases to permit familial matching (generally parent – child or sibling – sibling matching) has enabled DNA databases to be used to search for family members of a donor. Unlike traditional "direct" matching, familial matching tends to result in a list of potential family members which must then be investigated. Y-STR (STRs located on the male Y-chromosome) is also available in some jurisdictions and can also provide a potential match to a male relative. This ability leads to investigations of the feasibility of using Y-STRs to predict surnames and indeed has found some success with rare surnames (9). Some DNA databases now also facilitate matching using a specific pedigree tree. This enables the searching of a database using a number of more distant relatives. For example, where a close family member such as a parent, child or sibling is not available, a pedigree including a number of more distant relatives (cousins, aunts/uncles) may enable a match.

More recently, the introduction of Massively Parallel Sequencing (MPS) technology has raised the possibility of using DNA in other ways. These include ancestry testing (i.e. likely ethnic origin), phenotypic testing (the prediction of appearance traits, i.e. likely hair, eye and skin color) and genetic genealogy. Forensic DNA phenotyping and ancestry determination can provide investigative leads to trace unknown persons who are unidentifiable with current comparative DNA profiling. Some pigmentation traits are predictable with reasonably high accuracies giving investigators important information about the unknown individual and importantly excluding potential missing persons (10). DNA Phenotyping has been used to create composite images of the deceased persons and has assisted in a number of identifications (11).

The use of a genetic genealogy database for identification received intense media scrutiny after the GEDmatch Database was used to identify the Golden State Killer, a former police officer who evaded detection during his 10-year plus notorious killing spree from the mid-seventies to the mid-eighties in the United States (US). Genetic genealogist Barbara Rae-Venter was able to identify him as a suspect after a sample of his DNA was uploaded to GEDmatch. The resulting potential match to a distant relative provided investigators with information that eventually led to the suspect (12). However, as a result of this, media scrutiny and the potential privacy and ethical issues raised, many genealogy companies now have an "opt in clause" and only those who indicate they are willing for their DNA to be used by police can be tested. This will reduce the power of these databases to be used for the identification of unknown individuals.

Similarly, genetic genealogy was also used to identify the "Buckskin Girl" (named after the distinctive jacket she wore), 37 years after her death in Ohio, US. A sample from her remains was uploaded to GEDmatch after her case was taken on by the DNA Doe Project. This resulted in a potential match to a first cousin once removed. The DNA Doe Project has since gone on to make identifications in a number of other cold cases (13,14).

Forensic odontology (dentistry)

Forensic odontology combines the collection, management, evaluation, preservation and presentation of dental evidence, and its application to the legal system. The most common role of the forensic odontologist is the identification of missing or unknown persons and has proved to be extremely reliable over the years. Teeth are very resilient being protected by the orofacial structures and tissues and can survive most conditions of nature that may destroy other body tissues. Dental enamel is the hardest biological substance in the human body. However, successful and timely identification is largely dependent on the availability and accuracy of the antemortem dental record that can be compared with the post-mortem dental findings (15) (Figure 17.2a and b).

Any discrepancies between the two datasets must be explainable. A positive identification can be established from a few teeth or even a single tooth provided there are sufficient unique features. Additionally, teeth may provide a good source for DNA analysis.

Good quality dental records are an essential component of dental care, a medicolegal requirement and necessary for identification, but the quality of the records varies within countries and from country to country, as does the length of time the dentist must keep those records. Nowadays, records are mostly digital. Records may be obtained from a dental practice, dental hospitals, specialists and health centers. It is worth noting that medical departments may have information about the dentition from image capture for other conditions/diagnoses.

Post-mortem radiographs are invaluable for revealing "hidden" dental information including tooth-colored restorations (that may be overlooked in a clinical examination), root canal treatments, implants, signs of recent or old trauma (pins, wires and plates) and pathologies. Tooth and root/pulp chamber morphology, along with trabecular bone patterns, can all be visualized on radiographic images and used to compare with antemortem images. Post-mortem CT scanning is increasingly useful when available along with handheld portable X-ray machines which can be mains and battery operated (16). Dental implants are frequently used to replace missing teeth or entire dentitions and research has shown that dental implants can often be radiographically differentiated by company type. Implants have batch numbers which can often withstand high temperatures; it is unfortunate that they do not have individual serial numbers that associate them with a particular recipient (17). Jaws are not removed for examination except when other access methods are not possible. If removed (with appropriate authority) they should be carefully labeled and returned to the body.

If no antemortem record is available, the odontologist may assist other disciplines to narrow the population search by providing post-mortem information on dentition status, ancestry, behavioral habits (for example, grinding of the teeth as in bruxism), systemic disease, smoking status and dietary habits. Age estimation at the time of death is widely used (especially for children and young adults) to narrow the field of search and should be population and gender specific. Smiling photographs showing teeth (now readily available from social media) may provide valuable information about the anterior dentition and permit superimposition which can be an alternative antemortem dental source in cases with no dental records (18). All this

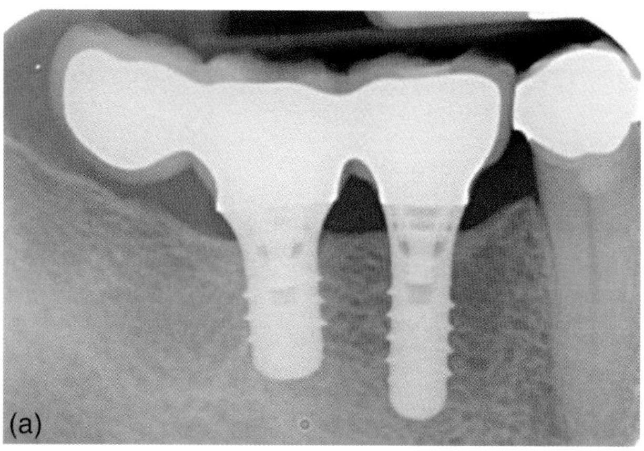

(a)

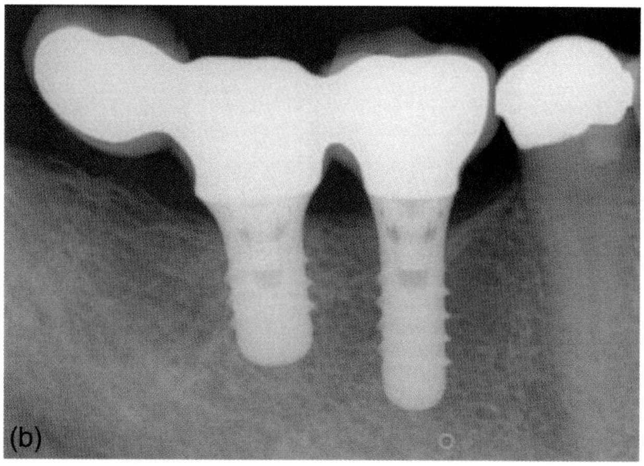

(b)

17.2 **(a)** Case 1: Antemortem radiograph – dental implants. **(b)** Case 1. Post-mortem radiograph – dental implants (Printed with permission from South Australian Coroner).

information will enable the creation of a post-mortem profile for the deceased.

Forensic anthropology

Where only skeletal remains are present, the expertise of a forensic anthropologist is invaluable through appraisal of ante- and post-mortem skeletal information. Forensic anthropology is concerned with the examination of material believed to be human to answer medicolegal questions, including those related to identification (19). The forensic anthropologist plays an important role in recovering and identifying fragmented human skeletal remains, differentiating human from non-human remains, establishing basic biological information such as the sex, age, and at times, the ethnic origin of the individuals, and confirming or denying the possibility of reassociating body parts for release to families.

However, where no anthropologist is available, the forensic pathologist should be able to make some general comments on the observed characteristics of the skeletal remains. The skeletal remains should be evaluated to determine whether they are human bones and whether one or more body is involved. Opinions should be expressed on the stature, age, sex and possible ancestry of the remains, particularly where the skull, long bones and pelvis are present. The findings should be carefully documented and photographed, and ideally, certain key parts should be retained for later examination where no local anthropologist is readily available.

Semi-scientific methods

Other techniques that may be utilized where routine methods fail to allow for positive identification include forensic artwork, craniofacial identification, including facial reconstruction and video-photograph and radiographic superimposition/subtraction. Facial reconstruction is a specialized technique, which may assist with a tentative identification of the remains and subsequent positive identification especially if antemortem dental records can be obtained and compared. With video-photo superimposition, a life photograph of a missing person is superimposed on a photograph of the unidentified skull, or the skull itself using video equipment. This technique is useful for exclusion (20).

IDENTIFICATION OF HUMAN REMAINS IN A MASS FATALITY/ DISASTER

Identification of human remains in a mass fatality/disaster setting requires a well-structured and planned approach. The aim of Disaster Victim Identification (DVI) is to ensure a scientific and reliable identification of each victim in a dignified and sensitive manner (*see* Chapter 96 – "Disaster Victim Identification"). It is essential that the examination of human remains, and the identification process, is undertaken by qualified and competent personnel (21).

When dealing with large numbers of fatalities, it is practical and sensible to use standardized, international forms (INTERPOL forms are widely used) and terminology to record all relevant ante- and post-mortem data which can be incorporated into computer software ready for the reconciliation (comparison) process.

A unique reference number is given to each body or body fragment, and this will stay with those remains throughout all identification stages until identification is finalized and ratified allowing for body release and repatriation. There is an ethical duty to observe and record all information and retain appropriate samples potentially relevant to identification (22). Recognizing that visual identification can be unreliable, the International Criminal Police Organization (INTERPOL) Disaster Victim Identification Guide recommends that human remains discovered at a mass fatality incident should be stored prior to appropriate formal identification and release. The methodology for identification is the same as for an individual case, with appropriate quality assurance, but large numbers of fatalities lead to a complex and challenging situation. Where fragmentation has occurred, DNA analysis of the remains may allow for reassociation of body parts. The different disciplines can pull together and share information to maximize the chance of identification and release of the remains to families or friends. Each incident should be assessed, and the most effective method(s) selected.

Debriefing of the teams is an essential step at the end of the deployment to better understand what worked well and what did not for future improvement. Mental welfare of the teams must always be considered.

MISIDENTIFICATION

Misidentification may result from commingling of remains, the distortion of identifying features by injury or post-mortem changes (such as muscular flaccidity and decomposition), the emotive state of the deceased's next of kin and changes in physical attributes of the decedent due to the passage of time or aging (2).

There are many reports of misidentification in cases of mass vehicular accidents, where the incorrect visual identification led to severe distress of misinformed relatives. As recently as 2018 in Canada, a junior ice hockey team was involved in a fatal accident when their bus, taking them to a game, collided with a truck leaving 16 dead. Two victims were incorrectly visually identified compounding this tragic incident as the team members looked similar after treating their hair with peroxide for the game and all were athletic young people. The mistake was rectified as soon as possible but caused further unnecessary distress for relatives.

CASE STUDIES

Case 1

A burned-out car was discovered in woodland with human remains in the rear seating area (Figure 17.3). Post-mortem examination revealed the body to be that of a young adult female. Despite the extreme fire damage, the posterior teeth and lower front teeth were well preserved (Figure 17.4). The deceased was identified as the owner of the burned vehicle and manner of death was suicide. The deceased was captured on CCTV purchasing a can of petrol and matches on the day of the fire and had a history of depression. Comparison of the good-quality antemortem and post-mortem dental information confirmed the identification within a few hours of the incident.

17.3 Case 1: Discovery of a burned car in woodland. (Printed with permission from New Zealand Police.)

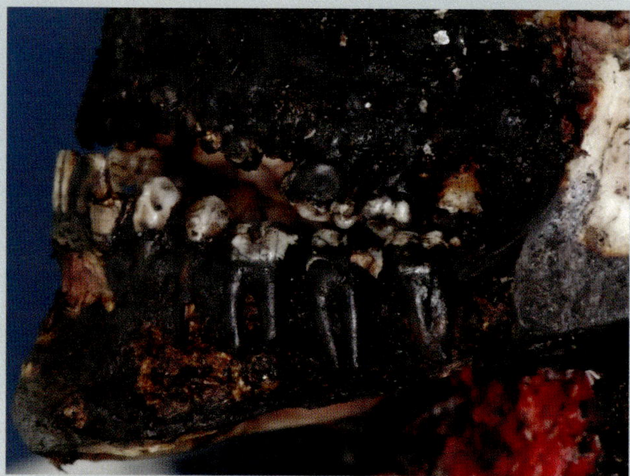

17.4 Case 1: Despite high temperature, soft-tissue and bone destruction, tooth detail and structure still present. (Printed with permission from New Zealand Police.)

CASE 2

The decomposed body of an unknown adult person was discovered in a shallow creek. Although extensive soft tissue loss and changes were present (Figure 17.5), a sutured scalp incision (Figure 17.6), and cranial burring (Figure 17.7) were observed at post-mortem examination, in addition to mandibular exostosis and evidence of previous dental work (Figure 17.8). The observation of the recent surgical intervention assisted with presumptive identification as recent surgical lists of local hospitals were searched to identify patients who underwent the described surgery. Despite the advanced decomposition, identity was subsequently positively confirmed with fingerprint examination (Figure 17.9).

17.5 Case 2: Extensive post-mortem soft-tissue loss.

17.7 Case 2: Cranial burring.

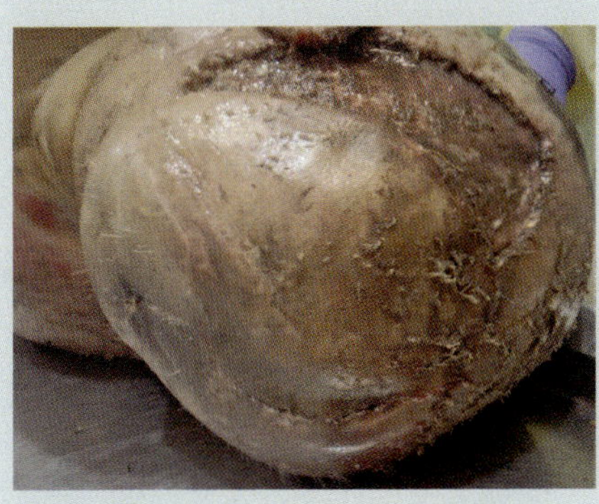

17.6 Case 2: Sutured scalp incision.

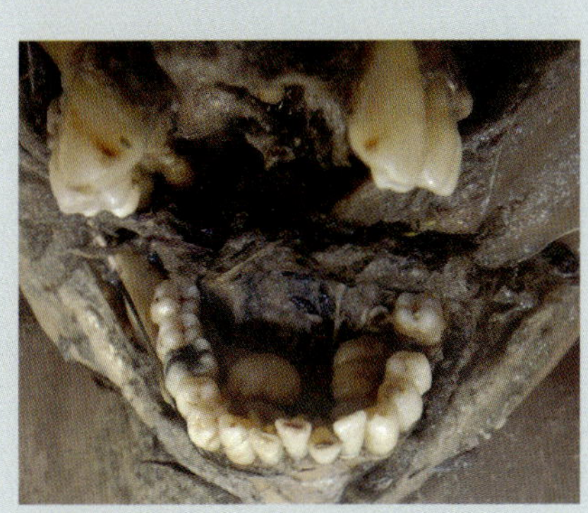

17.8 Case 2: Mandibular exostosis and evidence of previous dental work.

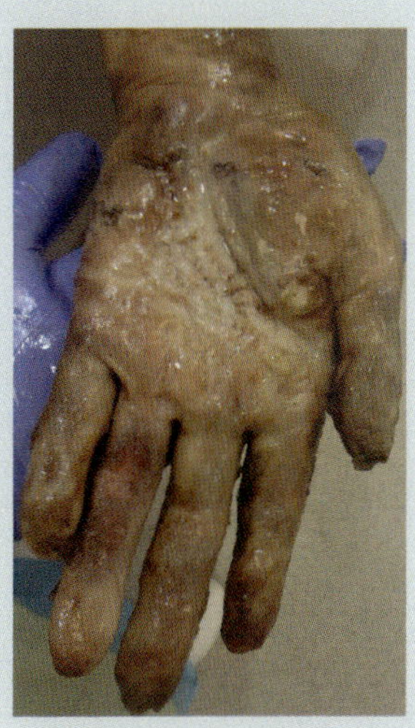

17.9 Case 2: Right hand with decomposition changes evident.

CONCLUSION

To maintain gold standards in identification, teamwork is hugely important; all disciplines have a role to play. Sharing information and following relevant identification protocols is crucial. The type of incident requiring the identification of human remains may determine which method will give the most accurate, timely and reliable results. Working together, there is a duty of care to the deceased maintaining a sensitive and dignified approach. For the sake of relatives, investigators and the judiciary, there must be a thorough and competent examination carried out by qualified and trained personnel who collect, preserve and interpret the evidence thereby minimizing distressing mistakes. The integration of new techniques, imaging and research can only improve the process.

REFERENCES

1. INTERPOL. DVI Guide, 2018. Available from: https://www.interpol.int/en/How-we-work/Forensics/Disaster-Victim-Identification-DVI (Accessed 25 April 2023).
2. Black S, Walker G, Hackman L, et al. *Disaster Victim Identification: The Practitioner's Guide*. Dundee: Dundee University Press; 2010.
3. Holobinko A. Forensic human identification in the United States and Canada: A review of the law, admissible techniques, and the legal implications of their application in forensic cases. *Forensic Sci Int* 2012; **222(1–3)**: 394.e1–13.
4. Mercer BM, Sklar S, Shariatmadar A, et al. Fetal foot length as a predictor of gestational age. *Am J Obstet Gynecol* 1987; **156(2)**: 350–5.
5. Tiemensma M, Phillips VM. The dilemma of age estimation of children and juveniles in South Africa. *S Afr Med J* 2016; **106**: 1061.
6. Brough AL, Morgan B, Rutty GN. Post-mortem computed tomography (PMCT) and disaster victim identification. *Radiol Med* 2015; **120**: 866–73.
7. Hargreaves-O'Keane M, Dixon J. Advances in Fingerprint Techniques. In: Mallett X, Blythe T, Berry R (eds), *Advances in Forensic Human Identification*. Boca Raton: CRC Press; 2014, pp. 305–34.
8. Schmidt CW, Nawrocki SP, Williamson MA, et al. Obtaining fingerprints from mummified fingers: a method for tissue rehydration adapted from the archaeological literature. *J Forensic Sci* 200; **45(4)**: 874–5.
9. King TE, Ballereau SJ, Schürer KE, et al. Genetic signatures of coancestry within surnames. *Current Biol* 2006; **16(4)**: 384–8.
10. Kayser M. Forensic DNA phenotyping: Predicting human appearance from crime scene material for investigative purposes. *Forensic Sci Int Genet* 2015; **18**: 33–48.
11. Serrano AC. Forensic DNA phenotyping: A promising tool to aid forensic investigation. Current situation. *Span J Leg Med* 2020; **46(4)**: 183–90.
12. Phillps C. The Golden State Killer investigation and the nascent field of forensic genealogy. *Forensic Sci Int Genet* 2018; **36**: 186–8.
13. Augenstein S. *"Buck Skin Girl" Case Break Is Success of New DNA Doe Project*. Forensic Magazine, 2018.
14. DNA Doe Project. *Success Stories*. DNA Doe Project Cases, 2021. Available from: http://dnadoeproject.org/project_category/success/ (Accessed 25 April 2023).
15. Hinchliffe J. Forensic odontology, Part 1. Dental identification. *Br Dent J* 2011; **210**: 219–24.
16. Forrest A. Forensic odontology in DVI: Current practice and recent advances. *Forensic Sci Res* 2019; **4**: 316–30.
17. Berketa J, James H, Marino V. Survival of batch numbers within dental implants following incineration as an aid to identification. *J Forensic Odonto-stomatol* 2010; **28(1)**: 1–4.
18. Reesu GV, Mânica S, Revie GF, et al. Forensic dental identification using two-dimensional photographs of a smile and three-dimensional dental models: A 2D-3D superimposition method. *Forensic Sci Int* 2020; **313**: 110361.
19. Blau S, Briggs C. The role of forensic anthropology in Disaster Victim Identification (DVI). *Forensic Sci Int* 2011; **205**: 29–35.
20. DiMaio VJM, Dana SE. Identification of Remains. In: DiMaio VJM, Dana SE (eds), *Handbook of Forensic Pathology*, 2nd ed. Boca Raton: CRC Press; 2007, pp. 29–38.
21. Toupenay S, Cheikh AB, Ludes B, et al. Forensic odontology identification response to terrorist attacks in Paris November 2015. *Forensic Sci Res* 2020; 5: 214–22.
22. Cordner S, McKelvie H. Developing standards in international forensic work to identify missing persons. *Int Rev Red Cross* 2002; 84: 867–83.

CHAPTER

18

Time of Death

Christopher M. Milroy

INTRODUCTION

Trying to identify what time an unwitnessed death has occurred has been a "holy grail" of forensic research. Much time and effort has been spent on researching how post-mortem changes may be used to try to pinpoint the time of death. It is noteworthy that the leading textbook on time since death is called ***Estimation of the Time Since Death***, indicating the lack of certainty in the state of the science, despite the comprehensive research that has been undertaken (1).

CHANGES IN THE EARLY POST-MORTEM PERIOD

Following death, autolysis of tissue occurs, and it is the process of breakdown of cells and cessation of the normal physiology after death that results in changes that can be utilized to try and give an estimate of the time since death in the early post-mortem period. These include hypostasis (livor mortis), rigor mortis, temperature-based methods, supravitality and biochemical changes.

Post-mortem hypostasis (lividity or sugillation)

When circulation ceases, blood will move under the forces of gravity (2). As a consequence, blood accumulates in the vessels in the dependant parts. The filling of the vessels with blood, which after death is de-oxygenated, imparts a purple or reddish-purple color to the adjacent skin, a change to which the terms hypostasis, lividity or sugillation are given, though sugillation is now archaic. Hypostasis and lividity are used interchangeably.

Pressure to even a mild degree is sufficient to prevent gravitation of the blood into the compressed areas of "contact flattening". When laid on the back, the body has pale areas over the shoulder blades, buttocks and calves (Figure 18.1). Corresponding areas will be present when the body lies face down. Contact flattening also occurs at sites of tight clothing worn at the time of death.

Hypostasis is characteristically purple because of deoxygenated blood. In carbon monoxide poisoning, the formation of carboxyhemoglobin, results in a cherry red color to blood. Cyanide and fluoroacetate poisoning are also associated with a red coloration. Methemoglobin formation, such as occurs in sodium nitrite poisoning, makes the blood appear more chocolate brown.

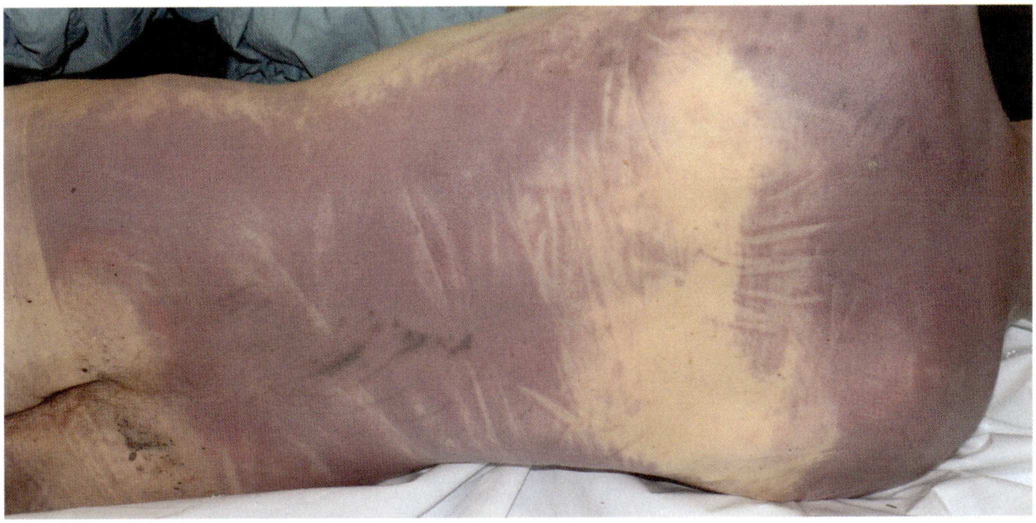

18.1 Post-mortem hypostasis with pressure pallor on the back.

DOI: 10.1201/9781003138754-20

Hypostasis typically begins within 30 minutes to 2 hours after death. It is less prominent in the anemic, the elderly or the very young when it may be difficult to identify. After 8–12 hours, hypostasis begins to remain fixed, so that lividity will no longer move under gravity if the body position is changed.

Hypostasis may be intense in dependant parts of the body and petechial hemorrhages may occur. A common finding in suicidal hangings is prominent hypostasis in the legs. If the head is in a dependant position, the congestion may be so intense as to obscure ante-mortem injuries. Colorimetry has been used to try to introduce more objective analysis of hypostasis but remains a research tool (3).

Rigor mortis (cadaveric rigidity)

Rigor mortis is the stiffening of skeletal muscle after death (Figure 18.2) and is a well-known phenomenon to medical and lay person alike (4,5). After death, energy sources will become depleted and ATP in muscle will be consumed but cannot be replaced. The actin-myosin complex will form, and muscle contraction will occur. There are four phases in the development of rigor mortis. In the first phase, sufficient ATP remains for cross-links to break down. In the second phase, cross-linking will only be reversed if oxygen or ATP is supplied, a situation that only exists in the laboratory. In the third phase, rigor mortis is fully developed and is followed by the fourth phase, when rigidity is lost, as a consequence of de-naturation of muscle.

The first scientific description of rigor mortis is attributed to Nysten in 1811 (4,5). A law named after him describes rigor mortis as developing in a descending order from the head, jaw muscles, neck, trunk and arms and finally those of the lower limbs. This was attributed to the distance between the muscle groups and the central nervous system. Shapiro challenged the concept of a descending order of rigor mortis (6). He pointed out that because rigor mortis is a physio-chemical process, it will occur simultaneously in all muscle groups, and that muscle size and joint structure dictate the onset of rigor mortis

Mallach analysed the literature between 1811 and 1960 and reported that the mean time for establishment of rigor occurred at 3 hours (+/– 2 hours), with complete rigidity in 8 hours, persisting for 57 hours (+/– 14), with resolution at 76 hours (+/– 32) (7).

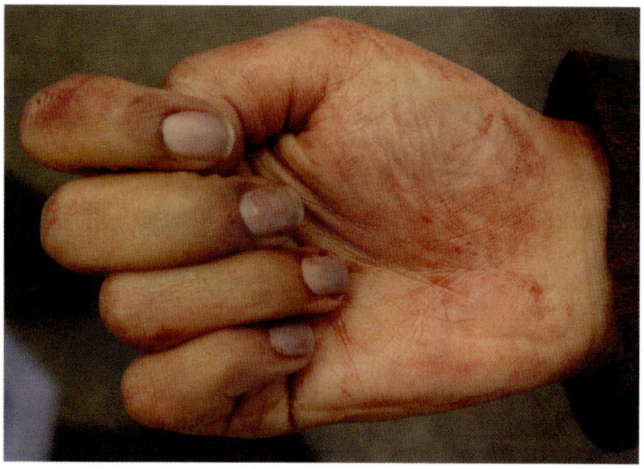

18.2 Rigor mortis causing stiffness in the fingers.

These findings show that the onset of rigor mortis is very variable and is influenced by a number of factors, including temperature, mode of death particularly with physical activity, and mechanism of death including poisoning and electrocution. Temperature is known to affect the onset of rigor mortis. Cold temperatures cause persistence of rigor mortis. All pathologists must be familiar with the body removed from a refrigerated environment after a few days where rigor mortis is still evident. Prolonged refrigeration, whether induced or environmental, can result in persistent rigor mortis for up to many days. Warm conditions will accelerate rigor mortis and the whole process to resolution may be over in a few hours. Freezing a body before the onset of rigor mortis will prevent the formation of rigor mortis. The body will be stiff due the formation of ice, but on thawing rigor mortis develops. Physical activity before death will increase the speed of development of rigor, and thus the resolution, because energy supplies will be lower than in resting muscle. Cadaveric spasm (instant rigor mortis) is the most extreme example of more rapidly developed rigor mortis (see below). Krompecher states that he has never encountered a case and nor had his colleagues (5). Polson and Gee stated they had only seen two cases in 20 years in their practice in Leeds, United Kingdom (UK) (4).

In young children, and particularly in infants, rigor mortis may be less discernible. Similarly, in people who are malnourished and wasted, rigor may be less pronounced and develop more quickly. Once rigor mortis has developed, it can be "broken" by moving the arms and legs. If this is done in the developing stage, rigor will reform to a greater or lesser extent, but once fully established the stretched limb will remain limp.

Temperature methods – cooling the body

Research on cooling the body and timing of death began in the nineteenth century (8). These studies continue and a large body of work has been produced in this area (9). According to Newtonian cooling, the rate an inorganic body cools depends on the temperature difference between the mass and the surrounding environmental temperature. Marshall and Hoare showed that the human body does not follow Newtonian principles in the first 12 hours after death (10–12). The core temperature of a dead human body may remain at a normal temperature for a number of hours after death. Although De Saram stated that this was 45 minutes (13), Shapiro found that this plateau could last for 4 hours (14). Marshall and Hoare described the plateau as lasting for up to 5 hours (10).

The actual core temperature at the time of death is usually unknown. Deaths may be associated with a higher temperature; for example, infections, pontine hemorrhage, heatstroke and drug-related deaths may all cause a raised body temperature before death. Deaths may be associated with a low temperature, including those where there is infection, hypothyroidism or environmental hypothermia.

With many victims of assault, death may occur after hours of incapacitation and so core temperatures may be low at death. Head injuries may affect thermoregulation and present clinically with low core temperatures.

A "rule of thumb" suggesting that bodies cool at 1.5°F is not accurate (15). In the later twentieth century, more sophisticated temperature methods were developed. Hengsse developed nomograms and computer-assisted programs based on the work of Marshall and Hoare (9). Hengsse's work takes account of the weight and clothing of the body and whether it is in still or moving air.

Rather than using rectal temperature, other authors have used the head temperature with microwave thermometry and the external auditory meatus, with infrared thermometry (16–19). The ear may be more easily accessible at a scene than the rectum. Unlike the rectum, ear temperatures do not show a lag period.

The eye and biochemical changes

The eye exhibits post-mortem changes including tache noire, the drying artefact of the exposed sclera, which occurs in the hours following death [15]. The color changes from red-brown to black giving the name tache noire – "black line" (Figure 18.3).

Ophthalmoscopy reveals "trucking" of the vessels, which typically occurs within one hour. Post-mortem clouding of the cornea can, however, prevent visualization.

Vitreous fluid is a standard fluid used in autopsy work (20). The utility of the fluid includes analysis for electrolytes. Changes in vitreous fluid contents, particularly potassium, have been analysed in the context of time of death (21). Potassium rapidly rises after death as red blood cells break down and release intracellular potassium. This means that blood potassium post mortem cannot be used as an indication of potassium toxicity but raises the possibility of using the vitreous concentration as an indicator of post-mortem interval. Hypoxanthine has also been studied. Cerebrospinal fluid changes have also been researched.

Supravitality

Attempts to use post-mortem electrical excitability of muscle were revived in the twentieth century by Prokop (22). Work indicates that a longer terminal period, as seen in clinical autopsy cases, results in a shorter period of excitability of muscles. In forensic pathology cases excitability may be longer. Those who have used the method recommend its use along with other methods, such as Hengsse's nomogram.

Stomach contents and time of death

In *Knight's Textbook on Forensic Pathology*, it is stated with respect to stomach contents that "with one exception, this controversial topic could be dismissed summarily" (15). The refers to the Canadian case of Steven Truscott. He was convicted in 1959, when age 14 years, of murdering Lynn Harper and was sentenced to death; his sentence being commuted to life imprisonment. An

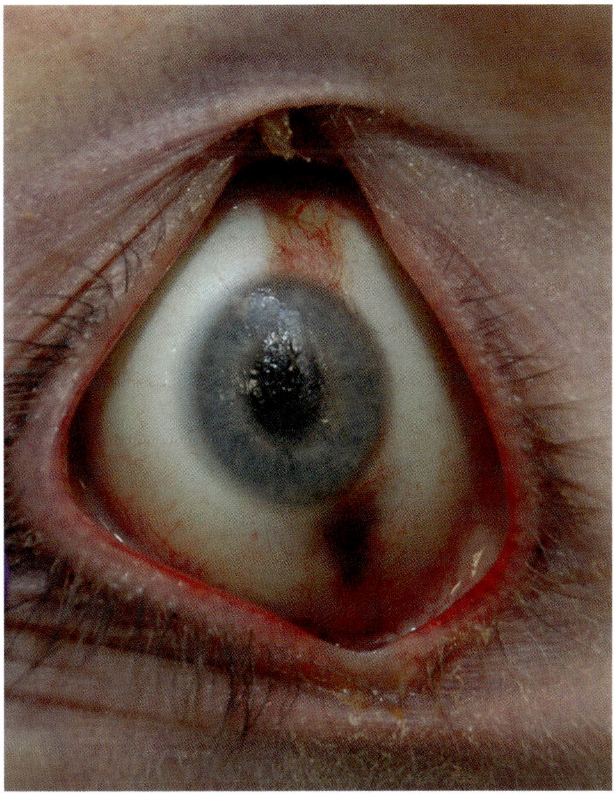

18.3 Tache noire: drying artefact of the eye – an early post-mortem change.

appeal was dismissed in 1966, but a further appeal in 2007 was successful (23). The original pathologist, based on stomach emptying time, had placed the time of death between 7 pm and 7.45 pm. The experts called by the defense (including Professor Knight) challenged the scientific validity of the estimation of the time of death. Along with entomological evidence, particularly the lack of insect activity, when it should have been present, based upon the prosecution's case, and other post-mortem changes, the conviction was finally quashed.

Immunohistochemistry

The use of immunohistochemical stains have been proposed with examination of thyroid and pancreatic hormones to estimate time of death. Madea and colleagues illustrate a case with the use of thyroglobulin and calcitonin stains along with glucagon and insulin staining to determine time of death, in combination with vitreous electrolytes (24). The absence of calcitonin staining indicated a post-mortem interval of at least days.

LATER POST-MORTEM CHANGES

Putrefaction

After the cooling stage, the body begins to visibly putrefy (4,15). Putrefactive changes make techniques used in the early post-mortem period unreliable or redundant.

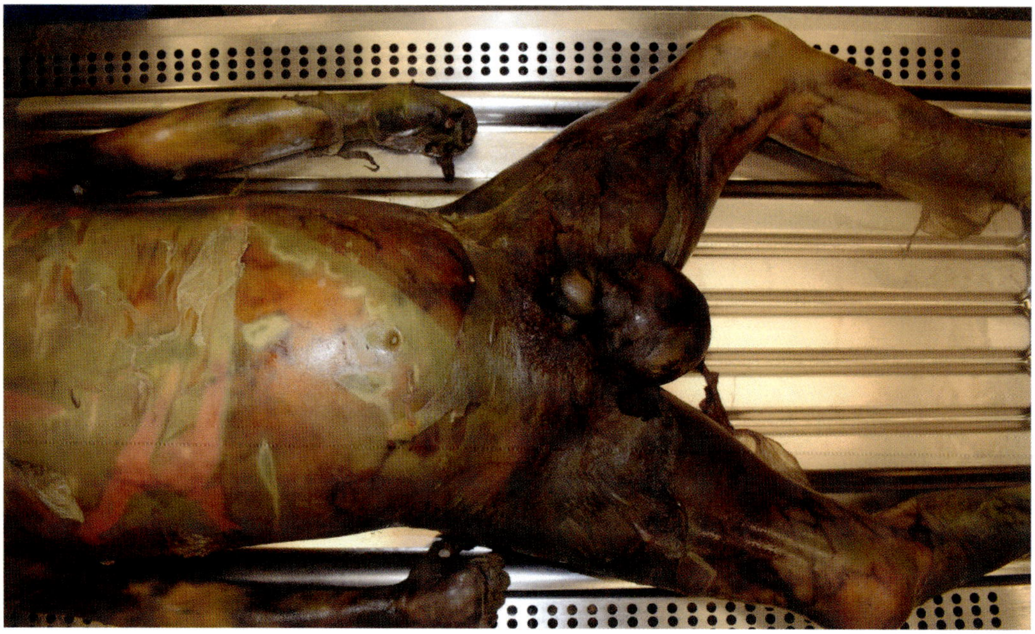

18.4 Putrefactive changes with green discoloration, skin slippage, and bloating.

Decompositional changes are brought about by bacterial (putrefaction) and enzyme activity (autolysis). The speed with which it is visible will depend on environmental conditions. In temperate climates, they are usually seen by three days (15). At higher temperatures, processes are accelerated. Low temperatures retard decomposition, which is of course the principle of refrigeration and freezing. Putrefactive changes are optimal at temperatures between 21–37°C (70–100°F). Refrigerators are maintained at 4°C.

The first visible sign of putrefaction is green or greenish-red discoloration of the skin of the anterior abdominal wall, normally beginning in the right iliac fossa. The coloration is due to the formation of sulph-hemoglobin. This spreads to involve the whole abdominal wall, chest and thighs and, in due course, the skin of the entire body. This takes up to one week in a temperate climate.

In the next phase, there is gas formation and the appearances of blisters of up to 10 cm diameter, which are filled with reddish watery fluid (Figure 18.4). As the epidermis separates, skin loosens giving rise to "skin slippage". At this stage, hair separates easily from the skin. Gas formation results in swelling of body cavities and general tumefaction of the skin. The face will blacken and become bloated, and the scrotum and penis often swell dramatically. With swelling, decomposing tissues are pushed out of the body causing purging of feces, urine and blood-stained fluid from body orifices. Such purging of blood-stained fluid may be mistaken for blood from an injury. This hemolysis is also reflected in internal tissues and can be difficult to distinguish from ante-mortem bleeding, particularly in the head and neck.

These changes may be modified by the action of insects and animals depending on the prevailing environmental conditions. Ultimately, the soft tissues will be removed to leave only the skeleton, unless mummification or adipocere formation occurs.

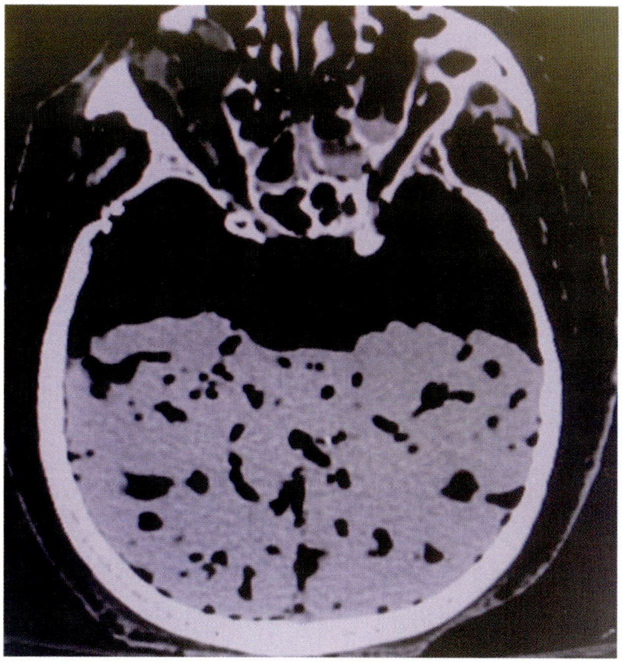

18.5 Post-mortem CT scan of the head in putrefaction with loss of brain substance and "Swiss cheese" appearance.

With the increased use of post-mortem CT scanning, striking putrefactive changes can be seen on imaging (Figure 18.5). This technology provides an avenue for more research on the development of putrefactive changes (25).

Forensic entomology

Using the knowledge of faunal succession of insects may provide useful information on the time since death. This requires specialist expertise. Absence of fauna may also

18.6 Extensive maggot (insect larvae) activity on a murder victim dumped in a field.

be an important observation, where it might otherwise be expected. Insect activity will vary with environmental conditions. The literature on forensic entomology has been steadily increasing (26–29). Insects will colonize bodies that they have access to, and the resultant destruction can be extensive (Figure 18.6).

Buried bodies and bodies in water will be exposed to different insect communities with a different faunal succession. Bodies in water may have been previously exposed on land before being dumped in water. Bodies that enter water may float, being exposed to non-aquatic fauna. Similarly, bodies that sink, but float with bloating may become exposed to terrestrial insects. Bodies immersed in salt water will have a different insect population to those exposed to fresh water ecosystems.

Adipocere

Adipocere is a variant of putrefaction where the body fats undergo hydrolysis and hydrogenation. The changes can result in preservation of the body for many years. The process may be seen along with other changes such as mummification and preservation in peat. While the changes are most prominent in subcutaneous fat, changes also occur in internal organs, notably the liver, kidneys and heart (Figure 18.7). While older authors stated that adipocere took 3–6 months to form, it is now accepted that it can be more rapid (4,15).

Mummification

The process of mummification is most often associated with the funeral practices of the ancient Egyptians (30). However, Egyptian mummies were embalmed and were different to bodies that have undergone natural mummification (4). A degree of natural mummification may be seen in bodies that have lain in dry conditions (Figure 18.8). Characteristically, the hands, feet and head will dry, and the tissues will become hard. Full mummification of a body in a temperate climate is rare, the most common situation being newborn/stillborn infants. Because a newborn infant is small and sterile, under appropriate dry conditions, the body will not putrefy, but will mummify.

Natural mummification has produced fascinating bodies of major historical interest, such as the Tarim mummies in China, and the Greenland mummies found at Qilakisoq (31,32). Bodies buried in very cold conditions may effectively "freeze dry" and remain remarkably preserved.

Preservation in permafrost

In 1845, Sir John Franklin led an expedition to discover the Northwest Passage in what is now Canada (33). All members of the expedition perished, but three crew members were buried in the Arctic. These graves were excavated in the 1980s and showed an extraordinary degree of preservation. In 1991, a much older body was found on the Austro-Italian border in a melting glacier 3200 meters above sea level (34). Carbon dating suggested the man, called Ötzi, died between 3365 and 2940 BCE.

Preservation in snow is well recognized by forensic pathologists who practice in areas such as Canada and Scandinavia, where winters are cold and prolonged. When snow melts in Spring, a missing body may be uncovered. Decompositional changes often develop rapidly after thawing.

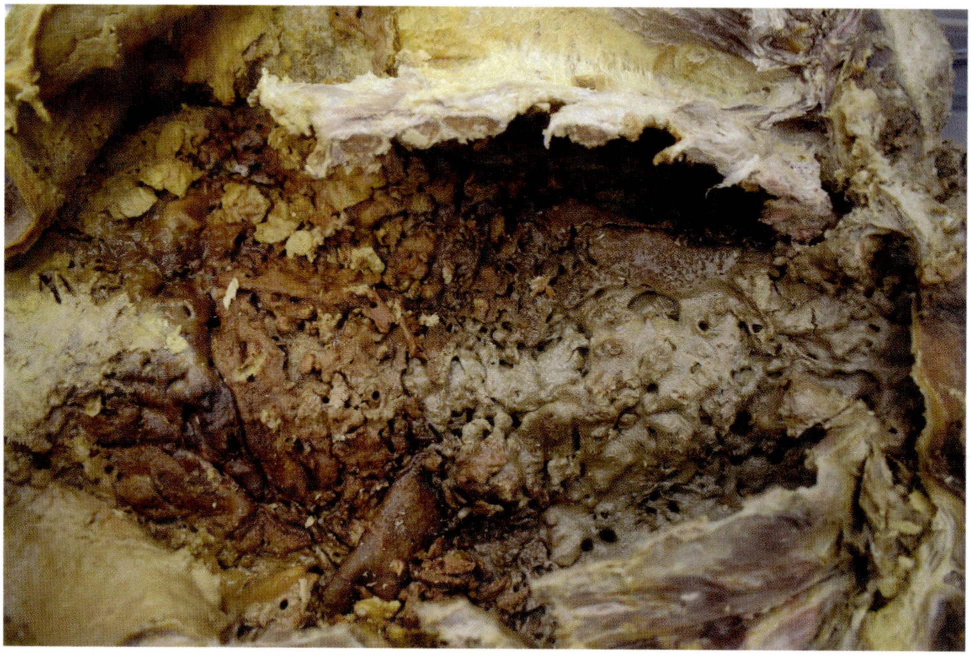

18.7 Adipocere formation in the organs of a man not seen for a month.

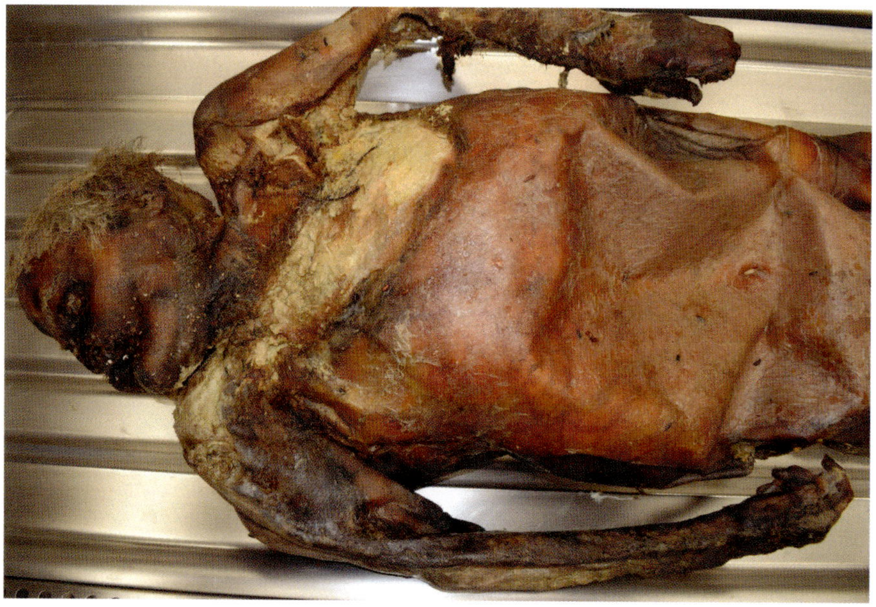

18.8 Mummification after one month in warm dry conditions.

Preservation in peat bogs

Peat is a type of soil found in wetlands and consists of a soft brown material composed of organic matter, in particular, a type of moss called *Sphagnum* moss. Modern peat bogs date from after the last ice age, less than 10 000 years ago. Lowland peat bogs may be 10–12 meters deep, with upland or blanket peat bogs being up to 3 meters deep. It is from lowland peat bogs that the famous bog bodies have been recovered. The phenomenon was brought to world attention by the Danish archaeologist Glob (35). In 1950, a man was found in Tollund Fen, central Jutland, Denmark. Tollund man, as he is now called, was 2000 years old, dating from the Iron Age.

Further interest in bog bodies was kindled when the body of an Iron Age Briton was found at Lindow moss in Cheshire in 1983 (36). Carbon dating placed his death in the Romano-British period. Lindow man is now preserved in the British museum. The previous year, a female skull had been found in the same area, resulting in a man confessing to the murder of his wife two decades before (37). Despite carbon dating indicating that the skull dated from the Iron Age, he was convicted

(*R v Reyn-Bardt*, Chester Crown Court, 1984). Modern victims of homicide, notably the Moors Murder victims were buried in peat bogs above Manchester and when found were well preserved (38).

Radiocarbon and radio-isotope dating

Carbon dating may have value in dating ancient bodies (39). It also has some utility in bodies exposed to atmospheric atomic testing after the Second World War which resulted in additional C14 in the atmosphere. This means that it is possible to use the "bomb peak" to radiocarbon date bodies and skeletons, though it requires careful analysis (40). Analysis of other radioisotopes have been proposed including ^{90}Sr, ^{210}Po and ^{210}Pb in dating skeletal remains (41).

DETERMINING TIME OF DEATH IN CASE WORK

The reality of case work is that most deaths do not require an accurate determination of the time of death. Where a time of death is an issue, there is a need for the pathologist to assess all of the available information not, for example, just the body temperature on its own, which may be of no value (24). Where expert information is required, such as entomology data, the specialist should be consulted before collection of specimens, where possible. In giving a time of death, current knowledge only allows an estimated range and dogmatic times, as given in the Truscott case can lead to miscarriages of justice.

REFERENCES

1. Madea B (ed). *Estimation of the Time Since Death*. London: CRC Press; 2015.
2. Madea B, Knight B. Postmortem Lividity. Hypostasis and Timing of Death. In: Madea B (ed), *Estimation of the Time Since Death*. London: CRC Press; 2015, pp. 59–62.
3. Vanezis P, Trujillo O. Evaluation of hypostasis using a colorimeter measuring system and its application to assessment of the post-mortem interval (time of death). *Forensic Sci Int* 1996; **78**(**1**): 19–28.
4. Polson CJ. The Signs of Death. In: Polson CJ, Gee DJ, Knight B (eds), *The Essentials of Forensic Medicine*, 4th ed. Oxford: Pergamon Press; 1985.
5. Krompecher T. Rigor Mortis. Estimation of the Time Since Death by Evaluation of Cadaveric Rigidity. In: Madea B (ed), *Estimation of the Time Since Death*. London: CRC Press; 2015, 41–58.
6. Shapiro HA. Rigor mortis. *BMJ* 1950; **2**(**4673**): 304.
7. Mallach HJ. Zur Frage der Todeszeitbestimmung. *Berl Med* 1964; **18**: 577–82.
8. Knight B, Madea B. Historical Review of Early Work on Estimating the Time Since Death. In: Madea B (ed), *Estimation of the Time Since Death*. London: CRC Press; 2015, 7–16.
9. Henssge C. Postmortem Body Cooling and Temperature-Based Methods. In: Madea B (ed), *Estimation of the Time Since Death*. London: CRC Press; 2015, 63–152.
10. Marshall TK. Estimating the time of death-the rectal cooling after death and its mathematical representation. *J Forensic Sci* 1962; 7: 56–81.
11. Marshall TK. Estimating the time of death-the use of the cooling formula in the study of postmortem cooling. *J Forensic Sci* 1962; 7: 189–210.
12. Marshall TK. Estimating the time of death-the use of body temperature in estimating the time of death. *J Forensic Sci* 1962; 7: 211–21.
13. De Saram GS, Webster G, Kathirgamatamby N. Post-mortem temperature and the time of death. *J Crim L Criminol* 1955; **46**: 562.
14. Shapiro HA. The post-mortem temperature plateau. *J Forensic Med* 1965; **12**(**4**): 137–41.
15. Saukko P, Knight B. The Pathophysiology of Death. In: Saukko P, Knight B (eds), *Knight's Forensic Pathology*, 4th ed. Boca Raton: CRC Press, 2016, pp. 55–94.
16. al-Alousi LM, Anderson RA, Land DV. A non-invasive method for postmortem temperature measurements using a microwave probe. *Forensic Sci Int* 1994; **64**(**1**): 35–46.
17. Baccino E, De Saint Martin L, Schuliar Y, et al. Outer ear temperature and time of death. *Forensic Sci Int* 1996; **83**(**2**): 133–46.
18. Rutty GN. The estimation of the time since death using temperatures recorded from the external auditory canal. *Forensic Sci Med Pathol* 2005; **1**(**2**): 113–23.
19. Laplace K, Baccino E, Peyron PA. Is infrared thermometry suitable for the determination of the time since death based on ear temperature? A comparative study of two measurement methods. *Int J Legal Med* 2021; **135**(**4**): 1669–74.
20. Coe JI. Use of chemical determinations on vitreous humor in forensic pathology. *J Forensic Sci* 1972; **17**(**4**): 541–6.
21. Madea B, Henssge C. Eye Changes After Death. In: Madea B (ed), *Estimation of the Time Since Death*. London: CRC Press; 2015, pp. 161–185.
22. Madea B. Supravitality in Tissues. In: Madea B (ed), *Estimation of the Time Since Death*. London: CRC Press; 2015.
23. Williams K, Milroy CM. The medicolegal issues surrounding the case of Steven Truscott: A forensic pathology perspective. *Acad Forensic Pathol* 2015; **5**(**2**): 273–9.
24. Madea B, Ortmann J, Doberentz E. Estimation of the time since death: Even methods with a low precision may be helpful in forensic casework. *Forensic Sci Int* 2019; **302**: 109879.
25. Smith KGV. *A Manual of Forensic Entomology*. London: Natural History Museum Publications; 1986.
26. Tomberlin JK, Benbow ME (eds). *Forensic Entomology: International Dimensions and Frontiers*. Boca Raton: CRC press; 2015.
27. Reibe S. Forensic Entomology. In: Madea B (ed). *Estimation of the Time Since Death*. London: CRC Press; 2015, pp. 249–258.
28. Byrd JH, Tomberlin JK (ed). *Forensic Entomology: The Utility of Arthropods in Legal Investigations*. Boca Raton: CRC Press; 2019.
29. David R (ed). *Egyptian Mummies and Modern Science*. New York: Cambridge University Press; 2008.
30. Mallory JP, Mair VH. *The Tarim Mummies*. New York: Thames & Hudson; 2000.
31. Hansen JP, Medlgaard J. *Greenland Mummies*. Washington DC: McGill-Queen's Press-MQUP; 1991.
32. Beattie O, Geiger J. *Frozen in Time: The Fate of the Franklin Expedition*. Greystone Books Ltd; 2017.
33. Paterlini M. Anthropology: The Iceman defrosted. *Nature* 2011; **471**(**7336**): 34–5.
34. Glob PV. *The Bog People: Iron Age Man Preserved*. London: Faber and Faber; 1969.
35. Turner RC, Scaife RG. *Bog Bodies. New Discoveries and New Perspectives*. London: British Museum Press; 1995.
36. Garrett G, Green MA, Murray LA. Technical method-rapid softening of adipocerous bodies. *Med Sci Law* 1988; **28**: 98.
37. Henriques M. Uncannily well-preserved bodies from the ancient world occasionally surface Northern Europe's bogs. Stranger even than their remarkable preservation is the disturbing manner of their deaths, 2022. Available from: https://www.bbc.com/future/article/20220907-the-mystery-of-the-human-sacrifices-buried-in-europes-bogs (Accessed 25 April 2023).
38. Rosendahl W, Doppes D. Radiocarbon dating. Basic Principles and Applications. In: Madea B (ed). *Estimation of the Time Since Death*. London: CRC Press; 2015, pp. 259–268.
39. Handlos P, Svetlik I, Horáčková L, et al. Bomb peak: Radiocarbon dating of skeletal remains in routine forensic medical practice. *Radiocarbon* 2018; **60**(**4**): 1017–28.
40. Maclaughlin-Black SM, Herd RJ, Willson K, et al. Strontium-90 as an indicator of time since death: A pilot investigation. *Forensic Sci Int* 1992; **57**(**1**): 51–6.
41. Swift B. Dating human skeletal remains: Investigating the viability of measuring the equilibrium between 210Po and 210Pb as a means of estimating the post-mortem interval. *Forensic Sci Int* 1998; **98**(**1–2**): 119–26.

CHAPTER

19

Age Estimation in the Deceased

Sara Tangmose Larsen, Chiara Villa, Marie Louise Jørkov and Niels Lynnerup

INTRODUCTION

The need for estimating the age of a deceased individual is a key element for investigations of human remains from mass disasters, unidentified bodies in different stages of decomposition and skeletonization, and deceased individuals without identification (1). It has been argued that the number of unidentified cadavers is increasing due to legal and illegal immigration (2). Moreover, as the climate changes, a future rise in immigration and mass disasters has been predicted (3).

The result of the age assessment, along with other post-mortem findings, may serve as a screening process in the identification of human bodies or body parts. Thus, a reliable age estimation is of great importance. Traditionally, methods for forensic age estimation are based on the best-preserved tissues, that is, dental and skeletal traits. Teeth are the hardest structures in the human body and can survive after everything else has decomposed (4). Age estimation methods range from mainly observational to destructive analyses of these hard tissues. Depending on the state of decomposition, these methods can sometimes be applied directly to exposed bones and teeth, or if soft tissue is present, specific bone structures and teeth can be dissected or biopted, and thus rendered available for direct study. More recently, the increasing use of post-mortem medical imaging allows for the various methods to be applied on images and visualizations derived from such imaging. Of course, imaging is also of great use when having to perform age estimation of the living, and imaging also allows the possibility of second opinions, independent of access to the remains. Furthermore, thanks to the introduction of CT scanners in many forensic institutes around the world (5–8) and the acquisition of whole-body CT scanning before the autopsy, we are seeing the creation of modern, up-to-date virtual collections. These collections can be used to re-calibrate methods for both sub-adults and adults that have been developed on more than 100-year-old collections and overcome the well-known problem of "age mimicry" (9). An example is "The New Mexico Decedent Image Database" that provides access to whole human body CT scans and associated metadata (10) or the "Skeletal Biology and Forensic Anthropology Virtual Osteological Database" housed at the Queensland University of Technology, a CT-scan dataset of modern Australian male and female individuals aged from birth to 75 years (11).

Generally, the assessment of a chronological age assumes that the biological age of an individual more or less follows the chronological age. The chronological age is our calendar age in years, while our biological age refers to how aging affects our body and how this can be observed or analyzed. Aging methods usually employ a system of stages or scores, or direct measurements, all of which then result in an estimated age interval. So-called atlas methods consist of comparing observed morphology directly to standardized images, which again should be indicative of a certain age or age range.

As mentioned by Cunha et al. (12), methods for age assessment need to be well defined or so well explained that they do not entail undue intra- or inter-observer error when applied. A general problem relates to how a given method, developed on a specific reference sample, in a certain decade of time, translates to other populations (12). Moreover, reference studies most often report the relationship between biological age-related traits and chronological age by means and standard deviation. Unfortunately, these means and standard deviations are affected by the age-composition of the reference sample. This bias is known as age-mimicry.

While the relationship between chronological and biological age is relatively strong for sub-adults due to growth changes, this relationship decreases with age after growth has finished. Hence, a reliable age may be difficult to obtain in adults. Due to the lack of strong correlation between a biological trait and age, the Study Group on Forensic Age Diagnostics (AGFAD) and Forensic Anthropology Society of Europe (FASE) recommend the use of as much information as possible, that is, to combine several traits in order to achieve more accurate age estimates with appropriate levels of uncertainty (12,13). This may challenge the age assessments in mass disasters where human remains are often incomplete. Moreover, statistical models that combine several age-related traits often result in overly simple estimation, for example by calculating a mean age range by compiling several reference studies. Ideally, age estimations should be assessed using models based on Bayesian statistics (14–17).

In adulthood, growth and development is completed and age estimation is generally based on degenerative

DOI: 10.1201/9781003138754-21

changes in the teeth and skeleton (18–22). Such changes do have some relationship with age but are more variable and may differ highly from chronological age, as they are influenced by factors such as genetic make-up, disease, nutrition and loading (23). As a result, these methods are less accurate and may require population specific references (12).

Several methods exist, both observational and destructive. Observational methods include different types of imaging (CT-, surface scanning) as well as an assessment of joint surfaces (rib-ends, pubic symphysis, auricular surface, acetabulum, cranial sutures). Destructive methods, for example bone or teeth histology, radiocarbon analyses (C14), protein racemization and DNA methylation analyses are more time-consuming and require access to laboratory facilities.

AGING SUB-ADULTS

The biological–chronological relationship is highly correlated in the growing skeleton and dental development (24) of sub-adults. Thus, features associated with bone growth such as the presence of ossification centers, epiphyseal closure, the dimensions of long bones (e.g. humeral and femoral length) and dental development such as mineralization and eruption are mostly used (24–26). Toward the end of skeletal growth and dental development, fewer age-related traits remain for age estimation. These include the development of the third molar tooth (27–30), closure of the sphenobasilar or sphenooccipital synchondrosis and frontosphenoidal suture (31), fusion of the sternal end of the clavicle (32) and the iliac crest epiphysis (33).

Bone age

Although mostly used in the living, the epiphyseal closure of bones in the left hand and wrist as seen on a radiograph, or more recent, non-ionizing methods such as Magnetic Resonance Imaging (MRI) (34) and sonographic (US) (35) can be used to assess the age of deceased, as was demonstrated in the Southeast Asian Tsunami on 26 December 2004 (36). The best-known method for assessing age from a hand-wrist radiograph is the atlas method of Greulich and Pyle, based on hundreds of serial radiographs from upper-middle-class white children enrolled in the Brush Foundation Study in Cleveland, Ohio, between 1931 and 1942 (37). The atlas comprises two sets of standard radiographs representing the median skeletal development at a given age (bone age) in males and females, ranging from 3 months to 18 years (females) or 19 years (males), separated by 6 months to 1 year between standards. Bone age is usually estimated by finding the closest resemblance between the radiograph at hand and the sex-specific standards of the atlas, which can be done within a few minutes (38,39). The atlas is still widely used and has been found to be valid as a reference for age assessment (40,41). At least two other methods have been proposed for medicolegal purposes, which include a combination of scores, which again relates to a corresponding age range or a mean age and standard deviations. These are the bone-specific techniques by Tanner Whitehouse (TW) (42,43) and Roche et al. (FELS) (44).

The fusion of the spheno-occipital synchondrosis has been studied on dry bone, either by direct inspection or histologically, at autopsies and by imaging modalities (radiographs and CT). Standards proposed by Scheuer and Black (45) state that females fuse between 11 and 13 years and males between 13 and 18 years. In dry bone, Shirley and Jantz found the earliest age at which fusion is complete was 13 years in females and 16 years in males, and the latest age at which the suture remains open was 13 years in females and 17 years in males (46). They argued that the onset of fusion corresponds closely with the onset of puberty (31).

The apophyses of the iliac crest fuses in adolescence and can be assessed in dry bone (46) and by the use of ionizing radiation (47). The stages of fusion of the apophyses indicates an age at – or above – 16 to 20 years, when the fusion is complete (46,47).

The clavicle is the last bone to ossify and the degree of ossification has been classified in both anatomical studies (46,48) and by use of imaging modalities (49,50). Using imaging, most methods are based on a 4- or 5-stage system depending on the inclusion of the assessment of the epiphyseal scar, and further subdivision of stages 2 and 3 by three stages (A, B and C) has been suggested (32). Several developmental variants of the clavicle have been described (51). Some of these are located at the sternal end and include accessory ossicles, asymmetric closure of the growth plate and varying shapes, for example funnel or handlebar-like (51,52). In approximately 5 percent of the clavicles, these developmental anomalies inhibit a stage to be assigned (32,53). Clavicle ossification varies greatly and hence, high accuracy age estimates cannot be obtained. However, at stage 4, a computed tomography (CT) study has reported that 95 percent of the included subjects (16–25 years) were above 21 years. Stage 5 has been said to indicate an age above 26 years (32). The minimum age reported at stage 3C is 19.5 years (32).

Dental age

Several methods are published on dental age assessment, but mainly comprise inspective methods based on evaluating deciduous and permanent teeth eruption (e.g. Nystrom [54]) or radiographic methods based on mineralization, using both the atlas method (55) and/or a system based on stages and scores(27,28,30,56). The Demirjian method assesses the developmental status of seven permanent mandibular teeth on the left side. Challenges due to missing teeth due to post-mortem decay of soft tissue around the teeth must be considered (36). Variations in the rate of dental maturation have been observed between different populations but is believed to be unaffected by environmental factors and diseases, and rather due to genetic differences (57). Excluding the third molars, the maturation of the dentition ends at the age of approximately 16 years (55).

The third molars are the only teeth still in development in the age range 15–24 years (58). However, the third molar is frequently absent, malformed or impacted (30). Absence is due to agenesis or extraction. The prevalence of agenesis of at least one third molar has been reported ranging between 5 percent and 40 percent among various populations (59). In approximately 5 percent of a population, agenesis of all four third molars may be anticipated (60). When available, the third molars are the most variable teeth in the dentition with respect to size, time of formation and time of eruption (58). The high variability of development is reflected by a standard deviation of age at each stage of development of approximately 2 years, making the 95 percent confidence interval (CI) around the mean ± 4 years (29). Still, third molars are an important biological marker in adolescence. Several staging methods to assess the degree of third molar development have been developed (61). Frequently used are the 8 stages (A–H) by Demirjian (56) or the 10 stages (C½–Ac) by Gleiser and Hunt, modified by Köhler (28). Precision and accuracy differ slightly among staging methods but have been reported best for Demirjian's 8 stages (62,63). Most studies report a 4–6-month earlier development of third molars in males than females, which is a unique feature of the third molar compared to other parts of the dentition and skeleton (30,61). Third molars fully develop over a range of 7–9 years, and of these, the root accounts for 4.5 years (mandibular) (30,61). The third molars located in the maxilla complete their development approximately 1–2 years ahead of the mandibular third molars (30,58).

Sexual dimorphism and secular trends

The growing skeleton fuses faster in females than males (37,45). Therefore, knowledge of the sex of a sub-adult may be of great importance for achieving a more reliable age. Depending on the state of preservation of the deceased, for example loss of soft tissue, this may be somewhat of a challenge. However, indications of the sex of the sub-adult may be obtained from clothing and/or accessories discovered as part of the crime scene investigation.

Moreover, the relationship between the onset of puberty/menarche and the fusion of the skeleton including the decreasing age at which these events occur may challenge the accuracy of age estimation methods (64). This is known as a secular trend and refers to the process of accelerated maturation over at least one generation (approximately 20–25 years) (65). The presence of a secular trend in bone age among sub-adults has been found in South Africa, Japan, China and Australia (66–69), and generally may increase the risk of overestimating the age. The mechanism underlying the secular trend has been suggested to refer to improved nutrition, healthcare, and socio-economic environment (66,70), but may also be due to genetic factors, such as increased geographic migration (71). Hence, the composition of the reference sample as well as the continuing testing of accuracy of these methods are of great importance (9).

AGING ADULTS

Degenerative changes

When growth and development is completed, most aging methods focus on the non-synovial joints and the changes in the bone joint surfaces as evaluated macroscopically. These changes relate to broad age categories, typically ranging 10 years or more. Non-synovial joints are found between the three bones making up the pelvis, between the sternal rib end and the rib cartilage and between cranial sutures (called synostoses). Several methods have been described to evaluate changes in these joints with age. Lovejoy et al. (72) described a method for the auricular surface of the sacroiliac joint, which generally becomes more porotic, pitted with loss of the undulating pattern and a more pronounced demarcation of the joint surface from the surrounding bone with age. This method has since been modified (73–76). The first method for assessing age from the symphyseal surface was published by Todd in 1920 (77), and has been revised several times since, for example by Suchey and co-workers (78,79). Using sternal rib ends, Işcan et al. (20) published a method whereby age-related changes could be observed, generally transitioning from a rather clear-cut demarcation between bone and cartilage to becoming more uneven with age, due to bony outgrowth and bone thinning.

In 1875, Broca described age-related trends in the ossification of the cranial sutures (80). While it seems that there is a relationship between age and the ossification of the cranial sutures, this method has proven less accurate. However, as the skull is often well preserved, this method is still used (81). An often-used method was developed by Meindl and Lovejoy (22).

Other skeletal features have been evaluated to estimate age-at-death, such as the entheseal changes of all the bones (82), and the alteration of the vertebrae end of the sacrum (83,84). Indeed, by looking at features of the entire skeleton it is possible to reach more accurate and precise age-at-death estimates, as demonstrated by Milner and Boldsen (85). Boldsen and colleagues are developing a method, called Transitional Analysis (86) that accounts for 62 skeletal traits in the newest version (TA3 Software [statsmachine.net]).

Radiographic methods

Radiographic methods, such as imaging of the proximal epiphyseal ends of long bones (humerus and femur) can be used to quantify the degree of trabecular bone loss, which relates to age (87,88). This method was first described on macerated bone (87) but may also be used on soft-tissue covered bone.

Aging changes on different bones have been evaluated using CT scanning and 3D models applying the traditional methods on the 3D bones or taking advantage of the information extracted from CT images (89). Indeed, the trabecular structure or the thickness of the cortical bones can be used to obtain information about age (among them Barrier et al., 2009; de Froidmont et al., 2013; Pasquier et al., 1999; Villa et al., 2013) (90–93). An interesting and promising approach is the mathematical one, until now, applied only to the joints of the pelvis (94–97).

Histologic

If possible, age can be assessed using histological investigations of teeth and bone. The Gustafson method, described in 1950 (98), assesses the amount of secondary dentin formation by odontoblasts in the pulp cavity of teeth. This can be seen both histologically and non-destructively using radiography and MRI, as it is associated with the volume reduction of the pulp cavity (99). In bones, Kerley (100) described a method of determining the age at death by counting the secondary osteons, osteon fragments, non-Haversian canals and the percentage of lamellar bone from the mid-shaft of the femur, tibia and fibula. The method has been criticized and revised since (101).

Radiocarbon and protein racemization

Radiocarbon dating is traditionally used in archaeological research to date skeletal remains that are of historical or prehistoric dates to indicate a time since death (102). The method utilizes the so-called bomb-pulse, a period with a heightened atmospheric content of 14C due to nuclear bomb testing during the Cold War, resulting in radical variations of the atmospheric 14C content during the last 50 years. Subsequent to the Test Ban Treaty in 1963, the concentration has decreased rapidly, mainly because the atmospheric 14C has diffused into the oceans, while radioactive decay (the half-life of 14C is 5730 years) is of minor importance (103). Since the change in concentration is significant even on a yearly basis, this allows very accurate dating. Carbon 14 is usually measured in the protein in bone or teeth. However, more recently, it has been shown that the amount of radiocarbon in the eye lens may be used to determine the time of birth (102). This method was illustrated in a specific case where the year of birth of three infants, stored in a deep freezer, was assessed. Radiocarbon dating of proteins in infants' eye lenses were used to date the formation of the lens crystalline and had an accuracy within 1–2 years (104).

Apart from radiocarbon analyses, protein racemization analyses also rely more directly on an absolute chronology. In 1975, it was shown that there is a relationship between the chronological age of an individual and the process of amino acid racemization in collagen from tooth enamel (105). Since then, racemization has been performed on other tissues such as skin, vertebral discs, arteries and corneas (106,107) and other organic elements such as wood (108) and textiles (109).

Several studies have explored the use of racemization of dentine amino acids to correlate age from the aging of the proteins (106,110–112). The basis of amino acid racemization as an aging technique is the measurement of the relative proportions of the L- and D-chiral forms or asymmetric center at the a-carbon atom in amino acids. In almost all living proteins, amino acids are present in the L-form with the exception of bacterial cell wall biopolymers, collectively termed peptidoglycan. When the organism dies, L-amino acids slowly convert to D-amino acids, which themselves spontaneously revert back to the L-form. This process is called racemization and stops when an equilibrium at 50 percent of each enantiomer is reached. The process is very slow and can take hundreds or thousands of years, depending on the amino acid residue, the sequence, and the temperature, and so on. The progress of the racemization process from the L-enantiomers to the D-enantiomer of a given protein may thus be a measure of the time elapsed since the protein was synthesized, provided that new protein synthesis does not occur and that the protein is metabolically stable. Hence, tissues with relatively no turn-over such as dental enamel and, as previously mentioned, the special proteins in the eye lens fibers, termed crystalline, can be used for this method (113).

DNA methylation

As we age, cells and tissue differentiate and change. Among these changes are epigenetic DNA methylation, which involves the addition of a methyl group to a cytosine nucleotide in cytosine/guanine regions, known as CpG islands (114). While DNA methylation from various tissues and body fluids have been investigated, there is scarcity of data using this method for assessing the age in deceased individuals (115).

The dental pulp is located in the central region of the tooth and is formed by a stromal tissue containing nerves, blood and lymphatic vessels as well as protected from external insults by hard tissues. The unique location and structure make it the preferred tissue for DNA analysis (114). DNA methylation on the dental pulp has shown promising results with an MAE (mean absolute error) between predicted and chronological age of 1.5–2.13 years for age-at-death estimation in adult individuals (1,114).

CONCLUSION

Although a wide range of methods exist for age estimation in the deceased, an accurate age estimate still cannot be obtained. Hence, the forensic pathologist or forensic anthropologist should evaluate which methods are best suited in each case, for example depending on the state of preservation, time required and access to laboratory facilities.

REFERENCES

1. Zapico CS, Ubelaker DH. Applications of physiological bases of ageing to forensic sciences. Estimation of age-at-death. *Ageing Res Rev* 2013; **12(2)**: 605–17.
2. Cattaneo C, Ritz-Timme S, Schutz HW, et al. Unidentified cadavers and human remains in the EU: An unknown issue. *Int J Legal Med* 2000; **113(3)**: N2–3.
3. Reuveny R. Climate-related migration and population health: Social science-oriented dynamic simulation model. *BMC Public Health* 2021; **21(1)**: 598.

4. Ubelaker DH. *Human Skeletal Remains: Excavation, Analysis, Interpretation.* Taraxacum, 1999.
5. Leth PM. The use of CT scanning in forensic autopsy. *Forensic Sci Med Pathol* 2007; **3(1)**: 65–69.
6. Poulsen K, Simonsen J. Computed tomography as routine in connection with medico-legal autopsies. *Forensic Sci Int* 2007; **171(2–3)**: 190–197.
7. Rutty GN, Morgan B, O'Donnell C, et al. Forensic institutes across the world place CT or MRI scanners or both into their mortuaries. *J Trauma* 2008; **65(2)**: 493–4.
8. Thali MJ, Yen K, Schweitzer W, et al. Virtopsy, a new imaging horizon in forensic pathology: Virtual autopsy by postmortem multislice computed tomography (MSCT) and magnetic resonance imaging (MRI): A feasibility study. *J Forensic Sci* 2003; **48(2)**: 386–403.
9. Bocquet-Appel JP, Masset C. Farewell to paleodemography. *J Hum Evol* 1982; **11(4)**: 321–3.
10. Daneshvari Berry S, Kroth PJ, Edgar HJH, Warner TD. Developing the Minimum Dataset for the New Mexico Decedent Image Database. *Appl Clin Inform* 2021; **12(3)**: 518–27.
11. Lottering N, MacGregor DM, Alston CL, et al. Introducing computed tomography standards for age estimation of modern Australian subadults using postnatal ossification timings of select cranial and cervical sites. *J Forensic Sci* 2016; **61**: S39–S52.
12. Cunha E, Baccino E, Martrille L, et al. The problem of aging human remains and living individuals: A review. *Forensic Sci Int* 2009; **193(1–3)**: 1–13.
13. Schmeling A, Grundmann C, Fuhrmann A, et al. Criteria for age estimation in living individuals. *Int J Legal Med* 2008; **122(6)**: 457–60.
14. Arge S, Wenzel A, Holmstrup P, et al. Transition analysis applied to third molar development in a Danish population. *Forensic Sci Int* 2020; **308**: 110145.
15. Boldsen JL, Milner GR, Konigsberg LW, Wood JW. Transition Analysis: A New Method for Estimating Age From Skeletons. In: Hoppa RD & JW Vaupel (eds). *Paleodemography: Age Distributions from Skeletal Samples.* Cambridge: Cambridge University Press, 2002; pp. 73–106.
16. De Tobel J, Fieuws S, Hillewig E, et al. Multi-factorial age estimation: A Bayesian approach combining dental and skeletal magnetic resonance imaging. *Forensic Sci Int* 2020; **306**: 110054.
17. Tangmose S, Thevissen P, Lynnerup N, et al. Age estimation in the living: Transition analysis on developing third molars. *Forensic Sci Int* 2015; **257**: 512.e511–17.
18. Brooks S, Suchey J. Skeletal age determination based on the os pubis: A comparison of the Acsadi-Nemeskeri and Suchey-Brooks methods. *Human Evolution* 1990; **5**: 227–38.
19. Buckberry J L, Chamberlain AT. Age estimation from the auricular surface of the ilium: A revised method. *Am J Phys Anthropol* 2002; **119(3)**: 231–9.
20. Işcan MY, Loth SR, Wright RK. Metamorphosis at the sternal rib end: A new method to estimate age at death in white males [Research Support, Non-U.S. Gov't]. *Am J Phys Anthropol* 1984; **65(2)**: 147–56.
21. Lovejoy CO, Meindl RS, Pryzbeck TR, Mensforth RP. Chronological metamorphosis of the auricular surface of the ilium: A new method for the determination of adult skeletal age at death. *Am J Phys Anthropol* 1985; **68(1)**: 15–28.
22. Meindl RS, Lovejoy CO. Ectocranial suture closure: A revised method for the determination of skeletal age at death based on the lateral-anterior sutures. *Am J Phys Anthropol* 1985; **68(1)**: 57–66.
23. Nawrocki SP. The Nature and Sources of Error in the Estimation of Age at Death from the Skeleton. In: Latham K, Finnegan M (eds). *Age Estimation of the Human Skeleton.* Springfield, IL: Charles C Thomas Pub Ltd; 2010, pp. 79–101.
24. Scheuer L, Black S. *The Juvenile Skeleton.* London: Elsevier; 2004.
25. Rissech C, Lopez-Costas O, Turbon D. Humeral development from neonatal period to skeletal maturity: Application in age and sex assessment. *Int J Legal Med* 2013; **127(1)**: 201–12.
26. Stull KE, L'Abbé EN, Ousley SD. Using multivariate adaptive regression splines to estimate subadult age from diaphyseal dimensions. *Am J Phys Anthropol* 2014; **154(3)**: 376–86.
27. Haavikko K. Tooth formation age estimated on a few selected teeth: A simple method for clinical use. *Proc Finn Dent Soc* 1974; **70(1)**: 15–19.
28. Köhler S, Schmelzle R, Loitz C, Puschel K. Development of the wisdom tooth as a criterion for age-determination. *Ann Anat-Anatomischer Anzeiger* 1994; **176(4)**: 339–45.
29. Liversidge HM, Marsden PH. Summary of: Estimating age and the likelihood of having attained 18 years of age using mandibular third molars. *Br Dent J* 2010; **209(8)**: 406–7.
30. Mincer HH, Harris EF, Berryman HE. The ABFO study of third molar development and its use as an estimator of chronological age. *J Forensic Sci* 1993; **38(2)**: 379–90.
31. Shirley NR, Jantz RL. Spheno-occipital synchondrosis fusion in modern Americans. *J Forensic Sci* 2011; **56(3)**: 580–5.
32. Kellinghaus M, Schulz R, Vieth V, et al. Forensic age estimation in living subjects based on the ossification status of the medial clavicular epiphysis as revealed by thin-slice multidetector computed tomography. *Int J Legal Med* 2010; **124(2)**: 149–54.
33. Norouzi M, Hanafi MQ, Gharibvand MM. Computed tomography-based age estimation of illiac crests calcification in 10–29-year-old individuals. *J Family Med Prim Care* 2019; **8(6)**: 1947–52.
34. Urschler M, Krauskopf A, Widek T, et al. Applicability of Greulich-Pyle and Tanner-Whitehouse grading methods to MRI when assessing hand bone age in forensic age estimation: A pilot study. *Forensic Sci Int* 2016; **266**: 281–8.
35. Mentzel HJ, Vilser C, Eulenstein M, et al. Assessment of skeletal age at the wrist in children with a new ultrasound device. *Pediatr Radiol* 2005; **35(4)**: 429–33.
36. Varkkola O, Ranta H, Metsaniitty M, Sajantila A. Age assessment by the Greulich and Pyle method compared to other skeletal X-ray and dental methods in data from Finnish child victims of the Southeast Asian Tsunami. *Forensic Sci Med Pathol* 2011; **7(4)**: 311–16.
37. Greulich WW, Pyle SI. *Radiographic Atlas of Skeletal Development of the Hand and Wrist.* Redwood City, CA: Stanford University Press; 1959.
38. Kemperdick HF. Determination of skeletal age in children of Western-Germany with normal and abnormal growth-development. *Fortschritte Der Medizin* 1981; **99(5)**: 152–6.
39. King DG, Steventon DM, O'Sullivan MP, et al. Reproducibility of bone ages when performed by radiology registrars: An audit of Tanner-and-Whitehouse-Ii versus Greulich-and-Pyle methods. *Br J Radiol* 1994; **67(801)**: 848–51.
40. Groell R, Lindbichler F, Riepl T, et al. The reliability of bone age determination in central European children using the Greulich and Pyle method. *Br J Radiol* 1999; **72(857)**: 461–4.
41. van Rijn R R, Lequin MH, Robben SGF, et al. Is the Greulich and Pyle atlas still valid for Dutch Caucasian children today? *Pediatr Radiol* 2001; **31(10)**: 748–52.
42. Tanner JM, Healy MJR, Goldstein H, Cameron N. *Assessment of Skeletal Maturity and Prediction of Adult Height (TW3 Method).* 3rd ed. Philadelphia: Saunders; 2001.
43. Tanner JM, Whitehouse RH, Cameron N, et al. *Assessment of Skeletal Maturity and Prediction of Adult Height (TW2 Method).* 2nd ed. London: Academic Press; 1983.
44. Roche A F, Chumlea W, Thissen D. Assessing the skeletal maturity of the hand-wrist: FELS method. *Am J Hum Biol* 1989; **1(2)**: 175–183.
45. Scheuer L, Black SMD. *Developmental Juvenile Osteology.* London: Academic Press; 2000.
46. Webb PAO, Suchey JM. Epiphyseal union of the anterior iliac crest and medial clavicle in a modern multiracial sample of American males and females. *Am J Phys Anthropol* 1985; **68(4)**: 457–66.
47. Lottering N, Alston-Knox CL, MacGregor DM, et al. Apophyseal ossification of the iliac crest in forensic age estimation: Computed tomography standards for modern Australian subadults. *J Forensic Sci* 2017; **62(2)**: 292–307.
48. Meijerman L, Maat GJR, Schulz R, Schmeling A. Variables affecting the probability of complete fusion of the medial clavicular epiphysis. *Int J Legal Med* 2007; **121(6)**: 463–68.
49. Tangmose S, Jensen KE, Lynnerup N. Comparative study on developmental stages of the clavicle by postmortem MRI and CT imaging. *J Forensic Radiol Imaging* 2013; **1(3)**: 102–06.
50. Tangmose S, Jensen KE, Villa C, Lynnerup N. Forensic age estimation from the clavicle using 1.0T MRI: Preliminary results. *Forensic Sci Int* 2014; **234**: 7–12.
51. Jurik AG. *Imaging of the Sternocostoclavicular Region.* Berlin Heidelberg: Springer-Verlag; 2007.

52. Keats ET. *Atlas of Normal Roentgen Variants That May Simulate Disease.* 6th ed. Maryland Heights, MI: Mosby; 1996.
53. Schulz R, Zwiesigk P, Schiborr M, et al. Ultrasound studies on the time course of clavicular ossification. *Int J Legal Med* 2008; **122(2)**: 163–7.
54. Nystrom ME, Ranta HM, Peltola JS, Kataja JM. Timing of developmental stages in permanent mandibular teeth of Finns from birth to age 25. *Acta Odontol Scand* 2007; **65(1)**: 36–43.
55. Alqahtani SJ, Liversidge HM, Hector MP. The London Atlas of tooth development and eruption. *Am J Phys Anthropol* 2010; **142(3)**: 481–90.
56. Demirjian A, Goldstein H, Tanner JM. New system of dental age assessment. *Human Biology* 1973; **45(2)**: 211–27.
57. Chaillet N, Nystrom M, Demirjian A. Comparison of dental maturity in children of different ethnic origins: International maturity curves for clinicians. *J Forensic Sci* 2005; **50(5)**: 1164–74.
58. Gunst K, Mesotten K, Carbonez A, Willems G. Third molar root development in relation to chronological age: A large sample sized retrospective study. *Forensic Sci Int* 2003; **136(1–3)**: 52–57.
59. Celikoglu M, Miloglu O, Kazanci F. Frequency of agenesis, impaction, angulation, and related pathologic changes of third molar teeth in orthodontic patients. *J Oral Maxillofac Surg* 2010; **68(5)**: 990–5.
60. John J, Nambiar P, Mani SA, et al. Third molar agenesis among children and youths from three major races of Malaysians. *J Dent Sci* 2012; **7(3)**: 211–17.
61. Levesque GY, Demirijian A, Tanguay R. Sexual dimorphism in the development, emergence, and agenesis of the mandibular third molar. *J Dent Res* 1981; **60(10)**: 1735–41.
62. Dhanjal KS, Bhardwaj MK, Liversidge HM. Reproducibility of radiographic stage assessment of third molars. *Forensic Sci Int* 2006; **159**: S74–S77.
63. Olze A, Bilang D, Schmidt S, et al. Validation of common classification systems for assessing the mineralization of third molars. *Int J Legal Med* 2005; **119(1)**: 22–26.
64. Cavallo F, Mohn A, Chiarelli F, Giannini C. Evaluation of bone age in children: A mini-review. *Front Pediatr* 2021; **9**: 580314.
65. Roche AF. Secular trends in human growth, maturation, and development: Introduction. *Monogr Soc Res Child Dev* 1979; **44(3–4)**: 1–120.
66. Hawley NL, Rousham EK, Norris SA, et al. Secular trends in skeletal maturity in South Africa: 1962–2001. *Ann Hum Biol* 2009; **36(5)**: 584–94.
67. Ranjitkar S, Lin Nih-Hung L, Macdonald R, et al. Stature and skeletal maturation of two cohorts of Australian children and young adults over the past two decades. *Aust Orthod* 2006; **22(11)**: 47–58.
68. So LL, Yen PK. Secular trend in skeletal maturation in southern Chinese girls in Hong Kong. *Z Morphol Anthropol* 1990; **78(2)**: 145–53.
69. Takai S, Akiyoshi T. Skeletal maturity of Japanese children in Western Kyushu. *Am J Phys Anthropol* 1983; **62(2)**: 199–204.
70. Schmeling A, Schulz R, Danner B, Rosing F. The impact of economic progress and modernization in medicine on the ossification of hand and wrist. *Int J Legal Med* 2006; **120(2)**: 121–6.
71. Roche AF, Davila GH. Associations between the rates of maturation and growth in the short bones of the hand. *Am J Phys Anthropol* 1970; **33(3)**: 349–355.
72. Lovejoy CO, Meindl RS, Mensforth RP, Barton TJ. Multifactorial determination of skeletal age at death: A method and blind tests of its accuracy. *Am J Phys Anthropol* 1985; **68(1)**: 1–14.
73. Buckberry JL, Chamberlain AT. Age estimation from the auricular surface of the ilium: a revised method. *Am J Phys Anthropol* 2002; **119(3)**: 231–9.
74. Falys CG, Schutkowski H, Weston DA. Auricular surface aging: Worse than expected? A test of the revised method on a documented historic skeletal assemblage. *Am J Phys Anthropol* 2006; **130(4)**: 508–13.
75. Hens SM, Rastelli E, Belcastro G. Age estimation from the human os coxa: A test on a documented Italian collection. [Research Support, Non-U.S. Gov't]. *J Forensic Sci* 2008; **53(5)**: 1040–43.
76. Osborne DL, Simmons TL, Nawrocki SP. Reconsidering the auricular surface as an indicator of age at death. *J Forensic Sci* 2004; **49(5)**: 905–11.
77. Todd TW. Age changes in the pubic bone. I. The male white pubis. *Am J Phys Anthropol* 1920; **3(3)**: 285–334.
78. Suchey JM, Brooks ST, Katz D. *Instructions for Use of the Suchey-Brooks System for Age Determination of the Female os pubis. Instructional Materials Accompanying Female pubic symphysial Models of the Suchey-Brooks System.* Fort Collins, Colorado: France Casting; 1988.
79. Suchey JM, Katz D. Application of Pubic Age Determination in a Forensic Setting. In: Reichs K, (ed). *Forensic Osteology*. Springfield, IL: Charles C Thomas Pub Ltd, 1998, pp. 204–236.
80. Stone JL. Paul Broca and the first craniotomy based on cerebral localization. *J Neurosurg* 1991; **75(1)**: 154–9.
81. Barszcz M, Wozniak K. Complete sagittal suture closure evaluation based on post mortem computed tomography. *Leg Med (Tokyo)* 2021; **52**: 101907.
82. Nolte M, Wilczak C. Three-dimensional surface area of the distal biceps enthesis, relationship to body size, sex, age and secular changes in a 20th Century American sample. *Int J Osteoarchaeol* 2013; **23(2)**: 163–74.
83. Belcastro MG, Rastelli E, Mariotti V. Variation of the degree of sacral vertebral body fusion in adulthood in two European modern skeletal collections. *Am J Phys Anthropol* 2008; **135(2)**: 149–60.
84. Rühli FJ, Muntener M, Henneberg M. Age-dependent changes of the normal human spine during adulthood. *Am J Hum Biol* 2005; **17(4)**: 460–9.
85. Milner G R, Boldsen JL. Skeletal Age Estimation: Where We Are and Where We Should Go. In: Dirkmaat DC (ed). *A Companion to Forensic Anthropology*. Chichester: John Wiley & Sons, Ltd; 2012, pp. 224–38.
86. Boldsen JL, Milner GR, Konigsberg LW, Wood JW. Transition Analysis: A New Method for Estimating Age from Skeletons. In: Hoppa RD, Vaupel JW (eds). *Paleodemography: Age Distributions from Skeletal Samples*. Cambridge: Cambridge University Press; 2002, pp. 73–106.
87. Barvencik F, Gebauer M, Beil FT, et al. Age- and sex-related changes of humeral head microarchitecture: Histomorphometric analysis of 60 human specimens. *J Orthop Res* 2010; **28(1)**: 18–26.
88. Lynnerup N, Thomsen I, Frohlich B. A non-invasive technique for age at death determination. *Med Sci Law* 1990; **30(4)**: 317–20.
89. Villa C, Buckberry J, Lynnerup N. Evaluating osteological ageing from digital data. *J Anat* 2019; **235(2)**: 386–95.
90. Barrier P, Dedouit F, Braga J, et al. Age at death estimation using multislice computed tomography reconstructions of the posterior pelvis. *J Forensic Sci* 2009; **54(4)**: 773–8.
91. de Froidmont S, Grabherr S, Vaucher P, et al. Virtual anthropology: A comparison between the performance of conventional X-ray and MDCT in investigating the trabecular structure of long bones. *Forensic Sci Int* 2013; **225(1–3)**: 53–59.
92. Pasquier E, De Saint Martin Pernot L, Burdin V, et al. Determination of age at death: Assessment of an algorithm of age prediction using numerical three-dimensional CT data from pubic bones. *Am J Phys Anthropol* 1999; **108(3)**: 261–8.
93. Villa C, Hansen MN, Buckberry J, et al. Forensic age estimation based on the trabecular bone changes of the pelvic bone using post-mortem CT. *Forensic Sci Int* 2013; **233(1–3)**: 393–402.
94. Biwasaka H, Sato K, Aoki Y, et al. Three dimensional surface analyses of pubic symphyseal faces of contemporary Japanese reconstructed with 3D digitized scanner. *Leg Med (Tokyo)* 2013; **15(5)**: 264–8.
95. Slice DE, Algee-Hewitt BF. Modeling bone surface morphology: A fully quantitative method for age-at-death estimation using the pubic symphysis. *J Forensic Sci* 2015; **60(4)**: 835–43.
96. Stoyanova D, Algee-Hewitt BF, Slice DE. An enhanced computational method for age-at-death estimation based on the pubic symphysis using 3D laser scans and thin plate splines. *Am J Phys Anthropol* 2015; **158(3)**: 431–40.
97. Villa C, Buckberry J, Cattaneo C, et al. Quantitative analysis of the morphological changes of the pubic symphyseal face and the auricular surface and implications for age at death estimation. *J Forensic Sci* 2015; **60(3)**: 556–65.
98. Gustafson G. Age determinations on teeth. *J Am Dent Assoc* 1950; **41(1)**: 45–54.
99. Timme M, Borkert J, Nagelmann N, et al. Age-dependent decrease in dental pulp cavity volume as a feature for age assessment: A comparative in vitro study using 9.4-T UTE-MRI and CBCT 3D imaging. *Int J Legal Med* 2021; **135(4)**: 1599–1609.

100. Kerley ER. The microscopic determination of age in human bone. *Am J Phys Anthropol* 1965; **23(2)**: 149–163.
101. Lynnerup N, Frohlich B, Thomsen JL. Assessment of age at death by microscopy: Unbiased quantification of secondary osteons in femoral cross sections. *Forensic Sci Int* 2006; **159**: S100–S103.
102. Lynnerup N, Kjeldsen H, Heegaard S, et al. Radiocarbon dating of the human eye lens crystallines reveal proteins without carbon turnover throughout life. *PLoS One* 2008; **3(1)**: e1529.
103. Spalding KL, Buchholz BA, Bergman LE, et al. Forensics: Age written in teeth by nuclear tests. *Nature* 2005; **437(7057)**: 333–4.
104. Lynnerup N, Kjeldsen H, Zweihoff R, et al. Ascertaining year of birth/age at death in forensic cases: A review of conventional methods and methods allowing for absolute chronology. *Forensic Sci Int* 2010; **201(1–3)**: 74–78.
105. Helfman PM, Bada JL. Aspartic-acid racemization in tooth enamel from living humans. *Proc Natl Acad Sci USA* 1975; **72(8)**: 2891–94.
106. Ritz-Timme S, Collins MJ. Racemization of aspartic acid in human proteins. *Ageing Res Rev* 2002; **1(1)**: 43–59.
107. Ritz-Timme S, Laumeier I, Collins MJ. Aspartic acid racemization: evidence for marked longevity of elastin in human skin. *Br J Dermatol* 2003; **149(5)**: 951–9.
108. Engel MH, Zumberge JE, Nagy B. Kinetics of amino acid racemization in *Sequoiadendron giganteum* heartwood. *Anal Biochem* 1997; **82(2)**: 415–22.
109. Moini M, Klauenberg K, Ballard M. Dating silk by capillary electrophoresis mass spectrometry. *Anal Chem* 2011; **83(19)**: 7577–81.
110. Griffin RC, Chamberlain AT, Hotz G, et al. Age estimation of archaeological remains using amino acid racemization in dental enamel: A comparison of morphological, biochemical, and known ages-at-death. *Am J Phys Anthropol* 2009; **140(2)**: 244–52.
111. Helfman PM, Bada JL, Shou MY. Considerations on the role of aspartic acid racemization in the aging process. *Gerontology* 1977; **23(6)**: 419–25.
112. Ohtani S, Yamamoto K. Age estimation using the racemization of amino-acid in human dentin. *J Forensic Sci* 1991; **36(3)**: 792–800.
113. Johnstone-Belford EC, Blau S. A review of bomb pulse dating and its use in the investigation of unidentified human remains. *J Forensic Sci* 2020; **65(3)**: 676–85.
114. Zapico SC, Gauthier Q, Antevska A, McCord BR. Identifying methylation patterns in dental pulp aging: Application to age-at-death estimation in forensic anthropology. *Int J Mol Sci* 2021; **22(7)**: 3717.
115. Dias HC, Cordeiro C, Real FC, et al. (2020). Age estimation based on DNA methylation using blood samples from deceased individuals. *J Forensic Sci* 2020; **65(2)**: 465–70.

CHAPTER

20

Medicolegal Autopsy

Bertrand Ludes

INTRODUCTION

A medicolegal autopsy usually constitutes the last examination of a deceased individual and the very last opportunity to document findings with the possibility of collecting adequate samples for laboratory investigations (1). To facilitate the work of the forensic pathologist, who is expected to provide an opinion regarding the causes and manner of death, post-mortem investigations must include examination of the crime scene or police records of these investigations, a review of the case history and, finally, the autopsy itself (2). The autopsy must include external examination and dissection, the microscopic examination of tissues and laboratory analyses such as toxicological, genetic or limnological screenings on bodily fluids or tissues. Nowadays, post-mortem CT (PMCT) examination is also proving a valuable adjunct to these investigations.

Definition

An autopsy can be defined as the detailed systematic external and internal examination of a corpse carried out by a pathologist and/or one or several medicolegal experts to ascertain the underlying and possible contributing causes of death, as well as the manner of death. To perform an autopsy, an authorization by the juridical or police authorities must be given. During the act, the necessary health and safety precautions must be taken, and medical ethical principles must be respected to guarantee the dignity of the deceased.

There are two main types of autopsies:

- The medicolegal or forensic autopsy, ordered by the competent legal authority to investigate sudden unexpected, suspicious, unnatural, or criminal deaths. These investigations are also performed for deaths in police custody or during imprisonment, or to identify unknown bodies. In most jurisdictions, the permission of the relatives is not required.
- The hospital or clinical autopsy, performed to investigate the extent of a known disease and the effectiveness of treatment. It can also be performed as part of a medical audit or for research purposes. The consent of the relatives is required unless the deceased has given consent before death.

Medicolegal autopsies have much broader goals than clinical autopsies and include as much information as possible about the scene of death and the circumstances of death. It consists, after the examination of the clothing (if found on the corpse), of a full external and internal examination of the body, including the dissection and investigation of all three body cavities (1).

An autopsy must be thought of as a complete process that does not only consist in the physical analysis, but also considers the presumed circumstances of death, including attendance at the scene where the body was found, reconstruction of the circumstances of death and the clinical/pathologic course of the causes of death.

HISTORIC BACKGROUND

The earliest recorded external examination of a dead body was performed in ancient China more than 2000 years ago and the development of ancient forensic medicine originated in the period of warring states (475–221 BCE) (3).

During the Song dynasty (AD 960–1279) official documents requested a written order for a post-mortem examination and reported the case to higher authorities. The procedure included external examination and proposed conclusions based on that examination. These documents had to be signed by the parties involved and certified by the official assigned to the case (1).

In continental Europe, the Justinian Code (AD 529–564) introduced the principle that the function of medical experts is to assist the judiciary by impartial interpretation and opinion (1).

As early as AD 800, Emperor Charlemagne asked judges to resort to doctors in criminal cases. Later, in the fourteenth century, the first forensic autopsy was performed in Bologna by Bartolomeo da Varignana on a body suspected of having been poisoned (4).

In 1532, the Constitutio Criminalis Carolina promulgated by Charles V had a major impact on the development of forensic medicine. Many of its provisions

DOI: 10.1201/9781003138754-22

brought about the indispensable expansion of the forensic discipline. At the same time, Ambroise Paré, the King's surgeon, took an interest in forensic medicine, the practice of autopsies and reflected on what medicine and surgery could bring to sixteenth-century justice (4).

The examinations were reported orally to judges and the surgeons also had to provide expertise regarding injuries to living persons.

Concerning the investigative dissection of a dead body, the earliest anatomic dissections took place in Alexandria, Egypt, around 320 BCE in the first known school of anatomy (1), and concerning medicolegal dissection, we can consider that the first ones were performed at the University of Bologna in Italy between 1266 and 1275 and, as mentioned previously, in France, by Ambroise Paré in 1562.

The practice of clinical autopsy took much longer to develop and first came to prominence after the introduction of the modern concepts of disease pathogenesis by Carl von Rokitansky (1804–1878) (1).

Forensic medicine took a new turn in the eighteenth century with the creation of scientific societies and specialized chairs of forensic medicine in several European universities. In the nineteenth century, the forensic autopsy was almost accepted by all and famous names in forensic medicine published reference works containing very precise clinical descriptions, particularly in France: *The Treaty of Legal Medicine* by Mathieu Orphila in 1830, and the *Precis of Legal Medicine* by Léon Thoinot in 1913 (4).

Scientific advances and discoveries of the twentieth century in various fields (toxicology, imaging, genetic identification, etc.) have contributed to significant advances in the practice of forensic medicine and in the application and adoption of accurate medicolegal autopsy protocols.

OBJECTIVES OF AN AUTOPSY

- Identify a body or record all the identification parameters to permit scientific identification
- Determine the cause of death (to record and describe all pathologic processes apparent in the deceased that could contribute to understanding the cause and circumstances of the death)
- In relevant cases, determine whether stillbirth or live birth has occurred
- Determine the mode of death; to determine how the death occurred, i.e. to draw conclusions about the cause of death and other medical and non-medical factors contributing to death
- Contribute to the reconstruction of the circumstances surrounding the death
- Determine the time of death
- Describe all external or internal abnormalities, malformations and diseases
- Record and describe external and internal injuries
- Sample biological fluids or tissues to allow ancillary investigations
- Take photographs and collect samples for evidential or teaching purposes
- Provide a full written report and expert interpretation of the findings
- Restore the body to the best possible cosmetic condition before release.

It should also be noted that the information obtained during the autopsy can be of further value in terms of public health. In fact, autopsy results can help to describe the causes of death more accurately, allowing for more adequate mortality statistics and may be used as an early-warning system for issues of public health and safety, contributing to the prevention of disease and accidents.

According to European recommendation R (99) 3 (5) about the harmonization of the indications of medico-legal autopsies, the following circumstances can be cited:

- Homicide or suspected homicide
- Sudden, unexpected death including sudden infant death
- Violation of human rights, suspicion of torture or any other form of ill treatment
- Suicide or suspected suicide
- Suspected medical malpractice
- Accidents (domestic, occupational or transportational)
- Technological or environmental disasters
- Occupational diseases and hazards
- Death in custody or associated with police or military activities
- Unidentified remains.

IMAGING TECHNIQUES BEFORE AUTOPSY

Post-mortem imaging is usually routine in most forensic institutes.

Classically, and historically, radiography has been employed to document the findings of the pathologist at the time of examination.

Natural normal or abnormal osseous findings may be documented, such as occult fractures of the extremities or the typical metaphyseal lesion in cases of likely physical abuse, namely child abuse. Radiologic imaging techniques are usually performed systematically before the dissection itself. Classical X-ray is appropriate in cases of bone fractures or with the presence of foreign bodies but new imaging techniques, such as PMCT and magnetic resonance imaging (MRI) allow the visualization and analysis of patterned injuries. These investigations are required for postoperative autopsies following the complications of anesthesia, surgical intervention or postoperative care.

The acceptance of traditional autopsies has decreased dramatically in the past few years, and it is useful to limit the practice of this invasive approach, namely by submitting bodies to post-mortem imaging, thus allowing for triage based, for example, on the presence of signs of the involvement of a third party, which constitute strong arguments in favor of a full autopsy (6).

Because of its ability to provide quick and complete documentation of the skeletal system and major parenchymal alterations, PMCT is the imaging technique most frequently applied in post-mortem forensic investigations.

In fact, PMCT is very useful in analyzing violent deaths, since it permits excellent visualization of skeletal traumatic lesions, intra-vascular gases and foreign bodies. This technique is not only noninvasive and nondestructive, but it also covers regions of the body that are not usually dissected during autopsy, such as the extremities and the soft tissues of the back and the spine.

Post-mortem MRI (PMMR) has also been implemented in post-mortem settings, but its use is usually limited to focused analysis (e.g. the study of the heart and brain).

PMCT angiography has also been introduced to differentiate soft-tissue interfaces and for the diagnosis of vascular lesions.

When these post-mortem imaging techniques are used exclusively however, no samples can be collected for histopathological, toxicological or microbiological analyses, although the introduction of post-mortem percutaneous biopsies could resolve this issue (7).

Another advantage of post-mortem imaging techniques is digitalization of the images, allowing the storage of data which can be analyzed by other experts if judges make this request, even years later if a case is reopened.

Three-dimensional (3D) images are also especially suitable for presentation in court during trial since they are more intelligible to non-medical experts. The frequency of requests for PMCT scanning varies from institution to institution and depends on the availability of the scanner inside the medicolegal department (7).

According to Flach and al. (8), PMCT is indicated in cases of gunshot wounds, blunt or sharp trauma, accidental death where a reconstruction of the event is desirable, in decomposed bodies or for identification purposes, namely in mass catastrophes where PMCT might greatly facilitate identification. PMCT angiography may be usefully added in case of natural death (such as acute aortic dissection, ruptured aortic aneurysm, etc.) or in traumatic deaths where parenchymal lesions are suspected and where unenhanced PMCT often fails to correctly document and identify such pathologic alterations (9).

Wang et al. (10) proposed combining forensic imaging and endoscopic investigations by thoracoscopy and laparoscopy to examine organs and tissues in the thoracic and abdominal cavities (coelioscopy) for post-mortem examination in cases where a diagnosis of drowning must be established. Concurrently, target tissues are also sampled for histological examination. This combined technique would likely be highly efficient at detecting hemothorax, hemoperitoneum, aortic injuries, as well as injuries of the liver, spleen and diaphragm.

In a multicentric study, Grabherr et al. (11) proposed that post-mortem examination should be performed in a stepwise manner, beginning with a thorough external examination of the body and the circumstances of death. Secondarily, a PMCT should be performed, since it may be sufficient to confirm a suspected cause and/or manner of death. PMCT is used here as a means of triage, because it helps to determine whether autopsy, PMCT angiography, targeted histological analysis, or any combination would best help to ascertain the cause and manner of death.

These authors suggest that PMCT angiography detects a greater number of important issues than autopsy, especially vascular and bone abnormalities; it is therefore the method of choice for vascular examination. For parenchymal and soft-tissue examination, autopsy and PMCT angiography detect similar findings, but PMCT alone is inferior. By combining autopsy and PMCT angiography, abnormalities are more likely to be detected and the quality of the post-mortem examination is thus increased.

AUTOPSY TECHNIQUES (15)

The medicolegal autopsy involves external and internal examinations of the three body cavities, the sampling of body fluids and tissues for ancillary investigations and the writing of a report.

External examination of the body should be carried out systematically and include the head, the neck, the trunk, the upper and lower extremities, the back of the body and must include:

- Observation of the clothing. Even if the pathologist does not perform a detailed examination of the clothing, they must identify damage such as cuts or bullet holes and establish the relations between those marks and the injuries observed on the body.
- The sex, age, build, height and weight, biogeographic group, nutritional state, skin and hair color and physical characteristics such as scars, tattoos or morphologic abnormalities.
- A description of post-mortem changes, especially the distribution and grading of *rigor mortis*, the distribution of post-mortem lividity and its apparent degree of fixation and hypostasis, as well as decomposition.
- The precise description of all bodily surfaces and orifices, length, density and distribution of hair, color of irises and sclerae, the presence or absence of petechiae or other injuries.
- The appearance of the ears and nose.
- The nature of the dentition.
- The presence of blood or vomit in both the nose and mouth.
- The presence of any foreign material, evidence of medical treatment or resuscitation (endotracheal or nasogastric tubes, airways or surgical marks).
- The description of the injuries must include a description of the location in relation to stable anatomic landmarks, indications of size, shape and color of the injury as well as the correct qualification of the injury in terms of blunt-versus-sharp force.

Internal examination includes examination of the body cavities and the organs *in situ*, followed by a description of the volumes and appearances of bodily fluids. After this step, the internal organs are removed, weighed, examined and samples are collected for further analyses. The investigation should describe the presence of gas, that is, pneumothorax, the presence of fluids, that is, effusions or exudates (the volumes of which must be measured) and finally the presence of foreign bodies.

Whether the internal organs are removed as a single block or in separate organ groups will depend on the practice and training of individual pathologists and the necessities of the case.

From a practical point of view, it is often best to remove the neck and chest organs as a single block and then, after ligating the jejunum, the liver, spleen, pancreas, stomach and duodenum can be removed as a separate block. The retroperitoneal tissues and the aorta are then removed, as well as the pelvic organs, with the appropriate dissection techniques (12).

A coronal incision across the top of the scalp from behind each ear may allow access to the brain and allow the pathologist to record, by exposure of the posterior subcutaneous scalp tissues, all subcutaneous scalp and galeal injuries.

The description must include the appearance of the internal surfaces and anatomic boundaries, as well as the location and external appearance of organs. All organs must be dissected after description of the outer appearance, the cut surface has also to be mentioned and the weight of the major organs should be recorded. The hollow organs must be opened, and their contents described and measured. All relevant vessels, arteries and veins should be dissected. All abnormalities must be described by location and size.

Photographs including the case number, a measuring device such as a ruler and a color code may be included in the autopsy files.

During the medicolegal autopsy, samples must be collected, according to national legislation, for ancillary investigations, such as the histological examination of the main organs, toxicological analyses of bodily fluids, such as peripheral blood, vitreous humor (for alcohol level, glucose, ketones, electrolytes), cerebrospinal fluid, bile, urine, the stomach contents, hair samples or other relevant tissues, (e.g. the lung, in cases of inhalation of volatiles).

Some small specimens can be sampled for various tests relevant to the case, that is, analyses in toxicology, biochemistry, microbiology, endocrinology, histology, anthropology, neuropathology, limnology and molecular biology. Small samples of internal organs examined are also retained to be included into histology blocks and slides for later examination.

Under French law, biological samples withdrawn during an autopsy cannot be returned to the families after analysis (4).

AUTOPSY REPORT

The medicolegal autopsy report is an essential part of the procedure and should be complete, detailed and comprehensible by non-experts. This report should include a discussion of the significance of all the findings made during the dissection. Where the findings are of an uncertain nature and there are several competing potential causes, the pathologist should attempt to give an opinion regarding their probability (1).

Attention must be given to the provision of the formal report within a reasonable timeframe, and it should be made available to the tribunal/courts, the next of kin and any legitimately interested parties.

The report should include all the information obtained during the autopsy, including negative findings, which may be as valuable as the positive findings.

The best way to write the report is to follow the dissection protocol and to start with the description of the lesions, before detailing the injuries caused to the chest wall, abdomen or head and finally describing the internal organs. In the discussion and conclusion, the autopsy findings must highlight the role of the lesions in the cause and manner of death.

Both the report and subsequent expert testimony in court should avoid giving opinions based on incomplete or inadequate scientific or medical analyses and must endeavor to refrain from favoring one party over another during the proceedings, a process that must include identifying possible unconscious biases.

The testimony of the pathologist in court is one of the most important phases of their work and all the required care and skill must be applied to this task (13).

It may also be suggested that, in accordance with good medical practice, all relevant observations and negative findings, as well as the samples, should be recorded in a way that would allow another pathologist to provide their own analysis and accurate conclusions concerning a case (13).

HANDLING THE FAMILY OF THE DECEASED AND OTHER ETHICAL CONSIDERATIONS

Autopsies may only be conducted in institutions (hospital, mortuaries, medicolegal institutes) that possess adequate facilities and safety procedures.

In a forensic pathology context, in which a deceased person's body has been taken out of the control of the relatives and an autopsy has been performed (often without the express consent of the next of kin) a heavy responsibility is placed on the forensic pathologist to ensure that the autopsy is carried out in a dignified way. Special care should be taken to ensure appropriate respect for the deceased person and the interests of the families. These obligations are often expressed in relevant legislation dealing with autopsies. In accordance with those obligations, the facilities and equipment destined to receive the bodies must be carefully considered. They must allow proper storage, the viewing of bodies by families and the reconstruction of bodies after the autopsy (13).

Informing the family

Before each forensic autopsy, it is essential that the relatives of the deceased be notified of their death, that an autopsy is to be carried out and that they understand what this means. The decision may cause additional pain for families, which we must all try to alleviate by showing humanity and respect, in our words and in our actions. In France, this concept is specified in article 230–28 of the CCP (14). The text does not specify by whom the information should be delivered. The role of the medical examiner is not to receive the families of the deceased. This role therefore falls to police officers. It is unacceptable that families still learn more about the death of their loved one from the media than from investigators. According to the French article 230–28 of the CPP (14), the summarized information to be provided relates to the fact and process of the autopsy and the collection of biological samples. At a minimum, families should be made aware of the location of the body of the deceased and when the body will be presentable. The samples only concern liquids and organ fragments (with exceptions) and that they will be destroyed at the request of the courts at the end of the legal proceedings (4).

CONCLUSION

The medicolegal autopsy is a technical act that is the responsibility of the forensic pathologist who performs it. A medicolegal autopsy must be performed thoroughly, according to strict protocols and in the presence of police officers. These autopsy protocols represent the minimum methods of investigations (description, photographic documentation, etc.), dissection and sample collection. There are specific procedures in certain cases which complete the basic protocols. It is essential to stress the importance of describing lesions using precise forensic vocabulary and anatomic landmarks. It is also imperative to take samples during this autopsy, which must include at least mandatory toxic and anatomopathological samples and additional samples according to the case (e.g. genetics in the event of an identification problem, diatoms in the event of suspected drowning).

Whatever the situation, the medicolegal autopsy must be performed according to ethical rules while respecting the body being examined. It is imperative to carry out the necessary investigations and to refrain from any unnecessary mutilation. At the end of the autopsy, the body must be reconstituted, certain disfiguring operations must possibly be masked by medical care devices (bandage, cotton net, etc.) and possible embalming treatments must be carried out. It is always necessary to provide supporting information to the family about the practice of the medicolegal autopsy so that the process is as transparent as possible.

REFERENCES

1. Saukko P, Pollak S. Autopsy, Procedures and Standards. In: Payne-James JJ, Byard RW, Corey TS, Henderson C (eds), *Encyclopedia of Forensic and Legal Medicine*, Vol 1. London: Elsevier; 2005, pp. 166–71.
2. Krous HF, Corey TS. Pediatric. In: Payne-James JJ, Byard RW, Corey TS, Henderson C (eds), *Encyclopedia of Forensic and Legal Medicine*, Vol 1. London: Elsevier; 2005, pp. 176–83.
3. Tao JJ, Cameron JM, Xu W. A brief history of forensic medicine in China. *The Criminologist* 1988, **12**: 67.
4. Delbreil M, Voyer M, Sapanet L. Leturmy. L'autopsie médico-légale au regard de la loi. *Presse Med* 2018; **47**: 339–48.
5. European recommendation R (99) 3, 2002. Available from: *http://prison.eu.org/recommandation-r-99-3-sur-l/* (Accessed 26 April 2023).
6. Bollinger SA, Thali MJ, Ross S, et al. Virtual autopsy using imaging: Bridging radiologic and forensic sciences. A review of the Virtopsy and similar projects. *Eur Radiol* 2018; **18**: 273–82.
7. Filograna L, Pugliese L, Muto M, et al. A practical guide to virtual autopsy: Why, when and how. *Semin Ultrasound CT MRI* 2018; **40**: 56–66.
8. Flach PM, Gascho D, Schweitzer W, et al. Imaging in forensic radiology: An illustrated guide for postmortem computed tomography technique and protocols. *Forensic Sci Med Pathol* 2014; **10**: 583–606.
9. Ross SG, Bollinger SA, Ampanozi G, et al. Postmortem CT angiography: Capabilities and limitations in traumatic and natural causes of death. *Radiographics* 2014; **34**: 830–46.
10. Wang Z, Ma K, Zou D, et al. Diagnosis of drowning using postmortem computed tomography combined with endoscopic autopsy. *Medicine (Baltimore)* 2020; **99**(**11**): e19182.
11. Grabherr S, Heinemann A, Vogel H, et al. Postmortem CT angiography compared with autopsy: A forensic multicenter study. *Radiology* 2018; **288**: 270–76.
12. Ferris JAJ. Autopsy, Adults. In: Payne-James JJ, Byard RW, Corey TS, Henderson C (eds), *Encyclopedia of Forensic and Legal Medicine*, Vol 1. London: Elsevier; 2005, pp. 183–92.
13. Cordner S, McKelvie H. Autopsy, Medico-Legal Considerations. In: Payne-James JJ, Byard RW, Corey TS, Henderson C (eds), *Encyclopedia of Forensic and Legal Medicine*, Vol 1. London: Elsevier; 2005, pp. 171–6.
14. Republique Francaise. *Code de procédure pénale*. Available from: https://www.legifrance.gouv.fr (Accessed 25 April 2023).
15. Geraut A. L'autopsie. In: Chariot P, Debout M (eds), *Traité de Médecine Légale et de Droit de la santé*. Paris: Vuibert; 2011, pp. 74–88.

CHAPTER

21

Hospital Autopsy

Julian L. Burton, Panagiota Kitsanta, Eu-Wing Toh, Kirsty L. Lloyd, Katie McDonald and S. Kim Suvarna

INTRODUCTION

The autopsy is the standard investigation to determine the cause of death (1–2). In addition, hospital autopsies have roles to play in quality assurance and audit of care (2–3), evaluating the positive and negative effects of treatment, the presence of occult pathology, collecting material for research and in teaching medical students (4) and doctors (1–3).

Autopsy practice can be broadly divided into two categories: hospital autopsies and medicolegal (or "forensic") autopsies. Hospital autopsies are typically performed by hospital-based histopathologists at the request of the attending clinician (who, in England and Wales, must be sufficiently confident in the cause of death that they can provide a Medical Certificate of the Cause of Death [MCCD]) and with consent obtained from the deceased's next of kin. By contrast, medicolegal autopsies are undertaken on the instruction of a legal authority such as a coroner or procurator fiscal and do not require consent of the next of kin. Medicolegal autopsies are conducted where the cause of death is not known, and/or where death may be due to an iatrogenic cause, the deceased's occupation, suicide, accident or unlawful actions of a third party. Regardless of the broad category, the autopsy examination might be conducted in a hospital mortuary or a public mortuary. We define the hospital autopsy as those examinations conducted at the request of clinicians under consent from the next of kin. As these examinations are performed at the request of, and ultimately for the education of, clinicians, the requesting clinicians should be invited to attend the hospital autopsy (or a review of its findings) wherever possible.

There may be little practical difference between the hospital and medicolegal autopsy in the post-mortem room. Both types of autopsies will include a review of available historic information, an external examination and some form of internal examination. Medicolegal autopsies may focus more on trauma and may be limited to an exploration of the cause(s) of death. By contrast, depending on the consent obtained, hospital autopsies may take a wider remit, exploring in depth all diseases found during the examination.

Studies from around the world have repeatedly and consistently demonstrated the value of the hospital autopsy in determining the cause of death in adults and children by revealing frequent discrepancies between clinical diagnoses and autopsy findings (5–16). In such studies, the autopsy is often considered to be the gold standard in death investigation (17), but we should be mindful that while autopsy is the standard, it is not quite so shiny. Autopsy practice frequently lacks quality assurance procedures, and opportunities to review autopsy findings may be limited. Nonetheless, the autopsy consistently reveals class I errors in approximately 10 percent of cases (17). Hospital autopsies have also played a pivotal role in delineating the pathology in newly recognized diseases. For example, autopsy studies have been essential in determining the cardiorespiratory, neurologic, gastrointestinal and renal pathologies caused by SARS-CoV-2 in the recent pandemic (18–23).

Hospital autopsy rates have declined markedly over the past 60 years in many countries (1–4,17,24,25) such that in some hospitals fewer than 1 percent of deaths are now followed by a hospital autopsy (25). The reasons for the hospital autopsy's decline are multifactorial (26). Clinicians may be reluctant to request autopsies because they perceive them to be unnecessary in an age of modern antemortem laboratory and radiologic investigation, because the results come too late to be of value, because gaining consent is onerous, and/or because they fear litigation if proven wrong (3,17,24). Pathologists may eschew autopsy practice, perceiving it to be unpleasant and/or unrewarding (3). For hospital managers, the autopsy is expensive (3). Relatives may feel that the deceased has already suffered enough or may have religious objections. Negative press and public scandals around autopsy practice might also dissuade relatives from granting consent (27) but a common reason why relatives do not give consent is that they are not asked (3,4).

Despite the marked decline in the hospital autopsy rate, there may be some cause for hope. Waidhauser et al. (28) demonstrated that autopsy rates could be improved from 0 percent to 35.8 percent at a center in Germany over a 10-year period by means of structured conversations with relatives and demonstrations of autopsy findings to clinicians. Other authors have had similar results, stressing the importance of engagement of clinicians by pathologists and structured engagement

DOI: 10.1201/9781003138754-23

with relatives (29,30). When such interventions are discontinued, however, autopsy rates tend to return to their baseline levels (31). The current global shortage of pathologists, with fewer pathologists electing to train in autopsy practice (2) and ever-rising workload pressures created by materials from the living, may mean that the capacity to increase the hospital autopsy rate no longer exists in all centers.

A detailed step-by-step description of how to perform a hospital autopsy would merit a book of its own(23,33) and falls outside the scope of this chapter. Instead, we consider the importance of a complete medical history and the role that digital and limited autopsies have to play before presenting an overview of key aspects of the evisceration, sample collection and dissection undertaken during hospital autopsies.

THE IMPORTANCE OF THE CLINICAL HISTORY

Clinical history taking is essential in achieving the most accurate diagnosis. The value of a comprehensive history at autopsy cannot be overstated; however the quantity and quality of the information varies enormously.

It is important to recognize that there are two types of historic information: factual and hearsay. Factual information comes from medical records, results of investigations undertaken in life and, to a certain extent, occupational and social circumstances. Hearsay is received from coroner's officers, the police, witnesses and so on. While these reports are indeed useful, they should be viewed with caution; a lay person's explanation to a police officer which is then interpreted by them may not be accurate. It is not uncommon for much of the history to be absent, for example, in those patients who function outside of conventional society with a nomadic lifestyle or a chaotic life due to drug and substance misuse where access to health services may not be joined up into the medical records.

The job of the pathologist is first to establish whether the case presented to them for examination is indeed appropriate for their level of expertise or speciality. For the purpose of this chapter, the pathologist must be satisfied that a hospital autopsy is appropriate and that referral to the appropriate medicolegal authority is not required. Once the case is accepted, then the gathering of data will be familiar to all doctors: circumstances prior to death (presenting complaint), past medical, drug, social, occupational and family history along with information about allergies.

From this initial assessment, decisions can be made with regard to the examination approach, the ancillary investigations that may be required (toxicology, microbiology, histology, frozen tissue for genetic analysis, etc.). The history allows the pathologist to predict which organs are most likely to provide supporting evidence of pathologic processes and the cause of death. The autopsy will play a role in confirming the presence, severity and sequelae of previously recorded diseases. The history may also influence dissection technique, for example, in a committed alcoholic one might anticipate gastrointestinal hemorrhage and therefore ensure that the esophagus remains intact with the stomach to allow for inversion and examination of varices. Where the history raises the possibility of infection or sepsis, the pathologist is guided to consider collecting samples for microbiological examination.

The history helps ensure the safety of the mortuary team. Information about potential hazard group 3 and 4 infections (or their risk factors) or hazardous material (radioactive beads, electronic or implanted sharps) is essential to carry out the correct risk assessment of each case (34).

The cause of death formulation is provided on the balance of probability. This is a low benchmark, and the history helps enormously with the specific question of why this person died at that moment, and not last week. Given the importance of the clinical history in the autopsy, waiting for the appropriate level of information prior to examining the body is reasonable.

THE ROLE OF PMCT/DIGITAL AUTOPSY EXAMINATION

The increasing role at autopsy of post-mortem computerized tomography (PMCT) has somewhat lagged behind computerized tomography (CT) for the living (35,36). PMCT is not a radical new development since plain radiographs have been used for skeletal surveys and identification of foreign bodies in forensic autopsies for decades. There has also been research and specialist radiology investigations on consent autopsy tissues including post-mortem coronary angiography using dye infusion and plain X-rays of stents (37).

Given that it is neither practical, nor indeed desirable, to autopsy the majority of the deceased in the United Kingdom (UK) (or indeed any another country) the question arises from the perspective of the epidemiologists, public health departments and various government agencies as to how to readily define non-certified deaths. From a pragmatic perspective, if societies are prepared to accept a statement as to the cause of death from the family or hospital doctor, based solely on a history and/or clinical assessment (38), then PMCT clearly provides additional information which can reassure the pathologist as to the accuracy of the cause of death (35,39).

In the UK, post-mortem imaging has developed initially from post-mortem magnetic resonance imaging (PMMR) driven by faith needs in Manchester. The religious desire for a body to be rapidly progressed after death to a defined death certificate allows prompt burial. The delays facing some relatives 20–30 years ago, awaiting autopsy investigation, pushed the coroner to accept post-mortem radiology as a solution, with this now being accepted legal practice (40). That some families did not want an open investigation was a further factor promoting the radiologic autopsy. It became evident that, in non-contrast studies on bodies, there were relative advantages of PMCT over PMMR and this has largely become the primary post-mortem investigation of choice (36,39).

The pathologist may wish to look at the radiology but, in most centers, current practice provides PMCT information from the radiologist in text form (41). Inasmuch as the background history from the family doctor and case summary from the various hospitals that have treated this individual are concerned, PMCT is simply another set of data which may guide one to a cause of death and/or focus one's attention on an area of the body which needs invasive study.

PMCT has a variety of advantages over conventional autopsy, perhaps with the most obvious being those of speed and simplification of body handling. Bodies can be placed into secure, leak-proof bags and examined by CT scan in a modern scanning unit, often within 15 minutes per body. If specialist tests are required, such as localized angiography or targeted needle biopsy of lesions within the body, the timings may be longer (42). Yet, even on unselected cases, the rapid progress of unselected bodies through the mortuary allows designation of cause of death and transfer to the funeral services for the bereaved in the majority of cases (41). It is stressed that, despite this positive statement, some open autopsies will be needed.

Many medicolegal authorities look for a cost advantage for running a PMCT service over a conventional mortuary and autopsy service. A conventional autopsy service has fixed costs of the mortuary buildings, staff, consumables and so-on, notwithstanding the caseload variables of consumables and tests. This has to be balanced against the costs of setting up a scanner unit, transporting bodies to/from an established radiologic service and the provision of other staff.

As indicated, given that not all causes of death may be resolved by PMCT, it must be realized that some mortuary activity will need to continue. It is therefore reasonable to expect that some degree of cost increase may be found, depending on the workload being seen in any mortuary. However, what is clear is that there is some financial benefit in the reduction in cases needing open autopsy. Those that merit such investigation often only require localized dissection and avoidance of the need to open all body compartments (41). This speeds up handling of the bodies and correspondingly allows the pathologist more time to focus on areas of complex pathology needing consideration.

From the workload planning viewpoint, the availability of PMCT images and reports, often 6–24 hours before starting an autopsy, allows clear consideration of the relevant areas for dissection and tests needed. It also may identify when to defer cases (should the PMCT reveal unexpected and/or suspicious injuries) (43). Overall, there is a time saving for body handling, diminished relatives' stress, some reduction in autopsy suite activity and protection of pathologist's time.

One might regard the post-mortem imagery as akin to histology. The PMCT produces a static image of the body, usually in two dimensions, although 3D-rendered images can provide particularly useful information when cases are being reviewed. Indeed, the opportunity for scans to be available for hospital mortality meetings and potentially available to courts in cases of criminal and civil claims cannot be underestimated (43). The images can be viewed in a non-emotive manner, unlike autopsy suite external and open dissection photographs.

It follows that, if there is a reduction in open autopsies, the traditional methods of training will be diminished (33) as there will necessarily be fewer bodies available for standard training practices. The experienced autopsy practitioner/trainer must therefore use their smaller pool of cases for open investigations with more creativity in order to train individuals at all stages of their career progression (44).

Looking at the ways one validates the progression of a trainee will need to be changed. Reliance on a simple "number of cases performed" is a poor discriminator as to trainee ability and competence. Yesteryear, practices of giving repeated basic cases to trainees did little to allow them to develop appropriate skills for the many pathologies and post-treatment cases that make up the bulk of complex autopsy practice. Training centers and national accreditation bodies must ensure that appropriate training and examination in PMCT autopsies exists for relevant certification before trainees move to established consultant practice (44).

FULL OR LIMITED AUTOPSY?

A full autopsy is generally expected to include a review of the available clinical information, an external examination, evisceration of thoracic, abdominal, pelvic and cranial cavities, and macroscopic examination of each organ. Limited autopsies require some invasive internal examination, perhaps coupled with PMCT. In some jurisdictions, a cause of death may be given if one is apparent after only an external examination (e.g. the view and grant system in Scotland), but these have a high error rate and will not be considered further here (45). The extent of a hospital autopsy will vary depending on the availability of PMCT and upon the consenting family's wishes.

While PMCT may reveal the cause of death, a limited invasive examination may still be necessary following the radiologic autopsy (46). This situation can arise when there is need to collect tissue samples, a need to distinguish between two differential diagnoses, or when a diagnosis not visualized on PMCT (e.g. pulmonary thromboembolism) is suspected in a particular body cavity. Obtaining samples for further investigations does not necessitate evisceration (47,48). Samples for microbiological and virological testing and for histopathologic examination can be obtained via needle biopsy (48,49). Bacteriological and virological swabs of the oropharyngeal and nasopharyngeal cavities can also be obtained (49). Samples for toxicological testing can be obtained via needle aspiration of bodily fluids (47). Where needed, percutaneous needle biopsies can be collected with palpation of masses, ultrasound (50) or PMCT guidance (51). The use of thoracoscopy, endoscopy, endovascular collection (52) and/or laparoscopy have been suggested, but these techniques are not widely available in mortuaries, and remain a research tool (52,53). The level of invasiveness will depend on the differential diagnosis as well as the pathologist concerned.

Advantages of limited autopsies include increased speed and societal acceptability as well as decreased risk to staff from biohazards. Disadvantages are, however, inherent in all stages of the process. There is a danger of missing significant pathology if there is a lack of relevant clinical or radiologic information before autopsy, or if testing does not show expected results. Lastly, there is a risk of deskilling consultants, trainees and anatomic pathology technicians if procedures are not regularly performed. The only available systematic review of minimally invasive techniques still expounds full conventional post mortems as the most accurate, with minimally invasive examinations that include biopsies as a close second (54).

The decision to perform a limited hospital autopsy will depend on the consent obtained, legal and procedural factors, the available clinical information, radiologic findings and the confidence of individual pathologists. One can change to performing a full autopsy at any time if there are unexpected findings. Flexibility of approach is key, both before and during the autopsy.

SAMPLE COLLECTION

Samples for histopathologic, toxicological, microbiological or genetic analysis are commonly collected during the autopsy in order to reach or refine a cause of death. The pathologist should consider what samples may be necessary before entering the mortuary, having considered the available clinical history, while having flexibility to modify their plan as the autopsy progresses. Often, there will only be one opportunity to collect adequate uncontaminated samples, and this is particularly true for samples collected for microbiological or toxicological analysis (49,55).

Samples of the heart, lungs, liver, spleen, pancreas, kidney, brain and of any identified lesion can be collected as dissection progresses for histopathologic examination.

Where death may be due to an infection, microbiological sampling is essential (55). A detailed consideration of which samples to collect in which clinical scenarios is outside the scope of this chapter. Samples of blood (preferably from the subclavian vein), urine, cerebrospinal fluid and swabs of the nasopharynx and/or oropharynx for bacteriological and virological studies are best collected prior to evisceration in order to reduce the risk of contamination by the gut microbiome (49). Fluid samples are collected using percutaneous needle puncture having first cleaned the skin with alcohol or alcohol-based solutions containing iodine or chlorhexidine (49,55). Tissue samples, for example of the lungs, spleen, heart and brain, and aspirates of bile or pus are best collected as soon as the body has been opened during evisceration and prior to other handling of the internal organs (49,55). Samples for microbiological study are collected using separate sets of sterilized instruments and are placed into sterile empty containers without fixative (49,55). Where the autopsy has been limited to one or more body cavities, or indeed to a minimally invasive autopsy with needle biopsy only, samples of solid organs can still be collected for microbiological study by percutaneous core biopsy (48). Even where there is considerable putrefaction or a prolonged post-mortem interval, such investigations may still yield pathogenic organisms of interest (55,56) but discussion with a microbiologist is recommended (55). Because the possibility of post-mortem bacterial contamination exists, correlation of microbiology results with those of antemortem cultures and post-mortem histology is recommended (55).

Approximately 5 percent of significant major pathologies at autopsy can only be diagnosed with the aid of histopathologic examination (14). Samples can be collected via needle biopsy or during the dissection of organs. Samples placed directly into tissue cassettes are then fixed in 10 percent neutral buffered formalin. Only rarely is it necessary to retain a whole organ. Washing of tissues at autopsy has been demonstrated not to impair histology (57). The samples collected will be guided by the clinical history and autopsy findings.

While commonly used in medicolegal autopsies, toxicology is of less relevance to hospital autopsies (because concerns over drug toxicity should prompt referral of the death to the appropriate medicolegal authority). Plain and preserved samples of femoral venous blood, urine, vitreous humor obtained prior to or during evisceration are the principal samples to be collected (2). It is better to collect the samples at the start of the autopsy and discard them than to reach the end of the examination and wish you had them.

As with toxicology, collection of samples for genetic testing is more likely to be a feature of medicolegal autopsies investigating sudden deaths. It still has a role in hospital autopsies, for example, when the clinical history or autopsy findings raise the possibility of an inherited heart disease (58). A 2 cm^3 sample of spleen or psoas muscle should be collected into an empty sterile container and submitted for DNA extraction and genome/exon analysis.

Digital photography has a valuable role to play in the autopsy, and pathologists should have a low threshold for photographing findings as the autopsy progresses.

EVISCERATION

The modern hospital autopsy requires adaptable techniques ranging from examinations limited to the chest, abdomen, pelvis or head, a full autopsy or combination of these.

Where a full invasive examination is to be performed, the body is opened using a Y-incision or (modified Y-incision) on the anterior torso (and neck), and a horizontal incision over the occipitoparietal scalp is employed to allow access to the calvarium. Where an invasive examination is to be limited to one or more body cavities of the torso, a vertical midline I-shaped incision is employed (59,60). The deep midline vertical skin incision starts at the sternal notch and extends to the symphysis pubis. This can be modified to end 10 cm below the xiphoid for a limited-to-chest approach or to start at this point and end at the pubis for an autopsy limited to the abdomen. The Patowary incision (61), which exposes both the anterior and posterior aspects of the torso and the calvarium, is rarely used.

The skin is reflected to expose the rib cage so that the skin flaps lie to the right and the left sides. Rib shears, an oscillating saw or a long-bladed serrated knife are used to divide the ribs in the midclavicular line, starting at the costal margin and working to the sternoclavicular joints (60). The anterior rib shield is removed to expose the thoracic organs. If the neck structures are required, these are exposed by reflecting the skin and incising the floor of the mouth from the mandible. The abdominal cavity is opened by a deep midline vertical incision through the skin, taking care not to puncture the intestines when opening the peritoneum (60).

Having opened the body cavities, the pathologist must determine which method to use to eviscerate the organs of the torso. A variety of eponymously named techniques exist (Table 21.1), with most pathologists in our center preferring a modified Y-incision and either the Letulle or Gohn techniques, in which the organs of the neck and torso are removed as one or two blocks (59,60). The techniques described by Virchow (62) and Rokitansky are rarely employed (though may have value where a limited autopsy is desired).

In the Letulle technique, the tongue, trachea and esophagus are pulled gradually toward the thorax and freed from the surrounding soft tissues in continuity with the thoracic aorta and large vessels, the lungs, mediastinum and heart. If the abdomen is not to be eviscerated the esophagus is cut at the level of the diaphragm and both the neck structures and the thoracic organs are removed as one piece. In the abdomen, the intestines are removed first, leaving behind the proximal jejunum and duodenum in continuity with the stomach. The rectum is cut distally at the level of the anterior peritoneal reflection with a circular knife cut. The pelvic organs are freed on either side by blunt dissection and transected distally. The diaphragm is incised circumferentially and the abdominal and retroperitoneal organs are dissected from their vertebral attachments and removed *en masse* with the pelvic organs as one block (60).

Having incised the occipital scalp, the scalp flap is reflected anteriorly over the face and posteriorly to the back, and the muscles are reflected. An oscillating saw is used to perform a circumferential craniotomy and the skullcap is removed, exposing the dura mater (60). The sagittal sinus is incised and examined, and then the dura mater is incised to expose the cerebral hemispheres. The cranial nerves and all the attachments of the meninges to the cranium are divided working antero-posteriorly and the brain is removed intact by severing the spinal cord just below the foramen magnum (63). The pituitary gland can be removed by making parasagittal incisions on either side of the sella turcica and then removing the posterior wall of the sella using a T-piece. The pituitary gland can be removed with a scalpel (60,63).

TABLE 21.1 Evisceration techniques (59,60,62)

Technique	Description
Gohn	The organs are removed as a series of blocks (brain, neck and thoracic organs, abdominal organs, pelvic organs)
Letulle	The organs are removed from the body as a single block, '*en masse*'
Rokitansky	The organs are dissected *in situ* and then removed in a series of blocks
Virchow	The organs are removed from the body one at a time to be dissected and examined

DISSECTION

While there is no single correct sequence for organ dissection, it is important that it is performed in a systematic and methodical manner (64). The authors' approach to dissection is to start with dissection of the organs of the retroperitoneum and pelvis, followed by the upper gastrointestinal tract, the thoracic block and ending with the brain. Each organ is weighed as it is removed from its surrounding tissues.

With the organ block positioned so that the posterior surface is uppermost, the abdominal aorta is opened down to the common iliac arteries, noting the condition of the intima and the patency of ostia of the main branches. The adrenal glands are identified and dissected. The perinephric fat and renal capsules are incised and removed. The ureters are freed by blunt dissection to the bladder. The kidneys are bisected, allowing inspection of their parenchyma, and the ureters are opened. The bladder (and prostate) is opened anteriorly with scissors via the urethra. The vagina is opened vertically with scissors and the uterus is bisected longitudinally. The ovaries are bisected in the coronal plane. It is rare that the fallopian tubes need to be opened (64,65).

Next, attention is focused on the upper abdominal organs. The spleen is lifted posteriorly and the gastrosplenic ligament divided to expose the lesser peritoneal sac and the pancreas. The pancreas is sliced. The spleen is removed, weighed and sliced. The esophagus is dissected free and opened longitudinally with scissors, the incision being extended along the greater curve of the stomach into the duodenum. Patency of the common bile duct is assessed by gently squeezing the gallbladder to express bile into the duodenum. The gallbladder is then dissected from the liver bed and opened longitudinally. The liver is separated from its vascular attachments, weighed and sliced. Where intestinal pathology is suspected, the small and large intestines can also be opened at this point along their antimesenteric borders (64,66).

Dissection of the thoracic block begins with opening of the pericardium to expose the heart, pulmonary trunk and aortic root. The pulmonary vasculature is identified, opened and inspected for thromboemboli. The heart is then freed from its vascular attachments.

The coronary arteries are incised at 3–5 mm intervals along their lengths. The heart can then be opened. First, three horizontal slices are made through the distal ventricles. The heart is then opened following the flow of blood (67). The trachea and main bronchi are opened posteriorly to the hilum of the lungs. The lungs are then separated from their hilar attachments and weighed. The lungs may then be bisected in the coronal plane, or the vessels and bronchi of the lungs can be opened from the hilum (64,68).

The brain is weighed and then the Circle of Willis is identified and dissected. The cerebellum and brain stem are removed and sliced. The cerebellum is then radially sliced. The cerebral hemispheres are sliced at 10–15 mm intervals and inspected (63,64).

AT THE END OF THE AUTOPSY

Once the dissection has been completed, and all samples required collected, the organs should be returned to the body so that it can be reconstructed by an anatomic pathology technician. The pathologist's attention then should turn to the provision of a timely complete autopsy report. The report should include the demographic details of the deceased, a brief synopsis of the clinical history, the findings of PMCT (if used) and then the findings of the external and internal examinations. Where further investigations, such as histopathology, microbiology, genetics and/or toxicology have been performed, the results should be included. The salient positive findings should be summarized, and then discussed to explain the cause of death.

REFERENCES

1. Burton J, Underwood J. Clinical, educational, and epidemiological value of autopsy. *Lancet* 2007; **369(9571)**: 1471–80.
2. Davis G. Forensic toxicology. *Clin Lab Sci* 2012; **25(2)**: 120–24.
3. Van den Tweel J, Wittekind C. The medical autopsy as quality assurance tool in clinical medicine: Dreams and realities. *Virchows Archiv* 2016; **468**: 75–81.
4. Burton J. The autopsy in modern undergraduate medical education: A qualitative study of uses and curriculum considerations. *Med Educ* 2003; **37**: 1073–81.
5. Aalten C, Samson M, Jansen P. Diagnostic errors; the need to have autopsies. *Neth J Med* 2006; **64**: 186–90.
6. Carlotti A, Bachette L, Carmona F, et al. Discrepancies between clinical diagnoses and autopsy findings in critically ill children: A prospective study. *Am J Clin Pathol* 2016; **146(6)**: 701–08.
7. Coradazzi A, Morganti A, Montenegro M. Discrepancies between clinical diagnoses and autopsy findings. *Braz J Med Biol Res* 2003; **36(3)**: 385–91.
8. González-Franco M, Ponce-Camacho M, Barboza-Quintana O, et al. Discrepancies between clinical and autopsy diagnosis, a study of 331 autopsies performed over a 7 year period. *Medicina Universitaria* 2012; **14(54)**: 16–22.
9. Friberg N, Ljungberg O, Berglund E, et al. Cause of death and significant disease found at autopsy. *Virchows Archiv* 2019; **475**: 781–8.
10. Issa V, Dinardi L, Pereira T, et al. Diagnostic discrepancies in clinical practice. An autopsy study in patients with heart failure. *Medicine (Baltimore)* 2017; **96(4)**: e5978.
11. McGoogan E. The autopsy and clinical diagnosis. *J R Coll Physicians Lond* 1984; **18(4)**: 240–43.
12. Ordi J, Castillo P, Garcia-Basteiro A, et al. Clinico-pathological discrepancies in the diagnosis of causes of death in adults in Mozambique: A retrospective observational study. *PLOS One* 2019; **14(9)**: e0220657.
13. Pastores S, Dulu A, Voight L, et al. Premortem clinical diagnoses and postmortem autopsy findings: Discrepancies in critically ill cancer patients. *Crit Care* 2007; **11**: R48.
14. Roulson J, Benbow E, Hasleton P. Discrepancies between clinical and autopsy diagnosis and the value of post mortem histology: A meta-analysis and review. *Histopathology* 2005; **47(6)**: 551–59.
15. Shojania K, Burton E, McDonald K, et al. Changes in rates of autopsy-detected diagnostic errors over time: A systematic review. *JAMA* 2003; **289**: 2849–56.
16. Tavora F, Crowder C, Sun C-C, et al. A comparison of university, community and private autopsy practices. *Am J Clin Pathol* 2008; **129**: 102–09.
17. Goldman L. Still necessary, even if occasionally not sufficient. *Circulation* 2018; **137**: 2686–88.
18. Elsoukarry S, Mostyka M, Dillard A, et al. Autopsy findings in 32 patients with COVID-19: a single institution experience. *Pathobiology* 2021; **88**: 56–68.
19. Falasca L, Nardacci R, Columbo D, et al. Postmortem findings in Italian patients with COVID-19: A descriptive full autopsy study of cases with and without comorbidities. *J Infect Dis* 2020; **222(11)**: 1807–15.
20. Hanley B, Naresh K, Roufosse C, et al. Histopathological findings and viral tropism in UK patients with severe fatal COVID-19: A post-mortem study. *Lancet Microbe* 2020; **1(1)**: E245–E53.
21. Maiese A, Manetti A, La Russa R, et al. Autopsy findings in COVID-19 related deaths: A literature review. *Forensic Sci Med Pathol* 2020; **7**: 1–18.
22. Sekhawat V, Green A, Mahadeva U. COVID-19 autopsies: Conclusions from international studies. *Diagn Histopathol* 2021; **27(3)**: 103–07.
23. Sperhake J-P. Autopsies of COVID-19 deceased? Absolutely! *Legal Med (Tokyo)* 2020; **47**: 101769.
24. Loughrey M, McCluggage W, Toner P. The declining autopsy rate and clinicians' attitudes. *Ulster J Med* 2000; **69(2)**: 83–9.
25. Turnbull A, Osborn M, Nicholas N. Hospital autopsy: Endangered or extinct? *J Clin Pathol* 2015; **38**: 601–04.
26. Byard R, Bourne A. The autopsy: A dying art? A paediatric perspective. *J Paediatr Child Health* 1990; **26**: 119–21.
27. Burton J, Underwood J. Autopsy practice after the "organ retention scandal": Requests, performance and tissue retention. *J Clin Pathol* 2001; **56**: 537–41.
28. Waidhauser J, Martin B, Trepel M, et al. Can low autopsy rates be increased? Yes, we can! Should postmortem examinations in oncology be performed? Yes, we should! A postmortem analysis of oncological cases. *Virchows Archiv* 2021; **478**: 301–08.
29. Haque A, Patterson R, Grafe M. High autopsy rates at a university medical center. What has gone right? *Arch Pathol Lab Med* 1996; **120(8)**: 727–32.
30. Lugli A, Anabitarte M, Beer J. Effect of simple interventions on necropsy rate when active informed consent is required. *Lancet* 1999; **354**: 1391–92.
31. Underwood J. The Future of the Autopsy. In: Burton J, Rutty G (eds), *The Hospital Autopsy: A Manual of Fundamental Autopsy Practice*, 3rd ed. London: Hodder Arnold; 2010, pp. 11–17.
32. Burton J, Rutty G. *The Hospital Autopsy: A Manual of Fundamental Autopsy Practice*, 3rd ed. London: Hodder Arnold; 2010.
33. Suvarna S. *Atlas of Adult Autopsy. A Guide to Modern Practice*, 1st ed. New York: Springer International Publishing; 2016.
34. Burton J. Health and safety at necropsy. *J Clin Pathol* 2003; **56(4)**: 254–60.
35. Roberts I, Benamore R, Benbow E, et al. Post mortem imaging as an alternative to autopsy in the diagnosis of adult deaths: a validation study. *Lancet* 2012; **379(9811)**: 136–42.
36. Smith A, Traill Z, Roberts I. Post mortem imaging in adults. *Diagn Histopathol* 2018; **24(9)**: 365–71.
37. Grabherr S, Djonov V, Yen K, et al. Postmortem angiography: review of former and current methods. *Am J Roentgenol* 2007; **188(3)**: 832–8.
38. Thomas L-M, D'Ambruoso L, Balabanova D. Verbal autopsy in health policy and systems: a literature review. *BMJ Global Health* 2018; **2018(3)**: e000639.

39. Inai K, Noriki S, Kinoshita K, et al. Postmortem CT is more accurate than clinical diagnosis for identifying the immediate cause of death in hospitalized patients: a prospective autopsy-based study. *Virchows Archiv* 2016; **469**(1): 101–09.
40. Chief Coroner. Guidance No 1. The Use of Postmortem Imaging (adults), 2016. Available from: https://www.judiciary.uk/wp-content/uploads/2013/09/guidance-no-1-use-of-port-mortem-imaging.pdf (Accessed 25 April 2023).
41. Suvarna S, Kitsanta P, Burton J. The effects of postmortem CT scanning all cases entering a UK public mortuary: a 3-month pilot. *J Clin Pathol* 2017; **70**: 903–04.
42. Roberts I, Traill Z. Minimally invasive autopsy employing post mortem CT and targeted coronary angiography: Evaluation of its application to a routine Coronial service. *Histopathology* 2014; **64**(2): 211–17.
43. Rutty G, Morgan B, Robinson C, et al. Diagnostic accuracy of post mortem CT with targeted coronary angiography versus autopsy for coroner-requested post mortem investigations: A prospective, masked, comparison study. *Lancet* 2017; **390**(**10090**): 145–54.
44. Suvarna S. The colour of autopsy training – from red … to black and white. *ACP News* 2017; 31–33.
45. Rutty G, Duerden R, Carter N, et al. Are coroners' necropsies necessary? A prospective study examining whether a "view and grant" system of death certification could be introduced into England and Wales. *J Clin Pathol* 2001; **54**(4): 279–84.
46. Burton J, Kitsanta P. Daily application of post-mortem computed tomography digital autopsy in a public mortuary. *Diagn Histopathol* 2020; **26**(8): 358–67.
47. Burton J. Standard and Special Tests. In: Suvarna S (ed), *Atlas of Adult Autopsy Practice: A Guide to Modern Practice*, 1st ed. New York: Springer International Publishing; 2016.
48. Saegman V, Cohen M, Burton J, et al. Microbiology in minimally invasive autopsy: best techniques to detect infection. ESGFOR (ESCMID study group of forensic and post-mortem microbiology) guidelines. *Forensic Sci Med Pathol* 2021; **17**(1): 87–100.
49. Burton J, Saegman V, Arribi A, et al. Postmortem microbiology sampling following death in hospital: an ESGFOR task force consensus statement. *J Clin Pathol* 2019; **72**(5): 329–36.
50. Weustink A, Hunink M, van Dijke C, et al. Minimally invasive autopsy: an alternative to conventional autopsy? *Radiology* 2009; **250**(3): 897–904.
51. Blokker BM, Weustink AC, Wagensveld IM, et al. Conventional autopsy versus minimally invasive autopsy with postmortem MRI, CT, and CT-guided biopsy: Comparison of diagnostic performance. *Radiology* 2018; **289**(3): 658–67.
52. Fan J, Tong D, Poon J, et al. Multimodality minimally invasive autopsy: A feasible and accurate approach to post-mortem examination. *Forensic Sci Int* 2010; **195**(**1–3**): 93–8.
53. Cacchione R, Sayad P, Pecoraro A, et al. Laparoscopic autopsies. *Surg Endosc* 2001; **15**(6): 619–22.
54. Blokker B, Wagensveld I, Weustink A, et al. Non-invasive or minimally invasive autopsy compared to conventional autopsy of suspected natural deaths in adults: a systematic review. *Eur Radiol* 2016; **26**(4): 1159–79.
55. Fernández-Rodríguez A, Burton J, Andreoletti L, et al. Post-mortem microbiology in sudden death: Sampling protocols proposed in different clinical settings. *Clin Microbiol Infect* 2019; **25**(5): 570–79.
56. Palmiere C, Vanhaebost J, Ventura F, et al. Cerebrospinal fluid PCR analysis and biochemistry in bodies with severe decomposition. *J Forensic Leg Med* 2015; **34**: 21–24.
57. Cotton D, Stephenson T. Impairment of autopsy histology by organ washing: A myth. *Med Sci Law* 1988; **28**(4): 319–23.
58. Ribeiro A, Coelho L, Puentes K, et al. Postmortem genetic testing: Clinical diagnosis is not ended by the patient's death. *Rev Port Cardiol (Engl Ed)* 2019; **38**(7): 503–09.
59. Menezes R, Monteiro F. *Forensic Autopsy*. StatPearls Publishing; 2020. Available from: https://www.ncbi.nlm.nih.gov/books/NBK539901/ (Accessed 25 April 2023).
60. Rutty G, Burton J. The Evisceration. In: Burton J, Rutty G (eds), *The Hospital Autopsy: A Manual of Fundamental Autopsy Practice*, 3rd ed. London: Hodder Arnold; 2010, pp. 115–35.
61. Patowary A. The fourth incision: A cosmetic autopsy technique. *Am J Forensic Med Pathol* 2010; **31**: 37–41.
62. Virchow R. *A Description and Explanation of the Method of Performing Post-Mortem Examinations*. London: J&A Churchill; 1876.
63. Burton J, Suvarna S. The Central Nervous System, with Eye and Ear. In: Suvarna S (ed), *Atlas of Adult Autopsy: A Guide to Modern Practice*, 1st ed. New York: Springer International Publishing; 2016, pp. 271–97.
64. Burton J, Rutty G. Dissection of the Internal Organs. In: Burton J, Rutty G (eds), *The Hospital Autopsy: A Manual of Fundamental Autopsy Practice*, 3rd ed. London: Hodder Arnold; 2010, pp. 136–58.
65. Suvarna S. Genitourinary and Breast Tissues, Including Preganancy. In: Suvarna S (ed), *Atlas of Adult Autopsy: A Guide to Modern Practice*, 1st ed. New York: Springer International Publishing; 2016, pp. 191–225.
66. Brown S, Suvarna S. Gastrointestinal and Hepatobiliary System. In: Suvarna S (ed), *Atlas of Adult Autopsy: A Guide to Modern Practice* 1st ed. New York: Springer International Publishing; 2016, pp. 161–90.
67. Sheppard M. Approach to the cardiac autopsy. *J Clin Pathol* 2012; **65**(6): 484–95.
68. Suvarna S. Thorax: Heart, Lungs, Mediastinum, and Pleura. In: Suvarna S (ed), *Atlas of Adult Autopsy: A Guide to Modern Practice*, 1st ed. New York: Springer International Publishing; 2016, pp. 65–160.

CHAPTER 22

Minnesota Protocol

Ritesh George Menezes and Alok Atreya

INTRODUCTION

"All human beings are born free and equal in dignity and rights" (1). Any unlawful death is a violation of the right to life, where the perpetrator should be made accountable. The Minnesota Protocol is a practical guideline to investigate unlawful, suspicious or potentially unlawful deaths occurring anywhere in the world (2). This protocol is followed throughout the world and has been translated into many different languages and is a standard protocol to be followed by death investigators in the following situations:

- Death caused by law enforcement personnel (army, police, paramilitary) who are either directed, permitted, or acquiesced to by the state
- Death caused by private military or security forces while exercising a state function
- Custodial death (either in prison or detention center)
- When the state fails to protect an individual or individuals from threats of violence which are foreseeable and caused by non-state agents.

The protocol stresses the prompt, effective, thorough, impartial and transparent investigation into such unlawful deaths.

OBJECTIVES OF THE MINNESOTA PROTOCOL

1. To formulate a standard and detailed guideline to investigate potentially unlawful deaths.
2. To observe the highest standard of professional ethics of the individual involved in the investigation.

HISTORY

The Philippine leader Benigno Aquino, while returning to his country after a 3-year stay in the United States, was shot dead as he stepped from the plane in 1983 (3). A small group of lawyers based in Minnesota, United States were concerned by this unlawful death of the opposition leader by armed military and the lack of accountability. They advocated for an unbiased investigation into such unlawful deaths holding the perpetrators accountable (4). However, there was no national or international guideline to investigate such cases. These lawyers, therefore, felt a need for a standard protocol. They formed the "Minnesota Lawyers International Human Rights Committee" and engaged local and international legal and forensic experts. After working for several years, they devised a standard draft which they presented at a conference in Wayzata, Minnesota in 1987. In 1989, it was endorsed by the United Nations (UN) General Assembly as the "UN Principles on the Effective Prevention and Investigation of Extra-Legal, Arbitrary, and Summary Executions". In 1991, the UN formally adopted the guidelines as the "United Nations Manual on the Effective Prevention and Investigation of Extra-Legal, Arbitrary, and Summary Executions", which is commonly known as the "Minnesota Protocol" (5). The manual was further revised in 2016, commissioned by the UN to meet the requirements of the twenty-first century with an official title "the Minnesota Protocol on the Investigation of Potentially Unlawful Death" (2016).

PROTECTION OF HUMAN RIGHTS IN MASS KILLINGS

Genocides or mass killings are usually undertaken to assume or consolidate political power, wealth and position. After an incident of genocide, the victims are either buried or disposed of in a secluded location. The families of those who are killed often do not know the fate of their loved ones, whether they are alive or dead, and if dead, where the body/remains are located. Such "ambiguous loss" occurs without official verification of life or death. Some families may hope for the return and others may perceive the lost person as dead. Without proof of finality and lack of the body/remains for final rituals, it becomes a story without an end. The families of the missing/disappeared are ignored, exploited, or swept under the rug for political reasons. The physical and

DOI: 10.1201/9781003138754-24

TABLE 22.1 Rights and obligations to the families of the missing or dead from armed conflicts

Rights/obligation	International Humanitarian Law: Rules (6)	Practice guidelines relating to the rule (6)
"With a view to the identification of the dead, each party to the conflict must record all available information prior to disposal and mark the location of the graves."	Rule 116: Accounting for the Dead. (Related Practice: Volume II, Chapter 35, Section E)	Article 4 of 1929 Geneva Conventions; Article 16 of 1949 Geneva Convention I
"Each party to the conflict must take all feasible measures to account for persons reported missing as a result of armed conflict and must provide their family members with any information it has on their fate."	Rule 117: Accounting for missing person. (Related Practice: Volume II, Chapter 36, Section A)	Article 32 and 33(1) of Additional Protocol I to the 1977 Geneva Conventions; Article 136–141 of 1949 Fourth Geneva Convention; Article 13(6) of 1992 UN Declaration on Enforced Disappearance
"Family life must be respected as far as possible."	Rule 105: Respect for Family Life. (Related Practice: Volume II, Chapter 32, Section Q)	Article 46 of the 1899 and 1907 of Hague Regulation; Article 27 of 1949 Geneva Convention IV; Article 10(1) of the 1966 International Covenant on Economic, Social and Cultural Rights; Article 11and 17 of the 1969 American Convention on Human Rights; Article 17 and 23 of the 1966 International Covenant on Civil and Political Rights; Article 38 of the 1874 Brussels Declaration
"Parties to the conflict must endeavor to facilitate the return of the remains of the deceased upon request of the party to which they belong or upon the request of their next of kin. They must return their personal effects to them."	Rule 114: Return of the Remains and Personal Effects of the Dead. (Related Practice: Volume II, Chapter 35, Section C)	Article 16 and 17: First Geneva Convention, 1864

psychological suffering of the family who does not know the fate of their loved ones is a humanitarian problem. As a result, there are international laws formulated to provide rights and obligations to the families of the missing or dead from armed conflicts (Table 22.1) (6).

It is the right of the family to know what happened to their missing loved ones in an armed conflict. Furthermore, it is their right to be united with them, if alive, and to mourn the loss with dignity and in accordance with beliefs and tradition, if dead. As per the Geneva Convention of 1949, there is an obligation to return the body/remains of the missing and forcibly disappeared individuals to their families (7). The "Minnesota Protocol" provides a conceptual and detailed framework to collect and gather information about missing individuals, managing the dead, and also to help to identify them and provide psychosocial healing to the family by resolving the tragedy. This humanitarian effort to help relieve human suffering as a result of extrajudicial mass killings is addressed by the protocol which utilizes advanced forensic science techniques to ensure the professionalism and dignified management of the dead and provide objective answers about the identity and fate of the missing. Some of the notable unlawful mass killings in history are listed in Table 22.2 (8–29).

INVESTIGATION INTO UNLAWFUL DEATHS

The investigation into unlawful killings or extrajudicial killings is similar throughout the world (30,31). As most of the unlawful killings are by armed police or military, the investigation might be influenced if a police inquest is being considered. Political influence is another factor that can hinder the investigation (32). Therefore, a magistrate or a judge is usually appointed by a government to lead an investigation. The International Committee of the Red Cross (ICRC) that monitors unlawful killings worldwide is involved in the investigation of unlawful deaths (6,33). The ICRC collects data of the missing and also collects other information by interviewing family members. In those countries where experts to conduct the investigation are lacking, the ICRC provides its own experts who will not only conduct the investigation but will also train local doctors for the future.

Ethical consideration

The first part of the "Minnesota Protocol" defines and describes the ethical principles to be followed during

TABLE 22.2 Some notable unlawful mass killings in history

Name and place	Time frame	Deaths
Great rebellion (Sepoy mutiny) in India (8–10)	1857 to 1858	More than 0.8 million people are believed to have been killed
Armenian genocide (World War I) in Armenia (11)	1915 to 1918	More than 1 million Armenian people are believed to have been killed
Genocide of the European Jews (The Holocaust) (11)	1941 to 1945	More than 6 million Jews are believed to have been killed
Bangladesh genocide (12,13)	1971	Nearly 3 million people are believed to have been killed
Cambodian genocide (14–16)	1975 to 1979	Around 1.5 to 2 million people are believed to have been killed
El Mozote massacre in El Salvador (17,18)	1981	More than 1000 people were killed with more than half of them children
Vukovar hospital massacre in Croatia (19–21)	1992	More than 420 patients were shot and buried in a mass grave
Massacre of Hutu in Congo (22,23)	1996 to 1997	More than 200000 are believed to have been killed
Kosovo war (24,25)	1998 and 1999	Around 1500 to 2000 people are believed to have been killed
Nepalese civil war (26,27)	1996 to 2006	More than 17000 people are believed to have been killed
Darfur genocide in Sudan (28,29)	2003 to date	More than 500000 people are believed to have been killed

an investigation into unlawful deaths. This protocol warrants a prompt, effective and impartial investigation which should be independently carried out without any undue influence or pressure. Any security personnel suspected of wrongdoing should not be allowed to be part of the investigating team. Institutional hierarchy and chain of command can influence the investigation process therefore the investigation should be conducted under the jurisdiction of a civilian court. Such investigations should be transparent to both the victim's family and the general public. There are cases of extrajudicial killings where autopsies were conducted and reports drafted in the favor of those involved in the killings (34). The victim's family and the general public have the right to information about the incident and therefore the factual findings and the progress of the investigation are to be shared with them.

Forensic investigation

The forensic investigation into unlawful deaths depends upon the following factors:

- Presence or absence of the body
- Knowledge and identification of the crime scene
- Condition of the body when found: intact, fragmented, decomposed or skeletonized
- Identification of the deceased.

In the case of burial, forensic investigation depends upon whether the body is intact or not (as in the case of fresh burial), partially skeletonized or completely skeletonized.

A thorough forensic investigation should then be carried out by a team of experts which should preferably include forensic pathologists, forensic anthropologists, forensic archeologists, forensic entomologists, forensic odontologists, human identification experts, forensic ballistics experts, digital data experts, facial reconstruction experts, and so on. A thorough and detailed investigation should include the following:

- Crime scene visit
- Identification of the grave(s)
- Exhumation
- Autopsy
- Examination of skeletal remains.

Crime scene visit

The crime scene should be identified with the help of local residents, family members, or any witnesses to the crime. The available physical evidence should be taken as a clue to identifying the crime scene such as clothes, bloodstains, spent bullet cases, disturbed vegetation, freshly dug soil, unusual heaping of the soil, changes in color of topsoil, and so on (35). Once a possible crime scene is identified, it should be cordoned off and unauthorized access restricted to avoid damage to, or loss of, evidence. Surface marking needs to be done with flagging of the physical evidence found. All the findings should be documented photographically. Any physical evidence found should be collected and labeled and preserved for further analysis by forensic experts. The chain of custody should be maintained during the transportation of any evidence with proper documentation and authorized signatures.

Identification of the grave

In cases of unlawful deaths, the perpetrators often dispose of bodies in a secluded location in an attempt to minimize the chances of recovery. Identification of the grave can be done with the clues obtained from interviews with family members, local residents of the neighborhood, or any potential witnesses (36). The circumstances and events prior to the disappearance of the victim, history, and other information obtained will help narrow down the location of the burial (37). Additionally, as mentioned above, the available physical evidence should be taken as a clue in identifying the crime scene (38).

Exhumation

Standard operating procedures should be followed for exhumation (35,39). There should be accurate and detailed documentation of the time, place, and names of all of the persons involved in the exhumation. Every piece of evidence found should be photographed, after which, it should be collected and labeled (40). The body should be exposed as clearly as possible and all the photographic evidence should be collected followed by detailed handwritten notes (41). Collection of evidence should also follow the standard procedure of packing, labeling and handover, maintaining the chain of custody at all levels (18). Once the body is removed, further deeper digging should be carried out to make sure that any physical evidence if present beneath the body is not missed.

Autopsy

The dead body or the fragmented body parts should undergo a detailed examination at a specified mortuary with at least the basic minimal facilities required to conduct an autopsy. Adequate photographs aid in thorough documentation and also serve as crucial evidence. Photographs should be taken for each and every injury. A ruled photographic scale should be placed with the autopsy identification number in all the photographs. The number and types of cameras used should be documented. Distant, medium-range and close-up photographs serve to show orientation and assist with identification. Photographs should be taken before and after unclothing and the cleaning of wounds. Every attempt should be made to identify the deceased at autopsy if the identity cannot be established by physical appearance. A meticulous autopsy should be done with detailed documentation of all of the injuries present (42). A pictorial body chart is preferred to note down all external and internal findings during an autopsy with the precise anatomic location. Radiologic investigation in the form of X-rays should be done in suspected firearm injury or any suspicious death where radiology would provide crucial evidence (18). Nevertheless, radiologic examination is advocated in all cases (43) and nowadays should include post-mortem CT (PMCT) examination if possible. Evidentiary material should be collected, properly labeled, and handed over to the investigating authority for further examination maintaining a proper chain of custody. Samples for DNA analysis, toxicology, entomology, and other necessary material for autopsy ancillary investigations should be collected and preserved as required in all cases (44). If possible, video recording of the autopsy procedure should be done, which could serve as evidence and also which can be later independently reviewed if required.

Examination of skeletal remains

When examining skeletal remains, the investigator should verify the tags, labels and seals. Once it is ascertained that all the necessary protocols are followed, and there has been no tampering with evidence, and the chain of custody has been maintained, examination of the skeletal remains can be conducted (45). The bones should be counted and then should be laid out on a table in anatomic order. The skeletal examination may provide crucial evidence including the minimum number of individuals, time since death, cause of death, and also the proper identification of the deceased by DNA analysis (44,46). In commingled bodies, the minimum number of individuals technique can be used to quantitatively estimate the minimum number of individuals in the assemblage (47). The degree of body fragmentation known as the fragmentation index can be used to understand the manner of death (48). Antemortem and post-mortem data can be compared at any time during the investigation to include or exclude any potential victim. Facial reconstruction can also be performed which may assist in identifying the deceased. The age of the individual can be estimated from the eruption pattern of the teeth in young individuals (49). The appearance and fusion of secondary epiphysis in the long bones can be used to estimate age in young adults (50). Cranial morphometry and fusion of cranial sutures are taken into account to estimate the sex and age in adults (51). As teeth resist putrefaction and are enclosed and preserved inside the oral cavity, they are considered as an important tool for the identification of an individual (52,53).

CONCLUSION

The "Minnesota Protocol" is a useful guide to follow in investigating unlawful deaths where human rights violation is suspected. This protocol is designed for a prompt, effective, thorough, impartial and transparent investigation into such deaths. From a pathologic perspective, this protocol details the conduct of exhumation, the autopsy and the preparation of a final report. In addition, information on the appropriate collection and documentation of evidence, and its examination in a scientific way is outlined.

REFERENCES

1. Universal Declaration of Human Rights [Internet]. United Nations; 1948. Available from: https://www.un.org/en/udhrbook/pdf/udhr_booklet_en_web.pdf (Accessed 27 April 2023).
2. The Minnesota Protocol on the Investigation of Potentially Unlawful Death (2016): The Revised United Nations Manual on the Effective Prevention and Investigation of Extra-legal, Arbitrary and Summary Executions [Internet]. New York and Geneva: Office of the High Commissioner, Human Rights, United Nations; 2017. Available from: https://www.ohchr.org/Documents/Publications/MinnesotaProtocol.pdf (Accessed 27 April 2023).
3. Hessbruegge J. Minnesota Protocol on the Investigation of Unlawful Death Gets a New Life. EJIL: Talk! [Internet]. 2017 May 26; Available from: https://www.ejiltalk.org/minnesota-protocol-on-the-investigation-of-unlawful-death-gets-a-new-life/ (Accessed 27 April 2023).
4. Prestholdt J. The Minnesota Protocol: Creating Guidelines for Effective Investigations. 2016 Feb 26; Available from: https://theadvocatespost.org/2016/02/26/minnestota_protocol/ (Accessed 27 April 2023).
5. Minnesota Protocol Revision of the UN Manual on the Effective Prevention and Investigation of Extra-Legal, Arbitrary and Summary Executions [Internet]. Office of the High Comissioner, Human Rights. Available from: https://www.ohchr.org/EN/Issues/Executions/Pages/RevisionoftheUNManualPreventionExtraLegalArbitrary.aspx (Accessed 27 April 2023).
6. International Committee of the Red Cross. International Humanitarian Law [Internet]. Cambridge: Cambridge University Press; 2005. Available from: https://ihl-databases.icrc.org/customary-ihl/eng/docindex/home (Accessed 27 April 2023).
7. The Geneva Conventions of 1949 and their Additional Protocols [Internet]. Geneva: International Committee of the Red Cross; 2010. Available from: https://www.icrc.org/en/doc/war-and-law/treaties-customary-law/geneva-conventions/overview-geneva-conventions.htm (Accessed 27 April 2023).
8. Dasgupta S. Remembering Gonoo: The Profile of an Adivasi Rebel of 1857. In: Pati B (ed). The Great Rebellion of 1857 in India: Exploring Transgressions, Contests and Diversities. London & New York: Routledge; 2010. pp. 32–45.
9. Pati B. The great rebellion of 1857: a historiography. *Contemp Perspect* 2007; **1(2)**: 166–72.
10. Sehrawat JS, Sankhyan D. Forensic anthropology in investigation of crimes against humanity: global dimensions and the mid-19th century Ajnala (India) massacre. *Forensic Sci Rev* 2021; **33(1)**: 38–65.
11. Melson R. Paradigms of genocide: The Holocaust, the Armenian genocide, and contemporary mass destructions. *Ann Am Acad Pol Soc Sci* 1996; **548**: 156–68.
12. Akmam W. Atrocities against humanity during the liberation war in Bangladesh: A case of genocide. *J Genocide Res* 2002; **4(4)**: 543–59.
13. Beachler D. The politics of genocide scholarship: The case of Bangladesh. *Patterns Prejudice* 2007; **41(5)**: 467–92.
14. Hinton AL. Agents of death: Explaining the Cambodian genocide in terms of psychosocial dissonance. *Am Anthropol* 1996; **98(4)**: 818–31.
15. Hinton AL. Why did you kill? The Cambodian genocide and the dark side of face and honor. *J Asian Stud* 1998; **57(1)**: 93–122.
16. Hinton AL. A head for an eye: Revenge in the Cambodian genocide. *Am Ethnol* 1998; **25(3)**: 352–77.
17. Medina RA, Binford L. Revisiting the El Mozote massacre: Memory and politics in postwar El Salvador. *J Genocide Res* 2014; **16(4)**: 513–33.
18. Scott DD. Firearms identification in support of identifying a mass execution at El Mozote, El Salvador. *Hist Archaeol* 2001; **35(1)**: 79–86.
19. Bloom JD, Sondorp E. Relations between ethnic Croats and ethnic Serbs at Vukovar general hospital in wartime and peacetime. *Med Confl Surviv* 2006; **22(2)**: 110–31.
20. Chapman B. Vukovar, Siege of, 1991. In: Hall RC (ed). *War in the Balkans: An Encyclopedic History from the Fall of the Ottoman Empire to the Breakup of Yugoslavia*. Santa Barbara: ABC-CLIO; 2014.
21. Alimpić M. The Vukovar hospital case from the perspective of a national investigative judge. *Int Rev Red Cross* 2014; **95(890)**: 267–86.
22. Okosun TY, Kibiswa N. Human rights violations and genocide in the Democratic Republic of the Congo. *Contemp Justice Rev* 2013; **16(4)**: 482–93.
23. Emizet KNF. The massacre of refugees in Congo: A case of UN peacekeeping failure and international law. *J Mod Afr Stud* 2000; **38(2)**: 163–202.
24. Freedman L. Victims and victors : Reflections on the Kosovo War. *Rev Int Stud* 2000; **26**: 335–58.
25. Cottey A. The Kosovo war in perspective. *Int Aff* 2009; **85(3)**: 593–608.
26. Gobyn W. From war to peace: The Nepalese Maoists's strategic and ideological thinking. *Stud Confl Terror* 2009; **32(5)**: 420–38.
27. Ko H. Child health impact of the Nepalese civil war. *Rev Dev Econ* 2021; **25(2)**: 694–711.
28. Totten S, Markusen E. The US government Darfur genocide investigation. *J Genocide Res* 2005; **7(2)**: 279–90.
29. Hagan J, Rymond-Richmond W, Barker P. The criminology of genocide: The rape and death of Darfur. *Criminology* 2005; **43(3)**: 525–62.
30. Groen WJM, Márquez-Grant N, Janaway RC, (eds). *Forensic Archaeology*. Chichester, UK: John Wiley & Sons, Ltd; 2015.
31. Enforced Disappearance and Extrajudicial Execution: Investigation and Sanction: A Practitioners Guide [Internet]. Geneva: International Commission of Jurist; 2015. Available from: http://www.icj.org/wp-content/uploads/2015/12/Universal-Enforced-Disappearance-and-Extrajudicial-Execution-PGNo9-Publications-Practitioners-guide-series-2015-ENG.pdf (Accessed 27 April 2023).
32. Djurić M, Pavlović T. Excavation of mass graves with Serbian context: Complexity of the political milieu. *Forensic Sci Int* 2021; **319**: 110657.
33. Guidelines for investigating deaths in custody [Internet]. Geneva: International Committee of the Red Cross; 2013. Available from: https://www.icrc.org/en/doc/assets/files/publications/icrc-002-4126.pdf (Accessed 27 April 2023).
34. Thomsen JL, Voigt J. Forensic medicine and human rights. *Forensic Sci Int* 1988; **36(1–2)**: 147–51.
35. Atreya A, Menezes RG, Acharya A. Hands-on training on exhumation: An approach to train forensic medicine residents in South Asia. *Med Leg J* 2022; **90(3)**: 166–8.
36. Ríos L, Ovejero JIC, Prieto JP. Identification process in mass graves from the Spanish civil war I. *Forensic Sci Int* 2010; **199(1–3)**: e27–36.
37. Ghaleb SS, Hassan DA, Elroby FA, Mogassabi KR, Alemam AA. Identification of victims from mass grave discovery near Benghazi, Libya. *J Forensic Leg Med* 2019; **67**: 24–7.
38. Martin V. A first world war example of forensic archaeology. *Forensic Sci Int* 2020; **314**: 110394.
39. Verano JW. Paleonthological analysis of sacrificial victims at the Pyramid of the Moon, Moche River Valley, Northern Peru. *Chungará (Arica)* 2000; **32(1)**: 61–70.
40. Ferrándiz F, Baer A. Digital memory: The visual recording of mass grave exhumations in contemporary Spain. Forum Qual Sozialforsch [Internet]. 2008; **9(3)**: Art.35. Available from: http://nbn-resolving.de/urn:nbn:de:0114-fqs0803351 (Accessed 27 April 2023).
41. Thannhäuser A, Szleszkowski Ł, Jurek T. Unidentified human remains discovered within Polish territory: Traces of the difficult history of the twentieth century. *Forensic Sci Int* 2021; **318**: 110608.
42. Menezes RG, Monteiro FN. Forensic Autopsy [Internet]. *StatPearls* 2021. Available from: http://www.ncbi.nlm.nih.gov/pubmed/30969723 (Accessed 27 April 2023).
43. Viner M. Overview of Advances in Forensic Radiological Methods of Human Identification. In: *New Perspectives in Forensic Human Skeletal Identification*. London: Elsevier; 2018. pp. 217–26.
44. Zupanič Pajnič I, Obal M, Zupanc T. Identifying victims of the largest second

world war family massacre in Slovenia. *Forensic Sci Int* 2020; **306:** 110056.
45. Forensic Identification of human remains [Internet]. Geneva: International Committee of the Red Cross; 2013. Available from: https://www.icrc.org/en/publication/4154-forensic-identification-human-remains (Accessed 27 April 2023).
46. Wedel VL, Galloway A (eds). *Broken Bones: Anthropological Analysis of Blunt Force Trauma*. 2nd ed. Springfield, Ill: Thomas; 2014.
47. Vaduvesković I, Djuric M. Mass grave complexity effects on the minimum number of individuals estimation. *Forensic Sci Med Pathol* 2020; **16(1):** 57–64.
48. Vaduveskovic I, Starovic A, Byard RW, Djuric M. Could a "body fragmentation index" be useful in reconstructing events prior to burial: case studies of selected primary and secondary mass graves from eastern Bosnia. *Leg Med (Tokyo)* 2020; **47:** 101766.
49. Hillson S. *Dental Anthropology*. Cambridge: Cambridge University Press; 1996.
50. Baker BJ, Dupras TL, Tocheri MW, Wheeler SM. *The Osteology of Infants and Children*. College Station TX: Texas A&M University Press; 2005.
51. Walker PL. Sexing skulls using discriminant function analysis of visually assessed traits. *Am J Phys Anthropol* 2008; **136(1):** 39–50.
52. Acharya AB, Sehrawat JS. Morphological dental trait examination of Ajnala skeletal remains and their possible population affinity. *J Forensic Odontostomatol* 2021; **1(39):** 24–34.
53. Sehrawat JS, Singh M. Application of trace elemental profile of known teeth for sex and age estimation of Ajnala skeletal remains: A forensic anthropological cross-validation study. *Biol Trace Elem Res* 2020; **193(2):** 295–310.

CHAPTER 23

Forensic Post-Mortem Imaging and Associated Technologies

Joey C.A. Hardy, Gisela de Heus, Wilma L.J.M. Duijst, Bartholomeus G.H. Latten, Paul A.M. Hofman and Rick R. van Rijn

INTRODUCTION

Radiology is a medical discipline focused on diagnostic imaging of the human body and image-guided interventions. Post-mortem radiology refers to the radiologic examination of a decedent. Clinical post-mortem radiology serves a purpose in healthcare and can play an important role in treatment evaluation and quality control. In forensic post-mortem radiology, a decedent is subjected to radiologic examination(s) to assist in forensic investigation and legal inquiry. Forensic post-mortem radiology may provide various details of interest to determine the (etiology of) an injury, the mechanism, cause, and manner of death, and a reconstruction of the possible course of events.

A BRIEF HISTORY OF FORENSIC RADIOLOGY

On November 8th 1895, Wilhelm Conrad Röntgen discovered X-radiation (i.e. X-rays), a discovery which was published in *Nature* on January 23rd 1896 (1,2). Already on February 7th 1896, the first use of radiography in forensics was reported. It concerned the victim of a gunfight in which the retained bullet could not be located by the surgeon (3). Having read about the discovery, Cox and Kirkpatrick decided to use this new technique to locate the bullet. Using a 45-minute exposure to X-rays, the flattened bullet was shown located between the tibia and fibula and was subsequently removed. Both the bullet, as well as the radiograph, served as evidence in the court case. Although the worldwide use of radiology in forensics continued, it was Gill Brogdon who with his book titled *Forensic Radiology*, really drew attention to this field when published in 1998. This book is still seen as the benchmark in forensic radiology and has set many radiologists toward a career in forensic radiology. The first presentations on the "Virtopsy" project led to a broader interest in forensic radiology. In 2001, at the 80th Annual Meeting of the German Society of Radiology, Dirnhofer gave a groundbreaking lecture entitled "from autopsy to virtopsy" (4). The initiators of this project Dirnhofer and Thali explained that

> *"The term VIRTOPSY was created from the terms virtual and autopsy: Virtual is derived from the Latin word "virtus", which means "useful, efficient and good". Autopsy is a combination of the old Greek terms "autos" (=self) and "opsomei" (=I will see). Thus, autopsy means "to see with one's own eyes". Because our goal was to eliminate the subjectivity of "autos", we merged the two terms virtual and autopsy – deleting "autos" – to create VIRTOPSY"* (5).

The use of cross-sectional imaging has led to a steep increase in the number of scientific publications, generating an evidence base for forensic computed tomography (CT) and magnetic resonance imaging (MRI) with a consequent increasing integration in legal medicine (Figure 23.1) (6). Several years later, professional societies were formed: in 2005, the International Association of Forensic Radiographers (IAFR) was founded followed in 2011 by the International Society of Forensic Radiology and Imaging (ISFRI) (7,8). The ISFRI aims to strengthen and develop the field of forensic radiology and imaging worldwide. In the last two decades, it has become evident that forensic radiology plays an important role in the post-mortem evaluation of bodies and that it should be an integrated part of the forensic workflow (9). Consequently, many forensic medicine departments use clinical imaging systems, have incorporated a CT-scanner in their facilities, or are planning to do so.

FORENSIC POST-MORTEM IMAGING TECHNIQUES

Post-mortem radiology is rapidly developing into a new sub-specialty (10,11). There are a variety of imaging techniques that are predominantly developed for clinical purposes, however, nowadays, some of them are being used in the field of forensics.

DOI: 10.1201/9781003138754-25

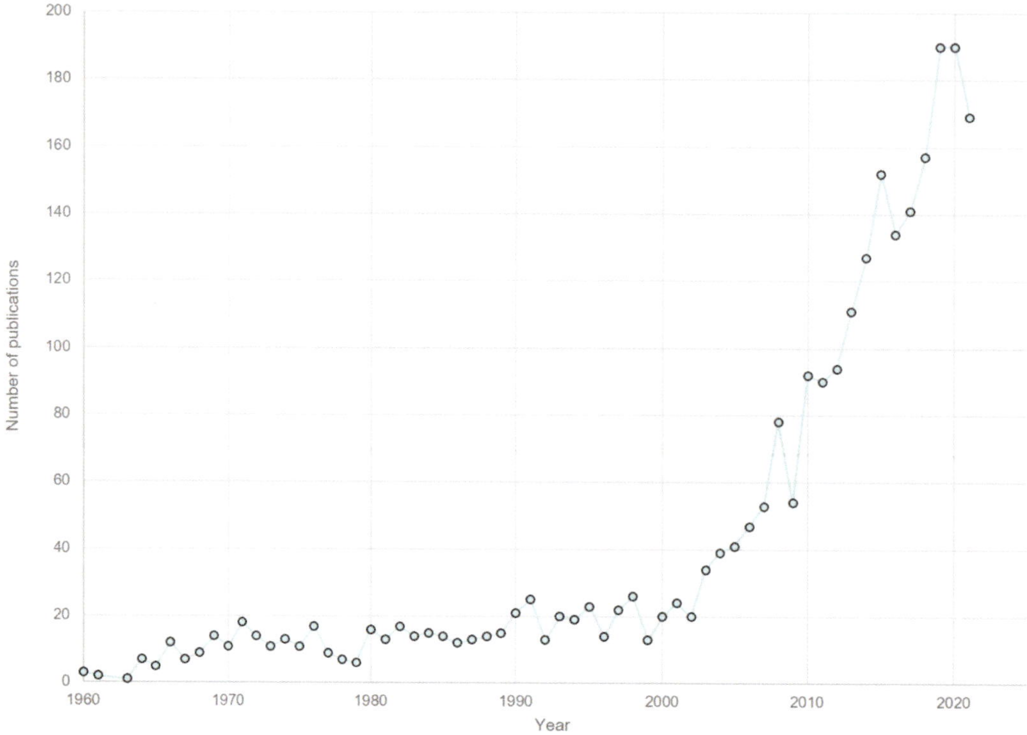

23.1 Between 1960 and 2021 a steep increase in the number of forensic radiologic publications can be seen (based on a Pubmed search - query: "forensic medicine" AND Radiography [Mesh]).

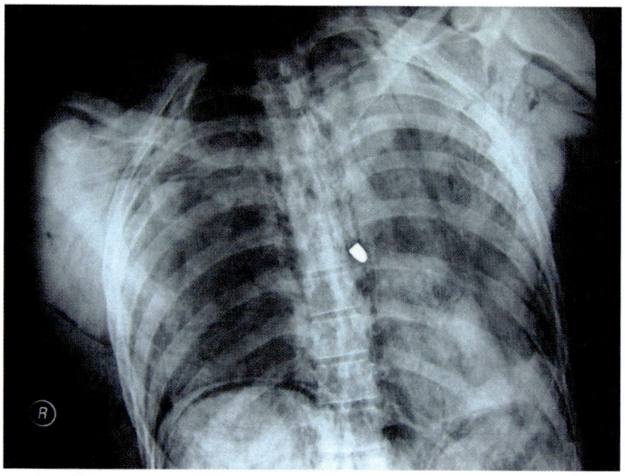

23.2 Conventional radiograph of a decapitated torso, note the retained bullet next to the spine on the left side (courtesy of V. Niehe, Department of Radiology, Groene Hart Ziekenhuis, Gouda, The Netherlands).

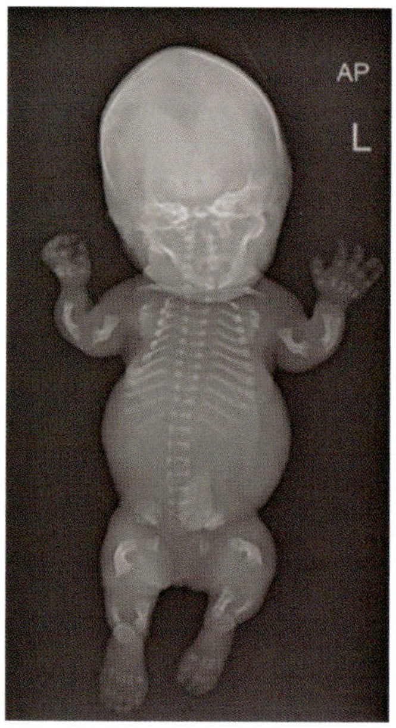

23.3 Due to abnormal findings on antenatal ultrasound, where a skeletal dysplasia was strongly considered, termination of pregnancy was performed. The post-mortem radiograph shows an exemplary case of thanatophoric dysplasia.

Conventional radiography

Conventional radiography was the first imaging modality used in a forensic context. For a long time, it was the most used modality in forensic medicine for both the living and deceased. In forensic casework, it is a technique most suitable for the detection of foreign bodies (e.g. metal objects, rocks), projectiles (bullets) and injuries to the skeletal system (Figure 23.2) (12). Nowadays, in forensic casework of adults, conventional radiography is often supplanted by post-mortem computed tomography (PMCT). However, it is still an essential part of the forensic work-up in deceased young children. In fetuses and neonates, conventional radiography can be used to assess the gestational age and to evaluate the presence of fractures and potential underlying skeletal disorders/dysplasias (Figure 23.3).

In infants and young children, conventional radiology is still used because of its high spatial resolution

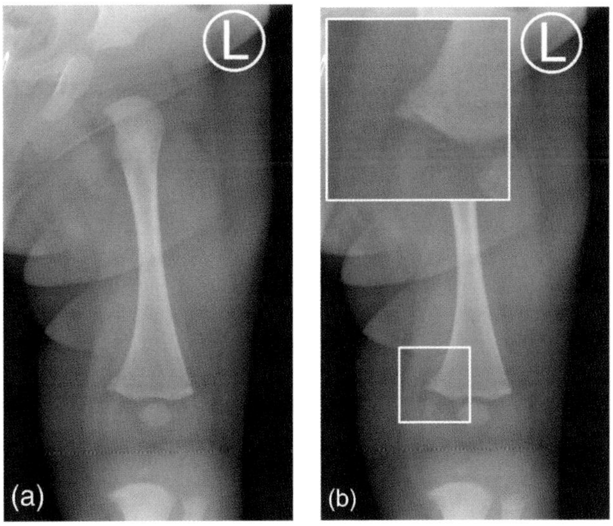

23.4 Post-mortem radiography in a deceased abused infant. (a) Skeletal survey shows a metaphyseal corner fracture (inset). (b) Due to the lower resolution the CT scan is false negative (inset).

compared to CT. This high resolution is essential for the detection of subtle fractures such as metaphyseal corner fractures (Figure 23.4 a&b). In all children under the age of 2 years, who die of an unnatural cause, a full skeletal survey should be obtained according to the guidelines of the Royal College of Radiologists (RCR) and the Society and College of Radiographers (SCoR) or the American College of Radiology (ACR) (13–15). Although there is an ongoing discussion whether a full-body CT could replace the skeletal survey, there is no evidence that this is sufficient. Doyle et al. performed a systematic review and found that there are no papers, in living children, supporting the use of whole body CT instead of a skeletal survey (16). So, until evidence to that effect is available the conventional skeletal survey will remain mandatory.

Finally, conventional radiography, using a mammography system or a dedicated X-ray specimen cabinet, can be used to obtain high-resolution images of autopsy specimens in forensic casework of both adults and children (Figure 23.5).

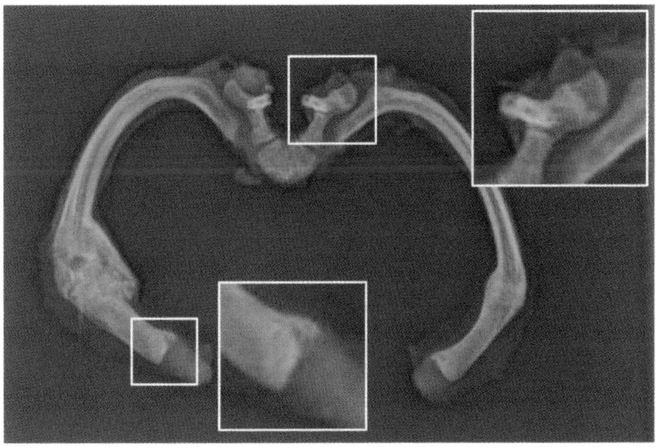

23.5 Specimen radiograph of the fourth rib of an abused infant. The post-mortem radiograph showed healing lateral rib fractures. The specimen radiograph shows an additional costochondral fracture on the right side (inset) and a healing fracture of the left transverse process (inset).

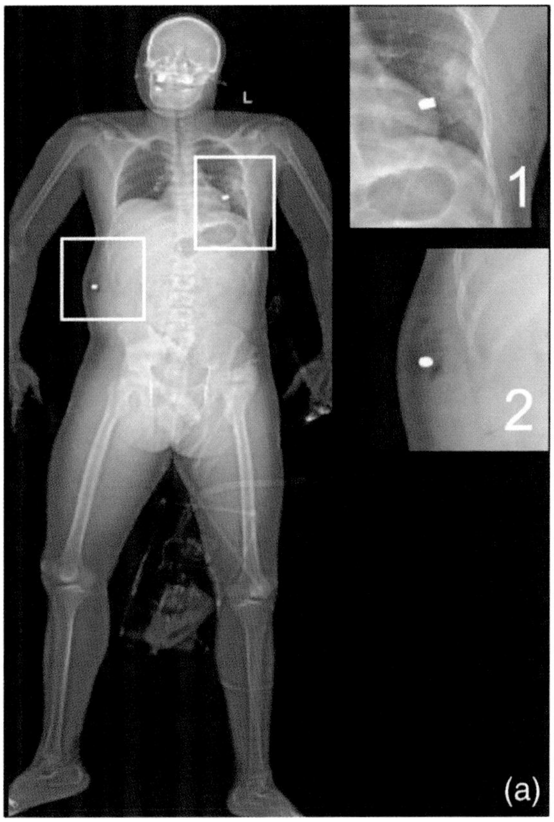

23.6 (a) Lodox scan of a gunshot victim. Two projectiles are visible on the anteroposterior scan, the bullet of the left side has penetrated the thorax, fracturing the sixth rib on the lateral side and causing focal pulmonary oedema (inset 1). The bullet on the right side is surrounded by subcutaneous air (inset 2).

Low-dose radiography

Since as early as 1999, a technique termed "Lodox/Statscan" has been applied in clinical tests for the screening of polytrauma patients. This technique, originally developed for the screening of diamond smuggling, can produce full-body images using low-dosage radiation in a matter of seconds. While radiation is not a particular issue in post-mortem investigations, other advantages of this technique such as its speed, ease of use, and comparatively low costs make it an interesting modality for forensic facilities where more advanced modalities and/or radiologists support are not available (17,18). The application of the Lodox system is beneficial in, for example, victim identification and localization of foreign bodies (Figure 23.6). Bernitz et al. showed that the Lodox scanner can be of use for identification purposes when other methods are not possible. For example, in cases where bodies are heavily decomposed, mutilated, and/or carbonized (19).

While more advanced imaging modalities are still the preferred method in forensic investigations, the use of

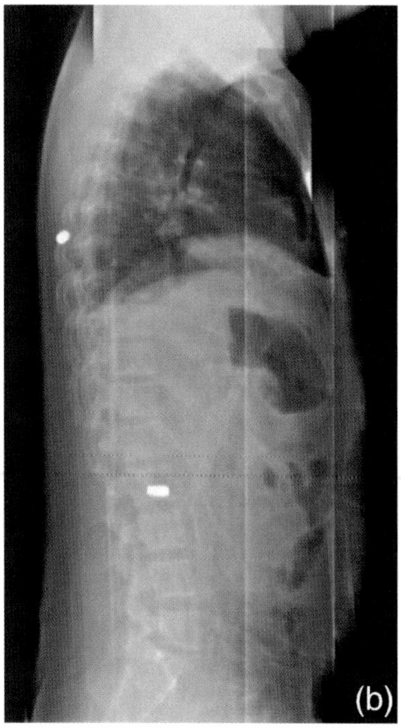

23.6 (b) The lateral radiograph shows that both bullets are located at the back of the patient (Courtesy of A. Speelman, Cape Peninsula University of Technology, Cape Town, South Africa).

the Lodox system can be an excellent alternative in the absence of those techniques.

Cross-sectional imaging techniques

Currently, the most commonly used radiologic examinations in forensic and legal practice are PMCT, post-mortem computed tomographic angiography (PMCTA) and post-mortem magnetic resonance imaging (PMMR) (20,21). These modalities are categorized as cross-sectional imaging techniques, meaning that they generate a stack of image "slices" that display the internal aspects of the body. Several reconstruction techniques can then be used to generate multiplanar and 3D image(s).

During post-mortem cross-sectional imaging, the body stays in a bag, in a supine position (22). This will prevent soiling and leakage of fluids and potential contamination of the body or scanner and loss of forensic evidence. To avoid unwanted manipulation of any forensic evidence, body sampling and collection of traces should be completed before scanning (22). The head and extremities are aligned (if possible), that is, face forward and arms and legs aligned to the body axis, to achieve optimal conditions for reviewing the images (22).

Post-mortem computed tomography

Similar to conventional radiography, CT utilizes X-rays to obtain images of the whole body (23). The acquired data are processed using various algorithms to generate the radiologic images, presenting tissue variances as typical radiologic appearances. These images can display soft tissues (e.g. muscles and subcutaneous fat), organ tissues (e.g. lung, liver and brain), and the skeletal system. As a rule of thumb, high-density tissues appear brighter (e.g. bone) than low-density tissues (e.g. lung) (Figure 23.7 a–e) (23).

Dual-energy CT is a relatively recently developed imaging technique. It utilizes two different X-ray spectra allowing the distinction between material or tissues based on different attenuation properties at different energy levels. This imaging modality is a promising technique in forensic investigations. For example, injuries to soft tissues not apparent on single-energy CT could potentially be visualized by dual-energy CT (24–26).

In a recently published systematic review and meta-analysis by Ampanozi et al., the diagnostic accuracy of PMCT, PMCTA, and PMMR was compared to autopsy in adults with diverse causes of death (27). Regarding PMCT, Ampanozi et al. found a pooled sensitivity of 65 percent (95% CI [0·51–0·77]) for soft-tissue and organ findings, 86 percent (95% CI [0·80–0·91]) for skeletal injuries, and 76 percent (95% CI [0·66–0·83]) for hemorrhages (27). Superficial injuries, such as skin abrasions, are less frequently detected by PMCT, thus, post-mortem imaging should always be combined with an external examination (28). Gas collections and high-density foreign objects (e.g. retained projectiles) are easily recognized on PMCT. In cases of major fatal trauma, post-mortem imaging frequently determines the extent of many injuries more accurately than an autopsy (28). Utilizing techniques such as multiplanar reconstruction and maximum intensity projection reconstruction, PMCT can generate a 3D reconstruction of cross-sectional images of the body. In doing so, the internal aspects and injuries of the body will be depicted following 3D relations.

For pediatric cases, the ISFRI and the European Society of Paediatric Radiology published an international guideline on PMCT (29). In fetuses, PMCT can be used to assess the gestational age (30). In the case of severely decomposed fetuses, PMCT in combination with a thorough external inspection and DNA sampling can replace a full autopsy.

Post-mortem computed tomography angiography

The unenhanced PMCT can be complemented by angiography (PMCTA). In this procedure, a contrast agent (with high density) is injected into the blood vessels. Several procedural protocols exist; however, this is usually accomplished by a small incision in the inguinal area, followed by cannulization of femoral blood vessels. Subsequently, boluses of contrast agent, often mixed with paraffin oil, are injected (31). In comparison to PMCT, the images benefit from a higher tissue contrast, which results in more apparent pathologies of soft tissues, internal organs and blood vessels (Figure 23.8 a&b) (20). Ruptured vessels can be identified by contrast extravasation, often enabling localization of the exact bleeding site. Studies included in the systematic review by Ampanozi et al. stated high sensitivities for PMCTA regarding the diagnosis of hemorrhage (ranging between 80% and 96%) (27). By means

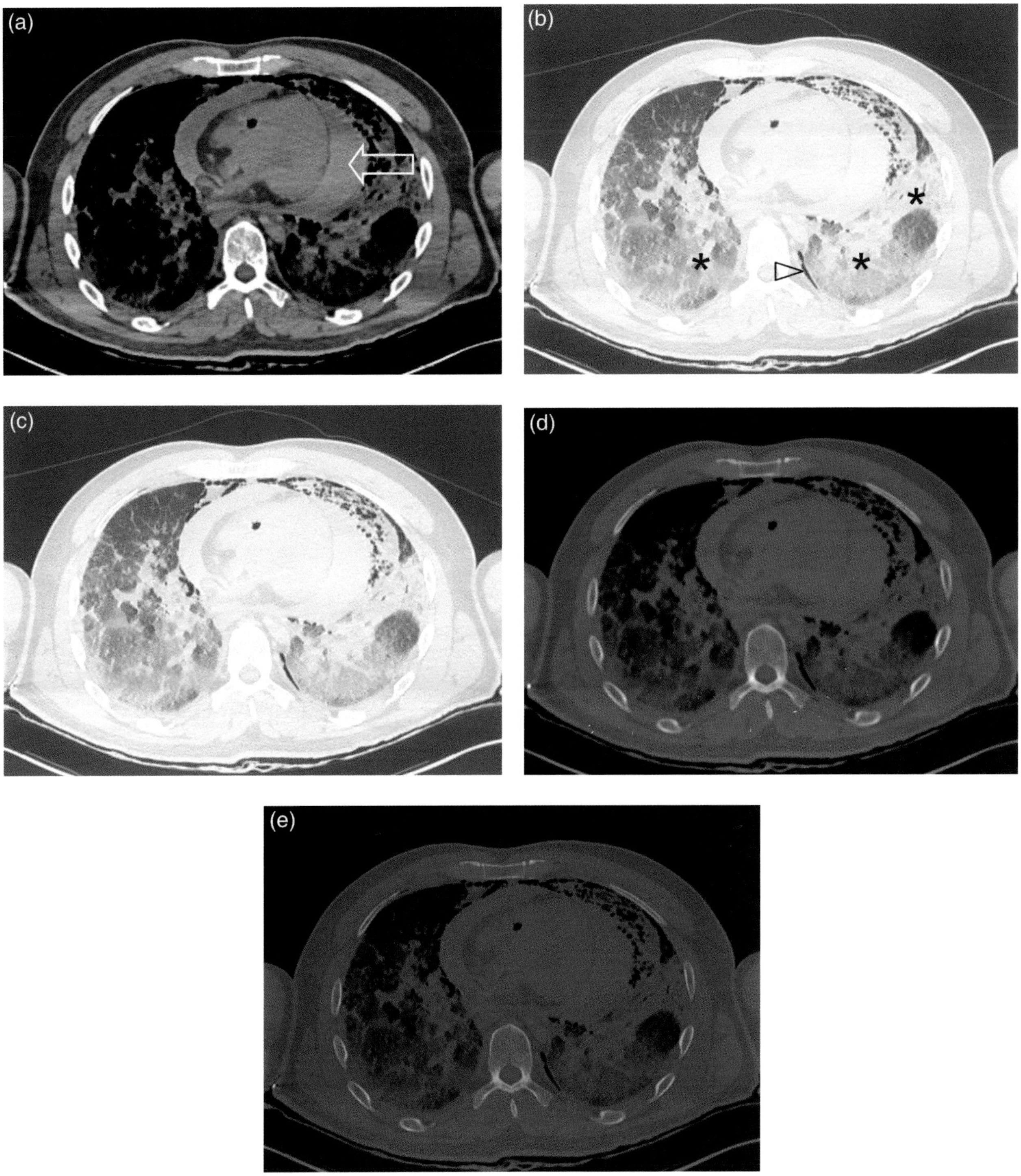

23.7 PMCT of the chest. (a) Reconstructed with a soft kernel and visualized with a soft-tissue window. This allows for the assessment of soft tissues. This example shows pericardial hemorrhage with fluid-fluid level (arrow). (b) Reconstructed with a soft kernel and visualized with a lung tissue window. This allows for the assessment of the lungs and air collections. This example shows bilateral post-mortem pulmonary abnormalities (asterisks) and a small pneumothorax (arrowhead). (c) Reconstructed with a bone kernel and visualized with a lung tissue window. This allows for the assessment of the lungs and air collections. Mark that the contours are sharper than in the soft kernel reconstruction. (d) Reconstructed with a soft kernel and visualized with a bone tissue window. This allows for the assessment of bone lesions. (e) Reconstructed with a bone kernel and visualized with a bone tissue window. Note that the contours are sharper than in the soft kernel reconstruction.

of a meta-analysis, researchers calculated a pooled sensitivity of 91 percent (95% CI [0.51 to 0.77]) for soft-tissue and organ findings (27). PMCT and PMCTA may demonstrate findings crucial for forensic investigation, particularly in cases of a traumatic manner of death (32). Additionally, PMCTA is performed in cases of presumed natural death in several countries, as it is also beneficial in several leading natural causes of death, such as fatal

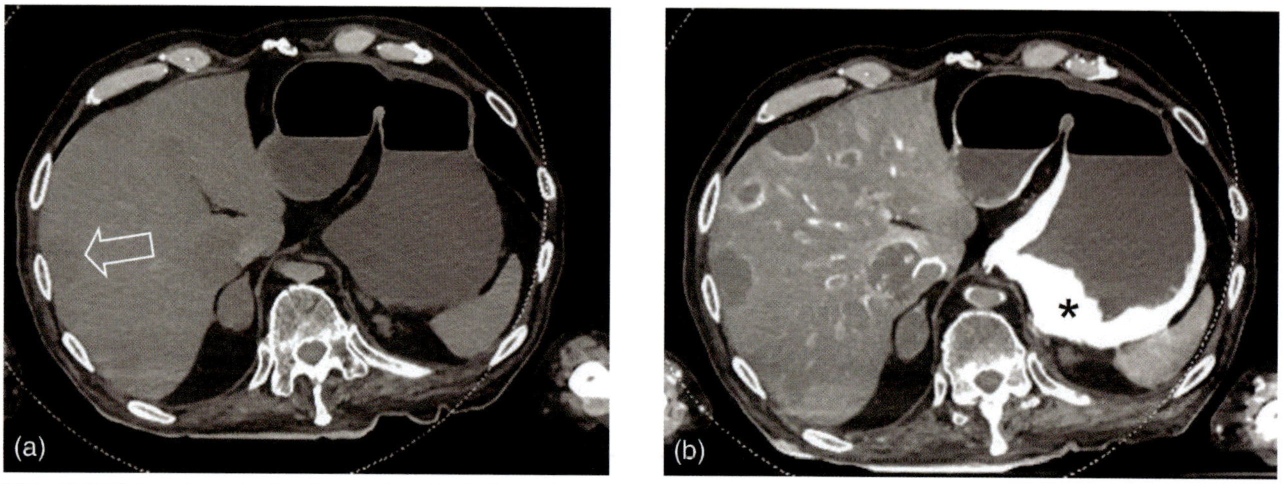

23.8 PMCTA in a donor to the Amsterdam Body Donation program. (a) Unenhanced CT shows a vague hypodense lesion in the liver. (b) PMCTA clearly shows multiple metastases in the liver. Due to the use of contrast mixed with water instead of polyethylene glycol extravasation into the stomach is seen (asterisk).

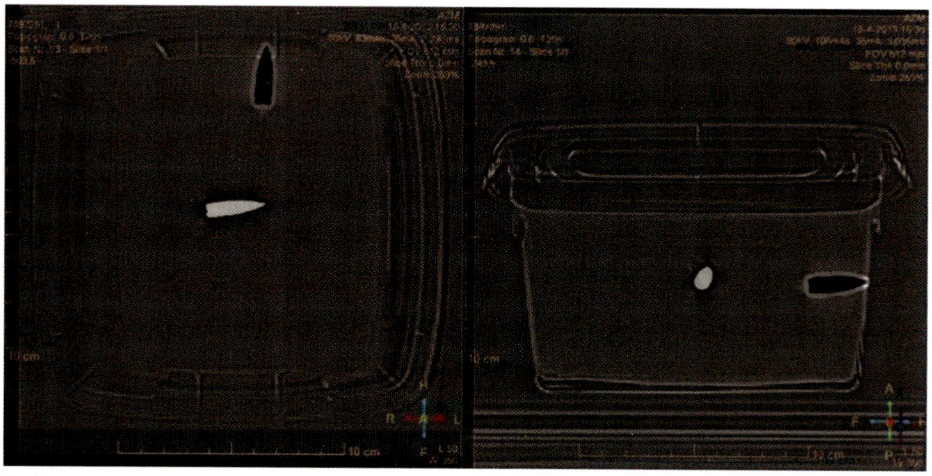

23.9 Upper view (***left***) and lateral view (***right***) of a CT of gelatine containing a projectile. The projectile before exposure to the magnetic field of the MRI is shown in ***white***; the position of the projectile after exposure to the MRI is shown in ***black***. A clear displacement of the projectile has occurred along the direction of the main axis of the static MRI field in combination with a rotation of the projectile (41). (Reprinted from Luijten M. et al.)

coronary thrombosis (20,33,34). At present, PMCTA is not routinely performed in all forensic medical centers due to several drawbacks, such as relatively high costs, the time required for procedures, and the necessity of trained personnel. In addition, contrast agents may leak into the organ parenchyma and body cavities possibly affecting the autopsy and subsequent toxicological and histologic analyses (35–37). However, the contrast agent's permeability varies across different solutions (38,39). Mixtures without or having negligible effects on subsequent examinations should be favored and body sampling for toxicological analyses before scanning is advised.

Post-mortem magnetic resonance imaging

In MRI, strong homogeneous magnetic fields, radiofrequency pulses, and natural magnetic properties of human tissues, especially those of hydrogen atoms which are abundantly present in the human body, are used to acquire images (40).

In forensic radiology, PMCT is followed by PMMR to an increasing extent. The application of PMMR for forensic and legal inquiries is a developing field. Before PMMR imaging, PMCT should ascertain that the body does not contain ferromagnetic objects (e.g. projectiles) to prevent any displacement under the influence of the MR-scanner's strong magnetic field, possibly distorting forensic evidence (Figure 23.9) (41). PMMR offers higher tissue contrast and spatial resolution than PMCT and is therefore mainly advantageous in evaluating fluid accumulation (e.g. hemorrhages) and injuries to soft tissues and internal organs (20). A potential low temperature of the body should be taken into account when evaluating PMMR images, as this negatively affects the contrast between tissues (42–45). PMMR images are usually acquired for a specific region of interest, as opposed to whole-body imaging in PMCT (20). The relatively high costs of PMMR (compared to PMCT) and the limited availability of modern

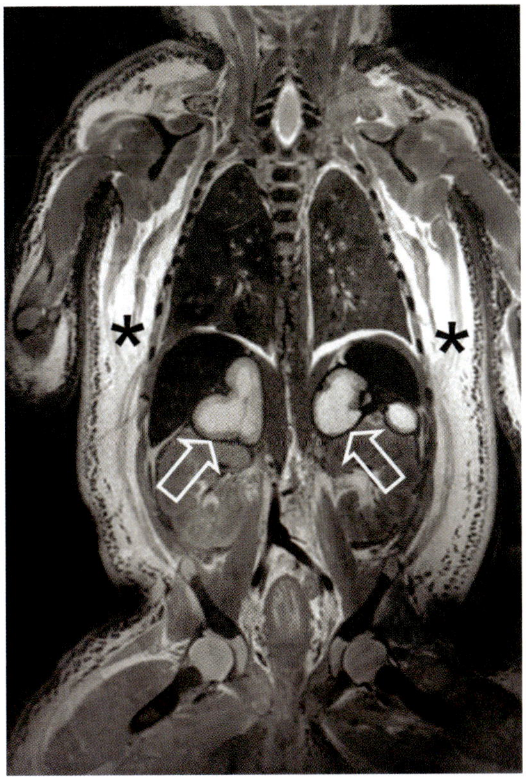

23.10 Premature neonate who died of persistent pulmonary problems. On coronal T2-weighted PMMR imaging bilateral adrenal hemorrhages (arrows) and extensive soft-tissue edema (asterisks) were seen. No cause of death was found on PMMR imaging.

imaging equipment in some facilities are potential drawbacks for large-scale employment of PMMR.

Most studies about pediatric PMMR have a strong focus on fetuses and neonates and their role in clinical minimal invasive autopsy (Figure 23.10) (46–50). In these studies, in which major congenital anomalies were a main cause of death, it has been shown that PMMR has high diagnostic accuracy, similar to that of the conventional autopsy. In the field of forensics, there has been little to no research into its value as an adjunct to the autopsy.

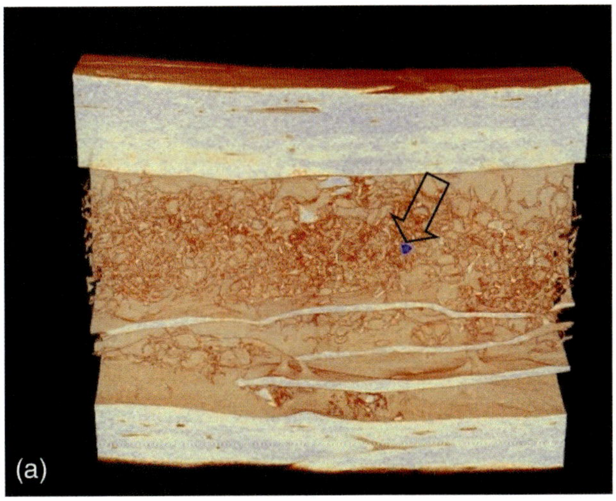

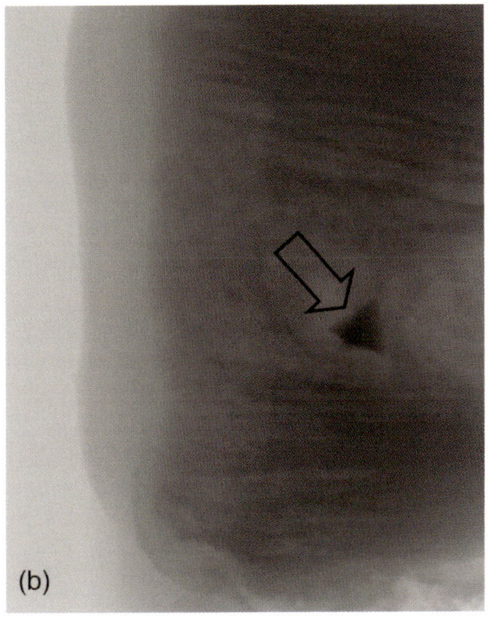

23.11 Micro-CT of metallic objects. **(a)** Metallic object in a human bone with order of magnitude millimeters (arrow). **(b)** Metallic object in an elbow with order of magnitude millimeters (arrow), later determined to be the tip of a knife.

FUTURE PROSPECTS

Several research groups have shown an interest in the potential role of modern imaging techniques in forensic and legal inquiries. The application of micro-CT, with its exceptional spatial resolution, presents a promising technology for these purposes (51). It may be employed, for example, to examine shape patterns in bone injuries (e.g. caused by a knife), to locate metallic particles (e.g. from a knife) and to evaluate the distribution of gunshot residue in entrance wounds (Figure 23.11 a&b) (51).

Three-dimensional multispectral full-body photogrammetry has been postulated as feasible to detect forensic evidence on the skin or object surfaces which are not visible to the naked eye using electromagnetic spectra beyond the visible spectrum (52). This technique can be used in conjunction with a CT-scanner making it possible to digitally look for latent evidence on the body (52).

Another important development is the use of post-mortem imaging in other fields of forensic science. In recent research, an algorithm was developed that accurately assessed time since death (i.e. post-mortem interval, PMI) based on the findings detailed by PMCT, the position of the body, and various environmental conditions (53). This new technique uses a 3D reconstruction of photographs and thermal images of the whole body as input for a new software program (Figure 23.12 a–c) (53,54). Variables such as clothing, weight, temperature of the body, and various environmental factors can be registered in this new software program. The program then calculates the cooling rate of the body using 3D reconstruction and in turn, more accurately than the currently used technique – the nomogram of Henssge – determines the post-mortem interval with a

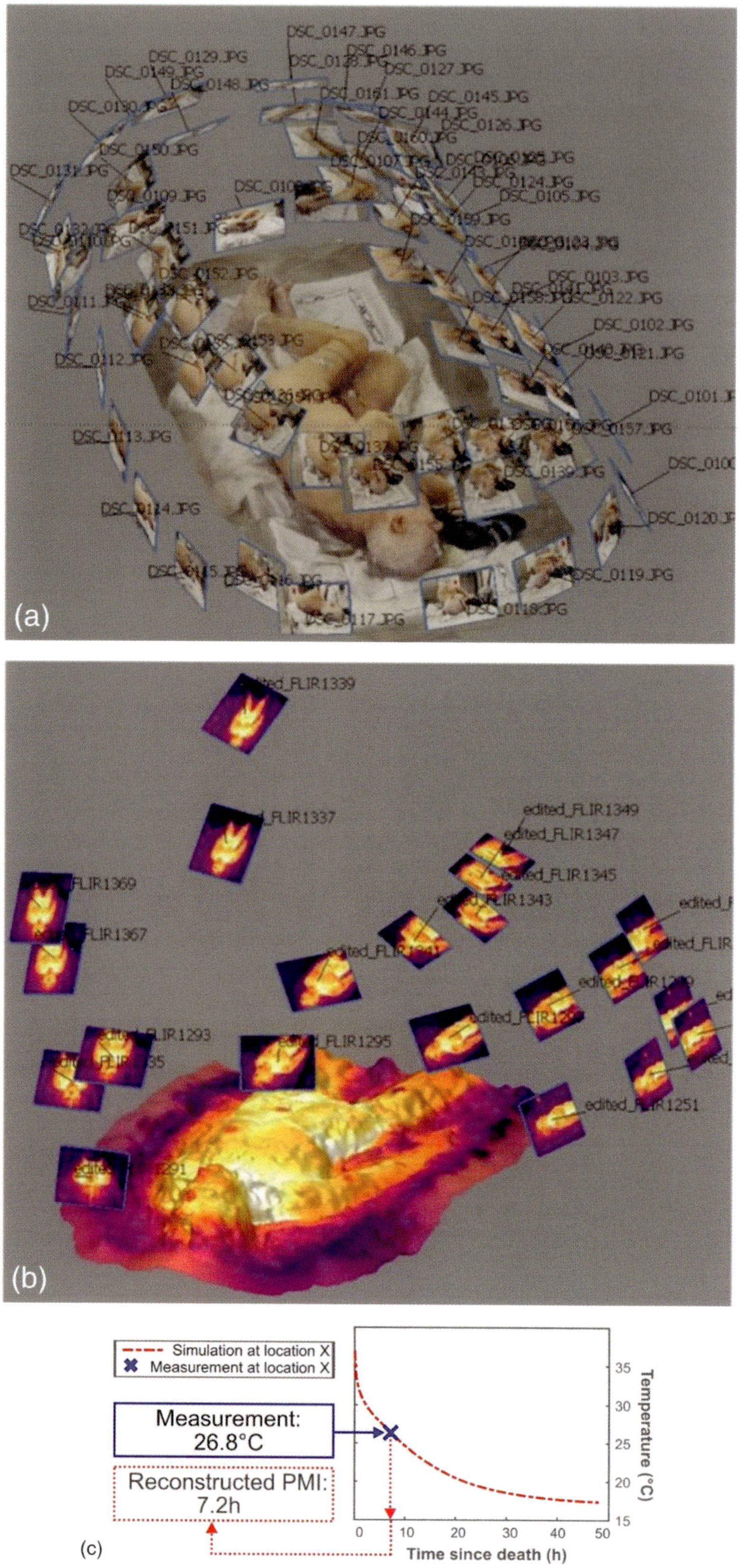

23.12 New technique for PMI estimation using 3D reconstruction of visible and thermal photographs. **(a)** Photographs of a body. **(b)** Thermal images of a body. **(c)** PMI simulation based on the input of photographs and thermal images. (Courtesy of Prof MCG Aalders, Msc PhD, Department of Biomedical Engineering and Physics, Amsterdam UMC, University of Amsterdam, the Netherlands.)

window of up to 45 minutes. This technique is still being validated in forensic casework, but it shows promising results making this a potential method for the future.

POST-MORTEM CHANGES AND DECOMPOSITION IN POST-MORTEM IMAGING

It is important to acknowledge that the main difference between post-mortem radiology and clinical radiology is the presence of radiologic signs of post-mortem changes and decomposition. These features may mimic disease or hinder image interpretation (55). It is therefore essential to have a general understanding of the decomposing body to adequately examine post-mortem images.

"Early radiological signs" of post-mortem changes

Due to the effect of gravity, blood and other body fluids will redistribute and accumulate in the lowest soft tissues, giving rise to the well-known "livor mortis". In post-mortem imaging, livor mortis can be noted as increased attenuation of the subcutaneous fat and dermis and should not be mistaken for subcutaneous edema resulting from trauma (56). A similar phenomenon occurs in the lowest parts of the lungs, often referred to as "internal livor mortis of the lungs" (Figure 23.13) (56). These can easily be misinterpreted as pneumonia, which will possibly result in a false conclusion about the cause of death. This pitfall, if relevant to the case at hand, could be overcome by the use of post-mortem ventilation that improves the visibility of pathology by lung expansion (57,58). A radiologist with knowledge about these post-mortem processes might be able to speculate about the predominant position of the body after death.

After death, blood coagulation and sedimentation will occur due to a lack of circulation. Blood cells and blood clots will settle at the lowest part of the blood vessels, creating a visible fluid-fluid level separating blood cells and serum (56). These findings should not be mistaken for aortic dissection or thromboembolism.

"Late radiological signs" of post-mortem changes

Late post-mortem changes result from putrefaction due to bacterial action, putrefactive gas formation and cellular decomposition (i.e. autolysis) (56). Gas accumulations in the intestinal walls, bile ducts, liver and eventually the hepatic blood vessels are often seen on post-mortem imaging and can be considered one of the first radiologic signs of advancing decomposition (Figure 23.14). This phenomenon is probably caused by intestinal gas and gas-producing bacteria that ascend along the bile ducts, the latter possibly facilitated by rapid autolysis of the pancreas and stomach (55). Gas collections will disseminate along (major) blood vessels and can easily be misinterpreted as a fatal air embolism. It has been suggested that gas distribution apparent on PMCT could be used to estimate the PMI, however, this method has not yet been validated (59). Over time, further decomposition will take place. Soft tissues and internal organs will undergo putrefaction, typically causing the symmetrical distribution of putrefactive gas accumulations. However, asymmetrical gas formation may result from underlying injury (e.g. lung laceration) or may occur when a body part is exposed to an environment that affects the rate of decomposition (e.g. partial submersion in water) (56). On further decay, soft tissues and organs will begin to fragment, degenerate, and eventually liquefy (Figure 23.15 a-d). At this stage, tissue and anatomic relations are significantly altered which affects

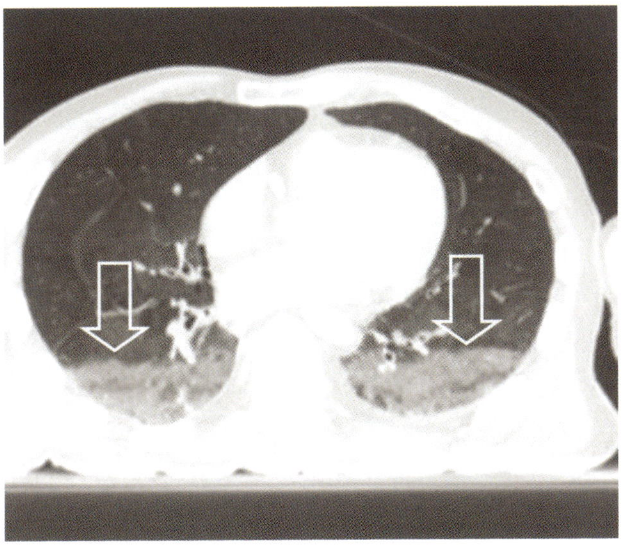

23.13 Livor mortis resulting in bilateral post-mortem pulmonary edema (arrows). Note the horizontal well-demarcated borders in keeping with a supine position after death.

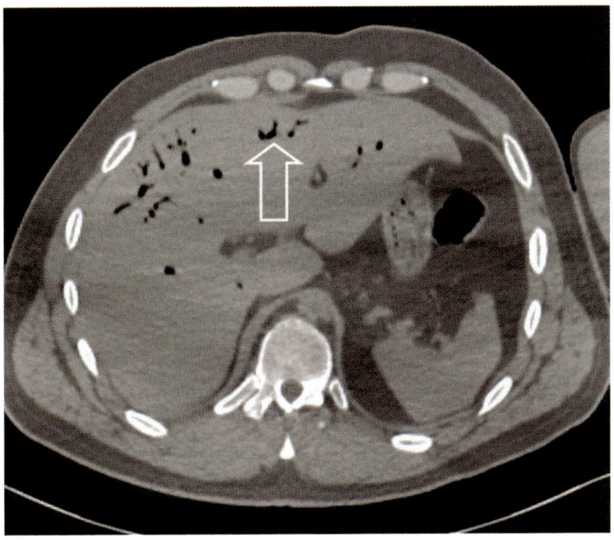

23.14 PMCT with gas in the portal veins (arrow). This is a normal post-mortem finding and can be visible within hours.

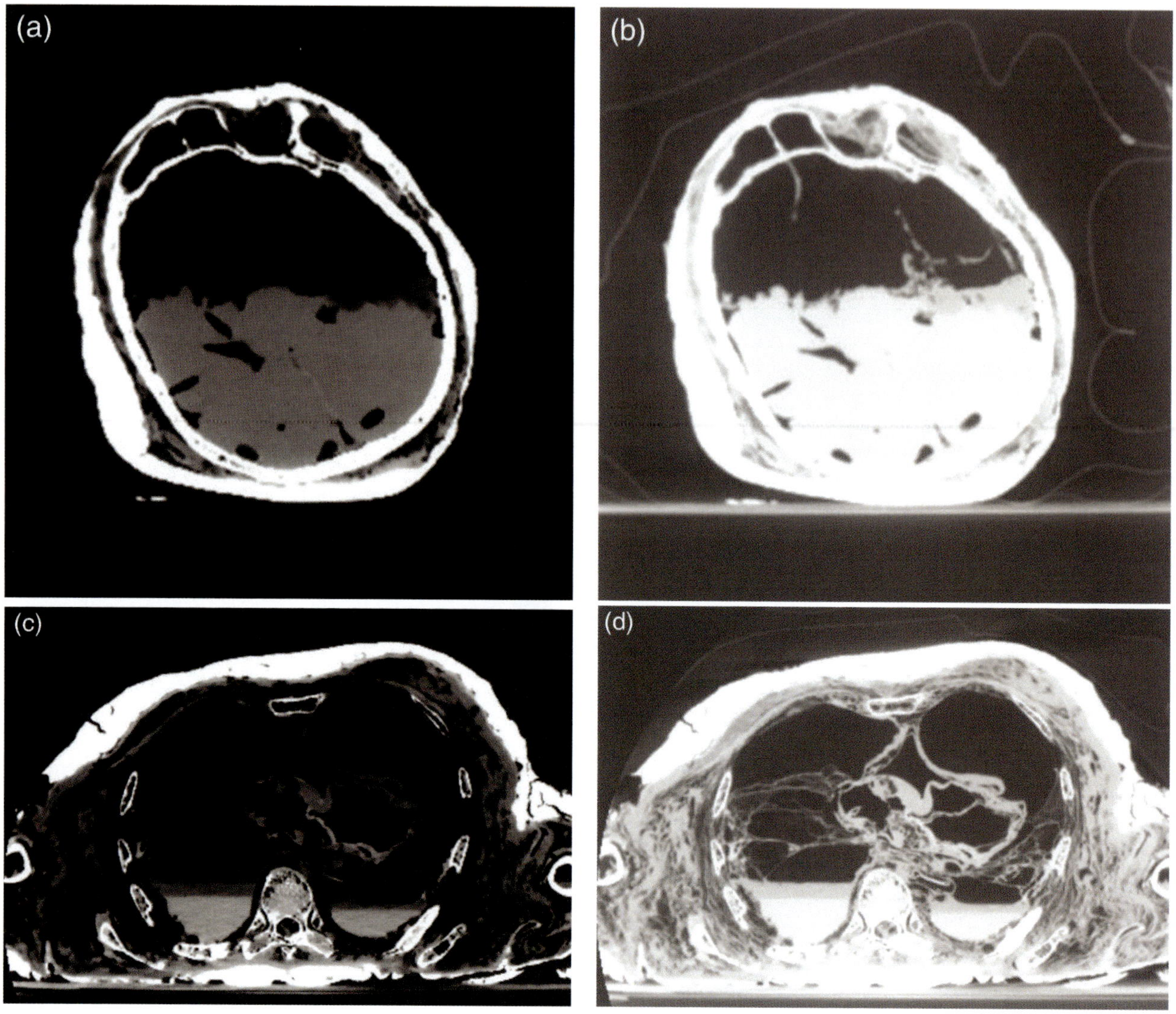

23.15 PMCT of a body of a donor exhumed several months after burial from the Sub-surface Taphonomy and Anthropology (ARISTA) facility (116). The dense matter surrounding the body is encrusted earth. Throughout the body, the organs show severe decomposition. The brain is liquefied (a), air is present in blood vessels and the intracranial cavity (b). The chest cavity shows fluid-fluid levels, with fatty content in the top layer (c). The heart and lungs are nearly completely decomposed (d).

the efficacy of post-mortem examinations. Radiologic signs that reveal the cause of death might be concealed or have completely disappeared due to decomposition (56). As a result of artefacts and the loss of tissue contrast, PMMR is not feasible in most cases of advanced decomposition. However, PMMR of the brain could be considered, as the opening of the intracranial cavity during autopsy might result in the complete disintegration of brain tissue due to liquefaction (60).

POST-MORTEM IMAGING IN FORENSIC CASEWORK

In every forensic post-mortem investigation, there are several main questions that must be answered, including: what is the identity of the deceased, when did the person die, what is the mechanism, cause and manner of death? Different experts in forensic investigation will have to collaborate to answer these questions. The following section will describe the application and associated pitfalls, limitations and benefits of imaging techniques in forensic post-mortem investigations in different case contexts.

External blunt force trauma

Blunt force trauma can be defined as any non-penetrating trauma to the body such as from traffic accidents, falling from heights, beating and kicking, being struck by firm dull objects, and so on. Injuries often encountered in cases of blunt force trauma include abrasions, lacerations, hemorrhages and fractures. Depending on the affected body part, varying imaging modalities can assist in the detection of these injuries. A variety of studies show, as previously mentioned, that PMCT performs particularly well in the detection of fractures, large areas of hemorrhage and gas accumulations (Figure 23.16 a&b)

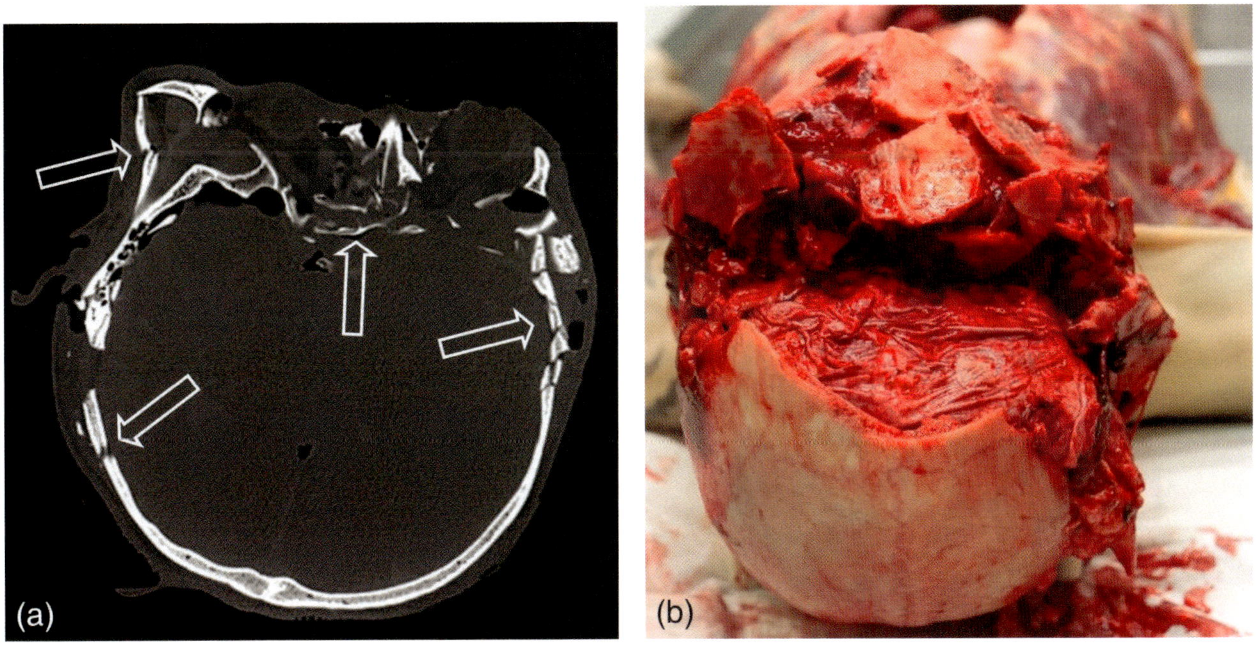

23.16 Victim of blunt force trauma. (a) PMCT of the skull with multiple skull and facial fractures (arrows). (b) Autopsy photograph of the skull.

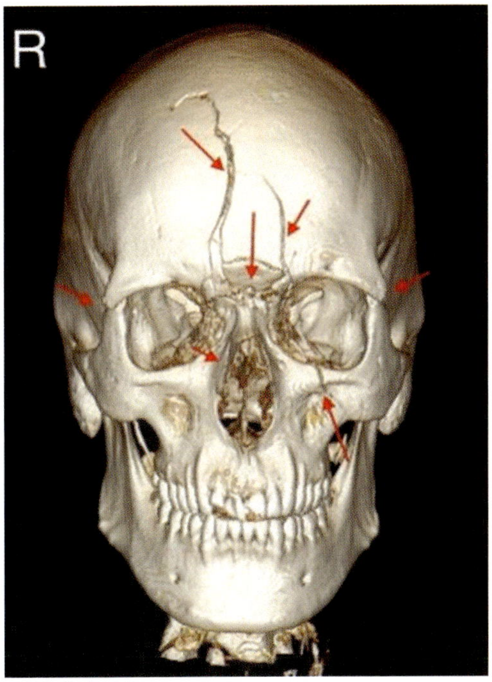

23.17 PMCT 3D-visualization of a road traffic victim's skull with multiple skull and facial fractures (arrows).

(27,61–65). Therefore, PMCT is a reliable modality for the detection of fractures, especially for structures that are challenging to access and are not routinely inspected during an autopsy (Figure 23.17) (27,61–66). For the detection of minor internal organ and soft-tissue injuries, conventional autopsy is still the preferred method (62). A less frequently used technique in the forensic context is PMCTA. This technique has been shown to detect more vascular lesions in cases of blunt force trauma which is one of the main weaknesses of other imaging techniques (20). Due to the diversity of encountered injuries in these cases, often a combination of techniques including non-imaging techniques is required to get a thorough assessment and determination of the cause of death.

In infants and children, blunt force trauma and acceleration/deceleration trauma can lead to clinical occult fractures. Although in the section on conventional radiology we stated that there is no evidence to replace the skeletal survey with PMCT, there are however publications on the use of CT for imaging dedicated to the skull and the ribs. Multiple publications have shown that a properly performed CT of the skull, with a 3D reconstruction, is superior in the detection of skull fractures in comparison to conventional radiology (67–72). The strongest voiced conclusion was by Martin et al. who stated '*Conventional radiographs (SRX) does not add further diagnostic information and can be omitted from the skeletal survey when CT with 3D reconstruction is going to be or has been, performed*' (69). This conclusion was based on a study of 104 paired conventional radiographs and CT scans of the skull in children with a mean age of 6.75 months (range 4 days to 2 years) of which 21 (20%) showed skull fractures. Two fractures on CT were missed on SXR and none on CT.

For rib fractures, there is overwhelming evidence that CT is superior to conventional radiography (Figure 23.18 a–e) (73–76). In the largest study to date, Shelmerdine et al. performed a diagnostic accuracy study in 25 paired post-mortem chest CT scans and chest radiographs; all images were read by 38 international radiologists (76). Overall, radiologists diagnosed three times as many rib fractures on chest CTs compared with chest radiographs (sensitivity 44·9% [95% CI 31·7–58·9] vs 13·5% [8·1–21·5]; difference 31·4% [23·3–37·8; p<0·001]). The radiologists also had a higher sensitivity for the correct

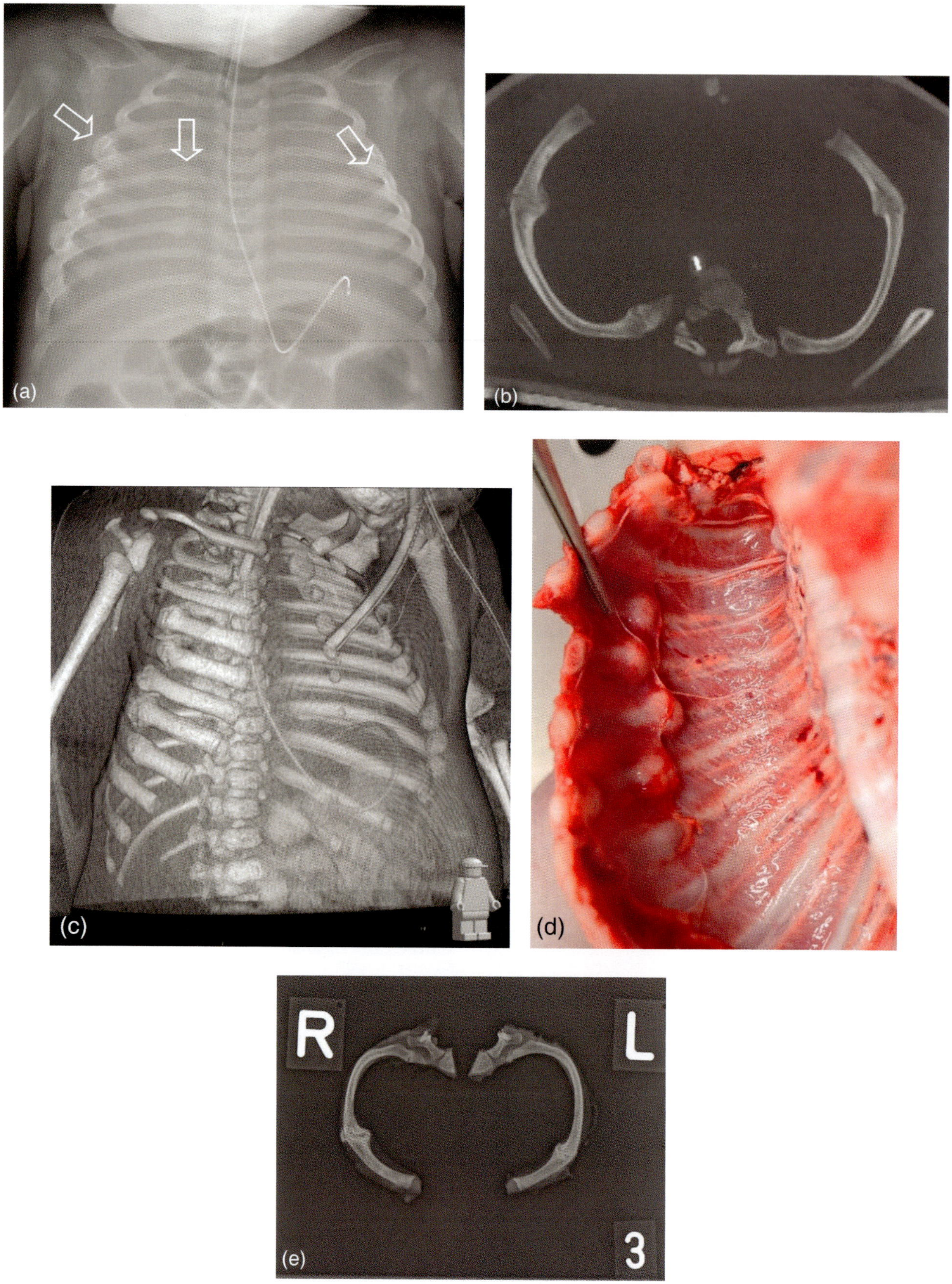

23.18 Fatally abused infant. **(a)** Post-mortem chest radiograph shows bilateral multiple healing lateral (right 3–7, left 3) and posterior (right 5–7) rib fractures (arrows). **(b)** Oblique axial reconstruction at the level of the third rib shows three rib fractures. **(c)** 3D reconstruction shows the lateral healing rib fractures. **(d)** At autopsy, the lateral healing rib fractures are clearly seen due to callus formation. **(e)** Specimen radiographs of the third ribs show no new findings. The use of lead letters is mandatory.

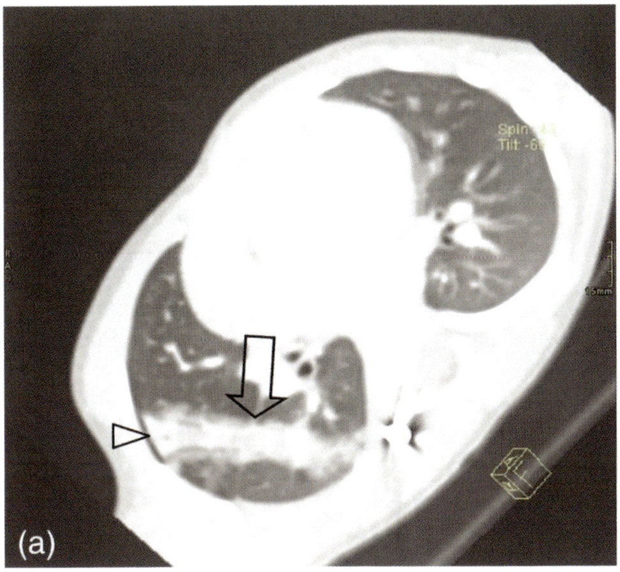

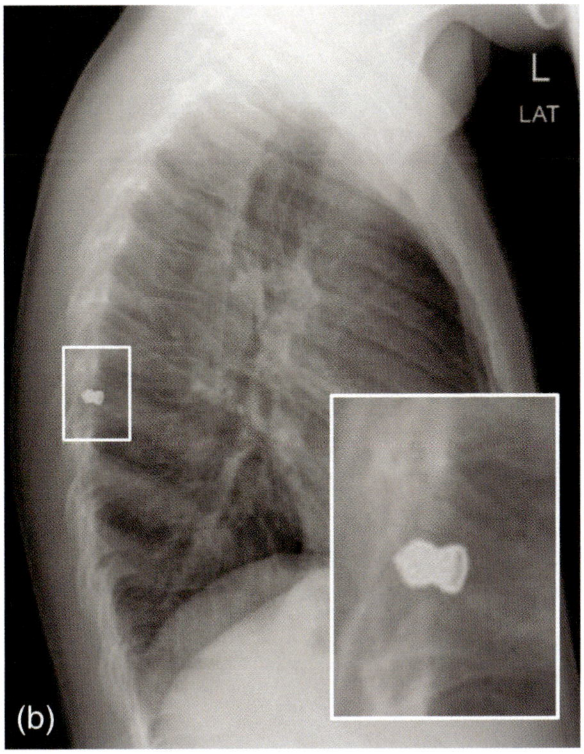

23.19 Young child shot with an airgun. (a) Oblique axial reconstruction of the chest CT shows the trajectory of the bullet (arrow), a small pneumothorax (arrowhead). (b) Follow-up chest radiograph shows the characteristic wasp-waisted shape of an airgun pellet (inset).

location of the rib fracture and had higher confidence when reporting chest CT. As in deceased children, the radiation dose is no issue, it can be argued that CT can replace skull and chest radiographs. However, there is currently insufficient evidence to date a rib fracture on CT imaging. In these cases, thus, conventional radiographs together with histology can still be useful.

Gunshot fatalities

A thorough radiologic examination of injuries in gunshot fatalities provides crucial insight for forensic investigation and subsequent legal proceedings. PMCT can assess whether the wound is caused by the entering or exiting of a projectile and depict the 3D projectile trajectory by examining the morphology of injuries to soft tissues, bones and internal organs (Figure 23.19 a&b) (77,78). For example, the inward or outward bevelling of a skull fragment in the case of a gunshot to the head indicates an entrance or exit wound, respectively (Figure 23.20) (78). In cases with multiple gunshot wounds, radiologic differentiation between several projectile trajectories and gunshot wounds can be cumbersome (77,78). However, in contrast to an autopsy, the process of reconstructing the projectile trajectory can be repeated using PMCT data, if necessary. On some occasions, it is possible to illustrate the most probable sequence of gunshot injuries to the body (79), for example, by following Puppe's rule, relying upon the fact that a fracture line will not cross a pre-existing fracture (80). The differentiation between entrance or exit wounds and depicting the 3D-projectile trajectory forms the basis for case reconstructions used to determine the most likely course of events within the stated margins of error (81,82). In selected cases, PMMR can be employed to further assess injuries to soft tissues and internal organs if PMCT confirms that the body does not contain ferromagnetic objects (e.g. projectiles). Based on perceived injuries, forensic post-mortem radiology can contribute to determining the cause of death in most gunshot fatalities (77,83).

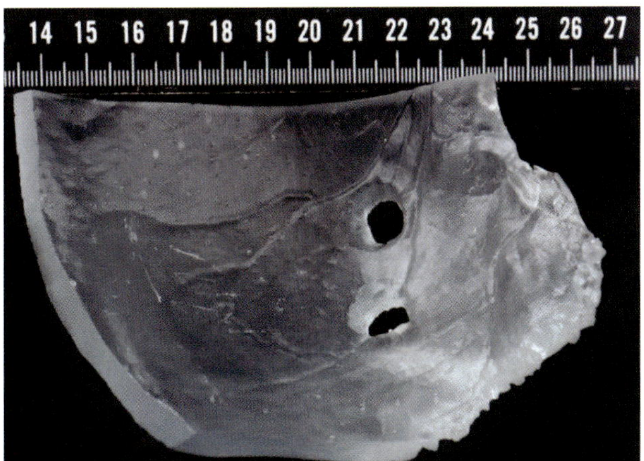

23.20 3D print of a skull bone with two bullet wounds. The inside is shown and note the bevelled edges of the entrance wounds. (Courtesy of S Decker, Department of Radiology, University of South Florida Morsani College of Medicine, Tampa, Florida, USA).

PMCT can also efficiently locate (fragments of) projectiles retained within the body (77). Moreover, if these are not detected, the possibility of a retained projectile is essentially excluded. Detecting retained projectiles could have implications for the examination of the crime scene, for example, if post-mortem imaging reveals a mismatch between found projectiles and cartridges (78). In addition, successfully locating retained projectiles will result in more opportunities for ballistic analyses as potentially more projectiles will be retrieved during the autopsy.

Stabbing fatalities

Injuries to soft tissues and internal organs due to stabbing and cutting can be accurately examined by PMCT, and even more so by PMMR (Figure 23.21 a–h) (23). In addition, PMMR is a reliable method to assess the wound channel (23), however, its efficacy compared to an autopsy examination remains to be investigated. Caution should be taken in determining the length of the injury-causing object as this does not necessarily correspond to the wound channel due to the elasticity of soft tissue. PMCT can depict cleaving injuries of bone and cartilaginous tissues which are frequently seen in stabbing injuries, providing clues to what type of sharp instrument is used (23). Examination of the wound morphology, however, remains the forensic pathologist's field of expertise (84). Nonetheless, forensic post-mortem radiology can contribute to determining the cause of death in stabbing fatalities, for example, by detecting a fatal air embolism or hemopericardium (23,84). Fragments of the injury-causing object, for example the tip of a knife, can be broken off when striking hard material (e.g. bone) and may be lodged in the victim's body. These can clearly be seen on PMCT and could guide the pathologist in the retrieval (85).

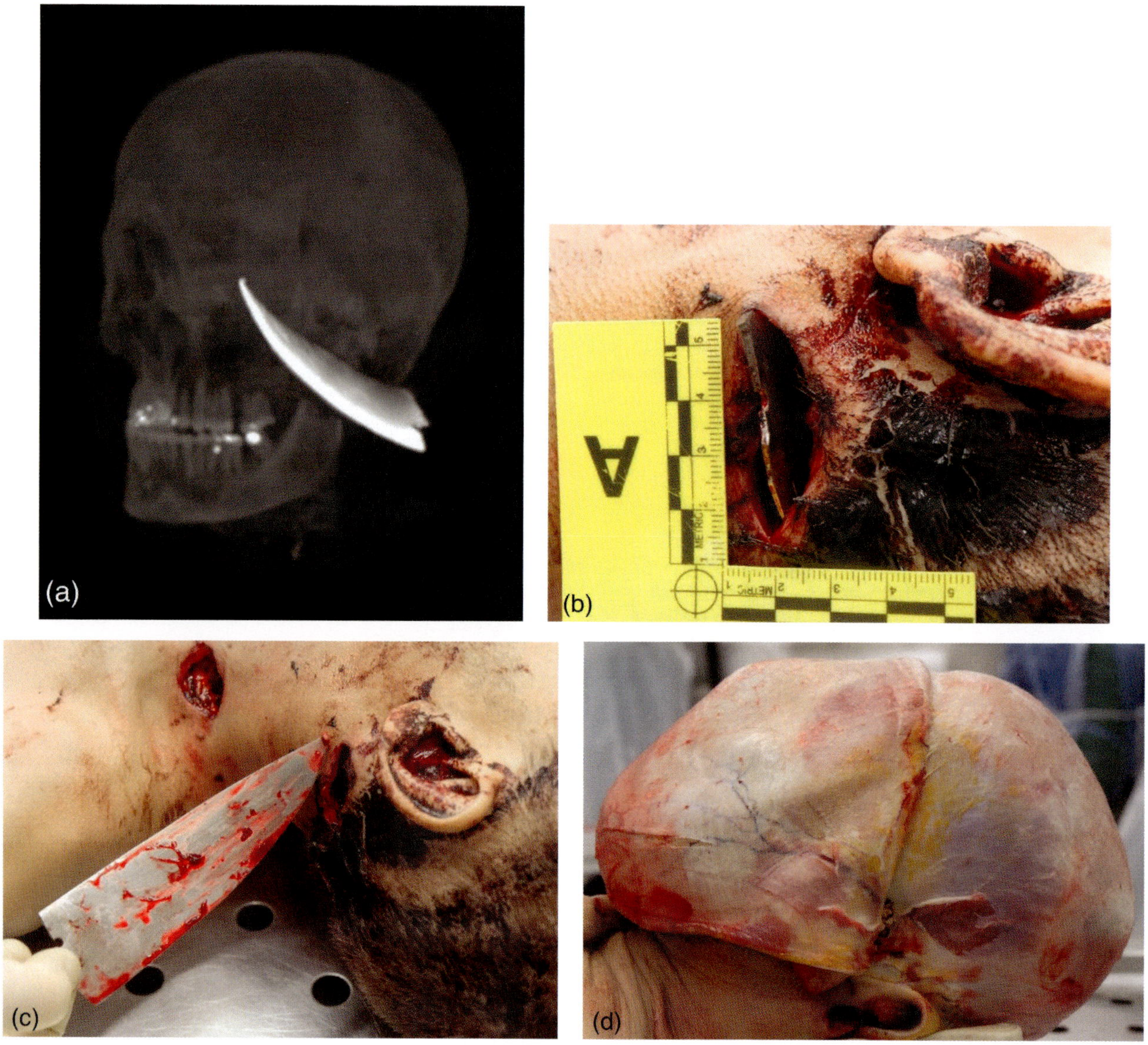

23.21 (a) Maximum intensity projection of a PMCT of a penetrating skull injury with the knife blade *in-situ*. (b) Autopsy photograph of knife blade *in situ* posterior from left ear. (c) Autopsy photograph of removed knife blade, posterior from left ear. (d) Autopsy photograph of the subcutaneous tissues on the left side of the skull.

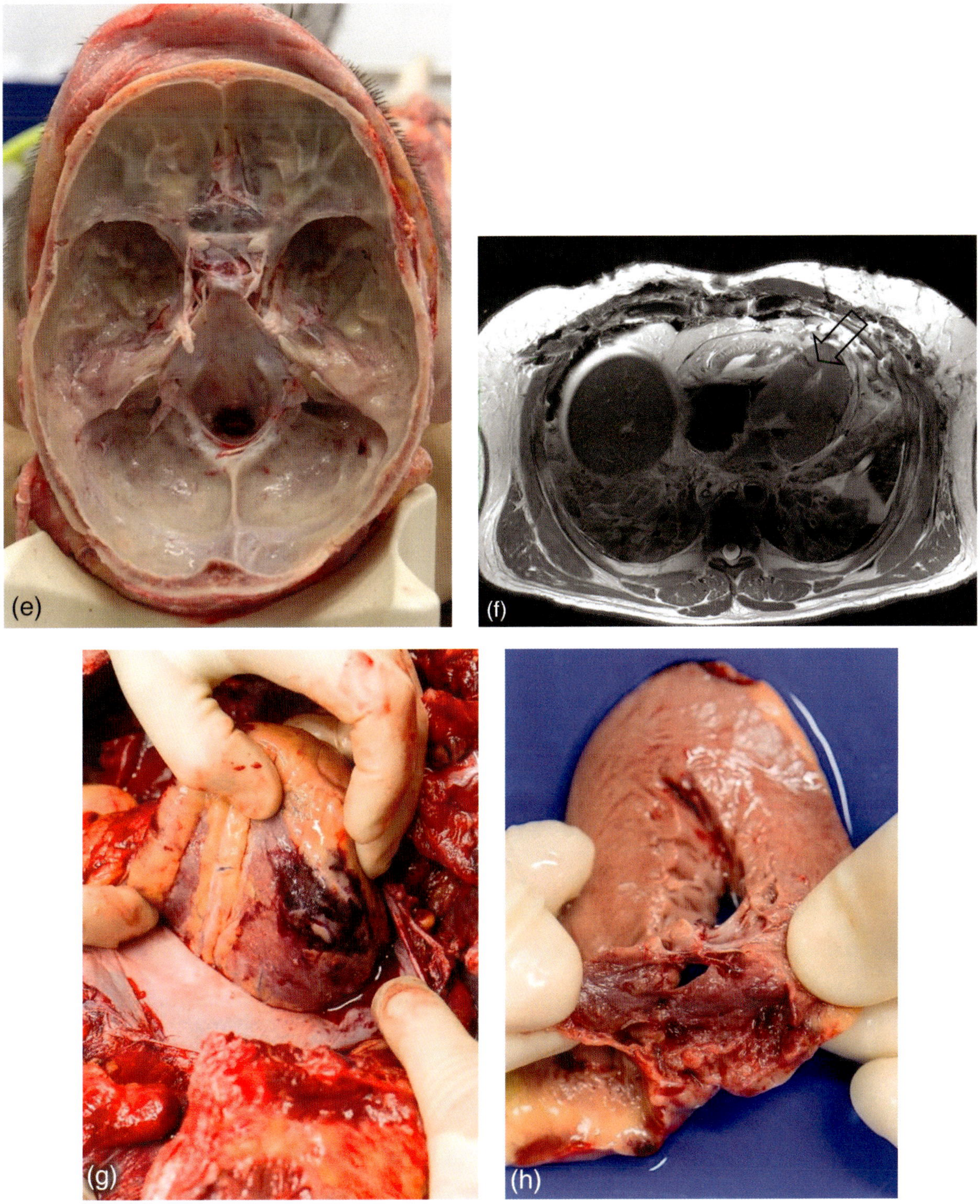

23.21 (e) Autopsy photograph of the skull base with absent trauma. (f) PMMR of the chest showing a penetrating injury through the chest wall and heart (arrows). (g) Autopsy picture of heart injury (externally). (h) Autopsy picture of heart injury (after dissection).

Strangulation

Strangulation is caused by external pressure on the neck and surrounding structures, either manually or with a ligature, which can cause numerous injuries. Frequently encountered injuries in cases of strangulation include fractures of the laryngeal skeleton, soft-tissue hemorrhages and gas accumulations. One of the strengths of forensic post-mortem imaging is the detection of fractures. Therefore, PMCT is frequently used in cases of (suspected) strangulation. A fracture of the second cervical vertebra, which occurs in hanging with a substantial drop (the hangman's fracture), may be detected using imaging techniques, particularly PMCT.

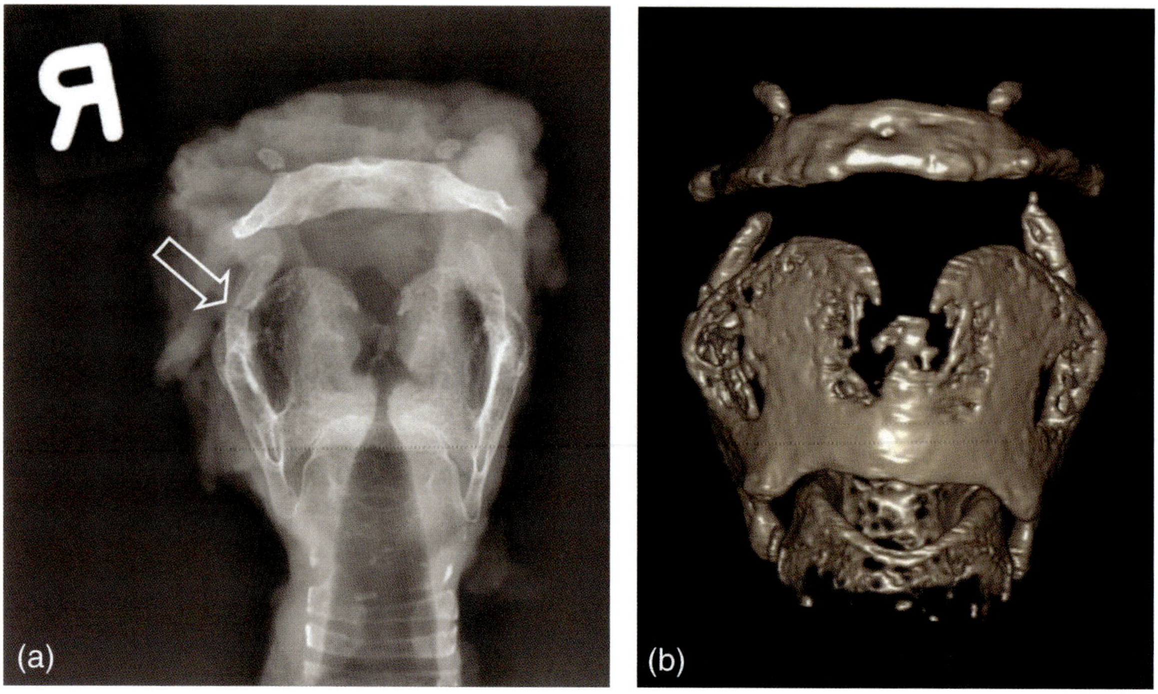

23.22 (a) Radiograph and (b) 3D CT of a resected hyoid-larynx complex with a fracture of the superior horn of the thyroid cartilage (arrow). Note the significantly higher resolution of the radiograph compared to the CT scan. (Courtesy of B de Bakker, MD PhD, Amsterdam UMC, University of Amsterdam, the Netherlands).

These types of fractures are also frequently detected in traffic accidents (86). However, the most common fractures encountered in strangulation cases are fractures of the hyoid bone and thyroid cartilage. International studies report comparable rates of detected fractures of the hyoid bone and thyroid cartilage between PMCT and autopsy (86,87). However, the presence of anatomic variations of the hyoid bone and thyroid cartilage makes the distinction between a fracture and an anatomic variation sometimes difficult. Soft-tissue hemorrhages are considered evidence of a recent fracture which can be used for the distinction between an anatomic variant and a fracture. Dating of a fracture, as well as the definite distinction between a fracture and an anatomic variant requires histologic examination. Soft-tissue hemorrhages in general are considered evidence of vitality. Hemorrhages are often missed by PMCT but can be reliably detected by PMMR or conventional autopsy (86).

PMCT is superior to conventional autopsy in the detection of gas. In cases of strangulation, a phenomenon called the gas bubble sign can occur which may be considered evidence of a laryngeal fracture (86). It is proposed that external forces on the neck induce a localized vacuum due to the expansion of enclosed tissue spaces which allows small gas bubbles to develop. Also, gas accumulations in the soft tissues of the neck or mediastinum, proposed to be the result of rupturing alveoli, are considered evidence of vitality and can be detected using PMCT but are generally not identified during an autopsy (86).

A study by Bakker et al. comparing three techniques of imaging, that is, hyoid-larynx reconstructions from initial PMCT, X-ray scan of explant, and CT scan of an explant with autopsy concluded that imaging of the explant of the hyoid-larynx complex can be considered to more reliably detect the number and location of fractures (88). Some studies report promising results for the detection of fractures in the hyoid-larynx complex using micro-CT, but because of the limited access to this technique, X-ray of the explant is the preferred technique (Figure 23.22 a&b) (90). It should be mentioned that histologic examination of the (suspected) fracture is still superior to imaging techniques (88). The combination of PMCT and PMMR can show the different features of strangulation, for example soft-tissue swelling, hemorrhage and fractures, but further studies will be needed to establish the relation to autopsy and histology (Figure 23.23 a–c).

Road vehicle fatalities

Traffic fatalities refer to incidents involving a collision of at least one vehicle (e.g. car, motorcycle, boat and/or aeroplane). They frequently concern pedestrians and cyclists, as these groups are particularly vulnerable. Their injuries might result from blunt force as well as penetrating trauma (Figure 23.24 a–c).

In addition to detecting injuries and (contributing to) determining the cause of death, an appraisal of the possible course of events is of particular importance in (road) traffic fatalities since this will most likely differentiate between a fatal accident or homicide. During these analyses, forensic post-mortem imaging addresses inquiries such as the direction of impact and the position of the body during impact (91–93). These inquiries call for a

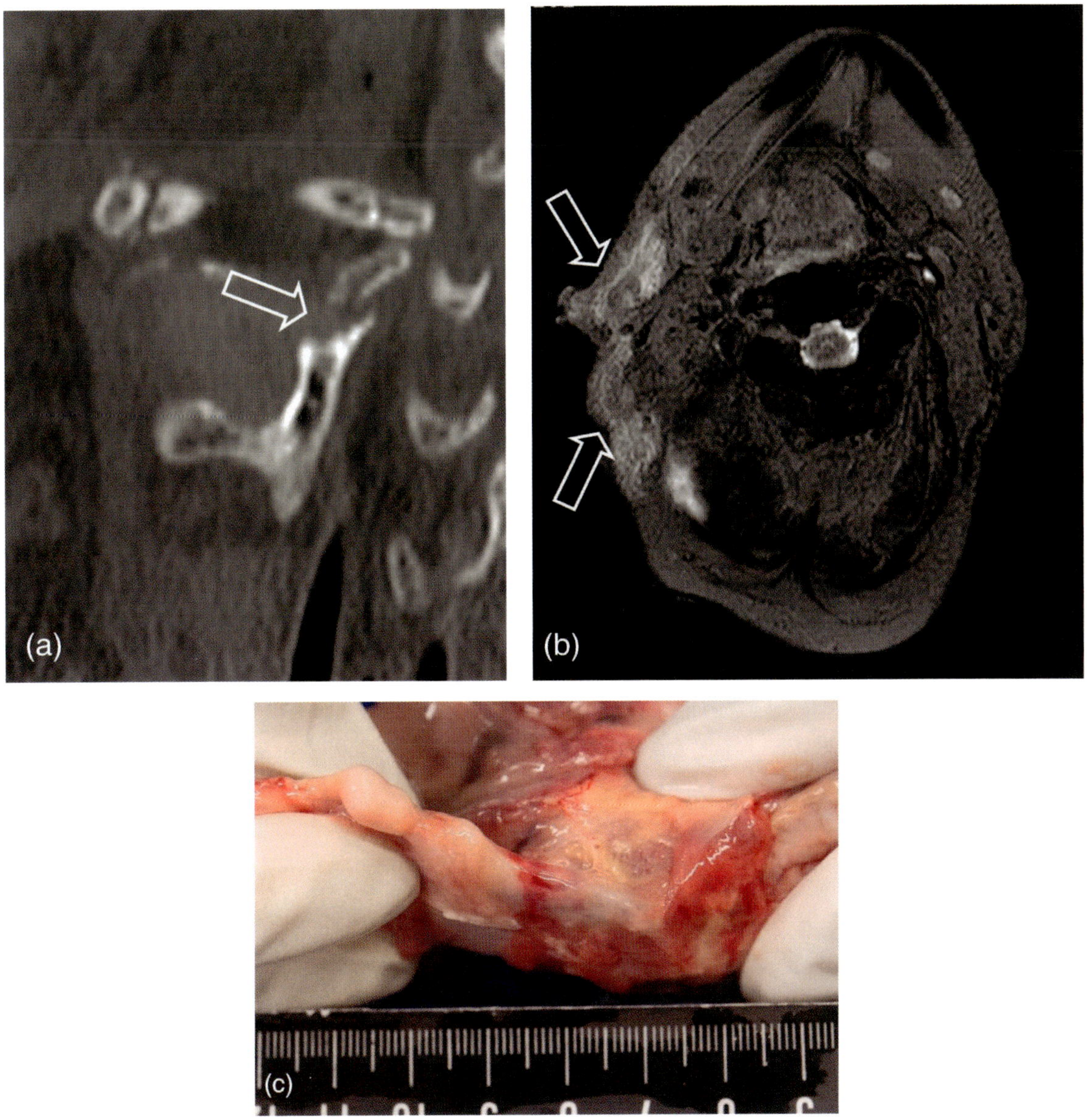

23.23 (a) PMCT multi-planar reconstruction of a thyroid fracture after strangulation (arrow). (b) PMMR of the neck with subcutaneous edema (arrows) after strangulation. (c) Autopsy photograph of fractured cornu superior of the thyroid cartilage, with bleeding.

close collaboration between medicolegal examiners and technical forensic investigators. A correlation between radiologic apparent (possibly patterned) internal injuries and digitalized depiction of the injury-causing vehicle is often an essential step in this reconstruction (94–96). An elaborate discussion about the techniques used to develop a 3D reconstruction of the (potential) crime scene to unravel the possible course of events is discussed in the section titled "Case reconstruction".

Undetermined death

In cases of undetermined deaths there are no apparent leads to the cause and manner of death or there is insufficient evidence to determine these after an initial (external) examination. In cases of undetermined deaths, a range of causes of death can be encountered making post-mortem imaging a valuable technique (Figure 23.25). For example, gases due to perforation of the bowel, skeletal pathologies and intracranial hemorrhages can be reliably detected by PMCT and myocardial infarction by PMMR (97). These techniques can also be of added value in cases of undetermined deaths to exclude injuries (28,97). Adding (targeted coronary) angiography to PMCT results in a higher proportion of diagnosed causes of death in cases of sudden adult fatalities (28,33). There are also particular causes of death for which the most often used imaging techniques are not suitable. Roberts et al. found that in a group with mainly sudden deaths of unknown cause referred to a coroner, post-mortem imaging techniques including PMCT and PMMR were inaccurate in determining the cause of death in case of ischemic heart

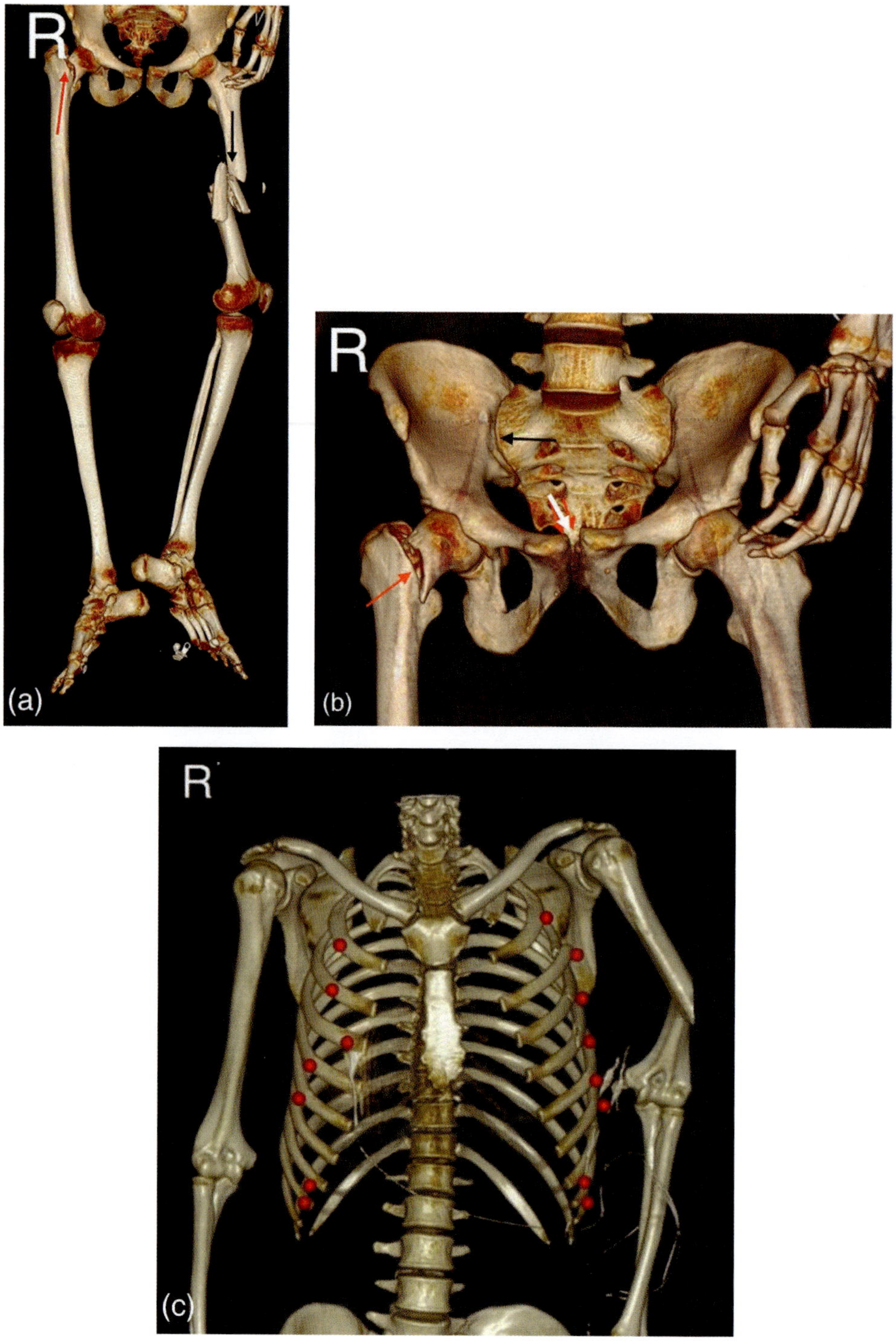

23.24 PMCT 3D-visualization of a road traffic victim with multiple fractures. (a) Femoral shaft fracture of the left leg (black arrow) and pertrochanteric femoral fracture of the right leg (red arrow). (b) Pertrochanteric femoral fracture of the right leg (red arrow), sacroiliac diastasis (black arrow), and symphysis pubis diastasis (white arrow). (c) Multiple rib fractures (red dots).

disease, pulmonary thromboembolism, pneumonia and intra-abdominal lesions (98). Because cardiovascular diseases are one of the most common causes of death in developed countries, this is a significant limitation of these techniques. This limitation can be partially overcome using a targeted coronary PMCTA (Figure 23.26) (31,99,100).

Disaster victim identification

In a mass casualty incident, one of the main objectives is rapid identification of the deceased (101). According to the International Criminal Police Organization (Interpol), the primary and three most reliable methods for the identification of the deceased include: DNA, fingerprints, and dental analysis (102). In the case of a mass casualty incident, the bodies might be severely mutilated or burned, often making it impossible to use one of these primary techniques. In these cases, other identification procedures can be used, including imaging techniques. Radiology reporting forms have therefore officially been incorporated into the INTERPOL Disaster Victim Identification (DVI) post-mortem (pink) forms (103). Conventional radiographs or PMCT could be employed for the primary assessment of the remains. These techniques may detect objects that are potentially hazardous to on-site investigators, indicate whether the remains belong to one or more victims, exclude non-human remains, and potentially recognize identifiable anatomic or medical landmarks in body parts (Figure 23.27 a&b). Vehicle-based mobile radiology units (e.g. CT-scanners) have successfully been used in mass casualty incidents in which the local radiologic equipment was inadequate (Figure 23.28) (104,105). Once retrieved by autopsy, medical devices, or implants (e.g. prosthetic hips) often lead to the victim's identity. If the primary assessment does not result in the identification of the deceased, a secondary radiologic survey is frequently employed in (various) anatomic position(s) to facilitate identification based on radiologic correlation (106). This step typically involves a comparison with antemortem images (e.g. dental radiographs), if available (Figure 23.29) (101,107). Three-dimensional reconstruction of dental radiographs has many advantages, but in the absence of this more advanced technology, it has been shown that the Lodox scanner can be an alternative (19,108). Corresponding radiologic appearances may provide sufficient evidence to establish the victim's identity but, if individual identification is not achievable,

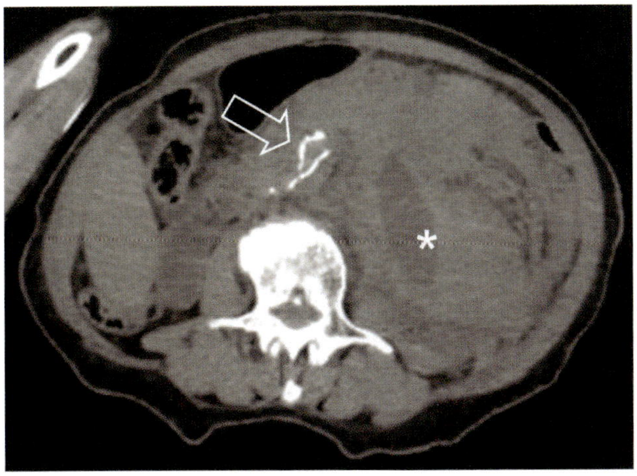

23.25 An unresponsive individual presented at an emergency department and despite resuscitation died. Although the cause of death was thought to be an out of hospital cardiac arrest, PMCT was performed. This showed a ruptured aortic aneurysm (arrow denotes the calcified collapsed wall of the aorta) with a massive retroperitoneal hematoma (asterisk) as the cause of death.

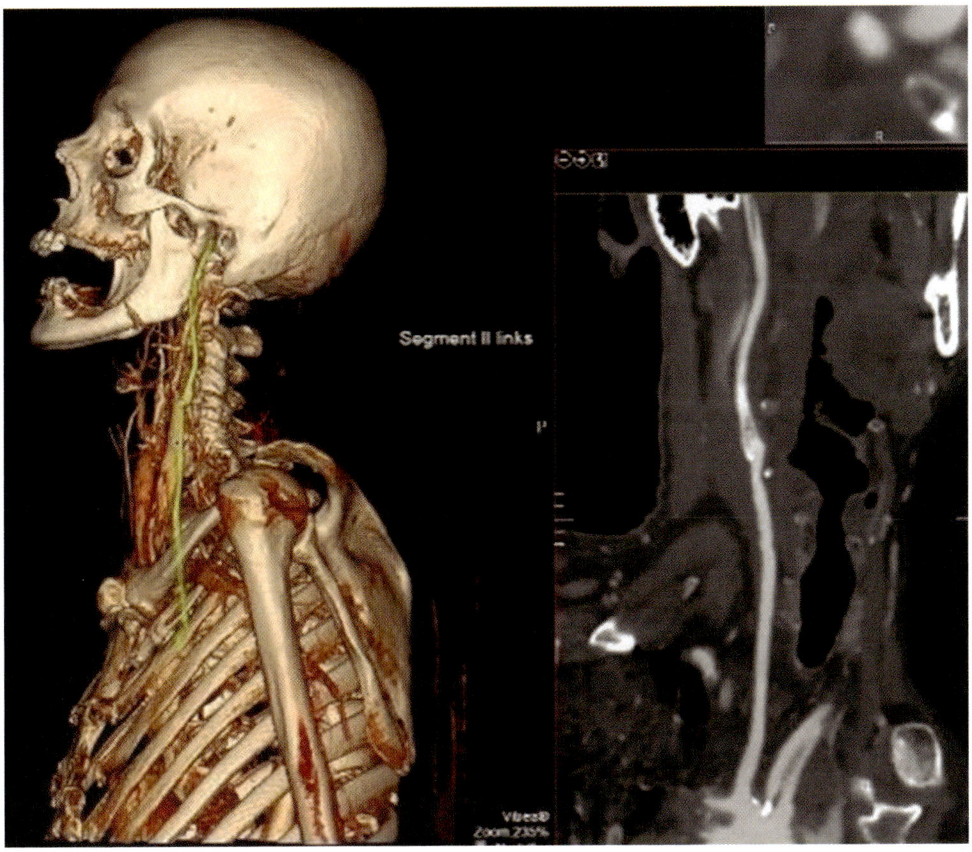

23.26 Multiplanar and 3D reconstruction of the carotid artery using PMCTA images.

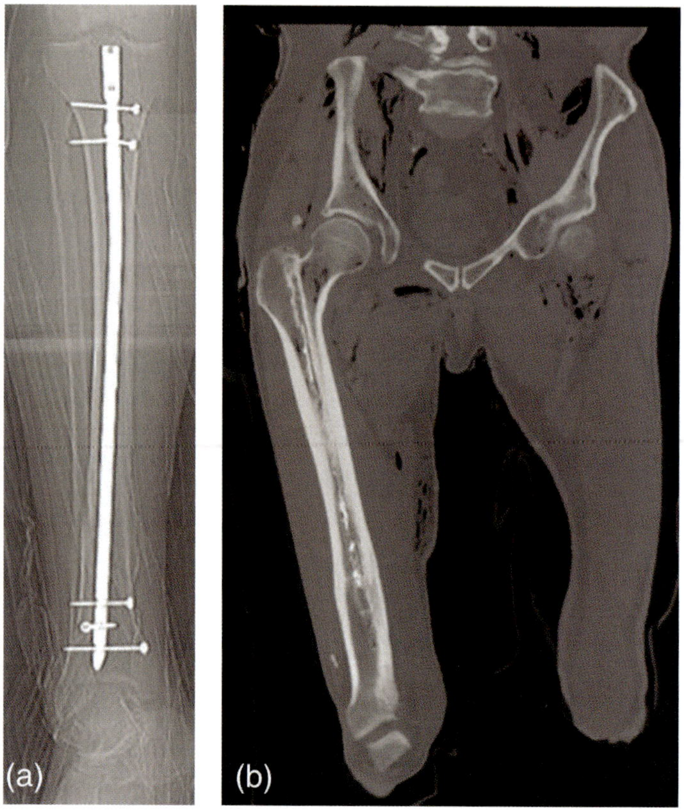

23.27 Coronal reconstructions of PMCTs showing intramedullary fixation rod (a) and an intramedullary scar after removal of a fixation rod (b). This information can be useful in an identification process.

23.28 Mobile CT unit, at the "Korporaal Van Oudheusden" military base in Hilversum, the Netherlands, used in the MH-17 disaster victim identification process (117).

post-mortem radiology can contribute to determining morphologic anthropologic parameters, for example, to establish the most likely sex, age and ethnicity (109).

Case reconstruction

Several techniques exist to generate a 3D reconstruction of cross-sectional (post-mortem) images of the body. Images acquired by PMCT are especially well-suited for this purpose. This enables, for example, the determination of a projectile trajectory, as previously discussed. These reconstructions can be readily understood by medical laymen and are therefore highly useful to police, criminal lawyers and judges (20).

Forensic investigators increasingly use visualization and reconstruction techniques to generate a virtual

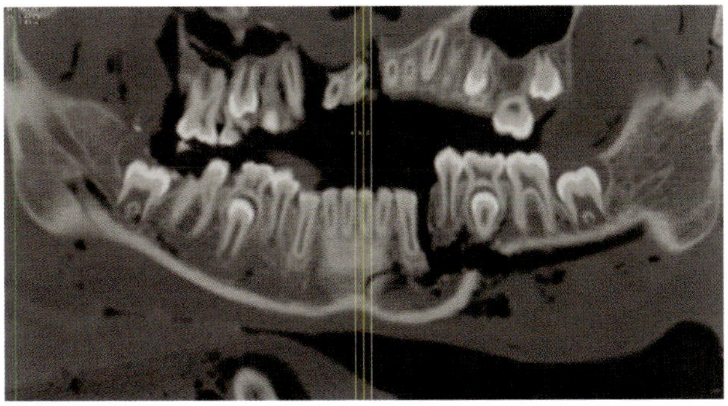

23.29 Reconstruction of an PMCT resembling an orthopantomogram. This can be used by the forensic dentist in an identification.

3D reconstruction of the potential crime scene, injury-causing objects, and sometimes even the suspect (20,94). A comprehensive discussion of the forensic imaging techniques used for this purpose goes beyond the scope of this chapter, however, the principles of frequently used techniques are discussed.

A body concealed by packaging can be considered a potential crime scene. In these cases, a PMCT can be used to examine the body and packaging material without unpacking. This might give crucial information to establish a systematic approach for unpacking, aiming to prevent loss of evidence and to ensure the investigator's safety (110,111). In digital photogrammetry, multiple photographs from various angles are digitally merged to reconstruct objects, which are depicted in their original colors. Surface scanning (i.e. 3DSS) allows reconstruction of an object based on the principle of triangulation, that is, the (deviated) reflection of light projecting on an (angled) surface. This technique is used if reconstructions of objects, traces or damage at the potential crime scene have to be depicted in high resolution. Digital photogrammetry and surface scanners can also be employed to show superficial injuries of the skin (e.g. abrasions or cuts) as these are often not apparent on 3D reconstructions of cross-sectional radiologic images due to limited image resolution (20,112). A laser scanner emits a vast amount of laser beams (i.e. point cloud) while rotating in a horizontal and vertical plane, measuring distances and angles of objects' surfaces reflecting the laser projections. This allows for a quick digitalization of the potential crime scene, also detailing nearby objects (94).

When forensic radiologists join forces with forensic investigators, the 3D reconstruction of internal and external findings of the body can be merged with the 3D reconstruction of the potential crime scene and relevant (injury-causing) objects (113). This will generate a dynamic 3D case reconstruction which allows for an examination of the likelihood of various forensic scenarios (94). To illustrate, forensic experts can, for example, evaluate the most likely position of the victim and the suspect in a gunshot incident or a road traffic incident (94) and correlate the observed injuries to the presumed injury-causing object, such as a vehicle or a stomping foot (114). These models can even be used to generate a virtual reality representation of the potential crime scene which allows for a virtual walkthrough of the potential course of events, even years after its manifestation (115).

COLLABORATION WITH FORENSIC PARTNERS

The diversity of forensic casework makes close collaboration between different specialities essential. Collaborations, for example with the forensic pathologist, forensic odontologist and forensic physicians have already been discussed. Every forensic speciality has its strengths and limitations. Collaborating with different partners and knowing each other's strengths and limitations makes it possible to determine the best strategy for each case.

In a guideline for post-mortem cross-sectional imaging in adults for non-forensic deaths from the Royal College of Pathologists and the Royal College of Radiologists, it is advised that clinicopathologic and radiologic findings are correlated to establish a multidisciplinary final post-mortem report (28). The authors of this chapter strongly encourage this workflow in a forensic setting.

REFERENCES

1. Röntgen WC. *Ueber eine neue Art von Strahlen, Gastgeber*. Physik-Med Ges Würzberg. 1895; December (132).
2. Röntgen WC. On a new kind of rays. *Nature* 1896; **53**: 253.
3. Cox J, Kirkpatrick RC. The new photography with report of a case in which a bullet was photographed in the leg. *Montreal Med J* 1896; **24**: 661.
4. Dirnhofer R. Von der Autopsie zur Virtopsie. *Rechtsmedizin* 2001; **11**: 137.
5. Thali MJ, Jackowski C, Oesterhelweg L, et al. VIRTOPSY – the Swiss virtual autopsy approach. *Leg Med (Tokyo)* 2007; **9(2)**: 100–4.
6. Aalders M, Adolphi N, Daly B, et al. Research in forensic radiology and imaging: Identifying the most important issues. *J Forensic Radiol Imaging* 2017; **8**: 1–8.
7. The International Association of Forensic Radiographers. History [cited 2022 23 august]. Available from: https://forensicradiography.com/index.php/about-us/history/ (Accessed 27 April 2023).
8. International Society of Forensic Radiology and Imaging (ISFRI). Strengthening and developing the field of forensic radiology and imaging worldwide [cited 2022 23 August]. Available from: https://isfri.org/ (Accessed 27 April 2023).
9. Ebert LC, Franckenberg S, Sieberth T, et al. A review of visualization techniques of post-mortem computed tomography data for forensic death investigations. *Int J Legal Med* 2021; **135(5)**: 1855–67.
10. O'Donnell C, Woodford N. Post-mortem radiology: A new sub-speciality? *Clin Radiol* 2008; **63(11)**: 1189–94.
11. Flach PM, Thali MJ, Germerott T. Times have changed! Forensic radiology: A new challenge for radiology and forensic pathology. *AJR Am J Roentgenol* 2014; **202(4)**: W325–34.
12. Re GL, Salerno S, Terranova MC, et al. Virtopsy and living individuals evaluation using computed tomography in forensic diagnostic imaging. *Semin Ultrasound CT MRI* 2019; **40(1)**: 67–78.
13. Wootton-Gorges SL, Soares BP, Alazraki AL, et al. ACR appropriateness criteria® suspected physical abuse—child. *J Am Coll Radiol* 2017; **14(5)**: S338–S49.
14. The Royal College of Radiologists (RCR) and the Society and College of Radiographers (RCoR). The radiological investigation of suspected physical abuse in children 2017 [cited 2022 23 august].

Available from: https://www.rcr.ac.uk/publication/radiological-investigation-suspected-physical-abuse-children (Accessed 27 April 2023).

15. American College of Radiology. ACR-SPR Practice Parameter for the Performance and Interpretation of Skeletal Surveys in Children [cited 2022 31 august]. Available from: https://www.acr.org/-/media/ACR/Files/Practice-Parameters/qct.pdf?la=en (Accessed 27 April 2023).
16. Doyle E, Dimmock M, Lee K, et al. A systematised literature review: Can low-dose whole-body computed tomography replace a radiographic skeletal survey when investigating paediatric non-accidental injury? *Forensic Imaging* 2021; **27**: 200481.
17. du Plessis M, Liebenberg L. Lodox®: the invaluable radiographic solution in the forensic setting. *Int J Legal Med* 2020; **134(2)**: 655–62.
18. Spies AJ, Steyn M, Prince DN, Brits D. Radiological detection of sharp force skeletal trauma: an evaluation of the sensitivity of Lodox in comparison to CT and X-ray. *Int J Legal Med* 2022; **136(5)**: 1417–30.
19. Bernitz H, Verster J. Lodox® digital imaging: A tool for dental identification in single and mass fatality situations. *S Afr Dent J* 2017; **72**(3): 118–21.
20. Grabherr S, Egger C, Vilarino R, et al. Modern post-mortem imaging: An update on recent developments. *Forensic Sci Res* 2017; **2(2)**: 52–64.
21. Rutty GN, Brogdon G, Dedouit F, et al. Terminology used in publications for post-mortem cross-sectional imaging. *Int J Legal Med* 2013; **127(2)**: 465–6.
22. Flach PM, Gascho D, Schweitzer W, et al. Imaging in forensic radiology: an illustrated guide for postmortem computed tomography technique and protocols. *Forensic Sci Med Pathol* 2014; **10(4)**: 583–606.
23. Thali M, Dirnhofer R, Vock P. *The Virtopsy Approach: 3D Optical and Radiological Scanning and Reconstruction in Forensic Medicine*. 1st ed. London: CRC Press; 2009.
24. Alkadhi H, Leschka S. Dual-energy CT: Principles, clinical value and potential applications in forensic imaging. *J Forensic Radiol Imaging* 2013; **1(4)**: 180–5.
25. Persson A, Jackowski C, Engström E, Zachrisson H. Advances of dual source, dual-energy imaging in postmortem CT. *Eur J Radiol* 2008; **68**: 446–55.
26. Ruder TD, Thali Y, Bolliger SA, et al. Material differentiation in forensic radiology with single-source dual-energy computed tomography. *Forensic Sci Med Pathol* 2013; **9(2)**: 163–9.
27. Ampanozi G, Halbheer D, Ebert LC, et al. Postmortem imaging findings and cause of death determination compared with autopsy: a systematic review of diagnostic test accuracy and meta-analysis. *Int J Legal Med* 2020; **134(1)**: 321–37.
28. The Royal College of Pathologists. Guidelines for post-mortem cross-sectional imaging in adults for non-forensic deaths 2021 [updated july; cited 2022 23 August]. Available from: https://www.rcpath.org/uploads/assets/666dbf95-de06-44ad-89c3b4e5f1ceab79/0de643ef-9afe-4c80-bbeb67f59f3b1257/G182-Guidelines-for-post-mortem-cross-sectional-imagingFor-Publication.pdf (Accessed 27 April 2023).
29. Shelmerdine SC, Gerrard CY, Rao P, et al. Joint European Society of Paediatric Radiology (ESPR) and International Society for Forensic Radiology and Imaging (ISFRI) guidelines: Paediatric postmortem computed tomography imaging protocol. *Pediatric Radiol* 2019; **49(5)**: 694–701.
30. Sieswerda-Hoogendoorn T, Soerdjbalie-Maikoe V, Maes A, van Rijn R. The value of post-mortem CT in neonaticide in case of severe decomposition: Description of 12 cases. *Forensic Sci Int* 2013; **233(1–3)**: 298–303.
31. Grabherr S, Doenz F, Steger B, et al. Multi phase post-mortem CT angiography: Development of a standardized protocol. *Int J Legal Med* 2011; **125(6)**: 791–802.
32. Grabherr S, Heinemann A, Vogel H, et al. Postmortem CT angiography compared with autopsy: A forensic multicenter study. *Radiology* 2018; **288(1)**: 270–6.
33. Rutty GN, Morgan B, Robinson C, et al. Diagnostic accuracy of post-mortem CT with targeted coronary angiography versus autopsy for coroner-requested post-mortem investigations: A prospective, masked, comparison study. *Lancet* 2017; **390(10090)**: 145–54.
34. La Russa R, Catalano C, Di Sanzo M, et al. Postmortem computed tomography angiography (PMCTA) and traditional autopsy in cases of sudden cardiac death due to coronary artery disease: A systematic review and meta-analysis. *La radiologia medica* 2019; **124(2)**: 109–17.
35. Jackowski C, Bolliger S, Aghayev E, et al. Reduction of postmortem angiography-induced tissue edema by using polyethylene glycol as a contrast agent dissolver. *J Forensic Sci* 2006; **51(5)**: 1134–7.
36. Grabherr S, Grimm J, Baumann P, Mangin P. Application of contrast media in post-mortem imaging (CT and MRI). *Radiol Med* 2015; **120(9)**: 824–34.
37. Rutty GN, Smith P, Visser T, et al. The effect on toxicology, biochemistry and immunology investigations by the use of targeted post-mortem computed tomography angiography. *Forensic Sci Int* 2013; **225(1–3)**: 42–7.
38. Grabherr S, Hess A, Karolczak M, et al. Angiofil-mediated visualization of the vascular system by microcomputed tomography: a feasibility study. *Microsc Res Tech* 2008; **71(7)**: 551–6.
39. Higgins S, Parsons S, Woodford N, et al. The effect of post-mortem computed tomography angiography (PMCTA) using water-soluble, iodine-based radiographic contrast on histological analysis of the liver, kidneys and left ventricle of the heart. *Forensic Sci Med Pathol* 2017; **13**(3): 317–27.
40. Pooley RA. Fundamental physics of MR imaging. *Radiographics* 2005; **25(4)**: 1087–99.
41. Luijten M, Haest I, van Kan R, et al. Can postmortem MRI be used to assess trajectories in gunshot victims? *Int J Legal Medicine* 2016; **130(2)**: 457–62.
42. Zech WD, Schwendener N, Persson A, et al. Temperature dependence of post-mortem MR quantification for soft tissue discrimination. *Eur Radiol* 2015; **25(8)**: 2381–9.
43. Persson A, Baeckmann J, Berge J, et al. Temperature-corrected postmortem 3-T MR quantification of histopathological early acute and chronic myocardial infarction: a feasibility study. *Int J Legal Med* 2018; **132(2)**: 541–9.
44. Adolphi NL, Gerrard C, Hatch GM, Nolte KB. The physical basis of poor fat/muscle contrast observed at low temperatures in post-mortem MR (PMMR) imaging. *J Forensic Radiol Imaging* 2014; **2(2)**: 101.
45. Adolphi N, Gerrard C, Hatch G, et al. Determining the temperature-dependence of tissue relaxation times (T1 and T2) for prospective optimization of post-mortem magnetic resonance (PMMR) image contrast. *J Forensic Radiol Imaging* 2013; **1(2)**: 80.
46. Arthurs OJ, Hutchinson JC, Sebire NJ. Current issues in postmortem imaging of perinatal and forensic childhood deaths. *Forensic Sci Med Pathol* 2017; **13(1)**: 58–66.
47. Thayyil S, Chandrasekaran M, Chitty LS, et al. Diagnostic accuracy of post-mortem magnetic resonance imaging in fetuses, children and adults: A systematic review. *Eur J Radiol* 2010; **75(1)**: e142-e8.
48. Thayyil S, Sebire NJ, Chitty LS, et al. Post-mortem MRI versus conventional autopsy in fetuses and children: a prospective validation study. *Lancet* 2013; **382(9888)**: 223–33.
49. Arthurs O, Guy A, Thayyil S, et al. Magnetic Resonance Imaging Autopsy Study (MaRIAS) Collaborative Group Comparison of diagnostic performance for perinatal and paediatric post-mortem imaging: CT versus MRI. *Eur Radiol* 2016; **26(7)**: 2327.
50. Addison S, Arthurs OJ, Thayyil S. Post-mortem MRI as an alternative to non-forensic autopsy in foetuses and children: From research into clinical practice. *Br J Radiol* 2014; **87(1036)**: 20130621.
51. Rutty G, Brough A, Biggs M, et al. The role of micro-computed tomography in forensic investigations. *Forensic Sci Int* 2013; **225(1–3)**: 60–6.
52. Kottner S, Schulz MM, Berger F, et al. Beyond the visible spectrum: Applying 3D multispectral full-body imaging to the VirtoScan system. *Forensic Sci Med Pathol* 2021; **17(4)**: 565–76.
53. Wilk LS, Hoveling RJ, Edelman GJ, et al. Reconstructing the time since death using noninvasive thermometry and numerical analysis. *Sci Adv* 2020; **6(22)**: eaba4243.
54. Wilk LS, Edelman GJ, Roos M, et al. Individualised and non-contact post-mortem interval determination of human bodies using visible and thermal 3D imaging. *Nature Commun* 2021; **12(1)**: 1–10.
55. Thali MJ, Viner MD, Brogdon BG. *Brogdon's Forensic Radiology*. London: CRC press; 2010.
56. Levy AD, Harcke HT, Mallak CT. Postmortem imaging: MDCT features of postmortem change and decomposition. *Am J Forensic Med Pathol* 2010; **31(1)**: 12–7.
57. Rutty GN, Biggs MJ, Brough A, et al. Ventilated post-mortem computed tomography through the use of a definitive airway. *Int J Legal Med* 2015; **129(2)**: 325–34.

58. Robinson C, Biggs MJ, Amoroso J, et al. Post-mortem computed tomography ventilation: Simulating breath holding. *Int J Legal Med* 2014; **128(1)**: 139–46.
59. Egger C, Vaucher P, Doenz F, et al. Development and validation of a postmortem radiological alteration index: The RA-Index. *Int J Legal Med* 2012; **126(4)**: 559–66.
60. Tschui J, Jackowski C, Schwendener N, et al. Post-mortem CT and MR brain imaging of putrefied corpses. *Int J Legal Med* 2016; **130(4)**: 1061–8.
61. Lin MJ, Barry N, Akusoba I, et al. Traditional autopsy versus computed tomography imaging autopsy in trauma: A case of "synergistic disagreement". *Surgery* 2016; **160(1)**: 211–19.
62. Jalalzadeh H, Giannakopoulos GF, Berger FH, et al. Post-mortem imaging compared with autopsy in trauma victims: A systematic review. *Forensic Sci Int* 2015; **257**: 29–48.
63. Grabherr S, Baumann P, Minoiu C, et al. Post-mortem imaging in forensic investigations: Current utility, limitations, and ongoing developments. *Res Rep Forensic Med Sci* 2016; **6**: 25–37.
64. Leth PM. Computed tomography in forensic medicine. *Danish Medl J* 2015; **62(6)**: 1–26.
65. Norberti N, Tonelli P, Giaconi C, et al. State of the art in post-mortem computed tomography: A review of current literature. *Virchows Arch* 2019; **475(2)**: 1–12.
66. Leth PM, Ibsen M. Abbreviated injury scale scoring in traffic fatalities: Comparison of computerized tomography and autopsy. *J Trauma Acute Care Surg* 2010; **68(6)**: 1413–16.
67. Culotta PA, Crowe JE, Tran Q-A, et al. Performance of computed tomography of the head to evaluate for skull fractures in infants with suspected non-accidental trauma. *Pediatric Radiol* 2017; **47(1)**: 74–81.
68. Sharp S, Patel S, Brown R, Landes C. Head imaging in suspected non accidental injury in the paediatric population. In the advent of volumetric CT imaging, has the skull X-ray become redundant? *Clin Radiol* 2018; 73(5): 449–53.
69. Martin A, Paddock M, Johns CS, et al. Avoiding skull radiographs in infants with suspected inflicted injury who also undergo head CT: "a no-brainer?". *Eur Radiol* 2020; **30(3)**: 1480–7.
70. Pennell C, Aundhia M, Malik A, et al. Utility of skull radiographs in infants undergoing 3D head CT during evaluation for physical abuse. *J Pediatr Surg* 2021; **56(6)**: 1180–4.
71. Orman G, Wagner MW, Seeburg D, et al. Pediatric skull fracture diagnosis: should 3D CT reconstructions be added as routine imaging? *J Neurosurg: Pediatr* 2015; **16(4)**: 426–31.
72. Cosgrave L, Bowie S, Walker C, et al. Abusive head trauma in children: radiographs of the skull do not provide additional information in the diagnosis of skull fracture when multiplanar computed tomography with three-dimensional reconstructions is available. *Pediatr Radiol* 2022; **52(5)**: 924–31.
73. Ringl H, Lazar M, Töpker M, et al. The ribs unfolded-a CT visualization algorithm for fast detection of rib fractures: Effect on sensitivity and specificity in trauma patients. *Eur Radiol* 2015; **25(7)**: 1865–74.
74. Sanchez TR, Grasparil AD, Chaudhari R, et al. Characteristics of rib fractures in child abuse: The role of low-dose chest computed tomography. *Pediatr Emerg Care* 2018; **34(2)**: 81–3.
75. Sanchez TR, Lee JS, Coulter KP, et al. CT of the chest in suspected child abuse using submillisievert radiation dose. *Pediatr Radiol* 2015; **45(7)**: 1072–6.
76. Shelmerdine SC, Langan D, Hutchinson JC, et al. Chest radiographs versus CT for the detection of rib fractures in children (DRIFT): A diagnostic accuracy observational study. *Lancet Child Adolesc Health* 2018; **2(11)**: 802–11.
77. Giorgetti A, Giraudo C, Viero A, et al. Radiological investigation of gunshot wounds: a systematic review of published evidence. *Int J Legal Med* 2019; **133(4)**: 1149–58.
78. Van Kan R, Haest I, Lahaye M, Hofman P. The diagnostic value of forensic imaging in fatal gunshot incidents: a review of literature. *J Forensic Radiol Imaging* 2017; **10**: 9–14.
79. Flach PM, Ampanozi G, Germerott T, et al. Shot sequence detection aided by postmortem computed tomography in a case of homicide. *J Forensic Radiol Imaging* 2013; **1(2)**: 68–72.
80. Viel G, Gehl A, Sperhake JP. Intersecting fractures of the skull and gunshot wounds. Case report and literature review. *Forensic Sci Med Pathol* 2009; **5(1)**: 22–7.
81. Riva F, Buck U, Buße K, et al. Error estimation on extracorporeal trajectory determination from body scans. *Int J Legal Med* 2022; **136(3)**: 729–37.
82. Kerkhoff W, Bolck A, Alberink I, et al. Pistol bullet deflection through soft tissue simulants. *Forensic Sci Int* 2018; **289**: 270–6.
83. Nolte KB, Lathrop SL. *Utility of Postmortem X-ray Computed Tomography (CT) in Supplanting or Supplementing Medicolegal Autopsies*. US Department of Justice; Office of Justice Programs, 2016. Available from: https://www.ojp.gov/library/publications/utility-postmortem-x-ray-computed-tomography-ct-supplanting-or-supplementing (Accessed 27 April 2023).
84. Schnider J, Thali M, Ross S, et al. Injuries due to sharp trauma detected by postmortem multislice computed tomography (MSCT): A feasibility study. *Legal Med* 2009; **11(1)**: 4–9.
85. Minoiu AC, Genet P, Mirea I, et al. Augmenting autopsy through MPMCTA in cases involving stabbing wounds. *Rom J Leg Med* 2019; **27(1)**: 22–7.
86. Gascho D, Heimer J, Tappero C, Schaerli S. Relevant findings on postmortem CT and postmortem MRI in hanging, ligature strangulation and manual strangulation and their additional value compared to autopsy: A systematic review. *Forensic Sci Med Pathol* 2019; **15(1)**: 84–92.
87. Decker LA, Hatch GM, Lathrop SL, Nolte KB. The role of postmortem computed tomography in the evaluation of strangulation deaths. *J Forensic Sci* 2018; **63(5)**: 1401–5.
88. de Bakker HM, Olsthoorn PC, Soerdjbalie-Makoe V, de Bakker BS. Comparison of post-mortem radiologic modalities to evaluate suspected neck violence. *Forensic Imaging* 2020; **21**: 200373.
89. de Bakker HM, Warmbrunn MV, van den Biggelaar P, et al. Fracture patterns of the hyoid-larynx complex after fatal trauma on the neck: Retrospective radiological postmortem analysis of 284 cases. *Int J Leg Med* 2020; **134(4)**: 1465–73.
90. Baier W, Mangham C, Warnett JM, et al. Using histology to evaluate micro-CT findings of trauma in three post-mortem samples: First steps towards method validation. *Forensic Science Int* 2019; **297**: 27–34.
91. Karger B, Teige K, Fuchs M, Brinkmann B. Was the pedestrian hit in an erect position before being run over? *Forensic Sci Int* 2001; **119(2)**: 217–20.
92. Buck U, Christe A, Naether S, et al. Virtopsy—noninvasive detection of occult bone lesions in postmortem MRI: additional information for traffic accident reconstruction. *Int J Leg Med* 2009; **123(3)**: 221–6.
93. Chatzaraki V, Thali MJ, Ampanozi G, Schweitzer W. Fatal road traffic vehicle collisions with pedestrian victims: forensic postmortem computed tomography and autopsy correlation. *Am J Forensic Med Pathol* 2018; **39(2)**: 130–40.
94. Buck U, Naether S, Räss B, et al. Accident or homicide–virtual crime scene reconstruction using 3D methods. *Forensic Sci Int* 2013; **225(1–3)**: 75–84.
95. Buck U, Naether S, Braun M, et al. Application of 3D documentation and geometric reconstruction methods in traffic accident analysis: With high resolution surface scanning, radiological MSCT/MRI scanning and real data based animation. *Forensic Sci Int* 2007; **170(1)**: 20–8.
96. Haest IIH, Kroll J, vand er Goes J, Hofman PAM. Why should we use radiology for the examination of deceased road traffic victims? EVU XXVI 2017–21 National Conference, Italy. 2017: 207–12.
97. Femia G, Langlois N, Raleigh J, et al. Comparison of conventional autopsy with post-mortem magnetic resonance, computed tomography in determining the cause of unexplained death. *Forensic Sci Med Pathol* 2021; **17(1)**: 10–18.
98. Roberts ISD, Benamore RE, Benbow EW, et al. Post-mortem imaging as an alternative to autopsy in the diagnosis of adult deaths: a validation study. *Lancet* 2012; **379(9811)**: 136–42.
99. Palmiere C, Lobrinus JA, Mangin P, Grabherr S. Detection of coronary thrombosis after multi-phase postmortem CT-angiography. *Leg Med (Tokyo)* 2013; **15(1)**: 12–18.
100. Brandt C, Leth PM. Post-mortem CT-coronary angiography. *Scand J For Sci* 2007; **13(1)**: 8–9.
101. Brough AL, Morgan B, Rutty GN. The basics of disaster victim identification. *J Forensic Radiol Imaging* 2015; **3(1)**: 29–37.
102. INTERPOL. INTERPOL Disaster victim identification guide [cited 2022 23 august]. Available from: https://www.interpol.int/How-we-work/Forensics/Disaster-Victim-Identification-DVI (Accessed 27 April 2023).
103. Rutty GN, Biggs MJP, Brough A, et al. Remote post-mortem radiology reporting in disaster victim identification: Experience gained in the 2017 Grenfell Tower disaster. *Int J Leg Med* 2020; **134(2)**: 637–43.

104. Rutty GN, Robinson CE, BouHaider R, et al. The role of mobile computed tomography in mass fatality incidents. *J Forensic Sci* 2007; **52**: 1343–9.
105. Khoo LS, Hasmi AH, Abdul Ghani Aziz SA, et al. MH17: The Malaysian experience. *Malays J Pathol* 2016; **38(1)**: 1–10.
106. Hofman P, Alminyah A, Apostol M, et al. Use of post-mortem computed tomography in disaster victim identification. Updated positional statement of the members of the disaster victim identification working group of the International Society of Forensic Radiology and Imaging; July 2019. *J Forensic Radiol Imaging* 2019; **19**: 100346.
107. Biggs M, Marsden P. Dental identification using 3D printed teeth following a mass fatality incident. *J Forensic Radiol Imaging* 2019; **18**: 1–3.
108. Jackowski C, Lussi A, Classens M, et al. Extended CT scale overcomes restoration caused streak artifacts for dental identification in CT-3D color encoded automatic discrimination of dental restorations. *J Comput Assist* 2006; **30(3)**: 510–13.
109. Brough AL, Rutty GN, Black S, Morgan B. Post-mortem computed tomography and 3D imaging: anthropological applications for juvenile remains. *Forensic Sci Med Pathol* 2012; **8(3)**: 270–9.
110. De Matteis M, Giorgetti A, Viel G, et al. Correction to: Homicide and concealment of the corpse. Autopsy case series and review of the literature. *Int J Legal Med* 2021; **135(3)**: 1115.
111. Haest IIH, Hofman PAM, Herbergs JPJ, et al. The application of CT for 3D visualization of concealed bodies. *Sci Justice* 2022; **62(4)**: 424–32.
112. Buck U, Buße K, Campana L, Schyma C. Validation and evaluation of measuring methods for the 3D documentation of external injuries in the field of forensic medicine. *Int J Legal Med* 2018; **132(2)**: 551–61.
113. Haest IIH, Herbergs J, Jelicic M, Nelen H. De inzet van forensische radiologie; van opsporing tot bewijsvoering Beschouwing vanuit een forensisch-radiologisch perspectief. *Expertise en Recht (E&R)* 2020; **5**: 161–170.
114. Thali MJ, Braun M, Buck U, et al. VIRTOPSY—scientific documentation, reconstruction and animation in forensic: individual and real 3D data based geo-metric approach including optical body/object surface and radiological CT/MRI scanning. *J Forensic Sci* 2005; **50(2)**: JFS2004290–15.
115. Sieberth T, Dobay A, Affolter R, Ebert LC. Applying virtual reality in forensics – a virtual scene walkthrough. *Forensic Sci Med Pathol* 2019; **15(1)**: 41–7.
116. Oostra R-J, Gelderman T, Groen WJM, et al. Amsterdam Research Initiative for Sub-surface Taphonomy and Anthropology (ARISTA) - A taphonomic research facility in the Netherlands for the study of human remains. *Forensic Sci Int* 2020; **317**: 110483.
117. MH17: zes aspecten van het strafrechtelijk onderzoek toegelicht [cited 2022 31 august]. Available from: https://boetebase.om.nl/mh17-ezine-juni2016/4-forensisch-onderzoek.html (Accessed 27 April 2023)

CHAPTER

24

Death from Natural Causes

Hans H. de Boer and Judith Fronczek

INTRODUCTION

Although differences between jurisdictions exist, most forensic pathologists are regularly confronted with deaths due to natural causes. Knowledge of the diagnostic features and effects of a large variety of natural diseases is therefore a prerequisite for every forensic pathologist. The potentially relevant diseases are, however, exceedingly numerous, even if one only focuses on the most common diseases or organ systems that are implicated in so-called "sudden" or "unexpected" natural death. Besides, selecting diseases for a general forensic pathology text is difficult, as the frequency in which they may be encountered differs between practitioners around the world. Therefore, it would be impossible to adequately cover all (potentially) relevant diseases over the course of just one chapter. Also, the rapid increase of our understanding of many of these diseases would quickly render such a chapter outdated. Table 24.1, however, summarizes key causes of sudden death related to specific organ systems to provide a background to the chapter (see also Figure 24.1).

This chapter therefore does not aim to provide a comprehensive overview of the key diagnostic features, differential diagnoses and clinical effects of the diseases that may result in death from natural causes. For this, the reader is referred to dedicated pathology textbooks, for instance those dedicated to cardiovascular pathology (1,2), thoracic pathology (3), neuropathology (4–6), and sudden death in the young (between 0 and 30 years of age) (7). Also, various excellent review papers can be used for this purpose, for instance on sudden cardiac death (8), the diagnosis and interpretation of cardiac hypertrophy (9), sudden unexpected death in epilepsy (SUDEP) (10) and the use of post-mortem biochemistry (11,12). Reference can also be made to other, more specific chapters in this book, for instance those on COVID-19 (Chapter 28), maternal deaths (Chapter 38), infant and childhood death (Chapter 37) and cardiac death (Chapter 58).

This chapter discusses the more general aspects of "death from natural causes". It especially focuses on those aspects that are less often addressed in forensic pathology texts but are still of considerable relevance. Firstly, why natural deaths are relevant for forensic pathologists is addressed, and why examination of such deaths is important for the community in which the forensic pathologist operates. Then the definition of "death due to natural causes" is explored, and the challenges that exist in classifying a death as such. Also, the meaning and use of the terms "sudden", "unexpected" and "unexplained" are discussed in more detail. Lastly,

TABLE 24.1 Key causes of sudden natural death

Cardiovascular system	Respiratory system	Central nervous system
Acute myocardial infarction	Acute epiglottitis	Meningitis
Myocarditis	Pneumonia	Encephalitis
Valvular heart disease	COPD[1]	Infarction
Hypertensive heart disease	Asthma	Hypertensive hemorrhage
Aortic dissection/rupture		Cerebral artery aneurysm
Vasculitis		Cerebral amyloid angiopathy
Genetic cardiomyopathies		Epilepsy
Ion-channelopathies		
Pulmonary thromboembolism		
Gastrointestinal system	**Endocrine system**	**Musculoskeletal system**
Esophageal varices	Diabetes mellitus	Necrotizing fasciitis
Gastric/duodenal ulcer	Addison's disease	Osteomyelitis
Gastric/intestinal volvulus	Thyroiditis	Rhabdomyolysis
Pancreatitis	**Genitourinary system**	**Systemic diseases**
Liver cirrhosis	Pyelonephritis	Metastatic disease
Cholecystitis/cholangitis	Cystitis	Sepsis
Ischemic bowel	Endometritis/salpingitis	Anaphylaxis
Appendicitis	Ectopic pregnancy	
Diverticulitis		

[1] Chronic obstructive pulmonary disease

DOI: 10.1201/9781003138754-26

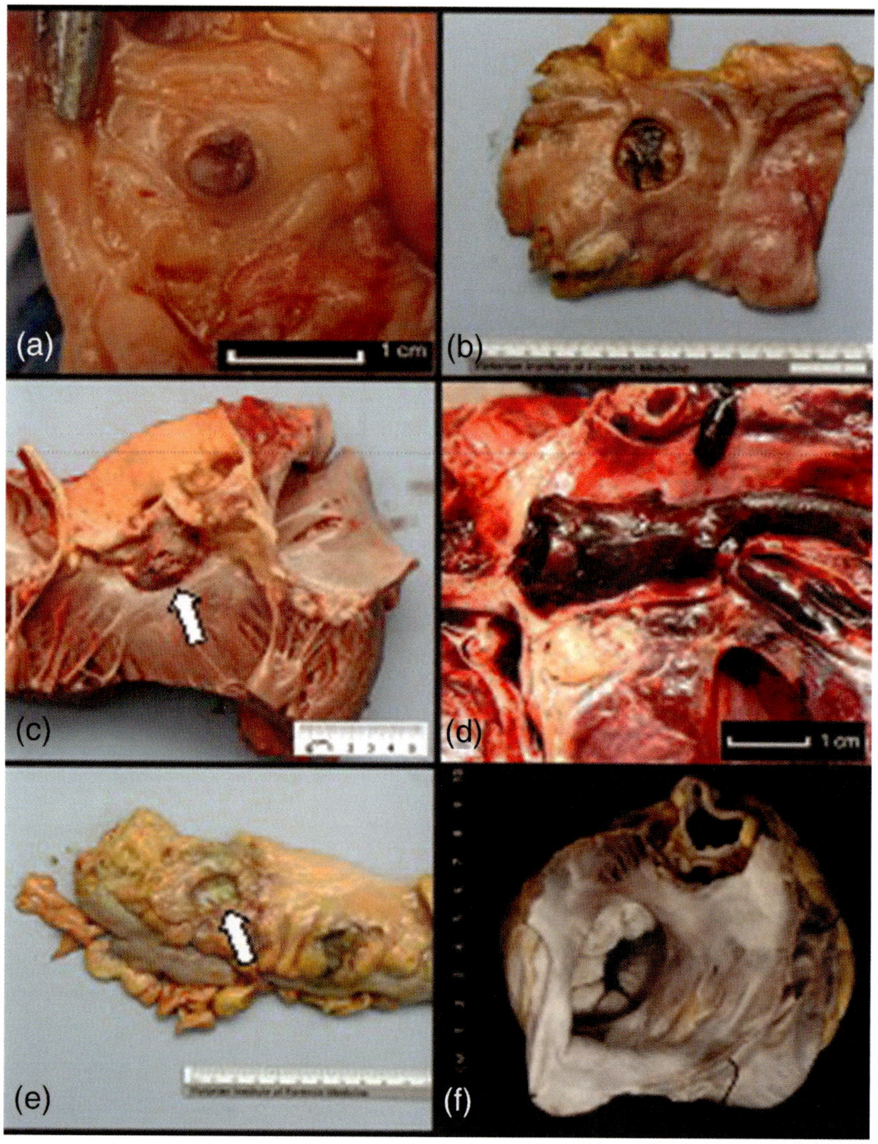

24.1 Examples of key causes of sudden natural death. (a) Thrombosis of the left anterior descending artery. (b) Duodenal ulcer, causing massive gastro-intestinal hemorrhage (not in image). (c) Infective endocarditis of the aortic valve (arrow). (d) Pulmonary thromboembolism. (e) Perforated diverticulitis (arrow). (f) Mitral valve insufficiency due to floppy mitral valve. (Photos (a–b) courtesy of Victorian Institute of Forensic Medicine. Photo (f) courtesy of Amsterdam University Medical Centre.)

consideration is given to the determination of the cause of death; something that can be very challenging in cases of chronic disease, when there may be interaction between trauma and disease, or when the autopsy findings are non-specific.

WHY IS DEATH FROM NATURAL CAUSES RELEVANT FOR FORENSIC PATHOLOGISTS?

The mandate and organization of a medicolegal death investigation system is usually based on a combination of socio-cultural, political and economic considerations. As a result, large differences exist between regions in the number and types of cases examined by a forensic pathologist, and in the number and type of cases that undergo a forensic autopsy. This affects the extent to which a forensic pathologist is confronted with natural disease, and which diseases this entails.

In the Netherlands, for example, the threshold for ordering a forensic autopsy is extremely high. The Netherlands has a population of approximately 17 million people, with an annual death rate of approximately 150 000 per year (13). Of those, only 200–250 cases are being referred annually for a forensic autopsy. The forensic pathologists at the Netherlands Forensic Institute (NFI) therefore deal almost invariably with suspicious deaths, while they are rarely confronted with deaths from natural causes. On the contrary, in most coronial systems, a legal obligation exists to examine all deaths in which the attending physician cannot formulate a reasonable cause of death (e.g. [14,15]). In such a context, deaths from natural causes represent the majority of forensic pathology cases.

Irrespective of these differences, knowledge of, and experience with, disease is a *sine qua non* for adequate forensic pathology, for a variety of reasons. For instance, most cases can only be reliably classified as being "natural" after an autopsy has been performed. Quite regularly, cases are deemed sufficiently suspicious to be referred to the forensic pathologist but eventually turn out to be the result of natural disease. It goes without saying that this requires a thorough understanding of the diagnostic features and lethal potential of a large variety of diseases, especially those that can lead to circumstances that mimic a homicidal death.

Many culpable deaths also present with a combination of natural disease and injuries. These cases can be extremely challenging, as it is incumbent upon the forensic pathologist not only to diagnose the disease(s) correctly but also to determine its relative contribution to the cause and mechanism of death. A common example is when severe injury and severe coronary artery atherosclerosis co-exist (e.g. [16,17]). Also, in deaths during restraint, the potential contribution of concomitant natural disease is often hotly debated (18,19).

Furthermore, questions of culpability are not limited to violent or unnatural deaths. In many legal cases, the correct diagnosis and interpretation of natural disease may be pivotal. Consider for instance the diagnosis of a metastatic mesothelioma in an individual with a history of work-related asbestos exposure (20). Pulmonary thromboembolism in a context of immobilization after a culpable event is another example (21). In such cases, rightful compensation hinges on an accurate tissue diagnosis, and the correct pathophysiological inferences.

Lastly, forensic pathologists have a role to play in the detection and reporting of diseases that may affect the next of kin of the deceased or the community. Reportable infectious diseases such as tuberculosis, botulism or COVID-19 are good examples of the latter. Examples of the former are inheritable cardiac diseases that predispose to sudden cardiac death, such as hypertrophic obstructive cardiomyopathy (HOCM), arrhythmogenic cardiomyopathy (ACM) and the so-called "channelopathies" (22,23). These disorders often display an autosomal dominant inheritance pattern, while their lethal potential can be mitigated by medication, or by the implantation of a pacemaker or an internal cardiac defibrillator (ICD). Recognition and appropriate follow-up can therefore literally save lives.

The diagnosis of inheritable or reportable diseases is an important point that argues for extending a medicolegal death investigation system beyond the examination of suspicious and unnatural deaths. Such a system also increases the reliability of cause of death statistics, which is indispensable for prevention. An efficient medicolegal death investigation system should therefore include at least some deaths due to natural causes. At the same time, autopsies are ideally limited to those cases in which the results prevent further morbidity and mortality. Finding the right balance proves to be challenging. In many jurisdictions where forensic autopsies are limited to suspicious death, forensic pathology expertise appears to be underutilized. In other words, additional public benefits can be gained by increasing the number of autopsies. Conversely, in many coronial medicolegal death investigations, public gains can be made by undertaking fewer autopsies. The use of post-mortem CT scans can assist with this (24–26).

WHAT IS A "DEATH FROM NATURAL CAUSES"?

Some thoughts must also be dedicated to what a "death from natural causes" actually is. This is relevant, since classifying a death as such may have important implications. For instance, in many jurisdictions, the legal official who is responsible for the medicolegal death investigation (e.g. the coroner or public prosecutor) has limited mandate or interest in examining natural deaths. Rather, they tend to focus their resources on unnatural causes of death such as homicides, suicides and accidents.

A natural death is usually defined as "a death that is solely due to disease", or "a death that arises solely or entirely from natural disease" (27,28). This definition is commonly accepted, irrespective of whether the forensic pathologist operates in a medical examiner's, coronial or another type of medicolegal death investigation system. Therefore, classifying a death as being from "natural causes" first requires the diagnosis of a natural disease that reasonably explains death. Secondly, non-natural contributions must be excluded.

On the surface this may seem straightforward, and in many cases it is. Many diseases have lethal potential, and it is therefore common to identify at least one that can reasonably explain death, considering the circumstances of the case. Note that in this regard, the number of diseases and their potential interactions do not complicate the issue. Also, the standard of proof is generally the "balance of probabilities". As such, classifying a death as natural is less demanding than ascertaining "the" cause of death.

Problems arise, however, when there is a non-natural element that might have contributed to the lethal mechanism. As many colleagues will recognize, excluding entirely such a possible contribution can be very challenging. As an example, consider a case of intra-axial cerebral bleeding due to amyloid angiopathy, when minor head trauma has occurred. The bleeding could have occurred spontaneously, causing a terminal collapse. Alternatively, the bleeding could have been elicited by the head trauma. Disentangling the causal chain in such cases may be impossible, and therefore, strictly speaking, the death cannot be classified as natural. This problem of causal direction can present itself in various ways (29).

In other cases, the contribution of an unnatural element can be so temporally distant that it may affect any perceived relevance, even when a causal relation with the immediate cause of death is firmly established. For instance, the negative health effects of smoking and chronic alcoholism are well-known, and they are commonly included as contributory factors, for instance when ascribing a death to the effects of liver cirrhosis or lung cancer. Such deaths are nonetheless usually classified as "natural".

Perioperative deaths, or deaths after other medical procedures, present challenges of their own. In the Netherlands, such deaths can be classified as natural (or actually: not unnatural) if the care provided was necessary for the treatment of a disease, and the treatment was adequately performed (27). In this context, known complications of treatment are regarded as an extension of the natural disease. A similar approach is proposed in Dorries et al. (30). Note how such a decision might require detailed knowledge of treatment indications, execution and complications; knowledge that is not always within the field of expertise of a forensic pathologist.

The above-mentioned limitations can be mitigated to some extent by considering the purpose of "natural death" classification. Its main aim is to differentiate between relevant cases and irrelevant cases, from a legal perspective. Interpreted as such, it is less essential to determine whether a death was "solely due to disease". Instead, it is important that a qualified medical professional advises whether the death "occurred entirely independent from any external factor of legal significance" (28).

"SUDDEN", "UNEXPECTED" AND "UNEXPLAINED" DEATHS

For most forensic pathologists, the most relevant diseases are those that result in deaths that can be referred to as "sudden", "unexpected" and/or "unexplained". These terms are also commonly used to group diseases based on their (presumed) etiology or their clinical presentation; sudden cardiac death (SCD), sudden unexpected death in epilepsy (SUDEP), sudden adult death syndrome (SADS), sudden infant death syndrome (SIDS) and sudden unexpected death in infancy (SUDI) are examples. The use of such terms allows for categorization of deaths for research purposes, public health statistics and preventative campaigns.

Defining a death as "sudden" can be problematic, and the term "sudden" is not necessarily interchangeable between these classification systems. SCD for instance, generally only includes deaths that occurred within one hour of symptom onset (31). In the International Classification of Disease (ICD-10) of the World Health Organization (WHO), however, "sudden" applies to deaths that occur within 24 hours of the onset of symptoms (32). Note that any such definition assumes that the death was preceded by observable symptoms. Also, it assumes that the moment of symptom onset is known. In a forensic context, however, such information is often unavailable. The challenges this poses have been reported before, both in the clinical (10) and the forensic pathology literature (33), and the matter can be complicated further if extensive medical intervention or resuscitation are taken into account. This is why the SUDEP classification for instance does not define a specific timeframe (10), while some authors have proposed that SCD could also apply to unwitnessed deaths in which the individual was known to be in apparent good health less than 24 hours before death (8).

Irrespective of which definition of "sudden" is used, one should be aware of its effect on the causes and mechanisms of deaths that it may include. Only a limited number of diseases can cause instantaneous death (within minutes) in an (apparently) previously healthy individual. The longer the time interval between symptom onset and death, the longer the list of potential causes of death. Most "sudden" death classifications therefore strongly recommend, or even require, a full autopsy. However, when contextual information is limited, or when no invasive autopsy is performed, "sudden death" can include a wide variety of diseases.

As with "sudden" deaths, "unexpected" deaths are of special interest since, in many jurisdictions, the unexpectedness of a death determines to a large part whether the case will be referred for medicolegal investigation. The term is again not without problems, however, which is largely due to its innate operator-dependency. In other words, what might be unexpected for bystanders, or for the next of kin of the deceased, may not be unexpected at all for a medical professional. From a philosophic point of view, it can be argued that no death can be entirely unexpected, and when applied to individuals of advanced age the term can have a somewhat odd connotation. The variability in its use has a direct bearing on the workload of forensic pathologists, who are frequently confronted with deaths that were deemed unexpected by non-medical professionals. Similarly, treating doctors may report a death as being unexpected, arguing that to their knowledge, the deceased had no relevant medical history. However, in a substantial portion of these cases, a review of the medical history reveals underlying diseases that reasonably can explain death. This once again highlights the importance of information on the medical context. Retrieving and sharing such information in a timely manner can frequently prevent a full forensic pathologic examination.

Deaths can be both unexpected and unexplained but note that these terms are not the same. This was also emphasized by Nashef et al. in 2012 (10), when they clarified that the term SUDEP relates to "unexpected" deaths, and not to "unexplained" ones. After all, deaths can be unexpected yet well-explained, while unexplained deaths do not necessarily happen unexpectedly. Also, the question to consider here is: "unexplained to whom"? Some authors suggest that the term should be reserved for deaths that remain unexplained after medical attention (34). In other words, the death must be unexplained to a medical professional. This would clearly set the "unexplained" deaths apart from other types of deaths. This definition is, however, not universally accepted.

DETERMINING "THE" CAUSE OF DEATH

The cause of death classifications form of the WHO requires identification of the direct cause of death (part 1) and any significant contributing factors (part 2). Within part 1, the immediate cause of death is given in 1a. This is the disease, injury or complication that occurred closest to the time of death and directly caused death. Preceding underlying disease or injury can be entered as 1b or, when there is another disease or injury underlying 1b, also in 1c. Reconstruction of this causal chain is relevant, as it helps to determine how many people die of a specific disease, but also what the most common lethal complications of a specific disease are (35).

Disentangling the fatal causal chain and determining which event should be classified as "the" cause of death, are among the most challenging tasks of a forensic pathologist. For a large part, this is because causality cannot be observed, only inferred. The general complexities of (inferring) causality, and how these translate to forensic pathology, has been discussed previously (29, 36–38), but these publications mostly focus on (potentially) culpable deaths, while the same issues can arise in natural deaths. In general, a causal chain is easier to infer when the autopsy findings are specific (i.e. the effect is specific for the antecedent disease) and the pathophysiologic chain of events presents over a short span of time. A good example would be a hemopericardium due to a ruptured left ventricle, resulting from myocardial infarction, caused by thrombotic occlusion of an atherosclerotic coronary artery. Oftentimes, however, non-specific autopsy findings preclude such a clear-cut pathophysiologic reconstruction.

This non-specificity of autopsy findings is a common problem, due to a variety of reasons. First, when examining the body, the forensic pathologist has to deal with a static end-state, representing the ultimate result of disease process(es) and the process of dying. The fact that many diseases interact, not uncommonly by common final pathways, complicates this further. Also, the diagnostic armamentarium of forensic pathologists is limited, and mainly focuses on anatomic/structural abnormalities. As a result, physiological, biochemical and metabolic abnormalities remain largely undetected. Furthermore, the complicating effect of post-mortem artefacts must be considered.

These limitations can cause a situation in which mutually exclusive explanations for the death co-exist, and no single cause or mechanism can be sufficiently elevated above all others. How does one then choose between the various options? A useful approach is to order them on the basis of their lethal potential, with diseases that are more directly lethal prevailing over diseases with less lethal potential (28,29). The abductive heuristic of William of Ockham ("Ockham's Razor") is also popular, which dictates that simple explanations prevail over more complex ones. However, though appealing, this principle is not infallible.

In the author's opinion, when confronted with a challenging case, the first step is to remember that possibility and probability are very different things. The fact that an explanation for the death cannot be excluded, does not necessarily make it relevant. Also, when determining the probability of an explanation in a challenging case, some degree of uncertainty must be accepted. After all, if everything was certain the case would not be challenging in the first place.

Furthermore, the considerations of the forensic pathologist should not be limited to the probability of the explanations or causes of death: the cost and benefit (the "utility") of the explanation must also be kept in mind. Some causes of death may be quite improbable, but the cost of falsely excluding them is very high. For instance, falsely excluding a genetically inheritable disease could have detrimental effects. Such improbable yet important explanations should not be mentioned in the cause of death but should be mentioned explicitly in the report.

Belief in the probability of an event and determining utility is ultimately subjective. Differences between practitioners may exist due to differences in knowledge, experience and creativity. Especially in challenging cases, it seems more appropriate to talk about "forming an opinion on" or "estimating" the cause of death, than to talk about "determining" the cause of death. Another useful realization is that the probability of a cause of death is not only dependent on forensic pathologic or even medical information. Other information, unknown to the forensic pathologist, may increase or decrease the probability, even to the extent where a cause of death is unequivocally excluded or confirmed. It is therefore helpful to accept that most autopsy reports are so-called "investigative" opinions: an expert opinion that can, and sometimes even should, incite additional investigation (39). Since the forensic pathologist cannot anticipate future information, it is often appropriate to classify a death as "unascertained" and discuss the relevant explanations, their (preliminary) relative probability, the reasoning that underpins this ranking, and possible leads for future investigation.

ACKNOWLEDGMENTS

The authors thank Dr Matthew Lynch of the Victorian Institute of Forensic Medicine for the various discussions which have assisted the writing of this chapter.

REFERENCES

1. Buja LM, Butany J. *Cardiovascular Pathology*. London: Academic Press; 2015.
2. Burke AP, Tavora F. *Practical Cardiovascular Pathology*. Philadelphia: Lippincott Williams & Wilkins; 2010.
3. Burke AP, Aubry M-C, Maleszewski J, et al. *Practical Thoracic Pathology: Diseases of the Lung, Heart, and Thymus*. Philadelphia: Lippincott Williams & Wilkins; 2016.
4. Gray F, Gray F, Duyckaerts C, De Girolami U. *Escourolle and Poirier's Manual of Basic Neuropathology*. Oxford: Oxford University Press; 2013.
5. Leestma JE. *Forensic Neuropathology*. London: CRC Press; 2014.
6. Love S, Perry A, Ironside J, Budka H (eds). *Greenfield's Neuropathology*. London: CRC Press; 2018.
7. Byard RW. *Sudden Death in the Young*. Cambridge: Cambridge University Press; 2010.

8. Basso C, Aguilera B, Banner J, et al. Guidelines for autopsy investigation of sudden cardiac death: 2017 update from the Association for European Cardiovascular Pathology. *Virchows Archiv* 2017; **471(6)**: 691–705.
9. Basso C, Michaud K, d'Amati G, et al. Cardiac hypertrophy at autopsy. *Virchows Archiv* 2021: **479(1)**: 79–94.
10. Nashef L, So EL, Ryvlin P, Tomson T. Unifying the definitions of sudden unexpected death in epilepsy. *Epilepsia* 2012; **53(2)**: 227–33.
11. Palmiere C, Mangin P. Postmortem chemistry update part II. *Int J Legal Med* 2012; **126(2)**: 199–215.
12. Palmiere C, Mangin P. Postmortem chemistry update part I. *Int J Legal Med* 2012; **126(2)**: 187–98.
13. Death and causes of death [Internet]. 2021. Available from: https://opendata.cbs.nl/statline/#/CBS/en/dataset/7233ENG/table?ts=1639535414331 (Accessed 27 April 2023).
14. The Chief Coroner's guide to the Coroners and Justice Act 2009. Accessed on 15 December 2021. Available from: https://www.judiciary.uk/publications/the-chief-coroners-guide-to-the-coroners-and-justice-act-2009/ (Accessed 27 April 2023).
15. Coroners Court of Victoria. Practice handbook: a legal practitioner's guide to the coronial system in Victoria. 2011. Available from: https://www.coronerscourt.vic.gov.au/sites/default/files/2018-11/practice%2Bhandbook%2B%28web%2Bversion%29%2B-%2Bmarch2012.pdf (Accessed 27 April 2023).
16. Turner SA, Barnard JJ, Spotswood SD, Prahlow JA. 'Homicide by heart attack' revisited. *J Forensic Sci* 2004; **49(3)**: JFS2003343–3.
17. Flannery FT, Oetgen CC, Oetgen WJ. Homicide by fright: The intersection of cardiology and criminal law. *Am J Cardiol* 2010; **105(1)**: 136–8.
18. Gill JR. The syndrome of excited delirium. *Forensic Sci Med Pathol* 2014; **10(2)**: 223–8.
19. Vilke GM, Payne-James JJ, Karch SB. Excited delirium syndrome (ExDS): Redefining an old diagnosis. *J Forensic Legal Medicine* 2012; **19(1)**: 7–11.
20. Graham MA, Roggli VL. Medicolegal aspects of asbestos I: Malignant mesothelioma and lung cancer. *Acad Forensic Pathol* 2013; **3(4)**: 386–406.
21. Gill JR. Medicolegal Evaluation of Fatal Pulmonary Thromboembolism. In: Tsokos, M (ed). *Forensic Pathol Reviews.* Totowa, NJ: Humana Press; 2005, pp. 285–302.
22. Fellmann F, Van El CG, Charron P, et al. European recommendations integrating genetic testing into multidisciplinary management of sudden cardiac death. *Eur J Hum Genet* 2019; **27(12)**: 1763–73.
23. Magi S, Lariccia V, Maiolino M, et al. Sudden cardiac death: Focus on the genetics of channelopathies and cardiomyopathies. *J Biomed Sci* 2017; **24(1)**: 1–18.
24. Nolte KB, Lathrop SL. *Utility of Postmortem X-ray Computed Tomography (CT) in Supplanting or Supplementing Medicolegal Autopsies.* US Department of Justice, 2016.
25. O'Donnell C, Rotman A, Collett S, Woodford N. Current status of routine post-mortem CT in Melbourne, Australia. *Forensic Sci Med Pathol* 2007; **3(3)**: 226–32.
26. Rutty GN, Morgan B, Robinson C, et al. Diagnostic accuracy of postmortem CT with targeted coronary angiography versus autopsy for coroner-requested post-mortem investigations: A prospective, masked, comparison study. *Lancet* 2017; **390(10090)**: 145–54.
27. KNMG. *Handreiking (niet-)natuurlijke dood.* 1st ed. 2016.
28. Madea B, Argo A. Certification of Death: External Postmortem Examination. In: Madea B, (ed). *Handbook of Forensic Medicine.* Chichester: John Wiley & Sons; 2014.
29. Pollanen MS. Deciding the cause of death after autopsy: Revisited. *J Clin Forensic Med* 2005; **12(3)**: 113–21.
30. Dorries C. *Coroners' Courts: A Guide to Law and Practice.* Oxford: Oxford University Press; 2014.
31. Semsarian C, Ingles J. Molecular autopsy in victims of inherited arrhythmias. *J Arrhythm* 2016; **32(5)**: 359–65.
32. World Health Organization. *The International Statistical Classification of Diseases and Health Related Problems ICD-10: Tenth Revision.* Vol 1: Tabular List: World Health Organization; 2004.
33. Markwerth P, Bajanowski T, Tzimas I, Dettmeyer R. Sudden cardiac death: Update. *Int J Legal Med* 2021: **135(2)**: 483–495.
34. Saukko P, Knight B. The Pathology of Sudden Death. In: *Knight's Forensic Pathology*, 4th ed. Boca Raton: CRC Press; 2015.
35. Madea B, Rothschild M. The post mortem external examination: Determination of the cause and manner of death. *Deutsch Ärztebl Int* 2010; **107(33)**: 575.
36. Cordner SM. Deciding the cause of death after necropsy. *Lancet* 1993; **341(8858)**: 1458–60.
37. Meilia PDI, Freeman MD, Zeegers MP. A review of causal inference in forensic medicine. *Forensic Sci Med Pathol* 2020; **16(2)**: 313–20.
38. Oliver WR. Inference in forensic pathology. *Acad Forensic Pathol* 2011; **1(3)**: 254–75.
39. De Boer HH, Fronczek J, Berger CEH, Sjerps M. The logic of forensic pathology opinion. *Int J Legal Med* 2022; **136(4)**: 1027–36.

CHAPTER 25

Pathophysiology of COVID-19

Aniello Maiese, Alice Chiara Manetti and Vittorio Fineschi

INTRODUCTION

SARS-CoV-2 (acute respiratory syndrome coronavirus 2) is an enveloped virus that belongs to the *Coronaviridae* family (1). Its genome is composed of a single-stranded, positive-sense RNA molecule that codifies for various proteins, including the spike protein (protein S). Protein S is a surface-located glycoprotein that contains the receptor-binding domain (RBD) and allows the virus entry into the cell, binding the angiotensin-converting enzyme 2 (ACE2) (2). Then, the protein S is primed by cellular proteases to allow further membrane fusion. The cellular transmembrane protease serine 2 (TMPRSS2) seems to be also involved (3). Once entered, SARS-CoV-2 replicates and transcripts its genome, assembling new viral particles. Type II alveolar cells express ACE2, partially explaining why SARS-CoV-2 has a pulmonary tropism (4). However, ACE2 is expressed in many other tissues, as well (5). The clinical manifestations of SARS-CoV-2 (so-called coronavirus disease 2019, COVID-19) are mainly respiratory and extremely variable, ranging from the absence of symptoms or fever with a mild cough, to severe pneumonia with acute distress respiratory syndrome (ARDS), and even death (6). Nevertheless, many authors have reported that other organs could be involved, such as the brain, heart, liver, kidney, skin and gastrointestinal (GI) tract. For example, Wong et al. recently found SARS-CoV-2 RNA in epithelial cells of various organs (7). Many authors have also suggested that SARS-CoV-2 triggers the so-called "cytokine storm", which is an extreme activation of the immune system with massive cytokine release, causing disseminated intravascular coagulation (DIC) and multiple organ failure (MOF) (8,9). Both clinical and post-mortem studies have shown that severe COVID-19 could be accompanied by thrombotic events (10,11,27–31). Furthermore, endothelial cells express the ACE2 receptor, suggesting a direct vascular involvement (12).

To further understand the pathophysiology of this multisystem disease, pathologic findings in each organ need to be investigated. Since December 2019, SARS-CoV-2 has spread all over the world, causing millions of victims. Nevertheless, knowledge about SARS-CoV-2-related pathologic features has not proportionally increased due to the lack of autopsy data. In this chapter, we aim to collect all of the available information, published so far, concerning autopsy and histopathologic findings of SARS-CoV-2 decedents, in order to highlight the potential pathophysiologic mechanisms that underlie this complex disease. It is also important to establish a standardized autopsy procedure to produce uniform and comparable data. Therefore, a proposal for the management of COVID-19 deaths is briefly provided in the next paragraph.

THE AUTOPSY IN SARS-CoV-2 DECEASED

There are no international guidelines concerning autopsy procedures for COVID-19 cases. When available, it is a fundamental requirement to obtain clinical information regarding both previous medical conditions and the most recent clinical course of the disease. The correlation between clinical and autopsy data is crucial to demonstrate a possible causal relationship between COVID-19 and death, as well as to investigate the correlation between different clinical manifestations and pathologic findings.

Prior to the autopsy, in a case of suspected COVID-19, post-mortem nasopharyngeal and oropharyngeal swabs for SARS-CoV-2 RNA detection are recommended (13, 14). The detection of gene sequences is obtained by the reverse transcription polymerase chain reaction (RT-PCR). Many variables influence the testing capacity of molecular tests, causing false-negative results (15). Post-mortem tests seem to be highly sensitive and specific when performed within a week of death (16). Nevertheless, positive post-mortem swabs have been obtained even 30–35 days after death, even in exhumed decomposed bodies (17–19). Our suggestion is to perform a molecular test in any case with an unknown medical history or suspicion of COVID-19 regardless of the post-mortem interval (PMI). The usefulness of a post-mortem swab is not only to make the operators aware of the contamination risk in case of positivity but also to direct the following autopsy procedure and further examinations. On the other hand, when the suspicion of a COVID-19-related death is strong, based on the clinical history, appropriate

DOI: 10.1201/9781003138754-27

preventive measures should be adopted, even if the post-mortem swab is negative.

Schröder et al. demonstrated that the risk of SARS-CoV-2 transmission from the deceased is low if safety measures are correctly adopted during the management of the body (20). It is important to mention that SARS-CoV-2 has been classified as a Hazard Group 3 (HG 3) pathogen, according to the classification of infectious biological agents provided by the Advisory Committee on Dangerous Pathogens (ACDP) (21). It means it "can cause severe human disease and may be a serious hazard to employees; it may spread to the community, but there is usually effective prophylaxis or treatment available". Virus transmission occurs through respiratory secretion, droplets, aerosols and direct contact (22). Several studies have also demonstrated that SARS-CoV-2 survives on inanimate surfaces, even if this route of transmission may be minimal (23,24). It is beyond the scope of this chapter to enumerate all of the hygiene precautions that must be undertaken in the management of COVID-19 infected bodies. Briefly, the autopsy room must conform to biosafety level 3 (BSL 3), and all the operators must adopt appropriate precautionary measures and appropriately wear personal protective equipment, to avoid environmental and self-contamination, as recommended for HG3 pathogens (25).

Another preliminary examination that may be performed before the autopsy is post-mortem computer tomography (PMCT) (25). PMCT is a valid ancillary technique that has many applications in forensic and clinical pathology (26,27). It is important to refer to a radiologist specialized in post-mortem examinations and to perform PMCT as soon as possible (<48 hours) as post-mortem artifacts may lead to misinterpretations (i.e. milk glass opacity due to dorsal hypostasis) (28). Even if there are only few studies on PMCT in COVID-19 deaths, the main radiologic findings seem to be ground-glass opacities (often multilobar and peripheral), multiple consolidations, "crazy-paving" patterns, traction bronchiectasis, and interseptal thickenings (10,29–33). However, these features are not specific for COVID-19 and so the autopsy should always subsequently be performed. Moreover, PMCT may miss other findings, such as pulmonary embolism, and cannot distinguish between primary and superinfected bacterial pneumonia (30).

Concerning the autopsy technique, in suspect or confirmed COVID-19 cases, we suggest performing an "*en bloc*" extraction of the cervicothoracic organs (cardiovascular-respiratory block) and then opening the pulmonary arteries from the pulmonary trunk to the pulmonary hilum, to evaluate the presence of pulmonary embolism. Then, the respiratory block should be separated from the cardio-aortic block and the respiratory tract should be opened from the larynx to the lower airways. A lower respiratory tract swab should also be performed (13). Keep in mind that the presence of SARS-CoV-2 RNA in the upper and lower respiratory tract does not prove a causal relationship between COVID-19 and the death if adequate clinical and/or pathologic findings are missing. The remaining autopsy procedure could be performed as the pathologist deems appropriate, considering the past and recent medical history if known.

With regard to the advisable organs samples that should be collected during the autopsy, we suggest at least the following: sections of the brain and the olfactory bulb in particular; the heart, a total of six samples (anterior, lateral, and posterior wall of the left ventricle, septum, free wall of the right ventricle, apex); the trachea, the bronchi, and perihylar lymph nodes, especially when enlarged; the lungs (at least two samples per lobe); the liver; the spleen; the GI mucosa, if ante-mortem GI symptoms are reported; the kidney; and the skin, if any cutaneous changes are present.

In addition to the traditional hematoxylin and eosin staining, immunohistochemical staining could be used, that is, to recognize the type of inflammatory cells present. Moreover, SARS-CoV-2 proteins and RNA could be identified on formalin-fixed paraffin-embedded tissues through immunohistochemistry (i.e. adopting antibodies against the nucleocapsid protein) or *in situ* hybridization (34). Furthermore, RT-PCR or electron microscopy (EM) could reveal the presence of viral RNA or viral particles within the cells, respectively, even if EM could not be specific and may lead to misinterpretation (35–37).

PATHOLOGIC FINDINGS IN COVID-19-RELATED DEATHS

Respiratory system

As noted, the main symptoms related to SARS-CoV-2 infection involve the respiratory system. Most infected patients experience mild symptoms, such as tiredness, fever and cough. However, a small percentage of patients, more often the elderly and those with comorbidities, manifest severe pneumonia and ARDS, with the need of intensive medical intervention (38).

Pulmonary findings are fundamental to attribute the cause of death to COVID-19 in the case of ARDS and to investigate how the virus affects the lungs. At gross examination, the lungs appear congested and stiff, red-maroon colored, with hemorrhagic areas (39). The lung weight is usually increased (>1000 g), which is consistent with data obtained from in-life CT scan quantitative analysis (40,41). In the airways, mucosal edema and thick mucus may be present, in particular if superimposed bacterial infection has occurred. Mediastinal, perihilar and peribronchial lymph nodes may be enlarged. Histologic examination of the lung reveals diffuse alveolar damage (DAD), both exudative and proliferative/organizing, with hyaline membranes and inflammatory cell infiltration (42–44). Inflammatory cells comprise neutrophils and macrophages, but also lymphocytes (T-cells), depending on the clinical stage of the disease (45). Immunohistochemical stains could be used to highlight different types of inflammatory cells. Reactive type 2 pneumocytes have also been described (43). DAD and interstitial damage cause blood-gas barrier alterations, reducing the ability of the lungs to exchange gases (46). Septal ruptures may lead to alveolar hemorrhages, both focal and diffuse, which further compromise gas exchange (44).

Pulmonary barotrauma induced by mechanical ventilation is another possible cause of DAD and septal rupture (47). So, it could be suggested that these changes depend on medical intervention rather than COVID-19 itself (47). The molecular demonstration of SARS-CoV-2 RNA presence in the lung parenchyma should be obtained to substantiate the causal relationship between lung histology and the viral infection. Many authors have demonstrated the presence of viral inclusions, as well as viral RNA (positive RT-PCR from parenchymal swab), in the lung parenchyma (48,49).

There could also be signs of superimposed bacterial infection (bronchopneumonia) with airspaces filled with neutrophils and histiocytes (42). Endothelial damage and vascular injury have also been reported in several cases, alongside alveolar capillary microthrombi and severe congestion (50–53). Endothelial injury to the alveolar capillaries contributes to fluid accumulation within the alveolar space and alters gas exchange (54).

When death occurs long after the symptom onset, fibrotic tissue may be seen within the lung parenchyma, leading to distortion of the normal architecture and honeycomb-like remodeling (44,55). Xu et al. demonstrated that the binding between SARS-CoV-2 and the ACE2 alters the expression of various molecules, such as transforming growth factor-beta (TGFB1), vascular endothelial growth factor A (VEGF A) and others, inducing fibrosis (56). However, there are still little data about long-term lung alterations. Pathologic features of underlying diseases should also be carefully evaluated since COVID-19 patients often have cardiovascular and/or pulmonary comorbidities, that is, chronic obstructive pulmonary disease (COPD), heart failure, asthma, emphysema and so on.

Cardiovascular system

Many clinical studies have also demonstrated cardiac involvement in COVID-19 infections (57). Since the beginning of the SARS-CoV-2 pandemic, the American College of Cardiology has published a clinical bulletin to warn clinicians about cardiac complications (58). The development of cardiac injury is related to higher mortality and morbidity (59). In addition, previous cardiovascular disorders are associated with a more aggressive clinical course and higher mortality rates (60). It is still not clear if cardiac involvement is due to direct viral damage. However, some researchers have demonstrated the presence of SARS-CoV-2 (RNA or viral particles) within the myocardium of COVID-19 patients (61–64). Precise epidemiologic data concerning myocarditis among these patients are still missing. Halushka et al. reported a prevalence of 7.2 percent, even if most of the cases were not functionally significant, and therefore the authors suggested the true prevalence could be less than 2 percent (65). An interesting case was presented by Gauchotte et al. regarding a 69-year-old man who died of cardiogenic shock (63). The autopsy revealed multifocal areas of macrophage and T-lymphocytic infiltration of the heart. The myocardium was also positive for SARS-CoV-2 using RT-PCR, while the lungs were negative and did not manifest any particular changes. The diagnosis was fulminant myocarditis. This case is significant as there was no lung involvement, suggesting that SARS-CoV-2 could directly affect the heart.

Concerning cardiovascular autopsy findings in COVID-19 cases, macroscopic examination of the heart usually does not reveal particular changes. It is possible to see right heart dilation as a consequence of pulmonary overload and evidence of previous conditions such as myocardial hypertrophy or fibrosis. Histologic examination may be more informative. Some authors have reported myocardial inflammatory changes, macrophage and lymphocyte infiltrate (as in the case previously described), and myocardial necrosis (61,66–68). The presence of microthrombi within the vessels was also demonstrated, alongside perivascular lymphocyte infiltrates (69–71). However, cardiac microscopic changes due to previous cardiovascular diseases, such as hypertensive cardiomyopathy, atherosclerosis, and chronic ischemic changes, are the most common findings (65). With respect to vessels involvement, the thrombotic risk seems to be augmented in COVID-19 patients and an increase in pro-coagulation markers has been highlighted (72). The prevalence of thrombotic events and coagulopathy varies from 20 up to 50 percent of severely ill patients (72,73). As already noted, SARS-CoV-2 affects the lungs but then induces an exaggerated inflammatory response with massive cytokines release ("cytokine storm"). Therefore, endothelial homeostasis between pro-thrombotic and anti-thrombotic stimuli seems to be altered causing vascular dysfunction and thrombotic manifestations (53,54,102–104). For these reasons, the pathologist needs to look for venous thrombosis and pulmonary embolism. In addition, endothelial cells express ACE2, suggesting direct endothelial involvement (74,75). In fact, viral inclusions have been identified within the endothelial cells (53). Moreover, widespread microthrombi appear to be one of the most common histologic findings in COVID-19, followed by perivascular inflammatory infiltrates of various organs.

Neurologic system

Neurologic manifestations in COVID-19 patients include olfactory and gustatory impairment without nasal congestion, headache, Guillan-Barré syndrome, stroke and meningoencephalitis (76–80). In particular, anosmia and dysgeusia are two of the most reported symptoms, varying from 59 up to 86 percent of cases (81). Olfactory dysfunction may be caused by direct olfactory nasal neuroepithelium or bulb involvement (82). As with other viruses, coronaviruses are neurotropic (83). The presence of SARS-CoV-2 RNA and virions within the olfactory bulb has indeed been proven (84). The axons of the neurons that compose the olfactory epithelium protrude through the cribriform plate and reach the olfactory bulb (85,86). Therefore, it has been suggested that SARS-CoV-2 could enter the central nervous system (CNS) through the olfactory epithelium (87). In this regard, Donegani et al. demonstrated that patients who manifested persistent anosmia even after COVID-19 recovery had a decrease in metabolic activity of the limbic cortex (88).

However, brain examinations conducted on COVID-19 decedents do not reveal any specific findings (89). Macroscopic evaluation of the brain may show swelling; ischemic and/or hemorrhagic lesions have also been reported (90). The most common brain histologic features are hypoxic changes, microglia activation and astrogliosis (91–94). The presence of non-specific findings seems to be in accordance with the result of the study conducted by Pedrosa et al., who demonstrated that SARS-CoV-2 does not replicate within the neurons (so-called non-permissive infection), even if it can still stimulate a local inflammatory response (95). Perivascular inflammatory infiltrates and microthrombi have been described in the brain as in other organs (96).

GASTROINTESTINAL TRACT

GI symptoms in COVID-19 are frequently described consisting of nausea, vomiting, abdominal pain, diarrhoea and, less often, GI bleeding (97,98). The presence of SARS-CoV-2 has been demonstrated in anal swabs and within stool specimens (99). Therefore, some authors have suggested that the feces may be an additional source of transmission (100). Studies concerning the correlation between the presence of GI manifestations and the severity of the disease have provided conflicting results (101). ACE2 is highly expressed in the GI mucosa, suggesting direct viral damage (102). Xiao et al. described the case of a 78-year-old man who developed bilateral COVID-19 pneumonia with ARDS (103). While he was hospitalized, he also manifested upper GI bleeding. He underwent an endoscopy and the only finding was esophageal mucosal injury. Mucosal samples were collected from various locations (esophagus, stomach, duodenum and colon), the histologic examination of which showed widespread lymphocyte and plasma cell infiltrates within the lamina propria and interstitial edema. The squamous epithelium of the esophagus also contained sporadic lymphocytes. Through immunofluorescent staining, the authors also highlighted the presence of SARS-CoV-2 in the GI epithelium. Livanos et al. reported the results of GI endoscopies in COVID-19 patients (104). No lesions were visualized, while SARS-CoV-2 was detected in the intestinal mucosa. Histologically, in seven cases out of seventeen, there were only limited inflammatory infiltrates, represented by lymphocytes or neutrophils. Overall, data concerning pathologic and histologic changes in the GI tract are not enough to draw any conclusions, even if a direct mucosal infection seems plausible.

Liver

Elevation of liver enzymes has been commonly reported and it may correlate with illness severity (101,105). Liver abnormalities are present even in patients with no pre-existing hepatic disease (106). Several mechanisms may be proposed to explain liver damage in COVID-19. Firstly, direct hepatic SARS-CoV-2 infection. However, hepatocytes barely express ACE2 (107). On the other hand, cholangiocytes do express ACE2 (108). SARS-CoV-2 presence in liver samples, both within the hepatocytes and endothelial cells, has been proven (109–112). Unfortunately, histology of the liver does not resolve this issue. To our knowledge, Sonzogni et al. conducted the most extensive work on liver histology published to date (111). They described T-cell infiltrates, Kupffer cell activation, portal vein endotheliitis, diffuse vascular alterations and intraluminal thrombosis. The authors related these findings to impairment of blood flow rather to direct viral damage. An alternative mechanism that could explain hepatic damage in COVID-19 is drug-induced injury. As known, paracetamol can be hepatotoxic, as well as hydroxychloroquine and azithromycin (113,114). A case of Tocilizumab-induced liver injury in a COVID-19 patient has been described (115). Another hypothesis is that liver damage is caused by the underlying inflammatory state. Cytokines can provoke hepatocellular cholestasis, as may occur in sepsis (116). Bile plugs have certainly been identified histologically (110,117). Lastly, respiratory and circulatory failure may induce hypoxia, leading to hypoxic hepatitis due to decrease in blood perfusion and oxygen supply with centrilobular necrosis (118). Various degrees of hepatic necrosis have been described in COVID-19 decedents (110,117). In particular, Schmit et al. reported centrilobular necrosis in 12 out of 14 autopsy cases of SARS-CoV-2 infected subjects (119). Another histologic finding is hepatic steatosis, both macro and microvesicular (110,111,117,119). Specifically, microvesicular steatosis could be associated with mitochondrial dysfunction (120). It may, however, be difficult to determine whether it should be considered as a pre-existing condition or a COVID-19 associated alteration.

KIDNEY

The prevalence of acute kidney injury (AKI) among patients hospitalized for COVID-19 is 28 percent, increasing to 46 percent in patients admitted to the intensive care unit (121). AKI seems to be associated with poor outcomes (122,123). Concerning the histologic aspect of the kidney in these patients, acute tubular necrosis with inflammatory infiltrates (macrophages and lymphocytes) has been described (124,125). In addition, Su et al. highlighted the presence of red cell aggregation within the peritubular and glomerular capillaries, causing lumenal obstruction, alongside hemosiderin granules and endothelial damage (124). Signs of pre-existing conditions, such as diabetic nephropathy and arteriosclerosis, have also been identified (124). The presence of viral RNA in the renal tissues has been proven and immunohistochemical staining has detected the virus within the tubular cell cytoplasm (48,52,125). ACE2 has been detected in the proximal tubule cells (126). However, the pathogenesis of AKI in COVID-19 patients is not clear. One hypothesis is that renal damage is secondary to rhabdomyolysis and pigmented casts have been seen on histologic examination correlating with elevated creatinine phosphokinase serum levels

(124,127). Rhabdomyolysis is described in COVID-19 patients in clinical reports and could be caused either by the virus itself, which could lead to myositis as in other viral infections, or be drug-induced (128–130). Hypoperfusion may lead to tubular injury as well. Diao et al. identified hypoxia-associated molecules in kidney samples of six COVID-19 patients (125). Furthermore, the cytokine storm may induce apoptosis and cellular death (131). It is reasonable to suppose that these pathologic mechanisms concur in causing tubular damage and AKI in SARS-CoV-2 infection.

SKIN

It is not uncommon for viral infections to cause alterations to the skin (132). Dermatologic manifestations in COVID-19 are heterogeneous and different authors have proposed various classifications (133–136). The following have been described: urticaria-like and morbilliform rash, dermatosis, varicella-like papulovesicular exanthem, purpuric papules (also defined as "vasculitic"), livedo reticularis and chilblain-like lesions (137–142). In order to understand the pathophysiology of SARS-CoV-2 infection, a deeper look into the histologic appearance of its skin manifestations may be interesting, especially related to those features that could be linked to systemic inflammatory and vasculitic processes.Chilblain-like lesions, also called acro-ischemic, are erythematous, purplish, sometimes blistering, patches located on the extremities. They are one of the most frequent skin manifestations of COVID-19 and mainly affect young adults and children (133,143–145). Keratinocyte necrosis, edema of the dermis, and perivascular lymphocytic aggregates are the main histologic features of these lesions (143,146–148). The pathogenesis of chilblain-like lesions may depend on the exaggerated cytokine release or endothelial damage, as the presence of perivascular lymphocytic infiltration suggests. The pro-thrombotic imbalance may also cause obliterative microangiopathy, as some authors have suggested (149). Both these mechanisms are consistent with the considerations already proposed about other organs' pathophysiology of COVID-19. Giavedoni et al. did not find an association between chilblain-like lesions and autoantibodies, suggesting that they are not auto-immune mediated (139). Immunohistochemistry allowed the visualization of SARS-CoV-2 within the endothelial cells of chilblain-like lesions, supporting a direct correlation between these lesions and the virus-induced endotheliitis. Livedo reticularis is another possible dermatologic manifestation in COVID-19 patients. It is considered to be the expression of venous hypercongestion and dilation due to arterial inflow or venous outflow decrease (150). Again, virus-mediated endotheliitis and microvascular thrombosis may be the cause of these changes (151). Microthrombi within the lumen of skin vessels have been seen (152). Purpura generally is the cutaneous manifestation of a vasculitic process (153,154). In COVID-19, it could be both generalized and localized and seems to be more common in aging patients (133,155–157). Histologically, leukocytoclasis and neutrophil and lymphocyte infiltration, alongside swollen endothelium, have been seen (155,158,159). In short, these three cutaneous features appear to be correlated to SARS-CoV-2-induced vasculitis.

As regards the remaining skin manifestations, histologic examinations described in the literature do not seem to enhance our understanding of the pathophysiology of COVID-19. Acantholysis, dyskeratosis, keratinocyte swelling and necrosis, and inflammatory infiltrates have been seen in cases of papulovesicular, measles-like, or urticaria-like rash (138,160–166).

CONCLUSION

In the light of the pathologic findings described above, COVID-19 is certainly a respiratory disease that can also affect multiple organs. Its pathophysiologic mechanisms are still partially unclear, especially those concerning extrapulmonary manifestations. However, the evidence of endotheliitis and microthrombosis in various tissues seems to prove the fundamental role played by endothelial involvement and coagulation dysregulation. Exacerbated inflammation with the release of a multitude of cytokines is another event that aggravates the clinical presentation, in particular in the case of vulnerable patients (the elderly and those with comorbidities).

In a recent paper the authors highlighted

> *"the morphological impact of the cytokine storm triggered by SARS-CoV-2 infection and the potent inflammatory response involved in the pathogenesis of COVID-19. The cytokines involved are a complex group of mediators, particularly pro-inflammatory cytokines such as IL-1β, IL-6, IL-15, and TNF-α, which are produced at sites of tissue inflammation… Further autopsy studies are needed to expand this evidence and highlight the pathognomonic signs of the disease, as well as to facilitate the establishment of standard practices for collection of autopsy and post-mortem data"* (167).

REFERENCES

1. Lu R, Zhao X, Li J, et al. Genomic characterisation and epidemiology of 2019 novel coronavirus: Implications for virus origins and receptor binding. *Lancet*. 2020; **395(10224)**: 565–74.
2. Hoffmann M, Kleine-Weber H, Schroeder S, et al. SARS-CoV-2 cell entry depends on ACE2 and TMPRSS2 and is blocked by a clinically proven protease inhibitor. *Cell* 2020; **181(2)**: 271–80.
3. Matsuyama S, Nao N, Shirato K, et al. Enhanced isolation of SARS-CoV-2 by TMPRSS2-expressing cells. *Proc Natl Acad Sci USA* 2020; **117(13)**: 7001–03.
4. Li G, He X, Zhang L, et al. Assessing ACE2 expression patterns in lung tissues in the pathogenesis of COVID-19. *J Autoimmun* 2020; **112**: 102463.
5. Zou X, Chen K, Zou J, et al. Single-cell RNA-seq data analysis on the receptor ACE2 expression reveals the potential risk of different human organs vulnerable to 2019-nCoV infection. *Front Med* 2020; **14(2)**: 185–92.

6. Struyf T, Deeks JJ, Dinnes J, et al. Signs and symptoms to determine if a patient presenting in primary care or hospital outpatient settings has COVID-19. *Cochrane Database Syst Rev* 2021; **2:** CD013665.
7. Wong DL, Klinkhammer BM, Djudjaj S, et al. Multisystemic cellular tropism of SARS-CoV-2 in autopsies of COVID-19 patients. *Cells* 2021; **10(8):** 1900.
8. Maiese A, Passaro G, Matteis A, et al. Thromboinflammatory response in SARS-CoV-2 sepsis. *Med Leg J* 2020; **88(2):** 78–80.
9. Li H, Liu L, Zhang D, et al. SARS-CoV-2 and viral sepsis: observations and hypotheses. *Lancet* 2020; **395(10235):** 1517–20.
10. Wichmann D, Sperhake JP, Lütgehetmann M, et al. Autopsy findings and venous thromboembolism in patients with COVID-19: A prospective cohort study. *Ann Intern Med* 2020; **173(4):** 268–77.
11. Klok FA, Kruip MJHA, van der Meer NJM, et al. Confirmation of the high cumulative incidence of thrombotic complications in critically ill ICU patients with COVID-19: An updated analysis. *Thromb Res* 2020; **191:** 148–50.
12. Hamming I, Timens W, Bulthuis ML, et al. Tissue distribution of ACE2 protein, the functional receptor for SARS coronavirus. A first step in understanding SARS pathogenesis. *J Pathol* 2004; **203(2):** 631–7.
13. Santurro A, Scopetti M, D'Errico S, Fineschi V. A technical report from the Italian SARS-CoV-2 outbreak. Postmortem sampling and autopsy investigation in cases of suspected or probable COVID-19. *Forensic Sci Med Pathol* 2020; **16(3):** 471–6.
14. Mao D, Zhou N, Zheng D. Guide to forensic pathology practice for death cases related to coronavirus disease 2019 (COVID-19) (Trial draft). *Forensic Sci Res* 2020; **5(1):** 1–7.
15. Feng W, Newbigging AM, Le C, et al. Molecular diagnosis of COVID-19: challenges and research needs. *Anal Chem* 2020; **92(15):** 10196–209.
16. Hall JA, Harris RJ, Emmett HE, et al. On the sensitivity and specificity of post-mortem upper respiratory tract testing for SARS-CoV-2. *J Infect Dis* 2021; **224(3):** 389–94
17. Beltempo P, Curti SM, Maserati R, et al. Persistence of SARS-CoV-2 RNA in post-mortem swab 35 days after death: A case report. *Forensic Sci Int* 2021; **319:** 110653.
18. Gabbrielli M, Gandolfo C, Anichini G, et al. How long can SARS-CoV-2 persist in human corpses? *Int J Infect Dis* 2021; **106:** 1–2.
19. Plenzig S, Holz F, Bojkova D, et al. Detection and infectivity of SARS-CoV-2 in exhumated corpses. *Int J Legal Med* 2021; **24:** 1–6.
20. Schröder AS, Edler C, Ondruschka B, et al. The handling of SARS-CoV-2 associated deaths: Infectivity of the body. *Forensic Sci Med Pathol* 2021; **17(3):** 411–18.
21. HSE. *The approved list of biological agents: Advisory Committee on Dangerous Pathogens*, 2021. Available from: https://www.hse.gov.uk/pubns/misc208.pdf (Accessed 27 April 2023).
22. Meyerowitz EA, Richterman A, Gandhi RT, Sax PE. Transmission of SARS-CoV-2: A review of viral, host, and environmental factors. *Ann Intern Med* 2021; **174(1):** 69–79.
23. Kanamori H. Rethinking environmental contamination and fomite transmission of SARS-CoV-2 in the healthcare. *J Infect* 2021; **82(1):** e17–e18.
24. Mondelli MU, Colaneri M, Seminari EM, et al. Low risk of SARS-CoV-2 transmission by fomites in real-life conditions. *Lancet Infect Dis* 2021; **21(5):** e112.
25. Fineschi V, Aprile A, Aquila I, et al. Management of the corpse with suspect, probable or confirmed COVID-19 respiratory infection: Italian interim recommendations for personnel potentially exposed to material from corpses, including body fluids, in morgue structures and during autopsy practice. *Pathologica* 2020; **112(2):** 64–77.
26. Cartocci G, Santurro A, Neri M, et al. Post-mortem computed tomography (PMCT) radiological findings and assessment in advanced decomposed bodies. *Radiol Med* 2019; **124(10):** 1018–27.
27. Ampanozi G, Thali YA, Schweitzer W, et al. Accuracy of non-contrast PMCT for determining cause of death. *Forensic Sci Med Pathol* 2017; **13(3):** 284–92.
28. Christe A, Flach P, Ross S, et al. Clinical radiology and postmortem imaging (Virtopsy) are not the same: Specific and unspecific postmortem signs. *Leg Med (Tokyo)* 2010; **12(5):** 215–22.
29. Ducloyer M, Gaborit B, Toquet C, et al. Complete post-mortem data in a fatal case of COVID-19: Clinical, radiological and pathological correlations. *Int J Legal Med* 2020; **134(6):** 2209–14.
30. Kniep I, Heinemann A, Edler C, et al. COVID-19 lungs in post–mortem computed tomography. *Rechtsmedizin (Berl)* 2021; **15:** 1–3.
31. De-Giorgio F, Cittadini F, Cina A, et al. Use of post-mortem chest computed tomography in Covid-19 pneumonia. *Forensic Sci Int* 2021; **325:** 110851.
32. Williams AS, Dmetrichuk JM, Kim P, Pollanen MS. Postmortem radiologic and pathologic findings in COVID-19: The Toronto experience with pre-hospitalization deaths in the community. *Forensic Sci Int* 2021; **322:** 110755.
33. Helmrich E, Decker L, Adolphi N, Makino Y. Postmortem CT lung findings in decedents with Covid-19: A review of 14 decedents and potential triage implications. *Forensic Imaging* 2020; 200419. doi: 10.1016/j.fri.2020.200419
34. Massoth LR, Desai N, Szabolcs A, et al. Comparison of RNA in situ hybridization and immunohistochemistry techniques for the detection and localization of SARS-CoV-2 in human tissues. *Am J Surg Pathol* 2021; **45(1):** 14–24.
35. Guerini-Rocco E, Taormina SV, Vacirca D, et al. SARS-CoV-2 detection in formalin-fixed paraffin-embedded tissue specimens from surgical resection of tongue squamous cell carcinoma. *J Clin Pathol* 2020; **73(11):** 754–7.
36. Zhao Y, Xia Z, Liang W, et al. SARS-CoV-2 persisted in lung tissue despite disappearance in other clinical samples. *Clin Microbiol Infect* 2020; **26(10):** 1424–25.
37. Goldsmith CS, Miller SE, Martines RB, et al. Electron microscopy of SARS-CoV-2: A challenging task. *Lancet* 2020; **395(10238):** e99.
38. Chen N, Zhou M, Dong X, et al. Epidemiological and clinical characteristics of 99 cases of 2019 novel coronavirus pneumonia in Wuhan, China: A descriptive study. *Lancet* 2020; **395(10223):** 507–13.
39. Maiese A, Manetti AC, La Russa R, et al. Autopsy findings in COVID-19-related deaths: A literature review. *Forensic Sci Med Pathol* 2021; **17(2):** 279–96.
40. Barton LM, Duval EJ, Stroberg E, et al. COVID-19 autopsies, Oklahoma, USA. *Am J Clin Pathol* 2020; **153(6):** 725–33.
41. Gattinoni L, Chiumello D, Caironi P, et al. COVID-19 pneumonia: Different respiratory treatments for different phenotypes? *Intensive Care Med* 2020; **46(6):** 1099–1102.
42. Borczuk AC, Salvatore SP, Seshan SV, et al. COVID-19 pulmonary pathology: A multi-institutional autopsy cohort from Italy and New York City. *Mod Pathol* 2020; **33(11):** 2156–68.
43. Calabrese F, Pezzuto F, Fortarezza F, et al. Pulmonary pathology and COVID-19: Lessons from autopsy: The experience of European pulmonary pathologists. *Virchows Arch* 2020; **477(3):** 359–72.
44. Mauad T, Duarte-Neto AN, da Silva LFF, et al. Tracking the time course of pathological patterns of lung injury in severe COVID-19. *Respir Res* 2021; **22(1):** 32.
45. Bösmüller H, Traxler S, Bitzer M, et al. The evolution of pulmonary pathology in fatal COVID-19 disease: An autopsy study with clinical correlation. *Virchows Arch* 2020; **477(3):** 349–57.
46. Dimbath E, Maddipati V, Stahl J, et al. Implications of microscale lung damage for COVID-19 pulmonary ventilation dynamics: A narrative review. *Life Sci* 2021; **274:** 119341.
47. Rouby JJ, Lherm T, Martin de Lassale E, et al. Histologic aspects of pulmonary barotrauma in critically ill patients with acute respiratory failure. *Intensive Care Med* 1993; **19(7):** 383–9.
48. Bradley BT, Maioli H, Johnston R, et al. Histopathology and ultrastructural findings of fatal COVID-19 infections in Washington State: A case series. *Lancet* 2020; **396(10247):** 320–32. Erratum in: *Lancet* 2020; **396(10247):** 312.
49. Schaefer IM, Padera RF, Solomon IH, et al. In situ detection of SARS-CoV-2 in lungs and airways of patients with COVID-19. *Mod Pathol* 2020; **33(11):** 2104–14.
50. Ackermann M, Verleden SE, Kuehnel M, et al. Pulmonary vascular endothelialitis, thrombosis, and angiogenesis in Covid-19. *N Engl J Med* 2020; **383(2):** 120–8.
51. Edler C, Schröder AS, Aepfelbacher M, et al. Dying with SARS-CoV-2 infection: An autopsy study of the first consecutive 80 cases in Hamburg, Germany. *Int J Legal Med* 2020; **134(4):** 1275–84. Erratum in: *Int J Legal Med* 2020; **134(5):** 1977.
52. Menter T, Haslbauer JD, Nienhold R, et al. Postmortem examination of COVID-19 patients reveals diffuse alveolar damage with severe capillary congestion and variegated findings in lungs and other organs suggesting vascular dysfunction. *Histopathology* 2020; **77(2):** 198–209.
53. Varga Z, Flammer AJ, Steiger P, et al. Endothelial cell infection and endotheliitis in COVID-19. *Lancet* 2020; **395(10234):** 1417–18.

54. Libby P, Lüscher T. COVID-19 is, in the end, an endothelial disease. *Eur Heart J* 2020; **41(32):** 3038–44.
55. Schwensen HF, Borreschmidt LK, Storgaard M, et al. Fatal pulmonary fibrosis: A post-COVID-19 autopsy case. *J Clin Pathol* 2020 Jul 28:jclinpath-2020–206879.
56. Xu J, Xu X, Jiang L, et al. SARS-CoV-2 induces transcriptional signatures in human lung epithelial cells that promote lung fibrosis. *Respir Res* 2020; **21(1):** 182.
57. Long B, Brady WJ, Koyfman A, Gottlieb M. Cardiovascular complications in COVID-19. *Am J Emerg Med* 2020; **38**(7): 1504–07.
58. American College of Cardiology. COVID-19 clinical guidance for the cardiovascular care team. 2020. Available from: https://www.acc.org/~/media/665AFA1E710B4B3293138D14BE8D1213.pdf (Accessed 27 April 2023).
59. Shi S, Qin M, Shen B, et al. Association of cardiac injury with mortality in hospitalized patients with COVID-19 in Wuhan, China. *JAMA Cardiol* 2020; **5**(7): 802–10.
60. Arentz M, Yim E, Klaff L, et al. Characteristics and outcomes of 21 critically ill patients with COVID-19 in Washington State. *JAMA* 2020; **323(16):** 1612–14.
61. Lindner D, Fitzek A, Bräuninger H, et al. Association of cardiac infection with SARS-CoV-2 in confirmed COVID-19 autopsy cases. *JAMA Cardiol* 2020; **5(11):** 1281–85.
62. Fox SE, Li G, Akmatbekov A, et al. Unexpected features of cardiac pathology in COVID-19 infection. *Circulation* 2020; **142(11):** 1123–25.
63. Gauchotte G, Venard V, Segondy M, et al. SARS-Cov-2 fulminant myocarditis: An autopsy and histopathological case study. *Int J Legal Med* 2021; **135(2):** 577–81.
64. Bulfamante GP, Perrucci GL, Falleni M, et al. Evidence of SARS-CoV-2 transcriptional activity in cardiomyocytes of COVID-19 patients without clinical signs of cardiac involvement. *Biomedicines* 2020; **8(12):** 626.
65. Halushka MK, Vander Heide RS. Myocarditis is rare in COVID-19 autopsies: Cardiovascular findings across 277 postmortem examinations. *Cardiovasc Pathol* 2021; **50:** 107300.
66. Basso C, Leone O, Rizzo S, et al. Pathological features of COVID-19-associated myocardial injury: A multicentre cardiovascular pathology study. *Eur Heart J* 2020; **41(39):** 3827–35.
67. Sang CJ 3rd, Burkett A, Heindl B, et al. Cardiac pathology in COVID-19: A single center autopsy experience. *Cardiovasc Pathol* 2021; **54:** 107370.
68. Jacobs W, Lammens M, Kerckhofs A, et al. Fatal lymphocytic cardiac damage in coronavirus disease 2019 (COVID-19): Autopsy reveals a ferroptosis signature. *ESC Heart Fail* 2020; **7**(**6**): 3772–81.
69. Pellegrini D, Kawakami R, Guagliumi G, et al. Microthrombi as a major cause of cardiac injury in COVID-19: A pathologic study. *Circulation* 2021; **143(10):** 1031–42.
70. Rapkiewicz AV, Mai X, Carsons SE, et al. Megakaryocytes and platelet-fibrin thrombi characterize multi-organ thrombosis at autopsy in COVID-19: A case series. *EClinicalMedicine* 2020; **24:** 100434.
71. Hanley B, Naresh KN, Roufosse C, et al. Histopathological findings and viral tropism in UK patients with severe fatal COVID-19: A post-mortem study. *Lancet Microbe* 2020; **1(6):** e245–e253.
72. Al-Ani F, Chehade S, Lazo-Langner A. Thrombosis risk associated with COVID-19 infection. A scoping review. *Thromb Res* 2020; **192:** 152–60.
73. Miesbach W, Makris M. COVID-19: Coagulopathy, risk of thrombosis, and the rationale for anticoagulation. *Clin Appl Thromb Hemost* 2020; **26:** 1076029620938149.
74. Bernard I, Limonta D, Mahal LK, Hobman TC. Endothelium infection and dysregulation by SARS-CoV-2: Evidence and caveats in COVID-19. *Viruses* 2020; **13(1):** 29.
75. McFadyen JD, Stevens H, Peter K. The emerging threat of (micro)thrombosis in COVID-19 and its therapeutic implications. *Circ Res* 2020; **127(4):** 571–87.
76. Jain R, Young M, Dogra S, et al. COVID-19 related neuroimaging findings: A signal of thromboembolic complications and a strong prognostic marker of poor patient outcome. *J Neurol Sci* 2020; **414:** 116923.
77. Montalvan V, Lee J, Bueso T, et al. Neurological manifestations of COVID-19 and other coronavirus infections: A systematic review. *Clin Neurol Neurosurg* 2020; **194:** 105921.
78. Caress JB, Castoro RJ, Simmons Z, et al. COVID-19-associated Guillain-Barré syndrome: The early pandemic experience. *Muscle Nerve* 2020; **62(4):** 485–91.
79. Asadi-Pooya AA, Simani L. Central nervous system manifestations of COVID-19: A systematic review. *J Neurol Sci* 2020; **413:** 116832.
80. Ren AL, Digby RJ, Needham EJ. Neurological update: COVID-19. *J Neurol* 2021; **268(11):** 4379–87.
81. Yan CH, Faraji F, Prajapati DP, et al. Self-reported olfactory loss associates with outpatient clinical course in COVID-19. *Int Forum Allergy Rhinol* 2020; **10(7):** 821–31.
82. Ralli M, Di Stadio A, Greco A, et al. Defining the burden of olfactory dysfunction in COVID-19 patients. *Eur Rev Med Pharmacol Sci* 2020; **24(7):** 3440–41.
83. Li YC, Bai WZ, Hirano N, et al. Coronavirus infection of rat dorsal root ganglia: Ultrastructural characterization of viral replication, transfer, and the early response of satellite cells. *Virus Res* 2012; **163(2):** 628–35.
84. Fabbri VP, Foschini MP, Lazzarotto T, et al. Brain ischemic injury in COVID-19-infected patients: A series of 10 postmortem cases. *Brain Pathol* 2021; **31(1):** 205–10.
85. Katoh H, Shibata S, Fukuda K, et al. The dual origin of the peripheral olfactory system: Placode and neural crest. *Mol Brain* 2011; **4:** 34.
86. Schwob JE. Neural regeneration and the peripheral olfactory system. *Anat Rec* 2002; **269(1):** 33–49.
87. Natoli S, Oliveira V, Calabresi P, et al. Does SARS-Cov-2 invade the brain? Translational lessons from animal models. *Eur J Neurol* 2020; **27(9):** 1764–73.
88. Donegani MI, Miceli A, Pardini M, et al. Brain metabolic correlates of persistent olfactory dysfunction after SARS-CoV-2 infection. *Biomedicines* 2021; **9(3):** 287.
89. Maiese A, Manetti AC, Bosetti C, et al. SARS-CoV-2 and the brain: A review of the current knowledge on neuropathology in COVID-19. *Brain Pathol* 2021; **31(6):** e13013.
90. Kantonen J, Mahzabin S, Mäyränpää MI, et al. Neuropathologic features of four autopsied COVID-19 patients. *Brain Pathol* 2020; **30(6):** 1012–16.
91. Reichard RR, Kashani KB, Boire NA, et al. Neuropathology of COVID-19: A spectrum of vascular and acute disseminated encephalomyelitis (ADEM)-like pathology. *Acta Neuropathol* 2020; **140(1):** 1–6.
92. Meinhardt J, Radke J, Dittmayer C, et al. Olfactory transmucosal SARS-CoV-2 invasion as a port of central nervous system entry in individuals with COVID-19. *Nat Neurosci* 2021; **24(2):** 168–75.
93. Al-Dalahmah O, Thakur KT, Nordvig AS, et al. Neuronophagia and microglial nodules in a SARS-CoV-2 patient with cerebellar hemorrhage. *Acta Neuropathol Commun* 2020 **8(1):** 147.
94. Matschke J, Lütgehetmann M, Hagel C, et al. Neuropathology of patients with COVID-19 in Germany: a post-mortem case series. *Lancet Neurol* 2020; **19(11):** 919–29.
95. Pedrosa CDSG, Goto-Silva L, Temerozo JR, et al. Non-permissive SARS-CoV-2 infection in human neurospheres. *Stem Cell Res* 2021; **54:** 102436.
96. Lou JJ, Movassaghi M, Gordy D, et al. Neuropathology of COVID-19 (neuro-COVID): Clinicopathological update. *Free Neuropathol* 2021; **2:** 2.
97. Zhang JJ, Dong X, Cao YY, et al. Clinical characteristics of 140 patients infected with SARS-CoV-2 in Wuhan, China. *Allergy* 2020; 75(7): 1730–41.
98. Menon T, Sharma R, Earthineni G, et al. Association of gastrointestinal system with severity and mortality of COVID-19: A systematic review and meta-analysis. *Cureus* 2021; **13(2):** e13317.
99. Gu J, Han B, Wang J. COVID-19: Gastrointestinal manifestations and potential fecal-oral transmission. *Gastroenterology* 2020; **158(6):** 1518–19.
100. Song M, Li ZL, Zhou YJ, et al. Gastrointestinal involvement of COVID-19 and potential faecal transmission of SARS-CoV-2. *J Zhejiang Univ Sci B* 2020; **21(9):** 749–51.
101. Cha MH, Regueiro M, Sandhu DS. Gastrointestinal and hepatic manifestations of COVID-19: a comprehensive review. *World J Gastroenterol* 2020; **26(19):** 2323–32.
102. Yan R, Zhang Y, Li Y, et al. Structural basis for the recognition of SARS-CoV-2 by full-length human ACE2. *Science* 2020; **367(6485):** 1444–48.
103. Xiao F, Tang M, Zheng X, et al. Evidence for gastrointestinal infection of SARS-CoV-2. *Gastroenterology* 2020; **158(6):** 1831–33.e3.
104. Livanos AE, Jha D, Cossarini F, et al. Intestinal host response to SARS-CoV-2 infection and COVID-19 outcomes in patients with gastrointestinal symptoms. *Gastroenterology* 2021; **160(7):** 2435–50.e34.
105. Bangash MN, Patel J, Parekh D. COVID-19 and the liver: Little cause for concern.

Lancet Gastroenterol Hepatol 2020; 5(6): 529–30.
106. Garrido I, Liberal R, Macedo G. Review article: COVID-19 and liver disease-what we know on 1st May 2020. *Aliment Pharmacol Ther* 2020; **52(2)**: 267–75.
107. Bertolini A, van de Peppel IP, Bodewes FAJA, et al. Abnormal liver function tests in patients with COVID-19: relevance and potential pathogenesis. *Hepatology* 2020; 72(5): 1864–72.
108. Nardo AD, Schneeweiss-Gleixner M, Bakail M, et al. Pathophysiological mechanisms of liver injury in COVID-19. *Liver Int* 2021; **41(1)**: 20–32.
109. Wang Y, Liu S, Liu H, et al. SARS-CoV-2 infection of the liver directly contributes to hepatic impairment in patients with COVID-19. *J Hepatol* 2020; 73(4): 807–16.
110. Lax SF, Skok K, Zechner PM, Trauner M. Pulmonary arterial thrombosis in COVID-19 with fatal outcome. *Ann Intern Med* 2021; **174(1)**: 139–40.
111. Sonzogni A, Previtali G, Seghezzi M, et al. Liver histopathology in severe COVID 19 respiratory failure is suggestive of vascular alterations. *Liver Int* 2020; 40(9): 2110–16.
112. McConnell MJ, Kawaguchi N, Kondo R, et al. Liver injury in COVID-19 and IL-6 trans-signaling-induced endotheliopathy. *J Hepatol* 2021; 75(3): 647–58.
113. Boeckmans J, Rodrigues RM, Demuyser T, et al. COVID-19 and drug-induced liver injury: A problem of plenty or a petty point? *Arch Toxicol* 2020; **94(4)**: 1367–69.
114. Olry A, Meunier L, Délire B, et al. Drug-induced liver injury and COVID-19 infection: The rules remain the same. *Drug Saf* 2020; **43(7)**: 615–17.
115. Muhović D, Bojović J, Bulatović A, et al. First case of drug-induced liver injury associated with the use of tocilizumab in a patient with COVID-19. *Liver Int* 2020; 40(8): 1901–05.
116. Geier A, Fickert P, Trauner M. Mechanisms of disease: Mechanisms and clinical implications of cholestasis in sepsis. *Nat Clin Pract Gastroenterol Hepatol* 2006; 3(10): 574–85.
117. Lagana SM, Kudose S, Iuga AC, et al. Hepatic pathology in patients dying of COVID-19: A series of 40 cases including clinical, histologic, and virologic data. *Mod Pathol* 2020; 33(11): 2147–55.
118. Henrion J, Schapira M, Luwaert R, et al. Hypoxic hepatitis: Clinical and hemodynamic study in 142 consecutive cases. *Medicine (Baltimore)* 2003; **82(6)**: 392–406.
119. Schmit G, Lelotte J, Vanhaebost J, et al. The liver in COVID-19-related death: Protagonist or innocent bystander? *Pathobiology* 2021; **88(1)**: 88–94.
120. Tandra S, Yeh MM, Brunt EM, et al. Presence and significance of microvesicular steatosis in nonalcoholic fatty liver disease. *J Hepatol* 2011; **55(3)**: 654–9.
121. Silver SA, Beaubien-Souligny W, Shah PS. The prevalence of acute kidney injury in patients hospitalized with COVID-19 infection: A systematic review and meta-analysis. *Kidney Med* 2021; 3(1): 83–98.e1.
122. Menon T, Sharma R, Kataria S, et al. The association of acute kidney injury with disease severity and mortality in COVID-19: A systematic review and meta-analysis. *Cureus* 2021; **13(3)**: e13894.
123. Cheng Y, Luo R, Wang K, et al. Kidney disease is associated with in-hospital death of patients with COVID-19. *Kidney Int* 2020; **97(5)**: 829–38.
124. Su H, Yang M, Wan C, et al. Renal histopathological analysis of 26 postmortem findings of patients with COVID-19 in China. *Kidney Int* 2020; **98(1)**: 219–27.
125. Diao B, Wang C, Wang R, et al. Human kidney is a target for novel severe acute respiratory syndrome coronavirus 2 infection. *Nat Commun* 2021; **12(1)**: 2506.
126. Mizuiri S, Ohashi Y. ACE and ACE2 in kidney disease. *World J Nephrol* 2015; **4(1)**: 74–82.
127. Bajema IM, Rotmans JI. Histological manifestations of rhabdomyolysis in the kidney. *Nephrol Dial Transplant* 2018; **33(12)**: 2113–14.
128. He YC, Chen F. Rhabdomyolysis as potential late complication associated with COVID-19. *Emerg Infect Dis* 2020; **26(9)**: 2297–98.
129. Singh B, Kaur P, Mechineni A, Maroules M. Rhabdomyolysis in COVID-19: Report of four cases. *Cureus* 2020; **12(9)**: e10686.
130. Beydon M, Chevalier K, Al Tabaa O, et al. Myositis as a manifestation of SARS-CoV-2. *Ann Rheum Dis* 2021; **80(3)**: e42.
131. Sarhan M, von Mässenhausen A, Hugo C, Oberbauer R, Linkermann A. Immunological consequences of kidney cell death. *Cell Death Dis* 2018; **9(2)**: 114.
132. Makino S, Yamaguchi F, Sata T, et al. The rash of measles is caused by a viral infection in the cells of the skin: A case report. *J Dermatol* 1994; **21(10)**: 741–5.
133. Genovese G, Moltrasio C, Berti E, Marzano AV. Skin manifestations associated with COVID-19: Current knowledge and future perspectives. *Dermatology* 2021; **237(1)**: 1–12.
134. Galván Casas C, Català A, Carretero Hernández G, et al. Classification of the cutaneous manifestations of COVID-19: A rapid prospective nationwide consensus study in Spain with 375 cases. *Br J Dermatol* 2020; **183(1)**: 71–77.
135. Potekaev NN, Zhukova OV, Protsenko DN, et al. Clinical characteristics of dermatologic manifestations of COVID-19 infection: Case series of 15 patients, review of literature, and proposed etiological classification. *Int J Dermatol* 2020; 59(8): 1000–09.
136. Gisondi P, PIaserico S, Bordin C, et al. Cutaneous manifestations of SARS-CoV-2 infection: A clinical update. *J Eur Acad Dermatol Venereol* 2020; **34(11)**: 2499–2504.
137. Piccolo V, Neri I, Filippeschi C, et al. Chilblain-like lesions during COVID-19 epidemic: A preliminary study on 63 patients. *J Eur Acad Dermatol Venereol* 2020; 34(7): e291–e293.
138. Gianotti R, Coggi A, Boggio F, Fellegara G. Similarities in cutaneous histopathological patterns between COVID-19-positive and COVID-19 high-risk patients with skin dermatosis. *Acta Derm Venereol* 2020; **100(15)**: adv00249.
139. Giavedoni P, Podlipnik S, Pericàs JM, et al. Skin manifestations in COVID-19: prevalence and relationship with disease severity. *J Clin Med* 2020; **9(10)**: 3261.
140. Marzano AV, Genovese G, Fabbrocini G. Varicella-like exanthem as a specific COVID-19-associated skin manifestation: Multicenter case series of 22 patients. *J Am Acad Dermatol* 2020; **83(1)**: 280–5.
141. Fernandez-Nieto D, Ortega-Quijano D, Jimenez-Cauhe J, et al. Clinical and histological characterization of vesicular COVID-19 rashes: A prospective study in a tertiary care hospital. *Clin Exp Dermatol* 2020; 5(7): 872–5.
142. Najarian DJ. Morbilliform exanthem associated with COVID-19. *JAAD Case Rep* 2020; **6(6)**: 493–4.
143. Colonna C, Monzani NA, Rocchi A, et al. Chilblain-like lesions in children following suspected COVID-19 infection. *Pediatr Dermatol* 2020; 37(3): 437–40.
144. Landa N, Mendieta-Eckert M, Fonda-Pascual P, Aguirre T. Chilblain-like lesions on feet and hands during the COVID-19 Pandemic. *Int J Dermatol* 2020; **59(6)**: 739–43.
145. Garrido Ruiz MC, Santos-Briz Á, Santos-Briz Á, et al. Spectrum of clinicopathologic findings in COVID-19-induced skin lesions: Demonstration of direct viral infection of the endothelial cells. *Am J Surg Pathol* 2021; **45(3)**: 293–303.
146. Kanitakis J, Lesort C, Danset M, Jullien D. Chilblain-like acral lesions during the COVID-19 pandemic ('COVID toes'): Histologic, immunofluorescence, and immunohistochemical study of 17 cases. *J Am Acad Dermatol* 2020; **83(3)**: 870–5.
147. Locatelli AG, Robustelli Test E, Vezzoli P. Histologic features of long-lasting chilblain-like lesions in a paediatric COVID-19 patient. *J Eur Acad Dermatol Venereol* 2020; **34(8)**: e365–e368.
148. Cordoro KM, Reynolds SD, Wattier R, McCalmont TH. Clustered cases of acral perniosis: clinical features, histopathology, and relationship to COVID-19. *Pediatr Dermatol* 2020; 37(3): 419–23.
149. Kaya G, Kaya A, Saurat JH. Clinical and histopathological features and potential pathological mechanisms of skin lesions in COVID-19: Review of the literature. *Dermatopathology (Basel)* 2020; **7(1)**: 3–16.
150. Rose AE, Sagger V, Boyd KP, et al. Livedo reticularis. *Dermatol Online J* 2013; **19(12)**: 20705.
151. Khalil S, Hinds BR, Manalo IF, et al. Livedo reticularis as a presenting sign of severe acute respiratory syndrome coronavirus 2 infection. *JAAD Case Rep* 2020; **6(9)**: 871–74.
152. Magro CM, Mulvey JJ, Laurence J, et al. The differing pathophysiologies that underlie COVID-19-associated perniosis and thrombotic retiform purpura: A case series. *Br J Dermatol* 2021; **184(1)**: 141–50.
153. Shavit E, Alavi A, Sibbald RG. Vasculitis: What do we have to know? A review of literature. *Int J Low Extrem Wounds* 2018; **17(4)**: 218–26.
154. Schreiner DT. Purpura. *Dermatol Clin* 1989; 7(3): 481–90.
155. Caputo V, Schroeder J, Rongioletti F. A generalized purpuric eruption with histopathologic features of leucocytoclastic vasculitis in a patient severely ill with COVID-19. *J Eur Acad Dermatol Venereol* 2020; **34(10)**: e579–e581.

156. García-Gil MF, Monte Serrano J, García García M, et al. Acral purpuric lesions associated with coagulation disorders during the COVID-19 pandemic. *Int J Dermatol* 2020; **59(9)**: 1151–52.
157. Karaca Z, Yayli S, Çalışkan O. A unilateral purpuric rash in a patient with COVID-19 infection. *Dermatol Ther* 2020; **33(4)**: e13798.
158. Larrondo J, Cabrera R, Gosch M, et al. Papular-purpuric exanthem in a COVID-19 patient: Clinical and dermoscopic description. *J Eur Acad Dermatol Venereol* 2020; **34(10)**: e570–e572.
159. Negrini S, Guadagno A, Greco M, Parodi A, Burlando M. An unusual case of bullous haemorrhagic vasculitis in a COVID-19 patient. *J Eur Acad Dermatol Venereol* 2020; **34(11)**: e675–e676.
160. Rodríguez-Jiménez P, Chicharro P, De Argila D, et al. Urticaria-like lesions in COVID-19 patients are not really urticaria: A case with clinicopathological correlation. *J Eur Acad Dermatol Venereol* 2020; **34(9)**: e459–e460.
161. Mahé A, Birckel E, Merklen C, et al. Histology of skin lesions establishes that the vesicular rash associated with COVID-19 is not 'varicella-like'. *J Eur Acad Dermatol Venereol* 2020; **34(10)**: e559–e561.
162. Amatore F, Macagno N, Mailhe M, et al. SARS-CoV-2 infection presenting as a febrile rash. *J Eur Acad Dermatol Venereol* 2020; **34(7)**: e304–e306.
163. Herrero-Moyano M, Capusan TM, Andreu-Barasoain M, et al. A clinicopathological study of eight patients with COVID-19 pneumonia and a late-onset exanthema. *J Eur Acad Dermatol Venereol* 2020; **34(9)**: e460–e464.
164. Tammaro A, Adebanjo GAR, Parisella FR, et al. Cutaneous manifestations in COVID-19: The experiences of Barcelona and Rome. *J Eur Acad Dermatol Venereol* 2020; **34(7)**: e306–e307.
165. Reymundo A, Fernáldez-Bernáldez A, Reolid A, et al. Clinical and histological characterization of late appearance maculopapular eruptions in association with the coronavirus disease 2019. A case series of seven patients. *J Eur Acad Dermatol Venereol* 2020; **34(12)**: e755–e757.
166. Trellu LT, Kaya G, Alberto C, et al. Clinicopathologic aspects of a papulovesicular eruption in a patient with COVID-19. *JAMA Dermatol* 2020; **156(8)**: 922–4.
167. Frisoni P, Neri M, D'Errico S, et al. Cytokine storm and histopathological findings in 60 cases of COVID-19-related death: from viral load research to immunohistochemical quantification of major players IL-1β, IL-6, IL-15 and TNF-α. *Forensic Sci Med Pathol* 2022; **18(1)**: 14–19. Erratum in: *Forensic Sci Med Pathol* 2022; **(18)1**: 120.

CHAPTER 26

Vehicular-Related Deaths

Vikas Meshram and Tanuj Kanchan

INJURIES SUSTAINED BY PEDESTRIANS

Pedestrians are the most vulnerable population to sustain fatal injuries in vehicular accidents. According to the World Health Organization's (WHO) Global status report on road safety 2015, pedestrians accounted for 22 percent of the total mortality from vehicular crashes (1, 2). The weight of the vehicle is a significant determinant for the severity of the injuries caused to the pedestrian. Hence the pattern and mechanism of injuries sustained by the pedestrian can be different in impact with motorcycle, light motor vehicle or heavy vehicle.

Injuries to pedestrians due to impact by a motorcycle

Impact by a motorcycle may cause external and/or internal injuries to a pedestrian that usually correspond to the site of impact and commonly involve the lower extremities. The injuries can be in the form of imprint abrasions, bruises, lacerations and fractures. The injuries to the upper extremities can also be observed due to a subsequent fall. Fatalities in such cases are frequently associated with injuries to the head, spine or any of the vital organs. Pelvic injuries and fractures of the femur can also be seen. Elderly persons are especially prone to such injuries due to increased bone fragility.

Injuries to pedestrians due to impact by a four-wheeler vehicle

The mechanisms of injuries sustained due to collisions between four-wheelers and pedestrians are complex. These depend on factors such as the speed of the vehicle, the weight of the vehicle, the direction of impact, the application of brakes of the vehicle before the collision, the height of the pedestrian, the direction of walking and the reaction of the pedestrian to the impending impact. Based on the chronology of the impact of a pedestrian with a vehicle and the subsequent impact against any other surface, these injuries are classified as primary impact injuries, secondary impact injuries and secondary injuries. In high-speed impact, primary injuries are more significantly observed, whereas secondary impact injuries are seldom present. In extremely high-speed impact, a person may fly over a vehicle and not sustain secondary impact injuries. However, the person may sustain severe injuries due to impact against a road due to the fall. In low-speed crashes, the proportion of secondary injuries is much higher.

Primary impact injuries

Primary impact injuries are sustained due to the first impact of the vehicle with the pedestrian. The site and pattern of these injuries are dependent on the relative position of the pedestrian and vehicle, the speed of the vehicle and the relative height of the impacting area of the vehicle. The projecting parts of the vehicle, such as the bumper, radiator grille, bonnet, headlight, and so on, are usually responsible for these impact injuries. The lower extremities are the most common site for primary impact injuries. In such collisions, the legs are accelerated in the direction of the vehicle, causing musculoskeletal injuries with imprint abrasions, contusions, lacerations and/or fractures. If a pedestrian is struck by a heavy vehicle with a higher front, the primary impact will be further up on the body. In such a scenario, injuries can be sustained to the pelvis, abdomen, chest, shoulder, spine or head. In collisions with light motor vehicles, the level of impact is usually below the center of gravity of the pedestrian, with the exception of children and individuals of short stature. In cases where the primary impact is above the center of the gravity of the body, the pedestrian will be pushed down and may be carried forward on the radiator grill or may even subsequently be run over. In a child pedestrian a triad of injuries comprising a fractured femoral shaft and thoraco-abdominal injuries on the side of impact with head injuries on the contralateral side have been observed, known as Waddell's triad.

Primary impact injuries caused by the bumper of light motor vehicles are often referred as "bumper injuries", which includes bumper fractures, wedge-shaped fractures of the tibia and fibula. The base of the wedge indicates the point of impact and the apex indicates the direction of the force. It is advisable to measure the level of the bumper injuries from the sole of the foot to correlate it with the height of the bumper of the alleged offending vehicle. The height of primary impact

DOI: 10.1201/9781003138754-28

injuries may not always correspond with the height of the bumper as braking may cause the front of the car to dip down; conversely, the front of the car may be elevated with acceleration. In short-statured persons or children, the bumper fracture may involve the femur. The pattern of bumper injuries also depends on the site of impact and whether the pedestrian was walking or running.

Secondary impact injuries

Secondary impact injuries are caused by subsequent impact against the vehicle following the initial crash. These injuries are usually more severe than primary impact injuries. The pattern of injuries is determined by the speed of the vehicle, make of the vehicle, the direction of the impact and relative movement of the pedestrian following the first impact. The speed of the vehicle is the major determinant of the pattern of the injuries produced.

The mechanism of characteristic secondary impact injuries is well-illustrated by impacts with light motor vehicles. In such crashes, the primary impact is below the center of the gravity of the pedestrian, resulting in the feet accelerating forward, with the body scooped up over the hood. Subsequently, the body may strike the hood, the vehicle's pillar, windshield, or roof, resulting in secondary impact injuries. The length of the hood and height of the bumper influence the scooping process and subsequent injuries. Head injuries are commonly observed due to secondary impact as the head may impact against the windshield, pillar or frame, sustaining bruises, lacerations, facial bone fractures, skull fractures and brain injuries. The site of secondary impact injuries is also influenced by the throwing distance following the primary impact. In high-speed impacts, the throwing distance is greater, hence the head may be spared from secondary impact. In some cases, the neck can be impacted against the frame, resulting in fracture-dislocation at the cervical spine and spinal cord injury. Besides head injury, injuries to the thorax, limbs and pelvis can also be due to secondary impact. Thoracic injuries can range from fractures of the ribs, flail chest, pneumothorax, hemothorax, contusion or laceration of lung and heart, or even fracture-dislocation of the thoracolumbar spine. In higher speed impact, knee and hand fractures are also commonly observed.

Secondary injuries

Following the vehicular impact, the body may be thrown clear of the vehicle, and may fall against the ground or any other surface. The injuries sustained by such impact are referred as secondary injuries. The pattern of injuries is influenced by the vehicle's speed, the type of impacting surface, the part of the body involved, and the clothing worn by the victim. Secondary injuries may or may not occur subsequent to secondary impact. In high-speed impacts, the throwing distance is greater, hence the body may be thrown completely clear of the vehicle. Secondary injuries can include abrasions, bruises, lacerations and fractures. Head injuries are more commonly observed, although fatal injuries to the chest, abdomen or spine may occur.

Run-over injuries

Run-over injuries are not uncommon in vehicular crashes. After the initial impact, the pedestrian may be run over by the same or another vehicle, and there can be involvement of one or more wheels. In such cases, tyre marks may be observed on the body surface, the pattern of which depends on the part of the body involved, the make of the wheel and the interposition of clothing. The pattern and dimensions of the tyre marks need to be documented and photographed to assist with the identification of the vehicle.

Other injuries associated with run-over accidents are stretch lacerations and graze abrasions. Stretch lacerations are caused by overstretching of the skin and are situated away from the area of compression, while graze abrasions are indicative of dragging and thus the direction of force. Run-overs may also result in extensive damage and disruption of the underlying organs due to direct as well as indirect pressure effects. There are documented cases of traumatic inguinal hernia following run-over accidents (3). Rarely, the intestine can also be herniated from an injury involving a remote part of the body such as the ankle (4). Run-over injuries involving the skull may cause severe crush injuries, compression of head and face, and, rarely, decapitation. Run-overs usually involve the smallest diameter, that is, the biparietal diameter of the head, causing fractures of the vault and base of the skull. Stretch lacerations may be present behind the ear. In a run-over accident involving a limb, the rotatory force of the tyre may cause avulsion of the skin from underlying bone. There may be detachment of the skin from the underlying subcutaneous tissue or within the subcutaneous tissue itself, resulting in the formation of cavitations, also called decollements (5). Limb injuries usually present with extensive soft-tissue damage and multiple fractures. Complete amputation of the limb may also occur.

Run-over injuries are mostly severe and are often fatal. The pediatric population is more vulnerable to run-over injuries. Although run-over injuries are mostly accidental, homicidal run-over cases have also been reported, particularly with the intention to disguise it as a road accident.

INJURIES SUSTAINED BY TWO-WHEELER RIDERS

Two-wheeler accidents are common, particularly in developing countries. This can be attributed to the increasing usage of these low-cost vehicles. Two-wheeler occupants include those riding pedal cycles, scooters, mopeds, motor bikes, and so on. Two-wheeler occupants are more vulnerable to sustaining injuries due to the inherently unsafe nature of such vehicles. According to the WHO Global status report on road safety 2015, almost half of the estimated 1.25 million deaths on the world's roads per year are among those with the least protection, that is, vulnerable road users (VRU), which include motorcyclists (23 per cent), pedestrians (22 percent) and cyclists (4 percent) (2). These accidents most commonly involve the younger age group, mostly between 15 and 34 years. Risky driving, craving for excitement, overconfidence and disregard for safety measures are among many factors contributing to increasing motorcycle accidents among youth (6–9). Although two-wheeler rider injuries have traditionally been described in the context of injuries sustained by motorcyclists, their pattern and extent may vary with different vehicle types and depending on whether the victim was driving the vehicle or was a pillion passenger.

A motorcyclist can sustain injuries due to collision with other motor vehicles or any stationary object, or from skidding or falling. Animal–vehicle collisions are also a not uncommon occurrence in developing countries. Two-wheeler accidents are often attributed to bad road infrastructure. The need for road barricades and adequate lighting along the roads has frequently been highlighted (10). The pattern of injuries sustained by motorcyclists can depend on many factors, such as the type of impact, type of vehicle involved, vehicle speed and use of safety helmets.

Motorcyclist injuries may result from a low-side crash, high-side crash, top-side crash and collision. In a low-side crash, the rider falls toward the low side of the leaning angle during a turn. In a high-side crash, the rider falls to the opposite side of a turn while trying to correct, causing the motorcycle to flip over and the rider to be thrown from the seat. The motorcycle suddenly decelerates in a top-side crash, and the rider flips over the handlebars. In a collision type of crash, the rider strikes a stationary object and is subjected to blunt trauma and deceleration forces (11).

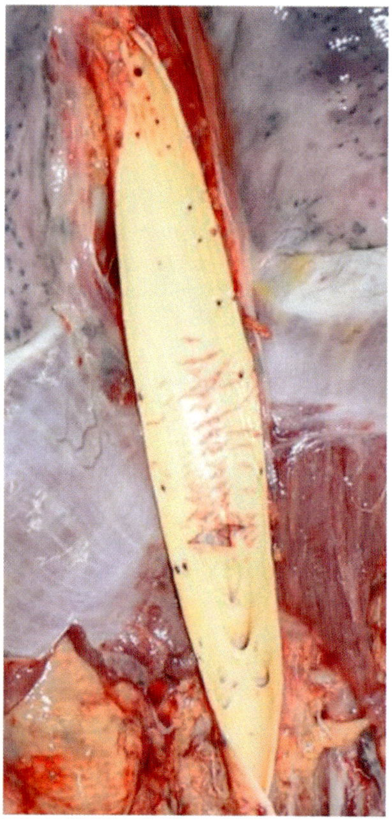

26.1 Inner surface of aorta showing multiple intimal tear in "ladder" pattern.

Head injuries are the leading cause of mortality in accidents involving a motorcycle. Head injuries are seen in all types of crash in which a rider can be thrown to the ground or collide against other vehicles or any static object, resulting in skull fractures and/or brain injuries. Skull fractures commonly occur in the temporoparietal region and base of the skull. In this regard, "motorcyclist fracture" is typically reported, in which the fracture line passes from the petrous part of the temporal bone, through the greater wing of the sphenoid of one side to the other through the pituitary fossa, thus dividing the skull into two parts that move independently like a hinge (Figure 26.1). Motorcyclist fractures may be associated with brain stem injuries. Rarely, ring fracture in the posterior cranial fossa around the foramen magnum can be observed following impact on the crown of the head. Internal brain injuries include intracranial hemorrhages, cortical contusions and/or lacerations. On occasion brain matter may extrude through a compound skull fracture. Pillion riders may fall off the back and sustain lacerations, mostly to the back of the head with fractures of the posterior cranial fossa.

Helmets are of paramount importance in preventing fatal head injuries among motorcyclists. The National Highway Traffic Safety Administration (NHTSA) data show that helmets reduce the risk of fatality to motorcyclists in the event of a crash by 29 percent and the risk of brain injury by 67 percent (12). Whiplash injuries to the neck may rarely occur due to sudden deceleration following impact resulting in hyperextension. There can be atlanto-occipital or atlanto-axial fracture-dislocations.

Besides the head, injuries to the limbs are commonly encountered in two-wheeler accidents. Lower limb injuries occur in low-side types of crashes, in which the lower limb gets trapped between the ipsilateral upper limb and the skidding motorcycle. In such cases, the injuries are mostly restricted to one side of the body. These limb entrapment injuries include abrasions, bruises, lacerations and fractures of the tibia, fibula and femur. Sometimes, tyre spoke injuries are also sustained in which severe soft-tissue defects, as well as injuries to the calcaneus and Achilles tendon, are seen (13–15). The foot can also be injured when a motorcycle rider, in anticipation of losing stability on a turn, reacts to an impending crash by stretching out his/her leg in an attempt to maintain balance. The foot may be injured due to hyper-dorsiflexion and external rotation (11). Motorcycle riders at high speed can also sustain shoulder fractures due to direct vertical impact against a fixed object. When a two-wheeler rider is thrown off the vehicle, he/she may extend the arms to brace against severe damage. In doing so, a fracture of the distal radius, also referred as "motorcycle radius injury", may be sustained (16,17). Sometimes, firmly holding the handlebar and locking the elbows may cause fracture-dislocation of the joints at the metacarpal and proximal phalanx, also referred as "motorcycle thumb" (18).

On occasion the protruding parts of a motorcycle such as the handlebars, projection levers or mirrors, and so on, may impact against the abdomen or groin causing rupture of the liver and spleen, with groin or genital injuries. Fuel tank injuries may occur when a motorcycle suddenly decelerates and the rider's momentum carries him or her forward, impacting the pelvis against the tank. It includes fractures of the pelvis and bladder injuries (19). Aortic injuries varying from intimal tears to rupture have been reported in motorcyclist accidents (20).

Tailgating accidents are not uncommon in a motorcycle crash. This is the type of rear-end collision in which a motorcycle crashes into a moving or stationary heavier motor vehicle from behind. The motorcyclist may sustain severe injuries to the head, shoulders and upper torso. In severe impacts, decapitation may occur. In side-on impacts with a heavy motor vehicle, the motorcyclist and/or the pillion passenger may be dragged under the heavy vehicle resulting in run-over injuries, which are similar to those described in run-over injuries sustained by pedestrians.

INJURIES SUSTAINED BY THE OCCUPANTS OF A MOTOR VEHICLE

Injuries to motor vehicle occupants are not uncommon in vehicular crashes. Factors influencing the mechanism and pattern of injuries include the speed of the vehicle, the position of the occupant in the motor vehicle, the type of impact, the reaction of the occupant to the impending impact, and the presence or absence of safety devices. Depending on the deployment and effectiveness of the safety devices, there may be variations in the spectrum of injuries. The pattern and extent of injuries may further vary in roll-over accidents, and this may depend upon multiple factors such as whether the roll-over was arrested or complete, whether the occupant was fastened by a seat belt or not, whether the roof was deformed or not, and whether the occupant was ejected out of the vehicle or not. Many injuries can occur due to the intrusion of various parts of the chassis into the interior of the vehicle. Safety modifications are now being made to the interior of vehicles, which include smoother surfaces, more easily breakable protruding parts and better cushioning, to reduce such injuries. Among vehicle occupants, fatalities are commonly reported in the drivers, followed by front-seat and rear-seat occupants.

Injuries to the driver

With a front-on collision, the vehicle decelerates while the driver is accelerated forward. The legs of the driver may strike against the fascia/parcel-shelf area of the car while the knees may impact the dashboard resulting in fractures of the patella and distal femur. Thus, drivers have higher chances of lower extremity injuries than front- and rear-seat passengers. Vehicular crashes in head-on collisions mostly involve the front of the driver's side, making drivers more vulnerable to impact against the dashboard with floor-pan intrusion and foot entrapment. With further momentum, the driver is impacted against the steering wheel, resulting in chest impact injuries.

The extent and severity of steering wheel impact injuries varies with the deployment of the seatbelt and airbags. Such injuries include transverse fractures of the sternum and ribs, and lacerations of the aorta, heart and liver. Lower abdominal injuries following steering wheel impact include contusions and lacerations of varying severity and frequency involving the mesentery, the small and large intestine and the spleen. Jejunal mesenteric tears are more common than ileal mesenteric tears from steering wheel injuries (21). Bruises, lacerations of the face, concussion and fractures of the facial bones may be seen when the head is impacted against a steering wheel. In rare cases, the heart can be completely avulsed from its attachments, particularly in a high-speed collision. Steering wheel impact injuries are more common in unbelted drivers, but they have also been documented in belted drivers. Injuries commonly reported in unbelted drivers are fractures of the ribs, and lacerations of the aorta, heart and liver, while in belted drivers, pulmonary contusions and aortic lacerations occur more often (22). As a result of this, modern designs have focused on making the steering wheel more hinged and collapsible to reduce impact trauma.

Unrestrained drivers may be driven forward with greater momentum, as a result of which the head may strike against the windshield, the rim of the windshield or the side pillar. Shattered pieces of the windshield can cause multiple, small, superficial, punctate lacerations of the head and face, referred to as "dicing injuries" or "sparrow foot lesions". Fragments of glass may be found embedded in these injuries. In high-speed impacts, the head may protrude through the windshield or the driver can be completely propelled out of the vehicle, particularly when unrestrained. Windshields these days are made up of laminated safety glass that is glued to the frame, a process that helps in keeping the fragments together, thus, providing some protection from windshield injuries.

Neck injuries are not uncommon in motor vehicle collisions. Cervical acceleration-deceleration is the predominant mechanism that results in whiplash injuries, which are more common in rear-end impact in which hyperextension of the cervical spine is followed by hyperflexion, than in frontal impacts. Whiplash injuries usually involve the neck muscles, vertebral discs, nerves and tendons. Fracture-dislocation of the cervical spine, particularly at the C6–C7 level or atlantooccipital dislocation may be seen in severe whiplash injuries. The head rest is the safety feature in the car meant to prevent sudden hyperextension.

Most of the injuries to the thoraco-abdominal region are caused by direct impact with the steering wheel as described above. Besides direct impact, injuries can also occur by acceleration-deceleration mechanisms. In this regard, aortic injuries are not infrequent. These injuries can range from intimal tear to complete transaction of the aorta. Aortic intimal tears are sometimes observed as multiple parallel tears in a step ladder pattern and hence are described as 'ladder-rung tears' or 'ladder tears' (Figure 26.2). The multiple mechanisms of aortic injuries can be sudden deceleration, shearing forces, osseous pinch or a sudden increase in intrathoracic pressure. The thoracic aorta is the most common site, but injuries to the abdominal aorta are also reported.

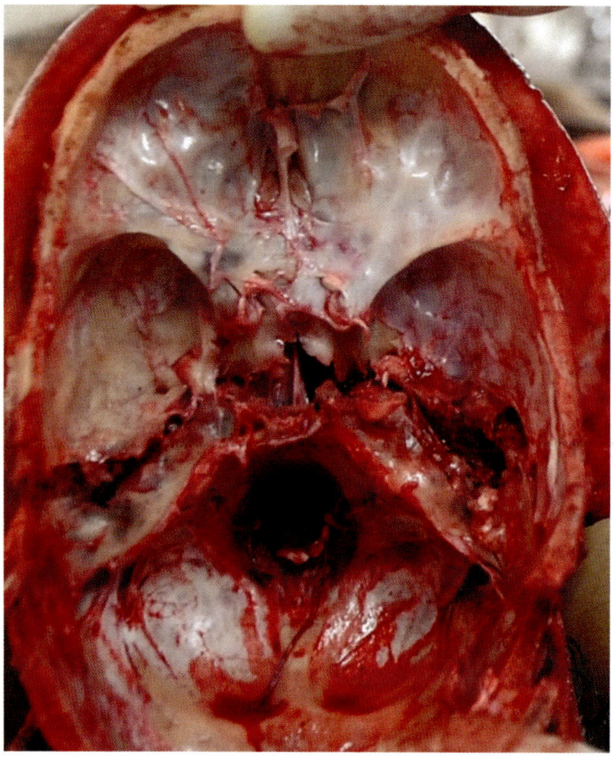

26.2 Hinge fracture of the skull.

Sometimes, a driver may firmly hold on to the steering wheel in anticipation of a collision to avoid the impact of the head and chest against the windshield and steering wheel. This may result in fractures to the wrists and forearms. Similarly, the feet can be firmly placed on the brakes with an extension of the lower limbs, which may result in dislocation of the hip joint and fracture of the neck of the femur.

Injuries to front-seat passengers

The pattern of injuries to the front seat occupants is very similar to that of the driver. The differences in the injury patterns are primarily due to the absence of a steering wheel on the passenger's side. This is associated with higher chances of the head striking against the windshield or frame, resulting in fatal head trauma, particularly in unrestrained passengers. Front seat passengers are also at a greater risk of sustaining trauma to the chest and abdomen. Impact against a dashboard or shelf edge may result in pelvic fractures. Injuries to the lower limbs occur if the thighs and knees strike against the parcel shelf area causing fractures of the distal femur and patella. Forward thrust can also cause fractures of the shafts of the tibia and fibula if the feet are trapped. There may be fracture-dislocation of the toes due to hyperflexion.

Injuries to rear-seat passengers

Rear-seat passengers are also prone to severe injuries. This can be attributed to lesser safety features in the rear seat compartment, the tendency of rear passengers to avoid fastening seat belts and lack of awareness of an imminent accident with the absence of evasive actions. Unrestrained rear-seat occupants may be thrown forward due to sudden deceleration and can strike against the back of the front seat and headrest. They can also be thrown over the front seat, and may even be ejected through the windshield. Traumatic brain injuries, trauma to the chest and abdomen and pelvic injury can occur in all such scenarios.

Seat belt injuries

A seat belt is one of the essential safety features designed to secure an occupant in place in a motor vehicle. Seat belts have a protective role against harmful movements following sudden deceleration, and in preventing impact against the interior of the car. They also prevent occupants from ejecting from a vehicle. Seat belts are known to reduce severe injuries and death by about a half in automobile crashes (23) and to considerably reduce the risk of facial, spinal and abdominal injuries. However, some studies have observed limited value in preventing head, neck, thoracic and limb injuries (24). Despite its protective value, the seat belt has also been associated with a spectrum of injuries that are referred as seat belt injuries. These injuries are commonly attributed to improper use of seat belts, particularly if they are ill-fitting or loose.

Seat belt injuries are more common in the pediatric population but have also been documented in adults. The 'seat belt' sign constitutes abrasion and bruising over the chest and abdomen underneath the seat belt area. It is often associated with underlying hemorrhage in the subcutaneous tissues and musculature. This can be due to the blunt force impact of the seat belt and the tangential movement of the skin. In addition, the intrabdominal contents may be crushed between the seat belt and vertebral column. The proximal jejunum and distal ileum are more vulnerable to such injuries as they are fixed and relatively immovable. The mesentery can often be contused or lacerated and there may be rupture of the liver, spleen and, less frequently, the pancreas and cecum. Hyperflexion of the spine over the belt as a fulcrum can result in a transverse fracture of the lumbar spine, the so-called Chance fracture. The triad of a seat belt sign, intrabdominal injuries, and lumbar fracture is referred as 'seat belt' syndrome.

Seat belt injuries may vary with a particular type of crash. For example, one study showed that renal injuries associated with seatbelt use mostly occurred in frontal and side-impact collisions (25). Lap belts have been mostly associated with abdominal, pelvic or spinal injuries. In contrast, three-point belts have been associated with injuries of the chest, heart, lungs, brachial plexus and major blood vessels in addition to abdomen-pelvic and spinal injuries (26,27).

Airbag injuries

Airbags are one of the most essential safety features deployed in the modern motor vehicle and reduce severe facial and head injuries. However, there have been documented cases of injuries sustained due to airbag deployment. Airbags use sodium azide, which is converted into nitrogen gas in milliseconds, causing rapid inflation. The stages of airbag deployment consist of an initial stage of punch out, mid-stage of catapult and final stage of bag slap. Injuries can occur in all the different stages of bag deployment.

The injuries documented in the punch out stage of bag deployment include atlanto-occipital dislocations, cervical spine fractures with brain stem transaction, cardiac, liver and splenic lacerations, diffuse axonal injuries, subdural and epidural hematomas and, rarely, decapitation. Fracture, degloving injury and amputation of the upper limb has also been observed. The mid-stage of deployment drives the head and neck rearward and can cause vascular injury, ligament tear, ruptured eyeballs and fracture of the cervical vertebrae. The final stage of a big slap mostly causes ocular injuries (28). Ocular injuries are among the most common injuries sustained due to airbags. External injuries consist of periorbital contusions and laceration, with hyphema and/or corneal abrasions. Corneal abrasion can be caused by contact with the bag or exposure to sodium azide. Serious ocular injuries consist of globe rupture, lens dislocation, retinal detachment and fractures. Glass pieces or frames of eyewear can also pierce the eye in occupants wearing glasses.

Airbag module covers are also propelled with airbag deployment and may cause severe injuries. Upper limb injuries are mostly reported due to impact with the module. These injuries include degloving injuries, fractures, dislocations and even amputations. Sometimes, the module may hit the face of the occupant, resulting in a fatal head injury.

MEDICOLEGAL INVESTIGATION OF VEHICULAR CRASHES

The majority of fatalities on the road are due to vehicular crashes. The various medicolegal issues involved in such cases include investigations of rash and negligent driving, hit and run cases and claims for insurance and compensation. Forensic investigations are also aimed at ruling out suspected homicide or suicide using a vehicle. The medicolegal investigations in vehicular impacts include an examination of the scene of the incident, the vehicles, the driver and other occupants, that can help in the reconstruction of the crash.

The investigating agency usually secures the scene of the incident. The scene is thoroughly searched for traces left by the vehicle and the victim. The extent of damage to any property or stationary objects such as a pole or road divider is noted. Skid marks, if found on the road, may provide information about the vehicle's speed, braking or sideways skid, that is, yaw mark. The pattern of the tyre mark may be analyzed for identification of the vehicle. The scene of incident is searched for any traces left by a vehicle such as glass pieces from a windshield, headlights or mirror, paint or any dirt from the under-surface of the vehicle, and any part that has broken off the vehicle. Traces of blood, clothing or footwear of the victims may also be found at the scene.

The vehicle involved in the crash should be examined for the extent of damage or missing parts. Any mechanical failure or engine failure should be ruled out. In impacts involving motor vehicles and pedestrians, the victims' traces, such as blood and clothing, hair, tissues, and so on, are searched for on the impacting surface and under-surface of the vehicle. In vehicular crashes, visible damage to the vehicle may help to explain the injuries sustained by the victim. Steering wheel impact results in steering wheel deformation, which can be useful in reconstruction. In run-over injuries or when a pedestrian is hit by a heavy motor vehicle, there may not be any visible damage to the vehicle. However, trace evidence from the victim or the scene of the accident left on the vehicle or material from the vehicle deposited over the body of the victim may help in clarifying the incident.

A detailed medicolegal examination is essential for both the survivors and the deceased in a vehicular crash. All of the injuries and trace evidence must be carefully documented and photographed. Clothes should be examined for damage, and trace evidence of mud, paint, grease, oil, pieces of glass and/or metals and so on should be documented. The pattern of damage to clothes may give some idea about impacting or protruding parts of a vehicle. The footwear of pedestrians should be examined following such events. Abrasive damage to the soles of both shoes may indicate that the person was upright and possibly still at the time of impact. Abrasive damage may be restricted to one sole if the person was walking. The pattern and distribution of injuries needs to be correlated with findings at the scene of a crash, the history, eyewitnesses accounts, and so on, for the reconstruction of the incident.

The examination of the driver is of paramount importance in fatal vehicular crashes. Intoxication and substance abuse among drivers remains one of the major reasons for vehicular crashes. In addition, medical conditions such as cardiac arrhythmias, acute coronary insufficiency, stroke, epilepsy, and so on, may cause or contribute to a crash. Drivers and pedestrians should also be examined for visual disturbances such as cataract and color blindness. The use of mobile phones while driving is one of the common causes of distracted driving and vehicular crashes. Thus, the driver's mobile phone data may provide vital clues in such cases. Helmets should be examined for the pattern and extent of damage in accidents involving two-wheeled vehicles.

In automobile crashes with multiple casualties, the identification of deceased persons is an essential task. This is often required in accidents with multiple vehicles or when a crash is followed by fire. There may be dismemberment and extensive burning of bodies in such cases and, hence, identification can be challenging.

Fatal vehicular crashes are a cause of great concern globally and require detailed medicolegal investigations. Road safety investigation can help to identify the cause of crashes and lead to measures for prevention. The data can also help in evaluation of vehicular and personal safety measures, road infrastructure and compliance to existing legislation.

REFERENCES

1. World Health Organization. Road traffic injuries. [cited 2022Feb2]. Available from: https://www.who.int/news-room/fact-sheets/detail/road-traffic-injuries (Accessed 24 April 2023).
2. World Health Organization. Global status report on road safety 2015. World Health Organization; 2018 [cited 2022Feb2]. Available from: https://www.afro.who.int/publications/global-status-report-road-safety-2015 (Accessed 24 April 2023).
3. Jadav D, Gorchiya A, Shekhawat RS, Kanchan T. Traumatic inguinal hernia: An uncommonly reported entity. *Med Sci Law* 2020; **60(4)**: 319–22.
4. Das S, Ravi K. Traumatic herniation of intestine through ruptured skin at the ankle. *Forensic Sci Med Pathol* 2021; **17(4)**: 734–7.
5. Stemberga V, Petaros A, Barisic A, Coklo M, et al. Car-to-pedestrian accident with a unique decollement injury. *Forensic Sci Int* 2013; **228(1–3)**: e67–70.
6. Heydari ST, Maharlouei N, Foroutan A, et al. Fatal motorcycle accidents in Fars Province, Iran: A community-based survey. *Chin J Traumatol/Zhonghua Chuang Shang ZaZhi* 2012; **15(4)**: 222–7.
7. López-Alvarenga JC, Vázquez-Velázquez V, Arcila-Martínez D, et al. Accuracy and diagnostic utility of the Hospital Anxiety and Depression Scale (HAD) in a sample of obese Mexican patients. *Rev Investig Clin Organo Hosp Enfermedades Nutr* 2002; **54(5)**: 403–9.
8. Zargar M, Khaji A, Karbakhsh M. Pattern of motorcycle-related injuries in Tehran, 1999 to 2000: A study in 6 hospitals. *East Mediterr Health J Rev* 2006; **12(1–2)**: 81–7.
9. Araqi E, Vahedian MO. Study on susceptible and damages from motorcycle accidents in Mashhad in 2005. *Horiz Med Sci* 2007; **13(1)**: 34–9.
10. Mohanty C, Radhakrishnan R, Jain M, et al. A study of the pattern of injuries sustained from road traffic accidents caused by impact with stray animals. *J Emerg Trauma Shock* 2021; **14(1)**: 23–7.
11. Petit L, Zaki T, Hsiang W, et al. A review of common motorcycle collision mechanisms of injury. *EFORT Open Rev* 2020; 5(9): 544–8.
12. NHTSA's National Center for Statistics and Analysis. Traffic safety facts. [cited 2022Feb8]. Available from: https://crashstats.nhtsa.dot.gov/Api/Public/ViewPublication/809908 (Accessed 24 April 2023).
13. Alicioglu B. Injuries associated with motorcycle accidents. *Acta Orthop Traumatol Turc* 2008; **42(2)**: 106–11.
14. Batista F, Silveira LO, Castillo JJAQ, et al. Epidemiological profile of extremity fractures in victims of motorcycle accidents. *Acta Ortopédica Bras* 2015; **23(1)**: 43–6.
15. Zhu YL, Li J, Ma WQ, et al. Motorcycle spoke injuries of the heel. *Injury* 2011; **42(4)**: 356–61.
16. Soldado F, Ghizoni MF, Bertelli J. Injury mechanisms in supraclavicular stretch injuries of the brachial plexus. *Hand Surg Rehabil* 2016; **35(1)**: 51–4.
17. Paryavi E, Gilotra MN, Johnson AJ, et al. Upper extremity injuries in motorcyclists: Implications for mortality and need for rehabilitation services. *J Trauma Acute Care Surg* 2015; **78(5)**: 1021–5.
18. Alexander C, Abzug JM, Johnson AJ, et al. Motorcyclist's thumb: carpometacarpal injuries of the thumb sustained in motorcycle crashes. *J Hand Surg Eur Vol* 2016; **41(7)**: 707–9.
19. Meredith L, Baldock M, Fitzharris M, et al. Motorcycle fuel tanks and pelvic fractures: A motorcycle fuel tank syndrome. *Traffic Inj Prev* 2016; **17(6)**: 644–9.
20. Otte D, Facius T, Klintschar M, Brand S. Investigations and injury mechanisms of aortic ruptures among vehicle occupants and vulnerable road users over time. *Int Res Counc Biomech Inj* 2006; 870–87.
21. Chen R, Gabler HC. Risk of thoracic injury from direct steering wheel impact in frontal crashes. *J Trauma Acute Care Surg* 2014; **76(6)**: 1441–6.
22. Wani I, Bhat RA, Wani S, et al. Isolated small bowel mesentery injury after steering wheel trauma. *Trauma Mon* 2012; **17(2)**: 279–81.
23. National Highway Traffic Safety Administration. Final regulatory impact analysis amendment to Federal Motor Vehicle Safety Standard 208. Passenger car front seat occupant protection. Washington, DC: US Department of Transportation, National Highway Traffic Safety Administration; 1984. Publication no. DOT-HS-806-572. [cited 2022Feb8]. Available from: https://crashstats.nhtsa.dot.gov/Api/Public/ViewPublication/806572 (Accessed 24 April 2023).
24. Fouda Mbarga N, Abubakari A-R, Aminde LN, Morgan AR. Seatbelt use and risk of major injuries sustained by vehicle occupants during motor-vehicle crashes: a systematic review and meta-analysis of cohort studies. *BMC Public Health* 2018; **18(1)**: 1413.
25. Kuan JK, Wright JL, Nathens AB, et al. American Association for the Surgery of Trauma Organ Injury Scale for Kidney Injuries predicts nephrectomy, dialysis, and death in patients with blunt injury and nephrectomy for penetrating injuries. *J Trauma Inj Infect Crit Care* 2006; **60(2)**: 351–6.
26. McGrath N, Fitzpatrick P, Okafor I, et al. Lap belt injuries in children. *Ir Med J* 2010; **103(7)**: 216–18.
27. Anderson PA, Rivara FP, Maier RV, Drake C. The epidemiology of seatbelt-associated injuries. *J Trauma Inj Infect Crit Care* 1991; **31(1)**: 60–7.
28. Duma SM, Rath AL, Jernigan MV, et al. The effects of depowered airbags on eye injuries in frontal automobile crashes. *Am J Emerg Med* 2005; **23(1)**: 13–19.
29. Buck U, Buße K, Campana L, et al. What happened before the run over? Morphometric 3D reconstruction. *Forensic Sci Int* 2020; **306**: 110059.

CHAPTER

27

Aviation Deaths

Matthew M. Orde

'There are two critical points in every aerial flight – its beginning and its end.'

Alexander Graham Bell, 1906 (1)

INTRODUCTION

The first recorded fatal aviation incident involved the crash of a Rozière balloon (a type of balloon that is inflated with hot air, but also has a separate compartment containing non-heated lifting gas, in this case hydrogen) during an attempted crossing of the English Channel near Wimereux, France, on 16 June 1785. The crash resulted in the death of the balloon's inventor, Jean-François Pilâtre de Rozier, and the other occupant, Pierre Romain (2). Since that time the field of aviation has expanded enormously, with 4.5 billion passenger flights globally on scheduled services alone in 2019 (pre-pandemic) and many more privately chartered and hobby flights (3). Thankfully, only very few flights end in disaster: in the same year there were 239 fatalities worldwide involving scheduled commercial flights on aircraft with a weight of more than 5.7 t, and the annual data for 2019 were skewed by 157 deaths in association with the crash of an Ethiopian Airlines Boeing 737 Max 8 (4). Notwithstanding their rarity, the potential for airborne incidents to impact others necessitates a careful approach in analyzing the likely cause.

The potential causes of air crashes are protean, and it is outside the scope of this review to provide anything other than the briefest of introductions to the topic. Factors that may be operative include: pilot error (the most common cause); pilot ill-health; other human error (notably by air traffic controllers and maintenance engineers); structural and mechanical flaws; malfunction of avionics equipment; issues with stowed cargo; meteorologic factors; and, rarely, sabotage. It is recognized, however, that the majority of serious air crash incidents do not stem from one single isolated issue, but rather from a chain of events that must occur in a certain sequence (5,6).

As well as identifying factors that may have contributed to the aircraft crash itself, and identifying a definitive cause of death of victims, autopsy data can be put to good use to help prevent future injury and deaths of a similar nature, whether by contributing to improved design of safety features, providing an opportunity to address structural aircraft flaws, prompting enhanced awareness of and screening for health issues in pilots and, on occasion, identifying features that suggest negligent and possibly criminal actions.

THE ROLE OF FORENSIC PATHOLOGY

The fundamental objective of air crash investigation is to identify information that may assist with crash sequence reconstruction and help elucidate the underlying cause, with a view to improving flight safety and preventing later occurrences of a similar nature. Medical examination of victims contributes to this process by providing information not only on injuries sustained but also on the identification of potentially incapacitating natural diseases that may be present, as well as facilitating analysis for the presence of intoxicating substances. Features suggesting contribution to a lethal outcome by post-impact fire and possibly a hostile post-crash environment may also be identified.

Autopsy data will be key in addressing the standard requirement to identify the answers to the questions 'Who? When? Where? How? And by what means?' with reference to both cause and manner of death. However, while a wealth of information will be uncovered during the investigation of any serious aviation incident, much of which will undoubtedly be of interest to various parties and potentially to subsequent legal proceedings, it is not the primary purpose of the air crash investigation to apportion blame or liability (7).

A MULTIDISCIPLINARY APPROACH

The pathologist will typically be required to work as part of a team, alongside coroners, other forensic specialists and, on occasion, forensic anthropologists, law enforcement agents and air crash investigators. Indeed, the mainstay of many investigations will ultimately prove to be the air crash investigation team, which may be a civilian unit or drawn from military personnel. However, many small aircraft crashes will only be attended to by

DOI: 10.1201/9781003138754-29

local first responders, law enforcement and death investigation personnel.

According to international law, domestic teams have primacy in the investigation of air crashes in that nation state. However, in incidents involving a flag-carrier of one nation operating in another, or in relation to overseas passengers, countries may wish for their own investigators to be deployed in addition to local operatives. On occasion there may also be interest from military authorities and industry, notably the aircraft manufacturer and the aircraft operator. In the case of incidents occurring in neutral territory, such as international waters, the international convention is that the country where the aircraft is registered should lead the investigation (8).

PREPARATION

The approach required will naturally depend upon the specifics of the incident. Key factors will be the type of aircraft involved, the location of the incident and the suspected number of victims. Where available, passenger manifests should be consulted (though with some circumspection and in the knowledge that these may be incorrect), and in the event of an air crash involving people on the ground, steps should be taken to ascertain as far as possible the probable number of people involved and, where possible, their likely identities. The pathologist will also need to satisfy themselves that they have the requisite authority to conduct an examination of human remains and that, where required, they have a valid licence to practise in the jurisdiction.

As well as benefiting from a general understanding of the principles of flight and the basics of aircraft control, there will often be value in the pathologist first gaining a little knowledge about the type of aircraft involved. The position of the wings (high wing versus low wing), the nature and location of the engines, the undercarriage, the seating configuration, and the position of the fuel tanks can all significantly affect the human outcome. Helicopters are generally considered to be somewhat less reliable than fixed wing aircraft, perhaps reflecting the increased number and complexity of moving parts, and the outcome can also be suboptimal when they crash by virtue of the location of the engine and/or fuel tank, which is frequently positioned above the passenger compartment. A brief review of recent weather patterns and the terrain that the aircraft was operating over will provide an insight into the conditions encountered by the aircraft during transit. An overview of the suspected incident scenario will assist pathologists as they formulate an approach – for example, was this a relatively slow speed stall into the ground on or shortly after take-off or on approach, or was this a high velocity controled flight into terrain?

As with any autopsy investigation, there is merit in first reviewing the medical histories of the parties involved, particularly those of the pilot and the co-pilot. Both pre-existing medical history and the actions of first attenders who may have attempted resuscitation should be considered. However, the absence of any notable past medical history and a "clean bill of health" documented in recent medical checks does not preclude the possibility of even somewhat advanced natural disease, as is evidenced by significant positive autopsy findings in many such instances. Antemortem dental records will naturally be of importance in instances where identification is to be made by comparative dental examination.

THE SCENE

Attendance at crash scenes can be incredibly informative for pathologists and is to be encouraged. Information obtained may assist with assessment of the origin of injuries, and provides a contextual framework for interpretation. Certainly, where there exists the possibility of functional compromise of human physiology stemming from the interaction between the body and other objects at the scene, such as mechanical asphyxia by way of compression of the body by adjacent structures, such a possibility may be overlooked unless consideration is given before extraction of the remains. Specific issues and concerns may also be flagged at an early stage, affording the pathologist the opportunity to direct the focus of the examination accordingly.

Standard equipment required for a scene visit would include:

- Notebook and pens/pencils
- Clipboard or similar
- Camera
- Identification tags/bracelets
- Indelible marker pen (although be aware that many indelible inks are soluble in volatile fluids such as kerosene/gasoline)
- Blank copies of any documents that may be required
- Bubble-wrap, adhesive tape, and cyanoacrylate ("super") glue
- Robust scissors and/or fabric cutters
- Forceps
- Retractable tape measure
- Assorted small specimen containers
- Body bags and/or other suitable containers/wrappings
- Personal protective equipment, including high particulate filtration face masks, eye protection, cut-resistant gloves and surgical gloves
- Carry bag/rucksack
- Appropriate dress and equipment for the conditions that are likely to be encountered, such as sunscreen, hat and raincoat as applicable.

The pathologist's main duties at the scene – after confirmation of the fact of death, if not already undertaken – will be the identification of human remains, documentation of the location of the remains in relation to the wreckage and other bodies, applying judgement as to the probable pairing of dissociated and possibly commingled body parts, and making an initial assessment of injuries and/or other pathology. In a setting where there are widely dispersed remains, the assistance of others, and on occasion a search team, may be required.

27.1 Two bodies *in situ* in an aircraft wreckage. (Image courtesy of Professor Ryan Blumenthal, Department of Forensic Medicine, University of Pretoria, South Africa.)

The *in-situ* examination of human remains should be undertaken in the context of adjacent structures, notably flight controls, seating, safety harnesses/mechanisms and hard surfaces, and also with consideration of structures that may previously have been in close contact with the body but have been obliterated by impact trauma and possibly the effects of fire, such as fabric harness straps (Figure 27.1).

Prior to departing the scene, the pathologist should supervise the labeling, extraction, packaging and transportation of bodies from the scene to the mortuary. Helpful guidance on numbering and labeling is provided in Annexure 13 (DVI Recovery Labels and Forms) of the INTERPOL Disaster Victim Identification guide (2018) (9). It is important that each body and each unattached body part is labeled individually. In instances of fragmented or heavily heat-damaged fragile remains, the risk of ongoing further fragmentation during extraction and/or transit can be limited by careful and judicious removal of the remains from the wreckage, wrapping of the head and/or other weakened areas with bubble-wrap and tape, and the application of cyanoacrylate ("super") glue to the teeth and/or charred areas of bone. Cyanoacrylate adhesive fluid penetrates charred bone and teeth prior to hardening, helping to preserve the tissue integrity and keeping loosened teeth in position in the jaw. Cyanoacrylate glues are readily available and have the advantage of being radiolucent, so do not materially hinder subsequent dental assessment and imaging (10).

HEALTH AND SAFETY

Multiple hazards that pose a potential risk to human health may be present at scenes of aircraft crashes. The forensic pathologist will often be the only or most senior medical person present at the scene of an aircraft crash, and as such has a duty not only to protect him/herself from the risk of harm but also to offer appropriate advice and guidance to other personnel present, particularly in relation to biological hazards. The site of the aircraft crash should not be approached until clearance has been provided by appropriate experts in attendance, typically fire crew and air crash investigators, and following the route of entry as advised.

Naturally, where human remains are present, particularly with the possibility of bodily fragmentation, there will be a risk of contamination with bodily fluids and tissues, with the associated risk of transmission of infectious disease. Fractured bone ends can be sharp and can be a risk to examiners.

Modern aircraft are composed of a variety of materials, which can pose a risk to health in a variety of ways. Potential hazards will include flammable and toxic materials, and on occasion there will be a risk of explosion, a risk that may be magnified due to the effects of physical trauma and/or heat. Such risk can be posed by objects such as: high-pressure vessels including tyres, hydraulic suspension, other hydraulic systems and fire extinguishers; compressed gas tanks; and explosive safety devices such as inflatable seatbelt restraints and ballistic parachutes. There may be sharp edges and unsecured heavy loads, and much of the air frame mass may itself be unstable. Modern lightweight composite materials can pose specific inhalational hazards, particularly when damaged with the generation of dusts. Radioactive compounds, such as depleted uranium for use as aviation counterweights, may be present. Spilled fuel may pose a risk of fire, as well as the potential for damage to skin and mucous membranes. Ground-based structures at the crash site and cargo items can add to the mix and may necessitate input from experts on hazardous materials; herbicidal and insecticidal substances may be present in association with agricultural aircraft. Military aircraft frequently pose additional hazards, including the presence of ejection seats, explosive canopies and unexploded ordnance (11).

THE POST-MORTEM EXAMINATION

Objectives and triage

The primary objective of the autopsy will be to identify and document all significant disease processes and injuries, in order to provide an evidential basis for subsequent analysis of the incident scenario, and to assist with future design of aircraft safety features. The decision as to which remains will be subjected to autopsy will naturally depend upon the circumstances, the questions that arise, the number of fatalities, available manpower, the

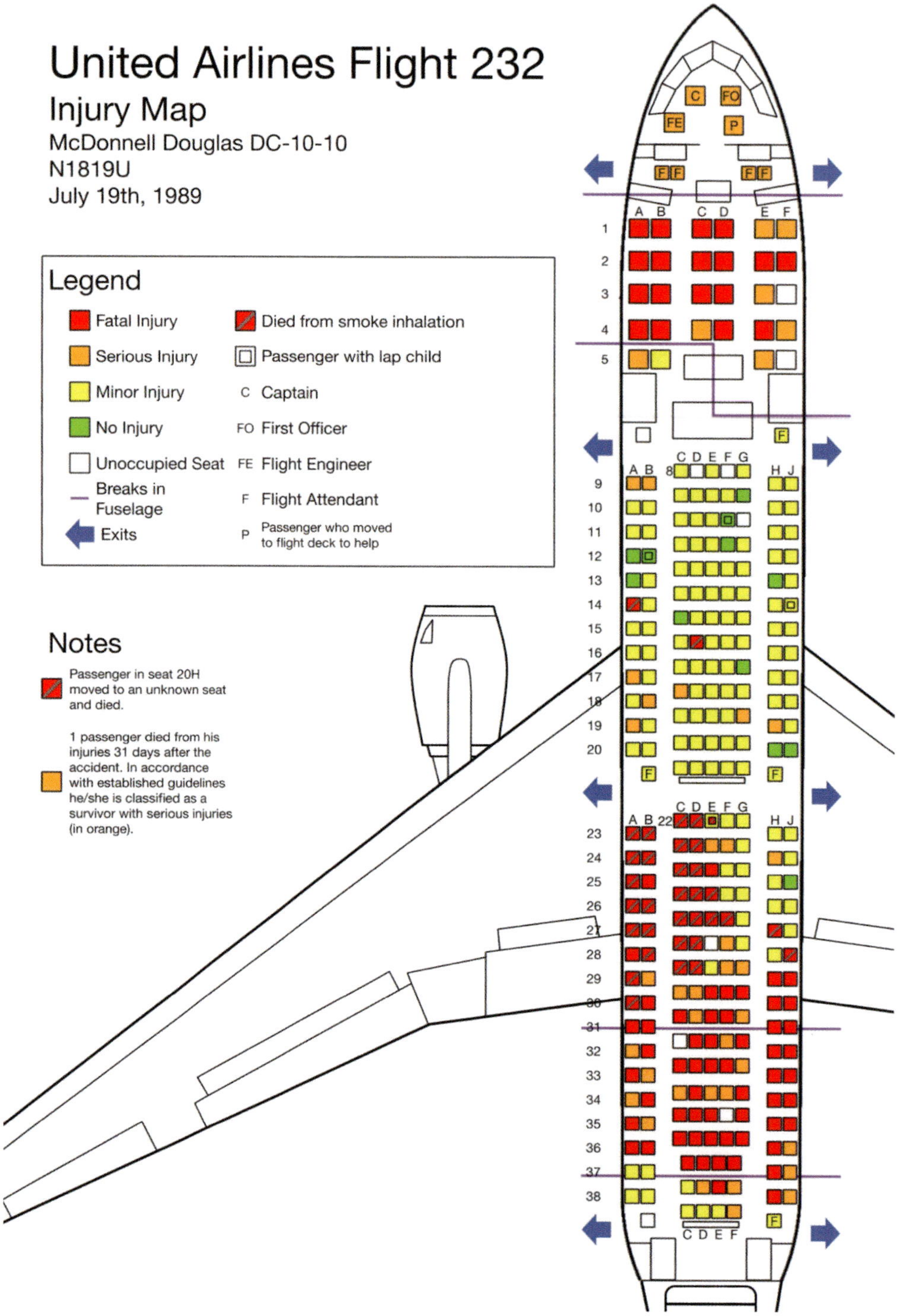

27.2 Seating plan and distribution of injuries, United Airlines flight 232; McDonnell Douglas DC-10–10, Sioux Gateway Airport, Sioux City, Iowa, USA, July 19, 1989. (Data derived from US National Transportation Safety Board, Aircraft Accident Report AAR-90/06; image attribution: Ardenau4, Wikimedia Commons.)

facilities available and religious and cultural concerns. Given the possibility that incapacitation by natural disease, injury or toxic effects may have been operative and potentially contributing to the incident, the pilot in charge (who typically occupies the front port/left seat in the cockpit) should *always* be autopsied. Should the aircraft have dual controls – as is the case with most civilian and many non-combat military aircraft – then the co-pilot (starboard/right seat) should also be subjected to autopsy, because he/she may have been in control of the aircraft at the material time, or otherwise have had input into the flight controls, and/or may have been involved with the navigation of the aircraft and communications. However, there is certainly also merit in examination of victims of air crash incidents other than the flight crew (12). Observations from post-mortem examination can offer assistance with assessment of factors that may have compromised potential survivability, such as safety harness failure, seat collapse or detachment, and features of smoke inhalation. The value of observations that can be derived from examination of non-aircrew victims and survivors is demonstrated well by the production of seating plans and injury maps, which provide an easy-to-comprehend visual demonstration of the distribution of patterns of injury and survivability in relation to various airframe structures, sites of damage and/or fire, and proximity to escape routes. See, for example, Figure 27.2, which shows a seating plan and injury map pertaining to the crash of United Airlines 232 in Sioux City, Iowa, USA, in July 1989. This incident stemmed from failure of the tail-mounted engine and associated loss of flight controls, which resulted in a crash landing in which the aircraft bounced several times and the fuselage broke into several pieces. A total of 112 of the 296 people on board died, most by way of injuries sustained in the impact; the majority of the survivors were seated toward the front of the aircraft. Of interest, 35 people in the middle section of the aircraft, directly above the fuel tanks, died from smoke inhalation in the post-crash fire, and of these, 24 had not sustained significant blunt-force injuries and could otherwise have potentially survived.

THE AUTOPSY PROCESS

The body should first be examined while it is still clothed and with personal effects still *in situ*, primarily in view of the fact that damage to the clothing and other surface objects can provide an indication of mechanisms of injury that may not be evident from examination of the underlying skin, but also because clothing and other items can modify the appearance of underlying bodily injuries. Protective headgear and the soles of footwear in particular merit close examination. The presence of glasses or contact lenses should be noted, as their wearing or absence may provide an indication of the visual acuity of the wearer at the time of the incident. While it is standard practice for bodies to be weighed after undressing, if bulky clothing, protective equipment or footwear is present, this should also be weighed.

An assessment of the external features of the body is then undertaken. With awareness that the ultimate significance attributed to even seemingly innocuous features – such as trivial injuries that perhaps indicate contact with certain airframe structures – will often not be known at the initial stages of the inquiry, the description of injuries and other observations should be made in detail. Any potentially patterned marks should properly attract particular attention.

Wherever possible, the autopsy should then proceed to full internal examination with evisceration of the cranial and thoraco-abdomino-pelvic cavities. Given the potential significance of disease conditions that pose a risk of incapacitation, the autopsy should be complete and thorough, and should include, for example, examination of the carotid arteries and the mucosal aspect of the gastrointestinal tract. There should be a low threshold for specific examination of the posterior neck to assess for injury to the cervical spine and atlanto-occipital articulation (13), and there may also be merit in dissection of the limbs to permit a detailed assessment for injuries that may indicate contact with flight control surfaces at the time of impact (see also the discussion of this point later in this chapter).

ANCILLARY STUDIES

Toxicological analyses of members of the flight crew should be considered mandatory, as any impairment due to the effect of alcohol or drugs can have potentially catastrophic consequences. Aircraft occupants may also be exposed to carbon monoxide and other exhaust fumes by way of inadvertent ingress into the passenger compartment, and carbon monoxide and other products of combustion in the event of fire.

Microbiological studies may aid interpretation of potentially infective pathology, although such an occurrence will of course be rare at least in relation to pilots and aircrew (14). Biochemical analyses will occasionally have value in the setting of aircraft incidents, with particular reference to the possibility of hypo/hyperglycamia which may be associated with diabetes mellitus, and ketoacidosis (15–17).

Consideration should also be given to the retention of fluids or tissue samples so as to permit genetic analysis. This has particular utility in the case of unidentified remains, and in circumstances that suggest the possibility of pilot incapacitation but where the autopsy fails to identify significant gross pathology and toxicological analyses do not provide a potential cause, thereby raising the possibility of an inherent arrhythmic cardiac disorder, possibly with genetic underpinnings.

AUTOPSY FINDINGS

Injuries and other non-natural Pathology

By their very nature, aircraft crashes are idiosyncratic events and each must be considered in light of the particular circumstances. There will certainly be a difference in the pathology findings dependent upon the horizontal and vertical pre-impact velocity vectors, the attitude of the aircraft at the time of impact, the specifics of the aircraft involved and any post-impact fire. It may be useful to consider the factors that come into play by referring to the so-called 'CREEP' framework:

- Container: compromise of the occupant-containing structure, whether by collapse or penetration by external objects
- Restraint: mechanisms used to limit movement of occupants and cargo
- Environment: potentially injurious objects located within the "strike zone" of the occupant

TABLE 27.1 Blunt force injuries and typical associated decelerative forces. ('G': the average accelerative force due to gravity acting upon a body at the earth's surface, ca 9.8 m/s^2.) (Source: Bellenkes et al. 2001 (18).)

Injury type	Typical associated decelerative force
Pulmonary contusion	25 G
Nose – fracture	30 G
Vertebral body – compression	20–30 G
Fracture dislocation of C1 on C2	20–40 G
Mandible – fracture	40 G
Maxilla – fracture	50 G
Aorta – intimal tear	50 G
Aorta – transection	80–100 G
Pelvis – fracture	100–200 G
Vertebral body – transection	200–300 G
Total body fragmentation	> 350 G

- Energy absorption: mechanisms designed to limit accelerative/decelerative forces, such as crumple zones, undercarriage and seat suspension, airbags, and elasticity of restraints
- Post-crash factors: such as fire and other hostile external environments; and also with consideration of exit routes (18).

In light of the extreme velocity of many aircraft, the potential for rapid uncontroled descent from altitude and the magnitude of deceleration forces (typically amounting to many 'G' – the average accelerative force due to gravity acting upon a body at the earth's surface, ca 9.8 m/s^2) encountered upon impact with the ground or other objects, air crash victims will frequently display features of multiple severe blunt force injuries, with extensive and multifocal bone fracturing and dislocation, and visceral and vascular lacerating injury. (See Table 27.1, which sets out the forces typically associated with a range of injuries.) Commonly encountered patterns of injury in aviation incidents share much in common with high velocity motor vehicle incidents and falls from height. Not infrequently, extremely disfiguring and fragmentary injuries may also be encountered.

The extensive nature of injuries frequently encountered in air crash fatalities can prove both confronting and challenging for the pathologist, especially those with only limited experience of multi-trauma deaths (19). A meticulous and systematic approach should be adopted in assessment and documentation of injuries, because the nature and pattern of injuries will be of importance not only in relation to determination of the cause of death, but may also provide assistance in piecing together the likely sequence of events leading up to and during the incident, and on occasion provide an

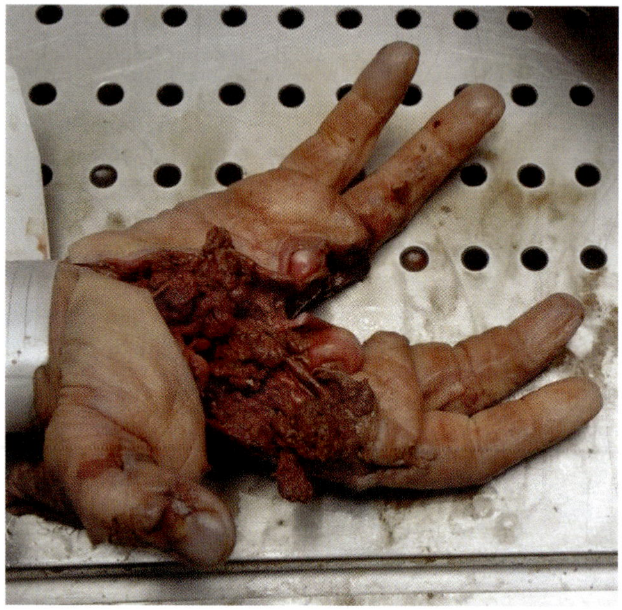

27.3 Typical palmar 'control surface injuries' – a putative but essentially non-specific marker of the victim having been in control of the aircraft at the time of impact. (Image courtesy of the National Center of Forensic Medicine, Affiliated to the Sackler Faculty of Medicine, Tel-Aviv University, Israel.)

indication of the potential for injury-associated incapacitation with resultant compromise of the victim's ability to make an effective escape.

The investigation into the air crash will naturally be informed by knowledge of who was operating or attempting to control the aircraft at the time the incident occurred, and such determination will on occasion provide insight into the sequence of events prior to impact. However, the location of human remains within the wreckage will not always provide a firm indication as to who was operating the aircraft at the time of the incident, because of the movement of bodies in association with the impact and the presence of dual controls in many aircraft. This issue has driven the search for specific injury characteristics, with most historic emphasis being placed on so-called "control surface" injuries. These have classically been described as including: lacerations to the palmar aspect of the hand and the web space between the first and second metacarpals; metacarpal fractures; wrist fractures/dislocations; fractures of the distal radius/ulna; foot and talar fractures; fractures of the distal tibia and fibula; and sometimes damage to the soles of the footwear (19). Such injuries reflect the operation of and transmission of impact/decelerative forces through the yoke/control column and rudders/foot brakes of the aircraft (see, e.g. Figure 27.3) (20,21). In fact, however, published data demonstrate only limited correlation between the presence of injuries of this nature and that individual having been in documented control of the aircraft at the time of the incident. For example, a 2007 study by Campman and Luzi, in which 42 pilot and 58 passenger fatalities from a mixture of fixed wing and rotary wing aircraft crashes were

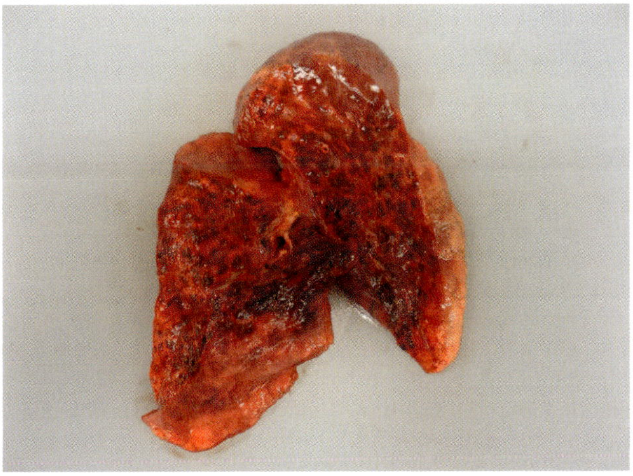

27.4 A sliced lung showing spotty peribronchial/peribronchiolar hemorrhage characteristic of hemoaspiration.

examined, demonstrated that identification of injuries of this nature had a sensitivity of 69 percent and a specificity of only 28 percent, and the positive and negative predictive values of presumed control surface injuries were both under 50 percent (22).

Specific assessment should also be undertaken for injuries that may be associated with restraint harnesses and other safety devices. Interpretation will require knowledge of the restraint and safety mechanisms present in the aircraft – frequently multipoint harnesses for cockpit occupants and other aircrew members, but often only lap straps for passengers and, occasionally, airbags.

Features that may assist in the determination of whether or not there may have been a survival period between the time of injury and death should also be sought. Key in this regard will be the presence and amount of associated hemorrhage, with significant hemorrhage generally indicating an antemortem origin. Signs of hemoaspiration, as evidenced by frothy blood in the airways and spotty "leopard-skin" pulmonary hemorrhage centered on bronchi/bronchioli in the lungs, can be a useful marker of at least a short survival period after injury with associated bleeding into the airways (Figure 27.4). The microscopic observation of fat and/or bone marrow embolism within the lung vasculature will provide similar assistance, indicating at least some ongoing circulation after the moment of injury, whether by intrinsic cardiac function or resuscitative chest compressions.

Due to the presence of abundant flammable fuel, post-crash fires are commonplace in aviation incidents, and fires may also break out in the air and potentially contribute to the development of the incident. The reader is directed to further discussion on the topic in Chapter 46, with specific reference to heat-related artefact that can mimic traumatic injury.

Other forms of "artefact" can also be a feature in aviation disaster victims by virtue of the location of the incident, such as a watery environment, post-mortem animal scavenging and predation and, on occasion, changes of decomposition which may reflect the remoteness of the crash site and an associated time delay before recovery of the remains. Contact with aviation fuel can also result in skin blistering and sloughing of the surface cutaneous layers, which on occasion may mimic burn injuries.

NATURAL DISEASE

The search for potentially incapacitating occult natural disease in pilots and other members of the flight crew is one of the key functions of the autopsy in aviation incidents, although such an event is a very rare occurrence, with a 2014 review of the literature indicating an incidence of in-flight incapacitation of pilots of 0.19–0.45 times/10^6 flights (23). A meta-analysis of publications on the topic involving airline pilots, spanning 1968 to 2000, indicates that the leading causes of pilot incapacitation were myocardial infarction, cardiac arrhythmias and epileptic seizures (24). This of course relates to the incidence of such disease in relation to incapacitation and death in the general community. There are, however, numerous potential other causes, ranging from gastroenteritis/diarrhoea, through ureteric colic, acute myocarditis and acute pulmonary thromboembolism, to cerebrovascular strokes. A distinction must be made between pathologic conditions that are identified at autopsy that raise the possibility of potential pilot incapacitation (such as stable coronary artery atherosclerosis), and conditions that would unequivocally have been incapacitating (such as a ruptured myocardial infarct or a catastrophic hypertensive intracerebral hemorrhage). Consideration must also be given to physiological causes of incapacitation that may not be evidenced by anatomic changes, such as syncope, arrhythmic disorders, diarrhoea, sneezing and somnolence.

POST-MORTEM IMAGING

Prior to or concurrent with examination by pathologists, there is most certainly merit in undertaking radiologic assessment of the remains if circumstances permit. Plain imaging provides limited assistance with the assessment of skeletal injury patterns and identification of radiopaque foreign materials. Computed tomography (CT) imaging is now becoming more accessible to practitioners in many countries, and in some jurisdictions mobile CT scanning devices may even be available for use at temporary morgue facilities. The plethora of data generated by these scanners in contrast to plain X-rays can be of immense value, and imaging can be conducted even before the body is removed from the body bag.

IDENTIFICATION AND MASS FATALITY INCIDENTS

Identification of deceased individuals is of course one of the cornerstones of forensic pathology practice. This is particularly so in the setting of multiple fatalities, and especially where fragmented and/or heat-damaged human remains may be encountered. The challenges of effectively managing an investigation into mass disaster incidents are frequently compounded by the glare of the media spotlight and intense political scrutiny.

The methods employed to identify victims will be case dependent and will be guided by the circumstances and the nature of the incident. As with the majority of deaths dealt with by the forensic pathologist, satisfactory identification of air crash victims can frequently be made by visual means, often by way of confirmation from a close relative or other acquaintance. However, in the case of disfiguring injuries and possibly heat damage, and in the context of multiple fatalities – where psychological stress experienced by relatives makes visual identification unreliable – there should be a very low threshold for seeking more reliable means of confirmation of identity. Consideration of personal traits such as skin color, hair color, tattoos, stature, features of disease and/or surgery, clothing and personal effects are typically not considered sufficient to provide independent identification. The INTERPOL Standing Committee on Disaster Victim Identification (DVI) provides assistance in this regard, indicating that the most reliable means are the three so-called primary identifiers: dental examination, fingerprints and DNA. Specific characteristics of prosthetic implants such as serial numbers, and the morphologic/radiologic appearances of surgical metalwork, when compared to antemortem data, can also be used to provide definitive identification (25,26).

Particular issues with identification of human remains can arise in the setting of extreme bodily fragmentation involving more than one individual in close proximity to another, with the potential for commingling. Heat damage will compound the problem. Larger body parts can typically be reliably united with the "parent" remains by persons with expertise in human anatomy, such as pathologists and/or forensic anthropologists. However, in some instances, where the tissue fragments are small or otherwise difficult to match up with other body parts, DNA analysis may be required to determine definitive confirmation of identity. Naturally, this can lead to a very expensive and time-consuming process, and often a pragmatic decision will need to be made regarding where to "draw the line".

Comparative dental examination forms the mainstay of identification in many air crash incidents, largely because the teeth are robust and incredibly resistant to the effects of traumatic injury, heat and decomposition. Examination can be made by both visual assessment and radiologic imaging, with comparison to antemortem dental records (26).

A detailed review of the identification of human remains and disaster victim identification is outside the scope of this chapter, and the reader is instead directed elsewhere for further information (see Chapter 17: 'Identification of the Deceased') (25).

FALLS TO EARTH AND OTHER LESS COMMONLY ENCOUNTERED AVIATION DEATHS

From time to time, individuals may accidentally fall or intentionally jump from flying or tethered aerial objects, and if their descent is uncontroled, or only partially controled, then impact with the ground poses a risk of extreme injury and death. However, notwithstanding the typical extreme magnitude of forces involved in such incidents, on occasion the external cutaneous marker of injury can be minimal to non-existent, particularly when the individual impacts a soft and forgiving surface such as snow or ploughed soil, and internal injuries to account for death may only be apparent upon internal autopsy examination and/or post-mortem radiologic imaging.

Lethal falls from height may be sustained by skydivers/wingsuit flyers/parachutists whose equipment fails, and unintentional falls from stowaways aboard aircraft, such as wheel-well occupants, who may fall at the time the undercarriage is lowered for landing on approach to the airport. Aircraft stowaways are also exposed to the risk of mechanical trauma, for example by way of interaction with the mechanism of retractable undercarriage, and to the effects of hypothermia and hypoxia during unprotected flight at high altitude.

Hot air balloons and dirigibles such as airships typically possess lower horizontal velocity and momentum than fixed wing and rotary wing aircraft, because their buoyancy does not depend upon rapid airflow over an aerofoil such as an aircraft wing or helicopter rotor blade. Should such aircraft impact to the ground, forces involved will therefore stem primarily from the vertical descent vector, and typically be less severe than that encountered in other forms of aviation because there may be some residual lift even though the aircraft is failing and falling to the ground. The extent of physical injuries sustained by persons on board will be modified accordingly.

Low-flying aircraft, including helicopters, fixed wing aircraft and balloons/dirigibles, are also exposed to the risk of strikes with ground-based objects such as power lines, high buildings and terrain, and birdlife. As well as the possibility of electrocution and possibly fire stemming from interaction with electrical cables, wire strikes may produce specific signs of damage to both the aircraft and occupants (28).

CONCLUSION

The pathologic investigation of aviation-associated fatalities plays an integral role in helping to determine the likely cause of the incident. Pathologic data are also key in assessment of the potential survivability of aircraft incidents and can help to drive future improvements in safety design. Even if there are no significant positive autopsy findings other than blunt force traumatic injuries, negative results can still be pivotal in the final assessment. Toxicological analyses are one of the key ancillary studies in relation to aviation death investigations.

While a rare occurrence, it is important to identify occult natural disease or other factors with the potential for incapacitation of pilots or other members of the aircrew, by way of morphologic appearances, toxicologic analyses and, on occasion, biochemical studies. Consideration should also be given to the possibility of arrhythmic cardiac disorders without discernible naked eye or light microscopic structural correlate, prompting the need for genetic analysis/molecular autopsy.

The pathologist will maximally fulfil their role if they work as part of a collaborative exercise involving other experts.

REFERENCES

1. Alexander Graham Bell, 1906.
2. Smeaton WA. Jean-François Pilâtre de Rozier, the first aeronaut. *Ann Sci* 1955; **11**(4): 349–55.
3. ICAO (International Civil Aviation Organization). Annual Report, 2019. The world of air transport in 2019. Available from: https://www.icao.int/annual-report-2019/Pages/the-world-of-air-transport-in-2019.aspx (Accessed 24 April 2023).
4. International Civil Aviation Organization. Accident statistics. Available from: https://www.icao.int/safety/iStars/Pages/Accident-Statistics.aspx (Accessed 24 April 2023).
5. US National Research Council. *Improving the Continued Airworthiness of Civil Aircraft: A Strategy for the FAA's Aircraft Certification Service*. Washington, DC: The National Academies Press, Washington; 1988.
6. Reason J. *Human Error*. Cambridge: Cambridge University Press; 1990
7. *Annex 13 (Aircraft Accident and Incident Investigation) to the Convention on International Civil Aviation (the 'Chicago Convention')*. International Civil Aviation Organization. Available from: https://applications.icao.int/postalhistory/annex_13_aircraft_accident_and_incident_investigation.htm:~:text=Annex%2013%20defines%20an%20accident,is%20classified%20as%20being%20missing (Accessed 24 April 2023).
8. *Annex 13 (Aircraft Accident and Incident Investigation) to the Convention on International Civil Aviation (the 'Chicago Convention'). Reference should also be made to applicable local death investigation legislation*. International Civil Aviation Organization. Available from: https://www.emsa.europa.eu/retro/Docs/marine_casualties/annex_13.pdf (Accessed 24 April 2023).
9. INTERPOL. Annexure 13: INTERPOL guidance: Numbering in disaster victim identification operations. 2018. Available from: https://www.interpol.int/content/download/5760/file/E%20DVI_Guide2018_Annexure13.pdf (Accessed 24 April 2023).
10. Griffiths CJ, Bellamy GD. Protection and radiography of heat affected teeth. *Forensic Sci Int* 1993; **60**(**1–2**): 57–60.
11. Australian Transport Safety Bureau, Australian Directorate of Defence Aviation and Air Force Safety. Hazards at aviation accident sites: Guidance for police and emergency personnel. 7th ed. 2017. Available from: https://www.atsb.gov.au/publications/2017/hazards-at-aviation-accident-sites/ (Accessed 24 April 2023).
12. Cullen SA, Turk EP. The value of postmortem examination of passengers in fatal aviation accidents. *Aviat Space Environ Med* 1980; **51**(**9, Pt 2**): 1071–3.
13. Snyder VS, Matshes EW. Assessment and diagnosis of trauma in the high cervical spine using dissection, radiography, computed tomography and magnetic resonance imaging. *Acad Forensic Pathol* 2014; 4(4): 532–44.
14. Lucas SB. The autopsy pathology of sepsis-related death. *Curr Diagnost Pathol* 2007; **13**: 375–88.
15. Palmiere C, Mangin P. Postmortem chemistry update part I. *Int J Legal Med* 2012; **126**(2): 187–98.
16. Palmiere C, Mangin P. Postmortem chemistry update part II. *Int J Legal Med* 2012; **126**(2): 199–215.
17. Hockenhull J, Dhillo W, Andrews R, et al. Investigation of markers to indicate and distinguish death due to alcoholic ketoacidosis, diabetic ketoacidosis and hyperosmolar hyperglycemic state using post-mortem samples. *Forensic Sci Int* 2012; **214**(**1–3**): 142–7.
18. Bellenkes A, Trenholm B, Jones N, et al. *The Naval Flight Surgeon's Pocket Reference to Aircraft Mishap Investigation*. North Atlantic Treaty Organization; Science and Technology Organization. 5th ed. Norfolk, VA, USA; 2001.
19. Cullen SA. *Injuries in Fatal Aircraft Accidents*. Paper presented at the RTO HFM Lecture Series on 'Pathological Aspects and Associated Biodynamics in Aircraft Accident Investigation', North Atlantic Treaty Organization; Science and Technology Organization, held in Madrid, Spain, 28–29 October 2004; Königsbrück, Germany, 2–3 November 2004, and published in Aspects and Associated Biodynamics in Aircraft Accident Investigation (RTO-EN-HFM-113). Educational Notes RDP. 2005. DOI: 10.14339.
20. Anderson HG. *The Medical and Surgical Aspects of Aviation*. London: Henry Frowde; 1919.
21. Krefft S. Who was at the controls when the fatal accident occurred? *Aerospace Med* 1970; **41**: 785–9.
22. Campman SC, Luzi SA. The sensitivity and specificity of control surface injuries in aircraft accident fatalities. *Am J Forensic Med Pathol* 2007; **28**(**2**): 111–15.
23. Huster KM, Müller A, Prohn MJ, et al. Medical risks in older pilots: a systematic review on incapacitation and age. *Int Arch Occup Environ Health* 2014; **87**(**6**): 567–78.
24. DeJohn CA, Wolbrink AM, Larcher JG. In-flight medical incapacitation and impairment of airline pilots. *Aviat Space Environ Med* 2006; 77(10): 1077–9.
25. INTERPOL Disaster Victim Identification Guide. 2018. Available from: https://www.interpol.int/content/download/589/file/18Y1344%20E%20DVI_Guide.pdf (Accessed 24 April 20233).
26. de Boer HH, Roberts J, Delabarde T, et al. Disaster victim identification operations with fragmented, burnt, or commingled remains: Experience-based recommendations. *Forensic Sci Res* 2020; 5(3): 191–201.
27. Hinchliffe J. Forensic odontology, Part 1. Dental identification. *Br Dent J* 2011; **210**(**5**): 219–24.
28. McConnell TS, Zumwalt RE, Wahe RE et al. Rare electrocution due to powerline contact in a hot-air balloon: comparison with fatalities from blunt trauma. *J Forensic Sci* 1992; 37(5): 1393–400.

CHAPTER

28

Custody and Restraint Deaths

Alfredo E. Walker

INTRODUCTION

The term 'death in custody' refers to a category of deaths in which the circumstances of the death place the decedent either in direct or indirect contact with law enforcement officers such as can occur during pursuit, apprehension or incarceration (1). The investigation of these deaths is complex and a uniform approach to their investigation and evaluation should be adopted by medical examiners, forensic pathologists and coroners to arrive at the correct certification of both cause and manner of death. Uniformity and consistency in the investigation of these deaths will ensure confidence in the independence of the investigating authority, the criminal justice system, and public health statistics by the general community (1). Deaths in custody have the potential to undergo great public scrutiny on how the fatal incident was (i) handled by law enforcement officials, (ii) investigated and (iii) managed by the medical examiner/forensic pathologist and coroner. It is for these reasons that a consistent approach **must** be adopted.

Ideally, the investigation of the circumstances of any death in custody **must occur** by an independent investigating agency such as the Special Investigation Unit (SIU) in the Province of Ontario, Canada (2), the Independent Office for Police Conduct and the Prison & Probation Ombudsman in the UK (4), or the Independent Policing Oversight Authority in Kenya (5). The SIU is a civilian law enforcement agency created in 1990. Its mission is to nurture public confidence in policing by making law enforcement officers accountable through rigorous scrutiny and independent investigation of their actions in cases that fall under SIU jurisdiction (2). The SIU has jurisdiction over municipal, regional and provincial police officers, special constables employed by the Niagara Parks Commission and peace officers with the Legislative Protective Service (2). The SIU is independent of any police service in Ontario and operates at arm's length from the Ministry of the Attorney General (2). Even though such organizations are independent, it is inevitable for their independence to be called into question at some time.

In 48 of the 58 counties in the state of California, USA, the duties of the sheriff intersect with the duties of the coroner (6). It is important to recognize that the coroner referred to in this chapter may well have different structure and function compared to other jurisdictions where a similar term is used (e.g. England & Wales – *see* "Chapter 12 – Principles of Investigation of War Crimes and Torture & Cruel, Inhuman and Degrading Treatment & Other Matters") The sheriff as coroner (sheriff-coroner) has the authority to both investigate and rule on cause and manner of death for deaths that may involve one or more of his/her deputies, or the death of a prisoner in a jail/prison under the sheriff's control (6). Apart from the obvious conflict of interest that arises from the overlapped functions of these two positions, a real potential for biased determinations exists. This fact was manifested in the removal of the medicolegal death investigation duties of a sheriff-coroner in San Joaquin County, California in 2018, following an investigation into the impartiality of his death certification in police-involved deaths (7). The investigation of that sheriff-coroner had been initiated by the county supervisors following the resignations of two forensic pathologists who had alleged that the sheriff-coroner had interfered with medicolegal death investigations and had pressured the two forensic pathologists to change their certifications of cause and manner in a case so that police officers were protected from any culpability (7). In that county and most other Californian counties, a forensic pathologist determines the cause of death for all sudden, suspicious or violent deaths **but** an elected sheriff-coroner decides on the manner of death (accident, homicide, suicide, natural or undetermined). In at least two cases, the sheriff had allegedly ignored the forensic pathologist's opinion that the manner of death should be classified as homicide and had certified them as accidents instead (7). An independent review of the sheriff-coroner system recommended that it be replaced by a medical examiner's office run by a board-certified forensic pathologist (8). This is a prime example of why a law enforcement agency should not investigate any death in which its personnel are involved.

The 2017 Position Paper of the US National Association of Medical Examiners (NAME) on Deaths in Custody made recommendations on the categorization, investigation, examination and reporting of such deaths (1). The critical information that should be gathered during the investigation includes enhanced autopsy procedures, guidance on death certification, parameters for statistical reporting and the release of information to the public (1).

DOI: 10.1201/9781003138754-30

The position paper proposed a definition of a death in custody as:

1. Any death that occurs under the perceived or physical control or restraint of a law enforcement officer, a correctional officer (including a private correctional officer), or an authorized employee or agent of a district juvenile secure facility or youth residential facility, including being:
    a. in pursuit
    b. under arrest
    c. in the process of being arrested
    d. detained
    e. in the process of being detained.
2. Incarcerated in, committed to, or on work release from a jail or correctional facility (including contract facility) or psychiatric hospital.
3. Committed to a juvenile secure facility.
4. Judicial executions.

Based on the results of a survey of the NAME membership, three categories of deaths in custody were offered: (i) pre-custody (pre-arrest), (ii) in-custody (from physical arrest to incarceration) and (iii) judicial executions.

PRE-CUSTODY DEATHS

Pre-custody (pre-arrest) deaths refer to any death in which the decedent perceived that there was restraint of his/her freedom of movement, as can occur during a casual street encounter, detention for questioning, chase (foot/vehicle) or verbal standoff with law enforcement officers (1). This category therefore includes all deaths that occur prior to the application of any physical restraint associated with the arrest, inclusive of non-lethal force such as pepper spray or conducted electrical weapons (CEWs) (*see* Chapters 85 and 86).

IN-CUSTODY DEATHS

This category refers to all deaths that occur within the interval from the point of physical contact with law enforcement officers to release from jail or prison (1). It covers all deaths that occur **whilst in actual physical custody** of the police, correctional services (both pre-trial and post-trial) or other agency. In-custody deaths can be further subclassified into five sub-categories:

1. Arrest
2. Transportation
3. Booking-in
4. Incarceration
5. Healthcare.

Arrest deaths refer to the sub-category of in-custody deaths that occur during a physical struggle that ensues during the attempted apprehension of an individual (1).

Transportation deaths refer to deaths that occur during the transportation of an individual from the scene of an incident to either a police station, jail or medical facility, with the latter also including transportation by ambulance (1).

The "booking-in phase" refers to the processing of an arrested individual who is being transferred from the custody of the arresting officer to a police station, jail, other temporary housing facility or correctional facility (1).

Incarceration deaths refer to deaths that occur following placement of an individual into a locked cell within a police station, jail or prison (1). The death of an individual who has been released from incarceration but may have died from injuries sustained while in custody is also classifiable as a death in custody and **must also** be investigated as a death in custody (1).

JUDICIAL EXECUTIONS

In jurisdictions where judicial executions are legal, the death of a sentenced individual by the state is classified as a death in custody (1). These judicial executions may be carried out by hanging, lethal injection, firing squad or electrocution (1). Local legislation in a particular jurisdiction will determine if these deaths fall under the jurisdiction of a medical examiner or coroner for investigation and even if the medical examiner/coroner does not have jurisdiction, they must still be classified as a death in custody (1). By definition, the manner of death in these cases is always classified as homicide since they are "*deaths at the hands of another*" but no criminal prosecution will ensue for those who carried out the court-mandated sentences since the executions were legally applied.

EXCITED DELIRIUM

Excited delirium (ED) or Excited Delirium Syndrome (ExDS) is a controversial entity that has been used to describe a constellation of signs and symptoms where a person who is acutely behaviorally disturbed displays violent behavior with a potentially fatal state of extreme agitation and delirium. The controversy highlights the differences in practice and usage between forensic pathologists using the term as a diagnosis for cause of death, and clinicians (e.g. first responders, emergency physicians, psychiatrists, and forensic physicians) who encounter patients who are acutely behaviorally disturbed and need to be able to distinguish between those who are simply violent and aggressive and those who need immediate medical care and intervention. The term was first used in 1985 in the *Journal of Forensic Sciences* journal article by Wetli and Fishbain who had described cocaine-induced psychosis and sudden death in seven recreational cocaine users (9).

ED has been invoked as a putative phenomenon to explain the death of an individual during physical interaction with law enforcement officers. It is typically diagnosed as a cause of death after the performance of a post-mortem examination in young, adult males who were physically restrained at the time of death, mostly by law enforcement personnel, with a disproportionate number being black (10,11). Agitated delirium/agitated delirium syndrome (AgDS) and Acute Behavioral Disturbance (ABD) are used in the literature as a synonym for ExDS. The various terms have been used interchangeably (11) by a number of different medical bodies in different jurisdictions. The risk factors for AgDS were identical to ExDS with the only exception being that ExDS was used almost exclusively in the post-mortem/forensic pathology literature where all cases were fatal, whereas both ExDS and AgDS have been both used in the clinical literature to describe the identical antemortem patient characteristics for both non-fatal and fatal cases (12). However, ExDS is far more likely to be used when aggressive restraint was applied, and the outcome is fatal (11). There is no existing evidence that ExDS is inherently lethal in the absence of aggressive restraint and only 2 percent of fatalities did not include a description of some form of restraint (11). There are no pathognomonic features to distinguish ExDS from AgDS.

Proponents of ED state that at-risk victims are those who use large quantities of stimulant drugs (cocaine or methamphetamine), are mentally ill (paranoid schizophrenia, manic depression), are non-compliant with their antipsychotic medications, exhibit bizarre behavior that precipitates telephone calls to the police, fail to respond appropriately to police presence with that failure necessitating the use of force to apprehend and continue to struggle during the apprehension (with apparent "superhuman" strength) despite attempts to restrain them, and appear impervious to pain. They frequently have acute drug intoxication (cocaine, methamphetamine, PCP and MDPV) (13), and are on antipsychotic medications which may increase the risk of death (14,15,16), in the context of many other factors such as positional asphyxia, hyperthermia, and/or catecholamine-induced fatal arrhythmias (13). ED in North America has become recognized as a police-related phenomenon and has been invoked as a cause of death in cases in which death had occurred during or shortly after restraint (physical, chemical, electric). The use of the term as a cause of death has not happened to the same extent in other jurisdictions. In other regions and jurisdictions, it has been used as a term by those working in psychiatric, emergency and clinical forensic medicine to identify those requiring immediate medical care rather than further restraint and detention, and may be a useful tool in preventing death, while accepting it is not a diagnosis.

The presentation of ED in the seven cases as described in the original journal article consisted of the progressive development of an acute onset of intense paranoia followed by bizarre and violent behavior that necessitated forcible restraint, frequently accompanied by unexpected strength and hyperthermia, with sudden fatal respiratory collapse that generally occurs within several minutes to an hour after being restrained (11). Five of the seven decedents had died in police custody and all seven had been restrained (six by police +/- assistance of bystanders and emergency room staff). All the decedents had died suddenly with respiratory arrest (17). Four of the seven decedents had been either "hog tied" or hobble restrained in the prone position which can impair breathing (17). The prone restraint was only mentioned in passing in the paper without any discussion of the role that restraint **may** have played in the deaths (17). This cohort of cases prompted the use of ED as a diagnosis, unique disease and cause of death without new scientific evidence to underpin this stance and in the years that followed, publications on cocaine-induced ED sought to seek new applications of the theory (17).

The bodies of 12 black women, who were presumed sex workers, had been discovered in the same geographic area in Miami between September 1986 and November 1988 (18). Almost all the decedents had low levels of cocaine on toxicologic screening and the majority of cases were classified as accidental deaths from cocaine intoxication. It was later suggested that these female decedents had died from the combination of sex and cocaine use with a claim that the post-mortem examinations had demonstrated conclusively that they had not been murdered. Without any evidential scientific basis, it was speculated that a combination of cocaine and a certain blood type found in black populations could have contributed to lethality through an unknown mechanism (17).

Despite police investigators' beliefs that a serial killer was responsible for the women's deaths, the theory that cocaine and orgasm produced lethal results continued to be promoted. Subsequent authors embraced the term and either modified its definition and criteria (11). Excited Delirium Syndrome (ExDS) was coined in 2006 by DiMaio and DiMaio (19).

At the end, a review of the initial 19 of those deaths by the Chief Medical Examiners, it was concluded that all were homicides (20). Fourteen of the cases which had initially been ruled accidents or unclassified were reclassified as homicides. Nine exhibited definitive signs of strangulation/asphyxiation with features of neck pressure in seven cases, pressure to the mouth in four and hemorrhages (petechiae) in the eyes (20,21). The reviewer was critical of the initial post-mortem examinations (22). All but one of the women were believed to have been killed by the same perpetrator (22,23). Charles Henry Williams, a convicted rapist, was identified as the primary suspect. He had been arrested in 1989 on an unrelated rape charge and was later charged with one of the murders but had died before he could stand trial (24).

There is substantial inconsistency about the use of the term. The phenomenon of ED has not received formal recognition by the medical fraternity. It is not recognized by the World Health Organization (WHO), the American Psychiatric Association (APA), the American Medical Association (AMA) or the American Academy of Emergency Medicine (AAEM) and it is not listed in the Diagnostic and Statistical Manual of Mental Disorders of the APA or the International Classification of Diseases (ICD) (25). It has however previously been accepted and referred to by medical bodies predominantly involved in the care and management of the acutely behaviorally disturbed and includes the American College of Emergency Physicians (ACEP) (26), the Royal College of Emergency Medicine, the Faculty of Forensic & Legal Medicine of the Royal College of Physicians, and the College of Paramedics.

A 2017 report from the United Kingdom (UK) on the independent review of deaths and serious injury in police custody recommended that ED should never be used independently as a term that communicates a cause of death and that this terminology should be avoided when communicating guidance to police officers (27).

In 2020, the UK Forensic Science Regulator (FSR) sought advice from the Forensic Pathology Specialty Group (FPSG) and Forensic Pathology Specialty Advisory Committee (SAC) of the Royal College of Pathologists and issued guidance on the diagnosis of ED (28). The guidance clearly stated that ED must not be used as a sole cause of death. It has invoked controversy since it has been applied in some cases where other important pathologic mechanisms such as positional asphyxia and trauma may have more appropriate descriptions.

The June 23, 2021 statement by the UK Royal College of Psychiatrists stated that it does not support the use of either excited or agitated delirium since no empirical evidential basis exists for the use of either term, and use of either term constitutes racial discrimination (29). However, a subsequent statement of July 16, 2021 indicated that, given the particular nature of the specific issues raised and the topic covered in the statement, the RCPsych had taken the decision to withdraw it, pending further consideration of the issues (29).

These conflicting opinions and references have resulted in further reviews being undertaken as to how these terms should be used including a proposed Delphi study; the study purpose of which is stated as "Management of ABD in the UK is currently the subject of debate. Many of the features used to identify patients at risk with presentations of ABD have emerged from publications focused on ED, which is not recognized as a diagnosis in the UK. In an effort to distinctly separate the UK presentation of ABD from the USA data on ExD, there is a clear need to establish consensus across stakeholder organizations regarding the identification of ABD in a UK setting, and to establish when and how ABD guidance should be applied."

A group of US-based neurologists wrote that the term ED is a misappropriation of medical terminology that is used by law enforcement officers to legitimize police brutality and retrospectively explain certain deaths that occur in police custody (12). As an alternative, "sudden death in restraint syndrome," was suggested by the UK Independent Advisory Panel on Deaths in Custody as a means of enhancing clarity (29).

Following the outcome of a 2009 internal review by a task force of the ACEP, ED was accepted by the organization as a real, unique syndrome (30). The leader of the task force commented that only two medical specialities, the coroner and emergency medicine physicians, are involved with the syndrome, and that it was only in the preceding two or three years that the general population had become aware of it. The descriptive symptoms of the alleged condition were attributed to agitation (usually), uncontrolable speaking/shouting usually, pacing/running without purpose, issuance of verbal and/or physical threats, profuse sweating, the appearance of being ill and lack of self-control. Often this diagnosis is ascribed in association with mental disorders or the use of stimulant drugs such as cocaine (31). Although the ACEP explicitly recognized ED as a medical diagnosis, its diagnostic criteria are considered unclear and to date no rigorous studies have been performed to validate it as a medical diagnosis.

In response to the ACEP's 2009 White paper, the 2020 position paper of the APA stated that although the concept of ED/ExDS has been invoked in a number of cases to explain/justify injury or death for those who have died in police custody, it has been disproportionally applied to black men (32). Despite the ACEP's explicit recognition of the entity as a medical condition, the criteria are unclear and no rigorous studies that validate ED as a medical diagnosis have ever occurred (32).

DSM-5 recognizes delirium, hyperactive type, but the symptoms of this condition differ in many ways from the symptoms typically attributed to ED (e.g. superhuman strength, impervious to pain, etc.). It was further noted that ExDS itself "*is too non-specific to meaningfully describe and convey information about a person.*" The conclusion was that "*excited delirium*" should not be used until a clear set of diagnostic criteria are validated.

Case descriptions of both ExDS and AgDS are unsystematic with almost all the published research on the topic being on retrospective case studies and series (33).

In 2021, the AMA issued policy guidance for the very first time that strongly opposed the use of ED following a special meeting of its House of Delegates (34). The guidance warned against the use of ED as a medical diagnosis. Specifically, the guidance confirmed the AMA's stance that the evidence did not support ED as an official diagnosis and opposed its use until a clear set of diagnostic criteria has been established. It denounced the use of ED as sole justification for the use of excessive force by law enforcement. It also advised against the application of certain pharmacological interventions to treat ED in the field, without a legitimate medical reason and solely for a law enforcement purpose. In that regard, it underscored the importance of emergency physician-led oversight of the associated medical emergencies in the field and opposed the use of sedative/hypnotic and dissociative drugs (such as ketamine) as an intervention for an agitated individual in a law enforcement setting, without a legitimate medical reason. In so doing, it recognized the risk that sedative/hypnotic and dissociative drugs possess in relation to an individual's age, underlying medical conditions, and potential drug interactions when used outside a hospital setting by a non-physician. Reports that illustrated a pattern of use of ED to justify pharmacological interventions when excessive police force was disproportionately applied in cases where black men died in law enforcement custody, were addressed. The new policy urged law enforcement officers and frontline emergency medical service personnel to participate in training overseen by EMS medical directors that includes de-escalation techniques and the appropriate use of pharmacological intervention for agitated individuals in out-of-hospital settings. Medical and behavioral health specialists were urged to serve as first responders and decision-makers in medical and mental health emergencies, instead of law enforcement officers. It called for the administration of any pharmacological treatments in an out-of-hospital setting to be undertaken in an equitable, evidence-based, anti-racist and stigma-free manner.

The understanding of the use of the terms AgD, ABD and ED are continually being reviewed and refined (*see also* "Chapter 72 – Acute Behavioral Disturbance and Excited Delirium Syndrome"). ED or ExDS is not a diagnosis and not a cause of death that should be used, but for clinicians the features it describes remains (as long as used appropriately) a means of identifying those at risk and directing toward appropriate medical intervention and thus saving lives. It is clear however that this debate will continue.

RESTRAINT

Restraint is employed in law enforcement to effect control of an individual to facilitate arrest. The appropriate methods to be utilized must strike an acceptable balance between minimization of the risk of injury or death while maximizing the effectiveness of achieving rapidity of control. There are two broad categories of restraint that can be employed: 1. Physical restraint and 2. Chemical restraint.

The modalities of physical restraint can be:

(i) **manual** (prone position with or without supplemental ligature application; neck holds or other methods to incapacitate),

(ii) **use of implements** (hand/leg cuffs/ligatures, restraint suits, spit hoods, batons),

(iii) **firearms** (standard weapons, impact rounds, Kevlar belts) and

(iv) **conducting electrical devices** (TASERs, stun guns).

The chemical modalities of restraint consist of the (i) use of lacrimal agents and chemical irritants (pepper spray) and (ii) sedative drugs.

Physical restraint

Physical restraint procedures can consist of the application of handcuffs to the wrists (either in front of or behind the body), ankles, prone positioning of the body, hog-tied/hobbled position, restraint of the extremities while in the prone position, the application of downward pressure on the back while in a prone position and the use of spit hoods.

The prone maximal restraint position (PMRP) refers to the hog-tied or hobble restraint position in which the subject is forced into the prone position and handcuffed at the wrists behind the back, shackled at the ankles with connection of the handcuffs to the ankle cuffs via a chain or other ligature.

Individuals have died while restrained in the prone position. "Manhandling" refers to the use of force in the form of blows to the body, submission or choke holds, tackling, use of the body weight of officer(s) to pin an individual down onto ground in a prone position. The outcome of restraint is dependent on its type, duration, the amount of force applied and the anatomic region of application (face, neck, torso and appendages). Individuals who die while being restrained in these positions would fulfill the criteria for positional asphyxia with a post-mortem diagnosis of restraint asphyxia (27, 35). The question to be answered is "Did cardiorespiratory collapse occur during active restraint or shortly thereafter?"

Spit hoods

A spit hood, spit mask, mesh hood, spit guard or spit and bite guard (SBG) is a restraint device that covers the mouth, face and head of a restrained person to prevent the assault of law enforcement officers, correctional officers and the public through spitting and/or biting (37). It consists of a breathable mesh (nylon in most cases) that loosely covers the face and head and is kept in place by an occluding elastic band around their neck. Some spit hoods have a plastic component that covers the nose and mouth. Although they have been used by law enforcement officers for years (often in jails and prisons), substantial controversy exists about their use, with often polarized views about their utility, safety, and encroachment on human rights between civil /human rights activists. The predominantly law enforcement proponents of their use highlight concerns about the risks of transmission of infection and subsequent need for prophylaxis by law enforcement professionals exposed to biological fluids (37). It has been stated that the infectious risk that spitting poses to law enforcement is often overstated. SBGs will not be used on subjects' who are either vomiting or bleeding from the mouth or nose. The device should only be applied when the subject is under control, whether through the use of multi-officer restraint techniques and/or handcuffs. Application of the SBG requires sufficient officers working together to safely control the subject. As with all restraint tactics, officers are reminded of the dangers associated with positional asphyxia and ABD, and any restraint should be for the minimum time possible in the circumstances.

Spit hoods can contribute to in-custody deaths in several ways. Their use, in conjunction with other restraints, can lead to asphyxiation. By covering a person's face, the mask makes it more difficult for first responders to monitor their breathing. At times, suspects might bleed or vomit into the mask, clogging the mesh so they are unable to breathe. An SBG should not be allowed to become saturated or filled with fluid or solids of any description. It is potentially dangerous to restrain a subject in the prone position with a spit mask *in situ*. In the wake of the death of an unarmed black man who died in Rochester, New York State in March 2020 after being hooded by police and held face down for two minutes following a call for help when he was in mental health crisis, Amnesty International condemned the use of spit hoods and stated that spit hoods are particularly dangerous when applied to an individual who is in distress (38).

Chemical irritants and lacrimal agents

The use of oleoresin capsicum (OC) spray devices (i.e. pepper spray, pepper mace, OC, capsaicin) by law enforcement to control suspects using sublethal force has raised the question whether exposure to capsaicin, a noxious irritant, can cause or contribute to unexpected sudden deaths in custody (39). Capsaicin stimulates nociceptors in exposed mucous membranes to produce intense pain, particularly involving the conjunctiva, and generates systemic physiologic and behavioral responses consonant with such extreme discomfort.

The International Association of Chiefs of Police (IACP) had issued an executive brief in 1994 on the use of OC which was based on the work of a task force which had been established to review the role of OC in precipitating death in arrestees in an excited state (40). Thirty incidents in the US between August 1990 and December 1993 were identified in which death had followed spraying with OC. The 30 cases shared some common characteristics in that all suspects behaved in a combative or bizarre manner, drugs or alcohol use was involved, OC spray was either ineffective or less than effective, other means of restraint were used, and all deaths occurred immediately or soon after the confrontation. The IACP review concluded that OC was not the cause of death or contributing factor in all 30 cases, but the subjects had died from asphyxia, drug-related factors, or drug-related diseases. The four leading causes of in-custody deaths include positional asphyxiation, cocaine intoxication, ED, and neuroleptic malignant syndrome (40). In contrast, Steffee et al. had determined that OC had been a contributing factor in unexpected in-custody deaths among those with ABD, particularly those with heart disease (39).

As with any other in-custody death, a thorough autopsy and toxicologic analysis, coupled with evaluation of the pre-mortem chain of events, post-exposure symptomatology, and the extent of natural disease processes, will help to reveal the role of OC spray as unrelated, contributory, or causative (39).

Chemical restraint and sedatives

The administration of therapeutic drugs is a means of intervention sometimes employed to treat subjects who exhibit ABD during apprehension, in scenarios in which intoxication with stimulant drugs, narcotics, ethanol or prescription medications are highly likely (41). Neuroleptic drugs (such as haloperidol) are used but can cause hypotension, prolongation of the QT interval and ventricular arrhythmias. Benzodiazepines are a better alternative to effect sedation in this scenario but can effect respiratory arrest, especially in the context of ethanol intoxication (41). As such, in the setting of putative ED and prone restraint, chemical restraint with either neuroleptic agents or benzodiazepines is potentially risky and requires careful medical supervision. As such, they should be employed cautiously and with full medical support to prevent an adverse outcome (41).

Ketamine, a dissociative anesthetic with potent sedative properties and a high rate of causing respiratory distress, is often administered to subjects who exhibit ABD with the most common adverse effects being respiratory-related events and hypersalivation (42). When administered in a controled environment for procedural sedation, ketamine is safe and well-tolerated with rare loss of airway or respiratory drive (42). However, pre-existing co-ingestant drugs may alter its pharmacological effect (43) and result in a fatal outcome of its administration (44). Intramuscular administration of ketamine to agitated subjects in a pre-hospital setting, in the context of concomitant cocaine intoxication, was associated with a statistically significant 5.75-fold increased rate of subsequent intubation in the emergency department (44). "Complications of ketamine administration following forcible restraint" was the ascribed cause of death of an unarmed 23-year-old black man in Aurora, Colorado in 2019, who had been stopped by police while walking home from a store in their response to a "suspicious person" report. He was administered ketamine and had suffered a cardiac arrest *en route* to hospital and died three days later.

Although ketamine has a role in the management of agitation in the pre-hospital setting, education of emergency personnel and utilization of ketamine protocols should be employed to aid in safe and effective pharmacotherapy and provide guidance on the management of adverse events (42).

PHYSICAL RESTRAINT

Sudden death of individuals who were clinically thought to have ED has occurred during physical restraint in the prone position (45,46) with restraint asphyxia being invoked as their cause of death. However, conflicting physiological studies have been used as the evidential base with some authors opining that it is unlikely that positional restraint is the only mechanism. As such, restraint asphyxia has not achieved universal agreement as a distinct pathological entity. Intuitively, it is not unreasonable to postulate that restricted ventilation superimposed on extreme, prolonged physical exertion with associated hypoxemia, lactic acidosis, catecholamine surge and hyperkalemia, are a potentially lethal combination, either alone or in combination with other significant factors such as pre-existent cardiovascular disease (gross/microscopic or genetic).

In their experimental study of healthy males, Chan et al. reported no clinically relevant changes in oxygen or ventilation in the restraint position (47). This study utilized healthy male volunteers aged 18–40 years who were exercised to achieve a heart rate of 167 bpm before they were restrained. However, a heart rate of 167 bpm cannot be considered maximal physiological stressing of the heart in an average person, since a tachycardia of 200 bpm is possible. Additionally, the findings of this study could not be extrapolated directly to the real-life situation where an individual exhibiting the putative features of ED is physically restrained in the prone position.

The study methodology could not take into account any underlying medical conditions, delirium, struggle and/or body position that can cause respiratory compromise. Thus, this and other studies on restraint asphyxia cannot accurately reproduce all the complex factors that operate in a typical law enforcement restraint scenario, such as extreme exhaustion, biochemical/metabolic derangements, cardiorespiratory disease, drug intoxication and body habitus.

Some of the authors of the 2009 ACEP publication included those who had published studies in the preceding decade which had attempted to demonstrate that virtually any level of restraint-related chest compression (up to 210 lbs) did not result in asphyxia (48). That publication was more concerned with the management of an agitated aggressive patient in the emergency room setting rather than fatal cases, but it inadvertently lent credibility to the proposal that fatal ExDS in the setting of restraint must involve an unidentifiable lethal pathophysiological mechanism. It also erroneously assumed that restraint-related asphyxia does not have the potential to alter cardiorespiratory function in an agitated patient such that it can cause death, a position that is not supported by other literature (11).

Strommer et al. reported on their comprehensive analysis of pooled data from all reported cases of ExDS and AgDS in the medical literature. A case database was created to include case demographics, mental illness, the use of force, drug intoxication and survival outcomes. The results determined that the most published current information indicated that some occult pathophysiological process is at play in ED deaths and no evidence exists to support ExDS as a cause of death **in the absence of restraint.** As such, **restraint-related asphyxia must be considered a more likely cause of death in the setting of aggressive restraint of someone who fits the profile of excited/agitated delirium.** The results indicated that ExDS is a diagnostic construct devoid of predictive value to distinguish it from AgDS, except for the presence of aggressive restraint and a high risk of death. The report also indicated that a diagnosis of ExDS and potentially fatal restraint are inextricably interwoven and although ExDS and AgDS are used interchangeably in the literature with largely identical presentations (12,49), the odds of an ExDS diagnosis were nearly 10 times greater that an AgDS diagnosis in the event of a fatality (8).

The authors determined there was no literature-based justification for the two separate diagnoses and recommended that ExDS be abandoned as a diagnosis to prevent systematic error in cause of death determinations (11). This recommendation was made since fatal ExDS is essentially AgDS with superimposed aggressive and potentially fatal restraint. It was further suggested that agitated delirium replace ExDS **in all instances,** with modification to reflect the degree of restraint used. The suggested modifications are (i) AgDS without restraint, (ii) AgDS with mild restraint and (ii) AgDS with aggressive restraint.

According to this, the ascribed manner of death in fatal cases of AgDS with restraint should be either homicide or undetermined but not natural or accident. It was proposed that the high frequency of aggressive restraint in ExDS is the most probable mechanism that was driving the association between ExDS and death (11). The most aggressive forms of restraint such as manhandling, handcuffing and hog/hobble tying increased the odds of an ExDS diagnosis by 7 and 29 times whereas a diagnosis of AgDS was only 2.5 times more likely to be diagnosed when less aggressive forms of restraint such as pepper spray, 4-point restraint and so on were used.

The 2021 publication of Steinberg reinforced the opinion that the precise role of physical restraints and their impact on respiratory physiology and cardiac output remains unclear. Although experiments attempted to reproduce the impact of prone restraint and PMRP on those parameters, those experiments were typically performed on healthy subjects in situations that could not replicate the exact conditions in which deaths have occurred. Since agitated individuals may be in a state of metabolic acidosis, restraint in the prone position may exacerbate the situation through inadequate ventilation and decreased cardiac output to result in pulseless electrical activity (PEA) and asystolic cardiac arrest (50).

Additionally, Steinberg stated that "restraint asphyxia" and "prone asphyxia" do not provide a correct description of the condition since positional and/or restraint-associated limitation of breathing and gas exchange are only part of the problem. "Prone restraint cardiac arrest" was offered as an alternative since in that setting, cardiac arrest occurs from a combination of factors that include high oxygen demand, a need for increased CO_2 removal, significant metabolic acidosis and significant decreases in both ventilation and cardiac output (50). Restraint in the prone position superimposed on pre-existent metabolic acidosis represents a potential physiologic catastrophe. This is supported by careful review of all publications which suggest that sudden death in agitated individuals who are restrained in the prone position, is most likely due to metabolic acidosis exacerbated by inadequate ventilation and decreased cardiac output. The combination of these derangements can lead to PEA or asystolic cardiac arrest which are commonly observed in cardiac arrest associated with asphyxia and metabolic acidosis (51). Asystole and PEA are the primary arrhythmias associated with the "4Hs and 4Ts." The 4Hs consist of hypoxia, hypo/hyperkalemia, hydrogen ion (acidosis), hypo/hyperthermia and hypovolemia. The 4Ts consist of tension pneumothorax, cardiac tamponade, thrombosis (coronary and pulmonary) and toxins (poisons). The probability of survival after asystole or PEA cardiac arrest is extremely low (estimated at 4.4%) even with attempted resuscitation (CPR), advanced cardiac life support (ACLS) and treatment of reversible conditions. The underlying causes of sudden cardiac death are primarily associated with the induction of ventricular fibrillation and ventricular tachycardia rather than asystole and PEA arrest.

Neck hold restraints

Neck hold restraints are employed by law enforcement officers to temporarily incapacitate or render an individual unconscious. For this, two types of neck holds can be employed, the choke hold or strangle hold. The choke hold refers to the application of enough pressure on the neck to restrict the airway. The stranglehold refers to effecting restriction of blood flow to the brain by applying pressure on both sides of the neck to compromise the carotid arteries (52). Tactics involve the application of force around the neck, pressure on the back of the torso while in the prone position, and knee-to-neck holds.

The human brain requires at least 15–20 percent of the total blood circulation with some parts of the brain being vulnerable to permanent ischemic injury when delivery drops to half of that (53). The carotid artery supplies 70 percent of the cerebral blood flow with the passage of 600–700 mL per minute (54). The most important mechanism for loss of consciousness is decrease in cerebral blood flow (55). Although there are many adaptive mechanisms to preserve cerebral perfusion (53,56), there is no failsafe for the bilateral loss of carotid arterial blood flow. Additionally, stimulation of the carotid sinus baroreceptors may cause bradycardia, hypotension and decreased cerebral blood flow (55). Loss of consciousness can occur with interruption of cerebral arterial blood supply for a minimum of 4 seconds with only 6 kg being necessary to compress the carotid arteries (57). 250 mmHg is required for collapse of the carotid artery whereas collapse of the trachea requires 6 times that (58).

Compression and occlusion of the carotid arteries have been demonstrated by both clinician and researchers to cause pathology. Studies in animal models have been used as stroke models (59). Mechanical compression of the carotid arteries can cause devastating disabling embolic strokes from dislodgement of atheromatous plaques in the arteries, seizures and death. Mechanical trauma of the cervical blood vessels can cause cardiologic and delayed neurologic sequelae (such as strokes) which can occur some time after an arterial dissection which makes it difficult to associate the stroke with the preceding chokehold (60).

The implication that there is a safe way for law enforcement officers to restrain using carotid manipulation or traumatic manipulation of cerebral blood flow in any form is false (60) as the potential for neurologic sequelae exists from oxygen deprivation, embolic risk from mechanism trauma of arterial wall and arrhythmia (60). Thus, the possibility of devastating consequences from the application of neck restraint is too high to merit its use under any circumstance (60). A 2021 publication by three neurologists stated that the current understanding of the brain, carotid neurophysiology and the clinical effects of carotid compression does not support the safe use of choke holds or strangleholds (60). However, proponents of neck restraint as a law enforcement restraint tactic claim that it is a safer and more humane alternative to other forms of pacification (40).

The correlation of post-mortem findings with historic accounts of an incident that includes neck compressions is critical to assessing the role (if any) played by the neck hold in causing death (61). If vascular compression from a neck restraint hold directly leads to death, unconsciousness will occur during the application of the hold with no return of consciousness on release (61). Purposeful activity or verbalization following release of the neck hold indicates that the neck hold did not directly cause death (61).

Some studies have suggested that the PMRP can induce changes on oxygen saturation following physical exertion and may be the basis of positional asphyxia and some arrest-related deaths (35,46,62) while later studies that used more sophisticated direct measurements reported that PMRP did not produce physiological respiratory compromise (47,48,63,64). It was reported that no clinically important limitations of metabolic or ventilatory function were seen in generally physically fit volunteers after 60 seconds of maximum struggling in the PMRP (65).

CONDUCTED ELECTRICAL WEAPONS

Electrical control devices use electricity to effect compliance through pain or incapacitation through neuromuscular mechanisms (61). Electrically induced pain compliance is the basis for the effectiveness of the stun gun (61) which carries a high voltage, low amperage current through relatively superficial tissue and stimulates pain fibers as it travels between two narrowly spaced electrodes which are directly applied to the skin surface, typically 2.5–5 cm (1–2 inches) apart (66). Cardiac capture but no ventricular fibrillation has been documented in pigs under experimental conditions although no adult human deaths have been ascribed directly to the electrical effect of a stun gun (61). For efficacy, a law enforcement officer needs to be in close proximity to the subject for direct application of the electrodes onto the skin. Stun guns can be ineffective against those with high pain tolerance or insensitivity.

Electricity has also been used to effect incapacitation through involuntary contraction of skeletal muscle by stimulation of alpha motor neurons in electromuscular disruption (61). Electricity is delivered via dart-like electrodes (probes) which are propelled from a device to which they are tethered, to facilitate delivery of an electric charge from a distance to ensure physical separation between the subject and law enforcement officer. The effectiveness of these CEWs is greater than 90 percent (61). Depressions of the skin, abrasions and contusions are possible injuries from the application of a stun gun, the latter accompanying an abrasion on forceful application (67–69).

Although numerous similar devices are on the market, the forerunner of current CEWs was designed in the 1970s as the "Thomas A Swift Electric Rifle" (TASER) and multiple iterations and models have been subsequently developed. Three modalities of effect exist: (i) the direct effect of the electrical current on the tissues, (ii) conversion of electrical injury to thermal injury and (iii) injuries sustained from falls precipitated by generalized muscular contraction (70). Handgun-like models have both probe deployment and stun gun modes. Currently, the most popular is the TASER X26 which was introduced in 2003. Activation by pulling the trigger results in deployment of a pair of probes by a blast of nitrogen. Both probes are tethered to the device by a conducting wire. The darts are propelled at a slightly offset angle to ensure separation. The device is most effective when the interprobe distance in around 35.5 cm which can be achieved from a target distance of 2.4–3 meters using a standard cartridge (71). The most commonly used cartridges have a maximum range of 6.4–7.6 meters but some models have a maximum range of 10.5 meters. However, the usual range of deployment is 3–4.5 meters (71). Embedding of the probes in the skin, subcutaneous fat and or clothing near the skin completes a circuit which allows passage of a current between the electrodes. The flow of the current stimulates alpha motor neurons which cause involuntary contraction of skeletal muscles and hence incapacitation. The observable effect of the involuntary muscular contraction will be influenced by the spread of the probes and the area of the body through which the current flows. Contraction of large muscle groups results in maximal incapacitation and prevents further aggressive behavior by the subject. A single pull of the X26 delivers an electrical discharge with a 5-second duration complex wave form. The typical injury is a simple puncture from the dart; an abrasion may also occur of the cylinder from which the probe projects, if it strikes the skin with sufficient force (69,72,73). Apart from these cutaneous injuries, secondary injuries from the discharge of a CEW are uncommon (61) but penetrating injuries of the eye and skull have been reported (74,75). Serious injuries and death from CEWs are rare but serious blunt force and fatality have occurred from falls associated with CEW-induced incapacitation. The fatalities were due to head injuries (61).

The potential impact of CEW exposure on respiratory and/or cardiovascular function has been the focus of several studies that involve human subjects. The available published data suggest that CEW exposures have minimal impact on these systems (76). No deaths or intensive care unit (ICU) admissions were recorded in a review of 26 CEW deaths in Paris (70). The first indirect glimpse of TASER's experience on cardiac effects was obtained from 650 000 of cases of human volunteer subjects from CEW training procedures with reports of insignificant changes in cardiac function (77).

A 2021 publication on the outcome of a systematic review of 33 studies on the use of CEWs found no evidence that electrical weapon exposure is associated with adverse health outcomes (78). However, most of the existing studies reviewed had recruited healthy and physically fit individuals and it is unlikely that the existing evidence constitutes a good representation of real-life field situations. Based on the published findings, the risk for adverse health outcomes due to CEW exposure is currently estimated as low but with the aforementioned caveat.

CONCLUSION

Accurate certification of cause and manner of death for certain categories of deaths in custody that involve agitation/delirium, physical exertion, the application of one/more modalities of physical restraint, chemical restraint, restraint in the prone position (with/without hog-tying/hobbling), application of force on the back of the torso, intoxication by stimulant drug(s), underlying psychotic psychiatric illness, and underlying natural disease that predispose to sudden cardiac death, remains a complex procedure and the approach to it must be evidence-based to ensure acceptable valid determinations. However, the issue of certifying arrest-related deaths in custody can be adequately addressed through preventive measures that must start with the education of law enforcement officers as to the inherent risks associated with the application of physical, irritant chemical, pharmacological and electrical restraints in individuals with acute behavioral disorders. Of specific importance, they must be informed that physical restraint of a subject in the prone position, PMRP or the application of a spit hood, must all be avoided and rather the subject should be placed in a seated position and handcuffed with their hands in front of them, attached to a belt (41).

REFERENCES

1. Mitchell RA, Diaz F, Goldfogel GA, et al. National Association of Medical Examiners Position Paper: Recommendations for the Definition, Investigation, Postmortem Examination, and Reporting of Deaths in Custody. *Acad Forensic Pathol* 2017; 7(4): 604–18.
2. The Special Investigations Unit of Ontario. Available from: *https://www.siu.on.ca/en/unit.php* (Accessed September 2023).
3. Independent Office for Police Conduct. What we do. Available from: https://www.policeconduct.gov.uk/about-us/what-we-do (Accessed September 2023).
4. The Prisons and Probation Ombudsman. Available from: https://www.ppo.gov.uk/ (Accessed September 2023).
5. The Independent Policing Overview Authority. Available from: https://www.ipoa.go.ke/ (Accessed September 2023).
6. California State Association of Counties. Available from: *https://www.counties.org/county-office/sheriff-coroner* (Accessed September 2023).
7. KQED. San Joaquin County Sheriff Stripped of Role in Death Investigations. Available from: *https://www.kqed.org/news/11664465/san-joaquin-county-sheriff-stripped-of-role-in-death-investigations* (Accessed September 2023).
8. Mitchell R, Jnr. *San Joaquin County Coroner Review and Audit*. April 10, 2018.
9. Wetli CV, Fishbain DA. Cocaine-induced psychosis and sudden death in recreational cocaine users. *J Forensic Sci* 1985; 30(3): 873–80.
10. American Psychiatric Association. Position Statement on Concerns About Use of the Term "Excited Delirium" and Appropriate Medical Management in Out-of-Hospital Contexts; 2020.
11. Strömmer EM, Leith W, Zeegers MP. The role of restraint in fatal excited delirium: a research synthesis and pooled analysis. *Forensic Sci Med Pathol* 2020; **16(4)**: 680–92.
12. Imam SF, Patel H, Mahmoud M, et al. Bath salts intoxication: a case series. *J Emerg Med* 2013; **45**: 361–5.
13. Grant JR, Southall PE, Mealey J, et al. Excited delirium deaths in custody: past and present. 2009; *Am J Forensic Med Pathol* **30(1)**: 1–5.
14. Garcia-Roberts G. *Is excited delirium killing coked-up, stun-gunned Miamians?* Miami New Times. Available from: https://www.miaminewtimes.com/news/is-excited-delirium-killing-coked-up-stun-gunned-miamians-6367399 (Accessed 22 September 2023).
15. Budhu J, O'Hare M, Saadi A. How "excited delirium" is misused to justify

police brutality. Brookings; August 10, 2020. Available from: https://www.brookings.edu/articles/how-excited-delirium-is-misused-to-justify-police-brutality/#:~:text=The%20problem%20is%20twofold%3A%20It,police%20aggression%20that%20is%20unwarranted. (Accessed 22 September 2023).

16. Kraines SH. Bell's mania. Am J Psychiatry 1934; **91(1)**: 29–40.
17. Physicians for Human Right Report 2022. Excited Delirium" and Deaths in Police Custody: The Deadly Impact of a Baseless Diagnosis. March 2022. Available from: *https://phr.org/our-work/resources/excited-delirium/* (Accessed 22 September 2023).
18. Walker A, Dewar H, *Cocaine-Sex Deaths in Dade Probed, Miami News*, Nov. 24, 1988. Available from: https://www.newspapers.com/search/?query=Cocaine-Sex%20Deaths%20Dade%20Probed&t=5565 (Accessed 22 September 2023).
19. DiMaio TG, DiMaio VJ. *Excited delirium syndrome cause of death and prevention*. Boca Raton: CRC Press, Taylor & Francis; 2006.
20. Goudreau, R. Coroner: Somebody Killed 19 women," *Miami Herald*, May 31.
21. Donnelly J. Suspect in Murder of Prostitutes Speaks Out, *Miami Herald*, May 9, 1993.
22. Gehrke G. *"18 Killings Leave Families Struggling with Uncertainty," Miami Herald*, Jun. 18, 1989; Barry Bearak, "Eerie Deaths of 17 Women Baffle Miami," *Los Angeles Times*, May 14, 1989. Available from: *https://www.latimes.com/archives/la-xpm-1989-05-14-mn-413-story.html* (Accessed 24 September 2023).
23. Tatiana M. With, *"Absence of justice: case closed on suspected killer of 32," Miami Herald*, Sept. 25, 1994.
24. AAEM Excited Delirium Statement." AAEM. Available from: https://www.aaem.org/statements/excited-delirium/ (Accessed 22 September 2023).
25. Excited Delirium Task Force. White Paper Report to the Council and Board of Directors on Excited Delirium Syndrome, American College of Emergency Physicians, Sep 10, 2009. Available from: https://www.prisonlegalnews.org/media/publications/acep_report_on_excited_delirium_syndrome_sept_2009.pdf (Accessed 22 September 2023).
26. Rt Hon Dame Elish Angiolini DBC, QC. Report of the Independent Review of the Deaths and Serious Injury in Police Custody, Jul 2017. Available from: https://assets.publishing.service.gov.uk/government/uploads/system/uploads/attachment_data/file/655401/Report_of_Angiolini_Review_ISBN_Accessible.pdf (Accessed 22 September 2023).
27. Forensic Science Regulator Guidance: The Use of 'Excited Delirium' as a Cause of Death; FSR-G-231, 2000. Available from: https://assets.publishing.service.gov.uk/government/uploads/system/uploads/attachment_data/file/929746/Excited_Delirium_Guidance_2.pdf (Accessed 22 September 2023).
28. Royal College of Psychiatrists. Statement on Acute Behavioural Disturbance (ABD). June 23, 2021. Available from: "Statement on Acute Behavioural Disturbance (ABD)". Royal College of Psychiatrists. June 23, 2021. Available from: *https://www.rcpsych.ac.uk/news-and-features/latest-news/detail/2021/07/16/follow-up-on-our-statement-regarding-acute-behavioural-disturbance-(abd)?searchTerms=excited%20delirium)* (Accessed 22 September 2023).
29. Baker D Making sense of 'Excited Delirium' in cases of death after police contact. *Policing: A Journal of Policy and Practice*. **12(4)**: 361–71.
30. Hoffman L. *ACEP Recognizes Excited Delirium Syndrome. Emergency Medicine News* 2009; **31(11)**: 4.
31. Sorelle R. (2010). "ExDS Protocol Puts Clout in EMS Hands". *Emergency Medicine News* 2020; **32** (10): 1,32. Available from: . *https://journals.lww.com/em-news/fulltext/2010/10000/exds_protocol_puts_clout_in_ems_hands.1.aspx* (Accessed 22 September 2023).
32. American Psychiatric Association. Council on Psychiatry and the Law. Position Statement on Concerns About Use of the Term "Excited Delirium" and Appropriate Medical Management in Out-of-Hospital Contexts. American Psychiatric Association. December 2020. Available from: *https://www.psychiatry.org/File%20Library/About-APA/Organization-Documents-Policies/Policies/Position-Use-of-Term-Excited-Delirium.pdf)* (Accessed 22 September 2023).
33. Gonin P, Beysard N, Yersib B, et al. Excited delirium: a systematic review. *Acad Emerg Med* 2018; **25**: 552–65.
34. AMA Press Release. New AMA policy opposes "excited delirium" diagnosis (2021). Available from: *https://www.ama-assn.org/press-center/press-releases/new-ama-policy-opposes-excited-delirium-diagnosis* (Accessed 22 September 2023).
35. O'Halloran RL, Frank JG. Asphyxial death during prone restraint revisited: a report of 21 cases. *Am J Forensic Med Pathol* 2000; **21(1)**: 39–52. Erratum in: *Am J Forensic Med Pathol* 2000; **21(2)**: 200. PMID: 10739225.
36. Savaser D, Chan TC. Positional and restraint asphyxia. In: Ross D and Vilke G (eds) *Guidelines for investigating officer-involved shootings, arrest-related deaths, and deaths in custody*. New York and London: Routledge, Taylor and Francis Group; 2017, pp 149–62.
37. Kennedy KM, Payne-James JJ, Payne-James GJ, et al. The use of spit guards (also known as spit hoods) by police services in England, Wales and Northern Ireland: to prevent transmission of infection or another form of restraint? *J Forensic Leg Med* 2019; **66**:147–54. PMID: 31306914.
38. Amnesty International. Use of spit hood in NY case illustrates systemic issues within police force. Available from: *https://www.amnestyusa.org/press-releases/use-of-spit-hood-in-ny-case-illustrates-systemic-issues-within-police-force/* (Accessed 22 September 2023).
39. Steffee CH, Lantz PE, Flannagan LM, et al. Oleoresin capsicum (pepper) spray and "in-custody deaths". *Am J Forensic Med Pathol* 1995;**16(3)**:185–92.
40. Granfield J, Onnen J, Petty C. Pepper spray and in-custody deaths (Executive Brief). Alexandria, VA: International Association of Chiefs of Police; March 1999.
41. Otahbachi M, Cevik C, Bagdure S, et al. Excited delirium, restraints, and unexpected death: a review of pathogenesis. *Am J Forensic Med Pathol* 2010; **31(2)**:107–12. PMID: 20190633.
42. Linder LM, Ross CA, Weant KA. Ketamine for the acute management of excited delirium and agitation in the prehospital setting. *Pharmacotherapy* 2018; **38(1)**:139–51. PMID: 29136301.
43. Solano JJ, Clayton LM, Parks DJ, et al. Prehospital ketamine administration for excited delirium with illicit substance co-ingestion and subsequent intubation in the emergency department. *Prehosp Disaster Med* 2021; **36(6)**: 697–701. PMID: 34551849; PMCID: PMC8607139.
44. Appelbaum PS. Excited delirium, ketamine, and deaths in police custody. *Psychiatr Serv* 2022; **73(7)**: 827–29. PMID: 35538746.
45. O'Halloran RL, Lewman LV. Restraint asphyxiation in excited delirium. Am J Forensic Med Pathol 1993; **14(4)**: 289–295.
46. Reay DT, Fligner CL, Stilwell AD et al. Positional asphyxia during law enforcement transport. *Am J Forensic Med Pathol* 1992; **13(2)**: 90–7. PMID: 1510077.
47. Chan TC, Vilke GM, Neuman T, et al. Restraint position and positional asphyxia. *Ann Emerg Med Ann Emerg Med* 1997; **30(5)**: 578–86.
48. Chan TC, Neuman T, Clausen J, et al. Weight force during prone restraint and respiratory function. *Am J Forensic Med Pathol* 2004; **25**:185–89.
49. Vilke GM, Payne-James J, Karch SB. Excited delirium syndrome (ExDS): redefining an old diagnosis. *J Forensic Leg Med* 2012; **19(1)**: 7–11. PMID: 22152441.
50. Steinberg A. Prone restraint cardiac arrest: A comprehensive review of the scientific literature and an explanation of the physiology. *Med Sci Law* 2021; **61(3)**: 215–26. PMID: 33629624.
51. Neumar RW, Otto CW, Link MS. et al. Part 8: Adult Advanced Cardiovascular Life Support: 2010 American Heart Association Guidelines for Cardiopulmonary Resuscitation and Emergency Cardiovascular Care. Circulation 2010; **122**: S729-S767.
52. Evstatieva M, Mak T. How decades of bans of police choke holds have fallen short. National Public Radio (NPR); June 2020. Available from: *https://www.npr.org/2020/06/16/877527974/how-decades-of-bans-on-police-choke-holds-have-fallen-short* (Accessed 22 September 2023).
53. Cipolla MJ. *The Cerebral Circulation*. San Rafael (CA): Morgan & Claypool Life Sciences; 2009. Available from: *https://www.ncbi.nlm.nih.gov/books/NBK53081/* (Accessed 23 September 2023).
54. Zarrinkoob L, Ambarki K, Wåhlin A, et al. Blood flow distribution in cerebral arteries. *J Cereb Blood Flow Metab*

2015; 35(4): 648–54. PMID: 25564234; PMCID: PMC4420884.
55. Mitchell JR, Roach DE, Tyberg JV, et al. Mechanism of loss of consciousness during vascular neck restraint. *J Appl Physiol (1985)* 2012;**112(3)**: 396–402. PMID: 22096121.
56. Neumann S, Burchell AE, Rodrigues JCL, et al. Cerebral blood flow response to simulated hypovolemia in essential hypertension: A magnetic resonance Imaging study. *Hypertension* 2019; **74(6)**: 1391–98. PMID: 31656098.
57. Yamasaki S, Takase I, Takada N, Nishi K. Measurement of force to obstruct the cervical arteries and distribution of tension exerted on a ligature in hanging. *Leg Med (Tokyo)*. 2009; 11(4): 175–80. PMID: 19364674.
58. Vilke GM. Neck Holds. In: *Sudden Deaths in Custody*. Totowa (NJ): Humana Press; 2006, pp. 15–37.
59. Zu QQ, Liu S, Xu XQ, et al. An endovascular canine stroke model: middle cerebral artery occlusion with autologous clots followed by ipsilateral internal carotid artery blockade. *Lab Invest* 2013; **93(7)**: 760-7. PMID: 23648562.
60. Berkman JM, Rosenthal JA, Saadi A. Carotid physiology and neck restraints in law enforcement: Why neurologists need to make their voices heard. *JAMA Neurol.* 2021; **78(3)**: 267–68.
61. Graham MA. Investigation of Deaths Temporally Associated with Law Enforcement Apprehension. *Acad Forensic Pathol* 2014; **4(3)**: 366–89.
62. Reay DT, Howard JD, Fligner CL, Ward RJ. Effects of positional restraint on oxygen saturation and heart rate following exercise. *Am J Forensic Med Pathol* 1988; **9(1)**: 16–18. PMID: 3354518.
63. Schmidt P, Snowden T. The effects of positional restraint on heart rate and oxygen saturation. *J Emerg Med* 1999; **17(5)**: 777–82. PMID: 10499689.
64. Parkes J. Sudden death during restraint: A study to measure the effect of restraint positions on the rate of recovery from exercise. *Med Sci Law* 2000; **40(1)**: 39–44. PMID: 10689860.
65. Michalewicz BA, Chan TC, Vilke GM, et al. Ventilatory and metabolic demands during aggressive physical restraint in healthy adults. *J Forensic Sci* 2007; **52(1)**:171–5. PMID: 17209931.
66. Robinson MN, Brooks CG, Renshaw GD. Electric shock devices and their effects on the human body. *Med Sci Law* 1990; **30(4)**: 285–300. PMID: 2263172.
67. Ho JD, Dawes DM. Conducted Electrical Weapon Drive-Stun Wounds. In: Ho JD, Daws DM, Kroll MW (eds). *Atlas of Conducted Electrical Weapons Wounds and Forensic Analysis*. New York: Springer; 2012; pp. 61–78.
68. Anders S, Junge M, Schulz F, Püschel K. Cutaneous current marks due to a stun gun injury. *J Forensic Sci* 2003; **48(3)**: 640–2. PMID: 12762539.
69. Graham M. Histopathology of Cutaneous Conducted Electrical Weapon Injuries. In: Ho JD, Daws DM, Kroll MW (eds). *Atlas of Conducted Electrical Weapons Wounds and Forensic Analysis*. New York: Springer; 2012; pp. 79–112.
70. Becour B. Conducted electrical weapons or stun guns: A review of 46 cases examined in casualty. *Am J Forensic Med Pathol* 2013; **34(2)**: 142–6. PMID: 23574872.
71. Dawes DM, Burns TJ. Extended Range Conducted Electrical Weapons. In: Ho JD, Daws DM, Kroll MW (eds). *Atlas of Conducted Electrical Weapons Wounds and Forensic analysis*. New York: Springer; 2012; pp. 113–29.
72. Dawes DM, Ho JD. Conducted Electrical Weapon Deployed Probe Wounds. In: Ho JD, Daws DM, Kroll MW (eds). *Atlas of Conducted Electrical Weapons Wounds and Forensic Analysis*. New York: Springer; 2012; pp. 47–60.
73. Kunz SN, Zinka B, Fieseler S, et al. Functioning and effectiveness of electronic control devices such as the TASER® M- and X-series: A review of the current literature. *J Forensic Sci* 2012; **57(6)**: 1591–4. PMID: 22515413.
74. Witherspoon SR, Lauer AK, Marinaro JL. Eye and Head Injuries. In: Ho JD, Kroll MW (eds). *TASER Conducted Electrical Weapons: Physiology, Pathology and Law*. New York, Springer; 2009; pp. 201–19.
75. Mangus BE, Shen LY, Helmer SD, et al. Taser and Taser associated injuries: A case series. *Am Surg* 2008; **74(9)**: 862–5.
76. Van Meenen KM, Lavietes MH, Cherniack NS, et al. Respiratory and Cardiovascular Response during Electronic Control Device Exposure in Law Enforcement Trainees. *Front Physiol* 2013; **4**: 78. PMID: 23616772.
77. TASER International 2008.
78. Baliatsas C, Gerbecks J, Dückers MLA, Yzermans CJ. Human health risks of conducted electrical weapon exposure: A systematic review. *JAMA Netw Open*. 2021; **4(2)**: e2037209. PMID: 33576818.

CHAPTER

29

Environmental Issues

Roger W. Byard

'Mother nature knows very well how to take revenge, so be careful before hurting her.'

INTRODUCTION

Accidents, illnesses and deaths may all be the result of adverse environmental conditions. Lethal outcomes may be directly due to weather conditions with hypothermia and hyperthermia being two well-recognized results of exposure to low and high temperatures. These may, however, occur in a variety of very different circumstances with hypothermic deaths being found in elderly recluses in urban situations during winter, in mountaineers trapped by avalanches and in individuals involved in commercial fishing who may have fallen overboard. Hyperthermic deaths again may occur in elderly urban dwellers during heat waves, or in manual workers exposed to high work environment temperatures or be associated with certain types of illicit drug taking. Although typical situations increase the risks of such events such as European winters for hypothermia and African deserts for hyperthermia, the range of locations where such deaths may be encountered is surprisingly varied and single locations may result in both types of death. Extreme (high or low) temperatures account for approximately 0.86 percent of total mortality (1). Animal-related deaths may also be a significant feature of certain environments such as snake attacks in poor rural African or Asian communities, or shark attacks in the sea.

29.1 Early processing of bodies in one of the many clearing stations set up following the 2004 South Asian tsunami.

Natural disasters may cause serious morbidity and mortality with large scale events such as the South Asian tsumani in 2004 resulting in the deaths of hundreds of thousands of individuals (Figure 29.1). In this situation, early deaths mostly resulted from drowning and trauma. Major disaster victim identification exercises are then required to locate, identify and repatriate the victims following such events.

It appears that there has been an increase over recent years in the numbers of natural events such as flooding, landslides, wild (bush) fires, cyclones, hurricanes, and typhoons most likely due to climate change (2–4). All of these will negatively impact upon local forensic services that are called upon to handle the bodies resulting in situations where even body storage may exceed regional capacities (Figure 29.2).

Changes in the environment may also cause or exacerbate natural diseases with the COVID 19 pandemic being a striking example of the effect that a new pathogen may have globally. The relationship of climate and weather to infectious diseases was, however, recognized many centuries ago by Hippocrates (5). Other established diseases are now spreading, with changes in temperatures facilitating the spread of insect vectors such as mosquitoes. This has resulted in increasing numbers of diseases such as malaria and dengue fever not only in areas previously regarded as endemic, but in multiple other sites. Air pollution and storms have been associated with exacerbations of underlying respiratory illnesses such as asthma and chronic obstructive airways disease (COAD), as well as cardiovascular illness. All of these have resulted in increased mortality rates.

HYPOTHERMIA

Hypothermia is defined as being present when the body temperature falls to below 35°C having a 70 percent

DOI: 10.1201/9781003138754-31

29.2 Temporary storage facilities that may be used to assist during disaster victim identification to store excess numbers of bodies include modified shipping containers.

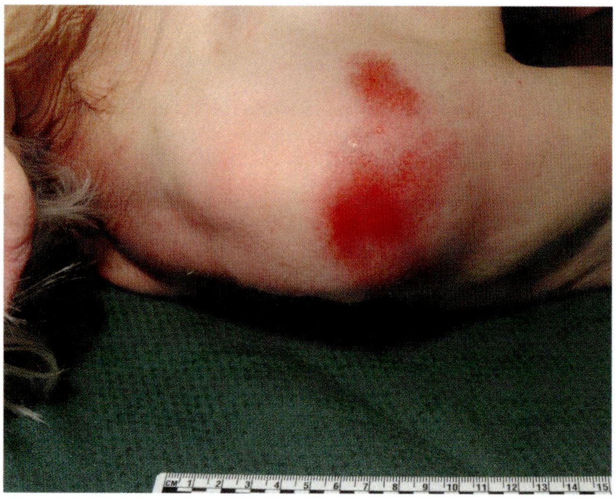

29.3 Reddening of the skin of the shoulder in a case of suspected hypothermia.

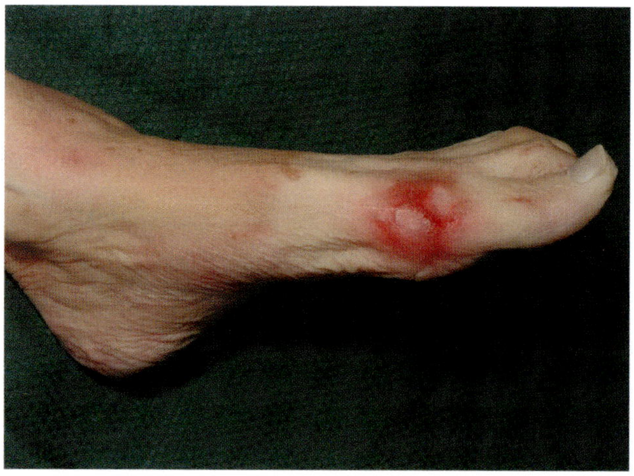

29.4 Reddening of the skin of the foot in a case of suspected hypothermia.

mortality rate for temperatures less than 30°C and 90 percent at 26°C (6). Death results from ventricular arrhythmias and electrolyte disturbances. Although often associated with low exterior environmental temperatures, it may also occur in the frail elderly in unheated houses and may be related to underlying organic diseases such as diabetes mellitus (7), or simply due to fuel poverty. The pathological diagnosis may not be straightforward as features such as pink skin discoloration over extensor surfaces (Figures 29.3 and 29.4) and Wischnewski spots in the stomach are variable (Figure 29.5) (8); the latter possibly requiring stress to develop, and are not necessarily diagnostic. Cold temperatures are responsible for more deaths than heat (7.29% compared to 0.42%) (1), although this comparator may evolve with climate change.

HYPERTHERMIA

Approximately 400 deaths occur in the United States per year due to extremely high temperatures with the most

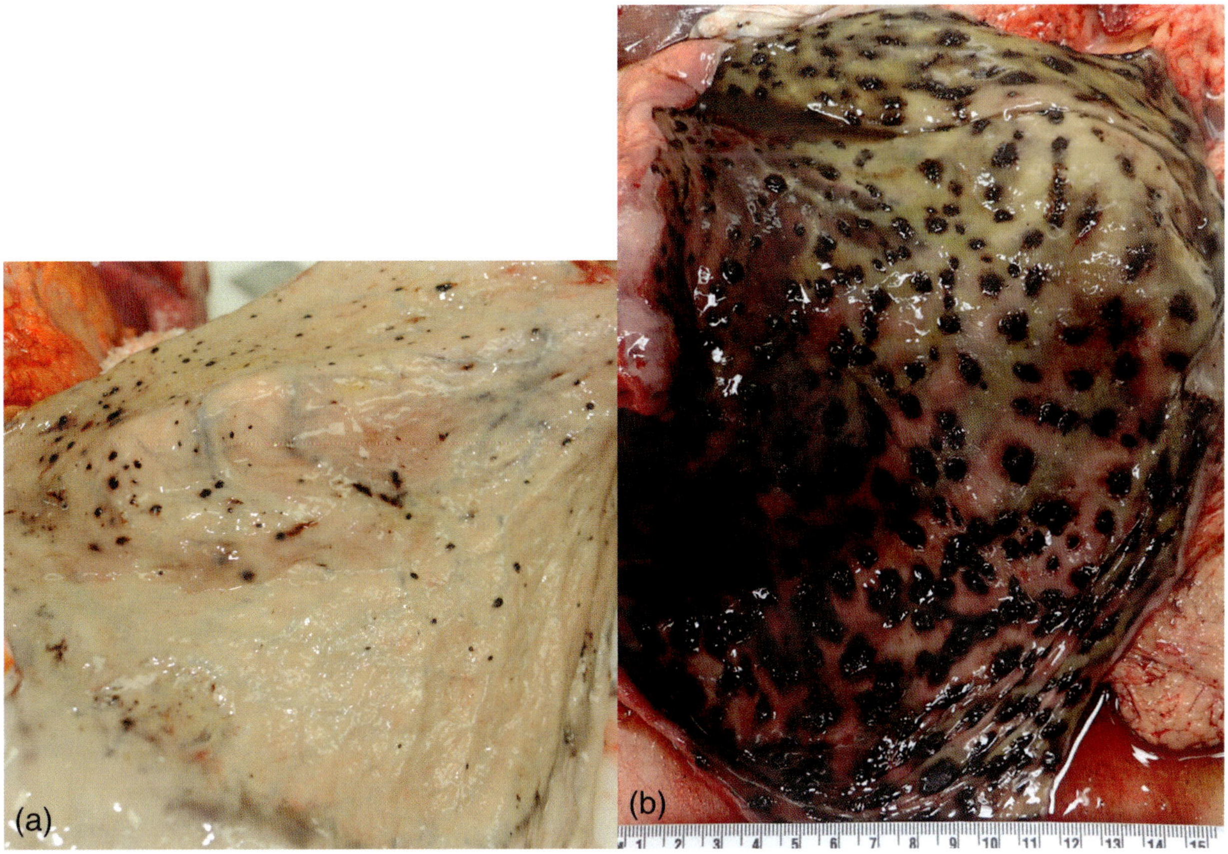

29.5 Wischnewski spots in cases of hypothermia may be few in number **(a)** or quite intense **(b)**.

vulnerable groups being those aged over 65 years, infants and children and those who are socially isolated/deprived and/or have pre-existing disease (9–12). A study of hospital admissions in California, United States, from 1999 to 2009 showed a 7 percent increase in admissions on the peak heat wave days accounting for 11 000 excess admissions due to extreme heat. Issues arose particularly in those with underlying respiratory and cardiovascular disease with dehydration, acute renal failure and heat-related and mental health issues (13). Extreme heat may also be associated with a greater number of adverse pregnancy outcomes (14). The 2021 heatwave in North America had a 69-fold increase in emergency department visits and more than 1000 excess deaths compared to previous years (15).

While a diagnosis of lethal hyperthermia requires a core temperature of ≥40.6°C with an environmental temperature >37.8°C, it is often difficult to establish with any confidence as these measurements may not be available at the time of autopsy. There are also no pathognomonic supporting features (16,17). Thus, the National Association of Medical Examiners has suggested that "heat-related death" is an appropriate term to use when hyperthermia is suspected but not proven (18).

Higher environmental temperatures have occurred in recent years with increased mortality from these elevated temperatures (17). An Excess Heat Factor has been proposed as a calculation which may assist as a way of predicting when there may be increases in heat related morbidity and mortality (19), in addition to the universal thermal climate index (UTCI) which integrates a variety of weather variables (20).

Hyperthermia may also result from certain cultural practices such as the use of saunas and sweat lodges (21) and may be exacerbated by the use of prescription medications including antidepressants, opioids and anticholinergics, and illegal agents such as cocaine and amphetamines. Athletes may also be at risk of heat-related illness and even fatal heat stroke (14,22–24).

In addition, it has been shown that there will be an increase in the death rate from less extreme increases in ambient temperatures. Specifically, it has been predicted that the mean global temperature increase of 1.8 to 4.0°C by 2100 will be associated in the United States with 8844–25 486 extra deaths annually from cardiovascular disease and between 2063 and 13 039 extra deaths yearly from stroke (9). Since the 1970s, average global temperatures have been increasing at approximately 0.2°C per decade (10).

ANIMAL ATTACKS

The nature and type of animal attacks depend on the location of the encounter and the types of animal involved. Terrestrial attacks by animals most often involve dogs with injuries resulting from combinations of blunt and sharp force trauma (26). However, lethal episodes may occur from animals as divergent as camels, buffalo, sheep, kangaroos, elephants and donkeys (27–30). Aquatic deaths may involve sharks or crocodiles (31,32). Other types of deaths may be caused by envenomation, poisoning or anaphylaxis occurring in both terrestrial and aquatic environments (33,34). Children who are traveling may be at risk of infections from bites and scratches as they are less likely to report exposures (35). The forensic investigation of such deaths has been described elsewhere (36,37).

NATURAL DISASTERS

Many natural disasters are interconnected with, for example, tsunamis and flooding accompanying earthquakes, and landslides following bushfires if there has been significant loss of forest cover. Increase in the incidence and severity of many of these events has been linked to elevated global temperatures and changes in rainfall and climate patterns (2). In recent years, there have been significant floods in Europe, Australia, Japan and China with wildfires in North America, Algeria, Greece, Turkey and Australia (15).

In the Asia-Pacific region between 1970 and 2011, it has been estimated that approximately two million people died as a result of natural disasters, accounting for 75 percent of all global disaster fatalities. The total number of deaths globally (from 10 009 extreme weather events listed in the Emergency Events Database) from 1969 to 2018 was 2 037 415 with 3 998 466 cases of disease (38).

The health impacts of natural disasters depend on the type of event, its severity and duration, and the effectiveness of advanced warning systems (39). A 50-year study of extreme weather events found that floods and tropical cyclones were the most commonly occurring events accounting for 47 and 30 percent of cases, with 39 percent of deaths due to tropical cyclones, 34 percent to droughts and 16 percent to floods. Forty-seven percent of cases of morbidity associated with such events were due to cold weather, 31 percent to floods and 18 percent to tropical cyclones (38).

EARTHQUAKES

Earthquakes result when seismic activity occurs as segments of the earth's crust move along fault lines. The resultant instability and movement of the earth's surface may result in hundreds of deaths when people are crushed or trapped in buildings that have collapsed. Other causes of injuries and deaths include landslides, debris flows, tsunamis and bridge collapses (40).

Deaths may be due to blunt and penetrating trauma, exsanguination or crush asphyxia (41). Upper airway occlusion may also result from inhalation of soil, sand or pulverized building material. Trapped survivors may succumb to dehydration or sepsis if wounds become infected and are unable to be treated, or to burns and smoke inhalation if fire breaks out. In cases of tsunamis or of dam breaches there may be deaths due to drowning.

There has also been a demonstrable increase in certain natural diseases associated with earthquakes which have included fatal myocardial infarction and sudden cardiac deaths as well as heart failure, stress cardiomyopathy, arrhythmias, hypertension, pulmonary embolism and stroke (42). Chronic physical and mental illness may also follow such events (43).

Earthquakes may also cause damage to nuclear power plants with leakage from the Fukushima nuclear facility in Japan following an earthquake in 2011 resulting in radiation levels in Tokyo reaching 20 times the usual background levels within days (44).

LANDSLIDES

The sudden movement of massive amounts of soil and debris downhill may result from natural and human activity including excessive rainfall with rising water levels, earthquakes, volcanic activity and deforestation (45). There has been an increase in the number of deadly landslides worldwide in recent years with 3876 landslides resulting in 163 658 deaths between 1995 and 2014. The two major factors involved in this were thought to be extreme rainfall and population distribution (2). In the United States, 25–50 people are estimated to die from landslides annually (46). Deaths occur from blunt and penetrating trauma and asphyxiation with contamination by soil or sand (47). Later health issues involving infectious diseases such as cholera associated with overcrowding, lack of clean drinking water and effective sanitation facilities with collapse of health infrastructure (48).

VOLCANOS

Volcanic eruptions occur when defects in the earth's crust allow the escape of molten rock (magma), rock fragments and gases. The major hazards to humans come from ash and rock missiles propelled by the explosion. The results of this are still graphically seen in Pompeii, Italy following the eruption of Mt Vesuvius in 79AD. In addition to this, deaths can be caused by pyroclastic and lava flows and volcanic gases (49). Thus deaths and injuries can be caused by extreme heat and rock projectiles, or asphyxiation from ash engulfment or inhalation of toxic gases such as hydrogen sulphide, sulfur dioxide, and hydrogen chloride/hydrochloric acid (HCl) (50). In addition, engine failure has been reported in aircraft when volcanic ash has blocked fuel nozzles or fused onto propellers or parts of the engine (51).

As well as exacerbating underlying respiratory illnesses, ash dispersed from a volcanic eruptions may also contaminate community water supplies, damage crops and buildings, and disrupt access to health services (52).

FLOODING

Large-scale flooding is seen in most parts of the world and represents the most common natural disaster with the highest death rate. It has accounted for 47 percent of recorded natural disasters affecting 2.3 billion people over the past 20 years (53). In 2016, 161 floods occurred globally (43% in Asia, 23% in the Americas and 12% in Europe), impacting more than 74 million people with 4720 deaths (54). It is estimated that 175 000 people died from floods from 1975 to 2001, a trend which appears to be increasing exacerbated by climate change; for example, while flooding from rivers currently affects approximately 21 million people per year this could increase to 54 million by 2030 (55). Individuals who drown in floods are either swept away by the current or are trapped in buildings or cars. Flooded rivers are a particular danger as fast-flowing water creates eddies and vortexes that can quickly suck swimmers under the surface (56). Flash floods after drought are another source of fatality (57).

During the clean-up phase after flood waters have subsided, deaths from electrocution and myocardial infarctions have been reported (58). In addition, contamination of water supplies by debris containing sewage, manure and dead animals/humans may cause disease. It may also be contaminated by organic and inorganic chemicals and gasoline and oil (44). Increases in diseases such as cholera and malaria are reported, particularly in poor, crowded areas with unhygienic living conditions (53,59).

CYLONES/HURRICANES/TYPHOONS

Cyclones, hurricanes and typhoons refer to rotating storm systems that have low-pressure centers with extremely strong winds and heavy rain. They may be associated with significant numbers of deaths and marked property damage. For example, Hurricane Katrina which struck the United States coast in 2005 killed approximately 1200 people and caused damage totalling $170 billion (60). Deaths occur from drowning and also from blunt trauma if an individual is struck by airborne objects. Later health effects are related to an increase in mold from flooding that may exacerbate allergies and respiratory conditions such as asthma and COAD (60).

TORNADOS

Occurring mostly in the midwestern and south central and eastern parts of the United States, tornados are violently rotating columns of air that are in contact with the ground. Each year approximately 1200 tornados occur in the United States resulting in 60–65 deaths, mostly in those with wind speeds greater than 267 kph. Between 1950 and 1994, there were over 4115 tornado-related deaths with the most vulnerable being elderly individuals with reduced mobility and underlying medical conditions. The majority of those killed directly by the tornado were impacted or cut by flying debris or were thrown into an object. Wounds sustained during tornados are particularly susceptible to Gram-negative infections due to soil that has been sucked up into the vortex (61,62).

TSUNAMIS

Tsunamis consist of huge "tidal" waves created by underwater earthquakes, landslides or volcanic eruptions (63). They have the capacity to cause massive destruction to coastal communities and the nearby hinterland as was witnessed in 2004 in Thailand and adjacent countries, and in 2011 in the Oshika Peninsula of Tōhoku of Japan, with many thousands of lives lost and injuries caused in both instances (64). Deaths are caused by drowning or by blunt or penetrating trauma due to high impact forces that occur when victims are being rapidly propelled through the water. Other complications relate to retained foreign bodies in soft tissues and aspiration pneumonia (65).

AVALANCHES AND SNOWFALLS

Avalanches refer to situations where a large amount of snow moves very rapidly downhill. Deaths may be due to blunt force trauma or, more often, to asphyxia when individuals are buried underneath the snow. It has been shown that over 85 percent of deaths in avalanches have been caused by chest compression and airway occlusion, with approximately 9 percent of victims succumbing to a combination of trauma and asphyxiation, and only 5.4 percent from trauma (66). Severe snowstorms may also be associated with deaths from temperature extremes, trauma and interference with the ability to seek medical care.

WILD (BUSH) FIRES

Wild, bush or brush fires refer to uncontroled conflagrations where grasslands, forests and vegetation are destroyed by fires, which sometimes extend into adjacent towns or cities (67). Although sometimes regarded as a natural disaster, most often caused by lightning strikes, many cases are either deliberately or accidentally initiated by human activity. Increasing numbers of such blazes are associated with extreme temperatures, high winds and low humidity and rainfall (68).

Deaths occur due to inhalation of products of combustion such as carbon monoxide, thermal injuries, oxygen deprivation, trauma associated with the fires or with attempts to escape, and exacerbation of underlying illnesses (13,68). In addition, there may be direct health consequences from the inhalation of bushfire smoke which may contain large amounts of particulate matter as well as aromatic hydrocarbons and aldehydes. This may be of particular significance to individuals such as fire fighters who may suffer repeated exposures (67,69). Wildfire smoke inhalation has been associated with exacerbations of COAD, asthma, ischemic heart disease and cardiac arrests (70). There may also be a risk of exposure to soil pathogens (71).

Difficulties are encountered in the forensic investigation of deaths due to wildfires as the death scenes may cover many hundreds of square kilometers with numerous victims necessitating coordinated Disaster Victim Identification (DVI) activities. Bodies may be incomplete due to the action of the fire or to post-mortem animal predation, and there may be contributions from trauma (e.g. falling trees) or natural diseases such as ischemic heart disease (68).

THUNDERSTORMS AND LIGHTNING STRIKES

Thunderstorms may be associated with high winds and flooding or lightning strikes which may threaten life. An additional complication is thunderstorm-triggered asthma which refers to increases in acute asthma attacks immediately after a thunderstorm due to high concentrations of airborne allergens at ground level (72). The allergens are usually grass pollens and the mechanisms by which they are concentrated are unclear with suggestions that these result from breakdown of pollens into respirable particles due to humidity and rainfall-induced osmotic shock being challenged in situations where rainfall and humidity were relatively low (73). It is possible that irritant biogenic volatile organic compounds may also be released from bursting grass pollens (74). In 2016 in Melbourne, Australia, there were 3365 excess respiratory-related presentations to emergency departments (a rise of 672%) within 30 hours of storms beginning, with 10 000 people requiring hospital treatment and 10 deaths (73).

Lightning refers to the discharge of static electricity during storms with currents of up to 200 000 amperes and voltages of one billion. Deaths may be due to a variety of factors involving electrocution from direct strikes, from touching or standing beside an object that has been hit, or from ground currents or blast injuries. (75).

AIR POLLUTION

The rates of air pollution have been increasing in many centers globally associated with increasing industrialization and climate change. Studies on heatwaves, particularly in Europe have shown that a synergistic effect exists between high temperatures and air pollution resulting in modifications of allergens causing reduction in lung function, exacerbation of chronic lung disease (including chronic bronchitis, emphysema and asthma) and premature deaths (76,77). Approximately 12–16 million people in the United States suffer from chronic obstructive pulmonary disease (COPD) with it ranked as the third leading cause of death. Patients with chronic lung diseases are susceptible to increased morbidity and mortality with even low levels of exposure to both indoor and outdoor air pollution (78).

Approximately 7 million deaths have been attributed to household and environmental air pollution involving ischemic heart disease, stroke, COAD, lung cancer and lower respiratory infections (79). The elderly may represent a particularly vulnerable group (80).

NATURAL DISEASES

As noted above, deaths from natural diseases increase after certain environmental changes with, for example, greater cardiovascular and pulmonary disease mortality associated with both high and low temperatures (78,81). Due to changes in climatic conditions and increased population movements, there have also been marked changes in the incidence and range of a number of infectious diseases such as West Nile, Ebola and Usutu viruses. Certain of these such as hantavirus and Ebola are lethal to humans (82–84). Ebola fever first emerged in 1976 and causes a highly lethal hemorrhagic fever characterized by profuse watery diarrhea resulting in severe dehydration, hypovolaemic shock and fatal multiorgan failure (85). It has been predicted that the resurgence in numbers of yellow fever cases may mark it as the likely cause of the next major pandemic (86). Infectious disease outbreaks are often a sequel to extreme weather events (59).

With increased tourism and air travel, infectious cases may now be encountered in any forensic practice, with for example, yellow fever, chikungunya and Zika viruses now being found in urban locations (87,88). In addition, the emergence of diseases such as HIV and COVID 19 have dramatically altered life in most countries around the planet. Epidemics may also follow natural disasters resulting in further loss of life due mainly to population displacement with crowding, lack of clean water and sanitation facilities, and lack of functional health services (89). Although viruses such as chikungunya usually have a low fatality rate, they may target vulnerable groups such as the very young and old and those with underlying cardiac, renal and hepatic diseases (90).

COVID-19

So much has been written on the COVID-19 pandemic that there is little need to reiterate material in this chapter. As is well known, COVID-19 is a coronavirus responsible for severe acute respiratory syndrome (SARS). It was first recognized in Wuhan, China, in late 2019 and has since spread around the globe causing millions of deaths (91,92). Breakthrough infections following full vaccinations are a current concern (93). The virus again serves to emphasize the vulnerability of the modern world to infection transmission via migration and travel (87).

TUBERCULOSIS

Tuberculosis (TB) is primarily a respiratory disease caused by *Mycobacterium tuberculosis*. While the mortality rate fell by 22 percent globally between 2000 and 2015, it still represents the major infectious cause of death (94). It has been suggested that there are two billion individuals globally who have latent infections that could represent a major health issue from reactivation (95). In addition, multi drug-resistant strains are increasing, including totally drug-resistant strains (96,97) which, combined with increasing immigration, tourism and population movements, could lead to a massive resurgence in numbers. Important issues for forensic pathologists include the fact that many cases may not be identified prior to death, partly due to the stigma attached to the disease resulting in failure to seek medical care, and to inaccuracies in imaging and clinical evaluation (94,98).

MALARIA

Malaria is a febrile disease caused by *Plasmodium* parasites transmitted by *Anopheles* mosquitoes. Severe cases are characterized by respiratory distress and altered consciousness with neurologic signs. In 2019, there were approximately 229 million cases of malaria globally with 409 000 deaths. It is predicted that there will be an increase in cases of malaria as climate change extends the habitat of *Anopheles* mosquitoes, with suggestions that the southern United Kingdom will be suitable for *Plasmodium vivax* transmission for two months of the year by 2030 (99). In Rwanda in the late 1980s. the infection rate with malaria increased threefold following heavy rainfall and warmer temperatures associated with the El Niño event of 1987–1988 (59).

DENGUE FEVER

Dengue shock syndrome is a febrile illness caused by a single-stranded RNA virus that is a member of the *flaviviridae* family which has an untreated mortality rate of more than 20 percent (100). Dengue hemorrhagic fever manifests as hypovolemic shock with metabolic acidosis, disseminated intravascular coagulation, hemorrhage and multiorgan failure. It is spread by mosquitoes and is the most common arthropod-borne viral disease of humans and one of the most rapidly evolving vector-borne infections, currently being reported from 129 countries (101).

A marked increase in cases has occurred globally since the 1980s due to increases in the size of poorly serviced urban areas, poor vector control and inadequate public health programs. Over the preceding 50 years, the incidence has increased 30-fold with approximately 50–100 million dengue infections worldwide annually including 22 000 deaths (102). There are no vaccines or antiviral drugs for treating dengue (100).

PLAGUE

Another re-emerging infectious disease is plague caused by the coccobacillus *Yersinia pestis*. There are three forms: bubonic, septicemic and pneumonic, all of which have high mortality rates (103). Plague is carried by rodent fleas and has been responsible for three major pandemics over six centuries with an estimated death rate of 200 million. As there is now multiple drug resistance with considerable genetic plasticity and no effective vaccines, plague could lend itself to use in biowarfare (104).

CONCLUSION

Changes in weather patterns and environmental temperatures have had profound effects in recent years on the severity and number of natural disasters and also on the spread and evolution of infectious diseases. Whatever the etiology of such climatic developments, there is no doubt that they are clearly associated with an increasing burden of morbidity and loss of life.

REFERENCES

1. Gasparrini A, Guo Y, Hashizume M, et al. Mortality risk attributable to high and low ambient temperature: A multicountry observational study. *Lancet* 2015; **386:** 369–75.
2. Haque U, da Silva PF, Devoli G, et al. The human cost of global warming: Deadly landslides and their triggers (1995–2014). *Sci Total Environ* 2019; **682:** 673–84.
3. Ebi KL, Hess JJ. Health risks due to climate change: Inequity in causes and consequences. *Health Aff* 2020; **39:** 2056–62.
4. Grobusch LC, Grobusch MP. A hot topic at the environment-health nexus: investigating the impact of climate change on infectious diseases. *Int J Infect Dis* 2021; **116:** 7–9.
5. Mills JN, Gage KL, Khan AS. Potential influence of climate change on vector-borne and zoonotic diseases: A review and proposed research plan. *Environ Health Persp* 2021; **118:** 1507–14.
6. Byard RW, Bright FM. Lethal hypothermia: A sometimes elusive diagnosis. *Forensic Sci Med Pathol* 2018; **14:** 421–3.
7. Bright F, Winskog C, Walker M, Byard RW. A comparison of hypothermic deaths in South Australia and Sweden. *J Forensic Sci* 2014; **59:** 983–5.
8. Bright F, Winskog C, Tsokos M, et al. Issues in the diagnosis of hypothermia: A comparison of two geographically separate populations. *J Forensic Leg Med* 2014; **22:** 30–2.
9. Mazidi M, Speakman JR. Predicted impact of increasing average ambient temperature over the coming century on mortality from cardiovascular disease and stroke in the USA. *Atherosclerosis* 2020; **313:** 1–7.
10. Weilnhammer V, Schmid J, Mittermeier I, et al. Extreme weather events in Europe and their health consequences: A systematic review. *Int J Hyg Environ Health* 2021; **233:** 113688.
11. Byard RW, Tsokos M. Forensic issues in cases of Diogenes syndrome. *Am J Forensic Med Pathol* 2007; **28:** 177–81.
12. Henderson SB, McLean KE, Lee MJ, Kosatsky T. Analysis of community deaths during the catastrophic 2021 heat dome: Early evidence to inform the public health response during subsequent events in greater Vancouver, Canada. *Environ Epidemiol* 2022; **6:** e189.
13. Rossiello MR, Szema A. Health effects of climate change-induced wildfires and heatwaves. *Cureus* 2019; **11:** e4771.
14. Ebi KL, Capon A, Berry P, et al. Hot weather and heat extremes: Health risks. *Lancet*. 202; **398:** 698–708.
15. Ebi KL. Managing climate change risks is imperative for human health. *Nat Rev Nephrol* 2022; **18:** 74–5.
16. Byard RW. Heat-related deaths. *Forensic Sci Med Pathol* 2013; **9:** 469–70.
17. Herbst J, Mason K, Byard RW, et al. Heat-related deaths in Adelaide, South Australia: Review of the literature and case findings: An Australian perspective. *J Forensic Leg Med* 2014; **22:** 738.
18. Donoghue ER, Graham MA, Jentzen JM, et al. Criteria for the diagnosis of heat-related deaths: National Association of Medical Examiners: Position paper. *Am J Forensic Med Pathol* 1997; **18:** 11–14.
19. Langlois NEI, Herbst J, Mason K, et al. Use of excess heat factor (EHF) to

predict the risk of heat related deaths. *J Forensic Leg Med* 2013; **20:** 408–11.
20. Ghada W, Estrella N, Ankerst DP, Menzel A. Universal thermal climate index associations with mortality, hospital admissions, and road accidents in Bavaria. *PLoS One* 2021; **16:** e025908.
21. Byard RW, Riches KJ. Dehydration and heat-related death: Sweat lodge syndrome. *Am J Forensic Med Pathol* 2005; **26:** 236–9.
22. Herbst J, Gilbert J, Byard RW. Urinary incontinence, hyperthermia and sudden death. *J Forensic Sci* 2011; **56:** 1062–63.
23. Byard RW, Gilbert J, James R, Lokan RJ. Amphetamine derivative fatalities in South Australia - is “Ecstasy” the culprit? *Am J Forensic Med Pathol* 1998; **19:** 261–5.
24. Byard RW, Summersides G, Thompson A. Muscle pallor: A macroscopic marker of cocaine-induced rhabdomyolysis. *Forensic Sci Med Pathol* 2011; **7:** 364–6.
25. Tsokos M, Byard RW, Püschel K. Extensive and mutilating craniofacial trauma involving defleshing and decapitation: Unusual features of fatal dog attack in the young. *Am J Forensic Med Pathol* 2007; **28:** 131–6.
26. Byard RW. Sheep-related deaths in forensic practice. *Aust J Forensic Sci* 2022; **54(3):** 401–5. Available from: https://doi.org/10.1080/00450618.2020.1846786 (Accessed 24 April 2023).
27. Gilbert JD, Byard RW. Camel-related deaths: A forensic overview. *Am J Forensic Med Pathol* 2021; **42:** 46–50.
28. Byard RW. Vehicle fatalities involving collisions with kangaroos. *Med Sci Law* 2021; **61:** 23–6.
29. Vuletic J, Byard RW. Death due to crushing by an elephant trunk. *Forensic Sci Med Pathol* 2013; **9:** 449–51.
30. Byard RW, Gilbert JD, Brown K. Pathological features of fatal shark attacks. *Am J Forensic Med Pathol* 2000; **21:** 225–9.
31. Sinton TJ, Byard RW. Pathological features of fatal crocodile attacks in northern Australia, 2005–2014. *J Forensic Sci* 2016; **61:** 1553–5.
32. Thien CM, Byard RW. Characteristics and relative numbers of lethal snake bite cases in medicolegal practice in central Myanmar: A five-year study. *J Forensic Leg Med* 2019; **63:** 52–5.
33. Tiemensma M, Byard RW. Fatal sea snake envenomation. *Am J Forensic Med Pathol* 2021; **42:** 401–4.
34. Muehlenbein MP, Angelo KM, Schlagenhauf P, et al. Traveller exposure to animals: A GeoSentinal analysis. *J Trav Med* 2020; **27:** 1–7.
35. Bury D, Langlois NEI, Byard RW. Animal-related fatalities Part I: Characteristic autopsy findings and variable causes of death associated with blunt and sharp trauma. *J Forensic Sci* 2012; **57:** 370–4.
36. Bury D, Langlois NEI, Byard RW. Animal-related fatalities Part II: Characteristic autopsy findings and variable causes of death associated with envenomation, poisoning, anaphylaxis, asphyxiation and sepsis. *J Forensic Sci* 2012; **57:** 375–80.
37. Keim ME. The epidemiology of extreme weather event disasters (1969–2018). *Prehosp Disaster Med* 2020; **35:** 267–71.
38. Hashim JH, Hashim Z. Climate change, extreme weather events, and human health implications in the Asia Pacific Region. *Asia Pac J Public Health* 2016; **28(2 Suppl):** 8S–14S.
39. Alexander D. The health effects of earthquakes in the mid-1990s. *Disasters* 1996; **20:** 231–47.
40. Bartels SA, VanRooyen MJ. Medical complications associated with earthquakes. *Lancet* 2012; **379:** 748–57.
41. Kloner RA. Lessons learned about stress and the heart after major earthquakes. *Am Heart J* 2019; **215:** 20–2.
42. Cammack F, Shipton EA. The Christchurch earthquake: Crush injury, neuropathic pain, and posttraumatic stress disorder. *Case Rep Med* 2013; **2013:** 973234.
43. Kelley T. Environmental health insights into the 2011 Tōhoku Japan earthquake disaster. *Environ Health Ins* 2011; **5:** 21–2.
44. Carrión-Mero P, Montalván-Burbano N, Morante-Carballo F, et al. Worldwide research trends in landslide science. *Int J Environ Res Public Health* 2021; **18:** 9445.
45. Pollock W, Wartman J. Human vulnerability to landslides. *Geohealth* 2020; **4:** e2020GH000287.
46. Hata M, Ichiba T, Okazaki Y. Sand injuries associated with the landslide. *BMJ Case Rep* 2020; **13:** e235254.
47. Musoke R, Chimbaru A, Jambai A, et al. A public health response to a mudslide in Freetown, Sierra Leone, 2017: Lessons learnt. *Med Public Health Prep* 2020; **14:** 256–64.
48. Newhall CG, Fruchter JS. Volcanic activity: A review for health professionals. *Am J Public Health* 1986; **76:** 10–24.
49. Heggie TW. Geotourism and volcanoes: Health hazards facing tourists at volcanic and geothermal destinations. *Travel Med Infect Dis* 2009; **7:** 257–61.
50. Heggie TW. Volcanoes and travel medicine. *Travel Med Infect Dis* 2010; **8:** 199–200.
51. Cuthbertson J, Stewart C, Lyon A, et al. Health impacts of volcanic activity in Oceania. *Prehosp Disaster Med* 2020; **35:** 574–8.
52. Suhr F, Steinert JI. Epidemiology of floods in sub-Saharan Africa: A systematic review of health outcomes. *BMC Public Health* 2022; **22:** 268.
53. Paterson DL, Wright H, Harris PN. Health risks of flood disasters. *Clin Infect Dis* 2018; **67:** 1450–4.
54. Lehman E. Extreme rain may flood 54 million people by 2030. *Sci Am* 2015; 5. Available from: https://www.scientificamerican.com/article/extreme-rain-may-flood-54-million-people-by-2030/:~:text=River%20flooding%20could%20affect%2054,are%20affected%20annually%20by%20floods (Accessed 24 April 2023).
55. Byard RW. Drowning deaths in rivers. *Forensic Sci Med Pathol* 2017; **13:** 388–9.
56. Yari A, Ostadtaghizadeh A, Ardalan A, et al. Risk factors of death from flood: Findings of a systematic review. *J Environ Health Sci Eng* 2020; **18:** 1643–53.
57. Pereira S, Zezere JL, Qaresma I, et al. Mortality patterns of hydro-geomorphologic disasters. *Risk Anal* 2016; **36(6):** 1188–210.
58. McMichael AJ. Extreme weather events and infectious disease outbreaks. *Virulence* 2015; **6:** 543–7.
59. Waddell SL, Jayaweera DT, Mirsaeidi M, et al. Perspectives on the health effects of hurricanes: A review and challenges. *Int J Environ Res Public Health* 2021; **18:** 2756.
60. Chiu CH, Schnall AH, Mertzlufft CE, et al. Mortality from a tornado outbreak, Alabama, April 27, 2011. *Am J Public Health* 2013; **103:** e52–e85.
61. Bohonos JJ, Hogan DE. The medical impact of tornadoes in North America. *J Emerg Med* 1999; **17:** 67–73.
62. Løvholt F, Pedersen G, Harbitz CB, et al. On the characteristics of landslide tsunamis. *PhilosTrans R Soc* 2015; **373:** 20140376.
63. Rutty GN, Byard RW, Tsokos M. The Tsunami. An environmental mass disaster. *Forensic Sci Med Pathol* 2005; **1:** 3–8.
64. Kaewlai R, Srisuwan T, Prasitvoranant W, et al. Radiologic findings in tsunami trauma: experience with 225 patients injured in the 2004 tsunami. *Emerg Radiol* 2007; **14:** 395–402.
65. McIntosh SE, Grissom CK, Olivares CR, et al. Cause of death in avalanche fatalities. *Wild Environ Med* 2007; **18:** 293–7.
66. Dennekamp M, Abramson MJ. The effects of bushfire smoke on respiratory health. *Respirology* 2011; **16:** 198–209.
67. Byard RW, Gilbert JD, Kostakis C, Heath K. Circumstances of death and diagnostic difficulties in brushfire fatalities. *J Forensic Sci* 2012; **57:** 969–72.
68. Reisen F, Brown SK. Australian firefighters' exposure to air toxics during bushfire burns of autumn 2005 and 2006. *Environ Int* 2009; **35:** 342–52.
69. Walter CM, Schneider-Futschik EK, et al. Health impacts of bushfire smoke exposure in Australia. *Respirology* 2020; **25:** 495–501.
70. Hauser N, Conlon KC, Desai A, Kobziar LN. Climate change and infections on the move in North America. *Infect Drug Resist* 2021; **14:** 5711–23.
71. Harun N-S, Lachapelle P, Douglass J. Thunderstorm-triggered asthma: What we know so far. *J Asthma Allerg* 2019; **12:** 101–8.
72. Venkateson P. Epidemic thunderstorm asthma. *Lancet Respir Med* 2022; **10(4):** 325–32.
73. Gibbs JE. Essential oils, asthma, thunderstorms, and plant gases: A prospective study of respiratory response to ambient biogenic volatile organic compounds (BVOCs). *J Asthma Allergy* 2019; **12:** 169–82.
74. Byard RW, Thu M, Gilbert JD. Cutaneous manifestations of lightning strike: Lichtenberg figures. *Forensic Sci Med Pathol* 2017; **13:** 390–3.
75. De Sario M, Katsouyanni K, Michelozzi P. Climate change, extreme weather events, air pollution and respiratory health in Europe. *Eur Respir J* 2013; **42:** 826–43.
76. Viegi G, Maio S, Pistelli F, et al. Epidemiology of chronic pulmonary disease: Health effects and air pollution. *Respirology* 2006; **11:** 523–32.
77. Hansel NN, McCormack MC, Kim V. The effects of air pollution and temperature on COPD. *J COPD* 2016; **13:** 372–9.
78. De Matteis S, Forastiere F, Baldacci S, et al. Issue 1 - “Update on adverse respiratory effects of outdoor air pollution”.

Part 1): Outdoor air pollution and respiratory diseases: A general update and an Italian perspective. *Pulmonology* 2022; **10:** S2531–0437.

79. Bentayeb M, Simoni M, Baiz N, et al. Adverse respiratory effects of outdoor air pollution in the elderly. *Int J Tuberc Lung Dis* 2021; **16:** 1149–61.
80. Peters A, Schneider A. Cardiovascular risks of climate change. *Cardiology* 2021; **18:** 1–2.
81. Filho WL, Ternova L, Parasnis SA, et al. Climate change and zoonoses: A review of concepts, definitions, and bibliometrics. *Int J Environ Res Public Health* 2022; **19:** 893.
82. Douglas KO, Payne K, Sabino-Santos G Jr, Agard J. Influence of climatic factors on human hantavirus infections in Latin America and the Caribbean: A systematic review. *Pathogens* 2021; **11:** 15.
83. Cárdenas G, Salgado P, Laura-Foronda E, et al. Neglected and (re-)emergent infections of the CNS in low-/middle-income countries. *Infez Med* 2021; **29:** 513–25.
84. Baseler L, Chertow DS, Johnson KM, et al. The pathogenesis of Ebola virus disease. *Ann Rev Pathol* 2017; **12:** 387–418.
85. Gabiane G, Yen PS, Failloux AB. Aedes mosquitoes in the emerging threat of urban yellow fever transmission. *Rev Med Virol* 2022: e2333.
86. Byard RW. Travel-related issues and the morgue. *Forensic Sci Med Pathol* 2015; **11:** 149–51.
87. Weaver SC, Charlier C, Vasilakis N, Lecuit M. Zika, Chikungunya, and other emerging vector-borne viral diseases. *Ann Rev Med* 2018; **69:** 395–408.
88. Watson JT, Gayer M, Connolly MA. Epidemics after natural disasters. *Emerg Infect Dis* 2007; **13:** 1–5.
89. Khongwichit S, Chansaenroj J, Chirathaworn C, Poovorawan Y. Chikungunya virus infection: Molecular biology, clinical characteristics, and epidemiology in Asian countries. *J Biomed Sci* 2021; **28:** 84.
90. Hanley B, Lucas SB, Youd E, et al. Autopsy in suspected COVID-19 cases. *J Clin Pathol* 2020; **73:** 239–42.
91. Chams N, Chams S, Badran R, et al. COVID-19: A Multidisciplinary review. *Front Public Health* 2020; **8:** 383.
92. Afshar MZ, Barary M, Hosseinzadeh R, et al. Breakthrough SARS-CoV-2 infections after vaccination: A critical review. *Hum Vaccin Immunother* 2022; **18(5):** 2051412.
93. Heath K, Byard RW. Tuberculosis-related stigma contributing to a "hidden" disease at autopsy. *Med Sci Law* 2019; **59:** 135–8.
94. Stephenson L, Byard RW. An atlas overview of characteristic features of tuberculosis that may be encountered at autopsy. *Forensic Sci Med Pathol* 2020; **16:** 143–51.
95. Sharma A, Machado E, Lima KVB, et al. Tuberculosis drug resistance profiling based on machine learning: A literature review. *Braz J Infect Dis* 2022; **26:** 102332.
96. Zumla A, Abubakar I, Raviglione M, et al. Drug-resistant tuberculosis: Current dilemmas, unanswered questions, challenges and priority needs. *J Infect Dis* 2012; **205:** S228–40.
97. Stephenson L, Byard RW. Issues in the handling of cases of tuberculosis in forensic practice. *J Forensic Leg Med* 2019; **64:** 42–4.
98. Kulkarni MA, Duguay C, Ost K. Charting the evidence for climate change impacts on the global spread of malaria and dengue and adaptive responses: a scoping review of reviews. *Global Health* 2022; **18:** 1.
99. Gilbert JD, Higgins G, Byard RW. Unexpected death due to dengue virus infection in a nonendemic area. *Aust J Forensic Sci* 2016; **48:** 323–5.
100. Leowattana W, Leowattana T. Dengue hemorrhagic fever and the liver. *World J Hepatol* 2021; **13:** 1968–76.
101. Byard RW. Lethal dengue virus infection: A forensic overview. *Am J Forensic Med Pathol* 2016; **37:** 74–8.
102. Byard RW. A forensic evaluation of plague: A re-emerging infectious disease with biowarfare potential. *Med Sci Law* 60(3): 200–5.

CHAPTER

30

Infant and Childhood Deaths

Irene Scheimberg and Marta C. Cohen

PERINATAL DEATH

Perinatal deaths are those occurring around the time of delivery. If the death occurs in hospital, it is fundamental that the pathologist has access to the obstetric record; and if the infant is born alive and dies a few hours or days later, also to the neonatal notes to reach a correct conclusion. The most important points to consider in cases of intrapartum death are the role of asphyxia and trauma in the causation of the infant's death. Timing of fetal death in relation to delivery may also be an important point in these cases. Finally, intrapartum lesions should always be considered in the differential diagnosis of possible child abuse in babies aged 2 months or less.

Assessing at post mortem whether an infant was alive at the time of delivery may be difficult, particularly if there has been a delay in retrieving the body, or if it has been affected by the environment (i.e. temperature, water immersion, damaged by predatory fauna, etc.). The factors that should be considered when assessing the probability that an infant has been born alive include: the presence or absence of maceration, the gestational age and fetal growth, the presence of congenital abnormalities, histologic and microbiological evidence of infection, and significant placental abnormalities (if it is available for examination) (1). The examination of the placenta is fundamental in all cases of perinatal and neonatal death.

Findings suggesting that the baby was stillborn are the presence of maceration, the presence of congenital malformations, or a large retroplacental hematoma, associated with subdural hemorrhage and petechiae on the lungs and other viscera related to placental abruption leading to a sudden rise of intracranial pressure (hence the subdural bleeding) and fetal asphyxia. Florid congenital pneumonia with the presence of polymorphonuclear leukocytes in the alveoli correlates with chorioamnionitis in the placenta and may be seen both in a stillborn fetus or in an early neonatal death.

Intrapartum vs intrapartum asphyxia

Intrapartum asphyxia occurs when there is impairment of gas exchange during labor which eventually results in hypoxia, hypercapnia and metabolic acidosis. There are many causes of intrapartum asphyxia (Table 30.1) that should be considered when investigating intrapartum fetal death. During normal labor, the fetus can withstand a temporary degree of asphyxia, which is rapidly reversed between contractions. The damage caused by the acidosis to the capillary vessels results in hemorrhage in many organs, including the dura mater (2). It is important to understand that the presence of subdural hemorrhage does not always indicate trauma and may be seen after normal vaginal

TABLE 30.1 Causes of intrapartum asphyxia*

Maternal conditions	Placental conditions	Umbilical cord conditions
Severe anemia	Placental infarction	Abnormal length
Malnutrition	Widespread villitis	Cord entanglement
Chronic renal failure	Villous edema	True knots
Heart disease	Abnormal maturation	Cord prolapse
Peripheral artery disease	FTV	Cord compression
Shock and hypoxia	Prolonged pregnancy	Cord stretching
Maternal hemorrhage	Placenta previa	Cord hematoma
Epilepsy	Vasa previa	Cord tear
Maternal lung disease	Placental abruption	Funisitis
Maternal diabetes	Circumvallate membranes	Vessel thrombosis
Aortic compression	Chorioamnionitis	Vessel aneurysm
Drug abuse	Utero-placental insufficiency	Velamentous insertion
Pregnancy cholestasis		Furcate/marginal insertion
Uterine rupture		Hypercoiled cord
Amniotic fluid embolus		

FTV: Fetal thrombotic vasculopathy.

* Modified from (4).

DOI: 10.1201/9781003138754-32

delivery (although is more prominent after prolonged second stage of labor (and in fact it has been reported in up to 46 percent of asymptomatic neonates) (3).

Intrapartum trauma includes any physical injury that occurs as a consequence of the birth process, some of which may result in death and are the ones discussed here. Severe birth trauma is now infrequent due to improved obstetric care, and most cases are associated with difficult deliveries. Many of the factors that predispose to intrapartum asphyxia also increase the risk of birth trauma; asphyxia is a predisposing factor and without a post-mortem examination it may be difficult to assess the relative contribution of intrapartum trauma and intrapartum asphyxia to the fetal or neonatal death. Asphyxia may also be a predisposing factor for trauma, and sometimes it may be difficult to decide whether asphyxia or trauma was the main cause of death (4). The other major predisposing factors are instrumental delivery, malpresentation, obstructed or prolonged labor, feto-pelvic disproportion, macrosomia, some fetal abnormalities, and epidural anesthesia. It is important to have detailed obstetric notes available at the time of doing the post-mortem examination. Prematurity is also a risk factor for trauma. Table 30.2 lists the risk factors and the related intrapartum injuries (Figure 30.1).

Skull fractures may occur in forceps and ventouse deliveries and occasionally in normal vaginal deliveries (see below).

Retinal hemorrhages may also be related to birth, with a reported incidence up to 50 percent. These hemorrhages often involve multiple areas and layers of the retina and optic nerve (5), have been reported even in a small percentage of cesarean sections and may last up to two months (6). As with subdural and intradural

TABLE 30.2 Risk factors and related intrapartum injuries*

Normal vaginal delivery	Caput succedaneum Cephalhematoma (rare) Skull fractures (rare) Retinal hemorrhage
Precipitate vaginal delivery	Subdural hemorrhage
Malpresentation (including breech)	Bruising and lacerations Occipital osteodiastasis Spinal injury
Vacuum (ventouse)	Caput succedaneum Subaponeurotic hemorrhage Skull fractures (rare) Retinal hemorrhage
Forceps	Bruising and lacerations Subaponeurotic hemorrhage Subdural hemorrhage Skull fractures Retinal hemorrhage
Rotational forceps	Occipital osteodiastasis Spinal injury

* Modified from (4).

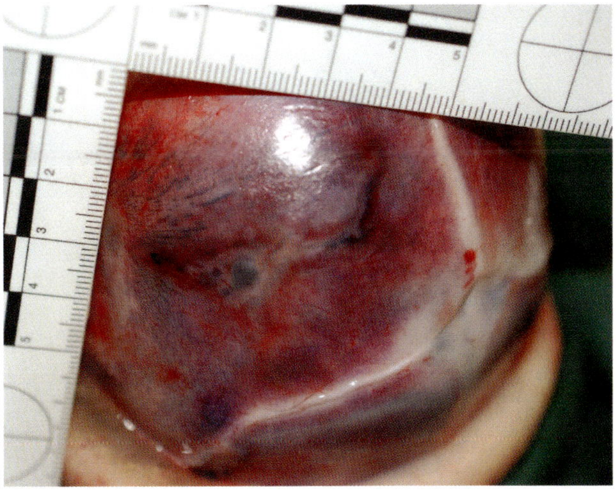

30.1 Depressed skull fracture at the post mortem of an infant with intrapartum death occurring involving a forceps-assisted delivery.

hemorrhages, a relationship with hypoxia in birth retinal hemorrhages without trauma has been proposed.

Infections

Intrauterine infections, acquired across the placenta, through vascular dissemination or by ascending infection, are a common cause of stillbirth and early neonatal death. Placental examination (including histologic sampling) must be part of the protocol of post-mortem investigation.

Neonatal infection is usually divided into early (within the first week after birth) or late (7+ days after birth). Some have divided it into very early (<24 hours), early (1–7 days) and late (8–28 +days); this may prove helpful in separating those likely and less likely to be due to infections acquired *in utero*.

Very early and early neonatal sepsis (EONS) are either present at birth or occur within the first few days after birth. Infections may be congenital, that is acquired *in utero* or during birth, such as herpes simplex type 2 infection in a mother who has a vaginal delivery with an active genital herpes infection. Those that occur within a few days of birth may still be acquired *in utero* or during birth but not become apparent until several days after birth. Those acquired after birth may be transmitted from the mother, a relative, from nursing staff or on occasions, from one neonate to another.

Late onset neonatal sepsis (LONS), as the name suggests, is acquired later, sometimes after the neonate has left the hospital. Late infections are community or family-acquired reflecting diseases present within the population.

METABOLIC DISORDERS

Inherited metabolic diseases (IMD) are caused by inherited defects in the enzymes/proteins or co-factors that metabolize proteins, carbohydrate and fat. These disorders are the result of molecular mutations/deletions that alter

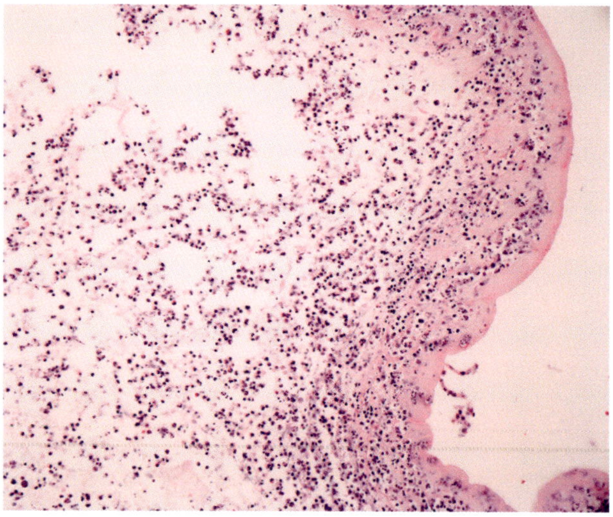

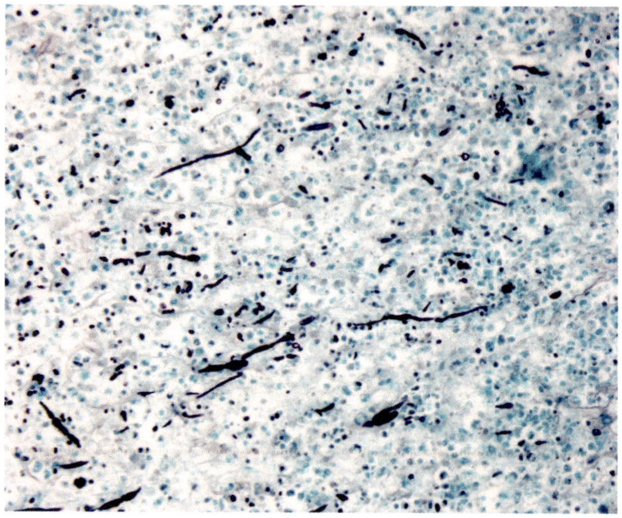

30.2 (a) Placental histology showing necrotizing acute chorioamnionitis (H&E x 200); (b) numerous hyphae are demonstrated on Grocott staining (x 400).

TABLE 30.3 Investigations in neonatal deaths

Cultures		
Nasopharyngeal swab	Bacteriology Virology	Always
Rectal swab	Bacteriology Virology	If suspicion of gastroenteritis
Lung tissue or swab	Bacteriology Virology	Always
Spleen tissue or swab	Bacteriology Virology	Always If suspicion of parvovirus
Liver	Virology	If suspicion of hepatitis
Heart	Virology	Always
Blood	Bacteriology	Always
CSF	Bacteriology Virology	Always
Stomach contents	Bacteriology	Newborn
Other investigations		
Biochemistry	Vitamin D and bone profile	If possible
Guthrie card	Metabolic investigations Other uses	Always
Urine	Metabolic investigations	If possible
Vitreous humor	Glucose, U+E	If necessary

metabolic pathways through deficient or absent activity of a protein (enzyme). Frequently, identified disease-associated gene variations are of the missense type with the potential to produce abnormal enzyme conformation due to misfolding (7,8). Most common types of IMD include defects of fatty acid oxidation and defects of ketogenesis (9). At post-mortem examination, the major gross features may include paleness of the liver, heart enlargement, swollen brain (in hyperammonemia), pericardial, pleural and peritoneal effusions, left ventricular hypertrophic cardiomyopathy or dilatation. Subendocardial fibroelastosis has often been described in many of the long-chain fatty acid oxidation defects (9–11).

INVESTIGATIONS IN NEONATAL DEATHS

Infection should be suspected in any neonatal autopsy, even in cases where clinicians believe that another condition had a primary role to play in the death, such as congenital heart disease. It may be a component in the development of hypoxic ischemic encephalopathy or significant brain injury peripartum, *in utero* or postnatally.

There is only one chance to investigate and exclude such infection and that is at the time of autopsy. Microbiology and virology swabs from the nasopharynx are the most important investigations before opening the body.

DEATHS IN INFANCY AND CHILDHOOD

Sudden unexpected death in infancy (SUDI) occurs in 0.5 per 1000 live births every year. A specific cause of death is identified in approximately 30 percent of cases (12).

SUDI is a death that was not anticipated as a significant possibility 24 hours before the death, including non-anticipated death occurring as a result of an acute illness, deaths from a previously known condition but not expected to lead to death, or deaths arising from a pre-existing condition not previously recognized. It usually includes those deaths resulting from accidental trauma or poisoning. After a detailed post-mortem investigation, a cause of death may be found for these unexpected deaths. Those infants whose cause of death is not known after a full detailed history, death scene investigation, full pathology using a standardized protocol and multiagency review are then described as sudden infant death syndrome (SIDS).

EXPLAINED NATURAL INFANT DEATH

A specific cause of death is found more frequently in neonates than in infants between 1 month and 1 year of age and in previously unwell infants compared to those who have been previously asymptomatic.

The most common specific causes of infant death are due to infections or cardiac disease. Diseases of other systems may also result in sudden death in infancy and the list of possible causes is very long (12–29,31,33–43). Many infants show more than one cause, particularly those with congenital conditions, some of which are only diagnosed after birth. Metabolic diseases are being diagnosed more frequently, especially when the appropriate samples are taken. Other causes include poisoning (intentional and accidental) and unwitnessed accidents. Metabolic causes, poisoning and accidents are discussed elsewhere.

Infections

Bacterial infection is a common cause of death in infancy; up to 25 percent of post-neonatal infant deaths are due to infections including overwhelming pneumonia, septicemia and meningitis. Group B *Streptococcus* (GBS), *Pneumococcus* and *Meningococcus* are common and can lead to very rapidly progressive infection in previously healthy infants. Disseminated intravascular coagulopathy (DIC) and acute tubular necrosis (ATN) may be identified in septic patients. Infants who die of a bacterial infection tend to be older than those whose death is unexplained. The most common pathogen identified is *Staphylococcus aureus*, followed by *Streptococcus pneumoniae*, ß-hemolytic *Streptococcus* and *Escherichia coli*.

Infants with bacterial pneumonia may present with non-specific symptoms of mild fever and malaise or may have minor respiratory symptoms. Inflammation may not be histologically prominent in the early stages and there may just be an eosinophilic exudate containing bacteria with scanty neutrophils. Bronchopneumonia with multiple foci in all lobes is more common than lobar pneumonia; in cases of *Pseudomonas* infection there may be necrotizing pneumonia.

Epiglottitis due to *Hemophilus influenzae* was once common, but since the advent of the Hib immunization it is now rare in the United Kingdom (UK). Whooping cough (due to *Bordetella pertussis)* infection in non-immunized infants can be particularly severe; it presents atypically without the classical cough but there is a high fever, a non-specific respiratory illness and an extremely high white cell count. At autopsy, inflammation in the lungs may be relatively mild, but there is alveolar epithelial necrosis and there is typically profound depletion of the lymphoid tissues (14).

Infants may present with primary septicemia from *Pneumococcus*, *Meningococcus*, group A or group B *Streptococcus* and occasionally from other microorganisms. In many cases, the origin of the sepsis cannot be identified. Infants with asplenia are particularly susceptible to pneumococcal septicemia and infants with functional asplenia may be perfectly well until a fatal episode (15). Hemophagocytosis can be seen in severe infections.

Other rare respiratory causes of SUDI include bacterial tonsillitis (16) and retropharyngeal abscess (17).

Bacterial meningitis can also cause infant morbidity and mortality. Symptoms are non-specific and the typical rash of meningococcal meningitis is not always present. Besides meningococcus, other organisms such as *Streptococcus pneumoniae* and *Hemophilus influenza* can cause bacterial meningitis. In fulminant infections, there may not be obvious inflammation on the brain surface. Bilateral adrenal hemorrhage is frequently found, not only with meningococcal infection but also with *Hemophilus* or *Pneumococcus*. The most common organism in neonatal meningitis is GBS. Coagulase negative Staphylococcus may also cause meningitis in neonates. In most cases, the causal microorganism can be isolated from blood and cerebrospinal fluid (CSF).

Other bacterial infections may present as SUDI in children with vague symptoms, particularly peritonitis. This occurs usually in infants with underlying pathology (meconium ileus, congenital bands, necrotizng enterocolitis, intussusception, volvulus, Hirschsprung disease, etc. (18). Patients with asplenia may develop primary peritonitis due to pneumococcal infection.

Positive bacterial cultures are common in post-mortem samples. In general, mixed cultures are likely to be due to post-mortem overgrowth or contamination. When a culture shows a single organism, careful correlation with histology and clinical presentation is paramount to decide if the cause of death is overwhelming infection or should be classified as unascertained (19).

Viral infections are less frequent as causes of sudden death in infants. The most important is viral myocarditis; pneumonitis and encephalitis can also be fatal.

Myocarditis can be congenital or acquired after birth. Congenital myocarditis may coexist with encephalitis. The causal viruses are generally enteroviruses, particularly Coxsackie virus type B. it is important to sample the myocardium and brain including the brainstem in suspicious cases. The infant may be non-specifically unwell for the first few days of life before collapsing. Enteroviruses can also cause myocarditis in older infants, together with many other viruses (adenovirus, cytomagalovirus [CMV], parvovirus B19), bacteria and other organisms. Post-neonatal myocarditis in infants presents frequently as SUDI (20). Macroscopic examination is usually non-specific and therefore histology is mandatory. Multiple samples should be taken from both ventricles and the septum (21). Histology shows cardiac myocyte damage and an inflammatory infiltrate (Figure 30.3a&b).

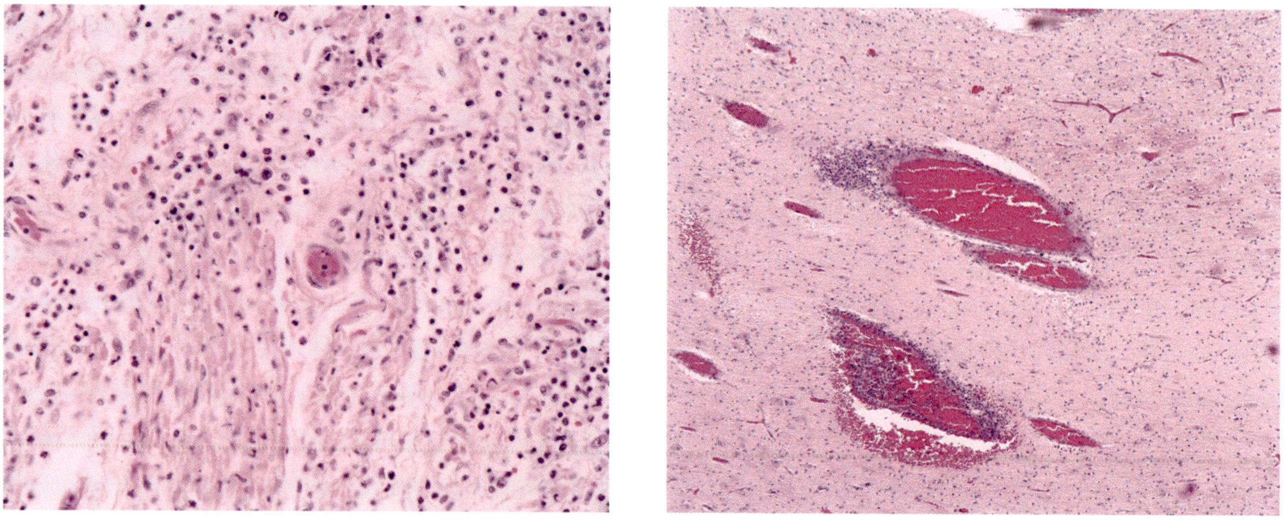

30.3 Term female who at day 8 of life was noted to be sleepy and not feeding well, and who on day 9 suddenly stopped breathing. At post-mortem examination, there was myocarditis with lymphocytic infiltrates and extensive myocardial necrosis (a) (H&E x 200); and encephalitis with perivascular lymphocytic infiltrates (b) (H&E x 200). Enterovirus was identified in the myocardium and the cerebrospinal fluid.

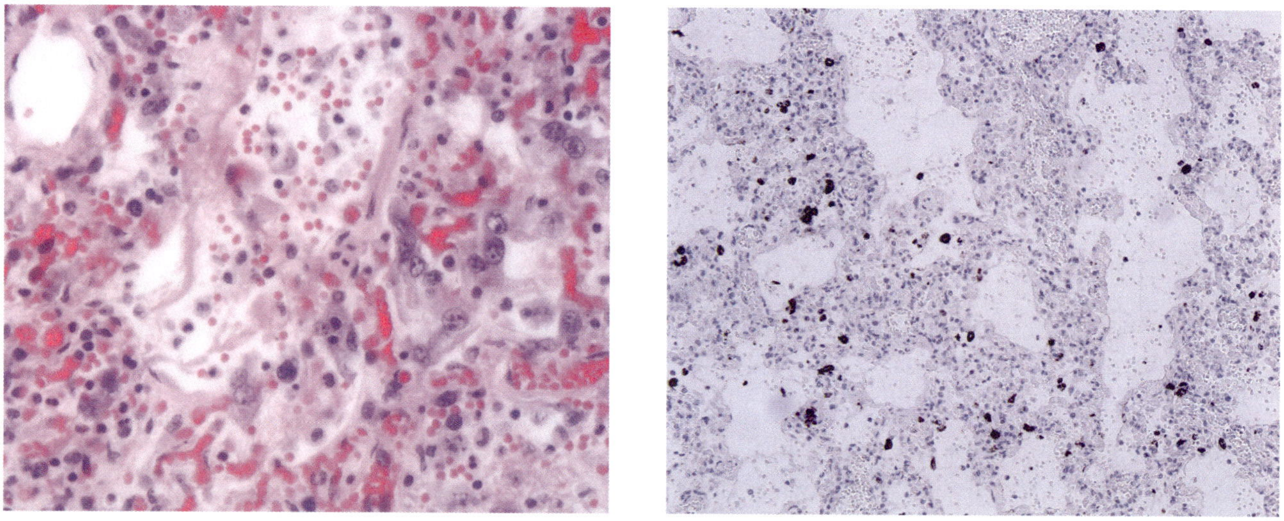

30.4 A 7-year-old child with an underlying neurodevelopmental condition who developed COVID-19 and died as a consequence of pneumonia complicated by Klebsiella infection. The lungs showed hyaline membranes and alveolar cell necrosis (a) (H&E x 600); SARS-CoV-2 was highlighted with immunohistochemistry (b) (x 100).

Interstitial pneumonitis, usually caused by viruses, is generally self-limiting but respiratory syncytial virus (RSV) may lead to apnaea in very young infants, particularly premature or those with congenital heart disease (22). Occasionally, rapidly progressive overwhelming viral infections may occur, particularly with enteroviruses and adenovirus and also with influenza H1N1. More recently, COVID-19: In the first year of the pandemic deaths from COVID-19 in children remained low, at 0.17 per 100 000 population, comprising 0.48 percent of the estimated total mortality from all causes in a normal year (23). Deaths were more common in older children and in those with underlying vulnerabilities (Figure 30.4a&b). In our center, we have performed a small number of autopsies in children with SARS-CoV-2 infection; in some cases coincidental and in others causing death in vulnerable children. Similar to our experience, other authors have described the presence of pneumonia, microthrombosis, myocarditis, colitis, encephalitis among other specific organs affected in COVID-19 (24).

In healthy children, SARS-CoV-2 may trigger a condition known as Pediatric Inflammatory Multisystem Syndrome Temporally Associated with SARS-CoV-2 (PIMS-TS). Although the majority of cases are between 9 and 16 years of age, infants as young as 3 months may develop PIMS-TS. SARS-CoV-2 is usually not isolated at presentation and most cases were previously healthy or with only mild symptoms in keeping with COVID-19, 4–6 weeks prior to presentation. The key laboratory features include: elevated C reactive protein, ferritin, neutrophils, D-dimer, troponin I, N-terminal pro B-type natriuretic peptide, with low lymphocyte count and vitamin D levels (25). It has been proposed that a host immune response to SARS-CoV-2 triggers an inflammatory response (cytokine storm).

At post mortem, cases of PIMS-TS do not show prominent pneumonia, and viral infection seems to mainly affect endothelial cells, mainly in cardiac and brain vessels, as well as in parenchymal cells of various tissues. Myocarditis, encephalitis, liver necrosis, microthrombi, lymphopenia and nephritis have been described in these cases (24).

Viral encephalitis is usually asymptomatic, or the infant may be non-specifically unwell and so it is particularly difficult to diagnose in immunodeficient children (26). Enteroviral encephalitis predominates in the first 3 months of life and herpes simplex is more common after 6 months. Other viruses that may cause encephalitis are other herpesviruses, adenovirus, measles, mumps and rubella (27). When the brainstem is affected, infants may present with a sudden collapse.

In cases of overwhelming infection, the possibility of an underlying immunodeficiency state should be considered and investigated, particularly in cases of viral or pneumococcal infection. Immunodeficiency should also be considered in case of disseminated BCGitis (28,29).

Cardiac disease

Around 10 percent of sudden infant deaths can be attributed to cardiac disease (30). Viral myocarditis has already been discussed. Eosinophilic myocarditis, which tends to occur in older children, can be associated with drug toxicity, infections or hypereosinophilic syndrome (31).

Undiagnosed congenital cardiac malformations remain a significant cause of sudden death despite advances in neonatal screening, particularly in the first week of life. Infants frequently have problems feeding and the parents describe them as not being quite well. Very often death is due to an observed collapse rather than a death in a cot. The commonest cardiac abnormalities that may result in infant death are truncus arteriosus, transposition of the great arteries, aortic stenosis/atresia and other causes of hypoplastic left heart syndrome. Other recognized causes are total anomalous pulmonary venous return and anomalous origin of the coronary arteries. Another rare condition that may result in sudden infant death is fibromuscular dysplasia of the coronary arteries. Fibrodysplasia may affect other arteries in the body and the vascular changes are often focal and segmental.

Another cause of sudden infant deaths, generally as an observed collapse, is cardiomyopathy. This can be hypertrophic or dilated. A possible underlying metabolic (glycogen storage disease, LCHAD) or mitochondrial disease should be investigated.

Noonan syndrome typically has hypertrophic cardiomyopathy. Severe vitamin D deficiency may present with dilated cardiomyopathy and, if not diagnosed, can be a cause of SUDI (32).

Other rarer causes of cardiomyopathy are mitogenic cardiomyopathy (32) and oncocytic (histiocytoid) cardiomyopathy. The former can be quite subtle, and the latter may be focal, so multiple samples should be taken (34). Endocardial fibroelastosis occasionally presents as SUDI (35).

Cardiac tumors may lead to arrhythmias and severe heart enlargement. Multiple rhabdomyomas raise the possibility of tuberous sclerosis; other tumors that can present as SUDI are cardiac fibromas, myxomas, myofibroblastic sarcomas and angiomyomas (36).

Finally, long QT syndrome (LQTS) is a group of disorders characterized by the prolongation of the QT interval on an echocardiogram. They are due to delayed cardiac repolarization as a result of mutations in genes coding for cardiac ion channels. These conditions may be inherited or occur *de novo* (37–40). Diagnosis at post mortem is problematic since there are no gross findings and so it is important to store appropriate tissue for DNA studies.

Respiratory tract

Structural malformation of the upper airways, such as choanal atresia, laryngomalacia and tracheomalacia can lead to respiratory obstruction and a careful examination of the respiratory tract is fundamental (41). Noisy breathing or stridor may have been apparent in life and the condition may be exacerbated by a respiratory infection. Pierre Robin syndrome may lead to sudden unexpected death (42).

Pulmonary vascular disease is generally associated with congenital heart disease but may occur in isolation or as part of syndromes such as Smith-Lemli-Opitz. In Williams syndrome, there is an association of abnormal peripheral pulmonary vessels and supravalvular aortic stenosis (43). In the neonatal period, alveolar-capillary dysplasia causes intractable pulmonary hypertension (44).

Respiratory failure may be due to neuromuscular diseases, including congenital myopathies, polymyositis, viral myositis, and anterior horn disease. The first diagnosis may be at post-mortem examination. As the disease may be confined to the diaphragm, it is important that this is sampled (45).

Malignancies

Various tumors (including those involving the heart that have been already mentioned) can present as SUDI. Among the undiagnosed solid tumor and hematological malignancies presented as sudden unexpected death are hepatoblastoma (46), juvenile myelomonocytic leukemia (47), hepatic hemangioendothelioma (48), oligodendroglioma, congenital mesoblastic nephroma, pleuro-pulmonary-blastoma and malignant hemangioendothelioma (49). Among hematologic malignancies described as causing SUDI are B-cell acute lymphoblastic leukemia and acute myelogenous leukemia (47).

Brain and central nervous system

Meningitis and encephalitis can be a cause of sudden death in infancy as discussed above. It is worth mentioning acute necrotizing encephalopathy, which is associated with viral infections such as Influenza A and B. Reported in children from 5 months to 10 years who

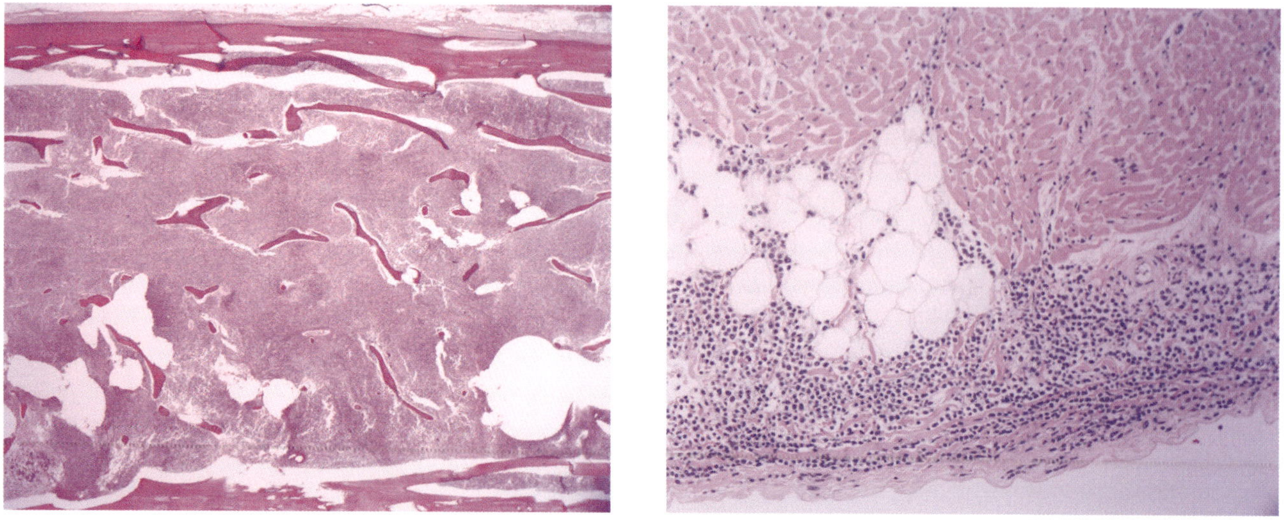

30.5 A teenager who was unwell for 48 hours before collapsing. The bone marrow was packed with a monoblastic leukemic infiltrate (a) (H&E x 20); blood vessels were distended due to the infiltrate, with focal leukemic cells in many organs (b) monoblastic cells infiltrating the pericardium (H&E x 200). SARS-CoV-2 was identified in the nasopharyngeal swab but this was interpreted as coincidental to the cause of death.

present with a respiratory illness followed by acute encephalopathy, it is associated with hepatomegaly and hepatic necrosis.

Strokes can also cause death in childhood and half of them occur in children with underlying problems such as cardiac disease.

Metabolic disease of the central nervous system (CNS), particularly lipid storage or mitochondrial diseases should be considered in infants who collapse unexpectedly or after stress such as an infection.

Epileptic seizures in children with known epilepsy may cause sudden death. In many of these cases, there may be no findings at post mortem. Death is more likely in infants with an underlying developmental disorder (50). Dravet syndrome is a recognized cause of SUDI in children over 1 year of age (51).

Dural hemorrhage is common in neonates and although less common, it can be seen in older infants in the absence of trauma (52). Older hemorrhages may rarely be seen in SIDS autopsies (53,54) and fresh subdural hemorrhage has been described in a case of resuscitated SIDS infant (55).

Intraventricular hemorrhages are typically associated with immature brains in premature infants.

Birth trauma, particularly after a difficult instrumental delivery, may result in skull fractures or occipital osteodiastasis. Skull fracture should be considered if there is cephalohematoma or subarachnoid hemorrhage. Most fractures are linear but depressed and complex fractures may occur. They can be seen not only with forceps but also with ventouse deliveries, and occasionally even in normal deliveries (56). Occipital osteodiastasis may occur when there is excessive occipital pressure during breech or instrumental delivery which causes tearing of the occipital venous sinuses or tentorium, with cerebellar edema and laceration (57,58). Histology of other organs may show cerebral tissue (GFAP positive) in blood vessels (59).

SIDS and SUDC

Sudden infant death syndrome (SIDS) is defined as the sudden unexpected death of an infant below the age of 1 year, with onset of the fatal episode apparently during sleep, which remains unexplained after a thorough investigation, including a complete autopsy, examination of the death scene, and review of the clinical history (60). Identified risk factors for SIDS include male sex, prematurity, low birth weight, prone sleeping position, smoking, young parents and low socioeconomic status (61).

Sudden unexpected death in childhood (SUDC) is the sudden death of a healthy child aged between 1 and 18 years of age which remains unexplained after reviewing the clinical history, circumstances of death, performance of a complete autopsy and ancillary testing (62,63). SUDC is most common between the ages of 1 and 4 and accounts for 1.3/100 000 deaths per year in this age range (64–66). The Centers for Disease Control estimates that SUDC is 50.7 to 600 times less common than SIDS, the leading cause of death in infancy (63).

The protocol of post-mortem examination in any death presenting suddenly and unexpectedly in an infant or a child should include the following steps:

1. Information gathering: clinical and family history, home visit (conducted jointly by a pediatrician and the police, both with expertise in the investigation of these cases). The social services and police registry should be checked.
2. Post-mortem examination instructed by the Coroner/Procurator Fiscal or equivalent jurisdiction: conducted as soon as possible by a pathologist with expertise in pediatric deaths.
3. Photographs of the front and back of the body, as well as any specific lesions. Weight and other measures compared with appropriate charts.

TABLE 30.4 Ancillary investigations to be conducted in all sudden deaths in infancy or childhood

Ancillary investigation	Specification	Specification
X -Ray	Full body	
Metabolic analysis	Blood spot (Guthrie Card) Urine for organic acids	Skin sample: Fibroblast culture to exclude FAO
Genetic analysis (including Whole Genome Sequencing if available)	Skin sample	
Nasopharyngeal swab	Virology	Bacteriology
Tracheal Swab	Virology	Bacteriology
Lung	Virology	Bacteriology
Blood	Virology	Bacteriology
Bowel content	Virology	Bacteriology
Toxicology	Full and preserved blood Vitreous Urine Stomach contents*	

FAO: Fatty Acid Oxidation Disorders.
* A sample can be kept frozen and sent if required.

TABLE 30.5 Minimum histology samples and special stains if necessary

Heart: 1 LV, 1 RV, 1 septum	Septum: levels & EVG
Lungs: 1 from each lobe hilum to periphery	EVG, Perls
Trachea with thyroid 1	
Larynx through epiglottis 1	
Gastro-esophageal junction 1	
Gastrointestinal tract: rectum 1, TI;1	
Liver: left lobe 1, right lobe 1	Reticulin, EVG, PAS, PAS-D
Spleen 1	
Pancreas 1 (consider longitudinal)	
Kidneys: right 1, left 1	
Adrenals: left 1, right 1	
Gonads	
Rib (right 5th or 6th) including costochondral, including chondrocostal junction	
Skeletal muscle: psoas & diaphragm	
Lymph nodes if relevant	
Pool of liver, kidney, heart and muscle	Oil red O
Brainstem: Medulla	
Pons	
Midbrain	
Cerebellum: Vermis	
Dentate nuclei (R&L)	
Cerebrum: Frontal cortex (R&L)	
Basal Ganglia (R&L)	
Hippocampi (R&L)	
Occipital cortex (R&L)	
Hypothalamus	

L: left; R: right; LV: left ventricle; RV: right ventricle; EVG: Elastic Van Gieson; PAS; Periodic Acid Schiff stain; PAS-D: Periodic Acid Schiff -Diastase.

4. A careful external examination should record general nutritional status and hygiene, any abnormal findings in the skin or any evidence of disease, evidence of malformations and evidence of medical intervention. A careful internal examination should identify any malformation, features of any disease (infection, tumor, etc.) and/or trauma.
5. Minimal ancillary investigations to be conducted are shown in Table 30.4. Any additional cultures should be considered if needed (for example: middle ear swab in otitis media, virology from the myocardium if myocarditis is suspected; etc.).
6. Tissue samples: See Table 30.5.
7. Clinical-pathological summary: This should include a careful review of the clinical history and autopsy findings including the ancillary investigations.
8. Multidisciplinary meeting to discuss the cause of death: chaired by a pediatrician, and with the attendance of the pathologist, police, ambulance team, emergency team involved in the resuscitation, general practitioner, etc.

REFERENCES

1. Cohen MC, Scheimberg I. Forensic aspects of perinatal deaths. *Acad Forensic Pathol* 2018; 8(3): 452–91.
2. Scheimberg I, Cohen MC, Zapata Vazquez RE, et al. Nontraumatic intradural and subdural hemorrhage and hypoxic ischemic encephalopathy in fetuses, infants, and children up to three years of age: Analysis of two audits of 636 cases from two referral centers in the United Kingdom. *Pediatr Dev Pathol* 2013; **16**(3): 149–59.
3. Rooks VJ, Eaton JP, Ruess L, et al. Prevalence and evolution of intracranial hemorrhage in asymptomatic term infants. *AJNR Am J Neuroradiol* 2008; **29**(6): 1082–9.
4. Scheimberg I, Arbuckle S, Holden S. Intrapartum and Neonatal Death. In: Cohen MC, Scheimberg I (eds). *The Pediatric and Perinatal Autopsy Manual.* Cambridge: Cambridge University Press; 2014.
5. Callaway NF, Ludwig CA, Blumenkranz MS, et al. Retinal and optic nerve hemorrhages in the newborn infant: One-year results of the Newborn Eye Screen Test Study. *Ophthalmology* 2016; **123**(5): 1043–52.
6. Hughes LA, May K, Talbot JF, Parsons MA. Incidence, distribution, and duration of birth-related retinal hemorrhages: A prospective study. *J AAPOS* 2006; **10**(2): 102–6.
7. Gregersen, N. Protein misfolding disorders: Pathogenesis and intervention. *J Inherit Metab Dis* 2006; **29**: 456–70.
8. Gregersen N, Bross P. Protein misfolding and cellular stress: An overview. *Methods Mol Biol* 2010; **648**: 3–23.
9. Cohen MC, Yap S, Olpin SE. Inherited Metabolic Disease and Sudden Unexpected Death. In: Payne-James JJ, Byard R (eds). *Encyclopaedia of Forensic and Legal Medicine*. 2nd ed. New York: Elsevier; 2015.
10. Olpin SE. Pathophysiology of fatty oxidation disorders and resultant phenotypic variability. *J Inherit Metab Dis* 2013; **36**: 645–58.
11. Gilbert Barness E, Barness L. *Metabolic Diseases: Foundations of Clinical Management, Genetics and Pathology.* Natick, MA: Eaton Publishing; 2000.
12. Howatson AG. The autopsy for sudden unexpected death in infancy. *Curr Diagn Pathol* 2006; **12**: 173–83.
13. Byard RW. *Sudden Death in the Young.* 3rd ed. Cambridge, UK: Cambridge University Press; 2010.
14. Sawal M, Cohen MC, Irazuzta JE, et al. Fulminant pertussis: A multicenter study with new insights into the clinico-pathological mechanisms. *Pediatr Pulmonol* 2009; **44**(10): 970–80.
15. Angelski CL, McKay E, Blackie B. A case of functional asplenia and pneumococcal sepsis. *Pediatr Emerg Care* 2011; **27**(7): 639–41.
16. Gerber JE. Acute necrotizing bacterial tonsillitis with Clostridium perfringens. *Am J Forensic Med Pathol* 2001; **22**(2): 177–9.
17. Coutlhard M, Issacs D. Retropharyngeal abscess. *Arch Dis Child* 1991; **66**: 1227–30.
18. Peres LC, Cohen MC. Sudden unexpected early neonatal death due to undiagnosed Hirschsprung disease enterocolitis: A report of two cases and literature review. *Forensic Sci Med Pathol* 2013; **9**(4): 558–63.
19. Prtak L, Al-Adnani M, Fenton P, et al. Contribution of bacteriology and virology in sudden unexpected death in infancy. *Arch Dis Child* 2010; **95**(5): 371–6.
20. Neagu O, Rodríguez AF, Callon D, et al. Myocarditis presenting as sudden death in infants and children: A single centre analysis by ESGFOR study group. *Pediatr Dev Pathol* 2021; **24**(4): 327–36.
21. Inwald D, Franklin O, Cubitt D, et al. Enterovirus myocarditis as a cause of neonatal collapse. *Arch Dis Child Fetal Neonatal Ed* 2004; **89**: F461–2.
22. Pickens DL, Schefft GL, Storch GA, Thach BT. Characterization of prolonged apneic episodes associated with respiratory syncytial virus infection. *Pediatr Pulmonol* 1989; **6**: 195–201.
23. Bhopal SS, Bagaria J, Olabi B, Bhopal R. Children and young people remain at low risk of COVID-19 mortality. *Lancet Child Adolesc Health* 2021; **5**(5): e12–e13. Erratum in: *Lancet Child Adolesc Health* 2021; **5**(5): e18.
24. Duarte-Neto AN, Cald EG, Gomes-Gouvêa MS, et al. An autopsy study of the spectrum of severe COVID-19 in children: From SARS to different phenotypes of MIS-C. *EClinicalMedicine* 2021; **35**: 100850.
25. White M, Tiesman B, Handforth J, et al. Paediatric inflammatory multisystem syndrome temporally associated with SARS-CoV-2 (PIMS-TS): The Evelina Experience. *Arch Dis Child* 2020; **105**(11): 1025–27.
26. Messacar K, Fischer M, Dominguez SR, et al. Encephalitis in US children. *Infect Dis Clin North Am* 2018; **32**(1): 145–62.
27. Modlin JF. Perinatal echovirus and group B coxsackievirus infections. *Clin Perinatol* 1988; **15**: 233–46.
28. Cohen MC, Drut R. Cytologic features of disseminated Bacillus Calmette-Guérin (BCG) infection. *Diagnost Cytopathol* 2001; **25**(2): 134–137.
29. Kourime M, Akpalu EN, Ouair H, et al. BCGitis/ BCGosis in children: Diagnosis, classification and exploration. *Arch Pediatr* 2016; **23**(7): 754–9.
30. Pryce JW, Weber MA, Ashworth MT et al. Changing patterns of infant death over the last 100 years: Autopsy experience from a specialist children's hospital. *J R Soc Med* 2012; **105**(3): 123–30.
31. Krous HF, Haaas E, Chadwick AE, Wagner GN. Sudden death in a neonate associated with idiopathic eosinophilic myocarditis. *Pediatr Dev Pathol* 2005; **8**: 587–92.
32. Scheimberg I, Perry L. Does low vitamin D have a role in pediatric morbidity and mortality? An observational study of vitamin D in a cohort of 52 postmortem examinations. *Pediatr Dev Pathol* 2014; **17**(6): 455–64.
33. Chang KT, Taylor GP, Meschino WS, et al. Mitogenic cardiomyopathy: A lethal neonatal familial dilated cardiomyopathy characterized by myocyte hyperplasia and proliferation. *Hum Pathol* 2010; **41**(7): 1002–8.
34. Andreu AL, Checcarelli N, Iwata S, et al. A missense mutation in the mitochondrial cytochrome *b* gene in a revisited case with histiocytoid cardiomyopathy. *Pediatr Res* 2000; **48**: 311–14.
35. Bennett MJ, Hale DE, Pollitt RJ, et al. Endocardial fibroelastosis and primary carnitine deficiency due to a defect in the plasma membrane carnitine transporter. *Clin Cardiol* 1996; **19**: 243–6.
36. Bryant VA, Booth J, Palm L, et al. Childhood neoplasms presenting at autopsy: A 20-year experience. *Pediatr Blood Cancer* 2017; **64**(9).
37. Schwartz PJ, Stramba-Badiale M, Segantini A, et al. Prolongation of the QT interval and the Sudden Infant Death Syndrome. *N Engl J Med* 1998; **338**: 1709–14.
38. Lahrouchi N, Raju H, Lodder EM, et al. The yield of postmortem genetic testing in sudden death cases with structural findings at autopsy. *Eur J Hum Genet* 2020; **28**: 17–22.
39. Raju H, Ware JS, Skinner JR, et al. Next-generation sequencing using microfluidic PCR enrichment for molecular autopsy. *BMC Cardiovasc Disord* 2019; **19**(1): 174.
40. Tester DJ, Wong LCH, Chanana P, et al. Cardiac genetic predisposition in sudden infant death syndrome. *J Am Coll Cardiol* 2018; **71**(11): 1217–1227.

41. Sivan Y, Ben-Ari J, Schonfeld TM. Laryngomalacia: A cause for early near miss for SIDS. *Int J Pediatr Otorhinolaryngol* 1991; **21:** 59–64.
42. Costa MA, Tu MM, Murage KP, et al. Robin sequence: Mortality, causes of death, and clinical outcomes. *Plast Reconstr Surg* 2014; **134(4):** 738–45.
43. Khairul Z, Kirsten H, Nicholson AG, Cohen MC. Abnormal muscularization of intra acinar pulmonary arteries in 2 cases presenting as sudden infant death (SIDS). *Pediatr Dev Pathol* 2017; **20(1):** 49–53.
44. Hung SP, Huang SH, Wu CH, et al. Misalignment of lung vessels and alveolar-capillary dysplasia: A case report with autopsy. *Pediatr Neonatol* 2011; **52(4):** 232–6.
45. Sundararajan S, Ostojic NS, Rushton DI, et al. Diaphragmatic pathology: A cause of clinically unexplained death in the perinatal/paediatric age group. *Med Sci Law* 2005; **45:** 110–14.
46. Pryce J, Kiho L, Scheimberg I. Sudden unexpected death in infancy associated with an epithelial-type hepatoblastoma in a 6-month-old infant. *Pediatr Dev Pathol* 2010; **13(4):** 338–40.
47. Somers GR, Smith CR, Perrin DG, et al. Sudden unexpected death in infancy and childhood due to undiagnosed neoplasia: An autopsy study. *Am J Forensic Med Pathol* 2006; **27(1):** 64–9.
48. Lunetta P, Karikoski R, Penttilä A, Sajantila A. Sudden death associated with a multifocal type II hemangioendothelioma of the liver in a 3-month-old infant. *Am J Forensic Med Pathol* 2004; **25(1):** 56–9.
49. Rajs J, Råsten-Almqvist P, Nennesmo I. Unexpected death in two young infants mimics SIDS: autopsies demonstrate tumors of medulla and heart. *Am J Forensic Med Pathol* 1997; **18(4):** 384–90.
50. Callenbach PM, Westendorp RG, Geerts AT, et al. Mortality risk in children with epilepsy: the Dutch study of epilepsy in childhood. *Pediatrics* 2001; **107:** 1259–63.
51. Cooper MS, Mcintosh A, Crompton DE, et al. Mortality in Dravet syndrome. *Epilepsy Res* 2016; **128:** 43–7.
52. Scheimberg I, Cohen MC, Zapata Vazquez R, et al. Non-traumatic intradural and subdural hemorrhage and hypoxic ischaemic encephalopathy in fetuses, infants and children up to 3 years of age: Analysis of two audits of 636 cases from two referral centers in the UK. *Pediatr Dev Pathol* 2013; **16(3):** 149–59.
53. Keeling J, Busuttil A. Sudden Unexpected Death in Infancy. In: Busuttil A, Keeling J (eds). *Paediatric Forensic Medicine and Pathology*. London: Edward Arnold; 2009, p. 218.
54. Rogers CB, Itabashi HH, Tomiyasu U, et al. Subdural neomembranes and sudden infant death syndrome. *J Forensic Sci* 1998; **43(2):** 375–6.
55. Krous HF, Haas EA, Chadwick AE, et al. Delayed death in sudden infant death syndrome: A San Diego SIDS/SUDC Research Project 15-year population-based report. *Forensic Sci Int* 2008; **176(2–3):** 209–16.
56. Hughes CA, Harley EH, Milmoe G, et al. Birth trauma in the head and neck. *Arch Otolaryngol Head Neck Surg* 1999; **125:** 193–99.
57. Wigglesworth JS, Husemeyer RP. Intracranial birth trauma in vaginal breech delivery: The continued importance of injury to the occipital bone. *BJOG* 1977; **84:** 684–91.
58. Dixit S, Jain A, Data S, Sinha N. Occipital osteodiastasis. *Indian Pediatr* 2010; **47:** 440–2.
59. Cox P, Silvestri E, Lazda E, et al. Embolism of brain tissue in intrapartum and early neonatal deaths: Report of 9 cases. *Pediatr Develop Pathol* 2009; **12:** 464–8.
60. Krous HF, Beckwith JB, Byard RW, et al. Sudden infant death syndrome and unclassified sudden infant deaths: A definitional and diagnostic approach. *Pediatrics* 2004; **114:** 234–8.
61. Byard RW, Krous HF. Sudden infant death syndrome: overview and update. *Pediatr Dev Pathol* 2003; **6:** 112–27.
62. Kinney HC, Chadwick AE, Crandall LA, et al. Sudden death, febrile seizures, and hippocampal and temporal lobe maldevelopment in toddlers: A new entity. *Pediatr Dev Pathol* 2009; **12:** 455–63.
63. Hesdorffer DC, Crandall LA, Friedman D, Devinsky O. Sudden unexplained death in childhood: A comparison of cases with and without a febrile seizure history. *Epilepsia* 2015; **56:** 1294–300.
64. Kinney HC, Armstrong DL, Chadwick AE, et al. Sudden death in toddlers associated with developmental abnormalities of the Hippocampus: A report of five cases. *Pediatr Dev Pathol* 2007; **10:** 208–23.
65. Crandall LG. Inexplicable child deaths: Medicolegal death investigation resources from the SUDC Foundation and the SUDC registry and research collaborative. *Acad Forensic Pathol* 2017; **7:** 24–6.
66. Krous HF, Chadwick AE, Crandall L, Nadeau-Manning JM. Sudden unexpected death in childhood: A report of 50 cases. *Pediatr Dev Pathol* 2005; **8:** 307–19.

CHAPTER

31 Maternal Death

Victoria Francis and Matthew Lynch

INTRODUCTION

Maternal deaths have long been recognized as a significant global health problem and while over recent decades, the number of maternal deaths has declined in developed countries, it remains a significant global health issue. Pregnancy-associated death should be considered in any unexpected death in a young woman. The approach to the maternal death autopsy will be addressed along with discussions of the more difficult conditions associated with maternal deaths.

Definitions

The World Health Organization (WHO) defines maternal deaths as the "number of female deaths from any cause related to or aggravated by pregnancy or its management (excluding accidental or incidental causes) during pregnancy and childbirth or within 42 days of termination of pregnancy, irrespective of the duration and site of the pregnancy" (1,2). A late maternal death is a maternal death that occurs more than 42 days but less than one year following the termination of pregnancy (1,2). The 11th revision of the ICD combines maternal and late maternal deaths into a "comprehensive maternal deaths" which also includes unintentional, accidental and incidental deaths (1,2).

There is a further subclassification of maternal deaths into direct or indirect deaths. Direct maternal or obstetric deaths are defined as those "resulting from obstetric complications of the pregnant state (pregnancy, labor and puerperium), and from interventions, omissions, incorrect treatment or from a chain of events resulting from any of the above" (1,2). An indirect maternal death results "from previous existing disease or disease developed during pregnancy and not due to direct obstetric causes but were aggravated by the physiologic effects of pregnancy" (1). More recently, deaths due to postpartum depression or psychosis are also classified as direct maternal deaths (3).

INDIRECT VS DIRECT DEATHS

It is important for all maternal deaths to be identified and analyzed for public health purposes, but this can be difficult in some cases, in particular, delayed maternal deaths may be difficult to capture in this process. Some of the classifications also may seem arbitrary – for example, whether a cardiomyopathy developed during pregnancy, is purely due to the pregnancy in isolation, or if it is the unmasking of an underlying condition in the setting of the physiological stress of pregnancy (3). Further, the effects of some conditions (for example, postpartum cardiomyopathy) may not manifest until months after delivery (4). There is also a probable under-reporting of some types of maternal deaths, such as those due to unsafe abortions, and also when the cause of death is misclassified or inaccurate (5).

Maternal deaths should be collated for appropriate categorization and analysis with an aim to prevent further deaths (6). In some countries, such as the United Kingdom (UK) and Japan, there are nationwide comprehensive and multidisciplinary review systems in which maternal deaths are reviewed and regular reports are published along with recommendations for improving care and preventing further morbidity and mortality (6,7). Some maternal deaths may not be identified in a Coronial system as they may not be reportable (for example, deaths due to malignancy or already diagnosed cardiovascular disorders). In Australia, National Maternal Mortality Data Collection is collected under the banner of the Australian Institute of Health and Welfare (AIHW) (8). Forensic pathology involvement in any multidisciplinary clinical groups discussing these deaths is strongly recommended.

Factors associated with increased risk of maternal death include increased maternal age, obesity, lower socio-economic status and ethnicity (9). In developed countries, women of non-white ethnicity are reported to have an increased risk of maternal death for various reasons including language barriers, medical care access and affordability and other multifactorial issues including endemic systemic racism (10).

APPROACH TO AUTOPSY IN MATERNAL DEATHS

As with any sudden or unexpected death in a young person, the approach to the maternal death autopsy needs to be thorough and well-documented (9,11,12). A comprehensive review of the medical records is required prior to undertaking the examination, particularly when the death has occurred during or following delivery (11). If relevant, placental and/or hysterectomy specimens

DOI: 10.1201/9781003138754-33

should be examined but if not available, hospital histology pathology reports and histology slides should be reviewed.

Post-mortem radiology, particularly post-mortem computed tomography (PMCT) is strongly recommended. There are certain cases in which PMCT is particularly useful to direct how the autopsy may proceed. For example, cases in which there is intracranial or thoracic hemorrhage seen on PMCT which may suggest a cause of death but internal autopsy investigation is still recommended to investigate any underlying cause of hemorrhage. CT angiogram may be considered in order to possibly identify the source of peritoneal or thoracic hemorrhage, although this may be balanced against the potential difficulties that arise from the artefact caused by contrast. PMCT with angiography is particularly useful in cases of splenic artery aneurysm rupture that may be associated with pregnancy. PMCT provides valuable information in deaths in which venous gas embolism is a potential cause of death to be able to identify intravascular gas and to provide comparative information (i.e. gas in the liver may represent decomposition rather than evidence of air embolism). In cases where medical treatment may be an issue, it may also be prudent for antemortem imaging to be reviewed by an independent radiologist.

A full (three cavity) autopsy examination should ideally be undertaken in these cases, depending on coronial permission and the next of kin's assent (9,11,12,15). Consideration should be given for more detailed neuropathologic examination or referral of organs (for example the placenta) to a histopathologist with a special interest in gynecologic pathology. Photography of relevant specimens (including macroscopic and histologic) should be recorded if possible. Examination and documentation of genital tract tears following delivery and potentially *en bloc* removal of the lower genital tract may be advisable in cases involving postpartum hemorrhage and potential genital tract trauma. Examination of the fetus should also be undertaken, and this most commonly involves an external examination including appropriate measurements to check growth (11,12).

In some cases where there may be an early pregnancy, it may be necessary to confirm pregnancy – while in more advanced pregnancies this should be straightforward, it is possible to test for the presence of β-HCG on post-mortem blood, vitreous and bile specimens (13,14). Toxicology, biochemistry and microbiology should be undertaken particularly in maternal deaths occurring out of hospital, but discretion may be applied depending on the circumstances and relevance to the case.

There are conditions that can cause direct maternal death throughout any stage of pregnancy including venous thrombosis (pulmonary thromboembolism), pre-eclampsia/eclampsia (although this most commonly occurs around parturition) and sepsis (although ascending infection is most common following delivery) and many of the potential causes of indirect maternal deaths (for example, epilepsy, asthma, cardiac conditions) may affect any stage of pregnancy (Table 31.1). The approach to autopsy may also vary depending on the deceased's stage of pregnancy and the circumstances surrounding the death (11) and these stages are discussed in the following paragraphs.

TABLE 31.1 More common causes of maternal death

Direct	
Condition	***Phase of pregnancy****
Ruptured ectopic pregnancy	Early
Gestational trophoblastic disease (including choriocarcinoma)	Early
Unsafe/illegal abortion	Early
Acute fatty liver of pregnancy	Late pregnancy
Obstructed labor	Peripartum
Puerperal sepsis	Postpartum/Any phase
Obstetric hemorrhage (incl. uterine atony, placental issues)	Peri- or post Postpartum
Venous thrombosis/pulmonary thromboembolism (PE)	Any phase
Amniotic fluid embolism	Peripartum
Anesthetic-related death	Peri- or postpartum
Vascular gas/air embolism	Peripartum (surgical delivery)
Pre-eclampsia/eclampsia/ hypertensive disorders	Late pregnancy/ peripartum
Postpartum cardiomyopathy	Postpartum
Suicide (Postpartum depression/ anxiety/psychosis)	Postpartum
Unascertained	Any phase
Uterine rupture	Later pregnancy/ peripartum
Coronary artery dissection	Postpartum
Indirect	
Morphologic/congenital cardiovascular disease	Postpartum/Any phase
SADS-MNH^	Postpartum/Any phase
PE (underlying thrombophilia)	Any phase
Epilepsy	Any phase
Asthma	Any phase
Sickle cell crisis	Any phase
Cancer (i.e. breast, gynecologic)	Any phase
Suicide (underlying mental health issues)	Postpartum/Any phase
Non-obstetric hemorrhage (i.e. ruptured aneurysm)	Any phase
Obesity related death	Any phase
HIV/AIDS	Any phase
Connective tissue disorders	Any phase
Systemic hypertension	Any phase
Community acquired sepsis/ infection (i.e. influenza/pneumonia)	Any phase
Diabetes mellitus-related deaths	Any phase
Homicide	Any phase

(Continued)

TABLE 31.1 (Continued)

Coincidental	
Accident	Any phase
Cancer (not worsened by or related to pregnancy)	Any phase
Drug-related deaths	Any phase

* *Most* common phase(s) of pregnancy.

^ Sudden Adult Death Syndrome in a person with a Morphologically Normal Heart.

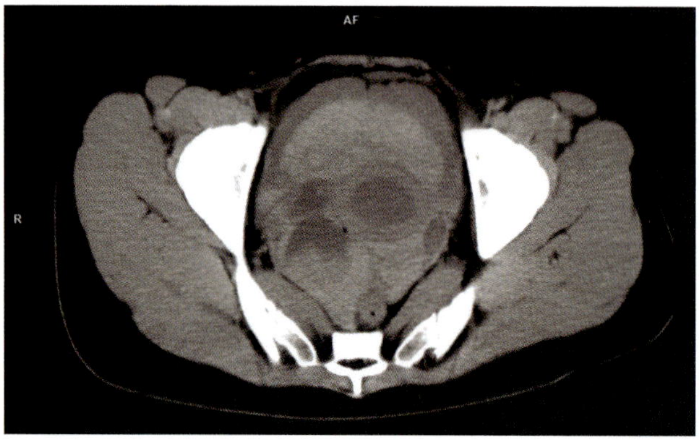

31.1 PM CT image of peritoneal hemorrhage due to ruptured tubal ectopic pregnancy.

DEATHS DURING PREGNANCY

The most common cause of direct maternal death in early pregnancy is a ruptured ectopic pregnancy. Ectopic pregnancy should be considered as the most likely cause of peritoneal hemorrhage in a young woman (Figures 31.1 and 31.2) whether she is known to be pregnant or not.

Trophoblastic disease (sometimes resulting in pulmonary embolization) is also reported in early pregnancy, particularly following treatment (16,17). Indirect and incidental maternal deaths are much more common than direct deaths (5) particularly around this phase of pregnancy, with causes varying from underlying cardiovascular or other conditions, motor vehicle accidents, suspicious deaths/homicides and drug-related deaths.

Death following legal or natural abortion is rare in developed countries with hemorrhage or infection being the most likely causes (Figures 31.3 and 31.4). Historically, in developed countries, a large proportion of maternal deaths were due to illegal abortions with common complications including sepsis or endotoxic shock, venous gas embolism, fat embolism, uterine rupture, or hemorrhage (17,18).

Maternal deaths associated with birth

Hemorrhage, sepsis, hypertensive disorders (including pre-eclampsia/eclampsia), fatty liver of pregnancy are some of the main conditions occurring around childbirth, but delivery may be expedited because of the presence of hypertensive conditions or fatty liver of pregnancy. Deaths during childbirth are the most common cause of direct maternal deaths in undeveloped countries and complications of obstructed labor, hemorrhage and sepsis are particularly common in these regions (5).

Anesthetic-related deaths, involving either spinal or general anesthetics, are also more common around delivery, but the incidence of these deaths has significantly decreased over the last few decades (7,15). The potential complications are the same as in non-maternal death related anesthetic complications and include anaphylaxis, neuro-axial/high spinal block, line or airway placement issues, incorrect agent administration or incorrect dosage, bronchospasm and aspiration (7,15).

Deaths due to hemorrhage around delivery can be difficult to diagnose during the autopsy and if death occurred during or following surgery, it is important to have all available surgical specimens for examination. The estimation of blood loss is often based on visual approximation which is dependent on multiple factors including the experience of the clinician and it should be also noted that the autopsy findings of exsanguination are non-specific and the post-mortem diagnosis is usually based on these non-specific autopsy findings, circumstantial evidence and in the absence of another competing cause of death. There is also the difficulty of interpreting degrees of blood loss in the setting of transfusion protocols. Transfusion itself also carries risk, in particular, risk of TRALI (transfusion related lung injury) (15). Often, amniotic fluid embolism is presented as a differential diagnosis in these cases and the difficulty in differentiating these entities is discussed below.

Delayed maternal deaths

Delayed maternal deaths are rarer, particularly in Australia, but these deaths may also be more difficult to identify as the deceased's maternal status is not always made clear in the available history. Psychiatric deaths, due to postpartum depression, anxiety or psychosis, would be the most common cause of reportable direct delayed maternal deaths. Cardiovascular conditions may also be more likely in this cohort (19).

Embolic maternal deaths

Embolism (due to thrombus, air, fat or amniotic fluid) is one of the commonest causes of cardiorespiratory arrest during pregnancy (15,20). Most embolic deaths are due to thrombosis, and it is important in the autopsy that examination of the pelvic vessels is undertaken. The differentiation of thromboembolic maternal deaths into direct or indirect categories may be arbitrary as up to 50 percent of patients with an underlying thrombophilia will be unmasked in the setting of an additional risk factor such as pregnancy (20), although thromboembolic deaths are generally classified as direct even with an underlying thrombophilia. Fat embolism may occur in pregnant women with sickle cell disease and rarely in the setting of fatty liver of pregnancy but the most common cause of fat emboli would be in the setting of trauma or cardiopulmonary resuscitation (15).

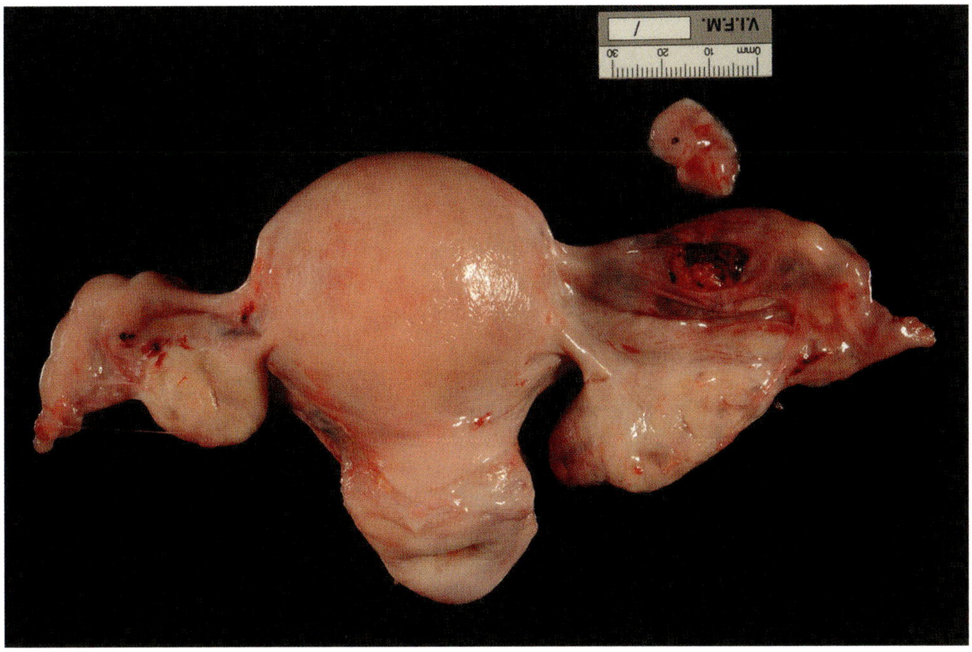

31.2 Ectopic pregnancy – Uterus with ruptured fallopian tube and separate fetus.

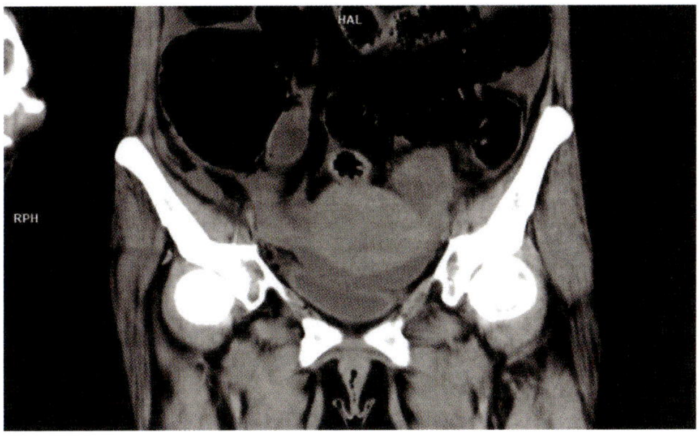

31.3 PM CT image of pelvic collection in the case of Group A Streptococcal ascending infection following spontaneous miscarriage.

The amniotic fluid embolism/anaphylactoid syndrome of pregnancy issue

Amniotic fluid embolism (AFE) is a rare but serious complication of pregnancy and delivery. The condition was first described in 1926 but the clinical importance of the condition was recognized in 1941 (21,22). The exact mechanism is unclear, but an immune-mediated cause appears to be the current theory with a systematic inflammatory response syndrome and an anaphylaxis-like response and more recent papers call the entity "anaphylactoid syndrome of pregnancy" although it should be noted that there is no elevation of tryptase in these cases (23). It is a clinical diagnosis which usually presents as a sudden, unexplained cardiovascular collapse with profound hypotension or hypoxemia and associated with disseminated intravascular coagulation (DIC), although the criteria to clinically diagnose the entity varies in different countries (23–25). It should also be noted that

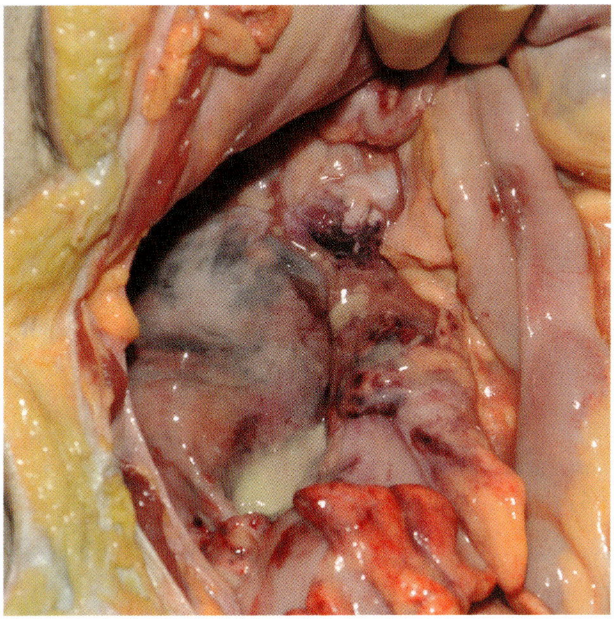

31.4 Autopsy images of pelvic collection in the case of Group A Streptococcal ascending infection following spontaneous miscarriage.

DIC may be secondary to various conditions, including sepsis, pre-eclampsia, uterine rupture (12) and even postpartum hemorrhage (26) but once DIC has developed it may be more difficult to confirm an underlying cause. Treatment of AFE is supportive and the survival rate has improved over time, particularly with early diagnosis and with appropriate intensive care unit support.

While some risk factors have been recognized such as increased maternal age, induced labor (any form but particularly with oxytocin infusion and instrumental delivery), no one risk factor has been categorically proven (12,25). Over the last two decades, research has been undertaken to try to identify how to more accurately diagnose the entity in the hospital setting. More recent studies have suggested two types of AFE with the more classical cardiopulmonary collapse type involving amniotic components within the maternal pulmonary vessels and a DIC which meets the clinical AFE criteria with postpartum hemorrhage of unknown etiology, uterine atony and with fetal components in the uterine vessels (27,28).

In the post-mortem setting, the diagnosis is made based on the clinical circumstances and on the presence of fetal material (usually squames) in the pulmonary vessels. Immunohistochemistry such as cytokeratin stains (AE1/AE3), Zn-CP1 (zinc coporphyrin) and/or sialyl-Tn (to highlight meconium) or Alcian blue (for intravascular mucin) may be helpful (12,27–28); CD88 to demonstrate complement activation. However, it should be noted that fetal material within the maternal circulation is not pathognomonic for AFE without an appropriate clinical history (22,29).

In several cases, AFE has been diagnosed in the setting of postpartum hemorrhage in which massive transfusion protocol has been initiated. While the presence of genital tract trauma and subsequent hemorrhage in the setting of delivery is a risk factor for developing AFE, it is difficult to ascertain whether AFE actually exists in these cases or if the blood loss in isolation may account for the collapse and subsequent death. A recent clinical study has attempted to differentiate postpartum hemorrhage from DIC-type AFE using a careful analysis of the clinical background and using a blood loss/fibrinogen ratio which is reportedly significantly higher in AFE (30). A careful and ideally multidisciplinary review of the events leading to the death is vital in these cases to allow for appropriate clinicopathologic correlation.

Vascular gas/air embolism

Venous gas embolism requires further discussion. The clinical diagnosis of this condition is unknown and potentially underdiagnosed clinically (20). According to Lignitz et al. (17), a minimum of 120 cm^2 of gas volume is required to cause fatal gas embolism and autopsy diagnosis is made based on macroscopic autopsy findings including a dilated right ventricle and gas bubbles within the coronary arteries and frothy blood detected in the inferior vena. Richter's method has been recently confirmed to be the more accurate in determining the presence of venous air embolism (31). In this technique, the skull, clavicles, sternoclavicular joints and subclavian vessels are kept intact to prevent the introduction of gas into the right heart. Once the ribs are cut, the pericardium is opened and pericardial sac is filled with water and the right ventricle or pulmonary artery is cut and the water inspected for bubbles (31).

Venous gas embolism has been put forward as a potential cause of maternal death in the setting of cesarian section, criminal abortion (as mentioned above) and has been reported in the literature involving vaginal insufflation in oro-genital sexual activity or drug taking activities (32–36) and, more recently, in the setting of uterine inversion and atonic hemorrhage (37) in which a young woman developed persistent uterine hemorrhage following delivery. In this case report (37), the patient underwent emergency laparotomy during which she suffered a cardiac arrest in the setting of massive manual compression and packing of the uterus. She was resuscitated and underwent a hysterectomy but the patient died following a second cardiac arrest. A post-mortem X-ray and CT scan were undertaken prior to autopsy which showed extensive arterial and venous gas emboli, although the time interval between the death and the post-mortem imaging is not specified. A sample of gas was aspirated from the right heart and tested by an aspirometer, apparently proving gas embolism (37).

Little has been published on the post-mortem diagnosis of vascular gas embolism and the use of imaging, particularly PMCT scan and thus critical examination of the diagnosis of vascular gas embolism with critical evaluation of the potential for artefact related to resuscitation or putrefaction or other post-mortem changes has not been critically discussed in the literature. A careful approach to these cases and the interpretation of the radiologic and autopsy findings would be recommended.

Unascertained maternal deaths

Maternal deaths in which there is no cause of death can be frustrating for all involved (15). While a proportion of these deaths may be attributable to underlying cardiac condition/channelopathy (known as sudden adult death syndrome in a person with a morphologically normal heart or SADS/MNH), and it may be possible to subsequently attribute the death to this with genetic testing and appropriate clinical genetic follow up for family members. There is a well-known association between congenital long QT syndrome and pregnancy, the mechanism thought to be related to the massive hormonal changes known to occur around these stages (19).

One of the most complex types of maternal deaths are those which occur days to weeks following a precipitating

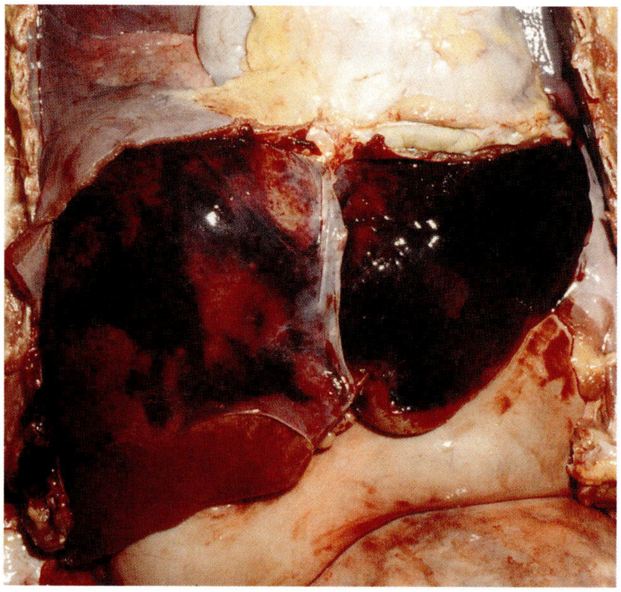

31.5 Ruptured subcapsular hepatic hematoma in a case of HELLP – *in situ* image of the liver with subcapsular hematoma.

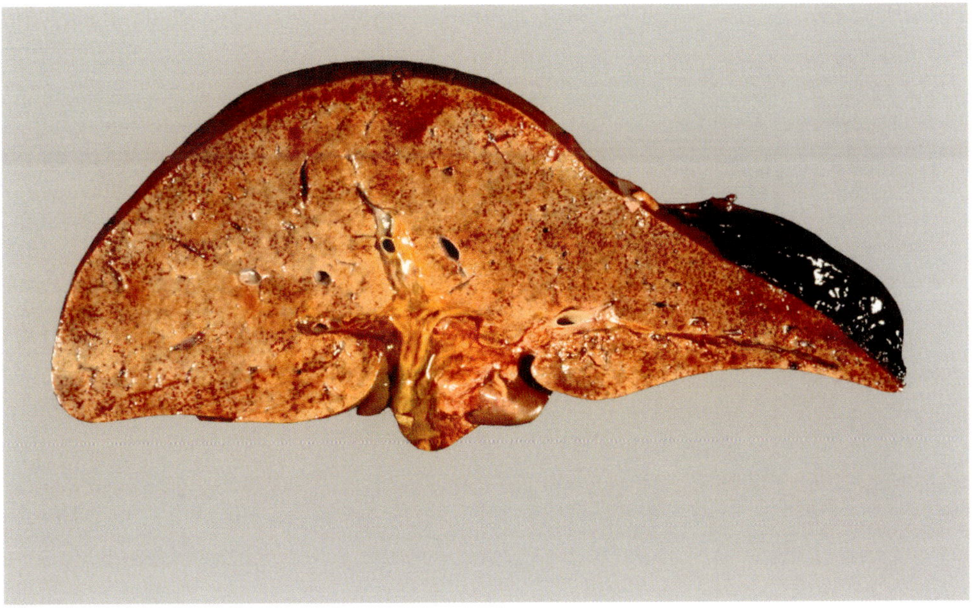

31.6 Ruptured subcapsular hepatic hematoma in a case of HELLP – cut surface of the liver with subcapsular hematoma.

arrest/event. These cases require extensive medical record review, detailed autopsy examination and clinicopathologic correlation which requires input from both the deceased's treating clinicians as well as specialists not involved with the deceased's treatment. Unfortunately in these cases, autopsy findings are heavily compromised by a period of survival and the findings usually involve post-arrest complications (aspiration pneumonitis, resuscitation injuries, hypoxic ischemic brain injury etc.) rather than any findings specific to the precipitating event (for example, in any cases of amniotic fluid, gas or fat embolism, these findings are unlikely to be found when death has occurred even hours to days following the precipitating event). Also, because the sequence of events in these cases may occur rapidly and medical records regarding the incidents are often written in retrospect and may sometimes be incomplete or potentially misleading. Underlying comorbidities such as WHO class III obesity further complicate these cases (15).

Pre-eclampsia/eclampsia

Pregnancy-associated hypertensive disease including pre-eclampsia, eclampsia and hemolysis, elevated liver enzymes, low platelet count (HELLP) are also a leading cause of global maternal and fetal morbidity and mortality and are defined as "pregnancy-specific disease characterized by new-onset hypertension, and proteinuria after 20 weeks of gestation that can progress to severe end-organ damage to the kidneys, liver, and brain" (38) (Figures 31.5 and 31.6).

Circulating antiangiogenic proteins and endothelial injury have been identified as underlying causes of the condition (38) and potential clinical presentations include gross intracerebral hemorrhage, pulmonary edema, renal impairment, placental damage, periportal vascular lesions in the hepatic circulation as well as a diastolic dysfunction syndrome (15). The placenta is the most important organ to examine histologically for proof of pre-eclampsia/eclampsia in the form of vascular and villous ischemic lesions (38–39). Endothelial damage in the renal glomeruli, liver and the cerebral white matter are included among the potential autopsy findings (38) but it can be difficult to precisely define why a woman with pre-eclampsia has died, particularly in the absence of gross intracerebral hemorrhage or evidence of HELLP (15).

CONCLUSION

The post-mortem examination of maternal death cases can be complex and requires careful documentation of autopsy and multidisciplinary clinicopathologic correlation findings in order to provide the deceased mother's family, clinicians and the wider community with relevant answers about the death and to work toward preventing future maternal deaths.

REFERENCES

1. Cresswell J. Maternal deaths. World Health Organization: Data/GHO/Indicator Metadata Registry List, 2021. Available from: https://www.who.int/data/gho/indicator-metadata-registry/imr-details/4622 (Accessed 4 April 2023).
2. World Health Organization. Trends in Maternal Mortality 2000 to 2017: Estimates by WHO, UNICEF, UNFPA, World Bank Group and the United Nations Population Division. Geneva: World Health Organization 2019. Available from: https://apps.who.int/iris/handle/10665/327596 (Accessed 24 April 2023).
3. Dada M. Maternal Deaths. In: Vanezis, P. (ed). *Essential Forensic Medicine*, 1st ed. Hoboken: John Wiley & Sons; 2020, pp. 363–9.

4. Buschmann C, Schmidbauer M, Tsokos M. Maternal and pregnancy-related death: Causes and frequencies in an autopsy study population. *Forensic Sci Med Pathol* 2013; **9**: 296–307.
5. Say L, Chou D, Gemmill A, et al. Global causes of maternal death: A WHO systematic analysis. *Lancet Glob Health* 2014; **2**(**6**): e323–33.
6. Wakasa T, Ishibashi-Ueda H, Takeuchi M. Maternal death analysis based on data from nationwide registration system in Japan (2010–2018). *Pathol Int* 2021; **71**: 223–31.
7. Knight M, Bunch K, Tuffnell D, et al. (eds). *Saving Lives, Improving Mothers' Care - Lessons learned to inform maternity care from the UK and Ireland Confidential Enquiries into Maternal Deaths and Morbidity 2016–18*. Oxford: National Perinatal Epidemiology Unit, University of Oxford; 2020.
8. Australian Institute of Health and Welfare. *Maternal deaths in Australia*. Cat. no. PER 99. Canberra: AIHW, 2020. Available from: https://www.aihw.gov.au/reports/mothers-babies/maternal-deaths-in-australia (Accessed 24 April 2023).
9. Millward-Sadler GH. The Maternal Autopsy. In: Burton J, Rutty G, (eds). *The Hospital Autopsy: A Manual of Fundamental Autopsy Practice*. 3rd ed. London: Hodder Arnold; 2010, pp. 204–215.
10. March of Dimes. *Maternal death and pregnancy-related death*, 2021. Available from: https://www.marchofdimes.org/complications/pregnancy-related-death-maternal-death-and-maternal-mortality.aspx (Accessed 24 April 2023).
11. Lucas S. *Guidelines on Autopsy Practice Scenario 5: Maternal death*. The Royal College of Pathologists 2010. Available from: https://www.google.com/search?q=Guidelines+on+Autopsy+Practice+Scenario+5%3A+Maternal+death&oq=Guidelines+on+Autopsy+Practice+Scenario+5%3A+Maternal+death&aqs=chrome..69i57.621j0j15&sourceid=chrome&ie=UTF-8 (Accessed 24 April 2023).
12. Garland J, Little D. Maternal death and its investigation. *Acad Forensic Pathol* 2018; **8**(**4**): 894–911
13. Fanton L, Bévalot F, Cartiser N, et al. Post mortem measurement of human chorionic gonadotropin in vitreous humor and bile. *J Forensic Sci*; **55**(**3**): 792–4.
14. Palmiere C, del Mar Lesta M, Fanton L, et al. Determination of human chorionic gonadotropin in postmortem samples in ectopic pregnancies. *J Forensic Sci* 2016; **61**(**1**): 234–7.
15. Lucas S. Difficult diagnoses in maternal death: The negative maternal autopsy. *Med Res Arch* 2020; **8**(**11**): 1–24.
16. Garner EI, Chang-Lee, WY, Lu KH, et al. Trophoblastic pulmonary embolization after hysterectomy for invasive complete mole: A case report. *J Reprod Med* 1999; **44**(**10**): 908–12.
17. Lignitz E, Kernbach-Wighton G, Henn V, et al. Death During Pregnancy. In: B. Madea (ed.) *Handbook of Forensic Medicine*. Chichester: Wiley Blackwell; 2014, 516–24.
18. Knight B. *Simpson's Forensic Medicine*, 11th ed. London: Arnold; 1997.
19. Asatryan B, Rieder M, Castilione A, et al. Arrhythmic risk during pregnancy and post partum in patients with long QT syndrome. *Herzschr Elektrophys* 2021; **32**(**2**): 180–5.
20. Gei AF, Vadhera RH, Hankins GDV. Embolism during pregnancy: Thrombus, air, and amniotic fluid. *Anesthesiology Clin N Am* 2003; **21**(**1**): 165–82.
21. Moore J, Baldisseri MR. Amniotic fluid embolism. *Crit Care Med* 2005; **33**(**10**): S279–85.
22. Sinicina I, Pankratz H, Pise K, et al. Forensic aspects of post-mortem histological detection of amniotic fluid embolism. *Int J Legal Med* 2010; **124**: 55–62.
23. Benson MD. Amniotic fluid embolism: The known and not known. *Obst Med* 2014; **7**(**1**): 17–21.
24. Benson MD. Current concepts of immunology and diagnosis in amniotic fluid embolism. *Clin Dev Immunol* 2012: **2012**: 946576.
25. Metodiev Y, Ramasamy P, Tuffnell D. Amniotic fluid embolism. *BJA Education* 2019; **18**(**8**): 234–8.
26. Collins P, Abdul-Kadir R, Thachil J. Management of coagulopathy associated with postpartum hemorrhage: Guidance from the SSC of the ISTH. *J Thromb Haemost* 2016; **14**(**1**): 205–10.
27. Tamura, N, Farhana M, Oda T, et al. Amniotic fluid embolism: pathophysiology from the perspective of pathology. *J Obstet Gynaecol Res* 2017; **43**(**4**): 627–32.
28. Paine Q, Hughes R. Anaphylactoid syndrome of pregnancy: An autopsy case report. *Am J Forensic Med Pathol* 2021; **42**(**2**): e10-e12.
29. Nakagami H, Kajihara T, Kamei Y, et al. Amniotic components in the uterine vasculature and their role in amniotic fluid embolism. *J Obstet Gynaecol Res* 2015; **41**(**6**): 870–5.
30. Matsunaga S, Masuko H, Takai Y, et al. Fibrinogen may aid in the early differentiation between amniotic fluid embolism and postpartum haemorrhage: A retrospective chart report. *Sci Rep* 2021; **11**(**1**): 8379.
31. Zolotarov P, Fraser R. Venous air embolism: Artefactual air entrapment and autopsy technique. *Int J Legal Med* 2020; **134**(**3**): 1033–36.
32. Collins KA, Davis GJ, Lantz PE. An unusual case of maternal-fetal death due to vaginal insufflation of cocaine. *Am J Forensic Med Pathol* 1994; **15**(**4**): 335–9.
33. Davies, DE, Digwood KL, Hilton JN. Air embolism during caesarian section. *Med J Aust* 1980; **1**: 644–6.
34. Fatteh A, Leach WB, Wilkinson CA. Fatal air embolism in pregnancy resulting from orogenital sex play. *Forensic Sci* 1973; **2**(**2**): 247–50.
35. Hill BF, Jones JS. Venous air embolism following orogenital sex during pregnancy. *Am J Emerg Med* 1993; **11**(**2**): 155–7.
36. Kim CS, Liu J, Kwon JY, et al. Venous air embolism during surgery, especially cesarean delivery. *J Korean Med Sci* 2008; **23**(**5**): 753–61.
37. Banaschak S, Janβen K, Becker K, et al. Fatal postpartum air embolism due to uterine inversion and atonic haemorrhage. *Int J Legal Med* 2014; **128**: 147–50.
38. Hecht JL, Ordi J, Carrilho C, et al. The pathology of eclampsia: An autopsy series. *Hypertens Pregnancy* 2017; **36**(**3**): 259–68.
39. Falco ML, Sivanthan J, Laoreti A, et al. Placental histopathology associated with pre-eclampsia: Systematic review and meta-analysis. *Ultrasound Obstet Gynecol* 2017; **50**(**3**): 295–301.

CHAPTER

32

Autopsies after Surgery and Percutaneous Interventions

Megan Jenkins, Patrick J. Gallagher and Russell J. Delaney

INTRODUCTION

The Lancet Commission on Global Surgery (1) reported that 313 million surgical procedures are performed worldwide each year. Further analysis suggested that 4.2 million people die within 30 days of surgery. Globally, postoperative deaths account for 7.7 percent of all deaths, ranking only behind ischemic heart disease and stroke. At least half of these postoperative deaths occur in low- and middle-income countries (LMIC) (2) where, for example, death rates after cesarean section (3) and surgery for cancer (4) are higher than in well-resourced countries.

Post-mortem examinations of patients who have died after surgical procedures or percutaneous interventions are some of the most challenging cases faced by autopsy pathologists. It is essential that they are performed to a high standard by clinical or forensic pathologists with a background understanding of the clinical aspects of perioperative care and a detailed knowledge of the associated pathology. This chapter is a revision and expansion of our previous publication (5). In Section 1, we describe the indications for, and the methods used, in postoperative autopsies. In Section 2, the important complications encountered in any postoperative autopsy are summarized and in Section 3, the pathologic features in specific procedures, particularly new percutaneous interventions and minimally invasive surgery.

SECTION 1: AUTOPSIES AFTER SURGERY AND PERCUTANEOUS INTERVENTIONS: GENERAL PRINCIPLES

REVIEW OF CLINICAL RECORDS

Thorough preparation is an essential part of any postoperative post-mortem examination. In most cases, the preceding clinical events will determine the examination approach and provide some direction for ongoing post-mortem investigations. While it might seem tempting to proceed with the autopsy at the earliest opportunity and review the clinical records at some subsequent date, this can mean that opportunities for targeted examination are missed and necessary investigations are neglected. For example, rapid deterioration following the administration of a drug should prompt the pathologist to investigate for anaphylaxis (6). Similarly, respiratory compromise following orthopedic surgery may require investigation for fat embolism or pulmonary cement embolism (7).

A complete record of all medical and surgical events corresponding to the perioperative period should be reviewed. As a minimum, this should include the admission notes, preoperative chart, anesthetic records, operation notes, drug charts, and postoperative medical, surgical and nursing records. It may be helpful to produce a timeline summarizing the clinical events. The pre- and postoperative biochemistry, hematology and microbiology results should be obtained, along with any relevant radiology and histology reports. In some cases, historic records may also be required.

The pathologist should familiarize themselves with the surgical procedure before commencing the autopsy. This may seem obvious, but surgical approaches and techniques evolve rapidly and it is virtually impossible for a pathologist to remain learned in such matters. Where the Coroner or Medical Examiner allows, it is often helpful to discuss the case with the clinicians who cared for the patient, particularly in a complex case. Alternatively, the advice of an independent specialist may be sought. Post-mortem photography is invariably beneficial and does facilitate subsequent presentation of the autopsy findings at the relevant morbidity and mortality meeting.

PURPOSE AND VALUE OF THE POST-MORTEM EXAMINATION

Perioperative deaths are often the subject of a medico-legal investigation by the Coroner or equivalent local authority. The principal purpose of the post-mortem examination in this setting is to provide an opinion regarding the medical cause of death. The autopsy

DOI: 10.1201/9781003138754-34

pathologist would be expected to perform a thorough post-mortem examination, document the findings, provide a clinicopathological interpretation of the findings and prepare a report for the instructing authority.

Perioperative deaths may be broadly classified into one, or occasionally, more of the following groups:

- Those caused directly by the disease or injury for which the operation was performed
- Those caused by a disease or abnormality other than that for which the surgery was performed
- Those caused by a complication or failure of the operation
- Those caused by a complication of the administration of an anesthetic

It is important therefore to consider the following in each case:

- The surgical procedure and its possible, likely or expected complications
- The severity of the underlying disease process and the correlation with the preoperative appearances
- The severity of any known or unknown pre-existing comorbid conditions that may have caused or contributed to death
- The method and nature of anesthesia

Some deaths following emergency or urgent surgical procedures for life-threatening disease or injury may be considered inevitable and unavoidable, for example major trauma, ruptured atherosclerotic abdominal aortic aneurysm. In other cases, it is important to consider the question of whether death would have been expected to occur at that particular time had the operation not been performed.

Often deaths are multifactorial. The original disease process, the burden of surgery, pre-existing comorbid medical conditions and the physiological changes of advancing age may all potentially contribute to the fatal sequence. It will often be necessary to carefully correlate the pathological findings with the clinical history so that detailed information beyond the medical cause of death can be provided.

The medicolegal investigation may consider whether the standard or quality of surgical intervention and perioperative medical care was adequate. This is likely to be outside the expertise of the autopsy pathologist unless there has been an obvious or catastrophic error. A further reason to provide detailed and accurate pathological data is that the post-mortem findings may be considered at a later date by an appropriate independent clinical specialist.

Discrepancies between clinical diagnoses and pathological findings

The perioperative post-mortem examination also has a vital role in the audit of clinical practice and diagnostic performance. Discrepancies between premortem clinical diagnoses and post-mortem findings can be categorized by the Goldman method (8) (Table 32.1). This classifies discrepancies according to the severity of the condition and the potential impact on therapy or survival had a diagnosis been made prior to death. Major discrepancies are primary causes of death and important underlying conditions. Minor discrepancies include unknown pre-existing, contributing diagnoses and related conditions. Major discrepancy rates of 15–31 percent have been reported (9–12). In our own study, the most common missed diagnoses were infections, ischemic heart disease and thromboembolic disease (12).

There is inevitable variation in the numbers of autopsies performed after surgical procedures. In the UK, a detailed National Confidential Enquiry into Perioperative Deaths (NCEPOD – later renamed the National Confidential Enquiry into Patient Outcome and Death) recorded an autopsy rate of 41 percent (89% on behalf of the Coroner and 11% hospital consented cases) (13). In five separate cardiac surgical centers, postoperative deaths were followed by autopsy in 24–86 percent of cases (14).

TABLE 32.1 Goldman classification of autopsy discrepancies

Major	Description	Illustrative example
Class 1	If known, would have altered management or prolonged survival	Significant area(s) of bronchopneumonia after abdominal surgery, not recognized in life
Class 2	If known, would not have altered management or prolonged survival. May have influenced decision to operate	An unrecognized metastatic carcinoma of the colon in a patient dying from heart failure after cardiac surgery
Minor		
Class 3	Related to terminal disease process but not directly related to death	An undiagnosed left ventricular mural thrombus in a patient who died from known congestive cardiac failure after surgical treatment for perforated appendicitis
Class 4	Unrelated diagnoses	Unrecognized non-metastatic prostate carcinoma in an elderly patient dying of pneumonia after a Hartmann's procedure for diverticulitis
Class 5	Complete agreement between premortem clinical diagnosis and post-mortem changes	The situation in at least two-thirds of clinical cases

The value of the examination may also be limited by its quality. Two recent reviews from the Sheffield group provided valuable guidelines on all aspects of postoperative examinations (15,16).

RADIOLOGY

Non-invasive radiologic techniques such as computerized tomography (CT) are increasingly used as an adjunct to the standard invasive post-mortem examination (17,18). In a perioperative death, radiologic investigation of possible cardiac air embolism (e.g. following procedures to the head and neck) or pneumothorax should be considered. If radiology is not available, then standard autopsy techniques of puncturing the heart and/or pleural cavities under water can identify these pathologies.

EXTERNAL EXAMINATION

Once the clinical history has been thoroughly reviewed, the pathologist should make a careful external inspection of the body. It should not be delegated to a mortuary assistant and should always be performed prior to any internal examination or evisceration (16). It should include general features such as peripheral edema, jaundice, signs of injury, signs of resuscitation and post-mortem changes.

In a perioperative case, particular attention should be paid to the operation site and medical devices. Ideally all medical devices should be left *in situ*, and the nature and location recorded. The position of significant invasive devices such as central venous cannulae and endotracheal tubes should be confirmed by dissection. This is especially important if they have been inserted during a period of attempted resuscitation immediately prior to death. If the position of a device is inappropriate, this should be recorded by photography. Sometimes there may be a request to remove an endotracheal tube prior to viewing by relatives. An acceptable compromise is to cut off the endotracheal tube at the level of the lips ensuring that the balloon remains inflated so that its true position can be documented later.

INTERNAL EXAMINATION

Post mortems after interventions or operations should be careful systematic examinations. The operation site should be carefully inspected and the location, length and orientation of the incision recorded. The method of wound closure and any external signs of hemorrhage, leakage or infection should be documented. The number and nature of any drains should be documented together with the nature and volume of any contents of the drainage bags. Any stomas should be assessed to determine their nature and viability. As far as possible this should be done with the organs *in situ*. Review of the surgical anatomy by the operating surgeon and pathologist in the autopsy room may be of considerable benefit. If logistically difficult, careful photography of technical complications may be valuable.

The amount of hemorrhage or fluid accumulation at the site of cutaneous access, the site of the intervention or the operative field should be measured as accurately as possible. The costal angles, subphrenic spaces, paracolic gutters and the pouch of Douglas should be examined before the lungs and intestines are removed. Hemorrhage is inevitable after major surgery but there is no simple way of assessing whether a hemorrhage is clinically significant. Heavily bloodstained fluid or 250–500 mL of blood is not uncommon in technically satisfactory operations. Details of transfusion, amounts of blood in drainage containers and reoperations for bleeding may be important. In general terms, fresh hemorrhage in excess of 1 litre is significant. Factors predisposing to intra- or postoperative hemorrhage include liver disease and coagulation disorders, obesity, increasing age, sepsis and blood transfusion during operations (*see* "Post-Procedure Hemorrhage" in Section 2 below for detailed discussion).

Pus or pus-like fluid is especially important and should be measured and swabbed. Post-mortem blood cultures or spleen swabs often grow contaminating organisms and should be interpreted with caution. Surgical anastomoses should be examined gently and carefully. Autolysed bowel is friable and anastomoses are easily torn by rough handling.

LABORATORY INVESTIGATIONS

Histology, biochemistry and microbiology

In the majority of forensic centers, histology is routinely taken after a postoperative autopsy. We strongly support this approach. Histology is valuable in many postoperative cases (19,20) and especially in:

- Confirming postoperative infections, especially pneumonia, and in diagnosing acute lung injury
- Identifying and dating suspected areas of myocardial infarction and coronary thrombosis
- The diagnosis of postoperative cerebral infarction
- Distinguishing residual tumor from postoperative changes, especially in the abdomen
- Assessing the extent of intrinsic renal disease in postoperative renal impairment
- Confirming postoperative complications such as small bowel infarction and pancreatitis.

Biochemistry and hematology have a strictly limited role in postoperative autopsies. Details of values recorded immediately before death are therefore especially important. Sodium, urea and creatinine can be measured in vitreous humour and β-hydroxybutyrate in blood or vitreous humor. Potassium, hemoglobin, WBC, platelets and other indices of coagulation cannot be reliably estimated after death. Post-mortem troponin estimations in blood and pericardial fluid can be helpful in the diagnosis of myocardial infarction but, as yet, the methods have not been validated in postoperative cases. The laboratory confirmation of anaphylaxis is described below.

A premortem positive blood culture is invaluable in establishing a diagnosis of postoperative septicemia. Many post-mortem blood cultures or spleen swabs grow contaminating organisms only. Careful inspection of the mucosal surface of the large bowel is necessary in patients receiving broad-spectrum antibiotics. Antibiotic induced (pseudomembranous) colitis due to *C. difficile* can be confirmed by stool culture.

AUTOPSY REPORT

A poor quality autopsy report can limit the value of an otherwise excellent examination. The report must be an accurate reflection of the post-mortem findings and include details of ancillary investigations such as toxicology and histology. It is useful to include a summary of the clinical history at the beginning of the report although it should be stressed that this is the pathologist's understanding of the case history based on the information available at that time.

The report should cover all the major organ systems as detailed in appropriate guidelines (16) and standard texts. The operation site should receive specific comment. If no abnormalities are present, a useful phrase is "All technical aspects of the procedure appeared satisfactory." Histological confirmation of significant findings is considered best practice, especially to confirm postoperative pneumonia and acute lung injury, and to accurately date myocardial and coronary artery changes.

Perhaps the most important component of the report is the clinicopathological correlation. This has been emphasized in two recent and detailed reviews (15,16). This brings together the clinical history and pathological findings and provides the basis by which the medical cause of death is explained. Besides the responsible medical staff, the report may be read by a variety of lawyers, by the patient's general practitioner and importantly by relatives of the deceased. It is therefore essential that the clinicopathological summary is clearly written and unexplained use of medical jargon avoided.

Postoperative deaths are frequently subject to medicolegal investigation by a Coroner or considered by a Medical Examiner. Ideally, the autopsy should be undertaken by a pathologist who is independent from the institution in which the surgery was conducted. This will negate any concerns regarding a conflict of interests. The examination findings should be reported to the Coroner or Medical Examiner in an objective manner and without unnecessary judgement. Deaths after surgery may be followed by an inquest. As with the written report, verbal evidence should be clear and concise and in a style of language that allows non-medical personnel to understand the often complex clinicopathological features. Opinion should be restricted to the specific area of expertise and clinical matters in particular should be deferred to the relevant expert. If the post-mortem examination process does reveal clear evidence of negligence or unacceptable practice then the responsible pathologist, in liaison with the Coroner or Senior Medical Examiner, should ensure the case is referred to the appropriate medicolegal authority.

SECTION 2: POTENTIAL COMPLICATIONS OF ANY OPERATIVE OR PERCUTANEOUS PROCEDURE

DEATHS DURING A PROCEDURE

Deaths due to anesthesia are uncommon with an estimated incidence of 0.5–0.8 per 100 000 anesthetics. A study encompassing around six million anesthetic episodes in Australia and New Zealand between 2003 and 2005 identified 24 deaths where it was considered reasonably certain that death was caused by anesthetic factors alone, 33 cases where there was some doubt and 55 cases where anesthetic and surgical factors were implicated (21). The physiological effects of an anesthetic however may contribute to death from other causes. There may be little in the way of positive findings in these cases and it is vital therefore to review the anesthetic charts to gain an understanding of the clinical history. The majority of autopsy pathologists will be unfamiliar with modern anesthetic techniques and therefore discussion of the case with an anesthetist prior to and after the autopsy is essential.

Complications in anesthesia-related deaths can be broadly categorized into those affecting the airway, including obstruction and equipment failure, those related to the anesthetic agents and their reversal, and those related to the complex cardiovascular changes associated with anesthesia (Table 32.2).

TABLE 32.2 Potential complications of anesthesia

Nature of Complication	Pathophysiological change	Comments
Airway related	Obstruction Malintubation Equipment failure, including disconnection	Equipment failure in ~0.25% general anesthetics, a combination of machine failure and human error (see reference 103)
Drug related	Dose-related respiratory depression Idiosyncratic reactions Acute anaphylaxis	Anticholinerase reversal associated with brady- and tachycardia (see reference 104)
Cardiovascular effects	Changes in blood pressure and heart rate Arrhythmias, including atrial fibrillation Cardiac arrest (see references 22 & 23)	Physiological changes include decreased vascular resistance, myocardial contractility and stroke volume and increased myocardial irritability

TABLE 32.3 Potential post-operative complications after surgery

Complication	Clinicopathological features	Pathological changes
Acute coronary syndromes	Postoperative tachycardia and hypotension. Typical pattern of chest pain uncommon. Risk factors include previous coronary heart disease, cardiac failure, renal impairment and diabetes. Most cases are NSTEMIs. Q waves in only ~12% of cases	Coronary artery narrowing but thrombotic occlusion uncommon (see text). Hemorrhagic infarction often close to areas of scarring
Gastrointestinal complications	Intestinal dilatation (postoperative ileus), intestinal perforation, anastomotic dehiscence, pancreatitis, acute non calculous cholecystitis	Intestinal dilatation with low-grade acute peritonitis. Sub phrenic, para colic or pelvic purulent effusions. Hepatic fatty change especially in diabetics. Abdominal wall bleeding after minimally invasive surgery
Hemorrhage	Large hemorrhages associated with tachycardia, decreased blood and pulse pressures, increased respiratory rate, anxiety and confusion	Collections of blood or blood-stained fluid close to operative site or in adjacent recesses. Precise site of hemorrhage seldom identified
Multiorgan failure	Long ITU stay, poor systemic perfusion with reduced renal function, acidosis and jaundice	Acute lung injury (ARDS) see text. Small intestinal necrosis, hepatic fatty change, pre-existent renal disease and occasionally renal cortical or tubular necrosis
Respiratory tract infection, bronchopneumonia and acute lung injury	Many risk factors including age >70 yrs, upper abdominal surgery, surgery for >3 hrs, blood transfusion, duration of mechanical ventilation, diabetes, previous stroke, obesity	Histology required for accurate diagnosis, especially in early stages of acute lung injury
Stroke	Uncommon after elective non major surgery but up to 10% in cardiac, vascular or neurosurgical procedures. Specialist stroke physicians involved in management	Detailed examination of brain and carotid arteries essential. Brain fixation and dissection by neuropathologist recommended, if stroke is the leading cause of death
Venous thromboembolic disease	Strong risk factors include active cancer, surgery for >30 min, bedridden for >3 days, trauma and fractures and surgery following an acute admission	Large often bilateral pulmonary artery thromboemboli (Figure 32.3). Small emboli, with or without infarcts unlikely to be the immediate cause of death. Confirm venous disease by lower limb dissection

ARDS: adult respiratory distress syndrome; NSTEMI: Non ST elevation myocardial infarct.

The most common mechanism of death is cardiac arrest (22,23) which may be multifactorial and more prevalent in those with pre-existing coronary artery disease or previous myocardial infarction. Possible underlying causes to be considered include hypoxia, decreased myocardial perfusion due to induction-related hypotension and/or bradycardia, and neurogenic causes such as laryngoscopy, intubation or surgical manipulation.

The airway should be considered as extending from the alveoli to the anesthetic equipment. Expert examination of the anesthetic equipment, including the machine, gas supply, connecting tubes and other devices, is mandatory in cases of possible equipment failure.

Esophageal intubation is uncommon but the position of an endotracheal tube should be confirmed by dissection in deaths occurring rapidly after induction. The airway can be obstructed by foreign material such as blood or vomit or foreign bodies such as teeth. However, the appearances should be interpreted with caution as movement of the body and resuscitation can produce artefact. Histological examination of the lungs may be of assistance in determining the significance of aspiration.

Anesthetic drugs, including those used in premedication and as muscle-relaxing agents, have the potential to cause respiratory depression in a dose-related manner and toxicology should be considered in deaths during anesthesia. Anesthetic gases will not be detected by standard toxicological techniques and retention of a lung for volatile gas analysis is unlikely to be helpful.

Thecal administration or an overdose of an epidural anesthetic may cause cardiorespiratory arrest. The administration site should be dissected carefully and a sample of cerebrospinal fluid should be retained for drug analysis (24).

The symptoms and signs of an anaphylactic reaction are highly variable. A classical presentation may include bronchospasm, laryngeal edema, hypotension and peripheral vasodilatation. The most common post-mortem finding is non-specific pulmonary edema and congestion (25). Histology of the upper airway may identify edema and an infiltrate of eosinophils. Blood should be retained for mast cell tryptase and specific IgE antibody analysis. Post-mortem results should however be interpreted with caution and with the assistance of a clinical immunologist as the quoted reference ranges often apply to live patients and mast cell tryptase levels may be elevated in non-anaphylactic deaths (26,27).

Malignant hyperthermia is a rare idiosyncratic reaction that can be associated with some anesthetic agents such as succinylcholine and halothane. It is characterized by a rapid rise in temperature. Autopsy findings are non-specific and the diagnosis can be confirmed by analysis of ante-mortem blood samples (24).

POST-PROCEDURE HEMORRHAGE

Excessive bleeding remains a major complication during and after many types of surgery (28) and, to a lesser extent, percutaneous interventions (29). It is important that the amount of hemorrhage and/or hemorrhagic fluid at the operative site should be carefully measured at autopsy. The site of operative drains should be recorded. As emphasized above, the costal angles, sub phrenic spaces, paracolic areas and pouch of Douglas must be examined before major organs are removed. The American College of Surgeons Committee on Trauma has devised a 4-grade classification of hemorrhagic shock based on the volume of blood loss and associated cardiovascular, respiratory and renal changes (30). Importantly for the autopsy pathologist, a loss of <750 mL is associated with few cardiovascular changes and a normal respiratory rate. **Consequently blood loss of less than about a liter is unlikely to be the primary cause of postoperative death.**

There are complex hemostatic changes in the perioperative period, especially in critical care (31) and after cardiopulmonary bypass and organ transplantation (32). These include coagulation abnormalities resulting from preoperative blood loss or intra-operative bleeding. To the best of our knowledge, these cannot be evaluated in post-mortem blood. Preoperative anemia is an established risk factor for perioperative hemorrhage, increased hospital stay and overall mortality (33). Preoperative hemoglobin levels should therefore be recorded. Liver, spleen and bone marrow histology are especially important in deaths associated with perioperative hemorrhage.

A recent clinical study from a leading center reported that important hemorrhage occurred in 2.1 percent of nearly 2000 pulmonary lobectomies (34). Risk factors included male gender, preoperative anemia, previous sternotomy and operative adhesions. No source of bleeding was identified in 44 percent of re explorations. **It is therefore not surprising that an exact source of postoperative hemorrhage is seldom identified at autopsy.** The approximate area that the bleeding arose from is usually obvious and should be documented photographically. Histology of these areas may demonstrate inflammation and suggest secondary hemorrhage.

CARDIOVASCULAR COMPLICATIONS

Major perioperative cardiovascular complications, such as myocardial infarction, cardiac arrest or congestive cardiac failure, account for at least one third of all perioperative deaths. The leading group of investigators suggest that worldwide 10 million patients have a significant

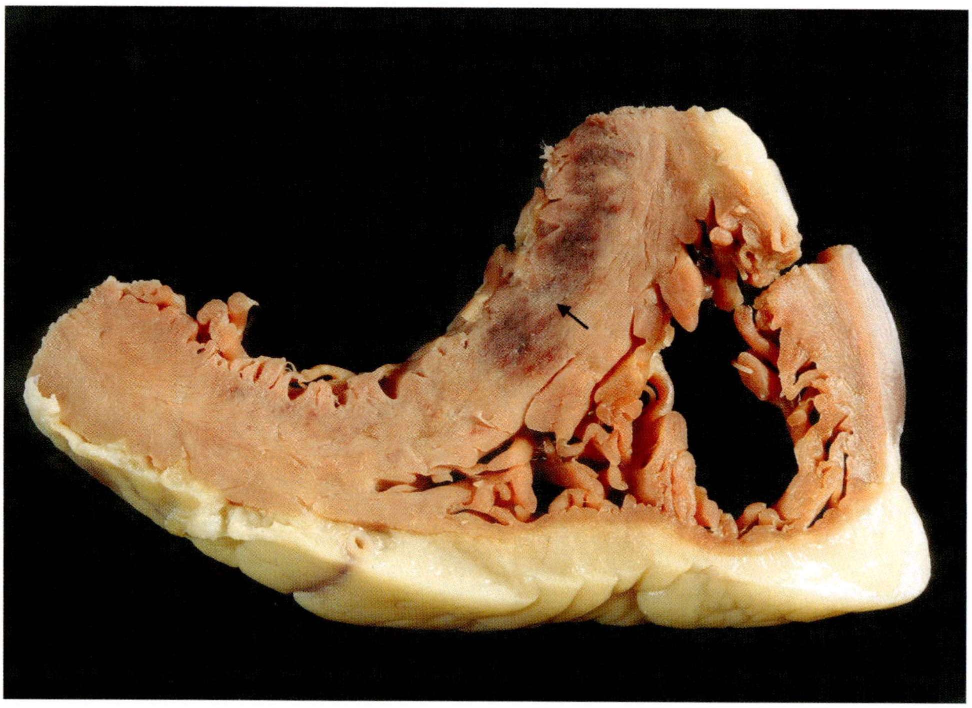

32.1 Postoperative myocardial infarction. An elderly and frail male died suddenly 4 days after an uncomplicated operation for acute diverticulitis. At post mortem there was some acute peritonitis. There was moderate non-occlusive coronary atherosclerosis and a small acute hemorrhagic largely sub endocardial septal infarct. A small area of scarring is arrowed. Clinical studies have demonstrated that >80% of postoperative infarcts are 'non Q wave' (35,36), the pathological counterpart of which is a sub endocardial infarct. In cases such as this, the cause of death is clearly multifactorial. Our report indicated that all technical aspects of the surgery were satisfactory and suggested as a cause of death. Diverticulitis with peritonitis ***and*** acute myocardial infarction.

postoperative cardiac complication each year (35). Predictably, pre-operative risk factors include a history of cardiac disease, especially coronary artery disease and cardiac failure, renal insufficiency and diabetes. Hypotension, tachycardia, hemorrhage, coagulation abnormalities and hypothermia are important intra-operative changes which can contribute to perioperative and postoperative myocardial ischemia. Some of these are a consequence of sympathetic stimulation during anesthesia or the operative procedures.

In the POISE study (Perioperative Ischemia Evaluation trial) over 8000 surgical patients in 190 centers in 23 countries were included. Five percent had a perioperative infarct but only about 35 percent had symptoms of cardiac ischemia and only 12 percent had Q waves, a feature which suggests a larger transmural or ST elevation myocardial infarct. Thirty-day mortality was 11.6 percent in patients who had an infarct but only 2.2 percent in those who did not (36).The risk of a perioperative infarct in a patient with a previous recent myocardial infarct is much increased but declines to a basal level of less than 10 percent after 6 months. The majority of perioperative infarcts are subendocardial rather than transmural. Many occur at or close to healed infarcts (Figure 32.1). Our experience is that coronary thrombi are uncommon in the relevant coronary artery. It is probable that postoperative tachycardia and coronary narrowing combine to produce critical ischemia and infarction. When the heart rate declines, perfusion becomes more normal. There is then reflow of blood into the infarcted area which becomes hemorrhagic (see below: Cardiac surgery and interventions).

WOUND AND SURGICAL SITE INFECTION

Surgical site infection is one of the most frequently encountered types of hospital-acquired infection and may follow even minor, minimally invasive procedures (37). It is therefore vital that the pathologist conducts a thorough external examination, ensuring they assess every site at which the skin has been breached. This includes all venous access sites and drain sites. Bacterial swabs of the wound and surrounding skin should be taken if there are signs of infection, such as erythema or swelling. Intravenous catheter tips can also be retained for culture (38).

Surgical wounds should also be explored, either during examination of the internal organs (if the surgical wound is located on the trunk) or else through adjacent incision of the skin, in order to investigate for deep infection or underlying abscess (39). Additional incisions should be kept to a minimum, with consideration given to the post-mortem reconstruction of the body.

Systemic sepsis

The fundamental challenge faced by the pathologist investigating a case of suspected sepsis is that it is a clinical syndrome, defined as life-threatening organ dysfunction caused by a dysregulated host response to infection (40). It is not possible to measure organ function after death. Post-mortem investigations must therefore be thorough and supported by microbiological testing. Sepsis may be inferred if the examination findings confirm infection and demonstrate acute organ damage that is deemed incompatible with baseline function.

There are no specific gross or microscopic post-mortem findings that reliably indicate sepsis.

Externally, a rash or hemorrhagic skin lesions may be evident (41). Joint swelling, particularly in patients with an orthopedic history, should be explored by incision. Examination of the internal organs may reveal the infective focus. Additional, non-specific macroscopic findings that can be seen in sepsis include pulmonary edema and congestion, dilatation of the cardiac ventricles, hepatomegaly (often the result of diffuse fatty change) and splenomegaly (42–45). Softening of the spleen is often interpreted by pathologists as a sign of sepsis, yet this is subjective, affected by decomposition and rarely described as a specific finding in published medical literature (46).

Microscopically, diffuse alveolar damage (DAD) and acute tubular injury are among the more commonly observed pathologies seen in sepsis deaths, though these findings may reflect a systemic inflammatory response rather than necessarily being due to infection (47,48). Complications of sepsis, such as disseminated intravascular coagulation (DIC) or septic emboli, may be evident and there may be features of end-organ hypoperfusion to suggest shock (e.g. hypoxic-ischemic encephalopathy, myocardial ischemia or hypoxic liver injury). Despite traditional assertions, the presence of acute splenitis is entirely non-specific (49).

Post-mortem microbiological samples should be taken at the earliest opportunity and under sterile conditions, where possible, to prevent contamination. The sampling approach will depend upon the surgical history and the suspected pathology. Blood culture (from the subclavian vein or heart) is essential. Any identifiable infection should also be sampled. When the focus of infection is unclear, as a minimum, the following should also be collected: cerebrospinal fluid (cisterna magna puncture), urine (suprapubic puncture) and upper airway swabs (viral and bacterial) (50). Tissue samples or swabs of the lung, liver, spleen, myocardium, adrenal glands and brain, should also be retained for culture. If present, samples of skin petechiae, pleural fluid, ascites, feces and pus can be retained. If antibiotic-associated pseudomembranous colitis is suspected, the large bowel mucosa should be inspected and *Clostridium difficile* infection investigated by means of stool culture. Tissue samples as opposed to swabs are required where fungal or viral disease is suspected. If there is a history of being immunocompromised, intravenous drug use or recent travel, atypical infections must also be considered and precautions taken.

Post-mortem analysis of concentrations of acute-phase proteins may be of some benefit. Notably, C-reactive protein and procalcitonin are relatively stable after death and can reliably indicate a hyperinflammatory state (51,52). In cases of suspected sepsis, the post-mortem findings should be evaluated with consideration to the recent surgical intervention and circumstances of death. If microbiological investigations return a positive result, it is important to consider the cultured organism within the context of the overall case, as not all cultured organisms are necessarily of pathological significance.

Postoperative pneumonia

Postoperative pneumonia is one of the most commonly encountered postoperative complications, particularly among patients who have undergone cardiothoracic or abdominal surgery (53). Additional risk factors for the development of postoperative pneumonia include cardiovascular disease, chronic lung disease, immunocompromise, old age, prolonged sedation, and poor lung function on preoperative pulmonary function tests. The majority of cases are caused by Gram-negative, aerobic bacteria such as those of the *Klebsiella*, *Enterobacter* and *Pseudomonas* species (54). Postoperative pneumonia may be further categorized as hospital-acquired pneumonia (HAP) or ventilator-associated pneumonia (VAP). HAP refers to any pneumonia that arises 48 hours or more after admission to hospital. VAP is a subtype of HAP that is more loosely defined, but essentially refers to pneumonia that develops after endotracheal intubation (55,56). Given the associated high mortality rate, it is not unusual to find pneumonia during post-mortem investigation of a postoperative death. Thorough histologic sampling is essential, including in those cases with an antemortem diagnosis of pneumonia.

Pneumothorax

Pneumothorax should be considered in any patient that has undergone cardiothoracic intervention, central vascular cannulation or mechanical ventilation (57). A simple method of investigation is to dissect the skin, subcutaneous tissues and muscles of the anterior and lateral chest wall away from the ribcage, ensuring that the intercostal muscles remain intact. Water is then poured into the space between these superficial chest wall structures and the ribcage. The pathologist can then puncture the lateral intercostal muscles underwater and observe whether bubbles escape the pleural cavity, indicating pneumothorax. This must be done prior to evisceration of the abdominal contents to ensure that the diaphragm is undamaged. However, post-mortem radiology is the gold standard method for investigation of pneumothorax.

Postoperative acute lung injury

Acute respiratory distress syndrome (ARDS) refers to a spectrum of clinical syndromes characterized by hypoxemia, poor lung compliance and bilateral, acute-onset, pulmonary opacities visible on pulmonary radiology (58). The syndrome results from some form of acute lung insult, whether that be directed upon the alveoli or pulmonary vasculature. There has been a great deal of work into understanding the pathophysiology of ARDS, particularly in recent years due to its association with SARS-CoV-2 infection. ARDS has many causes – those particularly relevant to the postoperative setting include: pneumonia, pulmonary contusion, aspiration of gastric contents ("direct" causes); and blood transfusion, cardiopulmonary bypass, extrathoracic trauma, reperfusion edema after cardiopulmonary bypass ("indirect" causes) (59–61). ARDS mortality rates have declined in recent decades, at least in part due to improvements in methods of mechanical ventilation. Nevertheless, ARDS is often seen in the postoperative period, typically occurring within a week of the clinical insult.

DAD is the histologic correlate of ARDS and can be seen in approximately 70 percent of patients with clinically severe ARDS (62). In DAD, the lungs are typically heavy (often weighing over 1 kg), firm, edematous but only focally hemorrhagic (Figure 32.2a). Accurate diagnosis requires histology and it is sensible routine practice to take one block from each lung lobe in every postoperative case. The "textbook" histologic appearance of DAD describes widespread hyaline membrane formation, type 2 pneumocyte hyperplasia and intra-alveolar aggregates of mixed inflammatory cells. These classic features are seldom seen in the postoperative setting. Instead, fibrin deposition within the alveolar spaces, alveolar wall necrosis accompanied by vasodilatation, patchy inflammation with lymphocytes, macrophages and occasional megakaryocytes are more typical of postoperative DAD (Figure 32.2b). Co-existing pneumonia is common.

Postoperative venous thromboembolism

Major surgery, especially prolonged surgery for active malignancy, is a strong risk factor for venous thromboembolism (VTE) (63). Surgical trauma is associated thrombocytosis with elevated levels of clotting factors (notably fibrinogen and prothrombin), thereby promoting a state of hypercoagulability. Surgical dissection and sometimes venous catheterization can cause endothelial injury; and perioperative immobilization precipitates venous stasis (54,65). Despite the routine use of VTE prophylaxis in all major surgical interventions, pulmonary embolism remains the most common cause of preventable death in the postoperative period and careful examination of the pulmonary arteries is an essential step in any postoperative post-mortem examination.

True thrombi are often adherent, at least in some areas, to the intimal lining of the pulmonary artery. The so-called "Lines of Zahn" help to distinguish a true thromboembolus from post-mortem clot (Figure 32.3) and histology can also be helpful in this situation. Ideally the deep calf veins, the femoral and iliac veins should be examined in all cases of pulmonary embolism. Although this may seem unnecessary at the time of autopsy, subsequent enquiries may focus on the clinical evidence for ante-mortem thrombosis. Determining the time of thrombosis formation may then be of considerable medicolegal importance. Fineschi et al. (66) and Mansueto et al. (67) provide a detailed description of the morphologic transformation and immunohistochemical profile of thrombi at various chronological stages. As is the case with any microscopic "dating" exercise, it is important to accept that this is not an exact science but can be used as a useful guide where necessary.

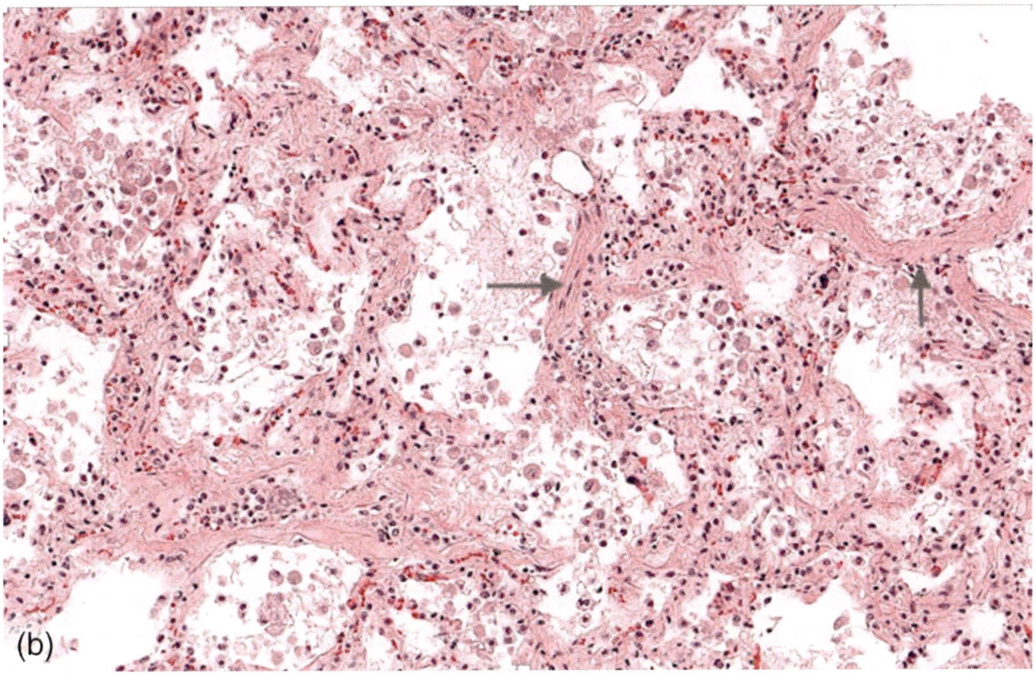

32.2 Acute lung injury. The patient in (a) was a teenage female who died 7 days after a road traffic accident. There was clinical and physiological evidence of severe acute lung injury. All lung lobes had a similar appearance with uniform congestion and focal areas of hemorrhage (arrow). Note that the pleural surfaces are normal. Acute lung injury is uncommon in children but may occur after complex operations. This patient had surgery for complex congenital heart disease in the past. (b) shows the typical histological changes of early acute lung injury. There is edema of the alveolar walls with widespread fibrin deposition (arrow). There is no significant acute inflammation but increased numbers of interstitial lymphocytes and macrophages. Small amounts of fibrin are present in alveoli. The patient was an elderly male who died 8 days after a colonic resection for carcinoma. Textbook descriptions of acute lung injury emphasise thick "hyaline membranes" and interstitial fibrosis but these are not prominent in acute postoperative deaths.

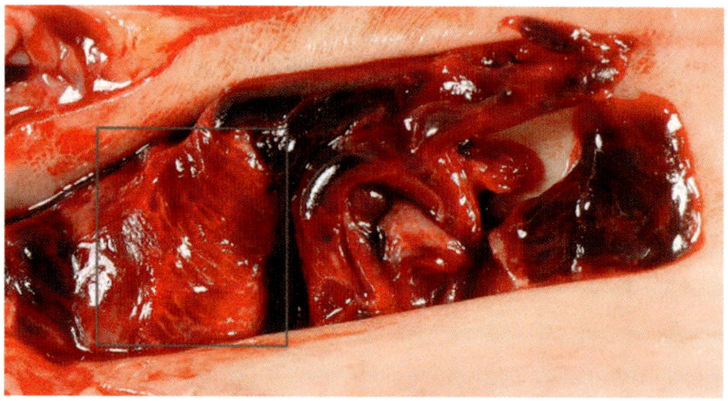

32.3 Pulmonary embolism. An elderly female died unexpectedly while recovering from surgery for pelvic injuries sustained in a road traffic collision. She was dyspnoeic in the period immediately before her death and had a respiratory alkalosis. The photograph shows a large coiled thromboembolus in the right pulmonary artery but there was also thrombus in the left artery. The boxed area shows prominent "Lines of Zahn" confirming that this is a true thrombus.

SECTION 3: CLINICO-PATHOLOGICAL ASPECTS OF SPECIFIC PROCEDURES

PERCUTANEOUS PROCEDURES

Some details of these procedures have been summarized in Table 32.4. Minor complications, such as localized hemorrhage around the insertion of a cannula are common and are seldom of clinical significance. Major complications, such as lung injury after insertion of a chest drain or peritonitis after placement of a feeding tube can cause or contribute to death. Detailed photography is essential in these cases.

Percutaneous coronary interventions

Pathologists who perform autopsies on patients who die after cardiovascular interventions should have a basic understanding of what these interventions involve and the possible complications. Ideally, they should speak with the responsible cardiologist before the autopsy, especially if the procedure was unusual or novel. Full details of all aspects of percutaneous cardiovascular procedures are published annually by the British Cardiovascular Intervention Society (BCIS) and are freely available on their website (68).

Recent reviews have detailed the advances in the design of coronary stents and their associated pathology (69) and the range of clinical and pathological complications associated with percutaneous coronary artery interventions (PCI) (29). Just over 100 000 PCIs are performed annually in the UK, the majority now as primary treatment for acute myocardial infarction (AMI). The BCIS reported a clinical "success rate" of 89 percent in 2019–20 and an overall mortality of 2 percent. As in all parts of the world, the mortality was greatest in patients with cardiogenic shock following AMI (35.3%), was 5.5 percent in primary PCI after AMI but 8.5 percent in "rescue" PCI

TABLE 32.4 Complications of percutaneous procedures

Procedure	Minor complications	Potentially significant complications
Central venous pressure line (CVP), peripherally inserted small bore catheters (PICC) and larger bore Hickman lines	Localized soft-tissue hemorrhages at point of insertion. May track into adjacent soft tissues, occasionally into pleural cavities	Occasional venous thromboses. Inadvertent carotid arterial puncture
Chest drains	Localized soft-tissue hemorrhage. Pneumothorax	Injury to heart, lung or great vessels causing hemothorax. Photographic documentation essential
Percutaneous endoscopic gastrotomy (PEG)	Uncommon. Even minor intestinal adhesions rare	Acute peritonitis, usually soon after insertion
Cardiac pacemakers	Uncommon. Post procedure pyrexia. Leads passing through the tricuspid valve may be positioned between chordae tendineae but without hemodynamic consequences. Lead tips may induce endocardial fibrosis. Although this is the desired result it may make subsequent replacement of the leads difficult	Right ventricular perforation with hemopericardium, often self-limiting. Endocarditis or thrombus formation requiring pacemaker replacement
Coronary arteriography, angioplasty and stenting	Localized hematomas at site of arterial puncture, now less common with radial artery access and femoral closure devices	Coronary artery dissection (now usually managed successfully) and coronary perforation. Early or late stent thrombosis
Insertion of covered stents (EVAR: endovascular aortic repair; TIPS: trans jugular intrahepatic portosystemic shunt)	Hemorrhage at access site	Injury to vessel wall by supportive struts. Occlusion of branch vessels and leakage of blood into the aneurysmal sac in aortic procedures (see text). Encephalopathy after TIPS, an indication for neuropathology

performed after failed thrombolysis for AMI. In contrast, mortality rates after elective PCI for stable coronary artery disease were only 0.2 percent. In overall terms, the major *clinical* complications of PCI were Q wave myocardial infarction (0.07%), non-Q wave myocardial infarction (0.1%), cerebrovascular accident (0.08%) and emergency coronary artery bypass grafting (0.04%).

Particular objectives of post-mortem examination after PCI are to examine the site(s) of coronary intervention, to estimate the size and age of acute and healed myocardial infarcts and to consider the possibility of contrast associated acute kidney injury. The full range of histological changes in coronary arteries containing drug-eluting stents have been described and illustrated in detail by Nakano et al. (70). However, in every day autopsy practice, the most relevant complications that should be excluded are traumatic coronary dissection, iatrogenic coronary thrombosis and coronary perforation. The stented segment of the coronary artery and the unstented coronary artery proximal and distal to the stent should be carefully dissected, photographed and examined histologically. With small sharp scissors, recently implanted stents can be easily opened and removed, allowing the coronary artery wall to be processed into paraffin blocks (Figure 32.4). Stents that have been in place for longer will be organized into the coronary artery wall and should be embedded in plastic (71). In our experience, the majority of acute myocardial infarcts in patients dying after PCI are >50 mm in dimension and, because of reflow following the intervention are hemorrhagic (Figure 32.5a). In occasional patients, a paradoxical pattern of progressive cardiomyocyte death follows a seemingly successful PCI (Figure 32.5b), so-called "myocyte reperfusion injury" (72). In all patients who die after PCI, detailed histology of normal and infarcted myocardium is recommended. Other major organs should be examined histologically. This is especially important when post-procedure increases in creatinine raise the suspicion of contrast induced kidney injury.

Aortic and aortic valve procedures

Two further percutaneous procedures are now in universal use, are inevitably associated with unexpected death and then require careful assessment and dissection at autopsy. Worldwide more than 500 000 transcatheter aortic valve implantations (TAVI) have now been performed. A recent report (73) describes an all-cause mortality of 2.6 percent within 30 days and 7.1 percent at one year. The most important complication leading to death soon after the procedure is (substantial) hemorrhage, but, as always, identifying the exact site of hemorrhage at autopsy is difficult. Other important complications are disabling stroke, new onset atrial fibrillation and myocardial infarction. The implanted valve should be examined first from

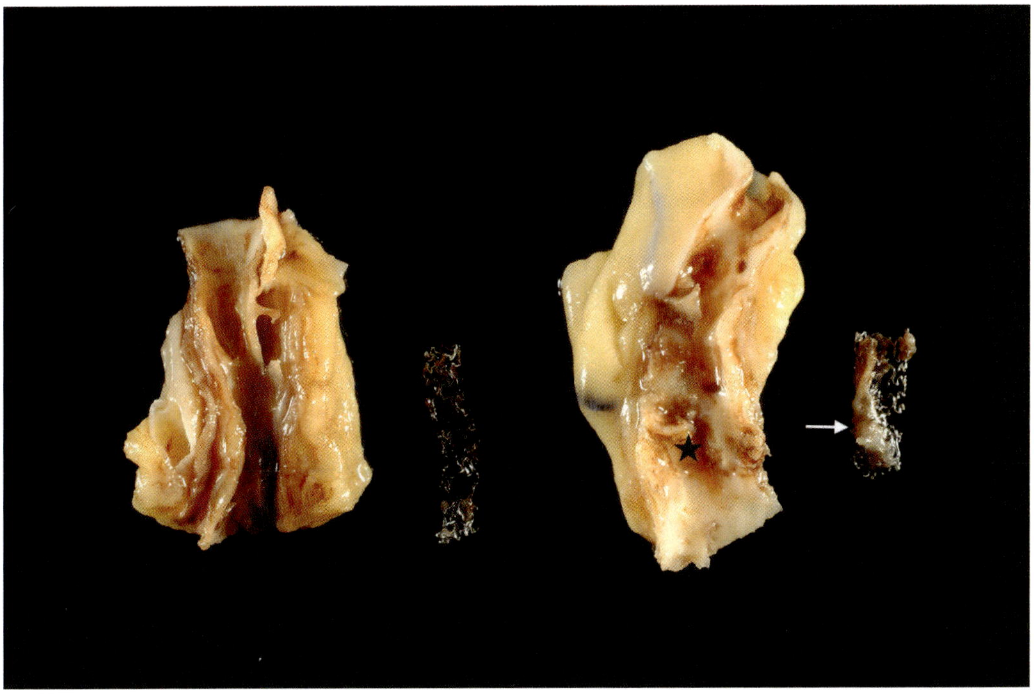

32.4 Coronary artery stents. A late middle-aged male died unexpectedly 4 months after elective coronary angioplasty and stenting. The stents had not become endothelized and were removed easily. The anterior descending artery (left image) was fully patent and the stent contained only a small amount of fibrous tissue. In contrast, there was significant partially occlusive atheroma (black star) in the right coronary artery (right image) and the stent was occluded by ingrowth of fibrous tissue (white arrow). The "bare metal stents" used in this case are now rarely used and have been replaced by drug-eluting stents. These reduce but do not fully prevent restenosis (see reference 69).

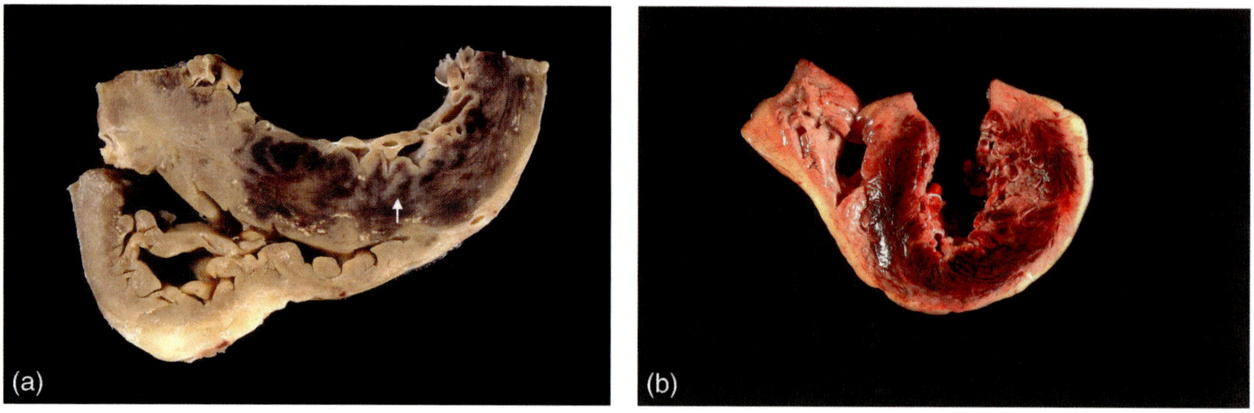

32.5 Acute myocardial infarction treated by percutaneous coronary intervention (PCI). In each case, all technical aspects of the procedure were satisfactory. The patient in (a) was an elderly male. He was in shock on admission and died 24 hours after PCI. There was a large anteroseptal acute infarct with a typically hemorrhagic appearance. Note small areas of headed fibrosis (white arrow), indicating previous ischemic injury. In contrast to the postoperative infarct shown in Figure 32.1, this is a large transmural infarct. The patient in (b) was a middle aged female who was admitted with chest pain. ECG showed a ST elevation anterior myocardial infarct. PCI was performed immediately but the patient's condition deteriorated progressively over the next 36 hours. The extensive pattern of hemorrhagic change indicates myocardial reperfusion injury, a rare and poorly understood complication of restoration of blood flow (see reference 72).

the aortic face. Photographs should document the exact site of insertion of the valve, the appearances of the adjacent coronary arterial ostia and the amount of hemorrhage in the different layers of the ascending aorta. The extent of coronary arterial atheroma and the presence of old or recent myocardial infarcts should be detailed in the report. As stroke occurs in ~4 percent of cases within 30 days, rising to 7.0 percent and 8.5 percent at one and two years (73), the brain should be expertly examined in all cases.

Endovascular aneurysm repair of the thoracic or abdominal aorta (EVAR) is now an acceptable alternative to open aortic surgery. It is associated with lower 30-day all-cause mortality and decreased morbidity. However, there are important complications and lifelong post-procedure surveillance may be required (74). So-called "endoleaks" are the result of failure of the intra-aortic device to completely exclude the aneurysm. This results in persistent blood flow into the aneurysmal sac. Radiologists have devised a detailed system of classification of endoleaks, using a variety of imaging methods. Most of these leaks occur at the proximal and distal placement points of the endovascular graft. At autopsy, it is these sites that should be examined with particular care. The exact position and appearance of the graft should be photographed as stent migration and endograft infection are recognized complications. Renal, lower limb and intestinal ischemia should be excluded (75).

CARDIOVASCULAR AND THORACIC SURGERY

Autopsies in patients dying after open heart surgery require careful attention to detail. Predictably, mortality is greater in emergency than elective operations and is highest in patients who have had a recent acute infarct, a major complication such as a ruptured interventricular septum or an aortic dissection (14). Additional significant risk factors include preoperative ventilation and/or ionotropic support, renal failure and an ejection fraction of <30 percent. However, two separate studies have reported a ~0.4 percent mortality rate in patients with low preoperative risk factor scores (76,77) confirming that all patients are at some risk. Many coronary artery bypass operations are now performed in high-risk subjects with extensive coronary atheroma, often on a background of diabetes or renal failure (78). The operation record will list the type of grafts used and the arteries that were bypassed. Grafts should be carefully examined for thrombosis, especially at the distal anastomosis (Figure 32.6). Any acute infarcts should be examined histologically for it is important to determine whether the infarct(s) occurred before or after the surgical procedure. Some degree of acute pericarditis is an almost inevitable complication of bypass surgery and is usually self-limiting (79). Pericardial effusions and constrictive pericarditis are rare but well recognized medium- and long-term complications (80,81). Hemorrhage is the major technical complication and is a particular problem in proximal aortic dissection or in repair of ruptured abdominal aneurysms. A number of audits of post-mortems after cardiac surgery have produced broadly similar findings. In the most recent study, cardiac failure was responsible for ~48 percent of deaths and multiorgan failure, with or without sepsis, for ~29 percent of deaths (82). Another reported that technical complications, especially hemorrhage, were responsible for ~10 percent of deaths and new information was obtained in 7–23 percent of cases. In up to 15 percent of cases, an exact cause of death was not determined (14). This is important because pathologists,

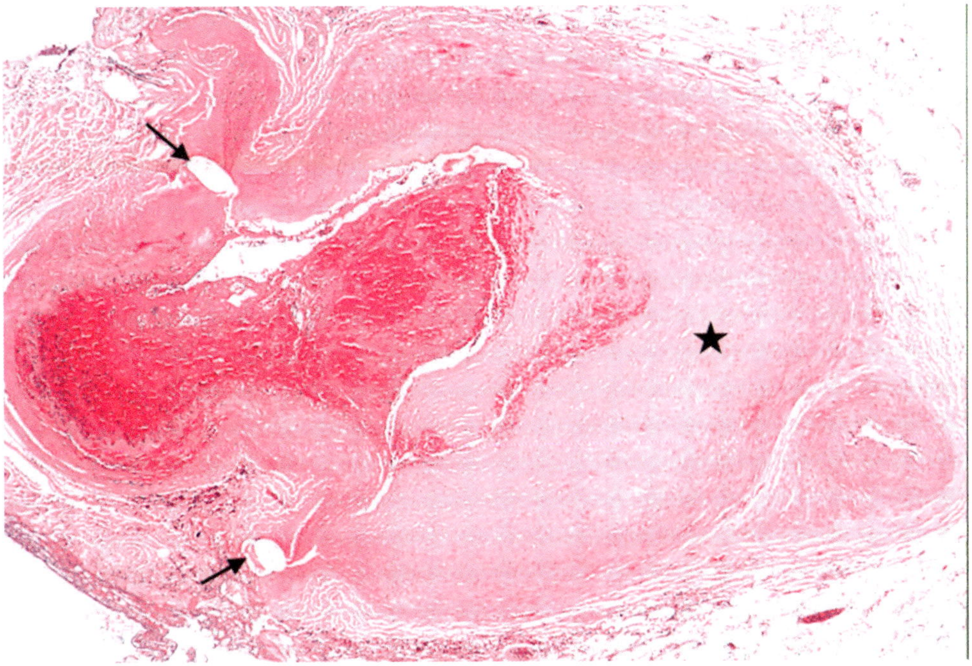

32.6 Coronary artery surgery. A histologic section taken through the distal anastomosis between a coronary artery (right) and a saphenous vein (left). Black arrows indicate sutures. The lumen is occluded by thrombus. A fibrolipid plaque in the coronary artery is indicated by a star. As far as possible, cardiac surgeons try to avoid making the anastomosis at the site of an atheromatous plaque.

surgeons and coroners must accept that a clear cause of death will not be found in a significant number of postoperative deaths. In many of these cases, the post-mortem findings suggest a sudden cardiac death but there may be little, if any, cardiac pathology (76). Mortality after open thoracotomy is 3–4 percent. Respiratory failure due to atelectasis, pneumonia and acute lung injury are the leading causes of both morbidity and mortality. Small pleural effusions are a common finding after thoracotomy and pneumothorax, chylothorax and broncho-pleural fistulae are additional complications (83). Significant postoperative hemorrhage was reported in 42 of 1960 lobectomy cases (2.7%), with 27 (1.4%) requiring reoperation (34). Atrial fibrillation is the most common cardiovascular complication. Video-assisted and robotic thoracic surgery are now the preferred approaches for lung cancer (84). Rare but significant complications include pulmonary arterial and pulmonary venous injury, conversion to unplanned pneumonectomies or lobectomies and tracheoesophageal fistulae.

COMPLICATIONS OF OPEN, LAPAROSCOPIC AND ROBOTIC GASTROINTESTINAL SURGERY INCLUDING BARIATRIC SURGERY

Increasingly, gastrointestinal (GI) and other abdominal surgeries are being performed using minimally invasive and now robotic methods (85). These techniques are associated with a faster patient recovery, though postoperative complications and mortality rates are broadly equivalent to those of open surgery. Invariably, major complications are more common following emergency surgery, which has a 30-day mortality rate five times higher than that of elective surgery (86). Perioperative SARS-CoV-2 infection is associated with high mortality, especially after cardiac and GI surgery (87). Thresholds for surgery during the COVID-19 pandemic should be higher than during normal practice, particularly in men aged 70 years and older.

Complications vary depending upon the surgical procedure and the post-mortem approach should be adapted accordingly. Perforation and pancreatitis should be considered following endoscopy, particularly if retrograde cholangiopancreatography has been performed, while gas embolism and trocar-induced trauma may complicate laparoscopic interventions. In some cases, it may be necessary to remove the intestines *en bloc* with the internal organs, particularly in a case that requires exploration of the celiac or mesenteric vasculature.

Anastomotic dehiscence is a common and often life-threatening complication of GI surgery, with death typically resulting from peritonitis and abdominal sepsis. Anastomotic dehiscence occurs most commonly following esophageal (5.7–14.3%) or colorectal (1.0–20.0%) anastomoses (88). Dehiscence following gastric, small intestinal and colocolonic anastomoses are infrequent. There are many risk factors attributed to anastomotic dehiscence, including male gender, obesity, malnutrition, corticosteroid use, chemo- or radiotherapy, smoking and atherosclerotic disease (89). Careful handling of the anastomosis site *in situ*, prior to evisceration, is vital in order to prevent post-mortem breakdown and perforation. For this reason, no part of the GI tract should be distended with water. The anastomosis should be examined histologically to determine the viability of the surrounding mucosa.

Post-mortem examination of an obese individual can be technically demanding. Obesity rates are rising worldwide and bariatric surgeries, such as gastric banding and Roux-en-Y gastric bypass, are increasingly performed with postoperative mortality rates as high as 5 percent (90). Anastomotic dehiscence, sepsis, hemorrhage, small bowel obstruction and VTE are the most frequently observed fatal complications (91). Major long-term complications of bariatric surgery include intra-abdominal adhesions, malnutrition and cirrhosis. Post-mortem should be undertaken in a mortuary with specialized bariatric facilities and with a sufficient number of assisting staff in order to facilitate a safe and complete examination.

DEATHS FOLLOWING ORTHOPEDIC SURGERY

Elderly patients, and especially elderly frail patients (92,93), often have decreased physiological reserve and pre-existing medical conditions that may increase the risk of postoperative death. Critical risk factors have been identified that increase the risk of postoperative orthopedic mortality – age greater than 70 years, hip fracture, chronic renal failure, congestive cardiac failure and chronic obstructive pulmonary disease. The risk of death increases significantly with an increasing number of risk factors (94). Surgical delay, Parkinson's disease, Alzheimer's disease, malignant disease and the use of cemented hemiarthroplasties have also been identified as increasing the risk of death following hip fracture surgery (95,96).

Cemented hemiarthroplasty and other orthopedic procedures that involve manipulation of the medullary canal may cause pulmonary fat or bone marrow embolism, cement emboli or acute anaphylaxis (19,97–99). These possibilities should be considered in any case of sudden cardiovascular collapse occurring during or soon after an orthopedic procedure. Significant pulmonary fat and/or bone marrow embolism can be suspected with standard H&E histological stains but ideally is confirmed by Oil red O staining of frozen lung tissue (7). Non-orthopedic causes of fat embolism syndrome are exceedingly rare and include pancreatitis, sickle cell disease, alcoholic liver disease, bone marrow harvest or transplantation, and as recently described after liposuction (99).

MATERNAL DEATH

Maternal death in the UK is defined as any death that occurs in pregnancy or within twelve months of birth. Death may be directly related to pregnancy, indirectly related (e.g. pre-existing heart disease exacerbated by pregnancy) or coincidental (100).

Postoperative maternal deaths occur principally following termination of pregnancy (TOP – "abortion") or cesarean section. The major complications from legal TOP relate to sepsis or perforation of the genital tract/abdominal viscera. Very careful inspection of the uterus and intestines is required and histology/microbiology would often be considered necessary (100,101).

"Criminal" or "unsafe" abortion occurs when the operator lacks the necessary skills and/or in an environment that does not meet appropriate medical standards. Criminal abortion is associated with a considerable risk of mortality especially in countries with a less well-developed system of medical/social care. In addition to sepsis and perforation, causes of mortality include toxic effects of chemicals (e.g. formalin, alcohol) and cardiac air embolism as a consequence of syringe insufflation of air (101). In these cases, strong consideration should be given to post-mortem radiology.

The risk of death following cesarean section is greater in low- and middle-income countries. The main cause of death is postpartum hemorrhage. A recent review of 196 studies from middle- and lower-income regions identified a risk of maternal death in women who had a cesarean section of 7.6 per 1000 (3). This is ~600 times greater than the Netherlands where deaths directly to and associated with cesarean section are 13 per 100 000. The direct causes relate to sepsis, hemorrhage and complications of anesthesia. The associated deaths include obstetric complications (principally hypertensive disorders), thromboembolic disease, amniotic fluid embolism and heart disease (102).

SUMMARY AND CONCLUSION

Post-mortem examination of patients dying after surgery or a percutaneous procedure is a key step in clinical audit and may have important medicolegal implications. It usually establishes a cause of death and may reveal clinically unsuspected conditions. Most deaths are the result of predictable natural causes such as pneumonia with or without acute lung injury, pulmonary embolism, acute coronary syndromes or cardiac failure. However, in up to 15 percent of cases an accurate cause of death is not established. The technique of post-mortem examination should be adapted to first demonstrate whether the anatomic result of the procedure has the expected appearances. Hemorrhage is the most important technical complication but only bleeding of more than a liter is likely to be the immediate cause of death. Histology has a valuable role in the diagnosis of cardiac and pulmonary disease and in the investigation of postoperative renal, hepatic and multi-organ failure. Percutaneous coronary interventions and minimally invasive and robotic surgery are now used routinely and pathologists must expect to encounter deaths after these procedures. In the final report, the clinicopathological aspects of the case should be summarized as accurately and clearly as possible. In particular, the certainty with which the cause of death was established should be discussed.

REFERENCES

1. Meara JG, Leather SJM, Hagander L, et al. Global Surgery 2030: Evidence and solutions for achieving health, welfare, and economic development. *Lancet* 2015; **386:** 569–624.
2. Nepogodiev D, Martin J, Biccard B. Global burden of postoperative death. *Lancet* 2019; **393:** 401.
3. Sobhy S, Arroyo-Manzano D, Murugesu N, et al. Maternal and perinatal mortality and complications associated with caesarean section in low-income and middle-income countries: A systematic review and meta-analysis. *Lancet* 2019; **393:** 1973–82.
4. GlobalSurg Collaborative and National Institute for Health Research Global Health Research Unit on Global Surgery. Global variation in postoperative mortality and complications after cancer surgery: A multicentre, prospective cohort study in 82 countries. *Lancet* 2021; **397:** 387–97.
5. Delaney RJ, Gallagher PJ. Deaths: Perioperative and Postoperative – Pathology. In: Payne-James JJ. and Byard R.W. (eds.) *Encyclopedia of Forensic and Legal Medicine*, 2nd ed, Vol. 2, pp. 105–113. Oxford: Elsevier; 2016.
6. Chambers D, du Parcq J, Sheldon J, *Guidelines on Autopsy Practice: Autopsy for suspected acute anaphylaxis (includes anaphylactic shock and anaphylactic asthma)*. London: Royal College of Pathologists; 2018.
7. Milroy CM, Parai JL. Fat embolism, Fat Embolism Syndrome and the autopsy. *Acad Forensic Pathol* 2019; **9:** 136–54.
8. Goldman L, Sayaso R, Robbins S, et al. The value of the autopsy in three medical eras. *N Engl J Med* 1983; **308:** 1000–05.
9. Mort TC, Yeston, NS. The relationship of pre mortem diagnoses and post mortem findings in a surgical intensive care unit. *Crit Care Med* 1999; **27:** 299–303.
10. Ooi A, Goodwin A.T, Goddard M, Ritchie A.J. Clinical outcome versus post-mortem finding in thoracic surgery: A 10 year experience. *Eur J Cardiothoracic Surg* 2003; **23:** 878–82.
11. Lee AHS, Borek BT, Gallagher PJ, et al. Prospective study of the value of necropsy examination in early death after cardiac surgery. *Heart* 1997; **78:** 34–38.
12. Delaney RJ, Gallagher PJ, The value of post-mortem examinations after surgery. *Ann R Coll Surg* 2005; **87(Supplement):** 106–08.
13. NCEPOD. *The 2002 report of the National Confidential Enquiry into Perioperative Deaths.* London: NCEPOD; 2002.
14. Hickling MF, Pontefract DE, Gallagher PJ, Livesey SA. Post mortem examinations after cardiac surgery. *Heart* 2007; **93:** 761–5.
15. Burton J. An approach to the autopsy examination of patients who die during surgery or in the post-operative period. *Diagn Histopathol* 2019; **25:** 436–43.
16. Burton J, Suvarna SK. *Guidelines on autopsy practice: Postoperative deaths.* Osborn M, (ed). London: Royal College of Pathologists; 2019.
17. Magnin V, Grabherr S, Michaud K. The Lausanne forensic pathology approach to post-mortem imaging for natural and non-natural deaths. *Diagnostic Pathol* 2020; **8:** 350–7.
18. Rutty GN, Morgan B, Robinson C, et al. Diagnostic accuracy of post-mortem CT with targeted coronary angiography versus autopsy for coroner-requested post-mortem investigations: a prospective, masked, comparison study. *Lancet* 2017; **390:** 145–54.
19. Bernardi FD, Saldiva PH, Mauad, T. Histological examination has a major impact on macroscopic necropsy diagnoses. *J Clin Pathol* 2005; **58:** 1201–04.
20. Roulson J, Benbow E W, Hasleton PS. Discrepancies between clinical and autopsy diagnosis and the value of post mortem histology: A meta-analysis and review. *Histopathology* 2005; **47:** 551–9.
21. Gibbs N. *Safety of anaesthesia: A Review of Anaesthesia-Related Mortality Reporting in Australia and New Zealand 2003 - 2005.* Melbourne: Australian and New Zealand College of Anaesthetists; 2009.
22. Ellis S, Newland MC, Simonson JA. Anesthesia-related cardiac arrest. *Anesthesiology* 2014; **120:** 829–38.
23. Moitra VK, Einav S, Thies K-C. Cardiac arrest in the operating room: Resuscitation and management for the anesthesiologist: Part 1. *Anesth Analg* 2018; **126:** 876–88.
24. Start RD, Cross SS. Pathological investigation of deaths following surgery, anaesthesia, and medical procedures. *J Clin Pathol* 1999: **52:** 640–52.
25. Pumphrey RSH, Roberts ISD. Post-mortem findings after fatal anaphylactic reactions. *J Clin Pathol* 2000; **53:** 273–6.
26. Edston E, Eriksson O, van Hage M. Mast cell tryptase in postmortem serum: Reference values and confounders *Int J Legal Med* 2007; **121:** 275–80.
27. McLean-Tooke A, Goulding M, Bundell C, et al. Postmortem serum tryptase levels in anaphylactic and non-anaphylactic deaths. *J Clin Pathol* 2014; **67:** 134–8.
28. Kalra SK, ThilagarB, Khambaty M, Manjarrez E. Post-operative anemia after major surgery: A brief review. *Curr Emerg Hosp Med Rep* 2021; **9:** 89–95.
29. Kandan SR, Johnson TW. Management of percutaneous coronary intervention complications. *Heart* 2019; **105:** 75–86.
30. Canon JW. Hemorrhagic shock. *N Engl J Med* 2018; **378:** 370–9.
31. Hunt BJ. Bleeding and coagulopathies in critical care. *N Engl J Med* 2014; **370:** 847–59.
32. Ghadimi K, Levy JH, Welsby IJ. Perioperative management of the bleeding patient. *Br J Anaesth* 2016; **117(S3):** iii18–iii30.
33. Clevenger B, Richards T. Pre-operative anaemia. *Anaesthesia* 2015; **70 (Suppl. 1):** 20–28.
34. Udelsman BV, Sonia M, Madariaga ML, et al. Incidence, aetiology and outcomes of major postoperative haemorrhage after pulmonary lobectomy. *Eur J Cardiothoracic Surg* 2020; **57:** 462–70.
35. Devereaux PJ, Sessler DI. Cardiac complications in patients undergoing major noncardiac surgery. *N Engl J Med* 2015; **373:** 2258–69.
36. Devereaux P, Xavier D, Pogue J, et al. Characteristics and short term prognosis of perioperative myocardial infarction in patients undergoing non-cardiac surgery: A cohort study. *Ann Intern Med* 2011; **154:** 523–8.
37. Berrios-Torres SA, Umscheid CA, Bratzler DW, et al. Centers for Disease Control and Prevention: Guideline for the prevention of surgical site infection. *JAMA Surg* 2017; **152:** 784–91.
38. Burton JL, Saegeman V, Arribi A, et al. Postmortem microbiology sampling following death in hospital: ESGFOR task force consensus. *J Clin Pathol* 2019; **72:** 329–36.
39. Badia JM, Casey AL, Petrosillo N, et al. Impact of surgical site infection of healthcare costs and patient outcomes: a systemic review in six European countries. *J Hospital Infect* 2017; **96:** 1–15.
40. Singer M, Deutschman CS, Seymour CW, et al. The third international consensus definitions for sepsis and septic shock. *JAMA* 2016; **315:** 801–10.
41. Stassi C, Mondello C, Baldino G, Spagnolo EV. Post-mortem investigations for the diagnosis of sepsis: a review of the literature. *Diagnostics* 2020; **10:** 849–74.
42. Yang QP, Lui WP, Guo LX, et al. Autopsy report of four cases who died from Streptococcus suis infection, with a review of the literature. *Eur J Clin Microbiol Infect Dis* 2009; **28:** 447–53.
43. Farofalo AM, Lorente-Ros M, Goncalvez G, et al. Histopathological changes of organ dysfunction in sepsis. *Intensive Care Med Exp* 2019; **7:** 45.
44. Sledzinska A, Mielech A, Krawczyk B, et al. Fatal sepsis in a pregnant woman with pyelonephritis caused by Escherichia coli bearing Dr and P adhesins: Diagnosis based on postmortem strain genotyping. *BJOG* 2011; **118:** 266–9.
45. Sinicina I, Matevossian E, Fischer F, et al. The petrified heart in sepsis. *Virchows Archiv* 2005; **447:** 875–8.
46. Palmiere C, Tettamanti C, Scarpelli MP, et al. The forensic spleen: morphological, radiological and toxicological investigations. *Forensic Sci Internat* 2018; **291:** 94–99.
47. Lucas S. The autopsy pathology of sepsis-related death. *Curr Diagn Pathol* 2007; **13:** 375–8.
48. Garofalo AM, Lorente-Ros M, Goncalvez G, et al. Histopathological changes of organ dysfunction in sepsis. *Intensive Care Med* 2019; **7:** 1–15.
49. Feig JA, Cina SJ. Evaluation of characteristics associated with acute splenitis (septic spleen) as markers of systemic infection. *Archiv Pathol Lab Med* 2001; **12:** 888–91.
50. Fernandez-Rodriguez A, Burton JI, Andreoletti L, et al. Post-mortem microbiology in sudden death: Sampling protocols proposed in different clinical settings. *Clin Microbiol Infect* 2019; **25:** 570–9.
51. Rorat M, Jurek T, Simon K. Post-mortem diagnosis in cases of sepsis. Part 2. Biochemical and morphological examinations. *Archives of Forensic Medicine and Criminology* 2015; **65:** 55–66.
52. La Russa F, Maiese A, Viola RV, et al. Searching for highly sensitive and specific biomarkers for sepsis: State-of-the-art in post-mortem diagnosis of sepsis through immunohistochemical analysis.

Int J Immunopathol Pharmacol 2019; **65:** 45–47.

53. Agostini P, Cieslik H, Rathinam S, et al. Postoperative pulmonary complications following thoracic surgery: are there any modifiable risk factors? *Thorax* 2012; **65:** 815–58.
54. Chughtai M, Gwam CG, Mohamed N, et al. The epidemiology and risk factors for postoperative pneumonia. *J Clin Med Res* 2017; **9:** 466–75.
55. Fitch ZW, Whitman GJR. Incidence, risk, and prevention of ventilator-associated pneumonia in adult cardiac surgical patients: a systemic review. *J Card Surg* 2014; **29:** 196–203.
56. Ottosen J, Evans H. Pneumonia: Challenges in the definition, diagnosis and management of disease. *Surg Clin North Am* 2014; **94:** 1305–17.
57. Miskovic A, Lumb AB. Postoperative pulmonary complications. *Br J Anaesth* 2017; **118:** 317–34.
58. ARDS Definition Task Force: Ranieri VM, Rubenfeld GD, et al. Acute respiratory distress syndrome: The Berlin Definition. *JAMA* 2012; **307:** 2526–33.
59. Dushianthan A, Grocott MPW, Postle AD, et al. Acute respiratory distress syndrome and acute lung injury. *Br Med J* 2011; **87:** 612–22.
60. Thompson BT, Chambers RC, Lui KD. Acute respiratory distress syndrome. *N Engl Med* 2017; **377:** 562–72.
61. Stephens RS, Shah AS, Whitman GJR. Lung injury and acute respiratory distress syndrome after cardiac surgery. *Ann Thorac Surg* 2013; **95:** 1122–29.
62. Thille AW, Esteban A, Fernández-Segoviano, et al. Comparison of the Berlin definition for acute respiratory distress syndrome with autopsy. *Am J Respir Crit Care Med* 2013; **187:** 761–7.
63. Khan F, Tritschler T, Kahn SR, Rodger MA. Venous thromboembolism. *Lancet* 2021; **398:** 64–77.
64. Gangireddy C, Rectenwalk JR, Upchurch GR, et al. Risk factors and clinical impact of postoperative symptomatic venous thromboembolism. *J Vasc Surg* 2007; **45:** 335–42.
65. DeFreitas DJ, Kasirajan K, Ricotta JJ, et al. Preoperative inpatient hospitalization and risk of perioperative infection following elective vascular procedures. *Ann Vasc Surg* 2012; **26:** 46–54.
66. Fineschi V, Turillazzi E, Neri M, et al. Histological age determination of venous thrombosis: A neglected forensic task in fatal pulmonary thrombo-embolis. *Forensic Sci Int* 2009; **186:** 22–28.
67. Mansueto G, Costa D, Capasso E, et al. The dating of thrombus organization in cases of pulmonary embolism: an autopsy study. *BMC Cardiovasc Disord* 2019; **19:** article number 250.
68. British Cardiovascular Intervention Society. *Audit report for 2019–20.* Available from: https://www.bcis.org.uk (Accessed 25 April 2023).
69. Torii S, Jinnouchi H, Sakamoto A, et al. Drug-eluting coronary stents: Insights from preclinical and pathology studies. *Nature Rev Cardiol* 2020; **17:** 37–51.
70. Nakano M, Otsuka F, Yahagi K, et al. Human autopsy study of drug-eluting stents restenosis: Histomorphological predictors and neointimal characteristics. *Eur Heart J* 2013; **34:** 3304–13.
71. Rippstein P, Black MK, Boivin M, et al. Comparison of processing and sectioning methodologies for arteries containing metallic stents. *J Histochem Cytochem* 2006; **54:** 673–81.
72. Hausenloy DJ, Yellon DM. Myocardial ischemia-reperfusion injury: a neglected therapeutic target. *J Clin Invest* 2013; **123:** 92–100.
73. Ranasinghe MP, Peter K, McFadyen JD, et al. Thromboembolic and bleeding complications in transcatheter aortic valve implantation: Insights on mechanisms, prophylaxis and therapy. *J Clin Med* 2019; **8:** 280–96.
74. Daye D, Walker TG. Complications of endovascular aneurysm repair of the thoracic and abdominal aorta: evaluation and management. *Cardiovasc Diagn Ther* 2018; **8 (Suppl 1):** S138–S156.
75. Maleux G, Koolen IM, Hete S. Complications after endovascular aneurysm repair complications after endovascular aneurysm repair. *Semin Intervent Radiol* 2009; **26:** 3–10.
76. Freed DH, Drain AJ, Kitcata J, et al. Death in low-risk cardiac surgery: The failure to achieve a satisfactory cardiac outcome (FIASCO) study. *Interact Cardiovasc Thorac Surg* 2009; **9:** 623–25.
77. Janiec M, Sartipy U. Death in low-risk cardiac surgery: Stockholm experience. *Interact Cardiovasc Thorac Surg* 2010; **11:** 547–9.
78. Arri SS, Patterson T, Williams RP, et al. Myocardial revascularisation in high-risk subjects. *Heart* 2018; **104:** 166–179.
79. Troughton RW, Asher CR, Klein AL. Pericarditis. *Lancet* 2004; **363:** 717–27.
80. Gaudino M, Anselmi A, Pavone, N, Massetti M. Constrictive pericarditis after cardiac surgery. *Ann Thorac Surg* 2013; **95:** 731–6.
81. Khana NK, Jarvela KM, Loisa EL, et al. Incidence, presentation and risk factors of late postoperative pericardial effusions requiring invasive treatment after cardiac surgery. *Interact Cardiovasc Thorac Surg* 2017; **24:** 835–40.
82. Němec P, Fila P, Štěrba J, Černošek J. Value of autopsy in cardiac surgery. *Cor Vasa* 2015; **57:** e91–e94.
83. Sengupta S. Post-operative pulmonary complications after thoracotomy. *Indian J Anaesth* 2015; **59:** 618–26.
84. Cypel M, Yasufuku K. Complications during minimal invasive thoracic surgery: are new surgeons prepared? *Lancet Oncol* 2018; **19:** 17–19.
85. Kyle H. Sheetz KH, Claflin J, Dimick JB. Trends in the adoption of robotic surgery for common surgical procedures. *JAMA Netw Open* 2020; **3:** e1918911.
86. Sørensen LT, Malaki A, Wille-Jørgensen P, et al. Risk factors for mortality and postoperative complications after gastrointestinal surgery. *J Gastrointest Surg* 2007; **11:** 903–10.
87. COVIDSurg Collaborative Mortality and pulmonary complications in patients undergoing surgery with perioperative SARS-CoV-2 infection: An international cohort study. *Lancet* 2020; **396:** 27–38.
88. Chadi SA, Fingerhut A, Berho M, et al. Emerging trends in the etiology, prevention, and treatment of gastrointestinal anastomotic leakage. *J Gastrointest Surg* 2016; **20:** 2035–51.
89. Kingham TP, Pachter HL. Colonic anastomotic leak: risk factors, diagnosis, and treatment. *J Am Coll Surg* 2009; **208:** 269–78.
90. Cummings PM, Le BH, Lopes BS. Postmortem findings in morbidly obese individuals dying after gastric bypass procedures. *Hum Pathol* 2007; **38:** 593–7.
91. Lucas SB. Autopsy following complications of bariatric surgery. *Histopathology* 2014; **65:** 290–1.
92. Treml J, Kroker PB. Orthopaedic surgery in the elderly. *Hosp Med* 2000; **61:** 417–19.
93. Castillo-Angeles M, Cooper Z. Jarman MP, et al. Association of frailty with morbidity and mortality in emergency general surgery by procedural risk level. *JAMA Surg* 2021; **156:** 68–74.
94. Bhattacharyya T, Iorio R, Healy WL. Rate and risk factors for acute inpatient mortality after orthopaedic surgery. *J Bone Joint Surg Am* 2002; **84:** 562–72.
95. Kilci O, Un C, Sacan O, et al. Postoperative mortality after hip fracture surgery: A 3 years follow up. *PLoS One* 2016; **11:** e0162097.
96. Huette P, Abou-Arab O, Djebara A, et al. Risk factors and mortality of patients undergoing hip fracture surgery: A one year follow-up study. *Sci Rep* 2020; 10: 9607
97. Kilci O, Un C, Sacan O, et al. Postoperative mortality after hip fracture surgery: A 3 year follow up. *PLoS One* 2016; **11:** e0162097.
98. Heine TA, Halambeck BL, Mark JB. Fatal pulmonary fat embolism in the early postoperative period. *Anesthesiology* 1998; **89:** 1589–91.
99. Cantu CA, Pavlisko EN. Liposuction induced fat embolism syndrome: A brief review and postmortem diagnostic approach. *Arch Pathol Lab Med* 2018; **142:** 871–5.
100. Millward-Sadler GH. Pathology of maternal deaths. In: Kirkham N, Shepherd N (eds). *Progress in Pathology* Vol 6. London: Greenwich Medical Media, 2003, pp. 163–85.
101. Saukko P, Knight B. Deaths associated with pregnancy. In: *Knight's Forensic Pathology*, 4th ed, London: CRC Press; 2015, pp. 437–46.
102. Kalliandis AF, Schutte JM, van Roosmalen J, et al. Maternal mortality after caesarean section in the Netherlands. *Eur J Obstet Gynecol Reprod Biol* 2018; **229:** 148–52.
103. Fasting S, Gisvold SE. Equipment problems during anaesthesia: Are they a quality problem? *Br J Anaesth* 2002; **89:** 825–31.
104. Shaydenfish D, Scheffenbichler FT, Kelly BJ, et al. Effects of anticholinesterase reversal under general anesthesia on postoperative cardiovascular complications: A retrospective cohort study. *Anesth Analg* 2020; **130:** 685–95.

CHAPTER

33

Drowning

Lilli Stephenson and Roger W. Byard

INTRODUCTION

Drowning accounts for approximately 7 percent of all unintentional injury-related deaths each year around the world (1). It can occur indoors or outdoors, in recreational, occupational or domestic settings including beaches, oceans, lakes, dams, lagoons, rivers, creeks, streams, spa/baths, swimming pools and, on the rare occasion, even in shallow containers such as paddling pools and buckets. The highest rates of drowning are among children, males and those unfamiliar with the risks associated with entering a body of water such as tourists (2,3). Children are at particular risk when they are exploring their environment as they often fail to appreciate possible dangers (4,5). They may not have the mental or physical capabilities to extract themselves from potentially lethal situations such as rainwater tanks (6) and may be at risk in baths from shared bathing or when using infant bath seats (7,8).

Other risk factors for drowning are access to open bodies of water, living in flood-prone areas, lower socioeconomic status, drug and/or alcohol intoxication and medical conditions such as epilepsy (1). For example, intoxication may play a role in drownings in inner city rivers located close to licensed premises and bars (9). Drownings are however significantly underreported due to the use of highly variable terminology in the literature; inconsistent recordings of causation; exclusion of intentional drownings and drownings associated with natural disasters (e.g. floods and tsunamis) and water transport accidents from overview statistics (10); and the difficulty that arises in definitely determining drowning as a cause of death. While the diagnosis of drowning may appear straightforward, it can be confounded by significant obstacles associated with the investigation of immersion deaths including environmental factors at the death scene, non-specific autopsy findings, and the lack of diagnostic signs and tests (11,12).

Definitions

The first difficulty that may be encountered in evaluating drowning in the literature is navigating the highly variable terminology used. Drowning is generally defined as "the process of experiencing respiratory impairment from submersion/immersion in liquid" with the potential outcomes of death, morbidity or no morbidity (1,10,13,14). In a forensic context, this definition can be applied to describe a drowning event with a lethal outcome (15,16). However, significant modifications have been required to improve the consistency and accessibility of forensic drowning terminology (17,18). Inconsistencies arise between clinical and forensic assessments, as drowning in a clinical context may not always be associated with a fatal outcome (i.e. near-drowning or non-fatal drowning). Idris et al. stated that a victim of drowning may live or die after the incident, "but whatever the outcome, he or she has been involved in a drowning incident" (13). This statement underpins a major issue in forensic drowning terminology, with open-ended definitions lacking distinctions between clinical and forensic incidents. The term "near drowning" has been applied to an event in which the victim survives for a period of time after the incident. While its use has been criticized, "near drowning" may be helpful in distinguishing between fatal and non-fatal drowning incidents and so assist in the standardization of mortality data (19). This is similar to the recent emphasis on strangulation and non-fatal strangulation, the latter of which has become much more widely understood by both clinicians and forensic practitioners.

Furthermore, it has been recommended that terms such as "dry/wet drowning", "secondary drowning", "active/passive drowning" and "delayed onset of respiratory distress" should be avoided (10) as some incidents do not comply with the standard definition of drowning (3). For example, "dry drowning" has been used to describe the small proportion of cases who do not exhibit aspiration of significant amounts of fluid. In the absence of fluid aspiration, a differential diagnosis may be more appropriate (20), for example: "death due to upper airway obstruction complicating immersion". While the nature of forensic drowning terminology has improved significantly over recent years, there is still room for clarification (18).

PATHOPHYSIOLOGY

The pathophysiological mechanisms underpinning drowning are multifactorial and to some extent depend on the drowning medium which may be salt water, fresh water, another type of liquid or no liquid at all as in cases of "dry drowning". For those who do not die immediately

DOI: 10.1201/9781003138754-35

following a near-drowning incident, death is often attributed to hypoxic-ischemic encephalopathy due to an extended period of submersion. Children are, however, known to be able to survive quite prolonged periods of submersion, particularly if the water is cold (21).

For saltwater drownings, aspiration of salt water into the lungs promotes the diffusion of fluid from the capillaries surrounding the alveoli into the lungs due to the osmotic gradient. The resultant formation of pulmonary edema or fluid accumulation in the lungs disrupts pulmonary surfactant which inhibits oxygen exchange, causing subsequent hypoxia and death (22).

Aspirating fresh water, however, results in water diffusing from the alveoli into the surrounding capillaries, resulting in increased blood volume and subsequent hemolysis (23). The underlying mechanism of death is attributed to cardiac arrythmias (22).

In cases of "dry drowning" and in the absence of fluid aspiration, the mechanism of death is thought to be hypoxia due to laryngospasm, pulmonary reflexes or cardiac arrest mediated by the parasympathetic nervous system (14,15,24).

SCENE INVESTIGATION

Difficulties often arise in the scene investigation of drowning deaths, particularly when this is outdoors. Often, bodies may not be discovered for an extended period of time due to reduced accessibility and discoverability, resulting in prolonged post-mortem intervals. This is particularly so for freshwater drownings in rivers resulting in greater likelihood of putrefaction (25). While all personnel involved in body retrieval and scene investigation may be hampered by particular locations, new technologies are being developed to assist in locating bodies submerged in water. For example, side-scan sonar technology utilizes sound frequencies to survey the sea floor to detect submerged objects and has become increasingly employed in forensic investigations to detect bodies and physical evidence (26,27).

Environmental factors such as water temperature and movement of the body from its point of entry by currents, wind, waves or tides may also affect the integrity and preservation of the body and possible associated physical evidence (28).

Animal predation can significantly alter identifiable features and signs of physical injury, often creating new wounds (29). Depending on the species involved (e.g. sea lice, sharks, fish, crocodiles or crawfish), evidence of animal predation may range from superficial tissue injuries to the complete removal of tissues and organs (29,30). If organs are removed in their entirety, this may impact upon the evaluation of underlying organic disease and/or toxicological analyses (31). Puncture wounds inflicted by fish or crocodiles can also be mistaken for self-inflicted wounds or wounds inflicted by an implement (29). It is also sometimes difficult to determine whether animal predation occurred prior to death and contributed to the fatality, or whether the animal(s) was merely feeding on post-mortem remains (29).

While colder water temperatures may assist in body preservation, accelerated rates of decomposition and putrefaction are observed in bodies recovered from rivers and other warm bodies of water due to higher water temperatures (25,32). For bodies retrieved from warmer water, it is recommended that the autopsy examination is conducted in a timely manner to prevent further post-mortem degradation (25). In domestic settings, there are examples of bodies discovered submerged in baths with initially warm or hot water which can interfere with estimations of time of death due to significantly accelerated decomposition. At death scenes where the water temperature is significantly low or high, it may also be helpful to record the temperature of the water (25).

AUTOPSY FINDINGS

While there are autopsy findings considered to be characteristic of drowning, it is important to note there are no definitive diagnostic features (33) (Table 33.1). Autopsy examination also becomes problematic once putrefactive changes have begun, which often disguises or removes features to support drowning (28).

External findings

External examination will often reveal wrinkling of the hands and/or feet in cases of prolonged immersion (also referred to as "washerwoman" hands), which can progress to sloughing of the epidermis to form a "glove" (Figures 33.1–33.3), a "plume" of foam around the nose (Figure 33.4), mud and debris in the mouth, and abrasions on the dorsal surface of the feet, hands and knees from dragging (current, waves or physical removal of the body) (14,28,34–36). As noted, this may have been confounded by the effects of decomposition and animal predation). The differentiation between abrasions and laceration caused by body movement against objects or surfaces in water, and those caused pre-immersion may often be unclear.

Internal findings

Autopsy signs reported in drowning include foamy edema fluid in the nasal passages, larynx, trachea and bronchi (Figures 33.5–33.7), pleural effusions, pulmonary edema and/or hemorrhage, dilation of the right side of the heart, fluid in the sinuses, middle ear or mastoid air cell hemorrhage, fluid in the stomach, reduced splenic volume and soft-tissue hemorrhage in the neck. For bodies that have been submerged and are discovered in a moist, low-oxygen environment (wet ground or mud), adipocere may also be present, formed from the hydrolysis of triglycerides within adipose tissue (37). The stomach may be filled with water (Wydler's sign) and the lungs may be hyperinflated (so-called emphysema aquosum) with surface indentations from pressure against the ribs and hemorrhagic Paltauf's spots (35,36,38–40). Inhalation of sandy water forming endobronchial sand

TABLE 33.1 Characteristic features of drowning

External	• Foam around the nose • Wrinkling of the hands and feet • Mud/debris in the mouth • Abrasions on the dorsal surface of feet, hands and knees
Auditory	• Middle ear/mastoid air cell hemorrhage
Respiratory	• Airway foam • Fluid in sinuses (Svechnikov's sign) • Pleural effusions • Pulmonary edema and/or hemorrhage • Increased lung volume • Hyperinflated lungs (emphysema aquosum) • Rib indentations on the lungs • Focal hemorrhage (Paltauf's spots)
Circulatory	• Differential staining of aortic root/pulmonary trunk • Dilation of the right side of the heart
Digestive	• Fluid in the stomach (Wydler's sign) • Superficial tears in the stomach mucosa (Sehrt's sign)
Other	• Neck hemorrhage • Reduced spleen volume • Adipocere

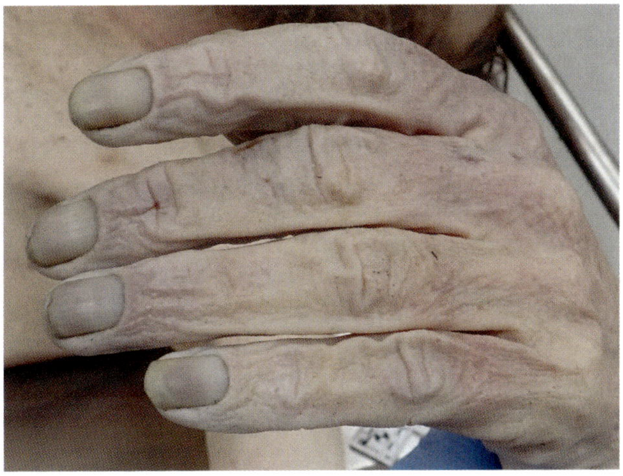

33.1 Subtle wrinkling of the skin of the fingers following immersion – so-called "washerwoman" changes.

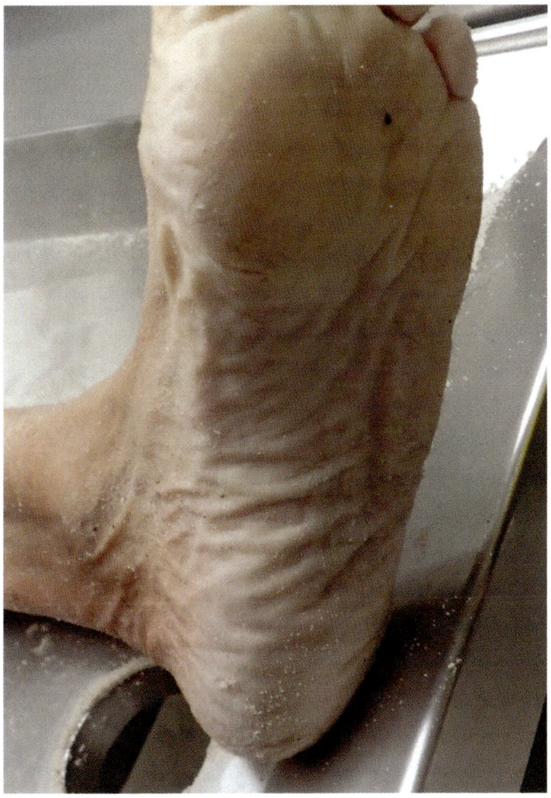

33.2 More pronounced "washerwoman" changes of the skin of the sole of the foot with adherent sand.

casts has been found in a wildlife forensic case indicating that drowning had occurred in turbulent water near to the shore (41).

Airway foam

The presence of foam in and around the airways is often considered a diagnostic feature of drowning. However, it is not a consistent finding in all drownings and is less likely to be observed with a prolonged post-mortem interval (42–45). Furthermore, the presence of foam within the airways is not necessarily supportive of drowning as it can be a produced by fluid that enters the lungs post mortem (47) and has also been observed with other causes of death such as drug toxicity and conditions with raised intracranial pressures (47). Conversely, the absence of foam cannot be used to exclude

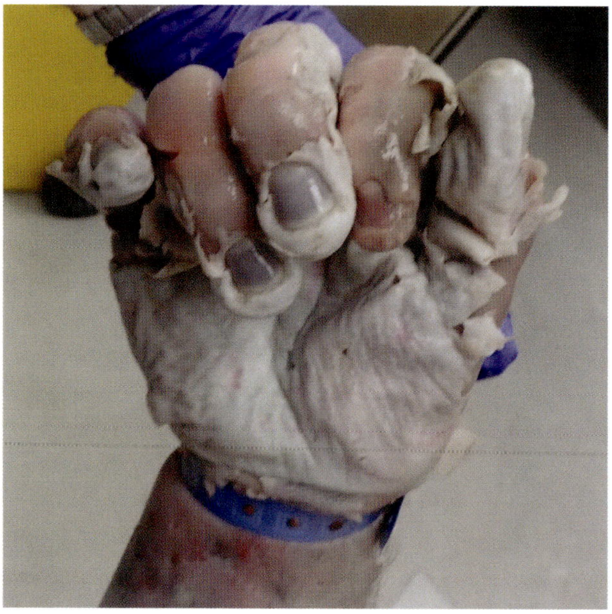

33.3 Washerwoman changes of the hand with maceration and skin removal from the fingers by post-mortem animal predation.

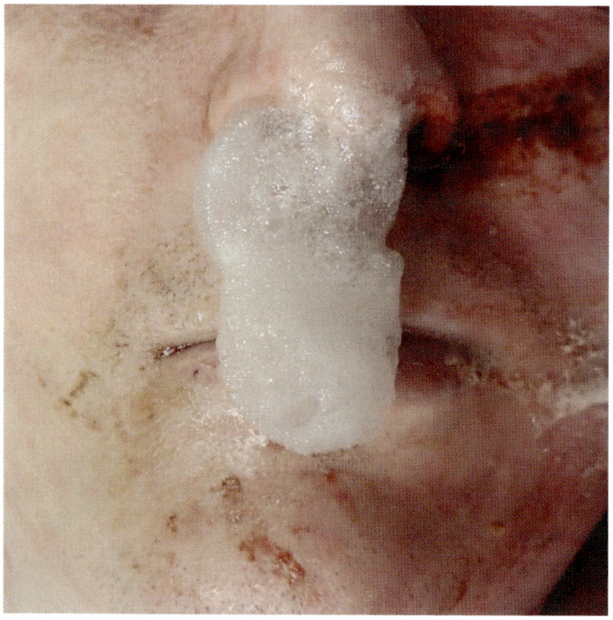

33.4 A plume of edema fluid that may be seen following drowning or drug overdose.

drowning. Airway foam could also be disturbed during attempted resuscitation and is also highly susceptible to environmental degradation (43,44,48).

Fluid in the sinuses

Fluid in the paranasal sinuses, nasal pharynx, oropharynx and trachea is a common finding in drowning deaths (49). The presence of fluid within the sphenoid sinuses in cases of drowning has been termed Svechnikov's sign (40,50). However, fluid in the sinuses cannot be used to confirm a diagnosis of drowning or to exclude other potential causes of death. Fluid in the upper airways is merely a sign of immersion and does not indicate whether fluid was aspirated before death or entered body spaces after death (14,49). In addition, fluid in the sinuses and trachea can be observed in other causes of death such as cardiac failure, burning and poisoning (51) or may simply be a result of post-mortem stasis of saliva or fluid (49).

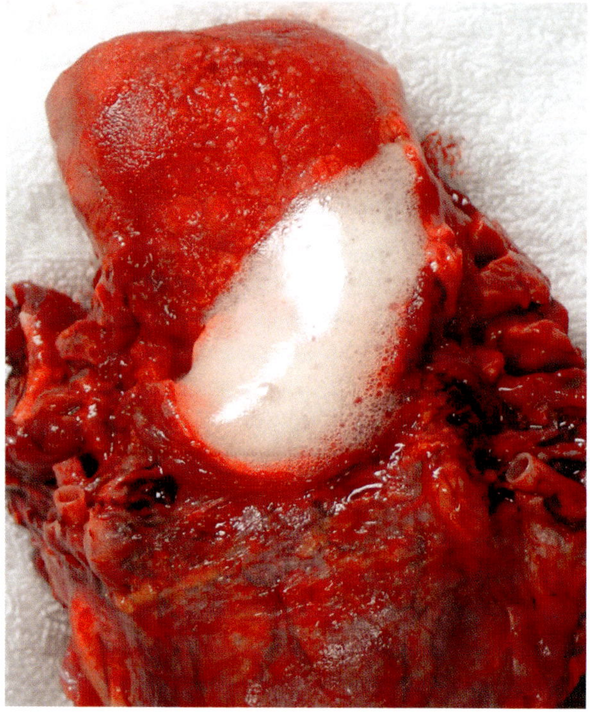

33.5 Filling of the glottis with foamy edema fluid.

33.6 Opening of the larynx to reveal foamy edema fluid.

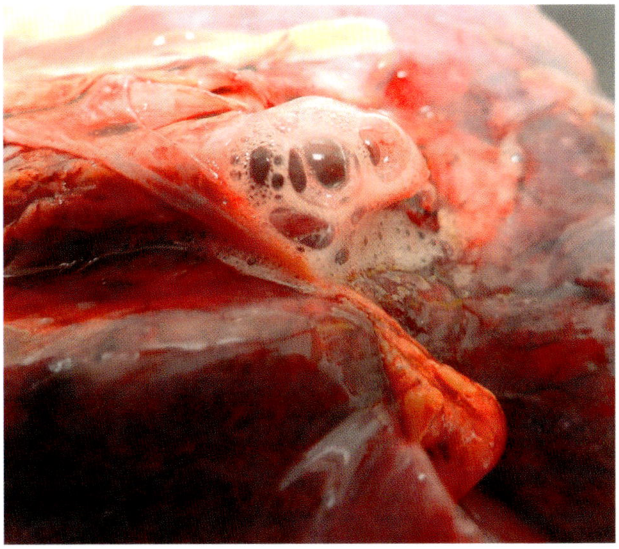

33.7 Bubbling of edema fluid from major bronchi after removal of the lung at autopsy.

Neck hemorrhage

Identification of intramuscular neck hemorrhage at autopsy is inconsistent and opinions vary on the usefulness of this post-mortem finding (35). The presence of neck hemorrhage has been reported sporadically in drowning deaths (14,36) and is thought to be a result of violent agonal movements and muscle contractions (36,52). It is important to avoid assuming that neck hemorrhage in a case of drowning is associated with inflicted pressure (35), although hemorrhage in the anterior aspect of the neck may indicate injuries from blunt force trauma or strangulation (36) and should raise suspicions of the involvement of a second party (38). Hemorrhage may also be observed on the posterior aspect of the esophagus and has been termed the Prinsloo Gordon artefact, a result of tissue dissection at autopsy (35,36,38).

Increased lung weight

Increased lung weight is often observed in cases of drowning due to aspiration of fluid, pulmonary alveolar damage and cardiac failure (53–55). However, there appear to be no significant differences in lung weights between salt and freshwater drownings (48).

Fluid in the stomach (Wydler's sign)

Wydler's sign has been taken as an indication of drowning, with the presentation of three layers of stomach contents that includes an upper layer of frothy material, a middle layer of fluid and a lower layer of dense semi-digested material (50,56,57). However, this finding is a relatively rare occurrence (57).

Pleural effusions

Early studies associated net decreases in lung weight with pleural effusions (48), however, this finding may be skewed by increased post-mortem interval (58,59).

Pulmonary hyperinflation (emphysema aquosum)

Aspiration of fluid can cause increased production of mucus and edema foam, blocking the airways and preventing effective expiration which results in pulmonary hyperinflation, in association with filling of alveoli with fluid (42). As the name suggests, the physical presentation is similar to the hyperinflation seen in emphysema patients, hence the name emphysema aquosum. Hyperinflation of the lungs increases pressure on the pleural cavity and pericardium, often resulting in imprints of the ribs on the surface of the lungs and Paltauf's spots (34–36,38–40).

Paltauf's spots

Paltauf's spots are irregularly shaped sites of hemorrhage in the lower lobes of the lungs observed in some cases of drowning (50,60–63). This effect was first described in 1888 by the medical examiner Arnold Paltauf (64), however, the exact incidence and significance of this finding has not been determined.

Changes to splenic volume

From as early as the nineteenth century, significantly reduced splenic weight, spleen-to-body weight ratio and spleen-to-liver weight ratios have been studied as potential indicators of drowning (65,66). It was initially concluded that a reduced weight of the spleen was the result of sympathetic stimulation induced by hypoxia (65). However, other authors have suggested that reduced spleen weight is non-specific and merely a post-mortem phenomenon rather than a pathophysiologic outcome of drowning (34,54,55). Thus, again the significance remains unclear.

"DIAGNOSTIC" SIGNS AND TESTS

Unfortunately, there are no reliable diagnostic tests that can distinguish between peri-mortem and post-mortem immersion. The earliest diagnostic markers involved analysis of body temperature and blood viscosity to determine time of death and the drowning medium involved (67), but these are no longer employed due to their limitations and lack of validation. However, previously dismissed methods are being re-assessed, in conjunction with the application of new techniques and technologies, to assist in the diagnosis of drowning (14).

Lung weight

Assessment of lung weight has previously been used to support a diagnosis of drowning, with variable success (68,69). Authors have reported significant differences in lung weight between drowning and other causes of death (61,70). However, the relationship between lung weight and submersion time, drowning medium and other post-mortem findings is still unclear. No correlation has been shown between the accumulation of pleural fluid and changes in lung weights despite being previously proposed as diagnostic markers (48,58). Several other hypotheses relating to correlations between lung weight and pleural transudate, and the lung-heart weight ratio and cause of death have been suggested (48,71), however, increased lung weight is not specific to drowning and is observed in other conditions (68,69,71).

Drowning index

A drowning index (ratio of lung-to-spleen weight) was proposed to differentiate drowning from other causes of death (55). It has been suggested that the index is only useful with a post-mortem interval of under two weeks, after which time post-mortem changes prevent meaningful assessment of organ weights (34,55,72). However, as noted above, the assessment of changes in lung and spleen weight in drownings is unreliable and so an index of the two measures may not provide any further useful information.

Diatoms

Diatoms are a large group of single-celled silicaceous algae found in fresh and salt water. In the process of drowning, diatoms may enter the circulation by diffusing through alveolar capillary membranes when water is aspirated (73). However, research aiming to demonstrate the usefulness of diatom testing in diagnosing drowning has been met with much controversy and criticism (40,73–77). It has been proposed that the presence of diatoms in sites such as bone marrow is indicative of water aspiration prior to death (78), however, diatoms may be absent in cases of confirmed drowning and may also be present in deaths attributed to other causes (40,79). Furthermore, a negative diatom test does not provide any useful information about the cause of death (80). As with other potential markers of drowning, diatom samples may be negatively impacted by ante- and post-mortem environmental changes and contamination which can occur via antemortem or post-mortem diatom penetration, entrance to the systemic circulation via open wounds, from resuscitation or during the sample preparation process (75,76). Thus, there are major limitations associated with diatom testing in the diagnosis of drowning (76).

Diatoms may, however, be useful in determining the entry site of a decedent if the body has drifted substantially from its point of origin with water currents, as diatom profiles vary significantly by geographic area and season (79). In cases where a body has drifted, the location of drowning can potentially be ascertained by comparing diatoms from a post-mortem sample with water samples of the area (79,81–85). For example, in a sample of 52 cases, diatom profile matching between samples of bone marrow and drowning medium was successful in 90 percent of cases (79).

Technologic advancements have also improved the reliability and sensitivity of diatom detection (77,86) through the application of polymerase chain reaction (PCR) (87–89). Thus, although the diagnosis of drowning cannot be made based on diatom testing alone, it may provide some support and assist in locating the site of drowning (40,77,85).

Electrolytes

Quantitative analysis of electrolyte levels has been proposed as a potential diagnostic marker for drowning, involving analysis of electrolytes in both blood and vitreous humor (90). In 1921, the Gettler Test which analyzed and compared chloride levels in the right and left heart ventricles was developed to diagnose drowning (91) but was later determined to be unreliable (80,92–94). A similar approach has been applied to the analysis of strontium levels, where a disparity of >75 percent in strontium levels between the right and left ventricles was thought to indicate saltwater drowning (95). However, this method is yet to be validated. Studies involving the analysis of magnesium and calcium levels have also produced inconsistent results (40,95).

While blood electrolyte studies have not yielded meaningful results, analysis of electrolytes in vitreous humor may assist in distinguishing freshwater and saltwater immersion (96–99). Vitreous humor as a sample site is ideal as it is less susceptible to the effects of decomposition and contamination (100). Levels of sodium have been found to be elevated in vitreous humor in saltwater drownings, with lowered levels in freshwater drownings (90). However, changes in vitreous humor sodium levels may also be influenced by other factors such as dehydration or increased dietary sodium intake (101). In submerged bodies, electrolyte levels have also been shown to change after a post-mortem interval of more than one hour due to post-mortem diffusion (93,97,99,102). Thus, electrolyte studies have also not proven particularly useful in the diagnosis of drowning, nor in distinguishing saltwater from freshwater drowning.

Aortic intimal staining

Differential staining of the intima of the aortic root compared to the pulmonary trunk has been identified in some cases of freshwater drowning (103–106). It was first described in the German literature as "hämoglobinimbibiert" (107,108) (Figure 33.8). The introduction of hypotonic fluid into the lungs with transudation into the circulation causes erythrocytes in the aorta to undergo lysis and discolor the aortic intima. However, this change has also been observed in deaths attributed to any organic condition that involves the lysis of erythrocytes (e.g. extensive burn injury or disseminated sepsis), although this usually involves both the aortic and pulmonary outflow tracts. Differential staining has also been observed in other conditions such as pulmonary embolism (109). The discoloration is only observed in a small proportion of freshwater drownings (105), more frequently in cases that have been recovered from the water relatively quickly (103). Some authors have argued for this type of staining to be a recognized marker of drowning, with examples of hemolytic staining extending into the endocardium of the left cardiac chambers (110).

Sehrt's sign

Sehrt's sign appears as superficial tears of the mucosa of the stomach, however, the underlying cause is still

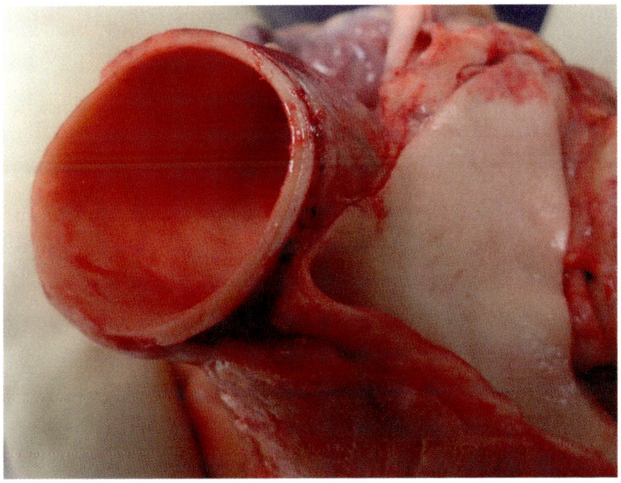

33.8 Differential staining of the aortic intima (red) compared to the pale pulmonary trunk in a case of freshwater drowning.

uncertain. The initial hypothesis by Ernst Theodor Sehrt was that they were caused by emesis of aspirated water (111,112). However, the more recent consensus is that it is a result of forceful chest compressions associated with resuscitation (113). This finding has not been widely reported in the literature therefore caution should be taken in its interpretation.

Computed tomography

Post-mortem medical imaging such as computed tomography (CT) is becoming increasingly recognized as a valuable, non-invasive investigative tool. While there are many limitations associated with using medical imaging to diagnose drowning, it can be useful to visualize areas that are otherwise anatomically inaccessible such as the paranasal sinuses (114). Application of whole-body CT has demonstrated several consistent pathologic changes in a significant proportion of drowning cases, but none that are specific to drowning (49,115). The lung appearance on CT varies greatly from airspace consolidation to a mosaic-type pattern (115,116), with further attempts made to classify lung appearances into three major categories; ground-glass opacities with thickened pulmonary interstitium, centrilobular distribution of ill-defined nodules along the airways or a combination of both (115–119). However, these appearances are not specific enough to drowning to definitively exclude other causes of death (114,120–122). Caution has also been advised when interpreting the significance of changes to the appearance and volume of organs deemed to be relevant in drowning (such as lungs and spleen) due to a lack of association between these changes and the mechanism of death (123).

Other tests

Early markers of drowning such as coldness of the body and hemodilution have since been proven to be unreliable (39,67). Microscopic changes within the alveoli have also been studied as a potential marker of drowning. It was thought that anthracotic pulmonary macrophages or asbestos bodies could be detected in left-sided heart blood in cases of drowning, but the results are again conflicting (124,125). Changes in pulmonary surfactant levels have also been studied but without useful practical applications (40).

ALTERNATIVE CAUSES OF DEATH

While it may appear reasonable to assume that a person found deceased in a body of water may have died by drowning, there are many other potential causes of death that require consideration. Therefore, a thorough autopsy examination is required to identify and assess the presence of biological disease and physical trauma which may corroborate or exclude drowning as the possible/probable cause of death (126).

Comorbidities

An individual can die from many other causes while in a body of water (natural or otherwise), or a disease or condition can precipitate a fall into water, or an individual may die on land only to end up immersed after death (121). Therefore, all injuries, comorbidities and toxicologic findings must be fully evaluated to accurately evaluate the cause of death.

Among many other organic conditions, individuals with epilepsy and ischemic heart disease are at increased risk of drowning (127,128). A study of immersion-related childhood deaths showed that approximately 10 percent of cases were associated with an organic illness including epilepsy, a bleeding arteriovenous malformation and a hypoplastic coronary artery (127). Similarly, the presence of a cardiac channelopathy such as long QT syndrome has been associated with a small proportion of drowning deaths (21,129). Conditions such as these may not have been identified prior to death, which makes a thorough autopsy with ancillary genetic studies even more important. An increased body mass index (BMI), while associated with increased cardiovascular morbidity, may actually assist in flotation due to increased amounts of adipose tissue (130).

Accidents

When drowning is associated with an activity (aquatic sports or SCUBA [self-contained underwater breathing apparatus] –diving) or physical injury, it can be difficult to determine which was causative and which was contributory. Craniocerebral or other physical trauma may contribute to a drowning death due to incapacitation of the individual through loss of consciousness. This is particularly relevant for cases of drowning where an individual has engaged in recreational activities in a shallow body of water with poor visibility (e.g. river, lagoon etc.) which can lead to head, neck and/or spinal injuries.

SCUBA diving has been associated with drowning deaths and may occur via several mechanisms. The most common causes of death include drowning, equipment faults and pressure-related trauma (barotrauma) (22).

The latter may cause particular post-mortem changes such as pneumothoraces that differ from a standard drowning due to pressure-related effects (22). Such deaths also require experts in the field to inspect and assess the equipment that was being used to determine the cause of the incident (22).

MANNER OF DEATH

An unwitnessed incident and/or one with an incomplete description of events, a lack of medical history, the presence of potentially fatal underlying comorbidities, significant physical injuries, lack of definitive pathologic signs and obscure toxicology findings all complicate determination of manner of death. A comprehensive medical history is often not available at the time of autopsy which may make interpretation of post-mortem and toxicology findings difficult. It may be difficult or impossible to definitively determine the manner of death if the incident is unwitnessed (17). CCTV and image recordings by witnesses on devices such as smartphones may all assist in clarifying events leading up to immersion. Thus, all records, comorbidities, injuries, autopsy and toxicology findings must be fully evaluated, and all manners of death considered. Certain features such as evidence of weighting of a body may be an indication of augmentation of a suicide method (131) or of disposal of a body following a homicide.

CONCLUSION

Inconsistent terminology, complex death scenes, non-specific pathology, and lack of definitive diagnostic markers continue to make drowning a persistently difficult diagnosis. It is crucial that all evidence available is used, in addition to a comprehensive post-mortem examination to determine events leading up to the immersion to ensure that wherever possible the correct diagnosis is made.

REFERENCES

1. World Health Organisation. Drowning: fact sheet [Internet]. Geneva, Switzerland; 2021 [cited 2021 September 30]. Available from: https://www.who.int/news-room/fact-sheets/detail/drowning. (Accessed 23 April 2023).
2. Stephenson L, Byard RW, van den Heuvel C, Peden AE. Fatal drowning among tourists and recently arrived individuals from overseas at South Australian Metropolitan beaches. *Aust J Forensic Sci* 2021; 5: 535–42.
3. Meddings D, Hyder AA, Ozanne-Smith J, Rahman A (eds). *Global Report on Drowning: Preventing a Leading Killer.* Geneva, Switzerland: World Health Organization; 2014.
4. Byard RW, Lipsett J. Drowning deaths in toddlers and preambulatory children in South Australia. *Am J Forensic Med Pathol* 1999; **20:** 328–32.
5. Byard RW. Drowning in childhood: An ongoing problem. (Invited editorial) *J Pediatr Int Care* 2012; **1:** 3–4.
6. Byard RW. Rainwater tank drowning. *J Forensic Leg Med* 2008; **15:** 533–4.
7. Byard RW, de Koning C, Blackbourne B, et al. Shared bathing and drowning in infants and young children. *J Paediatr Child Health* 2001; **37:** 542–4.
8. Byard RW, Donald T. Infant bath seats, drowning and near-drowning. *J Paediatr Child Health* 2004; **40:** 305–7.
9. Stephenson L, Stockham P, van den Heuvel C, Byard RW. Characteristic features of drowning deaths in an inner city river. *Leg Med* 2020; **47:** 101783.
10. Van Beeck EF, Branche CM, Szpilman D, et al. A new definition of drowning: towards documentation and prevention of a global public health problem. *Bull World Health Organ* 2005; **83:** 853–6.
11. Byard RW. Immersion deaths and drowning: Issues arising in the investigation of bodies recovered from water. *Forensic Sci Med Pathol* 2015; **11:** 442–4.
12. Stephenson L, Van den Heuvel C, Byard RW. The persistent problem of drowning: A difficult diagnosis with inconclusive tests. *J Forensic Leg Med* 2019; **66:** 79–85.
13. Idris AH, Berg RA, Bierens J, et al. Recommended guidelines for uniform reporting of data from drowning: The "Ustein style". *Circulation* 2003; **108:** 2565–74.
14. Lunetta P. Autopsy Findings: Drowning and Submersion Deaths. In: Payne-James J, Byard RW (eds). *Encyclopedia of Forensic and Legal Medicine.* 2nd edn. Vol 1. Oxford: Academic Press; 2016. pp. 315–22.
15. Lunetta P, Modell JH, Sajantila A. What is the incidence and significance of "dry-lungs" in bodies found in water? *Am J Forensic Med Pathol* 2004; **25:** 291–301.
16. Szpilman D, Bierens JJ, Handley AJ, Orlowski JP. Drowning. *N Engl J Med* 2012; **366:** 2102–10.
17. Byard RW. Immersion deaths and drowning: issues arising in the investigation of bodies recovered from water. *Forensic Sci Med Pathol* 2015; **11:** 323–5.
18. Schmidt AC, Sempsrott JR, Szpilman D, et al. The use of non-uniform drowning terminology: A follow-up study. *Scand J Trauma Resusc Emerg Med* 2017; **25:** 72.
19. Byard RW. Drowning and near drowning: Definitions and terminology (Letter). *Forensic Sci Med Pathol* 2017; **13:** 529–30.
20. Modell JH, Bellefleur M, Davis JH. Drowning without aspiration: Is this an appropriate diagnosis? *J Forensic Sci* 1999; **44:** 1119–23.
21. Byard RW. *Sudden Death in the Young.* 3rd ed. Cambridge: Cambridge University Press; 2010.
22. Prahlow J. Drowning. In: *Forensic Pathology for Police, Death Investigators, Attorneys, and Forensic Scientists.* New Jersey (US): Humana Press; 2010. pp. 433–48.
23. Byard RW, Cains G, Simpson E, et al. Drowning, haemodilution, haemolysis and staining of the aortic root: Preliminary observations. *J Clin Forensic Med* 2006; **13:** 121–4.
24. Noble CS, Sharpe N. Drowning: its mechanism and treatment. *Can Med Assoc J* 1963; **89:** 402–5.
25. Byard RW. Putrefaction: An additional complicating factor in the assessment of freshwater drownings in rivers. *J Forensic Sci* 2018; **63:** 899–901.
26. Schultz JJ, Healy CA, Parker K, Lowers B. Detecting submerged objects: The application of side scan sonar to forensic contexts. *Forensic Sci Int* 2013; **231:** 306–16.
27. Healy CA, Schultz JJ, Parker K, Lowers B. Detecting submerged objects: Controlled research using side-scan sonar to detect submerged proxy cadavers. *J Forensic Sci* 2015; **60:** 743–52.
28. Byard RW. Drowning deaths in rivers. *Forensic Sci Med Pathol* 2017; 13: 388–9.
29. Byard RW, James RA, Gilbert JD. Diagnostic problems associated with cadaveric trauma from animal activity. *Am J Forensic Med Pathol* 2002; **23:** 238–44.
30. Duband S, Forest F, Clemenson A, et al. Postmortem injuries inflicted by crawfish: morphological and histological aspects. *Forensic Sci Int* 2011; **206:** 49–51.
31. Byard RW. Major organ loss from post mortem animal predation: Issues arising from emptied body cavities. *Med Sci Law* 2022; **62:** 60–3.
32. Caruso JL. Decomposition changes in bodies recovered from water. *Acad Forensic Pathol* 2016; **6:** 19–27.
33. Moar JJ. Drowning: Postmortem appearances and forensic significance. A case report. *S Afr Med J* 1983; **64:** 792–5.
34. Wardak KS, Buchsbaum RM, Walyzada F. The Drowning index: Implementation in drowning, mechanical asphyxia, and acute myocardial infarct cases. *J Forensic Sci* 2014; **59:** 399–403.
35. Alexander RT, Jentzen JM. Neck and scleral haemorrhage in drowning. *J Forensic Sci* 2011; **56:** 522–5.

36. Carter N, Ali F, Green MA. Problems in the interpretation of hemorrhage into neck musculature in cases of drowning. *Am J Forensic Med Pathol* 1998; **19:** 223–5.
37. Byard RW. Adipocere: The fat of graveyards. *Am J Forensic Med Pathol* 2016; **37:** 208–10.
38. Spitz DJ. Investigation of Bodies in Water. In: Spitz WU, Spitz DJ, eds. *Spitz and Fisher's Medicolegal Investigation of Death*, 4th ed. Springfield: Charles C. Thomas; 2006, pp. 846–81.
39. Jeanmonod R, Staub, CH, Mermillod B. The reliability of cardiac haemodilution as a diagnostic test of drowning. *Forensic Sci Int* 1992; **52:** 171–80.
40. Piette MHA, De Letter EA. Drowning: Still a difficult autopsy diagnosis. *Forensic Sci Int* 2006; **163:** 1–9.
41. Byard RW, Machado A, McLelland D. Endobronchial sand casts: An unusual marker of saltwater inhalation in a juvenile pygmy sperm whale (*Kogia breviceps*). *Forensic Sci Med Pathol* 2011; **7:** 222–4.
42. Lunetta P, Penttila A, Sajantila A. Circumstances and macropathologic findings in 1590 consecutive cases of bodies found in water. *Am J Forensic Med Pathol* 2002; **23:** 371–6.
43. Reijnen G, Buster MC Vos, PJE, Reijnders UJL. External foam and the post-mortem period in freshwater drowning: results from a retrospective study in Amsterdam, The Netherlands. *J Forensic Leg Med* 2017; **52:** 1–4.
44. Ambade VM, Kukde HG, Malani A, et al. Decomposed and nondecomposed bodies retrieved from water: A comparative approach. *Med Sci Law* 2013; **53:** 12–18.
45. Henssge C, Althaus L, Bolt J, et al. Experiences with a compound method for estimating the time since death. II. Integration of non-temperature-based methods. *Int J Leg* 2000; **113:** 320–31.
46. Reijnen G, Vos P, Buster M, Reijnders U. Can pulmonary foam arise after postmortem submersion in water? An animal experimental pilot study. *J Forensic Leg Med* 2018; **61:** 40–4.
47. Dinis-Oliveira RJ, Santos A, Magalhães T. "Foam Cone" exuding from the mouth and nostrils following heroin overdose. *Toxicol Mech Methods* 2012; **22:** 159–60.
48. Kringsholm B, Filskov A, Kock K. Autopsied cases of drowning in Denmark 1987–1989. *Forensic Sci Int* 1991; **52:** 85–92.
49. Vander Plaetsen S, De Letter E, Piette M, et al. Post-mortem evaluation of drowning with whole body CT. *Forensic Sci Int* 2015; **249:** 35–41.
50. Dettmeyer RB, Verhoff MA, Drowning SHF. Homicidal Drowning. In: *Forensic Medicine, Fundamentals and Perspectives*. Heidelberg (Berlin): Springer; 2014, pp. 245–60.
51. Kawasumi Y, Kawabata T, Sugai Y, et al. Diagnosis of drowning using postmortem computed tomography based on the volume and density of fluid accumulation in the maxillary and sphenoid sinuses. *Eur J Radiol* 2013; **82:** e562–6.
52. Puschel K, Schultz F, Darrmann I, Tsokos M. Macromorphology and history of intramuscular haemorrhages in cases of drowning. *Int J Legal Med* 1999; **112:** 101–6.
53. Copeland AR. An assessment of lung weights in drowning cases: the Metro Date Country experience from 1978 to 1982. *Am J Forensic Med Pathol* 1985; **4:** 301–4.
54. Hadley JA, Fowler DR. Organ weight effects of drowning and asphyxiation on the lungs, liver, brain, heart, kidneys, and spleen. *Forensic Sci Int* 2003; **133:** 190–6.
55. Sugimura T, Kashiwagi M, Matsusue A, et al. Application of the drowning index to actual drowning cases. *Leg Med (Tokyo)* 2010; **12:** 68–72.
56. Nečas P, Hejna P. Eponyms in forensic pathology. *Forensic Sci Med Pathol* 2012; **8:** 395–401.
57. Gotsmy W, Lombardo P, Jackowski C, et al. Layering of stomach contents in drowning cases in post-mortem computed tomography compared to forensic autopsy. *Int J Leg Med* 2019; **133:** 181–8.
58. Yorulmaz C, Arican A, Afacan I, et al. Pleural effusion in bodies recovered from water. *Forensic Sci Int* 2003; **136:** 16–21.
59. Morild I. Pleural effusion in drowning. *Am J Forensic Med Pathol* 1995; **16:** 253–6.
60. Wang Z, Ma K, Zou D, et al. Diagnosis of drowning using postmortem computed tomography combined with endoscopic autopsy: A case report. *Medicine (Baltimore)* 2020; **99:** e19182.
61. Yang K, Choi BH, Lee B, Yoo SH. Bath-related deaths in Korea between 2008–2015. *J Korean Med Sci* 2018; **33:** e108.
62. Bohnert M, Ropohl D, Pollak S. Forensic medicine significance of the fluid content of the sphenoid sinuses. *Archiv fur Kriminologie* 2002; **209:** 158–64.
63. Hottmar P. The presence of fluid in the paranasal sinuses in comparison with other diagnostic signs of drowning. *Soudni lekarstvi* 1995; **40:** 34–6.
64. Paltauf A. Über den Tod durch Ertrinken. Wien [u.a.]: Urban & Schwarzenberg; 1888.
65. Haffner HT, Graw M, Erdelkamp J. Spleen findings in drowning. *Forensic Sci Int* 1994; **66:** 95–104.
66. Lunetta P, Modell JH. Macroscopical, Microscopical and Laboratory Findings in Drowning Victims. In: Tsokos M (ed) *Forensic Path Rev*. Vol. 3. New Jersey (US): Humana Press; 2005, pp. 3–77.
67. Caspar JL. *A Handbook of the Practice of Forensic Medicine Based Upon Personal Experience*. Vol. 2. *Thanatological Division*. Ch IV. Death from drowning. London; The New Sydenham Society; 1862, pp. 229–74.
68. Tse R, Garland J, Kesha K, et al. The potential diagnostic accuracy of autopsy lung weights, lung-heart ratio and lung-body ratio in drowning deaths. *Am J Forensic Med Pathol* 2018; **39:** 223–8.
69. Tse R, Garland J, Kesha K, et al. Combining postmortem vitreous sodium and chloride and lung-body ratio in aiding the diagnosing saltwater drowning. *Am J Forensic Med Pathol* 2018; **39:** 229–35.
70. Zhu BL, Quan L, Li DR, et al. Postmortem lung weight in drownings: a comparison with acute asphyxiation and cardiac death. *Legal Med (Tokyo)* 2003; **5:** 20–6.
71. Zhu BL, Quan L, Ishida K, et al. Lung-heart weight ratio as a possible index of cardiopulmonary pathophysiology in drowning. *Leg Med (Tokyo)* 2003; **5:** S295–7.
72. Nishitani Y, Fujii K, Okazaki S, et al. Weight ratio of the lungs and pleural effusion to the spleen in the diagnosis of drowning. *Leg Med (Tokyo)* 2006; **8:** 22–7.
73. Lunetta P, Penttilä A, Hällfors G. Scanning and transmission electron microscopical evidence o the capacity of diatoms to penetrate the alveolo-capillary barrier in drowning. *Int J Legal Med* 1998; **111:** 229–37.
74. Badu IK, Girela E, Beltrán CM, et al. Diatoms in forensic analysis: a practical approach in rats. *Med Sci Law* 2015; **55:** 228–35.
75. Di Giancamillo A, Giudici E, Andreola S, et al. Immersion of piglet carcasses in water-the applicability of microscopic analysis and limits of diatom testing on an animal model. *Leg Med (Tokyo)* 2010; **12:** 13–18.
76. Lunetta P, Miettinen A, Spilling K, Sajantila A. False-positive diatom test: a real challenge? A post-mortem study using standardized protocols. *Leg Med (Tokyo)* 2013; **15:** 229–34.
77. Zhao J, Liu C, Bardeesi ASA, et al. The diagnostic value of quantitative assessment of diatom test for drowning: An analysis of 128 water-related death cases using microwave digestion-vacuum filtration-automated scanning electron microscopy. *J Forensic Sci* 2017; **62:** 1638–42.
78. Krstic S, Duma A, Janevska B, et al. Diatoms in forensic expertise of drowning: A Macedonian experience. *Forensic Sci Int* 2002; **127:** 198–203.
79. Pollanen MS. The diagnostic value of the diatom test for drowning, II. Validity: an analysis of diatoms in bone marrow and drowning medium. *J Forensic Sci* 1997; **42:** 286–90.
80. Byard RW, Houldsworth G, James RA, Gilbert JD. Characteristic features of suicidal drownings: A 20-year study. *Am J Forensic Med Pathol* 2001; **22:** 134–8.
81. Ludes B, Coste M, Tracqui A, Mangin P. Continuous river monitoring of the diatoms in the diagnosis of drowning. *J Forensic Sci* 1996; **41:** 425–8.
82. Ludes B, Coste M, North N, et al. Diatom analysis in victim's tissues as an indicator of the site of drowning. *Int J Legal Med* 1999; **112:** 163–6.
83. Saukko P, Knight B. *Knight's Forensic Pathology*. 4th ed. Boca Raton: CRC Press; 2016.
84. Thakar MK, Singh R. Diatomological mapping of water bodies for the diagnosis of drowning cases. *J Forensic Leg Med* 2010; **17:** 18–25.
85. Lin CY, Yen WC, Hsieh HM, et al. Diatomological investigation in sphenoid sinus and lung tissue from cases of suspected drowning. *Forensic Sci Int* 2014; **244:** 111–15.
86. Kakizaki E, Yukawa N. Simple protocol for extracting diatoms from lung tissues of suspected drowning cases within 3 h: first practical application. *Forensic Sci Int* 2015; **251:** 179–85.
87. Rutty GN, Bradley CJ, Biggs MJ, et al. Detection of bacterioplankton using

PCR probes as a diagnostic indicator for drowning: the Leicester experience. *Leg Med (Tokyo)* 2015; **17:** 401–8.
88. Rácz E, Könczöl F, Tóth D, et al. PCR-based identification of drowning: Four case reports. *Int J Legal Med* 2016; **130:** 1303–7.
89. Rutty GN, Johnson C, Amoroso J, et al. Post-mortem computed tomography angiography coaxial cutting needle biopsy to facilitate the detection of bacterioplankton using PCR probes as a diagnostic indicator for drowning. *Int J Legal Med* 2017; **131:** 211–16.
90. Byard RW, Summersides G. Vitreous humor sodium levels in immersion deaths. *J Forensic Sci* 2011; **56:** 643–4.
91. Gettler AO. A method for the determination of death by drowning. *J Am Med Assoc* 1921; **77:** 1650–2.
92. Shkrum MJ, Ramsay DA. Bodies Recovered from Water. In: *Forensic Pathology of Trauma: Common Problems for the Pathologist*. New Jersey: Humana Press; 2007.
93. Farmer JG, Benomran F, Watson AA, Harland WA. Magnesium, potassium, sodium and calcium in post-mortem vitreous humour from humans. *Forensic Sci* 1985; **27:** 1–13.
94. Modell JH, Davis JH. Electrolyte changes in human drowning victims. *Anesthesiology*. 1969; **30:** 414–20.
95. Azparren JE, Cubero C, Perucha E, et al. Comparison between lung weight and blood strontium in bodies found in seawater. *Forensic Sci Int* 2007; **168:** 128–32.
96. Cala AD, Vilain, R, Tse R. Elevated postmortem vitreous sodium and chloride levels distinguish saltwater drowning (SWD) deaths from immersion deaths not related to drowning but recovered from saltwater (DNRD). *Am J Forensic Med Pathol* 2013; **34:** 133–8.
97. Tse R, Kuo TC, Kesha K, et al. Postmortem vitreous humor magnesium does not elevate in saltwater drowning when the immersion time is less than 1 hour. *Am J Forensic Med Pathol* 2017; **38:** 298–303.
98. Tse R, Kuo TC, Garland J, et al. Postmortem vitreous sodium and chloride elevate after 1 hour and magnesium after 2 hours in bovine eyeballs immersed in salt water. *Am J Forensic Med Pathol* 2018; **39:** 242–6.
99. Garland J, Tse R, Oldmeadow C, et al. Elevation of post mortem vitreous humour sodium and chloride levels can be used as a reliable test in cases of suspected salt water drowning when the immersion times are less than one hour. *Forensic Sci Int* 2016; **266:** 338–42.
100. Thevis M, Thomas A, Schänzer W, et al. Measuring insulin in human vitreous humour using LC-MS/MS. *Drug Test Anal* 2012; **4:** 53–6.
101. Ingham AI, Byard RW. The potential significance of elevated vitreous sodium levels at autopsy. *J Forensic Leg Med* 2009; **16:** 437–40.
102. Anne S, Tse R, Oldmeadow C, et al. Immersion of bovine eyeballs after 1 hour in seawater does not result in elevation of postmortem vitreous humour sodium and chloride levels. *Am J Forensic Med Pathol* 2016; **37:** 108–11.
103. Byard RW. Aortic intimal staining in drowning. *Forensic Sci Med Pathol* 2015b; **11:** 442–4.
104. Byard RW, Cains GE, Gilbert JD. Is haemolytic staining of the aortic root a sign of fresh water drowning? *Pathology* 2005; **37:** 551–2.
105. Tsokos M, Cains G, Byard RW. Hemolytic staining of the intima of the aortic root in freshwater drowning: a retrospective study. *Am J Forensic Med Pathol* 2008; **29:** 128–30.
106. Byard RW, Cains G, Tsokos M. Haemolytic staining of the intima of the aortic root – a useful pathological marker of freshwater drowning? *J Clin Forensic Med* 2006; **13:** 125–8.
107. Dettling J, Schönberg S, Schwarz F. *Lehrbuch der Gerichtlichen Medizin.* Basel: Karger; 1951.
108. Ponsold A. Ertrinken. In: Ponsold A (ed.) *Lehrbuch der Gerichtlichen Medizin einschliesslich der ärztlichen Rechtskunde und der Versicherungsmedizin.* Stuttgart: Thieme; 1957, pp. 375–87.
109. Byard RW. Differential intimal staining of the aortic root and pulmonary trunk following pulmonary thromboembolism. *Forensic Sci Med Pathol* 2019; **15:** 488–90.
110. Zátopková L, Hejna P, Janík M. Hemolytic staining of the endocardium of the left heart chambers: a new sign for autopsy diagnosis of freshwater drowning. *Forensic Sci Med Pathol* 2015; **11:** 65–8.
111. Sehrt E. Vorgang des Ertrinkens, seine Bekämpfung und Verhütung. *Münch Med Wschr* 1932; **31:** 1229.
112. Sehrt E. Zur Frage des Ertrinkungstodes und seiner Bekämpfung. *Münch Med Wschr* 1933; **20:** 762.
113. Buschmann CT, Schmid S, Tsokos M. Gastric mucosal lacerations in drowning: resuscitation artifact or sign of death by drowning ("Sehrt's sign")? *Forensic Sci Med Pathol* 2015; **11:** 312–13.
114. Kawasumi Y, Kawabata T, Sugai Y, et al. Assessment of the relationship between drowning and fluid accumulation in the paranasal sinuses on post-mortem computed tomography. *Eur J Radiol* 2012; **81:** 3953–5.
115. Christe A, Aghayev E, Jackowsku C, et al. Drowning: Post-mortem imaging findings by computed tomography. *Eur Radiol* 2008; **18:** 283–90.
116. Kim KI, Lee KN, Tomiyama N, et al. Near drowning: thin-section CT findings in six patients. *J Comput Assist Tomogr* 2000; **24:** 562–6.
117. Hourscht C, Christe A, Diers S, et al. Learning from the living to diagnose the dead: Parallels between CT findings after survived drowning and fatal drowning. *Forensic Sci Med Pathol* 2019; **15:** 249–51.
118. Verschakelen JA, De Wever W. *Computed Tomography of the Lung: A Pattern Approach*. Berlin: Springer; 2018.
119. Levy AD, Harcke HT, Getz JM et al. Virtual autopsy: Two- and three-dimensional multidetector CT findings in drowning with autopsy comparison. *Radiol* 2007; **243:** 862–8.
120. Hyodoh H, Terashima R, Rokukawa M, et al. Experimental drowning lung images on postmortem CT: Difference between sea water and fresh water. *Leg Med (Tokyo)* 2016; **19:** 11–15.
121. Van Hoyweghen AJ, Jacobs W, Op de Beeck B, Perizel PM. Can post-mortem CT reliably distinguish between drowning and non-drowning asphyxiation? *Int J Legal Med* 2015; **129:** 159–64.
122. Michiue T, Ishikawa T, Oritani S, et al. Forensic pathological evaluation of postmortem pulmonary CT high-density areas in serial autopsy cases of sudden cardiac death. *Forensic Sci Int* 2013; **232:** 199–205.
123. Okuma H, Gonoi W, Ishida M, et al. Comparison of volume and attenuation of the spleen between postmortem and antemortem computed tomography. *Int J Legal Med* 2016; **130:** 1081–7.
124. Locali RF, Almeida MD, Oliveira-Júnior IS. Use of histopathology in the differential diagnosis of drowning in fresh and salty water: an experimental model establishment in rats. *Acta Cir Bras* 2006; **21:** 203–6.
125. Betz P, Nerlich A, Penning R, Eisenmenger W. Alveolar macrophages and the diagnosis of drowning. *Forensic Sci Int* 1993; **62:** 217–24.
126. McEwen BJ, Gerdin J. Veterinary forensic pathology: drowning and bodies recovered from water. *Vet Pathol* 2016; **53:** 1049–56.
127. Smith NM, Byard RW, Bourne AJ. Death during immersion in water in childhood. Am *J Forensic Med Pathol* 1991; **12:** 219–21.
128. Bell GS, Gaitatzis A, Bell CL, et al. Drowning in people with epilepsy: how great is the risk? *Neurology* 2008; **71:** 578–82.
129. Lunetta P, Levo A, Laitinen PJ, et al. Molecular screening of selected long QT syndrome (LQTS) mutations in 165 consecutive bodies found in water. *Int J Legal Med* 2003; **117:** 115–17.
130. Byard RW. Body mass index (BMI) and saltwater drowning. *Am J Forensic Med Pathol* 2017; **38:** 304–5.
131. Stephenson L, van den Heuvel C, Byard RW. Weighted drownings: An example of augmentation or enhancement of a suicide method. *J Forensic Leg Med* 2020; **70:** 101914.

CHAPTER

34

Lethal Asphyxia

Roger W. Byard

INTRODUCTION

The term asphyxia is used when normal metabolic processes fail due to a lack of adequate tissue oxygenation. Hypoxia refers to incomplete oxygen deprivation and anoxia to situations where it is complete. Although historically the term derived from the Greek term for an absence of pulse (*asphuxia*: *a* – not; *sphuxis* – pulse) (1), the current forensic usage is for situations where oxygen delivery from the environment to organs and tissues is impaired, rather than on cardiovascular manifestations (2).

Earlier authors sometimes used the term asphyxia synonymously with respiratory arrest or apnoea that led to "want of aeration of the lungs" (3–5), referring to examples such as suffocation, choking, hanging or drowning. While the initial focus was on pulmonary failure it soon became apparent that more complex mechanisms were involved in some of these situations, with Taylor correctly pointing out in 1865 that death from hanging could occur without complete blockage of the upper airway (as has been subsequently observed in video recordings of hanging deaths). He hypothesized that compression of major neck vessels led to "apoplexy of the congestive kind" (6). Similarly, it is now recognized that deaths due to drowning may involve electrolyte disturbances from hemodilution, possible airway obstruction from laryngospasm and arrhythmias, in addition to environmental oxygen depletion (7). Asphyxial deaths may be due to accidents, homicides or suicides, or may be a complication of natural diseases.

CLASSIFICATION

Confusion may arise when lethal asphyxia may involve a number of different processes or mechanisms. For example, although the term "hanging" applies to a particular form of ligature strangulation where the force applied to the neck derives from the weight of the body, a number of quite different mechanisms may contribute to lethal hypoxia in these circumstances including airway narrowing, vascular compression and on occasion probable vagal inhibition (1).

A more physiological method of classifying asphyxia evaluates where critical oxygen depletion occurs, that is, 1) in the environment, 2) during transfer from alveoli to blood, 3) during transport in the blood, or 4) at the time of cellular uptake.

Decreased environmental oxygen

A critical reduction in the amount of oxygen in the surrounding air may be caused by one of two processes: displacement or consumption. Oxygen may be displaced in the air by other gases or by fluids. A classic example of oxygen displacement by gas involves methane or carbon dioxide which may accumulate in sewers or in wheat silos creating a lethal oxygen-poor environment (8). On occasion, this may result in multiple deaths. Canaries were once used in coal mines to detect odorless gas accumulation as they are more sensitive to lower levels and so acted as an early warning system.

The recent increase in deaths due to suicides using plastic bags filled with methane or nitrogen relies on both replacement of oxygen by inert gases and depletion of oxygen by breathing inside the bag (9,10). Deaths have occurred when a gas such as nitrous oxide is being used recreationally, for example, inadvertently causing reduced oxygen levels in a confined space such as a vehicle (1). Once inspired, oxygen levels fall to below 25 percent the effects are immediate with consciousness being lost within seconds and death within minutes if levels in inspired air are not restored (11). Although a variety of different pathophysiological processes contribute to death in drowning, displacement of oxygen by water is an important factor.

Consumption of oxygen may occur due to breathing within a sealed space such as an entrapped child in a refrigerator, or with a plastic bag over the head (with or without augmentation by inert gases) (12). Flash fires may be of such intensity that oxygen is rapidly consumed (1).

Although suicides in previous years using domestic gas resulted from the toxic effects of the gas, removal of these substances means that such deaths in a domestic setting now result from oxygen displacement (13). Similarly, the addition of catalytic converters to vehicles may result in less carbon monoxide being produced and so death may again be the result of asphyxia from oxygen displacement (14,15).

DOI: 10.1201/9781003138754-36

Decreased blood oxygenation

If the patency of the airways is compromised anywhere between the nose/mouth and the bronchioles, there may be a significant reduction in airflow to the alveoli resulting in impaired blood oxygenation. Smothering is an example of external airway occlusion where the nose and mouth are obstructed by a variety of methods/materials. This may involve placing a hand over the external airways in a case of deliberate infant/child smothering or using plastic wrap or cloth gags. Accidental smothering may occur if the face is pressed into soft but occlusive material such as sand or soil following a vehicle crash or in infants and young children who may become trapped in a plastic bag or have their airways obstructed from soft bedding (16–18).

Smothering should not be used for situations where the internal airways are obstructed by material that has been inhaled (19) as this is more correctly termed choking (Figure 34.1). The circumstances of choking deaths vary greatly and include accidents, suicides and homicides. Accidental choking occurs in the setting of so-called café coronary syndrome or bolus deaths where an individual chokes on food while eating. Predisposing factors include dementia, alcohol or drug intoxication and poor dentition. A wide range of ingested materials may obstruct the airways ranging from feces in the elderly with dementia, to parts of toys in children (20,21). It has also been described in certain animals (22). Cloth gags have been deliberately inhaled in cases of suicide, often in the mentally ill, or have been forced into the upper airway in homicides. A combination of smothering and choking may occur in individuals who have been accidentally or deliberately buried in fine soil. Occasionally, aspiration of blood into the airways may either follow craniofacial trauma or be the result of underlying organic disease (23). Airway occlusion may occur in hanging from direct pressure causing the trachea to collapse or when the tongue is lifted upward obstructing the oropharynx.

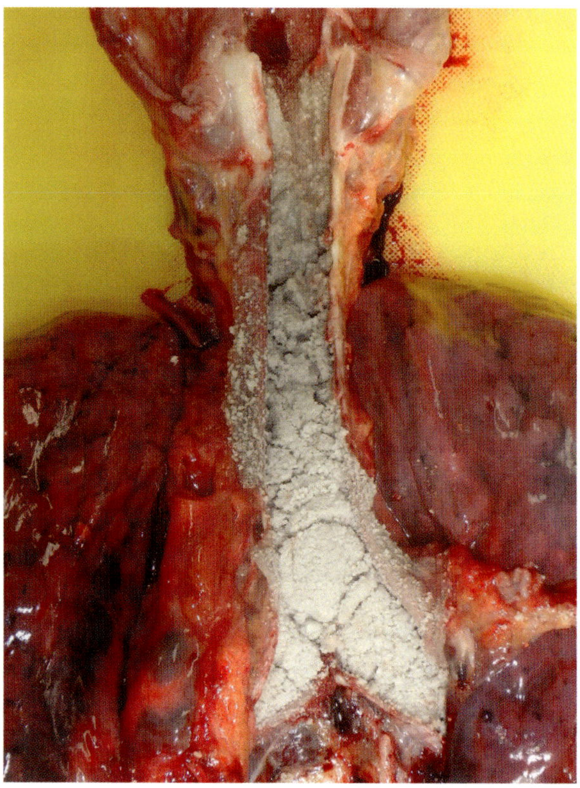

34.1 Choking from inhalation of perlite powder occluding the trachea and main bronchi in an industrial accident.

Airway patency may also be compromised by natural diseases including developmental lesions such as thyroglossal duct cysts, or benign or malignant tumors such as laryngeal hemangiomas or carcinomas (24,25). Infections that may cause critical airway narrowing can involve retropharyngeal abscesses, tonsillar enlargement and acute epiglottitis (26–29). The latter is usually a disease of the very young which has had a marked reduction in incidence following the use of *Hemophilus influenzae* vaccinations. Narrowed airways may also predispose to occlusion if sedatives such as narcotics are taken as muscle relaxation, pooling of tenacious secretions and reduced arousal may exacerbate the situation (30).

In certain situations, the airways may be patent but there is a failure of the chest bellows mechanism which is required to inflate the lungs by expanding the thorax. One example of this is positional asphyxia where the chest is splinted by an unusual position of the body (31). In these circumstances, the victim is not compressed as in crush asphyxia but is unable to inhale due to impairment of chest expansion and diaphragmatic movement. Child chimney sweeps in Victorian England were at risk of this if they slipped and became wedged tightly in narrow chimney spaces. William Wyer was sentenced in 1875 to 6 months hard labor for having caused the death of a boy, George Brewster who he sent into a chimney at Fulbourne Lunatic Asylum in the UK (33). An additional factor in positional asphyxia may be acute angulation of the neck often associated with alcohol intoxication (34). One of the features of positional asphyxia is that the victim does not extricate themselves from a dangerous situation due to impairment, or loss, of consciousness, lack of physical coordination or reduced strength. The very young may also not understand the dangers of a particular situation or have the physical strength or dexterity required to escape (18). Positional asphyxia may be predisposed to by certain neurologic conditions and also by a high body mass index (BMI), again due to reduced ability to move to safety (34).

The bellows function of the chest may also be compromised by trauma when there is a flail chest where multiple often bilateral rib fractures result in paradoxical movement of the chest wall. This may be exacerbated by a traumatic pneumothorax where there has been collapse of the lung parenchyma due to puncturing of the lungs or chest wall (1).

A related form of mechanical asphyxia involves crushing where the body is compressed under or by a weight. This classically occurs in crowd surges at football matches or concerts, in children trapped under heavy furniture that has tipped over while they are climbing, and in mechanics who are crushed while working under a vehicle that has slipped off a jack (35,36).

Blood oxygenation may also be decreased if the oxygen binding ability of hemoglobin is impaired. This most often occurs with exposure to carbon monoxide an odorless gas that derives from house fires or vehicle exhaust in cases of suicide (37). Charcoal burning barbecues have also recently been used as a source of carbon monoxide in suicide attempts. Leaking or faulty heaters or car exhaust systems may also be responsible for accidental deaths from carbon monoxide inhalation. Even quite low levels of environmental carbon monoxide may prove lethal as it has up to 250 to 300 times the binding affinity for hemoglobin compared to oxygen (11). Determining the lethality of a particular blood level of carbon monoxide requires consideration of the health status of the decedent. For example, although carbon monoxide concentrations should be greater than 50 to 60 percent to be lethal in an otherwise healthy adult, it may be as low as 25 percent in older individuals with comorbidities such as ischemic heart disease, congestive cardiac failure, anemia or chronic chest conditions (38). Sodium nitrite is another substance used in suicide that can bind to hemoglobin reducing its ability to transport oxygen (39).

Decreased transport of oxygen

Once blood has been successfully oxygenated in the lungs, it must be transported to target organs and tissues via the circulation. Significant narrowing of critically placed blood vessels may however impede blood flow and therefore cause tissue hypoxia. This most commonly occurs in cases of hanging or ligature strangulation. When pressure is applied to the neck from a ligature in hanging, the first effect is obstruction of venous return from the brain, and then interference with arterial flow to the cerebral circulation. This occurs before tracheal obstruction as the pressure required to compress the trachea is 7.5 times that needed to compress the jugular veins and three times that required to compress the carotid arteries (11). Vessel narrowing may critically reduce cerebral oxygenation causing anoxia, coma and death. This process has been observed to occur very quickly with loss of consciousness within seconds and cessation of respiration within minutes (40). Reduction in blood flow may also be exacerbated by underlying natural diseases such as cardiac failure.

Decreased cellular uptake/ utilization

Chemical asphyxia occurs if oxygen transfer into cells is prevented or if cellular metabolism of oxygen is impaired. Cyanide is a poison that interferes with cellular enzyme systems and carbon monoxide is also known to impair mitochondrial respiration (11).

Combinations of the above

Asphyxial deaths in a variety of situations often involve a number of different additive mechanisms. For example, a case of positional asphyxia in a morbidly obese individual may have an element of crush asphyxia if the diaphragm is compressed by the weight of viscera and adipose tissue. Infiltration of the soft tissues around the pharynx may also create an element of airway narrowing in such individuals. As noted, if an individual is buried in soil there may be a combination of smothering when the face is covered as well as choking if soil has been inhaled deep into the airways. There may also be an element of crush asphxyia if soil is compressing the chest and abdomen (41,42). The lethal effects of neck compression from hanging often result from the synergistic effects of vascular compression, possible vagal inhibition and upper airway occlusion from tracheal compression and elevation of the tongue. Plastic bag suicides with inert gases represent a type of augmented suicide involving smothering with the added effects of reduced environmental oxygen levels (12,43).

PATHOLOGIC FEATURES OF ASPHYXIA

In the early literature, a number of features at autopsy were considered diagnostic, or at least highly suggestive of asphyxia. These ranged from swelling of the face to lividity of the limbs, as well as foam around the mouth and evidence of discharge of feces, urine and semen (4). The heart was described as being "engorged" and blood was thought to be dark due to high levels of carbon dioxide (5). The so-called classic signs of asphyxia which included congestion and edema, fluidity of the blood, petechial hemorrhages, cyanosis and engorgement of the right heart have, however, been called by Adelson "an obsolete diagnostic quintet" (37).

Thus, it is now recognized that none of these findings are reliable and so the diagnosis of lethal asphyxia at autopsy can be problematic as there are no pathognomic features of acute hypoxia. The conclusion that an asphyxial event has occurred therefore requires synthesis of detailed scene information with any post-mortem markings or changes of the body. If there has been survival for some time after an asphyxial episode, changes of hypoxic ischemic encephalopathy may assist in establishing the diagnosis if there is evidence of neuronal nuclear pyknosis and cytoplasmic eosinophilia (44).

Petechial hemorrhages

Although petechial hemorrhages have been previously taken as reliable markers of asphyxial events, this is no longer believed to be the case. Petechiae represent pinpoint (arbitratily said to be 0.1 to 2 mm in diameter) collections of blood that may be observed in the conjunctivae, skin, sclera, and under serous membranes such as the pericardium and pleura. It is hypothesized that they

TABLE 34.1 Causes of decreased tissue/organ oxygenation

Reduced intake	Decreased environmental oxygen levels
Reduced transport	Decreased oxygenation/blood flow
Reduced uptake	Cellular toxins
Combinations	

are present in these tissues because there is less perivascular supporting tissue. Estimates of the time taken to develop petechiae are at least 15 to 30 seconds (38).

The underlying mechanisms resulting in petechiae have been debated, with proposals that they occur when there is an acute rise in vascular pressure from mechanical vascular obstruction or right heart failure, or that they arise from direct capillary damage with or without an associated blood coagulation disorder (45). Other authors have considered that there is no real evidence of endothelial damage and postulate instead that facial and conjunctival petechiae are "purely mechanical vascular phenomena, unrelated to asphyxia or hypoxia" and that their occurrence depends on "the degree of venous obstruction", inversely proportional to "arterial compression, at or above the level of the heart" (46). They have been attributed to bursting of peripheral venules after an acute rise in venous pressure (37). There is supportive circumstantial evidence for the mechanical theory, with petechiae being absent in choking deaths and only present on the face and conjunctivae in cases of plastic bag asphyxia when the bag has been firmly tied around the neck by a ligature (20,47,48). The capillary fragility test which relies on producing petechiae in the skin when a tourniquet is placed around the upper arm also blocks venous but not arterial flow (2).

Petechiae are not, however, sensitive or specific markers for asphyxia with an autopsy study finding them most often in natural deaths (39.2%), usually due to cardiovascular disease, followed by asphyxia, head injury and central nervous system conditions. In addition, not all deaths attributed to asphyxia had conjunctival petechiae (45); they may also develop after death and may be influenced by the position of the body, the BMI and the amount and distribution of lividity (38).

Manual strangulation is a situation where facial and conjunctival petechiae often occur, presumably due to significant intermittent pressure on cervical vessels. Crush asphyxia is usually associated with significant numbers of petechiae in the upper chest, neck and face (35) (Figure 34.2). The eyelids should always be everted to demonstrate petechiae on their inner surfaces (Figure 34.3). Dissection of the thyroid gland in these cases often shows it to be black in color due to intense congestion with marked engorgement of perifollicular capillaries that rupture into the colloid-producing blood islands (49,50) (Figure 34.4). Although it has been argued that petechiae in this situation arise purely from hypoxia, their geographic location and absence in other parts of the body that are subject to an equal degree of hypoxia would argue against this. In addition, their absence in skin compressed by tight fitting clothing shows that vascular engorgement is required (51). While recognizing that petechiae may be caused by conditions such as hematological disorders, sepsis or toxins, they tend to have a generalized distribution in these circumstances.

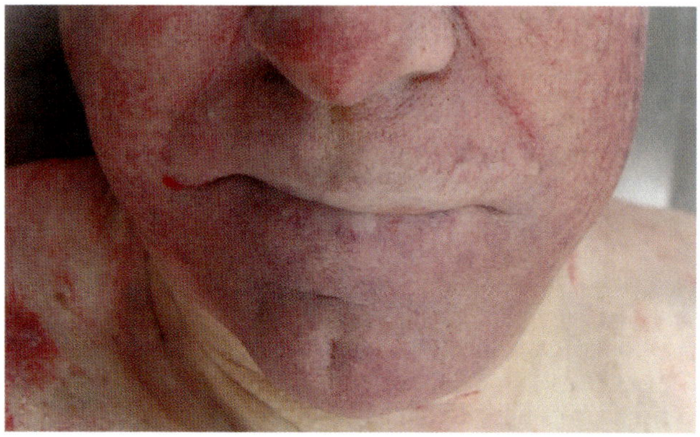

34.2 Intense congestion of the face with numerous facial petechiae in a case of crush asphyxia.

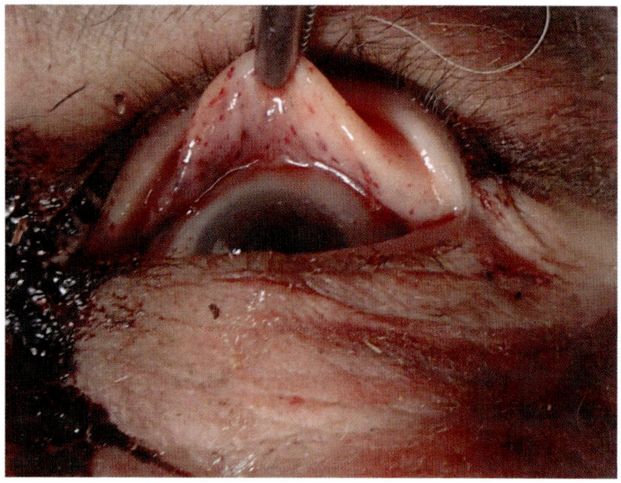

34.3 Petechial hemorrhages on the inner aspect of the eyelid in a case of crush asphyxia.

Other observations at autopsy

Many of the features noted in asphyxial deaths are not due to hypoxia per se but to the underlying causative pathophysiological mechanisms. For example, the intense congestion and edema of the face and head that occurs with crush asphyxia, sometimes with intense subconjunctival hemorrhage (Figure 34.5) and bleeding from the nose and ears (Figures 34.6 and 34.7), is not due to lowered oxygen levels but to obstruction of venous return. This may also be observed in manual or ligature strangulation but is less often seen in hanging where the weight of the body usually causes occlusion of both venous and arterial blood flow. This was very clearly stated by Casper over 150 years ago "How often do we read in purely theoretical authors of the violet, bluish-red, swollen countenance of those strangled! Nothing, however, is so erroneous as to suppose that everyone hanged has such an appearance." (52). Congestion and edema of the lungs and other organs are merely non-specific findings found in deaths from a vast number of natural and unnatural conditions and are probably simply due to terminal cardiorespiratory failure.

ISSUES AND FINDINGS AT THE SCENE AND AUTOPSY

Determination of the cause and nature of an asphyxial death requires evaluation of as much information as

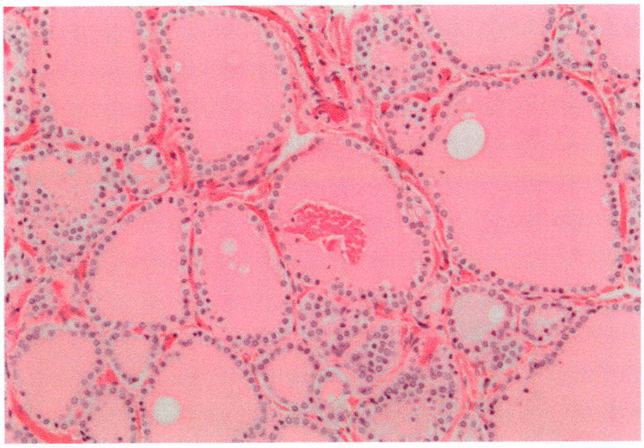

34.4 Rupture of a congested capillary into the colloid of a thyroid follicle producing a blood island in a case of crush asphyxia (H&E x 200).

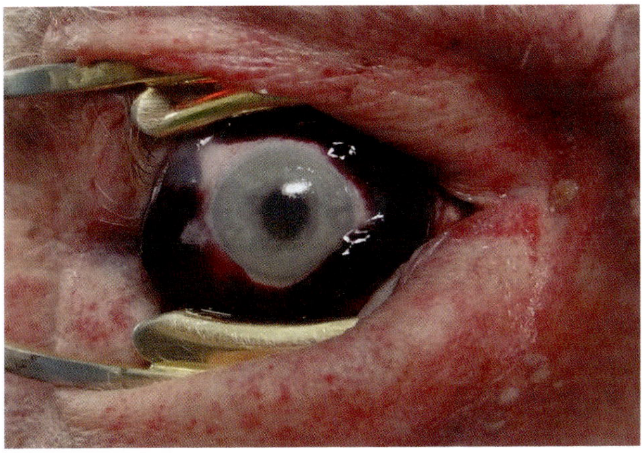

34.5 Intense subconjunctival hemorrhage in a case of crush asphyxia.

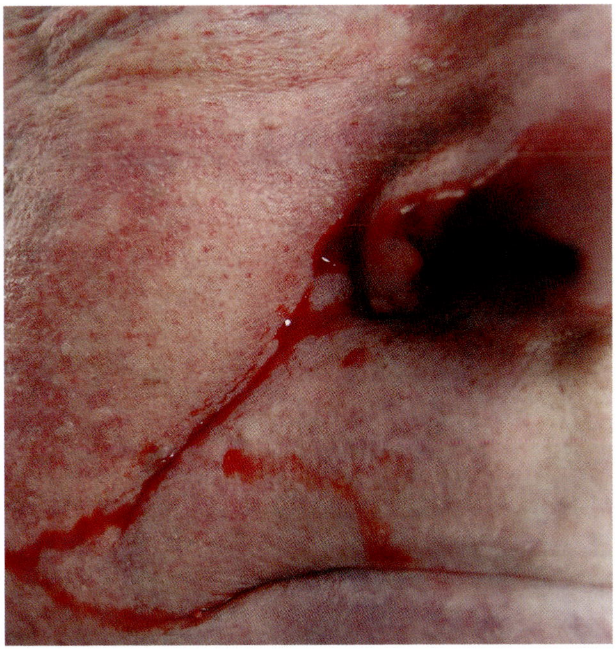

34.6 Bleeding from the nose in a case of crush asphyxia.

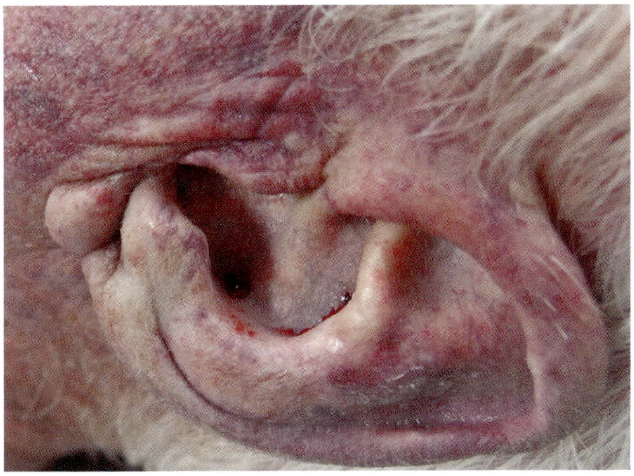

34.7 Bleeding from the ear in a case of crush asphyxia.

possible with careful documentation of characteristic scene and autopsy findings. Difficulties may therefore arise if scene findings have been altered. This may occur in infant wedging deaths in unsafe cots if parents or first responders have moved the body to facilitate assessment. It may inadvertently or deliberately occur if a plastic bag is removed and discarded in a case of plastic bag asphyxia, or if a piece of food or foreign material occluding an airway is removed during attempted resuscitation. In cases of autoerotic death, family members may try to remove evidence or disguise signs of solitary sexual activity. This includes removing bondage equipment, fetishist attire and pornographic images/literature (53–55). Typical scenarios are now described that may be found within the different pathophysiological classifications.

Decreased environmental oxygen

If death occurs rapidly from an inadequate supply of oxygen in the environment, there will usually not be any useful findings at the time of autopsy dissection. In industrial accidents or in deaths in sewers or wheat silos the presence of more than one decedent, however, points to likely environmental issues. Further deaths are sometimes described of those who have entered a dangerous area attempting a rescue. In these circumstances, evaluation of the death scenes with environmental gas measuring may detect low levels of oxygen or methane. The latter may also be identified on head space analysis of blood or tissues from the victims (8). Deaths in wheat silos may also occur from smothering and crush asphyxia if the victim has been buried (Figure 34.8).

Decreased blood oxygenation

Smothering on soft surfaces or by plastic bags usually leaves no markings on a body although if sufficient pressure has been applied to the face/head there may be abrasions or bruises on the inner aspects of the lips. If a gag has been used, there may be material inside the mouth and/or skin impressions on the cheeks. Damp or wet cloth applied to the nose and mouth is also less permeable to air flow than similar dry material. This may be a particular problem in infants who have regurgitated while lying face down on soft bedding. Careful evaluation of the death scene may provide vital clues in these circumstances.

A particular circumstance that illustrates difficulties in establishing a diagnosis of suffocation involves infants who are in a shared sleeping situation with adults. While many would classify these deaths as sudden infant death syndrome (SIDS) due to the lack of findings at autopsy there exists a considerable problem in excluding airway compromise due to smothering or compression which has led to a number of these deaths being classified as undetermined or unascertainable (56–58). Evidence that some of these deaths are not due to SIDS includes an equal sex ratio in the co-sleepers compared to the alone sleepers where the male-to-female ratio is 2:1 (59). The presence of neuropathological differences in the alone compared to the co-sleepers also argues in favor of different mechanisms. These include increases in glial fibrillary acidic protein (GFAP), β-amyloid precursor protein (β-APP), and terminal deoxynucleotidl transferase-mediated dUTP nick end labelling (TUNEL) (60,61). Other possibilities to consider are deliberate suffocation which may be a feature of cases of factitious illness by proxy (62), but again autopsy findings may be entirely nonspecific, although nail marks from pinching of the nose may sometimes be detected.

On occasion, suffocation may complicate other forms of death, as was observed in a series of petrol sniffing deaths from Central Australia. Although cardiac dysrhythmia initially appeared the most likely lethal mechanism, review of the autopsy findings showed circumferential markings around the nose and mouths of the decedents where the tins used to contain the inhaled volatiles had pressed into their faces cutting off the air supply (63).

Despite a clear history of choking on food or foreign objects often nothing is found within the airways at the time of autopsy. A variety of mechanisms may also be involved that can only be clarified at the time of post-mortem examination (64). Absence of material at autopsy is most often due to the airways being cleared by those attempting resuscitation, with discarding of the offending material. If ambulance personnel are involved, they may either retain the specimen for examination or provide a clear description of it for the pathologist. Useful ancillary investigations in such cases include toxicology and neuropathology. The finding of gastric contents within the airways should not be taken as firm evidence of pre-mortem aspiration, as gastric contents may be forced into the airways during attempted resuscitation and such material may enter the airways due to post-mortem movement of the body. In addition, 20 to 25 percent of individuals may aspirate food agonally, independent of the cause of death (11,65).

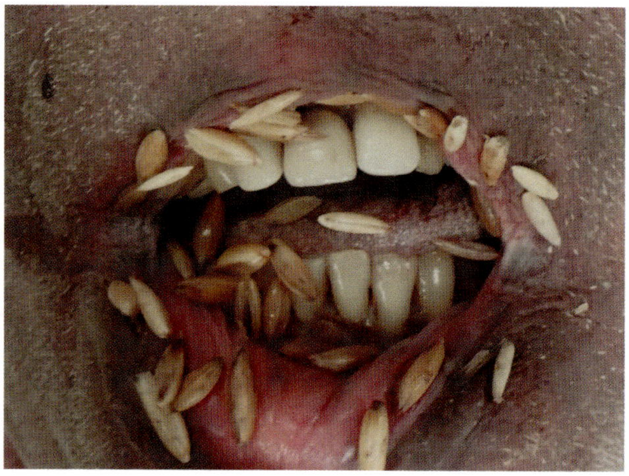

34.8 Wheat in the mouth in a case of crush asphyxia and smothering in an individual who slipped into a wheat silo and was buried. There was no wheat deeper within the airways.

The features of crush asphyxia at autopsy have been described, however additional useful information may be ascertained at autopsy, where patterned parchmented impressions may be observed on skin surfaces. Careful documentation with photographs and measurements will enable comparisons to be made to machinery or ground surfaces where the body was allegedly compressed.

One circumstance where external autopsy findings may be useful involves carbon monoxide toxicity in light-skinned individuals where there may be a characteristic "cherry pink" coloration of the skin (Figure 34.9), or of the nail beds and lips in darker-skinned individuals. Dissection may reveal a similar cherry pink color of skeletal muscles and some organs. If the case involves a suicide in a vehicle, there may be soot staining of the hands from handling of the exhaust pipe. Unfortunately, many cases show significant changes of decomposition due to delay in finding the body because of the isolated site that was chosen, and the high internal temperatures that may occur in vehicles (66). Confirmation of exposure to carbon monoxide can be obtained via toxicologic testing for carboxyhemoglobin (67). Sodium nitrite poisoning may also be suspected at autopsy if a body has characteristic blue-gray hypostasis (Figure 34.10) and brown discoloration of the blood (Figure 34.11).

Decreased transport of oxygen

Probably the most common scenario where oxygen transport is limited by vascular compression is hanging. Both homicidal and accidental hangings are rare compared to suicides, with hanging being the method of choice for self-termination in many countries (68). In typical cases of hanging, the decedent will be found suspended from a ligature at a home address or in an isolated area of woodland (sites that reduce the chances of discovery). The suspension point will be able to be accessed either by reaching upward or by using a chair or ladder (at autopsy, it is useful to measure the distance from the sole of the foot to the ligature mark in the anterior neck if reconstruction is subsequently needed). Rarely, the hands may be tied which could suggest a homicide, although it may be evidence of efforts to prevent self-extrication by loosely tying the knot and stepping through it. There may be abrasions to the backs of the hands from agonal movements, or to the body if it has fallen heavily as it is being cut down. Review of scene photographs may identify nearby objects that the body may have impacted. Consideration must also be given to the possibility of homicides staged as suicided (69,70,71).

Some discussion has occurred regarding the speed of incapacitation and death during suspension by hanging. It appears from case descriptions and video recordings of hanging deaths that loss of consciousness occurs very rapidly (within seconds) with death soon following (39). The major findings at autopsy are of a ligature around the neck (unless this has been removed) (Figure 34.12) overlying a parchmented mark (Figure 34.13) which rises to a 'V' at the point of suspension (Figure 34.14). The mark often has a pattern corresponding to the weave pattern of the ligature. However, if a broad ligature such as a sheet has been used, there may be minimal or only very subtle markings. This may also occur if the ligature has been padded with material such as a towel (72).

Other features at autopsy include protrusion of the tip of the tongue from the mouth with brownish desiccation. This occurs with lifting of the pharynx by the ligature. Facial and conjunctival petechiae are not common in hanging as pressure on the carotid arteries results in under perfusion of the face. The exception in this case occurs with low suspension due to intermittent pressure on cervical vessels. Dependent pooling of blood in the legs may occur with punctate interstitial hemorrhages, particularly when bodies have been hanging for some time.

Fractures of the hyoid bone and greater horns of the thyroid cartilage may be observed on post-mortem CT examination or on dissection, with the likelihood of this finding increasing with age as cartilage ossifies. Such fractures do not always occur, with a study of 40 suicidal hangings finding fractures in only 48 percent of cases involving the thyroid cartilage (23%), hyoid bone (10%) and a combination of both (15%) (73).

Neck fractures are a feature of judicial hangings with the classic "hangman fracture" representing bilateral fractures of the pars interarticularis of the second cervical vertebrae (the axis) caused by hyperextension and distraction injury (74). Such fractures may be predisposed to by the length of the drop, arthritic degeneration of the cervical spine and obesity (11). On occasion, long-drop hanging may result in decapitation (75). Hyperextension in hanging may also be the cause of Simon's sign (Figure 34.15) which refers to hemorrhage beneath the anterior longitudinal ligament overlying the intervertebral space in the lumbar region (76).

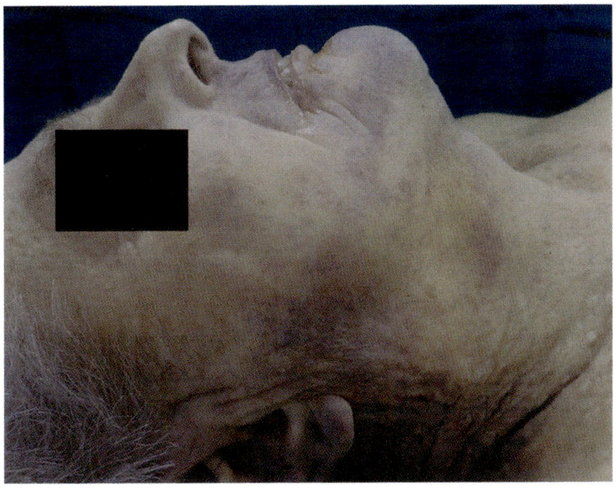

34.10 Typical blue-gray discoloration of the skin in a case of sodium nitrite toxicity.

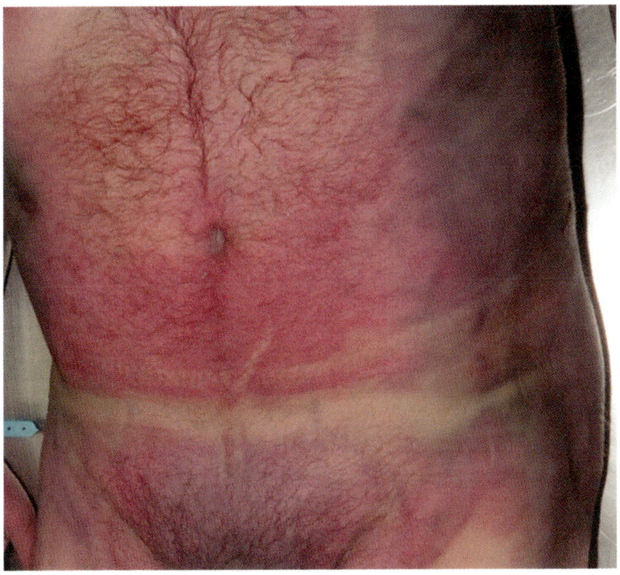

34.9 Typical cherry pink discoloration of the skin in a case of suicidal carbon monoxide toxicity with areas of blanching from clothing.

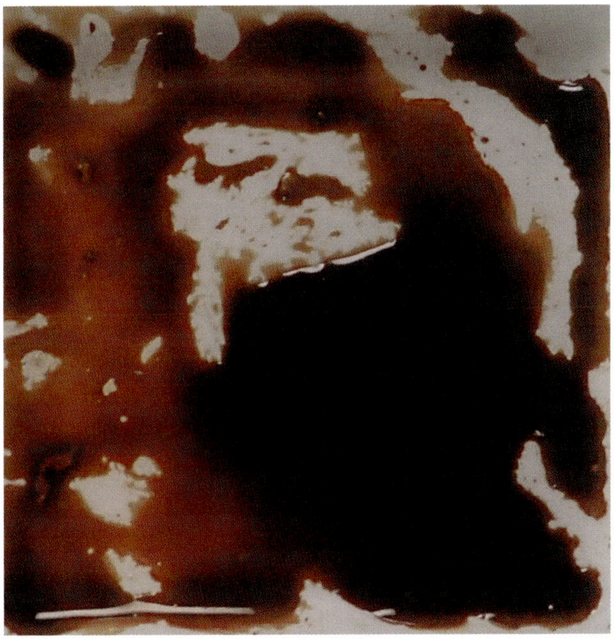

34.11 Typical brown discoloration of the blood in a case of sodium nitrite toxicity.

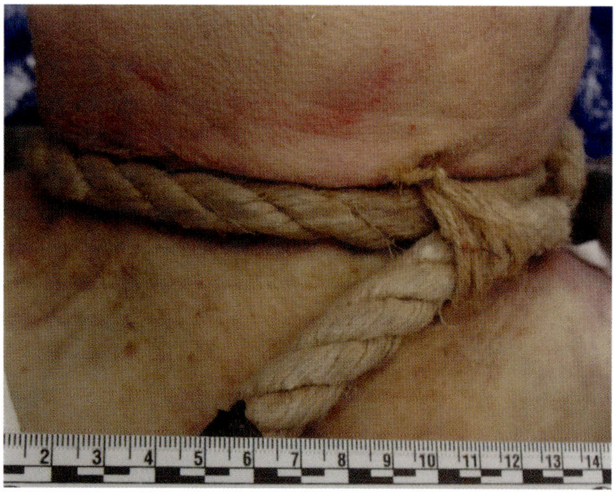

34.12 A ligature *in situ* around the neck in a case of suicidal hanging.

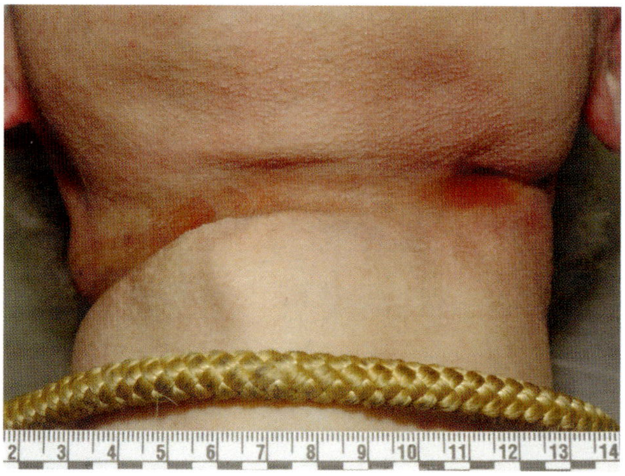

34.13 Removal of the ligature in a case of suicidal hanging showing a subtle weave pattern in the indentation that corresponded to the rope forming the noose.

Accidental hanging is more common in young children who are experimenting with ropes and in adolescents and adults who are engaging in autoerotic activities in the form of sexual asphyxia. As noted, the presence of sexual paraphernalia is an indication of the latter activity, also with the presence of a failed "fail safe" device that the decedent has previously relied upon (77). On occasion, it may be difficult to distinguish suicide from an accident in someone who has used similar equipment (78). The pathological findings of suspension may be more subtle in the very young (Figure 34.16) (79).

Manual strangulation may be associated with circular bruises from fingertips or linear abrasions from fingernail scratches, whereas ligature strangulation often results in a horizontal parchmented mark around the neck. In these cases, there is a greater likelihood of petechial hemorrhages of the face and conjunctivae as struggling of the victim may result in inconsistent pressure being applied to the carotid arteries. Careful layer dissection of the neck may reveal bruising of the soft tissues and strap muscles.

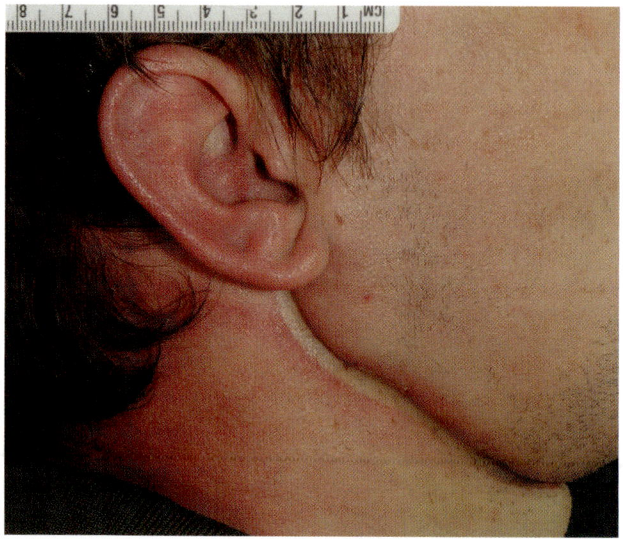

34.14 A typical ligature mark in hanging rising to a point of suspension over the occiput in contrast to the usual horizontal mark left by ligature strangulation.

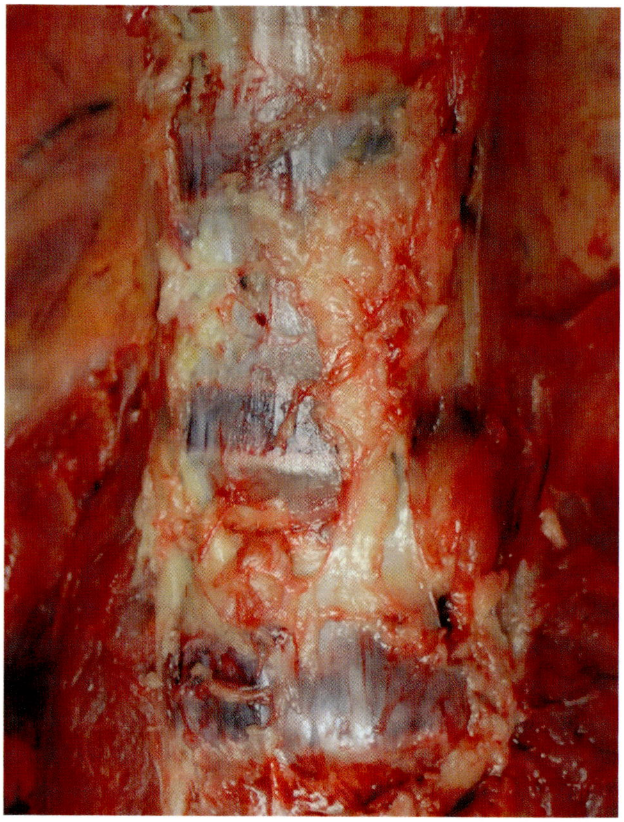

34.15 Characteristic hemorrhage beneath the anterior longitudinal ligament overlying the intervertebral space in a case of hanging, or Simon's sign.

The nature of sudden death during an altercation or involving police restraint has been the subject of quite intense debate. While there is no doubt that certain individuals may collapse during police restraint the roles of agitation, drug use, positioning and obesity have not been definitively determined (80). In some cases, however, contributing factors clearly involve crush asphyxia

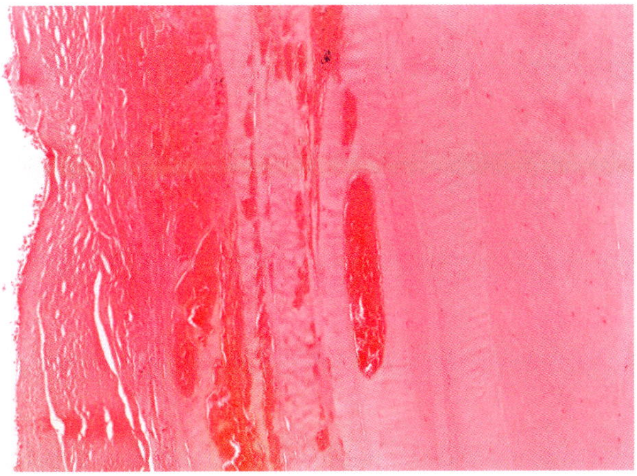

34.16 Histology of the anterior longitudinal ligament in a hanging case with a positive Simon's sign showing congestion and interstitial hemorrhage (H&E x 150).

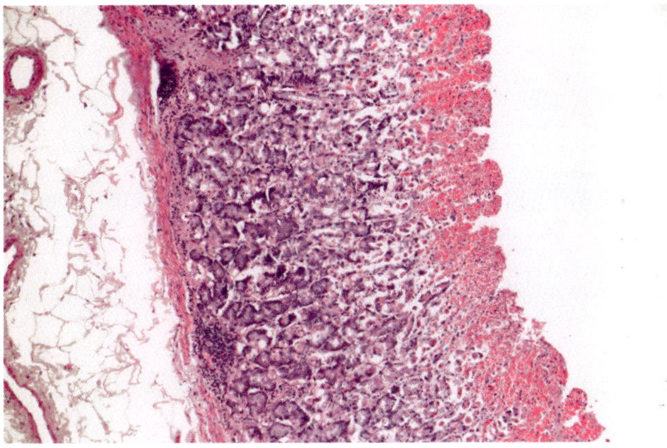

34.17 Acute hemorrhagic gastritis typical of acute cyanide poisoning (H&E x 150).

when police are lying on top of the victim, or neck compression. In the latter instance, a flexed arm may have compressed the carotid arteries bilaterally, the so called "carotid sleeper" or "sleeper hold", or an arm, baton or flashlight may have compressed the front of the neck and occluded the airway, the so called "bar arm". Lethal mechanisms may involve airway occlusion, carotid artery compression or perhaps carotid sinus reflex stimulation. At autopsy, there may be facial and conjunctival congestion with petechiae, and possible marks on the anterior aspect of the neck with bruising of underlying soft tissues, sometimes with fractures of the hyoid bone or laryngeal cartilages (81,82).

TABLE 34.2 Contribution of scene and autopsy findings to the diagnosis of asphysial deaths

Suffocation
Smothering
History and scene features/reconstruction (S)
Choking
History and scene features/reconstruction (S)
± Airway obstruction (A)
Compression
Mechanical/positional asphyxia
History and scene features/reconstruction (S)
± Skin markings
Crush asphyxia
History and scene features/reconstruction (S)
Craniocervical congestion (A)
Facial/conjunctival petechiae (A)
± Nasal and ear hemorrhage
± Skin markings/injuries
Neck compression
Ligature strangulation
± Scene features (S)
Ligature mark around neck (A)
± Facial/conjunctival petechiae (A)
Other injuries (A)
Manual strangulation
Bruising and abrasions around neck (A)
± Facial/conjunctival petechiae (A)
Other injuries (A)
Hanging
History and scene features/reconstruction (S)
Ligature/marks around neck (A)
± Facial/conjunctival petechiae (A)
Chemical asphyxia
± Scene features (S)
Toxicology (A)

S – scene; A – autopsy; ± – not always present.
(*Source*: (Adapted from Byard & Jensen [1])

Decreased cellular uptake/utilization

Hydrogen sulphide is a toxin that blocks cellular respiration. It is found in sewer gas and while small amounts have a classic smell of rotten eggs, in higher concentrations it is odorless. At autopsy, the brain may have a characteristic green discoloration (83). Another cellular toxin is hydrogen cyanide which may cause characteristic brick-red or pink coloration of lividity. Upon dissection, there may be corrosive gastritis with gastric hemorrhage (Figure 34.17), bright red coloration of the gastric mucosa and a smell of bitter almonds (38).

CONCLUSION

The diagnosis of an asphyxial event at autopsy requires careful integration of the history and scene examination with autopsy findings (Table 34.2) as there are no pathognomonic features of acute hypoxia. In fact, the "classic" signs of asphyxia of congestion and edema, petechiae, cyanosis, engorgement of the right side of heart and fluidity of the blood have been called an "obsolete diagnostic quintet". Typical cases of lethal asphyxia such as hanging, crushing, carbon monoxide toxicity and garrotting may incorporate a number of different pathophysiological mechanisms.

REFERENCES

1. Byard RW, Jensen L. Fatal asphyxial episodes in the very young: Classification and diagnostic issues. *Forensic Sci Med Pathol* 2007; **3:** 177–81.
2. Byard RW, Cains G. Lethal asphyxia: Pathology and problems. *Minerva Med* 2007; **127:** 273–82.
3. Giffen GH. *Students' Manual of Medical Jurisprudence and Public Health*. 2nd ed. Edinburgh: William Bryce; 1906.
4. Reese JJ. *Text-book of Medical Jurisprudence and Toxicology*. 7th ed. Philadelphia: P. Blakiston's Son & Co; 1906.
5. Mann JD. *Forensic Medicine and Toxicology*. 3rd ed. London: Charles Griffin & Co; 1902.
6. Taylor AS. *The Principles and Practice of Medical Jurisprudence*. London: John Churchill & Sons; 1865.
7. Stephenson L, Van den Heuvel C, Byard RW. The persistent problem of drowning: A difficult diagnosis with inconclusive tests. *J Forensic Leg Med* 2019; **66:** 79–85.
8. Byard RW, Wilson GW. Death scene gas analysis in suspected methane asphyxia. *Am J Forensic Med Pathol* 1992; **13:** 69–71.
9. Austin A, Winskog C, van den Heuvel C, Byard RW. Recent trends in suicides utilizing helium. *J Forensic Sci* 2011; **56:** 649–51.
10. Byard RW. Changing trends in suicides using helium or nitrogen: A 15-year study. *J Forensic Leg Med* 2018; **58:** 6–8.
11. DiMaio VJ, DiMaio D. *Forensic Pathology*. 2nd ed. London: CRC Press; 2001.
12. Byard RW, Simpson E, Gilbert JD. Temporal trends over the past two decades in South Australia in asphyxial deaths involving plastic bags or wrapping. *J Clin Forensic Med* 2006; **13:** 9–14.
13. Lester D. Effects of detoxification of domestic gas on suicides in The Netherlands. *Psychol Rep* 1001; **68:** 202.
14. deRoux SJ. Suicidal asphyxiation by inhalation of automobile emission without carbon monoxide poisoning. *J Forensic Sci* 2006; **51:** 1158–9.
15. Schmunk GA, Kaplan JA. Asphyxial deaths caused by automobile exhaust inhalation not attributable to carbon monoxide toxicity: study of 2 cases. *Am J Forensic Med Pathol* 2002; **23:** 123–6.
16. Byard RW, Tsokos M. Infant and early childhood asphyxial deaths: Diagnostic issues. In: *Forensic Pathology Reviews* Vol 2. Tsokos M, (ed). Totowa, NJ: Humana Press; 2005, pp. 101–23.
17. Byard RW. Hazardous infant and early childhood sleeping environments and death scene examination. *J Clin Forensic Med* 1996; **3:** 115–22.
18. Byard RW, Beal S, Bourne AJ. Potentially dangerous sleeping environments and accidental asphyxia in infancy and early childhood. *Arch Dis Child* 1994; **71:** 497–500.
19. Redpath M, Sauvageau A. An unusual case of smothering secondary to ingesting raw pet cat. *Am J Forensic Med Pathol* 2011; **32:** 190–2.
20. Wick R, Gilbert JD, Byard RW. Café coronary syndrome – fatal choking on food: An autopsy approach. *J Clin Forensic Med* 2006; **13:** 135–8.
21. Byard RW. Coprophagic café coronary. *Am J Forensic Med Pathol* 2001; **22:** 96–9.
22. Byard RW, Gilbert JD, Gibbs SE, Kemper CM. Cetacean café coronary. *J Clin Forensic Med* 2003; **10:** 85–8.
23. Tsokos M, Byard RW. Massive fatal aspiration of blood. Not always a result of trauma. *Am J Forensic Med Pathol* 2007; **28:** 53–4.
24. Kiho L, Byard RW. Acute fatal upper airway obstruction from an occult cavernous hemangioma of the larynx. *J Forensic Sci* 2015; **60 Suppl 1:** S93–6.
25. Byard RW, Heath K. Variable mechanisms of sudden and unexpected death in cases of occult carcinoma of the larynx. *Am J Forensic Med Pathol* 2021; **42:** 92–5.
26. Byramji A, Gilbert JD, Byard RW. Fatal retropharyngeal abscess: A possible marker of inflicted injury in infancy and early childhood. *Forensic Sci Med Pathol* 2009; **5:** 302–6.
27. Byard RW. Tonsillitis and sudden childhood death. *J Forensic Legal Med* 2008; **15:** 516–18.
28. Houldsworth G, James RA, Gilbert JD, Byard RW. Unexpected death in association with an occult posterior lingual abscess. *Legal Med* 2000; **4:** 221–3.
29. Byard RW. Unexpected death due to infectious mononucleosis. *J Forensic Sci* 2002; **47:** 202–4.
30. Byard RW, Gilbert JD. Narcotic administration and stenosing lesions of the upper airway: A potentially lethal combination. *J Clin Forensic Med* 2005; **12:** 29–31.
31. Byard RW, Wick R, Gilbert JD. Conditions and circumstances predisposing to death from positional asphyxia in adults. *J Forensic Legal Med* 2008; 15: 415–19.
32. Byard RW. Acute alcohol intoxication and lethal neck flexion. *Forensic Sci Med Pathol* 2022; **18(2):** 223–5.
33. Elworthy J, (ed). Chimney sweep from Ely workhouse whose death changed the law. Available from: https://www.elystandard.co.uk/news/education/22740723.chimney-sweep-ely-workhouse-whose-death-changed-law/ (Accessed 26 April 2023).
34. Byard RW. The relationship between positional asphyxia and increasing body mass index. *Leg Med* 2020; **43:** 101678.
35. Byard RW, Wick R, Simpson E, Gilbert JD. The pathological features and circumstances of death in lethal crush/traumatic asphyxia in adults: A 25-year study. *Forensic Sci Int* 2006; **159:** 200–5.
36. Byard RW, Hanson KA, James RA. Fatal unintentional traumatic asphyxia in childhood. *J Paediatr Child Health* 2003; **39:** 31–2.
37. Byard RW. Carbon monoxide: The silent killer. *Forensic Sci Med Pathol* 2019; **15:** 1–2.
38. Saukko P, Knight B. Suffocation and 'asphyxia'. In: *Knight's Forensic Pathology,* 4th ed. Boca Raton: CRC Press; 2016, pp. 353–68.
39. Benowitz N. Nitrates and nitrites. In: Olson K (ed) *Poisoning and drug overdose*, 7th ed. New York: McGraw Hill; 2018, pp. 339–40.
40. Gilbert J, Jensen L, Byard RW. Further observations on the speed of death in hanging. *J Forensic Sci* 2008; **53:** 1204–5.
41. Hanson K, Gilbert JD, James RA, Byard RW. Upper airway occlusion by soil: An unusual cause of death in motor vehicle accidents. *J Clin Forensic Med* 2002; **9:** 96–9.
42. Byard RW, Williams D, James RA, Gilbert JD. Diagnostic issues in unusual asphyxial deaths. *J Clin Forensic Med* 2001; **8:** 214–17.
43. Stephenson L, van den Heuvel C, Byard RW. Weighted drownings: An example of augmentation or enhancement of a suicide method. *J Forensic Leg Med* 2020; **70:** 101914.
44. Byard RW, Rutty G, Blumbergs P, et al. Lack of evidence for a causal relationship between hypoxic ischemic encephalopathy and subdural hemorrhage in fetal life, infancy and early childhood. *Pediatr Develop Pathol* 2007; **10:** 348–50.
45. Rao VJ, Wetli CV. The forensic significance of conjunctival petechiae. *Am J Forensic Med Pathol* 1988; **9:** 32–4.
46. Ely SF, Hirsch CS. Asphyxial deaths and petechiae: a review. *J Forensic Sci* 2000; **45:** 1274–7.
47. Haddix TL, Harruff RC, Reay DT, Haglund WD. Asphyxial suicides using plastic bags. *Am J Forensic Med Pathol* 1996; **17:** 308–11.
48. Athanaselis S, Stefanidou M, Karakoukis N, Koutselinis A. Asphyxial death by ether inhalation and plastic bag suffocation instructed by the press and the internet. *J Med Internet Res* 2002; **4:** e18.
49. Byard RW. Pathological changes in the thyroid gland in crush asphyxia. *Forensic Sci Med Pathol* 2013; **9:** 568–72.
50. Byard RW, Bellis M. Histological changes in the thyroid gland in cases of infant and early childhood asphyxia:A

preliminary study. *J Forensic Sci* 2016; **61:** 674–5.

51. Byard R. The brassiere "sign": A distinctive marker in crush asphyxia. *J Clin Forensic Med* 2005; **12:** 316–19.
52. Casper JL. *A Handbook of the Practice of Forensic Medicine Based Upon Personal Experience.* Vol II, *Thanatological Division.* London: The New Sydenham Society; 1862.
53. Byard RW, Hucker SJ, Hazelwood RR. Fatal and near-fatal autoerotic asphyxial episodes in women: Characteristic features based on a review of nine cases. *Am J Forensic Med Pathol* 1993; **14:** 70–3.
54. Byard RW, Hucker SJ, Hazelwood RR. A comparison of typical death scene features in cases of fatal male and female autoerotic asphyxia with a review of the literature. *Forensic Sci Int* 1990; **48:** 113–21.
55. Byard RW, Bramwell NH. Autoerotic death: A definition. *Am J Forensic Med Pathol* 1991; **12:** 74–6.
56. Byard RW, Hilton J. Overlaying, accidental suffocation and sudden infant death. *J SIDS Infant Mort* 1997; **2:** 161–5.
57. Mitchell E, Krous HF, Byard RW. Pathological findings in overlaying. *J Clin Forensic Med* 2002; **9:** 133–5.
58. Byard RW. Overlaying, co-sleeping, suffocation, and sudden infant death syndrome: The elephant in the room. *Forensic Sci Med Pathol* 2015; **11:** 273–4.
59. Byard RW, Elliott J, Vink R. Infant gender, shared sleeping and sudden death. *J Paediatr Child Health* 2012; **48:** 517–19.
60. Spinelli J, Byard RW, Van Den Heuvel C, Collins-Praino L. Medullary astrogliosis in sudden infant death syndrome varies with sleeping environment: evidence for different mechanisms of death in alone verses co-sleepers? *J Child Neurol* 2018; **33:** 269–74.
61. Collins-Praino L, Byard RW. Infants who die in shared sleeping situations differ from those who die sleeping alone. *Acta Paediatrica* 2019; **108:** 611–14.
62. Byard RW, Beal SM. Munchausen syndrome by proxy: Repetitive infantile apnoea and homicide. *J Paediatr Child Health* 1993; **29:** 77–9.
63. Byard RW, Chivell WC, Gilbert JD. Unusual facial markings and lethal mechanisms in a series of gasoline inhalation deaths. *Am J Forensic Med Pathol* 2003; **24:** 298–302.
64. Byard RW. Mechanisms of unexpected death in infants and young children following foreign body ingestion. *J Forensic Sci* 1996; **41:** 438–41.
65. Knight BH. The significance of the post mortem discovery of gastric contents in the air passages. *J Forens Sci* 1975; **6:** 229–34.
66. Byard RW, Farrell ER, Simpson E. Diagnostic yield and characteristic features in a series of decomposed bodies subject to coronial autopsy. *Forensic Sci Med Pathol* 2008; **4:** 9–14.
67. Austin A, van den Heuvel C, Byard RW. Differences in local and national database recordings of deaths from suicide. *Forensic Sci Med Pathol* 2017; **13:** 403–8.
68. Costa M, Silva BS, Real FC, Teixeira HM. Epidemiology and forensic aspects of carbon monoxide intoxication in Portugal: A three years' analysis. *Forensic Sci Int* 2019; **299:** 1–5.
69. Byard RW. Wills S. Neck protection in suicidal hanging. *Aust J Forensic Sci* 2016; **48:** 312–16.
70. Prahlow SP, Cohle S, Shattuck B, Prahlow JA. Homicides disguised as staged suicides. *Acad Forensic Pathol* 2020; **10(2):** 104–12.
71. Adair TW, Dobersen MJ. A case of suicidal hanging staged as homicide. *J Forensic Sci* 1999; **44(6):** 1307–9.
72. Howarth A. *Death in Bollywood: Who Killed Jiah Khan.* The Guardian. 1st October 20, 2017. Available from: https://www.theguardian.com/global/2017/oct/01/death-in-bollywood-who-killed-jiah-khan-crime-murder-suicide-investigation (Accessed 26 April 2023).
73. Green H, James RA, Gilbert JD, Byard RW. Fractures of the hyoid bone and laryngeal cartilages in suicidal hanging. *J Clin Forensic Med* 2000; **7:** 123–6.
74. Li X-F, Dai L-Y, Lu H, Chen X-D. A systematic review of the management of hangman's fractures. *Eur Spine J* 2006; **15:** 257–69.
75. Byard RW, Gilbert JD. Suicidal decapitation by hanging: A population-based study. *J Forensic Sci* 2018; **63:** 958–60.
76. Hejna P, Rejtarová O. Bleedings into the anterior aspect of the intervertebral disks in the lumbar region of the spine as a diagnostic sign of hanging. *J Forensic Sci* 2010; **55:** 428–31.
77. Byard RW. Autoerotic death: Characteristic features and diagnostic difficulties. *J Clin Forensic Med* 1994; **1:** 71–8.
78. Byard RW, Botterill P. Autoerotic asphyxial death: Accident or suicide? *Am J Forensic Med Pathol* 1998; **19:** 377–80.
79. Moore L, Byard RW. Pathological findings in hanging and wedging deaths in infants and young children. *Am J Forensic Med Pathol* 1993; **14:** 296–302.
80. Byard RW. Ongoing issues with the diagnosis of excited delirium. *Forensic Sci Med Pathol* 2018; **14:** 149–51.
81. Reay DT, Fligner C, Stillwell A, Arnold J. Positional asphyxia during law enforcement transportation. *Am J Forensic Med Pathol* 1992; **13:** 90–7.
82. Reay DT, Eisele JE. Law enforcement and neck holds. *Am J Forensic Med Pathol* 1986; **7:** 177–87.
83. Milroy C, Parai J. Hydrogen sulphide discoloration of the brain. *Forensic Sci Med Pathol* 2011; **7:** 225–6.

CHAPTER

35

Head Trauma Deaths

Colin Smith and Kevin Kinch

INTRODUCTION

Traumatic brain injury (TBI) is a leading cause of morbidity and mortality worldwide and accounts for over one-third of all injury-related deaths (1). Pathologists who undertake medicolegal autopsies will encounter TBI frequently and therefore must be familiar with the key clinical and pathological concepts. This chapter will outline the pathology associated with fatal head trauma in adults and children and offer practical guidance for postmortem examination in cases of death related to TBI.

EPIDEMIOLOGY

TBI is a significant global medical and socioeconomic problem. In the United States, there were approximately 2.87 million TBI-related emergency department visits, hospitalizations and deaths reported in 2014 (2). Children aged 0–4 years, adolescents aged 15–19 years, and adults over 65 years are the age groups most likely to sustain a TBI. Leading causes include falls, motor vehicle crashes (MVCs), struck by or against events and assaults (3). Recent data from Centers for Disease Control and Prevention (CDC) report 64 362 TBI-related deaths in 2020 (4). Suicide accounted for 35.5 percent of TBI-related deaths, falls 29.9 percent, MVCs 17 percent, and homicide 9.2 percent. TBI-related mortality was over three times higher in males than in females and rates of TBI-related deaths were highest in adults over 75 years. The leading cause of TBI-related death in this age group was falls, whereas in adults 15–34 years it was MVCs, and in children 0–17 years, homicide and MVCs were the most common mechanisms of injury (5). These data pertain to the United States but are broadly comparable with other developed countries, with some notable exceptions: in Europe, the leading cause of TBI-related death is falls (1), whereas in developing countries, where the TBI burden is greater, MVCs (6).

CLASSIFICATION

TBI is an injury to the brain caused by an external mechanical force. The severity of the injury and associated pathology depend largely on the magnitude of the force, its distribution, and the time over which it is applied. The force can be transferred to the brain through impact with the head or by linear or rotational acceleration of the head, or by a combination of both. The transfer of force causes tissue damage that manifests as various pathologies that can be subclassified as primary (occurring at the time of injury) or secondary (insults that evolve minutes/hours to days after primary injury), or as focal or diffuse, as defined by their location in the central nervous system (Table 35.1). This chapter will follow the neuropathological focal or diffuse classification as the authors consider this to correlate well

TABLE 35.1 Classification of TBI by injury type

	Focal injury	Diffuse injury
Primary injury	Scalp lesions Skull fractures Intracranial hemorrhage Intracerebral hemorrhage Cerebral contusions/lacerations	Diffuse traumatic axonal injury Diffuse vascular injury
Secondary injury	Focal brain swelling Focal ischemia Raised intracranial pressure and associated vascular changes	Diffuse ischemic brain injury Diffuse brain swelling

DOI: 10.1201/9781003138754-37

with clinical presentation and outcome, and to be most relevant to the pathology community. It is important to note, however, that no single classification system can adequately describe the full spectrum of clinical and pathological features, and neurobiology of TBI, and neuropathological findings should be correlated with the autopsy findings and circumstances of death.

PATHOLOGY

Focal injury

Lesions of the scalp and skull

Abrasions, contusions and lacerations of the scalp are caused by contact injury and are frequent but usually clinically insignificant findings in TBI. The location and type of injury, however, may provide a clue to significant underlying intracranial pathology: an occipital scalp contusion is typically associated with contusions of the frontal lobes and temporal poles (so-called contre-coup contusions); contusions around the mastoid process may be associated with traumatic subarachnoid hemorrhage (tSAH); and contusions overlying the temporal bone may be associated with an underlying fracture and extradural hematoma (EDH).

Skull fractures are common in TBI. Their prevalence increases with the severity of injury and incidence has been reported to be as high as 80 percent in fatal TBI cases (7). They can be classified as linear (most common) or depressed. Linear fractures are caused by impact with a flat surface where the force is distributed over a large surface area. They may be limited to the vertex or the base of the skull (basilar skull fracture). The latter can extend through the orbital roof of the frontal bone, or traverse the floor of the middle cranial fossa, following the petrous temporal bone or greater wing of the sphenoid bone into the pituitary fossa. If an individual sustains a severe blow to the side of the head, a hinge-type fracture can develop, whereby the fracture extends across the whole base of the skull.

Depressed fractures, where fragments of the inner table are displaced inward, are caused by focal impact. They are called compound if associated with a scalp laceration and penetrating if the dura mater is torn, and they are important sources of intracranial infection.

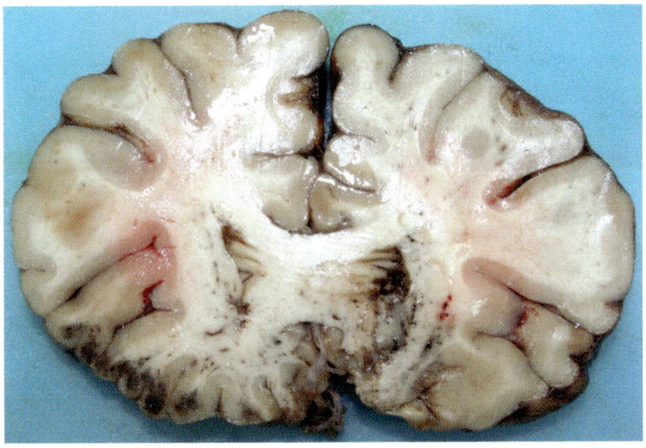

35.1 A coronal section of brain at the level of the genu of the corpus callosum showing acute cortical contusions involving the inferior aspects of both frontal lobes. On the left side, these extend into underlying superficial white matter, whereas on the right side, there is an associated laceration resulting in loss of the medial cortical tissues. These lesions indicate an impact head injury, the inferior frontal cortices striking the irregular bony structures of the anterior cranial fossa.

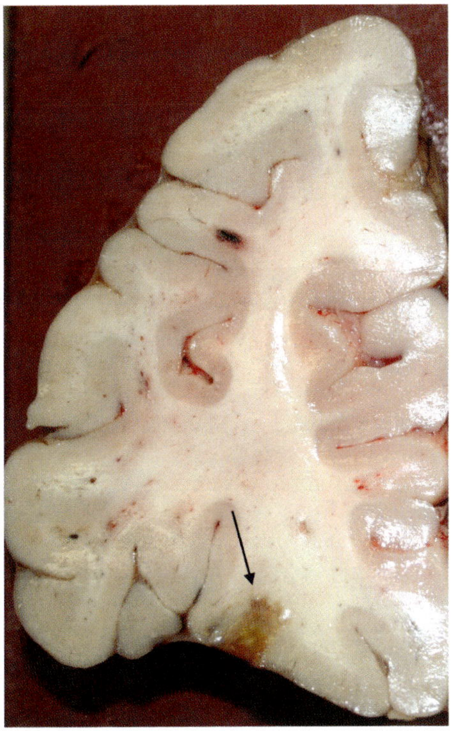

35.2 A coronal section through the left frontal lobe showing an old cortical contusion (arrow). There is loss of cortical tissue, the damaged tissue being replaced by a golden-brown gliotic scar within which hemosiderin-containing macrophages will be found.

Contusions and lacerations of the brain

Contusions are pathognomonic of impact TBI and are seen in a majority of fatal cases. They are a result of focal damage to small superficial cortical blood vessels caused when the brain impacts against the bony protuberances of the skull base. Acute contusions appear as punctate or confluent cortical hemorrhages (Figure 35.1) that can extend into underlying white matter and, in some cases, form a hematoma. Histologically, acute contusions are hemorrhagic, the hemorrhage being predominantly perivascular. They are most severe on the crests of gyri and have a characteristic distribution affecting the inferior rectus gyri and the orbitofrontal cortex, lateral and inferior aspects of the temporal lobes, temporal poles and perisylvian cortices. In severe TBI, there is often associated laceration of the pia-arachnoid and associated subdural hemorrhage (SDH). The combination of severe contusions, laceration and SDH constitutes a burst lobe and typically occurs in the frontal and temporal lobes. Contusions of the parietal lobes, occipital lobes and cerebellum are rare and usually underlie a fracture (8). Old contusions are characterized by focal cortical damage and atrophy and appear golden-brown due to hemosiderin deposition (Figure 35.2).

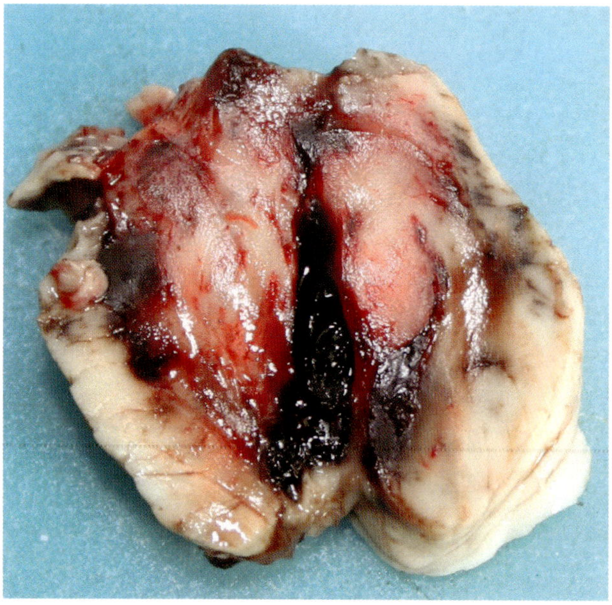

35.3 Extensive midline hemorrhage involving the midbrain from a case with an acute subdural hemorrhage in the supratentorial compartment acting as a space-occupying lesion and causing axial displacement and terminal brainstem hemorrhage (Duret hemorrhage). There is significant parenchymal damage associated with this bleeding.

Extradural (epidural) hematoma

EDH, a collection of blood between the skull and the dura, is seen in 5 to 22 percent of fatal TBI cases (9). In most cases, it results from a fracture in the squamous part of the temporal bone that has damaged the middle meningeal artery, but it can also occur in the occipital, frontal and posterior fossa regions, and, particularly in children, in the absence of a fracture (10). A series of 95 post-mortem cases reported falls as the leading mechanism of injury, followed by MVCs and assaults (11).

The hematoma expands quickly stripping the dura from the scalp to form a circumscribed, ovoid mass that indents and flattens the adjacent brain. In some cases, the source of the bleeding is venous, and the hematoma expands more slowly, over hours to days. A volume exceeding 40–50 mL is usually associated with raised intracranial pressure (ICP). A volume exceeding 100 mL is typically fatal and associated with deformation of the brain, midline shift, internal herniation and secondary brain stem hemorrhage (Duret hemorrhages [Figure 35.3]).

Though exceptional, non-traumatic causes of EDH have been described in association with paracranial infections, coagulopathies, vascular malformations and neoplasia. EDH can be seen in fire-related deaths, but these lesions are typically pink and spongy, differentiating them from dark-red traumatic EDH.

Acute subdural hematoma

Acute subdural hematoma (SDH) is seen in 20 to 63 percent of fatal TBI cases (Figure 35.4) (7,9). Most SDH are due to rupture of veins that bridge

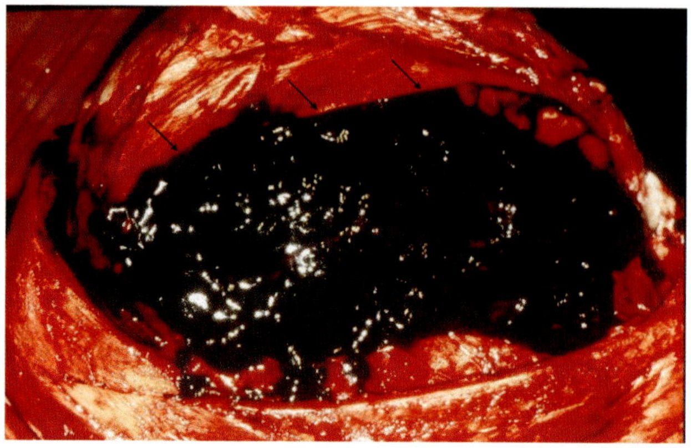

35.4 An acute subdural hematoma overlying the cortical convexity. The reflected edge of the dura is indicated by arrows. At post mortem, the dura would have been tense and bulging. The blood extends extensively over the cortical surface, unlike an extra(epi-)dural hematoma which remains much more localized.

the subdural space where they connect the cortical surface to the sagittal sinus (bridging veins), and to damage of blood vessels on the cortical surface in assciation with localized contusions. SDH can also be associated with extensive contusions causing an associated parenchymal hemorrhage (burst lobe). Common mechanisms of injury include falls and assaults (12). SDH is associated with high mortality (30–50%), and an important factor in determining prognosis is the extent of concomitant primary parenchymal brain damage, particularly contusions and lacerations (13,14). As with EDH, secondary brain damage is due to mass effect and raised ICP. There are several recognized non-traumatic causes of SDH, including ruptured vascular malformations, coagulation and hematological disorders, metabolic disorders and as a complication of neurosurgery (15). SDH is also well-recognized in the setting of congenital heart disease (16).

EDH and SDH are the most common cause of clinical deterioration in patients who experience a lucid interval, "talk and die", or "talk and deteriorate after injury" (17) particularly in the case of EDH, which can occur with minimal primary brain injury. The clinical complications associated with a hematoma are related to the size/volume of the lesion, the anatomic location, and the rapidity with which the hematoma develops. They can cause secondary complications associated with a space-occupying lesion (SOL), such as herniation (subfalcine, tentorial, tonsillar), axial displacement, brainstem hemorrhage and global ischemia.

Subarachnoid hemorrhage

Localized small volume subarachnoid hemorrhage (SAH) is common in cases of fatal TBI but is typically of little consequence in relation to the cause of death, beyond being a marker of TBI. However, SAH volume is a predicter of outcome, with increasing SAH volume being associated with a poorer outcome. In forensic pathology, however, tSAH is a specific entity caused by a blow to the neck or head that damages the vessels at the base of the brain (typically the intracranial portion of the vertebral artery as it crosses the dura) causing massive basal SAH. It is often the only pathology identified at post-mortem examination. In most cases, injury results from an assault, and it is particularly common in young intoxicated males (18). Collapse is rapid and death typically occurs within 24–48 hours (19). The precise mechanism of death is unclear. Hyperextension of the neck and the effect of massive basal SAH or localized traumatic damage disrupting cardiorespiratory centers in the medulla have been suggested (20).

When faced with extensive basal SAH at autopsy with a history detailing a temporal association between a blow to the neck or head followed by immediate collapse, the pathologist should consider the most likely explanation as being tSAH. However, the pathologist must consider and exclude spontaneous rupture of an aneurysm or vascular malformation by careful dissection of the cerebral blood vessels at autopsy, or by detailed pre-autopsy CT angiography (CTA). The intracranial vertebral arteries must be examined for damage *in situ* and removed for histologic examination.

Intracerebral hematoma

Traumatic intracerebral hematoma (ICH) is seen in around 15 percent of fatal TBI cases (9). They are often multiple and occur most commonly in the frontal and temporal lobes.

ICH likely results from the rupture of parenchymal blood vessels at the time of injury. In some cases, however, delayed traumatic intracerebral hemorrhage (DTICH) can develop a few hours to several days after injury (21), and this may have important medicolegal implications if the patient subsequently dies, for example, after an assault (22,23).

Traumatic basal ganglia hematoma is associated with severe TBI. Clinical studies have shown that in 60 to 94 percent of patients with traumatic basal ganglia hematoma, injury results from an MVC (24,25). They are thought to be due to rotational acceleration forces damaging the deep penetrating arteries. As such, concomitant lesions associated with rotational forces such as parasagittal white matter hemorrhage and diffuse traumatic axonal injury (TAI) are commonly seen (26). Outcome is poor and mortality has been reported to be as high as 59 percent (24).

Spontaneous causes of ICH include hypertension, rupture of a saccular aneurysm, hemorrhagic transformation of an ischemic stroke, and cerebral amyloid angiopathy (CAA). The latter is an important cause of lobar hemorrhage in older individuals, and CAA may make vessels more fragile and susceptible to TBI and also may also exacerbate traumatic bleeding (27).

Traumatic intraventricular hemorrhage

Traumatic intraventricular hemorrhage (IVH) is seen in around 10 percent of fatal TBI cases (28). It is associated with rotational forces and is frequently seen together with diffuse TAI. It is thought to be due to the rupture of small blood vessels in the fornix or septum pellucidum, periventricular veins, and choroid plexus. In some cases, it may represent an extension of a parenchymal hematoma or basal SAH.

Traumatic brain stem hemorrhage

Contusions and lacerations of the brain stem are usually associated with fractures of the foramen magnum and hyperextension of the neck. In extreme hyperextension of the neck, partial or complete pontomedullary or cervicomedullary avulsion can occur (pontomedullary rent) (29). This injury is often seen in pedestrian versus MVCs and motorcyclists involved in accidents. Individuals are unconscious at the time of injury and die within 24 hours.

Diffuse injury

Traumatic axonal injury and diffuse axonal injur

TAI is a common pathology in TBI associated with rotational acceleration injury. It comprises a spectrum of damage ranging from focal to diffuse that underlies a clinical spectrum ranging from mild concussion to immediate, prolonged coma resulting in death. The clinical and radiologic entity known as diffuse axonal injury (DAI) is associated with severe diffuse TAI, with focal hemorrhagic lesions in the parasagittal white matter, corpus callosum and dorsolateral quadrants of the rostral brain stem, and with a higher incidence of diffuse vascular injury, parasagittal white matter hemorrhage (30) and basal ganglia hematoma (26).

DAI is commonly seen in MVCs, falls from a significant height, and severe assaults (31–33). It contributes to at least 35 percent of fatal TBI cases (34), and in the absence of an intracranial SOL or global ischemic injury, it is the most common cause of post-traumatic coma, severe disability and persistent vegetative state (35,36).

In most cases, axons are damaged as a delayed consequence of an applied force (secondary axotomy) as opposed to being torn at the time of the injury (primary axotomy) (37). Three grades of diffuse TAI have been described. In grade 1, there is microscopic evidence of axonal damage in the white matter of the parasagittal cortex, corpus callosum, internal capsule, dorsolateral midbrain and pons, and cerebellar peduncles. In more severe TBI, there are focal hemorrhagic lesions in the corpus callosum (grade 2) and dorsolateral quadrants of the rostral brain stem (grade 3) in addition to widespread axonal damage. Though the grades correspond, roughly, with the severity of TBI and neurologic dysfunction, clinicopathological correlation between and within

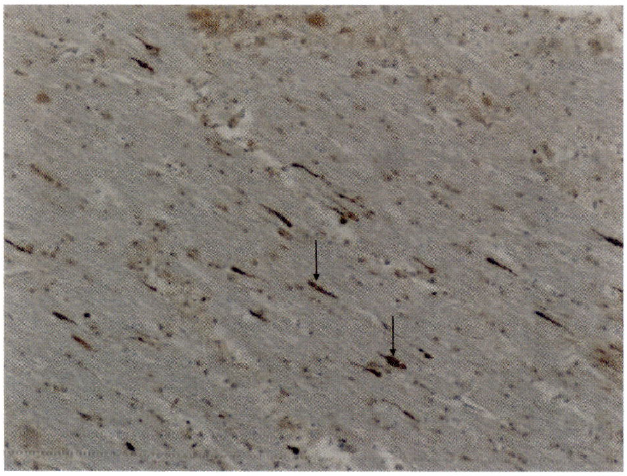

35.5 Diffuse traumatic axonal injury (TAI) highlighted by β-APP immunohistochemistry. There are a number of dark-brown axonal profiles indicating axonal injury, some of which show obvious axonal swelling and beading (two highlighted by arrows).

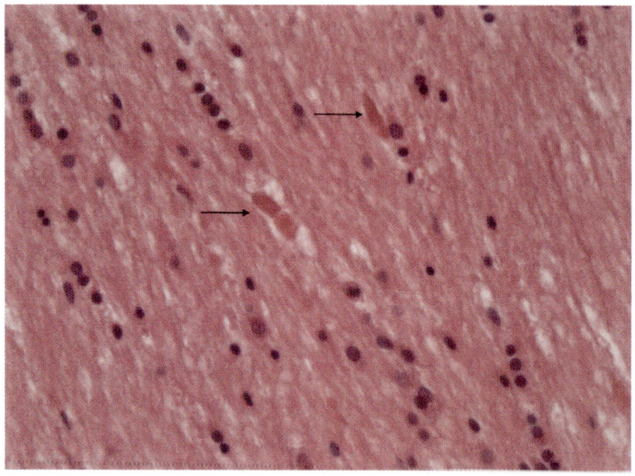

35.6 Eosinophilic retraction bulbs (balls) seen in the white matter of the corpus callosum. These typically require a survival time of at least 13 hours before they can be detected (H&E x40.)

grades is poor and inexact. For example, patients with grade 1 TAI can have a clinically mild, moderate, or, albeit less commonly, severe TBI, and fall within a spectrum of clinical presentation and outcome ranging from concussion and recovery to coma and death. Moreover, focal TAI (not involving the brain stem) is increasingly recognized and is likely associated with mild to moderate TBI, but the clinical consequences are unclear. The extent of brain stem pathology correlates most closely with prolonged coma and a poor clinical outcome.

Axonal damage is identified microscopically as varicosities along the length of an injured axon (Figure 35.5) or as a single swelling called an axonal retraction bulb (ARB). They appear eosinophilic or argyrophilic in hematoxylin and eosin (H&E) (Figure 35.6) or silver stained sections respectively, although a survival time of at least 13 hours is required before ARBs can be identified using these techniques (38). A more specific and sensitive marker of axonal injury is β-amyloid precursor protein (β-APP) immunohistochemistry (IHC). β-APP labels injured axons and can detect TAI in adults and children after a minimal survival time of 35 minutes (39,40). Immunoreactivity has been reported less than 35 minutes after injury and in cases described as dead at the scene, but staining is relatively subtle, with only occasional small granules and beaded axons in the white matter (41). The intensity of staining increases over 24 hours and is obvious for approximately 10–14 days after injury, but by 4 weeks immunoreactivity is usually absent (42). In long-term survivors, Wallerian degeneration of white matter tracts is highlighted by IHC for microglial cells (e.g. CD68) and immunoreactivity persists for years after injury (43). There is no literature relating to the timing of β-APP accumulation in other causes of immunostaining, such as after ischemic injury.

35.7 Immunohistochemistry for β-APP in a case with an acute subdural hematoma with midline shift. This image is from the corpus callosum and shows a classical vascular pattern of axonal damage, with an irregular linear pattern of immunostaining. In TAI, the pattern is much more localized or confined small groups of damaged axons (β-APP IHC x20).

It is confined important to note that β-APP is not diagnostic of TAI, and any process that causes axonal damage and disrupts the fast axonal transport system will cause β-APP to accumulate. It is important, therefore, when assessing a case of possible TBI, to be aware of other potential causes of widespread axonal injury, such as ischemia (44), hypoglycemia (45) and polydrug abuse (46). Ischemia, in particular, is almost ubiquitous in fatal TBI and can cause extensive β-APP accumulation throughout the white matter, but it is possible to differentiate TAI from ischemic axonal injury based on the pattern of β-APP immunoreactivity (Figure 35.7) (47). In ischemic damage, the axons show an ill-defined and

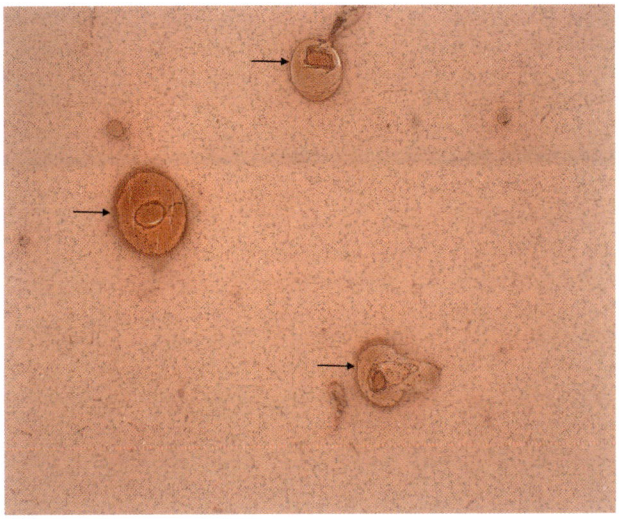

35.8 Diffuse vascular injury. Macroscopically petechial hemorrhages are seen, particularly in the frontal white matter, and microscopically there is perivascular hemorrhage (arrows) (H&E x10)

contiguous linear or geographic pattern not confined to individual white matter bundles. By contrast, in TAI axons are confined to individual, similarly orientated white matter bundles. In some cases, however, ischemic axonal injury is so extensive that it becomes impossible to comment on the presence, let alone the amount, of TAI. In such cases, it is sensible to consider the clinical history: extensive β-APP accumulation is unlikely to represent severe diffuse TAI if the patient had a lucid interval before death.

Diffuse vascular injury

Diffuse vascular injury is associated with severe rotational acceleration forces and is characterized by multiple petechial hemorrhages in the white matter, especially in the frontal and temporal lobes and brain stem. The pathology is thought to represent the shearing of small parenchymal blood vessels at the time of injury and is often seen in cases described as dead at the scene (7). Microscopic examination shows perivascular hemorrhages (Figure 35.8). As part of the spectrum of rotational injury, parasagittal white matter hemorrhage, subcortical hemorrhage and traumatic basal ganglia hematoma may also be seen in diffuse vascular injury.

Brain swelling

Brain swelling is common in fatal TBI, and increased ICP due to brain swelling is the most common cause of death in severe TBI (48,49). Brain swelling is due primarily to an increase in the water content of brain tissue (cerebral edema) (50), but an increase in cerebral blood volume (congestion) may also contribute. At autopsy, brain swelling is recognized by flattening of the gyri, sulcal effacement, ventricular compression, and midline shift if the swelling is unilateral. Swelling can be localized or diffuse. Localized swelling is associated with contusions, lacerations and ICH, and is caused by damage to the blood-brain barrier (BBB) that results in the leakage of plasma proteins, water and electrolytes out of blood vessels and into the white matter (vasogenic edema). Diffuse swelling of one cerebral hemisphere is often seen in association with an ipsilateral acute SDH. When the hematoma is evacuated, the hemisphere may swell. Exactly why this happens is not clear, but it is likely secondary to metabolic mismatch within the damaged tissue or ischemic injury, resulting in cytotoxic edema, and reperfusion of a non-reactive vascular bed. Diffuse swelling of both cerebral hemispheres can be seen in DAI and is a prevalent finding in fatal pediatric and adolescent head injury (51). The pathogenesis of this entity is unclear, but it is likely due to vasodilation and disruption to an immature BBB resulting in vasogenic edema.

Ischemic brain injury

Ischemic brain injury has been reported in over 90 percent of cases of fatal TBI (52). It is a consequence of reduced or absent cerebral perfusion secondary to raised ICP or cardiac arrest or a combination of both. The ischemic changes are most obvious in the cerebral cortex, striatum, thalamus, hippocampus and cerebellar Purkinje cells (53). If ischemia is mild and brief, then there is little cellular reaction and injury is restricted to neurons only (selective neuronal necrosis) resulting in nuclear pyknosis and cytoplasmic eosinophilia. This change requires a survival of several hours from the time of injury. If ischemia is severe and prolonged, and there has been survival of at least several days, damage involves all cells and the neuropil resulting in infarction.

Spinal cord trauma

Spinal cord injuries (SCI) are common, the prevalence ranging from 11.5 to 57.8 cases per million people in the population (54). The etiology of SCI varies between countries but MVCs, falls, sports-related injuries and assaults are consistent causes between studies (54). Closed SCIs are the commonest traumatic cord lesions in clinical practice and are associated with fracture or dislocation of the spine. Contusional SCI is typically associated with vertebral body fractures, in some cases with dislocation. Direct blunt force trauma to the spinal cord results in parenchymal hemorrhage and edema that causes fusiform swelling of the cord. Bleeding is initially petechial but these lesions coalesce to form more extensive hemorrhages, usually situated centrally within the spinal cord. Ischemia develops, resulting in central infarction of the cord. The tissue damage extends for several levels above and below the site of direct injury.

ABUSIVE HEAD TRAUMA IN INFANTS AND CHIDREN

Abusive head trauma (AHT) describes head injuries that are deliberately inflicted on infants and children (55). The CDC define AHT as injury to the skull or intracranial contents of an infant or child less than 5 years old caused by inflicted blunt impact, violent shaking, or both (56). It has a peak incidence in infants (less than 12 months old) and associated mortality is high (57–59). The most common clinical presentation is acute and severe neurologic impairment, respiratory compromise and seizures. SDH (usually thin film and bilateral), retinal hemorrhage (RH) and hypoxic-ischemic encephalopathy (HIE) are the hallmarks of AHT and would, until recently, have been considered pathognomonic of shaking. Other frequently observed injuries may include scalp contusions, lacerations and abrasions, skull fractures, parasagittal white matter hemorrhage, focal craniocervical TAI, diffuse brain swelling, cervical ligamentous/soft-tissue injury, cervical spinal cord injury, rib fractures, long-bone fractures and abdominal injuries.

SDH arising in a previously well infant or child is likely due to trauma and is found in most cases of AHT (60). Moreover, several prospective studies have shown a strong association of SDH with AHT compared with accidental trauma (61–65), an observation that has been corroborated in several robust clinical and radiologic peer-reviewed studies (66–68). The mechanism of SDH in AHT is attributed to traumatic rupture of bridging veins caused by inertial forces with or without impact.

RHs are rare in accidental injury. Most reports describe mild, predominantly unilateral, pre- or intraretinal hemorrhages in the posterior pole with no extension to ora serrata (69). By contrast, bilateral, severe multi-layered RHs that extend to the ora serrata are strongly associated with AHT (70,71). Perimacular retinal folds and traumatic retinoschisis have low sensitivity but high specificity for AHT, but these findings are not pathognomonic and have been described in cases of accidental severe crush head injury (72–74). Optic nerve sheath hemorrhages are significantly more common in AHT (69). The mechanisms of RH in AHT is thought to be due to traumatic damage to blood vessels caused by inertial forces, with or without impact, and a rapid rise in ICP.

HIE is a consequence of reduced or absent cerebral perfusion. It is seen in almost every case of fatal AHT and is the overriding mode of death. The most common cause is cardiorespiratory arrest. Other potential causes or contributing factors include seizures and brain swelling. The exact cause of cardiorespiratory arrest in this setting is likely multifactorial. In some cases, it may be due to craniocervical TAI resulting in apnea followed by hypoxia leading to cardiac arrest and circulatory collapse (75,76).

Over the last 20 years, a small number of researchers have proposed that hypoxia in infants and children can cause SDH and RH in the absence of trauma (77–82). But clear and robust evidence to support this hypothesis is lacking. Moreover, the findings of several pathological and radiologic studies do not support an association of SDH and HIE in infants and children (83–87) including neonates who have sustained perinatal asphyxia (88–90).

There are, of course, other causes for SDH and RH in infants and children that should be considered and excluded. In particular, it is important to distinguish between perinatal and neonatal SDH and SDH in infants and children. SDH is a common incidental finding in neonates that resolves spontaneously in the first few weeks of life (91–93). These low volume and clinically irrelevant perinatal SDH should be distinguished from the rare massive SDH seen in the perinatal period as a consequence of tears in the falx and tentorium due to trauma caused by instrumentation. The common small volume perinatal SDH is most likely due to the compressive forces of the uterus during labor. Intradural hemorrhage (IDH) is also a common finding in term and premature infants, particularly in parasagittal dura mater (94,95). They resolve spontaneously in a few months and are of no clinical significance. Similarly, RHs are common at birth. The incidence is highest in vacuum-assisted delivery and lowest in cesarean section. They are intraretinal and can be focal or widespread. Most resolve within two to four weeks without visual sequelae (96,97).

A diagnosis of AHT is *not* made automatically based on the presence of SDH, RH and HIE. But neither can it be excluded if one or more of these elements is absent. Making a diagnosis of AHT is a summative process that requires the collaboration of a multidisciplinary team, who must consider and correlate the findings of pertinent clinical, radiologic and laboratory investigations. The role of the expert pathologist, including the neuropathologist, ophthalmic pathologist, pediatric pathologist and forensic pathologist, is to describe the post-mortem findings and provide a balanced interpretation of those findings in the context of the case. His or her report is but one part of the overall investigation into the death of an infant or child with fatal TBI.

THE AUTOPSY

In cases of death related to TBI, the post-mortem can provide a detailed description of intracranial, intracerebral and spinal pathology associated with trauma and help to clarify the mechanism and timing of injury.

As with any post-mortem examination, knowledge of the deceased's medical history is important, but in cases of death related to TBI it is particularly useful to know about coagulopathy, hypertension and alcohol abuse. Intracranial hemorrhage may be delayed or exacerbated in a patient with a coagulation disorder. Spontaneous intracerebral hemorrhage can occur in patients with hypertension who may also have signs of significant blunt force head injury such as skull fracture, intracranial hemorrhage and contusions as a result of collapse. Alcoholics are prone to falls and may have evidence of old TBI including old contusions and chronic subdural hematomas. The former, if severe, is a risk factor for post-traumatic seizures (98) and the latter can rebleed spontaneously or following relatively trivial trauma. If the deceased died following a period of time in hospital, it is useful to know about radiologic findings and neurosurgical intervention. Lastly, it is important to be aware of other injuries and significant natural disease and to have as much background information as possible relating to the incident that caused the TBI as it allows the neuropathologic findings to be presented in context, without which it may be difficult to reach a conclusion.

The post-mortem examination should be performed in the standard way. A detailed description of the approach to an external and internal examination can be found in standard texts (99). Obviously, in cases of death related to TBI, particular attention should be given to injuries to the head and neck region. If there is suspicion of SCI, then the spinal column and cervical spine should be examined.

In most fatal head injury cases, the proximate cause of death is obvious. It is usually due to raised ICP secondary to intracranial hematoma, contusions, lacerations, infarction, or swelling, all of which can cause deformation of the brain, midline shift, internal herniation and secondary brain stem damage. In such cases, and in the setting of a witnessed and undisputed accident, macroscopic examination by an experienced pathologist is sufficient to provide a cause of death. If, however, there are likely to be criminal or legal proceedings, or the brain is almost entirely normal in appearance but there is a clear history of head injury, or the circumstances relating to the incident that caused the fatal head injury are unclear, referral for specialist neuropathological opinion is recommended and the whole brain should be retained for fixation (10% formalin). If a decision is made not to retain the brain, then it is prudent to discuss sampling with a neuropathologist. In general, for adult cases, a coronal slice of the cerebral hemispheres at the level of the posterior hippocampus/lateral geniculate body, a coronal slice anterior to this to include basal ganglia and anterior corpus callosum, a slice of the left and the right cerebellar hemisphere, a section of midbrain, pons and medulla, and dura with attached SDH and EDH together with any focal lesion(s) of concern is a reasonable protocol. If there is cervical spine injury, a small segment of cervical cord should be retained.

Histology is most useful in the assessment of diffuse injury (diffuse TAI, diffuse vascular injury and diffuse ischemic brain injury) or where the assessment of a focal lesion may provide information regarding the timing of an injury. The following protocol is recommended as part of the assessment of diffuse injury. The blocks should be taken from both the right and left side.

- **Block 1:** Frontal parasagittal white matter and anterior corpus callosum
- **Block 2:** Basal ganglia, including the internal capsule
- **Block 3:** Hippocampus (at the level of the lateral geniculate body)
- **Block 4:** Thalamus, including the internal capsule
- **Block 5:** Parietal parasagittal white matter and posterior corpus callosum
- **Block 6:** Parietal convexity
- **Block 7:** Pons, including the superior cerebellar peduncle
- **Blocks 8 and 9:** Cerebellum, including the middle cerebral peduncle

The blocks should be stained with H&E, and, where appropriate, β-APP. SDH and EDH attached to dura should be sampled and sampling should include different regions if more than one episode of bleeding is suspected. H&E, Perls and CD68 are useful stains to age the hematoma.

In pediatric head injury and suspected AHT, in addition to the above recommendations, the dura should be sampled from various locations and the brainstem, cervicomedullary region and the entire spinal cord should be examined and sampled thoroughly for focal lesions and axonal injury. The eyes should be removed with attached orbital contents and retrobulbar optic nerve so that it is possible not only to comment on the presence or absence of RH, but also the presence or absence of hemorrhage in the orbital fat and extraocular muscles and optic nerve sheath.

REFERENCES

1. Majdan M, Plancikova D, Brazinova A, et al. Epidemiology of traumatic brain injuries in Europe: A cross-sectional analysis. *Lancet Public Health* 2016; **1(2)**: e76–e83.
2. *Centers for Disease Control and Prevention Surveillance Report of Traumatic Brain Injury-related Emergency Department Visits, Hospitalizations, and Deaths—United States, 2014*. Centers for Disease Control and Prevention, U.S. Department of Health and Human Services; 2019.
3. Faul M, Xu L, Wald MM, Coronado VG. *Traumatic Brain Injury in the United States: Emergency Department Visits, Hospitalizations and Deaths 2002–2006*. Centers for Disease Control and Prevention. National Center for Injury Prevention and Control, Atlanta, GA; 2010.
4. Centers for Disease Control and Prevention. National Center for Health Statistics: Mortality Data on CDC WONDER. Available from: https://wonder.cdc.gov/mcd.html (Accessed 25 April 2023)
5. *Centers for Disease Control and Prevention Surveillance Report of Traumatic Brain Injury-related Deaths by Age Group, Sex, and Mechanism of Injury—United States, 2018 and 2019*. Centers for Disease Control and Prevention, U.S. Department of Health and Human Services; 2022.
6. Dewan MC, Rattani A, Gupta S, et al. Estimating the global incidence of traumatic brain injury. *J Neurosurg* 2018: 1–18.
7. Adams JH, Graham DI, Scott G, et al. Brain damage in fatal non-missile head injury. *J Clin Pathol* 1980; **33(12)**: 1132–45.
8. Adams JH, Doyle D, Graham DI, et al. The contusion index: A reappraisal in human and experimental non-missile head injury. *Neuropathol Appl Neurobiol* 1985; **11(4)**: 299–308.
9. Freytag E. Autopsy findings in head injuries from blunt forces. Statistical evaluation of 1367 cases. *Arch Pathol* 1963; **75**: 402–13.
10. Galbraith SL. Age-distribution of extradural haemorrhage without skull fracture. *Lancet* 1973; **1(7814)**: 1217–18.
11. Baykaner K, Alp H, Ceviker N, et al. Observation of 95 patients with extradural hematoma and review of the literature. *Surg Neurol* 1988; **30(5)**: 339–41.
12. Gennarelli TA, Thibault LE. Biomechanics of acute subdural hematoma. *J Trauma* 1982; **22(8)**: 680–6.
13. Leitgeb J, Mauritz W, Brazinova A, et al. Outcome after severe brain trauma due to acute subdural hematoma. *J Neurosurg* 2012; **117(2)**: 324–33.

14. Sawauchi S, Abe T. The effect of haematoma, brain injury, and secondary insult on brain swelling in traumatic acute subdural haemorrhage. *Acta Neurochir (Wien)* 2008; **150(6)**: 531–6; discussion 6.
15. Kemp AM. Investigating subdural haemorrhage in infants. *Arch Dis Child* 2002; **86(2)**: 98–102.
16. Lo WD, Lee J, Rusin J, et al. Intracranial hemorrhage in children: An evolving spectrum. *Arch Neurol* 2008; **65(12)**: 1629–33.
17. Reilly PL, Graham DI, Adams JH, Jennett B. Patients with head injury who talk and die. *Lancet* 1975; **2(7931)**: 375–7.
18. Gray JT, Puetz SM, Jackson SL, Green MA. Traumatic subarachnoid haemorrhage: A 10-year case study and review. *Forensic Sci Int* 1999; **105(1)**: 13–23.
19. Contostavlos DL. Isolated basilar traumatic subarachnoid hemorrhage: An observer's 25 year re-evaluation of the pathogenetic possibilities. *Forensic Sci Int* 1995; **73(1)**: 61–74.
20. Tatsuno Y, Lindenberg R. Basal subarachnoid hematomas as sole intracranial traumatic lesions. *Arch Pathol* 1974; **97(4)**: 211–15.
21. Sprick C, Bettag M, Bock WJ. Delayed traumatic intracranial hematomas--clinical study of seven years. *Neurosurg Rev* 1989; **12 Suppl 1**: 228–30.
22. Elsner H, Rigamonti D, Corradino G, et al. Delayed traumatic intracerebral hematomas: "Spät-Apoplexie". Report of two cases. *J Neurosurg* 1990; **72(5)**: 813–15.
23. Nanassis K, Frowein RA, Karimi A, Thun F. Delayed post-traumatic intracerebral bleeding. Delayed post-traumatic apoplexy: "Spätapoplexie". *Neurosurg Rev* 1989; **12 Suppl 1**:243–51.
24. Boto GR, Lobato RD, Rivas JJ, et al. Basal ganglia hematomas in severely head injured patients: Clinicoradiological analysis of 37 cases. *J Neurosurg* 2001; **94(2)**: 224–32.
25. Takeuchi S, Takasato Y, Masaoka H, et al. Traumatic basal ganglia hematomas: An analysis of 20 cases. *Acta Neurochir Suppl* 2013; **118**: 139–42.
26. Adams JH, Doyle D, Graham DI, et al. Deep intracerebral (basal ganglia) haematomas in fatal non-missile head injury in man. *J Neurol Neurosurg Psychiatry* 1986; **49(9)**: 1039–43.
27. Opeskin K. Cerebral amyloid angiopathy. A review. *Am J Forensic Med Pathol* 1996; **17(3)**: 248–54.
28. Matsukawa H, Shinoda M, Fujii M, et al. Intraventricular hemorrhage on computed tomography and corpus callosum injury on magnetic resonance imaging in patients with isolated blunt traumatic brain injury. *J Neurosurg* 2012; **117(2)**: 334–9.
29. Leestma JE, Kalelkar MB, Teas S. Pontomedullary avulsion associated with cervical hyperextension. *Acta Neurochir Suppl (Wien)* 1983; **32**: 69–73.
30. Adams JH, Doyle D, Graham DI, et al. Gliding contusions in nonmissile head injury in humans. *Arch Pathol Lab Med* 1986; **110(6)**: 485–8.
31. Adams JH, Doyle D, Ford I, et al. Diffuse axonal injury in head injury: definition, diagnosis and grading. *Histopathology* 1989; **15(1)**: 49–59.
32. Blumbergs PC, Jones NR, North JB. Diffuse axonal injury in head trauma. *J Neurol Neurosurg Psychiatry* 1989; **52(7)**: 838–41.
33. Chelly H, Chaari A, Daoud E, et al. Diffuse axonal injury in patients with head injuries: an epidemiologic and prognosis study of 124 cases. *J Trauma* 2011; **71(4)**: 838–46.
34. Gennarelli TA. Head injury in man and experimental animals: Clinical aspects. *Acta Neurochir Suppl (Wien)* 1983; **32**: 1–13.
35. Graham DI, McLellan D, Adams JH, et al. The neuropathology of the vegetative state and severe disability after non-missile head injury. *Acta Neurochir Suppl (Wien)* 1983; **32**: 65–7.
36. Kinney HC, Samuels MA. Neuropathology of the persistent vegetative state: A review. *J Neuropathol Exp Neurol* 1994; **53(6)**: 548–58.
37. Maxwell WL, Povlishock JT, Graham DL. A mechanistic analysis of nondisruptive axonal injury: a review. *J Neurotrauma* 1997; **14(7)**: 419–40.
38. Geddes JF, Whitwell HL, Graham DI. Traumatic axonal injury: Practical issues for diagnosis in medicolegal cases. *Neuropathol Appl Neurobiol* 2000; **26(2)**: 105–16.
39. Gorrie C, Oakes S, Duflou J, et al. Axonal injury in children after motor vehicle crashes: extent, distribution, and size of axonal swellings using beta-APP immunohistochemistry. *J Neurotrauma* 2002; **19(10)**: 1171–82.
40. Hortobagyi T, Wise S, Hunt N, et al. Traumatic axonal damage in the brain can be detected using β-APP immunohistochemistry within 35 min after head injury to human adults. *Neuropathol Appl Neurobiol* 2007; **33(2)**: 226–37.
41. Morrison C, MacKenzie JM. Axonal injury in head injuries with very short survival times. *Neuropathol Appl Neurobiol* 2008; **34(1)**: 124–5.
42. Graham DI, Smith C, Reichard R, et al. Trials and tribulations of using beta-amyloid precursor protein immunohistochemistry to evaluate traumatic brain injury in adults. *Forensic Sci Int* 2004; **146(2–3)**: 89–96.
43. Smith RP, Lam ET, Markova S, et al. Pharmacogene regulatory elements: From discovery to applications. *Genome Medicine* 2012; **4(5)**: 45.
44. Dolinak D, Smith C, Graham DI. Global hypoxia per se is an unusual cause of axonal injury. *Acta Neuropathol* 2000; **100(5)**: 553–60.
45. Dolinak D, Smith C, Graham DI. Hypoglycaemia is a cause of axonal injury. *Neuropathol Appl Neurobiol* 2000; **26(5)**: 448–53.
46. Büttner A, Rohrmoser K, Mall G, et al. Widespread axonal damage in the brain of drug abusers as evidenced by accumulation of beta-amyloid precursor protein (beta-APP): An immunohistochemical investigation. *Addiction* 2006; **101(9)**: 1339–46.
47. Reichard RR, Smith C, Graham DI. The significance of beta-APP immunoreactivity in forensic practice. *Neuropathol Appl Neurobiol* 2005; **31(3)**: 304–13.
48. Miller JD, Becker DP, Ward JD, et al. Significance of intracranial hypertension in severe head injury. *J Neurosurg* 1977; **47(4)**: 503–16.
49. Graham DI, Lawrence AE, Adams JH, et al. Brain damage in non-missile head injury secondary to high intracranial pressure. *Neuropathol Appl Neurobiol* 1987; **13(3)**: 209–17.
50. Marmarou A, Fatouros PP, Barzó P, et al. Contribution of edema and cerebral blood volume to traumatic brain swelling in head-injured patients. *J Neurosurg* 2000; **93(2)**: 183–93.
51. Graham DI, Ford I, Adams JH, et al. Fatal head injury in children. *J Clin Pathol* 1989; **42(1)**: 18–22.
52. Graham DI, Adams JH, Doyle D. Ischaemic brain damage in fatal non-missile head injuries. *J Neurol Sci* 1978; **39(2–3)**: 213–34.
53. Cole G, Cowie VA. Long survival after cardiac arrest: case report and neuropathological findings. *Clin Neuropathol* 1987; **6(3)**: 104–9.
54. Ackery A, Tator C, Krassioukov A. A global perspective on spinal cord injury epidemiology. *J Neurotrauma* 2004; **21(10)**: 1355–70.
55. Narang SK, Fingarson A, Lukefahr J. Abusive head trauma in infants and children. *Pediatrics* 2020; **145(4)**.
56. Parks SE, Annest JL, Hill HA, Karch DL. *Pediatric Abusive Head Trauma: Recommended Definitions for Public Health Surveillance and Research.* Atlanta, GA: Centers for Disease Control and Prevention. Atlanta, GA; 2012.
57. Duhaime AC. Demographics of abusive head trauma. *J Neurosurg Pediatr* 2008; **1(5)**: 349–50; discussion 50.
58. Keenan HT, Runyan DK, Marshall SW, et al. A population-based study of inflicted traumatic brain injury in young children. *JAMA* 2003; **290(5)**: 621–6.
59. Selassie AW, Borg K, Busch C, Russell WS. Abusive head trauma in young children: A population-based study. *Pediatr Emerg Care* 2013; **29(3)**: 283–91.
60. Hobbs C, Childs AM, Wynne J, et al. Subdural haematoma and effusion in infancy: an epidemiological study. *Arch Dis Child* 2005; **90(9)**: 952–5.
61. Bechtel K, Stoessel K, Leventhal JM, et al. Characteristics that distinguish accidental from abusive injury in hospitalized young children with head trauma. *Pediatrics* 2004; **114(1)**: 165–8.
62. Duhaime AC, Alario AJ, Lewander WJ, et al. Head injury in very young children: Mechanisms, injury types, and ophthalmologic findings in 100 hospitalized patients younger than 2 years of age. *Pediatrics* 1992; **90(2 Pt 1)**: 179–85.
63. Vinchon M, de Foort-Dhellemmes S, Desurmont M, Delestret I. Confessed abuse versus witnessed accidents in infants: comparison of clinical, radiological, and ophthalmological data in corroborated cases. *Childs Nerv Syst* 2010; **26(5)**: 637–45.
64. Matschke J, Voss J, Obi N, et al. Nonaccidental head injury is the most common cause of subdural bleeding in infants <1 year of age. *Pediatrics* 2009; **124(6)**: 1587–94.
65. Feldman KW, Bethel R, Shugerman RP, et al. The cause of infant and toddler subdural hemorrhage: a prospective study. *Pediatrics* 2001; **108(3)**: 636–46.
66. DiScala C, Sege R, Li G, Reece RM. Child abuse and unintentional injuries: a 10-year retrospective. *Arch Pediatr Adolesc Med* 2000; **154(1)**: 16–22.

67. Hymel KP, Makoroff KL, Laskey AL, et al. Mechanisms, clinical presentations, injuries, and outcomes from inflicted versus noninflicted head trauma during infancy: Results of a prospective, multi-centered, comparative study. *Pediatrics* 2007; **119**(5): 922–9.
68. Keenan HT, Runyan DK, Marshall SW, et al. A population-based comparison of clinical and outcome characteristics of young children with serious inflicted and noninflicted traumatic brain injury. *Pediatrics* 2004; **114**(3): 633–9.
69. Watts P. Abusive head trauma and the eye in infancy. *Eye (Lond)* 2013; **27**(**10**): 1227–9.
70. Bhardwaj G, Chowdhury V, Jacobs MB, et al. A systematic review of the diagnostic accuracy of ocular signs in pediatric abusive head trauma. *Ophthalmology* 2010; **117**(5): 983–92.e17.
71. Binenbaum G, Mirza-George N, Christian CW, Forbes BJ. Odds of abuse associated with retinal hemorrhages in children suspected of child abuse. *J AAPOS* 2009; **13**(3): 268–72.
72. Lantz PE, Sinal SH, Stanton CA, Weaver RG. Perimacular retinal folds from childhood head trauma. *BMJ* 2004; **328**(**7442**): 754–6.
73. Lueder GT, Turner JW, Paschall R. Perimacular retinal folds simulating nonaccidental injury in an infant. *Arch Ophthalmol* 2006; **124**(**12**): 1782–3.
74. Watts P, Obi E. Retinal folds and retinoschisis in accidental and non-accidental head injury. *Eye* 2008; **22**(**12**): 1514–16.
75. Bohn D, Armstrong D, Becker L, Humphreys R. Cervical spine injuries in children. *J Trauma* 1990; **30**(**4**): 463–9.
76. Koch LE, Biedermann H, Saternus KS. High cervical stress and apnoea. *Forensic Sci Int* 1998; **97**(**1**): 1–9.
77. Cohen MC, Scheimberg I. Evidence of occurrence of intradural and subdural hemorrhage in the perinatal and neonatal period in the context of hypoxic Ischemic encephalopathy: An observational study from two referral institutions in the United Kingdom. *Pediatr Dev Pathol* 2009; **12**(3): 169–76.
78. Geddes JF, Tasker RC, Hackshaw AK, et al. Dural haemorrhage in non-traumatic infant deaths: Does it explain the bleeding in 'shaken baby syndrome'? *Neuropathol Appl Neurobiol* 2003; **29**(1): 14–22.
79. Mack J, Squier W, Eastman JT. Anatomy and development of the meninges: implications for subdural collections and CSF circulation. *Pediatr Radiol* 2009; **39**(3): 200–10.
80. Scheimberg I, Cohen MC, Zapata Vazquez RE, et al. Nontraumatic intradural and subdural hemorrhage and hypoxic ischemic encephalopathy in fetuses, infants, and children up to three years of age: Analysis of two audits of 636 cases from two referral centers in the United Kingdom. *Pediatr Dev Pathol* 2013; **16**(3): 149–59.
81. Squier W, Mack J. The neuropathology of infant subdural haemorrhage. *Forensic Sci Int* 2009; **187**(**1–3**): 6–13.
82. Squier W. The "Shaken Baby" syndrome: Pathology and mechanisms. *Acta Neuropathol* 2011; **122**(5): 519–42.
83. Byard RW, Blumbergs P, Rutty G, et al. Lack of evidence for a causal relationship between hypoxic-ischemic encephalopathy and subdural hemorrhage in fetal life, infancy, and early childhood. *Pediatr Dev Pathol* 2007; **10**(5): 348–50.
84. Dubowitz DJ, Bluml S, Arcinue E, Dietrich RB. MR of hypoxic encephalopathy in children after near drowning: correlation with quantitative proton MR spectroscopy and clinical outcome. *AJNR Am J Neuroradiol* 1998; **19**(**9**): 1617–27.
85. Hurley M, Dineen R, Padfield CJ, et al. Is there a causal relationship between the hypoxia-ischaemia associated with cardiorespiratory arrest and subdural haematomas? An observational study. *Br J Radiol* 2010; **83**(**993**): 736–43.
86. Jaspan T. Current controversies in the interpretation of non-accidental head injury. *Pediatr Radiol* 2008; **38 Suppl 3**: S378–87.
87. Rafaat KT, Spear RM, Kuelbs C, et al. Cranial computed tomographic findings in a large group of children with drowning: diagnostic, prognostic, and forensic implications. *Pediatr Crit Care Med* 2008; 9(6): 567–72.
88. Baenziger O, Martin E, Steinlin M, et al. Early pattern recognition in severe perinatal asphyxia: a prospective MRI study. *Neuroradiology* 1993; 35(6): 437–42.
89. Barkovich AJ, Westmark K, Partridge C, et al. Perinatal asphyxia: MR findings in the first 10 days. *AJNR Am J Neuroradiol* 1995; **16**(3): 427–38.
90. Sie LT, van der Knaap MS, Oosting J, et al. MR patterns of hypoxic-ischemic brain damage after prenatal, perinatal or postnatal asphyxia. *Neuropediatrics* 2000; **31**(3): 128–36.
91. Looney CB, Smith JK, Merck LH, et al. Intracranial hemorrhage in asymptomatic neonates: Prevalence on MR images and relationship to obstetric and neonatal risk factors. *Radiology* 2007; **242**(**2**): 535–41.
92. Rooks VJ, Eaton JP, Ruess L, et al. Prevalence and evolution of intracranial hemorrhage in asymptomatic term infants. *AJNR Am J Neuroradiol* 2008; **29**(6): 1082–9.
93. Whitby EH, Griffiths PD, Rutter S, et al. Frequency and natural history of subdural haemorrhages in babies and relation to obstetric factors. *Lancet* 2004; **363**(**9412**): 846–51.
94. Friede RL. *Developmental Neuropathology*. New York: Springer-Verlag; 1975.
95. Croft PR, Reichard RR. Microscopic examination of grossly unremarkable pediatric dura mater. *Am J Forensic Med Pathol* 2009; **30**(**1**): 10–13.
96. Emerson MV, Pieramici DJ, Stoessel KM, et al. Incidence and rate of disappearance of retinal hemorrhage in newborns. *Ophthalmology* 2001; **108**(**1**): 36–9.
97. Hughes LA, May K, Talbot JF, Parsons MA. Incidence, distribution, and duration of birth-related retinal hemorrhages: a prospective study. *J AAPOS* 2006; **10**(**2**): 102–6.
98. Englander J, Bushnik T, Duong TT, et al. Analyzing risk factors for late posttraumatic seizures: a prospective, multicenter investigation. *Arch Phys Med Rehabil* 2003; **84**(3): 365–73.
99. Knight B, Saukko PJ. *Knight's forensic pathology*. 4th ed. Boca Raton: CRC Press, Taylor & Francis; 2016.

CHAPTER

36

Neck Trauma Deaths

Judith Fronczek and Hans H. de Boer

INTRODUCTION

From an anatomic perspective, the neck is a relatively narrow and unprotected part of the human body, which nonetheless contains many vital anatomic structures. Damage or injury to the airway, various major blood vessels and several neurologic structures (i.e. the carotid sinuses and the spinal cord) all have the potential to induce rapid death.

Fatal neck injury is commonly encountered in forensic pathology practice, and can be seen in the contexts of accidental, suicidal and homicidal deaths. The types of injury comprise compressive trauma, non-compressive blunt force trauma and sharp force trauma. This chapter provides an overview of the different types of fatal neck injury, the forensic pathology findings, and how these findings relate to the mechanism and manner of death. Strong emphasis is placed on the discussion of compressive trauma, including ligature strangulation and hanging, due to its frequency and sometimes challenging interpretation. For further reading on neck trauma, the monograph by Vanezis is recommended (1).

COMPRESSIVE TRAUMA

THE ANATOMIC BASIS OF AUTOPSY FINDINGS

The hyoid bone, thyroid cartilage and cricoid cartilage

The main structures that maintain an open proximal airway are the thyroid cartilage, the hyoid bone and the cricoid cartilage. Of particular forensic relevance are the structures that connect the thyroid cartilage and the hyoid bone, the horns or *cornuae*. The superior horns of the thyroid cartilage are located just below the greater horns of the hyoid bone and are connected by a fibrous membrane (thyrohyoid membrane). Due to their location and their relative gracility, these horns are prone to fracturing when force (most often compressive) is applied to the neck. Anatomic variants of the hyoid and laryngeal structures are common and include malunion of ossifications centers in the horns, extra chondroid fragments (*cartilago triticea*) in the thyrohyoid membrane, and underdeveloped horns (2). Previous trauma may also cause angulation of the horns. It is pivotal that these findings are not mistaken for injuries. Fractures of the thyroid cartilage and the cricoid (the upper tracheal ring just below the thyroid cartilage) are less common. They are, however, more commonly seen after blunt force trauma than compressive force to the neck (3). With advancing age, the horns of the thyroid cartilage and hyoid bone will calcify and become more brittle. In children and adolescents, when these structures are still mostly cartilaginous, fractures are almost never seen.

Damage to the thyroid cartilage, hyoid bone and cricoid cartilage is not lethal in itself, but rather is an indication of significant trauma to the neck. It is the concomitant compression or injury to other neck structures that comprises the lethal potential of neck trauma.

Veins and arteries

Both anterior compartments of the neck contain major veins and arteries which, with their soft, pliable walls, are easy to compress. Depending on the vessel type, applied force and duration of compression, this may result in rapid unconsciousness and death, and produce typical findings at autopsy. Although veins and arteries are discussed separately below, it should be remembered that isolated compression of veins or arteries is exceedingly rare, and that the effects of venous and arterial compression interact.

The jugular veins

Compression of the jugular veins will severely impede venous return from the head and neck to the body, rapidly causing signs of congestion. This development is enhanced if the carotid arteries are not fully compressed simultaneously. The neck and head above the occlusion will become congested within seconds after total occlusion. If the pressure increases enough for venules to burst, petechial hemorrhages will appear, especially in the soft tissues where these small vessels are less well-supported by surrounding connective tissue. Favored areas are the conjunctivae, the oral mucous membranes and, less commonly, the skin of the face (Figure 36.1a–c). Petechiae do not appear as quickly as the other congestive signs, but once present will remain visible (sometimes for days) after release. As such, they may be the only lasting sign

DOI: 10.1201/9781003138754-38

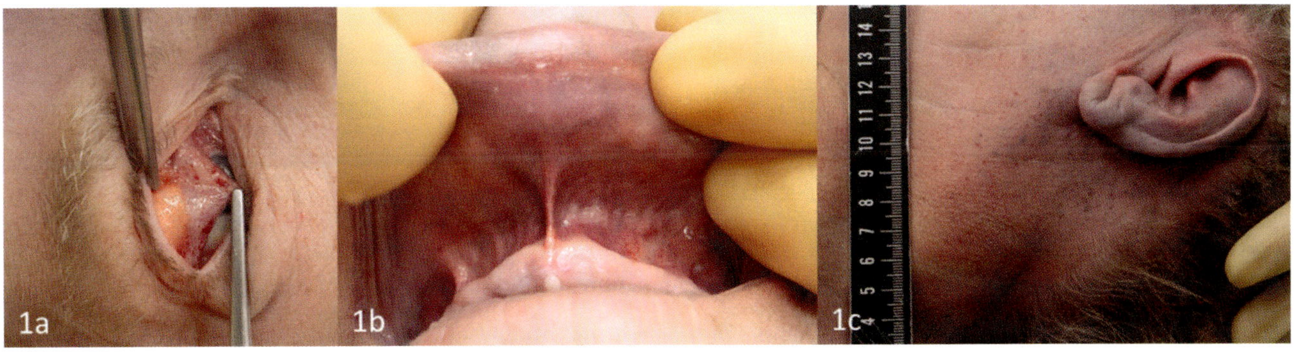

36.1 Petechial hemorrhages in the conjunctiva of the eye **(a)**, the mucosa of the lips **(b)** and the skin of the face and behind the ears **(c)** in a death due to manual strangulation. (Photos courtesy of the Netherlands Forensic Institute.)

of neck compression, not only in deceased individuals, but also in survivors.

It should be noted that congestion and petechial hemorrhages are by no means specific for compression of the neck. In essence, any substantial impediment to venous return from the head and neck can induce these "classical" features of asphyxia. Such instances include compressive force to the abdomen or chest (e.g. in the context of mechanical or positional asphyxia), pooling of blood (e.g. due to a head-down position), resuscitation, or even a sudden rise in pressure in the head due to forceful sneezing or during delivery at birth. The interpretation of petechial hemorrhages therefore requires careful consideration of contextual information.

The carotid arteries, including the carotid sinuses

Compression of the carotid arteries requires more force than compression of the jugular veins, due to a combination of their thicker vessel wall, their location deeper in the neck and their higher internal (blood) pressure. Total occlusion of both carotid arteries will limit the supply of oxygen-rich blood to the brain to such an extent that unconsciousness ensues after 10–30 seconds, and irreversible brain damage may occur after minutes (minimum approximately 4–5 minutes). When total occlusion of the carotid artery occurs, "classical" asphyxia signs will be absent, and the face will be pale, so-called "white asphyxia".

The common carotid artery wall near the bifurcation also contains nerve endings with baroreceptors (the carotid sinus or *sinus caroticus*), which monitor blood pressure and regulate cardiac output to maintain brain oxygenation. Pressure or tensile stress on these baroreceptors can induce tachycardia, bradycardia and syncope via the parasympathetic nervous system and the vagal reflex. These effects may contribute to the mechanism of death in neck compression cases.

In addition, compression of the baroreceptors has also been implicated as the cause of so-called "reflex cardiac arrhythmia/arrest", a term used by some to explain sudden death following neck compression with a lack of congestive features. However, although included in most forensic medicine or pathology textbooks as a potential mechanism of death (4,5), there are no published lethal cases in which death has been solely attributed to reflex cardiac arrest (6). On the other hand, reflex cardiac arrest has been described in clinical settings, namely bradycardia and cardiac arrest elicited by tension on extraocular muscles (oculocardiac reflex) or the abdominal wall (7,8). It seems prudent to only introduce reflex cardiac arrest as a potential mechanism of death when death remains unexplained after extensive investigation, and to do so with great caution. In most cases, the (non) existence of "reflex cardiac arrest" due to carotid baroreceptor compression is of limited significance.

Airways

With its rigid cartilaginous rings, the upper airway is relatively well-protected against obstruction due to external force. Death due to compression of the airways alone is therefore rare. In addition, due to the reserves of oxygen in the lungs and blood, limiting the air supply to the lungs is considered to present less (rapid) lethal potential than compression of veins and arteries.

Given the anatomic relation between the laryngeal structures, the tongue and the nasopharynx, indirect compression of the airways can also occur. When pressure is applied at or superiorly to the hyoid bone, the tongue is pushed against the roof of the mouth, occluding the (naso)pharynx. If sustained for a period of time, this blockage can contribute to hypoxemia.

In addition, the vertebral arteries, which travel through the cervical spine to the base of the skull, may be damaged. The intracranial part of the vertebral artery, however, is most vulnerable. Damage of the vertebral artery may result in basal subarachnoid hemorrhage.

Nowadays, with post-mortem imaging being more and more ubiquitous in forensic pathology practice, it has become indispensable for a rapid diagnosis of cervical spine injury.

TYPES OF FATAL NECK COMPRESSION

HANGING

Hanging is a specific type of ligature strangulation, in which the compressive force of the ligature to the neck is provided by the body weight of the deceased. The manner of death in most cases is suicide. Rarely, hanging occurs in the setting of an accident, that is, when subjects are unable to free themselves from a position in which the neck is entangled. This is usually seen in inebriated or otherwise impaired adults, or in children. Homicidal hangings are rare and are usually limited to those cases in which the victim is significantly smaller/weaker and/or is incapacitated, for instance due to intoxication. Infrequently, hangings are staged to cover up a homicide, for example, after ligature strangulation. If there are features at the scene that point toward some kind of paraphilia, for example sex toys, certain clothing/accessories, videos or photos with a sexual context, and/or mechanisms that facilitate near-hanging, an auto-erotic incident needs to be considered. Those cases are usually correctly classified as accidental, although some of them may represent suicide (see below).

In the forensic pathology literature, a distinction is made between typical vs atypical and complete vs incomplete hangings. In typical hangings, the point of suspension is located at the nape of the neck, although some authors include all cases in which the suspension is located behind the ears (5,9). In atypical hangings, the point of suspension is at any site other than the nape of the neck. Complete hangings constitute those in which the body is entirely suspended, while incomplete hangings are defined by the fact that some part of the body (most often the feet or legs) are still being supported. Incomplete hangings are very common, and in many such cases the suspension point is at quite a low level (e.g. doorknobs, radiators), with the deceased being found in a sitting, lying or kneeling position.

The classical asphyxia signs of congestion and petechial hemorrhages are variably present in hanging cases. Especially in complete, typical hangings, the deceased may rather have a strikingly pale face without petechiae. Some classical forensic pathology textbooks attribute this to the aforementioned "reflex cardiac arrest" (4). However, an alternative explanation is provided by bilateral total occlusion of the carotid arteries, limiting blood supply to the head and neck to such an extent that no congestion occurs (the aforementioned "white asphyxia"). In incomplete and atypical hangings, total compression of the carotids is less common, and signs of congestion are more often seen.

Close examination of the ligature mark is essential in each hanging case, as it may provide critical information about the method of hanging. During examination, the effects of post-mortem alteration on the ligature mark should be considered. The mark may initially only be visible as blanching in an area of post-mortem lividity. With time, the mark may become brown or red and parchmented in appearance. This is especially the case when the skin is abraded, due to use of a firm and structured ligature (i.e. a rope); such patterned ligature marks can often be compared to (potential) ligatures. The mark left by a wide, soft ligature can remain pale or be virtually invisible, making comparison much more difficult, if not impossible. Ligature marks ordinarily display a *punctum maximum*, that is, a location where the mark/injury is most severe. This is generally the lowest point of the mark and located on the opposite side of the suspension point (or *apex*). In incomplete hangings with a low point of suspension, the ligature mark may lie in an almost horizontal plane, and these features are less clear. Next to the ligature mark there may be abrasions, caused by gliding of the ligature over the skin in the process of suspension. A slipknot or slip-noose will usually result in a ligature mark around the full circumference of the neck, sometimes leaving an imprint of the knot at the suspension point. When a non-sliding knot is used, the ligature mark is usually deficient at the point of suspension. When the ligature encircles the neck more than once, skin folds between the loops may show red discoloration due to blood extravasation. Also, the skin above the ligature mark may show red discoloration as a result of hypostatic blood pooling. Both findings, as well as the ligature mark itself, are no proof of vitality (10).

Bruising, either in the skin or the subcutaneous tissues, is found in the minority of cases. If present, such hemorrhages are most frequently found at the origin of the sternocleidomastoid muscles (11), sometimes with rupture of muscle fibers (12). Other associated findings include fractures of the larynx, most frequently, the superior horns of the thyroid cartilage. These usually display minimal or no surrounding hemorrhage. The reported incidence of fractures varies significantly, which is believed to be in part due to different dissection techniques (12–14).

Some hanging cases present with abrasions on other parts of the body, mostly frequently on the arms and legs, caused by knocking into objects during the convulsive phase, one of the phases observed in filmed hangings (15). Scene information is instrumental for adequate interpretation of these findings. Hemorrhages can also be observed anteriorly to the intervertebral discs, most commonly of the lumbar spine. These "Simon's bleedings" are likely due to a combination of traction and spasms during the convulsive phase (16). In a minority of cases, tears in the intima of the carotid arteries can be seen. In case of a long-drop hanging, for instance, after jumps from heights or in judicial hangings, fractures of the cervical spine, or even decapitation may occur (17,18).

Sometimes, when the ligature has detached from the suspension point, it can be difficult to differentiate between hanging and other forms of ligature strangulation (see below). This is especially so in incomplete hangings, if the ligature mark lies in a horizontal plane. In these cases, a proper scene investigation is mandatory.

OTHER FORMS OF LIGATURE STRANGULATION

Other forms of ligature strangulation are most often homicidal, although suicidal ligature strangulation not involving hanging has been reported (10). Such suicides can only be successful if the ligature is applied in such a way that it does not release after loss of consciousness. Tie-wraps can serve this purpose, and the authors have examined a rare case of suicide in which a tight, thick rope was wound around the neck multiple times, causing it to remain in place. Accidental ligature strangulation is rare, and the circumstances will often readily point to the nonintentional nature of the death.

A particular type of ligature strangulation is so-called "garroting", sometimes also known as the "Spanish windlass". The terms strictly refer to the tightening of a ligature around the neck by twisting it with a lever, for instance a stick or rod. Historically, garroting was prevalent in the nineteenth century during robbery. The victim was approached from behind with a chain, rope or wire which was quickly tightened around the throat. The resultant abrupt collapse would allow the assailant to then tighten the ligature further with one or more turns. The term Spanish windlass was used as garroting, namely as a mode of judicial execution, albeit sometimes with the addition of a sharp spike that was forced into the back of the neck, penetrating the spinal cord (19,20). Both suicidal and accidental forms of garroting have been reported (21).

Most cases of ligature strangulation will display signs of asphyxia with congestion, edema and/or cyanosis of the skin above the ligature mark. Petechial hemorrhages are oftentimes florid, especially in the conjunctiva of the eyes, the oral mucosa surfaces and the facial skin. In severe cases, petechiae behind the ears, nose and ear bleeds, and hemorrhages in the tongue can also be observed. This has been termed the "masque ecchymotique". The extensiveness of these signs is a product of the dynamics of (homicidal) ligature strangulation as the continuous movement of perpetrator and victim precludes continuous occlusion of the carotids, while the bracing and resistance of the victim increase their intrathoracic pressure.

The historically described "classic signs" of asphyxia, comprising cyanosis, persistent liquidity of blood, petechiae, right-sided cardiac dilatation and visceral congestion, were dismissed as proof that death resulted from mechanical asphyxia in the second half of the twentieth century (22). The changes are so non-specific that they are also referred to as the "obsolete diagnostic quintet".

As in hangings, examination of the ligature mark and other injuries is essential to help determine the cause and manner of death. The mark may range from readily visible in case of a thin, structured and rigid ligature, to totally absent in case of wide, soft material. Suicidal cases usually have a single ligature mark, multiple ligature marks are more commonly seen in accidental and (most often) homicidal cases, due to reapplication of the ligature. Compared to hangings, the mark in homicidal cases is usually located lower on the neck, sitting in a horizontal plane or showing a downward slant. Exceptions to this rule may occur, but this is ordinarily only possible when the victim is much smaller or is positioned much lower than the perpetrator.

Additional superficial abrasions above and below the ligature mark may represent fingernail scratching, as a result of attempts of the victim to remove the ligature. A higher frequency of skin bruising, or subcutaneous and neck muscle hemorrhages is also seen in these cases (10). Fractures of the larynx and hyoid bone can occur: most frequently of the horns of the thyroid cartilage, less commonly of the hyoid bone, and rarely of the cricoid cartilage.

MANUAL STRANGULATION

The manner of death in manual strangulation is almost invariably homicide and is often seen in conjunction with other signs of injury. Strangling an unincapacitated adult requires considerable force and stamina, and this is reflected by the fact that women and children are the most common victims. Accidental cases are exceedingly rare but can occur in the context of sadomasochistic sexual practices (23,24).

As in non-hanging ligature strangulation, florid congestive signs are a common occurrence. This is because the grip of the perpetrator tends to occlude the jugular veins (continuously or intermittently), without totally occluding the carotid arteries. The grip of the perpetrator ordinarily results in abundant bruising of the neck, sometimes these are discoid, reflecting the fingertips of the perpetrator. They can be observed at every location of the neck, due to the dynamics of the process, but are most often observed in the laryngeal area, below the lower jaw, and at the sides of the neck. The nape of the neck is another common location. Such bruises are generally more widespread and more extensive than in all types of ligature strangulation. Exceptions however occur, for instance, in cases of a single grip in a relatively defenseless victim (10) (Figure 36.2a). Fractures of the larynx and/or hyoid bone are also encountered more often. Again, the superior horns of the thyroid cartilage are most often fractured (Figure 36.2b), but fractures of the hyoid bone are also common. Fractures of the thyroid and cricoid cartilage are rare, but more often seen than in ligature strangulation (3).

The injuries caused by the perpetrator can be compounded by the attempts of the victim to remove the perpetrator's hands. This may result in bruising, but often linear or curvilinear fingernail scratches are also present. However, since the perpetrator's hands could equally cause such markings, they cannot readily be interpreted as signs of struggle.

SEXUAL ASPHYXIA

A specific type of compressive neck trauma is sexual asphyxia. Without any awareness of the entity, these deaths could be mistakenly regarded as suicides, while most cases are accidental, although some cases of paraphilic suicide have been reported (25). Sexual asphyxia can be seen in the setting of auto-erotic practice, that is, only involving the victim, or in the setting of sadomasochistic practice, that is, including other individuals. The persistent interest of individuals into engaging in sexual asphyxia relates to the effects of cerebral oxygen deprivation, which is stated to increase the physical and emotional sexual response for some. Interestingly, autoerotic asphyxia deaths involving women are rare (26,27).

In most auto-erotic deaths, the scene readily suggests the context of the case, exhibiting paraphernalia including sex toys, typical clothing (e.g. fetishistic rubber, latex and lingerie), pornographic material, and so on.

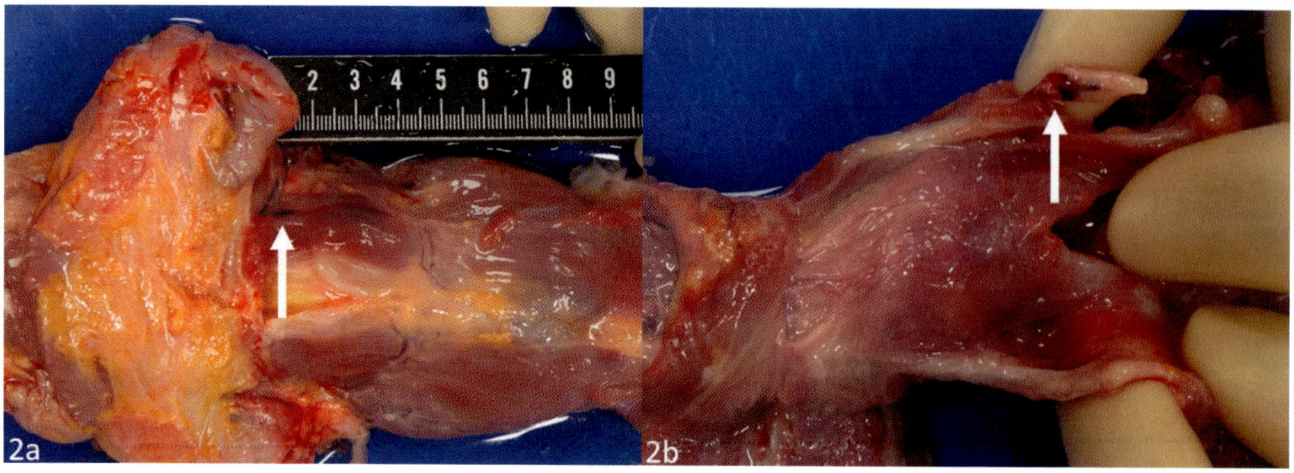

36.2 Internal findings in the same manual strangulation case depicted in Figure 36.1. (a) Layered dissection of the strap muscles in a bloodless field revealed only one small hemorrhage (arrow) in the left deeper neck muscle overlying the thyroid cartilage (*musculus thyrohyoideus*). (b) Examination of the thyroid cartilage revealed a fracture of the left cornu superior of the thyroid cartilage with surrounding hemorrhage (arrow). (Photos courtesy of the Netherlands Forensic Institute.)

There may be evidence of repetitive activity. On some occasions, ingenious complex neck compression devices have been constructed, incorporating a "fail safe" mechanism by which the user can free him or herself from the asphyxia-inducing apparatus (28). If the "fail safe" fails however, asphyxial death ensues. When more than one person is involved in the sexual act, intent, that is, homicidal strangulation, needs to be excluded. Depending on the ligature or device used, the findings are consistent with the findings in ligature strangulation. There are no specific external or internal findings. For further reading on auto-erotic deaths see Chapter 65.

NON-COMPRESSIVE BLUNT FORCE TRAUMA

The majority of cases with non-compressive blunt force trauma to the neck occur in the setting of motor vehicle crashes. Less frequently, they are found in the setting of falls, during sport activities, or assaults. Essentially, injuries can be classified as indirect and direct, with indirect injuries including hyperextension, hyperflexion and rotation of the neck. Depending on the mechanism, the type and location of injuries differs. Careful examination is therefore a powerful tool to help infer the mechanism of trauma. More so than in compressive trauma, external injuries may be minimal while internal injuries can be extensive. If external injuries are present, attention to patterned injuries is essential, for instance to identify stamping with a shoed foot.

Internally, the injuries are usually more severe and more extensive than with compressive forces. Also, the type and location of injuries is different. Displacement or even crushing of the structures that maintain the airway can occur, causing narrowing or obstruction of the air passages. In cases of traumatic disruption of the laryngeal structures, laryngeal nerves may also be damaged. Ligamentous and mucosal lacerations and hemorrhage may be encountered.

Injuries to vascular structures are much less often encountered. In older individuals, damage of an atheromatous artery can, however, lead to plaque rupture and thrombus formation. Damage of the vertebral artery may be the result of a fracture that runs through the transverse foramina of the 2nd to the 6th cervical vertebrae. Vertebral artery dissection or tearing can occur, due to blows or kicks to the side of the neck resulting in rotational forces. It is thought that the blood can track along the vessel and enter the cranial cavity, resulting in basal subarachnoid hemorrhage. However, some controversy exists as to whether cervical vertebral artery dissection is the actual cause of the subarachnoid hemorrhage or whether the subarachnoid hemorrhage has a different etiology (4).

Injuries to the spinal vertebrae can either be the result of direct impact to the vertebrae or indirect trauma. Indirect trauma can be sustained during acceleration/deceleration or due to trauma directed to other parts of the body, for instance to the skull or chest. The spinal cord, being contained within the cervical vertebral column, is arguably the most protected vital structure of the neck. Injuries to the spine and spinal cord are therefore generally only seen in cases of severe blunt force trauma, including acceleration-deceleration and rotational forces to the neck. Dislocation or fracture of the cervical vertebrae can impact the spinal cord. Depending on the location of the spinal cord injury, this may result in loss of vital functions, such as respiration and heart rhythm.

SHARP FORCE TRAUMA

After the chest, the neck is the most common part of the body to sustain fatal sharp force injuries. Although a knife is the most used implement, a variety of pointed or sharp implements can cause these injuries, for example glass, screwdrivers, fragments of a metal can, and so on. The manner of death can be homicidal, suicidal or accidental, although the latter are much rarer. In the authors' experience, suicidal cases often involve a psychiatric and/or toxicologic element. Forensic pathologists are often asked to differentiate between homicidal or suicidal sharp force. With an increase in the number of injuries, a homicide becomes more likely, especially when considering injuries on other body parts. "Defense-type" injuries are said to favor a homicidal death, while "hesitation wounds" point toward a suicidal death. These terms are however dangerously suggestive, since the terms already imply a specific type of intent, while their specificity and sensitivity are far from perfect. Accidental sharp force injuries to the neck are uncommon but are encountered in certain settings. One of the authors (JF) autopsied such a case of accidental sharp force injury: a woman who had been drinking wine at home, who tripped and fell on her broken wine glass, injuring her left common carotid artery in the process, causing hypovolemic shock.

For further discussion of sharp force death (*see* Chapter 41 – "Sharp Force Injuries").

Stab wounds

It was demonstrated in a prospective study that 20 percent of stab wounds to the neck were associated with significant injuries to vital structures (29). Of the vascular structures of the neck, the common carotid artery is most often injured, although injuries to the veins are also common (30). Both may cause rapid and life-threatening blood loss. Being protected by the cervical vertebrae, one could assume that the vertebral arteries are not frequently injured, but the authors have seen several cases of homicide in which posterior stab wounds severed vertebral arteries. Air embolism is another lethal mechanism that may result from severing of neck veins. Even if the blood vessels are not directly injured, tensile stretch may damage the endovascular lining, causing thrombosis and subsequent brain ischemia. With prolonged survival, a pseudoaneurysm may develop.

Direct sharp force injury to the airway can be lethal, most commonly by inducing blood inhalation and subsequent asphyxia.

Injuries to the spinal cord from sharp weapons are relatively uncommon, and, depending on the location of the injury, can lead to instantaneous loss of vital functions and death. In this respect, stab wounds that enter the neck laterally are more dangerous than stab wounds that enter posteriorly. Laterally oriented stab wounds may enter the spinal canal between two vertebrae; in posteriorly directed stab wounds, the implement can be deflected by the spinal processes (31,32). Most frequently, such stab wounds travel downward or in a horizontal plane (30). If a knife meets the osseous parts of the spinal column, it may leave grooves or scratches in the bone, or the tip may break and stay behind in the body. The retained piece of metal can then be fitted to the alleged weapon; a so-called "souche". By means of micro-trace analysis, it can be possible to profile the composition of the used weapon (33).

Incised wounds

Incised wounds to the neck are also called "slash" wounds or "cut-throat" wounds. Many textbooks describe a typical appearance of self-inflicted throat cuts, with the wound usually being higher on the non-dominant side of the individual, passing downward across the anterior neck to a lower point on the dominant side. Such injuries are also said to be deeper at the origin than at the end (4,34,35). There are however many exceptions to this much-repeated description, and the differentiation between homicidal or suicidal wounds can be very challenging (36–38).

Internally, incised wounds generally injure the same structures as in stab wounds. In a recent autopsy study, injury to an external jugular vein was most common, but also the trachea, carotid arteries and internal jugular veins were frequently injured (39).

REFERENCES

1. Vanezis P. *Pathology of Neck Injury*. Oxford: Butterworth-Heinemann; 1989.
2. de Bakker BS, de Bakker HM, Soerdjbalie-Maikoe V, Dikkers FG. Variants of the hyoid-larynx complex, with implications for forensic science and consequence for the diagnosis of Eagle's syndrome. *Sci Rep* 2019; **9**(**1**): 1–10.
3. Godin A, Kremer C, Sauvageau A. Fracture of the cricoid as a potential pointer to homicide: a 6-year retrospective study of neck structures fractures in hanging victims. *Am J Forensic Med Pathol* 2012; **33**(**1**): 4–7.
4. Saukko P, Knight B (eds). *Knight's Forensic Pathology*. Boca Raton: CRC Press; 2015.
5. Van de Voorde W. *Handboek Forensische Geneeskunde*. Brugge: Die Keure; 2010.
6. Schrag B, Vaucher P, Bollmann MD, Mangin P. Death caused by cardioinhibitory reflex cardiac arrest—a systematic review of cases. *Forensic Sci Int* 2011; **207**(**1–3**): 77–83.
7. Lynch MJ, Parker H. Forensic aspects of ocular injury. *Am J Forensic Med Pathol* 2000; **21**(**2**): 124–6.
8. Arnold RW. The oculocardiac reflex: A review. *Clin Ophthalmol (Auckland, NZ)* 2021; **15**: 2693.
9. Plattner T, Yen K, Zollinger U, et al. Differentiation of typical and atypicial hanging. *Rechtsmedizin* 2004; **14**(**4**): 266–70.
10. Madea B. *Handbook of Forensic Medicine*. Chichester: John Wiley & Sons; 2014.
11. Keil W, Forster A, Meyer HJ, Peschel O. Characterization of haemorrhages at the origin of the sternocleidomastoid muscles in hanging. *Int Journal Legal Med* 1995; **108**(**3**): 140–4.
12. Jayaprakash S, Sreekumari K. Pattern of injuries to neck structures in hanging: An autopsy study. *Am Journal Forensic Med Pathol* 2012; 33(**4**): 395–9.
13. Clément R, Guay J-P, Sauvageau A. Fracture of the neck structures in suicidal hangings: a retrospective study on contributing variables. *Forensic Sci Int* 2011; **207**(**1–3**): 122–6.
14. Zátopková L, Janík M, Urbanová P, et al. Laryngohyoid fractures in suicidal hanging: a prospective autopsy study with an updated review and critical appraisal. *Forensic Sci Int* 2018; **290**: 70–84.
15. Sauvageau A. Agonal sequences in four filmed hangings: analysis of respiratory and movement responses to asphyxia by hanging. *J Forensic Sci* 2009; **54**(**1**): 192–4.
16. Kleiber M, Koops E, Puschel K, et al. Pathology of hanging with special reference to vital reactions. *Beitr Gerichtl Med* 1982; **40**: 117–21.
17. Matschke J, Hildebrand E, Puschel K. An extraordinary case of death-Decapitation

via hanging in a murder-suicide. *Kriminalistik* 1999; **53(10)**: 687–8.
18. Pankratz H, Schuller E, Josephi E. Decapitation by hanging. *Arch Kriminol* 1986; **178(5–6)**: 157–61.
19. Damjanov I. *Knight's Forensic Pathology.* Boca Raton: CRC Press; 2004.
20. Johnson H. The essentials of forensic medicine. *J Clin Pathol* 1985; **38(9)**: 1083.
21. Maloney MS. *Asphyxiation: Death Scene Investigation.* Boca Raton: CRC Press; 2017, pp. 155–70.
22. Adelson L. *The Pathology of Homicide: A Vade Mecum for Pathologist, Prosecutor and Defense Counsel.* Springfield, IL: Charles C Thomas Pub Ltd; 1974.
23. Byard RW. Autoerotic death: Characteristic features and diagnostic difficulties. *J Clin Forensic Med* 1994; **1(2)**: 71–8.
24. Byard RW, Bramwell NH. Autoerotic death: A definition. *Am J Forensic Med and Pathol* 1991; **12(1)**: 74–6.
25. Byard R, Botterill P. Autoerotic asphyxial death-accident or suicide? *American J Forensic Med Pathol* 1998; **19(4)**: 377–80.
26. Byard RW, Hucker SJ, Hazelwood RR. A comparison of typical death scene features in cases of fatal male and female autoerotic asphyxia with a review of the literature. *Forensic Sci Int* 1990; **48(2)**: 113–21.
27. Byard RW, Hucker SJ, Hazelwood RR. Fatal and near-fatal autoerotic asphyxial episodes in women. *Am J Forensic Med Pathol* 1993; **14(1)**: 70–3.
28. Shields LB, Hunsaker DM, Hunsaker III JC. Autoerotic asphyxia: Part I. *Am J Forensic Med Pathol* 2005; **26(1)**: 45–52.
29. Demetriades D, Theodorou D, Cornwell E, et al. Evaluation of penetrating injuries of the neck: Prospective study of 223 patients. *World J Surg* 1997; **21(1)**: 41–8.
30. Vanezis P. *Pathology of Sharp Force Trauma.* Boca Raton: CRC Press; 2021.
31. Peacock W, Shrosbree RD, Key A. A review of 450 stabwounds of the spinal cord. *S Afr Med J* 1977; **51(26)**: 961–4.
32. Rubin G, Tallman D, Sagan L, Melgar M. An unusual stab wound of the cervical spinal cord: A case report. *Spine* 2001; **26(4)**: 444–7.
33. Palazzo E, Amadasi A, Boracchi M, et al. The detection of metallic residues in skin stab wounds by means of SEM-EDS: A pilot study. *Sci Justice* 2018; **58(3)**: 232–6.
34. Mason K, Purdue B. *The Pathology of Trauma.* Boca Raton: CRC Press; 1999.
35. Spitz WU, Spitz DJ, Fisher RS. *Spitz and Fisher's Medicolegal Investigation of Death: Guidelines for the Application of Pathology to Crime Investigation.* Springfield, IL: Charles C Thomas Pub Ltd; 2006.
36. Brunel C, Fermanian C, Durigon M, de la Grandmaison GL. Homicidal and suicidal sharp force fatalities: autopsy parameters in relation to the manner of death. *Forensic Sci Int* 2010; **198(1–3)**: 150–4.
37. Karger B, Niemeyer J, Brinkmann B. Suicides by sharp force: Typical and atypical features. *Int J Legal Med* 2000; **113(5)**: 259–62.
38. Racette S, Kremer C, Desjarlais A, Sauvageau A. Suicidal and homicidal sharp force injury: a 5-year retrospective comparative study of hesitation marks and defense wounds. *Forensic Sci Med Pathol* 2008; **4(4)**: 221–7.
39. Rao D. An autopsy study of 74 cases of cut throat injuries. *Egypt J Forensic Sci* 2015; 5(4): 144–9.

CHAPTER

37

Spinal Trauma Deaths

Jakob Matschke

INTRODUCTION

Although less common than craniocerebral trauma, spinal cord trauma (SCT) occurs worldwide with an annual incidence of approximately 23 cases per million persons. It mostly affects males in their 3rd decade or over 70 years of age. Causes are motor vehicle crashes, falls, interpersonal violence and recreational injuries. Since SCT often causes life-changing, debilitating conditions for patients, it poses a significant human, public health and economic burden worldwide. On average, patients with SCT show significantly lower life expectancies than persons without SCT. Mortality rates are significantly higher during the first year after injury than during subsequent years. Distinct from craniocerebral trauma, the neuropathology, and forensic issues of SCT have received comparatively little attention in the literature. After a brief overview on anatomic, epidemiologic, clinical, and biomechanical aspects of SCT, this chapter provides an in-depth discussion on the neuropathology and forensic issues of SCT.

ANATOMIC, EPIDEMIOLOGIC, CLINICAL AND BIOMECHANICAL ASPECTS

The spinal cord is an extension of the brain residing in the spinal canal of the vertebral column originating at the cervicomedullary junction and terminating at the conus medullaris and the fibres of the filum terminale. The nerve cells of the spinal cord are located centrally while the white matter tracts are to be found at the periphery. Each of the 31 segments of the spinal cord (8 cervical, 12 thoracic, 5 lumbar, 5 sacral and 1 coccygeal) holds an entering dorsal root and an exiting ventral root. In its relatively small cross-sectional area of around 1 cm, the spinal cord harbors basically all the motor, somatosensory and visceral innervation of the body from the head downward. Thus, injury to the spinal cord often causes devastating, life-changing neurologic conditions for patients. An acute injury with complete or almost complete severance of the spinal cord will result in complete flaccid paralysis (i.e. paraplegia or quadriplegia), in loss of sensation below the level of the lesion, and suspension of all reflex functions. This condition is commonly referred to as the first stage of spinal shock (areflexia), which usually after a period of a few weeks will turn into the second stage of heightened reflex activity (1–4). Clinically, the extent and severity of SCT or any other, non-traumatic, spinal cord injury is based on the assessment of sensory and motor function following the International Standards for Neurological Classification of Spinal Cord Injury (ISNCSCI) published by the American Spinal Injury Association (ASIA) (5).

The global incidence of SCT is estimated at about 23 new cases per 1 million persons each year (6–8). The figure varies considerably depending upon conditions in individual countries and regions, and variations in study design also need to be considered. While for Western Europe, the estimated median for new cases is around 16 per million persons each year, in North America the incidence rises to 40 (8). With 195.4 new cases per million persons each year, one of the highest reported incidences of SCT is from a regional orthopedic center in the West of Ireland (9).

SCT mainly affects males between 20 and 29 years of age and again in later life (70+). The male-to-female ratio is at least 2:1. In general, the cervical spine is most commonly involved in spine injuries. Motor vehicle crashes and falls account for most cases, followed by interpersonal violence (mostly gunshot wounds followed by stabbing), work-related accidents, and recreational injuries (10–16). Historically, much of our understanding of SCT comes from experiences during warfare (17–21).

SCT usually occurs with traumatic impact to the vertebral column, resulting in dislocation of bony components. Since the head and the neck form one functional-anatomic continuum, head loading often also implies neck loading; thus, the cervical spine is the most frequently injured segment of the spinal cord. Usually, one of the following mechanisms is involved: (i) persistent compression by displacement of osseous fragments; (ii) transient compression following hyperextension; (iii) distraction due to stretching or tearing of the vertebral column in the axial plane; (iv) laceration/transection by penetrating injuries or dislocation of sharp bone fragments (2,22,23). These changes cause the initial primary injury to the spinal cord, which as early as within minutes of the initiating traumatic event is followed by

DOI: 10.1201/9781003138754-39

secondary injuries. The latter comprise hypoxic-ischemic damage, disturbance in ionic homeostasis, excitotoxicity, free radical formation, calcium influx, and lipid peroxidation, leading to progressive tissue degeneration (22). In rare cases, injuries due to military firearms may cause concussive injury secondary to shock wave or temporal cavitation injury to the cord without actual primary pathomorphologic damage (20,24,25). In comparison with cranial epidural hematoma (EDH), significant space-occupying spinal EDH is exceedingly rare after SCT (26). Spinal EDH rather occurs spontaneously, in persons with coagulation disorders, due to vascular malformations, or as a complication of spinal manipulation therapy or similar procedures (27–31). Spinal subdural hematomas (SDH) may also result from extension of their cranial counterparts but may also occur on their own (32). The percentage of children with SCT is less than 5 percent of adult SCT (33). Due to the highly malleable properties of the vertebral column in children, spinal cord injury in children from birth up to 10 years of age might occur without radiologic or pathological signs of damage to the osseo-ligamentous apparatus of the vertebral column, a condition that has been given the acronym of SCIWORA, which stands for spinal cord injury without radiologic abnormality (34–37).

NEUROPATHOLOGY OF SPINAL CORD TRAUMA

In comparison with the huge body of literature on the neuropathology of craniocerebral trauma, the reader will find only very little concerning SCT. Fortunately, the basic principles of the neuropathology of brain trauma and its stereotyped reactions also apply to spinal trauma. Due to the intimate anatomic association between the vertebral column, the ligamentous apparatus and the spinal cord proper, the forensic pathologist is well advised to use post-mortem computed tomography (PMCT) before the removal of the spinal cord during autopsy, lest any traumatic changes go unnoticed (38,39). In addition, pre-mortem CT scans, if any, should be requested from the treating hospitals. Usually, in SCT, the cord may have suffered contusions with or without associated hemorrhage, compressive damage, lacerations, or transections (Figures 37.2 and 37.3). Damage may be mild, moderate, or

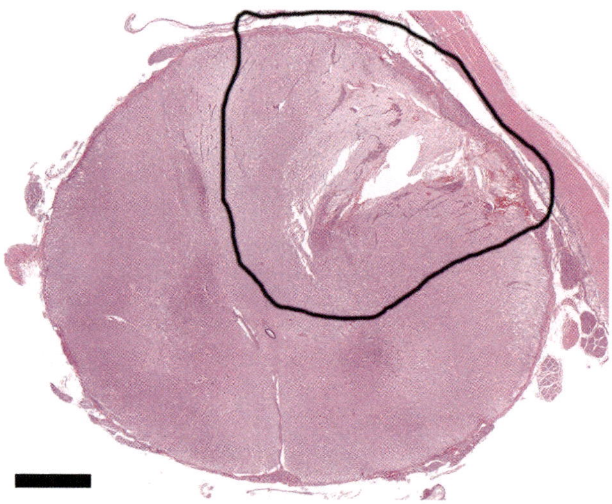

37.1 Transverse section of the cervical cord of a 13-week-old female infant who died 4 days after combined severe blunt head injury and abusive head trauma. The accused father declared that the infant fell from his arms after which he fell upon her and then gave her a “hard shake”, allegedly in an attempt to “resuscitate” her. The histopathological section clearly shows a superficial contusion (outlined), while the cervical vertebral column showed neither radiologic abnormalities in a CT scan nor pathomorphological findings during autopsy. (H&E stain, scale bar 1 mm.)

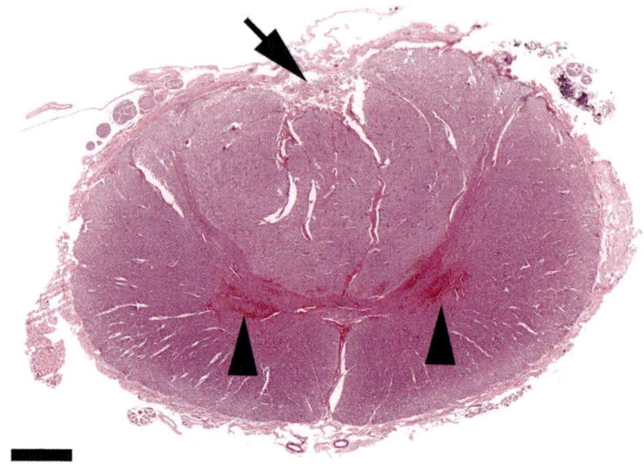

37.2 Transverse section of the upper cervical cord of an 88-year-old man who died 3 days after he slipped and fell backward. He sustained severe blunt head injury with a massive, fatal subdural hematoma and a fracture of the dens axis. The histopathological section shows a superficial contusion (arrow) and fresh hemorrhagic necrosis of the gray matter of the cord (arrowheads) due to secondary hypoxic-ischemic injury. (H&E stain, scale bar 1 mm.)

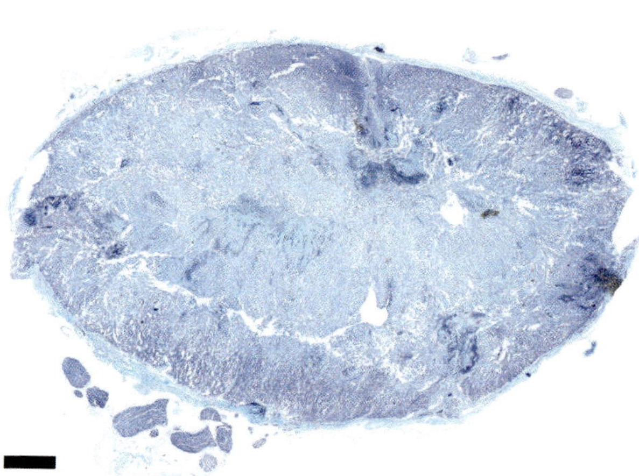

37.3 Transverse section of the upper cervical cord of a 57-year-old man who died 7 days after a motor vehicle crash with a head on collision at an estimated speed of 30–36 km/h. The man had not been wearing his seat belt and sustained a fracture of the dens axis due to employment of the airbag of the vehicle. The histopathological section shows a massive subtotal contusional injury. (Kluever-Barrera´s stain, scale bar 1 mm.) (Case from [72].)

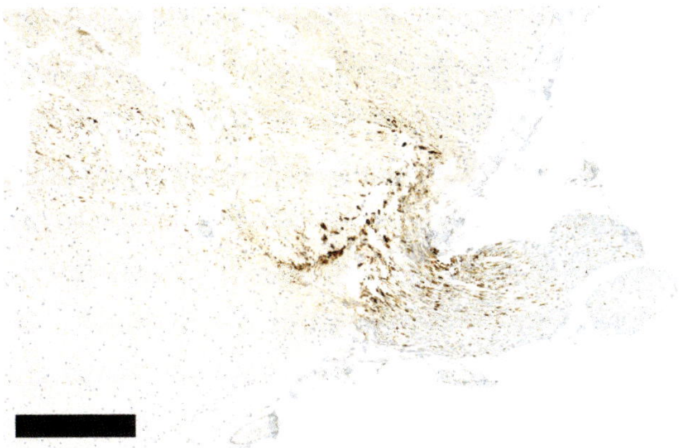

37.4 Dorsal root from the cervical cord of an 8-week-old female infant who died 3 days after a presumed shaking event by her father. The infant had been brought to the emergency department in extremis; further work-up showed bilateral thin subdural hematomas, optic nerve sheath bleeding bilaterally, extensive retinal bleeding in both eyes and diffuse hypoxic-ischemic encephalopathy. The histopathological section shows signs of focal traumatic axonal injury with grouped damaged axons immunopositive for amyloid-β precursor protein (APP) in the dorsal nerve root and the adjacent cord parenchyma. (Immunohistochemistry for APP, scale bar 250 μm.)

severe, and extend over multiple segments. Small amounts of extradural, subdural and subarachnoid hemorrhage are quite common in SCT, but, unlike meningeal hemorrhage in craniocerebral trauma, only rarely causes significant damage to the cord itself (40). Traumatic necrosis often involves the central parts of the cord, while an outer rim of white matter is preserved in a subpial location (41). Microscopically, granulocytes are found during the first 12–24 hours after the traumatic event and are followed by lymphocytes and macrophages over several days. Hemosiderin may be identified with Turnbull's stain after 3 days. Reactive astrocytes appear after about one week and can easily be identified with immunohistochemistry for GFAP. With survival over years, removal of necrotic debris may result in post-traumatic syringomyelia with a propensity to further enlarge over time (42–44). Avulsion of nerve roots may lead to the formation of post-traumatic amputation neuroma. Axonal damage can be seen in association with focal cord damage – that is, perilesional axonal injury (45) – after about 1 hour using immunohistochemistry for amyloid-β precursor protein (APP) highlighting axonal varicosities or axonal spheroids. Over time, secondary degeneration of ascending fibres usually leads to rarefication of the posterior columns above the level of the lesion, which can be visualized with myelin

TABLE 37.1 Selected cases of spinal trauma deaths with forensic implications from the literature

Sex	Age (years)	Cause of trauma	Mechanism of injury	Reference
F	2	MVA with airbag deployment	Occipitoatlantoaxial disarticulation with traumatic spinal cord separation	(73)
F	2	Non-accidental trauma with hyperextension of the spine	Tearing of anterior longitudinal ligament with diastases of vertebrae C5/C6	(74)
F	13	Fall during gym class striking head on a hurdle	Transmission of a concussive force through the reticular activating system	(75)
F	26	Homicidal stab wound	Transection of the cervical cord	(76)
M	29	MVA	Laceration of cervical cord facilitated by predisposing malformation (os odontoideum)	(77)
M	33	MVA with airbag deployment and expulsion of metal fragments of defective airbag	Transection of the cervical cord	(78)
M	47	Homicidal gunshot to the head	Cardiorespiratory arrest due to secondary concussive injury to spinal-medullary junction	(79)
M	Approx. 50	MVA as pedestrian	Transection of the cervical cord with expulsion of the cord through the oral cavity	(80)
M	56	Fall from the top of stacked hay bales on a farm	Transection of the cervical cord	(81)
M	57	MVA with airbag deployment	High cervical contusion due to dens fracture	(72)
M	60	Accidental strangulation	Dislocated fracture of vertebrae C2-C3 and impression of high spinal cord	(82)
M	65	Cyclist hit by vehicle	Ischemic injury of the cervical cord with predisposing congenital craniocervical malformation	(83)
M	67	MVA	Cervical spine injury due to disruption of the C5/6 discoligaments and intervertebral disc	(84)

stains such as Luxol fast blue or Kluever-Barrera´s. On the other hand, below the level of the lesion, degeneration of the descending tracts, most notably the pyramidal tract, will occur. In abusive head trauma in infants, the acceleration-deceleration forces during a violent act of shaking may result in focal traumatic axonal injury to nerve fibers of the cord or nerve roots (Figure 37.4).

For a more comprehensive review of the neuropathology of SCT, the reader is referred to the literature (15,40,41,46–53).

CAUSES OF DEATH AFTER SPINAL CORD TRAUMA

In comparison with persons without SCT, patients with SCT are two to five times more likely to die prematurely. Mortality risk is highest in the first year after injury and remains high compared to the general population. Patients with isolated SCT, who survive the first 24 hours after the initial event, succumb to systemic complications due to immobility because of motor paralysis and/or reduced reflexes. Although most of the deaths are multifactorial, the most common causes include (aspiration) pneumonia, sepsis with urinary tract infection, and pulmonary thromboembolism (54,55). In addition, patients with SCT may experience immune depression due to disruption of the connection between the CNS and the immune system, further favoring complicating infections (so-called spinal cord injury induced immune depression syndrome [56,57]). Of note, the rate of suicides in patients with SCT is higher than in the general population (58–60).

Death directly or exclusively because of SCT is rare. Patients with severe lesions above the 6th thoracic segment may suffer interruption of sympathetic vasomotor input leading to pooling of blood in the venous system and thus a decrease in venous return and cardiac output. This results in neurogenic shock, a potentially life-threatening condition (61–65). Furthermore, the syndrome of autonomic areflexia with loss of control over sympathetic responses might lead to arterial hypertension with the risk of delayed sudden death due to fatal intracerebral hemorrhage (66–71).

The literature contains a plethora of case reports discussing various forensic aspects of spinal trauma deaths (*see* Table 37.1 for selected cases).

REFERENCES

1. Atkinson PP, Atkinson JLD. Spinal shock. *Mayo Clin Proc* 1996; **71**(4): 384–9.
2. Dumont RJ, Okonkwo DO, Verma S, et al. Acute spinal cord injury, part I: Pathophysiologic mechanisms. *Clin Neuropharmacol* 2001;**24**(5): 254–64.
3. Nacimiento W, Noth J. What, if anything, is spinal shock? *Arch Neurol* 1999; **56**(8): 1033–5.
4. White RJ, Likavec MJ. Spinal shock: Spinal man. *J Trauma-Injury Infect Crit Care* 1999; **46**(5): 979–80.
5. Maynard FM, Bracken MB, Creasey G, et al. International standards for neurological and functional classification of spinal cord injury. American Spinal Injury Association. *Spinal Cord* 1997; **35**(5): 266–74.
6. Cripps RA, Lee BB, Wing P, et al. A global map for traumatic spinal cord injury epidemiology: Towards a living data repository for injury prevention. *Spinal Cord* 2011; **49**(4): 493–501.
7. Fitzharris M, Cripps RA, Lee BB. Estimating the global incidence of traumatic spinal cord injury. *Spinal Cord* 2014; **52**(2): 117–22.
8. Lee BB, Cripps RA, Fitzharris M, et al. The global map for traumatic spinal cord injury epidemiology: Update 2011, global incidence rate. *Spinal Cord* 2014; **52**(2): 110–16.
9. Roche SJ, Sloane PA, McCabe JP. Epidemiology of spine trauma in an Irish regional trauma unit: A 4-year study. *Injury* 2008; **39**(4): 436–42.
10. Chan CWL, Eng JJ, Tator CH, et al. Epidemiology of sport-related spinal cord injuries: A systematic review. *J Spinal Cord Med* 2016; **39**(3): 255–64.
11. de Barros TEP, Cristante AF, Marcon RM, et al. Gunshot injuries in the spine. *Spinal Cord* 2014; **52**(7): 504–10.
12. Jakoi A, Iorio J, Howell R, et al. Gunshot injuries of the spine. *Spine J* 2015; **15**(9): 2077–85.
13. Taylor TKF, Rutkowski SB, Jones RF, et al. Spinal cord injuries in Australian footballers. *Anz J Surg* 2003; **73**(7): 493–9.
14. Peacock WJ, Shrosbree RD, Key AG. A review of 450 stabwounds of the spinal cord. *S Afr Med J* 1977; **51**(26): 961–4.
15. Hayes KC, Kakulas BA. Neuropathology of human spinal cord injury sustained in sports-related activities. *J Neurotrauma* 1997; **14**(4): 235–48.
16. Osawa M, Satoh F, Hasegawa I. Acute death due to hyperextension injury of the cervical spine caused by falling and slipping onto the face. *J Forensic Leg Med* 2008; **15**(7): 457–1.
17. Kang DG, Lehman RA, Carragee EJ. Wartime spine injuries: Understanding the improvised explosive device and biophysics of blast trauma. *Spine J* 2012; **12**(9): 849–57.
18. Furlan JC, Gulasingam S, Craven BC. Epidemiology of war-related spinal cord injury among combatants: A systematic review. *Global Spine J* 2019; **9**(5): 545–58.
19. Lawless MH, Lytle EJ, McGlynn AF, et al. Surgical management of penetrating spinal cord injury primarily due to shrapnel and its effect on neurological outcome: A literature review and meta-analysis. *J Neurosurg-Spine* 2018; **28**(1): 63–71.
20. Baker GS, Daniels F. Concussion of the spinal cord in battle casualties. *J Neurosurg* 1946; **3**: 206–11.
21. Donovan WH. Donald Munro Lecture. Spinal cord injury: Past, present, and future. *J Spinal Cord Med* 2007; **30**(2): 85–100.
22. Alizadeh A, Dyck SM, Karimi-Abdolrezaee S. Traumatic spinal cord injury: An overview of pathophysiology, models and acute injury mechanisms. *Front Neurol* 2019; **10**: 25.
23. Rowland JW, Hawryluk GW, Kwon B, et al. Current status of acute spinal cord injury pathophysiology and emerging therapies: Promise on the horizon. *Neurosurg Focus* 2008; **25**(5): E2.
24. Patil R, Jaiswal G, Gupta TK. Gunshot wound causing complete spinal cord injury without mechanical violation of spinal axis: Case report with review of literature. *J Craniovert Jun Spine* 2015; **6**(4): 149–57.
25. Mirovsky Y, Shalmon E, Blankstein A, et al. Complete paraplegia following gunshot injury without direct trauma to the cord. *Spine* 2005; **30**(21): 2436–8.
26. Boukobza M, Guichard JP, Boissonet M, et al. Spinal epidural hematoma: Report of 11 cases and review of the literature. *Neuroradiology* 1994; **36**(6): 456–9.
27. Chan DTM, Boet R, Poon WS, et al. Spinal shock in spontaneous cervical spinal epidural haematoma. *Acta Neurochir* 2004; **146**(10): 1161–3.
28. Beatty RM, Winston KR. Spontaneous cervical epidural hematoma. A consideration of etiology. *J Neurosurg* 1984; **61**(1): 143–8.
29. Liu H, Zhang T, Qu T, et al. Spinal epidural hematoma after spinal manipulation therapy: Report of three cases and a literature review. *World J Clin Cases* 2021; **9**(22): 6501–9.
30. Vanichkulbodee A, Issaragrisil S, Inboriboon PC. Massage-induced spinal epidural hematoma presenting with delayed paraplegia. *Am J Emerg Med* 2019; **37**(4): 797.e1–.e4.
31. Abe T, Nagamine Y, Ishimatsu S, et al. Spinal epidural hematoma after stretch

exercise: a case report. *Am J Emerg Med* 2009; **27(7)**: 902.e1–2.
32. Nagashima H, Tanida A, Hayashi I, et al. Spinal subdural haematoma concurrent with cranial subdural haematoma: Report of two cases and review of literature. *Br J Neurosurg* 2010; **24(5)**: 537–41.
33. Reynolds R. Pediatric spinal injury. *Curr Opin Pediatr* 2000; **12(1)**: 67–71.
34. Pang D, Wilberger JE. Spinal cord injury without radiographic abnormalities in children. *J Neurosurg* 1982; **57(1)**: 114–29.
35. Pang D, Pollack IF. Spinal cord injury without radiographic abnormality in children: The SCIWORA syndrome. *J Trauma* 1989; **29(5)**: 654–64.
36. Pang D. Spinal cord injury without radiographic abnormality in children, 2 decades later. *Neurosurgery* 2004; **55(6)**: 1325–42.
37. Carroll T, Smith CD, Liu X, et al. Spinal cord injuries without radiologic abnormality in children: A systematic review. *Spinal Cord* 2015; **53(12)**: 842–8.
38. Uhrenholt L, Boel LWT. Contributions from forensic iimaging to the investigation of upper cervical fractures. *J Foren Sci* 2010; **55(6)**: 1598–602.
39. Makino Y, Yokota H, Nakatani E, et al. Differences between postmortem CT and autopsy in death investigation of cervical spine injuries. *Forensic Sci Int* 2017; **281**: 44–51.
40. Kakulas BA. Neuropathology: The foundation for new treatments in spinal cord injury. *Spinal Cord* 2004; **42(10)**: 549–63.
41. Kakulas BA. Pathology of spinal injuries. *Cent Nerv Syst Trauma* 1984; **1(2)**: 117–29.
42. Balmaseda MT, Wunder JA, Gordon C, et al. Posttraumatic syringomyelia associated with heavy weightlifting exercises: Case report. *Arch Phys Med Rehabil* 1988; **69(11)**: 970–2.
43. Jaksche H, Schaan M, Schulz J, et al. Posttraumatic syringomyelia: A serious complication in tetra- and paraplegic patients. *Acta Neurochir Suppl* 2005; **93**: 165–7.
44. McComas CF, Frost JL, Schochet SS. Posttraumatic syringomyelia with paroxysmal episodes of unconsciousness. *Arch Neurol* 1983; **40(5)**: 322–4.
45. Reichard RR, White CL, Hladik CL, et al. Beta-amyloid precursor protein staining of nonaccidental central nervous system injury in pediatric autopsies. *J Neurotrauma* 2003; **20(4)**: 347–55.
46. Dimitrijevic MR, Kakulas BA. Spinal cord injuries, human neuropathology and neurophysiology. *Acta Myol* 2020; **39(4)**: 353–8.
47. Hayes KC, Askes HK, Kakulas BA. Retropulsion of intervertebral discs associated with traumatic hyperextension of the cervical spine and absence of vertebral fracture: An uncommon mechanism of spinal cord injury. *Spinal Cord* 2002; **40(10)**: 544–7.
48. Kakulas BA, Jacobsen PF, Bedbrook GM. Acute spinal injuries. A clinico-pathological study. *Proc Veterans Adm Spinal Cord Inj Conf* 1973 **(19)**: 84–95.
49. Kakulas BA. The clinical neuropathology of spinal cord injury. A guide to the future. *Paraplegia* 1987; **25(3)**: 212–16.
50. Kakulas BA. A review of the neuropathology of human spinal cord injury with emphasis on special features. *J Spinal Cord Med* 1999; **22(2)**: 119–24.
51. Kakulas BA. The applied neuropathology of human spinal cord injury. *Spinal Cord* 1999; **37(2)**: 79–88.
52. Kakulas BA, Kaelan C. The neuropathological foundations for the restorative neurology of spinal cord injury. *Clin Neurol Neurosurg* 2015; **129 Suppl 1**: S1–7.
53. Ginsberg L. Disorders of the spinal cord and roots. *Pract Neurol* 2011; **11(4)**: 259–67.
54. DeVivo MJ, Kartus PL, Stover SL, et al. Cause of death for patients with spinal cord injuries. *Arch Intern Med* 1989; **149(8)**: 1761–6.
55. Kopp MA, Watzlawick R, Martus P, et al. Long-term functional outcome in patients with acquired infections after acute spinal cord injury. *Neurology* 2017; **88(9)**: 892–900.
56. Brommer B, Engel O, Kopp MA, et al. Spinal cord injury-induced immune deficiency syndrome enhances infection susceptibility dependent on lesion level. *Brain* 2016; **139(Pt 3)**: 692–707.
57. Prüss H, Tedeschi A, Thiriot A, et al. Spinal cord injury-induced immunodeficiency is mediated by a sympathetic-neuroendocrine adrenal reflex. *Nat Neurosci* 2017; **20(11)**: 1549–59.
58. DeVivo MJ, Black KJ, Richards JS, et al. Suicide following spinal cord injury. *Paraplegia* 1991; **29(9)**: 620–7.
59. Cao Y, Massaro JF, Krause JS, et al. Suicide mortality after spinal cord injury in the United States: injury cohorts analysis. *Arch Phys Med Rehabil* 2014; **95(2)**: 230–5.
60. Savic G, DeVivo MJ, Frankel HL, et al. Suicide and traumatic spinal cord injury: A cohort study. *Spinal Cord* 2018; **56(1)**: 2–6.
61. Guly HR, Bouamra O, Lecky FE. The incidence of neurogenic shock in patients with isolated spinal cord injury in the emergency department. *Resuscitation* 2008; **76(1)**: 57–62.
62. Mallek JT, Inaba K, Branco BC, et al. The incidence of neurogenic shock after spinal cord injury in patients admitted to a high-volume level I trauma center. *Am Surg* 2012; **78(5)**: 623–6.
63. Ruiz IA, Squair JW, Phillips AA, et al. Incidence and natural progression of neurogenic shock after traumatic spinal cord injury. *J Neurotrauma* 2018; **35(3)**: 461–6.
64. Kondo T, Saito K, Nishigami J, et al. Fatal injuries of the brainstem and/or upper cervical spinal cord in traffic accidents: 9 autopsy cases. *Sci Justice* 1995; **35(3)**: 197–201.
65. Schmidt P, Madea B. Reflex mechanisms of death in missile injuries of the neck. *Forensic Sci Int* 1994; **66(1)**: 53–60.
66. Comarr AE, Eltorai I. Autonomic dysreflexia/hyperreflexia. *J Spinal Cord Med* 1997; **20(3)**: 345–54.
67. Eltorai I, Kim R, Vulpe M, et al. Fatal cerebral hemorrhage due to autonomic dysreflexia in a tetraplegic patient: Case report and review. *Paraplegia* 1992; **30(5)**: 355–60.
68. Baguley IJ. Autonomic complications following central nervous system injury. *Semin Neurol* 2008; **28(5)**: 716–25.
69. Bycroft J, Shergill IS, Choong EAL, et al. Autonomic dysreflexia: A medical emergency. *Postgrad Med J* 2005; **81(954)**: 232–5.
70. Dolinak D, Balraj E. Autonomic dysreflexia and sudden death in people with traumatic spinal cord injury. *Am J Forensic Med Pathol* 2007; **28(2)**: 95–8.
71. Krassioukov AV, Furlan JC, Fehlings MG. Autonomic dysreflexia in acute spinal cord injury: An under-recognized clinical entity. *J Neurotrauma* 2003; **20(8)**: 707–16.
72. Hahn M, Dreimann M, Matschke J, et al. An airbag can also be fatal [article in German]. *Rechtsmedizin 2022*; **32**: 131– 135.
73. Cooper JT, Balding LE, Jordan FB. Airbag mediated death of a two-year-old child wearing a shoulder/lap belt. *J Forensic Sci* 1998; **43(5)**: 1077–81.
74. Dudley MH, Garg M. Fatal child abuse presenting with multiple vertebral and vascular trauma. *J Forensic Sci* 2014; **59(2)**: 386–9.
75. Davis GG, Glass JM. Case report of sudden death after a blow to the back of the neck. *Am J Forensic Med Pathol* 2001; **22(1)**: 13–18.
76. Savall F, Dedouit F, Mokrane FZ, et al. An unusual homicidal stab wound of the cervical spinal cord: A single case examined by post-mortem computed tomography angiography (PMCTA). *Forensic Sci Int* 2015; **254**: E18–E21.
77. Dempster AG, Heap SW. Fatal high cervical spinal-cord injury in an automobile accident complicating os odontoideum. *Am J Forensic Med Pathol* 1990; **11(3)**: 252–6.
78. Albalooshi YM, Sherif HM, Alzarooni SM, et al. Fatal automobile accident due to airbag misdeployment. *Int J Legal Med* 2021; **135(2)**: 565–72.
79. Demontis R, d'Aloja E, Manieli C, et al. Case report of sudden death after a gunshot wound to the C2 vertebral bone without direct spinal cord injury: Histopathological analysis of spinal-medullary junction. *Forensic Sci Int* 2019; **301**: e49–e54.
80. Viola L, Di Nunno N, Costantinides F, et al. Unusual neck lesion in a pedestrian caused by a road accident. *Am J Forensic Med Pathol* 2002; **23(1)**: 68–71.
81. Charlwood C, Byard RW. Potential dangers of hay bailing. *J Forensic Leg Med* 2014; **21**: 56–8.
82. De-Giorgio F, Grassi S, Miscusi M, et al. Cervical spine involvement in a challenging case of accidental strangulation. *Am J Forensic Med Pathol* 2019; **40(2)**: 156–9.
83. Aragaki Y, Takatsu A, Shigeta A. Unusual mechanism of lethal cervical spinal-cord injury in a case of atlantoaxial diastasis. *Int J Leg Med* 1993; **106(1)**: 41–3.
84. Okuda T, Shiotani S, Hayakawa H, et al. A case of fatal cervical discoligamentous hyperextension injury without fracture: Correlation of postmortem imaging and autopsy findings. *Forensic Sci Int* 2013; **225(1–3)**: 71–4.

CHAPTER 38

Chest and Abdominal Trauma

Roger W. Byard

INTRODUCTION

Injuries to the chest and abdomen can be caused by many types of trauma including blunt and sharp forces (the latter of which may cause penetrating injury), and these may result in serious organ or vascular damage causing fatality. Crushing or compression forces may also cause significant soft-tissue and solid organ parenchymal disruption. Structural differences between the chest and abdomen may result in different injuries arising from similar trauma. For example, the rib cage protects the chest organs from trauma as it has the greatest viscoelastic potential, so a greater velocity of deformation is required to cause injury. The upper abdomen has the next highest, followed by the lower abdomen (1,2). Alternatively, the bony thorax may facilitate penetration of the chest cavity by sharp objects such as knives that may readily pass through the splinted intercostal spaces.

Characteristic injuries to the chest and abdomen may vary with age. For example, acute or healing posterior rib fractures in infants are highly suggestive of forceful gripping. Similarly, a punch to a child's abdomen or stamping with a foot may result in typical midline injuries with liver lacerations, pancreatic transections and duodenal/mesenteric tears (3). These are high impact injuries also seen in road traffic collisions.

Indeed, the most common situation in civilian settings causing extensive blunt force trauma to the chest and abdomen is that of a vehicle crash which may involve both occupants and pedestrians. The nature of the injuries depends on a variety of factors including the speed of impact, the position of the victims, the type of vehicle and the characteristics of the victim such as age and physical condition (4,5). Lethal animal attacks, although far less common, may involve both blunt and sharp force trauma to the torso. Examples of blunt force trauma with organ disruption and crush asphyxia have involved elephants, buffalo and horses. Sharp force trauma may occur with aquatic animals such as sting rays or terrestrial animals such as buffalo (6,7). Biting may involve both sharp forces from teeth causing penetrating and avulsion injury and blunt forces from crushing, as may be seen following shark, dog or crocodile attacks (8,9).

CASPER'S SIGN

Casper's sign refers to the absence of external signs of trauma despite severe and often lethal internal injuries. It was named after Professor Johann Casper who was the Professor of Pathology in Berlin, Prussia, in the mid-nineteenth century (10). He stated that the phrase "traces of external injury wanting" used in public judicial notices respecting the finding of an unknown dead body may result in an assumption that there could be no significant internal injuries and so an autopsy would not be required. His conclusion was that "the actual truth is precisely the reverse" because of the elasticity and deformability of the skin which enables it to move with blunt trauma, rather than resisting it and sustaining injury (11).

This contrasts with internal organs which are not particularly elastic, and which are also tethered by fascia, ligaments and blood vessels rendering them susceptible to blunt trauma as they are unable to move out of the path of an intruding/impacting object, such as a motor vehicle, fist or boot (1). In the chest, the rib cage, although somewhat elastic (particularly in the young) will tend to fracture with high force injuries resulting in displaced fragments lacerating the heart and lungs. Deceleration injuries that may follow an impact with a vehicle interior during a crash or with the ground in a long-distance fall may also involve the aorta causing laceration or transection (Figure 38.1). Vehicle crashes may also cause multiple organ injuries within the chest with rib, sternal and spinal fractures. Within the abdomen, the liver, spleen, pancreas, mesentery and duodenum are vulnerable, particularly when tethered between the spine and the impacting force, sustaining lacerations (Figure 38.2) and parenchymal disruption with hemorrhage. Significantly, all of these injuries may occur without obvious external trauma (10).

CHEST TRAUMA

Blunt force trauma

This may result from impact with an object, or from the body impacting a solid or immovable surface such as the ground. The nature of the underlying injury depends

DOI: 10.1201/9781003138754-40

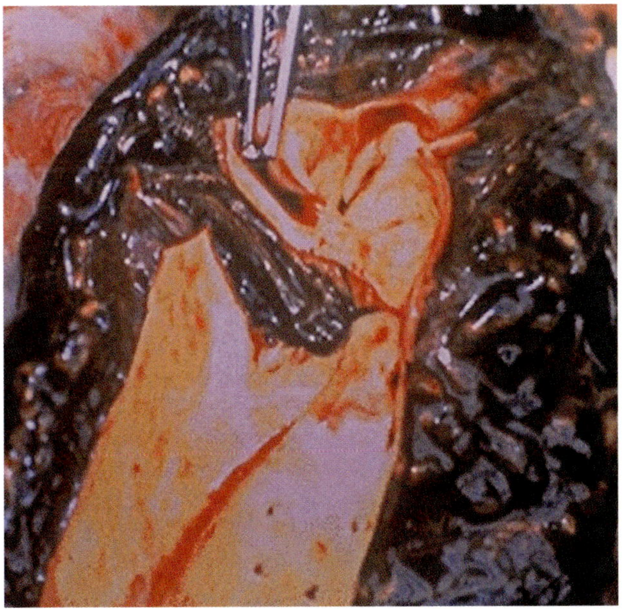

38.1 Typical laceration of the aorta with surrounding hemorrhage following decelerative trauma.

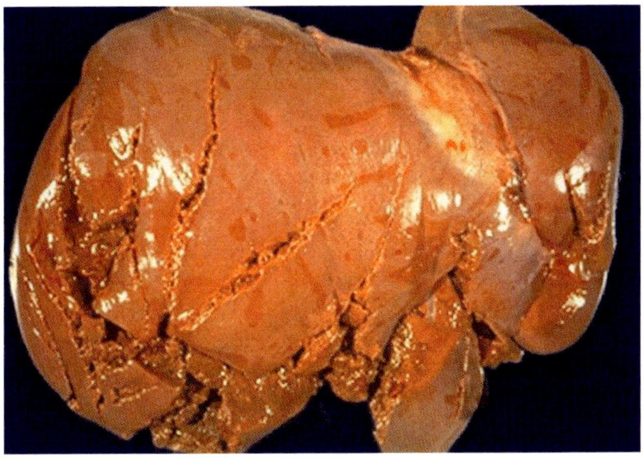

38.2 Multiple lacerations of the liver following a vehicle crash.

on the force of the blow or impact, the point of contact and the size of the impacting surface. For example, greater damage will be caused by a force of the same energy if it is localized rather than diffusely applied (1). The chances of underlying injury increase when there is greater mechanical compromise of tissues with the propagation of stress, shock and shear waves into the body cavities, as well as with the addition of possible crush injuries (12).

Injuries result from inward displacement which represents the primary mechanism of energy transfer. Animal studies have shown that mammalian torsos have very little rebound velocity when impacted by a blunt object which means that organ displacement after impact is rate dependent with both the magnitude and rate of body wall distortion determining the nature and severity of the resultant organ injury. Thus, organs may be quite resistant to marked inward displacement if the compressing force is slow, compared to a more rapid compression which may cause injuries with an internal displacement of only 3–4 cm (13). Prolonged compression may however certainly be associated with severe injury.

Stress (compression) waves associated with small but rapid distortions of tissue (strain) can cause injuries and are most often found with high-speed impacts. The lung, which is characterized by significant variations in density at air and tissue interfaces, may sustain tearing of capillaries because of these pressure differentials with intraalveolar and interstitial hemorrhage. Stress waves are generated by the inward movement of the body wall with the extent of injury being a function of the peak velocity of the body wall (12). Stress waves may also cause indirect injuries when they reflect off the mediastinum or bronchial surfaces resulting in a synergistic action and focal high pressures away from the site of impact. An example of this would be blunt force trauma to the lateral chest wall with the most severe injury occurring some distance away at the lung hilum.

The most common types of injuries associated with low-velocity impacts involve shear waves (12) which are transverse waves of longer duration requiring significant momentum with marked displacement of the body wall. Visceral trauma arises from impact of organs with nonelastic structures, stretching at the sites of attachment or asynchronous motion of adjacent connected structures. Within the chest cavity, shearing causes lacerations and contusions of the pulmonary hilum and the aorta at the ligamentum arteriosum.

Shock waves are found in explosions and are high-pressure, high-velocity waves that may cause subpleural and intraparenchymal lung hemorrhages (12).

Significant blunt force trauma to the chest is most often seen in civilian practice following motor vehicle crashes. At autopsy, there may be external indicators of injury with contusions, lacerations and brush abrasions from dragging (14). Patterned injuries may assist in determining the nature of the final impact with seat belt markings identifying vehicle occupants, and impressions from tyres or vehicle grills denoting pedestrians (15,16). Alternatively, an impacting blunt object may leave "tram track" (rail track) markings or patterns from its surface. Attempting to estimate the age of any bruises arising from blunt force impact should be undertaken with extreme caution as color changes are unreliable and histologic changes vary depending on the distance of the tissue sampling from the site of impact (17).

Dissection will often reveal subcutaneous and mediastinal bruising sometimes associated with rib fractures. Bilateral rib fractures may have resulted in a flail chest, and lacerations of the heart may be associated with a tense hemopericardium. Lacerations of the lung and aortic transections may have caused bilateral hemothoraces, the latter sometimes associated with fracture-dislocation of the thoracic spine. The aorta usually tears at the level of the ligamentum arteriosum as this marks the junction of the fixed thoracic aorta with the more mobile aortic arch and heart. Factors associated with aortic transection in vehicle crashes include high speed and impact on the decedent's side, with intrusion of the vehicle wall (18). With severe impact, there may be avulsion of the heart or lungs, the latter with tracheal transection and soft-tissue emphysema.

The assessment of possible blunt chest trauma must always be carried out with an understanding that many injuries may be caused by prolonged and forceful attempts at resuscitation (19). A review of the presenting history should therefore be undertaken with features such as parchmenting of the central chest with attached defibrillator pads and intravenous lines confirming that resuscitation had been attempted.

Commotio cordis

On occasion, blunt chest trauma may be associated with sudden collapse without any significant findings at autopsy. Termed "commotio cordis" this is a situation that occurs in adolescents playing sports who are hit in the chest with a baseball, cricket ball or hockey puck. Death is thought to be due to a lethal arrhythmia from cardiac concussion (20,21). Although this is the classical situation there appears to be no reason why similar fatal arrhythmias cannot occur in individuals with associated non-lethal chest trauma or underlying cardiovascular disease (22). Cases where there is bruising of the heart have been termed "contusio cordis".

Positional and crush asphyxia

Another situation where there may be minimal findings at autopsy occurs in cases of positional asphyxia where expansion of the thorax has been prevented by splinting of the chest wall, often due to wedging in a confined space. It may be associated with collapse from acute alcohol intoxication or an underlying medical condition (23). A related situation involves crush asphyxia where chest expansion is prevented by direct pressure onto the thorax. This is more likely to have findings at autopsy, sometimes with parchmented marks or bruises from the compressing object identified on external examination (24).

In addition, there is often intense congestion of the head, face and upper body with crushing associated with extensive areas of facial and conjunctival petechial hemorrhages. These may be absent under tight fitting clothing (25). There may also be prominent subconjunctival hemorrhages (Figure 38.3) with blood leaking from the nose and ears. Dissection of the neck may reveal a black thyroid gland with characteristic blood islands on histology (Figure 38.4) (26).

Sharp force trauma

Stab wounds to the chest usually indicate that a homicide has occurred (Figure 38.5) although such injuries may be found in suicides and may be multiple (27). Rarely, accidental stab wounds to the chest may occur. Apart from cartilage and bone, the tissue with the most resistance to penetration by a blade is the skin. In the chest, penetration may be assisted by underlying buttressing of the intercostal spaces by the ribs (28) (Figure 38.6). Deaths from stab wounds to the chest most often result from penetration of the heart (Figure 38.7), lungs or major vessels such as the aorta and are associated with pneumo- and hemothoraces and extensive mediastinal hemorrhage (Figure 38.8).

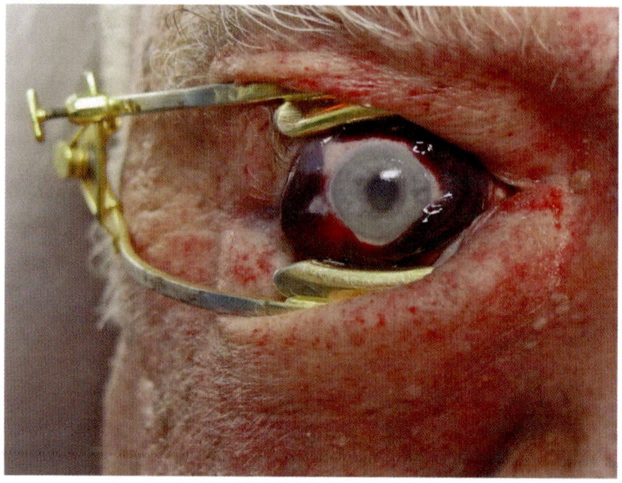

38.3 Subconjunctival hemorrhage in a case of crush asphyxia due to chest compression with surrounding petechiae.

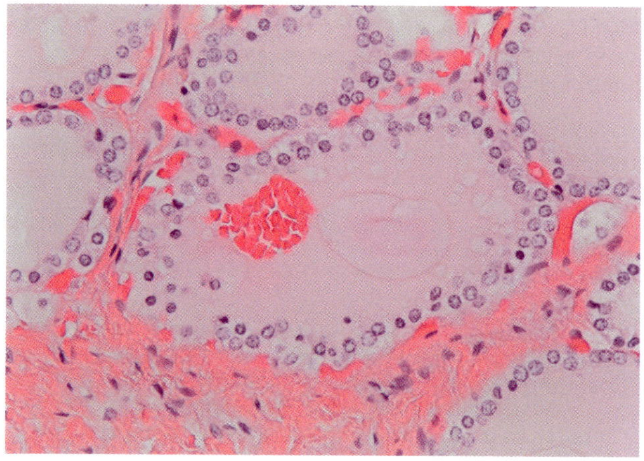

38.4 A blood island in the thyroid gland in a case of crush asphyxia due to rupture of a congested capillary (H&E x 150).

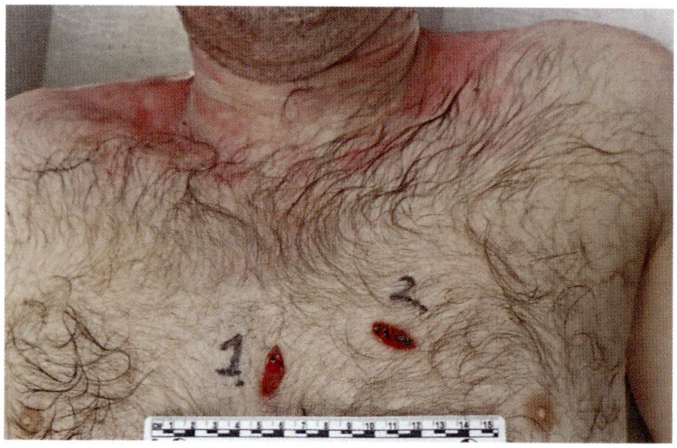

38.5 Stab wounds of the upper chest.

Post-mortem imaging prior to removal of a weapon may give a far more accurate determination of the direction of the wound than careful layer dissection, as elastic tissue recoil may obscure the true tract (29). In addition, identification of the tip of a knife that may have broken off when it impacted the vertebral column may be the most useful way of identifying the offending weapon.

38.6 Two stab wounds to the chest passing through the intercostal muscles between the ribs.

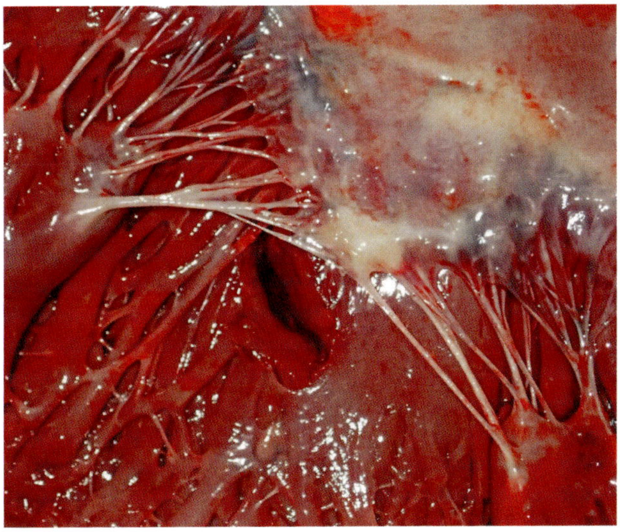

38.7 A stab wound to the heart beneath the mitral valve.

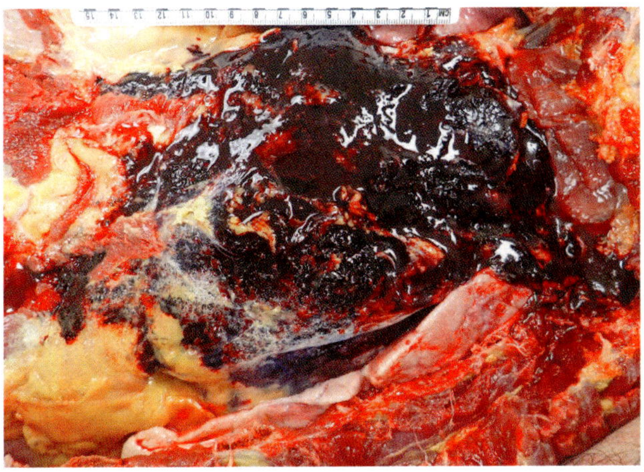

38.8 Marked anterior mediastinal hemorrhage due to stab wounds to the heart.

Firearm injuries

The characteristics of firearm injuries are described elsewhere in this text, however, gunshot wounds to the chest cavity may result in immediate incapacitation and death from organ disruption and hemorrhage. On occasion, delayed death may occur from air embolism. The nature of the tissue/organ damage depends on the type and calibre of the weapon, for example shotgun vs handgun, the range and the position of the perpetrator and victim.

ABDOMINAL TRAUMA

Blunt force trauma

As with the chest, blunt force abdominal trauma may be caused by a direct blow or by impact of the body against a solid object. Solid abdominal organs are generally more susceptible to the effects of blunt force trauma than are hollow organs with animal studies showing that injuries to the liver and spleen occur with lower impact forces than that required to damage hollow organs. A study of injuries sustained in vehicle crashes showed that the liver was the most vulnerable accounting for 38.2 percent of the injuries, followed by the spleen at 24.2 percent, and the kidneys at 13.7 percent. This compared to the intestines and urinary bladder which accounted for only 18.5 percent of the injuries (30). Hollow organs are, however, more susceptible to injury if they are filled with fluid or air. Vulnerable areas to blunt trauma include the root of the mesentery, the splenic pedicle and the liver at the falciform ligament (1) often associated with anterior abdominal wall bruising (Figure 38.9).

Hollow organs such as the intestines are most vulnerable to the effects of blast injuries from explosions resulting in submucosal and serosal hemorrhage and rupture, and these will be dependent on the nature of the blast.

Underlying medical conditions may increase the vulnerability of certain organs to blunt force trauma. A good example of this is the spleen which is predisposed to

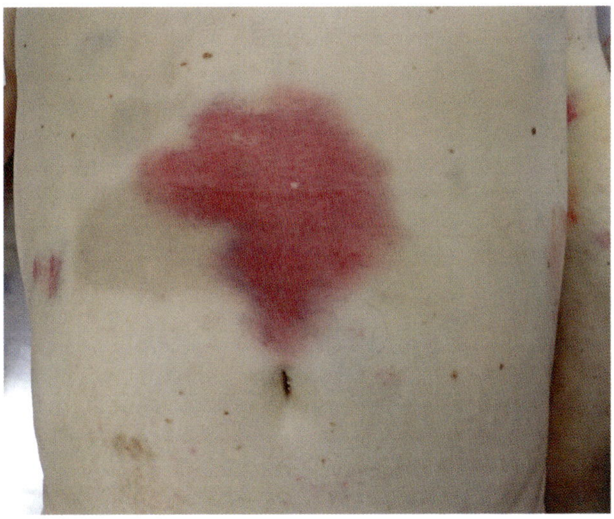

38.9 Bruising of the central abdomen due to blunt force trauma associated with underlying organ injuries.

rupture in individuals with splenomegaly from malaria or infectious mononucleosis (31). Splenic rupture following trauma may be delayed if there is hemorrhage underneath an intact capsule which may take some time to rupture. An indication in the history that splenic bleeding has occurred, is a record of pain referred to the tip of the shoulder.

Delayed death may also occur following abdominal trauma if there has been perforation of the intestine leading to leakage of intestinal contents with resultant peritonitis. Similarly, injury to the pancreas may lead to the development of lethal hemorrhagic pancreatitis.

Positional and crush asphyxia

Both positional and crush asphyxia can involve the abdomen and result in death. For example, if the body is positioned upside down (32) the abdominal viscera may compress the diaphragm and chest organs (Figure 38.10). Similarly, if there is significant external compression of the abdomen, upward displacement of organs will splint the diaphragm and prevent normal respiratory excursion. Typical signs such as facial and conjunctival petechiae (Figure 38.11) will be present at autopsy. These situations may be exacerbated by those with higher body mass index (BMI) as obese individuals may have difficulty extracting themselves from dangerous situations and the abdominal viscera may be heavier than normal (33). Crushing of the abdomen may sometimes be associated with extrusion of the intestines (Figure 38.12).

38.10 Upside-down suspension resulting in positional asphyxia in an obese male (arrow indicates where his shoe had become impaled on a fence that he was attempting to climb over).

Sharp force trauma

The abdomen is often targeted in homicidal sharp weapon attacks with multiple wounds being present. Careful layer dissection is required commencing with the skin and subcutaneous tissues, although it is recognized that removal of a knife may cause distortion of the original wound tract (29). When multiple wounds are present,

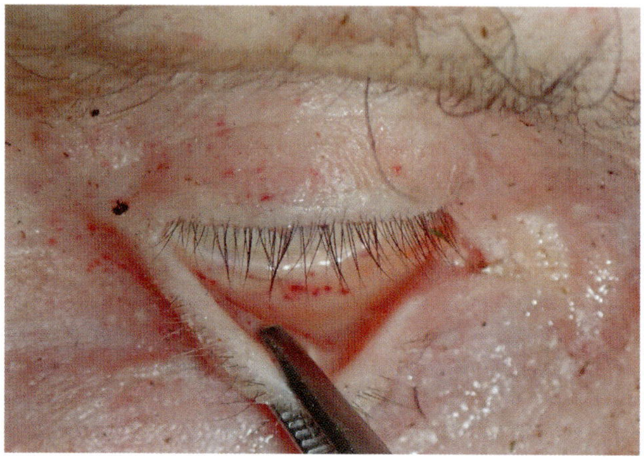

38.11 Petechiae on the inner aspect of the lower eyelid and surrounding skin in a case of crush asphyxia due to abdominal compression.

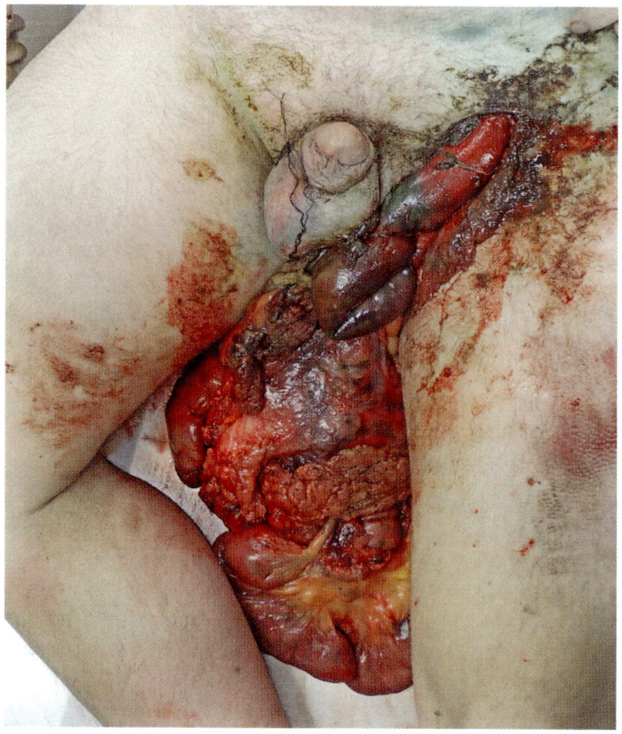

38.12 Tearing of the lower abdominal wall with herniation of loops of intestine following a crushing injury to the abdomen.

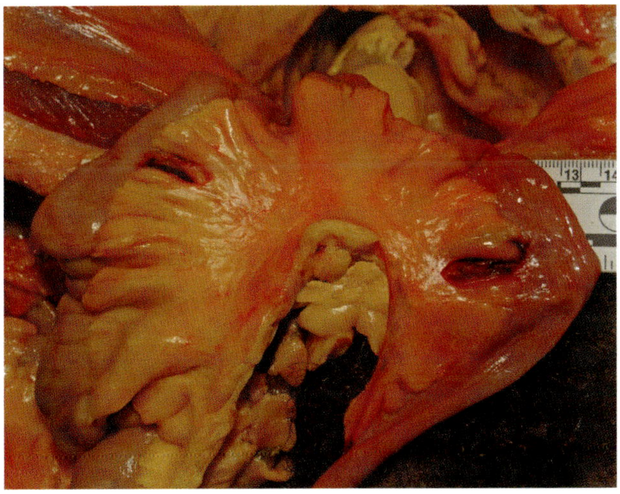

38.13 Stab wounds of the mesentery associated with significant hemorrhage.

it is imperative to determine the path and dimensions of each tract as they may have been caused by different weapons and/or perpetrators. It is also vital to accurately separate lethal wounds from non-lethal wounds.

Deaths often occur from stab wounds to the liver, spleen, kidneys, mesentery (Figure 38.13) and major vessels. The first indication of significant organ injury may be a large hematoperitoneum, although extensive retroperitoneal bleeding may also occur.

Firearm injuries

Gunshot wounds to the abdominal cavity may cause death from injury to organs such as the liver and spleen or to perforation of major vessels such as the aorta or the inferior vena cava. Examination of clothing or skin may be useful in determining range with close range wounds having soot soiling and tattooing. Post-mortem imaging is required to clearly demonstrate the location of projectiles which should be carefully extracted at autopsy without the use of metal equipment to prevent artefactual scoring of fragments.

CONCLUSION

Many types of trauma may result in lethal injuries to the contents of the chest and abdominal cavities. Meticulous autopsy dissection augmented by post mortem is required to determine the extent of the injuries and the involvement of specific organs, soft tissues and vessels. In addition, careful documentation of autopsy findings and appropriate evidence collection may be of key relevance in identifying or excluding possible weapons. Dissections may, however, be complicated by putrefactive changes in cases where there has been a prolonged post-mortem interval and post-mortem animal predation, which may preclude assessment of injuries if organs have been removed and cavities are empty (34).

REFERENCES

1. Byard RW. Accidents. Ch. 2. In: Byard RW. *Sudden Death in the Young*, 3rd ed. Cambridge: Cambridge University Press; 2010, pp. 7–82.
2. Liman ST, Kuzucu A, Tastepe AI, Ulasan GN, Topcu S. Chest injury due to blunt trauma. *Eur J Cardiothoracic Surg* 2003; 23: 374–8.
3. Byard RW, Heath K. Mesenteric fibrosis: A histologic marker of previous blunt abdominal trauma in childhood. *Int J Leg Med* 2010; **124:** 71–3.
4. Galan G, Penalver JC, Paris F, et al. Blunt chest injuries in 1969 patients. *Eur J Cardiothoracic Surg* 1992; **6:** 284–7.
5. Turk E, Tsang Y-W, Champenari A, et al. Cardiac injuries in car occupants in fatal motor vehicle collisions: An autopsy-based study. *J Forensic Legal Med* 2010; **17:** 339–43.
6. Langley RL. Animal-related fatalities in the United States: An update. *Wild Environ Med* 2005; **16:** 67–74.
7. Bury D, Langlois NEI, Byard RW. Animal-related fatalities Part I: Characteristic autopsy findings and variable causes of death associated with blunt and sharp trauma. *J Forensic Sci* 2012; **57:** 370–4.
8. Byard RW, Gilbert JD, Brown K. Pathological features of fatal shark attacks. *Am J Forensic Med Pathol* 2000; **21:** 225–9.
9. Sinton TJ, Byard RW. Pathological features of fatal crocodile attacks in northern Australia, 2005–2014. *J Forensic Sci* 2016; **61:** 1553–5.
10. Byard RW. How reliable is external examination in identifying internal injuries: Casper's sign revisited. *J Forensic Leg Med* 2012; **19:** 419–21.
11. Casper JL. *A Handbook of the Practice of Forensic Medicine based upon Personal Experience*, vol. 1, *Thanatological Division*. London; The New Sydenham Society. 1861; pp. 109–117.
12. Cooper GJ, Taylor DEM. Biophysics of impact injury to the chest and abdomen. *J Roy Army Med Corps* 1989; **135:** 58–67.
13. Stalnaker RL, McElhaney JH, Roberts VL. Human Torso Response to Blunt Trauma. In: King WF, Mertz HJ (eds) *Human Impact Response: Measurement and Simulation*. New York: Plenum Press; 1973, pp. 182–99.
14. Thompson M, Gilbert JD, Byard RW. Lethal "brush abrasions". *Aust J Forensic Sci* 2017; **49:** 479–82.
15. Byard RW. Shoulder-lap seatbelts and thoracic transection. *J Clin Forensic Med* 2002; **9:** 92–5.
16. Byard RW. Vehicular Locard's principle and patterned tire markings. *J Forensic Sci* 2022; **67**(2): 806–8.
17. Byard RW, Langlois NEI. Bruises: Is it a case of "the more we know the less we understand?" *Forensic Sci Med Pathol* 2015; **11:** 479–81.
18. Neschis DG, Scalea TM, Flinn WR, Griffith BP. Blunt aortic injury. *N Engl J Med* 2008; **359:** 1708–16.
19. Olds K, Byard RW, Langlois NEI. Injuries associated with resuscitation: An overview. *J Forensic Leg Med* 2015; 33: 39–43.
20. Maron BJ, Poliac LC, Kaplan JA, et al. Blunt impact of the chest leading to sudden death from cardiac arrest during sports activities. *N Engl J Med* 1995; **333:** 337–42.
21. Nesbitt AD, Cooper PJ, Kohl P. Rediscovering commotio cordis. *Lancet* 2001; **357:** 1195–7.
22. Marshall D, Gilbert J, Byard RW. The spectrum of findings in cases of sudden death due to blunt cardiac trauma: 'Commotio cordis'. *Am J Forensic Med Pathol* 2008; **29:** 1–4.
23. Byard RW, Wick R, Gilbert JD. Conditions and circumstances predisposing to death from positional asphyxia in adults. *J Forensic Legal Med* 2008; **15:** 415–19.
24. Byard RW, Wick R, Simpson E, Gilbert JD. The pathological features and circumstances of death of lethal crush/traumatic asphyxia in adults: A 25-five-year study. *Forensic Sci Int* 2006; **159:** 200–5.
25. Byard RW. The brassiere 'sign': A distinctive marker in crush asphyxia. *J Clin Forensic Med* 2005; **12:** 316–19.

26. Byard RW. Pathological changes in the thyroid gland in crush asphyxia. *Forensic Sci Med Pathol* 2013; **9:** 568–72.
27. Austin A, Guddat S, Tsokos M, et al. Multiple injuries in suicide simulating homicide. *J Forensic Leg Med* 2013; **20:** 601–4.
28. Saukko P, Knight B. The Pathology of Wounds. Ch 4. In: *Knight's Forensic Pathology*, 3rd ed. London: Arnold; 2004, p. 162.
29. Winskog C. Precise wound track measurement requires CAT scan with object in situ: How accurate is post-mortem dissection and evaluation? *Forensic Sci Med Pathol* 2012; **8:** 76–7.
30. Miller MA. Tolerance to steering wheel induced lower abdominal injury. *J Trauma* 1991; **31:** 1332–9.
31. Byard RW. Unexpected death due to infectious mononucleosis. *J Forensic Sci* 2002; 47: 202–4.
32. Heath KJ, Cala A, Byard RW. Metal railing fences and accidental deaths. *J Forensic Sci* 2018; **63:** 972–5.
33. Byard RW. The relationship between positional asphyxia and increasing body mass index. *Leg Med* 2020; **43:** 101678.
34. Byard RW. Major organ loss from postmortem animal predation: Issues arising from emptied body cavities. *Med Sci Law* 2022; **62:** 60–3.

CHAPTER 39

Musculoskeletal Trauma Deaths

Eva Keller and Peter Attila Gergely

INTRODUCTION

The musculoskeletal system (MSKS) of the human body is made up of bones, muscles, tendons, as well as soft tissues attached via ligaments, which support and connect the tissues and organs. Also known as the locomotor system, it is the main system allowing synchronized body movement, and providing protection for vital internal organs. Due to the complexity of the system, it can be affected by a wide range of conditions. In most cases requiring forensic examinations, Musculoskeletal Disorders (MSDs) are usually investigated in connection with injuries and disorders affecting the body's movement or MSKS. Patients will also present for disability evaluation, or in connection with traffic accidents requiring insurance medicine experts. The most common underlying factors in MSD cases include biomechanical, psychosocial, occupational or other factors. According to the WHO, musculoskeletal conditions comprise over 150 conditions affecting the locomotors system of individuals, which range from those that arise suddenly and are short-lived, such as fractures, sprains and strains, to lifelong conditions associated with ongoing functioning limitations and disability (1–4).

Apart from disabilities, MSDs also include traumatic musculoskeletal injuries that may lead to death either within a short time span or years after the incident. Trauma-related injuries are the third leading cause of death worldwide, and the majority of trauma-related deaths require forensic investigations in several EU countries (1,5).

Immediate deaths are mostly due to traumatic shock, or the consequence of multiple external and internal injuries, or later complications, such as embolism and infections; the forensic investigation process depends heavily on the manner of death, and also on the applicable local legal regulations.

Background

The medicolegal investigation of musculoskeletal trauma deaths (MSKTD) is based on the decision of the competent local authority; there is no uniform practice within the European Union as to which trauma-related deaths require a comprehensive judicial investigation, and which of them do not. Comprehensive investigation is generally accepted as required in homicide cases, hit-and-run accidents, some cases of suicide, or if there is a suspicion of suicide. Recently, special attention has been paid to traumatic deaths caused by major disasters or terrorist attacks.

Regarding traumatic injuries followed by short-term or long-term survival, the medicolegal death investigation process is based on the clinical findings, proper diagnosis, and depends on whether the prosecutor's office requests a complete autopsy or not.

Investigation of musculoskeletal trauma-related deaths

Traumatic deaths

Severe traumatic injuries can lead to death immediately, after a short hospital treatment, or after prolonged survival time.

Immediate deaths

These types of deaths may result from an extensive injury to the body, including brain damage, multiple fractures, or extensive soft-tissue or organ injuries. In the case of immediate death after a musculoskeletal trauma, a regular, medicolegal investigation protocol should be followed.

Forensic scene investigation

Prior to the initiation of death investigation, competent medical personnel should determine the occurrence of death. The next step is the crime scene briefing to the person in charge (e.g. sharing information on scene location, time, witnesses, and investigative strategy, etc.) (6). In principle, on-site death investigation of MSKS deaths involves:

- Documenting and photographing the undisturbed scene
- Gathering relevant physical evidence
- Making attempts to determine the time of death
- Ascertaining any post-mortem locations and finding out whether post-mortem movement of the body has occurred or not
- Providing detailed description of the injuries

DOI: 10.1201/9781003138754-41

At the site of the discovery of the body, special attention must be paid to the position and clothing. In addition, individual characteristic features are especially important when no identification card can be found. By recording all of these relevant details, photography of the scene provides permanent documentation. Besides these details, it should also be determined whether the death actually occurred where the body was discovered, or not.

Scene examination of a body by a forensic practitioner is a vital part of the forensic and medicolegal autopsy, since it can serve as an important source of information for subsequent investigation steps. Therefore, quality assurance of the investigations carried out on-site in conformity with the requirements set out in the ECLM guideline is a pre-requisite (6).

All the injuries found on the deceased must be described in detail, with numbers assigned to them. Each injury should be photographed with a measure. Apart from physical features, descriptions should also include references that allow for differentiation of injuries and grouping them according to whether they are recent or old lesions. In case of MSKS injuries, a detailed examination of the skin surface is extremely important to enable the recognition of potential patterned injuries or other signs of external force.

Due to longer post-injury survival, developments in emergency medical care services, the large variety of available modes of transportation, the availability of specialized care, and changes in criminal activity, today a body may be moved from its actual location of illness or injury to some other place. Post-mortem changes, however, should be carefully documented, as they are necessary for the exact determination of the cause and manner of death. Furthermore, they can provide information regarding the time of death, or can clearly indicate whether the body has been moved after death or not (7).

Summing up the essentials of scene investigation, Richard C. Harruff, MD, PhD, Associate Medical Examiner for the Department of Public Health in Seattle, Washington said: "A competent and thorough death-scene investigation provides the basis for a comprehensive medicolegal autopsy, and together the scene investigation and autopsy provide the basis for an accurate determination of cause and manner of death" (7).

Autopsy

Musculoskeletal injuries are often examined as a part of deaths related to major traumatic injuries. In such cases, conventional autopsies are carried out to identify the different injuries to the skin, to differentiate and describe open and closed injuries, including open or closed fractures, such as skull and vertebral fractures, long-bone fractures, or pelvic fractures, as well as penetrating injuries.

Considering the alterations caused by high-impact trauma to the body, the most common type of injury affecting the outer surface of the body, the skin and the soft tissues of the MSKS are blunt trauma injuries, including abrasions, contusions, lacerations, or tearing of the body parts. Unfortunately, many wounds caused by blunt trauma are not specific enough to make it possible to determine the object that has produced the injuries. By definition, an injury pattern is a predictable but non-specific injury having a characteristic distribution consistent with a particular traumatic event.

Transportation accidents related injuries

Road traffic crashes usually involve car drivers, passengers, cyclists, motorcyclists and pedestrians. The MSKS injuries suffered in road traffic crashes are characteristic of the vehicle involved in the impact. Vehicles have their own characteristic features, such as bumpers, lamps, tires, or any decorative parts, which can all cause a wide spectrum of injuries ranging from superficial lesions to serious life-threatening injuries. The actual magnitude of the injury depends on the type of the vehicle and the applied force, as well as the clothing worn during the accident, and the active and passive automotive safety systems, which play a major role in limiting injuries caused to the driver, passengers and/or pedestrians (8–10).

Apart from cars, heavy transports, such as buses, trams or trains may also cause accidents resulting in severe life-threatening injuries, or can cause immediate death on site, as a result of multiple major organ failure.

Other high-impact injuries

Other high-impact injuries of the MSKS include gunshot wounds, falls, blunt traumatic injuries, or a major catastrophic event such as earthquake or building collapse, which could lead to crushing and compression (11–13).

Blunt injuries with different objects

It is well known that perpetrators may use a wide range of tools during an attack. The impressions of these toolmarks on the skin can be identified by skin inspection, making use of 3D surface scanning or even computerized tomography (CT) (12,13).

In the above-mentioned cases, an imprint is formed locally due to the absorption of a critical amount of mechanical energy, which can permanently change the anatomic integrity of the affected site, creating a wound. Structural alteration may be the result of pulling apart (tension), pressing (compression) or applying differential forces (such as friction or shear). The relation between external (skin-related injuries) and internal trauma is clear evidence of the direct application of force (14).

Skin lesions, especially the patterns of the injuries, can be detected applying either a conventional method, for example with the help of a light microscope, or a new technique such as digital imaging of the body surface using a three-dimensional surface scanner (3SS) or photogrammetry. This method is commonly used in cases of reconstruction of traffic accidents, or to correlate injuries with the object suspected of causation (15,16).

Non-conventional autopsy techniques

Over recent decades, the use of post-mortem radiology techniques has become more accepted in forensic investigations. The application of state-of-the-art modalities (CT, MRI, cone-beam CT, X-ray examination) has a long history: in the past, radiology was used as an additional method in personal identity verification. Lately, an increased number of publications have demonstrated that these techniques are useful and – if they are carried out in high numbers – also relatively cost-efficient methods for other purposes, such as quality control in healthcare and legal examinations (15,16).

As radiology techniques allow for the visualization of the entire human body, they can sometimes serve as substitutes for an autopsy if less invasive examination is needed or in the case of an objection (for instance for religious reasons). These methods can be combined with non-invasive or partial autopsy examinations, especially in cases involving children. Also, for further toxicology and histology analysis CT or ultrasound-guided specimen sampling can be performed. The CT scan provides a great opportunity to collect medical data and special information for identification, to find foreign bodies, and perform screening before the autopsy. A full-body MRI scan can reveal the cause of death even in exhumed bodies. Also, these imaging devices are useful for trauma detection: full body scanning can reveal bone fractures, cranial trauma (epidural, subdural, subarachnoid hemorrhages, brain contusion), or even gases trapped between layers (e.g. subcutaneous emphysema, pneumoencephalon). Furthermore, the gases produced during the decomposition of the body can also sometimes be detected as an artifact. To complement the above, post-mortem CT (PMCT) angiography can be performed by using special X-ray sensitive compounds circulated artificially in the vessels (15–17).

Although the software programs of modern CT and MRI scanners can produce a 3D reconstruction of the body, they require much time and computing capacity, and the upper layer structures (usually the skin) and alterations will not be visualized in as much detail as in the case of a conventional 3D surface scanner as mentioned above (15–18).

Traumatic deaths after a short hospital treatment

After a short hospital stay, death may occur unexpectedly for the following reasons: air fat or septic embolism.

Air embolism

Major soft-tissue and organ trauma generally leads to injuries to the venous system. Open skull fracture, for example, can also cause air embolism when the underlying venous system is injured. Approximately 80–100 mL of air entering the venous system will result in clinical symptoms, and an amount of gas exceeding 200 mL will usually lead to a fatal outcome. As a consequence, vein rupture can occur accompanied by massive bleeding into the soft tissue; nevertheless, vein rupture can easily remain undetected.

Detection of air embolism requires special precautions at the beginning of the autopsy. The chest must be carefully opened not to cause vascular injury: it is usually done "under water" to detect air bubbles indicative of air embolism. Recently, it has been considered more accurate to use CT to identify air embolism (19–21).

Fat embolism/bone marrow embolism

Fat embolism (FE) or bone marrow embolism occurs when fat/bone marrow enters the systemic circulation from the bone marrow. This is especially evident after fractures, but also after intramedullary nailing of long-bone fractures, or the insertion of knee and hip prostheses. It occurs most frequently after lower extremity fractures and severe trauma, and less frequently after upper extremity fractures, rib fractures, or vertebral injuries. Massive soft-tissue trauma may lead to such embolism. In explosion victims, FE may also be due to soft-tissue damage.

Lung damage occurring as a result of FE is thought to be mediated by two mechanisms: mechanical occlusion of the pulmonary vasculature by fat globules, and the release of free fatty acids and other substances triggering an inflammatory cascade that further damages the vasculature. A combination of lung, brain and skin symptoms and signs occurs in up to 85 percent of cases. This is called fatty embolism syndrome, and it usually occurs within 12 to 24 hours following a traumatic event. An overall mortality of 5 to 15 percent has been reported (22).

Fat emboli are thought to pass from the pulmonary circulation to the systemic circulation through a probe patent foramen ovale (PFO), which is seen in 20 to 30 percent of the general population.

In the brain, the occluded vasculature may eventually lead to gross encephalopathy, localized cerebral edema and white-matter changes (23).

Post-mortem histopathological examination can easily confirm the diagnosis when fat stains are combined with routine histological sections, or with frozen sections for fat staining (e.g. with Sudan III stain test, or by applying the more suitable oil-red O stains). In the absence of fat stains, fat in vessels can be deduced from hematoxylin and eosin-stained sections of the lungs. In the process of developing paraffin sections fat is removed, but the dissolved fat globules leave vessels distended in the stained sections. However, use of fat stains has been reported to increase the diagnostic incidence (22,24,25).

Prolonged survival time related deaths in MSKS trauma

Sepsis

Sepsis is a life-threatening condition in which the body's reaction to infection causes injury to tissues and organs. It may follow suppression of the immune response.

There are several common signs and symptoms of sepsis including fever, increased heart rate, increased breathing rate, as well as confusion. In addition, symptoms related to specific infections may also develop, such as a cough accompanying pneumonia, or painful urination associated with genitourinary infections. Those who are very young or old or have a weakened immune systems might not experience any symptoms of a specific infection, and the body temperature may be low or normal instead of being elevated. Severe sepsis results in compromised organ function or insufficient blood flow, which can be identified by the presence of low blood pressure, high blood lactate or low urine output. Septic shock with low blood pressure often fails to improve after fluid replacement. Sepsis can be caused by a variety of pathogens including bacteria, viruses and fungi. Common locations for the primary infection include the lungs, brain, urinary tract, skin and abdominal organs.

Compartment syndrome

Acute compartment syndrome (ACS) is a potentially devastating condition associated with musculoskeletal trauma. The final common pathway is cellular ischemia resulting from increased tissue pressure within an osteofascial compartment. Compartment syndrome can occur as a result of several different causes including fractures, contusions, bleeding disorders, burns, trauma, post-ischemic swelling and gunshot wounds. Prompt diagnosis and treatment are essential in limiting patient morbidity and mortality. The diagnosis of compartment syndrome usually relies on clinical factors such as pain, pressure, paresthesia, paralysis and pulselessness (28,29).

The most common cause of ACS is tibial fracture ranging from 2 to 9 percent. After the foot, the second most common site for ACS is the forearm, but almost any compartment may be affected, including the arm, thigh, foot, buttocks, hands and abdomen.

Long-term inappropriate positioning of an unconscious patients may also contribute to ACS.

The prognosis of ACS depends on several factors including the severity of the injury, duration of ischemia, comorbidity and the time of fasciotomy (29,30).

As a result of delay in diagnosis, irreversible tissue ischemia may develop leading to potentially catastrophic nervous system deficits, muscle necrosis, ischemic contractures, infection, chronic pain, delayed fracture union, rhabdomyolysis, amputation or even death.

Rhabdomyolysis

Rhabdomyolysis (also known as pigment nephropathy) may develop after severe traumatic events including car accidents, fall from height, or building collapse. In the case of a traumatic origin, prolonged compression of the body due to long-term immobilization may also result in the compression of muscles, which can manifest in clinical symptoms including dark red or brown (also referred to as cola color) urine, decreased urination, elevated serum creatine kinase level (sometimes higher than 100 000 U/L), muscle swelling or stiffness. Damage to skeletal muscle cells leads to myoglobin proteinuria, tubular epithelial cell ischemia oxidative destruction of the tubules, or pigment cast formation, and, if not treated properly, may eventually result in death due to renal failure. The diagnosis can be confirmed microscopically via routine and myoglobin immunohistological staining, which may reveal acute tubular injury, show granular or pigmented casts in tubules, interstitial edema, or spared glomeruli (expanded mesangium with neutrophils and edema) (31–33).

Trauma induced coagulopathy – disseminated intravascular coagulation

In major traumas, hypovolemic shock is the leading cause of death; with hemorrhage accounting for approximately 40 percent of all trauma deaths (34).

Trauma-induced coagulopathy as well as disseminated intravascular coagulation (DIC) can be described as the *in vivo* activation of the coagulation system resulting in the intravascular deposition of fibrin and consumption bleeding. DIC is a serious hemostatic complication of trauma, and careful attention should be devoted to avoiding further complications; early intervention and proper treatment of DIC make it possible to prevent a fatal outcome. Treatment includes the surgical repair of injured body parts, improvement of shock, and the rapid and sufficient replacement of platelet concentrate, fresh frozen plasma and depleted coagulation factors (27,35–37).

Musculoskeletal injuries to the fetus

In pregnant women, intrauterine fetal injury most often occurs as a result of traffic accidents or suicide. Apart from that, any type of blunt trauma occurring as a result of domestic violence to the pregnant woman can also lead to placental abruption and subsequent miscarriage.

In some cases, due to the high force applied to the maternal abdominal region, the fetal skeleton itself may suffer damages including skull injuries accompanied by contusions, multiple fractures in the limbs, or spinal cord injury, which may lead to the death of the fetus (38).

Cooperation between experts – expert consultations

Forensic investigation requires teamwork, since in most cases the origin of the trauma requires further forensic investigation.

The opinion issued by the pathologist needs to be complemented by other examinations involving a radiologist, or other medical specialists such as trauma surgeons, internal medicine physicians, anesthesiologists, ICU staff, surgical pathologists, laboratory experts, microbiologists, geneticists and toxicologists.

Sometimes cooperation with other non-medical fields is also necessary. Depending on the assignment, working together with crime scene personnel, physicists or a forensic vehicle examiner is indispensable for the reconstruction of a trauma-related injury (39).

REFERENCES

1. Torgbenu EL, Nakua EK, Kyei H, et al. Causes, trends and severity of musculoskeletal injuries in Ghana. *BMC Musculoskelet Disord* 2017; **18**(1): 349.
2. Murray CJ, Vos T, Lozano R, et al. Disability-adjusted life years (DALYs) for 291 diseases and injuries in 21 regions, 1990–2010: A systematic analysis for the Global Burden of Disease Study 2010. *Lancet* 2012; **380**(9859): 2197–223.
3. Hsu JR, Mir H, Wally MK, Seymour RB. Clinical practice guidelines for pain management in acute musculoskeletal injury. *J Orthop Trauma* 2019; **33**(5): e158–e82.
4. Murray CJ, Barber RM, Foreman KJ, et al. Global, regional, and national disability-adjusted life years (DALYs) for 306 diseases and injuries and healthy life expectancy (HALE) for 188 countries, 1990–2013: Quantifying the epidemiological transition. *Lancet* 2015; **386**(10009): 2145–91.
5. Schmidt U, Oramary D, Kamin K, et al. Synergistic effects of forensic medicine and traumatology: Comparison of clinical diagnosis autopsy findings in trauma-related deaths. *World J Surg* 2020; **44**(4): 1137–48.
6. Cusack D, Ferrara SD, Keller E, et al. European Council of Legal Medicine (ECLM) principles for on-site forensic and medico-legal scene and corpse investigation. *Int J Leg Med* 2017; **131**(4): 1119–22.
7. Justice USDo. Death Investigation: A Guide for the Scene Investigator, 2011. https://www.ojp.gov/pdffiles1/nij/234457.pdf (accessed 29 April 2023).
8. Buck U, Buße K, Campana L, et al. What happened before the run over? Morphometric 3D reconstruction. *Forensic Sci Int* 2020; **306**: 110059.
9. Dempsey N, Blau S. Evaluating the evidentiary value of the analysis of skeletal trauma in forensic research: A review of research and practice. *Forensic Sci Int* 2020; **307**: 110140.
10. Töro K, Hubay M, Sótonyi P, Keller E. Fatal traffic injuries among pedestrians, bicyclists and motor vehicle occupants. *Forensic Sci Int* 2005; **151**(2–3): 151–6.
11. Senocak R, Tas H, Ureyen O, et al. Effects of weapon types, interventions, and transport times on complications in combat injuries to musculoskeletal system. *North Clin Istanb* 2019; **6**(1): 64–8.
12. Covey DC. Blast and fragment injuries of the musculoskeletal system. *J Bone Joint Surg Am* 2002; **84**(7): 1221–34.
13. Davis GJ. Patterns of injury. Blunt and sharp. *Clin Lab Med* 1998; **18**(2): 339–50.
14. Sparks L, Buris L. *Forensic Medicine: Diagnosis and Signs of Death/Special Autopsy Techniques/Injuries and Accidents/Wounds and Wound Healing/Sudden, Unexpected Death/Suffocation, Infanticide, Sexual Offences, Criminal Abortion/Paternity/Toxicology/Identification of Victims*. Heidelberg: Springer; 2012.
15. Grabherr S, Baumann P, Minoiu C, et al. Post-mortem imaging in forensic investigations: Current utility, limitations, and ongoing developments. *Res Rep Forensic Med Sci* 2016; **6**: 25.
16. Ahn JM, El-Khoury GY. Role of magnetic resonance imaging in musculoskeletal trauma. *Top Magn Reson Imaging* 2007; **18**(3): 155–68.
17. Buck U, Naether S, Braun M, et al. Application of 3D documentation and geometric reconstruction methods in traffic accident analysis: with high resolution surface scanning, radiological MSCT/MRI scanning and real data based animation. *Forensic Sci Int* 2007; **170**(1): 20–8.
18. Thali MJ, Braun M, Brueschweiler W, Dirnhofer R. 'Morphological imprint': determination of the injury-causing weapon from the wound morphology using forensic 3D/CAD-supported photogrammetry. *Forensic Sci Int* 2003; **132**(3): 177–81.
19. Williamson JA, King GK, Callanan VI, et al. Fatal arterial gas embolism: Detection by chest radiography and imaging before autopsy. *Med J Aust* 1990; **153**(2): 97–100.
20. Bajanowski T, West A, Brinkmann B. Proof of fatal air embolism. *Int J Leg Med* 1998; **111**(4): 208–11.
21. Zolotarov P, Fraser R. Venous air embolism: Artefactual air entrapment and autopsy technique. *Int J Leg Med* 2020; **134**(3): 1033–6.
22. Rothberg DL, Makarewich CA. Fat embolism and fat embolism syndrome. *J Am Acad Orthop Surg* 2019; **27**(8): e346–e55.
23. Bulauitan CS, Gupta R, Lopez Rowe V. Fat embolism, 2020. https://emedicine.medscape.com/article/460524-overview (accessed 29 April 2023).
24. Milroy CM, Parai JL. Fat embolism, fat embolism syndrome and the autopsy. *Acad Forensic Pathol* 2019; **9**(3–4): 136–54.
25. Fulde GW, Harrison P. Fat embolism--a review. *Arch Emerg Med* 1991; **8**(4): 233–9.
28. Mauffrey C, Hak DJ, Martin MP. *Compartment Syndrome: A Guide to Diagnosis and Management*. Cham: Springer; 2019.
29. Olson SA, Glasgow RR. Acute compartment syndrome in lower extremity musculoskeletal trauma. *J Am Acad Orthop Surg* 2005; **13**(7): 436–44.
30. Tillinghast CM, Gary JL. Compartment Syndrome of the Lower Extremity. In: Mauffrey C, Hak DJ, Martin IM (eds), *Compartment Syndrome: A Guide to Diagnosis and Management*. Cham: Springer; 2019, pp. 67–81.
31. Petejova N, Martinek A. Acute kidney injury due to rhabdomyolysis and renal replacement therapy: A critical review. *Crit Care* 2014; **18**(3): 224.
32. Esposito P, Estienne L, Serpieri N, et al. Rhabdomyolysis-associated acute kidney injury. *Am J Kidney Dis* 2018; **71**(6): a12–a4.
33. Plotnikov EY, Chupyrkina AA, Pevzner IB, et al. Myoglobin causes oxidative stress, increase of NO production and dysfunction of kidney's mitochondria. *Biochim Biophys Acta* 2009; **1792**(8): 796–803.
34. Curry N, Hopewell S, Dorée C, et al. The acute management of trauma hemorrhage: A systematic review of randomized controlled trials. *Crit Care* 2011; **15**(2): R92.
35. Hardaway RM. Trauma, sepsis, and disseminated intravascular coagulation. *J Intensive Care Med* 1995; **10**(3): 145–52.
36. Stanley M, Chippa V, Aeddula NR, et al. *Rhabdomyolysis*. Treasure Island: StatPearls; 2021.
37. Simmons JW, Pittet JF, Pierce B. Trauma-induced coagulopathy. *Curr Anesthesiol Rep* 2014; **4**(3): 189–99.
38. Safdari M, Safdari Z, Pishjoo M. Intrauterine fetal traumatic brain injury following motor vehicle accident; A case report and review of the literature. *Bull Emerg Trauma* 2018; **6**(4): 372–5.
39. Malewski H, Kurapka VE, Matulienė S, Navickienė Ž. Cooperation between law enforcement officers and forensic specialists. Diagnosis and possible improvements - a Lithuanian experience. *Arch Med Sadowej Kryminol* 2016; **66**(3): 182–210.

CHAPTER

40

Sports-Related Deaths

Roger W. Byard

INTRODUCTION

The term "sports-related death" has variably been used to refer to any death associated with competitive organized physical activities or with physical exertion related to improving fitness that usually has a defined set of rules (1). This chapter explores different sports that may have shared, or separate causes and mechanisms of death related to trauma occurring as an integral part of the particular activity, or to an underlying recognized or occult medical condition. The term "sport" has been deliberately kept quite broad to capture the range of both competitive and recreational activities involving exercise that may be associated with a lethal outcome as the separation may not be clear; for example, recreational fishing may sometimes involve competition and certain sporting activities such as downhill skiing or football may be undertaken for purely recreational purposes. Similarly, bungee jumping, snowboarding, extreme skiing, canyoning, surfing, skateboarding, skydiving, paragliding, rock climbing and mountain bicycling have all been labeled sports (2).

Unnatural deaths during sporting activities are most often accidental as in cases of head trauma from an unintentional impact with a baseball but may be homicidal in cases of persistent blunt trauma in boxing, occurring after a round has been declared over, or even suicidal as in cases of a skydiver deliberately failing to release a parachute. Traumatic deaths occur in sports in all age ranges (3).

Natural causes of deaths during sport also occur at all ages and may be due to recognized and treated underlying conditions such as asthma or coronary artery atherosclerosis, or to occult acquired disease such as viral myocarditis. Congenital conditions that may have been thought to have been adequately treated, such as surgically repaired cardiac malformations, can result in sudden death during sport, as may occult congenital conditions such as aortic stenosis.

SPECIFIC SPORTING ACTIVITIES

Football

Football is a classic contact sport where head and neck injuries may be sustained from impact with other players, the ground or goal posts. Acute head injuries may involve skull fractures with epidural or subdural hematomas (Figures 40.1 and 40.2) with cerebral contusions. Neck hyperextension may cause potentially lethal upper spinal cord and brainstem injuries (1).

Blunt head trauma can also cause concussion which is characterized by headache, confusion and amnesia, often with disturbances of vision and gait. It is now recognized that concussion, even without loss of consciousness, may represent a serious head injury with the potential for long-term neurologic problems (4). Such recognition has, for example, lead to a trial of removal of deliberate

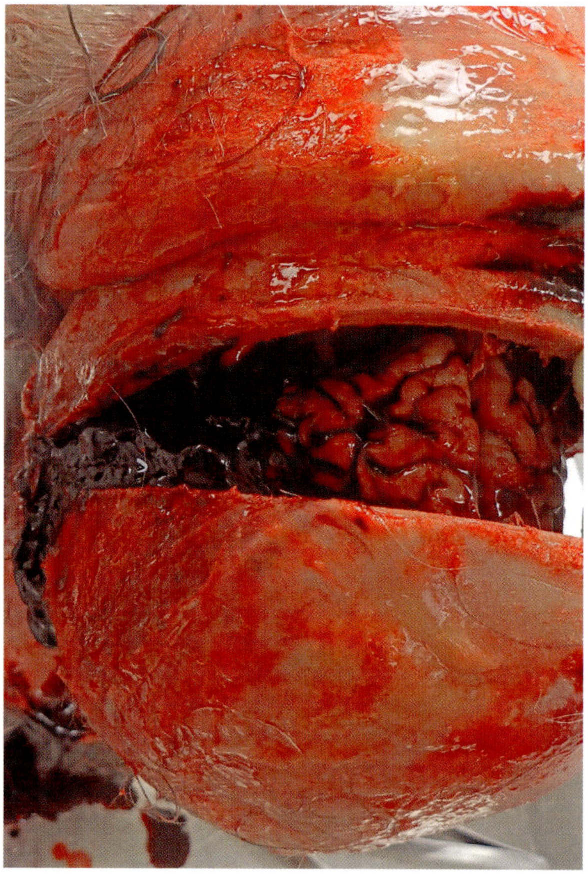

40.1 Opening of the skull may reveal a collection of subdural blood clot.

DOI: 10.1201/9781003138754-42

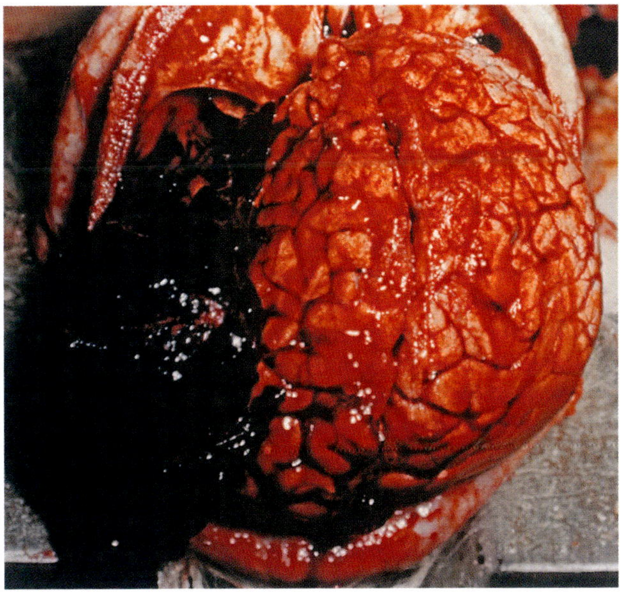

40.2 Another subdural collection of blood with midline shift following blunt craniocerebral trauma.

heading in football for under 12s by the UK Football Association (5). Importantly, it has also been recognized that the neurologic consequences of subsequent head trauma may be magnified, with separate episodes of trauma having a synergistic effect. That is, the effects are greater than the simple sum of the two (or more) impacts (6). This has been termed the second impact syndrome and is believed to involve the rapid development of cerebral swelling with herniation (7,8). Although protective head equipment in the form of helmets for some types of football reduces the incidence of head trauma it does not eliminate the possibility (8).

A consequence of repetitive head trauma may also be chronic traumatic encephalopathy (CTE) which was initially believed to be associated only with boxing but has now been found in American football players, hockey players and wrestlers. It has been associated with premature deaths in athletes, although the link with suicide has not been confirmed (1,9,10).

In summer, football players are susceptible to heat stroke, a condition characterized by hyperthermia (body temperature ≥40.6°C (105°F) with neurologic disturbances that include lethargy, delirium, disorientation and coma (11,12). While mild heat illness is common, more serious cases may be lethal if untreated. Since 1995, an average of three players a year in the United States have died from exertional heat stroke. Between 2000 and 2019 this included 40 high-school football players and at least 10 college football players (13,14). As most of these deaths have occurred during training and conditioning for the game, and not during play, the responsibility of coaches has been highlighted (13,14).

The autopsy diagnosis of a possible heat-related death is difficult as there are no diagnostic features, and environmental and core temperatures from the scene may not be available at the time of post-mortem examination (15). For this reason, the National Association of Medical Examiners in the United States has suggested using the term "heat-related death" for suspected cases where precise information is unavailable (16).

Boxing and wrestling

The majority of deaths arising from boxing matches are due to traumatic brain injury (TBI) involving subdural hematomas which may be followed by permanent neurologic injury and the development of CTE (17). Contusions and intraparenchymal hemorrhage may be associated with direct impact and also with cerebral acceleration/deceleration (18). An Australian study found however, that the rate of boxing-related deaths of 2.3 cases per million participant-years compared favorably with rugby league at 7.3, rugby union at 4.0 and Australian rules football at 3.2 (19).

While wrestling does not usually have lethal injuries, high cervical fractures may occur representing significant trauma (20). Wrestling has also been associated with the development of CTE (10).

Running

In addition to football, marked physical exertion from running in hot and humid conditions may also cause heat stroke with, for example, a death occurring in the 2001 Chicago Marathon in the United States (13).

Baseball, cricket and other ball games

Any ball game may be associated with blunt head trauma if a player is struck. A variety of injuries may occur ranging from simple soft-tissue trauma to potentially more sinister extradural hematomas with the classic "lucid interval" sometimes obscuring the diagnosis.

Commotio cordis is typically seen when a young player who has been struck in the chest by a baseball, cricket ball, lacrosse ball or hockey puck collapses and is unable to be resuscitated (21). It has been described as an instantaneous cardiac arrest caused by non-penetrating chest trauma with no resultant injuries identified at autopsy (22). Animal studies have shown that smaller size is related to an increased risk (23). (*See also* Chapter 38 on "Chest and Abdominal Trauma".)

Karate

The case of a 17-year-old male has been reported where sudden collapse followed a karate kick to the anterior chest. The differential diagnosis included cardioinhibitory reflex or commotio cordis (24). The cardioinhibitory reflex is characterized by a sudden reduction in blood pressure with decrease in cardiac output due to possible sympathetic/parasympathetic stimulation with vasodilation of the splanchnic vasculature (24). Commotio cordis is thought to arise when non-penetrating trauma causes cardiac electrical instability (21,25). Generally, fatalities are uncommon in martial arts such as kendo, kung fu and tae kwon do, and if they occur are

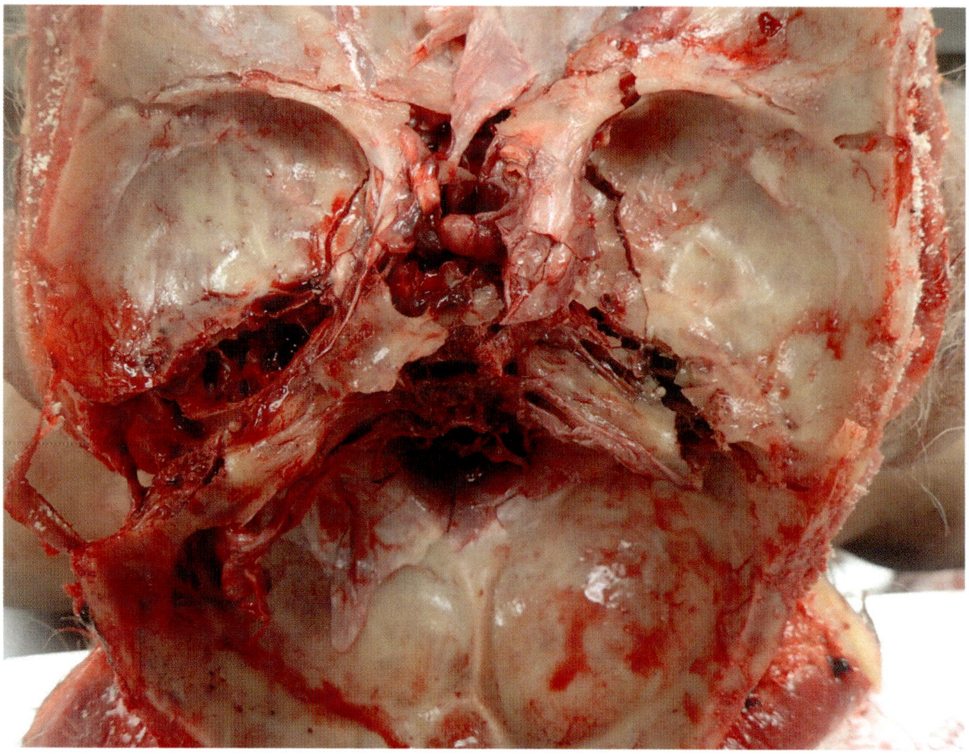

40.3 A hinge fracture of the base of the skull from significant blunt force craniocerebral trauma.

often related to head injury, blunt trauma or underlying illness (26–28).

Skiing and snowboarding

Deaths of skiers descending at speed down slopes most often arise from collisions with objects such as trees, rocks and other skiers with resultant blunt force trauma to the head/neck, chest and abdomen (Figure 40.3) (29). The two major risk factors are speed and loss of control (30). Children are at risk of lethal injuries while skiing due to their lack of experience and musculoskeletal immaturity; 67 percent of childhood skiing fatalities are due to head trauma with 4 to 10 percent associated with thoracoabdominal and spinal injuries (31).

Deaths in avalanches where a large volume of snow moves rapidly downhill may also be due to blunt force trauma or to asphyxia if the victim is buried beneath the snow. A study of a series of avalanche-related deaths found that only 5.4 percent of the cases died from trauma, 8.9 percent from a combination of trauma and asphyxiation, and the remaining 85.7 percent from a combination of suffocation from snow obstructing the airways and compressing the chest (32). Signs of traumatic asphyxia at autopsy include facial and upper body petechiae and subconjunctival hemorrhage (Figure 40.4). Ice masks, which refer to expired air freezing on the face, may also contribute to airway obstruction (33).

On occasion, a skier or snowboarder may fall headfirst into a space around a tree (a tree well), or into a deep drift. Deep spaces can form around tree trunks if the snow in the well melts or is scoured by the wind, or if the surrounding snow slides downhill. Death may occur quite rapidly in these circumstances from a combination of airway obstruction, positional asphyxia and rebreathing of carbon dioxide, rather than from hypothermia or trauma (33). Hypothermia (body temperature falling below 35°C) is always a risk factor in those participating in sports in areas with low environmental temperatures (34). This is suggested when Wischnewski spots are found at autopsy (Figure 40.5).

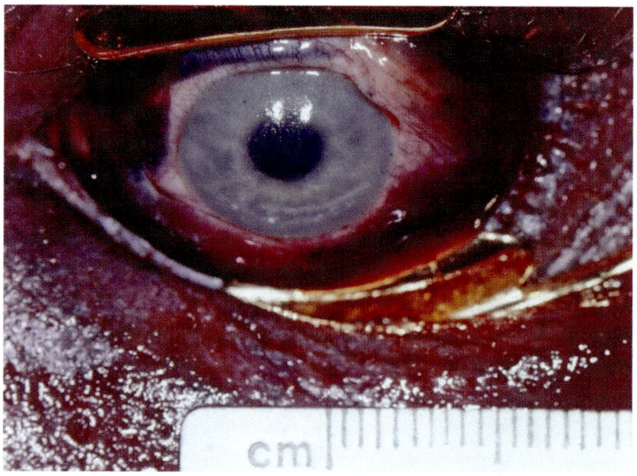

40.4 Extensive subconjunctival hemorrhages in a case of crush asphyxia with intense congestion of the face.

Snowboarding has been associated with higher rates of concussion than skiing (2), with cross-country skiing and sledging having low mortality rates compared to ski

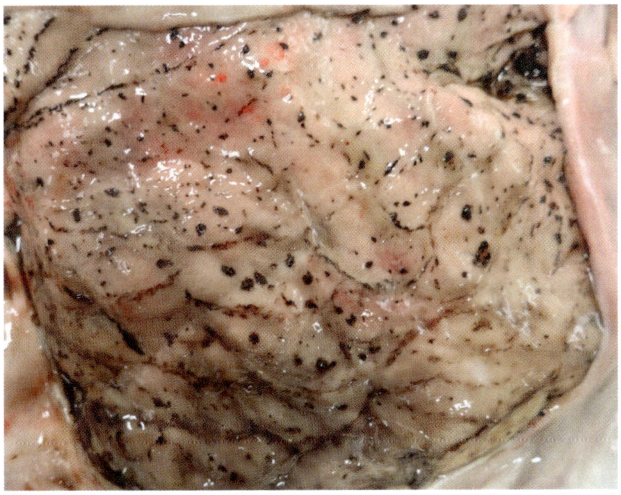

40.5 Numerous Wishnewski spots due to lethal hypothermia.

touring which exposes individuals to greater risks from avalanches (35).

Mountaineering, climbing and hiking

Mountaineers and hikers may sustain similar blunt force injuries to skiers, but these are mainly caused by falls. The types of injuries that may be observed at autopsy depend on the angle of the slope, the attempts of the falling individual and his/her partner to prevent or slow the descent, and the nature of the surface that is impacted. Average distances for fatal falls have been cited at 91 meters, compared to non-fatal falls of 9 meters (29). In a study of mountaineering fatalities in the United States, 34 percent of the deaths were caused by avalanches (36). A study from England and Wales in the 1980s found that mountaineering was one hundred times more dangerous than water sports or ball games and that, when exposure was taken into account, mountaineering was the most dangerous sport/leisure activity overall (37).

Hiking or climbing at high altitudes may also be associated with potentially lethal hypothermia which may be precipitated by a fall into a crevasse or tree well with immobilization (38). Hypothermia may also be a problem in those participating in ultra-endurance events where long-distance events over 42 km may involve traversing rugged wilderness terrain at extreme temperatures (34).

Unacclimatized climbers who ascend rapidly to high altitudes may develop high-altitude pulmonary or cerebral edema which may be lethal (39–41). Rock climbing at lower altitudes than mountaineering generally has a lower mortality rate (42). On occasion, significant injury and potentially death may occur from indoor wall climbing, although the risk is lower than for outdoor rock climbing, as it is for bouldering (ropeless climbing at low heights) (43,44).

The mortality rate of hikers is much less than that for climbers, with studies from Austria showing an average of 82 to 134 deaths in mountain hikers per year, with the majority (90%) being due to falls (46%) or sudden cardiac deaths from underlying medical conditions (44%) (42).

Other causes of death in wilderness areas may be related to animal attacks which vary depending on the geographic location; for example, lion and hippopotamus attacks characterize parts of Africa, compared to bear and cougar attacks in North America (45). Envenomation from snakes is an ever-present danger in many rural areas (46).

Parachuting, skydiving and jumping

Deaths from failed equipment may occur while parachuting or from miscalculation while sky diving. An analysis of 6.2 million jumps showed 0.57 deaths and 49 injuries per 100 000 jumps, with a five times greater risk of death in males. Of note 2.7 to 8.6 percent of these deaths have been attributed to suicides and not accidents (47). Careful assessment of the mental history of the decedent with a review of the circumstances of the jump, ideally with a psychological autopsy, may therefore be required to clarify the manner of these deaths. Lethal injuries are usually multiple involving the head, neck, torso and limbs (48).

Base jumping (building, antenna, span, e.g. a bridge, earth, e.g. a cliff) refers to jumping from heights with the use of a parachute to decelerate in the latter part of the fall. A mortality rate of one in 60 participants has made it six to 90 times more lethal than skydiving, with a Norwegian study showing that one death occurred for every 2317 jumps off the Kjerag massif (49,50). Most fatalities involve wingsuit jumps in mountains with inadequate parachute deployment or path miscalculation resulting in impact (51). At autopsy, multiple serious injuries are found due to ground and cliff strikes. Bungee jumping where the jumper is secured by an elastic cord around the ankles has occasionally been lethal when a ground strike has occurred (52).

Paragliding and hang gliding

Paragliding refers to the use of free-flying craft that were developed from parachutes where the pilot sits in a semi-recumbent position below the wing. Deaths have occurred with a mortality rate in Germany of 0.46 cases/1000 persons at risk. Issues associated with fatalities include strong winds, collapse of the paraglider, stalling, collisions with objects and mistakes during take-off and landing (42). In powered paragliding, an engine is strapped to the back of the pilot, however, it is unclear if this alters mortality compared to standard paragliding and hang gliding (53).

Hang gliding involves the use of a triangular wing supported by a cross bar and keel that has the pilot suspended underneath in a harness. Non-lethal and lethal accidents occur more often due to pilot error than equipment failure, with deaths resulting from head, neck and chest trauma. A characteristic injury is aortic transection from rapid deceleration (Figure 40.6). Occasionally, electrocution may occur if collision with power lines has occurred (54).

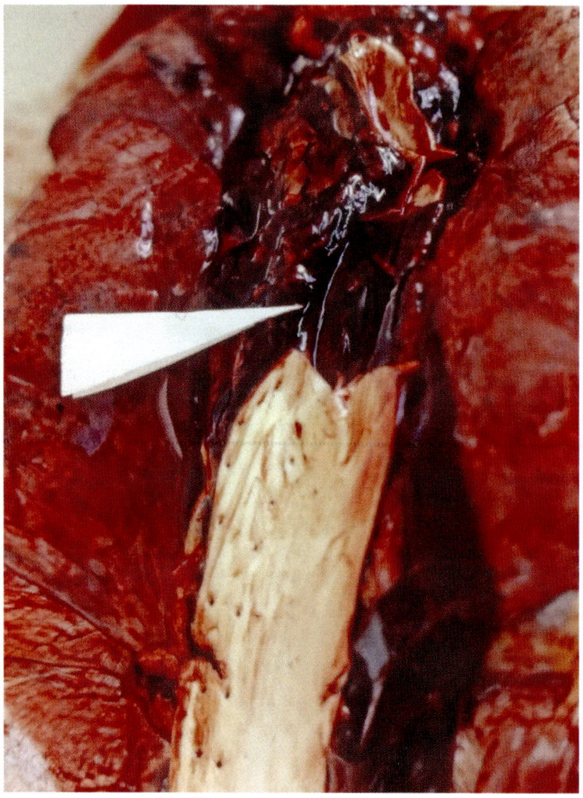

40.6 Aortic transection (arrow) with surrounding interstitial hemorrhage in a young hang glider who impacted the ground.

Horse riding

Equestrian sports are popular among children but are associated with significant injuries and even deaths, most commonly due to blunt head trauma (55). In professional situations of horse racing, jockeys are particularly at risk of serious injuries or fatalities from falling or being trampled. The fatality rate of horseback riding is actually higher than motorcycle or automobile racing, with concussion rates in jockeys of 13 percent exceeding levels found in American footballers and boxers (56). It was estimated that equestrian sports were responsible for 45 percent of sports-related TBI in a study from 2003 to 2012 in the United States (57). The most common injuries associated with horses involve falls (68%) followed by crushing (15%), kicking (8%) and trampling (5%) (58). Occasionally, strangulation by reins has occurred as well as being dragged by stirrups (56).

A study of sports and leisure activity fatalities in England and Wales from 1982 to 1988 found more deaths from horse riding (N = 98), compared to air sports (92 deaths), motor sports (86 deaths) and mountaineering (74 deaths). When exposure was taken into account, horse riding became the third most hazardous activity (33) with injuries related to equestrian activities accounting for 4.3 percent of all sporting injuries (59). Published data between 2006 and 2015 show that the number deaths occurring in a sports or athletic arena in the UK as a result of an accident remain low – around 20 per annum (60)

While injuries are often reported in rodeo riders, fatalities have not been well described in the literature. Trauma to the head and neck account for 10 to 29 percent of injuries with a rate of concussion cited as 3.4 per 1000 competitive exposures (61).

Cycling

Although countries such as Australia have seen increasing numbers of recreational cyclists on the roads in recent years, the number of cycling deaths has declined, indicating that safety programs have been effective (62) and also that cycling behavior in certain groups such as children has changed (63). A 12-year study of cyclist fatalities in South Australia found that 13 deaths (31%) were due to underlying medical conditions, predominantly ischemic heart disease. Traumatic deaths most often involved collisions with vehicles, with 95 percent of the victims being males having an average age of 47 years. Deaths were attributed to multiple injuries in 38 percent of cases and head trauma in 24 percent, with the remainder being due to chest and neck injuries (62). Non-fatal injuries tend to involve simple falls from the bicycle (64). Older individuals have a higher rate of delayed lethal complications such as pneumonia and pulmonary thromboembolism (65). It is no longer believed that exercise-associated collapse in prolonged endurance cycling is due to endotoxemia (66).

A subset of cyclists is mountain biker riders where off-road cycling occurs over rough terrain, often with specially designed bicycles. Serious injuries and deaths may occur usually involving blunt craniocervical and thoracic trauma, most often associated with the rider vaulting over the handlebars following rapid deceleration during a fast downhill descent. The death rate has however, only been reported at 3.5 per million mountain bikers. Risk factors for these types of incidents include an unstable surface and a lack of familiarity with the terrain (42).

Vehicle related

Competitive motor car and motorcycle racing are well recognized causes of lethal injuries following collisions. Less well recognized are golf carts, however, the incidence of golf cart-related crashes has been increasing with an estimated 48 255 golf cart-related injuries in the United States occurring between 2002 and 2005. This represents an injury rate of 4.14 per 100 000 of the population. The most common findings associated with TBI were skull fractures and subdural hematomas. In one study, the mean age was 36 years, 52 percent were males, alcohol was found in nearly one third, and one victim died (67). Lightning may be another rare cause of death in golfers and of other outdoor recreational activities.

Snowmobiles may be associated with fatalities due to blunt trauma from collisions or roll-overs or traumatic/asphyxial deaths from avalanches (68). First developed in the 1920s for moving supplies and people in regions of heavy snowfall, snowmobiling has become a "popular winter sport" for over 2 million people in North America alone, with machines reaching speeds in excess of 145 kph (90 mph) (69). This has resulted in approximately 14 000 injuries and 200 deaths per year with risk factors including alcohol consumption, driver inexperience, excess speed and poor judgement (69). Accidents involving children included collisions with fixed objects in 42 percent of cases and with motor vehicles in 35 percent (70), with deaths occurring predominantly from head and neck injuries (71). Similar issues arise with All Terrain Vehicles (ATVs).

Sailing

A number of recreational and sporting activities revolve around water. Sailing is an example of an activity that may be both recreational and competitive, although similar dangers exist for both types. Studies have shown that the majority of deaths related to sailing involve drowning (73%) due to either falling overboard (39–44%) or to having the vessel capsize (20–40%). The major risk factors for a lethal episode on the water are high winds (12–27%), alcohol consumption (10–15%) and operator inexperience (8%) (72). Hypothermia may be an issue in colder climates. Moving sailing boats with metal masts on land near power lines may also result in lethal electrocution.

Water skiing and boat racing

Water skiing and boat racing have both been associated with drowning but also with serious injuries from propellers accounting for more than one in 20 boating accidents, with a fatality rate of 15–23 percent. There is a higher risk of propeller injury in individuals who have fallen out of a boat compared to water skiers (73). Deaths occur from chop wounds causing deep lacerations to the chest or head, or from exsanguination, if major vessels have been severed (74). Shearing injuries have been caused by tow ropes (75). Victims may then drown if they have been incapacitated by their injury/ies (76).

The risk of death while power boating is directly linked to blood alcohol levels with the majority of lethal episodes being due to drowning, with only 18 percent involving collisions. This is in contrast to jet skis where deaths are mostly due to blunt trauma (Figure 40.7) (77).

Snorkelling and diving

Diving generally involves surface breathing (snorkelling), rebreather apparatus (recirculating underwater breathing) or SCUBA (self-contained underwater breathing apparatus). The main cause of death in diving fatalities remains drowning, with other causes including air embolism, decompression sickness, trauma and underlying natural diseases. Triggering events include exertion, buoyancy problems, disorientation, confusion and panic, with disabling events being rapid ascent, entrapment (for example with ropes) and cardiac conditions (78).

Deaths were associated with asphyxia (37%), cardiac issues (25%) and cerebral gas embolism/pulmonary barotrauma in one study of 126 scuba diving fatalities from Australia (79) (Figure 40.8). Underlying medical conditions causing or contributing to death are most often ischemic heart disease or arrhythmias (80). Trauma may include propeller injuries which can either

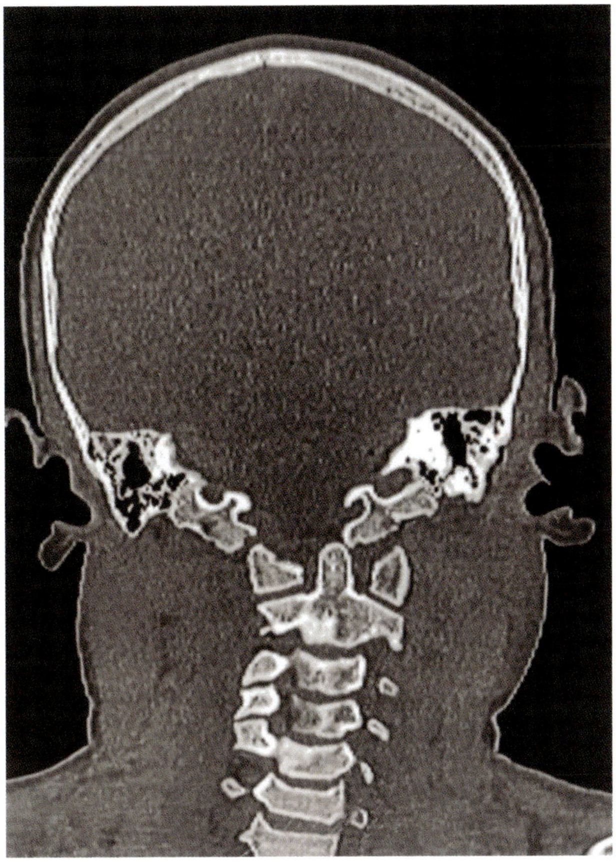

40.7 A post-mortem CT scan showing atlanto-occipital fracture-dislocation with marked neck swelling in a victim of a ski jet collision.

incapacitate or kill outright (76). If survival occurs for some time, central nervous system manifestations may develop (Figure 40.9).

The investigation of diving deaths should be multidisciplinary with careful evaluation of the diving plan, equipment used, water conditions (including wave heights and strength of currents) the diver's activities/actions, past medical history and diving experience (78,81), in addition to full autopsy examinations. Postmortem CT examination is a very useful technique for identifying air embolism (82).

Underwater activities may be associated with predator attacks which can involve saltwater crocodiles and sharks (83,84) (Figure 40.10). In Australia, over the period 1960 to 2017 there were 187 recorded shark attacks with 28 deaths, 13 of which involved snorkelers and 8 scuba divers. This is, however, a relatively small number of cases representing only 3 percent of diving fatalities over this 57-year period (84). Deaths in these cases result from dismemberment or hemorrhage from bites (85,86). Other dangerous animals that may be encountered in the sea include snakes, seals, sting rays, stone fish and jelly fish (45,46,87,88).

Fishing

Commercial fishing is associated with high rates of injury and death compared to recreational fishing as it involves heavy manual labor in all kinds of weather often on a

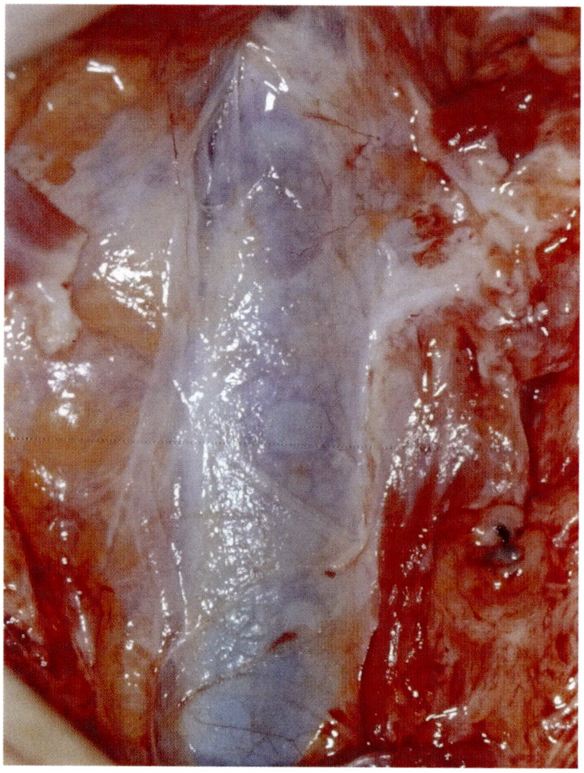

40.8 Air embolism may on occasion be visible at autopsy.

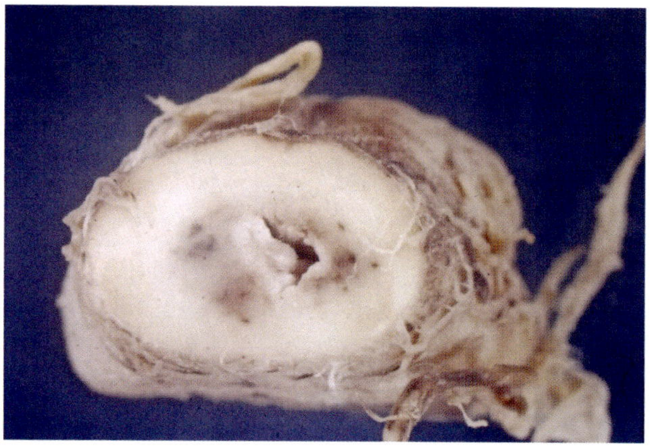

40.9 Cavitation of the central spinal cord in a case of decompression illness from diving.

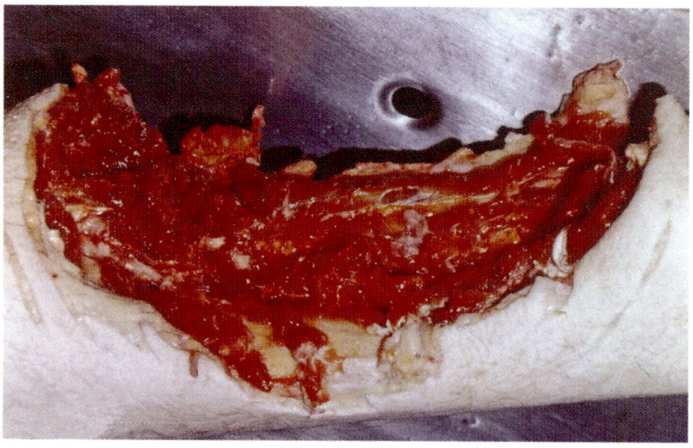

40.10 A large piece of thigh missing from a diver following a shark attack.

moving deck, and sometimes at night (89). While other forms of fishing may be regarded as purely recreational, fishing contests occur, and the International Game Fish Association has very clearly defined rules.

In Australia, rock fishing has been called the most dangerous sport in the country with 12 deaths per year occurring between 2004 and 2012 involving fishers who were swept off rocks by waves or who slipped and fell into the water and drowned (90). The concept that waders worn while fly fishing could fill with water and drag a fisher under has been disputed (90).

Injuries have been reported on commercial fishing boats from unrestrained large fish and, rarely, impact with a fish may also cause death during recreational fishing. This occurred in Northern Australia when a man who was fishing from a boat in Darwin harbour was side swiped by a leaping mackerel (91).

Swimming, diving and surfing

While swimming in rivers and the sea is generally recreational, surfing is both a recreational and competitive sport that may be associated with accidental drowning or injury, as may be recreational swimming where alcohol and inexperience play major roles (92). Surfing has been associated with neck fractures occurring 38 times more often than in skateboarders. Diving into shallow water may result in cervical spine fractures causing quadriplegia or even death (93). Collapse in individuals with LQT1 has been associated with swimming (94).

Canoeing, kayaking and rafting

Individuals who engage in activities involving traversing bodies of fresh water and in particular rivers, are all at risk of drowning and also in cold weather of lethal hypothermia. A problem with rivers is that there may be strong currents in the center of the waterway, without obvious white water or rapids, that create significant eddies and vortexes that can drag swimmers, or those who have fallen out of a craft, underwater very rapidly (95). In white water rivers, death from blunt head trauma from impact with submerged rocks may occur, as may underwater entrapment by rocks or trees; a problem that exists for both hard shell and inflatable boaters. Fallen trees are known as "strainers" as they tend to filter larger solid objects such as swimmers or their craft while allowing water to pass through. Equipment such as ropes may also contribute to underwater entrapment, which may also occur when large volumes of water recirculate at the base of waterfalls (96).

Flush drowning refers to a specific situation where an individual who is not entrapped or significantly injured dies having been swept down a turbulent river, usually while wearing appropriate flotation devices. The exact mechanism of death is unclear however it may be related to repeated episodes of immersion with inhalation of water possibly in association with low water temperatures (96). This may also occur in canyoning, or canyoneering where individuals navigate down a fast-flowing mountain stream in a gorge. There is again danger of

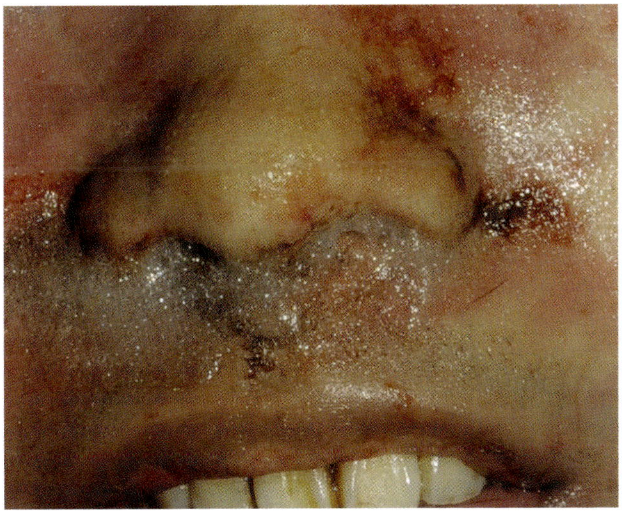

40.11 Foam around the nostrils in a drowning victim.

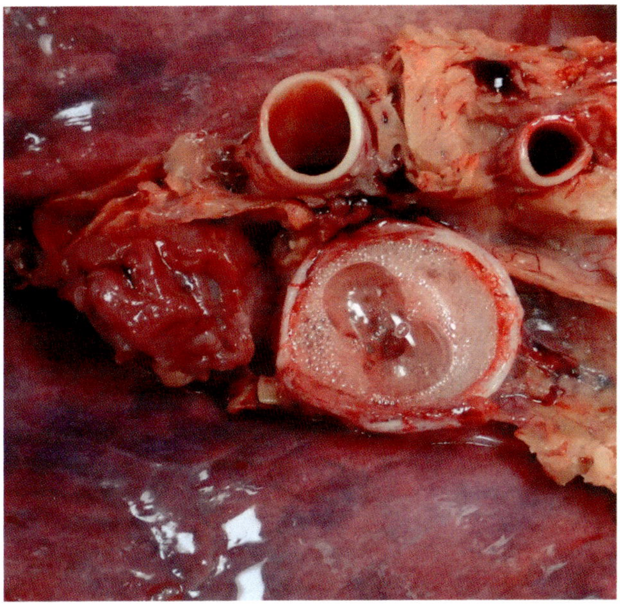

40.12 Marked foam in the airways of another drowning victim.

entrapment and of blunt trauma from collision with rocks.

The autopsy assessment of individuals who have drowned is often difficult and in rivers is made more complicated by a greater degree of putrefaction than in salt water due to difficulties in locating bodies and warmer water temperatures (97,98). Features such as foam in the nostrils (Figure 40.11) or airways (Figure 40.12), although characteristic, is not diagnostic.

Trampolining

While trampolining injuries are well-recognized in children, they have been increasing in adults. A study of 50 adults with trampoline-related injuries found seven to have cervical spinal injuries with one death (99).

Skateboarding

Although injuries are much more common than fatalities, deaths do occur associated with skateboarding, usually on roads. For example, in the United States between 2001 and 2015, 147 skateboarding deaths were recorded (100). Skateboarding has a higher rate of skull fractures compared to skiing, snowmobiling, surfing and mountain bike riding (2).

Sporting audiences

Deaths have been described in crowds at sporting events when the weight of the crowd has resulted in stadiums collapsing or where there has been a surge in the crowd with trampling and crush asphyxia (101,102). This occurred in The Hillsborough Football Stadium in Sheffield, United Kingdom, in 1989 resulting in 97 deaths (103). Rare deaths have also occurred in sporting crowds when signal rockets have been fired into a crowd causing fatal injuries (104).

Role of drugs

Toxicological screening should be performed in all cases of unexpected deaths during sports as performance-enhancing drugs such as amphetamines and other stimulants may lead to increased risk-taking behaviors, as well as being potentially arrhythmogenic (1).

Autopsy findings

In cases of blunt chest impact with no obvious injuries at autopsy, the likely cause of death is commotio cordis. However, this is a slightly contentious diagnosis as suggestions have been made that it can still be applied in cases where there are injuries such as rib fractures or underlying cardiovascular disease. This would expand the decedent group to include more than young athletes on the sports field (25,105). If there is bruising of the myocardium, this is termed contusio cordis.

Blunt thoracic trauma may be associated with significant disruption of the lungs, heart and major vasculature with avulsions and transections, often due to declarative forces. Additionally, blunt trauma may result in lacerations/tears from displaced fractured rib and sternal ends with resultant hemopericardium and hemothoraces (24). Caution may have to be exercised at autopsy in interpreting such findings, however, as forceful or prolonged attempts at cardiopulmonary resuscitation may have similar effects (106).

Blunt head trauma may result in lacerations and bruising of the scalp with underlying subgaleal hematomas, skull fractures and epidural, subdural and subarachnoid hemorrhage (Figure 40.13). Cerebral contusion may be on the side of the trauma with direct impact (coup) or on the opposite side in cases of declarative injuries from falling with a moving head striking a solid object such as the ground (contra coup) (1).

Blunt force abdominal injuries may be associated with liver and splenic lacerations with significant hemorrhage. Other organs at the site of impact may also be contused or lacerated. Penetrating trauma may cause deep vascular injuries (3,94).

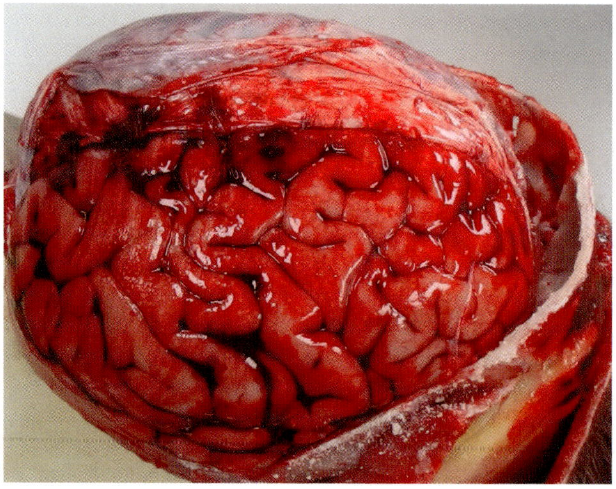

40.13 Gyral flattening with focal areas of subarachnoid hemorrhage following craniocerebral impact.

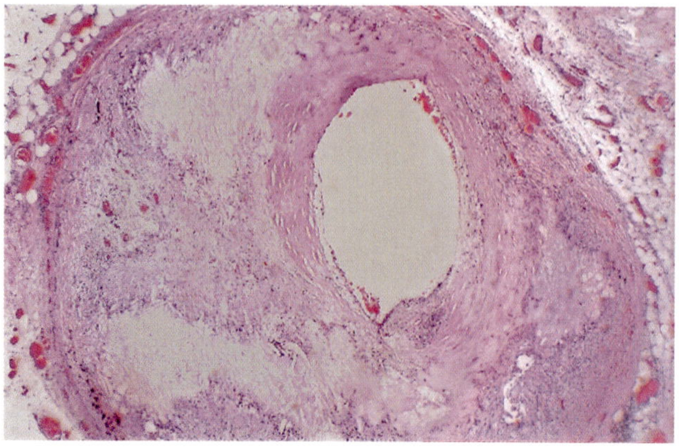

40.14 Marked stenosing atherosclerosis of the left anterior descending coronary artery in a case of sudden cardiac death without an occluding thrombus.

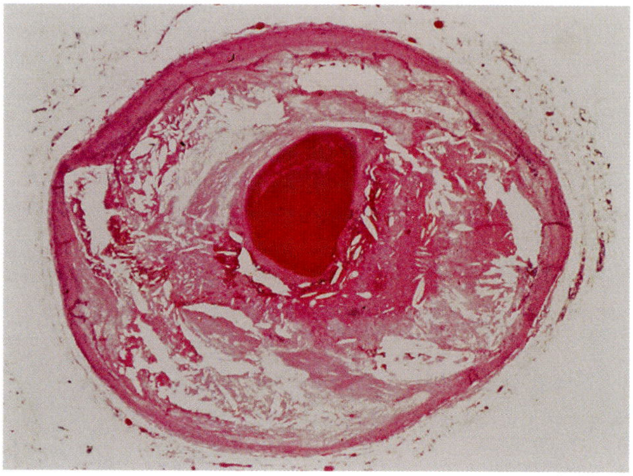

40.15 Similar stenosing atherosclerosis of the left anterior descending coronary artery as in Figure 40.14 but this time with an occluding thrombus.

NATURAL DISEASES ASSOCIATED WITH DEATH IN SPORT

Essentially, any medical condition that can cause sudden and unexpected death may result in death while engaging in sporting activities. As these have been described in detail in a number of review articles and textbooks (94), there is little need to describe their clinical and pathophysiological features in detail. While the risk of sudden death may be ever-present with many of these conditions, the temporal relationship to exertion and cardiovascular stress, with particularly high-energy sporting activities, clearly demonstrates the potential for an exacerbation of lethal mechanisms on the sporting field. A selection of medical conditions that may cause collapse and sudden death in sport are discussed below.

In a study of 18.5 million person-years of observation there were 74 sudden cardiac arrests, 58 of which occurred during non-competitive sports and the remaining 16 during competitive sports. The latter gave an incidence of 0.76 cases per 100 000 athletes with a 43.8 percent survival (107). There is a significantly greater risk of these events in middle-aged and older athletes compared to the young (108). In the United States, the activity most associated with sudden death in the young was basketball (109), whereas in Spain at all ages it was cycling (29%) and soccer (25.5%) (110). The issue of screening athletes for certain conditions prior to undertaking sporting activities is debated (111).

Ischemic heart disease

The classic case of sudden death during sports relates to ischemic heart disease involving a relatively fit middle-aged male who unexpectedly collapses while he is playing squash, engaged in an athletic run or bicycle riding (111,113). In a study of cycling fatalities over a 12-year period in South Australia, 13 of the 42 deaths (31%) were associated with collapse from an underlying medical condition of which 9 (69%) were due to coronary artery atherosclerosis (62). Often the major finding at autopsy is a single area of significant stenosis in the left anterior descending coronary artery, the so-called "widow-maker" (Figure 40.14), rather than an occluding thrombus (Figure 40.15). Other findings in the series of cyclists were anomalous coronary artery ostia, valvular heart disease and arrhythmogenic right ventricular cardiomyopathy (ARVC) (62).

Arrhythmogenic ventricular cardiomyopathy

This is a condition characterized by fibrofatty replacement in the right ventricle in particular, but also the left, that is associated with lethal arrhythmias and sudden death. It is inherited in an autosomal dominant manner with variable penetrance and expression and may be caused by mutations in chromosomes 1q42-q43, 2q32.1-q32.2, 3p23, 10p12-p14, 14q12-q22, 14q23-q24 and 17q21 (Naxos disease) (94). It has been responsible for 3 to 4 percent of sudden death or cardiac arrests in young athletes in the United States and France, and in 10 percent of athletes younger than 35 years in the United Kingdom, increasing to 24 percent in those older than 35 years (114).

Ion channel diseases

In certain circumstances, no morphologic abnormality may be found in a case of sudden death in an athlete which raises the possibility of an underlying channelopathy which includes Brugada syndrome, long and short QT syndromes and catecholaminergic polymorphic ventricular tachycardia. These may have associated genetic abnormalities and appropriate genetic testing and review is essential, often including family members (94).

Hypertrophic cardiomyopathy (HOCM)

This is a primary disorder of the myocardium caused by many hundreds of sarcomere protein gene mutations and is the most common genetic cardiovascular disease, occurring in approximately 1 in every 500 people (115). The most common mutations involve the β-myosin heavy chain (MYH7) and the myosin-binding protein C (MYBPC3) producing a profound increase in the size and weight of the heart due to myocyte hypertrophy (94). Considerable heterogeneity exists in the clinical and pathological presentations, even within the same family, and genotype often does not correspond to phenotype. Thus, although some cases may manifest in infancy with cardiac failure, others may remain occult until cardiac arrest occurs during a sporting activity. Although it has been asserted that it is the major cause of sudden cardiac death in athletes under 40 years of age (115), others have suggested that this may be overtaken by autopsy-negative cases presumably involving channelopathies (116). At autopsy, marked left ventricular hypertrophy is evident (Figure 40.16), sometimes with macroscopically observable myofiber disarray.

Myocarditis

Most often due to a viral infection of the heart due to cocksackie B4 virus with interstitial inflammation and myocyte necrosis, myocarditis predisposes to sudden death due to arrhythmias. Other viral agents include coxsackie A, influenza, polio and enteroviruses (1,88). Myocarditis should be suspected particularly in a young person who collapses while engaged in sports or athletics who has had symptoms and signs of a viral illness over the preceding days.

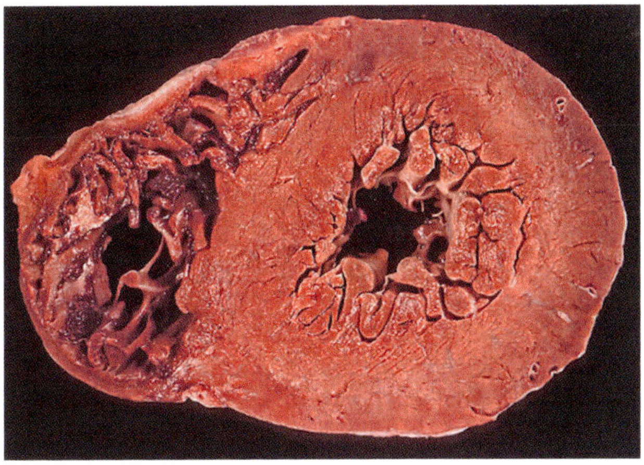

40.16 Marked concentric left ventricular hypertrophy in a case of hypertrophic cardiomyopathy.

Other cardiovascular conditions

Dilated cardiomyopathies have been associated with sudden death during sport, as have sarcoidosis and congenital heart disease (117,118). The latter includes occult anomalies such as aortic stenosis, coronary artery anomalies (Figure 40.17) and also treated cases where there is fibrous scarring from previous surgery (3). Arteriovenous

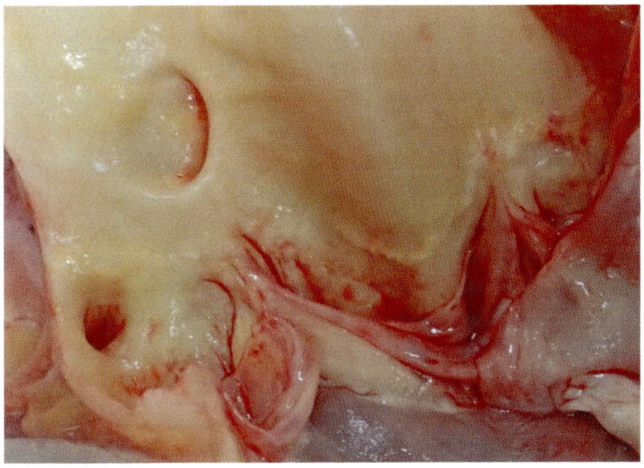

40.17 A ruptured berry aneurysm at the base of the brain (arrow) with subarachnoid and intraparenchymal hemorrhage.

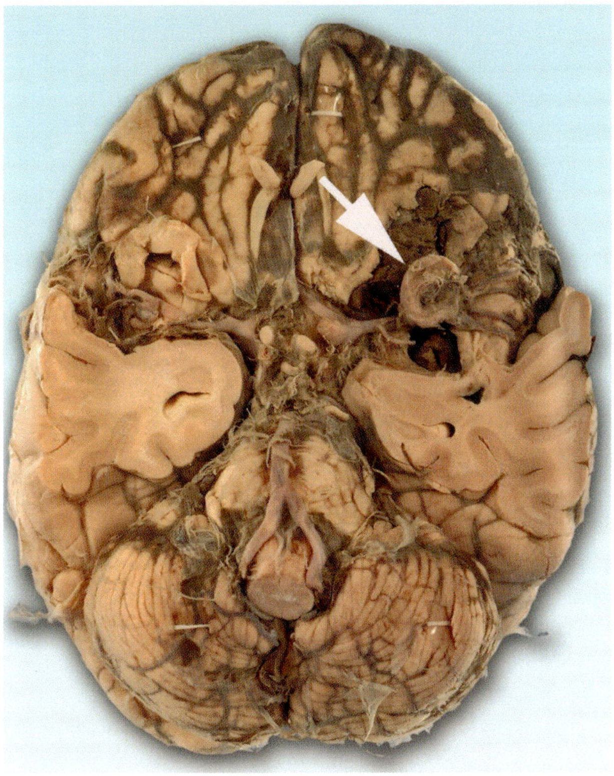

40.18 An anomalous coronary artery may cause sudden death during exercise at any age. Here, an anomalous right coronary artery can be seen above a normally situated left coronary artery ostium. The ostium of the anomalous vessel is slit-like due to a sharp angle of take-off of the vessel.

malformations of the brain and berry aneurysms (Figure 40.18) have been known to rupture during intense exercise such as weightlifting that are associated with increases in blood pressure (1). Pulmonary thromboembolism may result from immobility following leg injuries or may complicate knee surgery for sport-induced joint degeneration (Figure 40.19).

Connective tissue disorders

The most common connective tissue disorder associated with collapse during exertion is Marfan syndrome. Caused by mutations in the fibrillin gene, the typical Marfan phenotype is a tall thin individual with a long arm reach (as is often seen in basketballers), long fingers and toes (arachnodactly) a high-arched palate and pectus cavum. It may be associated with premature death from aortic dissection with rupture and/or cardiac tamponade and mitral valve prolapse due to myxomatous change (94).

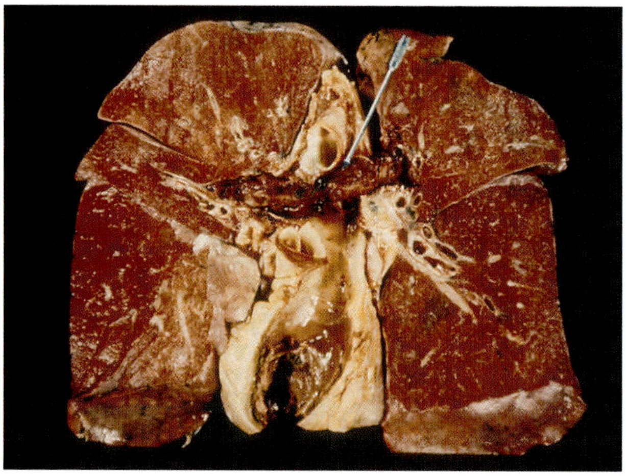

40.19 A large saddle pulmonary thromboembolus occluding the pulmonary outflow tract.

Sickle cell disease

Sickle cell disease is caused by replacement of glutamic acid by valine in the sixth position on the β-chain of the hemoglobin molecule. This results in decreased plasticity of red blood cells with elongation and "sickling". The cells are then no longer able to pass through normal vascular channels and are more susceptible to damage and are more likely cause blockage of vessels (94). Characterized by anemia, sudden death may occur from splenic sequestration, infection, stroke and pulmonary thromboembolism (119).

There is also a risk of sudden death during exertion in those with sickle cell trait, particularly among black American military recruits during exercise (120). The risk for this cohort is 28 to 40 times and occurs mostly in recruits over the age of 20 years. Exercise predisposes to venous hypoxia and acidosis, which, in combination with overheating, dehydration and hypotension, can result in lethal sickling (94).

Asthma

Bronchospasm due to asthma may significantly reduce air intake and limit activity. It may be induced by environmental irritants or allergens and also by exercise (121). At autopsy, the lungs will be hyperinflated obscuring the anterior surface of the heart, with mucus plugging (Figure 40.20) and basement membrane thickening with an eosinophilic infiltrate on microscopy.

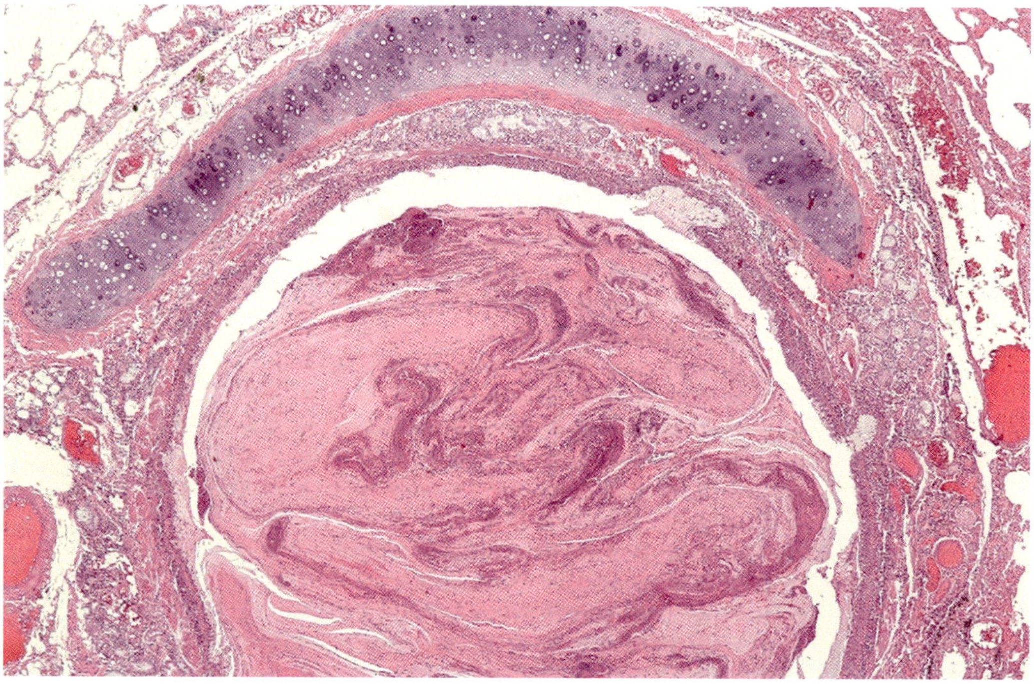

40.20 Mucus plugging of a small airway in a case of lethal asthma. At higher power, basement membrane thickening, and an eosinophilic infiltrate were observed.

It is now well recognized that sudden death due to an exacerbation of asthma may occur in both recreational and competitive athletes (122). Of note, up to 10 percent of high school athletes may have asthma, and in the 1996 Summer Olympic Games, it was reported in 50 percent of cyclists, 30 percent of swimmers, 25 percent of rowers and 18 percent of track and field athletes on the United States team (123).

There is also the possibility that the sporting environment an athlete is exposed to may cause or exacerbate asthma. For example, it has been shown that there is a higher rate of respiratory symptoms, airway inflammation and asthma in elite swimmers due to long-term exposure to pool chlorine (123,125).

Epilepsy

Individuals with epilepsy are at risk of physical injury if they have a seizure in high-risk situations such as driving (126). Children with epilepsy may also be at risk of drowning (127).

CONCLUSION

A wide range of injuries may cause death during sport, and the types of lethal trauma vary according to the activity and may be specific to the activity itself or apply to a range of sports. The possibility of occult or known organic disease is also a consideration when collapse occurs while an individual is engaged in sport, particularly when there is no history or evidence of physical injury, The correct determination of cause of death in these circumstances may be influenced by many factors and meticulous assessment is essential to ensure that relevant insurance, criminal or civil litigation issues are appropriately informed.

REFERENCES

1. Cina SJ, Cina JS. Deaths: Sports – Pathology In: Payne-James J, Byard RW (eds). *Encyclopedia of Forensic and Legal Medicine*. Vol 2. 2nd ed. Oxford: Academic Press; 2016; pp 135–42.
2. Sharma VK, Rango J, Connaughton AJ, et al. The current state of head and neck injuries in extreme sports. *Orth J Sports Med* 2115; **3**: 2325967114564358.
3. Byard RW, James RA, Gilbert JD. Childhood sporting deaths. *Am J Forensic Med Pathol* 2002; **23**: 364–7.
4. Erlanger DM, Kutner KC, Barth JT, Barnes R. Neuropsychology of sports-related head injury: dementia pugalistica to post-concussive syndrome. *Clin Neuropsychol* 1999; **13**: 1.
5. Football Association. Statement: heading in junior football. Available from: https://www.thefa.com/news/2022/jul/18/statement-heading-trial-u12-games-20221807 (Accessed 1 May 2023).
6. Webbe F, Barth J. Short-term and long-term outcome of athletic closed head injuries. *Clin Sports Med* 2003; **22**: 577–92.
7. Byard RW, Vink R. The second impact syndrome. *Forensic Sci Med Pathol* 2009; **5**: 36–8.
8. Cina SJ, Treika D. Sports-Related Injuries and Deaths. Ch 26 In: Collins KA, Byard RW, (eds). *Forensic Pathology of Infancy and Childhood*, New York: Springer Publishers; 2014, pp. 711–26.
9. Omalu BJ, DeKosky ST, Minister RL, et al. Chronic traumatic encephalopathy in a National Football League player. *Neurosurgery* 2005; **57**: 128–34.
10. Maroon JC, Winkelman R, Bost J, et al. Chronic traumatic encephalopathy in contact sports: A systematic review of all reported pathological cases. *PLoS ONE* 2015; **10**: e0117338.
11. Green H, Gilbert J, James R, Byard RW. An analysis of factors contributing to a series of deaths due to exposure to high environmental temperatures. *Am J Forensic Med Pathol* 2001; **22**: 196–9.
12. Bouchama A, Knochel JP. Heat stroke. *N Engl J Med* 2002; **346**: 1978–88.
13. Eichner ER. Heat stroke in sports: Causes, prevention, and treatment. *Sports Sci Exchange* 2002; **15**: 3.86
14. Eichner ER. Fatal exertional heat stroke in football: The coaches are the culprits. *Curr Sports Med Rep* 2019; **18**: 251–2.
15. Byard RW. Heat-related deaths. *Forensic Sci Med Pathol* 2013; **9**: 469–70.
16. Donoghue, ER, Graham MA, Jentzen JM, et al. Criteria for the diagnosis of heat-related deaths: National Association of Medical Examiners. *Am J Forensic Med Pathol* 1997; **18**: 11–14.
17. Miele VJ, Bailes JE, Cantu RC, Rabb CH. Subdural hematomas in boxing: the spectrum of consequences. *Neurosurg Focus* 2006; **21**: E10.
18. Constantoyannis C, Partheni M. Fatal head injury from boxing: A case report from Greece. *Br J Sports Med* 2004; **38**: 78–9.
19. Alevras AJ, Fuller JT, Mitchell R, Lystad RP. Boxing-related fatalities in Australia: A retrospective analysis of news media reports. *J Sci Med Sports* 2022; **25**: 25–30.
20. Kurup JKN, Jampani R, Mohanty SP. Catastrophic cervical spinal injury in an amateur college wrestler. *BMJ Case Rep* 2017; bcr2017220260.
21. Maron BJ, Poliac LC, Kaplan JA, et al. Blunt impact of the chest leading to sudden death from cardiac arrest during sports activities. *N Engl J Med* 1995; **333**: 337–42.
22. Nesbitt AD, Cooper PJ, Kohl P. Rediscovering commotio cordis. *Lancet* 2001; **357**: 1195–7.
23. Madias C, Maron BJ, Dau N, et al. Size as an important determinant of chest-blow–induced commotio cordis. *Med Sci Sports Exer* 2018; **50**: 1768–71.
24. de Froidment S, Lobrinus JA, Michaud K, et al. Cardioinhibitory reflex due to a karate kick. *Am J Forensic Med Pathol* 2015; **36**: 79–83.
25. Marshall D, Gilbert J, Byard RW. The spectrum of findings in cases of sudden death due to blunt cardiac trauma – 'commotio cordis'. *Am J Forensic Med Pathol* 2008; **29**: 1–4.
26. Oler M, Tomson W, Pepe H, et al. Morbidity and mortality in the martial arts: A warning. *J Trauma* 1991; **31(2)**: 251–3.
27. Barbesier M, Boval C, Desfeux J, et al. Acute fatal coronary artery dissection following exercise-related blunt chest trauma. *J Forensic Sci* 2015; **60(1)**: 233–5.
28. Caputo F, Barranco R, Fraternali, et al. Fatal intracerebral hemorrhage during "Muay Thai" in a 21-year-old man with undiagnosed acute myeloid leukemia: Spontaneous or posttraumatic hemorrhage? *Am J Forensic Med Pathol* 2020; **41(3)**: 213–216.
29. Windsor JS, Firth PG, Grocott MP, et al. Mountain mortality: A review of deaths that occur during recreational activities in the mountains. *Postgrad Med J* 2009; **85**: 316–21.
30. Morrow PL, McQuillen EN, Eaton LA, Bernstein CJ. Downhill ski fatalities: The Vermont experience. *J Trauma* 1988; **28**: 95–100.
31. Meyers MC, Laurent M, Higgins RW, Skelly WA. Downhill ski injuries in children and adolescents. *Sports Med* 2007; **37**: 485–99.
32. McIntosh SE, Grissom CK, Olivares CR, et al. Cause of death in avalanche fatalities. *Wild Environ Med* 2007; **18**: 293–7.
33. Van Tilburg C. Non-avalanche-related snow immersion deaths: tree well and deep snow immersion asphyxiation. *Wild Environ Med* 2010: **21(3)**: 257–61.
34. Procter E, Brugger H, Burtscher M. Accidental hypothermia in recreational activities in the mountains: a narrative review. *Scan J Med Sci Sports* 2018; **28**: 2464–72.
35. Niedermeier M, Gatterer H, Pococco E, et al. Mortality in different mountain sports acitivites primarily practiced in the winter season: A narrative review. *Int J Environ Res Pub Health* 2020; **17**: 259.
36. Christensen ED, Lacsina EQ. Mountaineering fatalities on Mt Ranier, Washington, 1977–1997: Autopsy and investigative findings. *Am J Forensic Med Pathol* 1999; **20**: 173–9.

37. Avery JG, Harper P, Ackroyd S. Do we pay too dearly for our sport and leisure activities? An investigation into fatalities as a result of sporting and leisure activities in England and Wales, 1982–1988. *Pub Health* 1990; **1046:** 417–23.
38. Bright F, Byard RW. Extremes of Temperature: Hypothermia. In: Payne-James JJ, Byard RW, (eds). *Encyclopedia of Forensic and Legal Medicine*. 2nd ed. Vol. 2. Oxford: Academic Press; 2016, pp. 486–95.
39. Westensee J, Rogé I, Van Roo JD, et al. Mountaineering fatalities on Aconcagua: 2001–2012. *High Alt Med Biol* 2013; **14:** 298–303.
40. Pennardt A. High-altitude pulmonary edema: Diagnosis, prevention, and treatment. *Curr Sports Med Rep* 2013; **12:** 115–9.
41. Luks AM, Swenson ER, Bärtsch P. Acute high-altitude sickness. *Eur Respir Rev* 2017; **26:** 160096.
42. Gatterer H, Niedermeier M, Poceco E, et al. Mortality in different mountain sports activities primarily practiced in the summer season: A narrative review. *Int J Environ Res Pub Health* 2019; **16:** 3920.
43. Schöffl VR, Hoffmann G, Küpper T. Acute injury risk and severity in indoor climbing: A prospective analysis of 515,337 indoor climbing wall visits in 5 years. *Wild Environ Med* 2013; **24:** 187–94
44. Schöffl V, Morrison A, Schwarz U, et al. Evaluation of injury and fatality risk in rock and ice climbing. *Sports Med* 2010; **40:** 657–79.
45. Bury D, Langlois NEI, Byard RW. Animal-related fatalities Part I: Characteristic autopsy findings and variable causes of death associated with blunt and sharp trauma. *J Forensic Sci* 2012; **57:** 370–4.
46. Bury D, Langlois NEI, Byard RW. Animal-related fatalities Part II: Characteristic autopsy findings and variable causes of death associated with envenomation, poisoning, anaphylaxis, asphyxiation and sepsis. *J Forensic Sci* 2012; **57:** 375–80.
47. Fer C, Guiavarch M, Edouard P. Epidemiology of skydiving-related deaths and injuries: a 10-years prospective study of 6.2 million jumps between 2001 and 2019 in France. *J Sci Med Sport* 2021; **24:** 448–53.
48. Peyron P-A, Margueritte E, Bacino E. Suicide in parachuting: A case report and review of the literature. *Forensic Sci Int* 2018; **286:** e8–13.
49. Westman A, Rosén M, Berggren P, Björnstig U. Parachuting from fixed objects: descriptive study of 106 fatal events in BASE jumping 1981–2006. *Brit J Sports Med* 2008; **42:** 431–6.
50. Soreide K, Ellingsen CL. Knutson V. How dangerous is BASE jumping? An analysis of adverse events in 20,850 jumps from Kjerag massif, Norway. *J Trauma* 2007; **62:** 1113–17.
51. Bouchat P, Brymer E. BASE jumping fatalities between 2007 and 2017: Main causes of fatal events and recommendations for safety. *Wild Environ Med* 2019; **30:** 407–11.
52. Søreide K. The epidemiology of injury in bungee jumping, BASE jumping and skydiving. *Med Sport J* 2021; **58:** 112–29.
53. Feletti F, Goin J. Accidents and injuries related to powered paragliding; A cross-sectional study. *BMJ Open* 2014; **4:** e005508.
54. Tongue JR. Hang gliding injuries in California. *J Trauma* 1977; **17:** 898–902.
55. Theodore JE, Theodore SG, Stockton KA, Kimble RM. Paediatric horse-related trauma. *J Paediatric Child Health* 2017; **53:** 543–50.
56. Byard RW. Lethal recreational activities involving horses: A forensic study. *Leg Med* 2020; **46:** 101728.
57. Winkler EA, Yue JK, Burke JF, et al. Adult sports-related traumatic brain injury in United States trauma centers. *Neurosurg Focus* 2016; **40:** E4
58. Clarke CN, Tsuei BJ, Butler KL. Equine-related injury: A retrospective analysis of outcomes over a 10-year period. *Am J Surg* 2008; **195:** 702–4.
59. Whitlock MR. Injuries to riders in the cross-country phase of eventing: The importance of protective equipment. *Br J Sport Med* 1999; **33:** 212–14.
60. Office for National Statistics. Accidental deaths that occurred in a sports or athletics area, England and Wales 2006 to 2015. Available from: https://www.ons.gov.uk/peoplepopulationandcommunity/birthsdeathsandmarriages/deaths/adhocs/006243accidentaldeathsthatoccurredinasportsorathleticsareaenglandandwales2006to2015 (Accessed 1 May 2023).
61. Meyers MC, Laurent CM. The rodeo athlete. Injuries: Part II. *Sports Med* 2010; **40:** 817–39.
62. Olds K, Byard RW, Langlois NEI. Injury patterns and features of cycling fatalities in South Australia. *J Forensic Leg Med* 2015; **34:** 99–103.
63. O'Donovan S, van den Heuvel C, Baldock M, Byard RW. Childhood cycling fatalities in South Australia before and after the introduction of helmet legislation. *Med Sci Law* 2020; **60(3):** 196–9.
64. Noakes TD. Fatal cycling injuries. *Sports Med* 1995; **20:** 348–62.
65. Fife D, Davis J, Tate L, et al. Fatal injuries to bicyclists: The experience of Dade County, Florida. *J Trauma* 1983; **23:** 745–55.
66. Moore GE, Holbein MEB, Knochel JP. Exercise-related collapse in cyclists is unrelated to endotoxemia. *Med Sci Sport Exer* 1995; **27:** 1238–42.
67. Simpson B, Shepard S, Kitagawa R. Golf cart associated traumatic brain injury. *Brain Injury* 2019; **33:** 1476–8.
68. Boyd J, Haegeli P, Abu-Laban RB, et al. Patterns of death among avalanche fatalities: A 21-year review. *CMAJ* 2009; **180:** 507–12.
69. Pierz JJ. Snowmobile injuries in North America. *Clin Ortho Rel Res* 2003; **409:** 29–36.
70. DeCou JM, Fagerman LE, Ropele D, et al. Snowmobile injuries and fatalities in children. *J Pediatr Surg* 2003; **38:** 784–7.
71. Rice MR, Alvanos L, Kenney B. Snowmobile injuries and deaths in children: A review of national injury data and state legislation. *Pediatrics* 2000; **105:** 615–19.
72. Nathanson A. Sailing injuries: A review of the literature. *Rhode Is Med J* 2019; **102(1):** 23–7.
73. Mann RJ. Propeller injuries incurred in boating accidents. *Am J Sports Med* 1980; **8:** 280–4.
74. Ihama Y, Ninomiya K, Noguchi M, et al. Fatal propeller injuries: Three autopsy case reports. *J Forensic Leg Med* 2009; **16:** 420–3.
75. Hummel G, Gainor BJ, Waterskiing-related injuries. *Am J Sports Med* 1982; **10:** 215–18.
76. Perilli G, Di Battista B, Motana A, et al. A rare case of a scuba diver's death due to propeller injuries of a desalination pump. *J Forensic Leg Med* 2015; **32:** 21–4.
77. Chalmers DJ, Morrison L. Epidemiology of non-submersion injuries in aquatic sporting and recreational activities. *Sports Med* 2003; **33(10):** 745–70.
78. Casadesús MP, Aguitte F, Carrera A, et al. Diving-related fatalities: multidisciplinary, experience-based investigation. *Forensic Sci Med Pathol* 2019; **15:** 224–32.
79. Lippmann J, Taylor D M. Scuba diving fatalities in Australia 2001–2013: chain of events. *Div Hyperbar Med* 2020; **50:** 220–9.
80. Lippmann J, Taylor D M. Medical conditions in scuba diving fatality victims in Australia 2001–2013. *Div Hyperbar Med* 2020; **50:** 98–104.
81. Ramnefjell MP, Morild I, Mørk SJ, Lilleng PK. Fatal diving accidents in Western Norway 1983–2007. *Forensic Sci Int* 2012; **223:** e22–6.
82. Dougherty S, Khorsandi M, Adelbai M, et al. Sudden death in a diver: A diagnostic conundrum. *Wild Environ Med* 2017; **28:** 225–9.
83. Sinton TJ, Byard RW. Pathological features of fatal crocodile attacks in northern Australia, 2005–2014. *J Forensic Sci* 2016; **61:** 1553–5.
84. Lippmann J. Fatal shark attacks on divers in Australia, 1960–2017. *Div Hyperbar Med* 2018; **48:** 224–8.
85. Byard RW, Gilbert JD, Brown K. Pathological features of fatal shark attacks. *Am J Forensic Med Pathol* 2000; **21:** 225–9.
86. Byard RW. James RA, Heath KJ. Recovery of human remains after shark attack. *Am J Forensic Med Pathol* 2006; **27:** 256–9.
87. Tiemensma M, Byard RW. Fatal sea snake envenomation. *Am J Forensic Med Pathol* 2021; **42:** 401–4.
88. Tiemensma M, Currie BJ, Byard RW. Jellyfish envenoming: Pediatric and geographic vulnerabilities. *J Forensic Sci* 2021; **66:** 2006–9.
89. Byard RW. Commercial fishing industry deaths: Forensic issues. *J Forensic Leg Med* 2013; **20:** 129–32.
90. Petrass LA, Blitvich JD, McElroy GK. Drowning deaths among anglers: are waders a contributing factor? *Int J Inj Cont Safe Prom* 2017; **24:** 131–5.
91. Tiemensma M, Byard RW. A recreational fishing death due to a jumping Spanish mackerel (*Scomberomorus commerson*). *Am J Forensic Med Pathol* 2021; **42(4):** 397–400.
92. Stephenson L, Byard RW. Drowning In: Payne-James JJ, Byard RW. (eds). *Forensic and Legal Medicine: Clinical and Pathological Aspects*. London: Taylor and Francis; 2002.
93. Voland C, Vilarino R, Grabherr S, et al. Fatal cervical spine injury from diving

accident. *Am J Forensic Med Pathol* 2015; **36:** 216–18.

94. Byard RW. *Sudden Death in the Young*. 3rd ed. Cambridge, UK: Cambridge University Press; 2010.
95. Byard RW. Drowning deaths in rivers. *Forensic Sci Med Pathol* 2017; **13:** 388–9.
96. Farstad DJ, Luttrell JM. Flush drowning as a cause of whitewater deaths. *Wild Environ Med* 202; **31:** 11–15.
97. Stephenson L, Van den Heuvel C, Byard RW. The persistent problem of drowning – a difficult diagnosis with inconclusive tests. *J Forensic Leg Med* 2019; **66:** 79–85.
98. Byard RW. Putrefaction: An additional complicating factor in the assessment of freshwater drownings in rivers. *J Forensic Sci* 2018; **63:** 899–901.
99. Arora V, Kimmel LA, Vu Kathy, et al. Trampoline related injuries in adults. *Injury Int J Care Inj* 2016; **47:** 192–6.
100. Fang K, Handy S. Skate and die? The safety performance of skateboard travel: A look at injury data, fatality data, and rider behaviour. *J Trans Health* 2017; **7:** 288–97.
101. Byard RW, Wick R, Simpson E, Gilbert JD. The pathological features and circumstances of death of lethal crush/traumatic asphyxia in adults: A 25-year study. *Forensic Sci Int* 2006; **159:** 200–5.
102. DeAngeles D, Schurr M, Birnbaum M, Harms B. Traumatic asphyxia following stadium crowd surge: stadium factors affecting outcome. *World Med J* 1998; **97:** 42–5.
103. Griffith R. Hillsborough part 2: Advance decisions and futile treatments. *Brit J Nurs* 2014; **23:** 672–3.
104. Alempijević D, Ječmenica D, Pavelić S, et al. Death caused by a signal rocket: Not an isolated case. *J Forensci Sci* 2008; **53:** 1172–3.
105. Byard RW. Commotio cordis (Letter). *N Engl J Med* 2010; **362:** 2229.
106. Olds K, Byard RW, Langlois NEI. Injuries associated with resuscitation: An overview. *J Forensic Leg Med* 2015; **33:** 39–43.
107. Landry CH, Allan KS, Connelly KA, et al. Sudden cardiac arrest during participation in competitive sports. *N Engl J Med* 2017; **377:** 1943–53.
108. Chugh SS, Weiss JB. Sudden cardiac death in the older athlete. *J Am Coll Cardiol* 2015; **65:** 493–502.
109. Endres BD, Kerr ZY, Stearns RL, et al. Epidemiology of sudden death in organized youth sports in the United States, 2007–2015. *J Athlet Train* 2019; **54:** 349–55.
110. Suàrez-Mier MP, Aguilera B, Mosquera RM, Sànchez-de-León MS. Pathology of sudden death during recreational sports in Spain. *Forensic Sci Int* 2013; **226:** 188–96.
111. Risgaard B, Tfelt-Hansen J, Winkel BG. Sports-related sudden cardiac death: how to prove an effect of preparticipation screening. *Heart Rhythm* 2016; **13:** 1560–2.
112. Turk EE, Riedel A, Püeschel K. Natural and traumatic sports-related fatalities: A 10-year retrospective study. *Br J Sports Med* 2008; **42:** 604–8.
113. Chappex N, Schlaepfer J, Fellmann F, et al. Sudden cardiac death among general population and sport related population in forensic experience. *J Forensic Leg Med* 2015; **35:** 62–8.
114. Patel V, Elliott P. Sudden death in athletes. *Clin Med* 2012; **12:** 253–6.
115. Alpert C, Day SM, Saberi S. Sports and exercise in athletes with hypertrophic cardiomyopathy. *Clin Sports Med* 2015; **34:** 489–505.
116. Asif IM, Harmon KG. Incidence and etiology of sudden cardiac death: new updates for athletic departments. *Sports Health* 2017; **9:** 268–79.
117. Dennis M, Elder A, Semsarian C, et al. A 10-year review of sudden death during sporting activities. *Heart Rhythm* 2018; **15:** 1477–83.
118. Van Camp SP, Bloor CM, Mueller FO, et al. Nontraumatic sports death in high school and college athletes. *Med Sci Sports Exer* 1995; **27:** 641–7.
119. Manci EA, Culberson, DE, Yang, Y-M, et al. Cause of death in sickle cell disease: An autopsy study. *Brit J Haematol* 2003; **123:** 359–65.
120. Kark JA, Posey DM, Schumacher HR, Ruehle CJ. Sickle-cell trait as a risk factor for sudden death in physical training. *N Engl J Med* 1987; **317:** 781–7.
121. DiDario AG, Becker JM. Asthma, sports, and death. *Allergy Asthma Proc* 2005; **26:** 341–4.
122. Becker JM, Rogers J, Rossini G, et al. Asthma deaths during sports: report of a 7-year exerience. *J Allergy Clin Immunol* 2004; **113:** 264–7.
123. Weiler JM, Layon T, Hunt M. Asthma in United States Olympic athletes who participated in the 1996 Summer Games. *J Allergy Clin Immunol* 1998; **102:** 722–6.
124. Fronczek J, Gilbert JD, Byard RW. Forensic issues arising in the assessment of chlorine-related deaths in a domestic setting. *Med Sci Law* 2021; **61:** 232–5.
125. Helenius I, Rytilä P, Sarna S, et al. Effect of continuing or finishing high-level sports on airway inflammation, bronchial hyperresponsiveness, and asthma: A 5-year prospective follow-up study of 42 highly trained swimmers. *J Allergy Clin Immunol* 2002; **109:** 962–8.
126. Krumholz A. Driving issues in epilepsy: past, present, and future. *Epilepsy Curr* 2009; **9(2):** 31–5.
127. Smith NM, Byard RW, Bourne AJ. Death during immersion in water in childhood. *Am J Forensic Med Pathol* 1991; **12:** 219–21.

CHAPTER

41 Sharp Force Injuries

Marianne Tiemensma and Roger W. Byard

INTRODUCTION

Accurate wound evaluation and description is one of the core functions of a forensic pathologist and clinical forensic physician. The definition of a skin wound, or injury relates to the mechanism(s) applied to the tissue that result in a characteristic appearance.

Traumatic skin injuries are broadly classified into blunt force, sharp force, or hybrid (combined blunt/sharp force) injuries.

Sharp force is a form of mechanical impact that causes injuries by means of pointed and/or sharp-edged instruments (1). Sharp force injuries can be inflicted by a range of pointed and/or sharp-edged objects including knives, forks, screwdrivers, scissors, broken glass, razor blades, swords, ice picks, pencils or pens, knitting needles, spears, arrows (Figure 41.1), machetes, axes, or any instrument with a relatively pointed or sharp edge.

Definitions

Sharp force trauma is defined as the "application of force to produce an injury which results in a clear division or separation of the skin and underlying tissues" (2). Sharp force injuries include incised wounds (also called "slashes"), stab wounds and therapeutic/diagnostic wounds.

An incised wound is typically caused by the slashing, swiping, or slicing movement of an edged or pointed implement across the skin, resulting in a wound with its surface length greater than the depth of the wound track into the tissue (Figure 41.2).

A stab wound results from a stabbing or thrusting movement of a sharp implement with the wound track greater than the surface length. The edges of the wound in the skin are sharp with relatively well-defined traumatic separation of the tissues, with no associated blunt force injuries (abrasion or contusion) (Figures 41.3 and 41.4). Stab and incised wounds have to be distinguished from lacerations, which are skin and tissue tears due to blunt force trauma. In contrast to the clean, well-defined wound edges seen in incised or stab wounds, lacerations show irregular edges, with connecting tissue strands ("bridging tissue"), and possibly associated blunt force injuries such as abrasions or contusions. A stab wound may imply that a weapon was taken to a scene.

Therapeutic/diagnostic wounds are surgical incisions made during emergency or elective diagnostic or therapeutic interventions, such as intercostal incisions related to chest drain placement, thoracotomy, or surgical cutdowns for vascular catheterization (Figure 41.5). These should be recognized to avoid misinterpretation, which can easily occur, particularly when medical paraphernalia were removed prior to post-mortem examination.

Hybrid injuries refer to injuries that display features of blunt and sharp force trauma, such as:

- **Chop wounds:** These are typically caused by a blow with a heavy object with at least one sharp edge such as a machete or an axe, and typically show a skin wound with an incised appearance with surrounding abrasion or contusion, and possible associated fracturing of underlying bone. Propeller injuries and machinery blades may also produce chop wounds with incision and laceration of tissues (3).
- **Blunt penetrating/perforating wounds:** These are injuries caused by cylindrical objects, such as a spear or a broken steel rod (Figure 41.6).
- **Sharp force injuries resulting from dog attacks:** Dog attacks can be classified under blunt force or sharp force trauma, however, there is an element of sharp force trauma involved in dog attacks, in addition to blunt force and/or crush injury (4,5) (Figure 41.7).

APPROACH TO THE EVALUATION OF SHARP FORCE INJURIES

Care should be taken to describe, measure, document and photograph all injuries, including evaluation and description of the overlying clothing. With the advance and increasing availability of post-mortem imaging in forensic practice, it is recommended that radiologic imaging should be obtained prior to post-mortem examination. This may aid in the detection of any hidden sharp implements and will assist in post-mortem diagnoses related to sharp force injuries, such as a hemo- or pneumothorax, or visceral injury. In addition, imaging may provide a more accurate assessment of the wound track than simple dissection once the weapon has been removed (6).

DOI: 10.1201/9781003138754-43

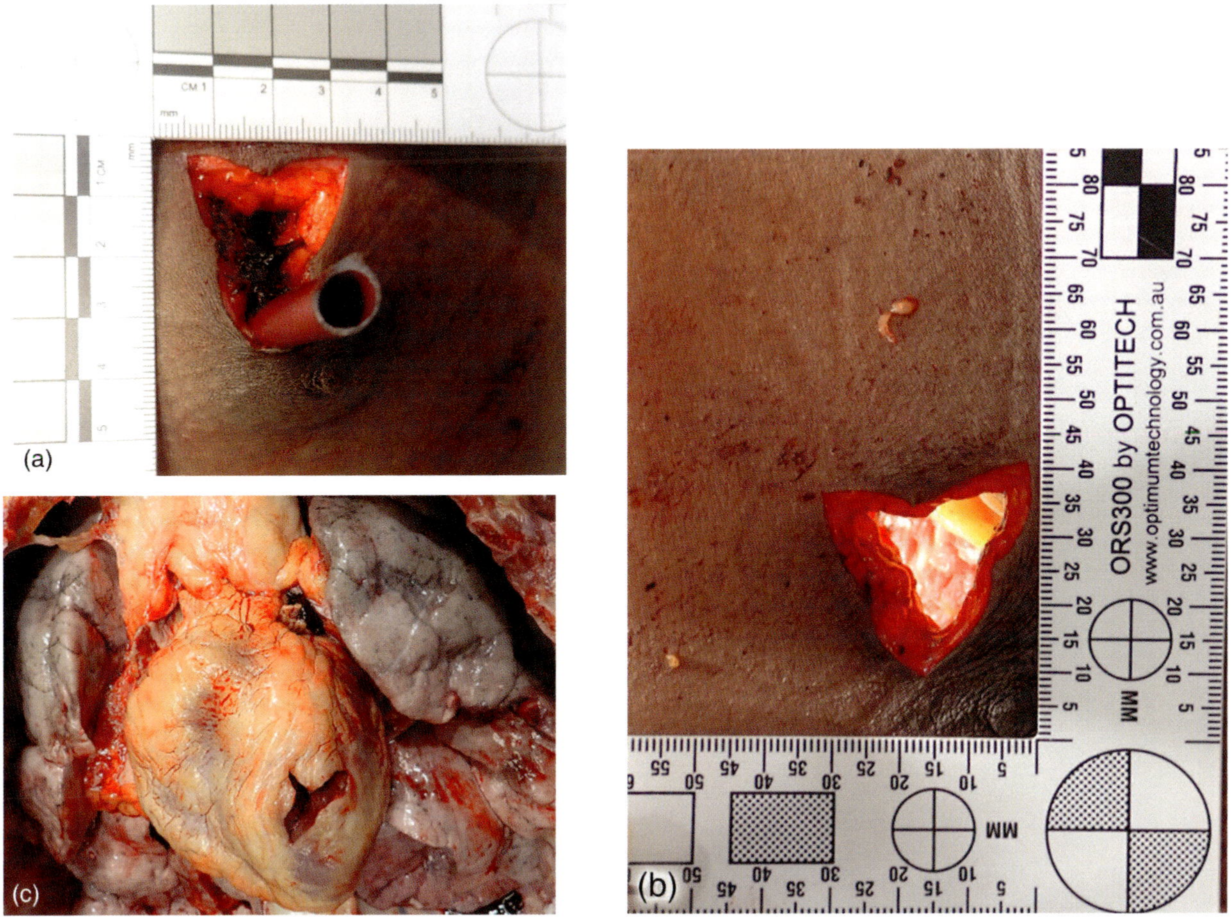

41.1 Penetrating crossbow arrow injury (fixed three-blade broadhead arrowhead), with the arrow *in situ* **(a)**, removed **(b)**, and demonstrating the underlying injury to the heart **(c)**.

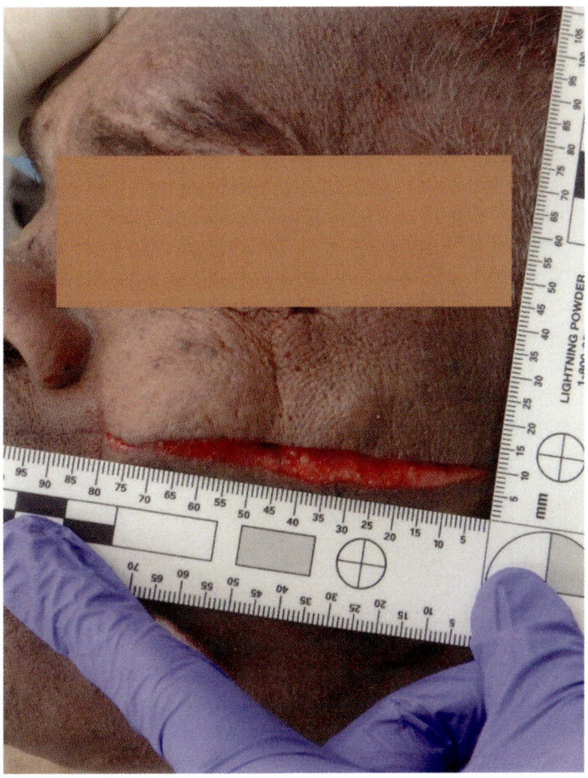

41.2 Slash wound across the left cheek.

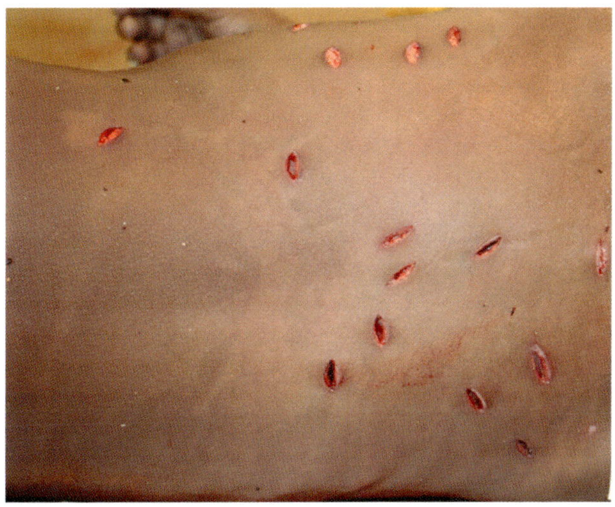

41.3 Multiple, almost identical stab wounds inflicted by the same weapon.

The description of sharp force injuries should include the number of stab wounds, exact anatomical location, and individual features (size and shape, orientation of the wounds), distinguishing features, and the underlying wound tracks (including the direction and approximated depth of the track, and documentation of injured tissue, viscera, and/or neurovascular structures). Each

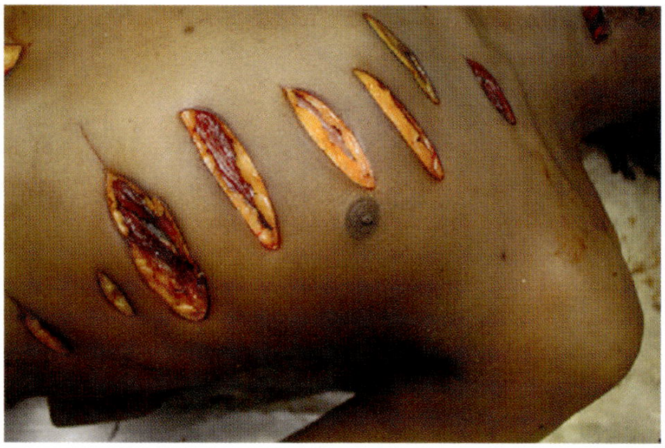

41.4 Multiple incised wounds with tailing of some wounds at the medial aspects, indicating superficial movement of the blade across the skin on withdrawal.

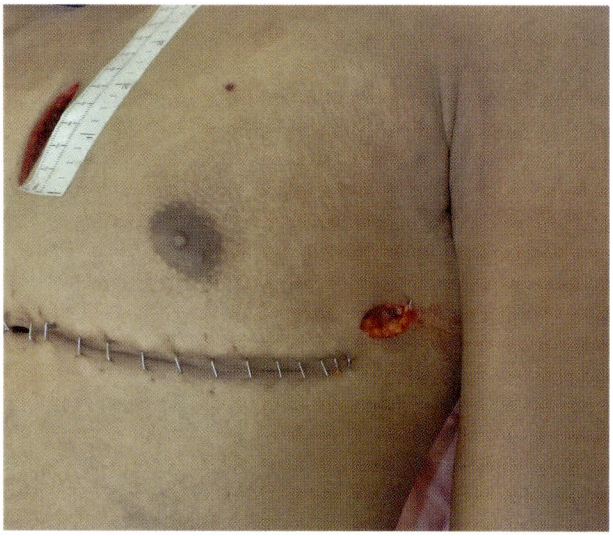

41.5 Therapeutic incisions (clipped thoracotomy and intercostal incision in the anterior axillary line) with an inflicted stab wound on the mid-anterior aspect of the chest.

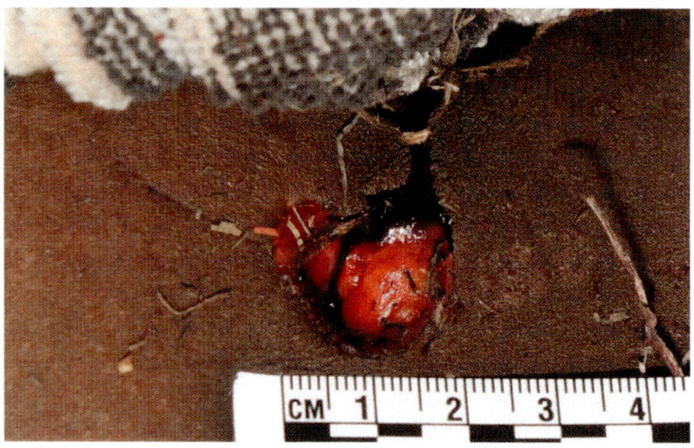

41.6 Blunt penetrating injury to the left lateral aspect of the torso (caused by a broken broom stick).

individual wound track should be described separately, except where multiple criss-crossing tracks are present that cannot be distinguished from each other with certainty. The depth of the wound track may be equal to,

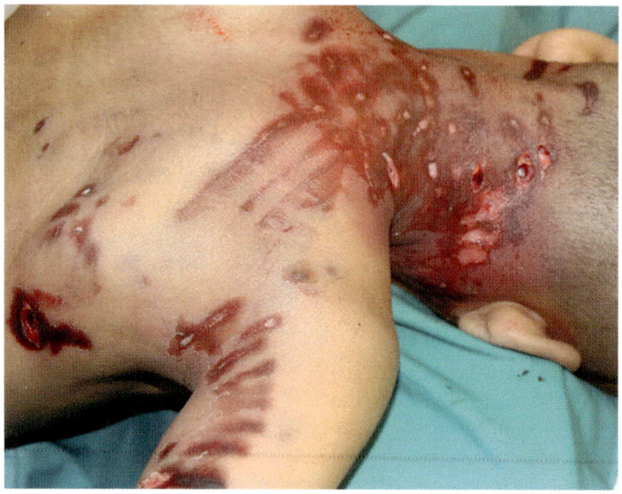

41.7 Dog attack. (Penetrating injuries with surrounding patterned abrasions from claw marks.)

less than, or greater than the length of the knife blade depending on the degree of force applied and resistance/elasticity of skin and tissues.

The shape of the weapon will influence the appearance of the skin wound. A stab wound inflicted by a single-edged knife typically shows a sharp or "V-shaped" end and an opposite blunted or squared-off end (Figure 41.8). Double-edged knife blades may produce wounds that are sharp or tapered at both ends. A hilt abrasion or contusion may be visible if the guard of the knife makes contact with the skin when the weapon has been driven into the body (Figure 41.9). A Phillips screwdriver may produce a circular wound with four equally spaced cuts or abrasions (Figure 41.10a and b). An attack with a serrated knife may result in fine serrations or saw-tooth markings on the skin, however, the absence of serrations does not exclude the possibility that the attack resulted from such a knife.

Extra care should be taken in cases where medical or surgical interventions were rendered prior to death or assessment, including review of the medical notes, to avoid misinterpretation of the findings. For example, a stab wound may be incorporated into a surgical incision, or early healing may have occurred, which will alter the original dimensions and appearance of the wound.

DNA comparisons between a victim, an assailant and a particular weapon may be crucial in establishing links and so suspected weapons must always be kept distant from autopsy examinations to avoid the possibility of inadvertent contamination.

MECHANISMS OF INJURY/DEATH

The potential effects resulting from sharp force injuries can be classified as acute and subacute/chronic (7).

Acute effects include:

- Hypovolemic shock from blood loss
- Cardiac tamponade

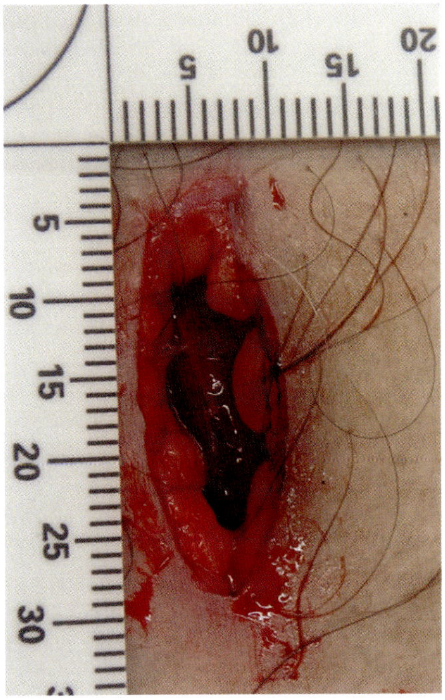

41.8 Stab wound caused by a sharp single-edged knife (V-shaped inferior margin and blunted/squared off superior margin).

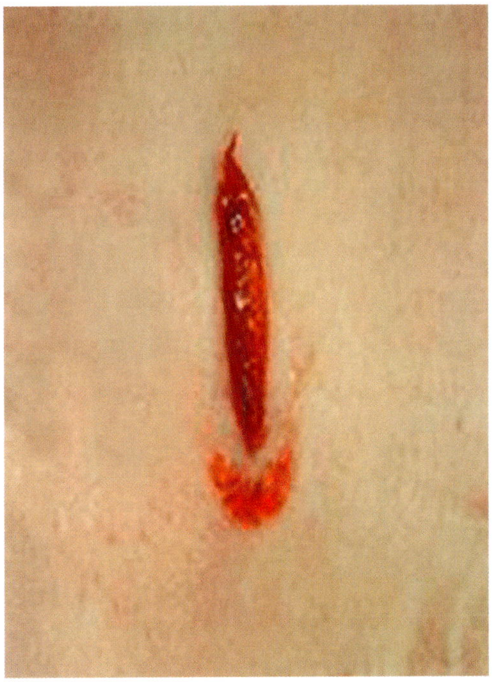

41.9 A deep stab wound with an abrasion from the knife hilt indicating that it had been inserted to the full length of the blade.

- Direct visceral injury with an effect on organ function such as the heart or spinal cord
- Air embolism
- Asphyxia from airway obstruction from hematoma
- Blood aspiration
- Pneumothorax
- Hemothorax

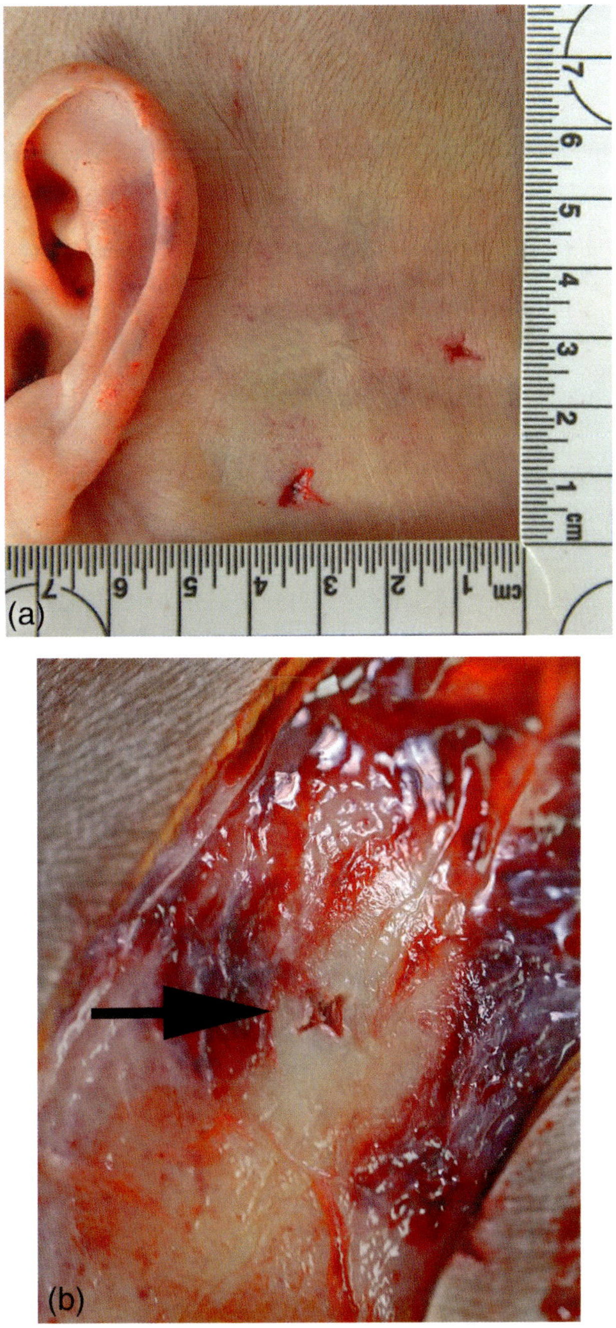

41.10 (a) Patterned cruciate stab wounds behind the ear from a Phillips head screw driver. (b) Removal of overlying soft tissues demonstrating a cruciate stab wound into the skull from a Phillips head screw driver (arrow).

Subacute and chronic complications include:

- Infection/sepsis
- Loss of, or diminished, function
- Aneurysm formation
- Arterial dissection
- Ischemia
- Fistula formation
- Herniation
- Adhesions
- Chronic inflammation

INJURIES PER BODY REGION

Head

Penetrating stab wound injuries to the head are rare occurrences in Western countries and occur almost exclusively in homicides, and typically in the presence of additional extracranial injuries (8). However, isolated penetrating sharp force injuries to the head are seen in other countries such as South Africa and Iran (9–11).

Although the adult skull usually offers an effective barrier, penetrating skull injuries can occur, typically in the context of a forcefully thrust sharp and rigid implement penetrating full-thickness through the adult skull, usually associated with a fixed position of the victim's head (8,12). The force required to penetrate the skull is much higher than the force needed to penetrate the skin (8). An intracranial stab wound with a knife can be easily identified when a characteristic slot fracture is observed. The skull defect produced by the weapon will match the width and thickness of the knife blade or screw driver (13). The blade of the knife may break when penetrating the skull, and it is recommended to perform radiological imaging prior to examination.

Primary injuries include vascular injury with hemorrhage, tissue damage and necrosis, with later potential complications of ischemia, aneurysm formation, and infection.

Neck

Stab wounds to the neck may result in injury to major blood vessels, the trachea, esophagus and spinal cord, with possible resultant acute effects from hemorrhage and exsanguination, air embolism, hemoaspiration and upper cervical spinal cord injury. Delayed complications include infection, arterial mural thrombosis with cerebral embolization and infarction, and aneurysm formation.

Chest

The chest is the region most commonly involved in fatal stab wounds. Injuries may include penetrating injuries of the heart and the great vessels, esophagus (with possible associated complications of mediastinitis, pyothorax and trachea-esophageal fistula), with injuries to the tracheobronchial tree, and lungs, with resulting acute effects including cardiac tamponade, exsanguination, hemo- and/or pneumothorax. Delayed complications following vascular injury include late hemorrhage, arteriovenous fistulas, false aneurysms and empyema (14–16). Penetrating wounds of the chest may also be associated with intra-abdominal injuries.

Abdomen

The most common abdominal regions affected by penetrating trauma involve the small intestine, large intestine, liver and intra-abdominal vasculature. Such injuries may pose an immediate threat to life due to profuse bleeding, however, delayed complications may include infection, particularly in the context of a perforated viscus, or fistulas. Stab wounds in the upper abdominal region may pose a threat of injury to the chest in addition to the abdomen depending on the direction of the stab wound track and the position of the diaphragm at the time of injury. Back and flank stab wounds have a greater risk of injury to retroperitoneal structures, such as the colon, kidneys, duodenum, aorta and inferior vena cava (17).

Extremities

Lethal penetrating sharp force injuries of the extremities may occur, usually as a result of injury to large blood vessels with resultant exsanguination. A rare complication following stab wound injury to the thigh is the development of acute compartment syndrome. This may occur when the pressure within an osseofascial compartment rises above the capillary perfusion gradient with impaired local circulation and resultant cellular anoxia, muscle ischemia, and death (18). On occasion, such stab wounds are found in traditional communities as a form of payback/reparation (19).

MANNER OF INJURY AND/OR DEATH

Sharp force injuries may be sustained in various circumstances, and the forensic evaluation of the injuries may assist in distinguishing between whether the injuries were self-inflicted (whether accidental or intentional) or non-self-inflicted.

Thorough circumstantial, scene, and death investigation and review of the medical history, including psychiatric history, should support the forensic wound evaluation to allow for an accurate classification of the manner of injury or death. The parameters should be considered to be indicative and not absolute, and integrated with the individual case, as many atypical features in both homicide and suicide cases have been reported (20). As with all suspected homicides, full toxicological evaluation of the protagonists is required.

Self-inflicted sharp force injuries

A number of "classic" characteristics have been ascribed in relation to self-inflicted sharp force injuries, however, it is important to note that these refer to the characteristics of groups or multiple injuries, and it may be impossible to determine the manner of injury where only a single sharp force injury is present. These features are not exclusive or diagnostic, but when present, may give an indication of self-infliction. Their absence does not exclude self-infliction, and their presence does not inevitably imply self-infliction (21). The more criteria that are fulfilled, the greater is the suspicion of a self-inflicted injury (22). Multiple self-inflicted stab wounds may, however, raise the possibility of homicide (23).

Characteristics include (21,22,24–27):

- **Anatomic location:**
    - The injuries have to be accessible to the victim's own hand, in order for the victim to reach the injured areas.
    - They are often located on the opposite side to the dominant hand.

- They avoid sensitive areas of the body, such as the eyes, lips, nipples, and genitalia, unless there is a serious underlying psychiatric illness.
- They involve common areas including the forearms, anterior or lateral thighs, forehead, cheeks, upper chest, and abdomen.

- **Number of injuries and their characteristics:**
  - The injuries are typically incised wounds or superficial stab wounds.
  - In the case of incised wounds, the wounds are regular, with an equal depth at origin and termination.
  - The incisions are often linear, and may be mildly curved, and may form geometric shapes, symbols, letters, or words.
  - The presence of hesitation wounds, which may comprise knife tip injuries, or superficial incised or stab wounds, which are typically parallel and multiple (28).
  - Hesitation marks are often seen in close proximity to the fatal wound (Figures 41.11 and 41.12).
- **Injury patterns:**
  - The injuries are usually grouped together, in parallel array, symmetrical, "mirror-image", or a "chess board" pattern.
- Overlying clothing is generally not involved.
- Other considerations:
  - Healed scars from previous physical suicide attempts or self-harm may be present (Figure 41.13).
  - Defensive injuries are usually absent or atypical.
  - Rare to see accompanying injuries of other types.

Non-self-inflicted sharp force injuries

The recognition of defensive injuries is important, as their presence suggests infliction by another person(s), and further indicate that the victim was conscious and mobile for at least part of the attack. Defensive wounds are typically inflicted because of a reflexive action of the victim trying to resist an attack. They are typically located on the ulnar or ventral/palmar aspect of the forearm or wrist, elbows, or palmar surface of the hand during a grasping motion in an attempt to grab the weapon (so-called "active" defensive wounds), or on the backs of the hands or fingers from non-grasping movements in attempt(s) to ward off a weapon (so-called "passive" defensive wounds) (Figure 41.14). Other features that support the likelihood that the injuries were inflicted by another include signs of a struggle with the presence of other non-sharp force injuries (29).

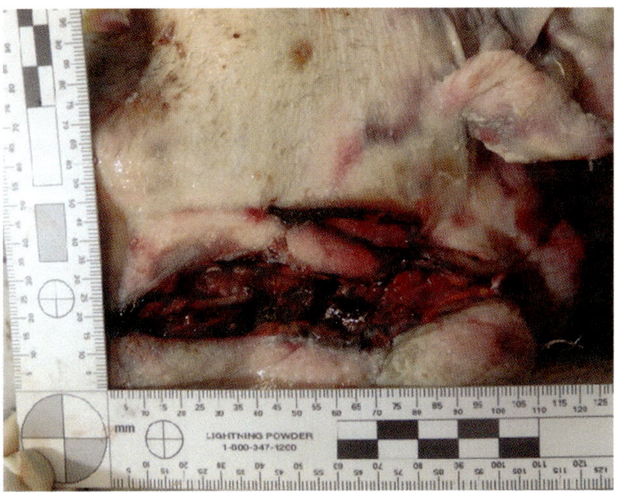

41.11 Deep self-inflicted incised wound to the neck with adjacent hesitation wounds.

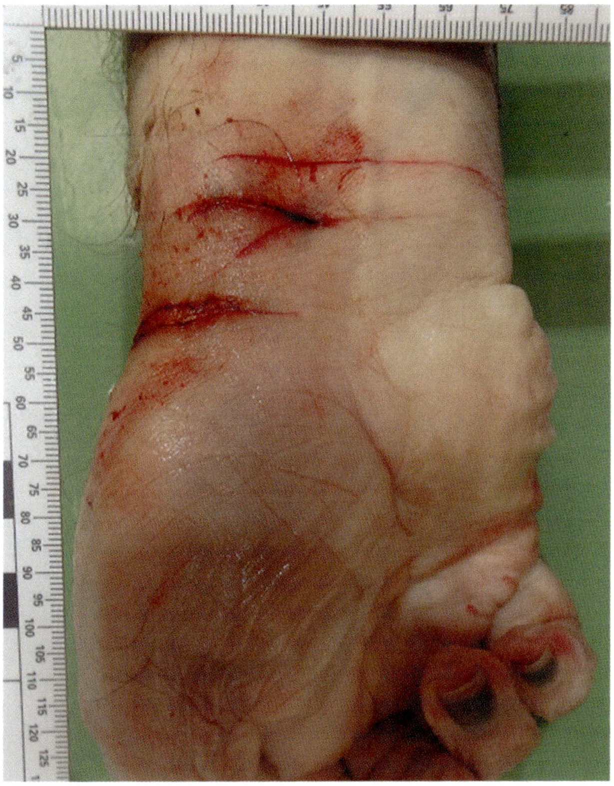

41.12 Parallel self-inflicted wounds to the right wrist.

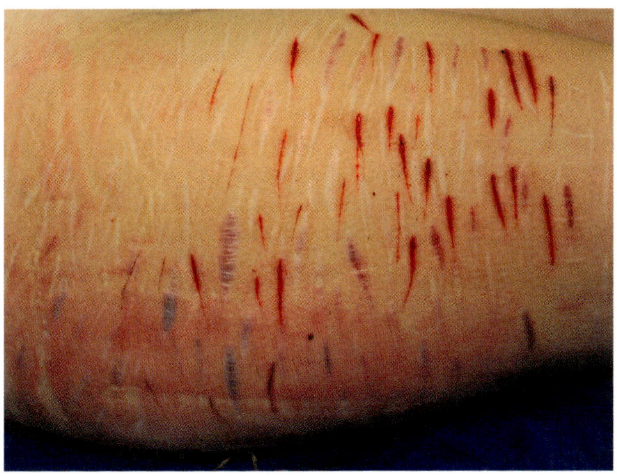

41.13 Healed and healing parallel self-inflicted superficial incised wounds of the lateral aspect of the right thigh.

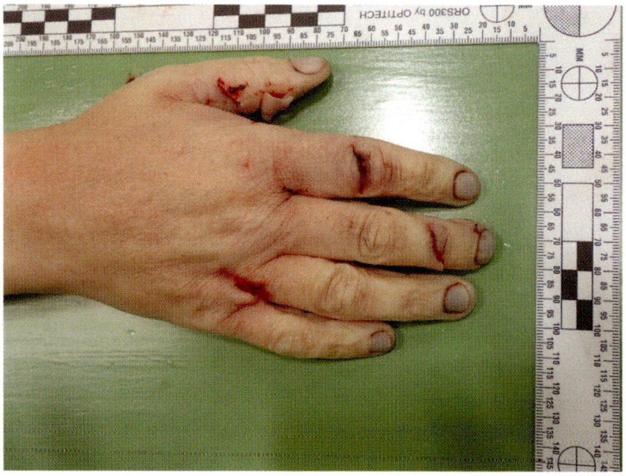

41.14 Defensive wounds to the right hand.

Accidental sharp force injuries

Accidental deaths resulting from sharp force injuries are considered to be quite rare, in contrast to accidental deaths resulting from other injuries, however; they do occur, with broken glass or some type of motorized machinery most commonly involved. Accidental sharp force injury fatalities are varied in their presentation, and features supporting the likelihood of an accidental nature of an injury include the involvement of overlying clothes, the presence of the weapon at the scene, and the absence of hesitation marks or defensive injuries. The most commonly reported accidental sharp force injury is a single stab wound (26,29). Other accidental wounds may arise from impalement, although the possibility of self infliction should still be considered (30,31). Accidental stab wounds may also occur during breaking and entering activities if windows are smashed to gain entry to a premises. These may range from single puncture wounds to quite large incised wounds (32,33).

DEGREE OF FORCE

The forensic physician or pathologist is often asked to comment on the degree of force required for an instrument to cause a penetrating injury. For penetration to occur, enough pressure is needed for the tip of the weapon to overcome the natural skin elasticity (34).

Caution has to be exercised when providing such an opinion, and it is impossible to exactly quantify the force exerted in a stabbing attack, although a qualitative assessment can be made, using comparative adjectives such as:

"Mild", "moderate", "considerable", or "severe" (35), or

"Slight", "moderate", "severe", "extreme" (36), or

"Weak", "weak/moderate", "moderate", "moderate/severe", "severe" (21).

The following variables should be considered carefully prior to attempting to qualify the likely degree of force required to cause a certain penetrating injury (4,35–37). It is not possible or appropriate to comment on the degree of force without having some information about the circumstances of the alleged injury and the characteristics of the implement (21).

Intrinsic properties of the object or weapon

- **Type of object/weapon**
  - Shape and size of the tip of the object:

    Most authors agree that the most important single factor is the fineness or sharpness of the point of the instrument used. The blade tip geometry, or sharpness of the blade plays a major role in the effect of stabbing incidents. If a pointed, sharp object is used, the amount of force is comparatively smaller than the force required to penetrate tissue with a blunt object that has a rounded blade tip.

    When blunt knives contact the skin, a much greater degree of elastic deflection of the skin is caused than for a sharp knife, and the critical contact stress for skin penetration may or may not be reached, depending on the degree of force applied to the knife.
  - Shape, size, and sharpness of the cutting blades:
    - Blade thickness: slender knives penetrate more easily than thicker blades. Knives with tapering blades are more effective at penetrating than knives with non-tapering blades.
    - Cutting edge sharpness: this helps continuous penetration once the skin has been breached.
    - The length of a flat blade (the longer the blade, the more force is needed to drive the blade in).

Velocity/speed of the weapon or object moving towards the target (Kinetic energy = $\frac{1}{2} mv^2$)

The higher the speed of contact, the greater force is applied, and the easier it is to penetrate the skin. If resistance is encountered during the movement of a weapon, for example, by full or partial restraint of the thrust of the attack, the velocity of the approaching weapon is reduced, and therefore so is the penetrating ability. Conversely, increasing the velocity of the blade increases the energy release rate of the skin, which results in a reduced rupture force, and increased ease of penetration (35).

Resistance

This includes resistance offered by penetrated tissues (e.g. skin, cartilage, or bone) and the resistance of any protective coverings (such as clothing) or intermediate objects between the weapon and the victim. Apart from cartilage and bone, skin has the highest resistance compared to underlying soft tissue and organ parenchyma.

Relative movements of the involved parties

A stabbing attack is a dynamic process that changes moment by moment. The victim may be moving toward, away from, or deflecting from the approaching weapon (7,21). Thus, the construct that is often proposed in court of the victim standing in a "sentry position" is somewhat artificial.

CONCLUSION

Sharp force injuries may present with a variety of manifestations that depend on many factors including the nature of the weapon(s), the relative positions of the assailant and victim, the specific form of the attack and the presence or absence of other types of trauma. For example, incapacitation by blunt force trauma to the head may be accompanied by multiple "coup de gras" type stab wounds to a particular area of the body (Figure 41.15). Careful documentation of stab wounds both at the death scene and at autopsy may be required to rule particular weapons in or out.

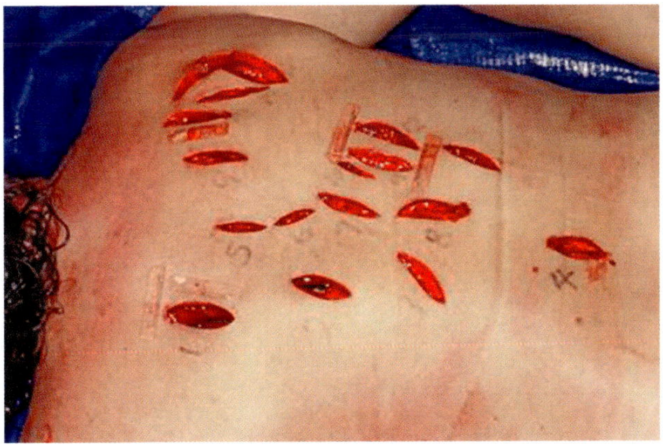

41.15 Multiple stab wounds in the back indicating that the victim had most likely been incapacitated at this stage of the assault.

REFERENCES

1. Bohner M, Huttemann H, Schmidt U. Homicides by Sharp Force. In: *Forensic Pathology Reviews* Vol 4. Totowa, NJ: Humana Press; 2004.
2. Vanezis, P. Pathology of Sharp Force Trauma. 1st ed. 2021. London: Taylor and Francis. Available from: https://www.perlego.com/book/2535014/pathology-of-sharp-force-trauma-pdf (Original work published 2021). (Accessed 1 May 2023).
3. Byard RW, Machado A, Woolford L, Boardman W. Symmetry – The key to diagnosing propeller strike injuries in sea mammals. *Forensic Sci Med Pathol* 2013; **9**: 103–5.
4. Prahlow J, Byard RW (eds). Sharp Force Injury Deaths. In: *An Atlas of Forensic Pathology*, New York: Springer Publishers; 2012, pp 573–631.
5. Bury D, Langlois NEI, Byard RW. Animal-related fatalities Part I: Characteristic autopsy findings and variable causes of death associated with blunt and sharp trauma. *J Forensic Sci* 2012; **57**: 370–4.
6. Winskog C. Precise wound track measurement requires CAT scan with object in situ: How accurate is post-mortem dissection and evaluation? *Forensic Sci Med Pathol* 2012; **8**: 76–7.
7. Payne-James J. Injury, Fatal and Nonfatal: Sharp and Cutting-Edge Wounds. In: *Encyclopedia of Forensic and Legal Medicine*, Vol 3. Amsterdam: Elsevier, 2016; pp. 244–56.
8. Bauer M, Patzelt D. Intracranial stab injuries: case report and case study. *Forensic Sci Int* 2002; **129**: 122–7.
9. Nathoo N, Boodhoo SS, Nadvi SS, et al. Transcranial brainstem injuries: A retrospective analysis of 17 patients. *Neurosurgery* 2000; **47**: 1159–62.
10. Nathoo N, Nadvi SS. Traumatic intracranial aneurysms following penetrating stab wounds to the head: Two unusual cases and review of the literatures. *Cent Afr J Med* 1999; **45**: 213–17.
11. Yarandi KK, Jelodar S, Khalatbari MR, et al. Stab wounds to the head; case series: Review of literature and proposed management algorithm. *Asian J Neurosurg* 2018; **13**: 754–9.
12. Bodwal J, Chauhan M, Behera C, Byard RW. An unusual patterned injury from homicidal craniocerebral impalement with a metal chair leg. *Forensic Sci Med Pathol* 2021; **17**: 327–9.
13. DiMaio VJ, DiMaio D. *Forensic Pathology*. 2nd ed. London: CRC Press; 2021.
14. Honda M, Tanioka T, Haruki S, et al. Thoracic esophageal injury due to a neck stab wound: A case report. *Surg Case Rep* 2021; **7(1)**: 126.
15. Oparah SS. Mandal AK. Operative management of penetrating wounds of the chest in civilian practice. Review of indications in 125 consecutive patients. *J Thorac Cardiovasc Surg* 1979; **77**: 162–8.
16. Sandrasagra FA. Management of penetrating stab wounds of the chest: An assessment of the indications for early operation. *Thorax* 1978; **33(4)**: 474–8.
17. Lotfollahzadeh S, Burns B. *Penetrating Abdominal Trauma*. [Updated 2022 Jun 3]. In: StatPearls [Internet]. Treasure Island (FL): StatPearls Publishing; 2022 Jan. Available from: https://www.ncbi.nlm.nih.gov/books/NBK459123/ (Accessed 1 May 2023).
18. Gillooly JJ, Hacker A, Patel V. Compartment syndrome as a complication of a stab wound to the thigh: A case report and review of the literature. *Emerg Med* 2007; **24**: 780–1.
19. Omond KJ, Charlwood C, Byard RW. Customary law, traditional punishment and death in the Aṉangu Pitjantjatjara Yankunytjatjara (APY) Lands of Central Australia. *Forensic Sci Med Pathol* 2016; **12**: 527–9.
20. De-Giorgio F, Lodise M, Quaranta G. et al. Suicidal or homicidal sharp force injuries? A review and critical analysis of the heterogeneity in the forensic literature. *J Forensic Sci* 2015; **60, S1**: C97–S107.
21. Payne-James JJ, Stark MM, Nittis M, Sheasby D. Injury Assessment, Documentation, and Interpretation. In: Stark MM (ed). *Clinical Forensic Medicine: A Physician's Guide*. 4th ed. Cham, Switzerland: Springer; 2020.
22. Heide S, Kleiber M. Self-inflicted injuries: A forensic medical perspective. *Deutsches Arzteblatt* 2006; **103(40)**: 2927–33.
23. Austin A, Guddat S, Tsokos M, et al. Multiple injuries in suicide simulating homicide. *J Forensic Leg Med* 2013; **20**: 601–4.
24. Byard RW, Heath KJ, Tsokos M. The symmetry of self mutilation and the chess board pattern. *Forensic Sci Med Pathol* 2013; **9(1)**: 106–107.
25. Karger B, DuChesne A, Ortmann CH, Brinkmann B. Unusual self-inflicted injuries simulating a criminal offence. *Int J Legal Med* 1997; **110(5)**: 267–2.
26. Prahlow JA, Ross KF, Lene WJW, Kirby DB. Accidental sharp force injury fatalities. *Am J Forensic Med Pathol* 2001; **22(4)**: 358–66.
27. Byard RW, Klitte Å, Gilbert JD, James RA. Clinicopathologic features of fatal self-inflicted incised and stab wounds: A 20-year study. *Am J Forensic Med Pathol* 2002; **23**: 15–18.
28. Racette S, Kremer C, Desjarlais A, Sauvageau A. Suicidal and homicidal sharp force injury: A 5-year retrospective comparative study of hesitation marks and defense wounds. *Forensic Sci Med Pathol* 2008; **4(4)**: 221–7.
29. Adelson L. *The Pathology of Homicide*. Springfield, IL: Charles C Thomas; 1974, pp. 319–77.

30. Byard RW. A forensic evaluation of impalement injuries. *Med Sci Law* 2018; **58:** 85–92.
31. Austin AE, Heath K, Gilbert J, Byard RW. Head impalement: An unusual form of suicide. *J Forensic Leg Med* 2012; **19:** 264–6.
32. Payne-James JJ, Jones RM. Simpson's Forensic Medicine. 14th ed. *Assessment, Classification and Documentation of Injury*. Boca Raton: CRC Press; 2019.
33. Byard RW. Lethal injuries occurring during illegal break-ins. *Am J Forensic Med Pathol* 2005; **26:** 121–4.
34. Byard RW. The 'break, enter and die' syndrome may involve significant injury to major neck vessels. *J Forensic Sci* 2011; **56 Suppl1:** S252–4.
35. Annaidh AN, Cassidy M, Curtis M, et al. A combined experimental and numerical study of stab-penetration forces. *Forensic Sci Int* 2013; **233(1–3):** 7–13.
36. Mason JK, Purdue BN. *The Pathology of Trauma*. 3rd ed. London: Arnold; 2000, p 135.
37. Hainsworth S. Cutting Crimes. *Ingenia* 2008; **37:** 38–43.

CHAPTER

42

Blunt Force Injuries and Death

Laura D. Knight and Katherine Callahan

INTRODUCTION

Blunt force injuries occur when a body is hit with an object or strikes against an object or surface, such as the ground. The transfer of kinetic energy from the relative movements of the object and the body results in damage to the body. The skin and tissues have significant elasticity and resilience, but when the force applied exceeds the tissue's ability to adapt, stretch, or resist, injury occurs. Types of blunt force injuries include abrasions, contusions, lacerations and fractures. Blunt force injuries are commonly encountered in autopsies and may or may not be the cause of death or a contributing factor in the death. They can also be sustained during resuscitation efforts, and it is important for the pathologist to recognize and not to misclassify these injuries.

The nature, depth and severity of blunt force injuries depend on several factors, including the amount of force applied, which can be considered in terms of the mass and velocity of the object (and/or of the body if moving/falling). The amount of time over which a force is delivered, the extent of surface area exposed to the force, the region of the body and condition/health of the tissues struck, nature of the object, and direction of force are also key factors. The heavier the object and the faster it is moving, the greater the severity of injury, as the amount of force delivered is directly related to the mass and the square of the velocity (force = 1/2 mass X velocity^2) of the impacting object. Mathematically speaking, velocity is more important than mass in the formula as a predictor of force. Acceleration takes into account the time over which a blow is delivered and can be expressed as change in velocity divided by elapsed time. A rapid blow over a small surface area will cause more severe and focally concentrated injury than a slower moving blow over a broader area. Direct blows delivered perpendicular to the body surface deliver maximal transfer of kinetic energy and result in greater injury than tangential, or glancing, blows. A fall in an osteoporotic elder with atrophy of muscle and adipose tissue will almost certainly result in more severe injuries than the same fall in a well-nourished young adult without underlying disease.

EXTERNAL BLUNT FORCE INJURIES

Abrasions

Abrasions, or scrapes, occur when the body encounters an object and the movement of the body, or the movement of the object, or a combination of both results in removal of the superficial layer of skin. Abrasions indicate a point of impact and may have a recognizable directionality with rolled up epidermis (superficial skin) at the terminal end of the wound. In Figure 42.1, the rolled up epidermis is designated with the black arrow, indicating that the directionality of the abrasion is from the top of the photo downward. Abrasions caused by tangential friction may be referred to as "brush" abrasions, and those specifically caused by contact with pavement may be called "road rash". Figure 42.2 demonstrates road rash on the back of a young man who was the ejected driver of a vehicle involved in a rollover collision. Parallel linear abrasions over wide areas of the body may also be caused by the dragging of a body over a rough surface (antemortem or post mortem).

Abrasions may be patterned, meaning that they have shape, size, and perhaps textural elements that can be matched to a particular object that created the injury; they are commonly seen in combination with patterned contusions. In a patterned injury, the force is typically

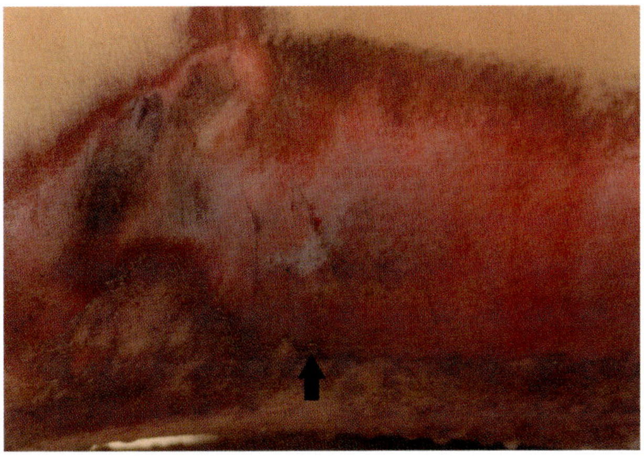

42.1 Abrasion with rolled epidermal edge (arrow).

DOI: 10.1201/9781003138754-44

applied at or near a right angle, rather than a glancing blow. The woman in Figure 42.3 was a pedestrian struck by a Ford F-150 truck. The patterned abrasion on the thigh is consistent with the grill on the front of the truck. Below the patterned abrasion is a large laceration with a comminuted fracture. Recognition of patterned injuries at the time of autopsy is key to appropriately photo-documenting these injuries with a right-angle odontological scale and collecting appropriate evidence, such as DNA swabs in suspected bite marks. The location and orientation of cutaneous blunt force injuries can also provide important information about the case. The woman in Figure 42.4a and b was the restrained front passenger of a vehicle involved in a single vehicle rollover collision. The abraded contusion at the base of the right side of the neck and the nearly horizontal contusion across the abdomen are consistent with injuries from a passenger-side seat belt.

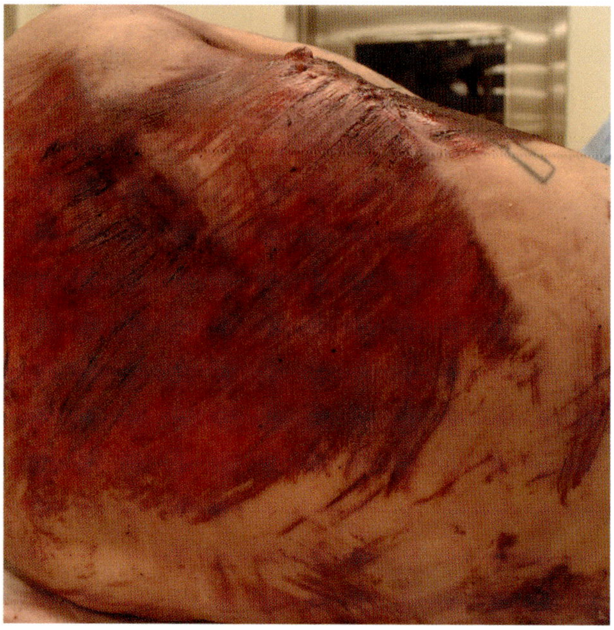

42.2 Road rash abrasions on the back of an ejected driver.

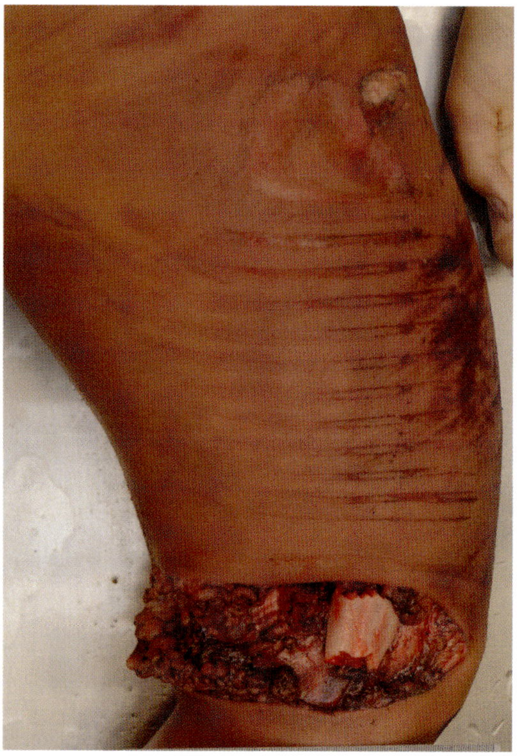

42.3 Patterned abrasion on a pedestrian's thigh consistent with a vehicle grill mark.

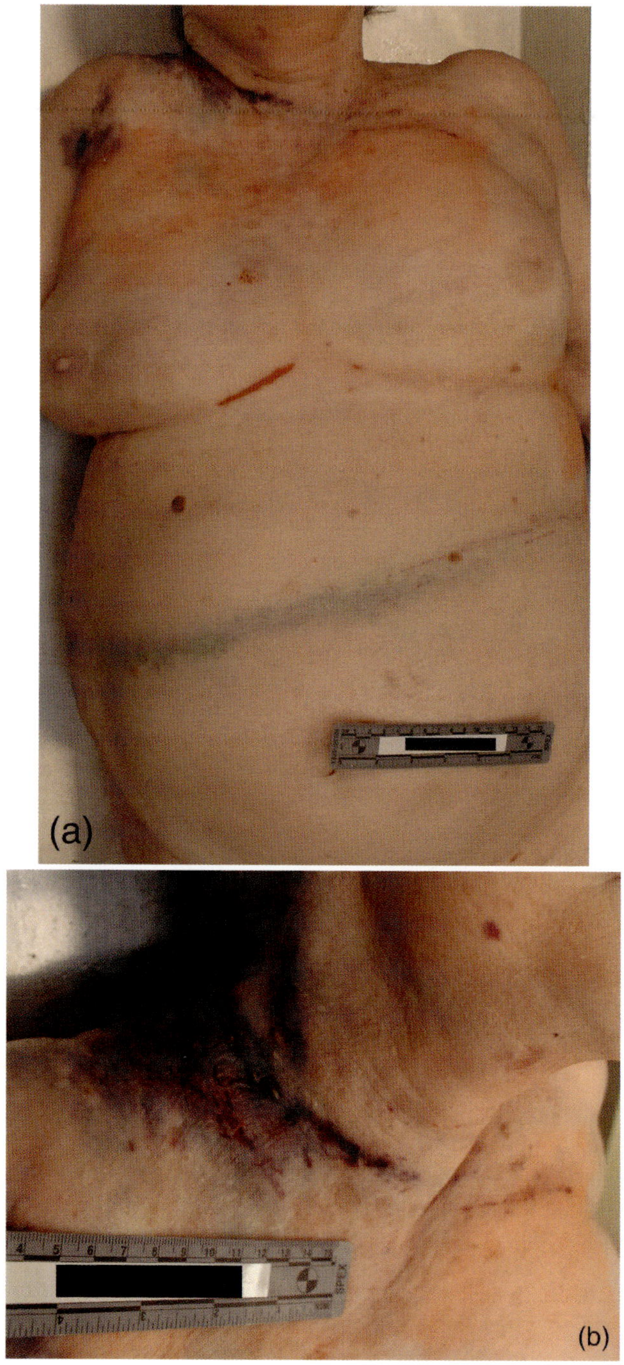

42.4 (a) Horizontal contusion of the abdomen consistent with lap restraint seat belt. (b) Abrasion-contusion of right neck in a band-like pattern consistent with a passenger-side restraint seat belt.

Abrasions can occur in the antemortem period and in the perimortem/post-mortem period. Antemortem abrasions exhibit a vital reaction resulting in a red-purple appearance. Perimortem/post-mortem abrasions can occur during resuscitation or during movement/transport of the body after death. Unlike antemortem abrasions, perimortem/post-mortem abrasions do not have a vital reaction and are yellow-orange (bloodless) and dried. They are often described as having the appearance of "parchment paper". Figure 42.5 shows a dried orange abrasion on the midline chest of a man with significant heart disease who was witnessed to collapse and underwent unsuccessful cardiopulmonary resuscitation. Figure 42.6 shows curvilinear, dried, orange, post-mortem abrasions on the right axilla of a woman who was strangled to death and then was moved into bed and posed in a peaceful sleeping position. Post-mortem abrasions are not uncommon, in contrast to the far less common post-mortem contusions.

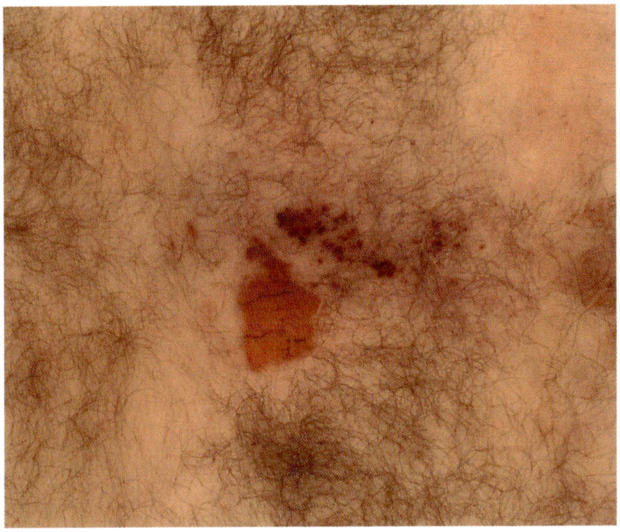

42.5 Patchy, orange, dried post-mortem abrasion on the chest sustained during cardiopulmonary resuscitation (chest compressions).

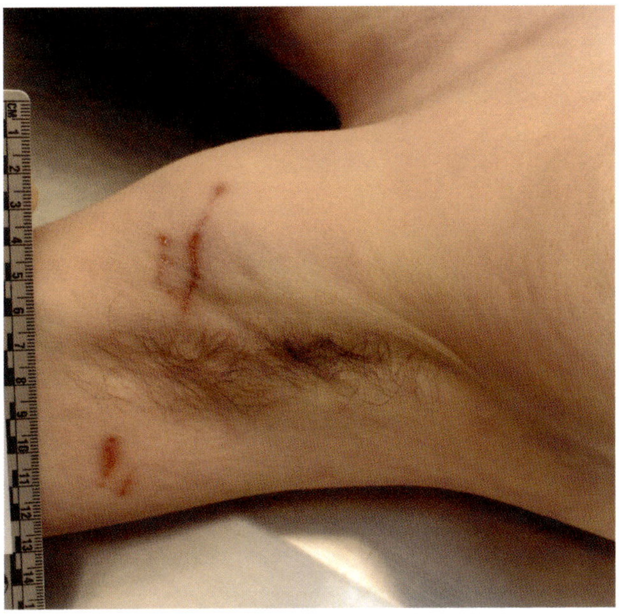

42.6 Curvilinear, dried, orange, post-mortem abrasions on the right axilla of a woman who was strangled to death and was then moved into bed and posed in a peaceful sleeping position.

Dating of abrasions using various techniques including histologic examination has been described in the literature (1–3). Many factors may alter the rate of healing, including individual variation, age, health, underlying diseases, depth of injury and so on. Attempts to age or date abrasions should be extremely cautious with only conservative estimates, perhaps limited to "acute" versus "healing" on the basis of gross examination only.

Contusions

Contusions, or bruises, occur when blunt impact tears blood vessels and results in extravasated blood in the surrounding tissue. (The term "ecchymosis", sometimes used interchangeably, is less specific and does not imply a particular etiology, whereas contusion by definition is due to blunt trauma.) In contusions, the superficial skin (epidermis) remains intact. It is important to note that contusions can occur in combination with abrasions and/or lacerations. Contusions often occur at the site of blunt impact but may also be located away from the site of impact from tracking of blood through tissues. On external examination, it may be difficult to differentiate a contusion from lividity or identify a contusion in an area of lividity. To aid in the identification of a contusion, an incision can be made in the skin. The hallmark of contusion is hemorrhage within the subcutaneous tissues. In contrast, lividity involves dependent congestion of intravascular blood and will not have frank tissue hemorrhage. Figure 42.7a shows a 62-year-old chronic alcoholic with contusions and lividity of the lateral right torso; Figure 42.7b (contusion and lividity with incisions) reveals hemorrhage in the underlying subcutaneous tissues in the area of the contusion (incision on right) and lack of hemorrhage in the subcutaneous tissue in the area of lividity (incision on left). Intense lividity can be associated with rupture of capillaries resulting in petechiae and Tardieu spots. Figure 42.8a shows a 52-year-old man who was found dead with his torso hanging off the side of a bed with the left side of his face resting on the floor. There is intense lividity with post-mortem Tardieu spots (dark purple discoloration) of the anterior neck and upper chest. An incision into the skin (Figure 42.8b) reveals hemorrhage limited to the dermis with lack of hemorrhage in the subcutaneous tissue. Contusions may be difficult to appreciate in dark-skinned individuals, and a flaying dissection of the skin may be necessary in certain cases (such as in-custody deaths or suspected child abuse) to thoroughly examine the subcutaneous tissue and deeper musculature for bruising that may not be apparent externally. Figure 42.9 shows contusions in the subcutaneous tissue of a toddler who died from inflicted blunt abdominal trauma. Additionally, in fair-skinned individuals, the underlying musculature may give the false appearance of indistinct contusion, particularly on the palms of the hands and dorsal surfaces of the feet. Incisions through the skin can confirm the presence or absence of a contusion. Figure 42.10a shows

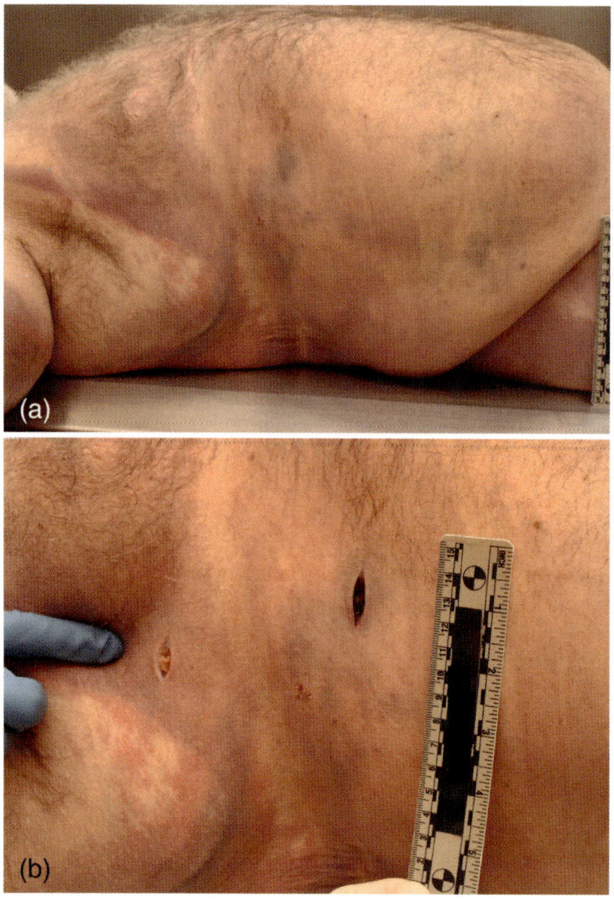

42.7 **(a)** Contusions and lividity on the lateral torso of a chronic alcoholic. **(b)** Diagnostic incisions into these areas demonstrating hemorrhage in the subcutaneous tissues at the contusion site, and lack of hemorrhage in the tissues where there is merely post-mortem lividity.

a 68-year-old fair-skinned woman with light purple discoloration in the antecubital fossa. An incision through the skin (Figure 42.10b) reveals unremarkable muscle without hemorrhage.

Post-mortem contusions are somewhat rare, but typically occur when there is post-mortem blunt trauma and dependent lividity can reach the area, as seen in Figure 42.11 depicting a small laceration and surrounding post-mortem contusion which occurred on this obese woman's forehead during body removal to a funeral home, following documentation of her atraumatic face and head in scene photographs prior to transportation. Post-mortem purple ecchymoses are also occasionally seen on the inner aspect of the arms, particularly in obese individuals, likely sustained during moving of the body for transport. Senile purpura, or ecchymoses, on the upper extremities of elderly individuals, by contrast, occur antemortem; the thin skin and lax supporting tissues allow tearing of vessels and associated subcutaneous bleeding to occur very easily with minimal trauma.

Contusions may be more prominent following autopsy and drainage of blood from the body; a second examination on the day following the autopsy may, therefore, be useful in identifying these.

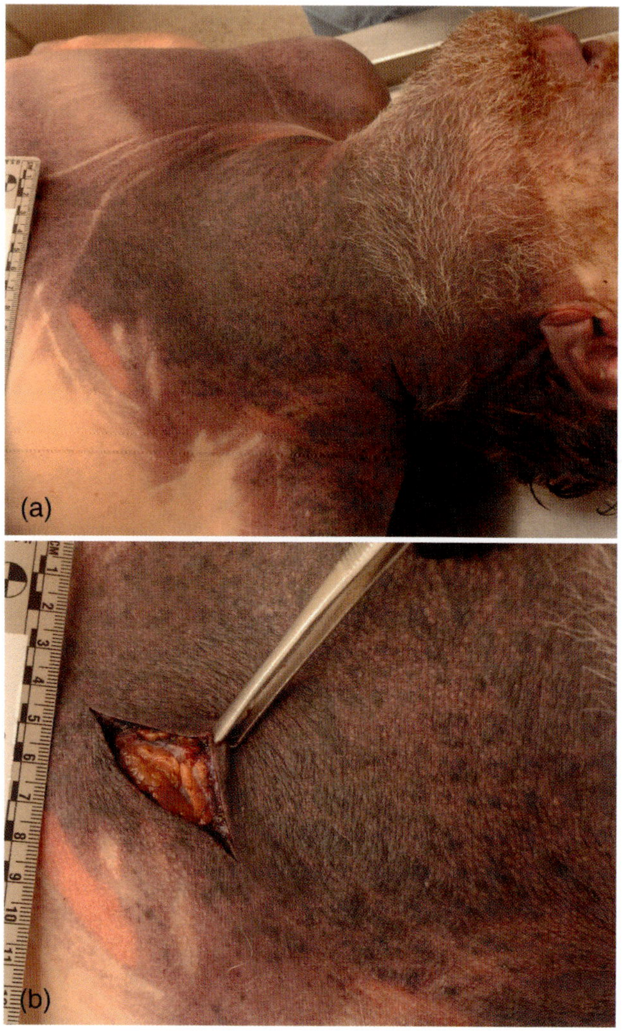

42.8 **(a)** Tardieu spots within areas of intense dependent lividity should not be mistaken for contusions. **(b)** Diagnostic incision into an area of Tardieu spots and lividity shows hemorrhage limited to the dermis and lack of hemorrhage in the subcutaneous tissues, in contrast to a contusion which typically shows hemorrhage in the subcutaneous tissues.

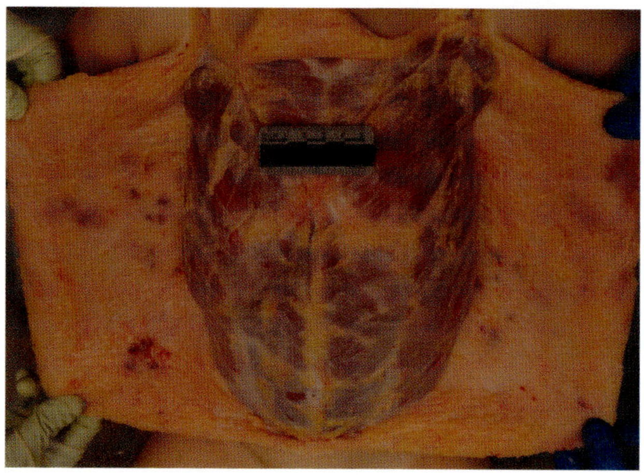

42.9 Flaying dissection of the skin, between subcutaneous and muscle layers, shows contusions in the subcutaneous tissues of a toddler who died from inflicted blunt abdominal trauma.

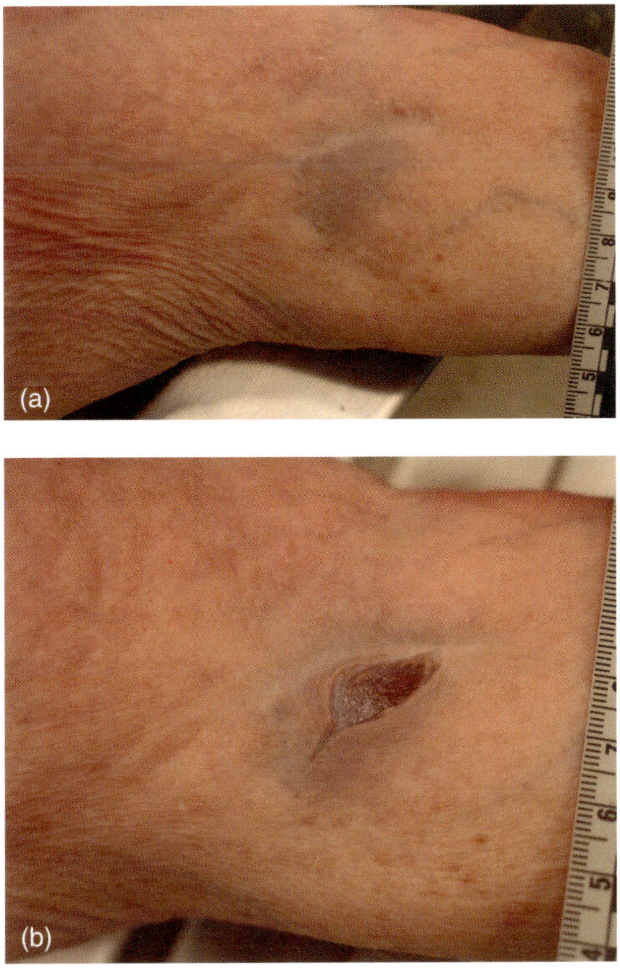

42.10 (a) Slight purple discoloration is appreciable in the central antecubital fossa. **(b)** Diagnostic incision into an area of discoloration shows no hemorrhage in the underlying muscle; this appearance should not be mistaken for contusion.

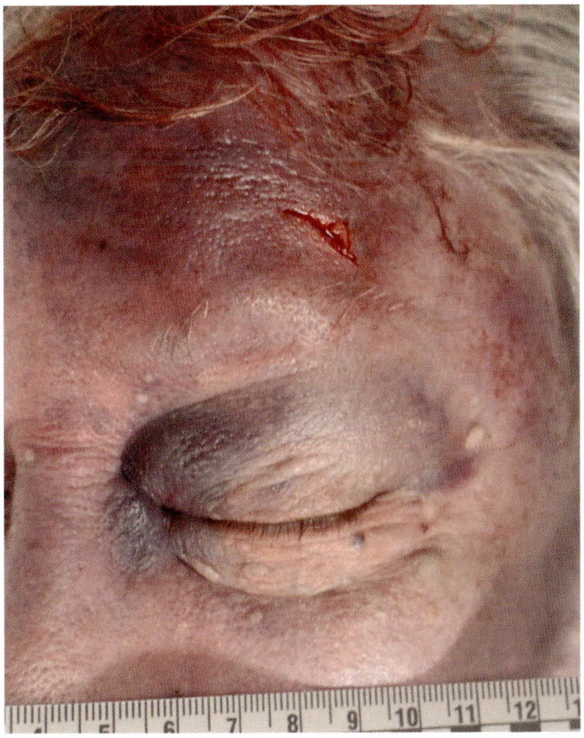

42.11 Post-mortem contusion and laceration due to injury sustained after death during transportation of the body; investigation was critical to confirm the post-mortem nature of the injuries.

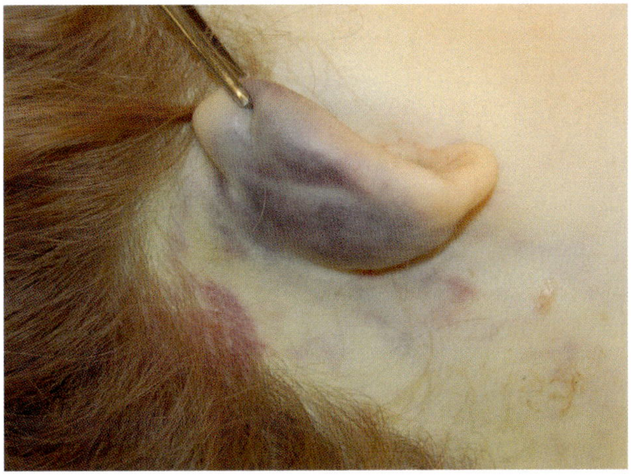

42.12 Battle's sign (ecchymosis at the post-auricular area), indicating basilar skull fracture.

Not all areas of bleeding beneath the skin are markers of direct blunt force to that location. Cutaneous ecchymosis may also be present as an indicator of internal trauma rather than a marker of direct force. Battle's sign (Figure 42.12) refers to ecchymosis at the post-auricular area over the mastoid process, indicating basilar skull fracture passing through the middle cranial fossa with associated rupture of the posterior auricular artery. "Raccoon eyes" refers to bilateral periorbital ecchymosis associated with extravasated blood descending from orbital plate fractures. The woman in Figure 42.13 sustained a self-inflicted gunshot wound to the head which resulted in orbital plate fractures and bilateral periorbital ecchymoses. Distinguishing periorbital ecchymosis from direct impact contusion of the orbit may be accomplished by correlating the presence or absence of orbital plate/frontal basilar skull fractures and examining the periorbital skin and eyebrow carefully for other cutaneous injuries (i.e. abrasions and lacerations).

The color of contusions can vary and usually changes with time and healing. Similar to the dating of abrasions, various methods to estimate the age, or date, contusions have been mentioned in the literature. These methods include visual observation (color), colorimetry, spectrophotometry, histologic examination and immunohistochemistry. In general, extreme caution should be used when estimating the age of a wound (4). The observation of yellow color has been reported to indicate that the bruise is not recent and is at least 18 hours old (5). However, the accuracy of the human eye is limited, and the ability to see the color yellow diminishes with age (6). Beyond simple appreciation of yellow color, overall dating of contusions by visual interpretation has been shown to have significant inter-observer variability, even among forensic experts (7). Figure 42.14 is an elderly man who experienced a mechanical ground level fall and sustained a left humerus fracture which was deemed non-operable.

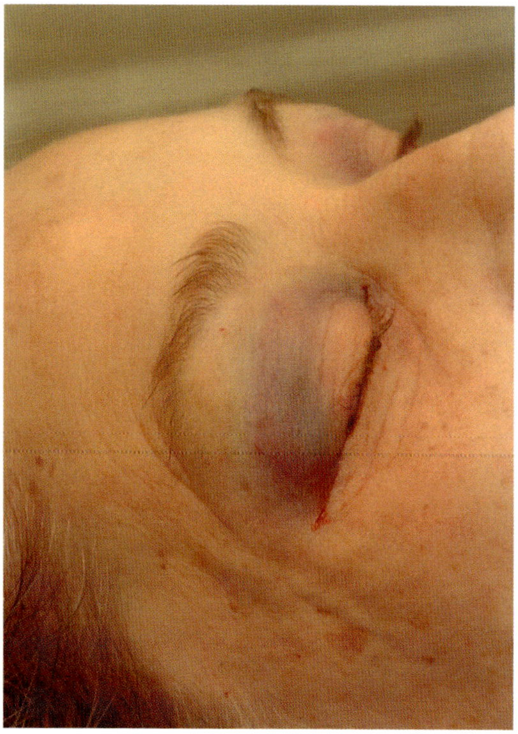

42.13 Periorbital ecchymosis due to orbital roof fractures.

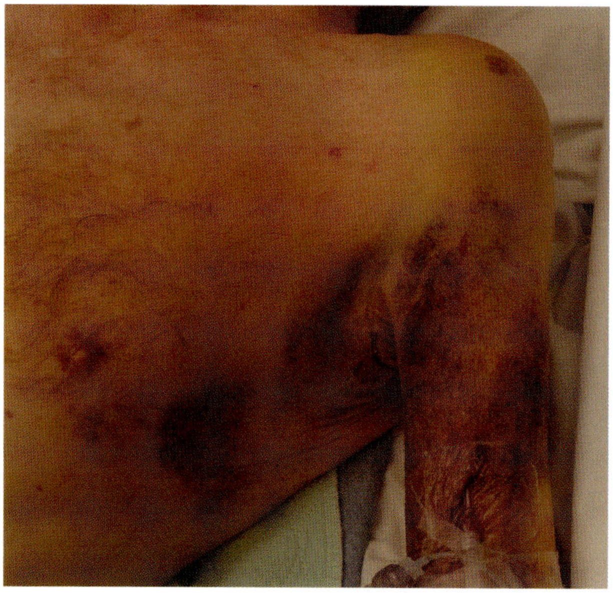

42.14 Yellow and green coloration in a 16-day old ecchymosis associated with humeral fracture in an elderly man.

He passed away sixteen days after the fall. Areas of the purple ecchymoses of the left arm, left axilla, and lateral left chest are starting to turn yellow and green in color. Color changes may vary in timing in the center of the contusion compared to the periphery; similarly, the histologic appearance of contusions may also vary depending on the proximity of sampling to the point of impact.

Contusions can be patterned, meaning that they have shape, size, and perhaps textural elements that can be matched to a particular object that created the injury; they may be seen in combination with patterned abrasions. Some examples of patterned contusions are bite marks, boot or shoe imprints, bumper hood ornament marks and tire tread marks on pedestrians, and so-called "tram track" contusions, which are parallel linear contusions with a central spared area of pallor resulting from being struck by a long, linear or cylindrical object (such as a baseball bat, baton, or edge of a wood board). Figures 42.15a and b are patterned contusions of a shoe imprint taken with an L-shaped odontology ruler.

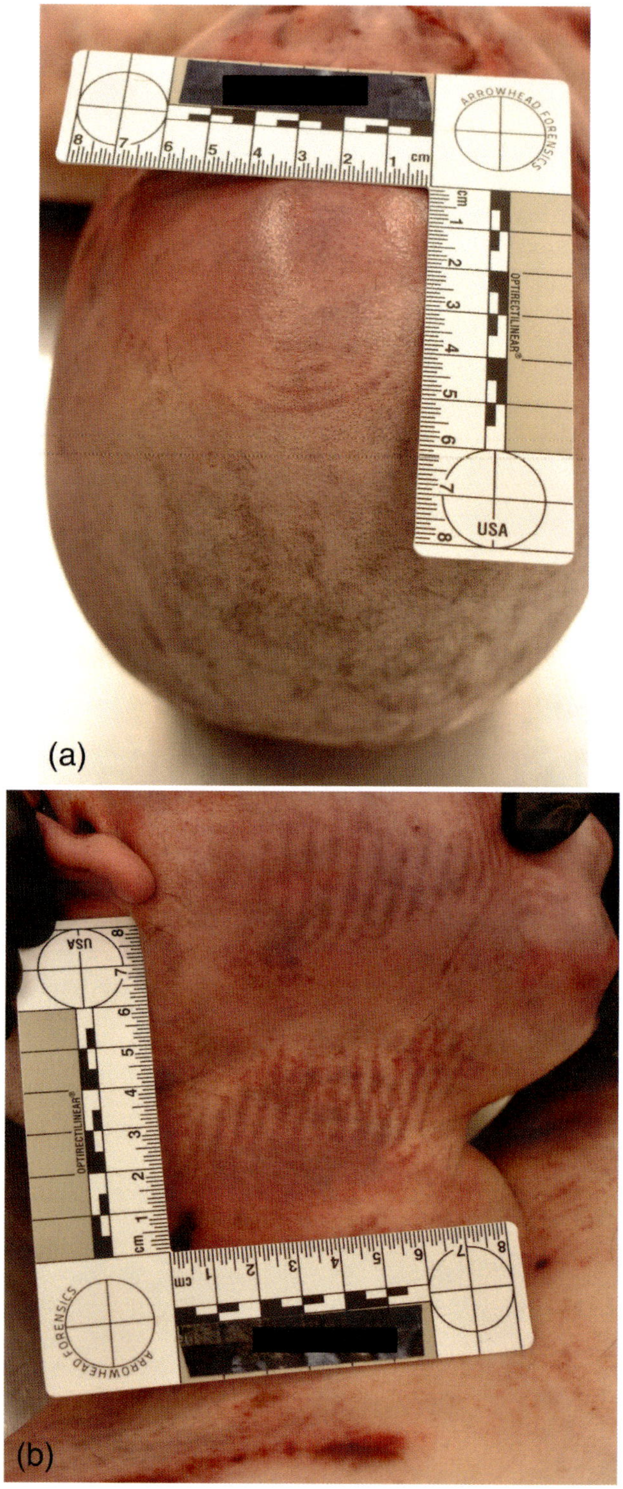

42.15 **(a)** Patterned contusion (shoeprint) on the front of the head consisting of concentric rings. **(b)** Patterned contusion of shoeprint(s) on the face and neck.

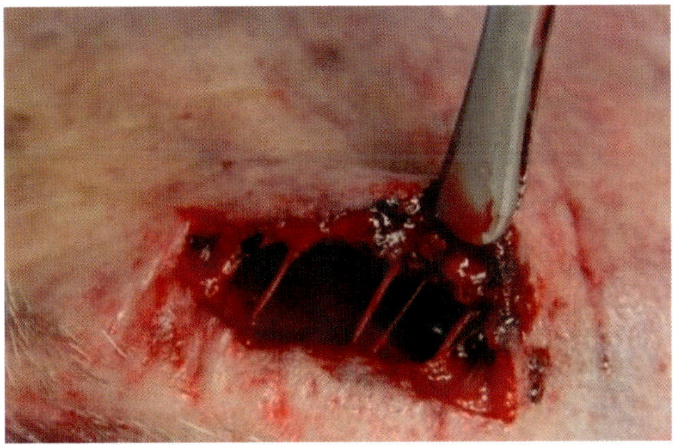

42.16 Tissue bridging in a laceration.

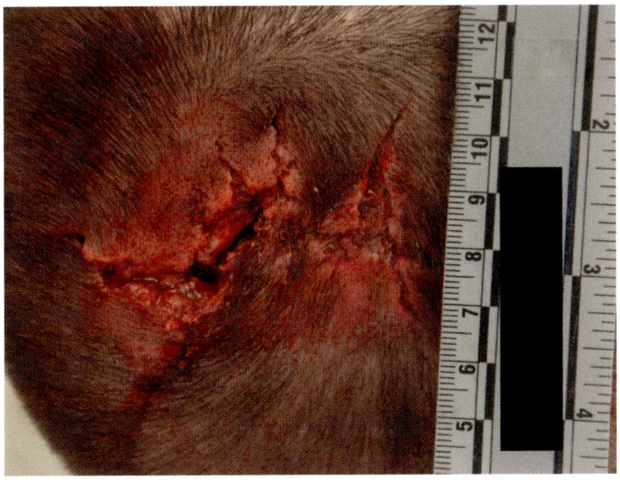

42.17 Stellate laceration with pink, abraded edges due to impact with concrete on the ground in a jump from a height.

Lacerations

Lacerations, or tears, occur when the force of an object impacting the body is greater than the elastic capacity of the skin and tissues. A laceration may be referred to by the layman as a "cut", but is a type of blunt force injury which should be distinguished from an incised wound which is a type of sharp force injury. In some cases, it might be difficult to differentiate lacerations from incised wounds. Unlike incised wounds, lacerations will have tissue bridging as seen in Figure 42.16, due to the greater elastic resilience of small nerves and blood vessels which remain spanning the laceration wound. Lacerations may have surrounding abrasion or contusion, and these features also aid in distinguishing lacerations from incised wounds. Lacerations may be stellate, irregular, linear, or curvilinear. Figure 42.17 shows an irregular laceration with abraded edges on the back of the head of a man who intentionally jumped from the ninth floor of a parking structure. Unlike abrasions and contusions which may recapitulate the pattern of a striking object, lacerations generally do not correlate with the shape of the striking object/surface (2). However, occasionally laceration shapes or patterns of array (such as paired lacerations from the claw end of a claw hammer) may suggest an object. Lacerations tend to occur over bony prominences, in areas where the skin is trapped between bone and a hard surface of impact.

Penetrating injuries may also mimic or have features overlapping lacerations. Blunt penetrating injuries, or puncture wounds, may have overlapping features of both blunt and sharp force trauma. Furthermore, chopping wounds created by heavy cutting implements, such as axes or hatchets, may have blunt trauma (abrasion and/or contusion) along the edges of an otherwise sharp force injury.

INTERNAL BLUNT FORCE INJURIES

Internal blunt force injuries may involve the musculoskeletal system, connective tissues, internal organs and/or body cavities. Classifications used on the exterior of the body, including the terms contusion and laceration, are also used to describe internal organ injuries, whereas abrasion generally refers only to the skin. References to various types of internal bleeding may include intramuscular hemorrhage or contusion, organ contusion or subcapsular hematoma, or collections of blood in body cavities (hemothorax, hemopericardium, hemoperitoneum and hemopelvis in the thoracoabdominal and pelvic regions; subdural, epidural or subarachnoid hemorrhage intracranially). The term fracture refers of course to a broken bone, whether complete or incomplete, displaced or not. Other commonly used terms in reference to internal injuries are utilized below, where appropriate, in describing the spectrum of injuries in each organ system. The introduction of postmortem CT (PMCT) examination has greatly facilitated the early identification and sometimes the evaluation of a range of internal blunt force injuries.

Heart and great vessels

Contusions of the heart are often epicardial, involving only the epicardial adipose tissue; cardiac contusions from more severe impacts may extend into the myocardium. Clinically, patients with myocardial contusion have elevated serum cardiac biomarkers and may have chest pain/soreness; they are at risk for significant cardiac arrhythmias and conduction disturbances (8). Rupture of the cardiac chambers usually occurs with high-energy blunt impacts, including motor vehicle collisions or falls from height, with death usually occurring at the scene. Atrial rupture is more frequent than ventricular rupture (9), and right-sided chamber ruptures are more frequent than left. Right atrial is the most common traumatic chamber rupture, followed by right ventricular (10). Ventricular rupture is more likely to occur when impact or compression occurs during late diastole, the phase of filling of the ventricular chambers, when they are most distended; in contrast, atrial rupture tends to occur when impact or compression is at late systole, when the atria are most distended (11). Hypotension and cardiac tamponade result (10). A strong correlation between sternal fracture and cardiac injuries was found by Türk and Tsokos in a study of blunt cardiac injuries due to falls from height, with sternal fractures present in 76 percent of cases involving heart injuries, and by contrast, only 18 percent of cases without heart injuries having sternal fractures (9). Pericardial laceration was overall the most common finding (45% of cases) in the falls from height (9). CPR-associated injuries of the heart are relatively rare but may include pericardial laceration and atrial or ventricular rupture, without or without associated rib or sternal fracture (12).

Commotio cordis describes a brief, low-energy impact to the precordium resulting in a lethal arrhythmia and sudden cardiac death (8). This is classically described in young, thin males struck in the chest during sports, particularly with a baseball or softball, and is one of the leading causes of sudden cardiac death in young athletes. The impact to the chest occurs during a vulnerable period of the cardiac electrical cycle (repolarization) and incites ventricular tachycardia or ventricular fibrillation (8). *Commotio cordis* may also occur at older ages following impact of the chest, such as with a steering wheel in a motor vehicle crash.

Coronary artery injury due to blunt trauma is uncommon but is described in the literature, and may include coronary artery dissection, laceration or aneurysm formation or rupture; thrombosis/occlusion is not typically seen (13). Angina, immediate or delayed myocardial infarction, or sudden death may be associated with this (8).

The aorta is commonly injured in high-energy acceleration-deceleration incidents, such as motor vehicle collisions, pedestrians struck by vehicles, and falls from heights. The aorta is most often injured at the isthmus, at a site just distal to the left subclavian ostium, due to the aortic arch being relatively more mobile than the fixed descending thoracic aorta (8). Blunt abdominal aortic injury is rare but reported, most frequently associated with motor vehicle collisions and spinal injuries in a large multi-center study (14). Aortic injury may range from intimal tears to intramural hematomas or pseudoaneurysm, full thickness laceration and complete rupture. Ruptures are far more frequent than dissections, which are more commonly associated with hypertension; both are associated with left-sided hemothorax. Figure 42.18 shows a complete aortic rupture at the classic location, just distal to the left subclavian ostium, with extensive periaortic hematoma, in an unrestrained driver involved in a motor vehicle collision; a 2.4-liter left hemothorax was also present. Ruptures of the aorta may be initially contained, covered by a thin layer of adventitia or hematoma, with subsequent delayed completion of the rupture when such fragile tissue gives way; this phenomenon should be considered when evaluating sudden unexpected deaths occurring hours or days after a survived motor vehicle collision. Additionally, other great vessels may be lacerated at their attachments to the heart/pericardium with acceleration-deceleration, most commonly the inferior vena cava in the authors' experience, resulting in hemopericardium. Rarely, a cardiac valve leaflet or chorda may rupture due to blunt chest trauma, with resultant acute valvular regurgitation (15).

Lungs, ribs and pleural cavities

Pulmonary contusions refer to bleeding into the pulmonary parenchyma following blunt impact or compression of the chest and may be associated with rib fractures.

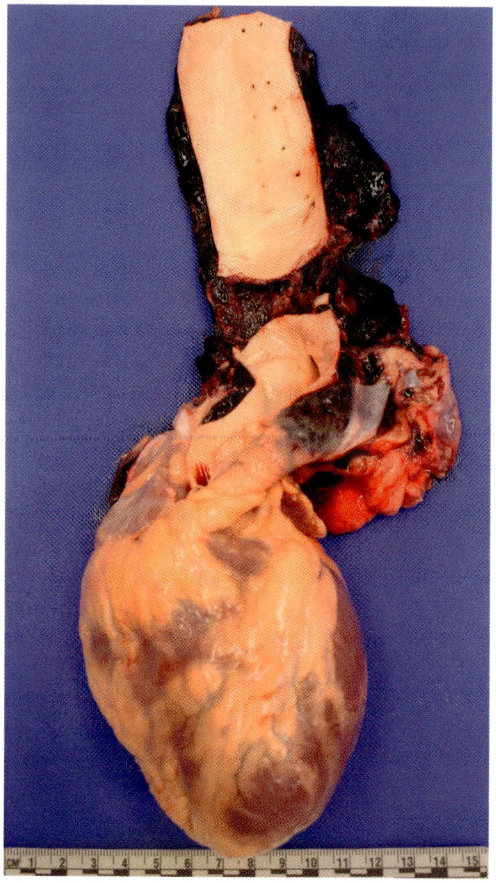

42.18 Complete aortic rupture (laceration) at the typical location, just distal to the left subclavian ostium, with extensive periaortic hematoma, in an unrestrained driver involved in a motor vehicle collision.

Displaced rib fractures with protruding bone within the pleural cavities may result in laceration of the parietal pleurae and may produce visceral pulmonary lacerations. The anterior, lateral, or posterior segments of the rib arcs may be fractured, depending on the direction and type of blunt force. Anterior and lateral rib fractures may commonly be associated with chest compressions from cardiopulmonary resuscitation. Posterior rib fractures in children are often inflicted injuries if another major source of trauma is not evident. However, posterior rib fractures have been reported in adults in association with the use of automated mechanical chest compression devices such as LUCAS, with rib fractures in general being the most common iatrogenic injury associated with these devices (16,17). A complete discussion of pediatric rib fractures is beyond the scope of this chapter. Two or more contiguous rib fractures with two or more breaks per rib defines the term flail chest, a serious condition in which a portion of the chest wall is destabilized by blunt trauma, resulting in respiratory insufficiency and paradoxical movement of the chest wall. Pneumothorax (the presence of air/gas in the pleural cavity, resulting in a collapsed lung) may be associated with flail chest, or with rib fractures in general, particularly if fractures are displaced, and can cause death if untreated. Tension pneumothorax refers to a pneumothorax in which the trapped air in the pleural cavity is under sufficient positive pressure to displace the mediastinal contents toward the opposite side, compromising cardiac function and compressing large vascular structures. Hemothorax refers to an accumulation of blood in the pleural cavity, the result of bleeding from the thoracic vasculature and/or organs.

Abdominopelvic organs

The abdominal solid organs are prone to lacerations with sufficient blunt force impact to the abdomen. The liver, kidneys, adrenal glands, pancreas and spleen all may be lacerated by blunt impacts or compression of the abdomen. The liver and spleen are the most commonly lacerated abdominal organs in motor vehicle collisions, in the authors' experience, and the most common causes of traumatic hemoperitoneum. Figure 42.19 demonstrates capsular laceration on the hilar aspect of the spleen *in situ*, with associated hemoperitoneum, sustained in a traffic collision. It is important to examine the spleen *in situ* prior to evisceration for such trauma, as artifactual tears of the capsule can occur during removal of the spleen particularly if the parenchyma is softened/diffluent due to post-mortem change. Though infrequent, the liver and spleen may also sustain lacerations due to compressions associated with cardiopulmonary resuscitation, which can lead to fatal outcomes even if patients are initially able to be resuscitated (12).

Subcapsular hemorrhages may occur in the liver due to blunt impact or compression, and also have been seen by the authors in association with cardiopulmonary resuscitation. Hemoperitoneum results from injuries such as lacerations that bleed freely from the surface of the organ; contained hemorrhages, such as subcapsular hematoma of the liver, do not typically cause hemoperitoneum (for which another cause should be sought in such cases).

The intestine and mesentery are also vulnerable to laceration or perforation, and diaphragmatic laceration (with herniation of abdominal contents through the diaphragmatic defect into the pleural cavity) can also occur. Midline structures, such as pancreas, mesentery and intestine, are vulnerable to injury (contusion, laceration, bisection) associated with compression between the spine and an object creating deep incursion of the abdomen. This is particularly true in children, where deep

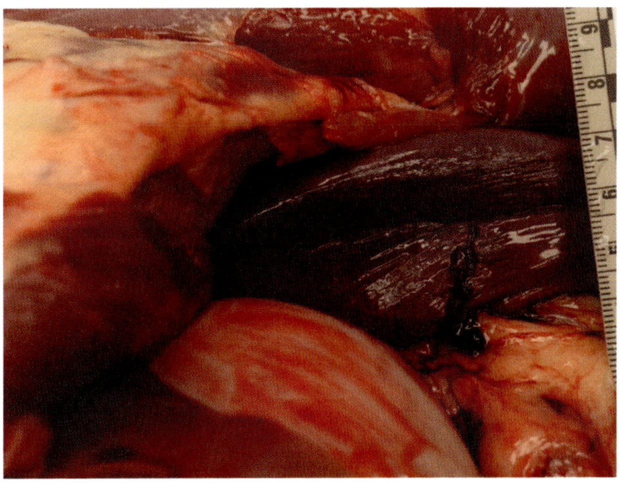

42.19 Spleen *in situ* with a capsular laceration on its hilar aspect, with associated hemoperitoneum.

incursion of the abdomen by a fist or foot can result in rupture of the duodenum with contusion or laceration of the pancreas (18). Rupture of the stomach is rare in cases of blunt force trauma to the abdomen. Venturing briefly into the pelvis, bladder rupture is typically associated with displaced pelvic ring fractures. In the case of ruptured hollow viscus organs, if death does not result immediately from bleeding and other injuries, delayed death from peritonitis may result if the injuries are unrecognized and go untreated. Additionally, injury of the pancreas can result in delayed death from pancreatitis and fat necrosis of the mesentery and omentum.

Severe, lethal blunt force trauma of the torso may be present without discernable injuries of the abdominal wall; this phenomenon has been referred to as Casper's sign (19). The skin's properties of elasticity and resilience allow it to resist injury, even while significant forces are transmitted to underlying musculoskeletal tissues and organs. Thus, the absence of external trauma of the abdomen is not an accurate predictor of the absence of significant internal trauma.

Head and neck

Blunt impacts of the head and neck can result in devastating injuries when sufficient force is transmitted. Skull fractures, cervical spine fractures or dislocations, facial bone fractures, intracranial hemorrhages and injuries of the brain may result, with associated high mortality rates. Abrasions and contusions of the scalp may be difficult to appreciate through the hair and so the hair may be shaved with clippers to facilitate examination and reveal the full extent of injuries of the external aspect of the head. Figure 42.20a shows the head of a fatally abused infant, shaved at autopsy for documentation of numerous scalp contusions. The scalp and facial skin are frequently injured in blunt traumas including assaults and traffic collisions, and the deep aspect of the scalp and outer surface of the skull should be carefully examined for interscapular or subgaleal (at the deep aspect of the galea aponeurotica) contusions. Reflection of the scalp should be carried out after the evisceration of the thoracoabdominal cavities and release of the blood in the aorta and common carotids, to avoid artifactual "hemorrhages" of the deep scalp. Figure 42.20b shows the reflected scalp of the infant seen in the prior figure, with innumerable deep scalp contusions. Figure 42.21 shows left-sided deep scalp and subgaleal contusion indicative of left frontal blunt impact in an unrestrained driver involved in a motor vehicle collision; there were no skull fractures. However, subgaleal hemorrhage may be seen overlying skull fractures.

Skull fractures occur when the force of blunt impact of the skull is sufficient to cause the bone to break. The type of fracture seen is dependent on the type of object striking the skull, as well as the surface area over which contact is made. Broad, flat surfaces of impact, such as the ground in a fall or a wide board, tend to produce linear or curvilinear fractures. More focal impacts, such as those made by a small but heavy object like the head of a hammer or a pointed rock, contacting a smaller surface area, are likely to produce depressed skull fractures, which may also be comminuted. Depressed skull

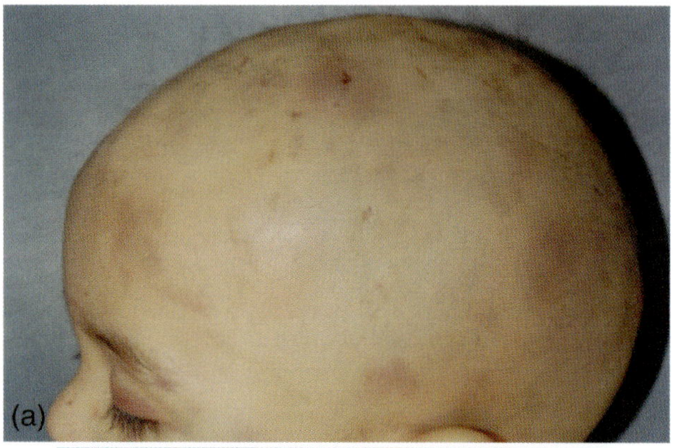

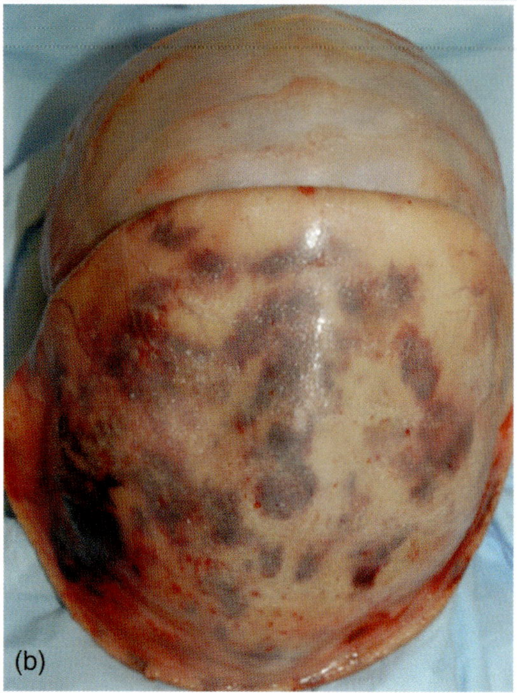

42.20 (a) Scalp of an infant with inflicted head injuries, with numerous contusions that otherwise would be difficult to appreciate without shaving the hair. (b) Reflected scalp of the same infant, showing innumerable deep scalp contusions.

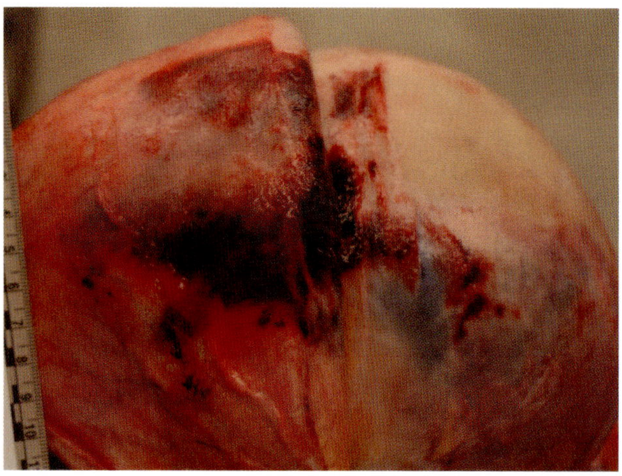

42.21 Deep scalp and galeal contusions sustained in a motor vehicle collision.

fractures do not typically occur with blows from fists; a single case report could be identified in the medical literature, in which the area of the temporoparietal skull involved by depressed fracture following a punch with a fist had undergone prior craniotomy and may have been weakened (20). Figure 42.22a illustrates a depressed frontal bone fracture extending into the superior orbital rim in a case of alleged assault with a rock; nasal bone fracture can also be appreciated. Figure 42.22b demonstrates bilateral periorbital contusions, in the same case, which were associated with both radiating fractures of the orbital plates in the basilar skull and direct facial trauma; Figure 42.22c shows one of the direct oculofacial injuries, fracture of the inferior right orbital rim (following a facial peel dissection) in this case. The brain beneath the depressed left frontal bone fracture was remarkable for cerebral laceration, contusion and subarachnoid hemorrhage seen in Figure 42.22d. Facial bone fractures, particularly involving the maxillary sinuses or nasal bones, may result in significant hemoaspiration.

Ring fractures occur in the basilar skull, surrounding the foramen magnum, in one of two scenarios, typically: either a forceful impact to the top of the head, such as a large heavy object falling on the individual from above; or to a fall from a height with impact on the ground directly on the top of the head. Hinge fractures of the skull refer to those that pass all the way across the basilar skull, often through the petrous temporal ridges, resulting in the anterior and posterior portions of the skull base being independently mobile, like a door hinge. Hinge fractures are indicative of severe blunt force and are typically seen in motor vehicle collisions.

In a case of the author's (LDK) of a charred body, significant blunt trauma of the head was able to be diagnosed, in conjunction with a forensic anthropologist and after extensive cleaning of the bones, from a small central remnant of unburned basilar skull shown in Figure 42.23. DNA evidence (blood) from the inside of the pants leg of the assailant matched the decedent, consistent with the decedent having been stomped/kicked to death. In blunt force trauma-related assaults, DNA evidence is highly likely to be significant, given the close proximity and likelihood of transfer of biological material, in comparison to gunshot-related homicides where there may be greater physical separation of victim and assailant.

The brain and intracranial cavity are also susceptible to injury from blunt impacts. Subdural and subarachnoid hemorrhages, epidural hemorrhage associated with skull fracture, and cerebral contusions may occur. *See also* Chapter 42 on forensic neuropathology/head trauma deaths.

Similarly, injuries of the cervical spine may cause death in blunt force trauma cases. Atlanto-occipital dislocations, atlanto-axial dislocations, and fractures of the high cervical vertebrae may cause rapid, near instantaneous deaths. Such severe injuries are frequently associated with high kinetic energy events, such as motor vehicle collisions. In a decedent involved in a traffic collision, consider a posterior neck dissection, with particular attention to the posterior arches of the first and second vertebrae, in cases in which insufficient injuries

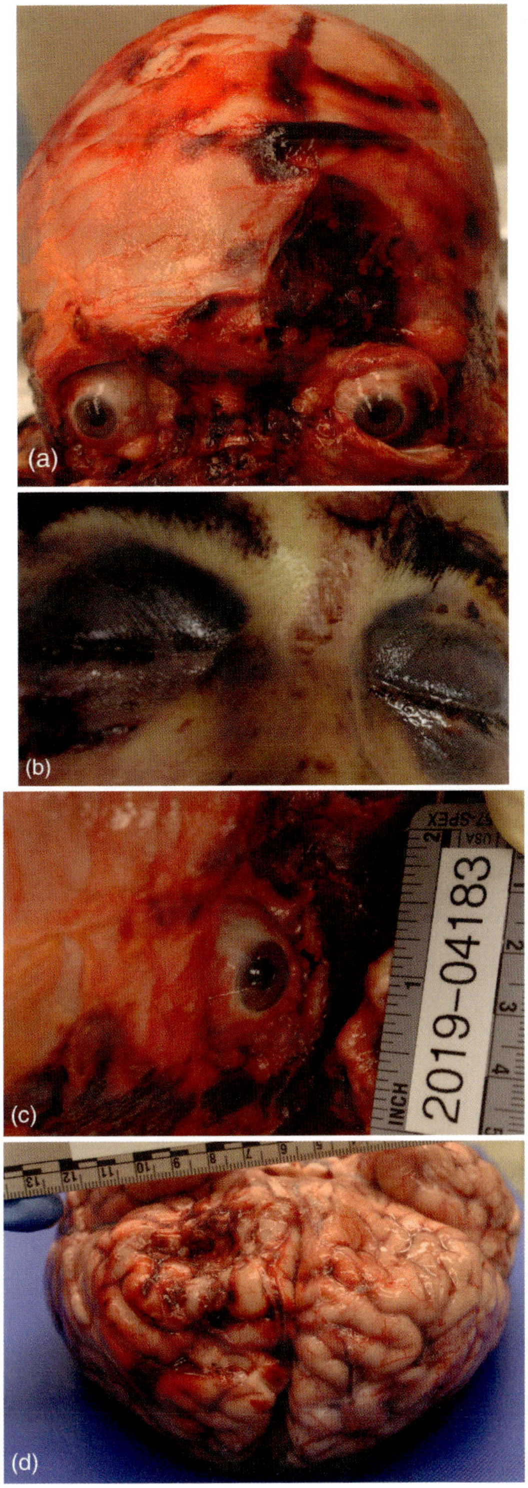

42.22 **(a)** Depressed left frontal bone fracture immediately above the left eyeball, due to assault with a rock, demonstrated on a facial peel dissection; nasal bone fracture can also be seen. **(b)** Purple periorbital contusions associated with facial trauma (healing laceration can be seen in and adjacent to the eyebrow, and bilateral orbital rim and wall fractures were present); fractures of the orbital plates were also present and may have contributed to the periorbital hemorrhages. **(c)** Fracture of the inferior right orbital rim, demonstrated by facial peel dissection. **(d)** The left frontal cerebrum beneath a depressed skull fracture showing laceration, contusion and subarachnoid hemorrhage.

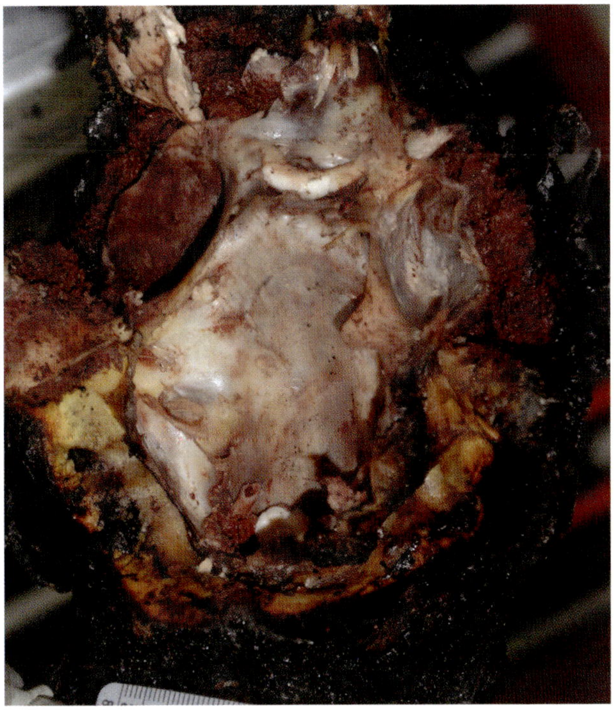

42.23 A focus of unburnt remaining central basilar skull in the charred body of a victim of a homicide due to blunt head trauma.

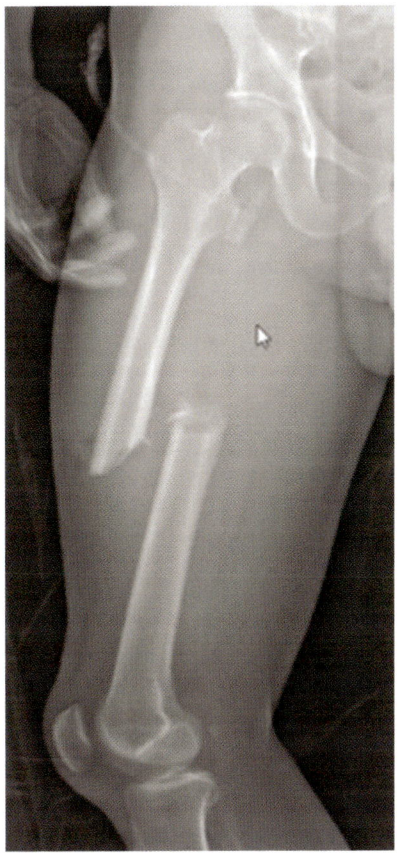

42.24 Slightly comminuted fracture of the right femur in a death due to traffic collision; gas (air) is seen in the soft tissue just lateral to the break, due to the compound nature of the fracture with overlying laceration of the skin and soft tissues.

are encountered during the "routine" autopsy to explain death. *See also* Chapter 43 on neck trauma deaths.

Musculoskeletal system/limbs/pelvis

Fracture of almost any bone in the human body can be caused by blunt force trauma. However, there are particular types and patterns of fractures seen with specific injury mechanisms which are worthy of highlighting. "Bumper fractures" in pedestrians struck by motor vehicles involve the bones of the lower extremities, often the tibia and fibula with low-profile sedans and cars but can involve the femurs and pelvis in large vehicles such as trucks. Pelvic fractures are seen with severe blunt force, such as motor vehicle collisions or falls from height, and when they involve the pelvic rim/circle of the pelvis, there are usually two or more fractures, as breaking a circle requires two breaks. Focal fractures of the acetabulum or a single pubic ramus may be seen in elderly falls. Fractures of the limbs and spine are seen in many types of blunt trauma, including motor vehicle collisions, simple ground level falls, ski accidents, falls from height and so on. A very lightly comminuted fracture of the right femur in a driver involved in a traffic collision is seen in the X-ray in Figure 42.24; gas in the soft tissue adjacent (lateral, in the figure) to the fracture on X-ray is consistent with a compound fracture, having associated laceration of the skin overlying the fracture from outward perforation by the deformed, fractured bone. An exhaustive treatment of limb fractures and their causes and types is beyond the scope of this chapter.

REFERENCES

1. Robertson I, Hodge PR. Histopathology of healing abrasions. *J Forensic Sci* 1972; **1**(1): 17–25.
2. Knight B, Saukko P. *Knight's Forensic Pathology*. 3rd ed. London: Arnold Publishers; 2004.
3. Raekallio J. Histological Estimates of the Age of Injuries. In: Perper JA, Wecht CH, (eds). *Microscopic Diagnosis in Forensic Pathology*. Springfield, Illinois: Charles C. Thomas Publisher; 1980, pp. 3–16.
4. Langlois NEI. Dating of Other Injuries in Children. In: Byard RW, Collins KA, (eds). *Forensic Pathology of Infancy and Childhood*. 1st ed, vol 1. New York: Springer; 2014, pp. 375–89.
5. Langlois NEI, Gresham GA. The ageing of bruises: A review and study of the colour changes with time. *Forensic Sci Int* 1991; **50**: 227–8.
6. Hughes VK, Ellis PS, Langlois NEI. The perception of yellow in bruises. *J Clin Forensic Med* 2004; **11**: 257–9.
7. Pilling ML, Vanezis P, Perrett D, Johnston A. Visual assessment of the timing of bruising by forensic experts. *J Forensic Legal Med* 2010; **17**: 143–9.
8. Bock JS, Benitez RM. Blunt cardiac injury. *Cardiol Clin* 2012; **30**(4): 545–55.
9. Türk EE, Tsokos M. Blunt cardiac trauma caused by fatal falls from height: An autopsy-based assessment of the injury pattern. *J Trauma* 2004; **57**(2): 301–4.
10. Asensio JA, Trunkey DD. Cardiac Injuries. In: *Current Therapy of Trauma and Surgical Critical Care*. Maryland Heights, MI: Mosby; 2008, pp. 304–15.
11. Wesson DE, Cox CS. Thoracic Injuries. In: Coran AG (ed). *Pediatric Surgery*. 7th ed. Maryland Heights, MI: Mosby; 2012, pp. 271–87.
12. Hashimoto Y, Moriya F, Furumiya J. Forensic aspects of complications resulting from cardiopulmonary resuscitation. *Legal Med* 2007; **9**: 94–99.
13. Marcolini EG, Keegan J. Blunt cardiac injury. *Emerg Med Clin N Am* 2015; **33**(3): 519–27.
14. Shalhub S, Starnes BW, Brenner ML, et al. Blunt abdominal aortic injury: A Western Trauma Association multicenter study. *J Trauma Acute Care Surg* 2014; **77**(6): 879–85.
15. Civil I. Thoracic Trauma. In: Sidebotham D, Mckee A, Gillham M, et al. (eds). *Cardiothoracic Critical Care*. Oxford: Butterworth-Heinemann; 2007, pp. 383–391.
16. Chun MJ, Zhang Y, Toraih EA, et al. Iatrogenic injuries in manual and mechanical cardiopulmonary resuscitation. *Am Surg* 2021; Available from: https://pubmed.ncbi.nlm.nih.gov/34645331/ (Accessed 1 May 2023).
17. Milling L, Mikkelsen S, Astrup BS. Characteristics of mechanical CPR-related injuries: A case series. *J Forensic Legal Med* 2020; **70**. Available from: https://doi.org/10.1016/j.jflm.2020.101918. (Accessed 1 May 2023).
18. Callahan K, Knight LD. The pancreas in child abuse. *Acad Forensic Pathol* 2018; **8**(2): 219–38.
19. Byard RW. How reliable is external examination in identifying internal injuries: Casper's sign revisited. *J Forensic Leg Med* 2012; **19**(7): 419–21.
20. Fenton TW, de Jong JL, Haut RC. Punched with a fist: The etiology of a fatal depressed cranial fracture. *J Forensic Sci* 2003; **48**(2): 277–81.

CHAPTER

43

Falls from Heights

Lorraine du Toit-Prinsloo and Rebecca A. Irvine

INTRODUCTION

Deaths due to falls constitute a significant proportion of forensic pathology practice. According to the World Health Organization, falls are the second leading cause of unintentional injuries causing death, and while there is an increased mortality in those over 70 years, mortality is also increasing in children and young adults (1), a growing concern also identified by the Centers for Disease Control and Prevention (2). Deaths due to falls are likely underreported, as a significant proportion are misclassified on death certificates as natural (3), or a fall is not specified in the circumstances (4). Falls are "a persistent risk to morbidity and mortality across all ages" (5).

Falls at work, those involving vulnerable individuals (especially the aged), those occurring in healthcare facilities, as well as sites of recurrent suicidal falls, are a significant focus of attention for policy, and prevention strategies by outside agencies.

Cases have been reported involving extreme and unexpected circumstances, such as BASE jumping (from a Building, Antenna, Span [bridge], or Earth [cliff], using a parachute requiring precise deployment) (6), and a suicide while parachuting (7). Balconing is the recent practice predominately involving young males jumping from a balcony to another balcony or pool, often in hotels, and is strongly associated with alcohol use (8).

Falls may reflect regional and cultural circumstances, from unprotected water wells in Tunisia (9), to falls from flat-top roofs where individuals sleep during hot seasons (10), to "wall falls" along the Mexico-New Mexico (US) border (11), to falls into irrigation canals in Japan (12).

Wilderness falls occur among outdoor enthusiasts, and generally the fatality rates are low, with one study reporting death in only 2 percent of fall cases, which is remarkable given that they tend to occur in remote areas (13). Falls sustained by rock climbers occur among young individuals who were close to the rock surface and resulted in extremity and soft-tissue injuries. In contrast, non-climbers who fell in the wilderness sustained more severe head injuries and required more rehabilitation after discharge (14). Zucher described 77 fatal falls in hikers in Switzerland, with more traumatic brain injuries (TBIs) occurring at elevations greater than 1800 m (15), and along with Faulhaber reported more falls during descent (16), which is more hazardous than ascent.

Trauma surgeons generally consider a vertical fall of more than 30 m as non-survivable, but there are exceptions. A young woman fell approximately 90 m, and then another 30 m; her survival was attributed to landing on her feet, the "ideal" body region of impact (17).

A wide variety of falls come to the attention of the pathologist, and any given case may represent an accident, suicide or homicide. Each case is unique in terms of the circumstances and the injuries sustained, and it is critical that the circumstances, scene and intrinsic factors are considered in every instance.

The following discussion will not include falls in the pediatric population and will not focus specifically on ground level /falls from a standing height.

MANNER OF DEATH

Homicide

Many death investigation systems require the pathologist to determine manner of death, a potentially difficult task in deaths due to falls.

While it is important to correctly ascribe the manner of death in falls from a height, it is critical that homicidal deaths are recognized as such to allow for appropriate investigation and examination. There are few studies available regarding findings in falls known to be homicidal. Rarely, is this distinction possible based solely on medical evidence, and accurate classification is dependent on the quality of the investigation. Rowbotham reported one case of a homicidal push from a height among 2743 fatal falls in Victoria, and concluded that homicide due to fall from a height is rare and associated with interpersonal violence situations (18).

While it is axiomatic that injuries not obviously in keeping with a fall are suspicious, or at least require explanation, there are few pathognomonic injuries of homicide. Injuries to palms may represent rope burns, or attempts to hold on, while bruising of the upper inner arms may represent grab marks. Damaged clothing in the groin region may be misinterpreted as evidence of sexual assault (19). Gentile reported a case of a fall from a window by an elderly man who had incised wounds on his neck and evidence of neck compression; having failed to die by incised wounds, he tied a rope (which

DOI: 10.1201/9781003138754-45

subsequently broke) around his neck to a heater and jumped out of a window (20).

The laryngohyoid complex is not necessarily spared in falls. Up to 9.4 percent of non-homicidal fall cases in one series showed laryngohyoid fractures; the incidence increased with height, age and concomitant cervical spine fractures. Fractures of the thyroid cartilage increased with concomitant clavicular and cervical spine fractures (21). Neck injuries, including hyoid bone fractures, may occur in up to one third of falls greater than 10 m (22).

In comparing homicidal blunt force injuries with those of a low-level fall, Lefevre noted that the former had more, and larger wounds, and that the "hat brim rule" for head injuries (that fall-related injuries should not lie above the hat brim line if the fall occurred from a standing position to the ground, without intermediary blows to the head) did not differentiate between them (23).

Another finding of concern for homicide is blunt force injuries on multiple surfaces without major trunk or extremity fractures, suggesting bludgeoning (19), and unexplained patterned, electrical or sharp force injuries (Figure 43.1a&b).

If injuries are present on multiple planes of the body, the scene should be examined for projecting surfaces or objects upon which the falling body may have impacted (Figure 43.2). Injuries should at least reflect the landing position of the body (Figure 43.3).

Ferguson evaluated 12 falls due to homicide and noted that they tended to occur in remote outdoor locations, were planned and motivated by gain. The assailant tended to have a controling relationship over the victim. Suspicious scene findings included signs of a struggle, and a barrier that could not be easily breached without a stepping mechanism. The authors reiterated that "... injury patterns and medical evidence were uncommonly used on their own to make manner of death determinations" (19).

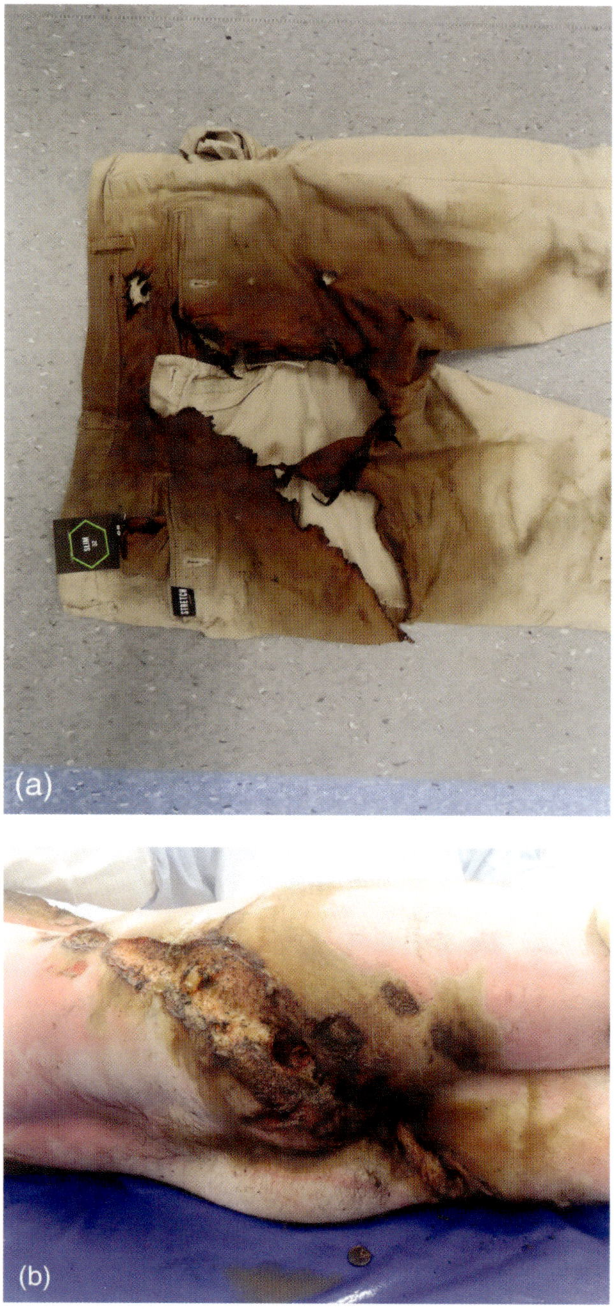

43.1 (a,b) A man jumped from a bridge and landed on the power cables above the train. He sustained high voltage electrical injury due to the fall.

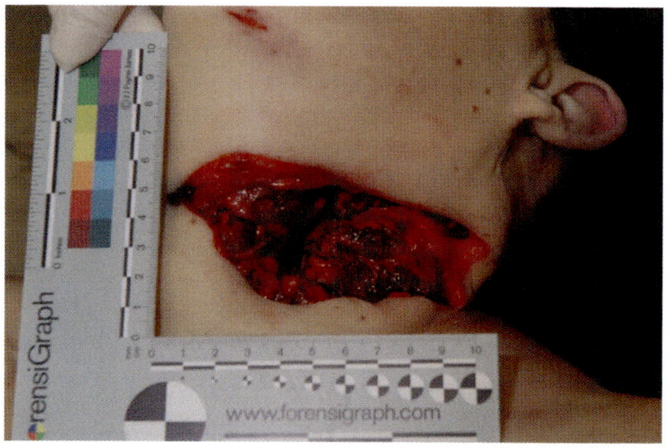

43.2 Originally considered a suspicious case, these images depict a female who fell from a ladder and sustained a large, incised wound to the right side of her neck due to a wallpaper scraper.

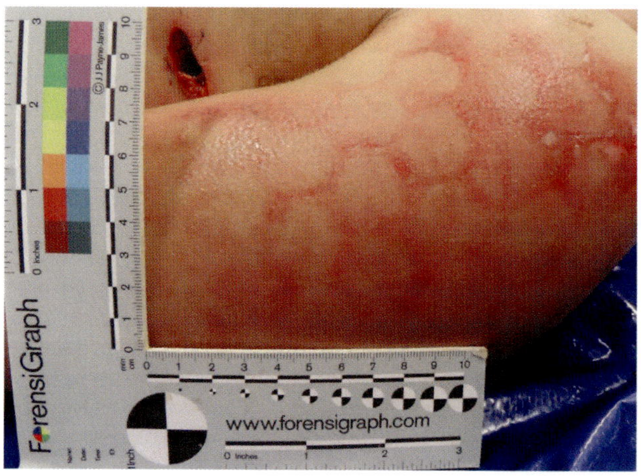

43.3 A tile pattern is clearly seen on the arm of the deceased who jumped from a balcony and landed on a tiled area surrounding a swimming pool.

TABLE 43.1 Circumstances of falls which may reflect manner of death (18–26,43,44)

Homicide*	Suicide
Signs of a struggle at top of height	Fall height (usually greater than accident)
Barrier above center of gravity, no stepping mechanism (also suicide)	Evidence of complex, planned suicide, supratherapeutic drugs
Isolated outdoor location (also suicide)	Disables security / rescue systems (e.g. parachute)
Staged scene / reporting: • Verbal false reporting of missing person • Offender "discovers" deceased • Alibi established • Body disposal, cleaning of biological evidence • Offender knowledge of site/map	Evidence of suicide pact, bodies bound together Residence (versus workplace) Possessions laid out at place of fall On-line search history (sit, methods)
Relationship with deceased • Deceased, usually female • Intimate relationship • Violent controling relationship with deceased • Motive sexual, anger, financial gain	How deceased accessed site Traditional risk factors (note, previous attempt, substance abuse, chronic medical conditions, mental health issues, triggers, etc.)
On-line search history (site, methods)	
How deceased accessed /brought to site	
Accident	
Extremely high-risk behavior (e.g. "balconing")	
Fall away from official trails in wilderness	
Faulty or unused / misused safety equipment	
Structural failure or hazard at site of fall	

* Note that these are based on very limited data

A fall from a height may disguise a homicide prior to pushing the deceased from a height. Aggrawal reported a case of a woman who was initially thought to have committed suicide by jumping from a height. Post-mortem examination showed the presence of a penetrating nail-gun injury of the head occurring prior to the fall, and the death was ruled a homicide (24).

Table 43.1 provides a summary of characteristics, with particular reference to the work of Ferguson (19), that may assist with determination that a fatal fall was a homicide.

Intentional vs unintentional falls

Choi analyzed characteristics in 8992 unintentional and 144 intentional cases of falls admitted to an Emergency Department. The most common age groups for unintentional falls were children and women over 65 years; most of this group was alive at discharge. The most common age group for intentional falls was 30 to 44 years, females slightly greater than males. In this group, most falls were greater than 4 meters. Slightly more than half of the cases were dead on arrival to hospital. More severe injuries were noted among the elderly, those with high school or greater education, greater fall height, women, and in association with alcohol use (25).

Obeid reviewed 291 intentional and 119 unintentional falls in New York City and demonstrated that those who died due to intentional falls were older, more likely female, fell from a greater height, and the injury profile included more hemorrhagic events, non-cervical vertebral fractures and visceral and pelvic injuries (26).

Suicide prevention measures at frequently used locations may consist of barriers, safety nets, early-warning devices and posted crisis contacts. These have been successful in Gap Park, Sydney, in reducing female, but not male jumping (27) (Figure 43.4a&b).

A barrier at the Bloor Viaduct in Toronto was deemed successful following a short-term rise of deaths at other bridges (28). Significant reduction was noted in 15 Swiss bridges and high structures with such measures in place (29), as well as in bridges in Norway (30), and bridges in Istanbul, linking Europe and Asia (31).

Accidental falls are often multi-factorial, and one approach is to consider the well-documented factors in

43.4 (a) One of Sydney's spectacular cliffs. (b) Suicide prevention strategies such as barriers are used at frequently used locations.

workplace falls (see below), as well as intrinsic factors such as intoxication and medical conditions (both also discussed below).

PATHOLOGIC FEATURES AND PATTERNS OF INJURIES IN FALLS

There are multiple published reports, some with impressively large cohorts, examining the correlation between fall height and manner of death, among other factors, with types and patterns of injuries (Table 43.2). Unfortunately, there is little consensus in the results. The pattern of injuries appears to be influenced by multiple factors, including weight, clothing, ground composition (deformability), landing position (22), body mass index (BMI) and sex (32).

Sikary presented a cautionary tale of two adults with a suicide pact (dyadic fall) who jumped from a 12-meter height with their wrists bound. The man landed on his head, while the woman landed on her feet. The injury patterns were totally different (33).

Velmahos examined spinal injuries in over 400 cases of falls; while 31 percent had spinal injuries, these tended to be at different levels, and 15 percent were non-contiguous. There was no correlation with the height of the fall (34).

Türk found that the most severe head injuries in a group dying from falls were at heights of less than 10 m, and greater than 25 m (22).

Concerning falls downstairs, Chatha found that older individuals were more likely to have injuries to all body regions, and more severe spinal injuries; intoxicated individuals sustained more head and neck injuries and tended to be younger (35). Bux reported in their series that 63.9 percent of fatal falls downstairs occurred at home, 53.5 percent were associated with alcohol use, and 42.8 percent were associated with severe natural disease (36).

In general, it appears that the height of the fall correlates with injury severity scores (37), suicidal falls tend to be from greater heights (25,38), and the number of fractures increase with fall height (22). In a study of fatal falls in New York City, individuals in falls of greater than 61 m were 12 times more likely to die on impact than those in falls of less than 7.6 m (26).

Casali reviewed 307 victims of falls and reported thoracic injuries in nearly all cases. An increase in the height of the fall was associated with more severe abdominal injuries (39).

In falls into water, external injuries may be relatively mild compared to internal injuries.

The point of impact can usually be determined by lateral predominance of injuries, or the classic skeletal injuries of landing upright such as tarsal, leg and pelvic fractures (40) (Figure 43.5a&b).

Impact decollement, or avulsion pocket, refers to traumatic avulsion of skin and subcutaneous fat from underlying muscle, and may indicate the point of impact. Atanasijevic reported on the incidence of decollement injuries in 375 cases of falls from a height up to 50 m. Decollement was not seen in cases where the decedent landed in a head-first position. Decollement was usually seen at the impact site, such as the side, back or buttocks. It was typically present with increased height of fall, and more in cases where the manner of death was deemed to be accidental (40).

Patterned injuries may identify the point of impact. Internal patterned injuries to the liver were described by Tattoli, consisting of linear contusions caused by compression of the rib cage into the liver capsule (Figure 43.6) (41).

Tattoli and Tsokos reported a remarkable patterned injury whereby compression of skin and soft tissue between the radius and ulna resulted in bruising on the skin of the forearm in a pattern outlining the bones (Figure 43.7) (42).

Some investigators have used specific systems to attempt to distinguish patterns of suicidal from accidental falls, such as the Berghaus 14-point scale with a reported accuracy of nearly 90 percent (43). Six of the points are based on the injured areas of the body. Using this system, Teresiński found that a suicide group had injuries in nearly all body regions, but no injury reliably differentiated the two; this tool was accurate for nearly 88 and 80 percent of suicides and accidents, respectively (44), but the erroneous indications (20% misclassified as suicide) and inconclusive categories (12% of suicides) would be unacceptable in many jurisdictions.

TABLE 43.2 Patterns of injuries in falls (22,26,39,40,86–88)

Head and neck	Abdominal
More common in falls from heights <7 m and >30 m	Liver most commonly injured
>30 m–no contrecoup injuries	In falls >15 m less cases have no abdominal injuries
Increase in complex skull fractures with an increase in height	Falls >40 m – hemoperitoneum less than 300 mL
Falls 3 m–15 m • Lacerations of the scalp • SAH with SDH most common injury seen • EDH alone is rare	Kidney injuries very rare according to some articles Mesentery and kidney injuries seen in falls from the 3rd–6th floor Bilateral kidney rupture in falls from 4th and 6th floor
More severe head injuries in falls <10 m and > 25 m	Liver and splenic lacerations in more than 50% of cases where the fall was >10 m in height
Neck injuries occurred in 33% of falls >10 m but did not occur in falls < 10 m	Pelvic fractures in 67% of falls >10 m (only 12% of falls <10 m) Pelvic fractures–50% of falls from 5th floor
Facial fractures increase in frequency with heights >12 m	Although the presence of abdominal injuries are generally low, they are associated with an increase in mortality
Chest	Intestinal root rupture present in approximately 25% of falls >10 m.
Increase in severity with increase in height	**Extremity/skeletal**
More rib fractures with increase in height	Abrasions very common
Frequency of heart and aortic lacerations not influenced by increase in height according to some publications	Long bone fractures are rare in falls from 3–6m included in this study
Falls from >25 m • Aortic rupture more common in falls >10 m (the majority of which occurred in the descending aorta) • Cardiac ruptures in 36% of cases >10 m • Lung injuries present in 62% of cases • Rib fractures in 78% of cases	Long bone fractures in 50% of those falling from the 6th floor Open long bone fracture in falls from the 8th floor Falls <3 m • <1.5 m: lower extremity (ox coxae and femur) fractures, appendicular fractures, upper extremity fractures are rare • Bilateral fractures are rare • 1.5–3 m: axial skeleton • Rib and skull fractures • Bilateral fractures occur more often
Pneumopericardium associated with bilateral pneumothorax Lung contusion and/or rib fractures–falls from 2nd floor Pulmonary or cardiac rupture–falls from the 7th floor Rib fractures seen in 90% of cases–seen more in people with a weight of >50 kg Injuries to the heart seen more with an increase in height and in decedents aged >60 years	Falls >3 m • More fractures of the appendicular and axial skeleton when the landing surface was non-deformable • Serial rib fractures hallmark of injuries in intentional jumpers from bridges • Upper extremities and pelvis injuries increase with an increase in height • Skull and C-spine fractures in >80% of cases
Most common findings in several publications	
Heights more than 15 m– two or more regions injured	
Most injuries occur with falls from 3– 6 m	
Authors differentiate between pattern of injury seen in falls vs other blunt force injury especially when the decedent is found next to a building and the circumstances were not witnessed.	

(*Continued*)

TABLE 43.2 (Continued)

Most common findings in several publications
Most common injuries –abrasions, bruises rare
Falls from the 5th floor associated with an increase in mortality
Injuries to the mesentery, kidneys and small bones of the upper extremity occurs in the threshold height of 3rd to 6th floor
Association with increased age and increase in the injuries to the mesentery, hip and kidney hilum
Increase in weight (>50 g) increase in injuries to the subtentorial brain, SDH, SAH and rib fractures
Increase in height associated with increased injuries to the heart, thoracic aorta, upper facial skull, liver, lung, jaw, cervical spine, diaphragm, sacroiliac joint and pubis symphysis
Increased height of fall–noncervical vertebral fractures, hemorrhagic events, liver, spleen, pelvis, lung, kidney and rib injuries
Falls from lower height–more intracranial hemorrhages
No injuries seen to the patella, fibula, tarsal, metatarsal or carpal bones

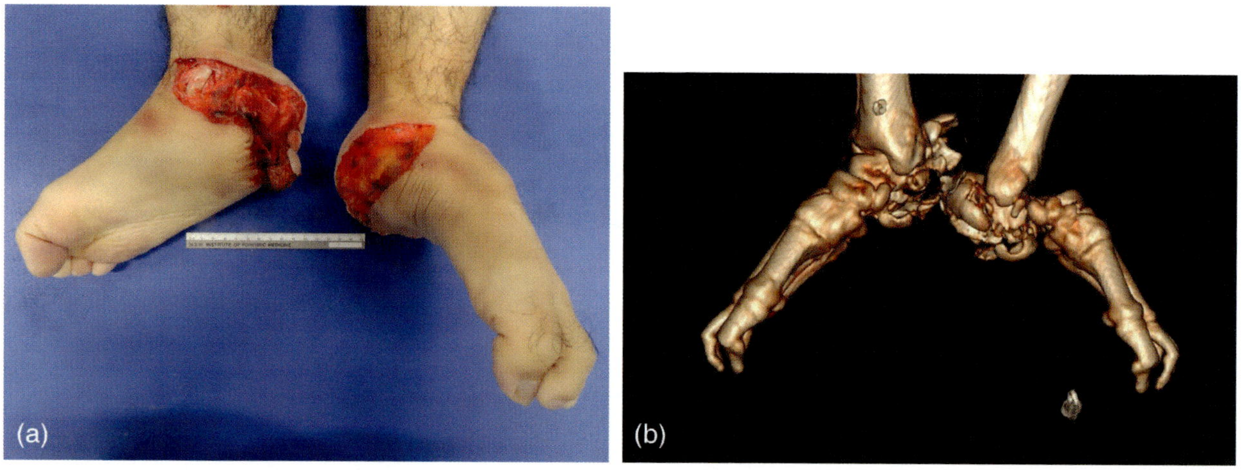

43.5 (a) Depicts the point of impact as the feet. The image shows large lacerations on the heels. The 3D reconstruction **(b)** shows the underlying comminuted fractures of the calcaneus.

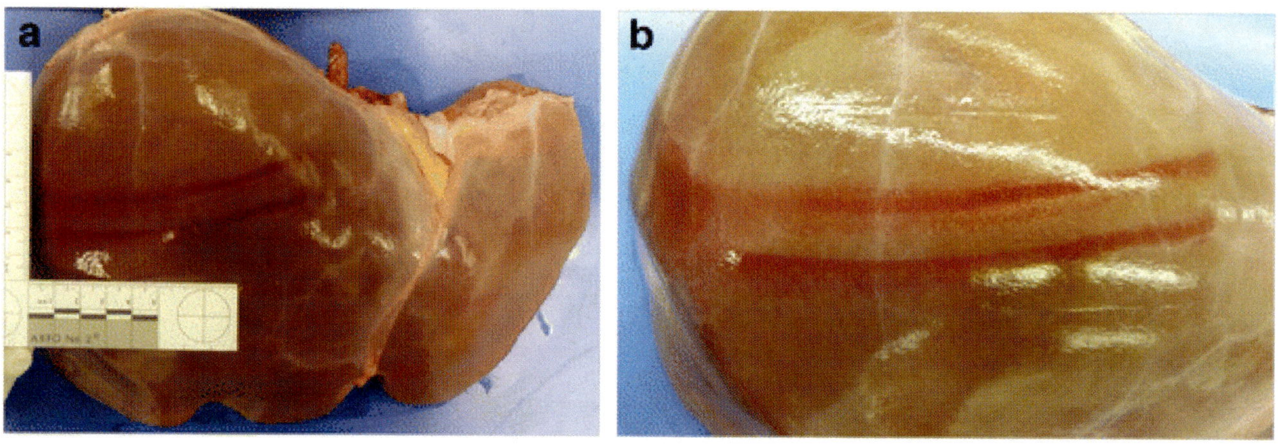

43.6 (a,b) "Tramline" bruising of the right liver lobe with an imprint of the ribs' shape (With permission from Springer Nature (Ref 41).

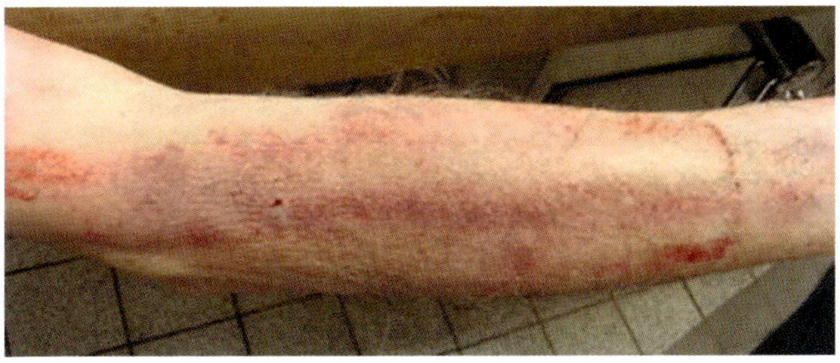

43.7 Parallel bruising along the posterior surface of the right forearm (With permission from Springer Nature [Ref 42]).

As Türk cautions, it is nearly impossible to reconstruct the circumstances of death based solely on injury pattern (22). As stated by Casali, great variability exists across all the available forensic literature concerning falls from a height (39). Table 43.2 presents injury patterns in falls from multiple publications; the tremendous variation in published results regarding falls should, however, be borne in mind.

POST-MORTEM EXAMINATION

Full internal examinations should be performed whenever possible. Natural disease may contribute significantly to death. Cecchetto reported myocardial sarcoidosis in a young woman who fell 9 m from a window, suggesting a possible natural cause for the fall (45). Puzovic reported the death of a construction worker who fell 3 m from scaffolding; full autopsy revealed that this was a COVID-19-associated death (46), and falls have also been reported as an atypical presentation in COVID-19-infected elderly individuals (47). Reported recurrent falls from unexpected conditions include hypothyroidism (48), odontoid pseudogout (49), a spinal meningioma (50), progressive subacute myelopathy due to nitrous oxide abuse (51), and (although obviously not identifiable at autopsy) stiff leg syndrome (52), and a woman with auditory hallucinations commanding her to fall down (53).

Role of imaging

Computed tomography (CT) imaging, if available, is an extremely useful tool to guide the post-mortem examination (54); it is, however, complementary as autopsy confirms and clarifies findings, and identifies injuries or conditions not apparent on imaging. Injuries, especially fractures, may be identified on imaging in areas not routinely assessed (limbs, cervical spine, pelvis, scapulae and paravertebral regions) and focus the examination. Fracture type, best seen on imaging, may provide information regarding the mechanism of the fall (54).

Importantly, imaging also provides a permanent objective record of injuries identifiable radiologically and is available for review in light of new information. Figures 43.8a and b are an example of 3D reconstruction of the skull and illustrate the complex skull fractures that may be sustained.

Figure 43.9 is a full body reconstruction showing all skeletal injuries. Such images may be useful in court proceedings as these images are not as confronting and potentially prejudicial as photographs.

Imaging may also indicate the presence of bony pathology which may contribute to the severity of injury, such as Paget disease of the bone or multiple myeloma.

The use of post-mortem magnetic resonance imaging (MRI) scan in traumatic cases was reviewed by Ross. The study reviewed 40 cases with six the result of falls from a height. MRI aided in the evaluation of soft-tissue trauma (such as subcutaneous hematomas), but the sensitivity was lower for traumatic lesions of the upper abdominal organs (especially the spleen). The authors concluded that MRI is a good adjunct to post-mortem examination, "especially to aid with accident reconstruction and second-opinion autopsies". Due to the cost of MRI, the authors proposed that a CT scan be used first as a screening tool (55).

Post-mortem CT angiography (PMCTA) may assist in the visualization of vascular injuries. Mokrane reported on three cases of fatal falls from a height where PMCTA assisted in indicating vascular injury, such as rupture of the internal carotid artery (56).

Toxicologic examination

Toxicologic examination (Table 43.3) is obviously an important adjunct to the post-mortem examination and may hold clues to the manner of death. Obtaining optimal specimens from bodies with extensive injuries may be challenging, especially with extravasated fluid specimens, but should be prioritized.

In a group of individuals with suspected suicides from falls, Fanton identified psychotropic medication in over half, and toxic drug concentrations in approximately 20 percent (57), suggesting planned complex suicides or amelioration of distress. Over half of non-occupational falls in adults are associated with alcohol use, which may be an actuating factor increasing the severity of at least TBIs (58). Schaffer et al. reported a positive blood alcohol concentration in more than 60 percent of unintentional falls from balconies (59). Drugs, especially benzodiazepines, have been identified in 77 percent of accidental falls, compared to only 39 percent of non-fall accidents (60). Peng documented the presence of psychotropic substances in 15.4 percent of cases of suicidal falls, 8.3 percent of accidental falls, and 5.6 percent of homicidal falls in Taiwan (61).

The use of sleep medications is noteworthy as a contributor to falls in community-dwelling older adults in the US (62).

Obscure causes of death

Occasionally, individuals suspected to have died of injuries related to a fall fail to show significant injuries on radiologic and standard post-mortem examination.

Certain serious injuries may be subtle and require additional examinations, such as posterior neck dissection for ligamentous injuries. Pontomedullary lacerations may be subtle and inapparent on imaging; Zivkovic reported these in about 15 percent of a series of death due to falls (63). Diffuse axonal injury may be difficult to demonstrate in the absence of a survival period. Other rare traumatic neurologic causes of sudden death include acute trauma-associated brainstem dysfunction ("*commotio medullaris*"), and subarachnoid hemorrhage associated with traumatic vertebral and basilar artery tears.

Hiquet reported suspected *commotio cordis* in an individual who fell onto wet sand (64), and Muacevic

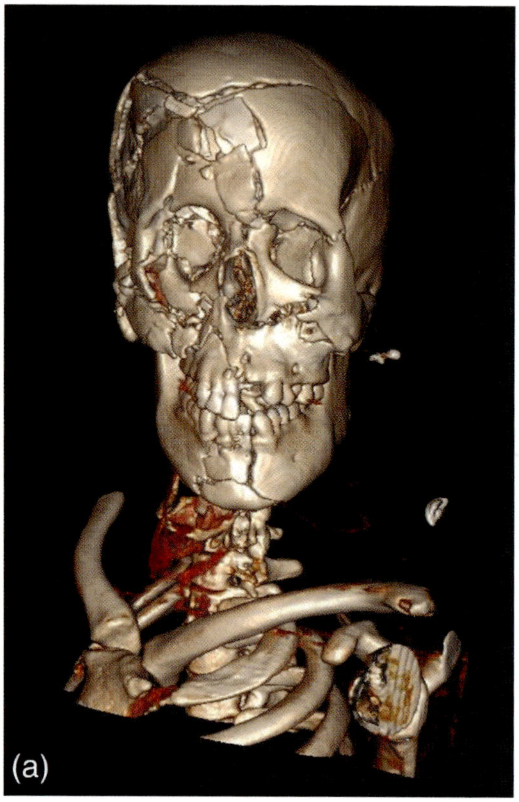

(a)

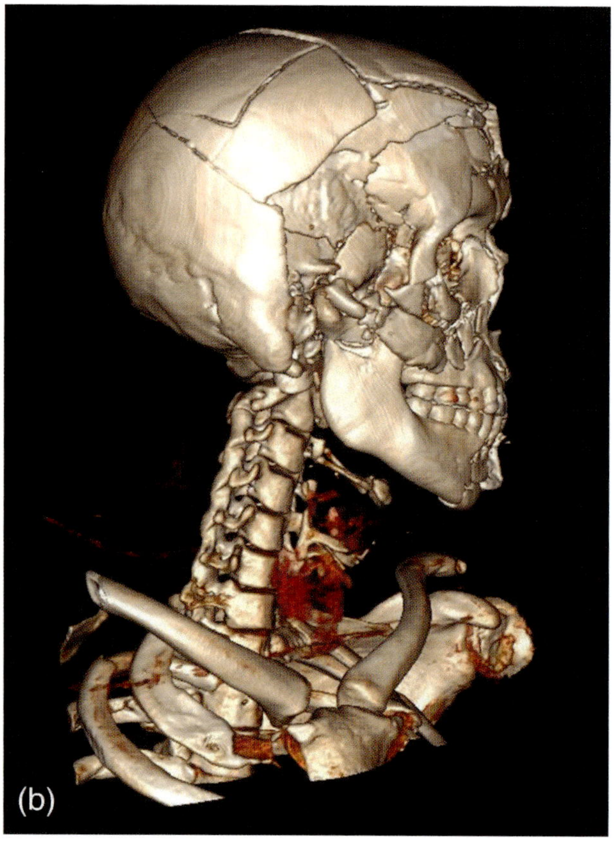

(b)

43.8 (a,b) A post-mortem CT scan with a 3D reconstruction of the skull demonstrating the complex skull fractures in a more detailed manner possible with simple description.

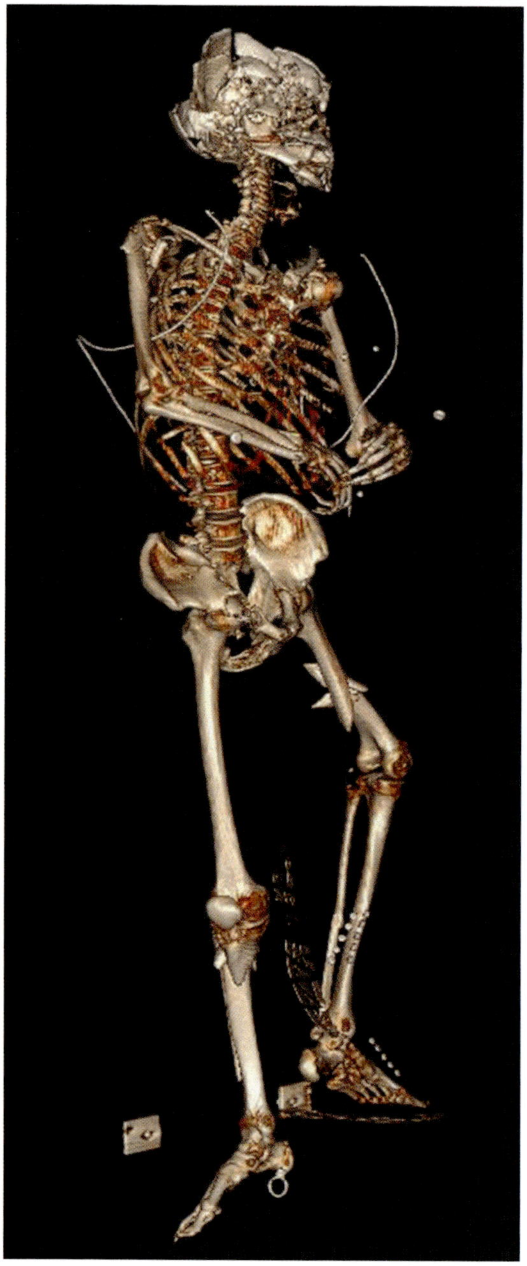

43.9 A full body reconstruction showing all injuries.

reported a cardiac contusion after a fall presenting as atrioventricular block (65).

The cause of death may relate to the scene of death. Individuals who land in water (which may be tidal) may have drowned, been stunned, or sustained a nonfatal injury such as an arm fracture which prevented self-rescue. The potential for perimortem or post-mortem injury from waves and rocks, and marine scavengers, complicates the determination of injuries causing, in contrast to following, death; in addition, injuries may be leeched by water resulting in a "post-mortem" appearance.

Environmental hypothermia, complications of prolonged immobility, and positional asphyxia are other considerations in individuals who are non-fatally injured. Behera reported a case of positional asphyxia in a man who fell in a bathroom, with occipital scalp lacerations raising the possibility of concussion (66).

SPECIAL CATEGORIES OF FALL DEATHS

Work related

Death occurring while at work (Table 43.4) is of particular interest to the Medical Examiner or Coroner (ME/C), and public agencies. A work-safety assessment/investigation is imperative in the evaluation of these cases. Falls at work are extremely common. In the construction industry, falls are the leading cause of serious injury (48%) and fatal injuries (30%) (67). In New York City, 13 percent of falls were found to be work-related, 4 percent of these due to improper use of safety equipment (26). In Australia, 11 percent of work-related deaths were attributable to falls, and mortality from these falls increased with age (68).

Factors in work-related falls have been extensively researched. The most common categories in construction include risky activities (incorporating individual characteristics, knowledge, health and sleep status); site conditions (such as lighting, equipment, breaks and organizational characteristics), weather conditions and agents (scaffolding and ladders in particular) (67). (See Table 43.4, adapted from Nadhim [67].)

Schoenfisch, demonstrated that falls were increased in construction industry workers with less than 10 union-years' experience (69). The industry often uses temporary and inexperienced employees.

Nadhim conducted a comprehensive literature review on fatal falls in the construction industry. The authors categorized the articles into two distinct groups. The first group reviewed earlier research (autopsy data including demographic data, location and height of the fall and the specific autopsy findings). The second group included strategies implemented to prevent falls. The authors

TABLE 43.3 Toxicological substances of possible significance in falls (57–62)
Alcohol
Psychoactive substances • Barbiturates • Benzodiazepines, sedative-hypnotics • Opioids (role actually unclear) • Neuroleptics • Amphetamines, stimulants • Cannabinoids • Hallucinogens • Anti-depressants
Antihypertensives, especially vasodilators
Anticoagulants / anti-platelet medications
Drugs of potential significance primarily because of indications • Anti-Parkinson agents • Iron (anemia) • Vitamin D (deficiency) • Cancer therapies • Medications for diabetes • Anti-epileptics used as such • Concentrated caffeine
Introduction of new medications, noncompliance and generally large number of medications prescribed
Supratherapeutic concentrations (suicidal intent, misuse or improper administration)

concluded that future research should include the use of cognitive mapping, and interviews with survivors of falls, to understand how these accidents occur and could be prevented (67). The Cochrane Work Group found that the quality of evidence was very low in a review of 17 injury prevention interventions in the construction industry (70).

Panuwatwanich studied the use of an "ambient intelligence system", a device able to detect when a worker is in a fall-risk area that raises an alarm to create awareness of risk (71).

Individuals vulnerable to falls

It is well established that, as a group, the elderly are at greater risk of falls, and have higher mortality associated with falls, although these are generally not falls from heights; older adult falls are projected to reach 100 000 per year in the United States (US) by 2030, with a recommendation to integrate screening for falls into clinical practice (72). Most jurisdictions consider these deaths reportable, and the manner of death accidental (Table 43.5).

Although the list of risk factors for falls in the elderly is extensive, it is worth review because these factors are not limited to that group (*See* Table 43.5, adapted from Kiel [73]). For example, Morris, while acknowledging that malignancies are increased in the aged, identified risk factors for the increased frequency of falls in individuals with malignancies, including fatigue, sarcopenia and the effects of treatment (such as neurotoxic chemotherapy-induced "chemo brain") (74,75).

Certain intrinsic conditions may have contributed to death and may warrant inclusion on a death certificate because they have aggravated injuries received in a fall, such as an expansive subdural hematoma occurring in the setting of medical anticoagulation. The same is true for non-therapeutic coagulopathies, such as in liver disease. Osteopenia or metabolic bone disease are risk factors for fractures. Rarely, local conditions may be vulnerable to trauma, such as herniae, hepato-splenomegaly, hydatid cysts and recent fractures or operative sites.

Falls in assisted-living facilities have occasionally resulted from assault by another resident, and should be considered homicides, although prosecution is obviously problematic.

Falls in hospitals

Falls remain distressingly frequent in healthcare settings, where multiple risk factors emerge, although they are again not usually from heights. Programs to prevent "never events" such as iatrogenic infections and pressure sores have been effective, but mixed results have been reported for the prevention of falls in hospitals (76). As this should be a safe environment where fall risk is carefully monitored, fatal falls in this setting particularly attract the interest of the Medical Examiner/Coroner.

TABLE 43.4 Considerations in workplace-related falls (26, 67–71)

Highest risk is construction industry • Scaffolding (including erection and dismantling), roofing, painting and decorating • Scaffolding, ladders are most frequent agents	Weather (heat/cold, rain, wind, fog, etc.) Site conditions (unprotected walkways, improper guardrails, slippery or sloped surfaces, etc.)
Age (direct relationship)	Ergonomics (environmental control, lighting, etc.)
Experience, including union years (usually indirect relationship)	Controlled access areas
Knowledge (education, skills, dexterity)	Organisation and management factors • Company size (small or medium may have short employment, high wages, contractors, sub-contractors etc.) • Safety standards / guidelines, training, equipment available and functioning • Project management (timelines, shiftwork, attitudes) • Learning from incidents, inspections, revisions • Prevention strategies (minimising hazardous agents, duration of exposure, fall protection programs, etc.)
Risky activities	Personal Protective Equipment (PPE) • Basic (harnesses, hard hats, masks, high-visibility articles, goggles, nets, etc.) • Ambient intelligence systems (improve awareness of immediate fall hazards) • Personal fall arrest systems
Physical disorders (depression, hypertension, heart disease, anaemia, diabetes, epilepsy, etc.)	Individual characteristics (fatigue, overconfidence, carelessness, ignore safety training, poor work practice, poor communication, language barriers, etc.)
Overweight (increases fatigue)	Alcohol and drug use

McErlean examined 190 falls in an Emergency Department; although over 95 percent resulted in no or minimal injury, the patients tended to be younger than in other healthcare settings. There was increased drug and alcohol use in these patients, and falls tended to occur during mobilization, especially with the use of the toilet (77).

Most falls in hospital involve the elderly, occur in medical units, are from low heights and result in minor injuries. Risk factors include admission after a fall, visual problems, frequent bathroom use and previous falls. In contrast, Trinh identified injuries in 45 percent of falls in hospital, approximately 10 percent of which were considered serious, especially head injuries (78). Kobayashi astutely pointed out that falls were increased in patients wearing slippers, as opposed to other footwear (79).

Hospital falls are not always accidental. A Swiss General Teaching Hospital was able to reduce suicidal jumps significantly by simply installing guard rails on windows (80). Chen reported that 8 percent of suicidal falls in Taiwan occurred in hospitals, with hospitals and shopping malls showing the greatest jumps per location (81).

ANALYTIC BIOMECHANICS

While it is the prerogative of the court to assess the scientific validity and admissibility of non-traditional sciences, the pathologist should at least be aware of the potential and limitations of this emerging field.

Most of these investigations involve the use of human models, and while some are quite complex (and costly), they are unable to precisely replicate human movement including dynamic components such as pushing or jumping, and movements to prevent, or during, a fall. Very lean or adipose individuals are not well represented by standard models, nor are individual organs and tissues (82).

The known physical parameters of an event may be limited, perhaps to only the landing position. Adamec attempted to analyze a case of an intoxicated individual who fell from a window, but the number and range of possibilities was so high that comprehensive analysis of all possible versions was not possible (82). Wach used models in falls on a staircase, but each fall was unique (83). Tsai noted that wind, even at a speed of 10 meters per second (which causes leaves to sway) can cause

TABLE 43.5 Individuals vulnerable to falls* (73–75)

Age**	Parkinsonism
Past history of falls • History of hip fracture predisposes to a second with attendant increase in mortality	Diffuse white matter lesions on MRI
Gait / balance/ coordination impairment and decreased muscle strength	Neurodegenerative conditions
Decreased vision (acuity, depth perception, contrast sensitivity, dark adaptation)	Peripheral neuropathy
History of cerebrovascular or cardiovascular disease	Seizures
Dizziness / syncope	Anemia
Orthostatic hypotension (antihypertensive treatment, dehydration)	Vitamin D deficiency (decreased muscle mass and strength)
Acute illness (especially fever, dehydration)	Bleeding tendency
Recent hospitalization, deconditioning	Mental impairment, emotional trauma, stress
Cognitive impairment, dementia, decreased executive functioning	Unfamiliar environment
Arthritis, chronic musculoskeletal pain (especially knee), and lower extremity muscle weakness	Long lie (unable to get up independently)
Abnormal BMI • Low: less muscle and fat to absorb energy, greater injury • High: decreased risk of trauma, but compromised balance, mobility	Footwear (thin, hard soles best [but seen as less comfortable]; bare feet, stockinged feet, increased heel height)
Cancer and its treatment	Environmental factors (slip / trip hazards, etc.)
Diabetes mellitus	Presence of ability / safety devices

*There is often impairment in multiple domains. **Age is associated with decline in proprioception, vestibular function, visual function, postural control, rate of muscle activation, etc. In general, age increases susceptibility to injury and complications during recovery.

horizontal displacement of an individual of up to 2 meters in a 30-meter fall. Wind speed varies by height, and especially between high rise and open structures such as bridges (84). Milaszkiewicz et al. tested a mathematical model in 109 cases in order to determine the height of the fatal falls. They concluded that the proposed formula resulted in a different height of the fall in 72.5 percent of cases (85).

With the advent of widespread closed-circuit television (CCTV) coverage, and early warning systems with the potential for videorecording at sites frequently associated with suicide, more information may be available in the future regarding the variables associated with falls from height.

At present, it appears results from analytic biomechanics should generally be interpreted with caution.

REFERENCES

1. World Health Organization. Falls [Internet]. 2021 April 26 [cited 2021 Aug 16] Available from: https://www.who.int/news-room/fact-sheets/detail/falls (Accessed 1 May 2023).
2. Centers for Disease Control and Prevention. Facts about Falls [Internet] 2021 Aug 6 [cited 2021 Aug 16] Available from: https://www.cdc.gov/falls/facts.html (Accessed 1 May 2023).
3. Schröder AS, Sperhake J. Quality of death certificates in hospitals. *Arch Kriminol* 2016; **238(5–6)**: 198–206.
4. Ellingsen CL, Ebbing M, Alfsen GC, Vollset SE. Injury death certificates without specification of the circumstances leading to the fatal injury: The Norwegian Cause of Death Registry 2005–2014. *Popul Health Metr* 2018; **16**(1): 20.
5. James SL, Lucchesi LR, Bisignano C, et al. The global burden of falls: global, regional and national estimates of morbidity and mortality from the Global Burden of Disease Study 2017. *Inj Prev* 2020; **26(Supp 1)**: i3–i11.
6. Rowbotham SK, Blau S, Hislop-Jambrich J. The skeletal trauma resulting from a fatal B.A.S.E jump: A case study showing the impact of landing feet-first under extreme vertical deceleration. *Forensic Sci Int* 2018; **286**: e20–e27.
7. Peyron P, Margueritte E, Baccino E. Suicide in parachuting: A case report and review of the literature. *Forensic Sci Int* 2018; **286**: e8–e13.
8. Segura-Sampedro JJ, Pineño-Flores C, García-Pérez JM, et al. Balconing: An alcohol-induced craze that injures tourists. Characterization of the phenomenon. *Injury* 2017; **48**(7): 1371–75.
9. Mlayeh S, Ben Abderrahim S, Haggui F, et al. Deadly falls into wells: A retrospective study of 72 autopsy cases from Kairouan, Tunisia. *J Forensic Sci* 2021; **66**(3): 934–9.
10. Turgut K, Sarihan ME, Colak C, et al. Falls from height: A retrospective analysis. World *J Emerg Med* 2018; **9**(1): 46–50.
11. Jackson NR, Lathrop S, Dvorscak L. Wall Falls: Blunt trauma sustained from border wall crossings. *Am J Forensic Med Pathol* 2021; **42**(3): 243–7.
12. Ichikawa M, Kuriyama A, Shirakura Y, Ikegami T. Health and economic burden of injurious falls into irrigation canals in Japan: A retrospective cohort study. *J Emerg Med* 2020; **59**(3): 424–31.
13. Bernard M, Martin MJ, Corsa J, et al. Into the wild and on to the table: A Western Trauma Association multicenter analysis and comparison of wilderness falls in rock climbers and nonclimbers. *J Trauma Acute Care Surg* 2020; **89(3)**: 570–5.
14. Bernard M, Wright R, Anderson H, Bernard A. Wilderness Falls: An analysis and comparison of rock climbers and nonclimbers. *J Surg Res* 2019; **234**: 149–54.
15. Zürcher S, Jackowski C, Schön CA. Circumstances and causes of death of hikers at different altitudes: A retrospective analysis of hiking fatalities from 2003–2018. *Forensic Sci Int* 2020; **310**: 110252.
16. Faulhaber M, Pocecco E, Niedermeier M, et al. Fall-related accidents among hikers in the Austrian Alps: a 9-year retrospective study. *BMJ Open Sport Exerc Med* 2017; **3**(**1**): e000304.
17. Weckbach S, Flierl MA, Blei M, et al. Survival following a vertical free fall from 300 feet: The crucial role of body position to impact surface. *Scand J Trauma Resusc Emerg Med* 2011; **19(1)**: 63.
18. Rowbotham S., Blau S. The circumstances and characteristics of fatal falls in Victoria, Australia: A descriptive study. *Aust J of Forensic Sci* 2017; **49**(4): 403–20.
19. Ferguson C, Sutherland T. Murder by pushing: An exploratory analysis of homicidal falls from a height. *Am J Forensic Med Pathol* 2018; **39** (3): 192–200.
20. Gentile G, Bianchi M, Boracchi M, et al. Forensic pathological considerations of a unique case of "complicated suicide". *J Forensic Sci* 2020; **65**(6): 2184–87.
21. Eş H, Şahin MF, Özdemir E. Laryngohyoid fractures in fatal nonhomicidal falls from a height. *Am J Forensic Med Pathol* 2017; **38**(4): 289–93.
22. Türk EE, Tsokos M. Pathologic features of fatal falls from height. *Am J Forensic Med Pathol* 2004; **25**(3): 194–9.
23. Lefèvre T, Alvarez JC, Lorin de la Grandmaison G. Discriminating factors in fatal blunt trauma from low level falls and homicide. *Forensic Sci Med Pathol* 2015; **11**(2): 152–161.
24. Aggrawal A, Pradhan M, Sreenivas M. Nail injury to the brain obfuscated by a fall from height: Homicide or suicide? A case report. *Med Sci Law* 2015; **55**(1): 40–43.
25. Choi JH, Kim SH, Kim SP, et al. Characteristics of intentional fall injuries in the ED. Am *J Emerg Med* 2014; **32**(**6**): 529–34.
26. Obeid NR, Bryk DJ, Lee T, et al. Fatal falls in New York City: An autopsy analysis of injury patterns. *Am J Forensic Med Pathol* 2016; **37**(2): 80–85.
27. Ross V, Koo YW, Kõlves K. A suicide prevention initiative at a jumping site: A mixed-methods evaluation. *EClinicalMedicine* 2020; **19**: 100265.
28. Sinyor M, Schaffer A, Redelmeier DA, et al. Did the suicide barrier work after all? Revisiting the Bloor Viaduct natural experiment and its impact on suicide rates in Toronto. *BMJ Open* 2017; **7**(5): e015299.
29. Hemmer A, Meier P, Reisch T, Seedat S. Comparing different suicide prevention measures at bridges and buildings: Lessons we have learned from a national survey in Switzerland. *PLoS ONE* 2017; **12**(1): e0169625.
30. Sæheim A, Hestetun I, Mork E, et al. A 12-year national study of suicide by jumping from bridges in Norway. *Arch Suicide Res* 2017; **21**(4): 568–76.
31. Yurtseven A, Üzün İ, Arslan MN. Suicides by jumping off Istanbul bridges linking Asia and Europe. *Am J Forensic Med Pathol* 2017; **38** (2): 139–44.
32. Çakı İE, Karadayı B, Çetin G. Relationship of injuries detected in fatal falls with sex, body mass index, and fall height: An autopsy study. *J Forensic Leg Med* 2021; **78**: 102113.
33. Sikary AK, Swain R, Dhaka S, et al. Jumping together: A fatal suicide pact. *J Forensic Sci* 2016; **61**(6): 1686–88.
34. Velmahos GC, Spaniolas K, Alam HB, et al. Falls from height: Spine, spine, spine! *J Am Coll Surg* 2006; **203**(5): 605–11.
35. Chatha H, Sammy I, Hickey M, et al. Falling down a flight of stairs: The impact of age and intoxication on injury pattern and severity. *Trauma* 2018; **20**(3): 169–74.
36. Bux R, Parzeller M, Bratzke H. Causes and circumstances of fatal falls downstairs. *Forensic Sci Int* 2007; **171(2–3)**: 122–6.
37. Dickinson A, Roberts M, Kumar A, et al. Falls from height: Injury and mortality. *J R Army Med Corps* 2012; **158**(2): 123–7.
38. Abder-Rahman H, Jaber MSO, Al-Sabaileh SS. Injuries sustained in falling fatalities

in relation to different distances of falls. *J Forensic Leg Med* 2018; **54**: 69–73.
39. Casali MB, Bruno CM, Battistini A, et al. The injury pattern in fatal suicidal falls from a height: An examination of 307 cases. *Forensic Sci Int* 2014; **244**: 57–62.
40. Atanasijevic T, Popovic V, Mihailovic Z, et al. Analysis of closed soft tissue subcutaneous injuries-"Impact Décollement" in fatal free falls from height: Forensic Aspect. *Am J Forensic Med Pathol* 2015; **36**(**3**): 145–8.
41. Tattoli L, Tsokos M, Buschmann C. Internal patterned injuries in trauma. *Forensic Sci Med Pathol* 2018; **14**(**1**): 123–6.
42. Tattoli L, Tsokos M. An unusual mechanism for patterned bruising in a fatal fall from a building. *Forensic Sci Med Pathol* 2014; **10**(**4**): 637–8.
43. Berghaus G. Mathematic-statistical discrimination between suicide and accident in falls from height. *Z Rechtsmed* 1978; **80**: 273–86.
44. Teresiński G, Cywka T, Milaszkiewicz A. Evaluation of possibilities of differentiating the causes of fatal falls from a height using the Berghaus scale. *Arch Med Sadowej Kryminol* 2016; 3(3): 141–8.
45. Cecchetto G, Viel G, Amagliani A, et al. Histological diagnosis of myocardial sarcoidosis in a fatal fall from a height: Histological diagnosis of myocardial sarcoidosis. *J Forensic Sci* 2011; **56**: S255–S258.
46. Puzović V, Baković M, Bubalo P, Mayer D. Accidental death from a fall from height at workplace turned out to be a COVID-19 death. *Forensic Sci Int: Reports* 2020; **2**: 100139.
47. Gawronska K, Lorkowski J. Falls as one of the atypical presentations of COVID-19 in older population. *Geriatr Orthop Surg Rehabil* 2021; **12**: 215145932199661.
48. Kwon KY, Lee M, Ju H, Im K. Older woman presenting with recurrent falls: An unusual manifestation of hypothyroidism. *Geriatr Gerontol Int* 2020; **20**(**1**): 87–88.
49. Brent A, Hartley R. An unusual cause of recurrent falls in an older gentleman. *BMJ Case Rep* 2010; **2010**(**oct11 1**): bcr0420102910.
50. Conesa D, Ferrer A, Torres A, et al. An unusual and reversible cause of falls: Spinal meningioma in an elderly woman. *J Am Geriatr Soc* 2013; **61**(**1**): 166–8.
51. Sleeman I, Wiblin L, Burn D. An unusual cause of falls in a young woman. *J R Coll Physicians Edinb* 2016; **46**(**3**): 160–2.
52. Michaud M, Gaudin C, Brechemier D, et al. An unusual cause of older adult falls: Stiff leg syndrome. *Eur Geriatr Med* 2013; **4**(**2**): 108–09.
53. Glauser M, Payman V. Falling for her psychiatrist: An unusual cause of falls in the elderly. *Int Psychogeriatr* 2016; **28**(**4**): 695–6.
54. Di Paolo M, Maiese A, dell'Aquila M, et al. Role of post mortem CT (PMCT) in high energy traumatic deaths. *Clin Ter* 2020; **171**(**6**): e490–e500.
55. Ross S, Ebner L, Flach P, et al. Postmortem whole-body MRI in traumatic causes of death. *Am J Roentgenol* 2012; **199**(**6**): 1186–92.
56. Mokrane FZ, Savall F, Rérolle C, et al. The usefulness of post-mortem CT angiography in injuries caused by falling from considerable heights: Three fatal cases. *Diagn Interv Imaging* 2014; **95**(**11**): 1085–90.
57. Fanton L, Bévalot F, Schoendorff P, et al. Toxicologic aspects of deaths due to falls from height. *Am J Forensic Med Pathol* 2007; **28**(**3**): 262–6.
58. Mosenthal AC, Livingston DH, Elcavage J, et al. Falls: Epidemiology and strategies for prevention. *J Trauma* 1995; **38**(**5**): 753–6.
59. Schaffer KB, Schwendig G, Nasrallah F, et al. Falls from a balcony while intoxicated: A new injury trend among young adults? *Inj Epidemiol* 2019; **6**(**1**): 4.
60. Acosta S, Andersson L, Bagher A, Wingren CJ. Drugs in fall versus non-fall accidents with major trauma: A population-based clinical and medico-legal autopsy study. *Forensic Sci Int* 2019; **296**: 80–84.
61. Peng TA, Lee CC, Lin JC, et al. Fatal falls from height in Taiwan. *J Forensic Sci* 2014; **59**(**4**): 978–82.
62. Nguyen K, Watanabe J. Association between sleep medications and falls and fall-related worries in community-dwelling older adults in the United States. *J Contemp Pharm Pract* 2019; **66**(**3**): 23–32.
63. Živković V, Nikolić S, Babić D, et al. Pontomedullary lacerations in falls from a height: A retrospective autopsy study. *J Forensic Sci* 2012; **57**(**3**): 654–7.
64. Hiquet J, Tovagliaro F, Gromb-Monnoyeur S. A fatal case of commotio cordis caused by an accidental fall on the beach. *J Forensic Leg Med* 2014; **21**: 22–23.
65. Muacevic A, Adler JR, Saleem M, et al. Story of an unfortunate fall: Cardiac contusion presenting with an atrioventricular block. *Cureus* 2019; **11**(**5**): e4650.
66. Behera C, Krishna K. Fatal positional asphyxia following a fall in bathroom. *Med Leg J* 2020; **88**(**3**): 169–71.
67. Nadhim EA, Hon C, Xia B, et al. Falls from height in the construction industry: A critical review of the scientific literature. *Int J Environ Res Public Health* 2016; **13**(**7**): 638.
68. Safe Work Australia. Work-related injuries and fatalities involving a fall from height, Australia [Internet]. 2013 Oct [cited 2021 Aug 16] Available from: https://www.safeworkaustralia.gov.au/system/files/documents/1702/falls-from-height.pdf (Accessed 1 May 2023).
69. Schoenfisch AL, Lipscomb H, Marshall S, et al. Work-related injuries among union drywall carpenters in Washington State, 1989–2008: Injuries among drywall installers. *Am J Ind Med* 2013; **56**(**10**): 1137–48.
70. Cochrane Work Group, van der Molen HF, Basnet P, et al. Interventions to prevent injuries in construction workers. *Cochrane Database Syst Rev* 2018; **2018**(**2**): CD006251.
71. Panuwatwanich K, Roongsrisoothiwong N, Petcharayuthapant K, et al. Ambient intelligence to improve construction site safety: Case of high-rise building in Thailand. *Int J Environ Res Public Health* 2020; **17**(**21**): 8124.
72. Houry D, Florence C, Baldwin G, et al. The CDC Injury Center's response to the growing public health problem of falls among older adults. *Am J Lifestyle Med* 2016; **10**(**1**): 74–77.
73. UpToDate® [Internet]. Kiel DP. Falls in older persons. 2021 Jul 12 [cited 2021 Aug 16]. Available from: https://www.uptodate.com/contents/falls-in-older-persons-risk-factors-and-patient-evaluation (Accessed 1 May 2023).
74. Morris R, Lewis A. Falls and cancer. *Clin Oncol (R Coll Radiol)* 2020; **32**(**9**): 569–78.
75. Jun MD, Lee KM, Park SA. Risk factors of falls among inpatients with cancer. *Int Nurs Rev* 2018; **65**(**2**): 254–61.
76. Bolton L. Preventing fall injury. *Wounds* 2019; **31**(**10**): 269–71.
77. McErlean DR, Hughes JA. Who falls in an adult emergency department and why: A retrospective review. *Australas Emerg Nurs J* 2017; **20**(**1**): 12–16.
78. Trinh LTT, Assareh H, Wood M, et al. Falls in hospital causing injury. *J Healthc Qual* 2020; **42**(**1**): 1–11.
79. Kobayashi K, Imagama S, Ando K, et al. Analysis of falls that caused serious events in hospitalized patients. *Geriatr Gerontol Int* 2017; **17**(**12**): 2403–06.
80. Mohl A, Stulz N, Martin A, et al. The "suicide guard rail": A minimal structural intervention in hospitals reduces suicide jumps. *BMC Res Notes* 2012; **5**(**1**): 408.
81. Chen Y, Gunnell D, Lu T. Descriptive epidemiological study of sites of suicide jumps in Taipei, Taiwan. *Inj Prev* 2009; **15**(**1**): 41–44.
82. Adamec J, Jelen K, Kubovy P, Lopot F, Schuller E. Forensic biomechanical analysis of falls from height using numerical human body models. *J Forensic Sci* 2010; **55**(**6**): 1615–23.
83. Wach W, Unarski J. Fall from height in a stairwell: Mechanics and simulation analysis. *Forensic Sci Int* 2014; **244**: 136–51.
84. Tsai WT, Hu CI, Chang CY. Effect of wind on horizontal displacement of fatal fall from a height. *J Forensic Sci* 2020; **65**(**1**): 255–8.
85. Milaszkiewicz A, Cywka T, Teresiński G. Verification of usefulness of the method for determining the height of fatal falls proposed by Lau et al. *Arch Med Sadowej Kryminol* 2019; **69**(**3**): 93–99.
86. Kohli A, Banerjee KK. Pattern of injuries in fatal falls from buildings. *Med Sci Law* 2006t; **46**(**4**): 335–41.
87. Rowbotham SK, Blau S, Hislop-Jambrich J, Francis V. Skeletal trauma resulting from fatal low (≤3 m) free falls: An analysis of fracture patterns and morphologies. *J Forensic Sci* 2018; **63**(**4**): 1010–20.
88. Rowbotham SK, Blau S. Skeletal fractures resulting from fatal falls: A review of the literature. *Forensic Sci Int* 2016; **266**: 582.e1–582.e15.

CHAPTER

44

Burns and Fire Deaths

Vladimir Živković and Slobodan Nikolić

INTRODUCTION

Human tissue survives in a relatively narrow range of temperatures between 20 and 44°C [1]). Even exposure to a temperature of 44°C for 5–6 hours would lead to necrosis of the epidermis, while only 3–5 seconds are sufficient at 60°C and only 1 second at 70°C (1,2).

Temperatures in house fires commonly range from approximately 500–650°C, usually not exceeding 700°C (3). The initiation and extension of a fire depends on several factors: an ignition source, a sufficient quantity of flammable material, as well as the presence of oxygen ("*no oxygen, no fire*") (3,4). In building fires, a temperature of 150°C may be reached within only 5 to 10 minutes, while in close confined spaces, a temperature of 250°C is reached in 5 to 6 minutes (4). Temperatures of 500°C, in building fires, may be reached only within 10 minutes (5). A sudden inflow of oxygen in a previously confined space may lead to sudden burst of flame called flashover, since the spontaneous ignition temperature of gases and other combustion product is reached, which is likely above 650°C (4), and it may occur after approximately 12 minutes in house fires (5). In airplane fires, temperatures may reach 1000°C, while in car fires they may rise to 1100°C, especially if fuel is present (4,7).

There are not many studies regarding the relation of duration of fire and the degree of body charring. A 1977 report by Richards reported that at 680°C within 10 minutes, the arms are badly charred, the legs after 14 minutes, the bones of the face and arms after 15 minutes, the ribs and skull after 20 minutes, the shin bones after 25 minutes, and the thighs with complete charring to bone within 35 minutes (5). Bohnert et al. (8) observed changes that occur during cremation, with temperatures between 670°C and 810°C. They observed that bodies showed a pugilistic attitude (Figure 44.1) after 10 minutes of exposure; after 20 minutes, the calvaria had lost soft tissue, with heat fractures of the external table. After 30 minutes, body cavities were visible with the shrinkage of internal organs, while extremities were significantly destroyed after 50 minutes, and the trunk broke apart after 90 minutes. Temperatures at the end of cremation reached between 800°C and 1200°C. After 2–3 hours from the beginning if cremation 1 to 3 kg of ashes were left (7–9).

Regardless of the fact that temperatures in house fires are similar (500–700°C) to temperatures during cremation (670–810°C), it is not common for a body to be completely destroyed during a house fire (9). In an extensive house fire, a human body will be severely charred (but not destroyed) in about 20 minutes (4). Factors which contribute to relative preservation of a body in a house fire compared to a cremation could be that house fires represent a less controled environment, with changes in temperatures and exposure to flame occurring during the conflagration. It is thus not easy to dispose of the body of a homicide victim by exposing it to house fire (10). Use of accelerants, such as gasoline, causes faster burning but limited body damage, unless massive quantities are used. The use of accelerants may also often lead to an explosion (11,12). Complete combustion is also uncommon in an accelerated fire in the open (3). It should be mentioned that "spontaneous" human combustion is nowadays regarded as a myth, since there is no scientific proof for this phenomenon, although in some cases a body can burn away virtually completely with minimal thermal destruction to the neighboring environment (13,14).

In the initial stages of a fire, the production of carbon-monoxide (CO) may be relatively low, but it rises with deficiency of oxygen, which is consumed by the fire (3,4). However, during a fire, the concentration of oxygen may be lower than atmospheric, especially in confined or poorly ventilated spaces, leading to incomplete burning and the formation of CO. The production of CO may be relatively low if the concentration of oxygen remains close to atmospheric, such as in bushfires or flashovers (15,16).

Besides CO, there are more than 400 different toxic substances present in smoke that can be inhaled during fires including hydrocyanic acid, acrolein, ammonia, bromofluorocarbons, isocyanates, nitrous gases, sulfur dioxide and hydrochloric acid (9). The effects of CO-Hb and cyanide are additive (3). Cyanide is formed mainly at high temperatures during the process of burning of nitrogenous materials such as polyurethane, polyamide and polyacrylonitrile, wool or silk (17). According to data from clinical medicine, cyanide (CN) or combined cyanide intoxication with CO is very common. Yet, in forensic medicine, CO is more regularly assessed than CN when the cause of death is being determined (17). The lethal level of blood cyanide is 5 mg/ml (3). Other

DOI: 10.1201/9781003138754-46

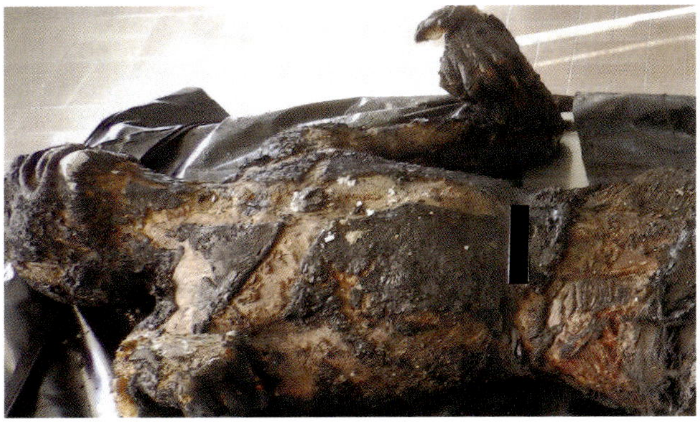

44.1 Pugilistic attitude in a fire victim.

toxic substances include nitric oxide, phosgene and more complex substances, which are released when plastic polymers are burned. Various toxic substances may also be released through the burning of structural components in houses and apartments including furnishings, upholstery, paints, lacquers and varnishes, since they are commonly composed of materials such as polystyrene, polyurethane, polyvinyl and other plastic materials (1).

Classification of burns

Thermal (heat) burns occur when some or all cells in the skin or other tissues are destroyed by high temperatures (18). Burns occur with exposure of the body to dry heat, that is, through contact with hot objects (contact burns) or flames. Exposure of the body to hot liquids, hot gases or steam causes scalds. Fires involving flames often damage unclothed areas of the body (head, hands, and legs), often singing hair, which becomes crinkly, brittle, and yellowish (9,19). In dry burns, clothing could have a protective effect against heat, unless it ignites when it may even contribute to the fatal outcome (20,21). On the contrary, hot fluids often soak the clothes, causing more severe injuries in areas in which close contact between clothes and skin exist (upper body and belt area), while singed hair is never present in scalding (19).

The extent of damage depends upon several factors, such as the temperature, the time for which the heat is applied and the ability of the body to deal with excess heat (1). The classification most commonly used in forensic medicine, the so-called traditional classification of burns divides them into four degrees. In recent years, this classification has often been replaced by a newer, surgical classification, which mostly overlaps with the previous categorization (1,3,9,19,22,23).

Superficial or first-degree burns: These are characterized by redness: erythema, without blistering (3,9,19,22). They are limited to the epidermis, which remains generally intact, although a small amount of desquamation may be present. This type of burn is not commonly detected at autopsy, since redness rapidly fades after death (3). Since this type of erythema represents a form of active hyperemia (it is histologically present as dilatation and congestion of dermal vessels), it is expected that blood may move by gravity into dependent area (3,9,23). Superficial burns may occur within a temperature range of 44–50°C (19).

Partial thickness or second-degree burns: These are characterized by blistering, accompanied by surrounding redness. Blisters form between the epidermis and dermis and are filled with serous or hemorrhagic liquid. These burns involve the superficial (papillary) dermis and/or the deeper, reticular dermis. Scarring may occur with survival when a significant portion of the epidermal appendages is destroyed (hair follicles, sweat and sebaceous glands), since these represent a source for re-epithelization (3,9,22). Partial thickness burns may occur within a temperature range of 50–70°C (19).

Full thickness or third-degree burns: These extend from the epidermis and dermis into subcutaneous fat and may also involve adjacent muscles (22). Pain is commonly absent since nerve endings in the skin are destroyed. The skin is firm and has a dry, leather-like appearance, usually white to yellowish-brown, sometimes with visible thrombosed blood vessels. Since skin appendages are destroyed, scarring also occurs (if a victim survives). Full thickness burns may occur with temperature above 62°C (19).

Fourth-degree burns or charring: In this situation, the skin and underlying tissues are severely damaged, often with exposure of bones, and black charring of soft tissues, organs and bones (9,19). This type of burn cannot be caused by hot fluids, hot gases or steam. Charring may occur with temperatures greater than 65°C, while with significantly higher temperatures so-called white charring of bones may occur (19).

The extent of burns, that is, total body surface area (TBSA) can be estimated using the *rule of nines* – the head and upper limbs each represent 9 percent, each side of the torso (front and back) and each lower limb represent 18 percent, while the surface of the neck or genital region represent an additional 1 percent. The surface of the hand also accounts for 1 percent (9,19). It should be kept in mind that, as children have proportionally bigger heads than adults, the TBSA is calculated differently: head and neck 18 percent, torso 18 + 18 percent, each arm 9 percent, each leg 14 percent.

The Burn index is an indicator of prognosis. It is obtained by adding age and TBSA of superficial and partial thickness (i.e. second- and third-degree) burns. A burn index lower than 80 carries a low mortality risk, a burn index between 80 and 120 carries an acute danger of a fatal outcome, while with a burn index higher than 120, survival is improbable. With the burn index reaching 100, the chance of survival is 50 percent, even with optimal treatment. Additionally, patients with deep burns of more than 30 percent of the TBSA have a poor prognosis, while survival is an exception in cases where the TBSA is higher than 50 percent (9,19).

Fire-related death in a hospital

The survival and clinical outcome of burn injuries depends on many factors, but the following three seem to be the most important in contributing to mortality: total body surface burnt >40 percent, age over 60 years (actually, burn index over 100) and injuries caused by inhalation of hot and toxic gases and fumes (4,22). Other prognostic factors include the depth of the burns (i.e. the percentage of third-degree burns), and underlying chronic respiratory and pre-existing disease (e.g. cardiovascular or other) and other conditions, such as smoking, alcohol or drug abuse (4). Determining the cause of death in cases where a burn patient survives, for a shorter or longer period of time may be challenging for a pathologist as many different complications may develop during hospital treatment that contribute to the fatal outcome.

The most common causes of death, especially in the early stages, include shock, sepsis and respiratory insufficiency (4,22). Sepsis is the leading cause of mortality and it can be caused by burn wound infection, pneumonia, urinary infection (due to the use of urinary catheters), infection of intravenous (IV) lines or infection of skin donor sites (4). Burn wounds represent an ideal site for infection: on one hand there is debris and serum which provide a good substrate for microorganism growth, and there is also impaired circulation which may block or hinder an effective immune response (22). These factors result in colonization by bacteria in practically all burns, and infection in many. The most common agent that causes infection is *Pseudomonas aeruginosa*, followed by antibiotic-resistant strains of other common hospital acquired bacteria, such as methicillin-resistant *Staphylococcus aureus* (MRSA), and also fungi, particularly Candida species (22).

Both burns and infections could lead to triggering of the systemic inflammatory response syndrome (SIRS) (4,9,22). This may lead to a very rapid (within hours) shift of body fluids to interstitial compartments, as a result of general impairment of vascular permeability, which may lead to additional hypovolemic shock, pulmonary edema and/or adult respiratory distress syndrome (ARDS) leading to respiratory insufficiency, and multiple organ failure, which are all possible imminent causes of death (4,22).

Injuries to the airways and lungs can occur either due to direct damage from high temperatures or to smoke inhalation. High temperatures may cause burns of the upper airways, epiglottis and laryngeal mucosa, even in the absence of facial burns (19). Cases of damage of the airways by eating hot food have been reported (24). Exposure of the airways to high temperatures may result in relatively rapid or delayed (up to 24 hours) edema of the laryngeal mucosa, caused by inflammation, which can (additionally) compromise breathing and cause respiratory failure, even if the initial exposure to a fire is survived; this may necessitate intubation (3,4,9).

However, with the exception of inhalation of steam and hot gases, high temperatures usually do not cause significant damage to the trachea and lower airways, as hot air is cooled during transit through the upper airways. With inhalation of dry air with a temperature of 350°C, the temperature in the larynx is between 159°C and 182°C, while there is no elevation in temperature at the bifurcation of the trachea. With a rise in the temperature of inhaled dry air to 500°C, the temperature also rises in the larynx to between 267°C and 327°C, but it also reaches 50°C at the bifurcation of the trachea (19). Such temperatures are, therefore, obviously sufficient to cause burn injuries and inflammation, more pronounced in the upper airways, but also in the lower airways. Humid hot air or steam inhalation causes damage at significantly lower temperatures (19). For example, a small number of breaths of humid saturated air at a temperature of 55°C may cause serious airway injury, while the maximum survivable breathing temperature is 150°C (4). Smoke inhalation or inhalation of other products of combustion, on the other hand, may affect the entire respiratory tract primarily interfering with the function of the respiratory epithelium and affecting normal airway clearance, as well as type II pneumocytes which produce surfactant. Microscopic examination of the upper airways may show elongation of cell nuclei or respiratory epithelium in a luminal direction, goblet-cell edema, mucosal edema with hyperemia, lymphangiectasis and hemorrhage (19,23). This thermal inhalation trauma may be of special importance when there is only minor or no inhaled soot as would be expected when the decedent is on fire on open ground (25). Traces of soot can be found macroscopically or microscopically usually within two days of exposure (4). Smoke inhalation injury may cause ulceration of the larynx and/or trachea, often requiring intubation or tracheostomy, that may be complicated by tracheobronchitis and pneumonia, or diffuse alveolar damage (DAD) (ARDS), which should be confirmed microscopically. Late complications (occurring weeks and months after injury) include stenosis of the glottis and subglottic area (4).

Complications of burns can be approximately divided into early (within the first week after initial injury) and late (more than week after initial injury). Relatively common early complications include different forms of inhalation injuries, wound infections (primarily *P. aeruginosa,* Gram-negative bacteria, and *S. aureus*), shock, kidney failure, pneumonia, paralytic ileus, but also neurologic complications due to CO toxicity such as basal ganglia necrosis, which may be observed at autopsy. Late complications are numerous, include most of the early complications and may depend on previous health status. These include systemic complications (shock, sepsis, disseminated intravascular coagulation [DIC], abscess formation, adrenal hemorrhage, viral infections, etc.), cardiovascular complications (acute myocardial infarct, infective endocarditis, suppurative thrombophlebitis, thromboembolism, etc.), pulmonary complications (pneumonia, DAD etc.), urinary tract complications (acute renal failure due to acute tubular or renal cortical necrosis, acute pyelonephritis, renal cortical infarcts due to renal artery thrombosis, etc.), gastrointestinal tract complications (gastric and duodenal ulcers – Curling's ulcers, ileus, gastric or colonic dilatation, ischemic enterocolitis, acute hemorrhagic pancreatitis, etc.), liver complications (acute liver failure, acute cholecystitis, etc.), and others (3,4,9,22).

The autopsy of a burn victim should include a thorough review of the clinical history, as well as the circumstances of the fire obtained from police or fire department investigators. External examination should include the extent and degree of the burns (with estimated percentages), with comment on the possible pattern of the burns. Also, all the medical procedures that were undertaken during hospital treatment should be described. Internal, along with microscopic examinations should be undertaken to describe changes to the major organs (and burns), necessary for determining the immediate cause of death. Other trauma should be ruled out. Microbiological post-mortem analyses are often not of great significance, due to their unreliability (3,4,9,26).

The significance of post-mortem CT in fire-related death

The role of post-mortem computed tomography (CT) is becoming increasingly significant in forensic practice regarding fire-related deaths. This method is a non-invasive, fast, highly sensitive and cost-effective complement to the autopsy. It also supplies permanent forensic evidence (27).

Post-mortem CT is especially useful in investigating air/gas distribution and content in body cavities and viscera (28). Thus, it is most helpful in detecting air embolism, pneumothorax, pneumomediastinum and subcutaneous emphysema, each of which may be present in fire-related deaths (27,29). Before an autopsy, it is a valuable add-on for detecting hidden signs of trauma, gas collections and foreign bodies, which may not be detected in conventional autopsies (27,29). Post-mortem CT in carbonized bodies may also reveal gunshot injuries, the trajectory and location of a foreign body (bullet, pellet, or similar), and facilitate the subsequent conventional autopsy (27,29,30).

It is also valuable for differentiating several potential forensic diagnostic pitfalls, including heat fractures. Thermal bone lesions have specific CT findings. One of the post-mortem CT signs of heat exposure is the mottled appearance ("*mottled lucency*") of the bone marrow, which reflects the progressive liquefaction of marrow fat under the influence of heat, present in the majority of burned bones (29,31). It is essential to differentiate heat fractures from fractures occurring during life. Trans-diploic fractures of flat bones are related explicitly to thermal mechanisms, as opposed to traumatic fractures, that are typically perpendicular to the bone surface and involve internal and external tables (31). The skull may show additional signs such as cortical network cracks, referred to as "*ancient Chinese porcelain*" by anthropologists, which represent longitudinal trans-diploic fractures. Splitting of the inner and outer table of the skull with the lifting of the outer table (*split diploë sign*), as well as delamination of the skull vault, which is due to the focal loss of the external table, may also be seen (29,31). In long bones of the extremities, heat fractures or amputations present with typically beveled ends often described as a "*flute-mouthpiece*" appearance, as cortices are directly exposed being uncovered by soft-tissue loss. Bilaterality in long-bone thermal fractures commonly exists in heat fractures, while in traumatic fractures, they are most commonly asymmetrical. Also, asymmetrical destruction of cortices may create a stair-step appearance at the extremity of bones (31).

CT examination can also differentiate blood from heat hematomas. This may have significance in an autopsy regarding the collection of fluid samples for toxicological screening (30). It also differentiates traumatic epidural bleeding from epidural heat-hematomas. The heat-hematoma is of low density and crescent-shaped, similar to a subdural hematoma in radiologic appearance, but often crossing the midline and detaching the venous sinus. In contrast, an epidural hematoma caused by trauma is dense, convex and lens-shaped (30). Of course, the gross appearance of heat-hematoma should not raise any problem regarding its origin to an experienced forensic pathologist.

It is a known fact that solid internal organs, such as the brain, liver, or lung, may dehydrate and shrink when they are directly exposed to heat. In such cases, post-mortem CT may show a typical dense border sign. In such cases, the autopsy findings would show thermal damage to the surface of the tissues and organs with blackening and stiffness (29).

Post-mortem CT can also help identify the deceased in cases of both individual and mass fire-related deaths (32,33). It can be used where traditional visual inspection techniques, fingerprinting, dental and DNA analysis are impossible. The identification process entails establishing a general biological profile by determining the deceased's age and sex, and if possible, eliciting more specific characteristics by detecting unique biological or physical features (32,33). Correlation of post-mortem CT findings with antemortem medical data of the alleged victim is necessary, with particular caution regarding the presence of internal medical devices such as vascular and orthopedic prostheses, dental fillings, surgical clips, pacemakers/defibrillators and intra-uterine devices, and so on (30).

The weaknesses of post-mortem CT are not insignificant, and it may fail to identify acute heart failure, intoxication and fatal gastrointestinal bleeding (27,29). Even more critical, post-mortem CT does not seem to be successful in the assessment of the number of cuts and stab wounds and also in detecting thermal injuries, such as blistering and charring of the skin and organs, the presence or absence of soot, and thermal damage in the airways. It is also unable to (solely) prove vitality during the fire and to determine it as a cause of death – the forensic autopsy's central question (27,29).

Post-mortem CT cannot be considered an alternative to the conventional autopsy but as a complementary method, which may be helpful in fire-related deaths in terms of determining either the main or associated causes of death (27,29,31).

It is yet unclear whether post-mortem magnetic resonance imaging (MRI) has a role in assessing fire-related deaths. Yet, some reports suggest that it may also help to detect soft-tissue lesions or changes that may be difficult to detect by macroscopic analysis, such as *globus pallidus* lesions in prolonged CO poisoning (34).

Fire-related death at the scene, without significant carbonization

The appearance of a body found at the site of fire may be quite varied, ranging from relatively undamaged to extensively charred, with significant disintegration.

The conclusion regarding the cause of death in bodies without significant charring is not usually a particularly difficult task for a pathologist. After autopsy, with or without microscopic examination, and toxicological analyses (for CO-Hb, the presence of cyanide, etc.) and with the exclusion of other types of trauma or disease that could be an immediate and undisputable cause of death, there are not too many options left for the possible cause of death. The causes of death due to fire and exposure to high temperatures come down to smoke inhalation and toxicity from CO in the majority of cases, as well as airway injury and local burns to the skin (1,9). The latter two findings are quite obvious at the autopsy. However, due to possibility of post-mortem burns, conclusions which would include them in the cause of death (contributory or main) require CO-Hb saturation analysis.

Alternatively, many victims of fires die without direct contact with the flames. CO has between 200 and 300 times greater affinity for hemoglobin than oxygen. The major effect of CO-Hb is to decrease the hemoglobin capacity for oxygen transportation. Besides this occupying effect, CO-Hb also reduces capacity through moving the curve of oxygen saturation of hemoglobin to the left, that is, there is also reduced oxygen release from hemoglobin to the tissues. The level of saturation of hemoglobin with CO in fatal cases is relatively broad, and is influenced by the rapidity of exposure, that is, the rate of rise in CO-Hb, as well as the individual's health status and age. Healthy individuals under 60 years of age rarely die with saturation levels below 50 percent. On the other hand, older individuals may die with CO-Hb concentration of 25 to 30 percent. Besides old age, with diseases such as anemia, coronary atherosclerosis or lung diseases such as emphysema, death may occur with significantly lower concentrations of CO-Hb (1). Concentrations of CO-Hb at least 10 percent are considered evidence that the victim was alive during the fire, as a post-mortem rise in CO-Hb concentration is not possible (1). However, the opposite is not necessarily true as concentrations of CO-Hb may be low or negative in rapid fires, especially caused by petrol, or in fires with sufficient oxygen influx (35). The cherry pink color in areas of hypostasis is a characteristic external autopsy sign of CO-Hb intoxication. The same color may be visible on internal examination, in muscles and blood, while other internal signs are non-specific. The cherry pink coloration is evident with a CO-Hb saturation of at least approximately 30 percent. With a saturation between 20 and 30 percent, experience, familiarity and adequate illumination are required for the coloration to be observed, and with a saturation of <20 percent no coloration is visible. In the presence of anemia in a victim, cherry pink coloration may be absent even with a high CO-Hb saturation (1).

In up to 10 percent of cases, death may occur even without an elevated CO-Hb or soot aspiration). In these cases, after the exclusion of a natural death or homicide, there are several additional, potential causes of death that include cyanide intoxication (confirmed by toxicological analyses), asphyxia caused by either oxygen depletion by the fire or due to a flashfire causing laryngeal or bronchial spasm or vagal reflex, heat shock due to redistribution of circulating blood to the skin, and heat rigor of thorax causing functional impairment to breathing (9).

Vital reactions in fire-related deaths

Determining the cause of death in bodies recovered from fires with signs of advanced charring (carbonization) may be challenging. On one hand, pathological changes and injuries may be partially or completely destroyed by high temperatures, while on the other, there are many heat artifacts that could be misinterpreted as injuries. That is why every forensic pathologist should be familiar both with vital reactions, and heat artifacts.

Vital reactions or vitality signs are findings at autopsy which are helpful in establishing whether the victim was alive at the time of the fire, which is one of the main issues in autopsy (9,19,26). Vitality signs in fire-related death include:

Smoke inhalation and rise in CO saturation: As discussed previously, concentrations of CO-Hb above 10 percent generally indicate that a victim was alive during the fire. Cigarette smokers may, however, have saturation up to 10 percent (1,3,9,36). In non-smokers, CO-Hb saturation does not normally exceed 3 percent (36). Also, a low saturation of CO-Hb does not exclude the possibility that the person was alive during a fire (35).

Soot inhalation: Respiration in close proximity to a fire causes soot inhalation. The presence of soot below the level of vocal cords, that is, in the trachea and main bronchi is a sign of vitality during a fire (Figure 44.2) (9,20,25,37). Massive soot aspiration may be present in closed settings such as inside an apartment, a house, or a car, and so on when oxygen depletion can cause increased development of soot. In cases of severely burnt bodies with opening of the trachea and the thoracic cavity, artificial findings of soot may be found. Histologically, soot may be found in the respiratory tract and the bronchi, often combined with extensive mucous secretion. Soot particles embedded in mucus are a proof of vitality (9,20). The presence of soot in the mouth and in the airways above the level of the vocal cords, with its

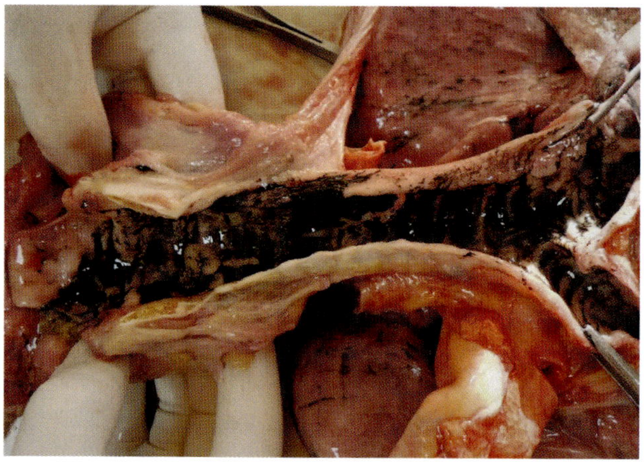

44.2 Soot inhalation in the larynx and bronchi.

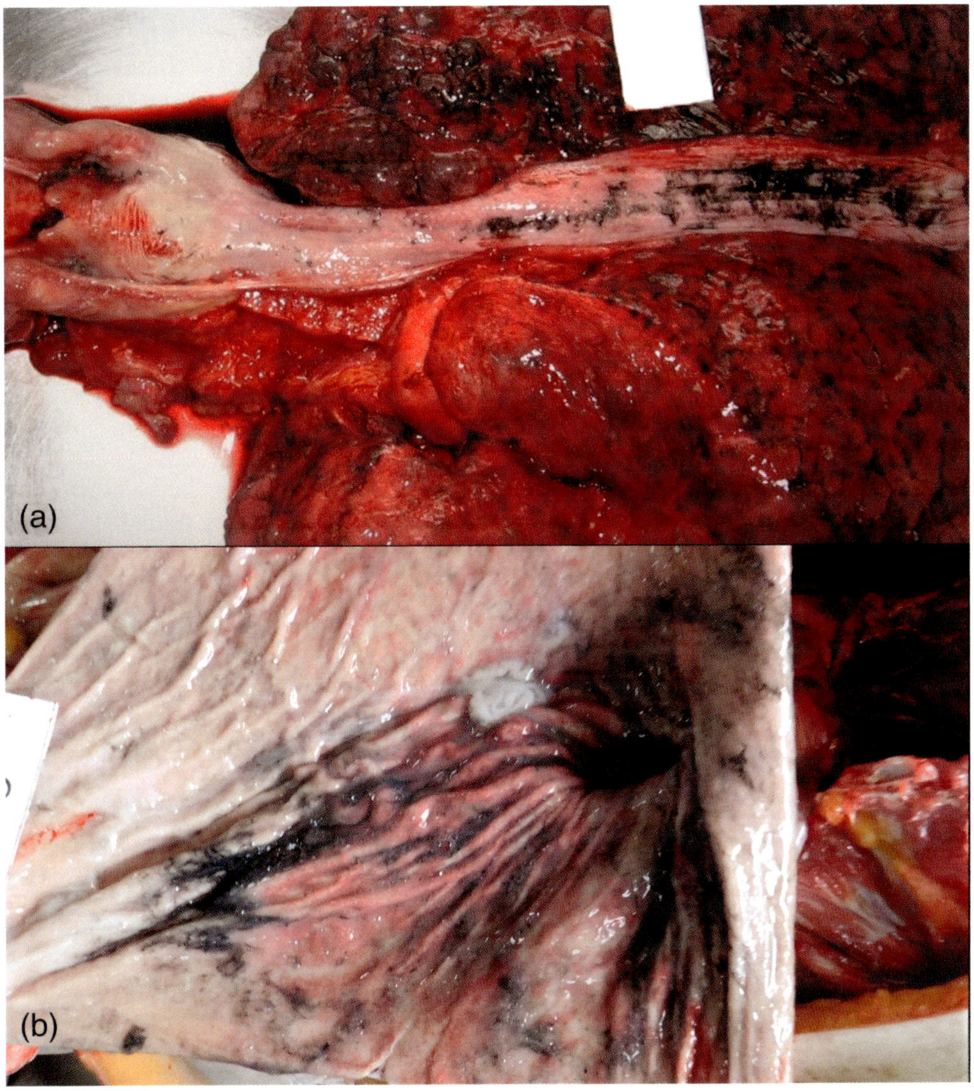

44.3 Soot swallowing in the esophagus (a) and stomach (b).

absence in lower parts, may be the consequence of passive accumulation of soot and in such cases cannot be regarded as a sign of vitality (3).

Soot swallowing: Swallowing is complex action, partially voluntary and partially reflex, which requires preserved function of the central nervous system (CNS). Thus, swallowing of soot, that is, the presence of soot in esophagus, stomach (Figure 44.3) and even duodenum implies that CNS function was preserved, that is, that the person was alive (3,9,19).

"Crow's feet" sign: In cases of sudden exposure to flames or great heat, while alive, victims may close their eyes tightly shut, producing a lateral line of skin at the canthi spared from thermal damage, or soot deposits (Figure 44.4). Other lines of skin spared from burning also suggest a final contraction of the facial muscles (19,38).

Inhalation trauma: As explained previously, exposure of the upper airways to hot air may cause injuries manifested at the autopsy by visible gross and microscopic changes (red and edematous mucosa of larynx and upper third of trachea, with hyperemia, lymphangiectasis and hemorrhages, etc.) (19,22).

Presence of foamy fluid in mouth, nostrils and airways: A plume of thick, white foam at the nostrils or mouth, having a relatively similar appearance to drowning cases, indicates continued breathing during a fire. Foam in the airways is caused by pulmonary edema and may be the result of smoke-induced bronchial irritation, systemic effects of CO intoxication, as well as heart failure due to the toxic effects of CO on cardiomyocytes (3).

Fat embolism refers to the presence of fat globules in the lung parenchyma and its peripheral circulation (pulmonary fat embolism) or in the systemic circulation – kidney, brain and heart, and so on. (systemic fat embolism) (39). In fire-related death, the presence of fat droplets in blood vessels of the lungs must be interpreted with caution, in the context of the presence or absence of possible blunt trauma and long-bone fractures (3). In the absence of such trauma, histologically detectable blockage of small blood vessels in the areas of branching (sausage- or antler-shaped fat droplets) may be regarded as being an intravital finding, since passive movement of fat droplets in the absence of circulation pressure does not occur due to high surface pressure of small vessels (with diameter 10 to 40 μm) (39). The presence of fat droplets (in cases without intravital fractures of long bones) in fire-related deaths seems to be a result of physicochemical alteration of fats normally present in the blood due to exposure to high temperatures (3).

Immunohistochemical staining may also be useful in determining vitality. Some papers suggest that expression of higher levels of fibronectin in the lung tissue of burn victims (in macrophages, fibroblasts, peribronchial tissue and vascular lumina) compared to cases with deaths unrelated to fire could be an indicator of an early intravital inflammatory response to fire damage (40). Similarly with heat shock protein 70 (Hsp70) which is expressed in different types of cells (primarily blood vessels, but also seromucous secretory cells, ciliated epithelial cells, smooth muscle cells and alveolar cells) in the epiglottis, the trachea, and the main and the peripheral bronchi (41). The value of these analyses is yet to be proven.

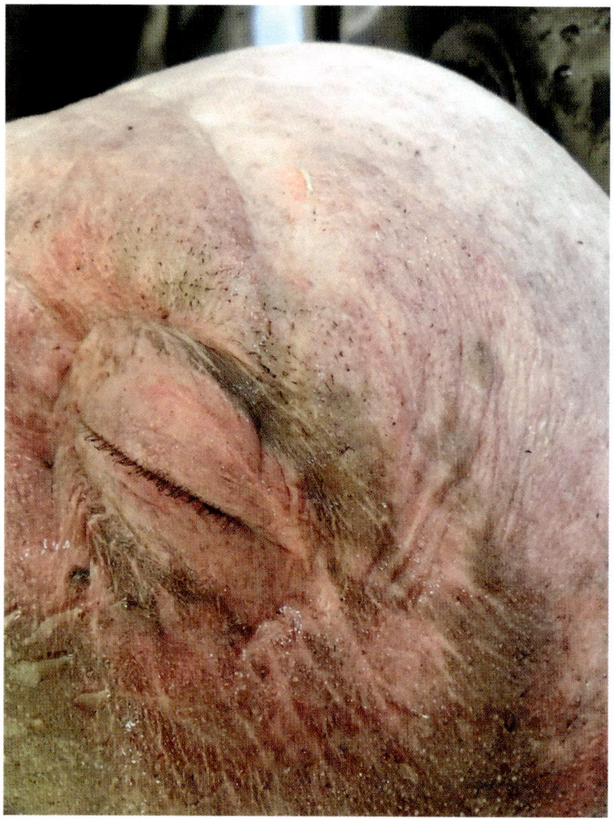

44.4 Linear transverse skin-folds spared from burns ("crow's feet") in the left temporal region.

Post-mortem heat artifacts in fire-related deaths

Post-mortem heat artifacts are the result of exposure of a body to high temperatures and do not represent injuries.

An ***epidural heat hematoma*** may appear on areas of the skull directly exposed to flame (Figure 44.5). This is not an extradural hematoma, but so-called epidural extravasate – an epidural accumulation of brick-red or brownish, brittle, spongy, foamy, dry or mud-like material, which is in contrast to the uniformly smooth dark-red appearance of an antemortem hematoma caused by mechanical trauma (9,20). This substance has elements of boiled blood, fluid and brain tissue extruded from the skull cavity due to heating with shrinkage and removal of dura mater from the skull (9).

A **pugilistic attitude** resembles the position of a boxer (Figure 44.1). During exposure to heat, skeletal muscle becomes shortened by dehydration and protein denaturation causing flexion of the extremities with the contraction of muscles and tendons – heat rigor. The flexor muscles, being bulkier than the extensors, contract more and force the limbs into a position of general flexion. Shoulder abduction, elbow and wrist flexion and incomplete leg extension, are typical, resulting in the so-called pugilistic attitude (3,9,10). Such appearance is more common when the body has been left in a supine position (3,9).

Tongue protrusion induced by heat occurs by similar processes (Figure 44.6). In bodies with severe charring, the charred tip or anterior third of the tongue projects through charred lips (19). The genioglossus is the major muscle of the tongue and is responsible for protruding (or sticking out) the tongue: by means of its inferior fibers, it draws the root of the tongue forward and protrudes the apex from the mouth. With heat exposure, the genioglossus muscle is shortened by heat, while shrunken skin also places additional pressure on the base of the tongue, all of which causes post-mortem tongue protrusion (10,42,43).

Skin splitting occurs as a result of shrinkage due to heat exposure and may cause opening of body cavities (Figure 44.7) (3,19). Skin splitting should be distinguished from antemortem cuts. Splits caused by heat invariably run parallel to the muscle fibers and straight and smooth (3,9). Thus, splits that run across muscle fibers cannot be caused by heat, but more likely by mechanical trauma (3). Post-mortem rupture of the abdominal

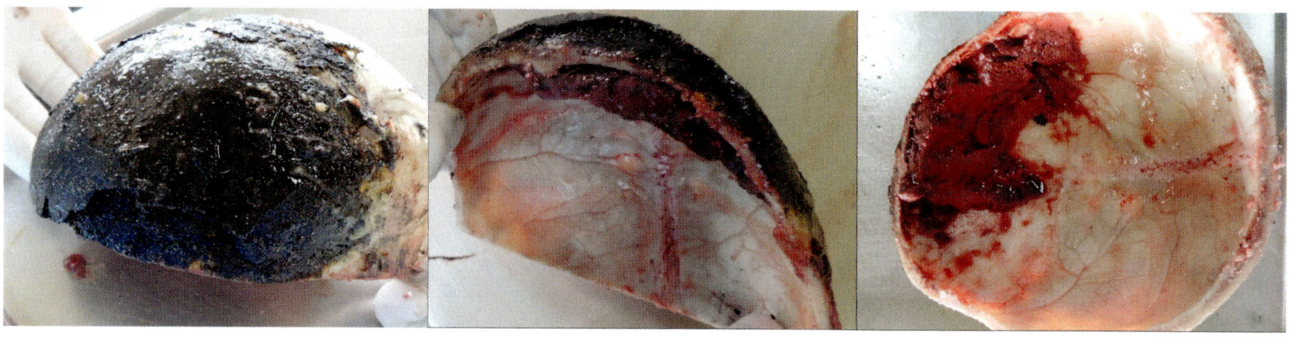

44.5 Heat hematoma in the frontal region. Note charring of outer surface of frontal bone.

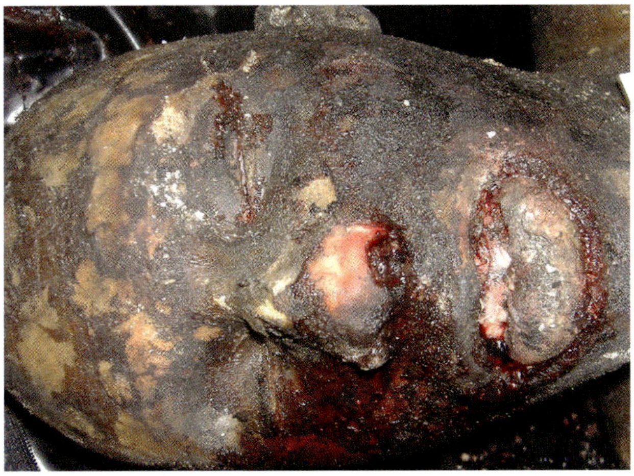

44.6 Protruded tongue in a burned body, with complete charring.

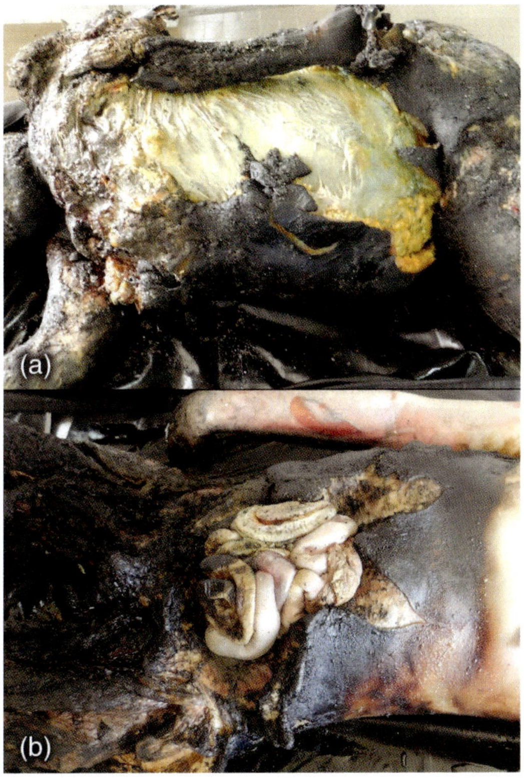

44.7 Partial (a) and complete (b) heat induced skin splitting, with opening of the abdominal cavity and protrusion of the intestines (b).

wall may cause herniation of intestinal loops (9). Splits may also occur in the epicranial aponeurosis, accompanied by shrinkage, causing the cranium to be stripped of soft tissues (19).

Heat blisters are post-mortem changes caused by changes in the content and distribution of tissue fluids, leading to vaporization of body fluids, leakage of fat in body cavities, vessels, or the heart, and leakage of fluid from the nose or mouth (9).

Heat fractures may develop in long bones as a result of shrinkage of skeletal muscles by the heat, which leads to undue pulling of tendons on bones. Post-mortem heat fractures may also occur in the skull. Such cracks usually occur in the temporal bones; they are rarely limited to the external tables, and sometimes may be bilateral. Such fractures have a characteristic appearance, with several lines radiating from a common center (starburst). These post-mortem fractures may be difficult to distinguish from antemortem fractures, caused by mechanical trauma. Although the edges of heat fractures may be more irregular and ragged, there is no absolute rule for distinguishing ante mortem from post-mortem (i.e. heat) fractures (3,44).

Coronary artery shrinkage: In charred bodies, due to fluid loss fixation of tissues and shrinkage of organs occurs. The rate of decomposition is slightly slower, due to heat-induced fixation of tissues. However, these changes may lead to misinterpretation of autopsy findings. One of the recent experimental studies suggested that heat exposure may cause significant coronary artery shrinkage which could be misinterpreted as antemortem coronary artery stenosis (45).

Manner of death in bodies recovered from fires

The manner of death in bodies recovered from fire is most commonly accidental, with the cause of death usually related to smoke (CO) inhalation or burns, as previously explained. However, the manner of death may, in some cases, be natural, when a natural death could be the cause of fire or merely coincidental, without any vital signs related to exposure to high temperature and fire. Suicidal self-immolation is rare and, in most instances, occurs in psychiatric patients (with schizophrenia) or as an act of political/social protest or demonstration. Self-immolation can be defined as the act of pouring a flammable liquid onto oneself and igniting it (46), sometimes in the form of complex suicide (44,47). It is usually performed in the open. Gasoline is most commonly used, but it may also involve the use of alcohol, methylated spirits, as well as kerosene, benzene and paraffin (46). It may also be performed as an acute emotional reaction or by persons with a fire fetish. Certain cultures and customs favor this type of suicide (10) and it is more common in Asia and Africa, particularly on the Indian subcontinent, where it may have ritual connotations, sometimes involving notions of purification by fire or sacrifice (46).

Homicidal arson, that is, causing death by means of fire is quite rare. Such events may take the form of intentionally intoxicating an individual (by alcohol or medications) and then igniting a fire, with the help of accelerants (petrol, alcohol, etc.), or even using fatal scalding of an intoxicated individual with hot liquid (19). If homicidal arson is suspected radiologic analyses before the autopsy may be helpful not only in determining presence of fractures or other injuries, but also for identification or determining the age of the victim (48). In cases where the perpetrator is found next to a victim in an accelerant-enhanced fire, it cannot be readily determined whether that is a murder-suicide or a murder-accident scenario (49).

One of the major forms of fire homicides, mainly present in India, Pakistan and Bangladesh, are so-called "dowry deaths" or "bride burning". Dowry refers to the transfer of goods, money and property to a bridegroom or his relatives from a bride's family as a condition of the marriage. The dowry is legally prohibited yet is still present and is regarded as a cause of significant violence against married women. One of the consequences of the dowry system has been the murder or abetted suicide of young wives. Most deaths are due to burning. Bride burning characteristically involves dousing a wife with flammable liquid (usually kerosene) and then setting her on fire. The victims rarely survive, and those who do are often severely and permanently scarred over much of their bodies. The total body area usually burnt ranges from 40 to 80 percent, with more than 75 percent of victims dying within 24 hours of the attack (50).

A variety of scenarios are possible when a body is found at the scene of a fire (51). Some tasks of the pathologist include determining the mechanism and manner of death, as well as establishing whether the victim was alive at the time of the event, whether there was any evidence of pre-existing injury or natural disease, and what was the most likely cause of death (51). One of the most important tasks at the autopsy is to exclude or confirm arson to conceal a homicide, that is committing homicide by other means, and then burning the body in an attempt to conceal the evidence. Because of this possibility, the autopsy of bodies with advanced charring should be performed with special care. The autopsy approach to such cases involves careful evaluation of the scene with particular attention being paid to the position of the victim, the presence of a container for an accelerant, and the pattern of the fire (51). The use of an accelerant should raise concerns (19). Wounds on the skin surface may often be obscured by heat artifacts (10). The presence of blood in the subdural space (in contrast to an epidural heat hematoma) or in the thoracic or abdominal cavities usually points to trauma unrelated to the fire (3,52), and further exploration of soft tissues for bruises or bones for fractures is required in such cases. Despite the external appearance of the body, internal organs are often relatively well preserved so that it is possible to follow injury tracts if present (10).

Identification of fire victims

Identification in cases where a body is preserved does not usually represent a problem. However, it may be difficult in cases of severe charring. The circumstances of the fire (e.g. known occupants of a dwelling), clothing and personal belongings (if preserved, even partially), preserved specificities of external body appearance (scars, deformities, tattoos, etc.) may be helpful. Charring, on the other hand, erases many of these features (4). The weight and length of the body are unreliable parameters due to shrinkage and vaporization (3). Pathological changes and surgical procedures (liver cirrhosis, missing appendix, surgical removal of a kidney, stomach esophagus, different surgical implants, cardiac pacemakers and defibrillators, etc.) could be of significant assistance (3). Radiological and dental analyses may be used, but these methods require adequate antemortem medical or dental records. Finally, DNA analysis may be useful, and in the absence of preserved soft tissue, teeth or bone may be sampled (3,4,9).

REFERENCES

1. Saukko P, Knight B, (eds). *Knight's Forensic Pathology*. 4th ed. Boca Raton: CRC Press; 2016.
2. Payne-James JJ, Jones R (eds). *Simpson's Forensic Medicine*. 14th ed. Boca Raton: CRC Press; 2020.
3. Spitz WU, Spitz DJ (eds). *Spitz and Fisher's Medicolegal Investigation of Death: Guidelines for the Application of Pathology to Crime Investigation*. 4th ed. Springfield, IL: Charles C Thomas; 2006.
4. Shkrum M, Ramsay D. *Forensic Pathology of Trauma: Common Problems for the Pathologist*. Totowa, NJ: Humana Press; 2007.
5. Richards NF. Fire investigation: Destruction of corpses. *Med Sci Law* 1977; **17**(2): 79–82.
6. Hill IR. An analysis of factors impeding passenger escape from aircraft fires. *Aviat Space Environ Med* 1990; **61**: 261–5.
7. Bohnert M, Rost T, Faller-Marquardt M, et al. Fractures of the base of the skull in charred bodies: Post-mortem heat injuries or signs of mechanical traumatisation? *Forensic Sci Int* 1997; **87**(1): 55–62.
8. Bohnert M, Rost T, Pollak S. The degree of destruction of human bodies in relation to the duration of the fire. *Forensic Sci Int* 1998; **95**(1): 11–21.
9. Madea B (ed). *Handbook of Forensic Medicine*; Chichester: Wiley Blackwell; 2014.
10. Nikolić S, Živković V. Protrusion of the tongue in bodies burned after death: Two cases of arson to cover homicide. *Med Sci Law* 2015; **55**(4): 300–3.
11. Bohnert M, Ropohl D, Pollak S. Clinical findings in the medico-legal investigation of arsonists. *J Clin Forensic Med* 1999; **6**(3): 145–50.
12. Heath K, Kobus H, Byard RW. Potential dangers of accelerant use in arson. *J Forensic Leg Med* 2011; **18**(2): 49–51.
13. Byard RW. The mythology of "spontaneous" human combustion. *Forensic Sci Med Pathol* 2016; **12**(3): 350–2.
14. Hejna P, Bohnert M, Janík M. Unique thermal destruction of the body following suicidal burning. *Forensic Sci Med Pathol* 2019; **15**(2): 262–6.
15. Byard RW, Gilbert JD, Kostakis C, Heath KJ. Circumstances of death and diagnostic difficulties in brushfire fatalities. *J Forensic Sci* 2012; **57**(4): 969–72.
16. Hirsch CS, Bost RO, Gerber SR, et al. Carboxyhemoglobin concentrations in flash fire victims: Report of six simultaneous fire fatalities without elevated carboxyhemoglobin. *Am J Clin Pathol* 1977; **68**(3): 317–20.
17. Stoll S, Roider G, Keil W. Concentrations of cyanide in blood samples of corpses after smoke inhalation of varying origin. *Int J Legal Med* 2017; **131**(1): 123–9.
18. WHO. *Burns*. Available from: https://www.who.int/news-room/fact-sheets/detail/burns (Accessed 3 May 2023).
19. Dettmeyer R, Verhoff M, Schuetz H. *Forensic Pathology: Fundamentals and Perspectives*. Heidelberg New York London: Springer; 2014.
20. Dolinak D, Matshes E, Lew EO. *Forensic Pathology: Principles and Practice*. Burlington: Elsevier; 2006.
21. Byard RW. Forensic features of clothing-related deaths: Historical and cultural aspects. *Am J Forensic Med Pathol* 2017; **38**(4): 318–22.
22. Kumar V, Abbas A, Aster J, (eds). *Robbins and Cotran Pathologic Basis of Disease*. 10th ed. Philadelphia: Saunders Elsevier; 2020.
23. Dettmeyer RB. *Forensic Histopathology: Fundamentals and Perspectives*. 2nd ed. Berlin: Springer; 2018.
24. Dalrymple A, Gilbert JD, Byard RW. Delayed fatal upper-airway obstruction

due to laryngopharyngeal burns and thermal epiglottis. *Med Sci Law* 2020; **60**(3): 223–6.
25. Madea B, Doberentz E, Jackowski C. Vital reactions: An updated overview. *Forensic Sci Int* 2019; **305**: 110029.
26. Byard RW. The autopsy evaluation of "straightforward" fire deaths. *Forensic Sci Med Pathol* 2018; **14**(3): 273–5.
27. Hueck U, Muggenthaler H, Hubig M, et al. Forensic postmortem computed tomography in suspected unnatural adult deaths. *Eur J Radiol* 2020; **132**: 109297.
28. Sogawa N, Michiue T, Ishikawa T, et al. Postmortem volumetric CT data analysis of pulmonary air/gas content with regard to the cause of death for investigating terminal respiratory function in forensic autopsy. *Forensic Sci Int* 2014; **241**: 112–17.
29. de Bakker HM, Roelandt GHJ, Soerdjbalie-Maikoe V, et al. The value of post-mortem computed tomography of burned victims in a forensic setting. *Eur Radiol* 2019; **29**(4): 1912–21.
30. Coty JB, Nedelcu C, Yahya S, et al. Burned bodies: Postmortem computed tomography, an essential tool for modern forensic medicine. *Insights Imaging* 2018; 9(5): 731–43.
31. Hammarlebiod S, Farrugia A, Bierry G, et al. Thermal bone injuries: Postmortem computed tomography findings in 25 cases. *Int J Legal Med* 2022; **136**(1): 219–27.
32. O'Donnell C, Iino M, Mansharan K, et al. Contribution of postmortem multidetector CT scanning to identification of the deceased in a mass disaster: Experience gained from the 2009 Victorian bushfires. *Forensic Sci Int* 2011; **205**(1–3): 15–28.
33. Nakamura M, Idota N, Shintani-Ishida K, et al. Simple, frequent indicator for personal identification-postmortem and antemortem abdominal computed tomography findings of a charred body. *Am J Forensic Med Pathol* 2020; **41**(1): 56–59.
34. Tsuneya S, Makino Y, Chiba F, et al. Postmortem magnetic resonance imaging revealed bilateral globi pallidi lesions in a death associated with prolonged carbon monoxide poisoning: A case report. *Int J Legal Med* 2021; **135**(3): 921–8.
35. Živković V, Nikolić S. Regarding the editorial "The autopsy evaluation of 'straightforward' fire deaths". *Forensic Sci Med Pathol* 2018; **14**(3): 419–20.
36. Hopper CP, Zambrana PN, Goebel U, Wollborn J. A brief history of carbon monoxide and its therapeutic origins. *Nitric Oxide* 2021; **111–112**: 45–63.
37. Bohnert M, Werner CR, Pollak S. Problems associated with the diagnosis of vitality in burned bodies. *Forensic Sci Int* 2003; **135**(3): 197–205.
38. Živković V, Damjanjuk I, Nikolić S. Is the phenomenon of "crow's feet" in cases of high-voltage accidents a vital reaction? *Forensic Sci Med Pathol* 2015; **11**(1): 145–6.
39. Nikolić S, Zivković V, Strajina V, et al. Lung fat embolism in a body changed by putrefaction: A hip fracture antemortem in origin. *Med Sci Law* 2012; **52**(3): 178–80.
40. Bohnert M, Anderson J, Rothschild MA, Böhm J. Immunohistochemical expression of fibronectin in the lungs of fire victims proves intravital reaction in fatal burns. *Int J Legal Med* 2010; **124**(6): 583–8.
41. Marschall S, Rothschild MA, Bohnert M. Expression of heat-shock protein 70 (Hsp70) in the respiratory tract and lungs of fire victims. *Int J Legal Med* 2006; **120**(6): 355–9.
42. Nikolić S, Živković V. Regarding the tongue protrusion as an indicator of vital burning. Much ado about nothing. *Int J Legal Med* 2015; **129**(2): 315–16.
43. Bohnert M, Hejna P. Tongue protrusion in burned bodies. *Int J Legal Med* 2016; **130**(5): 1253–5.
44. Bohnert M, Schmidt U, Perdekamp MG, Pollak S. Diagnosis of a captive-bolt injury in a skull extremely destroyed by fire. *Forensic Sci Int* 2002; **127**(3): 192–7.
45. Živković V, Cvetković D, Zaletel I, et al. The effects of elevated temperature on coronary artery dimensions. *Forensic Sci Int* 2020; **314**: 110390.
46. Alunni V, Grevin G, Buchet L, et al. An amazing case of fatal self-immolation. *Forensic Sci Int* 2014; **244**: e30–3.
47. Bohnert M, Rothschild MA. Complex suicides by self-incineration. *Forensic Sci Int* 2003; **131**(2–3): 197–201.
48. Fanton L, Jdeed K, Tilhet-Coartet S, Malicier D. Criminal burning. *Forensic Sci Int* 2006; **158**(2–3): 87–93.
49. Byard RW, Veldhoen D, Kobus H, Heath K. "Murder-suicide" or "murder-accident"? Difficulties with the analysis of cases. *J Forensic Sci* 2010; **55**(5): 1375–7.
50. Kaur N, Byard RW. Bride burning: A unique and ongoing form of gender-based violence. *J Forensic Leg Med* 2020; **75**: 102035.
51. Heath K, Kobus H, Byard RW. Potential dangers of accelerant use in arson. *J Forensic Leg Med* 2011; **18**(2): 49–51.
52. Nikolić S, Živković V. Fluid content protected lungs against heat, but not against carbon monoxide inhalation. *Forensic Sci Med Pathol* 2017; **13**(2): 265–6.

CHAPTER

45

Hypothermia

Jason Payne-James and Roger W. Byard

INTRODUCTION

Hypothermia is an unintentional drop of core temperature below 35°C. Annually, thousands die of primary hypothermia and an unknown number die of secondary hypothermia worldwide. It is a well-recognized cause of death in man although is likely underdiagnosed (1,2,3). In the living, diagnosis and assessment of the risk of cardiac arrest are based on clinical signs and core temperature measurement when available. Hypothermic patients with risk factors for imminent cardiac arrest (temperature <30°C in young and healthy patients and <32°C in elderly persons, or patients with multiple comorbidities), ventricular dysrhythmias, or systolic blood pressure < 90 mmHg) or who are already in cardiac arrest, need immediate resuscitation (4).

Hypothermia is usually caused by being in a cold environment. It can be triggered by a combination of factors, including prolonged exposure to cold (such as staying outdoors in cold conditions during sports or in a poorly heated room for a long time), rain, wind, sweat, inactivity or being in cold water. Deaths from exposure result from a combination of heat loss from radiation, convection, conduction, respiration and evaporation. Environmental temperatures below 10°C are generally sufficient to cause harmful hypothermia in vulnerable individuals. Many individuals suffer from and die of hypothermia even in temperate climates in winter. In marine disasters, hypothermia may be the cause of death rather than drowning. In cold seas and lakes in high latitudes, death from immersion may occur within a few minutes from sheer heat loss and before drowning can occur.

Otherwise healthy individuals may die from hypothermia caused by a cold environment. If a body gets cold, the normal response is to warm up by becoming more active, putting on more clothing or moving indoors. If exposure to the cold continues, other physiological processes will attempt to prevent any further heat loss. These processes include shivering (which keeps the major organs at normal temperature), restricting blood flow to the skin and releasing hormones to generate heat. Prolonged exposure to the cold will result in these processes failing to maintain body temperature. At this point, shivering stops and heart rate decreases. This can happen rapidly. Certain recreational activities place individuals at particular risk of developing hypothermia such as mountain climbing, skiing and sailing. Lifestyle commonly increases risk. For example, homeless individuals, and those who become intoxicated with drugs or alcohol may be at particular risk due to lifestyles (5). Alcohol consumption causes vascular dilatation and increased heat radiation, exacerbating the risk of hypothermia (6). Wind and rainfall increase the rate of drop in body temperature. The body may rapidly lose temperature when immersed in cold water, as water has a cooling effect that is 20–30 times that of dry air. Hypothermia may confer a protective effect on survival following cold water immersion, but survival may be accompanied by severe hypoxic brain injury. For some individuals, there may be an underlying medical cause (such as dementia, diabetes or thyroid dysfunction), or it may be associated with reduced mobility (7,8).

Hypothermia can be classified into mild (core temperature 32–35°C compared with a normal of 37°C), moderate (30–32°C), or severe (<30°C). Below a core temperature of 32°C, shivering ceases and thus this extra muscle activity will no longer generate heat, worsening the situation. Unconsciousness may occur between core temperatures of 27°C and 30°C, while ventricular fibrillation and apnea occur at core temperatures below 27°C.

Cold injury to the extremities may be severe enough to cause frost bite, which reflects tissue injury that varies in severity from erythema to infarction and necrosis following microvascular injury and thrombosis (9).

Hypothermia may cause behavioral abnormalities that can lead to death with scene findings that may appear suspicious. Paradoxical undressing is a phenomenon that describes the finding of partially clothed – or naked – individuals in a setting of lethal hypothermia. The pathophysiology of this is uncertain but it may reflect confusion and abnormal processing of peripheral cutaneous stimuli in a cold environment, leading the individual to perceive warmth and thus to shed clothing.

The phenomenon of "hide and die syndrome" describes the finding of a body that seems to have been concealed (e.g., under a hedge or in the corner of a room) often surrounded by disturbed furniture, vegetation, clothes or other artefacts (Figure 45.1). It is thought that this phenomenon reflects a terminal primitive "self-protective" behavior and may be more commonly observed where there is a slow decrease in core body temperature (10,11)

DOI: 10.1201/9781003138754-47

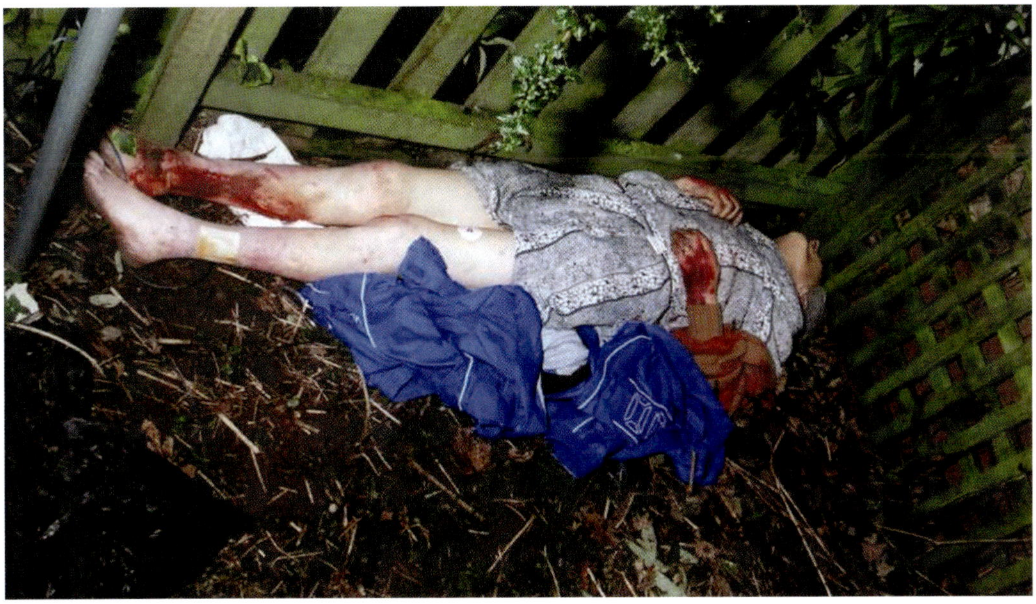

45.1 Elderly female with dementia who went missing from a care home and was found deceased partially clothed. Criminal activity must be excluded before any diagnosis of hypothermic death is made.

Pathophysiology

A reduction in core body temperature below normal levels has significant effects on thermoregulatory control and metabolic processes (12,13), with studies reporting a >70 percent mortality if the core temperature drops below 30°C, and 90 percent at 26°C (8). If the body is exposed to low environmental temperatures, the hypothalamus activates and initiates several counterregulatory mechanisms such as vasoconstriction and chemical thermogenesis (14–16). However, as the temperature declines further, heat loss exceeds heat production and thermoregulatory mechanisms begin to fail (17,18). Fatalities occur from various mechanisms including cardiac arrhythmias (e.g. ventricular fibrillation or asystole), often with accompanying myocardial ischemia, hypoxia, electrolyte abnormalities, and elevated catecholamine levels (8).

For forensic practitioners, the diagnosis of fatal hypothermia is (in the absence of any background information) often a considerable challenge because of the non-specific findings at post mortem, the subtlety of morphological features and wide variability of diagnostic findings. Additionally, the findings must take into account the need to exclude or determine whether criminal activity has taken place. The assistance given by having the core temperature of a decedent at the time of death cannot be underestimated and is often absent. This increases the need for full assessment of events leading up to the death (including the ambient temperature) which may rely upon other evidence such as witnesses, and CCTV and the exclusion of other factors.

Morphology

Table 45.1 shows the external and internal morphologic features of hypothermia. These features are neither specific nor diagnostic and there is wide variability in their frequency (1,19–21). Findings may include pink discoloration of the skin over the extensor surfaces of large joints, such as the elbows, knees and hips (Figure 45.2), acute pancreatic inflammation with fat necrosis, fatty change in cells of the heart, liver and kidneys, skeletal muscle hemorrhage, and vacuolization of renal tubular cells. Often considered the most significant finding is that of superficial gastric lesions, referred to as Wischnewski spots (22,23). In 1895, Wischnewski observed multiple dark-to-black superficial hemorrhagic lesions of the gastric mucosa in deaths due to hypothermia (Figure 45.3). Although not pathognomonic of hypothermia, Wischnewski spots are accepted as a reasonably reliable indicator of significantly reduced core temperature (1,3,20,23,24). Wischnewski spots vary in frequency, being found in 40–91 percent of cases in different series and may depend on circumstances of death, the duration of exposure to cold stimulus, an individual's reaction to cold stress and the resistance of the gastric mucosa to significantly decreased temperatures (20,21,25). The etiology of Wischnewski spots remains unclear but is considered to be multifactorial (26).

The extremities may exhibit frostbite, and this may be seen in those who have been in temperatures <0°C for a prolonged period. Frostbite is a severe ischemic injury which occurs due to tissue vascular damage after sub-zero temperature tissue exposure. Deep frostbite can result in necrosis which may be evident at post mortem (27).

Hypothermic deaths have been associated with a wide range of pancreatic effects.

These include:

- Raised serum amylase levels
- Necrosis of the pancreas
- Hemorrhagic pancreatitis, focal pancreatitis with necrosis of adipose tissue
- Marked congestion and interstitial hemorrhage
- Macroscopically visible pancreatic hemorrhages

TABLE 45.1 The external and internal morphological features of hypothermia

External feature	Description	Pathophysiology	Frequency	Specificity
Blistering of skin	Local blistering	Exposure to cold damages tissue	Unknown	Non-specific
Frost erythema	Pinkish, purple discoloration of skin over large extensor joints (elbow, knee and hip), sometimes projecting areas (ears, nose and male genitalia)	Unclear: — Pronounced vascular hyperemia in subepidermal soft tissue — Capillary damage — Damaged erythrocytes — Plasma/ hemoglobin leakage into tissues	Variable: 54-75%	Non-specific
Hematomas/ abrasions	Cutaneous lesions, reddening abrasions on elbows and knees	Terminal burrowing behavior prior to death	Variable: depends on circumstances of death	Non-specific
Internal feature	**Description**	**Pathophysiology**	**Frequency**	**Specificity**
Bright red blood and lividity	Blood appears bright red	Left shifting of oxygen-hemoglobin-dissociation curve	Case dependent decreased diagnostic value as these changes can occur post mortem	Non-specific
Hemorrhaging into core muscles	Specifically the iliopsoas muscle	Unclear; — Hypoxic damage — Diapedesis — Insufficient circulation due to hypothermia-induced vasoconstriction — Misbalance of decreased perfusion and oxygen requirement	Rare finding	Non-specific
Wischnewski ulcers	— Superficial hemorrhagic dark blackish brown "leopard skin" lesions of gastric mucosa — Necrosis with hematin formation — Characteristic linear pattern	Unclear; — Autolysis — Erythrocytes destroyed — Hemoglobin release — Disturbances of microcirculation — Involvement of tissue amines — Ischemic reperfusion — Increased capillary permeability and mucosal congestion	40–100% cases dependent on exposure, resistance to cold and the individual	Non-specific, however, most reliable feature of significantly reduced temperatures
Pancreatic changes	Acute/hemorrhagic pancreatitis. Patches of fat necrosis on organ surface, raised serum amylase levels, focal/ diffuse infiltration of leukocytes, inflammation, vacuolization adenoid cells	Unclear; — Thrombosis in microcirculation that results in ischemia and necrosis — Vacuolization due to impaired exocytosis and permeability	Variable 20–30%	Non-specific
Fatty changes	Heart, liver and kidneys	Unclear; possibly a result of energy depletion due to post shock-induced hypoxia — Tubular reabsorption following increased mobilization of triglycerides	Variable; case dependent	Non-specific
Vacuolization cells	Liver, pancreas, renal and adrenal cells	Loss of glycogen	Rare-variable	Non-specific

Source: Adapted from (57).

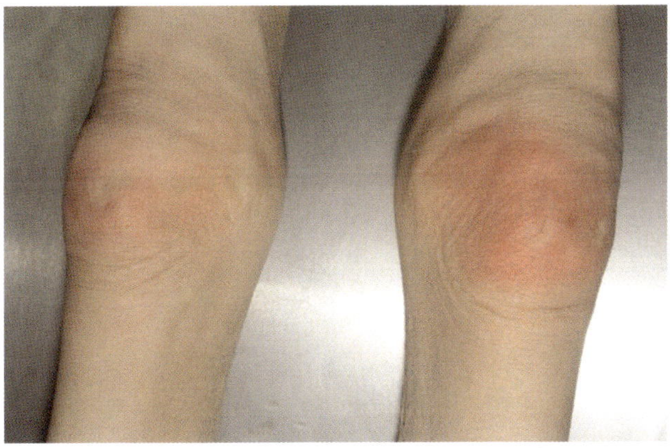

45.2 Pink discoloration over both knees in a case of lethal hypothermia. (With permission from 57.)

45.3 Wischnewski spots in the gastric mucosa in a case of fatal hypothermia producing a typical "leopard skin" effect. (With permission from 57.)

While acute pancreatitis has been identified in hypothermic adults (28–30,21), it is not diagnostic of such deaths and other causes of acute pancreatitis (e.g. alcohol misuse, cholelithiasis and shock must be excluded. Three possible mechanisms have been suggested for the relationship between acute pancreatitis and hypothermia that involved (28): ischemic pancreatitis, from the microcirculatory shock of hypothermia; hypothermia and acute pancreatitis, secondary to alcohol abuse; and severe pancreatitis as the primary disease with hypothermia resulting from social circumstances.

Etiology, incidence and prevalence

Various epidemiological studies of the morbidity and mortality of hypothermia have retrospectively reviewed data on hypothermic cases and have shown that exposure to significantly decreased temperatures is rarely the only contributory factor in these deaths (31–36).

Extremes of age are associated with increased morbidity and mortality associated with hypothermia (12,33,37–40). The elderly are also more susceptible to the effects of hypothermia due to failing biological mechanisms of temperature regulation, such as vasoconstriction and shivering, not being sufficient to maintain the balanced relationship between heat loss and heat production. A study from Japan showed that the prognostic factors for hypothermic death involved: age (≥75 years old), male sex, activities of daily living (needing total assistance), cause of accidental hypothermia (trauma, alcohol), Glasgow Coma Scale score, and potassium level (>5.5 mEq/L). The overall mortality rate was 24.5 percent (40). The elderly are also less able to discern cold temperatures due to possible autonomic nervous system dysfunction and may not dress appropriately, thus increasing body heat loss, and may be reluctant or be unable to spend money on heating (39,41,42,43). Frailty, particularly seen in the elderly, is associated with increased mortality in patients with hypothermia (44).

Cold weather injuries or harm are relevant concerns for children, in particular during winter sports and outdoor activities. For this high-risk population, there are two types of environmental cold injuries: freezing injuries and nonfreezing injuries. Frostbite is a freezing injury from direct contact with cold air or surfaces. The extent of injury depends on the depth to which the freezing extends. Hypothermia is a nonfreezing cold injury, and it can occur even when ambient temperatures are above freezing. Children may be unable to recognize the effects of hypothermia and indulge in unintended risky behaviors (45).

A wide range of natural diseases have been identified as predisposing factors to death from hypothermia (7,8,17,39,46). These diseases are often age related (34,39,43,47). Conditions contributing to hypothermia include hypothyroidism; diabetes mellitus; sepsis; stroke; and renal, heart, and liver failure (43,47,48).

Hypothermia in trauma patients is a common condition. It is aggravated by traumatic hemorrhage, which leads to hypovolemic shock. This results in a lethal triad of hypothermia, coagulopathy, and acidosis, leading to ongoing bleeding. Additionally, hypothermia in trauma patients can deepen through environmental exposure on the scene or during transport and medical procedures such as infusions and airway management (49).

All these conditions in some way affect thermoregulation, predispose to abnormal temperature control and regulation and thus have the potential to aggravate and enhance tissue damage induced by hypothermia (47). A confounding issue in the forensic evaluation of cases is that these and other conditions may mask the true mechanism of death (34,37). Conditions that affect cognitive function and mental illnesses such as schizophrenia, bipolar disorder, Alzheimer's disease and dementia are all risk factors for hypothermic deaths (37,50).

Alcohol intoxication is a well-known factor in certain hypothermic fatalities for a variety of reasons, occurring in up to 64 percent of cases in some series (6,50). Unsurprisingly, the frequent location of hypothermic deaths associated with alcohol intoxication has been outdoors with 40- to 50-year-old males being most susceptible (37,50).

Differences in percentages of males and females in various studies may be attributed to a variety of causes. Tanaka and Tokudome (50) reported a 91 percent incidence of hypothermic deaths in males, while Lim and Duflou reported a female predominance of 63 percent

(34). Sex differences in incidence may relate to variations in adiposity, muscle mass and metabolic responses between males and females (50–53).

The colder months of the year are known to be associated with an increase in death rates in those not accustomed to cold climates and are often associated with cardiovascular and respiratory illnesses in the elderly. This has ranged from 5 percent to 30 percent and is often referred to as excess winter mortality. Although hypothermic deaths contribute to this they are not limited to colder climates, with one study showing higher death rates from hypothermia in the warmer climate of South Australia (3.9/ 100 000) when compared with Sweden (3.3/100 000) (54). Fatal hypothermia remains a public health problem in warmer climates (34) and is often under-reported and under-recognized.

Hypothermia-related deaths account for the majority of weather-related deaths in the United States. Hypothermic deaths in New York City (NYC) and Houston were reviewed over a 10-year period, between January 2009 and July 2019. There were 139 hypothermia deaths in NYC with an average annualized rate of 1.7 per million. During this same period, there were 50 hypothermia deaths in Houston with an average annualized rate of 2.4 per million. Males were more likely to die of hypothermia compared to females in both cities. Hypothermia mortality in Houston was 66 percent higher than in NYC. No correlation was found between postcode poverty rates and hypothermia-related deaths. In this study, the most consistent autopsy finding was Wischnewski spots (56.6%), and the presence of alcohol was the most common toxicological finding (36.5%). The authors conclude that studies such as these can be used for preventive health education in appropriately targeted settings (55).

As yet, despite substantial knowledge about the pathophysiology and morphologic changes in hypothermic deaths and associated post-mortem findings having been recognized for decades, there is no absolute certainty in the post-mortem diagnosis of hypothermia. The search for specific single markers that will diagnose hypothermic deaths at post mortem continues with consideration of factors such as candidate biomarkers in brown adipose tissue of the deceased, but as yet this search is unsuccessful (56,57).

CONCLUSION

Hypothermia has a complex pathophysiology, and many factors contribute to morbidity and mortality. To diagnose hypothermia as a cause of death is a challenge, exacerbated by no absolute pathognomonic findings because of variation in the sensitivity, specificity and etiology of morphologic changes which may be seen. If the pre-death circumstances are unknown, the diagnosis becomes more of a challenge and can be testing for the forensic practitioner. The more information available about events leading up to the death and the recording of core body temperature can all assist in determining the correct diagnosis.

REFERENCES

1. Türk EE, 2010. Hypothermia. *Forensic Sci Med Pathol* 2010; **6**: 106–115.
2. Turk EE, Sperhake JP, Madea B, et al. 2006. Immunohistochemical detection of hemoglobin in frost erythema. *Forensic Sci Int* 2006; **158**: 131–4.
3. Mallet ML. 2002. Pathophysiology of accidental hypothermia. *Oxford J Med* 2002; **95**: 775–85.
4. Dettmeyer RB. *Hypothermia. Forensic Histopathology*. New York: Springer; 2011, pp. 165–71.
5. Dharmarajan TS, Widjaja D, 2007. Hypothermia in the geriatric population. *Aging Health* 2007; **3(6)**: Published online. Available from: https://www.futuremedicine.com/doi/full/10.2217/1745509X.3.6.735 (Accessed 1 May 2023).
6. Paal P, Pasquier M, Darocha T, et al. Accidental hypothermia: 2021 Update. *Int J Environ Res Public Health* 2022; **19(1)**: 501.
7. Zhang P, Wiens K, Wang R, et al. Cold weather conditions and risk of hypothermia among people experiencing homelessness: Implications for prevention strategies. *Int J Environ Res Public Health* 2019; **16(18)**: 3259.
8. Brändström H, Eriksson A, Giesbrecht Get al. Fatal hypothermia: An analysis from a sub-arctic region. *Int J Circumpolar Health* 2012; **71(0)**: 1–7.
9. Matz R. Hypothermia in diabetic acidosis. *Hormones* 1972; **3**: 36–41.
10. Zhou C, Byard RW, Armanni-Ebstein phenomenon and hypothermia. *Forensic Sci Int* 2011; **206**: e82–e84.
11. Rathjen NA, Shahbodaghi SD, Brown JA. Hypothermia and cold weather injuries. *Am Fam Physician* 2019; **100(11)**: 680–6.
12. Prahlow JA, Byard RW, *Hypothermia. Atlas of Forensic Pathology*. New York, NY: Springer; 2012, pp. 743 - 752.
13. Payne-James JJ Jones RM. *Hypothermia. Simpson's Forensic Medicine*. 14th ed. Boca Raton: CRC Press; 2019.
14. Reuler JB. 1978. Hypothermia: Pathophysiology, clinical settings and management. *Annals Int Med* 1978; **89**: 519–27.
15. Bristow G. 1984. Accidental hypothermia. *Can J Anaesth* 1984; **31(3)**: 52–55.
16. Caroselli CGA, Pisani A, Bruno G. 2009. Hypothermia: An under-estimated risk. *Int Emerg Med* 2009; **4**: 227–30.
17. Nirula R, Gentilello L. 2005. Detrimental Effects of Hypothermia. In: Tisherman SA, Sterz F, (eds). *Therapeutic Hypothermia*. Series: Molecular and Cellular Biology of Critical Care Medicine, Part 4. New York, NY: Springer; 2005, pp. 235 - 49.
18. Lonning PE, Skullberg A, Abyholm F. 1986. Accidental hypothermia: Review of the literature. *Acta Anaesthesiol Scand* 1986; **30**: 601–13.
19. Türk EE, Sperhake JP, Pueshel K, Tsokos M. An approach to the evaluation of fatal hypothermia. *Forensic Sci* 2005; **1**: 31–36.
20. Emslie-Smith D. Accidental hypothermia. *Lancet 2* 1958; 492–495.
21. Preuß J, Lignitz E, Dettmeyer R, Madea B. 2004. Fatty degeneration in renal tubule epithelium in accidental hypothermia victims. *Forensic Sci Int* 2004; **141**: 131–5.
22. Madea B, Tsokos M, Preuß J. Morphological findings, their pathogenesis and diagnostic value. *Forensic Pathol Rev* 2008; **5**: 3–21.
23. Wolf DA, Aronson J, Rajaraman S, Veasey SP. Wischnewski ulcers and acute pancreatitis in two hospitalized patients with cirrhosis, portal vein thrombosis and hypothermia. *J Forensic Sci* 1999; **44(5)**: 1082–85.
24. Bright F, Winskog C, Byard RW. Lethal hypothermia in South Australia (letter). *Med JA* 2012; **197**: 622.
25. Birchmeyer MS, Mitchell EK. 1989. Wischnewski revisited: The diagnostic value of gastric mucosa ulcers in hypothermic deaths. *Am J Forensic Med Pathol* 1989; **10(1)**: 28–30.
26. Sperhake HP, Rothschild M, Risse M, Tsokos M. Histomorphology of Wischnewsky Spots: Contribution to the Forensic Histopathology of Fatal Hypothermia. In: Oehmichen M (ed).

Hypothermia: Clinical, Pathomorphological and Forensic Features. Lubek: Schmidt-Romhild; 2004, pp. 211–20.
27. Hirvonen J. Necropsy findings in fatal hypothermia cases. *Forensic Sci* 1976; **8:** 155–64.
28. Sacco MA, Abenavoli L, Juan C, et al. Biological mechanisms behind Wischnewsky spots finding on gastric mucosa: Autopsy cases and literature review. *Int J Environ Res Public Health* 2022; **19(6):** 3601.
29. Joshi K, Goyary D, Mazumder B, et al. Frostbite: Current status and advancements in therapeutics. *J Therm Biol* 2020; **93:** 102716.
30. Foulis AK. Morphological study of the relationship between accidental hypothermia and acute pancreatitis. *J Clin Pathol* 1982; **35:** 1244–48.
31. Lin K, Ofori E, Lin AN, et al. Hypothermia-related acute pancreatitis. *Case Rep Gastroenterol* 2018; **12(2):** 217–23.
32. Khan MZ, Yousaf H, Jamil A, et al. Acute pancreatitis associated with hypothermia: An uncommon presentation. *Cureus* 2020; **12(6):** e8859.
33. Savides EP, Hoffbrand BI. Hypothermia, thrombosis, and acute pancreatitis. *BMJ* 1974; **1:** 614.
34. Thomas DR. 1988. Accidental hypothermia in the sunbelt. *J Gen Med* 1988; **3:** 552–4.
35. Herity B, Daly L, Bourke GJ, Horgan JM. 1991. Hypothermia and mortality and morbidity. An epidemiological analysis. *J Epidemiol Community Health* 1991; **45:** 19–23.
36. Lim C, Duflou J. 2008. Hypothermia fatalities in a temperate climate: Sydney, Australia. *Pathology* 2008; **41(1):** 46–51.
37. Danzl D, Pozos RS, Auerbach PS, et al. 1987. Multicenter hypothermia survey. *Ann Emerg Med* 1987; **16:** 1042–55.
38. McKee CM. 1989. Deaths in winter: Can Britain learn from Europe? *Eur J Epidemiol* 1989; 5(2): 178–82.
39. Taylor AJ, McGwin G, Davis GG, et al. 2001. Hypothermia deaths in Jefferson County, Alabama. *Inj Prev* 2001; **7:** 141–5.
40. Glickman EL, Caine-Bish N, Cheatham CC, et al. The influence of age on thermosensitivity during cold water immersion. *Wilderness Environ Med* 2002; **13:** 194–202.
41. Megarbane B, Axler O, Chary I, et al. Hypothermia with indoor occurrence is associated with a worse outcome. *J Intensive Care Med* 2000; **26:** 1843–49.
42. Wagner JA, Horvath S. Influence of age and gender on human thermoregulatory responses to cold exposures. *Am J Physiol* 1985; **85:** 180–6.
43. Takauji S, Hifumi T, Saijo Y, et al. Accidental hypothermia: Characteristics, outcomes, and prognostic factors-A nationwide observational study in Japan (Hypothermia study 2018 and 2019). *Acute Med Surg* 2021; **8(1):** e694.
44. Bright F, Winskog C, Byard RW. Wischnewski ulcers and hypothermia: Sensitive, specific or serendipitous? *Forensic Sci Med Pathol* 2013; **9:** 88–90.
45. Elbaz G, Etzion O, Delgado J, et al. Hypothermia in a desert climate: Severity score and mortality prediction. *Am J Emerg Med* 2008; **26:** 683–8.
46. Byard RW, Bright F, Winskog C. Reduced body mass index and lethal hypothermia. *Aust J Forensic Sci* 2014; **46:** 451–4.
47. Schimelpfenig SS, Jacobsen B. Pediatric environmental cold injuries. *Pediatr Rev* 2022; **43(8):** 449–57.
48. McKee CM. Deaths in winter in Northern Ireland: The role of low temperature. *Ulster Med J* 1900; **59(1):** 17–22.
49. Roeggla M, Holzer M, Roeggla G, et al. Prognosis of accidental hypothermia in the urban setting. *J Intensive Care Med* 2001; **16:** 142–9.
50. Maclean D, Murison J, Griffiths PD. Acute pancreatitis and diabetic ketoacidosis in accidental hypothermia and hypothermic myxoedema. *BMJ* 1973; **4:** 757–61.
51. van Veelen MJ, Brodmann Maeder M. Hypothermia in trauma. *Int J Environ Res Public Health* 2021; **18(16):** 8719.
52. Tanaka M, Tokudome S. Accidental hypothermia and death from cold in urban areas. *Int J Biometereol* 1990; **34:** 242–6.
53. Keatinge WR. The effects of subcutaneous fat and of previous exposure to cold on the body temperature, peripheral blood flow and metabolic rate of men in cold water. *J Physiol* 1960; **153:** 166–78.
54. Anderson GS, Ward R, Mekjavic IB. Gender differences in physio logical reactions to thermal stress. *Eur J Appl Physiol* 1995; **71:** 95–101.
55. Budd GM, Warhaft N. Body temperature, shivering, blood pressure and heart rate during a standard cold stress in Australia and Antarctica. *J Physiol* 1966; **186:** 216–232.
56. Bright F, Winskog C, Walker M, Byard RW. A comparison of hypothermic deaths in South Australia and Sweden. *J Forensic Sci* 2014: **59:** 983–85.
57. Dickinson GM, Maya GX, Lo Y, Jarvis HC. Hypothermia-related deaths: A 10-year retrospective study of two major metropolitan cities in the United States. *J Forensic Sci* 2020; **65(6):** 2013–18.
58. Zhang M, Wang N, Guo XS, et al. Candidate biomarkers in brown adipose tissue for post-mortem diagnosis of fatal hypothermia. *Int J Legal Med* 2022Sep 29. doi: 10.1007/s00414-022-02897-9. Online ahead of print.
59. Bright FM, RW Byard. Extremes of Temperature: Hypothermia. In: Payne-James JJ, Byard RW. *Encyclopedia of Forensic & Legal Medicine*. Cambridge, MA: Academic Press; 2016.
60. Byard RW, Bright FM. Lethal hypothermia: A sometimes elusive diagnosis. *Forensic Sci Med Pathol* 2018; **14:** 421–23.

CHAPTER

46

Heat Deaths

Nathan Milne, Christopher Day and Beng Beng Ong

INTRODUCTION

Heat production in the human body is derived from metabolism in the internal organs and muscular activity. Temperature homeostasis is regulated by the hypothalamus in the brain with loss of heat from conduction, convection, radiation and evaporation. When the environmental temperature is greater than the body temperature, the only means of losing heat is by evaporation.

Hyperthermia occurs when the body temperature is elevated above normal due to an inability of the body to regulate temperature. It differs from fever as the body temperature set point is unchanged.

Pathophysiology

The normal body response to heat is coordinated production of cell mediators from different cells to protect the body in response to the increase in temperature. The continuous exposure to heat and increase in body temperature will cause direct injury to the cells including the vascular endothelium, resulting in coagulopathy. Furthermore, there is increased cardiac output leading to distribution of blood to the peripheral circulation to facilitate loss of heat. The shift of blood from the splanchnic circulation increases the susceptibility of the gastrointestinal (GI) system to ischemia, especially in the vulnerable. This results in increased permeability of the gut, leading to leakage of toxins into the circulation. There is subsequent dysregulation of cell mediators, leading to encephalopathy and presentation of heatstroke (1).

Presentation

Heat-related illness can be considered as a spectrum, from minor heat illness to heat syncope and exhaustion to heatstroke, with the latter being potentially lethal (Table 46.1). The National Association of Medical Examiners (NAME) in the United States (US) defined a heat-related death as "*a death in which exposure to high ambient temperature either caused the death or significantly contributed to it*" (2).

TABLE 46.1 Classification of heat-related illness (7,8,30,33)

Category	Types
Mild	Heat edema Heat cramps Prickly heat
Moderate	Heat syncope Heat exhaustion
Severe	Heatstroke: • Classic • Exertional
Other forms	Drug induced hyperthermia syndromes • Malignant hyperthermia • Neuroleptic malignant syndrome • Serotonin syndrome • Sympathomimetic syndrome • Parkinsonism-hyperpyrexia syndrome • Baclofen withdrawal syndrome • Anticholinergic toxicity • Uncoupling of oxidative phosphorylation 'Excited delirium'

Risk factors for heat-related illness are summarized in Table 46.2. Extremes of age predispose to heat-related illness. Children have reduced heat tolerance due to factors that include a greater surface area to body mass ratio, an immature thermoregulatory system, a higher threshold for sweating and reduced sweat production (3). The natural aging process is associated with a greater risk of chronic disease, translating to an increased risk of heat-related illness (3). A study of heat wave-related deaths in France showed an increased risk of mortality from age 35 years that was most marked in those aged over 75 years (4).

Chronic disease, particularly cardiovascular disease, contributes to increased mortality. Other chronic conditions such as pulmonary disease, diabetes mellitus and obesity also impart increased mortality risk. Similarly, intercurrent acute illness or infection are risk factors.

Poor physical fitness, lack of acclimatization and insufficient hydration all render an individual at risk of a poorer outcome with excess heat exposure. Acclimatization involves physiological responses including increased cutaneous vasodilatation, increased sweating, reduced

DOI: 10.1201/9781003138754-48

TABLE 46.2 Risk factors for heat-related illness (1,7,8,51)

Extrinsic factors	
Environment	High temperature, heat wave High humidity Limited shade Limited water Limited airflow Entrapment
Restricted cooling	Excessive clothing or coverings Excessive protective equipment
Activity	Prolonged physical activity Insufficient breaks Insufficient hydration
Intrinsic factors	
General	Extremes of age Poor physical fitness Lack of acclimatisation Obesity Dehydration
Medical	Cardiovascular disease including hypertension Pulmonary disease Dermatological disease impairing cooling, including burns Diabetes mellitus Pre-existing acute illness Thyroid disease Psychiatric illness
Toxicological	Alcohol Drugs, prescribed • Anticholinergics • Antidepressants • Antihistamines • Antipsychotics • Benzodiazepines • Beta-blockers • Calcium channel blockers • Dietary supplements • Diuretics • Laxatives • Lithium • Neuroleptics • Phenothiazines • Thyroid agonists Drugs, illicit • Amphetamines • Cathinones • Cocaine • Heroin • Phencyclidine • Lysergic acid diethylamide

cutaneous and core temperature, and improved fluid balance and cardiovascular stability (3).

Mild heat-related illness

Heat edema is mild dependent swelling, most often involving the lower limbs. It results from cutaneous vasodilatation and typically resolves spontaneously but may be aided by elevation of the lower limbs. It may affect elderly non-acclimatized individuals who are active after a prolonged period of sitting, or healthy people arriving in a warmer climate (5).

Heat cramps are a manifestation of profuse sweating with inadequate replacement of fluid and electrolyte losses. Cramps usually occur in the context of intense exercise and profuse sweating, and are painful, involuntary spasms often involving the calves, but may also involve the thighs or shoulders (5).

Prickly heat (miliaria rubra) may also be referred to as "heat rash" or "sweat rash". It is a form of miliaria, a group of skin conditions in which there is obstruction of sweat from eccrine glands to the skin surface (6). Obstruction is at the level of the stratum spinosum and anhidrosis can ensue. It presents as an often pruritic, erythematous, papulovesicular rash that typically occurs at sites where clothing rubs the skin, such as the trunk and extremities, usually sparing the face.

Moderate heat-related illness

Heat syncope, also referred to as exercise-associated collapse, arises from the same mechanism as heat cramps. It is a vasovagal response to profound peripheral vasodilatation, intravascular volume depletion, reduced vasomotor tone and reduced venous return (7,8).

Heat exhaustion occurs when the body's thermoregulatory mechanisms are insufficient, and core body temperature rises to 38.3–40°C (101–104°F). It may be difficult to differentiate from early exertional heatstroke, to which it can progress if not recognized and managed (3). Signs and symptoms include pronounced sweating, cold and clammy skin, presyncope, headache, blurred vision, fatigue, malaise and GI symptoms (7,8). There is no altered mental state, which should be considered an indicator of heatstroke (7).

Severe heat-related illness (heatstroke)

Heatstroke can be subdivided into classic and exertional forms, which have certain differing features (Table 46.3). Presenting features are a core temperature of at least 40.6°C (105°F) in combination with an altered mental state. Signs of the latter include confusion, agitation, irritability, unusual behaviors and posturing, combativeness, hemiplegia, status epilepticus, coma, headache, ataxia and dizziness (5,9). Other possible evidence of heat stroke is hypotension, tachycardia, jaundice in cases of hepatic injury, coagulopathy, GI bleeding, disseminated intravascular coagulation (DIC), rhabdomyolysis and acute renal failure (9). Sweating is usually present in exertional heatstroke, but it may be absent in classic heatstroke, as there may be reduced sweat gland output in response to heat stress (1).

TABLE 46.3 Differentiating features of classic heatstroke from exertional heatstroke (1,8,9)

Feature	Classic heatstroke	Exertional heatstroke
Timing	Hot weather, heat wave	Can be any time
Age	Children, elderly	Adults, high school age
Health	Comorbidities	May be fit and well
Medications, drugs	Prescribed	Often none
Activity level	Sedentary	Active, strenuous
Onset	May be insidious e.g. days	Rapid e.g. hours
Sweating	May be absent	Usually present

Classic heatstroke typically affects vulnerable individuals such as children, the elderly and those with chronic illness. Other factors that have been reported are excessive clothing, acute alcohol intoxication, obesity, dementia, alcoholic liver disease, and lack of familiarity with environmental conditions (10). In addition, confinement to bed, not leaving the home daily, inability to self-care and psychiatric illness have been shown to be risk factors for death in heat waves (11). In fatal cases, this predilection for the vulnerable can complicate interpretation of death causation, particularly when pre-existing disease is sufficient to independently account for death.

It can also occur in hot environments in individuals not acclimatized to such conditions, especially in those with additional health factors (12).

Another circumstance of classic heatstroke is entrapment in a hot environment such as a motor vehicle, termed vehicular hyperthermia. This can affect anyone if there is no means of escape, but infants and toddlers are the usual victims, being less able to extricate themselves or gain assistance (13). Although deaths typically occur during hot weather, this is not a necessity, with deaths also occurring during cooler days (14). Vehicular temperature can exceed 41°C (105°F) even with an ambient temperature as low as 20°C (68°F) (15). Extreme temperatures can occur in hotter weather. A study conducted in Switzerland recorded a maximum vehicular temperature of 89.1°C (192.4°F) during summer with full sun exposure (16). Death can supervene quickly, with some deaths estimated to have occurred within less than half an hour (17).

Also, within the pediatric population, overheating or being over-dressed has been recognized as a risk factor for sudden unexpected death in infancy (18). It has been recommended that infants should be dressed in no greater than a single layer no more than would be appropriate for an adult in the same environmental conditions (19).

Fatal heat stroke has also been reported in association with hot microenvironments such as saunas, sweat lodges and beds with electric blankets (20,21,22).

Exertional heatstroke differs from classic heatstroke in that it is the result of strenuous physical activity, usually in hot weather. It can affect the physically fit, including athletes and those employed in physical occupations working in hot conditions such as military personnel, firefighters, miners and agricultural workers. It may occur in similar circumstances that have not previously caused heat-related illness (1). Deaths have been reported in the Australian outback after being stranded and walking (23). It shares risk factors with classic heatstroke with predisposing factors of acute and chronic illness, limited physical fitness and lack of acclimatization. Other risk factors are excessive clothing, pressure from self, peers or coaches, and the use of alcohol and stimulant drugs (1).

Hyperthermia has also been reported in the context of excited delirium (24).

Drug-induced hyperthermia syndromes

Malignant hyperthermia is a pharmacogenetic skeletal muscle disease that produces a potentially lethal hypermetabolic response following exposure to halogenated volatile anesthetics and depolarizing muscle relaxants. Three genes have been implicated that are involved in skeletal muscle calcium homeostasis (25). These include the *RYR1* gene located on chromosome 19q13. This encodes the ryanodine receptor, affecting calcium release channels in the skeletal muscle sarcoplasmic reticulum. The rise in myoplasmic calcium drives the hypermetabolic response that includes heat production with resultant hyperthermia. There is also increased carbon dioxide production, oxygen consumption and respiratory acidosis, and it can progress to multiorgan failure with complications including cardiac dysrhythmias, cell lysis, renal failure, hyperkalemia and DIC (26,27).

Neuroleptic malignant syndrome is associated with both typical and atypical antipsychotic medications; its features, in addition to hyperthermia, include diaphoresis, muscular rigidity, altered mental state and autonomic dysfunction (28). It has previously been reported to have a mortality rate of 10 percent, but this may have diminished with the development of new antipsychotic medications (29,30).

Serotonin syndrome presents clinically with hyperthermia, an altered mental state, autonomic hyperactivity and neuromuscular abnormalities following exposure to any drug that increases serotonin receptor activation (31). It can progress rapidly to cardiovascular collapse and death. Numerous drugs have been associated including selective serotonin-reuptake inhibitors, monoamine oxidase inhibitors, antidepressants (e.g. venlafaxine), valproate, lithium, analgesics (e.g. fentanyl, tramadol), antiemetics (e.g. ondansetron, metoclopramide), drugs of abuse (e.g. methylenedioxymethamphetamine, lysergic acid diethylamide) and supplements (e.g. tryptophan, St. John's wort, ginseng) (32).

Sympathomimetic syndrome results from psychostimulant drugs, for example, amphetamines, cocaine and cathinones. An excess of catecholamines results in and may present with, agitation, abnormal movements, delirium, hypertension and hyperthermia, the latter initially resulting from central dysregulation (33,34). It can progress with complications such as shock, renal failure, arrhythmia, myocardial infarction, stroke and death (30).

Withdrawal of intrathecal baclofen, a gamma-aminobutyric acid (GABA) agonist, has been associated with a withdrawal syndrome resembling malignant hyperthermia and neuroleptic malignant syndrome (30,35).

Parkinsonism-hyperpyrexia syndrome can similarly present with indistinguishable features in patients with Parkinson's disease and related disorders (30). It may result from reduction or cessation of dopaminergic medications, interruption of deep brain stimulation therapy, trauma, infection and GI illness (36).

Anticholinergic toxicity may induce hyperthermia by blocking acetylcholine-medicated receptors in sweat glands, causing anhidrosis and impaired heat loss. It typically follows overdose and although hyperthermia is usually only mild, complications may progress to include delirium, seizures and coma (30).

Uncoupling of oxidative phosphorylation by salicylates and dinitrophenol can lead to profound hyperthermia (33). Dinitrophenol has made a resurgence in recent years, being used as an unregulated weight loss agent, including in the body-building community (37,38).

Post-mortem findings

The findings are summarized in Table 46.4. Post-mortem findings are non-specific and varied. There is, however, a generally consistent description of pathological findings in autopsy series regardless of mechanism (classical versus exertional) of heat-related illness and also of age, occurring in both adult and child populations (39).

The constellation of findings is often dependent upon length of survival and typically reflect a systemic inflammatory response with subsequent multiorgan dysfunction.

In acute cases, the body temperature may be still raised if the post-mortem examination is conducted soon after death. There is usually accelerated post-mortem change, which ranges from rapid onset of rigor mortis to early decomposition change depending on the time of the post-mortem examination after death. The skin may show features of dehydration. Petechial hemorrhages may be seen on the conjunctival and skin surfaces (40,41). In some, there may be features of burns (blisters, redness and skin slippage) especially in extreme environmental temperature, from direct sunlight or contact with hot surfaces (Figure 46.1) (13,22,42). There may be no useful internal findings. Cerebral edema, pulmonary edema and visceral petechiae, most notably in the intrathoracic region, are most often identified internally (Figures 46.2– 46.4) (39,42,43). Contraction-band necrosis may be observed in the heart (21). The findings of skeletal muscle degeneration and breakdown usually described in malignant hyperthermia are not usually seen in deaths related to environmental hyperthermia (44). There are no pathognomonic features histologically, although it is claimed that the use of immunohistochemistry for heat-shock proteins can be useful in revealing early post-burn stages on the cutaneous surfaces (45). Importantly, accelerated decomposition may obscure the pathological changes present.

TABLE 46.4 Possible post-mortem findings in cases of heat-related deaths (8,21,40,41,42,52,53)

Skin	Evidence of burns – Superficial burns including blistering of the skin, hyperaemia Signs of dehydration – poor skin turgor, dry mucous membranes, sunken orbits
Visceral surface petechial hemorrhages	Pleural surface of lungs, epicardial surface of heart, serosa of intestines
Disseminated Intravascular Coagulopathy	Present in deaths with a period of survival, usually seen in the small blood vessels and capillaries of kidneys but may be present in other organs.
Accelerated decomposition	Affecting all organs and soft tissue.
Brain	Non-specific cerebral edema and vascular congestion. There may be focal petechial hemorrhages in the white matter
Intestines	Serosal and mucosal hemorrhages
Lungs	Pleural petechial hemorrhages Pulmonary edema and congestion Diffuse alveolar damage (period of survival)
Heart	Epicardial hemorrhages Subendocardial hemorrhage Contraction band necrosis
Kidneys	Hemorrhage within renal pelvis Acute tubular necrosis and myoglobin deposition in those with period of survival
Liver	Centrilobular necrosis
Pancreas	Acute pancreatitis.
Skeletal muscle	Pale and edematous on gross examination with hypercontraction bands, fibre degeneration and focal necrosis (usually in malignant hyperthermia)

Cases of more prolonged survival may have changes associated with multiorgan dysfunction. Features related to DIC are usually prominent, associated with hemorrhage in various organs including the brain, intestines, lungs and adrenal glands (Figures 46.5 and 46.6) (46). Other findings include acute tubular necrosis and rhabdomyolysis in the kidneys (Figure 46.7), and centrilobular necrosis in the liver (46,47).

Toxicology is an essential investigation. Certain medications, drugs and alcohol are known to predispose to hyperthermia and may directly cause drug-induced hyperthermia.

Further ancillary investigations are often not helpful. The post-mortem CT (PMCT) scan may demonstrate evidence of accelerated decomposition, observed as gaseous accumulation within organs and soft tissues,

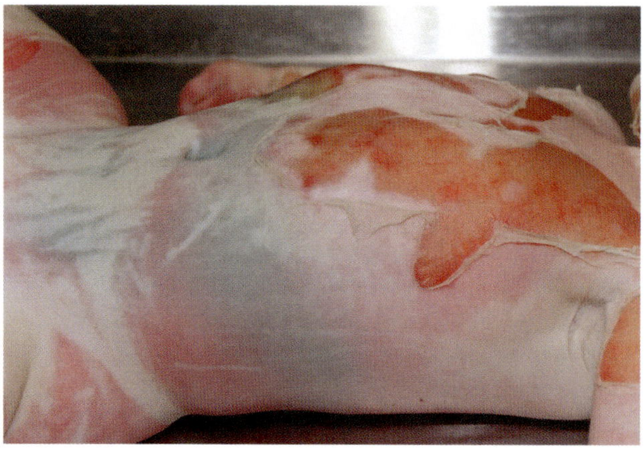

46.1 Skin slippage due to direct sun exposure in a child trapped in a car.

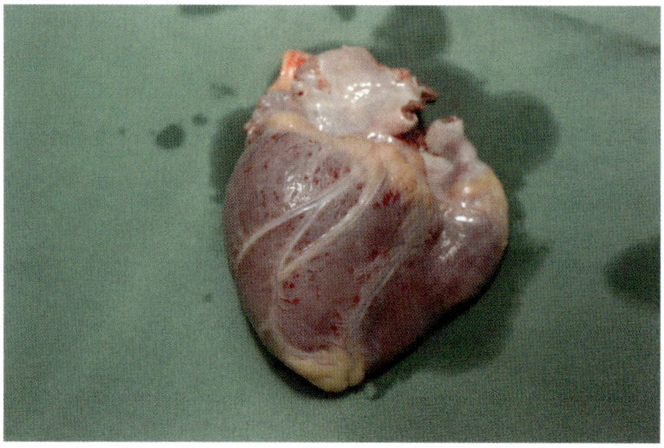

46.2 Intra-thoracic petechiae: Epicardial hemorrhages.

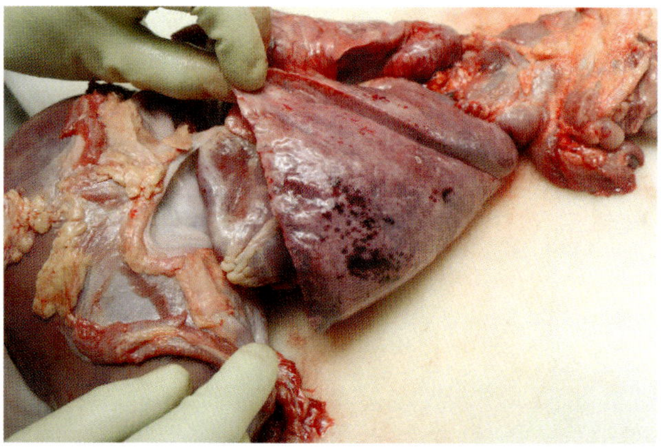

46.3 Intra-thoracic petechiae: Pleural hemorrhages.

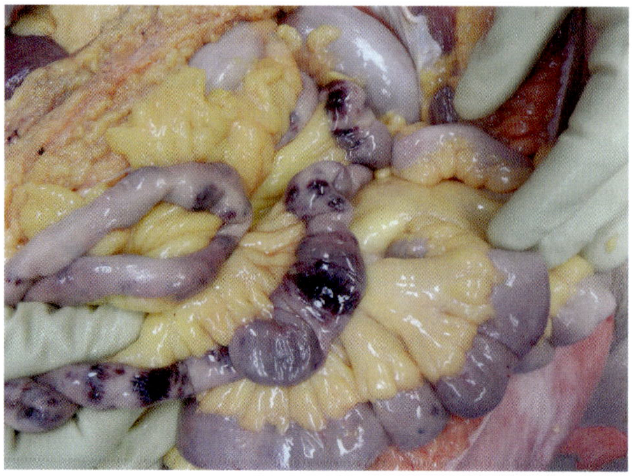

46.4 Serosal hemorrhages on the intestines.

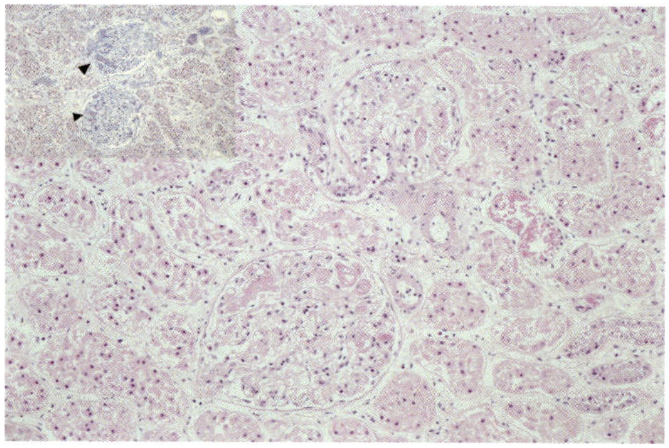

46.5 Glomerular capillaries showing the presence of fibrin. Inset: Fibrin is stained red with the use of Martius scarlet blue (MSB) stain (arrowheads).

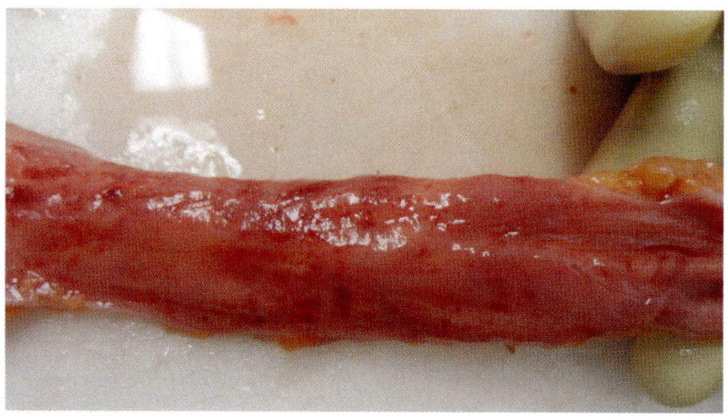

46.6 Hemorrhage in the mucosa of the small intestine.

greater than what would typically be expected based on post-mortem interval alone, but there is no specific feature related to hyperthermia. Post-mortem vitreous humor electrolyte biochemistry may show a dehydration pattern in acute deaths. This may not be present as deaths usually occur before significant dehydration has occurred. Myoglobin may be present in the urine in cases with a period of survival. A review of biochemical markers showed that it is not useful for post-mortem investigations of heat-related deaths (48).

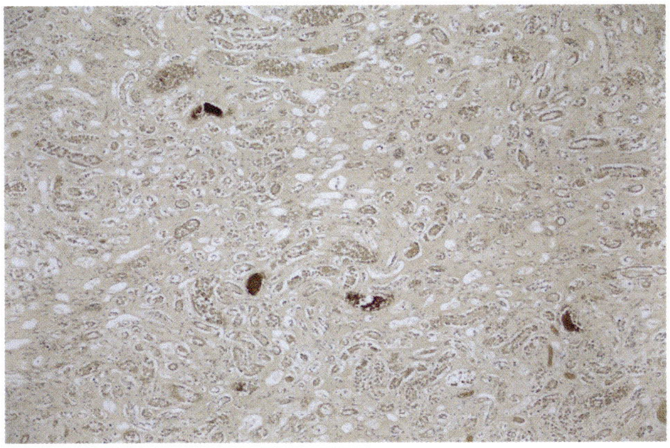

46.7 Positive immunohistochemistry stain for myoglobin in renal tubules of an individual with a 2-day survival and development of myoglobinuria.

An approach to post-mortem examination

Due to paucity of post-mortem findings, the diagnosis requires accurate assessment of both the scene and circumstances surrounding death. A cause of death due to hyperthermia or heatstroke can be made if the measured body temperature is recorded as more than 40.6°C (105°F). When there is absence of body core temperature at the time of death, the diagnosis should be considered if the environmental temperature at the time of collapse is high, and the circumstances are appropriate. Medical records in those who survived are especially useful as the clinical presentation usually includes body temperature at time of admission, symptoms of heatstroke (e.g. diaphoresis and altered mental state including seizures) and hospital investigation results showing DIC, raised muscle enzymes and abnormal liver function tests (46).

Apart from the non-specific findings of hyperthermia, it is important to document natural disease as it may increase the vulnerability of an individual to hyperthermia (49,50). Depending on the circumstances, the forensic pathologist may conclude natural disease to be the main cause of death, with heat-related illness being a significant contributing factor.

Of all ancillary investigations, toxicology is the most useful. Vitreous humor biochemistry showing a dehydration pattern may also be supportive in acute deaths.

CONCLUSION

In summary, the post-mortem findings are at best corroborative. A cause of death can be determined to be due to heat stroke if there is documented body temperature of >40.6°C (105°F) and a high environmental temperature at the scene. In cases with survival, corroborative medical history is essential to make the diagnosis. If there are no data available, it has been suggested that the term "heat-related death" can be used (2).

REFERENCES

1. Epstein Y, Yanovich R. Heatstroke. *N Engl J Med* 2019; **380**: 2449–59.
2. Donoghue ER, Graham MA, Jentzen JM, et al. Criteria for the diagnosis of heat-related deaths: National Association of Medical Examiners. Position paper. National Association of Medical Examiners Ad Hoc Committee on the Definition of Heat-Related Fatalities. *Am J Forensic Med Pathol* 1997; **18(1)**: 11–14.
3. Kenny GP, Wilson TE, Flouris AD, Fujii N. Heat Exhaustion. In: Romanovsky AA (ed). *Handbook of Clinical Neurology*, Vol 157. Amsterdam: Elsevier; 2018, pp. 505–29.
4. Fouillet A, Rey G, Laurent F, et al. Excess mortality related to the August 2003 heat wave in France. *Int Arch Occup Environ Health* 2006; **80**: 16–24.
5. LoVecchio F. Heat Emergencies. In: Tintinalli JE (ed). *Tintinalli's Emergency Medicine: A Comprehensive Study Guide*, 8th ed. New York: McGraw-Hill Education; 2006, pp. 1365–71.
6. Patterson JW. *Weedon's Skin Pathology*, 5th ed. Philadelphia: Elsevier; 2019, pp. 126–7.
7. Gauer R, Meyers BK. Heat-related illnesses. *Am Fam Physician* 2019; **99(8)**: 482–9.
8. Nixdorf-Miller A, Hunsaker DM, Hunsaker JC. Hypothermia and hyperthermia medicolegal investigation of morbidity and mortality from exposure to environmental temperature extremes. *Arch Pathol Lab Med* 2006; **130**: 1297–1304.
9. Glazer JL. Heat stroke. *BMJ Best Practice* 2018; **15(9)**: .
10. Green H, Gilbert J, James R, Byard RW. An analysis of factors contributing to a series of deaths caused by exposure to high environmental temperatures. *Am J Forensic Med Pathol* 2001; **22(2)**: 196–9.
11. Bouchama A, Dehbi M, Mohamed G, et al. Prognostic factors in heat wave-related deaths. A meta-analysis. *Arch Intern Med* 2007; **167(20)**: 2170–76.
12. Khogali M. Epidemiology of heat illnesses during the Makkah Pilgrimages in Saudi Arabia. *Int J Epidemiol* 1983; **12**: 267–73.
13. Quinton RA. Certification of vehicular hyperthermia deaths in the pediatric population. *Acad Forensic Pathol* 2016; **6(4)**: 657–62.
14. Grundstein A, Null J, Meentemeyer V. Weather, geography, and vehicle-related hyperthermia in children. *Geogr Rev* 2011; **101(3)**: 353–70.
15. Duzinski SV, Barczyk AN, Wheeler TC, et al. Threat of paediatric hyperthermia in an enclosed vehicle: a year-round study. *Inj Prev* 2014; **20**: 220–5.
16. Marty W, Sigrist T, Wyler D. Temperature variations in automobiles in various weather conditions. An experimental contribution to the determination of time of death. *Am J Forensic Med Pathol* 2001; **22(3)**: 215–19.
17. Booth JN, Davis GG, Waterbor J, McGwin G. Hyperthermia deaths among children in parked vehicles: An analysis of 231 fatalities in the United States, 1999–2007. *Forensic Sci Med Pathol* 2010; **6**: 99–105.
18. Ponsonby A-L, Dwyer T, Gibbons LE, et al. Thermal environment and sudden infant death syndrome: Case-control study. *BMJ* 1992; **304**: 277–82.
19. Task Force On Sudden Infant Death Syndrome. SIDS and other sleep-related infant deaths: Updated 2016 recommendations for a safe sleeping environment. *Pediatrics* 2016; **138(5)**: 11.
20. Kortelainen M-L. Hyperthermia deaths in Finland in 1970–86. *Am J Forensic Med Pathol* 1991; **12(2)**: 115–18.
21. Zhou Y, Li L, Liu L, et al. Heat stroke deaths caused by electric blankets: Case report and review of the literature. *Am J Forensic Med Pathol* 2006; **27**: 324–7.
22. Byard RW, Riches KJ. Dehydration and heat-related death: Sweat lodge syndrome. *Am J Forensic Med Pathol* 2005; **26**: 236–9.
23. Gun R. Deaths in Australia from work-related heat stress, 2000–2015. *Int J Environ Res Public Health* 2019; **16**: 3601.
24. Bunai Y, Akaza K, Jiang W-X, Nagai A. Fatal hyperthermia associated with excited delirium during an arrest. *Leg Med* 2008; **10(6)**: 306–9.
25. Riazi S, Kraeva N, Hopkins PM. Malignant hyperthermia in the post-genomics

era: New perspectives on an old concept. *Anesthesiology* 2018; **128(1)**: 168–180.
26. Ellinas H, Albrecht MA. Malignant hyperthermia update. *Anesthesiology Clin* 2020; **38**: 165–81.
27. Kim KSM, Kriss RS, Tautz TJ. Malignant hyperthermia. A clinical review. *Adv Anesth* 2019; **37**: 35–51.
28. Tse L, Barr AM, Scarapicchia V, Vila-Rodriguez F. Neuroleptic malignant syndrome: a review from a clinically oriented perspective. *Curr Neuropharamacol* 2015; **13**: 395–406.
29. Strawn JR, Keck PE, Caroff SN. Neuroleptic malignant syndrome. *Am J Psychiatry* 2007; **164(6)**: 870–6.
30. Caroff SN, Watson CB, Rosenberg H. Drug-induced hyperthermic syndrome in psychiatry. *Clin Psychopharmacol Neurosci* 2021; **19(1)**: 1–11.
31. Francescangeli J, Karamchandani K, Powell M, Bonavia A. The serotonin syndrome: from molecular mechanisms to clinical practice. *Int J Mol Sci* 2019; **20**: 2288.
32. Boyer EW, Shannon M. The serotonin syndrome. *New Engl J Med* 2005; **352**: 1112–20.
33. Jamshidi N, Dawson A. The hot patient: Acute drug-induced hyperthermia. *Aust Prescr* 2019; **42(1)**: 24–28.
34. McCormack D, Buckley NA. Psychostimulant poisoning. *Aust Prescr* 2006; **29**: 109–111.
35. Coffey RJ, Edgar TS, Francisco GE, et al. Abrupt withdrawal from intrathecal baclofen: Recognition and management of a potentially life-threatening syndrome. *Arch Phys Med Rehabil* 2002; **83**: 735–41.
36. Sarchioto M, Ricchi V, Melis M, et al. Dyskinesia-hyperpyrexia syndrome in Parkinson's disease: A heat shock-related emergency? *Mov Disord Clin Pract* 2018; **5(5)**: 534–37.
37. Holborow A, Purnell RM, Wong JF. Beware the yellow slimming pill: fatal 2,4-dinitrophenol overdose. *BMJ Case Rep* 2016. doi:10.1136/bcr-2016-214689.
38. Griffiths A, Milne N, Ong B, Watkins T. 2,4-Dinitrophenol overdose: Everything old is new again. *J Forensic Leg Med* 2021; **79**: 102148.
39. Adato B, Dubnov-Raz G, Gips H, et al. Fatal heat stroke in children found in parked cars: autopsy findings. *Eur J Pediatr* 2016; **175**: 1249–52.
40. Hiss J, Kahan T, Kugel C. Fatal and classical exertional heat stroke: Report of four cases. *Med Sci Law* 1994; **34(4)**: 339–43.
41. Byard R. Heat-related deaths. *Forensic Sci Med Pathol* 2013; **9**: 469–70.
42. Krous HF, Nadeau JM, Fukumoto RI, et al. Environmental hyperthermic infant and early childhood death. Circumstances, pathologic changes and manner of death. *Am J Forensic Med Pathol* 2001; **22(4)**: 374–82.
43. Nadesan, Chan SP, Wong CMM. Sudden death during jungle trekking: A case of heat stroke. *Malays J Pathol* 1998; **20(1)**: 49–54.
44. Ball CG, Herath JC. Earth, air, water and fire: Histopathology of environmental death. *Acad Forensic Pathol* 2018; **8(3)**: 641–52.
45. Fineschi V, Panrese F, Turillazzi E. Heat stroke in an incubator: An immunohistochemical study in a fatal case. *Int J Legal Med* 2005; **119**: 94–97.
46. Chao TC, Sinniah R, Pakiam JE. Acute heat stroke deaths. *Pathology* 1981; **13**: 145–56.
47. Kew M, Bersohn I, Seftel H, Kent G. Liver damage in heatstroke. *Am J Med* 1970; **49**: 192–202.
48. Palmiere C, Mangin P. Hyperthermia and postmortem biochemical investigations. *Int J Legal Med* 2013; **127**: 93–102.
49. Kortelainen ML. Hyperthermia deaths in Finland in 1970–1986. *Am J Forensic Med Pathol* 1991; **12(2)**: 115–18.
50. Siegler RW. Fatal heatstroke in a young woman with previously undiagnosed Hashimoto's thyroiditis. *J Forensic Sci* 1998; **43(6)**: 1237–40.
51. Pryor RR, Bennett BL, O'Connor FG, et al. Medical evaluation for exposure extremes: Heat. *Wilderness Environ Med* 2015; **26(4 suppl)**: S69–S75.
52. Li W, Zhang L, Liang Y, et al. Sudden death due to malignant hyperthermia with a mutation of RYRI: autopsy, morphology and genetic analysis. *Forensic Sci Med Pathol* 2017; **13**: 444–9.
53. Lifschultz BD, Donoghue ER. Forensic pathology of heat- and cold-related injuries. *Clin Lab Med* 1998; **18**: 77–90.

CHAPTER

47

Electrical Deaths

Roger W. Byard

INTRODUCTION

Electric currents may have a variety of different effects, ranging from minor non-lethal shocks without any tissue damage, to lethal cardiac arrhythmias. At autopsy, there may also be quite a variation in findings depending on the type and amount of current, and the area of contact. For example, a body electrocuted in a bath may have no physical injuries compared to others where there may be findings of classical targetoid burns. In a bath, resistance is markedly reduced due to the water, which also cools the skin preventing burns (1). High-voltage discharges may present with extensive burning and even charring of the body. The variability in findings may make the autopsy evaluation difficult and the diagnosis may depend on the integration of findings with a meticulous death scene investigation (2–4).

The nature of electricity

Electricity is caused by a flow of electrons between two points that have a potential difference. The flow is termed the current and is measured in amperes, with the potential difference between the two points being measured in volts. The amount of current flow is also dependent on the resistance of the material conducting the current, which is measured in ohms (2,3). The amount of current flowing increases with increasing potential difference and decreases with increasing resistance. The direct relationship between current (amperes) and potential (volts) and the indirect relationship with resistance has been encapsulated in Ohm's law and is expressed as: amperes = volts/ohms ($A = V/R$) (3,4).

A current can only pass through the body if a circuit has been completed, with the resultant effects and physical damage depending on the type of current, in addition to the size of the current, the voltage, and the resistance. In addition, other factors involved in the outcome include the amount of contact, the route of the current through the body and the duration of the incident (5). Current usually passes from the point of contact to the nearest earthed point which is often from hand to hand or from hand to foot.

Type of current

Electrical current may be either direct (DC) where the voltage is constant and the flow of electricity is in one direction or alternating (AC) where the voltage changes with a reversal in flow of the current. DC is not as dangerous as AC which may be lethal at lower current levels as it is more likely to cause tetanic spasm of muscles with gripping of wires and has a greater chance of causing cardiac arrhythmias. It has been estimated that AC is four to six times more likely to cause a lethal episode than DC (6,7).

Components of Ohm's Law

The most significant factor in a lethal electrocution is the amount of current flow, however, amperage is clearly related to both voltage and resistance. A current as low as 40 mA may result in loss of consciousness, with death occurring with currents of 50–80 mA or greater, after several seconds of exposure (7). The effects of different levels of current flow are summarized in Table 47.1.

Voltage may also have an effect, with deaths potentially occurring at low-voltages (<1000 V), high voltages (>1000 V) or with lightning (5,8). Contact with very low-voltages (i.e. <80 V) is very rarely lethal, although this may not be the case if there is prolonged contact, or there is increased moisture in the form of humidity which may decrease resistance (9,10). Most deaths are associated with voltages of 110 to 380 V which are typically found in home and work environments (11).

Deaths occurring from high voltages do not require the victim to come into contact with a conductor, as

TABLE 47.1 Clinical manifestations of electrical current (4)

1 mA	Barely perceptible tingle
16 mA	Current that can be grasped and released
16–20 mA	Muscular paralysis
20–50 mA	Respiratory paralysis
50–100 mA	Ventricular fibrillation
>2000 mA	Ventricular standstill

DOI: 10.1201/9781003138754-49

arcing through the air may occur. Such arcs may be associated with the generation of quite high temperatures (up to 5000°C) and so fatal mechanisms can involve either DC flow and/or deep burns (2). Other factors which may cause or contribute to death include falls if a victim is thrown because of muscle contractions/spasms.

The higher the resistance of a material, the lower the current flow will be for a similar voltage. Within the body, there is a wide range in levels of resistance, with the lowest being found in blood, mucous membranes, muscles and nerves compared to the highest in tendons, fat and bones (2,3). This means that different currents will traverse the body associated with the same voltage, depending on the specific tissues lying between entrance and exit points. The general internal resistance of the body has been estimated to lie between 500 and 1000 ohms. The skin may, however, act as a confounding factor, with dry skin having a resistance of 100 000 ohms, in contrast to skin that has been soaked by water or sweat having a resistance of only 1000 ohms (4,8,12). Calloused skin of the palms may have an even higher resistance. The low resistance and moisture of thin mucus membranes may put children at particular risk of severe orofacial injuries and/or death if they bite electrical leads or put them into their mouths (13,14).

Other factors

The longer there is contact between a victim and a circuit, the greater the chances are of a lethal event. For this reason, deaths have occurred with a potential as low as 24 volts when there has been contact for a number of hours (2). Conversely, a high-voltage electrocution may be survived if the victim was thrown away from the circuit by muscle spasms, as the duration of the contact is limited. On occasion, muscle spasm may have the opposite effect and prolong contact if the fingers flex and grip a conductor (2).

The route of an electrical current through the body may also have a significant effect, with lethal mechanisms more likely to be generated if current passes through the heart or brain (15,16).

Careful evaluation of the death scene is required as environmental factors may play a significant role in determining the lethality of a shock. For example, an individual in rubber shoes standing in a shower with an attached faulty earth line may not experience a shock that could be lethal for someone standing beside the shower on the wet floor in bare feet.

Lightning

Lightning may result in a specific form of electrocution. It represents a sudden discharge of static electricity during a storm that lasts between 0.0001 and 0.001 of a second and has currents of between 10 000 and 200 000 amperes, and voltages of between 20 million and 1 billion. Temperatures of up to 30 000°C may be generated (17,18).

Injuries occur from a variety of different mechanisms involving direct strikes, contact (when lightning hits an object that the victim was touching), side splash or flash (when the victim was standing beside a struck object), ground current (from current in the ground passing up into the victim) or blast injuries (17,19). A victim may be so highly charged from a lightning strike that they discharge an upward "streamer" (18). When a flash-over phenomenon occurs, electrical current from lightning passes over the surface of the body vaporizing surface water causing blast damage to clothing and shoes (4) which may suggest alternative possibilities to investigators such as blunt force trauma from a motor vehicle accident (20).

Rarely, deaths may occur indoors when a telephone is being used, with approximately one case/year occurring in the United States. Survivors may have deafness from ruptured tympanic membranes, ataxia, transient vertigo, neurologic deficits and convulsions (21–23). The effects of lightning are quite unpredictable with reports of only one person in a group that was struck suffering lethal injuries (24).

Lethal mechanisms

Deaths from electrocution may be caused directly by the electrical energy of the current, or by the secondary effects of burns or blunt trauma from falls initiated by the shock (12). Rapidly occurring deaths usually result from the passage of current through the body (25) with delayed deaths resulting from multiorgan complications due to the initial event (26).

Ventricular fibrillation: This is thought to be the most common cause of death occurring after electrical current passes through the heart. The exact etiology of the lethal arrhythmia is unclear; however, it is most likely due to the direct effect of current on cardiac myocytes, nodal tissues and conduction tracts (2).

Respiratory paralysis: This appears to be much less common than cardiac arrhythmias and occurs when current passes through the chest causing marked contraction of respiratory muscles, such as the intercostal muscles and diaphragm. This leads to anoxia with cardiac arrest and occurs more often with high-voltage contacts (3).

Respiratory center paralysis: This refers to a centrally mediated mechanism caused by current passing through the respiratory centers of the brainstem resulting in neuronal disruption. It may be induced directly by the electrical current or secondarily by heating (3).

Blunt force trauma: This may occur if a victim is thrown backward violently by muscle contractions induced by the shock.

Drowning: Incapacitation by electrocution may lead to drowning if a victim was already immersed in, or fell into, a body of water such as a swimming pool (26).

Findings at autopsy

Careful external examination of the body is required in all cases of suspected electrocution with meticulous examination of the hands and feet, including the palms, soles and web spaces. The upper extremity is most often the primary contact site (27,28). Burns of the fingers and palms may be obscured if finger flexion is maintained by rigor mortis (Figure 47.1). There are three main groups of injuries: those due to direct tissue damage from the electrical current, those caused by heat, and those due to trauma from muscle contractions with bone fractures, or from falls (29,30).

Skin

As the skin represents the interface between the victim and environmental forces, it often has the most useful markings to give an indication of possible causes of death. In the case of electrocution, the most typical lesions appear with low-voltage contacts as burns at entry and exit points. However, it should be noted that they are only found in 57 to 83 percent of cases as their development depends on a variety of factors including the amount of current, the voltage and the time of exposure. For example, in the case of a low current passing for only a short period of time, there may be no cutaneous markings (31,32).

If good contact has been maintained for some time, the electrical current will cause local heating of the skin with vaporization of fluid and blister formation. Once the current ceases, the blister will collapse with splitting of the epidermis. This results in a small, circumscribed and indurated crater with a gray or black center (from charring), surrounded by a ring of pallor from arteriolar spasm and coagulative necrosis (Figures 47.2 and 47.3). There may also be a peripheral zone of hyperemia with small vesicles (2). If the contact has been less firm and the voltage is higher, spark burns may occur due to arcing of current with small nodules formed from melted keratin. These two types of lesions often appear together but may also be produced after death. If death has occurred rapidly before a tissue inflammatory response has had time to occur it may not be possible, therefore, to separate ante- and post-mortem injuries (2,3).

It is often difficult to differentiate an entry from an exit burn, however, occasionally there may be a mark that matches the size and shape of a conductor such as a linear burn from a live wire, or evenly spaced burns from an electric plug (15). Patterned burns targeting specific parts of the body such as the genitalia may indicate torture or homicide.

Metallization occurs when tissue interacts with the metal of a conductor to form salts that deposit on the surface of the skin. If electrical arcing occurs, the skin may be coated with a layer of vaporized metal. Metallic residues may be identified chemically or by scanning electron microscopy (33).

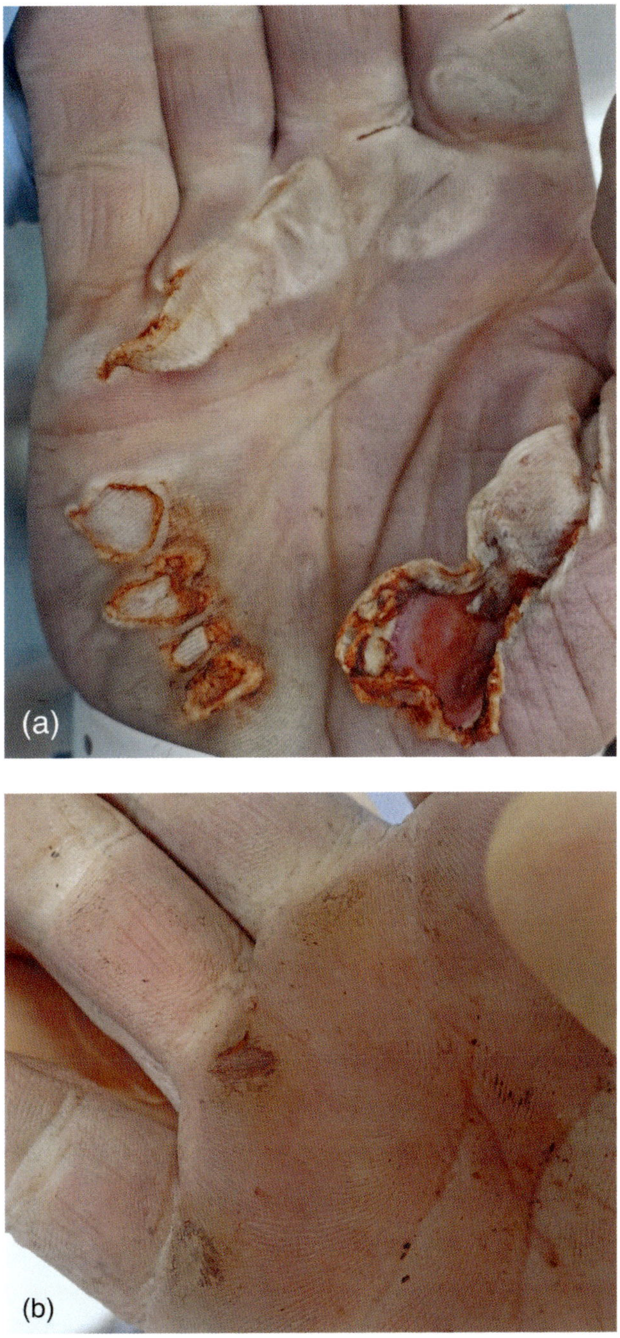

47.1 Opening fingers that are fixed and flexed from rigor mortis may reveal obvious deep electrical burns (a) or quite subtle lesions (b).

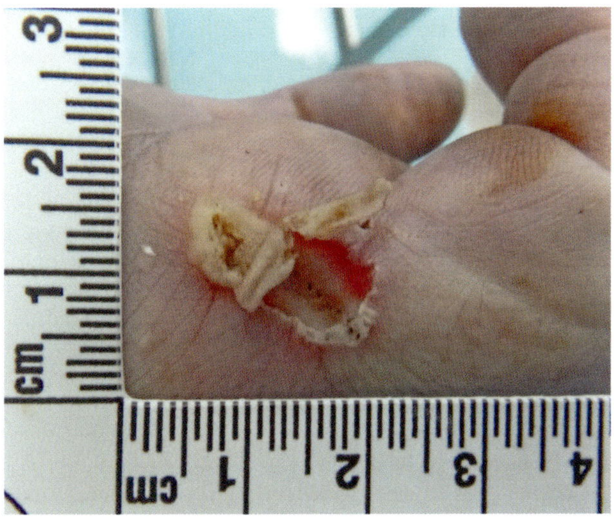

47.2 A typical electrical burn of the side of the hand showing central charring with surrounding pallor and a rim of hyperemic tissues with skin sloughing.

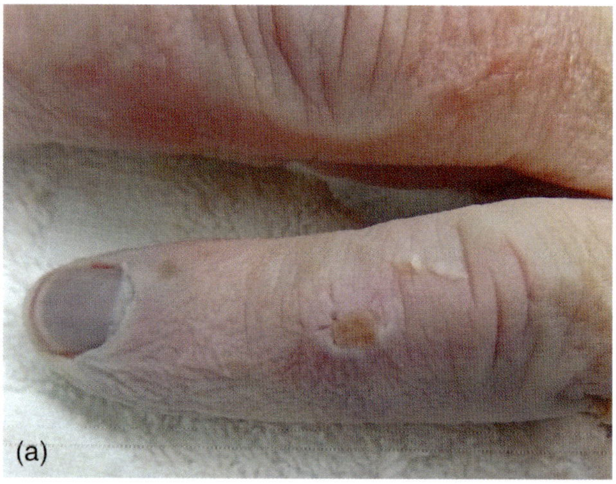

(a)

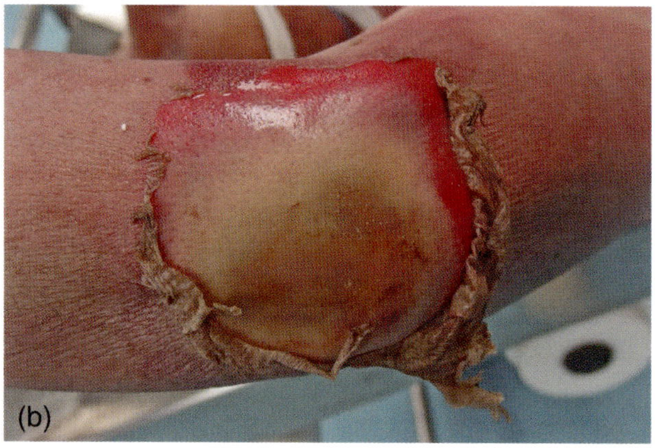

(b)

47.3 Electrical contact burns may be quite small and subtle **(a)** or much larger and more obvious **(b)**.

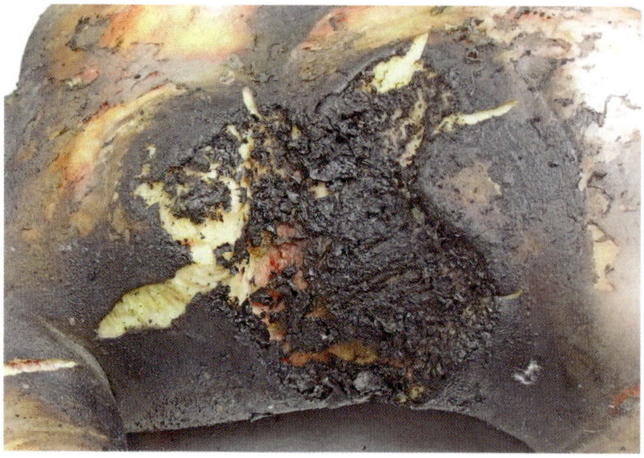

47.4 Extensive deep burning and charring characteristic of high voltage electrocution. In this case, contact had been made with high voltage overhead power lines.

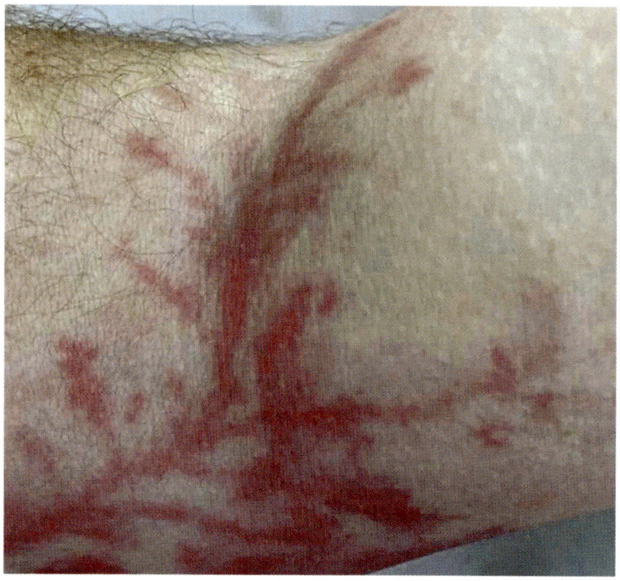

47.5 A typical Lichtenberg figure in a victim of lightning strike showing the characteristic ferning pattern associated with dermal erythema.

Deep burns with charring characterize high-voltage electrocutions that may be present on multiple areas of the body (Figure 47.4). Such lesions are often accompanied by spark burns from multiple current arcs causing a characteristic "crocodile skin" effect.

Lightning causes a specific type of cutaneous marking, so-called Lichtenberg figures, ferning or lightning prints. These consist of multiple, transient red-to-brown linear areas of erythema that develop within an hour and usually disappear by 24 to 36 hours (17) (Figure 47.5). Histology demonstrates nothing specific but dermal and subcutaneous vascular congestion. Red-cell extravasation appears unlikely as the lesions dissipate relatively quickly and so it is more probable that this is due to associated punctate burns from arcing (17,24). Linear burns that follow skin creases are more common than Lichtenberg figures. There may also be singeing of the hair and retinal detachments following a lightning strike (18).

Conjunctival and internal petechiae have been reported in up to three quarters of cases of electrocution in some series (31,32) but this is not always the case.

Histologically, the effects of electrical injuries are due to heat with no specific diagnostic features due to the current, despite claims in older textbooks. There may be a sharp border with normal skin with separation of the cells of the lower epidermis with microvesicle formation and coagulative necrosis extending into the dermis (15). Although cell nuclei show pyknosis and elongation with alignment, so called "nuclear streaming", this is no longer considered pathognomonic as it may be found in other types of burns and in hypothermia (34).

Other organs

While it has been stated that the heart may have scattered foci of myocardial necrosis with contraction bands and subendocardial hemorrhages, these are not specific findings (35). Injury to vascular intima and media may lead to later thrombosis, aneurysm formation or rupture if there is survival (12,29).

Falls precipitated by electricity-induced muscle contractions may be associated with visceral, soft-tissue and bony injuries. Fractures of long bones and vertebrae as well as joint dislocations may also be due to simple muscle spasms (4,30,36,37). In cases of marked heating from high-voltage electrocution there may be "osseous pearls" on the cortices of the burnt bones (15). Contraction bands in skeletal muscle are a reasonably common but non-specific finding (38) with intramuscular hemorrhage from prolonged current-induced muscle contractions rarely being observed (29). Changes within the brain are also non-specific and include petechial hemorrhages, edema, cellular vacuolization and demyelination (12,29). With survival, there may be long-term neurologic sequelae that include neurologic, cognitive and psychological impairments (39).

Manner of death

Accidents

The most common manner of death in electrocution is accidental, with it being the fifth leading cause of occupation-related death in the United States. Most often, the victim is a young male with death occurring during the summer months, associated with increased levels of outdoor activities. Possibly exertional sweating lowers skin resistance (11,32,40,41). Accidental electrocutions may occur more often in countries with suboptimal housing and electrical standards (15).

Low-voltage accidents are most often encountered in a domestic or work setting with high-voltage accidents occurring more often outdoors or with work-related activities. Autoerotic fatalities involving the use of an electrical stimulator are a distinct and unusual subgroup of accidental electrical deaths (42,43).

Suicide

Despite its ready availability in most domestic settings, suicide by electric current is uncommon. Generally, there are two groups: the first consists of individuals with a working knowledge of electricity such as electrical engineers or electricians who often use complicated time-delay systems (44), sometimes with drugs. The second group consists of individuals who opportunistically use electricity to suicide, such as those who drop a device such as a hairdryer or lamp into bath water (45,46) (Figures 47.6 and 47.7). With the use of safety switches this does not, however, always work (47). Deaths from electrocution in baths has been noted to sometimes be associated with unusual patterns of decomposition (48).

Homicide

Homicidal electrocution in most forensic practices is exceedingly rare although two homicides were found in 37 cases, and one homicide in 220 cases of electrical fatalities in two studies (8,31).

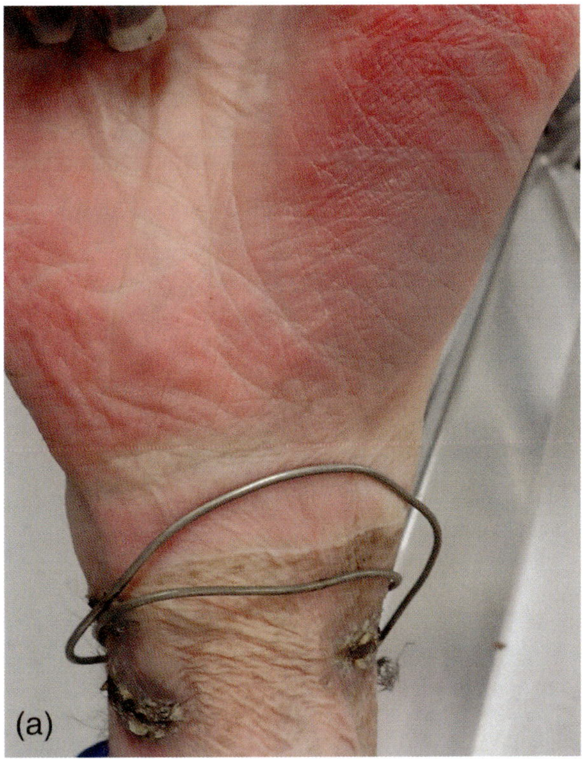

(a)

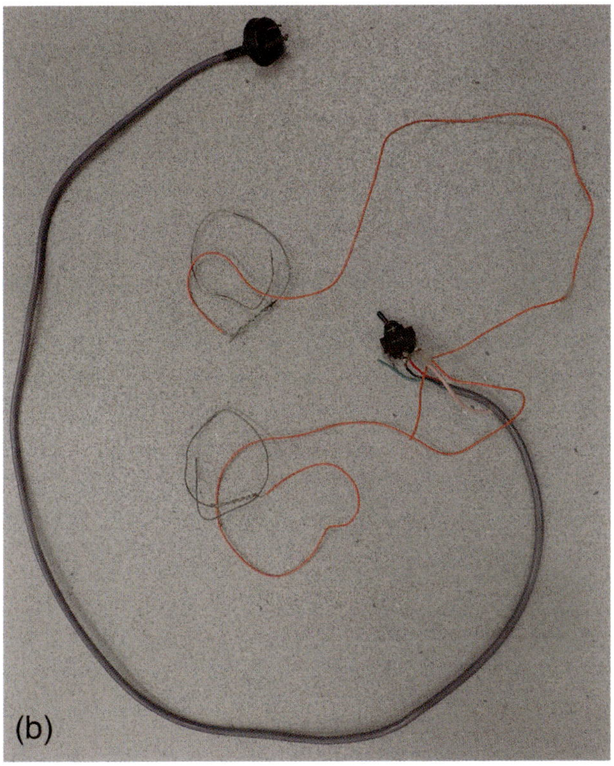

(b)

47.6 Wire wrapped around the wrist in a case of suicidal electrocution (a). Removal of the wires showed them connected to a plug (b) which was found inserted into a live socket at the scene.

The investigation of electrical deaths

The investigation of possible electrocution deaths may be an exceedingly complex activity which requires a team approach from the start. The death scene, once made safe, needs to be carefully documented with photographic/LIDAR documentation of the body, its surroundings and any nearby electrical devices, outlets or conductors (Figure 47.8). Workplace and electrical experts will need to provide a complete analysis of the

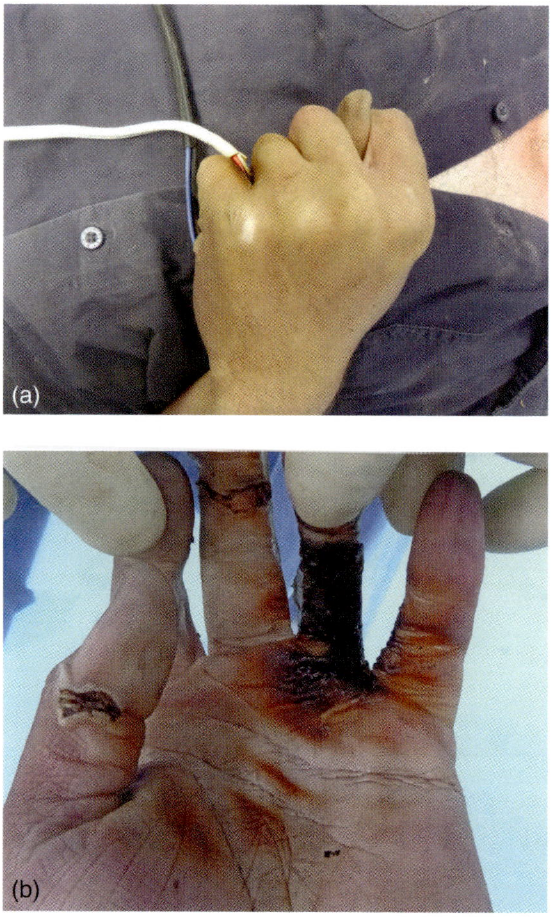

47.7 Live wires held in the hand in another suicidal electrocution (a). Opening of the fingers revealed typical electrical burns (b).

electrical circuitry within, and connected to, the building where the decedent was located, in addition to any equipment that was near the body, or that was being operated (8). The autopsy examination should include careful examination of the clothes and body surfaces for subtle electrical burns. Burns on clothing may correspond to metallic conductors and torn/burnt clothing and shoes may suggest a lightning strike (49). It is important to be aware that very rarely other conditions may convincingly mimic targetoid electrical burns (50).

The purpose of the pathological examination is also to look for evidence of underlying natural diseases such as cardiovascular conditions or epilepsy that may have predisposed the victim to coming in contact with live circuitry or may have reduced the victim's capacity to self-rescue or survive an electric shock. Toxicological studies of blood and fluids are essential, particularly in cases of workplace electrocutions.

The most problematic cases are often those where a body is presented to autopsy with a history of "collapse" or being "found dead", with no suggestion that there may have been an electrocution. If this is suspected, investigating officers will have to return to the scene and check for electrical devices. A history of screaming, swearing, or shouting followed by collapse may suggest that electrocution has occurred, with early development of rigor mortis occurring due to tetany from an electrical current (8).

Other problems arise when clear-cut cases of electrocution do not have any pathological findings, as in bathtub suicides where an unsubmerged body is found in a bath full of water beside a submerged electrical device. The scene findings of a suicide note, and a secured environment may be paramount in establishing the diagnosis.

47.8 Securing the workspace where an accidental electrocution occurred is essential to enable full testing of all electrical devices.

Other cases such as a middle-aged electrician with significant ischemic heart disease being found dead in a roof space should always raise the possibility of electrocution and electrical burns should be assiduously sought. As noted above, they may be quite small and hidden beneath clenched fingers from rigor mortis.

Certain cases may be even more difficult. For example, where a worker in a machine room in an industrial complex is found dead with typical skin markings of electrocution and no other traumatic injuries, toxicological substances or underlying organic illnesses are found that could have caused death. Thus, death is reasonably attributed to electrocution, but occupational health and safety investigations of the victim's and surrounding machinery reveal no faults. One possibility is survival for some time after an electric shock that may have occurred in some other part of the plant or that the fault was only intermittent. Clearly, the possibility of a live hazard being undetected is unacceptable as a not insignificant part of identifying electrocution as a cause of death lies in the need to protect others who may be exposed to the same dangerous environment or unsafe piece of equipment.

CONCLUSION

The assessment at autopsy of possible electrocution is complicated by the non-specificity and subtlety of lesions. Unfortunately, despite careful documentation and analysis of the death scene, assessment of the electrical safety of the building and any electrical equipment that was being used, and meticulous examination of all body surfaces, the answers may still not be straightforward. Electrocution should always, however, be suspected in any unusual work-related death.

REFERENCES

1. Goodson ME. Electrically induced deaths involving water immersion. *Am J Forensic Med Pathol* 1993; **14:** 330–3.
2. Wick R, Byard RW. Electrocution and the Autopsy. In: Tsokos M (ed). *Forensic Pathology Reviews,* Vol 5. Totowa, NJ: Humana Press; 2008, pp 53–66.
3. Wick R, Gilbert JD, Simpson E, Byard RW. Fatal electrocution in adults: A 30-year study. *Med Sci Law* 2006; **46:** 166–72.
4. Koumbourlis AC. Electrical injuries. *Crit Care Med* 2002; **30:** S424–30.
5. Mellen PF, Weedn VW, Kao G. Electrocution: A review of 155 cases with emphasis on human factors. *J Forensic Sci* 1992; **37:** 1016–22.
6. Budnick LD. Bathtub-related electrocutions in the United States, 1979–1982. *JAMA* 1984; **252:** 918–20.
7. Saukko P, Knight B. Electrical Fatalities. In: *Knight's Forensic Pathology*. 3rd ed. London: Arnold; 2004, pp 326–38.
8. Wright RK, Davis JH. The investigation of electrical deaths: A report of 220 fatalities. *J Forensic Sci* 1980; **25:** 514–21.
9. Marc B, Baudry F, Douceron H, et al. Suicide by electrocution with low-voltage current. *J Forensic Sci* 2000; **45:** 216–22.
10. Peng Z, Shikui C. Study on electrocution death by low-voltage. *Forensic Sci Int* 1995; **76:** 115–19.
11. Fatovich DM. Electrocution in Western Australia, 1976–1990. *Med J Aus* 1992; **157:** 762–4.
12. Leibovici D, Shemer J, Shapira SC. Electrical injuries: Current concepts. *Injury* 1995; **26:** 623–7.
13. Byard RW, Hanson KA, Gilbert JD, et al. Death due to electrocution in childhood and early adolescence. *J Paediatr Child Health* 2003; **39:** 46–8.
14. Yamazaki M, Bai H, Tun Z, et al. An electrocution death of an infant who had received an electrical shock from an uncovered oval shaped lamp switch in his mouth while in a hospital. *J Forensic Sci* 1997; **42:** 151–4.
15. al-Alousi LM. Homicide by electrocution. *Med Sci Law* 1990; **30:** 239–46.
16. Anders S, Tsokos M, Püschel K. Nachweis der Stromwirkung und des Stromweges im Körper. *Rechtsmedizin* 2002; **1:** 1–9.
17. Byard RW, Thu M, Gilbert JD. Cutaneous manifestations of lightning strike: Lichtenberg figures. *Forensic Sci Med Pathol* 2017; **13:** 390–3.
18. Blumenthal R. Lightning fatalities on the South African Highveld. A retrospective descriptive study for the period 1997–2000. *Am J Forensic Pathol* 2005; **26:** 66–9.
19. Ritneour AE, Morton MJ, McManus JG, et al. Lightning injury: A review. *Burns* 2008; **34:** 585–94.
20. Prahlow J, Byard RW, (eds). Electrical deaths. In: *An Atlas of Forensic Pathology*. New York: Springer Publishers; 2012, pp. 715–42.
21. Qureshi NH. Indirect lightning strike via telephone wire. *Injury* 1995; **26:** 629–30.
22. Andrews CJ. Telephone-related lightning injury. *Med J Aust* 1992; **157:** 823–6.
23. Kristensen S, Tveterås K. Lightning-induced acoustic rupture of the tympanic membrane: A report of two cases. *J Laryngol Otol* 1985; **99(7):** 711–13.
24. Resnik BI, Wetli CV. Lichtenberg figures. *Am J Forensic Med Pathol* 1996; **17:** 99–102.
25. Lee WR. The mechanisms of death from electric shock. *Med Sci Law* 1965; **18:** 23–28.
26. Bailey B, Forget S, Gaudreault P. Prevalence of potential risk factors in victims of electrocution. *Forensic Sci Int* 2001; **123:** 58–62.
27. Liu S, Yu Y, Huang Q, et al. Electrocution-related mortality: A review of 71 deaths by low-voltage electrical current in Guangdong, China, 2001–2010. *Am J Forensic Med Pathol* 2014; **35:** 193–6.
28. Von Caues S, Herbst CI, Wadee SA. A retrospective review of fatal electrocution cases at Tygerberg Forensic Pathology Services, Cape Town, South Africa, over the 5-year period 1 January 2008–31 December 2012. *S Afr Med J* 2018; **108:** 1042–5.
29. Anders S, Schulz F, Tsokos M. Ausgeprägte intramuskuläre Hämorrhagien vitaler Genese bei letaler suizidaler Strombeibringung. *Rechtsmedizin* 2000; **10:** 105–9.
30. Martinez JA, Nguyen T. Electrical injuries. *South Med J* 2000; **93:** 1165–8.
31. Karger B, Süggeler O, Brinkmann B. Electrocution: Autopsy study with emphasis on "electrical petechiae". *Forensic Sci Int* 2002; **126:** 210–13.
32. Hyldgaard L, Søndergaard E, Leth P. Autopsies of fatal electrocutions in Jutland. *Scand J Forensic Sci* 2004; **1:** 8–12.
33. Mondello C, Micali A, Cardia L, et al. Forensic tools for the diagnosis of electrocution death: Case study and literature review. *Med Leg J* 2018; **86:** 89–99.
34. Anders S, Matschke J, Tsokos M. Internal current mark in a case of suicide by electrocution. *Am J Forensic Med Pathol* 2001; **22:** 370–3.
35. Favia M, Mele F, Introna F, De Donno A. Morphological cardiac changes in electrocution deaths: A literature review. *Med Sci Law* 2021; **61(suppl):** 130–5.
36. Nekkanti S, Vijay C, Theja JSS, et al. An unusual case of simultaneous bilateral neck of femur fracture following electrocution injury: A case report and review of literature. *Orthop Case Rep* 2016; **6:** 70–2.
37. Bachhal V, Goni V, Taneja A, et al. Bilateral four-part anterior fracture dislocation of the shoulder: A case report and review of literature. *Bull NYU Hosp Jt Dis* 2012; **79(4):** 268–72.
38. Püschel K, Brinkmann B, Lieske K. Ultrastructural alterations of skeletal muscles after electric shock. *Am J Forensic Med Pathol* 1985; **6:** 296–300.
39. Yiannopoulou KG, Papagiannis GI, Triantafyllou AI, et al. Neurological and neurourological complications of

electrical injuries. *Neurol Neurochir Pol* 2021; **55**: 12–23.
40. Taylor AJ, McGwin G Jr, Davis GG, et al. Occupational electrocutions in Jefferson County, Alabama. *Occup Med* 2002; **52**: 102–6.
41. Taylor AJ, McGwin G Jr, Valent F, Rue LW 3rd. Fatal occupational electrocutions in the United States. *Inj Prev* 2002; **8**: 306–12.
42. Klintschar M, Grabuschnigg P, Beham A. Death from electrocution during autoerotic practice: Case report and review of the literature. *Am J Forensic Med Pathol* 1998; **19**: 190–3.
43. Shields LBE, Hunsaker DM, Hunsaker JC 3rd, et al. Atypical autoerotic death: Part II. *Am J Forensic Med Pathol* 2005; **26**: 53–62.
44. Chan P, Doflou JJ. Suicidal electrocution in Sydney: a 10-year case review. *J Forensic Sci* 2008; **53**: 455–9.
45. Bligh-Glover WZ, Miller FP, Balraj EK. Two cases of suicidal electrocution. *Am J Forensic Pathol* 2004; **25**: 255–8.
46. Fernando R, Liyanage S. Suicide by electrocution. *Med Sci Law* 1990; **30**: 219–20.
47. Byard RW, Williams D, James RA, Gilbert JD. Diagnostic issues in unusual asphyxial deaths. *J Clin Forensic Med* 2001; **8**: 214–17.
48. Fernando T, Winskog C, Byard RW. An unusual pattern of decomposition associated with suicidal electrocution in the bath. *J Forensic Sci* 2013; **58**: 1085–7.
49. Cherington M, Kurtzman R, Krider EP, Yarnell PR. Mountain medical mystery. Unwitnessed death of a healthy young man, caused by lightning. *Am J Forensic Med Pathol* 2001; **22**: 296–8.
50. Byard RW. Infiltrating carcinoma of the breast mimicking electrocution. *Forensic Sci Med Pathol* 2010; **6**: 71–2.

CHAPTER

48

Elder Abuse

Kim A. Collins and Julie Howe

INTRODUCTION

The World Health Organization (WHO) and the Center for Disease Control and Prevention (CDC) define an elder as a person who is 60 years of age or older. By 2050, 22 percent of the global population will be over 60 years of age (1). This equates to approximately two billion people. With recent advances in medicine and technology, people are living longer and living well. As of 2022, the life expectancy in the United States was 79 years; 76.1 years for men and 81.1 years for women (1). Unfortunately, many elders are abused, occurring in approximately one out of every six. Elder abuse was first described in 1975 when simultaneous reports of "granny battering" appeared (2–4). The American Medical Association defines elder abuse as an act or omission that results in harm or threatened harm to the health or welfare of an elder. Another definition is that elder abuse is any abuse or neglect of a person aged 60 years or older by a caregiver or another person in a relationship involving an expectation of trust that threatens his or her health or safety (5–8).

Six forms of elder abuse exist in the medical and scientific literature: neglect, physical abuse, sexual abuse, psychological abuse, financial and material exploitation, and violation of rights. This chapter will focus on neglect, physical abuse and sexual abuse (Figure 48.1) (1,9–11).

The aging body

To accurately assess signs of abuse in an elder, one must understand changes in the body that occur with aging. These changes may be due to the aging process itself, organic diseases, medications and/or therapies. In addition to other systems, the systems of the body that are particularly significant when examining elders are the skin and integument, musculoskeletal, urinary, gastrointestinal (GI) and the nervous systems.

Skin

The skin becomes more fragile with age. The epidermal thickness decreases and the epidermal-dermal interface flattens as dermal mucopolysaccharides and collagen decrease. The elastic and collagen fibers also become stiffer with decreased elasticity. Skin moisture decreases as the number of sweat glands reduce. The dermal vessels not only become more fragile but their number decreases. There is also a loss of subdermal adipose tissue (Figure 48.1).

Musculoskeletal and soft tissues

The muscles of the body atrophy and lose strength with a decrease in the number of myocytes and decreased regeneration. This is termed sarcopenia. Adipose tissue throughout the body also decreases. There is a reduction in cortical and trabecular bone with an increase in adipose tissue in the bone marrow (12). Decreased bone formation by osteoblasts and increased bone resorption leads to decreased bone density, osteopenia and osteoarthritis (12). This bone resorption also occurs around the teeth. Inactivity, decreased estrogen, decreased vitamin D production and decreased absorption of calcium lead to degenerative changes. Joint flexibility also decreases.

Gastrointestinal

Elders have a decreased sense of taste and smell, early satiety, and decreased GI mobility. Xerostomia, or dry mouth is common as the salivary glands atrophy. Certain medications can also result in xerostomia. Elders also have a decreased gag reflex and oromotor reflex. Within the stomach, there is a decrease in enzyme levels and gastric acid resulting in reduced absorption of nutrients including calcium, folate, iron, and vitamin B12 (13). Peristalsis is decreased, as is colonic water absorption. The liver decreases in size by 20 to 24 percent with a decreased hepatocyte ability to regenerate (13). There is also decreased hepatic perfusion. All of these factors may alter drug metabolism.

Urinary

The elder kidney has a decreased number of nephrons with hypertrophy of the remainder. Glomerulosclerosis, arteriosclerosis, tubular atrophy and interstitial fibrosis are also seen (13). This can result in decreased water absorption, sodium loss and decreased ability to concentrate urine. Decreased renal clearance of drugs can also be a problem.

DOI: 10.1201/9781003138754-50

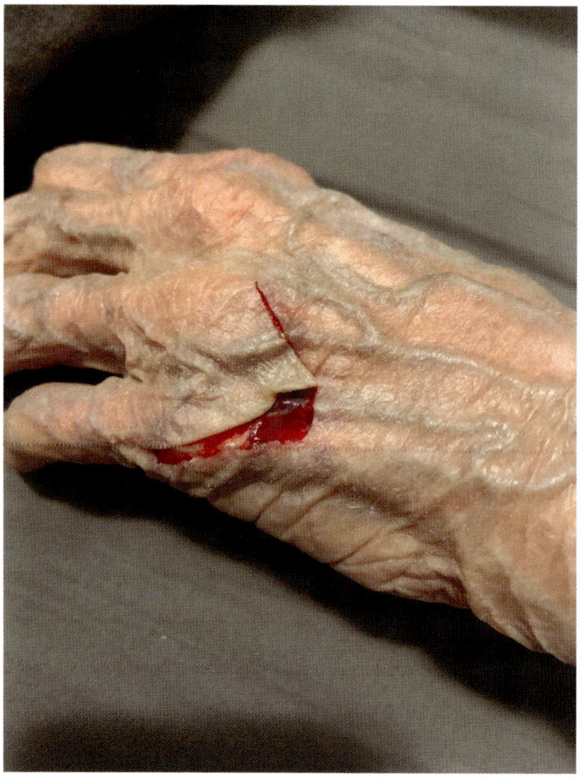

48.1 Laceration to dorsum of the hand after minor trauma.

TABLE 48.1 Signs suspicious for elder physical neglect
Decreased body weight
Decreased overall body adipose tissue
Skeletal muscle atrophy
Alopecia, brittle hair
Dental caries, periodontal disease, ill-fitting dentures
Poor hygiene
Pressure sore(s), especially untreated
Scaphoid abdomen
Protruding ribs and iliac crests
Winging scapula
Protruding occiput
Thin neck
Protruding joints with wrinkled skin
Wrinkled buttocks
Sunken orbits
Sticky serosal surfaces
Empty GI tract
Distended gallbladder
Fecal impaction – fecoliths
Reduced skin turgor, "tenting"

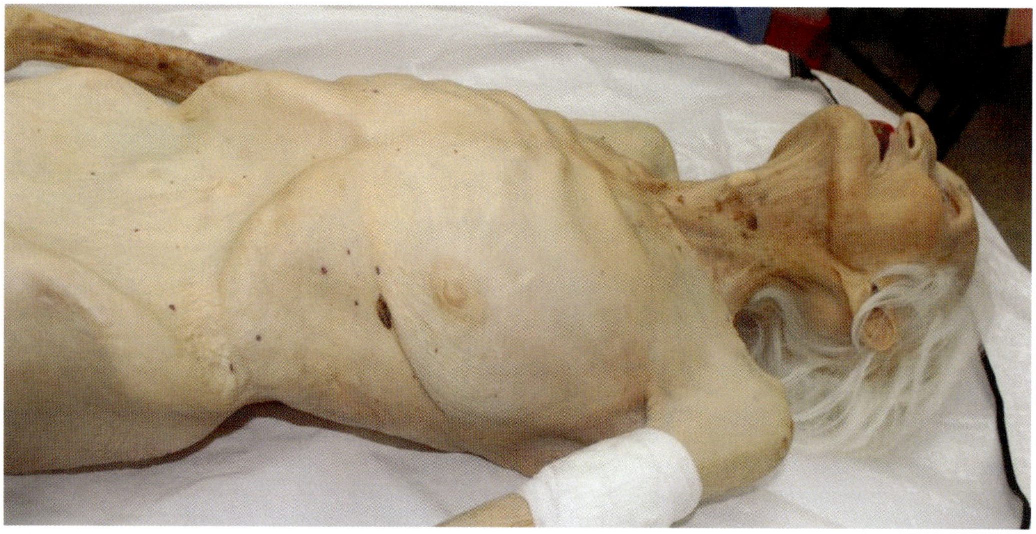

48.2 A case of starvation and malnutrition with scaphoid abdomen and prominence of ribs.

Nervous system

With age, the brain decreases in volume and weight, and in certain areas there is a decrease in the number of neurons and neuronal size. There is gray matter thinning and reduction of white matter (14,15). The peripheral nervous system is affected by diseases such as diabetes mellitus. Elders have decreased proprioception, so their gait, balance and skilled motor movements are impaired (13). Elders also have impaired temperature perception and regulation. Heat production is decreased, and cutaneous temperature control is impaired due to decreased numbers of dermal blood vessels. Also, vasodilation and vasoconstriction are decreased as is the shivering response. Visually, impaired depth perception and contrast sensitivity is noted (16). Elders experience loss of hearing acuity, especially high frequencies. Stiffening of the tympanic membrane and ossicular chain result in conductive changes (13).

Neglect

The most common form of elder abuse is neglect. Neglect is the failure to provide the basic care, goods and/or services which are necessary to ensure physical and psychological/emotional comfort (11,12). It is also defined as the failure of a caregiver or other responsible person to provide for an elder's basic physical, emotional, or social needs or failure to protect them from harm. Neglect can be active or passive. Active neglect is the willful failure to provide care. Passive neglect is the non-willful failure to provide care owing to the caregiver's ignorance, lack of skills, or his/her own failing health.

Elder neglect can manifest itself as starvation, malnutrition, dehydration, lack of medical treatment, poor hygiene and poor environmental hygiene.

Starvation is a condition marked by a severe lack of both nutrients and energy intake. Malnutrition is the lack of a proper balanced nutrient intake. Not only must a healthy diet be provided but it must be in the proper form such as soft, pureed, diabetic or assisted feeding. Dehydration results from a lack of proper body fluids. This can be due to lack of intake or excessive loss. The individual may not be provided enough hydration or hyperthermia/exposure may result in increased losses (Figure 48.2).

Poor hygiene may or may not be fatal. It is, however, a red flag for failure to provide adequate care and often accompanies other forms of neglect. Poor environmental hygiene encompasses infestation, dirty linen/clothes, squalor and filth and is usually associated with darkness and isolation.

A lack of medical care includes a poor diet based on a medical condition, lack of medication, lack of seeking medical treatment and neglecting wounds. Such wounds include pressure sores, also known as decubitus ulcers (Figures 48.3 and 48.4). It is reported that 95 percent of neglect victims have pressure sores (18). The pressure sore is a lesion of degenerating skin and underlying tissue caused by pressure on an area of decreased circulation resulting in ischemia and hypoxia to tissues. Pressure sores develop in the elder because of immobility or prolonged positioning, incontinence (urine and/or fecal), friction and shearing and are enhanced by peripheral vascular disease, venous stasis, diabetes mellitus, cachexia and malnutrition. Common areas of development are the sacral region, over the ribs, over the iliac crests, inner knees, heels, ankles and occiput (19–21). These are areas

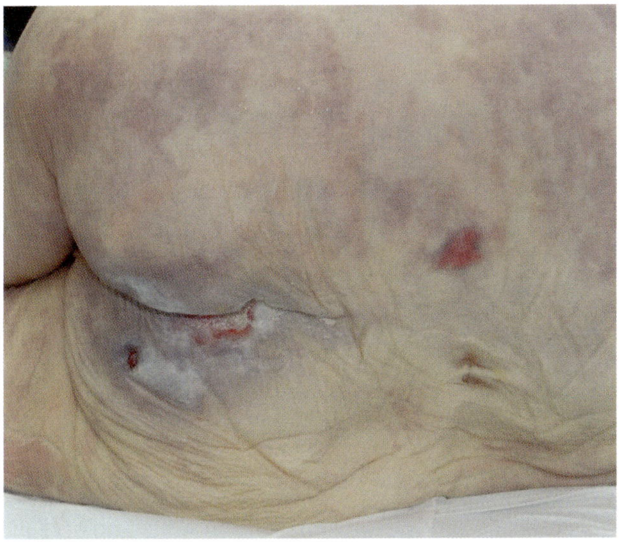

48.3 Pressure sore of the sacral area.

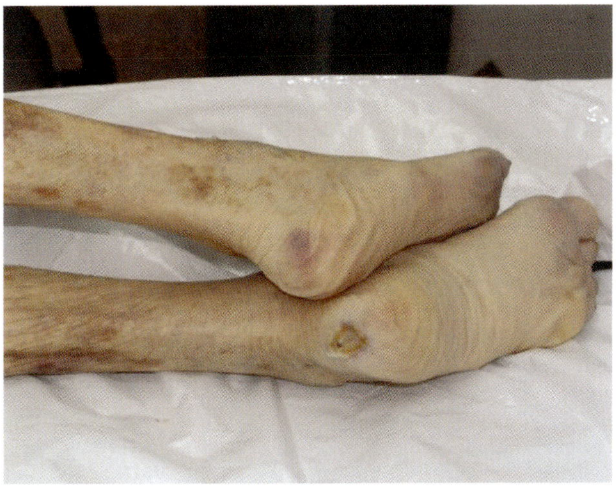

48.4 Pressure sore of the sacral area.

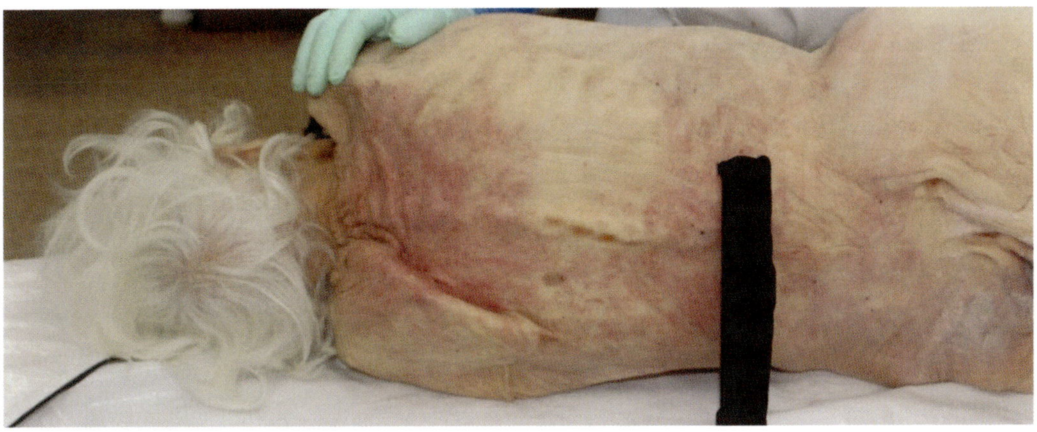

48.5 A thin elder with no pressure sores showing that pressure sores are not always inevitable.

of bony prominence especially in the underweight elder. Pressure sores are graded on a 1–4 scale (Table 48.2).

Preventative measures and treatment include repositioning every 2–3 hours, special mattresses, padding over prone areas, frequent changes of diapers and linens and proper wound treatment. Grades 3 and 4 are difficult to heal. However, it should be noted that pressure sores are not always inevitable (Figure 48.5). Also, these sores may be colonized with microorganisms leading to abscesses, osteomyelitis, bacteremia, pneumonia and sepsis (Figure 48.6). The mortality of a grade 4 pressure sore is approximately 50 percent (18–21).

TABLE 48.2 Pressure sore grades (18)

Grade 1	Non-blanchable erythema without a break in the skin
Grade 2	Superficial epidermal and dermal loss; partial thickness loss no deeper than the dermis; intact subcutaneous tissue
Grade 3	Full thickness involving the subcutaneous tissue
Grade 4	Ulceration, full thickness with loss of the skin and subcutaneous tissue and exposure of the skeletal muscle, tendon and/or bone and cartilage

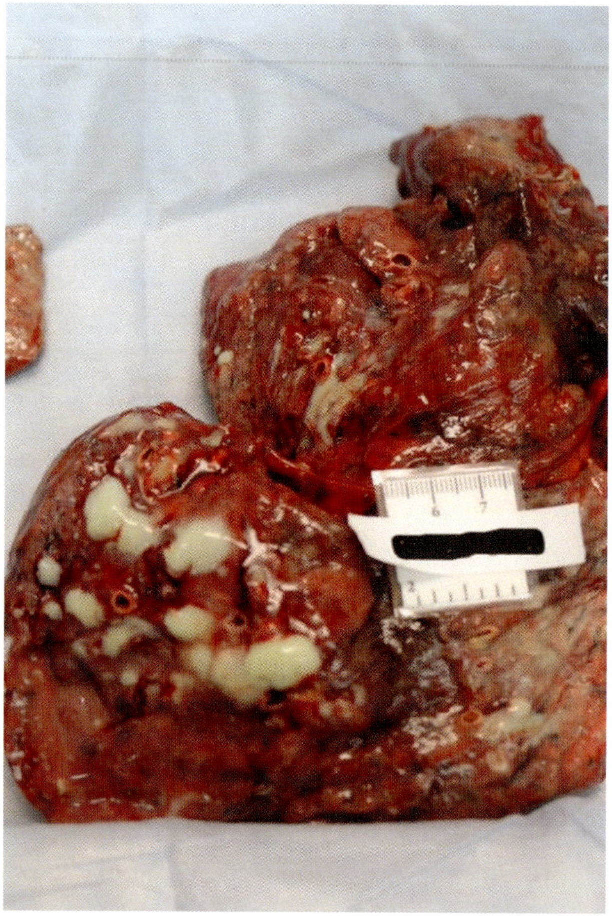

48.6 Gross cross section of lung with bronchopneumonia. The pneumonia is secondary to immunosuppression due to neglect.

Physical abuse

Physical abuse involves an action that is inflicted upon an individual with the purpose of causing injury and/or pain. Physical abuse is generally considered the most extreme form of elder maltreatment (18). Acts of physical abuse include slapping, kicking, pinching, other forms of blunt force trauma, bites, burns (especially palms, soles, genitals and buttocks), pulling of hair causing traumatic alopecia, improper use of restraints and improper administration of medication. Head trauma is the most serious type of physical abuse and carries the highest morbidity and mortality (Figures 48.7–48.10). Findings suspicious for elder abuse are listed in Table 48.3.

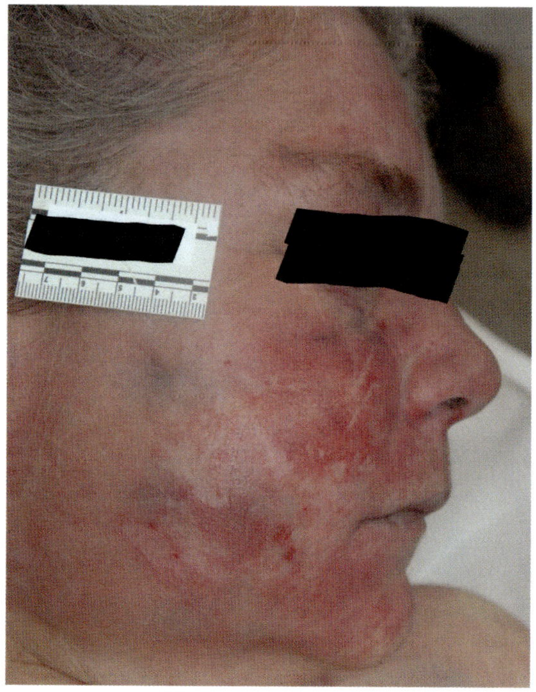

48.7 Blunt force trauma to the side of the face.

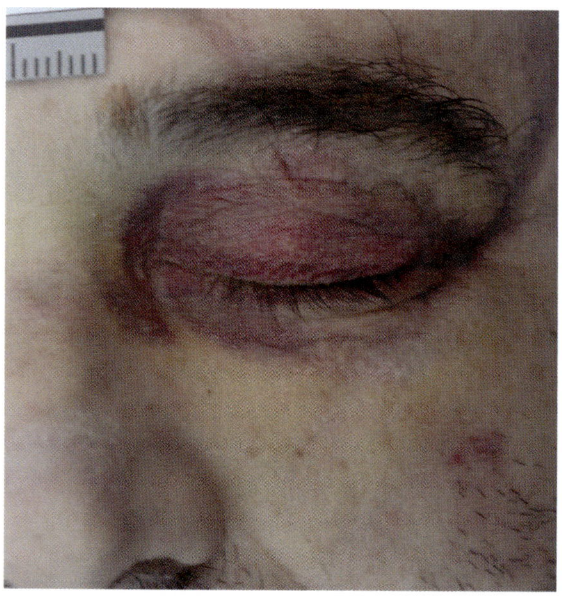

48.8 Periorbital contusion and zygomatic abrasion.

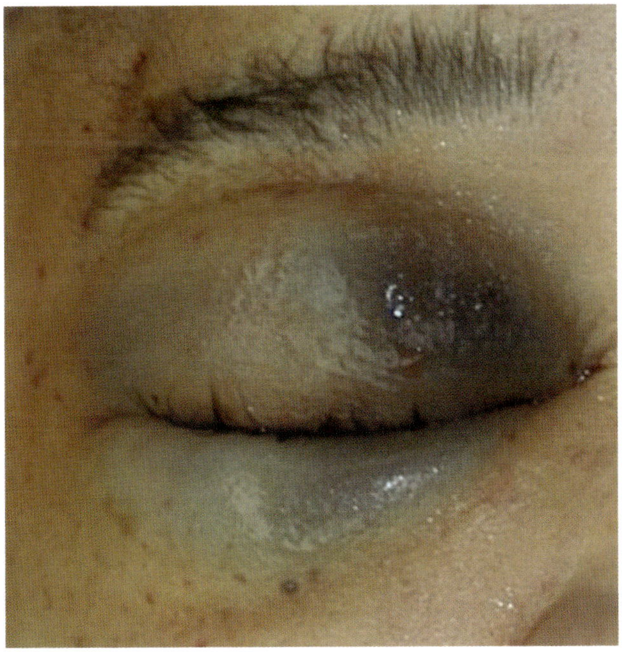

48.9 Periorbital contusion with swelling.

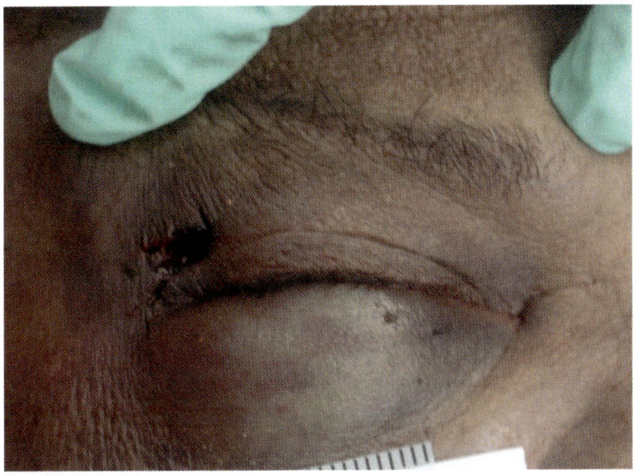

48.10 Periorbital contusion with brow laceration

TABLE 48.3 Findings suspicious for physical abuse (18)
Contusion to inner thighs or inner arms
Trauma to the ear/pinna
Nasal bridge injury (e.g. can occur while wearing glasses)
Periorbital ecchymoses
Facial or skull fractures
Injury to the mastoid process area, postauricular
Submental injury
Intraoral injury, perioral abrasions
Unusual alopecia pattern
Injury to the palms and soles
Cutaneous and muscular injury to the back
Injury to the buttocks (abrasion, burn, contusion)
Anal contusion, laceration
Breast abrasion, contusion, laceration
Vulva/vaginal abrasion, contusion, laceration
Scrotal/penile abrasion, contusions, laceration
Abrasion/contusion of the wrists or ankles (ligature marks)
Fracture to the femoral neck/humerus/vertebrae
Fractures to long bone shaft
Injury to the axillae (restraint use)
Pressure sores other than the lumbosacral area or heels
Untreated pressure sores
Stocking and glove patterned scalds, scalds to the back, scalds with immersion lines
Fecal impaction (neglect, dehydration, drug-related)
Poor hygiene
Numerous injuries of different ages, different planes of the body
Injuries not compatible with history
Delay in seeking medical treatment/absence of medical care

A difficult aspect in assessing elder physical abuse is distinguishing inflicted from accidental trauma. Due to the aforementioned changes in the elder related to aging, several entities may be suspicious for elder abuse but are actually mimickers. These are listed in Table 48.4.

Restraints

Physical restraints are used in elder for safety reasons (22). However, improper use or prolonged use can be abusive. Signs of improper use consist of abrasions to the wrists, ankles, or axillae. Pressure sores may also be indicative of improper use of restraints with prolonged positioning, especially of the back, lumbosacral area, heels and elbows (23). If tape is used as the method of restraint, loss of hair around the wrists or ankles and erythema in these areas may be seen. Another type of restraint is chemical restraint (23). This is seen in elders with dementia or who are combative and/or agitated. Toxicology can identify possible chemical restraints with a psychotropic drug. Toxicology is also useful in identifying a lack of prescribed medication.

Sexual abuse

It is a myth that elders are not sexually abused. Sexual abuse is an act of violence and control, and elders can be victims, as can any age group. However, the exact

TABLE 48.4 Mimickers of physical abuse (18)
Senile purpura, senile ecchymoses
Steroid purpura
Solar purpura, photoaged skin, fragile epidermis
Medical/alternative procedures such as cupping
Coagulopathy (liver disease, alcoholism, medication)
Autoimmune bullae
Hyperpigmentation secondary to medications
Contact dermatitis
Fixed drug reaction
Fracture secondary to a tumor
Fracture secondary to osteopenia or osteoporosis
Accidental fall with subdural hematoma
Rib and sternal fractures secondary to cardiopulmonary resuscitation
Fecal impaction secondary to narcotic use
Elevated drug levels due to impaired metabolism or excretion
Periorbital allergic "shiners"
Inflammatory bowel disease with anal involvement
Cutaneous reaction to a vaccination

TABLE 48.5 Mimickers of sexual abuse
Perineal excoriation due to poor hygiene
Perineal excoriation due to incontinence
Anal fissures, hemorrhoids
Post-mortem anal dilatation, scrotal drying
Cystocele
Inflammatory bowel disease
Fixed drug reaction
Contact dermatitis
Coagulopathies with easy bruising
Vaginal bleeding due to decreased estrogen
Vaginitis with increased pH
Vaginal lichen sclerosis

frequency is unknown for several reasons: elders often fear retaliation or institutionalization, decreased cognition/dementia may prevent reporting and underreporting. Investigators do not always consider sexual abuse in an elder, and medical personnel do not always consider or perform sexual assault examinations on elders (24–26). The victim is usually female, the perpetrator often male and the incident location is in the elder's residence. The female elder victim will often have genital injury, more often than their younger counterparts. Injuries result due to decreased pubic hair, reduced estrogen levels, vulvar atrophy, vaginal wall atrophy, dryness and thinning of the vaginal wall, decreased connective tissue and weakened pelvic structures. Extragenital injuries as seen in physical abuse may also be present with sexual assault. Due to the aging systems of the female elder, there are several entities that mimic sexual abuse (Table 48.5).

Residential care facilities

In the United States, over 5 percent of elders live in residential care facilities (27).Within these facilities, the aforementioned types of elder abuse may occur (17,23). Neglect can occur as in other types of elder residences. With physical abuse, the perpetrator may be a visitor or another resident but is usually an employee of the institution. The typical perpetrator is a young, less-educated employee in an institution with a high employee turnover (18,28). The elder is often mentally or physically vulnerable and often isolated with few family visits (28). The isolation and possible inability of the elder to report the abuse prevents discovery as does the fact that very few institutional elder deaths are investigated (23).

Medicolegal death investigation

While most deaths in the elderly are due to natural diseases, it does not exclude the requirement to rule out other causes. The need to report premature elder deaths to a medicolegal authority is often overlooked, as diseases of aging and physiology attributed to aging confound the picture and significantly complicate the determination whether death resulted from abuse or neglect (29). State statutes dictate reportable deaths and as such, the medicolegal death investigator may only respond to an elder death scene that is suspicious, has inconsistent information reported or is due to an unnatural death. Often, these deaths are signed out by the primary care physician who is not trained to recognize forensic markers, resulting in over-reporting of death due to natural causes (30–33).

The death investigation of an elder case can be more complex than other circumstances of death and requires a methodical approach to identify and document specific forensic markers, such as bruises, dehydration, poor hygiene, decubitus ulcers, fractures and deficient nutritional status, unique to this population that may hasten their death (34). Often, the cause is multifactorial and tends to present in an atypical or asymptomatic way making the diagnosis based on symptoms alone difficult. The natural physiological changes and diseases common in aging may also obscure indicators of abuse and neglect (23). In fact, the investigation is considered a crucial source of information and may be the only information available to the forensic pathologist besides the post-mortem evaluation (29).

The medicolegal death investigator needs to be familiar with the typical victim, scenario and perpetrator in these types of cases (23,35). The signs that will be most visible to the medicolegal death investigator are physical abuse, sexual abuse and physical neglect (36). Often, more than one type of abuse occurs simultaneously or repeatedly over time (37).

Medicolegal investigation

The investigation should include a home/scene investigation, review of medical records, medication and pharmacy record correlation, witness/neighbor/friend interview, interview of caretaker and communication with clinicians. Extensive information must be collected to help identify suspicious deaths, including medical/psychiatric/social/financial histories, environmental living conditions, degree of independence/autonomy, circumstances surrounding recent trauma, physical appearance of the body to include explanation of marks or injuries, presence and stage of pressure ulcers, neurological status, caregiver information, medication inventory and history of neglect or abuse (34). Circumstances at the time of death dictate whether an autopsy or ancillary tests will be performed, so obtaining information as expeditiously as possible is vital.

Medical history

The events leading up to, during, and following the death must be thoroughly documented and are critical to interpreting the findings derived and will dictate the extent of further investigation needed. Medical records alone, however, often do not provide adequate information for a medicolegal authority to determine if suspicious factors contribute to the death (20). Additionally, information may be inadequate due to the ongoing failure of physicians to recognize potential abuse and/or neglect despite increased awareness and laws mandating physicians to report suspected cases to an Adult Protective Service (APS) agency (29).

Clinicians may know family members or caregivers who attended visits with the decedent and can share any concerns or red flags that they might have. This information must be relayed to the forensic pathologist immediately.

Environment living conditions

Living conditions should be safe and clean. Utilities should be turned on and working. The ambient temperature should be documented and compared to the thermostat setting. Adequate and appropriate food should be found in the refrigerator and cabinets. Kitchen surfaces should be free from debris. Lighting should be appropriate and in working order. Improper and/or dirty clothing and linen, lack of linen, or the absence of appropriate bedding should be photographed after careful inspection. Absence of bedding is not normal and must be explained. The presence of human and/or pet excrement and poor sanitation should be noted as these are common signs of neglect. The medicolegal death investigator should document in both written form, and photographically, all findings and interview next-of-kin to confirm that these living conditions are not a matter of choice as seen in elders with Diogenes syndrome. Diogenes syndrome is considered a behavioral disorder that presents in the form of extreme self-neglect and can include social isolation, physical state of extreme neglect, hoarding and living in squalor with no lack of shame (38–40).

Decline in cognition may also contribute to poor or unsanitary conditions.

Psychiatric/Social history

Information about social, psychiatric and financial information should be obtained from the next-of-kin, caregivers and/or friends. Often, this information is unintentionally incorrect or incomplete. Recent hospitalizations, acute and chronic diseases, depression or recent withdrawal from loved one(s), disabilities and diet provide significant information for possible abuse.

Financial exploitation of the elderly, which is cited as the fastest-growing form of elder abuse, is usually perpetrated by family members. This may be evident in cases involving an elder parent and adult offspring or a new "best friend" at a residential care facility. Information about the decedent's overall financial status may especially play an important role when determining if an elder death is due to homicide. The recent loss of a spouse, relative or pet may be significant.

Falls

The CDC reports that more than one out of four elders fall each year and can result in injuries that require medical attention (41). One out of five falls causes a serious injury such as a broken bone or head injury and constitute the leading cause of unintentional death (41–44). More than 95 percent of hip fractures are caused by falling and falls are the most common cause of traumatic brain injuries (TBIs) in the elder population (41). As people age, natural physiological changes can occur that increase the risk of falling, such as decreased proprioception, decreased motor strength, cerebellar degeneration and impaired gait (23). It is important for the medicolegal death investigator to record the date, time and location of the fall, landing surface and the possibility of striking an intermediary object (e.g. piece of furniture) during the fall. All witnesses must be interviewed. Because environmental hazards may play a role in the cause of the fall, it is essential to also document information such as presence of throw rugs, wet floors, poor lighting, incorrect bed height, shoe type (if wearing), and improperly fitted or maintained wheelchairs. The majority of falls are due to accidents, but homicidal falls can also occur from pushing or shoving. Frailty and medications, including adverse-reaction to medication use, are of significance while evaluating the totality of circumstances. Nursing home residents make up an estimated 20 percent of deaths resulting from falls, which can be attributed to increased frailty (34,45).

Medications

The elderly take prescribed medications more frequently than any other age group. However, the aging process can affect how medications are absorbed, metabolized and excreted. Elders also have an increased risk for adverse reactions to medications. It is estimated that one-half to one-third of elders do not take their medications properly (34,46). Polypharmacy is common and may contribute to death. Obtaining and documenting a medication inventory is an essential component of the investigation, including medication name, prescribing physician, dose prescribed, date prescribed and number prescribed. A comparison of the number of pills present to the number that should be present in the container based on the dose and prescribing directions can indicate non-compliance with medications or overuse. Non-compliance must be explained. Undermedication can be seen when caretakers consume or sell an elder's medication (23). Overmedicating may occur to keep an elder unaware, and incapacitated and thus manageable (23,34). This is known as chemical restraint. Communication with the prescribing physician and pharmacy records will confirm the discovered medications and determine if any medication is missing. Absent or unfilled medications must be explained by the caretaker(s).

Pressure ulcers or other wounds

Pressure injuries are important indicators of the quality of care provided in an institution and can result in significant mortality and morbidity (47–49). As noted, pressure ulcers are most common in areas overlying bony prominences such as the sacrum/coccyx, heels or hips. Proper bedding and/or padding should be used to reduce the risk of or even prevent pressure ulcers (34). Lying in one position or sitting in wheelchairs for extended time without any movement increases the risk of developing a pressure ulcer. Certain diseases can also predispose to the formation and poor healing of pressure ulcers, such as diabetes mellitus, anemia, incontinence, and peripheral vascular disease or other poor circulatory conditions (23,33). Ninety-five percent of neglected elders have at least one pressure ulcer (23,33).

Care provider information

Complete information about antemortem functional status is required, including independence, competence and autonomy. Dependence on caregivers for activities of daily living or partial assistance, such as medication dispensing, is critical information. If the elderly requires mobility assistance, ensure that the wheelchair or walker are working properly. If a family member is caring for an impaired elder, they may be unable to adequately manage their caregiving responsibilities. Demented elders can be aggressive, belittling and demanding. The stress associated with providing care and assistance to frail and highly dependent elders is high and considered a leading contributor to elder abuse, especially if the elder is highly dependent on the caregiver. Slapping, hitting and pushing may occur in response to these stressful situations. Caregivers may become overwhelmed, frustrated and abusive because of the continuous caretaking demands posed. Document the length of time that the caregiver is involved in the elder's care. Independent spouses can carry a smoldering resentment to provide the care needed or when assessing the financial demands of placing their loved one in an institutional placement, resulting in abuse.

Residential care facilities

As the elder population continues to increase, so too will the number of elders who live in residential care facilities, including nursing homes, assisted-living facilities, skilled nursing centers and expanding other types of locations. The population of these care facilities includes patients with chronic and serious illnesses, including cardiovascular, pulmonary, cognitive and functional difficulties (50). Cases should be evaluated for the possibility of abuse, especially among patients who are highly dependent on care. Dementia is a leading risk factor for elder abuse as these patients may be extremely difficult to manage. The patients may be unable to voice their abusive situation or seek help and so they may appear distressed for unknown reasons because they are unable to verbalize the abuse.

Sexual abuse may also occur in this vulnerable population. Perpetrators are both male residents and direct care staff, some of whom assault the victim numerous times and/or assault multiple victims and have past criminal histories including sexual assault, psychiatric illness, and drug and/or alcohol dependence (51).

Because pressure ulcers are an indicator of quality of care, the presence and stage are critical factors to document. Pressure ulcers are not always preventable, and it is the responsibility of the facility to adequately document preventative measures, dates of treatment and all findings. A challenge for forensic pathologists in determining whether pressure ulcers were due to neglect is often lack of appropriate documentation (49).

As elders are expected to die from their chronic and numerous conditions, most deaths are not reported to a medicolegal authority. In the United States, only 20 states require mandatory reporting of suspected abuse to a medical examiner/coroner, leaving 31 states with no such mandatory reporting (23). As such, suspected cases of abuse and/or neglect are severely underreported and under identified; it may also be simply not possible to evaluate care to determine if it has been optimal. It may take the reporting by family members to law enforcement or other authorities to initiate an investigation.

Restraints

Physical or chemical restraints may be used to manage long-term care residents. Physical restraints include the use of belts, vests, soft ties, hand mitts, specialized chairs ("gerichair"), lap cushions, lap trays or tables and bilateral bedrails. They are intended to prevent an individual from moving or getting up and cannot be removed independently. They should be used in compliance with state licensing requirements, but are often used to punish, instill fear, or isolate an elder as a form of control (52). One study found that the incidence of restraint use in residents diagnosed with dementia was 48 percent, higher than patients with other diagnoses (53). Restraints should not restrict movement completely or cause entrapment. Causes of death have been reported due to incorrectly applied restraints or inadequate supervision while restrained (54).

Evidence of restraint use, method of restraint, length of time used and the restraint location on the elder's body must be documented both in written form and photographically.

Maltreatment

As with all medicolegal investigations, the person who last saw the elder or were in contact with them along with the person(s) who discovered the body must be interviewed. It is imperative to speak directly to the source and not to rely upon secondhand information to reduce the possibility of inaccurate material. If a caregiver is suspected of causing injury, witness accounts should be corroborated to prevent the offender from shifting responsibility to another (34).

Deaths rarely result from a single isolated incidence of abuse (34). Collaboration with outside agencies is, therefore, an integral part of an abuse and/or neglect investigation. Reports from APS, law enforcement and clinicians may establish a pattern of abuse (34). APS maintains records of past complaints and case information, including victims, perpetrators, household situations and income amount and sources (23).

CONCLUSION

People throughout the world are living longer and living better. Elders comprise a unique group of individuals with a different physiology, with different pathologies, who are frequently vulnerable and are too often victims of abuse. Understanding the changing pathophysiology of the elder is imperative to evaluating elder abuse. Abuse of elders, individuals aged 60 years and older, has become a global epidemic and the true incidence will be discovered only if we are aware and better investigate deaths in these individuals.

REFERENCES

1. 10 Facts on Ageing and Health. World Health Organization May 1, 2017. Available from: https://www.who.int/news-room/fact-sheets/detail/10-facts-on-ageing-and-health (Accessed 2 May 2023).
2. Kleinschmidt KC. Elder abuse: A review. *Ann Emerg Med* 1997; **30(4):** 463–472.
3. Baker AA. Granny battering. *Mod Geriatr* 1975; **5:** 20–24.
4. Burston GR. Granny-battering. *BMJ* 1975; **3:** 592.
5. Council on Scientific Affairs. Elder abuse and neglect. *JAMA* 1987; **257:** 966–971.
6. Rosenblatt DE. Elder abuse: What can physicians do? *Arch Fam Med* 1996; 5: 88–90.
7. Goldstein MZ. Maltreatment of elderly persons. *Psychiatr Serv* 1995; **46(12):** 1219–225.
8. Hall JE, Karch DL, Crosby AE. Elder Abuse Surveillance: Uniform Definitions and Recommended Core Data Elements for Use in Elder Abuse Surveillance Version 1.0. Atlanta, GA: National Center for Injury Prevention and Control, Centers for Disease Control and Prevention (US); 2016. Available from: https://www.cdc.gov/violenceprevention/pdf/ea_book_revised_2016.pdf (Accessed 2 May 2023).
9. Silverman TN. Abuse of the elderly through fraud and deception. *Psychiatr Hosp* 1983; **14(2):** 104–107.
10. Yon Y, Mikton CB, Gassoumis ZD, Wilber KH. Elder prevalence in community settings: A systematic review and meta-analysis. *Lancet* 2017; **5:** e147–156.
11. Collins KA, Bennett AT, Hanzlick R. Elder abuse and neglect. *Arch Intern Med* 2000; **160:** 1567–68.
12. Chen H, Zhou X, Fujita H, et al. Age-related changes in trabecular and cortical bone microstructure. *Int J Endocrinol* 2013; **2013:** 213234.
13. Ibrahim JE, Aitken G, Ranson DL. Pathophysiology of Aging. In: Collins KA, Byard RW (eds). *Geriatric Forensic Medicine and Pathology*. London: Cambridge University Press; 2020.
14. Lyons-Warren A, Lillie R, Hershey T. Short- and long-term spatial delayed response performance across the lifespan. *Dev Neuropsychol* 2004; **26:** 661–678.
15. Allen JS, Bruss J, Brown CK, Damasio H. Normal neuroanatomical variations due to age: The major lobes and a parcellation of the temporal region. *Neurobiol Aging* 2005; **26:** 1245–60.
16. Lord SR, Dayhew J. Visual risk factors for falls in older people. *J Am Geriatr Soc* 2001; **49:** 508–15.
17. Williamson AK. Non-Lethal Elder Abuse. In: Collins KA, Byard RW (eds). *Geriatric Forensic Medicine and Pathology*. London: Cambridge University Press; 2020.
18. Collins KA, Jaques R. Physical Abuse and Elder Homicide. In: Collins KA, Byard RW (eds). *Geriatric Forensic Medicine and Pathology*. London: Cambridge University Press; 2020.
19. Bryan CS, Dew CE, Reynolds KL, et al. Bacteremia associated with decubitus ulcers. *Arch Intern Med* 1983; **143:** 2093–95.
20. Galpin JE, Chow AW, Bayer AS, Guze LB. Sepsis associated with decubitus ulcers. *Am J Med* 1976; **61:** 346–50.
21. Heinemann A, Tsokos M, Puschel K. Medico-legal aspects of pressure sores. *Leg Med Tokyo* 2003; S263–266.
22. Bellenger E, Ibrahim J, Bugeja L, Kennedy B. Physical restraint death in a 13-year national cohort of nursing home residents. *Age and Ageing* 2017; **46:** 688--93.
23. Howe J, Collins KA, King P, Yeoman C. Investigation of elder deaths. *Acad Forensic Pathol* 2014; **4:** 290–304.
24. World Health Organization. *Elder Abuse*. Geneva. 2014. Fact Sheet No. 357. Available from: www.who.int/mediacentre/factsheets/fs357/en/ (Accessed 1 May 2023).
25. Cooper C, Selwood A, Livingston G. The prevalence of elder abuse and neglect: A systematic review. *Age and Ageing* 2008; **37(2):** 151–60.
26. Gibbs L, Mosqueda J. The importance of reporting mistreatment of the elderly. *Am Fam Phys* 2007; **75(5):** 628.
27. West LA, Cole S, Goodkind D, He W. 65+ in the United States: 2010. *US Census Bureau*. 2014; (June): 23–212.
28. Yon Y, Ramiro-Ganzalez M, Mikton CR, et al. The prevalence of elder abuse in institutional settings: A systematic review and meta-analysis. *Eur J Public Health* 2019; **29:** 58–67.
29. Kim L, Mitchell S, Dyer C. Do medical examiners determine elder mistreatment as a cause of death? *Forensic Sci Med Pathol* 2007; **3(1):** 9–13.

30. Drake SA, Akande A, Kelly PA, et al. Identifying gaps and improving investigation of fatal elder abuse and/or neglect. *J Forensic Sci* 2022; **66**: 2274–82.
31. Rosen T, Makaroun LK, Conwell Y, Betz M. Violence in older adults: scope, impact, challenges and strategies for prevention. *Health Aff* 2019: **38(10)**: 1630–7.
32. Schofield MJ, Powers JR, Loxton D. Mortality and disability outcomes of self-reported elder abuse: A 12-year prospective investigation. *J Am Geriatr Soc*. 2013: **61(5)**: 679–85.
33. Dong XQ, Simon MA, Beck TT, et. al Elder abuse and mortality: The role of psychological and social wellbeing. *Gerontol* 2011; **57(6)**: 549–58.
34. Howe J. Medicolegal Investigation of Elder Maltreatment and Death. In: Collins KA, Byard RW (eds). *Geriatric Forensic Medicine and Pathology*. London: Cambridge University Press; 2020.
35. Collins KA, Presnell. Elder homicide: A 20-year study. *Am J Forensic Med Pathol* 2006; **27**: 183–7.
36. Isaac C, Corneillson J, deJong J. An investigative tool for detecting elder abuse. *Acad Forensic Pathol* 2014; **4**: 524–31.
37. Collins KA. The underweight elder: Maltreatment, self-neglect, or normal aging? *Am J Forensic Med Pathol* 2013; **3(1)**: 40–45.
38. Byard R, Tsokos M. Forensic issues in cases of Diogenes syndrome. *Am J Forensic Med Path* 2007; **2**: 177–81.
39. Cipriani G, Lucetti C, Vedovello M, Nuti A. Diogenes syndrome in patients suffering from dementia. *Dialogues Clin Neurosci* 2012; **14**: 455–60.
40. Irvine JDC, Nwachukwu K. Recognizing Diogenes syndrome: A case report. *BMC Research Notes* 2014; **7**: 276.
41. Centers for Disease Control and Prevention. *Facts about falls*. Available from: https://www.cdc.gov/falls/facts.html (Accessed 3 May 2023).
42. Alexander BH, Rivara FP, Wolf ME. The cost and frequency of hospitalization for fall-related injuries in older adults. *Am J Public Health* 1992; **82(7)**: 1020–3.
43. Sterling DA, O'Connor JA, Bonadies J. Geriatric falls: Injury severity is high and disproportionate to mechanism. *J Trauma* 2001; **50(1)**: 116–19.
44. McMaughan DK, Phillips CD. In-hospital mortality and unintentional falls among older adults in the United States. *J Appl Gerontol* 2013: **32**: 923–35.
45. Centers for Disease Control and Prevention. Deaths from falls among persons aged 65 years or older: United States, 2007–2016. *Morbidity and Mortality Weekly Report* 2018: **67(18)**: 509–14.
46. Chisholm KM, Harruff RC. Elderly deaths due to ground-level falls. *Am J Forensic Med Pathol* 2010: **31(4)**: 350–4.
47. Smith, D. Pressure ulcers in the nursing home. *Am Intern Med* 1995: **123**: 433–38.
48. Park-Lee E. Pressure ulcers among nursing home residents: United States. *NCHS Data Brief* 2009: **14**: 1–8.
49. deJong J. Residential Care Facility Deaths. In: Collins KA, Byard RW (eds). *Geriatric Forensic Medicine and Pathology*.. London: Cambridge University Press; 2020.
50. Gruszecki AC, Edwards J, Powers RE, Davis GG. Investigation of elderly deaths in nursing homes by the medical examiner over one year. *Acad Forensic Pathol* 2004; **25**: 209–12.
51. Dayman G. Sexual Assault in Elders. In: Collins KA, Byard RW (eds). *Geriatric Forensic Medicine and Pathology*. London: Cambridge University Press; 2020.
52. National Research Council (US). In: Bonnie RJ, Wallace R, (eds). *Elder Maltreatment: Abuse, Neglect, and Exploitation in an Aging America*. The National Academies Press. Washington DC: 2003.
53. Bredhauer D, Becker C, Eichenr B, Koczy P. Factors relating to the use of physical restraints in psychogeriatric care: A paradigm for elder abuse. *Gerontol Geriat* 2005: **28**: 10–18.
54. Bellinger E, Ibrahim J, Bugeja L, Kennedy B. Physical restraint death in a 13-year national cohort of nursing home residents. *Age and Ageing* 2017; **45**: 688–93.

CHAPTER 49

Death by Suicide

Jan M. Gorniak and Gary L. Collins

DEFINITION AND INVESTIGATIVE ASPECTS

Suicide is a classification of manner of death defined as a death due to an intentional self-inflicted injury or poisoning that is meant to, or has an inherently high risk of, causing death. To describe it in a different way, the suicidal act(s) is/are designed to end the perpetrator's own life. (1) Methods of self-inflicted deaths may include physical injury, such as firearm injury; injury from sharp objects; falls from a height and asphyxial mechanisms, such as hanging or suffocation. Other methods of deaths involve the consumption or inhalation of a toxic agent or a consumption of a chemical compound in lethal quantities. Some methods may involve a combination of physical injury with an intoxicating agent.

The goal of the investigation of a death by suicide is to identify or confirm the actual cause of death. The cause of death is the illness or injury that results in the death and is listed as such on the death certificate. The conclusion that a death is by a suicidal act is based on a review of all of the circumstances of the death including the medical, social and psychiatric history of the victim, the method of death, information gathered from the scene and interviews with individuals with direct knowledge of the decedent, and the post-mortem examination of the decedent.

Predisposing factors

Characteristics or conditions that increase the chance that a person may try to take their life are risk factors, while warning signs are changes in or the presence of new behaviors. (Table 49.1 and Table 49.2). (2) Mental illness (depression, anxiety), substance abuse, and medical issues are the most common risk factors. The likelihood that an individual will attempt suicide is increased when they have multiple risk factors, especially if they exhibit several warning signs. Part of the death investigation of a suspected suicide should involve discussions with close relatives and friends to identify possible risk factors, warning signs, or triggers for the action.

TABLE 49.1 Risk factors for suicide

- Prior suicide attempts
- History of substance abuse
  - Drug
  - Alcohol
- Physical disability or illness
- History of a mental health condition
  - Depression
  - Anxiety
- Relationship problems
- Losing a friend or family member to suicide
- Recent death of a family member or a close friend
- Ongoing exposure to bullying behavior
- Access to harmful means

TABLE 49.2 Suicide warning signs

- Negative view of self
- Sense of hopelessness
- Isolation
- Aggressiveness and irritability
- Giving things away
- Making funeral arrangements
- Engaging in risky behaviors
- Self-harm behaviors (i.e. cutting)
- Drastic changes in mood and behavior

Methods of death

The common characteristic of all suicides is that, regardless of the life-ending method used, the process can be performed almost exclusively by the perpetrator, with little or no direct assistance from another individual. Death via physical trauma includes firearm injuries of the head or torso, hanging, incised wounds commonly to forearms and neck, stab wounds to anterior torso, falls from heights, such as from buildings or bridges, drowning by entering

DOI: 10.1201/9781003138754-51

TABLE 49.3 Methods of death in suicide

- Firearm injuries: Gunshot wounds, shotgun wounds
- Hanging
- Wounds by sharp objects
  - Stab wounds
  - Incised wounds
- Drowning/terminal immersion in water
- Blunt impact injuries/falls from height
- Death by poisoning
  - Ingestion of intoxicating chemical
  - Ingestion of a poison (e.g. sodium nitrate)
  - Inhalation of toxic agent (e.g. carbon monoxide, (Figure 49.5) hydrogen sulfide)
- Transportation related: Struck by train or automobile
- Self-immolation

rivers or bodies of water, or ingestion and/or inhalation of a toxic agent (Table 49.3). Some methods of death include the use of specialized equipment to generate toxic fumes. For example, the operation of a gasoline powered engine in a closed space, such as operating a car in a closed garage, possibly with a hose taped to the exhaust pipe leading to the interior of the car. Another example is lighting a charcoal grill in a sealed room or in a sealed car.

Chemical suicide, also known as "detergent suicide", is defined as the death resulting from the intentional mixing of common household chemicals specifically intended to create a toxic gas such as hydrogen sulfide (5). In many instances of chemical suicide, the chemical agents are mixed in a closed space such as a closet or a car. Other less common forms of suicidal deaths involving modes of transportation include stepping into the path of an oncoming train or lying across railroad tracks or driving an automobile into a fixed object or into a body of water, and self-immolation, the act of setting oneself on fire.

DEATH INVESTIGATION

The forensic death investigation of a suicide has three components. (3) They are:

- The report of death and review of the social and medical history of the decedent
- The review of the scene of the death if available
- The examination of the decedent

Report of death

The report of death will contain information about the decedent including the age, race and gender of the decedent and the presumed injury, cause of death or the mechanism of death. At the time of the report, the death investigator should gather as much information as possible about the decedent. Such information should include the date and time found, the date and time of pronouncement and the date and time last known to be alive. At the time of the initial report of death, or during subsequent follow up interviews or discussions with relatives or law enforcement officers, attempts must be made to document as much information about the deceased as possible, including possible risk factors.

Pertinent questions that must be asked and answered when a death by suicide is suspected include: (4)

- Any history of mental illness?
- Any history of chronic debilitating disease?
- Any medication for mental health conditions? If yes, determine compliance.
- Any hospitalizations for mental health conditions? If yes, voluntary or non-voluntary?
- Previous suicide attempts? When? How?
- Any history of substance abuse? What type? How often?
- Any history of alcohol use or abuse?
- Any history of domestic violence?
- Recent significant life changes? (Employment, financial, relationship, legal, etc.)

CASE EXAMPLE

The decomposing remains of an 18-year-old man were recovered from the bank of a river. He was reported missing two days prior when his car was discovered parked on a bridge that crossed the river. Personal belongings including his wallet and mobile telephone were found in his car. The car was fully operational. A search of the water below and nearby riverbank did not reveal his body. The death was presumed to be a drowning. Interviews with law enforcement officers and relatives did not identify any risk factors. The investigation confirmed that he was alone when last seen and that there were no drugs detected on toxicological analysis, thereby excluding the possibility that he may have been thrown from the bridge by another individual(s). It is important to note that, in many instances, an inciting factor may never be identified, in that the death investigator and family may never know "why" or be able to provide a reason for the individual's decision to end their life. In cases such as these, the manner of death is opined based on the exclusion of other possibilities. In the example given, there was no other explanation for a fully operational car to be found at the top of a bridge with the personal effects of the owner left inside the vehicle.

- Any upcoming dates of significance, such as the anniversary of the death of a spouse, child or loved one?
- Any suicide warning signs?
- Any recent cryptic telephone or text messages expressing love, regret, providing apologies or requesting forgiveness?
- Any reports of family or close friends dying by suicide?

Review of the scene of death

At the scene, it is important to document the position the decedent was found (Figures 49.1 and 49.2) the presence or absence of wounds/injuries, and whether the location is secure or easily accessible to the decedent and/or other individuals. Since the determination of intent is difficult, it is also critical to look for other indicators to the state of mind or health of the deceased.

Other findings to document include the presence of a suicide note/note of intention, the presence of drugs or drug paraphernalia, alcohol, medications for psychiatric disorders, documentation of medial/psychiatric history, and/or documentation to support other stressors such as a significant loss of a relationship or death, including cards or an obituary. It is important to identify evidence, such as receipts for recently purchased supplies such as a rope, extension cord, or a firearm, a broken belt near a point of suspension, significant items such as birthday cards, family photographs left arranged on a bed or table. There may be books on suicide; a review of the decedent's recent internet searches on their computer or mobile telephone may reveal searches for methods on how to die by suicide, or website information on obtaining items to end one's own life. The death investigator might find a printed card and or handwritten information for the suicide prevention hotline, suggesting the decedent may have reached out for assistance.

Examples of findings to note at the scene include:

- The position of the decedent
- The weapon or method used
- The presence of a suicide note/note of intention
- The condition of the location where death occurred
- Findings suggestive of alcohol consumption or chronic alcohol use
- The presence of apparent illicit drugs or drug paraphernalia
- Vehicle ignition in the 'On' position and the fuel gauge on empty
- Specific hazardous chemicals at the location including ease of access or recent purchase of specific hazardous chemicals

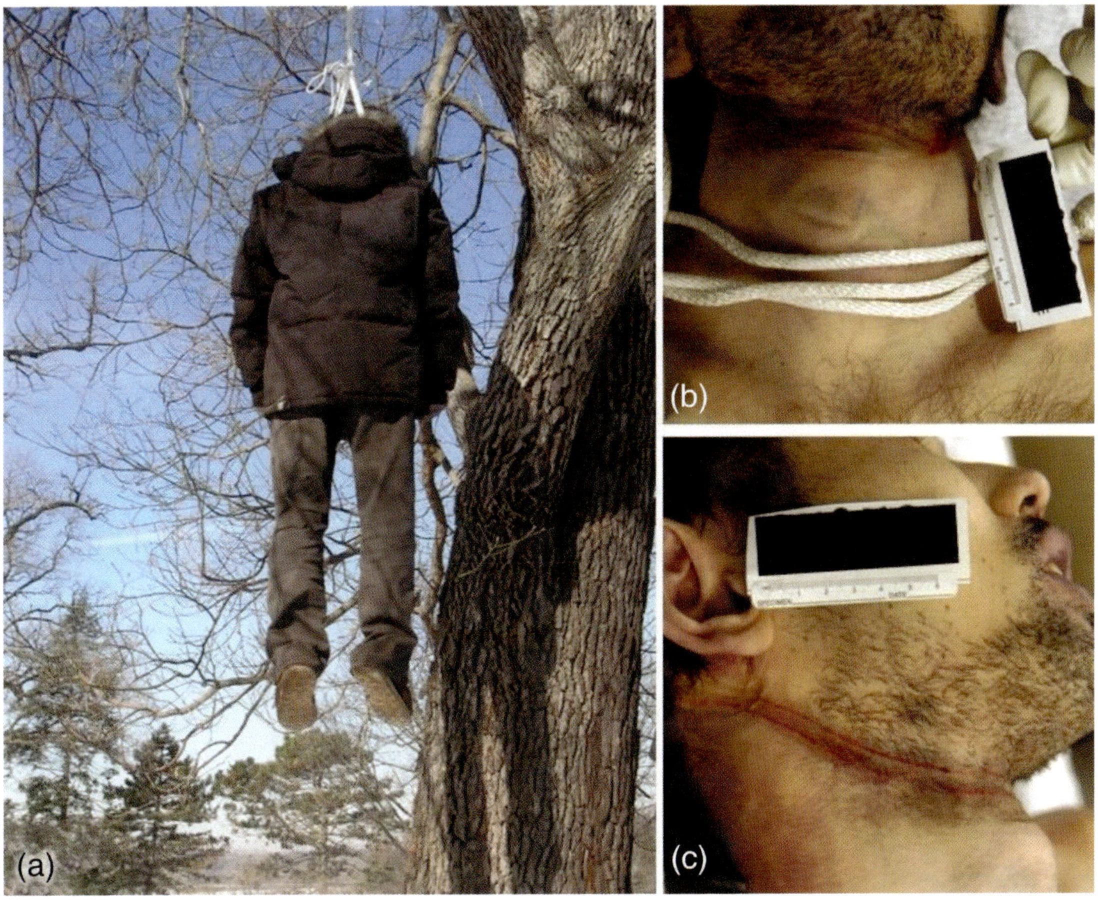

49.1 Hanging. **(a)** Example of full suspension. **(b)** and **(c)** Neck showing ligature furrow.

CASE EXAMPLE

The body of a 45-year-old man was found on a local walking trail with an apparent gunshot wound of his head. The weapon was found adjacent to the body. During a search of his pocket, a purchase receipt for the weapon was found. The receipt was dated the day prior to the discovery of the decedent.

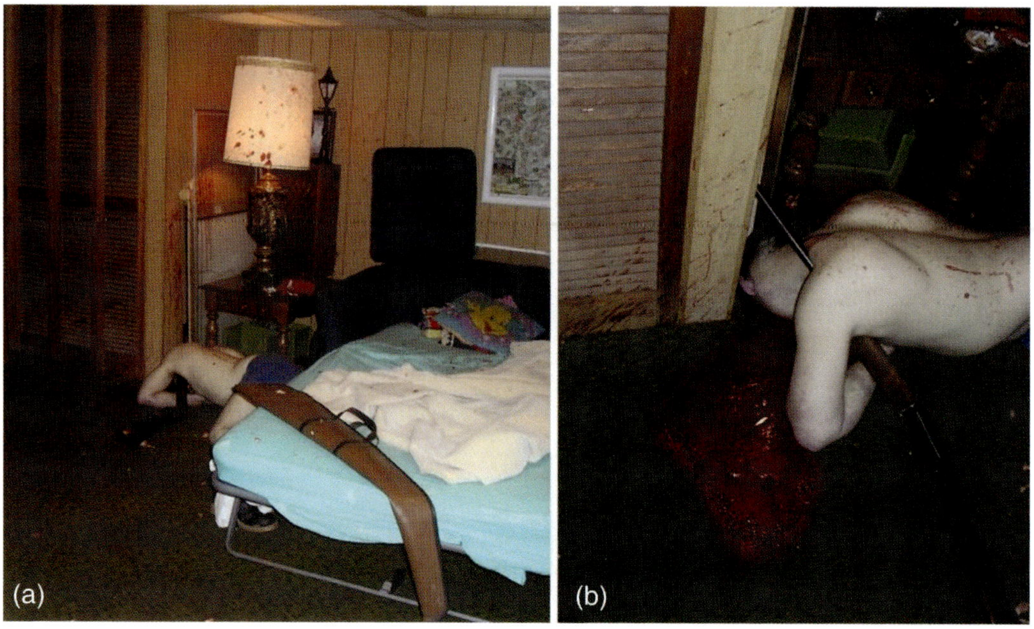

49.2 Scene findings from a victim of a self-inflicted shotgun wound.

- Review of recent internet searches that include suicide references or the presence of specific books with information about suicidal acts
- Posted notes or specific instructions on what to do with personal effects or with the decedent themselves (burial versus cremation)

Post-mortem examination

The post-mortem examination serves the purpose of confirming the identity of the decedent, documenting injuries, documenting natural disease processes, obtaining samples for toxicological analysis, collecting and preserving evidence and determining the cause of death (Table 49.3). Depending on the circumstances of the death, the post-mortem examination may be an external examination, limited examination (head or chest only), or complete autopsy with or without additional specialized dissections. Radiology may be performed, with or without the assistance of post-mortem CT (PMCT) scanning. Post-mortem examinations must include written and photographic documentation of the positive and negative findings.

Confirmation of the decedent's identity is imperative, especially if there are significant injuries or post-mortem changes that make visual identification not possible. The methods used for identification are beyond the scope of this chapter and are discussed elsewhere in the text.

The documentation of the terminal injury(ies) or other findings that support the cause of death will include documentation of wounds such as firearm injuries (Figure 49.3), sharp force injuries (Figure 49.4), or blunt force injuries. Of note, injuries found on the decedent may be acute and in the early stages of healing or there may be scars from prior attempts. What must be noted in the various wounds are the location and if the appearance of the injuries are such that it would be possible for the decedent to inflict the injuries to themselves. For example, self-inflicted gunshot wounds are commonly contact

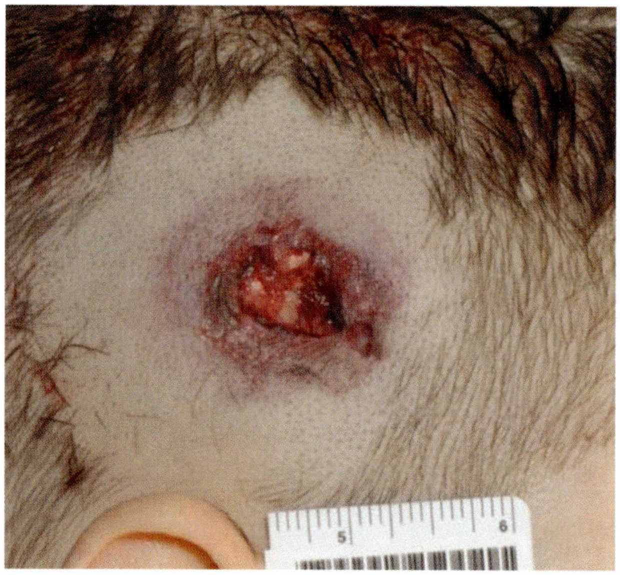

49.3 Contact gunshot wound of the head.

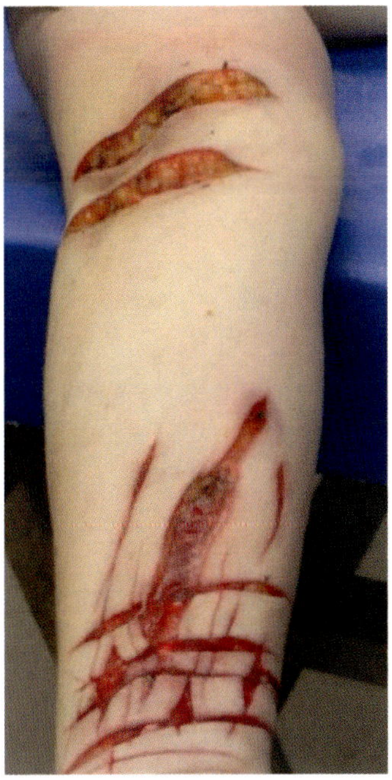

49.4 Incised wounds of right upper extremity.

49.5 Evidence of carbon monoxide poisoning. The end of the hose is attached to the muffler and located in the vehicle compartment.

(Figure 49.3) or close range and located in a position on the body that is easily accessible, such as the side of the head, center of the forehead, intraoral, underside of the lower jaw, or anterior chest. The presence of soot and/or stippling must be documented. A gunshot wound of the back is not supportive of a self-inflicted injury and raises the possibility of the involvement of another in the death (i.e. homicide).

Documentation of the findings may also include conducting measurements of the length of the body, weight and arm length (shoulder to tip of the index finger). Documentation of injuries should include detailed photographs with appropriate scales. In some instances, documentation of negative findings or absence of injury may be appropriate. For instance, in a hanging, the examiner should not necessarily expect to find other abrasions or contusions to the neck or other blunt force injuries of the rest of the body. In situations where a suspected death by suicide occurs in police custody, the post-mortem examination is very detailed and will consist of a full autopsy with extensive photographic documentation of the body inclusive of all positive and negative findings. Ideally, these findings can also be corroborated by PMCT.

TABLE 49.3 Objectives of the post-mortem examination

- Confirm the identification of the decedent
- Document injuries
  - Firearm injuries
  - Blunt impact injuries
  - Injuries caused by sharp objects (incised or stab wounds)
  - Findings of asphyxia
  - Injuries from prior attempts
  - Absence of injuries**
- Obtain samples for toxicological analysis
  - Blood
  - Vitreous fluid
  - Urine
  - Gastric contents
  - Tissues
- Retrieval of evidence
  - Bullets/projectiles
  - Trace evidence

**Absence of injuries is important when excluding physical assault by other(s) if the death is due to ingestion or inhalation of a toxic agent(s).

Suicides in children

Acts of suicide in children under the age of 13 are rare. The most common method used is hanging. The use of a firearm is also seen (6). It is important that the investigation documents possible risk factors and recent stressors. Particularly in this age group, looking at social media posts may reveal suicidal thoughts or plans. The post-mortem examination should document evidence or physical and/or sexual abuse. The certifying pathologist or coroner must be prepared to answer questions surrounding the possibility of intent and the evidence supports the determination that the death was intentional.

In-custody suicides

In-custody deaths, whether in the pre-arrest, arrest or post-arrest phase will be subject to increased scrutiny by the family of the decedent and the Department of Justice. As a result, it is imperative that all aspects of the death investigation be thorough so as to clearly document the cause of death and exclude any other possible causes of death. The authors recommend a full autopsy with examination and photographic

CASE EXAMPLE

A 35-year-old man barricaded himself in his residence after a domestic dispute wherein police were called. After several hours with no response from the individual, the police entered and found the decedent locked in a bathroom with a ligature produced by an electrical extension cord tightly secured around his neck. The ligature was tied to the handle of the bathroom door. Although the residence was secure and he was the only occupant of the house when breached, a full autopsy including, anterior and posterior neck dissections and examination of the subcutaneous tissues of the back and extremities was performed to document the absence of other findings. The day after the pronouncement of death, the family accused the police of being responsible for his death. The autopsy confirmed that there were no other wounds or findings of concern such as facial and conjunctival petechiae or contusions to his back or extremities. The medical examiner was able to adequately explain to the family how the death was due to the hanging, and that it was a suicide.

CASE EXAMPLE

A 45-year-old man is found dead in the driver's seat of a car with a single gunshot wound of the head. In the front passenger seat was his wife who was found with gunshot wounds of her head and torso. It was reported that earlier that day, he was witnessed to shoot a woman, who he was reportedly having an extramarital affair with, at her workplace. At the scene, the weapon was found on the floor of the driver's side. The post-mortem examination revealed the male decedent having a single penetrating contact gunshot wound of his head.

documentation of the structures of the head, neck and torso, along with posterior neck dissection, flay dissection of the back, buttocks, upper and lower extremities, with detailed toxicological analysis of collected samples (7).

Most in-custody suicides occur by means of hanging while incarcerated in jail or prison. In these types of deaths, the investigator must document the location of where the injury occurred (8). In those cases where the inmate/prisoner is transported from the facility and dies at the hospital, the investigator must conduct a scene investigation at the site where the injury/illness occurred. This is necessary to photograph the cell or area where the injury occurred, and any evidence that was present, such as ligature. Review of the inmate's medical records and the incident report is important and should be performed. As in other suicide deaths, suicide ideations, prior suicide attempts, and the presence of a suicide note/note of intention should be documented.

A police-involved shooting where an individual purposely engages with law enforcement to entice them to use deadly force (9). This is known as "suicide by cop". The suicidal individual typically has a weapon, firearm or knife, and is threatening to harm themselves. Law enforcement officers try to get them to place the weapon down. After numerous refusals, the individual points the weapons in the direction of the officers, forcing them to shoot the perpetrator in self-defense. In these instances, the manner of death is ruled homicide, not suicide.

Homicide – suicide deaths

There are situations in which there are one or more victim(s) of homicidal violence where the perpetrator has died of suspected suicide. These circumstances are usually seen in situations where the decedents were in a relationship. There may be a history of domestic violence and the relatives of the suspected homicide may report that the relationship was in disharmony or recently ended. With most combined homicide-suicide deaths, the decedents are usually found in the same location. Usually, the method of death is the same for both the homicide and suicide victims with death by firearm (gunshot or shotgun wounds) being the most common in the United States. In situations where there are both suspected homicide and suicide, the authors recommend conducting the medicolegal death investigation of the decedents as if they were homicides. The manner of death determination for the suicide victim will be made after the post-mortem examination following confirmation of the cause of death being self-inflicted, excluding other possible scenarios or causes of death.

CONCLUSIONS

Suicide is a classification of manner of death that is the result of an intentional self-inflicted injury or poisoning that is meant to cause death. Evidence of intent includes an explicit expression, such as a suicide note/note of intention or suicide ideations and previous attempts. Common methods of death may include trauma such as firearm injury, injury from a sharp object, fall from a height, hanging or the ingestion or inhalation of a toxic agent. Only after a thorough scene investigation, post-mortem examination, and knowledge of recent circumstances of the decedent's life can a determination of suicidal manner be made (10). The evidence gathered from the scene investigation, in conjunction with the information obtained from interviews with individuals with direct knowledge of the decedent is crucial. Viewing internet searches, online diaries, text messages and social media posts may reveal suicide ideations or plans to die by suicide. It is also essential for the medical examiner or coroner to review the medical, social and psychiatric history of the decedent in the determination of manner of death.

REFERENCES

1. Hanzlick R, Hunsaker JC, Davis GJ et al. A Guide for Manner of Death Classification. National Association of Medical Examiners; 2002. Available from: https://name.memberclicks.net/assets/docs/4bd6187f-d329-4948-84dd-3d6fe6b48f4d.pdf (Accessed 28 August 2023).
2. American Foundation for Suicide Foundation. Risk factors, protective factors, and warning signs. Available from: https://afsp.org/risk-factors-protective-factors-and-warning-signs (Accessed 28 August 2023).
3. Morii D, Miyagatani Y, Nakamae N, et al. Japanese experience of hydrogen sulfide: the suicide craze in 2008. *J Occup Med Toxicol* 2010; **5**: 28.
4. Wagner SA. Death Scene Investigation: A Field Guide. Boca Raton: CRC Press; 2017.
5. Cuyahoga County Medical Examiner's Office. Section III Scene Types. In Medicolegal Death Investigation A Step-by-Step Field Guide. 2017; pp. 18–19.
6. National Institute of Mental Health. Understanding the characteristics of suicide in young children, 2021. Available from: https://www.nimh.nih.gov/news/science-news/2021/understanding-the-characteristics-of-suicide-in-young-children. (Accessed 23 August 2023).
7. Mitchell Jr. RA, Diaz F, Goldfogel GA, et al. National Association of Medical Examiners Position Paper: Recommendations for the definition, investigation , postmortem examination, and reporting of deaths in custody. *Acad Forensic Pathol* 2017; **9(4)**: 604–18.
8. Carson EA. *Suicide in local jails and State and Federal prisons*, 1000-2019 – statistical tables. US Dept. of Justice, 2021.
9. Hutson HR, Anglin D, Yarbrough J, et al. Suicide by cop. *Ann Emerg Med* 1998; **32(6)**: 665–9.
10. Gorniak JM, Sudimack JR, Stanforth JR, et al. Hanging deaths with bound hands: what is the manner? *Am J Forensic Med Pathol* 2007; **28(3)**: 232–4.

CHAPTER 50

Homicides

Sebastian O. Sterling and Roger W. Byard

DEFINITION

The definition and laws involving homicide differ in each country, state, jurisdiction and territory around the world. Homicide may be defined as the unlawful killing of a person, including but not limited to murder and manslaughter. Terms may often be used interchangeably. Other forms of death, such as infanticide, neonaticide and femicide may also be classed by police as homicides (1).

MURDER VS MANSLAUGHTER

Within South Australia, Australia, murder and manslaughter are governed by the Criminal Law Consolidation Act 1935. For a person or persons to be guilty of murder, the victim must have died due to an unlawful act committed by the accused. This act must be found to have significantly contributed to their death. The key element in law is to establish an intent to kill or to cause grievous bodily harm to the victim, which may include evidence to suggest that the perpetrator was aware that it was probable that their act would result in death, harming or placing another person in danger with reckless indifference to their life (2).

Manslaughter, in contrast to murder, does not require intent to cause death or grievous bodily harm, nor does the defendant need to be aware that their actions would result in death. Manslaughter can be defined as voluntary or involuntary. Voluntary manslaughter is a less serious crime than murder due to the presence of mitigating circumstances, such as provocation. Involuntary manslaughter can result from the perpetrator deliberately exposing the victim to an unlawfully dangerous act but without the intent to kill, or when a victim dies as a result of a high level of criminal negligence, the actions of which are so reckless as to show a disregard for the life and safety of others (3).

EPIDEMIOLOGY

The rate of homicide in 2020 in the United States was 6.4 per 100 000 population, the highest it has been since 1998 (4). In contrast, between 2018 and 2019 in Australia homicide rates were 0.88 per 100 000, the second lowest ever recorded since the establishment of the National Homicide Monitoring Program (NHMP) in 1989. There has been a notable downtrend in the incidence of homicide in Australia since the 1980s. During 2018–2019, a total of 224 homicides were recorded, the highest numbers occurring in New South Wales (n = 81), Victoria (n = 45) and Queensland (n = 40).

There are, however, significant differences in homicide rates among different communities with, for example, homicide rates in indigenous Australian populations being consistently higher than for non-indigenous groups (5). Methods used in homicides also vary greatly between and among communities with firearms being favored in the United States and Israel compared to Australia and Samoa, where sharp force and blunt force trauma, respectively, predominate (6–8). The COVID-19 pandemic has also had different effects on homicide rates in different communities with both increases and decreases being reported often associated with intimate-partner violence (9).

The majority of homicides in Australia are classified as domestic (34%) and acquaintance (37%) homicides, with only 15 percent committed by a stranger and 13 percent classed as undetermined, due to the relationship between the victim and perpetrator being unknown, or to no perpetrator being identified. Male victims predominate in Australia with 68 percent, compared to females with 32 percent, which represents a consistent 2:1 male to female ratio throughout the years. However, intimate partner homicides comprise 62 percent of all domestic homicides. Women were the victims in 73 percent of intimate partner homicides committed during the period 2018–2019. Of the remaining domestic homicides, 13 percent were filicide (parent killing their own child), approximately 10 percent were parricide (the killing of one's parent) and 4 percent siblicide (the killing of a sibling), with the remainder being defined as homicide by another family member. Weapons were used in 88 percent of all homicides in Australia during this period, with over 40 percent involving a knife or other sharp objects. Only 18 percent of homicides utilized firearms and 16 percent used hands and/or feet to injure a victim (10). In cases of deaths due to homicides, attendance of a pathologist at the death scene is often required to assist in determining the likely cause and manner of death and to give advice on possible weapons used and the time of death (Figures 50.1 and 50.2). Alternatively,

DOI: 10.1201/9781003138754-52

50.1 Death scene evaluation may involve the assessment of bodies that have been left outside that may be subject to post-mortem animal/insect predation. In this instance, a body (arrow) was left lying beside a shed at an isolated farmhouse.

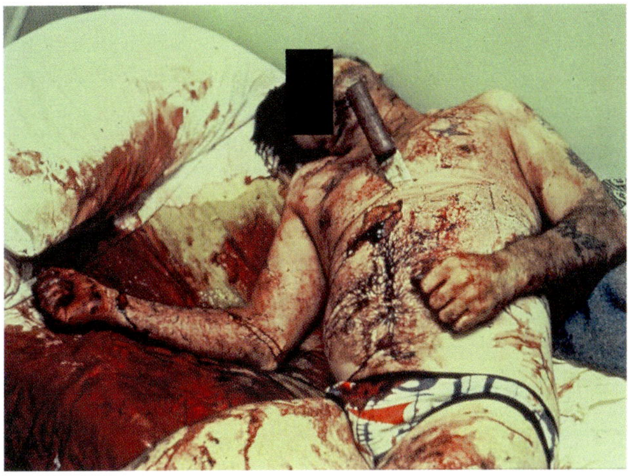

50.2 Crime scenes inside may be quite chaotic and soiled with fluids. The scene of a stabbing death shows the knife left embedded in the chest with considerable surrounding blood staining and pooling.

high-quality imaging taken at the time may assist if personal attendance is not possible.

BLUNT FORCE TRAUMA

Blunt force trauma is a leading cause of morbidity and mortality in those under the age of 35 years and ranked as the sixth leading cause of death worldwide. Blunt force injuries are the result of a direct contact between parts of the body and a blunt object (11). The most common causes of traumatic blunt force injuries are motor vehicle accidents (MVA) involving car-car or car-pedestrian impacts, assaults or sporting injuries. Within the elderly population, blunt force trauma is contributed to by falls, which are becoming of particular importance as societies age.

Trauma to the head with cerebral disruption and exsanguination are the most common causes of death due to blunt force injury; air embolism may be present if large veins have been traumatized (11). As blunt impact

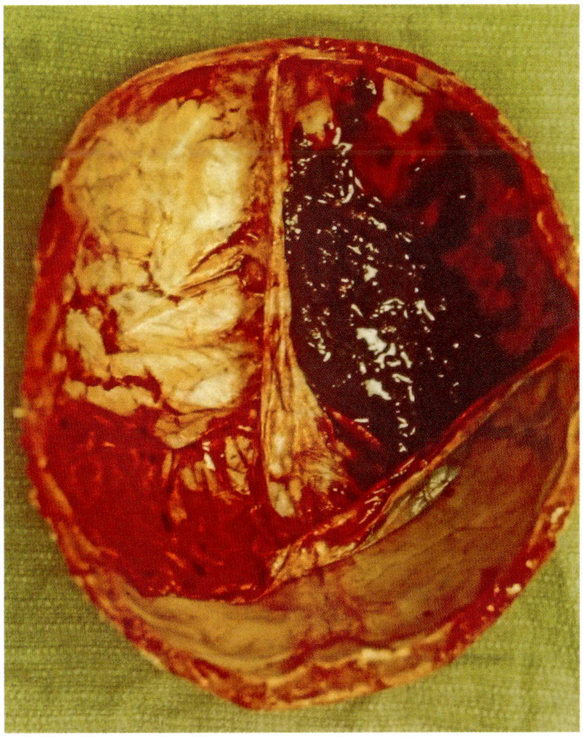

50.3 A left-sided subdural hematoma in a case of lethal inflicted blunt craniocerebral trauma.

injuries are common and result from a variety of different situations appropriate interpretation and classification of wounds is essential for accurate medicolegal testimony. Therefore, blunt force injuries have been subdivided into the following categories: contusions, abrasions, lacerations, fractures and avulsions (12).

Head injuries from inflicted trauma may range from superficial lacerations and subgaleal hematomas to skull fractures with intracranial hemorrhage. The latter includes epidural, subdural (Figure 50.3) and subarachnoid hemorrhage. These are often associated with cerebral swelling and contusions. A contusion on the same side as a subgaleal hematoma represents a "*coup*" injury from a direct blow compared to an injury on the opposite side which is "*contrecoup*" from deceleration. A typical example of the latter is a bruise over the occiput with contusions of the inferior aspects of the frontal lobes and temporal poles. This is in keeping with a fall and impact to the back of the head, rather than a frontal assault (13), a distinction that may have great significant in court (*see also* Chapter 35 – "Head Trauma Deaths".

Death may occur due to blood loss from lacerations particularly if there is an underlying bleeding disorder or anticoagulative medications. Delay in seeking medical attention may also be a contributing factor and so socially isolated alcoholics with liver disease are at particular risk. This may form part of the Diogenes syndrome (14) (*see also* Chapter 53– "Self-Neglect").

Concussion is now recognized as a potentially significant injury, and it may be associated with an additive effect if two or more episodes of blunt head trauma occur over time. Found in American footballers, this has been termed the "second impact" syndrome and it may result in rapid deterioration from cerebral edema (15). It has also been shown in animal studies that brain swelling following blunt head trauma occurs very rapidly and is biphasic, with initial swelling associated with vasodilation, that is followed by the development of cerebral edema from vascular leakage (16). The injury that is associated with a lucid interval is the epidural hemorrhage, where a skull fracture is associated with vascular compromise resulting in apparent recovery followed by gradual loss of consciousness as the enlarging area of hematoma peels the dura back from the skull (17,18).

Characteristics

A contusion consists of a collection of blood lying beneath intact epidermis which has leaked into the tissues due to rupture of vessels from significant mechanical impact. The term "contusion" is often used synonymously with "bruise", "hematoma" and "ecchymosis". The differentiation between these terms can be problematic due to inconsistent use throughout the literature. The terms "contusion" and "bruise" are often used interchangeably; however, bruises are sometimes used for injuries to the skin whereas contusions are restricted to internal organs (19). Hematomas often refer to collections of blood deeper in the tissues or within body cavities, such as the cranium, abdomen or thorax and are almost always associated with blunt trauma. Ecchymosis refers to discoloration of the skin, again due to extravasated blood, however, it may be remote from the site of trauma. The term bruising is generally used preferentially to ecchymosis in the clinical setting, as there is no essential difference between the terms. An example of this can be seen in classical periorbital ecchymosis caused by a fracture of the base of the skull (raccoon eye sign).

Abrasions, also referred to as scrapes, scratches or grazes, occur when the superficial epidermis is removed due to impact with an irregular surface such as asphalt (20). Locations of abrasions tend to be focused in the area of trauma, unlike contusions (bruises, ecchymoses), which have the ability to migrate due to blood tracking through tissue planes (21). Abrasions may be useful in determining the vector of impact in a forensic setting by close inspection of the epidermal tags produced by the tangential impacting force.

Laceration refers to tearing or splitting of the skin, due to significant blunt force impact, that often leaves subcutaneous tissue bridging and irregular wound margins (Figure 50.4) (22).

Fractures represent breaking of bone (or cartilage). Medically, there are a variety of eponymous fracture classifications described in the orthopedic and maxillofacial literature, depending on the location and mechanism, including the Weber classification for ankle fractures (23), Salter-Harris classification for pediatric growth plate fractures (24), or the Garden classification for hip fractures (25). However, in practical terms, fractures are classed as simple (closed) or compound (open) with further subdivisions being transverse, linear, oblique (with or without displacement), spiral, greenstick or comminuted. Simple fractures are fractures beneath intact

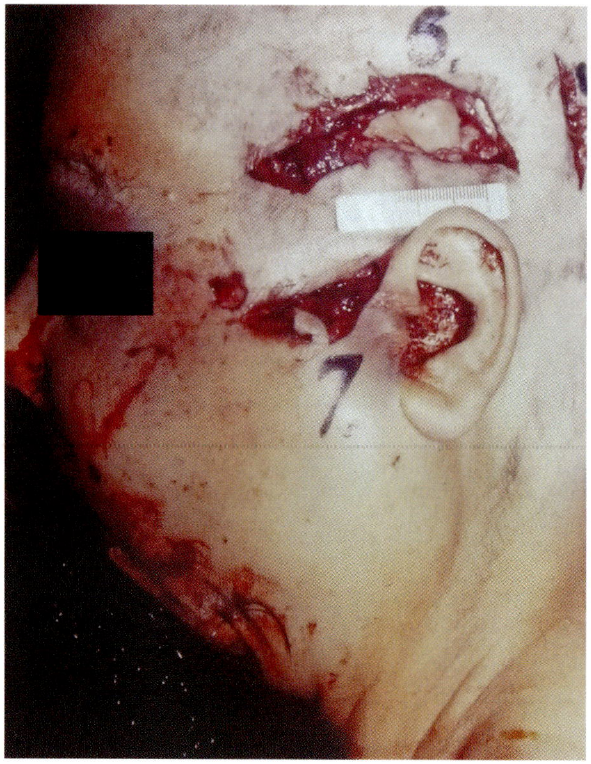

50.4 Blunt force trauma to the side of the head showing multiple irregular lacerations with irregular edges and associated underlying skull fractures.

dermis, in contrast to a compound fracture, where a laceration overlies the fracture, creating a direct communication between the skin surface and bone. Transverse, linear and oblique are terms used to describe the path of the fracture line. Transverse fractures run perpendicular to the length of a bone and oblique are angled.

Spiral fractures tend to be caused by rotational forces acting along the bone axis, commonly a result of sporting injuries, when the foot remains planted while the body rotates, or in cases of limb twisting in child abuse. It has been suggested that narrow trenches forming part of the defense system for Roman forts were designed to be difficult to see and result in spiral fractures of the leg when stepped into. Greenstick fractures are partial thickness fractures, where the cortex and periosteum on only one side is interrupted. This occurs when the bone tends to bend instead of separating into two separate pieces and is most commonly seen in children under 10 years of age due to their softer bone matrix prior to puberty (26). Fractures are classed as comminuted when the injury results in the bone fragmenting into multiple pieces.

Avulsion injuries refer to dismemberment resulting in the separation of an organ or body part from the body, predominantly due to blunt force. However, not all avulsion injuries are directly caused by blunt force trauma, as with Yabitsume (finger shortening), the ritualistic voluntary or involuntary self-amputation of the fingers, carried out by the Japanese mafia (yakuza or boryokudan) as a form of reparation for violations of the organization's code (27). Similar finger mutilation occurs in areas of Papua New Guinea as a mark of condolence at funerals. Commonly, avulsion injuries are a result of MVA. Although blunt force injuries have distinct subcategories, it is not uncommon for contusions to be present with lacerations, abrasions, fractures, or avulsion injuries.

Pathophysiology

A bruise can occur immediately following an injury, within approximately 15 to 20 minutes, or even days later (28). There is a common misconception that the color change of a bruise, from red, blue, black or green, can be accurately linked to its age, but this is incorrect (21,29,30). As macrophages are recruited to the site of injury and phagocytose erythrocytes, the enzyme heme-oxygenase initiates the initial breakdown of hemoglobin. Hemoglobin reduces to iron and biliverdin (a green pigmented compound). The latter is then rapidly converted to a yellow pigment, bilirubin, by biliverdin reductase (31). From the breakdown of hemoglobin and the establishment of bruise age, all that can be safely determined is that a bruise that is yellow is not recent (29,32,33), on condition that the contusion was not inflicted on a pre-existing injury. The time course for an inflammatory infiltrate to occur in a bruise is also very variable and is also skewed by the precise site of tissue sampling in relation to point of impact (34,35). It is now recognized that photographs cannot be used to date bruises with any accuracy, unless when corroborating presence or absence on known dates or times.

Abrasions and lacerations, depending on the severity, tend to undergo healing by second intention. Typically, the initial appearance of the wound is erythematous, due to tissue damage-induced vasoactive factor release, resulting in localized vasodilation. Scab formation and granulation tissues are produced as a natural bandage and healing mechanism, appearing brown in color (36,37). In the post-mortem state, the color of an abrasion may vary from bright red to black. A study by Vinay et al., concluded that, if used in conjunction with histopathological evaluation, examination with the naked eye could be used to date the age of such wounds (38).

It is becoming common practice to perform high-resolution post-mortem CT scans to help elucidate the cause of death and to evaluate the age of injuries in homicides. In relation to fractures, certain radiological features may help to date the injury, due to healing with callus formation which is initially fibrocartilaginous, followed by a bony callus (39). Features of fracture healing can be observed macroscopically, histologically, and also radiologically, to help estimate the approximate age of an injury. Widening of the fracture gap, with blurring of the margins are the first radiographic signs of healing, due to inflammation resulting in the resorption of dead bone, occurring between 10 and 14 days. As soft callus forms, a fluffy calcified appearance around the fracture site is often visible, in children this can occur as early as 10 days and around 2 weeks in adults. At around 7–8 weeks, signs of disuse osteoporosis can be observed, at the level of the fracture and distal to the fracture site, which more likely to be expected with fractures that have been immobilized (40). It should be noted, as with all situations where dating of a process is attempted post mortem, that although a standard series of stages is passed through in every case, there is marked idiosyncratic variability among individuals. For this reason, accurate dating of injuries and processes may not be possible based purely on the pathological or radiological findings (41).

Autopsy findings

Blunt force injuries in homicide are predominantly craniocerebral. In a study by Ambade and Godbole, (42), 80 percent of the study victims sustained blunt force head trauma, followed by upper limb and chest injuries. In some cases of blunt force injury, particularly with abrasions and contusions, there may be patterns which reflect the characteristics of the impacting object. For example, in a local hit-and-run case, the victim's leg showed contusions outlining the letter 'HOLD', corresponding to the car manufacturer, 'Holden'. Another example is the parallel, zig-zag pattern of contusions that may be seen on a victim's body which may match the footwear worn when used to inflict the injury. Blunt force injuries caused by linear objects result in the phenomenon of "negative imprinting" (43). This is when the object striking the skin causes a tear of marginal blood vessel around the edge of the object. If no bone underlies the afflicted area, the area under the object is spared of contusion resulting in a "tramline", "rail track" or "tram-track" appearance (44,45). Shaving of the head and other areas with body hair should be undertaken for not only blunt force injuries but also for sharp force and gunshot wounds (Figure 50.5) to adequately demonstrate and record the characteristics of the underlying injuries using rules and scales.

In some cases of death caused by blunt force injury there may be a complete absence of external signs of trauma. Lawyers in court may suggest that this is due to the inflicting trauma being minor and not significant enough to threaten life. However, this is incorrect as it is merely a manifestation of Casper's sign, where the skin elasticity and mobility prevent surface injury. This contrasts with fixed or rigid tissues which will sustain most

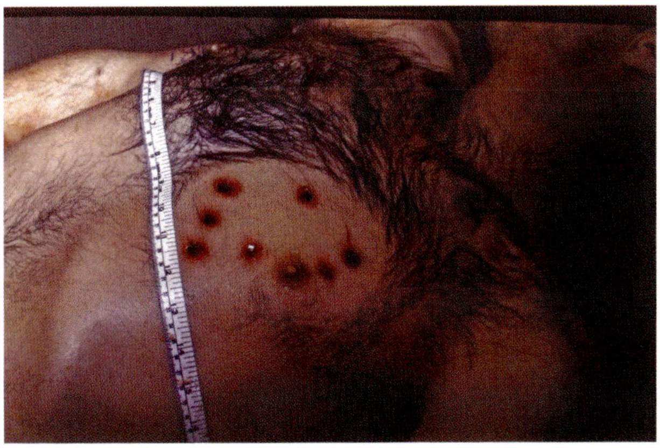

50.5 Shaving of chest hair better demonstrated wounds from shotgun pellets.

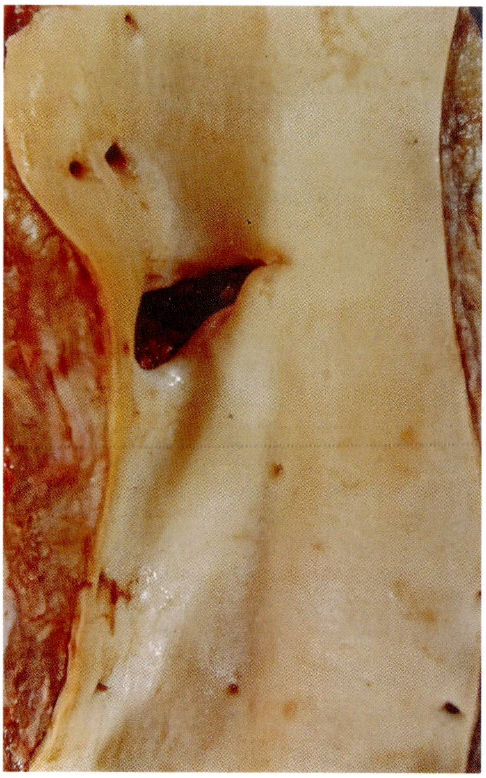

50.6 A stab wound of the aorta due to penetrating chest trauma from a knife.

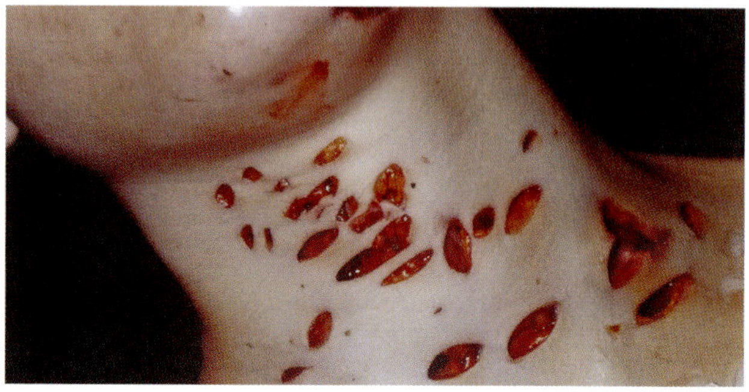

50.7 Multiple stab wounds to the anterior aspect of the neck with transection of major underlying arteries and veins.

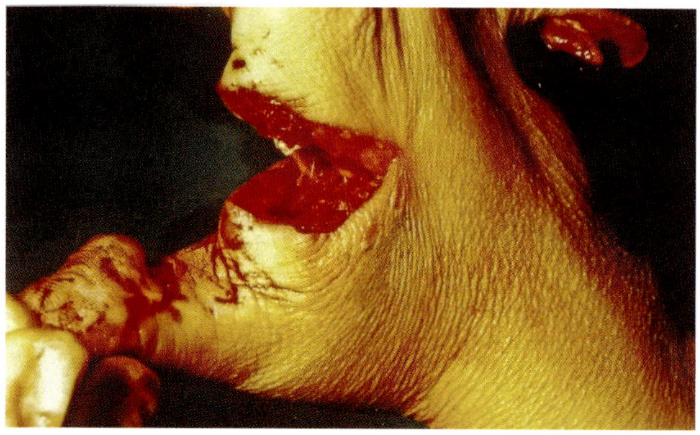

50.8 Defense wounds of the thumb and the base of the thumb sustained during an attack with a knife when the victim attempted to grab the weapon.

of the injury; hence the finding of significant internal injuries in the absence of any external signs of trauma (46,47).

SHARP FORCE TRAUMA

Sharp force trauma is simply defined as injury to tissues caused by an object with a sharp blade or pointed end. There are generally four subcategories of sharp force trauma which include incised, stab, chop and atypical wounds (48). The word "laceration" is often used erroneously by non-forensic healthcare professionals when referring to sharp force trauma. However, this is not correct as lacerations are due to crushing of tissues by the application of a blunt force (*see* Blunt Force Injury), whereas a "cut" is the result of sharp force (40). Deaths due to sharp force injuries usually occur because of exsanguination related to major vessel or organ injury (Figure 50.6). On occasion, air embolism may also contribute if, for example, major veins have been cut in the neck. Cases where multiple stab wounds have been inflicted, sometime after death, have been termed "frenzy" killing and suggest that the perpetrator was psychotic, knew the victim well, or was under the influence of drugs such as amphetamines (Figure 50.7). Even in cases of multiple stab wounds caution should be exercised as suicide may still be a possibility (50).

Incised wounds, also referred to as "cuts" or "slashes", are caused by sharp-edged objects slicing the skin (49). An example is a surgical incision with a scalpel. Wounds produced by a blade moving tangential to the skin are often longer than they are deep, with the deepest part being at the point of first contact. Some incised wounds may have wound tails or tags, which are superficial injuries caused by the blade moving on the skin (51). A general rule is that a tail is shorter and the wound deeper at the entrance point – due to the high pressure of the initial blow (52). Occasionally, tails may be used to estimate the direction of an inflicted wound however, when possible, this information should be used in conjunction with other soft-tissue injuries and/or clothing defects and interpreted cautiously.

Stab wounds, or "punctures" are caused by sharp pointed objects and are deeper than they are wide. The penetration mechanism is a crucial feature of a stab wound, with penetration being directly related to pressure *(P)*, which is due to force *(F)* over a particular area *(A)*.

$$Penetration \propto P = \frac{F}{A}$$

Stab wounds tend to terminate internally, only rarely having an exit wound. Exit wounds may be observed however in high-energy stab wounds such as from an arrow or wounds in the upper extremities, where the flesh thickness is less, or in defense wounds of the arms and hands. Defense wounds indicate that the victim was conscious during at least part of the attack (Figures 50.8–50.10). Apart from cartilage and bone,

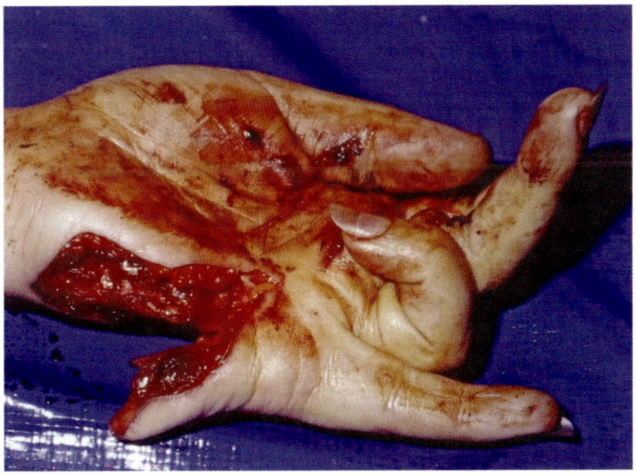

50.9 A deep defense wound of the hand from a sharp weapon.

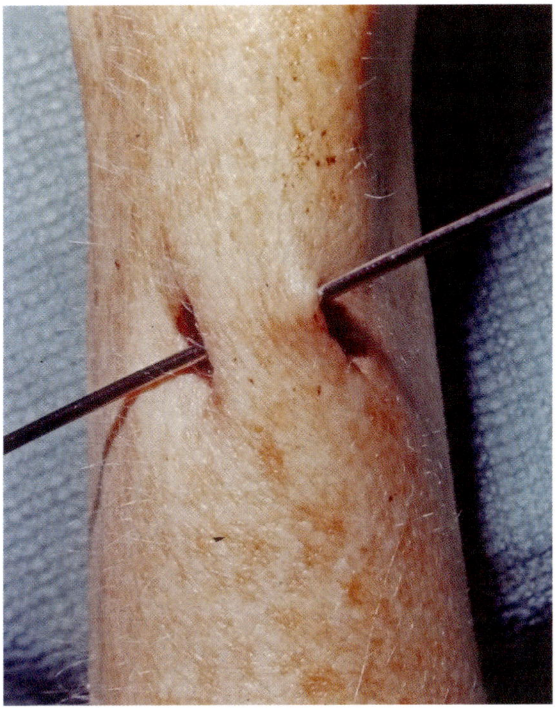

50.10 A through-and-through defense wound of the forearm with a probe delineating the tract.

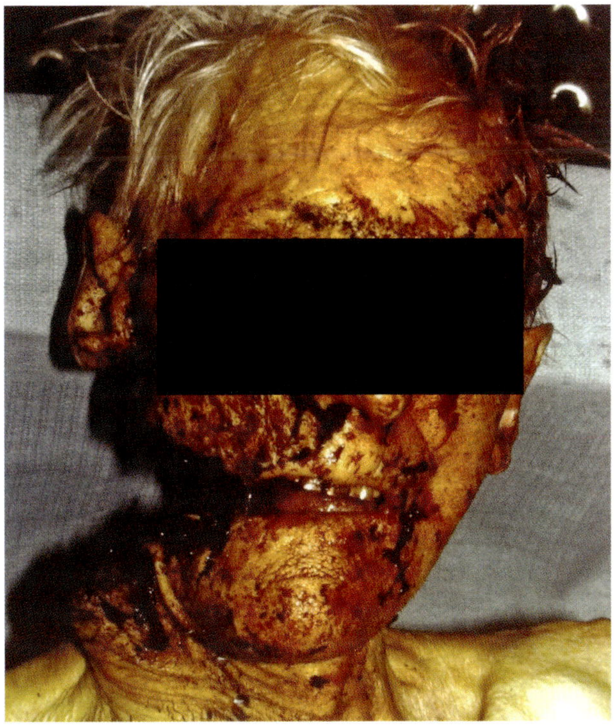

50.11 Severe trauma to the right side of the face from a chain saw.

skin has the highest resistance to stabbing, so that once the skin is breached, a sharp blade may penetrate relatively easily. The depth of penetration depends on the speed of the blow and the sharpness of the knife, not only on the force of application. It has been shown that fat padding in obese/morbidly obese individuals can protect viscera from injury in stabbing attacks (53).

Chop wounds are usually produced by heavy objects, which are relatively blunt with at least one sharp or sharpish edge, such as an axe, cleaver or machete (51). Due to the mixed blunt and sharp forces involved there tends to be a mixed injury pattern (54). Chop wounds often display a clean central area, where the skin has been impacted by the sharp edge of the blade. The surrounding wound margins are often less clean and regular due to both the thickness and/or the decreased sharpness of the blade peripherally. Surrounding contusions, abrasions or crushing injury may be observed around the wound. Due to the high-energy force applied by chop wounds, wound tails are typically absent with associated underlying fractures, particularly of the neck (55).

Atypical sharp force injuries are caused by other weapons such as scissors, broken glass or screwdrivers causing a variety of different wounds. An example of this can be seen with large tissue defects left by chain saws (Figure 50.11). Wounds inflicted by scissors may have two main patterns, depending on whether they are opened or closed on contact with the skin. A closed pair of scissors will produce a single entry point with a rhomboid or Z-shaped appearance (56). As expected, open scissors will produce two separate stab wounds, with a slightly widened angulated character separated by intact dermis (57). It is very important to clearly distinguish this from paired canine wounds that occur with dog bites. Injuries caused by broken glass, such as that from a broken bottle or tumbler ("glassing"), may have multiple stab wounds arranged in a circular pattern, matching the shape and diameter of the weapon (58), as may other unusual sharp-edged weapons (59).

Autopsy findings

Contrary to blunt force injuries where the majority are inflicted on the head, sharp force injuries are most commonly seen in the thorax and abdomen, followed by the upper limbs, lower limbs, head then neck (42). Due to the edge of the instrument used in sharp force injuries, skin bridging is almost never seen. The wound margins are cleanly divided, unlike that of a laceration, which can display ragged and irregular wound edges. Further evidence pointing to sharp force injury, is the presence of cut hairs around the wound, compared to the hairs around a laceration which tend to remain intact. Self-inflicted stab wounds and cuts are characterized by "hesitation" or "tentative" cuts which are superficial injuries adjacent to the major wound that represent initial attempts prior to the more serious wound creation. These are not typical of inflicted sharp force injuries (Figure 50.12). Self-inflicted wounds also tend to be symmetrical and parallel, often with scarring indicating previous episodes (Figure 50.13) (*see also* Chapter 83 – "Self-Injury"). If the weapon has hit bone, chipping or scoring may be seen more often than complete bone fractures, unless the wound is inflicted by heavy weapon, in the case of a chop injury. Radiological imaging may be very useful in identifying the tip of a blade that may have snapped off within bone which can then be used to match with possible weapons.

Stab wounds may not always have a clean, longitudinal entry wound as the knife penetrating the skin may undergo torsional forces, either by the perpetrator or by the movement of the victim during the confrontation. The wound entry points can then display peculiar shapes, more akin to the letters "V", "L" or "Y", or with splitting in the form of "fishtailing" (Figure 50.14) (22). Stab wounds can also be associated with localized contusional injuries. If a knife has been inserted to its hilt, a patterned impression may be left which can be helpful for weapon identification (60).

Although careful layer dissection is important at autopsy in an attempt to identify the direction of the blow, there are several important caveats. Firstly, the victim is seldom standing still in a "sentry position" during a knife attack unless restrained or otherwise immobilized. Similarly, the perpetrator is usually moving. For this reason, determining handedness of the perpetrator is not usually possible. Finally, post-mortem CT examination of knives within body cavities before autopsy dissection has clearly demonstrated that withdrawal of the blade from the body may result in elastic tissue and organs retracting back to their original anatomical position. Thus, a tangential knife wound may be in a quite different position at the time of dissection (61).

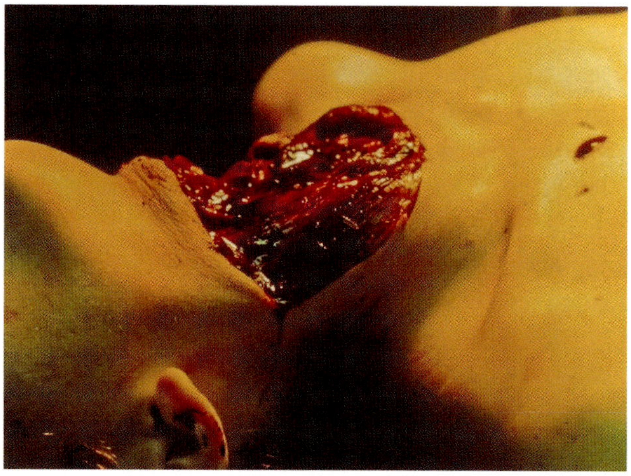

50.12 A stab wound to the chest with cutting of the throat with no evidence of "hesitation wounds".

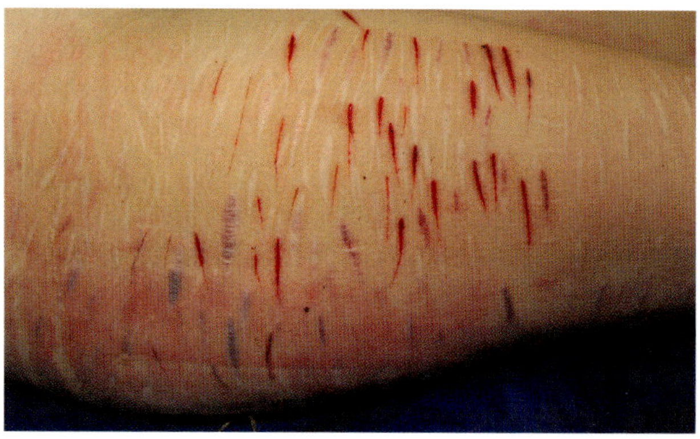

50.13 Multiple recent superficial and parallel self-inflicted wounds to the thigh of a young woman with extensive areas of previous scarring from similar injuries.

FIREARMS

In Australia, under the Firearms Act of 2015, a firearm is defined as a device that is designed to fire bullets, shot or other projectiles by the means of burning propellant, compressed air or other gases (62). In Australia during

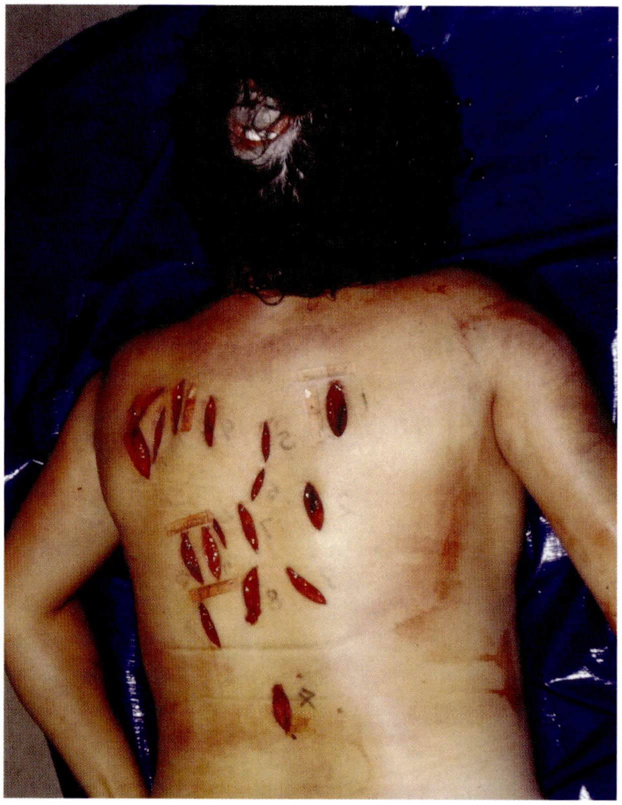

50.14 Multiple stab wounds to the back, some of which show "fishtailing". The laceration at the back of the head may suggest preceding incapacitating blunt force trauma.

2018–2019, approximately 16 percent of homicides utilized a firearm compared to the global average of 57 percent (63). Gunshot injuries are caused by any high-powered rifle, handgun or air rifle. Generally, gunshot injuries occur when only one projectile is fired at a time through a rifled barrel which has spiral grooves on the inner surface. In contrast, shotguns are smooth-bored weapons, generally with a wider diameter barrel capable of firing multiple, spherical lead pellets in one round (64).

Autopsy findings

Patterns seen on the skin after the infliction of a firearm wound can offer some insight into the type of weapon used and the distance between the victim and perpetrator. Shotgun contact wounds tend to display a single, circular entry wound that is approximately equal to the barrel bore size. The wounds will not have skin burning and soot deposit if a tight seal has been formed between the muzzle and skin if the barrel has been pressed firmly against the victim. However, if the barrel is placed over clothing, singeing of the fabric around the entrance wound may be present. Shotguns tend to cause massive injuries with marked tissue destruction (Figure 50.15).

Muzzle impression can be seen with close contact wounds from all types of firearms due to the blunt force pressure of the barrel on the skin causing a contusion/abrasion. Marking from shotguns may be double barrel – under-over or side-to-side – or single barrel (40,65). Close discharge shotgun wounds, where the barrel is not in direct contact with the skin, tend to be inflicted over clothing. In these circumstances, the clothing will collect a majority of the soot and absorb a significant proportion of the flame effects from the weapon discharge. As shotgun ammunition consists of a compacted mass of pellets, its dispersal is proportional to the distance from a target. At short distance, approximately 1–1.5 meters (3–5 feet), the pellets begin to spread before entering the body. These wounds have a large entry with a crenated (scalloped or "rat hole") appearance of the edges (49). At greater ranges, the central wound decreases in size and becomes surrounded by satellite wounds inflicted by the pellets. As distance is increased, the central defect will disappear completely and only pellet holes will be observed (66).

Gunshot wounds can be classified depending on muzzle velocity of the projectiles, being classified as either low- or high-velocity firearm injuries. The classification in the United Kingdom is based on the speed of sound in air (335 m/s) as a differentiator, and in the United States, on an arbitrary classification of 2000, 2500 or 3000 m/s (67,68). Wounds caused by gunshots tend to consist of a central tract or cavity, with a roughened perimeter, referred to as the abrasion collar or rim (69).

Gunshot wounds may be either entry or exit. Differentiation between entry and exit wounds can sometimes be complicated by the presence of multiple gunshot wounds. Usually, entry wounds tend to be smaller and more regular in diameter compared to exit wounds (70). Tissue will commonly show invagination into the wound entrance while the opposite is seen with exit wounds, with protrusion of underlying tissues (Figure 50.16). This may not, however, occur if the body was pressed against a firm surface as there will be shoring of the edges of wound.

Proximity of the weapon to the skin will determine the extent or not of muzzle burn, soiling, singeing and tissue reddening, from expelled gases. The presence of these features along with unburnt gun powder (tattooing/stippling) (Figure 50.17), abrasion rim and grease collar, can help identify an entry from an exit wound (71).

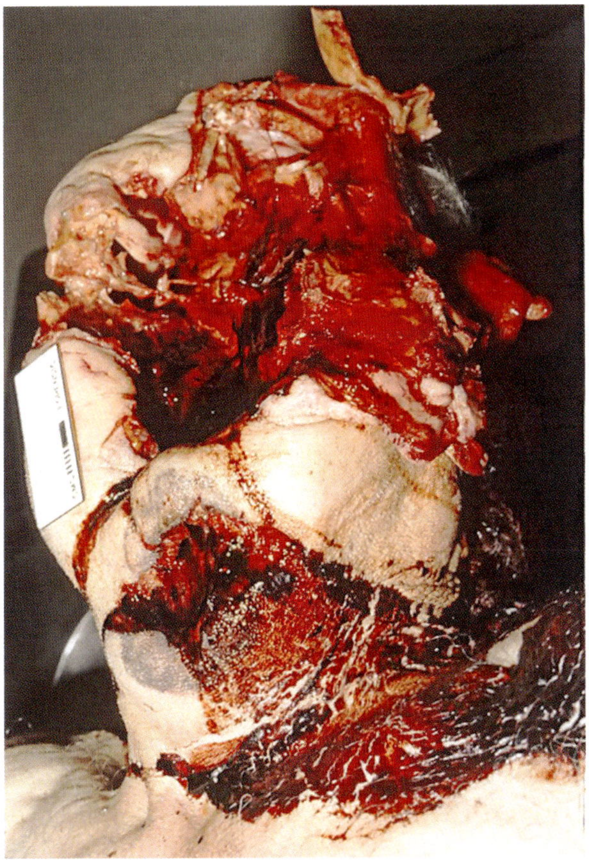

50.15 A shotgun injury to the head showing extensive traumatic disruption of the face, cranial cavity and brain with comminuted compound fracturing of the skull.

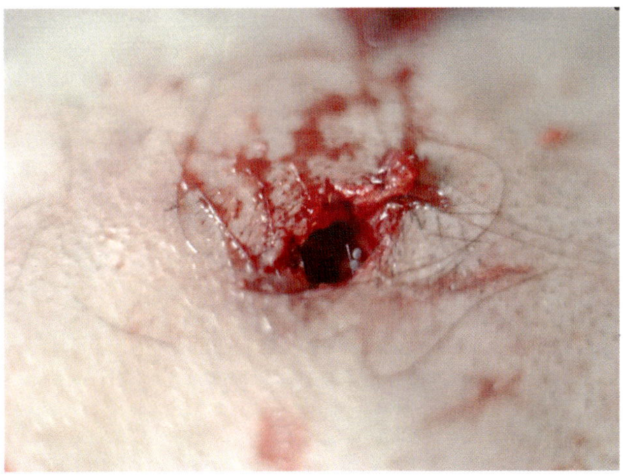

50.16 An irregular exit bullet wound with protruding tissue and no burning, soot soiling or tattooing.

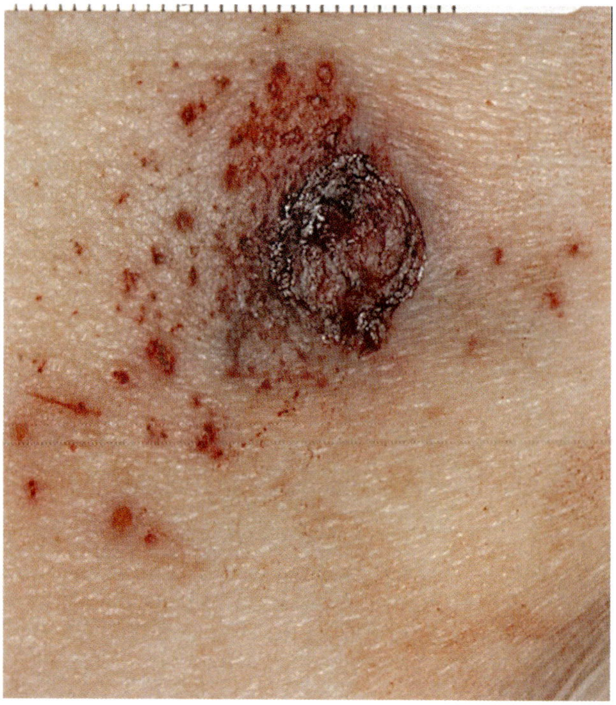

50.17 Elliptical stippling from an oblique angled gunshot.

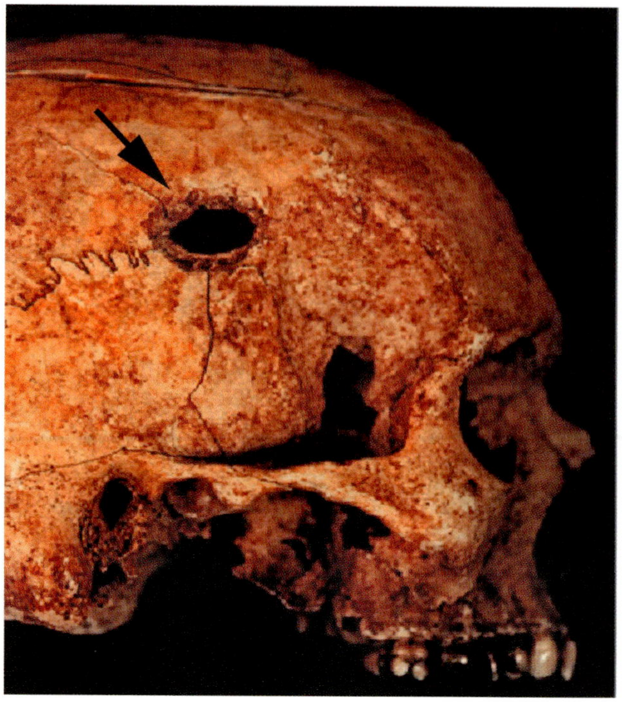

50.18 An exit wound on the right side of the skull with associated fractures showing typical external beveling.

An accompanying component of gunshot wounds is the sonic wave. This wave can have a disruptive effect on hollow viscera such as the intestine. The secondary effects caused by cavitation injury in some instances can be more detrimental than the bullet wound itself (72). These radial accelerations caused by the pressure wave can cause shear, stretch and compression forces to damage tissues distant from the main injury tract. This temporary cavitation phenomenon is more pronounced within uncompressible, solid organs (73,74).

Bullet wounds that pass through bones, especially long bones, tend to produce comminuted fractures. The transfer of energy, along with the cavitation forces, can produce significant bone fragmentation and displacement. Significantly high levels of energy can be passed onto bone fragments that can be dislodged into surrounding tissues and even ejected from the exit wound. In the case of multiple gunshot wounds to the head, it is possible to determine the sequence of these injuries utilizing Puppe's law. Originally published in the *Traumatische Todesursachen* in 1903, (75), Puppe's law was used to determine the sequence of skull fractures caused by blunt force injury. However, in 1988, Madea and Staak demonstrated that the principles could also be applied to multiple cranial fractures caused by gunshot wounds (76). In the skull, internal bevelling of the bony defect is found in entrance wounds, compared to external bevelling in exit wounds (Figure 50.18) (*see also* Chapter 61 – "Gunshot and Firearm Deaths").

One of the most important aspects of an autopsy examination in the case of a gunshot homicide is to correctly identify the number of wounds and projectiles. Post-mortem radiological examination is invaluable in finding projectiles which may have tracked some distance from an entry wound (Figure 50.19). It is also vital to carefully dissect out projectiles without handling with metal equipment so that the soft lead is not damaged thus facilitating examining and matching bullet striations with particular guns to enable estimation of the number and type of weapon used.

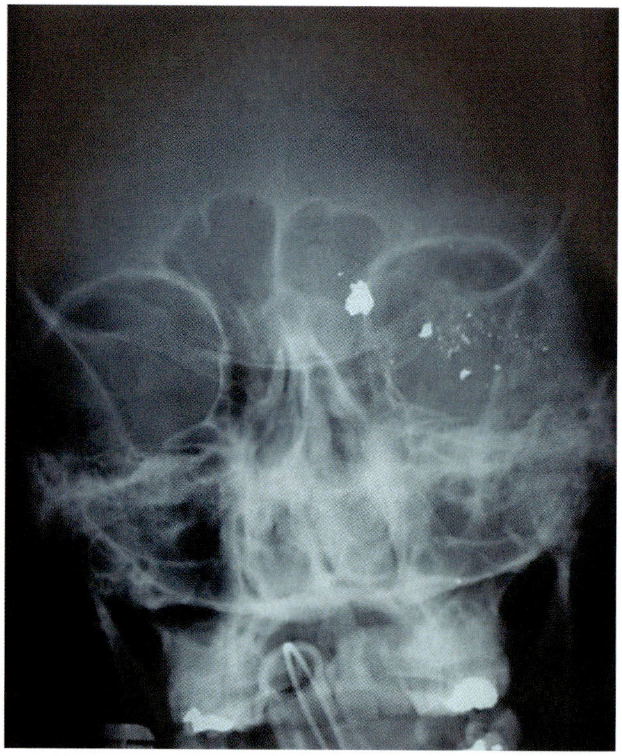

50.19 A post-mortem X-ray of the head showing fragments from a .22 bullet.

STRANGULATION

Homicides by strangulation are a relatively uncommon form of death. However, in the context of domestic homicides, sex-related murders and child killings, strangulation ranks as one of the more commonly observed methods of killing. Murder by strangulation is often subdivided into ligature strangulation – without suspension using a garrotte, and manual strangulation – using hands (77). Ligature strangulation is executed with a cord-like instrument, such as a rope, wire or chain. It was common practice between the fifteenth to the nineteenth centuries during the Spanish inquisition, where prior to the public ritual of penance, *auto-da-fé* ("act of faith"), the condemned heretics and apostates were killed by ligature strangulation (78).

The act of killing by strangulation usually requires a significant physical power differential between the perpetrator and the victim. For this reason, females rarely commit homicides in this matter due to the physical power required, with the exception being homicides that involve the death of a child.

PATHOPHYSIOLOGY

The mechanism behind death due to strangulation involves vascular compression and airway occlusion. The force required to close the airways by compression of the larynx is approximately 15 kg (33 lb), which is 7.5 times more than the force required to occlude blood vessels (≤2 kg, 4.4 lb) (79). Occlusion of the jugular venous return is responsible for the classical signs of congestion, cyanosis, edema and petechiae that characterize strangulation deaths, although these signs may also appear in survivors.

When compression is significant enough to cause bilateral occlusion of the more deeply set carotid arteries, which are largely obscured by the sternocleidomastoid muscles, almost immediate unconsciousness will occur. This is due to decreased blood supply to the brain with the vertebral artery co-lateral circulation being insufficient to maintain adequate cortical perfusion (80). Occlusion of the carotid circulation for four or more minutes results in permanent cerebral ischemic damage and inevitable death. Compression of the baroreceptors and carotid bodies, located at the bifurcation of the internal and external carotid arteries, may also cause bradycardia or cardiac arrest (81). The sequalae of events following decreased cardiac output is reduced cerebral perfusion, loss of consciousness, cerebral ischemia and inevitably death.

Other mechanisms involve direct compression of the larynx or trachea, or lifting of the larynx so that the root of the tongue presses against the soft palate and roof of the mouth (82). The question is often asked in court how quickly incapacitation and death may occur with strangulation. This may be difficult to answer as the force of strangulation may be intermittent due to both the victim and the perpetrator moving. In cases of hanging, it has been shown that consciousness may be lost within seconds with cessation of respiration within minutes (83).

Autopsy findings

Manual strangulation is characterized by oval, discoid bruising around the neck from finger pad pressure. These may be multiple or solitary. They range from 1 to 2 cm in diameter and may be found around the angle of the jaw and jawline or down to the clavicle due to a shifting grip during the attack. These may be associated with bruising over the upper chest, sternum and clavicles (84). An uneven distribution of bruises on the sides of the neck, with one or two on one side and clusters of bruises on the other, may suggest that one hand was used, however, this should be interpreted with caution as a shifting grip may cause a similar pattern (82). Abrasions caused by fingernail scratches may be seen and can be caused by either the perpetrator or the victim.

Ligature strangulation results in constriction of all components of the neck. The term garrotting is often used in reference to ligature strangulation. Garrotting was declared the sole method of civilian execution in Spain on the 28th of April 1828, with the last public garrotting occurring in May 1897. It was however, used up until the abolishment of the death penalty in the 1970s (85). The method utilized a rod within the ligature, to tighten the noose around the neck. This device was termed the "Spanish windlass" and may also be used during homicidal ligature strangulations to tighten the ligature. Ligatures around the neck may cut deeply into the skin if the tension is significant and can leave well-defined indentations sometimes showing the weave of the cord or pattern of the ligature. This may be useful in subsequently identifying the murder weapon. When softer fabrics such as a scarf or tie are used, the markings may be less well-defined making interpretation more difficult.

The bruising seen in the skin is often reflected internally in the platysma, sternocleidomastoid and neck strap muscles that should be examined by a meticulous layer dissection with photography (Figure 50.20). It is important to drain the venous blood before dissecting the neck to minimize post-mortem artefacts (86). This is most efficiently achieved by removal of the brain and viscera prior to dissection of the neck. Alternatively,

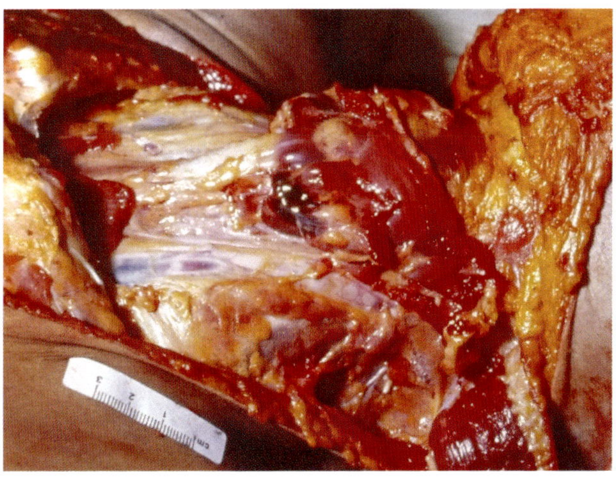

50.20 Circular bruising of the soft tissues of the anterior neck in a case of manual strangulation.

the internal jugular can be incised to allow for venous drainage before a detailed examination of the neck is undertaken.

It is becoming common practice to perform a high-resolution CT scan prior to autopsy to identify any fractures of the superior horns of the thyroid cartilage, the hyoid bone or rarely the cervical spine. Compression of the larynx by pressure bilaterally can deform the four cornuae (horns), which are responsible for maintaining airway patency. Within younger individuals, the horns are flexible and return to their resting positions once the pressure has been released, but in later years the horns begin to calcify and will fracture with pressure (87,88). Thus, the thyrohyoid ligament which holds the horns together should be carefully dissected to identify any fractures. Hemorrhage will often be present if there is a fracture. Bleeding in the front and sides of the larynx is also found in strangulation, however, special care must be taken in interpreting hemorrhage posterior to the larynx and pharynx, as this can be a post-mortem occurrence, termed the Prinsloo and Gordon artefact (89).

IMMERSION

When a body is found in water, death could be due to drowning or to a preceding natural or unnatural event and so may represent an accident, suicide or homicide. Unfortunately, the diagnosis of drowning is not easy and so the conclusion may be that the manner of death is undetermined (90) (*see also* Chapter 33 – "Drowning"). In the case of homicide, bodies are often placed in water as a means of disposal. Notable cases of immersion homicide have occurred within bathtubs. For example, George Joseph Smith, an infamous serial killer between 1912 and 1914, was responsible for murdering three of his eight wives in a series of homicides termed the "Brides in the Bath Murders". The murders were achieved by rapidly pulling the feet of the women to submerge their heads under the water (91). The autopsy findings in immersion deaths are discussed in detail elsewhere in this text.

ELECTROCUTION

Electrocution deaths occur when electric current passes through the body. Several factors are involved in determining the severity of tissue damage and outcome in individuals who receive an electric shock. These include current, voltage, resistance and duration. Current is equal to voltage over resistance and is measured in Amperes (amp) (92). During electrocution, an electrical path is created allowing for the passage of electrons through the body and vital organs. Current generally enters through the hands of an individual, most commonly due to handling of faulty electrical appliances. The current then leaves the body often through the feet, where the individual is earthed. The path through the body is determined by the line of least resistance, often taking the shortest route between the entry and exit.

While most deaths due to electrocution at all ages are accidental, occasional cases of suicide occur, with even fewer numbers of homicides (93–95). Dropping a live appliance into a bath with the victim may leave no discernible trace of electrical burns at autopsy due to the wide area of contact with the water. Research commissioned by the State of New York in the United States and carried out at Thomas Edison's laboratory concluded that AC current was a more humane method for executing criminals, which led to the establishment of the electric chair as a form of capital punishment. Alternating current is much more likely to cause a cardiac arrhythmia, such as ventricular fibrillation, and death, requiring only 100Ma for one fifth of a second (96); whereas high amperage DC, above 4A, is used to revert arrhythmias back into sinus during medical defibrillation.

Autopsy findings

Cutaneous features of electrocution may range from no lesions at all to complete avulsion injuries when extremely high energy is involved. Burns may be found at the entry point of the current (97) as a classic annular, raised gray/white ring with an umbilicated center and surrounding pallor and hyperemia. High-voltage discharges may produce multiple spark lesions producing a "crocodile-skin" effect.

POISONING

In previous centuries, poisoning was a not uncommon method of homicide with a third of all poisoning cases in the nineteenth century involving arsenic (98). However, as toxicological evaluation of blood and tissues became more sophisticated, poisons fell out of favor. Overall, murders by poisoning nowadays are extremely rare with a rate in the United States during the period of 1999–2005 of 0.26 cases/million/year (99). The symptoms of poisoning may simulate that of disease or may be non-specific which can lead to a delay in investigation and/or a misdiagnosis as to the cause and manner of death.

Autopsy findings

The autopsy findings in most cases of drug toxicity or poisoning are not specific and the diagnosis depends on toxicological analysis of body fluid. Samples of blood, urine, bile, cerebrospinal fluid (CSF), vitreous humor, stomach contents and, on occasion, intestinal contents may be collected for analysis. In special circumstances, when death from a volatile substance is suspected, head space analysis can be performed. A difficult situation may occur in the deaths of habitual drug users where it may not be possible to determine whether the dosage of a supplied drug was intentionally increased or whether the drug was administered by another (82) (*see also* Chapter 56 – "Poisoning").

NEGLECT

Homicide by neglect, in the context of caregiving, is the failure to provide sufficient nourishment, medical care or supervision, which results in decreased physical health and ultimately contributes to the victim's death. Those affected most by neglect are usually at the extremes of life as they are generally more vulnerable and reliant on the care of others. Child protection legislation in Australia states that:

> *"a person with the care and control of a child must not do an act, or fail to do an act, knowing (or recklessly disregarding) that the conduct may cause significant harm to a child from abuse (physical, sexual, emotional or psychological) or neglect"* (100).

Further defining neglect as:

> *"the person with parental responsibility to fail to provide a child... under his or her care with the 'necessities of life' – accommodation, food, clothing and access to healthcare and education"* (101).

Several studies have shown that the prevalence of child neglect ranges from around 1.6 percent to 4 percent of children (102–105), with approximately 1840 children dying from abuse or neglect in United States in 2019 (106). Changes have occurred over time for child homicides, with a local South Australian study showing that while the overall numbers of child homicides had decreased over the preceding decades, the number of nonlethal inflicted injuries had increased (107). Children may also be susceptible to inflicted injury by proxy (previously known as Munchausen syndrome by proxy) which may involve repetitive inflicted airway obstruction, poisoning or neglect (108) (*see also* Chapter 52 – "Neglect").

Autopsy findings

Starvation may form a subset of neglect which can be primary or secondary. Nutritional deficiencies can lead to infections, avitaminoses, skin disorders and nutritional edema (109). Subsequent dehydration and hypothermia are common manifestations contributing to death. Detailed discussion on pediatric autopsy is covered elsewhere in this text.

SEXUAL MURDERS

The definition of sexual homicide, also termed lust murder, sexual murder and erotophonophilia, is somewhat contentious (110), however, the general consensus is that for the homicide to be considered "sexual", evidence of sexual activity by the perpetrator must be present. This activity can occur before, during, after or throughout the event, ranging from acts such as masturbation to penetration of the victim (oral, anal or vaginal) (110). This activity may also be expressed symbolically through mutilation of the victim's genitalia (111). It is important, however, to differentiate post-mortem animal predation from antemortem sexual mutilation (112).

The motivation behind sexual murders includes the two major categories of anger and sadism (113). Anger-motivated murders tend to be retaliatory, grievance-motivated with unplanned, disorganized *modus operandi* and no premeditation. Sadistic sexual murders tend to display a more coordinated pattern with a focus on lust. Murder weapons and actions reflecting sadistic fantasies such as torture, restraints and retaining souvenirs are often seen in these types of homicides (114).

Autopsy findings

The autopsy findings in sexual murders can be similar to those seen in sexual assaults and so a standard external examination should be carried out to facilitate appropriate sample collection. Findings can be subdivided into perineal and whole body. The patterns of wounds may be organized or haphazard with genital injuries ranging from lacerations, bruises, swelling and bleeding within or around the vagina or anus and involving perineum. Common injuries include vulval/labial trauma, especially in children and tearing of the introitus of the vagina and lacerations around the anus. With significant force in younger children, a complete tear between the anus and vagina can sometimes be seen (82). Pelvic exenteration is the best method for demonstrating anogenital injuries at autopsy (Figure 50.21).

In addition, injuries may be found elsewhere with bruises around the lips and buccal surfaces which may show abrasions and lacerations from contact with teeth (82). Bite marks can often be seen around the neck

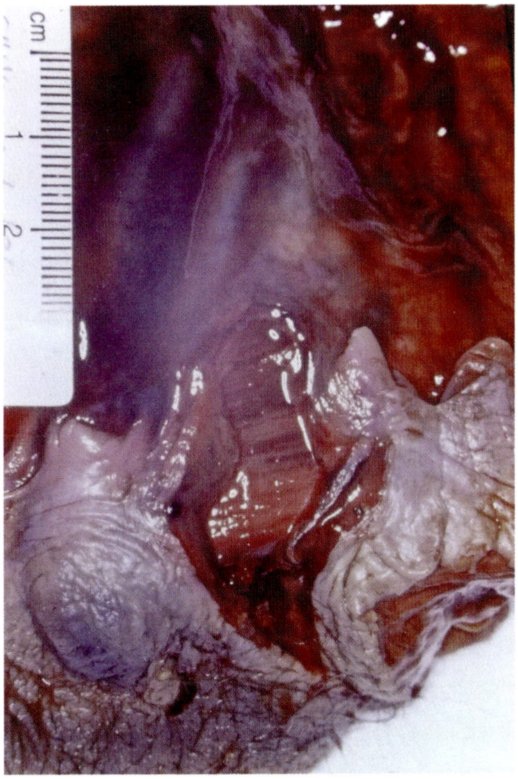

50.21 A deep mucosal tear in a case of sexual assault.

shoulder, breasts and buttocks. Circular or oval bruising patterns with small intradermal petechial hemorrhages can be seen with significant suction. These suction lesions can coexist with teeth indentations (115,116).

During a sexual assault, the breasts may be manipulated with force, resulting in discoid bruising. Bruising on the thighs and buttocks is also a common finding, due to a struggle between the victim and perpetrator when attempting intercourse. The inner aspect of the upper thighs is commonly bruised by forceful opening of the legs (115). The nails of the victim should be carefully examined for broken tips, trapped hairs or fibers in nail splits. Nails should be cut close to the nail junction for forensic analysis. Debris from under the nail can also be scraped out and collected and may contain DNA evidence of the assailant if scratched by the victim during the assault (117). In sadistic sexual assaults, stabbing and mutilation of sexual areas, especially the breasts, buttocks and perineum may be seen. Care should be taken to collect samples from the vagina and anus as well as surrounding clothing if any suspected blood or semen is present. As with the living victim, physical findings of sexual assault may be absent.

MASS MURDERS

The term mass murder has been defined by the Federal Bureau of Investigation (FBI) as the murder of four or more people during an event with no cooling-off period between murders (118,119). Mass murders can be carried out as terrorist attack, notably the Al-Qaeda September 11 attack in New York City, as part of a cult ritual as in Jim Jones' Peoples Temple murder-suicide deaths in 1978, or by individuals. Methods of mass killings can vary and include explosives, vehicles, poisons and most commonly firearms.

The interpretation of global data varies, with a study conducted by the Crime Prevention Research Center (CPRC) in 2015 in the United States concluding that Norway ranked the highest rate of mass shootings, with 1.88 deaths per million between the years of 2009 to 2015, with the United States ranking 11th (120). These data have been disputed as Norway's high ranking was skewed because of the Anders Breivik shooting of 77 people in 2011. Corrected median analysis of the data has resulted in the United States having the highest annual death rate per million people from mass public shootings between the years 2009 to 2015 (121). Another study by Lankford analyzed the mass shooting data from 171 countries between the years 1966 to 2012 and concluded that, although the United States only made up 5 percent of the world's population, it accounted for more than 30 percent of the mass shootings (122).

SERIAL KILLING

The definition of serial murders or "serial killing" differs among law enforcement officers, clinicians and academics depending on the number of victims involved, the methods used and the temporal aspects of the murders. The United States Congress defined serial murders as:

> *"The term 'serial killings'; means a series of three or more killings, not less than one of which was committed within the Unites States, having common characteristics such as to suggest the reasonable possibility that the crimes were committed by the same actor or actors."* (123).

The FBI National Center of the Analysis of Violent Crime in 2005 proposed the following definition:

> *"Serial murder: The unlawful killing of two or more victims by the same offender(s), in separate events."* (124).

Serial killing differs from mass murder as it tends to occur at multiple locations over a longer time. The motivation behind serial killings can vary greatly and includes anger, financial gain, ideology (i.e. terrorist groups attacking specific race or gender targets), power/thrill, psychosis and sexual gratification (125,126).

DOWRY DEATHS

Dowry death is the term used when husbands or their families kill young brides in countries where goods and money in the form of dowries have been part of a marriage transaction. Dowry deaths most often involve burning or hanging/strangulation, drowning and poisoning. Abetted suicide may occur where young women are encouraged to commit suicide by self-immolation or hanging. In 2015, 7634 women died due to dowry deaths, representing approximately 21 deaths per day in India (127). Honor killings, which refer to a specific form of homicide committed by family members toward a female, ostensibly to protect or restore a family's "honor", are discussed in detail elsewhere in the text.

LAPIDATION

Colloquially known as "stoning" or "Rajm", lapidation is a form of capital punishment where the victim is executed by being bombarded with stones. The practice of stoning is common in many countries in and around the Middle East, including Iran, United Arab Emirates, Qatar, Mauritania, Saudi Arabia, Yemen and Afghanistan, but has also been seen in some African and Asian countries. An example is Kelantan and Terengganu in Malaysia, where the approval of the Islamic criminal law in 1993 and 2002 respectively, allowed the practice of lapidation (128). Individuals subjected to stoning are commonly accused of adultery, however, homosexuality can also be a cause for this punishment (129). There are limited publications on the forensic findings of stoning, however, a paper published by Judd describes skull injuries from the impact of stones in Western Samoa (130). Most often, comminuted cranial vault fractures were present with dirt and debris contaminating the wounds.

CONCLUSION

A wide range of methods are used globally to cause the death of a fellow citizen ranging from firearms to knives and lapidation to incineration. Investigations of each type of homicide need to be comprehensive and follow standard procedures for both dissection and evidence retrieval and processing, with modifications where necessary for local conditions. While forming only a part of the overall investigation of murder, the pathological evaluation of cases has to be unbiased and substantial and robust enough to survive scrutiny and questioning in subsequent legal proceedings.

REFERENCES

1. Australian Bureau of Statistic. *Directory of Family, Domestic and Sexual Violence Statistics*. 2018. [Online]. Available from: https://www.abs.gov.au/ (Accessed 3 May 2023).
2. Government of South Australia. *Criminal Law Consolidation Act 1935*. [Online]. Available from: https://www.legislation.sa.gov.au/ (Accessed 3 May 2023)
3. Government of South Australia. *The Law Handbook South Australia*. 2000. [Online]. Available from: https://lawhandbook.sa.gov.au/ (Accessed 3 May 2023).
4. Mirabile F, Nass D. *New FBI Data is in: Murder rates in US cities, ranked*. 2018. [Online]. Available from: https://www.thetrace.org (Accessed 5 May 2023).
5. Temlett J, Byard RW. Homicide among Indigenous South Australians: A forty-year study (1969–2008). *J Forensic Leg Med* 2012; **19(8)**: 445–7.
6. Byard RW, Haas E, Marshall DT, et al. Characteristic features of pediatric firearm fatalities: Comparisons between Australia and the United States. *J Forensic Sci* 2009; **54(5)**: 1093–6.
7. Byard RW, Winskog C. Homicides in Samoa: A five-year study. *Aust J Forensic Sci* 2018; **50(4)**: 435–8.
8. Maiden NR, Hiss J, Gips H, et al. An analysis of the characteristics of thoracic and abdominal injuries due to gunshot homicides in Israel. *J Forensic Sci* 2016; **61(1)**: 87–92.
9. Byard RW. Geographic variability in homicide rates following the COVID-19 pandemic. *Forensic Sci Med Pathol* 2021; **17(3)**: 419–21.
10. Bricknell S, Doherty L. *Homicide in Australia 2018–19: Statistical report no. 24*. Canberra: Australian Institute of Criminology; 2021.
11. Simon LV, Lopez RA, King KC. *Blunt Force Trauma*. StatPearls. Treasure Island (FL): StatPearls Publishing; 2022.
12. Prahlow J. Blunt force injury deaths. *Forensic Pathology for Police, Death Investigators, Attorneys, and Forensic Scientists*. New York City: Springer; 2010, pp. 301–35.
13. Drew LB, Drew WE. The contrecoup-coup phenomenon. *Neurocrit Care* 2004; **1(3)**: 385–90.
14. Byard RW, Tsokos M. Forensic issues in cases of Diogenes syndrome. *Am J Forensic Med Pathol* 2007; **28(2)**: 177–81.
15. Byard RW, Vink R. The second impact syndrome. *Forensic Sci Med Pathol* 2009; **5(1)**: 36–8.
16. Byard RW, Gabrielian L, Helps SC, et al. Further investigations into the speed of cerebral swelling following blunt cranial trauma. *J Forensic Sci* 2012; **57(4)**: 973–5.
17. Khairat A, Waseem M. *Epidural Hematoma*. StatPearls. Treasure Island (FL): StatPearls Publishing; 2022.
18. Khairat A, Waseem M. *Epidural Hematoma*. 2021. [Online] Available from: https://pubmed.ncbi.nlm.nih.gov/30085524/ (Accessed 3 May 2023).
19. Capper C. The language of forensic medicine: The meaning of some terms employed. *Med Sci Law* 2001; **41(3)**: 256–9.
20. Shrestha R, Krishan K, Kanchan T. *Abrasion*. Treasure Island (FL): StatPearls Publishing; 2022.
21. Vanezis P. Interpreting bruises at necropsy. *J Clin Pathol* 2001; **54(5)**: 348–55.
22. Payne-James J. Injury, Fatal and Non-fatal: Sharp and Cutting-edge Wounds. *Encyclopedia of Forensic and Legal Medicine*. Philadelphia, USA: Elsevier; 2016, pp.244–56.
23. Kennedy JG, Johnson SM, Collins AL, et al. An evaluation of the Weber classification of ankle fractures. *Injury* 1998; **29(8)**: 577–80.
24. Brown JH, DeLuca SA. Growth plate injuries: Salter-Harris classification. *Am Fam Physician* 1992; **46(4)**: 1180–4.
25. Kazley JM, Banerjee S, Abousayed MM, Rosenbaum AJ. Classifications in brief: Garden classification of femoral neck fractures. *Clin Orthop Relat Res* 2018; **476(2)**: 441–5.
26. Atanelov Z, Bentley TP. *Greenstick Fracture*. Treasure Island (FL): StatPearls Publishing; 2022.
27. Bosmia AN, Griessenauer CJ, Tubbs RS. Yubitsume: Ritualistic self-amputation of proximal digits among the Yakuza. *J Inj Violence Res* 2014; **6(2)**: 54.
28. Randeberg LL, Winnem AM, Larsen EL, et al. In vivo hyperspectral imaging of traumatic skin injuries in a porcine model. *Int Society Optics Photonics* 2007.
29. Langlois NE, Gresham GA. The ageing of bruises: A review and study of the colour changes with time. *Forensic Sci Int* 1991; **50(2)**: 227–38.
30. Byard RW, Langlois NE. Bruises: Is it a case of "the more we know, the less we understand?" *Forensic Sci Med Pathol* 2015; **11(4)**: 479–81.
31. Lieberman M, Marks AD. *Marks' Basic Medical Biochemistry: A Clinical Approach*. Philadelphia: Lippincott Williams & Wilkins; 2009.
32. Langlois NE. The science behind the quest to determine the age of bruises: A review of the English language literature. *Forensic Sci Med Pathol* 2007; **3(4)**: 241–51.
33. Nash KR, Sheridan DJ. Can one accurately date a bruise? State of the science. *J Forensic Nurs* 2009; **5(1)**: 31–7.
34. Ross CG, Langlois NE, Heath K, Byard RW. Further evidence for a lack of reliability in the histologic ageing of bruises: An autopsy study. *Aust J Forensic Sci* 2015; **47(2)**: 224–9.
35. Byard RW, Wick R, Gilbert JD, Donald T. Histologic dating of bruises in moribund infants and young children. *Forensic Sci Med Pathol* 2008; **4(3)**: 187–92.
36. Guo S, Dipietro LA. Factors affecting wound healing. *J Dent Res* 2010; **89(3)**: 219–29.
37. Wallace HA, Basehore BM, Zito PM. *Wound Healing Phases*. Treasure Island (FL): StatPearls Publishing; 2022.
38. Vinay J, Harish S, Mangala GSR, Hugar BS. A study on postmortem wound dating by gross and histopathological examination of abrasions. *Am J Forensic Med Pathol* 2017; **38(2)**: 167–73.
39. Muire PJ, Mangum LH, Wenke JC. Time course of immune response and immunomodulation during normal and delayed healing of musculoskeletal wounds. *Front Immunol* 2020; **11**: 1056.
40. Davis KW, Yablon CM. *Fracture Healing*. 2021 [Online] Available from: https://www.statdx.com/document/fracture-healing/68d466bc-6262-4117-91ec-2a11030a3785 (Accessed 5 May 2023).
41. Byard RW. Timing: The Achilles heel of forensic pathology. *Forensic Sci Med Pathol* 2017; **13**: 113–14.
42. Ambade VN, Godbole HV. Comparison of wound patterns in homicide by sharp and blunt force. *Forensic Sci Int* 2006; **156(2–3)**: 166–70.
43. Tully J. *Skin Injuries: Can We Determine Timing and Mechanism?* Royal Childrens Hospital Melbourne. 2016. Available from: https://www.rch.org.au/uploadedFiles/Main/Content/vfpms/7_Jo_Skin%20injuries%20final_ni.pdf (Accessed 5 May 2023).
44. Pollak S, Saukko P. *Clinical Forensic Medicine - Overview*. 2nd ed. Amsterdam: Elsevier; 2013.
45. Fersini F, Govi A, Tsokos M, et al. Examples of tramline bruises in clinical forensic medicine. *Forensic Sci Med Pathol* 2017; **13(4)**: 508–10.
46. Byard RW. How reliable is external examination in identifying internal injuries: Casper's sign revisited. *J Forensic Leg Med* 2012; **19(7)**: 419–21.
47. Byard RW. Casper's sign in the elderly. *Med Sci Law* 2021; **61(4)**: 309–12.
48. Gitto L, Arunkumar P. *Autopsy & Forensics: Types of Injuries Sharp Force Injuries*. [Online] Available from: https://www.pathologyoutlines.com/topic/autopsysharpforce.html (Accessed 5 May 2023.
49. Prahlow JA, Byard RW. *Atlas of Forensic Pathology*. Philadelphia: Springer; 2012.
50. Austin AE, Guddat SS, Tsokos M, et al. Multiple injuries in suicide simulating homicide: report of three cases. *J Forensic Leg Med* 2013; **20(6)**: 601–4.

51. Prahlow JA, Denton J. *Forensic autopsy of sharp force injuries*. 2016. [Online] Available from: https://emedicine.medscape.com. (Accessed 5 May 2023).
52. Luna A, Solano C, Gomez M, Bañon R. Incised wound margins caused by steel blades. Scanning electron microscopy to determine wound direction. *Forensic Sci Int* 1989; **43(1)**: 21–6.
53. Omond KJ, Langlois NEI, Byard RW. Obesity, body mass index, and homicide. *J Forensic Sci* 2017; **62(4)**: 930–3.
54. Ong BB. The pattern of homicidal slash/chop injuries: A 10 year retrospective study in University Hospital Kuala Lumpur. *J Clin Forensic Med* 1999; **6(1)**: 24–9.
55. Gentile S, Kneubuehl BP, Barrera V, et al. Fracture energy threshold in parry injuries due to sharp and blunt force. *Int J Legal Med* 2019; **133(5)**: 1429–35.
56. Deps PD, Aborghetti HP, Zambon TL, et al. Assessing signs of torture: A review of clinical forensic dermatology. *J Am Acad Dermatol* 2020; S0190–9622(20)32619–0.
57. Catanese C. *Color Atlas of Forensic Medicine and Pathology*. Boca Raton: CRC Press; 2016.
58. Sauvageau A, Yesovitch R, Racette S. An unusual case of suicide by broken glass pierced through the buttocks. *Med Sci Law* 2005; **45(1)**: 81–4.
59. Bodwal J, Chauhan M, Behera C, Byard RW. An unusual patterned injury from homicidal craniocerebral impalement with a metal chair leg. *Forensic Sci Med Pathol* 2021; **17(2)**: 327–9.
60. Gitto L, Vullo A, Demari G. Identification of the murder weapon by the analysis of a typical pattern of sharp force injury. *Italian J Leg Med* 2012; **1(1)**: 4–14.
61. Winskog C. Precise wound track measurement requires cat scan with object in situ: how accurate is post-mortem dissection and evaluation? *Forensic Sci Med Pathol* 2012; **8(1)**: 76–7.
62. Government of South Australia. *Firearms Act 2015*. [Online] Available from: https://www.legislation.sa.gov.au (Accessed 5 May 2023).
63. United Nations. Global study on homicide - Understanding homicide. 2019. [Online] Available from: https://www.unodc.org/ (Accessed 5 May 2023).
64. Ordog GJ, Wasserberger J, Balasubramaniam S. Shotgun wound ballistics. *J Trauma* 1988; **28(5)**: 624–31.
65. Frost RE. *Forensic pathology of firearm wounds*. 2021. [Online] Available from: https://emedicine.medscape.com/ (Accessed 5 May 2023).
66. Molina DK, Wood LE, DiMaio VJ. Shotgun wounds: A review of range and location as pertaining to manner of death. *Am J Forensic Med Pathol* 2007; **28(2)**: 99–102.
67. Suneson A, Hansson HA, Seeman T. Peripheral high-energy missile hits cause pressure changes and damage to the nervous system: Experimental studies on pigs. *J Trauma* 1987; 27(7): 782–9.
68. Suneson A, Hansson HA, Seeman T. Central and peripheral nervous damage following high-energy missile wounds in the thigh. *J Trauma* 1988; **28(1 Suppl)**: S197–203.
69. Gujaral PB, Ajay B. Abrasion collar around shrapnel entry wound. *J Forensic Sci* 2017; **62(6)**: 1635–7.
70. Peonim V, Srisont S, Udnoon J, et al. Entrance and exit wounds of high velocity bullet: An autopsy analysis in the event of dispersing the mass rally in Bangkok Thailand, May 2010. *Leg Med* 2016; **23**: 10–16.
71. Shrestha R, Kanchan T, Krishan K. *Gunshot wounds forensic pathology*. 2021. [Online] Available from: https://www.ncbi.nlm.nih.gov/ (Accessed 5 May 2023).
72. Maiden N. Ballistics reviews: Mechanisms of bullet wound trauma. *Forensic Sci Med Pathol* 2009; 5(3): 204–9.
73. Sardiwalla I, Govender M, Matsevych O, Koto MZ. Indirect ballistic injury to the liver: Case report and review of literature. *Int J Surg Open* 2016; **5**: 23–6.
74. Hodnick R. Penetrating trauma wounds challenge EMS providers. *J Emerg Med Serv* April, 2012.
75. Puppe G. Traumatische Todesursachen. *Gerichtliche Medizin*. Jena: G Fischer, Zwölf Vortrage; 1903, pp. 65–84.
76. Madea B, Staak M. Determination of the sequence of gunshot wounds of the skull. *J Forensic Sci Soc* 1988; **28(5–6)**: 321–8.
77. Häkkänen H. Murder by Manual and Ligature Strangulation. In: Kocsis RN (ed). *Criminal Profiling: International Theory, Research, and Practice*. Totowa; Humana Press; 2007, pp. 73–87.
78. Reston Jr J. *Dogs of God: Columbus, the Inquisition, and the Defeat of the Moors*. New York City: Anchor; 2006.
79. Brouardel P. *La pendaison, la strangulation, la suffocation, la submersion*. Paris: Baillière; 1897.
80. Dunn RJ, Sukhija K, Lopez RA. *Strangulation injuries*. Treasure Island (FL): StatPearls. 2021.
81. Tontsch D, Alter P, Grimm W. Cardiac arrest following carotid sinus massage. *J Cardiovasc Electrophysiol* 2001; **12(11)**: 1331.
82. Saukko P, Knight B. *Knight's Forensic Pathology*. 3rd ed. Boca Raton: CRC Press; 2015.
83. Gilbert JD, Jensen L, Byard RW. Further observations on the speed of death in hanging. *J Forensic Sci* 2008; **53(5)**: 1204–5.
84. Yen K, Thali MJ, Aghayev E, et al. Strangulation signs: initial correlation of MRI, MSCT, and forensic neck findings. *J Magn Reson Imaging* 2005; **22(4)**: 501–10.
85. Gniger H. *A Spanish Anarchist, 26, Is Executed by Garroting*. 1974. [Online] Available from: https://www.nytimes.com/1974/03/03/archives/a-spanish-anarchist-26-is-executed-by-garroting-a-spanish-anarchist.html (Accessed 5 May 2023).
86. Sharma B, Harish D, Sharma A, et al. Injuries to neck structures in deaths due to constriction of neck, with a special reference to hanging. *J Forensic Leg Med* 2008; **15(5)**: 298–305.
87. Bhardwaj R, Tuli IP, PK MS, et al. Cricoid ossification mimicking an esophageal foreign body: A victim of overdiagnosis. *Dubai Med J* 2021; **4(1)**: 77–80.
88. Green H, James RA, Gilbert JD, Byard RW. Fractures of the hyoid bone and laryngeal cartilages in suicidal hanging. *J Clin Forensic Med* 2000; **7(3)**: 123–6.
89. Prinsloo I, Gordon I. Medico-legal section: Post-mortem dissection artefacts of the neck: their differentiation from ante-mortem bruises. *S Afr Med J* 1951; **25(21)**: 358–60.
90. Stephenson L, Van den Heuvel C, Byard RW. The persistent problem of drowning - A difficult diagnosis with inconclusive tests. *J Forensic Leg Med* 2019; **66**: 79–85.
91. Court G-BCC, Watson ER. *Trial of George Joseph Smith*. Toronto, Canada Law Book Company; 1922.
92. Ohm GS. *Die Galvanische Kette: Mathematisch*. Berlin: TH Riemann; 1827.
93. Byard RW, Hanson K, Gilbert JD, et al. Death due to electrocution in childhood and early adolescence. *J Paediatr Child Health* 2003; **39(1)**: 46–8.
94. Wick R, Gilbert JD, Simpson E, Byard RW. Fatal electrocution in adults: A 30-year study. *Med Sci Law* 2006; **46(2)**: 166–72.
95. Wick R, Byard RW. Electrocution and the Autopsy. In: Tsokos M (ed). *Forensic Pathology Reviews* Vol 5. Totowa, NJ: Humana Press; 2008, pp. 53–66.
96. Fish RM, Geddes LA. Conduction of electrical current to and through the human body: A review. *Eplasty* 2009; **9**: e44.
97. Payne-James J, Busuttil A, Smock W, Smock WS. *Forensic Medicine: Clinical and Pathological Aspects*. Cambridge: Cambridge University Press; 2003.
98. Acocella J. *Murder by Poison*. 2013. [Online] Available from: https://www.newyorker.com/ (Accessed 4 May 2023).
99. Shepherd G, Ferslew BC. Homicidal poisoning deaths in the United States 1999–2005. *Clin Toxicol (Phila)* 2009; **47(4)**: 342–7.
100. Government of Western Australia. Children and Community Services Act 2004 s101. Department of Justice. [Online] Available from: https://www.legislation.wa.gov.au/ (Accessed 5 May 2023).
101. Government of South Australia. Criminal Law Consolidation Act 1935 (SA) s 30. [Online] Available from: https://www.legislation.sa.gov.au/ (Accessed 5 May 2023).
102. Rosenman S, Rodgers B. Childhood adversity in an Australian population. *Soc Psychiatry Psychiatr Epidemiol* 2004; **39(9)**: 695–702.
103. Price-Robertson R, Smart D, Bromfield L. Family is for life: How childhood experiences within the family help or hinder the lives of young adults. *Fam Matters* 2010; **85**: 7–17.
104. Chu DA, Williams LM, Harris AW, et al. Early life trauma predicts self-reported levels of depressive and anxiety symptoms in nonclinical community adults: Relative contributions of early life stressor types and adult trauma exposure. *J Psychiatr Res* 2013; **47(1)**: 23–32.
105. Moore SE, Scott JG, Ferrari AJ, et al. Burden attributable to child maltreatment in Australia. *Child Abuse Negl* 2015; **48**: 208–20.
106. Children's Bureau. *Child abuse and neglect fatalities 2019: Statistics and Interventions*. [Online] Available from: https://www.childwelfare.gov/ (Accessed 5 May 2023).
107. Pilla M, van den Heuvel C, Musgrave I, Byard RW. Increasing incidence of nonlethal inflicted injuries in paediatric

homicides: A 45-year study. *J Forensic Leg Med* 2018; **59**: 4–7.

108. Byard RW, Beal SM. Munchausen syndrome by proxy: Repetitive infantile apnoea and homicide. *J Paediatr Child Health* 1993; **29(2)**: 77–9.
109. Henry Golden M. Nutritional and other types of oedema, albumin, complex carbohydrates and the interstitium: A response to Malcolm Coulthard's hypothesis: Oedema in kwashiorkor is caused by hypo-albuminaemia. *Paediatr Int Child Health* 2015; **35(2)**: 90–109.
110. Kerr KJ, Beech AR, Murphy D. Sexual homicide: Definition, motivation and comparison with other forms of sexual offending. *Aggress Violent Behav* 2013; **18(1)**: 1–10.
111. Meloy JR. The nature and dynamics of sexual homicide: An integrative review. *Aggress Violent Behav* 2000; **5(1)**: 1–22.
112. Byard RW. Implications of genital mutilation at autopsy. *J Forensic Sci* 2017; **62(4)**: 926–9.
113. Proulx J, Beauregard E, Cusson M, Nicole A (eds). *Sexual Murderers: A Comparative Analysis and New Perspectives*. Hoboken, NJ: John Wiley & Sons; 2007.
114. Edwards S. A crime scene approach to distinguishing sexual murderers. PhD thesis, Arts & Social Sciences: School of Criminology Simon Fraser University, 2019. Available from: http://summit.sfu.ca› files› iritems1› etd20074 (Accessed 5 May 2023).
115. World Health Organization. Assessment and examination of adult victims of sexual violence: WHO. [Online] Available from: https://www.who.int/ (Accessed 5 May 2023).
116. Kaur S, Krishan K, Chatterjee PM, Kanchan T. Analysis and identification of bite marks in forensic casework. *Oral Health Dent Manag* 2013; **12(3)**: 127–31.
117. Foran D, Lisa Hebda M, Doran A. Trace DNA from fingernails: Increasing the success rate of widely collected forensic evidence. 2015. [Online] Available from: http://www.ojp.gov (Accessed 5 May 2023).
118. Morton RJ. Serial Murder: Multi-disciplinary perspectives for investigators. 2008. [Online] Available from: https://www.ojp.gov/ (Accessed 5 May 2023).
119. Collins R. *Clues to mass rampage killers: Deep backstage, hidden arsenal, clandestine excitement*. The Sociological Eye. 2012. Available from: http://link.springer.com/article/10.1007/s11873-014-0250-2 (Accessed 5 May 2023).
120. Crime Prevention Research Centre. *Comparing Death Rates From Mass Public Shootings and Mass Public Violence in the US and Europe*. New York: Elsevier; 2015.
121. MacGuill D. Does the United States have a lower death rate from mass shootings than European countries? 2018. [Online] Available from: https://www.snopes.com/fact-check/united-states-lower-death-shootings/ (Accessed 5 May 2023).
122. Lankford A. Public mass shooters and firearms: A cross-national study of 171 countries. *Violence Vict* 2016; **31(2)**: 187–99.
123. United States Congress. Protection of children from sexual predators act. 1998. [Online] Available from: https://www.govinfo.gov (Accessed 5 May 2023).
124. Morton RJ. Serial murder: Multi-disciplinary perspectives for investigators. 2005. [Online] Available from: https://www.ojp.gov/ (Accessed 5 May 2023).
125. DeHart DD, Mahoney JM. The serial murderer's motivations: An interdisciplinary review. *Omega* 1994; **29(1)**: 29–45.
126. Leary T, Southard L, Aamodt M. Serial killers and intelligence levels: Variability, patterns, and motivations to kill. *N Am J Psychol* 2019; **21(4)**: 787.
127. Kaur N, Byard RW. Bride burning: A unique and ongoing form of gender-based violence. *J Forensic Leg Med* 2020; **75**: 102035.
128. Batha E. Stoning - Where does it happen? Thomson Reuters Foundation. 2013. [Online] Available from: https://news.trust.org/item/20130927172339-hoq1u/ (Accessed 5 May 2023).
129. Alasti S. Comparative study of stoning punishment in the religions of Islam and Judaism. *Justice Policy J* 2007; **4(1)**: 1–38.
130. Judd Jr CS. Skull injury from stoning--in Western Samoa and in history. *California Med* 1970; **112(4)**: 14.

CHAPTER

51

Cardiac Death

Antti Sajantila and Mikko I. Mäyränpää

INTRODUCTION

In case of a sudden death (SD), sometimes also referred to as sudden unexpected (natural) death (SUD), the forensic pathologist's task is to understand the main categories of disease that underlie such deaths, their mechanisms and risk factors, as well as to know how to examine and document these deaths. Cardiovascular diseases (CVD) represent the main cause of all deaths in developed countries, and account for a significant proportion of SDs. According to the Global Burden of Diseases (GBD) study, it accounts for approximately for one third of all deaths (1) and almost half of all non-communicable disease deaths (2).

The cardiovascular system, consisting of the heart and blood vessels, circulates blood throughout the body and supplies it with oxygen and nutrients. Problems in this system may lead to chronic diseases, which may lead to SD, even in symptomatic cases. The diseases are generally categorized into structural (e.g. arterial, myocardial, valvar and conduction system) or non-structural (toxic or genetic) diseases. Any severe disturbances, acute or chronic, in these systems may cause sudden cardiac death (SCD) (Tables 51.1 and 51.2). Despite advancements in prevention and treatment, SCD remains a leading cause of mortality and is responsible for almost half of all deaths from CVD (2). SCD show individual, age- and sex-dependent risk profiles (3,4) as well as well-defined general clinical risk factors, but there are also population and ethnic background level differences in SCD prevalence (5,6).

In this chapter, various diseases, and conditions underlying SCD are described with the consideration of the need for forensic pathologists in the realm of daily autopsy work.

DISEASES OF THE HEART VESSELS

The major cause for SCD globally, particularly for population over 50 years of age, is coronary artery disease

TABLE 51.1 Selected definitions related to sudden and unexpected natural deaths and sudden cardiac deaths

Sudden death (SD) or sudden unexpected (natural) death (SUD)	The World Health Organization's (WHO) definition of sudden death, according to the International classification of diseases, version 10 (ICD-10) is death, non-violent and not otherwise explained, occurring less than 24 hours from the onset of symptoms (7). In autopsy practice, sudden natural death is understood as an unexpected death, which occurs suddenly, and which cannot be attributed to external, violent or traumatic causes. Additionally, the deceased (a) was apparently in a good health prior to death, (b) suffered from a chronic disease, which according to clinical data was not expected to have a sudden outcome, and (c) died of natural cause with no witness.
Sudden cardiac death (SCD)	Multiple definitions have been employed for SCD in the literature, but generally it is used when (a) a congenital, or acquired, potentially fatal cardiac condition was known to be present during life, (b) autopsy identified a cardiac or vascular anomaly as the probable cause of death, or (c) no obvious extra-cardiac causes were identified in autopsy and therefore an arrhythmic even is the likely cause of death (2). For SCD, two levels of certainty have been suggested; firstly, established SCD is an unexpected death without obvious extra cardiac cause, occurring with a rapid witnessed collapse, or if unwitnessed, occurring within 1 hour after the onset of symptoms, and secondly, a probable SCD is an unexpected death without obvious extra-cardiac cause that occurred within the previous 24 hours (8).
Sudden unexplained death syndrome (SUDS)	SD of an individual over 1 year old with no autopsy performed (8). In cases of children under 1 year old, the term used in sudden unexplained death in infancy (SUDI) (9).
Sudden arrhythmic death syndrome (SADS)	SUDS with no findings after macroscopic and microscopic examination and toxicology screening in an autopsy (8,10,11). This is also known as 'negative autopsy' (12,13).

DOI: 10.1201/9781003138754-53

(CAD), and it is therefore one of the most common findings in the everyday autopsy practice. In addition, other diseases of heart vessels, which are of interest, are fatal complications of coronary vasculitis.

TABLE 51.2 Typical causes of sudden cardiac deaths in adults

Cause of death	Percentage of cases (%)[1]
Coronary atherosclerosis with acute thrombosis[2]	30–60
Coronary atherosclerosis with occlusion and myocardial hypertrophy (stable plaque >75% occlusion)	20–40
Dilated cardiomyopathy	10–20
Coronary atherosclerosis with occlusion and no myocardial hypertrophy (stable plaque <75 occlusion)	~10
Hypertrophic cardiomyopathy	3–5
Myocarditis	1–3
Sarcoidosis	1–3
Aortic stenosis	1–3
Aortic dissection	1–3
Arrhytmogenic cardiomyopathy	~1
Endocarditis	~1
Mitral valve disease	~1
Others	<1
No morphological change[3]	10–30

[1]Percentage varies by population and by study, and are approximates from several studies; [2]Includes acute myocardial infarction and myocardial ruptures; [3]Percentage is inversely correlated with age.

Coronary artery disease

CAD is also known as ischemic heart disease or atherosclerotic CVD, and denotes development of atherosclerotic plaque in the cardiac arteries. CAD manifests as myocardial infarct or ischemic heart disease with known clinical symptoms. Atherosclerotic lesions are initially intimal accumulations of lipid-laden inflammatory cells with proliferation of smooth muscle cells, which then accumulate connective tissue matrix including collagen, elastic fibers and proteoglycans, and deposition of intra and extracellular lipid (14).

Morphologically, the atherosclerotic plaques may be divided into two types, stenotic and non-stenotic plaques (15). Stenotic lesions tend to have thick fibrous caps, more fibrosis and calcification and smaller lipid cores. Non-stenotic lesions are more numerous than stenotic plaques. They are spread along the inner wall of coronary artery and tend to have large lipid cores. The fibrous caps are thin and therefore susceptible to rupture and thrombosis. Mostly atherosclerotic plaques are mixed and structurally between stenotic and non-stenotic types. The plaque development begins much earlier than the clinical signs become apparent with endothelial cell dysfunction, and the first symptom can lead to SCD. The endothelial cells lining the internal wall of the coronary artery lose their ability to properly regulate vascular tone and permeability. As a result, lipoprotein particles carrying cholesterol infiltrate the artery wall, triggering an inflammatory response by lipid-laden macrophage "foam cells." The artery's tunica media experiences smooth muscle cell proliferation, leading to wall remodeling and eventually narrowing of the lumen. This narrowing obstructs blood flow, causing ischemic heart disease. When the plaque surface ruptures and a blood clot is formed in the place, a myocardial infarction occurs. Downstream of the clot, blood flow is blocked and consequently oxygen deprivation leads to cell death (Figures 51.1–51.3).

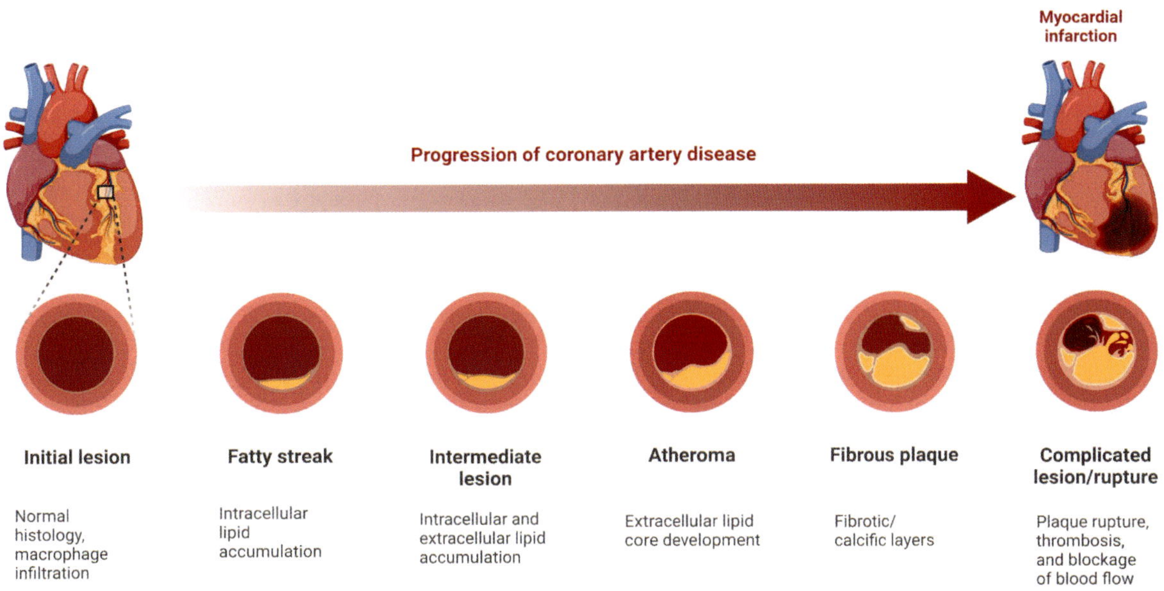

51.1 Development of atherosclerosis and myocardial infarction. The cross-sections of the coronary arteries are shown with the progression of atherosclerotic changes.

The severity and magnitude of CAD is illustrated by the fact that it remains one of the leading causes of premature deaths among the non-communicable diseases worldwide (16,17). Global age-standardized rates for SCD due to CAD declined during the last three decades, indicating that global increase (in absolute numbers) in CAD-related SCD have been due to population growth and aging (17). Epidemiological studies of CAD have identified several risk factors for CAD. These include age, male gender, smoking, elevated blood pressure, diabetes, obesity and a sedentary lifestyle, which are each independent risk factors for CAD and myocardial infarction (18). Risk factors that can be measured in the blood have also been described. These include particularly biomarkers for lipid metabolism, for example cholesterol and triglyceride (TG) metabolism (19,20). Large-scale cohort studies have shown a population level effect of lipid metabolism in CAD. The renowned North-Karelia (21), Framingham (22,23) and the Seven Country Studies (24) among others have shown that increased concentrations of circulating low-density lipoprotein (LDL) cholesterol, TG-rich lipoproteins and decreased high-density lipoprotein (HDL) cholesterol are independent risk factors of CAD.

CAD is a complex disease with environmental, lifestyle and inherited components. Early clinical observations from the 1950s (25) supported the notion that the risk of CAD is heritable. The inheritable nature was established in later studies for CAD (26) and its malicious consequences, primary cardiac arrest (27), myocardial infarction and SCD (28).

The notion of a "stable" CAD refers to patients who are diagnosed with CAD but have not suffered from a recent acute event. From the forensic pathologist's point of view, the concept is misleading since the patients are in a continuous risk of a major cardiovascular event and high risk of SUD.

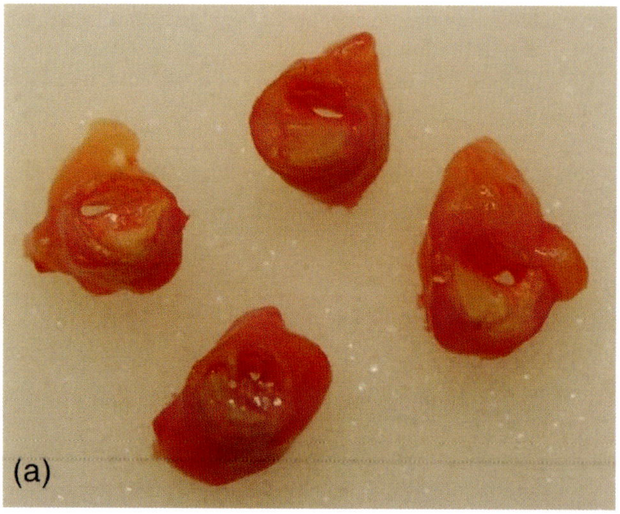

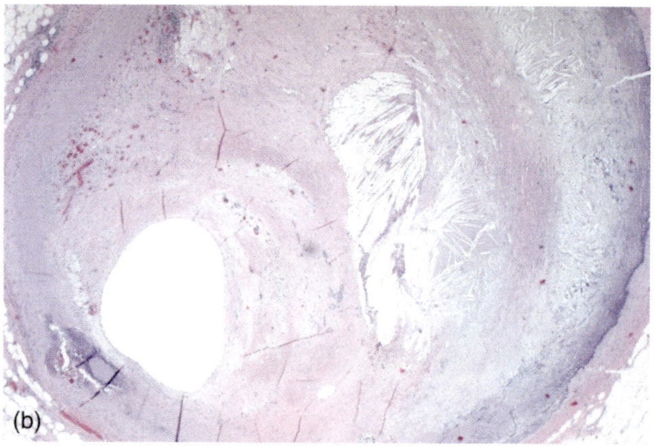

51.2 **(a)** A cross section along a stenotic atherosclerotic lesion. The lumen is obstructed with atheroma and fibrous plaque formation. **(b)** Hematoxylin-Eosin staining shows the same artery after EDTA-decalcification. Histological hallmarks, i.e. necrotic lipid core, plaque calcification, intimal thickening, luminal narrowing, plaque neovascularization and inflammation are all visible.

Vasculitis

Vasculitis is a group of generally uncommon diseases of generally unknown etiology (29). One typical feature of vasculitis is an inflammatory destruction of blood vessels, which can occur in any part of the vascular system and based on this, vasculitis has been divided into primary systemic vasculitis, secondary vasculitis, or isolated single-organ vasculitis.

Estimation of the incidence and prevalence of vasculitis is difficult, mostly due to the absence of reliable diagnostic criteria and the rarity of these conditions (29). Many classification criteria for vasculitis have been proposed. The categorization often used is the nomenclature and definitions established in the Chapel Hill consensus conferences (30,31). Key criteria of morphologic vasculitis work-up are vessel size, type of inflammation (granulomatous, necrotizing and/or leukocytoclastic) as well as the presence or absence of immune complexes and extravascular inflammatory changes. Based on these, the vasculitides are divided into large vessel vasculitis: Takayasu arteritis and giant cell arteritis; medium vessel vasculitis: polyarteritis nodosa, mucocutaneus lymph node syndrome (Kawasaki disease) and small vessel vasculitis: for example IgA-vasculitis (Henoch-Schönlein vasculitis), granulomatosis with polyangiitis (Wegener's granulomatosis) and eosinophilic granulomatosis with polyangiitis (Churg-Strauss granulomatosis) (Figure 51.4).

A curious epidemiologic and global pattern of vasculitides has been noticed. Firstly, vasculitis occurs mostly at the ends of the age spectrum, in young children and older adults. Mucocutaneus lymph node syndrome (Kawasaki disease) is mostly diagnosed in children aged <5 years, and it is most common in Japan and in children of Southeast Asian ancestry. In contrast, giant cell arteritis is the vasculitis of elderly individuals and found particularly in individuals of Northern European ancestry. Finally, Behçet syndrome has the highest prevalence along the ancient Silk Road, from the Mediterranean through the Middle East to East Asia.

Long-term consequences of vasculitis are, for example, vision loss, aneurysm formation, kidney failure and in rare cases, SD, particularly SCD. A histopathologic examination of the affected vessel is the gold standard for a diagnosis, although a definite diagnosis cannot always be made solely on histopathologic means. Often, a definite diagnosis is reached only in combination of histopathology and serology to clinical or autopsy data. Non-atherosclerotic narrowing of coronary arteries

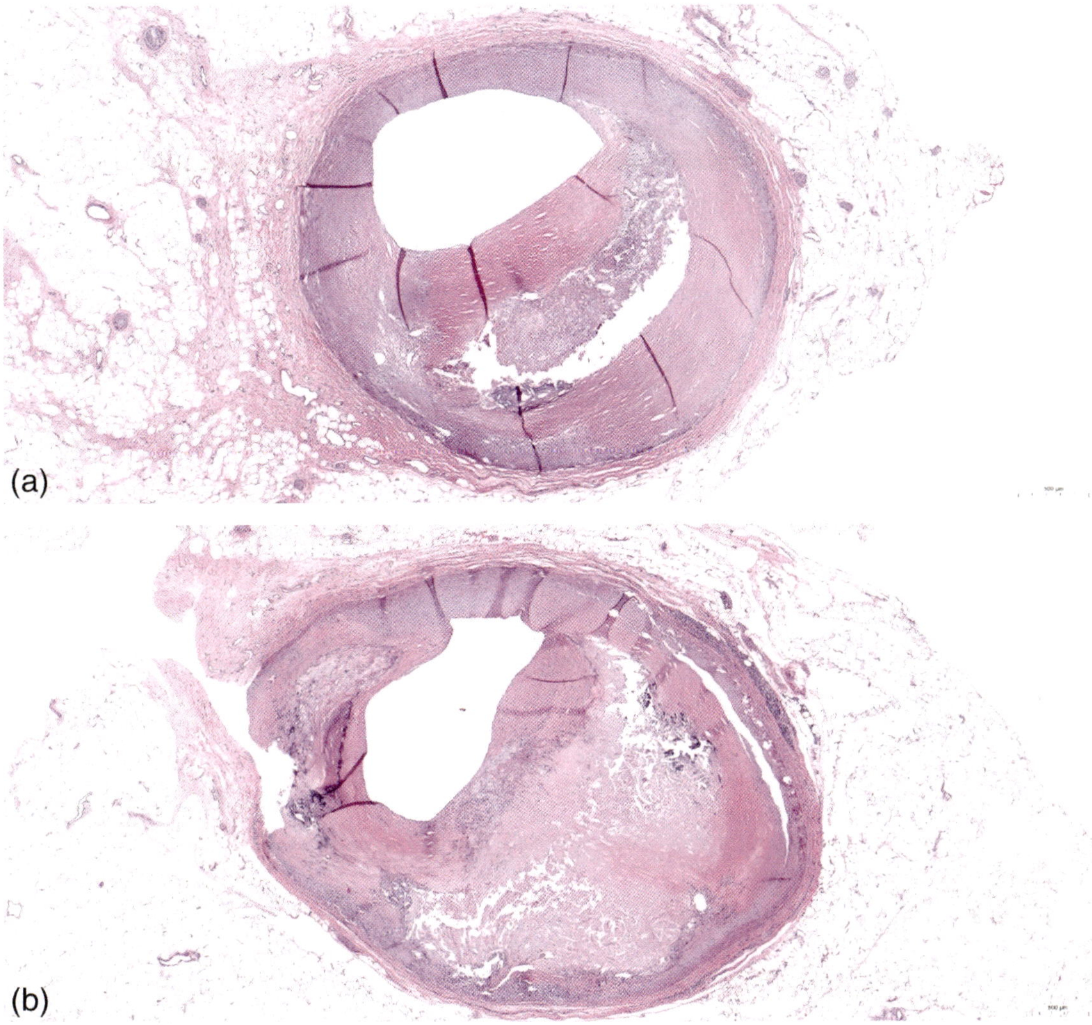

51.3 Typical microscopic views of coronary plaques. Histological hallmarks presented in section of two different autopsies (a and b) are necrotic lipid core, plaque calcification, intimal thickening, luminal narrowing and inflammation. Hematoxylin-Eosin staining.

accounts for a small amount (approximately 5%) of all fatal acute myocardial infarctions (32). Of those, coronary arteritis is responsible for a small portion and the condition has been examined in several case reports as an uncommon cause of death in non-atherosclerotic coronary diseases (33–38). According to these reports, SCD due to coronary arteritis is mostly associated with systemic vasculitis or systemic autoimmune diseases (e.g. Takayasu's arteritis), mucocutaneus lymph node syndrome (Kawasaki disease) in children, collagen vascular disease, hypersensitivity arteritis, eosinophilic granulomatosis with polyangiitis (Churg-Strauss granulomatosis) and granulomatosis with polyangiitis (Wegener's granulomatosis) as the most common forms of vasculitis affecting the coronary arteries (*see* Figure 51.4).

PERICARDIAL DISEASE

Pericardial disease, or pericarditis, is inflammation of any of the layers of the pericardium. The pericardium is a thin mesothelium lined sac that surrounds the heart and consists of an inner layer that envelopes the entire heart (visceral pericardium), middle fluid layer to prevent friction between the visceral pericardium and the outer layer made of fibrous tissue (parietal pericardium) (39).

Pericarditis is a common disorder that has multiple causes and is most commonly idiopathic. Generally, pericarditis may be caused by any process, which involves:

1. Bleeding into the pericardial space.
2. Leakage of plasma proteins into the pericardial space (e.g. myocardial inflammation or infarction or pneumonia adjacent to pericardium).
3. Physical factors and neoplasias causing pericardial cell irritation or bleeding or plasma protein leakage in the pericardium (e.g. drugs, irradiation, foreign material from surgical operations).
4. Infection/autoimmune inflammation of the pericardium (rheumatoid serositis, IgG4-associated constrictive pericarditis).

The main etiological categories of acute pericarditis are listed in Table 51.3.

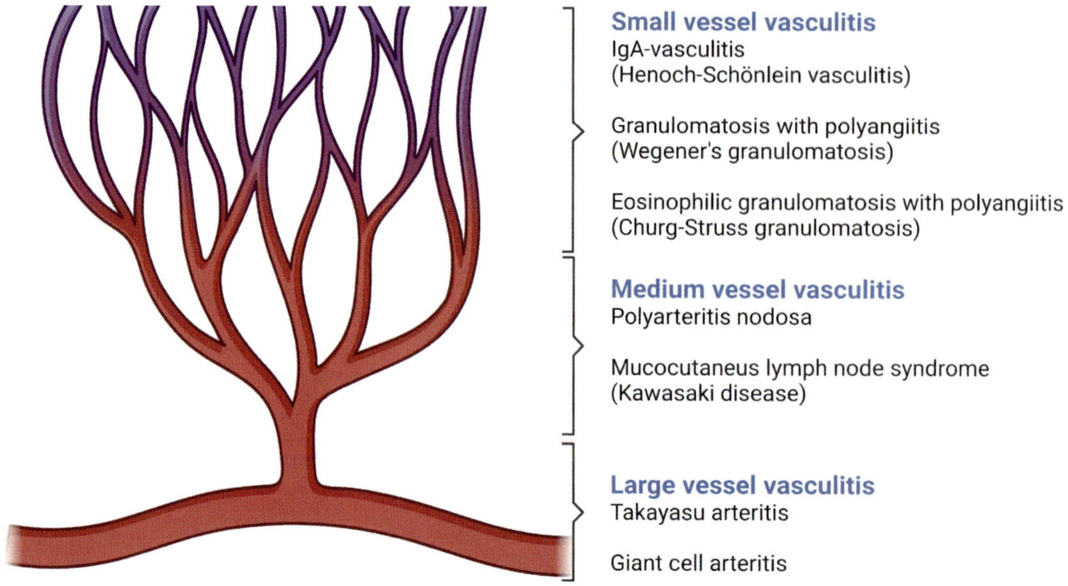

51.4 Vessel size involvement in vasculitis is taken into account in the nomenclature of the disease. There is considerable overlap with the nomenclature and the three main categories (large-, medium- and small-vessel vasculitis) are reported to affect any size of artery. Additional categories are variable vessel arteritis, which can affect any type of vessel, and Behçet syndrome (a blood vessel inflammation throughout the body).

TABLE 51.3 Etiology of acute pericarditis. Modified from (39)
Idiopathic pericarditis
Microbial pericarditis
Pericarditis related to vasculitis/connective tissues diseases
Pericarditis related to immunopathies and hypersensitivity
Pericarditis related to structural changes
Pericarditis related to metabolic condition
Neoplastic pericarditis
Traumatic pericarditis
Pericarditis and various syndromes

Although pericarditis is generally benign and self-limiting, it sporadically develops complications, such as pericardial effusion or constriction, which increases its mortality. In developing countries, tuberculosis is still a major cause of pericarditis (40). Men are in general at higher risk of obtaining pericarditis than women (41). A large epidemiologic study with close to 8000 patients diagnosed with viral or idiopathic pericarditis and with no underlying severe heart disease from Denmark, showed that there is an increased 5-year mortality risk after pericarditis, especially for women (42). The risk was higher especially during the first year after the disease.

Pericarditis can be acute or chronic. Cardiac tamponade is an important and potentially lethal complication of acute pericarditis, when progressing untreated (43). A chronic pericarditis often leads to thickened and scarred pericardium. This can make it difficult for the heart to expand with blood. The dissection of the pericardial sac can be tedious and requires good technical skills in these cases, so that the heart's structures remain intact for detailed evaluation.

DISEASES OF THE MYOCARDIUM

The myocardium is the middle muscular layer of the heart and lies between the endocardium and the outer epicardium. The myocardium is composed of cardiomyocytes, which are responsible for contractile function of the heart. The myocardial cells also provide a scaffold for heart chambers and conduct electrical impulse. Any acute or chronic disturbance of the myocardium may lead to a fatal loss of function and therefore to SCD. Below the main myocardial diseases are described from the SCD point of view.

Left ventricular hypertrophy

Left ventricular hypertrophy (LVH) is a stable, chronic pathological substrate for ventricular arrhythmias, cardiac failure and can lead to SCD (44). Due to the difficulties in differential diagnostics and interpretation related to LVH, the Association for European Cardiovascular Pathology (AECVP) recently made recommendations on common terminology and methodology to measure the heart weight, size and thickness as well as a systematic use of cut off values for normality by age, gender and body weight and height (45).

A spectrum of LVH, which is not classified as a cardiomyopathy, is a well-known finding to forensic pathologists in the autopsy. In evaluation of cardiac hypertrophy, measurements of the heart's weight, dimensions and chambers' thickness are recorded in autopsy. For practical reasons and cause of death certificate purposes it is important to note that LVH and cardiac hypertrophy in general, denote demarcation of a variety of disease entities. These include, for example, conditions due to

TABLE 51.4 Macroscopic and microscopic terms and definitions related to LVH

Term	Definition
Macroscopic	
Cardiomegaly	• A big heart upon visual judgement of the size • Transverse and longitudinal diameters can help
Cardiac hypertrophy	• Increased heart weight compared to normal predicted values (see subchapter "What is normal heart weight?")
Concentric hypertrophy	• Increased heart weight without cavity dilatation • Internal chamber diameter can help • The wall thickness is usually increased
Eccentric hypertrophy	• Increased heart weight without cavity dilatation • Internal chamber diameter can help • The wall thickness may be normal, increased, or decreased in eccentric hypertrophy
Symmetric LVH	• Almost equal thickness of the entire LV and septum
Asymmetric LVH	• The thickness is not uniform but increased either in the free wall or in the septum • The most frequent variant is asymmetric septal hypertrophy with septal-to-posterior wall thickness ratio ≥ 1.3
Microscopic	
Myocyte hypertrophy	• Increase in cardiac myocyte size • Nuclei are increased in size, irregular and hyperchromatic
Interstitial fibrosis	• Increased deposition of connective tissue in the interstitium without myocyte loss • Special connective tissue stains can be helpful
Replacement fibrosis	• Increased deposition of connective tissue following extensive myocyte loss • Special connective tissue stains can be helpful
Myocyte disarray	• Loss of normal alignment of cardiac myocytes, often arranged at oblique and perpendicular angles to each other • Can be either single myocyte or myocyte bundle disarray
Small vessel disease	• Marked medial and or intimal thickening of intramural arterioles (100–500 μm) wall with luminal stenosis • Special connective tissue stains can be helpful

chronic ischemia, pressure and volume overload, storage and infiltrative disorders and cardiomyopathies. Several gross morphologic features can indeed point to a specific diagnosis, such as concentric hypertrophy, obstruction with calcification of the aortic valve, other organ involvement and obesity. For specific diagnosis, appropriate histologic examination is needed. In case the cause of hypertrophy remains unexplained after in-depth macroscopic and microscopic examination, it is recommended to be classified as idiopathic LVH (45) (Table 51.4).

CARDIOMYOPATHIES

Cardiomyopathies are a class of myocardial diseases that cause close to half of the SCD in the young population. Hence, post-mortem diagnostics of cardiomyopathies is an important task in forensic pathology. The original description of cardiomyopathies date to the late nineteenth century with Fiedler's myocarditis (46), an isolated, non-ischemic myocardial disease, which was described in a series of deaths of young adults with cardiomegaly and heart failure, and an acute inflammation in the myocardium, which was unrelated to acute rheumatic fever, syphilis, tuberculosis, arteriosclerosis or septicemia. The ideas of inheritance and the term cardiomyopathy came into use around the 1950s with reports of familial unexplained cardiomegaly (47), and cases of idiopathic, non-coronary cardiomyopathies (48). Later, the WHO made an effort to make the first classification of the cardiomyopathies (49). Several updated definitions of cardiomyopathies, their treatment and diagnostics are available today, for example, the American Heart Association Classification of Cardiomyopathies (50), and the European Society of Cardiology Classification of Cardiomyopathies (51). According to those, cardiomyopathies can be grossly classified to hypertrophic cardiomyopathy (HCM), dilated cardiomyopathy (DCM), arrhythmogenic right ventricular cardiomyopathy (ARVC), restrictive cardiomyopathy (RCM) and a few acquired forms of cardiomyopathies, such as inflammatory cardiomyopathy (myocarditis) and peripartum cardiomyopathy. An important note on the diagnostics of cardiomyopathies is that they are solely or predominantly diseases of the heart muscle and secondary when myocardial involvement is associated with a multisystem disorder.

Hypertrophic cardiomyopathy

HCM is defined by the presence of myocardial hypertrophy in the absence of systemic diseases (e.g. amyloidosis and glycogen storage disease) and hemodynamic disorders, that could lead to the observed degree of hypertrophy (1–4,8,9). HCM is a disease in which there is a genuine myocyte hypertrophy, which increases ventricular wall thickness, instead of interstitial infiltration or intracellular accumulation of metabolite substrates (Figure 51.5). Often, a histological examination to demonstrate the myocyte hypertrophy is needed for the diagnosis of HCM. The typical patchy distribution of changes in most cardiomyopathies leaves the final diagnosis to be made reliably at post-mortem investigation.

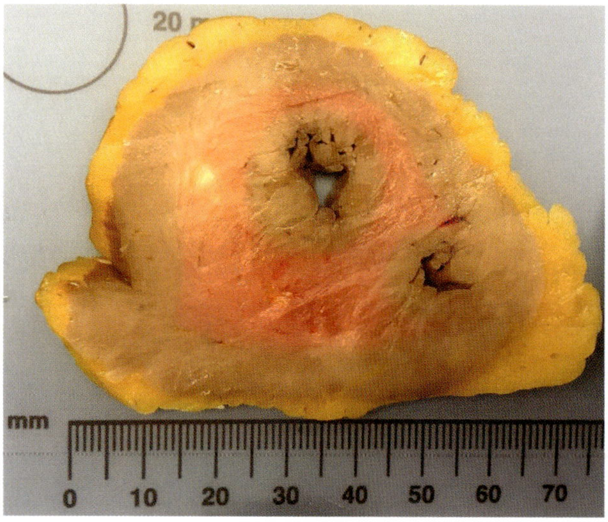

51.5 Hypertrophic cardiomyopathy. Cross section after formalin fixation.

The prevalence of HCM in the general population is approximately 1:500 (52). A familial, autosomal dominant pattern of inheritance has been observed, and has recently been shown to often be caused by mutations in the genes encoding cardiac sarcomere proteins. Most patients with sarcomeric protein gene mutations have an asymmetrical pattern of hypertrophy, with findings best seen in the interventricular septum as myocyte disarray. It should be noted that in addition to autosomal dominanant inheritance, also other, autosomal resessive and X-chromosome linked mutations may cause HCM-phenotype (e.g. listed in https://hpo.jax.org/app/browse/term/HP:0001639, and https://blueprintgenetics.com/tests/panels/cardiology/hypertrophic-cardiomyopathy-hcm-panel/). Left ventricular cavity size is regularly diminished. HCM is the most frequent cause of SCD in young people and competitive athletes (53).

Dilated cardiomyopathy

DCM is defined by the presence of left ventricular dilatation and left ventricular systolic dysfunction in the absence of hypertension or heart valve disease (abnormal loading) or CAD, which is considered severe enough to cause systolic deficiency. Right ventricular dilation and dysfunction may also be present.

The prevalence of DCM varies according to age and geography, but the overall prevalence in the general population is unknown. The most recent estimation of the DCM's prevalence is approximately twice the prevalence of HCM (~1/250 vs 1/500 individuals) (52). About 25 percent of the DCM cases in Western populations are familial and the inheritance pattern is mostly autosomal dominant (54,55), although other forms of inheritance have also been reported (56).

Familial disease should be suspected in cases of DCM-related SCD and a family history of cardiac deaths in young adults. Autosomal dominant DCM is caused by mutations in cytoskeletal, sarcomeric protein/Z-band, nuclear membrane and intercalated disc protein genes. In addition to the autosomal pattern, DCM is also associated with X-linked diseases, such as muscular dystrophies. DCM may also occur in patients with mitochondrial myopathies or inherited metabolic disorders. An acquired form of DCM may be associated with nutritional deficiencies, endocrine dysfunction and use of cardiotoxic drugs (57).

DCM can occur at a late stage following cardiac infection. Typical for this inflammatory DCM is the presence of chronic myocardial inflammation in association with left ventricular dilatation and functional defect. Histologic examination combined with immunohistochemistry staining of myocardium specimen is necessary for the diagnosis.

Peripartum cardiomyopathy (PPCM) is a form of acquired DCM with signs of cardiac failure during the last month of pregnancy or within 5 months of delivery (58). The underlying diseases for PPCM is suggested to be myocarditis, autoimmunity due to leakage of fetus' cells to mother and the hemodynamic stress of pregnancy. PPCM affects women of all ethnic groups, is independent from the number of pregnancies, strongly associated with gestational hypertension, twin pregnancy and occurs mostly with mothers older than 30 years of age.

Restrictive cardiomyopathy

RCM is a myocardial disorder resulting from myocardial stiffness leading to impaired ventricular filling (59). Affecting either or both ventricles, RCM may cause signs or symptoms of left or right heart failure. Arrhythmias and conduction disturbances are frequently encountered. RCM is difficult to define, since restrictive ventricular physiology occurs in a wide range of different pathologies. Definitions rely on a combination of clinically and morphologically defined parameters, relying on its restrictive ventricular physiology in the presence of normal or reduced diastolic volumes, normal or reduced systolic volumes, and normal ventricular wall thickness. Historically, systolic function was said to be preserved in RCM, but it is rare for contractility to be truly normal. Restrictive physiology can occur in patients with end-stage HCM and DCM.

RCM is a rare condition, and the exact prevalence of RCM is unknown. RCM may be idiopathic, familial, or result from various systemic disorders, in particular, amyloidosis, sarcoidosis, carcinoid heart disease, scleroderma and anthracycline toxicity. Familial RCM is often characterized by autosomal dominant inheritance, which in some families is caused by mutations in the *troponin I* gene; in others, familial RCM is associated with conduction defects, caused by mutations in the *desmin* gene. In some instances, familial disease can be associated with autosomal recessive inheritance or with X-linked inheritance (such as Anderson–Fabry disease). Genetic RCM is a severe disease with a high mortality rate (60).

Restrictive ventricular physiology can also be caused by endocardial pathology (fibrosis, fibroelastosis and thrombosis) that impairs diastolic function. These disorders can be subclassified according to the presence of eosinophilia into endomyocardial diseases with hypereosinophilia and endomyocardial disease without hypereosinophilia.

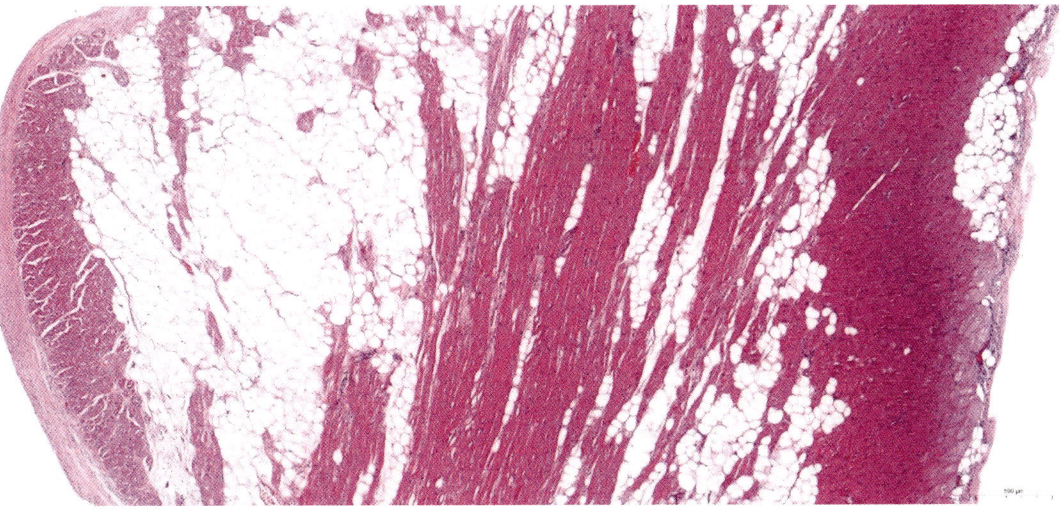

51.6 Typical fatty degeneration seen in the microscopical inspection of the right ventricle of the heart of ARVC patient. Hematoxylin-eosin staining.

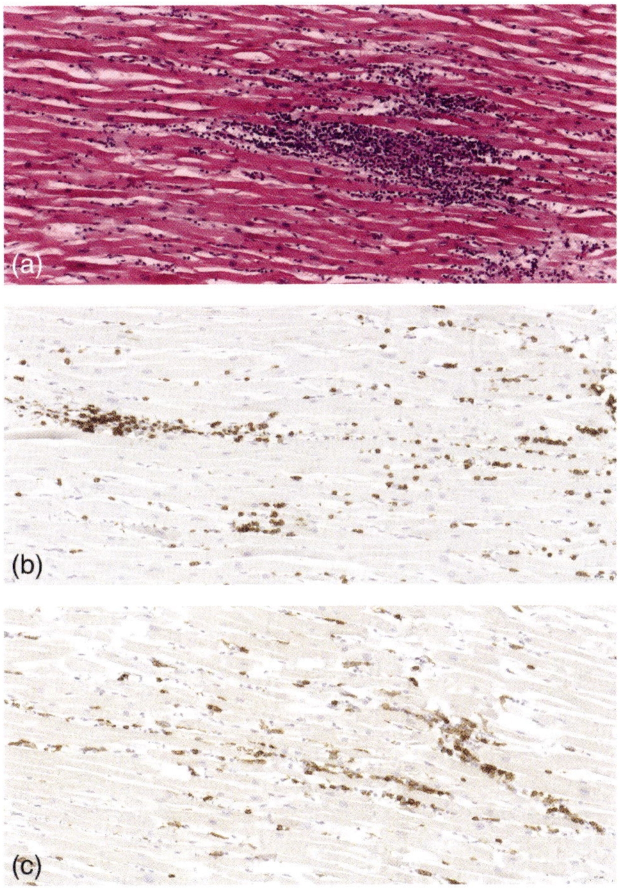

51.7 Inflammatory cell infiltrate in the heart of an ARVC patient. **(a)** Hematoxylin-eosin staining, **(b)** CD3 staining, **(c)** CD4 staining.

Arrhythmogenic right ventricular cardiomyopathy

ARVC is defined by the presence of progressive replacement of right ventricular myocardium with adipose and fibrous tissue in histologic examination and is often morphologically confined to a "triangle of dysplasia" comprising the right ventricular inflow, outflow and apex. In addition to the right ventricular fatty degeneration, inflammatory cells can also be seen in the microscopic examination (Figures 51.6 and 51.7). It is presented predominantly with arrhythmic disturbances. It was first described in the late 1970s and early 1980s and it is now frequently recognized to have biventricular involvement. The prevalence of ARVC is very low, for example in comparison to HCM or DCM (estimated prevalence 1:2000–1:5000) (61).

ARVC has been found more frequently as the cause of SD in young people in some areas of Europe. Also, other factors such as age, sex, electrophysiological features and cardiac imaging investigations all contribute to risk stratification. Autosomal recessive forms of ARVC are recognized, but most cases are caused by autosomal dominantly inherited mutations.

To date, altogether 16 genes have been associated with the ARVC phenotype, mostly those encoding desmosomal proteins: plakophilin-2 (PKP2), desmoglein-2 (DSG2), desmoplakin (DSP), and, rarely, desmocollin-2 (DSC2) and plakoglobin (JUP) (62). The non-desmosomal gene mutations have been found in single or isolated populations and mostly in single families. Candidate gene or linkage studies have also identified other cardiomyopathy/channelopathy-associated genes in patients with an ARVC phenotype, expanding the genetic and phenotypic spectrum of this disease. Despite these advances, the genetic cause of ARVC remains unknown for 40 to 50 percent of patients (62).

Left ventricular non-compaction

According to many reports, left ventricular non-compaction (LVNC) belongs to unclassified cardiomyopathies (51). LVNC is characterized by prominent left ventricular trabeculae and deep inter-trabecular recesses (Figure 51.8). As a consequence of these changes, the myocardial wall becomes thickened with a thin, compacted epicardial layer and a thickened endocardial

51.8 Non-compaction cardiomyopathy. Cross section. Note extensive trabeculation of the left ventricle.

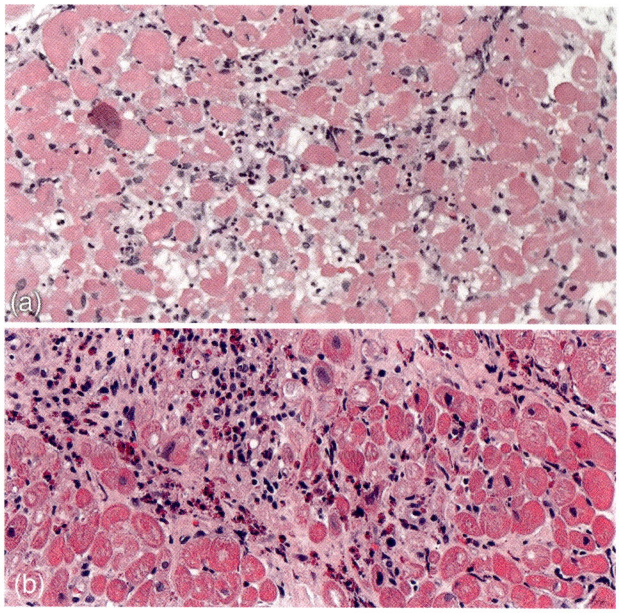

51.9 Light microscopic view in myocarditis. Haematoxylin-Eosin stainings. Cardiomyocyte damage with inflammatory cell infiltration are seen in the active phase of all types of myocarditis. After resolution of inflammation, myocardial fibrosis may be seen. **(a)** Lymphocytic myocarditis. In lymphocytic myocarditis infiltrates consist mainly of T-lymphocytes. **(b)** Eosinophilic myocarditis. Inflammatory infiltrates consisting mainly of eosinophils is typical for eosinophilic myocarditis. Degranulation of eosinophils may be extensive.

layer. LVNC is sometimes associated with left ventricular dilatation and systolic dysfunction (51,63).

The population prevalence of isolated LVNC is not known. LVNC is frequently familial, with around 25 percent of asymptomatic relatives having a range of echocardiographic abnormalities. Genes in which causative mutations have been identified and include X-chromosome linked *G4.5* encoding *taffazin*, *alpha dystrobrevin*, *ZASP*, actin and *lamin A/C*. It is not clear whether LVNC is a separate cardiomyopathy, or merely a congenital or acquired morphologic trait shared by many phenotypically distinct cardiomyopathies.

Takotsubo cardiomyopathy

Takotsubo cardiomyopathy also belongs to unclassified cardiomyopathies and is known as transient left ventricular apical ballooning syndrome. It is a transient regional systolic dysfunction which involves the left ventricular apex and/or mid-ventricle without a presence of obstructive coronary disease on coronary angiography. Originally described in Japan (64), the condition is also reported in Caucasian populations in Europe and North America (51). Cases typically occur in post-menopausal women, and the condition is associated with emotional or physical stress (65). Left ventricular function usually normalizes over a period of days to weeks and recurrence is rare. A similar type of transient myocardial dysfunction is also reported in patients with intracranial hemorrhage or other acute cerebral accidents, a phenomenon known as neurogenic myocardial stunning (51). The prognosis of Takotsubo cardiomyopathy is good, most patients recover fully, and the in-hospital mortality is around 1 percent (65).

MYOCARDITIS

Myocarditis, inflammation of the muscular portion of the heart, encompasses several different diseases with diverse etiologies (Table 51.5) and variable clinical presentations. The true estimate of the lifetime prevalence of myocarditis is not known, but population estimates range from 1 in 100 000 to 1 in 10 000. Autopsy studies report myocarditis in up to 12 percent of young victims of SCD and makes myocarditis as important a cause of SD as in the long-term in childhood cardiomyopathy (66).

The early definition of myocarditis, the Dallas criteria (67), required an inflammatory infiltrate and associated myocyte necrosis, which is not related to an ischemic event, be present on conventionally stained heart-tissue sections. The Dallas criteria were criticized, since they allowed variability in interpretation, and were of low sensitivity and prognostic value (68). Low prognostic value may be due to the fact that the Dallas criteria fail to differentiate mild myocarditis from the fulminant cases; fulminant myocarditis being relatively common with reported proportion 25–30 percent of the cases (69). Chow et al. (70) showed in a myocardial autopsy specimen from patients who had died with myocarditis that in a single sample histologic myocarditis was demonstrated only in 25 percent of samples and with >5 biopsy specimen, the Dallas criteria myocarditis was diagnosed in only approximately two-thirds of the diseased. A consensus reached for myocarditis (and related DCM) is that the diagnosis is based on conventional histopathology (Figures 51.9), immunohistochemical methods for inflammatory infiltrates added with molecular biological methods for persistence of viral genome(s) in endomyocardial biopsies. Idiopathic, autoimmune, infectious and drug-induced forms of myocarditis are now recognized (Table 51.5). To that end, some data suggest that patients in the "idiopathic" category suffer from myocardial inflammation due to persistent viral replication or post infectious autoimmune activation. It is noteworthy that inflammatory infiltrates are also seen in the myocardial specimens from patients with genetically confirmed cardiomyopathy (e.g. ARVD). The clinical importance of myocardial inflammatory cell infiltrates in these cases is poorly known. Some of the "idiopathic" category cases may belong to this group

In viral myocarditis, there is an initial direct invasion of the myocardium by cardiotropic viruses entering cardiomyocyte through receptor-mediated endocytosis. Enteroviruses, adenoviruses, cytomegaloviruses, human parvovirus-19, human herpesvirus 6 and severe acute respiratory syndrome coronavirus 2 are the main etiological factors in the pathogenesis of the viral myocarditis. Primary viral myocarditis includes several forms of myocarditis including fulminant, chronic active, eosinophilic and giant cell myocarditis (71). Seroepidemiologic and molecular studies linked coxsackievirus B to outbreaks of myocarditis from the 1950s through the 1990s. Later, the spectrum of viruses detected in myocarditis patients shifted from coxsackievirus B to adenovirus in the late 1990s and to parvovirus B19 and human herpes viruses (Epstein–Barr virus and human herpesvirus 6) as well as HIV (Table 51.5). All above-mentioned viruses are found in geographically diverse areas. Overall, viral myocarditis is associated with a long-term mortality of almost 20 percent at 4.7 years, and the presence of initial biventricular dysfunction is the best predictor of all-cause mortality. Other microbes, especially bacterial and protozoal myocarditis, are seen in geographically restricted regions.

Myocarditis may occur concomitantly with other cardiomyopathies and may have an adverse effect on the clinical course of the other condition. Myocarditis has been associated with clinical deterioration in HCM, and in such cases, evidence of a persistent viral genome may be identified in the myocardium. A high percentage of patients with ARVC or dysplasia have associated myocarditis; some of these cases are associated with a viral infection.

Sarcoidosis

Cardiac sarcoidosis is a granulomatous process detected in any part of the heart but is observed almost exclusively in the myocardium (Figure 51.10). The affected tissue may represent a minimal injury, as an incidental

TABLE 51.5 Etiological causes of myocarditis (summarized from various sources)

Infections	
Viral	Coxsackievirus, human immunodeficiency virus, echovirus, adenovirus, influenza, measles, mumps, parvovirus, poliovirus, rubella, varicella-zoster virus, herpes simplex virus, cytomegalovirus, hepatitis C virus, rabies virus, respiratory syncytial virus, vaccine virus, dengue virus, yellow fever virus
Protozoal	*Trypanosoma cruzi, Toxoplasma gondii*
Bacterial	*Brucella, Corynebacterium diphtheriae, Salmonella, Haemophilus influenzae, Mycoplasma pneumoniae, Neisseria meningitidis (meningococcus), Streptococcus pneumoniae, Staphylococcus, Mycobacterium, Neisseria gonorrhoeae (gonococcus), Vibrio cholerae*
Spirochetal	*Treponema pallidum, Borrelia, Leptospira*
Fungal	*Aspergillus, Candida, Cryptococcus, Actinomyces, Blastomyces, Histoplasma, Coccidioides*
Rickettsial	*Coxiella burnetii, Rickettsia rickettsii, Rickettsia tsutsugamushi*
Parasitic	*Trichinella spiralis, Echinococcus granulosus, Taenia solium*
Immunological	Alloantigens, heart transplant rejection, autoantigens (e.g. polymyositis), eosinophilic granulomatosis with polyangiitis (Churg-Strauss syndrome), celiac disease, Whipple disease, giant cell myocarditis, Kawasaki disease, systemic lupus erythematosus, systemic sclerosis, sarcoidosis, scleroderma, thrombocytopenic purpura
Drugs	Penicillin, sulfonamides, tetracycline, methyldopa, streptomycin, tricyclic antidepressants, thiazide diuretics, dobutamine, indomethacin
Toxic	Anthracyclines, catecholamines, amphetamines, cocaine, cyclophosphamide, 5-fluorouracil, trastuzumab, interferon, interleukin-2
Physical Agents and elements	Electric shock, radiation, hyperpyrexia, heavy metals, copper, iron, lead, arsenic, snake bite, scorpion bite, wasp and spider stings, phosphorus, carbon monoxide
Genetics	Inherited cardiomyopathies with immune-mediated pathogenesis (dilated and right ventricular cardiomyopathy)

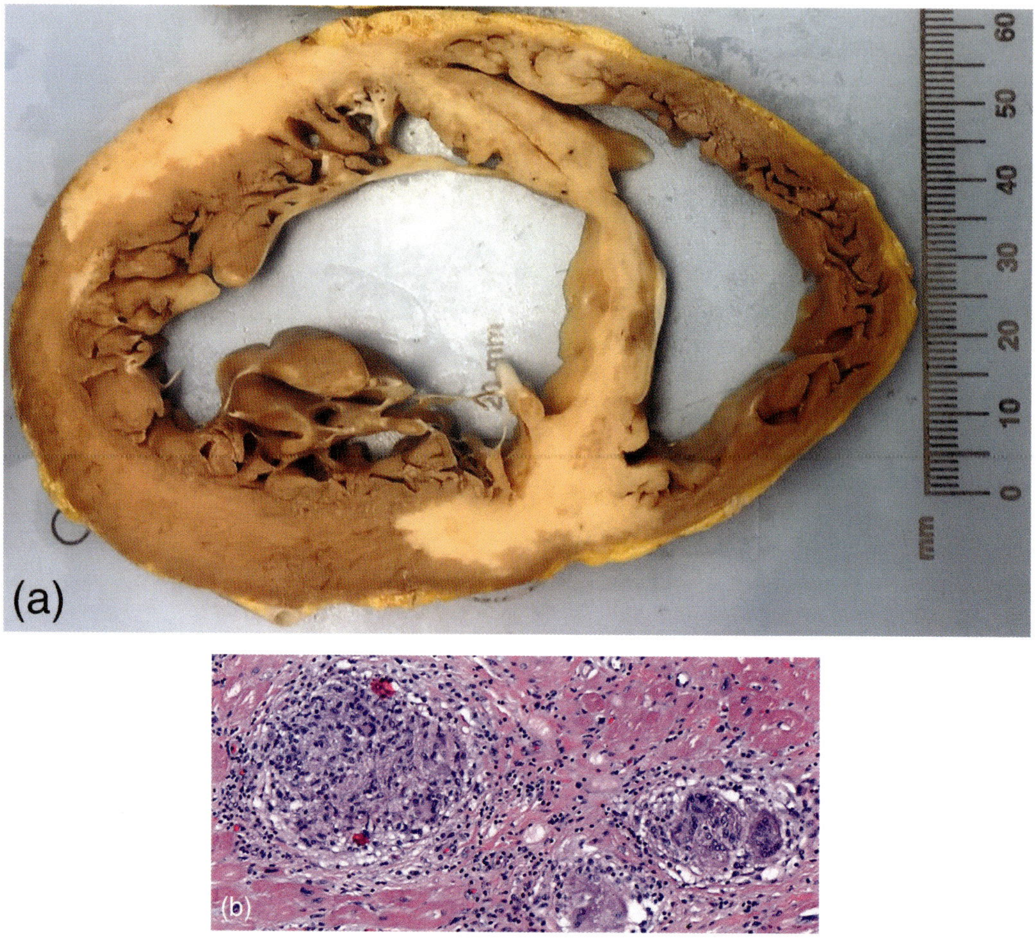

51.10 (a) Gross photo of myocardial sarcoidosis. Formalin fixed heart. Granulomatous and partly fibrotic lesions are seen in the interventricular septum and left ventricular wall as sharply demarcated white-tan regions. Histologically, this heart showed highly active sarcoid inflammation. **(b)** Cardiac sarcoidosis. Well-formed non-necrotizing epithelioid cell granulomas containing giant cells are the hallmark lesion in cardiac sarcoidosis. However, granulomas may be scarce and therefore hard to detect. Other inflammatory cell types such as lymphocytes and eosinophils are typically seen around sarcoid granulomas. In an autopsy setting, granulomas may be hard to detect for an unaware investigator as the giant cells lose their nuclei due to autolysis more rapidly than other cells (84).

finding or sustain extensive structural and functional disruption. Anatomic presence of sarcoidosis without clinical dysfunction is a typical feature of sarcoidosis. Despite intensive research, the etiology of sarcoidosis has remained a mystery (72), although recently certain genetic variants (e.g. SNPs in genetic neighborhood of *BTNL2*-, *HLA-DRB1*03*- and *HLA-DRB1*15*) have been associated with increased risk.

The incidence of sarcoidosis varies by geography and ethnic group. Incidence is 3 to 20 and 35.5 to 80 per 100 000 for whites and blacks, respectively (73). Curiously, the prevalence has been reported to be higher in Nordic countries than in other white populations (74). The disease is diagnosed usually in adults <40 years old (75).

Myocardial sarcoidosis was first described by Bernstein et al. in 1929 (76). In some instances, the first sign of myocardial sarcoidosis is sudden and unexpected fatality in a young person. The first such death was reported by Longcope and Fisher in 1941 (77). After this, more systematic clinical and autopsy studies of myocardial sarcoidosis were performed establishing that a myocardial involvement in systemic sarcoidosis is not as rare as previously known (77–82). Current understanding is that among fatalities from sarcoidosis cardiac involvement is likely responsible for 50 percent of cases (82). Prevalence of myocardial sarcoidosis is established to be around 15 to 25 percent in an autopsy series of individuals suffering from systemic sarcoidosis (79–83). Overall, it is estimated that sarcoidosis is fatal in 1 to 5 percent of cases (75).

Characteristic granulomatous finding with typical tight, naked, non-necrotizing and epithelioid granuloma in the myocardium raises the suspicion of sarcoidosis (Figure 51.10) (72). It is noteworthy that no clinical dysfunctions need to be present prior to death (83). Symptoms may be caused by mechanical interference with cardiac function either by a single lesion, which is in an unfortunate location or by a larger distortion of the normal anatomy. A challenge in the differential diagnostics is the giant cell myocarditis since it shares histopathologic and clinical features with myocardial sarcoidosis. Diagnostics, even after the autopsy, can be erroneous. The possibility that they represent different phenotypes of a single disease has been debated (84).

TUMORS OF THE HEART

According to the 5th edition of the WHO Classification of Thoracic Tumours (https://tumourclassification.iarc.who.int/home), the neoplasms of the heart are classified into benign, malignant and hematolymphoid tumors. Primary heart tumors begin in the heart tissue and may be of malignant or benign nature (85). Secondary heart tumors are metastatic (malignant). The prognosis depends on the type of tumor, its size and its location within the heart.

Clinical studies have shown that cardiac tumors are rare and an estimated 80 percent of cardiac tumors are benign. Primary heart malignancy is even more rare and affects less than 2/100 000 people annually. Primary neoplasia in the heart is a rare finding in autopsies, occurring with the frequency of 0.001 to 0.28 percent (86). Papillary fibroelastoma is the most common primary cardiac neoplasm (Table 51.6) (Figure 51.11). Due to improved recognition through higher-resolution imaging techniques, papillary fibroelastomas are found more often (85). Patients are typically 60–70 years old, with an age range of 42–80 years. No sex predilection has been observed for papillary fibroelastomas.

In adults, cardiac myxoma is the second most common primary cardiac neoplasm (Table 51.6). It is seen mostly in the age group of between 40 and 70 years, but it has been observed in all age groups. Cardiac myxomas occur twice as often in women as in men. More than 90 percent of cardiac myxomas arise in an isolated fashion.

Metastasis to the heart (or pericardium) represents a malignant neoplasia spreading from an extra-cardiac/ (or extra-pericardial) origin. The pericardium is the most frequently involved site of cardiac metastasis, accounting for 64 to 69 percent of all cardiac metastases. Epicardial (25–34%) and myocardial (29–32%) involvement represents the second and third most common sites of cardiac metastasis, respectively. Endocardial and intra-cavity metastases are rarely found in autopsy work (~3–5%). The importance of correctly identifying the cardiac neoplasia during the autopsy is in (a) determining the cause and the mechanism of death, and (b) assessing whether there are any underlying genetic conditions, such as LAMB (lentigenes, atrial myxomas, mucocutaneous myxomas, blue nevi) or NAME (nevi, atrial myxomas, myxoid neurofibroma. From the 25 percent of malignant tumors in heart about 75 percent are sarcomas (87) (Table 51.6).

TABLE 51.6 Tumors of the Heart

Benign tumors	
	Papillary fibroelastoma
	Cardiac myxoma
	Cardiac fibroma
	Cardiac rhabdomyoma
	Adult cellular rhabdomyoma
	Cardiac lipoma and lipomatous hypertrophy of the atrial septum
	Lipomatous hamartoma of the atrioventricular valve
	Hamartoma of mature cardiac myocytes
	Mesenchymal cardiac hamartoma
	Cardiac hemangioma
	Conduction system hamartoma
	Cystic tumor of the atrioventricular node
Malignant tumors	
	Cardiac angiosarcoma
	Cardiac leiomyosarcoma
	Cardiac undifferentiated pleomorphic sarcoma
	Other sarcomas that involved the heart
Hematolymphoid tumors	
	Cardiac diffuse B-cell lymphoma
	Cardiac fibrin-associated diffuse large B-cell lymphoma

Source: https://tumourclassification.iarc.who.int/home

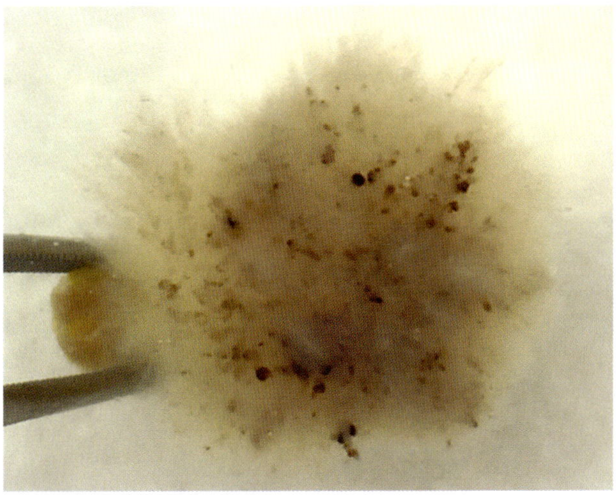

51.11 Gross photo of a papillary fibroelastoma in formalin. The delicate papillary structures collapse in air and are therefore best appreciated when the tumor is immersed in transparent fluid.

DISEASES OF HEART VALVES

The human heart has four valves; on the left side of the heart are the aortic and mitral valves, and on the right side are the pulmonic and tricuspid valves. Valvular heart diseases (VHD) are defined as any CVD process involving one or more of the four valves of the heart. Typically, the lesion or disease causes the valve not to open or close in VHD (Figure 51.12), and subsequently the workload of the myocardium increases leading to loss of function and life quality. VHD is divided in to left-side and right-side VHDs.

Left-side VHD includes aortic stenosis and regurgitation, and mitral stenosis and regurgitation. The etiology of the left-side VHD is mostly due to degenerative changes or rheumatic changes, but some of these are caused by endocarditis, inflammatory, congenital or ischemic causes. Right-side VHD includes tricuspid regurgitation, which is also partially considered to be physiological but can also be secondary due to right ventricular enlargement in, for example, pulmonary hypertension. The most common congenital cause of organic tricuspid regurgitation is Ebstein anomaly, though this is rare. Rheumatic disease can cause both tricuspid stenosis and regurgitation. Another right-side VHD is pulmonary valve disease, and it usually has a congenital etiology. It should be noted that VHDs can also be of mixed origin and affect multiple valves.

Globally, there is a substantial variation in the prevalence of VHD. In high-income countries, functional and degenerative diseases predominate the risk for VHD, whereas in low-income and middle-income countries predominance of rheumatic heart disease (RHD) is seen. Grossly speaking, RHD is the most common manifestation of VHD worldwide and affects approximately 41 million people, followed by degenerative mitral valve disease (24 million people) and calcific aortic stenosis (9 million people) (88). While the prevalence of RHD has remained stable, deaths from calcific aortic stenosis have increased. Also, other forms of acquired and congenital forms of VHD exist, but the epidemiologic data are limited.

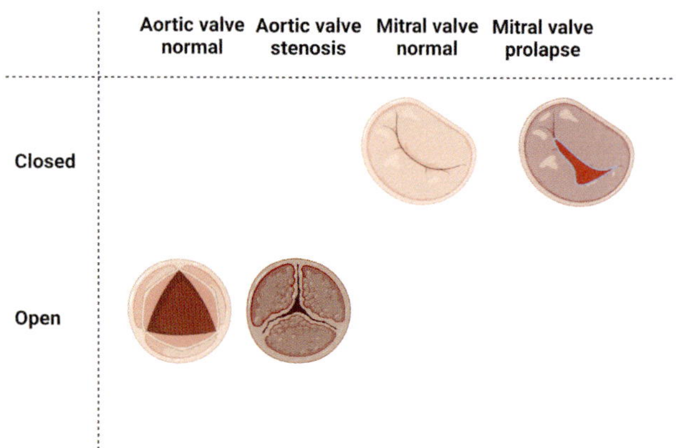

51.12 Examples of anatomic changes in the valvular heart diseases (VHDs) that are commonly seen in the autopsy. The left side VHDs are represented here by aortic and mitral valve stenosis of prolapse, leading to obstruction of blood flow or regurgitation, respectively.

VHDs occur largely as a consequence of aging (89), although they can also be of congenital origin or acquired as a result of a specific pathophysiological processes. VHD can also have a primary or secondary cause. Primary VHD relates to the disease in the valve itself, whereas secondary VHD results from pathology in other cardiac structures. For example, primary mitral regurgitation can be caused by leaflet prolapse or chordal rupture, whereas secondary mitral regurgitation is seen in patients with ischemic heart disease or cardiomyopathy. In these cases, left ventricular dilatation and remodeling result in distorted valve structure and function.

ENDOCARDIAL DISEASES

The endocardium is the innermost layer of the heart and lines the chambers and extends over projecting structures such as the valves, chordae tendineae and papillary muscles. Endocardial fibrosis, fibroelastosis and thrombosis are conditions considered as endocardial diseases and are typically further classified as endocardiac diseases with or without hypereosinophilia.

Hypereosinophilic syndromes are rare, occur typically in patients from 20 to 50 years, and present a heterogeneous group of disorders defined as continuous blood eosinophilia for over half a year and associated eosinophil-induced organ damage (89,90). Clinically, several organs can be damaged by an underlying blood cell-line disorder although not all patients show blood eosinophilia. In the case of cardiac involvement, the term eosinophilic (endo)myocarditis is used to describe cardiac damage caused by direct toxicity of circulating eosinophils. After the initial necrotic phase follows a thrombotic stage, in which thrombi develop on the ventricular endocardium, and the final fibrotic stage, which causes RCM and damage to atrioventricular valves. Autopsy findings include endocardial thickening with apical obliteration of one or both ventricles.

Tropical endomyocardial fibrosis is probably the most common type of RCM worldwide (91). The disease occurs predominantly in tropical regions and affects mostly children and adolescents. The etiology is unknown, but infection, autoimmunity and genetic predisposition have been suspected as causative or contributory parameters. After an initial period with febrile illness and pancarditis, a ventricular thrombosis affecting the apices and the subvalvular apparatus follows and later evolves to endocardial fibrosis. This is characterized by restrictive physiology, atrioventricular valve regurgitation and marked atrial dilation. Death results from complications of chronic heart failure but can occur suddenly from thromboembolism or arrhythmia.

Carcinoid syndrome is characterized by a typical cardiac lesion (carcinoid plaque), which is composed of smooth muscle cells, myofibroblasts and elastic tissue that forms a fibrous layer on the endocardial surface of the right ventricle and atrium, the valve leaflets and the subvalvular apparatus, including the chordae and papillary muscles (92).

Nonbacterial thrombotic endocarditis is characterized by platelet-fiber masses adherent to the mitral or aortic valves. These are seen in about 20 percent of patients with malignant tumors, especially mucin-producing adenocarcinomas, melanomas, leukemias and lymphomas. Nonbacterial thrombotic endocarditis is virtually always asymptomatic but occasionally is a source of systemic emboli. Because of the small size of many of the emboli, the first presentation is often with cerebral symptoms. Autopsy may reveal lesions that may otherwise not be found, and that may have been the source of systemic emboli.

GENETICS OF CARDIAC DEATH

A genetic risk of SCD is apparent from epidemiologic as well as from the autopsy studies. From those, it is also clear that the genetic susceptibility to SCD is greatest in young people and is mostly due to rare, monogenic forms of heart disease. These genetic traits are partially structurally recognizable or suspected, including premature CAD (e.g. in familial hypercholesterolemia) and cardiomyopathies, but some of them remain unexplained despite comprehensive dissection of the heart, and they belong to a group of sudden arrhythmic death syndrome, which may be challenging in the autopsy theater (8,93,94).

A substantial proportion of SCD in the young remains unexplained after comprehensive post-mortem evaluation, which is known as autopsy-negative sudden death (12,13). The heterogeneity of SCD, and difficulties in collecting large numbers of well-studied cases, have hindered the picture of the genetic architecture of SCD in the young. However, there has been a dramatic shift in the approach to rare and common cardiac disorders. Initial observations that SCD has a genetic predisposition were made in the late 1990s, when it was shown that a family history of sudden cardiac arrest (SCA) in a first-degree relative was an independent risk factor with the occurrence of myocardial infarction or SCA secondary to heart disease (rate ratio (RR) 1.57, 95 percent CI 1.27–1.95) (95). These findings were confirmed in studies from France (96), and Finland (97) confirming that SCD cluster in certain families.

About one-third of cases of SCD in children and young adults are due to structural disease, including cardiomyopathies (98,99). However, a previous cardiac diagnosis is typically present in only a small proportion of patients, SCD often being the first symptom (100,101). Thus, an autopsy has a pivotal role in the assessment of SCD, and specific guidelines should be followed (102) with a possibility for a cardio-histopathologists consultation (103). It should be noted that in about 40 to 50 percent of cases of SCD in the young the cause of death remains unknown after autopsy, indicating monogenic arrhythmia syndromes, for example long QT syndrome (LQTS), Brugada syndrome and catecholaminergic polymorphic ventricular tachycardia as a possible cause of death. These are characterized by abnormalities of myocardial electrical function detectable during life and the absence of overt structural abnormalities at autopsy (104,105).

Hereditary cardiomyopathies and arrhythmia syndromes are generally Mendelian autosomal dominant disorders with incomplete penetrance. They are caused by rare disease-causing variants in single genes. Therefore, rare variants are inherited, but they can be private to a family, that is, absent from other affected families or from the general population. The Genome Aggregation Database (gnomAD), ClinVar database (https://www.ncbi.nlm.nih.gov/clinvar) and HumanPhenotypeOntology-database (https://hpo.jax.org/app/), which contain genomic and phenotype data, clinical information and annotations of hereditary diseases. The prevalence of these conditions ranges from 1 in 500 (e.g. HCM) to 1 in 10 000 (short QT syndrome) individuals in the general population. Evaluation of first-degree relatives using genetic testing targeted to the genes linked to SCD and SADS is of utmost importance (8,98,101).

Genetic testing related to negative autopsies or suspected SCDs without structural changes observed in the heart have been coined as molecular autopsies (106). The current technology, using high-throughput DNA sequencing technologies, allows effective screening of over 100 genes related to SCDs or SADS (107,108).

Most genetic studies of cases of unexplained SCD have been retrospective, single-center studies and therefore biased. In addition, with the progressively extended gene panels, new previously undescribed variants were found, with difficulties for establishing variants' pathogenicity and in interpretation. A set of guidelines have been put forward to fill this need (109), and autopsy diagnostics now also rely on population, family and disease genomic data. On the basis of these criteria, variants are classified as being pathogenic, likely pathogenic, of uncertain significance, likely benign or benign. Unfortunately, most rare variants detected during a molecular autopsy using a large panel of genes fall into the category of variants of uncertain significance, which poses a practical problem (110).

Despite the current problems, practical and biological, it is clear that genetic testing in negative autopsy, and selected cases of apparent SCD is mandatory. The list of genetic mutations is increasing and therefore useless to list here. However, aid in the implementation exists in the current guidelines and expert consensus statements (8,111,112).

SELECTED TOPICS

In addition to the major topics in cardiac deaths dealt with above, there are specific topics that practical medicolegal specialists should be aware of in the autopsy context. The topics introduced here do not represent an exhaustive list but serve as examples of the variety of the issues in the realm of the autopsy theatre.

Chemically induced SCD

SCD can occur due to direct or indirect influence of chemicals on the heart. Best known are the effects of alcohol (ethanol), and some prescription medications as well as illegal drugs or a combination of these. The consequences are mostly a result of chronic use causing secondary cardiomyopathy, myocarditis or arrhythmia.

Chronic alcohol abuse can cause a DCM, which may be indistinguishable from other DCMs. Some individuals seem to be especially prone to alcohol induced cardiac toxicity (113) and others may experience SCD after their first ever exposure to alcohol due to predisposing mutation (114). Although the primary injury which causes alcohol-induced myocardial defect is not known, human and animal studies show a number of histologic-, subcellular and structural changes that occur in response to long-term heavy alcohol consumption (115). Several interrelated mechanisms may include oxidative stress, apoptotic cell death, impaired mitochondrial bioenergetics/stress, derangements in fatty acid metabolism and transport, and accelerated protein catabolism. Myocardial lesions in cases of the alcoholic DCM have been described and possibly this subgroup partly belongs to the group of inflammatory cardiomyopathies: in microscopic examination, hypertrophic cardiomyocytes with variable nucleus sizes dominate, and interstitial and endocardial fibrosis can occur with fiber ruptures (116,117). Individual cells may appear to be in necrosis with macrophage infiltration. Altogether, chronic inflammatory cardiomyopathy is an alternative histologic diagnosis, and therefore the anamnesis of chronic alcohol use is of importance with other organic signs of alcohol-related diseases, for example in the liver and pancreas. The effect of alcohol intake in the SCD cases is seen in large population-level studies. In a recent study analyzing a cohort of close to 6000 SCDs from northern Finland almost one-third had alcohol in their blood or urine, and from the vast majority (86%) of the SCDs occurred in the late-stage of alcohol inebriation, and approximately two-thirds of the cases had ischemic-heart disease, while one-third had a non-ischemic myocardial disease as the underlying cause of death (118).

Several prescription drugs have been associated with myocarditis, for example the antipsychotic drug, clozapine, is well known for its association with myocarditis (119). A recent analysis of data retrieved from the WHO pharmacovigilance database shows that altogether 62 drugs are associated with myocarditis (120). From those, two-thirds are categorized into five main pharmacologic classes (in descending frequency): antipsychotics, vaccines, antineoplastic-immunotherapies, salicylates and antineoplastic-cytotoxics. It is noteworthy that about 60 percent of these were not hitherto associated with myocarditis. Men are at greater risk to develop drug-related myocarditis with about 70 percent of reported cases, and those affected are on average from the young population (average age 35 years), and the delay till onset of the symptoms is around two weeks (15 days) (120). The death rate observed in this study is about 10 percent. There are a multitude of mechanisms suggested to cause drug-induced myocarditis. Vaccines (e.g. smallpox) are associated with autoimmunity-mediated myocarditis, seemingly secondary to vaccine-mimicry of myocardial antigens (121). For salicylates, direct myocardial toxicity, allergic reaction, hypersensitivity reaction or a humoral antibody response have been proposed. Eosinophilia is seen in antipsychotic and salicylate-associated myocarditis and immunosuppressive medications have been associated with fulminant lymphocytic myocarditis. Cytotoxic agents used in cancer therapy have direct cytotoxicity to cardiomyocytes. Immune oncologic therapies with immune checkpoint inhibitors may cause myocarditis – even fatal cases have been reported (122,123).

Drug-induced arrhythmia, or proarrhythmia, is the induction or exacerbation of cardiac arrhythmia associated with administration of a drug (124). It is well established that a large number of widely used medications may cause or exacerbate a variety of arrhythmias (125). These include antiarrhythmic agents, antimicrobial drugs, psychotropic medications, methadone, neurologic drugs and anticancer agents that can prolong the QT interval, provoke torsades de pointes, but also trigger other arrhythmias (e.g. bradycardia, atrial fibrillation/atrial flutter, atrial tachycardia, atrioventricular nodal reentrant tachycardia, monomorphic ventricular tachycardia, and Brugada syndrome). Most of the known drug-induced ventricular arrhythmias are related to drugs affecting cardiac repolarization; consequently, they prolong the QT interval and may cause fatal drug-induced torsades de pointes (126). Some of these arrhythmias (e.g. bradyarrhythmias, atrial and atrioventricular tachycardias) are significant due to their unpleasant, but rather non-serious symptoms, but some others (e.g. monomorphic ventricular tachycardia, Brugada syndrome, torsades de pointes) may result in SCD (125). Some of the mechanisms of arrhythmias are established for specific drug classes, but the mechanisms still remain poorly understood in many instances (127). A classical and historically perhaps the best known is digitoxin/digoxin leading sometimes to bradycardic cardiac arrhythmias in older people, despite its typical symptoms, due to the small therapeutic window and renal excretion (128).

Among illegal drugs with cardiac effects, cocaine, amphetamines and various new psychoactive substances (NPS) (e.g. MDMA, MDEA, α-PVP and MDPV, *see* curated list of NPSs https://www.unodc.org/LSS/Page/NPS) are the most used. The sympathomimetic effect of cocaine can cause hypertension, arteriosclerosis and spasms of the coronary arteries, with a consequent "cocaine cardiomyopathy" due to the chronic ischemia. Cocaine has also been reported to trigger a myocardial infarction and severe cardiac arrhythmia with ventricular fibrillation (129). The toxic effects of MDMA and MDEA are non-dose-dependent. The risk of sudden death for first-time users is relatively high, though the current data is limited (1:2000 to 1:50 000) (130). Various NPS cause indirect and possibly also direct effects on cardiomyocyte function (131), and association with acute myocardial infarction is also described (132).

Another area of chemicals relevant to autopsy practice are performance-enhancing drugs, also called doping agents. Cardiac effects are well described for anabolic steroids (133) as well as several other illustrative case-series have been reported on the use of anabolic steroids for non-medical indications and SCD (134–136). A list of "prohibited substances and methods" has been updated by the World Anti-Doping Agency (www.wada-ama.org). Also, many other performance-enhancing drugs are reported to be potentially arrhythmogenic (137).

External force induced SCD

External force affecting the thorax area can cause cardiac arrhythmia, rupture or other dysfunction leading to asystole. Various types of thorax traumas are a common finding in autopsy. These are classified as penetrating or non-penetrating and the injury patterns range from *commotio* and *contusio cordis* to ruptures of vessels and ventricles in blunt trauma or perforating injuries in sharp force or gunshot. As the force can vary and it can be of different origins and directions, the injuries can cause lesions solely to the heart, but also to the adjacent vital organs in the thoracic cavity, that is, the lungs or the large vessels. Cardiac deaths due to external force are also classified by injury patterns: blunt trauma causing *commotio* and *contusio cordis* or ruptures of vessels and ventricles or sharp force and gunshot causing perforations of the heart.

The mechanisms in the blunt, non-penetrating traumas are due to the compression of the chest. First, in falls from heights and traffic accidents, an abrupt, sudden delay of the body with filled heart ventricles, causes deceleration trauma in which the heart is pulled at the site of a large vessel with consequent rupture. Second, chest compression may simply lead to a sudden increase of ventricular pressure with subsequent rupture.

Fatal cardiac concussion and commotion have been reported with no gross injuries of the heart and no microscopic myocardial lesions (138,139). In such cases, immunohistochemical staining may reveal loss of myocardial myoglobin, CK-BB and CK-MM (140). However, loss of myoglobin may be prone to bias, and therefore positive staining is more reliable than loss of staining in this context. Typically, *commotio cordis* and subsequent death occurs immediately or after a short survival time and is related to a direct blunt force to the anterior (precordial) part of thorax during the myocardial repolarization with subsequent ventricular fibrillation. Blunt thoracic trauma can also have an effect on already damaged vessel walls, and trauma-induced plaque rupture with consequent bleeding or thrombus formation of the coronary arteries are conceivable.

Naturally, stabbing and gunshot wounds are clear penetrating injuries with a possibility of large destruction of the heart and its surrounding structures. Related to weapons, a controversy surrounds the possibility of the fatal effects of electro-muscular disruption (EMD) technology, also known as conducted energy devices (CEDs), which have become an accepted form of a so-called "less-lethal weapon" in crowd control. The literature of the cardiac effect and safety of these weapons is controversial (141).

Finally, iatrogenic injuries are a known risk during catheter examinations, for example coronary angiographies, coronary balloon dilatation and stent insertions. As a rare fatal complication, an acute coronary thrombosis with myocardial infarction or coronary wall rupture with subsequent acute pericardial tamponade can occur. In electroablation for cardiac arrhythmias, perforation of the heart wall at atrial level is a rare but typical risk. Complications of cardiopulmonary resuscitation procedures are well known and may also affect the heart (142,143).

What is normal heart weight?

Measuring the heart weight in autopsy is routine and the information is relevant in specific cases. However, it was realized already in the late nineteenth century that the interpretation of what is (in a range of) normal heart weight can be challenging, since there are many factors involved (144). These can be classified, on the one hand, to physiological and pathologic, and to individual, population-related and temporal factors, on the other. It is well established that gender, body dimensions (body-weight, body mass-index, body surface), age and diseases affect the weight of the heart (145–147). Men are known to have on average higher heart weight than women (148). Early observations showed that heart weight increases with body weight and age (149,150). Recently, it has been shown that the heart weight/body weight ratio has increased during the last century (150,151). The weight of the heart is affected by vascular and heart diseases, as well as obesity and cancer (145,147). Heart weight may also be markedly elevated by use of doping, especially anabolic androgenic steroids. Higher than expected liver and kidney weight is common among the anabolic androgenic steroid users. If use of anabolic steroids is suspected in a supposed cardiac death case, further studies are warranted.

In addition to the abovementioned factors, autopsy techniques also affect the recorded heart weight. Generally, the heart weight measurement is performed in at least three different dissection points: once the heart is dissected out of the pericardium (blood in the cavities), after the blood is removed or washed from the heart chambers or the heart is completely opened, washed and pat dried (152–154). The weight difference can be several percentages between each of the methods, and Lee and Byard (152) reported an extreme of 30.3 percent difference between the weight of the partially opened heart and that of the fully opened heart.

Based on the above, it is important to establish organ reference tables based on the local population of concern (147,151), combined with user-friendly technical support to help predict heart weight. Indeed, some interesting developments have been reported 155–159).

Similarly, data for organ weights in infants and young children have been reported as references for autopsy work (160,161).

CONCLUSION

SCD may result from a multitude of cardiac conditions, which may or may not reveal symptoms prior to death. In cases of non-apparent cardiac disease during the autopsy, a detailed cardio-pathologic examination is mandatory to disclose the underlying condition leading to sudden unexpected cardiac deaths, especially in young individuals. According to the international recommendations, these consist of detailed dissection of the heart and immunohistochemical staining of an extended set of samples from various anatomical parts of the heart, toxicological investigation and genetic analysis.

REFERENCES

1. GBD 2013 Mortality and Causes of Death Collaborators. Global, regional, and national age-sex specific all-cause and cause-specific mortality for 240 causes of death, 1990–2013: A systematic analysis for the Global Burden of Disease Study 2013 GBD 2013 Mortality and Causes of Death Collaborators. *Lancet* 2015; **385**: 117–71.
2. Townsend N, Wilson L, Bhatnagar P, et al. Cardiovascular disease in Europe: Epidemiological update 2016. *Eur Heart J* 2016; **37**: 3232–45.
3. Kannel WB, Wilson PWF, D'Agostino RB, Cobb J. Sudden coronary death in women. *Am Heart J* 1998; **136(2)**: 205–12.
4. Haukilahti MAE, Holmström L, Vähätalo J, et al. Sudden cardiac death in women: Causes of death, autopsy findings, and electrocardiographic risk markers. *Circulation* 2019; **139(8)**: 1012–21.
5. Becker LB, Han BH, Meyer PM, et al. Racial differences in the incidence of cardiac arrest and subsequent survival. *N Engl J Med* 1993; **329(9)**: 600–6.
6. Fender EA, Henrikson CA, Tereshchenko L. Racial differences in sudden cardiac death. *J Electrocardiol* 2014; **47(6)**: 815–8.
7. World Health Organization. *International Classification of Diseases (ICD-10)*. Geneva: World Health Organization; 2005.
8. Priori SG, Blomstrom-Lundqvist C, Mazzanti A, et al. 2015 ESC Guidelines for the management of patients with ventricular arrhythmias and the prevention of sudden cardiac death. The task force for the management of patients with ventricular arrhythmias and the prevention of sudden cardiac death of the Europe. *Europace* 2015; **17**: 1601–87.
9. Shipstone RA, Young J, Thompson JMD, Byard RW. An evaluation of pathologists' application of the diagnostic criteria from the San Diego definition of SIDS and unclassified sudden infant death. *Int J Leg Med* 2020; **134**: 1015–21.
10. Priori SG, Wilde AA, Horie M, et al. HRS/EHRA/APHRS CONSENSUS STATEMENT Executive summary: HRS/EHRA/APHRS expert consensus statement on the diagnosis and management of patients with inherited primary arrhythmia syndromes. *Europace* 2013; **15**: 1389–406.
11. Lahrouchi N, Raju H, Lodder EM, et al. Utility of post-mortem genetic testing in cases of sudden arrhythmic death syndrome. *J Am Coll Cardiol* 2017; **69(17)**: 2134–45.
12. Lawler W. The negative coroner's necropsy: A personal approach and consideration of difficulties. *J Clin Pathol* 1990; **43**: 977–80.
13. Cohle SD, Sampson BA. The negative autopsy: Sudden cardiac death or other? *Cardiovasc Pathol* 2001; **10(5)**: 219–22.
14. Ross R, Harker L. Hyperlipidemia and atherosclerosis. *Science* 1976; **193**: 1094–100.
15. Libby P, Theroux P. Pathophysiology of coronary artery disease. *Circulation* 2005; **111**: 3481–8.
16. Murray CJ, Lopez AD. Global mortality, disability, and the contribution of risk factors: Global Burden of Disease Study. *Lancet* 1997; **349(9063)**: 1436–42.
17. Roth GA, Mensah GA, Fuster V. The global burden of cardiovascular diseases and risks: A compass for global action. *J Am Coll Cardiol* 2020; **76(25)**: 2980–81.
18. Khera AV, Emdin CA, Kathiresan S. Genetic risk, lifestyle, and coronary artery disease. *N Engl J Med* 2017; **376(12)**: 1194–5.
19. Graham I, Cooney MT, Bradley D, et al. Dyslipidemias in the prevention of cardiovascular disease: Risks and causality. *Curr Cardiol Rep* 2012; **14**: 709–20.
20. Borén J, Chapman MJ, Krauss RM, et al. Low-density lipoproteins cause atherosclerotic cardiovascular disease: pathophysiological, genetic, and therapeutic insights: a consensus statement from the European Atherosclerosis Society Consensus Panel. *Eur Heart J* 2020; **41(24)**: 2313–30.
21. Puska P, Tuomilehto J, Salonen J, et al. Changes in coronary risk factors during comprehensive five-year community programme to control cardiovascular diseases (North Karelia project). *Br Med J* 1979; **2(6199)**: 1173–8.
22. Gordon T, Kannel WB, Castelli WP, Dawber TR. Lipoproteins, cardiovascular disease, and death. The Framingham study. *Arch Intern Med* 1981; **141(9)**: 1128–31.
23. Anderson KM, Castelli WP, Levy D. Cholesterol and mortality. 30 years of follow-up from the Framingham study. *JAMA* 1987; **257(16)**: 2176–80.
24. Verschuren WM, Jacobs DR, Bloemberg BP, et al. Serum total cholesterol and long-term coronary heart disease mortality in different cultures. Twenty-five-year follow-up of the seven countries study. *JAMA* 1995; **274(2)**: 131–6.
25. Gertler MM, Driskell MM, Bland EF, et al. Clinical aspects of coronary heart disease; an analysis of 100 cases in patients 23 to 40 years of age with myocardial infarction. *J Am Med Assoc* 1951; **146(14)**: 1291–5.
26. Pohjola-Sintonen S, Rissanen A, Liskola P, Luomanmäki K. Family history as a risk factor of coronary heart disease in patients under 60 years of age. *Eur Heart J* 1998; **19**: 235–9.
27. Friedlander Y, Siscovick DS, Weinmann S, et al. Family history as a risk factor for primary cardiac arrest. *Circulation* 1998; **97(2)**: 155–60.
28. Roncaglioni MC, Santoro L, D'Avanzo B, et al. Role of family history in patients with myocardial infarction. An Italian case-control study. GISSI-EFRIM Investigators. *Circulation* 1992; **85**: 2065–72.
29. Watts RA, Hatemi G, Burns JC, Mohammad AJ. Global epidemiology of vasculitis. *Nat Rev Rheumatol* 2022; **18(1)**: 22–34.
30. Jennette JC, Falk RJ, Andrassy K, et al. Nomenclature of systemic vasculitides. Proposal of an international consensus conference. *Arthritis Rheum* 1994; **37(2)**: 187–92.
31. Jennette JC, Falk RJ, Bacon PA, et al. 2012 revised International Chapel Hill consensus conference nomenclature of vasculitides. *Arthritis Rheum* 2013; **65(1)**: 1–11.
32. Waller BF, Fry ET, Hermiller JB, et al. Nonatherosclerotic causes of coronary artery narrowing--Part I. *Clin Cardiol* 1996; **19(6)**: 509–12.
33. Shields LB, Burge M, Hunsaker JC 3rd. Sudden death due to polyarteritis nodosa.*Forensic Sci Med Pathol* 2012; **8(3)**: 290–5.
34. Norita K, de Noronha SV, Sheppard MN. Sudden cardiac death caused by coronary vasculitis. *Virchows Arch* 2012; **460(3)**: 309–18.
35. Kajihara H, Tachiyama Y, Hirose T, et al. Eosinophilic coronary periarteritis (vasospastic angina and sudden death), a new type of coronary arteritis: report of seven autopsy cases and a review of the literature. *Virchows Arch* 2013; **462(2)**: 239–48.
36. Sakai K, Asakura K, Saito K, Fukunaga T. Sudden unexpected death due to coronary thrombosis associated with isolated necrotizing vasculitis in the coronary arteries of a young adult. *Forensic Sci Med Pathol* 2019; **15(2)**: 252–7.
37. Flossdorf S, Schiwy-Bochat KH, Teifel D, et al. Sudden death of a young adult with coronary artery vasculitis, coronary aneurysms, parvovirus B19 infection and Kawasaki disease. *Forensic Sci Med Pathol* 2020; **16(3)**: 498–503.
38. Bukiri H, Ruhoy SM, Buckner JH. Sudden cardiac death due to coronary artery vasculitis in a patient with relapsing polychondritis. *Case Rep Rheumatol* 2020; **2020**: 5620471.
39. M Lorbar M, Spodick DH. 'Idiopathic' pericarditis--the clinician's challenge [nothing is idiopathic]. *Int J Clin Pract* 2007; **61(1)**: 138–42.
40. Reuter H, Burgess LJ, Doubell AF. Epidemiology of pericardial effusions at a large academic hospital in South Africa. *Epidemiol Infect* 2005; **133(3)**: 393–9.
41. Kytö V, Sipilä J, Rautava P. Clinical profile and influences on outcomes in patients hospitalized for acute pericarditis. *Circulation* 2014; **130**: 1601–6.
42. Sigvardt FL, Hansen ML, Kristensen SL, et al. Risk factors for morbidity and mortality following hospitalization for pericarditis. *J Am Coll Cardiol* 2020; **76(22)**: 2623–31.
43. Yoshizane T, Yamamoto T, Hayashi H, et al. A case of primary bacterial pericarditis with recurrent cardiac tamponade. *J Nippon Med Sch* 2017; **84(3)**: 133–8.
44. Cunningham KS, Spears DA, Care M. Evaluation of cardiac hypertrophy in the setting of sudden cardiac death. *Forensic Sci Res* 2019; **4**: 223–40.
45. Basso C, Michaud K, Banner J, et al. Cardiac hypertrophy at autopsy on behalf of the Association for European Cardiovascular Pathology. *Virchows Arch* 2021; **479**: 79–94.
46. Fiedler A. Ueber akute interstitielle myokarditis. In: zu Dresden R (ed), *Festschrift zur Feier des funfzigjahrigen Bestehens des Stadtkrankenhauses zu Dresden-Friedrichstadt*, Part 2. Dresden: Wilhelm Baensch; 1899, pp. 3–24.
47. Evans W. Familial cardiomegaly. *Br Heart J* 1949; **11(1)**: 68–82.
48. Brigden W. Uncommon myocardial diseases: the non-coronary cardiomyopathies. *Lancet* 1957; **273**: 1243–9.

49. Brandenburg RO, Chazov E, Cherian G, et al. Report of the WHO/ISFC task force on the definition and classification of cardiomyopathies. *Br Heart J* 1980; **44**: 672–3.
50. Maron BJ, Towbin JA, Thiene G, et al. Contemporary definitions and classification of the cardiomyopathies: An American Heart Association Scientific Statement from the Council on Clinical Cardiology, Heart Failure and Transplantation Committee; Quality of Care and Outcomes Research and Functional Genomics and Translational Biology Interdisciplinary Working Groups; and Council on Epidemiology and Prevention. *Circulation* 2006; **113**: 1807–16.
51. Elliott P, Andersson B, Arbustini E, et al. Classification of the cardiomyopathies: A position statement from the European Society of Cardiology Working Group on Myocardial and Pericardial Diseases. *Eur Heart J* 2008; **29**: 270–6.
52. Hershberger RE, Hedges DJ, Morales A. Dilated cardiomyopathy: the complexity of a diverse genetic architecture. *Nat Rev Cardiol* 2013; **10**: 531–47.
53. Maron BJ, Shirani J, Poliac LC, et al. Sudden death in young competitive athletes. Clinical, demographic, and pathological profiles. *JAMA* 1996; **276**: 199–204.
54. Hershberger RE, Morales A, Siegfried JD. Clinical and genetic issues in dilated cardiomyopathy: a review for genetics professionals. *Genet Med* 2010; **12**: 655–67.
55. Burkett EL, Hershberger RE. Clinical and genetic issues in familial dilated cardiomyopathy. *J Am Coll Cardiol* 2005; **45**(7): 969–81.
56. Heliö K, Mäyränpää MI, Saarinen I, et al. GRINL1A complex transcription unit containing GCOM1, MYZAP, and POLR2M genes associates with fully penetrant recessive dilated cardiomyopathy. *Front Genet* 2021; **12**: 786705.
57. Brandenburg RO, Chazov E, Cherian G, et al. Report of the WHO/ISFC task force on the definition and classification of cardiomyopathies. *Br Heart J* 1980; **44(6)**: 672–3.
58. Honigberg MC, Givertz MM. Peripartum cardiomyopathy. *Br Med J* 2019; **364**: k5287.
59. Muchtar E, Blauwet LA, Gertz MA. Restrictive cardiomyopathy: Genetics, pathogenesis, clinical manifestations, diagnosis, and therapy. *Circ Res* 2017; **121**: 819–37.
60. Cimiotti D, Budde H, Hassoun R, Jaquet K. Genetic restrictive cardiomyopathy: Causes and consequences—an integrative approach. *Int J Mol Sci* 2021; **22**: 558.
61. Krahn AD, Wilde AAM, Calkins H, et al. Arrhythmogenic right ventricular cardiomyopathy. *JACC Clin Electrophysiol* 2022; **8**: 533–53.
62. Gandjbakhch E, Redheuil A, Pousset F, et al. Clinical diagnosis, imaging, and genetics of arrhythmogenic right ventricular cardiomyopathy/dysplasia: JACC State-of-the-Art Review. *J Am Coll Cardiol* 2018; **72**: 784–804.
63. Jenni R, Oechslin EN, van der Loo B. Isolated ventricular non-compaction of the myocardium in adults. *Heart* 2007; **93**: 11–15.
64. Dote K, Sato H, Tateishi H, et al. Myocardial stunning due to simultaneous multivessel coronary spasms: A review of 5 cases. *J Cardiol* 1991; **21**(**2**): 203–14.
65. Gianni M, Dentali F, Grandi AM, et al. Apical ballooning syndrome or takotsubo cardiomyopathy: A systematic review. *Eur Heart J* 2006; **27**: 1523–9.
66. McCarthy RE 3rd, Boehmer JP, Hruban RH, et al. Long-term outcome of fulminant myocarditis as compared with acute (nonfulminant) myocarditis. *N Engl J Med* 2000; **342**: 690–5.
67. Aretz HT, Billingham ME, Edwards WD, et al. Myocarditis. A histopathologic definition and classification. *Am J Cardiovasc Pathol* 1987; **1**: 3–14.
68. Baughman KL. Diagnosis of myocarditis: Death of Dallas criteria. *Circulation* 2006; **113**: 593–5.
69. Sharma AN, Stultz JR, Bellamkonda N, Amsterdam EA. Fulminant myocarditis: Epidemiology, pathogenesis, diagnosis, and management. *Am J Cardiol* 2019; **124**: 1954–60.
70. Chow LH, Radio SJ, Sears TD, McManus BM. Insensitivity of right ventricular endomyocardial biopsy in the diagnosis of myocarditis. *JACC* 1989; **14**: 915–20.
71. Pankuweit S, Portig I, Eckhardt H, et al. Prevalence of viral genome in endomyocardial biopsies from patients with inflammatory heart muscle disease. *Herz* 2000; **25**: 221–6.
72. Lagana SM, Parwani AV, Nichols LC. Cardiac sarcoidosis. A pathology-focused review. *Arch Pathol Lab Med* 2010; **134**: 1039–46.
73. Rybicki BA, Iannuzzi MC. Epidemiology of sarcoidosis: Recent advances and future prospects. *Semin Respir Crit Care Med* 2007; **28**(**1**): 22–35.
74. Lehtonen J, Uusitalo V, Pöyhönen P, et al. Cardiac sarcoidosis: phenotypes, diagnosis, treatment, and prognosis. *Eur Heart J* 2023; **44**(17):1495–1510.
75. Costabel U, Hunninghake GW. ATS/ERS/WASOG statement on sarcoidosis: Sarcoidosis Statement Committee, American Thoracic Society, European Respiratory Society, World Association for Sarcoidosis and Other Granulomatous Disorders. *Eur Respir J* 1999; **14**: 735–7.
76. Bernstein M, Konzelman FW, Sidlick DM. Boeck's sarcoid: Report of a case with visceral involvement. *Arch Intern Med* 1929; **4**: 721–34.
77. Longcope WT, Fisher AM. Effect of Schaumann's disease upon heart and its mechanisms. *Acta Med Scand* 1941; **108**: 529.
78. Ricker W, Clark M. Sarcoidosis: A clinicopathologic review of 330 cases, including 22 autopsies. *Am J Clin Pathol* 1949; **19**: 725–49.
79. Longcope WT, Freiman DG. A study of sarcoidosis - Based on a combined investigation of 160 case's including 30 autopsies from the Johns Hopkins Hospital and Massachusetts General Hospital. *Medicine* 1952; **31**: 1–131.
80. Gozo Jr EG, Cosnow I, Cohen HC, Okun L. The heart in sarcoidosis. *Chest* 1971; **60**: 379–88.
81. Silverman KJ, Hutchins GM, Bulkley BH. Cardiac sarcoid: A clinicopathologic study of 84 unselected patients with systemic sarcoidosis. *Circulation* 1978; **58**: 1204–11.
82. Iwai K, Tachibana T, Takemura T, et al. Pathological studies on sarcoidosis autopsy: I. epidemiological features of 320 cases in Japan. *Acta Pathol Jpn* 1993; **43**: 372–6.
83. Ekström K, Lehtonen J, Nordenswan H-K, et al. Sudden death in cardiac sarcoidosis: An analysis of nationwide clinical and cause-of-death registries. *Eur Heart J* 2019; **40**: 3121–8.
84. Ekström K, Räisänen-Sokolowski A, Lehtonen J, et al. Idiopathic giant cell myocarditis or cardiac sarcoidosis? A retrospective audit of a nationwide case series. *ESC Heart Fail* 2020; **7**: 1362–70.
85. Maraj S, Pressman GS, Figueredo VM. Primary cardiac tumors. *Int J Cardiol* 2009; **133**: 152–6.
86. Basso C, Valente M, Thiene G (eds). *Cardiac Tumor Pathology*. New York (NY): Springer Humana Press; 2013.
87. Vander Salm TJ. Unusual primary tumors of the heart. *Semin Thorac Cardiovasc Surg* 2000; **12**(**2**): 89–100.
88. Coffey S, Roberts-Thomson R, Brown A, et al. Global epidemiology of valvular heart disease. *Nature Reviews. Cardiology* 2021; 18: 853–3.
89. Nkomo VT, Gardin JM, Skelton TN, et al. Burden of valvular heart diseases: A population-based study. *Lancet* 2006; **368**: 1005–11.
90. Helbig G, Klion AD. Hypereosinophilic syndromes - An enigmatic group of disorders with an intriguing clinical spectrum and challenging treatment. *Blood Rev* 2021; **49**: 100809.
91. Sutter JS, Suboc TM, Rao AK. Tropical endomyocardial fibrosis. *JACC Case Rep* 2020; **2**: 819–22.
92. Srirajaskanthan R, Shanmugabavan D, Ramage JK. Carcinoid syndrome. *BMJ* 2010; **341**: c3941.
93. Semsarian C, Ingles J, Wilde AAM. Sudden cardiac death in the young: the molecular autopsy and a practical approach to surviving relatives. *Eur Heart J* 2015; **36**: 1290–6.
94. Lahrouchi N, Raju H, Lodder EM, et al. Utility of post-mortem genetic testing in cases of sudden arrhythmic death syndrome. *J Am Coll Cardiol* 2017; **69(17)**: 2134–45.
95. Friedlander Y, Siscovick DS, Weinmann S, et al. Family history as a risk factor for primary cardiac arrest. *Circulation* 1998; **97**: 155–60.
96. Jouven X, Desnos M, Guerot C, Ducimetière P. Predicting sudden death in the population: The Paris Prospective Study I. *Circulation* 1999; **99**: 1978–83.
97. Kaikkonen KS, Kortelainen ML, Linna E, Huikuri HV. Family history and the risk of sudden cardiac death as a manifestation of an acute coronary event. *Circulation* 2006; **114**: 1462–7.
98. Papadakis M, Sharma S, Cox S, et al. The magnitude of sudden cardiac death in the young: A death certificate-based review in England and Wales. *Europace* 2009; **11**: 1353–8.
99. Winkel BG, Gaardal Holst A, Theilade J, et al. Nationwide study of sudden cardiac death in persons aged 1–35 years. *Eur Heart J* 2011; **32**: 983–90.
100. Lahrouchi N, Raju H, Lodder EM, et al. The yield of postmortem genetic testing in sudden death cases with structural findings at autopsy. *Eur J Hum Genet* 2020; **28**: 17–22.
101. Hansen BL, Jacobsen EM, Kjerrumgaard A, et al. Diagnostic yield in victims of sudden cardiac death and their relatives. *Europace* 2020; **22**(**6**): 964–71.

102. Basso C, Aguilera B, Banner J, et al. Association for European Cardiovascular Pathology. Guidelines for autopsy investigation of sudden cardiac death: 2017 update from the Association for European Cardiovascular Pathology. *Virchows Arch* 2017; **471**: 691–705.
103. de Noronha SV, Behr ER, Papadakis M, et al. The importance of specialist cardiac histopathological examination in the investigation of young sudden cardiac deaths. *Europace* 2014; **16**: 899–907.
104. Schwartz PJ, Ackerman MJ, Antzelevitch C, et al. Inherited cardiac arrhythmias. *Nat Rev Dis Primers* 2020; **6**: 58.
105. Wilde AAM, Semsarian C, Márquez MF, et al. Developed in partnership with and endorsed by the European Heart Rhythm Association (EHRA), a branch of the European Society of Cardiology (ESC), the Heart Rhythm Society (HRS), the Asia Pacific Heart Rhythm Society (APHRS), and the Latin American Heart Rhythm Society (LAHRS).European Heart Rhythm Association (EHRA)/ Heart Rhythm Society (HRS)/Asia Pacific Heart Rhythm Society (APHRS)/ Latin American Heart Rhythm Society (LAHRS) Expert Consensus Statement on the state of genetic testing for cardiac diseases. *Europace* 2022; **24**: 1307–67.
106. Ackerman MJ, Tester DJ, Driscoll DJ. Molecular autopsy of sudden unexplained death in the young. *Am J Forensic Med Pathol* 2001; **22**: 105–11.
107. Hertz CL, Christiansen SL, Ferrero-Miliani L, et al. Next-generation sequencing of 34 genes in sudden unexplained death victims in forensics and in patients with channelopathic cardiac diseases. *Int J Legal Med* 2015; **129**: 793–800.
108. Hertz CL, Christiansen SL, Ferrero-Miliani L, et al. Next-generation sequencing of 100 candidate genes in young victims of suspected sudden cardiac death with structural abnormalities of the heart. *Int J Legal Med* 2016; **130**: 91–102.
109. Richards S, Aziz N, Bale S, et al. Standards and guidelines for the interpretation of sequence variants: a joint consensus recommendation of the American College of Medical Genetics and Genomics and the Association for Molecular Pathology. Assurance Committee. *Genet Med* 2015; **17**: 405–24.
110. Lahrouchi N, Raju H, Lodder EM, et al. Utility of post-mortem genetic testing in cases of sudden arrhythmic death syndrome. *J Am Coll Cardiol* 2017; **69**: 2134–45.
111. Fellmann F, van El CG, Charron P, et al. European recommendations integrating genetic testing into multidisciplinary management of sudden cardiac death. *Eur J Hum Genet* 2019; **27**: 1763–73.
112. Stiles MK, Wilde AMM, Abrams DJ, et al. 2020 APHRS/HRS expert consensus statement on the investigation of decedents with sudden unexplained death and patients with sudden cardiac arrest, and of their families. *Heart Rhythm* 2021; **18**: e1–e50.
113. Ware JS, Amor-Salamanca A, Tayal U, et al. Genetic etiology for alcohol-induced cardiac toxicity. *J Am Coll Cardiol* 2018; **71**: 2293–302.
114. Guimier A, Achleitner MT, Moreau de Bellaing A, et al. PPA2-associated sudden cardiac death: Extending the clinical and allelic spectrum in 20 new families. *Genet Med* 2021; **23**: 2415–25.
115. Alexandere CS. Electron microscopic observations in alcoholic heart disease. *Brit Heart J* 1967; **29**: 200–6.
116. Dettmeyer R, Reith K, Madea B. Alcoholic cardiomyopathy versus chronic myocarditis--immunohistological investigations with LCA, CD3, CD68 and tenascin. *Forensic Sci Int* 2002; **126**: 57–62.
117. Markwerth P, Bajanowski T, Tzimas I, Dettmeyer R. Sudden cardiac death-update. *Int J Legal Med* 2021; **135**: 483–95.
118. Holmström L, Kauppila J, Vähätalo J,et al. Sudden cardiac death after alcohol intake: classification and autopsy findings. Sci Rep 2022; 12: 16771.
119. Kilian JG, Kerr K, Lawrence C, Celermajer DS. Myocarditis and cardiomyopathy associated with clozapine. *Lancet* 1999; **354**: 1841–5.
120. Nguyen LS, Cooper LT, Kerneis M, et al. Systematic analysis of drug-associated myocarditis reported in the World Health Organization pharmacovigilance database. *Nat Commun* 2022; **13**: 25.
121. Cassimatis DC, Atwood JE, Engler RM, et al. Smallpox vaccination and myopericarditis: A clinical review. *J Am Coll Cardiol* 2004; **43**: 1503–10.
122. Wang DY, Salem JE, Cohen JV, et al. Fatal toxic effects associated with immune checkpoint inhibitors: A systematic review and meta-analysis. *JAMA Oncol* 2018; **4**: 1721–8.
123. Johnson DB, Balko JM, Compton ML, et al. Fulminant myocarditis with combination immune checkpoint blockade. *N Engl J Med* 2016; **375**: 1749–55.
124. Coughtrie AL, Behr ER, Layton D, et al. Drugs and life-threatening ventricular arrhythmia risk: Results from the DARE study cohort. *BMJ Open* 2017; **7**: e016627.
125. Tisdale JE, Chung MK, Campbell KB, et al. Drug-induced arrhythmias: A scientific statement from the american heart association. *Circulation* 2020; **142**: e214–e33.
126. Behr ER, Roden D. Drug-induced arrhythmia: Pharmacogenomic prescribing? *Eur Heart J* 2013; **34**: 89–95.
127. Mladěnka P, Applová L, Patočka J, et al. Comprehensive review of cardiovascular toxicity of drugs and related agents. *Med Res Rev* 2018; **38**: 1332–403.
128. Bremner WF, Third JL, Lawrie TD. Massive digoxin ingestion. Report of a case and review of currently available therapies. *Br Heart J* 1977; **39**: 688–92.
129. Kloner RA, Rezkalla SH. Cocaine and the heart. *N Engl J Med* 2003; **348**: 487–8.
130. Gore SM. Fatal uncertainty: Death-rate from use of ecstasy or heroin. *Lancet* 1999; **354**: 1265–6.
131. Zwartsen A, de Korte T, Nacken P, et al. Cardiotoxicity screening of illicit drugs and new psychoactive substances (NPS) in human iPSC-derived cardiomyocytes using microelectrode array (MEA) recordings. *J Mol Cell Cardiol* 2019; **136**: 102–12.
132. Lai TI, Hwang JJ, Fang CC, Chen WJ. Methylene 3, 4 dioxymethamphetamine-induced acute myocardial infarction. *Ann Emerg Med* 2003; **42**: 759–62.
133. Sullivan ML, Martinez CM, Gennis P, Gallagher EJ. The cardiac toxicity of anabolic steroids. *Prog Cardiovasc Dis* 1998; **41**: 1–15.
134. Luke JL, Farb A, Virmani R, Sample RH. Sudden cardiac death during exercise in a weightlifter using anabolic androgenic steroids: Pathological and toxicological findings. *J Forensic Sci* 1990; **35**: 1441–7.
135. Madea B, Grellner W, Musshoff F, Dettmeyer R. Medico-legal aspects of doping. *J Clin Forensic Med* 1998; **5**: 1–7.
136. Fineschi V, Riezzo I, Centini F, et al. Sudden cardiac death during anabolic steroid abuse: Morphologic and toxicologic findings in two fatal cases of bodybuilders. *Int J Legal Med* 2007; **121**: 48–53.
137. Furlanello F, Serdoz LV, Cappato R, De Ambroggi L. Illicit drugs and cardiac arrhythmias in athletes. *Eur J Cardiovasc Prev Rehabil* 2007; **14**: 487–94.
138. Green ED, Simson LR Jr, Kellerman HH, et al. Cardiac concussion following softball blow to the chest. *Ann Emerg Med* 1980; **9**: 155–7.
139. Frazer M, Mirchandani H. Commotio cordis, revisited. *Am J Forensic Med Pathol* 1984; **5**: 249–51.
140. Guan DW, Ohshima T, Jia JT, et al. Morphological findings of 'cardiac concussion' due to experimental blunt impact to the precordial region. *Forensic Sci Int* 1999; **100**: 211–20.
141. Zipes DP. Sudden cardiac arrest and death following application of shocks from a TASER electronic control device. *Circulation* 2012; **125**: 2417–22.
142. Bedell SE, Fulton EJ. Unexpected findings and complications at autopsy after cardiopulmonary resuscitation (CPR). *Arch Intern Med* 1986; **146**: 1725–8.
143. Machii M, Inaba H, Nakae H, et al. Cardiac rupture by penetration of fractured sternum: A rare complication of cardiopulmonary resuscitation. *Resuscitation* 2000; **43**: 151–3.
144. Arnold HD. Weight of the "normal" heart in adults. *J Boston Soc Med Sci* 1899; **3**: 174–84.
145. Kumar NT, Liestøl K, Løberg EM, et al. Postmortem heart weight: Relation to body size and effects of cardiovascular disease and cancer. *Cardiovasc Pathol* 2014; **23**: 5–11.
146. Wingren CJ, Ottosson A. Postmortem heart weight modelled using piecewise linear regression in 27,645 medicolegal autopsy cases. *Forensic Sci Int* 2015; **252**: 157–62.
147. Skurdal AC, Nordrum IS. A retrospective study of postmortem heart weight in an adult Norwegian population. *Cardiovasc Pathol* 2016; **25**: 461–7.
148. Dadgar SK, Tyagi SP, Singh RP, Hameed S. Factors influencing the normal heart weight--a study of 140 hearts. *Jpn Circ J* 1979; **43**: 77–82.
149. Smith HL. The relation of the weight of the heart to the weight of the body and of the weight of the heart to age. *Am Heart J* 1928; **4**: 79–93.
150. de la Grandmaison GL, Clairand I, Durigon M. Organ weight in 684 adult autopsies: New tables for a Caucasoid population. *Forensic Sci Int* 2001; **119**: 149–54.

151. Lucas SB. Derivation of new reference tables for human heart weights in light of increasing body mass index. *J Clin Pathol* 2011; **64**: 279–80.
152. Lee V, Byard RW. Variation in methods of cardiac dissection--a potential confounder in measuring cardiac weight at autopsy. *J Forensic Sci* 2013; **58**: 811–2.
153. Loper N, Garland J, Ondruschka B, et al. Significant differences in post mortem heart weight before and after dissection using the short-axis dissecting method. *J Forensic Sci* 2020; **65**: 1563–7.
154. Garland J, Kesha K, Glenn C, et al. The effects of drying the rinsed dissected heart on postmortem heart weight. *J Forensic Sci* 2022; **67**: 251–6.
155. Gaitskell K, Perera R, Soilleux EJ. Derivation of new reference tables for human heart weights in light of increasing body mass index. *J Clin Pathol* 2011; **64**: 358–62.
156. Vanhaebost J, Faouzi M, Mangin P, Michaud K. New reference tables and user-friendly Internet application for predicted heart weights. *Int J Legal Med* 2014; **128**: 615–20.
157. Centre universitaire romand de médicine légale (CURML) Heart weight calculator. Available from: https://calc.chuv.ch/Heartweight (Accessed 3 May 2023).
158. Wingren CJ, Ottosson A. Lund Forensic Medicine: Heartweight Calculator. Available from: http://lundforensicmedicine.com (Accessed 3 May 2023).
159. Feinberg Schoool of Medicine. Heart Weight Calculation Tool. Available from: https://labs.feinberg.northwestern.edu/webster/heart_weight/ (Accessed 3 May 2023).
160. Pryce JW, Bamber AR, Ashworth MT, et al. Reference ranges for organ weights of infants at autopsy: Results of >1000 consecutive cases from a single centre. *BMC Clin Pathol* 2014; **14**: 18.
161. Molina DK, Pinneri K, Stash JA, et al. Organ weight reference ranges for ages 0 to 12 years. *Am J Forensic Med Pathol* 2019; **40**: 318–28.

CHAPTER

52

Neglect

Jason Payne-James, Clifford Perera and Anil Aggrawal

INTRODUCTION

Neglect is observed in all age groups and communities across the globe to a variable extent. It has multiple medical, social, cultural and legal ramifications. Neglect existed throughout the ages of human development and commonly manifests in the modern era as a component of child and elder maltreatment or mistreatment. However, it includes a heterogenous group of vulnerable persons such as homeless adolescents/youth/adults, long-term detainees, prison inmates, refugees and asylum seekers, drug dependents, psychiatric patients, displaced persons, disabled persons and those who have been trafficked and those who are victims of modern-day slavery. Neglect and abandonment in their various forms are listed within the International Classification of Diseases (ICD-11) system of coding (1). Neglect is generally considered under definitions of abuse and is intricately associated with such behavior.

Neglect is a form of mistreatment by individuals resulting from inadequate attention, especially through carelessness or disregard for the needs of others. Neglect may also be wilful. Neglect is such a negative word, whether used as a noun or verb, and it always implies someone failed to do something and the results, or potential results, were somewhat devastating (2).

Neglect is defined or explained in a variety of ways in different jurisdictions and often refers to child abuse. The World Health Organization uses this definition: "*Child maltreatment is the abuse and neglect that occurs to children under 18 years of age. It includes all types of physical and/or emotional ill-treatment, sexual abuse, neglect, negligence and commercial or other exploitation, which results in actual or potential harm to the child's health, survival, development or dignity in the context of a relationship of responsibility, trust or power*". (3). It can be seen that this definition can apply to adults as well as children. The UK National Health Service provides broad examples when discussing abuse and neglect or vulnerable adults:

> "*Everyone has the right to live in safety, free from abuse and neglect. Abuse and neglect can occur anywhere: in your own home or a public place, while you're in hospital or attending a day centre, or in a college or care home. You may be living alone or with others. The person causing the harm may be a stranger but, more often than not, you'll know and feel safe with them. They're usually in a position of trust and power, such as a health or care professional, relative or neighbour....Neglect includes not being provided with enough food or with the right kind of food, or not being taken proper care of. Leaving you without help to wash or change dirty or wet clothes, not getting you to a doctor when you need one or not making sure you have the right medicines all count as neglect.*" (4).

Neglect is a heterogenous phenomenon and varies by type, severity and chronicity. It is beyond the simple equation of "caregiver" or "care provider" and "care receiver" interaction and cannot be explained fully without considering the timeline of events and the context of its occurrence.

The effects of neglect originate from the neglectful behavior of the person/s who are owing an official, social or moral responsibility of providing care (care giver/s) toward the affected person/victim (care receiver/s). Therefore, in very general terms, all forms of neglect other than self-neglect, may represent a breach of duty, or breach of responsibility and at its highest wilful, deliberate or criminal acts. In self-neglect, this responsibility moves to the affected person himself/herself, although failure to identify that someone is self-neglecting may in itself be a breach of duty or social responsibility and can result in criminal charges (5,6,7,8).

Diogenes syndrome refers to the combination of extreme self-neglect and excessive collecting with clutter and squalor, which may present in patients with dementia or other mental health conditions such as depression, obsessive-compulsive disorder, personality disorder and stress (9,10).

Any definition of neglect has its own limitations as one cannot use uniform standards to determine the effects of acts of omission on outcome when the standards of care that are considered acceptable may vary widely. Many of the questions raised by forensic practitioners with regard to consideration of neglect may be resolved in courts of law, but these too may struggle to make decisions in relation to evidence of neglectful acts.

DOI: 10.1201/9781003138754-54

For this chapter the following broad definition is used:

> "*Neglect is omission of desired, appropriate or required singular or multiple acts of care once or repeatedly. The determination of whether omission of the act or acts constitutes neglect will need to be determined according to the context by the relevant authorities, although the forensic practitioner may be required to provide an opinion.*"

The role of the forensic practitioner is to ensure that any harm or injury or fatality caused by any such omission is accurately and fully documented.

MEDICOLEGAL APPROACH TO NEGLECT

Neglectful behavior can be intentional or unintentional. Unintentional neglect will ultimately be judged by the courts along the lines of what a reasonable person could have or should have done to support or assist the neglect victim. The apparent neglectful conduct over a time may amount to breach of contract in civil and employment settings but, at its extreme, may represent criminal neglect if the failure to supervise, protect or provide care attains that level when applied to specific legislation enacted in specific jurisdiction. Therefore, in criminal neglect, the act of neglect may be considered intentional subject to proof at the relevant courts. The "intentionality" is a very difficult concept to assess and is not relevant in most neglect situations. The determination of intentionality is a matter for the court. The forensic practitioner's role is to provide the relevant evidence for the court to consider.

Most effects of neglect relevant to the forensic practitioner will be physical and psychological (emotional). Neglect is often woefully under documented in the elderly (11) and an under researched subject area in all communities, and all clinicians should be aware of the possibility and use screening protocols such as has been proposed in Emergency Departments (12). While abuse is generally mainly acts or acts of commission, neglect is mainly an act or acts of omission. Neglect and abuse can both be considered to be maltreatment.

Child neglect is often described as a component of child maltreatment which is an umbrella term to encompass both acts of commission and omission of caregivers. Child abuse and neglect are very often described together in literature making it difficult to identify the specific characteristics of child neglect, which is why the emphasis from the forensic practitioner's perspective must be to document and interpret based on the history available to them.

Neglect from a medicolegal perspective can often be considered under four main headings: clinical/pathological; psychological; criminological; and ethical and sociolegal considerations.

Neglect is necessarily an act or acts of omission, such as the failure to provide appropriate levels of shelter, nutrition, clothing or supervision or the failure to ensure that the child receives adequate healthcare or education over a period of time. Neglect can be a single event, such as in leaving a young child unsupervised in an unsafe setting, but often is a pattern of inadequate and/or unsafe care, such as the provision of inadequate food because of the parents' substance use or inability to provide due to poverty in the contemporary society.

Legal definitions are less precise than medical definitions in relation to neglect and child abuse and vary according to jurisdiction. In the USA, at the Federal level, the Child Abuse Prevention and Treatment Act has defined child abuse and neglect as "*any recent act or failure to act on the part of a parent or caregiver that results in death, serious physical or emotional harm, sexual abuse, or exploitation, or an act or failure to act that presents an imminent risk of serious harm*" (13).

Hayashi has highlighted the difficulties in making progress on psychological/emotional abuse and neglect without clarity about the definitions being used (in terms of their conceptual components) and the rationale for using the specific definitions chosen (14). In England & Wales, court cases have commented on aspects of neglect. In *R v Sheppard* [1981] AC394 the Court defined the meaning of wilful neglect to mean "deliberate" (15). The section made it an offense for anyone having care of a child to wilfully neglect the child "*in a manner likely to cause him unnecessary suffering or injury to health*".

In *R v Patel* [2013] EWCA Crim 965, the Court of Appeal (16) distinguished between the offenses contrary to section 1 of the Children and Young Persons Act (17) and section 44 of the Mental Capacity Act 2005 (18). The first case suggested that the "wilful neglect" is likely to result in unnecessary suffering or injury to health whereas in relation to the Mental Capacity Act it does not. The Court of Appeal stated:

> "*neglect is wilful if a nurse or medical practitioner knows that it is necessary to administer a piece of treatment and deliberately decides not to carry out that treatment, which is within their power but which they cannot face performing. … if the appellant was acting at a time of stress, that would be a matter which the judge could take into account at the time of sentence.*"

Thus, if a care worker wilfully neglects to do something which should be done in the treatment of a patient, the care worker could not escape liability on the basis that, even if the treatment had been administered, it would have made no difference to the well-being of the patient. The offence of "wilful neglect" became a specific offense under the Criminal Justice and Courts Act 2015 (CJCA 2015) (19) under which there is criminal liability where a person has been placed under the care of a medical professional in a hospital or care home (20), or under private home care (21). The definition of "wilful" amounts to intentional, reckless or reflects a "couldn't care less attitude". It was not felt necessary to define "wilful" in this legislation as it had a widely accepted meaning, established by case law. The legal formulation was provided in the case of *R v Sheppard* [1981] AC 394 HL (17) in which Lord Diplock held that:

> "*a man 'wilfully' fails to provide an adequate medical attention for a child if he either (a) deliberately*

does so, knowing that there is some risk that the child's health may suffer unless he receives such attention or (b) does so because he does not care whether the child may be in need of medical treatment or not."

There is no liability if a person who has genuinely failed to appreciate that, for example, the other person needed medical care, through for example personal inadequacy, is not guilty of the offense of wilful ill-treatment/neglect. The offense of wilful neglect is a conduct offense and the healthcare worker can be found guilty even if the intentional negligence did not cause any harm.

The Crown Prosecution Service in the England & Wales jurisdiction provides guidance to assist prosecutors in determining the most appropriate charge. Table 52.1 shows some of the definitions used (20).

Any definition of child neglect is subject to the values and norms of the community within which children and families live. The world being increasingly polarized related to resource allocation and quality of life, many families will continue to find it difficult to function at their optimal level, and marginal families will be unable to meet minimal expectations of the society for the care of their children.

EFFECTS OF CHILD NEGLECT

Strathearn and colleagues reviewed types of maltreatment from the Mater-University of Queensland Study of Pregnancy longitudinal prenatal cohort study spanning two decades (21). The associations of specific types of maltreatment with long-term cognitive, psychological, addiction, sexual health and physical health outcomes assessed in up to 5200 offspring at 14 and/or 21 years of age were compared and contrasted. Overall, psychological maltreatment (emotional abuse and/or neglect) was associated with the greatest number of adverse outcomes. Neglect, but not emotional abuse, was associated with having multiple sexual partners, cannabis abuse and/or dependence and experiencing visual hallucinations.

TABLE 52.1 Guidance to assist prosecutors in determining the most appropriate charge in the context of child abus

Definitions	
Age	Anyone under 18 is defined as a child or young person. This status and entitlement to services or protection is not changed even if a child or young person is 16 and is living independently, is in further education, is a member of the armed forces, is in hospital or in custody in the secure estate.
Abuse	This is a form of maltreatment of a child or young person. Someone may abuse or neglect a child or young person by inflicting harm, or by failing to prevent harm. Children or young people may be abused in a family, or in an institutional or community setting by those known to them or, more rarely, by others (e.g. via the internet). They may be abused by an adult or adults, or another child or young person or children or young people. Separate guidelines are available for youths in the legal guidance Youth Offenders.
	Child abuse includes physical, emotional and sexual criminal offences, as well as neglect, of a child. Such cases would normally include, for example: • parental assault where reasonable chastisement is not a defence; • sexual offences; • child homicides; • child cruelty, including neglect; • child prostitution; • harassment; • abandonment of a child; • forced marriage involving an under 18 year-old; • indecent images of children; • trafficked children; • familial abduction; and • non-recent child abuse where victim is now an adult.
Child cruelty, neglect and violence	
	Section 1(1) Children and Young Persons Act 1933 was amended on 3 May 2015, by Part 5 Section 66 of the Serious Crime Act 2015 to update and modernize some of the language. The amended version provides that the offence is made out if: • a person who has attained the age of 16 years; • who has responsibility for any child or young person under that age; willfully (i.e. intentionally or recklessly - see *R v Turbill and Broadway* [2013] EWCA Crim 1422); • assaults, ill-treats (whether physically or otherwise), neglects, abandons or exposes him, or causes or procures him to be assaulted, ill-treated (whether physically or otherwise), neglected, abandoned, or exposed; • in a manner likely to cause him unnecessary suffering or injury to health (whether the suffering or injury is of a physical or a psychological nature).

(Continued)

TABLE 52.1 (Continued)

Definitions
Child cruelty, neglect and violence
The offense covers a variety of conduct that can either together or separately amount to child cruelty. The four generally accepted categories are assault and ill-treatment, failure to protect, neglect and abandonment. The behavior necessary to establish the ill-treatment limb of the offence can be non-physical (for example a sustained course of non-physical conduct, including, for instance, isolation, humiliation or bullying, if it is likely to cause unnecessary suffering or injury to health). Section 1(2) provides that a person is deemed to have neglected a child or young person in a manner likely to cause injury to his health in either of the following situations: • Where a parent or person legally liable to maintain a child fails to provide adequate food, clothing, medical aid or lodging for the child or having been unable to provide the above failed to take steps to procure it to be provided; or • Where the cause of death for an infant under 3 years is suffocation (not being caused by disease or the presence of a foreign body in the throat or air passages) while the infant was in bed with some other person who has attained the age of 16 years and where that other person was under the influence of drink or a prohibited drug either when he went to bed or at any later time before the suffocation. Part 5 of the Serious Crime Act 2015 (Section 66) defines a "prohibited drug" for the purposes of section 1(2)(b); furthermore, it expands the reference to suffocation occurring in a bed, to include any kind of furniture or surface used for the purpose of sleeping.

Source: From Crown Prosecution Service.

Emotional abuse, but not neglect, revealed increased odds for psychosis, injecting-drug use, experiencing harassment later in life, pregnancy miscarriage and reporting asthma symptoms. Significant cognitive delays and educational failure were seen for both abuse and neglect during adolescence and adulthood confirming that child maltreatment, particularly emotional abuse and neglect, is associated with a wide range of long-term adverse health and developmental outcomes.

ELDER NEGLECT

As life expectancy increases, the phenomenon of the neglect of elderly persons is becoming more evident in the fields of both medicine and social care. The United States Older Americans Act Section 3002 provides definitions of several terms that are linked to the definition of elder abuse and neglect which are laid out as below (22):

> *"abuse" means the wilful—*
> *(A) infliction of injury, unreasonable confinement, intimidation, or cruel punishment with resulting physical harm, pain, or mental anguish; or*
> *(B) deprivation by a person, including a caregiver, of goods or services that are necessary to avoid physical harm, mental anguish, or mental illness.*
> *"elder abuse" means abuse of an older individual*
> *"older individual" means an individual who is 60 years of age or older.*
> *"neglect" means*
> *(A) the failure of a caregiver (as defined in paragraph 18(B)) or the fiduciary to provide the goods or services that are necessary to maintain the health or safety of an older individual; or*
> *(B) self-neglect. Elder neglect has been defined as "the failure of a caregiver or fiduciary to provide the goods or services that are necessary to maintain the health or safety of an older individual"*

Elder self-neglect is a global public health and human rights issue that threatens older people's health and safety. It commonly refers to refusal or failure to provide oneself with care and protection in areas of food, water, clothing, hygiene, medication, living environments and safety precautions. While prevalent, the status of self-neglecting individuals remains largely unclear, in particular within community-dwelling populations (23). Self-neglect is a significant international public health issue. Estimates suggest that there may be over one million cases per year in the United States. Aging populations will put more people at risk of self-neglect (24).

Lachs notes that consensus has arisen about the inclusion of five major types of elder: physical abuse, or acts carried out with the intention to cause physical pain or injury; psychological or verbal abuse, defined as acts carried out with the aim of causing emotional pain or injury; sexual abuse, defined as nonconsensual sexual contact of any kind; financial exploitation, involving the misappropriation of an older person's money or property; and neglect, or the failure of a designated caregiver to meet the needs of a dependent older person. Taking all these into account (based on epidemiological studies of community-dwelling people 60 years of age or older), an estimated overall prevalence of elder abuse of approximately 10 percent appears reasonable (25).

Many elderly individuals are entirely dependent upon their family for provision of physical and medical care. They die eventually at home and many others die in a healthcare setting including hospital, nursing home, assisted living, home healthcare or hospice. Knowledge about the healthcare environment and the associated level of independence of the elderly person concerned are important parameters to be evaluated with post-mortem findings when determining the final cause of death. Altendorf and colleagues noted that neglect of older people is common and may result in fatal and nonfatal outcomes (26). Normal changes of aging and disease-related symptoms may overlap with markers of neglect and lead to under-detection. A review was undertaken to delineate medical, psychiatric and pathophysiological indicators in the victim-identified in forensic case reports-to point out areas of overlap and raise awareness in healthcare professionals. Using the following search terms "neglect, elder, elderly, forensic, homicide", medical and forensic databases were searched. The authors found 11 publications with 25 cases, and these showed that neglect was associated with poor physical, psychological and mental health. Neglect can be a direct cause of death or contribute to a fatal outcome by exacerbating existing conditions. Red flags for neglect included malnutrition, dehydration, poor hygiene, untreated decubitus ulcers, hypothermia, contractures and an uncooperative caregiver. However, clear evidence of neglect may be masked due to age and disease-related changes.

It is evident that the prolonged state of abandonment (very poor hygiene, malnutrition and the lack of medical care), in subjects who are already vulnerable on account of their chronic diseases and advanced age, contributed to their physical decline and facilitated the onset of infections which, in the absence of proper treatment, proved fatal (27). A forensic pathologist needs to consider contextual variables and sublethal injuries in cases where the causal interpretations benefit from a more holistic approach. Otherwise, cases of elder neglect can go unnoticed and be certified as a simple natural death (28).

It is an essential part of such an assessment to explore and interpret the clinical evidence in medical and other healthcare or social care records of elderly deceased and the autopsy findings of such cases specially referred from a range of care facilities. This may require full disclosure of medical and nursing and care home records and review of accident and other incident reports. It should enable the forensic practitioner to identify long-standing neglect and the quality of life of the deceased.

TABLE 52.2 Some features which may be associated with neglect by another

The individual
Cognitive impairment
Intellectual disability
Chronic illness
Socially isolated
More advanced age
Personality disorder
The carer
Carer is dependent on individual for accommodation and finance
Carer has substance use issues
Carer has mental health issues
Carer has history of intimate partner violence or other abuse

TABLE 52.3 Some signs and symptoms which may be associated with but are not diagnostic of self-neglect or neglect by another

Decubitus ulcers (pressure areas on dependent or bony areas)
Poor oral hygiene
Malnutrition
Non-specific body pain and weakness
Nonadherence to medication regimen
Signs of dehydration (dry skin or mouth, diminished urine output)
Low mood
Delirium
Disease or condition that has worsened (possibly due to nonadherence to medication regimen)
Poor personal hygiene
Dirty clothing or bedding

Effects of elder neglect

Examples of some of the associations or predictors and effects of elder neglect are shown in Tables 52.2 and 52.3. Many features may also be present in the absence of neglect by self or another, which is in part why detection and diagnosis is challenging.

Advanced-stage or multiple pressure areas (also known as decubitus ulcers, or pressure sores) with signs of infection or poor care are evidence for medical neglect. The degree of injury is dependent on many factors but are predominantly injury to the skin and underlying tissue usually over a bony prominence, as a result of pressure, or pressure in combination with shear and/or friction (Figure 52.1). These are particularly associated with limited mobility, poor care and poor hygiene (such as prolonged lying in feces and urine) (Figure 52.2). A number of contributing or confounding factors are also associated with pressure ulcers. Untreated pressure areas are often sources of sepsis and can lead to fatal outcome. Multiple and advanced stage pressure areas may indicate neglect by carer, or where healthcare professionals are involved in treatment by doctors and allied health professionals. Documentation of pressure areas should include measurements of size, depth, location and staging. European and US national pressure ulcer advisory panels propose a 4-stage classification although there are a number of different means of grading or staging such lesions. It will be important to determine whether such pressure areas have been managed by healthcare professionals (such as trained nurses) or not utilizing internationally accepted consensus guidelines and for forensic practitioners to be aware of such guidelines (29–31). Decubitus ulcers with full thickness skin loss are most commonly associated with extensive tissue damage and necrosis. Devitalized tissue can present as either thick, moist, offensive, slough or dry hard eschar (Figure 52.3). Deep-tissue infection is a frequent complication of the deepest pressure ulcers. These ulcers need advanced hospital care. The deepest ulcers show full thickness of tissue loss, extending to underlying muscle tendon or even to

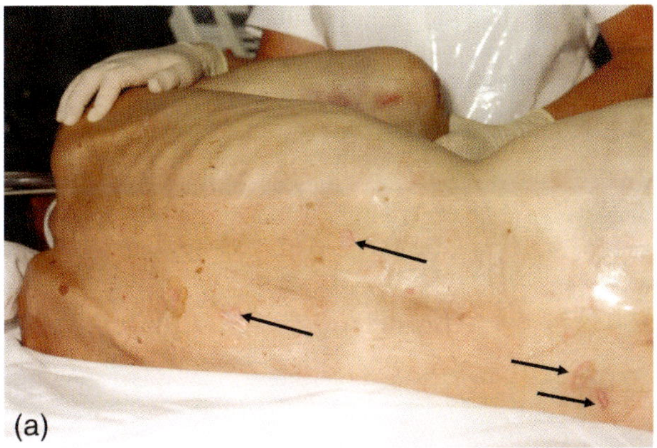

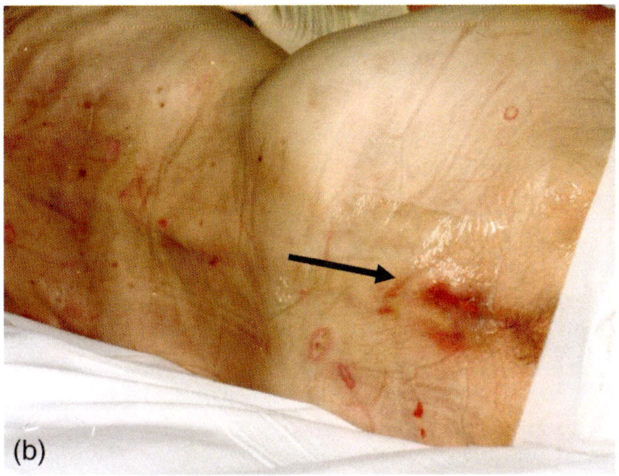

52.1 Multiple pressure areas on the back (a) and the sacrum (b) of a malnourished 55-year-old male with intellectual disabilities kept isolated by his family in the United Kingdom.

52.2 (a) A scene where an elderly female had been found deceased on the sofa to the left of the picture. She had not been moved by her carer for an unknown number or weeks. She had been moved by paramedic teams.

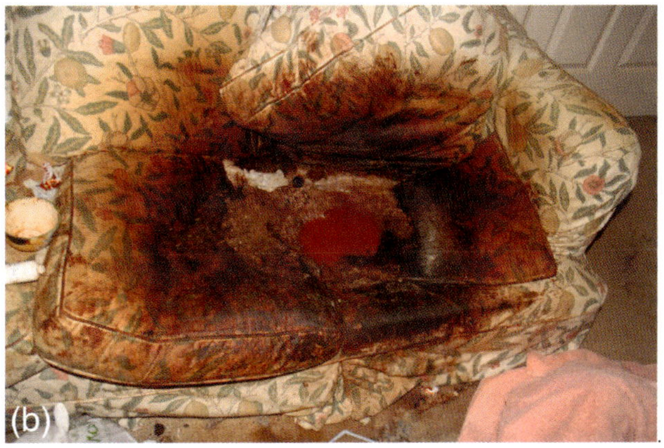

(b) A close up of the sofa with feces, urine and insect larvae in a pool where her body had been lying.

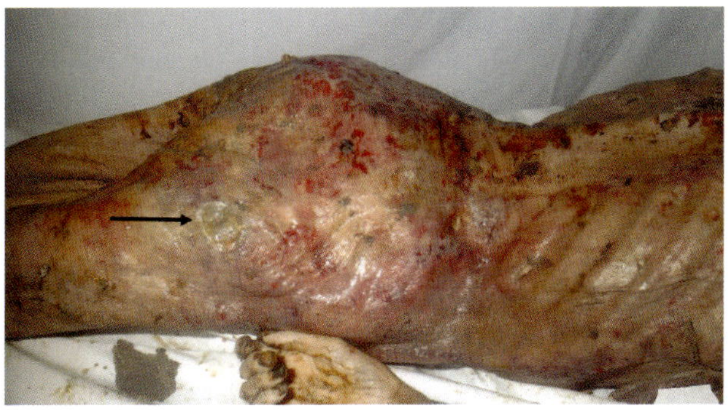

52.3 The body of a 70-year-old malnourished female found naked and deceased at her family home. She was known to have been exhibiting signs of life shortly before medical aid was called for. She had multiple confluent infected pressure areas, the deepest overlying her right greater trochanter. She had been immobile on her right side for several weeks.

bone (with osteomyelitis) and are often associated with undermining and tunneling. It is important when discussing and reviewing cases with colleagues that all involved are clear about the specific staging system being used. Eventually, the deep pressure ulcers of the deceased have become septic foci harboring harmful micro-organisms to the body. Pressure ulcers are typically colonized by multiple bacteria, even though there may be no clinical sign of infection. Pressure ulcers may act as reservoirs for multi-resistant bacterial strains. These ulcers are optimal sites for the growth of Gram-negative bacteria. Infected pressure ulcers can have many serious consequences, including heightened pain and anxiety, a deterioration in the patient's general condition and the detrimental effect on quality of life. The wound itself will increase in size, producing more exudate, slough and odor. An unresolved infection may ultimately lead to septicemia and death.

Psychological issues may be both the cause and consequences of neglect. At its most extreme in Diogenes syndrome, other aspects or behavior may be manifest. In all, there may be disorders of cognitive processes, such as reasoning and decision-making, sometimes caused by specific conditions (e.g. frontal lobe disorder) or other such as profound depression or dementia. Criminal liability of a caregiver can be supported when there is good evidence of some specific injury or trauma. As injuries are often non-specific and multiple it may be difficult to determine whether the injury (e.g. bruise, abrasion, laceration, fracture) is the result of abuse from direct blunt impacts as an assault, or neglect or accident. The forensic practitioner always needs to be bear in mind that evidence to support neglect often requires a

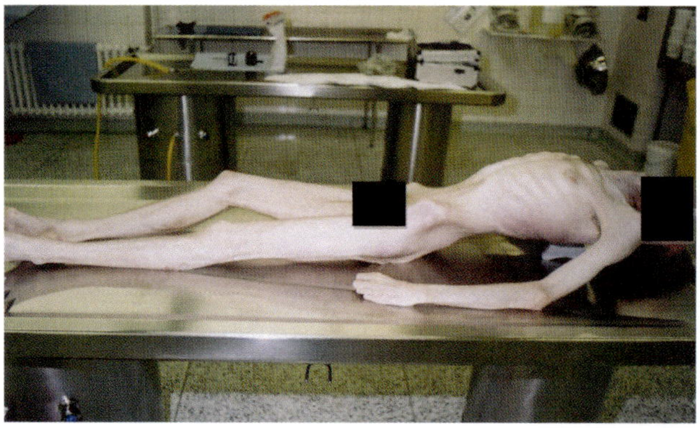

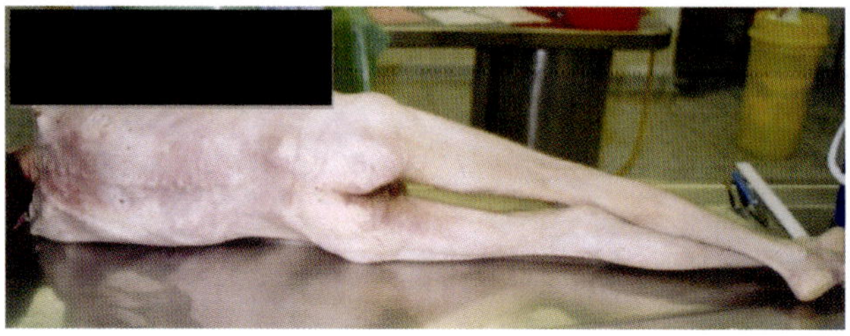

52.4 (a) A 44-year-old male died from malnutrition and a duodenal ulcer which had been causing persistent nausea and vomiting with weight loss for months. He had learning disabilities and his sibling carers did not seek medical help. (b) Muscle wasting and prominent bone structure (ribs, pelvis clavicle, verterbra) are obvious signs of malnutrition in this case.

pattern or chronicity associated with features such as unwashed garments, unkempt appearance and other signs of neglect such as untreated wounds, bedsores and poor dentition.

Malnutrition is often seen in neglect of elders and children (11,26) but not exclusively and those in their middle years may also be victims (Figure 52.4). In children, Burford and colleagues discussed the concept of malnutrition and medical neglect has been considered when anomalies are found during the assessment of nutrition in children are common in pediatric practice. The diagnosis of medical neglect requires several components including (a) harm, or risk of harm due to lack of recommended healthcare, (b) recommended care provides benefit significantly greater than potential risk, (c) caregiver understands the medical recommendations and (d) has access to the recommended care but fails to utilize it (32).

In addition, a victim's statement about lack of provision of food and other amenities available in the household may be relevant.

KEY ELEMENTS OF ASSESSMENT OF POSSIBLE NEGLECT VICTIMS

Physical examination

Forensic practitioners may need to assess living or deceased potential victims of neglect. Assessments may be undertaken by clinicians (commonly pediatricians or those working in older people's medicine dependent on the age of the subject) or pathologists. The main aim is to differentiate between natural diseases and those caused or exacerbated by neglect. However, when the assessment or post-mortem examination is undertaken, it is important to use a consistent approach. There are a number of published proforma and protocols which include: Screening tools for identification of elder abuse: a systematic review (33); the European Council of Legal Medicine (ECLM) Guidelines for the examination of suspected elder abuse (34); Diagnostic Tools in the Detection of Physical Child Abuse: A Systematic Review (35) and the Vulnerable Elder Protection Team: Initial experience of an emergency department-based interdisciplinary elder abuse program (36).

Key practical points within any assessment or post-mortem examination for neglect, or where neglect is suspected are noted below.

History taking

A full history must be obtained from the primary caregiver. Ask especially about his understanding of the nature of the patient's care needs. Enquire how well care has been provided. A detailed history may also be provided by others such as social workers, community nurses, mental health workers, care assistants, nursing or care home staff and friends or family. In the case of a death, it may be very important to visit the scene (Figure 52.5) and to review all medical, psychiatric, social care, nursing and care home records.

General examination

Assess whether the clothes are appropriate or not, and especially whether they are in consonance of the socioeconomic status of the family. Poor quality or damaged and dirty clothes and footwear in upper socio-economic strata may point to intentional neglect. Similarly, general hygiene and cleanliness. Poor dentition is a good indicator of poor or lax care. The state of finger and toenails may be relevant. These factors should be looked at in the context of the surrounding family or community. Look specifically for signs of any chronic illnesses, decubitus

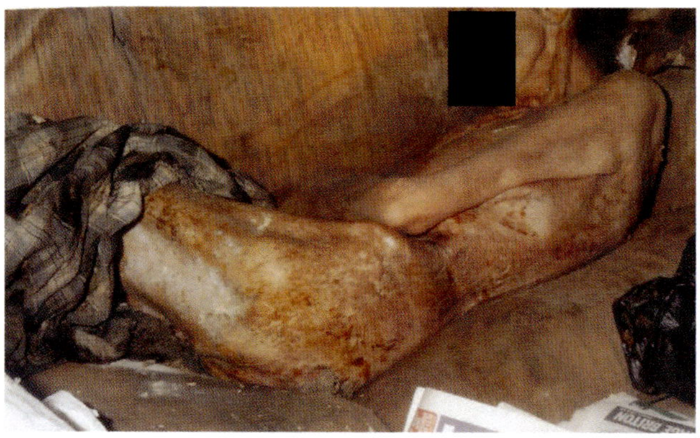

52.5 Scene of a 66-year-old deceased female who had not moved from the sofa on which she was found deceased for an indeterminate number of weeks.

ulcers and malnutrition. It will be appropriate to assess nutrition state using a nutrition assessment tool such as the Subjective Global Assessment (SGA) that refers to an overall evaluation of a patient's history and physical examination and uses structured clinical parameters to diagnose malnutrition. The SGA is known to be a reliable and valid tool that predicts morbidity and mortality associated with malnutrition (37).

Skin examination

Neglect can result in bedsores and infestations. It is useful to examine the skin for bedsores. A careful examination must be made especially over pressure points. A full external examination is essential (Figure 52.6).

Special investigations

Although clinical and pathological assessment may provide adequate evidence of features of neglect other investigations may be required to exclude or diagnose other forms of maltreatment (e.g. bone fracture) or identify other disease (e.g. infection, abscess) that may mimic or accompany neglect. If clinical examination has suggested malnutrition, then body-mass index (BMI) and albumin must be recorded. Toxicology may be appropriate to ensure appropriate therapeutic levels of prescribed medication are present and also to exclude administration of other substances. Other biochemistry may be appropriate to support clinical or pathological evidence of neglect such as hydration state (Figure 52.7).

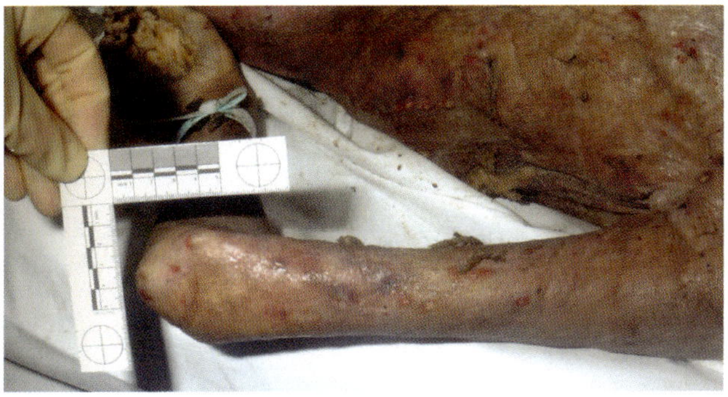

52.6 Pressure areas to the elbow with superficial and deeper ulcers. These must all be recorded as they may assist in determining how long the person had been immobile.

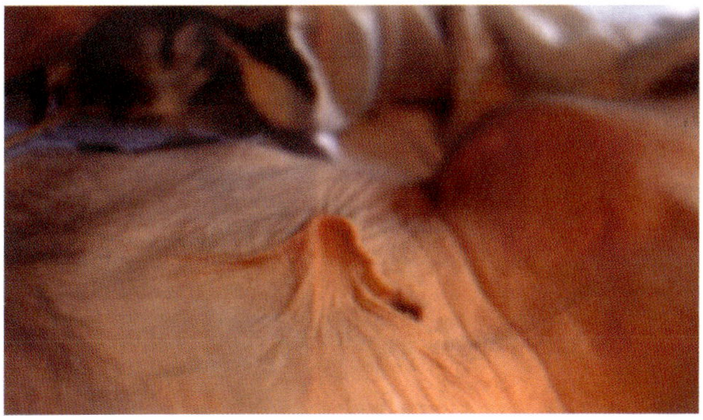

52.7 Extreme dehydration manifest by loss of elasticity from abdominal wall skin – note also the prominent iliac crest to the right of the image.

ETHICAL AND SOCIOLEGAL ASPECTS

Mandatory reporting

Most countries have some kind of legislation in place, where physicians, nurses, other healthcare workers, medical examiners and coroners must report all cases of neglect. There are multiple agencies that may be reported to which vary in different jurisdictions, but usually the agencies are police, other law enforcement organizations, child protection services or some other approved body. Omission of such reporting may lead to punishments, leading even to punishment. All concerned medical personnel must be well aware of the agencies to which they must report cases of neglect. Clear cases of neglect rarely present a problem, but it is those who have limited neglect features and apparently reasonable explanations for their condition that present the greatest problems of management. Forensic practitioners must have a low threshold for diagnosis and referral of neglect. Those who are healthcare professionals who have duties of confidentiality may need to take steps to ensure that they act in the best interests of patients for whom they consider neglect is a possibility.

CONCLUSION

Neglect is a broad term subject to a wide range of definitions and is often closely related to abuse and maltreatment. Extremes of age are the most likely group to suffer neglect but no age range is excluded. The causes and effects of neglect often overlap. Consideration should always be given whether in the clinical setting or at post mortem to the possibility of neglect, particularly in the presence of malnutrition and decubitus ulceration, and the forensic practitioner must be prepared to raise the issue with the appropriate local organizations at the earliest opportunity.

REFERENCES

1. World Health Organisation. International Classification of Diseases 11th Revision, 2022. Available from: https://icd.who.int/en (Accessed 9 May 2023).
2. Helfer RE. The neglect of our children. *Pediatr Clin North Am* 1990; **37(4)**: 923–42.
3. World Health Organisation. Child maltreatment, 2022. Available from: https://www.who.int/news-room/fact-sheets/detail/child-maltreatment (Accessed 9 May 2023).
4. National Health Service. Abuse and neglect of vulnerable adults, 2021. Available from: https://www.nhs.uk/conditions/social-care-and-support-guide/help-from-social-services-and-charities/abuse-and-neglect-vulnerable-adults/ (Accessed 9 May 2023).
5. BBC TV Live News Channel. Husband let wife starve to death, 2008. Available from: http://news.bbc.co.uk/1/hi/england/berkshire/7318610.stm (Accessed 9 May 2023).
6. Metro News. Daughter cleared of neglect after mum, 79, died in 'pool of urine and diarrhoea', 2018. Available from: https://metro.co.uk/2018/12/10/daughter-cleared-neglect-mum-79-died-pool-urine-diarrhoea-8228553/ (Accessed 9 May 2023).
7. BBC News. Jordan Burling: The teenager left to waste away, 2018. Available from: https://www.bbc.co.uk/news/uk-england-leeds-44643037 (Accessed 9 May 2023).
8. Liverpool Echo. Former Wirral nurse admits causing or allowing her elderly mum to die, 2011. Available from: https://www.liverpoolecho.co.uk/news/liverpool-news/former-wirral-nurse-admits-causing-3376663 (Accessed 9 May 2023).
9. Finney CM, Mendez MF. Diogenes syndrome in frontotemporal dementia. *Am J Alzheimers Dis Other Demen* 2017; **32(7)**: 438–43.
10. Proctor C, Rahman S. Diogenes syndrome: Identification and distinction from hoarding disorder. *Case Rep Psychiatry* 2021; **2021**: 2810137.
11. del Carmen T, LoFaso VM. Elder neglect. *Clin Geriatr Med* 2014; **30(4)**: 769–77.
12. Rosen T, Stern ME, Elman A, Mulcare MR. Identifying and initiating intervention for elder abuse and neglect in the emergency department. *Clin Geriatr Med* 2018; **34(3)**: 435–51.
13. CAPTA Reauthorization Act of 2010 (P.L. 111–320), 42 U.S.C. § 5101, Note (§ 3)
14. Hayashi M. Child psychological/emotional abuse and neglect: A definitional conceptual framework. *J Child Adolesc Trauma* 2022; **15(4)**: 999–1010.
15. *R v Sheppard* [1981] A.C. 394 Available from: https://vlex.co.uk/vid/r-v-sheppard-793906601 (Accessed 3 May 2023).
16. *R v Patel* [2013] EWCA Crim 965 Available from: https://www.lexology.com/library/detail.aspx?g=0bdea0b1-fcfb-4fa0-a063-7ae231e267ce (Accessed 3 May 2023).
17. Legislation.gov. Children and Young Persons Act 1933. Available from: https://www.legislation.gov.uk/ukpga/Geo5/23-24/12 (Accessed 9 May 2023).
18. Legislation.gov. Mental Capacity Act 2005. Available from: https://www.legislation.gov.uk/ukpga/2005/9/contents (Accessed 9 May 2023).
19. Legislation.gov. Criminal Justice and Courts Act 2015 (CJCA 2015). Available from: https://www.legislation.gov.uk/ukpga/2015/2/contents/enacted (Accessed 9 May 2023).
20. Crown Prosecution Service. The Code for Crown Prosecutors. Child Abuse (non-sexual) – prosecution guidance, 2022. Available from: https://www.cps.gov.uk/legal-guidance/child-abuse-non-sexual-prosecution-guidance (Accessed 9 May 2023).
21. Strathearn L, Giannotti M, Mills R, et al. Long-term cognitive, psychological, and health outcomes associated with child abuse and neglect. *Pediatrics* 2020; **146(4)**: e20200438.
22. Administration for Community Living. Older Americans Act 1975. Available from: https://acl.gov/about-acl/authorizing-statutes/older-americans-act (Accessed 9 May 2023).
23. Dong X. Elder self-neglect: Research and practice. *Clin Interv Aging* 2017; **12**: 949–54.
24. Day MR, Leahy-Warren P, McCarthy G. Self-neglect: Ethical considerations. *Annu Rev Nurs Res* 2016; **34**: 89–107.
25. Lachs MS, Pillemer KA. Elder abuse. *N Engl J Med* 2015; **373(20)**: 1947–56.
26. Altendorf A, Draper B, Wijeratne C, et al. Neglect of older people: Touching on forensic and pathophysiological aspects. *Gerontologist* 2020; **60(6)**: e449–e65.
27. Ventura F, Caputo F, Molinelli A. Medico-legal aspects of deaths related to neglect and abandonment in the elderly. *Aging Clin Exp Res* 2018; **30(11)**: 1399–402.
28. Paranitharan P, Pollanen MS. The interaction of injury and disease in the elderly: A case report of fatal elder abuse. *J Forensic Leg Med* 2009; **16(6)**: 346–9.
29. Litchford M. Putting the 2019 nutrition recommendations for pressure injury prevention and treatment into practice. *Adv Skin Wound Care* 2020; **33(9)**: 462–8.
30. Langemo D, Haesler E, Naylor W, et al. Evidence-based guidelines for pressure ulcer management at the end of life. *Int J Palliat Nurs* 2015; **21(5)**: 225–32.
31. Kottner J, Cuddigan J, Carville K. Pressure ulcer/injury classification today: An international perspective. *J Tissue Viability* 2020; **29(3)**: 197–203.
32. Burford A, Alexander R, Lilly C. Malnutrition and medical neglect. *J Child Adolesc Trauma* 2019; **13(3)**: 305–16.
33. Gallione C, Molin A, Cristina FVB, et al. Screening tools for identification of elder abuse: A systematic review. *J Clin Nurs* 2017; **26(15–16)**: 2154–76.
34. Keller E, Santos C, Cusack D, et al. European Council of Legal Medicine (ECLM) guidelines for the examination of suspected elder abuse. *Int J Legal Med* 2019; **133(1)**: 317–22.
35. Pavone V, Vescio A, Lucenti L, et al. Diagnostic tools in the detection of physical child abuse: A systematic review. *Children (Basel)* 2022; **9(8)**: 1257.
36. Rosen T. Elman A, Clark S, et al. Vulnerable elder protection team: Initial experience of an emergency department-based interdisciplinary elder abuse program. *J Am Geriatr Soc* 2022; **70(11)**: 3260–72.
37. Duerksen DR, Laporte M, Jeejeebhoy K. Evaluation of nutrition status using the subjective global assessment: Malnutrition, cachexia, and sarcopenia. *Nutr Clin Pract* 2021; **36(5)**: 942–56.

CHAPTER

53

Self-Neglect

Philip S.L. Beh and Thomas K.C. Foo

INTRODUCTION

With improved living conditions across the globe in the past decade, death due to poor socioeconomic status theoretically should be on the decline. This is, however, far from truth even in developed countries. Undignified deaths occur largely related to suboptimal environmental conditions particularly among vulnerable groups such as migrant workers and jobseekers, socially marginalized and elderly groups. Poverty is still alarmingly rampant and should not be underestimated by city administrators. Among those who succumb in isolated conditions, a particularly vulnerable elderly group can be identified (1). Other vulnerable groups include patients with mental illness and eccentric individuals who voluntarily neglect their basic needs. Those who are victims of criminal activities such as trafficking and modern-day slavery are also vulnerable. Forensic practitioners are presented with scenes of death suspicious of foul play which only upon further investigation will the long-standing nature of self-neglect be revealed (2). A comprehensive forensic approach should therefore be adopted to differentiate between a genuine foul play (3) or a non-suspicious event (4). The incidence and prevalence of these cases are likely to be underestimated due to lack of a proper reporting system and therefore is largely unknown to the public (5).

SELF-NEGLECT IN THE GERIATRIC POPULATION

Self-neglect is the inability or unwillingness to provide for oneself goods and services needed to live safely and independently to address their own basic physical, emotional and social needs (6). It can exist in an intentional or unintentional context. It may include lack of insight and capability to deal with personal health issues and environment. This is accompanied by a series of unsafe behaviors and poor decision-making that jeopardize the well-being of the individual. It is regarded as a risk factor of death (7). A list of risk factors of self-neglect is shown in Box 53.1. There are many distinguishing features of elder persons that render them to be particularly prone to the effects of self-neglect and ultimately present in a fatal outcome. In settings where access to free healthcare is not available, or funding is not available due to finances being directed toward other essentials, such as food or heating, basic medical need is often sacrificed. Living in a secluded location in the absence of proper support ensures that many preventative measures and timely intervention to address immediate health needs will not be met. It is not uncommon to find a death scene of filthy home environment filled with disused materials comprising of garbage, piles of hoarded items with abundance of rodents and cockroaches. Delayed discovery of cases due to isolation ensures that the body would likely be discovered in advanced putrefaction or in some settings and climates, mummified.

PSYCHOLOGICAL ASPECTS OF SELF-NEGLECT

Geriatric patients are not immune to psychiatric disorders as in other adults. Contributing conditions include schizophrenia, obsessive compulsive disorders and schizotypal personality disorders. Specific conditions include various neurodegenerative conditions, for example frontal lobe lesions and Alzheimer's dementia leading to cognitive impairment. Damage to strategic areas of the central nervous system results in abnormal neuropsychiatric presentations. Mood irritability may be a result of pathology involving the orbitofrontal region of the prefrontal cortex. Apathy is the emotional response when the medial-frontal cortex is damaged. The dorsofrontal region is responsible for planning and judgment (6). This altered mental status and decision-making capacity may contribute to failure in accessing appropriate medical care and neglecting physical ill health even when florid clinical symptoms have emerged. Behavioral changes also lead to social withdrawal and continual refusal of support and care, often super-imposed with atypical or anti-social behaviors. Further social isolation with poor relationship with neighbors, worsening physical health, lack of access to medication and food, alarming environment conditions of domestic squalor are the usual consequences. Patients may have a poor sense of worthiness believing that they can no longer contribute to the community and hence seriously affecting

DOI: 10.1201/9781003138754-55

communication within the social circle (8). Securing a precise behavioral analysis or psychological autopsy may be relevant during investigation to evaluate the contribution of self-neglect. In some settings, religion or culture may engender the belief that frugality will lead to irrational sacrifice and refusal to use available assistance. Elderly individuals feel that living is for the sake of younger members of the family, even though younger family members may have already moved away from home and achieved financial independence. Some do not want to be seen as a burden when they feel dependent on their offsprings (8). Intentional self-neglect dampening social contact involves eccentric individuals ignoring clear signals of dire medical and physical deterioration. This is problematic if they demonstrate a clear refusal to assistance challenging the ethical principle of respecting an individual's autonomy (self-determination). Whenever possible, their mental status and mental capacity should be assessed to ensure that decision-making is appropriate and not a function of mental health issues (9). This is contrary to the management of pediatric abuse and neglect which places primacy on children receiving adequate care and support. Social habits of chronic alcohol and drug abuse could contribute to the phenomenon of self-neglect.

Subclinical depression in the absence of florid psychiatric diagnosis is a significant factor of self-neglect. Patients are commonly bereaved, separated or divorced, chronically ill, socially isolated and suffering from the sequelae of adverse life events. These might motivate the individual to terminate one's life voluntarily. Instead of selecting methods that require planning and equipment, suicide in the domestic environment involves tools readily available, such as sharp-cutting instruments or ropes as ligature material. Alarming presentations such as incised wounds or atypical hanging posture may be challenging to the death investigators (12).

BOX 53.1 Risk factors of self-neglect

- Social isolation
- Suboptimal living environment
- Poor relationship with neighbors
- Lack of social network and support
- Family background: single, widow/er, offsprings living away
- Financial hardship
- Illiteracy
- Chronic comorbidities contributing to pain and frailty
- Neuropsychiatric conditions affecting insight and capacity
- Indulgence on risky behaviors, e.g. smoking, alcohol and drug abuse
- Presence of adverse life events, acute medical condition, accident or social event

CONTRIBUTION OF AGING IN SELF-NEGLECT

The elderly population is in a state of frailty which renders them vulnerable to stressors from reduced physiological reserves and comorbidities (10). Pathology of organ systems could contribute to self-neglect and present concomitantly (11). These might mimic findings of abuse and/or neglect by carers.

Fall, termed one of the "geriatric syndromes", especially in a domestic or care home environment, are a serious complication when medical support is not available in a timely fashion. They are the leading cause of trauma-related death globally in the elderly population. A long lie in particular rendering the subject susceptible to death from conditions such as hypostatic pneumonia, thromboembolism, rhabdomyolysis and acute kidney injury, starvation and sepsis (12). Aging individuals have deteriorated postural control characterized by worsening proprioception, impaired reflexes, poor muscle tone, postural sway and altered gait. Contributing medical conditions include orthostatic hypotension, degenerative joint diseases, foot problems, stroke, parkinsonism, peripheral neuropathy, peripheral vascular disease and atrophy of muscles due to disuse and deconditioning. Poor vision occurs as a result of impaired depth perception, contrast sensitivity, structural changes of lens and pupil, an increased incidence of glaucoma, cataract and age-related macular degeneration. Hearing loss occurs when there is stiffening of the tympanic membrane, ossicular chain pathology and presbycusis. These reduce the alertness to concealed dangers of underestimated home environment such as inappropriate design of furniture, beds, toilets, uneven stairs, steps and kerbs at entrances, obstacles on the floor, slippery bathtubs and poor lighting conditions (13). Polypharmacy, overmedications and side-effects of appropriate medication, for example antihypertensives, anticholinergics, sedatives, neuroleptics and anticonvulsants, can predispose to fall due to clouding consciousness, weakened balance and sensory input. Patients can develop complications owing to diminished metabolic reserve, osteoporosis or liver and renal insufficiency.

Disorders of swallowing, diminished cough reflex and increased risk of reflux (e.g. esophageal stricture, reduced peristalsis or hiatus hernia) leading to choking and aspiration are seen frequently in those with dementia. Patients with Parkinson's disease have delayed swallow reflex, prolongation of transit time in the pharynx and abnormal food bolus formation (13). A rapid and unexpected death can occur suddenly. Perianal conditions like anal fissure, hemorrhoids, abscess and rectal malignancy are prevalent among the elderly with fecal incontinence. Anatomic changes in pelvic floor muscles reduce bowel opening. Diabetes mellitus, hypothyroidism, hypercalcemia, together with reduced fluid intake and medications that reduce colonic transit, such as opiates, anticholinergic agents, calcium channel blockers, antipsychotics and iron supplements result in fecal impaction complicated by intestinal obstruction and aspiration (12).

Neuro-psychiatric diagnoses are prevalent among the elderly. Degenerative disorders of the cortex affecting executive functioning, memory, cognitive performance, subcortical dysfunction, vascular insult, nutritional deficiency, cerebrovascular accident, occult cerebral infection and trauma are etiologies of dementia. Patients can present with bizarre and inappropriate interaction with other individuals therefore missing opportunities for appropriate medical care (14). Acute change in pre-existing neurologic conditions encompass reversible dysfunction of organ systems, infections, drugs, injury, metabolic and electrolyte disturbances. Injuries are sustained under altered mental status, impaired judgement, agitation and lack of awareness to inanimate objects in the surroundings or during conflicts with people following abnormal personal contact (15).

Emaciated elderly patients with a decreased muscle mass and adipose tissue are at risk of hypothermia (16). The post-mortem diagnosis of hypothermia is a particularly challenging forensic issue when diagnostic uncertainty presents with the phenomenona of "hide and die syndrome" and "paradoxical undressing" following confusion of feelings of warmth in acute cerebral malfunction (11). On the other hand, certain medications, suboptimal indoor environment, decreased vasoconstriction with shrinkage of effective circulatory fluid compartment predisposes one to hyperthermia. It is seen more frequently in the context of environmental heat waves and reduced fluid intake (16).

With a strained cardiovascular system and reduced cardiac output secondary to hypertension, arterial overload, remodeling of heart chambers, senile degeneration of myocardial fibers and failure of conduction system, there would be reduced exercise tolerance and immobilization (13). Deep vein thrombosis and decubitus ulcers can be found in addition to chronic edema of lower limbs.

The number of viable nephrons and renal perfusion is decreased in aging subjects. There is abnormal renal handling of drugs and probable development of toxicity, complicated by effects of redistribution and contamination which could be difficult to interpret post mortem. Patients can be dehydrated with diuretic use, decreased thirst sensation, impaired reabsorption ability and concentrating power of urine (11).

Chest infections are more predisposed in the aged primarily as a result of structural alteration of chest wall cavity, compliance and co-existing kyphosis due to senile deformity of spine. Urinary tract infection occurs when there is asymptomatic bacteriuria and/or overdistension of bladder following detrusor muscle failure. An infected pressure sore is a consequence of malnutrition (13). Concomitant diabetes mellitus, chronic bronchitis, malignancies, poor dental and oral hygiene and use of steroids could convert an innocent looking infection into a fulminant sepsis.

Endocrine conditions like hypothyroidism and hypothalamic axis dysfunction contribute to overall ill-health. Changes in oral cavity, receding gums, exposure of tooth cementum, dental decay, periodontal conditions, xerostomia, alteration in smell and taste, incomplete mastication due to poor motor control of food bolus by tongue, abnormal absorption of carbohydrates and minerals will prevent proper intake of food and essential medications, worsening the overall health and nutrition of the individual (13). Other conditions like atrophic vaginitis mimic sexual abuse if there is unexpected postmenopausal bleeding (16). The integumentary system degenerates with atrophic skin, decreased epidermis, dermal fibroblasts and other cellular components, reduced elasticity and impaired sensation to touch and vibration (13). Suboptimal healing following accidental injuries and might confuse the investigators (17). Signs of self-neglect are listed in Box 53.2.

BOX 53.2 Signs of self-neglect

- Presence of treatable medical conditions at advanced stage, e.g. malignancy, intestinal obstruction, infections
- Unkempt appearance and unhygienic clothing
- Unshaven hair with facial sores and dystrophic nails
- Cachexia, contractures, dehydration, decubitus ulcers (18), perianal excoriation and heavy infestations (19)
- Untreated wounds and healing rib fracture
- Poor dental conditions, sore mouth (20)

CASE VIGNETTE

Police entered a public housing flat following a report to the management complaining of odd smell emitting from premises in the preceding days. Police gained entry and identified two bodies of an aged couple inside. The environment was humid and hot at around 33 degrees Celsius. The scene was in a state of disarray as a lot of space was occupied by groceries (Figure 53.1). It was packed with plastic bags of used and old clothing. There was no signs of ransacking or blood splatter identified. Lights and a fan were switched on indicating the couple likely passed away during nighttime. The bodies of the couple were in a state of advanced decomposition. A moderate amount of dark brownish serosanguinous fluid was present around the deceased. The husband was discovered sitting on the floor, leaning against a pile of boxes (Figure 53.2). His wife was lying in a prone position next to her husband (Figure 53.3). She was wearing a pair of spectacles with shattered lens. Her left foot was entangled between the legs of a toppled folding chair. At autopsy, both decedents weighed about 40 kg, showing generalized reddish and

(Continued)

CASE VIGNETTE (Continued)

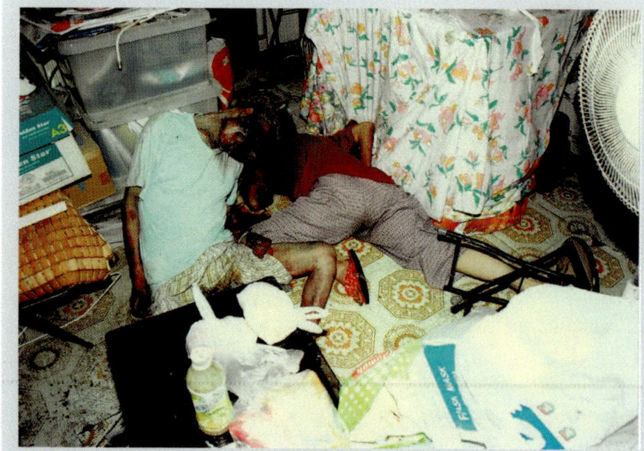

53.1 Scene of two elderly deceased who died at home with advanced putrefactive changes. The home was chaotic and there was hoarding of household items.

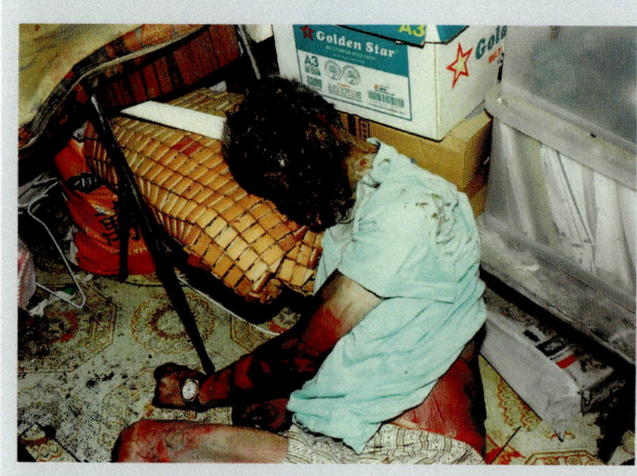

53.2 The male deceased.

greenish discoloration, slippage of epidermis, bloating of abdominal cavity and desiccation involving the face and anterior chest. Moderate amounts of maggots at various instar stages were identified. No recent external injuries were present. Decubitus ulcers were not found. Internal examination showed advanced putrefactive

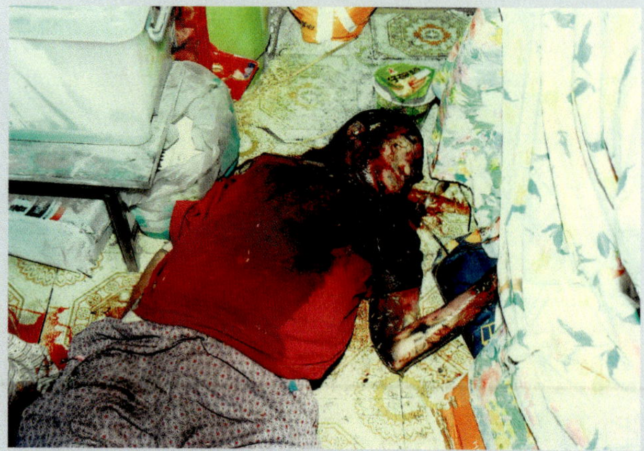

53.3 The female deceased.

changes of organs. Histological examination of viscera showed extensive loss of architecture due to autolysis. In addition, scattered myocardial fibrosis and severe coronary atherosclerosis were identified on the female deceased. Heavy consolidation changes of bronchopneumonia was identified in the male deceased. The stomach was empty while the gallbladder was distended, suggesting a state of fasting. Toxicology analysis was unremarkable. The time of death was estimated to be about three days prior to discovery based on the circumstances and post-mortem changes. Background investigation revealed financial dependence on social aid. Police revealed a record of the wife going missing one month previously and she was found wandering in the street late at night. The husband had a history of stroke and was dependent on his wife for care. The wife was said to have developed signs of early dementia. Both had become increasingly homebound and were last seen by a social worker one month previously. It was postulated that the wife collapsed suddenly first and being the sole caretaker of her spouse, the husband was unable to seek assistance and eventually died of chest infection.

DIOGENES SYNDROME

This case has illustrated elderly individuals dying in isolation known as Diogenes syndrome (21). It is also termed social breakdown syndrome, senile self-neglect, senile breakdown, senile squalor or social withdrawal in the elderly (22). Often, the cause of death is a natural disease condition but presented at a stage not amenable to medical intervention after failure to seek assistance. Typically, the home environment is in a state of extreme despair, filthy and occupied with unhygienic household items in disarray. Poverty and poor housing conditions are prevalent, and the deceased is tempted to hoard excessive items with a view to reuse them. Pre-existing psychiatric or neurodegenerative conditions account for deviated acts of hoarding unnecessary items known as "collectionism" or "syllogomania" (23). Autopsy examination invariably shows decomposition as death often goes unnoticed. Identity remains obscured in view of advanced decomposition and maggot infestations. Post-mortem injuries inflicted by domestic animals when aggressive pets started feeding on the body of the owner when food was not replenished. Rodents and insects producing post-mortem nibbling and trails of parchment-like abrasions may raise a suspicion of foul play (22). Antemortem injuries inflicted during a fall with bloodstain requires careful assessment of scene. One must differentiate from those inflicted as a result of abusive act or physical abuse (24) by elucidating relevant medical background (25), care regime and nutritional status (2). The disorganized home environment has to be distinguished from an illegal break-in and look for evidence of ransacking.

A variant of the syndrome illustrated clearly by the case example above is referred as *Diogenes a deux*, involving married couples living on a "closed" family system and inter-dependent on each other (26), succumbing in sequence when there was inadequate medical and vital support (1).

BOX 53.3 Features of death scene suggestive of self-neglect (21)

- Filthy and untidy environment with peeling paints, broken windows
- Presence of human excreta
- Unconsumed/prolonged storage of food
- Stacking of trash, papers and boxes obstructing hallways
- Neglect of safety risks, e.g. fire, poisoning and falls
- Lack of water supply
- Lack of bedding materials
- Absence of air conditioning or heating equipment

CONCLUSION

Self-neglect is regarded as the inability to provide the necessary means to meet the basic needs of oneself. It should be noted this condition presents in a spectrum of varying clinical severity. The lack of medical history, doubtful circumstances and an alarming presentation of the body often calls for a proper investigation. Efforts should be made to rule out criminal activity. Overlapping clinical features with neglect or maltreatment is the main differential diagnosis. Death investigators are obliged to scrutinize the background of the deceased, home environment, in consultation with a comprehensive forensic autopsy to formulate a reconstruction (Box 53.3). This issue concerns the realm of public health and contributing factors of health and social conditions need to be identified regarding preventive measures by implementing humane social measures at an early stage. The court may need to decide through an inquest on the manner of death and contributing factors related to a particular adverse outcome of the individual concerned.

REFERENCES

1. Cortellini V, Brescia G, Correa HS, et al. Living with the dead: A case report and review of the literature. *J Forensic Leg Med* 2019; **62**: 107–11.
2. Cuculic D, Sosa I, Petaros A. Decubitus ulcers and ligature marks as evidence in a homicide case. *Forensic Sci Int* 2015; **254**: e13–17.
3. Ortmann C, Fechner G, Bajanowski T, et al. Fatal neglect of the elderly. *Int J Leg Med* 2001; **114(3)**: 191–3.
4. Ventura F, Caputo F, Molinelli A. Medico-legal aspects of deaths related to neglect and abandonment in the elderly. *Aging Clin Exp Res* 2018; **30(11)**: 1399–402.
5. Pavlou MP, Lachs MS. Self-neglect in older adults: A primer for clinicians. *J Gen Intern Med* 2008; **23(11)**: 1841–6.
6. Dyer CB, Goodwin JS, Pickens-Pace S, et al. Self-neglect among the elderly: A model based on more than 500 patients seen by a geriatric medicine team. *Am J Public Health* 2007; **97(9)**: 1671–6.
7. Sauvageau A, Hunter BC. Self-neglect: Adaptation of a clinical tool to the practice of the medical examiner. *Am J Forensic Med Pathol* 2012; **33(3)**: 289–92.
8. Wu M, Peng C, Chen Y, et al. Nurses' perceptions of factors influencing elder self-neglect: A qualitative study. *Asian Nurs Res* 2020; **14(3)**: 137–43.
9. Abrams RC, Reid MC, Lien C, et al. The Abrams geriatric self-neglect scale: Introduction, validation and psychometric properties. *Int J Geriatr Psychiatry* 2018; **33(1)**: e73–84.
10. Dong X, Simon M, Fulmer T, et al. Physical function decline and the risk of elder self-neglect in a community-dwelling population. *Gerontologist* 2010; **50(3)**: 316–26.
11. Altendorf A, Draper B, Wijeratne C, et al. Neglect of older people: Touching on forensic and pathophysiological aspects. *Gerontologist* 2020; **60(6)**: e449–65.
12. Payne-James J. Fatal and Non-fatal Accidents. In: Collins KA, Byard RW (eds). *Geriatric Forensic Medicine and Pathology*. Cambridge: Cambridge University Press; 2020, pp. 72–86.
13. Ibrahim JE, Aitken G, Ranson DL. Pathophysiology of Aging: An Overview of Specific Pathophysiological Changes in Elders. In: Collins KA, Byard RW (eds). *Geriatric Forensic Medicine and Pathology*. Cambridge: Cambridge University Press; 2020, pp. 19–29.
14. Day MR, Mulcahy H, Leahy-Warren P, et al. Self-neglect: A case study and implications for clinical practice. *Br J Community Nurs* 2015; **20(3)**: 110–15.
15. Lee SM, Martino E, Bismark M, et al. Evidence to guide ethical decision-making in the management of older people living in squalor: A narrative review. *Intern Med J* 2022; **52(8)**: 1304–12.
16. Collins KA, Presnell SE. Elder neglect and the pathophysiology of aging. *Am J Forensic Med Pathol* 2007; **28(2)**: 157–62.
17. Akaza K, Bunai Y, Tsujinaka M, et al. Elder abuse and neglect: Social problems revealed from 15 autopsy cases. *Leg Med* 2003; **5(1)**: 7–14.
18. Heinemann A, Tsokos M, Püschel K. Medico-legal aspects of pressure sores. *Leg Med* 2003; **5**: S263–6.
19. Benecke M, Josephi E, Zweihoff R. Neglect of the elderly: Forensic entomology cases and considerations. *Forensic Sci Int* 2004; **146**: S195–9.
20. Petti S. Elder neglect: Oral diseases and injuries. *Oral Dis* 2018; **24(6)**: 891–9.
21. Byard RW, Tsokos M. Forensic issues in cases of Diogenes syndrome. *Am J Forensic Med Pathol* 2007; **28(2)**: 177–81.
22. Byard RW. Suicide and Social Isolation in Elders. In: Collins KA, Byard RW (eds). *Geriatric Forensic Medicine and Pathology*. Cambridge: Cambridge University Press; 2020, pp. 226–37.
23. Proctor C, Rahman S. Diogenes syndrome: Identification and distinction from hoarding disorder. *Case Rep Psychiatry* 2021; **2021**; 2810137.
24. Fox AW. Elder abuse. *Med Sci Law* 2012; **52(3)**: 128–36.
25. Howe J. Medicolegal Investigation of Elder Maltreatment and Deaths. In: Collins KA, Byard RW (eds). *Geriatric Forensic Medicine and Pathology*. Cambridge: Cambridge University Press; 2020, pp. 30–50.
26. Zuliani G, Soavi C, Dainese A, et al. Diogenes syndrome or isolated syllogomania? Four heterogeneous clinical cases. *Aging Clin Exp Res* 2013; **25(4)**: 473–8.

CHAPTER 54

Starvation

Burkhard Madea and Elke Doberentz

INTRODUCTION

Starvation is a rare cause of death in industrialized countries and may occur as a result of child abuse, fasting, insufficient nutrition or mental illness. However, there is still a high prevalence of undernutrition and death due to starvation in various regions worldwide. For example, the prevalence of undernutrition in various regions of the world from 2014 to 2016 was about 10 percent worldwide, 5 percent in developed countries and 20 percent in Africa. The diagnosis of death as a result of starvation is normally a simple *prima facie* diagnosis because the visual features of starvation are known from contemporary famines. If enough circumstantial evidence is present, the definitive diagnosis of starvation will not be doubted. Some examples of conditions that may result in death from starvation are as follows:

- Inability to eat (for example, as a result of natural diseases such as carcinoma of the esophagus)
- Voluntary refusal of food (fasting to death, hunger strike)
- Mental disease (anorexia nervosa, schizophrenia)
- Accidental entombment (colliery disasters)
- Deliberate withholding of food
- Neglect.

Both internal and external factors may lead to an identical clinical picture of cachexia (Figure 54.1).

Cachexia is defined as general wasting usually associated with severe chronic disease or malnutrition.

Malnutrition has been defined as a "state of nutrition in which a deficiency or imbalance of energy, protein, and other nutrition causes measurable adverse effects on body composition and function, and on clinical outcome from disease". In therapeutic terms, clinically important malnutrition may be defined as "a sufficiently severe state of undernutrition that measurable improvements in functional and clinical outcome result from nutritional intervention by natural or artificial means". After a few days without food and with loss of 5 percent of body weight there are detectable impairments of mental and physical function. These impairments increase after 10 to 15 percent weight loss. More than 35 percent weight loss is life threatening. Table 54.1 provides a useful glossary of terms for starvation.

In the developed world, malnutrition is usually the consequence of diseases which influence food intake, metabolism, or both. Using anthropometric criteria, between 10 and 40 percent of hospital admissions have been found to be undernourished. With prevalence rates varying from

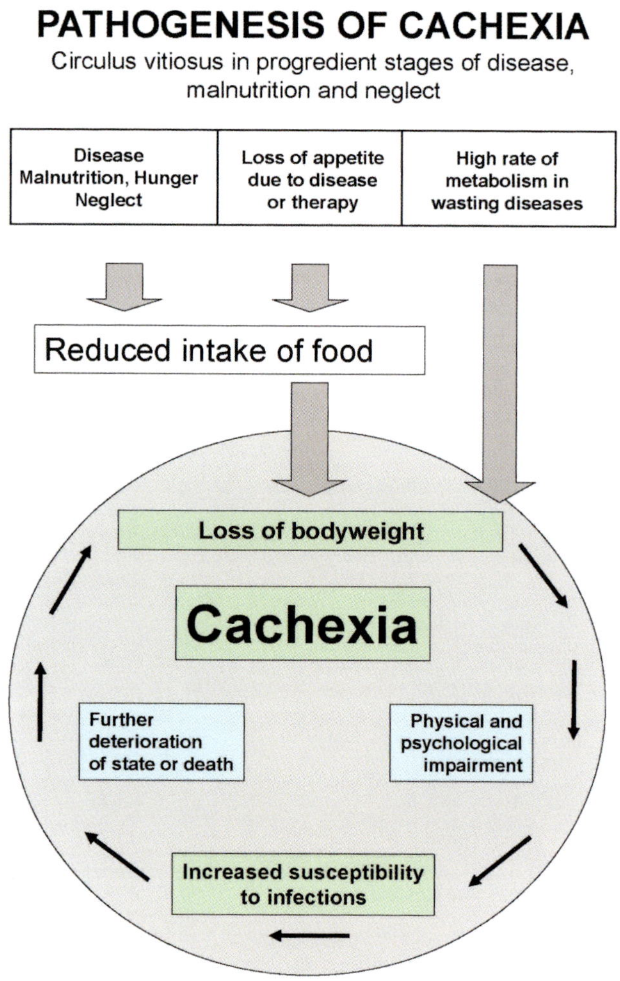

54.1 Pathogenesis of cachexia. Circulus vitiosus in progredient stages of disease, malnutrition and neglect.

DOI: 10.1201/9781003138754-56

TABLE 54.1 Glossary of terms for starvation

Body mass index	Body weight (in kg) divided by square of height (in m)
Cachexia	General wasting and emaciation, usually associated with severe chronic disease or malnutrition
Cachexia	Diagnostic criteria: Unintentional loss of body weight (≥5%) Body mass index <20 kg/m² in people aged <65 years <22 kg/m² in people aged >65 years Albumin concentration of <35 g/L Reduced fat-free body mass Increased cytokine concentrations (e.g. C-reactive protein)
Dehydration	Reduction or complete loss of water content
Failure to thrive	Children whose weight is significantly lower than the norms for their age
Fatal starvation	Death after long-standing food deprivation
Hypernatremic dehydration	Loss of body water not accompanied by a compensating sodium loss
Kwashiorkor	Severe form of malnutrition characterized by edema, anemia and impaired growth due to edematous protein–energy malnutrition
Malnutrition	Sufficiently severe state of undernutrition in which measurable improvements in function and clinical outcome result from a nutritional intervention by natural or artificial means. Any disorder resulting from a deficiency or excess of one or more essential nutrients that causes an unbalanced diet or inability to absorb or metabolize any nutrient
Marasmus	Non-edematous protein–energy malnutrition
Undernutrition	A state of nutrition in which a deficiency or imbalance of energy, protein, and other nutritional factors causes measurable adverse effects on body composition and function and on clinical disease outcomes. Inadequate nutrition due to a failure to ingest, absorb, or assimilate nutrients in adequate quantities
Physical neglect	Deprivation of necessary care including sufficient nourishment and hydration, not only in children but also in the elderly
Sarcopenia	Age-associated loss of muscle mass
Total energy expenditure (TEE)	Sum of resting energy expenditure (REE) required for maintaining the body at rest plus additional expenditure from physical activity
Tumor cachexia	General wasting and emaciation due to a malignant tumor
Protein energy malnutrition (PEM)	
Waterlow classification	Classification of PEM, that takes in account not only the body weight, but also the height and the weight expected for the actual height. Using this classification system it will become evident that these infants are not only light for their age but are also because of chronic malnutrition, impaired in their growth.

10 to 60 percent, malnutrition in acute hospitals has been acknowledged as a persistent problem in older adults worldwide. For instance, a cross-sectional, multicenter study in eight surgical wards in three Belgian hospitals revealed that a total of 107 patients (51.4%) were at risk of malnutrition. In patients older than 70 years. the risk of malnutrition increased up to 66 percent. This Belgian study confirmed the high risk of malnutrition in community living elders on admission to the hospital for selective surgery.

In a study from the United States (US) by Win et al., among 2252 veterans aged 65 years or older the prevalence of malnutrition was 15 percent (344/2252) and the prevalence of at risk for malnutrition was 40.3 percent (909/2252) (50).

Cachexia (*Gr. Kachexi'a; kako's bad; "e 'xis condition*) is a major cause of weight loss and increased mortality and affects more than five million people in the US (Table 54.2). Clinically, cachexia manifests with excessive weight loss in the setting of ongoing disease, usually with disproportionate muscle wasting (Table 54.3).

Mortality and morbidity rates from prolonged starvation, with or without injury, disease, or surgery, are increased in proportion to the degree of undernutrition. Cachexia from natural causes may be due to:

- Cancer, especially metastatic disease
- Infections (for example, tuberculosis or HIV infection)
- Old age (malnutrition, sarcopenia and cachexia in the elderly)
- Several other diseases such as chronic renal insufficiency, liver diseases, especially liver cirrhosis, endocrine diseases, diabetes).

Patients with pancreatic tumors or gastric cancer have a particularly high incidence of weight loss (83%)

TABLE 54.2 The number of persons in the United States with cachexia[1]

Disease	No. with disease	Cachexia	No. needing treatment
		%	
AIDS[2]	900 000	35	315 000
Cancer	1 368 000	30	410 400
COPD	16 000 000	20	3 200 000
Kidney failure	375 000	40	150 000
Rheumatoid arthritis	2 100 000	10	210 000
Heart failure	4 800 000	20	960 000
Nursing home	1 600 000	20	320 000

[1] Numbers are based on generally reported prevalence of disease and literature estimations of unintentional weight loss in these conditions. COPD, chronic obstructive pulmonary disease.

[2] The values may be too high in the era of the use of highly active antiretroviral therapy; some authors believe that 10% may be more appropriate.

TABLE 54.3 Diagnostic criteria for cachexia

Criteria
Unintentional weight loss (≥5%)
BMI
<20 in those aged <65 y
<22 in those aged ≥65 y
Albumin < 35 g/L (3.5 g/dL)
Low fat-free mass (lowest 10%)
Evidence of cytokine excess (e.g. elevated C-reactive protein)

TABLE 54.4 Incidence of weight loss in cancers of different sites

Tumor site	Incidence of weight loss (%)
Pancreas	83
Gastric	83
Esophagus	79
Head and neck	72
Colorectal	55–60
Lung	50–66
Prostate	56
Breast	10–35
General cancer population	63

Source: Mantovani G. *Cachexia and Wasting: A Modern Approach.* Milan Berlin Heidelberg New York: Springer Verlag Italia; 2006.

(Table 54.4). Tumor cachexia is caused by tumor products, production of cytokines such as tumor necrosis factor-α, catabolic metabolism with protein loss and lipolysis, and anorexia. In Germany in 2014, the mean age of death from cachexia due to HIV infection was 50.8 years, and the mean age of cachexia in the elderly was 87.1 years.

Anorexia nervosa is the most common eating disorder leading to death. A retrospective analysis of deaths from anorexia nervosa in the US revealed an average of 145 annual deaths and a rate of 6.73/100 000 deaths. The age and sex distribution suggests two fatal forms of anorexia nervosa: an early-onset form (89% women) and a later form (24% men). Twenty-nine deaths due to anorexia nervosa were reported in Germany in 2014.

The age and sex structure of the population have changed and will change dramatically in the past and future decades. People, especially women, are getting much older. With an increasing life span, age-related diseases such as dementia and cancer are also increasing.

As already mentioned, in the developed world, malnutrition is usually a consequence of diseases, which influence food intake, metabolism, or both. Diseases can of course lead to bed confinement, a risk factor for the development of pressure ulcers.

Therefore, in criminal acts involving starvation in which the cause of loss of body weight is suspected to be the result of deliberate withholding of food, the forensic pathologist must collect as much evidence as possible because the underlying cause of starvation (i.e. deliberate withholding of food or neglect), not the diagnosis of starvation itself, will be doubted in later proceedings. The distinction between cause and effect is of great importance when criminal charges are made.

In most cases, the victims of deliberate withholding of food are infants younger than 3 years and, more rarely, elderly or helpless people. Especially in infants, it is important not only to estimate the actual loss of body weight, but also to give an expert opinion as to whether a reduced body height may have been caused by chronic malnourishment. Classifications of protein–energy malnutrition (PEM) developed to estimate malnourishment in developing countries are of great value for such purposes.

ENERGY REQUIREMENTS AND NORMAL GROWTH

The total energy expenditure (TEE) is the sum of the resting energy expenditure (REE) required to maintain the body at rest (20–25 kcal/g body weight) plus the additional expenditure from physical activity. Energy intake in the form of carbohydrates (4 kcal/g), fat (9 kcal/g), and protein (4 kcal/g) needs to equal energy expenditure to maintain a stable body composition. Additionally, a minimum daily protein intake of 0.8 g/kg body weight is necessary. In the presence of disease, this requirement may rise to 1 g/kg body weight.

The daily energy requirement of humans above the basic metabolic rate mainly depends on the level of physical activity (Table 54.5).

Formulas used to calculate the basic metabolic rate are as follows:

- Harris–Benedict formula
  - Men: Basal metabolic rate in kcal/day = 66.47 + (13.7 × body weight in kg) + (5.0 × body height in cm) – (6.8 × age in years)
  - Women: Basal metabolic rate in kcal/day = 655.1 + (9.6 × body weight in kg) + (1.8 × body height in cm) – (4.7 × age in years)
- Empirical formula
  - Basal metabolic rate in kcal/day = body weight in kg × 25.

Energy requirements in healthy children are changing and age-dependent (Table 54.6). Energy requirements for boys and girls during the first year of life are presented in Table 54.7a–d.

The following rules of thumb can be used for normal growth.

Approximate average expected *weight* gain for a healthy term infant:

- 200 g/week in the first 3 months
- 130 g/week in the second 3 months
- 85 g/week in the third 3 months
- 75 g/week in the fourth 3 months
- Birth weight usually doubles by 4 months and triples by 12 months.

Body length:

- Increases by 25 cm in the first year
- Increases by 12 cm in the second year
- By 2 years, roughly half of adult height is attained.

TABLE 54.5 Daily calorie requirements in humans

Mode of energy turnover	Energy exchange	
Basic metabolic rate (body weight 70 kg)	F 6300 kJ/day	1500 kcal/day
	M 7100 kJ/day	1700 kcal/day
Basic metabolic rate plus leisure time requirement	F 8400 kJ/day	1900 kcal/day
	M 9600 kJ/day	2300 kcal/day
Basic metabolic rate for heavy workers	F 15500 kJ/day	3700 kcal/day
	M 20100 kJ/day	4800 kcal/day

F = female, M = male.

TABLE 54.6 Energy requirements in healthy children

Age	kcal/kg/day male/female
0 to <4 months	110
4 to <12 months	95
1 to <4 years	100
4 to <7 years	90
7 to <10 years	75
10 to <13 years	60/55
13 to <15 years	55/45
15 to <19 years	45/40

TABLE 54.7A Energy requirements of boys during the first year of life

Age in months	1985 FAO/WHO/UNU		2004 FAO/WHO/UNU		
	kJ/kg/day	MJ/day	kcal/day	kJ/kg/day	kcal/kg/day
0–1	519	2.166	518	473	113
1–2	485	2.387	570	434	104
2–3	456	2.494	596	397	95
3–4	431	2.380	569	343	82
4–5	414	2.546	608	340	81
5–6	404	2.674	639	337	81
6–7	397	2.730	653	329	79
7–8	395	2.845	680	330	79
8–9	397	2.936	702	330	79
9–10	414	3.058	731	335	80
10–11	418	3.145	752	336	80
11–12	437	3.243	775	337	81

FAO, Food and Agriculture Organization; WHO, World Health Organization; UNU, United Nations University.

TABLE 54.7B Energy requirements of girls during the first year of life

Age in months	1985 FAO/WHO/UNU		2004 FAO/WHO/UNU		
	kJ/kg/day	MJ/day	kcal/day	kJ/kg/day	kcal/kg/day
0–1	519	1.942	464	447	107
1–2	485	2.162	517	421	101
2–3	456	2.301	550	395	94
3–4	431	2.245	537	350	84
4–5	414	2.389	571	345	83
5–6	404	2.507	599	341	82
6–7	397	2.525	604	328	78
7–8	395	2.630	629	328	78
8–9	397	2.728	652	328	78
9–10	414	2.828	676	331	79
10–11	418	2.902	694	331	79
11–12	437	2.981	712	331	79

FAO, Food and Agriculture Organization; WHO, World Health Organization; UNU, United Nations University.

TABLE 54.7C Energy requirements of boys at 0 to 18 years of age, computed for a moderate level of physical activity

Age in years	1985 FAO/WHO/UNU		2004 FAO/WHO/UNU		
	kJ/kg/day	MJ/day	kcal/day	kJ/kg/day	kcal/kg/day
1–2	439	4.0	950	345	82
2–3	418	4.7	1125	350	84
3–4	397	5.2	1250	334	80
4–5	397	5.7	1350	322	77
5–6	377	6.1	1475	312	74
6–7	377	6.6	1575	303	73
7–8	326	7.1	1700	295	71
8–9	326	7.7	1825	287	69
9–10	326	8.3	1975	279	67
10–11	267	9.0	2150	270	65
11–12	267	9.8	2350	261	62
12–13	228	10.7	2550	252	60
13–14	228	11.6	2775	242	58
14–15	200	12.5	3000	233	56
15–16	200	13.3	3175	224	53
16–17	186	13.9	3325	216	52
17–18	186	14.3	3400	210	50

FAO, Food and Agriculture Organization; WHO, World Health Organization; UNU, United Nations University.

TABLE 54.7D Energy requirements of girls at 0 to 18 years of age, computed for a moderate level of physical activity

Age in years	1985 FAO/WHO/UNU		2004 FAO/WHO/UNU		
	kJ/kg/day	MJ/day	kcal/day	kJ/kg/day	kcal/kg/day
1–2	439	3.6	850	335	80
2–3	418	4.4	1050	339	81
3–4	397	4.8	1150	322	77
4–5	397	5.2	1250	310	74
5–6	356	5.6	1325	301	72
6–7	356	6.0	1425	289	69
7–8	280	6.5	1550	280	67
8–9	280	7.1	1700	268	64
9–10	280	7.7	1850	255	61
10–11	227	8.4	2000	243	58
11–12	227	9.0	2150	230	55
12–13	189	9.5	2275	218	52
13–14	189	10.0	2375	205	49
14–15	173	10.2	2450	197	47
15–16	173	10.4	2500	188	45
16–17	167	10.5	2500	184	44
17–18	167	10.5	2500	184	44

FAO, Food and Agriculture Organization; WHO, World Health Organization; UNU, United Nations University.

Head circumference:

- Increases by 1 cm/month in the first year
- Increases by 2 cm in the whole of the second year
- Will be 80% of adult size by 2 years.

(Note: Growth rates vary considerably among children; these figures should be used in conjunction with growth charts.)

CLINICAL STARVATION

Insufficient calorie intake compared with a person's requirements results in a negative energy balance with resultant loss of body weight. Malnutrition must be differentiated from undernutrition. Undernutrition is the intake of an insufficient quantity of food, whereas malnutrition is defined as feeding of inadequate quality. Symptoms and pathology of starvation have been comprehensively reported since World War II and are based on experiences and observations derived from the Nazi concentration camps. Starvation was also studied in the Minnesota Starvation Experiment of 1944–1945. This experiment was carried out by Dr Ancel Keys from the Laboratory of Physiological Hygiene at the University of Minnesota. For 12 weeks, volunteers received a standardized diet of 3200 calories a day. The food intake was then abruptly decreased from 3200 to 1570 calories a day. With this reduction in food intake, the starvation phase of the experiment had begun. Effects of the reduced food intake became quickly apparent in that the men showed a remarkable decline in strength and energy and felt constantly tired. After 6 months of starvation, the men had lost almost a quarter of their weight. In the rehabilitation phase, the volunteers increased their food levels.

The symptoms of starvation are generally constant and develop in a characteristic chronologic order:

1. Loss of well-being and experience of hunger, hunger pains and craving for food.
2. Apathy and fatigue.
3. Weight loss, more rapid in the first 6 months of starvation.
4. Pigmentation, cachexia and hypothermia.
5. Extreme lethargy, mental retardation and loss of self-respect.
6. Hunger edema.
7. Reduced resistance to infections in general; development of diarrhea and tuberculosis or other intercurrent infections.

Even in advanced stages of starvation, death may be sudden and unexpected; this has been documented in witness reports from concentration camps, as well as recent literature. The main clinical finding is extreme emaciation with loss of body weight (Figure 54.2). Loss of weight is first very rapid but becomes slower after approximately 3 months.

The significance of starvation in clinical, forensic, or medicolegal terms depends upon the degree of malnutrition or metabolic derangements induced, which in turn depend upon the severity and duration of starvation, and whether it is associated with exacerbating factors such as disease (Figure 54.3). Figure 54.3 shows the rates of weight loss with time in three different circumstances.

In patients with a normal premorbid weight, a loss of 5 percent body weight results in detectable impairments of

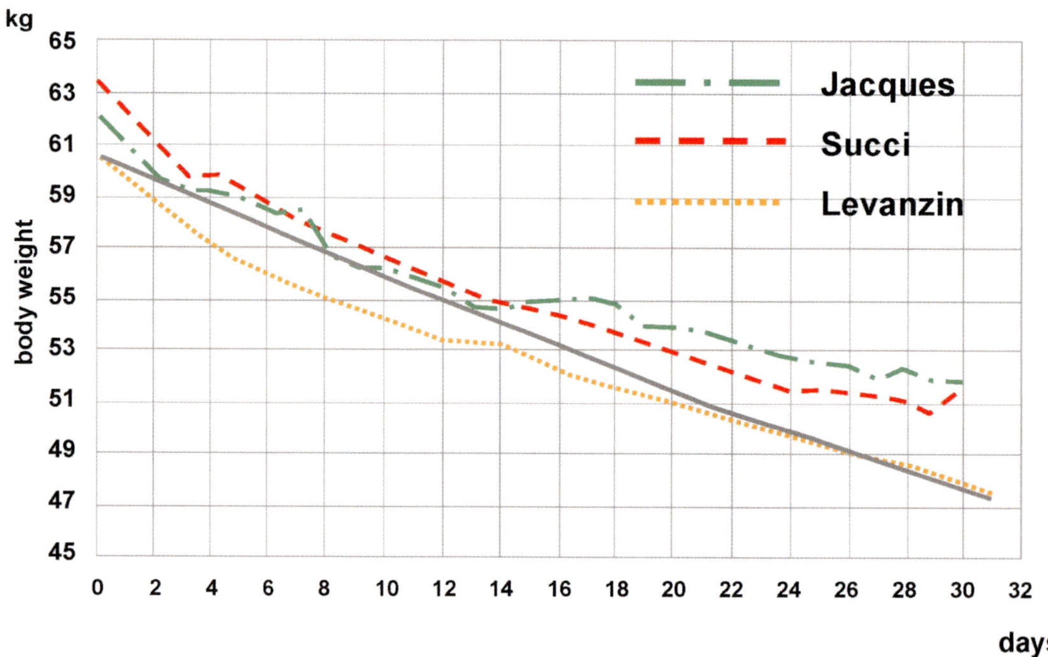

54.2 Loss of body weight in three male volunteers after complete withdrawal of food for 30 days (only water intake). After a stepwise loss of body weight within the first several days, the decrease in body weight was then retarded. The pulled-through line represents the calculated loss of body weight. (Modified according to Giese et al. [15].).

mental and physical function. After a loss of 10 to 15 percent body weight, nutritional intervention may be necessary. A loss of >35 percent body weight is life-threatening.

Figure 54.3 shows the percentage weight loss during semistarvation, total starvation and disease-associated starvation. Line 1 shows the more gradual slope derived from studies of normal young male volunteers who underwent semistarvation for 25 weeks (data from the Minnesota Starvation Experiment). The second steeper slope is derived from the Irish Republican Army hunger strikers who subjected themselves to total starvation for 70 days. By this time they had lost 38 percent of their body weight, and one-third died of undernutrition. The third and steepest slope represents

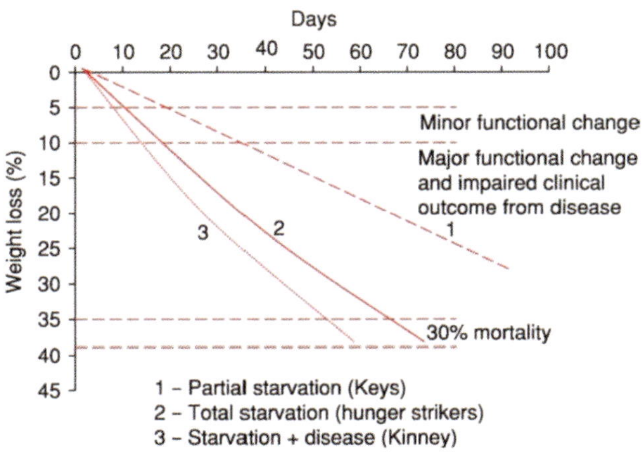

54.3 percentage weight loss during starvation, total starvation, and disease-associated starvation. (Reproduced from Allison 1992. [3]).

starvation combined with critical illness. A number of significant functional changes occur due to malnutrition. Some are shown in Figure 54.4. These figures are taken from studies of young male volunteers who underwent 20 weeks of semistarvation followed by a further 24 weeks of controled refeeding. Figure 54.4 shows changes in body composition, and Figure 54.5 shows changes in function as a percentage of their starting value. These figures show a progressive deterioration in mental and physical function. Changes in muscle function, immune function, wound healing, thermal regulation and endocrine function are summarized in Table 54.8.

According to Allison (3), the following degrees of starvation can be distinguished:

Fasting up to 72 hours

This induces physiological adaptations designed to conserve protein, and hence the mass and function of essential tissues and organs, while mobilizing reserves of fat. REE, after an initial rise, falls by 10 percent. Initially glucose is released from liver glycogen, but thereafter, essential glucose is provided by new glucose derived from conversion of protein, lactate and glycerol (gluconeogenesis). The brain, which normally derives its energy from glucose, adapts to metabolize ketones from liver fat metabolism, thereby reducing the necessity to convert protein to glucose. With longer periods of starvation, the metabolic rate falls further, *pari passu* with loss of lean mass. These adaptive mechanisms are overridden in the presence of acute illness or injury, which is characterized by increased metabolic rate and protein catabolism. Such short periods

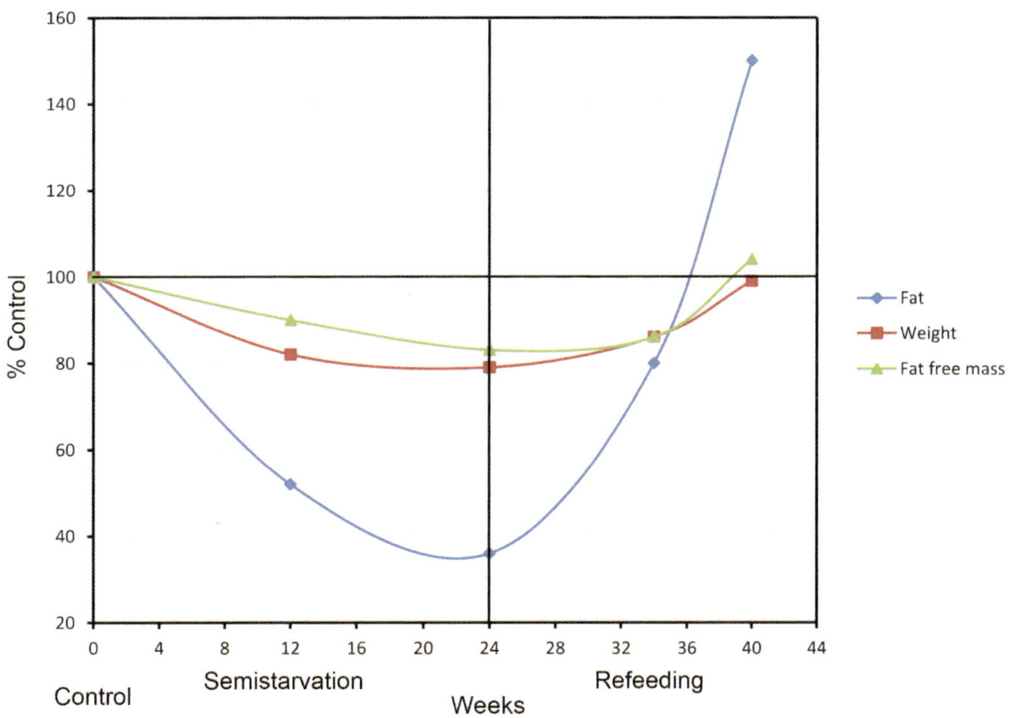

54.4 Body compositional changes (% starting value) in 12 male volunteers during 24 weeks of semistarvation followed by 24 weeks of controled refeeding. (Adapted from the data of Keys et al. reported by Allison 1992. [3]).

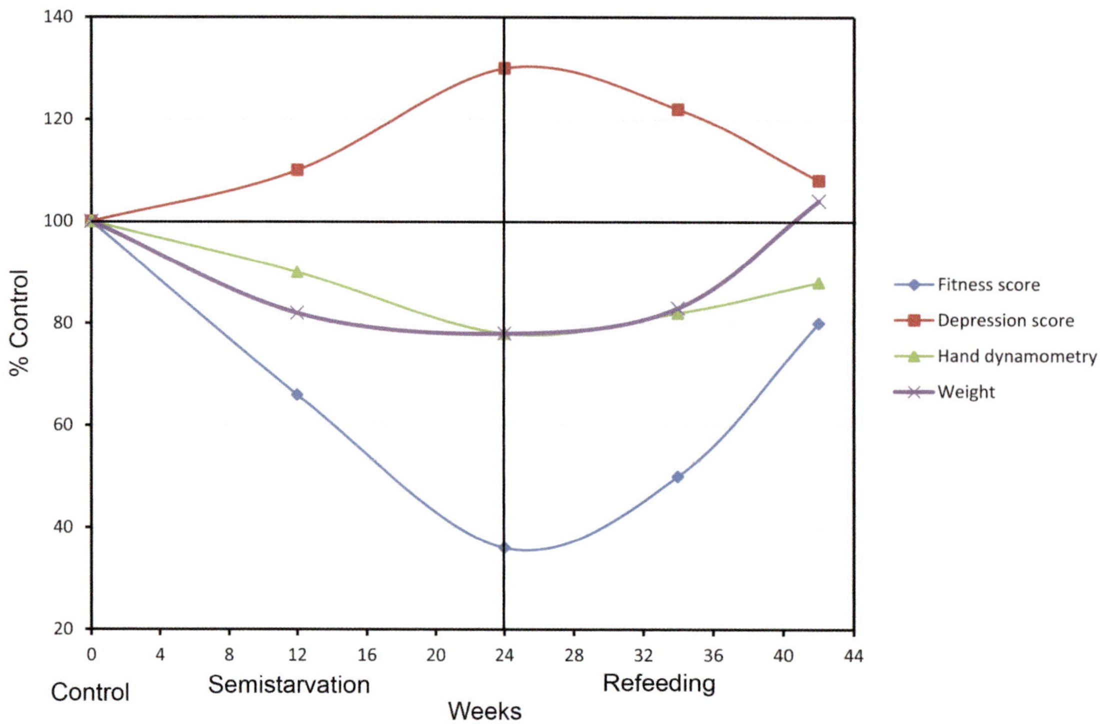

54.5 Changes (% in starting value) in weight, depression score, hand muscle strength, and fitness score in 12 male volunteers during 24 weeks of semistarvation followed by 24 weeks of controled refeeding. (Adapted from the data of Keys et al. reported by Allison 1992. [3]).

TABLE 54.8 Functional changes in cases of starvation

Impairment of mental and physical function		
Reduced vasoconstriction	→	Mild sensations of cold
Progressively diminished muscle strength	→	Respiratory capacity impaired
Reduced lymphocyte count, white cell function, immune responses	→	Predisposal to infections
Impaired wound healing	→	Impaired thermoregulation, undernourished individuals prone to hypothermia
Loss of cardiac muscle, impaired cardiovascular reserve, bradycardia, hypotension, electrocardiographic abnormalities		
Decreasing insulin levels	→	Lipolysis, ketosis, fat primary fuel
Reduced symphathoadrenal activity		
Decreasing sex hormone levels, discontinuation of menstruation below a BMI of 17 kg/m^2		
Increase in extracellular fluid volume as a percentage of body weight	→	Famine edema

of starvation result in less than 5 percent reduction in body weight, but identifiable, if small, reductions in function. Vasoconstriction to conserve heat is reduced, thereby impairing heat conservation in the body, an important consideration in cold environments. Mild sensations of cold, irritability, and loss of energy may be experienced. Reduced glycogen stores in liver and muscle also impair athletic performance. Short periods of starvation have also been shown to be important in patients undergoing surgery, in whom avoidance of starvation for more than 2 hours preoperatively, and for more than a few hours postoperatively, has been shown to improve outcome and the rate of recovery from operation.

Partial or complete starvation > 5 days with 5 percent weight loss

This results not only in the adaptive responses described above, but also in further impairment of mental and physical function. Individuals react by reducing their physical activity and hence TEE. Mood and muscle strength also deteriorate. If, however, sufficient food is reintroduced to maintain weight at its new level, the individual adapts to the new lower weight and function returns. However, if food intake continues to be inadequate, resulting in further weight loss, then clinically important reductions in function become apparent. It has been recommended by both American and European authorities that surgical patients should not be allowed to starve for more than 7 days postoperatively without feeding by natural or artificial means.

Starvation >7 days and weight loss >10 percent

With this degree of malnutrition or greater, several significant functional changes occur. Some of these are illustrated in Figures 54.4 and 54.5, taken from the studies of Keys and co-workers on young male volunteers who underwent 24 weeks of semistarvation, followed by an additional 24 weeks of controled refeeding (3). Expressing changes in body composition (Figure 54.4) and changes in function (Figure 54.5) as a percentage of their starting value, there is a progressive deterioration in mental and physical function as semistarvation continues and tissue is lost. With refeeding, restoration of fat mass is faster than that of lean mass, and there is a correspondingly slow return of mental and physical functions over many weeks. A large amount of detailed data has accrued in the literature concerning functional change due to starvation (Tables 54.9—54.13).

Especially if starvation is combined with critical illness, as it may be in elders, the time taken to reach a functionally significant or fatal weight loss may be halved. Starvation leads to an impairment of several mental and physical functions. For instance, muscle strength diminishes progressively, not only through reduced muscle mass but also through metabolic

TABLE 54.9 Clinical signs of malnutrition

Hair	Thinness, sparseness, easy removal
Face	Diffuse depigmentation, nasolabial seborrhea
Eyes	Conjunctival xerosis, corneal xerosis, keratomalacia, blepharitis
Lips	Angular stomatitis, angular scars, cheilosis
Tongue	Magenta tongue, glossitis
Gums	Spongy, bleeding
Glands	Thyroid enlarged, parotid enlarged
Skin	Xerosis, follicular hyperkeratosis, petechiae, ecchymoses, dermatosis
Nails	Koilonychia
Subcutaneous tissue	Edema
Muscular and skeletal system	Muscle wasting, osteomalacia
Liver	Hepatomegaly
Neurologic	listless, apathetic, mental confusion, irritability, sensory loss, motor weakness, loss of balance
Cardiovascular	Cardiac enlargement, tachycardia

Source: Mantovani G. *Cachexia and Wasting: A Modern Approach*. Milan Berlin Heidelberg New York: Springer Verlag Italia; 2006 (35).

TABLE 54.10 Clinical and anthropometric parameters in nutritional assessment

Clinical history	Physical examination	Anthropometric parameters
Involuntary diet restriction (poverty)	General appearance Skin, hair, nails	Height-weight ratio Body surface
Anorexia	Tongue, mucous membranes, Dentition	Wrist circumference (bone structure)
Inadequate diet (alcoholism, vegetarianism)	Muscle masses (temporal, proximal extremely)	Skin folds (fat mass)
Gastrointestinal symptoms (dysphagia, vomiting, diarrhea)	Eyes, loss of vision Neurologic system	Mid-arm muscle Circumference (lean mass
Chronic illness		

Source: Mantovani G. *Cachexia and Wasting: A Modern Approach*. Milan Berlin Heidelberg New York: Springer Verlag Italia; 2006 (35).

TABLE 54.11 Biochemical and immunological parameters in nutritional assessment

Biochemical assays	Immunological assays
Commonly available laboratory tests	Lymphocyte count
Nitrogenous balance	Skin tests to common recall antigens
Muscle proteins	C3-fraction
Plasma proteins (albumin, prealbumin, transferrin, retinol-binding protein, fibronectin)	
Vitamins and minerals	

Source: Mantovani G. *Cachexia and Wasting: A Modern Approach*. Milan Berlin Heidelberg New York: Springer Verlag Italia; 2006 (35).

TABLE 54.12 Biochemical parameters of nutrition

Nitrogenous balance
Muscle proteins
Plasma proteins: • Albumin • Prealbumin • Transferrin • Retinol-binding-protein
Vitamins and oligoelements
Basic chemical-clinical tests

Source: Mantovani G. *Cachexia and Wasting: A Modern Approach*. Milan Berlin Heidelberg New York: Springer Verlag Italia; 2006 (35).

TABLE 54.13 Concentrations of albumin, prealbumin and transferrin according to level of protein catabolism

Albumin (g/dL)	Normal >3.5	Slight depletion 2.8–3.5	Medium depletion 2.1–2.7	Severe depletion < 2.1
Prealbumin (mg/dL)	Normal 15–29	Slight depletion 10–15	Medium depletion 5–10	Severe depletion < 5
Transferrin (mg/dL)	Normal 250–300	Slight depletion 150–250	Medium depletion 100–150	Severe depletion < 100

Source: Mantovani G. *Cachexia and Wasting: A Modern Approach*. Milan Berlin Heidelberg New York: Springer Verlag Italia; 2006 (35).

effects which may have great significance in the elderly.

- Immune function is reduced (decreased lymphocyte count, white cell function, and immune responses).
- Wound healing is impaired. Furthermore, malnutrition is a risk factor for pressure sores.
- Thermoregulation is impaired. Heat conservation by cutaneous vasoconstriction is reduced.
- Pancreatic enzyme secretion is impaired.
- Malnutrition results in loss of cardiac muscle and impaired cardiovascular reserve. Bradycardia, hypotension, a 45 percent reduction in cardiac output, and electrocardiographic abnormalities were observed.

For the rapid screening of nutritional risk, the height, weight, and body mass index (BMI) are used (Tables 54.14 and 54.15). In adults, the BMI (weight in kilograms divided by height in meters squared) is the most commonly used measure of an individual's current nutritional status. Furthermore, anthropometric measurements such as mid upper-arm-circumference (MAC) and triceps skin fold (TSF) thickness give a measure of body composition or the proportions of residual fat and muscle. Simple tests like hand dynamometry for muscle strength or expiratory flow for respiratory function can also be applied (Table 54.16).

Laboratory tests for determining cachexia in older persons are shown in Table 54.17. A typical case of weight loss in older age is shown in Figure 54.6a–d.

TABLE 54.14 Body mass index: values of the body classes

0 = < 20.0 kg/m^2	Body mass deficit
N = 20.0–24.9 kg/m^2	Normal
1 = 25.0–29.0 kg/m^2	Moderate excess of weight
2 = 30.0–39.9 kg/m^2	Significant excess of weight
3 = > 40.0 kg/m^2	Very significant excess of weight

Source: Mantovani G. *Cachexia and Wasting: A Modern Approach*. Milan Berlin Heidelberg New York: Springer Verlag Italia; 2006 (35).

TABLE 54.15 Classification of malnutrition in adults by body mass index*

Body mass index (kg/m^2)	Nutritional status
≥18.50–24.99	Normal
17.00–18.49	Mild malnutrition
16.00–16.99	Moderate malnutrition
<16.00	Severe malnutrition

* WHO 1999 (49).

TABLE 54.16 Skin folds and methods of measurement

Triceps skin fold	On dorsal side of left arm relaxed, to medium point of humerus between olecranus and acromion, in vertical direction
Biceps skin fold	On median and front line of arm, at the point of measurement of arm circumference, in vertical direction
Subscapular skin fold	In left angle subscapular (1–2 cm under), in diagonal direction
Iliac skin fold	At the point of contact between axillary median line and iliac crest, in diagonal direction
Cheek fold	In the middle of line joining labial commissure to external auditory meatus
Meatus fold	Between auditory meatus and hyoid bone
Pectoral fold	On big pectoral muscle in correspondence of axillary front pillar, with arm extended laterally
Thoraci fold	Corresponding to tenth rib, on medium axillary line
Abdominal fold	Corresponding to third medial of line joining umbilicus to iliac spine front upper
Tight skin fold	At the medium point of line joining iliac spine front upper to rotula
Knee fold	Onto the rotula
Calf fold	Under popliteal cavity with leg semiflexed and fingers on the ground, on median back line, in vertical direction

Source: Mantovani G. *Cachexia and Wasting: A Modern Approach*. Milan Berlin Heidelberg New York: Springer Verlag Italia; 2006.

TABLE 54.17 Laboratory tests for determining cachexia in older persons

Test	Comment
Weight loss	Best test; < 5% in 3 months or 10% in 6 months
Body mass index	< 21 is highly suggestive
Midarm muscle or calf	Good indicators of loss of muscle mass muscle circumference
Albumin/prealbumin	Very low levels suggest cachexia or nephrotic syndrome or liver disease
Cholesterol	Low levels in cachexia

TABLE 54.17 (Continued) Laboratory tests for determining cachexia in older persons

Test	Comment
Hemoglobin	Anaemia usually coexists with cachexia
CD4 T-cells	Decreased in severe cachexia and starvation
C-reactive protein	Elevated in cachexia
Interleukin-2-receptors	Elevated in cachexia
Uric acid	Elevated in cachexia

Source: Mantovani G. *Cachexia and Wasting: A Modern Approach*. Milan Berlin Heidelberg New York: Springer Verlag Italia; 2006.

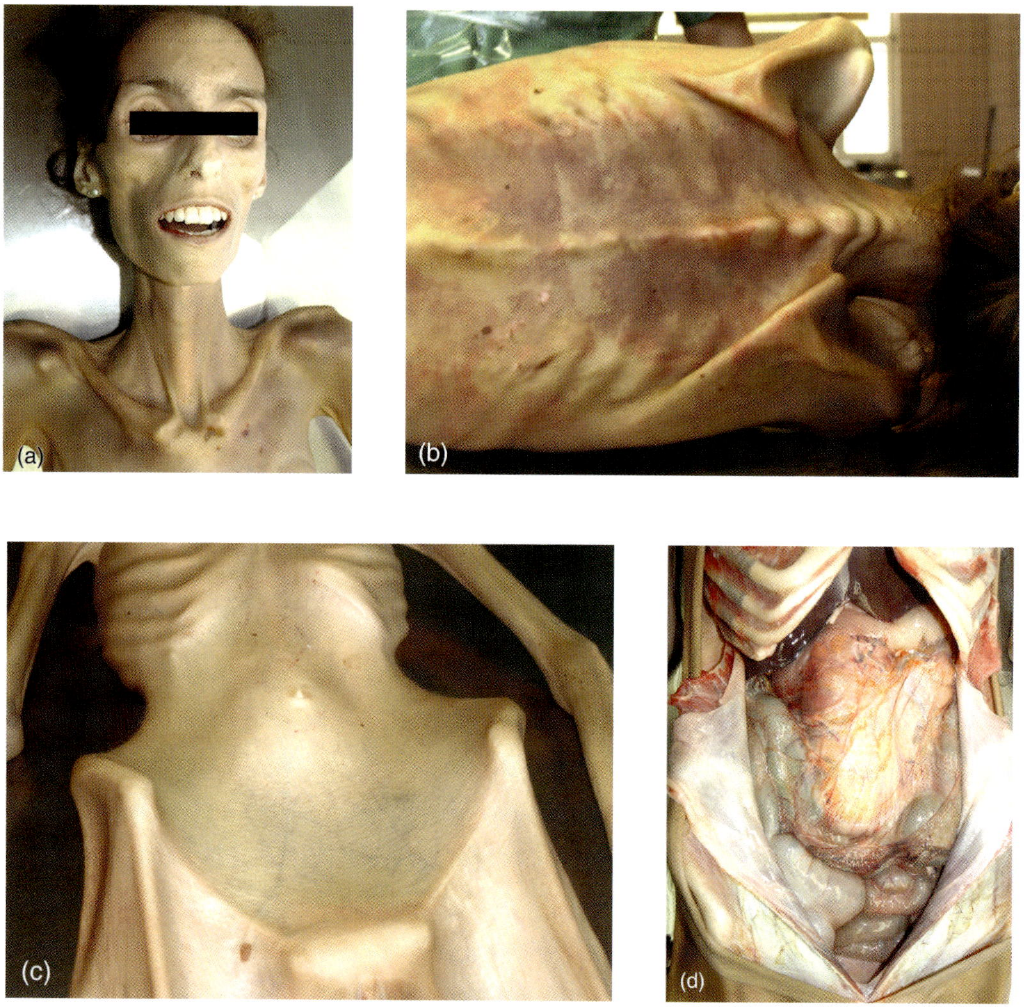

54.6 Typical autopsy findings in starvation are (a) emaciation with loss of Bichat's fat pad, sunken eyes, protruding bones, (b) and (c) complete loss of subcutaneous adipose tissue and (d) loss of adipose tissue of the mesenterium.

FATAL STARVATION

Most victims of fatal starvation are under the age of 1 year; however, older children may also be affected, especially disabled children. Children below the age of 3 years have only limited ability to obtain food or drink.

The main autopsy finding in cases of fatal starvation is extreme emaciation with loss of body weight and organ weights (Figure 54.7a–c, Table 54.18). Loss of body weight mainly results from the loss of subcutaneous adipose tissue and adipose tissue surrounding internal organs, atrophy of internal organs, and atrophy of muscles. Nearly all organs except the brain are reduced in weight (Table 54.19). Also quite characteristic is loss of the buccal fat pad (Bichat's fat pad). The skin becomes wrinkled due to the loss of subcutaneous adipose tissue. Additionally, sunken fontanelles and wrinkling of the

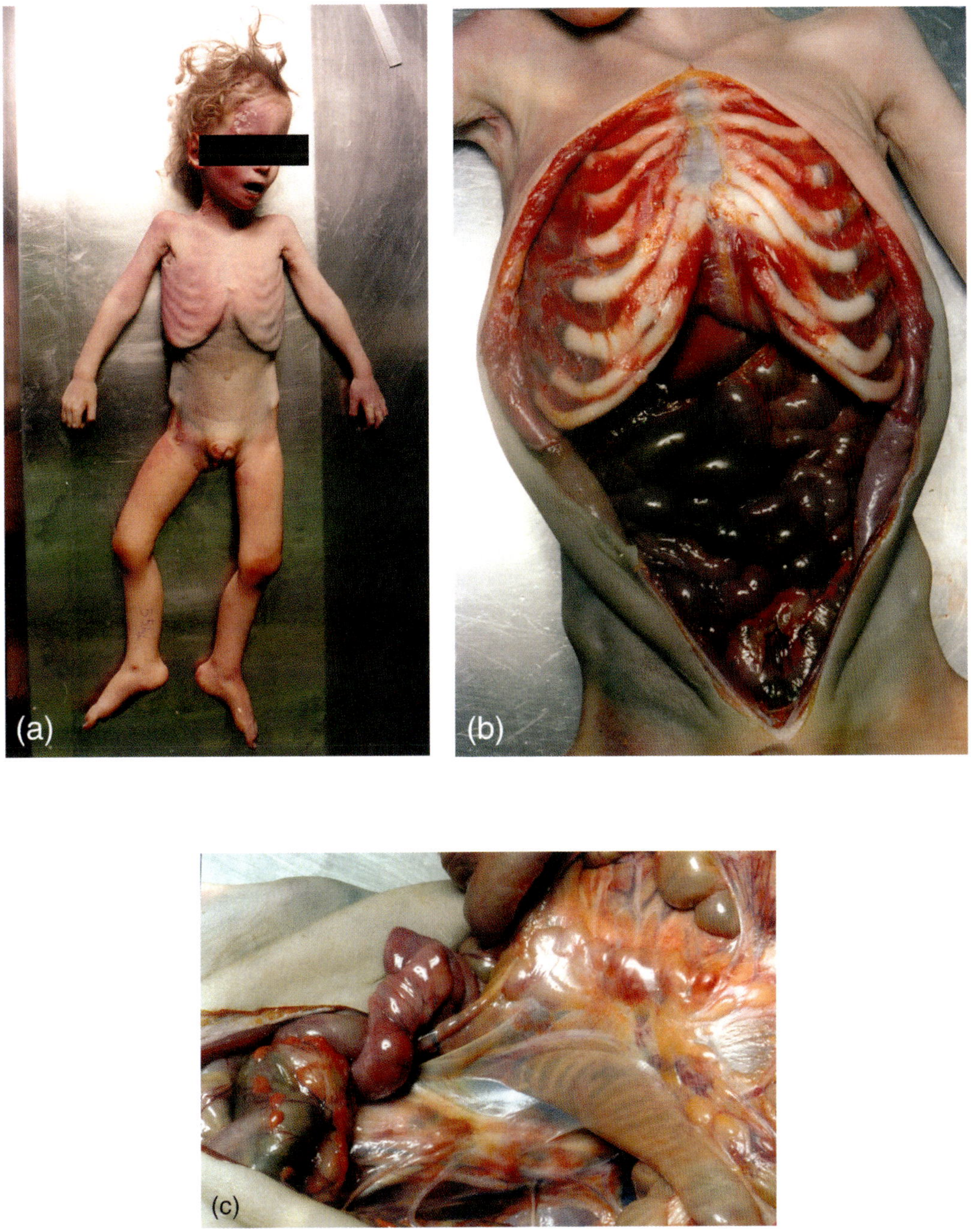

54.7 Main autopsy findings in starvation are **(a)** emaciation with loss of Bichat's fat pad, sunken eyes, protruding bones, **(b)** complete loss of subcutaneous adipose tissue and **(c)** loss of adipose tissue of the mesenterium.

skin, especially of the neck pad, can be found secondary to dehydration (Figure 54.8a,b).

Loss of about 35 to 50 percent of body weight may cause death. Atrophy of the endocrine and reproductive glands (testes) is quite characteristic in such cases. Mainly in infants, complete atrophy of the thymus is symptomatic; the lymph nodes also decrease in size.

The gallbladder is commonly distended because of the absence of food as the natural stimulant of bile excretion. The stomach and small bowel are normally empty, but the presence of extremely dry stool in the colon is another characteristic finding of fatal starvation. Foreign bodies may even be found in the colon, indicating that the starving person attempted to eat anything accessible prior to death.

TABLE 54.18 Gross autopsy findings in starvation/malnutrition

- Decreased body weight
- Decreased adipose tissue
- Decreased visceral adipose tissue
- Atrophied skeletal muscle
- Decreased organ weights
- Blue pallor of the skin, pale "semitranslucent" skin, thin sketched skin over the face
- Pressure sores
- Areas of hypopigmentation
- Dental caries
- Brittle hair
- Alopecia
- Protruding occiput
- Thin neck
- Sunken eyes
- Sunken cheeks/decreased buccal fat
- Protruding ribs
- Protruding vertebrae
- Protruding iliac crests
- Winging of the scapulae
- "Knobby knees" and joints
- Scaphoid abdomen
- Wrinkled skin over the joints and extremities
- Wrinkled skin and subcutaneous tissue over the buttocks
- Thinned walls of the stomach and intestines
- Empty gastrointestinal tract
- Distended and filled gallbladder
- Dehydrated feces, fecoliths
- Sticky serosal surfaces
- Tenting of the skin with dehydration
- Secondary infections

Source: Modified from Collins KA, 2010 (26).

TABLE 54.19 Loss of body weight and loss of weight of internal organs (%) in relation to normal weight for respective age group; 5 cases of fatal pediatric starvation

Case no.	Age	Body weight (kg)	Heart	Liver	Spleen	Kidney	Lungs	Brain
Case 1	3.0 months	53.3	7.4	25.0	68.7	40.4	36.0	+13.0
Case 2	2.3 years	54.0	37.0	37.0	24.0	46.0	30.0	+10.0
Case 3	2.5 years	60.0	25.0	54.0	57.0	45.0	–	15.0
Case 4	2.5 years	55.0	30.0	40.0	51.0	69.0	39.0	11.0
Case 5	2.5 years	52.0	46.0	46.0	43.0	33.0	52.0	10.0

See text for further details on the individual cases.

HISTOLOGY

In cases of starvation, histological investigations are very important to exclude concurrent causes of death or underlying diseases (e.g. malabsorption, malassimilation) as the cause of malnutrition. Histologic findings are non-specific in cases of pediatric starvation. Hepatic microvesicular steatosis due to protein deficiency is often found (Figure 54.9a&b). Besides thymic involution, microscopic findings such as the cytologic "starry sky" pattern, thymic calcification of Hassall's corpuscles, and fibrofatty replacement have been described. Furthermore, secondary siderosis due to protein deficiency in the spleen and liver can be found (Figure 54.10).

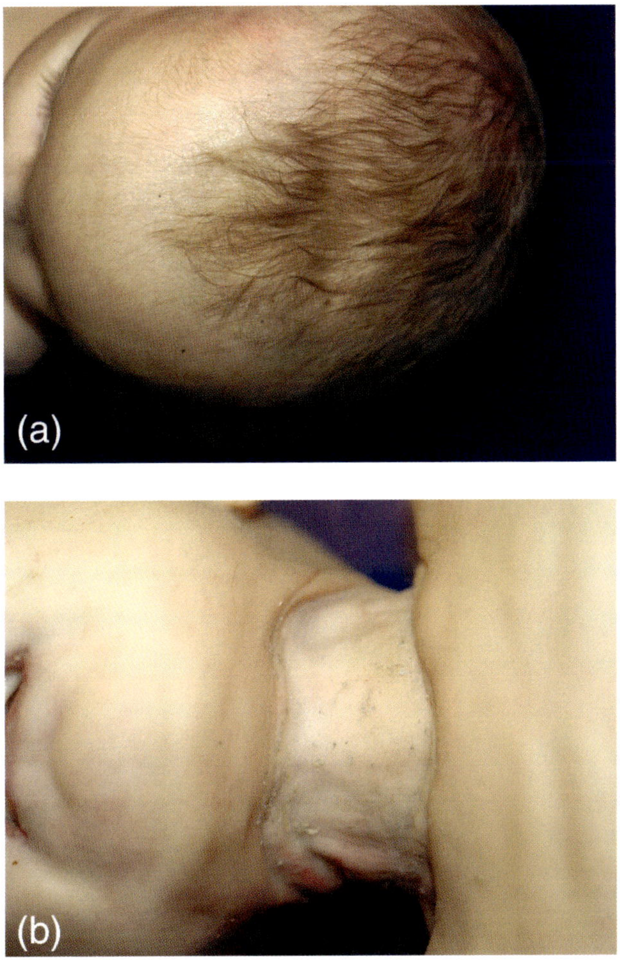

54.8 (a) Sunken fortanelles and (b) wrinkling of skin of the neck.

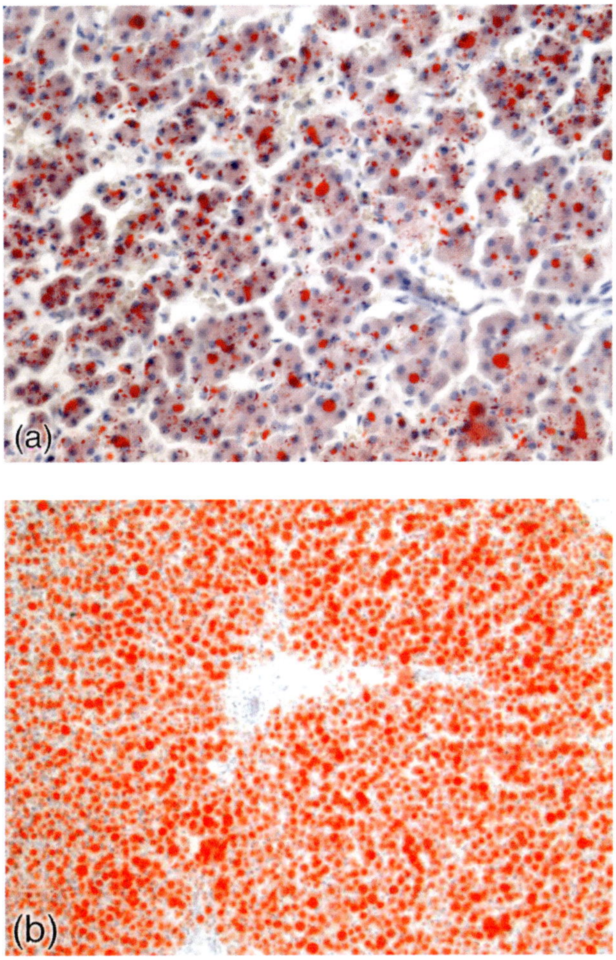

54.9 (a) Hepatic microvesicular steatosis and (b) massive steatosis.

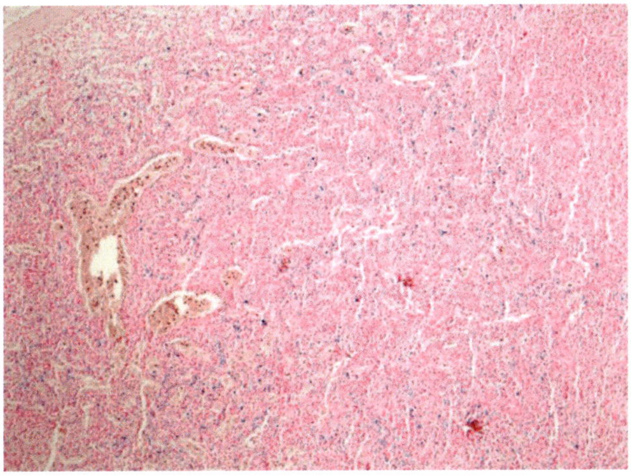

54.10 Secundary siderosis (spleen).

Post-mortem biochemical investigations of the vitreous humor (see below), toxicological investigations, microbiology and virology studies, and metabolic screenings must be carried out to rule out concurrent causes of death in cases of pediatric starvation.

METABOLIC DISEASES

Especially in children, blood and bile spotted on filter paper should be collected at autopsy for the post-mortem investigation of a possible underlying metabolic disorder. Blood specimens are collected in heparin-containing tubes. Bile should be spotted onto a filter paper card. Furthermore, liver specimens weighing approximately 1 to 5 g should be collected and frozen at −70°C as soon as possible. Skin and tendon specimens should be collected and placed in culture media for fibroblast culturing.

INVESTIGATION

A scene investigation must be carried out in all cases of pediatric starvation. An interview with the caregiver(s) is necessary to gather information on the personal history of abuse, eating disorders, psychopathology, and alcohol and drug use. Furthermore, the caregiver must be interviewed regarding the feeding history, formula preparation and medical history of the child (Table 54.20).

The World Health Organization (WHO) has recommended a checklist of points to be used when taking the child's medical history and conducting the physical examination. This checklist is quite useful worldwide, not only for the examination of cases of malnutrition in developing countries (Table 54.21). Some laboratory tests are also useful in the investigation of cases of pediatric malnutrition (Table 54.22). Many diseases may mimic pediatric dehydration and starvation and must be thoroughly investigated (Table 54.23). Organic diseases as a cause of malnutrition and dehydration must be ruled out. Medical history must be studied, and histological investigations are of utmost importance (Table 54.24).

Furthermore, malnutrition and failure to thrive may be unintentional in cases involving inexperienced and socially isolated mothers (Table 54.25). Unintentional

TABLE 54.20 Investigation of pediatric starvation/malnutrition

Routine investigation	Medical investigation
Interview of caregivers (personal history of abuse, eating disorders, psychopathology, alcohol and drug use, domestic violence, social skills)	Medical history (genetic conditions, growth history, endocrine disorders, caregivers' knowledge of normal growth and development, eating pattern, types of food available in the house)
Feeding history	Well-baby pediatric clinic records
Formula sample	WIC records
Manufacturer of formula for content and concentration	Charting of body measurements over time
Interview of siblings	Development over time
Interview of neighbors and family	Comparison of growth and development with family/social history
Determination of any changes in household; i.e. financial, new partner, drugs, etc.	
Social service records or social history	
Medical history	
Birth records	
Well-baby pediatric clinic records	
Home visit by health professional	

WIC, Women, Infants, and Children
Source: Modified from Collins KA, 2010 (26).

TABLE 54.21 Checklist for taking the child's medical history and conducting the physical examination

Medical history:

- Usual diet before current episode of illness
- Breastfeeding history
- Food and fluids taken in past few days
- Recent sinking of eyes
- Duration and frequency of vomiting or diarrhea, appearance of vomit or diarrheal stools
- Time when urine was last passed
- Contact with people with measles or tuberculosis
- Any deaths of siblings
- Birth weight
- Milestones reached (sitting up, standing, etc.)
- Immunizations

Physical examination:

- Weight and length or height
- Edema
- Enlargement of tenderness of liver, jaundice
- Abdominal distension, bowel sounds, "abdominal splash" (a splashing sound in the abdomen)
- Severe pallor
- Signs of circulatory collapse: cold hands and feet, weak radial pulse, diminished consciousness
- Temperature: hypothermia or fever
- Thirst
- Eyes: corneal lesions indicative of vitamin A deficiency
- Ears, mouth, throat: evidence of infection
- Skin: evidence of infection or purpura
- Respiratory rate and type of respiration: signs of pneumonia or heart failure
- Appearance of feces

Source: WHO 1999 (49).

TABLE 54.22 Laboratory tests

Test	Result and significance
Tests that may be useful	
Blood glucose	Glucose concentration of <54 mg/dl (3 mmol/l) is indicative of hypoglycemia
Examination of blood smear by microscopy	Presence of malaria parasites is indicative of infection
Hemoglobin or packed-cell volume	Hemoglobin of <40 g/l or packed-cell volume of <12% is indicative of very severe anemia
Examination and culture of urine specimen	Presence of bacteria on microscopy (or >10 leukocytes per high-power field) is indicative of infection
Examination of feces by microscopy	Presence of blood is indicative of dysentery Presence of *Giardia* cysts or trophozoites is indicative of infection
Chest X-ray	Pneumonia causes less shadowing of the lungs in malnourished children than in well-nourished children Vascular engorgement is indicative of heart failure Bones may show rickets or fractures of the ribs
Skin test for tuberculosis	Often negative in children with tuberculosis or those previously vaccinated with BCG vaccine
Tests that are of little or no value	
Serum proteins	Not useful in management, but may guide prognosis
Test for HIV	Should not be done routinely; if done, should be accompanied by counseling of the child's parents and result should be confidential
Electrolytes	Rarely helpful and may lead to inappropriate therapy

Source: WHO 1999 (49).

TABLE 54.23 Potential mimickers of pediatric dehydration and starvation/malnutrition

Potential mimickers of pediatric dehydration	Potential mimickers of pediatric starvation/malnutrition
• Diabetes mellitus • Diabetes insipidus • Chromosomal and genetic disorders/mental retardation • Neuromuscular incoordination • Metabolic disorders • Cystic fibrosis • Viral gastroenteritis • Congenital adrenal hyperplasia	– Oromotor abnormalities – Cleft palate – Pyloric stenosis – Celiac disease, short gut syndrome – Intestinal malabsorption, enzyme deficiencies – Cystic fibrosis – Glycogen storage diseases – Carcinoma, malignancy – Congenital heart disease – Cerebral palsy – Chromosomal and genetic diseases
	– Congenital heart diseases – Neurologic diseases – Immunodeficiencies – Side effects of therapies and prescribed medications – Chronic exposure to toxins and drugs – Rare metabolic diseases – Food allergy

Modified from Collins KA 2010 (26).

TABLE 54.24 Failure to thrive

Unintentional
• Breastfeeding difficulties
• Errors in formula preparation
• Poor diet selection
• Improper feeding technique
Organic diseases
• Cystic fibrosis
• Cerebral palsy
• HIV infection/AIDS
• Inborn errors of metabolism
• Celiac disease
• Renal disease
• Lead poisoning
• Major cardiac disease
Child neglect

Source: According to Block and Krebs, Pediatrics 2005:116;1234 (8).

failure to thrive may be seen in cases of inadequate nutrition, prolonged breastfeeding without adequate supplementation, overdilution of formulas, milk-free diets low in protein, homemade formulas with inappropriate composition, and cult diets.

CLASSIFICATION OF PEM

The anthropometrical data of starved persons and organ weights are routinely compared with those of a reference population. These data are the essential basis for the diagnosis of starvation. However, use of the reference values or percentile charts alone does not permit grading of the degree or stage of malnutrition.

Several classification systems have been established to estimate PEM in developing countries over the last few decades. Especially for forensic pathologists, these classifications are superior to percentile charts because anthropometrical data also allow an estimate of the degree of malnutrition. These gradings of PEM have been successfully applied to affected individuals in developing countries, but they may also be used to classify infantile malnutrition in cases of starvation due to deliberate withholding of food.

Attaining full-body measurements and organ weights is essential to appropriately relate the total body size and proportions to reference values. The body weight should not only be related to the expected weight for the respective age group. Classification systems developed for chronic PEM in developing countries should also be used because undernutrition is not always acute; it may be chronic (Table 54.25). Such classification systems may be especially helpful in distinguishing acute from chronic malnutrition. Simpler classifications such as the Wellcome classification or the Gomez classification of PEM use the expected weight for the respective age group as the standard (Tables 54.25– 54.27).

However, smaller infants will be lighter, and chronic and acute undernutrition cannot be distinguished from each other with these classification systems. Furthermore, infants who are tall for their age and have a reduced body weight would be classified as normal; accordingly, a chronic state of malnutrition cannot be recognized in such infants. Even with these issues, these classifications are already superior to reliance on percentile charts with respect to grading the degree of malnutrition.

The Waterlow classification of PEM takes into account not only the weight, but also the height and the expected weight for the height (Tables 54.25 and 54.27). Using this classification system, it becomes evident that malnourished infants are not only light for their age (loss of body weight of 50% of the standard value in the same age group), but also have impaired growth secondary to chronic malnutrition.

The data of 18 starved infants (the authors' cases and cases from the literature) whose state of nutrition was estimated using the Waterlow classification are presented in Table 54.28. The calculations shown in the table were based on measurements and weights determined at autopsy. In these cases, the actual body weight in relation to the expected body weight for the actual height indicated severe life-threatening malnutrition according to the Waterlow classification. Nearly all infants were far below the critical values for severe malnutrition presented in the literature. In all cases shown in Table 54.28, the actual weight in terms of the percent of the ideal weight for height is near or below 70 percent. Cut-off values for fatal starvation have not yet been described in the literature; on the one hand, only a few case reports on starvation using the Waterlow classification have been published, while on the other hand, the actual weight at time of death depends on various factors such as dehydration, infection and other conditions. Because most cases show a weight quotient of <70 percent, this may indicate the validity of grading starvation severity using the Waterlow classification. Four of the infants aged >1 year were stunted (height of <90 percent of normal height) for their respective age group, whereas most infants aged <1 year had a quotient of >90 percent. One may speculate that in older infants, undernutrition lasts longer (weight remains constant as a result of stunting),

TABLE 54.25 Classifications of PEM

WELLCOME CLASSIFICATION		
Body weight in relation to age	Without edema	With edema
60–80% <60%	Malnourishment Marasmic	Kwashiorkor Marasmic
GOMEZ CLASSIFICATION		
Body weight in relation to age (% of reference value)		
90–110	Normal	
75–89	Grade I: malnourishment (mild)	
60–74	Grade II: malnourishment (moderate)	
<60	Grade III: malnourishment (severe)	
WATERLOW CLASSIFICATION		
	Height (body height for age in %)	Body weight – height relation (weight related to height in %)
Normal	>95.0%	>90.0
Mild	87.5–95.0	80.0%–90.0
Moderate	80.0–87.5	70.0–8.00
Severe	<80.0	<70.0

TABLE 54.26 Simplified classification of PEM

	Body weight as % of standard*	**Edema**	**Deficit in weight for actual height**
Underweight child	80–60	0	Minimal
Nutritional dwarfing	<60	0	Minimal
Marasmus	<60	0	++
Kwashiorkor	80–60	+	++
Marasmic Kwashiorkor	<60	+	++

* Standard taken as 50th percentile of Harvard values (modified according to WHO, 1971)

TABLE 54.27 Grading of PEM

Stunting (chronic malnutrition)				
Grade	**0**	**1**	**2**	**3**
Actual height in % of normal height of respective age group	>95.0	95.0–87.5	87.5–80.0	<80.0
Wasting (acute malnutrition)				
Grade	**0**	**1**	**2**	**3**
Actual weight in % of normal weight for height	>80.0	90.0–80.0	80.0–70.0	>70.0

Information is based on the Waterlow classification. Using this TABLE, grading of both chronic malnutrition (stunting) and acute malnutrition (wasting) can be achieved.

TABLE 54.28 Data of 18 infants who died of starvation with estimation of a state of nutrition according to the Waterlow classification (application of the Waterlow classification)

Waterlow classification (grade)	Age	Sex	Actual height in cm	Normal height for respective age in cm	Actual height in % of normal height for resp. age	Actual weight in g	Normal weight in g (50% percentile for age)	Actual weight in % of normal weight	Ideal weight for height in g	Weight in % of ideal weight for height
Case 1	7 weeks	M	53 cm	58 cm	91.4	2010 g	4540 g	44	3900	51.5
Case 2	3 months	F	55 cm	59 cm	93,2	2570 g	5600 g	54.8	4500	57.1
Case 3	4 months	M	61 cm	59 cm	+ 3.4	4060 g	7000 g	58	6250	65
Case 4	5 months	M	61 cm	66 cm	92	4020Vg	7300 g	55	5800	69.3
Case 5	6.5 months	F	56 cm	68 cm	69.5	3400 g	7500 g	45	4800	70.8
Case 6	7 months	M	58 cm	70 cm	82.8	3520 g	7700 g	45	5000	70.4
Case 7	7 months	F	59 cm	68 cm	86.8	2720Vg	7700 g	35	5600	48.6
Case 8	8.5 months	F	53 cm	70 cm	75.7	2500Vg	8300 g	30	3900	64.1
Case 9	14 months	F	68 cm	76 cm	89.5	4740 g	10 300 g	46	8000	59.25
Case 10	2.4 years	F	86 cm	88 cm	97.7	6800 g	12 700 g	53.5	12 300	55.3
Cases 11 & 12 (twins)	2.5 years	M	79 cm	92.3 cm	85.6	6510 g	13 600 g	47.9	10 700	60.8
Case 12	2.5 years	M	79.5 cm	92.3 cm	86.1	6200 g	13 600 g	45.6	10 750	57.9
Case 13	2.5 years	M	78 cm	92.3 cm	84.5	5450 g	13 600 g	40.1	10 900	50
Case 14	9 years	M	118 cm	129 cm	91.5	21 300 g	31 000 g	68.7	28 100	75.8
Case 15	5 years	W	95 cm	112 cm	84.82	7375 g	18 700 g	39.44	13 900	53
Case 16	1.3 years	W	76Vcm	77 cm	98.7	5700 g	11 200Vg	50.89	9300	61.3
Case 17	7 years	W	105 cm	113 cm	92.9	9600 g	24 000Vg	40	20 110	47.74
Case 18	4 years	W	92.5 m	99 cm	93.4	14 500 g	16 600 g	77.5	15 190	95.46

whereas in younger infants, undernutrition causes death more rapidly without the possibility of compensation of body weight as a result of stunting.

MALNUTRITION IN ADOLESCENTS AND ADULTS

Severe malnutrition in adolescents and adults occurs in famine, situations of dependency (e.g. dependent elders), those with mental diseases (anorexia nervosa), and prisoners (hunger strikes) (Figure 54.6a—d). Malnutrition in adolescents and adults is often associated with other illnesses such as chronic infections, intestinal malabsorption, alcohol and drug dependence, liver disease, endocrine and autoimmune diseases, cancer and AIDS (WHO 1999) (49). In adults aged >18 years, malnutrition is classified using the BMI as an indicator. The BMI is defined as the body weight (in kg) divided by the square of the height (in m) (Table 54.29).

For adolescents (10–18 years of age), a WHO expert committee has recommended BMI-for-age as the indicator of thinness with a cut-off value of the <5th percentile. In such cases, or when nutritional edema exists, malnutrition should be diagnosed. For adolescents exhibiting stunting or a low height-for-age, the cut-off value is the <3rd percentile or below −2 SD of the median National Center for Health Statistics/WHO reference values (WHO 1999) (49).

Comparison of different criteria of defining acute malnutrition

Anthropometric variables such as weight, height and length are used to define an individual's nutritional status. Many classification systems have been developed worldwide, and cut-off points are used to define and classify malnutrition (mild, moderate, severe). These classification systems were originally established to describe syndromes of PEM in children in developing countries (Table 54.30a&b).

TABLE 54.29 Classification of malnutrition in adults by BMI*

BMI (kg/m²)	Nutritional status
≥18.50	Normal
17.00–18.49	Mild malnutrition
16.00–16.99	Moderate malnutrition
<16.00	Severe malnutrition

* WHO 1999 (49).

TABLE 54.30A Different criteria for defining acute malnutrition

Anthropometric criteria of failure to thrive
• Weight <75% of median weight for chronologic age (Gomez criterion)
• Weight <80% of median weight for length (Waterlow criterion)
• BMI for chronologic age <5th centile
• Weight for chronologic <5th centile
• Length for chronologic age <5th centile
• Weight deceleration crossing more than two major centile lines (centile lines used: 5, 10, 25, 50, 75, 90, and 95 from birth until weight within the given age group)
• Conditional weight gain = lowest 5% adjusted for regression toward the mean from birth until weight within the given age group

Source: Olsen et al., *Arch Dis Child* 2007; **92:** 109–14 [37].

TABLE 54.30B Criteria for defining acute malnutrition

Reference	Mild	Moderate	Severe
Gomez et al.	75%–90% standard weight	60%–74% standard weight	<60% standard weight
Tanner et al.		<5th percentile WFH	
Waterlow	80%–90% WFH	70%–80% WFH	<70% WFH
WHO		−3 < WFH SD score < −2	WFH SD score < −3

WFH: weight for height.
Source: Madea B. Starvation, dehydration, malnutrition and fatal neglect. In: *Handbook of Paediatric Forensic Pathology* [26].

Different anthropometric methods of classifying failure to thrive have been recommended to identify children at risk and determine the severity of malnutrition. Comparison of these anthropometric indices revealed that the methods vary widely in categorizing children, with some identified as moderately or severely failing to thrive using one method and normal or mild using another method.

The authors Olsen et al. conclude that there is no simple anthropometric measure that highlights the degree of risk for a child (37). Weight alone is the simplest and still most reasonable marker of failure to thrive. Olsen et al. compared seven criteria of failure to thrive (37). The concurrence among the criteria was generally poor, with more children identified by only one criterion. The positive predictive values of different criteria ranged from 1 to 58 percent. Altogether, no single measurement on its own seems to be adequate for identifying nutritional growth delay. We have quite good experiences with the Waterlow classification in cases of fatal starvation (see above).

Screening tool for the assessment of malnutrition in pediatrics

The Screening Tool for the Assessment of Malnutrition in Pediatrics (STAMP) has been validated in the UK as a nutritional screening tool for hospitalized children aged 2 to 16 years. The STAMP is a simple five-step tool developed by a team from Royal Manchester Children's Hospital and the University of Ulster. The STAMP provides a simple way of determining whether a child is at risk of malnutrition and provides guidance in developing a care plan according to the child's overall risk of malnutrition. The STAMP comprises five simple steps as shown in Table 54.31, with a breakdown of Step 1 shown in Table 54.32.

TABLE 54.31 STAMP screening form

Step 1 – Diagnosis				
Does the child have a diagnosis with any nutritional implications?	Score	1st screening	2nd screening	3rd screening
Definite nutritional implications	3			
Possible nutritional implications	2			
No nutritional implications	0			
Step 2 – Nutritional intake				
What is the child's nutritional intake?	Score	1st screening	2nd screening	3rd screening
No nutritional intake	3			
Recently decreased or poor nutritional intake	2			
No change in eating patterns and good nutritional intake	0			
3.75 pt				
Use a growth chart or the centile quick reference tables to determine the child's measurements	Score	1st screening wt: ht:	2nd screening wt: ht:	3rd screening wt: ht:
>3 centile spaces or ≥3 columns apart (or weight <2nd centile)	3			
>2 centile spaces or 2 columns apart	1			
0 to 1 centile spaces/columns apart	0			
Step 4 – Overall risk of malnutrition				
Add up the scores from the boxes in steps 1 to 3 to calculate the overall risk of malnutrition	Score	1st screening	2nd screening	3rd screening
High risk	≥4			
Medium risk	2–3			
Low risk	0–1			
Step 5 – Care plan				
What is the child's overall risk of malnutrition, as calculated in step 4?	Use management guidelines and/or local nutrition policies to develop a care plan for the child			
High risk	• Take action • Refer the child to a dietitian, nutritional support team, or consultant • Monitor as per care plan			
Medium risk	• Monitor the child's nutritional intake for 3 days • Repeat the STAMP screening after 3 days • Amend care plan as required			
Low risk	• Continue routine clinical care • Repeat the STAMP screening weekly while the child is an in-patient • Amend care plan as required			

Further information about the STAMP can be found at www.stampscreeningtool.org.

DURATION OF STARVATION

Published data concerning the duration of starvation until death refer mainly to adults, individuals who have undergone acute withdrawal of food and liquid until death, or infants with inborn malformations of the upper gastrointestinal tract. Based on these data, it seems possible to survive without food and drink for 8 to 21 days. If a person is only deprived of food, the survival time may even increase to about 2 months, although this is influenced by many other factors. According to observations of 10 young, previously healthy hunger strikers (mean age, 25.6 ± 0.7 years), the survival period until death varied from 53 to 73 days (mean, 61.0 ± 2.5 days) [2–4]. Notably, these data are

TABLE 54.32 Diagnosis table to be used to assign a score for step 1 of STAMP

Definite nutritional implications	Possible nutritional implications	No nutritional implications
• Bowel failure, intractable diarrhea	• Behavioral eating problems	• Day case surgery
• Burns and major trauma	• Cardiology	• Investigations
• Crohn's disease	• Cerebral palsy	
• Cystic fibrosis	• Cleft lip and palate	
• Dysphagia	• Celiac disease	
• Liver disease	• Diabetes	
• Major surgery	• Gastro-oesophageal reflux	
• Multiple food allergies/intolerances	• Minor surgery	
• Oncology on active treatment	• Neuromuscular conditions	
• Renal disease/failure	• Psychiatric disorders	
• Inborn errors of metabolism	• Respiratory syncytial virus	
	• Single food allergy/intolerance	

Source: STAMP, www.stampscreeningtool.org.

of limited value in cases of chronic starvation, especially in infants with premature birth and failure to thrive. A previous study showed that in infants with inborn malformations of the upper gastrointestinal tract (e.g. atresia of the esophagus), survival ranged from 3 to 4 days; in those with atresia of the small bowel or duodenum, survival generally ranged from 3 to 5 days, with a maximum of 10 days.

Physical condition prior to death

The medical records of affected infants must be reviewed to collect evidence of the duration of malnutrition, including body weight and height (*see* Table 54.9). A medical expert witness may be asked whether undernutrition of the respective child was recognizable (e.g. by caretakers, such as the parents or healthcare workers) during a certain time prior to death (usually days to weeks); if so, the caretakers would have been obliged to request medical advice and care. In such cases, it is recommended to extrapolate the time interval prior to death by considering that complete withholding of food results in a total body weight loss of about 0.7 to 1.0 percent per day. Using the Waterlow classification, the extrapolated body weight in relation to the ideal weight for height gives an impression of the severity of malnutrition. When withholding of food was not absolute in cases of chronic starvation, it can be assumed that the real body weight for the extrapolated time was lower.

Calculations have been recommended to determine the duration of starvation from the estimated caloric deficit. However, these calculations are based on several assumptions that may not be relevant to the case in question.

Severe malnutrition in adults occurs in famine, situations of neglect and dependency (e.g. dependent elders), those with mental diseases (anorexia nervosa), and prisoners (hunger strikes). Malnutrition in the elderly is often associated with other illnesses such as chronic infections, intestinal malabsorption, alcohol and drug dependence, liver disease, endocrine and autoimmune diseases, cancer and AIDS (WHO) (48). In adults aged 19 years of age and older, malnutrition is classified using the BMI (*see* Table 54.29).

Sarcopenia

"The sixth age shifts
Into the lean and slipper'd pantaloons
With spectacles on nose and pouch on side,
His youthful hose well sav'd, a world to wide
For his shrunk shank"

Shakespeare, *As You Like It*. Act II, Scene VII, lines 157–161

"...the shoulders, clavicles, chest and tights melt away. This illness is fatal ..." –

Hippocrates (460–370 BCE)

According to the International Working Group on Sarcopenia, sarcopenia, the age-associated loss of skeletal muscle mass and function, has considerable societal consequences for the development of frailty, disability, and healthcare planning (6,15,20) (Figure 54.11). A group of geriatricians and scientists from academia and industry met in Rome, Italy, on November 18, 2009, to arrive at a consensus definition of sarcopenia. The current consensus definition was approved unanimously by the meeting participants and is as follows: Sarcopenia is defined as the age-associated loss of skeletal muscle mass and function. The causes of sarcopenia are multifactorial and can include disuse, altered endocrine function, chronic diseases, inflammation, insulin resistance, and nutritional deficiencies (Figure 54.12; Table 54.33). Although cachexia may be a component of sarcopenia, the two conditions are not the same. The diagnosis of sarcopenia should be considered in all older patients who present

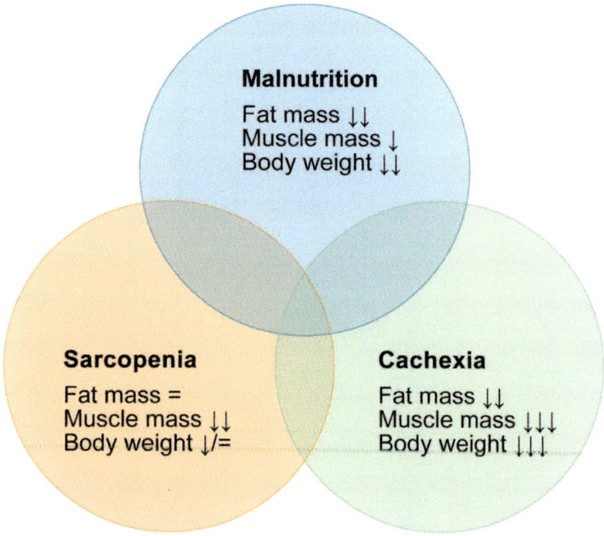

54.11 Overlap of malnutrition, cachexia and sarcopenia and their relevance for body weight and body composition.

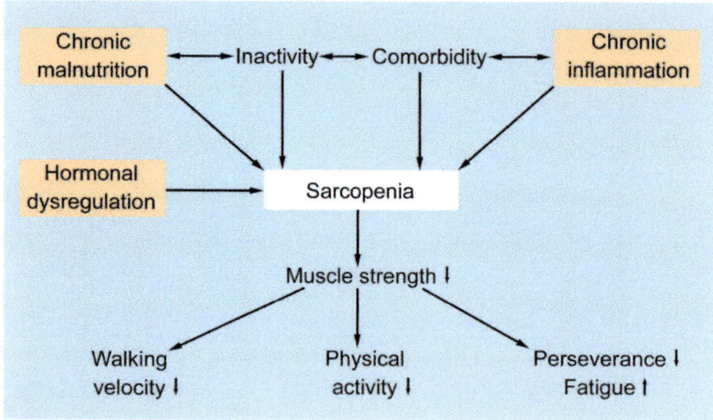

54.12 Causal factors and functional consequences of sarcopenia.

TABLE 54.33 Causes of sarcopenia
Aging
Physical inactivity
Anorexia
Decreased creatine intake
Peripheral vascular disease
Hypogonadism
Cytocine excess
Myostatin excess

Source: Mantovani G. *Cachexia and Wasting: A Modern Approach.* Milan Berlin Heidelberg New York: Springer Verlag Italia; 2006 (35).

TABLE 54.34 Initial patient presentation for evaluation of sarcopenia

- Noted decline in function, strength, "health" status
- Self-reported mobility-related difficulty
- History of recurrent falls
- Recent unintentional weight loss (> 5%)
- Post-hospitalization
- Other chronic conditions (e.g. Type II diabetes, CHF*, COPD**, CKD***, RA****, and cancer)

*CHF = chronic heart failure;
**COPD = chronic obstructive pulmonary disease;
***CKD = chronic kidney disease;
****RA = rheumatoid arthritis

with observed declines in physical function, strength, and/or overall health. Sarcopenia should specifically be considered in patients who are bedridden, cannot independently rise from a chair, or who have a measured gait speed less than 1 m/s^{-1}. Patients who meet these criteria should further undergo body composition assessment using dual energy X-ray absorptiometry with sarcopenia being defined using currently validated definitions. A diagnosis of sarcopenia is consistent with a gait speed of less than 1 $m{\cdot}s^{-1}$ and an objectively measured low muscle mass (e.g. appendicular mass relative to ht^2 that is ≤ 7.23 kg/m^2 in men and ≤ 5.67 kg/m^2 in women). Sarcopenia is a highly prevalent condition in older persons that leads to disability, hospitalization, and death (*see* Chapter 48 – "Elder Abuse").

The initial patient presentation to evaluate sarcopenia is shown in Table 54.34. Sarcopenia should be considered in patients who are bedridden, non-ambulatory, or who cannot rise from a chair unassisted (Table 54.35). In the consensus conference, there was an agreement that sarcopenia should be effectively targeted by assessing physical functioning in at-risk-patients. A comparison

TABLE 54.35 Targeting sarcopenia

- Assess patient for reduced physical functioning (or weakness)
- Consider sarcopenia in patients who are non-ambulatory or who cannot rise from a chair unassisted
- Assess habitual gait speed over a 4-meter course
- Patients with a habitual gait speed < 1.0 m/sec. should be considered for quantitative measurement of body composition by DXA

Source: Fielding RA, Vellas B, Evans WJ, et al. (15).

TABLE 54.36 Comparison of the major features of starvation, sarcopenia, cachexia and dehydration

	Starvation (Anorexia of aging)	Sarcopenia	Cachexia	Dehydration
Weight loss	++	+	+++	++
Loss of lean mass	+	+	+++	0
Loss of fat mass	++	0	++	0
Cytokine excess	+/-	+	+++	0
Albumin	-	0	--	0
Anaemia	+/-	0	++	0
Hypogonadism	+/-	+	++	0

Source: Mantovani G. *Cachexia and Wasting: A Modern Approach*. Milan Berlin Heidelberg New York: Springer Verlag Italia; 2006.

of the major features of starvation, sarcopenia, cachexia and dehydration is given in Table 54.36.

Immediate cause of death

The immediate cause of death in cases of starvation may be infectious complications, ventricular tachyarrhythmia, or hypoglycemic coma (41). Furthermore, starvation may be accompanied by dehydration as a cause of death (32).

MANIFESTATIONS OF CHILD NEGLECT

Physical neglect is defined as deprivation of necessary care, including sufficient nourishment and hydration. Manifestations of child neglect are as follows:

- Nonadherence (noncompliance) with healthcare recommendations
- Delay or failure to obtain healthcare
- Refusal of medical treatment
- Failure to thrive, food insecurity, hunger
- Drug exposure in newborns and older children
- Inadequate protection from environmental hazards
- Inadequate nurturance and affection
- Inadequate supervision, abandonment
- Inadequate hygiene
- Inadequate clothing
- Educational neglect.

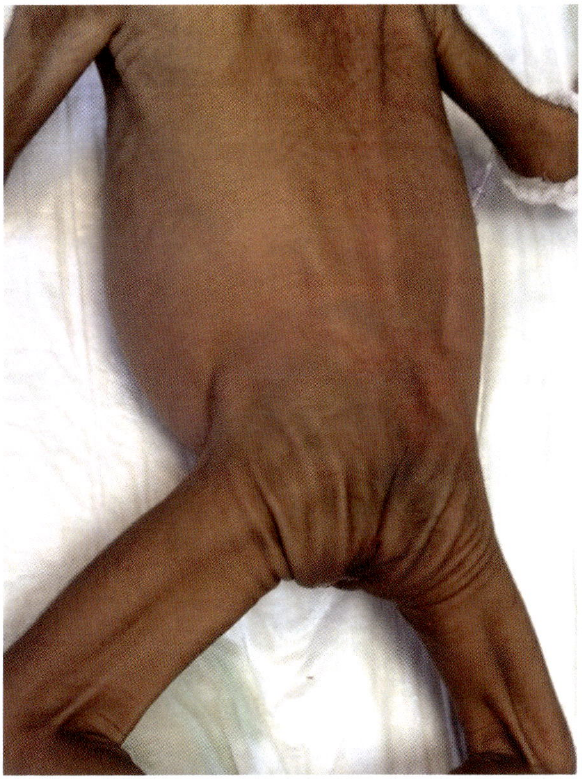

54.13 Cachexic 7-month-old female at hospitalization.

A case of child neglect with insufficient nourishment is shown in Figure 54.13 and Table 54.37.

Failure to thrive is often observed in neglected children. However, inadequate nutrition not only causes poor weight gain but also delayed development, abnormal behavior and disturbed social interactions.

TABLE 54.37 Comparison of body weight and height of reference values in a 7-month-old female infant with severe undernutrition

	Body weight	Body length	Head circumference
Birth	3.000 g (between 15th and 50th percentile)	49 cm (50th percentile)	34 cm (50th percentile)
Expected weight (50th percentile) for females at birth	ca. 3.200 g	49 cm	34 cm
Body weight in % of expected weight of females at birth	93.38%	100%	100%
Age of 2 months	3.540 g (<3rd percentile)	-	-
Expected weight for 2-month-old female (50th percentile)	5.200 g	-	-
Body weight in % of expected weight for 7-month-old female (50th percentile)	68.1%	-	-
Body weight at hospitalization at the age of 7 months	3.470 g (<3rd percentile)	58.5 cm (<3rd percentile)	38 cm (<3rd percentile)
Expected weight for 7-month-old female (50th percentile)	7.600 g	ca. 67.5 cm	42.8 cm
Body weight in % of expected weight for 7-month-old female (50th percentile)	45.7%	83.7%	88.8%
Ideal weight for height at the time of hospitalization	5.500 g	58.5 cm	-
Ideal weight for height in % at the time of hospitalization	63.1%	-	-

Risk factors for failure to thrive are as follows:

- Parental depression, stress, marital strife and divorce
- Parental history of abuse as a child
- Mental retardation and psychological abnormalities in the parent(s)
- Young and single mothers without social support
- Domestic violence
- Alcohol or other substance abuse
- Previous child abuse in the family
- Social isolation and/or poverty
- Parents with inadequate adaptive and social skills
- Parents who are overly focused on career and/or activities away from home
- Failure to adhere to medical regimens
- Lack of knowledge of normal growth and development
- Infants with low birth weight or prolonged hospitalization

Dehydration

A man weighing 70 kg consists of 60 percent water (42 L). Most of the water is found in the intracellular compartment (40% related to body weight), while interstitial and the intravascular water comprise 16 percent and 4 percent, respectively. Both body water and electrolyte metabolism are regulated within narrow ranges to maintain homeostasis. Loss of 15 percent of body water after acute dehydration and loss of >20 percent after longer-lasting dehydration is fatal. Although the extracellular space constitutes only one-third of the total body water, single water spaces are regulated mainly by the extracellular fluid compartment. Newborns and infants are extremely susceptible to dehydration; daily fluid intake and excretion accounts for 10 to 20 percent of body weight. Conversely, in adults, daily fluid intake and excretion accounts for just 3 to 4 percent of body weight. For a 7-kg infant, fluid exchange accounts for about 50 percent of the extracellular space, while in adults, this accounts for only about 14 percent. This means that in infants, half of the extracellular volume must be replaced daily, but only about 14 percent must be replaced in adults. The regulation of water–electrolyte metabolism may be reversibly or irreversibly disturbed in the following ways:

- Ambient factors (hemorrhage, thirst, hot environment)
- Diseases of the regulating organs (enteritis, renal insufficiency, burns, respiratory insufficiency)
- Diseases regulating endocrine organs (diabetes insipidus, Addison's disease)

However, external factors (e.g. ambient factors) are of utmost forensic importance, as in cases of hypertonic dehydration due to liquid deprivation, force-feeding of

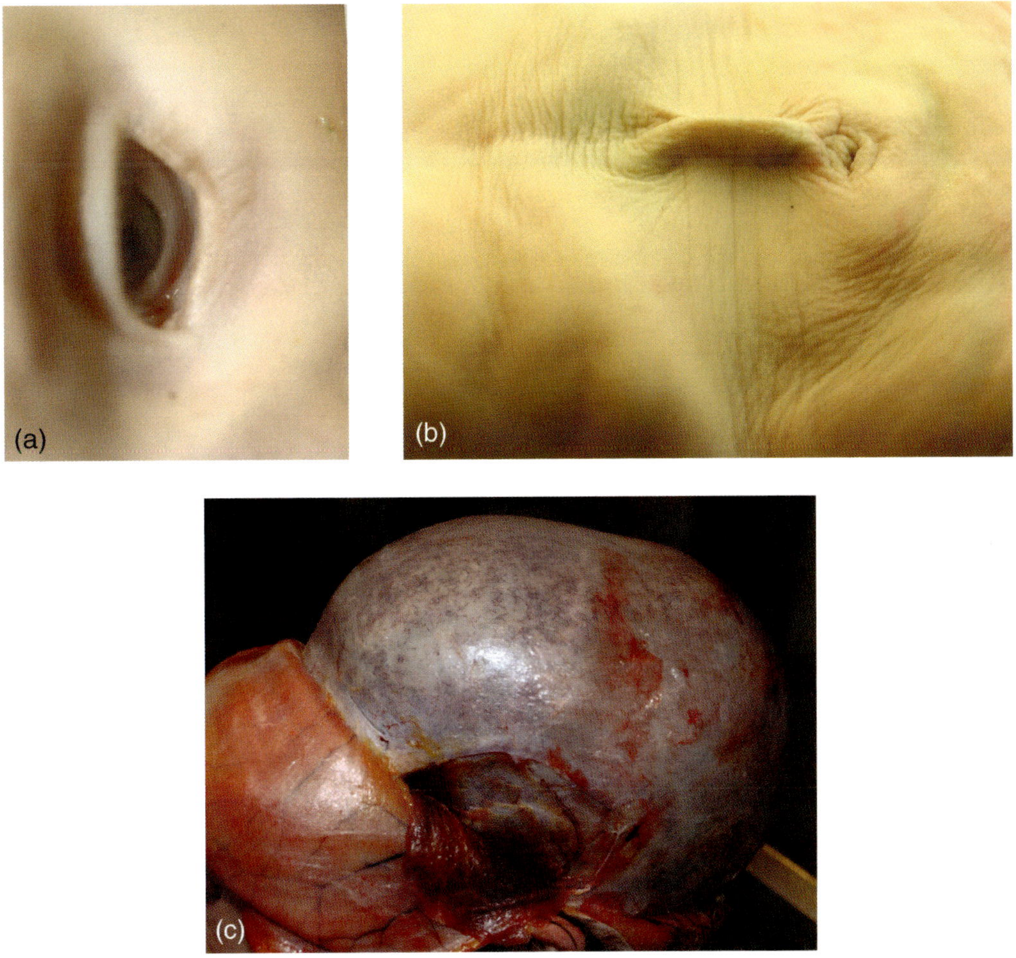

54.14 a–c Typical autopsy findings in hypertonic dehydration (a) Sunken eyes, (b) tinting of skin and (c) dry galea.

salt, or water intoxication. The classic autopsy findings that substantiate the diagnosis of hypertonic dehydration are as follows:

- Poor skin turgor
- Tinting of the skin
- Sunken eyes
- Dry galea and dry organ surfaces (Figure 54.14a–c).

Over the course of a lifetime, loss of body water results in elevation of sodium, chloride, and urea nitrogen levels in the blood; therefore, it can be easily diagnosed. A grading of dehydration based on clinical findings can be found in Table 54.38.

Dehydration pattern in vitreous humor

Because of post-mortem loss of selective membrane permeability, a diagnosis of serum electrolytes at the moment of death is not possible post mortem. Serum electrolyte concentrations at the moment of death are very well reflected in vitreous humor, and the characteristic dehydration pattern of elevated sodium, chloride and urea nitrogen can be diagnosed post mortem (Table 54.39) (10,11,32). In all cases of suspected dehydration, the vitreous humor should be analyzed to determine the cause of death. However, conclusions must be drawn carefully and based on the complete morphological and toxicological status.

CONCLUSION

Starvation may be of medicolegal importance if death results from the deliberate withholding of food.

- In infants, classifications to estimate protein-energy malnutrition (PEM) like the Waterlow classification could be used.
- Using such classification systems, grading of stunting and wasting can be achieved.
- Symptoms of starvation will be addressed as well as the forensic investigation of such cases.
- Furthermore, dehydration and the grading of dehydration based on clinical findings will be addressed.

TABLE 54.38 Grading of dehydration based on clinical findings

Degree of dehydration			
Clinical symptoms	Minimal	Mild to moderate	Severe
Turgor	Normal/slightly reduced	Reduced	Tenting of skin
Mucous membrane	Dry	Rough	Brittle
Behavior	Thirst, well, alert	Tachycardia, decreased blood pressure, sunken eyes, sunken fontanelles	Shock, rapid thready pulse, cyanosis, cold extremities, deep breathing, lethargy, unconscious, seizures
Urine production	Normal	Decreased	Missing
Loss of body weight			
Infant	<5%	5%–10%	>10%
Child	<3%	3%–6%	>6%
Expected fluid deficit (mL/kg body weight)			
Infant	<50	50–100	>100
Child	<30	30–60	>60

TABLE 54.39 Vitreous humor values

Antemortem abnormality	**Flame Photometry or SMA 6/60**	**Ektachem 400**	**Beckmann Astra**
Dehydration			
Sodium (mmol/L)	>155	>165	>155
Chloride (mmol/L)	>135	>125	>140
Urea nitrogen (mg/dL)	40–100	40–100	40–100
Low-salt condition			
Sodium (mmol/L)	<130	<135	<130
Chloride (mmol/L)	<105	<95	<110
Potassium (mmol/L)	<15	<15	<15

REFERENCES AND FURTHER READING

1. Adelsberger L. Medical observations in Auschwitz concentration camp. *Lancet* 1946; 1(6392): 317–319.
2. Adelson L. Homicide by starvation. The nutritional variant of the battered child. *JAMA* 1963; **186:** 458–60.
3. Allison SP. Starvation. In: Payne-James JJ, Byard RW (eds.) *Encyclopedia of Forensic and Legal Medicine*, Vol. 4, 1st ed. Amsterdam: Elsevier; 2005, pp. 130–6.
4. Allison SP, Madea B. Starvation. In: Payne-James J, Byard R (eds.) *Encyclopedia of Forensic and Legal Medicine*, Vol. 4, 2nd ed. Amsterdam, Boston: Elsevier; 2016, pp. 340–9.
5. Altun G, Akansu B, Altun BU, et al. Deaths due to hunger strike: Post-mortem findings. *Forensic Sci Int* 2004; **145:** 35–38.
6. Bauer JM, Wirth R, Volkert D, et al. Malnutrition, sarcopenia and cachexia in the elderly: From pathophysiology to treatment: Conclusions of an international meeting of experts, sponsored by the BANSS Foundation. *Dtsch Med Wochenschr* 2008; **133:** 305–10.
7. Beyon J. Hunger strike in Turkish prisons. *Lancet* 1996; **348:** 737.
8. Block RW, Krebs NF. American Academy of Pediatrics Committee on Child Abuse and Neglect & American Academy of Pediatrics Committee on Nutrition. Failure to thrive as a manifestation of child neglect. *Pediatrics* 2005; **116:** 1234–7.
9. Byard RG. *Sudden Death in the Young*. 3rd ed. Cambridge: Cambridge University Press.
10. Coe JI. Postmortem chemistries on human vitreous humor. *Am J Clin Pathol* 1969; **51:** 741–750.
11. Coe JI. Some further thoughts and observations on postmortem chemistries. *Forensic Sci Gazette* 1973; **4:** 2–5.
12. Collins KA. Intentional Starvation/Malnutrition and Dehydration in Children. In: Griest K (ed). *Pediatric Homicide: Medical Investigation*. Boca Raton, FL: CRC Press; 2010, pp. 169–85.
13. Davis JH, Rao VJ, Valdes-Dapena M. A forensic approach to a starved child. *J Forensic Sci* 1984; **29:** 663–9.
14. Doberentz E, Ortmann J, Horneff G, Madea B. Extreme form der chronischen Unterernährung eines Säuglings in Deutschland. *Rechtsmedizin* 2016; **26:** 308–12.
15. Fielding RA, Vellas B, Evans WJ, et al. Sarcopenia: An undiagnosed condition in older adults. Current consensus definition: prevalence, etiology, and consequences. International working group in sarcopenia. *J Am Med Dir Assoc* 2011; 12: 249–56.
16. Giese W, Hörstebock R. Allgemeine Pathologie des Exogenen Quantitativen Nahrungsmangels. In: Büchner F, Letterer E, Roulet F (eds). *Handbuch der Allgemeinen Pathologie*, Vol. 11, Part I, Berlin: Springer; 1962, pp. 446–591.

17. Gomez F, Galvan RR, Cravioto J, Frenk S. Malnutrition in infancy and childhood with special reference to Kwashiokor. *Adv Pediatr* 1955; **7:** 131–69.
18. Hewitt PL, Coren S, Steel GD. Death from anorexia nervosa: Age span and sex differences. *Aging Ment Health* 2001; **5:** 41–46.
19. Hobbs CJ, Hanks HGJ, Wynne JM. (1999) *Child Abuse and Neglect: A Clinicians Handbook*. 2nd ed. London: Churchill Livingstone; 1999.
20. International Working Group on Sarcopenia. Sarcopenia: An undiagnosed condition in older adults. Current consensus definition: Prevalence, etiology, and consequences. *J Am Med Dir Assoc* 2011; **12(4):** 249–57
21. Joosten KFM, Hulst JM. Prevalence of malnutrition in pediatric hospital patients. *Curr Opin Pediatr* 2008; **20:** 590–6.
22. Keys A. *The Biology of Human Starvation*. 2 Vols. Minneapolis: University of Minnesota Press; 1950.
23. Keys A, Brozek J, Henschel A, et al. *Experimental Starvation in Man*. Minneapolis: University of Minnesota Press; 1945.
24. Koletzko B, Cooper P, Makrides M, et al (eds). (2008) *Pediatric Nutrition in Practice*. Basel: Karger; 2008.
25. Leiter LA, Marliss EB. Survival during fasting may depend on fat as well as protein stores. *JAMA* 1982; **248:** 2306–07.
26. Madea B. Death as a result of Starvation. Diagnostic Criteria. In: Tsokos M (ed). *Forensic Pathology Reviews*. Vol. 2. Totowa, NY: Humana Press; 2005, pp. 3–23
27. Madea B. Starvation, Dehydration, Malnutrition and Fatal Neglect. In: Collins KA, Byard RW, (eds). *Handbook of Paediatric Forensic Pathology*. Berlin, Heidelberg, New York: Springer; 2014, pp. 667–98.
28. Madea B. Starvation. In: Payne-James J, Byard R (ed) *Encyclopedia of Forensic and Legal Medicine* Vol 4. 2nd ed. Amsterdam, Boston: Elsevier 2016, pp. 340–9.
29. Madea B, Michalk DV, Lignitz E. Verhungern infolge Kindesvernachlässigung. *Arch Kriminol* 1994; **194:** 29–38.
30. Madea B, Banaschak S. Remarks on: "percentile charts to determine the duration of child abuse by chronic malnutrition". *Forensic Sci Int* 1999; **105(3):** 191–4.
31. Madea B, Banaschak S. Verhungern. In: Brinkmann B, Madea B (eds). *Handbuch Gerichtliche Medizin* Bd. 1, Berlin Heidelberg New York: Springer; 2004, pp. 905–19.
32. Madea B, Lachenmeier DW. Postmortem diagnosis of hypertonic dehydration. *Forensic Sci Int* 2005; **155:** 1–6.
33. Madea B, Noeker M, Franke I. Child Abuse: Some aspects for neurosurgeons. In: Pickard JD (ed). *Advances and Technical Standards in Neurosurgery*, Vol 36. Vienna, New York: Springer; 2011, pp. 80–135.
34. Madea B, Ortmann J, Doberentz E. Forensic aspects of starvation. *Forensic Sci Med Pathol* 2016; **12:** 276–98.
35. Madea B, Doberentz E. Starvation, Dehydration, Malnutrition and Neglect. In: Byard RW, Collins KA (eds). *Geriatric Forensic Medicine and Pathology*. Cambridge: Cambridge University Press; 2020.
36. Mantovani G, Anker SD, Inui A, et al. *Cachexia and Wasting: A Modern Approach*. Milan, Berlin, Heidelberg, New York: Springer Italia; 2006.
37. Meade JL, Brissie RM. Infanticide by starvation: Calculation of caloric deficit to determine degree of deprivation. *J Forensic Sci* 1985; **30:** 1263–8.
38. Olsen EM, Petersen J, Skovgaard AM, et al. Failure to thrive: The prevalence and concurrence of anthropometric criteria in a general infant population. *Arch Dis Child* 2007; **92:** 109–14.
39. Raynor P, Rudolf CJ. Anthropometric indices of failure to thrive. *Arch Dis Child* 2000; **82:** 364–5.
40. Reece RM, Christian LW. *Child abuse. Medical Diagnosis and Management*. 2nd ed. Washington DC: American Academy of Pediatrics; 2009.
41. Rich LM, Caine MR, Findling JW, Shaker JL. Hypoglycaemic coma in anorexia nervosa. *Arch Intern Med* 1990; **150:** 894–5.
42. Rinaldo P. Postmortem investigations. In: Hoffmann GF, Zschocke J, Nyhan WL (eds). *Inherited Metabolic Diseases*, Berlin, Heidelberg: Springer; 2010, pp. 335–8.
43. Solarino B, Grattagliano I, Catanesi R, Tsokos M. Child starvation and neglect: A report of two fatal cases. *J Forensic Leg Med* 2009; **19:** 171–4.
44. Tanegashima A, Yamamoto H, Yada I, Fukunaga T. Estimation of stress in child neglect from thymic involution. *Forensic Sci Int* 1999; **102:** 173–80.
45. The Great Starvation Experiment 1944–1945. Available from: http://www.madsciencemuseum.com/msm/pl/great_starvation_experiment.
46. Tucker T. *Great Starvation Expermient. Ancel Keys and the Men who Starved for Science*. Minneapolis: University of Minnesota Press; 2007.
47. Waterlow JC. Classification and definition of protein-caloric malnutrition. *Br Med J* 1972; **2:** 566–9.
48. Waterlow JC. Note on the assessment and classification of protein-energy malnutrition in children. *Lancet* 1973; **302:** 87–89.
49. WHO *Management of Severe Malnutrition. A Manual for Physicians and Other Senior Health Workers*. Geneva: WHO; 1999.
50. Madea B, Doberentz E. (2022) Starvation and Neglect. In: *Handbook of Forensic Medicine*. 2nd ed. Chichester: Wiley; 2022, pp. 669–71.
51. Win AZ, Ceresa C, Arnold K, et al. High prevalance of malnutrition among elderly veterans in home based primary care. *J Nutr Health Aging* 2017; 21(6): 610–13.

CHAPTER

55

Drug Deaths

Olaf H. Drummer

INTRODUCTION

The widespread availability of drugs over the last decades has led to substantial increases in the numbers of deaths attributed to use of these substances. For example, in England and Wales there were 4400 drug poisoning deaths recorded in 2019 which is about 7.3 fatalities per 100 000 population (1). In Australia, the prevalence for the same year was similar with 1740 drug deaths (2).

The term "drug" refers to chemical substances legally prescribed by medical practitioners (and other suitably certified individuals), those available over-the-counter, as well as the huge number of drugs available from other (largely illegal) sources that include the Internet and street dealers. In many situations, drugs obtained legally can also be misused intentionally.

For many years, there were relatively few illicit drugs, comprising largely of heroin (diacetylmorphine), cocaine, some amphetamines, cannabis and a few others (ketamine, LSD, etc.). Over the last two decades, a large number of drugs termed novel, or new psychoactive substances (NPS) have entered the world drug markets. NPS include examples of drugs that mimic the actions of amphetamines (such as the cathinones), opioids, cannabis (e.g. synthetic cannabinoids) as well as alternate benzodiazepines. Many also show potent hallucinogenic activity.

While the toxicology and clinical outcomes of use of established illicit drugs is well known, that information is lacking for most of the NPS, other than their predicted likely effects based on their pharmacological class and occasional information from case reports of documented poisonings. The lack of medical and pharmacokinetic information on these newer drugs increases the complexity of interpretation in a case and may even mean a contribution from these drugs is uncertain.

In an acute fatal poisoning, the most toxic drugs are those that adversely affect the ability to breathe and the function of the heart. Drugs that affect breathing are most commonly the opioids and other central nervous system (CNS) depressant drugs, while drugs that can cause serious heart malfunction include the strong stimulants, although a number of medicinal drugs can cause arrythmias, among other changes, if used to excess.

For an effective toxicological investigation, the laboratory must be able to detect any (and all) relevant substance(s). Unless the laboratory has a well-developed methodology using sophisticated non-targeted mass spectral techniques that include high resolution mass spectrometry to identify true unknowns, these substances may be missed, particularly if they are only present in a community transiently and not on the local list of targeted screened drugs.

This chapter outlines the basis for determining a drug death and the factors that need to be considered in establishing a possible drug-caused death.

WHAT IS A DRUG DEATH?

A drug death can only be determined following an appropriate investigation. This investigation needs to include as full an account as possible of the circumstances of the death such as the scene of death and the events that led up to the death, including any relevant medical and personal history from medical, family or other witnesses. In particular, information on any medication and other drugs the decedent was known to be taking to help identify any drug-related contributions and also to ensure the toxicology laboratory includes these drugs (of relevance) in the analyses.

Ideally, this investigation would also include an autopsy to exclude other possible causes or contributors to the death. In some cases, particularly to accommodate wishes of the next-of-kin who may request a non-invasive approach, a combination of an external examination and imaging (e.g. CT or MRI), together with a review of their recent medical history and a thorough toxicological investigation, can be sufficient to identify if any comorbidities and non-obvious injuries are present (3,4).

It is essential that toxicology testing be as thorough as possible to include any drugs of relevance as indicated by the medical history and death scene but also to include a large range of other licit and illicit drugs (and other poisons) known to be available in the community. A large challenge is the availability of a large number of NPS that total in the hundreds and continue to increase. Nevertheless, without the ability to screen for as many of these NPS known to be present in a region, this will limit any conclusions that can be made in cases where a drug death is suspected, and little if any drugs of relevance have been detected.

DOI: 10.1201/9781003138754-57

For a drug to be considered as cause or contributor to death, it needs to be a drug not only capable of causing death in known amounts (or in the case of new drugs, believed to be capable of producing severe toxicity) but also consistent with the pathology/toxicology findings and the circumstances. This may seem obvious and potentially all substances are capable of causing death at sufficient doses, however, the toxicology and pathology findings need to considered within the known facts and context of the particular case.

Morphine and indeed other opioids are good examples, in that the concentration alone cannot be used to establish fatal toxicity, or not. The investigation would need to establish the likely source of morphine (e.g. prescribed morphine, or from use of heroin), witnesses to the death and/or associates that might know what the individual was doing, possible injection marks, their medical history and outcomes of a forensic medical procedure. The measurement of metabolites and other biomarkers, such as 6-acetylmorphine for heroin users, and analysis of other tissues should also be conducted by the laboratory, in particular, cases to understand the likely route of administration and possible relevance of the toxicology results.

In some situations, a death may occur many hours after administration of a drug that is capable of causing death, yet the concentration (in blood for example) may not be high and even be thought to be more consistent with non-fatal use. On-going elimination of drugs will occur in comatose states. For example, this can occur in deaths from a heroin injection; in which case, the detection of drug (and metabolite) in urine with knowledge of the context of the case and relevant pathology findings is essential.

DRUGS OF MOST INTEREST

The type of drugs that have the potential to cause death is huge; effectively almost all drugs have this capability depending on the dose and circumstance, however, the vast majority of these deaths comprise a relatively small number of poisons. Table 55.1 below shows examples of the most common types of drugs involved in fatal poisonings; however, this list does not contain all examples; this would cover a much larger and almost infinite list. Importantly, it shows that for most pharmacological classes drugs include both legal and illicit examples.

Also, this list does not include the long list of non-drug related poisons such as many of the industrial and agricultural poisons that occasionally feature in fatalities. Fortunately, in many countries, these are well controled and restricted from the general public, however they are much more common in developing countries (5,6). Another common poison seen globally is carbon

TABLE 55.1 Most common examples of drugs capable of causing a fatal poisoning

Pharmacological class	Most common drug examples
Alcohol (ethanol)	Usually from alcoholic drinks
Amphetamines and related stimulants	Methamphetamine, amphetamine (including dex-amphetamine), MDA, MDMA, MDEA, cathinone-based NPS (a-PVP, MDPV, methcathinone, ephylone etc.)
Cannabis (marijuana) and other cannabinoids	THC, CBD, NPS with cannabimimetic agonist activity (JWH-018, 5F-PB22, 5F-ADB, AB-PINACA, AB-FUBINACA etc.)
Cocaine	
Hallucinogens	Tryptamines (AMT, DMT, DiPT), NBOMe series (25C-, 25B-, 25H-, 25I- variants), 2C-series (FLY and dragonfly variants) and amino indanes (APB, MDAI)
Dissociates	Ketamine, methoxetamine, phencyclidine, 3-MeO-PCE etc.
Benzodiazepines and related hypnotics (Z-drugs)	Alprazolam, clonazepam, diazepam, flunitrazepam, lorazepam, nitrazepam, zolpidem, zopiclone and NPS-based benzodiazepines (flualprazolam, flubromazolam, phenazepam etc.)
Opioids	Heroin (diacetylmorphine), morphine, oxycodone, hydromorphone, fentanyl, methadone and NPS-based opioids (acetylfentanyl, furanylfentanyl, carfentanil, and the atypical opioids U-47700, MT-45, isotonitazene etc.)
Antidepressants	Tri-and tetra-cyclics (amitriptyline, doxepin, dothiepin, imipramine etc), serotonin reuptake (and noradrenaline) inhibitors (fluoxetine, citalopram, sertraline, venlafaxine etc.)
Other depressants	GHB

5F-ADB = methyl 2-{[1-(5-fluoropentyl)-1H-indazole-3-carbonyl]amino}-3,3- dimethylbutanoate; AB-FUBINACA = *N*-(1-amino-3-methyl-1-oxobutan-2-yl)-1-(4-fluorobenzyl)-1*H*-indazole-3-carboxamide; AB-PINACA = *N*-(1-amino-3-methyl-1-oxobutan-2-yl)-1-pentyl-1*H*-indazole-3-carboxamide; APB = 2-aminopropyl-benzofuran; AMT = a-methyl- tryptamine, DiPT = di-isopropyl-tryptamine, DMT = Dimethyl- tryptamine; 2C-series = substituted 2,5-dimethoxy-phenethylamines; CBD = cannabidiol; GHB = g-hydroxy-butyrate; 3-MeO-PCE = 3-methoxyeticyclidine; MDMA = 3,4-methylenedioxy-meth(yl)amphetamine; MDA = 3,4-methylenedioxy-amphetamine, MDEA = 3,4-methylenedioxy-ethylamphetamine; MDAI = 5,6-methylenedioxy-2-aminoindane; MDPV = 3,4-methylenedioxypyrovalerone; 5F-PB22 = quinolin-8-yl 1-pe ntyfluoro-1H-indole-3–8-carboxylate; a-PVP = a-pyrrolidinovalerophenone; D^9-THC = tetrahydrocannabinol; NBOMe = N-benzylmethoxy substituted phenethylamines.

monoxide. This originates predominantly both from incomplete combustion of coal and timber and emissions from motor vehicle exhaust and when inhaled will rapidly incapacitate and kill when persons are present in confined spaces (7).

POST-MORTEM ARTEFACTS

Once a person has died, a number of changes occur to the integrity and composition of tissues and fluids (including blood) that result in changes in the concentrations of drug. These changes are progressive and are both temperature and time dependent. Importantly, they are variable and largely unpredictable. Effectively, this means that in every case involving a decedent great care needs to be exercised to interpret quantitative drug findings, let alone other changes that can obscure any co-existing pathology.

In the case of blood, redistributive processes begin soon after death (probably within hours) and involve, among other changes, diffusion of a drug from a neighboring tissue containing a higher concentration to another as the integrity of cell walls is gradually lost. If muscle has a higher concentration than surrounding blood then diffusion can occur into pooled blood thus elevating the concentration. Conversely, the opposite can occur if the blood has a higher concentration than surrounding tissue. This latter phenomenon is very likely in the early phases of drug uptake and distribution when drug concentration in tissues is still rising after a recent dose. Other factors likely to play a role in changes in drug concentration are the various affinities of drugs to tissues and these may change with time.

Peripheral blood, such as that from femoral vessels, is least subject to redistribution after death and should be preferentially collected for analysis, whenever possible. These changes and others are summarized in Table 55.2. However, even peripheral blood may not represent the peri-mortem concentration. Examples of drugs that show the largest changes include many of the antidepressants and antipsychotics as well as THC and hydroxychloroquine to name a few examples (8,9). In contrast, the more hydrophilic drugs such as acetaminophen, morphine and less lipid soluble benzodiazepines (e.g. oxazepam, temazepam) tend to show relatively small changes.

While all drugs should be considered subject to redistributive changes after death, this phenomenon is usually greater for drugs with high lipid solubility and those with much higher tissue concentrations than circulating blood. Assessing changes that occur post mortem are difficult to quantify and often magnify if some time has elapsed from death to sampling. The most common method to assess the magnitude of these changes is to compare a peripheral blood concentration with blood obtained from the heart (ventricles), however, this supposes there has been no change peripherally, which cannot be assumed. Another method is comparing a blood specimen taken before death (in hospital) with one taken post mortem. Since this antemortem specimen is rarely taken just before (or just after) death pharmacokinetic processes occurring in life will operate and will affect the concentration before death has been certified. These changes can be both increases from on-going absorption or decreases due to metabolism and elimination.

While considerable knowledge of this phenomenon has occurred in the published literature, the extent that drugs undergo post-mortem changes is variable and cannot be estimated with any certainty in a particular case. This is further complicated by the dynamic nature of these changes. For example, studies have shown that depending on the time since death drug concentrations can both rise and fall over the days following a death. Examples include THC, anti-psychotics and antidepressants, but is likely to involve many other drugs as well (9–11).

In clinical situations, drug concentrations are usually measured in serum (or plasma) while, in death investigations, blood is usually collected. In most cases, the concentrations of drug are similar in these two specimens, however, for some drugs significant differences occur. For example, THC shows an almost 2-fold higher concentration in plasma compared to blood. Settling of blood during stasis will mean that the haematocrit can vary from one blood collection to another. This will further affect interpretation for drugs subject to significant differences in concentration in red blood cells and serum.

TABLE 55.2 Summary of key factors affecting post-mortem concentrations of drugs

Putrefactive changes	Stasis and changes in hematocrit Loss of tissue integrity (cell lysis) and liquefaction
Biodegradation	Action of anaerobic organisms (e.g. hydrolysis of acyl glucuronides; actions of esterases and nitroreductases, and sulfoxidation) Chemical instability of labile moieties
Incomplete distribution	Incomplete absorption and equilibrium in tissues
Redistributive changes	Diffusion of drug from neighboring tissues including lungs and gastrointestinal system
Changes in binding to macromolecules	Alterations in affinities of drugs to macromolecules and other binding sites with time
Preparation for transport and interment	Use of preservation materials such as embalming agents (alcohol, formaldehyde etc)

Changes in drug concentration are not limited to blood and include other fluids and solid tissues such as liver. Due to the proximity of the mesenteric vessels, the left lobe of the liver is more likely to exhibit elevated drug concentrations than the right lobe.

Putrefaction will produce further changes particularly as tissues degrade and liquify. When this occurs, quantitative results can no longer be interpreted.

While aerobic metabolism effectively stops soon after death, the presence of anaerobic bacteria from the gut can transform some drugs into metabolites. The most common examples are the nitrobenzodiazepines (nitrazepam, flunitrazepam and nimetazepam) which form the corresponding 7-amino-metabolite (12). S-oxidation of sulfur-containing drugs, such as thioridazine, and dothiepin also occurs post mortem forming the corresponding sulfoxide (and possibly sulfone). More common examples are acetylsalicylate (Aspirin), heroin and cocaine that are de-esterified by the ubiquitous esterases, as well as spontaneously due to chemical instability (13). Even labile conjugates, such as acyl glucuronides, can be degraded back to the non-conjugated form.

Vitreous humor and/or urine are useful specimens if the parent drug is sought because these specimens are less affected by bacterial action.

PHARMACOKINETIC CONSIDERATIONS

One of the more important issues in the interpretation of drug concentrations is establishing whether the decedent had developed any tolerance to the drug(s) in question. Repeated use of most drugs leads to the development of tolerance to the effects of the drug resulting in adaptation to adverse events, including toxicity. Opioids are prime examples, in which neuro-adaptation occurs with repeated regular use, such as prescribed therapeutic use of morphine. Acute doses of morphine over 20 mg can be toxic, whereas patients on regular treatment can tolerate doses over 1 gram daily without developing life-threatening toxicity. This is a result of pharmacodynamic changes associated with desensitization (among other factors) of opioid receptors, not because of increasing rate of elimination. Consequently, the higher tissue concentrations of morphine in chronic users does not necessarily mean that the drug has caused toxicity.

While it may not always be evident from the circumstances provided to the pathologist, it is strongly advised, whenever feasible, to seek out the decedent's recent past medical history. Obviously, scene investigations can also establish whether an overdose may have occurred, or not. Audits of any tablets or other types of medication, or containers of medications present at the scene, can assist in establishing the most likely scenario. Analysis of whole stomach contents can also assist in determining if an acute overdose occurred, although this will not always be useful if the death has been delayed.

The route of administration can also be an important consideration, particularly if intravenous (IV) use is a possibility. This is often the case for injecting heroin users, in which a bolus injection into a vein will lead to a surge of drug to target sites and can cause cardiorespiratory collapse, but not if the same dose has been infused slowly or even used by another route. Sudden death at the end of a needle will lead to high blood concentrations, but not in tissues. The higher bioavailability of drugs given IV, as compared to oral administration, is also a key factor in the risk of developing a serious adverse drug reaction. Drugs administered by nasal insufflation will also have high bioavailabilities since the drug bypasses the liver and the first-pass effect.

Drugs administered by smoking, such as cannabis (THC) and methamphetamine, will have high bioavailabilities, however, the yield of drug from the device is usually low due to inadequate volatilization and degradation of drug by heat.

PHARMACOGENOMIC CONSIDERATIONS

Pharmacogenomics in which genetic variations in people can lead to altered responses to drugs, as well as heightened adverse drug reactions, result from pharmacogenetic and/or pharmacodynamic variability.

The greatest number of severe outcomes relate to drugs affecting heart function (arrythmias and QT interval) and blood coagulation, although many other interactions are known (14). Importantly, a number of metabolizing enzymes are sometimes responsible for adverse drug effects. These include the phase 1 cytochrome P450 system (CYP complex) and the phase 2 processes involving glucuronidation and acetylation. Examples of drugs and some herbal preparations that are known to inhibit five key isozymes of the CYP superfamily of metabolizing enzymes are shown in Table 55.3.

TABLE 55.3 Some substances that inhibit CYP450 isozymes

Isozyme	Some key examples
1A2	Cimetidine, ciprofloxacin, fluvoxamine
2C9	Fluconazole, St. John's Wort, valproate
2C19	Fluconazole, fluvoxamine
2D6	Amiodarone, bupropion, chlorpromazine, fluoxetine, paroxetine, perhexiline, quinidine, ritonavir
3A4	Antifungals, clarithromycin, erythromycin, protease inhibitors, grapefruit juice

TABLE 55.4 Serotonin active drugs that cause Serotonin Syndrome particularly in combination with other serotonin-active drugs
Serotonin reuptake inhibitor antidepressants (fluoxetine, sertraline, citalopram, paroxetine)
Serotonin-noradrenaline reuptake inhibitors antidepressants (e.g duloxetine, mirtazapine, venlafaxine)
Older antidepressants (e.g. amitriptyline, nortriptyline, dothiepin)
Some opioids (fentanyls, meperidine, methadone, tramadol)
Monoamine oxidase A inhibitor antidepressant (e.g. moclobemide)
Metoclopramide, ondansetron and other "setrons" anti-emetic drugs
Triptan anti-migraine drugs (e.g. sumatriptan)
MDMA and MDMA-like NPS (butylone, 2C-I, MDPV, mephedrone, methylone, NBOMe etc)
Other drugs: Lithium, methylene blue, valproate, sibutramine, vilazodone

2C-I = 4-iodo-2,5-dimethoxy-phenethylamine; 5HT = serotonin; MDMA = 3,4-methylenedioxy-methylamphetamine; NPS = new psychoactive drugs; MDPV = 3,4-methylenedioxypyrovalerone; NBOMe = N-benzylmethoxy substituted phenethylamines;

Genetic diversity can also play some role in determining concentrations of drugs and their net effects with metabolizing rates for different enzymes ranging from being a normal metabolizer (NM), poor metabolizer (PM) or ultra-rapid metabolizer (UM). Of particular significance is the large percentage of UM for CYP2D6 in persons from Ethiopia (and other parts of the horn of Africa), and the high percentage of PM for N-acetyl transferase in Caucasians and Egyptians. The CYP2D6 isozyme shows one of the more diverse ranges of activities. PMs represent about 5 to 10 percent of the Caucasian population, about 1 percent of Asians but up to about 20 percent in some African populations, particularly those from the horn of Africa. UMs also show relatively large frequencies in some African countries. This is more of a problem in the metabolism of pro-drugs or drugs metabolized to active metabolites such as tramadol, codeine and oxycodone.

There are also drugs, and other substances, that induce enzyme activity. These are likely to reduce the concentration of parent drug, or in the case of prodrugs produce higher amounts of the active metabolite (15). While there are many examples of drugs that affect this family of metabolizing enzymes, and other enzymes such as those involved in glucuronidation, any substantial change in concentration and effect normally only occurs when a drug does not have alternate metabolising pathways and has a narrow therapeutic index.

Unfortunately, it is not common in death investigations to perform genetic analyses, however if a pharmacogenomic-related adverse event is suspected, there are laboratories that can perform this testing.

POLYDRUG USE

In about two-thirds of deaths suspected from use of drugs, the fatality is a result of the combined use of two or more psychoactive drugs. The most common drugs are combinations with excessive alcohol, although combinations with one or more of the CNS depressant drugs, such as opioids and benzodiazepines, are also relatively common. Combinations with cocaine and any one of the amphetamines with CNS depressants also increase the risk of serious toxicity.

Less common and sometimes difficult to identify are combinations of drugs that lead to significant adverse events, including sudden death when the concentration (and dose) of the drug appears to be in the therapeutic range. A review of 326 Victorian non-intentional drug toxicity cases identified over half the cases as having had possible major adverse interaction (16,17). Serotonin toxicity (ST, sometimes known as serotonin syndrome) was thought to occur in 8 percent of these cases. This type of drug toxicity occurs when two or more drugs capable of increasing serotonin levels in nerve terminals are used concomitantly (18). A large number of drugs have "serotonin" activity and include the serotonin reuptake inhibitor antidepressants, moclobemide (monoamine oxidase A inhibitor), some opioids (such as tramadol, meperidine, fentanyl), some anti-migraine drugs and dextromethorphan. MDMA use with another serotonin active drug has been a relatively frequent combination (19). A larger range of serotonin active drugs is shown in Table 55.4 including many of the NPS (20).

Unfortunately, ST is diagnosed clinically when the three features of mental-status changes, autonomic hyperactivity, and neuromuscular abnormalities are present, although these are not always present, or identified as present. Most commonly hyperthermia, hyperreflexia, tachycardia, convulsions, delirium and tremor are observed clinically (21).

THE MEDICOLEGAL EXAMINATION

An appropriate medicolegal examination of the body is essential in any death investigation, let alone those cases suspected of being drug caused. The investigation may involve a full autopsy or, depending on the circumstances and religious views, may involve non-invasive imaging, such as computerized tomography (CT) or magnetic resonance imaging (MRI) (22,23). These processes should determine whether other factors, such as natural disease or injuries, are likely to have contributed to the death.

SPECIMEN CONSIDERATIONS

While a number of specimens can be collected from decedents, the most common are blood and urine. Because of changes that occur post mortem, the collection of peripheral blood is preferred, such as the femoral region (leg). It is not advised to collect more than 10 mL of blood to avoid drawing blood from the abdominal vasculature. This volume should suffice since most laboratories analyze less than 1 mL in the initial tests conducted. The sampling blood vessel can be tied proximally to avoid contamination with abdominal blood, although it has been shown that this makes little difference when small volumes are collected by skin puncture (24). Ideally, blood should be taken at the earliest opportunity to try and minimize the degree of post-mortem changes. This includes the sampling of blood when the body is admitted to the mortuary, which may be well in advance of the autopsy.

Deaths that occur in hospital may have had blood collected for diagnostic testing; these can be very useful to obtain and analyze when their time in hospital has been many hours.

Other specimens can be useful depending on the case and any legal restrictions (25). Gastric contents are invaluable in cases of suspected acute overdoses to establish the actual content of drug (or poison) remaining in this organ at death. While substantial quantities of drug relative to its potency can reveal an overdose the absence of drug in the stomach contents could still mean an overdose occurred orally when the death has been delayed. Small quantities of drug (usually less than 1 mg) can also derive from the bile during agonal processes, hence any drug content in the stomach does not necessarily imply oral ingestion.

Urine should also be collected routinely and is mainly used for drug screens, particularly if sufficient volume of blood is not available, or past use of drugs is sought. This can be done by blind puncture of the bladder if an autopsy is not conducted.

Liver is a most useful specimen to analyze when the results in blood are equivocal. About 50 grams of liver should be collected from the right side of the organ particularly in cases where a possible drug death is suspected. A portion of this tissue can be readily homogenized in one or two volumes of water, or a neutral buffer. However, due to likely lower recoveries of drugs compared to blood it is imperative that matrix matching for calibrating standards occur using drug-free tissue, or to use the method of standard addition.

Vitreous humor is an ideal fluid for blood alcohol determinations, particularly if some putrefaction has occurred. The alcohol content of vitreous humor is normally slightly higher than that of blood if the blood alcohol has not been produced by bacteria, or blood has been contaminated with gastric contents.

Hair has proven to be a useful specimen in cases where regular prior exposure over weeks to months is important to establish. While a dose(s) cannot be determined from a hair result, segmental analysis of 0.5 to 1 cm sections (depending on length of hair and context) can give a history of use. On average hair grows about 1 cm per month but the rate can vary from almost half to almost double this rate. Banding of drugs close to the expected time(s) of administration is most common but sometimes maximum concentrations in segments may not align with the expected period. External contamination is also possible, particularly in persons living or working in areas where drug residues are present on surfaces, or where dust, smoke or aerosols are likely.

In cases of extreme putrefaction, other specimens may only be available (such as muscle, kidney, bone). While the laboratory can quantify any drugs detected their interpretation is particularly difficult.

INTERPRETATION

The interpretation of toxicology results is very much dependent on the circumstances of the case and the need to have an appropriate medicolegal examination of the deceased. Consequently, for a death to be considered as drug-caused, in part or wholly, the drugs detected (in their respective concentrations) must be not only capable of causing a death but also the context must be consistent with such a conclusion.

Unfortunately, except for some obvious drug overdoses, there is no simple process to determine if a drug is at a concentration that is clearly fatal. The effects of drugs are modified by many factors including dose, route of administration, presence of other drugs, and the presence of any significant natural disease or injury. Regular, if not daily use of drugs not only leads to buildup of concentrations but also leads to an adaptation (tolerance) to its effects. In post-mortem cases, the presence of possible artefacts such as distribution, redistribution and stability must always be considered, and it is never straightforward to assess their significance. For this reason, it is very difficult to provide a list of rules for interpretation of toxicological results.

There are also many drugs, including those commonly detected in cases, where there is little or no relation between a potentially fatal outcome and a tissue(s) concentration, whatever the circumstances. These drugs include, cannabis, cocaine and the amphetamines and likely most of the NPS. With these drug types, other reasonable causes of death need to be excluded before the drug(s) is considered as a direct cause.

The use of databases of toxic and fatal concentrations are only useful to provide a guide as to possible significance; rarely do they provide details of the context of the case and other comorbidities.

CONCLUSION

While drug deaths are all too common, the ability to determine this cause requires a lot more investigation than an interpretation of drug results in a biological specimen(s). The death requires not only a thorough toxicological investigation but also a detailed assessment of the circumstances of the death including a medicolegal investigation, which may include review of previous medical records, full autopsy or non-invasive radiological studies.

REFERENCES

1. Mahase E. Drug deaths: England and Wales see highest number since records began. *BMJ* 2020; **371:** m3988.
2. *Alcohol, tobacco & other drugs in Australia*. Canberra, Australia: Australian Institute of Health and Welfare; 2020. Contract No.: Cat. no. PHE 221.
3. Bolliger SA, Thali MJ, Ross S, et al. Virtual autopsy using imaging: Bridging radiologic and forensic sciences. A review of the Virtopsy and similar projects. *Eur Radiol* 2008; **18(2)**: 273–82.
4. Michaud K, Genet P, Sabatasso S, Grabherr S. Postmortem imaging as a complementary tool for the investigation of cardiac death. *Forensic Sci Res* 2019; **4(3)**: 211–22.
5. Alberreet MS, Ferwana MS, AlSalamah MA, et al. The incidence and risk factors of carbon monoxide poisoning in the Middle East and North Africa: systematic review. *J Health Inform Dev Ctries* 2019; **13(2)**.
6. Mattiuzzi C, Lippi G. Worldwide epidemiology of carbon monoxide poisoning. *Hum Exp Toxicol* 2020; **39(4)**: 387–92.
7. Hanley ME, Patel PH. *Carbon Monoxide Toxicity.* Treasure Island (FL): StatPearls; 2021.
8. Mantinieks D, Gerostamoulos D, Glowacki L, et al. Postmortem drug redistribution: A compilation of postmortem/antemortem drug concentration ratios. *J Anal Toxicol* 2020; **45(4)**: 368–77.
9. Chu M, Rago MD, Mantinieks D, et al. Time-dependent changes in THC concentrations in deceased persons. *J Anal Toxicol* 2020; **455(1)**: 1–7.
10. Saar E, Beyer J, Gerostamoulos D, Drummer OH. The time-dependant post-mortem redistribution of antipsychotic drugs. *Forensic Sci Int* 2012; **222(1–3)**: 223–7.
11. Brockbals L, Staeheli SN, Gascho D, et al. Time- and site-dependent postmortem redistribution of antidepressants and neuroleptics in blood and alternative matrices. *J Anal Toxicol* 2020; **45(4)**: 356–67.
12. Robertson MD, Drummer OH. Postmortem drug metabolism by bacteria. *J Forensic Sci* 1995; **40(3)**: 382–6.
13. Butzbach DM. The influence of putrefaction and sample storage on post-mortem toxicology results. *Forensic Sci Med Pathol* 2010; **6(1)**: 35–45.
14. Just KS, Dormann H, Schurig M, et al. Adverse drug reactions in the emergency department: Is there a role for pharmacogenomic profiles at risk?-Results from the ADRED study. *J Clin Med* 2020; **9(6)**: 1801.
15. Bahar MA, Setiawan D, Hak E, Wilffert B. Pharmacogenetics of drug-drug interaction and drug-drug-gene interaction: a systematic review on CYP2C9, CYP2C19 and CYP2D6. *Pharmacogenomics* 2017; **18(7)**: 701–39.
16. Pilgrim JL, Gerostamoulos D, Drummer OH. Deaths involving contraindicated and inappropriate combinations of serotonergic drugs. *Int J Legal Med* 2011; **125(6)**: 803–15.
17. Pilgrim JL, Gerostamoulos D, Drummer OH. The role of toxicology interpretations in prevention of sudden death. *Forensic Sci Med Pathol* 2012; **8(3)**: 263–9.
18. Boyer EW, Shannon M. The serotonin syndrome. *N Engl J Med* 2005; **352(11)**: 1112–20.
19. Pilgrim JL, Gerostamoulos D, Drummer OH. Deaths involving MDMA and the concomitant use of pharmaceutical drugs. *J Anal Toxicol* 2011; **35(4)**: 219–26.
20. Schifano F, Chiappini S, Miuli A, et al. New psychoactive substances (NPS) and serotonin syndrome onset: A systematic review. *Exp Neurol* 2021; **339**: 113638.
21. Prakash S, Rathore C, Rana K, Prakash A. Fatal serotonin syndrome: a systematic review of 56 cases in the literature. *Clin Toxicol (Phila)* 2021; **59(2)**: 89–100.
22. O'Donnell C, Woodford N. Post-mortem radiology: A new sub-speciality? *Clin Radiol* 2008; **63(11)**: 1189–94.
23. Ampanozi G, Halbheer D, Ebert LC, et al. Postmortem imaging findings and cause of death determination compared with autopsy: A systematic review of diagnostic test accuracy and meta-analysis. *Int J Legal Med* 2020; **134(1)**: 321–37.
24. Hargrove VM, McCutcheon JR. Comparison of drug concentrations taken from clamped and unclamped femoral vessels. *J Anal Toxicol* 2008; **32(8)**: 621–5.
25. Drummer OH. Good practices in forensic toxicology. *Curr Pharm Des* 2017; **23(36)**: 5437–41.

CHAPTER

56

Poison Deaths

Vikas Meshram, Alok Atreya, Utsav Parekh, Kewal Krishan and Tanuj Kanchan

INTRODUCTION

Poison is derived from the Latin word *potare*, meaning "to drink" (1). In French, the term "poison" means magic potion.

Poison is any substance that causes only toxic effects after exposure (1). However, this concept was discarded by Paracelsus some 500 years ago because any substance, when administered in large doses through a specific route, will cause adverse effects (1). A popular maxim formulated by Paracelsus considered as the "Father of Toxicology" states, "*In all things, there is a poison, and there is nothing without a poison. It depends only upon the dose whether a poison is a poison or not*" (1,2).

Professor Francis Edward "Taffy" Camps defined poison as "*any substance which when absorbed into the living body in sufficient quantity will cause ill-health, disease or death*". So, poisons include not only inorganic chemical substances but also food poisoning and envenomation. Food poisonings are accidental when they result due to a mistaken identity of edible food (e.g. poisonous mushroom, poisonous toad, aconite) and it can also occur due to toxins formed in the food or from the chemicals added as preservatives, additives, coloring or flavoring agents while envenomation is usually related to snake or scorpion bite and stinging by other animal species like Hymenoptera, results in an allergic or hypersensitivity reaction.

Mortality is one of the indicators of health in society. The International Statistical Classification of Diseases and Related Health Problems 10th Revision (ICD-10) has listed poisoning by drugs, medicaments and biological substances under T36-T50 (3). ICD-11 has coded the anaphylaxis by Hymenoptera venom under disease of the immune system whereas snake under reptile venom which is under non-medicinal substance (4).

HISTORICAL PERSPECTIVES

The Egyptian *Ebers Papyrus*, written circa 1550 BCE, describes the toxic effects of some poisons such as hemlock, opium and lead (1,5). In the fourth century BCE, Greek botanist Theophrastus described several dangerous plants in his book *De Historia Plantarum*. Poisons were classified into plants, animals and minerals during the first century AD by Greek physician Pedanius Dioscorides in his book *Materia Medica* (1). During the thirteenth-century AD, a Chinese book, *Hsi-yüan-lu*, was published. It is often referred to as the first textbook of Legal Medicine, was translated into several languages, and describes the investigation of homicides, including poisonings (1). Paracelsus in his book *Opus paramirum* proposed a theory that any disease was caused by the bodily imbalance of salt, mercury and sulfur (1,2). Mathieu Joseph Bonaventure Orfila, in 1813–1814, published a two-volume book on toxicology, which is considered the first book in Toxicology: *Traite´ de Toxicologie: Traite´ des poisons tires des regnesmine´ral, ve´ge´tal at animal outoxicologiege´ne´ra leconsidere'e sous Les rapports de la Physiologie, de la pathologie et la me'dicinelegale*. This book and analytical methods of detection of poisons in homicidal death recognized Mathieu Orfila as the "Father of Modern Toxicology"(1). The deaths from poison and poisoning are reported as early as 399 BCE. Table 56.1 lists some examples of historically significant poison deaths.

TOXICOEPIDEMIOLOGY OF POISON DEATHS

The global trends of poisoning show variations due to multiple factors. Poison Information Center and Hospital Information Systems are the common data sources on poisoning in various countries; for example, National Poison Information Service (NPIS) in the United Kingdom (6). However, not all countries have poison information centers. World Health Organization (WHO) reports that at 1st January 2021, 53 percent of member states had no poison centers (7). At the same time, the Poison Information Center and hospital information systems may not indicate the actual figures of poisoning. Hospital data may not include the cases of poisoned individuals not seeking treatment, thus underestimating numbers. Poison information centers may also overestimate the figures of poisoning by including the cases seeking only advice when actual exposure to poison has not occurred.

DOI: 10.1201/9781003138754-58

TABLE 56.1 Poison deaths: Historical cases

Year	Poison	Historical cases/Incidents
399 BCE	Hemlock	Socrates was poisoned for impiety against the pantheon of Athens, and corruption of the youth
30 BCE	Snake venom	Cleopatra VII, the last true pharaoh of Egypt killed herself with an Asp bite
1751	Arsenic	Mary Blandy poisoned her father
1850	Nicotine	Hippolyte Visart de Bocarmé poisoned his brother-in-law in Belgium
1856	Antimony	Dr William Palmer killed 15 people with Antimony
1858	Arsenic trioxide	21 people died after consumption of Arsenic adulterated sweets in Barford, England
1858	Gypsum	8000 infants died in a year after they were fed swill milk adulterated with plaster of Paris in the United States
1874	Copper Sulfate	Moreau, a 32-year-old Parisian, killed his two wives with copper sulfate, with the aim of receiving their dowry
1881	Aconite	Dr George Henry Lamson killed his brother-in-law by feeding him cake poisoned with Aconite
1932–1968	Methyl mercury	1784 people are believed to have died due to consumption of fish and shellfish contaminated with methyl mercury in Minamata bay, Japan
1934	Strychnine	Ethel Lillie Major killed her husband Arthur Major by mixing strychnine in his food
1941–1945	Cyanide	Roughly one million Jews were murdered in gas chambers during the great holocaust of World War II
1957	Insulin	A nurse named, Kenneth Barlow, killed his wife by insulin
1971	Methyl mercury	At least 459 people died due to the consumption of grain treated with methyl mercury in Iraq
1978	Ricin	Bulgarian national Georgi Markov was assassinated with a ricin pellet which was concealed in the umbrella tip
1978	Cyanide + Valium	Cult leader Jim James orchestrated the revolutionary suicide of 918 followers in Jonestown, Guyana
1984	Methyl isocyanate	At least 3787 people died due to gas leaked from industry in Bhopal, India
1988	Thallium	George Trepal killed his neighbor Peggy Carr by spiking her Coca-Cola bottles with thallium, in the USA
1999–2007	Cyanide	KD Kempamma is the first convicted female serial killer in India who poisoned at least six females with a motive of theft
2000	Diamorphine	Dr Harold Shipman murdered 15 of his patients by administering lethal doses of diamorphine
2002–2016	Cyanide	Jolly Joseph, a resident of Kerala, India, murdered six people of her family over 14 years with cyanide

There is also variation in the mortality rate of unintentional poisoning among different countries across the globe. As per the WHO statistics in 2019, the mortality rate of unintentional poisoning per 100 000 population varies widely being high in the Republic of Moldova, 5.45 and Somalia, 4.91 and low in countries like Brunei Darussalam, 0.001 and Saint Vincent & Grenadines, 0.005 (7). For the same time period, the rate was 0.26 in India, 0.33 in the UK, 0.51 in the USA, 1.79 in China, 2.82 in Central Africa and 3.81 in Russia (7).

Risk factors

Over time, several risk factors have been identified and reported according to the geographic, toxicological distribution and the manner of poisoning cases. The nature of poisoning will depend on what is available to the relevant population. Positive histories of psychiatric illness and previous poisoning, problems in relationships, marital discords, poor socio-economic conditions and unemployment are significant risk factors associated with adult admissions due to suicidal poisoning. The occupation of the person also bears correlation with the incidences of poisoning. Deliberate pesticide poisoning is commonly reported in agriculture farm workers, and they are also prone to snake bites. Industrial workers are prone to accidental exposure to toxic agents. Children are often vulnerable to accidental poisoning because of various risk factors like unsupervised playing, approachable placement, unsafe container designs, the color of the liquid, and mistaken identity in place of water.

Regional variations

The type and nature of poisoning differ in various geographic locations. It is based upon the manufacture, availability and accessibility of the poison. In North America and Western Europe, analgesics and psychotropes are the common poisons resulting in admission to hospital, whereas deaths occurring outside the hospital are mostly due to carbon monoxide. In Russia, the majority of the deaths due to poisoning are from alcohol, followed by carbon monoxide and pharmaceutical agents (8). In South Asian countries where the major occupation is agriculture, pesticide poisoning is more commonly encountered (9). Pesticides account for nearly 20 percent of suicidal deaths globally (10). A conservative estimate based on these data indicates that there were approximately 110 000 pesticide self-poisoning deaths each year from 2010 to 2014, comprising 13.7 percent of all global suicides. A sensitivity analysis accounting for underreporting of suicides in India resulted in an increased estimate of 168 000 pesticide self-poisoning deaths annually, that is, 19.7 percent of global suicides (11).

Age and sex variations

In the United States, unintentional poisoning in the pediatric population is commonly due to cosmetics and personal care products, whereas in the adult population, intentional poisoning is due to analgesics and sedatives (12). In 2019, the worldwide mortality rate of unintentional poisoning was 1.102/per 100 000 (13). When the gender-wise mortality rate was estimated for the same year, it was observed that the mortality rate in males worldwide (1.364/100 000) was much higher than that for females (0.824/100 000) (13). Similarly, the National Center of Health Statistics (NCHS) reported that drug-poisoning death rates were highest for the persons aged 35–44 years (35/100 000) in 2016, with the mortality rate for males being 26.2/100 000, which was almost double that of females 13.4/100 000 in the United States (14). Global burden of disease estimates by WHO report that 0.296 million deaths occurred in 2019 as a result of alcohol and substance use, of which 0.0623 million were females (15). Mortality due to carbon monoxide (CO) poisoning has been observed to be double in men than in women (16). It is estimated that more than half of the poisonous mushroom ingestion in the United States is by children under 6 years, where the total annual ingestion is around 6000 (17). In India, most of the deaths due to poisoning were observed in the 19–40 age group, with a male preponderance and overall sex ratio of 1.7:1 (18).

Seasonal variations

Seasonal variation can be attributed to multiple factors in different types of poison deaths. In South East Asian countries, most of the poisoning cases are reported in the summer season. This can be attributed to water scarcity leading to crop failure. Also, grain is preserved during the summer season for which pesticide agents are procured, leading to its easy availability (19). Incidences of CO poisoning peak during the winter when fossil fuel, firewood and gas heaters/geysers are used more frequently for heating purposes (15,20). Mushroom poisoning is also reported to show seasonal variations, with the peak poisoning incidences occurring during summer and autumn (21). Deaths due to snake envenomation peak during the summer and rainy seasons. They are rare during the winter when snakes go into hibernation. It is estimated that annual deaths due to snake envenomation range from 81 000 to 138 000 worldwide, most of which (45 900 deaths annually) occur in India alone (22). Venom-specific IgE present in Hymenoptera insect venom also shows seasonal variations (23).

Manner of poisoning

Dependent on the physical properties of the poison and the manner of exposure, whether intentional or non-intentional, death can be suicidal, homicidal or accidental. Twenty percent of global suicides are due to the consumption of insecticides, especially in the rural areas of low- and middle-income countries (24). National poison data system from the United States reported that between 2011 to 2018, there was a significant increase in self-poisoning (from 125% to 299%) among youths aged 10–15 years (25). Unintentional poisoning by common household products is more common in children (9,26,27). Accidental poisoning can occur when exposed to poisonous gases, especially carbon monoxide, released from automobiles and gas geysers (20,28). Misidentification and consumption of poisonous plants also lead to fatality (29,30). In homicidal poisoning, the perpetrator can try to disguise the homicide as natural death, suicide or even an accident. A successful homicidal poisoning is one where the victim doesn't suspect that the food or drink they are to consume contains poison. The victim's death, too, should not raise the suspicion of poisoning. The death should resemble a natural disease so as to escape further investigation. In this regard, the perpetrator can be a trustworthy acquaintance of the victim. The perpetrator should have access to the poison and know the route of administration so that it should not raise suspicion later. Homicide by poisoning, especially arsenic, was not uncommon during the eighteenth century, as mentioned in the first English language textbook of forensic medicine by Samuel Farr (31). The first reported case of murder by poisoning was in 1751, when Mary Blandy poisoned her father by adding arsenic to his food (31). In 1851, nicotine extract from tobacco leaves was used for homicide, which is also the first case where an exact proof of alkaloid was made in forensic medicine (32).

Poisons have also been used for execution. The death of Socrates in 399 BCE by consumption of hemlock is probably one of the oldest known cases of capital punishment by poisoning. Lethal injection as a form of capital punishment is justifiable homicide permitted by the legislature in countries like the United States and China (33,34). Mass poisonings have also been reported, which are mostly accidental and rarely homicidal.

MEDICOLEGAL INVESTIGATION INTO POISON DEATHS

Medicolegal investigation in poison death involves a multidisciplinary approach consisting of police/investigating officials, autopsy surgeons and toxicologists to investigate multiple aspects of the poisoning incident.

These include the information about the nature and circumstances of poisoning, examination of the scene of an incident, autopsy protocols to establish the cause of death and preservation of samples for toxicological analysis.

Examination of the scene of the incident can give a valuable clue regarding the manner of death. Suicidal poisoning can be readily identified by the presence of drug strip/case containing the poison in the vicinity. The presence of a suicide note further adds credence to the investigation. The history provided by the patient or their kin can give a clue to the manner of poisoning in cases of poisoning where medical attention is sought.

The type of poison can also give a clue about the manner of poisoning. Substances of abuse such as cocaine, heroin or even alcohol are often responsible for accidental death due to overdose. Pesticides are common agents used for suicide. There are instances of agents like arsenic, aconite, ricin, and so on, used for homicidal purposes because their properties are close to that of the ideal homicidal agent. Deaths due to snake bites are mostly accidental; however, there are also instances of homicidal snake bites.

Autopsy in poisoning deaths is done to look for the post-mortem signs of poisoning consistent with a suspected agent. It includes histopathology of the tissues to know the effects of poisons, and collection of the samples for qualitative and quantitative toxicological analysis. Autopsy features in certain poisoning are specific for the poison consumed or envenomation. Poisons with an affinity for a particular organ/system can be identified by its clinical manifestations and autopsy features. However, in many poisoning cases, autopsy features are non-specific or inconclusive. In all such cases, toxicological analysis at the FSL helps to confirm, or rule out, poisoning.

Histopathology of the organs can be helpful in the identification of the poison. In intravenous drug abusers, foreign body granuloma is seen scattered in the lung parenchyma due to the impurities in the abusive substance, also termed as "junkie lung" (35). Renal tubular degeneration with deposition of calcium oxalate crystals is seen in ethylene glycol poisoning (35). Hepatocellular necrosis is seen in poisoning due to paracetamol, chloroform and poisonous mushroom (35,36). Similarly, in the case of paraquat poisoning, the lungs will show hemorrhage and fibrosis along with necrosis of hepatic and renal cells (35).

The analytical toxicological analysis is essential in investigating poisoning death as it gives substantial proof of the poisonous/toxic agent involved. The qualitative and quantitative analysis of the poison helps not only to identify the substance but also to quantify the amount consumed. The analytical toxicological analysis includes a screening test and confirmatory test. The conventional screening tests include immunoassay, gas chromatography (GC), thin-layer chromatography (TLC), high-performance liquid chromatography (HPLC), capillary electrophoresis (CE), and so on. Confirmation and quantitative analysis are done mostly by mass spectroscopy (MS), atomic absorption spectroscopy (AAS), high-performance liquid chromatography with photodiode array detector (HPLC DAD), and so on.

TABLE 56.2 Indications for specific samples for toxicological analysis

Specimen	Circumstances
Heart	Cardiac poisons
Brain	Cerebral and spinal poisons, anesthetic agents
Spinal cord	Spinal poisons, anesthetic agents
Lungs	Volatile poisons
Uterus	Abortifacients
Skin with subcutaneous fat	Snake bite, injected poisons/drugs
Adipose tissue	Lipid soluble drugs, pesticides
Long bone	Heavy metals
Nails	Heavy metals, substance abuse
Scalp hair	Heavy metals, substance abuse
Bile	Drug screening, paracetamol
Vitreous humor	Alcohol, substance abuse
Pleural fluid	Alcohol
Pericardial fluid	Alcohol
Synovial fluid	Alcohol
Cerebrospinal fluid	Cerebral poisons, alcohol
Meconium, umbilical cord	*In-utero* drug exposure

It is essential to collect appropriate samples during autopsy for toxicological analysis. Blood is the most important analytical sample in forensic toxicology, which can facilitate the screening and quantification of many poisonous agents in a single analysis. In cases of suspected poisoning deaths by ingestion of a poisonous substance, stomach and intestines with their contents, sections of liver, kidneys and blood are preserved for toxicological analysis (37,38). Additionally, samples from organs such as the brain, spinal cord, lung, heart, adipose tissue, skin and bone are also preserved depending on the suspected poison (Table 56.2). With technical advancement, a lot of credence is laid on the toxicological profiling of the suspected poison/drug based on the analysis of biological fluids including blood, urine, bile, CSF and vitreous humor and so on. (37,38).

CONCLUSION

Poison deaths demand a detailed investigation by the law enforcement agencies, forensic pathologists and toxicologists, etc. to conclude on the nature of poisoning, and the cause and manner of death. Post mortems are conducted in poisoning deaths to look for the findings consistent with the alleged history of poisoning. Modern analytical techniques can make qualitative and quantitative analysis of the poison with precision to derive necessary conclusions.

Poison deaths are largely preventable. While safekeeping of the poisonous substances and adoption of safety measures can help in prevention of accidental poisoning deaths, restriction of the over-the-counter sale of drugs and poisonous substance can help to bring down the incidence of intentional poisoning.

REFERENCES

1. Lappas NT, Lappas CM. *Forensic Toxicology Principles and Concepts*, 2nd ed. New York: Elsevier; 2021.
2. Ball P. *The Devil's Doctor: Paracelsus and the World of Renaissance Magic and Science*. New York: Farrar, Straus and Giroux; 2006.
3. World Health Organization. International statistical classification of diseases and related health problems, 10th revision, 2016. Available from: https://apps.who.int/iris/handle/10665/246208 (Accessed 9 May 2023).
4. World Health Organization. International statistical classification of diseases and related health problems, 11th revision, 2022. Available from: https://icd.who.int/browse11/l-m/en (Accessed 9 May 2023).
5. Sigerist HE. *A History of Medicine*. New York: Oxford University Press; 1951.
6. National Poisons Information Service. Available from: https://www.npis.org/ (Accessed 9 May 2023).
7. World Health Organization. Poison control and unintentional poisoning. The Global Health Observatory, 2023. Available from: https://www.who.int/data/gho/data/themes/topics/indicator-groups/poison-control-and-unintentional-poisoning (Accessed 9 May 2023).
8. Jones AL, Dargan PI. Poisoning: Overview and Statistics. In: Payne-James J, Byard RW, Corey TC, Henderson C (eds), *Encyclopedia of Forensic and Legal Medicine*. Oxford: Elsevier Academic Press; 2005, pp. 1–9.
9. Peshin SS, Gupta YK. Poisoning due to household products: A ten years retrospective analysis of telephone calls to the National Poisons Information Centre, All India Institute of Medical Sciences, New Delhi, India. *J Forensic Leg Med* 2018; **58**: 205–11.
10. World Health Organization. One in 100 deaths is by suicide, 2021. Available from: https://www.who.int/news/item/17-06-2021-one-in-100-deaths-is-by-suicide (Accessed 9 May 2023).
11. Mew EJ, Padmanathan P, Konradsen F, et al. The global burden of fatal self-poisoning with pesticides 2006–15: Systematic review. *J Affect Disord* 2017; **219**: 93–104.
12. Poison Control. National Poison Control Call Statistics, 2021. Available from: https://www.poison.org/poison-statistics-national (Accessed 9 May 2023).
13. The World Bank. World Bank Open Data. Available from: https://data.worldbank.org/ (Accessed 9 May 2023).
14. National Center for Health Statistics. NCHS Data on Drug-poisoning Deaths, 2018. Available from: https://www.cdc.gov/nchs/data/factsheets/factsheet-drug-poisoning-H.pdf (Accessed 9 May 2023).
15. Vos T, Lim SS, Abbafati C, et al. Global burden of 369 diseases and injuries in 204 countries and territories, 1990–2019: A systematic analysis for the Global Burden of Disease Study 2019. *Lancet* 2020; **396(10258)**: 1204–22.
16. Mattiuzzi C, Lippi G. Worldwide epidemiology of carbon monoxide poisoning. *Hum Exp Toxicol* 2020; **39(4)**: 387–92.
17. Tran HH, Juergens AL. Mushroom Toxicity. StatPearls. 2021. Available from: http://www.ncbi.nlm.nih.gov/pubmed/30725796 (Accessed 9 May 2023).
18. Mittal C, Singh S, Kumar-M P, Varthya SB. Toxicoepidemiology of poisoning exhibited in Indian population from 2010 to 2020: A systematic review and meta-analysis. *BMJ Open* 2021; **11(5)**: e045182.
19. Chatterjee S, Verma VK, Hazra A, Pal J. An observational study on acute poisoning in a tertiary care hospital in West Bengal, India. *Perspect Clin Res* 2020; **11(2)**: 75–80.
20. Mohankumar TS, Kanchan T, Pinakini KS, et al. Gas geyser: A cause of fatal domestic carbon monoxide poisoning. *J Forensic Leg Med* 2012; **19(8)**: 490–3.
21. Cervellin G, Comelli I, Rastelli G, et al. Epidemiology and clinics of mushroom poisoning in Northern Italy: A 21-year retrospective analysis. *Hum Exp Toxicol* 2018; **37(7)**: 697–703.
22. Arnold C. Snakebite steals millions of years of quality life in India. *Nature* 2020. doi: 10.1038/d41586-020-03327-9. Online ahead of print.
23. Warpinski JR, Bush RK. Stinging insect allergy. *J Wilderness Med* 1990; **1(4)**: 249–57.
24. World Health Organization. Suicide, 2021. Available from: https://www.who.int/news-room/fact-sheets/detail/suicide (Accessed 9 May 2023).
25. Spiller HA, Ackerman JP, Spiller NE, Casavant MJ. Sex- and age-specific increases in suicide attempts by self-poisoning in the United States among youth and young adults from 2000 to 2018. *J Pediatr* 2019; **210**: 201–8.
26. Yates KM. Accidental poisoning in New Zealand. *Emerg Med* 2003; **15(3)**: 244–9.
27. Goto K, Kuroki Y, Shintani S, Kusakawa S. Accidental poisoning of children in Japan: A report from the Japan Poison Information Center. *Acta Paediatr Jpn* 1993; **35(3)**: 193–200.
28. Fisher-Hubbard AO, Appleford C, Kesha K, et al. Accidental carbon monoxide poisoning while driving: A case report with review of the literature. *Am J Forensic Med Pathol* 2018; **39(3)**: 270–2.
29. Ng WY, Hung LY, Lam YH, et al. Poisoning by toxic plants in Hong Kong: A 15-year review. *Hong Kong Med J* 2019; **25(2)**: 102–12.
30. Diaz JH. Amatoxin-containing mushroom poisonings: Species, toxidromes, treatments, and outcomes. *Wilderness Environ Med* 2018; **29(1)**: 111–18.
31. Watson KD. Poisoning crimes and forensic toxicology since the 18th century. *Acad Forensic Pathol* 2020; **10(1)**: 35–46.
32. Wennig R. Back to the roots of modern analytical toxicology: Jean Servais Stas and the Bocarmé murder case. *Drug Test Anal* 2009; **1(4)**: 153–5.
33. Paul NW, Caplan A, Shapiro ME, et al. Determination of death in execution

by lethal injection in China. *Camb Q Healthc Ethics* 2018; **27**(**3**): 459–66.
34. Denno DW. The lethal injection quandary: How medicine has dismantled the death penalty. *Fordham law Rev* 2007; **76**(1): 49–128.
35. Lau G, Lai SH. Forensic Histopathology, pp. 239–65, 2009. Available from: http://link.springer.com/10.1007/978-1-59745-110-9_13 (Accessed 9 May 2023).
36. Dettmeyer RB. Histopathology. In: Payne-James J, Byard RW (eds), *Encyclopedia of Forensic and Legal Medicine*. London: Elsevier; 2016, pp. 35–46. Available from: https://linkinghub.elsevier.com/retrieve/pii/B9780128000342002020 (Accessed 9 May 2023).
37. Dinis-Oliveira RJ, Vieira DN, Magalhães T. Guidelines for collection of biological samples for clinical and forensic toxicological analysis. *Forensic Sci Res* 2017; **1**(**1**): 42–51.
38. Flanagan RJ, Connally G, Evans JM. Analytical toxicology: Guidelines for sample collection postmortem. *Toxicol Rev* 2005; **24**(**1**): 63–71.

CHAPTER

57

Deaths from Sexual Activity

Evi Untoro, Putut T. Widodo and Jason Payne-James

INTRODUCTION

Deaths resulting from sexual activity may be natural, accidental or homicidal. It may sometimes be difficult to distinguish between these and, as with the living, whether the sexual activity was consensual or non-consensual. Participant and witness accounts may be extremely important in elucidating the cause of death.

Investigators in deaths where sexual motive or activity is suspected to have contributed will need to consider whether the sexual activity was the direct cause of death, or was it related to other factors. These factors are very wide-ranging and where others were involved in the sexual activity may include the need to consider whether the sexual activity itself was consensual and the injury sustained was an unexpected complication, whether drugs or alcohol caused death (and if so, were any of these administered unknowingly), whether the activity resulted in accidental death, and whether any party acted irresponsibly.

If the apparent sexual activity was solitary, was death intended or was it the result of accident, or has the apparent sexual activity been used to conceal homicide or suicide, or conversely has a homicide been concealed by the apparent sexual activity? Examples of such scenarios are reviewed and then a basic examination protocol outlined.

There are many available sources outlining the appropriate investigation practices for sexual crimes and these may be appropriate to different jurisdictions and the world region. In general, broad principles are similar (1–4). Sexual trauma deaths may generally be associated with penetrative sexual assault and homicide. Definitions of terms such as rape have been changed in recent years in many jurisdictions. For example, the US Federal Bureau Investigation (FBI) since 2017 has used the following definition of rape: "*penetration, no matter how slight, of the vagina or anus with any body part or object, or oral penetration by a sex organ of another person, without the consent of the victim*" (5). In Indonesia, rape in the article 285 of Indonesia Penal Code, "any person by using force or threat of force forces a woman to have sexual intercourse with him, out of marriage, shall, being guilty of rape, shall be punished in maximum imprisonment of twelve years." In Article 286 of Indonesia Penal Code, "any person who out of marriage, has carnal knowledge of a woman, of whom he knows that she is unconscious or helpless, shall be punished by maximum imprisonment nine years" (4). Rape is defined as sexual intercourse against a person's will by force or threat of force. These factors including the age of the victim and the perpetrator means the ability under law to give consent, mental capability, the use or threat of a weapon, physical injury to the victim, spousal or another legal relationship.

DEATHS ASSOCIATED WITH SEXUAL ACTIVITY

Bunzel and colleagues undertook a study which embraced non-natural deaths associated with sexual activity which occurred either with or without other involved persons using a German population (7). The study looked at the circumstances, sexual practices, and gender distribution of cases of non-natural death. The authors found over a 25-year period to 2017 0.45 percent (n = 74) of medicolegal cases were found to relate to sexual activities (0.45%). One female and 21 males had died in the course of autoerotic practices (group I, n = 22). Nine males and 14 females were undertaking sexual activity consensually (group II, n = 23), and 13 males and 16 females non-consensually (group III, n = 29). The mean age in group I was 45.4 years; in group II, 40.6 years; and in group III, 39.2 years. Most deceased were located in their own residence. There were many forms of stimulation including penetrative vaginal, anal and oral intercourse; insertion of foreign bodies; use of chemical substances; and tools for respiratory depression/hypoxia. Three deaths involved bondage and discipline, sadism and masochism (BDSM). Death due to strangulation was the main cause in group I, whereas intoxications were predominant in group II. Sharp force implements were mainly responsible for death in group III. Anogenital injuries were documented in all groups in approximately equal percentages. This study is helpful in showing the range of scenarios in which non-natural death connected to sexual activity may occur.

DOI: 10.1201/9781003138754-59

Asphyxia-related deaths are often the most difficult to determine as to whether these were accidental, suicidal or concealed homicide. Various reports explore the nature of these. A case of shibari, a double-hanging sexual asphyxia practice, which ended fatally for one of the two women involved emphasized the need to review the autopsy findings and alongside a psychiatric and psychometric evaluation of the surviving participant and emphasizes the risks of such practices (8). These are of particular relevance in the context of non-fatal strangulation (*see* Chapter 84 – "Non-Fatal Strangulation") and it seems possible that cases thought previously to be consensual sexual asphyxia that went wrong, were in fact homicides and this poses huge challenges for forensic practitioners and other investigators (9).

Accidental fatalities have been described such as a death from air embolism in a non-pregnant woman during consensual penile intercourse, in a position with the pelvis elevated above heart level. Air is thought to have entered the veins via a vaginal laceration, which occurred during digital foreplay (10).

Another case describes sudden vaginal bleeding and a cardiac arrest occurring in an 18-year-old female during consensual intercourse. Resuscitation procedures restored the cardiac function allowing admission to hospital, where two vaginal mucosal lacerations were diagnosed and sutured. A myocardial infarction was diagnosed with a patent foramen ovale. CT scan confirmed hypoxic brain damage with death occurring 2 days later, due to heart failure, cerebral anoxia and multiorgan failure. Autopsy confirmed the patent foramen ovale was considered as responsible for a paradoxical air embolism. The legal determination was that death occurred as a consequence of an unpredictable accident occurring during consensual intercourse without sexual violence (11).

Weisheng and colleagues describe a 27-year-old woman, gravida 1 para 0, who died 30 min after intercourse at the 16th week of gestation (12). The prenatal medical history had indicated the placental implantation position at the cervix. Autopsy revealed massive hemoperitoneum and a tumor in the placenta and myometrium on the anterior right side of the cervix. A transmural perforation was found from the tumor to the serosal surface of the cervix. The autopsy, histopathology and medical history indicated that her death was ascribed to the rupture of the cervix due to intraplacental choriocarcinoma (IC) after intercourse. The case indicated that placental implantation and tumor invasion might lead to the rupture of the uterus triggered by external forces in daily life.

Children are not exempt from death from sexual activity and these will include complications of abuse including physical injuries and infections that may result in mortality. Walong describes a case of pre-pubertal sexual abuse that presented as fatal pelvic inflammatory disease (PID) and peritonitis, whose diagnosis was incidentally made at autopsy (13). She had undergone surgery for management of peritonitis which was unsuccessful. The immediate cause of death was acute lung injury. Severe abdomino-pelvic peritonitis with PID was found on autopsy. Laboratory analysis suggested infection by *Neisseria gonorrhoeae*. The author emphasizes that a high index of suspicion is essential for appropriate diagnosis and management of such cases.

These examples all illustrate the need for meticulous investigation when death may be associated with prior sexual activity.

DRUG-FACILITATED SEXUAL ASSAULT DEATHS

Fatality associated with drug-facilitated sexual assault (DFSA) is well-recognized. The use of substances to render a victim susceptible to non-consensual acts is not new. Generally, drugs used for this purpose are often rapidly acting central nervous system (CNS) depressants that impair memory and mobility by intoxication (21) including Ethanol, alone or in combination with other substances (22–24). Examples of other substances include anti-histamines, benzodiazepines, Z-drugs, GHB (γ-hydroxybutyrate), ketamine and methylenedioxymethamphetamine. The risk of fatality in uncontroled administration of drugs with or without alcohol can be high.

Specific substances used may be responsible in isolation. Chloroform has been reported to cause fatality in a 13-year-old girl, where the cause of death was not immediately evident. Investigations showed that this was a case of a DFSA, which led to the girl's death and then to the suicide of the assailant. Post-mortem analysis revealed a blood concentration of 833.9 mg/L for the victim and analysis of chloroform in various fluids and viscera of the perpetrator showed that he had recently been handling the solvent (with concentrations in fat tissues 20 times higher than in his blood). This case emphasizes the need for searches for volatile substances in such investigations (25).

As the previous case shows, children are not exempt from fatal DFSA. Kintz and colleagues described a 14-year-old boy who was found dead at the home of a known sex offender (26). Autopsy findings were unremarkable with some pulmonary and visceral congestion. There was no evidence of violence, and no needle marks were found by the pathologist. Toxicological analyses demonstrated both recent and repetitive buprenorphine exposure in combination with nordiazepam. Buprenorphine concentrations were 1.1 ng/mL and 23 pg/mg in blood and hair, respectively. The boy's death was attributed to accidental asphyxia in a facilitated repetitive sexual abuse situation due to the combination of buprenorphine and benzodiazepines. The use of buprenorphine as a sedative drug was not challenged by the perpetrator.

In another case, a six-year-old girl died following sedation with gamma-hydroxybutyric acid (GHB) having been sexually abused by a relative. Samples of cardiac blood, bile, vitreous humor, liver, kidney, brain tissues and hair were analyzed by a LC–MS/MS method. Very high GHB levels were found in the proximal part of the hair sample (about 40.9 ng/mg). In distal segments of hair – up to 12 cm distant from the hair scalp – GHB concentrations were higher than the overall found endogenous range of 2–3 ng/mg. Police investigations revealed that the uncle had also administered GHB to the older half-sister. By exclusion of other causes of death and based on toxicology, autopsy and police investigations, a lethal intoxication with GHB could be confirmed (27).

Not all cases are what they appear to be initially. Busardo and colleagues (28) describe a case of a 21-year-old female sex-worker found deceased in a town square. Preliminary evidence suggested death associated with a DFSA. Two peripheral blood and two vitreous humor samples were collected for the purpose of GHB testing from the dead body at two different post-mortem intervals (PMIs): approximately 2 (t0) and 36 (t1) hours. The obtained results showed that, between t0 and t1, there was an increase of GHB concentrations in peripheral blood and vitreous humor of 66.3 percent and 8.1 percent, respectively and demonstrated GHB post-mortem production in the deceased and not *in vitro*, showing that vitreous humor is less affected than peripheral blood in GHB post-mortem production. The authors concluded that in cases of suspected DFSA, especially GHB-FSA, it is useful to collect not only blood but also other biological fluids and vitreous humor seems to be a valid complementary matrix for this purpose. This case showed that vitreous humour for GHB analysis was likely to be a more stable matrix in comparison to blood to avoid false positive results although what emerged from this single case, and the toxicological approach adopted for the case here reported, allowed the authors to exclude a GHB exogenous administration. After full investigation including a complete autopsy, serological, histological, toxicological and hematology analyses, a diagnosis of idiopathic hypereosinophilic syndrome (a myeloproliferative disorder characterized by persistent eosinophilia associated with damage to multiple organs) was made and the cause of death was due to a pulmonary eosinophilic vasculitis responsible for an acute respiratory failure.

AUTOEROTIC DEATHS

Chapter 58 describes autoerotic deaths in further detail but the investigator must be aware of the vast range of presentations of such deaths such as those described by Koops et al. which included (in a study of 40 deaths): (a) a 28-year-old firefighter who was found hanging under a bridge in a peculiar bound belt system (29). The autopsy and the reconstruction revealed signs of asphyxiation, feminine underwear and several layers of plastic clothing; (b) a 16-year-old dressed with feminine plastic and rubber utensils fixed and strangulated himself with an electric wire and (c) a 28-year-old male with progressive muscular dystrophy who was nearly immobile but persuaded a nurse to draw plastic bags over his body, close his mouth with plastic strips, and put him in a rubbish container where he died from suffocation. The latter case, in particular, emphasizes the need to consider the circumstances in every case and whether or not an accomplice might have been required (and if so, their contribution to the death). Such matters are particularly relevant and thorough investigation is required when considering cases such as the death of an MI6 agent in the UK whose naked body was found inside a locked holdall at his London flat. This is to be reviewed. No credible explanation has ever been provided (30).

ACCIDENTAL SEXUAL ACTIVITY DEATHS

There are a range of sexual activities where death may ensue but is neither expected nor intended. Emerging research has identified sexual activity while driving as a form of distracted driving. It includes an individual (the driver) who deviates resources from the primary task (driving) toward a secondary task (sexual activity). One study searched the internet from April to June 2020 for media reports in which sexual activities occurred within the cabin of a moving vehicle (31). A total of 106 unique and verified cases were identified from 2004 to 2020. The reports involved 76 male (71.7%) and 30 female drivers (28.3%), and there were 43 (40.5%) serious incidents that involved a crash and 23 fatalities (21.7%). In 17 (16.0%) incidents, their vehicle hit another car, and a pedestrian or cyclist was hit in three (2.8%) incidents. The risk of a serious incident was higher during oral sex or intercourse than solitary activities (i.e. masturbation). A total of 63 (59.5%) non-fatal incidents were identified, in which reports included accounts by witnesses or police regarding sexual activity while driving (10). Most data about the range of sexual activities while driving is based on self-reported data or media reports. Oviedo-Trespalacios and colleagues undertook content analysis of sexually explicit media (SEM) on a sample of 270 videos depicting real driving (32). Unsurprisingly, the results show that when engaging in sexual activity, drivers do not present safe vehicle control. Sexual activity imposes additional cognitive, physical and visual demands on the driver, thereby decreasing safety. Similar to other distractions, drivers engaging in sexual activity while driving appear to mitigate risks. With regard to the potential for legal sanctions, it appears that drivers may attempt to conceal sexual activity by reducing their visible nudity and minimizing interactions with other road users. Finally, mobile phones and cameras appear to interact with sexual activities while driving, by imposing potential restrictions on the range of sexual activities. For those investigating deaths involving transport, whether driver, passenger, other vehicle, or pedestrian the implications of such activity may have substantial legal, criminal, insurance and coronial consequences.

Sexual activity can result in death in many ways. A death in connection with zoosexuality (sexual intercourse between humans and animals) has been described of penetrating rectal injury associated with a rapidly progressive sepsis following sexual intercourse with a Maremma Sheepdog (33).

SEXUAL HOMICIDE DEFINITIONS

The definition of the nature of sexual homicide (murder) typologies is variable. For example, one study reviewed all empirical studies conducted between 1970 and 2016, relating >700 sexual murderers, to outline the overall patterns and motives underlying sexual murder. The authors identified with consistent three subtypes of sexual murder. They concluded that the term sexualized murder should be used to refer to those crimes in which killing is functionally related to the sexual element of the offense. Grievance murder refers to those murders driven by angry schema and an excessively aggressive response style. Rape murder involves only an indirect association between the sexual offense and killing (6).

Such classifications are often dependent on the discipline from which the authors derive and may not be used by those in other disciplines, although consistent definitions and classifications would assist when comparing the nature of such cases from different regions.

SEXUAL HOMICIDES

In a study from Scotland (14), the authors explored whether sexual homicide perpetrators differed from nonsexual homicide offenders in Scotland. Data from a national police database compared 89 male sexual homicide offenders who killed adult females with 306 male nonsexual homicide offenders. Sexual homicides appeared to be associated with indicators of instrumentality and sexual deviance and the authors concluded that sexual homicide offenders might be considered a distinct group of homicide offenders, with more similarities to sexual offenders than to other homicide offenders. A similar study from Scotland reviewing female sexual homicide offenders also suggested that they should also be seen as a distinct group of offenders, with specific characteristics and specific needs (15).

In France, the modus operandi and associated contextual and situational factors, of French serial sexual murderers (SSMs) was compared with nonserial sexual murderers (NSMs). Detailed data on the precrime, modus operandi, postcrime and victimology factors of 120 French sexual murderers (SSMs: n = 33; NSMs: n = 87) were compared. The authors found that the modus operandi of French SSMs was shaped by homicidal, sadistic and rape fantasies, while that of NSMs was shaped by the need to satisfy immediate, especially sexual, needs. In contrast, they noted that while the modus operandi of American and English NSMs is primarily shaped by general deviance, that of French NSMs appeared to be primarily shaped by sexual deviance (16).

A Chinese review explored the offender, victim and offense characteristics of Chinese sexual homicides. Fifty-nine cases from a 23 year-period to 2016 were studied and found that heterosexual assaults were far more prevalent in Chinese sexual homicides. Sexual murderers (average age 32.4 years) were predominantly male (97%), single (67%), secondary school educated (68%) and with no prior overall (80%) and sexual (88%) convictions. The victims were mostly female (83%) with a mean age of 35.35 years. The frequently observed offending patterns include strangers as victim choice (63%), sexual pleasure as primary motivation (49%) and personal weapons as murder weapon of choice (41%). Vaginal penetration was commonly observed sexual assault (88%) and victim body mutilation was also (47%) (17).

A study from the US explored 260 sexual homicides (207 nonserial and 53 serial) and identified 50 cases in which an offender (45 nonserial and 10 serial) inserted a foreign object into a victim's orifice. The foreign object insertion prevalence rate for the sexual homicide sample of cases was 19.2 percent. Nonserial offenders engaged in foreign object insertion at about the same rate (21.7%) as the serial offenders (18.8%). The authors considered that insertion behavior of the nonserial offenders reflects a level of sadism and deviancy which was comparable with the serial offenders, which may have possible prognostic implications for future behavior (18).

Object insertion (whether an erect penis, an object or a hand) can result in hollow organ rupture. Kovelman described a 45-year-old white woman who sustained devastating homicidal colorectal trauma that served as a primary cause of death in the setting of rape (19). She had sustained a 15 cm laceration of the anterior rectal wall and ultimately died of peritonitis and sepsis. Death from rectal perforation and sepsis in the setting of sexual assault remains rare but is of interest as it may present late, and not be recognized before fatality is inevitable – particularly when drug or alcohol intoxication is present.

The nature of injury can be horrific. Preuss and colleagues describe a 32-year-old woman found naked with signs of severe blunt trauma and oral, vaginal and anal penetration. At the crime scene, the intestine lay next to the woman without connection to the body. The perpetrator admitted fisting and inserting several objects into the vagina, anus and oral cavity. Following anal and vaginal insertion of the hands, large parts of the intestine were torn and pulled out through the anus and the vagina (20).

INVESTIGATING POSSIBLE SEXUAL ACTIVITY DEATHS

It is clear that, for many deaths, the link between the death and sexual activity may not immediately be apparent and that any forensic practitioner must be aware of the range of possibilities and implications related to sexual activity of the individual or others. Not all deaths will require criminal investigation and the forensic pathologist may frequently assist in the need for such involvement. Some cases will clearly have a sexual motive and for those the following provides key elements of any sexual homicide investigation and autopsy.

THE SCENE

The scene of the sexual trauma death victim when found, may represent the first scene or the second, third, or fourth and more, dependent on whether the perpetrator or other have moved the body from the site of death (Figure 57.1). The approach to the scene to assist in the investigation and to separate the cause and manner of death will require a multidisciplinary input which may include some or all of police, forensic scientist, forensic biologist, forensic pathologist and other forensic practitioners such as a forensic physician or nurse. It is essential to secure and map the scene, record still and moving images, document findings, using alternative light sources to identify possible biological liquid/stain (semen, sperm, blood, urine, feces, vomit substance and other liquids), and take samples from the scene and objects near the deceased for later laboratory analysis. If the victim presents with any ligatures or ties, the integrity of the knot needs to be maintained, as this may provide crucial evidence as to the identity of the perpetrator. Other investigations include sending the knot for fingerprinting or seeking DNA profiles from any epithelial cell recovered from the knot (34).

Sexual asphyxia

The differentiation between accidental death from autoerotic asphyxia or consensual sexual asphyxia, asphyxia suicide and nonconsensual sexual asphyxia can be one of the most challenging problems for forensic pathologists and investigators.

Thus, the deceased might have a neck ligature in place to induce cerebral hypoxia for sexual stimulation (placed by themselves or another) by occluding carotid flow/venous return to the brain but because of the failure or delay in loosening the tight ligature on their neck, accidental death occurred. This may be accompanied by a tie around the neck, wearing a mask and restraining the hands/using handcuffs, or tie the penis, and tie the legs or ankles, or tied to some mild heavy sack by the weight to make a voluntarily mechanism to tighten and loosen the ligature of the neck at will. There may be evidence of drug use (anesthesia agents and volatile substances) or plastic covering to the head and face, or low voltage electric cable to the penis, to enhance erotic sensations. Close review at the scene by the investigator may be very helpful in indicating whether this is homicide, accidental sexual masochism disorder (asphyxiophilia), or suicide (35). Failure to assess the scene may mean that vital evidence which would have assisted is lost or destroyed. Other paraphernalia at the scene, which may give an indication of events leading to death, include the fetish clothing (such as wearing female/male clothing, leather gear, wig and make up), pornography in view or pictures scattered around the body. This must all be documented.

Post-mortem examination

The post-mortem examination follows standard processes for the jurisdiction and is likely to include (once

57.1 The scene: imaging, documentation and sample collection for the laboratory.

the body has been taken to the mortuary), being weighed and measured, screened for COVID-19 virus, or X-ray to identify fibrosis of the lungs to diagnose the COVID-19 death (to obtain the level of Personal Protection Equipment [PPE]). Post-mortem CT scanning should be undertaken to identify trauma of soft tissues, fractures and other foreign objects that may be present in the body (e.g. dildo, bottle, other implements) (36). The body should then be photographed and documented and examined using mortuary light sources.

External examination

The examination must be a comprehensive head-to-toe assessment. Clothing of the deceased may have evidence of debris or vegetation attached that might identify the scene of death. Head, face, cheek, mouth and lips must be examined for sharp and blunt force trauma (direct or indirect) including bruises, abrasions, laceration on the buccal area from the mouth caused by heavily kissing or by pressure on the lips against the teeth; bite or bitemarks (examination and documentation should be undertaken with a forensic odontologist), using alternative light sources to identify saliva stains on the face, neck, shoulders, breasts, nipples, upper arms, lower arms, hands, fingers, abdomen, back, thighs, groin area, genitalia, buttocks, legs, feet and toes (Figure 57.2). Examine for injuries on the neck, caused by manual strangulation or ligature or other compressive forces, and fingernail marks. Look for anogenital signs such as bruises around the anus caused by finger pressure on the cleft of buttocks, or by forced penetration of the posterior vulva or anus. The vulva and anus must be examined: look for bruising, swelling, lacerations, blood or other discharge. Stains and other debris on pubic hair need to be recovered by combing and cutting the hair. Sample collection must be undertaken, ideally before moving or manipulating the body.

The body might have incised wounds, inflicted by the perpetrator before, during or after the sexual assault (Figure 57.3). Identify, whenever possible, whether these are ante- or post mortem. On the perineum area: the vulva and anus look for bruising, swelling, lacerations, blood and other discharge. Stain and other debris on pubic hair, comb the hair and take the sample collection before moving or manipulated the body. There may be visual evidence of second- or third-degree perineal tears between the vulva and anus (37).

Internal examination

A standard autopsy must be followed but with a separate internal examination on the perineum area. On opening the abdomen, photography and documentation of any

57.2 Body *in situ* showing incised wound to neck; abdominal sharp force trauma with intestine herniation; stab wounds on the right buttock.

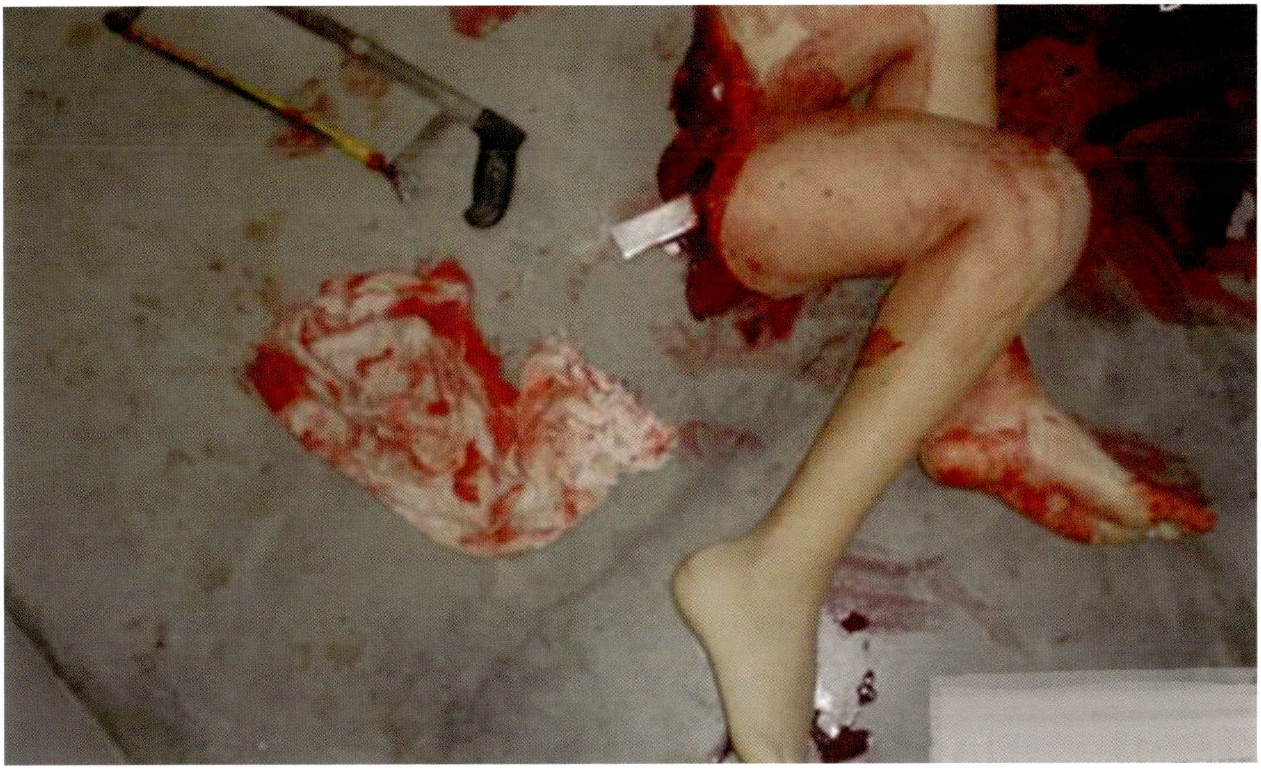

57.3 Mutilated body with manual handsaw following rape homicide.

wound or laceration of the vagina and cervix area which might be in continuity with the abdominal cavity which may have injuries to the internal organs. Rectal rupture may be present. Toxicological sampling is crucial and a urine sample is taken followed by examination of the pelvic organs detached on the autopsy on the anterior part of the pelvic and circumscribing the perineum. The vagina, cervix and the uterus are dissected on the non-injured area, with detailed examination and photography with all relevant genital anatomy being examined and sample collection following standard techniques. The histopathological sample collection were taken in this section. In some cases (e.g. with peritonitis or suspected child abuse) microbiological sampling may be relevant.

Sample collection

All jurisdictions will have their own standardized protocols for evidence retrieval and sample collection ensuring a robust chain of custody. Broad principles of recovery are explored below.

Anogenital samples should be collected before the external examination and before internal examination and during the autopsy findings (38). On the clothing, any debris/vegetation, stain of semen/ blood taken for sampling should be dried in room temperature and placed inside the evidence bag (39,40) (Figure 57.4).

Table 57.1 summarizes the samples which need to be considered.

All the cotton swabs are dried and placed in evidence bags (for the examination of semen, spermatozoa, DNA profile, sexual transmitted infection) complete the forms and send to the laboratory (39). The evidence bags must be accurately labeled: complete name with family name, date of birth (if the deceased's name is unknown: use the number of the sample and autopsy case number), date of the sample, type of sample, examiner name.

Semen/ seminal fluids and spermatozoa may be identified by using acid phosphatase test, even if the fabrics have been washed up to six times (41).

Toxicology is used to identify alcohol, drugs and others (42,43). The use of other substances in sexual assault cases is often region-specific and local toxicologists will be aware of particular drugs which should be screened for (43). Indonesia Penal Code Article 89 relates to the commission of violence involving a person in a state of unconsciousness or helplessness (4).

Antemortem examination

Finding bodies in situations which appear related to sexual activity poses a number of problems. Identification of the individual may be the least challenging part. It is helpful to seek more information about the individual from family, friends and colleagues. Unlike

1

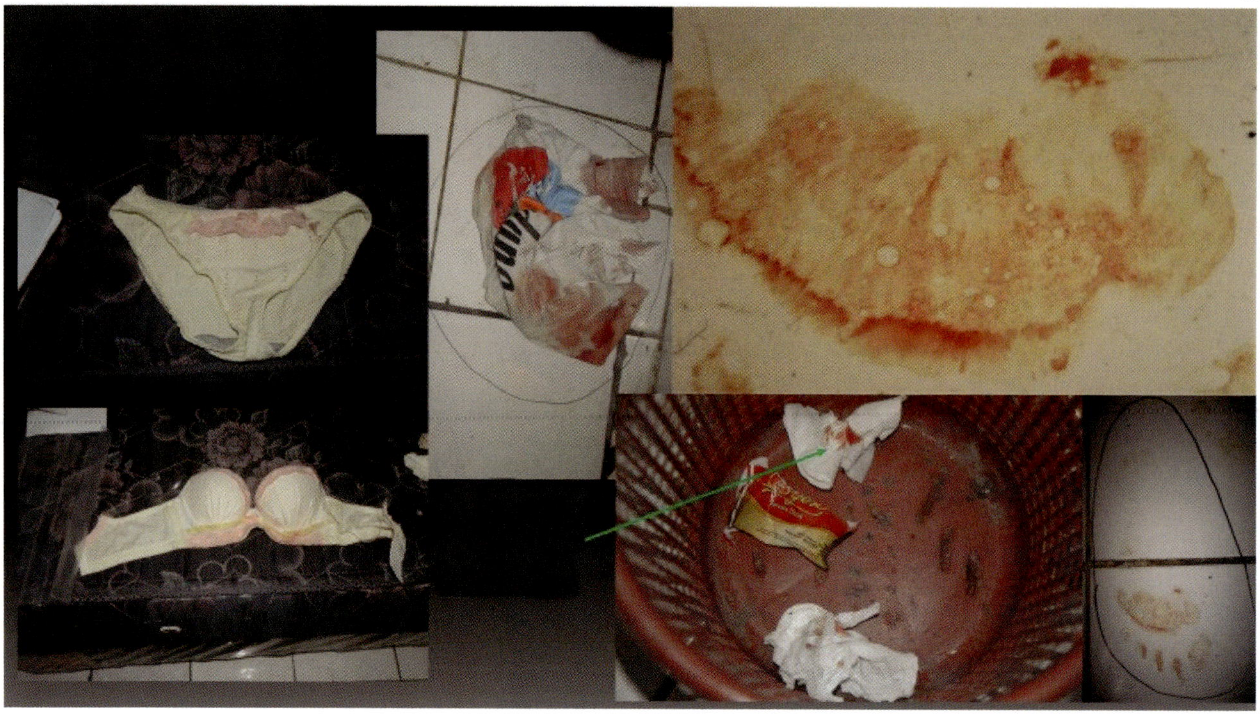

57.4 Relevant items that will require sampling an evidence collection. Bloodstain on the shirt and underwear, tissue in the waste bin and apparent bloody footprint on the floor.

TABLE 57.1 Range of samples that must be considered for recovery in sexual homicide cases
Samples from the body
Stains on head hair and pubic hair taken by cotton swab
Combed hair and pubic hair is cut and placed in separate evidence bags
Oral swabs taken by cotton swab for semen and DNA profiles of the victim and the perpetrator
Stains on the skin using cotton swab
Fingernail scrapings
Venous blood is taken for blood group, DNA profile and toxicology
Urine for pregnancy tasting, alcohol and/or toxicology examination
Bleeding/discharge of the vulva and anus
Female Cotton swabs on the margin vaginal orifice and interior of the vulva, margin and interior of the anus, mid-vagina open by speculum using cotton swab take the sample collection on the lower vaginal wall and upper vagina, cervix, and posterior fornix using cotton swabs to take the sample collections
Male Imaging, documentation and sample collection for the laboratory

Source: Adapted from (40).

non-sexual homicides, families and friends may be reluctant to disclose (or simply not be aware of) an individual's sexual preferences. It may also be that in cases of sexual asphyxia or autoerotic asphyxia that families or friends remove paraphernalia from the scene, or move the body, or change clothing out of perceived shame or embarrassment. Such interventions by friends or family may unintentionally alter the focus of the case on the part of the investigator resulting in vital and conclusive evidence being lost or disposed of before the police arrive and commence the scene examination.

CONCLUSION

Sexual activity death does not solely relate to sexual homicide but can include autoerotic activity, suicide, unintended consequences of both consensual and non-consensual sexual activity and deliberate criminal acts. The investigation of such deaths is often complex and in order to determine the cause of death and acts leading up to it, the expertise of forensic pathologists, forensic physicians, forensic scientist, crime scene investigators, child protection specialists, microbiologists and others may be required. These practitioners must be aware of the range of human sexual activity and how it might accidentally or deliberately, directly or indirectly lead to death, in order to best assist the investigating and legal authorities to come to the correct decision about the case to provide justice for the deceased and the bereaved and avoid miscarriages of justice.

REFERENCES

1. Holder E Jr, Robinson LO, Laub JH. Death investigation - A guide for scene investigator, 2011. Available from: https://www.ojp.gov/pdffiles/167568.pdf (Accessed 13 June 2023).
2. Vicks A. Regulating Medicolegal Death Investigations, Walden University, 2019. Available from: scholarworks.waldenu.edu/cgi/viewcontent.cgi?article=8788&context=dissertations (Accessed 13 June 2023).
3. Indonesia Law of Criminal Procedure, 1981. Available from: defensewiki.ibj.org/images/6/62/Indonesia_Law_of_Criminal_Procedure.pdf (Accessed 13 June 2023).
4. Indonesia Penal Code, 1999. Available from: www.icj.org/wp-content/uploads/2013/01/Indonesia-Penal-Code-1999-eng.pdf (Accessed 13 June 2023).
5. Federal Bureau of Investigation. Rape, 2017. Available from: https://ucr.fbi.gov/crime-in-the-u.s/2017/crime-in-the-u.s.-2017/topic-pages/rape (Accessed 13 June 2023).
6. Higgs T, Carter AJ, Tully RJ, Brown KD. Sexual murder typologies: A systematic review. *Aggress Violent Behav* 2017; **35**: 1–12.
7. Bunzel L, Koelzer SC, Zedler B, et al. Non-natural death associated with sexual activity: Results of a 25-year medicolegal postmortem study. *J Sex Med* 2019; **16**: 1547–56.
8. Roma P, Pazzelli F, Pompili M, et al. Shibari: double hanging during consensual sexual asphyxia. *Arch Sex Behav* 2013; **42**(**5**): 895–900.
9. Bauer K, Schön CA, Jackowski C. Fatal strangulation during consensual BDSM activity: Three case reports. *Int J Legal Med* 2021; **135**(**1**): 347–53.
10. Sadler DW, Pounder DJ. Fatal air embolism occurring during consensual intercourse in a non-pregnant female. *J Clin Forensic Med* 1998; **5**(**2**): 77–9.
11. Moreschi C, Da Broi U. Paradoxical air embolism through patent foramen ovale during consensual intercourse in a non-pregnant young female. *J Forensic Leg Med* 2009; **16**(**8**): 482–5.
12. Weisheng H, Shuang W, Yue L, et al. Fatal cervix rupture due to intraplacental choriocarcinoma triggered by sexual intercourse. *Int J Legal Med* 2020; **134**(**1**): 317–20.
13. Walong E. Mortality due to pelvic inflammatory disease with peritonitis with surgical intervention occurring in a sexually abused minor: A case report. *Forensic Sci Int* 2019; **1**: 100002.
14. Skott S, Beauregard E, Darjee R. Sexual and nonsexual homicide in scotland: Is there a difference? *Interpers Violence* 2021; **36**(**7–8**): 3209–30.
15. Skott S, Beauregard E, Darjee R. Female sexual homicide offenders: A descriptive and comparative study. *J Forensic Sci* 2019; **64**(**1**): 154–62.
16. James J, Proulx J, Vuidard E, et al. Sexual homicide in France. *Int J Offender Ther Comp Criminol* 2019; **63**(**9**): 1575–96.
17. Chan HCO, Li F, Liu S, et al. Sexual homicides in China: Exploring the offender, victim, and offense characteristics. *Int J Offender Ther Comp Criminol* 2019; **63**(**9**): 1517–37.
18. Koeppel S, Schlesinger LB, Craun SW, et al. Foreign object insertions in sexual homicide. *Int J Offender Ther Comp Criminol* 2019; **63**(**9**): 1726–37.
19. Kovelman I, Vey E, Schober J. Fatal anorectal trauma in the setting of sexual assault: Case report and literature survey. *Am J Forensic Med Pathol* 2010; **31**(**3**): 273–7.
20. Preuss V, Wöllner K, Vennemann B, et al. Fatal anogenital exenteration of the intestine. *Forensic Sci Med Pathol* 2022; **18**(**1**): 64–8.
21. Krasowski MD. Drug-Assisted Sexual Assaults: Toxicology, Fatality, and Analytical Challenges. In: Dasgupta A (ed), *Critical Issues in Alcohol and Drugs of Abuse Testing*, 2nd ed. London: Elsevier; 2019, pp. 225–36.
22. Kerrigan S. The use of alcohol to facilitate sexual assault. *Forensic Sci Rev* 2010; **22**: 15–32.
23. Couper FJ, Saady JJ. The use of miscellaneous prescription medications to facilitate sexual assault. *Forensic Sci Rev* 2010; **22**: 83–112.
24. Jenkins AJ, Stillwell ME. The use of over-the-counter medications to facilitate sexual assault. *Forensic Sci Rev* 2010; **22**: 75–82.
25. Richeval C, Allorge D, Lopez V, et al. Unusual case of drug-facilitated sexual assault using chloroform. *J Anal Toxicol* 2017; **41**(**3**): 256–7.
26. Kintz P, Villain M, Tracqui A, et al. Buprenorphine in drug-facilitated sexual abuse: A fatal case involving a 14-year-old boy. *J Anal Toxicol* 2003; **27**(**7**): 527–9.
27. Mehling LM, Johansen SS, Wang X, et al. Drug facilitated sexual assault with lethal outcome: GHB intoxication in a six-year-old girl. *Forensic Sci Int* 2016; **259**: e25–31.
28. Busardo FP, Portelli F, Montana A, et al. When a death apparently associated to sexual assault is instead a natural death due to idiopathic hypereosinophilic syndrome: The importance of gamma-hydroxybutyric acid analysis in vitreous humor. *Leg Med* 2017; **26**: 92–7.
29. Koops E, Janssen W, Anders S, Puschel K. Unusual phenomenology of autoerotic fatalities. *Forensic Sci Int* 2005; **147**: 65–7.
30. BBC News. MI6 'body-in-bag': Spy Gareth Williams' London flat death reviewed, 2021. Available from: https://www.bbc.co.uk/news/uk-wales-56158160 (Accessed 13 June 2023).
31. Oviedo-Trespalacios O, Phillips JG. Sexual activity while driving: A content analysis of media reports. *Transp Res Part F* 2021; **80**: 141–9.
32. Oviedo-Trespalacios O, Newton JDA, Demant D, et al. Understanding sexual activity while driving as a form of distracted driving. *Accid Anal Prev* 2022; **169**: 106621.
33. Virgilio E, Franzese E, Caterino S. Zoosexuality: An unusual cause of colorectal injury. *Acta Chir Belg* 2016; **116**(**5**): 316–18.
34. Mailhes J, Yarrarapu SNS, Callahan AL. *Sexual Assault Clothing Collection and Documentation*. Treasure Island: StatPearls Publishing; 2022.
35. Coluccia A, Gabbrielli M, Gualtieri G, et al. Sexual masochism disorder with asyphxiophilia: A deadly yet underrecognized disease. *Case Rep Psychiatry* 2016; **2016**: 5474862.
36. Lynch MJ, Woodford NW. The role of post-mortem imaging in preliminary examinations under the Coroners Act 2008 (Vic): A forensic pathologist's perspective. *J Law Med* 2014; **21**(**4**): 774–9.
37. Knight B. Death Associated with Sexual Offences. In: Knight B (ed), *Forensic Pathology*, 2nd ed. London: Oxford University Press; 1996, pp. 417–25.
38. Jones NS, Fornaro E (eds). 2019 National Institute of Justice Forensic Science Research and Development Symposium. Available from: https://www.ojp.gov/ncjrs/

virtual-library/abstracts/2019-national-institute-justice-forensic-science-research-and (Accessed 13 June 2023).

39. Ladd M, Seda J. *Sexual Assault Evidence Collection*. Treasure Island: StatPearls Publishing; 2022.
40. Bazinet M, Larose J, Noel S, et al. Data driven optimization of sexual assault case processing. *Forensic Sci Int Synerg* 2020; **2:** 164–72.
41. Nolan A, Speers SJ, Murakami J, et al. A pilot study: The effects of repeat washing and fabric type on the detection of seminal fluid and spermatozoa. *Forensic Sci Int* 2018; **289:** 51–6.
42. Mohr ALA, Logan BK, Fogarty MF, et al. Reports of adverse events associated with the use of novel psychoactive substances, 2017–2020: A review. *J Anal Toxicol* 2022; **46(6)**: 116–85.
43. The Center for Forensic Science Research & Education. Medicolegal Death Investigation. Available from: www.cfsre.org/research/forensic-toxicology/medicolegal-death-investigation (Accessed 13 June 2023).

CHAPTER

58

Autoerotic Deaths

Larissa Lohner and Jan-Peter Sperhake

INTRODUCTION AND DEFINITION

Deaths caused by autoerotic acts have been widely described in the forensic literature (1–29) and show a wide range of findings at the scene as well as on the deceased.

In erotic asphyxia ("asphyxophilia") (30), oxygen deprivation is induced to enhance sexual pleasure, using strangulation tools, airway occlusion by various devices (plastic bags, gags, latex or gas masks), chest compression, gas inhalation or a combination of these methods. Paraphilic objects may be present (5,19,31–35). In addition, the production of suffering or fear may be the goal of autoerotic acts (masochism) (36).

Autoerotic deaths are defined as unintentional deaths "that occur during individual, usually solitary, sexual activity in which a device, apparatus, or prop that was employed to enhance the sexual stimulation of the deceased in some way caused unintended death" (37).

Depending on the method, a distinction is made between "typical" and "atypical" autoerotic acts. Common, typical autoerotic practices include asphyxiation by strangulation/hanging, plastic bags, gas inhalation, and/or ingestion of chemical substances during autoerotic activity. Electrical stimulation, "body wrapping" (wrapping in foil), aqua-eroticum (35,38,39), foreign body insertion, or chest compression (atypical asphyxia) are often categorized as "atypical" methods in the literature and account for approximately 10 percent of all autoerotic deaths (13,24,31,41–44). A "typical autoerotic death" results from asphyxia by strangulation or hanging, whereas an atypical autoerotic death results from other asphyxia mechanisms (43,44).

In the United States and Canada with joint populations approaching 370 million, autoerotic deaths account for approximately 500 to 1000 cases per year (33,35,43–46). In Hamburg, the second largest city in Germany with a population of 1.8 million, 65 deaths with an autoerotic background have been forensically investigated in 35 years, including 7 deaths from internal causes during autoerotic acts (18,20,21). Sudden deaths from internal causes (e.g. myocardial infarction or stroke) during an autoerotic act are natural deaths and not autoerotic accidents in the strict sense although the legal outcome may vary dependent on jurisdiction (1,41). Overall, an unreported number of fatal autoerotic accidents can be assumed, since situations found may be misinterpreted or altered by relatives due to shame or embarrassment.

Basic knowledge of autoerotic accidents resulting in death is essential for the physician examining the deceased, since it is a non-natural death and thus in many countries there is an obligation to notify it to the police or other relevant authority. The physician may be expected to make an initial interpretation of the findings with regard to the possibility of third-party causation. Untrained observers – including police officers and other emergency services workers and first responders – may interpret bizarre situations in which the body is found as an indication of a mysterious ritual murder rather than an accidental suicide.

DEMOGRAPHICS

Men between the ages of 20 and 40 years are predominantly affected, with an age range of 9 to 87 years in published literature (2,5,11,16,18,21,24,31,35,40,43,44,47). Autoerotic deaths in women have been described much less frequently but occur sporadically (3,7,9,11,18,21,24,35,40,43,44,47,48). The accompanying scene for women is often less clear-cut and more characterized by the absence of typical objects, pornographic material, or "props." Particularly in women, homicide or death from internal causes should be ruled out with special care before an autoerotic accident is determined (7,36,45,48,49). In contrast to men, women are often found unclothed, with only a single ligature, and without bizarre devices; therefore, autoerotic accidents in women are less often recognized and therefore may be misinterpreted (49). Reasons for the small number of autoerotic deaths in women could be greater caution in the methods used, but also failure to diagnose in the field. However, the exact reasons remain unclear (3,9). It is likely that men are simply more prone to extreme forms of autoerotic activity.

DOI: 10.1201/9781003138754-60

DEATH SCENE

The scene in autoerotic deaths is usually described as bizarre. Victims are usually found alone in locked rooms, usually in their own homes, or in hidden public places with genitals exposed, fetish clothing such as latex clothing, and masks or women's underwear. In some cases, elaborate bondage and suspension devices are used, including intricate self-ties. The site of the activities is sometimes decorated with mirrors. Sadomasochistic paraphernalia such as chains, whips and barbed wire are also used (36). Pornographic material and sexually stimulating implements such as dildos, plugs and gags are frequently found in the environment. Often, there is evidence of previous sexual practices of this type at the site of the crime. In many cases, sophisticated self-rescue or fail-safe mechanisms had been constructed prior to the event. These include timers with devices to move the handcuff keys to an accessible position (14), or chairs designed to interrupt hanging (25). Other safety devices are used to control or relieve strangulation pressure and tension to reduce hypoxia (40). In rare cases, electrical devices are used for sexual stimulation. Self-restraint with electrical wires also occurs. The death scene is not infrequently misinterpreted, and often making a clear distinction between suicide, homicide and accident can be difficult. The scene should therefore be thoroughly investigated to rule out homicide or suicide – especially if the individuals are found unclothed and without any corroborating evidence (7). As hanging is the most common method of suicide (50), an autoerotic accident by hanging often cannot be distinguished from suicide beyond reasonable doubt. The involvement of a forensic pathologist on the part of the police can already help to clarify the situation at the death scene. The possibility that relatives or others have adjusted the scene at the place of death (e.g. by moving the body or removing autoerotic paraphernalia) because of shame and embarrassment should always be considered (14,19,21,24,26,34,35,41,43,51). It is believed that some asphyxial deaths were described in the literature as suicides before later being reinterpreted as autoerotic deaths (33,52,53).

CAUSES OF DEATH

Autoerotic acts can be fatal if self-induced oxygen deprivation occurs concurrent with failure to control the dosage of hypoxia or a self-rescue mechanism.

Strangulation: The most common cause of death in typical autoerotic accidents is asphyxiation due to strangulation (especially hanging) (7,11,18,24,35,43). Death occurs due to failure of "metered strangulation." At autopsy, the typical findings of strangulation by typical or atypical hanging are:

Airway covering and carbon dioxide rebreathing: The second most common cause of death in autoerotic accidents is asphyxia due to airway covering (7,11,18,24), often with a plastic bag or latex or gas masks, sometimes with airway closure by gagging. This leads to accumulation of carbon dioxide and consumption of oxygen. Autopsy signs of external and internal congestion (petechiae, emphysema) may be present.

Gas inhalation and intoxication: Due to the euphoric and aphrodisiac effects, volatile substances such as nitrous oxide (laughing gas; N_2O), alcohols, gasoline and ether are used for gas inhalation. These substances are readily available because they are used in nail polish removers, lacquer thinners and adhesives. The use of propane, butane or chloroform has also been described (21,33,36,43,54–56). Overdose with respiratory paralysis and cardiac arrhythmias can be fatal in these cases. In addition to gas inhalation, death can also result from intoxication with drugs or narcotics (e.g. ketamine) (6,42,57). A combination of the above methods has also been described (e.g. plastic bags and strangulation) (2,3,5,8,13,24,31,35,40,42,46,58). Toxicological studies to exclude or confirm are therefore strongly indicated. However, several studies have shown that narcotics, drugs and alcoholic beverages play a rather minor role among the total number of autoerotic accidents (21,43,44,59).

Electrical stimulation: Peripheral electrical stimulation to the genitals or erogenous zones results in a current flow that can be lethal. If the death scene has not been altered, it should usually be possible to reconstruct the mechanism forensically. Current marks may be visible at autopsy (19,44).

Foreign body insertion: According to the literature, deaths from foreign bodies inserted are rare and account for 1.2 percent of autoerotic deaths. Death may result from intra-abdominal injury or foreign body explosion (17).

Atypical asphyxia: Atypical asphyxia can occur by chest compression or by wrapping the body in plastic wrap ("body wrapping") or constriction with ropes (inverted suspension/abdominal ligature) (21,26,35).

Autoerotic drowning: Cases of autoerotic drowning are a rarity in the scientific literature. Asphyxia is produced by immersion in water. Concurrently, fear is experienced (38,39).

Overall, deaths caused by electrical stimulation, insertion of a foreign body, immersion in water or atypical asphyxia are less frequently described and belong to atypical autoerotic deaths (17,21,24,26,35,44).

EXTERNAL EXAMINATION OF THE BODY AND AUTOPSY

Autoerotic deaths exhibit considerable variability both at the site of discovery and at the corpse itself. An examination of the death scene, as well as a forensic external necropsy and autopsy, in combination with post-mortem computed tomography (if possible) are therefore of immense importance. The condition of the clothing (latex materials, fetish clothing, gas masks, gags) and any sexual aids present, as well as evidence of asphyxiation, can provide initial information. In bondage situations, the conditions should be documented in detail and the bondage material should be kept to be able to check and, if necessary, even exclude the possibility of self-infliction (60).

Autoerotic accidents are non-natural deaths, whereas death from internal causes during an autoerotic act should be classified as natural death. This distinction may also be of importance in insurance law but will, to some extent, vary according to jurisdiction. If the materials used (plastic bag, strangulation device) that ultimately led to death were intentionally used as part of the act, there is often no recognition in insurance law as an accidental death and thus no accident insurance benefit. If, on the other hand, death occurs accidentally during the autoerotic act, for example by tripping, there may be an insurer's obligation to pay benefits (34).

Since intoxication for example taking "poppers" (Amyl nitrite) can also occur in autoerotic acts, chemical-toxicological examinations and blood alcohol concentration screening and assay should be done and may influence interpretation of the findings (21,42).

AUTOEROTIC ACCIDENTS IN CHILDREN AND YOUNG ADULTS

Autoerotic acts occur not only in adults but also in adolescents and children (61,62). The earliest medically reported case of autoerotic death involved a 12-year-old boy in 1856 (63). Deaths during an autoerotic act often cannot be distinguished beyond doubt from suicide in adolescence, especially when no prior signs of suicidality have been noted and parents have had little access to their children's mental well-being. Particularly in the case of very young people, it should be borne in mind that the death scene may have been altered by the parents (61). Thus, especially in children, it can be very difficult to reliably distinguish early suicide, risky play behavior, copycat behaviors (e.g. from social media) and autoerotic activity.

CASE EXAMPLE 1

A 46-year-old man was found dead after he failed to show up for work. He was found in a kneeling position in front of the bathtub. There was an iron chain and rope attached to his neck, which was connected to the shower's mounting bar (Figure 58.1).

The body was fully clothed in latex, including latex stilettos. There was a leather mask on the head, a collar around the neck and a gag in the mouth. On the hands, were synthetic leather gloves, with the right thumb and the end phalanx of the right index finger exposed. The legs were tied with leather straps. The chain was locked at the neck with a brass padlock. Further along toward the shower rod was another brass lock. Through this, the chain was diverted to the buttocks. At the level of the shoulder blades, there was another brass lock, from which a chain around the hips led to a lock in the pubic area. Another chain led back to the lock on the back. On the back was another lock with a four-digit numerical code that held the other chains together. Through the shackle of the combination lock led the chain links of two handcuffs that fixed the hands behind the back (Figure 58.2).

The combination lock could be reached with the hands. A snap hook with eight keys was attached to the front neck area. The associated keys were attached to a keychain on the collar. A jack cable led from the laptop, which was located in the room above the sink and shower rod, to the head under the latex mask. Associated with this, were headphones that were inserted into the ear canals. The laptop was activated by the police officers. Now a computer voice announced a numerical code. This allowed the combination lock on the back to be opened. In the hallway in front of the bathroom was a floor lamp. The lamp's reflector was pointed into the bathroom and the power cord led into the bedroom, where it was connected to an electronic timer. Bondage clothing and various bondage objects were also found in the apartment. When the body was stripped during the autopsy, a red leatherette bodysuit, a black thong, nylon stockings, and two attached silicone breasts were revealed beneath the latex clothing. Under the leather mask were a latex hood and a latex swim cap. There was a plug in the anal canal. The forensic autopsy determined the cause of death to be suffocation by atypical hanging. Chemical-toxicological tests and a blood alcohol concentration determination were negative. A closer look at the elaborate restraint mechanism including a combination lock slightly above the hands raises the question whether this complicated setup was really intended as a self-rescue mechanism or whether another person should be involved here to open the combination lock by the announced code and free the man. The computer voice that was supposed to announce the code for opening the combination lock, in combination with the prepared gloves, suggested a self-rescue mechanism. The combination lock could be opened by him without sight, only by feeling the number wheels. However, in this case, an extraneous rescue by another person cannot be ruled out. Due to the conspicuous clothing, the sole sexual activity with induced oxygen deprivation and the rescue mechanism with numerical code and timer, this case was considered to be very likely a typical autoerotic accident, although third party involvement cannot be completely ruled out. However, no suspect was identified by the police in this regard.

(Continued)

CASE EXAMPLE 1 (Continued)

58.1 Typical autoerotic death scene from case 1 (From Institute of Legal Medicine, University Medical Center Hamburg-Eppendorf, Hamburg, Germany, 2016.)

58.2 Detail of hand cuffing from case 1. (From Institute of Legal Medicine, University Medical Center Hamburg-Eppendorf, Hamburg, Germany, 2016.)

CASE EXAMPLE 2

A 13-year-old boy was found hanged by his mother in a 3 m^2 room in their shared apartment. The body was dressed in a hooded sweatshirt with the hood pulled over the head and jeans with the fly open. Over the clothing, which was very tight around the neck, were a black nylon strap with a snap hook and a green cloth strap intertwined and lying on the left side of the neck to form a running noose. These were attached to a door hook. Also hanging from this hook was a lady's belt. The boy was hanging facing the door with the tips of his toes touching the floor. A total of three antenna cables were also used. One of them was loosely wrapped around the neck and knotted in the front area. Two others were used to tie the right wrist as well as the left ankle (Figure 58.3).

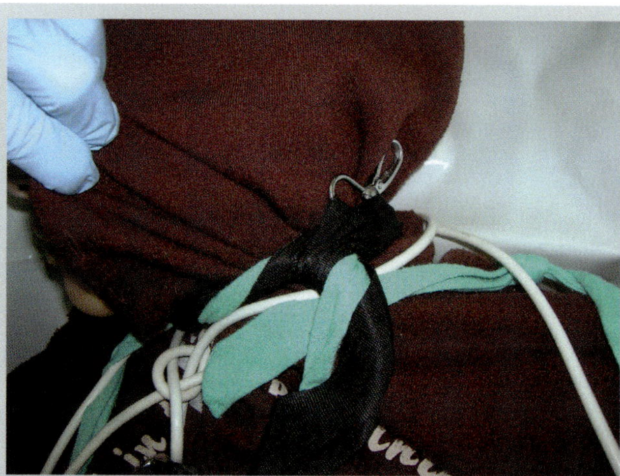

58.3 Bondage situation of the 13-year-old boy from case 2. (From Institute of Legal Medicine, University Medical Center Hamburg-Eppendorf, Hamburg, Germany, 2013.)

No medicolegal examination was conducted at the death scene. A suicide note was not found. There was a bikini top on the boy's bed that belonged to the mother. At autopsy, lividity appeared on the front and back of the legs. Single petechiae were visible on the eyelids and a distinct ligature mark was visible on the neck. There were constrictions on the right wrist consistent with the aerial cable. Post-mortem examination revealed discrete hemorrhages at the origin of the sternocleidomastoid muscles, hemorrhages at the anterior longitudinal ligament of the spine and pulmonary hyperinflation.

CASE EXAMPLE 2 (Continued)

From the medical history, it was known that the boy suffered from attention deficit disorder and apparently had no friends. He had also been psychologically abnormal in other ways, having engaged in sexually assaultive behavior toward his mother. He had often cuddled with his mother, fondled her breasts and masturbated in front of her. However, sexual intercourse allegedly never occurred. The boy had always seen his mother as a partner. He also turned over photos in the apartment because he felt he was being watched. The boy never expressed suicidal thoughts. The cause of death was hypoxic encephalopathy by hanging. The prosecutor did not order toxicological examinations and determination of blood alcohol concentration. A clear distinction between suicidal and autoerotic hanging could not be determined. The mental health issues, were considered to support death by suicide. However, the number of hanging devices in combination with the hand and foot restraints, which were not necessary for a suicidal hanging, could also be suggestive for an autoerotic act, especially in combination with the opening of the fly and the finding of the bikini top. This case illustrates the particular difficulties that may exist, especially in young people, in distinguishing between a suicide and an autoerotic accident.

TABLE 58.1 Criteria for the diagnosis of an autoerotic accident (4,32,33,37,43)

Criteria for the diagnosis of an autoerotic accident
Individual, solitary sexual activity
Inducing a lack of oxygen to increase sexual activity possibly in combination with a self-rescue mechanism
Failure of the oxygen-deficient mechanism (accident)
Sexually stimulating/ fantasy aids (e.g. pornographic material, dildos, plugs, latex clothing, bondage material)
Conspicuous decoration at the site (mirrors, cameras, narcotic bottles, "torture chamber")
No suicidal intent
Absence of signs of extraneous violence
Prior autoerotic practice
Exclusion of natural death

TABLE 58.2 Distinction between "typical" and "atypical" autoerotic accident (40,42,43,44)

Typical autoerotic accident	Atypical autoerotic accident
Asphyxia due to strangulation/ hanging	Electrical stimulation resulting in death
Asphyxia due to plastic bag	"Body wrapping" resulting in death
Asphyxia due to gas inhalation	Chest compression resulting in death (atypical asphyxia)
	Foreign body insertion resulting in death
	Autoerotic drowning (water immersion)

CONCLUSION

In conclusion, the death scene of an autoerotic death is often bizarre, and the death happens unexpectedly for the relatives. The diagnosis of an autoerotic death can only be made by combining the findings from the death scene examination (the finding situation is directional), post-mortem computed tomography, chemical toxicology analysis and autopsy. Nevertheless, the distinction between a suicide and an autoerotic accident may be difficult in some cases. The criteria in Table 58.1 may help in making the diagnosis. However, a homicide must be ruled out in all cases. In addition, a distinction should be made between an autoerotic accident and a natural death during sexual acts, particularly with regard to possible accident insurance benefits. Therefore, the finding situation must not be changed under any circumstances. An autoerotic accident/death is classified as a non-natural death.

REFERENCES

1. Baber Y, Bott E. Natural death in the setting of autoerotic practice. *Forensic Sci Med Pathol* 2016; 12: 174–7.
2. Bauer K, Schön CA, Jackowski C. Fatal strangulation during consensual BDSM activity: Three case reports. *Int J Legal Med* 2021; 135: 347–53.
3. Behrendt N, Buhl N, Seidl S. The lethal paraphiliac syndrome: Accidental autoerotic deaths in four women and a review of the literature. *Int J Legal Med* 2002; 116: 148–52.
4. Behrendt N, Modvig J. The lethal paraphiliac syndrome. Accidental autoerotic deaths in Denmark 1933–1990. Am J *Forensic Med Pathol* 1995; 16: 232–7.
5. Blanchard R, Hucker SJ. Age, transvestism, bondage, and concurrent paraphilic activities in 117 fatal cases of autoerotic asphyxia. *Br J Psychiatry* 1991; 159: 371–7.
6. Breitmeier D, Mansouri F, Albrecht K, et al. Accidental autoerotic deaths between 1978 and 1997 Institute of Legal Medicine, Medical School Hannover. *Forensic Sci Int* 2003; 137: 41–4.

7. Byard RW. Autoerotic death: A rare but recurrent entity. *Forensic Sci Med Pathol* 2012; 8: 349–50.
8. Byard RW. Manner of death associated with autoerotic practice. *Forensic Sci Pathol* 2016; 12: 236–7.
9. Byard RW. Female autoerotic asphyxia death: Features and issues. *Forensic Sci Med Pathol* 2017; 13: 107–9.
10. Byard RW, Botterill P. Autoerotic asphyxial death: Accident or suicide? *Am J Forensic Med Pathol 1998*; 19: 377–80.
11. Byard RW, Winskog C. Autoerotic death: Incidence and age of victims: A population-based study. *J Forensic Sci* 2012; 57: 129–31.
12. Capatina C, Hostiuc S, Dragoteanu C, et al. Autoerotic asphyxia hanging: Case presentation. *Rom J Leg Med* 2009; 3: 193–8.
13. Coluccia A, Gabbrielli M, Gualtieri G, et al. Sexual masochism disorder with asphyxiophilia: A deadly yet underrecognized disease. *Case Rep in Psychiatry* 2016; 2016: 5474862.
14. Doberentz E, Hülder J, Madea B. Autoerotische Asphyxie. Falldarstellung einer ungewöhnlichen Selbstfesselung. *Rechtsmed* 2012; 22: 39–44.
15. Eckhardt M, Shah K, Bois M, et al. Healed fracture of superior horn of thyroid cartilage in autoerotic asphyxia: An indication of prior activity? A case report utilizing 3D scanning and printing of the larynx. *Acad Forensic Pathol* 2018; 8: 170–9.
16. Halbach CS, Harrison AR, Broadbent TJ, et al. Erotic asphyxiation: May have you seeing double. *Am J Ophthalmol Case Rep* 2019; 13: 99–101.
17. Hejna P, Zátopkova L, Janík M. Rectal explosion: A strange case of autoerotic death. *Int J Legal Med* 2021; 135: 307–12.
18. Janssen W, Koops E, Anders S, et al. Forensic aspects of 40 accidental autoerotic deaths in northern Germany. *Forensic Sci Int* 2005; 147: 61–4.
19. Klintschar M, Grabuschnigg P, Alfred B. Death from electrocution during autoerotic practice: Case report and review of the literature. *Am J Forensic Med* 1998; 19: 190–3.
20. Koops E, Janssen W, Anders S, et al. Unusual phenomenology of autoerotic fatalities. *Forensic Sci Int* 2005; 147: 65–7.
21. Lohner L, Sperhake JP, Püschel K, et al. Autoerotic death in Hamburg, Germany: Autoerotic accident or death from internal cause in an autoerotic setting? A retrospective study from 2004–2018. *Forensic Sci Int* 2020; 313: 110340.
22. Lunetta P, Kriikku P, Tikka J, et al. Fatal a-PVP and amphetamine poisoning during a sauna and autoerotic practices. *Forensic Sci Med Pathol* 2020; 16: 493–7.
23. Nozomi I, Nakamura M, Tsuboi H, et al. Autoerotic asphyxia using a plastic bag loosely covering the head over a gas mask. *Leg Med* 2019; 38: 69–72.
24. Sauvageau A. A 25-year retrospective epidemiological study. *Am J Forensic Med Pathol* 2012; 33: 143–6.
25. Sauvageau A. Current reports on autoerotic deaths: Five persistent myths. *Curr Psychiatry Rep* 2014; 16: 430.
26. Schellenberg M, Racette S, Sauvageau A. Complex autoerotic death with full body wrapping in a plastic body bag. *J Forensic Sci* 2007; 52: 954–6.
27. Tattoli L, Solarino B, Tsokos M, et al. Two extraordinary autoerotic facilities. *Forensic Sci Med Pathol* 2017; 13: 102–6.
28. Tzikas A, Kornappel S, Püschel K. Autoerotic deaths and low socioeconomic status. Presentation of two cases. *Rechtsmedizin* 2016; 26: 53–5.
29. Ueno Y, Asano M, Nushida H, et al. Sexual asphyxia by hanging: A case report and a review of the literature. *Leg Med* 2003; 5: 175–80.
30. Money J, Wainwright G, Hinsburger D. The Breathless Orgasm: *A Lovemap Biography of Asphyxiophilia*. Buffalo, New York: Prometheus Book; 1991.
31. Gowitt GT, Hanzlick RL. Atypical autoerotic deaths. *Am J Forensic Med Pathol* 1992; 13: 115–19.
32. Hazelwood RR, Burgess AW, Groth AN. Death during dangerous autoerotic practice. *Soc Sci Med E* 1981; 15: 129–33.
33. Hazelwood RR, Dietz PE, Burgess AW. *Autoerotic Fatalities*. Lexington: Lexington Books; 1983.
34. Naeve W, Wittram S. *Tödliche Autoerotische Unfälle*. Karlsruhe: Verlag Versicherungswirtschaft e. V.; 1977.
35. Sauvageau A, Racette S. Autoerotic deaths in the literature from 1954 to 2004: A review. *J Forensic Sci* 2006; 51: 140–6.
36. Geserick G. Tödliche Unfälle bei autoerotischer (autosexueller) Betätigung. In: Madea B (ed), R*echtsmedizin. Befunderhebung, Rekonstruktion, Begutachtung*, 3rd Auflage. Berlin Heidelberg: Springer-Verlag; 2015, pp. 357.
37. Byard RW, Bramwell NH. Autoerotic death. A definition. *Am J Forensic Med Pathol* 1991; 12: 74–6.
38. Sauvageau A, Racette S. Aqua-eroticum: An unusual autoerotic fatality in a lake involving a home-made diving apparatus. *J Forensic Sci* 2006; 51: 137–9.
39. Sivaloganathan S. Aqua-eroticum: A case of auto-erotic drowning. *Med Sci Law* 1984; 24: 300–2.
40. Byard RW. Autoerotic death: Characteristic features and diagnostic difficulties. *J Clin Forensic Med* 1994; 1: 71–5.
41. Du Chesne A, Brinkmann B. Autoerotische Unfälle. In: Brinkmann B, Madea B (eds), *Handbuch gerichtliche Medizin*, Bd. 1. Berlin: Springer-Verlag; 2004, pp. 794–6.
42. Musshoff F, Padosch SA, Kroener LA, et al. Accidental autoerotic death by volatile substance abuse or nonsexual motivated accidents? *Am J Forensic Med Pathol* 2006; 27: 188–92.
43. Shields LBE, Hunsaker DM, Hunsaker JC. Autoerotic asphyxia: Part I. *Am J Forensic Med Pathol* 2005; 26: 45–52.
44. Shields LBE, Hunsaker DM, Hunsaker JC, et al. Atypical autoerotic death: Part II. *Am J Forensic Med Pathol* 2005; 26: 53–62.
45. Byard RW, Hucker SJ, Hazelwood RR. Fatal and near-fatal autoerotic asphyxia episodes in women. Characteristic features based on a review of nine cases. *Am J Forensic Med Pathol* 1993; 14: 70–3.
46. Nadesan K, Beng OB. Two cases of death due to plastic bag suffocation. *Med Sci Law* 2001; 41: 78–82.
47. Sauvageau A, Geberth VJ. Elderly victim: An unusual autoerotic fatality involving an 87-year-old male. *Forensic Sci Med Pathol* 2009; 5: 233–5.
48. Byard RW, Hucker SJ, Hazelwood RR. A Comparison of typical death scene features in cases of fatal male and female autoerotic asphyxia with a review of the literature. *Forensic Sci Int* 1990; 48: 113–21.
49. Byard RW, Bramwell NH. Autoerotic death in females. An underdiagnosed syndrome? *Am J Forensic Med Pathol* 1988; 9: 252–4.
50. Wu Y, Schwebel DC, Huang Y, et al. Sex specific and age-specific suicide mortality by method in 58 countries between 2000 and 2015. *Inj Prev* 2021; 27(1): 61–70.
51. Solarino B, Leonardi S, Grattagliano I, et al. An unusual death of a masochist: Accident or suicide? *Forensic Sci Int* 2011; 204: e16–19.
52. Auden GA. An unusual form of suicide. *J Mental Sci* 1927; 73: 428–30.
53. Lunetta P. Atypical suicides or the first undiagnosed autoerotic deaths in Europe? *J Forensic Leg Med* 2013; 20: 1010–1013.
54. Byard RW, Kostakis C, Pigou PE, et al. Volatile substance use in sexual asphyxia. *J Clin Forensic Med* 2000; 7: 26–8.
55. McLennan JJ, Sekula-Perlman A, Lippstone M, et al. Propane-associated autoerotic fatalities. *Am J Forensic Med* 1998; 19: 381–6.
56. Singer PP, Jones GR. An unusual autoerotic fatality associated with chloroform inhalation. *J Anal Toxicol* 2006; 30: 216–18.
57. Dickerson EM, Jones P, Wilkins D, et al. Complicated suicide versus autoeroticism. A case involving multiple drugs and a Porta-Potty. *Am J Forensic Med Pathol* 2013; 34: 29–33.
58. Idota N, Nakamura M, Tsuboi H, et al. Autoerotic asphyxia using a plastic bag loosely covering the head over a gas mask. *Legal Med* 2019; 38: 69–72.
59. Walsh FM, Stahl CJ, Unger HT, et al. Autoerotic asphyxial deaths: A medicolegal analysis of forty-three cases. *Leg Med Annu* 1977; 155–82.
60. Mueller B. *Gerichtliche Medizin*. Berlin: Springer-Verlag; 1953.
61. Henry RIF. Suicide by proxy: A case report of juvenile autoerotic sexual asphyxia disguised as suicide. A common occurrence? *J Clin Forensic Med* 1996; 3: 55–6.
62. Kirksey KM, Holt-Ashley M, Williamson KL, et al. Pediatric update: Autoerotic asphyxia in adolescents. *J Emerg Nurs* 1995; 21: 81–3.
63. Rosenblum S, Faber MM. The adolescent sexual asphyxia syndrome. J *Am Acad Child Psychiatry* 1979; 18: 546–8.

CHAPTER

59

Dowry Deaths and Honor Killings

Navpreet Kaur and Roger W. Byard

INTRODUCTION

Violence continues to be a major threat to the safety of women globally (1) occurring throughout life from before birth through infancy and childhood into adulthood (2). Common forms of violence against women include acts of domestic abuse, sexual harassment and assault, forced abortion and homicide. Culturally-focused violence includes acid attacks ("vitriolage"), breast ironing or flattening and genital mutilation. In order to be considered a specific act of violence against a woman the act must be committed solely because the victim is female. Dowry killing is one such crime and is regarded as a major public health problem in India (3).

THE DOWRY SYSTEM

The practice of dowry occurs in many cultures across the world, especially in South Asia (4), most commonly in countries with entrenched patriarchal systems where women are expected after marriage to live with or near their husband's family (3,5,6). Unfortunately the dowry system is a cultural practice that has led to the oppression, torture and murder of many women (7). While marriage is considered a sacrament in a number of cultures, dowry has no basis in religious practice, being merely a societal construct often reflecting the subordination of a woman to her husband and his family (8,9).

The dowry system dates back to Greco-Roman times and involves a bride's family transferring money, property and other goods to a bridegroom, his parents or his relatives as a condition of the marriage (3,9,10). Dowry was intended to be used as economic support for a newly married couple. The expansion of the Roman empire caused this system to be implemented in other parts of the world. Although the dowry system was also practiced in certain Western countries in medieval and early modern times (3,11) it is not found in European cultures and countries nowadays. It remains pervasive across the Brahmanical Hindu societies of South Asia. Traditionally, while dowry may have involved token gifts from friends and well-wishers, the "new dowry" (since the colonial period) often involves transfer of a considerable amount of money and consumer goods, as well as land. Unfortunately, failure to deliver an expected amount of gifts of a certain value is frequently accompanied by violence against recently married women (3,4). The exact incidence of dowry in India today is not clear and it has been suggested that it may also occur in Indian families who have migrated abroad (3).

Dowry deaths

Dowry violence is usually perpetrated by the husband and/or the parents-in-law in a bid to extract more gifts from the bride's family. Although the dowry price paid at the time of marriage may be significant, it is not uncommon for the demands from her husband and his family to increase after marriage. Failure to acquiesce to these requests frequently results in physical, mental or sexual violence. It has been estimated that as many as 25 percent of women have reported that their husbands and families were not content with the amount of dowry provided (3). The resultant inflicted violence has ranged from usual forms of domestic assault to extremes of slashing the genitalia or breasts with razors and burning alive with accelerants (12). Such deaths are termed "dowry deaths" in the Indian Penal Code (defined in section 304B) (13).

Most dowry death homicides involve burning, hanging/strangulation, drowning and poisoning. Another feature of dowry-related crime is abetted suicide where women are encouraged to commit suicide, often by self-immolation with kerosene, or hanging (3,7,14–20). It has been reported that 65 percent of dowry deaths occur within three years of marriage and that these have been classified as suicides in 67 percent of cases and homicides in the remainder (16).

The National Crime Records Bureau (NCRB) of India recorded a total of 8618 female deaths related to dowry disputes in 2011 (21), however, the Asian Women's Human Rights Council estimates that the practice of dowry is implicated in 25 000 deaths and maiming of women between the ages of 15 and 34 years in India every year (7). There was a 74 percent increase in dowry deaths from 1995 to 2007 with a 31 percent increase in dowry-related suicides. The number of dowry deaths increased by a further 2.7 percent from 2010 to 2011

DOI: 10.1201/9781003138754-61

associated with a 5.4 percent increase in cases of torture by husbands and relatives (22). In 2015, 7634 women died due to dowry harassment (9,23). In 2019, India reported that dowry death cases amounted to more than 7100. According to data released by NCRB up to 2019, approximately 21 women die every day across the country due to dowry-related crimes (24).

Dowry prohibition laws in India: Its ineffectiveness and possible remedies

The Dowry Prohibition Act of 1961 was the first attempt by the Government of India to curb the untoward use and consequences of dowries. The Dowry Prohibition Act 1961 Section 3 specifies that the penalty for giving or taking dowry does not apply to gifts that are given at the time of a marriage to the bride or bridegroom, when no demand for them has been made (25).

India's parliament under Section 304B of the Indian Penal Code has provided a legal definition of dowry deaths, which set the criteria for determining what type of domestic violence and homicide should be included (26).

According to this provision, a woman's murder at the hands of her husband and his family is classified as a dowry death only in instances where it meets five specified criteria:

- The death is caused by burns or bodily injuries
- The death occurs under abnormal circumstances
- The death occurs within 7 years of her marriage
- The victim was harassed or subjected to cruelty by her husband and/or his relatives
- The underlying cause of the death is connected to demands made by the husband or his relatives for dowry

Medical evidence in dowry deaths

Medical evidence plays a crucial role in assisting the courts to establish the likelihood of possible dowry deaths, especially in cases when the alleged crime has been committed in a secluded domestic situation and is being presented as a case of accidental death. This applies to both homicides and abetted suicides.

In situations of "bride burning" when a woman with significant burns is taken to a hospital, the police should be notified by the hospital authorities and a medicolegal investigation initiated. Standard procedure involves the police both attending the hospital to gather available information and witness statements, as well as securing the scene of the incident. When burns are so severe that they will result in death, a magistrate will be called to record a "dying declaration" that provides a witnessed account by the victim of the circumstances surrounding her burns. If necessary, the dying declaration may be taken by someone else, normally a doctor or police officer, if the magistrate is unable to record it due to the woman's rapid clinical deterioration (13).

The forensic evaluation of such cases should include a standard medicolegal autopsy with particular attention being paid to the presence of accelerant material on the clothing, body and hair, with headspace analysis of blood and/or lung tissues (9). Subsequently, the magistrate will hold an inquest, drawing on the dying declaration, the post-mortem findings and witness statements. Finally, the police will classify the death, taking advice from the results of the magistrate's inquest.

The inclusion of dowry deaths as a formal offense category in India reflects both an acknowledgement, and a means, of trying to deal with violence against women. Moreover, the emphasis on the accounts given by dying women themselves represents an effort to give them an authoritative voice, where they would clearly otherwise have none in bringing perpetrators to justice. In the expectation that she is likely to die, the victim may be presumed to have no vested interest in misleading the magistrate over the course of events leading to her demise. The testimony in her account is therefore granted special privilege (27), although the possibility of mistaken interpretation or deliberate misrepresentation must always be considered. However, the unfortunate fact remains that, despite increasing medicolegal and community attention and legislation, dowry-related violence is not uncommon in modern India.

HONOR KILLINGS

Honor killings refer to a specific form of homicide committed by family members toward a female, ostensibly to protect or restore a family's "honor" (27). There has been much debate on the validity of the term "honor" crime, however the Council of Europe has defined honor crimes as "crimes which are, or have been, justified by the perpetrator as unavoidable necessities to protect the honor of the family". Included under the umbrella of honor crimes are domestic violence, female genital mutilation, forced marriage and homicides. Elakkary used the term to describe all forms of violence against a female due to departure of her sexual activities from traditional cultural norms. This may be for an act as apparently simple as seeking separation or independence from her husband (28,29).

Honor is often considered to be the most important quality in a traditional society and so its presumed defilement is taken as the most serious corruption of a community's moral ethics. To redeem and resurrect tarnished honor may be perceived as the sacred duty of that particular group (30). It has been associated with violence, patriarchy and poverty (31).

The concept of honor may be gender specific. For example, in India a woman may traditionally be seen as the repository of a family honor as a daughter, wife and mother, while a male family member regulates this; that is, honor is presumed to be a female-linked commodity coupled with the male prerogative to ensure that she does not jeopardize its delicate balance (32,33).

Other reasons for honor killings of women include loss of virginity outside marriage, pre-marital pregnancy, infidelity, having unapproved relationships, refusing an arranged marriage, asking for a divorce, requesting custody of children after a divorce, leaving the family or marital home without permission, causing scandal or gossip in a community, falling victim to a rape, marriage out of caste, marriage by choice, homosexuality and inappropriate dressing (34,35). Giving birth to a female child may also incite violence due to the dishonor of not having a son (36).

Occurrence

Honor killings have been widely reported in countries/areas such as Iran, Turkey, Afghanistan, Iraq, Saudi Arabia, Egypt, Palestine, Jordan, Bangladesh, Algeria, Brazil, Ecuador, Morocco, Israel, Ethiopia, Somalia, Uganda, The Balkans, Sweden, Holland, Germany, Italy, Yemen and India (36). It is estimated by the United Nations Population Funds that as many as 5000 women and girls are killed by the members of their families and/or relatives each year in the name of "honor" around the world (36). Robert Linier however claims that the number 5000 is a marked under-representation and that it is closer to 20 000 (37). Certainly under-reporting is quite likely in impoverished and isolated rural areas.

In Jordan, a significant percentage of female homicides involve honor killings (39) and in Pakistan, which has some of the highest numbers of reported cases, honor killings accounted for more than 20 percent of all homicides (38). In rural and tribal areas of Pakistan, this is known as *karo-kiri* and occurs primarily for perceived pre- or extra-marital affairs (40).

In Turkey, the Human Rights Directorate reported that in Istanbul alone one honor killing per week was occurring with 1000 such deaths during the last 5 years. In the Iraqi city of Basra there were 47 killings in 2006 (41).

Perpetrators

In Pakistan, a study showed that 43 percent of the perpetrators were the victim's husband, 24 percent brothers and 12 percent other family members such as grandparents and uncles. While the majority of cases occurred in Muslim communities, cases were also reported in Hindu and Christian groups (38). Other communities where honor killings have occurred are Sikh, Druze and Jewish (42) prompting the proposal that the antecedents are more likely to be cultural than religious (38).

Perhaps most disheartening is the role the woman's own family plays in enabling the abuse to escalate. Once a woman is married in traditional communities societal notions of shame and family honor dictate that she cannot return to her parents' home. In India for example, in most cases, even after dowry-related abuse escalates, a woman is made aware that her father's home has been forever closed to her once she enters her marriage. The importance placed on family honor and the taboo against failed marriages dictates that "her own parents [are obligated to] refuse to take her back". In fact, the social stigma attached to unmarried women and divorced women is so strong that many parents would rather see their daughters dead than to have them separated from their abusive husbands (26).

Variable legal responses

In Pakistan, a perpetrator has been able to avoid legal consequences for his actions if he officially seeks forgiveness from the victim's family. However, in 2016, anti-rape and anti-honor killing legislation was approved (43). In certain Middle Eastern countries, however, leniency is also often shown to the perpetrators of honor crimes with Hadidi stating that, in Lebanon, the perpetrator of an honor crime may be "judged guilty but may not be imprisoned" (39). The Jordanian Penal Code, Articles 340 and 98, under "Excuses in Murder" states: "He who catches his wife, or one of his (female) ascendants, descendants or sisters with another in an unlawful bed, and he kills or wounds or injures one or both of them, will be exempt from any penalty or will benefit from a reduction of penalty" (42).

The 2009 Elimination of Violence Against Women Law in Afghanistan criminalized all forms of physical, sexual and emotional violence against women but failed to address honor killing (31). In Iran, Article 630 of the Penal Code permits a man who witnesses his wife "having sexual intercourse with another man to kill both of them if he is certain that his wife is a willing participant" (44). It appears that certain legislation from different countries represents state-sanctioned honor killing and makes international controls difficult to enforce.

In India in 2018, the Supreme Court gave a landmark ruling in the Writ Petition (Civil) No.231 of 2010, *Shakti Vahini v Union of India & others* that any attempt by Khap Panchayats (Assemblies of Village Elders) or any other assembly to prevent two consenting adults from marrying was illegal and preventive, remedial and punitive measures were delineated. This judgment followed a petition filed by a non-government organization Shakti Vahini in 2010 which sought to curb honor killings. The court held that "the criminal cases pertaining to honor killing or violence to the couple(s) shall be tried before the designated Court/Fast Track Court earmarked for that purpose. The trial must proceed on a day-to-day basis to be concluded preferably within six months from the date of taking cognizance of the offense. "We may hasten to add that this direction shall apply even to pending cases. The concerned District Judge shall assign those cases, as far as possible, to one jurisdictional court so as to ensure expeditious disposal thereof." The judgment also says that Khap Panchayats should not take the law into their own hands and cannot assume the character of a law implementing agency for that authority has not been conferred upon them under any law. Khaps are caste and community-based assemblies, usually comprising elderly men from the Jat community in the northern parts of India that have a say on several issues, including marriage, dowry and the education of children, based on traditional customs (45).

CONCLUSION

Thus, honor killings persist and in certain communities appear to be on the increase, in some cases, protected by legislation. However, in other countries such as India, legislative initiatives have been undertaken to confront this particularly heinous form of violence.

REFERENCES

1. Solotaroff JL, Pande RP. Violence against women and girls: Lessons from South Asia. South Asia Development Forum. World Bank Group, Washington, DC, 2014. Available from: https://openknowledge.worldbank.org/handle/10986/20153 (Accessed 10 May 2023).
2. Kapoor S. Domestic Violence Against Women and Girls. Magnitude of Problem. Florence: Innocenti Digest, No 6. UNICEF Innocenti Research Centre. United Nations International Children's Emergency Fund (UNICEF); 2000, pp. 4–7.
3. Menezes RG, Nagaraja SB, Krishna K, et al. Dowry Killings. In: Payne-James J, Byard RW (eds). *Encyclopedia of Forensic and Legal Medicine*, 2nd ed, Vol 2. Oxford: Academic Press; 2016, pp. 67–73.
4. Khanal K, Sen RS. The dowry gift in South Asia: An institution on the intersection of market and patriarchy. *J Econ Iss* 2020; **54**: 356–62.
5. Van Willigen J, Channa VC. Law, custom, and crimes against women: The problem of dowry death in India. *Hum Org* 1991; **50**: 369–77.
6. Dalmia S, Lawrence PG. The institution of dowry in India: Why it continues to prevail. *J Develop Areas* 2005; **38(2)**: 71–93.
7. Banerjee P. Dowry in 21st-Century India: The sociocultural face of exploitation. *Trauma Viol Abuse* 2014; **15**: 34–40.
8. Stone L, James C. Dowry, bride-burning, and female power in India. *Womens Stud Int For* 1995; **18**: 125–34.
9. Kaur N, Byard RW. Bride burning: A unique and ongoing form of gender-based violence. *J Forensic Leg Med* 2020; **75**: 102035.
10. Jethmalani R, Dey PK. Dowry deaths and access to justice. In: Jethmalani R (ed). *Kali's Yug: Empowerment, Law and Dowry Deaths*. New Delhi: Har-Anand; 1995, pp. 36–78.
11. UK Essays. Issue of the Dowry System in India, 2018. Available from: https://www.ukessays.com/essays/india/issue-of-the-dowry-system-in-india.php?vref=1. (Accessed 10 May 2023).
12. The Dowry System in India: Is the Trend Changing?, 2013. Available from: https://pulitzercenter.org/projects/dowry-system-india-trend-changing#:~:text=In%20India%2C%20it%20has%20its,the%20practice%20of%20dowry%20mandatory (Accessed 10 May 2023).
13. Belur J, Tilley N, Daruwalla N, et al. The social construction of 'dowry deaths'. *Social Sci Med* 2014; **119**: 1–9.
14. Kumar P, Sathyanarayana K, Sundaragiri S. An epidemiological study of dowry deaths in special reference to burns in Indian scenario: A medicolegal study. *Medico-Leg Update* 2017; **17**: 50–5.
15. Agarwal PK. Profile of dowry deaths in Garhwal region of Uttarkhand. *Medico-Leg Update* 2017; **17**: 224–6.
16. Sharma BR, Harish D, Gupta M, Singh VP. Dowry: A deep-rooted cause of violence against women in India. *Med Sci Law* 2005; **45**: 161–8.
17. Radhika RH, Ananda K. An autopsy study of socio-etiological aspects in dowry death cases. *J Indian Acad Forensic Med* 2011; **33**: 224–7.
18. Sabri B, Sanchez MV, Campbell JC. Motives and characteristics of domestic violence homicides and suicides among women in India. *Health Care Women Int* 2015; **36**: 851–66.
19. Mohanty S, Sen M, Sahu G. Analysis of risk factors of dowry death: A south Indian study. *J Forensic Leg Med* 2013; **20**: 316–20.
20. Lamb MR. Study of dowry deaths in northern Maharashtra Region. *Ind J Forensic Med Toxicol* 2019; **13**: 195–8.
21. Patil AP, Sangle JD, Chikhalkar B. Medico-legal autopsy study of alleged dowry deaths: A two year cross-sectional study. *Int J Forensic Med Toxicol Sci* 2020; **5**: 64–9.
22. Bhat M, Ullman SE. Examining marital violence in India: Review and recommendations for future research and practice. *Trauma Violence Abuse* 2014; **15**: 57–74.
23. Nigam C. 21 lives lost to dowry every day across India: Conviction rate less than 35 percent, 2017. Available from: https://www.indiatoday.in/mail-today/story/dowry-deaths-national-crime-records-bureau-conviction-rate-972874-2017-04-22 (Accessed 10 May 2023).
24. Abhiramy SM. What constitutes a developed society? Vismaya's death rakes up key questions, 2021. Available from: https://theprint.in/campus-voice/what-constitutes-a-developed-society-vismayas-death-rakes-up-key-questions/686749/ (Accessed 10 May 2023).
25. Srinivasan P, Lee G. The Dowry system in Northern India: Women's attitudes and social change. *J Marriage Fam* 2004; **66**: 1108–17.
26. Musa S. Dowry-Murders In India: The law & its role in the continuance of the wife burning phenomenon. *Northwest Interdisc Law Rev* 2012; **5(1)**: 227–45.
27. Belur J, Tilley N, Daruwalla N, et al. The social construction of 'dowry deaths'. *Soc Sci Med* 2014; **119**: 1–9.
28. Elakkary S. Deaths: Honor killings. In: Payne-James J, Byard RW (eds). *Encyclopedia of Forensic and Legal Medicine* 2nd ed, Vol 4. Oxford: Academic Press; 2016, pp. 74–9.
29. Elakkary S, Franke B, Shokri D, et al. Honor crimes: Review and proposed definition. *Forensic Sci Med Pathol* 2014; **10**: 76–82.
30. Rana MS. Honour killings is not caste, religion specific. *Mainstream* 2010; **51**: 28–31.
31. Gibbs A, Said N, Corboz J, Jewkes R. Factors associated with 'honour killing' in Afghanistan and the occupied Palestinian Territories: Two cross sectional studies. *PLoS ONE* 2019; **14**: e0219125.
32. Chowdhary P. *Contentious Marriages, Eloping Couples: Gender, Caste and Patriarchy in Northern India*. New Delhi: Oxford University Press; 2007.
33. Nabar V. *Caste as Woman*. New Delhi: Penguin Books. 1995.
34. Jan G, Munir K. Honour killing: A socio-legal analysis with special reference to district Srinagar of J&K. *Sociol Int J* 2018; **2**: 335–47.
35. Supreme Court of India. Shakti Vahini vs Union Of India on 27 March, 2018. Available from: https://indiankanoon.org/doc/92846055/?type=print (Accessed 10 May 2023).
36. Kaur N. *Acid Attacks on Women: A Socio Legal Perspective*. New Delhi: Satyam Law International; 2021.
37. Kaushal, K. No honour in honour killing: Comparative analysis of Indian traditional social structure vis-à-vis gender violence. *Ind J Wom Soc Change* 2020; **5**: 52–69.
38. Soldberg KE. Killed in the name of honour. *Lancet* 2009; **373**: 1933–4.
39. Hadidi M, Kulwicki A, Jahshan H. A review of 16 cases of honour killings in Jordan in 1995. *Int J Leg Med* 2001; **114**: 357–9.
40. Patel S, Gadit M. Karo-kari: A form of honour killing in Pakistan. *Transcult Psychiatr* 2008; **45**: 683–94.
41. Singh G. A study on honour related violence against women and its impact on their life, Department of Social Work, 2018. Available from: http://hdl.handle.net/10603/214127 (Accessed 10 May 2023).
42. Salameh HOG, Salameh RJ, Shwaiki M, Abder-Rahman H. Forensic medical aspects of femicide in Jordan. *J Forensic Leg Med* 2018; **56**: 90–3.
43. Fatimah H, Qadir TF, Hussain SA, Menezes RG. Pakistan steps up to remove "honour" from honour killing (letter). *Lancet* 2017; **5**: e145.
44. Pirnia B, Pirnia F, Pirnia K. Honour killings and violence against women in Iran during the COVID-19 pandemic (letter). *Lancet Psychiatry* 2020; **7**: e60.
45. National Human Rights Commission, India. Human Rights Newsletter, 2018. Available from: https://nhrc.nic.in/sites/default/files/2018_05_ENG.pdf (Accessed 10 May 2023).

CHAPTER 60

Femicide

Rossanna Cecchi, Vittoria Masotti and Matilde Sassani

INTRODUCTION

Femicide is the most extreme form of violence against women, that is their murder. It is a global scourge, and no country is spared from the phenomenon. In the last 20 years, there has been increasing public awareness, perhaps partially due to national and international campaigns and increasing use of social and other electronic media. This chapter reviews the definition of femicide, its forensic pathologic findings, legislative aspects and proposed risk factors.

A shared definition of femicide

Although the phenomenon of femicide is ubiquitous and widespread, it lacks a shared definition. International organizations have denounced the absence of a univocal definition as leading to an underestimation of the problem and to statistical data which are not fully representative and comparable (1,2). In addition, it is important to reach a consensus as forensic pathologists need objective and verifiable features of femicide during autopsies. This requires a methodologically shared protocol to autopsies, thus contributing to a post-mortem differential diagnosis of femicide from other forms of murders of women.

In 2022, an international interdisciplinary team gathered expertise in forensic pathology, penal law, neuroscience, psychiatry, sociology and statistics, to publish a contribution to the debate. They proposed a definition of femicide to be applied internationally by both forensic pathologists and legislators (3). The definition is "a murder perpetrated because of a failure to recognize the victim's right to self-determination" and is based on one of the funding principles of medical ethics, that is, autonomy. Based on this definition, femicides are instances in which a woman is killed because she refuses to comply with the requests or desires of the murder and this denial becomes the motive of the murder. On the contrary, there are cases that can be described as "female homicides", but not necessarily as femicides, for example, women killed in the context of robbery or drug dealing.

Forensic findings: Anatomy and number of lesions

To date, there are seven forensic pathology studies describing anatomic sites affected in female homicides (4–10). Table 60.1 is reproduced from (10) and summarizes their findings. All works showed that cases of female homicides are characterized by injuries primarily to the head, face, neck, upper limbs and chest. Only one work reported lesions specifically to "erogenous" areas (mouth, neck, pubis, perineum, buttocks and mammary region) as they may be regarded as a marker of intimate partner violence (10). A second work differentiated between intimate (114 cases) and non-intimate (106 cases) partner homicides and showed that, perhaps surprisingly, there was a higher proportion of lesions in the anogenital area in homicides perpetuated by non-intimate partners (6.6%) compared to intimate ones (1.8%) (4).

In addition, it can be argued that the presence of "overkilling" (i.e. the number and kind of lesions are significantly superior to those necessary to kill) can be considered a weak marker of femicide. Overkilling is not always present, but when identified, femicide must be considered in the differentials (10).

Forensic findings: Means and cause of death

The most common means used to murder women are gunshots, sharp objects, and blunt trauma although their relative proportion is dependent on geographic location, likely reflecting national legislation and local weapon availability. Table 60.2 is reproduced from (10) and summarizes the 18 studies published to date grouped by cause of death and geographic area. In most countries (United States, Canada, Brazil, Portugal and Jordan), firearm is the leading cause of death for murdered women (9,11–15). Notably, there was no female homicide perpetuated by gunshot in Taiwan, possibly reflecting a very stringent firearm legislation (4). In Taiwan, as well as Turkey and Egypt, sharp objects were the most common means of death (4,8,16); whereas reports

DOI: 10.1201/9781003138754-62

TABLE 60.1 Forensic pathology studies on murder of women. Anatomic site and erogenous zone affected, and the number of injuries are listed if available

STUDY	ANATOMIC SITE	EROGENOUS ZONE	NO OF INJURIES
Mathews S,et al. (2008) (17)	Unknown	Unknown	**Intimate femicide-suicide cases** **(=261)** Multiple injuries 41.1% Single injury 58.9% Undetermined 0.0% **Intimate femicide/non-suicide cases (=1088)** Multiple injuries 47.7% Single injury 46.9% Undetermined 5.6%
Fong WL, et al. (2016) (4)	**Intimate partner (n=114)** Face 56.1% Cranium 41.2% Neck 58.8% Chest 50.9% Abdomen 21.9% Back 25.4% Buttock 1.8% Upper limbs 53.5% Lower limbs 31.8% Ano-genitalia 1.8% **Non-intimate partner (n=106)** Face 65.1% Cranium 62.3% Neck 47.2% Chest 49.1% Abdomen 28.3% Back 22.6% Buttock 3.8% Upper limbs 66.0% Lower limbs 37.7% Ano-genitalia 6.6%	**Intimate partner (n=114)** Ano-genitalia 1.8% **Non intimate partner (n=106)** Anogenitalia 6.6%	Unknown
Giorgetti A, et al. (2022) (5)	**Fatal injuries (n=103)** Head 24.2% Neck 17.7% Chest 19.4% Multiple localization 38.7%	Unknown	One blow 24.2% Multiple blows 64.1% Multiple blows > 10 11.7%
Zara G, Gino S. (2018) (6)	Head, neck, face 53.6% Torso, chest and arms 23.4% Spread over entire body 23.0%	Unknown	Overkilling 40.7%

TABLE 60.1 (Continued) Forensic pathology studies on murder of women. Anatomic site and erogenous zone affected, and the number of injuries are listed if available

STUDY	ANATOMIC SITE	EROGENOUS ZONE	NO OF INJURIES
Salameh HOG, et al. (2018) (7)	**Fatal injury** Honor killings cases n=52 Chest 40% Bruising, lacerations or incised wounds on the arms 22% Intimate partner violence n=33 Head 46% Bruising, Lacerations or Incised wounds on the arms 6%	Unknown	Honor killings n=52 1 n=11 2–10 n=10 >10 n=29 Intimate partner violence n=33 1 n=16 2–10 n=6 >10 n=6
Karbeyaz K, et al. (2018) (8)	Head n=35 (23.6%) Chest n=82 (55.4%) Abdomen n=25 (16.9%)	Unknown	Unknown
Pereira AR, et al. (2013) (9)	**Fatal - Non fatal** Head n=25 (40.3%) – n=10 (28.6%) Face n=13 (21.0%) – n=16 (44.7%) Neck n=19 (30.6%) – n=15 (42.9%) Thorax n=30 (48.4%) – n=17 (48.6%) Abdomen n=10 (16.1%) – n=10 (28.6%) Upper limbs n=2 (3.2%) – n=26 (74.3%) Lower limbs n=2 (3.2%) – n=6 (17.1%)	Unknown	**Number - Fatal - Nonfatal** 1–2 n=8 (45.1%) – n=2 (5.7%) 2–9 n=26 (41.9%) – n=22 (62.9%) >10 n=8 (12.9%) – n=11 (31.4%)
Cecchi R, et al. (2023) (10)	N=46 Abdomen 39.1% Right lower limb 32.6% Left lower limb 23.9% Right upper limb 60.9% Left upper limb 56.5% Mouth 28.3% Head 54.3% Neck 69.6% Right thigh 32.6% Left thigh 23.9% Back 17.4% Pubis/ Perineum 8.7% Buttocks 15.2% Mammary region (R) 28.3% Mammary region (L) 32.6% Chest 43.5% Face 71.7%	Mouth n=13 28.3% Neck n=32 69.6% Pubis/perineum n=4 8.7% Buttocks n=7 15.2% Mammary region n=18 39.1%	**Multiple injuries** **n=21 45.7%**

TABLE 60.2 Forensic pathology studies on murder of women. Geographic area, murderer, motive, place and cause of death are listed if available

STUDY	GEOGRAPHIC AREA	MURDERER	MOTIVE	PLACE	CAUSE OF DEATH
Sabri B, et al. (2016) (11)	United States (Minnesota, Oregon, Texas, Washington, Wisconsin)	**Total cases = 123** Husband 53.2% Ex-husband 17.1% Partner (Unmarried) 17.1% Ex-partner unmarried 12.6%	Unknown	Unknown	**Intimate femicide-suicide cases (=35)** Gun shot 60% (n = 21) Sharp object 14.3% (n = 5) Unknown causes 8.6% (n = 3) Blow to the head 5.7% (n = 2) Multiple methods 5.7% (n = 2) Car accident 2.9% (n = 1) Decapitated 2.9% (n = 1) **Intimate femicide/ non-suicide cases (=88)** Sharp object 39.3% (n = 33) Gun shot 32.1% (n = 27) Strangulation 10.2% (n = 9) Others 9.4% (n = 8) Multiple methods 7.4% (n = 6) Run down with a vehicle 5.1% (n = 4) Bludgeoned with a hammer 3.6 (n = 3)
Jordan CE, et al. (2010) (22)	United States (Kentucky)	**Total cases: 148** **1. Age 13–65 n = 135** **2. Over 65 n = 13** Intimate partner 1.26.7%, 2.30.8% Ex-intimate partner 1.11.9%, 2.0.0% Family member 1.8.1%, 2.23.1% Acquaintance 1.3.7%, 2.7.7% Stranger 1.4.4%, 2.15.4% Missing/unknown 1.45.2%, 2.23.1%	Unknown	Unknown	Unknown

TABLE 60.2 (Continued) Forensic pathology studies on murder of women. Geographic area, murderer, motive, place and cause of death are listed if available

STUDY	GEOGRAPHIC AREA	MURDERER	MOTIVE	PLACE	CAUSE OF DEATH
Gillespie LK, et al. (2013) (12)	United States	**Total cases = 226** Husband 38.1% Boyfriend 30.1% Ex-boyfriend 15.9% Estranged husband 11.1% Ex-husband 4.9%	Unknown	Unknown	Gun shot 55.9% Sharp object 19.8% Person 14.4% Other 9.9%
Canadian Femicide Observatory for Justice and Accountability (13)	Canada	**Total cases = 128** **Known accused person = 72** Current/former partners 50% (Current legal spouse n = 12, Current common-law spouse n = 9, Current dating partner n = 6, Estranged legal spouse n = 3, Estranged common-law spouse n = 2, Estranged dating partner n=2, Not clear n = 2) Other family 26% Friends/ acquaintances 14% Strangers 10%	Unknown	**Private location n = 94**, 73% (victims or accused home, hotel rooms, unspecified residence) **Public location n = 17**, 13% (parks, streets, work place, inside vehicle) Unknown location n = 17, 13%	Gun shot 44% Sharp object 32% Beatings 13% Other methods 13%
Meneghel SN, et al. (2017) (14)	Brazil (Porto Alegre)	**Total cases = 64** Intimate 39/64 cases (Intimate: current or former partners – husbands, boyfriends, fiancées or dates) 25 not reported	Unknown	House 67.1% Public place 32.9%	Gun shot 50% Other (weapon/ suffocation) 50%
Fong, WL, et al. (2016) (4)	Taiwan	**Total cases = 220** **Intimate partner (n = 114)** Boyfriend 53.5% Husband 29.8% Ex-boyfriend 10.5% Ex-husband 6.1 **Non intimate partner (n = 106)** Relatives 34.9% Friend(s) 29.4% Other acquaintance(s) 29.4% Stranger(s) 6.6%	Unknown	**Intimate partner (n = 114)** Victim's home 58.8% Offender's home 9.6% Public places 7.0% Other 21.1% **Non intimate partner (n = 106)** Victim's home 54.7% Offender's home 9.4% Public places 8.5% Other 25.5%	**Intimate partner (n = 114)** Sharp object 52.6% Strangulation 27.2% Blunt force 13.2% Poison 2.6% Gun shot 2.6% **Non intimate partner (n = 106)** Sharp object 53.8% Strangulation 22.6% Blunt force 20.8% Poison 1.9% Gun shot 0.0%

(Continued)

TABLE 60.2 (Continued) Forensic pathology studies on murder of women. Geographic area, murderer, motive, place and cause of death are listed if available

STUDY	GEOGRAPHIC AREA	MURDERER	MOTIVE	PLACE	CAUSE OF DEATH
Salameh HOG, et al. (2018) (7)	Jordan	**Total cases = 100** Honor killings cases (n = 52) Brother 28 54% Father 7 13% Husband 5 10% Uncle 3 6% Cousin 3 6% Son 2 4% Unknown 4 7% **Intimate partner violence death (n = 33)** Husband n = 33 100%	Honor killings n = 52 52% Intimate partner violence n = 33 33% Quarrel n = 7 7% Other domestic violence, the woman having been killed by a son n = 5 5% Robbery n = 3 3%	Women's home 76% (94% for the Intimate partner violence death cases)	Gun 44% Sharp object 21% Blunt force 14 % Strangulation 8% Multiple weapons 6 % Burning 4 % Poisoning 3 %
Karbeyaz K, et al. (2018) (8)	Turkey	**Total cases = 148** Husband 48.6% Boyfriend 20.3% Ex-husband 16.9% Ex-boyfriend 8.1% Ex-fiancé 6,1%	Request of women to divorce/to break up with boyfriend 61.5% Jealousy (cheating claim) 15.5% Economic reasons 10.2% Unknown 12.8%	Unknown	Sharp object 49.3% Gun shot 39.9% Blunt force 6.8% Garotte 4.1%
Zaghloul NM, et al. (2019) (16)	Egypt	**Total cases = 93** Unknown 50.53% Husband 17.20% relative 17.20% caregiver 5.37% stranger 5.37% intimate partner 4.30%	Domestic arguments and fights 22.1% Followed by robberies 12.8% Sexual causes 8.1% Betrayal 4.7% Honor killing 3.7% Unknown 46.5%	Unknown	Sharp object 34.41% Other Blunt force 13.98% Gun shot 10.75% Throttling 10.75% Smothering 7.53% Strangulation 7.53% Burn 7.53% Falling from height 6.45% Electrocution n = 1 1.08%
Mathews S, et al. (2008) (17)	South Africa	**Total cases: 1349** **Intimate femicide-suicide cases (= 261)** Cohabiting partner 40.4% Boyfriend 28.8% Husband 30.8% Other 0.0% **Intimate femicide/ non-suicide cases (= 1088)** Cohabiting partner 55.5% Boyfriend 27.1% Husband 15.5% Other 1.9%	**Intimate femicide-suicide cases (= 261)** Argument 53.5% Alleged infidelity of victim 19.7% Female ended relationship 29.0% Other 1.3% **Intimate femicide/ non-suicide cases (= 1088)** Argument 54% Alleged infidelity of victim 19.7% Female ended relationship 8.4% Other 17.3%	Unknown	**Intimate femicide-suicide cases (= 261)** Gun shot 82.7% Sharp object 14.7% Blunt force 11.4% Strangled/ Asphyxiated 2.6% **Intimate femicide/ non-suicide cases (= 1088)** Sharp object 38.0 % Blunt force 40.7% Gun shot 18.1% Strangled/ Asphyxiated 3.9% Fire 1.4% Other 0.7% Drowning 0.5%

TABLE 60.2 (Continued) Forensic pathology studies on murder of women. Geographic area, murderer, motive, place and cause of death are listed if available

STUDY	GEOGRAPHIC AREA	MURDERER	MOTIVE	PLACE	CAUSE OF DEATH
Abrahams N, et al. (2013) (18)	South Africa	**Intimate femicide-suicide cases (n=1349(1999), n=1024(2009))** Intimate 50.2% (1999), 57.1%(2009) intimate: a current or former husband/ boyfriend, same-sex partner, or rejected would-be lover	Unknown	Unknown	**Intimate femicide-suicide cases (n=1349(1999), n=1024(2009))** Blunt force: 33.2% (1999), 29.5 % (2009) Gun shot: 30.6 % (1999), 17.4 % (2009) Sharp object: 33.2 % (1999), 31.4 % (2009) **Non intimate femicide-suicide cases (n=1335(1999), n=768(2009))** Blunt force: 21.2% (1999), 22.4 % (2009) Gun shot: 33.6 % (1999), 17.1 % (2009) Sharp object: 34.3 % (1999), 35.5 % (2009)
Meel B. (2018) (19)	South Africa	Unknown	Unknown	Unknown	**Total cases=1865** Gunshot (n=754) Sharp object (n=559) Blunt force (n=552)
Pereira AR, et al. (2013) (9)	Portugal	**Total cases=62** Marital 54.8% Common-law 24.2% Dating 11.3% Extramarital 9.7%	Context of separation of the couple 38.9% Jealousy 31.5% Conflicts 22.2%	Private residences 61.7% (n=37) Public places 35% (n=21)	Gun shot 45.2% Sharp object 27.4% Blunt force 14.5% Manual strangulation 4.8% Multiple methods 4.8% Heat trauma with burns 3.2%
Giorgetti A, et al. (2022) (5)	Italy (Bologna)	**Total cases=103** Current husband/ boyfriend 41.8% Family member 17.5 Previous husband/ boyfriend 16.5% Acquaintance 10.7% Lover 4.9% Customer 3.9% Student/employee 3.9% No relationship 0.8%	Passionate reasons 26.7% Familial problems 24.4% General crimes and robbery 22.2% Sexual femicides 4.4% Mental illness – victim 13.3% Mental illness – perpetrator 9%	Home 77.1% Hotel 4.2% Car 8.3% Road or abandoned place 10.4%	Gun shot 37.9% Sharp object 23.3% Blunt force 17.5% Strangulation 16.5% Toxic 2.9% Drowning 1% Thermal injury 0.9%

(Continued)

TABLE 60.2 (Continued) Forensic pathology studies on murder of women. Geographic area, murderer, motive, place and cause of death are listed if available

STUDY	GEOGRAPHIC AREA	MURDERER	MOTIVE	PLACE	CAUSE OF DEATH
Sorrentino A, et al. (2020) (23)	Italy	**Total cases = 1204** Husbands 33.8% Cohabitants 6.8% Ex-husbands 6.9% Ex-boyfriends 5.8% Boyfriends 3.6% Ex-cohabitants 3.4%	The inability to accept the end of the relationship 23.3% Jealousy between the partners 15.6% Escalation of violence started because of quarrels or conflicts in the couple 14.4% The presence of physical or mental illness of the author 12.9% The presence of physical or mental illness of the victim 7.2%	Unknown	Unknown
Vignali G, et al. (2021) (20)	Italy (Milano)	**Total cases = 82** Intimate partner 72% son or the grandson 9.3% The jealous client of a prostitute 9.3% An admirer 2.3% Son in law 1.2% Father 1.2%	Unknown	Unknown	Sharp object 34% Gun shot 20% Strangulation/ suffocation 17% Blunt force 14% Combined methods of murders 10% Burning 2% Drowning 2%
Moreschi C, et al. (2016) (21)	Italy (Udine)	**Total cases = 34** Current partners 44.1% Relatives 8.8% Ex-partners 5.9% Brother/Sister 5.9% Friends/ Acquaintances 5.9% Father 2.9% Strangers 11.8% Not identified 11.8% Killed by two people: Current partner and Relatives 2.9%	Perpetrators' mental disorder 23.5% Unknown 14.7% Related to the ending of their relationship 11.8% Trivial issues and Fighting 11.8% Robbery 8.8% Passion 8.8% Compassionate reasons (mercy killing) 5.9% Attempt to extort information 2.9% Jealousy 2.9%	Home 73.5% Countryside/ woodland 17.6% Street 2.9% Caravan 2.9% Unknown 2.9%	Sharp object 41.2% Gun shot 38.2% Asphyxiation 8.8% Physical aggression 5.9% Blunt force 5.8%
Zara G, Gino S. (2018) (6)	Italy (Turin)	**Total cases = 275** Known murderer 88.3% Stranger 11.6%	Passion killing 31.1% Family problems 18.7% Consequence of another crime 15.2% Predatory 14.0% Loss of control after a row or a refusal 13.6% Mental disorder 7.4%	Victim's or perpetrator's house 73.9% Public place (Car, Street, Countryside) 26.1%	Most common: gunshot, stab wounds, and strangulation

TABLE 60.2 (Continued) Forensic pathology studies on murder of women. Geographic area, murderer, motive, place and cause of death are listed if available

STUDY	GEOGRAPHIC AREA	MURDERER	MOTIVE	PLACE	CAUSE OF DEATH
Cecchi et al. (2023) (10)	Italy (Parma)	**Total cases=46** Partner 39.1% Not precise 23.9% Family 15.2% Ex-partners 10.9% Mother 2.2% Cohabitant of the mother 2.2% Other 6.5% **Femicide-Suicide cases** N=9 Same gun=6 Same knife= 1 1 Murder followed by suicide through precipitation 1 Murder followed by suicide through hanging	Pietas n=6, 13.0% Jealousy n=6, 13.0% The inability to accept the end of the relationship n=4, 8.7% Psychiatric pathology n=4, 8.7% Quarrel n=2, 4.3% Possession n=2, 4.3% Robbery n=1, 2.2% Shooting n=1, 2.2% Daughter murdered by Mother n=1, 2.2% Unknown n=19, 41.3%	home n=26, 56.5% car n=8, 17.4% farm n=4, 8.8% moat n=1, 2.2% unknown n=1, 2.2% hospital n=1, 2.2% park n=1, 2.2% guest-house n=1, 2.2% bridge n=1, 2.2% building n=1, 2.2% street n=1, 2.2%	Sharp object n=16, 34.8% Gunshot n=14, 30.4% Asphyxiation n=10, 21.7% Blunt force n=3, 6.5% Blunt force + Asphyxiation n=3, 6.5%

on Italy and South Africa show variable prevalence of gun shots, sharp objects and blunt trauma by geographic region and year (5,6,10,20,21,17–19).

Forensic findings: Perpetrators

Women are more likely to be murdered by their intimate current or previous partner or by someone they know (1,2). The relationship between the victim and perpetrator (reported in Table 60.2) is frequently defined as either "intimate" or "non-intimate" in an attempt to standardize analysis. This distinction often implies that femicide is equivalent to murder of a woman by a husband or (ex-) partner. There is an argument that this might be a too restrictive definition as other type of femicide (e.g. by another family member) might be left out as shown in several studies (4–6,10,13,15,16,20–22).

Forensic findings: Motives

The motive of the murder if frequently unknown, when revealed, pertains primarily to conflicts related to the emotional and relationship sphere (e.g. request of women to divorce/break up, jealousy) (5,6,8–10,17,21,23). In a proportion of cases, reference is made to a psychiatric disorder either of the victim and/or of the perpetrator (5,6,10,21,23).

Forensic findings: Place of murder

There are nine studies, to date, reporting the place of murder (Table 60.2). Most murders take place in the house (either of the victim or perpetrator) (4–6,9,10,13–15,21). This is, again, in line with women being more likely to be murdered by someone they know and who is part of their emotional/social sphere.

LEGISLATION IN COUNTRIES IN THE WORLD

Legislation on murders of women and, specifically, femicide are also very heterogeneous and dependent on whether a definition is recognized or not by the individual State. Table 60.3 summarizes available legislation by continent. Latin American Countries and Pakistan are the only ones with specific laws against femicide (24–26). Inevitably, there are country-specific conditions that shape the laws, with some defining femicide as the murder of a woman whereas other stating it is a murder motivated by hatred or contempt for women, by abuse of power, abuse in position of trust or abusive relationships. Lastly, there are laws which do not pertain specific to femicide, but include it in human trafficking, kidnapping, sexual violence and gang activity (24,25).

The view of supranational organizations

The United Nations (UN) Commission on Human Rights (27), in 2003, defined "violence against women", including their killing as "... any act of gender-based violence that results in, or is likely to result in, physical, sexual or psychological harm or suffering to women, including threats of such acts, coercion or arbitrary deprivation of liberty, whether occurring in public or in private life and including domestic violence, crimes committed in the name of honor,

TABLE 60.3 Worldwide legislation of femicide

The Americas
National criminal code provides specific provisions for femicide in Bolivia, Brazil, Colombia, Costa Rica, Dominican Republic, Ecuador, El Salvador, Guatemala, Honduras, Mexico, Nicaragua, Panama, Paraguay, Peru, Uruguay. In Chile there is an increase of applicable penalties for this crime (8).
In the United States there are no specific laws on femicide and the term is generally not commonly used (9).
Barbados, Belize, Canada, Saskatchewan, Cayman Islands, Trinidad and Tobago do not have a specific legislation on femicide (10).
Asia
East Countries like Japan, South Korea, Malaysia, Cambodia, Vietnam and Thailand, do not have specific legislations on femicide, nevertheless there are some laws concern stalking and marital violence (11–14).
In the Middle East and some South Asian countries, only Pakistan has a law providing specific penalties for acts committed against women in the name of traditional practices and honor-killing: the 2016 landmark amendment to the Code of Criminal Procedure, the Evidence Act and the Pakistan Penal Code (16).
Oceania
Oceanian countries, Australia, Fiji, Kiribati, Samoa and Toga, do not have specific legislation on femicide. In New Zealand, there are laws on domestic violence (10).
Africa
Gambia, Ghana, Kenya, Mauritius, Seychelles, Sierra Leone, Tanzania and Saint Helena do not have a legislation on femicide. Zambia violence against women have stronger penalties than the general criminal law (10).
Europe
No European Union Member State currently has a legal definition and laws on femicide (17). Italy, Germany and France provide for laws contrasting violence against women, but do not refer to their murder (19–23). Spain punishes specifically gendered motivations behind killings of women, for example because of hatred on the grounds of her sex.

crimes committed in the name of passion, trafficking in women and girls, traditional practices harmful to women, including female genital mutilation, early and forced marriages, female infanticide, dowry-related violence and deaths, acid attacks and violence related to commercial sexual exploitation as well as economic exploitation" (27).

On 16th September 2021, the European Parliament approved a Resolution to recognize and include femicide (defined as the murder of women) among the offenses listed in Article 83 of the Treaty on the Functioning of the European Union. In Article 83, femicide is added to the list of crimes to be fought on a common basis including trafficking in human beings, drugs and arms, cybercrime and terrorism (28).

In addition, numerous supranational organizations described and denounced the phenomenon of violence against women without referring specifically to their killing or to the term femicide.

In the UN Declaration on the Elimination of Violence Against Women of 20th December 1993, the General Assembly affirmed that violence against women is one of the crucial social mechanisms by which they are forced into a subordinate position to men (29). The 2002 World Report on Violence and Health of the World Health Organization (30) stated that violence is not a private matter, but is, instead, the result of complex causal factors that can cross national borders.

The Council of Europe, in the Istanbul Convention of 2011 on preventing and combating violence against women and domestic violence, discussed discrimination and violence against women without specifically defining femicide or having a separate section on their killing (31).

Social aspects proposed as risk factors

A few studies have assessed possible risk factors that can lead to the killing of a woman. In South Africa, Meel identifies numerous risk factors, mostly related to the culture of the place such as high alcohol consumption in both the victim and the perpetrator, the tendency to have multiple partners, high aggression and litigation, poverty, low economic possibilities, patriarchal culture, as well as the spread of firearms (32). In Italy, Moreschi et al. (21) identified as risk factors the possession of firearms and alcohol abuse (by the victim and/or aggressor) as well as mental health problems of the perpetrator. In Brazil, gender culture and structural violence are elements of risk, in addition to poverty and belonging to the Pentecostal religion (14). Of particular note, the authors documented that submission and resignation with respect to one's role (viewed as hierarchically subordinate) decreased the risk of being victims of femicide, whereas attempts to subvert traditional roles constituted a risk factor (14).

In the United States, JC Campbell noted that there are risk factors that have always applied, such as poverty and low socio-economic status, but there are also risk-conferring features that have emerged only recently, an example is living in overpopulated areas, as women are perhaps less likely to be able to escape violence (33,34). Unemployment and threats of harm to children are other risk factors. A perhaps counter-intuitive finding is that the risk of femicide appears to decrease when the aggressor has been subjected to previous arrests for violence

(33), a worrying discovery indicating that violence and warning signs are difficult to recognize and frequently go unnoticed by the criminal justice system.

There are, nonetheless, indicators foreshadowing femicides. Murders are frequently preceded by threats, intimidations and other aggressive behaviors. There can also be physical and psychological violence, including sexual abuse. A North American case-control study of 821 women in 10 cities (Baltimore, Huston, Kansas City, KS, Kansas City, MO, Los Angeles, New York, Portland, Seattle, St Petersburg, and Wichita), showed that women who reported having been followed or spied on are twice as likely to be victims of femicide (35).

A particularly dangerous situation, shown to increase the risk of femicide nine fold, is when a woman asks for a divorce and there are threats to harm own children by the future perpetrator (35).

It can, therefore, be concluded that stalking and the attitude to threats are strong risk factors that predispose the victim to be murdered (35).

CONCLUSION

The term femicide acquired for the first time a connotation of its own in 1973. It was defined as the killing of a woman by a man "for reasons of hatred, contempt, pleasure or sense of possession" by the sociologist and criminologist Diana EH Russell in "The politics of woman killing" (36). She notoriously summarized this gender murder definition as the "killing of a woman because she is a woman". Since then, the problem was initially framed as a sociological issue and only more recently there have been formal legislations and increasing attempts to characterize femicide from a forensic pathological point of view. In those endeavors, it is crucial to apply a standardized scientific method known to the international community to all cases of female murder in order to identify instances of femicide, inform the legislator, recognize risk factors and, ultimately, contribute to prevention.

REFERENCES

1. Weil S, Corradi C, Naudi M. *Femicide across Europe. Theory, research and prevention*. Policy Press, 2018. Available from: https://library.oapen.org/bitstream/handle/20.500.12657/28243/9781447347163.pdf?sequence=1&isAllowed=y (Accessed 10 May 2023).
2. United Nations Office on Drugs and Crime (UNODC). *Global Study on Homicide. Gender-Related Killing of Women and Girls*, 2019. Available from: https://www.unodc.org/documents/data-and-analysis/gsh/Booklet_5.pdf (Accessed 10 May 2023).
3. Cecchi R, Sassani M, Agugiaro G, et al. A medico-legal definition of femicide. *Leg Med (Tokyo)* 2022; **59**: 102101.
4. Fong WL, Pan CH, Lee JCL, et al. Adult femicide victims in forensic autopsy in Taiwan: A 10-year retrospective study. *Forensic Sci Int* 2016; **266**: 80–5.
5. Giorgetti A, Fais P, Giovannini E, et al. A 70-year study of femicides at the Forensic Medicine department, University of Bologna (Italy). *Forensic Sci Int* 2022; **333**: 111210.
6. Zara G, Gino S. Intimate partner violence and its escalation into femicide. Frailty thy name is "violence against women". *Front Psychol* 2018; **9**: 1777.
7. Salameh HOG, Salameh RJ, Shwaiki M, Abder-Rahman H. Forensic medical aspects of femicide in Jordan. *J Forensic Leg Med* 2018; **56**: 90–3.
8. Karbeyaz K, Yetis Y, Günes A, Msek US. Intimate partner femicide in Eskisehir, Turkey 25-year analysis. *J Forensic Leg Med* 2018; **60**: 56–60.
9. Pereira AR, Vieira DN, Magalhães T. Fatal intimate partner violence against women in Portugal: A forensic medical national study. *J Forensic Leg Med* 2013; **20(8)**: 1099–107.
10. Cecchi R, Masotti V, Sassani M, et al. Femicide and forensic pathology: Proposal for a shared medico-legal methodology. *Leg Med* 2023; **60**: 102170.
11. Sabri B, Campbell JC, Dabby FC. Gender differences in intimate partner homicides among ethnic sub-groups of Asians. *Violence Against Women* 2016; **22(4)**: 432–53.
12. Gillespie LK, Richards TN, Givens EM, Smith MD. Framing deadly domestic violence: Why the media's spin matters in newspaper coverage of femicide. *Violence Against Women* 2013; **19(2)**: 222–45.
13. Canadian Femicide Observatory for Justice and Accountability. #CallItFemicide Understanding sex/gender-related killings of women and girls in Canada, 2021. Available from: https://femicideincanada.ca/callitfemicide2020.pdf (Accessed 10 May 2023).
14. Meneghel SN, Rosa BARD, Ceccon RF, et al. Femicides: A study in Brazilian state capital cities and large municipalities. *Cien Saude Colet* 2017; **22(9)**: 2963–70.
15. Salameh HOG, Salameh RJ, Shwaiki M, Abder-Rahman H. Forensic medical aspects of femicide in Jordan. *J Forensic Leg Med* 2018; **56**: 90–3.
16. Zaghloul NM, Megahed HM. A descriptive medico-legal study of female deaths in Cairo governatorade, Egypt. *J Forensic Leg Med* 2019; **66**: 25–32.
17. Mathews S, Abrahams N, Jewkes R, et al. Intimate femicide-suicide in South Africa: A cross-sectional study. *Bull World Health Organ* 2008; **86(7)**: 552–58.
18. Abrahams N, Mathews S, Martin LJ, et al. Intimate partner femicide in South Africa in 1999 and 2009. *PLoS Med* 2013; **10(4)**: e1001412.
19. Meel B. Incidence of female homicide in the Transkei sub-region of South Africa (19932015). *J Forensic Leg Med* 2018; **56**: 75–9.
20. Vignali G, Franceschetti L, Merzagora I. A retrospective study on femicides assessed at the Institute of Legal Medicine of Milan. Are older woman at risk? *Forensic Sci Int* 2021; **325**: 110890.
21. Moreschi C, Da Broi U, Zamai V, Palese F. Medico legal and epidemiological aspects of femicide in a judicial district of north eastern Italy. *J Forensic Leg Med* 2016; **39**: 65–73.
22. Jordan CE, Pritchard AJ, Duckett D, et al. Relationship and injury trends in the homicide of women across the life span: A research note. *Homicide Stud* 2010; **14(2)**: 181–92.
23. Sorrentino A, Guida C, Cinquegrana V, Baldry AC. Femicide fatal risk factors: A last decade comparison between Italian Victims of Femicide by Age Groups. *Int J Environ Res Public Health* 2020; **17(21)**: 7953.
24. Carrigan M, Dawson M. Problem representations of femicide/feminicide legislation in Latin America. *Int J Crime Justice Soc* 2020; **9(2)**: 1–19.
25. Deus A, Gonzales D. *Analysis of Femicide/Feminicide Legislation in Latin America and the Caribbean and a proposal for a model law. United Nations Entity for Gender Equality and the Empowerment of Women*, 2018. Available from: https://lac.unwomen.org/en/digiteca/publicaciones/2018/12/analisis-legislacion-feminicidio-femicidio-modelo-de-ley (Accessed 10 May 2023).
26. US Department of State. Country Reports on Human Right Practices: Pakistan, 2021. Available from: https://www.state.gov/reports/2020-country-reports-on-human-rights-practices/pakistan/ (Accessed 10 May 2023).
27. UN Commission on Human Rights. *Commission on Human Rights Resolution 2003/45: Elimination of Violence against Women*, 2003. Available from: https://www.refworld.org/docid/43f3133b0.html (Accessed 10 May 2023).
28. European Parliament. Identifying gender-based violence as a new area of crime listed in Article 83(1) TFEU, 2019. Available from: https://www.europarl.europa.eu/doceo/document/TA-9-2021-0388_EN.pdf (Accessed 10 May 2023).
29. General Assembly resolution. Declaration on the Elimination of Violence against Women, 1993. Available from: https://www.un.org/en/genocideprevention/documents/atrocity-crimes/Doc.21_declaration%20elimination%20vaw.pdf (Accessed 10 May 2023).

30. Krug EG, Dahlberg LL, Mercy JA, et al. World report on violence and health of the world health organization, 2002. Available from: http://apps.who.int/iris/bitstream/handle/10665/42495/9241545615_eng.pdf;jsessionid=38439AF25C2A45F33808836E30EA4C2D?sequence=1 (Accessed 10 May 2023).
31. Council of Europe. Council of Europe Convention on Preventing and Combating Violence Against Women and Domestic Violence. Available from: https:rm.coe.int/168008482e (Accessed 10 May 2023).
32. Meel B. Incidence of female homicide in the Transkei sub-region of South Africa (1993–2015). *J Forensic Leg Med* 2018; **56**: 75–9.
33. Campbell JC. Helping women understand their risk in situations of intimate partner violence. *J Interpers Violence* 2004; **19**(**12**): 1464–77.
34. Campbell JC, Webster DW, Glass N. The danger assessment: Validation of a lethality risk assessment instrument for intimate partner femicide. *J Interpers Violence* 2009; **24**(**4**): 653–74.
35. McFarlane J, Campbell JC, Watson K. Intimate partner stalking and femicide: Urgent implications for women's safety. *Behav Sci Law* 2002; **20**(**1–2**): 51–68.
36. Russell DEH. Crimes against women: Proceedings of the international tribunal. International Tribunal on Crimes against Women. 1976, Brussels Belgium. In: Russell DEH, Radford J (eds). *Femicide: The Politics of Woman Killing*. New York: Twayne Publishers; 1992, p. 379.

CHAPTER

61

Gunshots, Firearm Deaths and Blast Trauma

Gert Saayman

INTRODUCTION

In a world where there are more than one billion firearms (most being in the hands of civilians) and where more than one-quarter of a million people die annually because of gunshot injuries (excluding war fatalities), forensic and other healthcare professionals must be aware of the nature, management and medicolegal implications of gunshot wounds (1,2). Most of these injuries and deaths take place in Central and North American countries, with firearm injuries now reported to be the leading cause of death among young people in the USA (3–5). Most gunshot injuries and fatalities are the result of interpersonal violence. For each fatality, there are approximately three non-fatal outcomes accounting for a significant percentage of the admissions at emergency medical facilities. Almost 100 000 such cases are seen annually at emergency medical centers in the US, with the overall annual cost of firearm injuries having been set al $557 billion (6–8). Irrespective of the manner or circumstance under which such injuries are sustained, criminal or other court proceedings may ensue, meaning that the proper initial (medicolegal) evaluation, management and documentation of these injuries could be vital to the administration of justice. To quote Samuel Farr, *"There is a kind of medical knowledge which is not so much concerned in the cure of diseases as in the detection of error and the conviction of guilt"* (9).

It is thus essential for first responders and other emergency medical personnel to have appropriate knowledge of such injuries. This chapter aims to assist healthcare professionals by outlining the basic principles of wound or terminal ballistics with medicolegal perspectives such as evidence management and appropriate documentation.

BASIC BALLISTICS

There are many different types of firearms and an even greater variety in the types of ammunition. Every weapon is made for a specific purpose and, for every firearm, there may be multiple types of ammunition, to be used in different settings for different purposes. Certain other weapons may produce injuries not dissimilar to those caused by firearms, such as humane killers (captive bolt pistols or bolt stunners), nail guns, crossbows, air guns, crude self-made weapons, as well as so-called less lethal weapons.

Overall, the study of ballistics may be divided into internal (weapon), exterior (flight) and terminal (including wound) ballistics and, thus a basic knowledge of the construction and functioning of weapons and ammunition, as well as bullet-flight perspectives, is necessary to better understand wounding caused by firearms (10).

Firearms can broadly be divided into rifled weapons and smooth bore weapons (shotguns). The former have spiral grooves and landings on the inside of the barrel, which imparts spin to the bullet, resulting in among other, greater gyroscopic stability and accuracy over longer distances. Smooth bore weapons (such as shotguns) typically fire multiple projectiles (shot pellets) simultaneously, the shot varying in size from approximately 1 mm (birdshot) to several millimeters (buckshot) in diameter, or even large, single slugs. Firearms are also broadly subdivided into handguns (such as pistols and revolvers) and shoulder weapons, according to their mode of use, although many hybrid or crossover forms may be found. In some countries, specific legislation defines the various categories of firearms according to *inter-alia* the presence of the shoulder stock and barrel length. Typically, rifles deliver bullets at greater speeds with greater accuracy over longer distances and are mostly designed for sporting use or military purposes. Pistols usually have a semiautomatic action (allowing for rapid self-loading or chambering of a next round, after successive shots) whereas carbines and military rifles may be used in semiautomatic or automatic fire mode – the latter being capable of delivering bursts of many bullets per second from one single trigger squeeze.

Manufacturers of distinct types of ammunition have specific objectives in mind when designing the cartridges or casings and the composition and configuration of bullets – there are hundreds of variations in the configuration and construction of cartridges and bullets (Figure 61.1). Variables include type, quantity and nature of propellant as well as shape and construction off the bullet itself – each of which have a direct or indirect influence on the internal, flight and terminal ballistics.

DOI: 10.1201/9781003138754-63

61.1 Ammunition variety. (From: https://www.americanfirearms.org/_next/image/?url=https%3A%2F%2Fcms.americanfirearms.org%2Fwp-content%2Fuploads%2F2023%2F01%2Ftmppw9_jlo2.jpg&w=1200&q=75.)

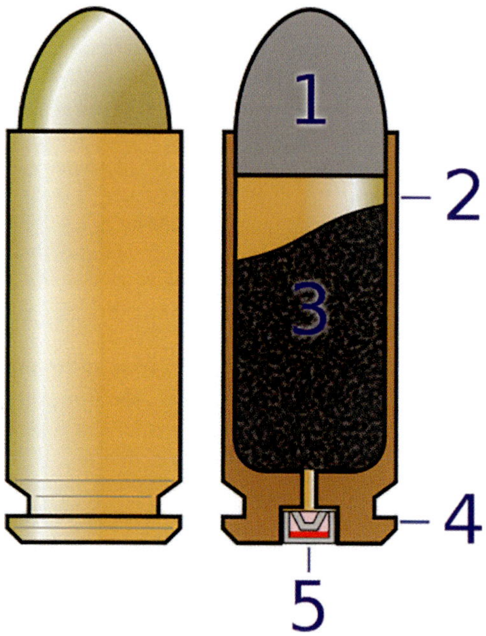

61.2 Cartridge construction. 1: Bullet (projectile); 2: Cartridge case; 3: Propellant (gunpowder); 4. Rim (for extracton of casing); 5. Primer (ignites the propellant). (From: https://en.wikipedia.org/wiki/Cartridge_%28firearms%29#/media/File:Cartridge_cross_section.svg).

61.3 Expanded hollow point bullet (Black Talon©).

When a shot is fired by squeezing the trigger of a weapon, a small (firing) pin strikes the base of the chambered cartridge, thereby activating the relatively unstable primer compound (usually comprised of a mixture of lead, antimony, barium and/or tetrazene), which then, in turn, ignites the propellant (a nitrocellulose compound) (Figure 61.2). Remnants of these primer and propellant powders may be deposited on the hands of a shooter and the body or clothing of a victim, when in proximity. The combustion of 1 g of modern smokeless powder may release up to 1000 mL of gas, and the extreme compression thus generated drives the bullet down the barrel of the weapon at great speed.

Clinicians and pathologists should be informed about basic concepts such as the caliber (cross-sectional diameter of the bullet, usually expressed in millimeters or inches), sharp-pointed or hollow-point construction and partial or full metal jacket configuration. So too, they should stay up to date with modern, specialized ammunition such as armor piercing and frangible bullets – all of that have bearing on the nature and severity of the wound which may be caused. Many commercially available bullets (such as the "Black

Talon"© and "Radically Invasive Projectile" (RIP©) have been specifically designed to cause maximal tissue damage) (Figure 61.3). In addition, regard must be had for the velocity of the bullet, which may vary from relatively low velocity (less than approximately 350 m/s) to medium velocity (350 to 500 m/s) and high velocity bullets, some of which may exceed speeds of 1000 m/s. Bullets may be somewhat unstable in-flight shortly after leaving the muzzle, where after the gyroscopic spin imparted by the rifling of the barrel may stabilize the projectile for a variable distance, when it may again become unstable (11). Concepts such as nutation, precession, yaw and tumbling of the bullet are important considerations in the field of external ballistics or flight ballistics and may play a role in wound assessment and/or shooting incident reconstruction (12). These concepts, and their roles in wound causation, are best understood by viewing images or clips made by stroboscopic and ultra-high-speed ballistic photography or videography (13).

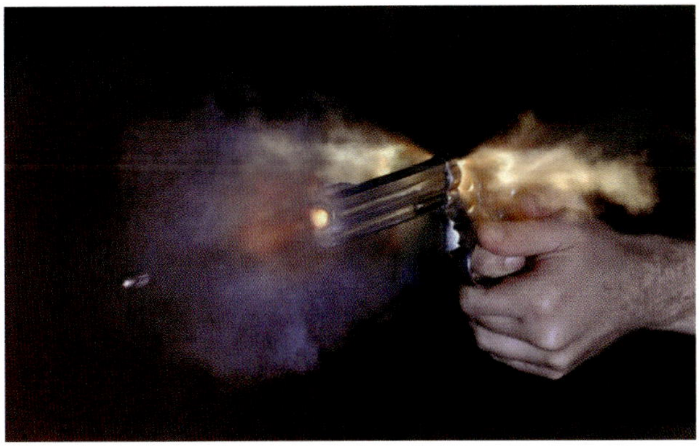

61.4 Revolver firing. Note also emissions from cylinder gap. (From: https://en.wikipedia.org/wiki/.38_Special#/media/File:Bullet_coming_from_S&W.jpg).

61.5 Zip gun.

Fundamental concepts in understanding gunshot injuries

From the perspective of injury causation and impact kinematics, the following are three fundamental concepts that facilitate the understanding of wound ballistics and help with the forensic medical evaluation of gunshot injuries:

- Gunshot wounds are ballistic injuries which in essence, represent a **hydrodynamic event** (in many respects, like a pebble being dropped into a pond). Kinetic energy is transferred from the projectile to the surrounding tissues or medium, causing multiple rapidly successive centrifugal and centripetal oscillations in pressure, like the back-and-forth ripples in a small pond, but lasting only for a few milliseconds in tissue. The measure and rapidity of such energy transfer will depend on (among other) velocity, mass, size, shape and behavior of the projectile (e.g. tumbling or fragmentation), all of which contribute to creating the temporary wound cavity and the residual permanent wound track. The nature of the target tissue (e.g. muscle tissue, parenchymal organ, hollow viscus, or bone) will also directly affect such energy transfer and final wounding outcome. Such transfer of energy may indeed result in damage to structures or tissues that were never in direct contact with the bullet (e.g. nerves or blood vessels several centimeters to the periphery). As the kinetic energy of a moving object is largely a function of its velocity (rather than its mass or caliber), small increments in the speed of a bullet may greatly increase the energy. It is nonetheless important to appreciate that the nature and gravity of wounding is essentially determined by the measure of kinetic energy transferred from the projectile to the tissue, rather than the inherent or total kinetic energy which a projectile may possess (14).
- **Not only a bullet leaves the barrel of a firearm when a shot is discharged.** Several other products are usually simultaneously expelled from the weapon, all of which may have a direct bearing on the nature and appearance of the inflicted injury and may include material deposited on the bullet during its passage through the barrel, burning and/or unburnt powder, heat or flames and hot gases (Figure 61.4). The assessment, detection and recording of these substances and features associated with such release, may be of greater significance from a medicolegal perspective (e.g. in determining the range of fire), than from a clinical or treatment perspective.
- **There exists a very wide range of firearms and an even wider range of ammunition** – from very sophisticated weapons and high-precision ammunition to crude self-made weapons (sometimes referred to as zip guns) and propellant mixes (Figure 61.5) (15). Every wound should thus be meticulously assessed and recorded for its specific individual and idiosyncratic features, for possible later correlation with additional information or postulated scenarios.

Classification and features of gunshot wounds

Many factors contribute to the physical appearance and morphologic features of gunshot wounds, including the type of weapon (whether it be one with a rifled barrel or smooth bore), the intrinsic kinetic energy of the projectile, the shape and construction of the projectile, flight ballistics and, of course, the type and nature of tissue constituting the target. Nonetheless, there are some features which may provide a relatively consistent and reliable basis upon which to differentiate between for example, entrance and exit wounds and even between distinct types of entrance wound. Emergency care physicians, trauma specialists and forensic medical practitioners should be familiar with these features, and should record their presence (or indeed, absence) to allow for contemporaneous or later informed opinion as to the primary nature of a particular wound. There may certainly be different approaches to the classification of gunshot wounds, but most will consider the same basic elements and morphological criteria. Knowledge of the various features commonly seen in gunshot wounds and in particular, the mechanisms which underlie their causation, will usually allow the observer to conclude the nature of the injury in question with a greater or lesser degree of certainty (12,16).

Entrance wounds

In most cases, gunshot wounds are the result of only the impact and penetration of the bullet itself. In such entrance wounds caused by relatively stable bullets, the hallmark features would be a central "punched out" defect (skin loss, partly due to disintegration and loss of skin and partly due to the elasticity of the skin), as well as the so-called collar of abrasion, the latter typically being a circumferential ring of abraded epidermis on the inner aspect of the perimeter of the wound (Figure 61.6). This feature is, in most cases, caused by the passage of the bullet (scraping away the superficial layers of the epidermis) and by radially displaced microscopic tissue fragments. It may be even more visible in persons with a dark skin, where the pigment layer of the epidermis may be denuded, resulting in a pink/white collar typically 2 to 3 mm in width, around the central defect. In some instances (usually associated with entrance of high-velocity sharp-point projectiles fired from military or sporting rifles), there may be no discernible collar of abrasion, but only small radial tears at the periphery of the wound defect. Similarly, entrance wounds to the palmar and plantar surfaces often do not display an obvious collar of abrasion. The visibility and appearance of this abrasion ring may be altered by desiccation of the wound edges, the presence of dried blood or insect or rodent predation. The skin surrounding an entrance wound may show variable degrees of discoloration due to bruising, depending on the anatomic site and the nature of the subcutaneous tissue. The absence of features which are deemed to indicate contact and/or intermediate-range entrance wounds, does not imply that the muzzle of the weapon was not near the target, as intervening objects (including clothing) may have altered the appearance.

Furthermore, entrance wounds have a somewhat indented appearance in most instances, with a central area of depression, and even some degree of inversion of the wound edges, and usually show no extrusion or herniation of soft tissue from the wound. A relatively rare but potentially important feature of entrance wounds is the grease collar or grime ring (also referred to as bullet wipe), which may be seen superimposed upon or adjacent to the collar of abrasion. This derives from material which may have been deposited on the surface of the projectile while still in the weapon (such as a mixture of grease, oil, grime or rust), that may be wiped from the bullet onto the skin – or even onto overlying items of clothing, especially if the latter is relatively sturdy and tightfitting (e.g. a taut leather jacket) (Figure 61.7). An eccentrically accentuated collar of abrasion may indicate an oblique angle of entry (from the side having a more prominent abrasion). In some cases, the bullet may only graze the skin, leaving only a superficial furrow, indicative of a tangential passage of the projectile. Bullets do not burn the skin upon entry as the temperature of the bullet is too low and passes through the skin too rapidly.

Contact wounds

Hard or full contact wounds

With contact wounds, the muzzle of the weapon is in full or flush contact with the target. If there is no intervening material (such as one or more layers of clothing), there will usually be either a full or an incomplete circular imprint abrasion of variable width, surrounding the penetrating skin defect, caused by the forceful blowback of skin against the muzzle of the weapon (Figure 61.8). This feature is typically more pronounced in areas

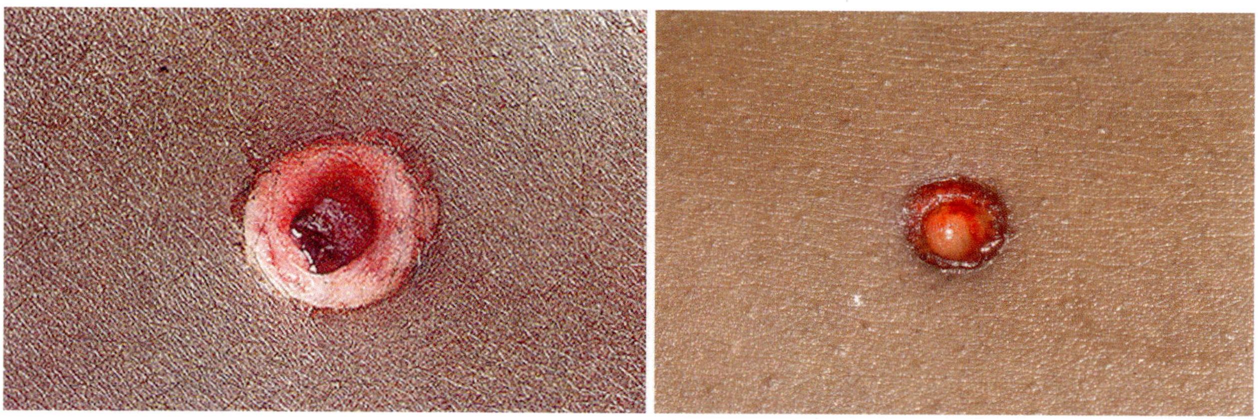

61.6 Examples of typical collar abrasions on entrance wounds.

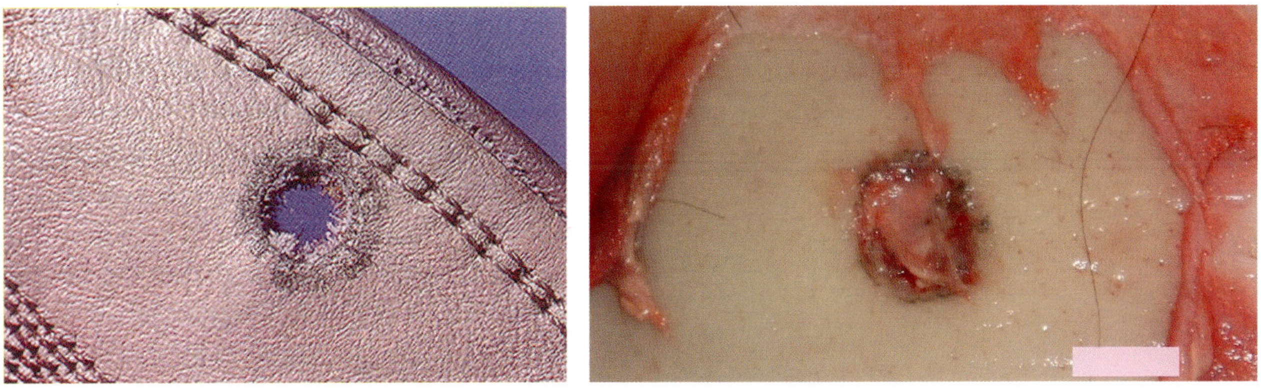

61.7 Bullet wipe – clothing and skull. Examples of grease collar or grime rings.

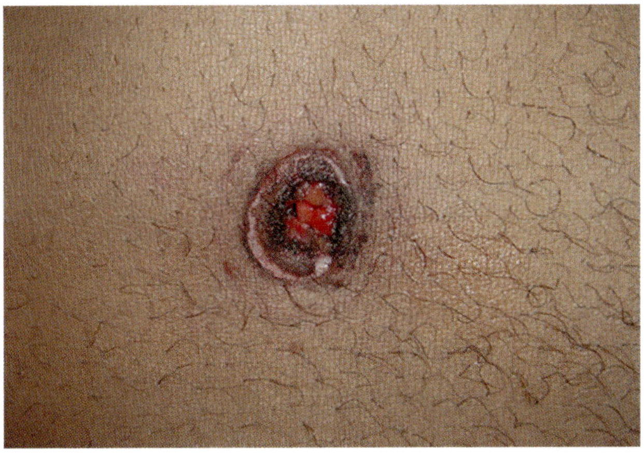

61.8 A contact wound modified by clothing with some blackening due to soot.

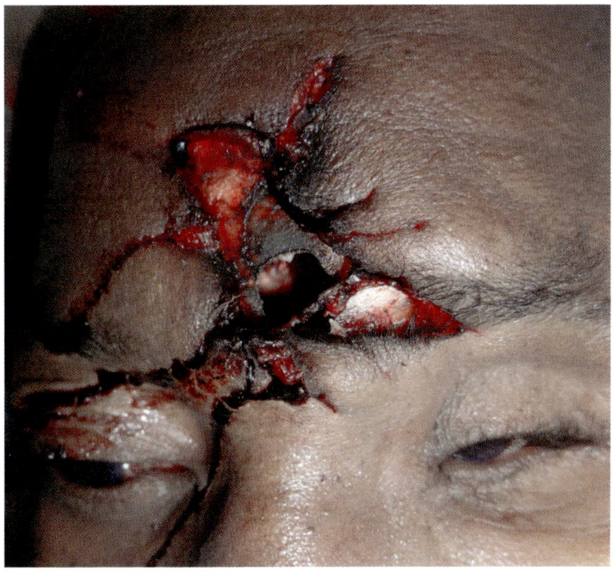

61.9 Contact wound to forehead.

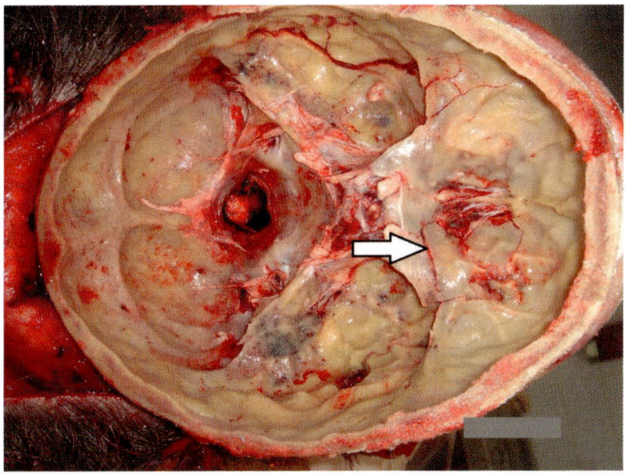

61.10 Orbital plate blowout caused by firearm discharge.

where the skin is fairly loose or supple, for example, the abdomen. In some cases, additional features such as an imprint of the pistol guide rod or the front (muzzle) sight may even be seen. A muzzle imprint abrasion is sometimes accompanied by some blackening and even searing of the immediately adjacent skin and subjacent tissues, due to the expulsion of propellant residue, flame and superheated gases. Propellant elements may be driven deeply into the tissues, causing extensive charcoal/black discoloration or tattooing. Occasionally, there may be an indistinct cherry-pink appearance of peri- and intralesional tissues, because of formation of carboxyhemoglobin. In certain anatomic areas (such as the scalp and over the sternum, where there is restricted subcutaneous space due to underlying bone), the expelled gases may cause very rapid outward (backward) ballooning of the skin that exceeds the elastic limits of the skin, typically resulting in a large, irregularly ruptured, or stellate defect (the various edges of which may be approximated to some extent) (Figure 61.9). At the same time, such highly compressed gases (expanding greatly and almost instantaneously upon leaving the muzzle) may then also be driven into confined underlying spaces, such as the cranial cavity, where they may have a destructive effect, such as blowout fractures of the orbital plates (Figure 61.10). In contact wounds of the head, careful inspection of the underlying periosteum and white bone may show tell-tale signs of soot discoloration even when this is not clearly visible on the skin. Small caliber, low kinetic energy projectiles however, may not result in such an overt stellate configuration of the wound, because of the lower volume of expelled gases (Figure 61.11).

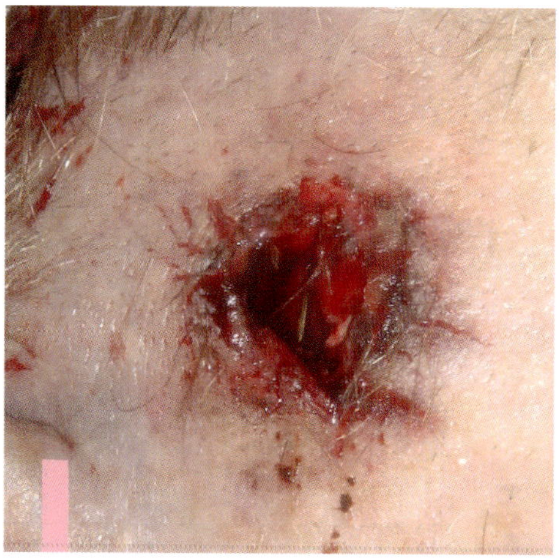

61.11 Contact wound to temple caused by small caliber, low kinetic energy projectile.

Partial or angled contact wounds

If the barrel of the weapon is not flush or in hard contact with the skin, this will allow for variable amounts of the gases that are expelled from the muzzle to escape into the atmosphere, with eccentrically accentuated deposition of soot and searing, an incomplete muzzle imprint and less likelihood of a large or stellate wound. In more hairy parts of the body (such as the scalp), there may be distinct singeing of hair – more noticeable when viewed under a magnifying glass. Indeed, many of the abovementioned features are best evaluated or confirmed with the use of a good light source (even a flashlight) and a magnifying lens. Where the muzzle of a weapon is held against intervening layers of clothing, discoloration, heat effects and irregular rupture of the material, may also be seen.

In case of contact or close-range wounding, the back spatter or blowback phenomenon may result in the retrograde displacement of tissue fragments and blood, which may then be found on the hand(s) of the shooter or the weapon in question (including the inside of the barrel) by careful examination or swabbing (17). It may thus be advisable to retain a blood or tissue sample from the victim for possible DNA analysis, for purposes of later comparison.

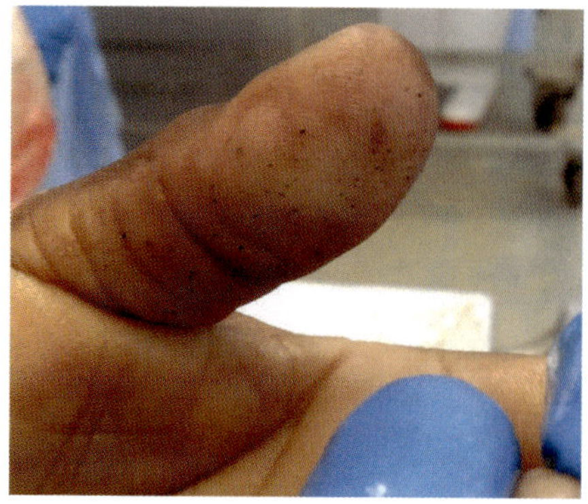

61.12 Tattooing – thumb caused by propellant residue. (Courtesy Dr R Blumenthal.)

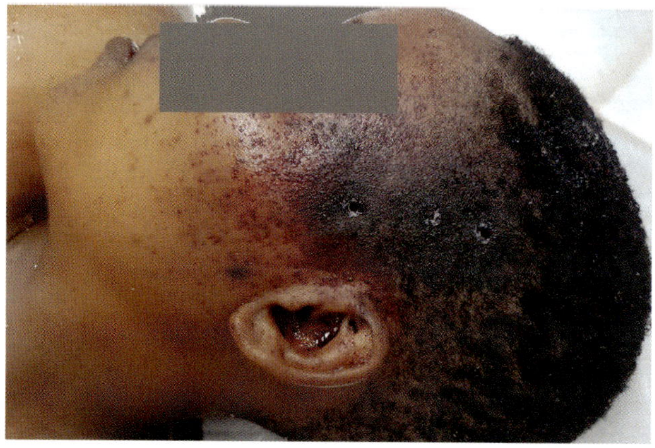

61.13 Tattooing and soot caused by gunshot residue, partially obscured in the scalp hair.

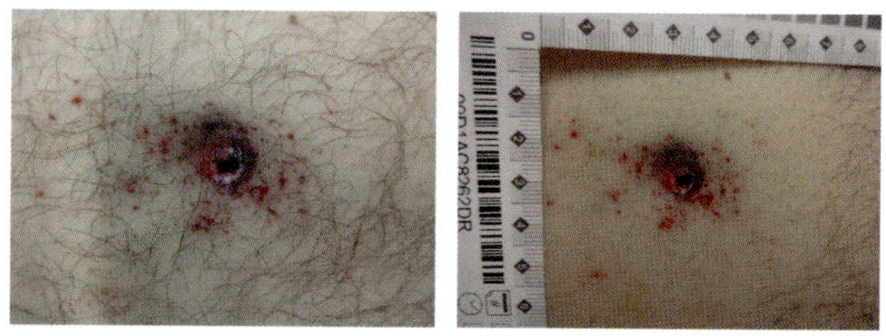

61.14 Powder tattooing and stippling to an abdominal wound – before and after shaving.

Intermediate range entrance wounds

If the muzzle of the firearm is in close proximity to the target (skin), unburnt or partially burnt propellant or residue, as well as flame/heat may contribute to the overall morphologic appearance of the wound, with features such as searing and singeing of hair, smoke and soot deposition and, in particular, the phenomenon of tattooing or stippling (Figure 61.11). The latter is caused by the superficial impregnation of the surrounding skin (or even items of clothing) by propellant residue, often leaving multiple reddish-brown stippled lesions of the skin, 1 or 2 mm in diameter; this being the hallmark of the so-called intermediate-range entrance gunshot wound (Figure 61.12). The maximum distance at which such features may be found will vary greatly, depending on among other things, the length of the barrel of the weapon, the type of ammunition and possible intervening objects (such as clothing). For most handguns and small arms, it is unlikely that such features will be readily visible if the weapon had been discharged at greater than 50 to 70 cm from the target (skin), although of course there may be exceptions to this rule. Tattooing may be difficult to identify in dark-skinned people or in hairy body parts, such as the scalp (Figure 61.13). The use of sophisticated investigative modalities such as alternative light sources and chemical means of detection, may however be used to find not only actual propellant particles but also chemical traces, with even greater ranges of fire. Powder tattooing or stippling is a somewhat robust phenomenon and will not readily be wiped away, in contrast to smoke/soot and gunshot residue deposits (Figure 61.14). Care must however be taken to differentiate true stippling from pseudo-tattooing, which may be due to various other causes, such as secondary projectiles from an intervening object (e.g. glass near the skin).

Atypical entrance wounds

Some entrance wounds do not have the typical features described above or may have additional unusual features, which may create uncertainty in the mind of the observer (18,19). These may include injuries caused by deformed or even partly fragmented bullets which strike the skin after piercing intermediary or intervening objects (for example, window panes, car doors, or items of clothing), often resulting in relatively large and irregularly shaped wounds with variable and non-symmetric collars of abrasion, or in more than one entrance defect (Figure 61.15). Such outcomes are perhaps most seen in cases where there is re-entry of the bullet after passing through one body part (e.g. the upper arm) before re-entry on the chest. Bullets which had become unstable in flight after traveling some distance (or after a ricochet from an object) may not strike the skin end-on, also causing such irregularly shaped defects. Tandem (piggy-back) bullets and unusual weapons or ammunition (such as bows and crossbows, kinetic impact projectiles or rubber bullets) may also result in atypical entrance wound features. This may also be the case where the bullet strikes the skin between skin folds (e.g. the axilla, gluteal cleft) or in a body orifice (e.g. external auditory opening), and the palmar or plantar web spaces (Figure 61.16). The overall appearance of entrance wounds and their surrounds may

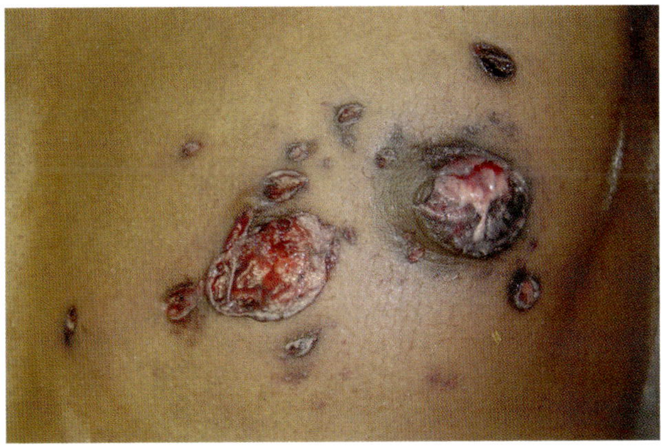

61.15 Atypical entrance chest wounds caused by fragmented projectile that had already passed through an intermediary target (vehicle door).

be further complicated by markings resulting from emissions associated with revolver cylinder gaps, silencers, muzzle brakes and flash suppressors (Figure 61.17) (16).

Exit wounds

Exit wounds tend to be larger than the corresponding entrance wound but are also more varied and unpredictable in size and shape. This is usually because the projectile may have become fragmented or misshapen due to impact with the target, but also because it has become unstable in flight, resulting in tumbling, thus causing an

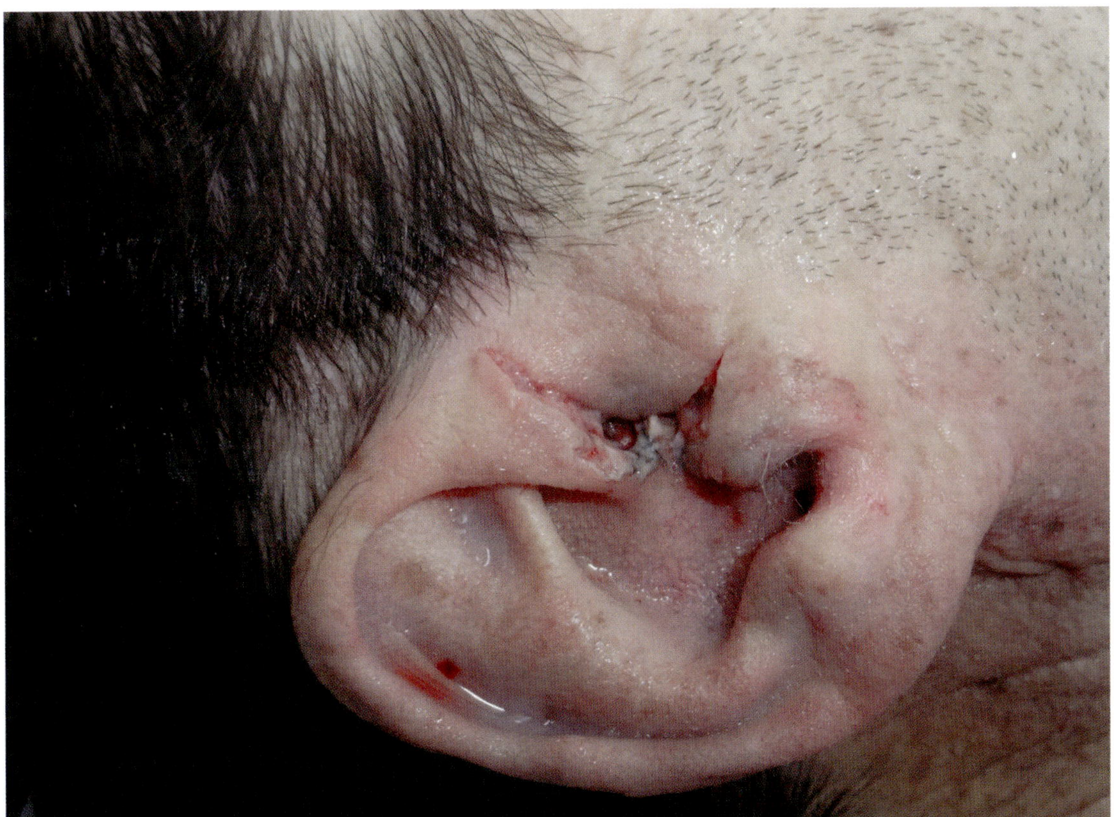

61.16 Atypical entrance wound to ear.

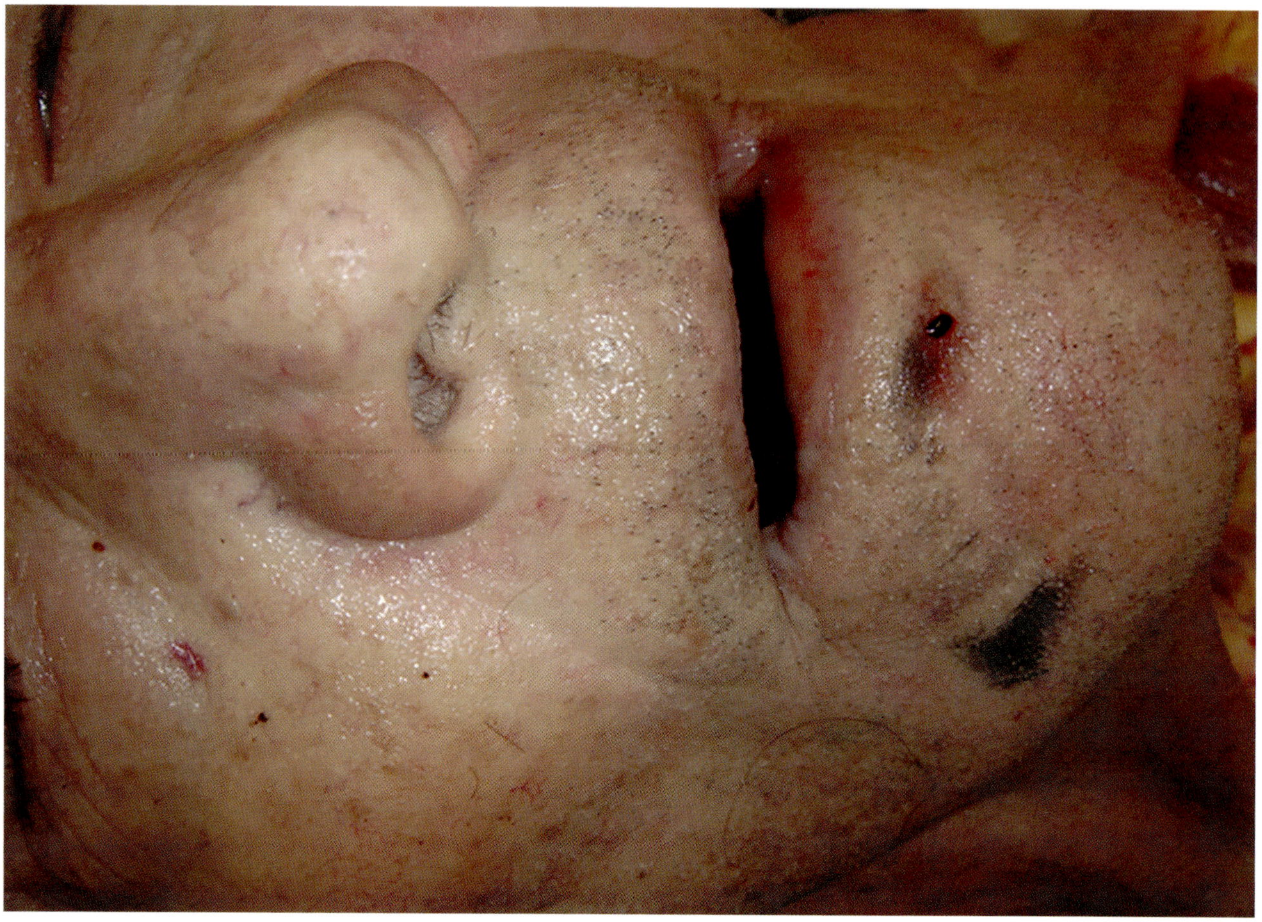

61.17 Gunshot residue emitted from cylinder gap of revolver discharged intra-orally.

irregular exit wound. Typically, there is no or minimal tissue loss of the skin (in contrast to most entrance wounds) so the wound edges are usually approximable, even being slit-like or similar in appearance to a stab wound. There may be more than one exit wound associated with a single entrance wound, due to bullet fragmentation or formation of secondary projectiles (e.g. bone splinters) (Figure 61.18). There is often eversion of the wound edges and extrusion or herniation of fibro-fatty subcutaneous tissue tags, pushed outward by the projectile and pressures within the wound cavity (Figure 61.19). In short, exit wounds may have almost any shape and may indeed, in many instances, be difficult to differentiate from entrance wounds, while in other cases, may be almost identical to stab wounds or lacerations. It is, however, very unusual to find a distinct collar of abrasion as so often seen at entrance wounds. The exception to this rule is the phenomenon of a "shored" exit wound, seen on the skin or body part where the bullet exits, is in firm contact with a supporting structure (such as a car seat,

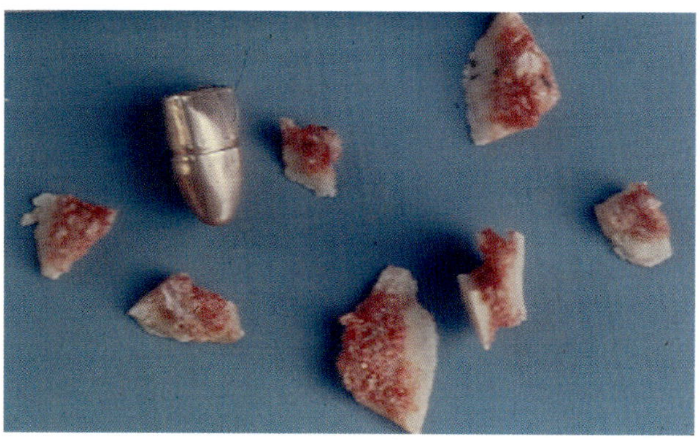

61.18 Bone fragments and bullet – the bone fragments can cause secondary projectiles created by the impact of the primary projectile (the bullet).

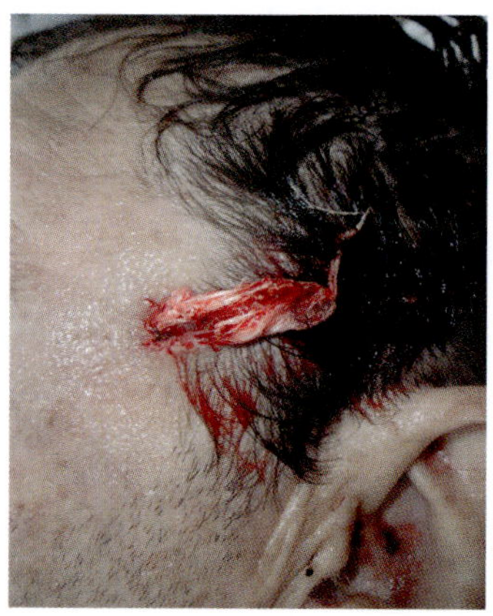

61.19 Exit wound at the temple with extrusion of intracranial contents.

floor or wall). This shores up the body tissue thus shoring up the body tissue and skin, resulting in an irregular and relatively pronounced surrounding area of bruising and abrasion of the skin. Shored exit wounds may also be found in association with wounds where there is exit and re-entry, for example, the inner aspect of the upper arm held firmly against the lateral aspect of the chest (20).

TEMPORARY AND PERMANENT WOUND CAVITIES AND THE WOUND TRACK

There is substantial variation in both shape and size of the temporary and permanent wound cavities, again depending on a multiplicity of factors such as the shape, configuration, velocity, gyroscopic stability and structural integrity of the projectile, as well as the elasticity and density of the affected tissues (12). Specialized texts will provide a detailed exposition of these parameters and associated variations in temporary and permanent wound cavities – much of which has been learned from studying the effects of bullets fired into gelatin blocks, used to simulate human tissue (Figure 61.20) (21). Wounds may be described as perforating (through and through) or penetrating (in the event of the bullet being retained within the body). In some cases, the cross-sectional measure of the temporary wound cavity may be 10 to 20 times larger than the caliber of the projectile, indicating the hydrodynamic nature of the event and the extreme kinetic energies which may be transferred to tissues. High-velocity bullets may thus have particularly destructive effects and result in damage to peripherally placed tissues (such as blood vessels and nerves) even though the latter were never in the path of the bullet

61.20 Gelatin block showing effects of bullet and pressure wave with expansion and cavitation (bullet traveling from right to left). (From: https://en.wikipedia.org/wiki/Ballistic_gelatin#/media/File:Aimed_Research_Sub-Microsecond_Photography_of_Federal_Power-Shok_100grn_.243.JPG.)

(Figure 61.21). It is not uncommon for a bullet to pass through the body or body parts, but ultimately not have sufficient kinetic energy to again pierce the skin in order to exit (notably over the back, where dense subcutaneous collagenous tissues may be found) – thus being retained immediately beneath the skin. Careful inspection and palpation will often reveal such "spent" bullets, which may then be easily removed by superficial dissection. An unusual phenomenon is that of a contour shot or track, sometimes seen when a relatively low-velocity bullet pierces the skin of (usually) the chest or head at an oblique angle but is then deflected by the subjacent bone to track beneath the skin around the trunk or head, where it may be found on the opposite side of the body – without having traversed the intervening structures. If initial radiographic screening is not routinely done, care should also be taken to inspect or preserve the clothing of victims, as bullets may quite often be retained there. In survivors with retained bullets or fragments thereof in

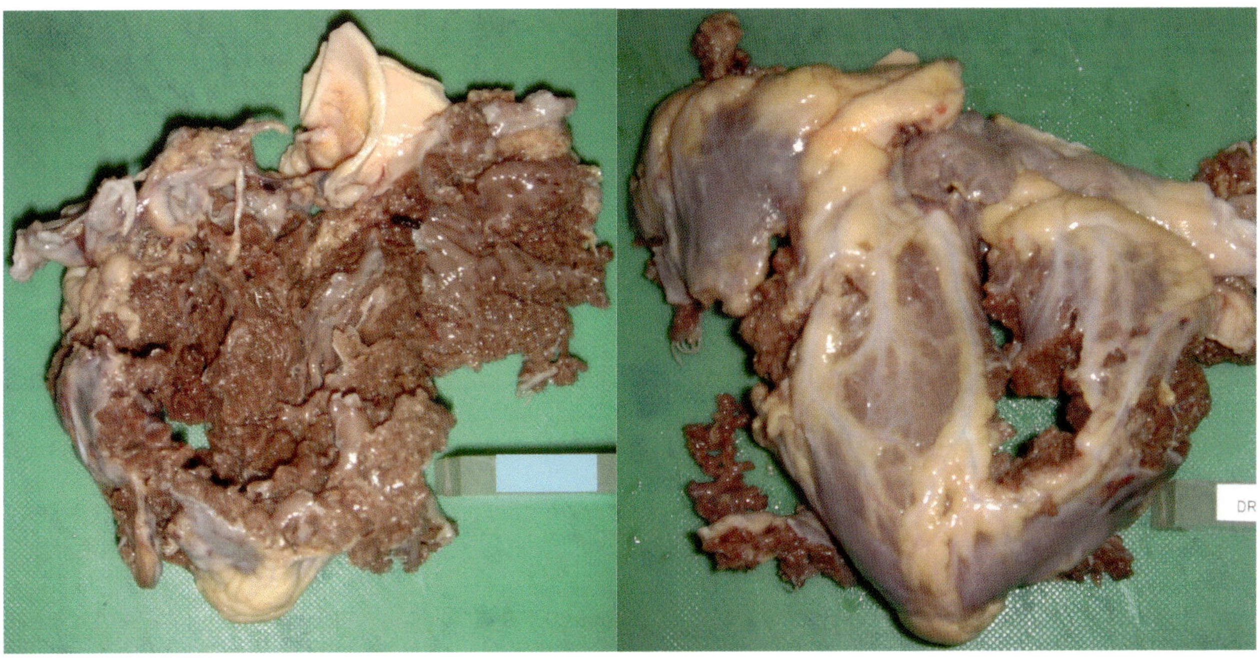

61.21 High velocity projectile injury of heart demonstrating the hydrodynamic nature of such events. (Courtesy Dr R Blumenthal.)

61.22 Bullets with striations which may have specific ballistic and forensic relevance. Also note entrapped tissue and/or fibers on projectile, presumably from target / victim.

the body, the possibility of plumbism or lead poisoning arises, in the longer term. Removed projectiles should be cautiously handled (without using metallic instruments) and packaged/sealed, labeled and managed in a manner which will ensure evidentiary integrity and maintenance of the chain of custody. The striations or grooves on the outer surface of such retrieved projectiles (caused when the bullet passes down the barrel) may disclose invaluable information to a ballistics expert, when comparisons are made using the integrated ballistic identification system, IBIS (Figure 61.22). Sophisticated radiographic imaging using computerized tomography scanning and magnetic resonance imaging, as well as low-dosage whole body digital scanning (such as Lodox©), is now available at many well-appointed forensic mortuaries, allowing for accurate review and reconstruction of wounds (22). This may provide additional information and greatly aid in the eventual explanation and presentation of findings in court proceedings. In facilities where firearm injuries are frequently seen, the Lodox© apparatus, has proved to be of great value, allowing for relatively rapid whole-body scanning to identify or locate bullelts or fragments, as well as fractures (Figure 61.23) (23). One rare phenomenon is that of the "disappearing bullet," where an entrance wound is present but no exit wound or retained bullet can be found. Unusual occurrences such as bullet embolization, migration of the bullet within body cavities or hollow organs such as the intestine, or even coughing up of a small caliber projectile from the lungs or airways (or regurgitation from the stomach) may then be the explanation. Such scenarios should be anticipated, particularly where whole-body radiography before autopsy does not reveal the presence of a bullet. It is quite common for small caliber, high-velocity sporting or military-type ammunition to disintegrate into multiple exceedingly small fragments upon striking hard objects or bone, making it difficult to retrieve individual fragments within a large and destructive wound. In such cases, the "snow-storm" appearance of multiple small fragments of only a millimeter or two in size, may be seen with radiography.

In some regions, it is not an uncommon phenomenon for victims with multiple gunshot wounds to be admitted to medicolegal mortuaries, particularly where gang warfare between rival groups is common, or where execution-style killings are involved. This may also be due to increasing availability and use of military type assault weapons (with automatic fire capacity) by criminals and paramilitary groups. In such cases, especially where dozens of wounds may be present, it may be difficult or even impossible to correlate specific entrance and exit wounds, or to reliably reconstruct wound tracks or shot sequences (Figure 61.24). Photography and line sketches to record or illustrate sites of injury as well as careful description of wounds nonetheless then

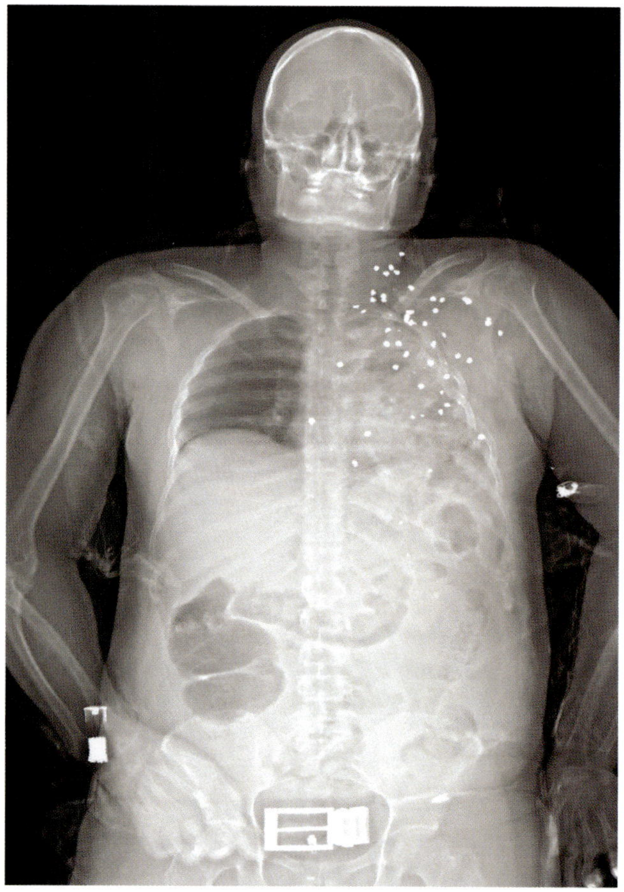

61.23 A Lodox© image of a shotgun wounding, with multiple pellets in the left upper chest region.

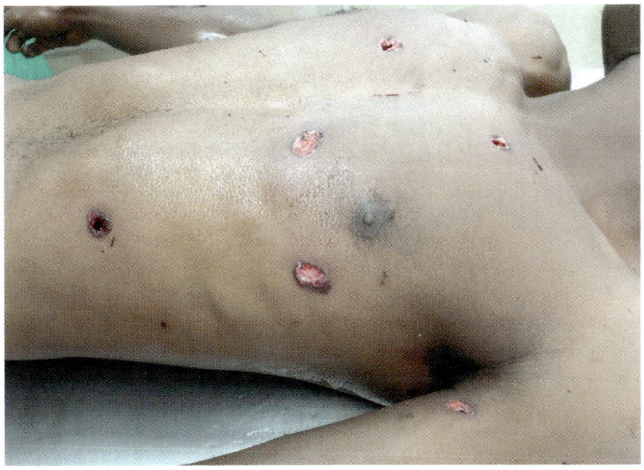

61.24 Multiple gunshot wounds cause difficulties in interpretation of wound tracks and directions.

remains important, to establish whether more than one type of weapon or ammunition may have been used, and whether close range discharges may be implicated. Where possible, prior full-body radiographic screening is an especially useful modality to determine the number, sites, type and possible fragmentation of projectiles.

GUNSHOT WOUNDS TO THE HEAD

Gunshot wounds to the head are commonly fatal and therefore often seen in forensic pathology practice. Some wound features associated with gunshot injuries of the head are worth further description. Beveling is a feature resulting from the tri-laminar construction of the skull, where the residual defect in the compact bone layers and diploe widens in the direction of the passage of the bullet – and may be a most reliable parameter to differentiate between entrance and exit wounds of the skull Figure 61.25). Bullets striking the skull at an oblique angle may create a variably beveled keyhole defect, from which the direction of travel of the bullet may also be deduced. Another useful indicator of a bullet entrance defect may be the presence of lead wipe on the edges of the defect in the outer table of the skull, or even the presence of impregnated soot and remnants of propellant in the adjacent bone and periosteum, in cases of contact or close-range discharge. There are many variations in the features and patterns of skull fractures associated with gunshot wounds, including blowout fractures of the orbital plates (resulting from hydraulic and/or buckling mechanisms and quite commonly encountered with contact gunshot wounds to the head). High kinetic energy projectiles striking the head (typically seen with military and sporting rifles) may result in severe destruction and fragmentation of the skull with traumatic extrusion of virtually the entire brain – sometimes referred to as the Krönlein phenomenon (Figures 61.26 and 61.27). In some cases, a stellate or relatively large, irregular wound may result from a bullet fired from a distance, when it strikes the head where there is subjacent bone – thus creating the impression of a contact gunshot wound. Careful inspection should however allow the observer to differentiate between the two as there will be no soot or powder discoloration in distant gunshot wounds (Figure 61.28).

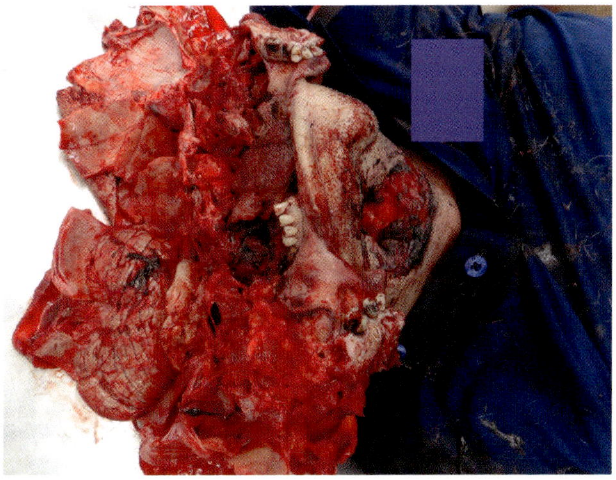

61.26 Massive tissue destruction following high-velocity submental contact wound.

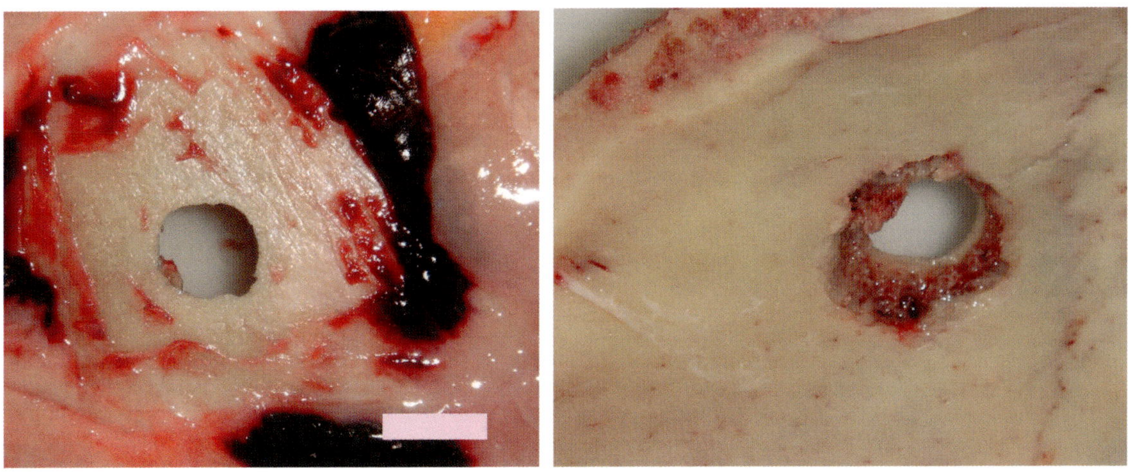

61.25 External and internal appearance of entrance wound to the skull showing marked beveling on inner aspect of the entrance wound.

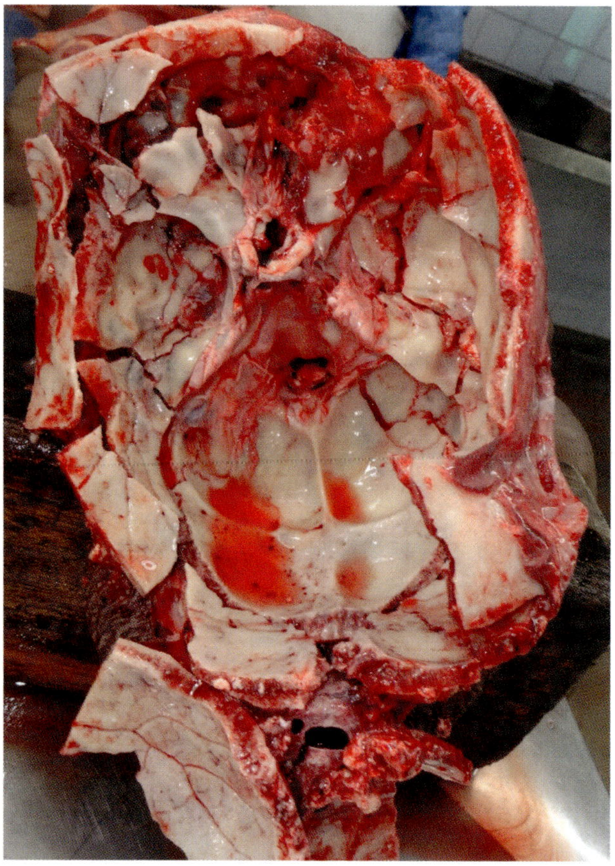

61.27 High-velocity bullet wound to the head resulting in brain evisceration (Krönlein phenomenon).

WOUNDS CAUSED BY OTHER OR UNUSUAL WEAPONS

Nail and stud guns, air guns, self-made firearms (zip guns), bows and crossbows, humane killer devices and less lethal weapons or kinetic energy devices (KEDs) all contribute to the hugely varied appearance of wounds seen in emergency or forensic practice. There appears to be a growing use of multiple types of KEDs in crowd or riot control and by security companies in certain parts of the world, with a great variation in the kinetic impact projectiles (KIPs) used in such weapons (25). These include plastic and rubber shotgun rounds, although the primary purpose of such weapons is to discourage or incapacitate one or more persons without a fatal outcome, most of these weapons may nonetheless result in serious or fatal injury when vulnerable parts of the body are struck (including for example, the temporal region of the skull, orbit, anterior part of the neck and precordial regions) (26,27).

Emergency physicians, as well as forensic medical practitioners, should in all cases contemplate the need for specialized investigations in respect of gunshot injuries. These may include the retention and later careful examination under controled, laboratory conditions and the swabbing of the hands or areas of skin around a wound to identify gunshot residue, or even (in fatal outcome cases) resection of skin tissue for purposes of stereomicroscopic or even histologic examination. The use of hand-held cordless digital microscopes within the autopsy suite may also be useful. High-quality forensic images may ultimately be extremely valuable from an evidentiary perspective. It is of course imperative that all bullets (or fragments thereof) found within or on the body of the victim, must be retained, carefully documented, and responsibly managed, for purposes of later evaluation by ballistic experts. The reconstruction of shooting incidents to determine (*inter-alia*) the flight path of bullets, muzzle to target distance or the sequence of shots, may help to clarify the circumstances surrounding a shooting, and to differentiate homicidal, suicidal and accidental events (27). The best results are obtained with an integrated approach, combining regard for physical evidence (including gunshot residue, type of weapon

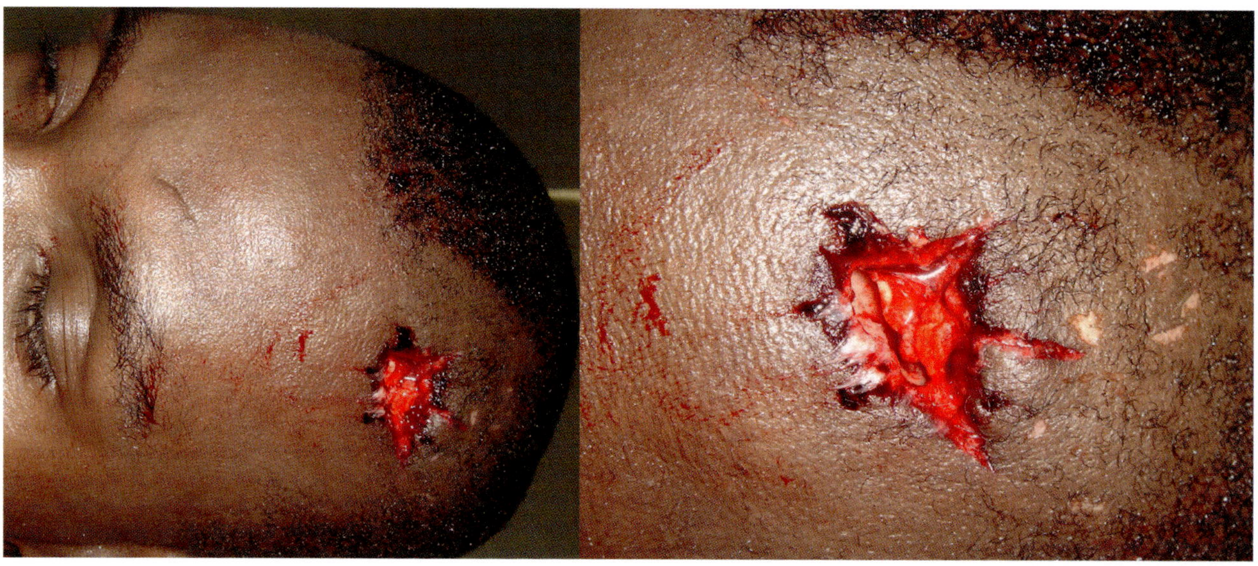

61.28 Distant gunshot wound to the head with stellate appearance – distinguished from a contact wound by absence of soot or powder residue.

and ammunition) and the post-mortem or medical findings. Although it may be a laborious and time-intensive exercise, it is important for forensic pathologists to participate in such investigations to gain insight into the technology and methodologies in use (including laser lights and smoke-filled rooms!), which will add to an overall better understanding of ballistics and in particular, wound ballistics (28,29).

Wounds caused by smooth-bore weapons

Firearms without rifling or grooves on the inside of the barrel are referred to as smooth-bore weapons and include shotguns and a variety of other military weapons such as artillery guns and mortars. There are many variations in the bore or gauge of shotguns, the most popular being the 12-gauge, 20-gauge and .410-bore barrels, also varied barrel configurations, including "side-by-side" and "over-and-under" placements, as well as combinations with rifled barrels. These guns typically fire multiple pellets at once, the latter mostly varying from approximately 2 to 5 mm in diameter, although single-shot slugs are also used. As these projectiles are neither spin stabilised nor aerodynamic, the effective range for most types of shot does not exceed approximately 50 m, although fatalities in humans can readily occur at greater distances, depending on shot size and the anatomic site involved. In some regions, shotguns are common, predominantly for sporting use (such as wing, skeet, or trap shooting). However, modified, or specialized pump action, short-barreled large-bore shotguns are commonly used in the security industry and perhaps increasingly so, in criminal activities.

At closer distances, shotguns may result in very destructive injuries among others due to the "billiard ball" effect, when multiple pellets strike the target and each other, dispersing in multiple directions. There is substantial variation in the construction of shotgun ammunition and the materials used, although in most cases, the mechanism of discharge is similar to cartridges used in rifled weapons. However, shot shells typically contain a plastic cup-like structure within the outer casing, in which the pellets are housed. The pellets are separated from the propellant by a disk-like wad (made from cardboard, cloth or plastic). Since the cup and wad are also discharged from the barrel of the weapon, these may also strike or penetrate the target in close range shots (Figure 61.29). From a forensic medical perspective, over and above the distinct nature and severity of shotgun injuries at close range, the most important consideration may be the determination of the approximate range of fire, based upon the degree of scatter of the pellets at variable distances (30). Contact or close-range shots may result in a relatively large entrance defect, with relatively smooth wound edges – and usually quite abundant discoloration due to smoke and propellant residue, as well as possible tattooing and searing. At progressively greater distances, the pellets may result in irregular scalloping of the wound edges, the wound then being likened to a "rat hole" or described as having a "cookie cutter" appearance (31). At several meters (depending on shot size and number of pellets), individual entry wounds may be seen, not dissimilar to other bullet entry wounds. Test shots fired with similar ammunition and weapon may yield a relatively accurate reconstruction of the probable muzzle to target distance, in a particular case. Because of their poor "penetrating power", shotgun pellets seldom result in exit wounds, except in close range discharge (Figure 61.30a&b).

It is standard protocol for forensic pathologists to approach the evaluation of decedents in a manner specifically intended to assess and address those issues and perspectives likely to shed light on the circumstances under which the injuries were sustained, and to anticipate the questions which may arise in later legal proceedings. However, this would not typically be the priority or approach by clinicians dealing with such victims. It is nonetheless vital for clinicians and emergency healthcare providers to also be mindful of these issues as there is a high likelihood of later legal proceedings, irrespective of a fatal or

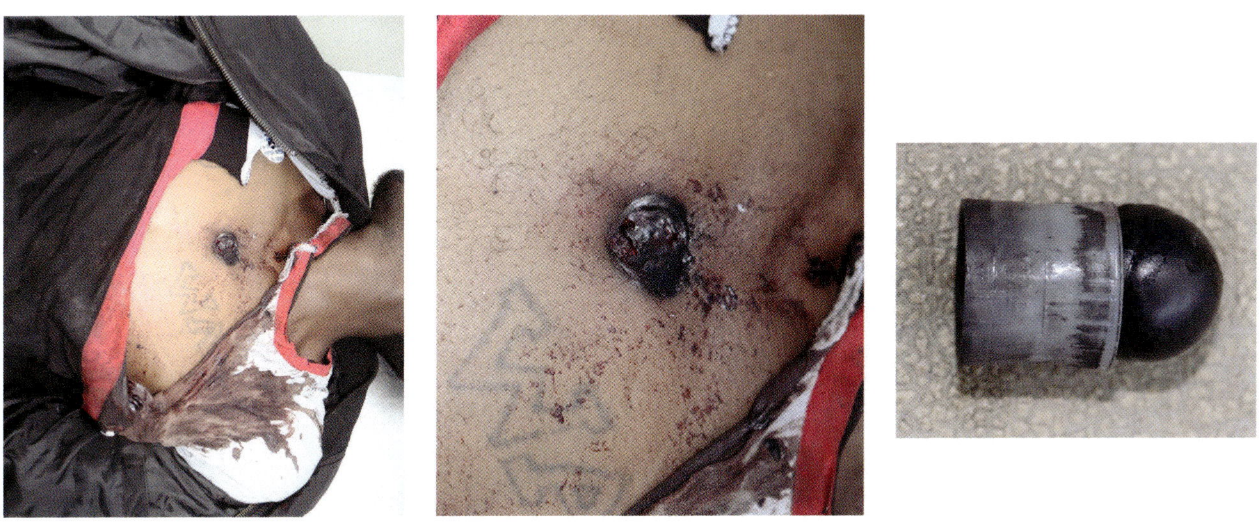

61.29 Shotgun entrance wound with single shot slug and cup present. (Courtesy of Dr SH Rossouw.)

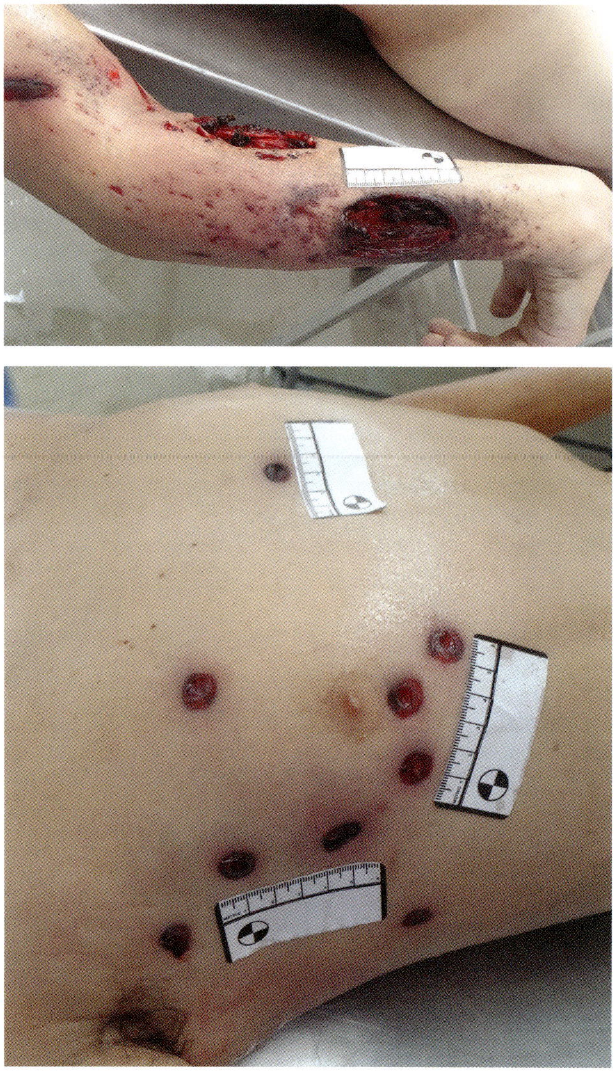

61.30 Shotgun wounds. **(a)** Close range discharge of shotgun through arm, **(b)** with re-entry of pellets to the chest.

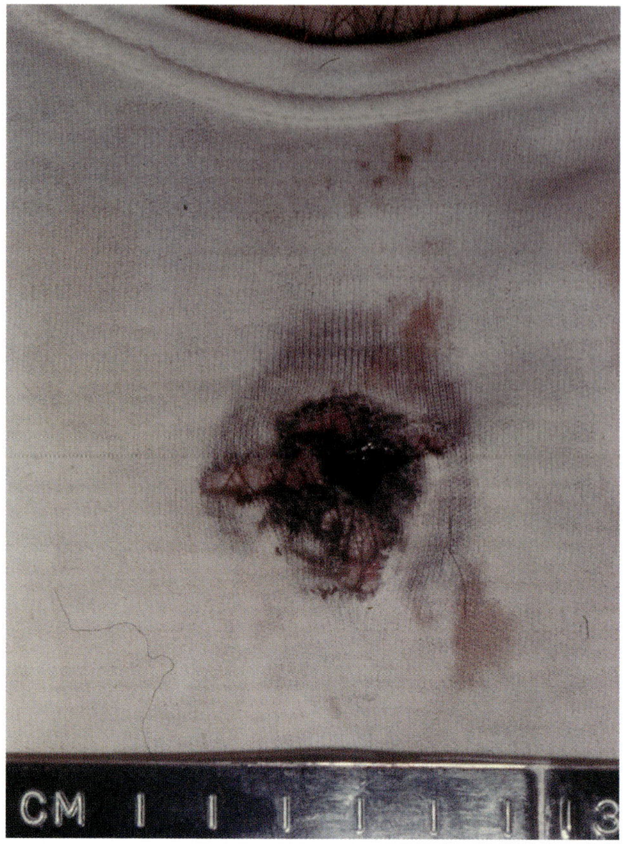

61.31 Undergarment showing gunshot residue indicative of close range discharge.

non-fatal outcome. Most patients who present to emergency rooms for treatment of firearm injuries do so following assault, as survival after intentional self-inflicted/suicidal injury with a firearm is rare. In a clinical setting, healthcare workers should thus consciously contemplate whether there are any legal or medicolegal imperatives or perspectives to be considered, even before assessment and management of the patient starts. At the scene of injury, or at the time of admission to an emergency room, there may be sparse, conflicting or incorrect information regarding the incident, and healthcare workers are advised not to assume and accept such preliminary information without reservation. Typical examples here would be the initial allegation that a victim had attempted to commit suicide or that an accidental shooting had taken place – versions quite often contested at a later stage. In practice, it is unfortunately the case that even police officers may fall into the trap of "premature closure" relating to the circumstances surrounding such cases, resulting in inadequate initial scientific investigation or recordings.

A moment of deliberate reflection is needed to consider the appropriate protocol and approach to ensure that these medicolegal perspectives are not neglected. It would thus be advisable to approach every patient (or decedent) with a suspected gunshot injury in anticipation of having to answer specific questions which may arise at later legal proceedings. In this regard, identifying and preserving evidentiary material (e.g. retaining items of clothing or protecting the hands of the victim – even at the scene of injury – for later gunshot residue swabbing, photography). It is common for emergency responders to remove and discard items of clothing or even cut through shirts or blouses, to expose the torso for placement of ECG leads or defibrillators, not realising that such items of clothing may harbor important physical evidence such as gunshot residue (Figure 61.31). In most cases, such unfavorable outcomes could probably be avoided without compromising the immediate management of the patient. An objective and meticulous assessment of the victim, seeking specifically to contemporaneously identify and record relevant features and to preserve evidentiary material, will serve the interests of the individual and society. Thus, when healthcare workers must attend to a patient who may have sustained a gunshot injury, they should briefly but consciously consider the following questions, over and above contemplating the medical management of the patient, to help serve the legal inquiry, which is likely to follow (often several months or years later). In short, the approach to a victim of interpersonal violence – seen from this perspective – should be like that of a crime-scene investigator. While some of the questions which are raised below can be addressed at a later stage with a view to completing the jigsaw puzzle, it may be very helpful for clinicians to be specifically cognizant of at least some of the relevant medicolegal perspectives right from the outset, as this may guide not only their assessment of the patient but also the way they contemporaneously record their findings.

COMMON QUESTIONS

Is it a gunshot wound?

Miscommunications, different versions and erroneous information regarding an incident may misdirect or even prejudice clinicians during the early stages of dealing with victims of violent injury. A stab wound inflicted by a star-bit screwdriver may result in an injury remarkably similar in appearance to an entrance gunshot wound caused by a smaller caliber bullet. In addition, victims of gunshot wounds may also have sustained injuries due to other forms of assault, vehicle accidents or falls.

How many gunshot wounds are there and how many projectiles may have struck the victim?

The total number of gunshot injuries (wounds) on the body may be significantly greater than the number of bullets that have struck the victim, as one projectile may result in multiple entrance and/or exit wounds. Can specific entrance and exit wounds be correlated?

Is it an entrance or an exit wound?

For obvious reasons, both from a clinical management view and for purposes of later legal proceedings, differentiating between entrance and exit wounds may be of vital importance. This may be of even greater relevance in instances where there are multiple wounds. An accurate and meticulous (contemporaneous) description of a wound by an attending emergency clinician may be of great value in cases where the patient subsequently undergoes treatment which may alter the appearance of the wound. This may include cleaning, debridement and suturing of the wound(s) or (if the patient survives the initial injury for a number of days), the intervening changes of inflammation, sepsis or healing in the wound – thereby precluding reliable conclusion as to the initial nature of the wound by even an experienced forensic pathologist who later examines and records such injuries.

What was the direction of the projectile when it struck the body and/or in its passage through the tissues?

The precise location of every wound should be carefully recorded and annotated with reference to the standard anatomic position. It only takes a moment to measure, not only the size of the wound (or even the dimensions of various components) but also its position relative to fixed reference points (e.g., height above the heel or distance from the midline). Careful inspection of the shape and other features of an entrance wound may, in some instances, allow for a reliable conclusion regarding the probable direction (relative to the site of impact), from which the projectile had come. Such objective measurements may later be of substantial value, when scene and/or shooting incident reconstruction is undertaken. Of course, the victim may have been in a different anatomic position at the time of sustaining the injury, as opposed to the time when being evaluated by the healthcare worker. By correlating what appear to be connected entrance and exit wounds, an approximate direction of travel within the body may be deduced, bearing in mind that there may have been an alteration in the initial direction (e.g. a projectile deflected by bone or fragmenting). Modern radiographic modalities may greatly facilitate such reconstructions, which may be of great value at later proceedings. This may be particularly useful in cases of multiple gunshots and/or where more than one type of firearm had been used (e.g. in the case of multiple assailants).

What was the probable position/positions of the victim at the time of sustaining the gunshot wounds?

Careful consideration of the anatomic sites of entrance and exit wounds, together with intervening wound tracks and contemplation of the type and nature of the firearm/ammunition in question, may often help with later reconstruction of the probable position of the victim at the time of sustaining the injury. A typical example would be the finding of an entrance and exit wound on the forearm or hand, seen in association with a re-entry wound to the chest or abdomen, suggesting that the forearm or hand had been positioned in front of the victim, perhaps in a defensive gesture. Careful consideration of various body positions to align entrance wounds, wound cavities and exit wounds, may later be used to support, or contest, versions provided by witnesses or an accused person.

Can any conclusion be drawn regarding the probable sequence of shots (when multiple gunshot injuries have been sustained)?

A contact wound to the head or several tightly grouped entrance wounds in a person with multiple other gunshot injuries, may suggest what amounts to a terminal "execution" of an already wounded person.

What was the range of fire (in other words, from what distance was the weapon discharged)?

Careful inspection of the clothing and the skin at the entrance wound may in many cases allow for a scientifically validated comment as to the probable range of fire, especially when the offending projectile is retrieved or where the firearm in question has been identified or made available. Specific wound features may be reliable indicators of a contact wound, a close-range wound or a shot fired from a distance. The nature and pattern of powder tattooing and smoke deposition on the clothing or skin may later be correlated with test shots fired from a similar weapon or with similar ammunition, yielding information used to validate or repudiate the versions of witnesses or accused individuals. Bearing in mind that features such as smoke and soot deposition, searing and tattooing, may be of an evanescent nature and if not recorded by initial observers, these may not be present or visible to a forensic pathologist who examines the decedent at a later stage. Where possible, specialized investigations should be performed or requested (e.g. using alternative light sources or doing chemical or other analyses to detect gunshot residue on skin or clothing).

What type of weapon and/or ammunition is implicated in the causation of the injury or injuries?

An experienced observer may be able to comment on the probable nature of the type of weapon and/or ammunition used to inflict a particular wound, based on the specific findings and features of the entrance and exit wounds or intervening wound track. While it may be more difficult and unreliable to make such an assessment in the living patient, modern imaging modalities may be especially useful in this regard. On the other hand, careful dissection, and assessment by the forensic pathologist in fatal outcome cases, may yield information which on occasion can allow for reliable conclusion as to the possible offending ammunition and/or type of firearm.

What was the (physical) capacity of the victim to act, after sustaining the injury?

The ability of an individual to continue with certain actions or activities after having sustained an injury, is often raised at later legal proceedings. For example, an accused pleading self-defense may state that the decedent had continued to pose a threat or had launched another assault, necessitating further shots, but this version may be repudiated by a finding that indicates the decedent would have been completely incapacitated by an initial shot.

Would rapid first aid or medical assistance have influenced the chances of survival and/or what was the probable survival period, after having sustained the gunshot injury?

A careful description of the nature and track of a wound, having regard also for the vital organs and structures affected, may allow for later comment as to the probable period of survival and/or whether immediate or rapid first aid may have presented an opportunity to effectively prevent a fatal outcome. In such cases, failure by an assailant to assist the victim or to request emergency medical support may be an aggravating factor at later legal proceedings.

What were the probable circumstances under which the injury was sustained – are there specific indicators to suggest the setting or manner of injury, such as self-inflicted injury, defensive or accidental injury?

A careful and open-minded assessment of one or more gunshot wounds based upon the cumulative features may allow an experienced forensic medical practitioner to express an opinion as to the possible setting or circumstance surrounding such an injury. Contact entrance wounds at the "sites of election" (including the frontal, temporal, intraoral, submental and precordial regions), typically implicate suicide, while self-inflicted wounds are very seldom seen on other parts of the face or neck (32). An unconventional grip on the firearm in some cases of self-inflicted injury may however result in wounds in unusual, and indeed confusing, sites.

What was the probable mechanism of death (pathophysiological processes resulting in death)?

In some cases, severe tissue destruction or involvement of vital organs or structures (e.g. the brain stem) may result not only in immediate incapacitation but even almost immediate death. In other cases, however, protracted bleeding, respiratory compromise due to aspiration of blood or even later cardiac tamponade (among others) may constitute the terminal pathophysiological derangements or mechanisms resulting in the eventual demise of the patient. Such considerations may be important in the overall assessment of the incident or case, perhaps in particular when the adequacy or correctness of (emergency) medical management of the victim is brought into question.

It is essential for the emergency healthcare worker or clinician to provide a full description of the various wound features, rather than simply recording or labeling a particular wound as being, for example, an entrance or a contact wound. It may be difficult to later validate or justify such a conclusion if the feature(s) upon which such a diagnosis was based were not contemporaneously recorded. Even if the attending emergency healthcare worker or clinician has only a relatively basic knowledge of ballistics and gunshot injuries but is mindful of the abovementioned perspectives and shows awareness and diligence in adequately documenting the findings and in preserving evidence, especially at the time of first clinical contact and evaluation, later legal review processes may be positively impacted (33). Critical evidentiary elements will be lost if emergency workers or nursing attendants remove items of clothing, clean, dress or even suture wounds before they are carefully assessed, recorded or photographed from a forensic medical perspective. Intervening changes of vital reaction (infection or inflammatory changes, crusting and desiccation of wound edges, infection, etc.), may, within hours, alter and obscure the initial nature of the

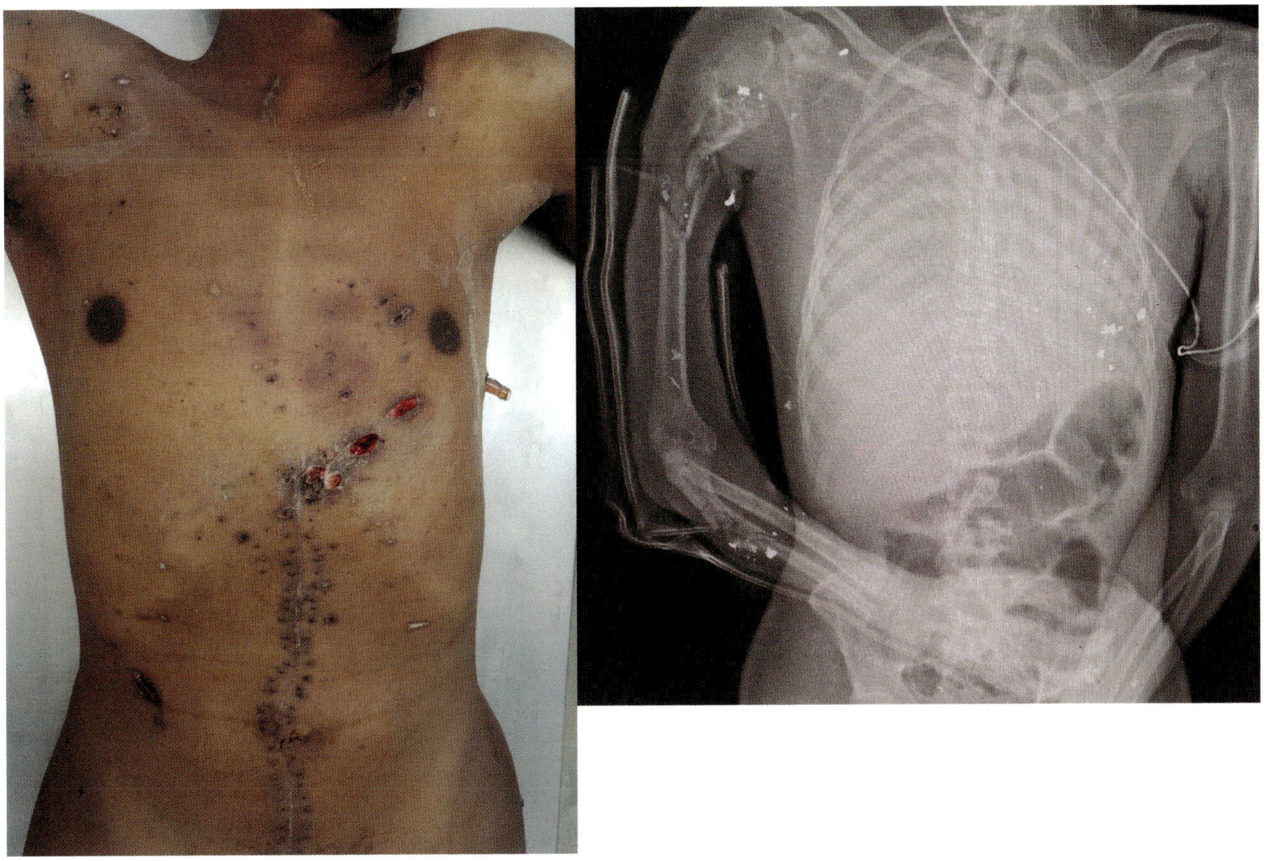

61.32 Wound healing and surgical intervention may complicate interpretation at a later stage.

wound, to the extent that even an experienced forensic pathologist will not then be able to reliably ascertain or comment upon the initial nature of the injury (e.g., distinguishing between an entrance as opposed to an exit wound) (Figure 61.32). Such duly documented findings may be all that stand between the justifiable conviction of a murderer or the acquittal of an accused who may have acted in self-defense.

DEATHS DUE TO BLASTS AND EXPLOSIONS

Fatalities due to explosions are seldom seen in routine forensic pathology practice. In a civilian setting, it has been reported that such deaths are most frequent in the industrial sector, associated with chemical explosions, fire, pressurized containers and arc flashes or blasts. In the US, fewer than 50 such fatalities are reported annually among construction workers (34). Certain industries, including the petrochemical, mining, transport and electrical sectors, appear to carry the greatest risk. Similarly, small numbers of such events have been reported from Australia. However, there is a general paucity of published data as few countries keep specific records of such fatalities. In contrast, fatalities specifically associated with explosive devices used in a military setting or associated with terrorist activity, are monitored, and reported on by various agencies. According to the United Nations, more than 11 000 civilians died in such explosions in 2021, the vast majority of these being in Afghanistan, Syria, Gaza, Yemen and Iraq (36). Overall, however, fatalities due to explosive weapons were reported from 57 countries. Globally, fatalities associated with terrorist activities (and notably, explosions) are on the increase, especially in Sub-Saharan Africa (37). In the US, between 13 and 27 deaths related to explosive devices have been recorded annually for the period 2017–2021 (38). In some countries and communities, the illegitimate acquisition and use of (usually commercial) explosives for use in criminal activities such as blasting of drop safes and automatic teller machines, as well as cash in transit heists, has also led to an increase in blast fatalities (Figure 61.33).

Although multiple and severe injuries (and indeed, multiple fatalities) may be seen in blast events that do not involve explosives, events where explosive devices are implicated typically produce more severe (and a greater spectrum of) injuries and pathologic features. A detailed discussion of diverse types of explosives and devices is beyond the scope of this chapter, but a distinction should broadly be drawn between low- and high-order as well as military ordnance explosives. The former (such as black powder, petrol bombs and "Molotov cocktails") explode by means of deflagration, generating subsonic velocities

61.33 ATM bombing.

of less than 1000 m/s, while high explosives (including, as examples, trinitrotoluene, nitroglycerin and Semtex) undergo detonation, yielding supersonic reaction velocities of well over 2000 m/s – even exceeding 8000 m/s (39). This discussion primarily addresses the effects of conventional barothermic explosive devices and does not extend to include the injuries and pathology associated with nuclear and other unusual types of explosions. Although so-called "dirty bombs" (also referred to as radiologic dispersal devices) may contain radioactive material, they are not classified as nuclear bombs and are still considered to be primarily of a barothermic explosive nature (40).

In detonations, the almost instantaneous release of so much energy results in over-pressurization and blast waves which may directly or indirectly damage human tissue. Subsonic blast waves do not usually directly cause substantial damage to human tissues, but supersonic blast/pressure waves may result in severe damage, more so where this blast wave is propagated through tissues of different densities or where an air/fluid or tissue/fluid interface is encountered. Therefore, with supersonic blasts, damage will be highly likely if the victim is in relative proximity to the reaction site, commonly injuring the middle ear, the lungs, eyes and hollow viscera (including the bowel). A multiplicity of other factors may be involved and complicate the mechanisms of injury causation associated with explosions, over and above detonation velocity and proximity to the blast point. These include shockwave reflection and propagation (where blasts take place in confined spaces such as buildings – usually amplifying and/or repeating blast wave related injury, as opposed to explosions in unconfined areas) (41,42). There are many forms of specialized munitions which may further complicate the mechanisms of injury causation associated with explosions. By way of example, the detonation of a cluster bomb scatters multiple bomblets (or submunitions) over a wide area, which then again detonate individually, causing damage over a much wider area (43). Other devices are designed to generate so-called explosively formed projectiles (EFPs), which may be capable of attaining velocities of 2000 m/s and penetrating several centimeters of steel, even at great distances (44).

Overall, injuries caused by explosions have been extensively reviewed and reported on and may be divided into four or five categories, although it may be difficult to specifically differentiate and/or separate such injuries in a particular case or event (*see also* Chapter 62). These include the following:

- **Primary blast injury** comprises barotrauma caused directly by the over-pressurization and propagation of blast wave in tissues of differential densities (as described above), with stretching and shearing of tissues and rupture of blood vessels. Although damage to the middle ear is the most common manifestation associated with this mechanism, blast lung is the injury most likely to result in fatal outcome (Figure 61.34). Such damage may not be macroscopically obvious at autopsy and is usually best confirmed with histologic evaluation. Systemic air embolism because of pulmonary parenchymal damage may also result in a relatively rapid fatal outcome, while diffuse alveolar damage and Acute Respiratory Distress Syndrome (ARDS) may also follow. Some authors also include the very severe injuries (such as gross destruction and traumatic dismemberment), seen in victims who were near the blast point, under the category of primary blast injury (Figure 61.35) (45–47).
- **Secondary blast injury** is the result of penetration by missiles (driven in almost all directions by the blast wave and moving at extreme velocities), comprising fragments or components of the explosive device itself as well as secondary objects such as debris, rocks, and glass (Figure 61.36). Some munitions are specifically constructed in a manner to maximize this kind of damage, including some improvised explosive devices (IEDs), such as pipe bombs, which have evolved to become the weapons of choice for many terrorist groups (Figure 61.37).

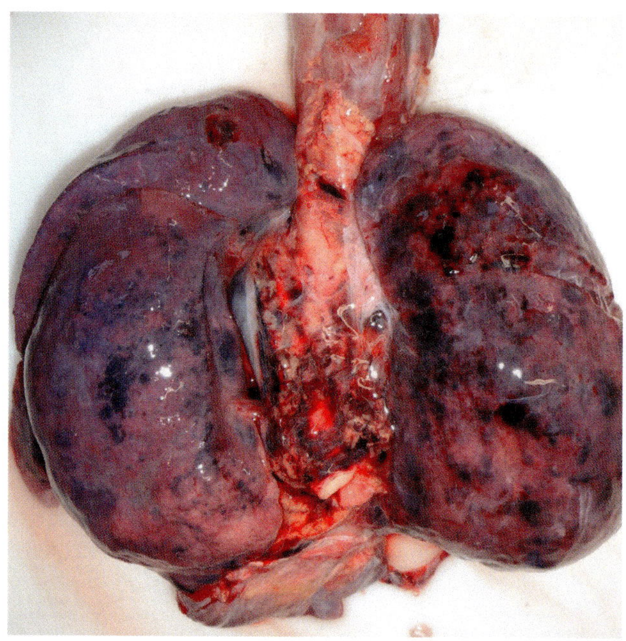

61.34 Primary injury – blast lung.

61.35 Traumatic dismemberment – generally classified as secondary blast injury.

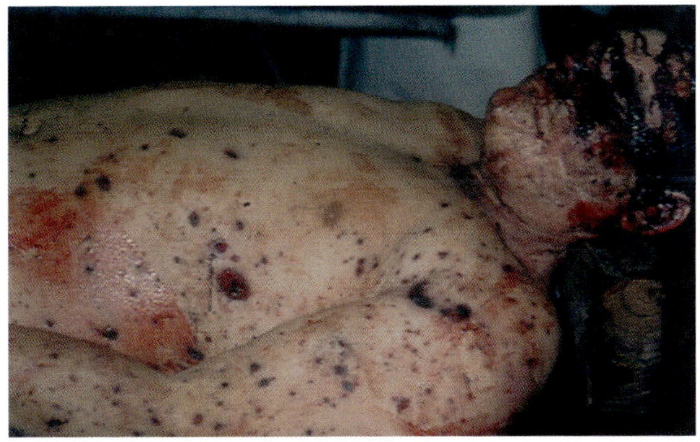

61.36 Secondary blast injury – multiple shrapnel wounds.

- **Tertiary blast injury** is the result of forceful displacement of the body against other objects, or from the disintegration and collapse of structures around the victim, resulting in severe mechanical or crush injury (Figure 61.38).
- **Quaternary blast injuries** include a variety of other injurious mechanisms and manifestations associated with blast events, such as thermal and radiation burns, mechanical asphyxia, myoglobinuria secondary to crush injury, ischemic cardiac lesions and more.
- **Quinary blast injury.** Few authors include this as a specific subset of blast-related injury but it has been used to accommodate diverse other or later effects or sequela associated with explosions, including a delayed hyperinflammatory response to chemicals or bacteria, sometimes incorporated in so-called "dirty bombs."

All victims of blast trauma should be approached based on having suffered multisystem trauma and that a wide range of injuries, insults and complications are likely to be present.

While most fatalities resulting from explosions may take place in countries or areas where full and proper medicolegal investigation of the incident and the victims may not be routinely undertaken, it remains important that pathologists develop and maintain appropriate protocols for managing such cases, in routine forensic pathology practice (48). The specific nature of a blast incident will determine the scope and complexity of the forensic medical and scientific investigation which is undertaken. Although rare events, suicide and accidental death may be more common in regions where commercial explosives are more available (e.g. mining communities) or where military ordnance from previous civil strife has not been properly disposed of or arms caches are dug up or recycled as scrap metal. In mass fatality events, or incidents involving dirty bombs or improvised devices, specialized investigative protocols may be required,

61.37 **(a)** Suicide vest with multiple ball-bearings and **(b)** Kevlar protective suit with multiple sites of damage.

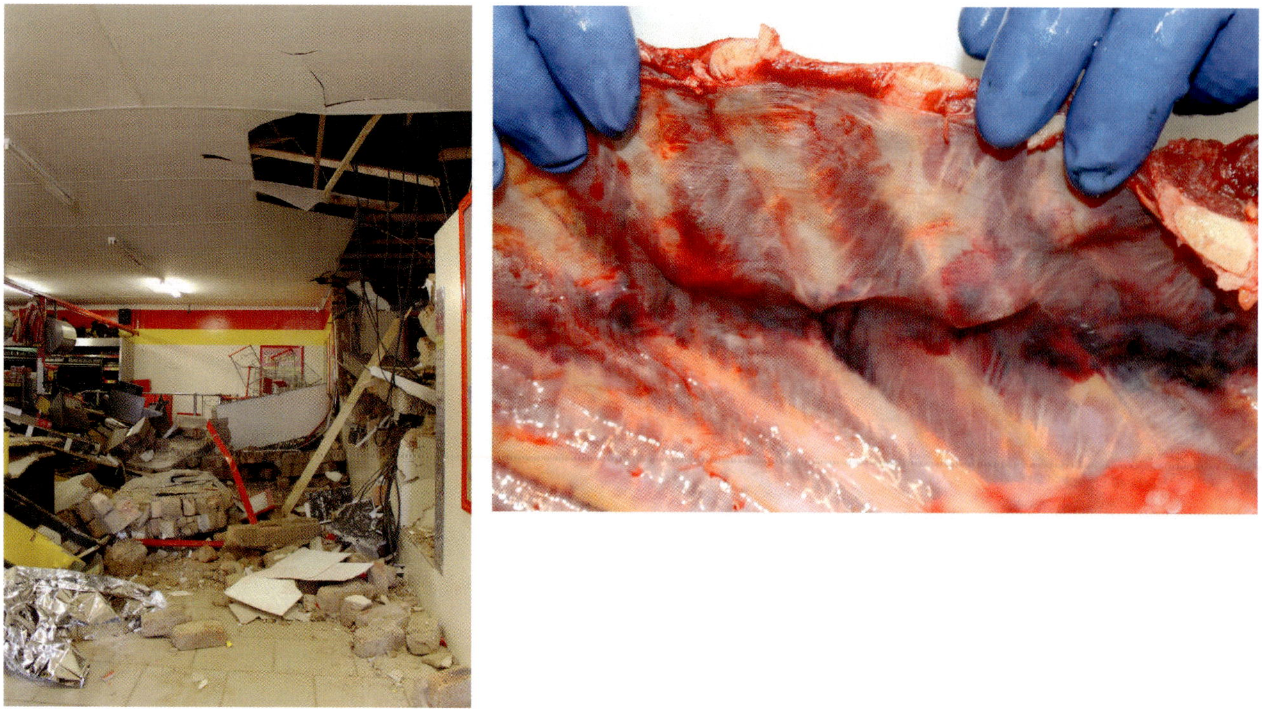

61.38 **(a)** Supermarket bombing and **(b)** rib fractures caused by building collapse (tertiary injury).

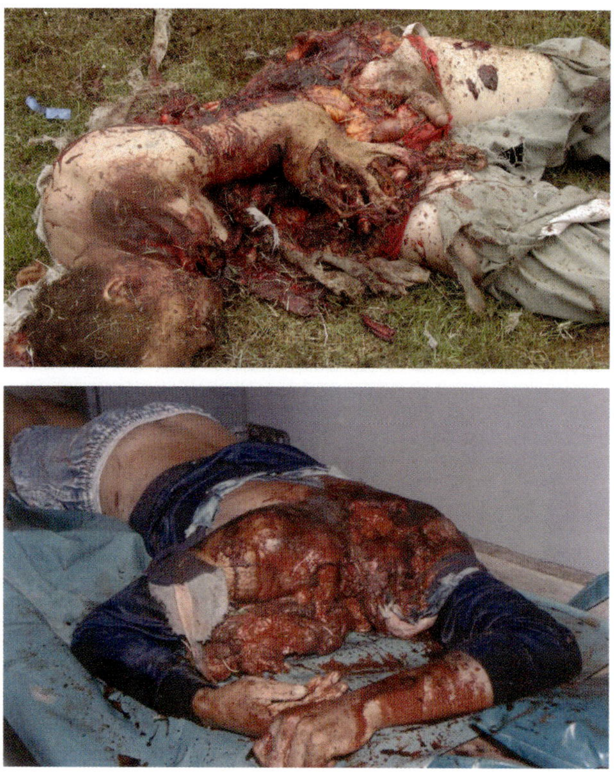

61.39 Suicide explosions create substantial difficulties in identification.

61.40 Beer hall and tavern – gas explosion.

including the deployment of forensic anthropologists as severe mutilation, and intermingling of body parts, will be likely and appropriate victim identification protocols will need to be followed (Figure 61.39). In all fatal blast events, the pathologist(s) should be part of initial briefings involving appropriate expertise and multiple agencies – including military personnel and blast or munitions experts (Figure 61.40). Scene attendance and mapping or photography, as well as collection of relevant samples and specimens should be undertaken in all cases, where possible. Safety considerations, at the scene and in the mortuary, should be of primary concern. Whole body post-mortem radiographic screening of bodies (preferably by means of PMCT or digital low-dose X-ray scanning) should be routinely undertaken to assist with victim identification and in revealing fractures, foreign bodies and injury patterns. Retrieved metallic or other particles, items of clothing and appropriate specimens or swabs should be submitted for further analysis to (among other) identify the explosive device, explosives residue and hazardous chemicals. Where relevant, forensic odontologic examination must be undertaken and tissues retained for DNA analysis. Routine toxicologic screening and histologic examination should furthermore be an integral part of such medicolegal investigations. Finally, it will also be best if the forensic pathologist participates in the eventual attempted reconstruction of the blast event, using all available and relevant information and expertise.

CONCLUSION

The immensity of the global firearm and munitions-related injury epidemic cannot be overstated. The large and ever-expanding diversity of ballistic and blast injuries and the often-complex biophysics associated with their causation, together with the multiplicity (and ever-increasing range) of firearm weaponry and explosive devices, requires clinicians, pathologists and forensic scientists to constantly revise their knowledge and understanding in this field. Such forensic knowledge and expertise may individually and collectively help in the administration of justice – and thus, to palliate the painful impact on society caused by these instruments of injury and destruction.

REFERENCES

1. Charlton E. There are more than 1 billion guns in the world and this is who owns them, 2019. Available from: https://www.weforum.org/agenda/2019/03/there-are-more-than-1-billion-guns-in-the-world-and-this-is-who-owns-them/ (Accessed 14 June 2023).
2. Karp A. Estimating global civilian-held firearms numbers, 2018. Available from: https://www.smallarmssurvey.org/sites/default/files/resources/SAS-BP-Civilian-Firearms-Numbers.pdf (Accessed 14 June 2023).
3. Rivara FP, Studdert DM, Wintemute GJ. Firearm-related mortality: A global public health problem. *JAMA* 2018; **320(8)**: 764–5.
4. Naghavi M, Marczak LB, Kutz M, et al. Global mortality from firearms, 1990–2016. *JAMA* 2018; **320(8)**: 792–814.
5. Goldstick JE, Cunningham RM, Carter PM. Current causes of death in children and adolescents in the United States. *N Engl J Med* 2022; **386(20)**: 1955–6.
6. Kaufman EJ, Delgado MK. The epidemiology of firearm injuries in the US: The need for comprehensive, real-time, actionable data. *JAMA* 2022; **328(12)**: 1177–8.
7. Kaufman EJ, Wiebe DJ, Xiong RA, et al. Epidemiologic trends in fatal and nonfatal firearm injuries in the US, 2009–2017. *JAMA Intern Med* 2021; **181(2)**: 237–44.
8. Everytown Report. The economic cost of gun violence, 2022. Available from: https://everytownresearch.org/report/the-economic-cost-of-gun-violence/ (Accessed 14 June 2023).
9. Farr S. Elements of Medical Jurisprudence; Or a Succinct and Compendious Description of Such Tokens in the Human Body as are Requisite to Determine the Judgment of a Coroner, and Courts of Law, in Cases of Divorce, Rape, Murder, &c: To which are Added Directions for Preserving the Public Health, 1788.
10. Rhee PM, Moore EE, Joseph B, et al. Gunshot wounds: A review of ballistics, bullets, weapons, and myths. *J Trauma Acute Care Surg* 2016; **80(6)**: 853–67.
11. Sellier KG, Kneubuehl BP, Haag LC. *Wound Ballistics and the Scientific Background*. Amsterdam: Elsevier; 1994.
12. DiMaio VJ. *Gunshot Wounds: Practical Aspects of Firearms, Ballistics, and Forensic Techniques*. Boca Raton: CRC Press; 2015.
13. Thali MJ, Kneubuehl BP, Dirnhofer R, Zollinger U. The dynamic development of the muzzle imprint by contact gunshot: High-speed documentation utilizing the "skin–skull–brain model." *Forensic Sci Int* 2002; **127(3)**: 168–73.
14. Stefanopoulos PK, Pinialidis DE, Hadjigeorgiou GF, Filippakis KN. Wound ballistics 101: The mechanisms of soft tissue wounding by bullets. *Eur J Trauma Emerg Surg* 2017; **43(5)**: 579–86.
15. Le Garff E, Delannoy Y, Mesli V, et al. Homemade firearm suicide with dumbbell pipe triggering by an air-compressed gun: Case report and review of literature. *Am J Forensic Med Pathol* 2015; **36(4)**: 257–61.
16. Denton JS, Segovia A, Filkins JA. Practical pathology of gunshot wounds. *Arch Pathol Lab Med* 2006; **130(9)**: 1283–9.
17. Schyma C, Baumann F, Madea B, Gotsmy W. Study of backspatter using high-speed video of experimental gunshots. *Forensic Sci Med Pathol* 2021; **17(1)**: 36–46.
18. Stone IC, Petty CS. Interpretation of unusual wounds caused by firearms. *J Forensic Sci* 1991; **36(3)**: 736–40.
19. Donoghue ER, Kalelkar MB, Richmond JM, Teas SS. Atypical gunshot wounds of entrance: An empirical study. *J Forensic Sci* 1984; **29(2)**: 379–88.
20. Dixon DS. Characteristics of shored exit wounds. *J Forensic Sci* 1981; **26(4)**: 691–8.
21. Carr DJ, Stevenson T, Mahoney PF. The use of gelatine in wound ballistics research. *Int J Leg Med* 2018; **132(6)**: 1659–64.
22. Norberti N, Tonelli P, Giaconi C, et al. State of the art in post-mortem computed tomography: A review of current literature. *Virchows Archiv* 2019; **475(2)**: 139–50.
23. du Plessis M, Liebenberg L. Lodox®: The invaluable radiographic solution in the forensic setting. *Int J Leg Med* 2020; **134(2)**: 655–62.
24. Pankratz H, Fischer H. Wound ballisticsof the Krönlein shot. *Zeitschriftfur Rechtsmedizin*. 1985; **95(3)**: 213–5.
25. Payne-James J, Jones RM (eds). *Simpson's Forensic Medicine*. Boca Raton: CRC Press; 2019.
26. Physicians for Human Rights. Kinetic impact projectiles, 2017. Available from: https://phr.org/wp-content/uploads/2020/06/PHR_INCLO_Fact_Sheet_Kinetic_Impact_Projectiles.pdf (Accessed 14 June 2023).
27. MacDonald JM, Kaminski RJ, Smith MR. The effect of less-lethal weapons on injuries in police use-of-force events. *Am J Public Health* 2009; **99(12)**: 2268–74.
28. Hueske EE. *Practical Analysis and Reconstruction of Shooting Incidents*. Boca Raton: CRC Press; 2005.
29. Haag MG, Haag LC. *Shooting Incident Reconstruction*, 2nd ed. Burlington: Academic press; 2011.
30. Breitenecker R. Shotgun wound patterns. *Am J Clin Pathol* 1969; **52(3)**: 258–69.
31. Ordog GJ, Wasserberger JO, Balasubramaniam SU. Shotgun wound ballistics. *J Trauma* 1988; **28(5)**: 624–31.
32. Blumenthal R. Suicidal gunshot wounds to the head: A retrospective review of 406 cases. *Am J Forensic Med Pathol* 2007; **28(4)**: 288–91.
33. Loots DP, Saayman G. Medicolegal perspectives of interpersonal violence: A review of first-contact clinical notes. *S Afr Med J* 2019; **109(10)**: 792–800.
34. McCann M. Fire and explosion deaths in construction, 2007. Available from: https://www.elcosh.org/record/document/1936/d000860.pdf (Accessed 14 June 2023).
35. Byard RW. Lethal explosions in a non-terrorist civilian setting. *Med Sci Law* 2018; **58(3)**: 156–8.
36. Reliefweb. Global Terrorism Index, 2022. Available from: https://reliefweb.int/report/world/global-terrorism-index-2022 (Accessed 14 June 2023).
37. Reliefweb. Explosive Violence Monitor, 2021. Available from: https://reliefweb.int/report/world/explosive-violence-monitor-2021 (Accessed 14 June 2023).
38. US Bomb Data Center (USBDC). Explosives Incident Report, 2021. Available from: https://www.atf.gov/file/166841/download (Accessed 14 June 2023).
39. US National Park Service Handbook for the Storage, Transportation, and Use of Explosives, 1999. Available from: https://www.nps.gov/parkhistory/online_books/npsg/explosives/Chapter2.pdf (Accessed 14 June 2023).
40. US Nuclear Regulatory Commission. Dirty Bombs, 2020. Available from: https://www.nrc.gov/docs/ML1814/ML18143B254.pdf (Accessed 14 June 2023).
41. Mathews ZR, Koyfman A. Blast injuries. *J Emerg Med* 2015; **49(4)**: 573–87.

42. Goh SH. Bomb blast mass casualty incidents: Initial triage and management of injuries. *Singapore Med J* 2009; **50(1)**: 101–6.
43. UN Office for Disarmament Affairs. Convention on Cluster Munitions. Available from: https://www.un.org/disarmament/convention-on-cluster-munitions/ (Accessed 14 June 2023).
44. Wilson JN, Lambert DE, Stewart JB. Explosively Formed Projectiles. S Air Force Research Laboratory. Available from: https://www.afrl.af.mil/ (Accessed 29 November 2022).
45. Wightman JM, Gladish SL. Explosions and blast injuries. *Ann Emerg Med* 2001; **37(6)**: 664–78.
46. DePalma RG, Burris DG, Champion HR, Hodgson MJ. Blast injuries. *N Engl J Med* 2005; **352(13)**: 1335–42.
47. Champion HR, Holcomb JB, Young LA. Injuries from explosions: Physics, biophysics, pathology, and required research focus. *J Trauma Acute Care Surg* 2009; **66(5)**: 1468–77.
48. Galante N, Franceschetti L, Del Sordo S, et al. Explosion-related deaths: An overview on forensic evaluation and implications. *Forensic Sci Med Pathol* 2021; **17(3)**: 437–48.

CHAPTER

62

Physiological Responses to Ballistic and Blast Injuries

Alexander Stoll, Sarah Watts, Henrietta Poon and Emrys Kirkman

INTRODUCTION

Forces that injure

When an explosive detonates, it generates an extremely rapid (effectively instantaneous) increase in pressure in the immediate vicinity of the explosion (1). This has a "knock on" effect on the surrounding air or water, transferring the high pressure as a wave outward faster than the speed of sound from the site of the explosion. The high pressure (called the peak overpressure) usually lasts only for thousandths of a second at any one point. The peak overpressure is followed by a rapid fall in pressure, often to sub-atmospheric levels, before returning to approximately normal. This is called the "shock wave". The magnitude of the peak overpressure falls as it travels away from the site of the explosion (1), initially by an inverse cube relation (doubling the distance reduces the pressure to one-eighth). Because the shock wave is a very brief event when using conventional explosives it does not cause an object or person to move any great distance (i.e. this is not the part of the explosion that "throws things around"). The shock wave can, however, cause serious injury.

Fragments (of the munition casing and pre-formed fragments contained within the device) and surrounding debris energized by an explosion are propelled outward and can collide with objects and people. In addition, the explosion usually gives rise to a very large volume of hot gas. This literally pushes air and debris outward and acts over a sufficiently long time course to throw people against other objects. This is called the "blast wind". The shock wave and the blast wind are sometimes collectively called the "blast wave". Finally, for those close to the explosion, there is also a large amount of heat, which can also cause injury.

Classification of blast injuries

Blast injuries are classified according to the forces causing the injury. There are five main categories (2,3). The original three categories were primary, secondary, and tertiary. Miscellaneous additional injuries from the explosive device give rise to quaternary and post-detonation environmental contaminants creating quinary categories, respectively (4).

1. Primary blast injuries result from the interaction of a shock wave with the body. Injury is largely confined to the air-containing organs, such as the lungs, bowel and ears, often without external signs of injury (5), although primary blast may also cause brain injury.
2. Secondary blast injury results from the impact of fragments and larger missiles accelerated by the blast (ballistic injuries). Injuries caused by these fragments can be penetrating or non-penetrating. This group accounts for the majority of explosion-related injuries.
3. Tertiary blast injury results from the acceleration of the whole body or parts of the body by the blast wave causing translational impacts of the body with the ground or other fixed objects, and/or traumatic amputation of body parts and stripping of tissue.
4. Quaternary blast injury represent a further group of miscellaneous injuries from exposure to an explosion, it includes flash burns, caused by radiant and convective heat, burns caused by combustion of the environment, crush syndrome, and the effects of noxious gaseous products (especially carbon monoxide) liberated in enclosed spaces.
5. Quinary blast injuries are the clinical consequences of "post detonation environmental contaminants" including bacteria (deliberate and commensal, with or without sepsis), radiation ("dirty" bombs) and tissue reactions to fuel and metals.

Altering factors

External factors, the nature of the environment where the victim is exposed to the explosion, as well as the

DOI: 10.1201/9781003138754-64

type of explosive/device, influence the balance of injuries received (6,7). If the explosion occurs within or near structures with surfaces that can reflect the shock wave, then the incidence of primary blast injury is likely to be higher than with an "open field" exposure. For example, the incidence of blast lung (primary blast injury) was high among the severely injured in the Madrid train bombings where the device was detonated within the train (8,9). Casualty analysis from Israel compared injuries among victims where both casualties and the explosive device were within buses, versus the situation where both were adjacent to buses (10). The study showed that the relative proportion of blast lung was higher in the "within-bus" group. The injuries within buses encompassed a spread of body regions including limbs and torso, with relatively few spinal injuries.

A different pattern of injury is present where the casualties are occupants of a structure and the explosion occurs outside, for example, when military vehicles are targets of an external explosion. Physical studies suggest that an external blast wave may diffract around a well-armored military vehicle, and reflect off the structure of the vehicle, rather than enter into the vehicle to cause primary blast injury. The rapid displacement of the vehicle, however, is likely to cause serious tertiary injuries to the occupants (11). This is confirmed in casualty analyses, which report extensive skeletal injuries, particularly to the limbs, spine and head in the most severely injured or fatalities (12,13). Primary blast injury such as blast lung is uncommon (13). This is referred to as "Underbody Blast" (UBB) where an explosive charge detonates underneath an armoured vehicle, with high accelerations over a short distance (14) accompanied by vertical loading to the occupants. It is thought that there are two main routes of transmission of the vertical load to the seated occupants of the vehicle (14); 1) through the feet and up the legs, and 2) through the pelvis and up the spine. This can cause extensive fractures in the foot, ankle and legs (15). The level and nature of the spinal fractures are in turn dependant on the initial rate of acceleration (16). The paucity of primary blast injuries described in these settings relate to explosions outside vehicles designed to protect the occupants from the primary and secondary blast injury (14). If the vehicles are only partially enclosed (or the hulls are breached) then blast lung injuries are also seen (17).

Internal (within the victim's body) altering factors include the physiological state and activity of the individual at the time of injury, tissues injured, degree and duration of hemorrhage, clinical interventions, quaternary injuries and, if present, the effects and responses to quinary blast injuries. Internal factors are complicated further by coagulopathies and inflammatory responses associated with trauma (including those directly associated with brain injury), the interaction between hemorrhage and tissue injury, and modification of these responses in response to primary blast.

PHYSIOLOGY AND PATHOPHYSIOLOGY

Although ballistic and/or explosive injuries will be specific to the incident and the individual(s) involved, the broad principles of injury and the physiological responses to these can be outlined.

The transfer of energy to tissues from a shock wave, shearing forces, penetrating wounds, including those associated with primary to tertiary blast injuries and ballistic injuries, can all damage vasculature. The degree of hemorrhage will be determined, in part, by the magnitude of forces, tissues involved, and the track of projectiles in the body.

"Simple" hemorrhage; the cardiovascular response

Hemorrhage is a leading cause of death in traumatic injury. Simple hemorrhage refers to bleeding where there is no accompanying major tissue damage. The loss of blood during hemorrhage results in reduced venous return, leading to reduced cardiac filling and thus reduced cardiac stroke volume. This causes a fall in arterial pulse pressure, which is detected by arterial baroreceptors, sensitive to changes in both the absolute pressure and rate of change of blood pressure, that is, pulse pressure (18).

In progressive simple hemorrhage, there is a biphasic physiological response to blood loss [19]). In Phase I, vagal inhibition and sympathetic efferent activity leads to reflex tachycardia, increased peripheral vascular resistance and thus maintenance of blood pressure (20,21). As hemorrhage progresses, however, and blood loss exceeds 20 to 30 percent of total blood volume, a depressor phase (Phase II) becomes apparent. This involves a vagally mediated bradycardia, a reduction in peripheral vascular resistance (19,22,23) and a marked fall in arterial blood pressure (Figure 62.1).

The compensatory Phase I is due to baroreceptor unloading. The decompensatory Phase II is not due to a failure of the baroreflex, since the latter's sensitivity is increased at this stage (24), nor is it a pre-terminal event (25,26), but rather it is due to the activation of additional reflex(es). The identity of the afferent limbs of these reflexes is uncertain (27,28), although the cardiac afferent C-fibers may be involved (*see* [29]). The end result in a conscious patient is pre-syncope followed by syncope. It is thought that this second phase of the response to hemorrhage confers some degree of protection since the bradycardia increases diastolic filling time resulting in a small increase in stroke volume and improved coronary perfusion (which principally occurs during diastole), although urgent action to restore venous return is needed for these casualties as they will quickly de-compensate.

Hemorrhage into cavities or tissues can also interfere with organ function. This type of bleeding can give rise to signs and symptoms associated specifically with the affected organ(s).

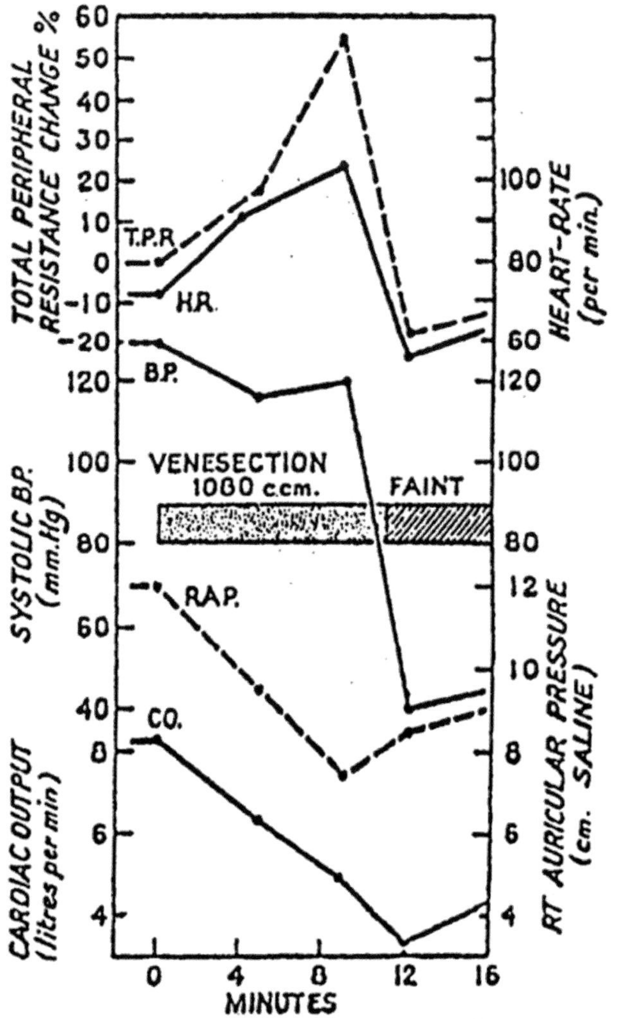

62.1 Effects of a progressive "simple" hemorrhage in a male volunteer showing a biphasic response. Blood was withdrawn by venesection until the subject fainted. TPR, total peripheral resistance; Syst BP, systolic arterial blood pressure; CO, cardiac output; Rt auric p; right atrial pressure (central venous pressure). (From Barcroft *et al.* (19).)

Shock

Shock is defined as the inability of oxygen delivery to meet tissue metabolic demand (30). At the whole body or organ level, oxygen delivery is the product of blood flow and arterial oxygen content, which in turn are influenced by vascular resistance, oxygen saturation and oxygen carrying capacity (hemoglobin concentration). At a microvascular level, shock can also be produced by a failure of local regulation of blood flow and consequently a mismatch of delivery and consumption in specific regions of an organ or tissue. Shock can also result from an increase in diffusion distance between the vasculature and the cells requiring oxygen (diffusion limited shock). This occurs in the case of edema resulting from either a severe inflammatory response or iatrogenic loading of tissues with fluid; for example over-resuscitation with crystalloid. All of these factors can contribute to shock in trauma.

Organs respond to reduced blood flow (e.g. due to hemorrhage) by extracting more oxygen from the available blood flow to maintain oxygen consumption. When this process can no longer compensate for reduced oxygen delivery by the blood, oxygen consumption starts to fall, and the organ is in "shock". The threshold at which oxygen consumption becomes dependent on oxygen delivery is the "critical oxygen delivery" and represents the point at which organs in the body start to suffer ischemic damage. There is evidence that activation of a neural nociceptive barrage normally associated with tissue damage elevates the whole-body critical oxygen delivery threshold and reduces a patient's overall ability to extract oxygen from the available cardiac output (31). This hastens the onset of shock and increases a patient's susceptibility to the metabolic effects of reduced oxygen delivery.

Tissue injury; the inflammatory response

Tissue injuries caused by an explosion and/or projectile(s) are also determined by the magnitude of the forces transferred to tissues, the tissues involved, volume of tissue affected and the wound track(s).

There is a growing interest in the immunologic response to traumatic injury, as this not only forms part of a defensive response to trauma but can also cause secondary problems and injuries for the patient. Skelton and Purcell have reviewed pre-clinical animal models, including references to the investigation of specific mediators (32).

Inflammation, due to the initial tissue damage at the time of injury, affects the progression of the response to injury. This is further confounded by hypoperfusion-induced ischemia, subsequent reperfusion injuries and immune dysfunction in critically ill patients. In summary, the inflammatory response to tissue injury and hemorrhage is initiated by the release of damage-associated molecular patterns (DAMPs) or alarmins, which lead to the activation of immune cells, the complement system, and cytokine release (Figure 62.2). The complex interaction between many pathways may, in severe injury, lead to the concurrent activation of systemic pro- and anti-inflammatory syndromes (systemic inflammatory response syndrome (SIRS) and compensatory anti-inflammatory response syndrome (CARS), respectively), which can pre-dispose to sepsis and multiple organ dysfunction syndrome (MODS) (32,33).

Initiated by DAMPs, but part of a milieu of catecholamines and reactive oxygen species, the pro-inflammatory actions are on 1) leukocytes (cause cytokine and reactive oxygen species production, proliferation and chemotaxis); 2) induction of the acute phase response, and 3) activation of endothelia (adhesion molecule expression, cytokine release, increased vascular permeability, and glycocalyx shedding). These actions initiate and propagate a pro-inflammatory state, including further tissue damage (32,34).

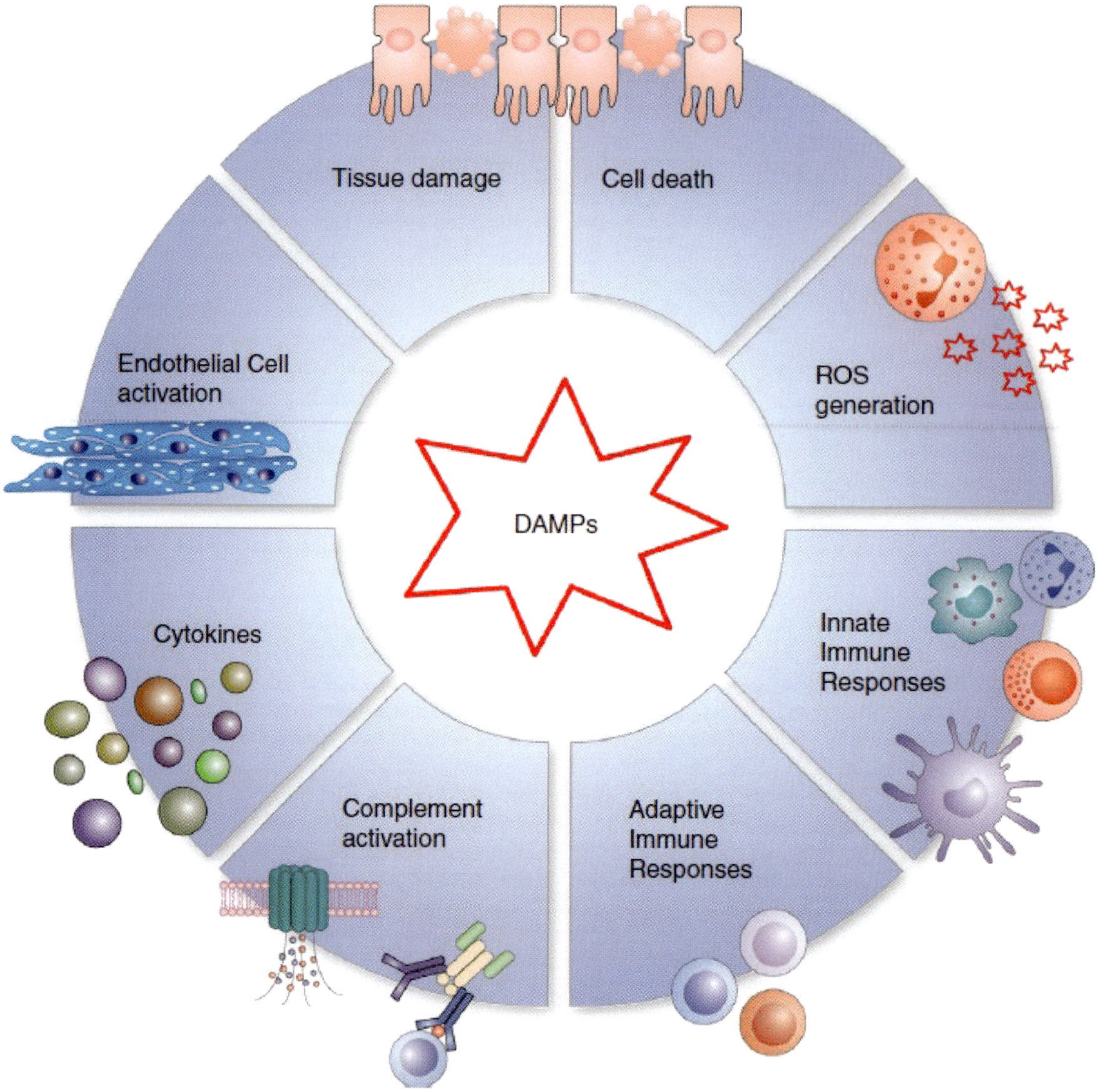

62.2 Damage associated molecular patterns (DAMPs) result in the activation of multiple inflammatory pathways. ROS: reactive oxygen species. (From Skelton and Purcell (32).)

Concomitantly, anti-inflammatory mediators are released, leading to states of immunosuppression. The neutrophil is an example of a leukocyte receiving and transmitting conflicting messages in the complex immune response to trauma. Pro-inflammatory signals result in the increased circulation, margination, extravasation and recruitment of neutrophils to injured tissue. Neutrophil degranulation, extracellular trap and cytokine release, and the generation of reactive oxygen species contribute to local tissue damage, clearance of debris, and propagation of inflammation. Meanwhile, release of juvenile neutrophils, and an altered neutrophil phenotype observed in trauma patients and *ex vivo* studies, exhibit changes in efficacy of these functions. A subset of neutrophils which suppress T-cell proliferation and function is also recognized. Further, lymphocytes are observed to become active and increase in number immediately following trauma, but this is followed by a lymphopenia. Together, these changes are thought to contribute to the increased risk of infection in trauma patients (32).

Tissue injury with haemorrhage; the cardiovascular response

When considering severe hemorrhage, there is often significant tissue injury. The resulting barrage of nociceptive signals from damaged musculoskeletal tissue elicit a profound change in the cardiovascular response that can have implications for shock, morbidity and mortality.

The biphasic cardiovascular changes elicited by a progressive "simple" hemorrhage are markedly attenuated by the presence of concomitant tissue injury (21). The initial increase in heart rate following a loss of 10 to 15 percent blood volume is reduced, and the vagal bradycardia following greater losses prevented. The attenuation of the heart rate changes normally associated with

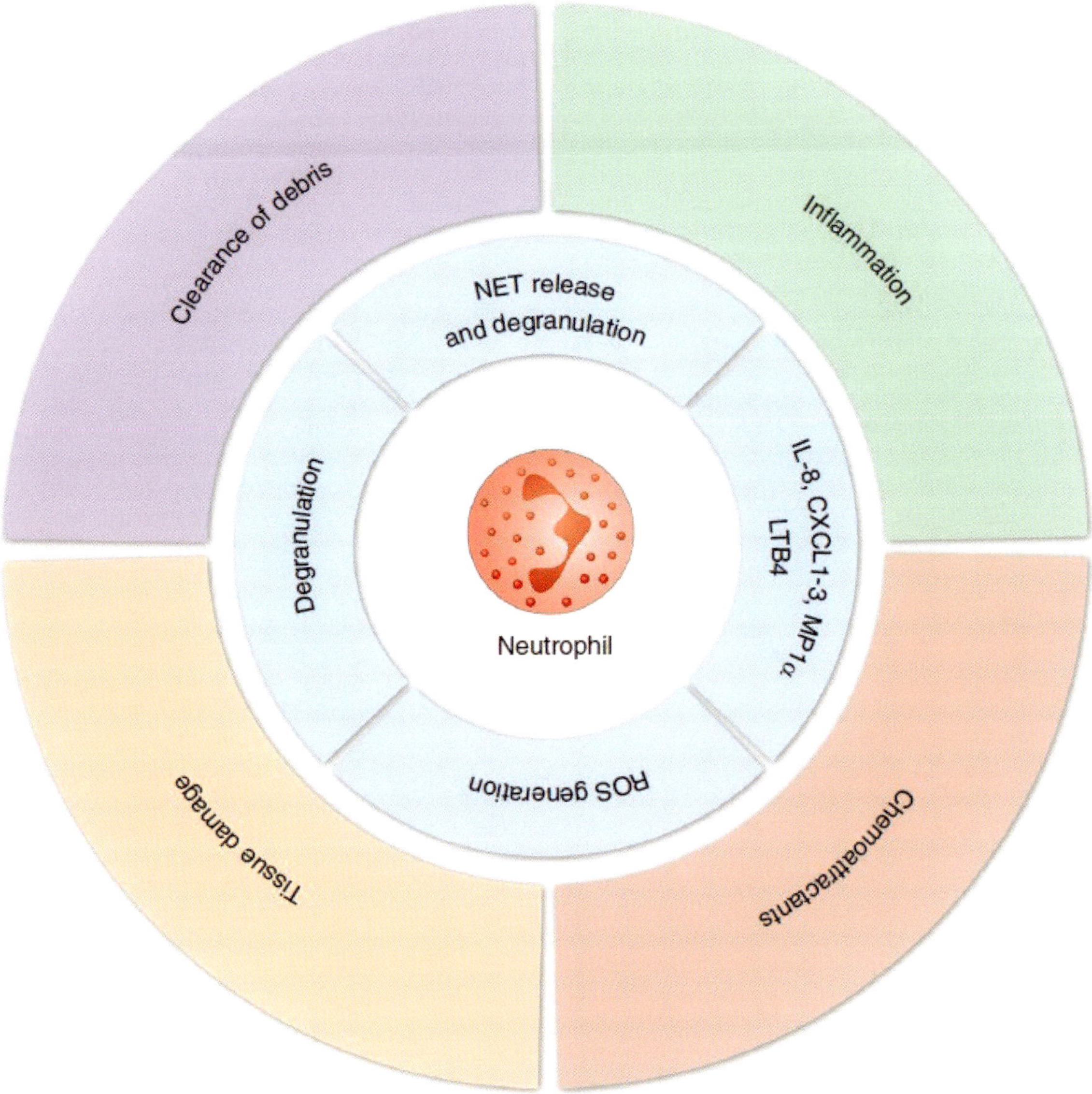

62.3 The diverse role of neutrophils in trauma can contribute to injury and repair. Abbreviations, clockwise from top: NET, neutrophil extracellular trap; IL-8, interleukin 8; CXCL1–3, chemokine C-X-C motif ligands 1–3; MP1α, monocyte chemoattractant protein 1α; LTB4, leukotriene B4; ROS, reactive oxygen species. (From Skelton and Purcell (32).)

blood loss seems to limit the hypotensive effects of a severe hemorrhage (21). However, a lower survival rate has been demonstrated in animals subjected to hemorrhage and concomitant electrical stimulation of the sciatic nerve (to simulate injury) compared to animals subjected to hemorrhage alone (35). It is possible that the better maintenance of blood pressure is achieved at the expense of intense peripheral vasoconstriction that further reduces blood flow, thus exacerbating shock and the severity of secondary (ischemic) injury.

It is possible that the splanchnic circulation may be selectively vulnerable to such ischemic damage. There is evidence that when hemorrhage is superimposed on a background of somatic afferent stimulation (to mimic injury) there is a relative redistribution of blood flow from the gut towards skeletal muscle (in-contrast to the pattern seen with simple hemorrhage) (36,37). This diversion of blood flow (oxygen delivery) away from metabolically active organs toward relatively inactive resting skeletal muscle may explain the increase in critical oxygen delivery elicited by somatic afferent nerve stimulation (31) since it effectively "wastes" a proportion of the cardiac output. Ischemic damage to the intestinal mucosa may lead to an increased inflammatory response (38,39), and possibly even increased intestinal permeability and enhanced translocation of endotoxin (40–42), which represent some of the pathophysiological consequences of shock.

Impairment in cardiac function and tissue oxygen delivery (shock) associated with blood loss is greater if the hemorrhage is superimposed on nociceptive nerve stimulation compared to hemorrhage alone (43). If the hemorrhage is superimposed on real rather than simulated tissue injury the tolerance to blood loss is further reduced (44).

Secondary tissue injury due to shock

Tissue injury/ischemia produces an increase in arterial blood pressure accompanied by a tachycardia (45). The increase in arterial blood pressure that accompanies injury is largely mediated by an increase in sympathetic outflow to the vasculature and a consequent increase in total peripheral resistance. There is a hierarchy of vascular beds affected by the increased resistance. In "simple hemorrhage" the hierarchy is thought to be skeletal muscle > vital organs (e.g. gut and kidney) >> brain, while in hemorrhage superimposed on musculoskeletal tissue injury (or the resulting nociceptive barrage) there is some evidence that the hierarchy may be vital organs > skeletal muscle >> brain (31,46). Therefore during hemorrhage, blood flow to the brain is initially protected at the expense of peripheral tissue, which suffers early ischemia to varying degrees depending on the circumstances. The fall in blood flow in most vascular beds (especially the periphery) contributes to shock and can lead to ischemic damage of these organs (35) and inflammation. The resulting spill-over of inflammation, especially from the periphery can contribute to the pathophysiology of shock and its sequelae such as multiple organ failure. Secondary tissue injury to individual organs include pathologic changes to the heart, lungs, gut, liver and kidneys, with cardiac, pulmonary and enteric pathophysiological consequences outlined below.

Heart

Cardiac dysfunction secondary to systemic inflammation is associated with DAMPs, complement activation, cytological structural alteration, and altered neuroendocrine function and cardiac metabolism associated with trauma (47). This is complicated further by pharmacological interventions and cardiac dysfunction associated with direct trauma to the heart, and the entanglement of the pathophysiology and pathogenesis of cardiomyopathies and cardiac dysfunction associated with injuries to the brain, burns, bone fractures, abdominal injuries, sepsis, and other acute physical or psychological stressors (47–51). Any functional disturbance to the heart could contribute to shock, morbidity and mortality, either acutely or in the period following initial survival of the insult and could compromise the response to resuscitation.

Lungs

The lung in shock has long been recognized ("wet lung" described in casualties of World War II) and its "grouping"with other acute lung injury/acute respiratory distress syndromes (ALI/ARDS) has been debated (*see* [52] and [53]). This is a syndrome wherein the lungs exhibit morphologic and functional derangement (hypoxemia, edema, reduced compliance, decreased functional residual capacity) as sequelae to indirect injury and including sepsis, shock, burns and mass transfusions (53). Secondary to systemic inflammation, the lungs receive mediators of inflammation hematogenously, resulting in changes centered on the alveolar capillaries (in contrast to direct injury which involves both the capillaries and alveolar septae/spaces) (54). Early morphological changes include leukostasis, endothelial swelling, interstitial edema and sometimes fat emboli. The consequence of these changes is the development of edema spilling over into the alveolar spaces as a result of compromise to the endothelial barrier (endothelial activation from inflammatory mediators and mediated by activated leukocytes) (54). The principal cause of hypoxemia in patients with acute respiratory distress syndromes is this loss of ventilation to fluid filled (and later fibrin lined) alveoli resulting in shunted blood flow (55).

Candidates for the mediation of indirect lung injury include (alone or together) neutrophils (and their dysregulation, causing bystander damage and release of inflammatory, including vasoactive, mediators), lymphocytes and dendritic cells (which have roles in regulation and resolution of the immune response), injury to epithelial cells (forming part of the barrier against fluid influx and mechanism of fluid efflux), injury to endothelial cells, and dysregulation of coagulation and fibrinolysis (53,56). The limited therapeutic approaches relate, in part, to the need for clarification of the mechanisms that eventually converge on the common syndrome of ALI/ARDS (53,57), and the need to tailor therapeutic interventions to the individual and the stage of pulmonary injury progression (58).

The issues are even more complex when other direct and indirect factors are considered which impact the lungs in trauma patients, including direct thoracic injuries, traumatic brain injury (*see* [59,60]), septic shock, substances toxic to the lungs (e.g. gastric content, exogenous chemicals and toxic gases), thermal injury (hot gases), and lung injury associated with mechanical ventilation (56,61–63).

Gut

The intense peripheral vasoconstriction has serious repercussions on splanchnic perfusion, resulting in ischemic morphological changes in the enteric mucosa and liver. An early morphological change is detachment and loss of villus epithelium at the villus tip which then descends down the length of the villus. The exposed "core" (lamina propria) of the villus may then disintegrate and the injury may then extend to reach the level of the villus crypts. The lacteals have a discontinuous lining to facilitate assimilation of larger substances into the lymph, but also means that the villus interstitial fluid equilibrates with the lacteal content, hence the efflux of protein-rich fluid observed in the enteric lumen when there is breakdown of the enteric barrier. Loss of protein-rich fluid into the lumen can also impact upon colloid oncotic pressure, contributing to edema formation locally and systemically, which can also worsen shock (64–66).

Recent work suggests that the inflammation associated with the mucosal injury (including microbial ingress across the damaged gut lining), releases DAMPs which reach the systemic circulation by means of the mesenteric lymphatics and contribute to the systemic inflammatory response by priming neutrophils and activating and injuring endothelial cells, including lung injury, and the systemic inflammatory response (67,68). The specific factors and DAMPs involved are an area of active research (68), for example, serine proteases (blocking of which reduced secondary lung injury in a rat model) (67), and mucin-2 (which may affect clotting) (69). Assimakopoulous and colleagues illustrate two "vicious cycles": the first involves compromised barrier integrity allowing bacterial translocation into submucosal tissue resulting in a local inflammatory response, further compromising barrier integrity. The second is the gut as a pro-inflammatory organ releasing DAMPs into the mesenteric lymph, damaging the lungs, releasing further DAMPs into the systemic circulation, resulting in SIRS, progressing to MODS and causing further intestinal barrier injury (68). The role of glycocalyx breakdown (69) and the microbiome (70) are being explored.

These factors may be confounded by therapeutic intervention, reperfusion injury, sepsis and MOF. Kidney (71–74) and liver (75,76) function are also impaired by hemorrhagic shock and may have a profound effect on outcome.

Tissue injury in response to resuscitation; ischemia-reperfusion

Local and systemic ischemia-reperfusion injury occurs in trauma patients and is a feature of the response to resuscitation. In addition to the reactive oxygen species, produced from activated neutrophils, tissue damage in ischemia-reperfusion injury generates further reactive oxygen species contributing to endothelial dysfunction. The generation of hypoxanthine during cellular hypoxia (reduced perfusion) depletes cellular second messenger cyclic adenosine monophosphate (cAMP) and subsequently reduces adenosine triphosphate (ATP) (77). This ATP deficiency leads to a series of events resulting in cellular membrane disintegration and DNA damage (77). Apoptosis and necrosis occur in prolonged hypoxic conditions, leading to irreversible tissue damage and the further release of DAMPs to activate the inflammatory response.

During reperfusion of ischemic tissue, the re-introduced oxygen reacts with hypoxanthine (accumulated during ischemia) to produce superoxide anion, which leads to the release of reactive oxygen species (hydroxyl ions) that further exacerbates cellular disturbance and the production of inflammatory mediators (77). Oxidative stress generated from ischemia-reperfusion induces an increased TLR4 surface expression, amplifying the inflammatory response and subsequent organ injury (78).

Coagulopathy in trauma

Trauma induced coagulopathy is now recognized as a serious secondary consequence of injury and the patient's (patho)physiological response to trauma (79–81). Trauma induced coagulopathy has an evolving pathology in the patient, often starting with the consequences of tissue hypoperfusion and developing through phases that can include the consequences of shock-driven acidosis, hypothermia, iatrogenic (and autogenic) hemodilution and factor consumption (79,81). Some authors also suggest an element akin to diffuse intravascular coagulation (DIC), without necessarily having tissue hypoperfusion (82). The initial phase of trauma-related coagulopathy is referred to as acute trauma coagulopathy (ATC), which manifests as attenuated coagulation early after injury.

The first phase of ATC, referred to by some authors, is thought to result from tissue hypoperfusion and is associated with the development of shock and increasing base deficit in the patient (81,83–88). However, it is not the acidosis associated with this shock *per se* that causes ATC, but rather an alteration in the endothelium leading to expression of thrombomodulin. The thrombomodulin interacts with thrombin to activate protein C, resulting in in simultaneous anticoagulation and fibrinolysis (79,83). Some have questioned the detail of this mechanism based on the kinetics of the changes (81). An additional concurrent or alternative mechanism involves damage to the glycocalyx, again driven by hypoperfusion and the sympatho-adrenal activation (89,90) that is an inherent part of the physiological response to hemorrhage and injury (19,31,37,46). The resulting release of a host of substances representing glycocalyx breakdown, including syndecan-1, soluble thrombomodulin and heparin-like substances, lead to autoheparinization (80) and an increase in aPTT (89). Irrespective of the precise mechanism, most authors agree that tissue hypoperfusion is a significant driver (79,81,86). The potential importance of early tissue hypoperfusion and burden of injury has been emphasized by the successful development of a pre-hospital predictive score (Trauma Induced Coagulopathy Clinical Score, TICCS) (91) which uses hypotension as a proxy for tissue hypoperfusion.

The second phase of ATC is related to resuscitation (81). Hemodilution, which is initiated by the physiological mobilization of interstitial fluid into the vascular space, is augmented by any asanguineous fluid given to the casualty with resultant dilution of clotting factors. The fall in hematocrit can also contribute to an alteration in clotting as a consequence of altered blood rheology (92,93). Finally, the acidosis that can be associated with shock and prolonged hypotensive resuscitation (most relevant when evacuation is delayed [94]) can also contribute to the coagulopathy by potentiating the effect of other mechanisms (95).

There is a complex interaction between the coagulation and inflammatory systems, with many common mediators. At present, our understanding of the interactions and interdependencies between the two systems are too rudimentary to allow anything but the most speculative of suggestions.

Another cause of coagulopathy is that caused by traumatic brain injury, affecting clinical outcome (96). Although the pathogenesis needs further investigation, it is considered to be associated with the release of brain-derived factors into the systemic circulation (97).

Predisposition to injury

The respiratory and gastrointestinal tracts are the principal internal organ systems with a direct interface between the internal and external environments, due to their common endodermal origin (98) and exchange functions. They are both predisposed to explosive injury as discussed below, and also result in clinical complications if there are breaches in their barrier function, in explosive or ballistic injury. The auditory tube and tympanic membrane also arise from the endoderm (98) and are predisposed to explosive injury as a result of the gas interface.

Respiratory pathology and pathophysiology

Ventilation and perfusion are carefully balanced in the healthy lung to optimize gas exchange across a very thin barrier (55). Explosive and ballistic injuries can alter the ventilation, perfusion and gas exchange by multiple mechanisms, including those listed in Table 62.1.

Primary blast injury to the lungs

Primary blast injury to the lungs is often referred to as "blast lung" and refers to pulmonary barotrauma (106). This is characterized by pulmonary contusion, rapid development of pulmonary edema and reduction in pulmonary gas transfer (94,107). A shock wave causes rupture of alveolar capillaries, and thus extravasation of blood and edema fluid into lung tissue (108,109), causing hemorrhagic foci, which can be substantial depending on the level of blast loading (110). Intrapulmonary hemorrhage and edema contribute to the initial respiratory compromise in blast lung (111) that is exacerbated by free hemoglobin and extravasated blood, which induce free-radical reactions and hence oxidative damage (111) and a pro-inflammatory response (112). Free hemoglobin can also potentiate an accumulation of inflammatory mediators and chemotactic attractants (113), together with DAMPs from the injured lung tissue (114), thereby amplifying the primary pathology.

A victim of explosive injury is likely to suffer a mixture of blast-related injuries. Secondary blast injuries account for the majority of blast injuries in survivors, particularly when the explosion has occurred in an open space, although about 11 percent of the seriously injured also exhibit blast lung (115,116). When the explosion occurs in a confined space, the proportion of seriously injured survivors exhibiting blast lung increases dramatically (8,9) because the shock wave can be amplified and reflected near solid structures. A casualty is likely to have extensive tissue damage and severe blood loss, and in a clinically significant minority, also have blast lung resulting in hypoxemia. Death may be immediate (excluding cases of body destruction close to the blast) due to air emboli, bone marrow (fat) emboli, and/or massive pulmonary contusion and hemorrhage (110,117).

Blast injury; the cardiorespiratory response

On thoracic exposure to a shock wave from an explosion, there is a cardiorespiratory response thought to be due to an autonomic (vagal) reflex, the afferent arm considered to include pulmonary C-fibers (118). This response

TABLE 62.1 Causes and mechanisms of altered ventilation, perfusion and/or gas exchange in ballistic and/or explosive injury (*see* (99–105) for detail on injuries).

Mechanism compromised	Potential causes in explosive and/or ballistic injury
Ventilation	Positional asphyxia or crushing
	Obstruction of conducting airways by debris or direct damage
	Thoracic wall injury e.g. flail chest
	Respiratory depression (*see* "Cardiovascular and respiratory responses to blast")
	Pneumo- and/or haemothorax
	Acquired atelectasis (collapse of parenchyma) and/or contusion
Perfusion	Shock
	Emboli (e.g. fat, bone marrow, gas)
	Cardiodepression (*see* "Cardiovascular and respiratory responses to blast")
Gas exchange	Hemorrhage within, or aspiration of blood into, airways
	Pulmonary edema
	Low oxygen atmosphere (e.g. smoke, carbon monoxide)
	Damage to respiratory tissues by hot and/or toxic gases from combustion
	Alveolar damage by primary blast injury and/or projectiles

is characterized by bradycardia, prolonged hypotension, and a short apnea (in survivors), which is followed by rapid shallow breathing (94). While the vagal reflex might explain the bradycardia and apnea (118,119), hypotension is likely to result from the interaction between reduced peripheral resistance and reduced cardiac output. It is postulated that the reduced peripheral resistance results from nitric oxide (a potent vasodilator and inflammatory mediator) released in the lung tissue (120–122), possibly having systemic reach (117). Meanwhile, reduced cardiac output is likely a result of reduced cardiac function (123), together with hypoxemia associated with the primary blast lung injury. These events (and other complicating factors) can modify the cardiovascular responses to hemorrhage and resuscitation (117).

Blast injury with hemorrhage; the cardiovascular response

The physiological response to blast with hemorrhage is complex. In experimental models, there appears to be either an inhibition of the baroreflex or an augmentation of the depressor reflex. Morphine can block the depressor (bradycardia and hypotension) reflex in "simple" hemorrhage, and also attenuates the effects of blast on the response to hemorrhage (resulting in a tachycardic response instead). This lends support to the theory that blast augments the depressor reflex (117,124).

Blast injury with hemorrhage; the response to resuscitation

Following arrest of massive bleeding, hypotensive resuscitation is advocated in pre-hospital resuscitation for the short-term support of casualties. This approach is a compromise to 1) maintain oxygen delivery and reduce the risk of physiological deterioration, but 2) minimize the risk of causing further bleeding by deliberately allowing blood pressure to remain below normal levels (117,125–129). Porcine experimental models have demonstrated, however, that this approach, in the presence of blast lung, increased mortality if extended beyond one hour. A switch from hypotensive to normotensive resuscitation at one hour was assessed, and improved outcomes significantly (117,130,131). This gave rise to a concept called "hybrid resuscitation" strategy which improved physiological outcomes in both pigs exposed to blast, tissue injury and hemorrhage and those with tissue injury and hemorrhage only, as a result of enhanced tissue oxygen delivery (117,131,132). In some circumstances, however, the hybrid approach may not be suitable, where there is a very high risk of re-bleeding when the resuscitation blood pressure target is elevated after an hour. An alternative approach in this circumstance is the provision of an elevated inspiratory oxygen fraction (FiO_2) (131). However, supplementary oxygen was not as effective in reversing shock as the hybrid resuscitation strategy, again emphasizing the impact and importance of the reduced blood flow in the cardiovascular response to blood loss.

Primary blast injury to the intestinal tract

The intestine is vulnerable to the effects of the blast wave because of the gas-tissue interface present. Primary blast injury to the gut has been categorized in different ways (7,133). A blast wave, particularly with immersed explosions, can result in intestinal injuries including perforation and hemorrhages (7,134,135). At the interface between different densities, stress waves cause direct tissue disruption. Cripps *et al.* also demonstrated that small bowel injury could be attenuated by decoupling the stress wave, while large bowel injury was not attenuated, suggesting the role of shear waves too (possibly because of restricted movement of the large bowel within the peritoneum compared to the small bowel) (135). The terminal ileum and cecum are areas of the gut most commonly affected by primary blast injury (7).

Immediate perforations of the intestinal wall can occur and associated hemoperitoneum and/or peritonitis (135), which can introduce an additional hemodynamic and inflammatory complication to the physiological response. Later perforation may also occur (133,135).

The inflammatory (including enteric nervous system) sequelae to these pathological changes have been suspected as contributory to the response since the early identification of primary blast injury to the intestine (see case reports and discussion by Webster et al. [134]).

Burn injuries associated with explosions

Burn injuries from explosions fall into the quaternary and the quinary injury classes. The heat of the explosion causes the former, while secondary fires resulting from the explosion cause the latter. Most explosions will generate a considerable amount of heat close to its origin. Burns can be caused by radiant heat and by hot gases. Cases with burns are likely to have been close to the origin of the explosion and have other serious injuries and a high fatality rate (136).

Approximately 10 percent of military casualties injured by explosion from a range of conflicts since the Second World War suffered burn injury (137,138). A 6-year retrospective study from a major burns unit in the UK considered blast-burn injury as being a relatively rare occurrence in civilian practice and consisted mostly of minor burns (139). Some incidents can have a disproportionate number of burn injuries, however. The incidence of burns from "homemade" explosives may be higher, with approximately 23 percent of casualties with heat and chemical burns being reported in a small series by the US Centers for Disease Control and Prevention (140). "Homemade" explosives are likely to be less reliable than commercial/military high explosives, and more likely to deflagrate (causing more heat and less explosion), while accidental explosion from powders can be associated with high incidences of burn injury that are often severe (approximately 40% of casualties in one report [141]).

TABLE 62.2 A suggested classification system for burn injuries from explosions adapted from Chukwu-Lobelu et al. (142).

Classification	Description
Primary (also considered a quaternary blast injury)	Burns from the thermal energy of the fireball. Associated with other serious injuries (occurs in the immediate vicinity of the explosion).
	Burns from radiant energy outside the range of the fireball. Flash burns of varying severity and may be associated with inhalation injury.
Secondary (also considered a quinary blast injury)	Burns associated with conflagration

A detailed analysis of the 7/7 terrorist bombings in the UK identified two main groups of victims with burn injuries (142). In survivors, the majority of burns were superficial and caused by radiant heat (flash burns), affecting exposed parts of the body (face, arms and legs) usually healing within 10 days. A wider range of burn injury was seen in non-survivors, encompassing the range of full thickness, partial thickness and flash burns. In a number of these casualties, there were also signs of inhalational injury, including singed nasal hair. Combining their evaluation of the 7/7 bombings with data from other events led the authors to suggest two classes of burn injuries from explosions as shown in Table 62.2.

Those closest to the origin of an explosion are more likely to suffer severe burn injury, and are also more likely to be non-survivors, often with other fatal injuries in addition to the burns (136).

Severe burn injuries elicit a profound pathophysiological response that includes massive and progressive loss of circulatory fluid volume, which in part is due to local and systemic inflammatory responses as well as direct damage to blood vessels (143,144). There is clear evidence of endothelial damage and shedding of syndecan-1 in burns patients, which is primarily associated with shock and inhalational injury (145). The endothelial damage and inflammation, in turn, contribute to a disruption of Starling forces and consequent extravasation of fluid from the microcirculation into the interstitial tissue, and development of edema (144). Recent developments in our understanding of blood and blood products as resuscitation fluids have led to the suggestion, via a potential effect on the endothelium, that they may provide a more effective resuscitation than crystalloids in burns patients (144). It has also been noted that burn patients with inhalation injuries generally require more resuscitation fluids than those without inhalation injury (146).

The inflammatory response in burn patients is particularly severe, distinguishing it from other trauma (143). The impact of the inflammatory response is wide-ranging, not only underpinning widespread edema, but also contributing to secondary damage in other organ systems, for example, secondary disruption of gut barrier function which occurs within hours of severe burn injury (147). The inflammatory response may also compromise cardiac function, leading to reduced contractility and to a degree of apoptosis in cardiac tissue (143), which can impair the response to resuscitation.

Combined blast and burn injury has been shown to result in more severe lung injury than that caused by blast, or burn, injury alone (148,149).

The central nervous system

The response of the central nervous system (CNS) to blast exposure has received an enormous amount of attention because it is unclear which of the forces associated with an explosion cause some of the more subtle injuries, or the route via which they are transmitted. In addition, we have no certainty which of the biological responses observed in models of blast injury are a specific consequence of blast exposure in human victims, or which ones are of pathological significance. The picture is further complicated in a multiply injured casualty, because the responses to, and consequences of, the other trauma can modify the CNS response to an insult (150–152).

Examples of candidate physical mechanisms, by which blast exposure could cause injury to the CNS, include direct coupling of the shock wave via the skull, rapid (but brief) acceleration and rotational forces and slower pressure changes, and "waves of pressure" transmitted to the CNS via the vasculature and cerebrospinal fluid (CSF) (150). A more controversial possibility includes cavitation and formation/collapse of nanobubbles in the CSF and brain tissue (153). Secondary mechanisms include the consequences of an increase in blood–brain barrier permeability (154), and inflammatory responses that originate elsewhere in the body (e.g. the lungs) impinging on the CNS (155), possibly facilitated by an altered blood–brain barrier.

An important driver for the research in this area is the concern that even mild blast exposure, particularly if repeated, may in some individuals have a long-lasting effect, or an effect that becomes apparent later in life. These include damage to white matter tracts (156,157) and accumulation of hyperphosphorylated tau into neurofibrillary tangles, leading ultimately (years later) to chronic traumatic encephalopathy (158). The early part of the tau pathology has been replicated in an animal model, where the tau phosphorylation is thought to be mediated by a mechanism involving substance P (159). Administration of a NK1 receptor antagonist after blast exposure in this murine model has been shown to attenuate the tau phosphorylation and early neurologic deficits (159), giving the possibility of a future treatment. However, we currently do not know the magnitude or the scope of the problem in individuals exposed to blast, or the relative numbers who suffer headaches that resolve after a few days (160) compared to those that go on to develop more serious, long lasting, consequences.

CONCLUSION

The physiological response to simple hemorrhage is biphasic. Phase I: tachycardia, increased peripheral vascular resistance and maintenance of arterial blood pressure. Phase II: following loss of 20 to 30 percent blood volume, bradycardia, reduced peripheral vascular resistance and reduced arterial blood pressure. Shock is the inability of oxygen delivery to meet tissue metabolic demand. In trauma, shock can be due to inadequate blood flow and/or oxygen content at the systemic or organ level, or at the microvascular level due to mismatches in delivery and consumption, and/or diffusion limited (edema).

Hemorrhage with accompanying tissue injury is typical in trauma. Inflammation is associated with traumatic tissue injury and secondary injury due to ischemia, and reperfusion. The resulting barrage of nociceptive signals can affect the cardiovascular response that can have implications for shock, morbidity and mortality. There is also a complex interaction between inflammatory responses and coagulopathy in trauma (ATC), complicated by therapeutic interventions.

Blast injuries are classified according to the forces causing injury: primary (interaction of the shock wave with the body), secondary (impact from material accelerated by the blast), tertiary (acceleration of the body or body parts), quaternary (other injuries caused by the explosive device), and quinary (consequences of post detonation environmental contaminants). The cardiovascular response to hemorrhage with blast injury is complex, further complicated by the profound effects of burns (if present) and the response to clinical intervention (resuscitation). The response of the CNS to blast exposure has received a lot of attention, and various putative mechanisms are subject to ongoing investigation. CNS injury can be associated with altered responses to haemorrhage, coagulopathy and inflammatory responses.

REFERENCES

1. Cullis IG. Blast waves and how they interact with structures. *J R Army Med Corps* 2001; **147**(**1**): 16–26.
2. Nelson TJ, Wall DB, Stedje-Larsen ET, et al. Predictors of mortality in close proximity blast injuries during Operation Iraqi Freedom. *J Am Coll Surg* 2006; **202**(3): 418–22.
3. Maynard R, Cooper G, Scott R. Mechanism of injury in bomb blasts and explosions. *Trauma* London: Heinemann; 1989.
4. Leggieri MJ Jr., Bieler D, Bjarnason S, et al. Environmental toxicology of blast exposures: Injury metrics, modelling, methods and standards. *J R Army Med Corps* 2019; **165**(1): 7–9.
5. Zuckerman S. Discussion on the problem of blast injuries. *Proc R Soc Med* 1941; **34**: 171–92.
6. Leibovici D, Gofrit ON, Stein M, et al. Blast injuries: Bus versus open-air bombings--a comparative study of injuries in survivors of open-air versus confined-space explosions. *J Trauma* 1996; **41**(**6**): 1030–5.
7. Owers C, Morgan JL, Garner JP. Abdominal trauma in primary blast injury. *Br J Surg* 2011; **98**(**2**): 168–79.
8. de Ceballos JP, Turégano-Fuentes F, Perez-Diaz D, et al. 11 March 2004: The terrorist bomb explosions in Madrid, Spain--an analysis of the logistics, injuries sustained and clinical management of casualties treated at the closest hospital. *Crit Care* 2005; **9**(1): 104–11.
9. Martí M, Parrón M, Baudraxler F, et al. Blast injuries from Madrid terrorist bombing attacks on March 11, 2004. *Emerg Radiol* 2006; **13**(3): 113–22.
10. Golan R, Soffer D, Givon A, Peleg K. The ins and outs of terrorist bus explosions: Injury profiles of on-board explosions versus explosions occurring adjacent to a bus. *Injury* 2014; **45**(**1**): 39–43.
11. Champion HR, Holcomb JB, Young LA. Injuries from explosions: Physics, biophysics, pathology, and required research focus. *J Trauma* 2009; **66**(5): 1468–77.
12. Vasquez KB, Brozoski FT, Logsdon KP, Chancey VC. Retrospective analysis of injuries in underbody blast events: 2007–2010. *Mil Med* 2018; **183**(**1**): 347–52.
13. Loftis KL, Mazuchowski EL, Clouser MC, Gillich PJ. Prominent injury types in vehicle underbody blast. *Mil Med* 2019; **184**(**1**): 261–4.
14. Salzar RS, Spratley EM, Henderson KA, et al. The mechanical response and tolerance of the anteriorly-tilted human pelvis under vertical loading. *Ann Biomed Eng* 2021; **49**(**11**): 2975–89.
15. Grigoriadis G, Carpanen D, Webster CE, et al. Lower limb posture affects the mechanism of injury in under-body blast. *Ann Biomed Eng* 2019; **47**(1): 306–16.
16. Sherman D, Somasundaram K, Begeman P, et al. Dynamic response of the thoracolumbar and sacral spine to simulated underbody blast loading in whole body post mortem human subject tests. *Ann Biomed Eng* 2021; **49**(**11**): 3046–79.
17. Singleton JA, Gibb IE, Bull AM, et al. Primary blast lung injury prevalence and fatal injuries from explosions: Insights from postmortem computed tomographic analysis of 121 improvised explosive device fatalities. *J Trauma Acute Care Surg* 2013; **75**(2): S269–74.
18. Angell James JE. The effects of altering mean pressure, pulse pressure and pulse frequency on the impulse activity in baroreceptor fibres from the aortic arch and right subclavian artery in the rabbit. *J Physiol* 1971; **214**(1): 65–88.
19. Barcroft H, Edholm OG, McMichael J, Sharpey-Schafer EP. Posthaemorrhagic fainting: Study by cardiac output and forearm flow. *The Lancet* 1944; **243**(**6294**): 489–91.
20. Secher NH, Bie P. Bradycardia during reversible haemorrhagic shock--a forgotten observation? *Clin Physiol* 1985; **5**(4): 315–23.
21. Little RA, Marshall HW, Kirkman E. Attenuation of the acute cardiovascular responses to haemorrhage by tissue injury in the conscious rat. *Q J Exp Physiol* 1989; **74**(**6**): 825–33.
22. Evans RG, Ludbrook J. Chemosensitive cardiopulmonary afferents and the haemodynamic response to simulated haemorrhage in conscious rabbits. *Br J Pharmacol* 1991; **102**(2): 533–9.
23. Ludbrook J, Ventura S. Roles of carotid baroreceptor and cardiac afferents in hemodynamic responses to acute central hypovolemia. *Am J Physiol* 1996; **270**(**5 Pt 2**): H1538–48.
24. Little RA, Randall PE, Redfern WS, et al. Components of injury (haemorrhage and tissue ischaemia) affecting cardiovascular reflexes in man and rat. *Q J Exp Physiol* 1984; **69**(4): 753–62.
25. Sander-Jensen K, Secher NH, Bie P, et al. Vagal slowing of the heart during haemorrhage: Observations from 20 consecutive hypotensive patients. *Br Med J (Clin Res Ed)* 1986; **292**(**6517**): 364–6.
26. Hoffman RL. Rupture of the spleen. A review and report of a case following abdominal hysterectomy. *Trans Pac Coast Obstet Gynecol Soc* 1971; **39**(0): 97–103.
27. Scherrer U, Vissing S, Morgan BJ, et al. Vasovagal syncope after infusion of a vasodilator in a heart-transplant recipient. *N Engl J Med* 1990; **322**(9): 602–4.

28. Shen YT, Knight DR, Thomas JX Jr., Vatner SF. Relative roles of cardiac receptors and arterial baroreceptors during hemorrhage in conscious dogs. *Circ Res* 1990; **66**(**2**): 397–405.
29. Evans RG, Ventura S, Dampney RA, Ludbrook J. Neural mechanisms in the cardiovascular responses to acute central hypovolaemia. *Clin Exp Pharmacol Physiol* 2001; **28**(**5–6**): 479–87.
30. Edwards JD, Shoemaker WC, Vincent JL. *Oxygen Transport: Principles and Practice*. Philadelphia: Saunders; 1993.
31. Kirkman E, Zhang H, Spapen H, et al. Effects of afferent neural stimulation on critical oxygen delivery: A hemodynamic explanation. *Am J Physiol* 1995; **269**(**6 Pt 2**): R1448–54.
32. Skelton JK, Purcell R. Preclinical models for studying immune responses to traumatic injury. *Immunology* 2021; **162**(**4**): 377–88.
33. Pugin J. How tissue injury alarms the immune system and causes a systemic inflammatory response syndrome. *Ann Intensive Care* 2012; **2**(**1**): 27.
34. Medzhitov R. Origin and physiological roles of inflammation. *Nature* 2008; **454**(**7203**): 428–35.
35. Overman RR, Wang SC. The contributory role of the afferent nervous factor in experimental shock; Sublethal hemorrhage and sciatic nerve stimulation. *Am J Physiol* 1947; **148**(**2**): 289–95.
36. Foëx BA, Kirkman E, Little RA. Injury (nociceptive afferent nerve stimulation) modifies the hemodynamic and metabolic responses to hemorrhage in immature swine. *Crit Care Med* 2004; **32**(**3**): 740–6.
37. Mackway-Jones K, Foëx BA, Kirkman E, Little RA. Modification of the cardiovascular response to hemorrhage by somatic afferent nerve stimulation with special reference to gut and skeletal muscle blood flow. *J Trauma* 1999; **47**(**3**): 481–5.
38. Wu WT, Lin NT, Subeq YM, et al. Erythropoietin protects severe haemorrhagic shock-induced organ damage in conscious rats. *Injury* 2010; **41**(**7**): 724–30.
39. Lee CC, Lee RP, Subeq YM, et al. Fluvastatin attenuates severe hemorrhagic shock-induced organ damage in rats. *Resuscitation* 2009; **80**(**3**): 372–8.
40. Deitch EA, Adams CA, Lu Q, Xu DZ. Mesenteric lymph from rats subjected to trauma-hemorrhagic shock are injurious to rat pulmonary microvascular endothelial cells as well as human umbilical vein endothelial cells. *Shock* 2001; **16**(**4**): 290–3.
41. Reino DC, Pisarenko V, Palange D, et al. Trauma hemorrhagic shock-induced lung injury involves a gut-lymph-induced TLR4 pathway in mice. *PLoS One* 2011; **6**(**8**): e14829.
42. Xu DZ, Lu Q, Adams CA, et al. Trauma-hemorrhagic shock-induced upregulation of endothelial cell adhesion molecules is blunted by mesenteric lymph duct ligation. *Crit Care Med* 2004; **32**(**3**): 760–5.
43. Rady MY, Little RA, Edwards JD, et al. The effect of nociceptive stimulation on the changes in hemodynamics and oxygen transport induced by hemorrhage in anesthetized pigs. *J Trauma* 1991; **31**(**5**): 617–21.
44. Rady MY, Kirkman E, Cranley J, Little RA. A comparison of the effects of skeletal muscle injury and somatic afferent nerve stimulation on the response to hemorrhage in anesthetized pigs. *J Trauma* 1993; **35**(**5**): 756–61.
45. Redfern WS, Little RA, Stoner HB, Marshall HW. Effect of limb ischaemia on blood pressure and the blood pressure-heart rate reflex in the rat. *Q J Exp Physiol* 1984; **69**(**4**): 763–79.
46. Kirkman E, Watts S. Haemodynamic changes in trauma. *Br J Anaesth* 2014; **113**(**2**): 266–75.
47. Weber B, Lackner I, Gebhard F, et al. Trauma, a matter of the heart-molecular mechanism of post-traumatic cardiac dysfunction. *Int J Mol Sci* 2021; **22**(**2**): 737.
48. Krishnamoorthy V, Mackensen GB, Gibbons EF, Vavilala MS. Cardiac dysfunction after neurologic injury: What do we know and where are we going? *Chest* 2016; **149**(**5**): 1325–31.
49. Cheah CF, Kofler M, Schiefecker AJ, et al. Takotsubo cardiomyopathy in traumatic brain injury. *Neurocrit Care* 2017; **26**(**2**): 284–91.
50. L'Heureux M, Sternberg M, Brath L, et al. Sepsis-induced cardiomyopathy: A comprehensive review. *Curr Cardiol Rep* 2020; **22**(**5**): 35.
51. Baker C, Muse J, Taussky P. Takotsubo syndrome in neurologic disease. *World Neurosurg* 2021; **149**: 26–31.
52. Fishman AP. Shock lung: A distinctive nonentity. *Circulation* 1973; **47**(**5**): 921–3.
53. Perl M, Lomas-Neira J, Venet F, et al. Pathogenesis of indirect (secondary) acute lung injury. *Expert Rev Respir Med* 2011; **5**(**1**): 115–26.
54. Schlag G, Redl H, Pretorius J. Morphology of the Lung as a Consequence of Direct and Indirect Trauma. In: Schlag G, Redl H (eds), *Pathophysiology of Shock, Sepsis, and Organ Failure*. Berlin: Springer-Verlag; 1993, pp. 161–75.
55. Petersson J, Glenny RW. Gas exchange and ventilation-perfusion relationships in the lung. *Eur Respir J* 2014; **44**(**4**): 1023–41.
56. Bakowitz M, Bruns B, McCunn M. Acute lung injury and the acute respiratory distress syndrome in the injured patient. *Scand J Trauma Resusc Emerg Med* 2012; **20**: 54.
57. Kasotakis G, Stanfield B, Haines K, et al. Acute respiratory distress syndrome (ARDS) after trauma: Improving incidence, but increasing mortality. *J Crit Care* 2021; **64**: 213–18.
58. Lewis KE, Stoll A, Watts S, Kirkman E. Relating ventilatory support and drug treatment strategies to the fundamental pathophysiology in COVID-19 illness. *Eur Med J* 2021; **6**(**2**): 25–35.
59. Kerr N, de Rivero Vaccari JP, Dietrich WD, Keane RW. Neural-respiratory inflammasome axis in traumatic brain injury. *Exp Neurol* 2020; **323**: 113080.
60. Kerr NA, de Rivero Vaccari JP, Abbassi S, et al. Traumatic brain injury-induced acute lung injury: Evidence for activation and inhibition of a neural-respiratory-inflammasome axis. *J Neurotrauma* 2018; **35**(**17**): 2067–76.
61. Wardle EN. Shock lungs: The post-traumatic respiratory distress syndrome. *Q J Med* 1984; **53**(**211**): 317–29.
62. Shaver CM, Bastarache JA. Clinical and biological heterogeneity in acute respiratory distress syndrome: Direct versus indirect lung injury. *Clin Chest Med* 2014; **35**(**4**): 639–53.
63. Walker PF, Buehner MF, Wood LA, et al. Diagnosis and management of inhalation injury: An updated review. *Crit Care* 2015; **19**: 351.
64. Haglund U. Hypoxic Damage. In: Schlag G, Redl H (eds), *Pathophysiology of Shock, Sepsis, and Organ Failure*. Berlin: Springer-Verlag; 1993, pp. 314–21.
65. Ackland G, Grocott MP, Mythen MG. Understanding gastrointestinal perfusion in critical care: So near, and yet so far. *Crit Care* 2000; **4**(**5**): 269–81.
66. Kvietys PR. *The Gastrointestinal Circulation*. San Rafael: Morgan and Claypool Life Sciences; 2010.
67. Deitch EA, Shi HP, Lu Q, et al. Serine proteases are involved in the pathogenesis of trauma-hemorrhagic shock-induced gut and lung injury. *Shock* 2003; **19**(**5**): 452–6.
68. Assimakopoulos SF, Triantos C, Thomopoulos K, et al. Gut-origin sepsis in the critically ill patient: pathophysiology and treatment. *Infection* 2018; **46**(**6**): 751–60.
69. Halbgebauer R, Braun CK, Denk S, et al. Hemorrhagic shock drives glycocalyx, barrier and organ dysfunction early after polytrauma. *J Crit Care* 2018; **44**: 229–37.
70. Appiah SA, Foxx CL, Langgartner D, et al. Evaluation of the gut microbiome in association with biological signatures of inflammation in murine polytrauma and shock. *Sci Rep* 2021; **11**(**1**): 6665.
71. Harrois A, Libert N, Duranteau J. Acute kidney injury in trauma patients. *Curr Opin Crit Care* 2017; **23**(**6**): 447–56.
72. Søvik S, Isachsen MS, Nordhuus KM, et al. Acute kidney injury in trauma patients admitted to the ICU: A systematic review and meta-analysis. *Intensive Care Med* 2019; **45**(**4**): 407–19.
73. Stene JK. Renal failure in the trauma patient. *Crit Care Clin* 1990; **6**(**1**): 111–19.
74. Lai WH, Rau CS, Wu SC, et al. Post-traumatic acute kidney injury: A cross-sectional study of trauma patients. *Scand J Trauma Resusc Emerg Med* 2016; **24**(**1**): 136.
75. Kholmukhamedov A, Czerny C, Hu J, et al. Minocycline and doxycycline, but not tetracycline, mitigate liver and kidney injury after hemorrhagic shock/resuscitation. *Shock* 2014; **42**(**3**): 256–63.
76. Karmaniolou, II, Theodoraki KA, Orfanos NF, et al. Resuscitation after hemorrhagic shock: The effect on the liver--a review of experimental data. *J Anesth* 2013; **27**(**3**): 447–60.
77. Keel M, Trentz O. Pathophysiology of polytrauma. *Injury* 2005; **36**(**6**): 691–709.
78. Powers KA, Szászi K, Khadaroo RG, et al. Oxidative stress generated by hemorrhagic shock recruits Toll-like receptor 4 to the plasma membrane in macrophages. *J Exp Med* 2006; **203**(**8**): 1951–61.
79. Asehnoune K, Faraoni D, Brohi K. What's new in management of traumatic coagulopathy? *Intensive Care Med* 2014; **40**(**11**): 1727–30.
80. Maegele M, Schöchl H, Cohen MJ. An update on the coagulopathy of trauma. *Shock* 2014; **41**: 21–5.
81. Cap A, Hunt B. Acute traumatic coagulopathy. *Curr Opin Crit Care* 2014; **20**(**6**): 638–45.

82. Hayakawa M, Gando S, Ieko M, et al. Massive amounts of tissue factor induce fibrinogenolysis without tissue hypoperfusion in rats. *Shock* 2013; **39**(6): 514–19.
83. Brohi K, Cohen MJ, Ganter MT, et al. Acute traumatic coagulopathy: Initiated by hypoperfusion: Modulated through the protein C pathway? *Ann Surg* 2007; **245**(5): 812–18.
84. Brohi K, Singh J, Heron M, Coats T. Acute traumatic coagulopathy. *J Trauma* 2003; **54**(6): 1127–30.
85. Chesebro BB, Rahn P, Carles M, et al. Increase in activated protein C mediates acute traumatic coagulopathy in mice. *Shock* 2009; **32**(6): 659–65.
86. Frith D, Goslings JC, Gaarder C, et al. Definition and drivers of acute traumatic coagulopathy: Clinical and experimental investigations. *J Thromb Haemost* 2010; 8(9): 1919–25.
87. Cohen MJ, Kutcher M, Redick B, et al. Clinical and mechanistic drivers of acute traumatic coagulopathy. *J Trauma Acute Care Surg* 2013; **75**(**1 Suppl 1**): S40–7.
88. Cheddie S, Muckart DJ, Hardcastle TC. Base deficit as an early marker of coagulopathy in trauma. *S Afr J Surg* 2013; **51**(3): 88–90.
89. Johansson PI, Stensballe J, Rasmussen LS, Ostrowski SR. A high admission syndecan-1 level, a marker of endothelial glycocalyx degradation, is associated with inflammation, protein C depletion, fibrinolysis, and increased mortality in trauma patients. *Ann Surg* 2011; **254**(2): 194–200.
90. Ostrowski SR, Johansson PI. Endothelial glycocalyx degradation induces endogenous heparinization in patients with severe injury and early traumatic coagulopathy. *J Trauma Acute Care Surg* 2012; **73**(1): 60–6.
91. Tonglet ML, Minon JM, Seidel L, et al. Prehospital identification of trauma patients with early acute coagulopathy and massive bleeding: Results of a prospective non-interventional clinical trial evaluating the Trauma Induced Coagulopathy Clinical Score (TICCS). *Crit Care* 2014; **18**(6): 648.
92. Valeri CR, Khuri S, Ragno G. Nonsurgical bleeding diathesis in anemic thrombocytopenic patients: Role of temperature, red blood cells, platelets, and plasma-clotting proteins. *Transfusion* 2007; **47**(**4 Suppl**): 206s–48s.
93. Eugster M, Reinhart WH. The influence of the haematocrit on primary haemostasis in vitro. *Thromb Haemost* 2005; **94**(6): 1213–18.
94. Kirkman E, Watts S. Characterization of the response to primary blast injury. *Philos Trans R Soc Lond B Biol Sci* 2011; **366**(**1562**): 286–90.
95. Cosgriff N, Moore EE, Sauaia A, et al. Predicting life-threatening coagulopathy in the massively transfused trauma patient: Hypothermia and acidoses revisited. *J Trauma* 1997; **42**(5): 857–61.
96. van Gent JAN, van Essen TA, Bos MHA, et al. Coagulopathy after hemorrhagic traumatic brain injury, an observational study of the incidence and prognosis. *Acta Neurochir (Wien)* 2020; **162**(2): 329–36.
97. Zhang J, Zhang F, Dong JF. Coagulopathy induced by traumatic brain injury: Systemic manifestation of a localized injury. *Blood* 2018; **131**(**18**): 2001–6.
98. Standring S, (ed). *Gray's Anatomy*, 42nd ed. Amsterdam: Elsevier; 2021.
99. Dick EA, Ballard M, Alwan-Walker H, et al. Bomb blast imaging: Bringing order to chaos. *Clin Radiol* 2018; **73**(6): 509–16.
100. Lichtenberger JP, Kim AM, Fisher D, et al. Imaging of combat-related thoracic trauma - blunt trauma and blast lung injury. *Mil Med* 2018; **183**(**3–4**): e89–e96.
101. Singh AK, Ditkofsky NG, York JD, et al. Blast injuries: From improvised explosive device blasts to the Boston Marathon bombing. *Radiographics* 2016; **36**(1): 295–307.
102. Yazgan C, Aksu NM. Imaging features of blast injuries: Experience from 2015 Ankara bombing in Turkey. *Br J Radiol* 2016; **89**(**1062**): 20160063.
103. Saukko P, Knight B. *Knight's Forensic Pathology*, 4th ed. Boca Raton: CRC Press; 2016.
104. Dettmeyer RB. *Forensic Histopathology*, 2nd ed. Berlin: Springer-Verlag; 2014.
105. Scott TE, Johnston AM, Keene DD, et al. Primary blast lung injury: The UK military experience. *Mil Med* 2020; **185**(**5–6**): e568–e72.
106. DoD Directive (DoDD) 6025.21E. Medical research for prevention, mitigation, and treatment of blast injuries. Available from: DoD Directive (DoDD) 6025.21E. Medical research for prevention, mitigation, and treatment of blast injuries. (Accessed 3 September).
107. Elsayed NM. Toxicology of blast overpressure. *Toxicology* 1997; **121**(1): 1–15.
108. Almogy G, Luria T, Richter E, et al. Can external signs of trauma guide management?: Lessons learned from suicide bombing attacks in Israel. *Arch Surg* 2005; **140**(4): 390–3.
109. Elsayed NM, Gorbunov NV, Kagan VE. A proposed biochemical mechanism involving hemoglobin for blast overpressure-induced injury. *Toxicology* 1997; **121**(1): 81–90.
110. Scott TE, Kirkman E, Haque M, et al. Primary blast lung injury - a review. *Br J Anaesth* 2017; **118**(3): 311–16.
111. Gorbunov NV, Asher LV, Ayyagari V, Atkins JL. Inflammatory leukocytes and iron turnover in experimental hemorrhagic lung trauma. *Exp Mol Pathol* 2006; **80**(1): 11–25.
112. Gorbunov NV, Elsayed NM, Kisin ER, et al. Air blast-induced pulmonary oxidative stress: Interplay among hemoglobin, antioxidants, and lipid peroxidation. *Am J Physiol* 1997; **272** (**2 Pt 1**): L320–34.
113. Gorbunov NV, McFaul SJ, Januszkiewicz A, Atkins JL. Pro-inflammatory alterations and status of blood plasma iron in a model of blast-induced lung trauma. *Int J Immunopathol Pharmacol* 2005; **18**(3): 547–56.
114. Li N, Geng C, Hou S, et al. Damage-associated molecular patterns and their signaling pathways in primary blast lung injury: New research progress and future directions. *Int J Mol Sci* 2020; **21**(**17**): 6303.
115. Smith JE. The epidemiology of blast lung injury during recent military conflicts: A retrospective database review of cases presenting to deployed military hospitals, 2003–2009. *Philos Trans R Soc Lond B Biol Sci* 2011; **366**(**1562**): 291–4.
116. Aboudara M, Mahoney PF, Hicks B, Cuadrado D. Primary blast lung injury at a NATO Role 3 hospital. *J R Army Med Corps* 2014; **160**(2): 161–6.
117. Kirkman E, Read MC. Management of Blast Related Injuries. In: Hutchings SD (ed), *Trauma and Combat Critical Care in Clinical Practice*. Cham: Springer; 2016.
118. Ohnishi M, Kirkman E, Guy RJ, Watkins PE. Reflex nature of the cardiorespiratory response to primary thoracic blast injury in the anaesthetised rat. *Exp Physiol* 2001; **86**(3): 357–64.
119. Irwin RJ, Lerner MR, Bealer JF, et al. Shock after blast wave injury is caused by a vagally mediated reflex. *J Trauma* 1999; **47**(1): 105–10.
120. Zunic G, Pavlović R, Malicević Z, et al. Pulmonary blast injury increases nitric oxide production, disturbs arginine metabolism, and alters the plasma free amino acid pool in rabbits during the early posttraumatic period. *Nitric Oxide* 2000; **4**(2): 123–8.
121. Zunić G, Romić P, Vueljić M, Jovanikić O. Very early increase in nitric oxide formation and oxidative cell damage associated with the reduction of tissue oxygenation is a trait of blast casualties. *Vojnosanit Pregl* 2005; **62**(4): 273–80.
122. Gorbunov N, Das D, Goswami S, et al. Nitric oxide (NO), redox signalling, and pulmonary inflammation in a model of polytrauma. *Free Radic Res* 2006; **15**: 19.
123. Harban F, Kirkman E, Kenward C, Watkins P. Primary thoracic blast injury causes acute reduction in cardiac function in the anaesthetised pig. *J Physiol Lond* 2001; **533**: 81.
124. Sawdon M, Ohnishi M, Watkins PE, Kirkman E. The effects of primary thoracic blast injury and morphine on the response to haemorrhage in the anaesthetised rat. *Exp Physiol* 2002; **87**(6): 683–9.
125. UK Defence Medical Education Training Agency (UDMET). Battlefield advanced life support. 2006.
126. National Institute for Clinical Excellence (NICE). Major trauma: assessment and initial management NICE guideline [NG39] Published: 17 February 2016 Available from: https://www.nice.org.uk/guidance/ng39 (Accessed 3 September 2023)
127. Bickell WH, Wall MJ Jr., Pepe PE, et al. Immediate versus delayed fluid resuscitation for hypotensive patients with penetrating torso injuries. *N Engl J Med* 1994; **331**(**17**): 1105–9.
128. Kowalenko T, Stern S, Dronen S, Wang X. Improved outcome with hypotensive resuscitation of uncontrolled hemorrhagic shock in a swine model. *J Trauma* 1992; **33**(3): 349–53.
129. Stern SA, Dronen SC, Birrer P, Wang X. Effect of blood pressure on hemorrhage volume and survival in a near-fatal hemorrhage model incorporating a vascular injury. *Ann Emerg Med* 1993; **22**(2): 155–63.
130. Garner J, Watts S, Parry C, et al. Prolonged permissive hypotensive resuscitation is associated with poor outcome in primary blast injury with controlled hemorrhage. *Ann Surg* 2010; **251**(6): 1131–9.
131. Kirkman E, Watts S, Cooper G. Blast injury research models. *Philos Trans R Soc Lond B Biol Sci* 2011; **366**(**1562**): 144–59.
132. Doran CM, Doran CA, Woolley T, et al. Targeted resuscitation improves

coagulation and outcome. *J Trauma Acute Care Surg* 2012; **72(4)**: 835–43.
133. Tatić V, Ignjatović D, Jevtić M, et al. Morphologic characteristics of primary nonperforative intestinal blast injuries in rats and their evolution to secondary perforations. *J Trauma* 1996; **40(3 Suppl)**: S94–9.
134. Webster DR, Ross AS, Alford EL. Immersion blast injuries of the abdomen. *Can Med Assoc J* 1943; **49(1)**: 1–4.
135. Cripps NP, Cooper GJ. The influence of personal blast protection on the distribution and severity of primary blast gut injury. *J Trauma* 1996; **40(3 Suppl)**: S206–11.
136. Cooper GJ, Maynard RL, Cross NL, Hill JF. Casualties from terrorist bombings. *J Trauma* 1983; **23(11)**: 955–67.
137. Wolf SE, Kauvar DS, Wade CE, et al. Comparison between civilian burns and combat burns from Operation Iraqi Freedom and Operation Enduring Freedom. *Ann Surg* 2006; **243(6)**: 786–92.
138. Popivanov G, Mutafchiyski VM, Belokonski EI, et al. A modern combat trauma. *J R Army Med Corps* 2014; **160(1)**: 52–5.
139. Patel JN, Tan A, Dziewulski P. Civilian blast-related burn injuries. *Ann Burns Fire Disasters* 2016; **29(1)**: 43–6.
140. Centers for Disease Control and Prevention (CDC). Homemade chemical bomb incidents - 15 states, 2003–2011. *MMWR Morb Mortal Wkly Rep* 2013; **62(24)**: 498–500.
141. Chen HC, Wu KP, Yen CI, et al. Management of major burns in 37 casualties of a colored powder explosion: Experience of the Linkou Burn Center in Taiwan. *Ann Plast Surg* 2019; **82(5)**: 512–19.
142. Chukwu-Lobelu R, Appukuttan A, Edwards DS, Patel HDL. Burn injuries from the London suicide bombings: A new classification of blast-related thermal injuries. *Ann Burns Fire Disasters* 2017; **30(4)**: 256–60.
143. Rae L, Fidler P, Gibran N. The physiologic basis of burn shock and the need for aggressive fluid resuscitation. *Crit Care Clin* 2016; **32(4)**: 491–505.
144. Gurney JM, Kozar RA, Cancio LC. Plasma for burn shock resuscitation: is it time to go back to the future? *Transfusion* 2019; **59(S2)**: 1578–86.
145. Welling H, Henriksen HH, Gonzalez-Rodriguez ER, et al. Endothelial glycocalyx shedding in patients with burns. *Burns* 2020; **46(2)**: 386–93.
146. Shah A, Pedraza I, Mitchell C, Kramer GC. Fluid volumes infused during burn resuscitation 1980–2015: A quantitative review. *Burns* 2020; **46(1)**: 52–7.
147. Wrba L, Palmer A, Braun CK, Huber-Lang M. Evaluation of gut-blood barrier dysfunction in various models of trauma, hemorrhagic shock, and burn injury. *J Trauma Acute Care Surg* 2017; **83(5)**: 944–53.
148. Chang Y, Zhang DH, Hu Q, et al. Usage of density analysis based on micro-CT for studying lung injury associated with burn-blast combined injury. *Burns* 2018; **44(4)**: 905–16.
149. Zheng XF, Zhu F, Fang H, et al. Management of combined massive burn and blast injury: A 20-year experience. *Burns* 2020; **46(1)**: 75–82.
150. Cernak I. Understanding blast-induced neurotrauma: How far have we come? *Concussion* 2017; **2(3)**: CNC42.
151. Bryden DW, Tilghman JI, Hinds SR 2nd. Blast-related traumatic brain injury: Current concepts and research considerations. *J Exp Neurosci* 2019; **13**: 1179069519872213.
152. Jarrahi A, Braun M, Ahluwalia M, et al. Revisiting traumatic brain injury: From molecular mechanisms to therapeutic interventions. *Biomedicines* 2020; **8(10)**: 389.
153. Marsh JL, Bentil SA. Cerebrospinal fluid cavitation as a mechanism of blast-induced traumatic brain injury: A review of current debates, methods, and findings. *Front Neurol* 2021; **12**: 626393.
154. Uzunalli G, Herr S, Dieterly AM, et al. Structural disruption of the blood-brain barrier in repetitive primary blast injury. *Fluids Barriers CNS* 2021; **18(1)**: 2.
155. Cernak I. The importance of systemic response in the pathobiology of blast-induced neurotrauma. *Front Neurol* 2010; **1**: 151.
156. de Lanerolle NC, Kim JH, Bandak FA. Neuropathology of traumatic brain injury: Comparison of penetrating, non-penetrating direct impact and explosive blast etiologies. *Semin Neurol* 2015; **35(1)**: 12–19.
157. Kim JH, Goodrich JA, Situ R, et al. Periventricular white matter alterations from explosive blast in a large animal model: Mild traumatic brain injury or "subconcussive" injury? *J Neuropathol Exp Neurol* 2020; **79(6)**: 605–17.
158. Dickstein DL, De Gasperi R, Gama Sosa MA, et al. Brain and blood biomarkers of tauopathy and neuronal injury in humans and rats with neurobehavioral syndromes following blast exposure. *Mol Psychiatry* 2021; **26(10)**: 5940–54.
159. Corrigan F, Cernak I, McAteer K, et al. NK1 antagonists attenuate tau phosphorylation after blast and repeated concussive injury. *Sci Rep* 2021; **11(1)**: 8861.
160. Tschiffely AE, Haque A, Haran FJ, et al. Recovery from mild traumatic brain injury following uncomplicated mounted and dismounted blast: A natural history approach. *Mil Med* 2018; **183(3–4)**: e140–e7.

SECTION

3

Clinical Forensic Medicine

CHAPTER

63

Roles and Responsibilities of Forensic Physicians

Jason Payne-James and Alex J. Gorton

INTRODUCTION

A forensic physician works within the field of clinical forensic medicine. The term "clinical" (implying living) is used to differentiate this aspect of forensic and legal medicine from forensic pathology (generally used to apply to those working with the deceased). Both forensic pathology and clinical forensic medicine can be considered parts of forensic and legal medicine. The role of the forensic physician and the development of clinical (living) forensic medicine has developed and expanded in the last three decades although the medical roles and functions have been present for centuries. Although definitions vary and the role and medical specialty may not be formally recognized by all medical establishments, the work undertaken is similar around the world. Definitions of clinical forensic medicine include from Denmark:

> *Clinical forensic medicine (CFM) is the discipline of performing clinical examinations of living victims of violence and their perpetrators for legal use* (1); from Germany – *Clinical forensic medicine does not only entail examination of patients after physical violence but also the option of clinical autopsies, e.g. after non-notifiable complications of medical interventions, after fatalities closely following medical interventions or fatalities as a result of injuries when the public prosecutor decides not to order a medicolegal autopsy* (2); from India – *Clinical Forensic Medicine ...deals with all medicolegal cases brought to the institution...prepares medicolegal reports, collect evidence, and supervises medicolegal issues... serves as a "one-stop center" for the victims of sexual assault* (3); from the USA – *Clinical forensic medicine is...the application of appropriate forensic practices and principles, heretofore reserved for use by the pathologist at autopsy, to living patients in a clinical setting...Living forensic patients include survivors of trauma and potentially catastrophic experiences resulting in injury* (4).

Payne-James and Stark stated: *Clinical forensic medicine may relate to any area in which medicine, law enforcement, and the judiciary come into contact* (5). This broad definition is similar to that made in one of the earliest references to the workload in contemporary medical literature to the term by Laidlaw in a review of 643 cases in 1960 (6) in which he describes "*A Clinical Forensic Medical Episode was defined as a case in which a doctor and a legal authority were concerned. The legal authorities in this context included the police, coroner, procurator fiscal, judge, recorder, National Society for the Prevention of Cruelty to Children, children's officer, duly authorised officer and the prison authorities.*"

Forensic physicians (then known as police surgeons and subsequently forensic medical examiners or forensic medical officers – *see* Chapter 1) were also working within the Metropolitan Police District of London, UK over a century ago, and publishing accounts about their workload (7).

Although the basis of clinical forensic medicine in any geographic locality has a strong emphasis on custodial medicine, sexual offense medicine and examination of complainants and suspects of crime it must be recognized that clinical forensic medicine is a continuously expanding area of medical specialty (often driven by factors such as other specialist areas of medicine wishing to draw a clear line between their therapeutic and medicolegal functions). Pollak (8) has identified other reasons for change:

> *The fields...covered by clinical forensic medicine are subject to time-related changes . . . Some fields of forensic sexual medicine (diagnosis of virginity, proof of criminal abortion) have become less important. . . . whereas victims of rape and sexual abuse continue to form a major part of the forensic examination material in the German-speaking countries. The evaluation of suspected physical child abuse has grown in importance since the 60s... More recently, medicolegal experts are increasingly confronted with further groups of persons: victims of domestic violence, abused/neglected seniors, refugees from countries where torture is used... new special field... is the estimation of age with regard to the criminal responsibility of suspects who have no identity papers or pretend to have none.*

DOI: 10.1201/9781003138754-66

TABLE 63.1 Key themes in clinical forensic medicine with which forensic physicians may be involved in the assessment of individuals

Age estimation	Miscarriages of justice
Elder abuse	Modern-day slavery
Female genital mutilation	Non-fatal strangulation
Honour crime	Prevention of deaths and harm in custody
Human trafficking	Prevention of DNA contamination in evidential sample collection
Intimate partner violence	Sexual assault examination
Less-lethal weapons	Supporting vulnerable individuals to participate in the criminal justice system equitably
Management of those arrested under terror legislation	Torture (cruel, inhuman and degrading treatment)
Management of those arrested under terror legislation	

Twenty years after Pollak wrote the above, Table 63.1 gives a list of contemporaneous matters which may relate to the role of the forensic physician when they are assessing patients and certain bodies may issue statements on such matters, such as on the appropriateness of virginity testing (9).

Clinical forensic medicine has clear structures in many countries even in those where it is not currently recognized as a speciality by medical regulatory bodies (e.g. United Kingdom, Australia) and, in others, it is included in the overall roles of those who are specialists in forensic medicine and for whom the clinical and pathologic elements are closely integrated (e.g. the Forensic Medicine MD in Sri Lanka) (10). In Europe, efforts are made to harmonize practice in both the clinical and pathologic aspects of legal and forensic medicine under the guidance of the European Council of Legal Medicine which has produced guidance on the matters such as the assessment of elder abuse (11).

RESPONSIBILITIES OF THE FORENSIC PHYSICIAN

A forensic physician when assessing a patient (in whatever setting) should be independent; non-judgmental; free from bias; and open to changing opinion when provided with additional evidence. Dependent on the reasons they are undertaking the assessment at the time; their roles may include either of (or both) patient care; undertaking forensic or legal functions. These two roles (if done competently) are to ensure: patient safety; prevention of death or harm; identification, recovery and documentation of evidence; and prevention of miscarriages of justice. A forensic physician must be mindful of and aware of ethical principles such as those outlined in the World Medical Association's Code of Medical Ethics (12). In particular and in the context of clinical forensic medicine:

4 *The physician must practise with conscience, honesty, integrity, and accountability, while always exercising independent professional judgement and*

5 *Physicians must not allow their individual professional judgement to be influenced by the possibility of benefit to themselves or their institution. The physician must recognise and avoid real or potential conflicts of interest. Where such conflicts are unavoidable, they must be declared in advance and properly managed maintaining the highest standards of professional conduct*

10 *The physician must never participate in or facilitate acts of torture, or other cruel, inhuman, or degrading practices and punishments*

13 *In providing medical care, the physician must respect the dignity, autonomy, and rights of the patient. The physician must respect the patient's right to freely accept or refuse care in keeping with the patient's values and preferences*

15 *The physician must respect the patient's right to be informed in every phase of the care process. The physician must obtain the patient's voluntary informed consent prior to any medical care provided, ensuring that the patient receives and understands the information needed to make an independent, informed decision about the proposed care. The physician must respect the patient's decision to withhold or withdraw consent at any time and for any reason*

22 *The physician must respect the patient's privacy and confidentiality, even after the patient has died. A physician may disclose confidential information if the patient provides voluntary informed consent or, in exceptional cases, when disclosure is necessary to safeguard a significant and overriding ethical obligation to which all other possible solutions have been exhausted, even when the patient does not or cannot consent to it. This disclosure must be limited to the minimal necessary information, recipients, and duration.*

23 *If a physician is acting on behalf of or reporting to any third parties with respect to the care of a patient, the physician must inform the patient accordingly at the outset and, where appropriate, during the course of any interactions. The physician must disclose to the patient the nature and extent of those commitments and must obtain consent for the interaction.*

The forensic physician must be aware of and familiar with their own relevant professional codes, guidance or regulations. For example in the UK, for doctors, this would be the General Medical Council's Good Practice (13), for nurses, the Nursing & Midwifery Council Code (14), and for paramedics, the Health & Care Professions Council (15). As for any medical specialist, it is appropriate for a forensic physician to have undergone appropriate training to develop relevant skills, competences and expertise. These requirements and standards will vary dependent on the jurisdictions in which that specialist works. If a doctor or other healthcare professional cannot adhere to the relevant codes or regulatory requirements, they will need to be prepared to justify their reasons why not.

Reasons why confidentiality might be breached might include (using England & Wales as an example): if required by law (e.g. mandatory reporting of female genital mutilation); if the patient consents; if justified in the public interest; if related to driving capabilities; reporting firearm and knife wounds; reporting serious communicable diseases; and reporting in relation to insurance or employment purposes.

In some settings, the legal system may permit actions to be undertaken without the individual's consent and on the instruction of a court. This places the forensic physician in conflict between their medical role and the duties which flow from that role, and their role as an employee where they may be seen to be refusing to undertake actions required by their employment. This was highlighted in an editorial in *The Lancet* in 1993 which states

> "*...doctors may be called upon to assist the authorities in their investigations by conducting medicolegal examinations... frequently have to cope with requests by detainees for treatment of medical conditions. These first two functions, those of medicolegal expert for the law enforcement agency and of treating doctor can be clearly defined and distinguished. A third function is much more problematic, the examination and treatment of detainees who allege that they have been mistreated by the police during their arrest, during interrogation, or during the various stages of police custody. In most countries these three functions are carried out by the same practitioner, who could be referred to colloquially as the "police doctor", although the official title may vary... This potentially conflicting combination of roles, together with inadequate training and supervision, gives rise to poor medical care and serious ethical dilemmas* (16)."

It is important that forensic physicians (and those with and for whom they work) understand these sometimes conflicting roles which can give rise to professional tensions. Intimate searches are an example from the England & Wales jurisdiction where police officers have the power to carry out intimate searches (e.g. vaginal, rectal) without consent when a person may have concealed anything that could be used to cause physical injury to the person or others. A doctor or nurse could carry out (and will often be asked to by the police) such a search but can only do so with the valid and informed consent of the patient. If searching for concealed drugs then only doctors or nurses can carry out such a search but must only do so with the valid and informed consent of the patient. Lack of understanding of the conflicts between law and medical ethics may lead to disagreements between police and healthcare professionals. Such issues can be handled sensitively when clear guidelines exist on how to approach such scenarios and recommendations have been published on intimate searches by the Faculty of Forensic & Legal Medicine of the Royal College of Physicians (FFLM) (*see* Figure 63.1) (17,18). Other areas of considerable concerns, but where medical ethics can be breached as a result of being required to perform or be complicit in legal sanctions including both judicial amputation and judicial killing, and being complicit in torture although these matters extend beyond the specialty of forensic medicine and into other specialties and health professions (19–23).

EXAMPLES OF SPECIFIC FUNCTIONS OF FORENSIC PHYSICIANS

In many jurisdictions, a substantial part of the workload will involve the assessment, documentation, management and interpretation of individuals who may be complainants or suspects in criminal matters such as assault, intimate partner violence, sexual offenses and non-accidental injury. This may include aspects of medical care (particularly for those in detention and in Sexual Assault Referral Centers (SARCs). The examinees may be adults and children. Each of these types of patient may have specific vulnerabilities (including being elderly, being refugees or asylum seekers) and often alcohol and drug misuse, mental health or intellectual disability may be over-represented (24–31).

Tables 63.2 and 63.3 provide typical functions and activities that forensic physicians may be required to undertake within their day-to-day workload. The nature of these functions will always be jurisdiction specific but there is now considerable commonality in many countries. The forensic physician's focus must be to minimize the risk of death or harm to their patient and to ensure appropriate assessment to make certain that their patient can undertake or be subject to relevant forensic processes (which might include interview, biological evidence collection, examination and documentation of injury). In order to do this, they must be aware of what risk factors need to be identified and managed and, where necessary, what advice may need to be given to law-enforcement personnel. Such advice may include regular monitoring of detainees (e.g. those with drug and/or alcohol intoxication) and being aware of those factors which increase the risk of someone coming to harm. Most deaths in the context of police custody (from the point of arrest) will relate to one or more of pre-existing natural disease, restraint techniques, alcohol or drug intoxication, alcohol (and occasionally drug) withdrawal and these may

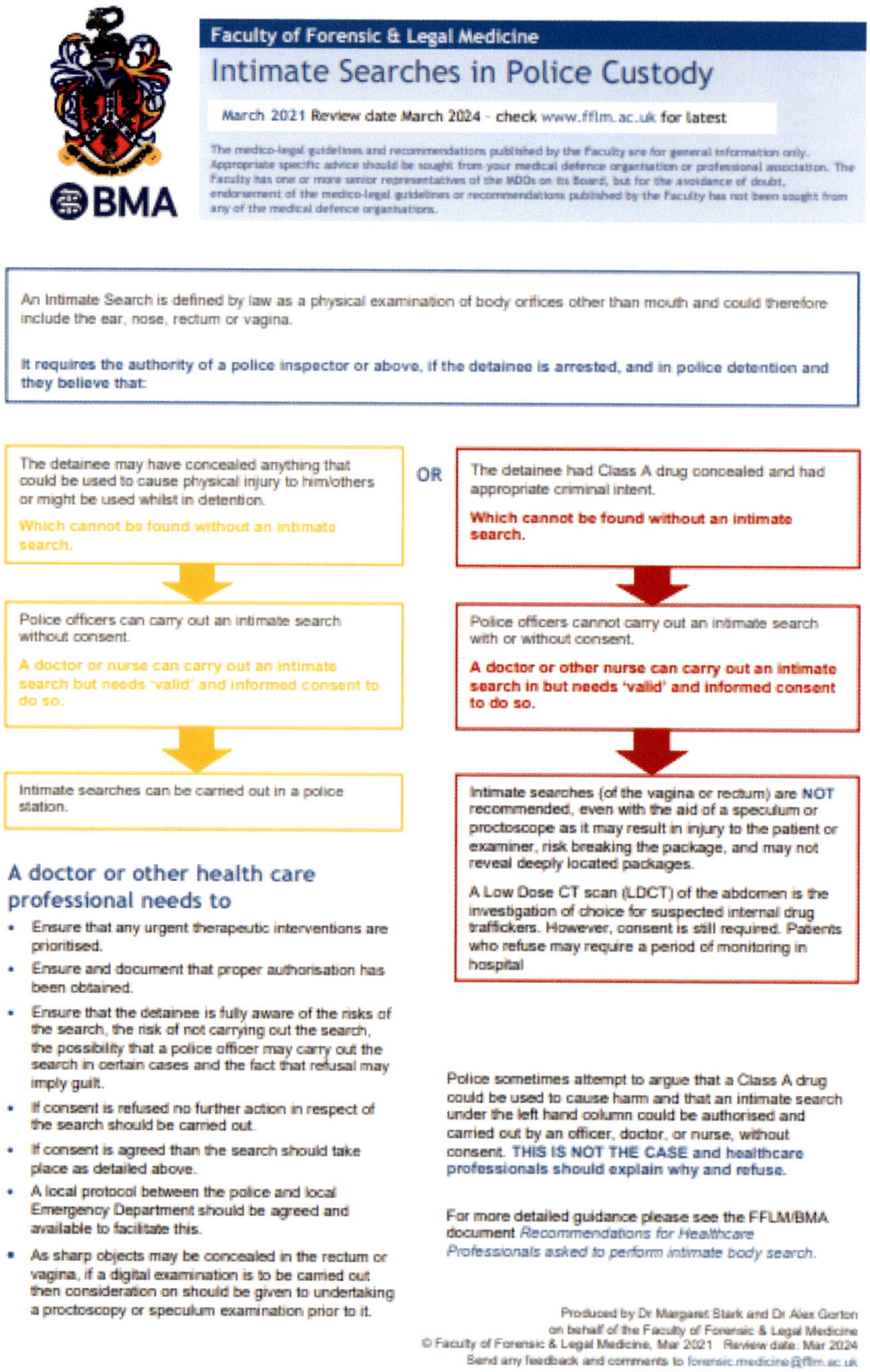

63.1 Guidelines for undertaking intimate searches in police custody (17).

also be in the presence of mental health crises. A small proportion will be because of deliberate, malicious or unlawful actions of law-enforcement personnel.

Studies have shown that rates of death vary by age and gender with some similarities across different countries and continents. There is a male dominance because the vast majority of persons taken into police custody are men. In the US, natural illness and disease progression such as heart disease and cancer were common causes of death along with high rates of suicide. In Europe, there is a predominance of non-natural deaths generally related to alcohol, drugs and medications, but suicide, injury and trauma are also common. Although systematic investigations of deaths in police custody are currently available for many countries (32), for example, the Independent Office for Police Conduct in England & Wales, the Independent Police Oversight Authority in Kenya (33,34), the differences in methodology and the lack of a uniform definition limits their comparability in terms of death rates. What is also impossible to determine is the

TABLE 63.2 What does a forensic physician do?

Forensic assessment of detainees in police custody
Forensic assessment of complainants • In Sexual Assault Referral Centers • In Hospitals/police custody/prison
Medical care of detainees in police custody
Medical care of complainants/victims • Child protection/safeguarding • Adult safeguarding • Intimate partner violence
Medical and forensic assessment of police personnel
Refugee and asylum seeker assessment • Immigration and removal centers • Torture and CIDT claims
Evidence to courts, tribunals, Coroners and others

The subjects highlighted in bold are common to most jurisdictions where forensic physicians (or any equivalent practising clinical forensic medicine) are present.

TABLE 63.3 Common activities that may be requested of a forensic physician in the police or judicial settings

Determine whether someone is • Fit to be detained • Fit to be released • Fit to be charged • Fit to transfer • Fit to be interviewed
Assess and treat alcohol and drug intoxication and withdrawal
Examine for road traffic offenses such as driving under the influence
Undertake intimate body searches for drugs or weapons
Document and interpret injuries • Adult • Child • Physical • Sexual • Non-accidental
Determine level or seriousness of injury
Take forensic samples
Undertake mental state examinations
Provide witness statements or medicolegal reports
Give live evidence to courts

relative effect of different access to healthcare in these settings, although a study from the UK clearly showed that forensic medical interventions prevented a number of likely fatalities (35).

Another element of care to which a forensic physician can contribute is in the context of acute behavioral disturbance (ABD) when it may be essential to differentiate between those who are resisting arrest and those who may be exhibiting features of treatable medical causes of such behavior. There is ongoing debate as to the terminology or sub-terminology applied and terms in addition to ABD including excited delirium syndrome (ExDS) or excited delirium (ExD) have been used successfully to identify early those requiring immediate medical treatment and avoid fatality, although the latter two terms are now being challenged. Without question, ExDS or ExD are not diagnoses but when identified as a constellation of signs, are an indication for immediate medical assistance. The debate on terminology will continue (36–44). Trained forensic practitioners can also advise on and monitor restraint techniques particularly in the context of potential prone or positional restraint (45–48).

Forensic physicians can also provide crucial advice at times of unexpected crises where risks to health of not only suspects and complainants may be present, but also to the forensic practitioners, allied health professionals, co-workers and law-enforcement colleagues. This was shown in the UK in the response to the COVID-19 pandemic when the FFLM developed early and evolving guidelines on the management of COVID-19 within police custody suites and within SARCs, at a time when the main medical establishment was focused on the broader health system (49).

In the UK, the FFLM publishes a wide range of guidance or recommendations on matters related to those working in clinical forensic medicine (50). Such guidance includes subjects such as care of suspects of assault in police custody, blood sampling in hospital for unconscious or incapacitated patients and management of head injury in custody. These are regularly revised. Table 63.4 provides further examples of such advice.

In the UK, the FFLM is tasked with publishing Quality Standards in Forensic Medicine which are intended to ensure that competent forensic physicians provide safe care for patients whether they are detainees in police custody or complainants/complainers of assault (51). There should be equivalence of healthcare and confidentiality in the custodial setting as compared to that enjoyed by patients in the outside community. Quality Standards have been developed in response to the recognition by the UK Home Office as the FFLM being responsible for the standards to be expected from all healthcare professionals involved in custody healthcare and forensic examination in response to the Violence Against Women and Children Taskforce Report (52) along with the Government's interim response, the FFLM should set those standards in conjunction with the Forensic Science Regulator (53). Standards can only be enforced if there is a training structure leading to qualification in a specialty which is why in the UK and Australia formal recognition

TABLE 63.4 Examples of Clinical Guidance & Recommendations from the UK Faculty of Forensic & Legal Medicine
Conducted Energy Device (CED): At a Glance Guidance for Clinicians Working in Police Custody (62)
Drug-Driving Competencies (63)
Frequently Asked Questions on Police Requests for Tests from Detainees in Custody for Sexually Transmitted Infections (64)
Guide to establishing urgency of sexual offense examination (65)
Proforma – Fitness for detention and interview (74)
Proforma – Forensic Examination: Adult Victim of Suspected Assault/Non-Accidental Injury (NAI) (67)
Proforma – Mental Health Act Assessment (68)
Provision of advice and help to those who have been raped or sexually assaulted abroad (66)
Recommendations – Consent from patients who may have been seriously assaulted (69)
Recommendations – Healthcare professionals asked to perform intimate body searches (18).
Recommendations – Labeling Forensic Samples (70)
Recommendations – Management of Epilepsy in Police Custody (71)
Recommendations – Managing blood-borne virus exposures in custody (72)
Recommendations for the examination of adult female suspects of sexual assault (73)

Source: www.fflm.co.uk

of, respectively, forensic & legal medicine and clinical forensic medicine as specialties is sought. Other routes of regulating aspects of clinical forensic medicine can be used, but in the absence of any substantive penalty if standards are not achieved, they may be toothless. The Forensic Science Regulator in the UK expressed concern with respect to SARCs in that "*some of those conducting the [sexual assault] examinations do not have the full range of competence to do so*" (54). Gorton and Stark (55) noted significant variability in the implementation of standards in both general forensic and sexual offense medicine for adults and children and there are significant areas of concern. This is explained by the inconsistency by which forensic medical services are provided within England & Wales and which may also account for complaints about healthcare professionals working in the SARC and custody settings (56,57). It is worth noting that within England & Wales the current commissioning model appears to be encouraging the removal of forensic physicians in favor of a nurse- and paramedic-only model which is at odds with recognized best practice in clinical care where a true multidisciplinary team minimizes risks and maximizes quality.

Absence of those with understanding of the duties of health professionals in such settings can lead to inappropriate care. In Spain in 2019, following widespread political protests in Catalonia, there were also numerous clashes between protesters and members of different Catalan and Spanish police forces, which ended with more than 600 people suffering injuries to varying degrees. Studies showed that of those arrested and who sustained injuries none of the detainees were informed of their right to a medical examination. Fifty percent of detainees reported access to medical examinations in police custody and, in all cases, this was carried out in primary healthcare centers with the presence of police in the examination room. In all cases, the report was given to the police instead of the detainee. The whereabouts of this documentation is unknown despite attempts from the detainees and their lawyers to obtain them. Thirty-one percent of detainees reported being medically examined in the courthouse, with police presence at all examinations. The results showed serious breaches of regional, national and international regulations emphasizing the need for ensuring that those in custody are assessed by trained forensic physicians who understand their duties (in particular of consent and confidentiality) to the patient (58).

When appropriately trained forensic physicians are managing the care of patients, they are in the position of being able to suggest or provide interventions that may benefit the health of the individual. A number of studies have possible benefits of such interventions particularly in the mental health, alcohol and substance misuse but suggest that further research is required (59,60). McKinnon and colleagues noted that innovations in police custody healthcare mainly relate to mental health. There remains a lack of rigorous research relating to interventions for physical health problems, protecting those at risk of substance withdrawal, and detainees with restraint or assault injuries. More research to improve the health of police custody detainees is needed addressing the high levels of morbidity and to facilitate health promotion and prevention activities (61).

CONCLUSION

Those working as forensic physicians (and associated healthcare professionals undertaking similar roles) in settings such as police custody, prison custody, SARCs, other detention locations and within justice systems have a unique and privileged access to settings in most areas where different types of patient safety issues and miscarriages of justice may occur. The clinical assessment, interpretation of findings, management and communication of that information to relevant authorities can only be done safely by a practitioner trained in that discipline. Absent inadequate training can adversely affect patient safety issues and increase the risks of miscarriages of justice. As such, forensic physicians need to work to recognized professional standards (as well as have the forensic competencies required). Forensic physicians are "gatekeepers" for fair and safe justice systems. There are well-defined standards for medical practitioners related to their duties to patients. These standards apply to all patients, irrespective of the clinical setting. There may be conflict between duties to the patient and duties to the employer. As a doctor, duties to the patient should always come before duties to the employer. This may not always be practical and, when conflicts arise, concerns may need to be escalated to senior colleagues or other monitoring bodies.

The funding of forensic medical services (whether in terms of pure healthcare or academic institutions or research) by governments (of any political persuasion) is generally poor when clinical forensic medicine is compared with other mainstream specialties such as cardiology or gastroenterology. The fate of those within the justice system (whether suspects or complainants) is often in part dependent on the quality of forensic medical services. It is difficult to understand why, but a cynic might argue that no political party sees investing money in justice systems, suspects and complainants of crime, as a vote winner. Irrespective of the politicians, those forensic physicians and allied healthcare professionals who work in clinical forensic medicine must ensure that they are aware of their duties and obligations to their patients and ensure that they fulfil them.

REFERENCES

1. Jakobsen LS, Jacobsen C, Lynnerup N, et al. Clinical forensic medicine in Eastern Denmark: Organisation and assessments. *Med Sci Law* 2020; **60**(2): 150–8.
2. Hammer U, Blaas V, Büttner A, et al. Autopsien mit Situs-Lehre in der klinischen Rechtsmedizin. *Chirurg* 2015; **86**: 1128–31.
3. Chaudhary B, Kumar P, Binaya S, Bastia K. Role of clinical forensic medicine unit in quality and standardization of medicolegal reports. *J Forensic Legal Med* 2020; **74**: 102007.
4. Rosenwald K, Hunsaker DM, Corey TS, Weakley-Jones B. Clinical forensic medicine introduction for healthcare providers. *J Ky Med Assoc* 2005; **103**(9): 433–5.
5. Payne-James J, Stark M. Clinical forensic medicine. *JAMA* 1996; **275**(**22**): 1725.
6. Laidlaw AJ. Clinical forensic medicine: An analysis of 643 cases. *J Coll Gen Pract* 1960; 3(2): 172–82.
7. Grant G. *The Diary of a Police Surgeon*. London: C Arthur Pearson Ltd; 1920.
8. Pollack S. Clinical forensic medicine and its main fields of activity from the foundation of the German Society of Legal Medicine until today. *Forensic Sci Int* 2004; 144(2–3): 269–83.
9. Independent Forensic Expert Group. Statement on virginity testing. *J Forensic Leg Med* 2015; **33**: 121–4.
10. Postgraduate Institute of Medicine, University of Colombo. Doctor of Medicine (MD) and board certification in forensic medicine, 2016. Available from: https://pgim.cmb.ac.lk/md-forensic-medicine-3/ (Accessed 11 May 2023).
11. Keller E, Santos C, Cusack D, et al. European Council of Legal Medicine guidelines for the examination of suspected elder abuse. *Int J Leg Med* 2019; **133**(**1**): 317–322.
12. World Medical Association. WMA International Medical Code of Ethics, 2023. Available from: https://www.wma.net/policies-post/wma-international-code-of-medical-ethics/#:~:text=The%20World%20Medical%20Association%20%28WMA%29%20has%20developed%20the,for%20the%20members%20of%20the%20medical%20profession%20worldwide (Accessed 11 May 2023).
13. General Medical Council. Good Practice Guidance, 2019. Available from: https://www.gmc-uk.org/ethical-guidance/ethical-guidance-for-doctors/good-medical-practice (Accessed 11 May 2023).
14. Nursing and Midwifery Council. The Code, 2015. Available from: https://www.nmc.org.uk/globalassets/sitedocuments/nmc-publications/nmc-code.pdf (Accessed 11 May 2023).
15. Health & Care Professions Council. Standards, 2023. Available from: https://www.hcpc-uk.org/standards/ (Accessed 11 May 2023).
16. Lancet. Editorial Three-faced practice: doctors and police custody. *Lancet* 1993; **341**(**8855**): 1245–7.
17. Faculty of Forensic & Legal Medicine. Intimate Searches in Police Custody Flow Chart, 2021. Available from: https://fflm.ac.uk/resources/publications/intimate-searches-in-police-custody-flow-chart/ (Accessed 11 May 2023).
18. Faculty of Forensic & Legal Medicine. Recommendations – Healthcare professionals asked to perform intimate body searches, 2021. Available from: https://fflm.ac.uk/resources/publications/recommendations-healthcare-profes sionals-asked-to-perform-intimate-body-searches/ (Accessed 11 May 2023).
19. Moszynski P. Sudanese doctors' role in judicial amputation "breaks medical ethics". *BMJ* 2013; **346**: f1253.
20. McColl H, Bhui K, Jones E. The role of doctors in investigation, prevention and treatment of torture. *J R Soc Med* 2012; **105**(**11**): 464–71.
21. Rix K. White coated healer or black coated executioner: Health professionals and capital punishment. *J Forensic Leg Med* 2013; **20**(**6**): 659–66.
22. Zimmers TA, Lubarsky DA. Physician participation in lethal injection executions. *Curr Opin Anaesthesiol* 2007; **20**(2): 147–51.
23. Pope KS. Psychologists and detainee interrogations: Key decisions, opportunities lost, and lessons learned. *Annu Rev Clin Psychol* 2011; 7: 459–81.
24. Rekrut-Lapa T, Lapa A. Health needs of detainees in police custody in England and Wales. Literature review. *J Forensic Leg Med* 2014; **27**: 69–75.
25. Addison M, Mcgovern R, Angus C, et al. Alcohol Screening and Brief Intervention in Police Custody Suites: Pilot Cluster Randomised Controlled Trial (AcCePT). *Alcohol* 2018; **53**(**5**): 548–59.
26. Arnold F, Chisholm J, Katona C, et al. Release arrangements for immigration detainees are medically unsafe. *BMJ* 2020; **368**: m15.
27. Sondhi A, Williams E. Health needs and co-morbidity among detainees in contact with healthcare professionals within police custody across the London Metropolitan Police Service area. *J Forensic Leg Med* 2018; **57**: 96–100.
28. Heide S, Chariot P, Green P, et al. Healthcare and forensic medical aspects of police detainees, suspects and complainants in Europe. *J Forensic Leg Med* 2018; **57**: 58–65.
29. Gandon V, Outh-Gauer S, Chariot P. The health of female arrestees in police cells: A descriptive study. *J Forensic Leg Med* 2018; **57**: 86–90.
30. Stark MM, Payne-James JJ. Provision of clinical forensic medical services in Australia: A qualitative survey 2011/12. *J Forensic Leg Med* 2014; **21**: 31–7.
31. Dorn T, Janssen A, de Keijzer JC, et al. Hospital referral of detainees during police custody in Amsterdam, The Netherlands. *J Forensic Leg Med* 2018; **57**: 82–5.
32. Heide S, Chan T. Deaths in police custody. *J Forensic Leg Med* 2018; **57**: 109–14.
33. Independent Office for Police Conduct. Website, 2020. Available from: https://www.policeconduct.gov.uk/ (Accessed 11 May 2023).
34. Independent Policing Oversight Authority. Website, 2022. Available from: https://www.ipoa.go.ke/ (Accessed 11 May 2023).
35. Teers R, Bucke T, Menin S, et al. Near Misses in Police Custody: A Collaborative Study with Forensic Medical Examiners in London: No. 10 (IPCC Research and Statistics Series). 12 Mar. 2008
36. Humphries C, Walker A. Retrospective cohort study of acute behavioural disturbance in police use of force reports. *J Forensic Leg Med* 2022; **93**: 102465.
37. Slocum S, Fiorillo M, Harding E, et al. In pursuit of inter-specialty consensus on excited delirium syndrome: a scoping literature review. *Forensic Sci Med Pathol* 2022. PMID: 36350497 Review
38. Martín-Ayuso D, et al. Death in custody in Spain: Excited delirium syndrome. Importance of a multidisciplinary approach. *J Forensic Leg Med* 2022. PMID: 35792399.
39. Sekhon S, Fischer MA, Marwaha R. *Excited Delirium*. Treasure Island: StatPearls Publishing; 2022.
40. Kim HK, Leonard JB, Corwell BN, Connors NJ. Safety and efficacy of pharmacologic agents used for rapid tranquilization of emergency department patients with acute agitation or excited delirium. *Expert Opin Drug Saf* 2021; **20**(2): 123–38.
41. Vilke GM, Payne-James JJ, Karch SB. Excited delirium syndrome (ExDS): Redefining an old diagnosis. *J Forensic Leg Med* 2012; **19**(**1**): 7–11.
42. Royal College of Emergency Medicine. Acute Behavioural Disturbance in Emergency Departments, 2022. Available from: https://rcem.ac.uk/wp-content/uploads/2022/01/Acute_Behavioural_Disturbance_Final.pdf (Accessed 11 May 2023).
43. Royal College of Psychiatrists. 'Acute behavioural disturbance' and 'excited delirium', 2022. Available from: https://www.rcpsych.ac.uk/docs/default-source/improving-care/better-mh-policy/position-statements/ps02_22.pdf?sfvrsn=63c6bcdc_6 (Accessed 11 May 2023).
44. Faculty of Forensic & Legal Medicine. Acute behavioural disturbance (ABD): guidelines on management in police custody, 2022. Available from: https://fflm.ac.uk/forensic-practitioners/acute-behavioural-disturbance-abd-guidelines-on-management-in-police-custody/ (Accessed 11 May 2023).
45. Hall C, Votova K, Heyd C, et al. Restraint in police use of force events: Examining sudden in custody death for prone and not-prone positions. *J Forensic Leg Med* 2015; **31**: 29–35.
46. Hall CA, McHale AM, Kader AS, et al. Incidence and outcome of prone positioning following police use of force in a prospective, consecutive cohort of subjects. *J Forensic Leg Med* 2012; **19**(2): 83–9.
47. Steinberg A. Prone restraint cardiac arrest: A comprehensive review of the scientific literature and an explanation of the physiology. *Med Sci Law* 2021; **61**(3): 215–26.
48. Campbell M, Dakin R, Stowe S, et al. Thoracic weighting of restrained subjects

during exhaustion recovery causes loss of lung reserve volume in a model of police arrest. *Sci Rep* 2021; **11(1)**: 15166.

49. Faculty of Forensic & Legal Medicine. COVID-19, 2020. Available from: https://fflm.ac.uk/resources/covid-19/ (Accessed 11 May 2023).
50. Faculty of Forensic & Legal Medicine. Resources, 2006. Available from: https://fflm.ac.uk/resources/ (Accessed 11 May 2023).
51. Faculty of Forensic & Legal Medicine. FFLM Quality standards in forensic medicine. 2022. Available from: https://fflm.ac.uk/resources/publications/fflm-quality-standards-in-forensic-medicine/ (Accessed 11 May 2023).
52. Taskforce on the Health Aspects of Violence Against Women and Children. Responding to violence against women and children - the role of the NHS, 2010. Available from: https://www.health.org.uk/sites/default/files/RespondingtoViolenceAgainstWomenAndChildrenTheRoleofTheNHS_guide.pdf (Accessed 11 May 2023).
53. GOV.uk. Forensic Science Regulator. Available from: https://www.gov.uk/government/organisations/forensic-science-regulator/about (Accessed 11 May 2023).
54. Forensic Science Regulator. Annual Report. 17 November 2019–16 November 2020, 2021. Available from: https://assets.publishing.service.gov.uk/government/uploads/system/uploads/attachment_data/file/950087/FSR_Annual_Report_2019-2020_Issue_1.pdf (Accessed 11 May 2023).
55. Gorton AJ, Stark MM. Quality standards in forensic medicine. *J Forensic Leg Med* 2022; **92**: 102436.
56. Kennedy KM, Payne-James GJ, Payne-James JJ, Green PG. Complaints against health care professionals providing police custodial and forensic medical/health care services in England, Wales and Northern Ireland - what do we know? *Med Sci Law* 2022; **62(3)**: 168–79.
57. Kennedy KM, Payne-James GJ, Payne-James JJ, Green PG. Provision of forensic healthcare services for police custodial settings in England, Wales and Northern Ireland: Current practice and implications for other services? *Med Sci Law* 2022; 63(3): 203–217.
58. Vivancos C, Rivera I. Medical examination of detainees in Catalonia, Spain, carried out in the presence of police officers. *Torture* 2020; **30(1)**: 49–53.
59. Newbury-Birch D, Ferguson J, Connor N, et al. A rapid systematic review of worldwide alcohol use disorders and brief alcohol interventions in the criminal justice system. *Front Psychiatry* 2022; **13**: 900186.
60. Lefèvre T, Denis C, Marchand C, et al. Multiple brief interventions in police custody: The MuBIC randomized controlled study for primary prevention in police custody. Protocol and preliminary results of a feasibility study in the Paris metropolitan area, France. *J Forensic Leg Med* 2018; **57**: 101–8.
61. McKinnon IG, Thomas S, Noga HL, Senior J. *Risk Manag Healthc Policy* 2016; **9**: 213–26.
62. Faculty of Forensic & Legal Medicine. Conducted Energy Device (CED): At a Glance Guidance for Clinicians Working in Police Custody, 2021. Available from: https://fflm.ac.uk/resources/publications/conducted-energy-at-a-glance-guidance-for-police-custody/ (Accessed 11 May 2023).
63. Faculty of Forensic & Legal Medicine. FFLM Drug-Driving Competencies, 2021. Available from: https://fflm.ac.uk/resources/publications/fflm-drug-driving-competencies/ (Accessed 11 May 2023).
64. Faculty of Forensic & Legal Medicine. Frequently Asked Questions on Police Requests for Tests from Detainees in Custody for Sexually Transmitted Infections, 2022. Available from: https://fflm.ac.uk/resources/publications/frequently-asked-questions-on-police-requests-for-tests-from-detainees-in-custody-for-sexually-transmitted-infections/ (Accessed 11 May 2023).
65. Faculty of Forensic & Legal Medicine. Guide to establishing urgency of sexual offence examination, 2022. Available from: https://fflm.ac.uk/resources/publications/guide-to-establishing-urgency-of-sexual-offence-examination/ (Accessed 11 May 2023).
66. Faculty of Forensic & Legal Medicine. Provision of advice and help to those who have been raped or sexually assaulted abroad, 2022. Available from: https://fflm.ac.uk/resources/publications/provision-of-advice-and-help-to-those-who-have-been-raped-or-sexually-assaulted-abroad/ (Accessed 11 May 2023).
67. Faculty of Forensic & Legal Medicine. Proforma – Forensic Examination: Adult Victim of Suspected Assault/Non-Accidental Injury (NAI), 2022. Available from: https://fflm.ac.uk/resources/publications/proforma-forensic-examination-adult-victim-of-suspected-assault-nai/ (Accessed 11 May 2023).
68. Faculty of Forensic & Legal Medicine. Proforma – Mental Health Act Assessment, 2022. Available from: https://fflm.ac.uk/resources/publications/proforma-mental-health-act-assessment/ (Accessed 11 May 2023).
69. Faculty of Forensic & Legal Medicine. Recommendations – Consent from patients who may have been seriously assaulted, 2022. Available from: https://fflm.ac.uk/resources/publications/recommendations-consent-from-patients-who-may-have-been-seriously-assaulted/ (Accessed 11 May 2023).
70. Faculty of Forensic & Legal Medicine. Recommendations – Labelling Forensic Samples, 2022. Available from: https://fflm.ac.uk/resources/publications/recommendations-labelling-forensic-samples/ (Accessed 11 May 2023).
71. Faculty of Forensic & Legal Medicine. Recommendations – Management of Epilepsy in Police Custody, 2022. Available from: https://fflm.ac.uk/resources/publications/recommendations-management-of-epilepsy-in-police-custody/ (Accessed 11 May 2023).
72. Faculty of Forensic & Legal Medicine. Recommendations – Managing blood-borne virus exposures in custody, 2022. Available from: https://fflm.ac.uk/resources/publications/recommendations-managing-blood-borne-virus-exposures-in-custody/ (Accessed 11 May 2023).
73. Faculty of Forensic & Legal Medicine. Recommendations for the examination of adult female suspects of sexual assault, 2022. Available from: https://fflm.ac.uk/resources/publications/recommendations-for-the-examination-of-female-suspects-of-sexual-assault/ (Accessed 11 May 2023).
74. Faculty of Forensic & Legal Medicine. Fitness for detention and interview, 2020. Available from: https://fflm.ac.uk/wp-content/uploads/2022/04/ARCHIVED-Pro-Forma-Fitness-for-Detention-and-Interview-June-2020.pdf (Accessed 6 September 2023).

CHAPTER 64

Role of the Sexual Offense Examiner

Rudo Masanzu and Sarah Hull

INTRODUCTION

Sexual assault is a crime of violence against a person's body and against their will. There are a range of crimes that, by statute, are classified as "sexual offenses". These cover non-consensual crimes, such as rape or sexual assault by touching or by penetration, child sexual abuse or grooming and crimes that exploit others for a sexual purpose be it in person or online.

The forensic medical examination of a victim or complainant (conventionally the term complainant is used prior to the outcome of court or judicial proceedings) of rape or sexual assault requires a trauma-informed, high-quality, sensitive and supportive approach for all victims, regardless of circumstances. Whenever possible, care for sexual assault victims needs to be standardized and based on the latest scientific evidence. The impetus should be for continual improvement in patient care standards as this aids justice in all its aspects and settings and, together with advances in research, education and training, will provide the highest standard of safe care for those who have experienced sexual violence in whatever form (1).

The expectation should always be that once an allegation or disclosure of a sexual assault is made, an appropriately skilled sexual offenses examiner will provide a timely and high quality forensic medical examination that will address the person's concerns, minimize further trauma, promote recovery, increase the likelihood of quality forensic evidence gathering, and support the criminal justice process. In this context, a forensic medical examination has been described as being an activity or process of observing, assessing, prioritizing, recording, collecting samples for scientific analysis, and documenting and interpreting injuries, with reference to sexual assault offenses (2). The term "patient" will be used throughout this chapter to refer to complainants, victims or survivors of sexual assault/violence. This chapter will emphasize the ideal functions and background of the sexual offenses examiner while recognizing that these may not always be achievable in some countries, regions and jurisdictions.

WHO IS AN SOE?

The term "sexual offense examiner" (SOE) is a generic term used to describe healthcare professionals who conduct forensic medical examinations on sexual assault patients. This includes appropriately trained doctors who may come from a range of specialist backgrounds (e.g. forensic physicians, forensic medical examiners, police surgeons, forensic gynecologists, pediatricians, general practitioners, genitourinary medicine practitioners, sexual and reproductive health practitioners), and nurses (e.g. forensic nurse examiners (FNEs), sexual assault nurse examiners (SANEs), appropriately trained emergency medicine and sexual health nurse practitioners, and forensic midwives) (3–6). The examination of pediatric sexual offense and child abuse cases is a highly specialized field and should ideally only be performed by healthcare practitioners with appropriate pediatric knowledge, skills, experience and training in the specialties of pediatric and adolescent gynecology and forensic medicine, namely consultant pediatricians and pediatric qualified doctors. In some countries and jurisdictions, this may be impractical, especially where there are shortages of pediatric-trained doctors. However, joint examinations by non-forensic pediatricians with non-pediatric experienced forensic practitioners can serve to provide a team approach to examine child sexual abuse cases. This pragmatic approach ensures the pooling of appropriate skills and knowledge in the best interests of the child. As an alternative in such cases, examinations may be done by specialist pediatric nurses and senior advanced practice nurses who have been trained to examine adolescent patients and to conduct joint examinations with pediatricians (6,7). In some localities, even this approach may be impractical, and consideration must be given to specific training of other health professionals.

In addition to having relevant qualifications, skills and experience, new SOEs must receive appropriate induction and training, with evidence of competency attainment before seeing patients independently. On completion of training, SOEs should have ongoing supervision and mentorship by a senior SOE as part of their continued professional development (CPD).

DOI: 10.1201/9781003138754-67

SOEs should be encouraged to obtain recognized qualifications within the field of forensic medicine. In the UK, such qualifications include licentiateship in sexual offenses medicine as offered by the Faculty of Forensic and Legal Medicine of the Royal College of Physicians [LFFLM(SOM)]. SOEs should also engage in regular peer review of cases to ensure calibration and consistency of decision making.

WHAT DOES AN SOE DO?

An SOE performs the forensic medical examination of a person who has disclosed or alleged a sexual assault. This entails gathering relevant medical and forensic information to guide the careful collection and documentation of forensic evidence and conducting a thorough but empathetic "top-to-toe" physical examination. This forensic medical examination also involves assessing for acute medical needs, providing treatment as needed, addressing non-acute medical needs, signposting to relevant agencies and making referrals to advocacy and support services.

Traditionally, the role of an SOE has been thought of as being a "dual role": a forensic role involving evidence collection for investigation and prosecution, and a therapeutic role covering care and medical treatment of the rape complainant (8,9). In practice, it is a multi-faceted and multi-skilled role (*see* Figure 64.1).

Conducting a thorough, compassionate and trauma-focused sexual assault forensic medical examination is a complex, time-consuming and niche procedure that requires adequate training and demands specific knowledge and expertise. A full examination can take two to three hours or longer to complete. Within the context of their role, an SOE must:

- Remember their obligation to the criminal justice system to remain objective and neutral
- Be cognizant of each patient's individual needs and circumstances, and adapt their approach sensitively and empathetically
- Make use of a trauma-focused approach for each case to mitigate re-traumatization of the patient and to help the patient feel "in control". During a sexual assault, traumatic stimuli are received by the body through the five senses. Re-traumatization then comes about when a situation, attitude, interaction or environment replicates the events or dynamic of the original trauma and triggers the overwhelming feelings and reactions associated with them (10). This can occur during a forensic medical examination, and promoting a sense of patient "control" is important as a means of mitigating potential re-traumatization
- Call upon clinical skills and knowledge to provide a holistic physical and psychological assessment which includes recognizing medical emergencies and possibly provision of treatment or onward referral for acute medical intervention
- Be knowledgeable about local and community services so that patients can be offered advocacy, ongoing psychosocial support, and information about agencies that can work with them in their recovery journey.

STAGES OF SEXUAL OFFENSES IN FORENSIC MEDICAL EXAMINATION

An SOE's role begins once they are made aware of an allegation or disclosure of a sexual offense. The SOE then needs to go through several stages to conduct the forensic medical examination (*see* Figure 64.2).

The case study below illustrates the complexity of the issues that can arise in the context of a forensic medical examination.

CASE STUDY 1

Maria is a 42-year-old single mother of three children aged 17 years, 11 years and 10 years. She had been in a relationship with a 34-year-old man for 18 months and they separated six months previously due to his controling and abusive behavior. Maria felt the relationship was having a negative effect on her children as her 10-year-old daughter had become withdrawn, which had become more noticeable after the man had moved in with her into the family home. Having not seen him for four months, Maria agreed to meet him to talk about their relationship. This ended up in an argument and he physically assaulted her. One week after this, he arrived at her home at 11pm wanting to apologize. She let him in as the children were asleep and she did not want to cause a commotion. Once inside, he became aggressive, physically assaulted her, and grabbed her by the neck choking her before penetrating her mouth, vagina and anus with his penis without use of a condom.

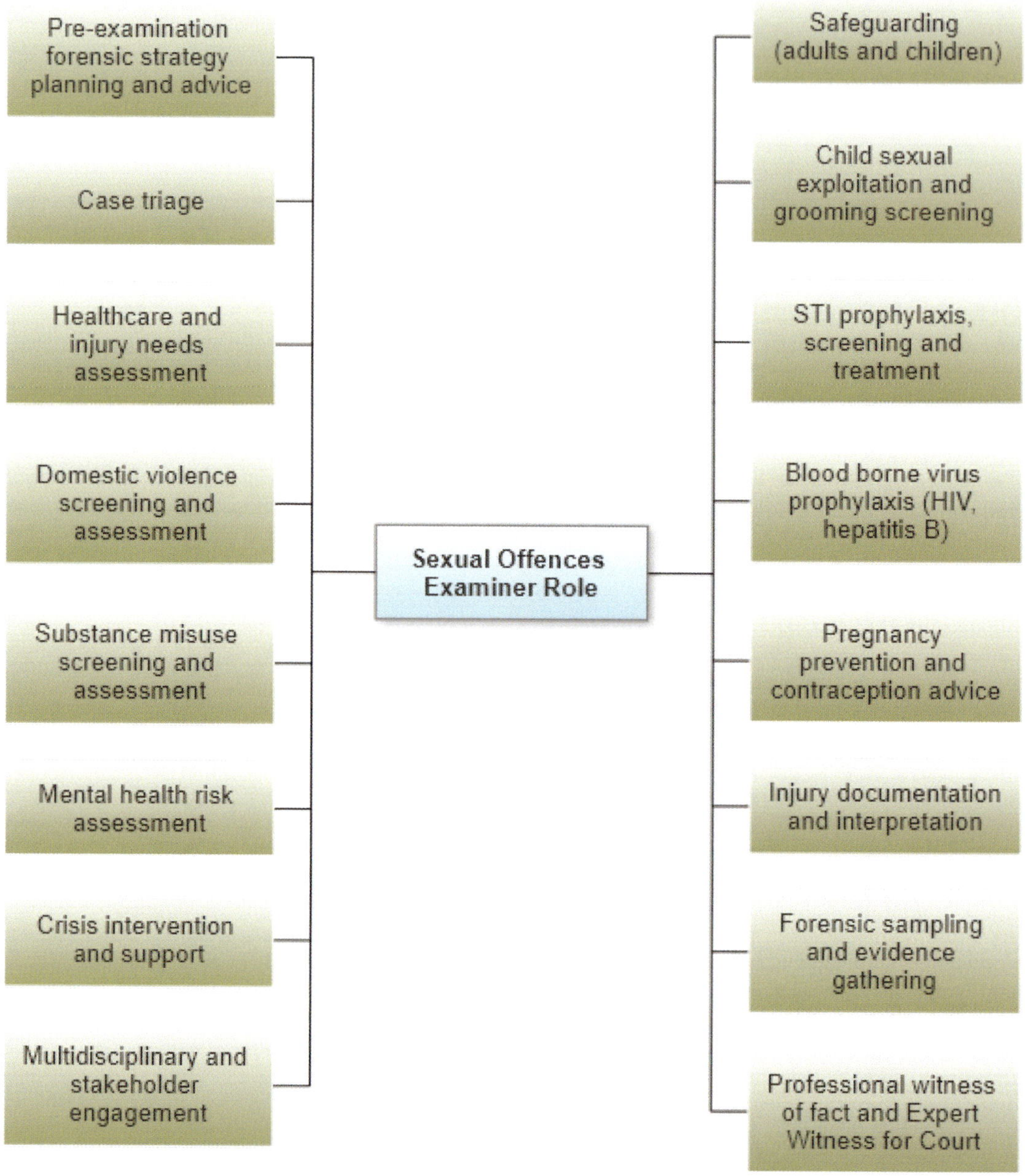

64.1 Roles of the Sexual Offenses Examiner.

64.2 Stages of a forensic medical examination.

The stages of the forensic medical examination detailed below serve as a guide for formulating a safe and appropriate way of managing this case, including an assessment of how some of the complex issues raised in the case study may be addressed.

Stage 1: Pre-examination – Referral and planning

The case referral may come from different sources, for example:

- The police or child abuse investigation team
- The patient (self-referral) or a friend/family member of theirs

- Primary care practitioner e.g. general practitioner/family doctor, sexual health center
- The Emergency Department
- Social services; or
- An advocacy organization.

Once the personal details of the patient have been obtained, the background and circumstances of the alleged offense are taken to establish the nature and type of the offense, the date(s), time(s)/timeframe and location of the alleged offense, and the alleged assailant's relationship to the patient. At this stage, it is also important to ascertain if a child was witness to or affected by the assault, and whether the alleged assailant might be a risk to a child. This enables early implementation of child protection measures – an essential component of safeguarding that focuses on protecting a child/children identified as suffering or likely to suffer significant harm (11). At this stage, it is also important to identify and address any potential safety issues for example if the alleged assailant has access to the home or is still at large.

If the patient reports any injuries, consideration should be given to referral to the Emergency Department for acute medical assessment and treatment as medical needs override forensic needs. Even if no injuries are reported, it is good practice to actively enquire about potential injuries, including asking about possible non-fatal strangulation (NFS), which is when a person has survived having pressure applied over their neck by a hand/s, forearm, a knee, a ligature or by any other means. This is important as NFS can be a cause of severe injury. Up to 40 percent of fatal strangulations have no external signs, with the majority of surviving victims having few or minor injuries (12) (*see also* Chapter 84–"Non-Fatal Strangulation"). If the patient has been sent to hospital for injury assessment or for medical intervention, liaising with the treating medical team is required to safely plan the timing and appropriateness of the forensic medical examination. In addition, screening for significant infections, for example SARS-CoV-2 and monkeypox, may also be necessary. Ascertaining whether there has been recent substance use (drugs or alcohol) is part of this initial assessment as the patient may possibly be intoxicated or withdrawing, and this may determine if they are medically fit to consent to the forensic medical examination. It is also important to make an assessment regarding any potential physical risks to staff, particularly in relation to self-referrers in the out-of-hours period when staffing levels are often limited.

The SOE also needs to anticipate supporting additional needs of the patient and so must screen for pre-existing mental health issues, learning disabilities and difficulties, other disabilities, medical issues, chronic dependency needs and also language needs (e.g. interpreter or sign language requirements). This may entail accessing the patient's electronic care records with their consent, or speaking with the patient's family practitioner/GP, mental health services, substance misuse services or social services.

At this first stage, the SOE will also give forensic advice to the police regarding early evidence collection such as collecting non-intimate samples for example mouth swabs, a mouth rinse sample, peri-oral swabs, hand swabs, fingernail samples, urine samples along with the toilet tissue used, and skin swabs. Guidance is given for the patient regarding preserving forensic evidence such as avoiding:

- Washing, bathing, showering and douching
- Wiping or cleaning the ano-genital area
- Brushing teeth or using a mouth wash; or
- Drinking fluids

and by retaining evidence such as:

- Tissues used
- Sanitary wear and tampons
- Clothing worn at the time of the alleged assault
- Bedding.

Once all of this has been done, the timing (Figure 64.3) and location for the forensic medical examination can then be decided. Ideally, this should be conducted in a specially dedicated forensic suite at a sexual assault referral center (SARC) or sexual assault treatment unit as this will minimize cross-contamination, enabling the best forensic evidence to be collected. The forensic suite environment should also be designed to minimize trauma to the patient. However, depending on the circumstances and the patient's needs, this examination may be carried out in a hospital, at a care home, in a mental health unit, in a secure setting such as a prison, or even at the patient's home. In the case of non-acute referrals, a clinic appointment can be organized at a time convenient to the patient.

Stage 2: Consent for the forensic medical examination

The patient must give their valid consent for the examination. Ideally, this should be in writing but verbal consent is acceptable. For consent to be deemed "valid", it must be:

- Given by a person who has the capacity to make the decision whether or not to have a forensic medical

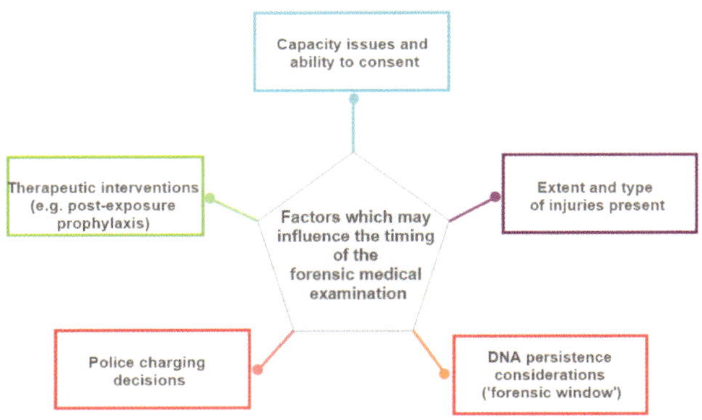

64.3 Timing of the forensic medical examination.

examination, i.e. they are able to understand and weigh up the pros and cons of the examination, and retain the information they are given
- Based on the person being given appropriate and adequate information about the nature and purpose of examination (i.e. "informed"); and
- Given voluntarily by that person with no coercion or pressure. It is important that the patient is aware that the examination is not something "done to them", but rather that they are involved in the process and that they feel that they have control.

Clinicians should be mindful of the relevant legislation, case law and professional guidance in their jurisdiction regarding consent and assessment of capacity.

There are many factors that can affect a patient's ability and capacity to give valid consent which include but are not limited to: the effects and side effects of prescribed and non-prescribed medicines, alcohol or substance intoxication or withdrawal, learning disabilities, cognitive impairment (e.g. dementia), mental health issues, physical injuries (e.g. concussion) and trauma and shock. In cases where the patient is temporarily incapacitated, for example due to alcohol/substance intoxication or shock, it may be appropriate to postpone the examination in whole or in part until the patient regains their capacity. In other cases, it may be appropriate to proceed following a "best interests" assessment.

The consent process should cover obtaining consent for:

- Forensic and medical history taking
- Physical "top-to-toe" examination
- Collection of forensic samples (which may include a sample of their own DNA for exclusion purposes) and clothing
- Collection of medical samples
- Recording contemporaneous notes, including a medical history, which may be disclosed to the court
- Use of anonymized data from the notes for audit, research and clinical governance purposes
- Photo-documentation, e.g. digital photographs or digital recordings of intimate and non-intimate areas (which may be used for evidence, diagnosis and/or training purposes)
- A report/statement being written based on this examination; and
- A copy of the notes being released on request from the police or for court purposes.

The patient must also be informed that any information recorded in the notes, details of the examination and any photographs or recordings taken during the examination may be required by the courts as evidence. The patient should also be advised that they may decline any part of the examination or stop the examination at any time. For safeguarding and public interest concerns, the patient must also be informed that if any concerns regarding their safety or the safety of others are identified, information may need to be shared with other services (e.g. social services or the police).

In the case of young children, additional considerations may apply in relation to consent. For example, in the UK, for children under the age of 13 years, consent should be obtained from the person who holds parental responsibility. For children between the ages of 13 to 16 years, clinicians should assess the competency of the child to provide consent using the Gillick competency test [*Gillick v West Norfolk and Wisbech Area Health Authority* [1986] AC 112] (see below). If a "Gillick competent" child refuses examination, this should be respected. If, however, the child is not Gillick competent, then the examination will proceed if it is determined to be in the child's best interest, in consultation with those who hold parental responsibility. In other jurisdictions, different principles for consent in child cases may apply. In special circumstances (e.g. due to significant discomfort/injuries), if a young child is unable to tolerate an examination, it may be appropriate to consider sedation. Such an examination should only be conducted in hospital premises in conjunction with the hospital medical team.

Gillick competency - Does the child understand:
the nature, purpose and risks of treatment
AND
the consequences of treatment, failure of treatment, alternatives and inaction?

Stage 3: History taking

It is recommended that standardized proformas for documenting the forensic medical examination are utilized in order to act as an aide memoire. This is advisable as examinations are often challenging and documentation is likely to be closely scrutinized as part of the criminal justice process. There should be a clear purpose for all documentation, and it is important that the SOE does not stray into the role of investigator.

The history of the alleged assault ("when, where, how, who") can be obtained from the police and then verified by the patient, or in the case of a self-referrer, can be obtained directly from the patient, all the while taking care as far as possible not to further re-traumatize the patient by making them relive the trauma. It is important to be aware that the story can often evolve as the effect of shock or intoxication wears off, and because of the effects of trauma on recollection of events. When new information, details or intelligence are provided by the patient, the SOE should document this verbatim and ensure that, as part of the debrief and handover, the police officer is informed of this. In the case of a child or a non-verbal patient, the history of the alleged assault may be given by a third party, for example, a person to whom the allegation was disclosed or who witnessed the incident.

Obtaining a history of drug and alcohol use around the time of the alleged assault is also important as this may have a bearing on the patient's ability to have given consent to the sexual act and may give an indication as to whether it may have been a drug-facilitated sexual assault (DFSA)/drug-facilitated crime. Part of the therapeutic assessment will involve assessing the patient regarding harmful use of alcohol, alcohol dependency and substance abuse, and signposting for support and early intervention as needed as this may help in their recovery.

To guide the forensic sampling strategy and to inform the forensic science laboratory analyzing the samples, factors that affect DNA retrieval and DNA persistence are documented as part of the post-assault history (Figure 64.4).

Stage 4: Examination

The examination room where the forensic medical examination is to be conducted must be forensically clean and secure. A trained chaperone whose main function is to support the patient, but who also plays the important role of safeguarding the patient and healthcare professional, should be present throughout the examination. This is often a crisis support worker or an appropriately trained nurse. The examination must be tailored to the individual and be developmentally appropriate. Moreover, the SOE should take time to carefully explain each part of the examination to the patient, remain alert to any signs of discomfort or distress, and be prepared to pause or stop the examination.

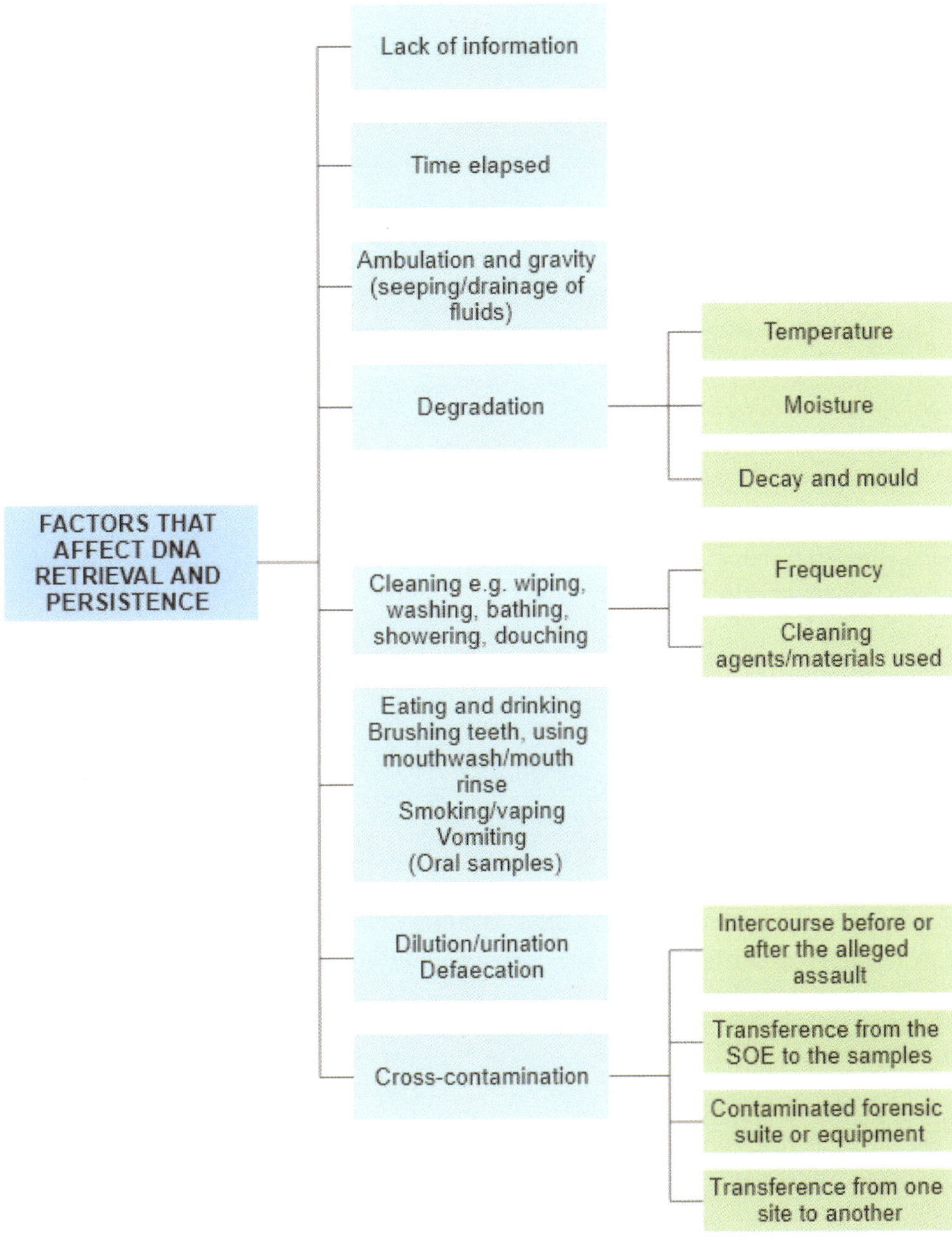

64.4 Factors affecting DNA retrieval and persistence.

Part of the general examination involves observation of demeanor and mental state, and a "top-to-toe" inspection for marks or injuries. All findings should be documented, whether positive or negative, including any limitations on the completeness of examination, for example, due to lack of consent or distress, or if the patient declines any part of the examination. Body charts and digital photography should be utilized for recording injuries. The patient should be encouraged to provide an explanation for any injuries and this should be recorded verbatim (Figure 64.5).

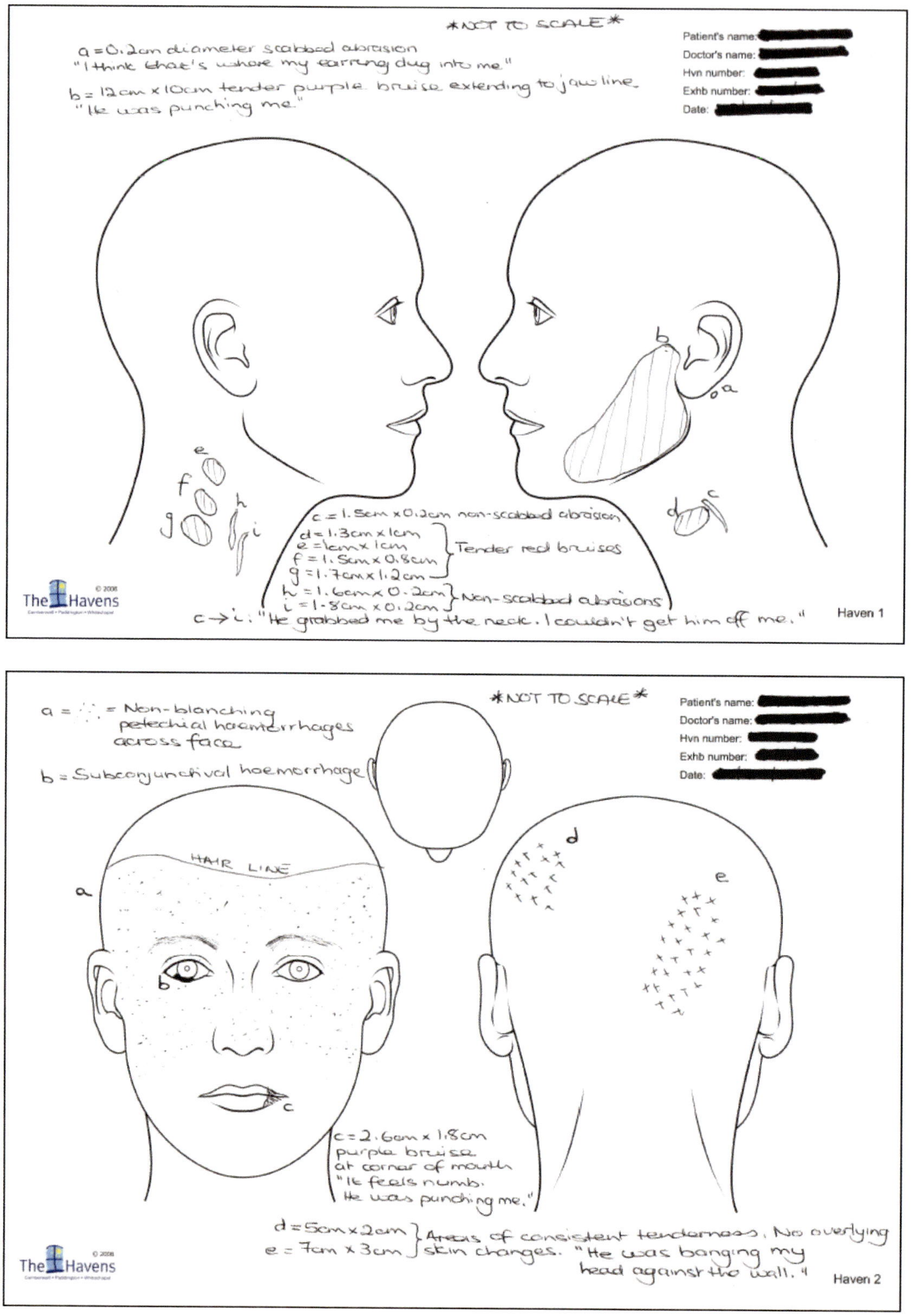

64.5 Body charts documenting injuries.

TABLE 64.1 Injury types

Blunt force	Bruise Abrasion Laceration
Sharp force	Incision Stab/penetrating wounds
Other	Burns Bites Erythema

While it is beyond the scope of this chapter to discuss all injury types and causation, Table 64.1 provides an overview of types of injuries (see also Chapter 75).

Key elements to document regarding injuries include:

- Type of injury
- Site
- Location/position relative to a fixed bony landmark
- Size (metric measurements i.e. centimeters or millimeters)
- Shape and orientation
- Color and appearance
- Degree of healing

Where injuries are present, it is also good practice to obtain photographs, as these can enhance and reinforce the written descriptions of injuries and the body charts produced, particularly for the criminal justice process. Careful and accurate documentation of injuries and their interpretation may indeed be crucial in corroborating the patient's account of events (13). There should be local arrangements regarding photography of injuries in non-intimate areas and whether this is provided by the police or by appropriately trained SOEs/clinicians. The SOE should be satisfied that consent has been obtained for imaging and that images are stored securely. In the case of ano-genital and intimate injuries, consent should be obtained for photo-documentation and recording of intimate images using a camera system such as a colposcope. Findings, interpretations and opinions should be documented in both the contemporaneous medical notes and in any subsequent statements written. The SOE should be competent in documenting and recording injuries, body diagrams and in interpreting injury findings.

Appropriate forensic samples should be taken in line with current scientific knowledge and practice using up-to-date recommendations for forensic specimens for example Faculty of Forensic and Legal Medicine (UK) forensic sampling guidance (14). It is the SOE's responsibility to ensure that these samples are labeled and packaged correctly, and that the chain of evidence is maintained.

Stage 5: Post examination – Aftercare and signposting

Following on from the examination, it is important to conduct a holistic needs assessment. This includes consideration of:

- Risk of pregnancy
- Risk of sexually transmitted infections
- Care and treatment of physical injuries
- Mental health and suicide risk assessment; and
- Need for signposting for further support e.g. counseling, advocacy, or substance abuse teams.

Extra-genital injuries are more common than genital injuries (15–17) and may require immediate medical attention. In the case of minor injuries, the SOE should be able to provide the necessary care. However, in the event of significant injuries such as head injuries or concerns arising regarding NFS, it may be necessary to refer onward to the Emergency Department for further assessment.

A pregnancy risk assessment and consideration of emergency contraception (hormonal contraception and copper intra-uterine device) should be undertaken for all women and for girls showing signs of pubertal development. The actual incidence of pregnancy following rape is unclear. Studies from the United States provide per incident as a result of rape pregnancy rates of between 5 to 7.98 percent vs 3.1 percent as a result of consensual sex (18). The most suitable method of emergency contraception will depend upon the individual patient and the time since unprotected sexual intercourse.

Survivors of sexual assault are at risk of acquiring sexually transmitted infections (STIs). Although STIs are frequently identified among both female and male sexual assault patients, it has not been found to be at higher rates than the rates found in non-sexual assault patients (19). It is important to conduct an individualized risk assessment to include prior knowledge of the alleged assailant and their risk factors. The diagnosis of a bacterial STI may be particularly relevant evidence in those who have not previously been sexually active or at the extremes of age. If the results of the STI screening are likely to have a medicolegal purpose, chain of evidence documentation is important. In other cases, it may be more appropriate to refer for sexual health screening at a future date. Risk assessment and prophylaxis for viral STIs such as HIV and hepatitis B should also be undertaken and appropriate follow up organized. As it has been shown that human papillomavirus (HPV) is associated with child sexual assault and indeed seems to behave as an STI (20), some centers advocate the use of HPV vaccination in accordance with national immunization guidelines in age appropriate pediatric and adolescent patients as a preventive measure in the post-sexual assault care setting (21).

The psychological impact of sexual violence should be considered and also the context of any underlying mental health problems and concerns regarding immediate and future safety, especially if the alleged assault took place in the person's home. All patients should have access to an Independent Sexual Violence Advocate (ISVA), or equivalent, to assist with co-ordination of ongoing care needs and support in navigating the justice process. Referral to counseling, psychology or psychiatric services should also be offered according to need, on a case-by-case basis.

THE SOE IN COURT

In many cases, the medical evidence only plays a minor part in the court process. However, in some cases, the medical evidence may play a pivotal role in determining guilt or innocence and may be a factor in matters relating to sentencing, meaning that the role of the SOE should never be taken lightly or casually. SOEs should be clear that their overriding responsibility is to the court and should familiarize themselves with the relevant legal process and ensure that they remain up to date in their clinical and forensic knowledge. If a statement for court is requested, the SOE should be clear on whether they are acting as a professional witness or as an expert witness (*see also* Chapter 14 – "Providing Evidence for Courts"). A well-constructed statement with carefully considered interpretation and opinion may avoid the requirement for attendance in court. Being called to court can be a time-consuming and, at times, a frustrating experience but it is essential to prepare beforehand by reviewing and being familiar with the case prior to giving live evidence.

DEVELOPING THE ROLE OF THE SOE

As advances in science and technology are made, the role of the SOE also develops. Research in this field of medicine will direct practice, inform forensic approaches and provide a better understanding of new ways of working that both serve and support patients better, while also better serving the criminal justice system. The skills base of the SOE has evolved over time from being merely a collector of forensic specimens from patients, to being a holistic, clinical forensic practitioner. As the understanding of injury patterns and healing in the context of sexual assault advances and the quality and nature of injury imaging and documentation evolves, the skill of interpreting findings by the SOE will also advance. SOEs will need to take a critical approach to their clinical and forensic practice to identify gaps in the evidence base in order to engage in research and quality improvement activities. This may involve networking with other SOEs and SARCs, multi-agency teams, and academic, clinical and other active researchers, all the while adhering to ethical practice, so that evidence-based strategies are developed and applied to enhance quality, safety and productivity, while keeping the patient's best interests at heart. Earlier forensic interventions and enhanced methods of forensic sample retrieval will improve the quality of forensic evidence and better serve the criminal justice system, thereby providing better outcomes for patients in terms of justice.

CONCLUSION

The SOE conducts the forensic medical examination of a person who has disclosed or alleged a sexual assault and gathers relevant medical and forensic information prior to collecting and documenting forensic evidence. This role involves assessing for acute medical needs, providing treatment as needed, addressing non-acute medical needs, signposting to relevant agencies and making referrals to advocacy and support services. This multi-faceted role requires skills that extend beyond just a forensic role and a therapeutic role in order to provide the holistic care needed by complainants of sexual assault. Following best-practice guidance in a trauma-focused manner helps attain the best standards of care for patients and helps promote positive outcomes.

REFERENCES

1. Jones H. Supporting victims of sexual assault: The forensic medicine doctor. *BMJ* 2021; **374**: n1946.
2. GOV.uk. Forensic Science Regulator. Sexual assault axamination: Requirements for the assessment, collection and recording of forensic science related evidence, 2020. Available from: https://assets.publishing.service.gov.uk/government/uploads/system/uploads/attachment_data/file/886562/116_Requirements_Sexual_Assault_Examination.pdf (Accessed 11 May 2023).
3. Du Mont J, White D. The uses and impacts of medico-legal evidence in sexual assault cases: A global review, 2007. Available from: https://apps.who.int/iris/handle/10665/43795 (Accessed 11 May 2023).
4. Cowley R, Walsh E, Horrocks J. The role of the sexual assault nurse examiner in England: Nurse experiences and perspectives. *J Forensic Nurs* 2014; **10**(2): 77–83.
5. Faculty of Forensic & Legal Medicine. FFLM Quality standards in forensic medicine general forensic medicine (GFM) and sexual offence medicine (SOM), 2022. Available from: https://fflm.ac.uk/resources/publications/fflm-quality-standards-in-forensic-medicine/ (Accessed 11 May 2023).
6. Faculty of Forensic & Legal Medicine. Quality standards for clinicians undertaking paediatric sexual offence medicine (PSOM), 2021. Available from: https://fflm.ac.uk/resources/publications/fflm-quality-standards-for-clinicians-undertaking-paediatric-sexual-offence-medicine-psom/ (Accessed 11 May 2023).
7. Herrmann B, Banaschak S, Csorba R, et al. Physical examination in child sexual abuse. *Dtsch Aerztebl Int* 2014; **111**: 692–703.
8. Petter LM, Whitehill DL. Management of Female Sexual Assault. *Am Fam Physician* 1998; **58**(4): 929–30.
9. World Health Organisation. Guidelines for medico-legal care of victims of sexual violence, 2003. Available from: https://apps.who.int/iris/handle/10665/42788 (Accessed 11 May 2023).
10. Subramanian S, Green JS. The general approach and management of the patient who discloses a sexual assault. *Mo Med* 2015; **112**(3): 211–17.
11. National Society for the Prevention of Cruelty to Children. Safeguarding Children and Child Protection, 2021. Available from: https://learning.nspcc.org.uk/safeguarding-child-protection (Accessed 11 May 2023).
12. De Boos J. Review Article: Non-fatal strangulation: Hidden injuries, hidden risks. *Emerg Med Australas* 2019; **31**(3): 302–8.
13. Crane J. Interpretation of non-genital injuries in sexual assault. *Best Pract Res Clin Obstet Gynaecol* 2013; **27**(1): 103–11.
14. Faculty of Forensic & Legal Medicine. Recommendations for the Collection of Forensic Specimens from Complainants and Suspects, 2023. Available from: https://fflm.ac.uk/resources/publications/recommended-equipment-for-obtaining-forensic-samples-from-complainants-and-suspects/ (Accessed August 2023) (Accessed 28 August 2023).
15. Sugar NF, Fine DN, Eckert LO. Physical injury after sexual assault: Findings of a large case series. *Am J Obstet Gynecol* 2004; **190**(1): 71–6.
16. Maguire W, Goodall E, Moore T. Injury in adult female sexual assault complainants and related factors. *Eur J Obstet Gynecol Reprod Biol* 2009; **142**(2): 149–53.

17. McLean I, Roberts SA, White C, Paul S. Female genital injuries resulting from consensual and non-consensual vaginal intercourse. *Forensic Sci Int* 2011; **204**(**1**): 27–33.
18. Coleman GD. Pregnancy after Rape, 2015. Available from: https://clinmedjournals.org/articles/ijwhw/international-journal-of-womens-health-and-wellness-ijwhw-1-004.php?jid=ijwhw (Accessed 16 May 2023).
19. van Rooijen MS, Schim van der Loeff MF, van Kempen L, de Vries HJC. Sexually transmitted infection positivity rate and treatment uptake among female and male sexual assault victims attending the Amsterdam STI Clinic between 2005 and 2016. *Sex Transm Dis* 2018; **45**(**8**): 534–41.
20. Unger ER, Fajman NN, Maloney EM, et al. Anogenital human papillomavirus in sexually abused and nonabused children: A multicenter study. *Pediatrics* 2011; **128**(**3**): e658–65.
21. Seña AC, Hsu KK, Kellogg N, et al. Sexual assault and sexually transmitted infections in adults, adolescents, and children. *Clin Infect Dis* 2015; **61**(**suppl 8**): S856–64.

CHAPTER 65

The Role of the Custody Nurse and Paramedic

Sean Carruthers

INTRODUCTION

This chapter will focus on the delivery of forensic healthcare within the police custody setting by nurses and paramedics in the UK. This involves the provision of healthcare and the undertaking of forensic processes for police detained persons (DP) (also referred to as prisoners or detainees). The terms custody healthcare, custodial medicine, forensic medical services and forensic healthcare may be used interchangeably. The roles of the custody nurse (CN) or paramedic in police custody are many and varied, as are their titles (e.g. custody nurse practitioner, forensic nurse practitioner, forensic nurse examiner, forensic paramedic, forensic paramedic practitioner). In this chapter, the CN and paramedic will be referred to as healthcare professionals (HCP).

The role of the HCP in custody is dependent on the healthcare provider in that police service; however, many of the roles are the same regardless of the police service or healthcare provider. This chapter will focus on the basic roles of the HCP. Additional roles unique to some areas may include Test on Arrest, Forensics Photography and Recognition of Life Extinct (ROLE). Test on Arrest is an initiative whereby the HCP assists the police in referring a DP (should they consent), who has tested positive for an illicit drug in custody, for a drugs awareness course in lieu of being charged for an offense. The charge must be low key, and the DP should be a first-time offender. If the offender agrees to this and is found to have been non-compliant in any way, then the original charge will be reinstated. This process has developed since 2012. Some additional roles may have been initiated by the Police & Crime Commissioner (PCC) for that area (over 40 police services in England & Wales), rather than the healthcare provider. PCCs are elected in areas of England & Wales and have responsibilities including how the area is policed and the police budget (1). Their priorities may be politically driven. Most police services in England & Wales have custody healthcare contracted out to private healthcare providers. Some are provided by the National Health Service, and a few have this facility provided directly by the police service. There is wide variation in how these services are delivered. In Scotland, this service is provided by NHS Scotland.

This chapter is intended to provide potential HCPs considering working in this area and those who may come into contact with them with an outline of the basic clinical roles not just from a clinical perspective, but also the core values and non-clinical skills required – especially the autonomous decision-making that the police will expect the HCP to deliver effectively.

FMEs (Forensic Medical Examiners – forensic physicians) and HCPs working in this area should provide healthcare of a standard that would be expected if the DPs were not in police custody and ensure appropriate monitoring of DPs, many of whom are vulnerable and from deprived backgrounds (*see* Chapter 63). They must also support the Criminal Justice System (CJS) in providing clinical assurances that DPs are fit and medically safe to continue their detention and to ensure that relevant forensic procedures can be undertaken.

THE HEALTHCARE PROFESSIONAL

For many years now HCPs have been embedded in police custody and have become an integral part of the multidisciplinary team (MDT) to manage the DP during the criminal justice pathway in police custody. This was formalized in the Police & Criminal Evidence Act 1984. Codes of Practice required (at para 9.5) the "custody officer to make sure a detainee receives appropriate clinical attention as soon as reasonably practical if the person:

(a) appears to be suffering from physical illness
(b) is injured
(c) appears to be suffering from a mental disorder
(d) appears to need clinical attention
and (at para 9.5A)
[this] applies whether or not individual requests it and whether or not they have been treated elsewhere (2)".

The HCP may be asked to carry out several different functions with respect to the DP, depending on their presentation, so that decisions and actions can be appropriately undertaken by the police.

DPs in custody following arrest have many different clinical needs. While sharing the same medical conditions as those not in custody, the management of those

DOI: 10.1201/9781003138754-68

conditions may be less than optimal due to the lifestyle choices and other vulnerabilities. There are a wide range of clinical challenges. The DPs may have medication to be administered during custody and the nature and dosing of that medication may be unclear, there may be problems of substance use (alcohol and licit and illicit drugs), they may be intoxicated – and the risks to safety may be compounded, for example, if there is a history of a head injury (HI). It can be argued that the main focus of the HCP, and indeed the police custody staff and interviewing officers, is preventing death or harm in police custody. Many DPs have potentially life-threatening medical conditions such as asthma, diabetes, heart disease and epilepsy. Some DPs may have a history of some self-injury and have suicidal ideation and, given the opportunity, some will act upon that. Some may consider suicide or other forms of self-injury after they leave custody.

During 2022/2023, the Independent Office for Police Conduct (IOPC) reported that there were 23 deaths in England & Wales in or following police custody (3) an increase in recent years.

Many clinical conditions can be managed in custody, but it must be emphasized that the medical facility in custody is not a mini-hospital or an adjunct of Emergency Department. Facilities for regular monitoring by an HCP and the range of equipment available to the HCP is limited, although all custody suites are equipped to manage Immediate Life Support. There is usually only one HCP in a custody suite with multiple prisoners so the clinical monitoring of DPs cannot be managed in custody as it can in the hospital setting where there are multiple clinical staff available. The DPs in custody are in a cell, sometimes with CCTV monitors, and are checked by (non-healthcare trained) Custody Detention Officers (CDOs) or gaolers regularly; however, it is in between checks that a DP may be most vulnerable.

FITNESS TO DETAIN

A request by the police to determine a DP's fitness to be detained in custody is one of the most common actions and possibly the most comprehensive element of the HCP interaction with a DP, and generally a detailed Clinical Assessment (CA) continues.

When a DP is arrested and brought into custody, the CDO undertakes a risk assessment to establish if there are any clinical or mental health (MH) issues that the custody staff need to be aware of. If there are, then they are referred to the HCP for assessment for Fitness to Detain (FTD). Peel (4) noted that most requests for the HCP to see a DP is to assess their fitness to detain. This provides the HCP the opportunity to establish the DPs clinical needs and record baseline observations which will be helpful for subsequent reviews. Gaining a meaningful assessment is to some extent being dependent upon the information provided by the DP to be reliable. This is not always the case, and inaccurate information regarding health may be provided for a variety of reasons. These may include drug-seeking behavior but may also include matters that the DP does not wish to disclose to police – for example, if they have hepatitis or HIV.

The HCP must be mindful that many DPs are not from the usual patient groups that they may see in other clinical settings, and they must be very aware that the HCP and police are dealing with, in many cases, individuals who may have a whole range of vulnerabilities that may modify their behavior.

HCPs in police custody must treat DPs as their patients, and their professional duties of consent and confidentiality apply as equally to DPs as they do to any other patient they would encounter. Dolphin (5) states and emphasizes that HCP's management of DPs must not discriminate against any DP on any grounds. All DPs are entitled to appropriate healthcare to the same standards as any other member of the public.

Certain organizations offer guidelines on all aspects of DPs' clinical management in police custody. The Faculty of Forensic and Legal Medicine of the Royal College of Physicians (FFLM), and the United Kingdom Association of Forensics Nurse and Paramedics (UKAFN) offer extensive guidelines and standards required on all the interventions the HCP have with DPs and provide numerous training courses. The FFLM has published guidance on the role of the HCP (6) along with UKAFN and the College of Paramedics and also quality standards for nurses and paramedics practicing general forensic medicine (7). These organizations do offer training either directly and, or, in conjunction with their affiliation with a number of UK universities who support these courses with the appropriate qualification. The UK College of Policing (CoP) also offers some relevant clinical and non-clinical training. Some of these training courses are appropriate to the custody setting and assist the HCP to provide the highest standard of healthcare unique to this setting (8).

DPs have a wide range of clinical issues to consider and these frequently include substance use and MH vulnerabilities. Most of the time the HCP can manage these conditions while ensuring the DP can progress on the criminal justice pathway without undue delay. The HCP's primary role is to ensure the health of the DP and ensure that potential harm, or even fatality are avoided. The HCP may have to make clear to police officers that this is their primary role, and that forensic matters may be secondary to this primary function. Once the FTD assessment is complete, it does not end there. That assessment may be reviewed at any time, and often is, particularly with those with vulnerabilities such as ongoing medical conditions, substance dependencies, MH issues, children and the elderly. Those with drug or alcohol dependencies regularly require reviews to assess their withdrawal levels and may require supportive medication during their time in custody. They are one of the groups of DPs who pose the greatest risk of death or harm in custody, whether due to acute intoxication or withdrawal. Assessments best undertaken in the medical room – where no CCTV is present, for reasons of medical confidentiality – although a CDO or gaoler may present in line of sight at the door for the safety of the HCP. Violence against HCPs can happen, and the HCP must be aware of this risk. This risk has long been recognized (9) and is a real possibility in police custody, so a different approach and situational awareness and management are required by the HCP. Violence or threats of violence may be related to a whole variety of causes including drug-seeking behavior, intoxication, frustration, dislike of police and acute MH crises. The HCP should be in a position and have the skills to generally de-escalate such situations.

As DPs are brought into custody, the HCP whenever possible can discreetly observe the DP during the booking-in stage so that they can get an initial snapshot of the DP's general health, well-being and presentation. Many are aggressive and argumentative stating they can't breathe, or they are withdrawing, or complaining of chest pain. Sometimes this may be an attempt by the DP to get out of custody for a trip to the hospital, or just to be as awkward as possible. As they are complaining of such, they may not present with signs congruent with their symptoms such as difficulty in breathing, objective drug withdrawals, or chest pain. It is at this point that the HCP can make a note documenting negatives and other visual observations that is, no shortness of breath or difficulty in breathing, well perfused and of good color, able to speak, argue and shout in full sentences with gusto, no abnormal breath sounds, bilateral chest movement, no guarding to pain, no facial expressions or body language congruent to pain or distress, independently mobile and fully weight bearing with good range of movement and power in all limbs, no MH crisis, and has capacity. This list of examples is not exhaustive, but the HCP must document these where appropriate to assist their decision making but also to provide a contemporaneous record of why they arrived at the decisions they did. For example, if the DP complains that the HCP did not give them an inhaler for their stated asthma attack then the HCP has a record, that their appearance and behavior did not appear to warrant it.

The DP will be seen by the HCP for a full CA, however, this initial snapshot of their presentation during booking-in may be useful for the HCP to bear in mind because when the DP is brought to the medical room for assessment, their presentation may change to match their complaint once they see the HCP. Most DPs, in the presence of a reasonable HCP treating them appropriately, will not feel the need to modify, exaggerate or falsify symptoms. If the DP's main issue is substance or alcohol dependence following the CA, the HCP may find the CA leaves them not indicated for supportive withdrawal medication. This may be determined via scales such as the Clinical Opiate Withdrawal Scale (COWS) (Figure 65.1) (10) and the Clinical Institute Withdrawal Assessment for Alcohol (CIWA) (Figure 65.2) (11) scores 0 or has a

Resting Pulse Rate: ________ beats/minute *Measured after patient is sitting or lying for one minute* 0 Pulse rate 80 or below 1 Pulse rate 81-100 2 Pulse rate 101-120 4 Pulse rate greater than 120	GI Upset: *over last 1/2 hour* 0 No GI symptoms 1 Stomach cramps 2 Nausea or loose stool 3 Vomiting or diarrhea 5 Multiple episodes of diarrhea or vomiting
Sweating: *over past 1/2 hour not accounted for by room temperature or patient activity.* 0 No report of chills or flushing 1 Subjective report of chills or flushing 2 Flushed or observable moistness on face 3 Beads of sweat on brow or face 4 Sweat streaming off face	Tremor *observation of outstretched hands* 0 No tremor 1 Tremor can be felt, but not observed 2 Slight tremor observable 4 Gross tremor or muscle twitching
Restlessness *Observation during assessment* 0 Able to sit still 1 Reports difficulty sifting still, but is able to do so 3 Frequent shifting or extraneous movements of legs/arms 5 Unable to sit still for more than a few seconds	Yawning *Observation during assessment* 0 No yawning 1 Yawning once or twice during assessment 2 Yawning three or more times during assessment 4 Yawning several times/minute
Pupil size 0 Pupils pinned or normal size for room light 1 Pupils possibly larger than normal for room light 2 Pupils moderately dilated 5 Pupils so dilated that only the rim of the iris is visible	Anxiety or irritability 0 None 1 Patient reports increasing irritability or anxiousness 2 Patient obviously irritable anxious 4 Patient so irritable or anxious that participation in the assessment is difficult
Bone or Joint aches *If patient was having pain previously, only the additional component attributed to opiates withdrawal is scored* 0 Not present 1 Mild diffuse discomfort 2 Patient reports severe diffuse aching of joints/ muscles 4 Patient is rubbing joints or muscles and is unable to sit still because of discomfort	Gooseflesh skin 0 Skin is smooth 3 Piloerrection of skin can be felt or hairs standing up on arms 5 Prominent piloerrection
Runny nose or tearing *Not accounted for by cold symptoms or allergies* 0 Not present 1 Nasal stuffiness or unusually moist eyes 2 Nose running or tearing 4 Nose constantly running or tears streaming down cheeks	Total Score ________ The total score is the sum of all 11 items Initials of person completing Assessment: ____________

Score: 5-12 mild; 13-24 moderate; 25-36 moderately severe; more than 36 = severe withdrawal

65.1 The proforma for the Clinical Opiate Withdrawal Scale (10).

low score. This assessment, along with the observational assessment from being booked-in may indicate that the DP may have embellished their presentation.

HCPs are the advocates of the DP's healthcare needs. The HCP must act in the best interests of the healthcare needs of the DP, and at the same time, be aware of the criminal justice pathway needs. If the DP is unwell and cannot be managed in custody, then transfer to the Emergency Department must be considered for further investigation and management. If this is the case, then the 24-hour detention clock which applies in England & Wales legislation will stop while they are away and recommence when they return to custody.

There are many components of consideration during the FTD assessment and much of this may determine their Fitness for Interview (FFI).

FITNESS FOR INTERVIEW

Once FTD is established, the DP will probably be taken back to the cell to await interview by the investigating officers. The police may request that their fitness to be interviewed (FTI) is established. During this time, they will be monitored by CDOs who will carry out routine observations which are defined by the College of Policing Authorized Professional Practice (APP) at four different levels shown in Table 65.1 (12) and generally determined by the custody officer taking into account advice from the HC. The APP also provides notes and comments as to the respective responsibilities of HCP and custody team.

Every officer or member of custody staff required to conduct close proximity supervision must be fully briefed by the custody officer with regard to their role, the needs

TABLE 65.1 Levels of observation of detainees*

Level 1: General observation

Following full risk assessment, this is the minimum acceptable level of observation required for any detainee. It includes the following actions:

- the detainee is checked at least every hour (the risk assessment is updated where necessary)
- checks are carried out sensitively to cause as little intrusion as possible
- if no reasonable foreseeable risk is identified, staff need not wake a sleeping detainee (checks of the sleeping detainee must, however, continue and if any change in the detainee's condition presents a new risk, the detainee should be roused)
- if the detainee is awake, staff should communicate with them

Level 2: Intermittent observation

Subject to medical direction, this is the minimum acceptable level for detainees who are under the influence of alcohol or drugs, or whose level of consciousness causes concern. It includes the following actions:

- the detainee is visited and roused at least every 30 minutes
- physical visits and checks must be carried out – CCTV and other technologies can be used in support of this
- the detainee is positively communicated with at frequent and irregular intervals
- visits to the detainee are conducted in accordance with PACE Code C Annex H

Level 3: Constant observation

If the detainee's risk assessment indicates a heightened level of risk to the detainee (for example self-harm, suicide risk or other significant mental or physical vulnerability) they should be observed at this level. It includes the following actions:

- the detainee is under constant observation and accessible at all times
- physical checks and visits must be carried out at least every 30 minutes
- CCTV is constantly monitored (other technologies can also be used)
- any possible ligatures are removed
- the detainee is positively communicated with at frequent and irregular intervals
- review by the HCP in accordance with the relevant service level agreement

The purpose of CCTV cell monitoring should be recorded in the custody record together with the name of the designated officer or member of custody staff who is responsible for the monitoring.

Officers and staff must consider issues of privacy, dignity and gender.

Level 4: Close proximity

Detainees at the highest risk of self-harm should be observed at this level. It must include the following actions:

- the detainee is physically supervised in close proximity to enable immediate physical intervention to take place if necessary
- CCTV and other technologies do not meet the criteria of close proximity observation but may complement it
- issues of privacy, dignity and gender are taken into consideration
- any possible ligatures are removed
- the detainee is positively communicated with at frequent and irregular intervals
- review by the HCP in accordance the relevant with service level agreement

*– taken from Authorized Professional Practice

Nausea and Vomiting
0 – No nausea or vomiting
1
2
3
4 – Intermittent nausea with dry heaves
5
6
7 – Constant nausea, frequent dry heaves and vomiting

Paroxysmal Sweats
0 – No sweat visible
1 – Barely perceptible sweating, palms moist
2
3
4 – Beads of sweat obvious on forehead
5
6
7 – Drenching sweats

Agitation
0 – Normal activity
1 – Somewhat more than normal activity
2
3
4 – Moderate fidgety and restless
5
6
7 – Paces back and forth during most of the interview or constantly thrashes about

Visual Disturbances
0 – Not present
1 – Very mild photosensitivity
2 – Mild photosensitivity
3 – Moderate photosensitivity
4 – Moderately severe visual hallucinations
5 – Severe visual hallucinations
6 – Extreme severe visual hallucinations
7 – Continuous visual hallucinations

Tremor
0 – No tremor
1 – Not visible, but can be felt at finger tips
2
3
4 – Moderate when patient's hands extended
5
6
7 – Severe, even with arms not extended

Tactile Disturbances
0 - None
1 – Very mild paraesthesias
2 – Mild paraesthesias
3 – Moderate paraesthesias
4 – Moderately severe hallucinations
5 – Severe hallucinations
6 – Extremely severe hallucinations
7 – Continuous hallucinations

Headache
0 – Not present
1 – Very mild
2 - Mild
3 - Moderate
4 – Moderately severe
5 - Severe
6 – Very severe
7 – Extremely severe

Auditory Disturbances
0 – Not present
1 – Very mild harshness or ability to frighten
2 – Mild harshness or ability to frighten
3 – Moderate harshness or ability to frighten
4 – Moderately severe hallucinations
5 – Severe hallucinations
6 – Extremely severe hallucinations
7 – Continuous hallucinations

Orientation and Clouding of the Sensorium
0 – Oriented and can do serial additions
1 – Cannot do serial additions
2 – Disoriented for date but not more than 2 calendar days
3 - Disoriented for date by more than 2 calendar days
4 – Disoriented for place/person

Cumulative scoring

Cumulative score	Approach
0 – 8	No medication needed
9 – 14	Medication is optional
15 – 20	Definitely needs medication
>20	Increased risk of complications

65.2 The proforma for the Clinical Institute Withdrawal Scale for Alcohol, Revised (CIWA-Ar) (11).

of the DP and the risks presented by the DP. They must be fully trained and equipped to respond accordingly. If there is a requirement to rouse, this must be done by a trained officer or member of staff. Any changes in the DP's condition must be brought to the CDO's attention immediately.

HCPs may work across different forces and be familiar with different categories or levels of observation. Custody managers should ensure that HCPs working within their force are aware of local procedures.

CHECKING OF VISITS AND ROUSING

Forces should have auditable systems that specifically inspect that staff adhere to observation levels. This should include using recorded CCTV to check timing of visits and rousing.

WRITTEN RECORD

Officers and staff must make a written record in the custody record following each and every visit/check/rousing completed for each DP.

The CDO must record the following in the custody record:

- The level of observation required for a DP (using consistent terminology within the record, for example level 1 or level 2 checks)
- The reasons for the decision
- Clear directions that specify the name and title of the persons carrying out the observations

HCPs should ensure that their recommendations for custody staff on the frequency of checks and/or any recommendations on the rousing of a DP are written in the custody record, in addition to being verbally passed on.

Officers and staff should not use the phrase "continue observations at the current level". HCPs and custody sergeants should specify the level of observation precisely at each review, to prevent any ambiguities.

Usually, the only intervention from the HCP during the sometimes-lengthy wait for the DP's interview is to review if the DP complains of withdrawals and offer supportive medication if indicated.

Those with alcohol dependence form the main group of DPs which require particular vigilance from the HCP – as they may not complain and suffer withdrawals in silence. Alcohol withdrawal can render some individuals unfit for interview, but most significantly acute alcohol withdrawal can be life threatening because of altered neurologic physiology. Potentially fatal seizure activity can be acute and manifest within hours of a DP's detention, even with the available medication in custody. This will not only make them unfit for interview, but also unfit for detention and require urgent transfer to the Emergency Department as this should be considered a medical emergency. Alcohol withdrawal is a well-recognized treatable cause of death in custody. Early recognition and treatment by the HCP can make management of the withdrawing alcoholic effective, by administering supportive medication and maintaining regular reviews. Management should, wherever possible, follow guidelines provided by the National Institute for Health & Care Excellence (13). More often than not, this is all that is required to enable the DP to remain FTD and FTI.

Other reasons that interviewing or custody officers may request a FTI could be a DP with acute or deteriorating MH issues. Many DPs do have MH issues sometimes associated with their lifestyles and choices, or indeed contributing to their lifestyles and choices, and sometimes apparent MH issues may be due to or exacerbated by drug or alcohol intoxication. If due to current drug or alcohol intoxication, they are unlikely to be FTI, and a period of time will be required to allow intoxicants to lower to an acceptable level before the HCP can determine if they are FTI. Certain individuals with vulnerabilities due to age, intellectual disabilities and MH issues may be FTI but need an additional safeguard of an Appropriate Adult (AA). The role of the AA is to safeguard the interests, rights, entitlements and welfare of children and vulnerable people who are suspected of a criminal offense, by ensuring that they are treated in a fair and just manner and are able to participate effectively (14). If MH issues are of more substantial concern, then consideration may be given to formal MH assessments by doctors with advice from the Approved Mental Health Professional (AMHP). The role of AMHP in the UK was created under section 18 of the Mental Health Act 2007 which amended the 1983 Act and made provision to replace the role of approved social worker (ASW).The role is broadly similar to the role of the ASW but is distinguished in no longer being the exclusive preserve of social workers and may be fulfiled by others including allied health professionals (15). Some police services have a Liaison & Diversion (L&D) Service consisting of MH nurses embedded within custody which is of great value to the HCP. Those custody suites without L&D can use the Local MH Services, and the duty AMHP should a Mental Health Act assessment be required.

It is the responsibility of the HCP to assess the mental state of the DP and how this manifests, and what action is required next. Interviewing and custody officers are reliant upon the advice of the HCP to determine the appropriateness of FTI, and what other steps need to be taken to address MH concerns.

FITNESS TO CHARGE AND FITNESS TO RELEASE

Fitness to charge the DP for an alleged offense needs to take into account similar considerations as FTI, as the DP in both cases must have capacity, and fully understand their situation. They may require an AA to be present at the time of charging.

There are some offenses which will automatically trigger the need for the HCP to undertake this assessment such as child sexual offenses, because of the increased risk of self-injury and death by suicide (16). Other reasons may be that the DP has deteriorating MH following interview and has expressed self-injury or suicidal ideation, regardless of the offense. Again, in this assessment, the HCP may consider signposting or referral to MH services as appropriate.

The above has described very briefly some of the roles of the HCP which form the basis of the first interactions that the HCP may have with DPs. These are the main components of focus to ensure that DP's welfare and clinical needs are met while in custody. All of the fitness assessment elements are fluid and require monitoring and reviewing regularly, even just to establish that they are still safe.

Other roles of the HCP focus on the purely forensic aspects of custodial medicine.

INJURY DOCUMENTATION

Injury documentation may be undertaken in written form and supplemented by body mapping using diagram templates. Increasingly, those undertaking custodial medicine will undertake photography to document injuries, and some police services areas have HCPs who have undertaken training in forensic photography and have the storage and data protection facilities and systems to undertake this method) The FFLM produces guidelines on appropriate photography (17).

INTIMATE BIOLOGICAL SAMPLING

Complainants of sexual assault will be examined at a Sexual Assault Referral Center (SARC) for examination. A suspect will be arrested and taken to the custody suite for investigation which may include biological sample taking and interview. In very general terms, swabs and samples taken from bodily orifices and intimate areas will be taken by the HCP with the consent of the DP. Clear guidelines as to the nature of care and sampling if suspects are provided and regularly updated by the FFLM (18). This requires authorization from an Inspector and consent from the suspect. The HCP must be satisfied that there are no clinical or MH contra-indications, and that the DP has capacity to consent following a full description of the procedure, so that the DP can give informed consent. Biological sampling may include penile swabs, pubic hair and blood for toxicology.

This procedure can be very emotionally traumatic for the suspect and requires a high degree of sensitivity in the approach from the HCP.

Prior the release of the DP, this will undoubtedly be preceded by the HCP and CDO confirming a fitness to release (FTR) due to the nature of the arrestable offense.

BLOOD SAMPLING FOR ROAD TRAFFIC CASES

Road Traffic Act (RTA) legislation is complex. The determination of the need for and request for blood samples in certain scenarios is proforma driven to assist the police officer undertaking the procedure and the HCP who may be requested to take the sample. This is a common reason for an HCP to provide written evidence, in the form of a statement or to give live evidence in court. Blood sampling under the RTA may be requested to take place within custody, or at the hospital. In certain circumstances, blood may be taken if the arrested person in hospital is unable to give consent, but is stored, and analyzed subsequently if consent has been given. If blood samples are required at the hospital, then the HCP with relevant training will attend (18). Treating clinicians at hospital may indicate they have no objections to the blood sampling taking place but do not take the samples themselves.

ATTENDANCE AT COURT

Any HCP should expect to give evidence at court regarding their examination of DPs. This could be regarding any of the interactions the HCP has had with the DP. Frequently, it will be in connection with blood sampling under the RTA.

Prior to being called for court, the HCP may have provided a witness statement at the request of the police. The HCP can be called by the prosecution or by the defense. In the latter case, this may be because there are matters that the defense wish to explore about the process itself, or because of queries raised by an expert witness. Often, these attendances to court are to clarify matters that may have been omitted from the witness statement.

This can be a very daunting experience for the HCP and for anyone unused to providing live evidence in court. It is because of this that the HCP really does need to have a good understanding of courtroom skills and etiquette. The HCP requires training in courtroom skills, and this is generally provided as an element in the Introduction to Clinical Forensic Medicine courses available. The HCP should ideally have this training before beginning their practice.

It is worth noting that an HCP should not generally form an opinion either in their statement, or verbally in court if they are not an expert in the field. The same

TABLE 65.2 Additional roles that certain HCPs with training may be asked to undertake

Welfare checks for children and vulnerable adults
Supply and/or administer medicines under Patient Group Directions*
Liaison with external agencies including: • Pharmacists • Social Services • Mental health services • Drugs and Alcohol Services • Homeless services
Recognition of life extinct (ROLE), if Ambulance Service, FME or patient's general medical practitioner is not available

* Patient group directions (PGDs) are written instructions to help supply or administer medicines to patients, usually in planned circumstances.

applies to forensic physicians. In general, when presenting evidence about a case seen in custodial healthcare practice, doctors, nurses and paramedics are acting as professional witnesses – they are simply reporting what they determined from their assessment, describing what injuries they documented, or what samples they took, and how. Opinion evidence can only generally be given by an expert witness who has had the opportunity to review all the evidence in a case but who did not necessarily examine the DP.

Table 65.2 identifies additional roles that certain HCPs with training may be asked to undertake.

A glossary of the main terms used in custody has been included Table 65.3.

TABLE 65.3 Glossary of terms and acronyms

AA	Appropriate Adult
AMHP	Approved Mental Health Professional
CA	Clinical Assessment
CDO	Custody Detention Officer
CJS	Criminal Justice System
CN	Custody Nurse
CoP	College of Policing
DP	Detained Person
FFLM	Faculty of Forensic and Legal Medicine.
FME	Forensic Medical Examiner
FNP	Forensic Nurse Practitioner
FTD	Fitness to Detain
FTI	Fitness to Interview
FTR	Fitness to Release
HCP	Healthcare Professional
HI	Head Injury
IOPC	Independent Office for Police Conduct
PACE	Police and Criminal Evidence Act 1984
PGD	Patient Group Direction
ROLE	Role of Life Extinct
RTA	Road Traffic Act
SARC	Sexual Assault Referral Center
UKAFN	United Kingdom Association of Forensic Nurses & Paramedics

CONCLUSION

The main universal roles standard to any police force have been described for HCPs working in custody healthcare. The extent of the role may be significantly broader dependent on the police service area and the healthcare provider.

This area of medicine is a very individual and unique area, unlike any other area – including Prison Nursing (although there are some similarities). Often the HCP is working alone and should have previous critical care experience, along with life experience to enable them to autonomously make decisions confidently and competently so that the police custody team can make decisions regarding the best way forward for that DP through the CJS. The HCP is the DP's advocate and, as such, must be able to act in the best clinical interest of the DP.

This clinical area is certainly not for all nurses and paramedics, which is understandable. It can, however, be extraordinarily rewarding as the HCP has a vital role in the multidisciplinary custody management of DPs and is often the one who spots the early clinical warning signs, understandably missed by police staff, which leads to early intervention thus avoiding serious illness, or even a death in custody. In addition to this, the HCP can, and sometimes does, provide some interaction and interventions that can make a difference to a DP's life for the better.

REFERENCES

1. Association of Police and Crime Commissioners. The role of the police & crime commissioner, 2023. Available from: https://apccs.police.uk/role-of-the-pcc/ (Accessed 16 May 2023).
2. Home Office. PACE Code C 2019. Requirements for the detention, treatment and questioning of suspects not related to terrorism in police custody, 2019. Available from: https://www.gov.uk/government/publications/pace-code-c-2019 (Accessed 16 May 2023).
3. Independent Office for Police Conducts. Deaths during or following police contact – statistics for England and Wales

2020/2021, 2021. Available from: https://www.policeconduct.gov.uk/deaths-during-or-following-police-contact-statistics-england-and-wales-202122#:~:text=In%20 2021%2F22%2C%20there%20 were,men%20and%20six%20 were%20women (Accessed 16 May 2023).
4. Peel M. Assessing fitness to detain in police custody. *Nurs Stand* 2015; 30(11): 43–9.
5. Dolphin S. *Healthcare in Police Custody for Healthcare Professionals*. Essex: Dolphin Books; 2018.
6. Faculty of Forensic & Legal Medicine. The role of the healthcare professional, 2021. Available from: https://fflm.ac.uk/wp-content/uploads/2021/02/ARCHIVED-The-Role-of-the-HCP-S-Fewkes-J-Smith-Dr-M-Stark-Jan-2019.pdf (Accessed 16 May 2023).
7. Faculty of Forensic & Legal Medicine. Quality Standards for nurses and paramedics. Available from: https://fflm.ac.uk/wp-content/uploads/2021/02/Quality-Standards-for-nurses-and-paramedics-J-Smith-Dr-M-Stark-and-Prof-I-Wall-Jan-2021.pdf (Accessed 16 May 2023).
8. College of Policing. College-run courses, programmes and other learning, 2023. Available from: https://www.college.police.uk/career-learning/learning/courses (Accessed 16 May 2023).
9. Schnieden V, Stark M, Payne-James J. Violence in clinical forensic medicine. *Med Sci Law* 1995; **35**(**4**): 333–5.
10. Wesson DR, Ling W. The clinical opiate withdrawal scale (COWS). *J Psychoactive Drugs* 2003; **35**(**2**): 253–9.
11. Sullivan JT, Sykora K, Schneiderman J, et al. Assessment of alcohol withdrawal: The revised clinical institute withdrawal assessment for alcohol scale (CIWA-Ar). *Br J Addict* 1998; **84**(**11**): 1353–7.
12. College of Policing. Detention and custody, 2023. Available from: https://www.college.police.uk/app/detention-and-custody (Accessed 16 May 2023).
13. National Institute for Health and Care Excellence. Alcohol-use disorders: diagnosis and management of physical complications, 2017. Available from: https://www.nice.org.uk/guidance.cg100/chapter/Recommendations#acute-alcohol-withdrawal (Accessed 16 May 2023).
14. National Appropriate Adult Network. What is an appropriate adult? Available from: https://www.appropriateadult.org.uk/ (Accessed 1 June 2023)
15. Legislation.gov.uk. Mental Health Act 2007, 2011. Available from: https://www.legislation.gov.uk/ukpga/2007/12/contents (Accessed 16 May 2023).
16. Phillips J, et al. *Non-natural deaths following prison and police custody. Data and practice issues. Equality and Human Rights Commission Research Report 106*. Sheffield Hallam University. University of Cambridge; 2016.
17. Faculty of Forensic & Legal Medicine. PICS Working Group. Guidelines on photography, 2022. Available from: https://fflm.ac.uk/wp-content/uploads/2020/03/PICS-Working-Group-Guidelines-on-Photography-Dr-Will-Anderson-Dec-2019.pdf (Accessed 16 May 2023).
18. Faculty of Forensic & Legal Medicine. Recommendations for the collection of forensic specimens from complainants and suspects, 2022. Available from: https://fflm.ac.uk/wp-content/uploads/2022/01/Recommendations-for-the-collection-of-forensic-specimens-FSSC-Jan-2022.pdf (Accessed 16 May 2023).
19. Faculty of Forensic & Legal Medicine. Drug-driving competencies, 2018. Available from: https://fflm.ac.uk/wp-content/uploads/2021/10/ARCHIVED-Drug-Driving-Competencies-Dr-Will-Anderson-Feb-2018.pdf (Accessed 16 May 2023).

FURTHER READING AND USEFUL WEBSITES

Advisory Council on the Misuse of Drugs (ACMD). Available from: www.gov.uk/government/organisations/advisory-council-on-the-misuse-of-drugs/ (Accessed 28 August 2023).

College of Policing. www.college.police.uk (Accessed 28 August 2023).

Faculty of Forensic and Legal Medicine of the Royal College of Physicians https://fflm.ac.uk (Accessed 28 August 2023).

Faculty of Forensic & Legal Medicine. Quality Standards for Nurses and Paramedics – General Forensic Medicine (GFM), March, 2021. https://fflm.ac.uk/resources/publications/fflm-quality-standards-for-nurses-and-paramedics-general-forensic-medicine-gfm / (Accessed 28 August 2023).

General Medical Council (GMC). www.gmc-uk.org (Accessed 28 August 2023).

Gorton A, Stark M. *Drug Driving Competencies*. Faculty of Forensics & Legal Medicine, 2018. Available from: https://fflm.ac.uk/wp-content/uploads/2021/10/FFLM-Drug-Driving-Competencies-Prof-M-Stark-Dr-A-Gorton-Oct-2021.pdf (Accessed 28 August 2023).

Nursing and Midwifery Council (NMC). https://www.nmc.org.uk/ (Accessed 28 August 2023).

Peel M. Alcohol Withdrawal: Introduction. *UK Association of Forensic Nurses and Paramedics*. Issue 14, Spring 2018.

Police and Criminal Evidence Act Code C – Revised Aug 2019. PCE Code C 2019 – https://www.gov.uk/government/publications/pace-code-c-2019 (Accessed 28 August 2023).

United Kingdom Association of Forensic Nurse and Paramedics. https://ukafn.org (Accessed 28 August 2023).

CHAPTER

66

Fitness to Detain & Fitness to Interview

Ian Francis Wall

FITNESS FOR DETENTION INTRODUCTION

This chapter will consider the detention of persons in police custody and refer to them as detainees (sometimes referred to as detained persons). In whatever jurisdiction the detention occurs, the basic principles of medical assessment are the same and the Istanbul Protocol (1) makes it clear that anyone detained in custody should receive healthcare of the same standard as they would have received were they not in custody. Furthermore, detainees also have the right to have prescribed medication continued while in custody, providing it is safe to do so.

Provision of healthcare in police custody has changed over the last several years and in the United Kingdom (UK), custodial healthcare is increasingly provided by nurses and paramedics and many police custody suites now have healthcare professionals resident in custody.

LIAISON WITH CUSTODY STAFF

Whether a doctor, nurse or paramedic examines the detainee, it is essential that the care and safety of the detainee should be paramount; any forensic issues are secondary. On arrival at the police station or place of detention, the forensic practitioner should obtain as much background information as possible and preliminary information should be obtained from the custody officer and custody record including the police risk assessment. Table 66.1 summarizes the information which should be obtained.

If the detainee has previously been in custody or has been seen by a forensic practitioner earlier in this detention, it is important to try and access relevant information and consideration should also be given to obtaining information from relatives, general practitioner (primary care physician) or other healthcare providers. In some jurisdictions and subject to consent, it is often possible to directly access a detainee's computerized health records, sometimes the complete health record or alternatively summaries of care.

The duration of detention will vary from jurisdiction to jurisdiction. In England and Wales, detention is governed by the Police and Criminal Evidence Act (PACE) legislation (2). Initial detention is limited to 24 hours before charge or production to court but the detention period is regularly reviewed at predetermined intervals with the maximum period of detention being 96 hours before charge or release. There are some differences in duration of detention for persons detained under terrorism legislation.

VENUE FOR THE ASSESSMENT

It is always preferable to examine a detainee in a medical room and consideration will need to be given to the use of a chaperone (3). However, it may be necessary in some circumstances to examine the detainee in a cell if there is a concern for the safety of the forensic practitioner. An example may be a detainee who is violent, and for whom it might only be possible to make observations through a cell door hatch. If a detainee refuses to come out of the cell for a medical assessment, the practitioner should go to the cell and speak to the detainee in person and clarify issues of consent, whether the detainee is actually refusing a medical assessment or indeed whether an assessment might be required on a best interests basis. All such contact should be documented contemporaneously.

CONSENT

After explaining the nature and purpose of the assessment, the practitioner should first establish consent and whether the detainee has capacity to consent to an examination taking into account factors such as the age of the detainee, current intoxication with drugs and/or alcohol, and mental health diagnoses. In an emergency situation, a practitioner may need to undertake an assessment and carry out any necessary treatment in the detainee's best interests. As well as a medical examination, consent from a person detained in custody may also need to include specific activities as shown in Table 66.2.

DOI: 10.1201/9781003138754-69

TABLE 66.1 Information to be sought prior to assessment of detainee
Reason for a clinical assessment
Time and reason for arrest
Whether any force was used during the arrest, e.g. handcuffs, batons, dogs, irritant sprays, conducted energy devices
Any warning markers that might be on police record systems
Whether anything relevant has been found on the detainee's person or property, e.g. prescribed or illicit drugs, drug paraphernalia, warning bracelets
If the detainee will be interviewed
Likely duration of the detention
Any specific concerns about the detainee's demeanor or behavior
Any concerns about risks to the personal safely of the forensic practitioner

TABLE 66.2 Activities for which consent should be sought from the detainee
Access to healthcare records
Taking forensic samples
Provision of a statement for court purposes
Contacting the detainee's GP
Making a safeguarding referral
Sharing information with other healthcare professionals and custody staff as necessary during the period of detention

HISTORY

A comprehensive medical history should be obtained which should include:

- Details of any current medical problems and whether an injury has been sustained and when.
- Past medical history and allergies.
- Past psychiatric history including any history of self-harm.
- Medication including prescribed, over-the-counter and illicit drugs noting the dose, duration and when each was last taken. For illicit drugs, it is also important to note the quantity taken on an average day and the route of administration.
- Alcohol intake including specific details of consumption in the last 24 hours and weekly alcohol intake. For those detainees who might be dependent on alcohol, enquiry should be made of any history of alcohol withdrawal symptoms including seizures.
- Educational and social history, the former being to assess for learning disabilities and difficulties.

Detailed contemporaneous notes should be made of the history. A proforma can be helpful (4).

Reliability of histories

It is known that some detainees, particularly those that misuse drugs, may not give reliable information, especially in terms of drug use. For a drug such as methadone, where risk of serious consequences of over prescribing can be fatal, it is important to try and obtain some form of external validation of the dose being prescribed. An explanation from the healthcare professional that they are independent of the police and building a rapport with the detainee is therefore important and may lead to more reliable information being given. One study (5) has shown that detainees with substance use disorders have negative perceptions of their medical care while in police custody.

Physical examination

The nature and extent of the clinical examination will partly depend on the history obtained and the circumstances relating to the arrest and detention. Best practice, as a minimum, should include:

- Assessment of conscious level and for any signs of drug or alcohol withdrawal.
- Measurement of pulse, blood pressure, oxygen saturation, respiratory rate, temperature and assessment of confusion. This would then allow the completion of the National Early Warning Score (NEWS2) (6).
- Measurement of pupil size and whether nystagmus is present.
- A brief assessment of mental state and self-harm risk.

In many circumstances, it will be necessary for a systems examination which might include examination of the heart, lungs, abdomen and a full neurologic examination or a more detailed assessment of mental state. If a history of use of force or injury has been obtained, body surfaces and joints should be examined and any injuries noted on body diagrams. Again, detailed medical notes should be made.

Assessment of any degree of alcohol or opiate withdrawal may be assisted by the use of the Clinical Institute Withdrawal Assessment for Alcohol (CIWA-Ar) (7) and the Clinical Opiate Withdrawal Scale (COWS) (8) respectively (*see* Chapter 65 – "The Role of the Custody Nurse and Paramedic"). Although the former has not been validated in the custody setting, it is useful as a baseline and particularly if the detainee requires repeat assessments. Significant levels of withdrawal will need treatment in the custodial setting to ensure the detainee remains fit for detention.

NEWS2 scores have been used in the acute hospital setting and have been shown to be effective with improved patient outcomes and lives saved (9). It has been suggested that the use of a modified score in the custody setting by non-medical police custody staff might help identify acutely unwell detainees. However, Miles and colleagues (10) studied a proposed Custody Early Warning Score (CEWS) and concluded "*The scoring systems that we assessed were not sensitive enough to identify health need in the detainee population, due to frequent, altered physiological parameters. Life-threatening conditions have low assessment scores, not reflective of the seriousness of medical conditions, nor the potential for rapid deterioration. Such scoring systems add little to the risk-assessment process, with low scores allowing for complacency and a false reassurance, when using a system designed for very different circumstances.*"

An assessment of mental state will help identify self-harm risk which is known to be increased (11) for a variety of reasons including during alcohol withdrawal, for sex offenders (12) and women during the early period of prison custody.

Management plan

At the conclusion of the medical examination the healthcare professional should give verbal advice to the custody officer responsible for the detainee's care as to whether the detainee is fit for detention and interview. The advice should be confirmed in writing (13) and should include levels of observation, any medical needs of the detainee, risk of self-harm and whether a medical review is necessary.

SPECIAL CONSIDERATIONS

Children and young people

The United Nations Convention on the Rights of the Child (UNHCR) (14) defines a child as everyone under 18, "unless under the law applicable to the child, majority is attained earlier". Age of consent may vary in different jurisdictions and the age of capacity to consent to medical as opposed to forensic examinations may also differ.

Special consideration needs to be given to children and young people in custody as they are likely to have complex needs and where there might be a risk of exploitation. Again, it will be important to take a detailed history of substance misuse particularly as poly drug use is common (15), and also any details of comorbid psychiatric problems such as attention deficit hyperactivity disorder (ADHD), and autistic spectrum disorder.

Attention will also need to be given to safeguarding the needs of the young person and a safeguarding referral must be made if there is concern that a child or young person is suffering or likely to suffer harm or is required by law.

Pregnancy and substance dependence

It is important to consider whether any female detainee of childbearing age might be pregnant, particularly if the woman has a history of alcohol or drug intoxication or withdrawal, in view of the risk to the fetus. With consent, a pregnancy test should be taken and the threshold for deciding whether a pregnant detainee should remain in police custody should be low. The FFLM (16) have identified a number of red flags which would require hospital assessment of the pregnant detainee.

Intellectual disabilities

The World Health Organization defines learning disability as "*a condition of arrested or incomplete development of the mind, which is especially characterised by impairment of skills manifested during the developmental period, skills which contribute to the overall level of intelligence, i.e. cognitive, language, motor and social abilities*". The term "intellectual disability" may also be used. This definition covers people with a broad range of disabilities and there is evidence that the identification of people with learning disabilities by police custody staff and custody healthcare staff is poor (17). Appropriate safeguards will need to be put in place to protect the detainee and these are considered in fitness to interview.

Persons detained on suspicion of terrorist offenses

Persons detained on suspicion of terrorist offenses pose special problems and are more likely to be detained for longer periods. In the UK, guidance on how these detainees should be managed has been based on the experience of doctors in Northern Ireland in "*The Troubles*" and it is recommended that detainees should have an automatic medical assessment on detention including a detailed assessment for any injuries plus a daily medical assessment and a medical assessment on any occasion they may need to leave the place of detention; this being partly to ensure that the detainee is not being subject to abuse or torture (18).

COMMON MEDICAL PROBLEMS

Cardiovascular disease

For any specific medical problem, a more detailed history should be taken and consideration given to making a physical examination of that system. Hypertension, heart disease and deep vein thrombosis (DVT) are common problems in the custody setting. Any prescribed medication should normally be continued and detainees allowed to keep their angina sprays with them unless they pose a self-harm risk. Any detainee with chest pain that is not relieved by an angina spray or lasts more than 15 minutes should be transferred to hospital via a 999 ambulance, not in the back of a police vehicle. It is important to be particularly cautious of a young detainee who develops chest pain, as it is known that cocaine misuse is associated with premature ischemic heart disease. Substance misuse detainees who inject drugs intravenously are at a high risk of DVT and pulmonary embolism.

Epilepsy

A history of seizures is common in the custodial setting and seizures can have numerous causes. A detailed history should be taken to include type of seizure, frequency of seizure, last seizure, triggers and any medications usually taken. It must also be noted if the seizures occur as a result of alcohol or benzodiazepine withdrawal.

As missed doses of anti-epileptic drugs may result in an increase in seizures, it is important to ensure that detainees receive their drugs in a timely manner. Any detainee who has a first-ever seizure or a second seizure while in custody should be transferred to hospital. The FFLM give detailed guidance on the management of detainees who have seizures including the management of an acute seizure (19).

Asthma

This can usually be managed in the custodial setting and again, asthma sufferers should normally be allowed to keep their asthma inhalers with them. If the asthma worsens, a detailed assessment is required including measurement of NEWS2 score, listening to the chest and measuring peak flow. A decision can then be made as to whether transfer to hospital is necessary.

Diabetes

It is recommended that all detainees who are diabetic should have a blood glucose measurement as soon as possible in their detention. A history will need to be taken to ascertain if the detainee's diabetes is managed by diet alone, medication or insulin. The level of diabetic control should be ascertained along with the presence of any diabetic complications. A clinical examination should then be undertaken with measurement of vital signs. Blood or urine testing for ketones should also be considered. A detailed management plan should be given to custody staff to include diet, medications/insulin requirements, symptoms and signs that might indicate that the diabetic control is deteriorating along with the need for blood glucose measurements and a medical review.

Two problems likely to be encountered are those of hypo- and hyperglycemia. If the blood glucose measures between 2 and 4 mmol/L glucose should be administered as either a drink, gel or carbohydrate foodstuff. For those who are unable to swallow or are unconscious, glucagon intramuscularly or glucose intravenously should be given. However, it must be remembered that detainees with chronic alcohol or liver problems may have poor glycogen stores and may not respond to glucagon. The healthcare professional should remain with the detainee until they are conscious and the management plan revisited.

Managing the detainee whose diabetes is treated with insulin can be problematic. Consideration should be given to supervising insulin injections. Most diabetics have their insulin before meals but the difficulty in the custodial setting is that detainees can sometimes be manipulative and refuse to eat after having insulin. It may therefore be advisable to encourage diabetics to eat first and then to administer their insulin. The FFLM (20) recommend that if the blood glucose is greater than 25 mmol/L and there is evidence of impairment of consciousness, confusion or concurrent infection, the detainee should be transferred to hospital. Safe practice would also mean that a detainee with a blood glucose greater than 30 mmol/L should also be transferred to hospital. Additionally, the FFLM guidance also gives advice on how detainees who are on Continuous Subcutaneous Insulin Infusion (insulin pumps) can be managed.

Mental health and self-harm

Mental health problems are very common in the custodial setting. In England and Wales, a mental disorder is defined as any disorder or disability of the mind (21). A risk assessment should be undertaken by the custody officer and this may identify a possible mental health problem following which the detainee should be seen by a healthcare professional. Mental illness and drug misuse often co-exist and the latter can cause a worsening of the mental state.

A mental state examination is important medicolegally; for example, a psychosis which may have been drug induced can have implications for fitness for interview. Following the initial assessment, it may be necessary for an opinion to be obtained from a psychiatrist. Special measures may need to be put in place to protect the individual, such as an "appropriate adult" who can advise the detainee during questioning to ensure that they understand what is happening and why.

Self-injury is particularly common in the custodial setting and an assessment of risk of self-injury should be made for all detainees. Measures should be put in place to minimize the risk with appropriate levels of observation, follow-up and if needs be, further assessment by a psychiatrist. A pre-release risk assessment may also be required.

Acute behavioral disturbance

Acute Behavioral Disturbance (ABD) is an umbrella a term for the clinical presentation of several conditions and may occur secondary to substance use, physical or mental illness. It has a wide differential diagnosis. In the past the term "Excited Delirium Syndrome" has been used for the extreme form of the condition but as many deaths have occurred in cases where there has been no evidence of delirium, it is considered best to concentrate on the recognition of ABD in general and how those most at risk of significant morbidity and mortality can be identified and managed. Detainees with this condition should not be brought to police custody but instead taken directly to a hospital Emergency Department (ED). However, the diagnosis should be suspected if a detainee exhibits the following physical signs: tactile hyperthermia, constant or near constant physical activity and extreme agitation/aggression. In this situation, immediate transfer to an ED by ambulance is mandatory. Consideration for a police vehicle transfer should only be considered if an emergency ambulance is not available. FFLM guidance (22) also gives advice about de-escalation and consideration of prescribing oral Lorazepam prior to transfer.

Dietary problems

Healthcare professionals may need to advise on detainees' dietary requirements which may be necessary for religious, cultural or medical reasons. This is particularly important for diabetics or those with specific dietary problems such as nut allergy.

Healthcare advice will also be required for detainees who refuse food and this can be problematic with insulin-dependent diabetics and especially those who might be detained for a prolonged period. It is recommended that persons detained on terrorism offenses should be weighed on detention and Body Mass Index calculated in case they go on a hunger strike.

Injuries

A history should be taken in relation to how any injury was sustained and whether it was sustained before, during or after arrest. Many injuries can be managed in the custodial setting but transfer to hospital may be required for wound toilet and closure or for X-rays.

A particular problem in custody is the detainee who has sustained a head injury (defined as any trauma to the head, other than superficial injuries to the face). Again, a detailed history of how the injury was sustained should be obtained with specific note of whether there has been any loss of consciousness, amnesia, vomiting and seizure. A physical examination should be carried out including, as a minimum, pupillary size/reaction, Glasgow Coma Score (or some other recognized level of consciousness), any obvious limb weakness, pulse, blood pressure and blood glucose along with documentation of the injury. The National Institute for Health and Care Excellence (23) has issued guidance on the assessment and early management of people who have sustained a head injury which has been adapted for the custody setting by the FFLM (24). It includes detailed guidance on history taking and advice for the custody officer as well as the detainee.

Conducted energy devices

A Conducted Energy Device (CED) is the generic term for devices commonly referred to as TASER™. A CED Joint Working Group (25) was established in 2020 and has produced detailed guidance of the clinical assessment and management of persons who have been subject to TASER™ discharge.

FITNESS FOR INTERVIEW INTRODUCTION

Healthcare professionals are often required to assess a detainee and give an opinion on fitness to interview (FTI). As fitness can change through the course of the period of detention, it is therefore important to ascertain the likely period of detention. A detainee might be unfit for a variety of reasons and a useful definition of when a detainee might be at risk in an interview is if (2):

- "Conducting the interview could significantly harm the detainee's physical or mental state
- Anything the detainee says in the interview about their involvement or suspected involvement in the offense about which they are being interviewed *might* be considered unreliable in subsequent court proceedings because of their physical or mental state."

The PACE Act Code C stresses that "*it is essential healthcare professionals who are consulted consider the functional ability of the detainee rather than simply relying on a medical diagnosis, e.g. it is possible for a person with severe mental illness to be fit for interview*". In addition, the guidance also advises the following should be considered:

- "How the detainee's physical or mental state might affect their ability to understand the nature and purpose of the interview, to comprehend what is being asked and to appreciate the significance of any answers given and make rational decisions about whether they want to say anything.
- The extent to which the detainee's replies may be affected by their physical or mental condition rather

than representing a rational and accurate explanation of their involvement in the offense.
- How the nature of the interview, which could include particularly probing questions, might affect the detainee".

False confessions

Individuals can be vulnerable for a variety of reasons and are at risk of making false or misleading statements to the police. If adequate safeguards are put in place, this will enable rebuttal of possible defense claims that any confession should be ruled inadmissible because the detainee was unfit for interview. In some jurisdictions, for example, Scotland, confession evidence alone cannot be used to secure a conviction but instead, corroboration is required.

There are various types of false confessions and psychologists have divided them into five different types: voluntary, accommodating-compliant, coerced-compliant, coerced-reactive and coerced-internalized. Knowledge of the main features of these different types of confession will enable healthcare professionals to recognize an individual who might be susceptible to one and to allow adequate safeguards to be put in place.

A voluntary false confession is one which has been given freely without any coercion or pressure from the interviewer. There are a variety of reasons why this might occur such as a psychotic individual who cannot distinguish fact from fantasy, to prevent investigation of a more serious crime or even a desire to be famous.

An accommodating-compliant is where an individual falsely confesses to a crime in an interview which is non-coercive because the detainee thinks it is important to believe what the police might be asserting borne out of a wish to be liked.

A coerced-compliant is where a person knows they have not committed a crime but falsely confesses when put under pressure during a police interview. Substance users are at risk of this type of confession. Again, there are several reasons why this might occur such as a desire to end the interview or be released from custody.

A coerced-internalized is where the individual falsely distrusts their own memory or has no memory of events and comes to accept a false scenario put to them by the police and believes that they have committed the crime.

A coerced-reactive confession is due to pressure from outside influences other than the police such as family, friends and acquaintances and may include the fear of consequences of not confessing.

ASSESSING FITNESS FOR INTERVIEW

It is therefore important to identify detainees who are vulnerable and who may be at risk of false confessions. Police custody detention and interview is a highly stressful situation and both the physical and mental health needs of the detainee must be assessed. FTI is a dynamic situation that can change with time and it will be necessary to advise on whether the person's condition might improve, change or be amenable to treatment and, if so, when. For example, treating a detainee's alcohol withdrawal may lead to a window of opportunity when the person is FTI; however, a person who has dementia may never be FTI. Identifying a vulnerable individual should then lead to advising on the risks of unreliability and consideration of what measures can be put in place to protect the detainee. In England and Wales an "Appropriate Adult" (AA) can be recommended whose responsibility is to safeguard the rights, entitlements and welfare of the vulnerable person.

Norfolk (26) advises that consideration needs to be given to the personality traits of the detainee and those factors that might increase the risk of a false confession (suggestibility, acquiescence and compliance), the health of the detainee, the characteristics of the interview (a person arrested on suspicion of murder is much more likely to be subject to challenging questioning and repeat interviews) and the totality of the circumstances.

The assessment should include:

- Background information
- General medical and psychiatric history
- Enquiry about drugs and alcohol
- Assessment of learning disability
- Enquiry about when the detainee last ate and slept
- Any social distractions, e.g. child care issues

An examination should then take place as described in fitness for detention above with a greater emphasis on mental state examination. At the conclusion of the assessment, the healthcare professional should then be able to conclude whether the detainee is FTI, for how long, whether any treatment is necessary and whether any special measures need to be put in place to safeguard the detainee.

Two important judgments have helped clarify the position in England and Wales and highlight the complexity of the issues and the need for a careful assessment of both physical and mental health problems. In *R v Aspinall* (27), the interviewee was a person with schizophrenia whose mental state was felt to be normal at the time of the interview which went ahead without an AA, the Court of Appeal held that even though Aspinall was lucid during interview, he should have been afforded the protection of an AA because he was vulnerable due to his mental health problems. In a different case (28), a detainee exhibiting mild drug withdrawal may still be FTI and the Court of Appeal held that the fact that an addict was withdrawing and might have a reason to confess does not necessarily render the confession unreliable. These judgments do mean that it is essential that a comprehensive assessment be made at the time of the interview.

CONCLUSION

Persons detained in police custody are vulnerable and often have complex physical and mental health problems. It is essential they have access to the same standard of care as persons not in custody.

A scheme for assessment of fitness for detention is outlined including liaison with other staff, the most appropriate place for assessment, consent, history taking, physical examination and the need for a management plan. Detainees who are especially vulnerable are discussed and access to helpful guidance documents are referenced.

A range of common medical problems that require particularly careful management or management that might be slightly different to those who are not in detention is outlined.

The problem of FTI and the risks of false confessions are also an important part of the management of detainees and a scheme for assessing fitness for interview is discussed.

REFERENCES

1. United Nations Human Rights, Office of the High Commissioner. *Istanbul Protocol: Manual on the Effective Investigation and Documentation of Torture and Other Cruel, Inhuman or Degrading Treatment or Punishment*, 2022. Available from: https://www.ohchr.org/sites/default/files/documents/publications/2022-06-29/Istanbul-Protocol_Rev2_EN.pdf (Accessed 17 May 2023).
2. Home Office. Police and Criminal Evidence Act 1984 (PACE). *Code of Practice for the Detention, Treatment and Questioning of Persons by Police Officers, 2019*. Available from: https://assets.publishing.service.gov.uk/government/uploads/system/uploads/attachment_data/file/903473/pace-code-c-2019.pdf (Accessed 17 May 2023).
3. General Medical Council. *Intimate Examinations and Chaperones*, 2023. Available from: https://www.gmc-uk.org/ethical-guidance/ethical-guidance-for-doctors/intimate-examinations-and-chaperones/intimate-examinations-and-chaperones#paragraph-8 (Accessed 17 May 2023).
4. Faculty of Forensic & Legal Medicine. *Fitness to Detain and Interview*, 2022. Available from: https://fflm.ac.uk/wp-content/uploads/2022/04/Fitness-for-detention-and-interview-Prof-I-Wall-April-2022.pdf (Accessed 17 May 2023).
5. Gregory M. Characteristics of drug misusers in custody and their perception of medical care. *J Forensic Leg Med* 2007; **14**; 209–12.
6. Royal College of Physicians. *National Early Warning Score (NEWS) 2: Standardising the Assessment of Acute Illness Severity in the NHS*, 2017. Available from: https://www.rcplondon.ac.uk/projects/outputs/national-early-warning-score-news-2 (Accessed 17 May 2023).
7. Sullivan JT, Sykora K, Schneiderman J, et al. Assessment of alcohol withdrawal: The revised clinical institute withdrawal assessment for alcohol scale (CIWA-Ar). *Br J Addict* 1989; **84(11)**: 1353–7.
8. Wesson DR, Ling W. The Clinical Opiate Withdrawal scale (COWS). *J Psychoactive Drugs* 2003; **35**(2): 253–9.
9. Care Quality Commission. *New Fundamental Standards; Part-3. The Standards*, 2018. Available from: https://www.cqc.org.uk/what-we-do/how-we-do-our-job/fundamental-standards (Accessed 17 May 2023).
10. Miles T, Webb V, Kevern P, et al. Custody early warning scores; Do they predict patient deterioration in police custody. *J Forensic Leg Med* 2020; **76**: 102069.
11. National Institute for Health and Care Excellence. Scope. Mental health of adults in contact with the criminal justice system: identification and management of mental health problems and integration of care for adults in contact with the criminal justice system. November 2014. Available from: https://www.nice.org.uk/guidance/ng66/documents/mental-health-of-adults-in-contact-with-the-criminal-justice-system-final-scope2 (Accessed 19 July 2023).
12. Independent Office for Police Conduct. *Deaths During or Following Police Contact: Statistics for England and Wales*, 2020–21. Available from: https://policeconduct.gov.uk/deaths-during-or-following-police-contact-statistics-england-and-wales-2020–21 (Accessed 17 May 2023).
13. Hannan M, Hearnden I, Grace K, Bucke T. *Deaths in or Following Police Custody: An examination of the cases 1998/99–2008/09*, 2010. Available from: http://data.parliament.uk/DepositedPapers/Files/DEP2012-1687/Deaths_In_Custody_Report_0811.pdf (Accessed 17 May 2023).
14. UNICEEF. *The United Nations Convention of the Rights of the Child*. Available from: https://downloads.unicef.org.uk/wp-content/uploads/2010/05/UNCRC_united_nations_convention_on_the_rights_of_the_child.pdf (Accessed 17 May 2023).
15. Sondhi A, Williams E. Health needs and comorbidity among detainees in contact with healthcare professionals within police custody across London Metropolitan Police Service area. *J Forensic Leg Med* 2018; **57**: 96–100.
16. Faculty of Forensic and Legal Medicine. *Management of the Pregnant Drug and/or Alcohol Dependent Patients in Police Custody*, 2020. Available from: https://fflm.ac.uk/wp-content/uploads/2020/12/ARCHIVED-Guidelines-Management-of-Pregnant-Drug-andor-Alcohol-Dependent-May-2013.pdf (Accessed 17 May 2023).
17. HMICFRS. *A Joint Inspection of the Treatment of Offenders with Learning Disabilities within the Criminal Justice System*, 2014. Available from: https://www.justiceinspectorates.gov.uk/hmicfrs/publications/joint-inspection-of-the-treatment-of-offenders-with-learning-disabilities-within-the-criminal-justice-system/ (Accessed 17 May 2023).
18. Faculty of Forensic & Legal Medicine. *Medical Care of Persons Detained under the Terrorism Act 2000*, 2022. Available from: https://fflm.ac.uk/wp-content/uploads/2020/12/Medical-Care-for-Persons-Detained-Under-the-Terrorism-Act-2000-TACT_May19.pdf (Accessed 17 May 2023).
19. Faculty of Forensic & Legal Medicine. *Management of Epilepsy in Police Custody*, 2022. Available from: https://fflm.ac.uk/wp-content/uploads/2022/10/ARCHIVED-Management-of-Epilepsy-in-Police-Custody-March-2019.pdf (Accessed 17 May 2023).
20. Faculty of Forensic & Legal Medicine. *Management of Diabetes Mellitus in Police Custody*, 2023. Available from: https://fflm.ac.uk/wp-content/uploads/2020/04/Management-of-Diabetes-in-Custody-Dr-K-Morrison-April-2020.pdf (Accessed 17 May 2023).
21. Legislation.gov.uk. Mental Health Act 2007. Available from: https://www.legislation.gov.uk/ukpga/2007/12/contents (Accessed 17 May 2023).
22. Faculty of Forensic & Legal Medicine. *Acute Behavioural Disturbance (ABD): Guidelines on Management in Police Custody*. Available from: https://fflm.ac.uk/wp-content/uploads/2022/10/ABD-Guidelines-on-Management-in-Police-Custody-Oct-2022.pdf (Accessed 17 May 2023).
23. National Institute for Health and Care Excellence. *Head injury: Assessment and Early Management*, 2019. Available

from: https://www.nice.org.uk/guidance/cg176 (Accessed 17 May 2023).

24. Faculty of Forensic & Legal Medicine. *Head Injury Advice Leaflet for Custody Officers, Goalers & Detention Officers*, 2023. Available from: https://fflm.ac.uk/wp-content/uploads/2019/12/Head-injury-warning-Advice-to-custody-officers-gaolers-detention-officers-Prof-J-Payne-James-and-Prof-P-Marks-Dec-2019.pdf (Accessed 17 May 2023).
25. Faculty of Forensic & Legal Medicine. *Conducted Energy device (TASER™): At a Glance Guidance for Police Custody*, 2022. Available from: https://fflm.ac.uk/wp-content/uploads/2021/08/CED-At-a-Glance-Guidance-for-Police-Custody-Aug-21.pdf (Accessed 17 May 2023).
26. Norfolk GA. Fit to be interviewed by the police: An aid to assessment. *Med Sci Law* 2001; **41**: 5–12.
27. *R v Aspinall* (Paul James) (1999) MHLR 12.
28. *R v Crampton.* Court of Appeal (Criminal division) (1990) *The Times Law Report*, 22 November 1990.

CHAPTER

67

Traffic Medicine

Margaret Stark and Vanita Parekh

INTRODUCTION

The report, *A Further Decade of Action for Road Safety 2021–2030* has been proposed by the UN General Assembly with the aim of preventing 50 percent of road traffic deaths and injuries. The number of road traffic deaths remains high with 1.35 million people killed every year and 50 million people injured worldwide. This initiative follows on from *The Decade of Action for Road Safety* over the period 2011–2020 (1). Table 67.1 describes the death rates from motor vehicle related collisions per jurisdiction (2).

TABLE 67.1 Estimated road traffic death rate (per 100 000 population), 2010/2019

Country	Death Rate 2010/2019
Australia	6.1/4.94
Brazil	22.5/16.05
Dominican Republic	41.7/64.6
France	6.4/5.13
Germany	4.7/3.78
New Zealand	9.1/9.57
Netherlands	3.93.98
Pakistan	17.4/13.01
Portugal	11.8/13.01
Russian Federation	18.6/12
South Africa	31.9/22.22
Spain	5.4/3.91
Sweden	3/3.14
Thailand	38.1/32.21
UK	3.7/3.21
USA	11.4/12.67
Vanuatu	16.3/14.86
Venezuela	37.2/39.02

TRAFFIC MEDICINE AS A MEDICAL SPECIALTY

Traffic medicine is a medical discipline concerning the prevention of harm from motor vehicle collisions and making driving as safe as possible. It includes many healthcare disciplines such as primary care, trauma surgery, ophthalmology, specialist medical physicians particularly sleep/respiratory, neurology, endocrinology, and occupational therapists; indeed almost all healthcare disciplines have a role to play from reporting unsafe drivers, to treating and managing those affected by motor vehicle collisions (3).

Police investigators, engineers, motor vehicle designers and researchers have a vital role to play in the prevention of harm and those undertaking traffic medicine roles must work collaboratively with experts from many fields of practice (4,5). Forensic medical practitioners may be required to provide advice and evidence in several settings including criminal, coronial and civil court systems, as well as to road transport authorities, driver licensing and insurance agencies.

A forensic physician may undertake many of the duties required in traffic medicine, other medical specialists may undertake some of these roles including:

- Attendance at the scene of motor vehicle fatalities, for the purposes of assisting police and other crash investigators particularly in medically related collisions and certifying life extinct
- Providing expert reports regarding the nature and significance of injuries sustained during motor vehicle collisions
- Providing evidence regarding the ability to be in proper control of a motor vehicle and to drive safely in the presence of a variety of medical conditions. This may include in criminal and coronial proceedings
- Providing evidence regarding the ability to be in proper control of a motor vehicle and to drive safely in the presence of a variety of medications and illicit substances, including alcohol
- Undertaking medical examination and collection of blood samples in drivers at the request of police. This may be used as evidence of impairment in criminal matters

DOI: 10.1201/9781003138754-70

- Proving opinion evidence on the potential medical reasons for failing to provide samples (breath, blood and/or urine) for analysis (6)

VEHICLE TYPES AND HUMAN ERROR

There are many types of motor vehicle, all of which can cause injury. By far the commonest contributing factor in motor vehicle collisions is human error (7); in 93 percent of investigated crashes 57 percent of those showed human error was the sole cause (8).

The nature and significance of injury is human and vehicle dependent. Vehicle design is constantly improving to minimize injury to drivers, passengers and pedestrians, design features include increases in structural integrity and passive measures such as seat belts and airbags.

To negate the effects of human error, vehicle safety features are rapidly emerging and developing such as anti-lock braking systems, electronic braking systems, electronic stability control, adaptive cruise control, autonomous emergency braking systems, lane departure warning and front underrun protection are rapidly becoming standard features in private and commercial vehicles.

WHAT ATTITUDES, KNOWLEDGE, SKILLS AND BEHAVIOR ARE REQUIRED FOR SAFE DRIVING?

Safe driving of a motor vehicle is a complex task requiring appropriate attitudes, knowledge, skills and behavior. Motor vehicles are potential weapons, acceptance of the danger associated with motor vehicles requires insight. Most jurisdictions require a knowledge base prior to driving which is assessed before the learning of practical on-road skills can be undertaken; with on-road experience the skills required for safe driving are consolidated. Aggressive and risk-taking behaviors are a common finding in collisions involving younger drivers (9,10).

Driving is a complex task which places demands on vision, rapid decision making, planning, tracking, vigilance, reaction time, coordination and gross motor activity. Most importantly, driving requires the ability to divide attention between several competing tasks such as steering a vehicle, observing, and obeying traffic signals and observing pedestrians simultaneously.

Preventable human factors in collisions pertinent to traffic medicine include:

- Alcohol use
- Drug use
- Fatigue
- Medical conditions including those affecting sensory input, executive and motor function. Certain medical conditions are reportable to most jurisdictional driver licensing authorities

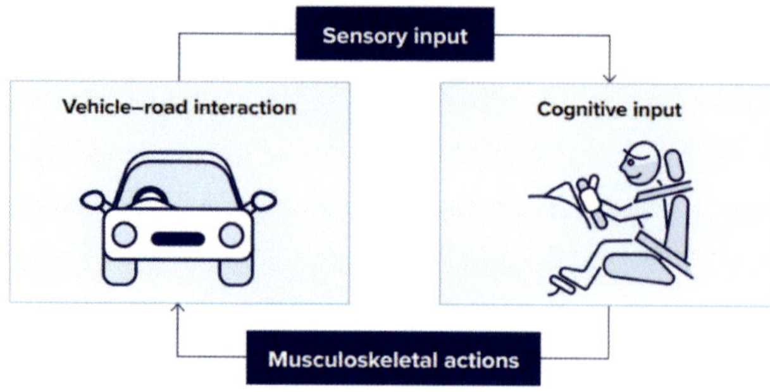

67.1 The driving task.

Figure 67.1 illustrates the fully functioning interactions between vehicle and human required for safe driving (11).

Collisions resulting in fatality are investigated by the coroner in most jurisdictions and the cause of these fatalities may be as the result of a driver with a medical condition. Independent bodies to medically assess drivers and who are separate from their treating medical practitioners engaged in a therapeutic relationship with the driver, exist in many jurisdictions. An independent assessment enables past medical history to be considered from the treating medical practitioners as well as information from other sources such as police and road transport authorities; a history of safe driving is not a future predictor of safe driving in the context of many medical conditions including dementia.

The recommendation of loss of a driver's license may be extremely distressing to the driver and their family and friends and quality assurance mechanisms must be in place that recognize the principles of fairness to the driver and the risk to public safety.

In the UK, the DVLA regularly update their advice to medical professionals (12). Other jurisdictions also undertake this function through their respective licensing agencies. Regulatory driver medical consultations involve the provision of consent by the driver to participate in the examination which includes the taking of a relevant medical history, history of driving (collision history, previous license restrictions, driving convictions, vehicle modifications and any on-road testing results), physical examination, medical information from other healthcare providers and reporting results of the consultation back to the regulatory authority.

Recommendations may be made for a practical driving assessment which involves putting the driver into a vehicle with a driving instructor and/or occupational therapist. Driving skills are then assessed while the person is driving on a public road. There are clinical situations that are clearly unsuitable for on-road assessments, such as significant visual impairment or significant cognitive impairment and this assessment is not recommended for these conditions as it has limited utility and risk to assessor and public safety (11).

TRENDS IN ALCOHOL AND DRUG USE WHEN DRIVING

Driving while impaired or under the influence of alcohol or drugs is a considerable risk factor for involvement in motor vehicle collisions. The type of substance consumed varies with local availability. Globally, jurisdictions have recognized the role of alcohol and other substances in causing motor vehicle collisions with legislation regarding aspects such as limits of blood-alcohol concentration while driving, presence and limit offenses for substances including alcohol (zero-tolerance, impairment, and *per se* or legal limits) and law enforcement strategies including roadside testing, blood sampling and refusal to participate in testing offenses.

The prevalence of alcohol and other drugs during driving has changed over time. There has been a steady increase in the prevalence of drivers who consume drugs while there has been a corresponding decrease in alcohol presence during driving in those involved in fatal collisions (13,14). The findings from fatal collisions (15) mirror the findings from self-reported drug and alcohol use while driving.

Alcohol

Alcohol use and driving

Table 67.2 lists the blood alcohol limits for various jurisdictions. Special drivers, e.g. commercial drivers, young drivers and other drivers in these jurisdictions may be subject to lower blood alcohol levels.

Alcohol is the commonest impairing substance detected following a motor vehicle collision (16–18). Although any person can be a drink driver, several characteristics (19) are more common in those who are involved in motor vehicle collisions, these are: (20–22)

- Males, women are less likely to report driving after alcohol consumption
- Younger age group between 25 to 34 years. Drivers under this age group are less likely to drive although inexperience and lower levels of driving skills increase their collision rates
- Higher levels of blood alcohol concentration
- Impulsivity and mental health issues
- Social networks with other drink drivers in the network
- Higher socioeconomic status
- Association with drug use in those who drink drive
- Recidivist drink driving. Many drivers who use alcohol have problematic drinking and this group is also overrepresented (23) in the recidivist drink-driving offender group. In response to tackle recidivist offenders, strategies have been developed in an effort to rehabilitate this group of offenders with a variety of measures such as:
    - Attendance at education courses
    - Relicensing following medical examination, blood testing
    - Alcohol interlocks (24) are breath analysis devices installed in a motor vehicle, where the

TABLE 67.2 Prescribed blood alcohol levels in various jurisdictions

Blood alcohol limit 80 mg of alcohol per 100 mL of blood	
Canada	United States
England	
Blood alcohol limit 50 mg of alcohol per 100 mL of blood	
Australia	Germany
Austria	Greece
Belgium	Italy
Bulgaria	Luxembourg
Denmark	Netherlands
Ireland	Spain
Finland	Scotland
France	
Blood alcohol limit 40 mg of alcohol per 100 mL of blood	
Lithuania	
Blood alcohol limit 20 mg of alcohol per 100 mL of blood	
Norway	Poland
Sweden	
Blood alcohol limit 0 (zero alcohol limit) mg of alcohol per 100 mL of blood	
Czech Republic	Russia
Hungary	Slovakia
Romania	Turkey

driver is required to supply a breath sample in the device before driving and also at random times during driving. Alcohol interlocks are useful in the prevention of driving under the influence by problematic alcohol drivers, however they are expensive, and methods of subversion have been described. A court order is generally required for enforcing use

- Criminality, mostly minor crime
- In urban areas with short distance travel

Alcohol, like most sedating substances, impairs the ability to drive safely through multiple mechanisms (25).

Reaction time

This is the time taken to respond to a particular situation. Alcohol produces impairment in responses and delays in reaction time, it further compounds the effects of fatigue.

Vision

Vision is a critical function required for the psychomotor tasks required for driving. Alcohol impairs the ability to track an object through disruption of the coordination of the eye muscles, this results in horizontal gaze nystagmus and is evident at blood levels of 0.05 percent and above.

Visual acuity is impaired by alcohol in 85 percent of subjects with blood-alcohol concentrations between 0.101 percent and 0.125 percent through ciliary muscle effects.

Diplopia occurs with alcohol and may occur at levels as low as 0.05 percent.

Impairments in color discrimination occurs from blood alcohol concentrations 0.09 percent.

Visual abilities are extremely sensitive to alcohol with nearly all subjects affected at concentrations of blood alcohol concentrations of 0.08 percent.

Executive functions including information processing as well as the ability to concentrate and undertake divided attention tasks is impaired to varying extents by alcohol, the effects become more pronounced with higher blood-alcohol concentrations.

Motor coordination is impaired by alcohol and is more pronounced at higher concentrations. Gross motor in-coordination may be demonstrated by slurred speech, staggering and unsteadiness.

Alcohol is the only substance for which there is a generally accepted relationship between blood concentrations and the risk of crashing and forms the basis of much blood-alcohol concentration-based legislation (26). Jurisdictional legislation defines cut-off levels, and penalties are afforded accordingly, however, there is a personal blood-alcohol range in which impairing effects evolve. Impairment in performance in a variety of skills occurs at the lowest measurable levels of alcohol concentration.

Following ingestion and absorption of alcohol, it is distributed in the water component of the body, the portion of body water varies between women and men and is the basis of the Widmark Factor. Absorption varies and is altered by the amount and type of food present in the stomach, the type of alcohol consumed and the rate of consumption. Peak blood-alcohol concentration occurs between 30 minutes and 2 hours after intake. Elimination of alcohol is mostly through metabolism in the liver and varies between 0.01 and 0.02 grams percentage per hour, higher metabolism occurs in chronic heavy drinkers (27).

Alcohol is a sedative drug with central nervous system (CNS) effects as well as other body effects. With increasing blood-alcohol concentration, the cerebral function is affected first, followed by midbra in functioning with the highest concentration in the hindbrain. This manifests by affecting sensation and perception, executive functioning and skilled performance particularly fine movement and short-term memory. Increasing impairment occurs with increasing blood-alcohol concentration.

Motor vehicle collisions and crash risk

Each driver when driving has a crash risk and a baseline risk; the risk of a collision may increase or decrease dependent on a number of factors including inexperience, teenage passengers, distraction when driving, excessive speed, alcohol and use of impairing substances and night driving (28).

Studies determining skills impairment are based on several methods including epidemiologic research, the largest being the Grand Rapids Study (26) driving simulators, off-road driving assessment and even on-road driving assessment. On-road assessment has significant limitations due to safety, ethical and legal reasons.

Testing methods for alcohol include:

- **Breath sampling** measures the amount of alcohol in breath and uses a constant ratio between expired alveolar air and blood concentration to provide a level. The ratio is defined in legislation is generally accepted at 1:2100.
- **Blood sampling** is still used to determine blood-alcohol concentration. Alcohol swabs used to clean the skin prior to blood sampling have no statistically significant effect on blood-alcohol concentration subsequently determined in the blood sample (29).
- **Hair sampling is** hair testing used in those with problematic alcohol use as proof of alcohol abstinence through hair EtG testing (30) and may be used with other methods such as biological sample testing and alcohol interlocks (31).

Blood and breath samples are taken following collisions; there is likely to be metabolism of alcohol in this time period and there may also be continued absorption of alcohol in this time period. Back calculation of alcohol levels may be undertaken to compensate for metabolism of alcohol although back calculation cannot compensate for alcohol that has not been absorbed at the time of collision, especially when the time between the collision and the consumption of alcohol is less than one hour. In a case where subsequent alcohol absorption may have occurred, there may be overestimation of the blood alcohol concentration (32).

The information required for calculation is:

- Time of blood sample collection (T1).
- Time of collision (T2).

- Difference in time between collision and collection of blood specimen (T1 minus T2) expressed in hours, that is conversion of the minutes to hours.
- Elimination rate per hour (R). In general, for the back calculation estimated should occur at three concentrations, low (0.01 g/dL), average (0.015 g/dL) and high (0.02 g/dL).
- Blood-alcohol concentration at the time of sample collection expressed as a percentage (B).
- The following formula is applied:

$$\text{Blood Alcohol concentration (BAC)} = (T1 \text{ minus } T2) \times R + B$$

The Widmark formula may be used to estimate blood-alcohol concentration based on the amount of alcohol consumed. It should be noted that there are many uncertainties in the Widmark (33–35) formula and many variations; women and older people (36) may have differences in their estimation of alcohol concentration

Widmark should be used cautiously, and estimations must contain appropriate caveats.

A simplified Widmark formula after Breakspere and Starmer is as follows:

$$BAC = \frac{G - \beta T}{r \times 10 \times W}$$

Where:
BAC = Blood-Alcohol Concentration in g%
G = Grams of alcohol consumed (75.8 g)
W = subject's weight in kilograms (55 kg)
T = Time in hours since drinking began (5.5 hours)
β = Metabolic rate (5–10 grams per hour)
r = Widmark's factor relating body mass and total body water
= 0.55 for women and 0.68 for men (0.55)

Drug use

Any substance with a psychomotor effect has the potential to affect the ability to drive safely. Alcohol, cannabis, opioids, stimulants particularly cocaine and methylamphetamine and sedating drugs, such as benzodiazepines, are the substances of greatest concern in road safety.

In general, prescribed medications for depression and affecting the CNS will cause maximum unsafe driving effects in the first 6 to 8 weeks of regular use. Intermittent use of substances does not enable tolerance for certain driving skills and hence has a greater effect on driving ability.

Recidivist offending (38) for drug drive offenses is as high as with drink driving.

The profile of drug drivers

There are characteristics which are commonly found in drug drivers; these are similar to those who drink drive and include:

- Criminal history, particularly of drug possession
- Younger age
- Males
- Drug use profile, THC (Delta-9-Tetrahydrocannabinnol), benzodiazepines, opiates)
    - It should be noted that prescription drugs (39,40) such as benzodiazepines and opiates may be more common in motor vehicle collisions
- Employment in the trucking and trade industries
- Mental health issues

Detection of substances in drivers involved in motor vehicle collisions in the non-post mortem setting

At present, there are several methods of sampling for substances from drivers; these are:

- Blood sampling
- Urine sampling
- Oral fluid samples
- Breath analysis, at present alcohol is the only substance measured by this method however validation is occurring for other substances

Sedative substances

Sedative substances impair the ability to drive safely especially in combination with alcohol. Sedative medications such as antipsychotics, anticonvulsants and sedating antidepressants affect driving ability, however, with regular and stable use, the effects on driving ability are minimized over 6 to 8 weeks; indeed, the crash risk may reduce as the patient's underlying medical condition becomes treated. Benzodiazepines, opiates and opioids increase crash risk in the first 6 to 8 weeks after commencing treatment and the development of tolerance. Again, this risk is markedly increased with the use of alcohol and other sedating drugs. Patients must be warned of the effects of sedating medication (14) on driving ability and the stabilization periods. Erratic or intermittent use of sedating substances is more likely to lead to unsafe driving.

Stabilization on opioid replacement therapy with methadone/buprenorphine induces tolerance to the sedating effects and patients can drive if their medication is taken as directed and no other psychoactive substances are consumed.

Stimulant substances

Epidemiologic data from those using methamphetamine (41) and cocaine show increased collision rates. Stimulant effects on driving include speeding, aggressive driving, risk taking, unsafe lane changing, overtaking and lack of adherence to red light signals. There is no substantial evidence of sustained improved performance following stimulant use. On a background of sleep deprivation or fatigue, stimulants may enhance performance; this does not occur in other groups. Indeed, stimulant use has an initial stimulatory phase which may be followed by a profound sudden onset phase of fatigue which may be dangerous if it occurs at the time of driving.

Use of a combination of substances

The use of more than one impairing substance (42) is a common finding in drivers following a collision. This also applies to alcohol and impairing substances, there is synergism between alcohol and cannabis producing greater effects of driving impairment (43,44) than either substance on its own due to the exertion of effects on executive functioning and psychomotor skills reflected in unsafe driving. Similarly, the use of more than one sedative drug causes more profound sedation and is reflected in unsafe driving.

Cannabis and driving

Delta-9-Tetrahydrocannabinol (often abbreviated to THC) produces its effects through specific cannabinoid receptors found in the central and peripheral nervous system. THC is the active drug found in cannabis (marijuana). Cannabis is usually smoked, and this causes the THC to be released into the blood stream. THC is lipophilic and quickly redistributes to the brain where it acts as a CNS depressant and hallucinogen with time to reach a baseline level of approximately 2 hours (45,46). Due to the pharmacokinetics, the concentration of THC in blood or oral fluid is not dependably related to impairment, however, the presence of THC at any level is associated with an increased crash risk (47). THC is not distributed from blood into saliva to any extent (48). Cannabis may affect driving ability, (49); effects include:

- Decreased car handling performance
- Motor in-coordination
- Impaired sustained vigilance
- Reduction in perceptive skills
- Slowing of reaction time
- Dulling of reflexes
- Impairment of time and distance perception
- Reduced capacity to respond quickly in stressful situations

Medicinal cannabis

Medicinal cannabis, which only contains cannabidiol, a non-psychoactive substance, does not affect the ability to drive safely. However, much illegitimately sourced medicinal cannabis contains delta-9-tetrahydrocannabinol which is psychoactive and impairs safe driving ability (50). In most jurisdictions, it is illegal to drive with the presence of delta-9-tetrahydrocannabinol regardless of the source. Other consequences of having the detectable presence of THC are: an increased risk of collisions, refusal of insurance, criminal liability or being charged with a presence offense.

Methylamphetamine, cocaine and driving

Cocaine and methylamphetamine are taken for their stimulant effects and have effects on driving. Different jurisdictions vary in their prevalence of use of these stimulants; however, on the whole, the effects on driving are similar. Both produce immediate effects including reduced fatigue, euphoria, positive mood, accelerated heart rate, elevated blood pressure, pupil dilation, increased temperature, reduced appetite, restlessness, behavioral disinhibition and short-term improvement in cognitive domains, including sustained attention. With long-term use, a psychotic condition causing paranoia may occur. These drugs may also affect judgement, the response to perceived danger, and may increase recklessness, aggression and risk taking. Methylamphetamine is not used for therapeutic purposes. Higher blood levels of methylamphetamine causes impairment in the ability of a driver to drive safely and are more likely to be associated with impairment.

The effects on driving include (41,51,52) erratic and inappropriate responses to the driving situation, speeding, increased lane movement, aggression, irrational or violent behavior. Sleep deprivation through the post-use sedation may occur following use of stimulant medications increasing crash risk (53).

Driver distraction, human factor, mobile device detection cameras

Driver distraction is increasingly recognized as a factor in collisions, with many deterrents in use such as mobile device detection and legislation to support conviction. Distraction is generally through one or more of four mechanisms including: driver not watching the road, the driver removing their hands from the steering wheel, noise and diversions from others in the vehicle, and thinking about other things rather than driving, for example observing the scene of another collision while driving by.

Fatigue and driving

Fatigue is a factor (54) in approximately 2.4 percent of fatal motor vehicle collisions.

In addition to feeling tired, the effects of fatigue on psychomotor function (55) include impairment of reaction time, divided attention tasks, tracking, vigilance and memory.

The effects of fatigue have some similarities with alcohol upon psychomotor function. Comparisons between crash risk from alcohol intoxication and fatigue (56,57) have been postulated with being awake for over 17 hours being equivalent to a blood alcohol concentration of 0.05 percent. As the hours of being awake increase, so does the level of impairment rising to an equivalent of 0.1 percent at 24 hours.

Exact levels of impairment in psychomotor function are disputed (58) however, a significant level of impairment occurs with fatigue.

Vulnerable road users

Alcohol use in drivers resulting in motor vehicle fatalities and injury is preventable. Correctly, much of the focus on prevention of injury in motor vehicle collisions is placed upon drivers who have consumed alcohol; pedestrians who consume alcohol represent many fatalities caused by motor vehicles. Alcohol impairs perception, judgement and coordination resulting in risk-taking behaviors such as crossing roads (59).

Alcohol is a factor in 50 percent of pedestrian fatalities, (60), with younger pedestrians involved at a higher proportion.

CONCLUSION

Drivers under the influence of alcohol and substances, and those with specific underlying medical conditions cause substantial harm from motor vehicles. Although jurisdictional licensing regulations vary, underlying medical conditions and their treatments may impact on the ability to drive safely. Assessing fitness to drive is a key preventative strategy used by traffic medicine specialists.

REFERENCES

1. World Health Organization. Decade of action for road safety, 2021. Available from: https://www.who.int/teams/social-determinants-of-health/safety-and-mobility/decade-of-action-for-road-safety-2021–2030 (Accessed 16 May 2023).
2. World Health Organization. Estimated road traffic death rate (per 100 000 population), 2021. Available from: https://www.who.int/data/gho/data/indicators/indicator-details/GHO/estimated-road-traffic-death-rate-(per-100-000-population) (Accessed 16 May 2023).
3. Seeger R. Verkehrsmedizin in der Grundversorger-praxis. *Ther Umsch* 2011; **68**(5): 235–41.
4. International Traffic Medicine Association. What is traffic medicine?, 2000. Available from: https://www.trafficmedicine.org/itma/what-is-traffic-medicine/ (Accessed 16 May 2023).
5. Royal College of Physicians Ireland. Available from: Traffic Medicine https://www.rcpi.ie/Healthcare-Leadership/National-Office-for-Traffic-Medicine (Accessed 2 June 2023).
6. Wall I, Stark MM. Traffic Medicine. In: Stark MM (ed), *Clinical Forensic Medicine. A Physician's Guide*, 4th ed. Cham: Springer Nature; 2020.
7. Treat JR, Tumbas NS, McDonald ST, et al. *Tri-Level Study Of The Causes of Traffic Accidents, Executive Summary, Indiana University, DOT HS 805 099*, Bloomington, IN: Indiana University; 1979.
8. Singh S. Critical reasons for crashes investigated in the National Motor Vehicle Crash Causation Survey. (Traffic Safety Facts Crash Stats. Report No. DOT HS 812 115). Washington, DC: National Highway Traffic Safety Administration, 2015.
9. Rolison JJ, Hanoch Y, Wood S, et al. Risk-taking differences across the adult life span: A question of age and domain. *J Gerontol B Psychol Sci Soc Sci* 2014; **69**(6): 870–80.
10. Lam LT. Factors associated with young drivers' car crash injury: Comparisons among learner, provisional, and full licensees. *Accid Anal Prev* 2003; **35**(6): 913–20.
11. National Transport Commission. Assessing Fitness to Drive, 2022. Available from: https://austroads.com.au/__data/assets/pdf_file/0022/104197/AP-G56-17_Assessing_fitness_to_drive_2016_amended_Aug2017.pdf (Accessed 16 May 2023).
12. GOV.uk. Assessing fitness to drive: a guide for medical professionals. Available from: https://www.gov.uk/guidance/assessing-fitness-to-drive-a-guide-for-medical-professionals (Accessed 16 May 2023).
13. Schumann J, Perkins M, Dietze P, et al. The prevalence of alcohol and other drugs in fatal road crashes in Victoria, Australia. *Accid Anal Prev* 2021; **153**: 105905.
14. Wollf, K. Driving under the influence of drugs. Report from the Expert Panel on Drug Driving, 2013. Available from: https://assets.publishing.service.gov.uk/government/uploads/system/uploads/attachment_data/file/167971/drug-driving-expert-panel-report.pdf (Accessed 16 May 2023).
15. Holló P, Henézi D, Berta, T. Comparison of self-reported and observed road safety performance indicators. *Period Polytech Transp* 2018; **46**(3): 117–21.
16. National Highway Traffic Safety Administration. Traffic Safety Facts, 2016. Available from: https://crashstats.nhtsa.dot.gov/Api/Public/ViewPublication/812450 (Accessed 16 May 2023).
17. Fell J. Approaches for reducing alcohol-impaired driving: evidence-based legislation, law enforcement strategies, sanctions, and alcohol-control policies. *Forensic Sci Rev* 2019; **31**: 161–84.
18. Hels T, Bernhoft IM, Lyckegaard A, et al. Risk of injury by driving with alcohol and other drugs, 2011. Available from: https://biblio.ugent.be/publication/1988746 (Accessed 16 May 2023).
19. Brubacher JR, Chan H, Erdelyi S, et al. Police documentation of drug use in injured drivers: Implications for monitoring and preventing drug-impaired driving. *Accid Anal Prev* 2018; **118**: 200–6.
20. Department for Transport. Reported Road Casualties in Great Britain, final estimates involving illegal alcohol levels, various years. Available from: https://www.gov.uk/government/statistics/reported-road-casualties-in-great-britain-final-estimates-involving-illegal-alcohol-levels-2020/reported-road-casualties-in-great-britain-final-estimates-involving-illegal-alcohol-levels-2020#:~:text=Final (Accessed 2 June 2023).
21. Sykes W, Groom C, Kelly, et al. *Road Safety Research Report No. 114 A Qualitative Study of Drinking and Driving: Report of Findings June 2010*. London: Department for Transport; 2010.
22. Beuret K, Corbett C, Ward H. Drinking among British women and its impact on their pedestrian and driving activities, 2014. Available from: https://www.reesjeffreys.co.uk/wp-content/uploads/2010/10/Drinking-among-British-Women-Social-Research-Associates.pdf (Accessed 16 May 2023).
23. Shaffer HJ, Nelson SE, LaPlante DA, et al. The epidemiology of psychiatric disorders among repeat DUI offenders accepting a treatment-sentencing option. *J Consult Clin Psychol* 2007; **75**(5): 795–804.
24. Parliamentary Advisory Council for Transport Safety. Alcohol interlocks – new PACTS research project, 2020. Available from: https://www.pacts.org.uk/2020/05/new-pacts-research-project-alcohol-interlocks/ (Accessed 16 May 2023).
25. Levine B, Caplan YH. Pharmacology and Toxicology of Ethyl Alcohol. In: Caplan YH, Goldberger BA (eds), *Garriott's Medicolegal Aspects of Alcohol*, 6th ed. Tuscon, AZ: Lawyers & Judges Publishing Company; 2015, pp. 31–4.
26. Borkenstein RF, Crowther RF, Shumate RP, et al. The role of the drinking driver in traffic accidents (The Grand Rapids Study). *Blutalkohol Alcohol Drugs Behavior* 1974; **11**: 1.
27. Jones AW. Alcohol its absorption, distribution, metabolism and excretion in the body and pharmacokinetic calculation, 2019. Available from: https://wires.onlinelibrary.wiley.com/doi/epdf/10.1002/wfs2.1340 (Accessed 16 May 2023).
28. National Institute of Child and Human Development. What risk factors do all drivers face? 2016. Available from: https://www.nichd.nih.gov/health/topics/driving/conditioninfo/risk-factors (Accessed 16 May 2023).
29. Tucker A, Trethewy C. Lack of effect on blood alcohol level of swabbing venepuncture sites with 70% isopropyl alcohol. *Emerg Med Australas* 2010; **22**(1): 9–12.
30. Marques PR, Tippetts AS, Yegles M. Ethylglucuronide in hair is a top predictor of impaired driving recidivism, alcohol dependence, and a key marker of the highest BAC interlock tests. *Traffic Inj Prev* 2014; **15**(4): 361–9.
31. Marques PR. Levels and types of alcohol biomarkers in DUI and clinic samples for estimating workplace alcohol problems. *Drug Test Anal* 2012; **4**(2): 76–82.
32. GOV.uk. Alcohol back calculation for road traffic investigation, 2020. Available from: https://www.gov.uk/government/publications/alcohol-back-calculation-for-road-traffic-investigations (Accessed 16 May 2023).

33. Searle J. Alcohol calculations and their uncertainty. *Med Sci Law* 2015; **55**(1): 58–64.
34. Gullberg R. Estimating the uncertainty associated with Widmark's equation commonly applied in forensic toxicology. *Forensic Sci Int* 2007; **172**: 33–9.
35. Barbour AD. Simplified estimation of Widmark "r" values by the method of Forrest. *Sci Justice* 2001; **41**(1): 53–4.
36. Bielefeld L, Auwärter V, Pollak S, et al. Differences between the measured blood ethanol concentration and the estimated concentration by Widmark's equation in elderly persons. *Forensic Sci Int* 2015; **247**: 23–7.
37. Breakspere R, Starmer G. *The Art of Sensible Drinking*. Ellsyd; 1984.
38. Parliamentary Advisory Council for Transport Safety. Drug driving: the tip of an iceberg? 2021. Available from: https://www.pacts.org.uk/news-and-publications/drug-driving-the-tip-of-an-iceberg-a-report-from-pacts/ (Accessed 16 May 2023).
39. Drummer OH, Yap S. The involvement of prescribed drugs in road trauma. *Forensic Sci Int* 2016; **265**: 17–21.
40. European Monitoring Centre for Drugs and Drug Addiction. Drug use, impaired driving and traffic accidents, 2014. Available from: https://www.emcdda.europa.eu/publications/insights/2014/drugs-and-driving_en (Accessed 16 May 2023).
41. Logan BK. Methylamphetamine and driving impairment. *J Forensic Sci* 1996; **41**: 457–64.
42. Mallik J, Johnston J, Goren N, et al. Drugs and driving in Australia. A survey of community attitudes, experience and understanding, 2007. Available from: http://www.onlinelibraryaddictions.stir.ac.uk/files/2017/07/Drugs_and_Driving_in_Australia_fullreport.pdf (Accessed 16 May 2023).
43. Sewell RA, James Poling J, Sofuoglu M. The effect of cannabis compared with alcohol on driving. *Am J Addict* 2009; **18**(3): 185–93.
44. Downey LA, King R, Papafotiou K, et al. The effects of cannabis and alcohol on simulated driving: Influences of dose and experience. *Accid Anal Prev* 2013; **50**: 879–86.
45. Huestis MA, Henningfield JE, Cone EJ. Blood cannabinoids. I. Absorption of THC and formation of 11-OH-THC and THCCOOH during and after smoking marijuana. *J Anal Toxicol* 1992; **16**(5): 276–82.
46. Meier U, Dussy F, Scheurer E, et al. Cannabinoid concentrations in blood and urine after smoking cannabidiol joints. *Forensic Sci Int* 2018; **291**: 62–7.
47. Drummer OH, Gerostamoulos J, Batziris H, et al. The involvement of drugs in drivers of motor vehicles killed in Australian road traffic crashes. *Accid Anal Prev* 2004; **36**(2): 239–48.
48. Heustis MA. Oral fluid testing for drugs of abuse. *Clin Chem* 2009; **55**(11): 1910–31.
49. Couper FJ, Logan BK. National Highway Traffic Safety Administration. Drugs and human performance fact sheets, 2004. Available from: https://www.nhtsa.gov/sites/nhtsa.gov/files/809725-drugshumanperformfs.pdf (Accessed 16 May 2023).
50. Arkell TR, Vinckenbosch F, Kevin RC, et al. Effect of cannabidiol and Δ9-tetrahydrocannabinol on driving performance: A randomized clinical trial. *JAMA* 2020; **324**(**21**): 2177–86.
51. Couper FJ, Logan BK. National Highway Traffic Safety Administration. Drugs and human performance fact sheets, 2004. Available from: https://www.nhtsa.gov/sites/nhtsa.gov/files/809725-drugshumanperformfs.pdf (Accessed 16 May 2023).
52. Gustavsen I, Morland J, Bramness JG. Impairment related to blood amphetamine and/or methylamphetamine concentrations in suspected drugged drivers. *Accid Anal Prev* 2006; **38**(3): 490–5.
53. Musshoff F, Madea B. Driving under the influence of amphetamine-like drugs. *J Forensic Sci* 2012; **57**(2): 413–19.
54. National Center for Statistics and Analysis. (2017, October). Drowsy Driving 2015 (Crash•Stats Brief Statistical Summary. Report No. DOT HS 812 446). Washington, DC: National Highway Traffic Safety Administration.
55. Williamson AM, Feyer AM. Moderate sleep deprivation produces impairments in cognitive and motor performance equivalent to legally prescribed levels of alcohol intoxication. *Occup Environ Med* 2000; **57**: 649–55.
56. Dawson D, Reid K. Fatigue, alcohol and performance impairment. *Nature* 1997; **388**: 235.
57. Williamson AM, Feyer AM. Moderate sleep deprivation produces impairments in cognitive and motor performance equivalent to legally prescribed levels of alcohol intoxication. *Occup Environ Med* 2000; **57**: 649–55.
58. Maruff P, Falleti MG, Collie A, et al. Fatigue-related impairment in the speed, accuracy and variability of psychomotor performance: Comparison with blood alcohol levels. *J Sleep Res* 2005; **14**(1): 21–7.
59. Dultz L, Frangos S. The impact of alcohol in pedestrian trauma. *Trauma* 2013; **15**: 64–75.
60. Lasota D, Al-Wathinani A, Krajewsk, P, et al. Alcohol and road accidents involving pedestrians as unprotected road users. *Int J Environ Res Public Health* 2020; **17**: 8995.

CHAPTER

68

Principles of Child Safeguarding

Jason Payne-James and Peter Green

INTRODUCTION

Safeguarding is the action taken to promote the welfare of children and protect them from harm and includes protecting children from abuse and maltreatment; preventing harm to children's health or development; ensuring children grow up with the provision of safe and effective care; and taking action to enable all children and young people to have the best outcomes. Child protection is part of that safeguarding process. Child protection focuses on protecting individual children who have been identified as being, or at risk of being, abused or maltreated and are suffering or are considered likely to suffer significant harm. Child protection procedures are standardized processes which should ensure a consistency of approach and care for each child requiring it (1). The terms abuse and maltreatment are often used interchangeably and inconsistently but the World Health Organization defines child maltreatment as the abuse and neglect that occurs to children under 18 years of age. It includes all types of physical and/or emotional ill-treatment, sexual abuse, neglect, negligence and commercial or other exploitation, which results in actual or potential harm to the child's health, survival, development or dignity in the context of a relationship of responsibility, trust or power (2). It is important for forensic physicians and allied forensic practitioners to understand which definitions are used in relation to their own practice within their own jurisdiction.

INTERNATIONAL INSTRUMENTS

Much of the current understanding and guidance on child safeguarding derives from the United Nations Convention on the Rights of the Child which was adopted and opened for signature, ratification and accession by General Assembly resolution 44/25 of 20 November 1989 entry into force 2 September 1990, in accordance with article 49 (3). It consists of 3 Parts and 54 Articles. All nations but the USA have ratified the convention.

Article 1 states that "*For the purposes of the present Convention, a child means every human being below the age of eighteen years unless under the law applicable to the child, majority is attained earlier.*". Reference to child protection is first made in Article 2 which states that

> "*1. Parties shall respect and ensure the rights set forth in the present Convention to each child within their jurisdiction without discrimination of any kind, irrespective of the child's or his or her parent's or legal guardian's race, colour, sex, language, religion, political or other opinion, national, ethnic or social origin, property, disability, birth or other status.*
> *2. Parties shall take all appropriate measures to ensure that the child is protected against all forms of discrimination or punishment on the basis of the status, activities, expressed opinions, or beliefs of the child's parents, legal guardians, or family members.*"

At Article 3, the Convention also introduces the principle of "best interests of the child" being a primary consideration in all actions concerning children, whether undertaken by public or private social welfare institutions, courts of law, administrative authorities or legislative bodies. Table 68.1 identifies other Convention Articles which may be of specific relevance to forensic practitioners within the context of the range of settings in which they may be involved with the assessment of children. A children's version of the Convention has been published which is available in multiple languages. Figure 68.1 gives an example of the English language version of the first 21 Articles (4).

MORBIDITY AND MORTALITY OF CHILDREN

It is believed that globally nearly three in four children – 300 million children – aged 2–4 years regularly suffer physical punishment and/or psychological violence at the hands of parents and caregivers. One in five women and one in 13 men report having been sexually abused as a child aged 0–17 years and 120 million girls and young women under 20 years of age have suffered some form of forced sexual contact. It is generally accepted that child maltreatment is often hidden and only a small proportion

DOI: 10.1201/9781003138754-71

TABLE 68.1A Metropolitan Police Service (UK) examples of what constitutes child maltreatment or abuse (8)

Physical abuse
- hitting, slapping, shaking or throwing
- burning or scalding
- inappropriate restraint or false imprisonment
- using physical force to discipline

Emotional abuse
- being made to feel inadequate, worthless or unloved
- being bullied, including over the internet (cyber-bullying)
- witnessing the abuse of others such as domestic abuse

Sexual abuse
- causing or inciting a child to watch or engage in sexual activities
- encouraging a child to behave in sexually inappropriate ways
- involving a child in the production of sexual images or videos
- grooming a child in preparation for abuse (including via the internet)

Neglect

Basic needs are persistently not being met by their parent or guardian. These needs include:
- adequate food, clothing and shelter
- protection from physical and emotional harm or danger
- adequate supervision (including not being left at home alone)
- access to appropriate medical care including dental treatment

TABLE 68.1B Examples of type of abuse (9)

Physical abuse
- Hit or punched
- Kicked
- Beaten by an object
- Shaken hard
- Cut or Stabbed on purpose
- Burnt by a hot object/liquid

Sexual abuse
- Someone exposed their genitals
- Made to pose naked
- Someone touched the genitals
- Made to touch other's genitals
- Made to have intercourse

Emotional abuse
- Insulted or criticized
- Been told they were "unloved"
- Been told "wish you had never been born/or were dead"
- Threatened to be hurt or killed
- Threatened to be abandoned/refused into home

of child victims of maltreatment ever receives support from health professionals. It is also well recognized that a child who has been maltreated or abused is more likely to abuse others as an adult (4). The UNICEF Report (6) *The State of the World's Children 2021, On My Mind* notes that children and young people report psychosocial distress that does not rise to the level of epidemiologic disorder but disrupts their lives, health and prospects for the future. An estimated 45 800 adolescents die from suicide each year and is the fifth most prevalent cause of death for adolescents aged 10–19. For adolescent boys and girls aged 15–19, it is the fourth most common cause of death, after road injury, tuberculosis and interpersonal violence. For girls aged 15–19, it is the third most common cause of death, and the fourth for boys in this age group. Mental health is intimately related to times of significant brain development, which can be affected by adverse childhood experiences (ACEs), such as physical and emotional

68.1 The Children's Version of the first 21 Articles of the Convention on the rights of the Child. (Unabridged version available from https://www.unicef.org/media/60981/file/convention-rights-child-text-child-friendly-version.pdf Also available in multiple languages.)

abuse, chronic neglect and violence. Exposure to at least four ACEs is strongly associated with sexual risk taking, mental health conditions and alcohol abuse; it is even more strongly associated with problematic drug use and interpersonal and self-directed violence. In the world's least developed countries, 83 percent of children experience violent discipline from caregivers and 22 percent are in a form of child labor. Among older children, absence from school or dropping out before finishing is linked to social isolation, which in turn can lead to mental health conditions, including self-harm, suicidal ideation, depression, anxiety and substance use. All of these are potential factors with which forensic physicians may become directly involved (6).

The State of the World's Children report also gives helpful comparative data on mortality rates of children at different ages and examples are shown in Tables 68.2 and 68.3.

Specifically, the report addresses comparative child protection issues. In particular, the report looks at factors reflected in the UN Convention on the Rights of the Child but adds in other important and significant comparators. These include the incidence of child labour, child marriage, birth registration, female genital mutilation, justification of wife-beating among adolescents, violent discipline and sexual violence in childhood. These data often assist in identifying where legal, regional, cultural, societal, ethnic and religious influence these findings. Examples are shown in Table 68.4. Forensic physicians should be aware of trends in their own locality.

There are four main categories of maltreatment which are relevant to the forensic practitioner: physical abuse; emotional abuse; sexual abuse and neglect and additionally fabricated or induced illness (FII) must be considered. FII is a clinical situation in which a child is, or is very likely to be, harmed due to parent(s) behavior and action, carried out in order to convince doctors that the child's state of physical and/or mental health and neurodevelopment is impaired (or more impaired than is actually the case). FII results in physical and emotional abuse and neglect, as a result of parental actions, behaviors or beliefs and from doctors' responses to these. The parent does not necessarily intend to deceive, and their motivations may not be initially evident (7). The Metropolitan Police Services lists examples of each of the main four categories to assist and these are shown in Table 68.1a (8). Table 68.1b lists examples of described abuse from a study from Sri Lanka (9). This study determined the prevalence of childhood physical, sexual and emotional abusive experiences among 1500 students (aged 18–19 years). Experiences of physical, sexual and emotional abuse and age at abuse, perpetrators, consequences and severity were assessed using a version of ISPCAN Child Abuse Screening Tool-Retrospective Version (ICAST-R) which was culturally adapted and validated by the authors for use among Sinhalese students.

The prevalence of the various forms of abuse during childhood was as follows: physical: 45.4 percent; sexual: 9.1 percent; emotional: 27.9 percent. The corresponding percentages of individuals categorized as having experienced severe or very severe abuse were as follows, physical: 0.3 percent (2/672); sexual: 4.05 percent (3/135); emotional: 8.8 percent (36/412). Physical abuse was more prevalent among male students (54.8% vs 38.3%) as was emotional abuse (33.9% vs 23.2%). Sexual abuse was more prevalent among female students (11.5% vs 6.4%). Parents and teachers were the commonest perpetrators of physical and emotional abuse. Most of the sexually abusive acts were committed by neighbors or strangers.

Barth and colleagues aimed to describe the current prevalence of child sexual abuse, taking into account geographic region, type of abuse, level of country development and research methods using studies published between 2002 and 2009 that reported CSA in children below 18 years (10). In 2012, they identified 55 studies from 24

TABLE 68.2 Number of under-5 deaths and under-5 mortality rate by country in 2019 (6).

Country	Annual number of under-5 deaths (thousands) 2019	Under-5 mortality rate (deaths per 1000 live births) in 2019		
		Median	Lower band	Upper band
Azerbaijan	3	20	13	32
Jordan	3	16	12	21
United Kingdom	3	4	4	4
France	3	4	4	5
Germany	3	4	4	4
Namibia	3	42	25	77
Kyrgyzstan	3	18	17	19
Gabon	3	42	27	68
Paraguay	3	19	10	39
Sri Lanka	2	7	6	9
Japan	2	2	2	3
Botswana	2	42	15	87

TABLE 68.3 Child mortality by country in 2019 (6).

Countries and areas	Under-five mortality rate			Annual rate of reduction in under-five mortality rate	Under-five mortality rate 2019		Infant mortality rate		Neonatal mortality rate			Mortality rate among children aged 5–14 years		Stillbirth rate		Annual rate of reduction in stillbirth rate	Under-five deaths	Neonatal deaths	Neonatal deaths as a percentage of under-five deaths	Deaths among children aged 5–14 years	Stillbirths
	1990	2000	2019	2000-2019	Male	Female	1990	2019	1990	2000	2019	1990	2019	2000	2019	2000-2019	2019	2019	2019	2019	2019
Sri Lanka	22	17	7	4.4	8	6	19	6	13	10	4	8	2	10	6	3.0	2,378	1,416	60	571	1,973
Ukraine	19	18	8	4.1	9	8	17	7	12	11	5	4	2	7	5	2.1	3,514	2,047	58	823	**1,853**
United Arab Emirates	17	11	7	2.1	8	7	14	6	8	6	4	3	2	8	5	2.8	750	398	53	178	**496**
United Kingdom	9	7	4	2.2	5	4	8	4	4	4	3	2	1	4	3	2.0	3,313	2,142	65	**613**	**2,358**
United Republic of Tanzania	165	129	50	5.0	54	47	100	36	40	34	20	28	11	25	19	1.6	103,222	42,814	42	18,812	40,480
United States	11	8	6	1.4	7	6	9	6	6	5	4	2	1	3	3	0.5	25,352	14,546	57	5,705	11,844

TABLE 68.4 Child protection issues by country in 2019 (6).

Countries and areas	Child labor (%)[H] 2012–2019[R]			Child marriage (%)[H] 2014-2020[R]			Birth registration (%)[H] 2011-2020[R]			Female genital mutilation (%)[H] 2012-2020[R]				Justification of wife-beating among adolescents (%)[H] 2014-2020[R]		Violent discipline (%)[H] 2012-2020[RR]			Sexual violence in childhood (%)[H] 2012-2019[R]	
										Prevalence		Attitudes								
	Total	Male	Female	Female		Male	Total	Male	Female	Women (Fa)	Girls (Fb)	Want the practice to stop (Fc)		Male	Female	Total	Male	Female	Male	Female
				Married by 15	Married by 18	Married by 18						Male	Female							
Spain	–	–	–	–	–	–	100 v	100 v	100 v	–	–	–	–	–						
Sri Lanka	1	1	1	1	10	–	97 x	97 x	97 x	–	–	–	–	–	54 x,y		–			
State of Palestine	9 x,y	11 x,y	8 x,y	1	13	–	99	99	99			–		–	18	90	92	88	4 y	2 y
Sudan	18	20	16	12	34	–	67	69	66	87	30	64 x	53	–	36	64	65	63	–	–
Suriname	4 y	5 y	4 y	9	36	20	98 y	98 y	99 v	–	–	–	–	8	6	87	89	86	–	–
Sweden	–	–	–	–	–	–	100 v	100 v	100 v	–	–	–	–	–	–	–	–	–	4 y	13 y
Switzerland	–	–	–	–	–	–	100 v	100 v	100 v	–	–	–	–	–	–	–	–	–	–	–
Uganda	18	17	19	7	34	6	32	32	32	0	1 x	–	83 x	53	58	85	85	85	1	5
Ukraine	3 y	3 y	3 y	0 x	9 x	4 x	100	100	100	–	–	–	–	2 x	2 x	61 y	68 y	55 y	–	2 x
United Arab Emirates	–	–	–	–	–	–	100 y	100 y	100 y	–	–	–	–	–	–	–	–	–	—	–
United Kingdom	–	–	–	–	0 y	–	100 v	100 v	100 v	–	–	–	–	–	–	–	–	–	1 y	7 y
United Republic of Tanzania	25	26	24	5	31	4	26	28	25	10	0	89 x	95	50	59	–	–	–	–	7

TABLE 68.5 UN Convention of the Rights of the Child Articles (3) which may have particular relevance to forensic physicians

Article 3	1. In all actions concerning children, whether undertaken by public or private social welfare institutions, courts of law, administrative authorities or legislative bodies, the best interests of the child shall be a primary consideration. 2. Parties shall ensure that the institutions, services and facilities responsible for the care or protection of children shall conform with the standards established by competent authorities, particularly in the areas of safety, health, in the number and suitability of their staff, as well as competent supervision.
Article 6	1. Parties recognize that every child has the inherent right to life. 2. Parties shall ensure to the maximum extent possible the survival and development of the child.
Article 12	1. Parties shall assure to the child who is capable of forming his or her own views the right to express those views freely in all matters affecting the child, the views of the child being given due weight in accordance with the age and maturity of the child. 2. For this purpose, the child shall in particular be provided the opportunity to be heard in any judicial and administrative proceedings affecting the child, either directly, or through a representative or an appropriate body, in a manner consistent with the procedural rules of national law.

countries. According to four predefined types of sexual abuse, prevalence estimates ranged from 8 to 31 percent for girls and 3 to 17 percent for boys. Nine girls and three boys out of 100 are victims of forced intercourse. Other studies published since identify on a regional basis what is known about such abuse. From Iran, it has been observed (11) that the prevalence of child sexual abuse is estimated to be 1.5 to 32.5 percent. The risk factors for child sexual abuse in Iran encompass substance abuse, low literacy and education, parents living separately and divorce, poverty and poor socioeconomic status and living in large families. Effective local interventions focused on parents and abused children have been conducted to raise awareness and prevent psychosocial harms as well as reduce aggression and physical and mental problems of children. However, existing laws do not specifically address child sexual abuse. From China (12), a meta-analysis that used the data from 131 734 participants showed no significant difference in the prevalence of childhood sexual abuse between Chinese men (9.1%) and women (8.9%). The prevalence of childhood sexual abuse in studies from mainland areas was significantly higher than that from Hong Kong/Taiwan. However, the author notes that the estimated prevalence of childhood sexual abuse in China also differed according to the definition of child sexual abuse, data collection method, year of data collection, and the mean age of participants at the time of assessment.

Lesser recognized features, which may be due to or part and parcel of types of previous child abuse, need to be considered by forensic physicians including eating disorders. Kimber and colleagues (13) reviewed the association between child emotional abuse (EA), emotional neglect (EN), and exposure to intimate partner violence (IPV) and adult eating-disordered behavior and eating disorders. They noted a Prevalence of EA and EN ranged from 21.0 to 66.0 percent, respectively. No prevalence information was provided in relation to child exposure to IPV. However, although there was a large proportion of adults with eating disorders or eating-disordered behavior report EA, EN, or child exposure to IPV, the authors emphasized there was a paucity of high-quality evidence about these relationships.

Child neglect has been studied in many countries. A study from Saudi Arabia (14) noted 309 cases of child neglect were diagnosed between 2015 and 2019. Mean age of victims was 4.4 ± 4.1 years, and 51.8 percent were male. Supervisory neglect was the most common form (63.1%), followed by medical neglect (39.2%), emotional neglect (6.8%), physical neglect (5.5%) and educational neglect (3.2%). Children between the ages of 1 and 3 years were 3.3 times more likely to be victims of supervisory neglect and girls were 4.5 times more likely to be victims of educational neglect. Children living with ≥4 siblings were 7 times more likely to be victims of physical neglect and 1.9 times of medical neglect. Worsening of underlying disease (30%) and internal injuries (23.5%) were the most common consequences of neglect. Mortality attributed to neglect was documented in 8 (2.6%) children. The authors concluded that although child neglect is common in Saudi Arabia, it has not been recognized as an important cause of morbidity and mortality of children and they recommended a national protocol that would help identify high-risk families for early detection and implementation of prevention programs.

Occasionally, novel factors may theoretically impact on risk of abuse. A study from the USA explored whether the COVID-19 pandemic had impacted on the levels of child physical abuse (15). Cases were identified for the period of April 1–June 30, 2020 (COVID-19) and compared to the identical period in 2019. There were no significant differences in child physical abuse cases between the time periods in the consortium as a whole or at individual hospitals. There were no differences between the study periods with regard to patient characteristics, injury types or severity, resource utilization, disposition, or mortality. In the initial stages of the pandemic apparent rates of new injuries related to child physical abuse did not increase early in the COVID-19 pandemic. However, the authors emphasize it is possible that under-reporting, under-detection, or delays in presentation of abusive injuries increased during the pandemic and thus long-term follow-up of subsequent rates and severity of child abuse is needed to assess for unrecognized injuries that may have occurred. The importance of the long-term follow-up has been shown by a further study from the US (16) which investigated factors associated with child maltreatment during the COVID-19 pandemic, including parental job loss. They found that parents who lost their jobs, were more depressed, and previously psychologically maltreated their children were more likely to psychologically maltreat during the pandemic. The authors concluded that job loss during the COVID-19 pandemic is a significant risk factor for child maltreatment.

The prevalence of child abuse however can be reduced and a study from Sweden (17) analyzed responses from school surveys in 2008, 2011, 2014 and 2017 in Södermanland County, Sweden with an average 5125 respondents per year, 15 and 17 years old. Identical questions were asked on exposure to violence and risk factors including parental employment, separated parents, disability or disease, foreign background and lack of adult support. Intimate partner violence was included at three occasions. The authors found that child physical abuse decreased significantly between 2008 and 2017. Of note, however, was that repeated abuse decreased to a lesser degree than abuse on one occasion.

CHILD PROTECTION PROCESS

Every jurisdiction should have its own child safeguarding policies and child protection processes. The document *Working Together to Safeguard Children* (1999) set out the process which should underpin initial enquiries under section 47 of the Children Act and this has subsequently been revised and updated on several occasions, the latest being in 2018. The current approach in the UK is outlined as an example in the flowcharts shown in Table 68.5 from the *Working Together to Safeguard Children Inter-Agency Guidance* published in July 2018 but developed from the initiatives referred to below (18).

The Children Act 1989 established the Principle of Paramountcy of the needs of the child and provided for statutory frameworks and guidance (19). In particular, the Act laid out that courts are required to act, in the child's best interests when considering the upbringing or the administration of a child's property ...or income arising from it. The Court should have regard to a list of items known as the "Welfare Checklist" which can be found in Section 1 Paragraph 3 of the Act. The Welfare Checklist is shown at Table 68.6. That Act also replaced the concept of parental rights with that of parental responsibility, reflecting Parliament's view that parenthood was a matter of responsibility not rights.

A subsequent Act (Children Act 2004) established that there would be an office of a Children's Commissioner, whose primary function is promoting and protecting the rights of children in England (2). The Children's Commissioner must, in particular, have regard to the United Nations Convention on the Rights of the Child in considering, for the purposes of the primary function, what constitutes the rights and interests of children (generally or so far as relating to a particular matter). It also reinforced or established a child-centered approach; Local Safeguarding Children Boards; a requirement for statutory agencies to co-operate; for Local Authorities to lead enquiries; and to develop local priorities and strategies. The 2004 Act also established Serious Case Reviews and a formal Child Death Overview Process. The National Institute for Health and Clinical Excellence published guidelines on Child Abuse and Neglect specifically aimed at ensuring that abuse and neglect in children and young people aged under 18 was recognized and responded to (NICE). It covers physical, sexual and emotional abuse and neglect and is intended to assist those whose work brings them into contact with children and young people to spot signs of abuse and neglect and to know how to respond. It also supports practitioners who carry out assessments and provides early help and interventions to children, young people, parents and carers (21). In 2017, The Children & Social Work Act emphasized the need for child safeguarding, learning from serious cases and from child deaths (22). It also repealed the local safeguarding children's board structures. Of real significance for healthcare practitioners, and in a departure from local authority lead processes, it made local health leaders responsible for local safeguarding arrangements in partnership with local police and local authority leaders. This new arrangement was given authority to function through local safeguarding children partnerships. The fact that educational authorities were not made statutory partners, given the high level of contact that children have with education, is still debated locally. Instead, they have been deemed to be "relevant agencies" and required to cooperate when called upon to do so, but do not share the legal responsibility.

A National Child Safeguarding Practice Review Panel has been established which identifies and reviews local safeguarding cases it judges to be complex, or of national significance with the aim of the review being to identify any improvements that should be made by safeguarding partners, or others, to safeguard and promote the welfare of children. This Panel publishes Annual Reports. In 2021, the Panel noted that between 1st January 2021 and 31st December 2021, there were 379 serious incidents notified to the Panel, relating to 398 children (23). Of those children notified in 2021, 156 (39.2%) died and 242 (60.8%) suffered serious harm; 325 children were affected indirectly by a serious incident; 252 (63%) were specified as male and 145 (36%) as female. Ethnicity was known for 354 of the 398 children. The majority of children were White British (61%) with Mixed and Black ethnicities at 11 percent each. The age distribution of these children showed a typical bi-modal pattern with a predominance of infants under the age of 1 (32%) and a second peak in the age group 11–15 (26%). Of the 398 children directly involved in a serious incident, 44 (11.1%) were already on a Child Protection Plan (CPP) at the time. Twenty-five of this group of children (56.8%) had been on a CPP at least once before. The number of children who had been on a CPP at some point prior to the incident was higher at 105 children (26.4%). There were 132 families of children recorded as open to Children's Social Care at the time of the serious incident (33.2%) and 266 families which were previously known to CSC (66.8%). Of the 132 families open to CSC at the time of the incident, 126 had had

Flow chart 1: Action taken when a child is referred to local authority children's social care services

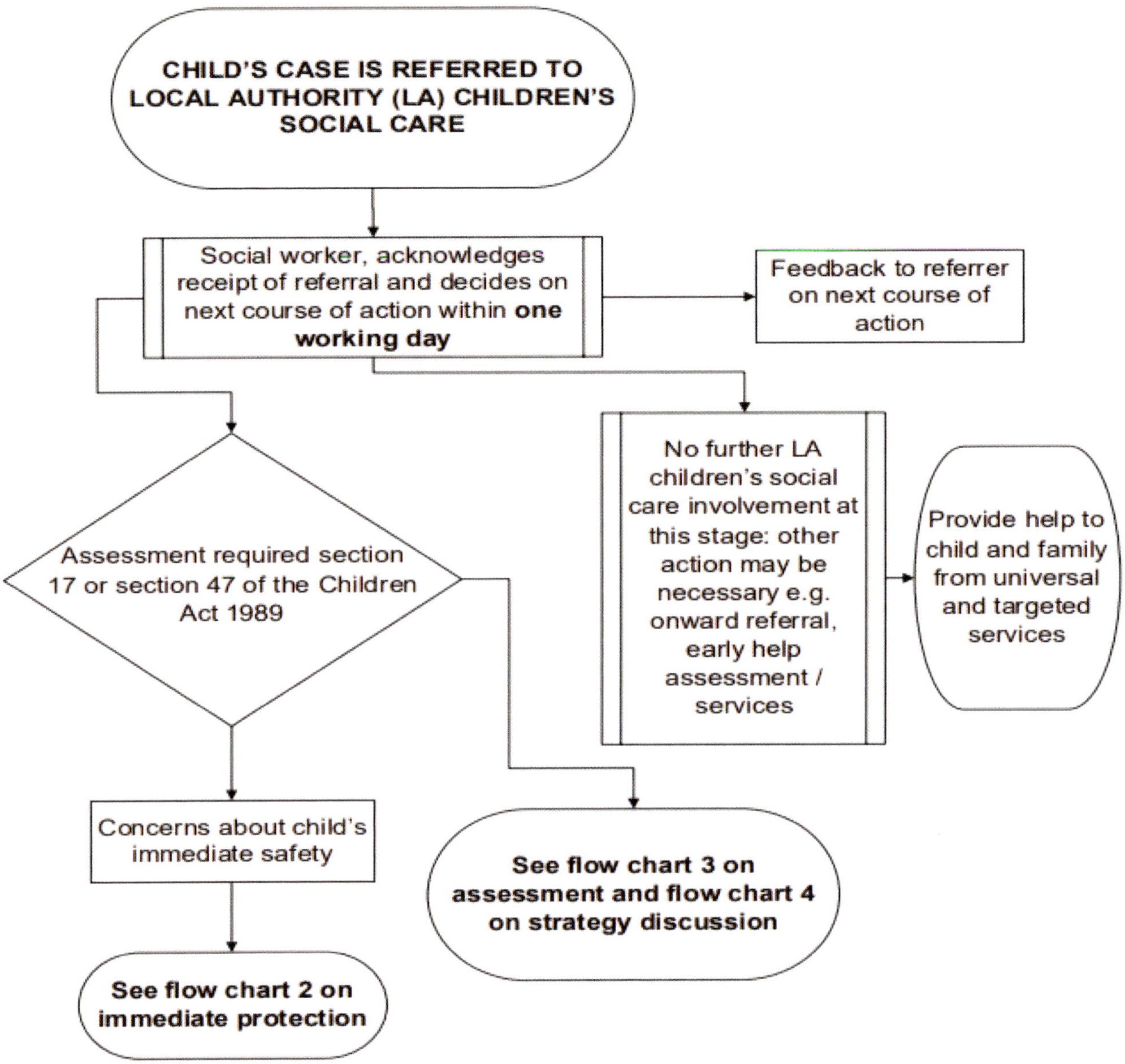

68.2 Flowcharts 1–3 outlining current process in England and Wales (18).

Flow chart 2: Immediate protection

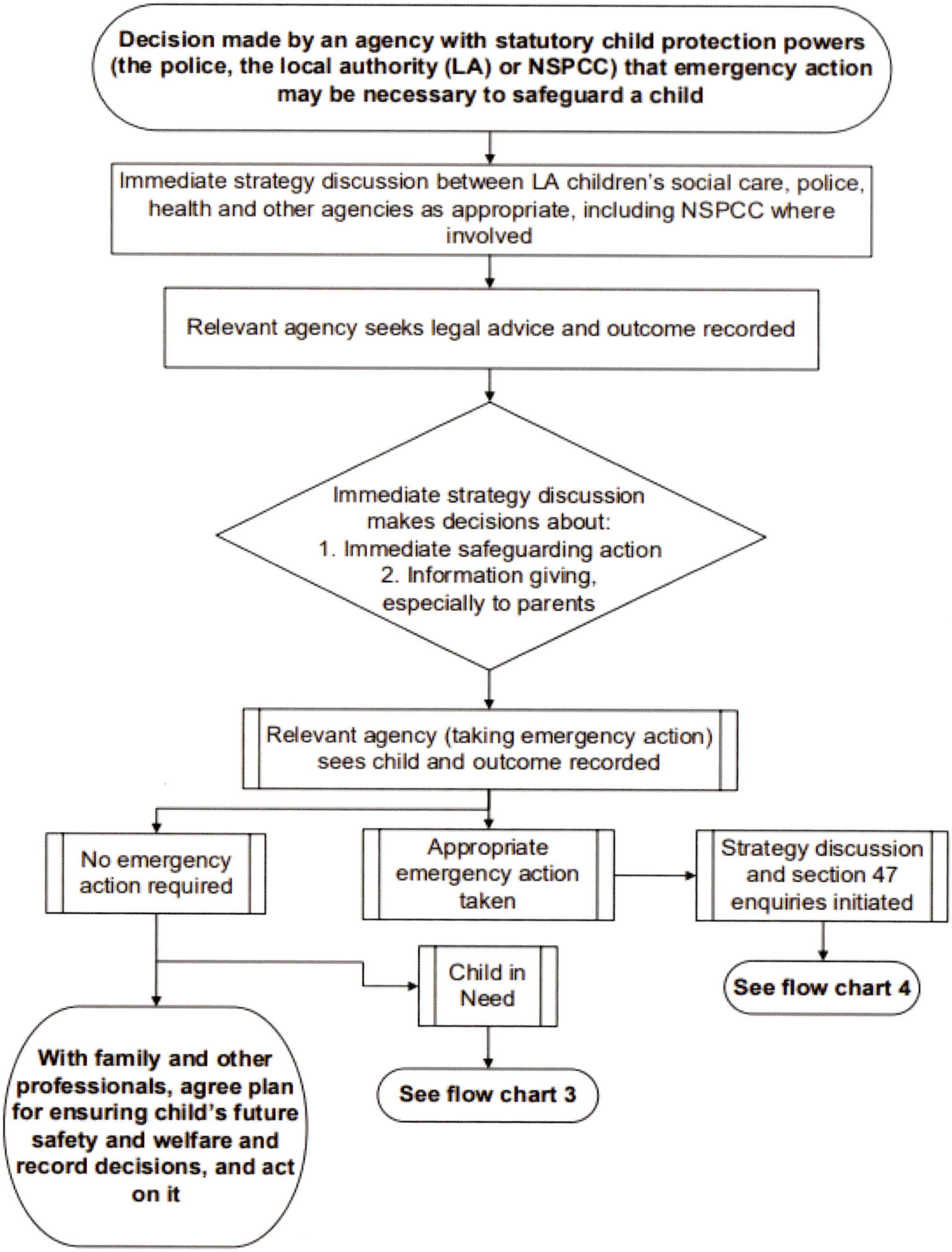

68.2 (Continued)

Flow chart 3: Action taken for an assessment of a child under the Children Act 1989

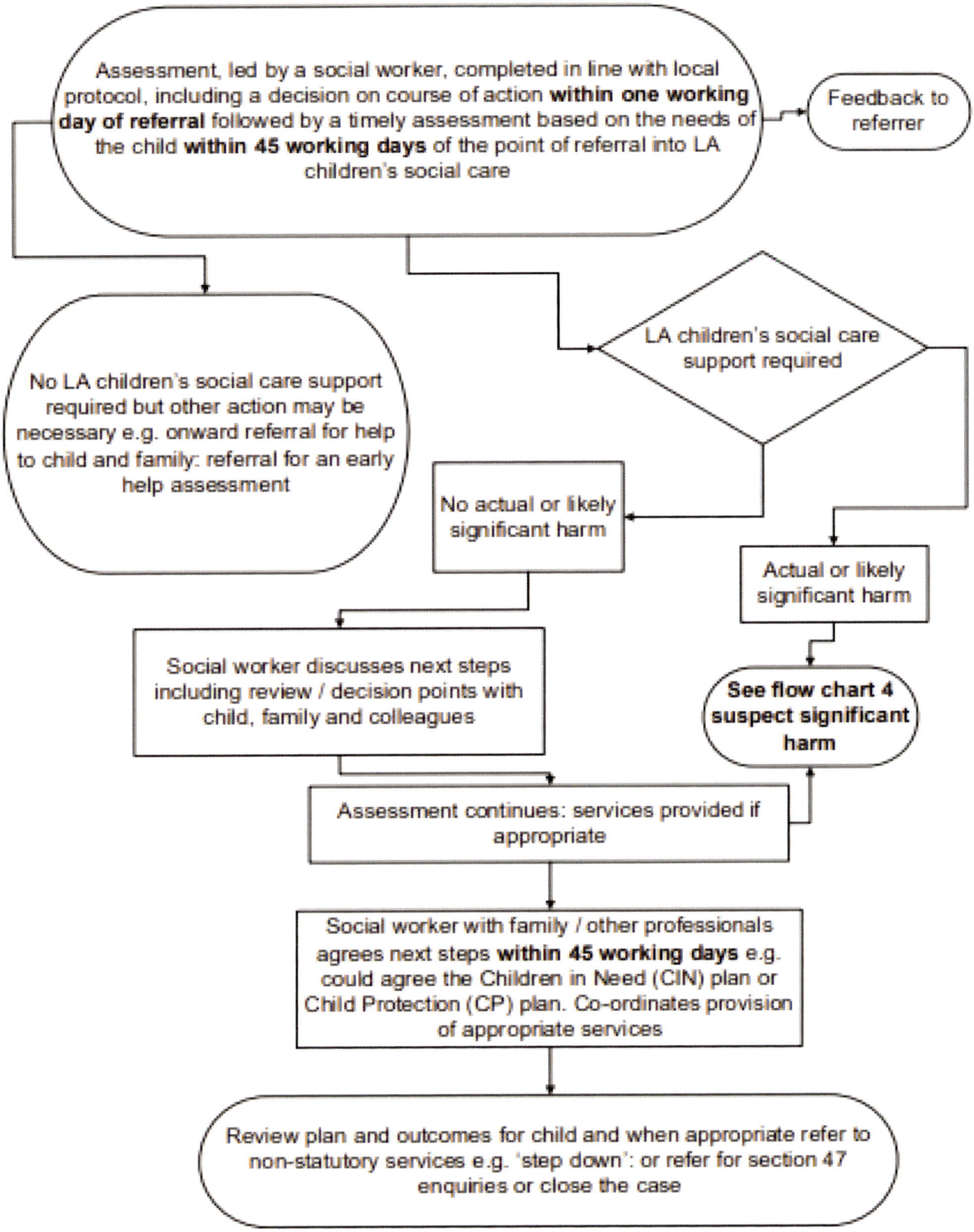

68.2 (Continued)

TABLE 68.6 The Welfare Checklist (as laid out in the Children Act 1989)

A court shall have regard in particular to:

- the ascertainable wishes and feelings of the child concerned (considered in the light of his age and understanding)
- his physical, emotional and educational needs
- the likely effect on him of any change in his circumstances
- his age, sex, background and any characteristics of his which the court considers relevant
- any harm which he has suffered or is at risk of suffering
- how capable each of his parents, and any other person in relation to whom the court considers the question to be relevant, is of meeting his needs
- the range of powers available to the court under this Act in the proceedings in question

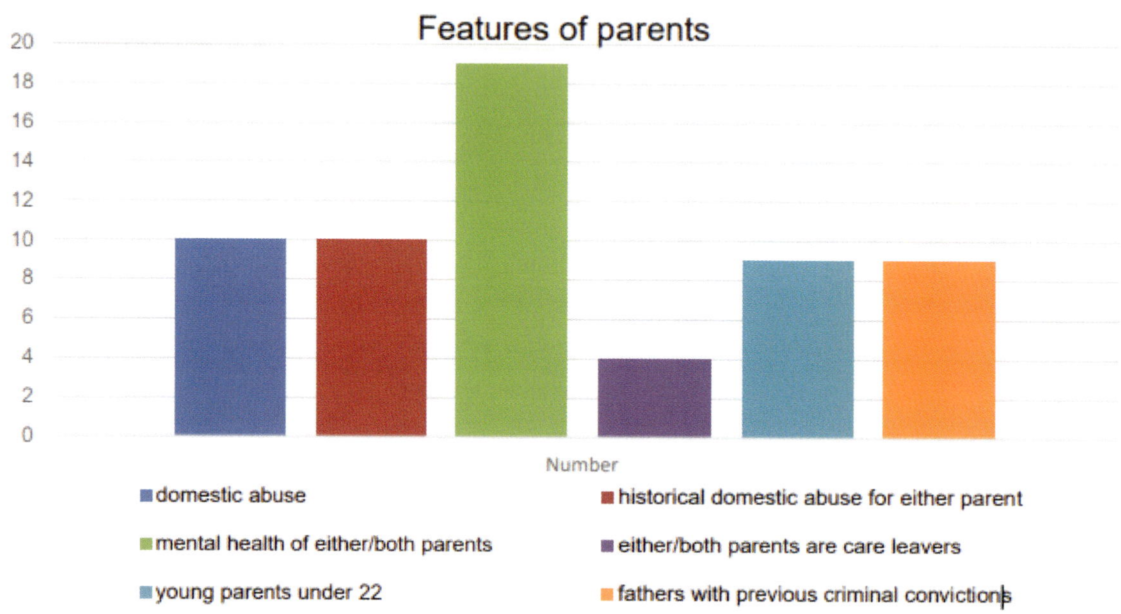

68.3 Findings from the National Review of Non-Accidental Injury in under 1s (24).

some involvement with the service at least once before (95.5%) although involvement may have been an assessment rather than being provided with other services. The Panel also publishes themed reviews. In April 2020, the Panel commissioned a national review of non-accidental injury in under ones. This review included all serious incident notifications and rapid reviews received since June 2018 of cases that met the criteria (24). The review found in the cohort of 23 babies, 19 were seriously harmed and four died. Of the four babies who died, all suffered head injuries/trauma and in three cases there were additional fractures. In three cases, there was evidence of historic injuries indicating injuries suffered on more than one occasion. Of the 19 babies that were seriously harmed, five babies suffered head injuries/trauma with additional fractures; three babies suffered head injuries/trauma; three babies suffered fractures and bruising; six suffered fractures and two suffered from ruptured frenulum's. Of the 19 babies who suffered serious harm, ten babies suffered injuries on more than one occasion. Of the 19 babies who were seriously harmed, five babies are thought to be likely to suffer long-term impairment. Other data from this review are shown in Figure 68.3.

For child deaths, specific statutory and operational guidance is available (25). This should provide national conformity and Figure 68.4 shows the number of death notifications received by the Child Deaths Overview Panels by months of death between 2019 and 2022 (26). In very general terms, the clinical healthcare team should notify the following within 24 hours (or the next working day) of the child's death: the Child Health Information System (CHIS); the NHS England CHIS system provides a comprehensive local record of a child's public health and community based healthcare; general practitioner (GP – primary care physician); the attending healthcare team should inform the child's GP of the fact and circumstances of the death, so that the GP is able to support the family; other professionals, as appropriate; community midwives, health visitor, school nurse, hospital/community medical team; CDR partners, via the local CDOP administrator (or equivalent; Mothers and Babies: Reducing Risk through Audits and Confidential Enquiries (MBRRACE-UK) (27); and Lead Reporter at the hospital of birth in the case of perinatal deaths (22+0 week's gestation to 28 days after birth) to complete the national perinatal mortality surveillance data. The reporting is undertaken

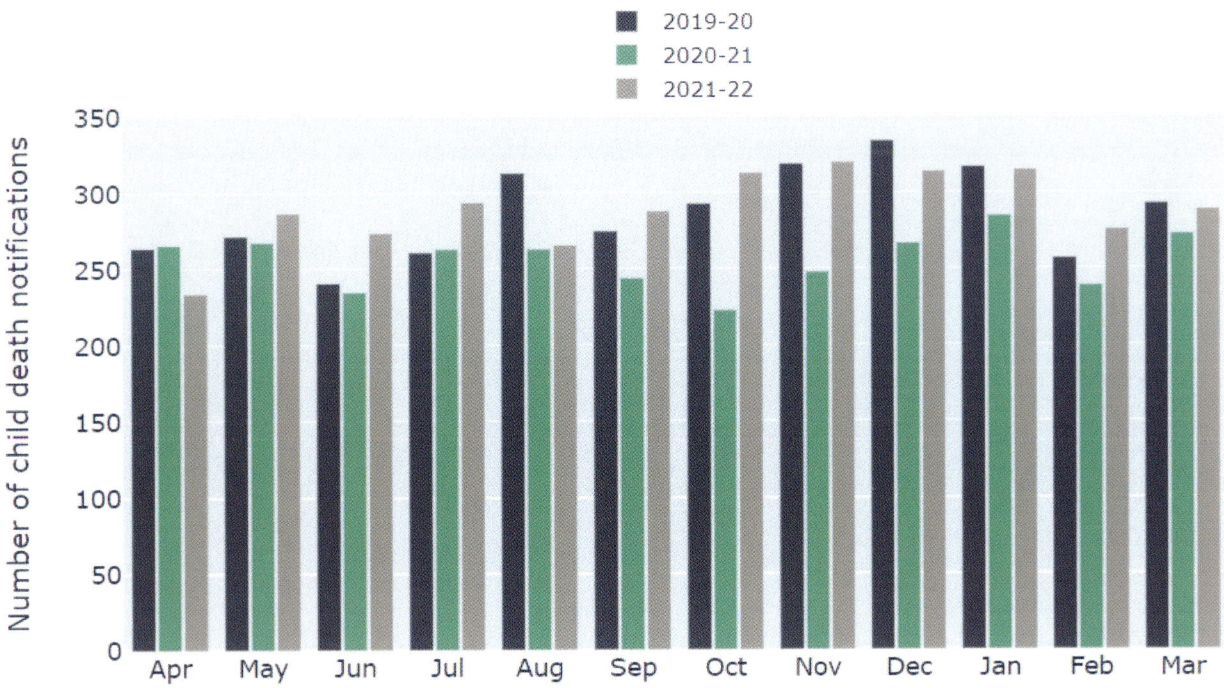

68.4 Number of child death notifications received by Child Death Overview Panels by month of death (26).

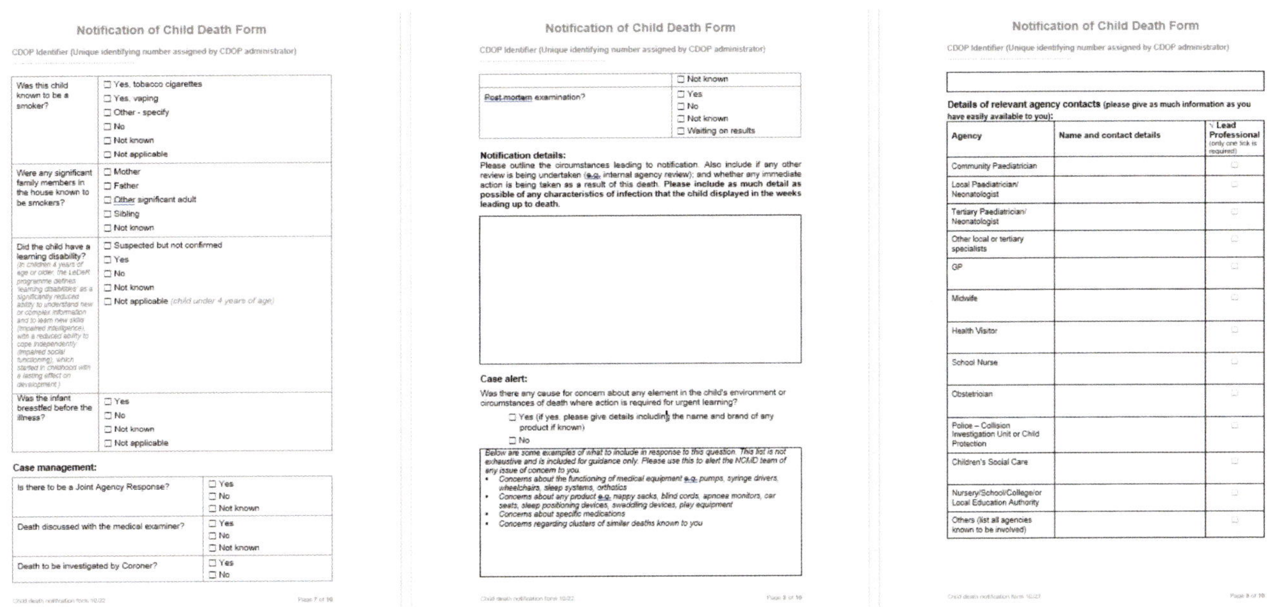

Notification of Child Death Form

CDOP Identifier (Unique identifying number assigned by CDOP administrator)

Was this child known to be a smoker?	☐ Yes, tobacco cigarettes ☐ Yes, vaping ☐ Other - specify ☐ No ☐ Not known ☐ Not applicable
Were any significant family members in the house known to be smokers?	☐ Mother ☐ Father ☐ Other significant adult ☐ Sibling ☐ Not known
Did the child have a learning disability? *(In children 4 years of age or older, the LeDeR programme defines 'learning disabilities' as a significantly reduced ability to understand new or complex information and to learn new skills (impaired intelligence), with a reduced ability to cope independently (impaired social functioning), which started in childhood with a lasting effect on development.)*	☐ Suspected but not confirmed ☐ Yes ☐ No ☐ Not known ☐ Not applicable *(child under 4 years of age)*
Was the infant breastfed before the illness?	☐ Yes ☐ No ☐ Not known ☐ Not applicable

Case management:

Is there to be a Joint Agency Response?	☐ Yes ☐ No ☐ Not known
Death discussed with the medical examiner?	☐ Yes ☐ No ☐ Not known
Death to be investigated by Coroner?	☐ Yes ☐ No

Notification of Child Death Form

CDOP Identifier (Unique identifying number assigned by CDOP administrator)

	☐ Not known
Post mortem examination?	☐ Yes ☐ No ☐ Not known ☐ Waiting on results

Notification details:
Please outline the circumstances leading to notification. Also include if any other review is being undertaken (e.g. internal agency review); and whether any immediate action is being taken as a result of this death. **Please include as much detail as possible of any characteristics of infection that the child displayed in the weeks leading up to death.**

Case alert:

Was there any cause for concern about any element in the child's environment or circumstances of death where action is required for urgent learning?

☐ Yes (if yes, please give details including the name and brand of any product if known)

☐ No

Below are some examples of what to include in response to this question. This list is not exhaustive and is included for guidance only. Please use this to alert the NCMD team of any issue of concern to you.
- *Concerns about the functioning of medical equipment e.g. pumps, syringe drivers, wheelchairs, sleep systems, orthotics*
- *Concerns about any product e.g. nappy sacks, blind cords, apnoea monitors, car seats, sleep positioning devices, swaddling devices, play equipment*
- *Concerns about specific medications*
- *Concerns regarding clusters of similar deaths known to you*

Notification of Child Death Form

CDOP Identifier (Unique identifying number assigned by CDOP administrator)

Details of relevant agency contacts (please give as much information as you have easily available to you):

Agency	Name and contact details	√ Lead Professional (only one tick is required)
Community Paediatrician		☐
Local Paediatrician/ Neonatologist		☐
Tertiary Paediatrician/ Neonatologist		☐
Other local or tertiary specialists		☐
GP		☐
Midwife		☐
Health Visitor		☐
School Nurse		☐
Obstetrician		☐
Police – Collision Investigation Unit or Child Protection		☐
Children's Social Care		☐
Nursery/School/College/or Local Education Authority		☐
Others (list all agencies known to be involved)		☐

68.5 Examples of part of the UK Child Death Reporting Form.

using standardized proforma issued by the Departments of Health & Social Care shown in Figure 68.5 (28).

CONCLUSION

The universal Rights of Children are well established and internationally accepted. Forensic physicians are very likely to encounter child maltreatment in many settings and need to be aware of local child protection and safeguarding processes. Forensic physicians must take responsibility for recognizing concerns, documenting them, sharing them with other agencies, biological sample taking, interpreting and presenting evidence to assist statutory processes. Child safeguarding can only work if public and professionals are educated about the signs, presentations and effects of child maltreatment (beyond visible injury). Public health campaigns are essential to ensure that children are enabled to disclose confusing, difficult or traumatizing experiences, and that it is safe for them to do so. Forensic physicians should work with local authorities, local police, local educationalists, public health teams, NGOs, the public and other healthcare professionals to advise, educate and train. Governments need to fund all bodies and organizations so that children can be supported. The forensic physician and allied practitioners working in these areas have the potential to change the outcome for a child who might be at risk of harm or death.

REFERENCES

1. National Society for the Prevention of Cruelty to Children. Safeguarding children and child protection, 2023. Available from: https://learning.nspcc.org.uk/safeguarding-child-protection (Accessed 16 May 2023).
2. World Health Organisation. Child maltreatment, 2022. Available from: https://www.who.int/news-room/fact-sheets/detail/child-maltreatment (Accessed 16 May 2023).
3. UNICEF. The United Nations convention on the rights of the child, 1990. Available from: https://www.unicef.org/child-rights-convention/convention-text (Accessed 16 May 2023).
4. UNICEF. Convention on the rights of the child: the children's version. Available from: https://www.unicef.org/sop/convention-rights-child-child-friendly-version (Accessed 16 May 2023).
5. World Health Organisation. Responding to child maltreatment: a clinical handbook for health professionals, 2022. Available from: https://www.who.int/publications/i/item/9789240048737 (Accessed 16 May 2023).
6. UNICEF. The state of the world's children 2021. On my mind. Promoting, protecting and caring for children's mental health, 2021. Available from: https://www.unicef.org/media/114636/file/SOWC-2021-full-report-English.pdf (Accessed 16 May 2023).
7. Royal College of Paediatrics & Child Health. Perplexing presentations (PP)/fabricated or induced illness (FII) in children – guidance, 2021. Available from: https://childprotection.rcpch.ac.uk/resources/perplexing-presentations-and-fii/ (Accessed 16 May 2023).
8. Metropolitan Police Service. What is child abuse? 2023. Available from: https://www.met.police.uk/advice/advice-and-information/caa/child-abuse/what-is-child-abuse (Accessed 19 May 2023).
9. Chandraratne NK, Fernando AD, Gunawardena N. Physical, sexual and emotional abuse during childhood: Experiences of a sample of Sri Lankan Young adults. *Child Abuse Negl* 2018; **81**: 214–24.
10. Barth J, Bermetz L, Heim E, et al. The current prevalence of child sexual abuse worldwide: A systematic review and meta-analysis. *Int J Public Health* 2013; **58**(3): 469–83.
11. Danaeifar M, Arshi M, Moghanibashi-Mansourieh A. Child sexual abuse in Iran: A systematic review of the prevalence, risk factors, consequences, interventions and laws. *J Inj Violence Res* 2022; **14**(3): 225–36.
12. Ma Y. Prevalence of childhood sexual abuse in China: A meta-analysis. *J Child Sex Abus* 2018; **27**(2): 107–21.
13. Kimber M, McTavish JR, Couturier J, et al. Consequences of child emotional abuse, emotional neglect and exposure to intimate partner violence for eating disorders: A systematic critical review. *BMC Psychol* 2017; **5**(1): 33.
14. AlFarhan M, AlMelhem J, ElMahadi A, et al. Child neglect in Saudi Arabia: The neglected form of child maltreatment. *Saudi Med J* 2022; **43**(6): 610–17.
15. Russell KW, Acker SN, Ignacio RC, et al. Child physical abuse and COVID-19: Trends from nine pediatric trauma centers. *J Pediatr Surg* 2022; **57**(2): 297–301.
16. Lawson M, Piel MH, Simon M. Child maltreatment during the COVID-19 pandemic: Consequences of parental job loss on psychological and physical abuse towards children. *Child Abuse Negl* 2020; **110**(**Pt 2**): 104709.
17. Kvist T, Dahllöf G, Svedin CG, Annerbäck EM. Child physical abuse, declining trend in prevalence over 10 years in Sweden. *Acta Paediatr* 2020; **109**(7): 1400–8.
18. HM Government. Working together to safeguard children. A guide to inter-agency working to safeguard and promote the welfare of children, 2018. Available from: https://assets.publishing.service.gov.uk/government/uploads/system/uploads/attachment_data/file/942454/Working_together_to_safeguard_children_inter_agency_guidance.pdf (Accessed 16 May 2023).
19. Legislation.gov.uk. Children Act 1989. Available from: https://www.legislation.gov.uk/ukpga/1989/41/contents (Accessed 16 May 2023).
20. Legislation.gov.uk. Children Act 2004. Available from: https://www.legislation.gov.uk/ukpga/2004/31/contents (Accessed 16 May 2023).
21. National Institute for Health and Clinical Excellence. Child abuse and neglect, 2017. Available from: https://www.nice.org.uk/guidance/ng76 (Accessed 16 May 2023).
22. Legislation.gov.uk. Children and Social Work Act 2017. Available from: https://www.legislation.gov.uk/ukpga/2017/16/contents (Accessed 16 May 2023).
23. GOV.uk. Child safeguarding practice review panel: annual report, 2021. Available from: https://www.gov.uk/government/publications/child-safeguarding-practice-review-panel-annual-report-2021 (Accessed 16 May 2023).
24. The Child Safeguarding Practice Review Panel. Fieldwork report: national review of non-accidental injury in under 1s, 2021. Available from: https://assets.publishing.service.gov.uk/government/uploads/system/uploads/attachment_data/file/1017227/National_Review_of_Non-Accidental_Injury_in_under_1s.pdf (Accessed 16 May 2023).
25. HM Government. Child death review. Statutory and operational guidance (England), 2018. Available from: https://assets.publishing.service.gov.uk/government/uploads/system/uploads/attachment_data/file/1120062/child-death-review-statutory-and-operational-guidance-england.pdf (Accessed 16 May 2023).
26. National Child Mortality Database. Child death review data release, 2022. Available from: https://www.ncmd.info/publications/child-death-review-data-release-2022/ (Accessed 16 May 2023).
27. MBRRACE-UK. Mothers and babies: reducing risk through audits and confidential enquiries across the UK, 2023. Available from: https://www.npeu.ox.ac.uk/mbrrace-uk (Accessed 16 May 2023).
28. GOV.uk. Child death reviews: forms for reporting child deaths, 2014. Available from: https://www.gov.uk/government/publications/child-death-reviews-forms-for-reporting-child-deaths (Accessed 6 September 2023).

CHAPTER

69

Substance Use in Short-Term Detention

Jason Payne-James and Alex J. Gorton

INTRODUCTION

For those who work in clinical forensic medicine settings, it is inevitable that a proportion of patients seen will be suffering from dependency on alcohol or other substances. These patients will be at risk of being intoxicated or withdrawing. Other patients (such as those frequenting hotels, public houses, clubs and bars) may not be dependent but may be acutely intoxicated with one or more substances including alcohol and other drugs. If those patients are detained in custody, or have been assaulted and require forensic medical assessments, their safety and well-being is in part dependent on the forensic physician or other forensic practitioner.

One single chapter can only provide an overview of such a vast topic and the authors would recommend those who regularly encounter patients who have substance use disorders take advantage of a dedicated text (1). Within the UK, a particularly useful resource is provided for clinicians via the UK Poisons Information Service especially their online clinical toxicology database (TOXBASE) (2).

In England & Wales, the Police and Criminal Evidence Act 1984 (3) and its Codes of Practice (4) indicate that the police must make sure a detainee receives appropriate clinical attention as soon as reasonably practical if they appear to be suffering from a physical illness or appear to need clinical attention.

In the majority of cases, those who are intoxicated, or drug or alcohol dependent, or apparently withdrawing from drugs or alcohol will be assessed by a forensic practitioner. This is reinforced by Authorized Professional Practice (APP) which is published by the College of Policing (5).

APP states with regard to those under the influence of drink or alcohol – "*Officers and staff must risk assess all detainees on arrival in custody and throughout their detention. Where a risk assessment shows that the person is not drunk and incapable but that they have a degree of impairment from alcohol or drugs, the minimum requirement is for level 2 rousing checks for all persons under the influence and subsequent escalation depending on the perceived level of intoxication. Even with level 3 and level 4 observation/supervision, rousing is still required at appropriate intervals*". Observation levels are range from 1–4 and these are described in Table 69.1. Police officers are advised that they must always consult an appropriate forensic healthcare professional (HCP) if: the risk assessment indicates that level 3 or level 4 monitoring is required; a person detained for an evidential breath test registers more than 150 micrograms of alcohol; a custody officer has particular concerns about a person who is believed to have consumed alcohol or drugs and has been physically restrained; the person experiences an epileptic seizure; and the detainee shows signs of alcohol withdrawal, especially delirium tremens (DTs). The police are further advised that if an HCP is not immediately available to assess a detainee who has had a seizure or has DTs, officers should immediately transfer the detainee to hospital. It is emphasized to the police that they should rouse detainees who are apparently under the influence of alcohol or other substances and this method of managing detainees who have consumed alcohol and/or drugs minimizes the possibility of missing a more serious underlying medical condition (such as intracranial hemorrhage or diabetic hypoglycemia).

The Independent Office for Police Conduct publishes annual statistics on deaths in police custody. In 2022/2023 there were 23 deaths in or following police custody, an increase of 12 from 2021/22, and the highest figure since 2017/18. Eight people were taken ill or were identified as being unwell in a police cell. Five were taken to hospital where they later died. Three people died in a police custody suite. Twelve people were taken ill at the scene of arrest. Eight people were taken to hospital, where they later died. Four people died at the scene. One man was taken ill in a police vehicle, and was taken to hospital where he died. One man died following release from police custody. The man had been taken to hospital after being charged and remanded. One man died after leaving police detention. His body was found after going missing from hospital while still in the care of police and awaiting a mental health assessment (7). The UK Government has noted that the majority of individuals who died in or following police custody in the most recent year had links to drugs and/or alcohol (8). This is in line with alcohol and drugs having been recognized as significant preventable causes of death around the world for many years (9–13).

All police and forensic HCPs in any country should therefore be aware of (a) the risks of alcohol and drugs use in custody and (b) that they often represent the largest group of potentially preventable deaths.

DOI: 10.1201/9781003138754-72

TABLE 69.1 Observation levels (6)

Level 1: General observation

Following full risk assessment, this is the minimum acceptable level of observation required for any detainee. It includes the following actions:

- the detainee is checked at least every hour (the risk assessment is updated where necessary)
- checks are carried out sensitively to cause as little intrusion as possible
- if no reasonable foreseeable risk is identified, staff need not wake a sleeping detainee (checks of the sleeping detainee must, however, continue and if any change in the detainee's condition presents a new risk, the detainee should be roused)
- if the detainee is awake, staff should communicate with them

Level 2: Intermittent observation

Subject to medical direction, this is the minimum acceptable level for detainees who are under the influence of alcohol or drugs, or whose level of consciousness causes concern. It includes the following actions:

- the detainee is visited and roused at least every 30 minutes
- physical visits and checks must be carried out – CCTV and other technologies can be used in support of this
- the detainee is positively communicated with at frequent and irregular intervals
- visits to the detainee are conducted in accordance with PACE Code C Annex H

Level 3: Constant observation

If the detainee's risk assessment indicates a heightened level of risk to the detainee (for example self-harm, suicide risk or other significant mental or physical vulnerability) they should be observed at this level. It includes the following actions:

- the detainee is under constant observation and accessible at all times
- physical checks and visits must be carried out at least every 30 minutes
- CCTV is constantly monitored (other technologies can also be used)
- any possible ligatures are removed
- the detainee is positively communicated with at frequent and irregular intervals
- review by the HCP

The purpose of CCTV cell monitoring should be recorded in the custody record together with the name of the designated officer or member of custody staff who is responsible for the monitoring.

Officers and staff must consider issues of privacy, dignity and gender.

Level 4: Close proximity

Detainees at the highest risk of self-harm should be observed at this level. It must include the following actions:

- the detainee is physically supervised in close proximity to staff to enable immediate physical intervention if necessary
- CCTV and other technologies do not meet the criteria of close-proximity observation but may complement it
- issues of privacy, dignity and gender are taken into consideration
- any possible ligatures are removed
- the detainee is positively communicated with at frequent and irregular intervals
- review by the HCP

Every officer or member of custody staff required to conduct close-proximity supervision must be fully briefed by the custody officer with regards their role, the needs of the detainee and the risks presented by the detained person. They must be fully trained and equipped to respond accordingly. If there is a requirement to rouse, this must be done by a trained officer or member of staff. Any changes in the detainee's condition must be brought to the custody officer's attention immediately.

HCPs may work across different forces and be familiar with different categories or levels of observation. Custody managers should ensure that HCPs working within their force are aware of local procedures.

DEMOGRAPHICS OF POLICE DETAINEES AND PREVALENCE OF DRUG USE

Numerous studies have shown that drugs and alcohol are over-represented in the detainee population (14–20). In a prospective study in London, UK of over 200 detainees, 33 percent were dependent on crack cocaine and heroin, 25 percent were dependent on alcohol and 17 percent on benzodiazepines.

This study did not take into account acute intoxication from other drugs (13). Many detainees will have associated mental health conditions and many will have chronic health conditions (e.g. diabetes, cardiac disease, chronic obstructive pulmonary disease, epilepsy) which, because of lifestyle may not be optimally managed, and concordance with, or access to, prescribed medication may be poor.

The high incidence of "general" healthcare issues and with associated "forensic" healthcare challenges put many detainees at increased risk of morbidity and mortality.

Use of drugs is widespread and spreads across age ranges. In England and Wales for the year ending June 2022 approximately 1 in 11 adults aged 16 to 59 years and approximately 1 in 5 adults aged 16 to 24 years reported using drugs in the previous year. Of adults aged 16 to 59 years 2.7 percent reported Class A drug use as did 4.7 percent of adults aged 16 to 24 years. There were no changes in the previous year drug use for the majority of individual drugs in the year ending June 2022 compared with the year ending March 2020, however, prevalence of ecstasy use fell from 1.4 percent to 0.7 percent in adults aged 16 to 59 years and from 4.0 percent to 1.1 percent in adults aged 16 to 24 years while prevalence of nitrous oxide use fell from 2.4 percent to 1.3 percent for adults aged 16 to 59 years and from 8.7 percent to 3.9 percent for adults aged 16 to 24 years.

While it may be tempting to speculate, it is not possible to know whether the decreases in the use of Class A drugs, ecstasy and nitrous oxide were as a result of social contact restrictions because of COVID-19. However 2.1 percent of adults aged 16 to 59 years and 4.3 percent of adults aged 16 to 24 years were classed as "frequent" drug users (i.e. had taken a drug more than once a month in the previous year) (21).

The proportion of those aged 11 to 15 years in England who had taken any drug (excluding novel psychoactive substances [NPS]) in the previous year was 10.4 percent (20). Cannabis is the most used drug in England and Wales; in the latest year, 7.4 percent and 16.2 percent of adults aged 16 to 59 years and 16 to 24 years, respectively, reported having used the drug in the preceding 12 months. Powder cocaine was used by 2 percent of those aged 16 to 59 years and 4 percent of those 16 to 24 years. NPS were used by 0.4 percent of adults aged 16 to 59 years and 0.9 percent of the 16 to 24 years group.

MANAGEMENT OF DRUG AND ALCOHOL USE IN CUSTODY

Widespread use of a range of drugs, often in association with alcohol, mean that the focus of the forensic practitioner is primarily to prevent harm (including death) as a result of intoxication or withdrawal from substances while in custody. The secondary role is to ensure that anyone who is dependent on, or suffering from the effects of, drugs or alcohol is fit enough to go through the police process safely, which may include sample taking, interview and identification processes. Those with substance use disorders, whether they are in police custody or not, should have access to appropriate quality and effective treatment. This will include full clinical assessment, identifying associated morbidities, identifying the degree and severity of dependence or intoxication with alcohol or drugs, identifying the need for medical intervention, and determining what (for both intoxication and withdrawal) the appropriate management is (including treatment or referral) to avoid, or minimize the risks of medical, psychiatric and/or procedural (legal or police) complications.

The UK Royal College of Psychiatrists and the Faculty of Forensic & Legal Medicine have produced a 5th edition of *Detainees with substance use disorders in police custody: guidelines for clinical management* (22). This publication outlines the principles of clinical management and the specific problems associated with specific drugs, outlining their effects. It also emphasizes the need for those forensic practitioners working in clinical forensic medicine to have skills appropriate to working with detainees with substance use disorders in police custody. The general principles espoused have been summarised and adapted in Table 69.2.

The priority must always be the clinical safety of detainees. It is important to be aware that those in custodial or Sexual Assault Referral Center (SARC) settings may not only use alcohol or a single drug as many will have polydrug use with or without alcohol. Excesses of either or use in combination may carry the risk of cardiorespiratory arrest (particularly if sedatives or opiates are present). It is also important to be aware of other sources of drug intake (if not admitted) and internal concealment of undeclared drugs carry the risk of fatality (23–25).

The management of those who are intoxicated should not be over-complicated. In very simple terms, if there are concerns about someone's degree of intoxication causing drowsiness or altered consciousness, the use of the PACE Codes of Practice Annex H (4) (*see* Table 69.3) enables an assessment to be done rapidly by the police and, if any detainee fails to meet any of listed criteria, an appropriate HCP assessment must be done or an ambulance must be called, as that person is not safe to remain in custody and requires formal clinical assessment and monitoring.

When assessing an individual in the context of drugs or alcohol use, in addition to a full medical history (which may include current complaints, relevant past medical, past surgical, past psychiatric, past sexual health and history), a detailed account of past and present drug and alcohol use should be obtained. Table 69.4 summarizes the essential aspects of such a history. The clinical examination should be thorough and, in particular, signs

TABLE 69.2 Skills suggested for forensic practitioners working with detainees in custody with substance use disorders

All clinicians have basic training in clinical forensic medicine

All clinicians working with detainees with substance use disorders must be able to:

- Take a comprehensive history
- Undertake a full multi-system clinical examination
- Assess mental state and be able to identify mental health conditions associated with substance use
- Identify and manage the signs and symptoms of drug and alcohol use, intoxication and withdrawal
- Safely and effectively prescribe medications
- Manage overdose
- Signpost to harm reduction interventions.

Be aware of:

- Particularly vulnerable groups and their management (e.g. those who are pregnant; those who are on prescribed medications)
- Forensic issues (e.g. sample collection, fitness to interview) and how they can be managed in the context of substance use disorder.

Source: Adapted from (22).

TABLE 69.3 Annex H – PACE Codes of Practice (4)

An immediate HCP assessment or ambulance attendance is required if the patient fails to meet any of the following criteria
Rousability – can they be woken? • Go into the cell • Call their name • Shake gently
Response to questions – can they give appropriate answers to questions such as: • What's your name? • Where do you live? • Where do you think you are?
Response to commands – can they respond appropriately to commands such as: • Open your eyes! • Lift one arm, now the other arm!
Remember to take into account the possibility or presence of other illnesses, injury, or mental condition; a person who is drowsy and smells of alcohol may also have the following: • Diabetes • Epilepsy • Head injury • Drug intoxication or overdose

TABLE 69.4 Key elements of a substance use history

Key elements
Type of substance used
Duration of substance use
Quantity taken per day, on an average/typical day and/or amount spent on substances
Frequency of use
Routes of administration (noting any sites of injection)
Sharing of needles and paraphernalia
Amount used in the past 24–48 hours
The time of the last dose(s)
Is currently receiving treatment and medication as part of an opioid substitution detoxification or maintenance program (OST)
Previous experience of withdrawal symptoms including physical and psychological consequences
Any history of treatment for misuse and its effectiveness

and symptoms of intoxication or withdrawal or chronic substance use should be sought. Figure 69.1 shows some examples of common clinical findings that may be of use in the overall assessment.

It is helpful and appropriate to use scoring systems in the case of alcohol and opiate dependence which have been validated for, or are considered appropriate in, the clinical forensic medicine setting.

BOX 69.1 Examples of conditions which mimic or may be mimicked by drug and alcohol intoxication and withdrawal

- Accidental prescribed drug overdose
- Bacteremia with rigours
- Deliberate but undisclosed drug overdose
- Diabetic ketoacidosis
- Encephalitis
- Hemorrhagic stroke
- Hypoactive delirium
- Hypoglycemia
- Hypothermia
- Hypoxia
- Intracranial bleed due to trauma
- Intracranial neoplasm
- Ischemic stroke
- Meningitis
- Neurosarcoidosis
- Post-ictal state
- Psychosis
- Sepsis

The Clinical Institute Withdrawal Assessment for Alcohol Scale-revised (CIWA-Ar) has been widely used and validated in hospitals to quantify the degree of withdrawal by documenting signs and symptoms exhibited or experienced by the patient.

It has not been formally validated in the detention setting but has become widely used as it allows the change in condition to be noted (26). It is shown in Chapter 65. Similarly, for those who are dependent on opiate drugs, the Clinical Opiate Withdrawal Scale (COWS) has proved valuable in the monitoring and confirming (or not) the degree of withdrawal symptomology experienced (27).

Both CIWA-Ar and COWS are used widely in the monitoring of the clinical condition of patients. Once a full history and clinical examination with the use of scoring systems, if appropriate, has been undertaken it may be possible to allot the patient into one of four groups (with respect to the signs and symptoms exhibited). These are – clinically stable; possibly withdrawing; possibly intoxicated with a final group where the signs and symptoms represent some other condition or pathology.

Figure 69.2 shows potential routes of actions once the assessment is complete. For those who are stable and who are not dependent on drugs, they may need no further assessment or, if there may be reasons (e.g. the need to assess for fitness to interview, or to assess for future withdrawal) for them to be reviewed at a fixed time. For those who are intoxicated, their management will depend on its degree and severity. This may range from simply allowing the effects to wear off, all the way through to the need for immediate resuscitation, ventilatory support and the use of reversal agents. Observations should be put in place taking into account clinical safety and need.

The Royal College of Psychiatrists guidelines for clinical management provides therapeutic guidelines for the treatment of withdrawal symptoms and examples of symptomatic treatments are shown in Table 69.5 and

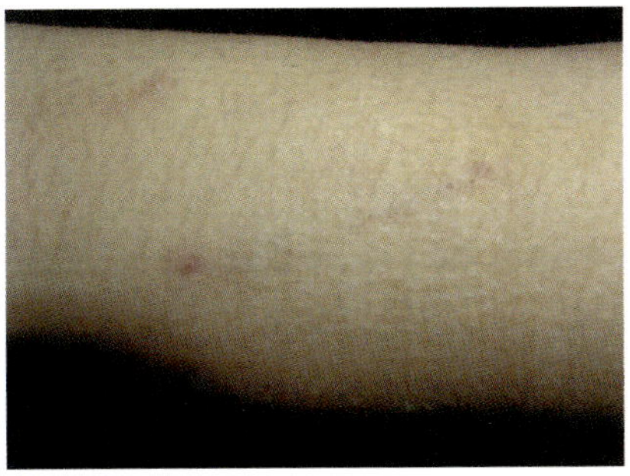

(a) Piloerection (gooseflesh) – sign of opiate withdrawal (note injection sites along line of vein).

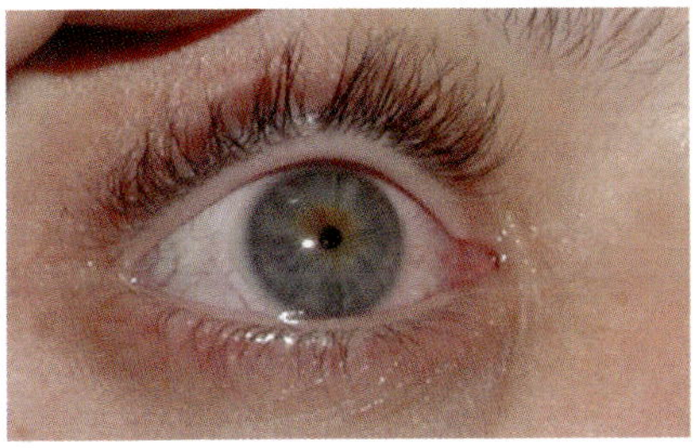

(b) Pinpoint pupil – caused by recent opiate use.

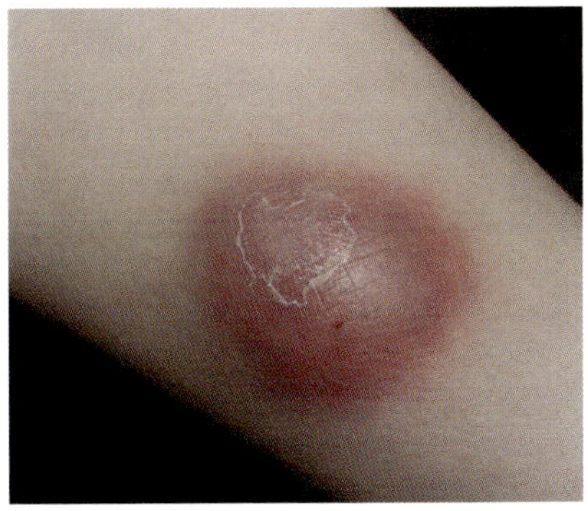

(c) Localized abscess at the site of intravenous injection in the forearm (note gooseflesh also present).

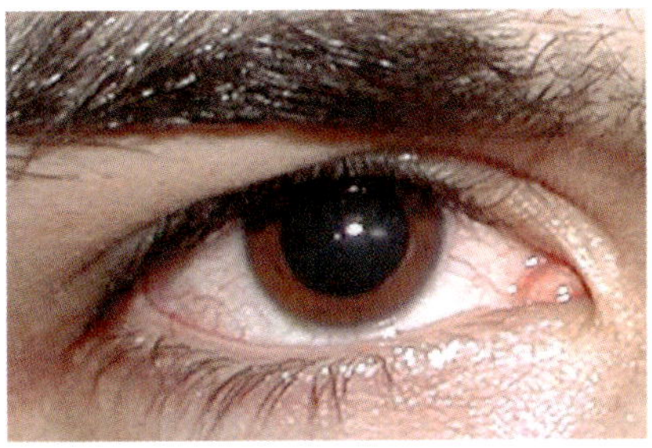

(d) Pupillary dilatation – consistent with alcohol or stimulant drug.

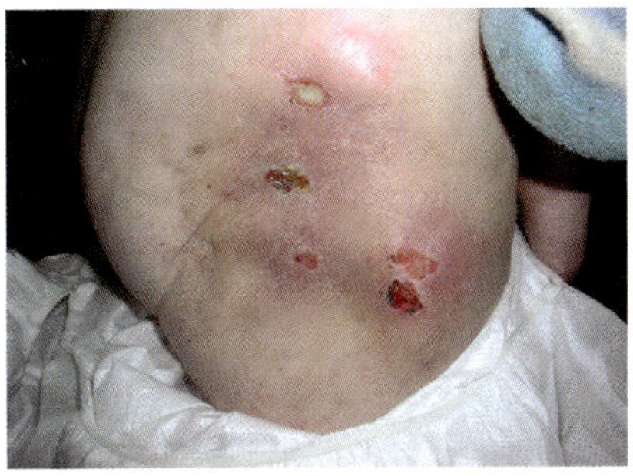

(e) Multiple **"skin-pop"** ulcers from injection sites to buttock.

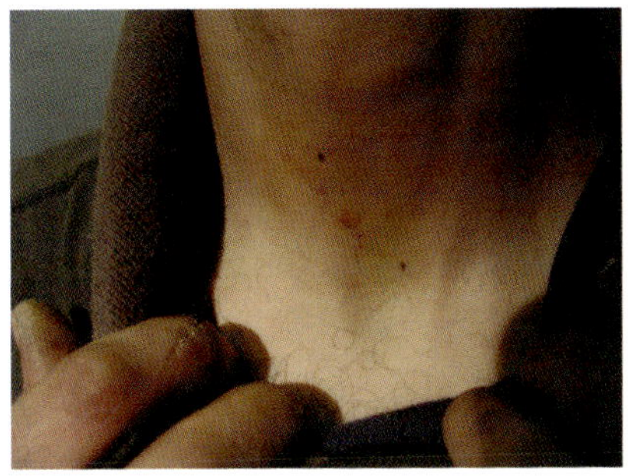

(f) Injection sites to neck.

69.1 Examples of possible clinical findings supporting substance misuse.

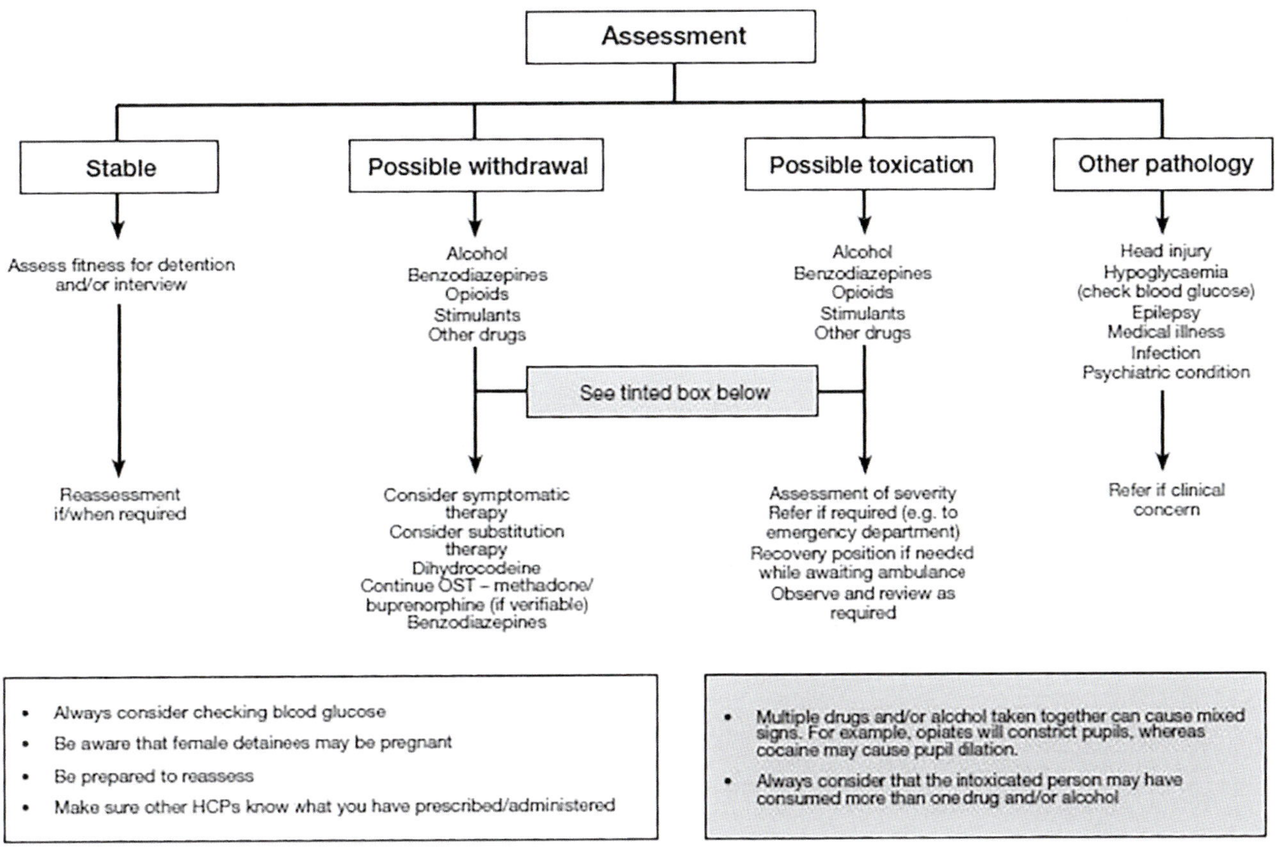

69.2 Proposed Assessment Protocol (as from 22).

substitution options are discussed at length within the 5th edition of *Detainees with Substance Use Disorders in Police Custody: Guidelines for Clinical Management* (22).

Every jurisdiction will have its own regulations and approach to the management of those who are under the influence of drugs and other substances, who are dependent on them, and who may be intoxicated by, or withdrawing from them. From the forensic physician and other forensic practitioner perspective, their duties should be to ensure the health and welfare of the individual, to identify risk factors which may lead to morbidity or death, and act on those risk factors. The actions may simply involve informing those who are responsible for the care (whether in custody, SARC or elsewhere) of the risks identified and ensuring that the advice given is followed through.

Sometimes (e.g. in cases of withdrawal) this may involve the administration of appropriate medication, adhering to appropriate prescribing guidelines, to allow the individual to be fully involved in the police or other process in which they are participating. Sometimes, it may involve lifesaving interventions when someone becomes acutely unwell (e.g. respiratory arrest after opiate intake).

Often it means ensuring that the person is directed to or referred to (after the current proceedings) to appropriate support (such as drug or alcohol teams).

Perhaps one of the most significant options is differentiating what has been perceived to be a drug or alcohol intoxication issue, and properly diagnosing a medical condition that requires immediate hospital referral.

Box 69.1 identifies a series of conditions which mimic or are mimicked by alcohol or drug intoxication or withdrawal, all of which may cause sudden death. There is a tendency to think of alcohol and drug intoxication in isolation, and to believe that each group of drugs will be readily identifiable by class signs and symptoms. This is rarely the case and the forensic practitioner must be aware that alcohol may be consumed with other sedative or stimulant drugs, many of whose actions and times of actions are known, but together are not. Additionally, with the advent of multiple NPS such as cathinones and synthetic cannabinoids whose use evolves and changes regularly and more recently widespread recreational use of nitrous oxide, the clinical effects of which are only now beginning to become recognized (28,29), it is essential that those who may have consumed alcohol and other substances have access to appropriate quality medical care that understand the wide range of presentations of the wide range of products available to the consumers. Forensic clinicians will find a useful resource for relevant NPS information at http://neptune-clinical-guidance.co.uk/ (30).

TABLE 69.5 Examples of symptomatic treatment options for opiate users (22)

Symptom	Drug	Administration
Vomiting	Metoclopramide	10 mg t.i.d. Not known to be harmful in pregnancy. Action antagonized by opioid analgesics. Caution, especially in young adults (15–19 yrs), extrapyramidal effects commonly occur
	Buccal prochlorperazine	3 or 6 mg (one or two 3 mg tablets) absorbed from buccal cavity twice daily. Useful if unable to retain oral medication
Abdominal cramps	Mebeverine hydrochloride	135-150 mg t.i.d., preferably 20 minutes before meals. Antispasmodic, not known to be harmful in pregnancy
	Hyoscine butylbromide	10-20 mg q.i.d. Smooth muscle relaxant Advised to avoid in pregnancy
Diarrhoea	Loperamide	Loperamide 4 mg initially followed by one after each loose stool; max 16 mg daily. An opiate receptor agonist which acts on the gut to reduce peristalsis, increases intestinal transit time and increases tone of the anal sphincter
	Paracetamol	Paracetamol 500 mg x two up to four times a day (max eight per day)
Minor aches and pains	NSAID such as ibuprofen	Ibuprofen 200–400 mg three to four times a day (Max 2.4 mg daily. Avoid in pregnancy especially third trimester)

CONCLUSION

The widespread use of alcohol and other substances means that many of the patients (whether detainees or complainants) seen within the clinical forensic medicine environment will be affected in some way by them. Many of these substances, alone or together, put the individual at health risk (of morbidity and fatality) but may also influence or compromise any associated investigation or court proceedings. It is essential that those with substance misuse disorders and police and other law-enforcement agencies are supported by forensic physicians and other forensic practitioners with the skills and expertise to properly assess, diagnose, manage and treat to prevent harm to the patient, to avoid preventable deaths in custody and minimize the risks of miscarriages of justice.

REFERENCES

1. Stark MM, Payne-James JJ, Scott-Ham M. *Symptoms and Signs of Substance Misuse*, 3rd ed. Boca Raton: CRC Press; 2015.
2. TOXBASE. Website, 2023. Available from: https://www.toxbase.org/ (Accessed 17 May 2023).
3. Legislation.gov.uk. *Police & Criminal Evidence Act 1984*. Available from: https://www.legislation.gov.uk/ukpga/1984/60/contents (Accessed 17 May 2023).
4. TSO. *Police & Criminal Evidence Act 1984. Codes of Practice for the Detention, Treatment and Questioning of Persons by Police Officers*, 2019. Available from: https://assets.publishing.service.gov.uk/government/uploads/system/uploads/attachment_data/file/903473/pace-code-c-2019.pdf (Accessed 17 May 2023).
5. College of Policing. *Alcohol and drugs, 2021*. Available from: https://www.college.police.uk/app/detention-and-custody/detainee-care/alcohol-and-drugs (Accessed 17 May 2023).
6. College of Policing. *Levels of Observation, 2021*. Available from: https://www.college.police.uk/app/detention-and-custody/detainee-care/detainee-care#levels-of-observation (Accessed 2 June 2023).
7. Independent Office for Police Conduct. *Annual deaths during or following police contact report - 2022/23*. Available from: https://www.policeconduct.gov.uk/publications/annual-deaths-during-or-following-police-contact-report-202223 (Accessed 28 August 2023).
8. GOV.uk. *Deaths in Police Custody: Progress Update, 2021*. Available from: https://www.gov.uk/government/publications/deaths-in-police-custody-progress-update/deaths-in-police-custody-progress-update-2021-accessible (Accessed 17 May 2023).
9. Aasebø W, Orskaug G, Erikssen J. Can deaths in police cells be prevented? Experience from Norway and death rates in other countries. *J Forensic Leg Med* 2016; **37**: 61–5.
10. Heide S, Chan T. Deaths in police custody. *J Forensic Leg Med* 2018; **57**: 109–14.
11. Heide S, Kleiber M, Hanke S, Stiller D. Deaths in German police custody. *Eur J Public Health* 2009; **19(6)**: 597–601.
12. Petschel K, Gall JA. A profile of deaths in custody in Victoria, 1991–1996. *J Clin Forensic Med* 2000; 7(**2**): 82–7.
13. Payne-James JJ, Green PG, Green N, et al. Healthcare issues of detainees in police custody in London, UK. *J Forensic Leg Med* 2010; **17**(**1**): 11–17.
14. Payne-James JJ, Keys D, Dean P. Drug misusers in police custody: A prospective survey. *J R Soc Med* 1994; **87**(**1**): 13–14.
15. Stark MM, Payne-James JJ. Provision of clinical forensic medical services in Australia: A qualitative survey 2011/12. *J Forensic Leg Med* 2014; **21**: 31–7.
16. Heide S, Chariot P, Green P, et al. Healthcare and forensic medical aspects of police detainees, suspects and complainants in Europe. *J Forensic Leg Med* 2018; **57**: 58–65.
17. Ceelen M, Dorn T, Buster M, et al. Health-care issues and health-care use among detainees in police custody. *J Forensic Leg Med* 2012; **19**(**6**): 324–31.
18. Hopkin G, Chaplin L, Slade K, et al. Differences between homeless and non-homeless people in a matched sample referred for mental health reasons in police custody. *Int J Soc Psychiatry* 2020; **66**(**6**): 576–83.
19. McKinnon IG, Thomas SD, Noga HL, Senior J. Police custody health care: A review of health morbidity, models of care and innovations within police custody in the UK, with international comparisons. *Risk Manag Healthc Policy* 2016; **9**: 213–26.
20. Office of National Statistics. *Drug Misuse in England and Wales: Year Ending June, 2022*. Available from: https://www.ons.gov.uk/peoplepopulationandcommunity/crimeandjustice/articles/drugmisuseinenglandandwales/yearendingjune2022#main-points (Accessed 17 May 2023).
21. NHS Digital. *Smoking, Drinking and Drug Use Among Young People in England, 2021*. Available from: https://digital.nhs.uk/data-and-information/publications/statistical/smoking-drinking-and-drug-use-among-young-people-in-england/2021 (Accessed 17 May 2023).
22. Royal College of Psychiatrists. *Detainees with Substance Use Disorders in Police Custody: Guidelines for Clinical management* (5th ed), 2020. Available from: https://fflm.ac.uk/wp-content/uploads/2020/12/college-report-cr227.pdf (Accessed 17 May 2023).
23. Busuttil A. Drug concealment in custody deaths--two cases. *J Clin Forensic Med* 1994; **1**(**1**): 35–7.
24. Havis S, Best D, Carter J. Concealment of drugs by police detainees: Lessons learned from adverse incidents and from 'routine' clinical practice. *J Clin Forensic Med* 2005; **12**(**5**): 237–41.
25. Norfolk GA. The fatal case of a cocaine body-stuffer and a literature review - towards evidence based management. *J Forensic Leg Med* 2007; **14**(**1**): 49–52.
26. Sullivan JT, Sykora K, Schneiderman J, et al. Assessment of alcohol withdrawal: The revised clinical institute withdrawal assessment for alcohol scale (CIWA-Ar). *Br J Addict* 1989; **84**(**11**): 1353–7.
27. Wesson DR, Ling W. The clinical opiate withdrawal scale (COWS). *J Psychoactive Drugs* 2003; **35**(**2**): 253–9.
28. Cohen L, Duroy D, Perozziello A et al. A cross-sectional study: Nitrous oxide abuse in Parisian medical students. *Am J Addict* 2023; **32**(**1**): 605.
29. Matsuda N, Wakakuri H, Uehara K, et al. A case of fever, impaired consciousness, and psychosis caused by nitrous oxide abuse and misdiagnosed as acute meningitis. *J Nippon Med Sch* 2022. doi: 10.1272/jnms.JNMS.2023_90-505. Online ahead of print.
30. NEPTUNE. *Neptune Clinical Guidance*. Available from: http://neptune-clinical-guidance.co.uk/ (Accessed 17 May 2023).

CHAPTER

70 Novel Psychoactive Substances

Dimitri Gerostamoulos and Matthew Di Rago

INTRODUCTION

In the last 15 years, the prevalence and detection of novel psychoactive substances (NPS) in medicolegal casework and in clinical presentations in hospitals has increased significantly. These drugs or chemicals have sometimes been termed new synthetic drugs or new psychoactive substances such that they could be differentiated from traditional drugs of abuse such as stimulants or opioids. While this may have been the case when first identified in 2008, the picture today is very different. Many of the NPS now detected are structurally quite different from the original drugs groups that they were supposed to mimic. The definition of NPS most widely adopted is that from the United Nations Office of Drugs and Crime (UNODC) is as follows "substances of abuse, either in a pure form or a preparation, that are not controled by the 1961 Single Convention on Narcotic Drugs or the 1971 Convention on Psychotropic Substances, but which may pose a public health threat"(1). Another significant change in the development of NPS is that the last 5 years has seen a shift in the potency and harm associated with these compounds, resulting in increased hospital admission and deaths. This chapter reviews the development and prevalence of NPS since they were first identified as well as the different classes of NPS, strategies required to detect these compounds and the challenges of interpretation when these compounds are detected in forensic and clinical casework.

BRIEF HISTORY OF NPS

The appearance of NPS on the illicit drug market first occurred in Germany in 2008. Initially identified as synthetic cannabinoids, many scientific studies subsequently attempted to characterize the specific agents in mixtures such as "spice" (2,3). The emergence of 1-Pentyl-3-(1-naphthoyl)indole (JWH-018) and other similar compounds resulted in many of these substances being controled legislatively or through individual bans as they were detected. This led to many new derivatives of molecules being synthesized in an attempt to evade legislative controls. The illicit drug market expanded significantly between 2009 and 2015, with many different types of compounds newly identified. Since that time, the number of new compounds has stabilized as more effective drug controls have been universally adopted across the world.

At the beginning of the NPS phenomenon, the range of substances initially detected were largely limited to synthetic cannabinoids and synthetic cathinones. However, these groups have expanded to include a range of centrally acting substances such as synthetic opioids, synthetic benzodiazepines, dissociatives and hallucinogens (4,5). The majority of NPS compounds are typically smoked, vaped, snorted or consumed orally as pills or tablets; they can also be injected and spiked onto blotter paper to avoid detection.

During the world pandemic (COVID-19), rapid increases in the consumption and detection of synthetic benzodiazepines and opioids has been observed. More potent drugs have been detected in clinical and forensic settings with many more presentations to emergency departments and deaths related to the consumption of these drugs. The detection of NPS varies globally with some countries reporting specific issues with certain classes of NPS. For example, the opioid phenomenon in North America has not been mirrored to the same degree in other parts of the world. Hundreds and thousands of deaths in the US have been attributed to synthetic opioids, largely dominated by potent fentanyl analogues (6,7). Illicit fentanyl markets have increased exponentially from 2009–2020 owing in part to increased drug potency requiring smaller volumes of drug production, as well as the US's dependency on opioids stemming from addiction to traditional opioids such as heroin and oxycodone. The estimated number of fentanyl derivatives detected exceeds 50 compounds (8).

In more recent times, many restricted pharmaceuticals have been the subject of counterfeit preparations. While not solely restricted to opioids (i.e. fentanyl laced medication), a number of potent synthetic benzodiazepines have been found in counterfeit preparations of traditional drugs such as diazepam and alprazolam. Substances such as etizolam, flualprazolam, clonazolam and many others have been found in high concentrations in counterfeit medications, often resulting in more potent medications being unknowingly consumed. The global lockdowns attributed to the pandemic have also resulted in many more drug preparations being delivered by

DOI: 10.1201/9781003138754-73

postal services rather than traditional means of accessing drugs through a dealer or distributor. NPS have also found popularity and accessibility through online dark web retailers such as Silk Road (shut-down in 2013), and its many predecessors. This kind of NPS supply is very difficult for law-enforcement to control as purchases of NPS on the dark web are usually made in cryptocurrency to ensure anonymity and untraceability, with small volumes of drug hidden among high-volume regular mail in the postal service.

CLASSES OF NPS

While it is not possible to document every NPS detected since 2010, there have now been over 1200 of these substances identified. There are many sources for up-to-date information in relation to the detection of these substances established as a result of increasing harms associated with these drugs or chemicals. Many of the commonly detected NPS are now scheduled drugs. New harmful NPS are regularly monitored and recommended for international control by the Expert Committee on Drug Dependence (ECDD) (9) convened through the World Health Organisation. The UNODC (10) has a dedicated portal on NPS which can provide timely information on detections of new drugs from around the world. Additionally, the European Monitoring Centre for Drugs and Drug Addiction (EMCDDA) (11) has contemporary information on illicit drugs and provides independent scientific evidence and analysis on drug-related harms. Finally, the US-based organization the Center for Forensic Science Research and Education (CFSRE) (12) collaborates with law enforcement, public health and public safety agencies to rapidly identify NPS and disseminate that information more broadly.

Synthetic cannabinoids

The largest number of NPS belong to the synthetic cannabinoids group. Approximately one-third of all NPS detected are classified as cannabinoids or, more specifically, synthetic cannabinoid receptor agonists. Many of these compounds were created by legitimate drug research groups attempting to find analogs of cannabis that could be used therapeutically to treat pain and other conditions. However, they have also been the subject of clandestine production fueling the NPS uptake and further development of more potent "spice" analogs.

When initially detected in 2008, many variants of synthetic cannabinoids were equivalent or greater in potency to delta-9-tetrahydrocannabinol (Δ9-THC). Compounds such as JWH-018, JWH-73 and JWH-210, developed by organic chemist John W. Huffmann (hence the JWH-naming convention), were more potent than Δ9-THC (some significantly more than others) which led to many reports of intoxications and deaths. Other similar compounds, such as AM2201 and HU-210, were also significantly more pharmacologically active than Δ9-THC (13). These early compounds were structurally similar to Δ9-THC, however, as new compounds were developed and chemically altered to avoid detection from regulatory agencies, the activity on human cannabinoid receptors was less predictable. The nomenclature and structures of synthetic cannabinoids and their subgroups was simplified in 2013 by the EMCDDA. The sheer number of synthetic cannabinoids resulted in substances being grouped according to their chemical structure, which was largely based on a number of essential structural elements including a core, a link, a ring and a tail enabling multiple points of chemical substitution (14). At least ten different subclasses of synthetic cannabinoids have been identified and continue to diversify as compounds appear and then disappear from drug markets (15) (Table 70.1).

From 2015 onwards, the synthetic cannabinoid market changed significantly with more potent cannabinoids being synthesized with increasing chemical complexity (16–18). The appearance of FUBINACA, PINACA, PICA and Cumyl-derivatives in the drugs markets have resulted in many more hospitalizations and deaths (19).

Synthetic cathinones

The next largest group of NPS are classified as synthetic cathinones or amphetamine-type stimulants and are compounds that mimic traditional drugs such as amphetamines (including ecstasy) and cocaine. Globally, there is an increasing demand for illicit stimulants with many countries now reporting significant uptake of these drugs for recreational use. Seizure data suggest that synthetic stimulants have increased significantly over the last decade (20).

While the stimulant market is currently dominated by methylamphetamine and cocaine, the range of stimulant drugs over the last 10 years has varied and has also been subject to jurisdictional differences. In order to avoid initial detection by law enforcement agencies, these NPS were also first labeled as "bath salts" or "plant food" and/or "research chemicals" (21). Drugs such as ephedrone (methcathinone), mephedrone (4-methymethcathinone) and methylone were first reported in 2007 in Israel followed by parts of Scandinavia, UK and Ireland (22). These derivatives were then followed by other stimulant subgroups such as pyrovalerones, notably methylenedioxypyrovalerone (MDPV) and α-pyrrolidinovalerophenone (α-PVP). Subsequent chemical modifications to many of these compounds led to an expanded range of more potent stimulants such as 4-methoxy-a-pyrrolidinovalerophenone (4-methoxy-a-PVP), ethylone (3,4-methylenedioxy-N-ethylcathinone) and ephylone (N-ethyl-pentylone) resulting in many emergency presentations and deaths (23–26).

Substances that were formulated many decades ago re-emerged in combination with other hallucinogenic type compounds (Figure 70.1). The work of chemist Alexander Shulgin was being reproduced by clandestine laboratories. The presence of 4-fluoro-amphetamine

TABLE 70.1 Summary of the classification of synthetic cannabinoids with selected example of common NPS

Drug Class	Example	Chemical Structure
Classical cannabinoids	Δ9-THC	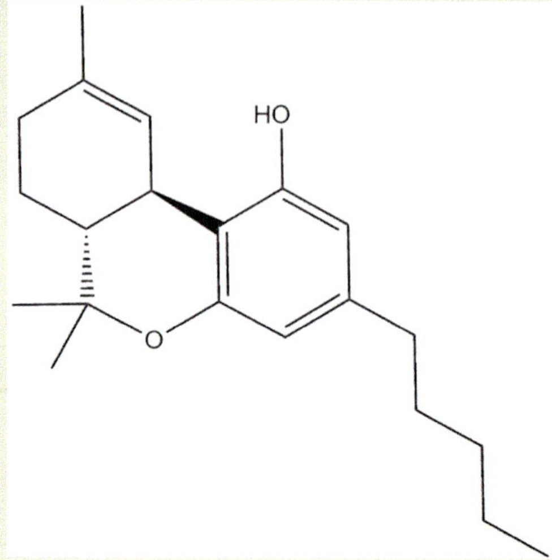
Non-classical cannabinoids (Cyclohexanols 3-arylcyclohexanols)	CP-47,497	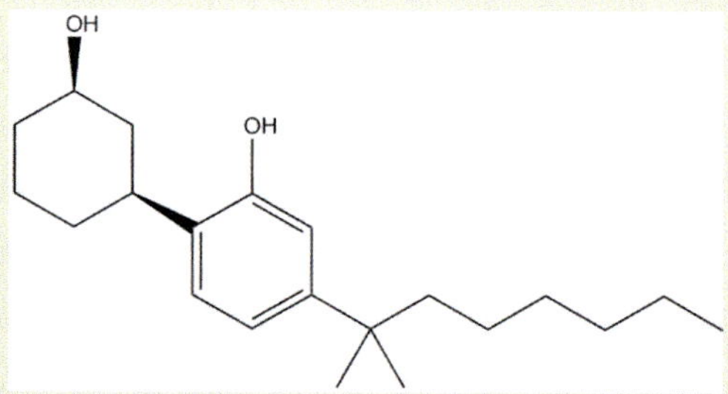
Hybrid cannabinoids (Classical and non-classical structures)	AM-4030	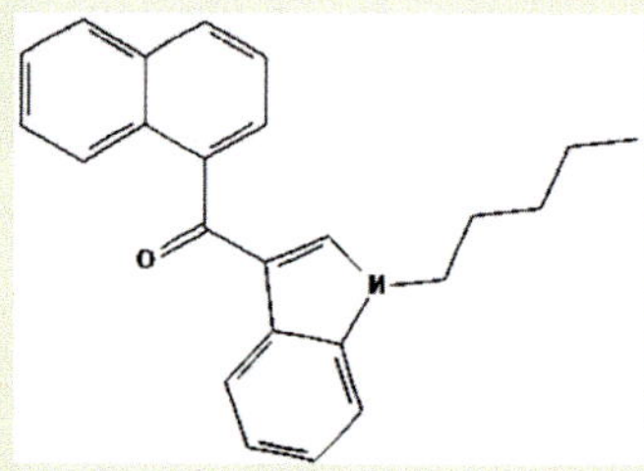
Aminoalkyndoles • naphthoylindoles • phenylacetylindoles • benzoylindoles • naphthylmethylindoles • cyclopropoylindoles • adamantoylindoles • indole carboxamides • indole carboxylates	JWH-018	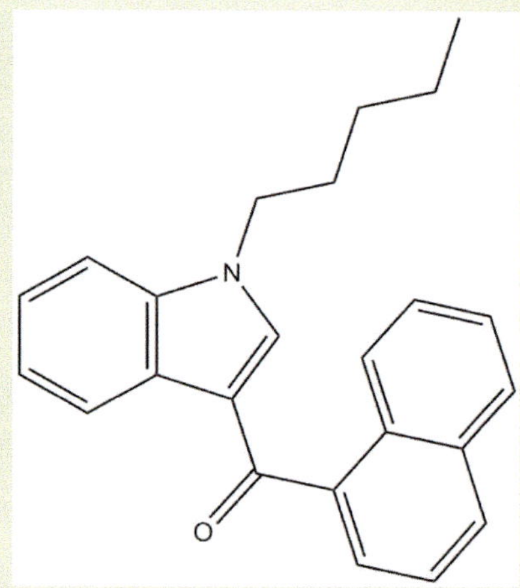

(Continued)

TABLE 70.1 (Continued) Summary of the classification of synthetic cannabinoids with selected example of common NPS

Drug Class	Example	Chemical Structure
	5F-PB-22	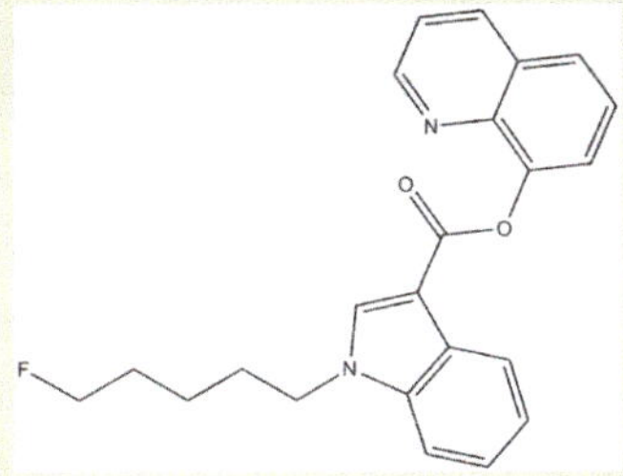
Aminoalkyndazoles (naphthoylindazoles indazole carboxamides)	AB-FUBINACA	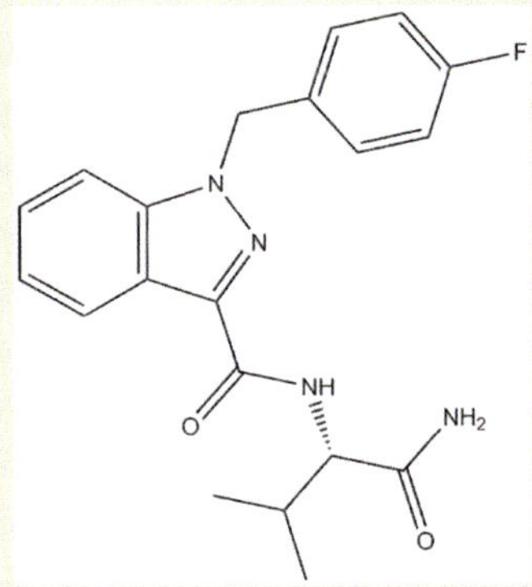
Eicosanoids	AM-356	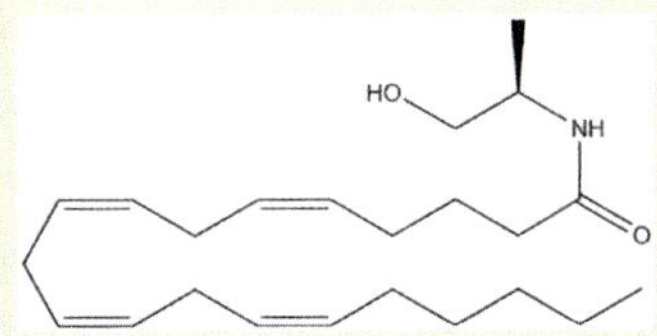
Others – range of other synthetic cannabinoids	CRA-13	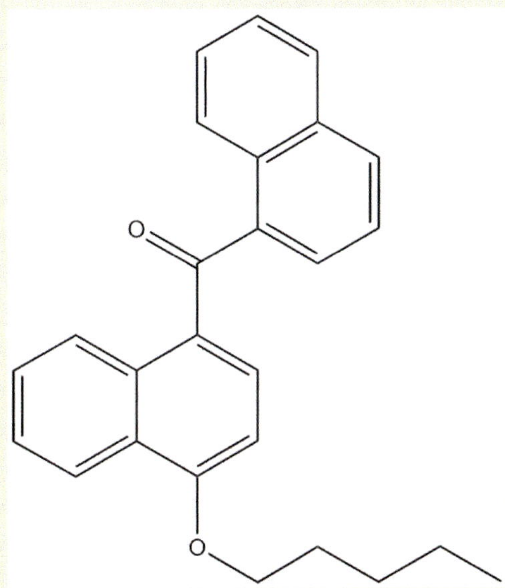

Source: Adapted from (70).

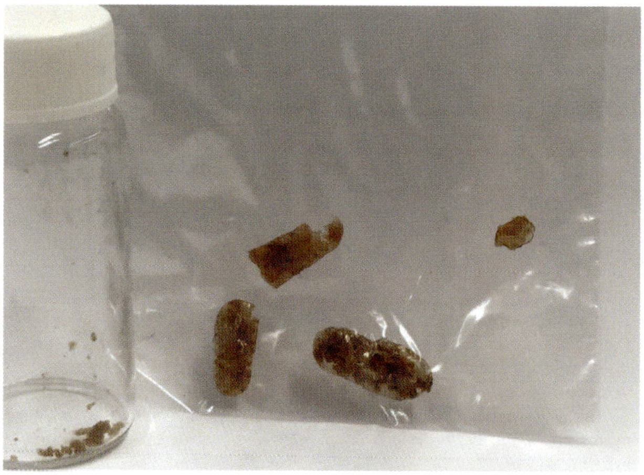

70.1 Example of synthetic drug preparation in forensic case – Ecstasy substituted as 4-fluoro-amphetamine and 25C-NBoMe.

and 25C-NBoMe 2-(4-chloro-2,5-dimethoxyphenyl)-N-[(2methoxyphenyl)methyl]ethanamine) substituted as fake ecstasy led to many deaths around Australia (27) and drug warnings in other countries. Other combinations with either NPS (28) or traditional drugs such as gamma-butyrolactone have resulted in hospitalization (29) or death (30).

Synthetic opioids

Many of the synthetic opioids discovered in the last 10 years have led to enormous numbers of deaths globally. The high rates of mortality in the USA have been driven by long-term dependency on pharmaceutical opioids and illicit heroin. Potent fentanyl-type analogs, older opioid agonists such as U-47700 and AH-7921 have all caused great harm in the USA and Canada. Traditional opioids such as tramadol continue to be highly problematic in many countries in Africa, while opioids such as codeine, methadone and oxycodone continue to be overrepresented in deaths involving regions such as Oceania.

Fentanyl derivatives such as acetyl-fentanyl, furanyl-fentanyl, butyryl-fentanyl and the highly potent carfentanil have been readily detected in emergency presentations (31) and post-mortem cases (32). These analogs vary in potency and can be hundreds of times more potent than morphine. They have been mixed with heroin and other stimulants or cutting agents and contaminants. These drugs can also be found in counterfeit medications such as oxycodone, hydrocodone (33), heroin (34) and other benzodiazepines (35). The emergence of fentanyl analogs shows no sign of decline with more potent opioids now prevalent not only in North America, but across the world. The prevalence of benzimidazole compounds – more commonly known as nitazenes – is now widespread and since 2019 multiple derivatives have emerged (36,37). Like many opioids, these compounds have high efficacy on opioid receptors (mu) and as such lead to significant respiratory depression (38).

Synthetic benzodiazepines

Synthetic benzodiazepines first began appearing in European drug markets in 2011. Compounds such as etizolam and phenazepam are considered as NPS despite the fact they have been legal medicines in countries such as Japan and Russia since the 1970s and 1980s.

As already mentioned, the sharp increase in detection of synthetic benzodiazepines in recent years has resulted in many identifications of drugs such as etizolam, clonazolam, flualprazolam, bromazolam and others. Counterfeit medications allegedly containing diazepam and alprazolam have been known to be entirely replaced with drugs such as etizolam, flubromazolam and flualprazolam or mixtures of these and other drugs (39) or other opioids such as U-47700 (40). While general pharmacological effects of legitimate benzodiazepines include sedation, muscle relaxation and control of anxiety, many of these highly potent synthetic versions can lead to agitation, excitement and increase in energy, thereby complicating the pharmacological picture. This is further complicated by the presence of other drugs especially opioids, stimulants and alcohol which can increase the risk of adverse effects (41) and death (42).

Other NPS

A range of other compounds have also been described as NPS and these typically include some of the traditional, older compounds which have been used by different community groups around the world. Classic hallucinogens such as psilocybin, mescaline, phencyclidine, lysergic acid diethylamide (LSD) and ayahuasca have increased in prevalence over the last decade (43). The global resurgence of dissociative type psychoactive substances such ketamine derivatives (e.g. deschloroketamine, 2-fluoro-2-deschloroketamine) have been widely reported in clinical and forensic casework.

Plant-based drugs such as khat (cathe adulis), kratom (mitragynine), salvia (salvia divinorum) have all been more readily detected (44). An extensive review of the current classification of NPS based on chemical structure has recently been proposed (5), however, the complex pharmacological properties and subsequent harmful outcomes of these substances remains challenging for clinical and forensic practitioners.

DETECTION OF NPS

The determination of NPS in biological fluids by either clinical laboratories or forensic organizations is an ongoing challenge largely due to the sheer magnitude of compounds and metabolites that need to be identified (45,46). Analytical methods must be able to detect low concentrations (usually ng/mL) which requires using liquid chromatography with mass spectrometry (LC/MS). Immunoassays and gas chromatography with mass spectrometry (GC/MS) do not have the requisite sensitivity nor analytical range to ensure adequate identification of NPS. It is not possible for one laboratory to detect all

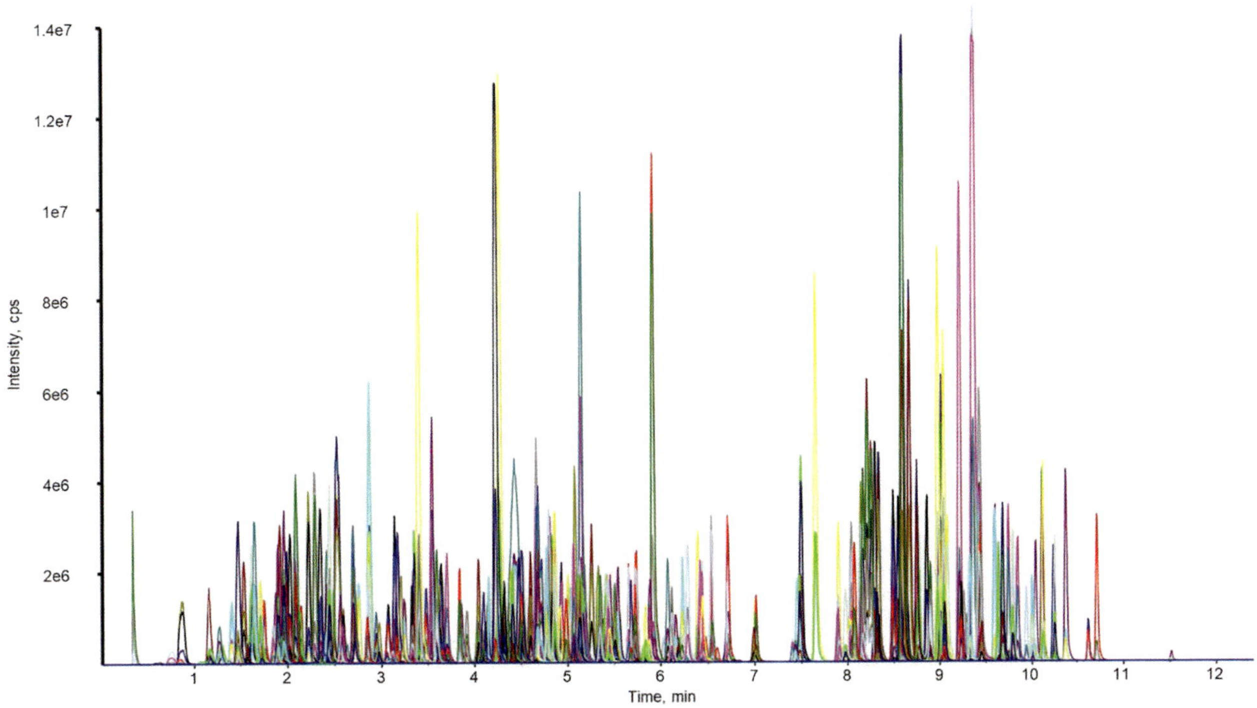

70.2 Example chromatogram of an SRM technique used for simultaneous screening and confirmation of a large panel of over 250 NPS. Each peak indicates detection of an analyte.

NPS and analytical methods need to be appropriately validated and more importantly be jurisdiction specific for compounds of interest.

Validation

Analytical methods developed for the detection and confirmation of NPS, or any other analyte, must undergo validation processes to ensure the applied technique is fit-for-purpose and to understand any analytical limitations. Analytical method validation involves systematic experimental investigation and documentation of method performance and must be performed before any technique can be applied to samples of interest. For example, a method must be investigated for interferences that may affect analyte detection such as common endogenous or exogenous compounds found in typical specimens that may interfere with analyte detection (Figure 70.1). This is particularly important given the danger of misidentification when measuring NPS due to minor differences in analyte chemical structures. Where an amount (concentration) of analyte is reported, a method must also have been evaluated for bias (difference in result from the "true" value) and precision (the variation in repeated measurements). At the time of writing, the most current guidelines for use in forensic toxicology are published by the American Academy of Forensic Sciences (47).

Immunoassay

Traditional systematic toxicological analyses typically use immunoassay-based techniques for fast broad-based screening of analytes or analyte classes in biological specimens. Once a positive finding is made, specimens are then subjected to a more specific detection method to confirm the identity and amount of compound detected. However, these techniques usually rely on specific antibody-substrate interactions designed to target chemical structures or binding sites common to analytes from a single drug class. Some techniques have been developed specifically for NPS detection, either targeting individual NPS or a common chemical structure common to a subclass of NPS. Rapid proliferation of NPS, often with subtle and unpredictable modifications to functional groups of existing compounds, may prevent detection via immunoassay techniques and, as a result, may not be a reliable technique for NPS detection (48–50).

Mass spectrometry

Mass spectrometer detectors (MSDs) are used for analyte detection based on molecular mass of a compound and are the gold-standard analytical toxicology detection technique. MSDs are usually coupled with chromatographic separation techniques such as gas-chromatography or liquid-chromatography to provide an analyte-specific chromatographic retention time and deliver a very high degree of identification power. MSDs can be tuned to a molecular mass of a specific analyte (derived from its chemical structure) and provide superb analyte detection limits and detailed spectrometric information. Triple quadrupole MSDs further enhance analyte identification by breaking targeted analytes into component chemical structures known as product ions (51). These "fingerprint"-like productions are specific to the analyte being measured and are used to confirm the presence of a specific compound in a sample. Operating the triple quadrupole MSD in this manner is known as selected-reaction-monitoring or SRM (*see* Figure 70.1). SRM techniques may target a single compound or methods may be developed to detect several hundred analytes in a single analytical run (52–56).

Triple quadrupole MSD techniques may also be coupled with high-resolution mass spectrometers (HR-MS) (Figure 70.3), such as time-of-flight (TOF) instrumentation. These detectors provide far superior mass resolving power through measurement of analyte travel time over a known distance. Using TOF, MSDs molecule transit time is directly related to its molecular mass where smaller molecules travel faster while larger molecules take longer to reach the detector. HR-MS instruments have several orders of magnitude and more mass-resolving power over standard triple quadrupole MSDs. HR-MS instruments may be used to collect information on all components of a sample mixture and produce incredibly data-rich scans, up to several gigabyte per sample. Through comparison of a response from an unknown sample to database of known mass-spectra, the identity of a compound may be confirmed with the highest confidence when all recommended identification criteria are met (57). Further, these datafiles may be re-interrogated for NPS in the future as new NPS are discovered.

Databases containing hundreds to several thousand compounds are commercially available for use with HR-MS instruments, however, these are usually specific to the instrument vendor (58–62). Laboratories may be able to curate their own databases through collection of NPS-certified reference material, however, the ever-increasing number of NPS can make this slow and expensive, and some NPS are often so novel a certified reference material is not yet commercially available. One approach has been to create a "crowd-sourced" database where participants from around the world contribute known HR-MS NPS spectra collected using instruments in their laboratory, and then other member laboratories may download these shared spectra, with a predicted retention time, for use in their own HR-MS screening techniques (63,64).

Interpretation of NPS in casework

The harms caused by NPS resulting in either hospitalization or death have been steadily increasing (65–67). Due to the transient nature of NPS supply and detection, there is limited research into most NPS detected in toxicological casework. NPS may be derived from published

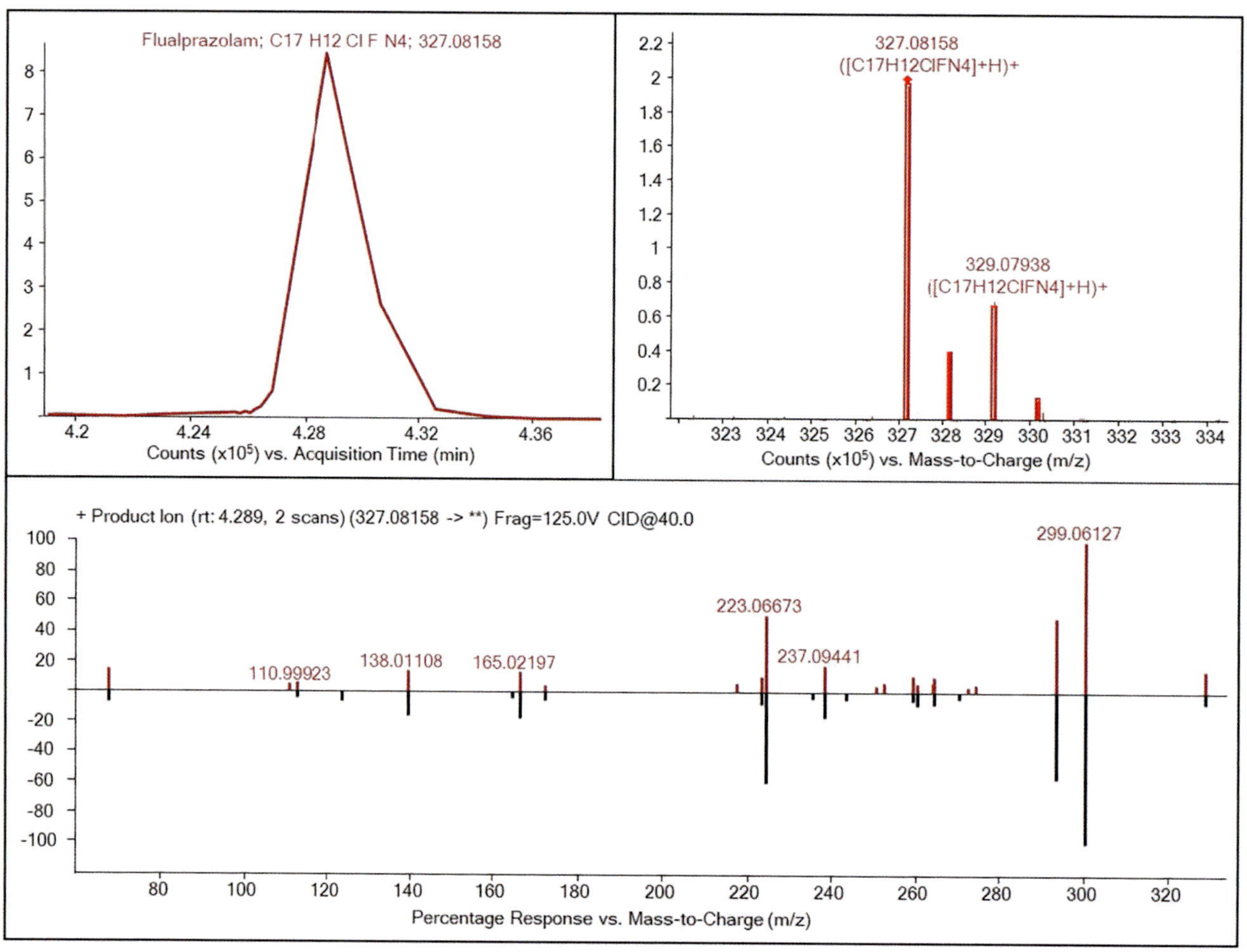

70.3 Example HR-MS confirmation of NPS benzodiazepine flualprazolam. Top left – chromatographic peak of parent molecule, Top right – overlaid observed/expected isotopic distribution, Bottom – Observed product ion spectra (red) compared to expected product ion spectra from database (black).

research papers investigating receptor binding studies for analogous compounds developed for medical treatment. Often, very little is known about these compounds before they emerge in the illicit market which makes interpretation of adverse effects and toxicity very difficult, particularly where multiple drugs are co-ingested. The research into NPS dose-related effects is further complicated due to ethical constraints administering drugs with unknown effects to volunteers. Even once approved, these types of studies are often very expensive to perform after which the NPS in question may not be detected again. Experts in the field have proposed that detection of an NPS is suitable for forensic casework and determination of the amount of drug present is not required (68). This is further evidenced by the lack of data for NPS surrounding metabolism, distribution, drug interactions, stability and, in the case of post-mortem casework, the phenomenon of post-mortem redistribution (69). As a result, caution must be taken when attempting to interpret the detection of NPS in forensic and clinical casework.

CONCLUSION

The number of NPS detected continues to increase around the world. In more recent times, these synthetic drugs have also demonstrated increased potency and likely associated harms resulting in either hospitalization or death. Defining the potential pharmacological interactions with other traditional illicit drugs as well as prescription medications remains challenging and relevant where multiple drugs are detected in casework. Demand and supply for traditional plant-based hallucinogenic compounds is also increasing (e.g. mushrooms, mitragynine) and must also be included in toxicology testing.

Analytically, many of these NPS require sophisticated instrumentation such as HR–MS to aid in identification. Often reference materials are not readily available and identification relies on co-operation between illicit drug chemists and toxicologists to better characterize these potentially harmful agents in clinical and forensic cases.

REFERENCES

1. Tettey JNA, Crean C, Ifeagwu SC, Raithelhuber M. Emergence, Diversity, and Control of New Psychoactive Substances: A Global Perspective. In: Maurer HH, Brandt SD (eds), *New Psychoactive Substances: Pharmacology, Clinical, Forensic and Analytical Toxicology*. Cham: Springer; 2018, pp. 51–67.
2. Auwärter V, Dresen S, Weinmann W, et al. 'Spice' and other herbal blends: Harmless incense or cannabinoid designer drugs? *J Mass Spectrom* 2009; **44**(**5**): 832–7.
3. Lindigkeit R, Boehme A, Eiserloh I, et al. Spice: A never ending story? *Forensic Sci Int* 2009; **191**(**1–3**): 58–63.
4. United Nations Office on Drugs and Crime. Regional diversity and the impact of scheduling on NPS trends, 2021. Available from: https://www.unodc.org/documents/scientific/GlobalSMART_25_web.pdf (Accessed 16 May 2023).
5. Zapata F, Matey JM, Montalvo G, García-Ruiz C. Chemical classification of new psychoactive substances (NPS). *Microchem J* 2021; **163**: 105877.
6. Hedegaard H, Miniño AM, Spencer MR, Warner M. Drug overdose deaths in the United States, 1999–2020, 2021. Available from: https://www.cdc.gov/nchs/data/databriefs/db428.pdf (Accessed 16 May 2023).
7. Volkow ND. The epidemic of fentanyl misuse and overdoses: Challenges and strategies. *World Psychiatry* 2021; **20**(**2**): 195–6.
8. Pichini S, Solimini R, Berretta P, et al. Acute intoxications and fatalities from illicit fentanyl and analogues: An update. *Ther Drug Monit* 2018; **40**(**1**): 38–51.
9. World Health Organization. Expert Committee on Drug Dependence (ECDD), 2023. Available from: https://www.who.int/groups/who-expert-committee-on-drug-dependence (Accessed 16 May 2023).
10. UNODC. Early warning advisory (EWA) on new psychoactive substances (NPS), 2023. Available from: https://www.unodc.org/LSS/Home/NPS (Accessed 16 May 2023).
11. European Monitoring Centre for Drugs and Drug Addiction. Website, 2023. Available from: https://www.emcdda.europa.eu (Accessed 16 May 2023).
12. The Centre for Forensic Science Research & Education (CFSRE) NPS Discovery. Available from: https://www.cfsre.org/nps-discovery (Accessed 28 August 2023).
13. Banister SD, Connor M. The Chemistry and Pharmacology of Synthetic Cannabinoid Receptor Agonists as New Psychoactive Substances: Origins. In: Maurer HH, Brandt SD (eds), *New Psychoactive Substances: Pharmacology, Clinical, Forensic and Analytical Toxicology*. Cham: Springer; 2018, pp. 165–90.
14. Presley BC, Gurney SM, Scott KS, et al. Metabolism and toxicological analysis of synthetic cannabinoids in biological fluids and tissues. *Forensic Sci Rev* 2016; **28**(**2**): 103–69.
15. Potts AJ, Cano C, Thomas SHL, Hill SL. Synthetic cannabinoid receptor agonists: Classification and nomenclature. *Clin Toxicol* 2020; **58**(**2**): 82–98.
16. EMCDDA. 25 years of early warning and response to new psychoactive substances in Europe, 2022. Available from: https://www.emcdda.europa.eu/ews25_en (Accessed 16 May 2023).
17. Malaca S, Busardò FP, Nittari G, et al. Fourth generation of synthetic cannabinoid receptor agonists: A review on the latest insights. *Curr Pharm Des* 2022; **28**(**32**): 2603–17.
18. Kronstrand R, Norman C, Vikingsson S, et al. The metabolism of the synthetic cannabinoids ADB-BUTINACA and ADB-4en-PINACA and their detection in forensic toxicology casework and infused papers seized in prisons. *Drug Test Anal* 2022; **14**(**4**): 634–52.
19. Navarro-Tapia E, Codina J, Villanueva-Blasco VJ, et al. Detection of the synthetic cannabinoids AB-CHMINACA, ADB-CHMINACA, MDMB-CHMICA, and 5F-MDMB-PINACA in biological matrices: A systematic review. *Biology* 2022; **11**(**5**): 796.
20. UNODC. Global synthetic drugs assessment, 2017. Available from: https://www.unodc.org/documents/scientific/Global_Drugs_Assessment_2017.pdf (Accessed 16 May 2023).
21. Baumann MH, Solis E, Watterson LR, et al. Baths salts, spice, and related designer drugs: The science behind the headlines. *J Neurosci* 2014; **34**(**46**): 15150–8.
22. Kelly JP. Cathinone derivatives: A review of their chemistry, pharmacology and toxicology. *Drug Test Anal* 2011; 3(7–8): 439–53.
23. Lee D, Chronister CW, Hoyer J, Goldberger BA. Ethylone-related deaths: Toxicological findings. *J Anal Toxicol* 2015; **39**(**7**): 567–71.
24. Krotulski AJ, Papsun DM, De Martinis BS, et al. N-ethyl pentylone (ephylone) intoxications: Quantitative confirmation and metabolite identification in authentic human biological specimens. *J Anal Toxicol* 2018; **42**(**7**): 467–75.
25. Blanco G, Vidler D, Roper C, et al. Acute toxicity from the synthetic cathinone N-ethylpentylone (ephylone) in the United Kingdom. *Clin Toxicol* 2021; **59**(**12**): 1270–3.
26. Kudo K, Usumoto Y, Kikura-Hanajiri R, et al. A fatal case of poisoning related to new cathinone designer drugs, 4-methoxy PV8, PV9, and 4-methoxy PV9, and a dissociative agent, diphenidine. *Leg Med* 2015; **17**(**5**): 421–6.
27. UNODC. Australia: "Ecstasy" capsules containing NPS are related to several deaths and severe intoxications in Melbourne, 2017. Available from: https://www.unodc.org/LSS/announcement/Details/48940b13-df58-4da2-a66b-d54a8f7362f7 (Accessed 16 May 2023).
28. Liveri K, Constantinou MA, Afxentiou M, Kanari P. A fatal intoxication related

to MDPV and pentedrone combined with antipsychotic and antidepressant substances in Cyprus. *Forensic Sci Int* 2016; **265**: 160–5.
29. Turcant A, Boels D, Helfer AG, et al. Acute combined poisoning with the new designer drug 4-methyl-N-ethyl-cathinone (4-MEC) and gammabutyrolactone (GBL): A case report with different analytical approaches for identification of some metabolites. *Toxicol Anal et Clin* 2014; **26(3)**: 119–27.
30. Pellegrini M, Bolino G, Varì MR, et al. A fatal chemsex case involving γ-butyrolactone and 4-methylethcathinone. *Drug Test Anal* 2019; **11(9)**: 1465–70.
31. Bäckberg M, Beck O, Jönsson K-H, Helander A. Opioid intoxications involving butyrfentanyl, 4-fluorobutyrfentanyl, and fentanyl from the Swedish STRIDA project. *Clin Toxicol* 2015; **53(7)**: 609–17.
32. Vohra V, Hodgman M, Marraffa J, et al. Fentanyl-and fentanyl analog-related deaths across five counties in Central New York between 2013 and 2017. *Clin Toxicol* 2020; **58(2)**: 112–16.
33. Sutter ME, Gerona RR, Davis MT, et al. Fatal fentanyl: One pill can kill. *Acad Emerg Med* 2017; **24(1)**: 106–13.
34. West H, Fitzgerald JL, Hopkins KL, et al. Trace residue identification, characterization and longitudinal monitoring of the novel synthetic opioid β-U10, from discarded drug paraphernalia. *Drug Test Anal* 2022; **14(9)**: 1576–86.
35. Green TC, Gilbert M. Counterfeit medications and fentanyl. *JAMA Intern Med* 2016; **176(10)**: 1555–7.
36. Vandeputte MM, Van Uytfanghe K, Layle NK, et al. Synthesis, chemical characterization, and μ-opioid receptor activity assessment of the emerging group of "nitazene" 2-benzylbenzimidazole synthetic opioids. *ACS Chem Neurosci* 2021; **12(7)**: 1241–51.
37. Vandeputte MM, Krotulski AJ, Walther D, et al. Pharmacological evaluation and forensic case series of N-pyrrolidino etonitazene (etonitazepyne), a newly emerging 2-benzylbenzimidazole 'nitazene' synthetic opioid. *Arch Toxicol* 2022; **96(6)**: 1845–63.
38. Palkovic B, Malcom NJ, McCorvy JD, et al. Nitazenes are potent mu-opioid receptor agonists with profound respiratory depression. *FASEB J* 2022; **36(S1)**.
39. Blakey K, Thompson A, Matheson A, Griffiths A. What's in fake 'Xanax'?: A dosage survey of designer benzodiazepines in counterfeit pharmaceutical tablets. *Drug Test Anal* 2022; **14(3)**: 525–30.
40. Nikolaou P, Katselou M, Papoutsis I, et al. U-47700. An old opioid becomes a recent danger. *Forensic Toxicol* 2017; **35(1)**: 11–19.
41. Helander A, Bäckberg M, Beck O. Drug trends and harm related to new psychoactive substances (NPS) in Sweden from 2010 to 2016: Experiences from the STRIDA project. *PLOS ONE* 2020; **15(4)**: e0232038.
42. Logan BK, Mohr ALA, Friscia M, et al. Reports of adverse events associated with use of novel psychoactive substances, 2013–2016: A review. *J Anal Toxicol* 2017; **41(7)**: 573–610.
43. Reinert JP, Colunga K, Etuk A, et al. Management of overdoses of salvia, kratom, and psilocybin mushrooms: A literature review. *Expert Rev Clin Pharmacol* 2020; **13(8)**: 847–56.
44. Orsolini L, Chiappini S, Corkery JM, et al. The use of new psychoactive substances (NPS) in young people and their role in mental health care: A systematic review. *Expert Rev Neurother* 2019; **19(12)**: 1253–64.
45. Simão AY, Antunes M, Marques H, et al. Recent bionalytical methods for the determination of new psychoactive substances in biological specimens. *Bioanalysis* 2020; **12(21)**: 1557–95.
46. Faro AFL, Di Trana A, La Maida N, et al. Biomedical analysis of New Psychoactive Substances (NPS) of natural origin. *J Pharm Biomed Anal* 2020; **179**: 112945.
47. American Academy of Forensic Sciences. Standard Practices for Method Validation in Forensic Toxicology. 2019. Available from: https://www.aafs.org/asb-standard/standard-practices-method-validation-forensic-toxicology (Accessed 28 August 2023).
48. Sundström M, Pelander A, Ojanperä I. Comparison between drug screening by immunoassay and ultra-high performance liquid chromatography/high-resolution time-of-flight mass spectrometry in post-mortem urine. *Drug Test Anal* 2015; 7(5): 420–7.
49. Nieddu M, Baralla E, Pasciu V, et al. Cross-reactivity of commercial immunoassays for screening of new amphetamine designer drugs: A review. *J Pharm Biomed Anal* 2022; **218**: 114868.
50. Gomila I, Leciñena MÁ, Elorza MÁ, et al. Detectability of dissociative psychoactive substances in urine by five commercial phencyclidine immunoassays. *J Anal Toxicol* 2019; **43(6)**: 497–503.
51. McLafferty FW. Tandem Mass Spectrometry. *Science* 1981; **214(4518)**: 280–7.
52. Di Rago M, Pantatan S, Hargreaves M, et al. High throughput detection of 327 drugs in blood by LC–MS-MS with automated data processing. *J Anal Toxicol* 2021; **45(2)**: 154–83.
53. Lee HK, Ho CS, Iu YPH, et al. Development of a broad toxicological screening technique for urine using ultra-performance liquid chromatography and time-of-flight mass spectrometry. *Anal Chim Acta* 2009; **649(1)**: 80–90.
54. Dulaurent S, Moesch C, Marquet P, et al. Screening of pesticides in blood with liquid chromatography–linear ion trap mass spectrometry. *Anal Bioanal Chem* 2010; **396(6)**: 2235–49.
55. Dresen S, Ferreirós N, Gnann H, et al. Detection and identification of 700 drugs by multi-target screening with a 3200 Q TRAP® LC-MS/MS system and library searching. *Anal Bioanal Chem* 2010; **396(7)**: 2425–34.
56. Liu H-C, Liu RH, Ho H-O, Lin D-L. Development of an information-rich LC–MS/MS database for the analysis of drugs in postmortem specimens. *Anal Chem* 2009; **81(21)**: 9002–11.
57. Meyer MR, Maurer HH. Review: LC coupled to low- and high-resolution mass spectrometry for new psychoactive substance screening in biological matrices – Where do we stand today? *Anal Chim Acta* 2016; **927**: 13–20.
58. Agilent. Forensic Toxicology PCDL for LC/TOF and LC/Q-TOF, 2022. Available from: https://www.agilent.com/en/product/liquid-chromatography-mass-spectrometry-lc-ms/lc-ms-application-solutions/forensic-toxicology-solutions/forensic-toxicology-pcdl-for-lc-tof-lc-q-tof (Accessed 17 May 2023).
59. Waters. Targeted and Non-Targeted Screening Using the Power of UNIFI, 2022. Available from: https://www.waters.com/waters/en_US/Toxicology-Screening/nav.htm?cid=134779723&locale=en_US (Accessed 17 May 2023).
60. ThermoFisher. mzCloud Mass Spectral Library, 2022. Available from: https://www.thermofisher.com/au/en/home/industrial/mass-spectrometry/liquid-chromatography-mass-spectrometry-lc-ms/lc-ms-software/mass-spectral-libraries/mzcloud-mass-spectral-library.html (Accessed 17 May 2023).
61. Bruker. Toxtyper®, 2022. Available from: https://www.bruker.com/en/products-and-solutions/mass-spectrometry/ms-solutions/toxtyper.html (Accessed 17 May 2023).
62. SCIEX. FORENSICS High Resolution MS/MS Spectral Library, 2022. Available from: https://sciex.com/products/spectral-library/hrms-forensics (Accessed 17 May 2023).
63. Mardal M, Andreasen MF, Mollerup CB, et al. HighResNPS.com: An online crowd-sourced HR-MS database for suspect and non-targeted screening of new psychoactive substances. *J Anal Toxicol* 2019; **43(7)**: 520–7.
64. Pasin D, Mollerup CB, Rasmussen BS, et al. Development of a single retention time prediction model integrating multiple liquid chromatography systems: Application to new psychoactive substances. *Anal Chim Acta* 2021; **1184**: 339035.
65. Deen AA, Claridge H, Treble RD, et al. Deaths from novel psychoactive substances in England, Wales and Northern Ireland: Evaluating the impact of the UK psychoactive substances act 2016. *J Psychopharmacol* 2021; **35(11)**: 1315–23.
66. Mohr ALA, Logan BK, Fogarty MF, et al. Reports of adverse events associated with use of novel psychoactive substances, 2017–2020: A review. *J Anal Toxicol* 2022; **46(6)**: e116–e85.
67. Tettey J, Raithelhuber M, Crean C, et al. Global synthetic drugs assessment, 2020. Available from: https://www.unodc.org/unodc/en/scientists/2020-global-synthetic-drugs-assessment_Global.html (Accessed 17 May 2023).
68. Gerostamoulos D, Elliott S, Walls HC, et al. To measure or not to measure? That is the NPS question. *J Anal Toxicol* 2016; **40(4)**: 318–20.
69. Zawilska JB, Andrzejczak D. Next generation of novel psychoactive substances on the horizon - A complex problem to face. *Drug Alcohol Depend* 2015; **157**: 1–17.

CHAPTER

71

Less-Lethal Restraint & Control

Jason Payne-James

INTRODUCTION

Restraint and control of individuals in law-enforcement settings or places of detention is often required for acute behavioral disturbance of individuals, in the presence of large crowds and at times of public protests. Such restraint and control frequently require use of force. There are many types of force or devices that may be used. The UK Prison Service summarizes the broad principle of use of force which is generally accepted in most settings by stating that the use of force by one person on another without consent is unlawful unless it is justified. The use of force will be justified, and therefore lawful, only: if it is reasonable in the circumstances; if it is necessary; if no more force than is necessary is used; and if it is proportionate to the seriousness of the circumstances (1). The 1990 United Nations Basic Principles on the Use of Force and Firearms by Law Enforcement Officials, the leading international instrument dedicated to regulating the use of force for law enforcement purposes, referred to less-lethal weapons (LLW) in two of its provisions (2). Basic Principle 2 called on Governments and law enforcement agencies to develop "*a range of means as broad as possible*", which

> "*should include the development of non-lethal incapacitating weapons for use in appropriate situations*". Principle 3 called for the development and deployment of LLW to be "*carefully evaluated in order to minimize the risk of endangering uninvolved persons*", and stipulated that their use "*should be carefully controlled*" (2).

More recently (3), the United Nations has defined LLW as

> "*Weapons designed or intended for use on individuals or groups of individuals and which, in the course of expected or reasonably foreseen use, have a lower risk of causing death or serious injury than firearms. Less-lethal ammunition may be fired from conventional firearms....the term includes conventional firearms when they are used to discharge less-lethal ammunition, but not when they are used to discharge conventional bullets or other ammunition that would be likely to result in life-threatening injuries*".

Concerns about police accountability have been explored in the Report "Police Less Lethal Force & Accountability: Monitoring Deaths in Western Europe" which emphasizes that

> "*In democratic societies, good policing depends on public consent and an acceptance of the legitimacy of the police. As events around the globe in 2020 have made evident, consent and legitimacy can be eroded when force is seen as unnecessary or excessive. The killing of George Floyd on 25 May after his arrest in Minneapolis initiated extensive media coverage of the use of force in policing across Europe, North America and beyond*" (4).

EXAMPLES OF METHODS OF RESTRAINT AND CONTROL AND THEIR CONSEQUENCES

There are many methods of restraint and control. Some, but not all, come under the international classifications of LLW. Examples are shown in Table 71.1 which also identifies those that are considered "less-lethal". When restraining and controling an individual (or individuals) law-enforcement personnel in any jurisdiction need to consider, is the method (or methods) I am using proportionate (i.e. is there a less risky option I can use) and do I know how to deal with any unintended consequences? The United Nations states

> "*Law enforcement officials shall receive appropriate initial and refresher training in the use and effects of any less-lethal weapons with which they have been equipped or deployed....Training should include information on the particular vulnerabilities of certain individuals to the effects of a particular weapon, and on how to identify especially vulnerable individuals. Trainees shall be made aware not only of the primary risk of injury arising from use of any less-lethal weapons with which they may be equipped but also of the secondary injuries that may result (for example, if a person against whom the weapon is used falls from an elevated position or onto a hard surface). These effects and risks should also be reflected in standard operating procedures.*" (2).

DOI: 10.1201/9781003138754-74

From the forensic practitioner's perspective, the UN Guidance also states

> "*Medical assistance shall be rendered to any injured or affected person at the earliest possible moment. The duty to assist applies without discrimination of any kind. Thus, assistance shall be duly provided, irrespective of whether the injured person is a suspected offender. Distinctions with regard to the medical assistance provided are justifiable only on medical grounds, such as the urgency of medical needs. Access to medical assistance should therefore be provided on the basis of the severity of the injury.*"

The UN (2) has developed an injury classification for LLWs as below. Injury is defined as

> "*Physical or physiological bodily trauma resulting from the interaction of the body with energy (mechanical, thermal, electrical or radiant, or due to extreme pressure) in an amount or at a rate of transfer that exceeds physical or physiological tolerance, or with toxic chemical substances*".

Moderate injury is an injury that is not life-threatening, but is more severe than a minor injury, such as a small cut, abrasion or bruise. Serious injury is an injury that is potentially life-threatening or life-changing and permanent blindness is classified separately as the irreversible and uncorrectable loss of vision in at least one eye, while serious visual disability is equivalent to visual acuity of less than 20/200 Snellen measured using both eyes. For the forensic physician and allied practitioners, the majority of injury seen will be mild to moderate. If restraint techniques go wrong or are misapplied the outcome may be a fatality.

Documentation of the effects of methods of restraint and control may be very significant in terms of long-term care and also the outcome of legal issues such as complaints against a law-enforcement agency. Examples of restraint methods and their medical and healthcare effects are given below. Chapter 86 – Conducted Electrical Weapons – reviews conducted energy devices (CEDs – also referred to as conducted energy weapons – CEWs).

TABLE 71.1 Examples of law-enforcement methods of restraint and control

Conflict resolution
Empty hand techniques
Handcuffs
Batons
Dogs
Horses
Chemical irritant sprays (tear gas) • Personal • Projectile
Incapacitants
Kinetic impact projectiles ('rubber bullets') • Baton rounds • Attenuating Energy Projectiles - AEPs
Other rounds
Conducted Energy Weapons • Taser (see Chapter 86)
Water cannon
Dazzle devices
Acoustic devices
Others

Those in italics are LLWs as defined by international convention.

Not all are currently permitted for use in all jurisdictions. Some methods and devices may be available to the general public lawfully and unlawfully.

Handcuffs

Three main means of handcuffing individuals exist: traditional handcuffs with two wrist pieces connected by a short chain; rigid cuffs whereby the two wrist pieces are connected by a bar and cannot move in relation to each other and plasticuffs or cable ties. In each case, overtightening or struggling by the restrained person or application of force (bending or twisting) by the restraining person may cause a range of injuries caused by direct and indirect pressure. The longer the cuffs are applied, the greater the chance of injury or prolonged complications. Rigid cuffs can result in direct angulation pressure to the bones of the wrist. The fixed connecting bar of the rigid handcuffs allows controled application of force across the wrist to gain control. Once applied, simple pressure against the wrist allows the single bar of the cuffs to release over the top of the wrist and close with a ratchet mechanism. If the individual is non-compliant and continues moving, the handcuffs can progressively tighten causing increasing pain and potentially increasing the risk of neurologic and skin damage.

Soft-tissue injuries may be produced by movement of the wrist within the handcuff, movement of the handcuff on the wrist or by the handcuff being too tight with a combination of blunt force injuries including reddening, abrasions, lacerations and bruising, particularly to the radial and ulnar borders of the wrists commonly being seen (*see* Figure 71.1). In cases of substantial struggling or extreme application of force, fractures (mainly to the ulna or radius) may be seen or need to be excluded. Sensory changes such as numbness or hyperesthesia in the distribution of the cutaneous nerves distal to the applied cuff is common but is generally transient for a few hours. Specific handcuff neuropathies have been described with single or multiple nerves being affected, dependent on a number of factors including the tightness of compression, the duration and the degree of struggle from the detainee and force applied by the law enforcement team. In most cases, the damaged nerves fully recover within a few weeks. Persistence of symptoms may require nerve conduction studies.

The most common neurologic problem acquired by US prisoners of war during Operation Desert Storm was handcuff neuropathy (5). Compressive neuropathy of ulnar, radial and median nerves have all been described and, in some cases, neurologic deficits persisted for years.

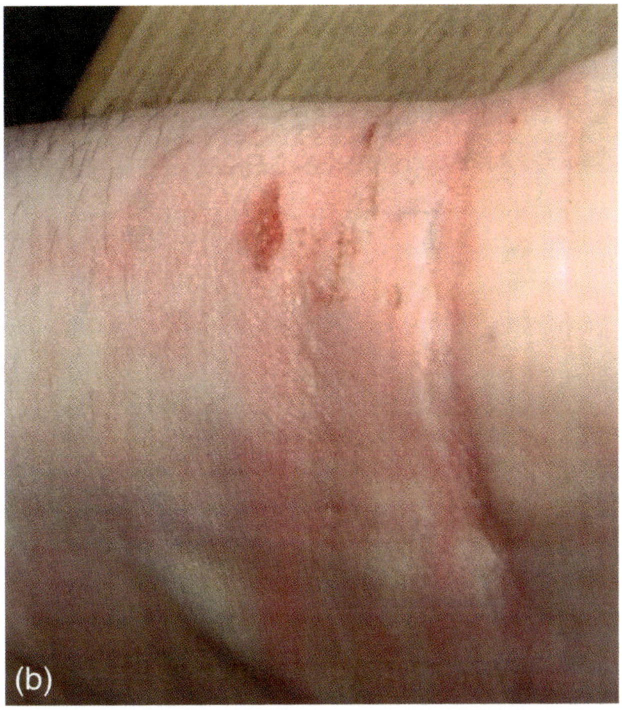

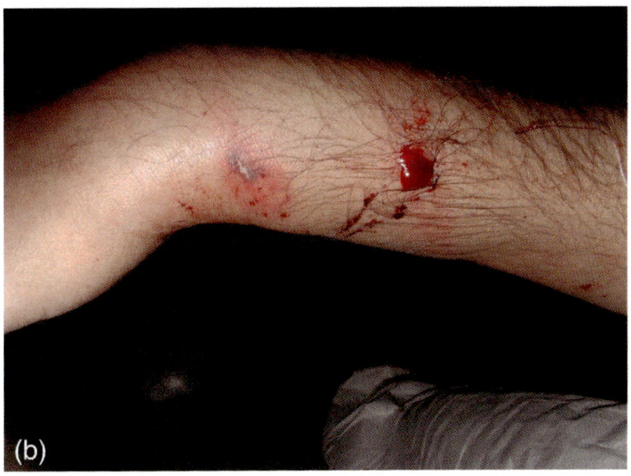

71.1 Examples of handcuff injury. **(a)** Reddening, superficial abrasion and imprint of cuffs following arrest. **(b)** Reddening, marked swelling and laceration causing bleeding to right lower forearm and wrist where cuffs had not been applied tightly, movement and struggle followed. There was an underlying ulnar styloid fracture.

Nerve conduction studies may be useful in diagnosis and excluding other causes. In one large study (6) of patients with a complaint of hand numbness, weakness, or paresthesias, attributed to overtightened handcuffs electrodiagnostic testing, revealed neuropathies due to overtightened handcuffs were detected in 22 superficial radial, 12 median and 9 ulnar nerves.

Chariot et al. (7) concluded that prolonged handcuffing associated with reduced conscious level and acute alcohol intoxication could be predisposing factors to handcuff neuropathy. In a study of 367 torture victims (8) 18.5 percent of the subjects had typical handcuff injuries, which were blunt trauma in nature around wrists or ankles. Ischemic monomelic neuropathy (IMN) is a rare type of ischemic neuropathy produced by the shunting of blood away from, or the acute non-compressive occlusion of, a major proximal limb artery. It consists of multiple mononeuropathies with axonal-loss that develop acutely and simultaneously in the distal portion of a limb. Ischemic neuropathies in a single limb are well-known in other settings such as following compression (casts or tourniquet use), proximal vascular procedures and thromboembolism. Ischemic dimelic neuropathy (IDN) has now been described in both upper limbs after plastic zip tie handcuffs had been applied (9). This report case highlights and increases awareness among physicians and security agencies to recognize IDN early, and take measures to prevent this rapidly developing neuropathy, by discouraging the use of plastic handcuffs. In a systematic review (10) in which a total of 16 studies involving 807 participants were included, a lesion to the superficial branch of the radial nerve was the most commonly reported injury noted in 82 percent (42/55) of hands examined. A total of 6 percent (5/77) of examined hands had bony injury, including three radial styloid fractures and two scaphoid fractures. Both studies on zip ties noted presence of handcuff neuropathy. The authors concluded that further studies of higher quality evidence are necessary to understand the effects of physical restraint on hand function and disability. The role of the forensic physician and allied healthcare professional is to ensure that signs and symptoms of handcuff injury are recorded accurately and, where necessary, referred for further neurologic investigation to minimize long-term complications.

Batons

Batons used by law-enforcement professionals globally have a variety of names, dependent on the region in the world, including truncheons, ASPs and night sticks. Most are rigid implements used to strike or as a threat of strike to exert control or restraint. Three typical baton types are used around the world with many variations: the three-part extendable gravity friction lock baton made of steel; acrylic patrol batons of different length, some with handles; and the wooden patrol baton. The long portion can be used for a direct strike, the baton can be held at both grip and long end and used to push back an individual and both ends can be used to the front and back to jab against someone.

Baton strikes of any kind result in blunt force injury with the entire range of blunt force injury being represented. The potential for injury will vary with the amount of energy transferred in a baton strike and may be dependent in part on the nature of the baton (11). When deployed, there are certain body targets that are classified into low, medium and high risk of injury areas. There are increased risks of serious or life-changing injury dependent on the target struck, and training is required to reduce these risks when batons are deployed. In evidential terms (e.g. with complaints of police assault) the patterned nature of some batons will result in patterned and identifiable injuries.

Areas of low injury potential (and thus primary targets) are legs (in the areas of the common peroneal, femoral and tibial nerves) and arms (in the areas of the radial and median nerves). Possible medical complications of strikes in these areas include reddening and bruising of the target area and transient motor dysfunction of the affected limb. The medium injury potential areas (and therefore should be avoided as primary targets) are knees and ankles, wrist, elbow, hands, upper arms and the clavicles. Potential medical complications include bone fractures, dislocation and soft-tissue damage at the points of impact. Higher injury potential areas (and which should not be targeted) are the head, neck/throat, spine, loins (kidneys), and abdomen (small bowel, stomach, liver, and pancreas). Potential complications include damage to intraabdominal structures, which could result in catastrophic hemorrhage or delayed peritonitis if the bowel is perforated. Tramline (railtrack) bruising or reddening is frequently seen in baton strikes. Routine baton strikes over bony structures can cause lacerations and bone fractures in addition to lesser blunt force injury. Strikes with the end of a baton are at risk of causing significant injury (e.g. rupture of eye). Forensic assessment is crucial after significant baton strike to ensure potential complications (e.g. intra-abdominal hemorrhage or perforation, and bony fracture) have been identified. Figure 71.2 shows examples of typical batons and baton injuries.

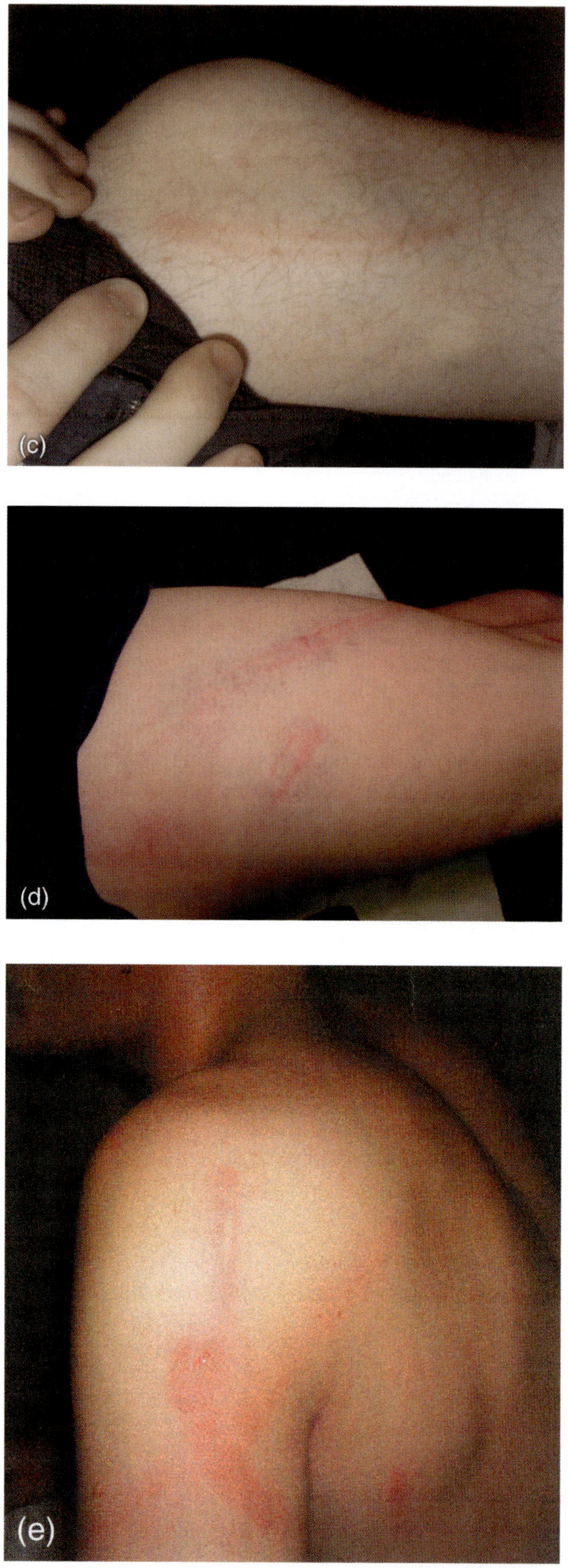

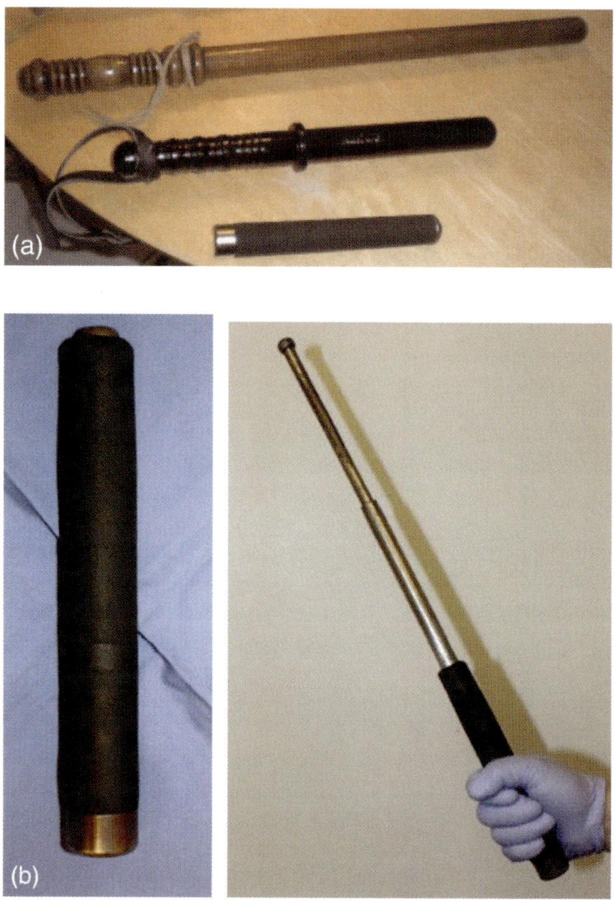

71.2 Examples of handcuff injury. **(a)** Range of batons used in law-enforcement – wooden, acrylic and extendable ASP. **(b)** Unextended and extended metal ASP baton. **(c)** Tramline (railtrack) bruising from baton strike to knee region. **(d)** Multiple baton strikes to outer thigh. **(e)** Multiple baton strikes to left upper arm and shoulder.

Chemical irritants

Restraint and control of detainees in the police setting can use a variety of methods of less-lethal force, including the deployment of irritant sprays (IS). These may be in the form of munitions or as personal IS (12). They may include CS, PAVA and pepper sprays among others. These were previously referred to as "incapacitant sprays". Personal IS augment the range of tactical options available to police officers confronted by aggressive or violent individuals or those with acute behavioral disturbance. These are supplied as hand-held personal issue devices. Such devices are increasingly used. Data from the UK showed that deployment of incapacitant sprays doubled from ~3500 to ~7000 in 2007–2011 (13). By 2022, the figure was over 12 000 (14). In the UK, both CS and PAVA spray are used. The effects of most IS are similar and are summarized in Table 71.2. Their predominant effects are lacrimatory, respiratory and dermatologic. Their effects may last

TABLE 71.2 Intended and expected effects of irritant sprays
Mouth
Clinical effects • stinging or burning sensation • nausea and vomiting (rare)
Management • symptomatic, based on clinical findings
Respiratory Tract
Clinical effects • nasal discomfort, pain & rhinorrhoea (<30 mins) • sneezing, coughing, sore throat • sore throat • shortness of breath • bronchospasm (rare) • laryngospasm (rare) • tracheitis • bronchitis (rare) • pulmonary edema may develop 12 to 24 hours after excessive exposure (rare) • Patients with pre-existing respiratory disease, such as asthma or bronchitis, are at greater risk of severe effects
Management • The majority of respiratory tract symptoms and signs (e.g. cough, dyspnea and chest tightness) should settle within 15–30 minutes after exposure • If there is evidence of bronchospasm that does not respond to simple bronchodilation refer urgently to hospital for assessment and treatment. • Longer-term respiratory symptoms necessitate review by a respiratory physician
Skin
Clinical effects • burning sensation & erythema (<24 hrs) • chemical burns, blistering • allergic contact dermatitis (rare - but law enforcement personnel regularly exposed to irritant spray may require changes in work practice – referral to Occupational Health teams should be made) • leukoderma (rare) • initiation or exacerbation of seborrheic dermatitis (rare) • aggravation of rosacea (rare)
Management • exposure to air and fan • exposure to fresh air will normally result in a significant recovery within 15–20 minutes • if reactions do persist beyond this period, then copious amounts of cool tap water should be used to flush remaining irritant from the face and skin • under no circumstances should warm water be used as this can reactivate irritants • treat chemical burns as thermal burns

(Continued)

TABLE 71.2 (Continued) Intended and expected effects of irritant sprays

Mouth
• topical steroids can be used for contact dermatitis • delayed skin irritation (due to MIBK), occurring 8 to 16 hours after exposure, is seen in a significant number; these symptoms can take up to one week to resolve • persistence of new skin conditions or aggravation of chronic conditions beyond 48 hours should be assessed by the person's GP and review by a dermatologist may be required
Cardiovascular effects
Clinical effects
• Pre-existing cardiac problems may be exacerbated by exposure • Angina may be precipitated in those with pre-existing cardiac conditions
Management
• Symptomatic treatment e.g. glyceryl trinitrate • Refer to hospital if any concerns at examination (e.g. persistent tachycardia, persistent chest pain, arrhythmias, hypertension, hypotension)

2–3 hours and if they persist beyond this time referral to appropriate specialists may be required (15,16). The agents currently used by police services in the UK are CS and PAVA (nonivamide). CS (CS O-chlorbenzylidene malonitrile, 5% solution) is dissolved in an organic solvent (methyl isobutyl ketone [MIBK]) to be used as a liquid aerosol with nitrogen as a propellant. The solvent evaporates leaving the CS particles to give their effects. PAVA (pelargonic acid vanillylamide, 0.3% solution [nonivamide]) is dissolved in a solvent of monopropylene glycol, ethanol and water and is also used in liquid aerosol form with nitrogen as a propellant. PAVA is a synthetic variant of capsaicin (the active ingredient of natural pepper). When delivered from personal IS devices, they are intended to be used to spray the face of a person at a distance of up to 3–4 meters, delivering the active chemical to the eyes, nose, mouth and skin. This can cause injury to the eyes, respiratory tract and skin. Individuals affected by chronic morbidities may be at higher risk of experiencing complications. Published data are limited with respect to the incidence and persistence of such complications with all irritants sprays. Longer exposure or exposure in confined spaces may result in enhanced or prolonged effects.

The broad principles of effect, treatment and management are the same for IS according to published clinical studies comparing the nature and incidence of their different effects. Chemical irritants can cause severe injury, permanent disabilities and, in rare cases, death. The true incidence of morbidity (and possible mortality) of IS remains unknown in the absence of prospective clinical studies of appropriate statistical power. The Faculty of Forensic & Legal Medicine publishes recommendations on the management of exposure to IS. CS and PAVA fail to affect about 10 percent of people exposed to spray (16). The reasons for this are varied and may include intoxication with other drugs or alcohol; mental health issues; or other causes of acute behavioral disturbance. Agitation may impede initial decontamination and increase the risks of secondary contamination of self or others. Other types of spray available include CN (Mace) (L-chloroacetophenone) and OC – Oleoresin Capsicum – which has active agents of 4 vanillyl fatty acid amides.

Prospective data on the effects of chemical IS are limited. Skin reactions have been reported (17–19) with contact allergy, leukoderma and exacerbation of sclerotic dermatitis and rosacea. Ocular damage has been reported including transient conjunctivitis and blepharospasm occurring a few seconds after exposure. Corneal damage, hyphema or vitreous hemorrhage have been described (21,22). Case reports have highlighted shortness of breath, sore throat and chest pain as the most common pulmonary complaints, which typically resolve within 30 minutes, with occasional incidents of bronchospasm and laryngospasm. Delayed pulmonary edema has been described. Acute laryngeal and bronchial obstruction is also seen due to vocal cord edema and extensive crusting at the glottic level, trachea and bronchi (23). A review of short- and long-term symptoms suggested there was no convincing evidence of long-term physical sequelae from exposure to CS spray (24) although the study was limited.

Kearney and colleagues studied the prevalence of and circumstances associated with symptoms suggestive of tissue injury beyond transient irritation in persons exposed to pepper spray by reviewing all human exposures to pepper spray reported to a poison control system between 2002 and 2011 (25). A total of 3671 cases met the inclusion criteria. Of these, 249 cases (6.8%) were found to have more severe symptoms that warranted a medical evaluation. There were no reported deaths. The cases with more severe symptoms most commonly involved the ocular (53.8%), respiratory (31.7%) and dermal (17.7%) organ systems. They found there was a low 1 in 15 potential risk for more severe adverse health effects in persons exposed to pepper spray that warranted a medical evaluation. The risk was highest when used for training of law enforcement personnel and involved severe ocular symptoms. This suggests that routine use of pepper spray for training of law enforcement or military personnel be reconsidered. Protective goggles may be an option when direct spraying into the face of trainees. Transport for medical evaluation should be considered for exposed persons that manifest persistent ocular or respiratory symptoms.

Haar et al. undertook a systematic review using PRISMA guidelines to identify injuries, permanent disabilities and deaths from chemical irritants worldwide between January 1, 1990 and March 15, 2015 (26). These included settings where such irritants were also delivered by munitions. They reported on 5131 people who suffered injuries, two of whom died and 58 of whom suffered permanent disabilities. Out of 9261 total injuries, 8.7 percent were severe and required professional medical management, while 17 percent were moderate and 74.3 percent were minor. Severe injuries occurred to all body systems, with the majority of injuries impacting the skin and eyes. Projectile munition trauma caused 231 projectile injuries, with 63 (27%) severe injuries, including major head injury and vision loss. Potentiating factors for more severe injury included environmental conditions, prolonged exposure time and higher quantities of chemical agent in enclosed spaces. They concluded that chemical weapons have significant potential for misuse, leading to unnecessary morbidity and mortality.

IS are in widespread use lawfully and unlawfully as they can easily be obtained online. Very little research work has been undertaken on the true incidence of side effects and long-term complications. The eyes, skin, respiratory and cardiovascular system may all be affected. There is no substantial body of research that links IS with increased risks of death. However, the area is under-researched and substantial morbidity may be found if looked at in a prospective study. First aid and removal from the source of spray as early as possible are key elements in reducing the potential mid- and long-term effects. The medical implications of the use of IS are poorly documented and available current data are based on case reports, small prospective case series, systematic reviews and retrospective data analyses (27).

Currently available data indicated that for exposure to any irritant spray each individual should be fully examined by a forensic physician or appropriately trained forensic practitioner with particular reference to eyes, oral and nasal cavity, cardiovascular, respiratory system and skin and plans made for subsequent reviewed if clinically indicated (16).

KINETIC ENERGY PROJECTILES

Kinetic energy projectiles means any type of device designed as less lethal, to be launched from any device as a projectile that may cause bodily injury through the transfer of kinetic energy and blunt force trauma. This blunt force trauma may cause penetrating injuries.

A number of firearms are adapted to fire projectiles (known by a variety of names and made of various substances and in various shapes and sizes such as plastic bullets, rubber bullets, baton rounds, attenuating energy projectiles (AEPs), bean bags and foam rounds) (*see* Figure 71.3). The names are not used consistently in the literature. In general, these projectiles are made out of materials of lower density than "normal" bullets, are larger and fired at lower velocities. The design, relatively large in size, low weight and low velocity is intended to reduce the risk of skin penetration while exerting severe pain on impact. This is intended to minimize severe or fatal injury. As with batons and IS, the intended usage and effect may be achieved, but others (including members of the public and law enforcement professionals) may sustain injury during deployment, or unintended injury of a severe nature, including fatality may be caused. The projectiles are frequently irregular cylinders made of rubber, plastic, wood, or foam, and can be as large as the full-bore diameter of the launcher. Projectiles may be single, or several fired at the same discharge (*see* Figure 71.4). Radiologic appearance may help determine the nature of the projectile (28). The UK Home Office currently permits the use of projectiles known as AEP. They are rarely fired in mainland UK (54 firings in almost 1000 deployments (14). Early reports after their introduction in the 1970s identified assorted oral and maxillofacial injuries (29). If they are to be deployed by law enforcement or other agencies, it is crucial that appropriate training is given in the deployment, the risks of injury and the aim points to be avoided.

The expected clinical effects can be considered to be those of any blunt force contact. However, despite the low velocity, the force of impact can be severe, and thus

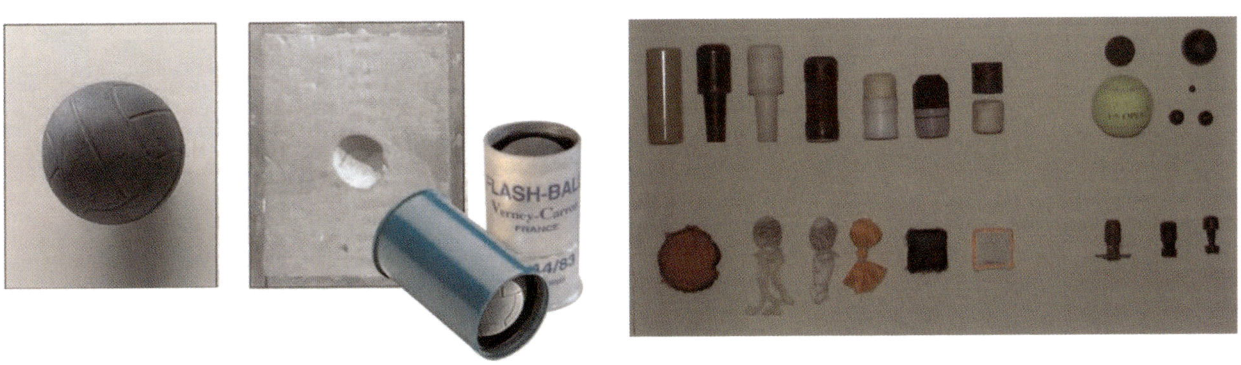

71.3 Examples of kinetic energy projectiles.

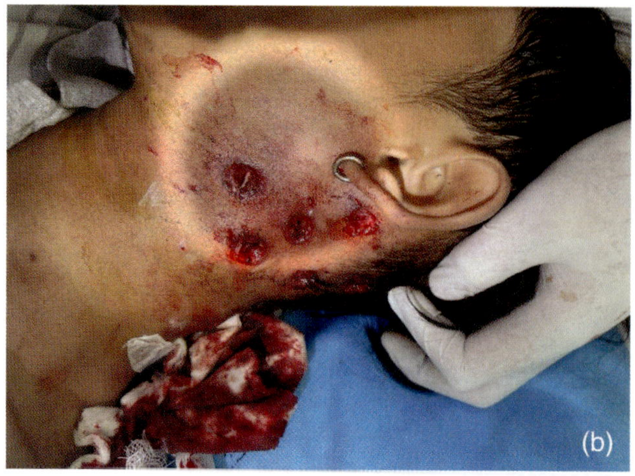

71.4 Three projectiles fired from a single 12-bore cartridge. In this example from Myanmar, two cartridges had been fired at close range to the left neck, **(a)** 12-bore cartridges each containing three rubber spherical projectiles. **(b)** Left side of neck with two cartridges each with three spheres discharged at close range.

the site of impact may result in considerable morbidity. Ritchie (30) described a series of 123 patients who attended a district general hospital in Belfast over a 14-year period from 1975, who had sustained 126 plastic bullet injuries, resulting in one death and several serious injuries. In another series of 201 patients, injuries were distributed randomly over the body surface and were mostly located in the limbs but also documented to the head, neck, and face, chest, back and abdomen. Ninety-three (61%) patients had blunt injuries and 59 (39%) penetrating ones. There were two fatalities – one after a penetrating ocular injury into the brain and one died indirectly, postoperatively. Parts of the body where there is underlying bone (e.g. the chest) may result in localized fractures such as ribs with co-morbidity such as hemo- or pneumothorax. Skull fracture has been described (31). Limb fractures have been described (32). Impacts to the soft tissues with no underlying bone (e.g. abdomen) have a risk of damage to the viscera (e.g. liver, spleen and gastrointestinal tract). Ocular injuries have been reported even with softer materials such as foam rounds (33). Testicular rupture has been reported (34). A Flashball is a kinetic energy projectile round used in France and reports of death due to *commotio cordis* have been documented (35). Both orbital and ocular injuries have also been documented with Flashballs (36). Sutter (37) described a series of ocular injuries in Switzerland caused by plastic bullets and, in one case, the injured eye was registered blind. In a study of predominantly beanbag injuries, Suyama et al. (38) identified significant visceral and soft-tissue injury in 27 subjects, including three subjects with the diagnoses of pulmonary contusion, liver laceration and Achilles tendon rupture. Amelot et al. (39) described a penetrating craniocerebral injury from a rubber bullet. Penetration into the ethmoid sinus has been described from a rubber bullet (40).

All these weapons can be accessed by the general public who will not be trained in appropriate use. Khonsari et al. (41) documented six patients who received treatment of facial injury due to rubber-bullet trauma from 2000 to 2008. They excluded injuries caused by law enforcement agencies. In five cases, the firearm had been used as an assault weapon and in one, the injury occurred in a self-defense situation. Substantial injuries were sustained involving fractures, penetration requiring facial skeleton reconstruction and removal of the eye. Figure 71.5 illustrates the clinical and radiologic findings in one case.

Impact rounds of all different types can result in serious and life-changing injury. Such weapons are available not only to lawful users such as law enforcement professionals (who may or may not use them appropriately) but also to the general public who may use them as weapons in a variety of settings. These weapons have the potential for high morbidity and mortality. All those who have sustained injuries from them should be appropriately medically examined to exclude occult, severe and potentially fatal injury (42). Many of those who sustained injuries will require substantial surgical intervention. Such are the concerns that in 2020, the American Academy of Ophthalmology called on domestic law enforcement officials to immediately end the use of rubber bullets and similar projectiles to control or disperse crowds of protesters (43).

MONITORING OF EFFECTS

The United Nations Principles indicate that LLWs will be monitored in terms of their use and effects by law enforcement agencies and states. That monitoring should include contextual information about the circumstances of use. It should be possible to identify the age, sex/gender, disability and ethnic group against or

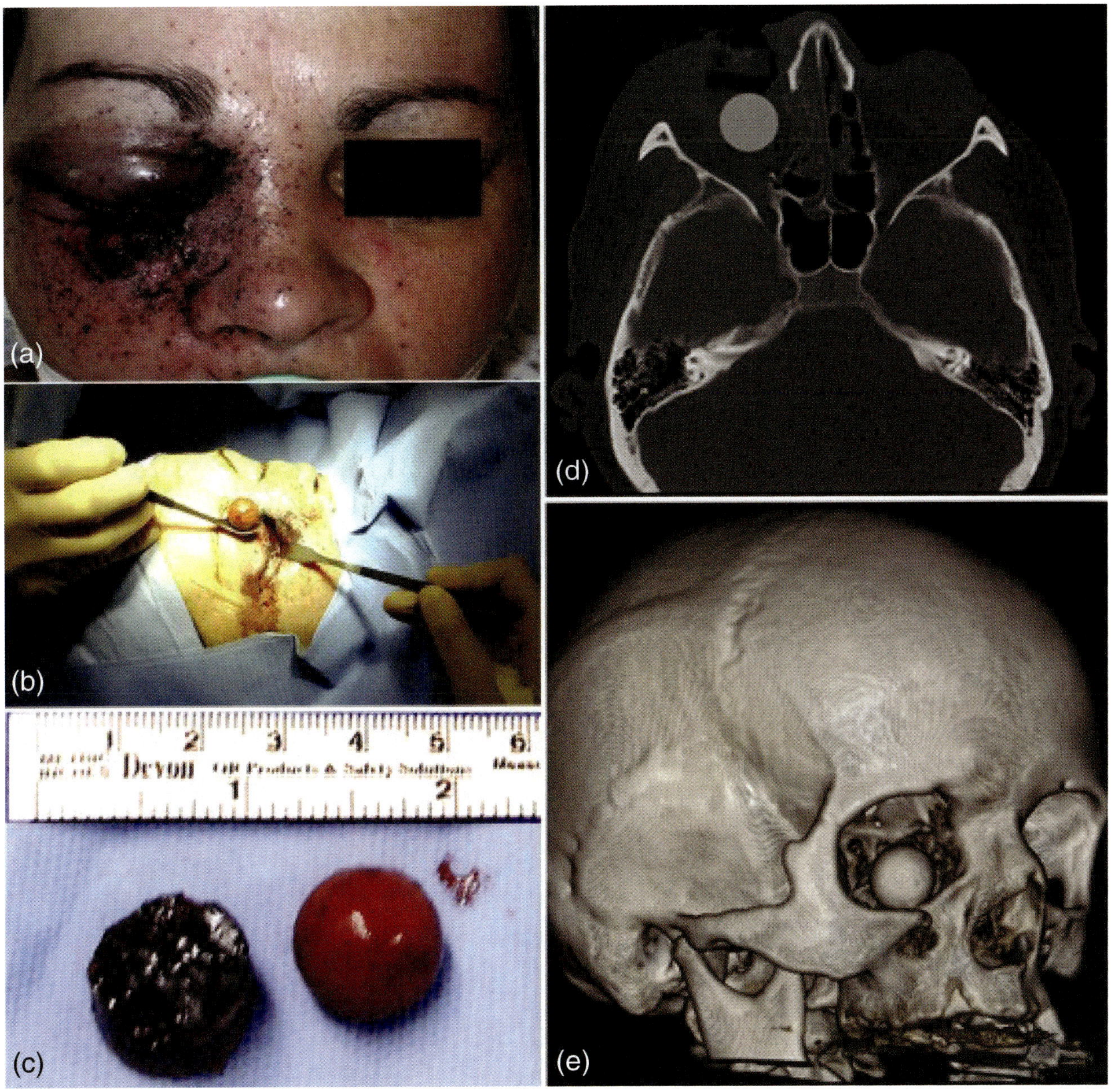

71.5 (a) Patient at admission, with extensive traumatic gunpowder tattoo and penetrating injury of the internal canthus; **(b&c)** the 18-mm rubber missile and the wad were extracted from the orbit; **(d)** the medial wall of the orbit and the right ethmoidal cells were fractured—the wad was visible anterior prior to the bullet; **(e)** 3D CT-scan showing the infero-medial intra-orbital localization of the rubber bullet; right zygoma and orbital floor fractures. (From [14].)

on whom the particular method is used and those data should be publicly available. Those data should include publicly available national statistics on deaths and serious injuries relating to different categories of LLWs. Few countries observe this guidance completely (2). The UK Government publishes annual Use of Force Statistics since 2017. These data have been collected from all 43 Home Office funded police forces and cover incidents where police officers have used force including: tactics used; reasons for using force; outcomes; injuries (to the officers and or the person involved); personal characteristics (age, gender, ethnicity and health conditions, as perceived by the reporting officer). Data from the year ending 31 March 2022 showed 608 164 recorded incidents in which a police officer used force (14). Restraint tactics (e.g. handcuffing, limb or body restraints, ground restraint) were the most common type of force used (79%). This is a similar proportion to the year ending 31 March 2021 (80%). The most common reason an officer used force was to protect themselves (70%); the most common impact factor was the person being under the influence of alcohol (39%). Almost half (44%) of "use of force" incidents involved males aged 18 to 34 (as perceived by the officer). This age and gender group

TABLE 71.3 Use of force tactics in England & Wales for which statistical data are published

A "use of force" incident is defined as a situation in which a police officer uses any of the following force tactics
Restraint tactics • handcuffing (compliant or non-compliant) • limb or body restraints • ground restraint
Unarmed skills • distraction strikes with hands and feet • pressure point and joint locks
Use of other equipment • a baton (including where it was drawn but not used) • irritant spray (including where it was drawn but not used) • spit and bite guard • shield (for example, person struck or pushed with a shield)
Less lethal weapons • Conducted Energy Device (CED), for example, TASER ® (including non-discharge uses) • Attenuating Energy Projectile (AEP), (including where it was drawn but not used)
Firearms • use of conventional firearms (including where it was aimed but not fired)
Other: • use of dogs (including where a dog was deployed but did not come into contact with, such as bite, the person) • other improvized tactics

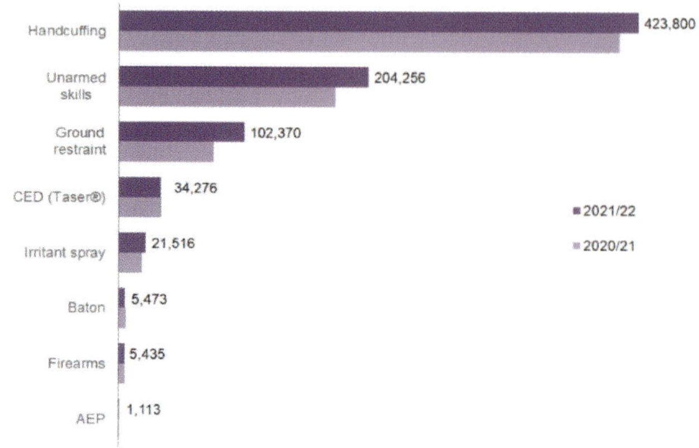

71.6 Number of times key tactics were used in "use of force" incidents, England & Wales, years ending 31 March 2021 and 31 March 2022. (From (14).)

had the highest rate of "use of force", (41 incidents per 1000 population). Table 71.3 summarizes the Use of Force Tactics in England & Wales for which statistical data are published. Figure 71.6 shows the breakdown of types of Use of Force in England & Wales. Table 71.4 shows the actual numbers and nature of deployment from 2021/2022 and identifies the number of children on whom these methods have been used. Bloom and Bloom (44) reviewed data from 2010 to 2019, to identify eye injuries caused by BBs and pellets, gas, air or spring-operated guns; and personal protective devices (PPDs) which included pepper spray, tear gas and bean bag guns. During the study period, 598 Emergency Department cases were associated with kinetic impact projectiles (n = 209) and PPDs (n = 389).

In the UK, monitoring of LLWs is undertaken by the Scientific Advisory Committee on the Medical Implications of Less-Lethal Weapons (45). SACMILL (and its predecessor DOMILL) provides independent advice to UK government departments and organizations on the biophysical, biomechanical, pathological and clinical aspects of LLW systems and issues independent statements on the medical implications of the use of specific LLW systems, when used in accordance with published operational guidance provided to users (46). It provides advice on the risk of injury from specific LLW systems striking specific areas of the body, in a format that will assist both those responsible for developing policy and for operational users to help make tactical decisions. For historical reasons, despite IS being considered less-lethal, it is does not currently come under SACMILL's remit. Increased use internationally highlights previously unrecognized concerns including possible effects on reproductive health (47).

CONCLUSION

Methods of restraint and control including LLWs are available to law-enforcement personnel and other agencies. Their use should be controled by appropriate training and by constant monitoring to ensure that their effects are not excessive and that morbidity and mortality is minimized. Despite robust international guidelines on the monitoring of use of data on morbidity and mortality are minimal in the context of the increasing use worldwide of all methods. All methods of restraint and control present risks of harm and fatality. Where such methods are deployed, it is essential that prospective monitoring and recording of adverse effects is undertaken. This is best done by forensic physicians and allied forensic professionals who are trained in the assessment of individuals exposed to restraint and control (whether classified as less-lethal or not).

TABLE 71.4 The numbers and nature of use of force tactics in England and Wales from 2021/2022

Type of force	Under 11 years	11–17 years	Total
Total restraint	**290**	**55 571**	**569 320**
Total handcuffing	114	41 198	423 800
Compliant handcuffing	40	24 552	263 602
Non-compliant handcuffing	72	16 130	154 459
Handcuffing not stated	2	516	5739
Limb/body restraints	72	4525	43 150
Ground restraint	104	9 848	102 370
Total unarmed skills	**362**	**21 874**	**204 256**
Total other equipment	**13**	**2318**	**36 108**
Total baton	2	416	5473
Baton drawn	2	298	3259
Baton used	0	111	2080
Baton not stated	0	7	134
Total irritant spray	2	1196	21 516
Irritant spray drawn	1	619	8798
Irritant spray used	1	572	12 541
Irritant spray not stated	0	5	177
Spit and bite guard	9	654	8281
Shield	0	52	838
Total less lethal weapons	**8**	**2748**	**35 389**
Total CED	8	2678	34 276
CED non-discharge	7	2454	29 378
CED discharge	1	100	3175
CED not stated [Note 6]	0	124	1723
Total AEP	0	70	1113
AEP drawn	0	61	987
AEP used	0	1	57
AEP not stated	0	8	69
Total firearms	**1**	**464**	**5435**
Firearms aimed	1	401	4880
Firearms fired	0	0	3
Firearms not stated	0	63	552
Total other	**138**	**4553**	**43 382**
Other/improvised	136	4215	40 602
Total dog use	2	338	2780
Dog deployed	2	270	2166
Dog bite	0	64	565
Dog not stated	0	4	49

Adapted from Table 71.2 Home Office "Police use of force statistics", England and Wales, April 2021 to March 2022 (14).

REFERENCES

1. HM Prison Service. Order number 1600. Use of force, 2015. Available from: https://assets.publishing.service.gov.uk/government/uploads/system/uploads/attachment_data/file/933347/use_of_force_-_pso-1600.pdf (Accessed 19 May 2023).
2. United Nations. Basic principles on the use of force and firearms by law enforcement officials, 1990. Available from: https://www.ohchr.org/en/instruments-mechanisms/instruments/basic-principles-use-force-and-firearms-law-enforcement (Accessed 19 May 2023).
3. United Nations. UN human rights guidance on less-lethal weapons and related equipment in law enforcement, 2020. Available from: https://www.ohchr.org/sites/default/files/Documents/HRBodies/CCPR/LLW_Guidance.pdf (Accessed 19 May 2023).
4. Rappert B, Adang O, Daillère A, et al. Police lethal force and accountability: Monitoring deaths in western Europe. Available from: https://lethal-force-monitor.org/downloads/police-lethal-force-report.pdf (Accessed 19 May 2023).
5. Cook AA. Handcuff neuropathy among U.S. prisoners of war from Operation Desert Storm. *Mil Med* 1993; **158(4)**: 253–4.
6. Grant AC, Cook AA. A prospective study of handcuff neuropathies. *Muscle Nerve* 2000; **23(6)**: 933–8.
7. Chariot P, Ragot F, Authier FJ, et al. Focal neurological complications of handcuff application. *J Forensic Sci* 2001; **46(5)**: 1124–5.
8. Ghaleb SS, Elshabrawy EM, Elkardawy M, et al. Retrospective study of positive physical torture cases in Cairo (2009 & 2010). *J Forensic Leg Med* 2014; **24**: 37–45.
9. Wali A, Hussain T. Devastating ischemic dimelic neuropathy after plastic zip tie handcuffs; Message for security agencies. *Ann Med Surg (Lond)* 2022; **78**: 103819.
10. Khan S, Mosa A, Clayton A, McCabe S. Hand and wrist injuries associated with application of physical restraints: A systematic review. *Hand (N Y)* 2022: 15589447221105548.
11. Roberts A, Nokes L, Leadbeatter S, Pike H. Impact characteristics of two types of police baton. *Forensic Sci Int* 1994; **67(1)**: 49–53.
12. Tidwell RD, Wills BK. *Tear Gas and Pepper Spray Toxicity*. Treasure Island: StatPearls Publishing; 2022.
13. Payne-James JJ, Rivers E, Green P, Johnston A. Trends in less-lethal use of force techniques by police services in England & Wales: 2007 - 11. *Forensic Sci Med Pathol* 2014; **10(1)**: 50–55.
14. GOV.uk. Police use of force statistics, England and Wales: April 2021 to March 2022, 2022. Available from: https://www.gov.uk/government/statistics/police-use-of-force-statistics-england-and-wales-april-2021-to-march-2022/police-use-of-force-statistics-england-and-wales-april-2021-to-march-2022#use-of-force-incidents-and-tactics12 (Accessed 19 May 2023).
15. Payne-James JJ, Smith G, Rivers E, et al. Effects of incapacitant spray deployed in the restraint and arrest of detainees in the Metropolitan Police Service area, London, UK: A prospective study. *Forensic Sci Med Pathol* 2014; **10(1)**: 62–8.
16. Faculty of Forensic & Legal Medicine. Irritant sprays: Clinical effects and management: Recommendations for healthcare professionals (forensic physicians, custody nurses and paramedics). Available from: https://fflm.ac.uk/wp-content/uploads/2021/02/ARCHIVED-Irritant-sprays-Dr-J-McGorrigan-and-Dr-J-Payne-James-December-2017.pdf (Accessed 19 May 2023).
17. Agrawal Y, Thornton D, Phipps A. CS gas – Completely safe? A burn case report and literature review. *Burns* 2009; **35(6)**: 895–7.
18. Hardwicke J, Satti U. Facial burns after exposure to CS spray. *Injury Extra* 2006; **37(3)**: 133–4.
19. Southward RD. Cutaneous burns from CS incapacitant spray. *Med Sci Law* 2001; **41(1)**: 74–7.
20. Euripidou E, MacLehose R, Fletcher A. An investigation into the short term and medium-term health impacts of personal incapacitant sprays. A follow up of patients reported to the National Poisons Information Service. *Emerg Med J* 2004; **21**: 548–52.
21. Carron P-N, Yersin B. Management of the effects of exposure to tear gas. *BMJ* 2009; **338**: b2283.
22. Shimada M, Young C, Tanen DA. Corneal ulcer associated with pepper spray exposure during military training. *J Emerg Med* 2012; **43(2)**: e149.
23. Karaman E, Erturan S, Duman C, et al. Acute laryngeal and bronchial obstruction after CS (o-chlorobenzylidenemalononitrile) gas inhalation. *Eur Arch Otorhinolaryngol* 2009; **266(2)**: 301–4.
24. Karagama Y, Newton J, Newbegin C. Short-term and long-term physical effects of exposure to CS spray. *J R Soc Med* 2003; **96**: 172–4.
25. Kearney T, Hiatt P, Birdsall E, Smollin C. Pepper spray injury severity: Ten-year case experience of a poison control system. *Prehosp Emerg Care* 2014; **18(3)**: 381–6.
26. Haar RJ, Iacopino V, Ranadive N, et al. Health impacts of chemical irritants used for crowd control: A systematic review of the injuries and deaths caused by tear gas and pepper spray. *BMC Public Health* 2017; **17(1)**: 831.
27. Payne-James JJ, Smith G, Rivers E, et al. Effects of incapacitant spray deployed in the restraint and arrest of detainees in the Metropolitan Police Service Area, London, UK: A prospective study. *Forensic Sci Med Pathol* 2014; **10(1)**: 62–8.
28. Manhas NS, Stahl D, Schellenberg M, Gholamrezanezhad A. Non-lethal weapon: Injury patterns and imaging correlates for firearm alternatives. *Clin Imaging* 2021; **79**: 165–72.
29. Sheridan SM, Whitlock RIH. Plastic baton round injuries. *Br J Oral Surg* 1983; **21(4)**: 259–67.
30. Ritchie A. Plastic bullets: Significant risk of serious injury above the diaphragm. *Injury* 1992; **23(4)**: 265–6.
31. Ali R, Poggi J, Doberstein CA, et al. Rubber bullet induced traumatic brain injury. *J Craniofac Surg* 2021; **32(6)**: 2189–92.
32. Dhar SA, Dar TA, Wani SA, et al. Pattern of rubber bullet injuries in the lower limbs: A report from Kashmir. *Chin J Traumatol* 2016; **19(3)**: 129–33.
33. Kim HJ, Ali S, Kelly LD. Ocular foam round injury: A case report and literature review. *Am J Ophthalmol Case Rep* 2021; **23**: 101149.
34. Kahle ME, Hamann KM, Sakher AA, et al. Testicular rupture following rubber bullet trauma case report. *Transl Androl Urol* 2021; **10(8)**: 3529–31.
35. Contargyris C, Peytel E. Commotio cordis après impact précordial de Flashballs. *Ann Fr Anesth Reanim* 2012; **31(5)**: 469–71.
36. Pinaud V, Leconte P, Berthier F, et al. Orbital and ocular trauma caused by the Flash-Balls: A case report. *Injury Extra* 2009; **40(9)**: 172–4.
37. Sutter FK. Ocular injuries caused by plastic bullet shotguns in Switzerland. *Injury* 2004; **35(10)**: 963–7.
38. Suyama J, Panagos PD, Sztajnkrycer MD, et al. Injury patterns related to use of less-lethal weapons during a period of civil unrest. *J Emerg Med* 2003; **25(2)**: 219–27.
39. Amelot A, Goutagny S, Ricome S, Peyre M. Penetrating craniocerebral injury caused by a rubber bullet questions the relative harmlessness of these weapons. *Am J Emerg Med* 2013; **31(3)**: 636.e5–636.e7.
40. Gross M, Regev E, Hamdan K, Eliashar R. Penetrating rubber bullet into the ethmoid sinus: Should the bullet be removed? *Otolaryngol Head Neck Surg* 2005; **133(5)**: 814–16.
41. Khonsari RH, Fleuridas G, Arzul L, et al. Severe facial rubber bullet injuries: Less lethal but extremely harmful weapons. *Injury* 2010; **41(1)**: 73–6.
42. Wahl P, Schreyer N, Yersin B. Injury pattern of the FlashBall: A less lethal weapon used for law enforcement: Report of two cases and review of the literature. *J Emerg Med* 2006; **21(3)**: 325–30.
43. American Academy of Ophthalmology. Nation's ophthalmologists condemn use of rubber bullets, 2020. Available from: https://www.aao.org/newsroom/news-releases/detail/nation-s-ophthalmologists-condemn-use-of-tear-gas- (Accessed 19 May 2023).
44. Bloom WR, Bloom TD. Epidemiology of eye injuries caused by personal protection devices and kinetic impact projectile weapons. *JAMA Ophthalmol* 2020; **138(12)**: 1318–19.
45. SACMILL, 2017. Available from: https://www.gov.uk/government/organisations/science-advisory-committee-on-the-medical-implications-of-less-lethal-weapons (Accessed 19 May 2023).
46. Scientific Advisory Committee on the Medical Implications of Less-Lethal Weapons (SACMILL). Statement on the medical implications of the TASER 7™ conducted energy device system, 2020. Available from: https://assets.publishing.service.gov.uk/government/uploads/system/uploads/attachment_data/file/911328/20200716_SACMILL_TASER_7_Medical_Statement_Final_HoC_ (Accessed 19 May 2023).
47. Hassan A, et al. (2023) More than tears: Associations between exposure to chemical agents used by law enforcement and adverse reproductive health outcomes. Availabe from: https://www.frontiersin.org/articles/10.3389/fepid.2023.1177874/full (Accessed 131023).

CHAPTER

72

Acute Behavioral Disturbance and Excited Delirium Syndrome

Christine A. Hall, William P. Bozeman and Gary M. Vilke

INTRODUCTION

While older historical references to severe agitation culminating in death exist, modern medical interest in the state of extreme psychomotor agitation combined with delirium began in the early 1980s when pathologists Wetli and Fishbain described subjects who died in a state of extraordinary agitation and delirium that was associated with only recreational use levels of cocaine. They coined the term Cocaine Excited Delirium and recognized a constellation of similar symptoms seen by those who died in that state (1,2). Twenty years ago, in 2001, Morrison and Sadler defined Excited Delirium as "... a state of extreme mental and physiological excitement, characterized by extreme agitation, hyperthermia, hostility, exceptional strength and endurance without apparent fatigue." (3).

In the almost 40 years since Wetli and Fishbain's original publication, a significant expansion of the literature has continued, primarily focused on the discussion of Excited Delirium (ExD)/Excited Delirium Syndrome (ExDS) in the prehospital environment but also shifting into the acute hospital care setting and the psychiatric literature (4–7). At the current time, ExD and ExDS are basically used as synonymous terms. Originally, ExD was used by medical examiners for death cases attributed to this condition. As emergency physicians also weighed in, particularly with the 2009 ACEP White Paper, the phraseology shifted to ExDS as most cases do not result in death and the constellation of symptoms that define the disorder is more consistent with a syndrome. Thus, for the remainder of this chapter the term used will be ExDS.

Despite ongoing debate regarding the specific criteria that make ExDS a diagnosis or not, it remains true that, in many cases of sudden unanticipated arrest related death (ARD), multiple clinical features are overwhelmingly similar and are also encountered with definable and consistent frequency in subjects of police interest who do not die (8–15). The identification of persons at risk, in order to mitigate that risk, has been the focus of epidemiologic study of ExDS features in police use of force events (8–14,16,17).

ACUTE BEHAVIORAL DISTURBANCE AND ExDS

In June 2021, the Royal College of Psychiatrists in the UK published a statement concerning the terms "Excited delirium" and "Acute Behavioral Disturbance (ABD)" that was subsequently withdrawn. It was withdrawn in part because emergency services personnel used the ABD/ExDS terminology to develop protocols to support the recognition of people suffering from or at risk for a physical health emergency. The development of such protocols is the intended point of the medical literature around ExDS to date. In 2022, the Royal College published its position statement on "ABD and Excited Delirium" (18). In that paper, the College of Psychiatrists opined that the terms "acute behavioral disturbance" ("ABD") and "excited delirium" ("ExDS") have been used to describe situations in which a person is extremely agitated and distressed, causing police and ambulance personnel to determine that restraint is required to stop the person from causing harm and to enable transport of the individual to an emergency department (ED) for treatment. The authors documented a description of an ABD referencing that the British Association of Psychopharmacology (BAP) and the National Association of Psychiatric Intensive Care and Low Secure Units (NAPICU) note the lack of unified definitions. An acute disturbance of behavior is described as:

> "an acute mental state associated with an underlying mental and/or physical disorder in the form of: (i) agitation and distress, which is excessive verbal or motor activity that may or may not lead to aggression or violence; or (ii) actual aggression or violence entailing harm, hurt or injury to another person, or damage to property regardless of whether it is verbally or behaviorally expressed, physical harm is sustained, or the intention is clear".
>
> Patel, Sethi et al., 2018 (18)

DOI: 10.1201/9781003138754-75

The term ABD is gaining popularity in the UK as a way to avoid using the term ExDS and to distance protocols from cited controversy regarding the development of the terminology beginning in the 1980s (18,20). While advocating for the term ABD and opining that "the term ExDS should never be used", the Royal College of Psychiatrists recognized that it is important clinicians are able to identify signs of a physical health emergency so that patients receive the right medical care quickly. Their statement further indicates that symptoms like a high temperature, rapid breathing, rapid pulse rate and extreme and sustained agitation represent a person who is likely in need of medical care (18). Their position statement also indicates that transport to an emergency care setting and rapid tranquilization or sedation should be considered for patients who do not respond to sustained attempts at de-escalation and for whom there is a serious concern of physiological collapse (18).

These are exactly the recommendations from current ExDS literature, aimed at detecting persons of perceived higher risk and providing for alternative monitoring and after care of subjects of police interest. ExDS literature describes a robust set of signs and symptoms, identifiable by non-medical personnel and studied in the population of interest that consistently describe a focused group that represents ~2 percent of 0.1 percent of policing (8–14,21,22).

The position statement of the Royal College of Psychiatrists maintains that all ExDS literature should be discarded and suggests that the triad model proposed by the Faculty of Forensic & Legal Medicine of the Royal College of Physicians might offer one such framework for identifying individuals at risk, "provided it is not accompanied by reference to unvalidated criteria drawn from 'ExDS' specific literature and there is guidance on assessing "extreme" agitation so as not to encompass distress without physiological deterioration" (18).

However, the term ABD is not formally defined and includes exceptionally broad indicators of its existence. There are no criteria that indicate a higher or lower likelihood of its presence, nor is there a body of literature in prehospital care that assesses its prevalence and outcomes. The vagueness of definition of ABD could apply to persons with a relatively mild behavioral disturbance and would thus not indicate individuals in medical distress. Even the Royal College of Psychiatry position statement suggests that the term be used as a noun in some clinical situations and an adjective in others, depending on a known outcome. This distinction is not useful in the moment when encountering a highly agitated person in a prehospital environment.

Stevenson and Tracy defined ABD as a potentially life-threatening syndrome of delirium, dysregulated physiologic responses and aggressive behavior (23). Those authors state that a lack of awareness about ABD means that it can be misrecognized as a more "generalized disturbance" which means the person may not be provided timely access to care. Stevenson indicated that ABD can be difficult to separate from what has been called an "angry man" episode. In their article, Stevenson and Tracy indicate that the main factors to consider when assessing and treating ABD are actually most of the published features of ExDS (23).

WHAT IS EXCITED DELIRIUM? SIGNS, SYMPTOMS AND INCIDENCE IN PREHOSPITAL ENVIRONMENTS

In 2004, the National Association of Medical Examiners (NAME) and, in 2009, the American College of Emergency Physicians (ACEP) determined that ExD was a definable medical condition with a higher risk of sudden unexpected death than individuals in a non-agitated state (9,13,24). Some authors have disagreed and insisted that ExD was a fabricated condition intended to explain death associated with conducted energy weapons, restraint position or vascular neck restraint, while others continue to assert that ExDS "only occurs" in the setting of police use of restraint or force (18,25–30).

There have been several position papers, reviews or statements abandoning the term ExDS or ExDS in favor of terms like ABD, Hyperactive Delirium or Autonomic Dysregulation (18,31,32). Suggestions for changes in taxonomy have occurred even as the authors recognize that police officers and first responders need a way to identify individuals in the prehospital environment who are not simply engaged in disruptive behavior but whose outwardly manifest behavior is indicative of mental and physiological disruption that requires urgent medical assessment and treatment rather than incarceration. The recent position statement by psychiatrists recognized that prehospital personnel require a list of "red flag symptoms" to guide their differentiation between unwanted behavior and medical illness (18).

Recently in the US, concerns have been raised that ExDS is a racist term as the original population of subjects were young black males in Miami using cocaine and many individuals diagnosed over the years have also been black. Many groups have denounced using the term, "excited delirium syndrome" (19,25). In their 2022 publication, the Royal College of Psychiatrists in the UK drew specific attention to concerns about racism in policing and use of force citing ExDS and ABD terminology as part of the problem. The authors stated that "the typical case of ABD is a black man in his thirties" (18). No published medical literature surrounding ExDS or even Hyperactive Delirium uses this description and none of the list of criteria for ExDS includes race/ethnicity (10,11,13,14,17,31).

It is important to be aware that not every person who is violent or resisting police officers is suffering from ExDS, and attribution of ExDS to explain every ARD is an inappropriate use of the literature surrounding ExDS. Additionally, black people are a minority of individuals with ExDS; the syndrome also affects white, Hispanic and Asian people. While discussions regarding racial issues in policing are outside the scope of this chapter, there has been documented disproportionate use of force in policing against people of color and it is true that a person's ethnic background has enormous impact on the experience of people interacting with policing and emergency health services (18). However, it is also true that people of color who require medical assessment, such as those who demonstrate signs of ExD, ought to be recognized as such and must have the same urgent access to medical care as individuals who are not visible minorities who have the same signs and symptoms. Again, the published criteria for ExDS are not race/ethnicity specific and are intended to identify any individual at higher risk of medical difficulty (9–11,13,17,31).

ACEP recently reviewed the literature associated with severely agitated individuals who die suddenly (31). ACEP rebranded the initial clinical presentation as "hyperactive delirium with severe agitation"; however, regardless of terminology, these terms are describing the same population of patients "marked by disorientation and aggressive words and/or actions, is an acute life-threatening medical condition that demands emergency medical treatment" (31).

Delirium is indicative of underlying pathophysiology that can represent a potential danger to survival if not definitively treated (33–41). Diagnostic definitions of delirium vary from source to source, but typically include being a syndrome characterized by an acute (minutes to days) transient disturbance in consciousness and cognition with disorientation, disorganized and inconsistent thought process, and inability to distinguish reality from hallucinations, including disturbances in attention, awareness and cognition not explained by a pre-existing neurocognitive disorder (42,43). The differential diagnosis for delirium is broad and includes many psychiatric and medical conditions, such as intoxication with and withdrawal from substances (35,37–40,44,45).

In hospital settings, regardless of why delirium is present, there is an increase in morbidity and mortality associated with it and much effort is dedicated to early detection and effective intervention for delirium (33–36,38,39,44–48). Delirium begins rapidly and evolves over the course of hours or days, its symptoms fluctuate and, based on the type of psychomotor symptoms displayed, delirium is categorized as hyperactive, hypoactive or mixed (i.e. presenting with periods of both hyper- and hypoactivity) (35,49,50).

The presence of delirium as a complicating factor in a patient's hospital care is captured through the use of ICD codes centered on delirium and agitation (38,39,47,51,52) (Table 72.1).

Delirium in the setting of isolated psychiatric disease is not the new, unfamiliar paradigm that many claim. "Bell's Mania", described in the 1840s, is the first known description of isolated psychiatric disease with delirium leading to death when untreated (54). Dr. Luther Bell, a psychiatrist at the McLean Asylum for the Insane in Massachusetts, documented patients with a subacute (2–3 week) onset of mania, progressing to violent behavior that required restraint. Fatigue and cardiovascular collapse occurred and 75 percent of patients died, with the deaths attributed to dehydration, metabolic and electrolyte derangements (5,54,55). Over the next decades, there were many reports of patient deaths in those who resided in long-term psychiatric facilities (56). The advent of antipsychotic medications and mood stabilizers in the 1960s led to much more effective management of psychomotor agitation and dopaminergic dysregulation. In the medical literature, publications surrounding these deaths in a state of excitation with delirium all but disappeared. More recently published, psychiatric illnesses associated with delirious states and excitation require immediate medical attention as death has occurred in hospital settings (3–5,36,57).

TABLE 72.1 ICD 9/10 codes for psychomotor agitation (53)

ICD9/10 code	Descriptor
799.2X	Abnormal
799.2AM	Psychomotor excitement
799.V	Psychomotor agitation
296.00 S	Manic excitement
307.9AD	Agitation
780.09E	Delirium
293.1 J	Delirium of mixed origin
292.81 Q	Delirium, drug induced
292.81 R	Delirium, induced by drug

The 1980s brought a new era in medical interest in ExD, when psychostimulants became more widely available in North America. Situated on the drug-trafficking route from South America to North America, Miami became the site of a new clinical experience involving cocaine. People came to the attention of police due to violent or aggressive aberrant behavior and then suddenly died. The prodrome of clinical symptoms Wetli and Fishbain described were remarkably consistent and the individuals died in a state of delirium associated with profound psychomotor agitation. Wetli and Fishbain named the entity they encountered "Cocaine Induced Excited Delirium" (1,58–60). Similar astonishing levels of psychomotor agitation with physiologic collapse have now been encountered with persons who have ingested other stimulant drugs including methamphetamine, MDMA, LSD, PCP, Bath Salts, Synthetic Cannabinoids and Flakka (61–72).

In contrast to suggested assessment algorithms that require knowledge of a person's medical history or previous response to treatment (18), historic patient information available to law enforcement officers or emergency medical services (EMS) providers is often unreliable, incomplete or unavailable. The most important first step when managing these severely agitated individuals is for law enforcement and prehospital personnel to recognize this presentation as a medical emergency rather than simply a violent and uncooperative individual. One of the main reasons for both law enforcement and paramedic agencies to be aware of ExDS is to optimize rapid transfer to an appropriate medical facility once patient and provider safety have been established so that appropriate treatment can be initiated. When the individual

TABLE 72.2 Characteristics of excited delirium (ExDS) (53)

Characteristic of ExD	Common sense definition
Naked/partially clothed	Self-explanatory
No response to police presence	Self-explanatory
Constant/near constant physical activity	Seems to never stop moving, pacing
Impervious to pain	Pain-mediated techniques ineffective
Does not fatigue	Fails to tire despite heavy physical exertion
Superhuman strength	Strength out of keeping with physical traits
Rapid breathing	Self-explanatory
Profuse sweating	Self-explanatory
Hot	Hot to the touch, does not rely on measurement
Glass attraction	Destruction of glass, mirrored surfaces

has been physically controled and can be brought to hospital, monitoring the individual for deterioration while investigating the underlying cause or diagnosis occurs concurrently with the management of the agitation and stabilization of underlying pathophysiology (8–10,13,14,22,38,39,73).

Presenting signs and symptoms of Excited Delirium Syndrome, when the National Institute of Medical Examiners (NAME) recognized ExDS as a diagnosis in 2004, the bulk of medical literature had centerd on retrospective analyses of those who had died. Thus, it was suggested that the presence of ExD was universally fatal. In 2009, the ACEP convened a task force to review the topic. ACEP joined NAME in recognizing ExDS as a diagnostic entity that discerned a higher level of risk for persons in that condition (13). The ACEP Committee reviewed the literature available at the time and recognized the set of clinical signs and symptoms documented in the medical literature as having been repetitively encountered in combination. These signs and symptoms are shown in Table 72.2.

ACEP reported that the presence of six or more concomitant features is consistent with a case of ExDS in the absence of another etiology. In contrast to NAME's previous consideration that ExDS was universally fatal (as was recently discussed in a position paper by the Royal College of Psychiatrists in the UK) (18), ACEP described that ExDS was not always fatal and more commonly was not (13). The literature has evolved in accordance with further epidemiologic study.

The signs and symptoms of ExDS originally described in the ACEP White Paper were prospectively examined across over 15 million police public encounters, of which 0.1 percent involved police use of force (10–12,21). Within use of force events, 1.8 percent will involve a person with six or more features of ExDS (9–14,21,58). It is unlikely that additional epidemiologic study will further refine this estimate. In short, the list of "red flag symptoms" that the Royal College of Psychiatrists of the UK recently called for (18), already exists and has been extensively studied in the population of interest. Based on the data, ExDS would be expected in at least 1 in 67 police use of force encounters. A very small minority (0.03%) of subjects of police use of force had all ten features of ExD (10–14,21). While violence is common when a police use of force occurs, the presence of violence alone does not discern between cases of ExDS and other violent presentations (10–12).

PATHOPHYSIOLOGY OF ExDS

There has been criticism of the term Excited Delirium Syndrome as a diagnosis because no specific consistent underlying pathophysiology has been determined. No specific blood test, laboratory study or radiographic evaluation can diagnose ExDS. The pathophysiology by which any delirium exists is generally unclear and commonly multifactorial, depending on interplay between predisposing risk factors, severity of underlying illness and the presence of comorbidities (34,35,74).

Evidence suggests that genetic factors, physiologic stressors, and disruptions in the neurotransmitters normally involved in cognitive function all have a role to play in any given case of delirium (35,75). Anticholinergic effects, dopaminergic excess, cytokines and inflammation and chronic stress resulting in increases in cortisol and other stress hormones have all been implicated in the generation of delirious states (35,38,39).

Dopamine is the neurotransmitter that regulates movement, hypothalamic function, higher cognitive function and positive behavior (movement, agitation, psychomotor activity). Dopaminergic excess contributes directly to delirium, which makes physiologic sense as disorders of dopamine transmission are accompanied by disorders in perception and cognition, such as psychosis and Parkinson's disease. Dopaminergic drugs (e.g. bupropion) are recognized precipitants of delirium, and dopamine antagonists (e.g. antipsychotic agents) are often used to effectively treat delirium symptoms (35,38,39). There is less published evidence regarding other neurotransmitters (such as norepinephrine, serotonin) although these neurotransmitters may generate their effects through interactions with the cholinergic and dopaminergic pathways.

Research in ExDS and ARDs have investigated the same pathophysiology of delirium for patients in prehospital settings to better understand why ExDS develops and why it is fatal for some. In post-mortem study, individuals who died with ExDS had anatomic changes in neurotransmitter receptor function that underpin cellular process changes (76–80). These changes result in unopposed sympathetic stimulation, resulting in metabolic stress.

Mash et al. have found that dopamine processing is altered significantly in persons who die in ExD (76–81). In a summary of Mash's works, chronic cocaine abusers

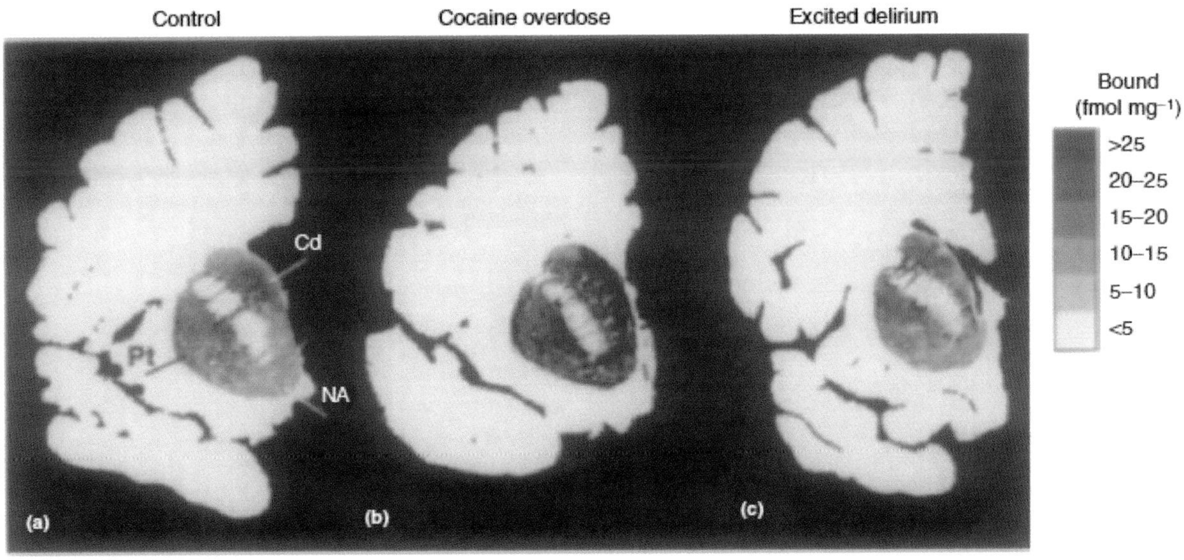

72.1 Abnormal dopamine uptake in the brain in ExDS. *In vitro* autoradiographic maps of [^{3}H]WIN 35 428 labeling of the dopamine transporter in coronal sections of the human brain from a representative **(a)** age-matched and drug-free subject, **(b)** a cocaine overdose victim and **(c)** a cocaine-related agitated delirium victim. The brain maps illustrate the adaptive increase in dopamine transporter density over the striatum in the cocaine overdose victims and the lack iof any apparent elevation in the victim presenting with agitated delirium. Since the dopamine transporter regulates the synaptic concentration of neurotransmitter, the lack of compensatory upregulation may result in a dopamine overflow following a cocaine "binge". Elevated synaptic dopamine with repeated exposures may kindle the emergence of agitated delirium syndrome. Gray scale codes are presented at the right and are matched for the range of density values across the groups (black = high densities; gray = intermediate; and light gray to white = low to background densities). Cd, caudate; NA, nucleus accumbens, Pt, putamen. (Reproduced from [82].)

have a compensatory increase in dopamine transporters to decrease the free dopamine in the synaptic cleft, and thus reduce the duration of post-synaptic receptor stimulation. However, victims of ExD have been documented to lack this adaptive change and its neuroprotective effect (78–80,82) (Figure 72.1). Serotonin is an independent modulator of dopaminergic neurotransmissions and Mash et al. demonstrated that ExDS victims did not display an upregulation of serotonin transporters within the substantia nigra, needed to manage excess dopamine transmission.

Evidence of dopaminergic excess is seen in individuals with delirium and is highly likely to be responsible for some of the features of ExDS as well as the metabolic collapse. Dopamine dysregulation is linked to psychosis and is also believed to have a significant role in thermoregulation through D1 and D2 receptor activity; an explanation for the extreme hyperthermia seen in some subjects with ExDS (10,13,77). Individuals who use stimulants have increased dopamine accumulation in the striatum and the nucleus accumbens. This accumulation is linked to the increase in psychomotor activity and the classic behaviors seen in stimulant users (83,84). Beneath the behavioral display seen in sympathomimetic use, sympathomimetic drugs have autonomic effects with increased heart rate, vasoconstriction, hypertension and hyperthermia. Cocaine, methamphetamine and amphetamine interact with the dopamine transporter, DAT, and alter its function, limiting reuptake of dopamine from the synaptic cleft, to further increase dopamine effect (83). The resultant catecholamine surge likely contributes to the superhuman strength, pain tolerance and failure to fatigue despite heavy physical exertion that is seen in ExDS. For individuals with undetected underlying genetic or acquired cardiac anomalies, the increased afterload and cardiac output, associated electrolyte imbalances, release of catecholamines, and autonomic changes in response to intense activity can trigger arrhythmia, syncope and sudden cardiac death (85,86).

Heat shock proteins and stress hormones

In initial studies evaluating heat shock proteins (HSPs), Mash et al. documented that HSPs were significantly elevated and dopamine transporters were decreased in post-mortem brain tissues in those persons who died in ExDS as compared to age-matched controls (77). Further study in deceased individuals by Johnson et al. in 2012 compared quantified gene transcripts in midbrain samples from a series of cocaine-related fatalities matched to drug-free controls. They found that while there was increase in HSP 70 expression in cocaine abusers, the increase was not correlated with the presence of ExDS, leading the authors to conclude that HSP expression was not a reliable cause of death in ExD (87).

An initial foray into HSP analysis, as well as stress hormones in 82 living individuals, was published in 2019. Vilke et al. conducted a multi-center prospective study of agitated patients (88). They evaluated three groups of patients: those with ExDS based on standard published criteria of six or more concomitant features of ExDS, those with acute agitation but who did not meet criteria for ExDS, and a control group who underwent exhaustive exercise followed by sham conducted energy weapon deployment in a laboratory setting. The authors found that cortisol was more elevated in ExDS as compared to the other groups. Both norepinephrine and dynorphin were elevated in the agitated and in the ExDS groups as compared to the exhaustive exercise followed by conducted energy weapons subjects. The clinical relevance of these findings is unclear and further study is needed to determine the implications of these findings (88).

Metabolic acidosis and lactic acidosis

Metabolic acidosis (MA) is an acid-base disorder characterized by a fall in blood pH due in part to a reduction of serum bicarbonate concentration. This can occur as a result of either the accumulation of acids (high anion gap MA) or the loss of bicarbonate from the gastrointestinal tract or the kidney (hyperchloremic MA) (89). In ExDS, the accumulation of acids (generating a significant anion gap) generates the acidosis. MA has multiple underlying causes, one of which is lactate production.

Lactate is known source of MA. When individuals are delirious, they can persist with heavy physical exertion that would normally be slowed in response to biofeedback, and physical exertion can go on for hours or days. Sustained physical activity can move the individual from aerobic metabolic states to anaerobic metabolic states at the cellular level. Lactate, or lactic acid, is produced from pyruvate as an end-product of glycolysis under anaerobic conditions (90). Lactate is produced in most tissues in the body, primarily in skeletal muscle, brain, intestine and red blood cells but, during stress, lactate is also produced in the lungs, white blood cells and splanchnic organs. During heavy exercise, the skeletal muscles produce the most excess circulating lactate, which usually normalizes in the absence of impaired hepatic metabolism (89–91).

High levels of lactate are associated with increased risk of death independent of organ failure and shock. Clinicians usually consider that MA with a pH less than 7.2 has a deleterious effect on hemodynamics and requires supportive care. Lactic acidosis can cause a reduction of cardiac contractility and vascular hyporesponsiveness to vasopressors through a variety of mechanisms (89–92). Mortality in acidosis can be extremely high (93).

Clinical signs of tissue hypoperfusion are often present, including severe hypotension, altered mental status, oliguria and tachypnea. Kussmaul respirations may be seen as the body attempts to compensate for the MA (89,90,92). It should be noted that subjects in a state of ExDS have altered mental status, and are often reported to demonstrate heavy breathing (Table 72.3).

TABLE 72.3 Adverse effects of severe acidosis (89).

Cardiovascular
• Decreased cardiac output
• Predisposition to cardiac arrythmias
• Hypotension due to an increase in peripheral vascular resistance
• Centralization of blood volume with increase in pulmonary vascular resistance
• Resistance to catecholamines
Central nervous system
• Decreased sensorium
Gastrointestinal
• Gastric atony
• Reduced hepatic blood flow
Metabolic
• Increased binding of oxygen to Hb with reduced oxygen delivery
• Reduction in ATP synthesis
• Insulin resistance
• Increase in ionized calcium levels

Rhabdomyolysis

Rhabdomyolysis is a common complication of heavy exercise, particularly in untrained individuals, although there are other causes of rhabdomyolysis (94). When rhabdomyolysis has occurred, some element of breakdown of skeletal muscle has happened and subsequent leakage of myoglobin, sarcoplasmic proteins (creatine kinase, lactate dehydrogenase, aldolase, alanine, and aspartate aminotransferase) and electrolytes into the extracellular fluid occurs. These elements can be measured in the blood and serum creatine kinase and is the most commonly used laboratory value to determine that rhabdomyolysis is part of the clinical picture. Rhabdomyolysis can be mild with low-level elevation of serum creatine kinase, to severe with associated medical emergencies such as the development of disseminated intravascular coagulation, acute kidney injury (AKI) and cardiac arrhythmias as complications of protracted and severe injury of muscle.

While there is not a specific serum level of serum creatine phosphokinase (CPK or CK) that defines the presence or categorization of rhabdomyolysis, many clinicians consider that a serum CPK level that is three–five times the upper limit of normal or approximately 1000 IU/L to define rhabdomyolysis that may require some level of treatment.

Rhabdomyolysis is one of the major causes of acute renal failure. If identified early, the prognosis of acute kidney injury with rhabdomyolysis is relatively benign. Heavy exertion as a result of delirium as well as physical struggle with the individual have been described as associated with sudden ARDs for individuals in a state of ExDS. Death can follow the development of rhabdomyolysis, although that death would not be anticipated to occur at the time of the physical exertion itself or within the short period following an altercation.

For law enforcement, for investigators and for triers of fact, the interpretation of serum chemistry and adverse events must consider the totality of the circumstance that generates the findings, being mindful of correlation versus causation.

ExDS MANAGEMENT

As ExDS is defined in part by agitation of the individual accompanied by some, or all, of strength out of proportion to physical appearance, constant or near constant physical activity often accompanied by MA, rhabdomyolysis, as well as the underlying physiologic effects of stimulant drugs including hyperthermia, hypertension and tachycardia, rapid treatment of the individual is essential to minimize the risk of fatality. Initiation of sedating medications can reduce the catecholamine/sympathetic tone engendered in the state of delirium including when underlying stimulant drugs use is present. Formal assessment and attempts at diagnosis and identification of the underlying etiologies of the delirium and its consequences can only occur with the individual in physical control.

Once individuals are recognized to be in a state consistent with ExDS, early intervention with sedative medications can help reduce activity that generates physiologic excitation leading to potentially fatal collapse (34,35,38–40,45,95).

Some position papers/reports indicate a poor appreciation for both the prehospital environment, the expertise of prehospital care agencies and their medical oversight as well as for the provision of emergency medical care in hospital. Many suggested protocols for the intervention and management of a highly agitated person prior to police restraint suggest evaluation of parameters that cannot be measured until control of the individual has been gained or that rely on information that is not readily available in most prehospital settings, reflecting referral and selection bias (18,23,30). Once physical control has been gained (voluntarily or involuntarily), then monitoring of the individual can and should begin. Assessments of heart rate, blood pressure and use of serial evaluation scores like National Early Warning Score (NEWS) as well as detailed medical investigation can only begin once the initial agitation has been successfully managed (18).

Prehospital administration of all medications occurs under the specific guidance of medical directors and the medical administration of emergency health services organizations and is not determined by policing administrations. Scientific and quality-based evaluation of the application and outcomes of those protocols is both necessary and a welcome addition to the medical literature surrounding the care of highly agitated people in the prehospital environment (18,30,37,41,50,96–107).

PHYSICAL CONTROL

For patients to be given sedation and/or be transported to a hospital to be assessed medically, they must be able to be under control. Many of the characteristics of ExDS make physical restraint methods used by law enforcement agencies less effective and possibly even injurious to both the subject and the applier of that force (11). Review of police use of force incidents involving subjects with ExD guide understanding of the complex scenario in which many force modalities are less effective.

The context in which police use of physical control occurs is important. Studies of police use of force document that use of force occurs in less than 0.1 percent of police public interactions (10–12,16,17,21,108). Police agencies have policies and procedures governing use of force and, while it is possible that some use of force is excessive and outside the bounds of written policy and procedure, not all use of force is excessive or as the result of inadequate de-escalation skills (18). Agencies whose use of force profile is higher than 0.1 percent of police public interactions, or who do not record and analyze the frequency and nature of use of force must be encouraged to understand, document and evaluate their use of force policies and practices.

Use of restraint and chemical restraint occurs in hospitals and other care institutions (3,18,74). Collaboration with oversight agencies, public interest groups, medical professionals, carers and families in the understanding of the context in which police use of force and how and when restraint occurs would provide for the development of protocols reflective of prehospital events without being affected by referral and practice biases (18,20,30).

The presence of ExDS features does change the nature of a use of force event. Baldwin et al. analyzed use of force data and accounted for the dynamic, violent nature of individuals presenting with ExD in whom police use of force occurred. Overall, Baldwin et al. found that the odds that a use of force intervention would be ineffective in ExDS was nearly 4:1 compared with other subjects requiring police use of force without ExDS (17). The odds of multiple use of force modalities being employed by law enforcement was five times higher in the presence of ExDS.

When subjects of police interest had six or more features of ExD, more officers were present at the scene and officers indicated that those with ExDS were likely to appear to them to be under the influence of drugs or alcohol, indicating that lone police officers responding to an individual with ExDS will require backup imminently and multiple officer involvement should be anticipated (17).

Use of force often results in injury to both subjects and officers (17). Officers were injured twice as often when situations involved ExDS compared with use of force events in other subjects (17).

Pharmacologic control/Sedation

Benzodiazepines

Benzodiazepines (diazepam, lorazepam, midazolam) have been used for decades and have been considered the mainstay of treatment in the management of delirium due to alcohol withdrawal and other delirious states. Benzodiazepines do not have the extrapyramidal effects of other agents, like major tranquilizers, but their usefulness outside of the management of gamma-aminobutyric acid (GABA)-mediated issues is unclear (39). Problems with this class of agents include long onset times, the need for redosing and respiratory depression. Close monitoring of respiratory and hemodynamic status is needed when using these agents.

Neuroleptics/Antipsychotics

Neuroleptic/antipsychotic medications are also commonly used for sedation. The precise pharmacologic action by which antipsychotic agents exert their calming effects is unclear but is most likely due to the inhibition of dopamine transmission (95). This inhibition is thought to reduce the positive, or outwardly visible, signs of delirium. There may also be an effect with the GABA system at high doses, and GABA mechanism activation usually results in negative symptoms (reduced activity) when atypical antipsychotics are given at high doses (95). At first glance, these mechanisms of action would have utility in the setting of ExDC. Two first-generation antipsychotics, haloperidol and droperidol, have minimal hemodynamic effects, almost no anticholinergic activity and do not interact with many other non-psychiatric medications significantly. However, they do have significant adverse effects including lengthening the QTc interval of the cardiac cycle, and cases of malignant dysrhythmia (Torsades des Pointes) have occurred. Both haloperidol and droperidol carry warnings regarding increased QTc intervals and, in 2007, the warning around droperidol was increased to an FDA black box warning. In addition to potential cardiac effects, first-generation antipsychotics carry risk of dystonia or neuroleptic malignant syndrome (38,95).

Even with these limitations, first-generation antipsychotics were favored as treatment for delirium until the mid 2000s. Both benzodiazepines and first-generation antipsychotics remain in sedation protocols for hospital EDs and EMS (9,73).

Phenothiazines and early dopamine receptor antagonists such as chlorpromazine (Thorazine®), are no longer indicated for the treatment of acute agitation. Compared to other first-generation antipsychotics, such as haloperidol, the phenothiazines cause more hypotension, more anticholinergic side effects, and lower the seizure threshold (38).

Second-generation, or atypical, antipsychotics developed in the last 30 years (such as olanzapine, quietapine and paliperidone) have become appealing for their effects as antagonists at the D2 receptor, and also for their antagonism of serotonin receptors, histamine, norepinephrine and other receptors thought to be involved in the generation of delirium. Second-generation antipsychotics carry less risk of adverse effects in general, particularly cardiac arrhythmia and neuroleptic malignant syndrome as well as the permanent adverse effects of tardive dyskinesia (38,95). Reviews of the use of atypical versus typical antipsychotics (haloperidol) found that they were at least equally efficacious (38).

Even if the evidence for use of antipsychotics were compelling, the slow onset of action makes the use of antipsychotics limited for immediate sedation in the setting of ExDS. With the goal of calming and reducing physical activity, the onset of action of most typical and atypical antipsychotics is too long to be of clinical relevance in ExDS (109).

Ketamine

While non-medical individuals often confuse modern use of ketamine with using a "veterinary medicine", ketamine has been used in EDs and hospitals worldwide for decades for many indications (100). Ketamine is an N-methyl-D-aspartate (NDMA) receptor antagonist that is known to produce analgesia at lower doses and a dissociative state at higher doses (37,41,46,96,100–102,105–107). In medical practice, the drug has gained much popularity for pediatric and adult procedural sedation, intubation and pain management, all of which occurs well outside the confines of anesthesiology practice; additionally, its emerging use in psychiatric applications demonstrates great promise (100).

For rapid sequence intubation, the production of a rapid, reliable onset of a dissociative state while preserving airway reflexes and even some bronchodilation makes ketamine an effective and desirable agent (100). Previous hospital-based trials noted that apnea with ketamine is very rare and respiratory related adverse events occur in less than 5 percent of individuals (109). These properties translate usefully into the consideration of ketamine as a chemical calming agent for agitated patients in hospital and prehospital environments (37,41,46,50,96,99–103,105,106).

Dissociative sedation ketamine given in the ED is usually defined as a dose of 3–5 mg/kg ketamine intramuscularly (IM), or 1–2 mg/kg intravenously (IV). Routes of administration of ketamine under a variety of indications/situations include intraosseous (IO), intramuscular (IM), intranasal (IN), and IV (50,96,105–107). In the prehospital setting with highly agitated patients, EMS typically use the IM route with the onset of action being approximately 3–4 minutes (109).

Concerns regarding serious adverse events with a dissociative sedation dose range led Mo et al. to study outcomes in an ED setting (97,103,104,107,110). In their study of ED visits, Mo et al. examined 210 events in which ketamine was used for sedation in the ED, 37 of those events included people with ExD. One of the 37 patients was intubated and 8 received oxygen supplementation (46). They found that dose range led to less intubation than in prehospital studies (some of which co-administered benzodiazepines) and had few toxicities, making dissociative sedation a viable option for ExD (46). Solano et al. (107) described an association between prehospital ketamine administration in ExD with concomitant illicit and prescription substance intoxication and subsequent ED intubation. In their cohort, patients treated with prehospital ketamine IM for ExD who had concomitant cocaine intoxication had a statistically significant 5.75-fold increased rate of subsequent intubation in the ED. When patients were intoxicated with other substances, there were no trends for intubation noted. Benzodiazepine co-ingestion was not a significant contributor to intubation rate when

TABLE 72.4 Medication treatment options (9)

Medication (trade name)	Administration routes	Typical dosing (mg)	Onset (min)	Duration (min)
Benzodiazepines				
Midazolam (Versed)	IN	5	3–5	30–60
	IM	5	10–15	120–360
	IV	2–5	1–5	30–60
Lorazepam (Ativan)	IM	4	15–30	60–120
	IV	2–4	2–5	60–120
Diazepam (Valium)	IM	10	15–30	15–60
	IV	5–10	2–5	15–60
Antipsychotics				
Haloperidol (Haldol)	IM	10–20	15–30	180–360
	IV	5–10	10	180–360
Droperidol (Inapsine)	IM	5	10–30	120–240
	IV	2.5	10	120–240
Ziprasidone (Geodon)[a]	IM	10–20	15–30	240
Olanzapine (Ziprexa)[a]	IM	10	15–30	24h
NMDA receptor agonist/Dissociative				
Ketamine (Ketaset, Ketalar)	IM	4–5 mg/kg	3–5	60–90
	IV	2–4 mg/kg	1	20–30

[a] Atypical antipsychotic medications.

EMS administration was controled for. Similarly, Cole et al. reported a small series of patients treated with Ketamine and more than half were intubated in the ED, including some who had received a second dose of sedative medication (50,97). In their study, more than one third of patients were intubated by the same physician, a significant confounder that likely represents individual provider practice. But in all studies using Ketamine in the ED, whether requiring intubation, supplemental oxygenation or not, there were no reported sudden cardiac arrests and deaths.

Combinations of agents have commonly been used for acute management of dangerous agitation. A summary of sedating agents, including typical doses, onset time and duration of sedative effects is reproduced here (Table 72.4).

An effective agent with a rapid onset of action is necessary to gain control of the individual and prevent the complications of severe agitation and metabolic abnormalities in ExDS that can result in cardiac arrest and death. It is intuitive that there can be interplay between ingested substances and any sedation regime. This relationship underscores the need for advanced medical assessment in hospital for patients with ExD once the subject is under physical and/or chemical control. Use of pharmacologic agents in the field makes further medical assessment mandatory and people who have been sedated must be transported for medical assessment in a hospital. Protocols involving prehospital sedation require cross-agency collaboration between law enforcement and EMS advanced life support units.

Outcomes

Some individuals with ExDS will die. Several reports have stated that people who have died have been "diagnosed" based on far fewer than six symptoms or when none of the features of ExDS existed (18,20,25). Misuse of published medical literature investigating specific findings, in application to circumstance not described in that literature does not obviate the original investigations nor confirm the original findings as erroneous. Not every in-custody death can be attributed to ExDS and investigators of police use of force events, as well as triers of fact, must be clear in their investigation of the signs and symptoms in each individual case. If fewer than six of the known published criteria of ExDS are present in the interval immediately prior to the death of a person in police custody, then investigators and triers of fact must consider and investigate alternate explanations.

Published literature around recognizing ExDS indicates that six or more of the ten published signs and symptoms of ExDS should be present to consider an individual to be in that state (9–11,13,14,16,17,21).

ABD guidelines are not as explicit, for example, the Royal College of Psychiatry of the UK position paper states "that most recent guidance issued by the Royal College of Emergency Medicine on 'ABD' offers a similar list of signs and symptoms as literature on 'ExD' but then notes that as few as one or two symptoms may be present in ABD" (18). In the US, several recent cases of ARDs have raised the issue of ExDS when the published features of ExDS were apparently not documented to be present. While it is true that not all persons with features of ExDS die, it is also true that not all persons who die are in a state of ExDS.

However, a definable number of individuals with features of ExDS do suddenly and unexpectedly die. In 2022, Baldwin reported a 5-year consecutive cohort using standardized reporting in a very large Canadian police agency that 11 725 use of force reports were generated out of 13.2 million police public interactions, an overall use of force rate of 0.09 percent (17). Of these, 3322 (31%) were perceived by officers to be emotionally disturbed. Approximately 10 percent (n = 1087) of use of force subjects displayed three or more features of ExDS and 1.8 percent (n = 197) of subjects displayed six or more features. Among these, 94.9 percent were male.

In prehospital research, including the most recent study by Baldwin et al., a very small number of subjects (n = 4; .04%) presented with all ten features of ExDS. Baldwin and previous authors have documented that the vast majority of subjects of police interest demonstrate few if any features of ExDS (10,11,16,21). There were a total of four deaths reported in the cohort of 197 ExDS subjects (2.0%; 95% CI 0.65 to 5.5; with Yates' correction) and all were violent and agitated and displayed many concomitant ExDS features. In other words, for people who were extremely agitated and delirious with six or more features of ExDS, as many as 1 in 18 could be at risk of sudden and unexpected death during a police use of force event (17). This is a refinement of Baldwin's previous estimate of 1 in 16 (12). These recent findings are somewhat lower than a previous report by Stratton et al. in 2001 in which an 8 percent mortality rate was calculated from a case series of subjects with ExDS who were restrained and medically treated (111). That retrospective study reviewed 18 deaths among 214 patients with ExDS.

Of note, the highest mortality rates (over 60%) have been seen in the subset of subjects with very high body temperatures (112,113). This has led to the general guidance that "Hyperthermia is a harbinger of death" in ExDS and that tactile or measured hyperthermia should prompt urgent and aggressive temperature management in a patient at high risk for sudden cardiovascular collapse and death (76).

What is still unknown is how many individuals in a state of ExDS do not come to the attention of law enforcement.

Following the first ACEP and NAME reports, concern has arisen over the use of ExD as a cause of death. While "Cause of Death" has been certified by medical examiners as ExDS in the absence of police involvement as well as when sudden ARD occurs, the determination of ExDS as a specific cause of death is now recognized as being controversial. Recognition that delirium is present invokes a need to assess and treat the person suffering the delirious state; and to subsequently determine underlying pathophysiology responsible for the delirious state.

Recent position statements and investigative reports have stated that ExD should not be used as a stand-alone term to identify cause of death (18,20,32).

SUMMARY

Knowledge and controversy surrounding ExDS continues to evolve. It should not be considered a diagnosis but a constellation of signs that may be the physical manifestation of a wide range of diagnoses. Regardless of what the clinical presentation is called, patients suffering from ExDS require urgent medical assessment and close monitoring for deterioration once physical control is gained. Persons identified in a state of ExDS need rapid control and early and aggressive administration of calming medications in order to be transported for medical assessment and to reduce the physiologic distress. The presence of many concomitant features of ExDS increases the need for urgent medical intervention, as such identification represents the first step in the care for the person suffering ExD, not the last. Even with appropriate therapy, there will continue to be deaths in this patient population.

Collaborative work across medical specialties, police agencies, prehospital first responders, care providers, families and interest groups is necessary to continue to advance understanding and mitigate risk for all persons affected.

Suggestions by mental health related experts and bodies, that mental health personnel be immediately available to attend prehospital scenarios and be directly involved in the de-escalation of highly agitated persons is noble and would be welcomed by police agencies and prehospital emergency personnel alike (18,23,30). Collaborative protocols will always be of value and there may be times when mental health personnel who know a specific patient can be brought to a scene emergently to be of assistance. However, many agitated persons are not already known to mental health professionals and many cases of agitation are related to stimulant drug abuse rather than an underlying mental health diagnosis. Unfortunately, the reality is that emergency response mental health teams are in short supply worldwide and the immediate availability of teams across a wide variety of policing and prehospital emergency care situations is at least decades away.

Lastly, it is incorrect to assume that all use of force events are a simple failure of de-escalation or that all use of police restraint is excessive.

REFERENCES

1. Wetli CV, Fishbain DA. Cocaine-induced psychosis and sudden death in recreational cocaine users. *J Forensic Sci* 1985; 30(3): 873–80.
2. Fishbain DA, Wetli CV. Cocaine intoxication, delirium, and death in a body packer. *Ann Emerg Med* 1981; **10(10)**: 531–2.
3. Morrison A, Sadler D. Death of a psychiatric patient during physical restraint. Excited delirium--a case report. *Med Sci Law* 2001; **41(1)**: 46–50.
4. Detweiler MB, Mehra A, Rowell T, et al. Delirious mania and malignant catatonia: A report of 3 cases and review. *Psychiatr Q* 2009; **80(1)**: 23–40.
5. Fink M. Delirious mania. *Bipolar Disord* 1999; **1(1)**: 54–60.
6. Sekhon S, Fischer MA, Marwaha R. *Excited Delirium*. Treasure Island: StatPearls Publishing LLC; 2022.
7. Lipsedge M. Excited delirium: A psychiatric review. *Med Sci Law* 2016; **56(2)**: 121–7.
8. Takeuchi A, Ahern TL, Henderson SO. Excited delirium. *West J Emerg Med* 2011; **12(1)**: 77–83.
9. Vilke GM, Bozeman WP, Dawes DM, et al. Excited delirium syndrome (ExDS): Treatment options and considerations. *J Forensic Leg Med* 2012; **19(3)**: 117–21.
10. Hall CA, Kader AS, McHale AMD, et al. Frequency of signs of excited delirium syndrome in subjects undergoing police use of force: Descriptive evaluation of a prospective, consecutive cohort. *J Forensic Leg Med* 2013; **20(2)**: 102–7.
11. Baldwin S, Hall C, Bennell C, et al. Distinguishing features of Excited Delirium Syndrome in non-fatal use of force encounters. *J Forensic Leg Med* 2016; **41**: 21–7.
12. Baldwin S, Hall C, Blaskovits B, et al. Excited delirium syndrome (ExDS): Situational factors and risks to officer safety in non-fatal use of force encounters. *Int J Law Psychiatry* 2018; **60**: 26–34.
13. Vilke GM, DeBard ML, Chan TC, et al. Excited Delirium Syndrome (ExDS): Defining based on a review of the literature. *J Emerg Med* 2012; **43(5)**: 897–905.
14. Vilke GM, Payne-James J, Karch SB. Excited delirium syndrome (ExDS): Redefining an old diagnosis. *J Forensic Leg Med* 2012; **19(1)**: 7–11.
15. Maher PJ, Walsh M, Burns T, Strote J. Prehospital resuscitation of a man with excited delirium and cardiopulmonary arrest. *Cjem* 2014; **16(1)**: 80–3.
16. Hall CA, McHale AM, Kader AS, et al. Incidence and outcome of prone positioning following police use of force in a prospective, consecutive cohort of subjects. *J Forensic Leg Med* 2012; **19(2)**: 83–9.
17. Baldwin S, Blaskovits B, Hall C, et al. Adverse outcomes in non-fatal use of force encounters involving excited delirium syndrome. *Police Pract Res* 2022; **23(3)**: 322–36.
18. Patel MX, Sethyi FN, Barnes RE, et al. Joint BAP NAPICU evidence-based consensus guidelines for the clinical management of acute disturbance: Deescalation and rapid tranquillisation. *J Psychopharmacol* 2018; 32(6): 601–40.
19. Royal College of Psychiatrists. College Position Statement PS 02/22 'Acute behavioral disturbance' and 'excited delirium', 2022. Available from: https://www.rcpsych.ac.uk/docs/default-source/improving-care/better-mh-policy/position-statements/ps02_22.pdf (Accessed 19 May 2023).
20. Physicians for Human Rights. "Excited Delirium" and Deaths in Police Custody: The Deadly Impact of a Baseless Diagnosis, 2022. Available from: https://phr.org/our-work/resources/excited-delirium/ (Accessed 19 May 2023).
21. Hall C, Votova K, Heyd C, et al. Restraint in police use of force events: Examining sudden in custody death for prone and not-prone positions. *J Forensic Leg Med* 2015; **31**: 29–35.
22. Ross DL. Factors associated with excited delirium deaths in police custody. *Mod Pathol* 1998; **11(11)**: 1127–37.
23. Stevenson R, Tracy DK. Acute behavioural disturbance: A physical emergency psychiatrists need to understand. *BJPsych Advances* 2021; **27**: 333–42.
24. Stephens BG JJ, Karch S, Wetli CV, Mash DC. National Association of Medical Examiners position paper on the certification of cocaine-related deaths. *Am J Forensic Med Pathol* 2004; **25(1)**: 11–13.
25. Saadi A, Naples-Mitchell J, da Silva Bhatia B, Heisler M. End the use of "excited delirium" as a cause of death in police custody. *Lancet* 2022; **399(10329)**: 1028–30.
26. Fiscella K, Pinals DA, Shields CG. "Excited delirium," erroneous concepts, dehumanizing language, false narratives, and threat to Black lives. *Acad Emerg Med* 2022; **29(7)**: 911–13.
27. Kunz SN, Þórðardóttir S, Rúnarsdóttir R. Restraint-related asphyxia on the basis of a drug-induced excited delirium. *Forensic Sci Int* 2018; **288**: e5–e9.
28. Truscott A. A knee in the neck of excited delirium. *Cmaj* 2008; **178(6)**: 669–70.
29. Strömmer EMF, Leith W, Zeegers MP, Freeman MD. The role of restraint in fatal excited delirium: A research synthesis and pooled analysis. *Forensic Sci Med Pathol* 2020; **16(4)**: 680–92.
30. American Psychiatry Association. Position statement on concerns about use of the term "excited delirium" and appropriate medical management in out-of-hospital contexts, 2020. Available from: https://www.psychiatry.org/getattachment/7769e617-ee6a-4a89-829f-4fc71d831ce0/Position-Use-of-Term-Excited-Delirium.pdf (Accessed 19 May 2023).
31. AHDT. ACEP Task Force Report on Hyperactive Delirium with Severe Agitation in Emergency Settings, 2021. Available from: https://www.acep.org/siteassets/new-pdfs/education/acep-task-force-report-on-hyperactive-delirium-final.pdf (Accessed 19 May 2023).
32. Angiolini E. Report of the Independent Review of Deaths and Serious Incidents in Police Custody, 2017. Available from: https://assets.publishing.service.gov.uk/government/uploads/system/uploads/attachment_data/file/655401/Report_of_Angiolini_Review_ISBN_Accessible.pdf (Accessed 19 May 2023).
33. Foertsch MJ, Winter JB, Rhoades AG, et al. Recognition, assessment, and pharmacotherapeutic treatment of alcohol withdrawal syndrome in the intensive care unit. *Crit Care Nurs Q* 2019; **42(1)**: 12–29.
34. Hshieh TT, Inouye SK, Oh ES. Delirium in the elderly. *Psychiatr Clin North Am* 2018; **41(1)**: 1–17.
35. Inouye SK, Westendorp RG, Saczynski JS. Delirium in elderly people. *Lancet* 2014; **383(9920)**: 911–22.
36. Jacobowski NL, Heckers S, Bobo WV. Delirious mania: Detection, diagnosis, and clinical management in the acute setting. *J Psychiatr Pract* 2013; **19(1)**: 15–28.
37. Kim HK, Leonard JB, Corwell BN, Connors NJ. Safety and efficacy of pharmacologic agents used for rapid tranquilization of emergency department patients with acute agitation or excited delirium. *Expert Opin Drug Saf* 2021; **20(2)**: 123–38.
38. Lonergan E, Britton AM, Luxenberg J, Wyller T. Antipsychotics for delirium. *Cochrane Database Syst Rev* 2007; (2): Cd005594.
39. Lonergan E, Luxenberg J, Areosa Sastre A, Wyller TB. Benzodiazepines for delirium. *Cochrane Database Syst Rev* 2009; (1): Cd006379.
40. Mainerova B, Prasko J, Latalova K, et al. Alcohol withdrawal delirium - diagnosis, course and treatment. *Biomed Pap Med Fac Univ Palacky Olomouc Czech Repub* 2015; **159(1)**: 44–52.
41. Mankowitz SL, Regenberg P, Kaldan J, Cole JB. Ketamine for rapid sedation of agitated patients in the prehospital and emergency department settings: A systematic review and proportional meta-analysis. *J Emerg Med* 2018; **55(5)**: 670–81.
42. American Psychiatric Association. *Diagnostic and Statistical Manual of Mental Disorders*, 5th ed. Washington DC: American Psychiatric Publishing; 2013.
43. Walls R HR, Gausche-Hill, M, Erickson T, Wilcox S. *Rosen's Emergency Medicine: Concepts and Clinical Practice*, 10th ed. Philadelphia: Elsevier; 2022.
44. Evered LA. Predicting delirium: Are we there yet? *Br J Anaesth* 2017; **119(2)**: 281–3.
45. Slooter AJC. Delirium, what's in a name? *Br J Anaesth* 2017; **119(2)**: 283–5.
46. Mo H, Campbell MJ, Fertel BS, et al. Ketamine safety and use in the emergency department for pain and agitation/delirium: A health system experience. *West J Emerg Med* 2020; **21(2)**: 272–81.
47. Émond M, Boucher V, Carmichael PH, et al. Incidence of delirium in the Canadian emergency department and its consequences on hospital length of stay: A prospective observational multicentre cohort study. *BMJ Open* 2018; **8(3)**: e018190.
48. Yue J, Tabloski P, Dowal SL, et al. NICE to HELP: Operationalizing National Institute for Health and Clinical Excellence guidelines to improve clinical

practice. *J Am Geriatr Soc* 2014; **62(4)**: 754–61.
49. Meagher DJ, Trzepacz PT. Motoric subtypes of delirium. *Semin Clin Neuropsychiatry* 2000; **5(2)**: 75–85.
50. Cole JB, Klein LR, Nystrom PC, et al. A prospective study of ketamine as primary therapy for prehospital profound agitation. *Am J Emerg Med* 2018; **36(5)**: 789–96.
51. Wongpakaran N, Wongpakaran T, Bookamana P, et al. Diagnosing delirium in elderly Thai patients: Utilization of the CAM algorithm. *BMC Fam Pract* 2011; **12**: 65.
52. Park SY, Lee HB. Prevention and management of delirium in critically ill adult patients in the intensive care unit: A review based on the 2018 PADIS guidelines. *Acute Crit Care* 2019; **34(2)**: 117–25.
53. Payne-James J, Byard R. *Encyclopedia of Forensic and Legal Medicine*, 2nd ed. Philadelphia: Elsevier; 2016.
54. Bell L. On a form of disease resembling some advanced stages of mania and fever but so contradistinguished from any ordinary observed or described combination of symptoms as to render it probable that it may be overlooked and hitherto unrecorded malady. *Am J Insanity* 1849; **6**: 97–127.
55. Cordeiro CR, Saraiva R, Côrte-Real B, et al. When the bell rings: Clinical features of Bell's mania. *Prim Care Companion CNS Disord* 2020; **22(2)**: 19102511.
56. DiMaio TG, DiMaio VJM. *Excited Delirium Syndrome: Cause of Death and Prevention.* Boca Raton: CRC Press; 2005.
57. Samuel E, Williams RB, Ferrell RB. Excited delirium: Consideration of selected medical and psychiatric issues. *Neuropsychiatr Dis Treat* 2009; **5**: 61–6.
58. Sztajnkrycer MD, Baez AA. Cocaine, excited delirium and sudden unexpected death. *Emerg Med Serv* 2005; **34(4)**: 77–81.
59. Ruttenber AJ, Lawler-Heavner J, Yin M, et al. Fatal excited delirium following cocaine use: Epidemiologic findings provide new evidence for mechanisms of cocaine toxicity. *J Forensic Sci* 1997; **42(1)**: 25–31.
60. Ruttenber AJ, McAnally HB, Wetli CV. Cocaine-associated rhabdomyolysis and excited delirium: Different stages of the same syndrome. *Am J Forensic Med Pathol* 1999; **20(2)**: 120–7.
61. Murray BL, Murphy CM, Beuhler MC. Death following recreational use of designer drug "bath salts" containing 3,4-Methylenedioxypyrovalerone (MDPV). *J Med Toxicol* 2012; **8(1)**: 69–75.
62. Penders TM, Gestring RE, Vilensky DA. Intoxication delirium following use of synthetic cathinone derivatives. *Am J Drug Alcohol Abuse* 2012; **38(6)**: 616–17.
63. Penders TM, Gestring RE, Vilensky DA. Excited delirium following use of synthetic cathinones (bath salts). *Gen Hosp Psychiatry* 2012; **34(6)**: 647–50.
64. Desharnais B, Dazé Y, Huppertz LM, et al. A case of fatal idiosyncratic reaction to the designer drug 3,4-methylenedioxypyrovalerone (MDPV) and review of the literature. *Forensic Sci Med Pathol* 2017; **13(3)**: 350–4.
65. Karch SB. Cathinone neurotoxicity ("The "3Ms"). *Curr Neuropharmacol* 2015; **13(1)**: 21–5.
66. Kesha K, Boggs CL, Ripple MG, et al. Methylenedioxypyrovalerone ("bath salts"), related death: case report and review of the literature. *J Forensic Sci* 2013; **58(6)**: 1654–9.
67. Murphy CM, Dulaney AR, Beuhler MC, Kacinko S. "Bath salts" and "plant food" products: The experience of one regional US poison center. *J Med Toxicol* 2013; **9(1)**: 42–8.
68. Zawilska JB, Kacela M, Adamowicz P. NBOMes-Highly potent and toxic alternatives of LSD. *Front Neurosci* 2020; **14**: 78.
69. Byard RW, Cox M, Stockham P. Blunt craniofacial trauma as a manifestation of excited delirium caused by new psychoactive substances. *J Forensic Sci* 2016; **61(6)**: 1546–8.
70. Allam S, Noble JS. Cocaine-excited delirium and severe acidosis. *Anaesthesia* 2001; **56(4)**: 385–6.
71 Dean BV, Stellpflug SJ, Burnett AM, Engebretsen KM. 2C or not 2C: Phenethylamine designer drug review. *J Med Toxicol* 2013; **9(2)**: 172–8.
72. Labay LM, Caruso JL, Gilson TP, et al. Synthetic cannabinoid drug use as a cause or contributory cause of death. *Forensic Sci Int* 2016; **260**: 31–9.
73. Brice JH, Pirrallo RG, Racht E, et al. Management of the violent patient. *Prehosp Emerg Care* 2003; **7(1)**: 48–55.
74. Burry L, Mehta S, Perreault MM, et al. Antipsychotics for treatment of delirium in hospitalised non-ICU patients. *Cochrane Database Syst Rev* 2018; **6(6)**: Cd005594.
75. Cerejeira J, Lagarto L, Mukaetova-Ladinska EB. The immunology of delirium. *Neuroimmunomodulation* 2014; **21(2–3)**: 72–8.
76. Mash DC. Excited delirium and sudden death: A syndromal disorder at the extreme end of the neuropsychiatric continuum. *Front Physiol* 2016; **7**: 435.
77. Mash DC, Duque L, Pablo J, et al. Brain biomarkers for identifying excited delirium as a cause of sudden death. *Forensic Sci Int* 2009; **190(1–3)**: e13–19.
78. Mash DC, Ouyang Q, Pablo J, et al. Cocaine abusers have an overexpression of alpha-synuclein in dopamine neurons. *J Neurosci* 2003; **23(7)**: 2564–71.
79. Mash DC, Pablo J, Ouyang Q, et al. Dopamine transport function is elevated in cocaine users. *J Neurochem* 2002; **81(2)**: 292–300.
80 Mash DC, Staley JK, Izenwasser S, et al. Serotonin transporters upregulate with chronic cocaine use. *J Chem Neuroanat* 2000; **20(3–4)**: 271–80.
81. Johnson MM, David JA, Michelhaugh SK, et al. Increased heat shock protein 70 gene expression in the brains of cocaine-related fatalities may be reflective of postdrug survival and intervention rather than excited delirium. *J Forensic Sci* 2012; **57(6)**: 1519–23.
82. Wetli CV, Mash D, Karch SB. Cocaine-associated agitated delirium and the neuroleptic malignant syndrome. *Am J Emerg Med* 1996; **14(4)**: 425–8.
83. Meyer MR. Toxicokinetics of NPS: Update 2017. *Handb Exp Pharmacol* 2018; **252**: 441–59.
84. Wolf ME. Regulation of AMPA receptor trafficking in the nucleus accumbens by dopamine and cocaine. *Neurotox Res* 2010; **18(3–4)**: 393–409.
85. Walker J, Calkins H, Nazarian S. Evaluation of cardiac arrhythmia among athletes. *Am J Med* 2010; **123(12)**: 1075–81.
86. Bosch C, Campuzano O, Sarquella-Brugada G, et al. A novel variant in RyR2 causes familiar catecholaminergic polymorphic ventricular tachycardia. *Forensic Sci Int* 2017; **270**: 173–7.
87. Johnson MM, David JA, Michelhaugh SK, et al. Increased heat shock protein 70 gene expression in the brains of cocaine-related fatalities may be reflective of postdrug survival and intervention rather than excited delirium. *J Forensic Sci* 2012; **57(6)**: 1519–23.
88. Vilke GM, Mash DC, Pardo M, et al. EXCITATION study: Unexplained in-custody deaths: Evaluating biomarkers of stress and agitation. *J Forensic Leg Med* 2019; **66**: 100–6.
89. Lim S. Metabolic acidosis. *Acta Med Indones* 2007; **39(3)**: 145–50.
90. Reddy AJ, Lam SW, Bauer SR, Guzman JA. Lactic acidosis: Clinical implications and management strategies. *Cleve Clin J Med* 2015; **82(9)**: 615–24.
91. Robergs RA, Ghiasvand F, Parker D. Biochemistry of exercise-induced metabolic acidosis. *Am J Physiol Regul Integr Comp Physiol* 2004; **287(3)**: R502–16.
92. Foucher CD, Tubben RE. *Lactic Acidosis*. Treasure Island: StatPearls Publishing; 2022.
93. Seheult J, Fitzpatrick G, Boran G. Lactic acidosis: An update. *Clin Chem Lab Med* 2017; **55(3)**: 322–33.
94. Stanley M, Chippa V, Aeddula NR, et al. *Rhabdomyolysis*. Treasure Island: StatPearls Publishing 2022.
95. Wilson MP, Pepper D, Currier GW, et al. The psychopharmacology of agitation: Consensus statement of the american association for emergency psychiatry project Beta psychopharmacology workgroup. *West J Emerg Med* 2012; **13(1)**: 26–34.
96. Ho JD, Smith SW, Nystrom PC, et al. Successful management of excited delirium syndrome with prehospital ketamine: Two case examples. *Prehosp Emerg Care* 2013; **17(2)**: 274–9.
97. Cole JB, Driver BE, Klein LR, et al. In reply: Ketamine is an important therapy for prehospital agitation - Its exact role and side effect profile are still undefined. *Am J Emerg Med* 2018; **36(3)**: 502–3.
98. Gerold KB, Gibbons ME, Fisette RE Jr, Alves D. Review, clinical update, and practice guidelines for excited delirium syndrome. *J Spec Oper Med* 2015; **15(1)**: 62–9.
99. Ho JD, Cole JB, Klein LR, et al. The hennepin ketamine study investigators' reply. *Prehosp Disaster Med* 2019; **34(2)**: 111–13.
100. Kitch BB. Out-of-hospital ketamine: Review of a growing trend in patient care. *J Am Coll Emerg Physicians Open* 2020; **1(3)**: 183–9.
101. Li M, Martinelli AN, Oliver WD, Wilkerson RG. Evaluation of ketamine for

excited delirium syndrome in the adult emergency department. *J Emerg Med* 2019; **58**(**1**): 100–5.
102. Linder LM, Ross CA, Weant KA. Ketamine for the acute management of excited delirium and agitation in the prehospital setting. *Pharmacotherapy* 2018; **38**(**1**): 139–51.
103. Olives TD, Nystrom PC, Cole JB, et al. Intubation of profoundly agitated patients treated with prehospital ketamine. *Prehosp Disaster Med* 2016; **31**(**6**): 593–602.
104. Parks DJ, Alter SM, Shih RD, et al. Rescue intubation in the emergency department after prehospital ketamine administration for agitation. *Prehosp Disaster Med* 2020; **35**(**6**): 651–5.
105. Scaggs TR, Glass DM, Hutchcraft MG, Weir WB. Prehospital ketamine is a safe and effective treatment for excited delirium in a community hospital based EMS system. *Prehosp Disaster Med* 2016; **31**(**5**): 563–9.
106. Scheppke KA, Braghiroli J, Shalaby M, Chait R. Prehospital use of i.m. ketamine for sedation of violent and agitated patients. *West J Emerg Med* 2014; **15**(**7**): 736–41.
107. Solano JJ, Clayton LM, Parks DJ, et al. Prehospital ketamine administration for excited delirium with illicit substance co-ingestion and subsequent intubation in the emergency department. *Prehosp Disaster Med* 2021; **36**(**6**): 697–701.
108. Bozeman WP, Stopyra JP, Klinger DA, et al. Injuries associated with police use of force. *J Trauma Acute Care Surg* 2018; **84**(**3**): 466–72.
109. Tran K, Mierzwinski-Urban M. CADTH Rapid Response Reports. In: Tran K, Mierzwinski-Urban M (eds), *Ketamine for Pharmacological Management of Aggression and Agitation in Pre-Hospital Settings: A Review of Comparative Clinical Effectiveness, Safety and Guidelines.* Ottawa: Canadian Agency for Drugs and Technologies in Health, 2019.
110. Burnett AM, Watters BJ, Barringer KW, et al. Laryngospasm and hypoxia after intramuscular administration of ketamine to a patient in excited delirium. *Prehosp Emerg Care* 2012; **16**(**3**): 412–14.
111. Stratton SJ, Rogers C, Brickett K, Gruzinski G. Factors associated with sudden death of individuals requiring restraint for excited delirium. *Am J Emerg Med* 2001; **19**(**3**): 187–91.
112. Gowing LR, Henry-Edwards SM, Irvine RJ, Ali RL. The health effects of ecstasy: A literature review. *Drug Alcohol Rev* 2002; **21**(**1**): 53–63.
113. U.S. Department of Justice. Study of deaths following electro muscular disruption, 2011. Available from: https://www.ojp.gov/pdffiles1/nij/233432.pdf (Accessed 19 May 2023).

CHAPTER

73

Child Abuse and Neglect

Jennifer Anne Sutherland Smith

INTRODUCTION

The World Health Organization categorizes child maltreatment into four types: emotional abuse, neglect, physical abuse and sexual abuse (1). The methods used to define, collect and collate data on these matters vary across continents but common trends in the last three decades indicate a decreasing rate of child homicide, sexual abuse and severe physical abuse but an increasing rate of cases categorized as emotional abuse (2–4). National cross-sectional survey data are only collected in the USA, Canada and the Netherlands and methodological flaws have been reported (4). Prior to the COVID-19 pandemic, rates of neglect, physical and sexual abuse were relatively stable (5–7) as were hospital data around rates of physical abuse (8). The reported co-existence of child maltreatment with domestic violence is almost 50 percent in some studies (5). Worldwide strategies are being implemented to reduce interpersonal violence, improve parenting skills, promote prosocial behaviors and create safe environments for children but despite these, adverse childhood experiences play a major role in the genesis of illness and poor health outcomes that cost billions (1,9,10).

Children can be abused in diverse ways (11,12). Physical forces can result in externally visible injuries but also internal injuries that can cause psychological harm, neurodevelopmental sequelae, persisting physical disability or death. Abused children can also fail to receive adequate shelter, nutrition and nurture and experience cruel and unreasonable punishments or a range of sexually abusive care-giver behaviors (11,12).

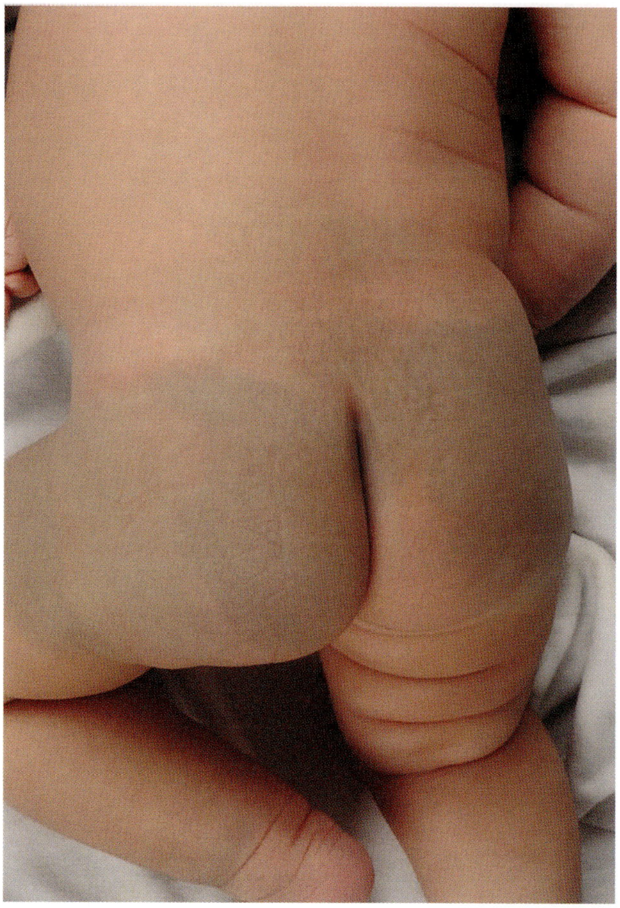

73.1 Dermal melanocytosis AKA “Mongolian blue spots”. This infant also had lesions on her ankles and shoulders.

Forensic clinicians play an important role in recognizing child abuse so that targeted interventions can protect abused and vulnerable children while avoiding misplaced accusations that harm caring parents. When evaluating suspected child abuse well-intentioned medical professionals can be influenced by bias, prioritizing advocacy over impartiality when a belief is formed that a child needs protection and fail to adhere to guidelines for investigation (13–16).

It is important that courts understand that the medical diagnostic process is often complex, multifaceted, requires information obtained from multiple sources, and is conducted over time as hypotheses are tested and modified. The medical evaluation of children’s injuries involves an open-minded, evidence-based assessment (17) of the anamnesis (the story provided to account for the injury), past medical and family histories, the child’s developmental capabilities, the examination findings, results of investigations and observed changes in the child’s clinical condition and test results. Radiologic and laboratory tests often provide vital information.

DOI: 10.1201/9781003138754-76

Scientific knowledge and methods of scientific enquiry thus form key elements of the medical evaluation of children's injuries.

THE INTERFACE BETWEEN PEDIATRIC MEDICINE AND THE LAW

Errors made by pediatric medical specialists have damaged experts' reputations and careers (18–20), contributed to miscarriages of justice (21,22), decreased confidence in medical experts' testimony (23–25) and reduced pediatricians' willingness to engage in medicolegal work (26–28). Significant miscarriages of justice have occurred, for example, because of misattribution of genital examination findings such as anal dilatation to sexual abuse (the Cleveland Inquiry) (29), misuse of statistics in relation to multiple deaths in one family (Sir Roy Meadow) (23,24), and misattribution of post-mortem findings to abusive head trauma (AHT) (Goudge inquiry) (22). Additionally, as the numbers of children subjected to ano-genital examinations increased, we learned that genital findings such as hymenal opening diameters, hymenal clefts, bands of tissue within the vaginal vestibule, pigmentary variations and peri-anal findings such as venous congestion have no forensic significance and are not signs of penetrative ano-genital trauma (12,30,31). It therefore seems wise that experts convey information to courts and child protection professionals about known diagnostic error rates, the confidence with which diagnostic conclusions are held and the scientific basis underpinning diagnoses (19,32,33).

Since the release in 2016 of the President's Council of Advisors on Science and Technology (PCAST) report on Forensic Science in Criminal Courts: Ensuring Scientific Validity of Feature Comparison Methods (32), courts and the professions have scrutinized the reliability and validity of many areas of forensic science (33,34) and some criticisms of the "matching" forensic sciences as "junk science" might be warranted. Pediatric medicine, however, is not a "feature comparison method". The diagnostic process involves more than "fast thinking" heuristics (35). Although concerns have been raised regarding the diagnostic processes around head injury, particularly the diagnostic consideration of AHT when a few specific findings are present (36), the consensus opinion is that AHT is "real" (37,38). Particular mention should be made of criticisms (39–42) of the Swedish Agency for Health Technology Assessment and Assessment of Social Service's report of a systematic review they performed "*to determine the diagnostic accuracy of the triad in detecting that an infant had been shaken*"(36) and the plethora of papers written by the SBU reviewers in defense of their actions and conclusions (43–45).

The remainder of this chapter deals with key forensic issues regarding medicolegally important injuries seen in abused children.

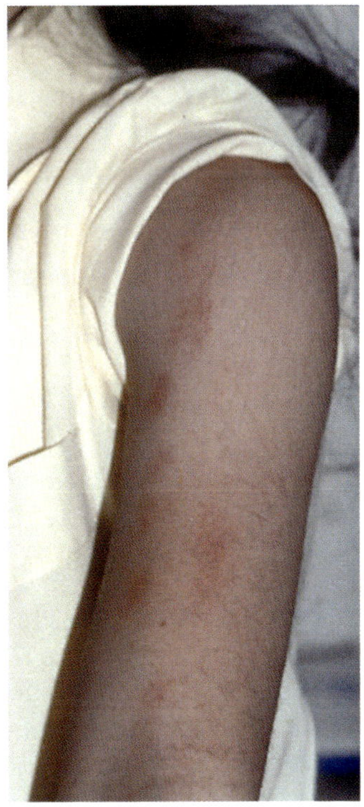

73.2 Bruising on the upper arm attributed to self-inflicted suction by a pre-teenaged girl who was practicing creating "hickeys".

BRUISES

Bruises move and evolve with time. Bruises are common injuries in childhood, frequently sustained by independently mobile children as a result of accidental falls and collisions (46–51). When bruising occurs as a result of accidental childhood trauma the bruises are usually few in number (1–3) small (< 1–2 cm) and located over bony prominences on knees, elbows and the front of the body (47,52,53). Inflicted bruises are more likely than accidentally acquired bruises to be large, multiple, clustered and associated with other injury types (53,54). Bruises on infants and children who are not independently mobile should generate concern about a possible nonaccidental cause (48,55,56). Even a single bruise on an infant aged 4 months or less warrants suspicion regarding an inflicted cause (48,57,58).

In children aged less than 4 years, the bruises' location on the body can generate concerns around child abuse. Bruising on the torso, ears and neck is particularly concerning (47,57,58). However, isolated small bruises located in the midline on the back over projecting bony spinous processes might be an exception. Additionally, bruises on the soft part of the cheek, over the angle of the mandible, around the eyes and over the sclera, and patterned shapes are seen more frequently in abused compared to accidentally injured young children (16,57,58). When trauma to the frenula is included, the mnemonic TEN4FACES p can be a useful tool to identifying bruises that might have been inflicted (58). It should be noted however that with a reported sensitivity of 69 percent

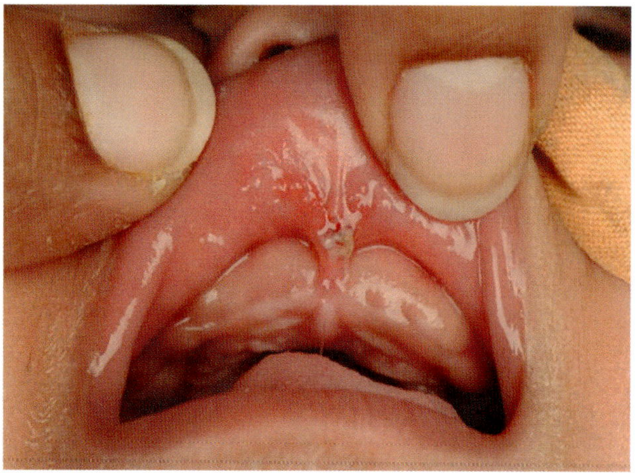

73.3 Frenulum laceration in an infant.

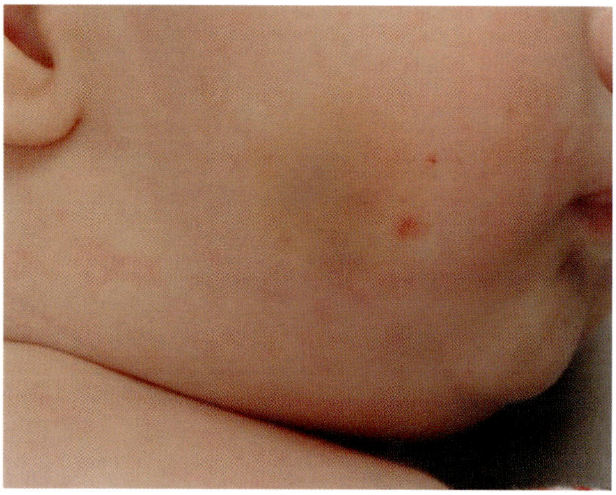

73.4 Bruising to the cheek and over the mandible in an infant. The TEN4FACESp mnemonic alerts clinicians to bruises that have a strong association with inflicted trauma.

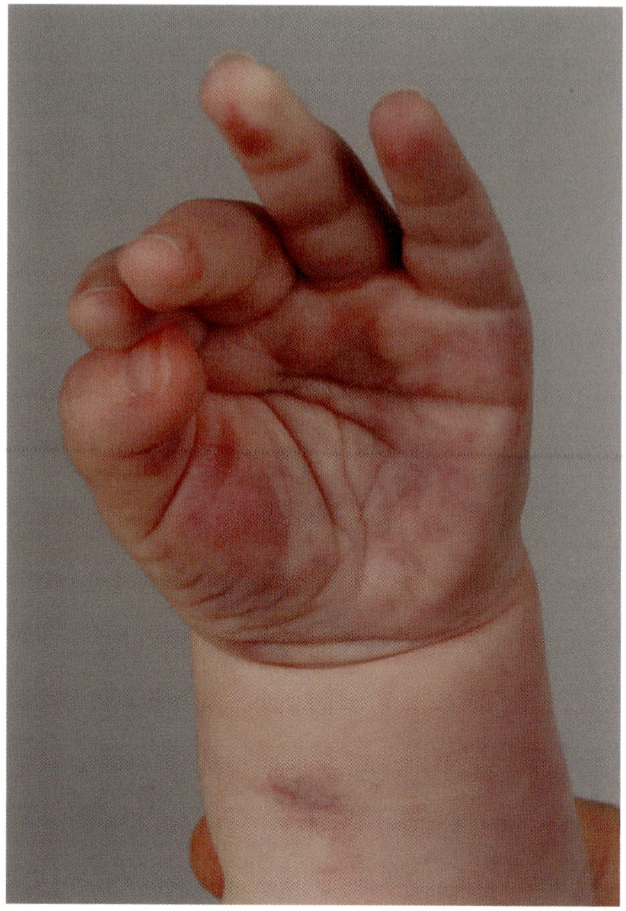

73.5 Bruising to the hand and forearm of an infant from firm squeezing of the infant's hand.

and specificity of 74 percent in one analysis and a sensitivity of 80.7 percent and specificity of 91.1 percent in another study, TEN4 categorization alone is not diagnostic (58,59). The TEN4FACESp bruising clinical diagnostic rule had a sensitivity of 95.6 percent and specificity of 87.1 percent, NPV of 98.8 percent and PPV of 63.9 percent in a validation study involving more than 2000 children aged less than 4 years (58).

Specific patterns of bruising within specified locations on the body can be observed after particular methods of infliction (60). For example, slaps to the face can result in variegated patterned bruising of the cheek that might contain obliquely oriented linear components and petechiae (61). Impacts to the ears can result in bruising to the scapha and concha as well as the helix and bruising can sometimes be seen on the posterior helix and scalp. These areas and tympanic membranes should be inspected when bruising to the ears is observed. Nose and oral cavities should be inspected searching for injuries such as septal hematoma, sublingual hematoma, intra-oral bruises, abrasions and lacerations. Spanking or slapping of the buttocks and lateral thighs can cause large areas of bruising that extend over lateral and posterior planes of the body, this may be patterned (61) and may result in parallel vertically oriented linear bruises either side of the natal cleft. Impacts from patterned implements may retain the shape of the object (61).

Petechiae are pinpoint-sized bruises which may coalesce to form larger areas of bruising. Petechiae are rarely seen following accidental trauma caused by impact but can be observed after small blood vessels rupture. Inflicted blunt force trauma such as slapping can cause petechiae and bruising in combination. Strangulation involving venous occlusion in the neck and venous occlusion of limbs can result in petechiae distal to the level of occlusion (i.e. a focal distribution is observed). Medical causes of blood vessel fragility and coagulopathy should be considered particularly when the distribution is more widespread or away from areas of trauma.

The age of bruises cannot be determined on the basis of color (53,62–64). The presence of the color yellow indicates causation likely occurred more than 18 hours to one day prior to observation (62,63). It should be noted however that individuals vary in their ability to perceive the color yellow (65,66), perception decreases with

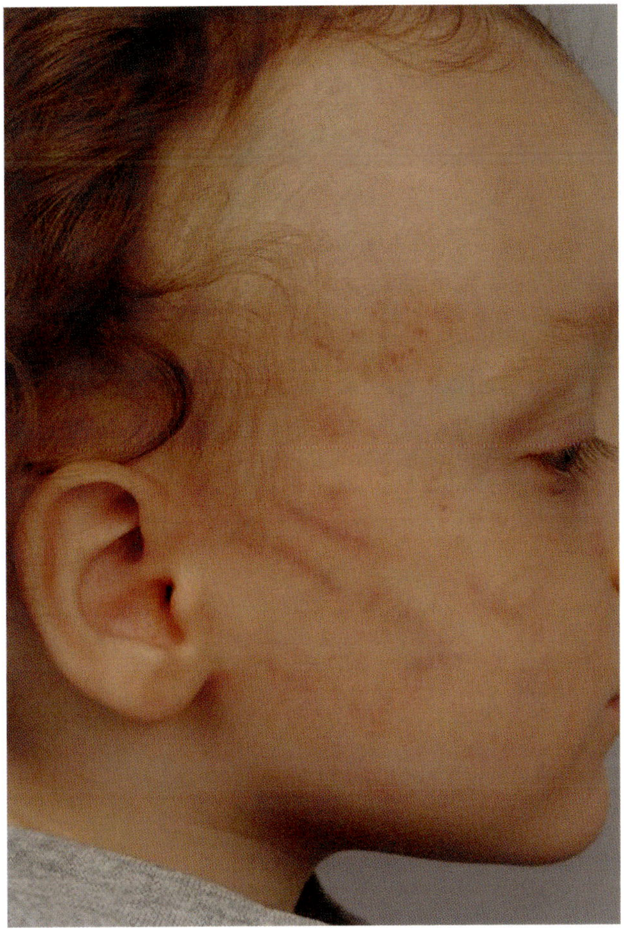

73.6 Slap marks to the cheek typically result in bruising containing linear elements angled obliquely. Ear, forehead and cheek bruising may also contain areas of petechial hemorrhage.

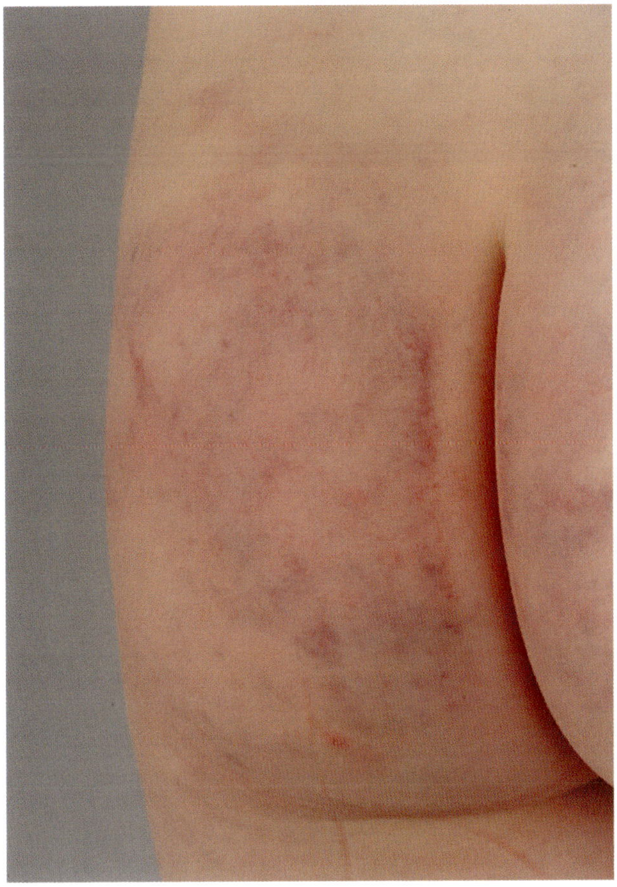

73.7 Spanking or slapping the buttocks can result in widespread patchy bruising to both buttocks with sparing of the natal cleft.

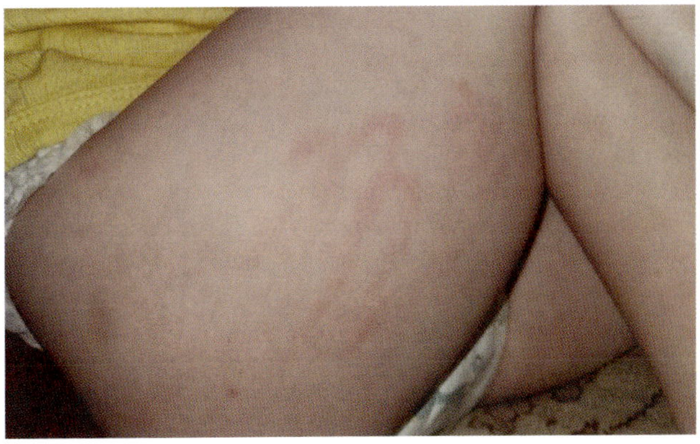

73.8 Slap marks (erythema, weal and flare) to the thigh.

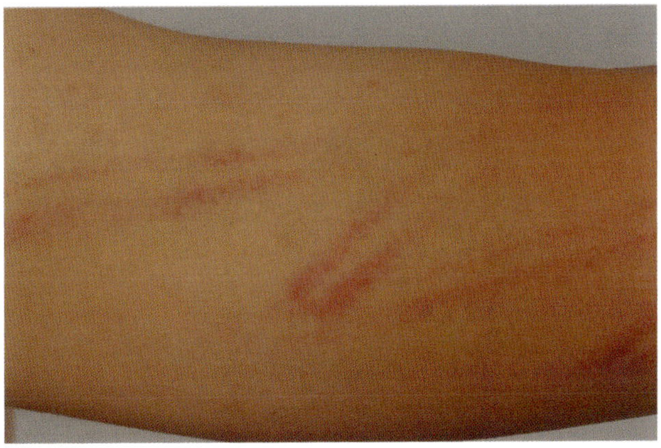

73.9 Tram-track patterned bruising inflicted by a thin linear object.

increasing age (66), and examiners describe colors differently (65,67). Examination conditions such as lighting, including alternative light sources, and children's cooperation might affect the examiners' ability to adequately examine bruises and, furthermore, photographs may not accurately reflect true color (63,65). In practical terms, the color of the bruise should not be used to determine its age, and bruises of the same age may present with different colors, and the colors of the bruise can be modified by the individual's skin tone.

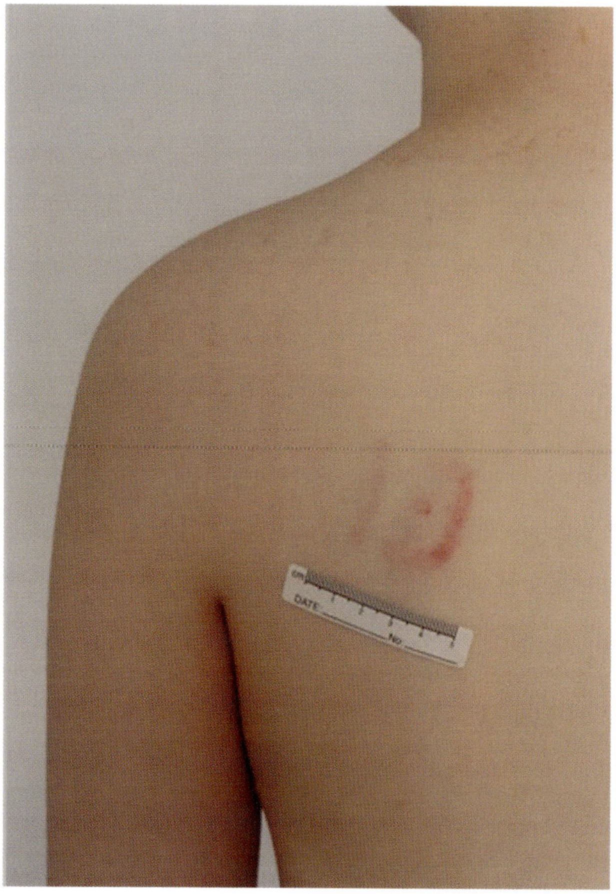

73.10 Imprint bruising in the shape of a belt buckle.

HUMAN BITES

Although human bites typically result in two opposing concave arcs, overall measuring 2–5 cm, with or without bruising and variations reflecting compression from individual teeth, human bites can also cause a variety of skin injuries including dragging abrasions, lacerations and, rarely, puncture wounds (68,69). Because bites often occur during dynamic events when both parties are moving relative to each other, the size and pattern of bite marks rarely form dental impressions of both dental arches. Toddlers frequently bite each other, typically on the arm (70). Some authors suggest that an inter-canine distance of less than 2.5 cm identifies child perpetrators (61,69) and that regularly spaced impressions are also more typical of child perpetrators (68). However, the reliability of these and other aspects of bite mark analysis has been harshly criticized (32,68). For example, the PCAST inquiry concluded, "*PCAST finds that bite mark analysis does not meet the scientific standards for foundational validity, and is far from meeting such standards*" (32). The identification of DNA from swabs at the site of bite marks may be useful in identifying assailants in some settings (68).

BURNS

Accidental burns in children, particularly scald burns, are common (71). The majority of accidental burns are scalds caused by pulling down hot liquids (resulting in a spill/splash/flow pattern involving the head, upper limb and upper torso resulting in irregular margins and irregular burn depth) or contact burns (from touching hot items such as hair straighteners, irons or ovens) affecting children less than 5 years old (71,72). Non-accidental burns in children can be caused intentionally or as a result of caregiver neglect (73).

Apart from AHT, intentional burns are the most likely injury to cause death or long-term morbidity. The prevalence of abusive burns is estimated to be 5.3 to 14 percent of children admitted to burns units highest for those aged 0–1 year. Scalds are the most common intentional burn injury (tap water is the most common causative agent) and contact burns are the second most common intentional burn injury (74).

Of children admitted to pediatric burns units, the reported percentages of non-accidental burns varies from 1.7 to 25 percent due to definitional and methodological variation (73). Compared to accidentally acquired burns of all categories, neglectful burns are associated with single-parent families, parental drug use, prior contact with child protection agencies, delayed presentation, lack of first aid and more skin grafting (73). The reported rates of pediatric admissions resulting from deliberate burning vary from 0.7 to 16 percent, with higher rates reported in the USA (73,75). Children admitted with intentionally inflicted burns tend to be younger than children who are accidentally burned, have scalds particularly immersion-patterned scalds with well-defined margins (e.g. glove and stocking patterned circumferential burns) and sparing of skin folds, burns on lower limbs, buttocks and perineum, larger burns, uniform and/or full thickness burns and additional injuries (72,75). Scalds attributed to abuse were more likely to be caused by hot water than food or beverages, to be symmetrical, to present with inadequate explanations or blaming of a sibling and to be triggered by soiling (72,76). Burns attributed to neglect are associated with inadequate supervision coupled with underestimation of children's developmental abilities, although it should be noted that children as young as 10–18 months can climb into a bath (77) and many parents are unaware of appropriate burn first aid (78).

Contact burns in children were the second most common type of burns in the ExSTRA study with most contact burns occurring to the legs (33.3%) arms (23.3%) and hands (21.7%) (72). Accidental contact burns commonly involve the hands touching a hot surface (71). Intentional non-scald burns frequently involve children older than 3 years, are located on their limbs, torso and backs of hands and were caused by cigarettes, irons, electrical heaters or appliances, hair dryers or curling tongs, chemicals, flames and other miscellaneous or undetermined causes (79). The shape of the causative object, multiple burns and injuries co-existing with other injuries generate concern regarding an inflicted non-scald burn (79). Contact burns caused by the deliberate application of the hot end of a lit cigarette are typically described as punched-out ulcers or deep craters (full thickness cigarette burns require an application of >1 sec) (80) and these may mimic or be mimicked by a range of traumatic and dermatologic conditions.

It has been suggested that occult bone injury be sought in children aged less than 2 years who have a

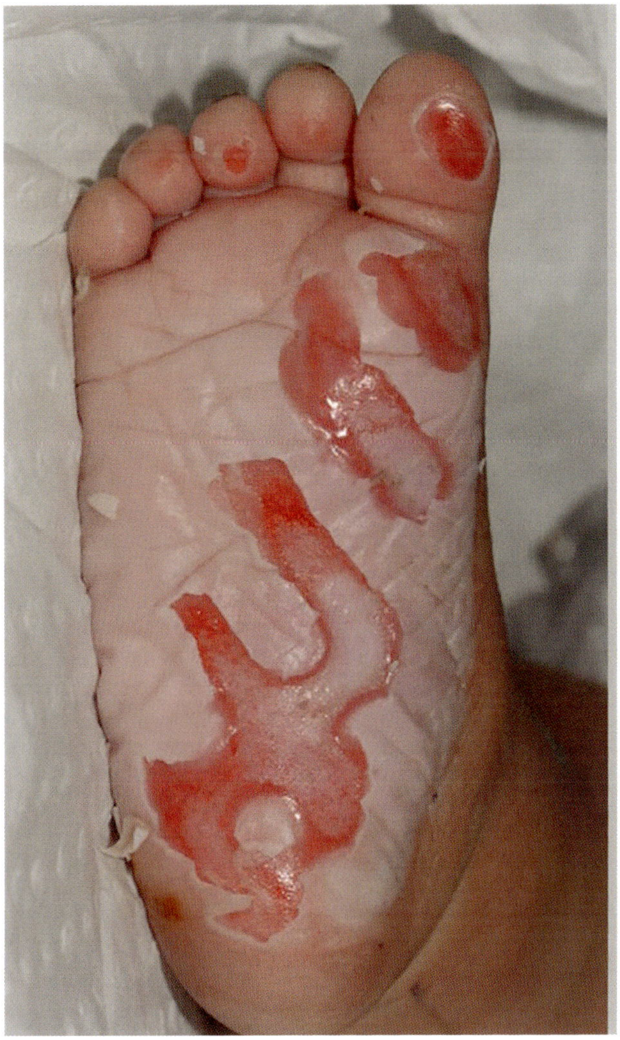

73.11 Contact burn to the sole of an infant's foot.

non-accidental burn but the rate of detection of occult fracture is lower than for other injuries (72,81). Positive skeletal survey findings have been reported in 1 to 14 percent of burn patients with wide variations between study methodologies and potential for circular reasoning (81). Neuroimaging is performed less commonly for children with suspicious burns than for children with other suspicious injuries, however, signs of AHT can be reported (as detected in 14.5% of the 25% of cases undergoing neuroimaging in the ExSTRA study) (72).

A prospective study of 2443 children (median age 2 years) demonstrated that implementation of the BuRN-Tool in four UK hospitals' Emergency Departments led to more discussions with senior Emergency Department staff and more referrals of <5 year-olds to children's social care because of safeguarding concerns (82). A score of 3 or more based on 8 variables had a sensitivity of 72.1, specificity of 82.7 and positive likelihood ratio of 4.2 (82).

FRACTURES

In infants and young children, some fractures occur as a result of abuse more commonly than accidents and vice versa (83–85). Similarly, some bones and some regions of bones are injured more frequently by abuse than accidents, however, no individual fracture location or pattern is pathognomonic of child abuse (83,85). Fractures in children are commonly the result of accidental falls and collisions, child abuse (fractures are the second most commonly detected abusive injury) (86), inherited and metabolic bone disease and birth trauma (85). Multiple fractures at different stages of healing generate suspicion about inflicted trauma and consideration of medical causes of bone fragility (12,85,87).

Classic metaphyseal lesion (CML) fractures are planar microfractures parallel to but not involving the physis of long bones, within the primary spongiosa layer of the distal metaphysis (88). This weak region of growing long bones is susceptible to injury from shearing forces such as might be exerted across the ends of long bones as infants' limbs flail when shaken or the ends of long bones are firmly grasped and manipulated (88). CMLs are typically seen in infants and children aged less than 2 years (84,88). In contrast, accidentally sustained fractures at the ends of long bones are more typically Salter-Harris type fractures involving the meta-epiphysis and are caused by falls and impacts that tend to exert forces along the long axis of bones (84,85).

It has been suggested by some that the radiographic appearance of CML fractures might be caused by metabolic diseases such as rickets or scurvy, not trauma (89). However, the overwhelming consensus view is that CML represent traumatic injuries (12,83,85,90,91). Evidence supporting a traumatic cause of CMLs includes (a) the ultrasound appearance of thickening, deformity and fractures of the metaphyseal bone collar, and irregularities and fracture lines in the zone of provisional calcification (92), (b) corresponding nuclear medicine bone scan regions of increased uptake of radionucleotide (93,94) or ^{18}F-NaF PET scan positivity (95), (c) MRI signs of soft-tissue edema, slippage of non-ossified epiphyseal centers or bone marrow edema (96) (d) CT reconstructed images of the thickened metaphyseal collar (97), (e) postmortem radiographs of excised bone and histologic confirmation of microfractures. Supportive evidence of a traumatic cause is provided by confessional studies (98). Additionally, in a study of 2890 young children with CMLs, 95.8 percent had at least one additional injury suggesting a common traumatic origin (99). A further study of 408 children suggested that such abnormalities are not commonly found in healthy infants and toddlers who have not suffered trauma (100).

Some authors have opined the existence of a transient state of bone fragility in infants (or perhaps some infants) (101,102), but evidence for this purported entity is lacking; the consensus opinion is that a "temporary brittle bone disease" of infancy does not exist (91,103). In the absence of biochemical abnormalities indicative of abnormal bone metabolism with radiologic findings indicative or supportive of metabolic bone disease, in young children a low serum Vitamin D level alone does not indicate a propensity to fracture (104–106). Ehlers-Danlos and hypermobility syndromes have been linked to childhood fractures (107,108) but the nature of the relationship is disputed (109–114). Genetic variants of unknown significance (VUS) that might be rare variants of osteogenesis imperfecta create genuine diagnostic challenges (115,116).

In infants, fractures of the ribs (117), particularly the postero-medial ribs, classic metaphyseal patterned fractures at the end of long bones in limbs, fractures of vertebrae, sternum, scapulae and digits are rarely attributed to accidents (83,84). In contrast, falls and other forms of accidental trauma are commonly cited to account for isolated distal radial buckle fractures (Colles fractures), supracondylar humerus fractures, distal tibial fractures in toddlers and mid-clavicular fractures (83).

Rarely, birth-related fractures of the femur and humerus can also result from vaginal-breech deliveries and difficult extractions during cesarean births (118). When rib fractures are caused by birth trauma, they can be associated with ipsilateral clavicular fractures (119,120). Skull fractures have been attributed to traumatic instrumental births but rarely to unassisted vaginal deliveries (119).

Single linear parietal skull fractures can occur as a result of accidental falls such as a fall from a carer's arms, infant products or buildings (121). They are also the most common abusive skull fractures. Infants are more likely than toddlers to sustain skull fractures after accidental falls, even from low heights, particularly when impacting a hard surface (122,123). Although complex skull fracture patterns generate suspicion regarding an abusive cause, complex skull fractures can occur as a result of accidents (124). Because skull fractures do not demonstrate radiographic signs of healing such as callus, and skull fractures can take months to heal, estimating the age of skull fractures is difficult (125). The absence of overlying scalp bruising does not exclude recent cranial impact and does not differentiate accidental trauma from abuse (126).

For long-bone fractures, estimates of the date of injury on the basis of radiologic investigations can usually only be made within broad categories such as "acute" (<1 week), "recent" (8–35 days) or "old" (>36 days) and should always be reviewed by a pediatric radiologist (83,86,127). Estimates of fracture-age can be useful in narrowing the window of timing of injury (128).

INTERNAL INJURIES

Significant injury to intrathoracic and intra-abdominal organs can occur in the absence of obvious injury to overlying skin and delays in diagnosis are common (129,130). Infants are particularly vulnerable to intra-abdominal injury (130–132). Hollow viscus injuries such as bowel perforation (particularly duodenal and proximal jejunal) and solid-organ injury such as pancreatic injury should generate suspicion regarding a non-accidental cause although inflicted injuries to liver and spleen are more common (129,132). In the 0–4 years age group, 15 percent of intra-abdominal trauma has been attributed to abuse (129). Co-existing head injuries and intrathoracic injuries are common (129). Alternative radiologic methods of investigation such as MRI and FAST (focussed abdominal sonography for trauma) are being used with increasing frequency in major pediatric trauma centers (132,133). Non-acutely, an unexplained bowel stricture or pancreatic pseudocyst should generate suspicion regarding past assault (129,130).

Inflicted intrathoracic injuries are not commonly reported and when they are detected, assault may be difficult to differentiate from injury inflicted during resuscitation. Pharyngeal and esophageal trauma may present with subcutaneous emphysema in a child who has non-specific symptoms of irritability, poor feeding, respiratory distress and oral bleeding or drooling (131).

HEAD TRAUMA

The US Centers for Disease Control and Prevention defines AHT as an injury to the skull or intracranial contents of an infant or young child (<5 years of age) due to inflicted blunt impact and/or violent shaking (134). Understanding of the pathophysiology of head trauma, particularly the neurometabolic cascades of brain injury (135) is informed by study of head trauma occurring as a result of accidents and abuse. The pathway from AHT to injury has rarely been documented in individual cases because randomized controled trials of AHT cannot be conducted for obvious ethical reasons. Several "nanny-cam" covert recordings exist of assaults, some of which resulted in head injury. Because of these limitations, epidemiologic techniques are used to determine causal relationships around AHT.

As data increase, predictive modeling regarding the medical diagnosis of AHT is becoming possible. Data around the sensitivity and specificity of clinical decision tools such as PediBIRN (136), PIBIS (137) and PredAHT2 (138) suggest that they may have clinical utility in cohorts of children similar to those used in tool development. Cluster analysis of head injured children supports current methodologies used in the forensic evaluation of pediatric neurotrauma (139).

Because infants and young children with head injuries often present with non-specific symptoms, injuries can be easily missed (140,141). In addition, in children with diagnosed AHT, evidence of prior injury is common (141,142). Features such as apnea and retinal hemorrhages (which correlate strongly), seizures, rib and long-bone fractures have a positive association with AHT (143).

Every forensic practitioner who evaluates pediatric head trauma should carefully consider the possibility of accidental trauma and medical mimics, including rare genetic and metabolic conditions (38,144).

SCALP INJURY

Impacts to the head may result in scalp bruising, swelling, abrasion, laceration and hematoma including bleeding beneath the galea aponeurotica (subgaleal

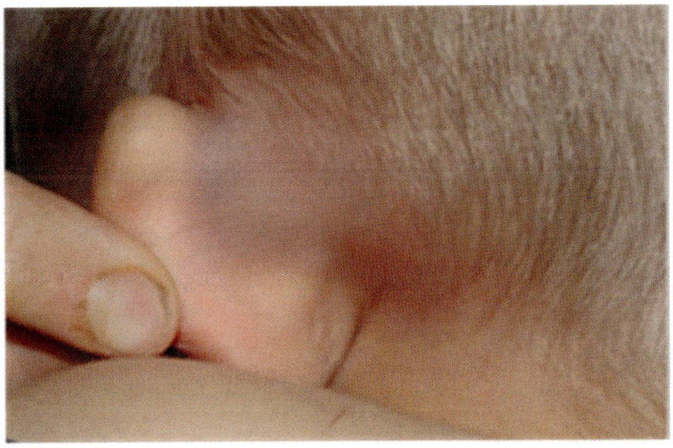

73.12 Blood from extensive scalp and subgaleal hematoma tracking to the posterior surface of the pinna.

hematoma) but external evidence of impact may be absent even in the presence of underlying skull fracture. Metz et al. reported scalp bruising in 5.5 percent, scalp soft-tissue swelling evident clinically in 73 percent and radiologically in 93 percent of 218 subjects when skull fracture was present (145). Impact onto a soft surface or fall dynamics that dissipate forces may result in no external sign of impact. Subgaleal hematoma, caused by rupture of emissary veins resulting in a collection of blood between the galea aponeurotica and skull-bone periosteum, produce large soft boggy swellings that may appear days following trauma (146). In infants, scalp swellings caused by trauma must be differentiated from spontaneous or delayed subaponeurotic collections of infancy (147,148) and scalp traction caused by hair pulling or braiding (149,150).

SKULL FRACTURE

Skull fractures can be described as simple (fractures with two terminal ends), complex (three or more terminal ends) and comminuted (an island of bone surrounded by fractured bone) (151). Fracture patterns are described as linear, curvilinear, stellate, diastatic, depressed or displaced (152). Because of the structural vulnerability of the infant skull, infants are more likely than toddlers to have skull fractures (125). Impact with a flat surface deforms (indents) the malleable infant skull that may fracture at the point of maximum out-bending (153).

Infant cadaver experiments performed last century demonstrated that a fall of 82 cm could result in skull fracture (154). More recent biomechanical and observational studies suggest that infant and toddler falls from a sitting height can occasionally result in skull fracture (123). The site and pattern of fracture does not differentiate AHT from accidents, however, abuse is more frequently diagnosed in infants with multiple skull fractures (155).

Estimating the age of trauma of skull fractures is challenging because fractures do not heal via periosteal reaction and callus formation (152) and healing can occur over months (156).

Extra-axial hemorrhage

Extradural hemorrhage in infants and young children is commonly caused by accidental impacts, especially accidental falls (157).

In contrast, subdural hemorrhage is the most frequently identified intracranial lesion attributed to AHT (38). Subdural hemorrhage is attributed to bleeding from delicate small bridging veins that traverse between cortical veins and the draining dural sinuses such that blood cleaves a space in the dural border cell layer (158). A recent survey of 43 neonatal infant and child autopsies found that the average number of bridging veins per brain was 54 (the largest number was 94) (159). The vast majority of subdural hemorrhages in infants and young children are caused by trauma, predominantly AHT (38). Accidental head trauma may result in evidence of impact and when subdural hemorrhages occur they can be of significant volume, compress underlying brain and may require drainage (160). Multicompartmental, multifocal, thin subdural hemorrhages over the cerebral convexities, falx and tentorium, particularly in the middle and posterior cranial fossa, are associated with medical diagnoses of AHT (38,158). Wittschieber et al. highlighted two important concepts; mixed-density subdural collections are not all caused by repeated trauma and hypodense subdural collections are not necessarily chronic (158). Mixed density subdural collections can be caused by a combination of hyperacute (i.e. active bleeding) and recent hemorrhage, blood mixed with CSF, blood separating into a cellular layer and supernatant fluid components, and a combination of acute and older hemorrhage (158). A fluid collection that is closer in density to CSF (albeit with proteinaceous components) may be the result of chronic subdural hemorrhage, CSF within the subdural space (the result of dural damage), an acute traumatic effusion or possibly (but unlikely) rupture of an arachnoid cyst (158,161). Furthermore, CT density and MRI intensity are only moderately useful in estimating the age of subdural fluid while "minimum age" estimates might have greater forensic utility (158).

Subdural hemorrhages associated with birth trauma are common, having a reported incidence of around 38 percent (in Rooks study 49% [162]), usually located posteriorly and are more frequently seen following vaginal delivery than cesarean births (163). Most resolve by one month of age (162).

Although "spontaneous" rebleeding and conversion of birth-related subdural hemorrhage to chronic subdural hemorrhages or hygroma has been suggested as a theory (158), case-related evidence of such phenomena is lacking. Rebleeding from areas of prior extra-axial hemorrhage is common with a reported incidence after AHT of 63.5 percent (164). Notably, rebleeding was clinically silent in almost all cases (161,164).

Subdural collections can occur as a result of accidental head trauma, birth trauma, infection (meningitis), coagulopathy, leukemia, and a range of rare medical conditions such as glutaric aciduria and Menkes syndrome (165). Mimics of AHT require careful consideration (166).

Acute subarachnoid hemorrhages and subpial hemorrhages may be seen in association with accidental and AHT. Retroclival epidural hemorrhage is frequently associated with ligamentous injury (stripping of the tectorial membrane as a result of flexion-extension forces) (167,168).

Enlargement of the subarachnoid space can be caused by chronic subdural hemorrhages or hygromas, disruption of the arachnoid-dural interface, prior trauma including AHT, parenchymal volume loss and post-traumatic communicating hydrocephalus (169). Tucker et al. observed an overall incidence of subdural collections in 5.6% of infants with benign enlargement of the subarachnoid spaces (BESS) (170). Adamsbaum suggests that incidental subdural collections are homogenous in density/intensity, located anteriorly, do not contain hemosiderin clots at the vertex, are not associated with tentorial or interhemispheric subdural hematoma, the brain parenchyma looks normal and the collections are clinically silent (171).

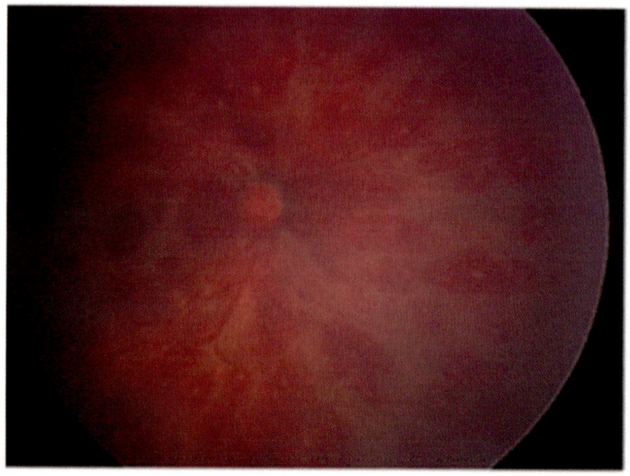

73.13 Extensive, too numerous to count, multilayered, retinal hemorrhages present in all 4 quadrants and all zones of the retina, extending to the periphery.

Parenchymal brain injuries

Intraparenchymal brain injuries caused by head trauma are the primary cause of mortality and morbidity in abused infants and toddlers. Diffuse axonal injury is generally attributed to apnea-induced hypoxic-ischemic injury (172) and possibly to injury directly caused by forces exerted during AHT (38).

Paroxysmal coughing and dysphagic choking have been described as "false mimics" of AHT whereas suffocation, strangulation and cardiac arrest can result in parenchymal brain injury that might be confused with AHT (172).

SPINAL TRAUMA

In Choudhary et al.'s 2014 study, cervical spine ligamentous injuries (nuchal, atlanto-occipital and atlanto-axial ligaments) were present in 78 percent of the AHT group, 46 percent of the accidental trauma group and 1% of the non-traumatic group (173). Spinal subdural hemorrhage is also more commonly detected following AHT compared to accidental trauma (174). In Rabbitt et al.'s study, spinal injury was detected in 59 percent of children investigated for suspected AHT and spinal subdural hemorrhage was associated with retinal hemorrhages ($p = 0.01$) and non-contact head injuries ($p = 0.008$) (175).

EYE INJURIES AND RETINAL HEMORRHAGES

Bruising around the eye and involving the eyelids, subconjunctival hemorrhage, direct trauma to the globe, retinal hemorrhages, traumatic retinoschisis and macular folds have been described in association with AHT (38,176). Retinal hemorrhages are reportedly associated with around 85 percent of diagnosed AHT (38,177). Eye examinations by an ophthalmologist should be conducted within 24–48 hours of admission when AHT is suspected (38,178,179). Bilateral, too-numerous-to-count, extensive, multilayered retinal hemorrhages extending to the ora serrata are strongly associated with AHT (38,176,178). Retinal hemorrhages that are few in number, located around the posterior pole and confined to a few retinal layers are relatively non-specific and have been described, albeit infrequently, in a wide range of medical conditions and accidental scenarios including occipital impacts (178,180). Accidental trauma sustained from falls from significant heights, motor vehicle accidents, occipital impacts, birth trauma and crush injuries to the head have been cited in rare instances as causes of severe retinal hemorrhages. Terson syndrome and Purtscher retinopathy also require consideration in the differential diagnosis (177). Vitreous hemorrhage may occur when blood breaks through the wall of a schisis cavity (177). Papilledema is uncommonly reported in association with AHT (approximately 10%) (177).

Traumatic retinoschisis is attributed to vitreo-retinal traction resulting from repeated rapid acceleration-deceleration forces (38).

Retinal hemorrhages typically do not worsen over time (179). Intra-retinal hemorrhages usually resolve in 1–2 weeks (32 days in one study and 58 days for one case of birth-related retinal hemorrhage in another) and too-numerous-to-count hemorrhages infrequently persist beyond a few days (179). Preretinal hemorrhages have been shown to persist for up to 111 days (179).

Birth-related retinal hemorrhages are common; reported in up to 13 000 of 56 200 newborns in the Soonchunhyang University Cheonan Hospital universal newborn eye screening (SUCH-NES) study (181). Retinal hemorrhages were more common after vaginal deliveries, 65 percent were bilateral and 35 percent were unilateral, 87 percent were intraretinal and zone III retinal haemorrhages were rare (0.03%) (181). Of the severe retinal hemorrhages 39 percent were re-examined monthly and of these, 4.4 percent persisted until 2 months of age (181).

CHILD AND ADOLESCENT SEXUAL ABUSE

The WHO 1999 defines child sexual abuse (CSA) as "*the involvement of a child in sexual activity that he or she does not fully comprehend, is unable to give informed consent to, or for which the child is not developmentally prepared and cannot give consent, or that violates the laws or social taboos of society*" (182). However, concepts and definitions vary across jurisdictions and research settings (183). CSA includes penetrative and genital contact forms of assault as well as non-contact abuse such as exhibitionism, exposing children to sexually explicit material and involvement in the production of child pornography. Sex trafficking (184,185), sexual exploitation of vulnerable children (186,187), grooming offenses (188) and technology facilitated child sexual assaults (189,190) are increasingly recognized. On the other hand, understanding normative sexual behavior at each developmental stage and across cultures has decreased concern regarding the forensic significance of some sexual behavior (191–194).

Counseling services for children with sexual behavior problems are expanding as peer-on-peer sexual assault rates increase, however few children with problematic sexual behaviors are themselves victims of sexual assaults (195). The LONGSCAN study reported sexually problematic behaviors in 21.6 percent of sexually abused children and only a 2-fold difference in rates of problematic sexualized behaviors between sexually abused and non-sexually abused cohorts (195). The Child Sexual Behaviour Inventory (CSBI) does not discriminate between sexually abused and non-abused children (196).

The medical evaluation of suspected child and adolescent sexual abuse has changed significantly over the last 30 years as knowledge increases around epidemiology, injury rates and characteristics, genital anatomy, sexually transmissible infections and dermatologic conditions affecting the genital area (197). Guidelines have been developed to assist health professionals to interpret ano-genital examination findings based on current evidence (198,199). Practitioners must be always be aware of current recommendations.

FABRICATED OR INDUCED ILLNESS BY CARER (FIIC)

One of the most curious ways in which a caregiver can abuse a child is to create the illusion that a child is ill or developmentally delayed or for the caregiver to act to make a healthy child unwell (200). Tully et al. describe FIIC as a phenomenon that occurs when a child's caregiver (typically the mother) elicits medical or psychological care for her child based on her need for the child to be recognized as more unwell or impaired than the child's actual state of health or well-being, resulting in actual or likely harm to the child (201). The child is thus subjected to unnecessary and harmful (or potentially harmful) medical and psychological interventions while the caregiver gains emotionally and sometimes financially from their interactions with health professionals (200). Yates and Bass reported 96.7 percent of their 796 perpetrators were female, 95.6 percent were the child's mother and 75.8 percent were married with a mean age of 27.6 years at the time of the child's presentation (202). The adult's deep-seated need to be seen as a "good parent", to receive emotional reward from others and to see one's-self as a martyr or victim are cited as psychological drivers of the adult's behavior (203). The quoted incidence is 0.5 to 2 per 100 000 children younger than 16 years (204). However some authors have suggested that the condition is more common although under-recognized and under-reported (201). The severity of harm to children occurs along a spectrum with overmedicalization and anxiety-driven excessive investigation of minor symptoms and signs at one end and fatalities resulting from induced illness (e.g. salt poisoning) at the severe end of the spectrum (204). The range of perpetrator behaviors can also occur across a spectrum that includes seeking unwarranted referrals to specialists, fraudulent production of documents and deliberate induction of illness or disability (200). Harm can be generated by caregivers providing misleading information to health professionals or withholding information, coaching others to falsely report symptoms or signs, simulating illness (e.g. contaminating a child's urine sample with blood) or by inducing illness in at least one of a myriad of ways (201,204). Health professionals are encouraged to recognize and respond to the "red flags" in a child-caregiver dyad that generate concern regarding fabricated or induced illness in a child (200,201,204). An accurate determination of fabrication or induction of illness often requires a collaborative approach between child protective services and health professionals to gather information about the child from a range of sources, recognizing that genuine illness may co-exist alongside fabrication and illness-induction (200). Meticulous appraisal of the child's complete medical records is usually required and a cautious approach should be taken to monitoring the safety of a child who has ongoing contact with a perpetrator (200,201).

CHILD NEGLECT

Definitions of child neglect vary across regions, but most definitions address the concept of parental omissions in care given adequate available resources. Legal definitions of child neglect vary significantly across jurisdictions as do the thresholds for protective interventions by state-based services (205). Child neglect is the category of child maltreatment most frequently documented by child protection services (206). Categories of child neglect include neglect of a child's physical needs (physical neglect), emotional, developmental and educational needs, medical and mental health needs, dental health, psychological well-being, and the need for supervision and moral guidance (205–207). Neglect of a child's physical environment (environmental neglect) may create hazards that incur risks to safety, health and development (205).

Child neglect is generally conceptualized using an ecologic model that has the child at the center of a family microsystem surrounded by their community (exosystem) that exists within a societal macrosystem (205).

Risk factors for child neglect are thus viewed as complex, interrelated and strongly influenced by societal factors that exacerbate disadvantage and increase vulnerability. Research suggests however that proximate factors are better predictors of child neglect than more distant societal factors and that parent-related risk factors such as a parental history of antisocial behavior, poor mental health and a past history of child abuse victimization correlate strongly with child neglect (205). Intergenerational transmission of patterns of neglectful parental behavior have also been reported (208). Screening young children using variables such as maternal history of physical neglect, maternal depression and substance abuse, stressful family circumstances and child-related factors that increase caregiving needs might identify children at higher risk of neglect (209).

Neglected children are at risk of malnourishment, suboptimal growth, physical injury, infestations and infections, periodontal disease, developmental delay, emotional and behavioral disorders of childhood and persisting difficulties relating to others (207). The clinical assessment of neglected children should therefore focus on the past (parental neglectful behaviors and evidence of harm to affected children) the present (categorizing how the parent is currently meeting the child's needs across multiple domains) and the future (predicting both changes in parenting capacity, if any, and the child's likely neurodevelopmental, health and behavioral outcomes if nothing changes). Clinicians concurrently assess parental behaviors with a focus on patterns of neglectful behavior and search for evidence of harm to children resulting from child neglect. A search for contributing factors might identify buffering, remediable or modifiable factors that will increase the likelihood of successful intervention to improve parenting. Welfare-based, strengths-based interventions for neglectful parents are generally favored over legal interventions that remove neglected children (207). However, clinicians should be aware that neglect can be fatal and irreversible neurodevelopmental harm can occur to neglected infants and toddlers.

Psychological abuse/Emotional abuse

Psychological abuse often co-exists with other forms of child abuse. The United Nations Convention of the Rights of the Child, Article 19, General Comment (GC)13: The right of the child to freedom from all forms of violence, includes subsection IV.a.21. which refers to a child's right to freedom from mental violence (210). Brassard, Hart and Glaser define mental violence as conveying to a child persistent messages that they are

> "*(a) worthless, unloved, unwanted, endangered or only of value in meeting another's needs, (b) scaring terrorizing and threatening, exploiting and corrupting, spurning and rejecting; isolating, ignoring and favoritism; (c) denying emotional responsiveness; neglecting mental health, medical and educational needs; (d) insults, name-calling, humiliation, belittling, ridiculing and hurting a child's feelings; (e) exposure to domestic violence; (f) placement in solitary confinement, isolation or humiliating or degrading conditions of detention; and (g) psychological bullying and hazing by adults or other children, including via information and communication technologies (IDTs) such as mobile phones and the Internet (known as "cyberbullying)*" (210).

Within countries where data are collected regarding types of psychological maltreatment or abuse, six categories of psychologically abusive caregiver behavior are commonly recognized (spurning, terrorizing, exploiting/corrupting, isolating, emotional unresponsiveness and effects of poor parental mental health, educational or medical neglect) (210).

Because there is no universal definition of psychological abuse, poor parenting is common and diagnosis hinges on third-party assessments of parent-child interactions, professional disagreements can arise regarding diagnosis, reporting thresholds and remediation (211). To further complicate the matter, specific harmful outcomes cannot be predicted other than in general terms (211) and evidence around effectiveness of interventions is lacking.

IMPACTS OF CHILD MALTREATMENT ON THE DEVELOPING BRAIN

The science around neurodevelopmental impacts of child maltreatment underpins policy and practice promoting early intervention to improve the life experiences of abused and neglected children. Persistent fear and anxiety, neglect and traumatic experiences such as sexual abuse and witnessing interpersonal violence can affect brain structure and function with long-term negative effects (212). Adverse childhood experiences, toxic stress and the influences of poverty and racism harm the developing brain with lasting impacts on physical and mental health (213).

CONCLUSION

Children can be abused in a myriad of ways impacting their physical and psychological health, growth, development, behavior and relationships. Symptoms and signs of child abuse range from obvious to occult signs of trauma only discovered after a thorough forensic investigation which includes consideration of medical conditions and accidents. Knowledge around the patterns of injury and clinical presentations associated with child abuse is increasing and clinical decision rules are proving useful. Courts are demanding medical testimony inclusive of information about test sensitivity, specificity, positive and negative predictive values, when known. Forensic practitioners must therefore remain well informed about advances in the field so they can inform courts of the strengths and limitations of the expanding evidence-base around child maltreatment.

REFERENCES

1. World Health Organisation. INSPIRE: Seven strategies for ending violence against children, 2016. Available from: http://www.who.int/violence_injury_prevention/violence/inspire/en/ (Accessed 19 May 2023).
2. Degli Esposti M, Humphreys DK, Jenkins BM, et al. Long-term trends in child maltreatment in England and Wales, 1858–2016: An observational, time-series analysis. *Lancet Public Health* 2019; **4**(**3**): e148–e58.
3. Roehrkasse AF, Wildeman C. Administrative data and long-term trends in child maltreatment: The prospects and pitfalls. *Lancet Public Health* 2019; **4**(**3**): e121–e2.
4. Jud A, Fegert JM, Finkelhor D. On the incidence and prevalence of child maltreatment: A research agenda. *Child Adolesc Psychiatry Ment Health* 2016; **10**(**1**): 17.
5. van Berkel SR, Prevoo MJL, Linting M, et al. Prevalence of child maltreatment in the Netherlands: An update and cross-time comparison. *Child Abuse Neglect* 2020; **103**: 104439.
6. Finkelhor D, Turner HA, Shattuck A, Hamby SL. Prevalence of childhood exposure to violence, crime, and abuse: Results from the national survey of children's exposure to violence. *JAMA Pediatr* 2015; **169**(**8**): 746–54.
7. Gilbert R, Fluke J, O'Donnell M, et al. Child maltreatment: Variation in trends and policies in six developed countries. *Lancet* 2012; **379**(**9817**): 758–72.
8. Wojciak AS, Butcher B, Conrad A, et al. Trends, diagnoses, and hospitalization costs of child abuse and neglect in the United States of America. *Int J Environ Res Public Health*. 2021; 18(14): 7585.
9. Bellis MA, Hughes K, Ford K, et al. Life course health consequences and associated annual costs of adverse childhood experiences across Europe and North America: A systematic review and meta-analysis. *Lancet Public Health* 2019; **4**(**10**): e517–e28.
10. Gilbert R, Widom CS, Browne K, et al. Burden and consequences of child maltreatment in high-income countries. *Lancet* 2009; **373**(**9657**): 68–81.
11. Reece RM, Christian C (eds). *Child Abuse: Medical Diagnosis & Management*, 3rd ed. Elk Grove Village: American Academy of Pediatrics; 2008.
12. Jenny C, Pierce MC (eds). *Child Abuse and Neglect: Diagnosis, Teatment, and Evidence*. St. Louis: Elsevier; 2011.
13. Hymel KP, Laskey AL, Crowell KR, et al. Racial and ethnic disparities and bias in the evaluation and reporting of abusive head trauma. *J Pediatr* 2018; **198**: 137–43.
14. Palusci VJ, Botash AS. Race and bias in child maltreatment diagnosis and reporting. *Pediatrics* 2021; **148**(**1**): e2020049625.
15. Jenny C, Hymel KP, Ritzen A, et al. Analysis of missed cases of abusive head trauma. *JAMA* 1999; **281**(7): 621–6.
16. Lindberg DM. To recognize child physical abuse early, frontline clinicians need subspecialty expertise. *JAMA Netw Open* 2021; 4(4): e215947.
17. Bennett CE, Christian CW. Clinical evaluation and management of children with suspected physical abuse. *Pediatr Radiol* 2021; **51**(**6**): 853–60.
18. Dyer C. Doctors in court. *BMJ* 2008; **337**: a975.
19. Skellern C. Medical experts and the law: Safeguarding children, the public and the profession. *J Paediatr Child Health* 2008; **44**(**12**): 736–42.
20. Craft A. Paediatricians and child protection. *Med Leg J* 2007; **75**(**2**): 55–62.
21. Turton J, Haines L. *An Investigation Into the Nature and Impact of Complaints Made Against Paediatricians Involved in Child Protection Procedures*. London: Royal College of Paediatrics and Child Health; 2007.
22. Iacobucci F, Hamilton G. The Goudge Inquiry and the role of medical expert witnesses. *CMAJ* 2010; **182**(**1**): 53–6.
23. Chadwick D, Krous H, Runyan D. Meadow, Southall, and the General Medical Council of the United Kingdom. *Pediatrics* 2006; **117**: 2247–51.
24. Mathews B, Payne H, Bonnet C, Chadwick D. A way to restore British paediatricians' engagement with child protection. *Arch Dis Child* 2009; **94**(**5**): 329–32.
25. Hey E. Suspected child abuse: The potential for justice to miscarry. *BMJ* 2003; **327**(**7410**): 299.
26. Dyer C. Lack of paediatric experts to testify in cases of suspected child harm is traumatising families, says judge. *BMJ* 2019; **367**: l6244.
27. Craft A. Child protection and paediatricians. *Clinical Risk* 2007; **13**(**3**): 92–5.
28. Neels A, Tuohy P, Elder D, on behalf of the Child Protection Clinical Network of the Paediatric Society of New Z. Training and confidence in undertaking child protection work as reported by New Zealand paediatricians. *J Paediatr Child Health* 2020; **56**(**1**): 107–13.
29. Summary of the Cleveland inquiry. *BMJ* 1988; **297**(**6642**): 190–1.
30. Pillai M. An evaluation of 'confirmatory' medical opinion given to English courts in 14 cases of alleged child sexual abuse. *J Forensic Leg Med* 2007; **14**(**8**): 503–14.
31. Pillai M. Genital findings in prepubertal girls: What can be concluded from an examination? *J Pediatr Adolesc Gynecol* 2008; **21**(**4**): 177–85.
32. President's Council of Advisors on Science and Technology. Forensic science in criminal courts: Ensuring scientific validity of feature-comparison methods, 2016. Available from: https://obamawhitehouse.archives.gov/sites/default/files/microsites/ostp/PCAST/pcast_forensic_science_report_final.pdf (Accessed 19 May 2023).
33. Edmond G, Martire KA. Antipodean forensics: A comment on ANZFSS's response to PCAST. *Aust J Forensic Sci* 2018; **50**(**2**): 140–51.
34. Vos EA. Using the PCAST Report to exclude, limit, or minimize experts. *Crim Just* 2017; **32**: 15.
35. Skellern C. Thinking fast and slow in the evaluation of injury plausibility in child protection. *J Paediatr Child Health* 2020; **56**(**9**): 1330–4.
36. Lynøe N, Elinder G, Hallberg B, et al. Insufficient evidence for 'shaken baby syndrome' - A systematic review. *Acta Paediatr* 2017; **106**(**7**): 1021–7.
37. Choudhary AK. The impact of the consensus statement on abusive head trauma in infants and young children. *Pediatr Radiol* 2021; **51**(**6**): 1076–8.
38. Choudhary AK, Servaes S, Slovis TL, et al. Consensus statement on abusive head trauma in infants and young children. *Pediatr Radiol* 2018; **48**(**8**): 1048–65.
39. Levin AV. The SBU report: A different view. *Acta Paediatr* 2017; **106**(**7**): 1037–9.
40. Narang SK, Greeley CS. Lynøe et al. - #theRestoftheStory. *Acta Paediatr* 2017; **106**(**7**): 1047–9.
41. Debelle GD, Maguire S, Watts P, et al. Abusive head trauma and the triad: A critique on behalf of RCPCH of 'Traumatic shaking: The role of the triad in medical investigations of suspected traumatic shaking'. *Arch Dis Child* 2018; **103**(**6**): 606.
42. Saunders D, Raissaki M, Servaes S, et al. Throwing the baby out with the bath water — response to the Swedish Agency for Health Technology Assessment and Assessment of Social Services (SBU) report on traumatic shaking. *Pediatr Radiol* 2017; **47**(**11**): 1386–9.
43. Lynøe N, Eriksson A. Hidden clinical values and overestimation of shaken baby cases. *Clin Ethics* 2019; **14**(**3**): 151–4.
44. Lynøe N, Eriksson A. Is focusing on the triad in suspected child abuse cases really irrelevant and of no practical use? *Acta Paediatr* 2018; **107**(**10**): 1675–6.
45. Lynøe N, Eriksson A. In order to ensure that evidence is unbiased it is sometimes necessary to retreat to the scientific ivory tower. *Forensic Sci Med Pathol* 2019; **15**(**1**): 164.
46. Pierce MC. Bruising characteristics from unintentional injuries in children: The 'green flag' study. *Arch Dis Child* 2017; **102**(**12**): 1097–8.
47. Pierce MC, Kaczor K, Aldridge S, et al. Bruising characteristics discriminating physical child abuse from accidental trauma. *Pediatrics* 2010; **125**(**1**): 67–74.
48. Pierce MC, Magana JN, Kaczor K, et al. The prevalence of bruising among infants in pediatric emergency departments. *Ann Emerg Med* 2016; **67**(**1**): 1–8.
49. Harris TS. Bruises in children: Normal or child abuse? *J Pediatr Health Care* 2010; **24**(**4**): 216–21.
50. Sugar NF, Taylor JA, Feldman KW. Bruises in infants and toddlers: Those who don't cruise rarely bruise. *Arch Pediatr Adolesc Med* 1999; **153**(**4**): 399–403.
51. Kemp AM, Dunstan F, Nuttall D, et al. Patterns of bruising in preschool children—a longitudinal study. *Arch Dis Child* 2015; **100**(5): 426–31.
52. Hibberd O, Nuttall D, Watson RE, et al. Childhood bruising distribution observed from eight mechanisms of unintentional injury. *Arch Dis Child* 2017; **102**(**12**): 1103–9.
53. RCPCH. Bruising: Systematic review, 2020. Available from: https://childprotection.rcpch.ac.uk/child-protection-evidence/bruising-systematic-review/ (Accessed 19 May 2023).

54. Maguire S, Mann MK, Sibert J, Kemp A. Are there patterns of bruising in childhood which are diagnostic or suggestive of abuse? A systematic review. *Arch Dis Child* 2005; **90**(2): 182–6.
55. Carpenter R. The prevalence and distribution of bruising in babies. *Arch Dis Child* 1999; **80**(4): 363–6.
56. Pierce MC, Smith S, Kaczor K. Bruising in infants: Those with a bruise may be abused. *Pediatr Emerg Care* 2009; **25**(12): 845–7.
57. Kaczor K, Pierce MC, Makoroff K, Corey TS. Bruising and physical child abuse. *Clin Pediatr Emerg Med* 2006; 7(3): 153–60.
58. Pierce MC, Kaczor K, Lorenz DJ, et al. Validation of a clinical decision rule to predict abuse in young children based on bruising characteristics. *JAMA Netw Open* 2021; **4**(4): e215832.
59. Kemp AM, Maguire SA, Nuttall DE, et al. Can TEN4 distinguish bruises from abuse, inherited bleeding disorders or accidents? *Arch Dis Child* 2021; **106**(8): 774.
60. Kos L, Shwayder T. Cutaneous manifestations of child abuse. *Pediatr Dermatol* 2006; **23**(4): 311–20.
61. Tsokos M. Diagnostic criteria for cutaneous injuries in child abuse: Classification, findings, and interpretation. *Forensic Sci Med Pathol* 2015; **11**(2): 235–42.
62. Maguire S, Mann MK, Sibert J, Kemp A. Can you age bruises accurately in children? A systematic review. *Arch Dis Child* 2005; **90**(2): 187–9.
63. Stephenson T. Ageing of bruising in children. *J R Soc Med* 1997; **90**(6): 312–14.
64. Langlois NEI, Gresham GA. The ageing of bruises: A review and study of the colour changes with time. *Forensic Sci Int* 1991; **50**(2): 227–38.
65. Munang L, Leonard P, Mok J. Lack of agreement on colour description between clinicians examining childhood bruising. *J Clin Forensic Med* 2002; **9**(4): 171–4.
66. Hughes VK, Ellis PS, Langlois NEI. The perception of yellow in bruises. *J Clin Forensic Med* 2004; **11**(5): 257–9.
67. Byard RW, Langlois NEI. Bruises: Is it a case of "the more we know, the less we understand?". *Forensic Sci Med Pathol* 2015; **11**(4): 479–81.
68. Sirakova MA, Debelle G. Identifying human bite marks in children. *Paediatr Child Health* 2014; **24**(12): 550–6.
69. Kemp A, Maguire SA, Sibert J, et al. Can we identify abusive bites on children? *Arch Dis Child* 2006; **91**(11): 951.
70. Garrard J, Leland N, Smith DK. Epidemiology of human bites to children in a day-care center. *Am J Dis Child* 1988; **142**(6): 643–50.
71. Kemp AM, Jones S, Lawson Z, Maguire SA. Patterns of burns and scalds in children. *Arch Dis Child* 2014; **99**(4): 316.
72. Pawlik M-C, Kemp A, Maguire S, et al. Children with burns referred for child abuse evaluation: Burn characteristics and co-existent injuries. *Child Abuse Negl* 2016; **55**: 52–61.
73. Chester DL, Jose RM, Aldlyami E, et al. Non-accidental burns in children—Are we neglecting neglect? *Burns* 2006; **32**(2): 222–8.
74. RCPCH. Burns: Systematic review, 2021. Available from: https://childprotection.rcpch.ac.uk/child-protection-evidence/burns-systematic-review/ (Accessed 19 May 2023).
75. Mullen S, Begley R, Roberts Z, Kemp AM. Fifteen-minute consultation: Childhood burns: Inflicted, neglect or accidental. *Arch Dis Child* 2019; **104**(2): 74.
76. Daria S, Sugar NF, Feldman KW, et al. Into hot water head first: Distribution of intentional and unintentional immersion burns. *Pediatr Emerg Care* 2004; **20**(5): 302–10.
77. Allasio D, Fischer H. Immersion scald burns and the ability of young children to climb into a bathtub. *Pediatr* 2005; **115**(5): 1419–21.
78. Davies M, Maguire S, Okolie C, et al. How much do parents know about first aid for burns? *Burns* 2013; **39**(6): 1083–90.
79. Kemp AM, Maguire SA, Lumb RC, et al. Contact, cigarette and flame burns in physical abuse: A systematic review. *Child Abuse Rev* 2014; **23**(1): 35–47.
80. Faller-Marquardt M, Pollak S, Schmidt U. Cigarette burns in forensic medicine. *Forensic Sci Int* 2008; **176**(2): 200–8.
81. Hicks RA, Stolfi A. Skeletal surveys in children with burns caused by child abuse. *Pediatr Emerg Care* 2007; **23**(5): 308–13.
82. Hollen L, Bennett V, Nuttall D, et al. Evaluation of the efficacy and impact of a clinical prediction tool to identify maltreatment associated with children's burns. *BMJ Paediatr Open* 2021; **5**(1): e000796.
83. Kleinman PK. *Diagnostic Imaging of Child Abuse*. Cambridge: Cambridge University Press; 2015.
84. Walker A, Kepron C, Milroy CM. Are there hallmarks of child abuse? I. Osseous injuries. *Acad Forensic Pathol* 2016; 6(4): 568–90.
85. Bilo R, Robber S, van Rijn R. *Forensic Aspects of Paediatric Fractures*. Berlin: Springer; 2010.
86. Marine MB, Forbes-Amrhein MM. Fractures of child abuse. *Pediatr Radiol* 2021; **51**(6): 1003–13.
87. RCPCH. Fractures: Systematic review, 2020. Available from: https://childprotection.rcpch.ac.uk/child-protection-evidence/fractures-systematic-review/ (Accessed 19 May 2023).
88. Kleinman PK, Marks SC, Blackbourne B. The metaphyseal lesion in abused infants: A radiologic-histopathologic study. *AJR Am J Roentgenol* 1986; **146**(5): 895–905.
89. Ayoub DM, Hyman C, Cohen M, Miller M. A critical review of the classic metaphyseal lesion: Traumatic or metabolic? *AJR Am J Roentgenol* 2014; **202**(1): 185–96.
90. Flaherty EG, Perez-Rossello JM, Levine MA, et al. Evaluating children with fractures for child physical abuse. *Pediatrics* 2014; **133**(2): e477–e89.
91. Jenny C. Evaluating infants and young children with multiple fractures. *Pediatrics* 2006; **118**(3): 1299–303.
92. Marine MB, Hibbard RA, Jennings SG, Karmazyn B. Ultrasound findings in classic metaphyseal lesions: emphasis on the metaphyseal bone collar and zone of provisional calcification. *Pediatr Radiol* 2019; **49**(7): 913–21.
93. Mandelstam SA, Cook D, Fitzgerald M, Ditchfield MR. Complementary use of radiological skeletal survey and bone scintigraphy in detection of bony injuries in suspected child abuse. *Arch Dis Child* 2003; **88**(5): 387.
94. Bainbridge JK, Huey BM, Harrison SK. Should bone scintigraphy be used as a routine adjunct to skeletal survey in the imaging of non-accidental injury? A 10 year review of reports in a single centre. *Clin Radiol* 2015; **70**(8): e83–e9.
95. Drubach LA, Johnston PR, Newton AW, et al. Skeletal trauma in child abuse: Detection with 18F-NaF PET. *Radiology* 2010; **255**(1): 173–81.
96. Perez-Rossello JM, Connolly SA, Newton AW, et al. Whole-body MRI in suspected infant abuse. *AJR Am J Roentgenol* 2010; **195**(3): 744–50.
97. Lawson M, Tully J, Ditchfield M, et al. Using computed tomography skeletal surveys to evaluate for occult bony injury in suspected non-accidental injury cases - A preliminary experience. *J Med Imaging Radiat Oncol* 2021; **66**(1): 41–8.
98. Adamsbaum C, De Boissieu P, Teglas JP, Rey-Salmon C. Classic metaphyseal lesions among victims of abuse. *J Pediatr* 2019; **209**: 154–9.
99. Thackeray JD, Wannemacher J, Adler BH, Lindberg DM. The classic metaphyseal lesion and traumatic injury. *Pediatr Radiol* 2016; **46**(8): 1128–33.
100. Eide P, Djuve Å, Myklebust R, et al. Prevalence of metaphyseal injury and its mimickers in otherwise healthy children under two years of age. *Pediatr Radiol* 2019; **49**(8): 1051–5.
101. Paterson CR. Temporary brittle bone disease: The current position. *Arch Dis Child* 2011; **96**(9): 901.
102. Miller ME, Hangartner TN. Temporary brittle bone disease: Association with decreased fetal movement and osteopenia. *Calcif Tissue Int* 1999; **64**(2): 137–43.
103. Pfeifer CM, Henry MK, Caré MM, et al. Debunking fringe beliefs in child abuse imaging: AJR expert panel narrative review. *Am J Roentgenol* 2021; **217**(3): 529–40.
104. Schilling S, Wood JN, Levine MA, et al. Vitamin D status in abused and nonabused children younger than 2 years old with fractures. *Pediatrics* 2011; **127**(5): 835–41.
105. Aldana Sierra MC, Christian CW. Vitamin D, rickets and child abuse: Controversies and evidence. *Pediatr Radiol* 2021; **51**(6): 1014–22.
106. Servaes S, States L, Wood J, et al. Rachitic change and vitamin D status in young children with fractures. *Skeletal Radiol* 2020; **49**(1): 85–91.
107. Holick MF, Hossein-Nezhad A, Tabatabaei F. Multiple fractures in infants who have Ehlers-Danlos/hypermobility syndrome and or vitamin D deficiency: A case series of 72 infants whose parents were accused of child abuse and neglect. *Dermatoendocrinol* 2017; **9**(1): e1279768.
108. Rolfes MC, Deyle DR, King KS, et al. Fracture incidence in Ehlers-Danlos syndrome - A population-based case-control study. *Child Abuse Negl* 2019; **91**: 95–101.
109. George MP, Shur NE, Peréz-Rosselló JM. Ehlers-Danlos syndrome: What the radiologist needs to know. *Pediatr Radiol* 2021; **51**(6): 1023–8.
110. Basalom S, Rauch F. Bone disease in patients with Ehlers-Danlos Syndromes.

Curr Osteoporos Rep 2020; **18**(2): 95–102.
111. Shur NE, Summerlin ML, McIntosh BJ, et al. Genetic causes of fractures and subdural hematomas: Fact versus fiction. *Pediatr Radiol* 2021; **51**(6): 1029–43.
112. Shur N. A case of broken bones and systems: The threat of irresponsible testimony. *Am J Med Genet A* 2019; **179**(3): 429–34.
113. Shur N, Tinkle B, Summar M, et al. Response to letter, broken bones, and irresponsible testimony: Enough is enough already: The flawed Ehlers-Danlos syndrome infant fragility theory should not rule. *Am J Med Genet A* 2019; **179**(12): 2335–7.
114. Paterson CR. Broken bones and irresponsible testimony? *Am J Med Genet A* 2019; **179**(12): 2333–4.
115. Canter J, Rao VB, Palusci VJ, et al. Interpreting osteogenesis imperfecta variants of uncertain significance in the context of physical abuse: A case series. *J Pediatr Genet* 2019; **8**(2): 63–8.
116. Pepin MG, Byers PH. What every clinical geneticist should know about testing for osteogenesis imperfecta in suspected child abuse cases. *Am J Med Genet C Semin Med Genet* 2015; **169**(4): 307–13.
117. Paine CW, Fakeye O, Christian CW, Wood JN. Prevalence of abuse among young children with rib fractures: A systematic review. *Pediatr Emerg Care* 2019; **35**(2): 96–103.
118. Fassier A, Gaucherand P, Kohler R. Fractures in children younger than 18 months. *Orthop Traumatol Surg Res* 2013; **99(1 Suppl)**: S160–S70.
119. Högberg U, Fellman V, Thiblin I, et al. Difficult birth is the main contributor to birth-related fracture and accidents to other neonatal fractures. *Acta Paediatr* 2020; **109**(10): 2040–8.
120. van Rijn RR, Bilo RA, Robben SG. Birth-related mid-posterior rib fractures in neonates: A report of three cases (and a possible fourth case) and a review of the literature. *Pediatr Radiol* 2009; **39**(1): 30–4.
121. Burrows P, Trefan L, Houston R, et al. Head injury from falls in children younger than 6 years of age. *Arch Dis Child* 2015; **100**(11): 1032–7.
122. Ibrahim NG, Wood J, Margulies SS, Christian CW. Influence of age and fall type on head injuries in infants and toddlers. *Int J Dev Neurosci* 2012; **30**(3): 201–6.
123. Hajiaghamemar M, Lan IS, Christian CW, et al. Infant skull fracture risk for low height falls. *Int J Legal Med* 2019; **133**(3): 847–62.
124. Metz JB, Otjen JP, Perez FA, et al. Are complex skull fractures indicative of either child abuse or major trauma in the era of 3-dimensional computed tomography imaging? *Pediatr Emerg Care* 2022; **38**(1): e200–e4.
125. Harper NS, Eddleman S, Shukla K, et al. Radiologic assessment of skull fracture healing in young children. *Pediatr Emerg Care* 2021; **37**(4): 213–17.
126. Metz JB, Otjen JP, Perez FA, et al. Fracture-associated bruising and soft tissue swelling in young children with skull fractures: How sensitive are they to fracture presence? *Pediatr Emerg Care* 2021; **37**(12): e1392–e6.
127. Messer DL, Adler BH, Brink FW, et al. Radiographic timelines for pediatric healing fractures: A systematic review. *Pediatr Radiol* 2020; **50**(8): 1041–8.
128. Karmazyn B, Marine MB, Wanner MR, et al. Establishing signs for acute and healing phases of distal tibial classic metaphyseal lesions. *Pediatr Radiol* 2020; **50**(5): 715–25.
129. Sheybani EF, Gonzalez-Araiza G, Kousari YM, et al. Pediatric nonaccidental abdominal trauma: What the radiologist should know. *Radiographics* 2014; **34**(1): 139–53.
130. Maguire SA, Upadhyaya M, Evans A, et al. A systematic review of abusive visceral injuries in childhood--their range and recognition. *Child Abuse Negl* 2013; **37**(7): 430–45.
131. RCPCH. Visceral injuries: Systematic review, 2018. Available from: https://childprotection.rcpch.ac.uk/child-protection-evidence/visceral-injuries-systematic-review/ (Accessed 19 May 2023).
132. Henry MK, Bennett CE, Wood JN, Servaes S. Evaluation of the abdomen in the setting of suspected child abuse. *Pediatr Radiol* 2021; **51**(6): 1044–50.
133. Scaife ER, Rollins MD, Barnhart DC, et al. The role of focused abdominal sonography for trauma (FAST) in pediatric trauma evaluation. *J Pediatr Surg* 2013; **48**(6): 1377–83.
134. Parks SE AJ, Hill HA, Karch DL. *Pediatric Abusive Head Trauma Recommended Definitions for Public Health Surveillance and Research*. Atlanta: National Center for Injury Prevention and Control; 2012.
135. Hung K-L. Pediatric abusive head trauma. *Biomed J* 2020; **43**(3): 240–50.
136. Hymel KP, Armijo-Garcia V, Musick M, et al. A cluster randomized trial to reduce missed abusive head trauma in pediatric intensive care settings. *J Pediatr* 2021; **236**: 260–8.
137. Berger RP, Fromkin J, Herman B, et al. Validation of the Pittsburgh infant brain injury score for abusive head trauma. *Pediatrics* 2016; **138**(1): e20153756.
138. Pfeiffer H, Cowley L, Kemp A, et al. Validation of the PredAHT-2 prediction tool for abusive head trauma. *Emerg Med J* 2020; **37**(3): 119–26.
139. Boos SC, Wang M, Karst WA, Hymel KP. Traumatic head injury and the diagnosis of abuse: A cluster analysis. *Pediatrics* 2022; **149**(1): e2021051742.
140. Jenny C. Analysis of missed cases of abusive head trauma. *JAMA* 1999; **281**(7): 621.
141. Laurent-Vannier A, Bernard JY, Chevignard M. High frequency of previous abuse and missed diagnoses prior to abusive head trauma: A consecutive case series of 100 forensic examinations. *Child Abuse Rev* 2020; **29**(3): 231–41.
142. Sirmai N, Garside L, Tzioumi D. Abusive head trauma in infants: Incidence and detection of prior brain injury. *Child Abuse Rev* 2020; **29**(3): 242–52.
143. RCPCH. Head and spinal injuries: Systematic review, 2019. Available from: https://childprotection.rcpch.ac.uk/child-protection-evidence/head-and-spinal-injuries-systematic-review/ (Accessed 19 May 2023).
144. Sidpra J, Chhabda S, Oates AJ, et al. Abusive head trauma: Neuroimaging mimics and diagnostic complexities. *Pediatr Radiol* 2021; **51**(6): 947–65.
145. Metz JB, Otjen JP, Perez FA, et al. Fracture-associated bruising and soft tissue swelling in young children with skull fractures: How sensitive are they to fracture presence? *Pediatr Emerg Care* 2021; **37**(12): e1392–e6.
146. Melhem N, Abrahamson E. Delayed onset of subgaleal haematomas associated with skull fracture following accidental head trauma. *Emerg Med J* 2013; 30: 877.
147. Stephan AM, Feldman KW, Otjen JP, Metz JB. Delayed subaponeurotic fluid collections: A benign cause of scalp swelling in infancy. *Pediatr Emerg Care* 2021; **37**(7): e408–e11.
148. Wang S, Drake J, Kulkarni AV. Management and outcome of spontaneous subaponeurotic fluid collections in infants: The Hospital for Sick Children experience and review of the literature. *J Neurosurg Pediatr* 2016; **18**(4): 442–7.
149. Edmondson SJ, Ramman S, Hachach-Haram N, et al. Hair today; scalped tomorrow: Massive subgaleal haematoma following sudden hair pulling in an adolescent in the absence of haematological abnormality or skull fracture. *J Craniofac Surg* 2016; **27**(5): 1261–2.
150. Onyeama CO, Lotke M, Edelstein B. Subgaleal hematoma secondary to hair braiding in a 31-month-old child. *Pediatr Emerg Care* 2009; **25**(1): 40–1.
151. Wiersema JM, Love JC, Derrick SM, et al. Standardized descriptive method for the anthropological evaluation of pediatric skull fractures. *J Forensic Sci* 2014; **59**(6): 1487–92.
152. Sidpra J, Jeelani NuO, Ong J, et al. Skull fractures in abusive head trauma: A single centre experience and review of the literature. *Childs Nerv Syst* 2021; **37**(3): 919–29.
153. Gurdjian ES, Webster JE, Lissner HR. The mechanism of skull fracture. *Radiology* 1950; **54**(3): 313–39.
154. Weber W. [Biomechanical fragility of the infant skull]. *Z Rechtsmed* 1985; **94**(2): 93–101.
155. Fingarson AK, Ryan M, Charleston E, Lorenz D. Single parietal skull fractures versus occipital fractures and multiple fractures in infants: Are there differences in history, findings, and determination of abuse? *Pediatrics* 2020; **146**(1): 2–3.
156. Harper NS, Eddleman S, Shukla K, et al. Radiologic assessment of skull fracture healing in young children. *Pediatr Emerg Care* 2021; **37**(4): 213–17.
157. Baş NS, Karacan M, Doruk E, Karagoz Guzey F. Management of traumatic epidural hematoma in infants younger than one year: 50 cases - single center experience. *Pediatr Neurosurg* 2021; **56**(3): 213–20.
158. Wittschieber D, Karger B, Pfeiffer H, Hahnemann ML. Understanding subdural collections in pediatric abusive head trauma. *Am J Neuroradiol* 2019; **40**(3): 388.
159. Cheshire EC, Malcomson RDG, Sun P, et al. A systematic autopsy survey of human infant bridging veins. *Int J Leg Med* 2018; **132**(2): 449–61.
160. Vinchon M, Defoort-Dhellemmes S, Desurmont M, Dhellemmes P. Accidental and nonaccidental head injuries in infants: A prospective study. *J Neurosurg* 2005; **102(4 Suppl)**: 380–4.
161. Hymel KP, Jenny C, Block RW. Intracranial hemorrhage and rebleeding in suspected victims of abusive head trauma:

Addressing the forensic controversies. *Child Maltreat* 2002; 7(4): 329–48.

162. Rooks VJ, Eaton JP, Ruess L, et al. Prevalence and evolution of intracranial hemorrhage in asymptomatic term infants. *Am J Neuroradiol* 2008; **29(6)**: 1082–9.
163. Nikam RM, Kandula VV, Yue X, et al. Birth-related subdural hemorrhage: Prevalence and imaging morphology. *Pediatr Radiol* 2021; **51(6)**: 939–46.
164. Wright JN, Feyma TJ, Ishak GE, et al. Subdural hemorrhage rebleeding in abused children: Frequency, associations and clinical presentation. *Pediatr Radiol* 2019; **49(13)**: 1762–72.
165. Squier W. The "Shaken Baby" syndrome: Pathology and mechanisms. *Acta Neuropathol* 2011; **122(5)**: 519–42.
166. Mankad K, Chhabda S, Lim W, et al. The neuroimaging mimics of abusive head trauma. *Eur J Paediatr Neurol* 2019; **23(1)**: 19–30.
167. Fiester P, Rao D, Andreou S, et al. Pediatric retroclival epidural hematoma in the acute trauma setting: A sign of tectorial membrane stripping injury. *AJR Am J Roentgenol* 2021; **216(6)**: 1641–8.
168. Gunda D, Cornwell BO, Dahmoush HM, et al. Pediatric central nervous system imaging of nonaccidental trauma: Beyond subdural hematomas. *Radiographics* 2019; **39(1)**: 213–28.
169. Caré MM. Macrocephaly and subdural collections. *Pediatr Radiol* 2021; **51(6)**: 891–7.
170. Tucker J, Choudhary AK, Piatt J. Macrocephaly in infancy: Benign enlargement of the subarachnoid spaces and subdural collections. *J Neurosurg Pediatr* 2016; **18(1)**: 16–20.
171. Adamsbaum C. Letter to the editor: Subdural collections and abusive head trauma. *J Neurosurg Pediatr* 2017; **19(5)**: 625.
172. Oates AJ, Sidpra J, Mankad K. Parenchymal brain injuries in abusive head trauma. *Pediatr Radiol* 2021; **51(6)**: 898–910.
173. Choudhary AK, Ishak R, Zacharia TT, Dias MS. Imaging of spinal injury in abusive head trauma: A retrospective study. *Pediatr Radiol* 2014; **44(9)**: 1130–40.
174. Garcia-Pires F, Jayappa S, Desai S, et al. Spinal subdural hemorrhage in abusive head trauma: A pictorial review. *Pediatr Radiol* 2021; **51(6)**: 980–90.
175. Rabbitt AL, Kelly TG, Yan K, et al. Characteristics associated with spine injury on magnetic resonance imaging in children evaluated for abusive head trauma. *Pediatr Radiol* 2020; **50(1)**: 83–97.
176. Christian CW, Levin AV. The eye examination in the evaluation of child abuse. *Pediatrics* 2018; **142(2)**: e20181411.
177. Binenbaum G, Forbes BJ. The eye in child abuse: Key points on retinal hemorrhages and abusive head trauma. *Pediatr Radiol* 2014; **44(S4)**: 571–7.
178. Levin AV. Retinal hemorrhage in abusive head trauma. *Pediatrics* 2010; **126(5)**: 961–70.
179. Binenbaum G, Chen W, Huang J, et al. The natural history of retinal hemorrhage in pediatric head trauma. *J AAPOS* 2016; **20(2)**: 131–5.
180. Atkinson N, van Rijn RR, Starling SP. Childhood falls with occipital impacts. *Pediatr Emerg Care* 2018; **34(12)**: 837–41.
181. Cho IH, Kim MS, Heo NH, Kim SY. Birth-related retinal hemorrhages: The Soonchunhyang University Cheonan Hospital universal newborn eye screening (SUCH-NES) study. *PLOS ONE* 2021; **16(11)**: e0259378.
182. World Health Organization. Report of the consultation on child abuse prevention, 1999. Available from: https://apps.who.int/iris/handle/10665/65900 (Accessed 19 May 2023).
183. Mathews B, Collin-Vézina D. Child sexual abuse: Toward a conceptual model and definition. *Trauma Violence Abuse* 2019; **20(2)**: 131–48.
184. Fedina L, Williamson C, Perdue T. Risk factors for domestic child sex trafficking in the United States. *J Interpers Violence* 2019; **34(13)**: 2653–73.
185. Greenbaum VJ, Dodd M, McCracken C. A short screening tool to identify victims of child sex trafficking in the health care setting. *Pediatr Emerg Care* 2018; **34(1)**: 33–7.
186. Bath EP, Godoy SM, Morris TC, et al. A specialty court for U.S. youth impacted by commercial sexual exploitation. *Child Abuse Negl* 2020; **100**: 104041.
187. Hampton MD, Lieggi M. Commercial sexual exploitation of youth in the United States: A qualitative systematic review. *Trauma Violence Abuse* 2020; **21(1)**: 57–70.
188. Winters GM, Jeglic EL. Stages of sexual grooming: Recognizing potentially predatory behaviors of child molesters. *Deviant Behav* 2017; **38(6)**: 724–33.
189. Mitchell KJ, Jones LM, Finkelhor D, Wolak J. Internet-facilitated commercial sexual exploitation of children: Findings from a nationally representative sample of law enforcement agencies in the United States. *Sex Abuse* 2011; **23(1)**: 43–71.
190. Rowse J, Mullane S, Bolt C, Gaya S, Tully J. Swipe right: The emergence of technology facilitated sexual assault in children and adults. *Pathology* 2021; **53**: S8.
191. Dewinter J, Vermeiren R, Vanwesenbeeck I, van Nieuwenhuizen C. Autism and normative sexual development: A narrative review. *J Clin Nurs* 2013; **22(23–24)**: 3467–83.
192. Mallants C, Casteels K. Practical approach to childhood masturbation--a review. *Eur J Pediatr* 2008; **167(10)**: 1111–7.
193. Araji SK. Preadolescents and Adolescents: Evaluating Normative and Non-normative Sexual Behaviours and Development. In: O'Reilly G, Marshall WL, Carr A, Beckett RC (eds), *The Handbook of Clinical Intervention with Young People who Sexually Abuse*. New York: Psychology Press; 2004, pp. 19–51.
194. Larsson I. Differences and similarities in sexual behaviour among pre-schoolers in Sweden and USA. *Nord J Psychiatry* 2000; **54(4)**: 251–7.
195. Allen B. Children with sexual behavior problems: Clinical characteristics and relationship to child maltreatment. *Child Psychiatry Hum Dev* 2017; **48(2)**: 189–99.
196. Vrolijk-Bosschaart TF, Verlinden E, Langendam MW, et al. The diagnostic utility of the child sexual behavior inventory for sexual abuse: a systematic review. *J Child Sex Abus* 2018; **27(7)**: 729–51.
197. Finkelhor D. *Sexually Victimized Children*. London: Simon and Schuster; 2010.
198. Adams JA, Farst KJ, Kellogg ND. Interpretation of medical findings in suspected child sexual abuse: An update for 2018. *J Pediatr Adolesc Gynecol* 2018; **31(3)**: 225–31.
199. Finkel MA, Giardino AP (eds). *Medical Evaluation of Child Sexual Abuse: A Practical Guide*, 4th ed. Itasca, Ill: American Academy of Pediatrics; 2019.
200. APSAC. Practice guidelines. Munchausen by proxy: clinical and case management guidance, 2017. Available from: https://docs.wixstatic.com/ugd/4700a8_3a615184374e4210b739f7b75721b567.pdf (Accessed 19 May 2023).
201. Tully J, Hopkins O, Smith A, Williams K. Fabricated or induced illness in children: A guide for Australian health-care practitioners. *J Paediatr Child Health* 2021; **57(12)**: 1847–52.
202. Yates G, Bass C. The perpetrators of medical child abuse (Munchausen Syndrome by Proxy) - A systematic review of 796 cases. *Child Abuse Negl* 2017; **72**: 45–53.
203. Bursch B, Emerson ND, Sanders MJ. Evaluation and management of factitious disorder imposed on another. *J Clin Psychol Med Settings* 2021; **28(1)**: 67–77.
204. Flaherty EG, Macmillan HL, Christian CW, et al. Caregiver-fabricated illness in a child: A manifestation of child maltreatment. *Pediatrics* 2013; **132(3)**: 590–7.
205. Mulder TM, Kuiper KC, Van Der Put CE, et al. Risk factors for child neglect: A meta-analytic review. *Child Abuse Negl* 2018; 77: 198–210.
206. Stoltenborgh M, Bakermans-Kranenburg MJ, Van Ijzendoorn MH. The neglect of child neglect: A meta-analytic review of the prevalence of neglect. *Soc Psychiatry Psychiatr Epidemiol* 2013; **48(3)**: 345–55.
207. Keeshin BR, Dubowitz H. Childhood neglect: The role of the paediatrician. *Paediatr Child Health* 2013; **18(8)**: e39–e43.
208. Assink M, Spruit A, Schuts M, et al. The intergenerational transmission of child maltreatment: A three-level meta-analysis. *Child Abuse Negl* 2018; **84**: 131–45.
209. Herrero-Roldán S, León I, Hernández-Cabrera JA, Rodrigo MJ. Improving early diagnosis of child neglect for a better response in healthcare settings. *Children* 2021; **8(10)**: 859.
210. Brassard MR, Hart SN, Glaser D. Psychological maltreatment: An international challenge to children's safety and well being. *Child Abuse Negl* 2020; **110**: 104611.
211. Baker AJL, Brassard MR, Rosenzweig J. Psychological maltreatment: Definition and reporting barriers among American professionals in the field of child abuse. *Child Abuse Negl* 2021; **114**: 104941.
212. Harvard.University. Center on the developing child. Neglect, 2022. Available from: https://developingchild.harvard.edu/science/deep-dives/neglect/# (Accessed 19 May 2023).
213. Shonkoff JP, Slopen N, Williams DR. Early childhood adversity, toxic stress, and the impacts of racism on the foundations of health. *Ann Rev Public Health* 2021; **42(1)**: 115–34.

CHAPTER

74

The Istanbul Protocol

Juliet Cohen

INTRODUCTION

The Istanbul Protocol (IP) is the *United Nations Manual on the Effective Investigation and Documentation of Torture and Other Cruel, Inhuman or Degrading Treatment or Punishment*, published by the Office of the UN High Commissioner for Human Rights (1). It was first produced in 1999, after more than three years of analysis, research and drafting by over 75 experts in law, health and human rights from around the world "to serve as international guidelines for the assessment of persons who allege torture or ill-treatment, for investigating cases of alleged torture and for reporting findings to the judiciary or any other investigative body." The "Istanbul Principles" in Annexe I of the document outline the minimum standards for States to follow in order to ensure the effective documentation of torture. The aim is for legal professionals and clinicians to understand how to gather and present symptoms and signs of torture that may serve as valid evidence in court. A second edition has been published in 2022 with updates in international law and the diagnostic reference criteria, as well as enhanced clinical content incorporating accumulated learning from practice. There are additional sections on investigation and documentation of torture of children and of LGBTI persons, on the role of healthcare professionals in documentation of torture in different contexts and on the required conditions for States' implementation of the IP.

INTERNATIONAL STANDING

The IP has been endorsed by the United Nations as guidance for how physical and psychological evidence of torture can be gathered and presented for any justice system.

While the IP is a non-binding document, international law obliges governments to investigate and document incidents of torture and other forms of ill-treatment and to punish those responsible in a prompt and impartial manner. The IP is a tool for doing so, and the UN Commission on Human Rights/ Human Rights Council (resolution of April 2003) (2) have strongly encouraged States to reflect upon the Principles in the IP in its Guidelines to EU Policy toward Third Countries on Torture and Other Cruel, Inhuman or Degrading Treatment or Punishment adopted by the General Affairs Council in 2001 (3). The EU guidelines mention that States should "establish and operate effective domestic procedures for responding to and investigating complaints and reports of torture and ill-treatment un accordance with the Istanbul Rules". The European Union Agency for Asylum (EUAA) recognizes the importance of the IP in the training and guidance it produces for immigration services in all Member States (4).

The central importance of the IP has been recognized in the field of asylum decision-making in the UK by the Home Office in their document *Medical Evidence in Asylum Claims* (5), and the courts (6). The Irish International Protection Appeals Tribunal (2017) recognizes the IP, stating at 5.1: "*The Tribunal expects all medico-legal reports in cases of alleged torture or ill-treatment to be carried out in accordance with the standards set down in the Istanbul Protocol.*" At 6.4, the document acknowledges that the report may also "*have a role as part of the credibility assessment.*"

The Supreme Court in its 2019 judgment on a Sri Lankan asylum seeker (7) recognized the importance of the IP in assessing evidence of torture "*In their difficult task of analyzing whether scars are the result of torture, decision-makers can legitimately receive assistance from medical experts who feel able to offer an opinion about the consistency of their findings with the asylum-seeker's account about the circumstances in which the scarring was sustained, not limited to the mechanism by which it was sustained.*"

IMPORTANCE FOR FORENSIC PRACTITIONERS

There are two key reasons that forensic practitioners can benefit from knowledge of the IP. The first is that forensic practitioners, who may come from a wide variety of professional backgrounds, may encounter torture survivors in their daily work. Victims of torture may be found in all places of detention including psychiatric institutes, immigration removal centers, prisons and police stations. Victims of torture may be British citizens who have suffered torture overseas, or asylum seekers and refugees.

DOI: 10.1201/9781003138754-77

It is likely that over 30 percent of asylum seekers have been torture victims (8), and a US meta-analysis suggests 44 percent of refugees have suffered torture (9).

All doctors have a duty to report torture (1,10), both where there is a risk that the individual may face further torture and to enable the individual to exercise their right to rehabilitation (11). Two new chapters in the 2022 edition of the IP set out the State's obligations to implement the IP and train health professionals, including those working in non-legal contexts, in how to fulfill their obligations to identify and document torture. This applies to those working with detainees in police custody, prison and immigration detention as well as other healthcare contexts.

The second reason for forensic practitioners to be aware of the IP is that it contains a wealth of general guidance on the holistic assessment of vulnerable persons who have suffered physical and psychological harm, and on how to give an objective and impartial opinion on the consistency of the allegations with the clinical findings made. Asylum decision makers in the UK are very familiar with the IP and, for example, its paragraphs 379–381 where a hierarchy of consistency of physical evidence is set out. This is shown in Table 74.1.

These consistency levels are now often used within the criminal setting. Asylum decision makers in the UK have come to expect medicolegal reports before them to utilize the IP guidance and refer to it, to the extent that reports not doing so may risk being given less evidential weight. The IP was referenced in recent key judgments such as *KV (Sri Lanka) v Secretary of State for the Home Department* [2019] UKSC 10 and *MN v The Secretary of State for the Home Department [2020] EWCA Civ 1746* both of which discuss the physician's role in assessing consistency of clinical findings with the person's account without straying into the decision maker's territory of overall credibility assessment.

In some circumstances, perhaps all that is required of the forensic practitioner is to confirm the presence and nature of an injury, for example, to determine if it is a burn or some other type of injury, but often the forensic practitioner has to provide additional assistance to the court or tribunal. This will include providing opinion not simply on injury classification but also to the *mode* of injury. How could this person sustain this particular injury? Is it from an assault, from an accident, from self-injury, or a medical or quasi-medical process? Is the person's account in keeping with the clinical findings? There has been some debate as to where the boundary lies between the role of the medical expert in this consideration, and that of the judge. It is accepted that the judge is the arbiter of the witness' credibility and matters of fact, but the medical expert can inform this decision because they have clinical knowledge, experience and expertise that a non-clinician lacks. The Supreme Court's decision on KV (7) was that it was not sufficient for the clinician to limit their opinion as to whether or not the scars identified were likely to be burns; their opinion was also required as to how a person could come by such particular burns on their arm and back.

In recent years, some forensic scientists adhering to Bayesian principles have asserted that an extremely formalized approach using explicitly quantified likelihood ratios is the only acceptable approach for expert communication to decision makers and have sought to impose this type of Bayesian approach in all forensic disciplines (12). Bayesian principles have utility in circumstances where likelihood ratios are supported by

TABLE 74.1 Levels of consistency used in the Istanbul Protocol (paragraphs 379–381)

379. The Istanbul Principles require clinicians to provide an "interpretation as to the probable relationship of the physical and psychological findings to possible torture or ill-treatment". At a minimum this should include an assessment of the level of consistency between all clinical evaluation findings and the allegations of torture or ill-treatment. If the clinician considers that there are clinical reasons for an inconsistent finding, this should be discussed.
380. The levels of consistency for such correlations are commonly expressed as follows: (a) "Not consistent with": the finding could not have been caused by the alleged torture or ill-treatment; (b) "Consistent with": the finding could have been caused by the alleged torture or ill-treatment, but it is non-specific and there are many other possible causes; (c) "Highly consistent with": the finding could have been caused by the alleged torture or ill-treatment and there are few other possible causes; (d) "Typical of": the finding is usually observed with this type of alleged torture or ill-treatment, but there are other possible causes; (e) "Diagnostic of": the finding could not have been caused in any way other than that described. The level of consistency denoted by "typical of" is not commonly used to assess psychological evidence of torture or ill-treatment as psychological findings tend to depend on individual factors. In addition, the level of consistency denoted by "diagnostic of" is used more frequently in the interpretation of physical evidence of torture or ill-treatment and is rarely used in the interpretation of psychological evidence.
381. Additional guidance on the interpretation of physical and psychological evidence of torture or ill-treatment is further elaborated in Chapters V and VI and Annex IV. While interpretations of physical and psychological evidence have some differences, both evaluations require clinicians to determine the level of consistency between all of the clinical evidence that the clinician has documented and the allegations of torture or ill-treatment. In some cases, the overall evaluation may report a higher level of consistency than each individual clinical finding, especially if there are many clinical findings that, when taken together, confirm the same conclusion. It is important to note that the highest level of consistency of an individual finding often determines the level of consistency for all of the clinical evidence.

validated empirical data such as the prevalence of blood type by race. However, such data do not exist in this field. The IP guidance on interpreting evidence of torture and ill treatment is modeled on the diagnostic process in clinical medicine. In fact, given that the task of diagnosis fits a Bayesian framework so well, some have argued that clinicians are natural Bayesians (13). But in practice, "*clinicians don't calculate a running tally of likelihood ratios as they evaluate patients. Rather, they incorporate each positive finding as 'somewhat more suggestive' of the disease and each negative test as 'somewhat less suggestive' and estimate the pre-test and post-test odds in qualitative rather than quantitative terms*" (13). The integration of prior probability or prevalence of torture based on their clinical experience and expertise about patterns of torture in a specific region is a key part of clinical diagnostics that allows them to estimate the likelihood of the diagnosis given the findings. The IP requires clinicians to consider not only the appearance of a single lesion, but the whole torture account, the pattern of the physical findings, the psychological findings, the person's background and past experiences and current stressors, and what is known of patterns of torture in their region. The use of likelihood ratios, as proposed by Robertson and Berger (14), would convey an unfounded level of precision in clinical interpretations of torture and create a duty for clinicians to disprove baseless alternative hypotheses that states advance to perpetuate and conceal torture practices.

Knowledge and expertise in assessment of the harm suffered, and its impact on the person, is critical in assisting that person to access the medical treatment they need and in properly documenting the harm suffered for any legal process they may be engaged in. While the IP was devised to focus on the investigation and documentation of torture and ill-treatment using the United Nations Convention against Torture and Other Cruel, Inhuman or Degrading Treatment or Punishment definition of torture (15) (Table 74.2), there is considerable clinical overlap in terms of the practical function of the IP with other forms of "physical, psychological sexual or gender-based violence" particularly in relation to the experiences of those seeking asylum (16). Some injuries are unique to specific torture methods and would be very unusual to find in a victim of criminal assault, such as scars from prolonged shackling, but many, especially those as a result of blunt force trauma, will have the same physical characteristics as criminal assault. The psychological impact of torture is linked to the experiences of fear and uncertainty, being powerless, in the control of the authorities and harmed by them, with nowhere to turn for help. The effect of torture methods is also to cause debility, degradation, disorientation, dread, dependency and fear. These effects can also be found in victims of trafficking, labor and sexual exploitation, and there is also some overlap in the effects of domestic and child abuse.

TABLE 74.2 UNCAT definition of torture
"Any act by which severe pain or suffering, whether physical or mental, is intentionally inflicted on a person for such purposes as obtaining from him or a third person information or a confession, punishing him for an act he or a third person has committed or is suspected of having committed, or intimidating or coercing him or a third person, or for any reason based on discrimination of any kind, when such pain or suffering is inflicted by or at the instigation of or with the consent or acquiescence of a public official or other person acting in an official capacity"

KEY PRINCIPLES OF THE ISTANBUL PROTOCOL

There are four key principles that are of great significance in the IP. They address absence of evidence, consideration of other possible causes for findings, the assessment of the potential of fabrication and the importance of the overall evaluation.

Firstly, the aphorism that "*absence of evidence is not evidence of absence*" is applicable to the IP which now states in paras 390–392:

> "390. *It is important to recognize limitations and potential misinterpretation or deliberate misuse of the Istanbul Protocol. While the Istanbul Protocol and its Principles may aid in the discovery of clinical evidence of alleged torture or ill-treatment, the absence of physical and/or psychological evidence of torture or ill-treatment, however, does not mean that it did not take place. Many factors may account for the absence of physical and psychological findings and documenting these factors can be useful in corroborating specific claims of torture or ill-treatment. Unfortunately, in some instances, parties accused of torture or ill-treatment have misinterpreted or deliberately misused the Istanbul Protocol by successfully arguing that they should be exonerated when physical or psychological findings are absent, for example in the absence of diagnostic criteria for PTSD. In such circumstances, misinterpretation or deliberate misuse of the standards enshrined in the Istanbul Protocol to disregard or conceal evidence of torture or ill-treatment may constitute a form of complicity or other forms of responsibility.*
>
> 391. *In such circumstances and in the courts of some countries, misinterpretation or deliberate misuse of such standards is likely to represent efforts by State officials to disregard or conceal evidence of torture or ill-treatment and, in some cases, prosecute individuals for making 'false allegations' against law enforcement officials. The inherent value of the Istanbul Protocol is its capacity to discover clinical evidence that may support specific claims of abuse. It is not a tool to prove that a hypothetical act did not take place.*
>
> 392. *In dismissing evidence of torture or ill-treatment, some courts have also rejected relevant clinical opinions by asserting incorrectly that they are beyond the remit or expertise of the clinician. On*

the contrary, as directed by the Istanbul Principles, all clinicians should always include opinions on the possibility of torture or ill-treatment in their medico-legal evaluations"

Paragraphs 393, 399 and 493 set out in further detail these important principles: that many acts of violence do not leave lasting physical evidence and that not every person who has suffered torture or other serious harm develops a recognized mental illness. Where there are clinical findings that can be linked to the ill-treatment, they provide support to the allegation, but a lack of such findings cannot be taken to indicate such ill-treatment did not occur. This has been specifically recognized in the context of victims of sexual assault, where physical injuries may be short-lived and fully resolved by the time the complainant comes to report the crime but is equally true of other assaults where the main physical injuries from blunt force trauma, for example, are likely to be bruising and abrasions that often resolve fully within days.

Secondly, other possible causes for the clinical findings should be considered and opinion given as to their relative likelihood. This principle is not only found in the IP, but is noted in Immigration Tribunal caselaw such as SA Somalia (6): "*if a (medical report) is to have any corroborative weight at all, it should contain a statement of the doctor's opinion as to consistency, directed to the particular injuries said to have occurred as a result of torture or other ill-treatment relied on as evidence of persecution*" and RT medical reports – causation of scarring (17): "*Where the doctor makes findings that there is a degree of consistency between the injuries/scarring and the appellant's claimed causes which admit of there being other possible causes (whether many, few or unusually few), it is of particular importance that the report specifically examines those to gauge how likely they are, bearing in mind what is known about the individual's life history and experiences.*"

Thirdly, the *assessment of fabrication* of the clinical findings is a routine part of an IP-guided examination – paragraphs 347–348: The physician should always try to identify possible exaggeration of fabrication, but "*keep in mind, however, that such fabrication requires detailed knowledge of physical and psychological evidence of torture that individuals rarely possess. Effective documentation of physical and psychological evidence of torture and ill-treatment requires clinicians to have a capacity to evaluate consistencies and inconsistencies in the report.*" Paragraphs 540–541 discuss the process of interpretation of psychological findings, in terms of their consistency with the alleged report of torture, whether the psychological findings are expected or typical reactions to extreme stress within the cultural and social context of the individual, where the individual is in the course of recovery, the impact of co-existing stressors and of physical conditions. Making the assessment of fabrication demonstrates the clinician's objectivity and impartiality, and their understanding of their duty to the Court.

Fourthly, the *overall evaluation of the clinical findings* is more important than the consistency of any one individual lesion or clinical finding (paragraph 383). The account of torture or other ill-treatment, acute and chronic symptoms relating to the torture and treatment received, together with the person's background, prior experiences and current health, is assessed for consistency with the clinical findings made in the examination (Annex IV of the IP). The overall number, appearance and distribution of physical lesions is important in this assessment. While a single small scar attributed to blunt trauma will likely be non-specific in appearance and will not be given a high consistency rating with an allegation of assault, especially if on a part of the body often injured accidentally, it is the case that 20 or 30 such scars scattered across the body of a person who has no occupational reason for such injuries, and on parts of the body not usually injured accidentally, will be given a much higher consistency rating.

Additional key areas of guidance within the Istanbul Protocol

Medical ethics and forensic practice

Clinicians may have conflicting responsibilities due to the circumstances of their employment, particularly those employed by the police, armed services or prison system. The interests of their employers may be in conflict with the best interest healthcare needs of their patients. The IP guidance paragraph 173 is that "*Whatever the circumstances of their employment, all health professionals have a fundamental duty to act in the best interests of the people they examine and treat. They cannot be obliged by contractual or other considerations to breach their core ethical obligations or compromise their professional independence. They must make an unbiased assessment of the patient's health interests and act accordingly.... In situations in which institutional pressure is brought to bear on a health professional, they should ensure they have mechanisms to resist such pressure, report it to their professional body and escalate their concerns about the health of their patients if their recommendations are not followed.*"

In all cases where health professionals are acting for another party, they have an obligation to ensure this is understood by the patient – they must identify themselves to the patient and explain the purpose of any examination or treatment and seek informed consent for this. In practical terms, this engages the healthcare professional working in, for example, an immigration removal center, where detention is administrative and there are safeguarding processes to protect vulnerable persons from being harmed by the detention itself, such that the practitioner can recommend the patient be released. Healthcare professionals must ensure they retain their independence and act only in their patients' best interests in assessment of vulnerability to harm from continued detention.

Forensic practitioners may have to make other assessments of a patient's vulnerability, for example, to consider if they are unfit for interview, or regarding transfer to a hospital from a police station, and must be guided always by these ethical duties above any institutional pressure from their employers.

Other potential sources of dilemma arising from conflicting obligations are discussed in the IP paragraphs 173–182, including reporting information that may be a breach of confidentiality, respecting patient autonomy and seeking informed consent for assessments required by the authorities.

Working with interpreters

The IP gives guidance on working with interpreters, (paragraphs 219, 296–298) which, in a multicultural society, is an important skill. Many people whose first language is not English may have basic fluency in English but find it difficult to describe emotions or complex events. When the content of the assessment is about highly sensitive experiences such as sexual violence, disclosure may be inhibited by a lack of fluency, but may also be inhibited if the person does not have trust that the interpreter will maintain their confidentiality. This is especially important if they are from the same community – interpreters should be professionals – friends or family members should not be used except in an emergency. The gender of the interpreter may also be important, perhaps more important to the patient than the gender of the clinician, as it is the interpreter to whom they are speaking. People should be asked if they would like an interpreter and if they have a preference for their gender. The clinician should speak directly to the patient, and not speak about the patient to the interpreter. The interpreter should translate exactly what is said and not summarize or edit the response to a question. Rather than have a side-conversation with the patient, they should advise the clinician if the meaning of a question or answer is unclear.

Memory and disclosure

Autobiographical memory is subject to considerable variability and this variability is increased for memories of trauma. More and different details may be recalled in successive accounts, with the omission of other details (18). Survivors of torture and other traumatic experiences may have an overly general memory of the experience, gaps in their memory, or other difficulties in recalling and recounting the specific details of their experiences.

This may be due to:

- Factors of the torture itself, such as drugging, blindfolding or periods of unconsciousness
- Fear of placing themselves or others at risk
- Lack of trust in the interviewer or interpreter
- Psychological impact of the experiences themselves

Anyone who feels they are still vulnerable to further harm from the perpetrator, such as victims of trafficking or of domestic abuse is particularly likely to have fears about disclosing their experiences.

Memory storage and hence retrieval may be impaired due to the high emotional arousal during traumatic experiences, resulting in high cortisol levels and poor or fragmented storage of the memory. Painful emotions such as guilt and shame associated with the memory may further affect recall, increasing "avoidance". Avoidance is a symptom of post-traumatic stress disorder (PTSD) where the person avoids talking about or recalling their traumatic experiences because of the distressing emotions re-experienced each time that they do so. They may even deny the experiences occurred at all. Dissociation can occur during a traumatic event, or as a result of triggers to recalling it, and makes the person cut off or unaware of events. Denial, avoidance and dissociation can all act as conscious or unconscious protective coping mechanisms and the physician needs to build trust and rapport and be cautious in their approach to minimize distress and facilitate the disclosure of such experiences.

Experiences of head trauma or asphyxia may impair the storage of memory at the time of the traumatic events. Later, conditions may develop that further impair recall of trauma memories including PTSD, depression, anxiety, insomnia (18).

Cultural sanctions can also affect disclosure, for example, a person may only feel able to disclose to someone the same gender as them, but it cannot be assumed for example that a man would prefer to disclose sexual violence to a male doctor. They may feel more at ease with a female doctor. Cognitive interview techniques that can assist in facilitating further disclosure are reviewed in the IP paragraphs 338–341.

Assessment of inconsistencies between an account (whether that given to the doctor or in the documents provided to them such as witness statements and interview records), and the clinical findings, needs therefore to bear all of the above factors in mind. There may be important clinical factors that can account for the inconsistencies. Paragraph 347 in the IP states "*...Although the individual may not be able to provide the details desired by the interviewer, such as dates, times, places, frequencies and exact identities of perpetrators, a broad outline of the alleged traumatic events will emerge and stand up over time. In a judicial context, differences in the narrative obtained over time may be interpreted as influencing the credibility assessment; therefore, it is imperative that the testimony presented by the evaluator includes a discussion about how variability and inconsistency should be interpreted.*"

Specifically in relation to disclosure of sexual violence (paragraphs 274–276), it is now recognized that this may be long-delayed, with many victims choosing never to report the crime. For example, UK data show for 2019–2020, fewer than one in six (16%) female victims and fewer than one in five (19%) male victims aged 16 to 59 years of sexual assault by rape or penetration since the age of 16 years reported it to the police (19). There may be clues such as gaps in the narrative or euphemisms such as "they did what they wanted to", or "red flag" symptoms such as compulsive washing of the genitals, unexplained vomiting or uro-genital symptoms, and self-harming behavior. The clinician needs to be mindful of their own responses to the person's distress and disclosure in order that they do not themselves contribute to or collude with a desire for avoidance and non-disclosure. Disclosure may be intensely distressing and raise the person's risk of self-harm or suicide. Victims may fear being blamed or punished if what has happened to them becomes known in their family or community, so risk assessment for both harm to self or from others must be made.

The effect of sexual orientation and gender identity must not be overlooked and is addressed in part in paragraphs 281–282:

"281. *Both victims and perpetrators of torture or ill-treatment can be of any sexual orientation or gender and, though often discussed together, sex, gender and sexual orientation are each different from one another. Sexual orientation refers to inherent emotional, romantic and/or sexual attraction to other people.*

Gender identity refers to how individuals perceive themselves and what they call themselves. Individuals who self-identify with any from a wide and varied spectrum of non-heterosexual orientations are often referred to as lesbian, gay, bisexual, transgender and queer persons. Intersex persons are those who are born with sex characteristics (including genitals, gonads and chromosome patterns) that do not fit typical binary notions of male or female bodies. These individuals, as well as those who find themselves in the process of questioning, exploring or beginning to understand their sexual orientation, are all at increased risk of torture and ill-treatment. In cases in which the alleged victims do not conform to the traditional binary notion of gender (including transgender, intersex and gender non-conforming persons), interviewers should acknowledge the stated gender identity of interviewees and use their preferred name and gender pronouns accordingly (see paras. 599–601 below).

282. *It is important to differentiate between sexual and gender-based torture and abuse. Sexual torture includes verbal, emotional and physical acts of a sexual nature with the intention of producing physical and psychological suffering. In gender-based torture, the gender identity and/or sexual orientation of the persons involved play a key role in the abuse. Both sexual and gender-based torture are reliant on the power dynamics involved and can change based on the social, cultural and religious context. Even if no explicit sexual assault is alleged, many forms of torture have sexual or gendered aspects that must be considered in the evaluation.*"

Paragraph 276 states "*Gender norms are entrenched in most societies and both the victims' own ideas of their sexual orientation and gender identity and the views of the society in which they live may be inextricably bound up in the impact of the sexual violence experience for them and influence disclosure. Sexual violence toward men highlights the victim's vulnerability and powerlessness, challenging and conflicting with their ideas of masculinity. Perceptions of sexuality, procreative ability and gender identity may also be challenged (20). The response of submission or freezing, the association of male rape with homosexual pleasure, and the lack of recognition and services for sexual violence toward men may significantly affect disclosure in men (21). In women, social stigma and concerns about 'losing one's honor' and/or being outcast from the family or community, are often entrenched in societies and influence disclosure. Sexual violence toward homosexual men or women similarly has unique impacts on the victims and distinct challenges regarding disclosure that must be considered and mitigated.*"

Assessment of consistency

In paragraph 379 (see also IP Principles 6b iv and Annex IV, XIII,) "*the Istanbul Protocol Principles require clinicians to provide an 'interpretation as to the probable relationship of the physical and psychological findings to possible torture or ill-treatment.' At a minimum this should include an assessment of the level of consistency between all clinical evaluation findings and the allegations of torture or ill-treatment. If the clinician considers there are clinical reasons for an inconsistent finding, this should be discussed.*" These consistency levels are outlined in Table 74.1.

The Istanbul Principles require the clinician to provide an interpretation as to the possible relationship to torture or ill-treatment of not only physical signs and psychological findings, but also acute and chronic symptoms, diagnostic test results, photographs and prior medical evaluations. Consideration of the correlation of symptoms may be of particular importance when methods of torture or ill-treatment have been used that leave no lasting physical evidence, such as asphyxia, electric shocks, suspension and stress positions.

In correlating the consistency of physical lesions, the physician should consider each individual examination finding with the attribution given, and if there is a finding that one is inconsistent, discuss if there are possible clinical reasons for this. Paragraph 420 states: "*Sometimes a group of similar lesions or lesions with the same attribution can be considered together and a level of consistency applied to the group as a whole. The clinician should consider possible causes of the physical findings as suggested by the evidence, for example, torture or other deliberate harm, accidental injury, skin disease, medical procedures, cultural medical care, ritual scarification, self-harm, and deliberate infliction to fabricate evidence of injury. It is common for there to be attribution of some physical findings on the body to causes other than torture, such as accidental injury, or for there to be physical findings for which the person cannot recall the cause. An individual may innocently mistake a physical finding for torture (e.g. striae distensae on the lower back) because they did not notice it before the alleged torture or ill-treatment but only afterward, when there is pain at the site or it is pointed out by the examining doctor.*"

Accidental injuries should be distinguished as far as possible from those caused deliberately. They are likely to differ in distribution from those caused by assault, being most often found on the parts of the body exposed rather than protected by clothing, and in first contact with the ground or hard surfaces in a fall. The expected number of accidental injuries and their location is also influenced by the person's occupational history. On the face of it, for example, it is not unusual for an individual to have one or two small scars from accidental injuries, but as the number of such lesions increases, so the chance of them all being due to accidents correspondingly decreases.

For some cases, it may also be important to consider self-injury, which may include cutting, burns such as with cigarettes, molten wax, or other heat source, banging the head or punching the wall. Victims of torture may disclose these injuries readily, and may explain that this is in response to, or as a way of coping with, the persisting pain of their torture. Others may find it difficult to disclose self-harming as it is associated with shame and stigma. The most severe injuries may be associated with severe mental health conditions including psychosis. Paragraph 423 of the IP: "*Deliberate injury for secondary gain is rare and such injuries tend to be superficial, of a single mechanism of causation, on accessible body parts and poorly congruent with the history, examination findings and timeline. Signs of injuries in unusual locations and a diffuse spread of injuries all suggest torture, as does the finding of multiple injury types – blunt force injury, sharp force and burn injury. The overall evaluation of all the physical evidence together with the psychological evidence and in the context of the account given is key to the consideration of fabrication.*"

Perhaps the most important principle in the IP is that the interpretation of injury should be a holistic one. This encompasses all of the key guidance that the level of consistency assessment and consideration of the relative likelihood of other possible causes should be made by considering:

- All of the clinical findings, physical and psychological
- Background, history, symptoms acute and chronic, treatment received and recommended
- Clinical reasons for inconsistencies.

CONCLUSION

The IP provides detailed guidance on the investigation and documentation of torture and other ill-treatment, and on the holistic assessment of any vulnerable victim of physical or psychological harm. Assessment of specific levels of consistency, for interpretation of the probable relationship between the physical and psychological findings, assists the practitioner to give an objective and impartial expert opinion on allegations of torture and other ill-treatment. The guidance is critical for forensic practitioners preparing reports for asylum applicants who may be victims of torture, and its value is increasingly recognized in documenting the harm suffered by victims of trafficking, domestic abuse, child abuse and criminal assault.

REFERENCES

1. United Nations Human Rights. Istanbul protocol. Manual on the effective investigation and documentation of torture and other cruel, inhuman or degrading treatment or punishment, 2022. Available from: Istanbul-Protocol_Rev2_EN.pdf (ohchr.org) (Accessed 22 May 2023).
2. UN Commission on Human Rights. Commission on human rights resolution 2003/32: torture and other cruel, inhuman or degrading treatment or punishment, 2003. Available from: http://www.refworld.org/docid/43f313310.html (Accessed 22 May 2023).
3. European Union. Guidelines to EU policy towards third countries on torture and other cruel, inhuman or degrading treatment or punishment, 2001. Available from: www.refworld.org/docid/3e2fac757.html (Accessed 22 May 2023).
4. European Asylum Support Office. EASO practical guide: Evidence assessment, 2015. Available from: https://easo.europa.eu/sites/default/files/public/EASO-Practical-Guide_-Evidence-Assessment.pdf (Accessed 22 May 2023).
5. Home Office. Medical evidence in asylum claims, 2022. Available from: https://assets.publishing.service.gov.uk/government/uploads/system/uploads/attachment_data/file/1100831/Medical_evidence_in_asylum_claims.pdf (Accessed 22 May 2023).
6. England and Wales Court of Appeal (Civil Division). SA (Somalia) v. Secretary of State for the Home Department, 2006. Available from: https://www.refworld.org/cases,GBR_CA_CIV,47ac1e802fe.html (Accessed 22 May 2023).
7. The Supreme Court. KV (Sri Lanka) (appellant) v Secretary of State for the Home Department, 2019. Available from: https://www.supremecourt.uk/cases/docs/uksc-2017-0124-judgment.pdf (Accessed 22 May 2023).
8. Kalt A, Hossain M, Kiss L, Zimmerman C. Asylum seekers, violence and health: A systematic review of research in high-income host countries. *Am J Public Health* 2013; **103(3)**: e30–42.
9. Higson-Smith C. Updating the estimate of refugees resettled in the United States who have suffered torture, 2016. Available from: cvt.org/sites/default/files/SurvivorNumberMetaAnalysis_Sept2015_0.pdf (Accessed 22 May 2023).
10. United Nations Office on Drugs and Crime. The United Nations standard minimum rules for the treatment of prisoners (the Nelson Mandela rules), 2015. Available from: https://www.unodc.org/documents/justice-and-prison-reform/Nelson_Mandela_Rules-E-ebook.pdf (Accessed 22 May 2023).
11. United Nations Human Rights. Basic principles and guidelines on the right to a remedy and reparation for victims of gross violations of international human rights law and serious violations of international humanitarian law, 2005. Available from: https://www.ohchr.org/en/instruments-mechanisms/instruments/basic-principles-and-guidelines-right-remedy-and-reparation (Accessed 22 May 2023).
12. Lund SP, Iyer H. Likelihood ratio as weight of forensic evidence: A closer look. *J Res Natl Inst Stand Technol* 2017; **122**: 1–32.
13. Gill CJ, Sabin L, Schmid CH. Why clinicians are natural bayesians. *BMJ* 2005; **330(7499)**: 1080–3.
14. Robertson B and Berger C. Interpreting evidence of torture. *Med Law Rev* 2019; **27(4)**: 687–95.
15. United Nations Human Rights. Convention against torture and other cruel, inhuman or degrading treatment or punishment, 1984. Available from: https://www.ohchr.org/en/instruments-mechanisms/instruments/convention-against-torture-and-other-cruel-inhuman-or-degrading (Accessed 22 May 2023).
16. The United Nations Refugee Agency. Detention Guidelines, 2012. Available from: https://www.unhcr.org/uk/sites/uk/files/legacy-pdf/505b10ee9.pdf (Accessed 22 May 2023).
17. Asylum and Immigration Tribunal/Immigration Appellate Authority. RT (medical reports - causation of scarring) Sri Lanka v. Secretary of State for the Home Department, 2008. Available from: refworld.org/cases,GBR_AIT,47ac1c7c2.html (Accessed 22 May 2023).
18. Cohen J. Errors of recall and credibility: Can omissions and discrepancies in successive statements reasonably be said to undermine credibility of testimony? *Med Leg J* 2001; **69**: 25–34.
19. Office of National Statistics. Sexual offences in England and Wales overview: Year ending March 2020, 2021. Available from: Sexual offences in England and Wales overview – Office for National Statistics (ons.gov.uk) (Accessed 22 May 2023).
20. The United Nations Refugee Agency. Working with men and boy survivors of sexual and gender-based violence in forced displacement, 2012. Available from: https://www.refworld.org/pdfid/5006aa262.pdf (Accessed 22 May 2023).
21. Bullock CM, Beckson M. Male victims of sexual assault: Phenomenology, psychology, physiology. *Am J Psychiatry Law* 2011; **39(2)**: 197–205.

CHAPTER

75

Injury Documentation & Assessment

Jason Payne-James

INTRODUCTION

Injuries need to be documented for many reasons and, in different jurisdictions, forensic practitioners and others will be responsible for classifying (establishing the nature of the injury) and grading (determining the severity of) the injury (both new and old). The forensic practitioners should be able to assess, document and interpret visible injuries, wounds, cutaneous marks or scars which have been sustained as a result of trauma or violence. Errors of interpretation may be caused by inadequate or poor assessment (1,2).

Violence is manifest in many ways, whether interpersonal, part of armed conflict, civil war, military intervention, or accident, torture and maltreatment or terrorism occuring worldwide. There may be clinical reasons such as using prognostic indices to determine likely clinical outcome and risk of death; to determine the severity of the injury; to determine the nature of the medical management and to determine long-term prognosis. Injuries may need to be assessed for occupational and employment purposes – for example, to determine if someone can return to their previous work, or to assess adjustments that the employer may have to make. Injury may need to be assessed for insurance purposes as well as for medicolegal purposes in both the criminal and civil setting. Irrespective of the reason, accurate and appropriate documentation is required so that relevant parties, including other health professionals, can easily understand the clinical findings. Unfortunately, outside the world of forensic and legal medicine this is rarely done well. Often opportunities to document injury at an early stage are missed, which makes later interpretation more difficult.

In the forensic setting injuries are classified to assist courts. Table 75.1 lists some of the reasons injuries need to be classified in criminal cases.

The term injury is used widely and is important to consider what the term embraces. The International Classification of Diseases 11 (ICD-11) defines (at para 22) "*Injury, poisoning or certain other consequences of external causes*" with the description "*... injury means physical or physiological bodily harm resulting from interaction of the body with energy (mechanical, thermal, electrical, chemical or radiant, or due to extreme pressure) in an amount, or at a rate of transfer, that exceeds physical or physiological tolerance.*

Injury can also result from lack of vital elements, such as oxygen. Poisoning by and toxic effects of substances are included, as is damage of or due to implanted devices. Injury usually has rapid onset in response to a well-defined event (e.g. a car crash, striking the ground after falling, drinking a strongly alkaline liquid, an overdose of a medication, a burn sustained during a surgical procedure).

These events are often referred to as external causes of injury. The injurious energy can, however, originate from the injured person and/or from his or her immediate environment (e.g. a person running on a hot day sustains heat exhaustion), and injury can be caused by the injured person (i.e. intentional self-harm). Injury includes manifestations that are evident immediately after onset, which may persist or not, and manifestations that first become evident at a later date." (3). The ICD definition is of use as it covers most areas of work that forensic practitioners (whether from a pathological or clinical background) encounter in their professional work.

TABLE 75.1 Examples of reasons why injuries need to be documented and classified in criminal cases

• Accidental or inflicted?	• To compare different accounts of causation
• Defense or offense?	• To determine cause of death
• Determine cause of injury	• To determine the consistency of accounts
• How old is the injury?	• To exclude normal anatomic variants
• How was the inflicting object or implement used or wielded?	• What was the nature of the inflicting object or implement?

DOI: 10.1201/9781003138754-78

CLASSIFICATION SYSTEMS THAT CAN BE ADAPTED TO FORENSIC SETTINGS

Authors have proposed standardized reporting classification systems in a number of areas including sports and some specific injury types such as muscle (5), forensic pathology and forensic sciences (6,7). These do not however solely focus on injury.

As the ICD is the foundation for identifying health trends and statistics worldwide and provides unique codes for injuries, diseases and causes of death and a common terminology that allows health professionals to share health information internationally, it may provide a route for standardization (8).

All forensic medicine texts provide terminology and classification of injuries but these are not standardized, and although there used to be substantial variation, they now appear much more aligned. Forensic practitioners have not historically used a common framework for injury documentation, classification and interpretation and the new ICD-11 may provide future opportunity for international collaboration and interpretation.

Figure 75.1 and Figure 75.2a–c give examples of injuries to the thorax and how they can be coded under ICD-11.

Other classifications can be adapted for use in forensic practice. The Bureau of Labor Statistics (BLS) developed the Occupational Injury and Illness Classification System (OIICS) to characterize occupational injury and illness incidents and was originally released in 1992 (8). The BLS redesigned OIICS in 2010 with subsequent revisions in 2012.

The OIICS includes four hierarchical coding structures which included 1) the nature (principal characteristic(s) of the injury or illness; 2) part of the body affected (the part of the body directly affected by the previously identified nature or injury or illness; 3) source and secondary source (the objects, substances, equipment and other factors that were responsible for the injury or illness incurred by the worker or that precipitated the event or exposure, 4) event or exposure (the manner in which the illness or injury was produced or inflicted by the source of injury or illness) (8).

This coding structure could also be applied to the forensic pathology and clinical forensic medicine settings.

The Manual on the Effective Investigation and Documentation of Torture and Other Cruel, Inhuman or Degrading Treatment or Punishment (generally known as the Istanbul Protocol – IP) was first published in 1999 and a second edition was published in 2022 (9). The IP uses a hierarchy to determine how consistent marks, scars and injuries are when compared with the accounts given as to how they were caused in the context of torture or ill-treatment.

Table 75.2 shows an adaptation of these consistency levels for use in the forensic pathology and clinical forensic medicine settings. This can be used in the context of criminal cases to assist courts in interpreting marks, scars and injuries, and can be helpful when different accounts of causation are given. Features that would be necessary for such a standardized international reporting protocol for classifying injuries in medicolegal cases are suggested in Table 75.3. This would be in addition to the written descriptions, body diagram and imaging.

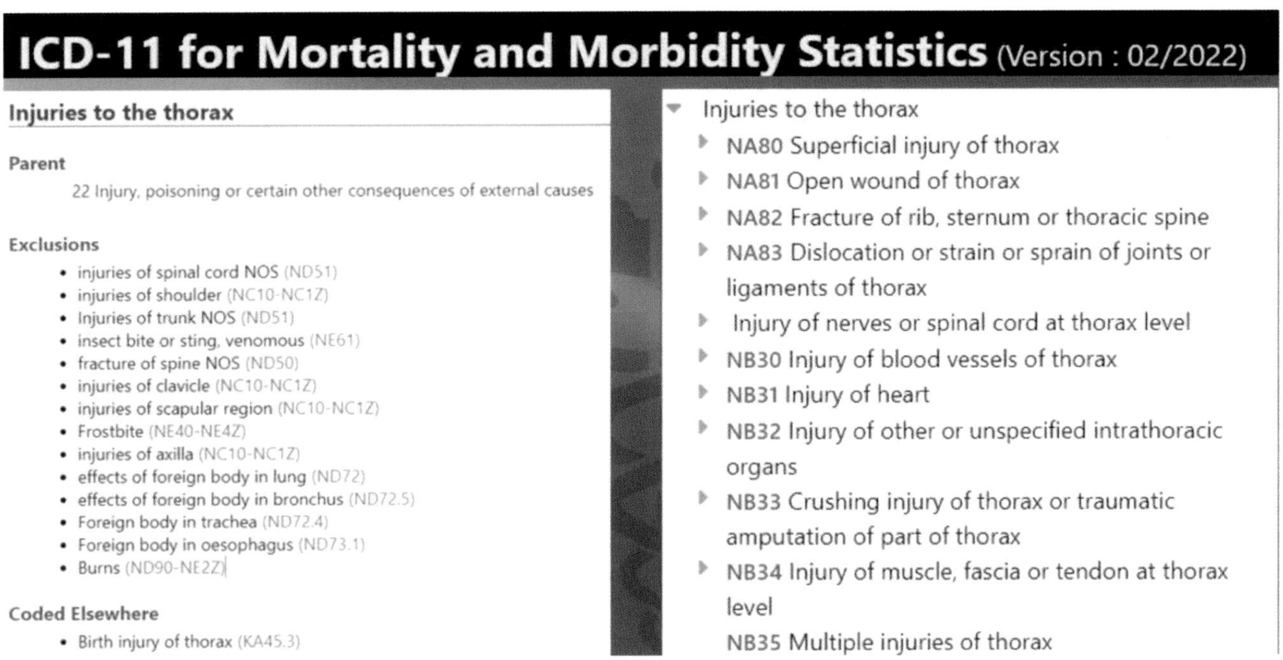

75.1 Example of ICD-11 coding for injuries to the thorax.

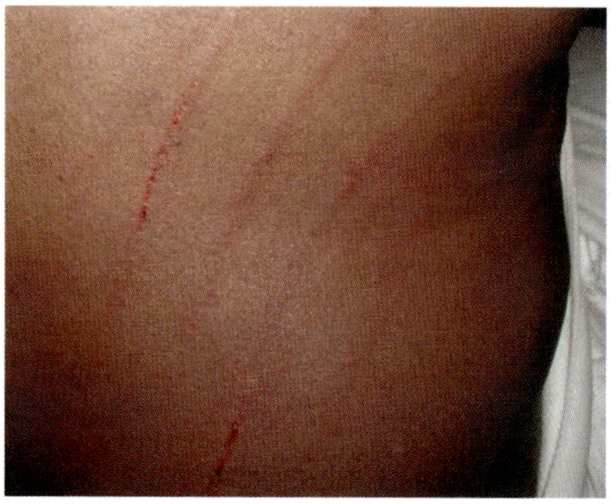

75.2 Examples of ICD coding of thoracic injuries (see also Figure 75.1). **(a)** Superficial linear fingernail abrasions – ICD-11 Code - NA81.

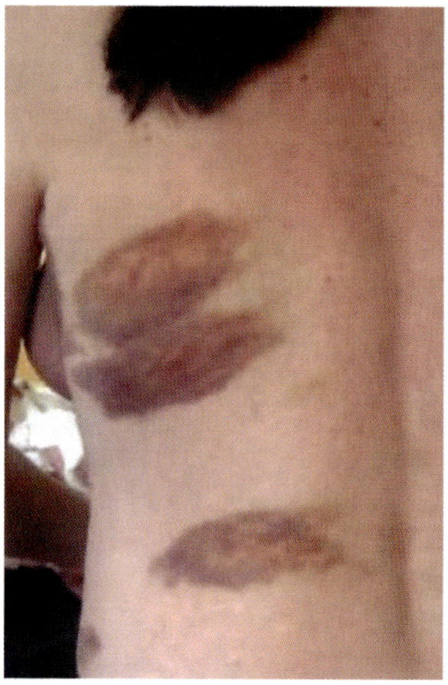

75.2 (b) Multiple blunt force injuries to thorax – ICD-11 Code – NB35 and ND5Y "Other specified injuries to unspecified part of trunk, limb or body region. Trunk blunt injury".

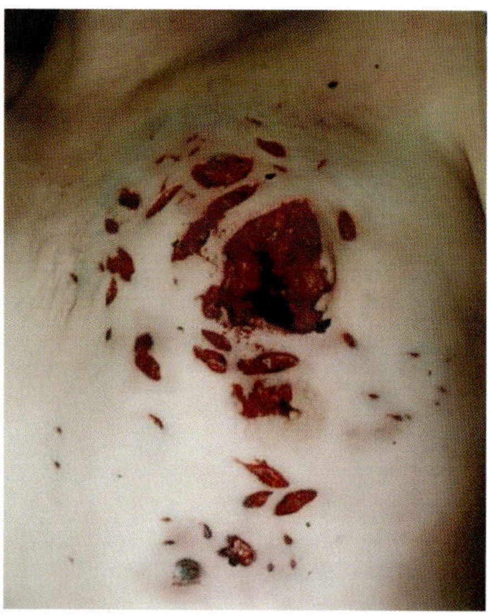

75.2 (c) Multiple stab wounds to thorax – ICD Code – NA31 – NB25 and PE3Z – "Assault by being cut or pierced by other or unspecified sharp object".

TABLE 75.2 Levels of consistency for use when considering injuries, scars and cutaneous marks in the criminal setting (adapted from the Istanbul Protocol "levels of consistency" between clinical findings and accounts given for torture and Ill-treatment 5 (f)

Not consistent with	Findings could not have been caused in the manner alleged
Consistent with	Findings could have been caused in the manner alleged but they are non-specific and there may be many alternative explanations
Highly consistent with	Findings could have been caused in the manner alleged and there are only a few other possible explanations
Typical of	Findings are those that would be expected in the manner alleged but other causes might need to be considered
Diagnostic of	Findings could not have been caused in any way other than in the manner alleged

TABLE 75.3 Suggested features that should be included in a standardized forensic medical international reporting protocol for classifying injuries, marks and scars in medicolegal cases. Such a protocol can be contributed to by more than one practitioner

• Applicable to forensic pathology and clinical forensic medicine	• Considers possible implements or methods of causation
• Applicable to minor injury	• Considers the key elements of the accounts provided (e.g. defendant, complainant, witness)
• Applicable to severe injury	• Considers other evidence (e.g. body worn video, CCTV)
• Applicable to fatality	• Explores the consistency of accounts
• Consistent terminology	• International Classification of Diseases 11 code
• Consistent classification	• Provides overall conclusions
• Provides prognosis (if the subject is living)	

Table 75.4 shows a proforma for such a protocol which combines elements of some of the systems mentioned to ensure capture of relevant information for injury or any injuries, marks or scars found in any forensic setting.

TABLE 75.4 Proposed table format for injury, mark or scar documentation in the forensic setting. A table would be created for each injury and adapted for additional accounts of causation

Feature	Examples
Nature	Size, shape, color, orientation, unique features
Anatomic location	Ear, liver, spleen, ribs, pelvis, femur, scalp
Injury Classification (with associated ICD-11 code)	Incised, blunt, crush, burn, grip, non-fatal strangulation
Factors or implement or object responsible for injury	Hand, shod foot, baseball bat, knife, broken bottle, car, vehicle, crush, RTC, manual strangulation
Summary of event described (witness 1)*	The manner in which the injury or illness was produced or inflicted by the source of injury
Consistency of account 1 described	Use consistency levels shown in Table 75.3
Summary of event described (witness 2)*	The manner in which the injury or illness was produced or inflicted by the source of injury
Consistency of account 2 described	Use consistency levels shown in Table 75.3
Prognosis	Cosmetic, functional, likelihood of recovery
Overall conclusions	

*Rows should be added for additional accounts or summaries from additional evidence (e.g. body worn video, CCTV) and the consistency levels also recorded.

INJURY, CUTANEOUS MARK AND SCAR DOCUMENTATION

Assessment and documentation of cutaneous marks, injuries or scars is intended to assist in determining or corroborating causation which is often the essence of medical evidence in courts and tribunals.

The forensic practitioners' role may also be to explain the clinical relevance of absence of visible injury or marks following trauma. The interpretation of the causes of wounds, scars, and injuries should be undertaken by those with forensic expertise, as there may be many factors involved in such interpretation.

That interpretation is often assisted by access to and review of other evidence including ambulance records, hospital records, operative notes, photographic images, body worn video, CCTV and personal devices such as smartphones. It is essential that the descriptions of what is seen are clear and unambiguous and that terminology is correct.

Terms that may be used in general conversation such as wound, cut or laceration may have specific forensic medical meanings and may impact on interpretation. For example, in England and Wales, the word "wound" requires evidence of a break in the continuity of the skin. A scratch is insufficient, there needs to be a breach in the whole of the skin (10). This definition may affect both the nature of any criminal charge brought and the subsequent sentence if convicted.

Non-forensic clinicians whose prime aim is to treat the patient may not accurately record injury at the time it presents, which may pose difficulties for later interpretation in court. Geriatricians, pediatricians, primary care physicians, gynecologists and emergency medicine specialists and allied health professionals working in those areas are typical of those who may treat patients with apparent injuries and who are victims of crime that may become the subject of argument within court proceedings. There is a strong argument to obtain early assessment of injuries by forensic practitioners who will not be involved in the therapeutic care, to ensure the best evidence is recorded.

The assessment and documentation of injury requires the taking of an appropriate history from the patient (or complainant or suspect) and undertaking an appropriate physical examination.

The findings of the history and examination should be recorded contemporaneously, clearly, and unambiguously. If a case goes to court, all such documentation (e.g. contemporaneous medical notes – handwritten or electronic – including body diagrams, images) will be reviewed by others including forensic practitioners, lawyers, judges and juries.

Consent for the assessment, and subsequent productions should always be sought from the person being examined. A full, standard medical history and examination should always be undertaken as a basis for the forensic assessment. The forensic practitioner will be aware that false or vexatious allegations can be made and other accounts may become available later. Forensic practitioners will be aware of their need to be unbiassed, independent and non-judgemental. There are specific elements which should always be considered when taking a history for injury assessment and these are summarized in Table 75.5.

Each injury, cutaneous mark or scar should be considered separately. Specific times should be sought for each. The nature or the weapon used can be very helpful when assessing injury as particular implements may cause recognizable, identifiable injuries (e.g. police batons, knuckledusters, machete, Stanley knife, footwear).

Documentation of injuries will be in a variety of formats, including written descriptions, hand-drawn notes, annotated proforma body diagrams, and photographic or as moving images. If photographic images are supplied, it is absolutely essential that the quality of the images adds to, rather than detracts from, the evidence and a variety of studies have explored the nature of images, and guidelines for photography should be adhered to (11).

It is useful for forensic practitioners to have undergone training in forensic photography. Figure 75.3 gives

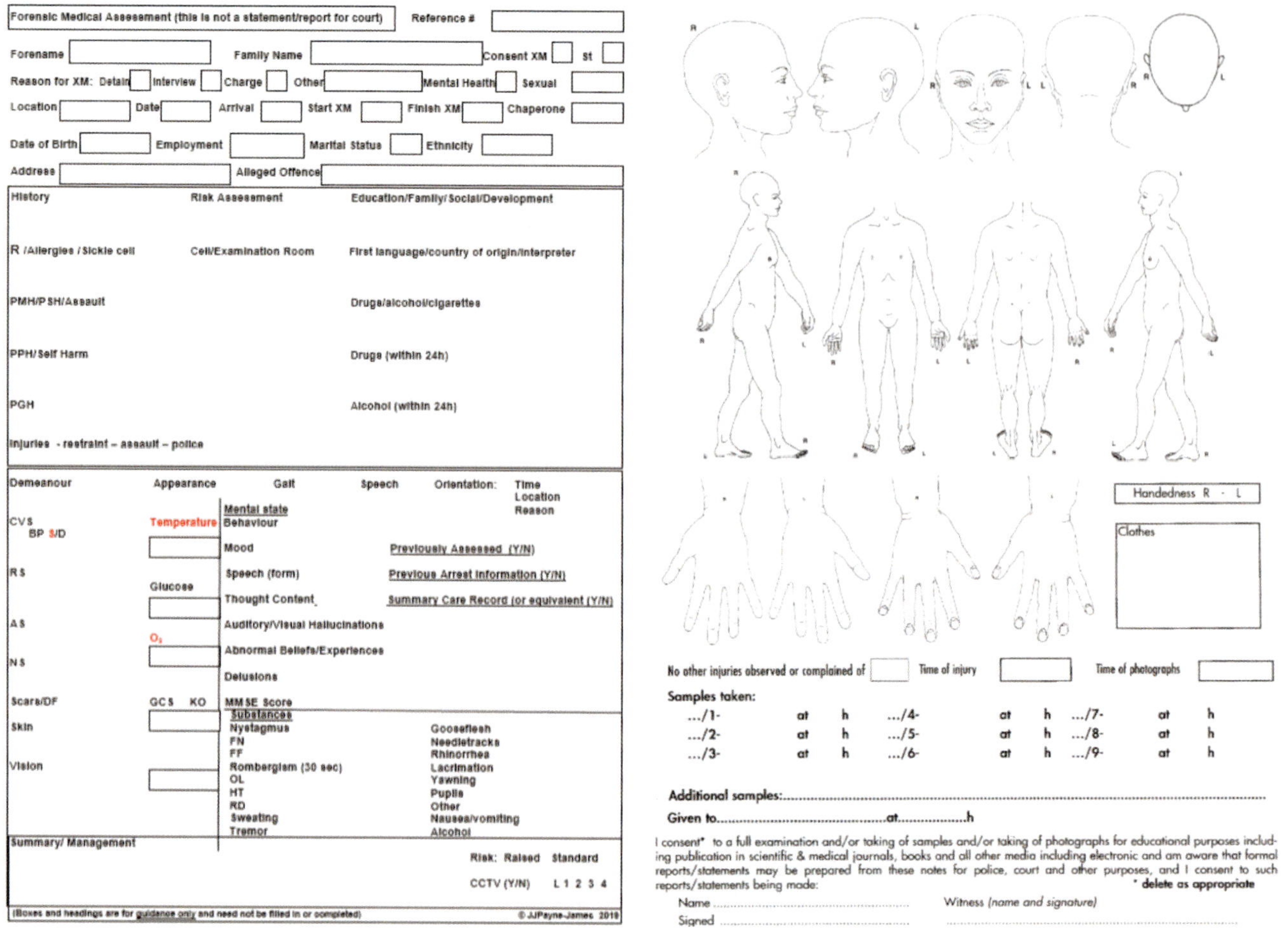

75.3 An example of single-sheet, two-sided document for history and examination.

an example of single-sheet, two-sided document for history and examination. Figure 75.4 gives examples of body diagrams that may be more appropriate for recording of multiple or complex injuries. Table 75.5 shows the detail which may be required when documenting each injury.

Apps are now available on smartphones and tablets that can allow documentation of injury, body diagram production, and photographic documentation, which accurately geolocates and times the examination and outputs an editable document (e.g. ForensiDoc®).

Pre- and post-treatment examination and photography is often very useful. Photographs should always be undertaken with rules and color scales to allow proper comparison at a later date. A range of rules and color chart are available at www.forensigraph.co.uk and the importance of accurate measurement is particularly significant when trying to assess injuries with clear measurable patterns.

Table 75.6 provides a simple classification which embraces most injury types. Some examples of the most common injury types are discussed below or in their relevant chapters. In very general terms, certain injuries such as bruises and abrasions can be divided into "non-specific" – where the nature of the bruise or abrasion in isolation doesn't give a clear indication of the cause, and "patterned" where a pattern of the impacting object or weapon or surface may be replicated as a bruise or abrasion. In these cases, it is particularly important that accurate measurements are taken so that injury and weapon can be compared. Most injuries are non-specific.

Sharp force

Sharp-force injuries are those injuries caused by any object, weapon, or implement with cutting edges or points (e.g. knives, scissors, and broken glass). Sharp-bladed implements can create different types of cuts including incised, stab and slash wounds. An incised wound describes a clean-edged wound that divides tissue.

Stab wounds and slash wounds are types of incised wounds, having been caused by a sharp edge. Certain bladed implements – for example, axes, machetes and meat cleavers – can create deep wide wounds due to their sharpness, shape and weight.

The term "chop" wounds may be used. Some such implements are blunt and although theoretically are cutting instruments, may only inflict blunt impact-type

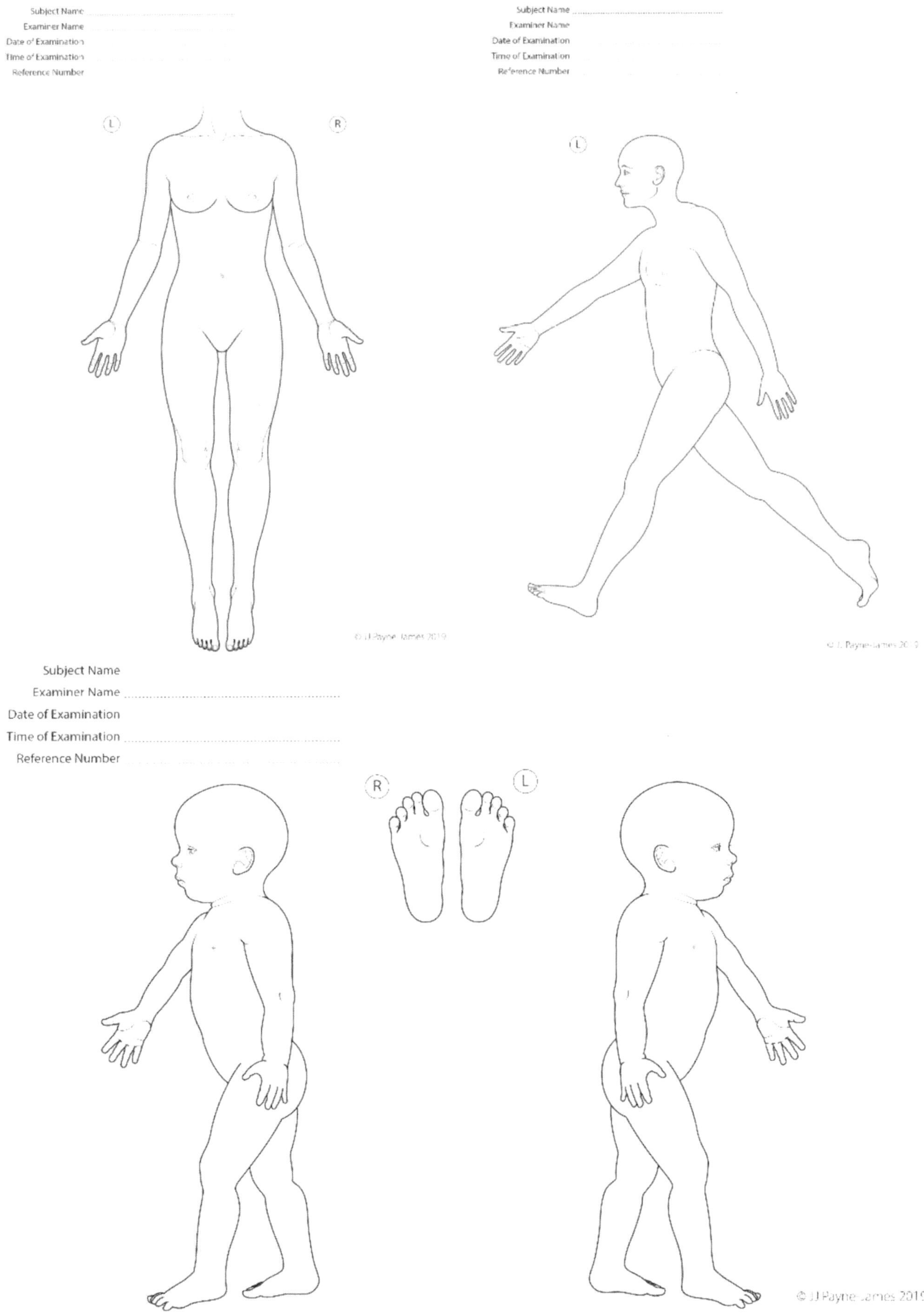

75.4 Examples of body diagrams for recording of multiple or complex injuries.

TABLE 75.5 Essential elements of a history for injury assessment

• How was the injury sustained?	• Are there any regular activities which may account for the injuries (e.g. employment, sport)
• When was the injury sustained?	• Are there medications which may influence interpretation? (e.g. anticoagulants, steroids)
• Was there an object or weapon?	• Is the handedness of complainant and suspect known?
• Is it available?	• Were drugs or alcohol used? (by complainant and suspect)
• Has injury been treated?	• Was clothing worn that may influence interpretation?
• Are there pre-existing illnesses which may influence interpretation? (e.g. Ehlers Danlos, eczema)	• Does the patient need to be reassessed subsequently? (to assess evolution of injury)

TABLE 75.6 Characteristics to be assessed at examination for each injury, cutaneous mark, or scar (optional and dependent on history)

• Location (anatomic – measure distance from landmarks)	• Shape
• Presence of pain?	• Pattern
• Presence of tenderness?	• Color
• Reduced mobility?	• Orientation
• Type of injury, mark or scar (e.g. bruise, laceration, abrasion, scabbed wound, mature scar)	• Possible age
• Size (use metric values)	• Possible causation

injuries. This may also apply where the impact is made, not by the cutting part but another, for example, the back of an axe or the side of the blade.

The term laceration (splitting of skin following blunt impact) is often wrongly used by non-forensic practitioners in the setting where bladed instruments have been used.

The degree of force required to penetrate skin and underlying structures (which may include fat muscle and fibrous tissue) and bone with sharp implements such as knives or scissors or other sharp-edged implements is predominantly dependent on the characteristics of the implement, including sharpness, numbers of cutting edges, pointedness and length of blade.

The degree of force required to inflict an injury may be described as any of – weak, weak/moderate, moderate, moderate/severe and severe. However, even with sharp implements, the force required to penetrate skin is generally at least moderate. Two types of injuries predominate – stabbing and slashing (or slicing). They may often be seen together. With stabbing – the wound tends to be deeper than it is wide. However, a stabbing motion directed where there is underlying bone, may not be. With slashing – a blade is drawn across a surface and the wound may be wider than it is deep. An oblique slash or slice may result in tissue loss or formation of tissue flaps. As slash cuts may run across different surfaces or curvatures of the body, they may be of varying depth throughout their length.

Many wounds are a combination of both. For all wounds, the depth of penetration will be dependent on the anatomic site of any injury, the characteristics of the implement (as described above) and any additional factors such as the type or nature of overlying clothes (law-enforcement personnel may wear stab vests). Clearly, this may also affect the depth of penetration as will other factors including, for example, whether an individual is obese or fat and whether there are underlying bones.

Figure 75.5 shows examples of typical sharp force injury in the living and includes diagrams of typical profiles of stab or penetrating wounds which may give some indication of the nature of the weapon used.

Blunt force

Blunt force, blunt contact, or blunt impact injuries are those injuries generally caused by objects without sharp

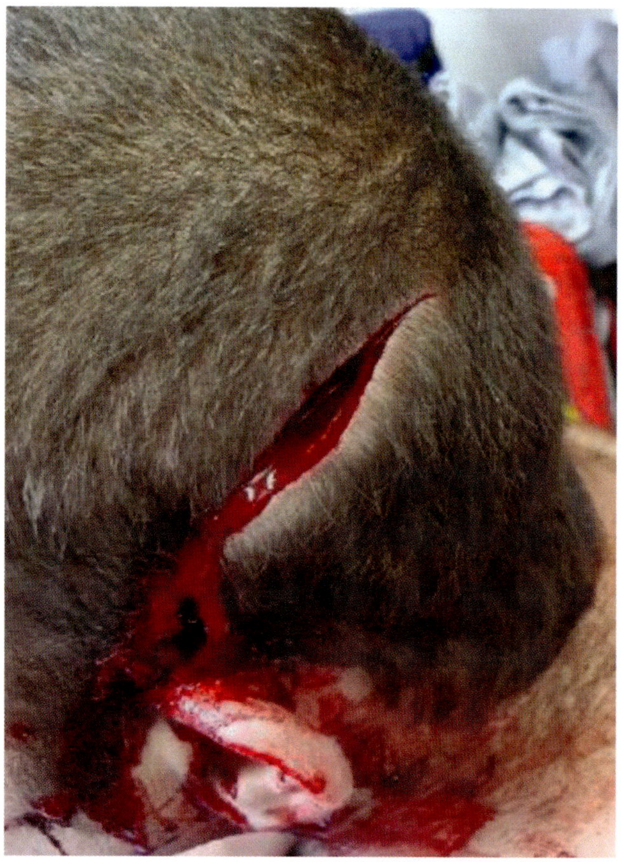

75.5 Examples of sharp force injury. (a) Slash wound. A slash wound caused by a kitchen knife drawn across the scalp (the skull was not penetrated). Note the clean regular edges and the linearity.

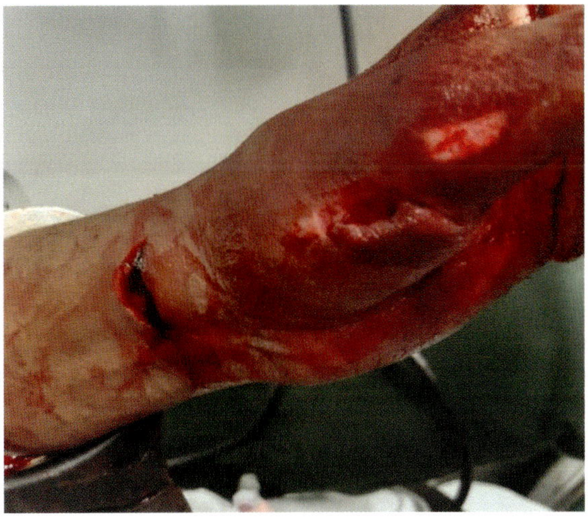

75.5 (b) Slice wound. A wound to the left thenar eminence where a sharp kitchen knife has sliced obliquely across the skin surface removing an area of skin and creating an irregular flap. Another incised wound is seen at the wrist.

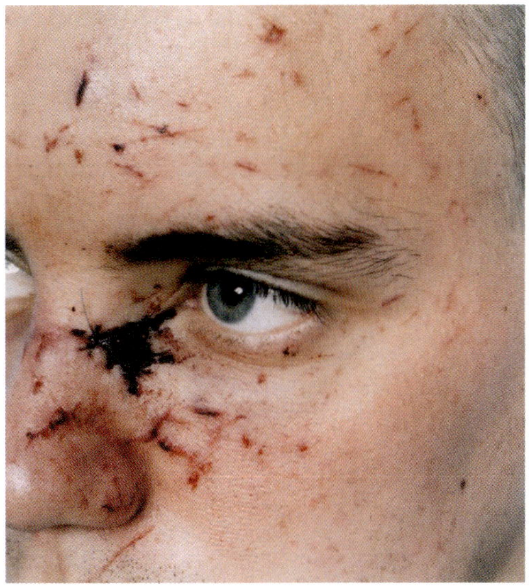

75.5 (e) Glassing. Multiple small, incised satellite wounds caused by glass breaking on impact at left side of nose.

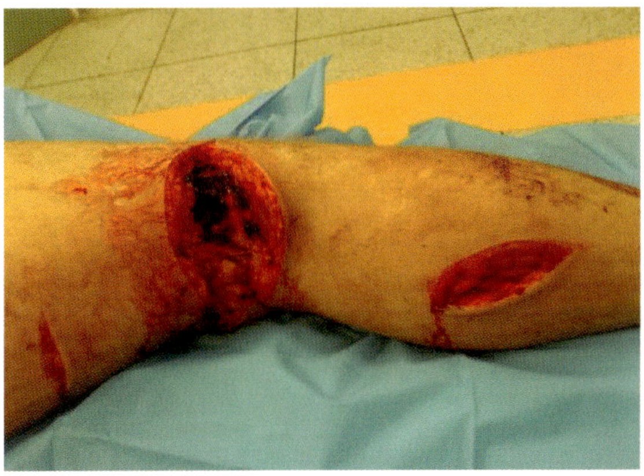

75.5 (c) Chop wounds. Two wounds to the back of the thigh and calf caused by two blows with a sharp machete. These may be indistinguishable from wounds caused by a sharp knife if cartilage and bone are not involved.

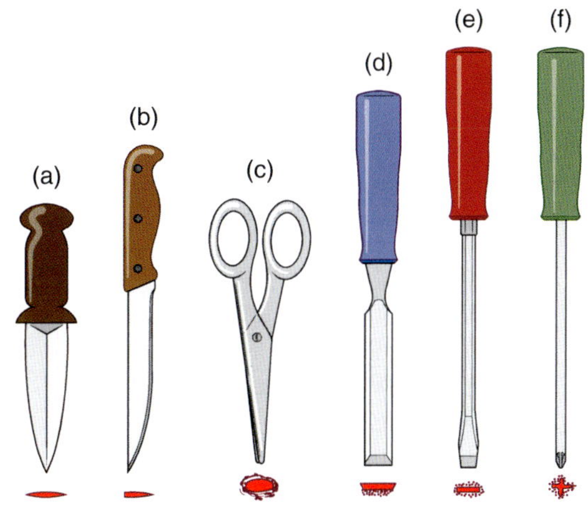

75.5 (f) Diagrammatic representation of a variety of implements capable of stabbing or penetrating skin and the typical wound appearance. Bladed implements will tend to have clean wound edges. a: double-edged knife; b: single edged knife (note 'fish-tail appearance); c: scissors (note possible irregular, abraded, bruised, lacerated or macerated edges); d: chisel (note same features as c); e: flat-head screwdriver (note same features as c); f: cross-head screwdriver (note same features as c).

75.5 (d) Amputation with heavy knife. A knife (shown) which weighed 160 g amputated a hand at the wrist with a single impact – the arm was raised In a defensive manner at the time.

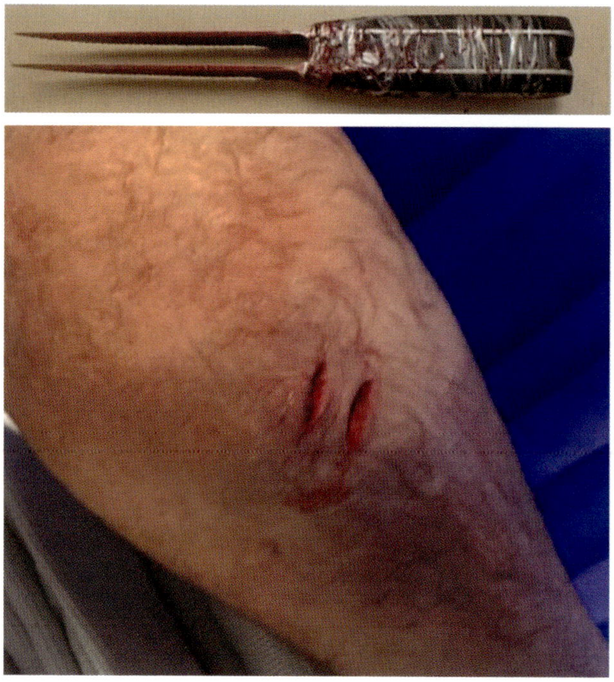

75.5 **(g)** Stab wounds. Two parallel stab wounds to the leg, caused by two identical knives taped together at the handle; the implement used is shown above.

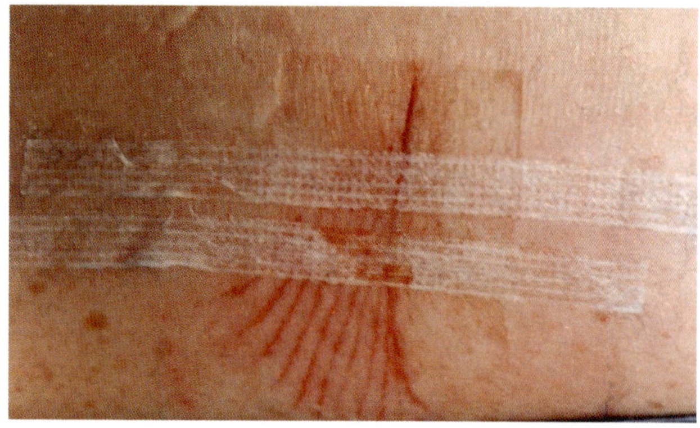

75.5 (h) An incised patterned wound. A superficial incised wound has been closed with Steri-Strip but a fan-like pattern of linear abrasion shows that the weapon used had a serrated edge.

or cutting edges such as fists, hands, feet, baseball bat, truncheon, hammers, metal bars and plastic drink bottles. These can all be used to hit an individual. There are many other examples of how a blunt injury can be sustained. An individual can fall and strike an object (e.g. brick wall or pavement) causing blunt impact injury.

An individual can walk into an object and cause blunt impact injury. An individual can be pushed into or against an object causing blunt impact injury. A car or train can impact an individual causing blunt impact injury. An individual can sustain blunt force injury in a car roll-over. Falling from a height may cause blunt force injury. Most people sustain impacts in our activities of daily life, at work, at leisure and during sport. Blunt-force injury also represents a common cause of serious injury and death.

From a forensic standpoint, even the most minor injury may have extreme forensic importance. Minor or superficial injuries may be overlooked or ignored by non-forensic healthcare professionals whose primary role is to assess, treat and manage injuries incurred in any setting. Initial forensic documentation of injury, however, can show patterns or configurations that can help assist courts and tribunals to understand the causation of injuries.

Such injuries may allow the examiner to interpret many factors surrounding their production, such as the instrument involved, the direction and duration of impact, and the minimum number of impacts. A clear understanding of blunt force injuries and their causation allows the medical professional to interpret the forces and events that cause them (1). Table 75.7 shows the range of injuries that can be caused by blunt force contact and Figure 75.6 illustrates typical blunt force injuries in the living.

A common question asked (particularly with bruises) is whether it is possible to identify a specific time or timeframe to the infliction of an injury (*see also* Chapter 16 – "Aging of Injuries in the Living and Deceased"). It is rarely possible to precisely time or date when they were caused in the absence of witnessed evidence. Injuries inflicted shortly before examination (in both living and deceased) will show no clinical or pathologic evidence of healing.

The physiological healing process (whether of blunt or sharp force injury) may be modified the site of injury, the force applied, the severity of tissue damage, infection and previous treatment. These can all make assessment of the age of a wound difficult. Bruises often become more prominent some hours or even days after infliction because of diffusion of blood closer to the skin surface; on occasion, a recent deep bruise may be mistaken for an older, more superficial lesion.

Bruises resolve over a variable period ranging from days to weeks. Many bruises exhibit multiple colors. Langlois and Gresham showed that a bruise with a yellow color was more than 18 hours old and that the colors red, blue and purple/black could occur anytime within 1 hour of bruising to resolution (up to 21 days in the study) (13). However, it should also be recognized that additional factors (due to color reproduction and color perception) make even the 18-hour timeframe questionable as studies have shown that estimation of bruise age from color photographs is unreliable – as the color values are not accurate and there is also interobserver variability in color matching both *in vivo* and in photographic reproductions. Studies show that, in children, no evidential value for aging of bruises should be put on color and this principle realistically is also applicable to adults (11–15). Considerable research continues in this field (in living and deceased) including using histologic, biochemical, hematological and photographic techniques but as yet no practical means of accurately aging injury in human subjects is readily available (16–22).

TABLE 75.7 Classification of injuries

Blunt force
• Wheals and erythema (reddening)
• Bruises (also known as contusions, ecchymosis – these terms are not now needed)
o Non-specific
o Patterned
• Hematoma (a fluctuant collection of liquid blood)
• Petechiae (small hemorrhages - size not necessarily relevant as these vary rapidly and can become confluent)
• Abrasions (grazes)
o Non-specific
o Patterned
• Scratches
• Point abrasion
• Lacerations (differentiated from sharp force cuts by the presence of other elements of blunt force and skin-bridging across the wound edges)
Sharp force
• Incisions
• Slash/slice
• Stab
• Chop
• Glassing
Burns (*see* Chapter 44)
• Contact
• Flame
• Chemical
Firearms (*see* Chapter 61)
Bites (*see* Chapter 92)
• Human
• Animal
Self-injury (*see* Chapter 83)
Exposure (*see* Chapters 44, 45, 46)
• Heat
• Cold

Burns

Burns are caused by the transfer of energy from a physical (e.g. hot water, an iron, a heated object) or chemical (e.g. bleach or acid) source into living tissues that causes disruption of their normal metabolic processes and commonly leads to irreversible changes that end in tissue death.

Burns may cause simple burning or extend to deep charring of tissue including muscle and bone. There are three main categories of burn used in the clinical setting, full thickness (destroying the full thickness of skin) and partial thickness which divide into superficial and deep. Very superficial burns – for example those caused by sunburn – may simply cause reddening with mild blistering that may occur after 12–18 hours.

After 5–10 days, the damaged layers of cells peel off without residual scarring. Partial thickness burns destroy the whole of the epidermis and possibly part of the next cellular layer – the dermis. Superficial partial-thickness burns result in fluid production which lifts off the dead epidermis forming blisters and subsequently scabs. Sensory nerves are damaged and the burn is very painful. New epithelium grows quickly and the burn heals in 10 to 14 days with little or no scarring.

Deep partial thickness burns are often less painful as nerve endings are destroyed and scarring is likely to be marked if the wound is allowed to heal spontaneously without skin grafting. Full-thickness burns destroy all skin elements and may require substantial reconstructive surgery.

The skin can tolerate a high surface temperature as it is able to dissipate heat rapidly. However, if the rate of absorption of heat exceeds dissipation rate, then burn injury will occur when the temperature arises high enough to disrupt cellular processes.

Little local cellular damage occurs with a surface skin temperature below 44°C unless exposed for > 6 minutes.

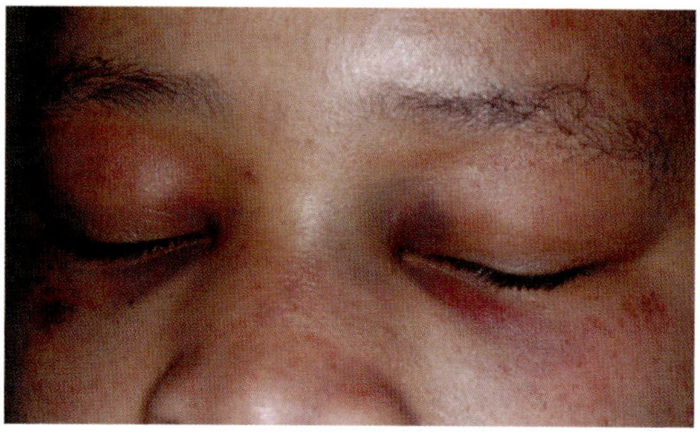

75.6 Examples of blunt force injury. (a) Bilateral periorbital bruising caused by impact to nose. This is a "non-specific" injury. The causative implement or object cannot be determined by the medical findings.

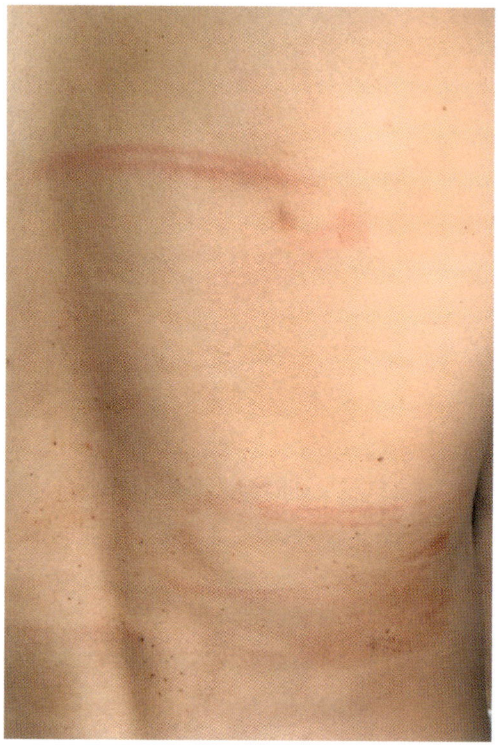

75.6 (b) Tramline (railtrack) bruising to back from beating with rigid stick. This is a typical "patterned" injury.

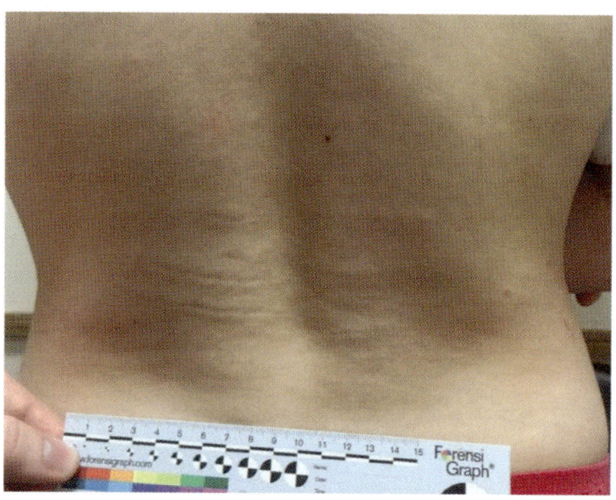

75.6 (c) Adolescent striae to back mimicking multiple impacts from a linear object injury.

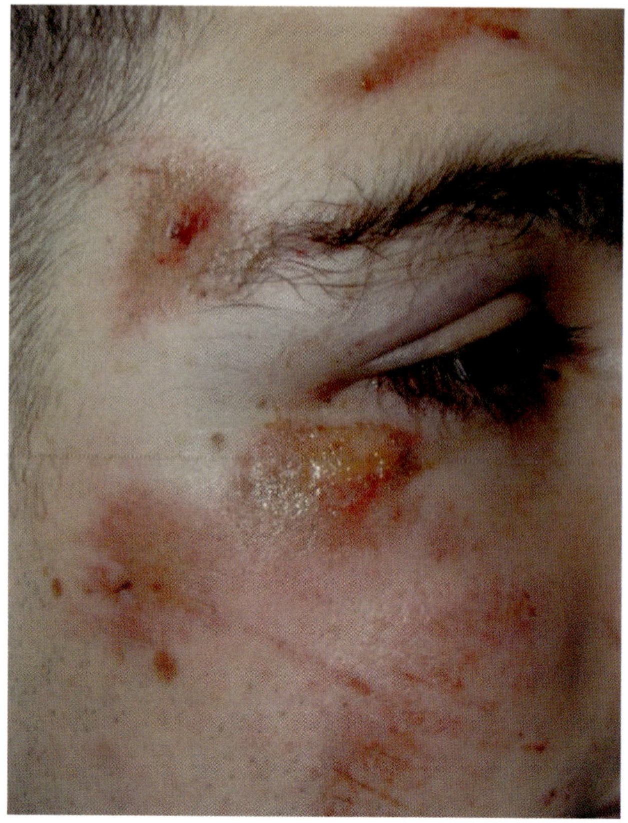

75.6 (d) Abrasions, erythema and bruising to face following multiple kicks with shod foot.

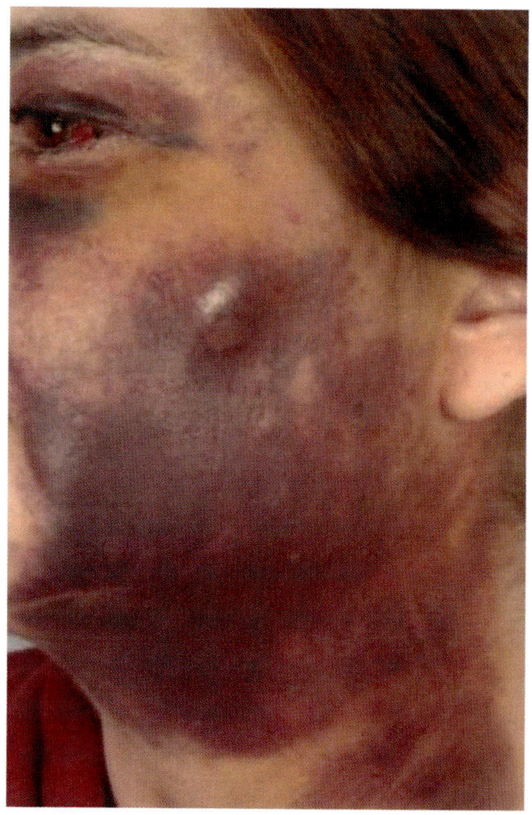

75.6 (e) Extensive coalesced bruising to face and neck following multiple punches.

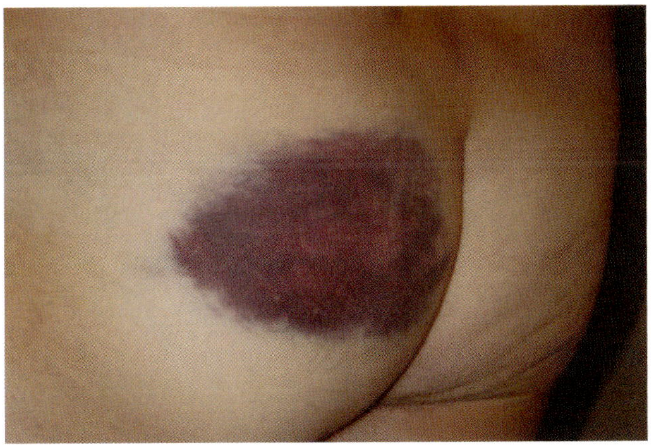

75.6 (f) Localized non-specific bruise to left buttock from fall backwards from ~15 meters (no underlying fracture).

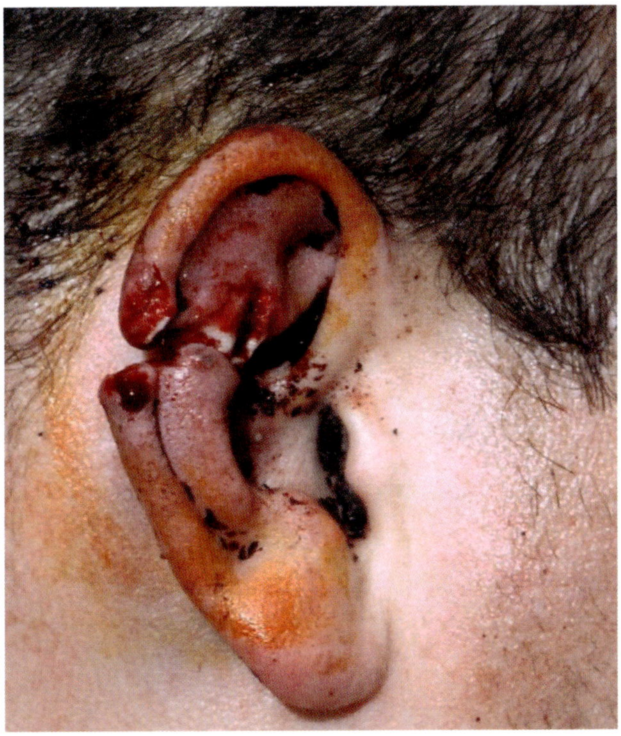

75.6 (g) Laceration to right ear (irregular margins with exposure of cartilage and bruising and swelling) caused by direct impact with baseball bat (skin bridging not visible in this image).

Skin surface exposed to temperatures in the range 44–51°C can suffer increased damage for a limited exposure time with the rate of cellular destruction doubling with each degree rise in temperature.

The epidermis is rapidly destroyed above 51°C and full-thickness skin destruction above 70°C. The degree of damage is therefore related to temperature and for how long something is applied to the skin.

Without knowing one variable, it is not possible to estimate the others. Cutaneous burns can result in many ways, each with their own individual characteristics of edge and base, but with overlap.

For thermal burns, whether a burn results, and the burn degree (depth) will primarily depend on the temperature of the injuring agent and duration of exposure. Contact burns occur when a hot, often metal, surface touches the skin.

These are the most common non-scald burns seen in abused children (23). The burn edges tend to be well demarcated and take the shape of part, or all, of the hot surface. The base tends to be uniform in depth if the surface is flat, and often deep; depending on the temperature and duration of contact. If there is pressure of a flat surface over an anatomically convex area of skin, the burn may be deepercentrally.

The hot surface may be fixed (e.g. a cooking utensil). Clear patterns may be seen. Flames burn at hundreds of degrees Celsius and cause cutaneous burns very quickly. Small, very localized flame burns result from small flames, for example, from a candle or cigarette lighter and often cause centrally deep and circular burns. Fluid burns (such as boiling water) may show flow patterns and sparing where clothing is worn.

Burn injuries are very difficult to age, especially without knowing the initial depth and mechanism. If blisters are present and intact, the burn is likely to be recent. Signs of cellulitis usually take around 48 hours to appear. Superficial partial-thickness injuries are usually healed within one week, and deep dermal injuries within three weeks. Figure 75.7 provides some examples of burn injury in the living.

Defensive injuries

Defensive injuries are those that may typically be seen when an individual has tried to defend themselves against an attack (whether with or without a weapon) and are part of the natural reaction to protect head, face and chest and to disarm an assailant or resist injury. Defense injuries may be present in any type of assault. If the individual being attacked is very young or frail, or intoxicated or already injured by an assault, they may be less able to defend themselves.

Defense injuries are present because, for example, when attacked with blunt objects, most individuals will

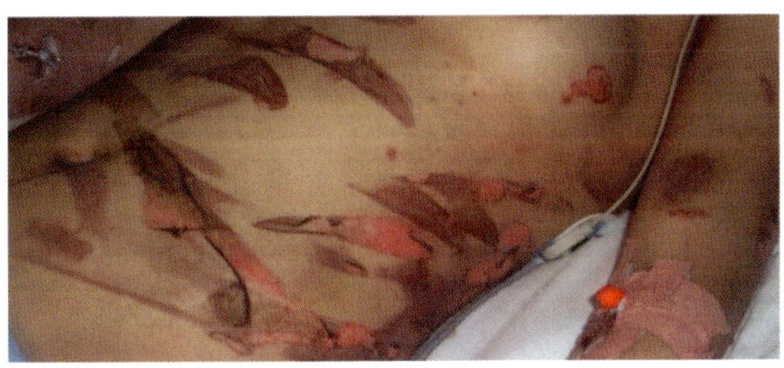

75.7 Examples of burn injury. (a) Partial-thickness contact burns. Knife heated on gas hob repeatedly applied to skin surface. Knife blade pattern can be seen and could be matched against the weapon used..

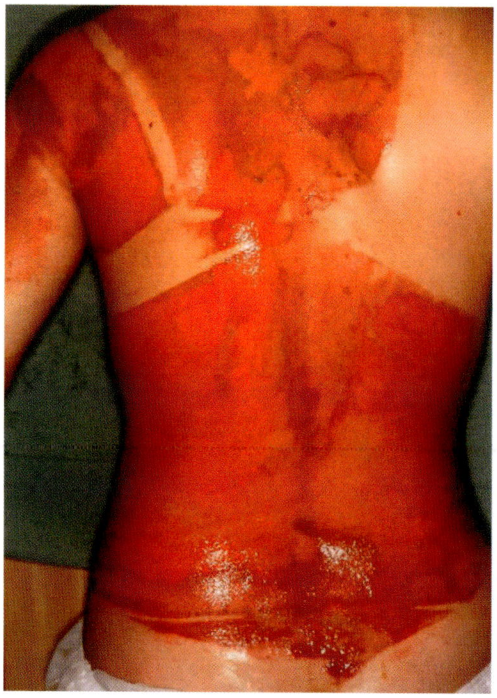

75.7 (b) Partial-thickness scald burns from boiling water. Sparing of skin where clothing worn.

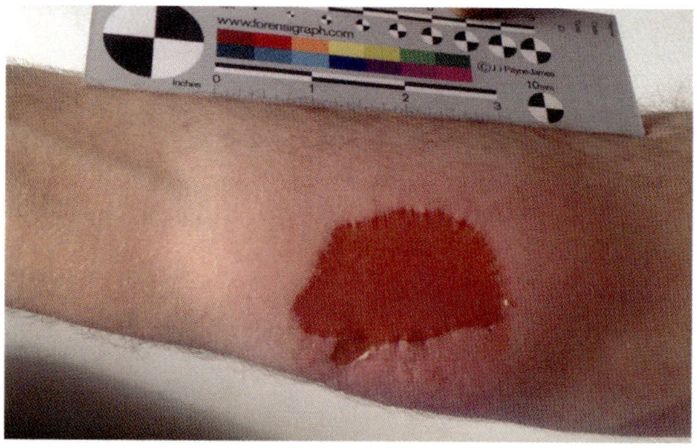

75.7 (c) Contact burn with hot kettle. Flexor aspect right forearm. Partial thickness and well delineated, note extensive swelling and surrounding reddening.

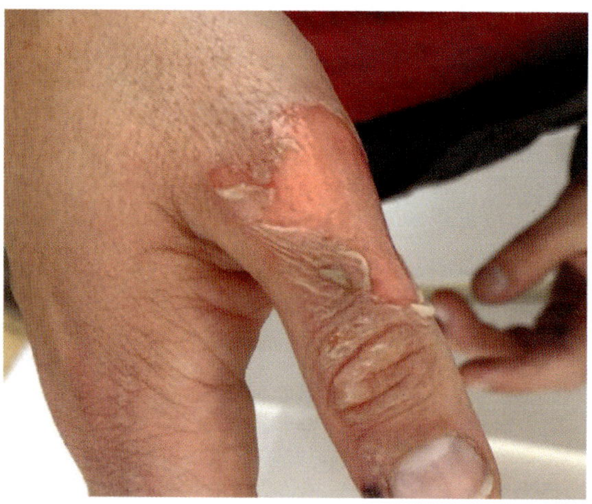

75.7 (d) Partial-thickness flame burn with deroofing of blister from burning methylated spirits – approximately 40 minutes after burn.

attempt to protect eyes and head and neck by raising arms, flexing elbows and covering the head and neck.

As a result, the exposed surfaces of the arms become the impact point for blows. The extensor surface of the forearms (the ulnar side) may receive blows, the lateral/posterior aspects of the upper arm, and the dorsum of the hands. Similarly, the outer and posterior aspects of lower limbs and back may be injured as an individual rolls into a ball, with flexion of spine, knees and hips to protect the anterior part of the body.

In sharp blade attacks, the natural reaction may be to try and disarm the assailant – by grabbing the blade or trying to knock it away. This can result in cuts to the palm and ulnar aspect of the hand. On some occasions, the hands or arms may be raised to protect the body against the stabbing motion resulting in stab wounds to the defense areas. In blunt force attacks, the injuries sustained usually take the form of bruises if the victim is being punched or kicked, but there may also be abrasions and/or lacerations depending on the nature of any weapon used. A single fracture of a forearm bone may be caused if the arm is raised to intercept a weapon about to strike the head. If the victim is lying on the ground while being assaulted, he or she will tend to curl up into a fetal position to protect the face and the front of the trunk, particularly from kicks. In these circumstances, defensive bruising is likely to be seen on other surfaces of the trunk and limbs. Examples of defense injuries are shown in Figure 75.8.

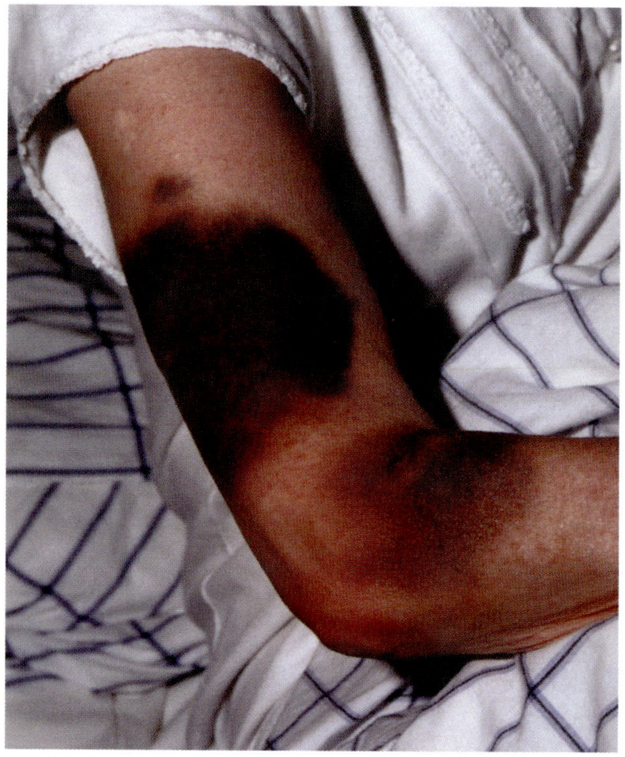

75.8 Examples of defensive injury. (a) Extensor forearm bruising. Bruising to extensor aspect of right forearm and upper arm (lifted to protect against assault from blunt implement).

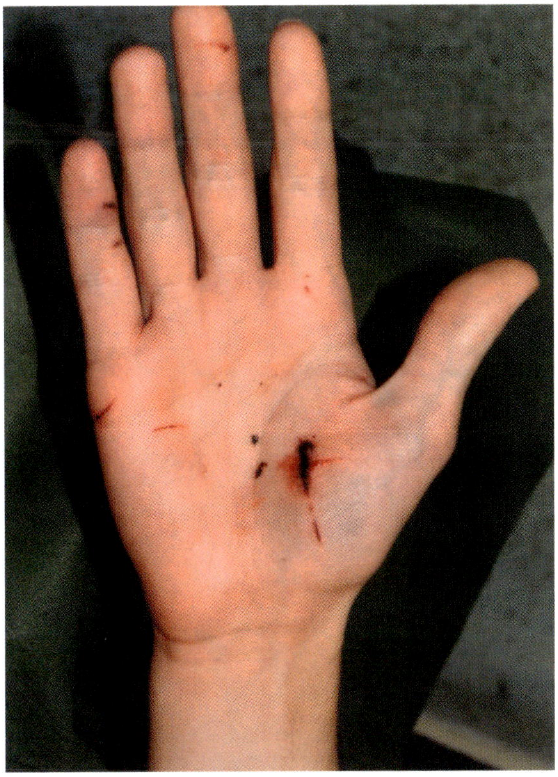

75.8 (b) Defense wounds to hand. Right (dominant) hand used to fend off assault from knife. Stab wound to thenar eminence and smaller incised wounds caused by contact with blade.

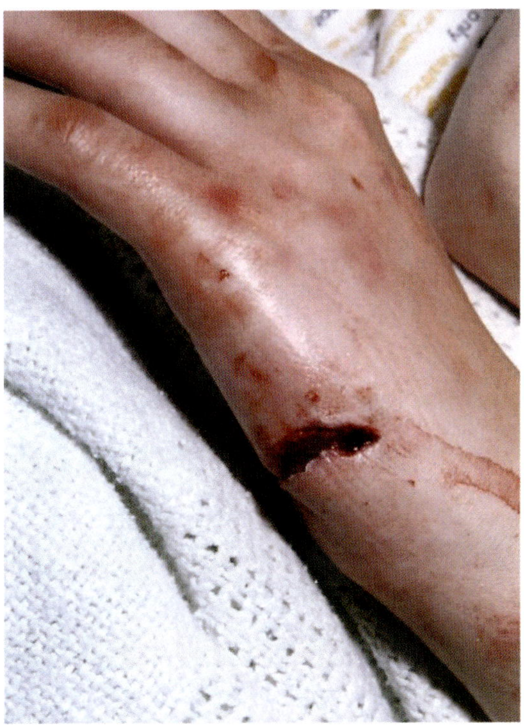

75.8 (c) Defensive chop wound to extensor aspect of left hand caused by trying to prevent a machete strike.

CONCLUSION

Any forensic healthcare professional should be able to document and classify injuries, marks or scars in a way that is unambiguously understood by, and can be interpreted by, other healthcare professionals and explained to those who are not forensic practitioners (e.g. courts, judges, juries, prosecuting authorities, defense lawyers, coroners and law-enforcement professionals).

In the medicolegal setting, injury classification has different functions. For criminal law, it is to determine the means of causation and the severity, on which the penalty will be determined and to determine whether there is any defense. Additionally, it may be to determine whether a suspect could have carried out the actions said to have taken place.

For civil law, it is to determine causation and liability (individual, corporate) and to determine long-term prognosis and financial compensation. Those working as forensic practitioners should have the skills and expertise to make these assessments and present the finding to courts or tribunals. Consideration should be given to developing a standardized international format for documenting injuries, marks and scars, to ensure that all relevant evidence is retrieved and available to the justice system.

Such a "forensic medical classification of injury" for all medicolegal purposes needs to be established for use by forensic and non-forensic healthcare professionals. The nature of injury classification will be dependent on what purpose it is intended for and may be jurisdiction dependent. Ideally, documentation should be in written, body diagram, and image form – each complementing the other. The interpretation may include medical diagnosis, seriousness of injury, management and long-term prognosis although some aspects of these may be matters for courts in some jurisdictions.

TABLE 75.8 Range of injuries caused by blunt force (force may be direct or indirect)

• No injury	• Localized hematoma
• Tenderness	• Abrasions
• Pain	• Lacerations (cuts)
• Reddening	• Organ rupture
• Swelling	• Organ avulsion
• Bruising (including petechiae)	• Fractures

REFERENCES

1. Gall J, Payne-James J. Injury Interpretation: Possible Errors and Fallacies. In: Gall J, Payne-James JJ (eds), *Current Practice in Forensic Medicine*. Chichester: Wiley; 2011, pp. 239–71.
2. Payne-James JJ, Stark MM, Nittis M, Sheasby D. Injury Assessment, Documentation, and Interpretation. In: Stark MM (ed), *Clinical Forensic Medicine: A Physician's Guide*, 4th ed. Cham: Springer; 2020, pp. 127–58.
3. World Health Organisation. ICD-11 for mortality and morbidity statistics. Injury, poisoning or certain other consequences of external causes. Available from: https://icd.who.int/browse11/l-m/en#/http%3a%2f%2fid.who.int%2ficd%2fentity%2f435227771 (Accessed 14 June 2023).
4. Mueller- Wohlfahrt H-W, Haensel L, Mithoefer K, et al. Terminology and classification of muscle injuries in sport: The Munich consensus statement. *Br J Sports Med* 2013; **47**: 342–50.
5. Meilia P, Herkutanto, Atmadja DS, et al. The PERFORM-P (Principles of evidence-based Reporting in FORensic medicine-pathology version). *Forensic Sci Int* 2021; **327**: 110962.
6. Cecchi R, Cusack D, Ludes B, et al. European council of legal medicine (ECLM) on-site inspection forms for forensic pathology, anthropology, odontology, genetics, entomology and toxicology for forensic and medico-legal scene and corpse investigation. *Int J Legal Med* 2022; **136(4)**: 1037–49.
7. World Health Organisation. International classification of diseases (ICD 11), 2018. Available from: https://www.who.int/news/item/18-06-2018-who-releases-new-international-classification-of-diseases-(icd-11) (Accessed 14 June 2023).
8. Centers for Disease Control and Prevention. Occupational injury and illness classification system, 2021. Available from: https://wwwn.cdc.gov/wisards/oiics/ (Accessed 14 June 2023).
9. United Nations Human Rights. Istanbul protocol: Manual on the effective investigation and documentation of torture and other cruel, inhuman or degrading treatment or punishment, 2022. Available from: https://www.ohchr.org/en/publications/policy-and-methodological-publications/istanbul-protocol-manual-effective-0 (Accessed 14 June 2023).
10. JJC v Eisenhower [1984] QB 331.
11. Faculty of Forensic & Legal Medicine. PICS Working Group. Guidelines on photography, 2022. Available from: https://fflm.ac.uk/wp-content/uploads/2020/03/PICS-Working-Group-Guidelines-on-Photography-Dr-Will-Anderson-Dec-2019.pdf (Accessed 14 June 2023).
12. Stephenson T, Bialas Y. Estimation of the age of bruising. *Arch Dis Child* 1996; **74(1)**: 53–5.
13. Langlois NEI, Gresham GA. The ageing of bruises: A review and study of the colour changes with time. *Forensic Sci Int* 1991; **50**: 227–38.
14. Munang LA, Leonard PA, Mok JYQ. Lack of agreement on color description between clinicians examining childhood bruising. *J Clin Forensic Med* 2002; **9(4)**: 171–4.
15. Maguire S, Mann MK, Sibert J, Kemp A. Can you age bruises accurately in children? A systematic review. *Arch Dis Child* 2005; **90**: 187–9.
16. Royal College of Paediatrics and Child Health. Child Protection Evidence. Systematic review on Bruising, 2020. Available from: https://childprotection.rcpch.ac.uk/wp-content/uploads/sites/6/2021/02/Child-Protection-Evidence-Chapter-Bruising_Update_final.pdf (Accessed 14 June 2023).
17. Mesli V, Le Garff E, Marchand E, et al. Determination of the age of bruises using a bilirubinometer. *Forensic Sci Int* 2019; **302**: 109831.
18. Ren K, Wang L, Wang Y, et al. Wound age estimation based on next-generation sequencing: Fitting the optimal index system using machine learning. *Forensic Sci Int Genet* 2022; **59**: 102722.
19. Trefan L, Harris C, Evans S, et al. A comparison of four different imaging modalities - Conventional, cross polarized, infra-red and ultra-violet in the assessment of childhood bruising. *J Forensic Leg Med* 2018; **59**: 30–5.
20. Grossman SE, Johnston A, Vanezis P, Perrett D. Can we assess the age of bruises? An attempt to develop an objective technique. *Med Sci Law* 2011; **51(3)**: 170–6.
21. Scafide KN, Sheridan DJ, Downing NR, Hayat MJ. Detection of inflicted bruises by alternate light: Results of a randomized controlled trial. *J Forensic Sci* 2020; **65(4)**: 1191–8.
22. Barington K, Agger JF, Nielsen SS, et al. Gross and histopathological evaluation of human inflicted bruises in Danish slaughter pigs. *BMC Vet Res* 2016; **12(1)**: 247.
23. Maggioni L, Maderna E, Gorio MC, et al. The frequently dismissed importance of properly sampling skin bruises. *I Leg Med (Tokyo)* 2021; **50**: 101867.
24. Royal College of Paediatrics and Child Health. Child protection evidence – Burns, 2022. Available from: https://childprotection.rcpch.ac.uk/child-protection-evidence/burns-systematic-review (Accessed 14 June 2023).

11\. Stephenson T, Bialas Y. Estimation of the age of bruising. *Arch Dis Child* 1996 **74(1)**: 53–5.

12\. Langlois NEI, Gresham GA. The ageing of bruises: a review and study of the colour changes with time. *Forensic Sci Int* 1991; **50**: 227–238.

13\. Munang LA, Leonard PA, Mok JYQ. Lack of agreement on color description between clinicians examining childhood bruising. *J Clin Forensic Med* 2002; **9(4)**: 171–174.

14\. Maguire S, Mann MK, Sibert J, Kemp A. Can you age bruises accurately in children? A systematic review. *Arch Dis Child* 2005; **90**: 187–189.

15\. Royal College of Paediatrics & Child Health. Child Protection Evidence. Systematic review on Bruising. Child-Protection-Evidence-Chapter-Bruising_Update_final.pdf March 2020 Available from: https://childprotection.rcpch.ac.uk/wp-content/uploads/sites/6/2021/02/Child-Protection-Evidence-Chapter-Bruising_Update_final.pdf (Accessed 260923).

16\. Mesli V, Le Garff E, Marchand E, et al. Determination of the age of bruises using a bilirubinometer. *Forensic Sci Int* 2019; **302**: 109831. doi: 10.1016/j.forsciint.2019.05.047.

17\. Ren K, Wang L, Wang Y, et al. Wound age estimation based on next-generation sequencing: Fitting the optimal index system using machine learning. *Forensic Sci Int Genet* 2022; **59**: 102722.

18\. Trefan L, Harris C, Evans S, et al. A comparison of four different imaging modalities - Conventional, cross polarized, infra-red and ultra-violet in the assessment of childhood bruising. *J Forensic Leg Med* 2018; **59**: 30–35.

19\. Grossman SE, Johnston A, Vanezis P, Perrett D. Can we assess the age of bruises? An attempt to develop an objective technique. *Med Sci Law* 2011; **51 (3)**: 170–6.

20\. Scafide KN, Sheridan DJ, Downing NR, Hayat MJ. Detection of inflicted bruises by alternate light: Results of a randomized controlled trial. *J Forensic Sci* 2020; **65(4)**: 1191–1198.

21\. Barington K, Agger JF, Nielsen SS, et al. Gross and histopathological evaluation of human inflicted bruises in Danish slaughter pigs. *BMC Vet Res* 2016; **12(1)**: 247.

22\. Maggioni L, Maderna E, Gorio MC, et al. The frequently dismissed importance of properly sampling skin bruises. *I Leg Med (Tokyo)* 2021; **50**: 101867.

23\. Royal College of Paediatrics & Child Health. Child Protection Evidence. Systematic review on burns. Available from: https://childprotection.rcpch.ac.uk/child-protection-evidence/burns-systematic-review October 2021 (Accessed 11 September 2023).

CHAPTER

76

Imaging of Trauma in the Living

Curtis E. Offiah

INTRODUCTION

Trauma, sometimes serious and multiple, constituting major trauma, is common and may require life-saving interventions. Trauma remains the biggest cause of death in people aged less than 45 years old in the United Kingdom; a significant proportion of survivors are left with permanent disability. Radiologic imaging is central to the management of traumatic injuries of varying degrees of severity. In the acute setting, this radiologic imaging takes the form of computed tomography (CT) imaging, particularly in the more severe degrees of trauma, sometimes additional magneitc resonance imaging (MRI) and/or plain radiography (X-rays), particularly in levels of traumatic injury that are not considered in the major trauma category.

ADVANTAGES

Radiologic imaging performed primarily with the aim of directing medical or surgical management of injuries of a victim, also details mechanism of injury, wound profile and potential causation when evaluated from a specialist forensic perspective by a forensic radiologist. Clinical radiologic imaging, if available, therefore provides a wealth of information for forensic purposes at an early and, importantly, at a later stage. The soft-tissue and bone injury patterns evident on CT scans performed on victims of blunt trauma can give indication of mechanisms of trauma and age of trauma while such imaging performed on victims of penetrating trauma (sharp force penetrating trauma such as knife wounds and projectile penetrating trauma such as gunshot wounds) on emergency hospital admission can also provide detail on trajectory of penetrating trauma as well as, for example, entry versus exit wounds on victims of perforating bullet injuries.

LIMITATIONS

When the radiologist evaluates and interprets scans, it is the source data (i.e. the axial hundreds or thousands of images) that are evaluated for injuries as well as coronal and sagittal reconstructions of this axial source data set of images. CT scans can, if of adequate resolution, be used to create three-dimensional (3D) image reconstructions (volume-rendered and surface-rendered reconstructions) which can be a useful way of presenting soft-tissue injuries and fractures of the axial and appendicular skeleton to the non-radiologist or lay-person. However, it is vital to understand that whenever source data acquired in clinical imaging such as CT scans is post-processed or manipulated in any way, particularly 3D reconstructions, vital clinical and forensic radiologic information within such data (i.e. the source data) will be lost (1).

A final potential limitation of any cross-sectional radiologic imaging relates to the way in which the scan parameters are set up and performed (sometimes referred to as the *scan protocol*). In imaging of major trauma in the living, there are evidence-based guidance protocols recommended – for example, in the United Kingdom, scan protocol recommendations are provided by the Royal College of Radiologists (2) which can mitigate the occurrence of suboptimal imaging at certain hospitals and scans of reduced resolution for example. However, this is not uniform across all hospitals throughout the United Kingdom (3–5).

Plain X-rays

Plain X-rays are also termed plain radiographs; these are projections most frequently used in the initial diagnosis and evaluation of appendicular skeletal fractures and some axial skeletal fractures where the injury is at the milder end of the spectrum. They may also be used in the follow-up of fractures. While of limited sensitivity (and specificity), for more complex fractures and more severe fractures compared to cross-sectional imaging modalities such as CT imaging and MRI, plain X-rays remain a central and essential part of clinical management of non-major trauma and are also of significant value in forensic radiology (Figures 76.1 and 76.2).

Types of cross-sectional radiologic imaging

In the acute trauma setting, this falls largely into two types of scan or imaging modalities – CT scanning and

DOI: 10.1201/9781003138754-79

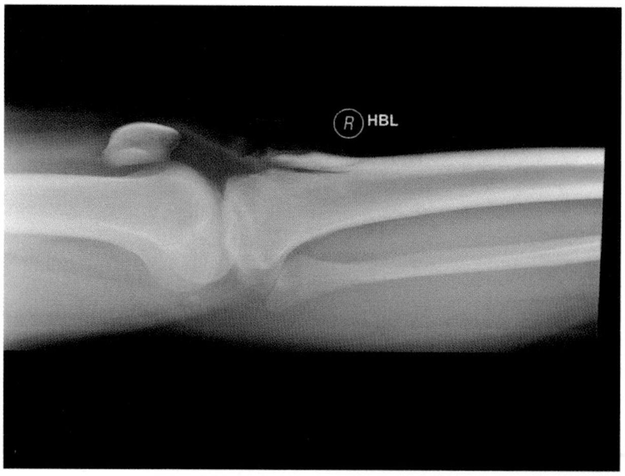

76.1 Lateral plain X-ray of the right knee demonstrates chop injury to the right knee inflicted with a machete in a male subject to an assault. Fracture through the proximal anterior tibial bone and overlying soft-tissue injury are demonstrated.

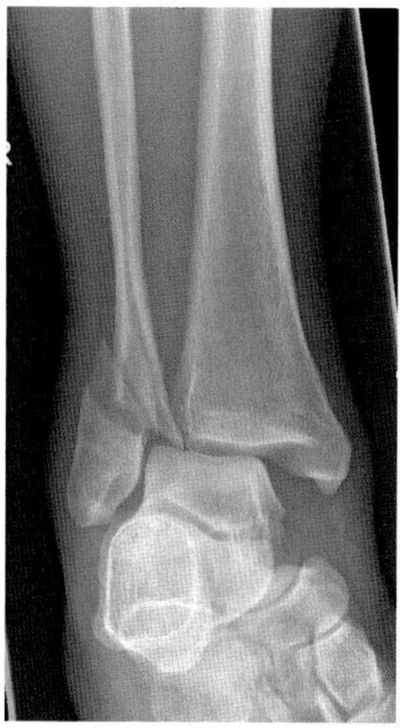

76.2 Frontal plain X-ray projection of the right ankle of a young adult male involved in an altercation sustaining fracture dislocation of the right ankle, consistent with external rotational force applied to a right foot fixed in the supinated (inwardly inclined) position at the time the twisting mechanism was sustained. The fracture appearances are not consistent with inflicted blunt impact trauma as alleged by the individual.

MRI scanning. Most cross-sectional imaging of this nature will be in the form of CT scanning – both for the surviving victim of trauma as well as for post-mortem imaging of fatalities.

THE BASICS

CT scanning

CT is the work-horse for imaging of traumatic injuries in the twenty-first century for clinical management and treatment of the majority of significant acute traumatic injuries of victims and, secondly, for extracting forensic radiologic findings relating to those injuries, where requested, or deemed helpful to the forensic investigation of such injuries. There have been significant advances in CT technology (in particular, multi-detector technology) over the last decade which make CT scanning central to the clinical (and subsequently forensic) evaluation of various traumatic injuries. The technique involves volume acquisition of a stack of axial slices of the body or region of the body using X-ray tubes and an array of aligned detectors. The acquired images are translated into a gray-scale. In the live patient, intravenous (IV) contrast can be injected into the patient/victim to identify significant vascular injury, active hemorrhage and increase the sensitivity and specificity of identification of visceral injury. The inherent disadvantage of CT scanning is that it utilizes ionizing radiation (X-rays) with all of the potential hereditary and deterministic side effects associated with ionizing radiation exposure. However, where the benefits to the patient/victim surpass the potential risks, such as in major trauma, CT scanning will be undertaken. The advantages of CT scanning are that it is a fast-imaging modality and is particularly sensitive and specific in the setting of trauma (6,7).

MRI scanning

MRI is an imaging modality based on the application of radiofrequency pulses to the body having placed the patient/victim in a high strength magnet (typically 1.5 Tesla or 3 Tesla). The radiofrequency pulses applied within the magnetic field causes movements of protons in the tissues of the body which will subsequently emit energy when they return to their normal position when the radiofrequency pulse ceases (8). The energy emitted is captured (in k-space) and, using mathematic algorithms, converted to an image. The main advantages of MRI scanning is that it does not use ionizing radiation and it has inherently superior contrast resolution for soft-tissue interrogation than CT scanning. The disadvantage and significant limiting factors of MRI scanning in the acute trauma imaging setting is that it is slower (comprehensive scanning of a body region can take approximately 20 to 30 minutes), it is not as sensitive or specific for identification of acute fractures as CT scanning and patients/victims with ferromagnetic substances within them (such as certain metals) such as certain types of pacemakers or bullets or knife tips cannot be imaged in MRI scanners because of the magnetic field strength. Patients who are intubated and require ventilatory anesthetic equipment (containing metal components) can only be imaged in specialist (typically) tertiary hospital radiology departments where specially adapted MRI-compatible equipment (such as adapted anesthetic machines) are available. Nevertheless, there are frequent situations where victims of severe trauma may subsequently (after CT imaging) require an MRI scan such as urgent evaluation of severe traumatic spinal injuries or certain cases of severe traumatic brain injury (TBI). Cost analysis of fixed CT and MRI scanners involves consideration of scanner purchase costs, building and siting costs, installation costs of the scanner as well as purchase costs of the associated software, maintenance and repair costs of the scanners and operating costs including staffing costs by radiographers/scanning technicians and running costs. There is an approximately 3- to 4-fold greater cost of a fixed MRI scanner compared to fixed CT scanner.

TYPES OF TRAUMA

There are a number of ways of categorizing traumatic injuries but a simple and broad division is between blunt force trauma (such as vehicular collision injuries or inflicted third-party assault or intimate partner abuse) and penetrating force trauma (such as stab injuries or gunshot injuries) and blunt force injury (although there are other types of frequently encountered soft-tissue injury such as chemical injury or thermal/fire-related injury which do not fall into either of these two broad categories). This broad categorization also allows useful observation of national statistics in any particular country and trends in overall violent crime. In the United Kingdom, the Crime Survey of England and Wales (Office of National Statistics) estimated approximately 1.5 million incidences of violence for the survey year ending March 2022. While the role of radiology in the assessment of trauma is too expansive a subject to detail comprehensively in this chapter, some examples of where clinical trauma radiology and imaging as a day-to-day clinical/medical subspecialty (particularly at the more severe end of the spectrum of trauma) impacts forensic medicine of trauma in the living, with a view to injury causation and correlates, will be provided in broader terms to offer an overview and understanding of radiology in forensic medicine.

Blunt trauma

The most common type of fatal and non-fatal trauma remains blunt force injury. The occurrence and extent of injury depends on the amount of force sustained. The primary role of CT imaging in the living in the setting of trauma is to direct treatment to preserve or save life or direct appropriate treatment to limit morbidity related to traumatic injuries. The radiologic imaging assessment used for medical and surgical management also offers the opportunity for forensic radiologic interpretation of such scans (9).

Suspected TBI related to blunt force mechanisms is a frequent occurrence in accidental and non-accidental trauma in infants and in adults (Figures 76.3–76.5). Non-enhanced (or non-contrast) CT head scan is critical for the triage of such patients to image intracranial pathology. This imaging modality has the advantage of speed and accessibility and sensitivity for depicting injuries that require neurosurgical intervention such as large volume space-occupying hematoma, herniation or evolving infarction (10–12).

CT imaging also has the advantage of detection of craniofacial fractures, for example, (Figures 76.6 and 76.7) or in the setting of severe blunt trauma to the head or neck, identification of craniocervical junction or subaxial cervical spine fractures. Craniofacial fractures can be life-threatening or life-changing depending on the associated damage of neighboring structures such as vascular and neural structures but also due to secondary association with traumatic injury to other sites such as critical vascular structures in the neck (e.g. the vertebral arteries or common carotid or internal carotid arteries. Craniofacial fractures with skull-base extension may also cause and result in such traumatic vascular (dissection) injury of the internal carotid arteries as they traverse the carotid canal through the skull base or of the vertebral arteries as they traverse the foramina of the craniocervical junction vertebrae and enter the foramen magnum just below and at the skull base respectively.

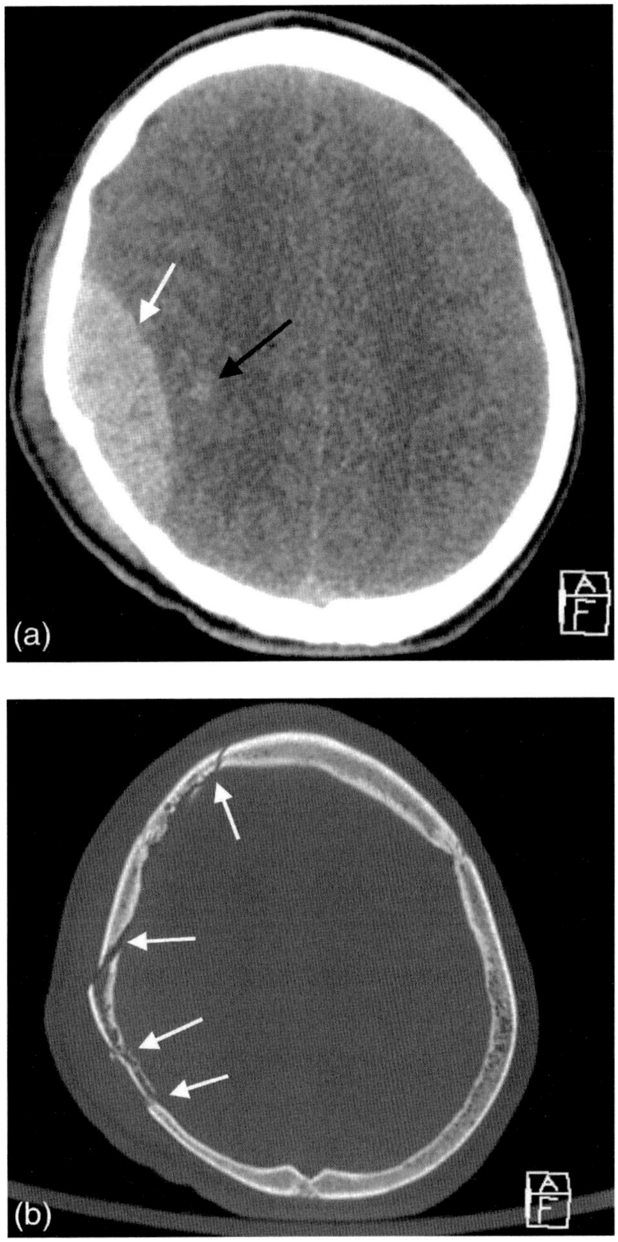

76.3 (a) Axial CT head image (on soft-tissue windows) of victim of blunt trauma to right side of the head following assault showing large extradural hematoma (white arrow) and subjacent cortical and subcortical hemorrhagic brain parenchymal contusions (black arrow) and severe mass effect. Note overlying scalp soft-tissue hematoma. **(b)** Axial CT head image (on bone windows) of the same victim showing extensive fracture of the overlying skull vault (arrows) with involvement of middle meningeal vessel channels in the affected skull vault.

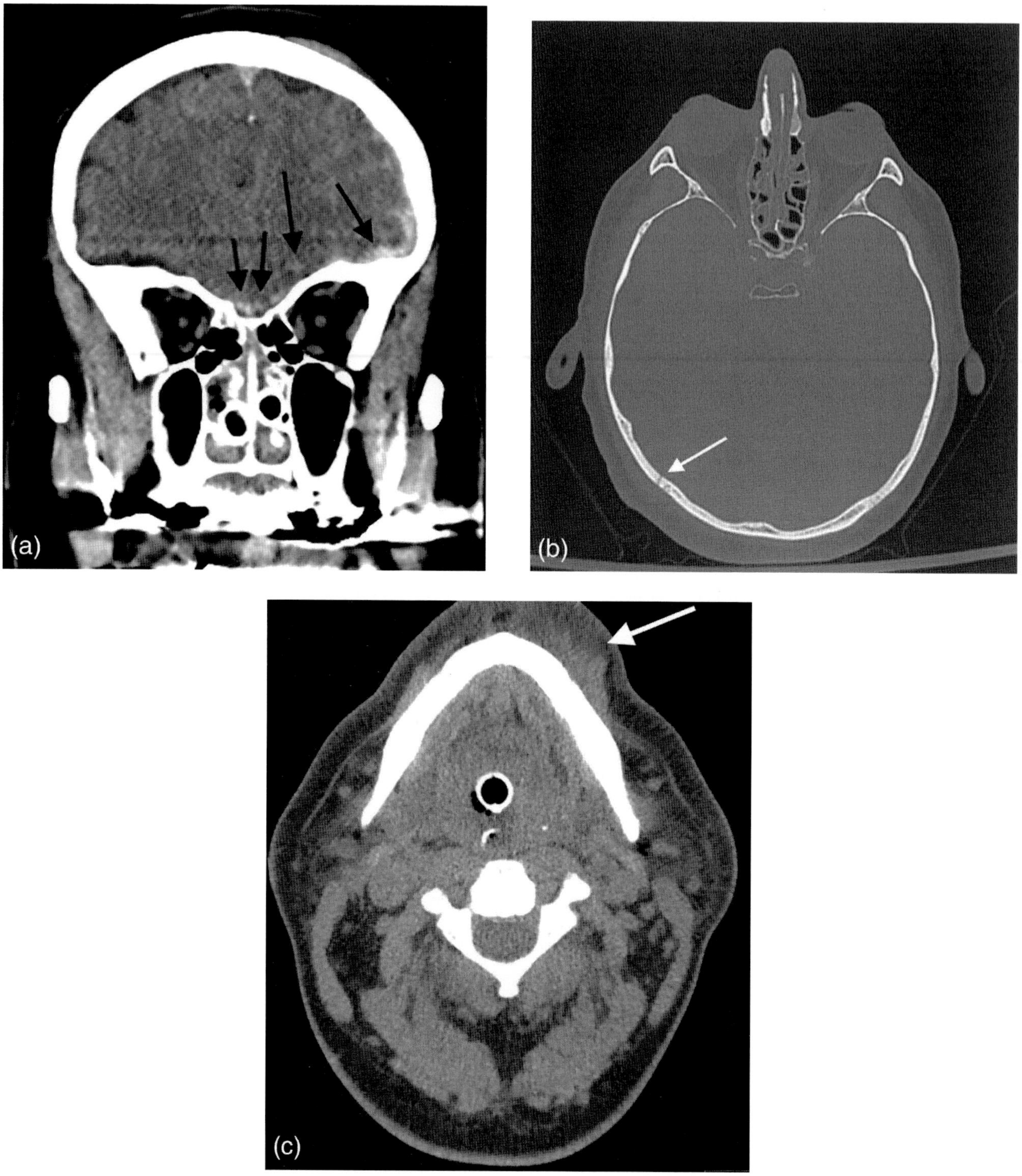

76.4 CT images of victim of one-punch head injury. **(a)** Contrecoup frontobasal hemorrhagic brain parenchymal contusions (black arrows) and traumatic subarachnoid hemorrhage (black arrows); **(b)** there is fracture (white arrow) of the posterior skull vault at the coup site of blunt traumatic impact against the ground; **(c)** left lower facial soft-tissue hematoma indicates the site of the inflicted punch to the left side of the jaw (white arrow).

Many craniocerebral and craniofacial blunt traumatic events may be associated with significant evidence-based risk to the craniocervical spine and sub-axial cervical spine and forms the basis of many national head injury assessment guidelines and recommendations in different countries (in the United Kingdom, this is the diagnosis and early management of head injury guidelines issued by the National Institute of Health and Care Excellence [NICE]). In the acute emergency setting, as well as a CT head scan, a CT scan of the cervical spine will also be performed on the trauma victim (13,14). Isolated blunt traumatic injury to the neck may also necessitate CT

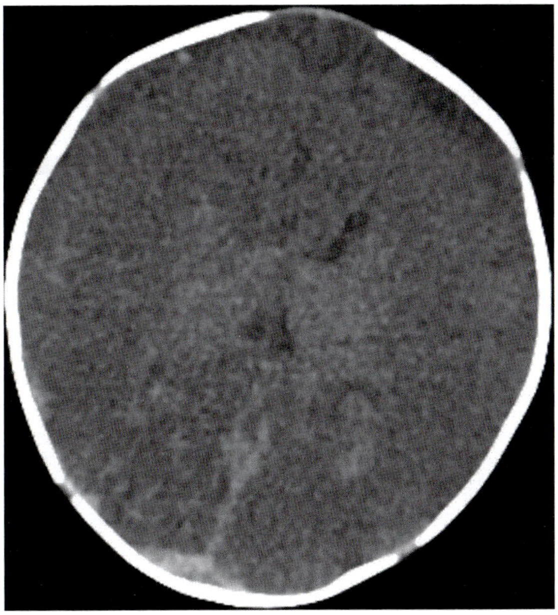

76.5 10-week-old baby with evidence of abusive head trauma on CT scan. There is acute bilateral subdural hemorrhage, intraventricular hemorrhage and subarachnoid hemorrhage as well as secondary severe hypoxic ischemic encephalopathy with loss of gray-white differentiation throughout the cortex.

scan of the cervical spine in the acute emergency setting. Where there is risk to the critical vessels of the neck, in cases of significant blunt craniofacial trauma or blunt neck trauma, a specific CT-imaging protocol called CT angiography using IV contrast allows evaluation of the integrity of these vessels and identification of any transection (more frequently in the setting of sharp force penetrating trauma) or occlusive or non-occlusive traumatic vascular dissection injury of these vessels which may then pose risk to upstream brain perfusion (with potential for infarction).

Blunt traumatic impacts to the anterior neck, be it due to accidental motor vehicular trauma or physical assault, may result in laryngeal fractures with life-threatening airway compromise either from laryngeal airway distortion or endolaryngeal submucosal hemorrhage and bleeding into the laryngeal airway. CT imaging may be performed in the acute setting specifically to evaluate the laryngo-tracheal cartilaginous skeleton for fractures and dislocations or laryngo-tracheal separation, or laryngo-tracheal damage may be identified on acute CT imaging performed to evaluate the cervical spine where cervical spine injury is suspected clinically (15).

Victims subject to non-fatal manual or ligature strangulation and near-hanging with ligature/noose, whether self-inflicted, or third-party inflicted, may be referred for emergency acute CT imaging of the neck if clinical concern exists. While most surviving victims are managed conservatively without imaging, many will undergo acute CT imaging. Acute CT scanning of victims as well as on acute and, where required, subacute MRI scanning, may demonstrate not only the ligature marking or furrowing on the skin surface, but also subcutaneous/subdermal soft-tissue contusion in the superficial fascia and deep cervical fascia including the deep cervical fascia surrounding the carotid sheaths as well as the strap muscles of the neck (16,17) (*see also* Chapter 84, "Non-Fatal Strangulation"). Laryngeal fractures or hyoid bone fractures will also be demonstrated on CT imaging, particularly in adult victims where the laryngeal cartilaginous skeleton has begun to calcify (Figure 76.8).

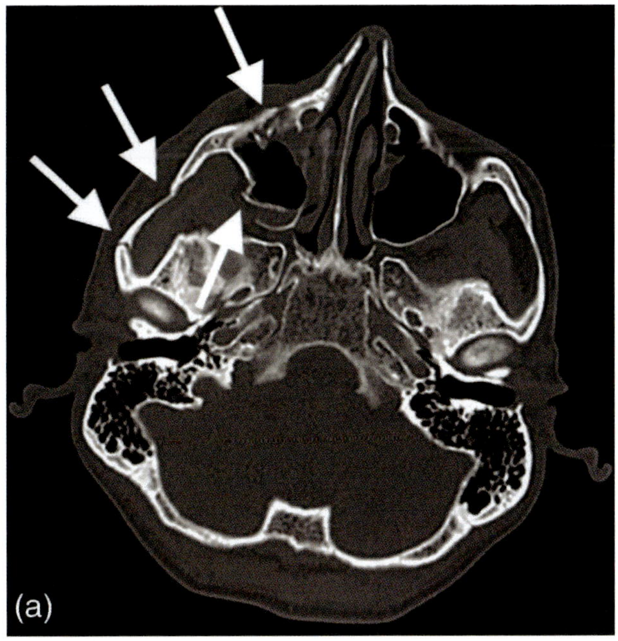

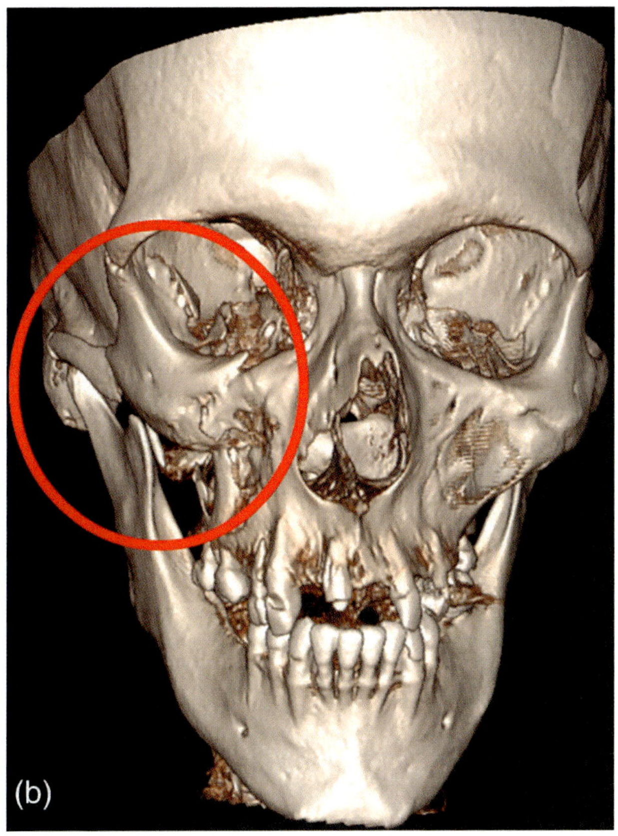

76.6 Adult male victim of assault with **(a)** axial CT image demonstrating some of the fractures of the right zygomatico-maxillary "quadripod" fracture (sometimes termed "tripod" fracture) sustained; **(b)** volume rendered reconstruction (3D reconstruction) of the fracture (annotated with red oval).

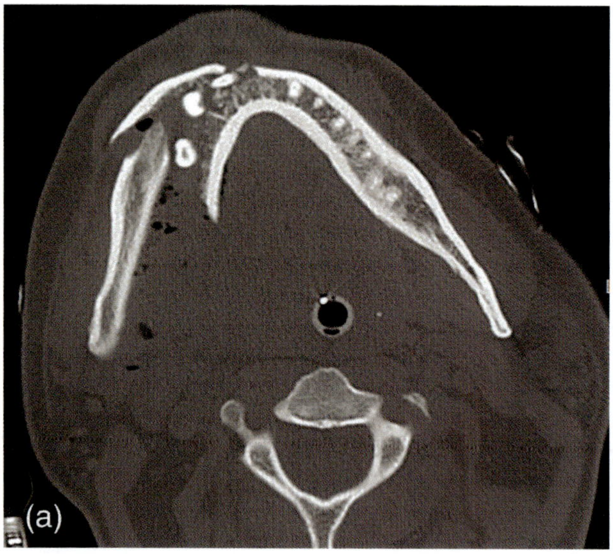

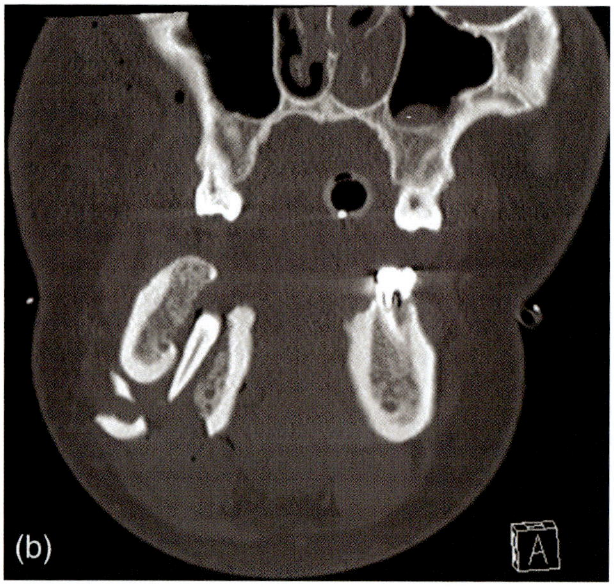

76.7 Victim of assault with severe mandibular fractures and associated avulsed dental trauma with some teeth displaced into fracture sites of the anterior (parasymphyseal) right body of the mandible demonstrated on **(a)** axial and **(b)** coronal CT images.

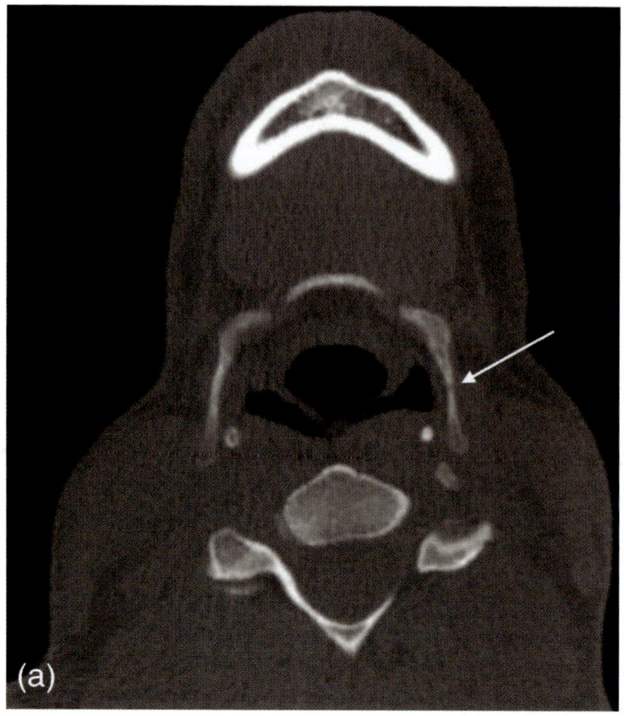

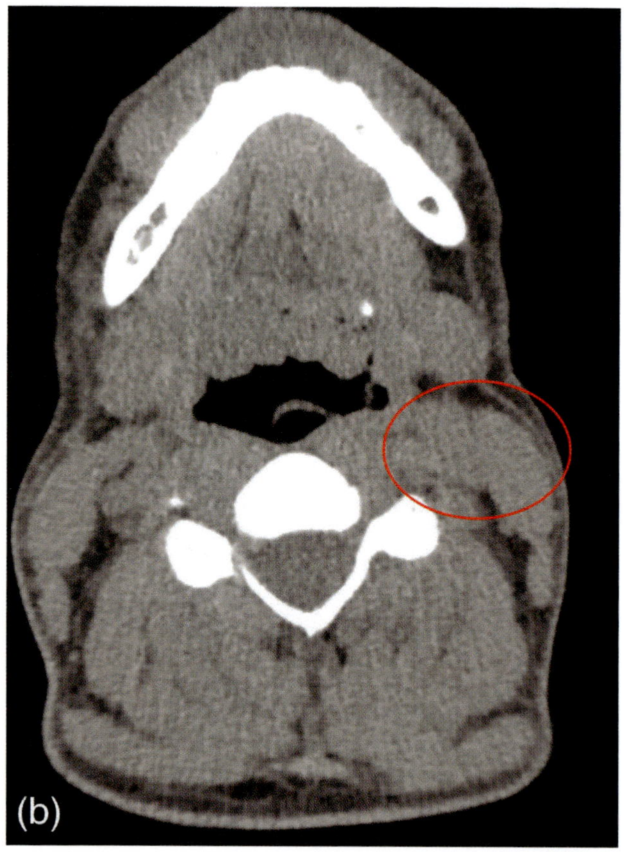

76.8 Middle-aged female adult victim of attempted strangulation. **(a)** Axial CT images demonstrate undisplaced fracture of the left greater horn of the hyoid bone (white arrow) and **(b)** loss of normal deep cervical fascia planes (compare abnormal left side to normal right side deep soft-tissue planes) in keeping with localized traumatic hematoma in the left deep cervical fascia overlying region of the left hyoid bone fracture (annotated with red oval).

Thoracic, abdominal and pelvic blunt force traumatic injuries are common manifestations of accidental and non-accidental blunt trauma particularly where such trauma is at the more severe end of the spectrum. Acute CT imaging will frequently be required to assess the nature of injuries, injury severity and the most appropriate management and treatment of those injuries (Figures 76.9–76.11) (18,19). The CT scan coverage of the chest and/or abdomen and/or pelvis also allows essential evaluation of the thoracic spine and/or lumbar spine and/or the pelvic bones for fractures (Figure 76.12).

Blunt traumatic injury to the spine carries a significant risk to life and risk of significant morbidity in survivors. Where significant fracture is identified in acute CT imaging of the cervical spine of thoracic of lumbo-sacral

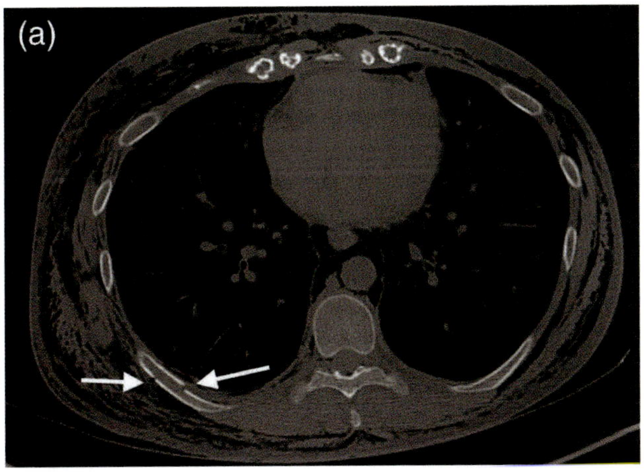

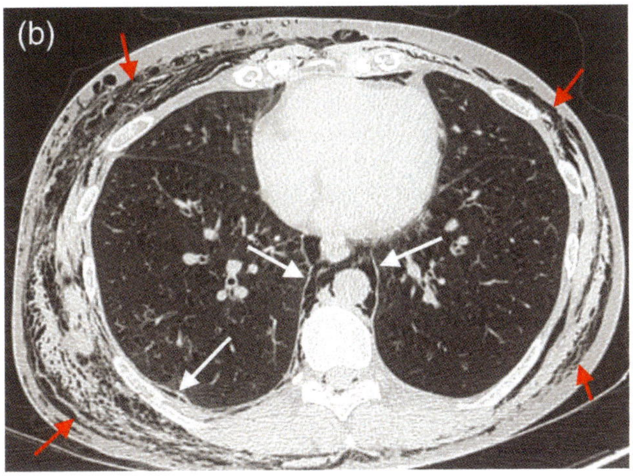

76.9 Elderly male subject to assault sustaining **(a)** fracture of the posterior segment of a lower right rib (white arrow) and **(b)** severe secondary soft-tissue emphysema (red arrows) and shallow right pneumothorax and pneumomediastinum (white arrows).

spine or, even in the absence of fractures, there is pertinent neurologic abnormality evident on clinical examination. MRI of the spine may be performed to look for evidence of spinal cord injury such as contusion or laceration or compressive accumulation of traumatic hemorrhage within the spinal canal (epidural or subdural hemorrhage) or ligamentous injury raising the possibility of spinal instability (Figure 76.12b) or nerve root avulsion (e.g., motorcyclists involved in high-speed collisions where brachial plexus injury may be sustained). The sensitivity and specificity of MRI far exceeds CT imaging for close evaluation and radiologic diagnosis of such neural injury.

Penetrating trauma

In the United Kingdom, according to the Office of National Statistics, the Crime Survey for England and Wales ending March 2020 determined that the most common method of killing, for both male and female victims was by a sharp instrument. The volume of victims of sharp force trauma encountering radiologic imaging, typically CT scanning, is considerable, particularly in the major trauma centers. These victims may or, sadly, may not survive but therein exists a wealth of forensically extractable information in the emergency hospital admission CT scans undertaken on victims of inflicted sharp force trauma (20).

Any area of the body can obviously be subject to sharp force penetrating trauma. Incised wounds (cuts) and stab wounds are examples of sharp force injuries (21–23). A slash wound is essentially an incised wound caused by a sharp-edged instrument such as a knife moving across the skin surface. While distinction is typically made between sharp force injury and blunt force injury, some injuries overlap and exhibit a combination of the two such as machete or axe injuries (chop injuries) and sometimes "glassing" injuries.

With the advances in multi-detector (multi-slice) CT imaging, the forensic radiologic evaluation of sharp force injuries has expanded significantly in addition to the clinical diagnostic evaluation (4,16,26,27). In the acute sharp force injury setting, acute emergency CT scanning of the victim is frequently undertaken as part of medical/surgical management. Most frequently, this CT imaging will be performed on the head in cases of craniocerebral penetrating trauma or on the craniofacial region in cases of orbito-facial sharp force penetrating trauma or on the neck in cases of stab injuries to the neck. In cases of craniocerebral penetrating trauma or neck penetrating trauma, CT angiography will be utilized to assess critical vascular damage such as vessel transection and active hemorrhage, vascular dissection injury and pseudoaneurysm formation and traumatic arteriovenous fistula formation (28,29). Stab wound tracks, as well as tissue and organ injury, can be evaluated on this acute CT imaging as part of forensic wound profiling of directionality/trajectory as well as the life-threatening nature of the stab wound (30). Wound tracks can be depicted in the live victim by assessing, not only characteristic skin surface wounds, but also hematoma along the wound track which may be accompanied by soft-tissue emphysema extending along the wound track and active bleeding from small or critical blood vessels captured on contrast-enhanced CT scans performed on the live victim (Figure 76.13).

Non-fatal gunshot injuries (i.e. those which are not immediately fatal) will frequently undergo emergency CT scanning on presentation to the Emergency Department of a hospital or Trauma Center. The use of non-contrast CT imaging of the brain, together with CT angiography of the brain, will frequently be required in cases of craniocerebral gunshot injuries (Figure 76.14); the latter to evaluate the frequently occurring intracranial vascular injury component and any active vascular bleeding site as well as prognostication. Global hypoxic ischemic encephalopathy may be present where the brainstem has been directly involved or "stunned" by the secondary shockwaves initiated by a closely related bullet wound track and perforating craniocerebral bullet injuries or bullet wound tracks that have transgressed more than one lobe or more than one hemisphere of the brain carry a poorer survival prognosis (28). With gunshot injuries to the neck, acute CT angiography of the neck is performed to evaluate the cervical spine for penetrating injury but also the critical vessels of the neck as well as

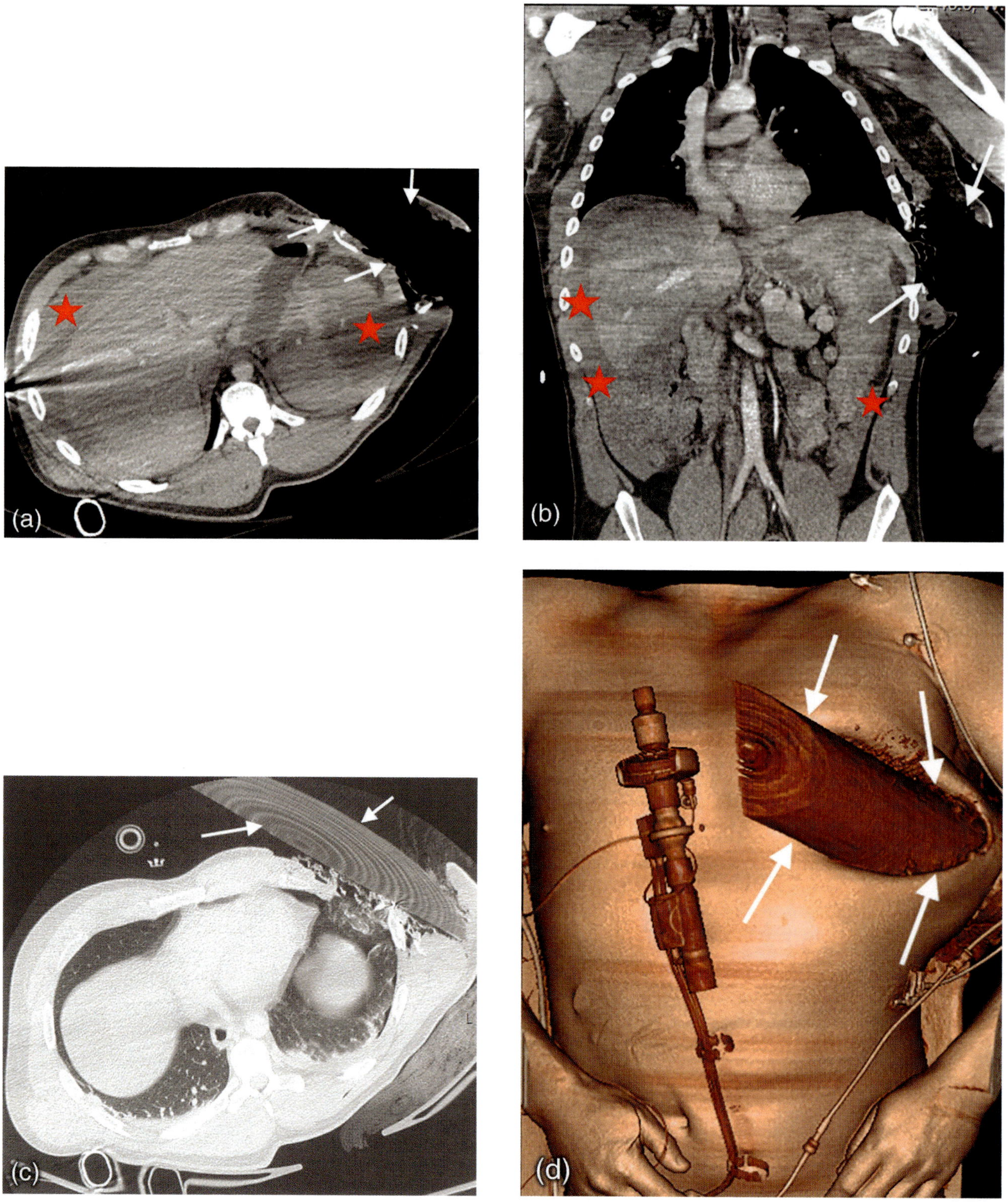

76.10 Middle-aged male fell from a height during a work accident sustaining impalement injury of the left chest. **(a)** and **(b)** show severe intra-abdominal hemorrhage and splenic injury present (stars) and left lateral chest wall injury associated with large wooden pole (white arrow) which is more discernible on **(c)** "lung windows" because of the air within the wooden pole (white arrow) and the appearances on **(d)** volume-rendered (3D) reconstruction (anesthetic ventilation tubing is lying on the front of the chest to the right of the wooden pole).

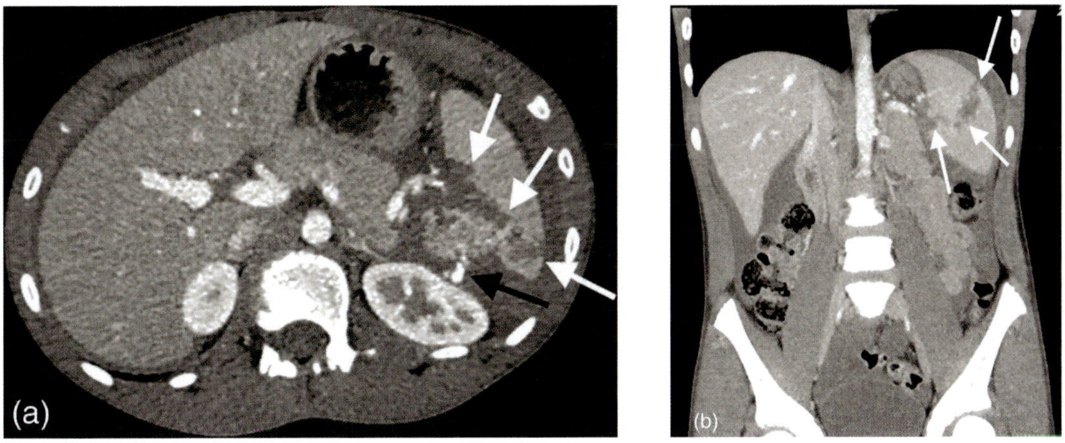

76.11 Teenager sustained fall from a skateboard with **(a)** axial and **(b)** coronal CT image demonstrating high-grade splenic laceration (white arrow) with active bleeding into the abdomen. There is pancreatic tail injury also present. Active extravasation of contrast on this contrast-enhanced CT scan (black arrow) indicates active bleeding from traumatic dissection injury of a splenic arterial vessel.

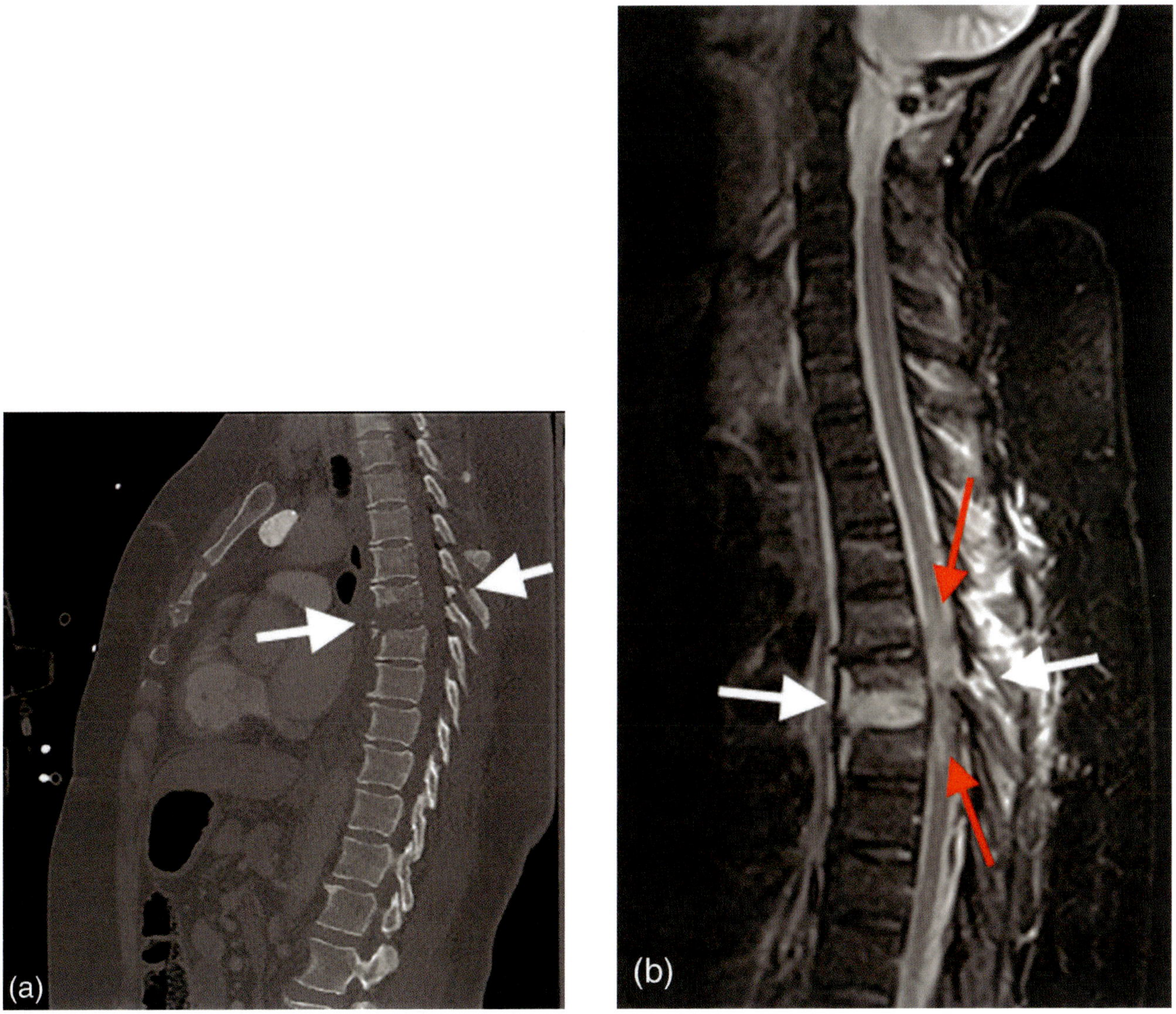

76.12 Middle-aged female crushed against a wall by a vehicle which reversed accidentally. **(a)** CT scan demonstrated severe unstable three-column injury – a Chance fracture (white arrows) of the thoracic spine which indicates high-grade spinal injury; **(b)** sagittal STIR MR image demonstrates severe spinal cord injury and cord laceration (red arrows).

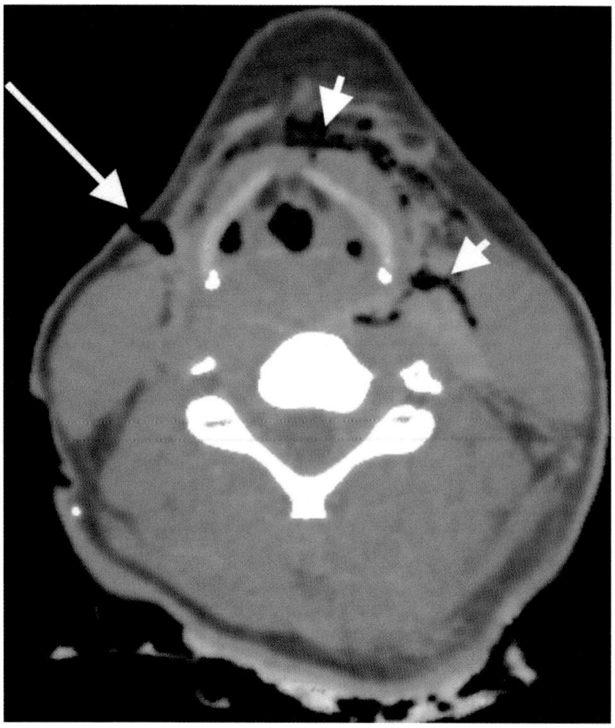

76.13 Adult male victim of stab injury to the right anterolateral neck (zone 2). Axial CT image demonstrates stab wound entry (long white arrow) and areas of soft-tissue emphysema (short white arrows) caused by penetration of the larynx and pharynx (not shown) by the stab wound track.

the laryngopharynx (29). Imaging can be affected somewhat by the frequently occurring bullet fragmentation which produces streak artefacts on CT scanning caused by the metal fragments and this can obscure neighboring radiologic detail. With gunshot injuries to the chest, abdomen or pelvis, contrast-enhanced CT acquisitions are used (similar to those used in blunt trauma radiologic evaluation) and this assists evaluation of vascular injury and areas of active bleeding. Not infrequently, the limbs may sustain bullet injuries, and where focussed and severe, acute emergency CT angiography of the limb may be performed if (similar to penetrating trauma of the neck, chest, abdomen of pelvis) active hemorrhage is not profound and uncontrolable and *immediately* life-threatening requiring immediate transfer to the operating theater without any emergency imaging – so-called Code-Red situations. There is an absolute contraindication of MRI of firearms injuries in the acute setting because of the specific metallic nature and composition of most bullets which may move within the body of the victim when subject to the strong magnetic fields associated with MRI scanners.

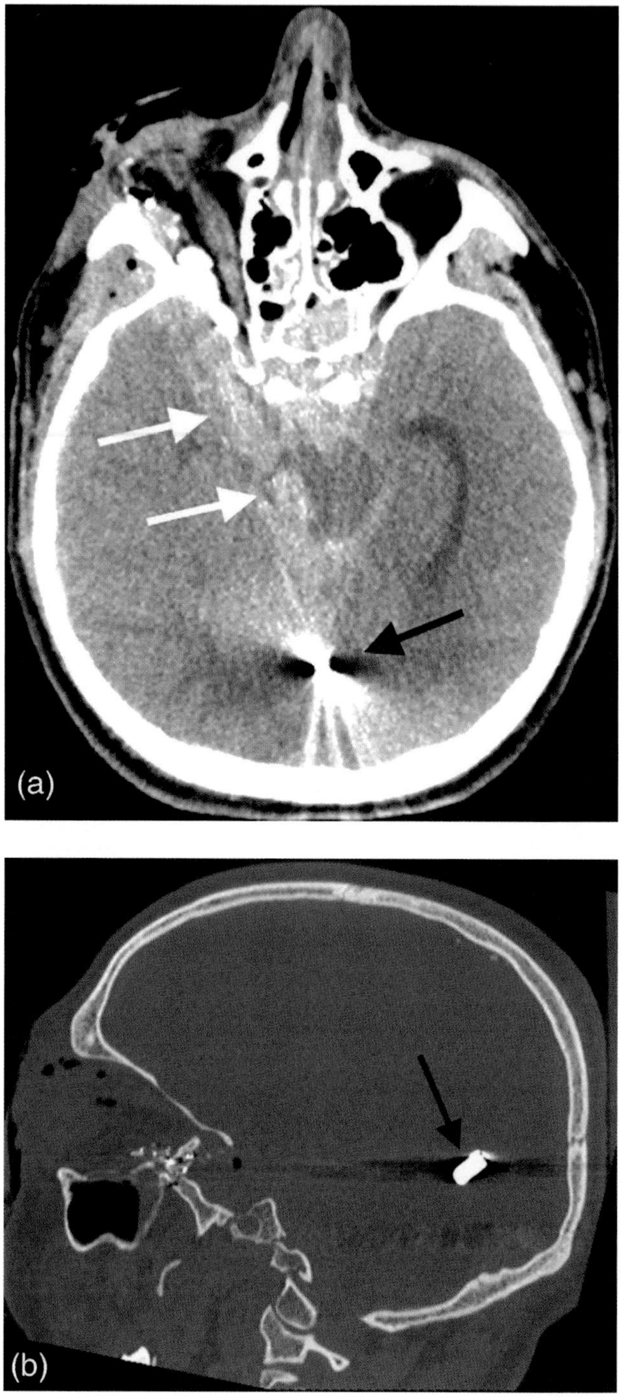

76.14 Young adult male victim of orbito-cranial penetrating gunshot injury to the head demonstrated on **(a)** axial CT image with entry through the right orbit and severe hemorrhagic brain injury and hemorrhagic bullet wound track through the right side of the brain including the brainstem (white arrows) and **(b)** sagittal oblique CT image showing bullet (black arrow) located within the right occipital lobe producing streak artefact because of its metallic nature.

CONCLUSION

Radiologic imaging is a central part of the clinical management of victims of trauma of all degrees. This may take the form of plain X-rays and/or CT imaging and/or, in certain cases MRI. In trauma at the more severe end of the spectrum, victims will all invariably be subject to some form of CT scanning which is the most frequently utilized imaging modality for these victims admitted to hospital emergency departments. While such emergency imaging is performed to facilitate the rapid diagnosis and treatment of injuries sustained by the victim, the existence of such imaging should always be borne in mind given its value to the forensic investigation pathway and may be crucial in corroborating or clarifying clinical findings.

REFERENCES

1. Borowska-Solonynko A, Solonynko B. The use of 3D computed tomography reconstruction in medico-legal testimony regarding injuries in living victims - Risks and benefits. *J Forensic Leg Med* 2015; 30: 9–13.
2. RCR. *Standards of Practice and Guidance for Trauma Radiology in Severely Injured Patients*, 2nd ed. London: Royal College of Radiologists; 2015.
3. Grassberger M, Gehl A, Puschel K, Turk EE. 3D reconstruction of emergency cranial computed tomography scans as a tool in clinical forensic radiology after survived blunt head trauma – report of two cases. *Forensic Sci Int* 2011; **207**: e19–e23.
4. Aromatario M, Cappelletti S, Bottoni E, et al. Weapon identification using antemortem CT with 3D reconstruction, is it always possible?-- A report in a case of facial blunt and sharp injuries using an ashtray. *Leg Med (Tokyo)* 2016; **18**: 1–6.
5. Bauer M, Polzin S, Patzelt D. The use of clinical CCT images in the forensic examination of closed head injuries. *J Clin Forensic Med* 2004; **11**(**2**): 65–70.
6. Prokop M. General principles of MDCT. *Eur J Radiol* 2003; **45**: 4–10.
7. Rydberg J, Buckwalter KA, Caldemeyer KS, et al. Multisection CT: scanning techniques and clinical applications. *Radiographics* 2000; **20**(**6**): 1787–806.
8. Pooley RA. AAPM/RSNA physics tutorial for residents: Fundamental physics of MR imaging. *Radiographics* 2005; **25**(**4**): 1087–99.
9. Schuh P, Scheurer E, Fritz K, et al. Can clinical CT data improve forensic reconstruction? *Int J Legal Med* 2013; **127**(3): 631–8.
10. Schweitzer AD, Niogi SN, Whitlow CT, Tsiouris AJ. Traumatic brain injury: Imaging patterns and complications. *RadioGraphics* 2019; **39**(**6**): 1571–95.
11. Mutch CA, Talbott JF, Gean A. Imaging evaluation of acute traumatic brain injury. *Neurosurg Clin N Am* 2016; **27**(**4**): 409–39.
12. Parizel PM, Philips CD. Traumatic Neuroemergency: Imaging Patients with Traumatic Brain Injury—An Introduction. In: Hodler J, Kubik-Huch R, von Schulthess G (eds), *Diseases of the Brain, Head and Neck, Spine 2020–2023*. Cham: Springer; 2020 pp. 87–101.
13. Dreizin D, Letzing M, Sliker CW, et al. Multidetector CT of blunt cervical spine trauma in adults. *RadioGraphics* 2014; **34**(**7**): 1842–65.
14. Offiah CE, Day E. The craniocervical junction: Embryology, anatomy, biomechanics and imaging in blunt trauma. *Insights Imaging* 2017; **8**(**1**): 29–47.
15. Go JL, Acharya J, Branchcomb JC, Rajamohan AG. Traumatic neck and skull base injuries. *RadioGraphics* 2019; **39**(**6**): 1796–807.
16. Yen K, Vock P, Tiefenthaler B, et al. Virtopsy: Forensic traumatology of the subcutaneous fatty tissue; multislice computed tomography (MSCT) and magnetic resonance imaging (MRI) as diagnostic tools. *J Forensic Sci* 2004; **49**(**4**): 799–806.
17. Levy AD, Harcke HT. *Essentials of Forensic Imaging: A Text-Atlas*. Boca Raton: CRC Press; 2011.
18. Oikonomou A, Prassopoulos P. CT imaging of blunt chest trauma. *Insights Imaging* 2011; **2**(**3**): 281–95.
19. Soto JA, Anderson SW. Multidetector CT of blunt abdominal trauma. *Radiology* 2012; **265**(3): 678–93.
20. Tarani S, Kamakshi SS, Naik V, Sodhi A. Forensic radiology: An emerging science. *J Adv Clin Res Insights* 2017; **4**: 59–63.
21. Payne-James J, Jones R, (eds). *Simpson's Forensic Medicine*, 14th ed. Hoboken: CRC Press; 2019.
22. Di Maio VJM, Di Maio DJ. *Forensic Pathology*, 2nd ed. Boca Raton: CRC Press; 2001.
23. Mason JK, Purdue BN. *The Pathology of Trauma*, 3rd ed. London: Oxford University Press; 2000.
24. Schmidt U, Pollak S. Sharp force injuries in clinical forensic medicine--findings in victims and perpetrators. *Forensic Sci Int* 2006; **159**(**2–3**): 113–18.
25. Bohnert M, Hüttemann H, Schmidt U. Homicides by Sharp Force. In: Tsokos M (ed), *Forensic Pathology Reviews*, Vol 4. Totowa: Humana Press; 2006.
26. Yen K, Ranner G, Dirnhofer R. Clinical Forensic Imaging. In: Thali M, Dirnhofer R, Vock P (eds), *The Virtopsy Approach: 3D Optical and Radiological Scanning and Reconstruction in Forensic Medicine*. Boca Raton: CRC Press; 2009, pp. 363–78.
27. Woźniak K, Moskała A, Rzepecka-Woźniak E. Imaging for homicide investigations. *Radiol Med* 2015; **120**(**9**): 846–55.
28. Offiah C, Twigg S. Imaging assessment of penetrating craniocerebral and spinal trauma. *Clin Radiol* 2009; **64**(**12**): 1146–57.
29. Offiah C, Hall E. Imaging assessment of penetrating injury of the neck and face. *Insights Imaging* 2012; **3**(**5**): 419–31.
30. Humphrey C, Kumaratilake J, Henneberg M. Characteristics of bone injuries resulting from knife wounds incised with different forces. *J Forensic Sci* 2017; **62**(**6**): 1445–51.

CHAPTER

77

Imaging of Suspected Non-Accidental Injury

Curtis E. Offiah

INTRODUCTION

Terminology in non-accidental injury (NAI) often changes and can be confusing. For example, NAI of the child has had and still has a number of synonyms such as "child abuse" for example. NAI of the head is currently medically termed "abusive head trauma" (AHT). The investigation and diagnosis of NAI of the child is a complex diagnostic pathway requiring input from various medical specialties at the center of which are the specialties of pediatrics, radiology, ophthalmology and neurology. However, frequently the opinions of other medical specialties such as neurosurgery, dermatology, toxicology and forensic & legal medicine (both clinical and pathological) will be required. In addition, many associated support and investigative agencies or bodies (such as police, local authorities, social services) may play a central role in the forensic aspects of investigation of such injury.

The first description of child physical abuse was by the French forensic physician Ambrose Tardieu in 1860 (1). Subsequently, it was the American pediatric radiologist John Caffey who spearheaded the concept in the twentieth century, publishing a description of six infants with long-bone fractures and subdural hematoma in 1946 postulating that these injuries were inflicted (2). He subsequently described the metaphyseal fracture which remains a specific indicator of NAI (3). Kempe and colleagues coined the term "battered child syndrome" describing metaphyseal fractures and other injuries typical of NAI in the child (4). The shaking mechanism of abusive head injury was first proposed by Guthkelch (5) and this was cemented by the research of Paul Kleinman and colleagues contributing to current understanding of the pathomechanisms of injury in non-accidental trauma (6–15).

NAI of the child is a global issue with a prevalence throughout all countries and across all socioeconomic groups and cultures. Children may be abused in a family or in an institutional or community setting by those known to them or, more rarely, by others. Child abuse is a broad church but is typically defined in four main categories 1) emotional abuse, 2) physical abuse, 3) sexual abuse and 4) neglect *(see* Chapter 73 – "Child Abuse and Neglect"). The Office of National Statistics in the United Kingdom (UK) which provides regular crime surveys for England and Wales estimated that one in five adults aged 18 to 74 years experienced at least one form of child abuse (which included emotional abuse, physical abuse, sexual abuse [16,17]).

This chapter focuses on physical abuse for which imaging is a cornerstone of diagnosis and investigation. The Crime Survey of England and Wales estimated, as of 31 March 2019, 4170 children in England (3 per 10 000) were subject to a Child Protection Plan and, in Wales, a further 285 children (5 per 10 000) were on the Child Protection Register for physical abuse (17). In the same survey, of the 209 serious incident notifications relating to deaths of children in England, physical abuse by a parent, carer or another family member was the cause of death in 28 of the 209 deaths (13%) (17).

The diagnosis of NAI may have significant legal consequences. Given that all medical professionals are duty bound to report all cases of suspected NAI, it is imperative that the diagnosis always remains on the radar of any medical professional encountering children in their daily practice. For radiologists, this means the need to recognize certain imaging injury in specific pediatric population groups as being significant and thus raising the possibility of NAI. It also means that imaging protocols and pathways must be optimized for the investigation of such patients and that there is familiarity with national guidelines for the appropriate diagnostic workup and management of such cases.

SKELETAL INJURIES

Fractures are common in abused children, second only to cutaneous bruising. Fractures are rarely life-threatening but indicative of the mechanism of injury. It is critical to identify specific types of fractures which are associated with NAI and therefore mandate recognition by the radiologist.

Most childhood fractures are accidental. Fractures become less common with decreasing age and in the non-ambulant (18–20). In inflicted skeletal injuries, fractures often occur in the absence of overlying bruising (21–23). A study looking at the epidemiology of victims

DOI: 10.1201/9781003138754-80

of skeletal injuries in NAI identified 67 percent of parents were unemployed and the mother was identified as the abuser in 50 percent of cases (24). The frequency of fractures in cases of NAI is variably reported as between 9 percent and 55 percent (25–34).

It is important to understand that there are significant differences between the patterns of non-accidental fracture injury occurring in infants compared to those occurring in older children and that the skeletal response to the responsible forces are different in infancy compared to childhood. For example, rib fractures and metaphyseal fractures of the tubular bones/long bones are common in the first year of life while long-bone diaphyseal fractures are more common in older children. The most common fractures in NAI involve long bones, ribs and skull.

The plain radiograph (X-ray) serves as the initial imaging approach for children suspected of having been subject to abusive trauma because osseous injuries are second only to pure soft-tissue injuries (such as bruising) as indicators of abuse (35). The identification of healing fractures is also imperative as it may be an indication of failure of the carer of the child to expeditiously present the child to medical assessment, raising concern for potential inflicted abuse or neglect.

Discussion of skeletal injuries will be limited to the more pathognomonic fractures of NAI of the infant as more detailed discussion is beyond the scope of this chapter. Discussion of the AHT will also be limited to the commoner pathognomonic neuroradiologic appearances as more detailed discussion is beyond the scope of this chapter.

Metaphyseal fractures of the long bones

The most specific of all the injuries of NAI is the metaphyseal fracture. It was first described by the pediatric radiologist John Caffey in 1957 (3) and is generally considered to be pathognomonic of abuse. Kleinman et al. described the classic metaphyseal lesions (7,10–13) which are evident in up to 50 percent of abused infants less than 18 months of age (7,36). Hence, the classic metaphyseal lesion is highly specific for NAI of the child but is present in half or less than half of cases. The classic metaphyseal lesion is seen almost exclusively in children under 2 years of age and occurs most often in the distal femur, proximal tibia, distal tibia and the proximal humerus (6,10–13,36). The classic metaphyseal lesion consists of a series of microfractures occurring across the metaphysis and the fracture line is orientated parallel to the growth plate, that is, perpendicular to the long axis of the diaphysis indicative of a shearing injury mechanism across the bone end which is a highly unusual biomechanical force for the long bone to obtain. Such a force is created by manual to-and-fro movement of the extremities such as by holding and shaking held by the feet or hands or shaking an infant held by the chest. These fractures will usually heal if the infant survives associated injuries. Correlative pathologic description of the histologic changes associated with the classic metaphyseal lesion is beyond the scope of this chapter but the radiologic appearances correlate closely with the histologic appearances. Radiologically, the classic metaphyseal lesion appears as a lucency within the metaphysis close to the growth plate involving all or only part of the width of the metaphysis and more or less perpendicular to the long axis of the diaphysis. The peripheral fracture site may sometimes be more discernible and the appearances of this region of fracture fragment related to the fracture line have been coined “corner fracture” and “bucket handle” fracture (the latter because the appearance sometimes resembles the handle of a bucket). These terms have therefore become synonymous with skeletal long-bone fractures occurring as a result of NAI but are basically a descriptive radiographic manifestation of the classic metaphyseal lesion (Figure 77.1). Healing of the classic metaphyseal lesion can be difficult to identify on plain radiographs (X-rays) because histologically, periosteal reaction with callus formation and subperiosteal new bone formation are less frequent with these fractures, however, what can sometimes be identified is focal or diffuse widening of the physis (the region of the growth plate) into the metaphyseal region. Nevertheless, follow-up radiography after a 2-week interval may therefore make these fractures more discernible (Figure 77.2).

As with all aspects of NAI, despite the importance of identifying such injuries, there are important differential diagnoses which should be excluded such as osteogenesis imperfecta and skeletal dysplasias and metabolic bone disease (such as rickets for example) (Figure 77.3).

Rib fractures

In the absence of metabolic bone disease, rib fractures in infants are highly unusual partly because of the highly deformable nature of the pediatric skeleton including the rib cage. Rib fractures in infants are therefore strongly associated with NAI. A tight hold or grip around the chest of the infant by adult hands produces forces which may fracture the anterior and lateral and posterior segments of the ribs. Fractures of the first rib are considered pathognomonic of NAI. It is rare for rib fractures to occur due to birth injury (37,38) and, if birth-related, tend to occur in babies born in the large weight range and babies born of difficult deliveries. Posterior rib fractures are particularly specific for NAI (*see* Figures 77.1 and 77.2). The posterior ribs are attached to the vertebral body of the same level and the ipsilateral transverse process of the vertebra of the same level. Squeezing of the chest causes this posterior rib to be levered over the ipsilateral transverse process resulting in a ventral cortical fracture or complete fracture of the full width of the posterior part of the rib (39–42). Such a pathomechanism is not a feature of traumatic biomechanical forces or iatrogenic biomechanical forces (such as chest compressions performed as part of cardiopulmonary resuscitation).

Radiologically, acute rib fractures will appear as lucent linear areas across the rib and may be complete

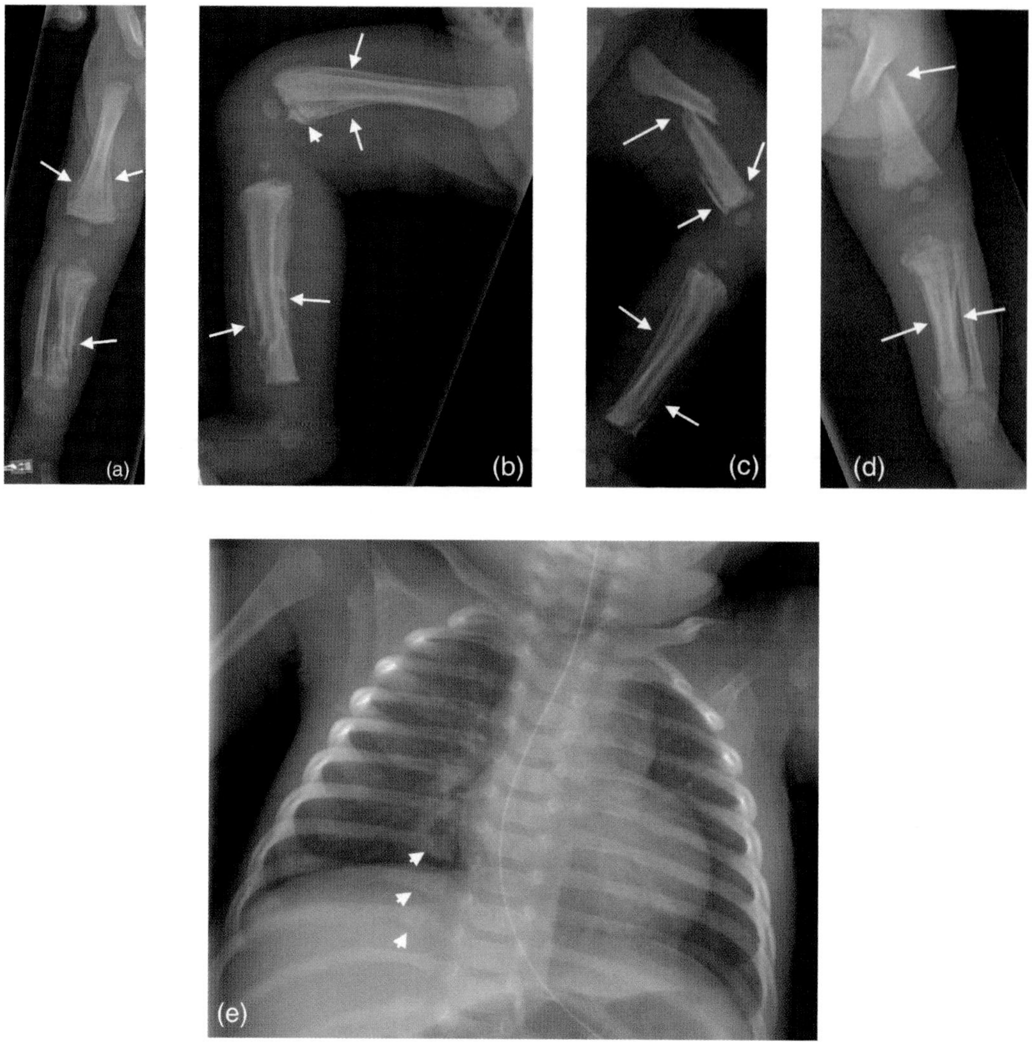

77.1 51-day-old baby girl victim of repeated physical child abuse. **(a)** Frontal projection showing healing fractures affecting the femur and tibia. There is also classic metaphyseal lesion of the femur evident; **(b)** Lateral projection of right lower limb showing healing fractures affecting the femur and tibia. There is also classic metaphyseal lesion of the femur also evident; **(c)** Projection of the left lower limb showing recent displaced fracture of the diaphysis of the left femur and healing classic metaphyseal lesion of the distal left femur. There is also healing fracture of the left tibia; **(d)** Projection of the left lower limb showing the displaced recent fracture of the diaphysis of the left femur and healing classic metaphyseal lesions of the distal femur and distal tibia; **(e)** Chest-X-ray showing healing fractures of the posterior right 8th, 9th and 10th ribs.

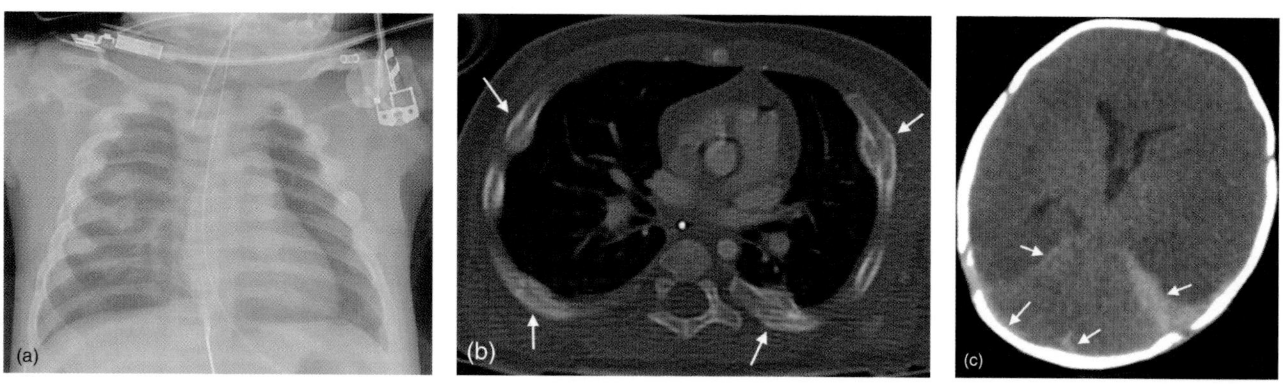

77.2 3-month-old baby boy victim of NAI from confirmed shaking mechanism. **(a)** Chest X-ray shows multiple healed fractures affecting the left and right ribs and suspected recent fracture on the right; **(b)** axial image of CT chest scan performed as part of acute presentation confirms multiple healed and fractures bilaterally (white arrows) and recent fractures were also present (not shown); **(c)** axial image of CT brain scan performed as part of the acute presentation demonstrates recent left cerebral hemispheric convexity subdural hemorrhage and recent right cerebral convexity subdural hemorrhage and recent subdural hemorrhage overlying the cerebellum (white arrows) and severe global hypoxic ischemic injury.

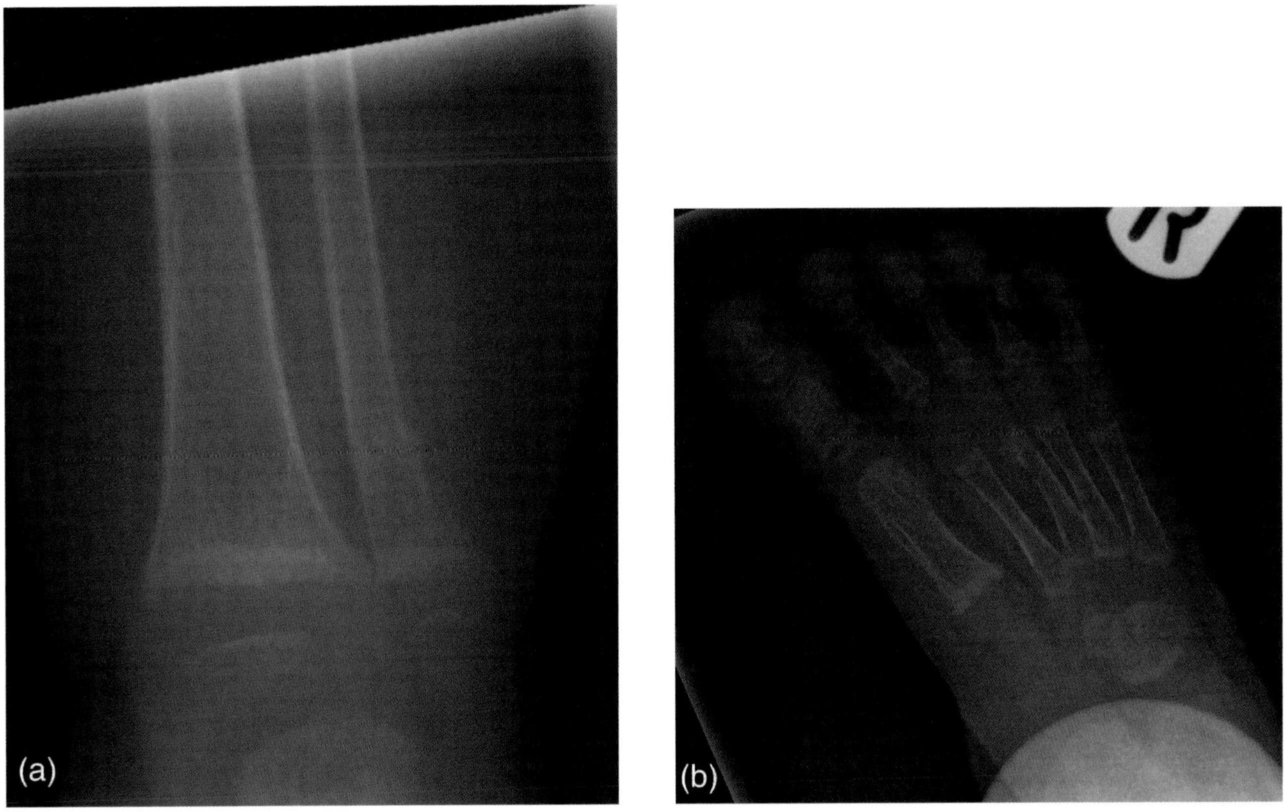

77.3 22-month-old female baby admitted with failure to thrive and failure to walk and suspected NAI subsequently but radiologic appearances of the skeletal survey demonstrated rickets bone changes and secondary rachitic fractures subsequently confirmed on biochemical screening and exhaustive socio-medical history excluded non-accidental history. **(a)** Projection of left lower leg demonstrates healing fracture of the distal left fibula and osteopenia and radiologic appearances of the metaphyses consistent with rickets; **(b)** Projection of right foot demonstrates healing fracture of the distal 3rd metatarsal bone secondary to rickets and rachitic bone changes.

or incomplete. The posterior rib fractures may be difficult to discern on plain radiographs of the chest because they may be non-displaced, superimposed on adjacent structures such as the transverse process or are obliquely orientated relative to the trajectory of the X-ray beam. As healing occurs, changes consistent with an underlying fracture may become discernible as subperiosteal new bone and callus formation (*see* Figure 77.2). Follow-up radiography after a 2-week interval may therefore make these fractures more visible (43).

Other fractures

Virtually every type of fracture has been described in NAI and therefore any fracture has the potential to be of an inflicted etiology (*see* Figures 77.1 and 77.2). The conflicting issue in causation is that once a child can walk, he or she is capable of *accidentally* sustaining significant injury.

Spiral long bone fractures and vertebral fractures imply mechanisms of force that are atypical in infants and are uncommon in infants sustaining accidental injury from falls. Hence, spiral fracture in a non-ambulatory child is highly suggestive of NAI. In contrast, accidental spiral fractures of the tibia (the "toddler's fracture") are relatively common once a child is walking even with no memorable antecedent traumatic episode. Any spinal fracture without a good history of accidental trauma is suggestive of NAI. Thoracolumbar compression fractures may occur with a shaking mechanism.

Aging of fractures on plain radiography

Aging of fractures is frequently asked of a radiologist but remains an inexact science despite a number of good quality studies (44,45). Evaluation of whether a fracture is in the healing phase can be made by a pediatric radiologist experienced in the assessment of NAI who may be able to indicate whether such healing fractures are in the early or mature stage of healing. However, such changes (and therefore such evaluation) is not applicable to skull fractures, spine fractures and some classic metaphyseal lesions. Subperiosteal new bone formation is typically observed between 4 and 21 days following injury; calcified callus is seen by 4 weeks and may be seen as early as 2 weeks; complete bridging of a fracture line resulting in loss of fracture line lucency may be evident at 10 to 21 days but may take up to 10 weeks; soft callus formation may be discernible at 10 to 21 days following injury while hard callus formation between 14 to 90 days and remodeling may be evident between 3 months and 2 years (44). Infants heal more quickly than older children and adults.

ABUSIVE HEAD TRAUMA

This is the commonest form of NAI leading to death in children less than 1 year of age (46–49). In children under 2 years of age, it accounts for 80 percent of deaths from head injury (46). It includes a spectrum of mechanisms of injury including impact of the head of the infant with a stationary object such as a wall, direct inflicted blow or blows to the head such as punches or alternating acceleration-deceleration mechanism to the head of the infant such as shaking (Figures 77.4 and 77.5). The infant is at particular risk of traumatic brain injury (TBI) as a result of shaking due, at least in part, to the relative size and weight of the head compared to the rest of the body and the relatively undeveloped strength of the neck musculature at this age. The outcome of infants subject to AHT is worse than for age-matched infants who have sustained accidental head injury. Developmental and mental retardation and disability are common sequelae of abusive head trauma in surviving infants.

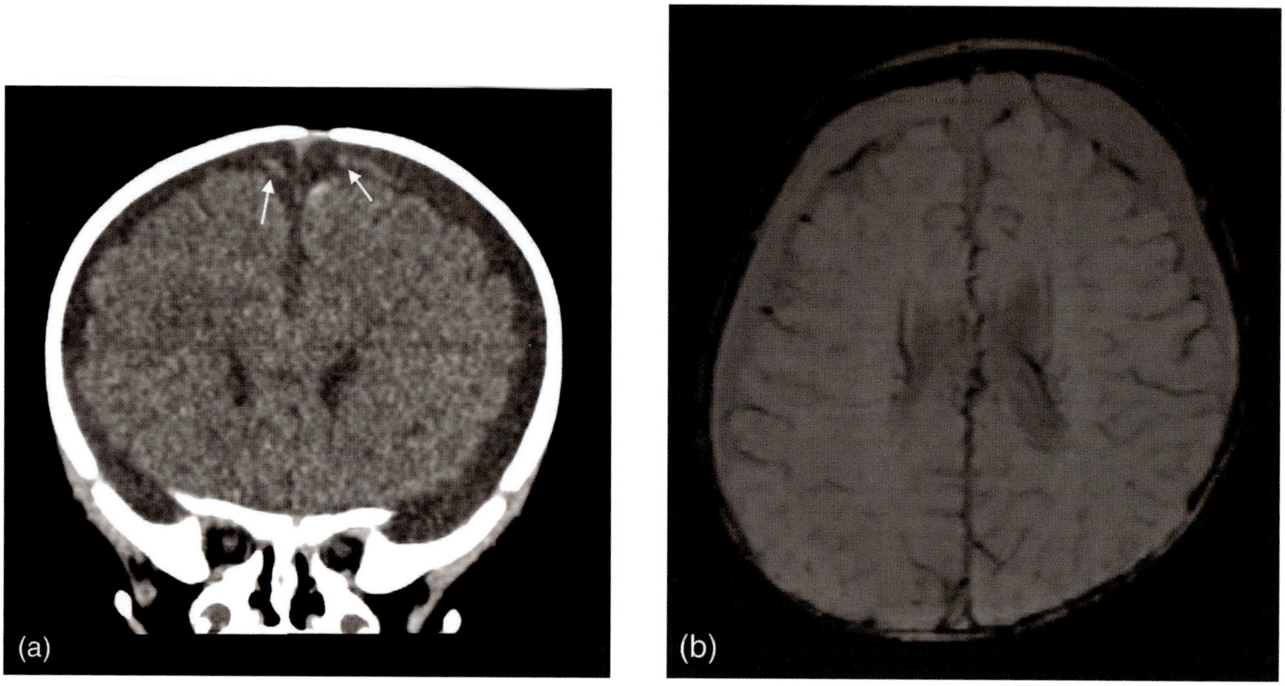

77.4 3-month-old male infant with acutely encephalopathic presentation with features of NAI on imaging. **(a)** Axial image of CT head scan shows bilateral recent hemorrhagic subdural collections over both cerebral hemispheres including interhemispheric with bridging vein thrombosis evident (white arrow); **(b)** axial image of MRI brain scan sequence confirms bilateral hematohygromata.

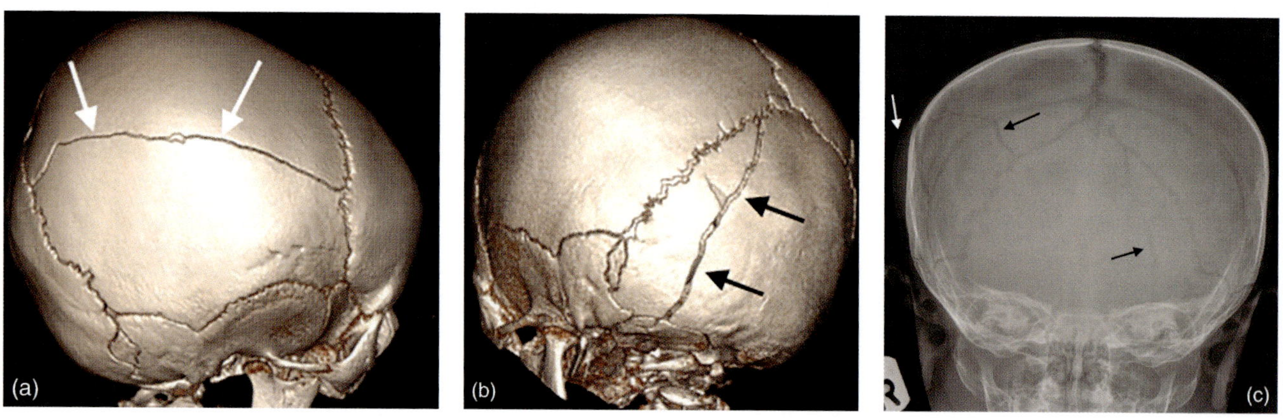

77.5 9-month-old male infant presented by carer with scalp swelling and bruising on right side of head related to suspected AHT. **(a)** volume rendered (3D) CT image of skull demonstrated right parietal skull fracture (arrow); **(b)** volume rendered (3D) CT image of skull demonstrated right parietal skull fracture also revealed a second separate distinct complex fracture of the left occipital bone; **(c)** plain X-ray image of the skull performed as part of subsequent skeletal survey demonstrating radiographic appearances skull fractures (black arrows) and scalp hematoma (white arrow).

Skull fractures

Isolated linear skull fractures are low in specificity for AHT occurring in accidental and NAI. The presence of a skull fracture may or may not be associated with intracranial trauma such as hemorrhage. It is proposed that the deformability (i.e. in-bending) of the infant skull injures the subjacent brain and meninges without fracture. Skull fractures result from contact blunt trauma. The velocity of the object striking the skull or of the skull striking a stationary object (such as in a fall) determines the magnitude of the contact force and the likelihood of fracture; the surface area and type of surface contacted will influence whether skull fracture will occur; a small contact are and sufficient velocity will result in a depressed skull fracture. However, the infant skull is more deformable and therefore relatively resistant to fracture. An important consideration in relation to fractures of the infant skull is that skull fractures are not rare in household trauma but significant underlying brain injury (with the exception of extradural hematoma) is rare in household trauma. It is rare for severe brain injury and even death to occur from witnessed short falls (50–52). Scalp or forehead soft-tissue swelling may be absent even in the presence of an acute fracture and therefore lack of soft-tissue swelling should not be taken as an indicator that the fracture is not recent (i.e. is non-acute) (53–55). The skull fracture types more likely to be associated with AHT are multiple fractures, fractures that cross sutures and bilateral fractures (Figure 77.5) (56–60). One of the most important factors in identifying a fracture that is likely the result of AHT is a contradictory or inconsistent history from the caregiver/caregivers of the infant. Skull fracture is one of the fracture sites occurring in NAI which is extremely difficult to age reliably and therefore caution should be exercised in terms of attempting to date skull fractures. CT scans of the head are mandatory in evaluation of NAI and the skull bones and scalp soft tissues should be scrutinized on high-resolution images for evidence of recent scalp injury, old, healed scalp injuries and skull fractures with multi-planar reconstructions and volume rendered 3D reconstructions (Figure 77.5).

Extra-axial hemorrhagic fluid collections

Subdural hemorrhage and subarachnoid hemorrhage are common in AHT. Extradural hematoma is much more often caused accidentally than by infliction and may result from relatively short falls. One of the commonest sites of subdural and subarachnoid hemorrhage in AHT is adjacent to the falx in the region of the interhemispheric fissures which is typically the result of shear injury of bridging veins in these locations (Figure 77.4). Specific features of hemorrhage and thrombosis of these bridging veins is of high specificity for AHT (of the acceleration-deceleration shaking type of mechanism) (55) although it may be caused by severe accidental trauma such as a fall from significant height or motor vehicle collision.

Dating hemorrhagic fluid collections requires caution and the experience of an expert pediatric neuroradiologist familiar with the forensic assessment of such injuries as the attenuation characteristics of subdural collections can be deceptive. High-density subdural collections are consistent with recent hemorrhage but low-density collections can occur as a result of recent injury because of traumatic tearing of the arachnoid mater and, similarly, mixed-density collections can occur in the acute setting as a result of hematohygroma formation (Figure 77.4). An important consideration in the causation of subdural hemorrhagic collections is birth-related trauma (subdural blood is common after delivery regardless of the mode of delivery) but should resolve by 4 to 6 weeks. Other non-abusive causes of subdural collections should be excluded in the work-up of such infants such as inherited coagulopathies (such as clotting factor deficiencies) and metabolic disorders such as glutaric aciduria type 1 or Menke's disease, for example.

Other intracranial injuries that can occur in the setting of AHT are cortical contusions and lacerations and shear injury such as traumatic focal and diffuse axonal injury and parenchymal clefts. As a result of secondary mechanisms, the infant brain may also suffer significant extensive hypoxic ischemic encephalopathy, (i.e. hypoxic ischemic brain injury) which may be associated with significant morbidity and mortality (*see* Figures 77.2 and 77.4).

Imaging evaluation of the spine is mandatory in AHT: the acceleration-deceleration mechanism is frequently associated with spinal injury which may be ligamentous or osseous (vertebral) or intraspinal with intradural or epidural hemorrhage or affecting the cranio-cervical junction ligamentous and muscle and fascial soft tissues or the prevertebral soft tissues, all of which may be evident on MR imaging (61) adding further credence to an abusive head trauma causation and seen in up to 60 percent of cases (62–64) (Figure 77.6).

VISCERAL INJURIES

Visceral injuries are estimated to account for up to 4 percent of all abusive injuries but are responsible for 12 percent of all deaths related to NAI (30,65,66). This is likely to be an underestimation however as much of these data are drawn from studies undertaken before the widespread use of CT imaging. Such injuries are typically delayed in presentation as the children may not be presented for medical attention until peritonitis, sepsis or hemodynamic collapse has occurred. Hence, abdominal injuries, for example, are not the commoner forms of NAI but are of high mortality. Visceral injuries include intrathoracic injuries such as lung contusion and lung laceration, cardiac laceration and fatal *commotio cordis* (44,67–69), lacerations and contusions

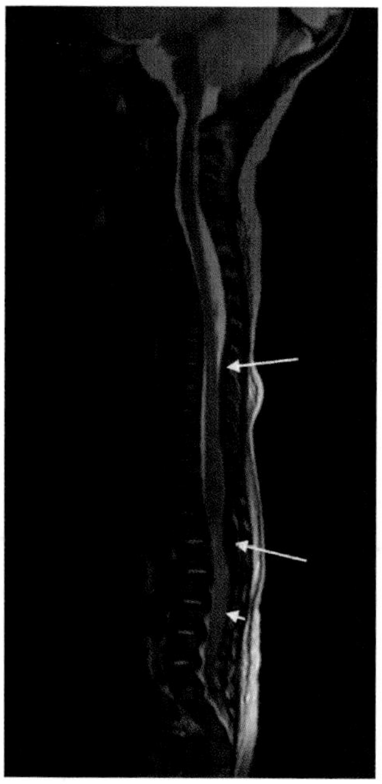

77.6 5-week-old female infant presenting with features of AHT (images not shown). Sagittal MR image of the spine demonstrating intraspinal epidural hematoma (long arrows) and intradural hemorrhage in the lumbar spine (short arrow) which is a frequent association with AHT. There were also soft-tissue changes affecting the suboccipital muscles and the prevertebral fascia consistent with AHT (images not shown).

and rupture of the stomach, small and large bowel, pancreas, liver, spleen, adrenal glands, kidneys and bladder. None of the visceral injuries is as specific for NAI as the classic metaphyseal lesion or posterior rib fractures or interhemispheric extra-axial (subdural and subarachnoid) hemorrhage.

IMAGING GUIDELINES

There are specific imaging guideline algorithms, protocols and diagnostic pathways established by Colleges of Radiologists throughout the world where NAI is suspected or warrants exclusion. In the UK, such guidelines are published by the Royal College of Radiologists (in collaboration with the Royal College of Paediatrics and Child Health) which is a living document and undergoes timely updates (70). Central to these guidelines is the skeletal survey which is a specific series of X-rays of the axial and appendicular skeleton as well as CT imaging of the head and MR imaging of the brain and whole spine (70). All radiologists involved in the assessment of NAI will be familiar with these guidelines and the protocol associated with these imaging investigations.

CONCLUSION

Radiology plays a central role in the investigation of NAI. However, such radiologic imaging interpretation is the remit of the specialist or expert pediatric radiologist and pediatric neuroradiologist familiar with the interpretation of such imaging. Given the high morbidity and mortality associated with NAI, it behoves all medical practitioners involved in the assessment of infants and children to be aware of the red flags that may indicate NAI. The forensic medical investigation of NAI is a multi-disciplinary investigation as well as a multi-agency investigation on a larger scale incorporating social services and police among others. However, medically, imaging assessment forms only one part of the investigation but at the basis of all of this is the "story" or "history" given by the caregiver. Any inconsistency should be thoroughly interrogated but with care and compassion.

REFERENCES

1. Tardieu A. Etude medico-legale sur les services et mauvais traitments exerces sur des infants. *Ann Hyg Publ Med Leg* 1860: 13: 361–98.
2. Caffey J. Multiple fractures in the long bones of infants suffering from chronic subdural hematoma. *Am J Roentgenol Radium Ther Nucl Med* 1946; **56**: 163–73.
3. Caffey J. Some traumatic lesions in growing bones other than fractures and dislocations: Clinical and radiological features. *Br J Radiol* 1957; **30**: 225–38.
4. Kempe CH, Silverman FN, Steele BF, et al. The battered-child syndrome. *JAMA* 1962; **181**: 105–12.
5. Guthkelch AN. Infantile subdural haematoma and its relationship to whiplash injuries. *Br Med J* 1971; **2**: 430–1.
6. Kleinman PK, Marks SC, Blackbourne B. The metaphyseal lesion in abused infants: A radiologic-histopathologic study. *Am J Roentgenol* 1986; **146**: 895–905.
7. Kleinman PK, Marks SC Jr, Richmond JM, Blackbourne BD. Inflicted skeletal injury: A postmortem radiologic-histopathologic study in 31 infants. *Am J Roentgenol* 1995; **165**: 647–50.
8. Kleinman PK, Marks SC Jr, Spevak MR, et al. Extension of growth-plate cartilage into the metaphysis: A sign of healing fracture in abused infants. *Am J Roentgenol* 1991; **156**: 775–9.
9. Kleinman PK, Raptopoulos VD, Brill PW. Occult nonskeletal trauma in the battered-child syndrome. *Radiology* 1981; **141**: 393–6.
10. Kleinman PK, Marks SC Jr. A regional approach to the classic metaphyseal lesion in abused infants: The proximal humerus. *Am J Roentgenol* 1996; **167**: 1399–403.
11. Kleinman PK, Marks SC Jr. A regional approach to classic metaphyseal lesions in abused infants: The distal tibia. *Am J Roentgenol* 1996; **166**: 1207–12.
12. Kleinman PK, Marks SC Jr. A regional approach to the classic metaphyseal lesion in abused infants: The proximal tibia. *Am J Roentgenol* 1996; **166**: 421–6.
13. Kleinman PK, Marks SC Jr. A regional approach to the classic metaphyseal lesion in abused infants: The distal femur. *Am J Roentgenol* 1998; **170**: 43–7.
14. Kleinman PK, Brill PW, Winchester P. Resolving duodenal-jejunal hematoma in

abused children. *Radiology* 1986; **160**: 747–50.

15. Kleinman PK, Marks SC. Vertebral body fractures in child abuse: Radiologic-histopathologic correlates. *Invest Radiol* 1992; **27**: 715–22.
16. Office of National Statistics: Child abuse in England and Wales: March 2020, 2020. Available from: https://www.ons.gov.uk/peoplepopulationandcommunity/crimeandjustice/bulletins/childabuseinenglandandwales/march2020 (Accessed 22 May 2023).
17. Office of National Statistics. Child physical abuse in England and Wales: Year ending March 2019, 2020. Available from: https://www.ons.gov.uk/peoplepopulationandcommunity/crimeandjustice/articles/childphysicalabuseinenglandandwales/yearendingmarch2019 (Accessed 22 May 2023).
18. Loder RT, Feinberg JR. Orthopaedic injuries in children with nonaccidental trauma: Demographics and incidence from the 2000 Kids' Inpatient Database. *J Pediatr Orthop* 2007; **27(4)**: 421–6.
19. Leventhal JM, Martin KD, Asnes AG. Incidence of fractures attributable to abuse in young hospitalized children: Results from analysis of a United States database. *Pediatrics* 2008; **122(3)**: 599–604.
20. Clarke NMP, Shelton FRM, Taylor CC, et al. The incidence of fractures in children under the age of 24 months – in relation to non-accidental injury. *Injury* 2012; **43(6)**: 762–5.
21. Peters ML, Starling SP, Barnes-Eley ML, Heisler KW. The presence of bruising associated with fractures. *Arch Pediatr Adolesc Med* 2008; **162(9)**: 877–81.
22. Maguire S, Mann M. Systematic reviews of bruising in relation to child abuse – what have we learnt: An overview of review updates. *Evid Based Child Health* 2013; **8(2)**: 255–63.
23. Harper NS, Feldman KW, Sugar NF, et al. Examining siblings to recognize abuse Investigators. Additional injuries in young infants with concern for abuse and apparently isolated bruises. *J Pediatr* 2014; **165(2)**: 382–8.
24. Krishnan J, Barbour PJ, Foster BK. Patterns of osseous injuries and psychosocial factors affecting victims of child abuse. *ANZ J Surg* 1990; **60(6)**: 447–50.
25. Ebbin AJ, Gollub MH, Stein AM, Wilson MG. Battered child syndrome at the Los Angeles County General Hospital. *Am J Dis Child* 1969; **118(4)**: 660–7.
26. Galleno H, Oppenheim WL. The battered child syndrome revisited. *Clin Orthop Relate Res* 1982; **162**: 11–19.
27. Herndon WA. Child abuse in a military population. *J Pediatr Orthop* 1983; **3(1)**: 73–6.
28. Kogutt MS, Swischuk LE, Fagan CJ. Patterns of injury and significance of uncommon fractures in the battered child syndrome. *Am J Roentgenol Radium Ther Nucl Med* 1974; **121(1)**: 143–9.
29. Lauer B, Broeck ET, Grossman M. Battered child syndrome: Review of 130 patients with controls. *Pediatrics* 1974; **54(1)**: 67–70.
30. Merten DF, Radkowski MA, Leonidas JC. The abused child: A radiological reappraisal. *Radiology* 1983; **146(2)**: 377–81.
31. Ryan MG, Davis AA, Oates RK. One hundred and eighty-seven cases of child abuse and neglect. *Med J Aust* 1997; **2(19)**: 623–8.
32. Belfer RA, Klein BL, Orr L. Use of the skeletal survey in the evaluation of child maltreatment. *Am J Emerg Med* 2001; **19(2)**: 122–4.
33. Day F, Clegg S, McPhillips M, Mok J. A retrospective case series of skeletal surveys in children with suspected non-accidental injury. *J Clin Forensic Med* 2006; **13(2)**: 55–9.
34. McMahon P, Grossman W, Gaffney M, Stanitski C. Soft-tissue injury as an indication of child abuse. *J Bone Joint Surg* 1995; **77(8)**: 1179–83.
35. Christian CW. Committee on Child Abuse and Neglect, American Academy of Pediatrics. The evaluation of suspected child physical abuse. *Pediatrics* 2015; **135**: e1337–e54.
36. Worlock P, Stower M, Barbor P. Patterns of fractures in accidental and non-accidental injury in children: A comparative study. *Br Med J (Clin Res Ed)* 1986; **293**: 100–2.
37. Hartmann RW Jr. Radiological case of the month. Rib fractures produced by birth trauma. *Arch Pediatr Adolesc Med* 1997; **151**: 947–8.
38. Rizzolo PJ, Coleman PR. Neonatal rib fracture: Birth trauma or child abuse? *J Fam Pract* 1989; **29**: 561–3.
39. Kleinman PK, Marks SC, Adams VI, Blackbourne BD. Factors affecting visualization of posterior rib fractures in abused infants. *Am J Roentgenol* 1988; **150**: 635–8.
40. Kleinman PK, Marks SC, Spevak MR, Richmond JM. Fractures of the rib head in abused infants. *Radiology* 1992; **185**: 119–23.
41. Kleinman PK, Schlesinger AE. Mechanical factors associated with posterior rib fractures: Laboratory and case studies. *Pediatr Radiol* 1997; **27**: 87–91.
42. Kleinman PK, Marks SC Jr, Nimkin K, et al. Rib fractures in 31 abused infants: Post-mortem radiologic-histopathologic study. *Radiology* 1996; **200**: 807–10.
43. Lonergan GJ, Baker AM, Morey MK, Boos SC. From the archives of the AFIP. Child abuse: Radiologic-pathologic correlation. *Radiographics* 2003; **23(4)**: 811–45.
44. O'Connor JF, Cohen J. Dating Fractures. In: Kleinman PK (ed), *Diagnostic Imaging of Child Abuse*, 2nd ed. St. Louis: Mosby; 1998, pp. 168–77.
45. Prosser I, Maguire S, Harrison SK, et al. How old is this fracture? Radiologic dating of fractures in children: A systematic review. *Am J Roentgenol* 2005; **184**: 1282–6.
46. Bruce DA, Zimmerman RA. Shaken impact syndrome. *Pediatr Ann* 1989; **18**: 482–92.
47. Keenan HT, Runyan DK, Marshall SW, et al. A population-based study of inflicted traumatic brain injury in young children. *JAMA* 2003; **290**: 621–6.
48. Girard N, Brunel H, Dory-Lautrec P, Chabrol B. Neuroimaging differential diagnoses to abusive head trauma. *Pediatr Radiol* 2016; **46**: 603–14.
49. Fernando S, Obaldo RE, Walsh IR, Lowe LH. Neuroimaging of nonaccidental head trauma: Pitfalls and controversies. *Pediatr Radiol* 2008; **38**: 827–38.
50. Nimityongskul P, Anderson LD. The likelihood of injuries when children fall out of bed. *J Pediatr Orthop* 1987; **7**: 184–6.
51. Duhaime AC, Alario AJ, Lewander WJ, et al. Head injury in very young children: Mechanisms, injury types, and ophthalmologic findings in 100 hospitalized patients younger than 2 years of age. *Pediatrics* 1992; **90**: 179–85.
52. Claydon SM. Fatal extradural hemorrhage following a fall from a baby bouncer. *Pediatr Emerg Care* 1996; **12**: 432–4.
53. Kleinman PK, Spevak MR. Soft tissue swelling and acute skull fractures. *J Pediatr* 1992; **121**: 737–9.
54. Block RW. Child abuse: Controversies and imposters. *Curr Probl Pediatr* 1999; **29**: 249–72.
55. Barnes PD, Robson CD. CT findings in hyperacute nonaccidental brain injury. *Pediatr Radiol* 2000; **30**: 74–81.
56. Patterson RH, Burns WA, Jannotta FS. Complications of external cardiac resuscitation: A retrospective review and survey of the literature. *Med Ann Dist Columbia* 1974; **43**: 389–94.
57. Billmire ME, Myers PA. Serious head injury in infants: Accident or abuse? *Pediatrics* 1985; **75**: 340–2.
58. Merten DF, Osborne DR, Radkowski MA, Leonidas JC. Craniocerebral trauma in the child abuse syndrome: Radiological observations. *Pediatr Radiol* 1984; **14**: 272–7.
59. Meservy CJ, Towbin R, McLaurin RL, et al. Radiographic characteristics of skull fractures resulting from child abuse. *Am J Roentgenol* 1987; **149**: 173–5.
60. Hobbs CJ. Skull fracture and the diagnosis of abuse. *Arch Dis Child* 1984; **59**: 246–52.
61. Offiah CE, Day E. The craniocervical junction: Embryology, anatomy, biomechanics and imaging in blunt trauma. *Insights Imaging* 2017; **8(1)**: 29–47.
62. Choudhary AK, Bradford RK, Dias MS, et al. Spinal subdural hemorrhage in abuse head trauma: A retrospective study. *Radiology* 2012; **262**: 216–23.
63. Choudhary AK, Ishak R, Zacharia TT, Dias MS. Imaging of spinal injury in abusive head trauma: A retrospective study. *Pediatr Radiol* 2014; **44**: 1130–40.
64. Jacob R, Cox M, Koral K, et al. MR imaging of the cervical spine in non-accidental trauma: A tertiary institution experience. *Am J Neuroradiol* 2016; **37**: 1944–50.
65. Kirks DR. Radiological evaluation of visceral injuries in the battered child syndrome. *Pediatr Ann* 1983; **12**: 888–93.

66. Ng CS, Hall CM, Shaw DG. The range of visceral manifestations of non-accidental injury. *Arch Dis Child* 1997; **77**: 167–74.
67. Cumberland GD, Riddick L, McConnell CF. Intimal tears of the right atrium of the heart due to blunt force injuries to the abdomen: Its mechanism and implications. *Am J Forensic Med Pathol* 1991; **12**: 102–4.
68. Cohle SD, Hawley DA, Berg KK, et al. Homicidal cardiac lacerations in children. *J Forensic Sci* 1995; **40**: 212–18.
69. Baker AM, Craig BR, Lonergan GJ. Homicidal commotio cordis: The final blow in a battered infant. *Child Abuse Negl* 2003; **27**: 125–30.
70. Royal College of Radiologists. The radiological investigation of suspected physical abuse in children, 2017. Available from: https://www.rcr.ac.uk/publication/radiological-investigation-suspected-physical-abuse-children (Accessed 22 May 2023).

CHAPTER
78
Evidential Sampling

Margaret Stark and Maria Nittis

INTRODUCTION

Evidence is collected and analyzed to assist investigators to piece together a crime, to determine what happened, who may have been present as well as corroborating a person's version of events. If evidence is insufficient, investigations may stall; if contradictory, charges may be dismissed or withdrawn; if sufficient and a suspect can be identified, cases may progress down judicial avenues. Evidence collection processes must therefore be robust and able to withstand scientific and legal challenge. While evidence may include video footage and other articles from crime scenes, this chapter focuses on the types of evidence (often biological), other than statements/version of events and documentation of injury, which might be collected from complainants and suspects.

ROLE OF FORENSIC MEDICAL EVIDENCE IN LEGAL OUTCOMES

The practice of modern day medical forensic examinations and collection of "rape kits" largely originated in the late twentieth century (1,2). Many attempts have been made to ascertain the role of the forensic medical examination and evidence collection when looking at judicial outcomes. What is clear is that it is a very complicated issue influenced sometimes by a variety of factors including the characteristics of the complainant, different jurisdictional requirements, time between assault and presentation for assessment, presence or absence of injury, analysis techniques, samples collected and arguments around consent or lack thereof. What might constitute pivotal evidence in one case might be considered inconsequential in another (3).

"*The findings from a medical examination performed fairly soon after an alleged sexual assault may be very important forensically or may be virtually irrelevant in contributing to an assessment of what occurred in the incident at issue.*" (4).

What appears to be universal, however, is the low rate of convictions in sexual assault/rape cases, when compared to other assault crimes.

A Danish study (5) attempted to assess the significance of forensic clinical examinations on the judicial assessment of rape complainants. Of the 184 forensic examinations undertaken of rape complainants, a suspect was unable to be identified in 41 cases (22.3%). Of the 143 cases where a suspect could be identified, 29 (n = 29/184; 15.8%) resulted in no charges being laid; in 71 cases (n = 71/184; 38.6%) charges were withdrawn, and 43 cases (n = 43/184; 23.4%) progressed to court. Thirty cases (n = 30/184; 16.3%) resulted in a conviction with 13 being acquitted.

Johnson et al. (3) observed that stranger and non-stranger rape cases might need to be processed differently. The major emphasis in stranger cases relates often to identification whereas, for others, it might be simply to support the allegation of sexual contact. Not surprisingly, therefore, DNA evidence was perceived by prosecutors as being particularly helpful when it rebutted defendant's denial of sexual contact (6). It may provide particularly telling information in those cases where a person is so incapacitated as to have no memory of a sexual act having occurred. District Attorneys in the USA reported that they sometimes used DNA evidence, even when not particularly probative: "*because it confirms the correct person is being prosecuted, it communicates the victim's and prosecution's seriousness, and it meets jury expectations in trials.*" (6)

Know your lab – know your numbers

The Education and Research Subcommittee of the Association of Police Surgeons, in collaboration with the Forensic Science Service and the Association of Chief Police Officers (ACPO), produced the first evidence collection guidelines in the United Kingdom (UK) in 1997. The Faculty of Forensic and Legal Medicine (UK) established the Forensic Science Subcommittee in 2006 with membership from forensic examiners, forensic scientific services and the police. This group produces recommendations for the collection of forensic specimens twice yearly (7). In 2011, a similar committee was established in New South Wales, Australia, to do the same. Both groups rely heavily upon local and international

DOI: 10.1201/9781003138754-81

literature as well as the results coming from local laboratories. Regularly reviewed and updated recommendations/guidelines ensure consistency, currency of practice and help identify knowledge gaps that need to be filled by future research.

The quality of the local information is dependent upon a number of factors including specific and relevant information being provided by the forensic examiner and police to the laboratory; quality collection and analytical procedures that decrease the risk of contamination; transparency of the results to forensic examiners for quality purposes (8); identification of items tested and not tested including the reasons for doing so; funding (e.g. is the laboratory limited to the number of items that can be tested, do they have autonomy over which items are tested, are they paid for each item, is the laboratory a private or government entity); is the laboratory and are the examiners undertaking and publishing their own research?

Important also, is an understanding of the number of evidence kits collected in any jurisdiction versus the number of kits submitted for testing. It is easy to assume that once a complainant has submitted themselves to what is often a lengthy process, the evidence collected will automatically be tested. In Detroit, USA, approximately 11 000 untested sexual assault kits were located in a police storage unit (9) and conservative estimates of untested US kits is in the order of hundreds of thousands (9). In some cases, there are suggestions that police view the evidence that can be obtained from these kits as a confirmatory check requested by prosecutors for cases going to court, but not as part of an investigation to determine if there should, in fact, be a prosecution (10).

Just-in-case collections

These relate to evidence collection from sexual assault/rape complainants when there is uncertainty about whether to involve police. The underlying purpose is to provide a complainant with additional time to make this decision. Sometimes, these kits are submitted for laboratory analysis but, in many cases, they remain untested. The value of increased time to make decisions needs to be balanced against the potential loss of additional evidence which might include evidence from the crime scene including discarded tissues, condoms, DNA, fingerprints and closed-circuit television (CCTV). Text messages and other social media communication might be lost. Evidence that has been collected, if not stored appropriately, might degrade. Witness statements and recollections might become tainted with time delays. There is the potential that a sex offender may be left in the community. All these risks should be communicated to the complainant to help inform their decision about just in case collections.

Early evidence

Early Evidence is the term often given to evidence collected (usually) by someone other than a forensic practitioner and prior to a formal forensic assessment. It may include a mouth rinse, mouth swabs, peri-oral swabs, urine collection and tissue wipes. These collections are undertaken in an effort to preserve evidence that might otherwise be lost due to time delays or an inability to undertake a more formalized forensic medical/nursing examination. This evidence might be self-collected or collected by a health professional with limited, if any, forensic training.

Urine is often an easy sample to collect and has been noted to be particularly useful when looking for spermatozoa. A Finnish study (11), with 88 female participants, looked at post-coital (consensual) urine samples. In 86 of the first post-coital urine samples, Y-DNA was detected in 96.5 percent (n = 83). After 24 hours, Y-DNA was measurable in 40.9 percent (n = 9/22) with one positive sample at 52.5 hours. Some samples were still positive on the 6th to 10th void. Spermatozoa were detected in 84.1 percent (n = 37/44) of first void urine samples. This was significantly higher than a 2014 Australian study where 35 percent of first void samples were positive for sperm (12). It should be noted that the Australian study was performed on sexual assault complainants.

Consideration, when compiling such kits, should be given to those samples that might have limited persistence such as spermatozoa in oral cavities, DNA from digital penetration of either the vagina or anus, drugs in blood samples, and body samples from pre-pubertal children. Consider also, the ability to collect underclothing and brassieres.

Contamination reduction and chain of evidence

Reducing the risk for contamination of the evidence or crime scene is an integral component of evidence collection (13). When undertaking forensic evidence collection, attention should be paid to the environment in which the examination is undertaken as well as to the items used to assist with the collection process (14). Dedicated examination rooms are the gold standard but, it is recognized, this is not always possible in busy hospitals, when patients require additional and ongoing medical care or when undertaken in custodial facilities (*see also* Chapter 87 – “Female Genital Mutilation”).

Ethylene oxide is a gas most commonly used for sterilization of evidence kits to a point where they might be considered “DNA free”. It is important, as a forensic practitioner to know your evidence kit if one is available. The practitioner should know what elements of the kit are “DNA free” and what are not. All items should ideally be single use where possible. Additional sterilization with ethylene oxide would further ensure there was little chance of foreign DNA. Procedures to reduce the risk of contamination should be documented and made available to the court, if required, including anything that may have occurred to compromise the process.

“Chain of evidence” is a log that outlines the sequential handlers of the evidence, from collection to distribution of results. This may be open to scrutiny by other legal teams and subject to challenge in court and it is important that this is maintained.

What evidence to collect

A variety of biological samples can be collected (blood, semen, saliva, urine, feces, "vaginal material", hair). Other samples such as clothing and apparently foreign material may also be identified and collected. Sometimes, only a limited history (or no history at all) is available and then evidence collection is usually determined by the time elapsed since assault; choosing those samples that may still return a positive sample (sperm or DNA). Most commonly, sample choice may depend upon the history provided by the complainant or the police. This, however, is not always accurate, as demonstrated by a 1992 study from New Zealand. Forty complainants (38% of the sexual assault victims) reported ejaculation having occurred, but seminal fluid was only detected in thirty-four. Of more interest, were the 16 complainants (15%) who reported there had been no ejaculation. Seminal fluid was detected in seven. "*The main conclusion that can be drawn from the work presented here is probably not surprising. It is that victims of alleged sexual assault may not remember accurately if penetration or ejaculation took place during the assault.*" (15)

Slides

Slides (smears) are generally made by either the forensic practitioner or by the laboratory scientist when a swab, targeting spermatozoa, is collected. Slides are made to assist with a selection of downstream DNA testing options (autosomal testing if sperm are seen versus Y-STR testing if sperm are not); to observe sperm quantity and morphology (intact vs non-intact sperm) to assist with time since intercourse estimates, and for the identification of sperm to provide additional information regarding the biological fluid likely responsible for a positive DNA profile or to corroborate a version of events (16).

Female genital swabs

It is recommended that standardized collection sets are adopted when sampling anatomic areas. Swabs from additional sites can be added (or removed), dependent upon the history of the case. For example, in Australia and the UK, sampling of the female genitalia following a history of penile vaginal penetration includes swabs taken from the vulva, low vagina, high vagina and endocervical regions. In the UK, it is suggested that perianal swabs be collected when there is a history of penile vaginal penetration (even without a history of anal penetration). Ensure that the area to be sampled for each of these areas is consistent. Twenty years ago in New South Wales, Australia, it was discovered that vulval swabs were being collected from multiple different anatomic areas until this process was standardized.

Cut-off time periods for sampling should be established and reviewed regularly in collaboration with the testing laboratory. At the time of writing, the cut-off time period for female genital sampling following suspected penile vaginal intercourse is 4 days in Victoria (Australia) (17), 5 days in New South Wales (Australia) (18) and 7 days in the UK (7).

Forensic Science Ireland examined 1450 cases between 2000 and 2007. Analysis of 3508 vaginal swabs revealed that detection of sperm decreased significantly after 18 hours. It decreased again after 48 hours. When beyond 96 hours, the likelihood of observing sperm was thought to be extremely low (19).

Sperm Elution™, a method for increasing the recovery of spermatozoa from swabs, has been observed in one study, reviewing data from swabs collected between 2009 and 2015, to significantly increase the time since intercourse in which sperm can be detected. Although hampered by limited case numbers submitted more than three days post intercourse, 16–20 percent of cases 4 to 6 days after intercourse were positive for sperm (n = 124) and 7 percent of cases (n = 28) at 6 to 7 days (20). Of course, these extended time periods may be of little benefit if the legal argument revolves less around the act and more about whether or not there was consent at the time.

Time periods for sampling and female genital sampling sites may change when the history suggests penetration by something other than a penis. As cunnilingus (licking or sucking of the female genitalia) generally results in penetration to a lesser extent than penile penetration, less samples are often collected, and these are usually limited to the more external anatomy. In New South Wales (NSW), the suggested sampling sites include the external labia (over the outer aspect of the labia majora, i.e. hair bearing skin segment) and vulva (up to 24 hours post assault; up to 48 hours if the victims haven't washed) (18); in Victoria, it is the external labia and vulva (up to 24 hours even if washed) (17).

Where there is suggestion of licking of skin, it may be possible for the laboratory to test for human α-amylase to corroborate the presence of saliva. This is not always done for vaginal samples or on underpants as they may sometimes provide false positive results (i.e. α-amylase positive even in the absence of saliva) as demonstrated by an in-house validation study that found approximately 29 percent α-amylase positive low vaginal swabs when not expected and on testing of new underpants, worn for 12 hours, by pre-pubescent, post-pubescent and post-menopausal females (21).

When allegations concern digital vaginal penetration, cut-off time periods shorten. In the UK, it is suggested that vulval, low vaginal and high vaginal swabs be collected up to 48 hours post assault, regardless, if the complainant has washed (7). In NSW external labial and vulval samples can be collected until 12 hours post-assault and only if the person has not washed. Low vaginal samples, however, may be collected up to 12 hours post-assault even if the patient has washed (18). In Victoria, samples may be collected from the external labia, vulva and low vagina up to 24 hours, regardless of urination, but only if the complainant has not washed (17).

Research into the persistence of DNA following digital penetration is not extensive. A study in 2015 (22) utilized eight couples who undertook digital vaginal penetration for a period of five minutes. A swab was taken from the vagina at various time intervals: 1-, 6-, 12, 24- or 72-hours post-penetration. They were advised to undertake normal daily activities. Predictably, the number of alleles obtained decreased with time although one couple had 72-hour swabs with 20+ alleles, with Y-STR testing, thought in part way due to her pregnancy status.

A UK study (23), using Sperm Elution extraction, looked at 47 sexual assault/rape cases (either penile vaginal or digital vaginal or both) where testing had already been negative for sperm, there had been no history of prior intercourse in the preceding 10 days and collection of samples had occurred within 48 hours of the alleged assault; 75 samples were accepted. Ten of the cases produced ≥ 10 Y-STR alleles. This occurred when there was an allegation of penile vaginal penetration (up to 48 hours prior to sampling); of digital vaginal penetration (up to 12 hours prior to sampling), and when there was an allegation of both (up to 48 hours prior to sampling).

Similar research (24) in Australia in 2019, demonstrated that it was possible to obtain full profiles from samples taken from the genital tract up to 44 hours post-assault when tests for semen were negative. Research was conducted on casework samples.

A Norwegian study in 2019 (25) reviewed 1126 samples for DNA, presumed to be recovered from the epithelial cells left by the alleged offender. DNA was positive on samples collected from external genitalia (up to 12 hours) and from skin and penile swabs (up to 48 hours). An internal vaginal sample was positive at 72 hours and two more were positive after 48 hours.

Transgender sampling

Although it is beyond the scope of this chapter to deal comprehensively with transgender sampling, given the individuality of circumstances that may present, the following aims to provide some overarching guidance or considerations that should assist the forensic practitioner.

Gender identity is now understood to be a spectrum rather than a binary assignment. It is acknowledged that there can be a marked incongruence between a person's assigned gender (at birth) and their experienced or expressed gender (26).

Cisgender Person is the term used when a person's sex, assigned at birth, matches their gender identity. In other words, there is no incongruity about their gender.

Transgender Person is the term used where there is some degree of incongruence.

Trans(gender) Man/Male is someone who was assigned as a female at birth who identifies as a male.

Trans(gender) Woman/Female is someone who was assigned as a male at birth who identifies as a female.

Any surgical intervention undertaken to align a person's physical attributes with their identified gender is referred to as either Confirmation or Affirmation surgery. It may be appropriate to ask about any medical transition that has occurred, in order to determine the most appropriate forensic sampling.

Vaginoplasty (for Transgender Women) can be undertaken in a number of different ways. Penile inversion vaginoplasty (often considered the gold standard) requires the skin of the penis to remain attached, inverted to become the lining of the vagina and inserted into a cavity created between the urethra and the rectum. Part of the glans becomes the clitoris. The urethra is shortened. The labial tissue is formed from the scrotum and tissue near the base of the penis (27).

If, during the examination and after forensic sampling, the urethra is not easily identifiable, a gloved finger can be inserted into the vaginal vault. Look superiorly for another opening. The size of the urethral opening should be approximately the same as for a cisfemale (28).

Hair removal pre-surgery is important otherwise there may be hair growth within the vaginal vault.

While there are many potential complications, vaginal strictures are common. There may be loss of depth of the vaginal vault (27).

Intestinal vaginoplasty requires taking a section of the bowel for use as the neo-vagina. The most common side effect appears to be stenosis at the introitus. Excessive discharge (often a transient problem) and persistent malodor have been reported in some cases (27).

Neo-vaginal canals do not self-lubricate with arousal. Neo-vaginal skin may tear more easily (27).

Treatment for sexually transmitted infections should be the same as for ciswomen (28).

Phalloplasty is often done in stages with 6 or more months between each. A flap of skin, for the new penis, is often harvested from the latissimus dorsi area (27).

Clothing

It has long been recognized that DNA can be transferred to clothing. In particular, underclothing worn immediately following rape/sexual assault and brassieres worn after licking/touching of the breasts.

Australian researchers (29) used a 45 kg dummy, wearing bra and underpants, subjected it to various activities by volunteers which included removing the undergarments, simulating digital vaginal penetration, grabbing the breast area under the bra and grabbing the breast over the bra in order to determine the best sampling sites. Removing underclothing showed maximal touching over the outer sections (the part of the underclothing normally in contact with the hips); removing the bra showed maximal contact over the back strap and clasp; simulated digital penetration showed maximal contact over the interior front when it was done with the dummy lying face up but, when performed with the dummy lying face down, contact sites on the underclothing were spread out over a larger surface area particularly over the lower crotch area and back of the underclothing; when groping the breast under the bra, not surprisingly, maximal contact was over the inner brassiere cup and externally on the perimeter of the bra cups. This study emphasizes the importance of obtaining a forensic history that details, where possible, what clothes were worn, who removed them and how were they removed. Additionally, if underclothing was put on following an assault inside out or back to front, this information should be provided to the lab.

Persistence of DNA on clothing has been well established (note semen-stained blue dress belonging to Monica Lewinsky). Research that examines semen-stained garments that have been washed multiple times is limited. One study (30) looked at multiple fabrics (cotton, terry towel, satin, nylon, lace and polar fleece) stained with semen. While all returned +ve alkaline phosphatase testing prior to washing, only cotton returned a weak positive result and only after the first wash. Positive testing for sperm was related, in the authors' opinion, to the material's knitted construction. Polar fleece and lace, with looser knit construction, were less likely to return positive sperm results after washing. Cotton and terry towel (100% cotton), with tighter weave patterns, showed the greatest retention with sperm being identified up to the sixth wash.

In the literature, there is also a case report (31) of recovering DNA from a skirt, stained by semen, that had since been dry cleaned and worn for a year prior to testing.

Condom evidence

Lubricant is commonly added to condoms to prevent sticking and are of two main types: polydimethylsiloxane (PDMS) and polyethylene glycol (PEG). If looking for trace evidence of either, it is important to obtain a relevant history from the complainant as to recent use of condoms, external lubricants or other medical vaginal treatment, for example vaginal ovules. Both PDMS and PEG can be found in some liquid soaps and shampoos (32). Sampling follows similar principles to that for DNA collections. Obviously, lubricant should not be used for the examination prior to sampling for condom residue (32).

Oral samples

Oral samples may include peri-oral swabs, oral swabs and/or mouth rinse. Of 554 oral swabs, collected in NSW, 84 had been collected less than 24 hours after the assault and sperm were detected in 4.2 percent and in none collected after 24 hours had elapsed. Of 104 oral rinses that were analyzed, 17 tested positive for sperm (16.3%). Of the 71 peri-oral swabs (around the outer lips) that were tested 13 were positive for sperm (18.3%). When tested for DNA, sperm positive oral swabs produced DNA profiles in 60.9 percent of cases; sperm positive oral rinses produced DNA profiles in 70.6 percent of cases and in sperm positive peri-oral swabs DNA profiles were generated in 75 percent (16).

A Norwegian study (25) noted that 11 percent of 71 oral swab samples were positive for the detection of spermatozoa up to 12 hours following the assault. No oral sample examined after this time period was positive.

Menstrual blood

Determination of a bleeding source during menstruation has traditionally relied upon siting blood originating from the cervical os, during speculum examination. This is not always possible. Sometimes blood stains can be found on clothing and determining the source of the blood can have forensic significance and assist with reconstructing an event.

As menstrual blood is a mixture of blood and cellular tissue, it has different concentrations of proteins, cholesterol, hemoglobin and bilirubin than that found in peripheral blood (33). Spectroscopy has been used to differentiate menstrual blood from peripheral blood and methods for determining time since deposition (up to 2 years) have been described (34,35).

Rectal and anal samples

Peri-anal, anal and rectal samples may be required. A 2019 Norwegian study which reviewed analysis of 17 rectal swabs, with allegations that might suggest the possibility for recovering DNA from deposited epithelial cells, noted that all were negative. Sperm that provided DNA from rectal swabs was only detected up to 35 hours post-assault, and there was only one case beyond 24 hours (25). The Irish Forensic Science Laboratory, when reviewing results obtained from anal samples, indicated that it was unlikely for sperm to be detected on internal anal swabs beyond 24 hours (19).

In NSW, recommendations are for collections of peri-anal and anal swabs up to 48 hours post-assault (18). Likewise, in Victoria, samples can be collected up to 48 hours but not if defecated or washed (17). The UK Faculty of Forensic & Legal Medicine Recommendations suggest anal sampling up to 72 hours post-assault, even if a condom is worn. There are also recommendations for peri-anal sampling up to 7 days post-penile vaginal penetration, with or without anal intercourse and with or without use of a condom (7).

Skin

Samples for the recovery of body fluids, cellular material and other visible trace evidence may be taken from hands and other areas of skin as required by the history of the incident. Time periods for collection often depend upon the donor fluid/tissue suspected, for example semen, blood, epithelial cells or saliva. There is a strong case, until genomics has developed to such a stage to enable the efficient detection of the source of donor DNA, to advise the laboratory of the potential source. Although not absolute, it would provide additional information when deciding cut-off times when sampling the skin for various substrates.

In NSW, skin can be sampled up to 12 hours (when looking for DNA from epithelial cells) and the patient has not washed (18). In Victoria, it is 24 hours and only if the patient has not washed (17). The UK recommends collections within 48 hours though, if the examinee has not washed, then consideration should be given to a longer timeframe (7).

If the substrate is thought to have been saliva, blood or semen, the recommendation in NSW extends to 48 hours regardless of whether washed or not and extended to 7 days if not washed (18). In Victoria, it is 72 hours if not washed (17).

Fingernails

Collection of nail evidence is not standardized. A 2014 study from the USA observed that "*neither MEs (Medical Examiners) nor SANEs (Sexual Assault Nurse*

Examiners) knew whether their practice for nail evidence collection was useful, much less optimal, nor had they ever received feedback on such evidence from crime laboratories." (36).

Although different jurisdictions recommend different methods, the UK advise the swabbing of nails (37,38) with specific nail swabs, stating that this is recommended over clippings unless comparison with a broken fingernail found at scene is necessary (7).

In NSW, the recommendation is to collect either clippings, swabs, or both, up to 48 hours only if the offender and victim were not previously known to each other or in an intimate relationship (18). Victoria recommends swabbing and differentiates between suspects and complainants, recommending a time limit of 24 hours for a complainant if the offender is a stranger. This extends to 5 days for a suspect (17).

Consideration in many cases is given to the relationship between the complainant and the offender. When in an intimate relationship, it might be commonly expected to find the other's DNA beneath fingernails. Malsom et al. (39) sampled fingernails from 12 couples on three separate occasions and found reportable mixed DNA profiles in 17 percent.

Penile

Swabs from the shaft and external foreskin (if present) and coronal sulcus, internal foreskin and glans, may recover body fluids, DNA and other material, even if a condom has been used. Timescales recommended for taking these samples vary between 48 and 72 hours. Research evidence suggests up to 24 hours (40,41) but forensic scientists in the UK advise that positive results of female DNA on penile swabs can be obtained after 48 hours and so recommend a longer time scale for sampling.

Hair

Recovery of foreign particles such as fibers and other hairs, body fluids/contact DNA and control hair samples may be required from head or pubic hair (42). Techniques include combing, swabbing, low adhesive tape (the latter may be more efficient than combing) (43) and cutting. Visible foreign particles/hairs can be removed with forceps.

Toxicology

Where substance use is suspected (drugs or alcohol) urine should be taken as soon as possible, potentially by a first responder and followed up with a blood sample. Timescales for the samples vary but ideally blood should be taken within 48 hours of the incident and urine up to five days (44). Glass bottles, in some jurisdictions, are required for both the collection of blood and urine, based on the theoretical loss of a small amount of THC (tetrahydrocannabinol) which can be absorbed into the plastic of the transport container. This should be balanced against the known difficulty with glass, both with transporting glass vials and testing in the laboratory and their potential to shatter resulting in the loss of the entire sample. Containers should not be overfilled as, increasingly, samples are frozen and fracture when defrosted. Blood tubes should contain both potassium oxalate (anticoagulant) and sodium fluoride preservatives if testing for alcohol concentrations.

Hair (head) for toxicology can be taken, if relevant in delayed presentations, 4–6 weeks after the date of interest up to 6 months. Occasionally, nail clippings can be used for drug analysis. These are specialized collections and are not undertaken in many laboratories. Prior to collection, the examiner should acquaint themselves with the recommended process (including use of specialized kit) and ensure there is a laboratory willing and able to undertake this type of testing.

CONCLUSION

It is essential that forensic practitioners have training in the field of evidence collection prior to taking on the role. This is to ensure they are competent and capable to manage the complex cases that present in the clinical forensic medical arena. All forensic practitioners must be familiar with contemporary best practice guidelines and recommendations generally and specifically within their own jurisdiction.

REFERENCES

1. Clarke MDB. Metropolitan Police Sexual Offences Examination Kit. In: *Rape. The New Police Surgeon*. Ed McLay WDS R. Association of Police Surgeons of Great Britain
2. Campbell R, Ma W, Javorka M, et al. Why do sexual assault survivors seek medical forensic exams and forensic evidence collection? Evolving patterns of service needs in a state-wide study. *Psychol Violence* 2021; **11**(3): 264–75.
3. Johnson D, Paterson J, Sommers I, et al. Use of forensic science in investigating crimes of sexual violence: Contrasting its theoretical potential with empirical realities. *Violence Against Women* 2021; **182**(2): 193–222.
4. Edwards J. Medical examination of sexual assault victims: Forensic use and relevance. *JOB* 2003; **15**(8): 65–66.
5. Kjaerulff MLBG, Bonde U, Schmidt Astrup B. The significance of the forensic clinical examination on the judicial assessment of rape complainants – developments and trends. *Forensic Sci Int* 2019; **297**: 90–9.
6. Alderson M, Cross TP, Vlajnic M, et al. Prosecutor's perspectives on biological evidence in sexual assault cases. *J Interpers Violence* 2021; **36**(7–8): 3880–902.
7. The Faculty of Forensic & Legal Medicine. Recommendations for the collection of forensic specimens from complainants and suspects, 2023. Available from: https://fflm.ac.uk/resources/publications/recommendations-for-the-collection-of-forensic-specimens-from-complainants-and-suspects/ (Accessed 24 May 2023).
8. Nittis M, Stark MM. Evidence based practice: Laboratory feedback informed specimen collection in NSW. *J Forensic Leg Med* 2014; **25**: 38–44.
9. Campbell R, Fehler-Cabral G, Pierce SJ, et al. Changing the criminal justice system response to sexual assault: An empirical study of a participatory action research project. *Am J Community Psychology* 2021; **67**: 166–78.
10. Campbell R, Fehler-Cabal G, Bybee D, et al. Forgotten Evidence: A mixed methods study of why sexual assault

kits (SAKs) are not submitted for DNA forensic testing. *Law and Human Behavior* 2017; 41(5): 454–67.
11. Joki-Erkki M, Tuomisto S, Seppanen M, et al. Urine specimen collection following consensual intercourse – A forensic evidence collection method for Y-DNA and spermatozoa. *J Forensic Leg Med* 2016; 37: 50–4.
12. Smith DA, Webb LG, Fennell AI, et al. Early evidence kits in sexual assault: An observational study of spermatozoa detection in urine and other forensic specimens. *Forensic Sci Med Pathol* 2014; **10**: 336–43.
13. Forensic Science Regulator. The control and avoidance of contamination in forensic medical examinations, 2020. Available from: https://assets.publishing.service.gov.uk/government/uploads/system/uploads/attachment_data/file/912748/207_DNA_Anti-_Contam_SARC__Custody_Issue_2_Final.pdf (Accessed 24 May 2023).
14. The Faculty of Forensic & Legal Medicine. Recommended equipment for obtaining forensic samples from complainants and suspects, 2023. Available from: https://fflm.ac.uk/resources/publications/recommended-equipment-for-obtaining-forensic-samples-from-complainants-and-suspects/ (Accessed 24 July 2023).
15. Hook SM, Elliot DA, Harbison SA. Penetration and ejaculation; forensic aspects of rape. *N Z Med J* 1992; **105(929)**: 87–9.
16. Nittis M, Cochrane C, Hughes R, et al. Preparing semen slides in cases of sexual assault: Do they who smear first smear best? *J Forensic Leg Med* 2021; **79**: 102130.
17. Victorian Institute of Forensic Medicine. *CFM Circular 66 – Specimen cut off times*, — July 2021
18. NSW Police Force/NSW Government Health. *Guidelines for the collection of forensic specimens from complainants and suspects* Version 20 DOCCFMU01, June 2021.
19. Casey DG, Domijan K, MacNeill S, et al. The persistence of sperm and the development of time since intercourse (TSI) guidelines in sexual assault cases at Forensic Science Ireland, Dublin, Ireland. *J Forensic Sci* 2017; **62**(3): 586–92.
20. Owers R, Davidson G, McDonald A, et al. Time since intercourse (TSI) data from a large-scale casework study of penile-vaginal penetration allegations using Sperm Elution™. *Forensic Sci Int* 2018; **288**: 10–13.
21. Sari D, Hitchcock C, Collins S, et al. Amylase testing on intimate samples from pre-pubescent, post-pubescent and post-menopausal females: Implications for forensic casework in sexual assault allegations. *Aust J Forensic Sci* 2020; **52(6)**: 618–25.
22. Sween KR, Quarino LA, Kishbaugh JM. Detection of male DNA in the vaginal cavity after digital penetration using Y-chromosome short tandem repeats. *J Forensic Nurs* 2015; **11**(**1**): 33–40.
23. McDonald A, Jones E, Lewis J, et al. Y-STR analysis of digital and/ or penile penetration cases with no detected spermatozoa. *Forensic Sci Int Genet* 2015; **15**: 84–9.
24. Henry J, Scandrett L. Assessment of the Yfiler® Plus PCR amplification kit for the detection of male DNA in semen-negative sexual assault cases. *Sci Justice* 2019; **59**: 480–5.
25. Fonneløp AE, Johannessen H, Heen G, et al. A retrospective study on the transfer, persistence and recovery of sperm and epithelial cells in samples collected in sexual assault casework. *Forensic Sci Int Genet* 2019; **43**: 102153.
26. American Psychiatric Association (ed). *DSM-5-TR Diagnostic and Statistical Manual of Mental Disorders*, 5th ed. Washington DC: American Psychiatric Association Publishing; 2013.
27. Loren S, (ed). *Gender Confirmation Surgery: Principles and Techniques for an Emerging Field*. Cham: Springer; 2020.
28. Hanley K, Wittenberg H, Gurjala D, et al. Caring for transgender patients: Complications of gender-affirming genital surgeries. *Ann Emerg Med* 2021; **78**(3): 409–15.
29. Ramos P, Handt O, Taylor D. Investigating the position and level of DNA transfer to undergarments during digital sexual assault. *Forensic Sci Int Genet* 2010; **47**: 102316.
30. Nolan A, Speers SJ, Murakami J, et al. A pilot study: The effects of repeat washing and fabric type on the detection of seminal fluid and spermatozoa. *Forensic Sci Int* 2018; **289**: 51–6.
31. Ogawa H, Hiroshige Y, Yoshimoto T, et al. STR genotyping from a dry-cleaned skirt in a sexual assault case. *J Forensic Sci* 2018; **63(4)**: 1291–7.
32. Burnier C, Massonnet G. Pre-analytical considerations of condom traces: A review of composition, background, transfer and persistence. *Forensic Sci Int* 2019; **302**: 109861.
33. Mistek-Morabito E, Lednev IK. Discrimination of menstrual and peripheral blood traces using attenuated total reflection Fourier transform-infrared (ATR FT-IR) spectroscopy and chemometrics for forensic purposes. *Anal Bioanal Chem* 2021; **413**: 2513–22.
34. Doty KC, Munro CK, Lednev IK. Predicting the time of the crime: Bloodstain aging estimation for up to two years. *Forensic Chem* 2017; **5**: 1–7.
35. Wojtowicz A, Weber A, Wietecha-Posluszny R, et al. Probing menstrual bloodstain aging with fluorescence spectroscopy. *Spectrochim Acta A Mol Biomol Spectrosc* 2021; **248**: 119172.
36. Hebda LM, Doran AE, Foran DR. Collecting and analyzing DNA evidence from fingernails: A comparative study. *J Forensic Sci* 2014; **59**(**5**): 1343–50.
37. Foran D, Hebda LM, Doran A. Trace DNA from fingernails: Increasing the success rate of widely collected forensic evidence, 2015. Available from: https://www.ojp.gov/pdffiles1/nij/grants/249534.pdf (Accessed 24 May 2023).
38. Oz C, Zamir A. An evaluation of the relevance of routine DNA typing of fingernail clippings for forensic casework. *J Forensic Sci* 2000; **45**(**1**): 158–60.
39. Malsom S, Flanagan N, McAlister C, et al. The prevalence of mixed DNA profiles in fingernail samples taken from couples who co-habit using autosomal and Y-STRs. *Forensic Sci Int Genet* 2009; **3**: 57–62.
40. Cina SJ, Collins KA, Pettenati MJ, et al. Isolation and identification of female DNA on post-coital penile swabs. *Am J Forensic Med Pathol* 2000: **21**; 97–100.
41. Farmen RKB, Haukeli I, Ruoff P, et al. Assessing the presence of female DNA on post-coital penile swabs: Relevance to the investigation of sexual assault. *J Forensic Leg Med* 2012: **19**; 386–9.
42. Exline DL, Smith FP, Drexler SG. Frequency of pubic hair transfer during sexual intercourse. *J Forensic Sci* 1998; **43**; 505–8.
43. Salter MT, Cook R. Transfer of fibres to head hair, their persistence and retrieval. *Forensic Sci Int* 1996: **81**(**2**); 211–21.
44. United Nations Office on Drugs and Crime. Guidelines for the forensic analysis of drug facilitating sexual assault and other criminal acts, 2011. Available from: https://www.unodc.org/unodc/en/scientists/guidelines-for-the-forensic-analysis-of-drugs-facilitating-sexual-assault-and-other-criminal-acts_new.html (Accessed 24 May 2023).

CHAPTER

79

Minimizing DNA Contamination

John A.M. Gall

INTRODUCTION

DNA analysis is now a well-established procedure within the forensic laboratory and improvements in the technology have increased the sensitivity of the kits used. As a result of this increased sensitivity of detection, even greater care needs to be exercised in the collection of forensic specimens to avoid contamination with DNA from other sources. Collection of these specimens is generally undertaken by doctors and other healthcare professionals within the forensic and legal medicine healthcare setting – and it is this group to whom the content of this chapter is particularly directed. This chapter discusses how inadvertent or accidental contamination may occur and provides advice on how this contamination may be minimized. Deliberate contamination is not discussed. For completeness and, as a reminder of the overall processing of any forensic DNA specimen, a brief outline of the DNA detection process is provided. This chapter will not provide either a detailed account of or discussion of DNA detection and analysis (*see* Chapter 95 – "DNA Analysis in Forensic Investigations"). There are many sources of information on the DNA detection process including its evolution and current profiling techniques (1,2) and of the future directions in this field (3).

The development of DNA profiling has been a major leap forward in criminal investigations and plays a primary role in paternity testing and victim identification, particularly following natural disasters and war. At one point, and perhaps still in some quarters, it attained perceived infallibility status (4–6) but there are many sources of error. To be clear, although DNA profiling is a very powerful weapon in the fight against crime, it is not infallible. Within criminal jurisdictions, it has been used not only to convict offenders but also to exonerate those incorrectly convicted of a crime. Unfortunately, its fallibility has also led to some significant miscarriages of justice where a person has been falsely found guilty of a crime for which they did not commit. Although there is a significant emphasis on DNA profiling, it is not a replacement for competent crime investigation. DNA profiling is merely an additional tool available to the crime investigator. For any DNA that may be found at a crime scene (and this includes on an individual), the question as to how it may have arrived at that scene needs consideration. Locard's Exchange Principle applies equally to DNA in that the perpetrator of a crime will leave some DNA at the crime scene and will also take some DNA with them away from the crime scene. The crime scene, however, may also contain DNA from innocent and unconnected sources and this presents a challenge for the investigators to distinguish between DNA from an innocent source (including the victim) from that of the offender. In keeping with Locard's Exchange Principle, forensic practitioners, be they medical practitioners, nurses or scientists, who collect forensic samples at the crime scene, similarly have the potential to contaminate the crime scene and the collected forensic specimens with their own DNA. It is this contamination from the innocent and the specimen collectors that this chapter will consider. The aim of forensic specimen collection is to successfully collect the offender's DNA with a minimization of contamination. Unfortunately, given the nature of crime scenes, it is not always possible to completely avoid unintended contamination of the specimens collected.

WHERE IS DNA FOUND?

Like all living entities, the human body consists predominantly of nucleated cells that contain an individual's DNA. The DNA is identical in each cell from the same person. Not all cells in the body contain a nucleus and important examples of this include the keratinized, a nucleated covering layer of the skin called the stratum corneum, hair shafts and red blood cells. Most other cells within the body do contain a nucleus. As the stratum corneum does not contain a nucleus, it may be expected that cells from this layer will not contain DNA. Research has shown that this is not the case and that DNA profiles may be retrieved from objects touched by a person (7,8). Although cells of the stratum corneum do not contain a nucleus, they do contain single-stranded DNA which can be detected using current DNA profiling (9). Interestingly, this and nucleus-free, or cell-free, nucleic acid (CNA) accounts for a significant proportion of the DNA found in sweat (10). DNA, therefore, may be deposited by a person touching any object with their skin. Depositors of flakes of keratinized skin may include the victim, offender, crime scene investigators, forensic practitioners, and anyone else who may enter the crime scene – and who may have entered the scene before it became a crime

DOI: 10.1201/9781003138754-82

scene. Similarly, body secretions and excretions will also leave either cellular DNA (i.e. DNA within a cell or cellular material) or CNA. Both secretions and excretions (e.g. sweat, vaginal fluid, saliva, semen, urine) contain cells/cellular material and thus DNA or CNA and will produce a DNA profile. Given the potential multiple sources of DNA within a crime scene, the potential for contamination is significant.

THE DNA DETECTION PROCESS

The technique for DNA profiling was initially developed in the mid-1980s by Sir Alec Jeffreys and his team (11) who used this technique to assist in the identification and conviction of a rapist and murderer of two teenage girls in Leicestershire. Their technique was slow and required sizable amounts of DNA unlike the techniques of today. The process required the use of radioactive-labeled complimentary DNA sequences (multi-locus probes) within segments of DNA cut with restriction enzymes. These fragments were subjected to electrophoresis to isolate those of differing sizes and then visualized following exposure to an X-ray plate. During the 1980s and early 1990s, there were two major scientific developments that enabled more accurate DNA profiling even from small quantities and fragmented segments of DNA. One development was the polymerase chain reaction (PCR) by Kary Mullis in 1983 and the other was the discovery of polymorphic microsatellites within the genome known as short tandem repeats (STRs). PCR effectively mimics DNA replication in the body and enables minute amounts of DNA sequences to be rapidly reproduced to provide millions (or more) of copies of the original sample to provide sufficient quantities of DNA to allow analysis in detail. STRs are repeated sequences of 2–5 nucleotides (usually 4) and, because unrelated people have different numbers of repeat units, these units are used to discriminate between individuals. Using increasing numbers of STI loci increases the likelihood that a DNA sample is from a specific individual. The units are targeted within the isolated DNA fragments, replicated to usable quantities using PCR, isolated using electrophoresis, detected by fluorescent probes and subsequently analyzed.

Once the laboratory receives a forensic specimen for DNA profiling, the process involves:

- Extracting the DNA from cells and cellular debris
- Removing any inhibitors of the PCR process (these may include proteins, enzymes, urea, bile and salts)
- Selection of an appropriate DNA sequence for amplification, incorporating a fluorescent probe for later detection, and amplification of that sequence (PCR)
- Separation of the different sized DNA molecules using electrophoresis
- Visualization (using the fluorescent probe) to create a profile
- Interpretation (if there are limited amounts of DNA, DNA from multiple individuals, the DNA is fragmented/degraded, or artifact is present, interpretation may be difficult and the profile becomes either unusable or in need of further analysis)
- Statistical evaluation

The laboratory requires DNA samples from both the victim and alleged offender to enable full matches to be made. Further complicating this process is the potential presence of extraneous DNA from innocent parties including the forensic specimen collector. DNA may be in high quantities and that from the alleged offender in very low quantities, a situation that will hinder the interpretation of the profile obtained.

Most laboratories analyzing crime scene DNA specimens utilize commercially available STR multiplex kits with loci relevant to their population that usually includes a gender locus. Analysis utilizing these kits is rapid and may take between 90 and 120 minutes (excluding the time required for specimen selection and result interpretation and evaluation). There are also DNA identification systems that target areas on the Y chromosome (for all males along the same paternal line). Mitochondrial DNA may also be analyzed that will similarly identify individuals with the same maternal line.

The potential for contamination of a DNA sample is significant not only during the collection process but also during the subsequent processing within the laboratory. At the point of collection, the DNA present may be in very small amounts and may be poorly preserved either at the scene or during subsequent transportation to the laboratory. The crime scene may contain DNA from one or more offenders and victims and, as PCR will amplify minute numbers of molecules, any contamination may lead to potentially false-positive results and subsequently a potentially misleading analysis.

DOES DNA CONTAMINATION OCCUR?

As outlined above, what may be a minute fragment of contaminating DNA within a forensic specimen may, following PCR, become a large volume of DNA that may adversely affect the detection and analysis of the alleged offender's DNA, assuming that it was present and has also been collected. It is essential to realise that this is not a theoretical concept but one that has occurred in the past and probably occurs on a far more regular basis than we are aware of. Contamination has been documented to occur both at, or even before, the point of specimen collection and during subsequent analysis within the laboratory (12).

One high-profile case that illustrates the importance of ensuring that specimens are collected using certified DNA-free equipment, and the ease with which contamination may occur and confound an investigation, is that of the Phantom of Heilbronn, so named following the murder of a female police officer in Heilbronn in 2007 (13,14). DNA profiling had shown that this female criminal had committed a multitude of crimes over a 15-year period in locations across Austria, France and Germany. It was not until March 2009, when re-examining the case of an unidentified deceased person that the identity of the Phantom was discovered. A DNA profile was obtained from the unidentified person's fingerprints and this DNA profile contained that of the Phantom. This seemed improbable given that the unidentified person died in 2002 and the Phantom committed crimes after 2002. Additional swabs were taken from the fingerprints and found not to contain the Phantom's DNA profile. Further investigative work revealed that the identified DNA was that of an innocent female worker on the production line for cotton-tipped swabs that had been used by multiple law enforcement agencies in Europe for forensic specimen collection.

Another high-profile case, also showing the ease with which contamination may occur, led to the criminal conviction and jailing of an innocent person. In 2008, a young Somalian male, Farah Abdulkadir Jama, was convicted of the rape of a 48-year-old female on the sole basis that his DNA had been identified on a single slide and swab collected during the forensic examination of the victim. The female victim had attended a nightclub, consumed a large volume of alcohol and was found unconscious in a toilet cubicle that had been locked from the inside. Suspecting a possible sexual assault, she was taken to a dedicated sexual assault examination suite and a standard forensic medical examination and collection of forensic samples was undertaken by a trained forensic medical officer. Mr Jama's DNA was found on a single swab taken from the endocervical region of the victim but not identified on other vaginal swabs. Mr Jama claimed that he had not actually attended the nightclub where the alleged assault had occurred and there was no evidence tendered during his trial to suggest otherwise. Despite this, Mr Jama was found guilty and served approximately 15 months of his sentence prior to being acquitted by the Court of Appeal. An enquiry was undertaken (15) and although the actual source of contamination was not specifically identified, it was presumed that it occurred within the clinical examination suite as the examining doctor had, the day previously, examined another female who had engaged in sexual activity with Mr Jama, an activity that had not led to any charges being laid. It was presumed that Mr Jama's DNA had inadvertently contaminated perhaps the slide and/or swab used the following day for the sexual assault examination. Not surprisingly, this resulted in the development and implementation of a single-use forensic medical examination kit (i.e. evidence recovery kit) to prevent a similar error occurring at some stage in the future.

Decontaminants

Before considering how to minimize DNA contamination, consideration of DNA denaturation is required as any item used to collect forensic specimens (including solutions used) and to handle forensic specimens needs to be DNA free. Experience also shows that there is a misunderstanding among many forensic clinicians between sterilization and DNA denaturation. Sterilization is designed to remove micro-organisms. It does not denature DNA. Thus, standard sterilization processes are totally unsuitable for DNA decontamination.

What then is useful? A number of studies have been undertaken to ascertain the most effective way of decontaminating surfaces and equipment both within the clinical and laboratory settings (for a more detailed account see Gall and Syndercombe Court (12). Water, 70 percent ethanol and detergents, the usual solutions for cleaning and wiping down surfaces, do not decontaminate those surfaces sufficiently for the PCR application (16,17). Radiation (beta and gamma), ethylene oxide, sodium hypochlorite and autoclaving have been shown to be effective but not under the procedures used for sterilization. Beta and gamma radiation, for example, require a dose of 25 kGy for sterilization whereas in excess of 50–60 kGy is required for DNA denaturation. Instruments generally require exposure to ethylene oxide for between 30 minutes and 10 hours for sterilization whereas DNA denaturation requires at least 6–12 hours. Autoclaving is used for sterilization but the process is usually at a temperature of 121–134°C at a pressure of 15–30 psi for 3–15 minutes. For DNA denaturation using autoclaving, a temperature of 121°C at a pressure of 15 psi is required for a time of 120 minutes, far longer (by at least 8 times) than that required for standard sterilization. UV light (254 nm) has sometimes been used within the clinical setting. Although it is a useful adjunct to decontamination, its efficacy is poor, and the times required for decontamination are long and directly related to the distance the light is from the surface being decontaminated. Further, it is unsuited for decontaminating instruments and equipment and, if it was to be used, only has a role for the decontamination of surfaces.

Based on studies to date, the most appropriate DNA decontaminants are ethylene oxide for equipment and, for surfaces, trolleys some equipment, either sodium hypochlorite alone or sodium hypochlorite followed by rinsing or wiping with DNA/CNA free water. It generally isn't the role of the clinician to supervise decontamination using ethylene oxide but for completeness, exposure of swabs and instruments for at least 12 hours appears necessary (18,19).

Sodium hypochlorite is not a sterilizing agent but an effective disinfectant and bleaching agent that denatures DNA. It is readily available as a household liquid bleach in concentrations of 5 to 10 percent. As it is a strong oxidizing agent, it can liberate toxic gases (e.g. chloramines and chlorine gas) that have a potential occupational health and safety implication (20). It is also corrosive which may render it unsuitable for use with instruments such as colposcopes and cameras. Determining the optimal cleaning process has varied with time. Earlier studies (16,21,22) suggested concentrations of at least 3 percent (w/v) hypochlorite and immersion for at least 15 minutes for successful surface decontamination. A study by Ballantyne and co-workers (23) demonstrated that the use of a 1 percent solution of sodium hypochlorite left for 5 minutes followed by wiping with 70 percent ethanol effectively removed all DNA from surfaces. More recently, Kampmann and co-workers (17) showed that cleaning services with water, 96 percent ethanol, and water followed by 96 percent ethanol was effective in removing most, but not all, traces of amplifiable DNA.

These cleaning methods were not, however, as effective as using sodium hypochlorite. They used two solutions of 3 to 6 percent and 0.9 to 1.8 percent and both proved to be effective, the lower concentration of hypochlorite being more ideal as it minimized any likelihood of adverse exposure to poisonous gases. Based upon these studies, the optimal surface cleaning agent within a clinical setting would be a 1 percent sodium hypochlorite sprayed on a surface followed by wiping with DNA/CNA free water.

Minimizing contamination from a clinical perspective

When failures occur, standard operating procedures must be reviewed and modified to ensure that those failures do not recur. The wrongful imprisonment of Mr Jama following inadvertent DNA contamination resulted in an enquiry and subsequent modifications to the way in which clinical forensic procedures were undertaken. This resulted in the development of guidelines for the cleaning and decontamination of clinical forensic examination suites initially by the then Australasian Association of Forensic Physicians (AAFP). This Association has been incorporated into the Faculty of Clinical Forensic Medicine of the Royal College of Pathologists of Australasia who have provided a more detailed guideline on cleaning and decontamination (24). The Faculty of Forensic and Legal Medicine of the Royal College of Physicians, London, similarly produced guidance on cleaning and decontamination of examination suites but this task is now provided by the United Kingdom Forensic Science Regulator (25). Although there are undoubtedly other organizations with similar guidelines, the above two are readily available online and provide a very good template that may be modified/updated to accommodate local jurisdictions. As the potential for DNA contamination increases with the increasing sensitivity of the DNA profiling kits, it is essential that any organization collecting forensic specimens for DNA profiling must have a set of guidelines that outline how best to minimize DNA contamination and are followed by the forensic specimen collectors. Such guidelines are essential not only in preserving the interests of the victim but also to reassure the investigative and judicial system that the risks of contamination are actively being minimized and that the quality of the forensic specimens obtained are optimal.

Irrespective of which template may be used to develop a local protocol for minimizing DNA contamination at the point of sampling, or in those cases where a set of guidelines are being devised independently of these templates, there are some general and more specific issues that need consideration and/or incorporation into any set of guidelines. Based upon the original AAFP guidelines, consideration should include the principles listed in Tables 79.1–3.

TABLE 79.1 General principles for reducing the risk of contamination
• Although the alleged victim is effectively a "crime scene", it is important to remember that they are first and foremost a "patient" and they should be accorded appropriate professional, non-judgemental care. The location of the forensic medical examination should be welcoming and comfortable, and the forensic medical examination itself and all specimen collection should be undertaken with care and sensitivity to not further traumatize the patient.
• The victim's medical and emotional care has absolute priority over the collection of forensic specimens. In some circumstances, this may compromise the collection of forensic specimens.
• Cleaning and decontamination procedures have two roles, one is infection control and the other is DNA decontamination. Both must be safe and effective.
• The choice of the DNA decontaminant and the decontamination procedure must be effective against cellular DNA. Occupational health and safety issues regarding the decontaminant used will need consideration in relation to the safety of the examining clinician, attending nurses, the cleaning staff, the victim and those accompanying the victim. The choice of a DNA decontaminant must not affect the PCR laboratory process. Because some DNA decontaminants are corrosive (e.g. sodium hypochlorite) they may be inappropriate for the decontamination of all parts of the examination suite and equipment such as colposcopes and cameras.
• All items (e.g. swabs, slides, containers) used for specimen collection need to be certified as being DNA/CNA free.
• No swab for DNA specimen collection should come in contact in any way with any surface or object other than the sample site on the patient and the interior of the swab's protective sheath.
• Ideally, examination suites should contain a minimum of equipment with desks and furniture that can be easily cleaned using a DNA decontaminant. Curtains should be kept to a minimum and the floor should be of a firm, sealed surface (not carpeted). The suites should be appropriately proportioned to enable unimpeded movement for the examination and specimen collection.
• Non-dedicated (i.e. used for other purposes) clinical examination suites should be decontaminated prior to each use. In cases where a dedicated clinical examination suite is used, conditional upon access being limited and it being used solely for the purposes of examinations requiring DNA specimen collection, decontamination post use may be satisfactory without a subsequent need to re-decontaminate prior to use.
• Access to the examination suite should be limited to the examining doctor/nurse, the victim and their chaperone/support person. Other persons (e.g. police, child protection personnel, friends and family of the victim) should not be allowed into the examination suite and any interview with these persons should be undertaken in a separate room.

(Continued)

TABLE 79.1 (Continued) General principles for reducing the risk of contamination
• Cleaning and decontamination of clinical examination suites should be undertaken by cleaners with appropriate training and using equipment dedicated to that suite.
• In the clinical setting, it is not possible to completely prevent DNA contamination. The purpose of implementing DNA decontamination guidelines is to minimize the potential for contamination.
• Periodically, testing of specific sites for DNA profiles within a cleaned dedicated examination suite should be undertaken.
• Alleged victims and offenders should not be examined in the same clinical examination suite.
• Victims should not be transported to the examination suite in the same vehicle(s) used to transport offenders.

TABLE 79.2 Principles for DNA decontamination of work surfaces and equipment
• The surfaces upon which specimens and the content of the evidence recovery kits are placed should be cleaned with a suitable DNA decontaminant. Similarly, the examination couch, patient chairs, forensic examiners chair and desk, examination lights and windowsills should also be cleaned with a suitable DNA decontaminant. The choice of this solution will be based upon how free of DNA that the surface needs to be. Current research would indicate that a 1% sodium hypochlorite solution sprayed on the surface and then wiped clean with a water-moistened tissue or cloth (both the water and cloth/tissue must be DNA/CNA free) is sufficient.
• Equipment such as examination lights, colposcopes and cameras used during the examination should have the surfaces that are likely to be touched by the examiner covered by plastic disposable protective covers or sheets (which also need to be certified DNA/CNA free).
• Non-disposable equipment that is safe for use with sodium hypochlorite may need to be decontaminated by soaking in a 3% sodium hypochlorite solution for 15 minutes and then dried with a DNA-free wipe.

TABLE 79.3 Principles for cleaning forensic examination rooms
• For dedicated forensic examination rooms, cleaning should be undertaken after each forensic examination and include damp dusting of all surfaces. When sequential forensic examinations are undertaken requiring the collection of forensic specimens for DNA analysis, a cleaning of the room between examinations must occur.
• For non-dedicated forensic examination rooms, cleaning should be undertaken immediately prior to the forensic examination and be thorough including damp dusting of all surfaces.
• Cleaning must include the handles of doors and of cupboards.
• The cleaning should be undertaken by suitably trained staff wearing fresh clean gloves and a fresh clean gown (i.e. freshly cleaned gloves and gown that are put on specifically to clean the forensic area) so as to minimize transfer of contaminants including DNA from other parts of the facility to the examination room.
• The cleaning equipment (e.g. mops, cloths, etc) should be disposable and only used once. Alternatively, non-disposable cleaning equipment should be dedicated to the forensic facility and not used elsewhere in the health facility.
• Before use, all non-disposable cleaning equipment either should be or should have been thoroughly cleaned (or thoroughly cleaned after the last use).
• Removal of soiled materials and refuse from examination suites after each use is essential and either clean linen or new disposable bed, pillow and other covers must be used for each examination.

PROTECTION OF THE FORENSIC PRACTITIONER

It is essential to minimize the potential for the forensic practitioner to contaminate specimens either with their own DNA or extraneous DNA. The wearing of personal protective clothing should be undertaken within the limitations of appropriate patient management, particularly in the case of young children. As a minimal requirement, the forensic practitioner should wear a clean gown and gloves. Double or triple or more gloving enables easy changing of gloves between different parts of the examination by simply removing the outer layer of gloves. The use of face masks and hair and beard covers is recommended to prevent the spread of the examiner's DNA.

Evidence recovery kits

The use of sealed, dedicated, single-use evidence recovery kits (called examination kits in some jurisdictions) is recommended. These should be quality controled and their production subject to rigorous standards and monitored. On completion of the examination, unused items within the kit should be discarded or alternatively used for other purposes within the facility other than forensic DNA specimen collection. It is essential that any equipment used for forensic DNA specimen collection is certified DNA/CNA free.

Logs and access

A log should be kept of all usage of dedicated forensic examination rooms. This log should document the date, time and purpose of all entries to the room and of all persons who enter the room including cleaning staff. For dedicated forensic examination rooms only, access to the room must be restricted and the room must be kept locked when not in use.

Gloves, linen and protective clothing

When conducting forensic medical examinations, beyond the items used to collect forensic specimens, gloves are the most likely item to come in contact with both the victim's and offender's DNA if it is on the victim. The gloves, therefore, are a potential source of contamination not only of items within and about the clinical examination room but elsewhere in the facility. Too often, forensic examiners leave their gloves on after touching the victim and then move about the examination suite touching other objects including door handles and then return to the victim wearing the same gloves. Similarly, gloves may be donned and used to touch various items in the examination suite (or elsewhere in the facility) before touching the victim. Both situations may lead to DNA contamination. Gloves should be worn for a specific purpose and then removed. This point cannot be emphasized more strongly. Placing multiple gloves on at the beginning of an examination often simplifies the changing of gloves between various activities and thus reduces the potential for DNA contamination.

While on the issue of gloves, and this also applies to any linen and protective clothing used in the facility, it may not be DNA/CNA free. Sterile surgical gloves may also not be DNA/CNA free. As occurred with the Phantom of Heilbronn, boxes of multi-packaged gloves may not be DNA/CNA free (26) which, in turn, may lead to DNA contamination. Not all commercially provided disposable items as well as items provided within a hospital facility such as linen cannot be assumed to be DNA/CNA free. Before using these items, it is important to ensure that they are certified DNA/CNA free and to establish they are from a recognized and approved supplier.

DNA elimination databases

Many jurisdictions hold national DNA databases. In many jurisdictions, health professionals and scientists are required to have their own DNA profile recorded on a separate national DNA database. This enables any contaminating DNA to be easily identified and excluded from the forensic investigation. There have been some concerns about this, and some forensic practitioners have expressed reservations regarding the security, privacy and possible misuse of such a database. The logic for such a database has many advantages conditional upon safeguards being in place and would enable early identification of unintentional or accidental contamination. Anyone requested to submit their DNA profile to a database should do so only in circumstances where they are assured appropriate safeguards are in place. A written contract should be entered into with the agency managing the database that stipulates what the profile will be used for and that it will not be used for other purposes without the prior written consent of the donor. Ideally, this database should be separate to any criminal database and penalties must be in place for any misuse of the information stored.

CONCLUSION

DNA "fingerprinting" is a very sensitive analytical tool for the investigation of crime scenes. Contamination of these scenes, which include the victims of crime, with extraneous DNA may either complicate or invalidate these investigations. In order to minimize DNA contamination of forensic specimens, especially from victims, appropriate procedures should be developed by the examining health facility. These procedures should ensure evidential forensic specimens are collected by and into DNA-free items. The examination room for the collection of these specimens should contain minimal furniture and both the room and furniture cleaned before use. Instruments and benches/trolleys should be cleaned using an appropriate DNA decontaminant. Appropriate protective clothing should be worn by the forensic examiner. Although absolute DNA decontamination is not possible, implementation of suitable DNA decontamination procedures helps to reduce suboptimal and, at times, misleading forensic analysis.

REFERENCES

1. Syndercombe-Court D. DNA Analysis: Current Practice and Problems. In: Gall JAM, Payne-James JJ (eds), *Current Practice in Forensic Medicine*. Chichester: Wiley; 2011, pp. 193–237.
2. Roewer L. DNA fingerprinting in forensics: Past, present, future. *Investig Genet* 2013; 4: 22.
3. Syndercombe-Court D. DNA: Current Developments and Perspectives. In: Gall JAM, Payne-James JJ (eds), *Current Practice in Forensic Medicine*, Vol 3. Chichester: Wiley; 2022, pp. 109–42.
4. Koehler JJ. Error and exaggeration in the presentation of DNA evidence. *Jurimetrics* 1993; 34: 21–39.
5. National Research Council. *The Evaluation of Forensic DNA Evidence*. Washington DC: National Academy Press; 1996.
6. Thompson WC. Forensic DNA Evidence. In: Black B, Lee P (eds), *Expert Evidence: A Practitioner's Guide to Law, Science and the FCJ Manual.* St Paul: West Group; 1997, pp. 195–266.
7. van Oorshot RA, Jones MK. DNA Fingerprints from fingerprints. *Nature* 1997; 387: 767.
8. Balogh MK, Burger J, Bender K, et al. STR genotyping and mtDNA sequencing of latent fingerprints on paper. *Forensic Sci Int* 2003; 137: 188–95.
9. Kita T, Yamaguchi H, Yokoyama M, et al. Morphological study of fragmented DNA on touched objects. *Forensic Sci Int Genet* 2008; 3: 32–6.
10. Quinones I, Daniel B. Cell free DNA as a component of forensic evidence

recovered from touched surfaces. *Forensic Sci Int Genet* 2012; **6**: 26–30.
11. Jeffreys AJ, Wilson V, Thein SL. Individual-specific 'fingerprints' of human DNA. *Nature* 1985; **316**: 76–9.
12. Gall JAM, Syndercombe-Court D. DNA Contamination – A Pragmatic Clinical View. In: Gall JAM, Payne-James JJ (eds), *Current Practice in Forensic Medicine*, Vol 2. Chichester: Wiley; 2016, pp. 1–34.
13. BBC News. 'DNA bungle' haunts German police, 2009. Available from: http://news.bbc.co.uk/2/hi/europe/7966641.stm (Accessed 14 June 2023).
14. Himmelreich C. Germany's phantom serial killer: A DNA bungle, 2009. Available from: http://content.time.com/time/world/article/0,8599,1888126,00.html (Accessed 14 June 2023).
15. Vincent FHR. Inquiry into the circumstances that led to the conviction of Mr Farah Abdulkadir Jama, 2010. Available from: http://netk.net.au/DNA/Jama.pdf (Accessed 14 June 2023).
16. Champlot S, Berthelot C, Pruvost M, et al. An efficient multistrategy DNA decontamination procedure of PCR reagents for hypersensitive PCR applications. *PloS ONE* 2010; **5**: e13042.
17. Kampmann M-L, Børsting C, Morling N. Decrease DNA contamination in the laboratories. *Forensic Sci Int Genet* 2017; **6**: 577–8.
18. Shaw K, Sesardic I, Bristol N, et al. Comparison of the effects of sterilisation techniques on subsequent DNA profiling. *Int J Legal Med* 2008; **122**: 29–33.
19. Archer E, Allen H, Hopwood A, Rowlands D. Validation of a dual cycle ethylene oxide treatment technique to remove DNA from consumables used in forensic laboratories. *Forensic Sci Int Genet* 2010; **4**: 239–43.
20. International Programme on Chemical Safety (IPCS). Sodium hypochlorite, 1998. Available from: https://inchem.org/documents/pims/chemical/pim495.htm (Accessed 14 June 2023).
21. Kemp BM, Smith DG. Use of bleach to eliminate contaminating DNA from the surface of bones and teeth. *Forensic Sci Int* 2005; **154**: 53–61.
22. Schwark T, Poetsch M, Preusse-Prange A, et al. Phantoms in the mortuary – DNA transfer during autopsies. *Forensic Sci Int* 2012; **216**: 121–6.
23. Ballantyne KN, Salemi R, Guarino F, et al. DNA contamination minimisation – finding an effective cleaning method. *Aust J Forens Sci* 2015; **47**: 428–39.
24. RCPA. Cleaning/decontamination of forensic examination suites, 2017. Available from: https://www.rcpa.edu.au/getattachment/0a069dc3-baf0-4ffa-ad1d-851292758fe5/CleaningDecontamination-of-Forensic-Examination-Su.aspx (Accessed 14 June 2023).
25. Forensic Science Regulator Guidance. The control and avoidance of contamination in forensic medical examinations, 2020. Available from: https://assets.publishing.service.gov.uk/government/uploads/system/uploads/attachment_data/file/912748/207_DNA_Anti-_Contam_SARC__Custody_Issue_2_Final.pdf (Accessed 14 June 2023).
26. Daniel R, van Oorschot RAH. An investigation of the presence of DNA on unused laboratory gloves. *Forensic Sci Int: Genet Suppl Series* 2011; **3**: 45–6.

CHAPTER

80

Findings after Sexual Assault – Adult

Vanita Parekh and Angela Williams

INTRODUCTION

In this chapter the terms victim, patient and complainant are used interchangeably.

Despite what is often presented in popular culture such as crime scene TV shows, victims of sexual assault do not fit into one stereotyped category. Victims of sexual violence may be women, men, people of different sexual and gender identities, cultures, socioeconomic backgrounds, ages, professions and perspectives. The forensic medical approach allows for high-quality medical and forensic care in all circumstances, and encourages reporting, accessibility of service, a non-judgmental and non-discriminatory forensic medical and legal practice.

DEFINITION OF SEXUAL VIOLENCE

The World Health organization (WHO) defines sexual violence as:

> *"Any sexual act, attempt to obtain a sexual act, unwanted sexual comments or advances, or acts to traffic or otherwise directed against a person's sexuality using coercion, by any person regardless of their relationship to the victim, in any setting, including but not limited to home and work" (1).*

Sexual violence is often defined by the behavioral characteristics of one person(s) used to exert power (sexually orientated) over another person(s), rather than any specific legal definition. Typical behaviors described in research include:

- Sexual harassment
- Sexualized bullying
- Unwanted kissing and sexual touching
- Sexual pressure and coercion
- Sexual assault including rape

Many organizations, agencies and jurisdictional legislation, nationally and internationally, have defined sexual assault and/or rape. This chapter will refer to the Australian Bureau of Statistics (ABS) definitions (2–4) to guide the commentary. It follows that sexual assault is:

> *"An act of a sexual nature carried out against that person's will, through the use of physical force, intimidation or coercion. It includes rape (sexual penetration without consent), attempted rape, aggravated sexual assault (sexual assault with a weapon), indecent assault, penetration by objects and forced sexual activity that did not end in penetration. Unwanted sexual touching and incidents that occurred before the age of 15 are not included."*

The above behaviors may intrude on the health and welfare of the victim immediately, as well as having adverse physical and psychological sequelae even into the long term.

The impacts to the health and welfare of individuals can be characterized as:

- **Physical** including injury, Sexually Transmitted Infections including HIV, pregnancy.
- **Psychological** consequences such as being hyperalert, PTSD, nightmares, flashbacks, depression, eating disorders, anxiety, low self-esteem, substance misuse.
- **Emotional reactions** such as shame, guilt, fear, self-blame, embarrassment, grief reactions (numbness, sadness, anger, shock and disbelief and denial).
- **Social and community**. These may also affect close family and friends, including isolation, and vulnerability.
- **Financial** on the person and communities.
- **Responses to ongoing and new events** including ongoing safety concerns.

While it is acknowledged the above impacts are adverse in nature, it is also acknowledged that there can be recovery following sexual assault.

BARRIERS TO REPORTING AND EFFECTS ON FINDINGS AFTER SEXUAL ASSAULT

Victims often report sexual assault to police, healthcare services, counseling services, workplaces or friends/family. Barriers to reporting sexual assault are well described by victims and reported in literature. They include personal

DOI: 10.1201/9781003138754-83

factors such as not recognizing that sexual assault has occurred, shame, embarrassment, not wanting others to know, being blamed by self or others, protection of self and family. Systemic factors (5) such as not recognizing sexual assault, lack of knowledge or confidence in the process of reporting, mistrust of law enforcement and the justice systems, often result in delays. The delay in reporting may impact forensic medical findings following sexual assault.

CLINICAL FORENSIC MEDICAL EXAMINATON

Forensic practitioners undertaking clinical assessments are tasked with providing both the forensic and the medical aspects of care for a victim of sexual assault. The elements are outlined in Table 80.1 below, which provides a summary of forensic and medical components of the forensic medical examination (FME). The majority of FMEs are undertaken in the relatively acute setting; usually within 5 days of the incident depending on jurisdictional timeframes and limitations in evidentiary value of forensic samples. The limited timeframe for an FME can be explained by the exponential loss of forensic evidence over time and the change to, or disappearance of, injuries as time passes (*see* Chapter 78 – "Evidential Sampling").

Prior to undertaking an FME, the examining clinician must rule out the presence of emergency or life-threatening injuries and/or conditions the treatment of which will take precedence over the forensic elements of

TABLE 80.1 Summary of the forensic and medical components of the forensic medical examination

Forensic	Medical
• Consent for evidential purposes • Assessment of injuries (or absence)	• Immediate assessment of life-threatening or significant injury • Consent for therapeutic purposes
Targeted Forensic History • Events & Incident • Potential sites of contact • Alcohol and other Drugs (AoD) • Covert substance administration • Past history of violence and risk factors for future violence	History • Past history including medical, surgical and psychiatric conditions • Medications • Risk of medical consequences/sequalae from injuries • Sexually Transmitted Infection (STI) acquisition • Psychological well-being
Forensic Examination • Body examination for injury (presence or absence) • Genital examination	Examination and assessment • Emergency medical needs • Mental health • Pregnancy • STI including HIV • Pre-existing medical conditions and normal variations
Injury documentation • Forensic medical record and note absence of any injuries • Forensic photography	Documentation • Medical records • Letters of medical referral
Evidence collection • Chain of custody • Body evidence • Clothing • DNA evidence • Photography	Specimen collection • Baseline STI screening including swabbing for penetrated sites (oral, vaginal and anal) and baseline serology for HIV, Syphilis, Hepatitis B. Hepatitis C if indicated • Other (e.g. wound infection microbiological swabs)
Toxicology • Urine or blood	Consider medical, psychological and social safety implications for the patient
Injury interpretation • Classification of injury • Mechanism of injury • Injury causation • Patterns of injury • Opinion	Treatment • STI • Provision of Emergency Contraception (EC) • Counseling • Alcohol and Drug • Mental health referral and counseling • Surgical referral
Provision of evidence • Medicolegal report • Expert evidence in court	Referral for ongoing medical care or immediate medical treatment: Emergency Department, Sexual Health, General Practice, Substance use program, social work and family violence services

an examination. Priority injuries/conditions in this context include:

- Significant bleeding, burns, open wounds or broken bones
- Genital bleeding
- Head, chest or abdominal injury
- Non-fatal strangulation
- Altered conscious states for any reason (head injury, intoxication, hypoglycemia)
- Surgical interventions (e.g. foreign body in anus or vagina, emergency surgery)
- Acute mental health crisis

It may be appropriate with consent of the individual (or acting in their best interests), and with the collaboration with treating doctors, to manage a forensic examination in concurrence with emergency medical treatment or even surgery, where evidence collection may occur in Intensive Care Units, resuscitation areas or the operating theater. However, the provision or nature of medical care in these circumstances should not be delayed or compromised by the FME.

The clinical examination is guided by the forensic practitioner in accordance with the details of the request, the nature of the complaint, the presentation of the patient and with consideration of the forensic value of doing so. The examination will only proceed on the basis of consent from the patient, or in the absence of such consent, from an appropriate alternative, or absence of an appropriate alternative, acting in the patient's best interests. Forensic specimens are collected under chain of custody to ensure evidence integrity (6).

The purpose of the forensic examination is not directly related to answering the question of whether a sexual assault occurred; rather, this is the role of the ultimate decision makers in the relevant jurisdiction. While the examination might elicit a basis for the forensic practitioner to provide an expert opinion on related questions (what caused the injury, was the person intoxicated, was there evidence of penetration) other issues of primary legal interest such as consent, are not generally within the realm of the forensic practitioner. The FME is recognized as positively contributing to the decision of prosecutors in taking the matter to court (7).

RESPONSES TO SEXUAL VIOLENCE

Exposure to sexual and interpersonal violence may result in several immediate physiological, physical and psychological responses commonly associated with intense fear or threat to safety. These responses (voluntary and involuntary) may occur in isolation or in combination. None of these responses imply that consent has been provided by the complainant. All of these responses affect injury patterns or lack of injury.

There is no standard response or predictable response to sexual and interpersonal violence; crisis is an extremely variable event for each individual. Each individual person and the individual set of circumstances before them will shape their acute responses to sexual and interpersonal violence. Responses are inherent reactions, some conscious some subconscious/automatic, and based on experiences and observations of the past.

Victims often describe thinking that they reacted in a very different manner to how they thought they would react in a harmful situation (e.g. they thought they would fight but found they froze).

Despite common assumptions that the fight and flight responses would be the most frequent victim responses, the freeze and surrender responses are more commonly described by victims of sexual and interpersonal violence.

Ultimately, a person experiencing an adverse event or acute crisis, such as sexual and interpersonal violence, will respond with the aim of self-preservation. Some responses will be voluntary, others involuntary.

Follow up of injury should include assessment of emerging and healing injuries; findings from this follow up may have an evidentiary value.

The immediate responses to sexual and interpersonal violence are shown in Table 80.2.

INJURY DETECTION FOLLOWING SEXUAL ASSAULT

Media reporting is a factor in generating community belief and expectations of findings and responses following sexual assault (14–17). While the community may expect physical violence and resultant injuries are common in sexual assault, it is often the opposite that occurs in reality. Both genital and non-genital injuries are relatively uncommon findings. Some of this may be explained by the fact that many victims know their offenders, that the main weapons are the hands or threats of the perpetrator, or that victims will act/react in a way that reduces the risk of injury, violence, pain and other adverse consequences, while ensuring self-preservation and survival.

General body injury

The presence of body injury following an assault is dependent on many factors. An expectation of injury is not reliable. In some circumstances, significant force may result in no externally observable injury; in others, light forces culminate in large obvious wounds or bruises. Injuries are influenced by the degree of force, the body part involved, the victim's reaction (no reaction to fighting back), the type of force (sharp vs blunt) and patient factors (age, consciousness, medications, conditions etc) (Table 80.3).

Where injuries are observable, they can be classified as bruises, abrasions, lacerations, incisions, bites and burns; some being non-specific as to their causation and others with a pattern or feature characteristic to the mechanism of injury.

The forensic practitioner should undertake an FME using a systematic approach to examining the patient from head to foot. This includes scalp, behind and within

TABLE 80.2 Immediate responses to sexual and interpersonal violence

Response	Freeze (8–11)	Fight or flight (12,13)	Surrender and/or Negotiate
Nature of response	This fear response to sexual and other interpersonal violence (e.g. family violence) is where a person feels unable to move or paralyzed and is also known as tonic immobility[1]	The fight response involves a person fighting back in response to a perceived harm and similar to the flight response The flight response is an attempt to escape from the actual or perceived threat of sexual and interpersonal violence	The surrender response involves a person acquiescing in response to sexual and interpersonal violence; this may be with negotiation, for example, the use of condoms, timing or location
Mechanism	The exact mechanisms of the freeze response have not been determined in humans. There are neural correlates within animal models. The mechanism of the freeze reactions is probably mediated through acetylcholine, adrenalin and noradrenalin, cortisol, serotonin as well as the amygdala; all appear to have key roles (2,3)	The response is based upon the sympathetic nervous system response	These responses involve conscious decision making to acquiesce in an attempt to minimize harm
Features of response	Features of this response include: the person appears to be awake with their eyes open with periods of closure and may have pupillary dilation, may be unable to move or call out, may have a resting tremor, have decreased responsiveness to stimulation		
Examples of response	Examples of this type of response are of feeling unable to breathe, think or move, time standing still or feeling frozen with fear	Examples of the flight response are of jumping out of cars, trying to escape, trying to get dressed, trying to alert other people or retreating to corners or hiding under blankets (5)	Examples of this response are to submit to sexual and interpersonal violence for fear of harm or death, suggesting the use of a condom to prevent sexually transmitted infections, positioning of the pelvis to prevent pain, doing what the assailant tells them to do in the hope this will allow them to get out alive by avoiding the expected harm and staying silent to prevent exposure to children in another room. Other anecdotal examples include asking to be able to make a phone call, call an ambulance or getting money as an opportunity to obtain assistance
Impact on injury pattern	There may be no or minimal physical injury present when complainants freeze in response to sexual and interpersonal violence, as with all the responses to sexual and interpersonal violence	There are studies that show where a victim has tried to fight back or defend themselves that minor injuries may be more prevalent. Body injury may occur at the sites of the application of force. Defense injuries may occur including across a variety of anatomic planes especially in areas that people use to defend vulnerable areas of their bodies, e.g. head. Common areas of injury are the back of the forearms, upper arms, upper outer thighs and hands. Injuries to the palms of the hands can also occur when complainants attempt to grab hold of weapons. Defense wounds may also occur on other parts of the body when the victim is in a prone, supine or fetal	

80

TABLE 80.2 (Continued) Immediate responses to sexual and interpersonal violence

Response	Freeze (8–11)	Fight or flight (12,13)	Surrender and/or Negotiate
		position. Defense injuries vary in their type depending on the nature of the application of the force e.g. sharp or blunt force (6) Injury patterns that may be seen in the flight response include from falls involving the kneecap and hands may also involve the wrist and palm of the hand. The types of injury include abrasions, lacerations and bruises generally as a result of the application of blunt force and movement. There may be no or minimal physical injury present when complainants have the fight or flight response to sexual and interpersonal violence.	
Notes	In a study of 298 women, 70% reported significant tonic immobility with 48% reporting extreme tonic immobility during the assault determined by psychological analysis after the reported sexual assault. Tonic immobility was associated with the development of post-traumatic stress disorder and severe depression at 6 months after the reported events. Previous trauma history and psychiatric treatment history were associated with the tonic immobility response. In addition to tonic immobility, significant fear was reported in 81% of the study population (4)		

TABLE 80.3 Genital injuries

Factor	Influence	References
Nature of assault and contact between the accused(s) and the victim	Type of assault Type of force and degree of impact Number of assailants Features of the penetrating object(s) Size and anatomy of the orifice involved	
Timing of examination	Wound healing Specimen collection	(23)
Examination	Practitioner knowledge and experience Equipment, lighting and techniques Naked eye vs microscopic visualization Direct light or room lighting Dyes or contrast other forensic	(23)
Examination facility	ICU vs dedicated sexual assault examination room	
Characteristics of the victim	Elasticity of the genital tissues Submission or reaction of the victim Age Conscious state Ethnicity Presence/absence of lubrication General health etc.	(24–28)

the ears, in the mouth, under the arms, the bikini line area and the sole of the foot. The nature of the case, the wishes of the patient, and the circumstances of the presentation may mean a comprehensive examination is not immediately possible. These limitations to a complete examination should be documented in the clinical record. Depending on the scenario, a secondary consultation may be necessary as injuries such as bruises may evolve and develop.

Photographs may be taken as an adjunct form of documentation and often assist the investigators and court in their fact finding and decision making. If photography is undertaken, it must be undertaken by a trained forensic photographer, following standard forensic photographic principles (18). Photographs should be considered as adjuncts to detailed notetaking and injury descriptions using body maps. Chain of evidence requirements also apply to photographic images and the clinician examiner must ensure the integrity of any contemporaneous images. Different jurisdictions will have different protocols. The same applies to genital or other intimate site photography. There are a range of injuries that may require forensic assessment and raise questions regarding interpersonal and intimate partner violence. The challenge in respect of sexual assault is the need to determine whether such findings have been sustained in consensual or non-consensual settings. Medical evidence can only assist in a minority of cases. The nature of injuries encountered include:

Bite marks: commonly found on the breast and neck areas but may be found on any accessible area of the body. The injury features may be used by forensic odontologists in their appraisal of the injury. The site of the bite mark should be sampled for DNA analysis and emerging forensic techniques, for example microbial concurrence for use in the detection of the offender.

Suction bruising: Suction bruises often known in lay terms as "love-bites" and "hickeys" are areas of localized patches of bruising caused by suction forces applied to the skin sufficient to cause disruption to the blood vessels to result in bruising. DNA may be recovered from offender saliva left at the site of the suction bruise.

Patients may not notice the presence of bite and suction marks in areas that are not able to be viewed directly.

Imprint marks: Imprints in the form of patterned bruises and or abrasions from overlying clothing or from objects applied with blunt force.

Fingertip bruising: During restraint, fingertip bruises may be found on the upper arms or inner thighs, as a cluster of ovoid bruises, often said to be approximately 1–2 cm in diameter but can be larger. Thumb imprints may or may not be present on the other side of the arm or leg.

Defense injuries: These are sustained in the effort to protect oneself. Defense injuries may occur including across a variety of anatomic planes especially in areas that people use to defend vulnerable areas of their bodies, for example the head. Common areas of injury include the hands, extensor surface of the forearms, upper arms and upper outer thighs. The locations of these injuries occur when these areas of body are used to protect vulnerable areas of their bodies, for example head or abdomen. Injuries to the palms of the hands can also occur when complainants attempt to grab hold of weapons, for example a knife (*see also* Chapter 75).

NON-FATAL STRANGULATION

Non-fatal strangulation is increasingly recognized as a feature of reported sexual assaults especially in victims reporting an assault by an intimate partner (19,20).

The experience of non-fatal strangulation by a partner increases the risk of subsequent homicide by almost 7.5 times (21).

It is important to use correct terminology when defining non-fatal strangulation: strangulation as external neck compression, suffocation as covering of the mouth and nose, and choking as internal airway obstruction. Many victims will describe being choked rather than experiencing non-fatal strangulation.

Compression to the neck and the injuries that occur as a result are serious and potentially life-threatening. The neck contains several vital structures including major blood vessels that supply the head and the brain, the trachea, the esophagus and the spinal column. Compression of the neck can lead to temporary or permanent damage to any or all of these structures and the organs they supply. A significant proportion of victims will have no external signs of injury following non-fatal strangulation. However, despite the absence of external signs of injuries, there may be significant and life-threatening damage to internal-underlying structures.

Non-fatal strangulation, mechanism, symptoms and signs are discussed in Chapter 92 – "Non-Fatal Strangulation."

GENITAL INJURY

It is well documented that a penetrative event (vaginal or anal) with a body part or object may not result in a visible injury in the genital area.

Where genital injury has been studied, the findings are difficult to compare because of differing research methods (22). Whether an individual sustains injury is dependent on any one or more of the following factors including but not limited to those listed in Table 80.3.

Where genital injuries are seen on FME, they may indicate trauma and/or depending on their location, be suggestive of a penetrative event. However, it is unlikely that examination findings will allow a clinician examiner to be sure about the object used to penetrate based solely on the location of the injury. A notable exception is making an opinion as to whether the object was (or was not) a sharp implement based on the type of injury observed.

While most observable genital injuries are minor and heal without consequence within a short timeframe, in some circumstances, genital injuries will require urgent medical intervention. A signal for the clinician examiner is the presence of genital bleeding in the absence of a history of menstruation. Suspicion should be high in cases of penetration using a large object (fist, objects with sharp or rough surfaces) and where the victim suggests the immediate onset of pain and/or bleeding occurs. These circumstances warrant consideration as to when and where the examination occurs and if therapeutic gynecological or surgical involvement is required.

Examiners should also take a systematic approach to examining the genital area whereby an external visual examination is conducted first and then observations are made of internal genital anatomy. In most cases, a speculum examination will assist, and relevant specimen collection should occur simultaneously. The common types of genital injuries can be characterized by the TEARS acronym (29) representing:

- Tears (lacerations)
- Ecchymoses (bruises)
- Abrasions
- Redness and swelling

However, depending on the nature of the case, it is also important to document bites, burns or incised wounds. Normal anatomy ought to be documented and so to the presence (or absence) of skin conditions, coexisting infections, inflammatory responses or other localized diagnoses (e.g. Bartholin's cyst, labial adhesions) (30).

Given the restricted value of interpreting genital injury, one prime purpose for taking genital photography is for peer review purposes. Care should be taken with the security of these sensitive images and distribution.

Genital injury may occur in both consensual and non-consensual sexual activity. Some studies show higher prevalence of genital injury in those reporting sexual assaults in comparison to consensual sexual activity (31,32). However, this has been subject to further recent refinement. McLean and colleagues (31) concluded that most complainants of rape will not sustain any genital injury, although women are three times more likely to sustain a genital injury from an assault than consensual intercourse. However, the medical findings cannot determine whether the individual is in the consensual or assault group. A more recent study (33) had the aims of identifying the constellation of genito-anal injury-related characteristics that most effectively discriminated between consensual sexual intercourse and sexual assault in females when controling for intercourse-related variables. After controling for race/ethnicity, age and time between intercourse and examination, logistic regression analyses showed that the presence of an external genital tear increased the odds of non-consensual intercourse more than two times (adjusted odds ratio [AOR] = 2.70, 95 percent CI = 1.28–5.56). Logistic regression analyses also showed that the odds of non-consensual sexual intercourse were significantly greater with a lower prevalence and frequency of external and internal genital redness, lack of condom use and lubrication and presence of anal penetration. The authors concluded that external genital tears occurred more frequently in the non-consensual sample and increased the odds of non-consensual intercourse more than two times. Anal tears, swelling and ecchymosis and anal penetration were markers for non-consensual intercourse and should increase suspicion for lack of consent. However, in a detailed comment in reply to the publication of this paper and with regard to external genital tears it was stated (34)

> "*One of the authors' main conclusions is that an external genital tear is a marker for non-consent. We find this conclusion flawed. In raw numbers 24% of non-consensual penetrations resulted in an external genital tear against 20% of consensual penetrations, by itself not statistically significant. Significance arose in a logistic regression model, resulting in an adjusted odds ratio of 2.7 that penetration was non-consensual in the presence of an external genital tear. The model controlled for age, race and time between penetration and examination. The finding is of no use to the forensic practitioner, because the authors do not elaborate on the specific influence of confounders. What is the exact effect of race? Age? Time? – and in particular how are the effects interacting or modifying the overall conclusion. The correct conclusion should be that genital injury can NOT discriminate.*" The authors further state (after discussion of other aspects of the Sommers & Fargo paper) "*The valid conclusions from this paper should be that any kind of genital-anal injury is common following consensual and non-consensual sexual intercourse. It should be stressed that extrapolation from group significance to single case significance is not a valid extrapolation in forensics or in most other medical specialties.*"

Oliphant (35) and colleagues' study confirms that the majority of women will have a normal genital examination following a report of sexual assault.

For the forensic practitioner, this debate emphasizes that (a) genito-anal injury may be seen in both consensual and non-consensual contact and (b) generally the nature of the injury does not assist in determining consensuality or non-consensuality. Finally, it is important for courts and decision makers to be aware that it is only the minority of individuals who will sustain injury after penetrative sexual contact.

Genital injury and population-based studies

Population-based studies cannot be applied to individual cases. The lack of injury or presence of injury cannot be used to determine the nature of consent provided by the complainant. Genital injuries can, however, be used to corroborate the history given by the complainant and their presence should enhance a comprehensive investigation by law enforcement.

The presence of genital injury is associated with decisions to take cases to trial (36) and successful prosecution (37) findings of guilt from juries (38) and jail sentences (39).

The detection of genital injury is an issue for the medicolegal system and not for the medical care of a patient except in significant injury requiring medical intervention.

Collection of specimens for DNA purposes

Specimen collection for the purpose of sampling DNA from deposited semen, blood, saliva or skin cells occur concurrently with the FME. DNA itself is not observable macroscopically and therefore sampling is done according to the patient history, deposit location or, in some cases, blindly (e.g. where no history can be obtained if the patient is or was unconscious).

Collection of specimens for toxicologic analysis

Drug Facilitated Sexual Assault (DFSA) is defined as a sexual act in which the victim is unable to give or rescind consent due to intoxication with alcohol and/or drugs that have been self-administered (opportunistic DFSA) or covertly administered by the perpetrator (predatory DFSA) (40). Differences in the types and prevalence of substances used to facilitate sexual assault vary internationally, however, alcohol is the commonest substance used to facilitated sexual assault (41,42).

Alcohol may be consumed voluntarily, consumed with added alcohol giving a higher dose or mixed with other substances.

Many other substances may be utilized to facilitate sexual assault often with the substances having sedative effects, benzodiazepines (the most commonly detected substance after alcohol), Z-drugs, antihistamines and tetrahydrocannabinol are some of the many substances that have been detected following sexual assault.

A history should be taken from the patient with questions directed at symptoms suggestive of substance ingestion, these include (43):

- Onset of effects, this may be immediate or delayed, however most substances have rapid elimination generally within 72 hours
- Feeling dizzy or lightheaded
- Gastrointestinal effects such as nausea and vomiting.
- Relative lack of alcohol ingestion
- Body temperature changes such as sweating or shivering
- Visual disturbance including blurred vision
- Complete or incomplete memory loss

Apparent findings of intoxication should be documented by the examining clinician such as confusion, impairment of gross motor coordination through slurring of speech, balance and gait abnormalities. In this instance, a decision should be made on undertaking the clinical FME at another time within DNA time and toxicology collection frames. Stimulant substances (42) may be used to facilitate sexual assault.

MEMORY AND SEXUAL ASSAULT

It is not unusual for memory to be affected during and after a sexual assault, especially in circumstances explained by alcohol (44,45), drugs and other substances, head injury, loss of consciousness and non-fatal strangulation. This may affect the history taking and goes some way to explain inconsistencies in recollection of events.

SEXUALLY TRANSMISSABLE INFECTIONS

Baseline testing for sexually transmissible infections (STIs) at the initial forensic medical assessment should be considered for all cases of sexual violence especially if post sexual assault prophylaxis is to be provided. Standard screening tests for STIs following sexual violence are used. The tests used should reflect the local epidemiology of infections, the nature of the sexual contact that occurred and any factors which may affect the likelihood of STI transmission.

Screening for STIs and Blood-Borne Viruses (BBV) should be considered and should include tests for chlamydia, gonorrhoea, trichomonas, syphilis, HIV, hepatitis B&C whether the patient is symptomatic or not. Routine screening for herpes simplex virus (HSV) and human papilloma virus (HPV) is not recommended in asymptomatic patients. Testing and management of STIs should be undertaken with the patient's consent as this will enable the best possible medical care to be provided.

At present, there is limited evidentiary value to determine source transmission due to current testing technologies. Testing methods are available that identify specific subtypes which may have an evidential value; however, these are not routinely employed and specialist advice from reference laboratories must be sought.

Following sexual assault, baseline testing for STIs may be undertaken. There are two possible explanations for a true positive result, these are:

1. The infection was contracted pre-assault *(Prevalent infection).*
2. The infection was contracted because of the assault *(Incident infection).*

Partner notification in both instances should be part of the medical care provided and use of local health services should be considered to enable complete notification. If the patient is managed by referral, continuity of care through documented handover may assist the patient and legal process.

PREGNANCY AS A RESULT OF SEXUAL VIOLENCE

For female patients in their reproductive years, pregnancy may result following sexual assault. Emergency contraception should be considered in all cases of sexual assault where conception and unwanted pregnancy may be a possibility. Patients may not be aware of the risk of pregnancy or the options to minimize this risk. Provision of accurate information regarding pregnancy risk and emergency contraception or referral to an immediately accessible provider should be undertaken.

In the instance where pregnancy results from sexual assault, maternal testing, products of conception from miscarriage of termination of pregnancy or from the birth of a child may undergo DNA analysis to determine the paternal donor.

PSYCHOLOGICAL EFFECTS

Patients having experienced sexual assault require a multidisciplinary team approach to deliver holistic health and welfare care. Advocacy and counseling services should be made available to every patient as an adjunct to the Forensic Medical process.

Patients may present for examination with significant emotional or psychological trauma overtly presenting as panic, shock or crying, while others appear to remain calm and in control, perhaps even sleeping. Furthermore, the correlation between the severity of the trauma and the resultant emotional response is poor, and often influenced by drugs, alcohol, sleep deprivation, the presence of support people and the timing of the consultation. The fact there is no standard reaction or response is often not well understood and expectations of family, friends or even healthcare workers may interfere with the delivery of a comprehensive service. What is well known, is that there is no set way to act or react following a sexual assault and that the clinician examiner must use their skills and experience to navigate unknown territory to be able to conduct the required elements of the FME.

The psychological consequences of sexual violence should not be underestimated. Assistance and referral to a psychiatrist, psychologist or counselor should be considered for every person who has experienced sexual violence. Medical certificates should be considered as an adjunct therapeutic option following sexual assault.

SEXUAL ASSAULT IN VULNERABLE GROUPS

Most published literature addresses female victims, patients and complainants of sexual violence. However, men are also sexually assaulted and make up a significant minority of complainants and require a tailored medical forensic medical approach. Men who have sex with men appear to be at higher risk of sexual assault. Those who identify as transgender also appear to be at higher risk of experiencing sexual violence (46,47). There are many other factors which increase vulnerability to sexual violence and include physical, intellectual and mental health conditions, use of alcohol and other substances and a history of childhood abuse.

UK data (48) show that for the year ending March 2020 there were 773 000 adults aged 16 to 74 years who were victims of sexual assault (including attempts) in the last year, with almost four times as many female victims (618 000) as male victims (155 000).

Men tend to report sexual assault and violence less which may be due to a variety of factors including shame, embarrassment, denial and masculine stereotypes (49). Reporting may also be delayed directly impacting on forensic evidence collection. Forensic medical services should ensure they are able to provide a high-quality forensic examination for males.

A tailored approach to the FME of each individual is necessary, taking into account the standard forensic elements described above (history, examination, specimen collection and medical care).

CONCLUSION

Sexual violence is experienced by people across the social spectrum and may result in significant immediate and long-term consequences for their physical and mental health, social interactions and overall well-being. Forensic evidence collection including DNA and toxicology collection and injury interpretation may assist in the legal process, should it be entered into with the patient's permission. It is imperative that, in each case, the forensic examiner undertakes the dual role of the forensic examiner; that is firstly to address the immediate physical and psychological health needs of the person and secondly to attend to an FME to enable the provision of the best possible care for the patient.

REFERENCES

1. World Health Organization. Violence against women – Intimate partner and sexual violence against women. Geneva, World Health Organization, 2011 in Understanding and addressing violence against women. Available from: https://www.who.int/publications/i/item/WHO-RHR-12.37. (Accessed July 2023).
2. Australian Bureau of Statistics. Women's safety Australia, 1996. Available from: https://www.abs.gov.au/ausstats/abs@.nsf/PrimaryMainFeatures/4128.0?OpenDocument (Accessed 24 May 2023).
3. Australian Bureau of Statistics. Recorded crime - victims, Australia, 2012. Available from: https://www.abs.gov.au/ausstats/abs@.nsf/lookup/4510.0Media%20Release12012 (Accessed 24 May 2023).
4. Australian Bureau of Statistics. Crime victimisation, Australia, 2012. Available from: https://www.abs.gov.au/ausstats/abs@.nsf/Lookup/4530.0Explanatory+Notes12010-11 (Accessed 24 May 2023).
5. Lievore D. Non-reporting and hidden recording of sexual assault: An international literature review, 2003. Available from: https://www.aic.gov.au/sites/default/files/2020-05/non-reporting-and-hidden-recording-of-sexual-assault-an-international-literature-review.pdf (Accessed 24 May 2023).
6. Linden JA. Care of the adult patient after sexual assault. *N Engl J Med* 2011; **365**: 834–41.
7. Kjærulff MLBG, Bonde U, Astrup BS. The significance of the forensic clinical examination on the judicial assessment of rape complaints - developments and trends. *Forensic Sci Int* 2019; **297**: 90–9.
8. Gallup GG. Tonic immobility: The role of fear and predation. *Psychol Record* 1997; **27**: 41–6.
9. Roelofs K. Freeze for action: Neurobiological mechanisms on animal and

human freezing. *Philos Trans R Soc B* 2017; **372:** 20160206.

10. Seo C, Guru A, Jin M et al. Intense threat switches dorsal raphe serotonin neurons to a paradoxical operational mode. *Science* 2019; **363(6426):** 538.
11. Moller A, Sondergaard HP, Helstrom L. Tonic immobility during sexual assault: A common reaction predicting post-traumatic stress disorder and severe depression. *Acta Obstet Gynecol Scan* 2017; 96: 932–8.
12. Nijenhuis ERs. Vanderlinden J, Spinhoven P. Animal defensive reactions as a model for trauma-induced dissociative reactions. *JTS* 1998; 11(2): 251 quoting Albach 1993.
13. Powers RA, Sipson SS. Self-protective behaviors and injury in domestic violence situations: Does it hurt to fight back? *J Interpers Violence* 2012; 27(17): 3345–65.
14. World Health Organization (WHO). Preventing intimate partner and sexual violence against women. Taking action and generating evidence, 2010. Available from: https://apps.who.int/iris/bitstream/handle/10665/44350/9789241564007_eng.pdf?sequence=1&isAllowed=y (Accessed 24 May 2023).
15. Everland WP. The Impact of News and Entertainment Media on Perceptions of Social Reality. In: Dillard JP, Pfau M (eds), *The Persuasion Handbook: Developments in Theory and Practice*. Thousand Oaks: Sage Publications; 2002, pp. 691–727.
16. Sutherland G, McCormack A, Pirkis J, et al. Media representations of violence against women and their children: Final report. Available from: https://www.anrows.org.au/publication/media-representations-of-violence-against-women-and-their-children-final-report/ (Accessed 24 May 2023).
17. Schwark S. Visual representations of sexual violence in online news outlets. *Front Psychol* 2017; **8:** 774.
18. Faculty of Forensic & Legal Medicine. PICS Working Group Guidelines on Photography, 2019. Available from: https://fflm.ac.uk/wp-content/uploads/2020/03/PICS-Working-Group-Guidelines-on-Photography-Dr-Will-Anderson-Dec-2019.pdf (Accessed 24 May 2023).
19. Zilkens RR, Phillips MA, Kelly MC, et al. Non-fatal strangulation in sexual assault: A study of clinical and assault characteristics highlighting the role of intimate partner violence. *J Forensic Leg Med* 2016; **43:** 1–7.
20. White C, Martin G, Schofield AM, Majeed-Ariss R. 'I thought he was going to kill me': Analysis of 204 case files of adults reporting non-fatal strangulation as part of a sexual assault over a 3-year period. *J Forensic Leg Med* 2021; **79:** 102128.
21. Glass N, Campbell J, Block CR, et al. Non-fatal strangulation is an important risk factor for homicide of women. *J Emerg Med* 2008; **35**(3): 329–35.
22. Kennedy KM. Heterogeneity of existing research relating to sexual violence, sexual assault and rape precludes meta-analysis of injury data. *J Forensic Leg Med* 2013; **20**(5): 447–59.
23. Lincoln C. Genital injury: Is it significant? A review of the literature. *Med Sci Law* 2001; 41(3): 206–16.
24. White C, McLean I. Adolescent complainants of sexual assault: Injury patterns in virgin and non-virgin groups. *J Clin Forensic Med* 2006; 13(4): 172–180.
25. Polous CA, Sheridan DJ. Genital injuries in postmenopausal women after sexual assault. *J Elder Abuse Negl* 2008; 20(4): 323–35.
26. Templeton DJ. Sexual assault of a post-menopausal woman. *J Clin forensic Med* 2004; 12: 98–100.
27. Ramin SM, Satin AJ, Stone IC Jr. et al. Sexual assault on postmenopausal women. *Obstet Gynecol* 1992; 80(5): 860–4.
28. Sommers MS, Zink T, Baker RB et al. The effects of age and ethnicity on physical injury from rape. *JOGNN* 2006; 35(2): 199–207.
29. Slaughter L, Brown CR, Crowley S, Peck R. Patterns of genital injury in female sexual assault victims. *Am J Obstet Gynecol* 1997; **176**(3): 609–16.
30. Sommers MS, Schafer JC, Zink T, Hutson L, Hillard P. Injury patterns in women resulting from sexual assault. *Trauma Violence Abuse* 2001; **2**(3): 240–58.
31. McLean I, Roberts S A, White C, Paul S. Female genital injuries resulting from consensual and non-consensual vaginal intercourse. *Forensic Sci Int* 2011; **204(1–3):** 27–33.
32. Lincoln C, Perera R, Jacobs I, Ward A. Macroscopically detected female genital injury after consensual and non-consensual vaginal penetration: a prospective comparison study. *J Forensic Leg Med* 2013; **20**(7): 884–901.
33. Sommers MS, Fargo JD. Discriminating between consensual intercourse and sexual assault: Genital-anal injury pattern in females. *J Forensic Leg Med* 2021; **79:** 102138.
34. Astrup BS, Kreiner S, Lauritsen J. Comment to the article: Discriminating between consensual intercourse and sexual assault: Genital-anal injury pattern in females. *J Forensic Leg Med* 2021: **81**; 102201.
35. Oliphant J, Nicolson B, Coomarasamy C, et al. A retrospective observational study of genital findings in adult women presenting to a New Zealand Adult Sexual Abuse Assessment and Treatment Service following an allegation of recent sexual assault. *J Forensic Leg Med* 2021; **86:** 102301.
36. Kjærulff MLBG, Bonde U, Astrup BS. The significance of the forensic clinical examination on the judicial assessment of rape complaints - developments and trends. *Forensic Sci Int* 2019; **297:** 90–9.
37. Rambow B, Adkinson C, Frost TH, Peterson GF. Female sexual assault: Medical and legal implications. *Ann Emerg Med* 1992; **21**(**6**): 727–31.
38. Gray-Eurom K, Seaberg D, Wears R. The prosecution of sexual assault cases: Correlation with forensic evidence. *Ann Emerg Med* 2002; **39**: 39–46.
39. Penttila A, Karhumen PJ. Medicolegal findings among rape victims. *Med Law* 1990; **9**(1): 725–37.
40. Grela A, Gautam L, Cole MD. A multi-factorial critical appraisal of substances found in drug facilitated sexual assault cases. *Forensic Sci Int* 2018; **292**: 50–60.
41. Scott-Ham M, Burton FC. Toxicological findings in cases of alleged drug facilitated sexual assault in the United Kingdom over a three-year period. *J Clin Forensic Med* 2005; **12**: 175–86.
42. García MG, Pérez-Cárceles MD, Osuna E, Legaz I. Drug-facilitated sexual assault and other crimes: A systematic review by countries. *J Forensic Leg Med* 2021; **79:** 102151.
43. Busardò FP, Varì MR, di Trana A, et al. Drug-facilitated sexual assaults (DFSA): A serious underestimated issue. *Eur Rev Med Pharmacol Sci* 2019; **23**(**24**): 10577–87.
44. Perry PJ, Argo TR, Barnett MJ, et al. The Association of Alcohol-Induced Blackouts and Grayouts to Blood Alcohol Concentrations. *J Forensic Sci* 2006; **51**: 896–9.
45. White AM. What happened? Alcohol, memory blackouts and the brain. *Alcohol Res Health* 2003; **27**(**2**): 186–96.
46. Fernández-Rouco N, Fernández-Fuertes AA, Carcedo RJ, et al. Sexual violence history and welfare in transgender people. *J Interpers Violence* 2017; **32**(**19**): 2885–907.
47. Ybarra ML, Goodman KL, Saewyc E, et al. Youth characteristics associated with sexual violence perpetration among transgender boys and girls, cisgender boys and girls, and nonbinary youth. *JAMA Netw Open* 2022; **5**(**6**): e2215863.
48. Office of National Statistics. Sexual offences in England and Wales overview: Year ending March 2020, 2021. Available from: https://www.ons.gov.uk/peoplepopulationandcommunity/crimeandjustice/bulletins/sexualoffencesinenglandandwalesoverview/march2020 (Accessed 24 May 2023).
49. Office for National Statistics. Crime survey for England and Wales, 2021. Available from: https://www.crimesurvey.co.uk/en/HomeReadMore.html (Accessed 24 May 2023).

CHAPTER 81

Findings after Sexual Abuse – Children

Stephen Boos and Heather Williams

INTRODUCTION

Sexual assault of children is a substantially different issue than sexual assault of adults. In most jurisdictions, there is an age below which consent for sexual contact cannot be granted, making any sexual act on younger children an act of sexual assault. Sometimes penetrative acts, "sexual assault" and "rape," are differentiated from non-penetrative acts, "indecent acts." Sexual involvement with a child by a person who is charged with their care is often defined as a separate crime from sexual assault, "sexual abuse." In addition to sexual contact sustained by force, coercion, or facilitated by drugs, we will define sexual abuse to include all situations when a child or adolescent is engaged in sexual activities that they cannot comprehend, for which they are developmentally unprepared and unable to give informed consent, and/or when there is a violation of the legal or social taboos of society (1). Most delayed assessments and many acute assessments of child sexual abuse identify no relevant physical findings and produce no physical evidence, making historic evidence the most common finding after child sexual abuse. Much of what this chapter covers is summarized in the US National Protocol for Sexual Assault Forensic Examinations—Adults/Adolescents and the US National Protocol for Sexual Abuse Forensic Examinations—Pediatric (2,3).

EPIDEMIOLOGY

Child maltreatment is a pervasive issue that embraces all demographics. Recent reports from the World Health Organization (WHO) estimate that 1 in 5 women and 1 in 13 men have been sexually abused as a child (4). In a recent meta-analysis assessing global prevalence, Africa had the highest prevalence rate of child sexual abuse (34.4%), followed by Asia (23.9%), America (10.1%) and Europe (9.2%) (5). The most recent National Child Abuse and Neglect Data System (NCANDS) annual report, from the US Department of Health and Human Services, shows that US state child protection agencies substantiated about 61 000 cases of child sexual abuse in 2018. With fewer than half of states reporting, 877 cases of child sex trafficking were reported (6).

Official figures are likely to underestimate sexual abuse rates because of factors such as social taboo, variability in definitions of abuse, and delays in disclosing or reporting abuse. While NCANDS reported 77 941 cases of sexual abuse in 2006, the National Incidence Study of Child Abuse and Neglect (NIS-4), an active surveillance tool in the US, reported 135 300 in the same timeframe (7,8). The tendency to undercount may be particularly problematic for phenotypic males, due to a myriad of reasons including programs' focus on females and the stigma often associated with sexuality and sexual abuse (9,10). There appears to be a decreasing incidence of child sexual abuse since the early 1990s (6,7,9). This has been attributed to improved social conditions, economic prosperity, public recognition, and prevention programs (9,11).

PRESENTATION

Disclosures and recantations of sexual abuse

Studies have shown that only 30 to 40 percent of adult survivors of child sexual abuse ever disclosed their abuse, and approximately 75 percent of sexually abused children wait at least one year before disclosing (12,13). Males and younger children are generally less likely to disclose abuse than females and older children or adolescents (9,14). Children may fail to disclose abuse due to a lack of understanding of the abusive events, childhood amnesia, emotional influences and active attempts to forget the abuse-related memories (15). Children who are abused by family members living in the home and those who do not feel supported or believed by their caregivers are more likely to delay or withhold disclosures (14,16).

False reports of sexual abuse and assault are rare, only accounting for approximately 1 to 3 percent of all reports (17). While studies have shown a lack of significant association between false allegations of sexual abuse and custody disputes, these cases do present unique challenges (18,19). False allegations may arise from the child, the child in collusion with a caregiver, or from the caregiver alone (17).

Studies have shown that retraction of a prior disclosure, "recantation," occurs in 4 to 22 percent of cases of suspected sexual abuse, with one study finding over

DOI: 10.1201/9781003138754-84

90 percent of recantations were later re-affirmed (9,13,20–22). Retraction may be influenced by multiple factors with an important element being the timing of the interview. A child may retract if he or she does not feel supported after family members have had a chance to respond to the disclosure (9).

Physical symptoms

Physical symptoms vary depending on the child's age, timing of presentation in relation to the abuse, and if injuries were sustained during the abuse. Symptoms may occur due to emotional harm, physical injuries, administration of drugs to facilitate abuse, sexually transmitted infections (STIs) or pregnancy (9).

Many traumatized children have no behavioral or somatic symptoms. Symptoms that do manifest may be non-specific: enuresis, encopresis, somatic complaints such as headache, abdominal or genital pain, ADHD, anxiety, dissociative reactions, aggression, regression and depression. These presentations are often confused for other health problems of childhood. Such "masked" presentations are more common following a chronic history of sexual abuse, males and an immediate family member as the abuser (24).

Sexualized behaviors or sexual play are common during childhood but sometimes result from sexual abuse. Some sexualized behaviors may be developmentally appropriate (touching their own genitals or attempting to view another's genitals) diminishing after 5 years of age. Problem sexualized behaviors occur when the actions are developmentally inappropriate or include intrusive sexual acts, coercion, distress or explicit re-enactment of explicit adult sexual acts. These behaviors warrant further consideration for additional mental health or behavioral concerns and family dysfunction, including child sexual abuse. Factors that increase expression of these behaviors include abuse at a younger age, an abuser who is an immediate family member and abuse that includes penetration (25).

STIs are one of the most forensically significant findings of sexual abuse. Children can present with dysuria, discharge, genital ulcers, genital growths or other signs and symptoms. STIs are frequently asymptomatic in children. Asymptomatic infection is particularly likely with oral and anal infections (23).

Special considerations

Drug facilitated sexual assault

Drug facilitated sexual assault (DFSA) is defined as "offenses in which victims are subjected to non-consensual acts while they are incapacitated or unconscious due to the effects of alcohol and/or drugs and are therefore prevented from resisting and/or are unable to consent." (26) Commonly detected substances include Rohypnol, other types of benzodiazepines (e.g. Xanax), alcohol, opiates and gamma-hydroxybutyric acid (GHB). Clinical manifestations of DFSA may include intoxication out of proportion to alcohol or drugs consumed, flashes of memory or no memory of events at all, and incongruencies in events such as finding clothing inside out or waking in an unexpected location (9,27). Adolescent females are at the highest risk for DFSA and may present while they are still acutely intoxicated (28).

Commercial sexual exploitation of children

Child sex trafficking and commercial sexual exploitation of children (CSEC) are overlapping terms describing "crimes of a sexual nature committed against children and adolescents that involve exploitation for financial or other gain" (29). These crimes include trafficking for sexual purposes, prostitution, sex tourism, mail-order-bride trade, early marriage, stripping, pornography, performing in sexual venues, "survival sex" and engaging in sexual acts for money or perceived excitement or adventure. Trafficking does not require travel from one physical location to another and does not require the use of force, fraud, coercion, deception, or other abuses of power if the child is under the age of 18 (29,30). Children may be reluctant to say or fail to recognize that they are being exploited, making the true prevalence of CSEC difficult to determine (30,31). The actual prevalence is likely higher than most data collecting systems show, with one study revealing that 9 to 28 percent of runaway/homeless youth experienced some form of CSEC (29,32). CSEC increases the risk for severe adverse health effects such as violence-related injuries, STIs, pregnancy, untreated chronic health problems, substance abuse complications and trauma-related mental health problems (33).

Pornography

US Federal law defines child pornography as any visual depiction of sexually explicit conduct involving a minor (34). The internet's easy accessibility, perceived anonymity and affordability have contributed to the increase in child sexual abuse material (CSAM) or "child porn" cases over the past several years (35). A survey in Canada found that 67 percent of children and adolescents depicted in CSAM felt that the distribution of their images impacted them differently than the actual sexual abuse depicted in the images (36). The majority of CSAM material depicts phenotypic females, but when it contains phenotypic males, they tend to be younger and involved in more explicit or egregious abuse. Prepubertal males and females are at higher risk to be depicted in CSAM (37). Due to variations in sexual maturity characteristics among children as they age, it can be very difficult to make any estimation of the age of a child depicted in CSAM based solely on the observation of the images (which may be of very variable quality) unless he or she is prepubertal or in the very early stages of puberty (9).

Assailants

Most individuals who commit sexual abuse are male and are known to the child (38,39). Men who commit sexual abuse outside of the home account for a small number of assailants but tend to abuse larger numbers of individual children (40). Assailants may be "preferential child molesters" or "situational child molesters" (41). Preferential child molesters have a sexual preference toward children, and many of them meet the diagnostic criteria for pedophilia in the Diagnostic and Statistics Manual of the American Psychiatric Association (DSM-5) (42). Situational child molesters are commonly family members or live in the home with the child and do not usually have a sexual preference for children (43). While childhood sexual abuse may be a risk factor for perpetrating as an adult, only a fraction of adult assailants were sexually abused as children (44). According to Finkelhor's precondition model, four conditions must be met before sexual abuse can occur: the assailant must have motivation to sexually abuse, overcome internal inhibitors, overcome external inhibitors, and overcome the resistance of the child (45). Grooming is typically a gradual process where the assailant progresses from seemingly minor sexual talk and touches to build a relationship eventually resulting in inappropriate sexual contact between the two. This type of behavior is utilized by both situational and preferential child molesters (9).

Evaluation

The primary aim of the medical evaluation of child sexual abuse is to guide preventive and treatment interventions directed at resulting injury, disease and emotional trauma. Collection of forensic evidence is a secondary aim, though it may support legal proceedings that protects the child from further harm. When faced with a clear suspicion of non-acute sexual abuse in a child with no acute symptoms, it is reasonable for a clinician to defer all evaluation to other settings and other professionals dedicated to the evaluation of child sexual abuse. Special evaluation centers exist in many countries. In the US, for example, there is a system of children's advocacy centers (CACs) in almost every county. The CAC model utilizes a forensic interviewer to obtain the history from the child so the multi-disciplinary team (MDT) of professionals involved in the case can work together to make decisions in the best interest of the patient and reduce the number of times the child is interviewed about the abuse. The information obtained in this interview guides medical and mental health management of the patient and aids in the investigation. CACs often provide courtroom preparation, victim advocacy and case management (46).

Medical history

An appropriate medical history is often the most significant part of the assessment. Important elements of this history include a timeline of the events, sexual acts attempted and completed, age of the alleged assailant, relationship to the alleged assailant, location of the reported event, any possible witnesses or other children who may have been abused, signs and symptoms of physical injury, any behavioral symptoms or changes and any child utterances with their antecedents. These may be revealed by the child, the accused or non-offending caretakers. Objectivity is always key, but particularly when assessing cases involving contentious custody issues where assessment explores exaggeration or fabrication of the alleged abuse while also protecting the patient. Separating the patient from potential assailants is vital to obtain valid disclosures of abuse (17).

The caregiver's history is especially important with pre-verbal and young children unable to articulate concerns for themselves. Caretakers, however, are not neutral observers and their agendas and fears may result in inferences being reported as facts, the specificity of children's statements being inflated, and suggestive caretaker questioning being unreported. Infrequently, the historian may be the assailant, or have ulterior motives to protect the abuser or to fabricate allegations of abuse. A special case of this occurs with CSEC. When a child is accompanied by a non-relative, a distant relative, or romantic partner; when the accompanying adult will not let the child speak alone or dominates the history taking; or when the accompanying adult seems to control or monitor the child, CSEC should be considered.

Children are often capable of providing important history themselves, but younger children are less likely to provide spontaneous disclosures than older children (47). Age and developmental capabilities, influence what information can be obtained (9). Medical providers evaluating children for sexual assault or abuse are often discouraged from trying to take a history directly from the child. In the US, the National Children's Alliance has made limiting the number of times a child is interviewed a system wide goal (48). However, while multiple interviews run the risk of conflicting histories, suggestion or re-traumatization of the patient, single interviews may lead to incomplete disclosures of abuse. Children are known to provide thorough partial or incremental disclosures (49). Guidelines on medical assessment in these circumstances mention the importance of the child's own history (50–52). Children may have history that caretakers are unaware of including the type of sexual contact, timing of the most recent event, physical symptoms, mental health concerns such as self-harm and suicidal ideation, consensual sexual activity, idiosyncratic details such as words used by the assailant and sensory details, such as how something tasted or felt. Finding the balance can be difficult. Table 81.1 illustrates a recommended approach to medical history taking (53).

Documentation of a child's history or a caretaker's report of their discussions with the child, are more useful when both the questions asked and the child's answer is written down. Verbatim answers should be in quotes. Some medical providers audio or video record the medical history. Medical providers who do so must ensure appropriate security and protection of such recordings.

Physical examination

The child's demeanor and response to the examiner, observations of whether the caregiver believes the child or appears supportive and observations of interactions between the caregiver and child may all provide important information related to the case. The emotional care of the child and approach to examinations should be guided by these observations, which may reveal problematic relationships between the child and accompanying adult.

TABLE 81.1 Approach to a child's medical history

Circumstances	Approach *Example Questions*
Child actively disclosing	Encourage elaboration, obtain clarification *Tell me more, tell me everything that happened.* *You said "he touched you" who is he, where did he touch?*
Parent reports child statements	Request reiteration *Your mom says she brought you because you told her something. Tell me what you said so I can take care of you.*
Child brought for symptoms or injuries	Request explanation *Your mom says that you are having problems, tell me about them. How did that happen? What started that?*
Other children, particularly older children	Open ended request for history *I am your doctor today, my job is to take care of your body, and to try to keep you healthy, happy and safe. Tell me about anything that I need to take care of today.*
Non disclosing or non-responsive children, particularly younger children	Forego additional history DO NOT mention a concept that will be the object of contention such as a suspected assailant or act. DO NOT ask about "good touch" and "bad touch."

A general, whole-body physical examination begins the process (50), starting with the least challenging procedures to reassure the child and to identify the need for support and distraction. All skin surfaces, the sclerae and conjunctivae and the oral, nasal and ear cavities should be examined for injury. Injuries, scars and marks should be noted, described, measured and photographed (*see* Chapters 75 and 91 – "Injury Documentation *and* Interpretation and Forensic Photography"). Between one-half and one-third of sexually assaulted adolescents have non-genital injuries (54–56). The likelihood of injuries is related to the relationship to the assailant, the reported acts and the interval between assault and examination (55). Some injuries or injury patterns are suggestive of non-accidental or inflicted causation (57–59) (*see* Chapter 73 – "Child Abuse and Neglect"). Similarly, extraneous material and adherent or dried substances should be recorded. If a Sexual Assault Evidence Kit (SAEK) is to be used, samples must be collected according to standardized protocols (*see* Chapters 78 and 79 – "Evidential Sampling" and "Minimizing DNA Contamination").

Anogenital examination begins with preparation of the patient. Children aged 12-years and older should formally assent to their examination and, in some jurisdictions, may consent to their examination in the absence of a guardian. A younger child's resistance to examination should be seen and respected as failure to assent. Medication-facilitated examination for forensic reasons alone is highly discouraged. Anxiolysis, sedation or anesthesia may be appropriate to facilitate examination by vaginoscopy, proctoscopy or sigmoidoscopy to fully define the scope of injury, or to allow for necessary surgical repair.

Support by a parent, another mature individual, or child life specialist can be very helpful. Distraction with videos, videogames, bubbles, toys and virtual reality may be useful. Constant communication can help a child anticipate and accommodate to the examination. Some adolescents and older children benefit from seeing what the examiner is seeing on a video monitor (60,61). A multi-method examination is used to fully view externally visible genital findings. Techniques are illustrated in Figure 81.1.

Concerning non-surgical findings in phenotypic females may be further assessed using water flotation. Labial traction is used with some anteriorly directed forces to pull the posterior fourchette up as a dam. Sterile water or normal saline is then instiled into the vestibule, floating the hymeneal membrane upward. Following puberty, swabs may be used to manipulate the hymeneal membrane to explore its anatomy. Using swabs on a pre-pubertal child, however, will result in an unpleasant burning or stinging sensation. For more complex hymeneal anatomy, a larger globular object may be placed in the vagina of some post-pubertal phenotypic females, pressed against the posterior vaginal wall, and then drawn outward, against the inner surface of the posterior hymen. This technique was originally described using a Foley catheter, with the balloon inflated with 5–10 cc of water. An alternative technique uses a scopette (oversized swabs designed for rigid endoscopy) covered with the finger of an exam glove.

The anal examination may be accomplished in supine knee-chest position, with the child on their back and their knees drawn up to their chest, in the prone knee-chest positions, or in lateral lying position with gluteal separation. In a relaxed child, dilation may occur, sometimes revealing the pectinate line, the canals of Morgagni, the anal mucosa or the rectal vault. If dilation to the rectum occurs, the diameter and duration should be noted and the presence of stool in the rectum evaluated.

The application of a nuclear dye, most commonly toluidine blue, is reported to increase sensitivity to superficial laceration and abrasion. False positives from retention in crevices and precipitated dye and the

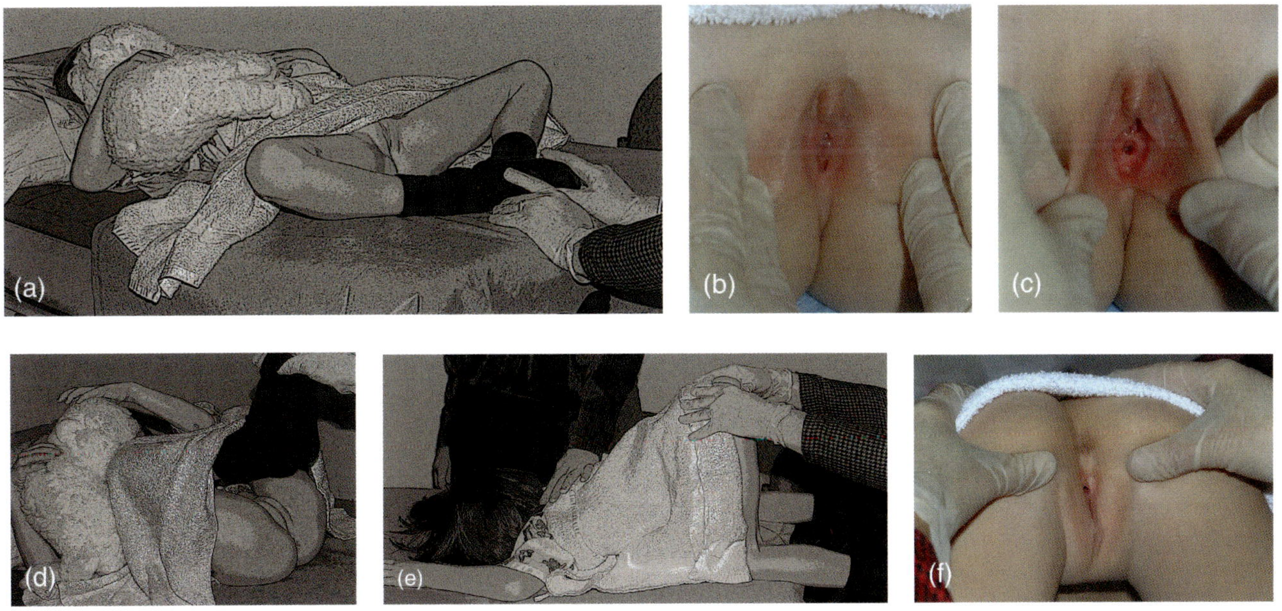

81.1 Physical examination techniques in child sexual abuse. (a) The supine frog-leg position. This position is used in the genital examination with the following two techniques for exposing the inner vulva. **(b)** Labial separation. **(c)** Labial traction, traction is primarily toward the examiner along the axis of the vaginal canal, though some separation and anterior or posterior traction may occur. **(d)** The supine knee-chest position. This position is principally used for the peri-anal examination. **(e)** The prone knee-chest position. This position is used for the peri-anal examination and for the genital examination. **(f)** Position of the hands in prone knee-chest genital examination. The thumbs lie between the lower labia majorae and the buttocks and are drawn apart. The entire hand is then rotated posteriorly/superiorly.

inconvenience of stocking the dye and the procedure itself have resulted in much less use of this technique, though it still appears in the literature.

Significant acute anogenital findings include erythema and swelling, petechiae, ecchymoses and lacerations of varying depths. There has been substantial debate about whether the occurrence or degree of injury can distinguish a sexual assault from consensual sex (consensuality being dependent on age of consent within the jurisdiction). In adolescents, there is clear indication that genital injuries, including severe injury such as vaginal laceration, can occur from consensual sex (63). The most common sites for female genital injury are the fossa navicularis (the posterior vestibule between the hymen and the posterior fourchette), the hymen, the labia minorae and the posterior fourchette. The most common types of injury are laceration, abrasion, erythema and bruising although these terms are not always used consistently (54,55,64). Following anal penetration, anal lacerations, erythema and bruising may be seen (55,64). Articles clearly reporting on acute examinations of children or very young women report positive anogenital findings in from 29 to 83 percent of examinations (54–56,64–67). The child's age, prior sexual experience, reported sexual acts, use of a lubricant, prior use of alcohol or drugs, relationship to the assailant, time from assault to examination and the definition of what constituted a relevant injury all influence the likelihood of findings (55,56,64–68).

The significance of findings in the delayed examination have been subject to substantial debate and revision over time (51,69,70). A group of ten experts in the field of child maltreatment provided guidance on the timing of the exam and how to interpret medical findings (70). This has become the standard for interpreting findings throughout much of the US, and elsewhere and is summarized in Table 81.2. Another widely used consensus document is "The Physical Signs of Child Sexual Abuse: An evidence-based review and guidance for best practice" published in May 2015 [2nd ed.] by the Royal College of Paediatrics and Child Health and represents a consensus with the American Academy of Pediatrics, the Faculty of Forensic & Legal Medicine and the Royal College of Physicians. A 3rd edition will be published in 2023/2024.

In the phenotypic female, the finding with the greatest relationship to past penetrating trauma is transection of the posterior hymenal membrane (Figure 81.2). While deep notches to the posterior hymen are not described in studies of normal pre-pubertal children, defining what constitutes "deep" has methodologic issues. Near-transections, with trivial residual hymenal rim and a substantial focal change in hymenal rim width are highly likely to be post-traumatic changes. A perforation or fenestration through an otherwise intact hymenal rim had been reported as a rare indication linked to prior hymenal trauma. Vaginal discharge is more common in abused phenotypic females. but also seen in the non-abused population (69,71,72). Measurements of hymeneal orifice diameter and the width of a smooth but narrow hymen are unreliable and their relationship to past trauma is, at best, suspect (71). Scars of the fossa navicularis and posterior fourchette are felt to be rare and may be difficult to distinguish from other midline findings such as linea vestibularis (73). Anal findings, perhaps, present even greater difficulty (74–76). Authors disagree on the relationship between peri-anal tags and anal trauma and anal tags are reported in 11 percent

TABLE 81.2 2018 Updated approach to interpretation of medical findings in suspected child sexual abuse (70)

SECTION 1: PHYSICAL FINDINGS

A. Findings documented in newborns or commonly seen in non-abused children.* *These findings are normal and are unrelated to a child's disclosure of sexual abuse.*

Normal variants

1. Normal variations in appearance of the hymen
    a. Annular: hymenal tissue present all around the vaginal opening including at the 12 o'clock location
    b. Crescentic hymen: hymenal tissue is absent at some point above the 3 to 9 o'clock locations
    c. Imperforate hymen: hymen with no opening
    d. Micro-perforate hymen: hymen with one or more small openings
    e. Septate hymen: hymen with one or more septae across the opening
    f. Redundant hymen: hymen with multiple flaps, folding over each other
    g. Hymen with tag of tissue on the rim
    h. Hymen with mounds or bumps on the rim at any location
    i. Any notch or cleft of the hymen (regardless of depth) above the 3 and 9 o'clock location
    j. A notch or cleft in the hymen, at or below the 3 o'clock or 9 o'clock location, that does not extend nearly to the base of the hymen
    k. Smooth posterior rim of hymen that appears to be relatively narrow along the entire rim; may give the appearance of an "enlarged" vaginal opening.
2. Periurethral or vestibular band(s)
3. Intravaginal ridge(s) or column(s)
4. External ridge on the hymen
5. Diastasis ani (smooth area)
6. Peri-anal skin tag(s)
7. Hyperpigmentation of the skin of labia minora or peri-anal tissues in children of color
8. Dilation of the urethral opening
9. Normal midline anatomic features
    a. Groove in the fossa, seen in early adolescence
    b. Failure of midline fusion (also called perineal groove)
    c. Median raphe (has been mistaken for a scar)
    d. Linea vestibularis (midline avascular area)
10. Visualization of the pectinate/dentate line at the juncture of the anoderm and rectal mucosa, seen when the anus is fully dilated
11. Partial dilatation of the external anal sphincter, with the internal sphincter closed, causing visualization of some of the anal mucosa beyond the pectinate line, which may be mistaken for anal laceration

B. Findings commonly caused by medical conditions other than trauma or sexual contact. *These findings require that a differential diagnosis be considered, as each may have several different causes.*

12. Erythema of the anal or genital tissues
13. Increased vascularity of vestibule and hymen
14. Labial adhesion
15. Friability of the posterior fourchette
16. Vaginal discharge not associated with a sexually transmitted infection
17. Anal fissures
18. Venous congestion or venous pooling in the peri-anal area
19. Anal dilatation in children with pre-disposing conditions, such as current symptoms or history of constipation and/or encopresis, or children who are sedated, under anesthesia or with impaired neuromuscular tone for other reasons, such as post-mortem.

C. Findings due to other conditions, which can be mistaken for abuse.

20. Urethral prolapse
21. Lichen sclerosus et atrophicus
22. Vulvar ulcer(s), such as aphthous ulcers or those seen in Behcet's Disease
23. Erythema, inflammation, and fissuring of the peri-anal or vulvar tissues due to infection with bacteria, fungus, viruses, parasites, or other infections that are not sexually transmitted
24. Rectal prolapse
25. Red/purple discoloration of the genital structures (including the hymen) from lividity post mortem, if confirmed by histologic analysis.

TABLE 81.2 (Continued) 2018 Updated approach to interpretation of medical findings in suspected child sexual abuse (70)

SECTION 1: PHYSICAL FINDINGS

D. No expert consensus regarding degree of significance. *These physical findings have been associated with a history of sexual abuse in some studies, but at present, there is no expert consensus as to how much weight they should be given, with respect to abuse. Findings 27 & 28 should be confirmed using additional examination positions and/or techniques, to ensure they are not normal variants (findings 1i, 1j) or a finding of residual traumatic injury (finding 37)*

26. Complete anal dilatation with relaxation of both the internal and external anal sphincters, in the absence of other predisposing factors such as constipation, encopresis, sedation, anesthesia and neuromuscular conditions
27. Notch or cleft in the hymen rim, at or below the 3 o'clock or 9 o'clock location, which extends nearly to the base of the hymen, but is not a complete transection. (This is a very rare finding that should be interpreted with caution unless an acute injury was documented at the same location.)
28. Complete cleft to the base of the hymen at the 3 or 9 o'clock location

E. Findings caused by trauma. *These findings are highly suggestive of abuse, even in the absence of a disclosure from the child, unless the child and/or caretaker provides a timely and plausible description of accidental anogenital straddle, crush or impalement injury, or past surgical interventions that are confirmed from review of medical records. Findings that may represent residual/healing injuries should be confirmed using additional examination positions and/or techniques.*

1) Acute trauma to genital/anal tissues

29. Acute laceration(s) or bruising of labia, penis, scrotum, or perineum
30. Acute laceration of the posterior fourchette or vestibule, not involving the hymen
31. Bruising, petechiae, **or** abrasions on the hymen
32. Acute laceration of the hymen, of any depth; partial or complete
33. Vaginal laceration
34. Peri-anal laceration with exposure of tissues below the dermis

2) Residual (healing) injuries to genital/anal tissues

35. Peri-anal scar (a very rare finding that is difficult to diagnose unless an acute injury was previously documented at the same location)
36. Scar of posterior fourchette or fossa (a very rare finding that is difficult to diagnose unless an acute injury was previously documented at the same location)
37. Healed hymenal transection/complete hymen cleft – a defect in the hymen below the 3 to 9 o'clock location that extends to or through the base of the hymen, with no hymenal tissue discernible at that location.
38. Signs of female genital mutilation (FGM) or cutting, such as loss of part or all of the prepuce (clitoral hood), clitoris, labia minora or labia majora, or vertical linear scar adjacent to the clitoris (Type 4 FGM)

SECTION 2: INFECTIONS

A. Infections not related to sexual contact

39. Vaginitis caused by fungal infections such as Candida albicans, or bacterial infections transmitted by non-sexual means, such as *Streptococcus* sp., *Staphylococcus* sp., *E. Coli*, *Shigella* or other Gram-negative organisms
40. Genital ulcers caused by viral infections such as Epstein-Barr virus or other respiratory viruses

B. Infections that can be spread by both non-sexual and sexual transmission. *Interpretation of these infections may require additional information, such as mother's gynecologic history (HPV) or child's history of oral lesions (HSV), or presence of lesions elsewhere on the body(Molluscum) which may clarify likelihood of sexual transmission. After complete assessment, a report to Child Protective Services may be indicated in some cases. Photographs or video recordings of these findings should be taken, then evaluated and confirmed by an expert in sexual abuse evaluation to ensure accurate diagnosis.*

41. Molluscum contagiosum in the genital or anal area. In young children, transmission is most likely non-sexual. Transmission from intimate skin-to-skin contact in the adolescent population has been described.
42. Condyloma acuminatum (HPV) in the genital or anal area. Warts appearing for the first time after age 5 years may be more likely to have been transmitted by sexual contact
43. Herpes Simplex Type 1 or 2 infections in the oral, genital or anal area

C. Infections caused by sexual contact, if confirmed by appropriate testing, and perinatal transmission has been ruled out.

44. Genital, rectal or pharyngeal *Neisseria gonorrhea* infection
45. Syphilis
46. Genital or rectal *Chlamydia trachomatis* infection
47. *Trichomonas vaginalis* infection
48. HIV, if transmission by blood or contaminated needles has been ruled out

SECTION 3: FINDINGS DIAGNOSTIC OF SEXUAL CONTACT

49. Pregnancy
50. Semen identified in forensic specimens taken directly from a child's body

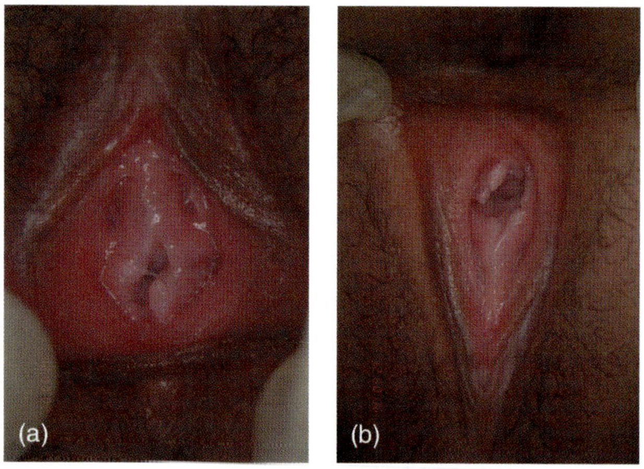

81.2 Hymeneal transection in a post pubertal phenotypic female, delayed examination. **(a)** Supine lithotomy, labial traction. **(b)** Prone knee-chest.

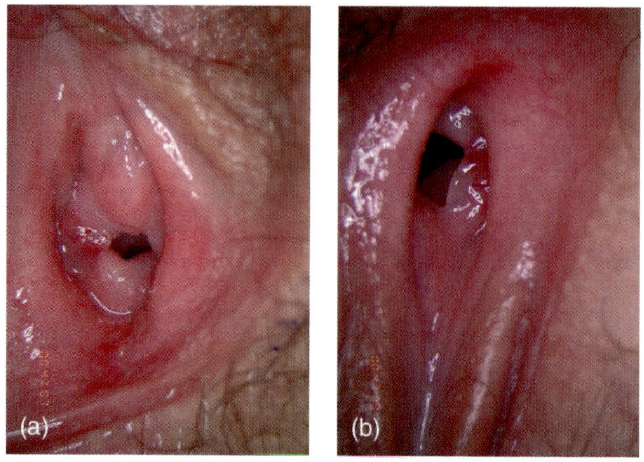

81.3 Hymeneal contusion without laceration. This lesion is likely to disappear without a trace within a week or two. **(a)** Supine lithotomy, labial traction. **(b)** Prone knee-chest.

of non-abused children (75–77). Where reported, anal scars associate strongly with reported anal penetration but the reported identification of anal scars varies substantially between studies (74,75). Terminology is inexact and fissures, lacerations, tears and splits are used interchangeably in many clinical and forensic settings. Fissures and deeper lacerations associate with trauma, but studies appear to have mixed acute with delayed exams (75,76). Small fissures are a common finding in non-abused children, often associated with a history of constipation, and unlikely to be informative in a clearly delayed examination. Degrees of dilation of the anal sphincter have been reported as associates of prior anal penetration. Although there is strong statistical association in case-control studies, dilation has been described in over half of normal children selected for non-abuse (75–77). Studies reporting these findings appear to have used a side lying examination technique, possibly accounting for the difference. Many experts will not cite anal dilation unless it occurs early, persistently, to a diameter >2.5 cm and in the absence of visualized stool. It is essential that any forensic practitioners ensure they are familiar with the latest consensus opinion and are aware of any significant new studies related to genito-anal injury or abnormality after sexual contact.

Demonstrable post-traumatic changes are rare in the non-acute sexual abuse examination. Not all types of sexual abuse involve penetration or contact likely to cause physical injury. From 17 to 71 percent of acute examinations have no demonstrable post-traumatic findings (54–56,64–67). Nearly half of adolescents and young adults do not report an acute rape within the first week, often delaying for years or never telling at all (78–82). Delay in disclosure allows acute injuries to heal prior to examination. Some findings, such as erythema, edema, petechiae and small abrasions may resolve within hours (51,55,66) (Figures 81.3 and 81.4). Some significant injuries heal without leaving identifiable post-traumatic residua (83–89) (Figures 81.5 and 81.6). Only lacerations of the posterior hymen extending into adjacent tissues are highly likely to heal with persistently identifiable residua, the

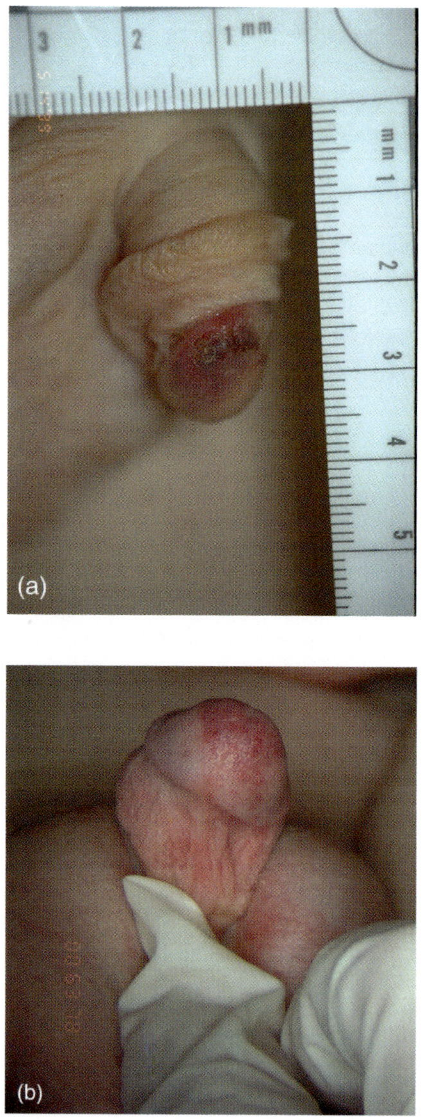

81.4 Penile hematoma. This lesion is likely to disappear without a trace within a week or two. **(a)** Right dorsal view. **(b)** Ventral view.

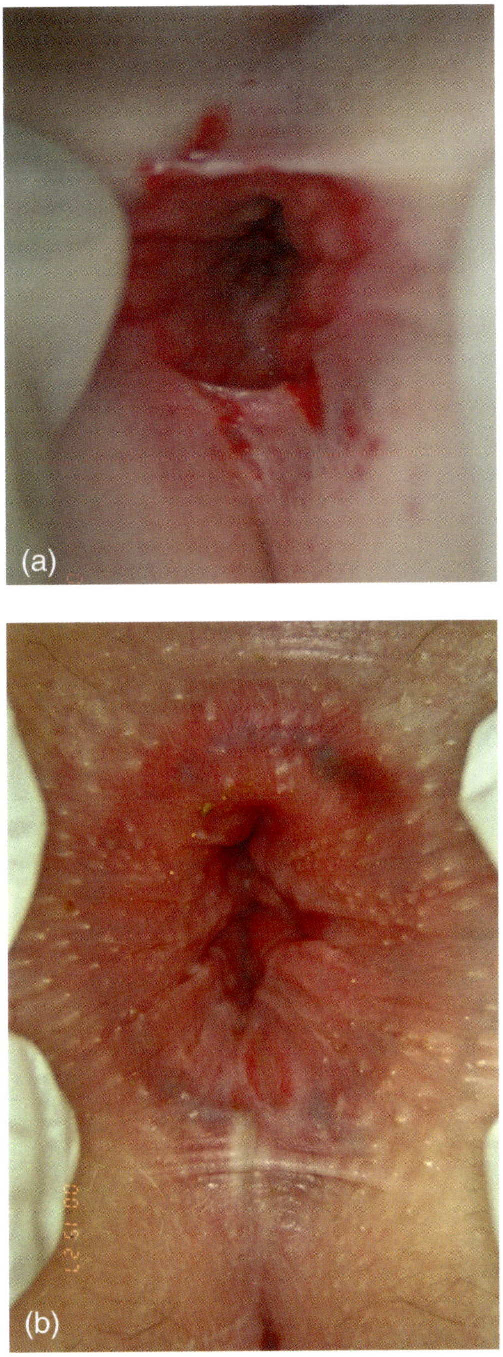

81.5 Acute and healing peri-anal lacerations. **(a)** Acute examinations, note lacerations at the 12:00, 5:30 and 6:30 positions. **(b)** Repeat examination after two weeks, note the development of visible bruising from initially inapparent deeper tissue injury. The lacerations at 12:00 and 6:30 are resolved and the laceration at 5:30 is barely visible at this point.

hymenal transection (87) (Figure 81.7). Articles clearly reporting on delayed examinations report normal or non-specific variant anogenital findings in from 44.7 to 97.5 percent of children (60,71,72,90,91). Normal examination has been reported in case series of pregnant adolescents and children whose abuser confessed to penetration (92,93).

Medical laboratory testing

Medical testing is performed in medical laboratories to guide the medical evaluation and treatment of patients. Medical laboratories adopt careful procedures to properly match specimens and results with patients for purposes of care, but do not necessarily maintain a strictly documented chain of custody, as is done with all evidence collected for purely forensic purposes.

Pregnancy testing is performed in the evaluation of acute sexual assault or abuse on potentially fertile phenotypic females for multiple reasons. If there is the possibility of a desired pregnancy, the patient may wish to forego post-coital contraception. If there is no prior sexual relationship with the assailant, it is emotionally beneficial to know of an existing pregnancy so that later discovery of pregnancy does not create confusion about paternity. If sexual assault or abuse does result in pregnancy, the products of conception, whether terminated or carried to delivery, will provide incontrovertible evidence of sexual intercourse and genetic evidence to identify the assailant. By the time of anticipated menses, urine pregnancy tests are 98 percent sensitive. Blood tests may be positive several days earlier (94).

Medical toxicology testing is performed to guide management of children with impaired level of consciousness or unusual behavior. Many medical toxicological tests are performed by immunoassay and suffer from issues of cross reactivity (95,96). Confirmatory testing by liquid-gas chromatography and mass spectroscopy can eliminate issues of cross reactivity and can evaluate for toxins not in the immunoassay panel, when needed (97,98).

The decision to undertake STI testing has many facets (2,99,100). For children with no legitimate potential of prior sexual contact the implications of an STI in the acute setting are limited to prior sexual assault or abuse, or detection of the STI in the residual secretions of the assailant. Intravaginal sampling of young children is discouraged, and some have indicated that the discomfort of STI testing may dissuade testing in the acute setting (99). In the delayed assessment, selective testing has been suggested (3,99,100). Testing is recommended for adolescents, particularly sexually active adolescents; circumstances with elevated risk such as assault by a stranger, an assailant with known STI, known STI in family members, or assault in a community with high STI prevalence; children with symptoms consistent with STI or with a known index STI; and children with history or physical evidence to indicate sexual penetration. The advent and growing acceptance of nucleic acid amplification testing (NAAT) has made universal testing for *Neisseria gonorrhea*, *Chlamydia trachomatis*, and *Trichomonas vaginalis* straightforward.

Preferred suggested testing methods are summarized in Table 81.3 (*see also* Chapter 90 – "Sexually Transmitted Infection Following Sexual Assault").

The interpretation of STIs as evidence for past sexual contact must consider their low prevalence in sexually abused children, and the possibility of non-sexual transmission, including during birth (101,103,104). The recommendations of the US Centers for Disease Control (USCDC), adopt the long-standing recommendations of the American Academy of Pediatrics Council on Child

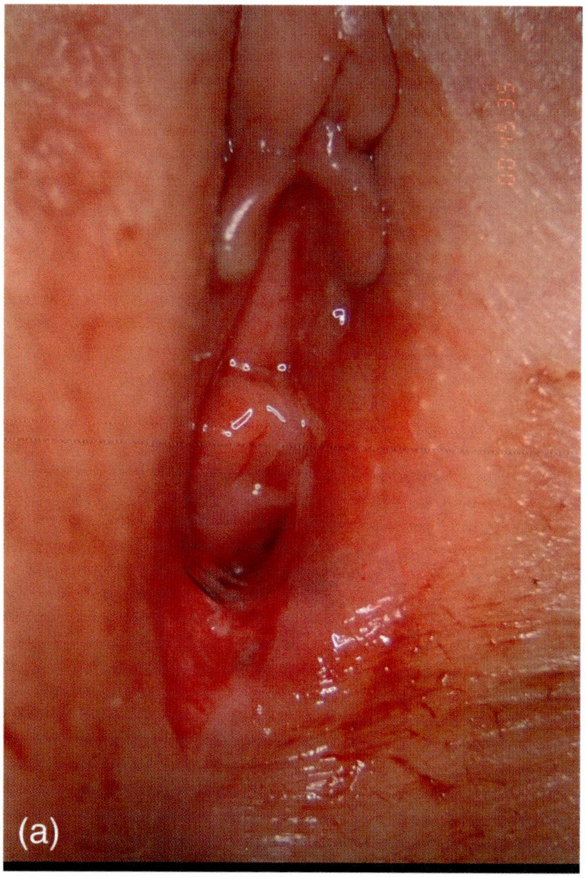

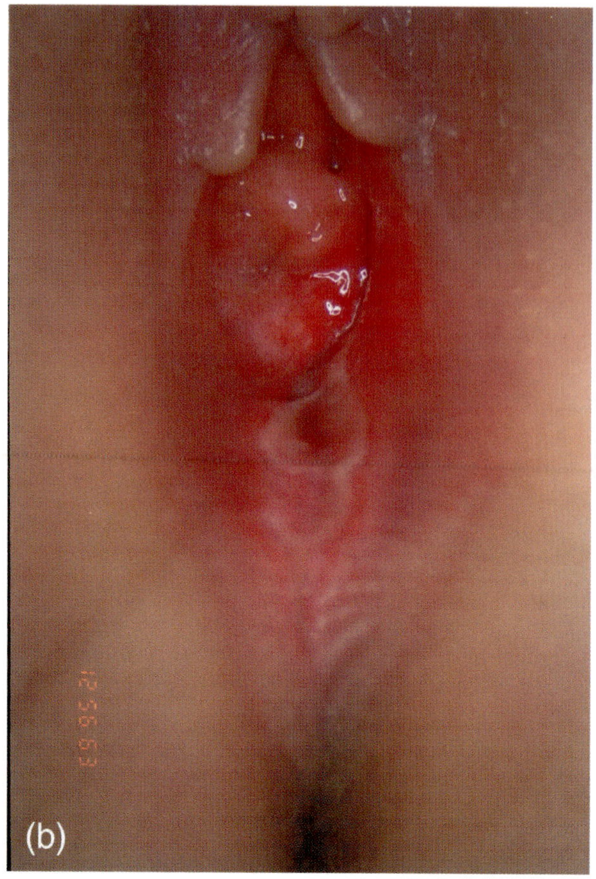

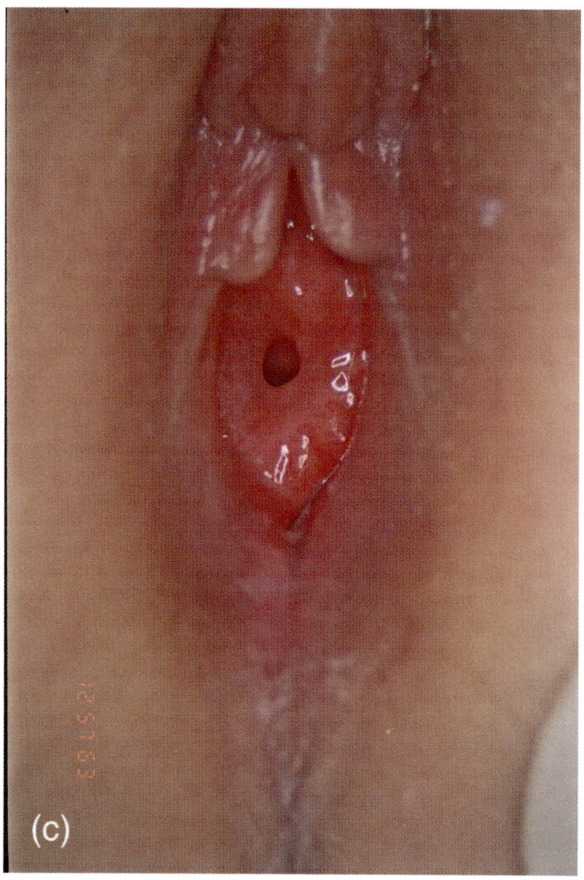

81.6 Laceration of the posterior fourchette. **(a)** Acute injury, deep laceration in the posterior fourchette and posterior vestibule, the hymen is not fully visible and has blood clots or petechiae on its posterior rim. **(b)** Injury after three days, note granulation of the laceration. **(c)** Injury after three weeks, changes to the posterior fourchette are very limited and will likely disappear, the hymen is completely normal.

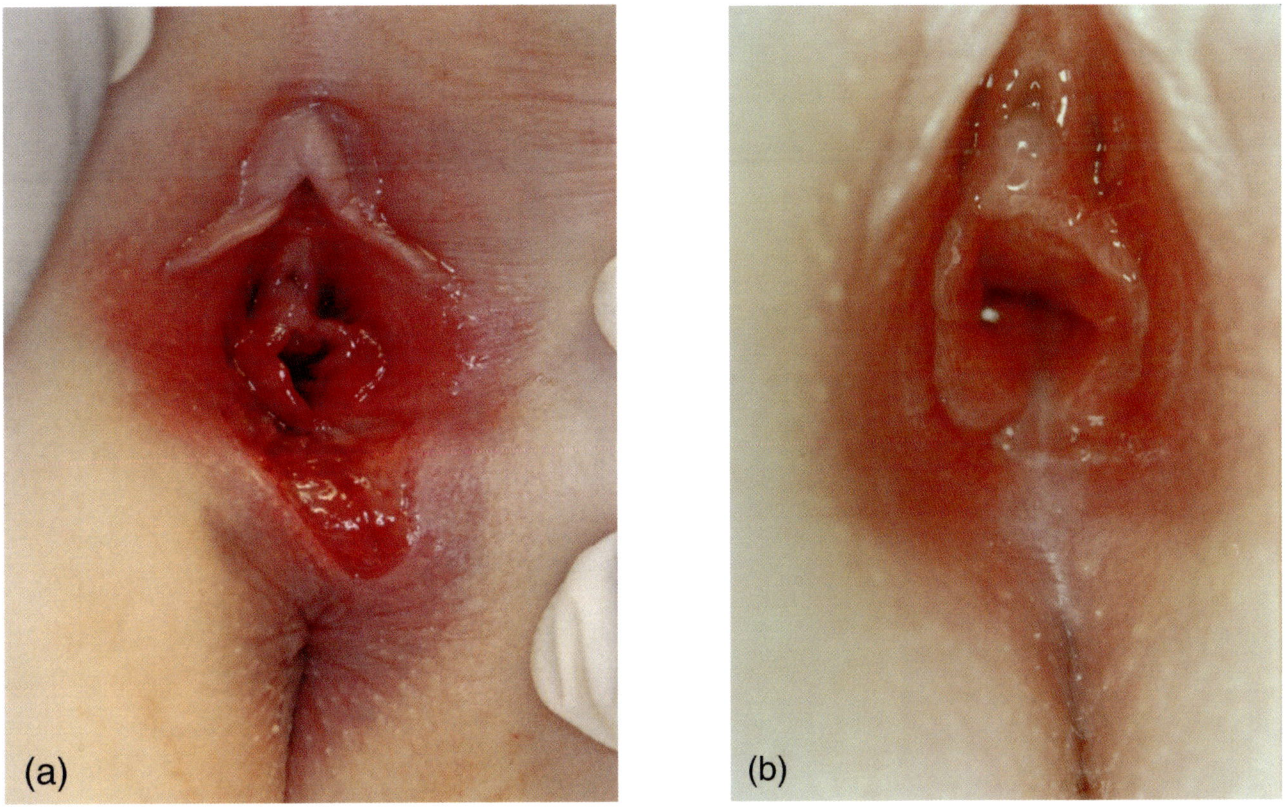

81.7 Laceration of the hymen, extending into adjacent tissues. **(a)** Acute examination with fresh laceration. **(b)** Two weeks later, a full transection of the posterior hymen is seen, there is some pallor but no obvious scarring in the posterior vestibule and posterior fourchette.

TABLE 81.3 Testing and interpretation of STI in pediatric sexual abuse

STI	Test	Site	Specimen	Confirmation*/ Follow-Up	Concern for abuse****
Chlamydia trachomatis	NAAT	Genitals	Dirty urine: pre- and post-pubertal females and males Swab: post-pubertal females only	Alternative target NAAT recommended. Can be performed on same sample Follow-up test in 2 weeks if acute assault/abuse	Diagnostic
		Pharyngeal/Anal	Swab		
Neisseria gonorrhoeae	NAAT	Genitals	Dirty urine: pre- and post-pubertal females and males Swab: post-pubertal females only	Alternative target NAAT recommended. Can be performed on same sample Follow-up test in 2 weeks if acute assault/abuse	Diagnostic
		Pharyngeal/Anal	Swab		

(Continued)

TABLE 81.3 (Continued) Testing and interpretation of STI in pediatric sexual abuse

STI	Test	Site	Specimen	Confirmation*/ Follow-Up	Concern for abuse****
Trichomonas vaginalis	Culture **	Genitals	Swab	Confirmation with second sample culture or alternative test of original sample recommended	Diagnostic
	NAAT***	Genitals	Dirty urine: pre- and post-pubertal females and males Swab: post-pubertal females only	Limited recommendations for this population Alternative sample confirmation testing is common practice	
HIV	ELISA (Ab/Ag Test)	Serum	Blood	Follow-up testing at 6 weeks and 3 months	Diagnostic
Hepatitis B	HBsAg	Serum	Blood	Follow-up testing at 6 weeks and 3 months	Non-specific
Syphilis	Nontreponemal test (VDRL or RPR)	Serum	Blood	Nontreponemal tests are confirmed with treponemal tests (e.g. TP-PA and rapid treponemal assays)	Diagnostic
	Darkfield exam and molecular test for *T. pallidum*	Genital and extra-genital lesion exudate or tissue	Swab	These tests are considered definitive methods for diagnosis	
HSV	NAAT or culture for Type 1 or 2 HSV	Genital and extra-genital lesions	Swab (base of unroofed lesion)	Diagnosis based on clinical findings and results of swab/serum testing. No routine confirmatory testing indicated	Suspicious
	Type-specific HSV Abs	Serum	Blood		
HPV	Clinical diagnosis	Genital and extra-genital lesions	n/a	Tests are available for detecting oncogenic types of HPV but are not indicated for females <25 years or general STI screening	Suspicious Likelihood of sexual abuse increases with age at diagnosis ‡ DNA type is non-contributory †

* Confirmatory tests are recommended for pre-pubertal patients due to high forensic significance related to the low prevalence of infection in that population.

** Recommended by the CDC. Most sensitive test that is readily available.

*** Limited recommendations regarding positive tests and confirmation testing in this population. Benefits of increased sensitivity and ease of collection over culture and wet-mount specimens (70).

**** Per AAP COCAN and USCDC if neonatal transmission is excluded and rare vertical transmission or transmission through transfusion is unlikely (50,99).

‡ Ref. 105, 106.

† Ref. 107.

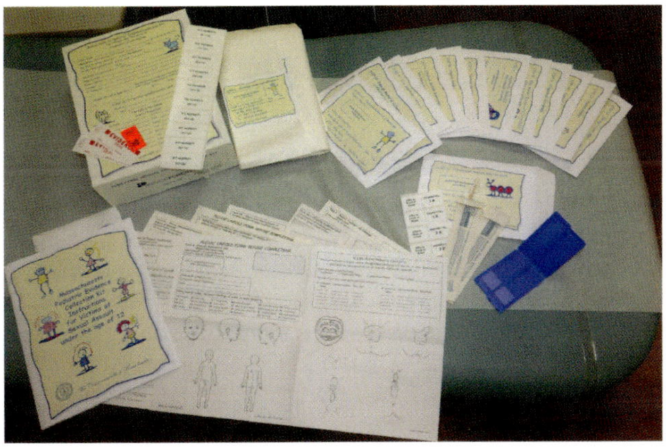

81.8 Sexual assault evidence kit. The many forms and envelopes of the kit are arrayed on the exam table. The instruction book is seen to the left and an open form for documenting exam findings on body diagrams is in the center foreground. The anogenital specimens envelope is opened, revealing the cotton tipped swabs used for evidence collection, and microscope slides to be prepared when collecting the kit.

Abuse and Neglect (AAP-COCAN) that gonorrhea, syphilis, HIV, chlamydia, and trichomonas be considered diagnostic for sexual abuse after neonatal transmission is excluded and rare vertical transmission or transmission through transfusion is unlikely (50,99). These recommendations are summarized in Table 81.3.

Sexual assault evidence kit

Sexual assault evidence kits (SAEKs) are used to ensure the integrity of biological sample evidence collected following complaints of sexual assault (Figure 81.8). A strict chain of custody is maintained for forensic evidence, from collection in the medical setting to processing in the crime lab. Forensic evidence is not necessary for, and does not contribute directly to, the medical assessment and care of a patient. Patient well-being may be enhanced, however, when successful legal handling results in protection of a child or participating in a legal process benefits mental health. Though this may all be self-evident, it is stated here because the first step in collecting an SAEK is obtaining consent from the child or their guardian, and this all forms a part of informed consent. Patients are required to provide consent for both the medical assessment and forensic evidence collection portions of their sexual assault assessments. Parental consent should be obtained for young victims unable to understand the process, but practitioners should stop at any point in time if the victim declines or is unable to tolerate the assessment, regardless of age. Practitioners should wait until a victim is coherent and able to provide consent if he or she presents intoxicated (3,9). The windows of opportunity for collection of appropriate biological samples (e.g. vaginal and anal swabs, blood and urine for toxicology, hair samples) varies according to the nature of assault, and the time since the incident. Recommendations for sampling, and the theory behind the recommendations are explored in Chapter 78 – "Evidential

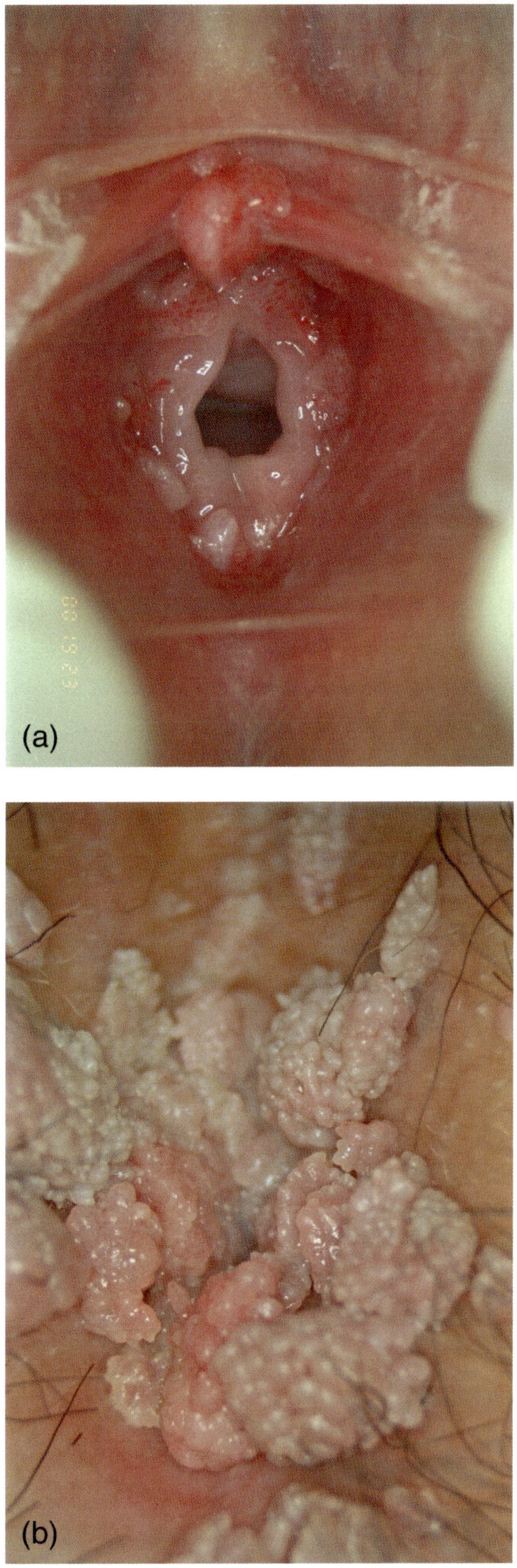

(a)

(b)

81.9 Genital condyloma. **(a)** Mucosal lesions in a pre-pubertal phenotypic female. **(b)** Typical post-pubertal condyloma accuminata.

Sampling". This explains the time limitations on certain sample sites so that unnecessary and potentially distressing sampling can be avoided. It should be noted when applying the adult recommendations, however, that for pre-pubertal children, the return of evidence drops off dramatically after 24 hours (108–111).

CONCLUSION

In evaluating the potential child victim of a sexual crime, difficulties in obtaining forensically relevant information arise from immaturity of the child, appropriate intimate access by the most common assailants, and delays in presentation that decrease the likelihood of either anatomic or trace evidence. Systems evaluating these children must cope with these challenges while maintaining the well-being of the child at the center of the evaluation. Child-centric protocols rely on thoughtful consideration of biological and emotional maturity, variation in social norms, and cross-disciplinary coordination. Approaches developed in the investigation of sex crimes against adults require substantial adaptation, if they are to optimize both the likelihood of legal success and the long-term wellness of the child.

REFERENCES

1. Kellogg N, American Academy of Pediatrics Committee on Child Abuse and Neglect. The evaluation of sexual abuse in children. *Pediatrics* 2005; **116**: 506–12.
2. US Department of Justice. A national protocol for sexual assault medical forensic examinations: adult/adolescent, 2013. Available from: https://www.ojp.gov/pdffiles1/ovw/228119.pdf (Accessed 25 May 2023).
3. US Department of Justice. A national protocol for sexual abuse medical forensic examinations: pediatric, 2016. Available from: https://www.justice.gov/ovw/file/846856/download (Accessed 25 May 2023).
4. World Health Organization. Child maltreatment, 2022. Available from: https://www.who.int/news-room/fact-sheets/detail/child-maltreatment (Accessed 25 May 2023).
5. Pereda N, Guilera G, Forns M, Gómez-Benito J. The prevalence of child sexual abuse in community and student samples: A meta-analysis. *Clin Psychol Rev* 2009; **29**(4): 328–38.
6. US Department of Health & Human Services. Child Maltreatment, 2019. Available from: https://www.acf.hhs.gov/cb/report/child-maltreatment-2019 (Accessed 25 May 2023).
7. US Department of Health & Human Services. Child Maltreatment, 2006. Available from: https://www.acf.hhs.gov/sites/default/files/documents/cb/cm06.pdf (Accessed 25 May 2023).
8. US Department of Health and Human Services. Fourth national incidence study of child abuse and Neglect (NIS-4). Report to Congress, 2010. Available from: https://www.childhelp.org/wp-content/uploads/2015/07/Sedlak-A.-J.-et-al.-2010-Fourth-National-Incidence-Study-of-Child-Abuse-and-Neglect-NIS-4.pdf (Accessed 25 May 2023).
9. Jenny C. *Child Abuse and Neglect: Diagnosis, Treatment, and Evidence.* Philadelphia: Saunders/Elsevier; 2011.
10. Holmes G. See no evil, hear no evil, speak no evil: Why do relatively few male victims of childhood sexual abuse receive help for abuse-related issues in adulthood? *Clin Psychol Rev* 1997; **17**(1): 69–88.
11. Finkelhor D, Jones L. Why have child maltreatment and child victimization declined? *J Soc Issues* 2006; **62**: 685–716.
12. London K, Bruck M, Ceci SJ, Shuman DW. Disclosure of child sexual abuse: What does the research tell us about the ways that children tell? *Psychol Public Policy Law* 2005; **11**(1): 194–226.
13. Elliott DM, Briere J. Forensic sexual abuse evaluations of older children: Disclosures and symptomatology. *Behav Sci Law* 1994; **12**(3): 261–77.
14. Hershkowitz I. Delayed disclosure of alleged child abuse victims in Israel. *Am J Orthopsychiatry* 2006; **76**(4): 444–50.
15. Sjöberg RL, Lindblad F. Limited disclosure of sexual abuse in children whose experiences were documented by videotape. *Am J Psychiatry* 2002; **159**(2): 312–14.
16. Lawson L, Chaffin M. False negatives in sexual abuse disclosure interviews. *J Interpers Violence* 1992; **7**(4): 532–42.
17. Oates RK, Jones DPH, Denson D, et al. Erroneous concerns about child sexual abuse. *Child Abuse Negl* 2000; **24**(1): 149–57.
18. Sarles RM. Filial dependency and recantation of child sexual abuse allegations. *Yearbook of Psychiatry and Applied Mental Health*. 2008; **2008**: 19–20.
19. Rieser M. Recantation in child sexual abuse cases. *Child Welfare* 1991; **70**: 611–21.
20. Sorenson T, Snow B. How children tell: The process of disclosure in child sexual abuse. *Child Welfare* 1991; **70**: 3–15.
21. Bradley AR, Wood JM. How do children tell? The disclosure process in child sexual abuse. *Child Abuse Negl* 1996; **20**(9): 881–91.
22. Coulborn Faller K, Henry J. Child sexual abuse: A case study in community collaboration. *Child Abuse Negl* 2000; **24**(9): 1215–25.
23. Hammerschlag MR. Sexually transmitted diseases in sexually abused children: Medical and legal implications. *Sex Transm Infect* 1998; **74**(3): 167–74.
24. Hunter RS, Kilstrom N, Loda F. Sexually abused children: Identifying masked presentations in a medical setting. *Child Abuse Negl* 1985; **9**(1): 17–25.
25. Kellogg N. Sexual behaviors in children: Evaluation and management. *Am Fam Physician* 2010; **82**(10): 1233–8.
26. LeBeau MA. *Drug-Facilitated Sexual Assault: A Forensic Handbook*. San Diego: Academic Press; 2001.
27. Bechtel LK, Holstege CP. Criminal poisoning: Drug-facilitated sexual assault. *Emerg Med Clin North Am* 2007; **25**(2): 499–525.
28. McGregor MJ, Ericksen J, Ronald LA, et al. Rising incidence of hospital-reported drug-facilitated sexual assault in a large urban community in Canada. *Can J Public Health* 2004; **95**(6): 441–5.
29. Barnert E, Iqbal Z, Bruce J, et al. Commercial sexual exploitation and sex trafficking of children and adolescents: A narrative review. *Acad Pediatr* 2017; **17**(8): 825–9.
30. Institute of Medicine, National Research Council. *Confronting Commercial Sexual Exploitation and Sex Trafficking of Minors in the United States*. Washington DC: The National Academies Press; 2013.
31. Stanley N, Oram S, Jakobowitz S, et al. The health needs and healthcare experiences of young people trafficked into the UK. *Child Abuse Negl* 2016; **59**: 100–10.
32. Greene JM, Ennett ST, Ringwalt CL. Prevalence and correlates of survival sex among runaway and homeless youth. *Am J Public Health* 1999; **89**(9): 1406–9.
33. The American Professional Society on the Abuse of Children. The commercial sexual exploitation of children: The medical provider's role in identification, assessment and treatment, 2013. Available from: https://www.apsac.org/_files/ugd/4700a8_57342ba449214e86a20aff48aaf4fc7f.pdf (Accessed 25 May 2023).
34. The United States Department of Justice. Child pornography, 2020. Available from: https://www.justice.gov/criminal-ceos/child-pornography (Accessed 25 May 2023).
35. Cooper A, Delmonico DL, Burg R. Cybersex users, abusers, and compulsives: New findings and implications. *Sex Addict Compulsivity* 2000; **7**(1–2): 5–29.
36. Canadian Centre for Child Protection. Survivor's Survey Executive Summary, 2017. Available from: https://www.protectchildren.ca/pdfs/C3P_SurvivorsSurveyExecutiveSummary2017_en.pdf (Accessed 25 May 2023).

37. National Center for Missing & Exploited Children. Child sexual abuse material, 2023. Available from: https://www.missingkids.org/theissues/csam (Accessed 25 May 2023).
38. Fagan PJ. Pedophilia. *JAMA* 2002; **288(19)**: 2458.
39. Finkelhor D, Ormrod RK. Factors in the underreporting of crimes against juveniles. *Child Maltreat* 2001; **6**(3): 219–29.
40. Salter A. Predators, pedophiles, rapists, and other sex offenders: Who they are, how they operate, and how we can protect ourselves and our children. *Br J Criminol* 2004; **44(6)**: 986–8.
41. Lanyon RI. Theory and treatment in child molestation. *J Consult Clin Psychol* 1986; **54(2)**: 176–82.
42. Ciccarelli SK, White JN. *Psychology: DSM 5*. Boston: Pearson; 2014.
43. National Center for Missing & Exploited Children. Child molesters: A behavioral analysis. For professionals investigating the sexual exploitation of children, 2010. Available from: https://www.missingkids.org/content/dam/missingkids/pdfs/publications/nc70.pdf (Accessed 25 May 2023).
44. Hanson RK, Slater S. Sexual victimization in the history of sexual abusers: A review. *Ann Sex Res* 1988; **1(4)**: 485–99.
45. Finkelhor D. *Child Sexual Abuse: New Theory and Research*. New York: Free Press; 1984.
46. Children's Bureau. Forensic interviewing: A primer for child welfare professionals, 2017. Available from: https://www.childwelfare.gov/pubPDFs/forensicinterviewing.pdf (Accessed 25 May 2023).
47. Oates K. Can we believe what children tell us? *J Paediatr Child Health* 2007; **43(12)**: 843–7.
48. National Children's Alliance. Our Model, 2021. Available from: https://www.nationalchildrensalliance.org/ (Accessed 25 May 2023).
49. Olafson E, Lederman C. The state of the debate about children's disclosure patterns in child sexual abuse cases. *Juv Fam Court J* 2006; **57(1)**: 27–40.
50. Jenny C, Crawford-Jakubiak JE, Committee on Child Abuse and Neglect, American Academy of Pediatrics. The evaluation of children in the primary care setting when sexual abuse is suspected. *Pediatrics* 2013; **132**: e558–e67
51. Adams JA, Kellogg ND, Farst KJ, et al. Updated guidelines for the medical assessment and care of children who may have been sexually abused. *J Pediatr Adolesc Gynecol* 2016; **29**: 81–7.
52. Crawford-Jakubiak JE, Alderman EM, Leventhal JM, et al. Care of the adolescent after sexual assault. *Pediatrics* 2017; **139**: e20164243.
53. Marchant R, Carter J, Fairhurst C. Opening doors: Suggested practice for medical professionals for when a child might be close to telling about abuse. *Arch Dis Child* 2020; **106**: 108–10.
54. Jones JS, Rossman L, Wynn BN, et al. Comparative analysis of adult versus adolescent sexual assault: epidemiology and patterns of anogenital injury. *Acad Emerg Med* 2003; **10**: 872–7.
55. Sugar NF, Fine DN, Eckert LO. Physical injury after sexual assault: Findings of a large case series. *Am J Obstet Gynecol* 2004; **190**: 71–6.
56. Feeney H, Chiaramonte D, Campbell R, et al. Anogenital and physical injuries in adolescent sexual assault patients: The role of child-offender relationship, alcohol use, and memory impairment. *J Forensic Nurs* 2017; **13**: 52–61
57. Pierce MC, Kaczor K, Lorenz DJ, et al. Validation of a clinical decision rule to predict abuse in young children based on bruising. *JAMA Netw Open* 2021; **4**: e215832.
58. Crumm CE, Brown ECB, Thomas Smith S, et al. Evaluation of an emergency department high-risk bruising screening protocol. *Pediatrics* 2021; **147**: e2020002444.
59. Kemp AM, Maguire SA, Nuttall DE, et al. Can TEN4 distinguish bruises from abuse, inherited bleeding disorders or accidents? *Arch Dis Child* 2021; **106**(8): 774–9.
60. Palusci VJ, Cyrus TA. Reaction to videocolposcopoy in the assessment of child sexual abuse. *Child Abuse Negl* 2001; **25**: 1535–46.
61. Mears CJ, Heflin AH, Finkel MA, et al. Adolescents' responses to sexual abuse evaluation including the use of video colposcopy. *J Adolesc Health* 2003; **33**: 18–24.
62. Fan SM, Grigorian A, Chaudhry HH, et al. Female pediatric and adolescent genitalia trauma: A retrospective analysis of the National Trauma Data Bank. *Pediatr Surg Int* 2020; **36**: 1235–41.
63. Frioux SM, Blinman T, Christian CW. Vaginal lacerations from consensual intercourse in adolescents. *Child Abuse Negl* 2011; **35**: 69–73.
64. Adams JA, Girardin B, Faugno D. Adolescent sexual assault: Documentation of acute injuries using photo-colposcopy. *J Pediatr Adolesc Gynecol* 2001; **14**: 175–80.
65. White C, McLean I. Adolescent complaints of sexual assault; Injury patterns in virgin and non-virgin groups. *J Clin Forens Med* 2006; **13**: 172–80.
66. Drocton P, Sachs C, Chu L, Wheeler M. Validation set correlates of anogenital injury after sexual assault. *Acad Emerg Med* 2008; **15**: 231–8.
67. Gallion HR, Milam LJ, Littrell LL. Genital findings in cases of child sexual abuse: Genital vs vaginal penetration. *J Pediatr Adolesc Gynecol* 2016; **29**: 604–11.
68. McNair SM, Boisvert L. Prevalence of adult female genital trauma after acute sexual assault: The need for a universal definition of genital trauma. *J Forensic Nurs* 2021; **17**(3): 140–5.
69. Berkoff MC, Zolotor AJ, Makoroff KL, et al. Has this prepubertal girl been sexually abused? *JAMA* 2008; **300**: 2779–92.
70. Adams JA, Farst KJ, Kellogg ND. Interpretation of medical findings in suspected Child sexual abuse: An update for 2018. *J Pediatr Adolesc Gynecol* 2018; **31(3)**: 225–31.
71. Berenson AB, Chacko MR, Wiemann CM, et al. A case-control study of anatomic changes resulting from sexual abuse. *Am J Obstet Gynecol* 2000; **182**: 820–34.
72. Anderson B, Thimmesch I, Aardsma N, et al. The prevalence of abnormal genital findings, vulvovaginitis, enuresis and encopresis in children who present with allegations of sexual abuse. *J Pediatr Urol* 2014; **10**: 1216–21.
73. Kellogg ND, Parra JM. Linea vestibularis: A previously undescribed normal genital structure in female neonates. *Pediatrics* 1991; **87**: 926–9.
74. Pierce AM. Anal fissures and anal scars in anal abuse-are they significant? *Pediatr Surg Int* 2004; **20**: 234–338.
75. Myhra AK, Adams JA, Kaufhold M, et al. Anal findings in children with and without probable anal penetration: A retrospective study of 1115 children referred for suspected sexual abuse. *Child Abuse Negl* 2013; **37**: 465–74.
76. Hobbs CJ, Wright CM. Anal signs of child sexual abuse: A case control study. *BMC Pediatr* 2014; **14**: 128.
77. McCann J, Voris J, Simon M, Wells R. Perianal findings in prepubertal children selected for nonabuse: A descriptive study. *Child Abuse Negl* 1989; **13**: 179–93.
78. Bicanic IAE, Hehenkamp LM, van de Putte EM, et al. Predictors of delayed disclosure of rape in female adolescents and young adults. *Eur J Psychotraumatol* 2015; **6**: 25883.
79. Smith DW, Letourneau EJ, Saunders BE, et al. Delay in disclosure of childhood rape: results from a national survey. *Child Abuse Negl* 2000; **24**: 273–87.
80. Alaggia R, Collin-Vezina D, Lateef R. Facilitators and barriers to child sexual abuse (CSA) disclosures: A research update (2000–2016). *Trauma Violence Abuse* 2019; **20**: 260–83.
81. McElvaney R, Moore K, O'Reilly K, et al. Child sexual abuse disclosures: Does age make a difference? *Child Abuse Negl* 2020; **99**: 104121.
82. Wallis CRD, Woodworth MD. Child sexual abuse: An examination of individual and abuse characteristics that may impact delays of disclosure. *Child Abuse Negl* 2020; **107**: 104604.
83. Finkel MA. Anogenital trauma in sexually abused children. *Pediatrics* 1989; **84**: 317–22.
84. McCann J, Voris J, Simon M. Genital injuries resulting from sexual abuse: A longitudinal study. *Pediatrics* 1992; **89**: 307–17.
85. McCann J, Voris J. Perianal injuries resulting from sexual abuse: A longitudinal study. *Pediatrics* 1993; **91**: 390–7.
86. Heppenstall-Heger A, McConnell G, Ticson L, et al. Healing patterns in anogenital injuries: A longitudinal study of injuries associated with sexual abuse, accidental injuries, or genital surgery in the preadolescent child. *Pediatrics* 2001; **112**: 829–37.
87. McCann J, Miyamoto S, Boyle C, Rogers K. Healing of hymenal injuries in prepubertal and adolescent girls: A descriptive study. *Pediatrics* 2007; **119**: e1094–e106.
88. McCann J, Miyamoto S, Boyle C, Rogers K. Healing of nonhymenal injuries in prepubertal and adolescent girls: A descriptive study. *Pediatrics* 2007; **120**: e1000–e11.
89. Berkowitz CD. Healing of genital injuries. *J Child Sex Abus* 2011; **20**: 537–47.
90. Adams JA, Harper K, Knudson S, Revilla J. Examination findings in legally confirmed child sexual abuse: It's normal to be normal. *Pediatrics* 1994; **94**: 310–17.
91. Gallion HR, Milam LJ, Littrell LL. Genital findings in cases of child sexual abuse: Genital vs vaginal penetration. *J Pediatr Adolesc Gynecol* 2016; **29**: 604–11.

92. Kellogg ND, Menard SW, Santos A. Genital anatomy in pregnant adolescents: "Normal" does not mean "nothing happened." *Pediatrics* 2004; **113**: e67–e9.
93. Muram D. Child sexual abuse: Relationship between sexual acts and genital findings. *Child Abuse Negl* 1989; **13**: 211–16.
94. Chard T. Pregnancy tests: A review. *Hum Reprod* 1992; 7: 701–10.
95. Zell-Kanter M. Preventing errors in patient management: The emergency department clinician and the toxicology laboratory. *Semin Diag Pathol* 2009; **26**: 2–6.
96. Wu AHB. Limitations of point-of-care testing in the ED or ICU: A role for regional centralized toxicology laboratories. *Clin Pharmacol Ther* 2010; **88**: 295–8.
97. Maurer HH, Meyer MR. High-resolution mass spectrometry in toxicology: Current status and future perspectives. *Arch Toxicol* 2016; **90**: 2161–72.
98. Van Wijk SMR, Goodnough R, Colby JM. Mass spectrometry in emergency toxicology: Current state and future applications. *Crit Rev Clin Lab Sci* 2019; **56**: 225–38.
99. Workowski KA, Bachmann LH, Chan PA, et al. Sexually transmitted infections treatment guidelines, 2021. *MMWR Morb Mortal Wkly Rep* 2021; **70(4)**: 1–187.
100. Sena AC, Hsu KK, Kellogg N, et al. Sexual assault and sexually transmitted infections in adults, adolescents and children. *Clin Infect Dis* 2015; **61**: 856–64.
101. Black CM, Dreibe EM, Howard LA, et al. Multicenter study of nucleic acid amplification tests for detection of *Chlamydia trachomatis* and *Neisseria gonorrhoeae* in children being evaluated for sexual abuse. *Pediatr Infect Dis J* 2009; **28**: 608–13.
102. Kellogg, ND, Melville JD, Lukefahr JL, et al. Genital and extragenital gonorrhea and chlamydia in children and adolescents evaluated for sexual abuse. *Pediatr Emerg Care* 2018; **34**: 761–6.
103. Girardet RG, Lahoti S, Howard LA, et al. Epidemiology of sexually transmitted infections in suspected child victims of sexual assault. *Pediatrics* 2009; **124**: 79–86.
104. Hammerschlag MR, Guillen CD. Medical and legal implications of testing for sexually transmitted infections in children. *Clin Microbiol Rev* 2010; **23**: 493–506.
105. Sinclair KA, Woods CR, Kirse DJ, Sinal SH. Anogenital and respiratory tract human papillomavirus infections among children: Age, gender, and potential transmission through sexual abuse. *Pediatrics* 2005; **116**: 815–25.
106. Unger ER, Fajman NN, Maloney EM. Anogenital human papillomavirus in sexually abused and nonabused children: A multicenter study. *Pediatrics* 2011; **128**: e658–e65.
107. Braun SA, Silling S, Schloer SM, et al. Human papillomavirus-type distribution in anogenital lesions of prepubertal children. *J Eur Acad Dermatol Venereol* 2021; **35**: 1219–25.
108. Christian CW, Lavelle JM DeJong AR, et al. Forensic evidence findings in prepubertal victims of sexual assault. *Pediatrics* 2000; **106**: 100–4.
109. Palusci VJ, Cox EO, Shatz EM, Schultze JM. Urgent medical assessment after child sexual abuse. *Child Abuse Negl* 2006; **30**: 367–80.
110. Girardet R, Bolton K, Lahoti S, et al. Collection of forensic evidence from pediatric victims of sexual assault. *Pediatrics* 2011; **128**: 233.
111. Thackeray JD, Hornor G, Benzinger EA, Scribano PV. Forensic evidence collection and DNA identification in acute child sexual assault. *Pediatrics* 2011; **128**: 227–32.
112. Homes MM, Resnick HS, Kilpatrick DG, Best CL. Rape-related pregnancy: Estimates and descriptive characteristics from a national sample of women. *Am J Obstet Gynecol* 1996; **175**: 320–5.
113. Saldanha N. Use of short acting reversible contraception in adolescents: The pill, patch, ring and emergency contraception. *Curr Prob Pediatr Adolesc Health Care* 2018; **48**: 333–4.
114. Gemzell-Danielsson K, Marions L. Mechanism of action of mifepristone and levonorgestrel when used for emergency contraception. *Human Reprod Update* 2004; **10**: 341–8.
115. Updated guidelines for antiretroviral postexposure prophylaxis after sexual, injection-drug use, or other nonoccupational exposure to HIV – United States, 2016. *MMWR Morb Mortal Wkly Rep* 2016; **65**: 458.
116. Kellogg ND, Parra JM. The progression of human papillomavirus lesions in sexual assault childs. *Pediatrics* 1995; **96**: 1163–5.
117. Andrews G, Corry J, Slade T, et al. Child sexual abuse. In: Ezzati M, Lopez AD, Rodgers A, Murray CJL (eds), *Comparative Quantification of Health Risks: Global and Regional Burden of Disease Attributable to Selected Major Risk Factors.* Geneva: World Health Organization; 2003, pp. 1851–940.
118. Hailes HP, Yu R, Danese A, Fazel S. Long-term outcomes of childhood sexual abuse: An umbrella review. *Lancet Psychiatry* 2019; **6**: 830–9.
119. Cowan A, Ashai A, Gentile JP. Psychotherapy with survivors of sexual abuse and assault. *Innov Clin Neurosci* 2020; **17**: 22–6.
120. Wamser-Nanney R. Maternal support following childhood sexual abuse: Links to parent-reported children's outcomes. *Child Abuse Negl* 2017; **67**: 44–53.

CHAPTER 82

Sexually Transmitted Infections Following Sexual Assault

Karen E. Rogstad

INTRODUCTION

Sexually transmitted infections (STIs) are infections that are primarily passed on through person-to-person sexual contact (1). They cause a variety of clinical diseases but can be asymptomatic (1–3). In the context of sexual assault, they can be transmitted during the assault but may be pre-existing in the victim. The methodology for testing for STIs has changed dramatically in recent years which has impacted on the sensitivity and specificity of tests (4) and how they can be used in a legal context. It has also resulted in testing being less invasive and therefore less traumatic and more acceptable to victims and also to forensic practitioners.

There have also been advances in the prevention of STIs following assault and in particular for post-exposure prophylaxis for HIV (5) as well as vaccination against Hepatitis B and Human papillomavirus (HPV) (4).

The presence of STIs and their significance in medico-legal cases is fraught with difficulties. In adults, the presence of an STI can be used as evidence of assault or used to bring into question the previous sexual behavior of the victim and discredit them. In the case of children, an STI may be the first indicator of sexual assault/abuse or used to link a perpetrator to victim (6); however, the possibility of transmission vertically, or fomite transmission can be used to argue against sexual transmission and a false diagnosis of sexual abuse can have major long-term repercussions on the child, parents or carers and other children in the family.

WHAT IS AN STI?

STIs are those bacteria, viruses or protozoa that are predominantly passed through sexual intercourse (1). The predominant bacterial STIs worldwide are *Chlamydia trachomatis* (Chlamydia, Lymphogranuloma venereum), *Neisseria gonorrhoea* (gonorrhoea), *Treponema pallidum* ssp *pallidum* (syphilis), Herpes simplex type 1 and 2, well as *Mycoplasma genitalium*, *Haemophilus ducreyi* (chancroid) and *Klebsiella ganulomatis* (Donovanosis/granuloma inguinale) (2).

There are also other infections where sexual transmission can occur but it may not be the main way of transmission.

PREVALENCE OF STIs

There are more than 1 million cases of STIs acquired worldwide every day and each year there are an estimated 374 million new infections with chlamydia, gonorrhoea, syphilis and trichomona (7). In addition, more than 500 million people aged 15 to 49 years are estimated to have a genital infection with Herpes simplex virus (HSV) (7). Prevalence varies for different STIs in different economies. Generally, STI prevalence is higher in less well-resourced countries and health systems.

STIs have a direct impact on sexual and reproductive health for many reasons including through stigmatization, infertility, cancers and pregnancy complications. STIs can also increase the risk of HIV.

Drug resistance, particularly for gonorrhea, is a major obstacle to reducing the burden of STIs worldwide (7).

The incidence and prevalence of STIs post sexual assault is therefore difficult to generalize. Data collection is also difficult as most sexual assaults are not reported.

There are some data on children but this varies according to whether, for example, it was stranger assault or on-going familial abuse. In children aged 0–12 years who were sexually abused gonorrhea was found in 0–4 percent, and for chlamydia in 3 percent and 12 percent (6).

DISEASES CAUSED BY STIs

It is important to diagnose STIs in those who are the victims of assault as they can have long-term serious and life-threatening consequences. Consequences can

DOI: 10.1201/9781003138754-85

be physical or psychological and, as well as affecting the patient themselves, if left undiagnosed and untreated there can be onward transmission to current or future sexual partners. STIs can affect fertility and pregnancy and the neonate of a female victim, or the victim's partner.

Presentations of all STIs can be varied and may be asymptomatic, present with a classical history or cause non-specific symptoms. Similarly, the physical presentation may include no clinical signs, non-diagnostic signs, some signs that strongly suggest the diagnosis and sometimes where the clinical diagnosis is enough and further tests are not required.

Gonorrhea

Gonorrhea is caused by the bacterium *Neisseria gonorrhoeae* (NG). In men, it causes a urethral discharge 2–5 days after infection. In women, it causes vaginal discharge which usually presents later than in men. If left untreated, gonorrhea in men can lead to epididymo-orchitis (inflammation of the epididymis and testes) resulting in scrotal pain which can be unilateral or bilateral. In women, the infection is present on the cervix and can then ascend into the uterus and fallopian tubes, resulting in endometritis with intermenstrual and post-coital bleeding, pelvic inflammatory disease (PID), and ectopic pregnancy. PID is a serious condition and can cause infertility and ectopic pregnancy which is a life-threatening emergency. Ectopic pregnancy can occur soon after infection or months or years later as a result of damaged fallopian tubes. Gonorrhea infection of the rectum, either through direct sexual contact (men and women) or through spread of infection from vagina to rectum without anal intercourse (in women) may also cause proctitis with anal discharge and occasionally pain. Infection of the pharynx is usually asymptomatic but can cause a sore throat. Infection of the eyes resulting in a purulent conjunctivitis can occur through autoinoculation.

Systemic effects and effects on pregnancy and the neonate of *N. gonorrhoeae* may be very significant (1,2).

Chlamydia and lymphogranuloma venereum

Chlamydia trachomatis (CT) is a bacterium that has different serovars causing different clinical diseases. In the context of STIs, serovars D-K cause what is known as chlamydia infection, and types L1–L3 cause lymphogranuloma venereum (LGV).

Chlamydia causes the same symptoms, clinical signs and complications as found in gonorrhea, though usually presents later (1–2 weeks in men) and can persist longer if not treated.

The systemic effects and effects on pregnancy and the neonate of *C. trachomatis* are described in detail in specialist publications.

LGV used to be found in tropical regions but, in recent years, has become endemic in some communities of men who have sex with men (MSM). The classical presentation in heterosexual men and women is a genital ulcer and lymphadenopathy.

In MSM, the usual presentation is tenesmus, rectal discharge and bleeding and painful proctitis. Long-term complications of the bowels are serious including strictures, fistulas and abscesses of the bowels and genital tract and elephantiasis.

Syphilis

Treponema pallidum spp *pallidum* (TP) causes syphilis, a serious infection which, if untreated, can cause severe neurologic or cardiovascular complications, usually many years later. Initial infection causes a genital, anal or oral ulcer which is usually painless and may not be noticed, 9–90 days after infection. This is followed by secondary syphilis 6 weeks to 6 months later (4–8 weeks after primary infection) which has multiple methods of presentation including rash, lesions of the mouth or genitals (mucous patches, condylomata lata), fever, lymphadenopathy, meningovascular or ocular symptoms and signs (8). Long-term complications include cardiovascular effects and neurosyphilis (9). Recent or longer term untreated infection in a pregnant woman results in serious and life-threatening complications to fetus and child (10). Almost 1 million pregnant women were estimated to be infected with syphilis in 2016, resulting in over 350 000 adverse birth outcomes including 200 000 stillbirths and newborn deaths (7).

Substantial information on systemic effects, effects on pregnancy and the neonate or long-term complications of *T. pallidum* is available (1–3).

Genital herpes

Genital herpes is caused by the Herpes simplex virus either type 1 or 2. In the past, type 1 was associated with oral infection and type 2 with genital infection, but now particularly in developed countries, 50 percent of genital infections may be caused by type 1 (2).

It causes a single or multiple penile, vulval or anal blisters which break down to ulcers and are exquisitely tender. There may be severe dysuria due to urine passing onto vulval blisters or because of urethral ulcers in a male. It can cause recurrent disease, usually less severe, which is non-curable. Recurrent disease in the context of sexual assault can be extremely psychologically distressing, as a recurrence, suppressive treatment or the need to take on going precautions to prevent transmission to current or any future partner including disclosure, is a reminder of the assault and re-traumatizing. Infection in a pregnant woman can cause neonatal infection at delivery resulting in severe neurologic injury and death of the neonate.

Further information on systemic effects, effects on pregnancy and the neonate, long-term complications, counseling including future disclosure to partners and psychologic distress of *H. simplex* is available in specialist publications (1–3).

Genital warts

HPV usually types 6 and 11 cause visible warts on the genital and perianal area, but often there is subclinical infection where the virus is present and can be transmitted but there are no clinical signs. Genital warts are unsightly and cause psychological distress (11) particularly in the context of sexual assault as although they can be treated (which may take months) they cannot be cured. They can present typically 6 weeks after exposure but can often be months or years after infection. The virus can be passed on to current or future partners irrespective of the presence of visible lesions. They usually don't cause any significant physical complications. Types 16, 18, 33 and others are also sexually transmitted, do not cause visible warts, but can have long-term life-threatening complications years later as they can cause cervical, penile, anal, vulval and laryngeal cancer (3). HPV infection is associated with 570 000 cases of cervical cancer in 2018, and over 311 000 cervical cancer deaths each year (7).

The incidence of genital warts has dramatically reduced in recent years in those countries with a vaccination program, but these are mainly in wealthier nations such as Australia and England & Wales (12).

Further information on effects on pregnancy and the neonate or long-term psychological and malignant complications is available (1–3).

Trichomonas

Trichomonas vaginalis is a protozoal infection which causes vaginal discharge and vulval soreness in women. However, in men, it is asymptomatic and is usually not detectable on testing of men, but they can pass it on to female partners.

Human immunodeficiency virus, Hepatitis A, B and C

Human immunodeficiency virus (HIV) can cause an acute seroconversion illness with flu-like /glandular fever like symptoms 4–6 weeks after infection, possibly with severe neurologic or respiratory complications. However, it may not present for years later with the complications of immunodeficiency and Acquired Immunodeficiency Syndrome (AIDS). If not diagnosed early and treatment offered, there is high risk of onward transmission to current or new sexual partners and the neonate.

The Hepatitis viruses A, B and C can be sexually transmitted. Risk of transmission is greater in MSM, or where there is no Hepatitis A or B vaccination program.

Hepatitis B and C have a significant risk of acute and long-term life-threatening complications including fulminant hepatic failure in the short term and liver cirrhosis and hepatocellular carcinoma in the long term.

Diagnosis of Hepatitis C can allow early treatment (13) where available to cure infection and prevent onward transmission.

Further information on systemic effects acutely and long-term complications HIV and Hepatitis A, B and C is available from specific publications (1–3).

Other sexually transmitted infections

Granuloma inguinale and chancroid are found more often in tropical areas and present with genital ulcers and or lymphadenopathy. Scabies (*Sarcoptes scabiei*) and "crabs" (*Phthirus pubis*) are sexually transmitted infestations. Genital molluscum, due to the virus *Molluscum contagiosum*, are sexually transmitted (compared with in children where it affects the face and is through close non-sexual contact).

There are many other infections that can be passed on sexually such as Ebstein Barr virus.

For further information on these please refer to a specialist text (1–3).

TRANSMISSION OF STIs

Adults

Transmission in adults of GC, CT, TV, genital warts, genital herpes and syphilis are through sexual contact. New HIV infection in adults is usually sexually transmitted or through injecting drug use. Blood or blood products transmission is rare where there is a good screening program of blood products. Transmission through medical or surgical interventions is also now rare and if the practitioner has undetectable viral load on treatment is not thought to occur at all.

Hepatitis A, B and C may be transmitted sexually or through non-sexual routes.

Transmission in the context of sexual assault is dependent on the STI itself (its transmissibility), the type of sexual assault, use of violence and the prevalence of STIs in the community and the individual demographics of the perpetrator. Prevalence therefore is affected by geographic region, economic issues, poverty, sexual behavior, access to healthcare and sexual mixing. In a high prevalence area for a particular STI, the perpetrator is more likely to be infected and therefore transmit an STI. STIs are more prevalent in certain groups, for example, young people and adults (GC, CT, TV), MSM (GC, LGV, HIV, syphilis, Hepatitis A,B,C).

Significance of STIs in adults

An STI can be pre-existing in someone who has been sexually assaulted. Unfortunately, this is sometimes used to discredit the victim and draw aspersions on their character. In some cases, testing of the victim is not undertaken because of this. A pre-existing STI should never be used in this way of victim blaming.

The presence of an STI in a victim can be evidence of an assault if they were previously not sexually active in general or at that site. If also found in the alleged assailant it may be possible to use it to link the perpetrator to the assailant, particularly if the infective organisms show similar or identical characteristics. This varies for each STI.

Children

Various routes have been proven or proposed for acquisition of STIs in children. This is a highly complex and emotive area with a limited evidence base (6).

It can be vertical (mother to child *in utero*, at delivery or through breast feeding) or through child sexual abuse (CSA) which includes sexual assault and child sexual exploitation (CSE). Other methods have also been proposed such as autoinnoculation, non-sexual transmission through routine care, through fomite transmission such as towels and so on.

In considering the most likely route of transmission of an infection that can be sexually transmitted, consideration must be given to the presence or absence of infection in the mother during pregnancy, the age of the child, whether the child is voluntarily sexually active and the presence or absence of infection in parents, siblings and other relatives, carers and those with access to the child. Voluntary sexual activity must be considered in the light of the legal age of consent in a country, and possible CSE. CSE may be indicated based on age differential, power imbalance, position of trust, sex for gifts including safety and emotional support. The definition of CSE is given in Box 82.1 (14). A child/young person may consider they are consenting to sexual activity, or the perpetrator may state that consent was given or implied, but no child can consent to their own sexual exploitation.

CSE is CSA and STIs in a child must therefore be considered in this context. A young person may be voluntarily sexually active with another young person while also being sexually exploited by one or more other people.

Significance of STIs in children: Sexually transmitted infections as a marker of child sexual abuse

In the past, expert opinion was used to advise if an STI was due to CSA or not, without a sound scientific basis. Many of the older papers and research in this area of STIs in children used inadequate testing methodology, did not consider CSA as a possibility, did not clearly assess for abuse, use control groups and used circular arguments (6). The *Physical signs of child sexual abuse: an evidence- based review and guidance for best practice* 2nd edition was published in 2015 by the Royal College of Paediatricians, The Royal College of Physicians (London), the Faculty of Forensic and Legal Medicine and The American Academy of Pediatrics (6). It is a consensus document and was an update of the 2008 edition. It is the only systematic evidence-based review on the significance of STIs in CSA. It discusses testing and has guidance for good practice. Widely known as "The Purple Book", it is considered the definitive evidence base and is widely used in child protection and legal cases. An updated version is currently under development which will be available online from the Royal College of Paediatrics and Child Health (RCPCH) (15). For each STI it reviews the evidence base, has key messages, an evidence statement and lists issues for clinical practice.

Current evidence shows that outside the neonatal period (and also may need to be considered within the neonatal period) for children with infection with ano-genital *Neisseria gonorrhoeae* and *Chlamydia trachomatis*, sexual transmission is the most likely mode of transmission and there is no evidence for a cut-off age for vertical transmission. In children selected for gonorrhea, sexual abuse was reported in 36 to 83 percent of 0–12 year olds; and for chlamydia sexual transmission was reported in 75 and 94 percent of 0–12 year olds. For anogenital warts, the evidence shows a significant proportion (12–58%) have been sexually abused (15).

Urgent referral to child protection services is recommended for any pre-pubertal child/child under 13 years with GC, CT, genital herpes, TV if over 6 weeks old, and syphilis depending on infection stage and evidence of other transmission modes. Sexual transmission should be considered as a possibility for HIV, Hepatitis B and C, and HIV where other transmission routes have been excluded. For all infections, the presence of infection in the mother does not preclude sexual transmission to the child. For children 13 years or over, it is recommended that referral to child protection services is considered on a case-by-case basis. A more recent study shows that the presence of a bacterial STI in a child 13–15 years old is associated with an increased risk of CSE (16), which would also require a referral to child protection services in the UK. Recent research has shown ophthalmic GC or CT has been found in sexually abused children (17). This is an area requiring further research.

BOX 82.1 The definition of child sexual exploitation (CSE) from Working Together to Safeguard Children (2018) (14)

Child sexual exploitation is a form of child sexual abuse. It occurs where an individual or group takes advantage of an imbalance of power to coerce, manipulate or deceive a child or young person under the age of 18 into sexual activity (a) in exchange for something the victim needs or wants, and/or (b) for the financial advantage or increased status of the perpetrator or facilitator. The victim may have been sexually exploited even if the sexual activity appears consensual. Child sexual exploitation does not always involve physical contact; it can also occur through the use of technology.

DIAGNOSIS OF STIs

In the past, the diagnosis of STIs in assault victims required specialized testing which was invasive and usually needed to be done by specialists in STIs/within specialized STI services. Testing in this context ran the risk of re-traumatizing the victim, more than one examination and seeing different specialists.

In recent years, as a result of the development of nucleic acid tests (NAATS) and near patient testing, non-invasive and self-taken tests are an option which do not require an STI specialist and can be done in remote settings, and some can be processed at the site of care and results given within a few minutes or hours. However, care must be taken about instructions for tests and there needs to be an understanding of the limitations of each test with regard to positive and negative predictive values and the need for confirmatory testing for some. Additionally, the clinician must be clear why they are doing the test. If it is to be used for possible medicolegal evidence of an assault and/or to link a victim to a perpetrator, then a chain of evidence is recommended (18). If there is no chain of evidence then the test could be repeated with a chain of evidence if infection is found and treatment has not yet been given.

Positive samples from victim and perpetrator can be further assessed to determine association using antibiotic sensitivity testing and detailed investigation of the genotype for *N. Gonorrhoeae*, and genomic sequencing, for example, for HIV.

In interpreting results of tests that are to be used in medicolegal cases, advice should be taken from a practitioner familiar with the implications of findings.

Tests recommended for victims depend on their availability, age, type of assault and time since the assault.

Regarding testing, timing and repeat testing local, national or international guidance should be adhered to, such as that of Australia for Asia–Pacific region (19), British Association of Sexual Health and HIV (BASHH) for the UK (18,20) and Center for Disease Control (CDC) for the USA (4).

Tests taken immediately after assault may identify pre-existing infection in the victim, or there may be infection present, for example, in the semen of the assailant. For women, testing should include a high vaginal swab (HVS) or vulvo-vaginal swabs (VVS) for GC and CT, and urine tests for GC and CT in men. Pharyngeal and rectal swabs for both GC and CT should also be considered depending on the nature of the assault and pre-existing sexual risk for STIs. For those transitioning gender or who have transitioned, swabs should be on anatomic sites rather than their gender identification but this needs to be done with sensitivity, and as for all testing, with informed consent.

TV testing on a VVS or HVS using PCR can be done if there is a high community prevalence or in the presence of abnormal vaginal discharge and/or vulval soreness. If PCR is not available, then wet-ground microscopy is necessary to diagnose TV. Testing should be repeated for GC and CT 2 weeks post last assault. HIV, Hepatitis B and C testing should be done at initial presentation usually on venous blood but a point of care test (POCT) can be used for HIV. This would give a baseline to determine if someone was infected from the assault, and would also assist in identification of pre-existing infection so that treatment could be offered. STI testing should not be deferred to follow-up visits as many victims do not attend for follow up. Tests for HIV need to be repeated 4 to 6 weeks after assault if 4th generation antigen/antibody testing is used and at 12 weeks if older tests are used or there is a very high risk for infection.

Hepatitis B and C testing should be performed at baseline and then at 3 and possibly 6 months. If there is very high risk for Hepatitis C infection, then viral load PCR testing can be used within the first 3 months, which becomes positive much earlier than antibodies (15).

Blood testing for syphilis, HIV, Hepatitis B and C can be performed on venous blood or finger prick testing, or for some cases via specialized oral tests.

It is essential that there are systems in place to check for positive results and ensure this is communicated to the victim and linked to treatment and any on-going necessary care. Any positive gonorrhea test should have culture performed to assess for antimicrobial resistance (although this may not be possible in some and especially resource-poor settings).

All tests should be performed after obtaining verbal consent.

STI testing in children

The same principles apply as for adults, though non-invasive testing should be used whenever possible. Reference should be made to national or regional guidelines as with adults, for example BASHH guidelines on the Management of Sexually Transmitted Infections in Children (20) and CDC guidelines (4).

See Table 82.1 for a summary of recommended tests in adults and children.

TABLE 82.1 Tests for sexually transmitted infections post sexual assault and possible timings

Sample site and test type	Test	Timing of test	Female	Male	Female pre-pubertal child	Male pre-pubertal child
Vulvo-vaginal swab NAAT/PCR	CT, GC +/-TV	Immediate and 2 weeks post last assault	X			
Vulvo-vaginal or vulval swab NAAT/PCR	CT, GC, +/-TV	Immediate and 2 weeks post last assault			X	

(Continued)

TABLE 82.1 (Continued) Tests for sexually transmitted infections post sexual assault and possible timings

Sample site and test type	Test	Timing of test	Female	Male	Female pre-pubertal child	Male pre-pubertal child
First-pass urine NAAT	GC, CT	Immediate and 2 weeks post last assault		X		X
Oral swab NAAT	GC, CT	Immediate and 2 weeks post last assault	X	X	X	X
Rectal swab NAAT	GC, CT	Immediate and 2 weeks post last assault	X	X	X	X
Swab of genital ulcer PCR*	Syphilis, Herpes simplex 1&2	Immediate	X	X	X	X
Venous blood or finger prick sample	HIV, syphilis +/- Hepatitis B & C	Immediate and 4–6 weeks post last assault, plus 12 and 26 weeks (see main body text)	X	X	X	X

* Specialist tests required if *Haemophilus ducreyi* or *Klebsiella granulomatis* suspected.

PREVENTION AND TREATMENT OF STIs POST SEXUAL ASSAULT

After a sexual assault, there is a short time period in which an intervention can occur to prevent the acquisition of an STI or modify its progress. These fall into four categories: (1) vaccination; (2) post-exposure prophylaxis for HIV; (3) epidemiologic treatment; and (4) early identification linked to treatment.

Vaccination

Vaccination against Hepatitis B can be given to those not previously vaccinated. This should take into account prevalence in the community, and also possible future risk behavior for acquisition. Ideally, it should be offered to all those not vaccinated. It can be initiated up to 6 weeks post assault. A super accelerated course is recommended in the UK of immediate vaccination repeated at days 7, 21 and 1 year or an accelerated course of immediate vaccination followed by repeat at 1, 2 and 12 months (8). Other areas recommend a schedule of immediate, 1 and 6 months. Schedules will vary for children and local guidelines should be used for adults and children. Vaccination against Hepatitis A could also be considered where there is a high risk of acquisition, for example MSM. Vaccination against HPV both oncogenic and non-oncogenic types could be considered for those unvaccinated. Even if a person has already been infected with one HPV type, it is unlikely they will have been infected with all types. There is no evidence if this intervention prevents infection but is recommended in some guidelines for certain groups, for example in the US, CDC recommends HPV vaccination for female and male survivors aged 9–26 years who have not been vaccinated or are incompletely vaccinated at the time of the initial examination, with follow-up doses administered at 1–2 months and 6 months after the first dose (4). The cost of vaccination may not make this possible and may be a health inequality issue where some may be able to pay and others who cannot are unable to access it.

Post-exposure prophylaxis against HIV

This is an established practice for adults post sexual assault, according to risk criteria including type of assault (with receptive anal sex being the highest risk), prevalence in the community, HIV status of assailant and, if positive, if they are on HIV treatment and virologically suppressed (in which case, prophylaxis is not required). Guidance is available from the British HIV Association (BHIVA) (5) and CDC (4). Treatment consists of three anti-retroviral drugs (ARVs) started immediately and at least within 72 hours of the assault and continued for 1 month. Testing for HIV should be done at baseline but treatment should not be postponed while waiting for the result. Patients must be suitably counseled regarding risks of medication and possibility of resistant virus developing. Testing for HIV acquisition must be repeated 4–6 weeks and 12 weeks post completion of therapy. If the victim is found to be already positive then there should be discussion about maintaining them on treatment to control their HIV and referral into care.

Epidemiologic treatment

Some guidelines recommend providing antibiotics for GC, CT and sometimes TV as prophylaxis against infections developing (4) or its consideration (18). If this is to be done, ideally, there should still be testing prior to medications starting.

Identification of STI and linkage to treatment

Testing for STIs, and repeat testing as required, followed by access to appropriate therapy can prevent the development of complications associated with GC, CT, TV, syphilis and HIV. If the patient has had sexual intercourse post assault, prior to a positive result and treatment being given, then partner notification of their sexual partner(s) should be undertaken to enable them to access testing and treatment and prevent reinfection of the victim. This needs very careful handling as their sexual partner may not know of the assault and it could put the patient at risk of domestic violence, relationship breakdown and stigmatization.

Recent developments in Hepatitis C treatment make early diagnosis linked to treatment an option (13).

CONCLUSION

STIs are an essential consideration when managing adults, young people and children who have been sexually assaulted.

STIs can have serious physical and psychological sequaelae, both in the victim, their current or future sexual partner and current or future pregnancies and neonates. Testing is simple and non-invasive. Testing for BBVs can be done on venous blood or finger prick testing.

Interventions can be used to prevent acquisition of infection such as post-exposure prophylaxis for HIV and Hepatitis B vaccination. If prophylactic antibiotic treatment is given, testing and chain of evidence should occur prior to this.

The presence of an STI can be helpful in medico-legal cases. The presence of an STI can also be the first indicator of sexual assault, particularly in a child or vulnerable adult, including those who are pre-verbal or non-verbal. Interpretation of the diagnosis of an STI in a child requires specialist expertise and the most recent version of *RCPCH Physical Signs of Child Sexual Abuse* should be referred to.

REFERENCES

1. Rogstad KE (ed). *ABC of Sexually Transmitted Infections*. London: BMJ Books; 2011.
2. Holmes KK, Sparling PF, Stamm W, et al. (eds). *Sexually Transmitted Diseases*, 4th ed. New York: McGraw-Hill; 2008.
3. Rogstad KE, (ed). Sexually Transmitted Infections and HIV & AIDS. Medicine Available from:https://www.Medicine-journal.co.uk (Accessed 13 September 2023).
4. Workowski KA, BachmannL H, Chan PA, et al. Sexually transmitted infections treatment guidelines, 2021. *MMWR Recomm Rep* 2021; **70**(**4**): 1–167.
5. Asanti K, Bhagani S, Boffito M, et al. UK guideline for the use of HIV post-exposure prophylaxis. HIV Med 2022; 23(5): 494–545.
6. Royal College of Paediatrics and Child Health. The Physical signs of child sexual abuse. An evidence-based review and guidance for best practice, 2015. Available from: https://childprotection.rcpch.ac.uk/resources/physical-signs-of-child-sexual-abuse/ (Accessed 31 May 2023).
7. World Health Organisation. Sexually transmitted infections, 2021. Available from: https://www.who.int/news-room/fact-sheets/detail/sexually-transmitted-infections-(stis) (Accessed 31 May 2023).
8. Baughn RE, Musher DM. Secondary syphilitic lesions. *Clin Microbiol Rev* 2005; **18**(**1**): 205–16.
9. Gonzalez H, Koralnik IJ, Marra CM. Neurosyphilis. *Semin Neurol* 2019; **39**(**4**): 448–55.
10. Woods CR. Syphilis in children: Congenital and acquired. *Semin Pediatr Infect Dis* 2005; **16**(**4**): 245–57.
11. Mortensen GL. Long-term quality of life effects of genital warts - a follow-study. *Dan Med Bull* 2010; **57**(**4**): A4140.
12. Public Health England. Sexually transmitted infections (STIs): Annual data tables, 2021. Available from: https://www.gov.uk/government/statistics/sexually-transmitted-infections-stis-annual-data-tables (Accessed 31 May 2023).
13. European Association for the Study of the Liver. EASL recommendations on treatment of hepatitis C: Final update of the series. *J Hepatol* 2020; **73**(**5**): 1170–218.
14. Department for Education. Child sexual exploitation. Definition and a guide for practitioners, local leaders and decision makers working to protect children from child sexual exploitation, 2017. Available from: https://assets.publishing.service.gov.uk/government/uploads/system/uploads/attachment_data/file/591903/CSE_Guidance_Core_Document_13.02.2017.pdf (Accessed 31 May 2022).
15. Royal College of Paediatrics and Child Health. Website, 2023. Available from: https://www.rcpch.ac.uk (Accessed 31 May 2023).
16. Ward C, Hughes G, Mitchell HD, Rogstad KE. Association between STI and child sexual exploitation in children under 16 years old attending sexual health clinics in England: findings from a case-control study. *Sex Transm Infect* 2019; **95**(**6**): 412–15.
17. Reading R, Rogstad K, Hughes G, Debelle G. Gonorrhoea, chlamydia, syphilis and trichomonas in children under 13 years of age: National surveillance in the UK and Republic of Ireland. *Arch Dis Child* 2014; **99**(**8**): 712–16.
18. Cybulska B, Forster G, Welch J, et al. UK national guidelines on the management of adult and adolescent complainants of sexual assault, 2011. Available from: https://www.bashhguidelines.org/media/1079/4450.pdf (Accessed 31 May 2023).
19. Australian STI management Guidelines. Adult sexual assault, 2021. Available from: https://sti.guidelines.org.au/populations-and-situations/adult-sexual-assault/ (Accessed 31 May 2023).
20. Ashby J, Browne R, Dwyer E, et al. BASHH national guideline on the management of sexually transmitted infections and related conditions in children and young people, 2021. Available from: https://www.bashhguidelines.org/media/1294/children-and-yp-2021.pdf (Accessed 31 May 2023).

CHAPTER

83

Self-Harm

John A.M. Gall and Jason Payne-James

INTRODUCTION

Self-harm (also referred to as self-injurious behavior; self-inflicted injury; intentional self-injury; deliberate self-harm) is common throughout all societies and its range of severity varies from minor to severe and, in some cases, fatal outcomes. It can be manifest in many ways (often hidden) such as cutting, burning, overdosing, scratching, biting, hair pulling and bone fracture. Not all acts of self-harm are considered socially unacceptable although what may be acceptable in one society may not be acceptable in another. Self-flagellation causing significant tissue damage and bleeding is a Christian practice found in some but not all Christian societies. Ritual genital mutilation of males and/or females is acceptable and expected in some cultures but unacceptable and even unlawful in others. Most parts of the body may be subjected to some form of mutilation in one society or another. The eyes and anus are the only sites that seem to be generally excluded from socially accepted mutilation (1). Within western cultures, tattoos and body piercings have become common, a situation that has markedly changed from the mid-twentieth century. The extent of piercings and tattoos may exceed, however, acceptable norms and fall into the abnormal. This determination may be dependent on the person's culture, religion, ethnic and social background.

Beyond socially accepted forms of self-harm, there are pathologic forms of self-harm that often require the involvement of a forensic practitioner, be they a forensic physician, forensic pathologist or psychiatrist (general and/or forensic). There is a wide spectrum of self-harm injuries with equally diverse motivations. Those engaging in these practices may be classified into five separate, but not mutually exclusive, groups and include:-

- Successful suicide
- Survivors of a potentially lethal suicide attempt
- Individuals making a "cry for help"
- As a feature of a mental health condition
- Impulsivity initiated by drugs and alcohol
- Malingerers

Although these groups may overlap, they essentially fall into two categories:

- Where there is a clear suicidal ideation; and
- Where suicidal ideation is minimal if present at all

From a mental health perspective, severe injury is more likely associated with schizophrenia or psychotic depression while lesser injury is more likely associated with personality disorders (2). Generally, and excluding most forms of socially sanctioned bodily manipulation, self-harm is associated with some form of psychopathology (3,4).

Completed suicides tend to be assessed by forensic pathologists but, in some jurisdictions, forensic physicians may be involved. Survivors of potentially lethal suicide attempts, those making a "cry for help" and persons with mental health conditions may be seen by forensic physicians and allied forensic healthcare professionals in custody but may also be seen within emergency departments or primary care centers.

Such patients will need assessment, appropriate immediate management and appropriate referral which should be to a mental health professional. The forensic physician may also encounter those who use self-harm as a means to falsely allege being a victim of crime to embellish and enhance their allegations or do so for some form of secondary gain. This may result in costly inappropriate police investigations and individuals being falsely charged for crimes they have not committed.

The types of perceived gain for these persons varies considerably but includes claims for compensation, revenge, to escape prosecution, to claim some form of advantage in adverse situations such as in the custodial system, to gain financial benefits, and to divert attention.

In the previous edition of *The Diagnostic and Statistical Manual of Mental Disorders* (DSM IV TR) (5), this group fitted within the definition of malingering which was defined as the "*intentional production of false or grossly exaggerated physical or psychological symptoms, motivated by external incentive such as avoiding military duty, avoiding work, obtaining financial compensation, evading criminal prosecution or obtaining drugs.*"

DOI: 10.1201/9781003138754-86

Although malingering has been removed from the index of the 5th edition of this manual (*DSM-5*) (6), the section remains together with other entities in the chapter titled: *Other Conditions that may be a Focus of Clinical Attention*. The term is retained in this chapter but authors recognize the term can be stigmatizing. These patients may be particularly challenging to assess as they may present with either the "classical" or atypical features of self-harm. Unfortunately, there is no specific diagnostic feature for self-harm and the diagnosis relies upon a thorough history, clinical examination and interpretation of findings.

INCIDENCE OF SUICIDE AND SELF-HARM

Estimating the extent of self-harm is particularly difficult as non-fatal self-harm injury is not reported. It is estimated that more than 700 000 people die from suicide each year with attempted suicide being significantly higher than the suicide figure (7). It is a leading cause of death worldwide and estimated to account for 1.3 percent of all deaths. Globally, in 2019, the World Health Organization (WHO) reported that the suicide rate was higher by a factor of 2.3 times in males (12.6 per 100 000) than females (5.4 per 100 000). For that year, it was the fourth leading cause of death among 15–29 year-olds for both males and females after road injury, tuberculosis and interpersonal violence.

As reported by the World Health Organization, suicide is not just a first-world problem but a global phenomenon with over 77 percent occurring in low- and middle-income countries (7,8). In 2019, the suicide rates in Africa (11.2 per 100 000) Europe (10.5 per 100 000) and Southeast Asia (10.2 per 100 000) were higher than the global average of 9.0 per 100 000. The Eastern Mediterranean region had the lowest suicide rate (6.4 per 100 000). Looking at the age-standardized suicide rates for males, the African region had the highest rate (18.0 per 100 000) followed by Europe (17.1 per 100 000) and then the Americas (14.2 per 100 000). This contrasted with the rates for females with the South-East Asia region being the highest (8.1 per 100 000).

The WHO publication also looked at changes in suicide rates at the time. In the 20-year-period between 2000 and 2019, the global suicide rate decreased by 36 percent with notable decreases in the European region (47%) and the Western Pacific Region (49%). Unfortunately, suicide rates in the Americas increased during this period reaching 17 percent.

Even with a death, accurate estimation globally is difficult as the available figures may be either misreported or underreported in many countries. The quality of reporting of suicide numbers is poor in some countries and may be biased in others. This is due to suicide contravening religious, cultural (association with a stigma) and legal traditions in those countries. Reported suicide cases are but the tip of the iceberg. Although suicide attempts and self-harm may present to hospitals and primary care services, there is an unknown number of "hidden" cases of attempted suicide and self-harm (9). There are estimates for non-suicidal self-harm ranging from 2.6 to 1100 per 100 000 and lifetime prevalence rates ranging from 720 to 5930 per 100 000 (10) but there are no actual international figures for those who self-harm. Most forensic physicians will frequently see those who have self-harmed and a study in police custody in London, UK noted that 7.1 percent had previously been sectioned under the Mental Health Act 1983 and 16.7 percent had previously intentionally self-injured (11). Self-harm is a common occurrence within all societies and it is important to be able to carefully consider each case to ascertain the nature harm that may be identified.

INJURY TYPES ASSOCIATED WITH SELF-HARM

The methods used and subsequent injuries sustained by each of the categories of self-harm vary and are listed in Table 83.1.

Although analyses have been undertaken of the methods of suicide in some individual countries, very little information is available with respect to the methods of suicide on an international basis and particularly a comparison of methods between international cultural groups.

Ajdacic-Gross et al. (12), in a unique study, undertook an overview of international patterns of suicide methods. Despite limitations associated with the collection of accurate data, this group utilized the World Health Organization International Classification of Diseases (10th revision; ICD-10) encoded mortality database to classify the different suicide methods.

As not all countries reported their mortality data to the ICD-10 standard, some countries were excluded, such as those from the African continent (with the exclusion of South Africa), and those with small populations. The data did, however, include 56 countries and covered the period 1994–2005. ICD–10 coding for suicide did enable differentiation of suicide methods into those due to a pesticide or unspecified poison, other poisons, hanging, drowning, firearms and explosives, and jumping from a height. Analyses were undertaken of suicide methods per country as well as internationally.

Hanging was the most common method of suicide in most countries analyzed, although a number of variations were noted in those countries where other major methods of suicide were available. For example, firearm suicide was the most common method in the United States of America and prevalent in Argentina, Switzerland and Uruguay.

Interestingly, only men use this method in Switzerland. Poisoning with pesticides was predominant in rural Latin American countries, Asian countries and Portugal

TABLE 83.1 More common types of injuries associated with the two categories of self-harm

Suicide and attempted suicide	Injuries where suicidal intent is minimal if present at all	
	General injuries	**More severe injuries associated with significant mental health disorders**
Poisons	Drug "overdoses"	Incising
Pesticides	Bruising	Amputations (ears; genitalia; fingers)
Carbon monoxide	Abrasions	Eye gouging
Drug overdoses	Biting	
Drowning	Burns	
Shooting	Banding (including the use of ligatures)	
Explosions	Insertion of foreign bodies	
Electrocution	Ingestion of foreign bodies	
Road injuries		
Rail injuries		
Immolation		
Jumping from heights		
Hanging		
Incising		
Stabbing		
Asphyxia		

particularly among women. Poisoning with drugs was common for women in Canada, Nordic countries and the United Kingdom. Males in these countries also frequently used this as a means of suicide. Hanging and firearm suicide was more frequent among men whereas less violent methods of poisoning or drowning tended to occur with women.

When considering the international comparisons, hanging, pesticide and firearms dominated country-specific suicide patterns. Important alternative methods included jumping from a height and poisoning predominantly from drugs. Their analysis indicated that although hanging is the most common method of suicide, this changes when the use of pesticides or firearms is more readily available.

Similar international data on the methods used for self-harm where suicide is not the intent do not exist. There are, however, several studies on the patterns of self-harm in specific population groups but how representative these findings are of the general population is questionable given biases associated with reporting.

Manzoor et al. (13) analyzed the data from three major hospitals in Lahore catering for pediatric cases between January 2000 and December 2010. They found that males self-harmed by injuring the wrist utilizing a sharp-edged weapon or, as an alternative, a blunt weapon whereas females tended to use a sharp-edged weapon.

FEATURES OF SELF-HARM

In the absence of either an admission of self-harm or witness accounts, there are no diagnostic features of self-harm. This may prove challenging when death has occurred and any witness has not come forth. In these cases, a determination is required as to whether the death was that of suicide, homicide or misadventure.

A consideration of all the facts and circumstances leading to the cause of death, the death scene and examination of the body becomes particularly important in arriving at a final opinion. For those those who have sustained injuries and are alive, there are a number of "classical" features, which together, may suggest that the injuries have been caused by self-harm (13,14). They include:

- Usually not fatal (in cases where suicide is not the intention)
- Tend to be superficial or minor (Figure 83.1)
- Often multiple and parallel (Figure 83.2)
- Tend to be of a single injury type (Figure 83.3)
- Generally consist of abrasions or incisions rather than bruises or lacerations
- Often all injuries are of a similar severity (Figures 83.4)
- Usually involve non-vital structures such as the cheeks, forehead, chest, abdomen, and upper and lower limbs but tend not to involve the eyes and nipples
- Present on accessible sites
- Presence of tentative (or hesitation) injuries (Figure 83.5)
- Old healed or healing scars in similar sites (Figure 83.6)
- Overlying clothing is often spared
- An absence of defensive injuries

These "classical"| features are presented in Table 83.2 with some additional comments in relation to their appearance.

In most cases of self-harm where the person is alive, the individual will admit to having caused the injuries themselves. This may not always occur in the early phase of the medical assessment but, with a suitably professional and compassionate approach, the individual may disclose at some point. This does not always happen.

There are situations where aspects of a particular case raise concerns of causation and the managing service (e.g.

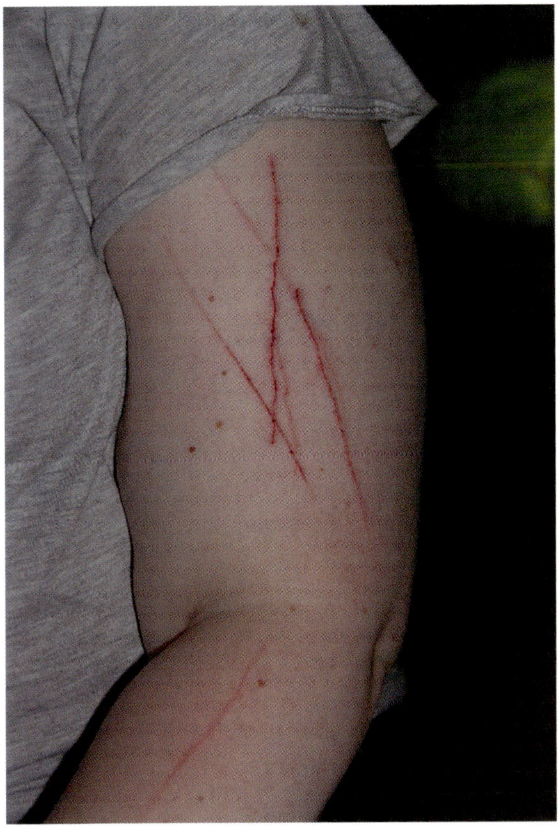

83.1 Superficial linear scratches from a pointed object not penetrating the full skin thickness.

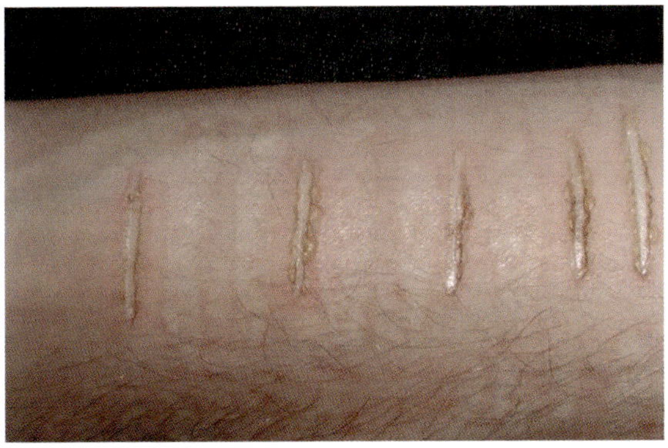

83.3 Multiple linear fresh burns caused by application of a heated knife. Pale mature scars in the same orientation can be seen between the fresh burns, these are old burns of a similar nature to the new injuries.

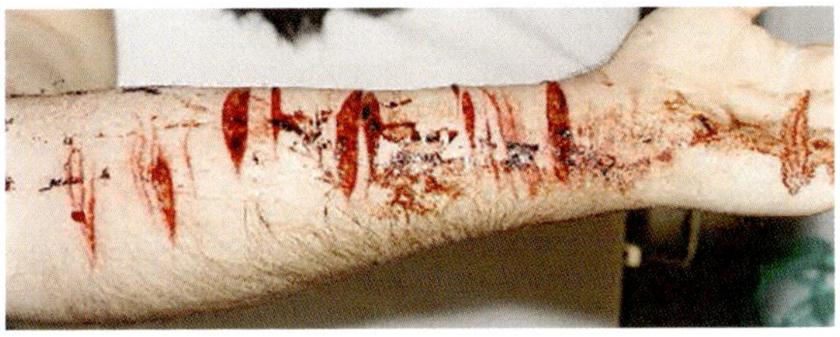

83.4 Deeper parallel incised wounds across the volar aspect of the forearm most of a similar depth and severity.

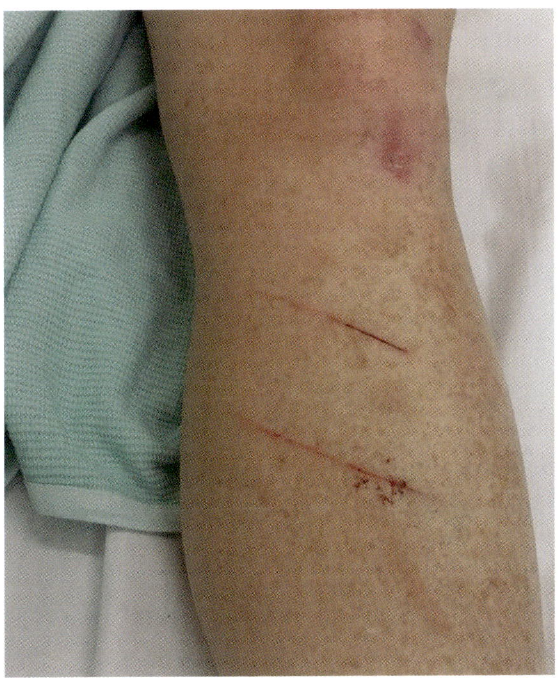

83.2 Parallel superficial incisions.

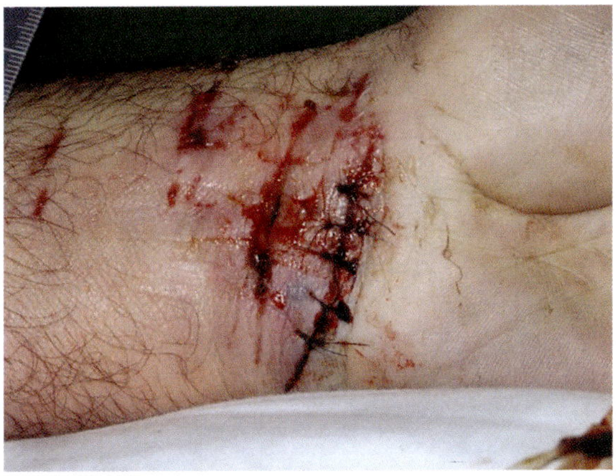

83.5 Multiple parallel incised wounds. The smaller ones are "tentative!" or "hesitation" injuries.

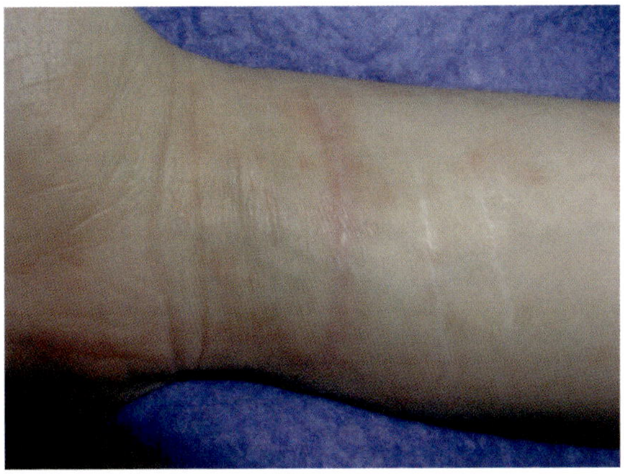

83.6 Transverse pale pink (more recent) scar and two pale scars (older) on the volar aspect of the right wrist.

police; child protection; treating medical practitioner) will request a forensic physician to review the case. This request may be to ensure patient safety while in custody so that it can be taken into account at risk assessment or it may be to obtain an opinion as to whether the injury is true assaultative injury or possible self-harm. These are cases where the injured person either denies having self-harmed or gives an account that conflicts with the appearance of the wound or the account of witnesses.

After considering all the information available (i.e. circumstances from third parties; witness accounts; information from the patient), and examination of the patient and examination of the implement or implements allegedly used to cause the injury, a decision regarding the probability of self-harm may be determined. In some circumstances, relevant information may be missing and a reliance upon the factors outlined in Table 83.2 may be necessary to provide an opinion. If reliance is placed upon these "classical" features, it is not necessary for all of the characteristics to be identified. Frequently, only some of these characteristics are present and it is only in rare circumstances that all features are present. The absence of either a particular characteristic or several characteristics does not preclude self-harm. The converse equally holds in that the presence of characteristics of self-harm does not necessarily imply or confirm self-harm.

Consideration of the "classical" features of self-harm becomes quite pertinent when dealing with the group of patients where secondary gain is the motive. Assessing this group may be quite challenging. Importantly, the injuries are usually not fatal and tend to be superficial or minor in nature.

The types of injuries sustained are usually abrasions, incisions and burns. Bruises and lacerations are uncommon although bruising from pinches or biting may be identified. All the injuries tend to be of a single type (i.e. all abrasions, all incisions or all burns) and are usually located on a part of the body that is readily accessible.

The injuries, therefore, tend to be located on the opposite side of the body to hand dominance (i.e. for right-handed persons, the injuries tend to be localized on the left-hand side of the body). In the case of abrasions and incisions, injuries tend to be parallel or near parallel and all are of similar appearance and severity. In the case of incisions, tentative injuries may be present.

These injuries tend to be more superficial and shorter than the subsequent injuries but, in some cases, may progress from a tentative and shallow incision to a deeper and more significant incision. The injuries usually involve non-vital structures such as the cheeks, forehead, chest, abdomen and upper and lower limbs, hands and lower lateral back but tend not to involve the eyes, nose, mouth, ears and areola. Interestingly, the thighs and legs are less frequently involved. The genitals may be involved in cases of alleged sexual assault. In some cases, old healed or healing scars in similar sites may be identified.

TABLE 83.2 Injury characteristics that may be associated with self-harm (Modified from 15)

Characteristic	*Additional comments*
Usually not fatal	Non-intentional fatalities may occur
Tend to be superficial or minor	More severe injury may be caused, particular in those with a significant psychiatric disorder
Often multiple and parallel	If there is more than one abrasion or incision, the injuries are of similar appearance, style and orientation. Typically self-inflicted incised injuries are more superficial, numerous, and similar than those sustained in an assault from another person, where the natural reaction of the assaulted person is to avoid repeated injury. More than one similar injury should raise an index of suspicion as to the possibility of self-infliction
Tend to be of a single injury type	More than one similar injury should raise an index of suspicion as to the possibility of self-infliction
Generally consist of abrasions or incisions rather than bruises or lacerations	
Often all injuries are of a similar severity	More than one similar injury should raise an index of suspicion as to the possibility of self-infliction
Usually involve non-vital structures such as the cheeks, forehead, chest, abdomen, and upper and lower limbs but tend not to involve the eyes and nipples	
Present on accessible sites	Sites less accessible (e.g. the middle of the back) are less likely. Injuries tend to be grouped or found on the contralateral side to the patient's handedness. A right-handed person will tend to inflict harm on the left-hand side of the body and vice versa
Tentative injuries may be present	Smaller or lesser injuries grouped with the main injuries suggest initial "tentative" attempts at self-harm
Old healed or healing scars in similar sites	Old healed scars in similar sites, scars of different ages in similar sites and slow-healing injuries. These may indicate previous attempts and repeated attempts of self-harm
Overlying clothing is often spared	For presumably economic reasons, self-harmers tend to spare the overlying clothing of where they inflict the injury especially in cases of malingering
An absence of defensive injuries	

Defensive injuries (*see* Chapter 75 – "Injury Documentation and Assessment") are absent. Importantly, and a feature that may often assist in making an assessment, the overlying clothing is often spared. Clothing worn at the time of an alleged assault is an important part of any assessment. If an alleged assault has occurred where foreign material may be expected to be on the clothing and the clothing is in pristine condition, questions would need to be raised as to the validity of the allegation. Environmental conditions may also be relevant (e.g. rain). Similarly, when a person alleges an assault with a weapon that has caused skin injuries such as abrasions and incisions yet the overlying clothing is undamaged, then this too raises questions regarding the veracity of the allegations.

IMPORTANCE OF IDENTIFYING SELF-HARM

It is particularly important to be able to identify cases of self-harm. Firstly, from a forensic perspective, the correct identification of self-harming will reduce the likelihood of an innocent person being falsely charged and the potential of wrongful conviction.

In addition, it prevents unnecessary time being spent on investigations by law-enforcement personnel and others with the associated costs involved. The second and equally important aspect is that often there is a need to care for and treat the individual.

Recognition of patterns of self-harm seen in both the community and those incarcerated may permit arrangements to be made for assessment and review with mental health or related services to treat any of the predisposing factors for self-harm. Early recognition of non-fatal attempts at self-harm may prevent a successful attempt at suicide in the future. This is an area of great significance, for instance, for prison officials where the profile of those incarcerated may be exactly those of individuals more likely to self-harm. A young female, for example, given a prison sentence may be at particular risk of self-harming and, if the risk factors have been identified, then processes can be put in place to attempt to reduce the risk of self-harm occurring.

Case Studies 83.1 and 83.2 presented here include both suicide and non-suicidal injuries and include the relatively severe to that of a more minor nature.

CASE STUDY 83.1

Case Study 83.1 relates to a young Korean male who was living away from his family and by himself. On the night of his death, neighbors could hear him screaming out very loudly, banging on the floor and intermittently speaking and singing in Korean.

This occurred for about 15–20 minutes before finally ceasing. On the following morning, he was found deceased with a number of significant stab and incised wounds to the abdomen and lower limbs, all on the anterior aspect of the body (Figure 83.7).

What appeared to be tentative injuries were also identified on the body. There were no defensive injuries and no evidence of intrusion into his unit or of a fight within the unit. The knife used to inflict the injuries was identified as a long bladed, single-edged, kitchen knife. The location and angulation of the injuries, if self-inflicted, would fit with a right-handed person which the subject was. Examination of his computer found documentary evidence of his being depressed.

He had come to understand the concept of and the perfection of his God and felt this was now expressed through him. Beyond this, there was no known history of psychiatric problems. Although the initial appearances were not that of anticipated self-harm, careful assessment of the injuries, an absence of defensive injuries, no evidence of an intruder within the subject's unit, and finding documented evidence regarding his depression, loneliness and disappointment with his few friends, assisted in making an assessment of suicide.

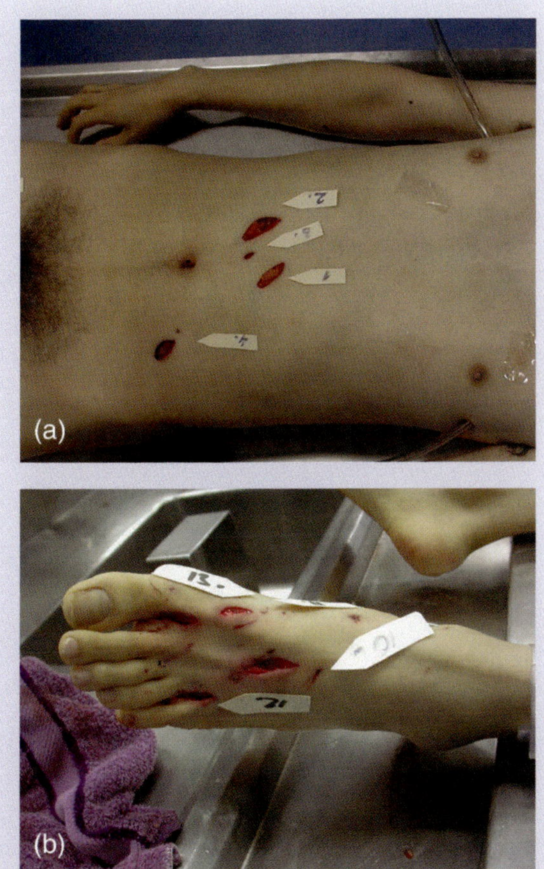

83.7 Suicide by what appeared to be a ritualized stabbing. Injuries were to the anterior part of the body involving the abdomen and lower limbs. **(a)** Only one injury was fatal and this was a stab wound that penetrated the inferior vena cava. **(b)** Some possible tentative injuries are shown (black arrows).

CASE STUDY 83.2

Case 2 relates to a teenage female who alleged that she was assaulted with a knife. She was traveling on a bus and alighted at a bus stop where there was an unknown male standing. Having walked a short distance, she noted that the male was following her. He allegedly grabbed her and tried to engage her in conversation.

He then grabbed her shoulders and tried to kiss her. She punched him in the face twice, a struggle ensured and the male produced a flick knife from his pocket. With the blade exposed, the male then allegedly lifted up the complainant's clothing (three layers) and allegedly "cut" her four times to the abdomen with the knife. The assailant decamped when other people approached. An opinion was requested by police as to whether the injuries sustained were as alleged. As is sometimes the case, the opinion needed to be based on photographs provided as the subject was not available for examination. The injuries sustained consisted of almost parallel areas of erythema extending from approximately the mid-line laterally with what appeared to be a single small abrasion toward the midline that had bled (Figure 83.8).

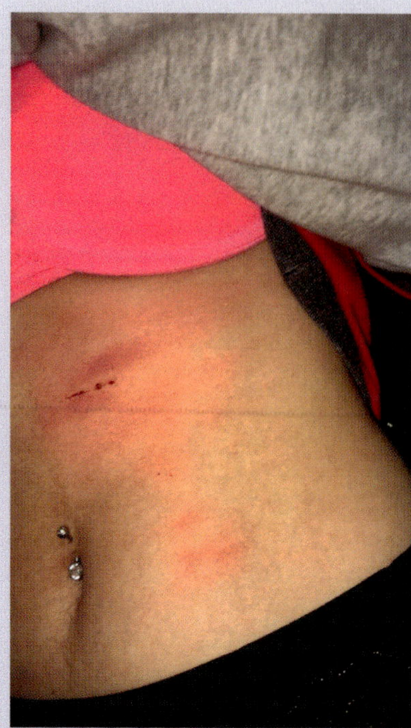

83.8 Areas of abdominal erythema/bruising on a teenager who alleged she was assaulted by an unknown male after alighting a bus. The assailant allegedly lifted up her clothing and "cut" her four times. The injuries shown in the photograph do not fit with the allegations.

Similar linear red markings were present near the umbilicus. No other injuries were identified. The bruises/erythema fitted more with blunt trauma from possibly the subject's own fingers although, in the absence of seeing the knife, it was difficult to exclude to blunt end of the knife handle being used for this purpose. The blade of the knife could certainly have caused the single abrasion identified but given the overall appearance of the injuries and the history, although limited, the injuries were highly suggestive of self-harm. Further details about the case were unavailable and it is uncertain what the particular secondary gain may have been.

CASE STUDY 83.3

Case Study 83.3 is of a middle-aged lady who alleged that she was assaulted by a male offender who hit the left side of her face with such force to cause her to fall over a lounge chair and onto the floor. He has then "cut" her multiple times with a serrated knife (steak knife). As a result, she sustained a number of linear abrasions to her left face, anterior neck, right and left anterior shoulders, anterior chest and breast and right proximal forearm (Figure 83.9). The injuries were similar in appearance suggesting that they were inflicted by the same or similar implement. All were of a similar depth. On her left shoulder, was an "H"-shaped group of abrasions. The lady was right-hand dominant and the location and direction (determined by skin tags) of the abrasions fit with self-harm from a right-handed person. Of note, despite being struck very forcefully to the left face, there was an absence of bruising and other possible blunt force injuries to support this allegation. Although it was not possible to completely exclude that these injuries were sustained as alleged by the subject, there was a high probability that the abrasions were self-inflicted.

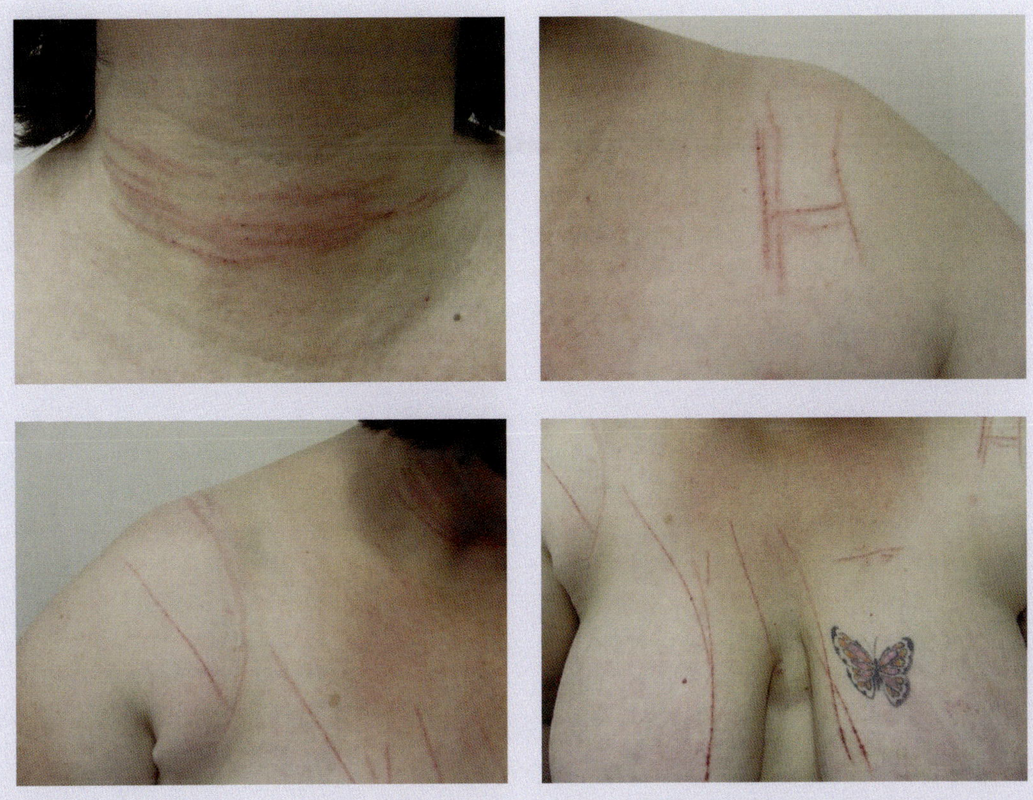

83.9 A female who alleged she had been assaulted with a serrated knife. Series of abrasion/incision-like injuries on the anterior upper left shoulder forming an "H" -like pattern. All injuries appear to be of similar severity. She sustained a number of linear abrasions to her left face, anterior neck, right and left anterior shoulders, anterior chest and breast and right proximal forearm some of which are shown. The injuries were similar in appearance suggesting that they were inflicted by the same or similar implement. All were of a similar depth.

AN APPROACH TO THE FORENSIC ASSESSMENT OF SELF-HARM

The management of cases of potential self-harm can be complex and much will depend upon the circumstances of the case to determine the approach taken. In some cases, there is either little or no uncertainty as the event was witnessed or the patient claims to have engaged in the self-harming activity.

Regarding the latter, care needs to be taken to ensure that the patient is being honest as there may be reasons for somebody to make a false and misleading claim. The greatest challenge is dealing with those cases where self-harm is engaged in for some form of secondary gain. The patient, in these cases, is usually the only person who knows the full facts of the case and will generally provide a history of events which they feel is compatible with the injuries they have caused.

Complicating this group are those who may have been assaulted but feel the injuries they have sustained are unconvincing for the events that occurred and then embellish their injuries by adding to the injuries already sustained during the actual assault. Unfortunately, there is no specific diagnostic criteria to determine self-harm in this group of patients.

In brief, maintaining an open mind, gathering all the necessary and available information, obtaining a thorough history from the patient, undertaking a competent and thorough medical examination, and considering all the options will result in an opinion either supportive or unsupportive of self-harm.

A schematic approach to the assessment is shown in Figure 83.10. For this group of people who self-harm, the following information, if available, needs to be gathered to enable the formulation of an opinion:

- Details of the events from police and witnesses
- Medical and psychiatric history from the patient or available medical records
- Handedness
- Details from the patient of the alleged assault and how the injuries were sustained
- Details of the weapon used
- Details of clothing worn by the patient during the alleged assault (ensure that damaged clothing corresponds to the location of injuries sustained on the body and that the damage to the clothing is compatible with the implement used)
- Relevant details regarding location and environmental factors (e.g. wet/dry; inside/outside; nature of services such as the grass, carpet, dirt; temperature)

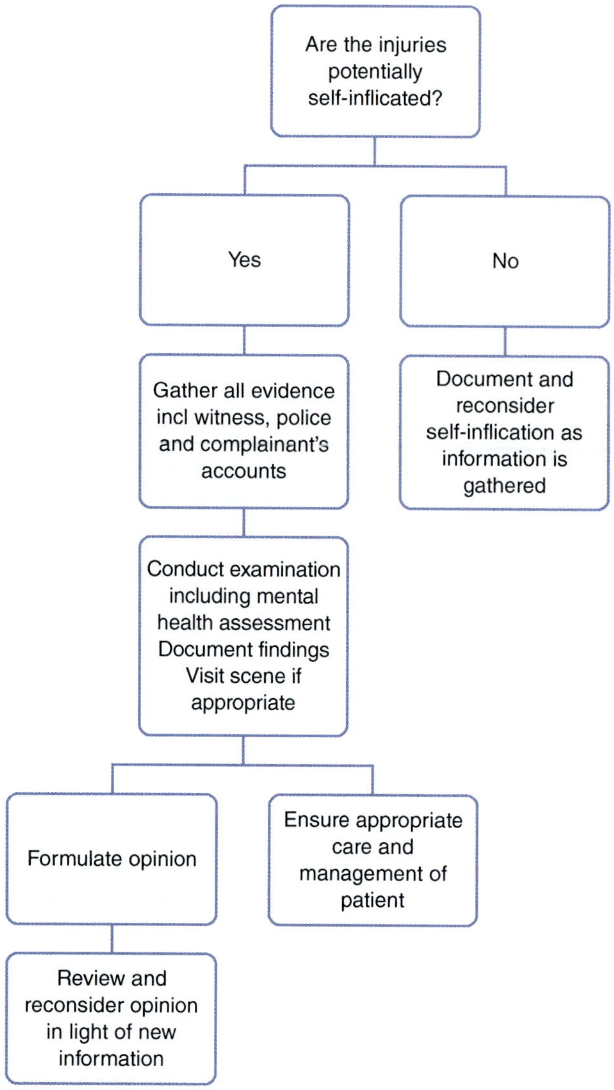

83.10 Flowchart of an approach to the assessment of possible self-harm. (Modified from [2])

A thorough but directed medical examination needs to be undertaken with consideration of the injuries sustained and the likely causes of those injuries. Once all the facts have been gathered, an opinion, arrived at by deductive reasoning, may be formulated. There will be cases where it is not possible, based on the available evidence, to determine whether the injuries are the result of self-harm. It is vital that the opinion is based solely on deductive reasoning and the facts and is not influenced by external pressures. In keeping with quality and appropriate healthcare, for cases where a mental health issue is suspected, appropriate follow-up care must either be provided or arranged.

CONCLUSION

Self-harm is not an uncommon event and is one encountered frequently within emergency departments and by psychiatrists managing acute psychiatric conditions.

There is a group of patients who engage in self-harm for secondary gain and it is this group, in particular, that necessitates the involvement of the forensic physician. Although there are features supportive of the probability of an injury occurring as a result of self-harm, there are no specific diagnostic features. To determine whether an injury or injuries is the result of self-harm, particularly in the group where secondary gain is the objective or where there is no witness account and the person may be deceased, requires a very careful consideration of the circumstances, consideration of the person's medical history, a thorough examination of the injuries and then a careful analysis to enable the formulation of an opinion as to the potential likelihood of self-harm.

REFERENCES

1. Favazza A. *Bodies Under Siege. Self-mutilation, Nonsuicidal Self-injury, and Body Modification in Culture and Psychiatry*, 3rd ed. Baltimore: Johns Hopkins University Press; 2011.
2. Gall J, Goldney R, Payne-James JJ. Self-inflicted Injuries and Associated Psychological Profiles. In: Gall J, Payne-James J (eds), *Current Practice in Forensic Medicine*. Oxford: Wiley-Blackwell; 2011, pp. 273–90.
3. Skegg K. Self-harm. *Lancet* 2005; **366**: 1471–83.
4. Klonsky ED. The functions of self-injury in young adults who cut themselves: Clarifying the evidence for affect-regulation. *Psychiatry Res* 2009; **166**: 260–8.
5. American Psychiatric Association. *Diagnostic and Statistical Manual of Mental Disorders*, 4th ed. Washington DC: American Psychiatric Association; 2000.
6. American Psychiatric Association. *Diagnostic and Statistical Manual of Mental Disorders*, 5th ed. Washington DC: American Psychiatric Association; 2013.
7. World Health Organization. Suicide worldwide in 2019, 2019. Available from: https://www.who.int/publications/i/item/9789240026643 (Accessed 31 May 2023).
8. World Health Organization. Suicide, 2021. Available from: https://www.who.int/news-room/fact-sheets/detail/suicide (Accessed 31 May 2023).
9. World Health Organization. Practice manual for establishing and maintaining surveillance systems for suicide attempts and self-harm, 2016. Available from: https://www.who.int/publications/i/item/practice-manual-for-establishing-and-maintaining-surveillance-systems-for-suicide-attempts-and-self-harm (Accessed 31 May 2023).
10. Welch SS. A review of the literature on the epidemiology of parasuicide in the general population. *Psychiatr Serv* 2001; **52**(3): 368–75.
11. Payne-James JJ, Green PG, Green N, et al. Healthcare issues of detainees in police custody in London, UK. *J Forensic Leg Med* 2010; **17**(1): 11–17.
12. Ajdacic-Gross V, Weiss MG, Ring M, et al. Methods of suicide: International suicide patterns derived from the WHO mortality database. *Bull World Health Organ* 2008; **86**: 726–32.
13. Manzoor S, Husain U, Jawaad I, et al. Self-inflicted injuries among young age group in Lahore, Pakistan. *Pakistan J Med Health Sci* 2022; **16**: 389–91.
14. Gall JAM, Boos SC, Payne-James JJ, Culliford EJ. *Forensic Medicine: Colour Guide*. Edinburgh: Churchill Livingstone; 2003.
15. Gall JAM, Payne-James JJ. Deliberate Self-harm Patterns: Patterns of Injury. In: Payne-James JJ, Byard RW (eds), *Encyclopedia of Forensic and Legal Medicine*, 2nd ed. Vol 2. Oxford: Elsevier; 2016: 183–9.

CHAPTER

84

Non-Fatal Strangulation

Jason Payne-James

INTRODUCTION

Strangulation in which death is the outcome (absent of any other factors) is "fatal strangulation" (FS). Survivors of strangulation have experienced "non-fatal strangulation" (NFS).

NFS is widely recognized in intimate-partner violence (IPV) settings. In recent years, it has become recognized that it may well be a precursor to fatal assaults. In a number of jurisdictions, legislation and prosecuting authorities have already recognized this and have introduced protocols to ensure that the more appropriate charging standards (and thus sentences) apply.

Glass and colleagues (1) examined NFS by an intimate partner as a risk factor for major assault and attempted or completed homicide for women. Comparing NFS among complete homicides and attempted homicides (n = 506) and an otherwise abused control group (n = 427) prior NFS was associated with greater than six-fold odds (odds ratio [OR] 6.70, 95 percent confidence interval [CI] 3.91–11.49) of becoming an attempted homicide, and over seven-fold odds (OR 7.48, 95 percent CI 4.53–12.35) of becoming a completed homicide confirming NFS as an important risk factor for homicide of women.

Monckton Smith (2) identified three reasons why NFS should be considered a separate offense in England & Wales. Firstly, Intimate Partner Homicide (IPH) has a strong relationship to domestic abuse and coercive control with "high risk markers" strongly associated with future homicide and serious harm. NFS is one of the strongest markers because people who use strangulation are more dangerous. Secondly, it is a traumatic, and effective way to exert the ultimate control and leave the victim in no doubt that their life has been threatened. NFS should not be considered a spontaneous and angry assault, but it is more likely to be a controled and determined threat. The California District Attorneys' Association published a document on "The Investigation & Prosecution of Strangulation Cases" in 2020 in which is stated (3):

> *As prosecutors, we have a responsibility to do something about it. We cannot continue to hear the words "he choked me" and treat these types of assaults like we would a slap or a punch. The difference between life and death in most strangulation assaults is only a matter of seconds. Prosecutors have a unique opportunity to stop most stranglers before they kill, but we must seize that opportunity in order to prevent homicides.*

Strack and colleagues (4) described 300 strangulation cases reviewed by the San Diego City Attorney's Office. The predominance of cases were by manual strangulation. This is a broad term and sometimes poorly understood. The California District Attorneys Guidance for investigators published information to assist victims (and investigators) in describing the method by which force was applied. That diagram is reproduced (Figure 84.1) but only addresses manual and upper limb techniques. Ligature application is an additional means of causing NFS although less common that manual strangulation.

The importance of a forensic medical assessment by a trained clinician was clear as the study showed that the nature of training of police may have led them to overlook symptoms of strangulation (including pain, difficulty in breathing and difficulty in swallowing) described by victims, but also by not recognizing that absence of symptoms (67%) and (50%) signs did **not** exclude strangulation. The lack of recognition that "absence of evidence" is not "evidence of absence" means that opportunities for higher level (and appropriate) criminal prosecutions were missed.

In England & Wales, NFS is now a separate offense under the Domestic Abuse Act 2021 with a potential prison sentence of 5 years (5). The definitions used are broad – "*Strangulation or suffocation…[if a person] intentionally strangles another person…or… does any other act …that…affects [the other person's] ability to breathe.*" These definitions will thus include the application of a ligature and means of externally occluding air passages.

NFS AND ASSAULT

Although there is much greater awareness of NFS nowadays, its importance and the difficulties in identifying or confirming such an allegation has been recognized for decades.

DOI: 10.1201/9781003138754-87

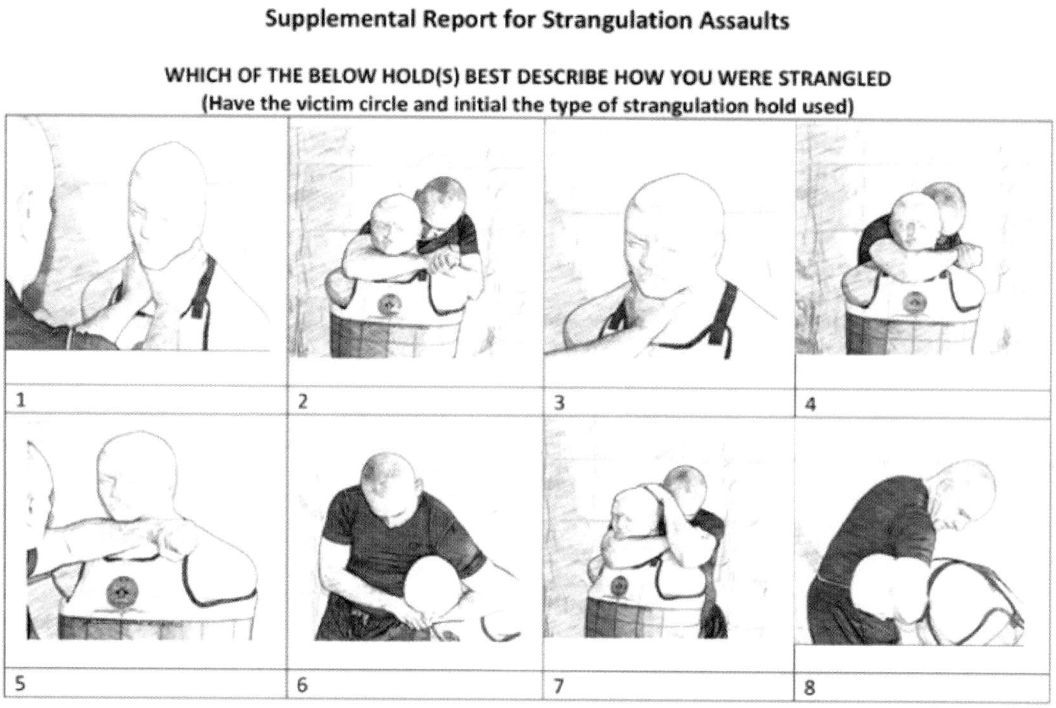

84.1 Supplemental report for strangulation assaults. (From Detective Alex Smith, Los Angeles County Sherrif's Department.)

Iserson wrote in 1984 "*in the ambulatory patient arriving with the complaint of near-strangulation, but with few, if any, signs or symptoms, care must be taken to evaluate the possibility that no strangulation had taken place*" (6).

In the forensic setting and in court the issue of the severity of strangulation may become a key element in the case. This is a difficult area, as fatality may occur after strangulation in the absence of visible injury. As the significance of NFS is better recognized, a number of studies have noted the incidence or presence of evidence of NFS.

McQuown and colleagues (7) reviewed the prevalence of strangulation in patients surviving sexual assault (SA) and domestic violence (DV), identified the presence of lethality risk factors in intimate partner violence, and assessed differences in strangulation between SA and DV populations. Three hundred and fifty-one of the overall study group (n = 1542–23%) reported strangulation in 23 percent during their assaults. The prevalence of strangulation was 38 percent with DV and 12 percent with SA. Most of the intimate partner encounters with strangulation had significant risk for lethality and they found that those patients presenting who were survivors of DV were more likely than SA patients to sustain strangulation.

Zilkens and colleagues (8) reviewed 1163 women attending a Sexual Assault Referral Center (SARC) in Western Australia over a 6-year-period from 2009 to 2015. An increased injury severity in women assaulted by intimate partners was identified and it had been previously noted (9) that women sexually assaulted by their intimate partner, have a very high risk of NFS. Of the 1163 subjects in the 2017 study 15 (1.3%) had physical signs of NFS and a history of NFS but were not referred to hospital. These were classified as moderate injuries. 13 (1%) with severe NFS findings required referral to hospital (including neck/throat pain, pain and/or difficulty in swallowing, vocal changes, shortness of breath, linear neck abrasions, non-petechial bruising neck, subconjunctival hemorrhages).

In the 2016 study, the authors found (n = 1064) 79 (7.4%) alleged NFS during the SA. Of women assaulted by an intimate partner, 22.5 percent gave a history of NFS compared to less than 6 percent of women assaulted by other assailant types. Of all SAs with NFS, intimate partners were the assailant in 58.2 percent of cases (9).

A retrospective review of 158 women in Jordan subject to non-fatal violence from their husbands showed that 19 (8%) sustained bruises or abrasions to their neck, although the authors observed that it was unclear if these occurred in the setting of attempted strangulation or if they were sustained randomly as part of a general assault emphasizing the need to ensure for formal forensic medical assessment (10).

In Taiwan (11), of the 220 adult femicide victims recruited, 114 were killed by intimate partners and 106 were killed by non-intimate partner offenders. The most common site of injuries in the intimate partner group and the non-intimate partner group was the neck and the upper limbs, respectively. The most common causes of death after sharp force injury in both groups was strangulation (27.2 and 22.6% respectively).

Strangulation is well-represented as a cause of violent death in women. Unal and colleagues (12) in a series of autopsy studies from Istanbul established that strangulation represented 8.4 percent of deaths and that the majority were perpetrated by spouse or boyfriend in the home. Data from Portugal (13) showed that 4.8 percent of fatal intimate partner violence against women in Portugal was by manual strangulation.

White and colleagues (14) undertook a retrospective study to identify the prevalence of NFS in patients presenting to the SARC and explore the characteristics of patients reporting NFS compared to those who did not. Of the 2196 adults 9.28 percent were NFS cases. The study found that the prevalence of NFS was 18.9 percent where the alleged perpetrator was a partner or ex-partner. For NFS cases, 96.6 percent (n = 197) of the patients were female and the alleged perpetrator was male in 98 percent (n = 200) of the NFS cases. In 27 percent (n = 55) of the NFS cases, the patient said that the alleged perpetrator had also strangled them on a previous occasion. An attributable injury to NFS affecting the neck or above was seen in 46.6 percent. NFS cases reporting loss of consciousness was 15.7 percent (n = 32), 8.8 percent (n = 18) were incontinent of urine and 2 percent (n = 4) incontinent of feces as a result of the NFS. Over one-third of the patients (36.6%) thought they were going to die during the NFS. Visible NFS injuries are not the norm yet fear of death is not uncommon.

Bugeja and colleagues (15) have identified the overlap between NFS signs and symptoms and those of COVID-19 infection and emphasize that red-flag findings traditionally interpreted by forensic clinicians as potential evidence of NFS, could represent a concurrent or alternative diagnosis of COVID-19 infection, again emphasizing the need for a full forensic medical assessment.

Table 84.1 shows signs and symptoms documented in a series of published studies related to NFS. The Table also shows the variation in how such signs and symptoms are documented and reinforces the need for the development of consensus terminology in describing NFS. Pending this, published studies must clearly outline the definitions or interpretations they are using or referring to.

A comparison of signs and symptoms that published consensus guidance documents from different countries on NFS advise may be observed in Table 84.2. There is variation between the guidance, but with considerable overlap, probably reflecting the range of effects of NFS rather than inadequacies in guidance and reinforces the requirement for detailed history taking and physical examination by forensic physicians and appropriately trained allied health professionals.

Whatever description is used, this must be supplemented by appropriate standard forensic photography including the use of both color scales and rules (i.e. determine nature, size, color or relative color) (q6). Extreme caution should be exercised in making any definitive interpretation in the absence of appropriate medical assessment combined with appropriate quality of photography (17). Certain standards are advised for photographic documentation of injuries in order to minimize the risks of misinterpretation (18).

TABLE 84.1 Examples of studies recording signs and symptoms in NFS cases and noting differences in terminology used

Study		**Strack GB et al. (4) (n = 300)**	**Plattner et al. 2005 (n = 134) (33)**	**Shields LBE et al. 2010 (n = 102) (32)**	**Zilkens RR et al. 2016 (8) (n = 79)**	**McQuown C et al. (7) (n = 351)**	**Spungen et al. 2023 (29) (only identified location of injury) (n = 580)**
Symptoms							
	Neck/throat pain				46.8		
	Neck tender on palpation				34.2		
	Pain and/or difficulty in swallowing				19	3	
	Pain with swallowing					31	
	Difficulty with swallowing			25		27	36.4
	Vocal changes				15.2		36.6
	Hoarseness			21			
	Difficult speaking						
	Shortness of breath		20	14	8.9	47	
	Loss of consciousness		11	38	8.9		29.8
	Difficult breathing			39			43.6
	Felt dizzy/faint		10	13	8.9		
	Blurred vision				2.5		
	Urinary incontinence		3	6	1.3		7.1

(Continued)

TABLE 84.1 (Continued) Examples of studies recording signs and symptoms in NFS cases and noting differences in terminology used

Study		Strack GB et al. (4) (n = 300)	Plattner et al. 2005 (n = 134) (33)	Shields LBE et al. 2010 (n = 102) (32)	Zilkens RR et al. 2016 (8) (n = 79)	McQuown C et al. (7) (n = 351)	Spungen et al. 2023 (29) (only identified location of injury) (n = 580)
	Fecal incontinence			3			
	Involuntary defecation/ urination					8	
	Pain on talking				1.3		
	Loss of memory			Undetermined		10	
	Loss of voice or voice change						21
	Nausea and/or vomiting						
	Persistent throat pain						
At least one symptom					67.1		
No symptoms			5.22				
Signs	Linear abrasions - neck				31.7		
	Abrasions			40			
	Petechiae – site not specified		21	15			
	Petechial bruising – upper neck/facial				21.5		
	Non-petechial bruising - neck				17.7		
	Bruising			54			
	Subconjunctival hemorrhage				3.8		
	Petechiae in conjunctivae				2.5		
	Soft-tissue swelling - neck			18	1.3		
	Injury to neck					57	
	Redness/discoloration			26			
At least one sign					50.6		
No signs			5.22	13			
Physical exam findings present							
	Face						24.3
	Eyes/eyelids						12.6
	Nose						7.8
	Ears						8.1
	Mouth						29.1
	Head						11.6

TABLE 84.1 (Continued) Examples of studies recording signs and symptoms in NFS cases and noting differences in terminology used

Study		Strack GB et al. (4) (n = 300)	Plattner et al. 2005 (n = 134) (33)	Shields LBE et al. 2010 (n = 102) (32)	Zilkens RR et al. 2016 (8) (n = 79)	McQuown C et al. (7) (n = 351)	Spungen et al. 2023 (29) (only identified location of injury) (n = 580)
	Neck						57.2
	Under chin						20.2
	Chest						22.8
	Shoulders						20

Source: Adapted from (31).

TABLE 84.2 NFS guidance from different organizations identifying signs and symptoms which may be identified (where terminology differs, the best equivalent has been used) (31)

Guideline	Sign or Symptom (these may be observed at the time of the assault or subsequently)	Royal College of Pathologists of Australasia: Clinical Forensic Assessment and Management of NFS – January 2018 (30)	Faculty of Forensic & Legal Medicine of the Royal College of Physician: Non-fatal Strangulation: in physical and sexual assault – 2023 (31)	California District Attorneys Association (CDAA) and the Training Institute on Strangulation Prevention Investigation and Prosecution of Strangulation Cases – 2020 (3)
Symptoms				This list is taken from the Table which provides a summary of the locations on the body where investigators may find signs of strangulation and/or suffocation and the Table below provides a summary of what symptoms to look for when trying to identify internal injury symptoms on a victim who has reported being strangled or who is believed to have been strangled.
Direct	Neck pain	Y		Y
	Dysphagia	Y	Y	Y
	Cough	Y	Y	Y
	Hoarseness/hoarse voice/"hot potato voice"	Y	Y	Y
	Loss of consciousness	Y	Y	
	Unable to speak		Y	Y
	Dribbling/drooling		Y	Y
	Vomiting/nausea		Y	Y
Indirect	Urinary incontinence	Y	Y	Y
	Fecal incontinence	Y	Y	Y
	Dizziness/lightheaded	Y	Y	Y

(*Continued*)

TABLE 84.2 (Continued) NFS guidance from different organizations identifying signs and symptoms which may be identified (where terminology differs, the best equivalent has been used) (31)

Guideline	Sign or Symptom (these may be observed at the time of the assault or subsequently)	Royal College of Pathologists of Australasia: Clinical Forensic Assessment and Management of NFS – January 2018 (30)	Faculty of Forensic & Legal Medicine of the Royal College of Physician: Non-fatal Strangulation: in physical and sexual assault – 2023 (31)	California District Attorneys Association (CDAA) and the Training Institute on Strangulation Prevention Investigation and Prosecution of Strangulation Cases – 2020 (3)
	Headache	Y	Y	Y
	Memory loss	Y	Y	Y
	Auditory change	Y	Y	
	Visual change	Y	Y	
	Behavioral change			Y
	Agitation/ combativeness			Y
	Seizure	Y	Y	
Respiratory	Difficulty in breathing	Y	Y	Y
	Shortness of breath	Y	Y	
	Hyperventilation		Y	Y
	Stridor		Y	
	Can't breathe			Y
Signs				
	Subconjunctival hemorrhage	Y		Y
	Petechiae in skin above the level of compression/ application of force	Y	Y	Y
	Petechiae in mucosa above the level of compression/ application of force	Y	Y	
	Swelling of face	Y		
	Swelling of tongue	Y		
	Swelling of lips			Y
	Mouth and tongue mucosal trauma		Y	
	Reddening (hyperemia) to the neck	Y	Y	Y
	Reddening to the face			Y
	Bruises	Y	Y	
	Abrasions (grazes)	Y	Y	
	Scratches (fingernails of assailant or victim)	Y	Y	Y
	Ligature marks	Y		Y

TABLE 84.2 (Continued) NFS guidance from different organizations identifying signs and symptoms which may be identified (where terminology differs, the best equivalent has been used) (31)

Guideline	Sign or Symptom (these may be observed at the time of the assault or subsequently)	Royal College of Pathologists of Australasia: Clinical Forensic Assessment and Management of NFS – January 2018 (30)	Faculty of Forensic & Legal Medicine of the Royal College of Physician: Non-fatal Strangulation: in physical and sexual assault – 2023 (31)	California District Attorneys Association (CDAA) and the Training Institute on Strangulation Prevention Investigation and Prosecution of Strangulation Cases – 2020 (3)
	Vaginal bleeding		Y	
	Epistaxis		Y	Y
	Fractured nose			Y
	Bleeding from external auditory meatus			Y
	Reduced Glasgow Coma Score		Y	
	Subcutaneous (surgical) emphysema		Y	
	Carotid bruits		Y	
	Hyoid bone, thyroid and laryngeal cartilage injury		Y	
Red Flags (necessitating referral to ED or ENT specialist)				
	Reduced Glasgow Coma Score		Y	
	Use of ligature	Y		
	Loss of consciousness	Y	Y	
	Loss of control of bowel or bladder	Y	Y	
	Difficulty or pain in swallowing	Y	Y	
	Voice change	Y	Y	
	Difficulty breathing	Y	Y	
	Neck pain	Y		

COMPLICATIONS OF NFS

Apart from recorded symptoms and visible signs, NFS also has well-documented morbidity. Direct pressure to the neck can cause visible damage to the skin surface but also directly and indirectly to underlying structures which may present immediately or later.

In general, the greater the surface area of the object applying the pressure, the less likelihood of focal external, visible injuries such as bruises at the site of the applied pressure. This may not be the case if other objects, or material (e.g. clothing, watches, bracelets) are present between the neck and the object applying the force.

Bichard and colleagues (19) undertook a systematic review reviewing pathologic, neurologic, cognitive, psychological and behavioral outcomes of NFS in domestic and sexual violence. Pathologic changes included arterial dissection and stroke. Neurologic consequences included loss of consciousness, which may represent mild acquired brain injury, seizures, motor and speech disorders, and paralysis. Psychologic outcomes included

Post-Traumatic Stress Disorder (PTSD), depression, suicidality and dissociation. Cognitive and behavioral sequelae which included memory loss, increased aggression, compliance and lack of help-seeking were described less frequently.

Valera (20) and colleagues have noted women who had experienced strangulation-related alterations in consciousness (AIC) performed more poorly on a test of long-term memory (p<.03) and had higher levels of depression (p<.03) and post-traumatic stress symptomatology (p<.02) than women who had not experienced strangulation-related AIC. Women who had experienced strangulation also performed more poorly on a measure of working memory. Another study has explored frequent and recent NFS and choking during sex and found that recent, frequent exposure to partnered sexual strangulation is associated with different neural activation patterns during verbal and visual working memory tasks compared to controls, suggesting that being choked/strangled during sex may modify the allocation of neural resources at increasing levels of cognitive load (21).

Rarer complications of NFS may (a) result in failure to recognize that the complication is related to NFS, or (b) present late. Examples include prolonged non-cardiogenic pulmonary edema and adult respiratory distress syndrome after attempted strangulation (22) in a patient who presented with cerebral irritability with multiple sites of bruising and petechial hemorrhage consistent with manual strangulation. Hemodynamic stroke has been documented after manual strangulation (23).

Carotid dissection has been described, not initially recognized as being due to strangulation but both of which resulted in devastating neurologic sequelae (24). The authors emphasized that sudden neurologic deficit in young adults without pathologic history should always include a carefully detailed history of previous violence or strangulation, even if the strangulation is only a single attempt, and that NFS should be considered in the differential diagnosis of stroke in at-risk patients.

Figures 84.2–84.6 show examples of features of NFS and summarizes of the victim's account given at the time. Features are hugely variable and visible abnormalities change rapidly over a short period of time which is why early and detailed forensic medical assessment and documentation is essential. The importance of forensic quality images is reflected in some of these images where detail may be unclear and unambiguous due to (for example) poor lighting, focus, positioning or failure to observe basic forensic photographic rules. Often complainants, witnesses (including law enforcement personnel) take images with smart phones or other devices. Sometimes they may be adequate, most often they are not if basic forensic photography principles are not applied.

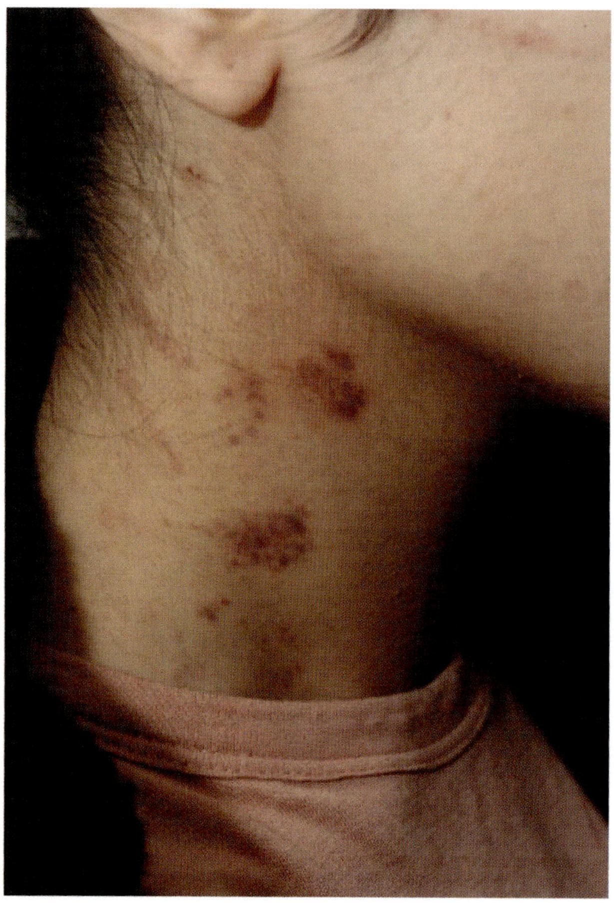

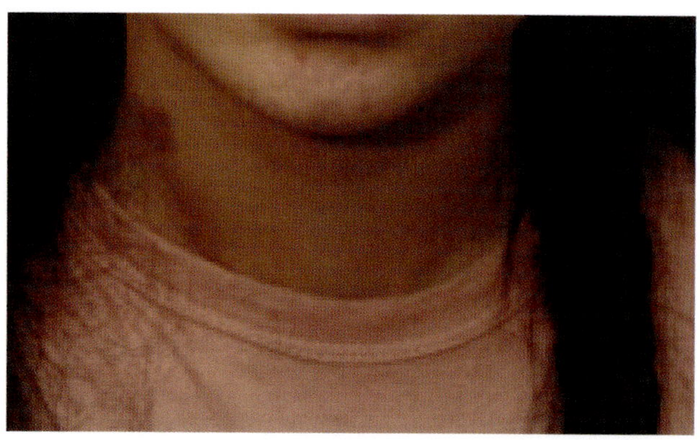

84.2 33-year-old female with bruising to the right side of the neck consistent with finger marks following manual strangulation. She believed it was a one-handed compression.

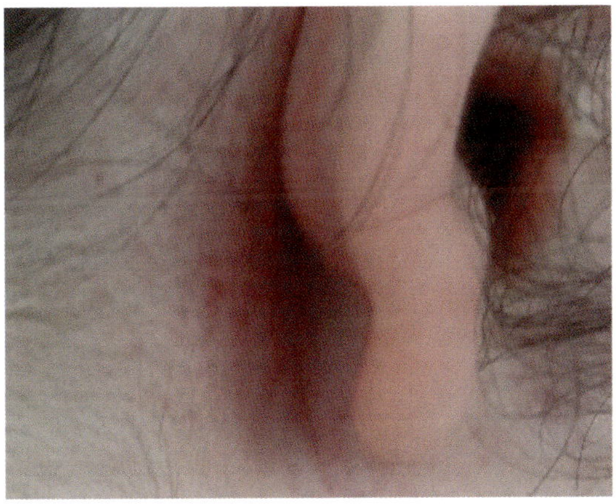

84.3 Image quality is poor but petechial hemorrhage is present on the scalp skin behind the right ear 4 hours after the assault. The victim said she was grabbed around the throat in a choke hold – him behind her and his arm around her neck but couldn't remember if she passed out.

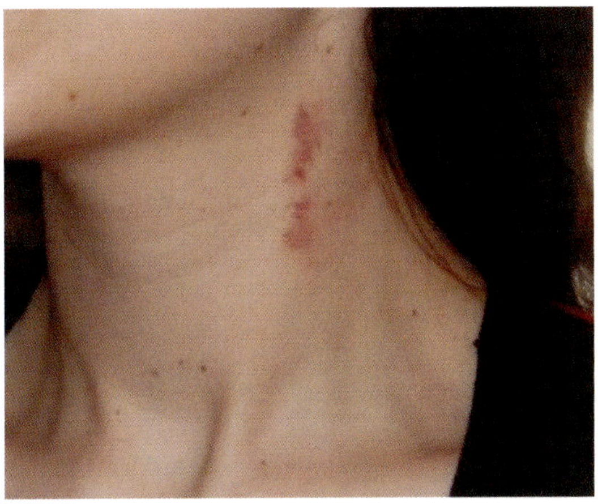

84.4 37-year-old female who was the victim of manual compression to the neck. Image (24 hours after the allegation) shows a mottled linear bruise, with petechial elements running down the anterior border of the left sternocleidomastoid muscle. She recalled "his left hand up to my face/throat and I could feel the palm of his hand on the underside of my chin…his thumb pressing very hard on my windpipe and he continued pressing very hard…within a few seconds, I had lost consciousness." She noted that she had urinated. It may be difficult to differentiate between bruises caused by manual compression and love-bites (hickeys).

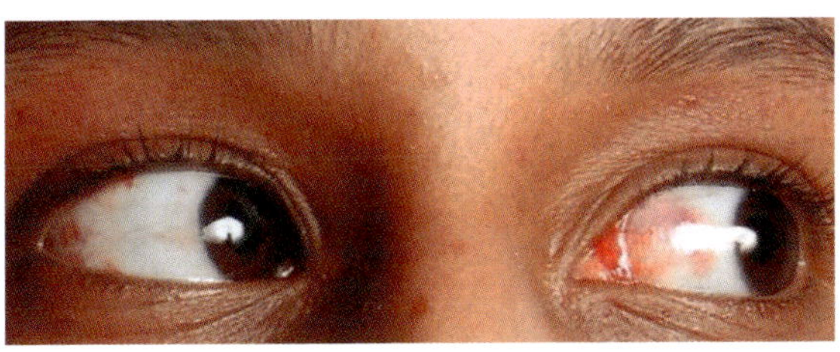

84.5 31-year-old female who describes being strangled (with no specific detail of nature). The image shows left scleral hemorrhage which initially presented as four petechial hemorrhages in the medial aspect of the left eye. After 8 hours (when this image was taken) this had coalesced into the visible hemorrhage seen. In the right eye ~5 petechial hemorrhages are seen. She said that when he strangled her she passed out and didn't know what happened after that. When she recovered, she had difficulty in breathing.

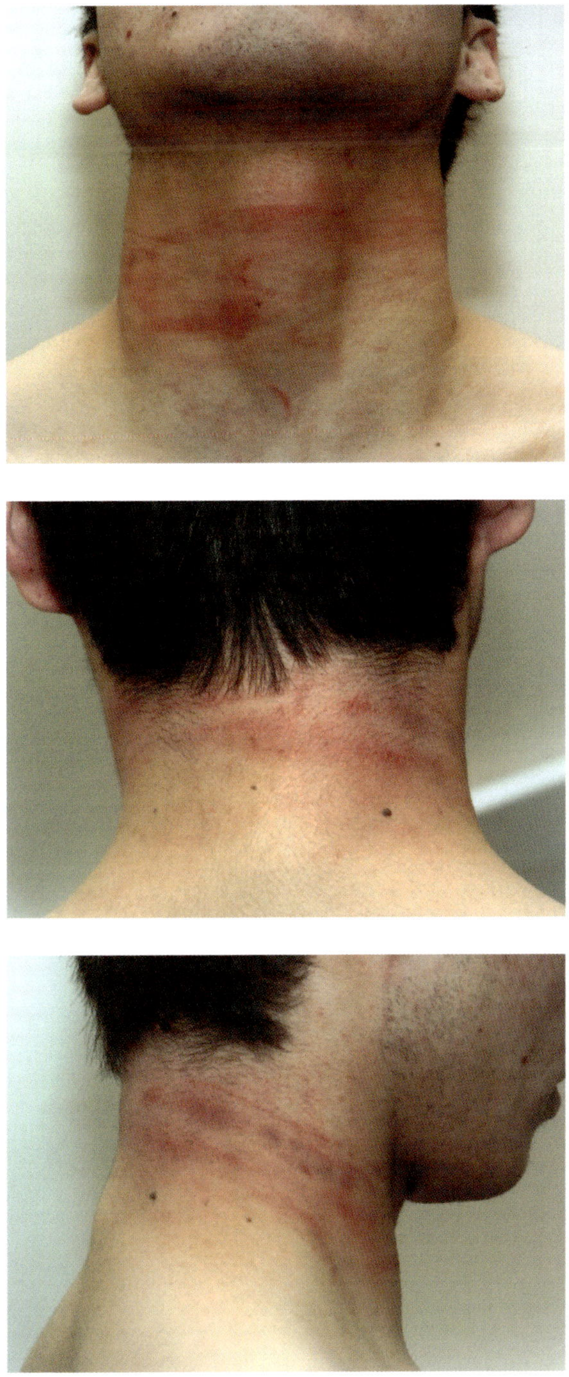

84.6 46-year-old male who was strangled with a ligature which he attempted to resist. The ligature marks, extensive and circumferential, may be seen where a victim has attempted to remove the ligature. Areas of irregular linear abrasion, consistent with fingernail abrasions from the victim's own nails as he tried to remove the ligature while struggling with his assailant. He said suddenly the assailant "*was holding a thin black electric wire around my neck getting tighter and tighter…I put my hands up to the lead to try and get it off my neck….as the wire was getting tighter and tighter …could not speak, the wire was too tight around my throat… was so tight it was impossible for me to get my fingers between the …could not breath[e …next thing I remember is N shaking my shoulder telling me to wake up….my head felt very heavy….was in a lot of pain in my neck….couldn't breathe[e] properly or speak….. realised I had fainted.*"

MANAGEMENT OF NFS

The management of cases of NFS should be divided into two main parts, both of which overlap. From a medical perspective, it is essential to exclude current or potential long-term complications of the neck injury and any accompanying other injury. This requires a full history and detailed examination with any injuries documented in written, body diagram and appropriate image capture (still and moving) form using rules and color scales (e.g. ForensiGraph™). This may be done with an app such as ForensiDoc™ using a smart device. It is recommended that all those undertaking such examinations should have forensic photographic training if their access to professional police or clinical photographers is limited. From a legal perspective, it is essential to ensure that all relevant evidential material is collected at the time. This may include documentation of symptoms and signs, requesting appropriate investigations which may corroborate findings and undertaking evidential biological sampling.

Otorhinolaryngological or emergency department referral may be relevant in those with hoarseness or dysphagia or any of the other red flags shown in Table 84.3, for further investigation. Virtual CT endoscopy may have a role (25).

RADIOLOGIC IMAGING IN NFS

From a clinical perspective, it is important to determine whether further investigations or treatment are required in addition to documentation of injury. Visible evidence of manual strangulation can and should be documented in written, body diagram and photographic/moving image form. In addition to concerns about possible structural anatomic damage, absence of visible injury with the presence of neck symptoms may also require further investigation. In fatal cases, neck dissection as part of the post mortem may provide further information (e.g. bruising to strap muscles) but such information obviously will not be available for NFS. Consideration should therefore be given to the use of other imaging modalities to identify and corroborate accounts where there is no external sign of injury.

CT is the most widely used modality for assessing the extent of neck injuries from blunt trauma to the neck and this can be supplemented by CT angiography. Christe and colleagues (26) reviewed 56 NFS cases comparing clinical forensic medical findings with MRI findings when attempting to determine whether the NFS was life-threatening or non-life-threatening. They concluded that MRI had a role to play in identifying life-threatening NFS when compared with clinical assessment and was better than CT for diagnosing soft-tissue injury.

Gascho and colleagues (27) emphasized that the radiation exposure of CT may not be justified in the NFS setting if symptoms are not severe. MRI may be more appropriate in the forensic or medicolegal setting to document non-externally visible injury. In a study of 195 cases of NFS subject to MRI a variety of abnormalities were found and these are summarized in Table 84.3.

A study which attempted to identify the handedness of an assailant in such cases by assessing trauma-induced

TABLE 84.3 MRI findings in 195 cases of NFS (27,32)

Superficial Tissue Zone	Number of subjects	% of subjects
Intracutaneous hemorrhage	22	11.3
Subcutaneous hemorrhage	56	28.7
Platysma hemorrhage/swelling	29	14.9
Middle Tissue Zone		
Lymph node hemorrhage	36	18.5
Intramuscular hemorrhage	29	14.9
Deep Tissue Zone		13.3
Peri-laryngeal fluid accumulation	26	13.3
Rare Findings		
Odema/hemorrhage of the salivary glands	12	6.2
Parapharyngeal hemorrhage	9	4.6
Glottis/vocal cord edema	7	3.6
Thyroid hemorrhage	2	1
Blood serum level in the glottis space	1	0.5
Fluid accumulation in the vessel/nerve sheath	1	0.5
Laryngeal fracture	1	0.5

edema of the cervical muscles associated with the handedness of the perpetrator, in cases of manual strangulation, concluded that measurement of differences between left and right cervical muscle volume does not allow for a conclusion concerning the probable handedness of the perpetrator (28).

The role of MRI is unclear at present. MRI should be considered when there is an absence of external visible findings in cases of NFS and for a joint radiology and forensic medical opinion to be provided summarizing those findings. Prospective studies in this area will more clearly define when an MRI should be undertaken.

For clinicians, it is of great importance that anyone presenting with visible neck signs (irrespective of a previous history) undergo an appropriately detailed assessment to exclude NFS. Those who are alleging NFS should always be examined by a forensic physician. Those presenting with symptoms (e.g. hoarseness, dysphagia) after assault should similarly be examined. Consideration must also be given to radiologic imaging to corroborate findings. Consideration must also be given if this occurs outside the police or forensic setting to ensure referral to police, safeguarding or domestic violence agencies to ensure that those at risk are properly identified and supported.

CONCLUSION

The significance of NFS is now well-recognized. It is important that all healthcare professionals (e.g. forensic practitioners, SARC practitioners, Emergency Department practitioners, primary care practitioners), law enforcement professionals, safeguarding professionals and any who come into contact with instances of NFS understand (a) its implications, (b) the importance of accurate and unambiguous documentation of the signs and symptoms present, (c) in the absence of visible signs, recognize when further investigations such as MRI be helpful and (d) know to whom to refer to ensure that relevant evidence is captured and interpreted appropriately. Education strategies need to be developed that include public health messages reaching out to potential and actual victims providing safe environments for them to be assessed and their injuries documented and managed appropriately.

REFERENCES

1. Glass N, Laughon K, Campbell J, et al. Non-fatal strangulation is an important risk factor for homicide of women. *J Emerg Med* 2008; **35(3)**: 329–35.
2. Monckton Smith J. Non-Fatal Strangulation. A summary report on data collected from SUTDA Survey, 2020. Available from: https://sutda.org/wp-content/uploads/Non-fatal-strangulation-word.docx (Accessed 31 May 2023).
3. California District Attorneys Association. Investigation and Prosecution of Strangulation Cases, 2020. Available from: https://www.familyjusticecenter.org/wp-content/uploads/2020/09/Strangulation_2020-Online-Version.pdf (Accessed 31 May 2023).
4. Strack GB, McClane GE, Hawley D. A review of 300 attempted strangulation cases Part I: Criminal legal issues. *J Emerg Med* 2001; **21(3)**: 303–9.
5. Legislation.gov.uk. Domestic Violence Act 2021. Strangulation or suffocation: Consequential amendments, 2021. Available from: https://www.legislation.gov.uk/ukpga/2021/17/schedule/2/enacted (Accessed 31 May 2023).
6. Iserson KV. Strangulation: A review of ligature, manual and postural neck compression injuries. *Ann Emerg Med* 1984; **12**: 179–85.
7. McQuown C, Frey J, Steer S, et al. Prevalence of strangulation in survivors of sexual assault and domestic violence. *Am J Emerg Med* 2016; **34**: 1281–5.
8. Zilkens RR, Phillips MA, Kelly MC, et al. Non-fatal strangulation in sexual assault: A study of clinical and assault characteristics highlighting the role of intimate partner violence. *J Forensic Leg Med* 2016; **43**: 1–7.
9. Zilkens RR, Smith DA, Kelly MC, et al. Sexual assault and general body injuries: A detailed cross-sectional Australian study of 1163 women. *Forensic Sci Int* 2017; **279**: 112–20.
10. Abedr-Rahman H, Salameh HO, Salameh RJ, et al. Role of forensic medicine in evaluating non-fatal violence against women by their husbands in Jordan. *J Forensic Leg Med* 2017; **49**: 33–6.
11. Fong W-L, Pan C-H, Lee J, et al. Adult femicide victims in forensic autopsy in Taiwan: A 10 year retrospectivce study. *Forensic Sci Int* 2016; **266**: 80–5.
12. Unal EO, Koc S, Unal V, et al. Violence against women: A series of autopsy studies from Istanbul, Turkey. *J Forensic Leg Med* 2016; **40**: 42–6.
13. Pereira AR, Vieira DN, Magalhaes T. Fatal intimate partner violence against women in Portugal: A forensic medical national study. *J Forensic Leg Med* 2012; **20**: 1099–107.
14. White C, Martin G, Schofield AM, Majeed-Ariss R. 'I thought he was going to kill me': Analysis of 204 case files of adults reporting non-fatal strangulation as part of a sexual assault over a 3 year period. *J Forensic Leg Med* 2021; **29**: 102128.
15. Bugeja L, Rowse J, Cunningham N, Parkin JA. Non-fatal strangulation and COVID-19 common symptoms and signs: Considerations for medical and forensic assessment. *Forensic Sci Med Pathol* 2022; **18(2)**: 165–9.
16. Payne-James JJ, Hawkins C, Bayliss S, Marsh N. Quality of photographic images for injury interpretation: Room for improvement? *Forensic Sci Med Pathol* 2012; **8(4)**: 447–50.
17. Gall J, Payne-James JJ. Injury Interpretation – Common Errors. In: Gall J, Payne-James JJ (eds), *Current Practice in Forensic Medicine*. Chichester: Wiley; 2011.
18. The Faculty of Forensic & Legal Medicine. PICS Working Group Guidelines on Photography, 2020. Available from: https://fflm.ac.uk/resources/publications/pics-working-group-guidelines-on-photography/ (Accessed 31 May 2023).
19. Bichard H, Byrne C, Saville CWN, Coetzer R. The neuropsychological outcomes of non-fatal strangulation in domestic and sexual violence: A systematic review. *Neuropsychol Rehabil* 2022; **32(6)**: 1164–92.
20 Valera EM, Daugherty JC, Scott O, Berenbaum H. Strangulation as an acquired brain injury in intimate-partner violence and its relationship to cognitive and psychological functioning: A preliminary study. *J Head Trauma Rehabil* 2022; **37(1)**: 15–23.
21. Huibregtse ME, Alexander IL, Klemsz LM, et al. Frequent and recent non-fatal strangulation/choking during sex and its association with fMRI activation during working memory tasks. *Front Behav Neurosci* 2022; **16**: 881678.
22. Murphy PG, Jackson E, Kirollos R, et al. Adult respiratory distress syndrome after attempted strangulation. *Br J Anaesth* 1993; **70**: 583–6.
23. Clarot F, Vaz E, Papin F, Proust B. Fatal and non-fatal bilateral delayed carotid artery dissection after manual strangulation. *Forensic Sci Int* 2005; **149**: 143–50.
24. Neto HS, Neville IS, Beer-Furlan A, et al. Hemodynamic stroke caused by strangulation. *Int J Clin Exp Med* 2014; 7(9): 2932–35.
25. Becker M, Leuchter I, Platon A, et al. Imaging of laryngeal trauma. *Eur J Radiol* 2014; **83**: 142–54.
26. Christe A, Oesterhelweg L, Ross S, et al. Can MRI of the neck compete with clinical finding in assessing danger to life for survivors of manual strangulation? A statistical analysis. *Leg Med* 2010; **12**: 228–32.
27. Gascho D, Heimer J, Thali MH, Flach PM. The value of MRI for assessing danger to life in nonfatal strangulation. *Forensic Imaging* 2020; **22**: 200398.
28. Marty M, Dobay A, Ebert L, et al. MRI segmentation of cervical muscle

volumes in survived strangulation: Is there an association between side differences in muscle volume and the handedness of the perpetrator? A retrospective study. *Diagnostics (Basel)* 2022; **12**(3): 743.

29. The Royal College of Pathologists of Australia. Clinical forensic assessment and management of non-fatal strangulation, 2018. Available from: https://www.rcpa.edu.au/getattachment/59a67b0e-ca6b-4686-a81f-14a1a15e70fe/Clinical-Forensic-Assessment-and-Management-of-Non.aspx (Accessed 31 May 2023).
30. Spungen HH, Bryan KM, Sachs CJ, Wheeler MJ. Symptoms and physical exam findings in sexual assault-related non-fatal strangulation. *West J Emerg Med* 2022; **23**(2): 268–75.
31. Faculty of Forensic & Legal Medicine. Non-fatal strangulation: In physical and sexual assault, 2023. Available from: https://fflm.ac.uk/wp-content/uploads/2020/03/Non-fatal-strangulation-in-physical-and-sexual-assault-Dr-C-White-Dr-M-Stark-Dr-B-Butler-March-2020.pdf (Accessed 31 May 2023).
32. Payne-James JJ. Non-fatal Strangulation. In: Gall JA, Payne-James JJ (eds), *Current Practice in Forensic Medicine*, 3rd ed. Chichester: Wiley; 2022.

CHAPTER

85

Crowd Control Techniques: Perspectives on the Type and Use of Weapons by Police Around the World

Matthew McEvoy, Neil Corney and Rohini J. Haar

INTRODUCTION

The use of coercive means by police against public protests remains both commonplace and controversial. Dramatic scenes of bloodied civilians and clouds of tear gas provoke outrage among many, and the growth of citizen journalism, social media and mobile technology means that such scenes frequently reach a wide audience, often in real time. Between 2019 and 2023, small protests, demonstrations and mass protest movements were met with state-sanctioned police violence and excessive use of force in many countries, including Belarus, Bolivia, Chile, Colombia, France, Hong Kong, India, Iran, Lebanon, Nigeria, occupied State of Palestine, Peru, Sri Lanka, Sudan and Thailand, among others (1,2). Black Lives Matters protests shook the United States (US) and spread around the world, frequently facing the kind of police violence and repression that spurred the protests in the first place (3).

During 2020, there were large protests against government responses to the COVID-19 pandemic in at least 26 countries, with all regions affected (4).[i] The economic fallout from the pandemic was predicted to exacerbate existing political instability and poverty (5), and this has been borne out, for example in 2022, with widespread protests against economic hardship in Sri Lanka (6). The illegal invasion of Ukraine by Russia on February 24, 2022 resulted in unprecedented economic impacts, including disruption to energy supply and financial instability. Shrinking economies and restricted access to credit will lead to cuts to social services and increases in taxes, impacting on the standard of living in all affected countries. In addition, the level of inequality between rich and poor is likely to increase even further. The growing climate crisis and more frequent and severe natural disasters will lead to resource scarcity, population movements and further political unrest. The combination of these major factors is likely to lead to increased protests and protest movements, and violent responses from repressive state authorities, in all regions (2). These trends, in turn, may see a range of weapons, including less lethal weapons, used with ever greater frequency and in larger quantities (7).

Set against this backdrop, it is crucial that medical professionals are familiar with those weapons most frequently used, the manner in which they are being used, and the associated health risks and treatment options. This chapter focuses on "less lethal weapons" also, known as "crowd control weapons" and these terms are used interchangeably in this chapter. These are weapons which, in the course of expected or reasonably foreseen use, carry a lower risk of causing death or serious injury than firearms (8). While less lethal weapons are being used with greater frequency to police assemblies, it is important to note that in a significant number of countries, firearms loaded with conventional bullets or other ammunition likely to cause life-threatening injuries are still widely used in the context of public gatherings. For example, in April 2022, Sri Lankan security forces reportedly used live ammunition during protests against the government, killing at least two people (6). Similarly, lethal weapons are frequently used in conjunction with less lethal ones to devastating effect, as exemplified by the Myanmar security forces' deadly reaction to anti-coup protests in the first quarter of 2021 when tear gas, rubber bullets and live ammunition were fired into crowds at the same time.

In Myanmar, Sri Lanka and many other places, unaccountable and excessive use of force by security forces, including use of less lethal weapons, is resulting in large numbers of deaths and serious injuries. Such injuries include thousands of instances of life-changing disfigurement and disability every year worldwide. The less lethal weapons industry continues to evolve apace and new technologies are being developed and marketed for

[i] For a mapping of incidents of excessive force under COVID-19 restrictions see https://omegaresearchfoundation.org/covid.php.

DOI: 10.1201/9781003138754-88

law enforcement use. Notwithstanding this, the types of weapons most frequently used to police public gatherings, and whose use continues to cause serious injuries and death, have essentially remained technologically unchanged and been in use for decades, and evidence suggests their use is increasing. This chapter will explore recent trends in the use of striking weapons, kinetic impact projectiles, chemical irritants and stun grenades.

This chapter does not discuss the legal constraints on the use of force in great detail. Nevertheless, it is important that forensic professionals are aware that there are international human rights instruments and standards by which law enforcement agencies must abide. Demonstrations are protected as fundamental human rights within the rights to freedom of expression and of peaceful assembly and of association. These rights are enshrined most clearly in the Universal Declaration of Human Rights and the International Covenant on Civil and Political Rights (ratified by more than 173 states). The national laws of nearly every country include some language on protection of demonstrations, marches, protests and other assemblies. The protections are not absolute–threats to public safety are commonly noted as reasons to restrict these rights (e.g. by dispersing a demonstration). Permit and notification requirements, rules on timings, location, or disruptions also frequently limit the full exercise of the right. Police responses to demonstrations which are frequently politicized can be affected by identity bias (based on the personal or group identities, race, gender, profession or class of the demonstrators) or viewpoint bias (based on the opinion and/or standpoints of demonstrators). The UN *Code of Conduct for Law Enforcement Officials* (9) and the *Basic Principles on the Use of Force and Firearms by Law Enforcement Officials* (10) set out key rules and principles for public security officials. The UN *Human Rights Guidance on Less Lethal Weapons in Law Enforcement* (8) also presents more detailed guidance on the use of some of the weapons discussed in this chapter.

Forensic professionals should also be aware that the link between excessive force and torture and other cruel, inhuman or degrading treatment or punishment (hereinafter, "torture and other ill-treatment") is well established, even when the act is perpetrated outside of custodial settings. The European Court of Human Rights has consistently held that "recourse to physical force which has not been made strictly necessary by a person's own conduct is in principle an infringement of the [prohibition of torture and other ill-treatment]", including in the context of a public assembly (11). When a participant in a public assembly resorts to violence, they may forfeit their right to the freedom of peaceful assembly, but they retain their rights to be free from torture and other ill-treatment, and to life, for all human rights violations (12). As discussed below, less lethal weapons are frequently used by law enforcement officials to violate these rights, whether it be unnecessarily, to discriminate against or punish those not engaged in violence, or disproportionately against those who are.

It is not the responsibility of forensic or healthcare professionals to determine whether a particular incident amounts to torture and other cruel, inhuman or degrading treatment or punishment, or was unlawful. However, accurate forensic evidence can play a vital role in helping legal professionals to determine whether the use of force was lawful and if the elements of the crime of torture are present. Effective documentation of the use of weapons, including through implementation of the Istanbul (13)[ii] and Minnesota (14) Protocols, is key to achieving accountability for individual cases of abusive use of force. On a more systemic level, where medical evidence corroborates multiple allegations of problematic practices, or weapons causing a disproportionate amount of harm, this can help to effect change in policy and practice by law enforcement officials. An updated report by PHR, INCLO and Omega, *Lethal in Disguise*, examines the use and abuse of less lethal weapons and suggests that to 1) protect health and 2) ensure meaningful human rights protections, there must be additional controls across design, development, and procurement of less lethal weapons, as well as on the range of processes involved: training, deployment, post-deployment procedures and accountability (15).

Before discussing the types of less lethal weapons most frequently used to police public assemblies, we will first take a step back and consider several contextual interlinked issues which frequently result in inappropriate or unsafe weapons, equipment and tactics being deployed by law enforcement officials.

CONTEXTUAL ISSUES

While the use of force by law enforcement officials is governed by international law and policing norms and standards, the weapons and equipment they utilize are not. There are no international technical, manufacturing, testing, performance or trade standards for less lethal weapons (16). This absence has resulted in a very wide range of products being marketed directly to law enforcement, some of which are inherently unsuitable and should be prohibited (e.g. spiked batons and shields or weighted restraints), and others with widely varying performance characteristics, resulting in unacceptable risk of injury (e.g. multiple impact projectiles, or high concentration chemical irritant sprays). While no international standards exist, some states have national standards for some weapons, for example, the UK has a technical standard for personal chemical irritant spray (17) and the US National Institute of Justice maintains a performance standard for handcuffs and standards for certification (18,19). The absence of international standards, administered by globally recognized standards authorities, continues to result in law enforcement agencies often having to rely on manufacturer data and company marketing alone.

Secondly, selection and testing of less lethal weapons prior to deployment can reduce the risk of subsequent harms. However, such processes are often inadequate or absent in states with fewer policing resources, resulting in inappropriate or dangerous weapons being deployed.

[ii] Please note that the updated version of the Istanbul Protocol was published in 2022.

The UN Guidance clearly establishes states' responsibility to take a precautionary approach and conduct testing, ideally by an independent body, of all less lethal weapons and law enforcement equipment prior to its procurement and the equipping of law enforcement officials (8). Testing should evaluate the effects of all reasonably likely or expected uses of the weapons, and particular consideration should be given to assess the potential effects on persons who may be especially at risk, for example children, the elderly, pregnant persons and the medically unwell. Ongoing monitoring of injuries caused by less lethal weapons is crucial in providing data to feed back into the testing and selection process, as well as to inform changes in policy, procedure and guidelines for use.

Thirdly, the trade in law enforcement equipment is poorly regulated by states, resulting in inappropriate goods being transferred to abusive regimes, where they may be used to commit human rights abuses. Many states do not control the trade (import and export) of law enforcement equipment, beyond those classified as "conventional arms", such as small arms, ammunition and certain chemical irritants (20). This often excludes such goods as pepper and tear-gas sprays, kinetic impact projectile munitions, electric shock weapons, water cannon, batons and restraints, as well as other weapons used in policing public assemblies. There have, however, been important advances made in this area including at EU and most recently internationally level (21). Such trade control standards are a vital component in controlling the trade (and use) of less lethal weapons.

A fourth key cause underlying violent policing of protests is the militarization of public security that has occurred in response to perceived "new threats", particularly terrorism and drug trafficking (22). Militarization of public security encompasses both military personnel carrying out law enforcement duties, and the use of military tactics and equipment by law enforcement officials. The inherent differences between the military and law enforcement paradigms mean that this blurring of roles, tactics and equipment can be problematic. Where soldiers are primarily trained for combat and to kill enemy combatants, law enforcement officials must instead fulfill their duty "by serving the[ir own] community and by protecting all persons against illegal acts, consistent with the high degree of responsibility required by their profession" (9).

The crossover of military equipment to law enforcement is not a new, or small-scale, phenomenon. Perhaps the most high-profile and sustained example of this transfer is the US Department of Defense's *1033 Program*, which facilitates the acquisition of military equipment by law enforcement agencies throughout the US. Under this program, since 1997, over 8000 law enforcement agencies have acquired more than $7.2 billion of military equipment, including armored vehicles, assault rifles, ammunition, and night-vision goggles and equipment which has no legitimate domestic law enforcement function, for example, bayonets (23). Figure 85.1 is illustrative of the type of transformation many police forces have undergone, with traditional uniforms being replaced by military-style fatigues, helmets and combat boots, and assault rifles being carried routinely rather than exceptionally.

85.1 Law enforcement officials attired in military-style uniforms with armored vehicles. (Source: Jamelle Bouie, "swat team, fully assembled". August 13, 2014. Ferguson, Missouri. [CC BY 2.0].)

Not all military equipment is inherently unsuitable for law enforcement. For example, specialist equipment such as stun grenades, high-powered firearms, and armored vehicles may be appropriate in exceptional circumstances, such as certain anti-terrorist operations. It does become problematic, however, when such equipment is deployed in other settings, such as public protests, where heavy displays of force may be disproportionate, can elevate tensions (8) and can lead to unnecessary injuries or loss of life.

Finally, police training on managing crowds and using crowd control weapons is often inadequate and focuses on protecting property, rather than on their fundamental human rights obligations and strict limits on use of force. While police may receive extensive training and re-training on firearms, they frequently receive less than one or two hours of total training on the use of a range of crowd control weapons from pepper spray to projectiles. As new weapons are added to police arsenals, each with different uses, firing ranges, safety profiles and potential injuries, there is rarely adequate additional training, or refresher training, and a lack of minimum proficiency standards. Moreover, especially in states healing from a colonial past, police are often trained based on mentalities, laws and policies entrenched in the era of Empire and colonization, rather than with a mission to support the communities they live in and serve.

Having considered some of the reasons participants in public assemblies are frequently exposed to unnecessary or disproportionate force, it is now time to examine how such force is meted out.

LESS LETHAL WEAPONS

Kinetic impact/striking weapons

Hand-held kinetic impact weapons, also known as striking weapons, include a range of specially manufactured batons and truncheons. Sticks and clubs are also widely used by law enforcement, and the use of short and long whips (sjamboks) (Figure 85.2) in some countries has also been documented.

Apart from the hands or feet, batons are the oldest type of weapon in use by law enforcement. They are ubiquitous worldwide due to their low cost. The visual message from an officer wielding a baton is universally understood, it is a sign of authority and indicates that pain will result if they strike.

Specially manufactured weapons can be made of rubber, wood, plastic or metal. They vary in width and length, from 20 cm for close use, up to 2 m for greater stand-off distance. Batons can be straight, extendable/expandable (collapsing to a short length for ease of carrying or concealment), or side-handled (commonly referred to as a tonfa). Longer batons are able to deliver greater impact energy, increasing the risk of serious injury. Use of over-arm strikes or from an elevated position, such as from a police horse, or standing on a police vehicle, increases the risk of fatal head injuries caused by baton strikes.

Other hand-held kinetic impact weapons may be made of natural materials, such as the bamboo cane "lathi" in India, or the rattan cane used in various Asian jurisdictions.

Batons and striking weapons can be used offensively or defensively. They are used by law enforcement officials to strike a subject to cause physical pain or to threaten physical pain in order to force them to comply or to deter them from an action. Such weapons should only ever be used on the larger muscle groups on the limbs; even then, striking weapons can cause severe bruising, lacerations and broken bones, especially if the joints are targeted or hit. They can also be used defensively by law enforcement officials as a blocking instrument, for instance, to protect themselves from blows from assailants. The use of a baton, and the force inflicted, is greatly dependent on the individual user, and is dependent on their height, strength, technique (e.g. side or over-arm strikes), and their training and oversight.

Batons are also used as a tool of restraint, including to hold limbs. Dangerous and potentially lethal "neck holds" or "carotid holds" using batons have been used by law enforcement officials to detain and subdue individuals. At least one EU-based company is known to have trained law enforcement officials in countries including Togo, Georgia and India in such neck restraints using

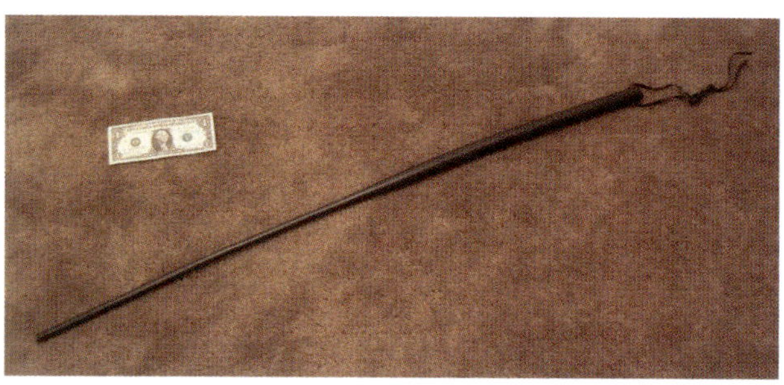

85.2 Plastic sjambok "A 90 cm (3 ft) plastic sjambok used by South African Police". (December 30, 2005. Ontario, Canada. "CC BY-SA 3.0. Source: OwenX".)

batons (24). The UN Guidance states that neck holds should "not be employed, as they present an especially high risk of death or serious injury as a result of compression of large blood vessels or the airway" (8).

The United Nations *Resource Book on the Use of Force and Firearms in Law Enforcement* (hereafter UN *Resource Book*) specifies that:

> "*Given the range of functions that a baton can have training in baton use is an essential part of a law enforcement agency's effort to develop capacity to differentiate the use of force depending on the law enforcement objective and the threat encountered. A baton is not expected to be lethal in the case of proper use.*" (25)

However, in accordance with international human rights law and policing standards on minimum use of force, any more than one single strike from a baton may amount to excessive use of force, which is always unlawful. Officers should re-assess the need for any further strikes after each strike, to make sure additional force is strictly necessary and proportional. Nonetheless, media images and footage of protests often show law enforcement officials repeatedly striking and beating people, often individuals who are on the ground, or chasing people while repeatedly striking them, including on the head.

Health concerns

Batons and other such weapons can cause serious injury and death. The most severe injuries often result from strikes to the head and face which can result in traumatic brain injuries (TBIs) (from skull fractures or internal bleeding), or trauma to the face resulting in deformities, facial fractures, eye trauma or cranial nerve trauma. Other body systems can also be impacted by the blunt trauma, such as chest injuries (rib fractures, punctured lungs, and cardiac injuries), abdominal injuries (such as internal bleeding, bruising or tears), musculoskeletal injuries (such as spinal cord injuries, nerve injuries and bleeding), not to mention the psychological toll of beatings. While bruising and contusions are common after baton use, all lesions must be carefully examined to ensure that deeper injuries are not present. The risks to health are increased when batons are used to strike the same individual multiple times or when the target is not able to shield themselves or maintain a defensive position (e.g. while handcuffed). If they are required, batons should only ever be used on the larger muscle groups on the limbs; even then, striking weapons can cause severe bruising, lacerations and broken bones, and permanent injuries, especially if the joints are targeted. Strikes should also be controled and carefully aimed in order not to impact sensitive body parts, including face, joints and the kidney area. Blows to the head and face should be prohibited; a single strike to the head can result in concussion, deformities, traumatic head injury or death.

In caring for those who have been struck by kinetic impact weapons, the fundamentals of trauma care are the best approach. Clinicians should manage obvious physical trauma as appropriate for the organ system affected. For minor injuries such as ecchymosis, applying cold compresses and mild analgesics such as acetaminophen may be helpful. For injuries to the head, face and other vulnerable or delicate body parts such as the neck, genitalia or hands, immediate medical attention is recommended. Clinicians should evaluate for internal bleeding, especially for any pain that feels different from a temporary bruise, or for symptoms such as blood in the urine, swelling, severe pain or difficulty moving or breathing.

Global context

In a major study documenting the misuse of striking weapons and batons worldwide, published in September 2021, Amnesty International, with assistance from Omega Research Foundation, verified over 188 videos of incidents of the misuse of striking weapons including police batons, lathis (long sticks), sjamboks (rigid whips) and improvised weapons in 35 countries, covering all regions of the globe. This highlighted examples of striking weapons, including police batons frequently used for torture and other ill-treatment, including excessive use of force, both in places of detention and outside of custodial settings including violent crackdowns on mass protests in countries as diverse as Belarus, Colombia, France, India and Myanmar (26). The following examples illustrate the widespread and contemporary nature of such abusive practices.

In Nigeria, protests began across the country on October 8, 2020, with calls for the authorities to disband and abolish the Special Anti-Robbery Squad (SARS), a police unit that had been widely reported to have been involved in abusive use of force. Human rights monitors and NGOs reported widespread excessive use of force against peaceful protestors, including severe beatings inflicted by officers using both police batons and sticks, often with multiple officers beating an individual on the ground (27).

In Belarus, Amnesty International reported numerous accounts of torture and other ill-treatment following post-election protests in August 2020, and many of these cases involved the misuse of batons or truncheons by security forces. Katsyaryna Novikava told Amnesty International that she had been detained for 34 hours at the Center for Isolation of Offenders, where she saw that the entire yard of the facility was filled with arrested men who had been forced to lie down in the dirt. Inside the center, dozens of men were told to strip naked and get down on all fours while officers kicked and beat them with truncheons (28). The OSCE also reported the widespread and systematic use of beatings with police batons for punishment of journalists, protestors and civilians (29).

In the US, during the 2020 nationwide Black Lives Matter and anti-police violence protests, human rights monitors reported the widespread abusive use of batons to beat protestors. Such violence included incidents where police, standing above a crowd on police vehicles, used batons to beat people's heads. This violence often occurred when no threat existed or when protestors were detained in a police cordon or "kettle" and unable to escape (30).

In Iran, widespread protest erupted in September following the death of Mahsa Amini aged 22, who was arrested for wearing an improper hijab. She was severely beaten by religious morality police and died later in hospital, although the Iranian coroners' report stated it was not a result of the beating (31). The violent security force responses to the protests included widespread use of beatings, for example, including the death of 16-year-old Nika Shakarami, whose skull was reportedly severely damaged with injuries consistent with being struck repeatedly on the head (32).

Whips have also been used in certain states, such as by the Central Cossack Battalion in Moscow, who attacked and whipped peaceful protestors in May 2018 (33). The Council of Europe's Committee for the Prevention of Torture reported that journalists were also attacked with whips at the same event (34). Long plastic or animal hide whips (sjamboks), as shown in Figure 85.2, have been used during the policing of COVID-19 restrictions in South Africa, where reporters filmed police assaulting civilians with sjamboks (35), and in Uganda, where police were photographed using whips to "clear" market vendors (36).

CHEMICAL IRRITANTS

A typical image in media reports of the policing of assemblies or protests shows streets filled with clouds of white or off-white/yellow smoke, or police using aerosol sprays against individuals or crowds. These are two examples of chemical irritants, one of the most widely used less lethal weapons in law enforcement worldwide, with almost every country using some form of chemical irritant weapon.

Chemical irritants are highly potent substances that produce sensory irritation and pain in the eyes, skin and upper respiratory tract. These properties are utilized to deter individuals from violence, disperse crowds or otherwise gain compliance with police orders through the infliction of pain. The chemicals most commonly used are the irritant agents CN or CS – often called tear gas (although the pure chemical substances are solids at operational temperatures) – and the inflammatory agents OC/Pepper or PAVA – often called pepper spray. A number of other irritant agents, such as CR, are marketed and held by states, but are not commonly encountered (37).

They are delivered via a wide range of methods and means. These include handheld aerosol sprays, weapon fired spray, shoulder-worn and backpack sprayers, handheld or vehicle mounted smoke generators or foggers, hand-thrown grenades, weapon-launched projectiles and grenades, as well as via water cannon and more recently via unmanned air or ground vehicles. Handheld aerosol sprays range in size from 25 mL to 500 mL, sometimes more, while shoulder-worn and backpack-style sprayers and smoke generators generally have a much larger capacity and can cover a wider area often in a very short time. Hand-thrown and weapon-launched projectiles/grenades and water cannons can be used from greater ranges and can be used to contaminate a wide area.

A particular issue with the majority of chemical irritant sprayers/foggers is that they have no dose control or cut-off trigger mechanism to control the amount dispersed. Under international laws of law enforcement, only the minimum amount of force should be used (and only when strictly necessary and proportionate to the threat) and force must cease when the threat from the individual ceases. In operational practice, law enforcement officials are expected to use the minimum "effective dose", that is, one very short burst of spray, and then re-assess the threat. However, sprays are frequently continually discharged at individuals or groups, dispersing large quantities of chemical irritant of unknown concentration. Design changes to sprayer equipment, to introduce "dosing" triggers that release only small quantities with each trigger pull, might help overcome this issue but are not generally in use at the time of this writing.

A range of factors can determine their effects including: the type of chemical agent and means of delivery used, the location and environmental conditions in which they are used (heat, humidity) and the concentration and quantity of irritant. The amount of active irritant agent in products available to law enforcement officials varies widely, and manufacturers will often offer a range of percentages for any given product or offer custom fills for customers. This results in those using, affected or treating the affected not knowing what amount of chemical irritant has been delivered, or can lead to speculation and confusion as to the type of irritant being used, and may also result in unusual medical effects being encountered. For example, PepperBall, a commonly used compressed gas launcher system, which delivers chemical irritant via 0.68 caliber plastic encapsulated projectiles, advertises a range of projectiles with a wide range of percentage of irritant: "VXR LIVE-X a more concentrated formula, containing approximately 10× the PAVA of the VXR LIVE projectile" (38).

Small handheld sprays are often deployed by law enforcement officials, intended to be used to temporarily deter or disorientate individuals at very close range (0–3 m). Chemical irritants are indiscriminate in nature, and the UN Special Rapporteur on the Rights to Freedom of Peaceful Assembly and of Association has warned that they fail to differentiate "between demonstrators and non-demonstrators, healthy people and people with health conditions" (39). Even the use of small, handheld sprays risks affecting innocent bystanders in a public gathering. Meanwhile, the UN has stressed that means of delivery for wider areas should only be used "for dispersing groups that present an immediate and direct threat and when conventional methods of policing have been tried and have failed or are unlikely to succeed" (25).

Health concerns

Commonly known as "tear gas" and "pepper spray", chemical irritants are most frequently linked to sudden onset and severe burning sensations and tearing in the eyes, pain on exposed skin, vomiting, coughing and restricted breathing (40). When a person comes into contact with a chemical irritant, it mixes with moisture on the skin, eyes and respiratory and oral tracts, and activates the TRPA1 and TRPV1 pain receptors located in the peripheral nervous system. Within seconds, exposed skin will feel a painful burning sensation, the eyes will be painful and tear up, resulting in blepharospasm (eyelid spasm characterized by frequently blinking) and difficulty keeping the eyes open. As the chemical is breathed in, it will irritate the oral and lung linings, causing pain, coughing and sensations of respiratory distress. Those affected frequently feel anxiety and panic.

Certain groups particularly at risk from the effects of chemical irritants, and for whom it may be life-threatening, include older people, children, people who are pregnant or people with respiratory problems. According to the American Academy of Pediatrics, "Children are uniquely vulnerable to physiological effects of chemical agents. A child's smaller size, more frequent number of breaths per minute and limited cardiovascular stress response compared to adults magnifies the harm of agents such as tear gas." (41).

The half-life of most chemical irritants is short and the symptoms are transient, lasting less than an hour after exposure ends for most people, although for some people the effects can be more severe, long lasting and cause ongoing health impacts (42). However, in settings of excessive use such as the use of chemical irritants in enclosed spaces (where the irritant cannot disperse) or prolonged exposure (when people cannot escape), the dose-exposure will increase, resulting in exacerbated harm (43). In some cases, these higher doses have been known to cause significant lung injury, gastrointestinal distress, corneal burns and even death. The European Court of Human Rights has recognized that large doses of pepper spray "may cause necrosis of tissue in the respiratory or digestive tract, pulmonary edema or internal hemorrhaging" (44). In addition, repeated exposure to CS agent can result in hypersensitivity reactions, with allergic responses worsening with each exposure.

Chemical irritant projectiles and grenades, launched from a variety of weapons, can cause significant trauma, acting as "bullets" or explosive grenades (45,46). When they explode in close proximity to an individual, there are risks of burns, shrapnel and explosive trauma. Because grenades are large, and dense, when the canister itself strikes an individual, it can cause trauma ranging from bruising to facial and limb fractures to internal bleeding to brain injury and death. Despite being widely available and used for nearly a century, there are few studies establishing the safety of chemical irritants, and none on newer compositions. Almost all reports and studies on chemical irritants note the need for more research, as well as the lack of statistically significant prospective clinical studies on the morbidity and mortality of the relevant weapon.

The use of chemical irritants during the COVID-19 pandemic has increased the risk of adverse medical effects due to COVID-19's effect on breathing and the lungs, as well as the risk of infection through induced coughing or sneezing, particularly for those in detention (47). In 2020, the American Thoracic Society called for a moratorium on the use of tear gas and other chemical agents deployed by law enforcement against protestors participating in demonstrations, citing "the lack of crucial research, the escalation of tear gas use by law enforcement, and the likelihood of compromising lung health and promoting the spread of COVID-19" (48). In the US, nearly 1300 medical professionals stated their opposition to the use of chemical irritants, which "could increase the risk of COVID-19 by making the respiratory tract more susceptible to infection, exacerbating existing inflammation, and inducing coughing" (49).

An area of increasing importance, but where no clinical studies have yet been published, is the growing awareness of the effects of chemical irritants on different human bodies and reproductive health. Reports have suggested that there may be a relationship between use of tear gas and miscarriage (1). Following the widespread use of large quantities of chemical irritants during Black Lives Matter and other protests in the US in summer 2020, media reports emerged of physiological effects for people who menstruate (50–52). While stress and other factors may play a role, the lack of research limits the understanding of these phenomenons.

Most symptoms of chemical irritant exposure should resolve spontaneously within an hour of the end of exposure. There is modest evidence to suggest that tear gas (CS) exposure is best treated with fresh air or copious amounts of water irrigation but pepper spray might be best treated with soap and water (as it is an oil-soluble compound). While there are anecdotal reports of a variety of substances helping with symptoms, there is little evidence to support their use. Nevertheless, antacids such as Maalox are commonly used around the world for symptomatic relief. Exposed individuals should attempt to remove contaminated clothing and those with contact lenses should remove them immediately. Individuals with severe respiratory symptoms, prolonged palpitations, blisters/burns or with any symptoms lasting longer than an hour should seek medical attention. Anyone with blunt trauma from the canister, especially to the head or face, should also seek immediate medical attention.

Global context

International human rights bodies have created strict standards concerning the use of chemical irritants. The UN Guidance states that chemical irritants, including those delivered via handheld sprays, should only be used when there is an imminent threat of injury, and warns against repeated or prolonged exposure to irritants (8). The UN *Resource Book* also recommends against chemical irritants being used against the same people several times in a short time period, or in confined spaces (25).

National policing, medical and practitioner bodies should offer advice to medical and other professionals who may have to treat or come into contact with those affected by chemical irritants. International policing standards require law enforcement officials to "ensure that assistance and medical aid are rendered to any injured or affected persons at the earliest possible moment" (10). It is therefore vital that full details of any chemical irritants used are known and published (53).

In a major study documenting the misuse of tear gas worldwide, published in June 2020 (updated in February 2021), Amnesty International with assistance from Omega Research Foundation verified over 500 videos of more than 100 events in some 31 countries and territories where tear gas has been misused (54). Incidents included cases of security forces firing projectiles and grenades into cars, inside a school bus and in hospitals, residential buildings, metro stations and shopping centers, as well as directly at individuals, and against others in confined spaces, as well as excessive quantities being fired.

The use of grenades that explode to disperse the chemical irritant has resulted in serious injuries. For example, in France the GLI-F4 exploding tear gas grenade containing TNT was eventually withdrawn in early 2020 following numerous serious injuries, where individuals had their hands blown off, or were injured by shrapnel from the exploding grenade (55). The GLI-F4 was replaced with the GM2L, which used a pyrotechnic charge rather than TNT to explode and disperse irritant and was stated to be a safer alternative. However, its use has continued to result in serious injuries, including, in December 2020, a participant at an assembly in Paris who had his fingers blown off when he touched the grenade as it exploded (56).

Direct firing of grenades at individuals can result in serious injuries or death. Such launched projectiles or grenades should never be fired directly at persons, they are designed to be launched into open areas to land on the ground and disperse chemical irritant. However, their use against individuals continues to be reported, including, for example, the death of Haykel Rachdi in Tunisia, who died of his injuries after reportedly "being struck on the head by a police tear gas canister" (57). Particularly horrific injuries and deaths were reported in Iraq in 2019, when "anti-riot police" and other security forces in Baghdad fired grenades, referred to by local people as "smokers", directly at individuals. The 40 mm military grade, heavy, Iranian- and Serbian-manufactured grenades caused severe injuries and many deaths when the metal projectiles impacted and penetrated the skull (58,59).

The use of large quantities of chemical irritant has increasingly been reported, either by the firing of tear gas projectiles and grenades, or dispersal using sprayers and other equipment.

A major new report by Physicians for Human Rights, INCLO and Omega Research Institute has identified nearly 120 000 people with chemical irritant injuries in the medical literature over the past 30 years. Of those, at least 5246 had severe injuries requiring medical interventions or a hospital stay (15).

During escalating protests in 2019 in Hong Kong, police used chemical irritants in large quantities, firing 800 tear gas projectiles in a single day, and in some cases in confined spaces. For example, on 11 August 2019, police fired multiple rounds of tear gas inside the Kwai Fong Mass Transit Railway station, a confined space with limited exits (21). Tunisian police used large amounts of launched tear gas cartridges during unrest in the city of Tataouine between 23 and 26 June 2020. Volunteers reportedly collected and counted almost 18 000 cartridges from the city after the operation had finished. People were affected in hospitals, places of worship and their homes, with at least 180 people reportedly admitted to hospital for emergency treatment after inhaling tear gas and 26 others were injured when struck with tear gas projectiles (60).

In 2020, Federal Agents from the Department of Homeland Security were deployed to protect federal property in Portland, Oregon under "Operation Diligent Valor". Protests occurred over many weeks and federal agents repeatedly deployed massive quantities of chemical irritants and smoke including via thermal foggers, as shown in Figure 85.3 – hand-held devices producing large volumes of tear smoke from water or oil-based solutions, as well as from "smoke pots" – open pots of burning incandescent substance (believed to be HC – Hexachloroethane) that produced dense clouds of gray/white smoke. Protesters reported a wide range of respiratory and/or reproductive health impacts after attending protests and being exposed to the chemical irritants, including unusual effects on menstrual cycles (61,62).

In 2021, mass protests took place across Colombia, as people protested the economic situation and demanded employment and better housing, health and education. Security forces, particularly the Mobile Anti-Riot Squad (Escuadrón Móvil Antidisturbios, ESMAD), responded to the largely peaceful demonstrations with excessive and unnecessary force including large quantities of tear gas projectiles and grenades. On April 30,. 2021 in Cali, ESMAD officers were filmed chasing protesters, including knocking them to the ground and firing tear gas at point blank range (54).

On the evening of October 1, 2022, a football match between Arema and Persebaya in the Kanjuruhan Stadium in Malang, East Java, ended in defeat for Arema. Arema supporters invaded the pitch and attacked both players and police. The police began firing tear gas projectiles, including directly into the stands. The tear gas caused supporters to panic and attempt to flee the ground, heading to the exits, some of which were locked. The panic and stampede caused by the tear gas resulted in a crush. At least 132 people died, including 32 children and two police officers, and over 600 were injured (63,64).

KINETIC IMPACT PROJECTILES

Kinetic impact projectiles (KIPs) are commonly referred to as rubber or plastic bullets, but they can also be made from other materials including wood, metal composite or plastic/PVC (metal projectiles are considered lethal and not covered here). "Less lethal" ammunition can contain single or multiple projectiles including, for example, pellets, balls, blocks, cylinders, or fabric bags filled with pellets ("bean bags").

Due to their indiscriminate effects and the danger they present, the Commissioner for Human Rights of the Council of Europe has expressed concern at the unsuitability of certain weapons that are increasingly used for the policing of protests. In this context, she stated that the number of serious injuries caused by the use of KIPs was "particularly striking" (65).

There is some divergence between international human rights standards on the lawful threshold for using KIPs. The UN Guidance states that they should only be used to strike a violent individual posing "an imminent threat of injury" (8). Both the ODIHR *Human Rights Handbook on Policing Assemblies* and the UN *Resource Book* impose a stricter standard, however, stating KIPs should only be used against individuals posing an immediate threat of *serious* injury or death (25,66).

These international human rights instruments also share important commonalities. All state that KIPs should only be used to target individuals posing a threat, not groups, and that the use of ammunition containing multiple projectiles, such as those shown below in Figure 85.4, does not comply with international human rights standards due to their inherent lack of accuracy. Both the UN Guidance and the *ODIHR Handbook* stipulate that KIPs should only be aimed at the lower abdomen or legs (8,67), and this is complemented by the *Resource Book* which states that they should not be fired at sensitive parts of the body, "in particular the head, neck, chest and groin" (25).

Health concerns

KIPs are designed to cause blunt, non-penetrative trauma, but they can perforate the skin, causing internal bleeding

85.3 Federal law enforcement agents use a thermal fogger during a Black Lives Matters protest. (*Source:* © Doug Brown, ACLU of Oregon. July 29, 2020. Portland, Oregon, USA.)

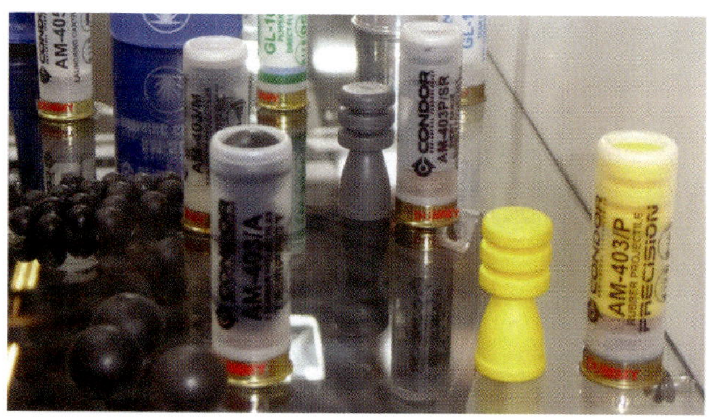

85.4 Examples of multiple projectiles (left) and single projectiles (right). (*Source:* © Omega Research Foundation. June 2018. Paris, France.)

or penetrating vital organs, particularly when fired from close range or at sensitive areas of the body, particularly the head, face, eyes or genital area (67). Especially when fired from close range, KIPs can cause serious injury or death. Most police guidelines recommend aiming at the chest and abdomen or at the legs. But, even at close range (when their velocity can approach that of live ammunition), the weapons are often difficult to aim and many projectiles have been found to be inaccurate and inconsistent (68,69). Depending on their characteristics and the manner in which they are used, projectiles can easily hit the head, neck or face, or can ricochet and strike bystanders or unintentional targets anywhere on a body. At long ranges, many KIPs are so inaccurate that they tend to impact indiscriminately.

KIPs can and have caused serious injuries, disability and death. In a recent report by Physicians for Human Rights, INCLO and Omega Research Institute, a systematic review of 45 research papers over 30 years, reported on more than 4000 people injured by KIPs with at least 1245 sustaining permanent injuries (15). Significant injuries were found in all body systems including bruising and lacerations of the skin, contusions and bone fractures, internal bleeding, liver, heart and kidney penetration (with subsequent organ failure or death) and neurovascular injuries. KIP trauma to the head has caused blunt trauma resulting in internal bleeding and in a number of cases, has penetrated the skull. Head injury results in TBI, hemorrhagic strokes and permanent disability. Another key injury is when KIPs strike the eye. Given their large size and the fragile bony structure and supple eye tissues, ocular injuries frequently result in permanent vision loss. The systematic review cited above identified 1885 ocular injuries resulting from KIP trauma ([15], p. 39). While poorly studied, the mental health impacts of KIP exposure may include stress and anxiety, as well as a possible chilling effect on attending future demonstrations (3).

Some characteristics of KIPs can potentiate injury. The use of dense material, such as metal, for instance, can exacerbate the risk of penetration and injury. Projectiles incorporating metal, such as rubber-coated metal bullets (used by Israeli forces in the Occupied Palestinian Territories), projectiles with metal fragments (used in several contexts including in Chile) and bean-bag rounds (used in the US and elsewhere) are well known to cause significant injuries, especially when fired at close range. Ammunition dispersing multiple projectiles at once, two to many dozens, cannot be aimed at a single target, and can hit multiple people or sites of the body, causing variable and indiscriminate injury.

Global context

In the Brazilian state of Pernambuco in 2017, a Military Police officer shot Edvaldo da Silva Alves in the thigh with a KIP during a peaceful protest. The projectile was fired from a distance of less than 5 m, resulting in penetration. Although the projectile was surgically removed from the victim's body, he later died of a general infection caused by his injuries (70).

In March 2022, Luis Paulo da Silva Pereira was shot twice in the face by prison authorities with a rubber projectile while an altercation was happening between the prison authorities and the prisoners, at the Centro de Progressão Penitenciária (CPP), in the Federal District of Brazil. The prison authorities also refused to provide him with medical help after he asked and he had to undergo reconstructive plastic surgery, leaving his face permanently disfigured (71,72).

Factors such as insufficient use of force reporting internally by law enforcement agencies and a lack of transparency regarding the use of force data that is compiled, make it difficult to measure trends relating to the use of less lethal weapons over time. The context-specific information available nonetheless seems to indicate KIPs are increasingly being used for the policing of protests.

The use of KIPs known as "Plastic Baton Rounds" against protesters by the Royal Ulster Constabulary and the British Army was "the most controversial aspect of public order policing" during the Troubles in Northern Ireland (73). According to the Patten Report, between 1981 and 1999 over 56 000 plastic baton rounds were fired by the police and the army, resulting in 11 deaths Ireland (73), of the 17 overall caused by rubber or plastic impact projectiles. Over 18 years, this averages out to approximately 8.5 rounds being used every day. In 1981, the year when most plastic baton rounds were fired, 29 695 rounds were used in total (74), averaging out to 81 per day.

In recent years, law enforcement officials in several countries have used even greater numbers of KIPs against protesters, including in response to mass protests that occurred in Chile in late 2019. Responding to an access to information request, the *Carabineros de Chile* revealed that they fired 151 288 shotgun cartridges containing 12 pellets each between 18 October and December 31, 2019 (76). Thus, on average, 2017 rounds were fired per day during this period. Similarly, in recent years, French police have responded to Yellow Vest protests with large quantities of less lethal weapons. The Council of Europe Commissioner for Human Rights reported that from November 17, 2018, when the protests began, to February 4, 2019, police fired 12 122 40 mm KIPs (76),[iii] an average of 152 per day. Although France and Chile are both much larger countries than Northern Ireland, it is still striking that use of KIPs in both countries so clearly exceeded use during even the most difficult times during the Troubles.

Although such data are often not collected or made publicly available, Omega's experience monitoring the use of force indicated that the use of large quantities of KIPs to police protests is not limited to these two cases. Assuming that these cases are, to an extent, representative of other examples, it is useful to look more

[iii] French police were also reported to have used 4942 stingball grenades, exploding grenades with multiple small hard rubber pellets, which are expelled at high velocity in a random pattern.

closely at the type of projectiles being used in Chile and France, how they are being used and the consequences of their use.

During the 2019–2020 protests in Chile, police used 12-gauge shotgun cartridges containing 12 small balls or pellets each. The National Human Rights Institute reported that 460 protesters suffered ocular injuries, with 35 people suffering either burst eyeballs or losing an eye (77). A medical study into cases of ocular trauma treated at the Eye Trauma Unit in Hospital del Salvador, Santiago, between 18 October and 30 November 2019, found that 182 (70.5%) of 259 patients had been injured by KIPs, all of which were multiple projectile rounds (78). Of the 182 patients whose injuries were caused by KIPs, 33 had total blindness in the affected eye and 90 had severe visual impairment or were blind at first examination (78).

As reports of large numbers of eye injuries emerged, there was international condemnation, but also intense domestic scrutiny as to the nature and use of the projectiles. For instance, a study carried out by the Faculty of Physical and Mathematical Sciences of the University of Chile revealed that the projectiles contained just 20 percent rubber, with the other 80 percent made up of silica, barium sulphate and lead (79). According to Viviana Meruane, Director of the Department of Mechanical Engineering, this composition provides added hardness and energy, "which significantly increases the damage caused by the projectiles" (79).

In response, the Carabineros issued a public statement, stating that they had carried out their own study in the Carabinero's Crime Laboratory following the publication of the independent one (80). The results of this second study were not published, but the public statement indicated that they also showed that the composition of the projectiles differed from the manufacturer's datasheet. The statement announced that the use of this ammunition would be suspended for crowd control. Such a statement suggests that the Chilean authorities were not previously aware of the composition of the projectiles they were using, because they had not carried out their own tests, independent of the manufacturer. The UN Guidance, however, requires states to carry out tests prior to procuring less lethal weapons, and these tests should be "based on impartial legal, technical, medical and scientific expertise and evidence" (8).

It subsequently became apparent that at least some testing had, in fact, been carried out by Chilean authorities. A classified 2012 study commissioned by the *Carabineros* was leaked to the media, showed that authorities were aware that kinetic impact ammunition containing multiple projectiles was both inaccurate and risked causing serious injury, including ocular injuries (81). The study recommended that its use be limited to distances greater than 30 meters and that the point of aim should always be the lower half of the body. At the same time, the study demonstrated the inaccuracy of these projectiles, with just two of the 12 projectiles striking the target when fired from 30 meters.

It is important to underline the fact that the inaccuracy of these projectiles does not preclude the possibility that they were also used unlawfully. The high number of ocular injuries during the Chilean protests suggests that the upper part of the body was repeatedly targeted, running counter to the recommendations made in the 2012 study. In such cases, kinetic impact ammunition was not being used to merely disperse protesters, but also to inflict additional harm.

During the Yellow Vest protests, French police used various types of kinetic impact ammunition, but the use of one particular kind, launched 40 mm projectiles, was the cause of widespread public anger. The *Lanceur de balles de défense* (*LBD*), also called the GL06 by the Swiss manufacturer B&T, is the 40 mm launcher most commonly used by French law enforcement. Although B&T markets a range of 40 mm ammunition[iv], this was not adopted by the French Government when the launcher was introduced, and French law enforcement mainly use 40 mm ammunition manufactured by the French company SAE Alsetex (part of the Etienne Lacroix Group).

Unlike the shotgun ammunition used in Chile, the 40 mm ammunition used in France contains single projectiles. These 40 mm KIPs are designed to impact head on, with the foam nose absorbing the energy upon impact and thereby reducing injuries, but the prevalence of serious injuries presented may indicate that they do not always do that.

The types of ammunition in use are designed to be launched from different ranges, with the longer-range ammunition containing more propellant. The French Ombudsperson (Défenseur des droits) has called for the use of this weapon system to be prohibited during public gatherings, in part due to the difficulty of determining the range and assessing the risk of hitting bystanders, as people are usually grouped and mobile in such a context (82). As with other KIPs, there is an increased risk of serious injury or death when rounds are used from close range or impact sensitive parts of the body (e.g. head or upper body). In January 2019, the Ombudsperson reported that use of the LBD was the cause of or implicated in 18 of the 45 complaints he had received of "extremely serious injury" or "permanent mutilation".

STUN GRENADES

Stun grenades, also known as "flashbangs" and "distraction" or "disorientation" devices, are explosive devices that can be either hand-thrown or weapon-launched. Upon detonation, they emit an extremely loud noise and/or bright flash(es) of light. The flash causes temporary blindness for several seconds by activating photoreceptor cells in the eye (15). The loud blast can cause temporary loss of hearing and loss of balance, as well as a sense of panic (15). Some stun grenades have ridges to limit their movement after

[iv] SIR [Safe Impact Round], SIR-X [Safe Impact Round - extended range], dye marking, impact CS, impact OC, rubber shot, muzzle blast OC, ballistic smoke, ballistic CS and muzzle blast CS.

85.5 Hand-thrown stun grenades. (© Omega Research Foundation. November 2017. Paris, France.)

detonation, while other types move around and have multiple explosions, causing loud blasts and bright flashes. The casing on some stun grenades has several circular cut-outs, such as those shown in Figure 85.5, to allow the sound and light from the explosion through. Some types also disperse chemical irritants and/or KIPs. The intensity of the noise and flash emitted varies from manufacturer to manufacturer. Some manufacturers market grenades with rubber casing as suitable for indoor use (83). Others claim that their grenades emit less heat upon detonation, lowering the fire risk, or are designed not to move upon detonation (84).

Health concerns

Like all explosive devices, stun grenades carry the risk of blast injury. They are designed to carry some explosive material in combination with pyro-technic material that creates loud sounds and bright lights. Blast injury results from the pressure waves caused by the blast on ambient air. As the proximity of a person or group of people to the explosion increases, so too does the risk of serious injury or death. The primary blast can cause injuries to the ear drum and lung membranes, especially when they discharge in close proximity to an individual. Secondary blast can cause blunt and penetrating injury from the explosion and fragmentation of the device itself. Some stun grenades can produce high-velocity fragments when they explode, which can have sufficient energy to cause serious injury or death. Safer grenades split, rather than fragment. Tertiary blast can cause blunt and penetrating trauma such as fractures and head trauma from pushing people into solid objects or entraining projectiles in the blast wave; and quaternary blast can result in burns, smoke inhalation, crush injuries from a resulting stampede or psychiatric trauma. The UN Guidance states that "the use of pyrotechnic flash-bang grenades directly against a person would be unlawful" (8).

There are case reports where defective or poorly designed weapons have exploded in officers' hands. Used in enclosed spaces, stun grenades can cause fires, smoke inhalation and serious burns in addition to blast injuries. A 2015 Propublica investigation reports in more than 50 cases of death and serious injury from law enforcement use of stun grenades (many of them when they were launched into residential spaces) (85).

The risk is lowered when grenades are rolled along the ground, rather than thrown or launched. This was tragically evident in the death of Remi Fraisse, who was killed during a protest against the construction of a dam in France in October 2014. A stun grenade thrown by the French Gendarmerie reportedly exploded near his back, severing his spinal cord and killing him (86).

As blast injuries have variable effects, early medical attention should be sought for any injuries to the head/face or other sensitive body parts such as the genitalia or hands. Burns, blisters and skin injuries should be treated as explosive injuries, irrigated and dressed. Prolonged hearing or vision loss would require in-depth evaluation for tympanic membrane rupture or globe rupture as a result of blast pressure or foreign bodies.

Global context

Originally designed as a training aid to simulate explosions, stun grenades were initially adopted for use by military special forces units, and later, by law enforcement special weapons and tactics (SWAT) teams, during room clearance or hostage situations. In some countries, stun grenades have become more widely used by law enforcement personnel for crowd-control purposes. When used in the context of a public gathering, the aim is to disorient those present and cause them to disperse. Use in this context carries with it an increased risk of secondary injuries from falls, as the detonation of stun grenades risks causing panic or stampedes among large groups of people. States may need to re-assess their use of stun grenades during public gatherings in light of the recent UN Human Rights Committee General Comment on the right of peaceful assembly, which states "when [less lethal] weapons are used, all reasonable efforts should be made to limit risks, such as causing a stampede or harming bystanders" (87).

Stun grenades were used in the law enforcement response to large protests that erupted against the contested results of the Belarusian presidential election in August 2020. UN High Commissioner for Human Rights Michelle Bachelet denounced the "heavy crackdown" this prompted, with police using "unnecessary and excessive force against largely peaceful protesters" (88). Large numbers of stun grenades were reportedly used during the first days of the protests, leading to many serious injuries (89).

The Belarusian security forces used several types of stun grenade, including the Russian-manufactured SV-1319 Viyushka (90), which, upon detonation, emits a loud bang, a bright flash of light, and 750 rubber pellets with a diameter of 7.5 mm. According to company information, these grenades produce a sound not less than 130 decibels measured at a distance of 10 meters from the explosion (91).

In Belarus, stun grenades were reportedly used directly against crowds of people, exploding at thigh height or lower (89). Serious injuries reportedly included broken bones in the finger, foot and calf. In in one instance, a man's foot was reportedly ripped off when a stun grenade exploded near him (89). Many protesters were injured by fragments of exploded stun grenades (92), including serious injuries such as pneumothorax (89) and some people also suffered ear drum damage (93).

Stun grenades were also previously used against large crowds of peaceful protesters in Yerevan, Armenia, on July 29, 2016. Police reportedly both launched and threw stun grenades into groups of peaceful protesters, with grenades exploding and emitting thick smoke and loud blasts, resulting in injuries to dozens of protesters and several journalists (94). Eleven people, injured during the protests, spoke to Civil Society Platform monitors; of those, seven had been injured by stun grenades, including one protester who suffered second-degree burns to 16 percent of her skin, including her face (95). The use of stun grenades led to injuries including first- and second-degree burns, fragmentation wounds and one protester reportedly lost an eye after being hit by fragments (96).

Human Rights Watch reported on the impact of a stun grenade exploding near a man's feet shortly after he joined the protest (94):

> *"He was briefly blinded by thick smoke and felt severe pain in his head. As he struggled to flee, he saw that his pant legs were almost entirely burned and his legs were covered in blood. [The individual] has 30 lacerations and first- and second-degree burns covering both legs. Doctors removed five plastic fragments from the stun grenade from his legs. He was not able to walk normally at the time of the interview."*

OTHER LESS LETHAL WEAPONS

There are a wide range of other less lethal weapons and devices in use, although perhaps not as commonly observed as those covered above, all would merit thorough examination, but a lack of space prevents it here. Water cannons are becoming more prevalent globally, due in part to lower cost arising from manufacture in China and South Korea (96), but also from more modern designs (97). There are reports that water cannons are being further weaponized by adding dye, chemical agents or foul-smelling contaminants to exert secondary impacts. Injury intensity is based on the pressure, distance, duration and composition of the water stream. Direct injury from the water jets is rare but include loss of the eyes and facial fractures (98). Secondary effects include being knocked over, pushed off high ground, or objects being entrained in the water stream impacting the body. Acoustic and optical devices are increasingly encountered. Acoustic devices were introduced for warning or as loud hailers, however some have "warning tones" at high-frequency or sound pressure levels, which can lead to hearing loss (99). Optical devices that interfere with an individual's vision are designed to warn or to dazzle (100). They have the potential to cause irreversible sight loss.[v] Dogs and horses are also commonly deployed in crowd control settings where dog bites, trampling by horses and other traumas have been observed/documented when confronted by these animals (100). An emerging issue in crowd control weaponry is the use of remote drone technology, either for surveillance of crowds or for deployment of lethal and less lethal weapons. Surveillance using drone or other remote technology is growing in recent years, with the potential to identify and later arrest or persecute demonstrators. The use of chemical irritant projectiles or grenades via drone has been increasingly reported and an increasing number of manufacturers offer such systems (101), underscoring the need for consistent monitoring of such technological developments.

Any use of firearms against peaceful protesters is unlawful under international human rights law and policing standards. The use of firearms to disperse a crowd is unlawful in all circumstances (87). Law enforcement officers in a number of states, including Israel (102) and India (103), assert that their use of firearms to launch bullets or pellets is a "less lethal" use of firearms. However, in these cases, safer alternatives are available which would not result in such devastating, life-long and life-limiting punitive injuries, and such use amounts to unlawful use of force.

CONCLUSION

The vast majority of public assemblies pass off peacefully and many do not even require the presence of law enforcement officials. Where police or other law enforcement officials are present, their primary duty is to facilitate, respect and protect the exercise of fundamental rights, enabling the assembly to take place as intended and minimizing the potential for injury to any person or damage to property (87). Nonetheless, in many countries, policing of assemblies is politicized, and there is also a tendency to label entire assemblies as violent and use less lethal weapons to disperse them. In cases of assemblies which may be non-peaceful, and where force against those who are violent may be justified, there is often no attempt to distinguish between individuals engaged in unlawful conduct and others exercising their right to peaceful assembly. Sporadic instances of violence by individuals in an assembly does not mean the whole

[v] See B.E. Meyers range of GLARE products: https://bemeyers.com/glare-la-9-p.

assembly can be classed as violent, and non-violent individuals still retain their rights which must be protected. The obligation to prioritize non-violent means of conflict resolution is frequently ignored in such circumstances.

There are various factors that contribute to law enforcement officials continuing to use excessive and arbitrary force to police assemblies, but one crucial issue is impunity. Impunity is, in turn, facilitated by a series of inter-related causes. These include unprofessional and permissive police cultures, weak use of force protocols, inadequate training, an absence of effective, independent oversight mechanisms, allegations of police abuse being investigated by the same agency, overly close relationships between police and prosecutors, and a lack of knowledge among judges and other legal professionals concerning international use of force standards and the technical characteristics of the weapons used by law enforcement agencies.

Reliable forensic evidence is of fundamental importance to addressing impunity and achieving accountability for the excessive or arbitrary use of force. As such, we encourage medical and forensic professionals to ensure they have up-to-date knowledge of the characteristics of less lethal weapons used in the jurisdictions where they practice, the techniques used for their employment, and the risks associated with their use. Professional bodies representing forensic professionals should offer training and support on these matters, complementing other training on the implementation of the Istanbul and Minnesota Protocols.

ACKNOWLEDGEMENT

Figures 85.1 (CC BY 2.0.) and 85.2 (CC BY-SA 3.0) are provided by permission of Creative Commons license. Figure 85.3 is reproduced by kind permission of the photographer, Doug Brown, ACLU of Oregon. Figures 85.4 and 85.5 are from the Omega Foundation.

REFERENCES

1. Sollom R, Atkinson H. *Weaponizing Tear Gas: Bahrain's Unprecedented Use of Toxic Chemical Agents Against Civilians*. Cambridge: Physicians for Human Rights; 2012.
2. Institute for Economics & Peace. Global peace index 2022: Measuring peace in a complex world, 2022. Available from: https://www.visionofhumanity.org/wp-content/uploads/2022/06/GPI-2022-web.pdf (Accessed 20 June 2023).
3. Physicians for Human Rights. Shot in the head, 2020. Available from: https://storymaps.arcgis.com/stories/29cbf2e87b914dbaabdec2f3d350839e (Accessed 20 June 2023).
4. Carothers T, Press B. The global rise of anti-lockdown protests—and what to do about it, 2020. Available from: https://www.worldpoliticsreview.com/articles/29137/amid-the-covid-19-pandemic-protest-movements-challenge-lockdowns-worldwide (Accessed 20 June 2023).
5. Institute for Economics & Peace. COVID-19 and peace, 2020. Available from: http://visionofhumanity.org/reports (Accessed 20 June 2023).
6. Amnesty International. Penalized for protesting: Sri Lanka's crackdown on protestors, 2022. Available from: https://www.amnesty.org/en/latest/news/2022/09/sri-lanka-authorities-crackdown-on-protest-rights-must-end/ (Accessed 20 June 2023).
7. Amnesty International. Protect the protest: Amnesty International launches global campaign to confront unprecedented worldwide threat to the right to protest, 2020. Available from: https://www.amnesty.org/en/latest/news/2022/07/protect-the-protest/ (Accessed 20 June 2023).
8. United Nations. UN human rights guidance on less-lethal weapons and related equipment in law enforcement, 2020. Available from: https://www.ohchr.org/Documents/HRBodies/CCPR/LLW_Guidance.pdf (Accessed 20 June 2023).
9. United Nations. Code of conduct for law enforcement officials, 1980. Available from: https://digitallibrary.un.org/record/10639?ln=en (Accessed 20 June 2023).
10. United Nations. Basic principles on the use of force and firearms by law enforcement officials, 1990. Available from: https://www.ohchr.org/en/instruments-mechanisms/instruments/basic-principles-use-force-and-firearms-law-enforcement (Accessed 20 June 2023).
11. European Court of Human Rights. *Izci v Turkey*, 2013. Available from: https://hudoc.echr.coe.int/tur#{%22itemid%22:[%22001-122885%22]} (Accessed 20 June 2023).
12. Kiai M, Heyns C. Joint report of the Special Rapporteur on the rights to freedom of peaceful assembly and of association and the Special Rapporteur on extrajudicial, summary or arbitrary executions on the proper management of assemblies, 2016. Available from: https://digitallibrary.un.org/record/831673?ln=en (Accessed 20 June 2023).
13. United Nations Human Rights. Manual on the effective investigation and documentation of torture and other cruel, inhuman or degrading treatment or punishment, 2022. Available from: https://www.ohchr.org/sites/default/files/documents/publications/2022-06-29/Istanbul-Protocol_Rev2_EN.pdf (Accessed 20 June 2023).
14. United Nations. The Minnesota protocol on the investigation of potentially unlawful death, 2016. Available from: https://www.ohchr.org/sites/default/files/Documents/Publications/MinnesotaProtocol.pdf (Accessed 20 June 2023).
15. International Network of Civil Liberties Organizations (INCLO), Physicians for Human Rights (PHR) and Omega Research Foundation. (2023) Lethal in Disguise 2: How Crowd-Control Weapons Impact Health and Human Rights, 2023. Available from: https://phr.org/our-work/resources/lethal-in-disguise-2/ (Accessed 11 September 2023).
16. Dymond-Bass A, Corney N, Casey-Maslen S. Weapons Testing and Review. In: Casey-Maslen S (ed), *Weapons Under International Human Rights Law*. Cambridge: Cambridge University Press; 2014, pp. 411–47.
17. United Kingdom Home Office. CAST standard for police chemical irritant sprays: CS and PAVA, 2014. Available from: https://assets.publishing.service.gov.uk/government/uploads/system/uploads/attachment_data/file/337910/standard-police-irritant-sprays-2314.pdf (Accessed 20 June 2023).
18. US National Institute of Justice. Minimum scheme requirements to certify criminal justice restraints described in NIJ standard 1001.00, 2017. Available from: https://www.ojp.gov/pdffiles1/nij/250566.pdf (Accessed 20 June 2023).
19. US National Institute of Justice. Criminal justice restraints standard NIJ standard 1001.00 revision A, 2019. Available from: https://www.ojp.gov/pdffiles1/nij/253876.pdf (Accessed 20 June 2023).
20. The Wassenaar Arrangement. Export controls for conventional arms and dual use goods and technologies, munitions list, 2020. Available from: https://www.wassenaar.org/app/uploads/2020/12/Standalone-Munitions-List_2020.pdf (Accessed 20 June 2023).
21. Omega Research Foundation and Amnesty International. Ending the torture trade: The path to global controls on the 'tools of torture', 2020. Available from: https://omegaresearchfoundation.org/sites/default/files/uploads/Publications/Ending%20the%20Torture%20Trade%20-%20The%20Path%20to%20Global%20Controls%20on%20the%20

%27Tools%20of%20Torture%27.pdf (Accessed 20 June 2023).
22. Centro de Estudios Legales y Sociales. The internal war: How the fight against drugs is militarizing Latin America, 2018. Available from: https://www.cels.org.ar/militarizacion/pdf/theinternalwar.pdf (Accessed 20 June 2023).
23. Barrett B. The Pentagon's hand-me-downs helped militarize police. Here's how, 2020. Available from: https://www.wired.com/story/pentagon-hand-me-downs-militarize-police-1033-program/ (Accessed 20 June 2023).
24. Omega Research Foundation and Amnesty International. Tackling the trade in tools of torture and execution technologies, 2017. Available from: https://omegaresearchfoundation.org/sites/default/files/uploads/Publications/Ending%20the%20torture%20trade%20WEB%20version.pdf (Accessed 20 June 2023).
25. United Nations. Resource book on the use of force and firearms in law enforcement, 2017. Available from: https://www.ohchr.org/Documents/ProfessionalInterest/UseOfForceAndFirearms.pdf (Accessed 20 June 2023).
26. Amnesty International. Blunt force: Investigating the misuse of police batons and related equipment, 2021. Available from: https://www.amnesty.org/en/latest/research/2021/09/blunt-force/ (Accessed 20 June 2023).
27. Human Rights Watch. Nigeria: Crackdown on police brutality protests, 2020. Available from: https://www.hrw.org/news/2020/10/16/nigeria-crackdown-police-brutality-protests (Accessed 20 June 2023).
28. Amnesty International. Belarus: Mounting evidence of a campaign of widespread torture of peaceful protesters, 2020. Available from: www.amnesty.org/en/latest/news/2020/08/belarus-mounting-evidence-of-a-campaign-of-widespread-torture-of-peaceful-protesters/ (Accessed 20 June 2023).
29. Benedek, W. OSCE Rapporteur's report under the Moscow mechanism on alleged human rights violations related to the presidential elections of 9 August 2020 in Belarus, 2020. Available from: https://www.osce.org/files/f/documents/2/b/469539.pdf (Accessed 20 June 2023).
30. Human Rights Watch. "Kettling" protesters in the Bronx. Systemic police brutality and its costs in the United States, 2020. Available from: https://www.hrw.org/report/2020/09/30/kettling-protesters-bronx/systemic-police-brutality-and-its-costs-united-states (Accessed 20 June 2023).
31. Reuters. Iranian coroner says Mahsa Amini did not die from blows to body, 2022. Available from: https://www.reuters.com/world/middle-east/iranian-coroner-says-mahsa-amini-did-not-die-blows-body-2022–10–07/ (Accessed 20 June 2023).
32. The Guardian. Mother says police beat daughter to death in Iranian protests, 2022. Available from: https://www.theguardian.com/world/2022/oct/08/mother-says-police-beat-daughter-to-death-in-iranian-protests (Accessed 20 June 2023).
33. Gershkovich E. Those guys with whips? They're cossacks meant to keep you safe at Russia's World Cup, 2020. Available from: https://www.themoscowtimes.com/2018/05/28/those-guys-with-whips-theyre-cossacks-meant-to-keep-you-safe-at-russias-world-cup-a61599 (Accessed 20 June 2023).
34. Safety of Journalists Platform. Journalists detained and assaulted at inauguration protests, 2018. Available from: https://www.coe.int/en/web/media-freedom/detail-alert?p_p_id=sojdashboard_WAR_coesojportlet&p_p_lifecycle=2&p_p_cacheability=cacheLevelPage&p_p_col_id=column-1&p_p_col_count=1&_sojdashboard_WAR_coesojportlet_alertPK=35676217&_sojdashboard_WAR_coesojportlet_cmd=get_pdf_one (Accessed 20 June 2023).
35. Reddy M, Allison S. Police use sjamboks and rubber bullets to enforce Hillbrow lockdown, 2020. Available from: https://mg.co.za/article/2020-03-31-police-use-sjamboks-and-rubber-bullets-to-enforce-hillbrow-lockdown/ (Accessed 20 June 2023).
36. Olewe, D. Coronavirus in Africa: Whipping, shooting and snooping, 2020. Available from: https://www.bbc.co.uk/news/world-africa-52214740 (Accessed 20 June 2023).
37. Organisation for the Prohibition of Chemical Weapons. Report of the OPCW on the implementation of the convention on the prohibition of the development, production, stockpiling and use of chemical weapons and on their destruction in 2018, 2019. Available from: https://www.opcw.org/sites/default/files/documents/2019/12/c2404%28e%29.pdf (Accessed 20 June 2023).
38. PepperBall. VXR Live-X. Available from: https://pepperball.com/projectiles/vxr-live-x/ (Accessed 20 June 2023).
39. Kiai M. Report of the special rapporteur on the rights to freedom of peaceful assembly and of association, 2012. Available from: https://digitallibrary.un.org/record/730973?ln=en (Accessed 20 June 2023).
40. Haar RJ, Iacopino V, Ranadive N, et al. Health impacts of chemical irritants used for crowd control: A systematic review of the injuries and deaths caused by tear gas and pepper spray. *BMC Public Health* 2017; **17**(1): 1–14.
41. Kraft CA. AAP Statement in response to tear gas being used against children at the U.S. southern border, 2018. Available from: https://www.aap.org/en/news-room/news-releases/aap/2018/aap-statement-in-response-to-tear-gas-being-used-against-children-at-the-us-southern-border/ (Accessed 20 June 2023).
42. Centers for Disease Control and Prevention. Facts about riot control agents interim document, 2018. Available from: https://emergency.cdc.gov/agent/riotcontrol/factsheet.asp (Accessed 20 June 2023).
43. United Nations Committee against Torture. Concluding observations on the second and third periodic reports of Bahrain, 2017. Available from: https://digitallibrary.un.org/record/1306835?ln=en (Accessed 20 June 2023).
44. European Court of Human Rights. Oya Ataman v. Turkey, 2007. Available from: https://hudoc.echr.coe.int/fre#%7B%22itemid%22:[%22001-78330%22]%7D (Accessed 20 June 2023).
45. European Court of Human Rights. Abdullah Yasa and Others v. Turkey, 2013. Available from: http://hudoc.echr.coe.int/eng?i=001-122368#{%22itemid%22:[%22001-122368%22]} (Accessed 20 June 2023).
46. Organization for Security and Co-operation in Europe. Guide on law enforcement equipment most commonly used in the policing of assemblies, 2021. Available from: https://www.osce.org/odihr/491551 (Accessed 20 June 2023).
47. Omega Research Foundation. Lowering the risk - Curtailing the use of chemical irritants during the COVID-19 pandemic, 2020. Available from: https://omegaresearchfoundation.org/sites/default/files/uploads/Publications/Position%20Paper%20with%20logo.pdf (Accessed 20 June 2023).
48. American Thoracic Society. Tear gas use during COVID-19 pandemic irresponsible; Moratorium needed, says American Thoracic Society, 2020. Available from: https://www.thoracic.org/about/newsroom/press-releases/journal/2020/tear-gas-use-during-covid-19-pandemic-irresponsible-moratorium-needed,-says-american-thoracic-society.php (Accessed 20 June 2023).
49. Greiner A, Laviana A, Stewart AW, et al. Open letter advocating for an anti-racist public health response to demonstrations against systemic injustice occurring during the COVID-19 pandemic, 2020. Available from: https://drive.google.com/file/d/1Jyfn4Wd2i6bRi12ePghMHtX3ys1b7K1A/view (Accessed 20 June 2023).
50. Slisco A. Tear gas may have led to abnormal menstrual cycles in Seattle and Portland, 2020. Available from: https://www.newsweek.com/tear-gas-may-have-led-abnormal-menstrual-cycles-seattle-portland-1529912 (Accessed 20 June 2023).
51. Stunson M. Protesters complain of unexpected side effect from tear gas: Period changes, 2020. Available from: https://www.miamiherald.com/news/nation-world/national/article244212707.html (Accessed 20 June 2023).
52. Nowell C. Protesters say tear gas caused them to get their period multiple times in a month, 2020. Available from: https://www.teenvogue.com/story/protestors-say-tear-gas-caused-early-menstruation (Accessed 20 June 2023).
53. Faculty of Forensic & Legal Medicine. Irritant sprays: Clinical effects and management, 2021. Available from: https://fflm.ac.uk/wp-content/uploads/2021/02/Irritant-sprays-clinical-effects-and-management-Dr-J-McGorrigan-Prof-J-Payne-James-Jan-2021.pdf (Accessed 20 June 2023).
54. Amnesty International. Tear gas: An investigation, 2020. Available from: https://teargas.amnesty.org/ (Accessed 20 June 2023).
55. Breeden A. France to stop using TNT-loaded tear gas grenades, 2020. Available from: https://www.nytimes.com/2020/01/27/world/europe/france-tear-gas-grenades.html (Accessed 20 June 2023).
56. SudOuest.fr. Loi sécurité globale : un manifestant a eu les doigts arrachés

par une grenade samedi à Paris, 2020. Available from: https://www.sudouest.fr/politique/gerald-darmanin/loi-securite-globale-un-manifestant-a-eu-les-doigts-arraches-par-une-grenade-samedi-a-paris-1642105.php (Accessed 20 June 2023).
57. Cordall SS. 'Things are getting worse': Tunisia protests rage on as latest victim named, 2021. Available from: https://www.theguardian.com/global-development/2021/jan/27/things-are-getting-worse-tunisia-protests-rage-on-as-latest-victim-named (Accessed 20 June 2023).
58. Hoz SS, Aljuboori ZS, Dolachee AA, et al. Fatal penetrating head injuries caused by projectile tear gas canisters. *World Neurosurg* 2020; **138**: e119–e23.
59. Amnesty International. Iraq: Iranian tear gas grenades among those causing gruesome protester deaths, 2019. Available from: https://www.amnesty.org/en/latest/news/2019/10/iraq-gruesome-string-of-fatalities-as-new-tear-gas-grenades-pierce-protesters-skulls/ (Accessed 20 June 2023).
60. Amnesty International. Tunisia: Authorities must investigate excessive use of force in Tataouine, 2020. Available from: https://www.amnesty.org/download/Documents/MDE3027472020ENGLISH.pdf (Accessed 20 June 2023).
61. Edelson JM, Simon KK, Cady NS, Holmes E. Complaint for declaratory and injunctive relief, 2020. Available from: https://aclu-or.org/sites/default/files/field_documents/nepa_federal_tear-gas_lawsuit.pdf (Accessed 20 June 2023).
62. Samayoa M. Lawsuit accuses Homeland Security of violating environmental law with Portland tear gas deployment, 2020. Available from: https://www.opb.org/article/2020/10/21/lawsuit-accuses-homeland-security-of-violating-environmental-law-with-portland-tear-gas-deployment/ (Accessed 20 June 2023).
63. Tempo.Co. Football disaster death toll rises as one fan dies from multiple head trauma, 2002. Available from: https://en.tempo.co/read/1644308/football-disaster-death-toll-rises-as-one-fan-dies-from-multiple-head-trauma (Accessed 20 June 2023).
64. The Guardian. Indonesia football stadium disaster: Police chief sacked as investigation launched, 2022. Available from: https://www.theguardian.com/world/2022/oct/03/indonesia-football-tragedy-questions-mount-over-police-response (Accessed 20 June 2023).
65. Mijatović D. Human rights comment: Shrinking space for freedom of peaceful assembly, 2019. Available from: https://www.coe.int/en/web/commissioner/-/shrinking-space-for-freedom-of-peaceful-assembly?inheritRedirect=true (Accessed 20 June 2023).
66. Organisation for Security and Cooperation in Europe. Human rights handbook on policing assemblies, 2016. Available from: https://www.osce.org/files/f/documents/c/5/226981.pdf (Accessed 20 June 2023).
67. Haar RJ, Iacopino V, Ranadive N, et al. Death, injury and disability from kinetic impact projectiles in crowd-control settings: A systematic review. *BMJ Open* 2017; 7(**12**): e018154.
68. Kenny J, Heal S, Grossman M. *The Attribute-Based Evaluation (ABE) of Less-Than-Lethal, Extended-Range, Impact Munitions*. National Institute of Justice; 2001.
69. Kenny J, Heal S, Kaufman P, Hughes E. An Attribute Based Evaluation II (ABE-2) of Less-Lethal Impact Munitions. National Institute of Justice; 2007.
70. Folha de Pernambuco. Polícia conclui que Caso Itambé foi homicídio, 2017. Available from: https://www.folhape.com.br/noticias/policia-conclui-que-caso-itambe-foi-homicidio/29761/ (Accessed 20 June 2023).
71. Globo. Detento fica ferido depois de ser atingido no rosto por bala de borracha, 2022. Available from: https://g1.globo.com/df/distrito-federal/df2/video/detento-fica-ferido-depois-de-ser-atingido-no-rosto-por-bala-de-borracha-10388665.ghtml (Accessed 20 June 2023).
72. Globo. Preso fica com rosto desfigurado após ser atingido por bala de borracha em presídio, no DF, 2022. Available from: https://g1.globo.com/df/distrito-federal/noticia/2022/03/15/preso-fica-com-rosto-desfigurado-apos-ser-atingido-por-bala-de-borracha-em-presidio-no-df.ghtml (Accessed 20 June 2023).
73. The Independent Commission on Policing in Northern Ireland. A new beginning: Policing in Northern Ireland, 1999. Available from: https://cain.ulster.ac.uk/issues/police/patten/patten99.pdf (Accessed 20 June 2023).
74. O'Halloran M. 6,000 plastic bullets fired since Drumcree stand-off, 1996. Available from: https://www.irishtimes.com/news/6-000-plastic-bullets-fired-since-drumcree-stand-off-1.67516 (Accessed 20 June 2023).
75. Weibel Barahona M, Jara M. Carabineros revela que disparó 104 mil tiros de escopeta en las primeras dos semanas del estallido social, 2020. Available from: https://ciperchile.cl/2020/08/18/carabineros-revela-que-disparo-104-mil-tiros-de-escopeta-en-las-primeras-dos-semanas-del-estallido-social/ (Accessed 20 June 2023).
76. Mijatović D. Memorandum on maintaining public order and freedom of assembly in the context of the "yellow vest" movement in France 2019. Available from: https://www.coe.int/en/web/commissioner/-/maintaining-public-order-and-freedom-of-assembly-in-the-context-of-the-yellow-vest-movement-recommendations-by-the-council-of-europe-commissioner-for- (Accessed 20 June 2023).
77. Instituto Nacional de Derechos Humanos. Reporte general de datos sobre violaciones a los derechos humanos, 2020. Available from: https://www.indh.cl/bb/wp-content/uploads/2020/04/Reporte-INDH-19-de-marzo-de-2020.pdf (Accessed 20 June 2023).
78. Rodríguez Á, Peña S, Cavieres I, et al. Ocular trauma by kinetic impact projectiles during civil unrest in Chile, 2020. Available from: https://www.nature.com/articles/s41433-020-01146-w?utm_source=feedburner&utm_medium=feed&utm_campaign=Feed%3A+eye%2Frss%2Fcurrent+%28Eye+-+Issue%29 (Accessed 20 June 2023).
79. Jorquera EP, Palma HR. Estudio de Perdigón. Investigación U. de Chile comprueba que perdigones usados por Carabineros contienen solo 20 por ciento de goma, 2019. Available from: https://www.uchile.cl/noticias/159315/perdigones-usados-por-carabineros-contienen-solo-20-por-ciento-de-goma (Accessed 20 June 2023).
80. Rozas Córdova MA. Declaración pública del director general de carabineros, 2019. Available from: https://twitter.com/Carabdechile/status/1196950642159476737/photo/1 (Accessed 20 June 2023).
81. Carabineros de Chile. Disparos con escopeta antidisturbios, con empleo de cartuchería con perdigón de goma y sus efectos en la superficie del cuerpo humano, 2012. Available from: https://policehumanrightsresources.org/carabineros-de-chile-disparos-con-escopeta-antidisturbios-con-empleo-de-cartucheria-con-perdigon-de-goma-y-sus-efectos-en-la-superficie-del-cuerpo-humano (Accessed 20 June 2023).
82. Toubon J. Décision du défenseur des droits n°2019–029, 2019. Available from: https://juridique.defenseurdesdroits.fr/doc_num.php?explnum_id=18403 (Accessed 20 June 2023).
83. Condor Tecnologias Nao Letais. GB-707. Available from: https://www.condornaoletal.com.br/gb-707/ (Accessed 20 June 2023).
84. Pacem Defense. GR-60. Available from: https://www.lesslethal.com/products/tld005-detail (Accessed 20 June 2023).
85. Angwin J, Nehrring A. *Hotter Than Lava*. Propublica; 2015. Available from: https://www.propublica.org/article/flash-bangs (Accessed 12 September 2023).
86. Désarmons-les. Rémi Fraisse, tué par les gendarmes à Sivens le 26 octobre 2014, 2018. Available from: https://desarmons.net/index.php/2018/01/09/retour-sur-la-mort-de-remi-fraisse-le-26-octobre-2014/ (Accessed 20 June 2023).
87. United Nations. General comment No. 37 on article 21 (Right of peaceful assembly), 2020. Available from: https://www.ohchr.org/en/documents/general-comments-and-recommendations/general-comment-no-37-article-21-right-peaceful (Accessed 20 June 2023).
88. United Nations Office of the High Commissioner for Human Rights. Bachelet condemns violent response of Belarus to post-electoral protests, 2020. Available from: https://www.ohchr.org/en/press-releases/2020/08/bachelet-condemns-violent-response-belarus-post-electoral-protests?LangID=E&NewsID=26162 (Accessed 20 June 2023).
89. Boika A, Litavrin M, Skovoroda Y, et al. Brutalised Minsk: How Belarusian police beat protesters, 2020. Available from: https://mediazona.by/article/2020/11/03/minsk-beaten-en (Accessed 20 June 2023).
90. AbraxasSpa. Russian less-lethal grenades used by Alpha, SOBR and other units in Minsk, 2020. Available from: https://twitter.com/AbraxasSpa/status/1293485090283159552 (Accessed 20 June 2023).
91. Rosoboronexport. Viyushka: Combined effect hand grenade. Available from: http://roe.ru/eng/catalog/special-weapons-and-ammunitions/non-lethal-grenades/vyushka/ (Accessed 20 June 2023).

92. Karmanau Y. Police break up protests after Belarus presidential vote, 2020. Available from: https://apnews.com/article/alexander-lukashenko-belarus-international-news-elections-riots-d310c4f9811b31e44fa5536bb826cc5e (Accessed 20 June 2023).
93. Mardilovic A. Комбинированная травма. Минчанка, получившая осколочное ранение от светошумовой гранаты, стала подозреваемой по уголовному делу, 2020. Available from: https://mediazona.by/article/2020/09/08/kombinirovannaya-travma (Accessed 20 June 2023).
94. Human Rights Watch. Armenia: Excessive police force at protest, 2016. Available from: https://www.hrw.org/news/2016/08/01/armenia-excessive-police-force-protest (Accessed 20 June 2023).
95. International Partnership for Human Rights. Beaten, burnt and betrayed: Armenians awaiting accountability for police violence, 2016. Available from: https://iphronline.org/wp-content/uploads/2016/09/Beaten-Burned-and-Betrayed-Armenia-report-Sept-2016.pdf (Accessed 20 June 2023).
96. Jino Motors. Titan-15. Available from: http://www.jinomotors.com/sub/product/list.php?idx=1 (Accessed 20 June 2023).
97. Albert Ziegler. PSV 9000. Available from: https://www.ziegler.de/de/produkte/sonderfahrzeuge/Spezielle%20Fahrzeuge/psv (Accessed 20 June 2023).
98. Grimley N. Blinded German man urges Boris Johnson not to bring water cannon to London, 2014. Available from: https://www.bbc.co.uk/news/uk-26226926 (Accessed 20 June 2023).
99. B.E. Meyers. Website. Available from: https://bemeyers.com/ (Accessed 20 June 2023).
100. Organisation for Security and Cooperation in Europe. Guide on law enforcement equipment most commonly used in the policing of assemblies, 2021. Available from: https://www.osce.org/files/f/documents/4/7/491551_0.pdf (Accessed 20 June 2023).
101. ISPRA. Riot control drone system, 2022. Available from: https://www.ispraltd.com/Riot-Control-Drone-System.html (Accessed 20 June 2023).
102. United Nations Commission of Inquiry on the 2018 protests in the Occupied Palestinian Territory. Report of the detailed findings of the independent international Commission of inquiry on the protests in the Occupied Palestinian Territory, 2019. Available from: https://www.un.org/unispal/wp-content/uploads/2019/06/A.HRC_.40.CPR_.2.pdf (Accessed 20 June 2023).
103. Office of the United Nations High Commissioner for Human Rights. Update of the situation of human rights in Indian-administered Kashmir and Pakistan-administered Kashmir from May 2018 to April 2019, 2019. Available from: https://www.ohchr.org/Documents/Countries/IN/KashmirUpdateReport_8July2019.pdf (Accessed 20 June 2023).

CHAPTER

86

Conducted Electrical Weapons

Mark W. Kroll and Gary M. Vilke

INTRODUCTION

The most critical fact for understanding the conducted electrical weapon (CEW) (sometimes referred to as conducted electrical devices or conducted energy devices [CEDs]) is that the CEW is an electronic muscle stimulator (1–4). Misconceptions about this have led to misunderstanding of the effects of these weapons. The primary difference between the therapeutic muscle stimulator and the CEW is that the CEW uses short sharp probes to create the connection while the muscle stimulator uses adhesive electrodes (4).

Those probes cause the most common demonstrated serious complication – penetrating eye injuries (5–7).

The probes also introduce the theoretical risk of electrocution in the event of a probe contacting the ventricular epicardium in a slender individual (BMI <22) with a skin-to-heart distance of <12 mm (8).

Some CEW models utilize a very short high-voltage arcing phase to generate a connection through the air in order to deliver the current to a heavily clothed individual. The low-charge arcing phase has no effect on the muscle contractions and is thus irrelevant to the physiology and pathology (9). Unfortunately, the presence of this small arc has led to the misconception that the CEW is a high-voltage source leading some practitioners to confuse the effects with those of powerlines and lightning strokes, which is unfortunate as a typical CEW delivers 2 watts of power compared to 30 kW from a powerline connection (10).

Human electronic control with the CEW has gained widespread acceptance as a preferred law enforcement intermediate force option. There have been over 4.2 million field uses of CEWs and over 6 million uses including training. "Presentation" compliance is 75–85 percent in that the threat of CEW use alone usually halts belligerent activity (11–13). Subject mortality is reduced by 2/3 compared to other use of force techniques thus substantially lowering the ARD (arrest-related death) rate (14,15). Subject injuries, requiring medical attention, have been shown to be reduced by 80 percent (16).

The short-duration electrical pulses applied are intended to stimulate the Type A-α motor neurons that control skeletal muscle contraction, but with minimal risk of stimulating myocardium. This typically leads to a loss of regional muscle control and can result in a fall to the ground to end a potentially violent confrontation or suicide attempt (17–19).

FATAL COMPLICATIONS

Traumatic brain injury and cervical fractures

With sufficient probe spread (30 cm in the front or 20 cm in the back) an uncontroled fall to the ground is likely (17). The most significant hazard associated with a fall is the possible head impact on the ground that can lead to severe or fatal injuries of the head or cervical spine (20,21).

With an effective probe connection, especially to the back, the extensors of the thorax and hips tend to dominate thus often causing a backward fall for the standing person. Forward falls have lower risks of life-threatening injuries compared to backward falls (22). A severe impact on the face causes fractures (nose, orbitals, and jaw) at moderate force levels resulting in energy absorption and a reduction of the resulting head acceleration similar to the function of crush zones in an automobile body. For backward falls, the greater stability of the occiput region leads to higher accelerations and a higher risk of intracranial injuries including coup and contrecoup contusions as well as subdural hematomas. The head impact velocity in falls from a standing position can reach values exceeding 6 m/s (22,23). Such impact on a solid surface can cause severe or fatal injuries.

There were 16 deaths reported from traumatic brain injury (TBI) due to CEW-induced falls as of 2015 (21). The age of the fatal-fall subjects was 46 ± 14 years which is significantly higher than that of ARDs in general (compared to Ho with 35.7 ± 9.8, n = 162, p = .0002) (24). Since then there have been five additional fatalities from induced falls given a total of 21 cases as of July 2021. There have been two deaths reported from cervical fractures caused by a CEW-induced fall (21). This gives a total of 23 fatalities from CEW induced falls.

DOI: 10.1201/9781003138754-89

Ignition of flammable fumes

The second largest fatality risk is with the ignition of flammable fumes – almost always gasoline. Fresh gasoline has a lower explosive limit (LEL) of 1.4 percent. This means that a mixture that is 98.6 percent air and 1.4 percent vapor is barely explosive. Surprisingly, this concentration level (1.4%) is not considered acutely toxicologically dangerous but in the "recreational" intoxication range for gasoline sniffers (25,26). The upper explosive limit (UEL) is 7.6 percent and thus gasoline, *per se*, is not explosive. With a CEW arc *seconds* after pouring gasoline in the clothes, Clarke found that the vapors were overly concentrated (>7.6%) and there was not enough air for combustion (27). With a shock *minutes* after pouring gasoline in the clothes, the vapors were under-concentrated (<1.4%) and there was not enough gas vapor for combustion. The probes had to be right in the area of the gasoline-soaked clothing and the shock delivered 30–60 seconds after the soaking to reliably ignite the fumes.

The minimum ignition energy (MIE) is 0.24 mJ which occurs at the "optimal" concentration between the lower and upper limits. This is lower than the ≈ 1 mJ of the popular TASER X26(E) (AXON Enterprises, Scottsdale, Arizona, USA) CEW probe-wire connection and thus the fumes are easily ignited by the arc in the "needle-eye" at the back of the probe with an optimal concentration (Figure 86.1). A challenge in recognizing the danger is that officers and subjects begin to be desensitized to the odor of gasoline within 1 minute of being around it (28).

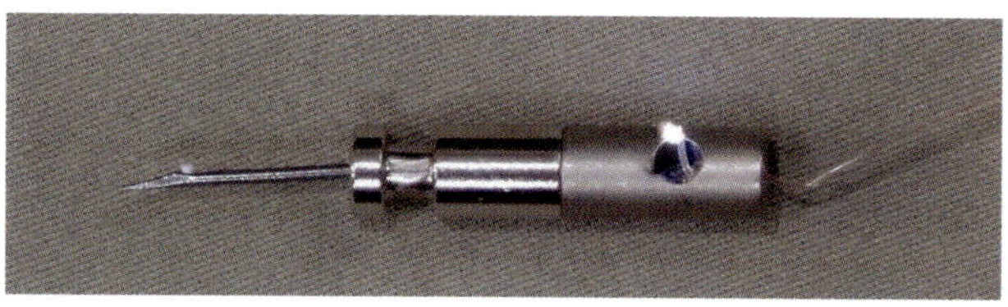

86.1 Arcing TASER probe.

There are other liquids that have similar explosive capabilities, but they have never produced a fatal case outside of a tragic double fatality incident with a home full of methane natural gas. Butane and its isomer, isobutene, are present in cigarette lighters. Oleoresin capsicum (pepper or OC) aerosol often uses flammable propellants, such as isopropyl alcohol, ethanol and methyl isobutyl ketone. A few OC aerosols use nitrogen or other non-flammable propellants. Many of the OC aerosols labeled as "non-flammable" can actually be ignited by a CEW (29). Most of these develop a small flame that is unlikely to produce a severe burn injury. Plastic cigarette lighters carried in a front or rear pocket are often ignited but there is only a single case of a moderate burn injury as the amount of fuel is small (30).

The MIE for each substance is given in Table 86.1. The ignition energy increases rapidly for concentrations not centered between the higher and lower explosive limits (31). This can explain why many electrical weapon probe deployments do not cause an explosion even in the presence of a given fuel.

The published literature reports six fatal burns (four petrol and two methane) from CEW ignition as of 2015 (30). Since that publication, there have been three deaths, all of whom had gasoline on their clothing in suicide threats. This gives a total of nine fatal fire deaths reported.

Vulnerable populations

There are certain groups more vulnerable to the effects of the CEW, although these groups are typically misidentified. Surprisingly, illegal drugs tend to make electrocution more difficult. For example, cocaine is a strong sodium channel blocker and it *increases* the electrocution threshold in swine and canines (32,33). Methamphetamine also appears to slightly increase the threshold for electrical sensitivity in sheep (34). The most common intoxicant seen in police work is alcohol and this has been studied with electrical weapons in a

TABLE 86.1 Relevant flammable substances

Substance	LEL	UEL	MIE (mJ)	Fatal cases	Source or usage
Petrol	*1.4%*	*7.6%*	*0.24*	*9*	Motor vehicles, arson, suicide, sniffing
Methane	*5%*	*15%*	*0.21*	*2*	Natural Gas
Isobutane	*1.8%*	*9.5%*	*0.009*	*0*	Spray-paint propellant, lighter fluid
Ethanol	*3.3%*	*19%*	*0.23*	*0*	Spray-paint propellant, OC spray propellant
Isopropyl alcohol	*2%*	*12%*	*0.65*	*0*	OC spray propellant
Methyl isobutyl ketone	*1%*	*8%*	*0.21–0.53*	*0*	OC spray propellant

crossover clinical study (35). Extreme chronic alcohol abuse (36% of caloric intake being ethanol) lowered the ventricular fibrillation (VF) threshold in a canine model (36).

Interactions with drug-intoxicated patients are well studied with large data. Strote found that 94 percent of CEW subjects had a history of drug or alcohol abuse or a psychiatric diagnosis (37). This implies that there have been over 4.2 million such subjects that received an electrical weapon exposure. There have been no demonstrated electrocutions in this group (38–40). Of the 180 patients for which toxicology was available immediately after the CEW application, Strote found that 71 percent were positive for illegal drugs. Most common was cocaine (40%), multiple drugs (33%) and depressants (26%) (37). A large Canadian forceful-arrest study found that 82 percent of the subjects were being affected by alcohol, drugs, or emotional disturbance (41). Ho et al. studied the outcomes of CEW usage with 2452 mentally ill subjects and found that this prevented several shootings and there were no electrocution deaths (42).

That is also consistent with 140 years of electrical injury and electrocution research which has never suggested or demonstrated any susceptibility or increased risk with mental illness. Mental health does not affect how electricity affects the body. Obese people are protected somewhat from electrocution because fat is an electrical insulator (43).

Theoretically, current from the CEW application could travel from the pacemaker housing down a pacing lead into the heart and induce an arrhythmia. This remains an extremely unlikely theoretical concern as a typical pacemaker patient is 80 years old and this age group tends not to fight with police (44). There is a single report of a pacemaker patient having rapid asymptomatic pacing during a CEW application arising from a prison riot (45,46).

The experience of over 6 million human exposures (including training exposures) and 20 years of research defines the vulnerable population.

The allergy analogy

Medications affect human beings individually in many different ways and a given medication might only work well on about half of people because of our genetic differences (47). Very importantly, a tiny amount of a specific drug or even peanuts can trigger the body's immune response which then responds, attacks the body and causes damage.

Electricity does not cause allergic reactions and it does not care about the subject's genotype. The only pathology that appears to lower the electrocution VF threshold is coronary artery disease and that has a mild effect that will be discussed later (48). This pathology is relatively uncommon in ARDs. On the other hand, due to long-term stimulant and alcohol abuse, cardiomyopathies are relatively common in ARD cases (49–51). However, cardiomyopathy patients do *not* have an increased susceptibility to electrocution (52).

Due to the notoriety of the CEW, occasional unique case reports appear that attempt to link an unusual ARD to the electrical weapon (53). Such reports suffer from the classic limitations of case reports and are not supported by later publications (54). The fatality risks supported by data remain with the falls and fires (15).

NON-FATAL COMPLICATIONS

Penetrating eye injuries

The typical CEW has a single laser sight that approximately aligns with the top probe. The lower probe is launched at a separation angle of 6–12° below the laser line depending on the model (Some newer models also have a laser light that provides the lower probe path). The requirement, of a 30 cm spread on the front, adds to the risk of a probe contacting the face, especially if the subject ducks to "avoid" the probes (17).

Globe rupture can be expected ($p = 0.5$) when the eye is within 6 m of the CEW muzzle and decreases with an increasing distance (5). Some of the penetrating eye injuries involve only a perforation by the dart portion of the probe. As of 2017, there had been 29 reported penetrating eye injuries out of 3.44 million field uses (7). The risk of enucleation or unilateral blindness was 69 ± 18 percent, partial blindness was 19 ± 15 percent and normal vision after surgical correction was 8 percent. Surgical correction can restore normal vision in some cases. The mean age was 31.1 ± 12.1 years which is consistent with the typical CEW-force recipient (32.0 ± 10.7) (37).

Non-fatal fall and fire injuries

Bozeman reported two non-fatal head injuries from falls – that resolved without neurosurgical intervention or long-term sequelae – out of 1201 CEW uses for a rate of 0.17 percent (95%CI: 0.05–0.61%) (55). More severe non-fatal head injuries were reported in the Mangus case-series with the worst appearing to be a case with a basilar skull fracture, right subarachnoid hemorrhage, and left-sided epidural hemorrhage necessitating craniotomy (20).

As of 2015, there were four major burn injuries (by American Burn Association definition) from CEW ignition (30). Since that publication, there have been four additional cases reported, all of whom had gasoline on their clothing, for a total of eight non-fatal major burn injury cases reported.

Rhabdomyolysis and acidosis

There have also been several case reports published noting vertebral bone injuries during CEW training use that have been attributed to the strong muscle contractions of the back muscles in individuals with osteoporotic bones (56,57).

The safety margin of modern electrical weapons is best appreciated by the increasing acceptance of electrical muscle stimulation for weight loss and muscle toning. Popular, US FDA-approved, muscle stimulators deliver more current than the TASER® brand muscle stimulators for the typical resistance range of 500–1000 Ω (4) (Figure 86.2).

The upper safety limits can be seen by the results from the Bodytec® (Miha, Gersthofen, Bayern, Germany) whole-body "workout" system which delivers a total current of nearly 48 mA (58) (Figure 86.3a&b). If a TASER® brand muscle stimulator were to have all four probes in the body it could deliver 3 mA, and thus, the Bodytec system delivers about 16 times as much current.

A typical Bodytec therapy session is 15 minutes compared to 15 seconds for the typical TASER electrical-weapon application. The only complications reported for the Bodytec system have been rhabdomyolysis and none were severe enough to require dialysis (59,60).

Since the therapeutic muscle stimulation sessions are *minutes* versus *seconds* and deliver about 16 times as much total current, rhabdomyolysis is not expected with applications of electrical weapons. This has been demonstrated in multiple clinical trials evaluating the

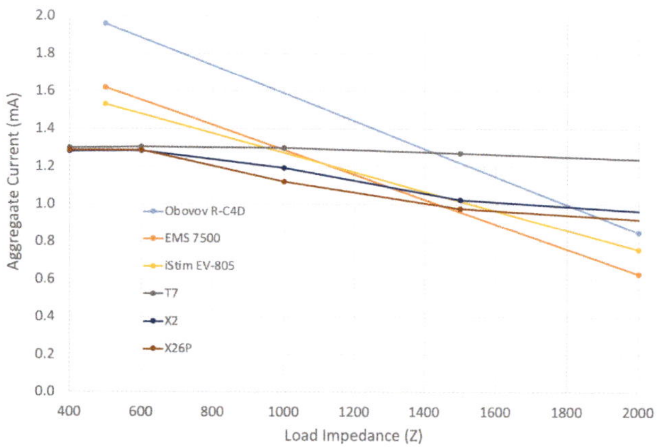

86.2 CEW EMS output plots.

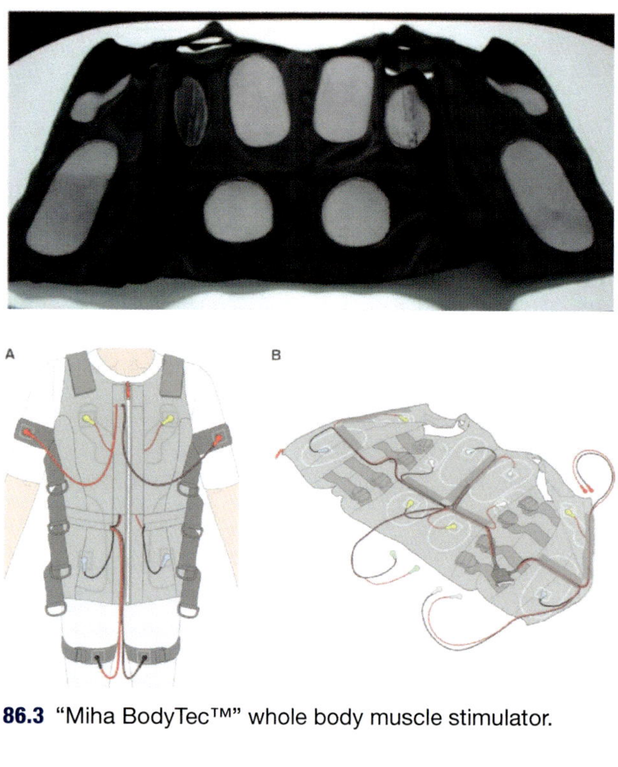

86.3 "Miha BodyTec™" whole body muscle stimulator.

physiologic effects of CEWs in humans, which have found only clinically insignificant increases in creatine kinase, myoglobin and other markers (61–64).

ELECTROCUTION RISK

Electrocution primer

Electrocution is a death caused by an application of electrical current to the human body. "Electrocution" in this context does not include a death from secondary trauma such as an electrical worker being startled by a shock and falling off a ladder and dying from a head injury.

Low-power electrocution is essentially synonymous with the induction of VF. On the other extreme, a lightning discharge can cause substantial acute and chronic neural effects leading to temporary asystole and ventilatory arrest (65–68). Eventually, cardiac activity and spontaneous circulation typically returns. In some cases, ventilatory arrest persists, and the hypoxia will lead to asystole or pulseless electrical activity from the systemic acidosis after a few minutes (65). Andrews used a sheep lightning model and found initial asystole followed by perfusing arrhythmias and ending with permanent asystole (69). Karobath reported both VF and asystole in his swine model of lightning strikes (66). Both asystole and VF have been reported in humans with lightning strikes with a typical progression of temporary asystole to VF which then finally deteriorates into asystole after approximately 30 minutes (67,68).

The original hypothesis (1880s) for electrocution was fatal acidosis induced by muscle contractions and induced ventilatory arrest. The acidosis *from ventilatory arrest* theory was popular in the later 1800s but Jones questioned this based on witnessed human accidents in 1895 (70). Fatal acidosis *from ventilatory arrest* was demonstrated by Cunningham in the 1890s in dogs but only with 10 minutes of continuous currents just below those required for VF but sufficient to cause ventilatory arrest (71). This is irrelevant to CEWs since they do not cause ventilatory arrest (72–76). Oliver and Bolam then did animal experiments which showed that electrocution was due to an immediate cardiac arrest, in their 1898 paper (77). In 1899, Prevost and Battelli published their landmark paper showing that electrocution was caused by VF (78). Over a century of electrocution research has never demonstrated one single death from electrically induced acidosis from muscle contractions.

In summary, in the context of the CEW, electrocution is synonymous with the induction of VF.

Safety standards

The basic international electrical safety standard (IEC 60479 series) has thresholds for perception, pain, muscle contractions, ventilatory arrest and fatalities with the fatal levels being set at the VF threshold (79,80). All present TASER brand CEWs deliver less than 2 W which is far less than the 5–7 W allowed by the Underwriters Laboratories (UL) electric fence standard (UL-69) (81). They also satisfy the conservative IEC (International

TABLE 86.2 ANSI CPLSO-17 output limits

	Raw charge (μC)	Normalized charge (μC)	Pulse rate (Hz)	Normalized aggregate current (mA)
Minimum	40	60	17	1.15
Maximum	125	120	30	2.2

TABLE 86.3 AC currents and their typical effects

AC Current (mA)	Effect
1500	Nerve Damage
1000	
500	Cardiac Arrest Probable
200	
100	Cardiac Arrest Possible
50	Interference w Breathing
20	
16	X2 CEW (AC Equivalent)
15	Male No-let-go threshold
10	Muscle Contractions Begin
5	Pain Sensation
1.1	Male Hand Perception
0.7	Female Hand Perception

Electrotechnical Commission) and European (Cenelec) 2.5 W electric fence limit (82–84). CEWs sold in the USA and UK all satisfy the ANSI electric fence standard limits for power, electrical charge, and aggregate current (85).

There is also an electrical standard designed specifically for the CEW: ANSI CPLSO-17 (86). It requires certain minimum outputs for effectiveness and has maximum limits for safety as shown in Table 86.2. All TASER brand CEWs satisfy this standard (87). There are other (non-TASER) brands of CEWs which do not satisfy the above safety standards but that does not necessarily imply that they have electrocution risks (88,89).

The typical clinical effects of various AC currents are shown in Table 86.3. The 1.8 mA of aggregate pulsed DC current for the TASER X2 CEW is equivalent to 16 mA AC due to the 9X "currency conversion" between DC pulses and steady AC current (90). This level is substantially lower than the 40 mA IEC safety limit used with residual current limiters which are designed to prevent VF internationally. TASER brand CEWs thus satisfy all relevant electrical safety standards (91,92).

A limitation, with applying electrical safety standards, is that they are largely based on *external* skin contact. However, the heart is very close to the skin in the 4th or 5th left parasternal intercostal spaces with a distance as little as 10 mm from *right* ventricular myocardium to the skin surface in a thin adult (93). The apex can also be this close but that is less relevant to electrocution since the *left* ventricle (and apex) is much thicker and hence has a higher VF threshold (94,95). Hence, the electrical safety standards imply an upper bound of ≈10 mm for the dart to heart distance (DTH) for VF induction. Therefore, a probe penetrating the skin directly over the right ventricle could theoretically induce VF even while satisfying these safety standards if the probe was nearly touching the ventricular epicardium (within 4 mm). Horowitz found that the induction of VF in humans by right-ventricular epicardial bursts required pulse charges of 97 μC (= 24.3 mA • 4 ms) which suggests that the 100 μC typical CEW charge would have to be delivered almost directly to the epicardium (48). For this reason, the relevant animal and human testing focuses on the critical DTH for the tip of the probe.

Animal cardiac studies

Due to longer QT intervals, shorter repolarization times and intramural Purkinje fibers, the swine heart is 3x more electrically sensitive than that of humans and goes into VF more easily than humans, thus swine are not good models for determining VF thresholds in humans (96–100).

Some small swine have had VF induced with a CEW probe very close to the heart. These studies demonstrate that the theoretical risk of electrocution is confined to very small or very thin humans. The largest swine electrocuted by a CEW was reported by Valentino et al. and weighed 36 kg (101). The levels of dangerous currents scale with body mass just like a drug dosage. Since swine are three times as sensitive to electrical current (as humans) we can translate the Valentino 36 kg pig to a 12 kg human (100). This calculation uses a direct proportion relationship for VF threshold to the body mass. Some authorities argue that the VF threshold scales with the *square root* of body mass (102). With such a relationship the Valentino pig is equivalent to a larger 21 kg human. Using this more conservative calculation, the best animal model evidence suggests that the risk of CEW electrocution is limited to humans with a body mass under 21 kg (46 lb).

Wu et al. evaluated probe spacings of 2–12 mm and found that the probe tip, had to be 5.8 ± 2.0 mm from the epicardium with an X26(E) to induce VF. The return (reference) dart was placed in the inferior part of the abdomen and no myocardium was in a straight vector between the electrodes (103). This refuted the common misperception that a "transcardiac vector" was relevant to the CEW electrocution risk. Other swine studies have also refuted the transcardiac hypothesis (104). Lakkireddy et al. also tested close probe spacings to the heart (12–23 mm) without inducing VF with an X26(E) and demonstrating an 8-fold safety margin in ≈ 35 kg swine (32,105). Based on the

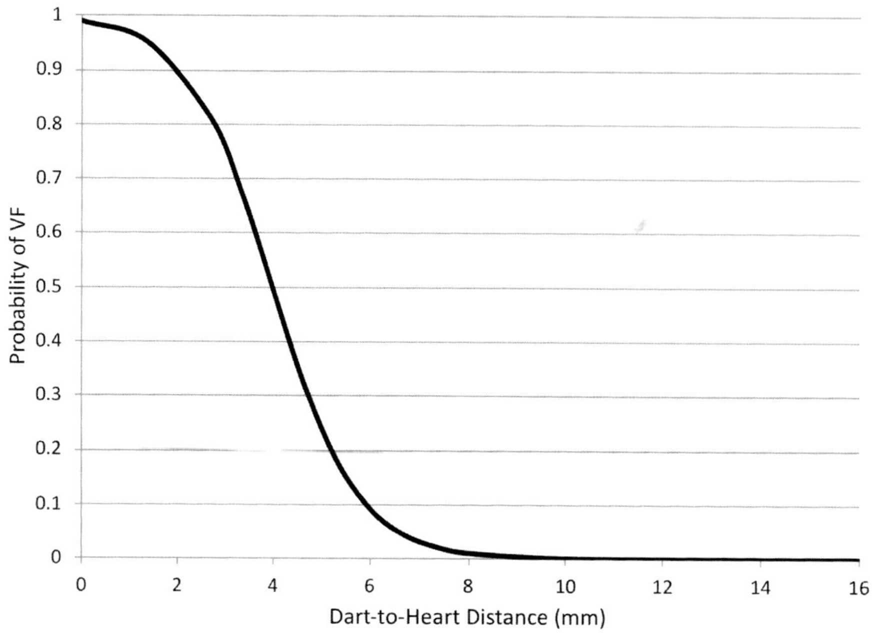

86.4 Probability VF vs DTH Webster Lakkireddy data.

Lakkireddy (12–23 mm) and Wu results, the probability of inducing VF in swine based upon DTH can be estimated by logistic regression as shown in Figure 86.4 (103,106).

The critical DTH in humans is less than that in swine since swine are more sensitive to external currents inducing VF (107). Coronary artery disease and metabolic acidosis will also lower the VFT threshhold (48,108).

Because of the human anatomy, this small DTH is very unlikely in a normal adult but could be possible in small children. A prospective study of CEW usage in minors (by age) found no complications beyond probe punctures (109). Risk calculations, using a distribution of body habitus and echo and CT-scan data have been performed (8,110). Ultimately, the VF risk in adult humans is estimated to be approximately 1 in 3 million field probe uses (106).

Human cardiac clinical studies

There have been 66 humans monitored continuously during a discharge with precordial CEW probes (Table 86.4). There was no VF induction but a single case of asymptomatic cardiac pacing in 2009 in a volunteer with pectus excavatus. That was with an experimental prototype CEW which was never manufactured. The margin between cardiac pacing and the induction of VF is quite high and typically about 12:1 (111). Thus, these clinical data suggest a very low risk of VF induction even with precordial probes.

A major manufacturer has warned against placing probes in the chest for three reasons: 1) risk of eye injury, 2) decreased effectiveness with the lower probe in the abdomen versus in the thigh, and 3) risk of electrocution with a probe touching the heart. Several organizations have suggested that the cardiac risk concern was exaggerated.

In 2011, the National Institute of Justice, after a 5-year panel review, concluded that "current research does not support a substantially increased risk of cardiac arrhythmia in field situations, even if the CED darts strike the front of the chest... There is currently no medical evidence that CEDs pose a significant risk for induced cardiac dysrhythmia in humans when deployed reasonably" (112). The American Academy of Emergency Medicine CEW guidelines agrees that electrocution might be a theoretical risk but has not yet definitively occurred: "There has not been a documented case of CEW-induced lethal VF that has withstood close scrutiny; whether it is theoretically possible is controversial and beyond the scope of this review" (113).

Diagnosis

Objective criteria can be given for an electrocution diagnosis in a CEW incident as shown in Table 86.5. Asystole (flatline) and PEA (pulseless electrical activity) are not inducible with electrical stimulation (114). Asystole is rarely confused by EMS personnel – and almost never if multiple leads are used (115). Electrically induced VF does not deteriorate to asystole in <20 minutes (116–118) and the median time in swine is 34 minutes (119). The delay is longer with chest compressions (120).

The best evidence suggests that electrocution in a human would require that the tip of the probe be within ≈ 4 mm of the epicardium (outer part of the heart). Induction of VF is not an issue with the drive stun as no probe penetrates the skin to get sufficiently close to the heart. A probe in the sternum is considered too far away as the sternum is an insulator in adults (121,122). With any chest compressions, defibrillation has a ≥ 90 percent success rates up to 10 minutes of electrically induced VF – with three or fewer shocks (123). Hence, the failure of prompt defibrillation to convert to a sinus rhythm essentially rules out an electrical cause for VF. After a cardiac arrest, normal

TABLE 86.4 Human testing with precordial probes and continuous monitoring

Author	n	Exposure (s)	Monitoring	Pacing	VF
Stopyra (127)	3*	5	Electrogram	0	0
Dawes (128)	10	5	Echo	0	0
Ho (129)	53	10	Echo	1	0

*Stopyra had four subjects but the pacemaker prevented recording in a single case.

TABLE 86.5 Diagnosis of electrocution by CEW. Each criterion must be satisfied

	Item	Notes
1	Presenting rhythm is VF (114).	Asystole and PEA are not inducible (114).
2	Dart-to-epicardial distance is ≤ 4 mm (103).	The critical DTH is 5.8 ± 2.1 mm in swine (103).
3	No documented pulse after CEW application.	When a pulse is detected, this has a 95% accuracy (130,131).
4	Cessation of normal breathing within 60 seconds of CEW application (124,125).	
5	Cessation of agonal breathing within 6 minutes of CEW application (125,126).	Commonly referred to as "dying gasps" and not confused with normal breathing.
6	If defibrillation (up to 3 shocks) is attempted within 10 minutes (or 14 minutes with CPR) it is successful (123).	Electrically induced VF is defibrillated with a 90% success rate at 10 minutes with any chest compressions (123).

breathing ceases in 12–60 seconds (124,125). However, some subjects can have "agonal" breathing (dying gasps) for up to 6 minutes (126).

A notable finding in many ARD autopsy reports is the opinion that the electrical current from a CEW "contributed" to an ARD. This is a curious finding as it has been long established that electrocution is a stand-alone cause of death with only trivial interactions with other pathologies. Most textbooks on forensic pathology have a chapter on electrocution and report the required electrical currents (typically 100 mA AC RMS), yet none of them list dyssynergies with other conditions.

CONCLUSION

A CEW is an electronic muscle stimulator and many approved muscle stimulators deliver more current than the TASER brand muscle stimulators. The primary difference between the therapeutic muscle stimulator and the CEW is that the CEW uses short sharp probes to create the connection while the muscle stimulator uses adhesive electrodes.

All present TASER brand CEWs deliver less than 2 W which is less than the various international electric fence limits of 2.5–7.0 W and satisfy the ANSI electric fence standard limits for power, electrical charge and aggregate current. These CEWs also satisfy the ANSI CPLSO-17 standard designed specifically for the CEW.

Fatal complications of CEW use include burns and a theoretical risk of electrocution in the event of a probe contacting the ventricular epicardium in an extremely slender individual. Theoretically, the current from a CEW application could travel from a pacemaker housing down the pacing lead into the heart and induce an arrhythmia but this has not yet occurred.

REFERENCES

1. Adams C, Scott W, Basile J, et al. Electrically elicited quadriceps muscle torque: A comparison of 3 waveforms. *J Orthop Sports Phys Ther* 2018; **48**(3): 217–24.
2. Vromans M, Faghri P. Electrical stimulation frequency and skeletal muscle characteristics: Effects on force and fatigue. *Eur J Transl Myol* 2017; **27**(4): 6816.
3. Nussbaum EL, Houghton P, Anthony J, et al. Neuromuscular electrical stimulation for treatment of muscle impairment: Critical review and recommendations for clinical practice. *Physiother Can* 2017; **69**(5): 1–76.
4. Kroll M, Perkins P, Chiles BD, et al. Output of electronic muscle stimulators: Physical therapy and police models compared. *Conf Proc IEEE Eng Med Biol Soc* 2021; **43**: 1264–8.
5. Kroll MW, Ritter MB, Kennedy EA, et al. Eye injury from electrical weapon probes: Mechanisms and treatment. *Am J Emerg Med* 2019; **37**(3): 427–32.
6. Moysidis SN, Koulisis N, Rodger DC, et al. TASER injuries to the eye and ocular adnexa: The management of complex trauma. *Ophthalmol Retina* 2018; **3**: 258–69.
7. Kroll MW, Ritter MB, Kennedy EA, et al. Eye injuries from electrical weapon probes: Incidents, prevalence, and legal implications. *J Forensic Leg Med* 2018; **55**: 52–7.
8. Kroll MW, Lakkireddy D, Rahko PS, Panescu D. Ventricular fibrillation risk estimation for conducted electrical weapons: Critical convolutions. *Conf Proc IEEE EMBC* 2011; **33**: 271–7.
9. Comeaux JA, Jauchem JR, Cox DD, et al. Muscle contraction during electro-muscular incapacitation: A comparison between square-wave pulses and the

TASER® X26 Electronic control device. *J Forensic Sci* 2011; **56**: 95–100.
10. Kroll MW, Panescu D. Physics of Electrical Injury. In: Ho JD, Dawes DM, Kroll MW (eds), *Atlas of Conducted Electrical Weapon Wounds and Forensic Analysis*. New York: Springer; 2012, pp. 25–45.
11. Stevenson R, Drummond-Smith I. Medical implications of Conducted Energy Devices in law enforcement. *J Forensic Leg Med* 2020; **73**: 101948.
12. Grove N, Grove C, Peschel O, Kunz S. Welfare effects of substituting traditional police ballistic weapons with non-lethal alternatives: Medico-economic comparative study. *Rechtsmedizin* 2016; **26(5)**: 418–24.
13. den Heyer G. An analysis of the effectiveness and use by the New Zealand Police of the TASER from 2009 to 2017. *Int J Police Sci Manag* 2020; **22(4)**: 356–65.
14. Ferdik FV, Kaminski RJ, Cooney MD, Sevigny EL. The influence of agency policies on conducted energy device use and police use of lethal force. *Police Q* 2014; 17(4): 1098611114548098.
15. Kroll M, Brave M, Pratt H, et al. Benefits, risks, and myths of TASER® handheld electrical weapons. *Hum Factors Mech Eng Def Saf* 2019; **3(1)**: 7.
16. Taylor B, Woods DJ. Injuries to officers and suspects in police use-of-force cases: A quasi-experimental evaluation. *Police Q* 2010; **13(3)**: 260–89.
17. Ho J, Dawes D, Miner J, et al. Conducted electrical weapon incapacitation during a goal-directed task as a function of probe spread. *Forensic Sci Med Pathol* 2012; **8(4)**: 358–66.
18. Criscione JC, Kroll MW. Incapacitation recovery times from a conductive electrical weapon exposure. *Forensic Sci Med Pathol* 2014; **10(2)**: 203–7.
19. Ho J, Dawes DM, Kunz SN, et al. A comparative study of conducted electrical weapon incapacitation during a goal-directed task. *Forensic Sci Med Pathol* 2020; **16(4)**: 613–21.
20. Mangus BE, Shen LY, Helmer SD, et al. Taser and taser associated injuries: A case series. *Am Surg* 2008; **74(9)**: 862–5.
21. Kroll MW, Adamec J, Wetli CV, Williams HE. Fatal traumatic brain injury with electrical weapon falls. *J Forensic Leg Med* 2016; **43**: 12–19.
22. Hajiaghamemar M, Seidi M, Ferguson JR, Caccese V. Measurement of head impact due to standing fall in adults using anthropomorphic test dummies. *Ann Biomed Eng* 2015; **43**: 2143–52.
23. Hamel A, Llari M, Piercecchi-Marti M-D, et al. Effects of fall conditions and biological variability on the mechanism of skull fractures caused by falls. *Int J Leg Med* 2013; **127(1)**: 111–18.
24. Ho JD, Heegaard WG, Dawes DM, et al. Unexpected arrest-related deaths in america: 12 months of open source surveillance. *West J Emerg Med* 2009; **10**(2): 68–73.
25. Drinker P, Yaglou C, Warren MF. The threshold toxicity of gasoline vapor. *J Ind Hyg Toxicol* 1943; **25**: 225–32.
26. Sandmeyer EE. Aromatic Hydrocarbons. In: Patty FA, Clayton GD, Clayton FE, Battigelli MC (eds), *Patty's Industrial Hygiene and Toxicology*. New York: John Wiley & Sons; 1985.
27. Clarke C, Andrews SP. The ignitability of petrol vapours and potential for vapour phase explosion by use of TASER® law enforcement electronic control device. *Sci Justice* 2014; **54(6)**: 412–20.
28. Pryor GT, Steinmetz G, Stone H. Changes in absolute detection threshold and in subjective intensity of suprathreshold stimuli during olfactory adaptation and recovery. *Percept Psychophys* 1970; **8**(5): 331–5.
29. Myers C, Wyant R, Burns T. TASER SAFE, OR FLAMMABLE? *Law Officer Magazine* 2007: 38–41.
30. Kroll M, Ritter M, Williams H. Fatal and non-fatal burn injuries with electrical weapons and explosive fumes. *J Forensic Leg Med* 2017; **50**: 6–11.
31. Zabetakis M. Flammability characteristics of combustible gases and vapors, 1924. Available from: https://www.osti.gov/servlets/purl/7328370/ (Accessed 16 June 2023).
32. Lakkireddy D, Wallick D, Ryschon K, et al. Effects of cocaine intoxication on the threshold for stun gun induction of ventricular fibrillation. *J Am Coll Cardiol* 2006; **48(4)**: 805–11.
33. Tisdale JE, Shimoyama H, Sabbah HN, Webb CR. The effect of cocaine on ventricular fibrillation threshold in the normal canine heart. *Pharmacotherapy* 1996; **16(3)**: 429–37.
34. Dawes DM, Ho JD, Cole JB, et al. Effect of an electronic control device exposure on a methamphetamine-intoxicated animal model. *Acad Emerg Med* 2010; **17**(4): 436–43.
35. Moscati R, Ho JD, Dawes DM, Miner JR. Physiologic effects of prolonged conducted electrical weapon discharge in ethanol-intoxicated adults. *Am J Emerg Med* 2010; **28(5)**: 582–7.
36. Patel R, McArdle JJ, Regan TJ. Increased ventricular vulnerability in a chronic ethanol model despite reduced electrophysiologic responses to catecholamines. *Alcohol Clin Exp Res* 1991; **15(5)**: 785–9.
37. Strote J, Walsh M, Angelidis M, et al. Conducted electrical weapon use by law enforcement: An evaluation of safety and injury. *J Trauma* 2010; **68(5)**: 1239–46.
38. Goudge S. The health effects of conducted energy weapons: The Expert Panel on the Medical and Physiological Impacts of Conducted Energy Weapons. Available from: https://www.prisonpolicy.org/scans/council_canadian_academics/The%20Health%20Effects%20of%20Conducted%20Energy%20Weapons.pdf (Accessed 16 June 2023).
39. Kroll MW, Lakkireddy DR, Stone JR, Luceri RM. TASER electronic control devices and cardiac arrests: coincidental or causal? Case reports. *Circulation* 2014; **129(1)**: 93–100.
40. Zipes DP. TASER electronic control devices can cause cardiac arrest in humans. *Circulation* 2014; **129(1)**: 101–11.
41. Hall CA, Votova K, Heyd C, et al. Restraint in police use of force events: Examining sudden in custody death for prone and not-prone positions. *J Forensic Leg Med* 2015; **31**: 29–35.
42. Ho JD, Dawes DM, Johnson MA, et al. Impact of conducted electrical weapons in a mentally ill population: A brief report. *Am J Emerg Med* 2007; **25(7)**: 780–5.
43. Maffiuletti NA, Morelli A, Martin A, et al. Effect of gender and obesity on electrical current thresholds. *Muscle Nerve* 2011; **44(2)**: 202–7.
44. Kroll MW, Luceri RM. Estimation of pacemaker and ICD interaction with electrical weapons: Italy demographics of electronic control recipients. *ResearchGate* 2016: 7.
45. Cao M, Shinbane JS, Gillberg JM, et al. Taser-induced rapid ventricular myocardial capture demonstrated by pacemaker intracardiac electrograms. *J Cardiovasc Electrophysiol* 2007; **18(8)**: 876–9.
46. Kroll M, Luceri RM, Calkins H. A very interesting case study involving a TASER conducted electrical weapon (CEW) used on a patient with a pacemaker. *J Cardiovasc Electrophysiol* 2007; **18(12)**: 29–30.
47. Tu YH, Hsu JC. Multiple comparisons of drug efficacy between subgroups defined by genetic polymorphisms. *Stat Med* 2012; **31(24)**: 2892–903.
48. Horowitz LN, Spear JF, Josephson ME, et al. The effects of coronary artery disease on the ventricular fibrillation threshold in man. *Circulation* 1979; **60**(4): 792–7.
49. Awtry EH, Philippides GJ. Alcoholic and cocaine-associated cardiomyopathies. *Prog Cardiovasc Dis* 2010; **52(4)**: 289–99.
50. Karch SB. Introduction to the forensic pathology of cocaine. *Am J Forensic Med Pathol* 1991; **12(2)**: 126–31.
51. Karch SB, Stephens BG. Drug abusers who die during arrest or in custody. *J R Soc Med* 1999; **92(3)**: 110–13.
52. Swerdlow CD, Olson WH, O'Connor ME, et al. Cardiovascular collapse caused by electrocardiographically silent 60-Hz intracardiac leakage current. Implications for electrical safety. *Circulation* 1999; **99(19)**: 2559–64.
53. Plenzig S, Verhoff MA, Gruber H, Kunz SN. Aspiration-related pneumonia after Taser exposure - A multiple causations mechanism. *Forensic Sci Int* 2021; **326**: 110906.
54. Karch SB. Peer review and the process of publishing of adverse drug event reports. *J Forensic Leg Med* 2007; **14(2)**: 79–84.
55. Bozeman WP, Hauda WE 2nd, Heck JJ, et al. Safety and injury profile of conducted electrical weapons used by law enforcement officers against criminal suspects. *Ann Emerg Med* 2009; **53(4)**: 480–9.
56. Sloane CM, Chan TC, Vilke GM. Thoracic spine compression fracture after TASER activation. *J Emerg Med* 2008; **34**(3): 283–5.
57. Winslow JE, Bozeman WP, Fortner MC, Alson RL. Thoracic compression fractures as a result of shock from a conducted energy weapon: A case report. *Ann Emerg Med* 2007; **50(5)**: 584–6.
58. USFDA. Miha bodytec II clearance, 2019. Available from: https://www.accessdata.fda.gov/scripts/cdrh/cfdocs/cfpmn/pmn.cfm?ID=K182519 (Accessed 16 June 2023).
59. Stollberger C, Finsterer J. Side effects of whole-body electro-myo-stimulation. *Wien Med Wochenschr* 2019; **169(7–8)**: 173–80.
60. Finsterer J, Stollberger C. Severe rhabdomyolysis after MIHA-bodytec(R)

electrostimulation with previous mild hyper-CK-emia and noncompaction. *Int J Cardiol* 2015; **180**: 100–2.
61. VanMeenen KM, Cherniack NS, Bergen MT, et al. Cardiovascular evaluation of electronic control device exposure in law enforcement trainees: A multisite study. *J Occup Environ Med* 2010; **52(2)**: 197–201.
62. Dawes DM, Ho JD, Sweeney JD, et al. The effect of an electronic control device on muscle injury as determined by creatine kinase enzyme. *Forensic Sci Med Pathol* 2011; **7(1)**: 3–8.
63. Kroll MW, Witte KK, Ritter MB, et al. Electrical weapons and rhabdomyolysis. *Forensic Sci Med Pathol* 2020; **17(1)**: 58–63.
64. Ho JD, Miner JR, Lakireddy DR, et al. Cardiovascular and physiologic effects of conducted electrical weapon discharge in resting adults. *Acad Emerg Med* 2006; **13(6)**: 589–95.
65. Kagiyama Y, Hill JL, Gettes LS. Interaction of acidosis and increased extracellular potassium on action potential characteristics and conduction in guinea pig ventricular muscle. *Circ Res* 1982; **51(5)**: 614–23.
66. Karobath H, Redtenbacher M, Hofecker G, et al. Zur Frage der Todesursache Beim Blitzunfall. *MMW Munch Med Wochenschr* 1977; **119**: 29–32.
67. Cooper M, Andrews CJ, Holle RL, et al. Lightning-Related Injuries and Safety. In: Auerbach PS, Cushing TA, Harris NS (eds), *Wilderness Medicine*, 7th ed. Philadelphia: Elsevier; 2017, pp. 71–117.
68. Kroll MW, Walcott GP, Ideker RE, et al. The stability of electrically induced ventricular fibrillation. *Conf Proc IEEE EMBC* 2012; **34**: 6377–81.
69. Andrews CJ. *Studies in Aspects of Lightning Injuries*. Queensland: University of Queensland; 1993.
70. Jones HL. The lethal effects of electrical currents. *Br Med J* 1895; **1(1783)**: 468–70.
71. Jex-Blake A. Death by electric currents and lightning. *Br Med J* 1913; **1**: 425–603.
72. Ho JD, Dawes DM, Chang RJ, et al. Physiologic effects of a new-generation conducted electrical weapon on human volunteers. *J Emerg Med* 2014; **46(3)**: 428–35.
73. Dawes DM, Ho JD, Reardon RF, et al. The physiologic effects of multiple simultaneous electronic control device discharges. *West J Emerg Med* 2010; **11(1)**: 49–56.
74. Dawes DM, Ho JD, Reardon RF, Miner JR. The cardiovascular, respiratory, and metabolic effects of a long duration electronic control device exposure in human volunteers. *Forensic Sci Med Pathol* 2010; **6(4)**: 268–74.
75. Vilke GM, Sloane CM, Suffecool A, et al. Physiologic effects of the TASER after exercise. *Acad Emerg Med* 2009; **16(8)**: 704–10.
76. Vilke GM, Sloane CM, Bouton KD, et al. Physiological effects of a conducted electrical weapon on human subjects. *Ann Emerg Med* 2007; **50(5)**: 569–75.
77. Oliver T, Bolam RA. Cause of death by electric shock. *Br Med J* 1898; **1(1933)**: 132–5.
78. Prevost J, Battelli F. La mort par les dècharges èlectriques. *Rev Med Suisse Romande* 1899; **19**: 545–74.
79. International Electrotechnical Commission. *Effects of Current on Human Beings and Livestock - Part 1: General Aspects*, 5th ed. Geneva: IEC; 2016.
80. International Electrotechnical Commission. *Effects of Current on Human Beings and Livestock - Part 2: Special Aspects*, 5th ed. Geneva: IEC; 2020.
81. UL 69: Electric Fence Controllers. 2003.
82. Kroll MW, Perkins PE, Panescu D. Electric fence standards comport with human data and AC limits. *Conf Proc IEEE EMBC* 2015; **37**: 1343–8.
83. International Electrotechnical Commission. *Household and Similar Electrical Appliances - Safety - Part 2–76: Particular requirements for electric fence energizers*. Brussels: IEC; 2006.
84. Nimunkar AJ, Webster JG. Safety of pulsed electric devices. *Physiol Meas* 2009; **30(1)**: 101–14.
85. ANSI. *Electric Fence Energizers*. Bristol: estandards.net; 2020.
86. Scherr C, de Carvalho AC, Belem LJ, et al. Cardiovascular effects of SPARK conducted electrical weapon in healthy subjects. *Int J Cardiol* 2016; **225**: 123–7.
87. ANSI. *Electrical Characteristics of ECD's and CEW's*. Bristol: estandards.net; 2017.
88. Chiles BD, Nerheim MH, Brave MA, et al. Electrical weapon charge delivery with arcing. *Conf Proc IEEE Eng Med Biol Soc* 2018; **2018**: 2234–9.
89. Mattei E, Censi F, Calcagnini G. Electrical stun gun and modern implantable cardiac stimulators: Update for a new stun gun model. *Health Phys* 2021; **120(3)**: 344–9.
90. Walcott GP, Kroll MW, Ideker RE. Ventricular fibrillation threshold of rapid short pulses. *Conf Proc IEEE EMBC* 2011; **33**: 255–8.
91. Panescu D, Nerheim M, Kroll M. Electrical safety of conducted electrical weapons relative to requirements of relevant electrical standards. *Conf Proc IEEE Eng Med Biol Soc* 2013; **35**: 5342–7.
92. Panescu D, Nerheim M, Kroll MW, Brave M. New conducted electrical weapons: Electrical safety relative to relevant standards. *Conf Proc IEEE EMBC* 2017; **39**: 2185–90.
93. Rahko PS. Evaluation of the skin-to-heart distance in the standing adult by two-dimensional echocardiography. *J Am Soc Echocardiogr* 2008; **21(6)**: 761–4.
94. Horowitz LN, Spear JF, Moore EN. Relation of the endocardial and epicardial ventricular fibrillation thresholds of the right and left ventricle. *Am J Cardiol* 1981; **48(4)**: 698–701.
95. Spear J, Horowitz L, Moore E. Relationship of endocardial and epicardial ventricular-fibrillation thresholds of right and left-ventricles. *Am J Cardiol* 1977; **39(2)**: 274.
96. Allison JS, Qin H, Dosdall DJ, et al. The transmural activation sequence in porcine and canine left ventricle is markedly different during long-duration ventricular fibrillation. *J Cardiovasc Electrophysiol* 2007; **18(12)**: 1306–12.
97. Brave MA, Lakkireddy DR, Kroll MW. Validity of the small swine model for human electrical safety risks. *Conf Proc IEEE EMBC* 2016; **38**: 2343–8.
98. Hamlin RL, Burton RR, Leverett SD, Burns JW. Ventricular activation process in minipigs. *J Electrocardiol* 1975; **8(2)**: 113–6.
99. Kano M, Toyoshi T, Iwasaki S, et al. QT PRODACT: Usability of miniature pigs in safety pharmacology studies: Assessment for drug-induced QT interval prolongation. *J Pharmacol Sci* 2005; **99(5)**: 501–11.
100. Walcott GP, Kroll MW, Ideker RE. Ventricular fibrillation: Are swine a sensitive species? *J Interv Card Electrophysiol* 2015; **42(2)**: 83–9.
101. Valentino DJ, Walter RJ, Dennis AJ, et al. Taser X26 discharges in swine: Ventricular rhythm capture is dependent on discharge vector. *J Trauma* 2008; **65(6)**: 1478–85.
102. Geddes LA, Cabler P, Moore AG, et al. Threshold 60-Hz current required for ventricular fibrillation in subjects of various body weights. *IEEE Trans Biomed Eng* 1973; **20(6)**: 465–8.
103. Wu JY, Sun H, O'Rourke AP, et al. Taser blunt probe dart-to-heart distance causing ventricular fibrillation in pigs. *IEEE Trans Biomed Eng* 2008; **55(12)**: 2768–71.
104. Dawes DM, Ho JD, Moore JC, Miner JR. An evaluation of two conducted electrical weapons and two probe designs using a swine comparative cardiac safety model. *Forensic Sci Med Pathol* 2013; **9(3)**: 333–42.
105. Lakkireddy D, Wallick D, Verma A, et al. Cardiac effects of electrical stun guns: Does position of barbs contact make a difference? *Pacing Clin Electrophysiol* 2008; **31(4)**: 398–408.
106. Kroll MW, Lakkireddy D, Rahko PS, Panescu D. Ventricular fibrillation risk estimation for conducted electrical weapons: Critical convolutions. *Conf Proc IEEE Eng Med Biol Soc* 2011; **33**: 271–7.
107. Chilbert M. Standards and Rationale. In: Reilly J (ed), *Applied Bioelectricity: From Electrical Stimulation to Electrical Pathology*. New York: Springer; 1998, pp. 454–501.
108. Gerst PH, Fleming WH, Malm JR. A quantitative evaluation of the effects of acidosis and alkalosis upon the ventricular fibrillation threshold. *Surgery* 1966; **59(6)**: 1050–60.
109. Gardner AR, Hauda WE 2nd, Bozeman WP. Conducted electrical weapon (TASER) use against minors: A shocking analysis. *Pediatr Emerg Care* 2012; **28(9)**: 873–7.
110. Panescu D, Kroll MK, Brave MA. Cardiac fibrillation risks with TASER conducted electrical weapons. *Conf Proc IEEE EMBC* 2015; **37**: 323–9.
111. Ideker RE, Dosdall DJ. Can the direct cardiac effects of the electric pulses generated by the TASER X26 cause immediate or delayed sudden cardiac arrest in normal adults? *Am J Forensic Med Pathol* 2007; **28(3)**: 195–201.
112. US Department of Justice. Study of deaths following electro muscular disruption, 2011. Available from: https://www.ojp.gov/pdffiles1/nij/233432.pdf (Accessed 16 June 2023).
113. Vilke G, Chan T, Bozeman WP, Childers R. Emergency department evaluation after conducted energy weapon use: Review of the literature for the clinician. *J Emerg Med* 2019; **57(5)**: 740–6.

114. Zima E, Gergely M, Soos P, et al. The effect of induction method on defibrillation threshold and ventricular fibrillation cycle length. *J Cardiovasc Electrophysiol* 2006; **17**(4): 377–81.
115. Cummins RO, Austin D Jr. The frequency of 'occult' ventricular fibrillation masquerading as a flat line in prehospital cardiac arrest. *Ann Emerg Med* 1988; **17**(8): 813–17.
116. Robertson PG, Huang J, Chen KA, et al. Increased cycle length during long-duration ventricular fibrillation is caused by decreased upstroke velocity as well as prolonged refractoriness. *Heart Rhythm* 2009; **6**(3): 378–84.
117. Worley SJ, Swain JL, Colavita PG, et al. Development of an endocardial-epicardial gradient of activation rate during electrically induced, sustained ventricular fibrillation in dogs. *Am J Cardiol* 1985; **55**(6): 813–20.
118. Wiggers CJ. Studies of ventricular fibrillation caused by electric shock: I. *Am J Physiol* 1930; **92**: 223–39.
119. Kroll MW, Walcott GP, Ideker RE, et al. The stability of electrically induced ventricular fibrillation. *Conf Proc IEEE Eng Med Biol Soc* 2012; **34**: 6377–81.
120. White RD, Goodman BW, Svoboda MA. Neurologic recovery following prolonged out-of-hospital cardiac arrest with resuscitation guided by continuous capnography. *Mayo Clin Proc* 2011; **86**(6): 544–8.
121. Panescu D, Kroll M, Iverson C, Brave M. The sternum as an electrical shield. *Annu Int Conf IEEE Eng Med Biol Soc* 2014; **2014**: 4464–70.
122. Panescu D, Kroll MW, Brave M. New conducted electrical weapons: Thoracic cage shielding effects. *Conf Proc IEEE EMBC* 2017; **39**: 2191–6.
123. Kroll MW, Fish RM, Calkins H, et al. Defibrillation success rates for electrically-induced fibrillation: Hair of the dog. *Conf Proc IEEE Eng Med Biol Soc* 2012; **34**: 689–93.
124. Haouzi P, Ahmadpour N, Bell HJ, et al. Breathing patterns during cardiac arrest. *J Appl Physiol* 2010; **109**(2): 405–11.
125. Zuercher M, Ewy GA, Otto CW, et al. Gasping in response to basic resuscitation efforts: Observation in a swine model of cardiac arrest. *Crit Care Res Pract* 2010; **10**(36): 1–7.
126. Clark JJ, Larsen MP, Culley LL, et al. Incidence of agonal respirations in sudden cardiac arrest. *Ann Emerg Med* 1992; **21**(12): 1464–7.
127. Stopyra JP, Winslow JE, Fitzgerald DM, Bozeman WP. Intracardiac electrocardiographic assessment of precordial TASER shocks in human subjects: A pilot study. *J Forensic Leg Med* 2017; **52**: 70–4.
128. Dawes DM, Ho JD, Reardon RF, Miner JR. Echocardiographic evaluation of TASER X26 probe deployment into the chests of human volunteers. *Am J Emerg Med* 2010; **28**(1): 49–55.
129. Ho JD, Dawes DM, Reardon RF, et al. Human cardiovascular effects of a new generation conducted electrical weapon. *Forensic Sci Int* 2011; **204**(1–3): 50–7.
130. Bahr J, Klingler H, Panzer W, et al. Skills of lay people in checking the carotid pulse. *Resuscitation* 1997; **35**(1): 23–6.
131. Dick WF, Eberle B, Wisser G, Schneider T. The carotid pulse check revisited: What if there is no pulse? *Crit Care Med* 2000; **28**(**11 Suppl**): N183–5.

CHAPTER

87

Female Genital Mutilation

Hazel I. Learner and Deborah Hodes

INTRODUCTION

The World Health Organization (WHO) defines Female genital Mutilation (FGM) as all procedures that involve partial or total removal of the external female genitalia, or other injury to the female genital organs for non-medical reasons (1).

The WHO classifies FGM into four types (Table 87.1). United Nations Children's Fund (UNICEF) use a different classification system for FGM which while less anatomically precise compared to the WHO system is simpler to understand and is therefore used for self-reported data collection. UNICEF has three types of FGM (2). "Flesh removed" which includes WHO type 1 & 2. "Sewn closed" referring to infibulation which includes WHO type 3. "Cut, no flesh removed/nicked" which includes WHO type 4.

Studies and reports with self-reported data need to be treated with caution and include detailed methodology. Individuals may not be aware they have been cut, or they may be unsure of what was actually done – particularly if FGM was performed at a young age (3). Some may not disclose due to the personal nature of the questioning and may fear the repercussions of reporting due to the potential illegal status of FGM (depending on country of residence and where FGM was performed).

The universal application of the term "mutilation" which conveys disfigurement, scarring and psychological trauma has been questioned as imprecise, inaccurate, misleading, harmful, ethnocentric and sexist (4). The term Female Genital Mutilation/Cutting (FGM/C) speaks to the culturally driven nature of FGM/C and that the practice is perpetuated by those who themselves have been victims and cut as children. This chapter will as such refer to FGM/C.

BACKGROUND TO THE PRACTICE OF FGM/C

The first record of FGM/C dates from the time of the Pharaohs and it is now a deeply rooted tradition practiced by specific ethnic groups in Africa, Asia and the Middle East as well as a few other countries.

No religious scriptures mandate FGM/C, although practitioners often use religion to justify the misconception that it is necessary. FGM/C-practicing communities are from many religious faiths including Christianity, Judaism, Islam and Animism. A potential factor in the conflation of FGM/C as an Islamic requirement is that FGM/C is often referred to as Sunna or Sunnah. Sunnah describes the Prophet's recommended practice rather than a description of cutting or circumcision.

In some cultures, FGM/C is performed as part of a ceremonial rite of passage to adulthood, such as the secret Sierra Leone tradition of Bondo Bush described by an adult teacher (Figure 87.1). Justifications include social pressure and social acceptance, preparation of a girl for adulthood and marriage, removal of "unclean" body parts, to reduce libido and ensure chastity, to cement or maintain cultural identity, protect virginity and the family honor. Genital appearance and genital hygiene may also be perceived reasons.

In communities where FGM/C is almost universally performed, the social conventions allow the persistence of FGM/C. An uncut woman would risk themselves and their family becoming ostracized. In communities where there are minimal opportunities for women beyond the role of wife or mother, there are strong financial motivations for FGM/C to persist unquestioned.

While FGM/C can be regarded as a form of female suppression and machination of the patriarchy, FGM/C is generally organized and performed by females. It is important to acknowledge that those involved with the performance of FGM/C will generally believe that they are acting in a child's best interest while also preserving cultural traditions and social norms (5), and may also be earning a living from the persistence of the practice.

Despite many internationally recognized laws against FGM/C, lack of validation in Islam and global advocacy to eradicate the practice, it remains embedded in many cultures (2).

PREVALENCE OF FGM/C

Over 200 million girls and women worldwide are estimated to have been subjected to FGM/C. This figure from UNICEF is based on national representative data from 30 countries (6).

DOI: 10.1201/9781003138754-90

TABLE 87.1 Types of FGM

	Description	Diagram
Type 1	Partial or total removal of the clitoral glans, and/or the clitoral hood (prepuce) *Variations:* Type Ia, removal of the clitoral hood only Type Ib, removal of the clitoral glans and clitoral hood	
Type 2	Partial or total removal of the clitoral glans and the labia minora, with or without removal of the labia majora *Variations:* Type IIa, removal of the labia minora only Type IIb, partial or total removal of the clitoral glans (clitoral hood may also be affected), and the labia minora Type IIc, partial or total removal of the clitoral glans, labia minora and the labia majora	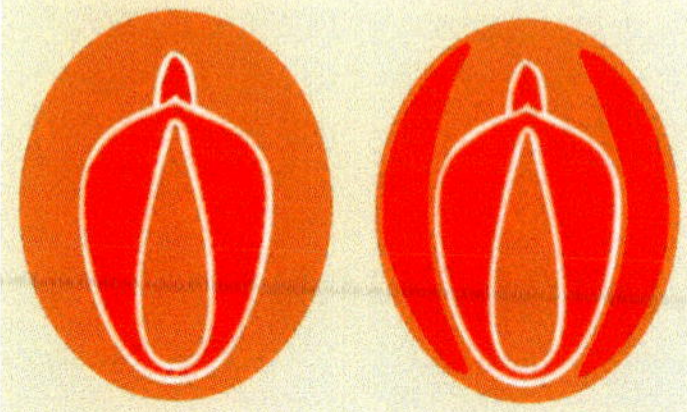
Type 3	Infibulation Narrowing of the vaginal orifice with the creation of a covering seal by cutting and appositioning the labia minora and/or the labia majora, with or without excision of the clitoris (infibulation) *Variations:* Type IIIa: removal and apposition (sometimes through stitching) of the labia minora with or without excision of the clitoral glans (clitoral hood may also be affected) Type IIIb: removal and apposition of the labia majora (sometimes through stitching), with or without excision of the labia minora, clitoral glans (clitoral hood may also be affected)	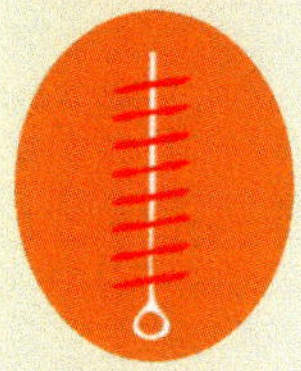
Type 4	This includes all other harmful procedures to the female genitalia for non-medical purposes, e.g. pricking, piercing, incising, scraping and cauterizing the genital area	

Before 2015, the estimated incidence of FGM/C was 125 million across 29 countries. The inclusion of Indonesia data dramatically altered the statistics on FGM/C and further highlighted that FGM/C was a global rather than solely an African concern.

FGM/C prevalence rates have dropped by one quarter, however, despite this reduction the incidence of FGM/C is increasing due to population growth (7,8). FGM/C prevalence and type varies between countries and regions. Prevalence appears to have reduced more significantly (in relative terms) in countries with lower initial prevalence compared to countries with higher initial prevalence (6).

Generally, FGM/C practice is declining more rapidly in urban compared to rural areas (9–11).

This partially reflects the protective value of education – girls are less likely to undergo FGM/C if their mothers have had any schooling. Indonesia, however, sees higher prevalence in urban areas and in the richest quintile (11).

FGM/C practicing communities are concentrated in sub-Saharan African countries from the Atlantic coast to the horn of Africa and Indonesia, but FGM/C has been described in countries including Colombia, Iran, India, Pakistan, Thailand and Russia. The type of FGM/C practice varies across ethnicities (rather than restricted by nation's boundaries) and generations (2).

Most women in Africa have had FGM/C with flesh removed (i.e. WHO type 1 or 2). Type 3 FGM continues to be practiced throughout much of sub-Saharan Africa, and this prevalence has increased in Chad, Mali and Sierra Leone (12). Most girls in South East Asia have had type 4.

Just as types of FGM/C and the rationale for FGM/C differs between communities so does the age that FGM/C is typically performed. FGM/C is nearly always performed in childhood and is typically performed on girls aged 2 to 15 years (2).

Global migration means that FGM/C is not limited to countries where it is traditionally practiced (8).

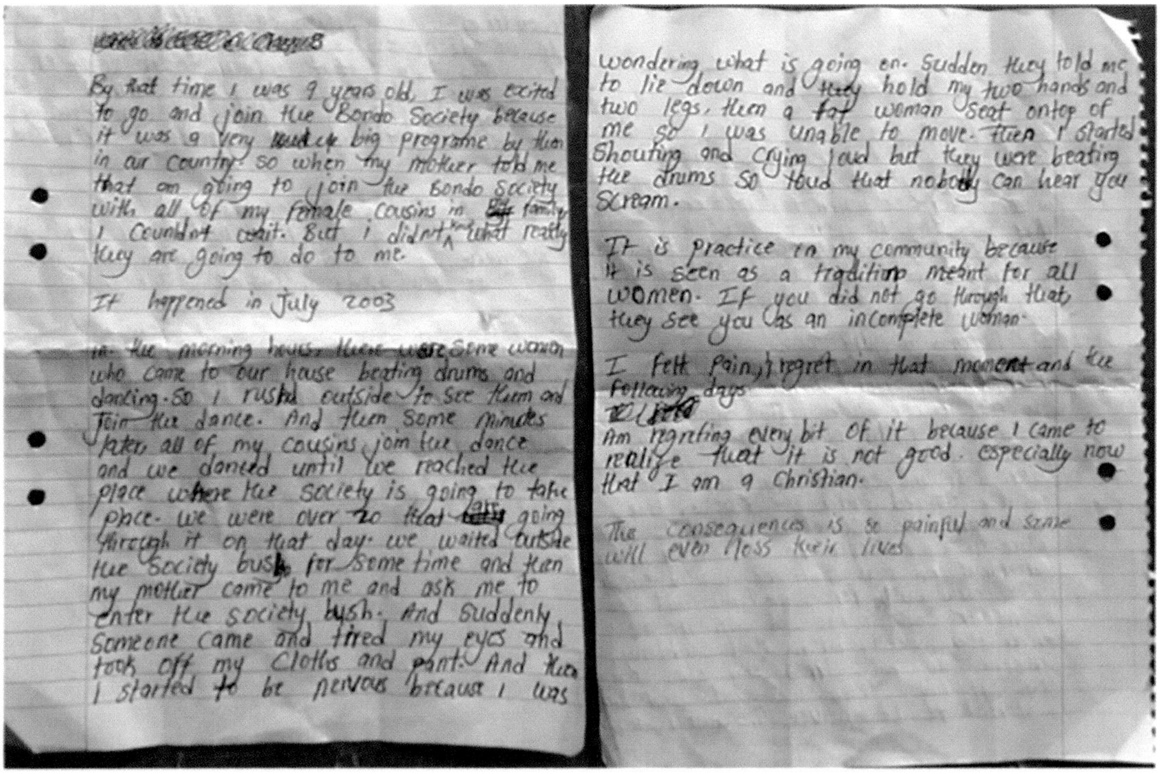

By that time I was 9 years old, I was excited to go and join the Bondo Society because it was a very big programe by them in our country so when my mother told me that am going to join the Bondo Society with all of my female cousins in family I couldn't wait. But I didn't know what really they are going to do to me.

It happened in July 2003

In the morning hours there were some women who came to our house beating drums and dancing. So I rushed outside to see them and join the dance. And then some minutes later all of my cousins join the dance and we danced until we reached the place where the society is going to take place. We were over to that going through it on that day. We waited outside the society bush for some time and then my mother came to me and ask me to enter the society bush. And suddenly someone came and tired my eyes and took off my cloths and pant. And then I started to be nervous because I was wondering what is going on. Sudden they told me to lie down and they hold my two hands and two legs, then a fat woman seat ontop of me so I was unable to move. Then I started shouting and crying loud but they were beating the drums so loud that nobody can hear you scream.

It is practice in my community because it is seen as a tradition meant for all women. If you did not go through that they see you as an incomplete woman.

I felt pain, regret in that moment and the following days

Am regreting every bit of it because I came to realize that it is not good. especially now that I am a Christian.

The consequences is so painful and some will even loss their lives

87.1 Letter from a teacher describing her experiences (author Miss Isatu Bangura, published with permission).

Research suggests that migrants from FGM/C practicing communities are likely to oppose the practice and that migration in itself facilitates attitude change to disagreeing with FGM/C (13). However, researchers also acknowledge the silence around FGM/C discussions in migrant populations due to the taboo nature of discussing FGM/C as well as the illegality (14).

It is estimated that there are 600 000 women and girls who have undergone FGM/C in the EU; 513 000 in the United States and 53 088 in Australia (15) and such indirect estimates through extrapolations are often too reductive and misrepresentative (16,17). These figures are often sensationally misreported. Typically, extrapolations rely on census data in combination with FGM/C prevalence for country of birth. This methodology has limitations as immigrants are typically more educated (protective against FGM/C) and does not reflect shifts in attitude to FGM/C with migration. Furthermore, immigrants are often under-enumerated in censuses.

At-risk estimations do not reflect empiric evidence of numbers seen (18). In the UK and Ireland, 103 children under 16-years-old with FGM/C were reported by the British Paediatric Surveillance Unit over a 2-year period compared to estimates of 65 000 girls aged 13 and under at risk of FGM. Of those reported in the study, 58 percent had had either type 1 or type 2, 8 percent type 3 and 21 percent type 4 (with13% not classified). The global picture of FGM/C was reflected with 70 percent of the 103 having had FGM/C in Africa with others from Europe, West Asia and South-East Asia (19).

CONSEQUENCES OF FGM/C

As described above, there is wide variation in the practice of FGM/C and, as such, there are variations in the ongoing health consequences of FGM/C and it is important to note that not all women will live with these sequelae.

Immediate consequences of FGM/C include death through hemorrhage or infection. Where non-sterile instruments are used, there is a risk of blood-borne infections (HIV, Hepatitis B and C, Syphilis). Acute urinary retention can be complicated related to pain or urethral trauma. If the child was restrained or held down during the FGM/C, they may have suffered physical traumas such as fractures or dislocations.

Long-term complications can include issues with urination; recurrent infections or slow urinary stream in those with urethral injury or type 3 FGM. Those with type 3 FGM may present with urinary incontinence from urine refluxes into the vagina and fistula.

FGM/C is associated with increased maternal and perinatal risks with childbirth including episiotomy, hemorrhage from vaginal trauma or uterine atony, instrumental delivery and cesarean delivery. FGM/C has been linked to an increased risk of stillbirth (20).

Physical causes of sexual problems include a reduction or loss of clitoral/labial sensation, painful vaginal penetration due to a narrowed or scarred introitus. Scarring and/or inclusion cysts can cause vulval irritation.

Psychological sequelae can include depression, anxiety, post-traumatic stress disorder (PTSD), low self-esteem and psychosexual problems. The surgical option for clitoral reconstruction is relatively novel. There is, however, limited evidence for clitoral reconstruction surgery's efficacy at improving physical, sexual, psychosocial and esthetic concerns following FGM/C (21).

A consequence of the drive to end FGM/C has seen migrant populations from FGM/C-practicing communities stigmatized as perpetrators of child abuse through FGM/C. This can lead to reduced motivations to seek healthcare due to the increased focus – or "fixation" on whether they have or have not been subjected to FGM/C previously. Healthcare providers need to be sensitive to the potential of FGM/C or potential sequela of FGM/C without detracting from the issue the women wanted help with or feeding into a narrative of self-deprecatory body image (mutilated) or the lack of capacity for sexual pleasure (14,22,23).

However, this acknowledgement of the othering effect of FGM/C safeguarding on migrant women shouldn't diminish the psychological effect of FGM/C of survivors living in FGM/C prevalent countries. While in some areas and cultures FGM/C may be a social norm, this does not protect against the development of PTSD or other psychological issues (24).

MEDICALIZATION OF FGM/C

Medicalization of FGM/C has increased over the years for many reasons including increase in family wealth and the perception that it is better and safer for the girl. Medicalized FGM/C refers to when a healthcare practitioner performs FGM/C with the use of antiseptics, anesthetics, analgesia and surgical instruments. This may be in a healthcare setting and sometimes alongside a traditional practitioner. Medicalized FGM/C can also refer to a re-infibulation (25).

A medicalized form of FGM/C has been reported in one quarter of people reporting FGM/C. It is concentrated in Africa (in particular, Egypt and Sudan) but reported worldwide (26). It potentially reflects a response to initiatives to end FGM/C with the perception that medicalized FGM/C reduces the health risks associated with FGM/C (2).

The expansion of medicalized FGM/C potentially undermines efforts to stop FGM/C. There is limited evidence considering harm reduction with medicalized FGM/C versus that performed by a traditional practitioner (27) and certainly risk remains. In 2020, the death of a 12-year-old Egyptian girl from medicalized FGM/C was widely reported, Nada Hassan Abdel-Maqsoud bled to death following FGM/C at a private clinic (28).

ACTION TO STOP FGM/C

In the 1950s, female genital circumcision was first discussed within the United Nations Commission on Human Rights. Subsequent increasing awareness through programs, meetings and conferences led, in 1997, to a joint statement from the WHO, United National Population Fund (UNFPA)and UNICEF which detailed the human rights violated by FGM and called upon national governments to take action to eradicate the practice (1).

In 2007, UNFPA and UNICEF launched a joint program to accelerate the abandonment of the practice (29).

In 2008, WHO issued a statement on the elimination of FGM/C. Subsequently, in 2012, the UN General Assembly adopted a resolution on the elimination of FGM/C and, in 2015, this was set as a sustainable development goal (SDG) for 2030 (30).

The WHO published guidelines in 2016 on the management of health complications from FGM/C with the guiding principles of accessible quality healthcare, that all stakeholders should be working to primary prevention of FGM/C, and that medicalization of FGM/C is never acceptable (31).

Local campaigns – generally NGO supported – initially focused on educating communities on the health consequences of FGM/C. Subsequently, more integrative approaches were employed including re-framing coming-of-age celebrations with the elimination of the cutting aspect and providing retraining as compensation to traditional cutters. Community empowerment programs help to dismantle social norms of FGM/C and highlighting FGM/Cs violation of human rights.

Global resolutions and local campaigns represented milestones for campaigns against FGM/C and also led to an increasing number of countries legislating against FGM/C, most recently Sudan in April 2020 (32). However in Africa, of the 29 countries, three still have no law: Sierra Leone, Mali and Mauritiana.

In England, there has been an evolution in legislation against FGM/C (Box 87.1).

BOX 87.1 FGM & Law: England & Wales

1985 Female Circumcision Prohibition Act

Illegal for a UK national or permanent resident to mutilate the whole or any part of a girl or woman's genitalia. Illegal to aid, abet, counsel or procure the carrying out of FGM in the UK.

2003 Female Genital Mutilation Act

Illegal to arrange for FGM to be carried out abroad, even in countries where the practice may be legal.

2012 Health and Social Care Act 2012

From 2015, clinicians are required to mandatory record FGM when recognized in patients (irrespective of age). Data submitted to the FGM Enhanced Dataset which quarterly releases data. These figures are often misrepresented as new cases rather than historic cases newly reported.

2015 Serious Crime Act – Amended Terms of 2003 FGM Act

Mandatory reporting to police of under 18s with FGM.
FGM protection orders.
Parents can be prosecuted for failing to protect their daughter from FGM.
Anonymity of victims of FGM for life.

BOX 87.2 Criminal trials of FGM in England

2015

In 2012, a junior doctor performed a Ventouse vaginal delivery with an episiotomy for a women who had undergone type 3 FGM in Somalia as a child. She had had pre-pregnancy de-infibulation. A small incision made by the junior doctor through a band of anterior scar tissue obscured the urethra and prevented catheterization. A single suture was placed anteriorly for hemostasis, and this suture formed the basis of the prosecution case that it was FGM. The junior doctor was of South Asian ethnicity and not from an FGM practicing culture. The trial took two years to come to court during which time the junior doctor was unable to practice. They were acquitted within 30 minutes of jury deliberation.

2018

Allegations made that a father (taxi driver of Somali origin) told his passenger he had arranged FGM for his daughter now aged 6. Daughter (and sisters) were examined by local safeguarding pediatrician, and subsequently referred to dedicated children's FGM clinic. Normal examination with colposcope, no evidence of FGM. The father was accused of "child cruelty" and the witness (taxi passenger) revealed to be a member of an FGM activist group working closely with the police. The judge described the protection evidence as "wholly inconclusive'"and ordered the jury to find father innocent.

The case had a clear detriment upon relations with the Somali British community locally.

2018

A 16-year-old girl alleged that aged 10-years-old, her father brought someone to the house to cut her.

She was held down and her genitals were cut on two occasions about 3 weeks apart. This was done as a punishment as he thought she has stolen money. She was seen in a dedicated children's FGM clinic and examination identified scarred labia minora with full thickness defects consistent with the history given. Classified as type 4 FGM.

The child was questioned on the witness stand in court, with a subsequent ruling that FGM had been performed but that there was an inability to rule on who performed or facilitated this. The father was ruled not guilty of FGM or of other offence of child cruelty.

2019 successful protection of 2003 FGM Act

A 3-year-old admitted to A+E with vulva trauma and acute blood loss requiring surgical repair of lacerations to clitoris and both labia. Neither parent was from an FGM practicing culture and the mother herself was not a victim of FGM. The parents claimed that the child fell astride a kitchen cupboard door although there was no forensic evidence of any blood on the cupboard door or floor. The child was examined at a dedicated children's FGM clinic within a few days of emergency surgery and findings were consistent with type 2 FGM. The child and brother were placed in foster care. The trial was criticized for allowing witchcraft accusations to be submitted as evidence and the validity and ethics of the evidence from the girl and her older brother (aged 10 at the time of trial) was also questioned. The mother was found guilty and sentenced to 14 years imprisonment.

The first successful prosecution of FGM/C in the UK came 34 years after FGM/C was specifically legislated against, this followed two previous trial acquittals (Box 87.2) (33).

While evidence is lacking to support media representation of FGM/C rates occurring in the UK, it is important to consider limits to why prosecutions are rare.

Victims may not wish to give evidence to incriminate their family, or they may be too young to recall. Where FGM/C occurs outside of the UK, evidence will be harder to gather although, since 2015, the parents can be prosecuted for not protecting their daughter even if they had not arranged it.

Further, there is a disparity between the legal definition of FGM/C and the diversity of type 4 FGM/C, which in family courts, some cases have been ruled as not mutilating. In a UK case heard in the family court in 2016, the judge stated "I am satisfied that if A has undergone FGM it would have been type IV" and "I'm equally satisfied that type IV FGM will very often not fall within the ambit of criminal law for that requires mutilation" (34).

The most recent FGM/C legalization in 2015, also reframed legislation to include protective measures with the FGM Protection Orders. These constitute a range of protective measures, that the Judge deems necessary and include restricting contact with people who have been identified as potential facilitators for FGM/C or removing a child's passport to prevent foreign travel.

DIAGNOSIS AND MANAGEMENT OF FGM/C

An FGM/C assessment should be conducted by a multidisciplinary (MDT) team with experience in FGM/C in a suitable setting. Presentation can reflect the potential sequelae of FGM/C (Box 87.3). Children and young people under 18 years of age should be seen by a pediatrician with an expertise in examination of the genitalia.

Clinicians should appreciate that consultation findings, especially in children, may be used as evidence in court and that they themselves may requested to attend. In adult women, clinical outcomes may become evidence in asylum application cases or historic FGM/C prosecutions. Therefore, an understanding of the laws surrounding FGM/C and implementing the principles of forensic and legal medicine are essential for those involved with FGM/C clinical assessments. Optimal consultations include appropriate interpreting services (with the patient's preferred gender of an interpreter) and, where possible, psychological support integral to an FGM/C consultation to debrief and identify on-going psychology needs.

Parents attending with their child may also need psychological support following the assessment due to being survivors themselves.

History of FGM/C

As with any health consultation a general medical, surgical, sexual, obstetric and social history should be taken (Box 87.4). As taking a history of FGM/C can be triggering, questions should be put sensitively.

BOX 87.3 FGM/C clinic referral indications

An individual with a history of FGM/C:

- Wants to gain understanding of their body and what happened to them as a child
- Has worries about starting a sexual relationship
- Has worries about delivery
- Has worries about cervical cytology screening
- Needs a way to access informed services to help manage vulval, menstrual, urinary, sexual, psychological symptoms
- Requires clinical confirmation to support asylum application
- Raises child safeguarding concerns

Children at risk of FGM/C - with suspicion of FGM/C

BOX 87.4 FGM/C history questions

- Patient's ethnicity and religion
- Rural or urban upbringing and educational level
- Immigration route/ travel history
- Family history and attitudes to FGM/C

- What age were they when FGM/C was performed?
- Do they remember what happened? Or are they retelling what they understood to have happened to them?
- Was there any social occasion surrounding the FGM/C? e.g. Ceremony, holiday
- Where was it done?
- Were they alone or in a group? (Were there any complications with anyone else?)
- Do they know who organized the FGM/C?
- Was there any deception around the FGM/C?
- Were their parents aware and accepting?
- Do they know what happened? i.e. UNICEF classification
- Where potential FGM, was this a cut? A prick? Caustic substances rubbed/inserted into the vagina? (Were they instructed to stretch their labia?)
- What tools were used?
- Do they know who performed the FGM/C? A traditional practitioner? A healthcare professional (e.g. doctor, midwife or nurse)?

- Were they restrained? How?
- Was there any cleaning or painkillers involved?
- What was done to help control bleeding? Were there dressings/topical remedies applied? Were their legs bound?
- What happened afterward; were they given antibiotics?
- Do they remember any acute complications? For example, pain, bleeding, issues with urination, other injuries?

Current health issues related to FGM/C

- Sleep disturbance/flashbacks
- Urinary symptoms
- Menstrual problems
- Vulval discomfort and care
- Sexual issues
- Pregnancy and complications
- History of re-infibulations

TABLE 87.2 Istanbul criteria

Level of consistency	Description
Not consistent	The physical/psychological finding could not have been caused by the trauma described
Consistent	The physical/psychological finding could have been caused by the trauma described, but it is non-specific and there are many other possible causes
Highly consistent	The physical/psychological finding could have been caused by the trauma described, and there are few other possible causes
Typical of	This is an appearance that is usually found with this type of trauma, but there are other possible causes
Diagnostic of	This appearance could not have been caused in any way other than that described

Specifics for pediatric FGM/C assessment

Children should be reviewed within a few weeks to help minimize delay with safeguarding investigations and proceedings.

Children should be reviewed in a pediatric setting rather than adult services. Whether the child is involved in the history taking depends on the child's age, developmental stage and the child's preference. It is important to understand why the child has been referred for FGM/C assessment. If there is suspicion rather than a disclosed history of FGM/C, it is particularly important to understand that child's family and cultural background, specifically the family history and attitude to FGM/C.

Examination – pitfalls

An FGM/C assessment on a child should be led by a pediatrician experienced with forensic genital examination. Forensic genital examination for child sexual abuse (CSA) is typically focused on the introitus, hymen and anus rather than the close labial and clitoral examination required for FGM/C assessment and so some may be less familiar with subtle FGM/C signs. Clinicians assessing for FGM/C must be aware of age changes in vulval development which is less covered in medical education compared to penile and scrotal development (Box 87.5) (35).

Never assume that the accompanying adult with the child is a parent, always clarify who is accompanying them.

The child's parent/carer(s) can be present at all stages unless the young person has capacity and does not wish for their parent/ caregivers to be present. Alternatively, if the medical assessment is part of a court order, judicial direction may have ordered that the parents/care-givers cannot be present.

The child's social worker can clarify the home situation and child safeguarding issues.

Younger children can be reassured by seeing on a doll what to expect from the examination. Younger children can also have their genital examination in the context of a general health check with a top-to-toe approach.

Examining for FGM/C can be challenging. Despite not undergoing a type 3 FGM, those who have had type 2 may have with adhesions opposing where the left and right labia were cut.

Type 4 FGM/C may only have subtle signs or have no discernible physical signs on later examination. Therefore, a normal genital examination does not exclude FGM/C. FGM/C type 4 can be confirmed based on a history rather than physical findings. The examination findings should be described along with a genitalia body map in the health record.

Examination with a video colposcope will ensure adequate lighting, magnification and photo-documentation. Findings should systematically detail the presence (or absence) and appearance of vulval structures, that is, clitoral hood, glans, palpable body, labia minora, labia majora, urethral meatus, introitus and perineum. Video recordings must be stored securely and anonymized – following local guidelines for storage of intimate images.

A summary of the clinical findings can inform an FGM/C diagnosis using the WHO classification system. It is sensible to apply Istanbul Protocol language (36) (Table 87.2

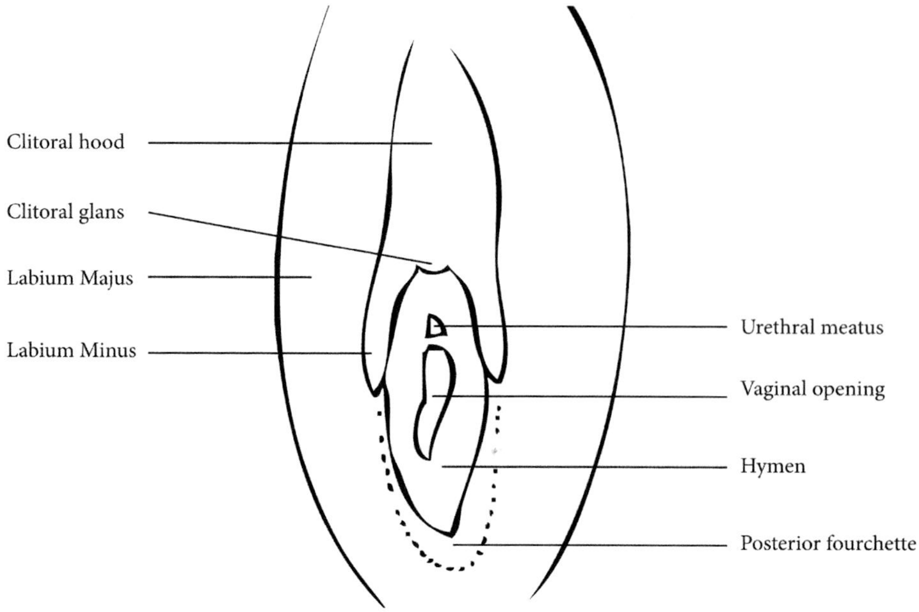

87.2 Pre-pubertal vulval anatomy. The vulval appearance will differ according to age and pubertal status. The pre-pubertal labia minora are small extensions inferior to the clitoral hood and can be mistaken as absent (average 3.2 mm width with 6.1 mm length). The clitoris is small (average diameter 4.6 mm and palpable/visible body length 7.7 mm). The glans may or may not be visible without gently retracting the clitoral hood.

With puberty and rising estrogen levels, there is an increase in subcutaneous fat deposition with the mons pubis and labia majora becoming fuller. The labia minor increases in length and width. More than 50% of adult women have visible labia minor protruding from the labia majora. Pigmentation alterations lead to labia minor color changes particularly along the labia mineral edges. The labia minor can develop a smooth or serrated edge and can develop bifid anteriorly. Asymmetrical development is not unusual with puberty.

and *see also* Chapter 82 – "Sexually Transmitted Infections Following Sexual Assault") bearing in mind that the medical record of the assessment could become medical evidence in court.

ACUTE PRESENTATION OF POTENTIAL FGM/C

Immediate complications of FGM/C can mean that a child will present to emergency health services with genital injuries, hemorrhage, or signs of sepsis. FGM/C training is therefore essential for any clinicians working with children as their initial assessment will form part of the medical evidence, if subsequent prosecution procedures.

Where unstable, the child's immediate clinical care must be prioritized but with a view for safeguarding and thorough documentation (which may need to be completed retrospectively). When clinically stable, a detailed history of injury mechanism should be taken from the parents/care-givers and the child themselves, if developmentally capable.

If emergency surgery is required for genital trauma and hemorrhage, then photographs at stages during the procedure are helpful, that is, before cleaning, before suturing and after suturing. Parental written consent for photographs should be taken, however, if no one with parental responsibility is available then photographs may be taken if deemed to be in the child's best interest.

When FGM/C is strongly suspected in an acute context, then social care and police should be involved as soon as clinically safe to do so.

Investigations and surgical management

Serology testing for blood-borne viruses is recommended with confirmation that the patient/family is happy for these results to be shared with their GP.

Depending on patient's symptoms a mid-stream urine or ultrasound scan of the pelvis may be indicated and potentially onward referral to urology or gynecology and so on.

The findings and type of FGM/C will indicate whether de-infibulation or excision of inclusion cysts can be offered. De-infibulation in older adolescents or adults can be performed in an outpatient setting with local anesthetic. But the explanation, and procedure itself, should be conducted sensitively as the experience could be triggering.

If there is more extensive scarring, an inclusion cyst, or patient preference, any of these, can mean that the procedure is planned as a day case under GA.

Young people typically defer de-infibulation until ready to start a sexual relationship. In pregnant women, de-infibulation can be performed electively as an antenatal procedure or intrapartum before delivery. There is no evidence to recommend either but an antenatal elective procedure will ensure that the procedure should be performed by someone experienced in de-infibulation.

Discussion with patient

A summarizing medical report should be sent to the referrer, general practitioner and patient or family. The findings should be explained and implications discussed with the child as age appropriate. Psychological support may be needed as well as further management and liaison with social care and police. Where no FGM/C is identified at pediatric assessment, then consider and list the risk factors to help direct potential safeguarding measures.

An FGM/C assessment is an opportunity to reinforce and support a family from an FGM/C-practicing community's anti-FGM/C stance. The clinic may help direct older members of the family who have survived FGM/C to have clinical reviews themselves or access FGM/C survivor support groups and charities such as FORWARD (37).

The consultation may also help to educate and empower a family on health risks of FGM/C and the legal status of performing or arranging FGM/C in that country.

Some countries have introduced FGM/C-specific child protection schemes where a child's FGM/C risk is documented and flagged in their health records (38).

CONCLUSION

All clinicians should be aware of FGM/C and their country's legal and mandatory reporting requirements. Patients should be sensitively asked about potential FGM/C without assumptions.

Patients with a history of FGM/C, or children with suspected FGM/C, should be referred to specialist clinics to help diagnose, support, educate and manage any long-term complications.

REFERENCES

1. World Health Organization. Eliminating female genital mutilation: an interagency statement, 2008. Available from: https://www.who.int/publications/i/item/9789241596442 (Accessed 21 June 2023).
2. United Nations Children's Fund, Gupta GR. Female genital mutilation/cutting: A statistical overview and exploration of the dynamics of change. *Reprod Health Matters* 2013; **21**(**42**): 184–90.
3. Elmusharaf S, Elhadi N, Almroth L. Reliability of self-reported form of female genital mutilation and WHO classification: Cross sectional study. *BMJ* 2006; 333(7559): 124.
4. Earp BD, Johnsdotter S. Current critiques of the WHO policy on female genital mutilation. *Int J Impot Res* 2021; **33**(**2**): 196–209.
5. Gaffney-Rhys R. Female genital mutilation: The law in England and Wales viewed from a human rights perspective. *Int J Hum Rights* 2020; **24**(**4**): 457–82.
6. UNICEF. Female genital mutilation country profiles, 2019. Available from: https://data.unicef.org/resources/fgm-country-profiles/ (Accessed 21 June 2023).
7. UNICEF. Female genital mutilation/cutting: A global concern, 2016. Available from: https://data.unicef.org/resources/female-genital-mutilationcutting-global-concern/ (Accessed 21 June 2023).
8. UNICEF. A decade of action to achieve gender equality: The UNICEF approach to the elimination of female genital mutilation, 2020. Available from: https://www.unicef.org/documents/decade-action-achieve-gender-equality-unicef-approach-elimination-female-genital (Accessed 21 June 2023).
9. Batyra E, Coast E, Wilson B, et al. The socioeconomic dynamics of trends in female genital mutilation/cutting across Africa. *BMJ Glob Health* 2020; **5**(**10**): e003088.
10. Weny K, Silva R, Snow R, et al. Towards the elimination of FGM by 2030: A statistical assessment. *PloS One* 2020; **15**(**10**): e0238782.
11. Population Reference Bureau. Female genital mutilation/cutting: Data and trends, 2017. Available from: https://www.prb.org/wp-content/uploads/2017/02/FGMC_Poster_2017-1-1.pdf (Accessed 21 June 2023).
12. Koski A, Heymann J. Thirty-year trends in the prevalence and severity of female genital mutilation: A comparison of 22 countries. *BMJ Glob Health* 2017; **2**(**4**): e000467.
13. Wahlberg A, Johnsdotter S, Selling KE, et al. Baseline data from a planned RCT on attitudes to female genital cutting after migration: When are interventions justified? *BMJ Open* 2017; **7**(**8**): e017506.
14. Dixon S, Agha K, Ali F, et al. Female genital mutilation in the UK-where are we, where do we go next? Involving communities in setting the research agenda. *Res Involv Engagem* 2018; **4**(**1**): 1–8.
15. Equality Now. Female genital mutilation/cutting: A call for a global response, 2020. Available from: https://www.equalitynow.org/resource/female-genital-mutilation-cutting-a-call-for-a-global-response/ (Accessed 21 June 2023).
16. Creighton SM, Samuel Z, Otoo-Oyortey N, et al. Tackling female genital mutilation in the UK. *BMJ* 2019; **364**: 15
17. Macfarlane A. Misleading use of FGM statistics compounds concerns about their reliability. *BMJ* 2019; **364**: 927.
18. Bindel J. An unpunished crime: The lack of prosecutions for female genital mutilation in the UK, 2014. Available from: http://www.womensgrid.org.uk/news/?p=2792 (Accessed 21 June 2023).
19. Hodes D, O'Donnell NA, Pall K, et al. Epidemiological surveillance study of female genital mutilation in the UK. *Arch Dis Child* 2021; **106**(**4**): 372–6.
20. Sylla F, Moreau C, Andro A. A systematic review and meta-analysis of the consequences of female genital mutilation on maternal and perinatal health outcomes in European and African countries. *BMJ Glob Health* 2020; **5**(**12**): e003307.
21. Jordal M, Sigurjonsson H, Griffin G, Wahlberg A. The benefits and disappointments following clitoral reconstruction after female genital cutting: A qualitative interview study from Sweden. *PloS One* 2021; **16**(**7**): e0254855.
22. Johnsdotter S. The impact of migration on attitudes to female genital cutting and experiences of sexual dysfunction among migrant women with FGC. *Curr Sex Health Rep* 2018; **10**(**1**): 18–24.
23. Karlsen S, Carver N, Mogilnicka M, et al. 'Putting salt on the wound': A qualitative study of the impact of FGM-safeguarding in healthcare settings on people with a British Somali heritage living in Bristol, UK. *BMJ Open* 2020; **10**(**6**): e035039.
24. Behrendt A, Moritz S. Posttraumatic stress disorder and memory problems after female genital mutilation. *Am J Psychiatry* 2005; **162**(**5**): 1000–2.
25. Kimani S, Shell-Duncan B. Medicalized female genital mutilation/cutting: Contentious practices and persistent debates. *Curr Sex Health Rep* 2018; **10**(**1**): 25–34.
26. Shell-Duncan B, Njue C, Moore Z. Trends in medicalisation of female genital mutilation/cutting: What do the data reveal? 2018. Available from: https://knowledgecommons.popcouncil.org/cgi/viewcontent.cgi?article=1570&context=departments_sbsr-rh (Accessed 21 June 2023).
27. Leye E, Van Eekert N, Shamu S, et al. Debating medicalization of female genital mutilation/cutting (FGM/C): Learning from (policy) experiences across countries. *Reprod Health* 2019; **16**: 158.
28. Michaelson R. FGM doctor arrested in Egypt after girl, 12, bleeds to death, 2020. Available from: https://www.theguardian.com/global-development/2020/feb/03/fgm-doctor-arrested-in-egypt-after-girl-12-bleeds-to-death Accessed August 2021 (Accessed 21 June 2023).
29. UNICEF. UNFPA-UNICEF joint programme on the elimination of female genital mutilation, 2023. Available from: https://www.unicef.org/protection/

unfpa-unicef-joint-programme-eliminating-fgm (Accessed 21 June 2023).
30. United Nations. Transforming our world: The 2030 agenda for sustainable development, 2021. Available from: https://sdgs.un.org/2030agenda (Accessed 21 June 2023).
31. World Health Organization. WHO guidelines on the management of health complications from female genital mutilation, 2016. Available from: https://www.who.int/publications/i/item/9789241549646 (Accessed 21 June 2023).
32. UNICEF. Sudan enters new era for girl rights with criminalization of FGM, 2020. Available from: https://www.unicef.org/mena/press-releases/sudan-enters-new-era-girl-rights-criminalization-fgm (Accessed 21 June 2023).
33. Samuel Z. *Female Genital Mutilation: Law and Practice.* Bristol: LexisNexis; 2017.
34. BAILII. Case No: ZW16C00313 & ZW16C00501, 2016. Available from: https://www.bailii.org/cgi-bin/format.cgi?doc=/ew/cases/EWFC/OJ/2016/B103.html&query=(.2016.)+AND+(EWFC)+AND+(B103) (Accessed 21 June 2023).
35. Akbiyik F, Kutlu AO. External genital proportions in prepubertal girls: A morphometric reference for female genitoplasty. *J Urol* 2010; **184(4)**: 1476–81.
36. United Nations Human Rights. Manual on the effective investigation and documentation of torture and other cruel, inhuman or degrading treatment or punishment, 2022. Available from: https://www.ohchr.org/sites/default/files/documents/publications/2022-06-29/Istanbul-Protocol_Rev2_EN.pdf (Accessed 20 June 2023).
37. FORWARD. Website, 2021. Available from: https://www.forwarduk.org.uk/ (Accessed 21 June 2023)
38. NHS Digital. Female genital mutilation - Information sharing, 2021. Available from: https://digital.nhs.uk/services/female-genital-mutilation-information-sharing (Accessed 21 June 2023).

CHAPTER

88

Herbal Medicines

Roger W. Byard

INTRODUCTION

Approximately 70–80 percent of the global population utilizes non-Western medicine which includes herbal therapies (1–3). For example, in India, Ayurvedic and Unani systems extensively use plant products, with more than 7000 species of medicinal plants being found in Chinese therapeutic systems. The popularity of herbal remedies has been increasing in Western communities as it is believed that these products are safer than prescribed drugs because they are "natural". This is in spite of a lack of understanding of their specific effects, possible harmful interactions of their ingredients and inconclusive evidence for their efficacy (4). It is well-recognized that a number of toxic substances present within herbal remedies may cause serious illness and even death (Table 88.1).

It was estimated that £300 million was spent in Europe on herbal therapies with a 10 percent increase in spending in the United States (3) where an estimated 30 percent of patients may now use herbal remedies. This use is often not reported to treating physicians either because the preparations are not regarded as potentially dangerous or due to a desire to control personal therapy and/or a fear of disapproval by medical practitioners (5–8). Tourist holidays are now being crafted around visits to herbal health centers (9) and Chinese herbal preparations have been promoted to both prevent and treat COVID-19 without supportive data (10). Such preparations may also be sold as dietary supplements rather than as drugs (11).

It would seem illogical, however, to assume that any agent that has a therapeutic effect would also not have the potential for a therapeutic side effect. Also, the profile of herbal medicine use has shifted in recent decades from a village-based cottage industry (Figures 88.1 and 88.2) (12) to a multibillion-dollar global business, often without adequate quality assurance. It has been shown that herbal preparations such as St John's Wort may have a similar pattern of adverse drug reaction reporting to drugs used to treat depression such as fluoxetine (13).

One of the issues with herbal remedies is lack of regulation, with access available to many products without prescriptions. Problems that may arise have been attributed to "non-medically qualified healers, lack of product standards, undeclared ingredients, non-disclosure of usage and long-term medication" (14).

Lack of accurate documentation of ingredients, variability in batch-to-batch concentrations and doses, adulteration with prescription drugs, contamination with toxins, and specific and idiosyncratic herb-herb and herb-drug side effects (Table 88.2) may all have significance in medicolegal cases. However, a history of herbal therapy is rarely obtained in forensic investigations and attending police officers and crime scene personnel do not routinely document herbal preparations when they are compiling a report on an unexpected death. In addition, the detection of organic substances is not part of routine forensic toxicology screening and may fail even if a material is suspected due to low levels of a particular agent or to lack of an established methodology (15,16). Thus, the potential role of herbal preparations in causing or exacerbating illness, or to contributing to a toxic event is often simply unknown (17). Perhaps a solution to this problem would be to create a separate sub-discipline of forensic herbal toxicology. This chapter outlines some of the medical and medicolegal issues that have arisen with herbal therapies.

POTENTIAL PATHOPHYSIOLOGICAL SIDE EFFECTS

Herbal medicines have not uncommonly had anticholinergic effects most often due to components of the Datura plant (15). However, this may occasionally arise from the substitution of other herbs that contain atropine, or atropine-like substances. Certain compounds may contain liquorice which has altered steroid metabolism resulting in hypertension and hypokalemia (7). Spontaneous intracerebral hemorrhage, seizures, intraocular and intracerebral hemorrhage have complicated the ingestion of *Ginkgo biloba* (1).

Hepatotoxicity is an increasingly recognized side effect of herbal therapy and is being documented more and more often by liver transplant services (18). A wide spectrum of manifestations may occur, ranging from medically unimportant transiently elevated serum liver enzyme levels to lethal hepatic failure with necrosis.

DOI: 10.1201/9781003138754-91

TABLE 88.1 Potential medical side effects of certain herbal remedies*

	Herbal therapy
Hepatitis	*Aristolochia* species, germander (*Teucrium chamaedrys*)
Hepatic veno-occlusive disease	Skullcap (*Scutellaria laterflora*), Comfrey (*Symphytum officinale*)
Liver failure	Kava (*Piper methysticum*), pennyroyal (*Mentha pulegium*), *Syo saiko to*, *Jin bu huan*, *Ma huang*
Hemorrhage, with seizures	*Ginkgo biloba*
Anticholinergic effects	*Datura*

* Adapted from Byard (1).

88.1 A herbalist in front of her store selling medicines and dried llama fetuses in a market in La Paz, Bolivia.

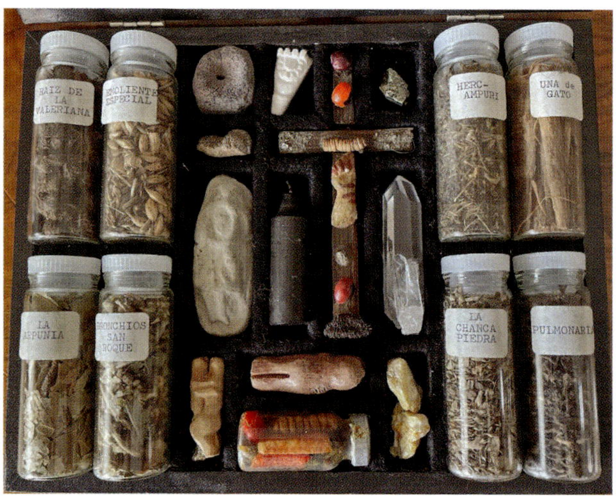

88.2 A collection of amulets, crystals and herbs from the witchcraft market in La Paz, Bolivia, used to treat an array of conditions ranging from renal stones to epilepsy and infertility.

TABLE 88.2 Causes of dangerous ingredients within traditional herbal medicines*

Inadequate processing
Addition of toxic substances
Inadvertent
Pesticides/herbicides
Chemicals
Heavy metals
Microorganisms/insects
Mycotoxins
Deliberate
Heavy metals
Organic toxins
Substituted herbs
Inadvertent
Mistaken identification
Deliberate
Cost cutting
Drug adulteration
Deliberate
Prescription drugs

* Adapted from Byard (1).

Although liver injury is most often caused by hepatotoxins that are integral to these substances, the possibility of herb–herb and herb–drug interactions must also be considered (see below) (18–20).

Hepatitis has resulted from the ingestion of a variety of herbs including germander (*Teucrium chamaedrys*) and *Aristolochia* species. Pennyroyal (*Mentha pulegium*), *Jin bu huan*, *Syo saiko to*, *Ma huang*, kava (*Piper methysticum*) and a Chinese herbal medicine known as "eternal life" have occasionally all resulted in fulminant liver failure requiring transplantation, and on occasion death (21,22). Skullcap (*Scutellaria laterflora*) and comfrey (*Symphytum officinale*) may cause hepatic veno-occlusive disease (5,20).

Infants have an increased vulnerability to herbal toxicity due to their low body weight and immature hepatic detoxification systems (23). There may also be other effects such as that of *Chuenlin* which may increase the risk of kernicterus-induced brain damage by displacing bilirubin from plasma proteins thus increasing free bilirubin concentrations. *Chuenlin* is administered to newborns to "remove toxic products of pregnancy" (7). If a child is found to have extensive liver necrosis at autopsy, herbal medicines should be considered rather than just possible drug and pesticide effects.

Herbs may also cause significant cardiovascular decompensation with arrhythmias, hypotension, hypertension, arteritis, pericarditis, cardiac failure and myocardial infarction (2). Central nervous system (CNS) and locomotor disorders may involve muscle weakness, movement disorders, cerebrovascular events and seizures (24) (Table 88.3).

TABLE 88.3 Summary of significant illnesses and conditions related to herbal therapy*

Liver disease	liver failure
Cardiovascular disease	cardiac arrhythmias, hypo/hypertension, cardiac failure, myocardial infarction, arteritis, pericarditis, transplant rejection
Gastrointestinal disease	nausea, vomiting, diarrhea
Lung disease	asthma
Renal/Genitourinary disease	urinary retention, interstitial nephritis, renal failure, transplant rejection
Neurological disease	confusion, coma, kernicterus, seizures, intracerebral hemorrhage/stroke, intracranial hemorrhage, encephalitis
Hematologic disease	agranulocytosis, anemia
Endocrine/metabolic disease	hyperthyroidism, hypoglycemia, hyperglycemia, pseudohyperaldosteronism
Heavy metal poisoning	acute toxicity, encephalopathy
Miscellaneous	anaphylaxis, carcinogenesis, postoperative hemorrhage

* Adapted from Byard (1).

ISSUES WITH INADEQUATE PROCESSING

The preparation of herbal remedies often requires specific steps to ensure that the material has been cleaned and preserved with removal of any components that may be toxic. Residual toxic material may have significant side effects, as has been observed in many cases of aconite poisoning in China. Aconite is often sold in a dry form which must be rehydrated and then boiled to reduce side effects. Failure to adequately do this may result in cardiac arrhythmias and heart failure (7,25).

Accidental contamination

As the ingredients for herbal remedies come from a variety of often-unspecified locations and environments there is always the possibility of accidental contamination from a wide range of substances. Cultivated herbs have been shown to be contaminated with pesticides including those that may be banned in the country of sale. Included among these is dichlorodiphenyltrichloroethane or DDT, a colorless and tasteless insecticide which has been associated with vomiting and seizures in high dose and is a possible carcinogen (26). Other contents of concern have included herbicides, mycotoxins, insects and microorganisms that have come from incorrect processing or faulty storage (27).

Heavy metal contamination

Inadvertent exposure of herbs to heavy metals may arise from contamination in fields or from storage in tainted environments (3). However, on occasion, heavy metals such as lead, thallium, arsenic, nickel, zinc, cadmium, mercury, copper, iron and manganese have been deliberately added to herbal medications due to a misplaced belief in their efficacy (28). In an early study by Ko, published in 1998, arsenic was found in 36 preparations obtained from 251 Asian herbal products purchased in California and the United States, with mercury in 35, and lead in 24 (29). A later study of 3320 Chinese medicines screened between 1990 and 2001 showed that 138 contained heavy metals at levels above legal limits (30). A mass spectrometry study of 26 traditional Chinese medicines purchased in South Australia showed arsenic, lead and cadmium contamination, with one having greater than 10 times the acceptable limit of arsenic (30).

As the manufacture of herbal medicines is unregulated, there may be quite high and potentially lethal concentrations present with documented episodes of acute mercury and lead poisoning, the latter with encephalopathy (3,7). Children may be particularly vulnerable with resultant developmental delays (23). For example, case studies have been reported of a five-year-old boy who developed arsenic poisoning following treatment of retinoblastoma with a traditional Indian remedy (31), and lead poisoning in another young boy given "Tibetan Herbal vitamins". It was estimated that he had consumed approximately 63 g of lead over four years (32).

Addition of other toxic substances

A range of toxic plant and animal substances may also be added to herbal medicines. An example is *Chan su* which is used to treat boils, palpitations and sore throats. It contains venomous secretions derived from the skin and auricular glands of Chinese toads (*Bufo melanostictus Schneider* or *Bufo bufo gargarzinus Gantor*). The secretions contain bufadienolides which have a digoxin-like effect that may cause cardiac arrhythmias, seizures or coma (8,16,33). Injection of *Chan su* may be fatal (16).

Substitution of ingredients

Accidental substitution of herbs may occur for a variety of reasons that may simply involve inadvertent misinterpretation of names listed in original texts. This may not be helped by multiple or regional names being used for the same herb, or different preparations having the same name (1). Examples of this include androgenization of newborns who were administered Chinese silk vine rather than Siberian ginseng (34). The incorrect use of *Podophyllum emodi* instead of *Gentiana species* may cause podophyllin poisoning with hepatic, renal and gastrointestinal problems and permanent neurologic damage (7).

A more egregious situation involves the deliberate substitution of one herb for another often for financial reasons or convenience due to the expense or scarcity of the original ingredient (35). Substituted herbs may be inappropriate for a number of reasons apart from not being the correct therapeutic agent. An outbreak of rapidly progressive interstitial nephritis with terminal renal failure in Belgium is a good example of the potential consequences. This occurred when *Stephania tetranda* was replaced by *Aristolochia fangchi* in a weight-loss preparation exposing purchasers to the nephrotoxic effects of aristolochic acid. Urothelial carcinoma *in situ* has also been identified in 40 percent of cases of Chinese–herb nephropathy (36–38). Sometimes ginseng is adulterated with cheaper herbs such as *Rauwolfia serpentia* (reserpine) and *Mandragora officinarum* (scopolamine) (7).

Adulteration with pharmaceutical drugs

A simple but often illegal method for ensuring the effect of a herbal preparation is to adulterate it with a pharmaceutical drug that has a known effect. This has resulted in the addition of non-steroidal anti-inflammatory drugs (NSAIDs) to herbal arthritic remedies, theophylline, antibiotics and steroids to herbal asthma remedies and anticonvulsants to herbal anti-epileptic remedies, to name but a few. Of great concern is that the dosage of these drugs is unregulated with potentially dire consequences (39).

A number of years ago Huang et al. studied herbal preparations in Taiwan and found that, despite this being illegal in that country, 23.7 percent contained undeclared drugs and 52.8 percent of these had two or more adulterants (40). Issues that arise if the nature and dose of the added drugs is not declared include problems with allergies to antibiotics or contraindications such as sildenafil in an individual with ischemic heart disease. Unfortunately, at the time of autopsy, there may be no indication that such drugs had been taken.

Other examples in the literature include phenytoin poisoning and coma in a patient with epilepsy who had not been prescribed the drug. Drug toxicity had arisen from the ingestion of a Chinese herbal preparation that was touted as having only pure Chinese medicines that would control seizures with no mention of any prescription drugs on the packaging (41). Undeclared phenylbutazone has caused aplastic anemia and occult glyburide significant hypoglycemia (8).

A study of 61 patients from Hong Kong who had consumed traditional herbal preparations containing concealed steroids showed that seven (11.5%) required admission to intensive care with two dying within 30 days of presentation. Thirty-eight had complications due to the steroid adulterant (42). A further study from Hong Kong of 404 cases referred for toxicological analysis revealed there were 1234 adulterants consisting of legal and illegal drugs and animal tissues. Sixty-five percent of the patients had adverse clinical outcomes with the three most common presentations being Cushing syndrome, psychosis and hypoglycemia (43).

Reports in the literature have documented augmentation of herbal products with many drugs including antihistamines, aminopyrine, aspirin, bromhexine, chlordiazepoxide, diazepam, diclofenac, glibenclamide, hydrochlorothiazide, indomethacin, mefenamic acid, paracetamol, phenacetin, phenylbutazone, phenytoin, steroids and theophylline (7,44).

A recent study from Australia has shown that 53 percent of 49 analgesic and anti-inflammatory herbal medicine preparations were contaminated or adulterated with undeclared ingredients. Pharmaceutical adulterants included ephedrine and atropine. Of the 26 contaminated samples, 19 (73%) were made in Australia (45). An earlier study from the same group examined 135 herbal medicines used for diet, weight loss and cardiovascular health and again found pharmaceutical adulteration with undeclared stimulants such as ephedrine, synephrine and caffeine (46).

Adulteration with pharmaceutical agents is certainly not, however, always an issue, with a detailed study of nine Vietnamese herbal preparations revealing no evidence of synthetic pharmaceuticals, herbicides or pesticides (47).

Herb–herb interactions

The concomitant use of multiple herbal agents has been termed "polyherbacy" to reflect the potential problems that may arise from herb–herb interactions (48). A case that illustrates this issue was that of a 43-year-old woman who developed fulminant liver failure requiring transplantation, but which was ultimately fatal, following the ingestion of 12 herbal agents. These were *Astragalus propinquus*, *Codonopsis pilosula*, *Paeonia* sp., *Atractylodes macrocephala*, *Pueraria* sp., *Poria cocos*, *Dioscorea opposita*, *Patriniae*, *Psoralea corylifolia*, *Alpinia katsumadai*, *Glycyrrhiza uralensis* and *Dolomiaea souliei* sp., a number of which have been associated with hepatotoxicity (18).

Herb–drug interactions

Just as herbal products may interact with other herbs, they may also have effects on drugs (Table 88.4), such as increasing or limiting their actions, or increasing their absorption and decreasing their clearance (49,50). Herbal products may also act in combination with drugs causing quite idiosyncratic effects (6,51).

St John's Wort (*Hypericum perforatum*) is an example of a herbal product that may have significant effects on a range of drugs by inducing several cytochrome P450 enzymes and the transporter protein P-glycoprotein. This may cause intermenstrual bleeding in women taking the oral contraceptive pill, reduce the anticoagulative effects of warfarin and interfere with the action of cyclosporine thereby contributing to acute organ transplant rejections (11). It may also increase the effects of selective

TABLE 88.4 Potential herb–drug interactions*

Herbal agent	Potential interactions
Asian ginseng (*Panax ginseng*)	Potentiates the side effects of monoamine oxidase inhibitors
	Decreases the effects of immunosuppressive agents
	Increases the effects of oral hypoglycemic agents
	Has an additive effect with benzodiazepines
St John's wort (*Hypericum perforatum*)	Results in intermenstrual bleeding in women taking oral contraceptives
	Decreases the anticoagulative effect of warfarin
	Interferes with the action of cyclosporine causing acute transplant rejection
	Decreases the bioavailability of amitriptyline, theophylline, methadone, digoxin, indinavir (HIV-1 protease inhibitor)
Garlic (*Allium sativum*)	Increases the liver toxicity of paracetamol
	Enhances the effects of oral hypoglycemic agents
	Increases the incidence of bleeding in patients prescribed anticoagulants
Evening primrose and borage oils (contain gamolenic acid)	Reduces seizure thresholds in epileptics
	Interferes with the actions of certain antiepileptic medications e.g. phenytoin
Dong quai, Devil's claw, ginseng and *Dan shen*	Increases the action of warfarin

* Adapted from Hu (50)

serotonin-reuptake inhibitors (SSRIs) and tricyclic antidepressants leading to serotonin syndrome (39). St John's Wort may also significantly impact upon the bioavailability of many drugs including amitriptyline, indinavir (an HIV-1 protease inhibitor), digoxin and theophylline. Reducing the bioavailability of methadone may lead to the re-emergence of withdrawal symptoms (52–54).

Asian ginseng (*Panax ginseng*) has enhanced the adverse effects of monoamine oxidase inhibitors, as well as having an additive effect with benzodiazepines, increasing the effects of oral hypoglycemic agents, and reducing the effects of immunosuppressants (55).

Gamolenic acid, which lowers the seizure threshold in epileptics, may be found in evening primrose and borage oils and so may counteract the effects of routine antiepileptic drugs. The anticoagulative effects of warfarin may be enhanced by preparations such as Devil's claw, ginseng, Siberian ginseng, *Dan shen* and *Dong quai*, which therefore may predispose to hemorrhage (54). Spontaneous bleeding may also occur with preparations that interfere with the actions of vitamin K or platelets (49). Garlic (*Allium sativum*) is known to increase the risk of bleeding with anticoagulants as may ginkgo (*Ginkgo biloba*) (1).

Garlic has also increased the hepatotoxicity of paracetamol and enhanced the effect of oral hypoglycemic agents (52). Also, herbal compounds containing furanocoumarins have been shown to increase the hepatoxicity of paracetamol in cell culture studies (19) which may explain cases of acute liver injury in the presence of apparently low levels of paracetamol (56). Recently, the possibility of flavonoids contributing to statin-induced myopathies has been raised (57).

ISSUES WITH SURGERY

The American Society of Anesthesiologists has recognized the potential problem of herb–drug interaction and, for this reason, recommends that herbal medicines should be ceased at least two weeks prior to surgery (54). A review of herbal preparations found that only eight were potentially dangerous in the perioperative period but noted that they represented 50 percent of all single herb preparations of the 1500 to 1800 herbal medicines sold in the United States (58). Specific problems that may impact upon surgery are summarized in Table 88.5.

Problems may also arise when herbal products cause abnormalities in laboratory results by increasing or reducing concentrations of prescribed drugs, by direct hepatotoxicity or by interfering with immunoassays. The extent of the interference caused by cross-reactivity between herbs and drugs varies depending on the assay method used (54,59).

PROBLEMS WITH IDENTIFICATION

Organic toxins are not routinely checked for in standard forensic toxicological screening and may be extremely difficult to detect even when a substance is strongly suspected of being involved in a death due to levels that may be below or borderline for laboratory methodology (15,16). In addition, active ingredients may be degraded during storage and related plant species may have similar chemical profiles. The types of analytical techniques that may be used have included capillary electrophoresis,

TABLE 88.5 Potential issues with certain herbal remedies

Ginkgo	Increased risk of hemorrhage due to inhibition of platelet activating factor
Garlic	Increased risk of hemorrhage due to inhibition of platelet aggregation and increased fibrinolysis
The side effects of both of the above may be increased in the presence of drugs that inhibit platelet aggregation	
Echinacea	Allergic reactions, immunosuppression, reduced efficacy of immunosuppressants
Ephedra	Increased risk of myocardial and cerebral ischemia; intra-operative hemodynamic instability due to reduction of endogenous catecholamines; ventricular arrhythmias with halothane; potentially lethal interaction with monoamine oxidase inhibitors
Kava	Possible exacerbation of sedative effects of anesthetic agents
Valerian	Possible exacerbation of sedative effects of anesthetic agents
Ginseng	Hypoglycemia; increased risk of hemorrhage due to inhibition of platelet aggregation; reduction of anticoagulation properties of warfarin
St John's Wort	Effects on drugs through the cytochrome P450 system as noted above

gas and high-performance liquid chromatography, and ultra-violet, infra-red, nuclear magnetic resonance and mass spectroscopy, with X-ray diffraction and combined high performance liquid chromatography-mass spectroscopy and gas chromatography-mass spectroscopy (1,3). In recent years, techniques such as next generation DNA sequencing have proven extremely useful in identifying plant species and subspecies (30,60).

IMPACT ON ENDANGERED AND DOMESTIC SPECIES

The overharvesting of medicinal plants for herbal preparations is known to be endangering the survival of certain species (61,62). In addition, it is not uncommon for animal products to be added to herbal preparations with an estimated 13% of traditional Chinese medicines containing animal derivatives, which are often undeclared. These include endangered species such as the snow leopard (*Panthera uncia*) which was identified in a herbal preparation bought over-the-counter at a market in Adelaide, Australia, despite there being no mention of leopard in the ingredients list (30,63). Other endangered species used in traditional preparations include pangolins to treat skin diseases and improve circulation, and mole rats and tigers to treat arthritis (63). It has also been reported that domestic animals have been given herbal preparations, sometimes with fatal consequences (64).

FAILURE TO ACCURATELY LIST AND DESCRIBE INGREDIENTS

It is not uncommon for the contents of herbal preparations to either be incomplete or not accurately listed on the packaging. For example, in a study of herbal medicines available on the internet or over-the-counter in South Australia 59 of 99 products (60%) registered with the Australian Register of Therapeutic goods (ARTG) had different ingredient concentrations on their website compared to their ARTG listing (65).

A problem with undeclared or inaccurately listed ingredients is that of allergy, either to drugs such as antibiotics, or to fillers such as nuts and wheat. The latter may be of significance to gluten intolerant patients (45,46). Vegans may be unaware of the 13% of traditional Chinese medicines that contain animal products (61).

FORENSIC IMPLICATIONS

The potential medicolegal significance of herbal preparations is underappreciated with a number of problems arising, often associated with the situations outlined above (Table 88.4). These range from establishing what the lethal levels of active ingredients may be (and detecting them), to ascertaining whether an individual died with the herbal substance or from it. In the latter instance, an issue may be establishing what the possible lethal mechanisms were. This is often exacerbated by the lack of pathologic findings at autopsy (15,66).

Determining the exact composition of herbal agents may be difficult as ingredients listed on packages may bear no relationship to content and so do not assist in determining possible dosage. Also, Internet sales do not help in controling unregulated material.

Other problems may involve determining the effect of a herbal treatment on underlying organic illness. For example, lethal hemorrhage from a gastric ulcer may have been caused by an unsuspected herbal anti-arthritic medication adulterated with undeclared steroids and NSAIDs; something that would probably not be tested for. Other more complex medicolegal issues arise if herbal therapies have been chosen to augment or replace conventional treatment. Patients with organ transplants who suffer lethal rejection may have been taking herbal preparations that counteract anti-rejection medication. Children may die of treatable malignancies if their parents had opted for herbal rather than chemotherapy. As the terminal manifestations of uncontroled malignancy may be horrific, questions about duty of care and the possibility of legal and moral liability must be considered. The role of herbal remedies in poor or unexpected surgical or medical outcomes should also be considered.

CONCLUSION

Herbal therapies are becoming increasingly popular in many communities and will have been used by more and more decedents presenting for medicolegal evaluation. Despite this, there remains a dearth of information on their role in morbidity and mortality in the community. To address this issue, it would be useful to document herbal preparations, in addition to legal and illicit drugs, found at death scenes and to consider the possibility of herbal actions at autopsy. Until this information is available, the range and nature of potential side effects of herbal therapies will remain unclear. Questions that have been asked are:

- Are herbal therapies involved in lethal outcomes in forensic practice?
- If this is the case, how common is this problem?
- How is this best investigated? (17)

REFERENCES

1. Byard RW. A review of the potential forensic significance of traditional herbal medicines. *J Forensic Sci* 2010; **55**: 89–92.
2. Ernst E. Serious adverse effects of unconventional therapies for children and adolescents: A systematic review of recent evidence. *Eur J Pediatr* 2003; **162**: 72–80.
3. Chan K. Some aspects of toxic contamination in herbal medicines. *Chemos* 2003; **52**: 1361–71.
4. Farrington R, Musgrave I, Byard RW. Evidence for the efficacy and safety of herbal weight loss preparations. *J Integ Med* 2019; **17**: 87–92.
5. Byard RW, Musgrave I, Maker G, Bunce M. What risks do herbal products pose to the Australian community? *Med J Aust* 2017; **206**: 86–90.
6. Stickel F, Patsenker E, Schuppan D. Herbal hepatotoxicity. *J Hepatol* 2005; **43**: 901–10.
7. Brazier NC, Levine MAH. Drug-herb interaction among commonly used conventional medicines: A compendium for health care professionals. *Am J Therap* 2003; **10**: 163–9.
8. Chan TYK, Chan JCN. Chinese herbal medicines revisited: A Hong Kong perspective. *Lancet* 1993; **342**: 1532–4.
9. Dasgupta A. Review of abnormal laboratory test results and toxic effects due to use of herbal medicines. *Am J Clin Pathol* 2003; **120**: 127–37.
10. Farrington R, Musgrave I, Nash C, Byard RW. Potential forensic issues in overseas travellers exposed to local herbal products. *J Forensic Leg Med* 2018; **60**: 1–2.
11. Byard RW, Musgrave I. Does herbal therapy for COVID-19 have implications for forensic practice? *Forensic Sci Med Pathol* 2021; **17**: 377–8.
12. Ernst E. Risks of herbal medicinal products. *Pharmacoepidem Drug Saf* 2004; **13**: 767–71.
13. Byard RW. The witchcraft market of La Paz. *Doctors Rev* 1987; **10**: 58–9.
14. Hoban C, Byard RW, Musgrave I. A comparison of patterns of adverse drug reactions to St John's Wort and fluoxetine during the period 2000–2013. *Clin Exp Pharmacol Physiol* 2015; **42**: 747–51.
15. Ernst E. Toxic heavy metals and undeclared drugs in Asian herbal medicines. *Trends Pharmacol Sci* 2002; **23**: 136–9.
16. Byard RW, James RA, Felgate P. Detecting organic toxins in possible fatal poisonings – a diagnostic problem. *J Clin Forensic Med* 2002; **9**: 85–8.
17. Kostakis C, Byard RW. Sudden death associated with intravenous injection of toad extract. *Forensic Sci Int* 2009; **188**; e1–5.
18. Byard RW, Musgrave I. Herbal medicines and forensic investigations. *Forensic Sci Med Pathol* 2010; **6**: 81–2.
19. Gilbert JD, Musgrave I, Hoban C, Byard RW. Lethal hepatocellular necrosis associated with herbal polypharmacy in a patient with chronic hepatitis B infection. *Forensic Sci Int* 2014; **241**: 138–40.
20. Britza S, Musgrave I, Byard RW. Paracetamol (acetaminophen) hepatotoxicity increases in the presence of an added herbal compound. *Leg Med* 2020; **47**: 101740.
21. Pittler MH, Ernst E. Systematic review: Hepatotoxic events associated with herbal medicinal products. *Aliment Pharmacol Ther* 2003; **18**: 451–71.
22. Skoulidis F, Alexander GJM, Davies SE. Ma huang associated acute liver failure requiring liver transplantation. *Eur J Gastroenterol Hepatol* 2005; **17**: 581–4.
23. Webb AN, Hardiker W, Cranswick NE, Somers GR. Probable herbal medication induced fulminant hepatic failure. *J Paediatr Child Health* 2005; **41**: 530–1.
24. Farrington R, Musgrave I, Byard RW. Potential adverse outcomes of herbal preparation use in childhood. *Acta Paediatrica* 2019; **108**: 419–22.
25. Ernst E. Serious psychiatric and neurological adverse effects of herbal medicines – a systematic review. *Acta Psychiatr Scand* 2003; **108**: 83–91.
26. Ko R. Safety of ethnic & imported herbal and dietary supplements. *Clin Toxicol* 2006; **44**: 611–6.
27. Leung KS-Y, Chan K, Chan C-L, Lu G-H. Systematic evaluation of organochlorine pesticide residues in Chinese Materia Medica. *Phytother Res* 2005; **19**: 514–8.
28. Halt M. Moulds and mycotoxins in herb tea and medicinal plants. *Eur J Epidemiol* 1998; **14**: 269–74.
29. Ko RJ. Adulterants in Asian patent medicines (letter). *N Engl J Med* 1998; **339**: 847.
30. Yee SK, Chu SS, Xu YM, Choo PL. Regulatory control of Chinese proprietary medicines in Singapore. *Health Pol* 2005; **71**: 133–49.
31. Coghlan ML, Maker G, Crighton E, et al. Combined DNA, toxicological and heavy metal analyses provides an auditing toolkit to improve pharmacovigilance of traditional Chinese medicines (TCM). *Sci Rep* 2015; **5**: 17475.
32. Muzi G, Dell'omo M, Madeo G, et al. Arsenic poisoning caused by Indian ethnic remedies. *J Pediatr* 2001; **139**; 169.
33. Moore C, Adler R. Herbal vitamins: Lead toxicity and developmental delay. *Pediatrics* 2000; **106**: 600–2.
34. Barry TL, Petzinger G, Zito SW. GC/MS comparison of the West Indian aphrodisiac "Love Stone" to the Chinese medication "Chan Su": Bufotenine and related bufadienolides. *J Forensic Sci* 1996; **41**: 1068–73.
35. Awang DVC. Maternal use of ginseng and neonatal androgenization (letter). *JAMA* 1991; **266**: 363.
36. Zhao Z, Yuen JPS, Wu J, Huang W. A systematic study on confused species of Chinese Materia Medica in the Hong Kong market. *Ann Acad Med Singap* 2006; **35**: 764–9.
37. Vanhaelen M, Vanhaelen-Fastre R, But P, Vanherweghem J-L. Identification of aristolochic acid in Chinese herbs. *Lancet* 1994; **343**: 174.
38. Debelle FD, Vanherweghem J-L, Nortier JL. Aristolochic acid nephropathy: A worldwide problem. *Kidney Int* 2008; **74**: 158–69.
39. Cosyns JP, Jadoul M, Squifflet JP, et al. Urothelial lesions in Chinese-herb nephropathy. *Am J Kidney Dis* 1999; **33**: 1011–7.
40. Huang WF, Wen K-C, Hsiao M-L. Adulteration by synthetic therapeutic substances of traditional Chinese medicines in Taiwan. *J Clin Pharmacol* 1997; **37**: 344–50.
41. Lau KK, Lai CK, Chan AYW. Phenytoin poisoning after using Chinese proprietary medicines. *Hum Exp Toxicol* 2000; **19**: 385–6.

42. Chong YK, Ching CK, Ng SW, Mak TW. Corticosteroid adulteration in proprietary Chinese medicines: A recurring problem. *Hong Kong Med J* 2015; **21**: 411–16.
43. Ching CK, Lam YH, Chan AY, Mak TW. Adulteration of herbal antidiabetic products with undeclared pharmaceuticals: A case series in Hong Kong. *Br J Clin Pharmacol* 2012; 73: 795–800.
44. Ernst E. Adulteration of Chinese herbal medicines with synthetic drugs: A systematic review. *J Internal Med* 2002; **252**: 107–13.
45. Hoban CL, Musgrave IF, Byard RW, et al. Combined liquid chromatography-mass spectrometry and next-generation DNA sequencing detection of adulterants and contaminants in analgesic and anti-inflammatory herbal medicines. *Pharm Med* 2020; **34**: 49–61.
46. Crighton E, Coghlan ML, Farrington R, et al. Toxicological screening and DNA sequencing detects contamination and adulteration in regulated herbal medicines and supplements for diet, weight loss and cardiovascular health. *J Pharm Biomed Anal* 2019; **30**: 112834.
47. Hoban C, Nash C, Musgrave IF, Byard RW. An analysis of Vietnamese traditional herbal medicines for prescription and non-prescription drugs, herbicides and pesticides. *Aust J Forensic Sci* 2018; 50: 514–20.
48. Ness J, Johnson D, Nisly N. "Polyherbacy": Herbal supplements as a form of polypharmacy in older adults. *J Gerontol A Biol Sci Med Sci* 2003; **58**: M478.
49. Samuels N. Herbal remedies and anticoagulant therapy. *Thromb Haemost* 2005; **93**: 3–7.
50. Hu Z, Yang X, Ho PCL, et al. Herb-drug intractions. A literature review. *Drugs* 2005; **65**: 1239–82.
51. Hoban CL, Byard RW, Musgrave IF. Analysis of spontaneous adverse drug reactions to echinacea, valerian, black cohosh and ginkgo in Australia from 2000 to 2015. *J Integ Med* 2019; **17**: 338–43.
52. Izzo AA, Ernst E. Interactions between herbal medicines and prescribed drugs. A systematic review. *Drugs* 2001; **61**: 2163–75.
53. Awang DVC, Fugh-Berman A. Herbal interactions with cardiovascular drugs. *J Cardiovasc Nurs* 2002; **16**: 64–70.
54. Dasgupta A, Bernard DW. Herbal remedies. Effects on clinical laboratory tests. *Arch Pathol Lab Med* 2006; **130**: 521–8.
55. Ernst E. The efficacy of herbal medicine – an overview. *Fund Clin Pharmacol* 2005; **19**: 405–9.
56. Yoon E, Babar A, Choudhary M, et al. Acetaminophen-induced hepatotoxicity: A comprehensive update. *J Clin Transl Hepatol* 2016; **4**: 131–42.
57. Zechner J, Britza SM, Farrington R, et al. Flavonoid-statin interactions causing myopathy and the possible significance of OATP transport, CYP450 metabolism and mevalonate synthesis. *Life Sci* 2022; **291**: 119975.
58. Ang-Lee M, Moss J, Yuan CS. Herbal medicines and perioperative care. *JAMA* 2001; **286**: 208–16.
59. Chow L, Johnson M, Wells A, Dasgupta A. Effect of the traditional Chinese medicines Chan Su, Lu-Shen-Wan, Dan-Shen and Asian ginseng on serum digoxin measurement by tina-quant (Roche) and synchron LX system (Beckman) digoxin imunoassays. *J Clin Lab Anal* 2003; **17**: 22–7.
60. Byard RW, Musgrave I, Hoban C, Bunce M. DNA sequencing and metabolomics: new approaches to the forensic assessment of herbal therapeutic agents. *Forensic Sci Med Pathol* 2015; **11**: 1–2.
61. Kala CP. Status and conservation of rare and endangered medicinal plants in the Indian trans-Himalaya. *Biol Conserv* 2000; **93**: 371–9.
62. Sheng-Ji P. Ethnobotanical approaches of traditional medicine studies: some experiences from Asia. *Pharmaceut Biol* 2001; **39**: 74–9.
63. Byard RW. Traditional medicines and species extinction: Another side to forensic wildlife investigation. *Forensic Sci Med Pathol* 2016; **12**: 125–7.
64. Byard RW, Musgrave I. The potential side effects of herbal preparations in domestic animals. *Forensic Sci Med Pathol* 2021; **17(4)**: 723–5.
65. Blacksell L, Byard RW, Musgrave IF. Forensic problems with the composition and content of herbal medicines. *J Forensic Leg Med* 2014; **23**: 19–21.
66. Sklerov J, Levine B, Moore KA, et al. A fatal intoxication following ingestion of 5-methoxy-N,N-diethyltryptamine in an ayahuasca preparation. *J Anal Toxicol* 2005; **29**: 838–41.

SECTION

4

Forensic Science and Related Specialties

CHAPTER 89

Principles of Crime Scene Management

Isobel Colclough

INTRODUCTION

Effective crime scene management is critical to the success and reliability of forensic science and its application in criminal and civil justice systems. The information available, initial assessment and subsequent preservation and security of the incident scene, and evidential material contained within, determine the scope and parameters of the crime scene examination, while effective strategies for the recording and recovery of evidence should optimize forensic opportunities. The actions of first responders and crime scene investigation personnel have considerable impact on the availability of forensic evidence and the integrity and continuity of exhibits presented in courts of law. The management and co-ordination of technical activities undertaken to search for, identify, record, recover and protect evidence in a methodical and systematic manner should ultimately ensure that every submission to forensic units examining material from the scene is received in the best possible condition for examination. Sampling, handling, packaging and documentation of forensic exhibits should prevent any interference, loss or addition of material and provide an audit trail that details the responsibility for and security, transfer and storage of evidence from the point of recovery to the point at which it leaves the control of the Crime Scene Investigation Unit (CSIU). The overriding duty of all forensic practitioners is to the court and the administration of justice (1) and impartiality and the absence of bias in the processing of crime scenes and recovered material must be assured. Training promoting awareness of cognitive biases, regular review of scene examination strategies with these in mind, and consideration of more than one hypothesis in the interpretation of crime scenes should be employed to ensure a balanced and unbiased approach to crime scene examination. Reporting should be detailed and unambiguous and present only the facts of observations and scene examinations for the consideration of the courts.

This chapter provides an overview of the nature of crime scenes, the roles and responsibilities of personnel conducting crime scene examinations, the decision-making process for deployment of Crime Scene Investigators (CSI) and the importance of the forensic awareness of first responders and effective early action at incident scenes. The principles of crime scene management from the point of view of investigators and forensic practitioners will be addressed, including the development of effective scene examination strategies and strategies for the submission of evidence recovered for further forensic examination and analysis in order to optimize forensic opportunities in criminal investigations.

WHAT IS A CRIME SCENE?

Any location, vehicle, individual or item associated with a criminal offense and with the potential to yield forensic evidence pertinent to that offense can be considered a crime scene. There is no formal classification system for crime scenes, although they may be defined by physical description, for example indoor, outdoor, vehicle, victim, suspect or weapon, or as primary (the site where the most serious elements of the offense took place or the majority of forensic evidence is concentrated) or secondary (sites of associated offenses or sources of material transferred from the primary scene, for example a victim or suspect or their vehicle or address, or by offense or activity type, for example burglary, robbery, abduction, sexual assault, murder, deposition, and so on. The only reliable constant is that no two crime scenes are the same and, to ensure optimum outcomes, each must be examined methodically and systematically according to a scene specific strategy based on observation, the information available and the objectives of the investigation.

Crime scene investigation responsibilities and roles

In basic terms, the role of CSI personnel is to search for, recognize, identify, assess, preserve, record, recover, protect, transport and store potential forensic evidence. A more holistic view of the CSI role within police forces recognizes that it goes beyond purely evidence-based functions to include community support and a focus on victims and their ability to cope with crime, providing advice and reassurance, critical thinking, objectivity and problem-solving using reasoning and thought, and legal and investigative comprehension (2).

DOI: 10.1201/9781003138754-93

Crime Scene Investigation personnel tend to work at different levels, dependent on the requirements of the investigating body or police force.

The first tier or entry level CSI (usually designated Volume Crime Scene Investigator or VCSI) is employed in the forensic investigation of volume crime types such as simple burglaries, vehicle crime and criminal damage and other frequently encountered tasks such as injury photography. Competency must be demonstrated in core skills such as: photography; enhancement and recovery of fingerprints, palm and plantar impressions (also referred to as friction ridge detail or FRD), footwear and tool marks; identification and recovery of items and deposits likely to provide DNA profiles; whole item recovery including clothing and items requiring chemical treatment or laboratory methods to enhance potential marks or impressions; trace evidence recovery (fibers, hairs, glass, paint, etc.); and the application of simple strategies to ensure evidence is recorded and recovered using the most appropriate procedures and in the correct sequence. The VCSI will work independently in most cases, notifying investigating officers of outcomes on completion of the scene examination and advising on submission of forensic exhibits when required.

The next tier, and in most cases forming the majority of crime scene investigation personnel within a unit or organization, is usually designated CSI, Crime Scene Examiner (CSE) or Scenes of Crime Officer (SOCO), although there are Forensic Investigators and Scientific Support Officers with the same role and responsibilities. Terminology varies in different countries and jurisdictions. Competency must be demonstrated in the application of the core skills of the VCSI to all types of crime and additional skills applied in the recovery of evidence types associated with serious and major crime, including murder, arson, firearms offenses, sex offenses and serious and organized crimes such as manufacture and distribution of controled substances. The CSI will often work independently, making decisions and developing scene examination strategies in consultation with investigating officers for serious offenses and providing advice relating to the submission of forensic material for further processing.

The next tier is almost always designated Crime Scene Manager (CSM) and may or may not be responsible for supervising a CSIU in addition to managing the forensic response to major incidents. Competency must be demonstrated in the application and co-ordination of techniques employed in the forensic investigation of the full spectrum of crime types encountered by the investigating body or police force. The CSM is also expected to have a basic understanding of a wide range of forensic disciplines and recognize features of the crime scene requiring examination, assessment, evaluation and/or interpretation by forensic scientists and subject matter experts. Working closely with the Senior Investigating Officer (SIO) and other relevant specialists, the CSM will develop and apply strategies for the examination of the crime scene, any deceased individuals within and post-mortem examination(s), victim(s), suspect(s) and secondary scenes such as vehicles and addresses associated with victim(s) or suspect(s). Strategies must address the objectives of the investigation of the incident and be signed off by the SIO prior to implementation. The crime scene examination will be completed by CSIs, who will apply the scene examination strategy and assist scene-going specialists in recording and recovering evidence, under the direction of the CSM. Examinations of victims, suspects and secondary scenes will be carried out by different CSIs under the remote direction of the CSM to prevent cross-contamination between individuals and locations. The CSM should attend investigation team briefings and review existing strategies when new information is received, making amendments as required and agreed by the SIO.

Finally, a Crime Scene Co-ordinator (CSC), usually an experienced CSM with responsibility for the supervision of a CSIU, may be appointed to oversee the forensic response to complex major incidents, with multiple scenes, victims and/or suspects, and linked series of serious offenses. In Major Incident investigations, the CSC can be the CSM of a scene associated with the incident but, where possible for complex cases, a CSC based in the Major Incident Room (MIR) alongside the SIO and Major Incident Team is preferable. With access to real-time information and intelligence to inform forensic investigation strategies, and as a point of contact for all CSMs to communicate forensic findings to investigators, the CSC can ensure an effective and efficient forensic response. The CSC is well placed to develop scene examination strategies to exploit opportunities to associate individuals with each other and scenes and to maintain equipment, vehicle and personnel matrices to avoid cross-contamination between scenes.

INITIAL RESPONSE TO REPORTS OF A CRIME

Once a report of crime has been received, the assessment of whether a forensic response is required will be different for Volume Crime and Serious or Major Incidents. In the case of Volume Crime, the assessment may be made by a call taker, crime recording officer or a uniformed police officer attending the scene to take a report of crime. These individuals should have received training in forensic awareness and identify the potential for recovery of forensic evidence based on the information received from the victim of crime, or person reporting on their behalf, or their observations at the location where the offense took place. They should also provide advice in relation to preserving the scene and any potential evidence present. A request for CSI attendance will be made and the circumstances and information provided will be reviewed by a CSI who will contact the victim or attending officer, if necessary to gather further information, and decide if a scene visit is required. If there is a clear opportunity to obtain forensic evidence that will contribute to identifying those responsible, a CSI will be deployed to the scene.

In the case of Serious or Major Incidents, police officers will be deployed to the scene and having dealt with any immediate issues, for example administering first aid, securing witness accounts, detaining suspects, or gaining control of the situation, assess the forensic opportunities before contacting the CSIU to request a scene visit, where appropriate. It is a necessity that the First Officer Attending (FAO) the scene of a reported crime recognizes what, if any, crime has been committed and identifies, locates and properly preserves evidence (3). Scene security and preservation of evidence may be achieved by removing or excluding members of the public, victims and suspects from the area and restricting further access to the scene by setting supervised cordons or supervising entry and exit points if the area is contained within buildings. A scene log should be created to restrict access to authorized personnel only and record any actions taken at the scene prior to arrival of crime scene practitioners and detectives. For serious incidents, the scene log may be recorded in the Pocket Notebook (PNB) of the FAO and be limited to details of initial observations, individuals present on arrival (including victims, witnesses, or suspects/offenders) and persons entering the scene with entry and exit times. If the incident is complex or has the potential to develop into a Major Incident (e.g. victim likely to die from injuries sustained), a separate scene log document should be commenced and all information from PNB entries added. For Major Incidents, the scene log is a formal document which prompts recording of the officer maintaining the log, scene and offense details, observations, scene parameters and a sketch of the scene, weather and environmental conditions and actions taken by the FAO(s), any medical practitioners in attendance and other agencies such as the fire service. Once established, the scene log is used to record each entry to the scene with details of the purpose of entry, the Personal Protective Equipment (PPE) worn on entry and whether the individual entering is included on Contamination Elimination Databases (CED - fingerprints and DNA). Authority to enter the scene can only be granted by the SIO or CSM (4). Control of fire scenes will remain with the Fire and Rescue Services (FRS) until all possibility of reignition is eliminated, although police cordons may also be set in a wide perimeter around the scene.

FAO OR FIRST RESPONDERS

Forensic awareness among first responders to incidents of crime is critical to the success of forensic investigations. Failure to recognize and preserve forensic material or identify activity that might lead to the transfer of material between suspects, victims, property, vehicles and crime scenes could be catastrophic to investigations of all types of crime. Conversely, failure to recognize circumstances where the transfer of evidential material is unlikely leads to the misdirection of forensic resources, potentially detracting from the quality of service to appropriately allocated incidents through delay and time pressures. First responders, call takers, Police Community Support Officers (PCSOs) and uniformed police officers, fall outside the control of forensic units and their forensic awareness training is variable. Forensic units are likely to deliver the input but have little influence on its duration and frequency. Initiatives, including attachments of new police officers and call takers to CSIUs for training and development, are rarely compulsory and often lost to competing demands for limited resources to maintain day-to-day operations in policing. One recent study highlights the inefficient use of forensic science on an international scale and points to insufficient training of investigators in forensic awareness as a long-standing contributing factor (5). Accreditation of CSIUs under IEC/ISO 17020:2012 (6) will place further pressure on police forces to improve in this area but does not extend beyond the interface between policing units and forensic units and, as such, is not compelling.

THE GOLDEN HOUR

The Golden Hour refers to the principle that "effective early action can result in securing significant material that would otherwise be lost to the investigation" (4). There are often many demands made on the FAOs attending incident scenes and the circumstances may be shrouded in confusion caused by the activities or distress of individuals present at the time of the offense or arriving shortly afterward. It is vital that early witness accounts are obtained and other opportunities, such as viewing available CCTV images, are seized promptly, to identify direction of travel and descriptions of offenders and key witnesses and the presence and location of critical evidential material so that it can be secured and preserved for forensic recovery.

BUILDING BLOCK PRINCIPLES OF MAJOR INVESTIGATIONS

The "Murder Investigation Manual", produced by the Association of Chief Police Officers (ACPO, now the National Police Chiefs' Council, NPCC) of England and Wales in 2006 (4), outlines five "Building Block Principles" that underpin all major investigations:

- Preservation of life
- Preserve scenes
- Secure evidence
- Identify victim
- Identify suspects

These principles should be considered in the management of the forensic investigation of major incidents and the development of scene examination strategies to ensure the objectives of the investigation are met.

Preservation of life is paramount and the impact on forensic opportunities is secondary to administering first aid, admission of medical practitioners into the scene and the removal of the victim for transfer to medical facilities. The potential loss of, or interference with, forensic material can be mitigated by the actions of the FOA in recording details of the scene prior to any medical intervention and aspects of the scene altered by this intervention, including movement of the victim and surrounding items. If possible, the FAO should identify a route into and out of the scene that is unlikely to have been used by the victim(s) or offender(s) and ensure that this is used by all first responders. This Common Approach Path (CAP) will limit disturbance or damage to evidence and can be reviewed and adjusted, if necessary, by CSIs on arrival. Where issued to police officers, body worn video devices can provide detailed information regarding the initial actions of FAOs and medical practitioners. Failure to identify the impact of medical intervention on the scene can lead to misinterpretation of the circumstances of the incident, for example, the assumption that disturbance of items within the scene is due to a struggle between victim(s) and offender(s), and result in unnecessary and time-consuming examinations. The CSM should liaise with first responders in all instances to gather or check information relating to these activities and use it to inform the development of scene examination strategies.

Preserve scenes once again relies heavily on the actions of the FOA and further highlights the importance of training for uniformed officers in forensic awareness and appropriate actions taken at the crime scene to prevent loss or contamination of forensic material. The removal of individuals and animals from the scene, application of supervised cordons and instigation of a Scene Log is essential. Protection of the scene or items within from the elements should be undertaken by the first crime scene personnel in attendance except in extreme circumstances where loss of critical evidence might occur before they arrive. Cordons or scene boundaries should be set to prevent access to any area that may contain forensic material and care should be taken to resist the temptation to use natural boundaries and consider the possibility of items being discarded over walls, fences or hedges by offenders leaving the scene. It is always advisable to place cordons beyond what is thought to be the extent of areas of forensic interest as a later expansion of the cordoned area can lead to issues with the integrity of evidence recovered after being unprotected for any period. Cordons can be reduced following review by the CSM and SIO when appropriate.

Secure evidence refers to witnesses, other individuals and vehicles present or seen to leave the scene and CCTV, mobile phone or dash-cam footage that may have recorded relevant events around the time of the incident. Access to witness accounts and this footage can prove invaluable in enabling the development of targeted strategies for the examination of the crime scene and prevent time-consuming, speculative examinations.

Identify victim is often relatively easy to achieve based on information from the victim, witnesses or relatives present during the incident or at the scene or identification documents in the victim's possession. When the identity of a deceased victim is unknown, and missing persons enquiries fail to produce any potential candidates, there are forensic techniques and specialisms that can be employed. If the deceased has been involved in crime or is thought to be an immigrant, their fingerprints (and DNA in the case of a criminal history) may be included on a biometric database and identification can be achieved in a relatively short time. In cases where the deceased is in the advanced stages of decomposition, fingerprints may still be recognizable, medical implants, if present, are traceable in most cases and odontology and anthropology can provide information that may assist in reducing the pool of candidates or confirm identification when the pool of candidates is reduced by other investigative means.

Identify offenders is the priority in any Major Incident investigation and the forensic evidence is often an essential contributor to a successful outcome. Offenders may be known to surviving victims or witnesses or located by investigators through enquiries or CCTV. Whether or not this is the case, crime scene examination will be required to attempt to secure forensic material that will corroborate identification or identify unknown offenders.

CRIME SCENE MANAGEMENT

There are several stages in the forensic investigation of crime scenes and they are summarized in "Modules in a Forensic Science Process" published by the International Laboratory Accreditation Cooperation in 2014 (7), a document published to provide guidance to forensic units seeking accreditation under the International standards IEC/ISO 17020 (6) and IEC/ISO 17025 (8). Of the nine modules included, the first six are most relevant to Crime Scene Management, shown in Table 89.1, and are examined in more detail.

TABLE 89.1 Modules in a forensic science process most relevant to crime scene management
• Initial discussion regarding scene of crime attendance
• Undertake initial actions at the scene of crime
• Develop a scene of crime investigation strategy
• Undertake scene of crime investigation
• Assess scene of crime findings and consider further examination
• Interpret and report findings from the scene of crime
The remainder are more representative of forensic examinations undertaken by forensic scientists at the crime scene or in a laboratory:
• Examination and testing
• Interpretation of the results of examinations and tests
• Report from examinations and tests including interpretation of results.

Source: Adapted from (8).

Initial discussion regarding scene of crime attendance

This effectively refers to preparing to attend the crime scene and begins with establishing the appropriate authorities are in place for the CSI to attend the location in question and seize items relating to the incident under investigation. When available, permission is sought from the victim or property owner to attend their premises, vehicle or person to carry out a scene examination and remove items for evidential purposes. In cases where this permission cannot be obtained, for example, locations associated with suspects, and a warrant is required, the CSI or CSM must have appropriate authorization to undertake scene examinations. In the UK, this may include delegated authority from the Chief Constable of the relevant police force, issued under Section 38 of the Police Reform Act 2002, for specific scene-going staff roles in Scientific Support Units.

Information to be gathered before attending scenes of crime includes details of the location, crime type reported, individuals present or known to be involved, any warnings allocated on police systems in relation to the location or associated individuals, for example drug supply or use, previous violent offenses or presence/possession of weapons, the circumstances of the incident and extent of the scene. Details of any known hazards presented by the scene should be obtained and, if available, generic risk assessments consulted.

In the case of Major Incidents, the CSM should establish, where possible, the actions taken by FAOs in relation to securing the scene and preserving evidence, the availability of CCTV or other footage that might assist in devising scene examination strategies, the weather forecast and environmental factors to be taken into consideration when determining the resources and equipment required at the scene, for example, scene tents, screens, welfare facilities, PPE other than standard issue, lighting, stepping plates or ladders, and whether a Rendezvous Point or Control Point has been appointed. Names and contact details of key personnel such as the SIO and FAO should be obtained and arrangements made for briefings at the scene or prior to attending to inform scene assessment and strategies. Consideration should also be given to the personnel likely to be required at the scene. The extent, nature and complexity of the incident scene and secondary scenes, vehicles and individuals as evidence sources may not have been identified in the early stages but, where they have, the CSM should be considering the availability of Scientific Support Staff, including CSIs, Imaging Specialists, Forensic Enhancement Laboratory (FEL) personnel and Forensic Specialists from internal or external Forensic Science Providers. Where there is a clear requirement for additional personnel, they can be tasked with attending the scene or notified of the likely requirement for their attendance pending further scene assessment on arrival. Any limitations in the availability of resources, for example, the ongoing examination of scenes associated with concurrent Major Incident investigations, should be noted, and considered in the strategy setting phase of the forensic investigation.

Undertake initial actions at the scene of crime

On arrival at the crime scene, the priority of the CSI or CSM is the health and safety of everyone present. A risk assessment must be completed to identify hazards and put in place actions to remove or mitigate the risk of harm from those hazards. In the case of volume crime, this may be a very simple process and involve steps to reduce the potential of illness or injury using PPE, to prevent contact with biological material or protect from sharps such as broken glass. There may be hazards associated with the location of the incident such as the presence of asbestos in building materials or chemicals used in industrial processes carried out at the site, in which case, there may be risk assessments in place for employees for reference or generic risk assessments held by the CSIU relating to materials frequently encountered at crime scenes. If in any doubt regarding safety at the scene, where the necessary risk assessment is outside the experience and knowledge of the CSI, advice must be sought before commencing the examination and, on occasion, it may be necessary to withdraw and arrange to revisit when the scene can be made safe or forego the examination entirely based on health and safety concerns. The list of potential hazards at Major Incident scenes is extensive and removal or mitigation may involve steps as drastic as demolition of buildings, or parts thereof, to remove the risk of structural collapse. The CSM should be trained in risk assessment and be aware of resources available to enhance safety at incident scenes, such as specialist or enhanced PPE, safe access teams, Mountain Rescue Services and aerial access platforms used by the FRS. The risk assessment should include actions taken to mitigate risk or remove the hazard and actions to be taken in the case of injury or harm occurring and be communicated to all personnel entering the scene. It should be included in the CSM's record or log and is a dynamic process to be reviewed at regular intervals and on discovery of further hazards as the scene investigation progresses.

An initial assessment of the scene is carried out by the CSI or CSM and should include gathering further information and checking accounts of victims, witnesses and the FAO and a review of the measures put in place to secure the scene and preserve evidence. At Major Incident scenes, the CSM should be briefed by the SIO and FAO of any updates to the information passed initially and cordons and any CAP established by the FOA should be reviewed. Cordons may be increased, reduced or altered as required, recording the rationale for doing so and any resulting issues with integrity of newly included parts of the scene and evidential material within, and a CAP established, if not already in place. It is not uncommon with outdoor scenes to establish an inner and outer cordon, with the inner cordon applied to the area containing a concentration of potential forensic evidence and enabling the area between cordons to be searched by appropriately trained officers once any obvious evidential material has been recovered and while the inner cordon is still being processed by forensic personnel.

The initial assessment of the scene should not be biased by prior information and care should be taken to consider alternatives to the opinions and accounts provided. ABC is a common acronym used by police officers and CSIs and variable in its extension to a version of:

- Assume nothing
- Believe nothing
- Challenge everything

Much work has been done recently to explore the potential impact of cognitive bias on forensic processes (9,10), and prior information has been found to influence the interpretation of a crime scene in a study involving 58 experienced CSIs (11). It should be noted, however, that the same traces were secured by all participants independent of the prior information. Selective perception, expectation, confirmation and anchoring bias and shifting the burden of proof from the investigator to the suspect are considered to negatively affect criminal investigations based on a study in 2015 (12). Recommendations are made to include training for investigators to recognize cognitive fallacies and exchange experiences with investigative peers on a regular basis. The Forensic Science Regulator's Code of Conduct for Forensic Practitioners (1) requires all to "act with honesty, integrity, objectivity and impartiality" and organizations must demonstrate that their structure, policies and procedures support this to achieve accreditation under either IEC/ISO 17020 (6) or IEC/ISO 17025 (8). It has been suggested that CSIs should not be briefed regarding the story or stories circulating at the time of their arrival at the scene (13). While this might be possible in some volume crime incidents, it is impractical and likely to stretch resources beyond the reasonable when dealing with the vast range of locations and circumstances encountered. It is necessary, in most cases, to target scene examinations based on information available to avoid the inefficiencies and inhibiting cost of examinations inherent in collecting every possible source of forensic material at a scene. The CSI, CSM and Forensic Scientist should, however, always consider the evidence that should be expected if the accounts received are accurate and, if they are not, seek to establish the presence of material that both supports and contradicts initial information to achieve a balanced and comprehensive scene examination strategy. Forensic scientists (and investigators), unlike other areas of scientific investigation, must also consider the possibility of deliberate, planned deception (13). An initial walkthrough at Serious and Major Incident scenes is used to identify areas and items of forensic interest in relation to establishing the course of events and the accuracy of accounts and information received.

At volume crime scenes, the victim should be asked to describe the circumstances of the offense and indicate any areas where the offender(s) is thought to have been, the prior location of items stolen or removed from the scene and items the offender may have handled or left behind. The CSI should check whether anyone has accessed the scene or areas of interest within since the offense, who has legitimate access to the areas for elimination purposes and when these areas were last cleaned. A visual examination should then take place to assess the scene and identify forensic opportunities. The use of a good quality, even, white light source to search and examine surfaces in the scene may reveal marks, smears, small spots of blood, fibers, hairs, or other trace evidence which should be noted for recovery according to the sequence outlined in the subsequent scene examination strategy. Areas suitable for fingerprint examination should also be noted for examination following recovery of any DNA sources, trace evidence, relevant items and visible marks.

Develop a scene of crime investigation strategy

The strategy setting phase of scene investigations may encompass the following questions:

- What has happened?
- Where did it happen?
- When did it happen?
- How did it happen?
- Who was involved?
- Why did it happen? (7).

Fisher's Techniques of Crime Scene Investigation (14) configures the "6Ws" (what, where, how, who, when and why) as the six points of the "Investigative Star" and describes them as providing the strongest framework for the planning and conduct of the investigation of a crime scene in themselves and via their interrelationships. All evidence targeted in the scene examination should address one or more of the questions outlined above or provide contextual information that may be useful to the investigation, for example lifestyle indicators such as drugs paraphernalia or blood staining thought to be unrelated to the incident in question but indicative of previous violent acts, injury or disease.

The type and extent of searches included in scene examinations should be determined by the aims and objectives of the investigation, the location and terrain and the information available. Those involved should be appropriately trained and provided with a clear brief regarding target material and action to be taken in the event of finds.

While standard operating procedures (SOPs) may apply to the recovery of individual evidense types and physical items associated with an offense, scene examination strategies must be applied to a scene or item with multiple evidence types present. A methodical and systematic approach to evidence recovery must be demonstrated and is essential to maximize forensic opportunities and ensure the evidence recovered is relevant and robust under the scrutiny of the courts.

In general, the scene examination strategy should take into consideration the objectives of the investigation in selecting and prioritizing evidence recovery. The procedures involved in evidence recovery should be considered and applied beginning with the least destructive methods and applying destructive procedures after other material of forensic value has been recovered. Legitimate access to items and areas examined for forensic purposes must be considered and names and elimination samples (DNA, fingerprints, footwear impressions) obtained wherever possible.

A crime scene examination strategy must consider the following:

Anticontamination measures. These should be determined at the outset and may include, but not be limited to, use of appropriate PPE (e.g. mask and double gloves as a minimum for DNA recoveries), the use of clean drop sheets on which to place equipment and consumables used in the scene, cleaning equipment prior to taking it into the scene and before replacing in the vehicle after use, minimizing the equipment and consumables carried into the scene, wiping or changing outer gloves between each DNA recovery and discarding unused consumables to prevent contamination of stock in vehicles with material from the scene. Large equipment items used repeatedly at incident scenes, such as stepping plates and scene tents, should be subject to a documented and monitored cleaning regime between incidents and securely stored to prevent contamination after cleaning. Packaging seals and labeling of each exhibit should be completed before moving on to the next and gloves should be cleaned or changed regularly to prevent transfer of material between items.

Fixing the scene

Note taking, sketches and photography are used in combination to document the scene as found and prior to any interference or evidence recovery in serious and major crime. Demonstrating the integrity of all evidence recovered during the investigation is essential and accurate and comprehensive recording from the outset should ensure the honesty and accountability of forensic recoveries submitted in evidence in courts. Major Incident scenes should be recorded in full using still photography and video and utilizing other photographic techniques such as 360-degree photography, 3D laser scanning or photogrammetry where they might assist those specialists and officers unable to attend the scene and provide context in court presentations. Crime Scene Surveyors (Plan Drawers) should also be employed to locate evidence within the scene and the scene within a larger area or in relation to other locations of interest to the investigation on plans or maps.

While general photography of the whole scene is not necessarily required for all volume crime scenes, photography and sketches are used to provide context, that is, orientation and location of evidence in relation to scene features. The recording of evidence prior to any processing and without scales and labels assists in demonstrating its integrity.

Vulnerable or fragile evidence

Evidence at risk of loss or damage due to the weather, environment or activity in the scene should be recovered at the earliest opportunity. This might include visible fibers or hairs snagged on catches on a point-of-entry window or lightweight items at risk of being blown away outside or when doors are opened. Fiber tape lifts, if required, should also be recovered early as should marks in powdery deposits or substrates that might easily be damaged or disturbed. Sampling for the presence of accelerants or explosives residues should be carried out as soon as possible to prevent loss of volatile components.

Critical items

In addition to the early recovery of vulnerable or fragile evidence at Major Incident scenes, it may be that critical items are identified, with the potential to quickly address investigation objectives. Examples might include a blood-stained weapon with potential fingerprints, DNA or trace evidence relating to both the victim and offender or fingerprints thought to belong to the offender in the blood of the victim. If present, such items should be recovered as a priority and fast-tracked to the appropriate Forensic Unit(s) for examination.

DNA sources; whole item, stains and targeted sampling of likely sources of cellular DNA. The ability to obtain profiles from very small amounts of cellular material makes DNA recoveries from crime scenes susceptible to contamination from many sources. To minimize opportunities for this to occur, DNA evidence is generally the first consideration in forensic strategies once vulnerable and critical evidence has been secured. Whole item recovery is generally preferable and small items with no other potential evidence types associated, such as cigarette ends and chewing gum, are good examples, however, where there is a possibility of fingerprints or dental impressions, for example, it is necessary to recover DNA from the item first and at the crime scene, wherever possible without deterioration or damage to the potential marks. There is greater recognition, now, of the contamination risks associated with opening packaging to further examine items in locations other than accredited laboratories conforming to the requirements of ISO 17025 (8) or recognized equivalent. In the UK, the Accreditation of Forensic Service Providers Regulations 2018 came into force on 25th March 2019 and requires all dactyloscopic data (FRD examinations) and DNA profiles requested in relation to the prevention, detection or investigation of criminal offenses to be provided using an accredited forensic service provider. Failure to recover DNA from an item that can be processed in its entirety at the scene or submitted for marks examination directly after recovery of DNA will lead to unnecessary delays and additional costs associated with submission to an accredited laboratory to separate the evidence types in the interim. Exceptions exist when dealing with major crime, for example, an item likely to be included in the interpretation of blood (or other body fluids) or fiber distribution.

Trace evidence

Samples such as glass from windows or drinking vessels broken during the offense, soil, paint and other trace materials that may have transferred to or from offenders or their possessions should be included in the strategy for recovery. Paint associated with tool impressions and trace evidence associated with footwear marks should be sampled after the mark has been recorded using scaled photographs and lifting or casting if required. Representative sampling should be considered where large quantities of the same material subjected to the same conditions are present. The possible presence of fingerprints, blood and other DNA or trace evidence should be considered before collection and packaging.

Portable items related to the incident or bearing potential latent marks or visible marks and impressions. Items handled, moved or introduced to the scene by offenders should be considered for fingerprint powder examination or laboratory-based examination techniques, if suitable surfaces are present and potential DNA and trace evidence have been recovered or ruled out. In general, non-porous smooth or lightly textured surfaces are examined using fingerprint powders or chemical treatments such as cyanoacrylate ("superglue") fuming. Items and surfaces suitable for powdering should be preserved for examination once all other evidential material has been removed from the scene to prevent contamination during the powdering process. Items for submission to an FEL should be packaged to prevent damage to or loss of potential marks and removed from the scene. Porous items such as paper and cardboard will absorb moisture in deposited marks, making them more robust for transfer to the FEL but consideration should be given to potential indented writing, if relevant, or stability of friable deposits when selecting packaging and any visible marks should be photographed with scales prior to packaging. Extraneous forensic material, DNA and fingerprints should be considered at the point of recovery of digital devices for examination by Forensic Digital Investigators.

Visible marks and impressions on fixed surfaces

Where partial or complete marks suitable for comparison are visible on fixed surfaces in the scene, they should be photographed with scales prior to any attempt to enhance visible and latent detail.

Application of powders and chemical treatments for the development and enhancement of marks or impressions. Usually, the final stage of any scene examination is the powdering or chemical treatment of surfaces and items free from other evidence types within the scene, to enhance visible or latent marks or stains. At volume crime scenes, this is generally limited to application of fingerprint powders but at major crime scenes, FEL officers may attend to apply chemical treatments to fixed surfaces unsuitable for powder examination. Contextual photography of enhanced marks for comparison should be completed prior to scaled photography and lifting or casting of the marks for comparison with suspect or elimination sets or database searches.

Where partial marks or stains have been recorded already, subsequent recording of the same after enhancement should clearly indicate the enhancement technique used and be cross referenced to previous images for clarity. Where sequential treatments are applied, the sequential steps should be clear in the exhibit referencing and recording and all images of the same marks or stains at the different stages of enhancement should be cross referenced to avoid duplication of work.

Volume crime scene strategies

For volume crime, the scene assessment and subsequent examination strategy is usually relatively straightforward, however, the variability of scenes, circumstances and forensic opportunities requires the strategy to be documented with rationale for the selection of techniques applied and sequence of evidence recovery. It is essential that any deviations from expected sequence of recoveries and SOPs applied to recovery methods are documented and justified. The investigative objective in most volume crime is to identify the offender and associate them with the offense and the extent of the examination is dictated by the known circumstances. For example, if a suspect is detained in custody and their clothing and a screwdriver in their possession secured, fiber tape lifts at the point of entry and tool marks and associated paint samples, if present, should be recovered for comparison in addition to any footwear marks, fingerprints and DNA that may be attributable to the offender. If there are no suspects detained, and the scene does not form part of a suspected series of offenses with an overarching linking strategy in place, fibers and tool marks are unlikely to be recovered and priority will be given to footwear marks, fingerprints and DNA. Volume crime scene examination strategies should be proportionate and realistic in terms of likelihood of positive outcomes and efficient use of resources.

Serious crime scene strategies

Scene examination strategies for serious crime scenes are usually devised and implemented by an experienced CSI. They are based on the objectives of investigators using the same principles as applied to volume crime but considering more offense specific evidence types, for example search for semen in sex offenses or ballistic material in firearms offenses and might involve more speculative sampling of potential DNA sources, toolmarks and trace evidence. Forensic scientists and specialists may be consulted in relation to evidence collection and submission and scene recording but are unlikely to attend the scene.

Major Incident scene strategies

Major Incident scene strategies are frequently more complex in nature and must take into consideration the needs of relevant Forensic Scientists and other specialists required to attend the scene. Discussion between the CSM, SIO, Forensic Scientists and other scene-going specialists such as the pathologist or Forensic Fire Investigators must take place to establish priorities and negotiate strategies balanced to optimize forensic yield. Care must be taken to apply procedures in a sequence that does not compromise any other forensic material present, wherever possible. The SIO will ultimately decide on the strategy to be employed, making decisions aligned with the priorities of the investigation where conflict arises between the needs of different forensic disciplines. It is good practice to ensure that the minimum number of people required to undertake effective examination of the scene are admitted (15) and detailed planning, careful time management and clear communication are essential. The impact of each examination method on the scene and other opportunities to recover evidence must be considered in devising the scene examination strategy. Specialist examinations such as High-Intensity Light Sources (HILS) to search for body fluids and trace evidence or chemical enhancement of surfaces to detect cleaning activity or blood stains on dark backgrounds may be required. These processes require blackout conditions to visualize and record results and consideration must be given to potential evidence around windows and doors beforehand and, in the case of chemical applications, the potential for contamination of nearby surfaces with wet chemicals should be addressed prior to application. If Blood Pattern Analysis (BPA) (*see also* Chapter 97) is required at the scene, all items within the range of the blood distribution should be left *in situ* until this is complete, including the body or bodies, if present, and speculative tape lifting and swabbing of exposed skin of deceased individuals in the scene can be time consuming and delay post-mortem examinations.

All forensic personnel should understand their role and responsibilities and those of other team members and systems should be in place to ensure every stage of a sequential examination is completed before the next commences. Scene and exhibit referencing conventions must be agreed and communicated to all personnel prior to documentation and recovery of evidence to ensure consistency and avoid confusion in case review and when devising forensic submissions strategies. Separate strategies may be required for the examination of deceased individuals *in situ* and at post-mortem examinations. The examination of surviving victims, suspects and associated vehicles and locations will be the subject of further scene examination strategies and forensic examination strategies and logistics may need to be negotiated with forensic units for critical items in urgent submissions. Scene examination strategy is a dynamic process and new information relating to the incident under investigation should prompt a review. If amendments are made, they should be communicated to all personnel promptly and clearly.

Undertake scene of crime investigation

Implementation of scene examination strategies should follow SOPs for technical activities and rationale should be documented for any deviations. Personnel should have demonstrated competence to the required level for the nature of the investigation or technical activities employed in the scene examination and regular review of progress and checking of work completed should take place.

Detailed contemporaneous notes should be made throughout the scene examination and observations, opinions, decisions made, information received (with source), instructions given and significant conversations should be included with timings. Notes should include details of areas examined within the scene and areas excluded with reasoning. All evidence recovered should be listed with detailed descriptions of items and locations to enable accurate reconstruction of the scene (in combination with photographs and sketches) by forensic practitioners not present at the time of the examination. Descriptions of evidence and locations should correspond with those on exhibit labels and this consistency should be maintained in any records and reports produced later to prevent any suggestion of irregularity in the chain of custody. Asset numbers of equipment used, such as scales, camera, SD cards and lenses, should be recorded and batch numbers of consumables such as fingerprint powders and reagents for presumptive testing and outcomes of positive and negative control tests with identifiers for positive reference samples. This enables quality control and tracking of cases that may be affected by equipment faults or damage or contaminated consumables, should they occur.

When the scene examination is completed, a review of the strategy should take place to ensure all relevant material has been secured. At Major Incident scenes, the CSM will usually walk through the scene with the SIO at the conclusion of the examination to review findings against scene examination strategies and investigation objectives and determine whether any further examination is required before the scene is released.

Assess scene of crime findings and consider further examination (forensic strategy)

This is the point at which a forensic strategy is determined for the investigation and decisions are made in relation to the further examination of material recovered from crime scenes. Most police forces use a case assessment and interpretation model to ensure best value is obtained from the available forensic resources and the needs of the Criminal Justice System are met (16). Forensic Submissions Units rely on the information provided regarding the circumstances of the case, victim, suspect and witness accounts, an overview of the evidence available, data relating to the expected outcomes of forensic examinations and the likelihood of those outcomes to assist in meeting the needs of the investigation to make objective decisions on whether to authorize submission of evidence to forensic units for further processing. The forensic budget is a finite resource with which the police force or investigating body must attempt to meet the scientific needs of all casework. Forecasting based on crime profiles, combined with supervision and strict procedures relating to authorization of forensic submissions, afford some control of budgets but constant monitoring of casework trends in terms of frequency of requests for each type of examination must also take place to identify potential shortfall and redistribute surplus.

The submission of evidence for further examination is dependent on whether a suspect or suspects have been identified or detained and whether the evidence available has the potential to identify suspects and/or provide conclusive links or associative evidence only. The individualizing characteristics of fingerprints, DNA and footwear marks are more likely to yield results that will conclusively eliminate or associate an individual or their shoes with a crime scene and are likely to be given priority over fibers or glass samples due to the potential for these to be duplicated in other locations in the wider environment. However, if multiple sources of associative evidence are recovered from the crime scene and suspect, their presence in combination becomes less statistically probable and may be sufficient to persuade a court of the involvement of the suspect. The level of the offense, priorities of the investigating body or police force and cost of examinations must be balanced in determining whether to authorize forensic submissions and, in most cases, the cost and timescales involved in trace evidence examinations are inhibitive in low priority investigations.

If there are no suspects, any FRD or DNA samples that could be reasonably expected to relate to an offender will be submitted for inclusion on the relevant database to establish whether they correspond with DNA profiles held for known individuals or unidentified profiles from other crime scenes. Where more than one sample is available from the scene, the quality and quantity of useful material in each sample, location found and number of individuals thought to be involved should be considered when deciding which should be included in the submission. Inclusion on databases will depend on whether sufficient information is present in the sample for automated searches and after comparison with any elimination samples taken from victims and other individuals with legitimate access to the scene. If suspects have been detained and DNA and fingerprints taken, samples will be submitted for direct comparison prior to inclusion on databases.

Footwear marks may be coded for inclusion on a footwear database but this is usually limited to class characteristics for intelligence purposes and a full comparison of individualizing features will only take place if footwear has been seized from suspects and screened for sufficient similarity to justify expert analysis and evaluation.

Forensic submissions from volume and serious crime

It is the responsibility of the investigating officer to prepare submissions forms and provide all relevant information for the consideration of Forensic Submissions Officers when seeking authorization for forensic examination of material recovered in the case. If fingerprints or DNA have been recovered, further submissions may be delayed pending outcomes of database searches or comparison as the results may have an impact on the value of examination of further material. Where multiple options exist in the range of forensic material available, CSIs and/or Forensic Submissions Officers should be consulted for advice in relation to the most appropriate examinations in terms of optimizing outputs. Results obtained from forensic examinations may clearly eliminate or implicate suspects or prompt a request for further submissions if the threshold for progression of the case against suspects is not met and additional forensic material is available. In the latter case, consultation with prosecution services and Forensic Submissions Officers should take place to determine whether the threshold is achievable with expected outcomes of further examinations, bearing in mind the best evidence is most likely to have been submitted to examination already.

Forensic submissions from Major Incident investigations

At the earliest opportunity after recovery of all evidence from scenes associated with a Major Incident, a Forensic Strategy meeting should be arranged with all relevant parties from the Major Incident Team, Scientific Support Services and Forensic Service Providers to review all exhibits and develop a strategy for the submission of selected items for further analysis and evaluation. An overview of the incident background and circumstances and accounts from victims, suspects and witnesses should be provided and the strengths and weaknesses of the case identified. Details of any elements of the investigation that are already corroborated by CCTV, digital data analysis, multiple independent witnesses or the results of urgent submissions of critical evidence should be provided. Scene observations and possible interpretations and initial findings from specialist examinations carried out at scenes and medical or post-mortem examinations should be included. The outstanding objectives of the investigation should be clearly defined and each item of evidence assessed in terms of potential contribution to achieving them, individually or as part of a combined submission. Opportunities to test both prosecution and defense hypotheses with forensic examinations should be identified. If there is confidence in the strength of the evidence secured already in the investigation, a Crown Prosecution Service (CPS) representative might be invited to advise regarding the quantity and nature of evidence required to reach the threshold for prosecution.

In complex investigations, the number of exhibits collected can run to hundreds or even thousands. The forensic strategy process can be protracted and meetings can run into days. Results may not meet expectations, failing to meet the threshold for prosecution, raising further questions or changing the direction of the investigation entirely and further investigation and forensic strategy meetings will be required to identify additional rounds of submissions until the case is considered ready for court or the forensic opportunities run out.

Interpret and report findings from the scene of crime

Formal reporting of crime scene examinations will usually take the form of a Statement and should contain only direct observations and a factual record of the examination conducted, the evidence recovered and continuity or chain of custody information. Opinion, interpretation and hearsay evidence may be included in personal contemporaneous notes and shared with investigators and other forensic personnel but only the facts of the examination should be presented to the court. Crime Scene Investigation personnel are not considered expert witnesses and evaluation and interpretation of scenes and evidence should be based on proven scientific methods of examination and analysis by competent experts in the appropriate field to meet the requirements of the relevant legislation, for example, The Criminal Procedure Rules 2020, Part 19, sets out the requirements relating to expert evidence in England and Wales. The Forensic Science Regulator (FSR) in the UK has produced guidance on the content of non-expert technical statements (17) and includes the requirement for all practitioners to declare compliance or non-compliance with the FSR Code of Conduct for Forensic Science Practitioners. The guidance also states that although there is no legal requirement to include a description of any accreditation held by the organization employing the witness, the CPS desires such declarations to facilitate compliance with The Accreditation of Forensic Service Providers Regulations 2018. If included, it should be made clear which methods applied are included in the scope of accreditation and which are not. A statement submitted in evidence to the court should be free from jargon and technical references, clear and comprehensive in content in order that lay persons or jurors can understand the scene, the examination that took place and the evidence recovered. It should be peer reviewed prior to submission to the court to ensure the content is appropriate and accurate and all the necessary information, declarations and signatures are present (18).

CONCLUSION

The quality of forensic material recovered from crime scenes is critical to the success or failure of forensic science in criminal investigations (19). The purpose of crime scene management is to ensure that the integrity and continuity of evidence from crime scenes is assured from the outset and that every forensic exhibit reaches the laboratory or examining forensic unit in the best possible condition for the intended examination and analysis (20). Attention to detail, a sound understanding of forensic principles and competence in all aspects of evidence recording and recovery are essential and the ability to innovate and solve problems is required to deal with the variety of circumstances, locations and environmental factors encountered. Understanding the policies and priorities of the investigating body or police force and the investigation objectives of the case when developing scene examination strategies leads to effective and efficient use of forensic resources. Effective anticontamination measures and careful and appropriate sampling, handling, packaging, transport and storage of forensic evidence should maximize forensic yields. Comprehensive contemporaneous documentation of crime scenes, crime scene examinations and evidence recovered should form the basis of clear and accurate statements submitted in evidence and combined with demonstrating the integrity and continuity of exhibits should, in most cases, result in CSI evidence being accepted without the need to attend court in person. Accreditation of CSIUs to an internationally recognized standard and compliance with the Code of Conduct for Forensic Science Practitioners should further reassure courts of the reliability of CSI evidence.

Crime Scene Management and the co-ordination of the forensic response to Major Incident investigations is complex and requires a working knowledge and understanding of criminal investigations and the diverse disciplines employed in forensic science. Effective communication and negotiation skills, planning and organization, and management of time and resources are essential to achieving the best possible outcomes of crime scene examinations associated with the investigation of Major Incidents.

REFERENCES

1. Forensic Science Regulator. Codes of Practice and Conduct for Forensic Science Providers and Practitioners in the Criminal Justice System, FSR-C-100, Issue 7, 2021. Available from: www.gov.uk (Accessed 28 June 2023).
2. Chowdhury M. Beyond bagging and tagging - An empirical investigation into the roles, designations and responsibilities of crime scene practitioners. *Sci Just* 2021; **61:** 271–9.
3. Monckton-Smith J, Adams T, Hart A, et al. *Introducing Forensic and Criminal Investigation.* London: SAGE Publications Ltd; 2013.
4. Association of Chief Police Officers. *Murder Investigation Manual.* Wyboston, Bedfordshire: National Centre for Policing Excellence; 2006.
5. Wullenweber S, Giles S. The effectiveness of forensic evidence in the investigation of volume crime. *Sci and Just* 2021; **61:** 542–54.
6. The British Standards Institution. *Conformity assessment - Requirements for the operation of various types of bodies performing inspection. BS EN ISO/IEC 17020:2012.* London: BSI Standards Limited; 2012.
7. International Laboratory Accreditation Cooperation. *Modules in a Forensic Science Process. ILAC-G19:08/2014.* Silverwater, New South Wales, Australia: ILAC; 2014.
8. The British Standards Institution. *General requirements for the competence of testing and calibration laboratories. BS EN ISO/IEC 17025:2017.* London: BSI Standards Limited; 2018.
9. Kukucka J, Kassin SM, Zapf PA, et al. Cognitive bias and blindness: A global survey of forensic science examiners. *J Appl Res Mem Cogn* 2017; **46:** 452–9.
10. Cooper G S, Meterko V. Cognitive bias research in forensic science: A systematic review. *Forensic Sci Int* 2019; **297:** 35–46.
11. van den Eeden CAJ, de Poot C, van Koppen PJ. Forensic expectations: Investigating a crime scene with prior information. *Sci Just* 2016; **56:** 475–81.
12. Ditrich H. Cognitive fallacies and criminal investigations. *Sci Just* 2015; **55:** 155–9.
13. Jamieson A. A rational approach to the principles and practice of crime scene investigation: I. Principles. *Sci Just* 2003; **44:** 3–7.
14. Tilstone WJ, Hastrup ML, Hald C. *Fisher's Techniques of Crime Scene Investigation.* Boca Raton : CRC Press; 2013.

15. Forensic Science Regulator. *The Control and Avoidance of Contamination in Scene Examination Involving DNA Evidence Recovery*, Issue 2, 2000. Available from: www.gov.uk (Accessed 28 June 2023).
16. Association of Chief Police Officers. *Forensic Submissions Good Practice Guide*. National Policing Improvement Agency; 2012.
17. Forensic Science Regulator. *Non-Expert Technical Statement Guidance, FSR-G-225, Issue 2*. London: Crown Copyright; 2020.
18. Millen P. Crime scene investigation – A defence perspective. *Sci Just* 2004; **44:** 104–106.
19. Sutton R, Trueman K. *Crime Scene Management, Scene specific methods*. Chichester: John Wiley and Sons; 2009.
20. Chowdhury M. A broken system? Examining the perilous state of quality assurance in crime scene practice. *Sci Just* 2021; **61:** 564–72.

CHAPTER

90

Biological, Chemical and Radioisotope Trauma and Associated Personal Protective Equipment

Mark Byers, Stevan R. Emmett and Peter G. Blain

INTRODUCTION

Since the end of the "Cold War", the threat of a total chemical, biological, radiologic and nuclear (CBRN) conflict has receded. The collapse of the Iron Curtain and the break-up of the Warsaw Pact may have led to a closer understanding between some of the former protagonists and scientists, but this collapse has destabilized the former geopolitical certainties as has been shown by recent events in Ukraine and other geographic regions. The break-up of the USSR has led to the loss of CBRN material, while theft, espionage and looting in failing states has increased the prevalence of these materials hidden in general society. There has also been an increase in the threat from global terrorism as illustrated by the use of nerve gas in Japan, anthrax spores in the USA, the rise of Al Qaeda and ISIS.

There is nothing new about the use of CBRN assets as weapons. The Tartar hordes catapulted plague-infected bodies over the besieged walls of Kaffa in 1345. The British used biological weapons in 1754 against Native Americans when they distributed blankets from smallpox-infected patients. Chlorine was first used in 1915 by the Germans at Ypres and mustard gas, again at Ypres, in 1918. The Rajneesh Cult, followers of the Bhagwan Shree Rajneesh, caused 751 casualties by releasing *Salmonella typhimurium* in Wasco, Oregon in 1984 and in 1995 the Aum Shinrikyo cult successfully released sarin nerve agent in the Tokyo subway system after a covert release in Matsumoto in 1994 and two previous, but ineffectual attacks using *Botulinum* toxin in 1990 and anthrax in 1993. The sarin attack caused 12 deaths and over 3000 casualties; 10 percent of whom were healthcare workers.

In 1979 at Sverdlovsk in the USSR, there was an unexplained outbreak of anthrax, which led to speculation of an accidental release. In recent times, there have been a series of attempts by individuals to use ricin as a poison, the occasional use of cyanide as a weapon, in Iraq Al Qaeda frequently used chlorine as a weapon and in Syria there has been reported use of crude mustard and the nerve agent sarin.

Georgi Markov was a Bulgarian journalist who worked as a broadcaster for the BBC World Service. He was very critical of the Bulgarian government in his radio programs and was regarded by them as a serious political threat. On 7 September 1978, Markov was waiting on Waterloo Bridge in London to catch a bus. He felt a sharp pain in the back of his thigh caused by a man waiting behind him who had, apparently accidentally, poked him with the tip of his umbrella. Markov ignored it but that evening became seriously ill with a marked fever. His condition deteriorated and he was admitted to hospital. Markov mentioned the incident on the bridge to his physicians. Despite supportive treatments, he died three days later.

As the cause for Markov's death was undetermined, an extensive autopsy was conducted. Initially, some form of poisoning was suspected to be the cause of death. Of significance, where the umbrella had punctured his leg a tiny (1.52 mm diameter) spherical pellet was found. The pellet was made of platinum and iridium and had two 0.35 mm holes drilled into it. UK experts in toxicology suspected Markov might have been poisoned by ricin, the highly toxic protein found in castor beans. This was confirmed by chemical analysis and toxicology testing.

The perpetrators of this assassination were never identified, although the Bulgarian secret service, assisted by the Soviet KGB, was widely blamed. Apparently, they had attempted to assassinate Markov on two previous occasions.

The Muslim fundamentalist sect Da'esh has taken this a step further in Syria, starting with chlorine and moving on to home-produced mustard gas. Both sides in the conflict have been accused of using sarin gas, although the Syrian Government's use seems unequivocal.

With North Korea's change in Supreme Leader, there has been a resurgence in their development of nuclear weapons, and they now hold at least five nuclear devices and the ability to produce many more. The State also

DOI: 10.1201/9781003138754-94

sanctioned the use of VX nerve agent to assassinate the Leader's half-brother and they are thought to possess vast stockpiles of anthrax, plague, sarin, mustard and VX in addition to their nuclear weapons. They are believed to have an active chemical and biological weapons program.

The Russian State is believed to have killed Alexander Litvinenko, with the radioisotope polonium^{210}. Litvinenko was a former KGB officer who had become very critical of the Russian leadership and had moved to the UK. On 1 November 2006, Litvinenko became unwell and was admitted to Barnet General Hospital in London and later moved to the Intensive Care Unit at University College Hospital. The cause for his illness was initially not determined and a range of potential poisons, including thallium, toxins and cytotoxic drugs was considered. Eventually, an earlier suggestion of ingestion, rather than irradiation, was confirmed when the radionuclide Polonium^{210} was detected in his urine. Polonium^{210} is primarily an alpha emitter with a high specific activity. Somehow Litvinenko had ingested the radionuclide, and this was now destroying vital cellular processes in his tissues.

Litvinenko had met with two former colleagues early on the day he became ill. They had tea in a hotel room and moved on for lunch at Itsu, a sushi restaurant in Piccadilly, London. Subsequent monitoring found traces of an alpha emitter, confirmed to be Polonium^{210}, everywhere the group had visited. The chemical signature of this polonium specifically identified it as originating from a nuclear reactor in Russia. The police investigation found the only credible explanation was that the Russian state was, in some way, involved in Litvinenko's murder.

More recently, the Russian GRU reportedly deployed the deadly nerve agent novichok on two separate occasions as an assassination tool in European countries in 2018 and 2020. The first target in the UK was a former GRU officer, Sergei Skripal. Fortunately, the early recognition that the clinical features in Skripal, and his daughter, suggested anticholinesterase poisoning led to the analytical detection of a novichok series compound in their blood and the provision of the appropriate medical treatment and care. Both survived the poisoning. There is an ongoing investigation into this poisoning and that of two unconnected members of the public who were poisoned by contact with pure novichok compound in a discarded perfume dispenser.

The potential for State and Non-State Actors to use CBRN weapons remains an extant threat and all those involved in forensic and legal medicine should have a basic understanding.

TYPES OF BIOLOGICAL WEAPONS

Biological weapons (BW) are naturally occurring diseases that:

- can be easily disseminated or transmitted from person to person
- result in high mortality/morbidity and thus impact on public health and healthcare systems
- have a major impact on a country's economic well-being and stability

BWs are classified as:

- Category A diseases which include anthrax, botulism, plague and smallpox (*see* Table 90.1).
- Category B diseases which are less easy to disseminate and less lethal and these include diseases such as glanders, melioidosis, Q Fever and ricin toxin.
- Category C diseases which are potentially debilitating

TYPES OF CHEMICAL WEAPONS

"A *Chemical Weapon* is a *chemical* used to cause intentional death or harm through its toxic properties" (1).

For convenience these are classified into six toxidromes:

- Acids and alkalis
- High-potency fentanyl analogs (carfentanil, remifentanil)
- Asphyxiants (e.g. cyanide)
- Vesicants (e.g. mustards and lewisite)
- Nerve Agents (e.g. G-series, V-series and the novichoks)
- Lung damaging agents (e.g. chlorine and phosgene gas)

TABLE 90.1 Potential biological warfare agents

Category A	Category B	Category C
Bacillus anthracis	*Coxiella burnetii*	Nipah virus
Clostridium botulinum toxin	Brucellae	Hanta virus
Yersinia pestis	*Burkholderia mallei*	Drug-resistant tuberculosis
Variola major	*Burkholderia pseudomallei*	Yellow fever
Francisella tularensis	Alpha viruses	Tick-borne encephalitis
Filoviridae (Ebola) Arenaviridae (Lassa)	Toxins (ricin, SEB, conotoxin)	

Source: Center for Disease Control and Prevention: Bioterrorism agents/disease. https://emergency.cdc.gov/agent/agentlist-category.asp

Acids, alkalis and opioids are now ubiquitous in society.

TYPES OF RADIOLOGIC WEAPONS

It has generally been considered that the use of a nuclear weapon is unlikely (although currently this risk level may have changed) but the use of radioactive isotopes and materials as terrorist weapons is a real possibility. Radioactive Dispersal Devices (RDDs) are designed to disseminate radioactive material over an area to cause harm and deny access to an area and Radiation Exposure Devices (REDs) are unshielded sources designed to expose people to high doses of radiation.

TYPES OF PERSONAL PROTECTIVE EQUIPMENT

Disease-causing agents enter the body by means of ingestion, injection, skin absorption or inhalation. To protect the body from disease the individual needs a barrier. This is achieved by wearing a protective ensemble that provides protection from inhalation, injection, contact and percutaneous absorption. A respirator protects the airway and usually the eyes and face, and a coverall suit protects the skin. The type of Personal Protective Equipment (PPE) is controversial and there is no universally accepted standard. Although no readily available combination of PPE protects against all hazards, personnel should be protected as much as possible commensurate with their task. There is a compromise that must be made between visibility, dexterity, mobility, physiological burden, communication and the environment to allow the individual to carry out their roles within the level of PPE chosen. In addition to standard precautions, transmission-based precautions should be used.

The American system of PPE classification is proscriptive, but has the advantage of being easy to understand, and classifies levels of protection from A to D (2).

- Level A is the highest level of protection with a fully encapsulated chemically resistant suit with a full-face self-contained breathing apparatus. The suit must be capable of withstanding any chemical that is encountered.
- Level B is similar to level A but there is less skin protection.
- Level C has chemical resistant material and an air purifying canister respirator.
- Level D is the lowest level with no respiratory protection and coveralls only.

In the UK, PPE regulations are covered by the Personal Protective Equipment Regulation (EU) 2016/425 (3). and guidance can be found from the Health and Safety Executive paper (4).

BIOLOGICAL AGENTS AS WEAPONS

Biological agents are not easy to produce or disseminate and require a high level of training to handle safely. Clues to their release include an outbreak of non-endemic or unusual disease, the presentation of a disease or sudden onset of atypical disease in a large number of people with the same symptoms at the same time. These are summarized in Table 90.2. Genetic engineering of natural biological organisms could alter their pathogenicity, incubation periods and clinical syndromes but evidence so far suggests virulence is not enhanced. Resistance to antimicrobial drugs and vaccines could also be engineered (5). But whatever is done to these diseases they all fall into one of three dissemination categories:

- Contact
- Droplet
- Aerosol

And it is these three categories that define the level of PPE required.

TABLE 90.2 Signs of deliberate release of a biological weapon (6)
• Occurrence of a sudden unusually large outbreak
• High infection rate
• Unexpected severity of disease
• Disease limited to a discrete population
• Evidence of an unusual route of exposure
• Disease in an atypical geographic locale
• Disease occurring outside normal transmission seasons
• Disease occurring in the absence of usual vector
• Simultaneous outbreaks of multiple diseases
• Unusual organism strains
• Unusual antimicrobial sensitivity patterns
• Disparity in attack rates among persons indoors and outdoors
• Terrorist claims
• Intelligence reports
• Discovery of unusual munitions

SAMPLE COLLECTION

The collection and handling of pre-morbid samples is useful. Possible samples include a full blood count, arterial gases and biochemistry as standard, nasal and throat swabs, blood and urine for cultures and toxin assays and serum serology. Standard techniques of culture, PCR, ELISA and DNA/RNA sequencing will be guided by the clinical picture. Samples should be handled as would any high-threat disease sample with appropriate risk reduction controls in place and investigated in appropriate containment facilities. The highest level of biosecurity are the level 3 and 4 facilities (7) as laid down in national legislation. Biosafety level 3 is appropriate for work involving microbes which can cause serious and potentially lethal disease via the inhalation route, whereas Biosafety level 4 is the highest level of biosafety precautions and is appropriate for work with agents that could easily be aerosol-transmitted within the laboratory and cause severe to fatal disease in humans for which there are no available vaccines or treatment (8).

AUTOPSY

The infectious autopsy, or high-risk autopsy, is defined as the post-mortem examination of a decedent who has had, or is likely to have had, a serious infectious disease that can be transmitted at autopsy (9).

While conducting a post-mortem, clinicians can reduce their risk of occupational infections by following the policy of standard precautions:

- All cadavers should be treated as potentially infectious and disposed of appropriately. A bespoke CBRN body bag allows the containment and evacuation of CBRN contaminated bodies and their safe disposal.
- All surfaces and equipment contaminated should be treated as potentially infectious.
- All fluid and tissue specimens should be considered potentially infectious.
- Post-mortem procedures for all patients should include complete protective wear for anybody who is at risk of fluid or tissue contamination.
- Instruments and surfaces contaminated during post-mortem procedures should be decontaminated appropriately.
- All specimens should be placed in a sealed and leak-proof container and labeled appropriately.

It will be impossible to guarantee zero-risk from sharps, but all precautions should be taken. Appropriate gloves, arm, body, face and respiratory tract protection should be worn commensurate with the risk of disease. Needles must not be re-capped, scalpels should be disposable and round-tipped, blunt-tipped scissors should be routine and an oscillatory saw with a vacuum attachment should be used.

CHEMICAL AGENTS AS WEAPONS

There are six well-recognized CBRN Chemical Toxidromes (10). Clinically, they can be differentiated using the Quick History, Quick Look, Quick CRESS system which has been adopted by NATO and other emergency responders.

The Quick History of a chemical attack includes:

- Multiple casualties with similar non-traumatic symptoms and signs
- Unusual taste, smell or mist
- Unexplained dead animals
- Unexplained constellation of symptoms including altered vision, eye pain, headache, breathlessness, chest tightness, excessive secretions and nonthermal burns
- Any unusual or unexplained symptoms, signs, morbidity or mortality

The Quick Look is a rapid focused initial assessment of a casualty for signs of trauma and intoxication. The recognition of a chemical toxidrome is initially based upon the clinical signs of the common chemical warfare agents using Conscious level, Respiratory pattern, Eyes, Secretions and Skin (CRESS) signs (Table 90.3). In a mass incident, the deployment of a "Clinical Scout", with the First Responders, to assess and feedback clinical signs to healthcare personnel, would suggest the likely causative agent, facilitate biological sampling and enable early administration of medical countermeasures.

Acid and alkalis (corrosive chemicals)

These compounds cause corrosive coagulative or liquefactive burns. They are more likely to be encountered in criminal events although the use of white phosphorus has been described in the Syrian conflict.

Opioids

The identification and treatment of an opioid casualty is well documented, although the toxidrome of decreased consciousness, pupillary constriction and respiratory depression can be confused with the anticholinesterase toxidrome as occurred in the initial assessment of the Skripal poisonings in 2018. While the recreational use of opioids is commonplace, the use of high-potency long-acting opioids has not occurred in terrorist actions. The forensic identification of opioid substances and casualties is, however, well documented in other texts.

DUBROVKA THEATER SIEGE IN MOSCOW

In October 2002, 50 armed Chechen rebels entered the Dubrovka Theater in Moscow and took around 900 people hostages. Chechen women, the so-called "black widows", were positioned around the auditorium with explosive devices.

Fifty-seven hours into the siege, Russian Spetnaz troops became involved. In the auditorium, one survivor recalled seeing a gray mist descending on to the hostages. As this mist entered the auditorium, the black widows and the hostages were rendered unconscious by the gas. Spetnaz troopers shot the Chechen men who were gathered in the theater reception area. Medical emergency responders had access to antidotes to treat the hostages affected by the incapacitant gas, but these were outside and not rapidly administered. This oversight led to the death of some hostages, who had either

TABLE 90.3 CRESS signs

Agent	Consciousness	Respirations	Eyes	Secretions	Skin
Nerve	Depressed consciousness or unconscious	Increased	Constricted (Miosis)	Increased (lacrimation, rhinorrhea, salivation, bronchial secretions)	Diaphoretic
Cyanide	Depressed consciousness or unconscious	Increased	Normal	Normal	May be flushed or cyanotic when advanced shock
Chlorine phosgene (delayed effects)	Normal (unless asphyxia causes loss of consciousness)	Increased	Normal	Increased (lacrimation, rhinorrhea, salivation) Delayed fluid in lungs at very high doses	Normal
Vesicants	Normal	Increased if vapor	Normal	Increased (lacrimation, rhinorrhea, salivation) Delayed fluid in lungs at very high doses	Normal initially
Opioid incapacitating agent	Depressed consciousness or unconscious	Decreased	Constricted (Miosis)	Normal	Normal
Anticholinergic incapacitating agent	Agitated	Normal or increased	Normal or dilated (mydriasis)	Decreased	Dry and hot
Riot control agents	Normal	Normal or increased	Normal	Lacrimation, rhinorrhea, salivation	Normal

stopped breathing, or mechanically obstructed their airway. At least 129 civilians died during the storming of the theater and of those rescued, 245 were hospitalized, eight in a serious condition. In total, more than 750 hostages were rescued alive.

Following pressure from Western governments, the Russian government revealed that "*a fentanyl-based substance was used to neutralize the terrorists.*" Clothing from British members of the audience was analyzed at the Defence Science and Technology Laboratory (DSTL) in the UK. Traces of carfentanil and remifentanil were identified.

Many lessons were learned from this use of fentanyl analogs as incapacitants. One was the difficulty of targeting with a safe but effective dose and controling the duration of exposure, especially with the rapidity of effect by the inhalation route. In the auditorium, there was a steep concentration gradient for the aerosols depending on location and so a difficulty managing the level and duration of exposure. Added to this was the inability of drowsy/unconscious victims to flee exposure and limit the dose received. The deployment was totally indiscriminate and significantly compromised the safety of those exposed, who varied from children through to the old, and healthy to those with pre-existing morbidities.

Naloxone is the non-selective competitive opioid receptor antagonist that antagonizes all opiate and opioid effects, but to varying degrees. Respiratory depression is reversed but sedation less completely. Naloxone has a short duration of action (some 20 to 30 min) and may need to be administered as repeated bolus doses or an infusion, as many opioids are longer acting. Naloxone is available for emergency clinical use as 400 μg, 2 mg and 5 mg pre-filled syringes. A nasal spray (2 mg naloxone) is increasingly available for use by law enforcement officers and first responders. Naltrexone and nalmefene are longer acting opioid receptor antagonists.

Asphyxiants

The simple asphyxiants either displace oxygen and form a non-respirable atmosphere (e.g. noble gases such as argon) or prevent oxygen reaching the tissues as with carbon monoxide forming carboxyhemoglobin. However, in CBRN, the asphyxiants generally comprise cellular poisons, notably cyanide and hydrogen sulfide.

Cyanide poisoning is due to the impairment of oxidative phosphorylation, a process whereby oxygen is used in the production of cellular energy sources in the form of ATP (adenosine triphosphate). Part of this process is transfer of electrons from NADH to oxygen, via a series of electron carriers. This is catalyzed by the cytochrome oxidase enzyme system in the mitochondria and is impaired by the inhibition of cytochrome oxidase a3 by cyanide. The resulting chemical combination results in rapid loss of the effectiveness of the enzyme and tissue utilization of oxygen is inhibited with impairment of vital functions.

Hydrogen sulfide is another cytochrome a3 poison. At high concentrations, hydrogen sulfide becomes toxic by binding to and inhibiting cytochrome C oxidase in the electron transport chain, the last complex in the chain prior to ATP synthesis.

Methods of detection include colorimetric assays such as the Prussian blue test, the pyridine-barbiturate assay and the taurine fluorescence-HPLC but, like all colorimetric assays, these are prone to false positives. More sensitive mass spectrometer assays are considered very sensitive.

Hydrogen sulfide poisoning is most frequently encountered in chemical suicides and cyanide is most commonly found in industrial accidents.

Vesicants

The common vesicants are sulfur mustard (mustard gas) and the arsenical based lewisite. Mustard is colorless and almost odorless (may smell of garlic/onions). At room temperature, it is a liquid with low volatility, and it is very stable during storage. The melting-point for pure mustard agent is 14.4 °C. It has been mixed with lewisite in some types of ammunition in a ratio of 2:3 producing a mixture with a freezing-point of -26 °C.

The toxic effects of mustard are due to its ability to rapidly covalently bind, especially to macromolecules such as proteins and DNA. The mustard compound readily eliminates a chloride ion by intramolecular nucleophilic substitution to form a cyclic sulfonium ion. This very reactive intermediate tends to cause permanent alkylation of the guanine nucleotide in DNA, which prevents cellular division and generally leads directly to cell death (11). Mustard agent can destroy a large number of different substances in the cell by means of alkylation and thereby influence numerous processes in living tissue.

Pure lewisite is an oily, colorless liquid, while impure lewisite is amber to black. It remains a liquid at low temperatures and is persistent in colder climates. It has the odor of geraniums. Lewisite damages skin, eyes and airways by direct contact. It inhibits many enzymes, in particular those with thiol groups, such as pyruvic oxidase, alcohol dehydrogenase, succinic oxidase, hexokinase and succinic dehydrogenase. The exact mechanism by which lewisite damages cells is not known. Mustard-lewisite mixture shares the vesicant properties of lewisite and the DNA alkylation and cross-linking properties of mustard.

Those exposed to lewisite can develop refractory hypotension known as Lewisite shock, as well as some features of arsenic toxicity. Lewisite causes physical damage to capillaries, which become leaky and can lead to hypovolemia.

Nerve agents

Nerve agents (NAs) are highly toxic. They are chemically similar to organophosphate pesticides and exert their biological effects by inhibiting acetylcholinesterase (AChE) enzymes. G-type agents are clear, colorless and tasteless liquids that are miscible in water and most organic solvents. GA (tabun) has a slightly fruity odor, and GD (soman) has a slight camphor-like odor. VX is a clear, amber-colored, odorless, oily liquid. It is miscible with water and soluble in all solvents. The novichoks consist of a group of NAs that can be solid or liquid and are highly toxic. Most nerve agent vapors are heavier than air.

GA was synthesized in 1936 and GB (sarin) 2 years later. GD was synthesized in 1944 and VX was synthesized in the early 1950s. Although related organophosphate chemicals are used in medicine, pharmacology and agriculture, these are nowhere as toxic as the NAs. The novichoks were developed by the Russians between 1970s to 1990s to circumvent the Chemical Weapons Convention and were first mentioned in a book by Vil Mirzayanov (12). They were reportedly more lethal than VX.

NAs are alkyl phosphonic acid esters. Tabun has a cyanide group while sarin and soman have methyl phosphorofluoridate groups. These NAs have a unique bond that is not found in OP pesticides and is very resistant to hydrolysis. VX contains sulfur. All the NAs are liquid at room conditions, tasteless and odorless and potentially volatile. G agents' densities are the same as water and evaporate at about the same rate. The freezing points are around 0°C and the boiling point is around 150°C. G agents rapidly spread on skin. G agents are released from clothing for about 30 minutes after vapor contact. In contrast, V agents are more oily, similar to engine oil. Due to the oily nature, VX is more effectively absorbed through the skin. The novichoks are not well described but are related to the other NAs. They come in liquid or solid form and are also organophosphate based poisons.

The main mechanism of action is irreversible inactivation of AChE (a process called "aging") at the cholinergic synapses leading to an accumulation of toxic levels of acetylcholine (ACh) at the synaptic junctions. This over stimulates the cholinergic pathway and consequently desensitizes the cholinergic receptor site. The toxidrome is one of overstimulation of the acetylcholine neurotransmitter systems and is pathognomonic of NA poisoning.

Lung-damaging agents

Lung-damaging agents (LDAs) affect the lungs and airways. They include traditional "choking" agents, such as chlorine, phosgene, diphosgene and chloropicrin, and some blistering agents, such as sulfur mustard, lewisite and phosgene oxime.

Agents are divided into three types depending on which part of the respiratory tract is largely affected:

- Upper Airway Agents: Affect large airways
- Intermediate Airway Agents: Affects the bronchi and bronchioles
- Small Airway Agents: Affect small airways and the small air sacs of the lungs (alveoli)

In simplistic terms, the traditional LDAs, ammonia, chlorine and phosgene dissolve in lung secretions depending on their solubility. Ammonia is very soluble and affects the upper airways, chlorine is of intermedial solubility and affects the intermediate-sized airways and phosgene is relatively insoluble but, once it is dissolved, rapidly hydrolyses. These agents form their respective acids which lead to burns, a chemical pneumonitis and frank pulmonary edema. The vesicants also cause significant burns as they do when in contact with skin.

PPE FOR CHEMICAL AGENTS

PPE needs to match the threat. In a field situation, exposure to a contact hazard, such as VX, needs good physical protection. If there is a respiratory hazard, then a chemical protective respirator with the appropriate canister will be required. However, once the casualty is fully decontaminated, there is little threat from them. The threat from off-gassing (the release of active agent from the casualty) is probably only relevant when a patient has ingested the poison as in aluminium phosphide poisoning or ingested a cyanide compound. NAs, mustards and asphyxiants are tightly bound to the tissues. Mustard blisters are sterile, although with lewisite, which has never been used in warfare, blisters contain active lewisite. Generally, when dealing with decontaminated chemical casualties, only standard precautions are necessary.

RADIATION

It is worth reiterating the difference between irradiation and contamination. An irradiated casualty has been exposed to a radiation source, whereas a contaminated casualty has radioactive material on or in them (incorporated) and remain radioactive until the source is removed. The only threat to forensic personnel is from an active source.

Types of ionizing radiation

These include charged alpha and beta particles, uncharged neutrons or high-energy electromagnetic radiations such as X-rays and gamma rays. When they interact with atoms, energy is transferred leading to ionization, which can lead to molecular damage. The clinical effects of different forms of radiation depend upon their range in air and tissue penetration.

Alpha particles are heavy and can travel only a few centimeters in air. They are easily absorbed by most materials and stopped by tissue paper or the outer layers of human skin. They generally only cause disease if ingested and incorporated into cells, as in the case of Alexander Litvinenko. Universal precautions will be effective.

Beta particles are high-energy, high-penetration electrons and dangerous. They are typically blocked by a thin aluminium plate but, if in the body, can continue to pose a threat to personnel.

Gamma radiation are short wavelength electromagnetic waves that impart high energy as they pass through a body.

Dosage and exposure

The dose of radiation is based upon the energy absorbed by a unit mass of tissue and is measured in Grays (Gy), with 1 Gy representing 1 Joule/kg. To take account of different types of radiation and in the sensitivity of various tissues, weighting factors are used to produce a unit of effective dose, measured in Sieverts (Sv). This value reflects the absorbed dose weighted for the damaging effects of the particular form of radiation and is most valuable in evaluating the long-term effects of exposure.

Effects of radiation exposure

Effects on the individual are classified as either deterministic or stochastic.

Deterministic effects

Deterministic (threshold) effects show increasing severity as dose increases above a threshold level. Tissues with actively dividing cells, such as bone marrow and gastrointestinal (GI) mucosa, are particularly sensitive to ionizing radiation. Lymphocyte depletion is the most sensitive marker of bone marrow injury and, after exposure to a fatal dose, marrow aplasia is a common cause of death. However, GI mucosal toxicity may cause earlier death due to profound diarrhea, vomiting, dehydration and sepsis (acute radiation sickness). Eye exposure can result in cataract and the skin is susceptible to radiation burns. Irradiation of the lung and central nervous system (CNS) may induce acute inflammatory reactions, pulmonary fibrosis and permanent neurologic deficit. Bone necrosis and lymphatic fibrosis characteristically follow regional irradiation, such as in therapy for breast cancer.

Stochastic effects

Stochastic (chance) effects show increasing probability of occurring as dose increases. Carcinogenesis represents a stochastic effect. With acute exposures, a leukemia may arise after an interval of around 2–5 years and solid tumors after an interval of about 10–20 years. Thereafter, the incidence rises with time. An individual's risk of developing cancer depends on the dose received, the time to accumulate the total dose and the interval following exposure.

PPE and radiation

A casualty that has been irradiated requires use of normal standard PPE only, as there is no threat to personnel due to radiation. Those with alpha particle irradiation do not pose a huge threat due to the ease in protecting against alpha particles, but it is common sense to protect the skin and respiratory tract. Beta radiation does pose a threat and careful attention should be given to exposure and dose, limiting radiation by limiting time of exposure, maintaining a safe distance whenever possible and employing sufficient shielding (Time-Distance-Shielding). Advice from radiation protection professionals is essential when dealing with radiation.

CONCLUSION

The risk of a deliberate release of a chemical, biological or radioactive (CBR) agent in a conflict has risen following recent deployments by state and non-state actors. Terrorist use has also become more likely. It is important to rapidly determine the nature of the agent used in a deliberate incident so that appropriate medical countermeasures can be provided. Knowledge of the toxic and pathologic effects are important in such evaluations and for the healthcare emergency response to an event. They also must be applied in preparedness planning of the resources, such as medical countermeasures (drugs and vaccines) and PPE, that need to be held in stockpiles or rapidly available to First Responders. There remains the unknown threat of a novel agent with clinical effects not easily characterized and suitable mitigating treatments not obvious. In cases of an unusual illness distinction between accidental or deliberate causation will inform the overall response although clinical management may be similar. In all CBR incidents, self-protection using appropriate PPE is essential and, where necessary, decontamination of the casualty prior to admission to a healthcare facility.

REFERENCES

1. OPCW. Definition of a chemical weapon. Available from: https://www.opcw.org/our-work/what-chemical-weapon. (Accessed 23 August 2023).
2. US Dept of Labor. Occupational Safety and Health Administration. Regulations (Standards – 29 CFR). Available from: https://www.osha.gov/laws-regs/regulations/standardnumber/ (Accessed 23 August 2023).
3. European Parliament. Regulation (EU) 2016/425. Personal Protective Equipment. Available from: https://www.legislation.gov.uk/eur/2016/425/contents# (Accessed 28 August 2023).
4. HSE. Managing infection risks when handling the deceased. Guidance for the mortuary, post-mortem room and funeral premises, and during exhumation, 2018. Available from: https://www.hse.gov.uk/pubns/books/hsg283.htm (Accessed 28th August 2023).
5. Alibeck K, Handelman S. Biohazard. New York: Rando House; 1998.
6. Pavlin JA. Epidemiology of bioterrorism. *Emerg Infect Dis* 1999; 5: 528–30.
7. European Parliament. Directive 2000/54/EC of the European Parliament and of the Council of 18 September 2000 on the protection of workers from risks related to exposure to biological agents at work. Available from: https://www.legislation.gov.uk/eudr/2000/54/data.pdf (Accessed 28 August 2023).
8. US Dept of Health and Human Services. Biosafety in microbiological and biomedical laboratories, 6th edn. Available from: https://www.cdc.gov/labs/BMBL.html (Accessed 28 August 2023).
9. Claydon SM. The high risk autopsy. Recognition and protection. *Am J Med Pathol* 14(3): 253–6.
10. Ciottone GR. Toxidrome recognition in chemical-weapons attacks. *N Eng J Med* 2018; 378(17): 1611–20.
11. Mirzayanov VS. State Secrets: An Insider's Chronicle of the Russian Chemical Weapons Program. Parker, CO: Outskirts Press; 2008.

CHAPTER

91

Forensic Photography of Injuries

Sam Evans

INTRODUCTION

Photography is an internationally recognized method for the digital capture of various forms of forensic evidence. Protocols and workflows have been put in place across multiple jurisdictions to ensure that forensic imaging complies with legal frameworks (1,2). These protocols discuss key elements that are essential for good practice, namely, keeping an intact chain of evidence and the faithful reproduction of the scene. Many forensic disciplines employ digital imaging to record visual evidence, such as footwear and fingerprint analysis. However, this chapter will focus on the image capture of skin injuries and intends to present a set of protocols to inform a range of professionals in the correct imaging techniques for injuries seen in a forensic context.

Forensic photographs must be of a high standard to enable any subsequent analysis and/or presentation to court. Therefore, when photographing injuries, it is important to correctly capture the digital likeness of the physical evidence that is present in the injury (such as the pattern of the causal implement). The digital representation of the location, size, shape and the color of the injury that has been captured by a camera and presented on a screen are all affected by the quality of equipment and methods employed to image the injury. Forensic professionals, such as pathologists and odontologists, have employed forensic imaging techniques for many years to aid in investigations (3,4), however, errors in technique can influence outcomes. For example, both the shape and size of the injury can be greatly affected by visual (5) and physical distortion (6,7), thus have an impact on the digital measurement of injuries. To further compound errors in analysis, research has (8,9) demonstrated that the properties of skin and the diffuseness of the bruise can lead to misinterpretation of the evidence. In spite of these issues, it has been shown that physical measurement is subject to a greater degree of imprecision (10–12).

In some instances, there may be a distinct pattern present in the injury that can give the practitioner a link to the causal implement. In this case, both the injury and implement should be imaged employing the same methodology to enable digital measurement and comparison. It should be noted that practitioners should use caution when employing matching techniques as the distortion mentioned above will have an impact on measurements collected (13). Furthermore, it is important to state that all measurements have some level of uncertainty, and no measurement is free of error (14).

Nonetheless, the methods set out here intend to limit errors in technique and enable practitioners to obtain the best possible images.

EQUIPMENT

The current gold standard for imaging injuries is to use professional grade digital cameras (digital single lens reflex, DSLR) with the use of good-quality lenses. As poor quality equipment can cause optical aberrations, it is recommended that sub-standard equipment should only be used when there is no other choice (13,15). Precision is required in the sharpness of the focus and the framing of the object in the center of the image. The consistency of the color and the tonal range are equally important and best results are achieved by using DSLRs. Devices such as camera phones have improved greatly in recent years, however, these cameras lack the ability to override the automatic controls, preventing the operator from fully controling the camera settings. Furthermore, the limited tonal range can affect the appearance of subtle injuries, such as bruises, making it more difficult to discern between the damaged and healthy skin.

Care must also be taken to eliminate any unwanted or distracting shadows, only the correct use of electronic flash can achieve the desired effect.

Consideration of the end product of digital imaging is needed, whether it is in the form of a digital print or the on-screen image as there is great variability in the color representation of the injury.

The reproducibility of color between the practitioner's computer and that of others (such as the court) is unreliable. The same image on different monitors can look very different if the monitors are not professionally calibrated. Further variability can be introduced when the digital image is printed, and often the printed image does not represent what appears on screen. This imprecision of color representation could cause bias in certain queries, such as attempts to age a bruise via its color.

DOI: 10.1201/9781003138754-95

Cameras

There are many manufacturers of DSLR cameras. Canon™ and Nikon™ appear to be the most commonly used by forensic photographers. Both companies provide a range of suitable cameras, lenses and flash systems. The latest DSLR cameras have very high pixel counts, which is a constantly evolving process, so there is little point in specific recommendations. As the power of the computer processor will inevitably increase and change over time, so will the sensitivity and capabilities of the sensor in the digital camera. Although the quantity of pixels is very important to the amount of information recorded by the camera it is only partly responsible for a high-quality image. The dynamic range and pixel noise are also important, as these elements affect small details, particularly at high magnifications. For amateur photographers entry level or mid-range DSLR cameras are perfectly suitable for the majority of practitioners. One exception will be when a camera is needed to be used in low light environments without an electronic flash. For example, when attaching a DSLR to a microscope, entry level cameras have a pixel-to-noise ratio that, when set to a high ISO, create significant noise and grain in the image, which may obscure relevant information.

Lens

DSLR cameras can interchange different types of lenses. The quality and build of the lens is an important factor in capturing the right levels of detail. The right lens will reduce the amount of photographic distortion (not considering operator error). Lenses used with DSLRs mostly fall into two categories: Prime or Zoom, which have varying focal lengths, and most are not suitable for use when photographing injuries. The focal length relates to the distance between the film plane (the digital camera sensor) and the focal point of the lens (the optical center of the end of the lens). The focal length is usually measured in millimeters. Prime lenses have a fixed focal length, for example, a 105 mm lens can provide the fine detail that may be needed to demonstrate any individual details seen in the injury. Zoom lenses do not have fixed focal lengths and instead have a range, such as an 18 to 55 mm lens which is commonly supplied with a camera when sold as a kit. Zoom lenses should be avoided when photographing injuries as, when using a zoom lens, the operator can often change the focal length without realizing causing inconsistencies in the size of the object between frames. Furthermore, changing the position of the zoom lens to a short focal length may introduce visual aberrations, such as barrel and pincushion (curvilinear) distortion (16). A lens with a focal length less than 50 mm (non-full frame sensors increase the focal length) will start to introduce some barrel distortion, which creates a sphere-like distortion of the image (Figure 91.1). However, visually obvious distortion may only be apparent to the inexperienced viewer when very short focal lengths (<20 mm) are used.

On occasion, it is necessary to take images at a close distance; at this point, a lens with macro capability is required. Such a lens allows the operator to focus on an object inches from the skin. Some non-SLR cameras, such as compact cameras or mobile phones with an attachment may have a macro function, however, this often only works when the zoom lens is set to a short focal length, thus giving barrel distortion. Some high-quality micro-system cameras may be fitted with adequate lenses suitable for photography of injuries. However, to maintain consistency, it is advantageous to use lenses that have markings on the barrel of the lens that relate to magnification ratios or distance in meters or in feet, thus ensuring the object remains the same size in the frame in each image.

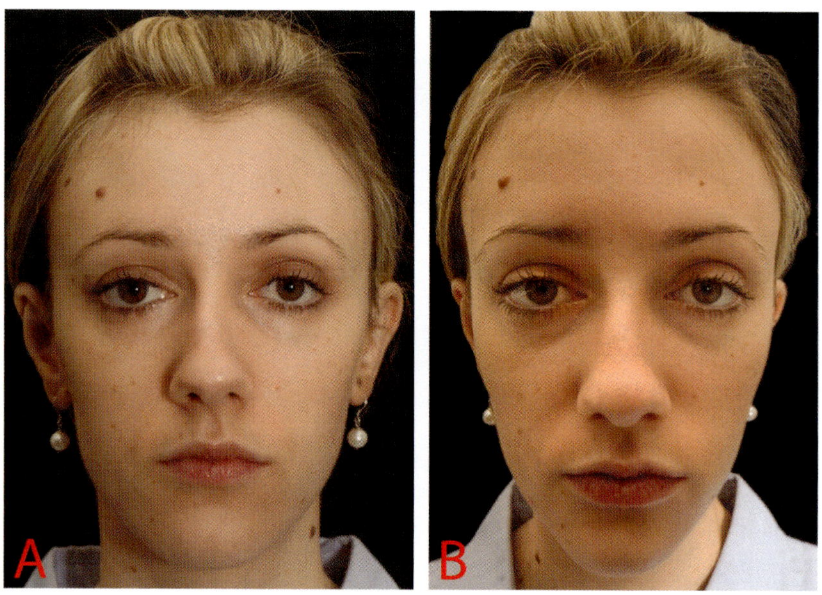

91.1 Demonstration of barrel distortion caused by the use of a short focal length lens. **(A)** was produced using a 60 mm lens, image **(B)** was produced using a 20 mm lens.

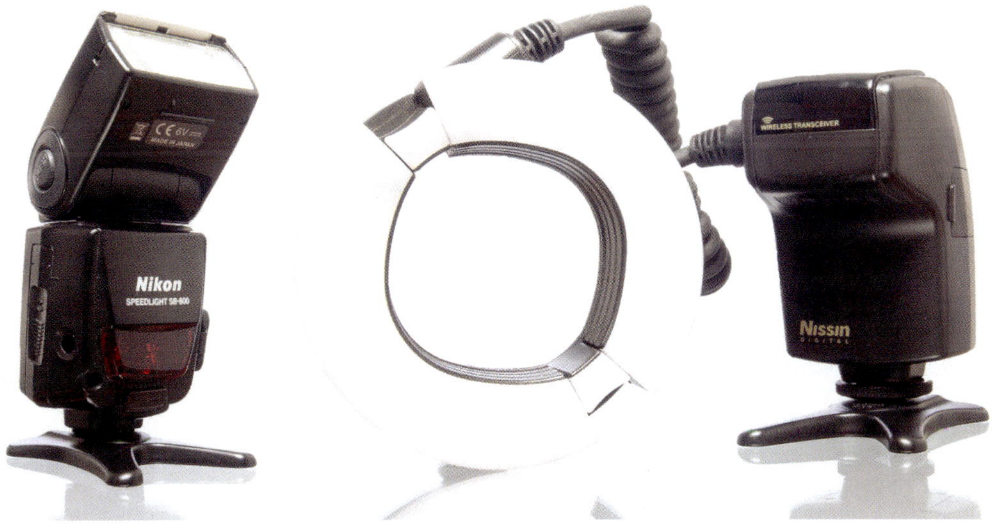

91.2 Images of suitable flash devices.

Flash

When photographing injuries, it is strongly recommended that flash devices be used (Figure 91.2). Many cameras have a built–in flash, and these flashes are generally either too weak to illuminate a large injury or in a position that cause unwanted shadows and overexposure, which may then obscure important information by either covering the injury in shadow or creating too many highlights. There are a variety of flash units available, however, a single-side mounted flashgun or ring-flash are suitable for photographing injuries for both close up and location images.

Metric scale

A rigid scale is essential for the photography of injuries in a forensic context. The ABFO No. 2 scale (17) allows the investigator to collect consistent measurements of the injuries. The scale must be placed correctly and photographed next to the injury, to ensure the subsequent measurements have minimal error. To undertake digital measurement via software such as Adobe® Photoshop® the digital ruler must be calibrated. To calibrate the digital ruler, the operator must use the scale in the photograph as a baseline. Therefore, it is imperative to follow the specific guidelines listed later in this chapter. Research has shown that some caution should be applied when using scales for forensic analysis (18). Any non-specific rulers used will have very small variations in the measurements printed and thus could introduce a subtle bias in the measurements.

An accurate color chart

In forensic photography, the use of color charts is routinely used to accurately color balance the whole image and thus color in the injury itself (1). To ensure correct color calibration in the image via a computer, a small mini-color chart will be the most practical to use. Good quality color charts will have the Red, Green and Blue (RGB) value (0–255) for each color with the accompanying documentation. Using image-editing software, the operator can color balance the image(s) by employing the color chart to calibrate the white balance tool. For consistent results, a color chart should be visible in every image that is taken, as slight changes in the distance between the flash and the subject will have an influence on the brightness within the image and thus will create slight variance in the color. However, placing a color chart in every image may be impractical in some cases. If need be, the gray squares on the ABFO No. 2 scale can be used for color calibration. Alternatively, rigid scales with a color chart included can be used (only if such charts have been printed to the correct RGB value).

It should be stated that, because there are many variables to account for, it would be inadvisable to use photography as a tool to interpret color and to correlate any forensic significance to the color of the injury, especially in terms of aging (19). However, the use of a color checker chart is vital when using cross-polarized imaging (this will be discussed later in the chapter).

Digital image file formats

All digital information must be processed, and how this information is processed can influence the final presentation of the image. In regard to digital images, it is important to have a process that limits any change to the appearance of the injury within the image.

The type of file format can have an impact on the image quality; this is usually reflected in the color representation, displayable dynamic range, and increased pixilation. An image that has been heavily compressed will often lose fine detail in shadows and display a reduced tonal range and this will affect subtle color and tonal differences in the image.

Different file formats have varying levels of digital compression. Compression here refers to the act of reducing the file's size in megabytes. This is done by the removal of pixels from the image, thus data is lost. However, The Select Committee on Science and Technology Fifth Report (1998) (20) suggested that there should not be a strict command for any particular file format:

"*We recommend that evidence should not necessarily be inadmissible because it does not conform with some specific technological requirement.*"

A particular format cannot be insisted upon as technology will inevitably advance and develop. However, it is important to state that file formats that use high levels of compression should be avoided.

"*Using an appropriate file format to capture different scenes without compromising the image quality*" (1).

The lossless (small amount of compression) type of format used by the camera will most likely either be the Tiff (Tagged Image File Format) or a RAW image format. Each camera manufacturer has its own proprietary RAW image format/digital negative. At the time of writing, two commonly used examples are the Canon RAW version (CRW & CR2) and the Nikon electronic format (NEF). The ability to use RAW image files is an important component for forensic analysis, as it gives an unfettered image, comparable to the negative used in traditional photography. Police forces in the United Kingdom use Nikon's NEF format the 16-bit NEF file (the original/ first copy) as the Nikon NEF file cannot be manipulated or overwritten. The NEF file can only be saved as a working copy in a different format, for example an 8-bit Tiff or the Lossy (heavy compression) JPEG (Joint Photographic Experts Group). It is important to set the camera to capture images at the highest quality (least amount of compression) setting so the greatest amount of detail and tonal range can be gathered; if files need to be compressed at a later date for electronic delivery, then they should be done on a working copy, thus preserving the original image.

Camera maintenance

With heavy use, the DSLR camera will need some form of maintenance. Due to the nature of the DSLR interchangeable lens system, it is inevitable that fragments of dust will get onto the various components, such as the sensor. Pieces of dust will appear as very small marks/ spots in the photograph and may, on occasion, obscure parts of the injury. Removal of the dust can be a difficult procedure and should be performed by those who are experienced in such tasks. The chances of dust getting onto the components can be reduced if care is taken when the lens is changed. It is recommended that lenses are removed or changed only when absolutely necessary.

Verify camera date and time

The camera must be set to the correct time and date, so this information is embedded within the digital image(s) as metadata. This is important in terms of evidence integrity, ensuring that the time and date in the image(s) metadata does not conflict with information given in any written statements made. The metadata can be accessed in databases or image-editing software. When noting the date and time, make clear distinction between creation and modified date.

Camera operation and image sequence

A fundamental component in the process of photographing injuries that may be used for forensic analysis and presentation to court, is the correct positioning of the camera to relation to the injury.

The forensic analysis and measurement of injuries is severely affected by distortion of the injury shape. This distortion can be categorized into two types of distortion, primary and secondary (6). Primary distortion is due to the processes at the time of impact, which includes two categories, dynamic (the interaction of the implement and skin) and tissue (such as stretching and swelling of the skin). Secondary distortion is broken down into three categories:

- Time-related changes
- Body position
- Photographic distortion (7)

Only photographic distortion presents itself as a variable that the operator can directly influence. If the photography is done correctly, photographic distortion can be reduced.

Research has shown that if a wound or feature on the body is photographed at more than 15 degrees (5) off set from the perpendicular (Figure 91.3), then distortion will change the pattern being investigated. There are three main types of photographic distortion prevalent in photographing patterned injuries, described in detail by Johansen and Bowers (21) and demonstrated below. To try and avoid such error the following steps in correct "camera to scale to injury" placement should be adhered to.

Type 1 distortion

When taking photographs, the sensor (and the lens) of the camera must be perpendicular to the plane of the injury. If the photographer fails to do this, then Type 1 distortion will take place. This is called angular distortion. Angular distortion can change the shape of the bruise, for example, making a circle more elliptical, thus changing the appearance of the bruise.

The use of a 60 mm lens with the DSLR might make it easier to obtain images that are perpendicular to the injury and the scale. Less distance would be required to stay at the correct position than using a 105 mm lens. However, it should be noted that using a 105 mm lens might be preferable if the photographer needs to have a safer working distance.

Type 2 distortion

The scale must be placed on the surface of the skin (Figure 91.4). This will ensure the scale is on the same plane as the injury. If the scale is not on the same plane as the injury, then there will be Type 2 distortion. This type of distortion will make it impossible to get accurate measurements due to perspective distortion.

(a)

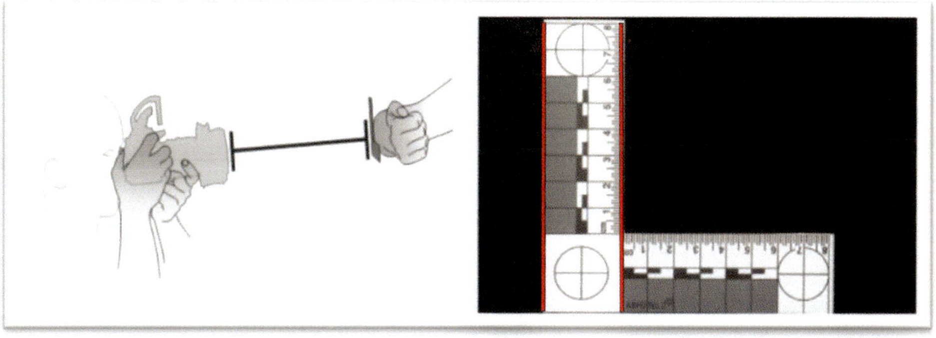

(b)

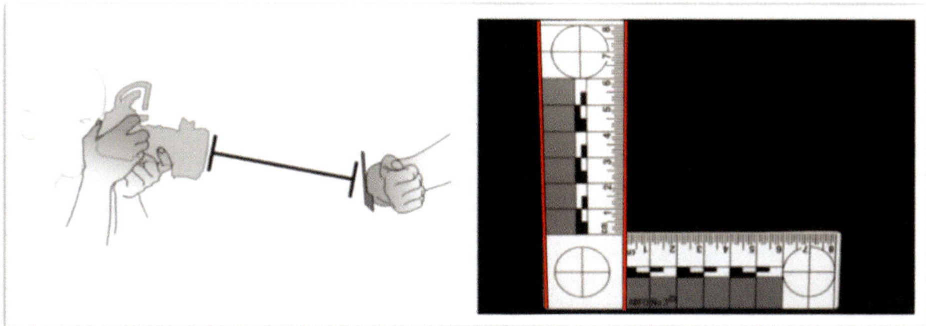

91.3 **(a)** Correct positioning with limited distortion produced. **(b)** Incorrect positioning with Type 1 distortion (angular).

(a)

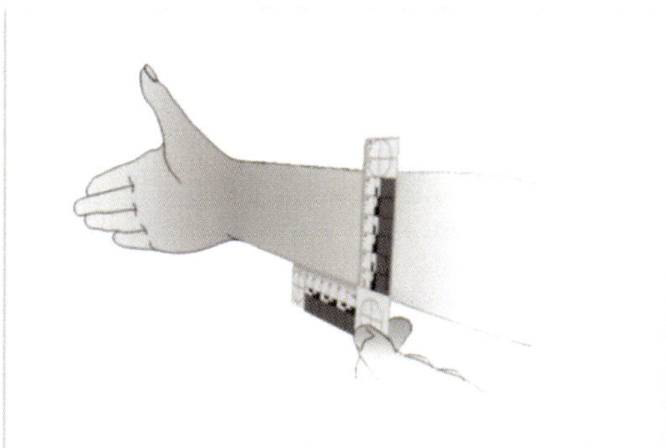

(b)

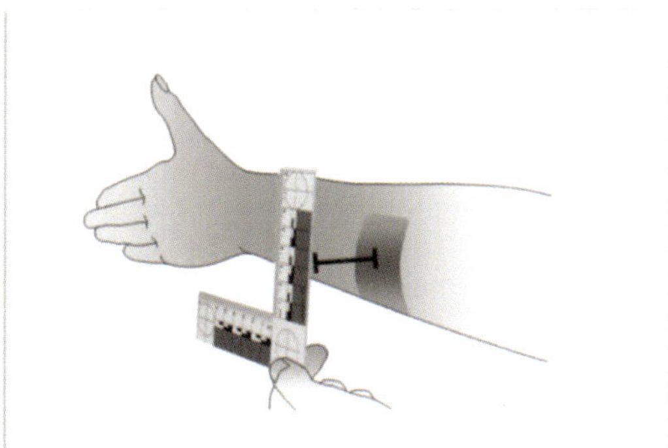

91.4 **(a)** Correct positioning – No distortion produced. **(b)** Incorrect positioning – Type 2 distortion.

Types 3 and 4 distortion

Applying too much pressure when it is placed next to the injury can warp a portion of the scale (Figure 91.5). Furthermore, if the scale is tilted, it will also introduce error (*see* Figure 91.4). Like Type 2, these factors have

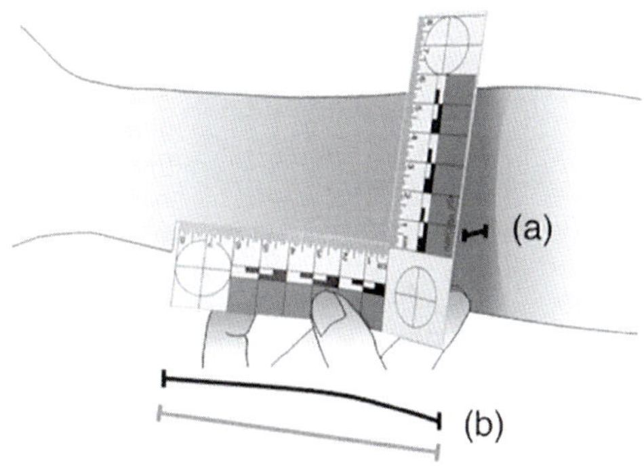

91.5 Incorrect handling of scale.

an impact on the use of the scale as a calibration tool for subsequent digital measurements.

When using the ABFO No. 2 scale, it is important to include all the circles to help the operator identify any angular distortion present in the image. It has been mentioned in some research studies (21) that such distortion can be digitally corrected. However, any digital "correction" of an image with angular distortion may result in the interpolation of the pixels. If interpolation takes place, then the digital evidence falls under the banner of "Reconstruction". According to the National Policing Improvement Agency (1) guidance, reconstruction can only be applied as a graphic interpretation and cannot be presented as a true image. Thus, any conclusion made from measurements regrading size is inadmissible. As mentioned by the National Policing Improvement Agency (1):

> "non-affine (local) transformation tools are offered and may be used arbitrarily to alter all or portions of an image. However, no mathematical description

of what is changing in an image is provided to the operator when using these tools. Results from this study indicate that it is not advisable to perform arbitrary alterations to an image of a bite mark".

This means it is difficult for the operator to know if the changes made are actually representing the true digital render of the injury. If the operator intends to correct for angular distortion with the use of the circles, further issues arise as the scale and the bruise are three-dimensional (3D) structures in 3D space, however the photograph is analyzed in two-dimensional space (2D). It will be difficult to know from analyzing the circles, if there is angular distortion along the vertical axis, and also distortion along the horizontal axis. Any geometric correction, using the circles in the photograph, would have to factor in both 2D (Euclidean) and 3D (non-Euclidean) geometry. To this effect, Procrustean geometric shape analysis has been used in face-shape analysis (22), however, such work inevitably involves approximation (23). Therefore, it is advisable to use caution when applying geometric restoration to the image of a bruise. Without a thorough understanding of the digital process involved, and a knowledge of the true distance between the camera and the injury, the operator may present unreliable results.

SEQUENCE OF IMAGES OF THE INJURY

This list of images to capture, and in what order, should be followed for best practice:

- Image of person's ID (patient label, consent form, etc.).
- The image of ID is needed to link images of injuries to the person being photographed.
- Location shot showing bruise and identifying anatomic area, without a scale.
- Close-up shots of the injury, including the whole of the scale (all three circles of ABFO No. 2 scale must be shown, helping identify any angular distortion). The scale should not obscure any part of the injury.
- If on a curved surface, then multiple views (at least three) will be needed.

When photographing a bruise on a curved surface, such as the edge of a forearm or bicep, it is vital that the photographer takes images from at least three different angles (Figure 91.6). The camera must remain perpendicular to the injury and scale for all images. For example, if the injury is curved around an arm, then the scale must be moved around the curve, ensuring that it is on the same focal plane as the impact site.

Detail shots if required

Detail shots might need to be taken if individual marks can be seen and are of good evidential value. Areas on small parts of the body such as fingers, ears and nose might benefit from more detailed views.

Images using photographic filters

Alternate methods of illumination may be used to record the bruise in addition to unfiltered photographs.

Image of persons' ID

This image is helpful to maintain the integrity of the sequence for the chain of evidence.

In some situations, it may be relevant to photograph the alleged causal implement for matching purposes. If this is the case, then the same method as illustrated above should be employed. To ensure continuity, the striking surface of the implement and injury should be photographed at the same magnification and with the accompanying scale placed appropriately within the image.

AUDIT TRAIL OF DIGITAL IMAGES

It is important to maintain an audit trail of every change made to an image from the moment it is first captured on a camera to the time when it is presented in court. In this way, it can be demonstrated that the image presented in court can be reproduced from the original image using a sequence of recognized processes that are repeatable.

Firstly, all images taken at the scene should be uploaded to an appropriate safe place, that is not freely accessible. None of the images should be deleted (even mistakes), as this illustrates an unbroken chain of evidence. If the images require any post processing, such as color balancing or changing the brightness, then working copies should be made from the digital negative. It is important to ensure that all changes made to the image are recorded either as separate paper notes or stored in the images metadata. Professional software packages, such as Adobe Photoshop

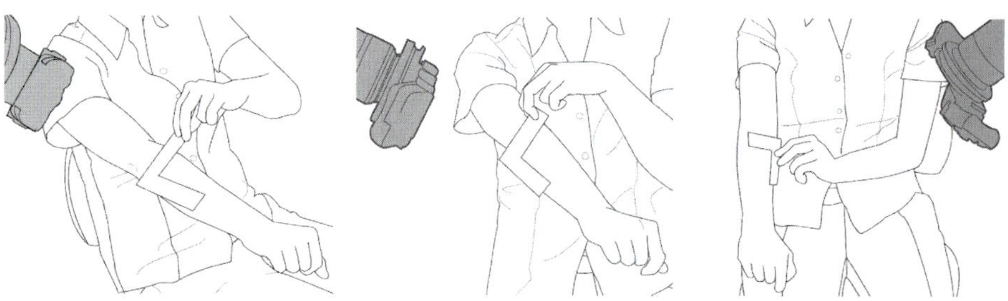

91.6 Position of camera to injury at different angles to move around the curve of the body.

are equipped with the facility to store changes made in the image via the metadata as a digital log (24, 25).

ALTERNATIVE IMAGE MODALITIES

3D image capture

The issues of distortion of the injuries, shape and size (from angular distortion and scale placement) described earlier in this chapter which are caused by the use of 2D cameras, are rendered obsolete by the use of 3D optical devices. Using 2D cameras can cause problems for the accurate representation of depth and the correct placement of scale. It has been proposed that 3D image capture is more precise, accurate and robust than other forms of recording injuries and that it should therefore be explored as an alternative method (5,26–28). A 3D device does not need to use a rigid scale as it is pre-calibrated and the operator does not need to concern themselves with issues regarding angular distortion.

There are several types of optical 3D capture devices that have been used for forensic and clinical applications, however, stereo photogrammetry is relatively easy to use and inexpensive compared with other 3D devices. Photogrammetry uses two images taken at slightly different positions and at a fixed distance. This can be done using three methods:

1. Two cameras that take two or more images simultaneously.
2. One camera taking two or more images at different positions.
3. One camera using a stereo lens. This is a lens that splits the image in two, creating two images that have been taken at two slightly different angles.

Each of these methods employ well-known triangulation techniques to mathematically quantify the position of the object imaged in space. Employing one camera with a stereo lens will produce the most consistent method and is the most commonly used. With the development of digital photography and advanced computing, 3D reconstructions of the object can be quickly created and analyzed in associated software. Research has shown that such devices can be comparable in accuracy to that of structured light scanners and laser scanners (29,30). Measurement of the injury can be performed using 3D imaging software to a greater level of precision (5).

Alternative light methods

There has been some suggestion that utilizing cameras that have been adapted to capture infrared and ultraviolet light, may elicit relevant information not visible to the naked eye, from injuries such as bruises (31). It is well known that the appearance of a bruise varies according to the breakdown of the bruise and the subsequent healing process. These changes may affect the absorbance and fluorescence properties of the skin (32). Thus, there is a theoretical possibility that the bruise may be visualized differently and at different stages of healing, depending on what wavelength of light is used. However, at present, research has yet to prove conclusively that IR and UV offer a robust option in identifying information of forensic significance that is not available in the visible spectrum. While some have put forward the benefit of such technology (31,33–36), more recent research has suggested that both IR and UV offer limited information (Figure 91.7) compared to standard imaging (35,37). However, in the same study, Trefan et al. (38) did show that cross-polarized imaging allowed for greater definition of the boundary edge of the bruise. Cross-polarized

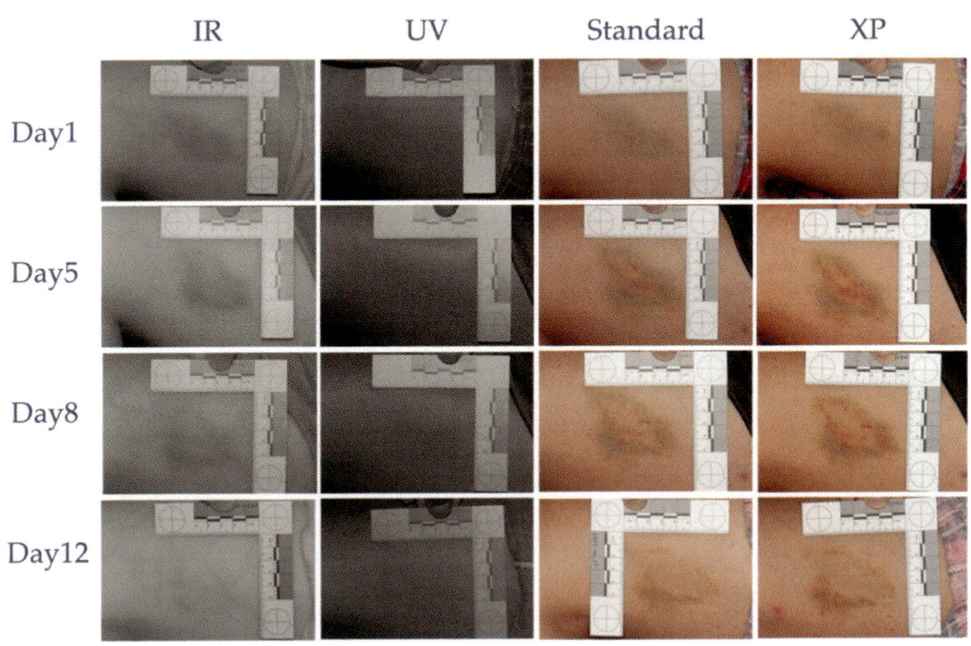

91.7 Sequence of images taken of the same bruise over 12 days. With infrared (IR), ultraviolet (UV), unfiltered conventional photography (Standard) and cross-polarized (XP). (Images used with permission from the study by Trefan [38].)

imaging utilizes commercially available photographic polarizing filters that are placed over the camera lens and flash. This simple technology eliminates glare from the electronic flash, which can obscure parts of the injury. This is particularly useful when photographing highly reflective injuries.

CONCLUSION

Forensic photographs must be of a high standard to enable analysis and for presentation to court. The digital representation of the injury is affected by the quality of the equipment used and methods employed. Consistent results are achieved by using DSLRs with suitable lenses and flash units.

To reduce shape distortion of the injury, care should be taken to ensure the camera is perpendicular to the injury with the scale appropriately placed; this is particularly important when digital measurements of the injury are collected. 3D photography should be considered the gold standard for the image capture of injuries in forensic medicine, as this approach all but eliminates shape distortion. To date, IR and UV offer limited information that is not already available with standard imaging. However cross-polarized imaging has shown some promise, particularly with injuries that are highly reflective.

REFERENCES

1. National Policing Improvement Agency. Practical Advice on Police use of Digital Images, 2007. Available from: http://library.college.police.uk/docs/acpo/police-use-of-digital-images-2007.pdf (Accessed 21 June 2023).
2. US Department of Justice. FBI Laboratory 2005 Report, 2005. Available from: https://archives.fbi.gov/archives/about-us/lab/lab-annual-report-2005/fbi-lab-report-2005-pdf (Accessed 21 June 2023).
3. Levy BP, Hipp JD, Balis UJ, Yagi Y. Potential applications of digital pathology and image analysis for forensic pathology. *Acad Forensic Pathol* 2012; **2**(**1**): 74–9.
4. Adams C, Carabott R, Evans S. *Forensic Odontology: An Essential Guide*. Chichester: Wiley Blackwell; 2013.
5. Evans ST, Jones C, Plassmann P. 3D imaging for bite mark analysis. *Imaging Sci J* 2013; **61**(**4**): 351–60.
6. Sheasby DR, Macdonald DG. A forensic classification of distortion in human bite marks. *Forensic Sci Int* 2001; **122**: 75–8.
7. Bowers CM, Pretty IA. Expert Disagreement in Bitemark Casework. *J Forensic Sci* 2009; **54**(**4**): 915–18.
8. Bush MA, Bush PJ, Sheets HD. Statistical Evidence for the similarity of the human dentition. *J Forensic Sci* 2011; **56**(**1**): 118–23.
9. Bush MA, Bush PJ, Sheets HD. A study of multiple bitemarks inflicted in human skin by a single dentition using geometric morphometric analysis. *Forensic Sci Int* 2011; **211**(**1–3**): 4–11.
10. Perednia DA, White RG, Schowengerdt RA. Localization of cutaneous lesions in digital images. *Comput Biomed Res* 1989; **22**(**4**): 374–92.
11. Evans S, Jones C, Plassmann P. 3D imaging in forensic odontology. *J Vis Commun Med* 2010; **33**(**2**): 63–8.
12. Lawson Z, Nuttall D, Maguire S, et al. Clinical photography of bruises: Measurement variability and image modality preference. *Arch Dis Child* 2011; **96**(**1**): 93–4.
13. Evans S, Baylis S, Carabott R, et al. Guidelines for photography of cutaneous marks and injuries: A multi-professional perspective. *J Vis Commun Med* 2014; **37**(**1–2**): 3–12.
14. Klapetek P. 2014. *Motivation 1 0*. doi: 10.1016/B978-1-45-573058-2.00001-2.
15. Biggs PR, Evans ST, Jones MD, Theobald PS. Development of a methodology for the standardisation and improvement of "Smartphone" photography of patterned bruises and other cutaneous injuries. *Sci Justice* 2013; **53**(**3**): 358–62.
16. Langford MJ. *Advanced Photography: A Grammar of Techniques*. London: Royal College of Art; 1975.
17. Hyzer WG, Krauss TC. The bite mark standard reference scale--ABFO No. 2. *J Forensic Sci* 1988; **33**(**2**): 498–506.
18. Payne-James JJ, Hawkins C, Baylis S, Marsh NP. Quality of photographic images provided for injury interpretation: Room for improvement? *Forensic Sci Med Pathol* 2012; **8**(**4**): 447–50.
19. Maguire S, Mann MK, Sibert J. Can you age bruises accurately in children? A systematic review. *Arch Dis Child* 2005; **90**(**2**): 187–9.
20. Parliament.uk. Science and technology - Fifth report, 1998. Available from: https://publications.parliament.uk/pa/ld199798/ldselect/ldsctech/064v/st0501.htm (Accessed 21 June 2023).
21. Johansen RJ, Bowers CM. Digital Analysis of Bitemark Evidence. Forensic Imaging Institute; 2000.
22. Sheets HD, Bush MA. Mathematical matching of a dentition to bitemarks: Use and evaluation of affine methods. *Forensic Sci Int* 2011; **207**: 111–18.
23. Popat H, Richmond S, Benedikt L, et al. Quantitative analysis of facial movement – A review of three-dimensional imaging techniques. *Comput Med Imaging Graph* 2009; **33**: 377–83.
24. Cardini A. Missing the third dimension in geometric morphometrics: How to assess if 2D images really are a good proxy for 3D structures? *It J Mamm* 2014; **25**(**2**): 73–81.
25. Hoerricks, J. Forensic photoshop - a comprehensive imaging workflow for forensic professionals, 2008. Available from: https://books.google.co.uk/books?id=jMDZZwEACAAJ (Accessed 21 June 2023).
26. Evans S, Noorbhai S, Lawson Z, et al. Contrast enhancement of bite mark images using the grayscale mixer in ACR in Photoshop®. *J Forensic Sci* 2013; **58**(3): 804–10.
27. Blackwell S, Taylor RV, Gordon I. et al. 3-D imaging and quantitative comparison of human dentitions and simulated bite marks. *Int J Leg Med* 2007; **121**: 9–17.
28. Thali, MJ, et al. VIRTOPSY—scientific documentation, reconstruction and animation in forensic: Individual and real 3D data based geo-metric approach including optical body/object surface and radiological CT/MRI scanning. *J Forensic Sci* 2005; **50**(**2**); 1–15.
29. Martin-De Las Heras S, Valenzuela A, Javier Valverde A, et al. Effectiveness of comparison overlays generated with DentalPrint© software in bite mark analysis. *J Forensic Sci* 2007; **52**(**1**): 151–6.
30. Urbanová P, Hejna P, Jurda M. Testing photogrammetry-based techniques for three-dimensional surface documentation in forensic pathology. *Forensic Sci Int* 2015; **250**: 77–86.
31. Camison L, Bykowski M, Lee WW, et al. Validation of the Vectra H1 portable three-dimensional photogrammetry system for facial imaging. *Int J Oral Maxilofac Surg* 2018; **47**(**3**): 403–10.
32. Wright FD, Golden GS. The use of full spectrum digital photography for evidence collection and preservation in cases involving forensic odontology. *Forensic Sci Int* 2010; **201**: 59–67.
33. Tetley C. The photography of bruises. *J Vis Commun Med* 2005; **28**(**2**): 72–7.
34. Vogeley E, Pierce MC, Bertocci G. Experience with wood lamp illumination and digital photography in the documentation of bruises on human skin. *Arch Pediatr Adolesc Med* 2009; **156**: 265–8.
35. Rowan P, Hill M, Gresham GA, et al. The use of infrared aided photography in identification of sites of bruises after evidence of the bruise is absent to the naked eye. *J Forensic Leg Med* 2010; **17**(**6**): 293–7.
36. Lawson Z, Nuttall D, Young S, et al. Which is the preferred image modality for paediatricians when assessing photographs of bruises in children? *Int J Leg Med* 2011; **125**(**6**): 825–30.
37. Garcia JE, Wilksch PA, Spring G, et al. Characterization of digital cameras for reflected ultraviolet photography; Implications for qualitative and quantitative image analysis during forensic examination. *J Forensic Sci* 2013; **59**(**1**): 1–6.
38. Trefan L, Harris C, Evans S, et al. A comparison of four different imaging modalities – Conventional, cross polarized, infra-red and ultra-violet in the assessment of childhood bruising. *J Forensic Leg Med* 2018; **59**: 30–5.

CHAPTER

92

Forensic Odontology

Denice Higgins and Harry Perkins

INTRODUCTION

Forensic odontology has been described as "that branch of dentistry which in the interest of the law deals with the proper handling and examination of dental evidence and the proper evaluation and presentation of such evidence" (1). Although the scope of forensic odontology is considerably broader, the layperson will be most familiar with the involvement of the profession in identification of deceased persons following a major disaster with multiple fatalities or in homicide cases which have a high public interest. Beyond personal identification of unknown remains, forensic odontologists are also involved in other matters such as the assessment and examination of injuries caused by teeth, age estimation in both living and deceased individuals, assessment of oral facial injuries following accidents or assaults and the provision of expert opinions on dental evidence as requested. They will often work intimately with numerous stakeholders in a multidisciplinary approach including police officers, members of the court and fellow scientists such as forensic anthropologists and pathologists. Consequently, a forensic odontology practitioner not only needs a sound understanding of the natural sciences and the fundamentals of dental practice but must also understand the legal systems, the law and relevant jurisdictional legislation, as well as have an in-depth knowledge of oral and dental anatomy and pathology.

Although isolated cases of identification using the dentition have been reported as occurring earlier, the practice of forensic odontology is often said to have commenced with the identification of the victims of the Bazar de la Charité fire which occurred in 1897 in Paris, France (2,3). The practices of forensic odontology have changed substantially since this time to keep abreast with newer technologies and increased pressure for forensic practices to be more solidly based in verifiable science. The development of forensic odontology practices has been influenced by specific jurisdictional requirements, pressures from the legal profession, criticisms of sciences applied, changing technologies and the validation of new approaches with these factors continuing to encourage improved future practices based on the best available scientific data.

IDENTIFICATION

The deceased have a basic humanitarian and legal right to be identified with the opportunity for their remains to be put to rest in a respectful manner (4). Dental information, along with DNA and fingerprint data, is one of the three primary identifiers often required in numerous jurisdictions for cases of unknown human identification (5). Relying on pattern recognition within matched antemortem and post-mortem data sets, these identification techniques consider all persons as having individualizing features that, when compared, set them apart from all others. The overall result of any analysis of these features, in conjunction with the skills of the examiner and supporting scientific knowledge, is dependent on the probative value of the pattern, that is the amount of detail in the pattern and the rate of occurrence of the features observed within the population. Dental comparison of antemortem and post-mortem data sets is an accepted method of human identification with the rationale being that there is not only individual variation in the morphologic features of the teeth and jaws, but that introduced features such as dental restorations and iatrogenic artefacts produce further variation between individuals. The complete adult human dentition consists of 32 teeth all having five surfaces (Figure 92.1), and with the potential for variability within each from underlying genetic and post-eruptive environmental factors, a great many combinations of dental patterns can exist (6,7). Features routinely considered available for comparison during dental identification include the presence or absence of teeth, individual tooth morphology, the position of each tooth within the jaws, the location, shape and composition of numerous forms of dental restorations and prothesis, pathologies, oral anatomy as well as maxillary and frontal sinus morphology.

Supporting the use of dental information in identification cases is the comparatively robust availability of antemortem data in most developed countries. As many people in these countries have attended an oral health professional in their lifetime, it is often possible to access known and trusted antemortem dental records. Additionally, as teeth are the hardest structures in the human body with a high resistance to peri- and post-mortem destruction, surviving features allow for probative post-mortem

DOI: 10.1201/9781003138754-96

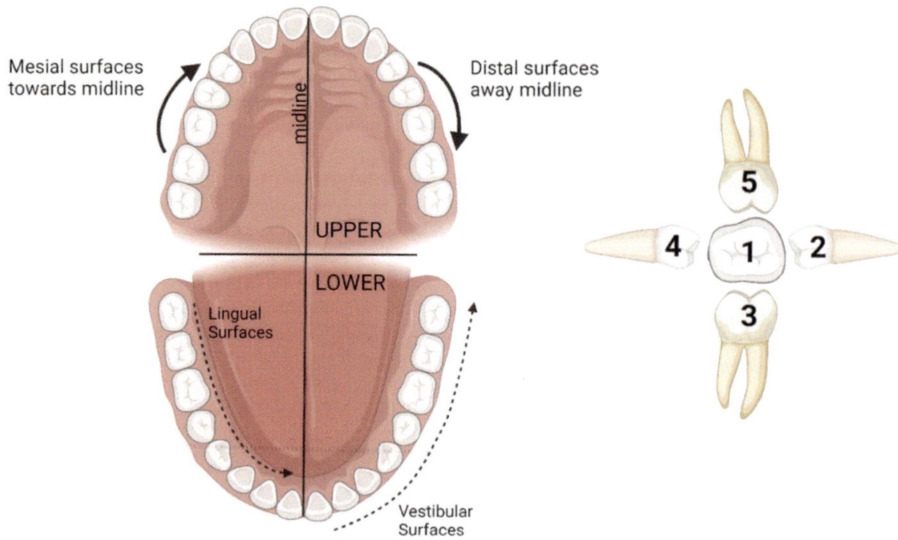

92.1 32 teeth present within the upper and lower arches of the oral cavity with the five surfaces of a dental crown being: 1. Occlusal; 2. Mesial; 3. Vestibular; 4. Distal; 5. Lingual. (Created with BioRender.com)

dental information to be collected and examined. As a consequence, dental features are likely the only surviving biometric datapoints available for reliably identifying incinerated, decomposed, skeletonized and fragmented remains (8).

Dental identification can be broken down into three main phases: antemortem, post mortem and reconciliation, focusing on the analysis of available dental data with the goal to form an opinion on a person's identity based purely on those data.

The antemortem phase involves the collection, collation and interpretation of dental, medical and personal records that can be used as a source of information regarding an individual's dentition during life. This may include any information that reliably depicts features of the teeth or oral and facial structures such as written dental records, dental radiographs, dental casts, dental scans, dental photographs, medical imaging of the head and neck area and personal photographs. Antemortem dental data may cover multiple decades of an individual's life with records created by numerous practitioners via varying record systems and hence careful consideration is needed when determining the probative value of the information. Records from multiple sources over a long period may demonstrate potentially conflicting information which will require careful consideration and verification. In routine casework, when a deceased individual is located, there is frequently circumstantial evidence suggesting the identity of that individual, allowing attempts by forensic investigators to locate any comparative antemortem data. A significant issue for accessing antemortem dental data is often the lack of knowledge of where an individual may have attended a dentist while alive as well as the routine culling of records performed by dental practices after a prescribed period. Although no comprehensive dental record databases exist in most countries, online radiology databases can often be a useful tool for sourcing antemortem imaging or for determining which dental clinic an individual may have attended while alive. No comparison is possible without antemortem records and, in these situations, an opinion regarding identification cannot be formed. In the circumstances of long-term missing persons, the proactive collection and archiving of any available antemortem records can substantially aid in an identification outcome. This is especially relevant if a body is later found after a considerable period.

The post-mortem phase involves collecting dental or oral data from unidentified human remains which may vary in presentation due to peri- or post-mortem damage or change. Fragmentation as well as loss of soft tissues from decomposition can result in dislodgment of teeth from jaws limiting the amount of available data for comparison. For cases such as incineration where dental information may present the best chance of identification, the protection of any evidence is paramount with damage to oral structures during transit potentially resulting in a further loss of probative data (9,10). Forensic odontologists provide training and facilitate support for investigators on relevant techniques to protect dental structures during transit and, on occasion, are requested to attend a scene to view remains directly (9). Post-mortem dental data can be collected via computed topography imaging, plain film radiography, photography, and written notes from a physical examination. The information collected is collated, the greater the number of individualizing features present in the dentition and the more unusual these features are, the higher will be the probative value of the evidence collected. In the absence of a presumptive ID post-mortem information can be used to add to a profile of the individual which may reduce the number of missing persons considered. Dental and orofacial information can provide data regarding ancestry, age, sex and potentially global region where the individual received dental treatment.

The reconciliation phase involves the comparison of the information collected within the two formed data sets, antemortem and post-mortem, which can include an assessment of the imaging created, as seen in Figure 92.2. Between the creation of these two datasets, there exists a period of time in which changes may have occurred

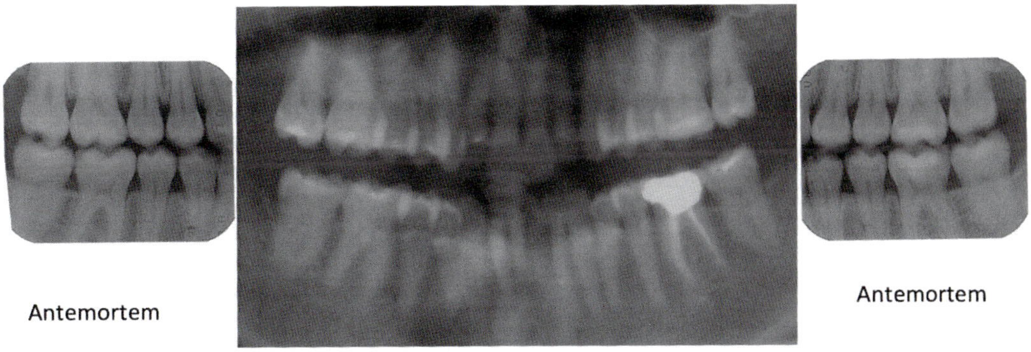

92.2 Comparison of images requires reconciliation of differences which may be caused by a number of factors. In this instance, the AM image was taken 16 years prior to the PM image and the radiography techniques used differ between the datasets. In this instance, reconcilable differences would be considered to be due to lack of recency of AM data, further dental treatment, poor quality of PM image and radiographic angulation differences.

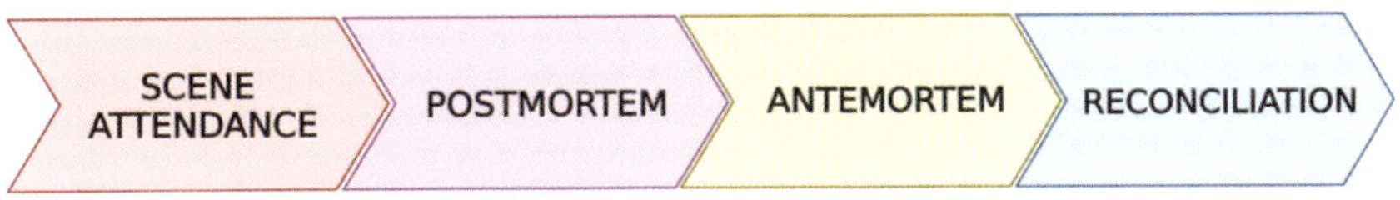

92.3 The four phases of DVI procedures as per INTERPOL guidelines. (Created with BioRender.com)

within the individual's dentition. These two data sets must be carefully compared to determine the presence of discrepant features and whether these discrepancies can be reconciled. Common causes of reconcilable discrepancies between the two data sets include a lack of antemortem detail and recency, the progression of dental disease, peri- or post-mortem damage, antemortem charting errors and nomenclature or terminology variation between practitioners. Discrepant features that cannot be reconciled, such as a tooth present in the post-mortem remains that is definitively shown as absent in the antemortem record, would lead to the presumed identity being excluded. If all discrepant features can be reconciled, then it is the expert's job to determine the value of the comparative features. Unusual and rare features have a higher evidentiary value then commonly occurring features; however, when possible, numerous accumulated points of comparison are often considered within all available information to increase the evidentiary weight of the opinion. Most recently new forms of 3D imaging are being considered as these forms of records potentially provide greater amounts of data regarding hard- and soft-tissue features than traditional 2D information (11,12). Dental identification requires a team approach for quality control and the validation of case outcomes. Ideally. all case work is peer-reviewed in that opinions formed are the production of two practitioners making an independent analysis of the data (5), with over confidence or errors in judgment having wide ranging consequences.

DISASTER VICTIM IDENTIFICATION

A disaster can be defined as a serious disruption of the functioning of a community involving widespread human, material, economic, or environmental losses and impacts, which exceeds the ability of the affected community to cope using its own resources. Disaster Victim Identification (DVI) is the term given to procedures used to identify deceased victims of a multiple casualty event and are not specific to forensic odontology practice. In most countries, DVI is ostensibly a police operation with support from various forensic specialists (5). The process of DVI is a team effort and, like a complex timepiece, the correct function of every cog whether large or small is important, with large-scale international disasters often requiring co-ordination and collaboration across numerous jurisdictions and disciplines. A multiple casualty event may be natural or man-made (deliberate or accidental) and can be classed as open or closed. A closed event is one in which a manifest or log exists of the individuals involved in the disaster, whereas an open event involves multiple unknown persons. Although logistical differences exist in these situations, in either case, the International Criminal Police Organisation (INTERPOL) recognizes four phases involved with DVI procedures.

1. Scene attendance, examination, and evidence collection
2. Post-mortem examination
3. Antemortem data collection and collation
4. Reconciliation (5) (Figure 92.3)

In some situations, secondary identifiers, or circumstantial evidence such as property may be used to supplement identification efforts, or it may be all that is available to indicate identification. Ultimately identification is determined by the Coroner or a reconciliation board once all information from the different specialties and police has been received and considered. The unpredictability of disaster events requires ongoing training and upkeep in the skills and knowledge required for forensic odontologists to fulfill their responsibilities when needed. As such, preparedness for a DVI event is the most important factor having a major impact on the success and timing of resolution of identification processes. Timely resolution of the identification process is a benefit not only to the families of the deceased but also to the involved governments and communities.

DNA AND THE FORENSIC ODONTOLOGIST

DNA comparison is an important biometric analysis not only as it allows positive correlation with an individual but in cases where no antemortem comparative data for the individual is available, comparison can be made with close biological relatives. If there is no presumptive identity, DNA can allow for generation of profiling information, such as phenotypic and ancestry informative data to narrow the search for identity (13–15). In situations like disaster events, DNA in organic tissues can be damaged by environmental and destructive forces such as high temperatures, moisture, UV irradiation and physical trauma reducing the yield of genetic information possible. In these circumstances, DNA will often be sampled from surviving teeth as the required organic tissues are physically protected by both the highly mineralized dental structures and the surrounding jawbones and oral soft tissues (16,17). An experienced odontologist will be able to determine which tooth, if any, within an individual's dentition would be the most appropriate choice for sampling (18).

Considerations not only include which tooth is likely to contain the best sample of DNA but also the impact of tooth destruction on dental comparison for identification and the emotional well-being of the next of kin (18). A tooth should only be removed from the jaw once the implications have been considered and radiographic and photographic recording has been completed. Indiscriminate removal of teeth for DNA analysis should be avoided, as not only may they subsequently be required for dental identification processes, but their retention may be significant to the next of kin, especially when limited remains are available for repatriation (18).

AGE ESTIMATION

An estimation of an individual's chronological age may be useful in a forensic context to add to a profile of an unknown deceased or in the case of the living for civil or criminal investigations. Chronological age is the measure of the time of existence of a person since their birth. Not only is this measure of age an integral part of a person's identity, but it is also important in our society due to numerous social and legal ramifications. Different societies will impose restrictions to participation in certain activities based on age including education, entering the workforce, voting, driving, alcohol consumption, eligibility to receive social welfare benefits and criminal prosecution (19–21). Generally, a person's chronological age can be ascertained from a record of their birth; however, sometimes there is no record as in the case of an immigrant from a third-world country where documentation of birth is not practiced or in the case of an individual whose identity cannot be determined.

Fortunately, in these cases where no record of an individual's date of birth is available, forensic odontologists can provide an estimation of age based on the stage of biological maturation of dental structures. Biological maturity can be divided into four physiological divisions: somatic, skeletal, sexual and dental. From examination of the stage of maturity, estimations of chronological age can be determined. The reliability of the estimate formed will be influenced by the degree of correlation that exists between the biological age examined and true chronological age and the level of error associated with the calculation. Numerous population-based studies have been undertaken with dental maturation being shown to have the highest degree of correlation with chronological age in comparison to other biological indicators (21). These studies have noted that dental age is relatively independent of somatic, skeletal, or sexual age and has also been shown to be the biological age least affected by extrinsic factors such as nutrition (22). This, and the highly resistant nature of teeth to destruction, makes evaluation of the state of dental development a valuable tool for age estimation in both the living and deceased.

Prior to adulthood, during the stages of development, a number of predictable changes occur within the dentition that can be utilized to estimate age. In all instances, age estimates are provided within a range of potential outlying measures, with improved confidence seen the younger the specimen with the number of predictable dental changes reducing throughout development. Once full-tooth maturation is complete in adulthood, dental indicators of age are not as clear-cut as during development when the formation, calcification, eruption and exfoliation of the teeth can be observed radiographically, histologically or clinically. Although structural and chemical changes in the teeth of an adult can be utilized to estimate their time span of existence in the mouth, only highly variable physiologic and pathologic degenerative patterns exist visually to make assessments by.

Estimation of age not only has forensic applications but is also used in clinical settings where dental or skeletal age may be compared to chronological age as an aid to formulating treatment plans in areas such as pediatrics, endocrinology and orthodontics and can be of value in anthropologic studies. Due to the legal consequences, forensic odontologists are likely to be more cautious in their estimations applying multiple methodologies to form an opinion.

PATTERNED INJURY ANALYSIS

Bite marks are considered patterned injuries as they potentially reflect the physical shape and characteristics of the object that caused them. The American Board of Forensic Odontology (ABFO) defines a bite mark as being "a representative pattern left in an object or tissue by the dental structures of an animal or human" (23). Like all patterned injuries, bite marks display both class and individual characteristics. Class characteristics can help differentiate between human and nonhuman bite marks due to the difference in the dental formula and oral morphometrics between species. Individual characteristics can help distinguish between individuals and may allow the experienced practitioner to exclude an individual from having caused the injury. The ABFO describes a human bitemark as "a circular or oval patterned injury consisting of two opposing (facing) symmetrical U-shaped arches separated at their bases by open spaces. Following the periphery of the arches are a series of individual abrasions, contusions, and/or lacerations reflecting the size, shape, arrangement and distribution of the class and individual characteristics of the contacting surfaces of the human dentition" (23). In the past, particularly in the USA, the probative value of bite-mark evidence has been overstated in legal proceedings leading in some cases to serious miscarriages of justice (24). Bite mark analysis is ostensibly a pattern-matching exercise with clear limitations due to the many factors that can influence the appearance of an injury (25). Unknown factors in bite injuries such as level of pressure, placement of victim and suspect, as well as differences in epidermis quality including skin elasticity and healing capability have been shown to potentially influence the case outcome. Further to this, despite improvements in image collection seen through technological advancements, unknown distortions can be present in 2D representations of 3D anatomic features impacting assessments made (25). As a result of these recognized issues, most recent changes to the ABFO recommendations indicate that an opinion formed regarding bite injuries should only exclude or fail to exclude a suspect rather than attribute causation (23); a point generally accepted globally. A recommended workflow for patterned injury analysis is shown in Figure 92.4. Bite marks or dental impressions can also be found in inanimate objects including foodstuffs (26–28). These materials may more accurately record the pattern of the biting surfaces of the teeth than human skin, but the issue remains as to how unique this pattern is to a particular individual. Hence, caution would suggest to exclude or not exclude would still be the only outcome likely from an assessment (25).

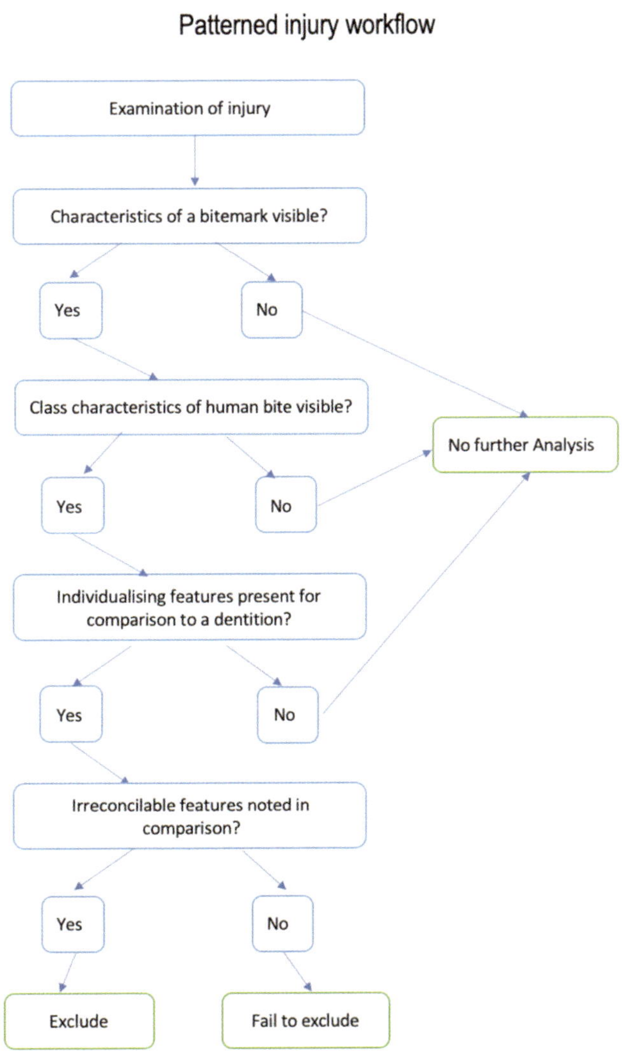

92.4 Patterned injuries casework decision-making workflow.

COMPARATIVE DENTAL ANATOMY

As teeth are independent features that can be removed from the jaw naturally or by force, assessment can often be required on a singular tooth to ascertain whether it is human or not and whether removal from the jaw was potentially suspicious, for example, as the result of an assault. This can be important in cases when suspected human material is found and timely assessments must be made to protect a potential crime scene and any further evidence. An in-depth knowledge of dental anatomy can allow the forensic odontologist to determine the likely species of a tooth sample to assist police in these enquiries.

Different animal species, including humans, display different patterns within their dentitions. Variations between species include jaw and tooth shape and size, the number and spacing of teeth present and the crown and root morphology. These differences also allow some level of differentiation between bitemarks made by different animals, for example, allowing a great white shark to be differentiated from other members of the shark family (29,30) and a fur seal can be differentiated from a dog when looking at a bite injury on a fairy penguin. A forensic odontologist may also be asked to aid in distinguishing animal from human bites in cases of injury to people but also in cases of injury to animals. Examination of bite marks on threatened species of animals can help in conservation efforts by identifying the perpetrators such as feral or other native animal species (31).

OTHER EXPERT ODONTOLOGY OPINIONS

Being qualified dental practitioners with further training in legal proceedings, forensic odontologists are best placed to provide expert witness testimony on evidence relating to the teeth and oral structures in a range of both civil and criminal cases.

Bone and soft-tissue injury interpretations are largely the remit of the forensic pathologist in the deceased and of the oral maxillofacial surgeon in the living; however, the training and expertise of the forensic odontologist makes them well placed to advise on injuries specific to the dentition. This may be required to support or disprove a victim/witness statement or in the living for claims of compensation to restore a damaged dentition. Personal injury claims involving the dentition can only be settled fairly if a considered opinion of the implications of the injury is provided to the court. This includes consideration of pain and suffering and long-term consequences of the injury such as treatment options, prognosis and potentially lifelong associated costs. With experience in evaluating evidence and in expert testimony, forensic odontologists can also be called on to give an opinion in cases of alleged dental malpractices or fraud relating to dental insurance claims. In reviewing case files for malpractice, as in all casework, an odontologist needs to be well-versed with the current scientific literature relating to the subject at hand.

CONCLUSION

Dental information has numerous potential applications in forensic casework, especially in the field of human identification. It can be said with some degree of confidence that humans will always have teeth, hence, there will always be the need for the recognition, examination, documentation, preservation, interpretation and analysis of dental data in relation to judicial or coronial investigations. Future forensic odontology practices will be dependent on evolving technologies and research. The introduction of neural network pathways and machine learning (ML) concepts into the field raises the potential for existing processes to be automated, reducing the perceived influence of human error. Even though technology may change how dental evidence is analyzed in the future a forensic expert will still be required to appropriately interpret this information.

REFERENCES

1. Keiser-Nielsen S. Forensic odontology. *Int Dent J* 1968; **18**(3): 668–83.
2. Hill IR. *Forensic Odontology: Its Scope and History*. Belgium: Academische Cooperatief; 1984.
3. Luntz LL. History of forensic dentistry. *Dent Clin North Am* 1977; **21**(1): 7–17.
4. Black S. Forensic Human Identification. In: Thompson T, Black S (eds), *Forensic Human Identification An introduction*. London: CRC Press; 2007, pp. 457–500.
5. INTERPOL. Disaster Victim Identification (DVI). Available from: https://www.interpol.int/How-we-work/Forensics/Disaster-Victim-Identification-DVI (Accessed 21 June 2023).
6. Adams BJ. Establishing personal identification based on specific patterns of missing, filled, and unrestored teeth. *J Forensic Sci* 2003; **48**(3): 487–96.
7. Martin-de-Las-Heras S, Valenzuela A, Luna Jde D, Bravo M. The utility of dental patterns in forensic dentistry. *Forensic Sci Int* 2010; **195**(1–3): 166.e1–5.
8. Pretty IA, Sweet D. A look at forensic dentistry-Part 1: The role of teeth in the determination of human identity. *Br Dent J* 2001; **190**(7): 359–66.
9. Berketa J, Higgins D. Stabilisation of dental structures of severely incinerated victims at disaster scenes to facilitate human identification. *J Forensic Leg Med* 2017; **51**: 45–9.
10. Berketa J, Higgins D. The use of gelling agents to preserve burnt teeth within the dental alveoli for dental human identification - a study utilising sheep mandibles. *Forensic Sci Med Pathol* 2021; **17**(1): 72–7.
11. Reesu GV, Woodsend B, Mânica S, et al. Automated Identification from dental data (AutoIDD): A new development in digital forensics. *Forensic Sci Int* 2020; **309**: 110218.
12. Simon B, Lipták L, Lipták K, et al. Application of intraoral scanner to identify monozygotic twins. *BMC Oral Health* 2020; **20**(1): 268.
13. Draus-Barini J, Walsh S, Pośpiech E, et al. Bona fide colour: DNA prediction of human eye and hair colour from ancient and contemporary skeletal remains. *Investig Genet* 2013; **4**(1): 3.
14. Walsh S, Liu F, Wollstein A, et al. The HIrisPlex system for simultaneous prediction of hair and eye colour from DNA. *Forensic Sci Int Genet* 2013; **7**(1): 98–115.
15. Zaumsegel D, Rothschild MA, Schneider PM. A 21 marker insertion deletion polymorphism panel to study biogeographic ancestry. *Forensic Sci Int Genet* 2013; **7**(2): 305–12.
16. Alvarez Garcia A, Munoz I, Pestoni C, et al. Effect of environmental factors on PCR-DNA analysis from dental pulp. *Int J Leg Med* 1996; **109**: 125–9.
17. Sweet DJ, Sweet CH. DNA analysis of dental pulp to link incinerated remains of homicide victim to crime scene. *J Forensic Sci* 1995; **40**(2): 310–14.
18. Higgins D, Austin JJ. Teeth as a source of DNA for forensic identification of human remains: A review. *Sci Justice* 2013; **53**(4): 433–41.
19. Bassed R, Ranson D. Age determination of asylum seekers and alleged people smugglers. *J Law Med* 2012; **20**(2): 261–5.
20. Solheim T, Vonen A. Dental age estimation, quality assurance and age estimation of asylum seekers in Norway. *Forensic Sci Int* 2006; **159**: 56–60.
21. Taylor J, Blenkin M. Age Estimation and Odontology in the Living. In: Black S, Aggrawal A, Payne-James J (eds), *Age Estimation in the Living*. West Sussex: Wiley-Blackwell; 2010, pp. 176–201.
22. Ubelaker DH. *Sex, Stature and Age Human Skeletal Remains, Excavation, Analysis, Interpretation*, 3rd ed. Washington DC: Taraxacum; 1999.
23. American Board of Forensic Odontology. Diplomates Reference Manual, 2016. Available from: http://abfo.org/wp-content/uploads/2016/03/ABFO-Reference-Manual-03162016.pdf (Accessed 21 June 2023).
24. Innocence Project. Wrongful convictions involving unvalidated or improper forensic science that were later overturned through DNA testing, 2016. Available from: https://www.innocenceproject.org/wp-content/uploads/2016/02/DNA_Exonerations_Forensic_Science.pdf (Accessed 21 June 2023).
25. Forrest A, Soon A. Bite Marks. In: Taylor JA, Kieser JA (eds), *Forensic Odontology Principles and Practice*. West Sussex: Wiley Blackwell; 2016, pp. 228–85.
26. McKenna CJ, Haron MI, Brown KA, Jones AJ. Bitemarks in chocolate: A case report. *J Forensic Odontostomatol* 2000; **18**(1): 10–14.
27. Nambiar P, Carson G, Taylor JA, Brown KA. Identification from a bitemark in a wad of chewing gum. *J Forensic Odontostomatol* 2001; **19**(1): 5–8.
28. Sweet D, Hildebrand D. Saliva from cheese bite yields DNA profile of burglar: A case report. *Int J Legal Med* 1999; **112**(3): 201–3.
29. Cirillo G, James H. Pattern association--a key to recognition of shark attacks. *J Forensic Odontostomatol* 2004; **22**(2): 47–8.
30. Nambiar P, Brown KA, Bridges TE. Forensic implications of the variation in morphology of marginal serrations on the teeth of the great white shark. *J Forensic Odontostomatol* 1996; **14**(1): 2–8.
31. James HAA, Taylor JA, Freak MJ. A case of bitten bettongs. *J Forensic Odontostomatol* 2002; **20**(1): 10–2.

CHAPTER

93

Forensic Toxicology

Marianne Arnestad and Liliana Bachs

INTRODUCTION

Forensic toxicology is the use of toxicological knowledge to help to interpret technical evidence regarding the presence and effects of drugs and poisons in the implementation of laws or administrative rules involving sanctions (1).

Table 93.1 shows the areas of practice where forensic toxicology is most often applied.

Toxicological analysis involves the detection, identification and quantitation of toxicologically relevant substances and the interpretation of the results. For all purposes, the results of the forensic investigation involve proving the presence of substances in biological specimens, including securing chain of custody, screening and confirmation of drugs and poisons, interpretations of the results and giving expert witness statements to be used in courts.

TOOLS IN TOXICOLOGICAL ASSESSMENT

Standards/guidelines in forensic toxicology

The practice and context of forensic toxicology differs among countries depending on their different legal systems, and developing international standards and guidelines has proven a difficult task. Guidelines within forensic toxicology are most often related to analytical practices within the laboratory. There are some guidelines and standards for forensic toxicological analysis in general and for specific situations, such as workplace drug testing and driving under the influence of drugs and alcohol (2). However, such guidelines have for the most part been set up by different organizations in different countries or laboratories, many of which are now outdated with regard to new technology and the emerging new drugs of abuse. In addition, guidelines on the therapeutic and toxic levels of drugs, as previously maintained by The International Association of Forensic Toxicologist (TIAFT – www.tiaft.org), are no longer available as there are too many aspects to consider in order to be able to standardize. In order to obtain a good quality in the laboratory work, certification by an accreditation body is highly recommended. Standards for a good quality laboratory involve education of personnel, continuous improvements in routines and technology, and a good quality control where the validity of testing results is monitored by external quality assurance programs and an active nonconformance management system (3).

Chain of custody

Chain of custody is applied in forensic toxicology in order to take precautions against tampering or mix-ups with the samples. Chain of custody involves documentation of all stages from sampling to reporting of the results. An analytical result is worthless if uncertainties regarding the identity of the donor or the measurement of the drug detected are questioned (4).

Samples should be collected under observation and identity of the donor checked. The time and date of the sampling must be registered, and the sample tubes should be sealed and labeled with the same case ID as the laboratory form. The sample should be kept locked

TABLE 93.1 Common areas where forensic toxicology is used

Human performance and behavioral toxicology
• Driving under the influence of drugs
• Drug-facilitated crime
• Drug-facilitated sexual assaults
Post-mortem toxicology
• Cause of death (drug related?)
• Use of drugs involved in manner of death
• Impairment prior to death
Forensic drug testing
• Testing of prisoners
• Workplace testing
• Child welfare/social services
• Sports testing

DOI: 10.1201/9781003138754-97

in a room with access control until forwarded to the laboratory. Control of correct case IDs need to follow all aliquots removed from the original sample in the laboratory. Screening and confirmation analysis should be performed in a separate aliquot from original sample so as to prevent mistaken identity.

Analytical methods in forensic toxicology (testing methodologies)

In forensic toxicology, where results are most often used to impose sanctions, it is essential that the analysis provides a high standard of proof. Two different analyses are therefore most often required, the first normally a screening test to establish the presence of a drug. If the screening test is positive, a confirmatory test is performed.

Screening is performed by qualitative (often immunoassay) or semi-quantitative methods (chromatographic). Qualitative screening provides high sensitivity to drug or group of drugs analyzed but moderate specificity. Cross-reactions with other substances can occur so that positive results indicating specific drugs must be confirmed by an alternative analytical technique. For unique identification and confirmation of presumed positive specimens gas/liquid chromatography (GC/LC/HPLC) combined with mass spectrometry (MS) methodology is applied. Confirmation analysis measures specific drugs and metabolites as well as the amount of drug present in the matrix analyzed (1). For all methods applied, there is a limit to how small amounts of drugs can be detected, given as a level of detection (LOD). For practical purposes, a level of quantification (LOQ) is also given by the laboratory (5).

Choosing the matrix

It is essential that the relevant specimen is collected depending on the nature of the case (4). Within post-mortem toxicology and human performance toxicology, a blood specimen is the preferred medium. Levels of drugs in blood can be used to determine level of impairment, intoxication or cause of death. Blood, however, has a short detection time for many drugs (hours/few days). Urine can determine a wide selection of drugs, poisons and their metabolites and often has higher drug concentrations and longer detection time (days/weeks). Urine is therefore utilized in forensic drug testing and can also be useful as a screening specimen. More recently, saliva has appeared as an alternative to urine within forensic drug testing. Similar to urine, it is non-invasive sampling with the added advantage of easier monitoring of the sampling. As for urine, saliva has proven useful in proving use of drugs ingested but, for some drugs, has a somewhat shorter detection time than urine (Figure 93.1). Hair testing can give an even longer detection window (months depending on hair length) and thereby provide a history of exposure to drug or poison. However, interpretation of findings in hair is laden with contamination issues.

In post-mortem cases, several other matrixes are utilized, such as heart blood, vitreous humor, cerebrospinal fluid (CSF), pericardial fluid, gastric content, muscle, liver, lung, brain and other organ samples. However, peripheral blood samples are considered the gold standard, and a blood sample is often needed in order to determine possible cause of death.

DRUGS AND POISONS MOST COMMONLY TARGETED

Finding the cause of intoxication or poisoning can depend on choosing the right repertoire. The repertoire chosen will depend on the type of case, knowledge of possible drugs or poisons involved as well as clinical information if available.

Within human behavioral testing, the repertoire consists of drugs of abuse and others known to cause impairment/intoxication. The groups of drugs most often targeted are alcohols, cannabinoids, benzodiazepines, amphetamines, cocaine, opioids and othercentral nervous system (CNS) depressants and some hallucinogens. Such a repertoire is also most often applied within forensic drug testing. In order to determine cause of death a wider repertoire is needed, and a screening of hundreds of drugs (both illicit and therapeutic drugs) and non-drug poisons is most often applied.

Interpretations

Interpretation of the analytical result is a major challenge in forensic toxicology. Depending on the case in question,

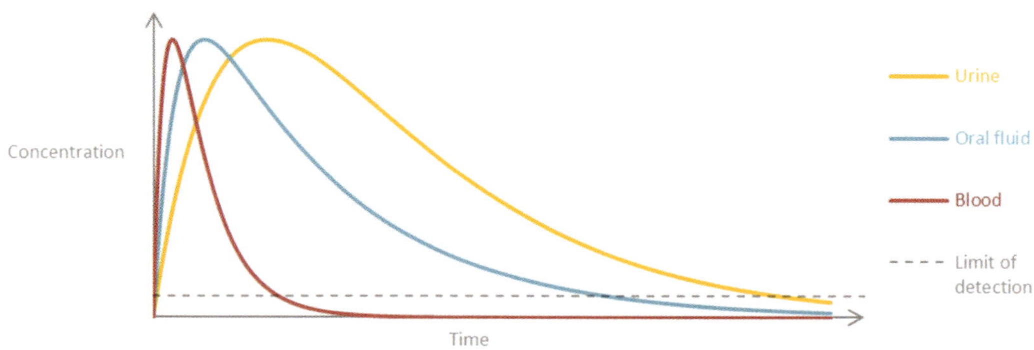

93.1 Illustration of concentration/time curves for the same drug in different matrices.

interpretation is complex, and consideration must be given to the information on the circumstances (4).

The purpose of sampling and the limitations of the results for the interpretation have to be clearly established. To interpret the results, one needs to have knowledge of the various routines for testing including properties of different matrixes, detection times of different drugs in the different matrixes, analytical issues such as cut-offs, methodology, the donor's use of drugs prior to sampling and methods of manipulation/use of adulterants.

Interpretation is also challenging due to a lack of robust scientific information for many drugs on questions such as what is a lethal dose and how long are drugs detected in different specimens? Interpretation also depends on accumulated experience which is often case specific.

Questions raised for the toxicologist to consider in non-fatal cases are:

- What has been ingested? (victim/perpetrator)
- When was the drug ingested?
- How much drug was ingested?
- Ingested drug's influence on behavior during course of event? (intoxication, level of consciousness, aggression, toxicity, drug-induced psychosis etc.)

Back calculations

Back calculation is one of the most useful tools to estimate a concentration if there is a substantial time lapse between the sampling and the event reported (e.g. driving under the influence or sexual assault). Its use demands an in-depth knowledge of the drugs kinetic properties, and most calculations may easily be disputed. The specific drug and the concentration range we use in back calculation will define if the elimination is a 1st- or 0-order kinetics. For example, ethanol has 1st-order kinetics up to 0.02 percent and then 0-order kinetics above that. Many drugs have similar patterns but not all in the range of concentrations usually encountered. For gamma hydroxybutyrate (GHB) as an example, the shift-point between 1st- and 0-order kinetics is poorly documented but, within the range, one can find in recreational use of the drug. Other drugs have this shift point at toxic levels. Even if there is a drug and concentration range found to be within the 1st-order kinetics, choosing the half-life is crucial for the result. For surprisingly many drugs, the terminal half-life found in the literature is based on data from very few individuals. As has been said, all half-lives are wrong, but some are useful (6). For example, applying a terminal half-life is not always the best choice when working within the first hours after intake, even if one takes absorption time into account. Presenting estimative intervals rather than one figure estimate, and a cautious presentation of the calculations, more as orienting examples than final results, is a wise approach.

Toxicological evaluation in post-mortem specimens

Post-mortem toxicology presents its own problems. Only minutes after death, several processes occur that can affect drugs concentrations, making interpretation difficult and sometimes almost impossible. But even though post-mortem drug concentrations will never accurately reflect the concentration prior to death, this does not mean they are not useful. The difficult interpretation begins with knowledge of post-mortem changes in the body and the faith of certain drugs due to such changes. Using only compilations of drug concentrations in living plasma to interpret post-mortem values in whole blood can never lead to any good (7,8).

Post-mortem artefacts are a major challenge. Such artefacts can be due to circumstances surrounding the death, changes in the body during the post-mortem period and properties of the drug itself. Post-mortem artefacts can be due to ante- and pre-mortal factors (such as treatment prior to death, pharmacokinetic principals in critically ill patients, death occurring before distribution equilibrium is reached), post-mortem changes in the body (such as time from death till sampling, resuscitation, transportation, decomposition), sampling artefacts (such as contamination), post-mortem changes in the matrices sampled (such as hemolysis, clotting), post-mortem redistribution, post-mortem decomposition, formation or metabolism of drugs and instability of drugs in post-mortem tissues and in blood after sampling. Post-mortem redistribution especially has been described as a toxicological nightmare (9), with a diffusion of drugs from high to lower concentrations in the body occurring within hours after death.

Peripheral blood is the matrix of choice in order to determine and interpret post-mortem drug concentrations; however, a difficult interpretation may be made easier if other matrixes, such as urine, vitreous humor, muscle and so on are sampled and available for analysis. Also, it must not be forgotten that a meaningful interpretation relies on the quality of the specimen collected.

For many drugs, there is a major overlap between therapeutic, toxic and lethal concentrations. Therefore, no post-mortem drug concentration can be interpreted on its own, without knowledge of circumstances surrounding the case in question. The interpretation relies on information on the circumstances of death and autopsy findings. Without knowledge of the case, the toxicologist has no hope of giving a meaningful and valid interpretation. Results and the interpretation of these can provide vital information on possible cause of death, as well as helping to explain the circumstances surrounding the death. All those involved in interpreting or needing to understand the significance of post-mortem findings must be made very aware of the challenges of post-mortem drug concentrations, so that the results are not misunderstood or misinterpreted.

Toxicological evaluation in violent and sexual crimes

Involvement of alcohol and other drugs of abuse in violent behavior and sexual crimes is highly prevalent. The potential effect of drugs on behavior may be of interest during the investigation or in court, and the police may require toxicological samples from the perpetrator or the victim after violent crimes. Time between the crime and the sample taking may be long, thus low concentrations of drugs, and alternative specimens such as hair may be of interest for the interpretation.

DRUGS OF ABUSE AND VIOLENCE

Acts of violence are highly multifactorial with prominent social and psychological components. The proof of a causal association between drug intake and violent behavior is elusive for many drugs, both epidemiological and experimental. Nevertheless, violent behavior and drug abuse share neurobiological mechanisms and behavioral traits that make associations between drugs and violence highly relevant.

From a neurobiological aspect, an increased dopaminergic transmission in the mesolimbic area and a reduced transmission in the prefrontal cortex are key features that concur in the acute effect of drugs and in the changes leading to addiction as well as in violent behavior.

Several behavioral features of acute intoxication, withdrawal or effects caused by chronic use of drugs are relevant for understanding why use of some drugs is linked to aggressive responses. Three of them are of special relevance:

- Reduced working memory capacity. When evaluating, if other individuals pose a potential threat, aggressive features are more salient than non-aggressive features. The latter may not be taken in consideration due to low working memory capacity, leading to biased decision-making.
- Reduced activity in the anterior cingulate area influences the capacity to foresee negative consequences in the future and underestimates the effect of negative consequences in the past, also affecting decision-making.
- Some drugs, especially in high doses and/or with chronic use may impair the ability to recognize emotions in other people's faces, and hence misinterpret others' intentions (10). Alterations in the recognition of anger and sadness are related to aggression and hostility, and alterations of fear processing can impair adequate categorization and recognition of risky scenarios. Neuropsychological studies support that the measures of quantity and duration of drugs used significantly predict poorer discrete emotions recognition.

When it comes to the individual effects of drugs, there is some experimental evidence for the direct association between intake and aggressive responding for several groups of drugs. In spite of numerous potential confounders, both individual and contextual factors, that hamper the study of causal association between drugs and aggression, we can draw some conclusions from the literature.

Alcohol is the drug most clearly associated to higher degree of aggression. Increased aggressive responses have been assessed especially for blood-alcohol concentrations around 0.08 percent or higher in both experimental and epidemiologic studies (11). Engaging in violent episodes has been related to the frequency and the amount of drug consumption. Some studies have also shown a linear association between blood-alcohol concentrations and aggression, especially when alcohol levels are in the rising limb. Alcohol, especially in moderate doses, reduces anxiety levels and may reduce the fear for the consequences of aggressive behavior. This mechanism has also been proposed for aggressive behavior seen in some sedating drugs, in addition to the three aforementioned cognitive features.

Reduction of anxiety is a key effect of benzodiazepines. Benzodiazepines are widely used as drugs of abuse at supra-therapeutic doses. Several experimental studies have shown a higher level of aggressive responses after acute, and some after chronic use of benzodiazepines at different doses (12). Individuals with personality traits low in the anxiety axis seem to react to benzodiazepines with higher aggression levels than individuals with high anxiety traits (13).

The same mechanisms as for benzodiazepines may apply for z-hypnotics (zopiclone, zolpidem), but there is a lack of experimental studies focused on aggression and z-hypnotics. Another rare side effect of z-hypnotics and especially zolpidem is parasomnias (sleep walking) with complex behavior. These episodes may also include criminal behavior and there have been several cases where the defense has pledged sleep walking in violent crimes or driving under the influence. Zolpidem is by far the drug most often involved in these episodes (14). The core signs of sleep walking that differentiate it from drug intoxication are abrupt onset, short duration, no signs of motor impairment and a strong reduced consciousness including inability to understand and interact with others.

The association between cannabis and aggression is less clear. It is widely accepted that chronic cannabis users perform worse in decision-making studies, including response control, and some epidemiologic studies have shown an association between cannabis and violence (15). Aggression is nevertheless a prominent feature of cannabis-induced psychotic episodes as discussed below.

The association between stimulants (amphetamine, methamphetamine and cocaine) and aggression is widely documented, both observational and self-reported (16). Stimulants increase self-confidence and reduce behavioral inhibition, typically increasing risk-taking behavior. However, the causal relation is not well established. As for cannabis, aggression is a common feature of stimulant psychosis. Milder psychotic symptoms such as suspiciousness or feeling of danger are far more common in stimulant users than full blown psychotic episodes and may also trigger aggression. Several studies point at the neurotoxic effect of stimulants on the serotonin system, as background for the association between long-term stimulant use and aggression.

DRUGS OF ABUSE AND PSYCHOSIS

Aggressive behavior is a common feature of drug-induced psychosis. The experience of psychotic symptoms is surprisingly prevalent among drug users in general, and the prevalence increases with the severity of the substance use disorders in interaction with the individual vulnerability (17). Psychotic symptoms may follow acute drug impairment or may be one of the features of abstinence.

Crimes committed in psychotic states may mitigate a judicial sentence, but that is usually not the case when the psychotic state is caused by a voluntary intake of drugs. The toxicologist may be asked provide evidence about these matters.

Drugs of abuse most frequently associated to psychosis during acute impairment are hallucinogens, stimulants and cannabis. Psychosis is also a typical feature of severe alcohol abstinence and can also occur in benzodiazepine withdrawal.

Drug-facilitated sexual assault

Voluntary consumed alcohol is the most prevalent drug found in toxicological investigations of drug-facilitated sexual assault, but the perpetrators may also give the victim drugs that compromise the capacity to consent to sexual relations. The most frequent drugs used are CNS depressants, for example benzodiazepines, GHB, ketamine or anticholinergics as scopolamine. The task for the toxicologist is first to detect the drug and secondly to estimate the degree of impairment at the time of the incident and help the court to determine drugs effects on the victim's consciousness and memory. The preferred specimen is blood to perform back calculations and assess its effects, but often the time elapsed between the aggression and the sample limits the choice to urine or even hair.

Toxicological evaluation in cases of driving under the influence

Driving under the influence of alcohol is considered one of the most important factors for motor vehicle crashes worldwide, however, over the past years, attention has been drawn to an increasing number of cases where other, licit or illicit, drugs are involved (18). The non-alcoholic drugs most often found to be involved in suspected driving under the influence cases are amphetamines, cannabis, benzodiazepines and opioids (19). Numerous studies have determined a correlation between blood-alcohol level and level of impairment of functions relevant for driving, so that at a relevant blood-alcohol level a set of behaviors can be expected on a population level. Most countries around the world have, based on such research, legislation in place regarding limits for driving under the influence of alcohol. In the last few years, as a consequence of more focus on non-alcoholic drugs importance for reduced driving skills, several countries are also introducing legal limits for such drugs.

Toxicological evaluation in forensic drug testing

Forensic drug testing aims at determining drug intake through the presence of drugs rather than its effects, in the implementation of laws or administrative rules involving sanctions. Typical areas are workplace, prisons, social services, child protection, family courts or proving abstinence from drugs in reinstatement of a revoked driver's license. Because the objective is mainly to identify if a drug has been ingested, specimens with longer detection times are preferred. The one most used has been urine but oral fluid arises as a good alternative, with similar detection times for many drugs and without violating the intimacy of the observed urine sampling. Hair samples are also utilized.

The job of the toxicologist in determinations in urine may involve several aspects; one is the determination of which drug has been ingested, given the metabolites present in urine, and eventually when the intake has occurred. Another may be if the findings can be attributed to legally prescribed medication. One example of the latter is amphetamine, where chiral analysis may determine if the amphetamine has been ingested as a racemic mixture (typical for illegal supplies) or as dextroamphetamine (more typical for medical amphetamine preparations).

In this field, the organization requiring the test may have their own demands regarding the repertoire of drugs to be tested for according to their internal rules.

CONCLUSION

Forensic toxicology involves the detection, identification and quantitation of toxicologically relevant substances and the interpretation of the results to aid medicolegal investigation of deaths, poisonings or drug use. Both advanced analytical toxicology and pharmacokinetic/pharmacodynamic expertise are pivotal for optimal results. The main fields of interest are human performance and behavior, post-mortem investigations and forensic drug testing.

The task includes many aspects; measuring drugs in different biological matrixes, determining the ingested drug and time of the ingestion, evaluating changes in drug concentration under storage or after death, and providing an overview over possible effects on human behavior on tasks, from driving to rape or murder.

REFERENCES

1. Levin B (ed). *Principles of Forensic Toxicology*, 2nd ed. Washington DC: AACC Press USA; 2006.
2. Penders J, Verstraete A. Laboratory guidelines and standards in clinical and forensic toxicology. *Accred Qual Assur* 2006; **11**: 284–90.
3. Chung H, Choe S. Challenges in forensic toxicology. *Aust J Forensic Sci* 2019; **6**: 665–73.
4. Drummer OH. Toxicology: Overview. In: Payne-James J, Byard RW (eds), *Encyclopedia of Forensic and Legal Medicine*, 2nd ed. Amsterdam: Elsevier; 2016, pp. 615–21.
5. Druid H. Retstoksikologi. In: Thomsen JL (ed), *Retsmedicin, Nordisk lærebog.* Copenhagen: Fadl's forlag; 2004, pp. 395–410.
6. Wright JG, Brody A. All half-lives are wrong, but some are useful. *Clin Pharmacokinet* 2001; 40(4): 237–44.

7. Skopp G. Artifacts are an inherent part of postmortem toxicology. *TIAFT Bull* 2010; **40**: 7–17.
8. Drummer OH. Postmortem toxicology of drugs of abuse. *Forensic Sci Int* 2004; **142**: 101–13.
9. Pounder DJ, Jones GR. Post-mortem drug redistribution – a toxicological nightmare. *Forensic Sci Int* 1990; **45**: 253–63.
10. Miller AM, Bershad AK, de Wit H. Drug effects on responses to emotional facial expressions: Recent findings. *Behav Pharmacol* 2015; **26**(**6**): 571–9.
11. Duke AA, Giancola PR, Morris DH, et al. Alcohol dose and aggression another reason why drinking more is a bad idea. *J Stud Alcohol Drugs* 2011; **72**(**1**): 34–43.
12. Albrecht B, Staiger PK, P Hall, et al. Benzodiazepine use and aggressive behaviour: A systematic review. *Aust N Z J Psychiatry* 2014; **48**(**12**): 1096–114.
13. Wilkinson CJ. Effects of diazepam (valium) and trait anxiety on human physical aggression and emotional state. *J Behav Med* 1985; **8**(**1**): 101–14.
14. Stallman HM, et al. Medication induced sleepwalking: A systematic review. *Sleep Med Rev* 2018; **37**: 105–13.
15. Norström T, Rossow I. Cannabis use and violence: Is there a link? *Scand J Public Health* 2014; **42**(**4**): 358–63.
16. Kuypers K, Verkes RJ, van den Brink W, et al. Intoxicated aggression: Do alcohol and stimulants cause dose-related aggression? A review. *Eur J Neuropsychopharmacol* 2020; **30**: 114–47.
17. Smith MJ, Thirthalli J, Abdallah AB, et al. Prevalence of psychotic symptoms in substance users: A comparison across substances. *Compr Psychiatry* 2009; **50**: 245–50.
18. Drummer OH, Gerostamoulos J, Batziris H, et al. The involvement of drugs in drivers of motor vehicles killed in Australian road traffic crashes. *Accid Anal Prev* 2004; **36**(**2**): 239–48.
19. Mørland J. Driving under the influence of non-alcoholic drugs. *Forensic Sci Rev* 2000; **12**: 79–105.

CHAPTER

94

Forensic Microbiology

Antti Sajantila and Bruce Budowle

INTRODUCTION

As a whole, forensic microbiology is a complex, multidisciplinary field comprised of an ensemble of experts and from disciplines such as microbiology, genetics, bioinformatics, forensic science, immunology, population genetics, biochemistry, molecular biology and epidemiology. These support a number of service-oriented bodies and organizations such as legal medicine, public health, law enforcement, policy makers and intelligence agencies.

The current scopes of research and practical applications in forensic microbiology are rapidly expanding (Table 94.1). The field is quite comprehensive and this chapter focuses only on some of these emerging topics to acquaint the readership with the remarkable capabilities that are now possible and hopefully to motivate others to pursue careers in this exciting discipline.

FORENSIC MICROBIOLOGY

There has been a long history of microbiology, used by pathologists, long before the inception of the discipline of forensic microbiology (1–6). Louis Pasteur and Robert Koch, known as the fathers of microbiology, developed fermentation and bacterial culturing using artificial mediums for reproduction of microbes (1–4). Due to their seminal work, culture services, the gold standard of microbe identification, became available in clinical medicine in the 1890s (5–8). The value of identifying associated microorganisms in post-mortem investigation was addressed by Achard and Phulpin who, in 1895, reported on the origins of the microorganisms found in dead bodies (9). Thereafter, the general value, sampling techniques, antemortem–post-mortem comparisons and interpretation issues of usage of microbiology in autopsy work have been mainstream (10–20). The fundamental concepts and challenges, as well as models for use of post-mortem microbiology, were delineated in such studies.

TABLE 94.1 Examples of research topics and practical applications in forensic microbiology

Investigation of the cause of death
Estimation of post-mortem interval
Tracking of infectious agents in suspected biocrimes and acts of bioterrorism
Transmission of pathogens related to forensic or medicolegal queries
Characterization of body fluids and identification in criminal cases
Linkage of a crime scene or a victim with the assailant
Estimation of geographic origins of unidentified cadavers
Investigations of forensic archeology and mass graves

Early forensic microbiology work focussed on determining the specific etiologic agent behind the infectious death by sampling infectious foci in various organs. These studies addressed many challenges related to the post-mortem use of newly developed methods in bacteriology. First, to understand the post-mortem succession of opportunist bacteria, a study of multi-organ sampling at the autopsy was performed (18). Second, the possibility of false positive results and/or sample contamination and the importance of correct sampling techniques to avoid these confounding issues were investigated (11). Third, it was imperative to assess microbial differences between samples taken antemortem, that is, during hospital treatment, and those taken post-mortem at autopsy to effect reliable interpretations of the obtained data (12).

Today, forensic microbiology is at the dawn of a new era, due in part to the aforementioned technical developments over the past decade that foster laboratory analyses, but also to the paradigm-changing modern understanding of the human body. Humans are composed not only of their own (human) cells, but according to this new concept, far more of the cells responsible for the human body ecosystem are of microbial origin.

Recently, high-throughput DNA-sequencing technologies opened new avenues for detailed understanding of the human microbiome in general (21,22), and, subsequently, created new possibilities in forensic microbiology (Table 94.2 and references therein). Since 2005, high-throughput DNA-sequencing methods (23,24), also known as massively parallel sequencing or next-generation sequencing (NGS), and versatile bioinformatics tools have made it possible to identify and characterize

DOI: 10.1201/9781003138754-98

targeted or full-genome sequences of the vast human microbiome. This capability made two major advancements possible. First, the seemingly monumental task of sequencing of the first entire human genome, concurrently achieved by the public funded Human Genome Project (HGP) (25) and by a privately funded group (26). Second, and even more important, was the finding that humans, during and after birth, quickly gain over one million additional genes via the establishment of their microbiomes, which are contributed to by at least the same amount, if not an order of magnitude greater number, of microbial cells than the human cells of a body. For example, the data show that a vast majority of commensal bacteria, ~10^{14} cells, reside in the human colon, followed by ~10^{12} bacteria residing in and on the skin, and the rest of the body housing less than 10^{12} bacteria. In addition to the bacteria, our microbiome consists of a multitude of eukaryotes, archaea, bacteria and viruses, the proportion and distribution of which is only now being realized. These data stem from the ongoing Human Microbiome Project (HMP) (27) (https://www.hmpdacc.org), originally based on the medical community's interest on the part the human microbiome may and does play in health and disease. Within the HMP, the collection and characterization of the diversity and function of the human microbiome has constantly increased (21,22). Some of the above-described milestones for the development of forensic microbiology are listed in Table 94.2.

TABLE 94.2 Important milestones in forensic microbiology supporting legal-medicine and public health from 1860s to 2020

Year	Major finding, observation or phenomenon	Authors (Reference)
1860	Liquid medium invented for bacterial culture	Pasteur (1–3)
1881	Solid medium invented for bacterial culture	Koch (4)
1895	First post-mortem microbiology study	Achard and Phulpin (9)
1904	Concept of post-mortem transmigration	Gradwohl (10)
1916	Concept of agonal spread	Fredette (11)
1964	First study of post-mortem microbiology in a large cohort (>2000 cases)	Carpenter and Wilkins (14)
1965	Concept of sterile autopsy	O'Toole et al. (15)
1974	Study of clinical importance of post-mortem microbiology	Koneman and Davis (19)
1992	First use of HIV[1] sequence analysis in transmission case in a dental practice	Ou et al. (28)
1994	First use of HIV sequence analysis in a rape case	Albert et al. (29)
1998	Development of MLST[2] technique	Maiden et al. (30)
2001	Anthrax letter attacks in USA	Bush et al. (31)
2000s	Development of DNA-barcoding	Hebert et al. (32)
	Development of metabarcoding	Taberlet et al. (33)
	Development of metagenomics	Tyson et al. (34)
	Development of HTS[3] technologies	Margulies et al. (23)
		Shendure et al. (24)
2007	Human Microbiome Project	Turnbaugh et al. (27)
2010	Use of phylogenetics for source of transmission in a rape case	Scaduto et al. (35)
2010	Use of metagenomics in detection of biological stains	Brenig et al. (36)
2010	Use of bacteria to detect vaginal fluid	Fleming and Harbison (37)
2010	Use of skin bacterial communities for identification	Fierer et al. (38)
2013	Use of phylogenetics for the timing of an intentional transmission of HCV[4]	González Candelas et al. (39)
2013	Concept of microbial clock for PMI[5]	Metcalf et al. (40)
2014	Foundation of the ESGFOR[6] study group	www.escmid.org
2015	Persistent viruses detected in human bone	Toppinen et al. (41)

[1] HIV= Human immunodeficiency virus; [2] MLST = Multilocus sequence typing; [3] HTS = High-throughput sequencing; [4] HCV = Hepatitis C-virus; [5] PMI = Post-mortem interval; [6] ESGFOR = ESCMID[7] Study Group of Forensic and Post-mortem Microbiology; [7] European Society of Clinical Microbiology and Infectious Diseases.

FORENSIC MICROBIOLOGY IN THE AUTOPSY CONTEXT

A fundamental component of specific microbes or microbial communities in the context of a forensic pathology is the difference between antemortem and post-mortem presence or absence of microbes. The balance between co-existing human and microbial cells of the human microbiome ecosystem is a necessity for a healthy physiological and homeostatic status of an individual. The mutual relationship of the human host and commensal microflora is also an integral part of the complex immunologic system and resistance safeguard against pathogenic and opportunistic microbes (42–44). An invading pathogen can disrupt this balance, and an infection with varying (or no) clinical signs is born. Body orifices (eyes, nose, mouth, genitals and anus) or open wounds and injuries are the typical routes for pathogens to enter the body.

Any emerging microbial disease, especially those that cause local epidemics or pandemics, are of grave concern to public health and also to the medicolegal and forensic pathology communities. Post-mortem microbial diagnostics is mostly directed by the analysis of generally known – or specific, regionally prevailing – and potentially lethal microbes. The detection of the microbes in post-mortem investigation is mainly based on screening the spectrum of known life-threatening microbes (45). The 2019 coronavirus disease (COVID-19) pandemic showed that new microbes can rapidly lead to a health emergency with high transmission and age-dependent death rates (46). The ability to rapidly identify the strains or variants spreading in a community or communities is highly important, since it allows epidemiologic tracking of transmission (47), helps in vaccine development (48,49) and aids generally to the understanding of microbial evolution (50).

Diagnostic finding, post-mortem artefact or contamination?

An underlying concept of forensic microbiology related to autopsy work is that the microbiota on the body and its close environment are different from those of the microbial system in the body. These two entities are separated as the epinecrotic microbiome and the thanatomicrobiome, respectively (Figure 94.1).

In general, post-mortem metamorphosis of the microbial flora may have such an effect that the comparison of post-mortem microbiome to that of antemortem turns into a meaningless effort. As the post-mortem interval (PMI) increases, the greater the possibility is for alterations of the microbiome (51). In practice, particularly in a corpse with advanced putrefaction, the post-mortem components of the microbiome are combinations of antemortem and post-mortem microbiomes and are often inseparable. Due to this phenomenon, post-mortem microbiology findings can be an outcome of various processes, and careful attention to these issues is of utmost importance for potential cause of death interpretations. Microbial findings in a post-mortem sample representing an infectious, or potentially fatal agent, causing or contributing to death, may thus need a consideration of alternate explanations for the presence of the microbes. The major critique toward a genuine positive finding is that the microbes found in the body post-mortem are, in fact, not real findings, but artefacts due to the:

- Agonal spread of microbes
- Post-mortem translocation of microbes
- And/or a contamination of these events

All these factors, alone or in combination, may lead to a false positive or false negative interpretation of the microbial findings from the samples obtained post-mortem.

A genuine positive finding is a case in which microbes infect the target organ(s) or body fluid(s) antemortem, in proximity to the death. However, the presence of microbes in the sample, obtained during the autopsy, does not necessarily imply a fatal infectious disease. For example, depending on the infective agent, bacteremia can occur without clinical symptoms or evidence of infectious foci and tissue damage. When the bacteremia or sepsis occurred prior to death with associated symptoms, and an infectious agent was detected post-mortem, the infection can be considered as the cause or a contributing factor to death. The combination of symptoms, signs of a specific infectious disease antemortem, and detection of infective focus and inflammation in the corpse post-mortem, provide more weight to the presence of the specific microbe. However, as many of the deaths in the forensic pathology realm are not witnessed and often there are no recent medical records available, the suspicion of infectious death may arise unexpectedly during the autopsy.

The concept of "agonal spread" was introduced in 1916 by JW Fredette (11). His idea was that the bacteria invade the blood circulation during the agonal period or resuscitation attempt. This "terminal infection" is thus due to artificial bacterial invasion into the bloodstream, and therefore, despite the bacterial growth in collected samples, no sign of inflammation or tissue and organ damage would be observed post-mortem. The basis for this phenomenon is that during the agonal period, the integrity of the mucosal surfaces is damaged by ischemia or hypoxia, permitting different microbial species to leak into blood and internal organs. Regarding bacteria, this invasion arises from the epinecrotic microbiome, where microbes naturally exist.

If agonal spread were to occur, the microbial analysis will likely reflect a mixture of pathogen(s) (if there is an infectious agent) and commensals. Thus, the observed findings in the thanatomicrobiome are rather a consequence than the cause of death. The study by Fredette (11) consisted of 119 autopsies, in which 77 negative and 42 positive cultures were obtained. In 31 of the 42 positive cases (74%), he found only one microbe, and in 11/42 positive cases, he found two microorganisms (26%). He also found the *Streptococci* were the typical "terminal invaders." The drawback of his study (and many others in the field) was the small cohort size: Fredette (11) had antemortem microbial data on only 14

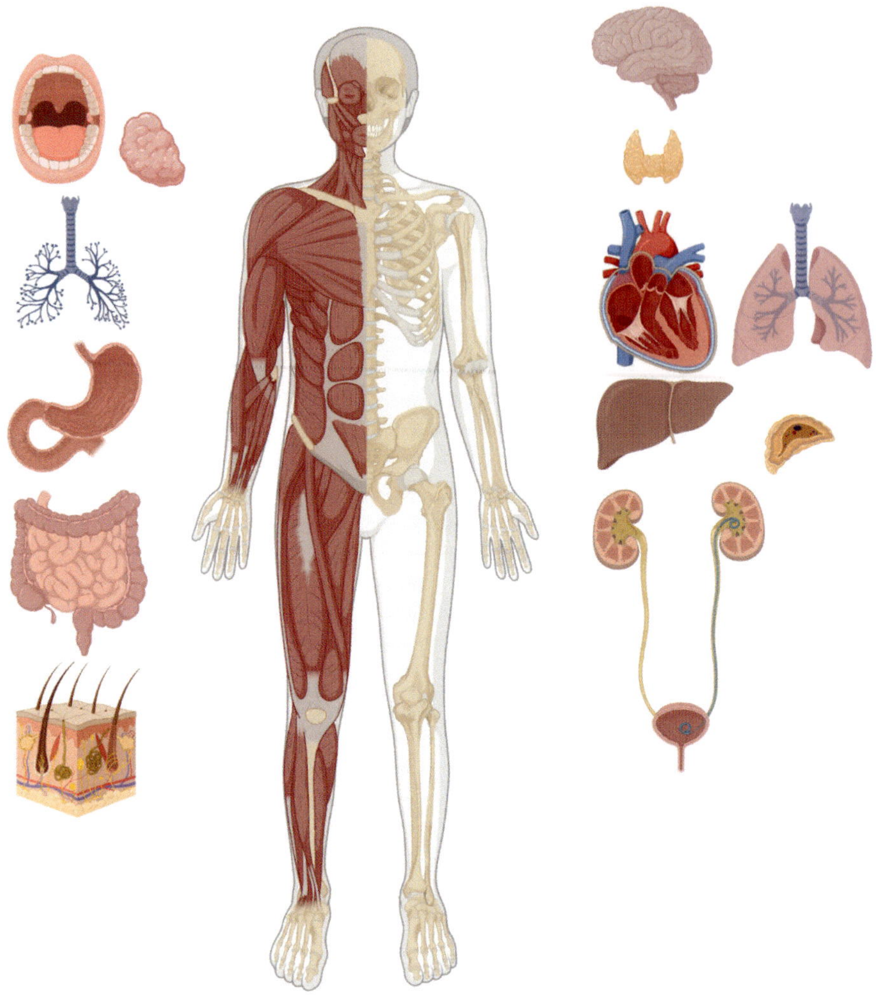

94.1 The human post-mortem microbiome. The **epinecrotic microbiome** consists of microorganisms residing in and on skin and body orifices, including the mouth and organs within it, respiratory tract, and gastrointestinal tract. The **thanatomicrobiome** includes microorganisms residing in all internal organs without anatomic access from the surrounding environment. (Created with BioRender.com.)

cases, out of which 8 showed no growth and 4 cases showing no post-mortem growth. Thus, antemortem and clinical contexts were not critically evaluated or not considered significant for post-mortem interpretation. Studies with larger datasets were presented by Koneman and Davis in 1974 (19) and Smith et al. in 1975 (52), who also considered agonal spread as a possibility. Koneman and Davis (19) performed 396 autopsies over a 2-year period, yielding 1428 isolates of microorganisms. In 42 percent of the samples, a single species was cultured, and in 8 percent there were three or more recovered. They concluded that there is a minimal post-mortem spread or contamination. Smith et al. (52) carried out a prospective study over three years and sampled 20 children who died of complications due to 2nd- and 3rd-degree thermal injuries. Microbes (bacteria and fungi) were deemed to have contributed to death in 17 out of 20 (85%) cases. They found that the antemortem and post-mortem microbiologic findings from cardiac blood and pulmonary tissues correlated "reasonably well with clinical and anatomic judgements of cause of death." The agonal spread seemed to have a rather small overall impact in post-mortem cases. However, the studies presented here were based on microbial culture and thus only those microorganisms amenable to culture were detected. As a consequence, many other potential causal pathogens may have been missed, and we now know that cultures provide a limited picture of the antemortem and post-mortem microbiomes.

Post-mortem translocation can follow when the blood circulation ceases and there is post-mortem damage of the mucosal surface, which allow microbes to pass through membranes into the blood, tissues or organ systems. This phenomenon was first described in 1904 by Gradwohl (10), and his study gained support based on a large study with 2033 cases by Carpenter and Wilkins in 1964 (14). The latter authors found that the positivity in cultures increased from 20 percent to 40 percent as the PMI increased.

A similar finding was obtained from *in vitro* experiments performed by Kellerman et al. in 1976 (53), who studied the post-mortem kinetics of the migration of intestinal bacterial flora to the peritoneal cavity. They showed that bacteria can transmigrate through an intact human intestinal wall, beginning about 15 hours post-mortem, with *Staphylococcus aureus*, Gram-negative bacilli and spore-forming Gram-positive bacilli gradually increasing in numbers.

A very recent study using molecular genetic methods also supports that post-mortem migration can occur. Tuomisto et al. (54) showed, by bacterial culturing and real-time quantitative PCR, a time-dependent post-mortem bacterial migration into several organs (liver, mesenteric lymph nodes, pericardial fluid, and portal and peripheral veins) in 33 autopsies with a post-mortem period of 1–7 days. These authors concluded that first choices for post-mortem bacterial investigation (less than 5 days post-mortem) are pericardial fluid and liver samples.

Contamination is a known concern for any laboratory work. In the case of forensic microbiology and autopsy, the bacteria can be inoculated into the specimen during the sampling process. Typically, commensal bacteria from the skin can appear in the organ sample as a false positive finding due to inadequate sampling as a result of contamination. The potential for contamination can be reduced by practicing "sterile autopsy" (15,17). This approach includes sterile morgue facilities (e.g. mimicking a surgical operation theater) with bodies cleaned and staff wearing personal protective equipment similar to that used during surgical operation, and autopsy dissections performed with controled airflow and use of sterile surgical instruments. The PMI was kept short (<20 hours), and samples were cultured in a manner similar to microbiological analysis of living patients. O'Toole et al. (15) and Minckler et al. (17) showed that 1) aseptic autopsy procedures minimize contamination, and thus 2) positive cultures with clinically known pathogens were more likely to represent a true infection as a post-mortem finding.

A necessity to avoid or minimize post-mortem contamination in autopsy facilities and sample handling has led to development of standards of practice. These standards include the following measures:

- The body should be transferred to cooled storage (+4 to +6°C)
- Unnecessary movement of the body should be avoided
- An autopsy should be performed within 24–48 hours after death
- An autopsy room should be clean with good ventilation
- Autopsy procedures and sampling should be performed in as sterile an environment as possible
- Samples should be transported to the laboratory in appropriate transport media (15,17,55,56)

Examples of cause-of-death investigation types

The identification of pathogens that may cause a fatal disease can be quite useful. The value of a post-mortem microbiologic investigation in such fatalities is, for example, to establish the diagnosis, to validate the antemortem diagnostics, to discover novel pathogens, and to form microbiologic sources for future studies, epidemics or pandemics. However, analyses can be challenging in the clinical setting for several reasons. First, a fatal disease may progress too quickly to allow proper sampling of a specimen(s) for diagnostics. Typically, a patient arriving at an emergency room in extremis, and who dies shortly after can be left without diagnostic procedure or the samples are sub optimally collected for diagnosis. As such, death is classified as sudden, unexpected death and a post-mortem investigation is needed to establish the cause of death including microbiologic tests if infection is suspected. Second, finding of the infection focus or foci in the body may take time, and if the site(s) is found, obtaining a specimen directly from it can be challenging. Third, in chronic situations, secondary infections may confound the clinical picture and mask the causative pathogen.

In general, the use of microbiology in investigations of the cause of death is a time-honored practice. Microbiological samples have been taken from the deceased and assayed with simple methods for detection of many infective agents, for example, *Mycobacterium tuberculosis, Haemophilus influenzae*, morbillivirus and poliovirus. In the routine autopsy context, the most typical diseases in adults considered in determining infections as a cause of death are related to pneumonia, sepsis and meningitis. In children, pneumonia is still a global problem, but microbiological tests are also routinely used in the investigation of children and neonates in cases of sudden infant death syndrome (SIDS). Of particular interest have been a number of viruses such as enteroviruses, adenoviruses, Epstein–Barr viruses, and parvovirus B19, which have been found in SIDS cases (57). Also, mRNA of parvovirus B19 has been found in adult patients suffering from heart failure (58). However, mere presence of viruses, or their components, does not mean causation, and it remains to be seen whether these findings are causal of diseases (or even death), innocent bystanders in the human body, or even play a part of our normal, balanced virome (59).

Since post-mortem microbial succession negatively affects the assessment of causality of death, it is important to characterize this process prior to the autopsy in cause-of-death investigations, that is, during the PMI. Hurtado et al. (51) showed that diagnostic use of microbial methods of autopsy material is reliable at least up to 24 hours after death. They also noted that the proportion of some bacteria (e.g. *Enterobacteriaceae* and *Pseudomonas* spp.) as etiological agents of fatal infections might be overestimated. In their study, they observed that increasing PMIs were associated with an increase in the number of different bacteria identified.

Other types of deaths of medicolegal relevance may also benefit from forensic microbiologic investigations. For example, bodies found in an aqueous environment still represent a diagnostically difficult task regarding potential drowning even in the hands of an experienced medicolegal specialist. Cadavers found in various aqueous environments (60,61) can be analyzed with forensic microbiological methods to potentially determine manner of death. The earliest microbiological testing for putative drowning was the so-called diatom test (62,63), which originally was based on the chemical or enzymatic disruption of the cellular material of diatoms and the subsequent identification of diatom species based on their characteristic shell morphology. It is likely that parallel to enzymatic or chemical analysis of diatoms, metabarcoding combined with high-throughput sequencing technologies will become an alternative or an adjunct to the diatom test for the cause-of-death investigation in suspected drowning cases (64).

Risk of pathogen transmission during autopsy to morgue personnel

Many infections can be transmitted through direct inoculation during autopsy. Biological contaminants in autopsy room facilities or forensic laboratories may infect personnel working with cadavers or cadaveric material, which is a serious health concern (similar to nosocomial infections in hospitals). The most important of these infectious agents include *Mycobacterium tuberculosis, Neisseria meningitides* (meningococcus), hepatitis B and C, and some more scarce or local infective agents, such as viruses that cause hemorrhagic fevers (55,56,65–67).

In order to avoid contamination and the risk of infection personal protection and autopsy theater infrastructure are of paramount importance. For personal protection, the essentials include well-trained autopsy techniques and PPE (including but not necessarily limited to vision shields, protective glasses, particulate filter respirators, and thin Kevlar-enhanced cut-resistant protective gloves) which are effective and recommended. Also, safety protocols and autopsy checklists have been proposed (68). For the infrastructure, autopsy facilities should be designed to reduce risk of contamination and infective agent transmission. For practical autopsy work, special practices and guidelines to reduce contamination should be implemented.

If all the above-mentioned procedures are in place, the risk of obtaining a severe disease while performing an autopsy or subsequent sample handling can be very low. Although incidences of emergency situations and even halting laboratory workflow have been reported (69), the risk of autopsy personnel to acquire an infectious disease during their work appears relatively low compared with some other healthcare professionals and is related to the infectious disease prevalence in the area of work (70).

OTHER APPLICATIONS OF FORENSIC MICROBIOLOGY

Estimation of post-mortem interval

Estimation of the PMI in forensic medicine is traditionally based on police investigation of the movements and contacts of the deceased prior to death, laboratory tests and body temperature measurements (71). The effect of PMI on bacterial cultures has also been studied (72). Establishing the PMI is critical in a number of death investigations. However, current techniques are susceptible to a range of errors, biases and uncertainties. For example, forensic entomology is widely used to assess the PMI, but errors in interval estimation can range from days to months. Microbial succession analysis may provide an alternate method for estimating PMI. Metcalf and colleagues showed recently that post-mortem microbial community changes are dramatic, measurable and repeatable in a mouse model system, allowing PMI to be estimated within approximately 3 days over 48-day intervals (40). In another study, Metcalf et al. used deep microbial community characterization, community-level metabolic reconstruction and soil biogeochemical assessment to understand the factors governing microbial community assembly during decomposition of human corpses (73). They found a suite of microbes (mainly bacteria and fungi) that contribute to nitrogen cycling and a reproducible network of decomposers. Importantly, these microbial decomposers emerge on predictable time scales and are ubiquitous and in low abundance. Thus, metagenomic analyses could be a promising approach for PMI assessment in selected circumstances.

Bioterrorism and other biocrimes

It has been two decades since the anthrax letter attacks of 2001 in the United States (31,74), which increased awareness of global vulnerability to bioterrorism and biocrime. The United States, as well as the rest of the world, was woefully unprepared to perform the necessary forensic genomics analyses at the time for attribution purposes. Nonetheless, using Sanger sequencing, the full genomes of the *Bacillus anthracis* strain found in the letters (i.e. Ames) and several morphology variants discovered during culture (75) were sequenced, which was laborious, quite costly and computationally challenging. However, that work ushered in the field of microbial forensics to build a forensic capability in order to assist investigations of bioterrorism and biocrime (76,77). Such events, that shake the safety and security of society, require rapid response and high resolution, with highly sensitive, targeted forensic work, even if the capabilities at the time were only partially validated (78,79). Since then, science has made great leaps to enable the analysis of microbiological evidence associated with bioterrorism, biocrimes, hoaxes or the accidental release of a biological agent or toxin for attribution purposes. Most noted is the implementation of NGS and other related high-throughput technologies being used to rapidly identify infectious agents or toxins to protect the public and assist victims as well as generate evidence to help identify perpetrators of such crimes. Whether the result of a crime or that of natural causes, the same tools can be used to pinpoint cause and source of an event (i.e. epidemiologic investigation). However, the forensic investigation may require higher resolution and individualization to limit the findings to a single origin (80). In addition, other molecular epidemiologic analyses have occurred in, for example, outbreaks of cholera after the earthquake in Haiti in 2010 (81) and sprouts contaminated with *Escherichia coli* O104:H4 strain in Germany (82). In 2019, the pandemic caused by SARS-CoV-2 spread from Wuhan, China. Researchers have been trying to determine the origin of the virus (83,84), and how it spreads and mutates throughout communities, countries and the world (47). These latter cases were not due to bioterrorism but illustrate the enormous impact a pathogen can have on society. It is evident that a threat for bioterrorism is taken seriously and nucleic acid detection-based technologies such as NGS allow for rapid diagnosis of a pathogen even if it has not been encountered previously. It should be noted that there are also non-nucleic acid-based testing procedures developed to address certain situations, such as methods to reconstruct how a bioweapon was produced, proteomics (85), toxin detection using immunoassays (86) or mass spectrometry (87), and stable isotope analyses (88).

CLINICAL FORENSICS INVESTIGATIONS

In the clinical setting, forensic microbiology has been reported in cases of transmission of infective agents in rape and the rare cases of medical malpractice, in which medical personnel were suspected to infect their patients intentionally or accidentally. The basis of molecular epidemiologic investigations of transmission events of human infectious agents is the use of molecular phylogenetics. The sequence data from a source are compared to those of the target(s), suspect(s) and/or victim(s), and other reference samples. The questions that may be answered in such cases depend naturally on the infectious agent (DNA/RNA sequences), the number of suspects, the number of victims, databases of reference samples, the analytic tools and the molecular models employed.

The first case reported using molecular analysis was a suspected transmission of human immunodeficiency virus (HIV) in a dental practice due to malpractice (28). Later rape cases (29,89), and other suspected criminal activities (35,90–92) were investigated by analyzing parts of the HIV genome. These early investigations involved relatively few transmission events over a short time period. Although strong support for relatedness between HIV samples obtained from the suspect and victims was attained, the direction of transmission between the evidence sample pairs was often unclear. The use of more advanced phylogenetic methods was better demonstrated in a report of two cases, where the paraphyly of HIV was used to establish the direction of transmission, and thus the source of infective agent could be inferred (35).

A large epidemiologic investigation of a suspected infection of 270 patients with hepatitis C virus (HCV) by an anesthetist in Spain was reported in 2013 (39). Using molecular-clock analysis, it was determined that the origin of transmissions was older than in the earlier cases (25 years at the time of the case) and involved a large number of victims (more than 300 candidate patients potentially associated with the original source of infection) treated in one of two hospitals and infected with HCV. For the first time, a molecular clock was used to estimate the date of various transmission events. In court, these data were compared with those obtained from the documents and testimonies. In two out of three cases, the molecular data estimates were congruent with other epidemiologic and forensic data.

LABORATORY METHODS

The laboratory analytics in forensic microbiology have been undergoing transformation and continue to transform to a new era with the development of metagenomics, targeted analyses and high-throughput sequencing technologies. The HMP has shown that microbes are ever-present in and on the human body. Some species are copious and/or easy to detect by culturing, but the vast majority are unculturable, and therefore some essential strains may escape detection by traditional means. The new molecular techniques developed during the last decade have proven to be vital to current forensic microbiology practices, as they obviate the need for culture methods for pathogen detection. The laboratory methods that have been in use in forensic microbiology are discussed below.

Microbial cultures

The method of bacterial culture was originally invented by Louis Pasteur in 1860 (1–3) and later by Robert Koch (4) in the 1881 (Table 94.2). Culture is still the gold standard in microbiology diagnostics and serves as the basis for the choice of antibiotic treatment.

In a culture, the microorganisms reproduce in a specific medium under controled conditions and can be isolated and identified morphologically or by a variety of serologic, immunologic, or chemical-based techniques. The microorganisms can be cultured on liquid medium contained in flasks or in solid media, such as agar, in petri dishes or tubes. Cultures for various microorganisms have different qualities and specificities. For selective growth of bacterial species, the cultures contain specific additives (nutrition and cofactors), whereas virus cultures rely on specific host cells for virus multiplication. International microbial culture collections are maintained and are resources to distribute strains among scientists, serve the scientific community for research and are available as clinical diagnostics in special or rare cases (6–8). Even with the new molecular technologies and their demonstrated advantages, culturing remains as the widely used diagnostic tool for medically relevant microbial infections. A limitation of use of culturing in the context of post-mortem investigation is that it requires a viable microbe which may not be accessible, and the microbe must be culturable. For other forensic applications, such as a bioterrorism attack, where the microbes may not be viable, culturing would not be feasible. For either situation, a drastic limitation is the time required for culturing which may not be suitable for a proper response time and only known microbes can be detected.

Nucleic acid detection and analysis

For medicolegal and judicial purposes, it is desirable to have a rapid diagnostic for microbe detection in autopsies, in cases where infectious disease putatively has a role in the cause of death, for forensic investigations in general, and as part of the public health response system. In fact, medical doctors performing autopsies are part of the sentinel system to detect the first signs of serious infectious disease. The same data can also be of great importance for epidemiologic surveys with community interest. For effective and timely data production, DNA (or RNA)-level analytic capabilities are a necessity, and there are manifold reasons why DNA (RNA)-level analysis is preferable over the traditional culturing. First, a positive or negative result of a suspected microbe can be obtained in an expeditious manner by direct amplification (e.g. PCR) of specific target regions of the targeted microbe's genome. Second, a hierarchical analysis of multitude of microbial genomes present in a sample can be accomplished by DNA/RNA-sequencing specific regions (e.g. by DNA barcoding). Third, microbial whole-genome analysis is possible using the state-of-the-art high-throughput DNA/RNA-sequencing technologies, which allow, in combination with bioinformatics analysis, in theory detailed examination of all microbial species and their quantitative and qualitative relationships in a questioned sample. Fourth, an important application is the enrichment of molecular signatures of the microbes, which allows detection and analysis of trace quantities of microbes in a sample.

Polymerase chain reaction

The polymerase chain reaction (PCR) is an *in vitro* enzymatic assay that generates millions to billions of copies of targeted DNA sequences (93,94). The specificity of the targeted amplification and the million to billion-fold amplified copies promote high sensitivity of detection which allow microscopic amounts of the target genomes to be detected. After PCR amplification, the targeted products are analyzed using various downstream methods. These methods include, for example, analysis of specific restriction sites, size separation of amplicons, enzymatic cleavage of specific nucleotide sequences, and hybridization by complementary DNA strands (or probes) (Table 94.3).

PCR with intercalating dyes (102), 5′ exonuclease assay (TaqMan) (103), molecular beacons (104), scorpion primers (105) and dye-labeled oligonucleotide ligation (106) are sophisticated and streamlined technologies which allow detection of microbial DNA directly during the PCR, and thus can enable rapid detection with the ancillary benefit of reducing contamination risk. The limiting factor with such real-time detection systems is that only a few targets (i.e. microbial genes or anonymous sequences) can be analyzed simultaneously.

While PCR-based technologies afford notable advantages, there are limitations that must be taken into consideration to effectively analyze forensic microbiology samples. First, inhibition of the amplification during PCR is a common phenomenon due to chemicals that are co-purified with nucleic acids. Therefore, additional sample cleanup or enrichment of microbes prior to PCR may be needed, making the procedure more laborious and longer as well as more susceptible to contamination (107). Alternatively, additives to buffers used in downstream analyses may overcome some effects of inhibition. Second, a sample may consist of several species or heterogeneous strains, which may compete for the reagents (primarily primers and dNTPs) that may lead to unbalanced PCR amplification products or result in no amplification of the desired target. The original Sanger DNA-sequencing method (108), used routinely until about a decade ago, did not offer sufficient resolution to characterize complex, post-mortem samples which often consist of numerous and wide-ranging microbial sequences. Most importantly, none of these traditional PCR-based methods had the capability to analyze "the

TABLE 94.3 Typical laboratory methods used after PCR-amplification for microbial DNA analysis

Year	Technology	Author(s) (reference)
1985	Restriction fragment length polymorphism analysis	Saiki et al. (93)
1987	Gel electrophoresis	Mullis and Faloona (94)
1988	Ligase-mediated gene detection	Landegren et al. (95)
1989	(Reverse) dot blot arrays	Saiki et al. (96)
1990	Primer extension or mini-sequencing assay	Syvänen et al. (97)
1991	Capillary electrophoresis	Schwartz et al. (98)
1992	Mass spectrometry	Schieltz et al. (99)
1994	High-performance liquid chromatography	Oefner et al. (100)
1995	DNA-chip array systems	Schena et al. (101)
2005	PCR enrichment-based next-generation sequencing	Margulies et al. (23)
		Shendure et al. (24)

unknown" sample; specifically designed primers to *a priori* known target regions are required for the amplification process. Therefore, if the assay is not designed for the etiologic agent, the result will be negative and possibly an incorrect conclusion may arise. Targeted PCR-based assays are not well suited for routine forensic microbiology or large-scale epidemiologic screening since they require *a priori* knowledge to design the primers for targeted amplification.

Multilocus sequence typing

The principle of multilocus sequence typing (MLST) is simple: the technique involves PCR amplification followed by DNA sequencing of relative short fragments (~400–500 bp) of several housekeeping genes (30). In MLST, the different sequence variations within a housekeeping gene observed across various bacterial species are assigned allele designations. The combination of alleles from the targeted housekeeping genes define an allelic profile characteristic of a species. The number of genes analyzed for genetic differences depends on the degree of discrimination desired for the microbes. The degree of relatedness of isolates is determined by the genetic similarity of allelic profiles housed in a database. The comparison and interpretation processes rely heavily on bioinformatics for final assessment. The MLST technique was originally developed for diagnostics of *Neisseria meningitidis*, the etiologic agent for meningococcal meningitis and septicemia (30), but later it was successfully used to identify a wide range of healthcare-related microorganisms, such as *Campylobacter*, *Staphylococcus aureus*, *Streptococcus pyogenes* and *Candida albicans*. The advantages of MLST are that it is highly unambiguous and portable, allows material and data exchange among laboratories, and can be automated for high-throughput data production. A limitation of the practical use of MLST is that because housekeeping genes are conserved, it lacks the necessary resolution and hence discriminatory power needed in forensic and epidemiologic investigations.

Barcoding

DNA barcoding (32) is a specifically designed targeted PCR amplification for attribution purposes. DNA barcoding uses primers targeting designated part(s) of a specific gene or genes common to all members of a kingdom, and the method identifies an organism to the species level by database searches or phylogenetic methods (32,109). The method has gained an international status with proponents (110) supporting an Internet-based informatics workbench system for taxonomists; The Barcode of Life Data System (boldsystems.org) (111–113), although there are some critics (114).

Barcoding of microbes is based on microbial phylogeny and taxonomy primarily using the 16S rRNA gene (111), but multiplex barcodes have also been used extensively. The Ribosomal Database Project (RDP) (http://rdp.cme.msu.edu) was created to provide detailed ribosome-related data to the scientific community (115,116). The current version of RDP provides online data analysis, 16S rRNA-derived phylogenetic trees, and aligned and annotated 16S rRNA sequences. RDP consists of close to 3.5 million 16S rRNA sequences. The 16S rRNA gene is useful for this purpose since it is highly conserved, and a DNA barcode can be created for numerous bacterial species. It has been widely studied to assess bacterial phylogenies (117), and it is a useful marker for screening of clinical microbiology samples for infectious agents (118). The 16S rRNA gene is also a marker of interest for identifying human hosts based on their microbiomes for forensic applications (40,119).

Metabarcoding

The idea of the original DNA barcoding analysis was to assess one species at a time that would be processed to the sequence level using a selected genomic region. In practice, DNA extraction was followed by PCR amplification using defined primers and subsequent Sanger sequencing to determine the underlying sequence of the targeted region. In metabarcoding (120), DNA from all the microbes in a specimen is extracted and a specific target(s) is enriched (e.g. using PCR, molecular inversion probes or hybrid capture-based approaches, see for example [121], all microorganisms present in the sample, after which the many short-targeted gene fragments are sequenced by NGS for taxonomic identification. The different enrichment steps are designed to accommodate the chemistry of the various NGS platforms and be amenable to potentially degraded samples. These technologies also allow multiple bulk samples to be analyzed simultaneously using specifically indexed short sequences (also known as barcodes) for each sample. The simultaneously analyzed samples' sequence data can be sorted using bioinformatics tools, and the DNA barcode reference database can be searched to facilitate species identification. This technical approach has been called metagenomics (Figure 94.2).

In general, metabarcoding is a set of techniques, with an objective to determine the makeup of a microbial population that can be found in a specified environment and studied in the context of its community (122). When using the latest high-throughput sequencing chemistry and platforms, the benefits of metagenomics approaches are that they allow 1) large-scale genomic analysis in order to obtain the maximum resolution for species identification, and 2) different samples to be sequenced simultaneously. Sophisticated bioinformatic pipelines are needed to select, clean, parse and make quality checks on the sequence output, and identify the species in the reference database(s). In forensic microbiology, metagenomics is highly suited to identify the "unknown(s)" from samples in which multiple species of importance can be expected to be detected or in samples that are highly complex and the potential causal agent is not the most abundant species.

The most reliable way to define the microbes in any sample is to analyze the full or partial genomes at the sequence level so that even close species can be resolved. There have been three waves of advancements in the nucleic-acid sequencing technologies that have made possible and, at the same time, changed the effectiveness,

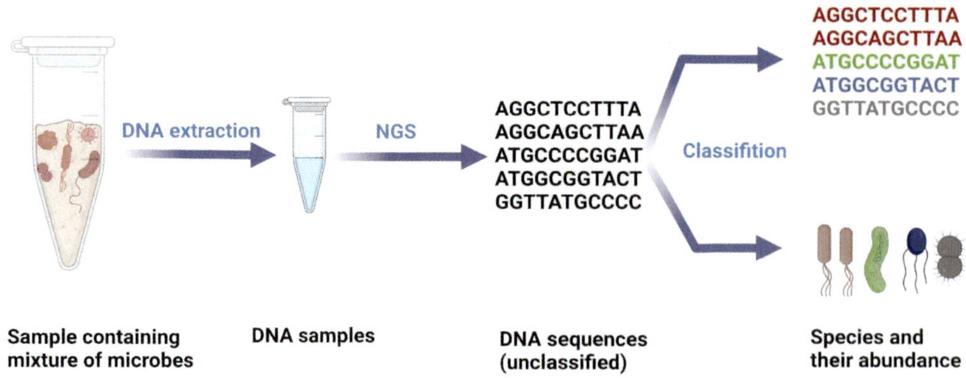

94.2 Simplified laboratory process of metagenomic microbial DNA analysis using next-generation sequencing (NGS). The result is expressed as the microbial species classification and the abundance of each microbe. (Created with Biorender.com.)

scale and speed of how molecular level signature are obtained for basic science and diagnostics that we know today.

High-throughput nucleic acid-sequencing technologies

In 1977, Sanger and his co-workers developed the first DNA-sequencing method using a chain-termination procedure (108), which became the standard until the 2000s. This first-generation DNA-sequencing method (Sanger sequencing) relied on electrophoretic separation of DNA strands of different lengths produced in the assay, and on radioactive labeling and autoradiography to detect the fragments (108, 123). The method was developed further by the change to fluorescently labeled sequencing primers (124,125) or dideoxy terminators (126) and electrophoresis in a semi-automated capillary-based instrument as opposed to manual slab gel formats (127).

In the early 2000s, several novel high-throughput DNA-sequencing chemistries and commercial platforms were developed (128). These technologies are known as the NGS, massively parallel sequencing (MPS) or more generally as second-generation sequencing methods. The great advantages of these NGS technologies over the Sanger sequencing method is that they have substantially higher throughput and are highly scalable such that an entire genome of specific or a variety of species can be sequenced in a single run. But just as importantly, is that the speed, cost and labor of sequencing dropped dramatically with NGS which enabled such analyses to be implemented into routine diagnostic laboratories.

The general process of NGS is that the genome(s) is fragmented into small DNA pieces, which have various short segments added to facilitate cloning of the fragments and to prepare these fragments for sequencing, and all prepared fragments are cloned in a massively parallel fashion *in vitro*. Subsequently, the cloned fragments are sequenced, again, in a massively parallel fashion, using chemistry applicable to the system the laboratory obtained. In NGS, a multitude of fragments are individually and simultaneously sequenced. Millions to billions of sequences are randomly generated then are "patched" together to reconstruct the original target or genome through use of bioinformatics (128,129).

A third wave of DNA-sequencing technologies are based on single-molecule detection chemistries and platforms, such as PacBio (130,131) and Nanopore sequencing (132,133). These technologies have the capability of a real-time detection of single-DNA molecules and no DNA-template amplification or enrichment are needed, although enrichment can be applied if desired. In theory, the third-generation technologies reduce copy errors generated by the amplification process, sequence-dependent biases and information loss, which have been related to the second-generation NGS platforms (128,134,135). However, they have their own rates of sequencing error that are typically higher than those of the second-generation technologies.

Many microbes, especially viruses, consist of an RNA-genome. RNA molecules can also be sequenced using NGS-modified chemistries (136), and these methods have been applied for single-cell RNA sequencing (137). RNA sequencing has not yet been used widely in forensic microbiology, but its usefulness can be anticipated. Indeed, degraded samples have been successfully analyzed from dead RNA-viruses in human tissues in the ancient DNA research (e.g. 1918 influenza pandemic) (138) to reconstruct the epidemiology of, for example, past pandemics. There are a number of infectious agents where RNA sequencing could be critical for today's epidemiologic investigations, including Ebola hemorrhagic fever, Severe Acute Respiratory Syndrome (SARS), Middle East Respiratory Syndrome (MERS), rabies, common cold, influenza, hepatitis C, HIV, West Nile fever, polio, measles, and perhaps as the best current example, COVID-19/SARS-CoV-2.

STANDARDS AND STANDARDIZATION

In order to be of diagnostic and judicial value, the methods applied in forensic microbiology need to have standards and be standardized. As described above, the efforts toward this goal have been ambitious in the early history of post-mortem work by some authors. A new systematic effort is currently underway at an organizational level. In 2014, the European Society of Clinical Microbiology and Infectious Diseases (ESCMID) (139) created a study group for forensic and post-mortem microbiology (ESGFOR). The ESGFOR has the aims 1) to promote standardization and research in the field of forensic microbiology, and 2) to establish European guidance for standardized microbiological sampling, testing methods and interpretation of results in forensic investigations. In addition, ESGFOR promotes cooperation among microbiologists, pathologists and other specialists with shared common interests in public health and prevention of preventable causes of death. ESGFOR also engages in scientific studies on post-mortem standardization (140).

Methodological validation is a critical point before applying any method to case work. Validation is the process that:

- Assesses the ability of procedures to obtain reliable results under defined conditions
- Rigorously defines the conditions required to obtain the results
- Determines the limitations of the procedures
- Identifies aspects of the analysis that must be monitored and controled
- Forms the basis for development of interpretation guidelines to convey the significance of the findings (78)

In forensic microbiology, it is important to note that the data, even produced post-mortem, are sensitive information that can affect health, life and freedom at an individual, family and community level. The information can also aid making policy decisions and actions taken by governments on a larger, societal scale. Taking that perspective, results obtained in each step, including the limitations of the technology, of the analyses (collection, transfer, technology used, and interpretation) must be understood. Budowle et al. (78) stressed that failure to properly validate a method or to misinterpret the results from a microbial forensic analysis or process may have unwanted consequences. For more specific and sophisticated laboratory techniques, Budowle et al. (79) described criteria for validation of high-throughput DNA-sequencing procedures. The criteria are common to the endeavors such as those for human genome sequencing and clinical diagnostics. Three common areas of these new technologies include:

- sample preparation
- sequencing
- data analysis; and these criteria are defined for each specific application

It is noteworthy that the possible number of microorganisms used as potential bioweapons is large, and even an experienced forensic pathologist may never have encountered any or all of these microorganisms and also may never have been involved in a criminal investigation. These limitations raise the need for forensic pathology institutions to have resources to establish practices, diagnostics and chain of custody. In case such a suspicion rises, the sample integrity is critical and thus correct sampling, packing, storage and transport procedures need to be carefully described and, when possible, customized according to the tissue type and suspected agent. Failures in this regard may promote post-mortem growth of commensal or environmental microbes or degrade and damage the sample. The process is increasingly complicated if the causative agent is not the one suspected during sampling. Currently, no universally applicable protocol(s) exists, and more studies are needed to develop effective ones.

CONCLUSION

Forensic microbiology relies on the key concepts that were founded in the later nineteenth and early twentieth centuries for post-mortem cause-of-death investigations. The arrival of new molecular, high-throughput DNA/RNA-sequencing technologies and concomitant bioinformatics tools, which have been developed in the first decades of the twenty-first century, and continue to be developed at quite rapid speeds, have made it possible to address many of the challenges posed in the early works of post-mortem microbiology.

The new areas of forensic microbiology extend now from autopsy work to, for example, bioterrorism, transmission of infective agents in rape and medical malpractice cases and provenance of unidentified cadavers. The forensic microbiology community benefits greatly from the international HMP, its progress in understanding of the human (living) microbiome and the crosstalk between human host cells and the microbiome resident in and on tissues and organ systems. Recently, the analytical capacity has progressed in forensic microbiology from bacteria-oriented studies to also include the analysis of human viruses (i.e. the virome) with new and interesting prospects. Overall, it is likely that with all the advancements of technology forensic microbiology is gaining new impact in forensic medicine and forensic sciences on a grander scale.

REFERENCES

1. Pasteur L. Mémoire sur la fermentation appelée lactique. *Ann Chim Phys* 1858; 58: 323–26.
2. Pasteur L, Joubert J, Chamberland C. La théorie des germes es ses applications à la médecine. *Bull Acad Med* 1878; 7: 432–53.
3. Pasteur L. De l'extension de la théorie des germes à l'étiologie de quelques maladies communes. *C R Acad Sci* 1880; 90: 1033–44.
4. Carter KC. translator. *Essays of Robert Koch*. Connecticut: Greenwood Press; 1987.
5. Uruburu F. History and services of culture collections. *Int Microbiol* 2003; 6(2): 101–3.
6. Boundy-Mills K, Hess M, Bennett AR, et al. The United States culture collection network (USCCN): Enhancing microbial genomics research through living microbe culture collections. *Appl Environ Microbiol* 2015; **81**(**17**): 5671–4.
7. Casaregola S, Vasilenko A, Romano P, et al. An information system for European culture collections: The way forward. *Springerplus* 2016; **5**(**1**): 772.
8. Bonnet M, Lagier JC, Raoult D, Khelaifia S. Bacterial culture through selective and non-selective conditions: The evolution of culture media in clinical

microbiology. *New Microbes New Infect* 2020; **34**: 100622.
9. Achard C, Phulpin E. L'envahissement des organs par les microbes pendant l'agonie et apres la mort. *Arch Med Exp* 1895; 7: 25–47.
10. Gradwohl R. Importance de l'examen bacteriologique pratique sur les cadavres. *Ann Inst Pasteur* 1904; **18**: 767–73.
11. Fredette J. Bacteremias in the agonal period. *J Lab Clin Med* 1916; **2**: 180–8.
12. Giordano A, Barnes A. Studies in postmortem bacteriology: Value and importance of cultures made postmortem. *J Lab Clin Med* 1922; **7**: 538–46.
13. Burn C. Postmortem bacteriology. *J Infect Dis* 1933; **54(3)**: 395–403.
14. Carpenter H, Wilkins R. Studies in autopsy bacteriology. *Arch Patol* 1964; 77: 73–81.
15. O'Toole W, Saxena H, Golden A, Ritts R. Studies of postmortem microbiology using sterile autopsy technique. *Arch Pathol* 1965; **80(5)**: 540–7.
16. Wood WH, Oldstone M, Schultz RB. A re-evalutation of blood culture as an autopsy procedure. *Am J Clin Pathol* 1965; **43**: 241–7.
17. Minckler T, Newell G, O'Toole W, et al. Microbiology experience in collection of human tissue. *Am J Clin Pathol* 1966; **45**: 85–91.
18. Roberts FJ. A review of postmortem bacteriological cultures. *Can Med Assoc J* 1969; **100(2)**: 70–4.
19. Koneman E, Davis M. Postmortem bacteriology. 3. Clinical significance of microorganisms recovered at autopsy. *Am J Clin Pathol* 1974; **61**: 28–40.
20. Kurtin J. Studies in autopsy bacteriology. *Am J Clin Pathol* 1958; **30**: 239–43.
21. Huttenhower C, Gevers D, Knight R, et al. Structure, function and diversity of the healthy human microbiome. *Nature* 2012; **486(7402)**: 207–14.
22. Methé BA, Nelson KE, Pop M, et al. A framework for human microbiome research. *Nature* 2012; **486(7402)**: 215–21.
23. Margulies M, Egholm M, Altman WE, et al. Genome sequencing in microfabricated high-density picolitre reactors. *Nature* 2005; **437(7057)**: 376–80.
24. Shendure J, Porreca GJ, Reppas NB, et al. Accurate multiplex polony sequencing of an evolved bacterial genome. *Science* 2005; **309(5741)**:1728–32.
25. Lander ES, Linton LM, Birren B, et al. Initial sequencing and analysis of the human genome: International human genome sequencing consortium. *Nature* 2001; **412(6846)**: 565–6.
26. Craig Venter J, Adams MD, Myers EW, et al. The sequence of the human genome. *Science* 2001; **291(5507)**: 1304–51.
27. Turnbaugh PJ, Ley RE, Hamady M, et al. The human microbiome project. *Nature* 2007; 449(7164): 804–10.
28. Ou CY, Ciesielski CA, Myers G, et al. Molecular epidemiology of HIV transmission in a dental practice. *Science* 1992; **256(5060)**: 1165–71.
29. Albert J, Wahlberg J, Leitner T, et al. Analysis of a rape case by direct sequencing of the human immunodeficiency virus type 1 pol and gag genes. *J Virol* 1994; **68(9)**: 5918–24.
30. Maiden MCJ, Bygraves JA, Feil E, et al. Multilocus sequence typing: A portable approach to the identification of clones within populations of pathogenic microorganisms. *Proc Natl Acad Sci* USA 1998; **95(6)**: 3140–5.
31. Bush LM, Abrams BH, Beall A, Johnson CC. Index case of fatal inhalational anthrax due to bioterrorism in the United States. *N Engl J Med* 2001; **345(22)**: 1607–10.
32. Hebert PDN, Cywinska A, Ball SL, Dewaard JR. Biological identifications through DNA barcodes. *Proc R Soc Lond* 2003; **270**: 313–21.
33. Taberlet P, Coissac E, Pompnon F, et al. Towards next-generation biodiversity assessment using DNA metabarcoding. *Mol Ecol* 2012; **21**: 2045–50.
34. Tyson GW, Chapman J, Hugenholtz P, et al. Community structure and metabolism through reconstruction of microbial genomes from the environment. *Nature* 2004; **428**: 37–43.
35. Scaduto DI, Brown JM, Haaland WC, et al. Source identification in two criminal cases using phylogenetic analysis of HIV-1 DNA sequences. *Proc Natl Acad Sci* USA 2010; **107(50)**: 21242–7.
36. Brenig B, Beck J, Schütz E. Shotgun metagenomics of biological stains using ultra-deep DNA sequencing. *Forensic Sci Int Genet* 2010; **4(4)**: 228–31.
37. Fleming RI, Harbison S. The use of bacteria for the identification of vaginal secretions. *Forensic Sci Int Genet* 2010; **4(5)**: 311–15.
38. Fierer N, Lauber CL, Zhou N, et al. Forensic identification using skin bacterial communities. *Proc Natl Acad Sci USA* 2010; 107(14): 6477–81.
39. González-Candelas F, Bracho MA, Wróbel B, Moya A. Molecular evolution in court: Analysis of a large hepatitis C virus outbreak from an evolving source. *BMC Biol* 2013; **11**: 76.
40. Metcalf JL, Wegener Parfrey L, Gonzalez A, et al. A microbial clock provides an accurate estimate of the postmortem interval in a mouse model system. *Elife* 2013; **2**: 1–19.
41. Toppinen M, Perdomo MF, Palo JU, et al. Bones hold the key to DNA virus history and epidemiology. *Sci Rep* 2015; 70(1): S81.
42. Belkaid Y, Hand TW. Role of the microbiota in immunity and inflammation. *Cell* 2014; **157(1)**: 121–41.
43. Rooks MG, Garrett WS. Gut microbiota, metabolites and host immunity. *Nat Rev Immunol* 2016; **16(6)**: 341–52.
44. Zheng D, Liwinski T, Elinav E. Interaction between microbiota and immunity in health and disease. *Cell Res* 2020; 30(6): 492–506.
45. Andersen BM. Dangerous Microbes. In: Andersen BM (ed), *Prevention and Control of Infections in Hospitals*. Cham: Springer; 2019, pp. 1021–8.
46. O'Driscoll M, Ribeiro Dos Santos G, Wang L, et al. Age-specific mortality and immunity patterns of SARS-CoV-2. *Nature* 2021; **590(7844)**: 140–5.
47. Gudbjartsson DF, Helgason A, Jonsson H, et al. Spread of SARS-CoV-2 in the Icelandic population. *N Engl J Med* 2020; **382(24)**: 2302–15.
48. Scarselli M, Giuliani MM, Adu-Bobie J, et al. The impact of genomics on vaccine design. *Trends Biotechnol* 2005; **23(2)**: 84–91.
49. Krammer F. SARS-CoV-2 vaccines in development. *Nature* 2020; **586**: 516–27.
50. Brockhurst MA, Colegrave N, Rozen DE. Next-generation sequencing as a tool to study microbial evolution. *Mol Ecol* 2011; **20(5)**: 972–80.
51. Hurtado JC, Quintó L, Castillo P, et al. Postmortem interval and diagnostic performance of the autopsy methods. *Sci Rep* 2018; 8(1): 16112.
52. Smith RF, Linares HA, Jorgensen JH. Bacteremia and postmortem microbiology in burned children. *Am J Clin Pathol* 1975; **63(4)**: 502–8.
53. Kellerma G, Waterman N, Scharfenberger M. Demonstration in vitro of postmortem bacterial transmigration. *Am J Clin Pathol* 1976; **66(5)**: 911–15.
54. Tuomisto S, Karhunen P, Vuento R, et al. Evaluation of postmortem bacterial migration using culturing and real-time quantitative PCR. *J Forensic Sci* 2013; **58(4)**: 910–16.
55. Andrion A, Pira E. What's new in managing health hazards in pathology departments. *Pathol Res Pract* 1994; **190(12)**: 1214–23.
56. Nolte KB, Taylor DG, Richmond JY. Biosafety considerations for autopsy. *Am J Forensic Med Pathol* 2002; **23**: 107–22.
57. Dettmeyer R, Baasner A, Schlamann M, et al. Role of virus-induced myocardial affections in sudden infant death syndrome: A prospective postmortem study. *Pediatr Res* 2004; **55(6)**: 947–52.
58. Pietsch H, Escher F, Aleshcheva G, et al. Detection of parvovirus mRNAs as markers for viral activity in endomyocardial biopsy-based diagnosis of patients with unexplained heart failure. *Sci Rep* 2020; **10(1)**: 22354.
59. Pyöriä L, Pratas D, Toppinen M, et al. Unmasking the tissue-resident eukaryotic DNA virome in humans. *Nucleic Acids Res* 2023; **51(7)**: 3223–39.
60. Lunetta P, Penttilä A, Sajantila A. Circumstances and macropathologic findings in 1590 consecutive cases of bodies found in water. *Am J Forensic Med Pathol* 2002; **23(4)**: 371–6.
61. Lunetta P, Smith GS, Penttilä A, Sajantila A. Unintentional drowning in Finland 1970–2000: A population-based study. *Int J Epidemiol* 2004; **33(5)**: 1053–63.
62. Lunetta P, Penttilä A, Hällfors G. Scanning and transmission electron microscopical evidence of the capacity of diatoms to penetrate the alveolo-capillary barrier in drowning. *Int J Legal Med* 1998; **111(5)**: 229–37.
63. Lunetta P, Miettinen A, Spilling K, Sajantila A. False-positive diatom test: A real challenge? A post-mortem study using standardized protocols. *Leg Med* 2013; **15(5)**: 229–34.
64. Liu M, Zhao Y, Sun Y, et al. Diatom DNA barcodes for forensic discrimination of drowning incidents. *FEMS Microbiol Lett* 2020; **367**: 145.
65. Burton JL. Health and safety at necropsy. *J Clin Pathol* 2003; **56**: 254–60.
66. Flavin RJ, Gibbons N, O'Briain DS. Mycobacterium tuberculosis at autopsy - exposure and protection: An old adversary revisited. *J Clin Pathol* 2007; **60(5)**: 487–91.

67. Fritzsche FR, Ramach C, Soldini D, et al. Occupational health risks of pathologists - results from a nationwide online questionnaire in Switzerland. *BMC Public Health* 2012; **12(1)**: 1054.
68. Shkrum MJ, Kent J. An autopsy checklist: A monitor of safety and risk management. *Am J Forensic Med Pathol* 2016; **37(3)**: 152–7.
69. Bhattacharjee Y. Biodefense: Army halts work at lab after finding untracked material. *Science* 2009; **323(5916)**: 861.
70. Puro V, De Carli G, Petrosillo N, Ippolito G. Risk of exposure to bloodborne infection for Italian healthcare workers, by job category and work area. *Infect Control Hosp Epidemiol* 2001; **22(4)**: 206–10.
71. Henssge C, Madea B. Estimation of the time since death. *Forensic Sci Int* 2007; **165(2–3)**: 182–4.
72. Morris JA, Harrison LM, Partridge SM. Practical and theoretical aspects of postmortem bacteriology. *Curr Diagnostic Pathol* 2007; **13(1)**: 65–74.
73. Metcalf JL, Xu ZZ, Weiss S, et al. Mammalian corpse decomposition. *Science* 2016; **351(6269)**: 158–62.
74. Keim P, Budowle B, Ravel J. Microbial *Forensic Investigation of the Anthrax-Letter Attacks*. In: Budowle B, Schutzer S, Breeze R, Keim P, Morse SA (eds), Microbial Forensics, 2nd ed. Amsterdam: Academic Press; 2011, pp. 15–25.
75. Read TD, Salzberg SL, Pop M, et al. Comparative genome sequencing for discovery of novel polymorphisms in Bacillus anthracis. *Science* 2002; **296(5575)**: 2028–33.
76. Budowle B, Schutzer SE, Einseln A, et al. Building microbial forensics as a response to bioterrorism. *Science* 2003; **301**; 1852–3.
77. Hawley RJ, Eitzen EM. Biological weapons – a primer for microbiologists. *Annu Rev Microbiol* 2001; 55: 235–53.
78. Budowle B, Schutzer SE, Morse SA, et al. Criteria for validation of methods in microbial forensics. *Appl Environ Microbiol* 2008; **74**: 5599–607.
79. Budowle B, Connell ND, Bielecka-Oder A, et al. Validation of high throughput sequencing and microbial forensics applications. *Investig Genet* 2014; **5**: 9.
80. Price EP, Seymour ML, Sarovich DS, et al. Molecular epidemiologic investigation of an anthrax outbreak among heroin users, Europe. *Emerg Infect Dis* 2012; **18(8)**: 1307–13.
81. Chin C-S, Sorenson J, Harris JB, et al. The origin of the Haitian cholera outbreak strain. *N Engl J Med* 2011; **364(1)**: 33–42.
82. Grad YH, Lipsitch M, Feldgarden M, et al. Genomic epidemiology of the Escherichia coli O104:H4 outbreaks in Europe, 2011. *Proc Natl Acad Sci U S A* 2012; **109(8)**: 3065–70.
83. Kucharski AJ, Russell TW, Diamond C, et al. Early dynamics of transmission and control of COVID-19: A mathematical modelling study. *Lancet Infect Dis* 2020; **20(5)**: 553–8.
84. Zhou P, Yang X, Wang X, et al. A pneumonia outbreak associated with a new coronavirus of probable bat origin. *Nature* 2020; **579**: 270–3.
85. Armengaud J. The proteomics contribution to the counter-bioterrorism toolbox in the post-COVID-19 era. *Expert Rev Proteomics* 2020; **17(7–8)**: 507–11.
86. Pöhlmann C, Elßner T. Toxins multiplex immunoassay techniques for on-site detection of security sensitive toxins. Available from: www.mdpi.com/journal/toxins (Accessed 22 June 2023).
87. Bragg WA, Lemire SW, Coleman RM, et al. Detection of human exposure to saxitoxin and neosaxitoxin in urine by online-solid phase extraction-liquid chromatography-tandem mass spectrometry. *Toxicon* 2015; **99**: 118–24.
88. Kreuzer-Martin HW, Jarman KH. Stable isotope ratios and forensic analysis of microorganisms. *Appl Environ Microbiol* 2007; **73(12)**: 3896–908.
89. Lemey P, Van Dooren S, Van Laethem K, et al. Molecular testing of multiple HIV-1 transmissions in a criminal case. *AIDS* 2005; **19(15)**: 1649–58.
90. Birch CJ, McCaw RF, Bulach DM, et al. Molecular analysis of human immunodeficiency virus strains associated with a case of criminal transmission of the virus. *J Infect Dis* 2000; **182(3)**: 941–4.
91. Machuca R, Jørgensen LB, Theilade P, Nielsen C. Molecular investigation of transmission of human immunodeficiency virus type 1 in a criminal case. *Clin Diagn Lab Immunol* 2001; 8(5): 884–90.
92. Metzker ML, Mindell DP, Liu XM, et al. Molecular evidence of HIV-1 transmission in a criminal case. *Proc Natl Acad Sci U S A* 2002; **99(22)**: 14292–7.
93. Saiki RK, Scharf S, Faloona F, et al. Enzymatic amplification of beta-globin genomic sequences and restriction site analysis for diagnosis of sickle cell anemia. *Science* 1985; **230(4732)**: 1350–4.
94. Mullis KB, Faloona F. Specific synthesis of DNA in vitro via a polymerase-catalyzed chain reaction. *Methods Enzymol* 1987; **155**: 335–50.
95. Landegren U, Kaiser R, Sanders J, Hood L. A ligase-mediated gene detection technique. *Science* 1988; **241(4869)**: 1077–80.
96. Saiki RK, Walsh PS, Levenson CH, Erlich HA. Genetic analysis of amplified DNA with immobilized sequence-specific oligonucleotide probes. *Proc Natl Acad Sci U S A* 1989; **86(16)**: 6230–4.
97. Syvänen A-C, Aalto-Setälä K, Harju L, et al. A primer-guided nucleotide incorporation in the genotyping of apolipoprotein assay. *Genomics* 1990; **8**: 684–92.
98. Schwartz HE, Ulfelder K, Sunzeri FJ, et al. Analysis of DNA restriction fragments and polymerase chain reaction products towards detection of the AIDS (HIV-l) virus in blood. *J Chromatogr* 1991; **559(1–2)**: 267–83.
99. Schieltz DM, Chou C-W, Luo C-W, et al. Mass spectrometry of DNA mixtures by laser ablation from frozen aqueous solution. *Rapid Commun Mass Spectrom* 1992; **6(10)**: 631–6.
100. Oefner PJ, Huber CG, Puchhammer-Stockl E, et al. High-performance liquid chromatography for routine analysis of hepatitis C virus cDNA/PCR products. *Biotechniques* 1994; **16(5)**: 898–899.
101. Schena M, Shalon D, Davis RW, Brown PO. Quantitative monitoring of gene expression patterns with a complementary DNA microarray. *Science* 1995; **270(5235)**: 467–70.
102. Higuchi R, Dollinger G, Walsh P, Griffiths R. Simultaneous amplification and detection of specific DNA sequences. *Biotechnol* 1992; **10(4)**: 413–17.
103. Holland PM, Abramson RD, Watson R, Gelfand DH. Detection of specific polymerase chain reaction product by utilizing the 5'---- 3' exonuclease activity of Thermus aquaticus DNA polymerase (ofigonucleotide probe/human immunodeficiency virus). *Proc Natl Acad Sci U S A* 1991; **88(16)**: 7276–80.
104. Tyagi S, Kramer FR. Molecular beacon probes that fluoresce on hybridiztion. *Nat Publ Gr* 1996; **14(3)**: 303–8.
105. Whitcombe D, Theaker J, Guy SP, et al. Detection of PCR products using self-probing amplicons and fluorescence. *Nat Biotechnol* 1999; **17(8)**: 804–17.
106. Chen X, Livak KJ, Kwok PY. A homogeneous, ligase-mediated DNA diagnostic test. *Genome Res* 1998; **8(5)**: 549–56.
107. Vutukuru MR, Sharma DK, Ragavendar MS, et al. A rapid, highly sensitive and culture-free detection of pathogens from blood by positive enrichment. *J Microbiol Methods* 2016; **131**: 105–9.
108. Sanger F, Nicklen S, Coulson AR. DNA sequencing with chain-terminating inhibitors. *Proc Natl Acad Sci USA* 1977; **74(12)**: 5463–7.
109. Savolainen V, Cowan RS, Vogler AP, et al. Towards writing the encyclopaedia of life: An introduction to DNA barcoding. *Philos Trans R Soc Lond B Biol Sci* 2005; **360(1462)**: 1805–11.
110. Schindel DE, Miller SE. Benefits of DNA barcoding. *Nature* 2005; **435**: 17.
111. Woese CR, Fox GE, Zablen L, et al. Conservation of primary structure in 16S ribosomal RNA. *Nature* 1975; **254(5495)**: 83–6.
112. Woese CR, Fox GE. Phylogenetic structure of the prokaryotic domain: The primary kingdoms. *Proc Natl Acad Sci U S A* 1977; **74(11)**: 5088–90.
113. Ratnasingham S, Hebert PDN. BOLD: The barcode of life data system: Barcoding. *Mol Ecol Notes* 2007; 7(3): 355–64.
114. Ebach MC, Holdrege C. DNA barcoding is no substitute for taxonomy. *Nature* 2005; **434**: 697.
115. Olsen GJ, Overbeek R, Larsen N, et al. The ribosomal database project. *Nucleic Acids Res* 1992; 20: 2199–200.
116. Maidak BL, Cole JR, Parker CT, et al. A new version of the RDP (Ribosomal Database Project). *Nucleic Acids Res* 1999; **27**: 171–3.
117. Schloss PD, Handelsman J. Status of the microbial census. *Microbiol Mol Biol Rev* 2004; **68(4)**: 686–91.
118. Clarridge JE. Impact of 16S rRNA gene sequence analysis for identification of bacteria on clinical microbiology and infectious diseases. *Clin Microbiol Rev* 2004; **17**: 840–62.
119. Goga H. Comparison of bacterial DNA profiles of footwear insoles and soles of feet for the forensic discrimination of footwear owners. *Int J Legal Med* 2012; **126(5)**: 815–23.
120. Ji Y, Ashton L, Pedley SM, et al. Reliable, verifiable and efficient monitoring of biodiversity via metabarcoding. *Ecol Lett* 2013; **16(10)**: 1245–57.

121. Mamanova L, Coffey AJ, Scott CE, et al. Target-enrichment strategies for next-generation sequencing. *Nat Methods* 2010; **7(2)**: 111–18.
122. Garrido-Cardenas JA, Manzano-Agugliaro F. The metagenomics worldwide research. *Curr Genet* 2017; **63**: 819–29.
123. Sanger F. The early days of DNA sequences. *Nat Med* 2001; **7(3)**: 267–8.
124. Smith LM, Fung S, Hunkapiller MW, et al. The synthesis of oligonucleotides containing an aliphatic amino group at the 5′ terminus: Synthesis of fluorescent DNA primers for use in DNA sequence analysis. *Nucleic Acids Res* 1985; **13**(7): 2399–412.
125. Ansorge W, Sproat BS, Stegemann J, Schwager C. A non-radioactive automated method for DNA sequence determination. *J Biochem Biophys Methods* 1986; **13**(6): 315–23.
126. Prober JM, Trainor GL, Dam RJ, et al. A system for rapid DNA sequencing with fluorescent chain-terminating dideoxynucleotides. *Science* 1987; **238(4825)**: 336–41.
127. Swerdlow H, Gesteland R. Capillary gel electrophoresis for rapid, high resolution DNA sequencing. *Nucleic Acids Res* 1990; **18**(6): 1415–19.
128. Shendure J, Balasubramanian S, Church GM, et al. DNA sequencing at 40: Past, present and future. *Nature* 2017; **550(7676)**: 345–53.
129. Loman NJ, Pallen MJ. Twenty years of bacterial genome sequencing. *Nat Rev Microbiol* 2015; **13**: 787–94.
130. Levene HJ, Korlach J, Turner SW, et al. Zero-mode waveguides for single-molecule analysis at high concentrations. *Science* 2003; **299(5607)**: 682–6.
131. Eid J, Fehr A, Gray J, et al. Real-time DNA sequencing from single polymerase molecules. *Science* 2009; **323(5910)**: 133–8.
132. Branton D, Deamer DW, Marziali A, et al. The potential and challenges of nanopore sequencing. *Nat Biotechnol* 2008; **26**: 1146–53.
133. Deamer D, Akeson M, Branton D. Three decades of nanopore sequencing. *Nat Biotechnol* 2016; **34**: 518–24.
134. Heather JM, Chain B. The sequence of sequencers: The history of sequencing DNA. *Genomics* 2016; 107: 1–8.
135. Mardis ER. DNA sequencing technologies: 2006–2016. *Nat Protoc* 2017; **12(2)**: 213–18.
136. Marioni JC, Mason CE, Mane SM, et al. RNA-seq: An assessment of technical reproducibility and comparison with gene expression arrays. *Genome Res* 2008; **18**(9): 1509–17.
137. Tang F, Barbacioru C, Wang Y, et al. mRNA-Seq whole-transcriptome analysis of a single cell. *Nat Methods* 2009; **6**(5): 377–82.
138. Taubenberger JK, Reid AH, Krafft AE, et al. Initial genetic characterization of the 1918 "Spanish" influenza virus. *Science* 1997; **275**(5307): 1793–6.
139. The European Society of Clinical Micobiology and Infectious Diseases (ESCMID) Available from: www.escmid.org/research_projects/study_groups/study_groups_a_f/forensicpostmortem_microbio (Accessed 3 July 2023)
140. Fernández-Rodríguez A, Cohen MC, Lucena J, et al. How to optimise the yield of forensic and clinical post-mortem microbiology with an adequate sampling: A proposal for standardisation. *Eur J Clin Microbiol Infect Dis* 2015; 5(**34**): 1045–57.

CHAPTER

95

DNA Analysis in Forensic Investigations

Denise Syndercombe-Court

INTRODUCTION

Since Alec Jeffreys discovered minisatellites in the genome that could be used to produce a virtually unique DNA "fingerprint" (1), DNA technology has been used in civil and criminal justice (CJ) to assist in questions of human identification, enabling perpetrators of crimes to be brought to justice and resolve complex kinship issues.

The early DNA fingerprints, visualized as a series of bands through the use of multilocus probes, proved difficult to interpret and required high (microgram) concentrations of DNA from a single-person source, limiting its usefulness. Modifications to look at a series of single locus probes (2), present only once in a single genome, allowed investigation of mixtures, but it was the combination of the polymerase chain reaction (PCR) (3) and short tandem repeat (STR) loci (4) that has led to the DNA "profile" that continues to form the mainstay of DNA analysis worldwide today. Not only can complex mixtures be analyzed, but it can also be achieved with picogram quantities of DNA – at around a 100-thousand-fold reduction in DNA quantity.

This chapter explores STR typing as applied to criminal cases, including complex mixtures. Applying this methodology to the male Y chromosome has proven exceptionally useful in sexual assault. New technologies that sequence the small, repeated blocks of DNA sequences through massively parallel sequencing will be introduced, as will the application of sequence variations to provide intelligence to assist in cold cases and disaster victim identification (DVI) in both nuclear and mitochondrial DNA. Beyond and more broadly, modifications to the DNA molecule can help answer other unresolved questions, as can the wider comparison of inherited elements across the genome when combined with genealogic information.

THE HUMAN GENOME

The human genome consists of pairs of chromosomes, one of each of the pair being inherited from the individual's respective parents. There are 22 pairs of autosomes (non-sex chromosomes) and an X and Y chromosome, consisting of a sequence of purine (adenine [A] and guanine [G]) or pyrimidine (cytosine [C] and thymine [T]) nucleotides (bases) bound covalently to a sugar phosphate backbone; the covalent bonding helps maintain the sequence along the DNA strand. There are three billion bases in a single copy; only about 2 percent code for proteins, dependent on the sequence of the nucleotides, while the remaining is termed non-coding yet includes a variety of regions that regulate chromosome structure and control gene expression. It is the non-coding DNA that is normally used in forensic analysis.

Each DNA strand is accompanied by a complementary sequence with A and T pairing, and G and C pairing, held together with hydrogen bonds, forming base pairs (bps). The configuration of the bonding provides the helical structure of the molecule (Figure 95.1). In its natural state in the cell, DNA is almost always double-stranded, but it can be separated by enzymes *in vivo*, and this is necessary for replication to occur. Separation of the strands exposes the bases and these can then act as a template for the formation of a new strand from more nucleotide subunits.

Separation of the strands can also be facilitated *in vitro* by an increase in temperature, for example, and it is this process that is utilized in the PCR process, enabling areas of DNA to be copied, a process extensively used in DNA science. The PCR amplification process involves the use of "primers", which are short complementary DNA sequences that bind to a selected area of the single DNA strand, providing a locus for the DNA polymerase enzyme, with free nucleotides in the mix, to produce a copy of the opposite strand, annealing as the temperature cools and producing a copy of each strand. Repeating the process doubles the amount of DNA in each cycle until the available materials are consumed. Introduction of a fluorescent tag at one end of the primer ensures that the colored tag is carried through the PCR process, enabling subsequent detection of the copied sequence.

SHORT TANDEM REPEATS (STRs)

A large proportion of the DNA molecule consists of repeated sequences of variable lengths. Short tandem repeats (STRs) are of particular interest in forensic analysis because the block sequence is very short (Figure 95.2), typically consisting of between (commonly

DOI: 10.1201/9781003138754-99

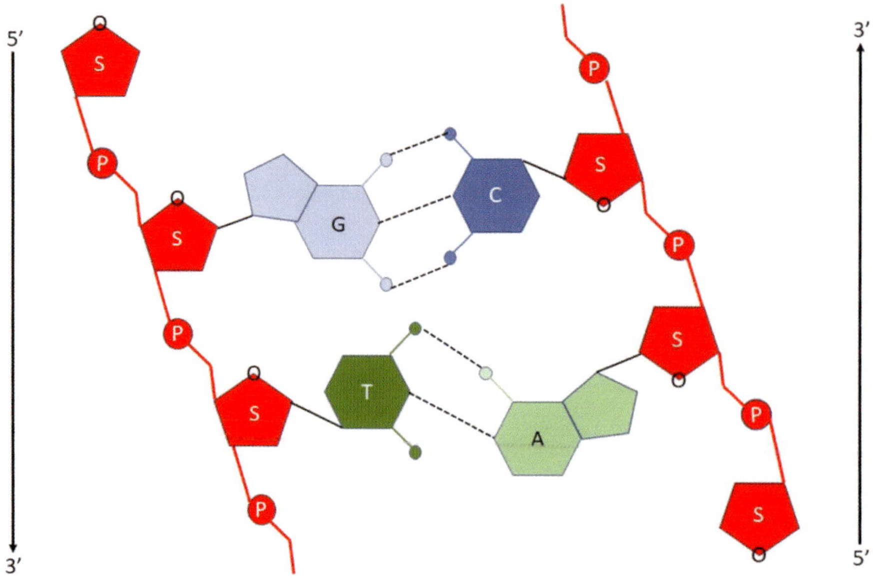

95.1 Chemical structure of the DNA double helix. S: 2-deoxyribose sugar and P: negatively charged phosphate group linked covalently with phosphodiester bonds. G: guanine and A: adenosine, purine nucleotides that form hydrogen bonds with C: cytosine and T: thymine, pyrimidine nucleotides, respectively, forming two linked antiparallel strands.

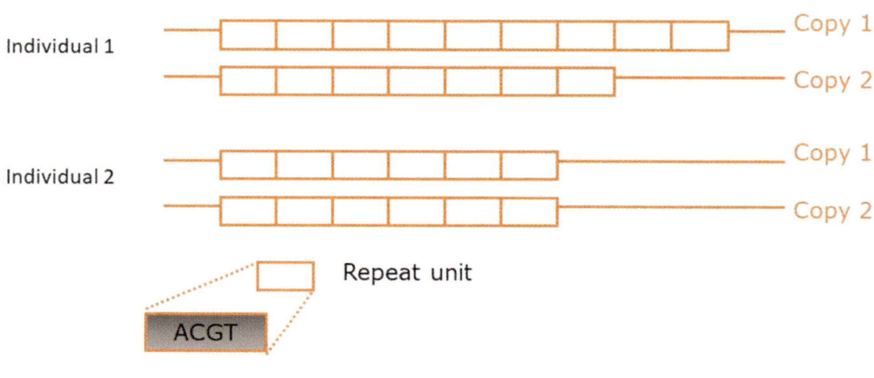

95.2 Illustration of a short tandem repeat locus in a chromosome pair from two individuals. Blocks of 3–5 nucleotides are repeated in tandem; the number of repeated sections being defined as alleles. Individual 1 is heterozygous for two alleles, 7 and 9; individual 2 is homozygous for a pair of 6 alleles.

four nucleotide bases) with the total sequence of tandemly repeated tetranucleotides, the STR, being between about 200 to 500 bp in length. This is important for forensic analysis because often the DNA obtained from a crime scene has degraded, due to hydrolytic cleavage of the sugar in the backbone, or the nucleoside base from environmental factors such as heat, light and moisture with accompanying bacterial growth. All these factors serve to break up the DNA strand such that only short fragment lengths survive to be analyzed.

STRs for forensic use are chosen because, at the selected locus, they are polymorphic in all populations, inherited independently (normally on different chromosomes, or perhaps on different arms of the same chromosome), robust when being multiplied, able to be multiplexed (analyzed together) with other loci, display limited copy artefacts, and have a low mutation rate (5).

Although there may also be some sequence variation within repeat regions, the different polymorphic types (alleles) are named after the number of repeat blocks. For example, the genotype at the region of the DNA illustrated in Figure 95.2 in individual 1 has alleles 7 and 9 and can be said to be heterozygous at this locus, whereas individual 2 appears to have inherited the 6 allele from each parent and is said to be homozygous.

DNA profiling has been used extensively since the Forensic Science Service (FSS) in 1994 developed a multiplex of four STR loci, shortly after being extended to six loci used until 1999, and then replaced by a ten locus test (SGM Plus), which was used until 2014 when the currently applied DNA17 test, consisting of 16 STR loci, and a sex marker, was introduced with the aim of making more of the individual loci as short as possible to enable better identification even if the sample is degraded.

Fluorescently labeled DNA STR fragments produced after amplification are separated and detected using capillary electrophoresis which can detect alleles that differ in length by one bp. Evolutionary processes over time lead to mutations that can produce microvariants, in which not every repeat unit has the same number of nucleotide bases. For example, the TH01 STR has a commonly observed 9.3 which consists of a collection of nine 4-nucleotides plus one unit that has only 3-nucleotides.

Essential to the analytic process is the ability to visualize the results of the PCR targeted amplification. This is facilitated through incorporation of different fluorescent dyes into the primers, which are then multiplied up along with the target DNA and can be detected electronically within an instrument. Fluorescently labeled target amplicons of varying lengths are separated by electrokinetic injection (because DNA molecules are charged) as they move through a very fine long glass capillary. An argon ion laser detector excites the fluorescent dye as it passes through a point in the capillary and the instrument collects information about the time of detection (which is proportional to the length of the fragment being detected) and the wavelength of the fluorescence, which identifies the dye and therefore also the sequence being targeted (6).

Addition of known-sized DNA fragments, labeled with a different dye, in the form of a size standard added to each sample allows calibration of the output to provide the fragment size in bp, and running standard samples alongside one that contains all of the common alleles (an allelic ladder) enables the sizes to be aligned to named alleles, in the form of an electropherogram (Figure 95.3). Most multiplexes also include a sex determinator. Amelogenins are proteins associated with enamel development. There are two virtually identical genes located on the X and Y chromosomes, with one of them having a 6 bp deletion. Targeting this area facilitates determination of sex in the STR analysis, which is revealed by two peaks for males and a single peak for females. Because, in some populations, a deletion of this region on the Y chromosome is observed that would, otherwise, suggest that the profile has originated from a female, the newer STR multiplexes often include STRs or other markers on the Y chromosome that are more distant in order to confirm a male origin.

THE UK NATIONAL DNA DATABASE

Introduced in 1995, the UK National DNA Database (NDNAD), part of the Forensic Information Databases Service (FINDS) was the first national DNA database and is one on the most significant innovations in fighting crime in recent history, providing more than half a million matches to unsolved crimes.

It consists mainly of two databases: profiles of autosomes of DNA from known individuals (CJ samples) with the associated sex indicator, and crime scene DNA data. The Police and Criminal Evidence Act (PACE) 1994 allows the collection of DNA from people suspected of committing a recordable offense, or stopped in relation to a question of terrorism, and from any sample associated with a scene of crime. The database can only be used for prevention or detection of crime, prosecution of a crime, or identifying a deceased person. The different parts of the database are compared daily and matches reported back to the supplying laboratory, who will report this to the police.

The Protection of Freedoms Act (PoFA) 2012, brought in as a result of the S and Marper appeal to the European Court of Human Rights (7) ensures that all CJ samples (distinct from profiles) are destroyed within six months and profiles are only held for a maximum of three years unless the individual has been convicted of a crime, with a few exceptions based on the seriousness of a particular crime or the age of the convicted person.

Key to the success is having a large number of people on the database. Currently, around 6.1 million individual's profiles, (accounting for replicates), around 10 percent of the population, are held on the reference database although this is biased toward the lower age range males in the population. Non-white individuals are, controversially, disproportionately represented.

If there is a complete match between the CJ profile and that from a crime scene sample, a full match is declared. Statistical assessments of allele frequencies allow scientists to say that it is around one billion times more likely that the profile has originated from the named individual than another unknown person unrelated to that individual. This statistic is known as a likelihood ratio (LR). Many crime scene profiles, however, have fewer designated alleles because of degradation leading to partial profiles and a lower LR, reducing the strength of evidence that a particular individual has contributed.

LOW LEVEL DNA

DNA analysis from a few cells such as might be deposited through touch, provides its own challenges due to stochastic effects which may lead to loss of alleles from a profile. This can be caused by an unequal sampling of the alleles in the early part of the PCR process, resulting in some alleles being over-represented and others being under-represented. This produces locus imbalance or total loss of the allele; the latter being known as drop-out.

DNA CONTAMINATION

Contamination of a DNA sample with DNA from another source is obviously problematic and may be overt or seen only at a very low level within an analysis (drop-in). The high sensitivity of DNA analysis today means that the unwanted presence of only a few cells from another source can be detected, producing an apparent mixture within a sample. Being able to differentiate this contamination from a true mixture is important and measures to avoid potential contamination are vital.

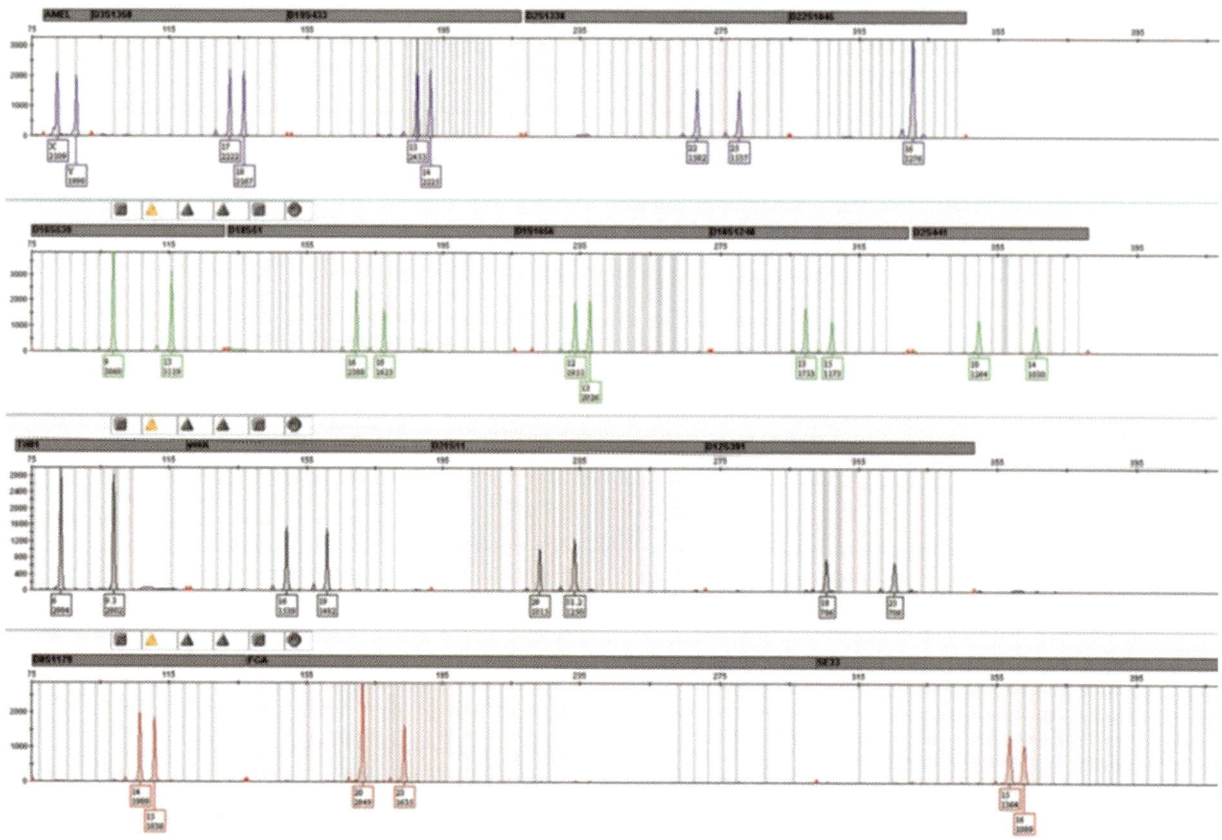

95.3 Electropherogram of a DNA-17 profile from a male consisting of 16 STRs and the amelogenin sex indicator.

DNA MIXTURES

The aim of a forensic scientist when analyzing material collected from a crime scene is to find profiles of interest to the police. Inevitably, the material recovered can also include DNA from innocent people and adventitious transfer from innocents must always be considered when interpreting the data.

The attribution of DNA components to a particular individual can sometimes be problematic. Figures 95.4 and 95.5 show two examples of mixtures, typical of the casework that a scientist will be asked to interpret.

In Figure 95.4, the mixture is recognized by the presence of more than two alleles at any one locus (one individual can provide a maximum of two alleles), and the very unbalanced pairs of loci in some areas. It is not possible to say that there is DNA from only two people in the mixture because more people could have provided the same alleles and their individual contribution will be hidden under the peak. Examination of the profile, however, reveals some more prominent components and it may be possible to suggest that these have come from one individual, in this case most likely a female.

In contrast, in Figure 95.5, the mixture is much more complex and it is not possible to separate out the individual profiles. Here, the Y component is at least as strong as the X component, suggesting that the mixture is predominantly from males but a female could not be excluded with any certainty as that individual may have only contributed a small amount to the mixture and, anyway, all profiles are vulnerable to "stochastic" processes that produce imbalance, especially in cases where the DNA is of poor quality or low in quantity.

In order to analyze DNA mixtures without interpretive bias, scientists will typically employ probabilistic statistical approaches that will consider the likely number of contributors along with their likely respective contributions and profiles (8).

SEQUENCED DNA FOR FORENSIC ANALYSIS

While STRs have been the mainstay of forensic DNA typing for many years, developments in sequencing technology are finding a place in forensic analysis (9). Variations in sequences between individuals are described as single-nucleotide polymorphisms (SNPs).

Sequencing was traditionally undertaken using Sanger sequencing, developed in the late 1970s. Massively parallel sequencing (MPS) is a technologic innovation in which DNA is fragmented, producing a "library" of fragments that ligate to complementary sequences of DNA bound to a substrate, such as to a glass slide (Figure 95.6), or to a bead in an emulsion. Miniaturization enables many millions of fragments to be bound and amplified in parallel, producing a cluster of identical single-stranded copies

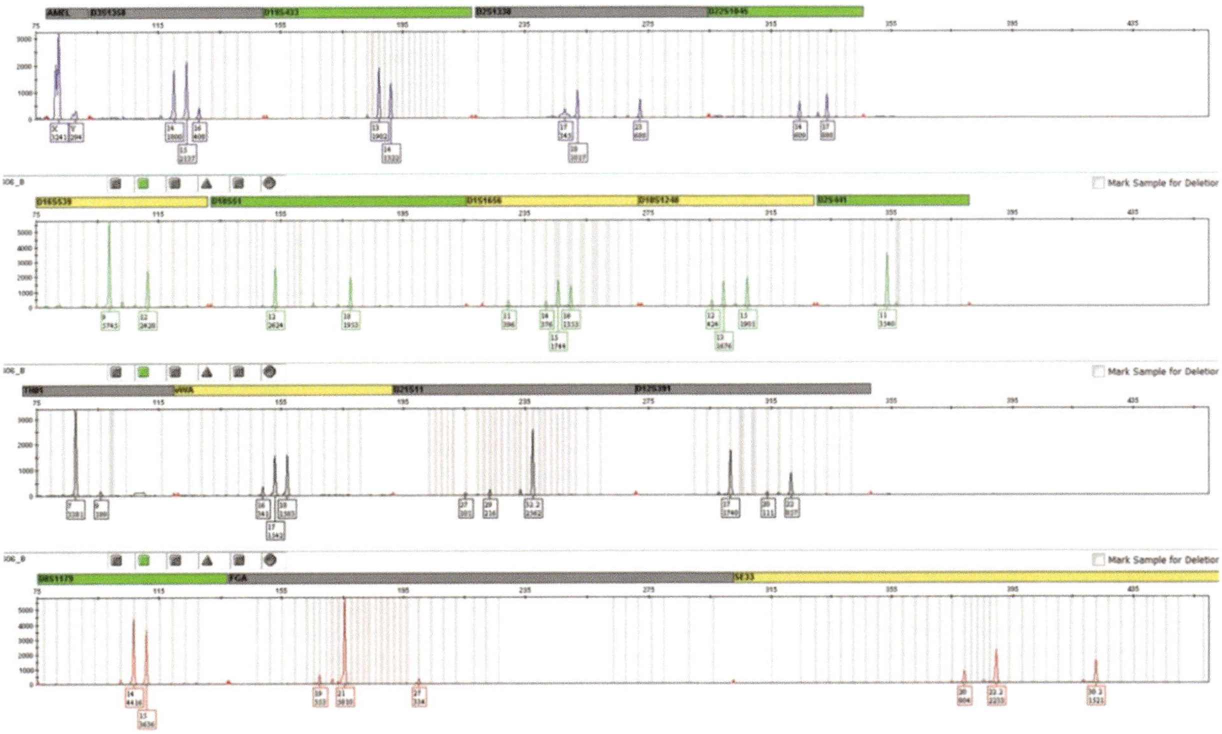

95.4 Electropherogram of a mixture of DNA from at least two individuals with a major female contributor and including at least one male.

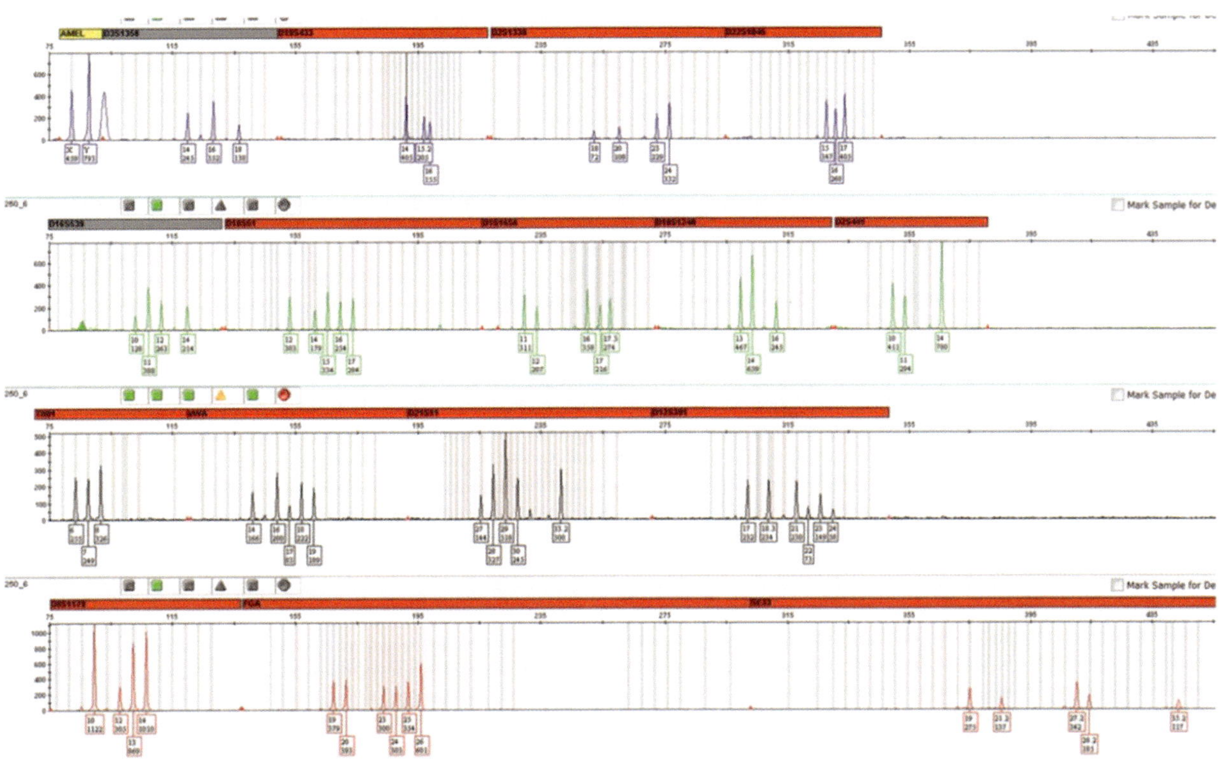

95.5 Electropherogram of a complex mixture of DNA from at least three individuals including at least one male.

of the fragment. "Sequencing by synthesis" (SBS) of the single-stranded fragment copies is enabled in two different ways. Nucleotides are sequentially exposed to the single strand along with polymerase enzyme and the sequence detected by release of a fluorophore, or a change in pH when a nucleotide binds to the strand.

Sequencing of STRs using MPS techniques has enabled a significant increase in allelic variants to be

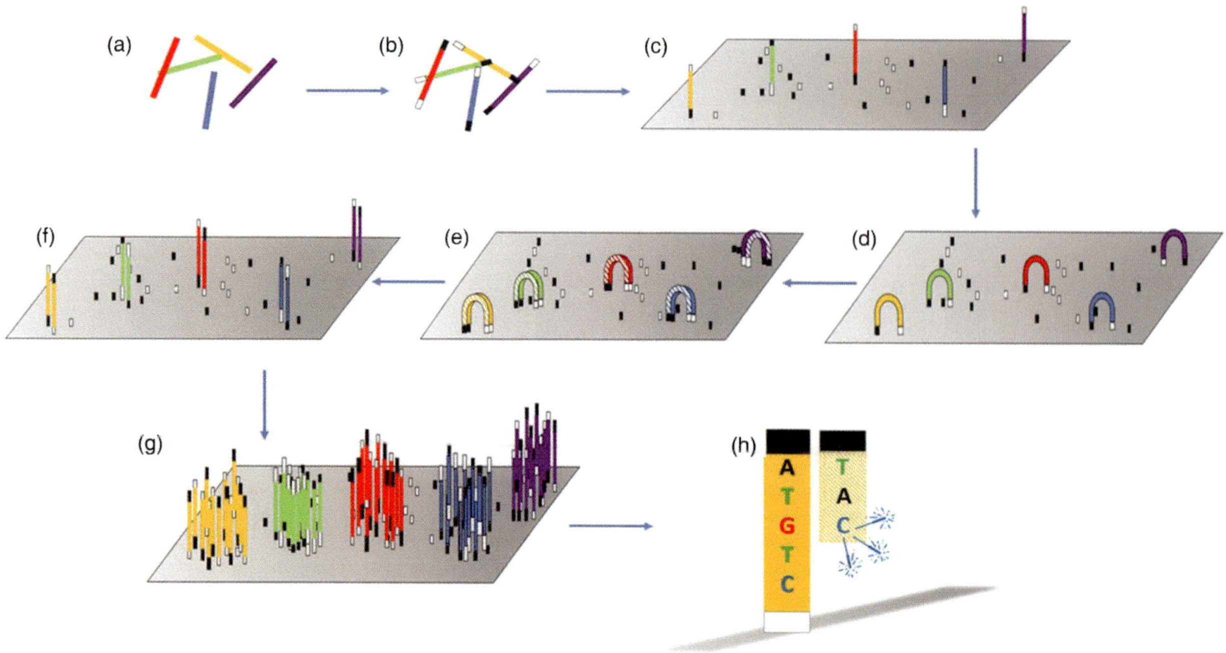

95.6 Schematic of massively parallel sequencing (MPS) methodology using Illumina technology. **(a)** DNA is fragmented into short strands; **(b)** adaptors annealed to the fragment ends; **(c)** fragments bind to a glass surface loaded with complementary primers to the adaptors; **(d)** DNA strands anneal to the primers on the glass surface, forming a bridge; **(e)** the bridge strand is amplified, creating a copy; **(f)** the strands dissociate; **(g)** repeated bridge formation, amplification and dissociation facilitates the development of clusters; **(h)** nucleotides in each strand in the clone are sequenced (sequencing by synthesis) and detected with a nucleotide-dependent release of fluorescent at binding.

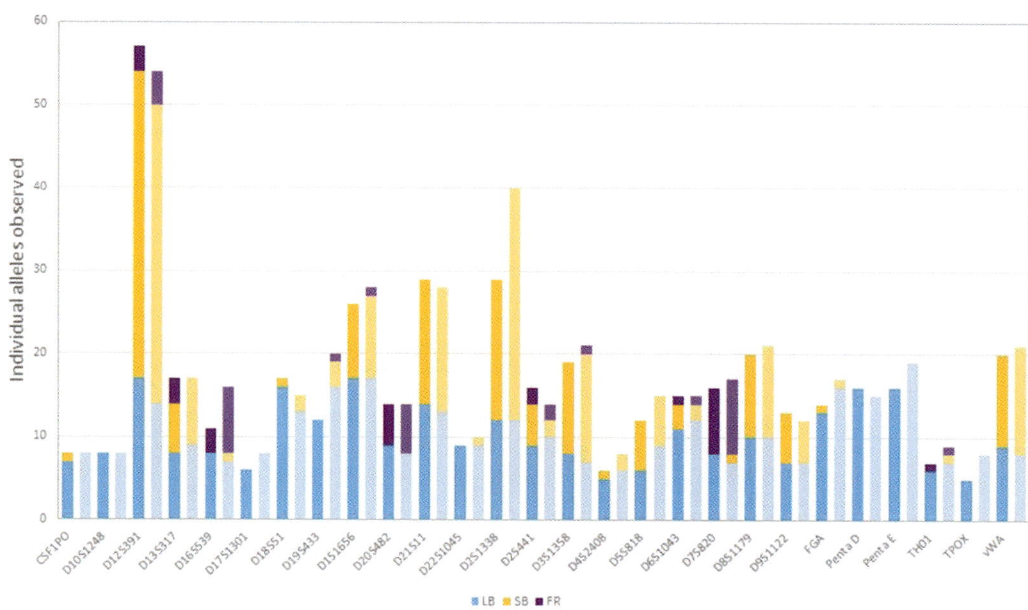

95.7 Variable increase in alleles in different STRs when assessed by length-based (LB), adding sequence-based (SB) variants and further addition of flanking region (FR) alleles.

identified (10) and allowed examination of variation within the flanking region of the repeats.

The number of additional alleles seen is very variable, dependent on the locus (Figure 95.7). One of the least variant loci, TPOX, present in databases for historic reasons, remains relatively invariant even when sequenced and D18S51, generally considered a useful polymorphic locus, shows little increase in allelic variation on sequencing. This is in contrast to loci such as D12S391 and D21S11 which more than double the number of sequence-based alleles in the repeat region; other loci, such as D7S820, D16S539 and D20S482 have limited sequence variation in the repeat region but much higher than normal flanking region variation.

LINEAGE MARKERS

The Y chromosome

The Y male, sex-determining, chromosome, as it is inherited only by males from their fathers, is almost identical down the patrilineal line, although single-step (one number difference) mutations are not infrequently observed. The STR markers on the Y chromosome can only be considered as one combined set (a haplotype) because the separate STRs are inherited together. Nevertheless, analysis of STRs on the Y chromosome has an important role in both forensic and kinship analysis (11). Its primary use in forensic examination is in sexual assault, particularly in cases where there has been no ejaculation or in azoospermic males in which plentiful DNA from the female predominates in the autosomal profile mixture, whereas analysis of the Y chromosome can occur without any inhibition from the female material. It can also assist in deciphering the minimum number of males participating in a "gang rape". Y chromosome analysis can be particularly helpful in missing person investigations and mass disaster identification. The YHRD database (12) maintains a collection of forensically validated haplotypes and can be used to estimate the frequency of a particular haplotype.

The X chromosome

X chromosomes are more complex than other lineage markers. Normal males have one X chromosome and so will pass this to their daughters only. Females will pass one of their two X chromosomes to all of their children. There are, therefore, some family relationships where X chromosome analysis can be useful: mother–son, mother–daughter, father–daughter, paternal grandmother–granddaughter. X chromosome analysis is not often undertaken but it is particularly useful in some circumstances where one of the parents is not available, in cases of incest, and in missing persons and mass disasters (13).

Mitochondrial DNA

Most of the human genome is located within the cell nucleus. However, within the cytoplasm lies a small circular genome found within organelles known as mitochondria. The majority of these organelles have originated from the mother because it is she who donates the egg; the sperm, fertilizing the egg, donates mainly nuclear DNA within the sperm head.

Mitochondria are dedicated to produce energy within the cell and, on average, cells contain around 500 mitochondria. The large number of mitochondrial genomes, in comparison with nuclear genomes, means that in situations where nuclear DNA analysis is not possible because of damage or degradation, such as in ancient remains, or in single hairs where there is no root present, mitochondrial sequence analysis can be successful.

The circular molecule consists of about 16539 bp which transcribe 37 genes within a coding region and a 1122 bp control region or D-loop (Figure 95.8). The D-loop is more variable (because it does not code for important genes) and is the region which is routinely mainly targeted in forensic analysis. Historically, scientists would sequence two hypervariable areas, known as HVS I and HVS II, but increasingly the whole of the control region is targeted. Bases are numbered from a particular position within the control region and changes that differ from the revised Cambridge Reference Sequence (rCRS) are recorded in forensic casework. The EDNAP mitochondrial DNA population database (EMPOP) was initiated in 2006 to provide the forensic community with a high-quality database (14).

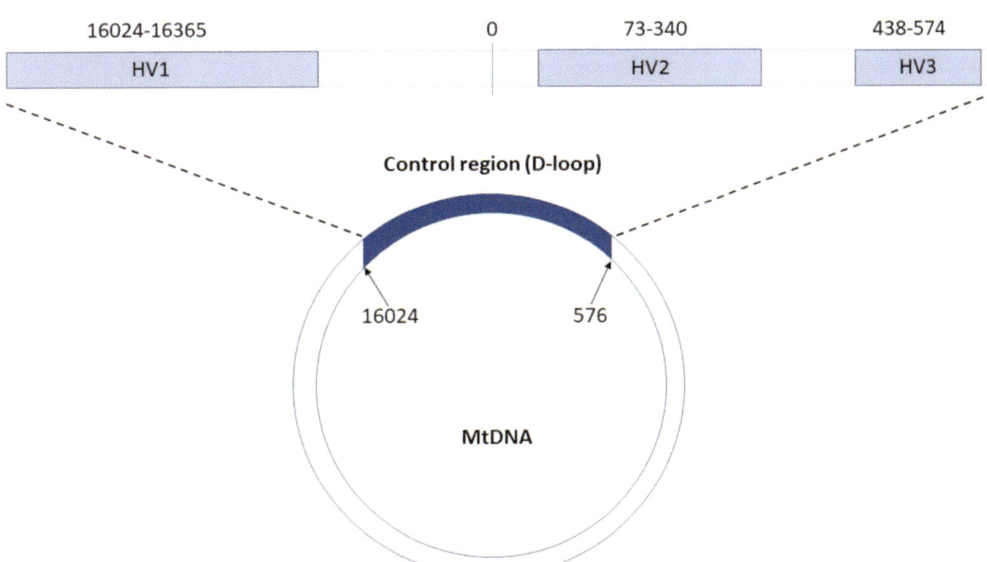

95.8 Schematic diagram of the circular mitochondrial DNA molecule with its approximately 16365 base pairs. Sanger sequencing generally targets the more variable D-loop, or control region. Sometimes only parts of the control region are sequenced, in particular the regions HV1 and HV2.

Newer techniques that use a "capture" method to target and enrich mitochondrial DNA in an MPS approach have led to increased sensitivity in degraded samples.

Forensic DNA phenotyping

In the absence of a database identification to name a potential suspect whose DNA is found at a crime scene, forensic geneticists are questioning what other information can be recovered from the DNA profile. Forensic DNA phenotyping (FDP) consists of a set of methodologies to infer information about externally visible characteristics (EVCs) of an individual (15) but can also include the often linked concept of someone's biogeographic ancestry (BGA) and the not so often included chronologic age. All may offer valuable intelligence to criminal investigations and the identification of missing persons. While none of these techniques are expected to be used in a court of law, they are framed as intelligence information to support a criminal investigation (16).

Externally visible characteristics

The most successful of these have led to a collection of SNP markers to predict eye, hair and skin color, known as HIrisPlex-S (17). Nevertheless, these predictions perhaps do not achieve the levels of certainty that we come to expect from DNA used in identification. They are, inevitably, somewhat limited because of the requirement of being able to conduct these tests with limited forensic material. Achieving area under the curve (AUC) measurements of around 0.95 for blue or brown eyes are achieved, but intermediate colors are more difficult with an AUC of around 0.75 (where an AUC of 1.0 predicts with certainty).

Hair color prediction is not quite as good with AUCs around 0.92 for red hair, 0.85 for black hair, 0.81 for blonde hair and 0.75 for brown hair. Genetic understanding of graying, and the age-dependent darkening of hair color, remains unsolved.

Much of the variation in eye and hair color is seen within the European populations but much less is known about skin color variation as this requires large studies of global populations. Good predictions have been achieved using HIrisPlex-S in some populations but accurate estimates in some Asian populations will need the inclusion of new SNPs to assist.

Biogeographic ancestry

The prediction of BGA continues to be controversial with significant concerns being expressed in relation to misinterpretation of the information and discrimination, such that in some countries its practice is prevented in law. It is important for practitioners to consider the level of resolution that is realistic in a forensic context so that there is a reasonable balance between informativeness and over-simplification when interrogating the complex distribution of contemporary human diversity (18). Panels of markers that include SNPs, microhaplotypes (linked SNPs) and sequenced STRs in different population sets currently enhance a basic continental tool. STRUCTURE (19) is a commonly used tool in this analysis that assists in population assignment and discovery of mixed ancestry.

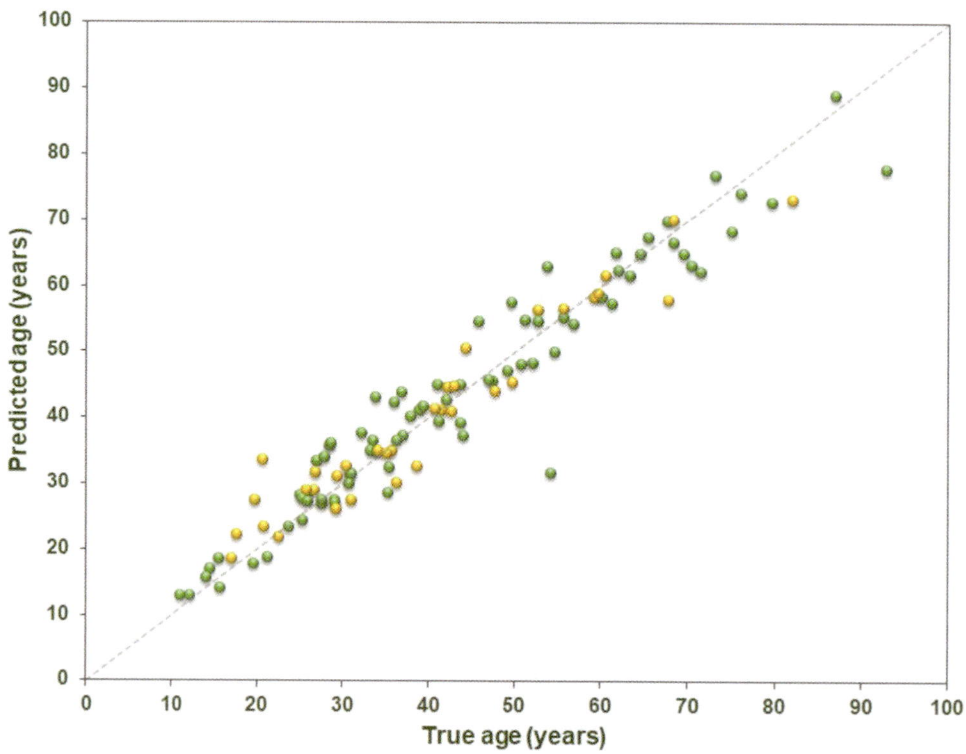

95.9 Epigenetic prediction of chronologic age using 11 age-dependent methylation of CpG residues with an absolute error of 3.3 years. Yellow dots – samples from people of varying age used to develop the model; green dots – samples tested in the model.

Age

Assessment of an individual's chronologic age has been undertaken using a variety of social and anthropomorphic assessments but prediction from a forensic trace relies on an epigenetic approach in which the change in ratio of molecular modification of the DNA molecule (in particular methylation of the cytosine residue) can form a signature of increasing age (20). As with other forensic tools, the ability to produce an accurate prediction needs to be weighed against the number of markers that can be utilized when there are only trace amounts of DNA available. Figure 95.9 shows the results of a developed model from just 11 methylation markers (in green) assessed with a test set of data (in yellow) that has produced an average error of 3.3 years.

Cell type identification

In addition to information about the person, knowledge of the cellular origin of forensic stains is often useful to the investigator. Although there are chemical tests for the presumptive inference of body fluids such as blood, saliva and semen, molecular approaches have taken this further to include differentiation of venous and menstrual blood, and identification of vaginal mucosa, for example (21). These tools mainly use the expression of messenger RNA, microRNAs, identification of particular microbial species and determination of methylation levels.

Analysis of biological trace to identify the donor of any DNA recovered can sometimes erroneously lead to an assumption of its cellular source where the presence of a body fluid is also detected. Linking these is not straightforward and, in some circumstances, can be of importance, not only in mixed body fluid stains but also when the stains appear to be from a single body fluid. The combined use of coding SNPs with body fluid-specific mRNA transcripts has provided a new approach to this problem (22).

FORENSIC INVESTIGATIVE GENETIC GENEALOGY

On April 24, 2018, a 72-year-old former police officer, Joseph James DeAngelo, was arrested and charged with eight counts of first-degree murder and, in June 2020, he pleaded guilty to multiple counts of murder, kidnapping and rape between 1973 and 1986. Variously known as the East Coast Rapist and the Original Night Stalker crime scene DNA had, in 2001, identified that they were one and the same; in 2013, he was first referred to as the Golden State Killer. He was identified through the use of a direct-to-consumer (DTC) commercial genealogic database (23).

DNA genealogy approaches use the power of many thousands of SNPs across the genome that support shared stretches of DNA across chromosomes, the amount of sharing being proportional to the relationship distance between pairs of individuals. It is the popularity of family history research, empowered by DNA, and the public availability of this data, that has, perhaps inevitably, led to its use to attempt to solve criminal cases.

While the identification and arrest of a serial killer has been welcomed worldwide, the potential invasion of people's privacy and the use of their DNA for a purpose other than what they gave their consent for, has caused considerable concern (24). Nevertheless, the procedure has been widely used in the US. Since the identification of Joseph James DeAngelo around 500 cases have been, or are being, investigated with this approach in the US principally, mostly to investigate unsolved crimes of serial and sexual violence (25). Unsurprisingly, most of the suspects identified were of European ancestry as that group form the bulk of submissions to the genealogy databases.

CONCLUSION

Since the birth of forensic genetics in the mid-1980s, human identification continues to evolve, using the considerable knowledge since the human genome was sequenced in 2003 along with the development of new chemistries, miniaturization and statistical tools to the point where only a few cells can be analyzed and provide reliable results, even within complex matrices.

In the years to come DNA, both nuclear and mitochondrial, and associated forms of RNA will provide more answers to uncertainties, such as those posed by activity level questions, as well as provision of better phenotypic information. DNA testing will become more efficient with translation to reliable onsite investigation of crime scene material becoming a reality, and non-human genetic information will come to the fore offering further intelligence to the CJ system. Alongside these advancements, we will become better at considering the use of these new tools in an ethical framework in order to continue to pursue CJ with the public on our side.

REFERENCES

1. Jeffreys A, Wilson V, Thein S. Individual-specific 'fingerprints' of human DNA. *Nature* 1985; **316**: 76–9.
2. Wong Z, Wilson V, Patel I, et al. Characterization of a panel of highly variable minisatellites cloned from human DNA. *Ann Hum Genet* 1987; **51**: 269–88.
3. Mullis K, Faloona F, Scharf S, et al. Specific enzymatic amplification of DNA in vitro: The polymerase chain reaction. *Cold Spring Harb Symp Quant Biol* 1986; **51**: 263–73.
4. Edwards A, Civitello A, Hammond HA, Caskey CT. DNA typing and genetic mapping with trimeric and tetrameric tandem repeats. *Am J Hum Genet* 1991; **49**: 746–56.
5. Butler JM. Genetics and genomics of core short tandem repeat loci used in human identity testing. *J Forensic Sci* 2006; **51**: 253–65.

6. Butler JM. Fundamentals of DNA Separation and Detection. In: Butler J (ed), *Fundamentals of Forensic DNA Typing*. San Diego: Elsevier Academic Press; 2010, pp. 175–203.
7. Council of Europe. *S. and Marper v The United Kingdom*, 2008. Available from: https://rm.coe.int/168067d216 (Accessed 22 June 2023).
8. Bieber FR, Buckleton JS, Budowle B, et al. Evaluation of forensic DNA mixture evidence: Protocol for evaluation, interpretation, and statistical calculations using the combined probability of inclusion. *BMC Genetics* 1985; **17**: 125.
9. Ballard D, Winkler-Galicki J, Wesoły J. Massive parallel sequencing in forensics: Advantages, issues, technicalities, and prospects. *Int J Legal Med* 2020; **134**: 1291–303.
10. Devesse L, Ballard D, Davenport L, et al. Concordance of the ForenSeq™ system and characterisation of sequence-specific autosomal STR alleles across two major population groups. *Forensic Sci Int Genet* 2018; **34**: 57–61.
11. Kayser M. Forensic use of Y-chromosome DNA: A general overview. *Hum Genet* 2017; **136**: 621–35.
12. Willuweit S, Roewer L. The new Y chromosome haplotype reference database. *Forensic Sci Int Genet* 2014; **15**: 43–8.
13. Garcia FM, Bessa BGO, Dos Santos EVW, et al. Forensic applications of markers present on the X chromosome. *Genes (Basel)* 2022; 7(**13**): 1597.
14. Parson W, Dür A. EMPOP-a forensic mtDNA database. *Forensic Sci Int Genet* 2007; **1**: 88–92.
15. Kayser M. Forensic DNA phenotyping: Predicting human appearance from crime scene material for investigative purposes. *Forensic Sci Int Genet* 2015; **18**: 33–48.
16. Scudder N, Robertson J, Kelty S, et al. A law enforcement intelligence framework for use in predictive DNA phenotyping. *Aust J Forensic Sci* 2019; **51**: 1–4.
17. Chaitanya L, Breslin K, Zuñiga S, et al. The HIrisPlex-S system for eye, hair and skin colour prediction from DNA: Introduction and forensic developmental validation. *Forensic Sci Int Genet* 2018; **35**: 123–35.
18. Phillips C. Forensic genetic analysis of bio-geographical ancestry. *Forensic Sci Int Genet* 2015; **18**: 49–65.
19. Porras-Hurtado L, Ruiz Y, Santos C, et al. An overview of STRUCTURE: Applications, parameter settings, and supporting software. *Front Genet* 2013; **29**(**4**): 98.
20. Aliferi A, Sundaram S, Ballard D, et al. Combining current knowledge on DNA methylation-based age estimation towards the development of a superior forensic DNA intelligence tool. *Forensic Sci Int Genet* 2022; **57**: 102637.
21. Sijen T. Molecular approaches for forensic cell type identification: On mRNA, miRNA, DNA methylation and microbial markers. *Forensic Sci Int Genet* 2015; **8**: 21–32.
22. Ingold S, Dørum G, Hanson E, et al. Assigning forensic body fluids to donors in mixed body fluids by targeted RNA/DNA deep sequencing of coding region SNPs. *Int J Leg Med* 2020; **134**: 473–85.
23. Phillips C. The Golden State Killer investigation and the nascent field of forensic genealogy. *Forensic Sci Int Genet* 2018; **36**: 186–8.
24. Syndercombe Court D. Forensic genealogy: Some serious concerns. *Forensic Sci Int Genet* 2018; **36**: 203–4.
25. Dowdeswell TL. Forensic genetic genealogy: A profile of cases solved. *Forensic Sci Int Genet* 2022; **58**: 102679.

CHAPTER

96

Disaster Victim Identification

Peter Juel Thiis Knudsen

INTRODUCTION

Identification of the living and the dead is part and parcel of the work of medical personnel. In the medical setting, this may include unconscious victims of accidents or patients suffering from dementia or psychiatric conditions which prevent them from giving information about their identity. In such living cases, the principles used are similar to the main subject of this chapter, Disaster Victim Identification (DVI).

Disasters may take many forms. Although the nature and cause of the disaster may vary (e.g. flood, earthquakes, tsunamis, air crash, ships lost at sea, terrorist attacks) the principles of DVI are the same.

PRINCIPLES OF IDENTIFICATION

Identification of the living or the dead is based upon the comparison of antemortem and post-mortem information. In the routine identification of the dead by the police, the comparison is usually made by the next-of-kin or close associates of the person presumed dead by comparing their recollection of her or him with the physical evidence of the deceased presented to them in the mortuary. This process works in most cases but when in doubt, and always in events with more than one casualty, the principle of primary identifiers should be adhered to. This principle should be applied, even in simple cases, when in the past perhaps a decomposed body found in the apparent place of residence with identification papers in the pockets would have been accepted as sufficient proof of identity.

Primary and secondary identifiers

For several decades, the concept of primary and secondary identifiers has been the golden standard for DVI work. Based upon the practical experience and the technologic advances during those years, the international DVI community as represented by the INTERPOL DVI Conference (1), has established that for the safe identification of deceased person in a mass casualty situation one of the three primary identifiers is required. These are fingerprints, also known as Friction Ridge Analysis, dental examination (Forensic odontology) and DNA-typing. If these are not available, then secondary identifiers such as personal effects found on the decedent, or medical findings provided by a partial or full autopsy (in some cases supplemented by an anthropologic examination) are needed (2).

The principles and the practical aspects of this are found in the INTERPOL DVI Guide, which provides continually updated state-of-the-art information for those performing DVI for the first time (3).

Friction ridge analysis

The use of friction ridge analysis and later imprints from hands or feet, was suggested by several scientists at the end of the nineteenth century, particularly Francis Galton (4), and is now widely used in police investigation. Friction ridge analysis has been used for the identification of airline passengers, some national identification systems for security entry admission and as a secure and effective means of accessing phones, laptops and other devices (5).

In some settings, fingerprints are not limited to the fingertips but may include the palm prints. Plantar prints have also been used and are recorded in the Royal Danish Air Force for possible DVI purposes.

Antemortem fingerprints may be obtained from national ID-data, or from biometric passport data, but in those countries where fingerprints are not easily accessible or recorded, other sources must be found. The classical source is police records, but this may be limited to persons who have committed or are being investigated for crimes, and not all crimes permit the storage of the fingerprints. This is a country or jurisdiction specific issue, and similar principles apply for DNA. Alternative sources are the home or the workplace of the deceased, but in this case a family member or colleague, who uses the same items or tools, may also have to give their fingerprints, which may present problems.

Post-mortem fingerprints are generally obtained by the police with newer methods such as scanning being used routinely in the living in airports all over the world.

Various systems are available for the comparison between antemortem and post-mortem fingerprints, the Automated Fingerprint Identification System (AFIS) being the best known (5). AFIS allows the examiner to

DOI: 10.1201/9781003138754-100

find several likely matches, which may then be compared manually. If the fingerprint being searched for is in the AFIS, the identification may be done in an hour or two depending on the quality of the material.

Forensic odontology

The role of odontology in identification is discussed in Chapter 92 in further detail, but one of the advantages of teeth is that they are very resistant to the processes that degrade the body, such as decomposition, trauma or fire.

Dental identification is divided into antemortem (AM) and post-mortem (PM) procedures, as is to be expected. The collection of AM information, which is often in the hands of the police, should always be supported by a forensic odontologist.

The PM work of the dentist consists of a detailed examination and recording of the teeth. The findings are recorded according to the nomenclature used nationally and when foreigners may be among the victims, an international nomenclature such as used by INTERPOL in the DVI forms (Figure 96.1) should be employed (6). The INTERPOL DVI Form has been designed to accommodate a digitized recording of the findings to compare many casualties (7).

In DVI, the dental diagram is used for screening among casualties, and the identification is routinely made from X-rays or CT scans. To secure a certain identification of an unknown corpse, several findings must be recorded; they must all comply with the AM information and there must be no discrepancies (8,9).

DNA analysis

Chapter 95 explores DNA analysis in further detail, but the development of DNA-typing for identification in the last half-century has supplemented the two classical primary identifiers and is, in many circumstances, the only method by which identification is possible. There are several advantages of DNA-analysis compared to the other two, most importantly that it is not necessary, albeit best, to have the DNA-type from the casualty directly.

In a setting such as that of fingerprints, the DNA-type may be available from persons who have been forced to deliver a mouth-swab test, as they have had to give their fingerprint. If the DNA-type is not directly available, it is possible with varying degrees of certainty, to use the DNA-types of close biological relatives to provide a probable DNA-type, that can be used for identification.

In the AM situation, the DNA-type is sought from tissue samples in a pathology biobank, from FTA-cards (a filter paper for collection of biological samples for genetic analysis) kept for medical purposes or from military or police personnel in countries where this is a standard procedure. The DNA-type of the missing person assumed to be a casualty may be found by using personal belongings, such as toothbrushes or combs, but this may be a less reliable source.

In the PM situation, the selection of material for DNA-typing will depend on the time since the incident and the state of the body in general. If the incident is recent and the body is well preserved, a smear from the

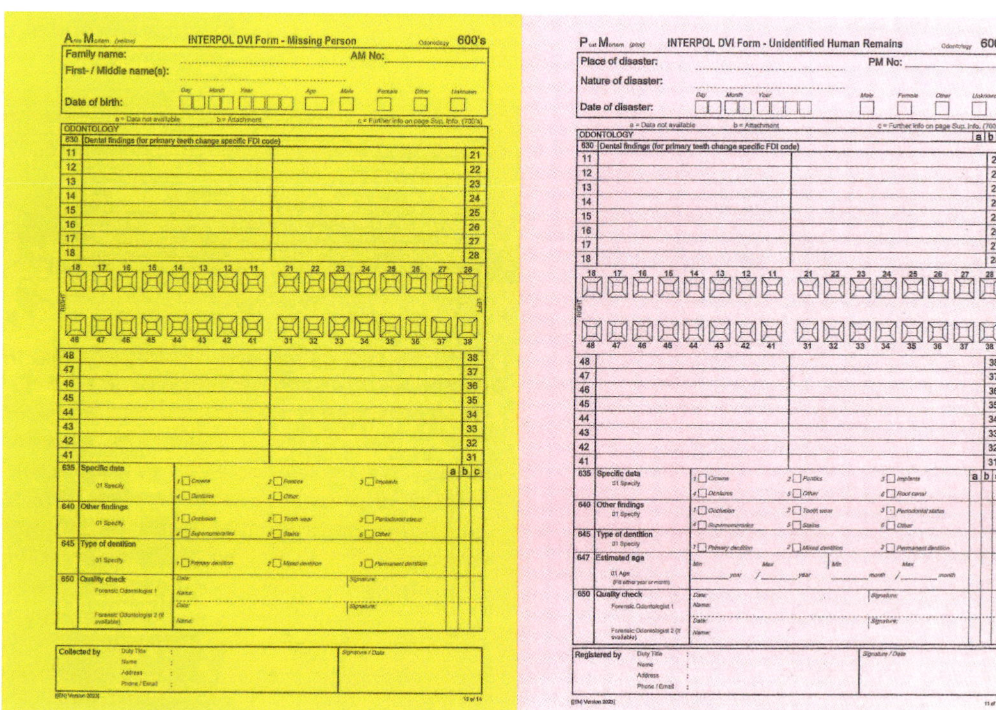

96.1 The pages from the INTERPOL DVI Forms showing one of the odontology pages. Similar pages to record clothing, effects, pathology, fingerprints, DNA-types and anthropology are included in the forms, that are designed to be used with the Plass Data program.

mucous membranes in the mouth is the most advantageous. The smear is transferred to an FTA-card which can be processed very rapidly in the laboratory. In a mass casualty situation, contamination is the major risk in DNA-typing. In case of "old" bodies, bone is the material of choice and can provide a DNA-type even after many years. The AM and PM DNA-types may be compared manually, when a single body must be identified but, in DVI situations, electronic processing is the method of choice (10,11).

Personal data/medical findings

There are external and internal findings which may contribute to the identification of the deceased if the primary identifiers are not successful. AM information is best obtained from next-of-kin and from medical records. The accessibility of those may vary from country to country and there may be legal constraints. Family members, primary care physicians and hospital medical records may all be valuable sources of information.

Specific external congenital features as well as external acquired features may be known to the relatives and may be very distinctive. Malformations and major tumors may be known to the next-of-kin, and they may have previous photographs corroborating these. Piercings and tattoos will often be known about or be visible, but some are in intimate parts of the body and the details of many may not be known by surviving family members. Photographic images again may be very useful in corroborating features found on the deceased. Surgical scars (e.g. from cosmetic surgery or cancer surgery) may be unique to that individual and family members or medical records may corroborate.

Internal features may be very useful but, in most cases, medical records are needed to provide hard evidence for the pathologist to make full use of them. Details necessary for identification must be documented by the medical records. It is also important to gain access to X-rays or CT scans. All implanted material will carry some batch and/or type number, which should be expected to be noted in the medical records. The serial number of pacemakers or some prostheses can be crucial for identification.

In principle, the remains of the deceased should be retained securely until the identity of all is safely established, but this is not always possible for ethical and practical reasons. In most cases, a post-mortem CT scan (PMCT) will be helpful with which to compare AM radiology (12,13). If the body is fragmented or skeletonized, the expertise of an anthropologist may be required (14,15).

Evidence/clothing

These items are such that are found by, on or attached to the body. They are useful in narrowing the field but can only rarely in isolation confirm identity. They are not unique identifiers and may cause misidentification and in DVI will have little relevance, since personal effects may be comingled. AM information about clothing, jewelery, watches, and spectacles may be inaccurate.

Effects found near the body carry little evidential value but can be used to give the police an idea who the deceased is. Evidence found on the body, but not inserted (piercings) is of more interest in terms of identification and police investigation. If the effects do not belong to the decedent, but to someone else, how did they get there? The relatives may be able to provide information of which documents such as driving license, credit or debit cards or membership cards the decedent was carrying, and if these are found on a person, the suspicion that it may by the decedent rises. Relatives may be able to provide specific information about possessions, for example inscriptions on rings, manufacturer of a watch, mobile phone or objects with serial numbers.

Items must be secured by the authorities and detailed records are made to ensure that nothing is lost to the relatives and for the identification process. The pathologist will keep a summary of items found at autopsy, but full details must be recorded by the relevant authorities.

ORGANIZATION OF DVI

The essence of DVI is teamwork. The authorities will appoint the lead agent, usually the police or prosecutor and the forensic pathologist, forensic odontologist or forensic geneticist must resign to work in a subordinate role, quite different to what she or he is used to in the daily departmental or institute setting. Authorities are assumed to have built up an organization, to respond at short notice, locally or abroad. This organization must be able to handle the collection of bodies or body parts, the AM information collection, the PM procedures, and the reconciliation process where the AM and PM information is compared, and the identification confirmed by the proper authorities.

Pre-disaster planning

Field Marshall Helmuth von Moltke stated: "Kein Operationsplan reicht mit einiger Sicherheit über das erste Zusammentreffen mit der feindlichen Hauptmacht hinaus" ["*No plan of operations extends with any certainty beyond the first contact with the main hostile force*"] (16). DVI planning must be flexible and must be directed at a range of scenarios.

There needs to be an agreed process for the operation with defined requirements and timelines for the police, forensic pathologists, forensic odontologists and forensic geneticists. With appropriate planning, a DVI operation should be able to be initiated within 24 hours.

Planning must include the ability to mobilize trained personnel and their equipment at short notice. The principles of mobilization apply to all relevant personnel including scientific (forensic pathologists, odontologists, anthropologists and geneticists) as well as police (pressure ridge analysts/fingerprint) experts.

Forensic pathologists and anthropologists will be used to handling identification, usually in the form of full autopsies. They must be trained in the handling of many fatalities in a short time and in often imperfect conditions. They need to be familiar with up-to-date identification software, such as the INTERPOL standard system ("Plass Data") (7).

Medical experts will usually bring their own personal equipment, but it may be necessary for the police to fund one or more spare sets for emergencies. This includes not only the pathologist's scalpels and forceps but also the expensive handheld digital X-ray equipment of the odontologist. A mobile CT scanner is very useful, and since it is probably not used by forensic pathologists as part of their daily work, planning must include borrowing one from the medical authorities or the military, including the trained personnel to use it. Common to all is the need for up-to-date portable computers with a reliable, secure internet connection.

ANTEMORTEM PROCEDURES

There must be plans for a center to collect the AM information. The AM Center must be staffed by experienced police officers, including fingerprint experts, with pathologists, odontologists, geneticists and anthropologists being available at short notice for advice and action.

POST-MORTEM PROCEDURES

The conduct of the PM procedures is a question of law and logistics. The responsible legal authority must decide the extent of autopsy, based on the legislation of the host country but considering the requirements of the countries of the foreign casualties, if any. In the case of man-made disasters such as accidents or crimes with many casualties, the requirement will, in most cases, be for full forensic autopsies, and the identification of the deceased will be integrated herein. In the case of a natural disaster such as the Thai tsunami, the authorities may have the options of full autopsies, partial autopsies with an emphasis on identification, relevant information or a pure identification autopsy, which means fingerprints, dental examination and/or DNA-typing. This decision will often be dependent on the location, number of fatalities and resilience of the relevant personnel. Common to all this is that a location must be identified where the necessary ID procedures can be prepared and undertaken. This location will require resources such as lighting, heating/air-conditioning, water, waste disposal and security.

Full autopsy

A full autopsy requires many resources, is time consuming and requires a substantially better environment than partial or ID autopsies. For legal or religious reasons, the latter may be preferable and more appropriate than a full autopsy.

The main advantages of the full autopsy, preferably with PMCT, is that all the procedures necessary for identification are included, and that both the primary and secondary identifiers are represented. A partial or ID-autopsy may provide inadequate information and it may then be necessary to perform a second autopsy if inconclusive. Inadequate initial examinations meant that after the Thai tsunami many bodies were examined three times (17).

A full forensic (medicolegal) autopsy, described in detail in Chapter 20 "Medicolegal Autopsy", gives the forensic odontologist access to perform the dental examination under optimal conditions and the forensic pathologist can obtain all the samples necessary for the forensic genetic investigation, dependent on the condition of the body, such as buccal or organ swabs, blood, muscle, teeth and/or bone. The forensic autopsy also makes it possible to use the secondary identifiers such as sequelae of disease, piercings and cutaneous features such as tattoos, which may support or establish the identity. The PMCT may reveal implants that might otherwise have been missed, especially in a fragmented or decomposed body.

Partial autopsy

Partial autopsy, as was employed during the Thai tsunami, means aiming for some specific anatomic structures in addition to the external examination and the primary identifiers (17). The advantage of the partial autopsy is that time consuming procedures such as opening the skull which are deemed to contain few clues to the identification are avoided. The decision on the type of autopsy must be made after consideration of all factors but also with a good knowledge of the predominant diseases or conditions of the presumed dead. It is up to the DVI management to decide the appropriate organ systems to examine or which organ to look for. During the Thai tsunami, it was decided to look for the gall bladder, the appendix and the uterus (in the female), since these organs were deemed most likely to have been removed in the victim population of 50/50 European/Australian and Thai descent. If PMCT is also employed, implants or sequelae from operations such as clips for sterilization operations or laparoscopic cholecystectomy will not be missed. In some cases, it is justifiable to do a full autopsy to identify implants that may be crucial such as pacemakers, ICDs or orthopedic implants that may carry a serial number.

ID autopsy

In countries with limited resources, an autopsy procedure looking solely for primary identifiers may be the only alternative to a mass burial of unidentified corpses. Fingerprints or pressure ridge analysis can be performed without invasive procedures by police officers without the need for full autopsy facilities. Dependence on fingerprints as the sole primary identifier means that there must be certainty that all the assumed dead have had their fingerprints taken. This is the case in those countries where one or more fingerprints are stored in a central identification database, often combined with passport or national ID-card. In case of a mixed list of victims, where some may have the fingerprints in a database while others may be foreigners, one of or both the other two primary identifiers should be utilized. The ID autopsy is sufficient if only identification is required and if the risk that none of the primary identifiers are conclusive, is accepted.

Reconciliation

AM and PM information are compared in the reconciliation process. This is the immediate precursor of the formal identification and writing of the medical certificate of cause of death and must be aligned with the national requirements. It is best to have a decision beforehand about which primary and/or secondary identifiers are considered necessary for the identification. The personnel on the reconciliation board may be police officers and lawyers with no or only very little practical knowledge of DVI, so it is necessary to present the evidence in a manner that will allow non-healthcare professionals in a DVI setting to understand the procedure. The final decision on identification is a matter for the Reconciliation Board and the officials will be legal personnel.

National versus international operations

National DVI operations are most often conducted by the countries themselves and only rarely has assistance from INTERPOL or another foreign organization been required.

With disasters involving victims of two or more different nationalities problems are bound to appear. The presence or absence of representatives from the relevant countries of the victims can make the difference between a smooth operation and one which is marred by misunderstandings and lack of trust. The INTERPOL DVI Guide emphasizes that in the case of victims of more nationalities, all relevant countries should be invited to send personnel to help the local authorities. Diplomatic issues such as the belief that other countries are interfering with the internal affairs of the host country, or that DVI personnel would present a security risk, can become an issue if not anticipated at an early stage.

The presence of non-nationals in the DVI operation should not be perceived as an external quality control mechanism but as an offer to the country in which the incident has taken place to provide the vital AM information and assist with country specific matters in the PM procedure. In accidents such as the Air France 447 with 31 different nationalities, no one person will be able to keep track of cultural and language specific findings (18). The guests from other countries will provide support and information of great value but need to be aware of their respective roles.

THE ROLE OF INTERPOL

INTERPOL is the chief player in the international cooperation in DVI and has developed procedures to react quickly if member states want help (1). This ranges from cases with a comparatively small number of casualties in an incident in a country with no tradition for DVI to the largest peace-time modern DVI operation, the Asia tsunami, with over 200 000 victims. The INTERPOL DVI organization consists of three major assets:

- A conceptual paper, the DVI Guide, which outlines the principles along which the INTERPOL thinks DVI operations should be conducted (3)
- The DVI Forms, which are the basis for documenting the casualties (6), on paper or using a computerized program, such as the DVI System International® ("Plass Data"), by the Danish firm KMD A/S (7)
- For immediate support, the Incident Response Teams (IRT) from INTERPOL HQ, who can at short notice go to the assistance of countries that do not have the experience of, or resources for, a full DVI operation. The IRT will report to the INTERPOL DVI Unit which will then handle requests for help or offers from nations to provide help. INTERPOL must in this as in any other activity rely on countries that are willing and able to provide equipment and personnel.

EXPERIENCE FROM DISASTERS

Large international disasters

The two major disasters in which DVI have played a prominent part in recent years are the 9/11 attack on New York in 2001 and the Asian Tsunami of 26th December 2004. They differ in origin, the former being a man-made disaster, while the latter was a natural disaster. Both were open disasters, and both were complicated by the many nations being represented. The 9/11 disaster was regarded as an Act of War and, unsurprisingly, was conducted as a USA operation exclusively.

The Asian Tsunami was complex in different ways. The disaster spread all over the coasts of the Indian Ocean and the highest number of victims by far were in the Banda Aceh region in Indonesia with DVI only performed in selected cases. In Thailand, the national authorities immediately realized that they did not have the resources to conduct a proper DVI operation, and therefore looked for someone to help them. The Australian DVI organization was close at hand, had been tested in the Bali bombings some years before and the Australian Government would willingly lend their support. Local DVI work started in a completely disorganized fashion, where independent single nations or groups of nations sent teams that worked according to their own standards thus being of little help in the big picture (Figure 96.2).

Several victims were identified by visual identification, but the dangers of inaccurate identification by this method was not always recognized.

96.2 The Wat Bang Muang site in the last days of December 2004. Examinations were initially done on the ground and only later were tables provided by and for the Scandinavian team. Approximately 1200 victims were brought to this site.

96.4 The "Field Mortuary" by NORMECA AS erected near the Phuket International Airport provided ample working room for six lines, two in each row of containers with lighting, running water and air conditioning. The lines were for fingerprints (nearest to the camera), pathology and odontology in that order.

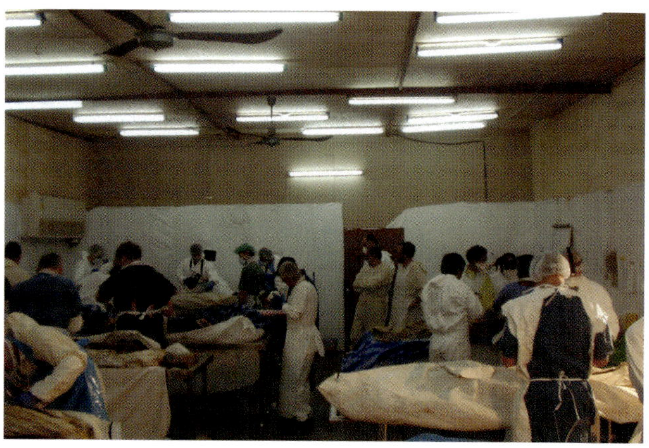

96.3 The morgue in Takua Pa. Desperately crowded but attempts at air conditioning and running water. Tables were rationed so every nation represented could get a chance to do what they came for.

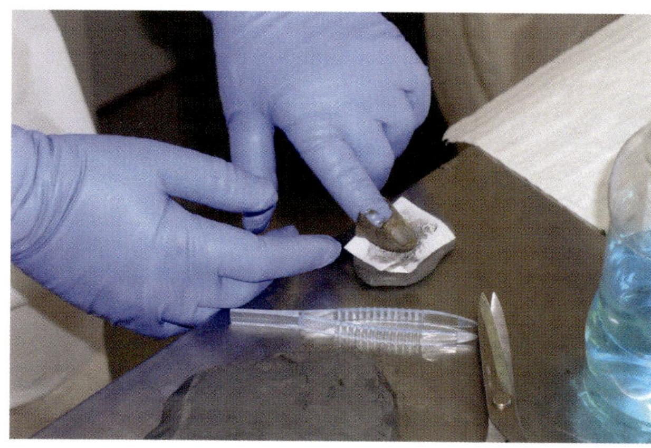

96.5 When bodies had been in the water for some time the epidermis of the fingertips could be removed *in toto* and placed on the gloved finger of the fingerprint expert to make the print.

During the first weeks and months an organization led by the Thai police and the Australian experts was built up in initially three sites (Figure 96.3) and with the erection of the Norwegian sponsored Mobile Forensic Medicine Center by NORMECA AS, which started work around 1st February 2005, the DVI work was focussed there, avoiding the complication of having three different sites (Figures 96.4–96.6).

Identification was done strictly according to the INTERPOL guidelines, facilitated by the fact that the foreign countries with most fatalities – Germany and Sweden – are active in the INTERPOL DVI organization (17).

Small international disasters

The crash of the Air France AF 447 from Rio de Janeiro to Paris on 1st June 2009 involved many different nations, in the comparatively small number of people on an international airliner (18). It happened over the sea and thus required rescue and recovery operations. In such an event, there are several parties involved:

- The owner of the airplane
- The country of the airplane
- The country of departure
- The country of its destination
- The geographic location of the crash
- The relatives of the deceased

It was most likely that the crash had happened in or close to Brazilian territorial waters, and it thus became the responsibility of Brazil to lead the search, and when the crash site was located, the bodies found on the surface were brought to the nearest large Brazilian city, Recife. The local authorities, in conjunction with the national authorities of Brazil and France, established a DVI organization that was joined by experts from some of the nations that had many casualties on board. Since

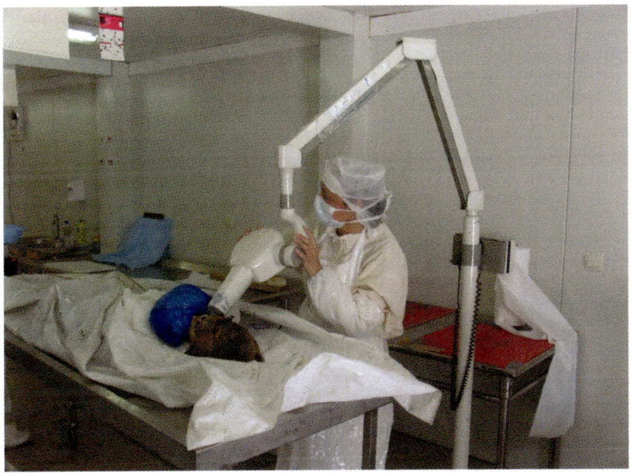

96.6 Each line had their own X-ray camera, so the bottle-neck in the radiology department in the Takua Pa morgue was eliminated. The forensic odontologist is seen taking the crucial bite-wing X-rays.

both Brazil and France adhere to the INTERPOL standards, and are prominent in the Interpol DVI Conference, cooperation was conducted smoothly. When later victims were collected from the seabed by a French naval vessel, the identification was continued in France.

With a French airplane involved, it was natural that the French authorities would handle the bulk of the AM data collection. The adherence to INTERPOL standards and the experience of working with a digitized database and data handling tool, the DVI System International®, in Thailand some years previously meant that the collection of data was much simplified. This would have been much more difficult if two or more different systems were used, particularly if no "translation" had been done beforehand.

National disasters

Disasters that take place in one country only, and which are not transportation accidents, such as natural disasters in remote areas, do not need or indeed carry the burden of international cooperation or lack of the same. The country in question may decide to limit the use of the INTERPOL primary identifiers to those most likely to be profitable in that country's setting, or which are most acceptable to the population from a cultural of religious point of view. In some of the large natural or transportation disasters in the Far East, it was decided to rely only on DNA-typing since dental AM data were scant or non-existent as were fingerprints. Not all the countries of this world can provide staffing and funding for the collection and processing of the tissue samples in a large disaster, so the cooperation with other countries or international organizations such as INTERPOL, the International Commission of the Red Cross or Crescent (19), or similar may be necessary to achieve the desired results.

CONCLUSION

The successful handling of the identification of victims in a large disaster depends upon the proficiency of the PM teams, but equally on the AM data collection and the management of the operation. PM data collection is a finite process, consisting of autopsies, dental examination, fingerprinting and the sampling for DNA-typing. In reports from disasters, it is often mentioned that important AM information was, for several reasons, much delayed, which is difficult to explain to relatives, who see the teams go home and then expect to have their loved ones being identified and given back to them. It is necessary to handle the press in a professional and efficient way and communicate the processes necessary to the speedy and certain identification of the victims.

If one were to suggest improvements to the handling of disasters from the DVI point of view a frequent complaint is the lack of exercises, that may show up deficiencies in the plans that seem so perfect. As has been said so often: "If you don't practice, you can't do it" and it is therefore necessary to involve the DVI community in whatever exercises are put on in the individual countries. The job is not over when the last survivor has been found. The sorrow of the relatives can be lessened, but never removed, by the knowledge that their loved ones have been found and that they may lay them to rest, secure in the knowledge that they are the right ones in the right place.

REFERENCES

1. Sweet D. INTERPOL DVI best-practice standards-An overview. *Forensic Sci Int* 2010; **201**: 18–21.
2. Schuliar Y, Knudsen PJT. The role of forensic pathologists in mass disasters. *Forensic Sci Med Pathol* 2012; **8**: 164–73.
3. Interpol. Disaster Victim Identification Guide 2018. Available from: https://www.interpol.int/en/How-we-work/Forensics/Disaster-Victim-Identification-DVI (Accessed 7 September 2023).
4. Galton, F. *Finger Prints*. London: MacMillan and Co; 1982.
5. McRoberts, A. (ed). *The Fingerprint Source Book*. Washington: National Institute of Justice; 2011.
6. Interpol. Disaster Victim Identification Forms, 2023. Available from: https://www.interpol.int/en/How-we-work/Forensics/Disaster-Victim-Identification-DVI (Accessed 7 September 2023).
7. Andersen L. DVI System international: Software assisting in the Thai tsunami identification process. *J Forensic Odonto-stomatology* 2005; **23**: 19–25.
8. Berketa JW, James H, Lake AW. Forensic odontology involvement in disaster victim identification. *Forensic Sci Med Pathol* 2012; **8**: 148.
9. Forrest A. Forensic odontology in DVI: Current practice and recent advances. *Forensic Sci Res* 2019; **4**: 316–30.
10. Prinz M, Carracedo A, Mayr WR, et al. DNA Commission of the International Society for Forensic Genetics (ISFG): Recommendations regarding the role of forensic genetics for disaster victim identification (DVI). *Forensic Sci Int Genet* 2007; **1**(**1**): 3–12.
11. Montelius K, Lindblom B. DNA analysis in disaster victim identification. *Forensic Sci Med Pathol* 2012; **8**: 140.
12. Brough AL, Morgan B, Rutty GN. Postmortem computed tomography (PMCT) and disaster victim identification. *Radiol Med* 2015; **120**: 866–73.
13. Sidler M, Cakckowski C, Dirhofer R, et al. Use of multislice computed tomography in disaster victim identification –

Advantages and limitations. *Forensic Sci Int* 2007; **169**: 118–28.
14. Mundorff AZ. Integrating forensic anthropology into disaster victim identification. *Forensic Sci Med Pathol* 2012; **8**: 131.
15. de Boer H, Blau S, Delabarde T, Hackman L. The role of forensic anthropology in disaster victim identification (DVI): Recent developments and future prospects. *Forensic Sci Res* 2019: **4**: 303–15.
16. von Molkte, HKB. *Molktes Militärische Werke: Die Tätlichkeit als Chef des Generalstabes der Armee im Frieden.* Munich: E.S. Mitter; 1900.
17. Schou MP, Knudsen PJT. The Danish disaster victim identification effort in the Thai tsunami – organisation and results. *Forensic Sci Med Pathol* 2012: **8**: 125–30.
18. Schuliar Y, Chapenoire S, Miras A, et al. A new tool for coding and interpreting injuries in fatal airplane crashes: The crash injury pattern assessment tool application to the Air France flight AF447 disaster (Rio de Janeiro Paris), 1st of June 2009. *J Forensic Sci* 2014; **59**: 1263–70.
19. Tidball-Binz M. Managing the dead in catastrophes: Guiding principles and practical recommendations for first responders. *Int Rev of the ICRC* 2007; **89**: 421–42.

CHAPTER

97

Blood Pattern Analysis

Sue Carney-Gannon

INTRODUCTION

Blood Pattern Analysis (BPA) considers the characteristics of blood stains at crime scenes and on exhibits to provide information about the actions leading to their deposition. BPA may be used in postulating a sequence of events that might be responsible for the blood findings, or in a criminal trial context, to differentiate between the versions of events asserted by prosecution and defense. In some cases, BPA findings may exclude the proposition put forward by one side and provide compelling evidence to support that of the other.

Unlike forensic science disciplines whose application has been co-opted from some other field, BPA is relevant only in a forensic context. However, it is influenced by multiple fields, using techniques from fluid dynamics (1–3), considering such factors as force, viscosity, surface tension, movement, direction and contact, and prompting developments in image capture (4), scanning technology (5), and analysis software (6,7).

Of all the forensic science specialisms, BPA is uniquely visual. Practitioners view bloodstains at close quarters, often in cramped conditions, hampered by the restrictions and discomforts of protective clothing. Training is overwhelmingly hands-on, based on the reproducible results of experiment. The creation of blood distributions and the observation of their formation are key for learning and research. A thorough BPA examination is methodical, requiring care and patience, detailed observation and the accurate recording of information with labels and measurements. It is complex and time-consuming. Training, casework experience (8), and consideration of casework context are vital for an objective and balanced interpretation. Despite this grounding in science, BPA has been labeled subjective (9). A prominent BPA expert suggests this is a misconception, unwittingly encouraged in two ways by the actions of practitioners:

- Historically, by opining at crime scenes without disclosing their supporting reasoning
- Failing to sufficiently document the conceptual development of BPA in the scientific record (10)

Despite this, the scientific record is not devoid of BPA. The prejudicial view of the discovery of blood is referenced throughout early law and literature. Scientific articles dating back to the nineteenth century demonstrate the origins of the specialism, but their descriptions of bloodstains are often problematic in that no consistent classification of blood patterns had yet been developed. The 1895 work of Piotrowski, "*Concerning Origin, Shape, Direction and Distribution of the Bloodstains following Head Wounds Caused by Blows*" (11), while brutal in its use of live rabbits, which he subjected to various bludgeonings, was also groundbreaking in its recognition of the directionality of airborne stains and their relevance to cast-off patterns resulting from blood flung off moving objects (12).

The work of Hans Gross, "*Handbook fur Untersuchungsrichter als System der Kriminalistik*" contained extensive details on the role of blood patterns in the investigative process, considering their collection, documentation and evaluation. It was considered the authoritative text of the time and an English translation, "*Criminal Investigation*", was published by J. Collyer Adam in 1924 (12).

The 1914 works of Haberda and Ziemke recognize many of the features included in modern BPA classifications. Haberda in particular, recognizing the importance of practitioner experience and warning of the limitations of interpretation (12). The work of Balthazard (13) was influential in the 1930s in considering trajectories of blood, and in understanding the importance of the ratio of length to width of bloodstains in determining the angle with which a blood drop has impacted a surface – the basis of modern techniques (12).

In 1966, Dr Paul Kirk delivered expert testimony (14) in a retrial of the 1955 case of *State of Ohio v Samuel Sheppard*, in which the defendant was accused of bludgeoning his wife, Marilyn Reese Sheppard, to death. Sheppard had been convicted at his original 1955 trial and served 10 years of a life sentence prior to the 1966 retrial. Dr Kirk's evidence, based on his examination of the crime scene, discussed the handedness of the perpetrator, and established the relative positions of the perpetrator and deceased at the time of the bludgeoning. It was considered instrumental in Sheppard's exoneration and is cited as a moment of acceptance and validation of BPA by a criminal justice system (11). This recognition of the specialism heralded what might be considered the modern era of BPA.

DOI: 10.1201/9781003138754-101

Professor Herbert MacDonnell is proclaimed by many as the father of modern BPA (11), and he is credited with creating the first comprehensive BPA training program. His 1971 publication, "*Flight Characteristics and Stain Patterns of Human Blood*" (15), co-authored with Lorraine Bialousz, is based on studies recreating blood distributions observed at crime scenes.

This chapter is intended not as an instruction manual for practitioners, but rather as a tour of the specialism for those who are familiar with the effects of injury, via a selection of injury-causing actions frequently encountered in criminal casework. The aim will be to consider the types of blood patterns that might be observed on the clothing and body of the injured party, those of the perpetrator, any weapons or objects involved and the material environs. These considerations are designed to provide an eclectic description of blood pattern types and will refer to case examples where these have been significant. They should not however be considered exhaustive. That is far beyond the scope of a single chapter, and a number of detailed texts (11,12,16,17) are available on the subject.

FUNDAMENTALS

To most effectively discuss the potential outcomes of the injuries in the examples that follow, it will be useful to provide some fundamental principles here as a basis for understanding.

An arrangement of bloodstains in an identifiable pattern can be defined as a blood distribution. Blood distributions can be broadly categorized according to how they came to be formed:

- Contact with a source of wet blood
- Blood becoming airborne due to the application of force, causing the formation of blood drops which subsequently land on a surface
- The flowing and pooling of liquid blood

Much of the terminology recommended by the Scientific Working Group on Bloodstain Pattern Analysis (SWGSTAIN) is defined by how the various stain types and patterns are formed (18). This is by far the most widely used approach, although other groups advocate for a mechanism-free nomenclature (19).

Contact stains

Contact-type bloodstains may be instructive in providing information about the bloodstained surface or object that made the stain, perhaps by revealing a shape or pattern. Such features might be indicative of a weapon or other object, although it should be understood that such an imprint is often partial, and its value also lies in the identification of the corresponding object. Such features may, in turn, suggest activities that took place during the incident. For example, circular marks in blood on a surface within the scene of an extensive and fatal beating, in conjunction with findings from two different wine bottles, bearing the perpetrator's fingerprints in blood, and with bloodstained bases, which matched the shape of the circular marks, suggested to investigators that the perpetrator had likely drunk the contents of these bottles after blood had been shed, that is, during or after the violent acts. Bloody fingermarks are a common observation at scenes and on exhibits that may be instructive in suggesting particular actions within the context of a case, even if no fingerprints can be identified from the stains.

Contact-type blood patterns might also indicate movement within the location of an incident, for example, the swipe pattern caused by bloodstained hair brushing a surface. It is not unusual to observe fabric marks in blood, which are potentially the source of other trace evidence such as fibers, and whose deposition may have altered other bloodstains at the scene (Figure 97.1).

Airborne blood: Single drops

The airborne blood distributions also provide information about the mechanisms that led to their deposition and are classified in that vein. Knowledge of the behavior and characteristics of single blood drops is required to identify these distributions, and investigation of the single blood drop is a popular place to begin the practical aspects of BPA training. Through a series of experiments designed to examine changing variables, the BPA trainee quickly learns that the characteristics of an airborne stain are affected by characteristics of the drop: its volume, speed, the distance traveled, the angle traveled relative to the recipient surface and by characteristics of the recipient surface. These are fundamentals of BPA.

Blood drops are spherical. Distorted slightly by movement and air resistance, nevertheless, blood drops falling due to gravity onto smooth flat surfaces form circular stains, referred to as spots of blood. The tightness of a blood drop is influenced by the ratio of red cells to plasma, which affects the extent to which the blood drop spreads on contact with a surface (20). The size of the blood drop is also a factor, larger blood drops

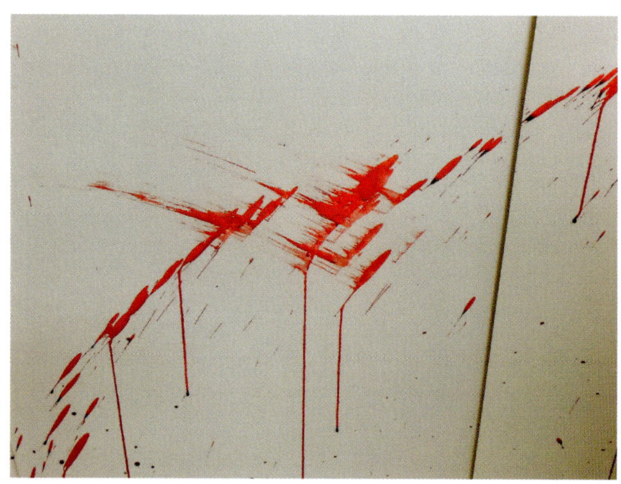

97.1 Projected stains affected by a wipe caused by hair and clothing, generated during BPA student training.

resulting in larger blood spots. The definition of "blood spot" here is significant, and its use by experts in casework reports implies that the blood under discussion has, at some point, been airborne. Factors such as the shape and dimensions of the site where blood drops are forming will affect the size of the drops produced, and hence, the size of the resultant blood spots. Generally, a pointed surface such as the tip of a knife tends to allow blood drops to form readily, resulting in a more frequent release of smaller drops compared to the larger volume drops that take longer to overcome surface tension and break away from the main source of wet blood dripping from a flatter surface (21,22).

As the height from which a blood drop falls increases, so too does the size of the resultant spot, up to the height from which the blood drop reaches terminal velocity and no longer accelerates due to gravity, at which point, spot size reaches its maximum. Given these findings, subsequent studies show that, as one might expect, an increase in the velocity with which blood drops travel also correlates to an increase in diameter of resultant spots (23).

The nature of the blood-receiving surface is a significant factor in the appearance of the resultant blood stain (24). Rough and textured surfaces cause a blood drop to break up and fragment on landing, resulting in stains with a disrupted edge to various degrees. These appearances range from a roughly circular stain with a scalloped edge on near smooth surfaces to stains that are overwhelmingly distorted and unrecognizable as circular on uneven surfaces. Frequently, small portions of the drop break away and are flung outward from the main stain in directions dictated by surface texture, even on relatively smooth surfaces, to form spines emanating from the edge of the parent stain, and what is termed secondary or satellite spatter (25) (Figure 97.2).

These effects are often pronounced by the qualities of some fabrics (26), with the additional effect that fabric's absorbent properties may mean that blood drops have no chance to spread across these surfaces, resulting in far smaller stains than might be expected (27). Some fabrics demonstrate effects counter to these expectations due to such factors as dyeing or other surface treatments, causing blood to wick in the direction of the fabric weave (28), or in some cases, separation of plasma from the other blood constituents. Such fabric effects may render identification of airborne blood impossible, or at the very least a source of debate and potential controversy within a case (29).

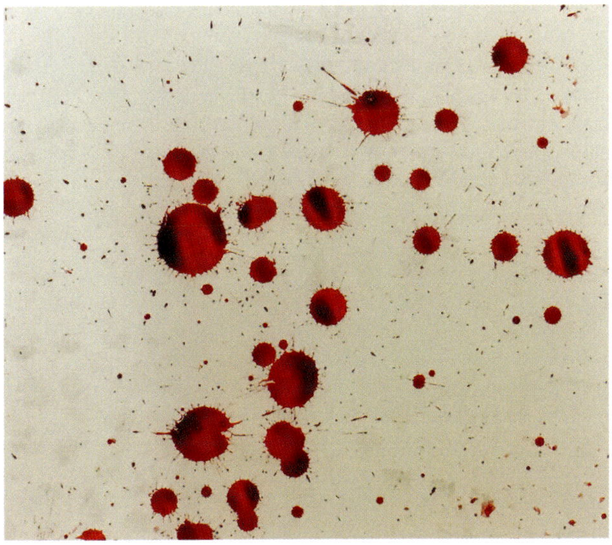

97.2 Blood spots on paper exhibiting spines and satellite spatter, generated during BPA student training.

The direction in which blood drops are traveling relative to the recipient surface has a marked effect on the shape of the resultant stain (13). As discussed previously, blood drops falling at 90 degrees to the recipient surface, that is, falling vertically due to the effects of gravity, produce circular stains. If blood is being acted upon by other forces, then its direction of travel may not be perpendicular to the recipient surface. As the angle of a blood drop's trajectory becomes more acute relative to the recipient surface, the resultant stain becomes more elliptical, increasing in elongation inversely to the size of this angle, and involving the additional morphology resulting from wave cast off. Wave cast off is defined as "*A small blood drop that originates from a parent drop of blood due to the wave-like action of the liquid in conjunction with striking a surface.*"

This is easiest to demonstrate in training using blood dripping vertically onto a surface angled through various degrees, although the effects are the same when blood travels through non-vertical trajectories. As the angle decreases, the morphology of resultant stains goes through a "bear claw" stage, (Figure 97.3) and at the extremes of angle, resembles an elongated exclamation mark; wave cast off producing the dot (Figure 97.4).

The ability to calculate angle led to the development of various models for estimating the location of the source of airborne blood spots within the crime scene. The most basic of these methods is known as stringing (30,31), and as the name suggests, uses string to extrapolate the trajectories of multiple blood drops to determine an area of convergence (32), thus indicating a location within the scene where a force was applied to wet blood, that is, the likely location an injury was inflicted. The inaccuracies of stringing, in failing to account for the effects of gravity on what are ultimately curved trajectories of blood drops, must be accounted for by the practitioner as a manageable limitation, which has the effect of suggesting a slightly higher than actual height of the injury-causing action. Despite this, the technique is extremely useful in scene reconstruction, and this limitation rarely affects the analyst's ability to infer a potential sequence of events, where there is sufficient information in the blood findings. The time-consuming and impractical nature of stringing has led to the development of various software packages for use in the calculation of blood drop trajectories (6).

Airborne distributions

A collection of associated blood spots, thought to have been deposited by a single event, is termed a spatter distribution. Knowledge of the properties of single blood drops, particularly in indicating direction, allow the identification of distinct distributions that can be

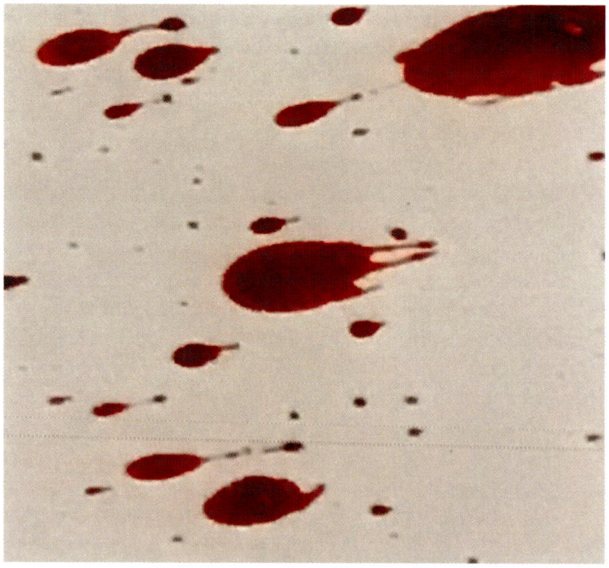

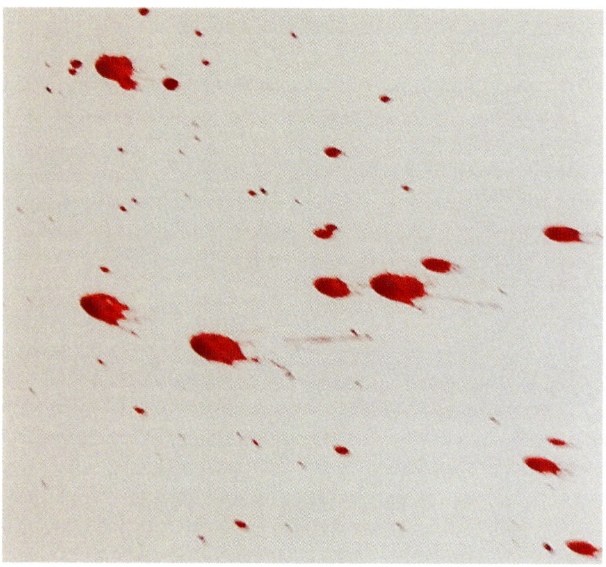

97.3 Directional bloodstains exhibiting a "bear claw" appearance from impact spatter, generated during BPA student training.

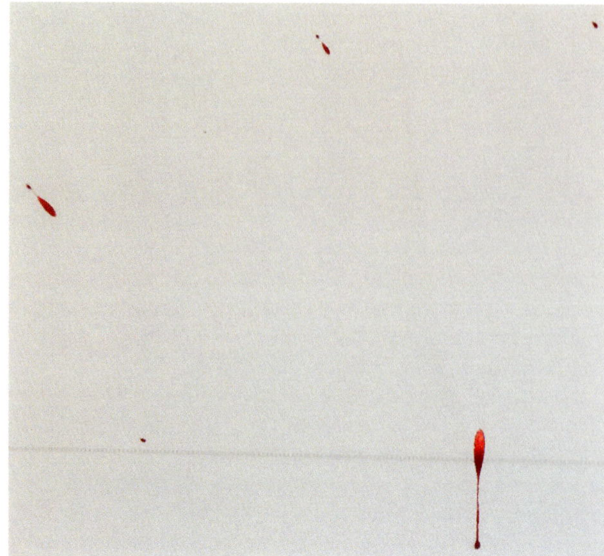

97.4 Elongated, elliptical bloodstains demonstrating wave cast off, generated during BPA student training.

attributed to the different types of action causing blood to become airborne. The airborne blood distributions can be broadly separated into those caused by:

- An impact into wet blood – impact spatter
- Blood being flung from a moving object – cast off
- Blood dripping due to gravity – passive drips and drip trails
- Blood being forced from the body under pressure – projected stains/spurts.

The criteria used to describe and identify specific blood distributions in modern BPA are based on those devised by Anita Wonder in her 2001 work, "*Blood Dynamics*" (16). These can be summarized as follows:

- Shapes of the whole pattern
- Alignment of spatters with regard to the whole pattern
- Alignment of spatters with regard to other spatters
- Distribution of sizes of spatters
- Distribution of numbers of spatters

Based on these criteria, an **impact spatter** (33) pattern can be described as fan, wedge, trapezoid or starburst-shaped. Individual spatters radiate from a specific area or source (the thin end of the fan, wedge, or trapezoid, or the center of a starburst-shaped distribution) indicating directionality away from the source. They contain a wide range of different-sized spatters that decrease in density in the direction of movement of the blood, away from the source. It is also useful to note here that generally, larger blood drops have the capacity to travel further than smaller drops. The shape of the pattern will be influenced by the nature of the site of the impact, the amount of wet blood at the site of the impact, the positions of the parties involved relative to each other and to their surroundings, the dimensions of the implement used to cause the impact and the speed and force of the blow (Figure 97.5).

Cast-off blood distributions (34,35) are linear or columnar, following the path of the moving object from which the blood is being released. Sometimes the swing of a weapon follows a curved path, and this would likely be reflected in the shape of any cast-off distribution generated from that swing. Individual spatters are parallel to the linear orientation of the pattern and to each other. The range of size of spatters may be small, spatter being of fairly uniform size and density throughout the distribution and indicating uniform directionality (Figure 97.6).

It is not unusual in cases of bludgeoning for multiple cast-off patterns to overlay each other. Often, stains are observed that indicate opposing directions, caused by blood drops being cast off during both the forward and backward swings of a weapon. Such distributions, particularly those observed on ceilings, are often referred to as "inline staining" by practitioners. On some occasions,

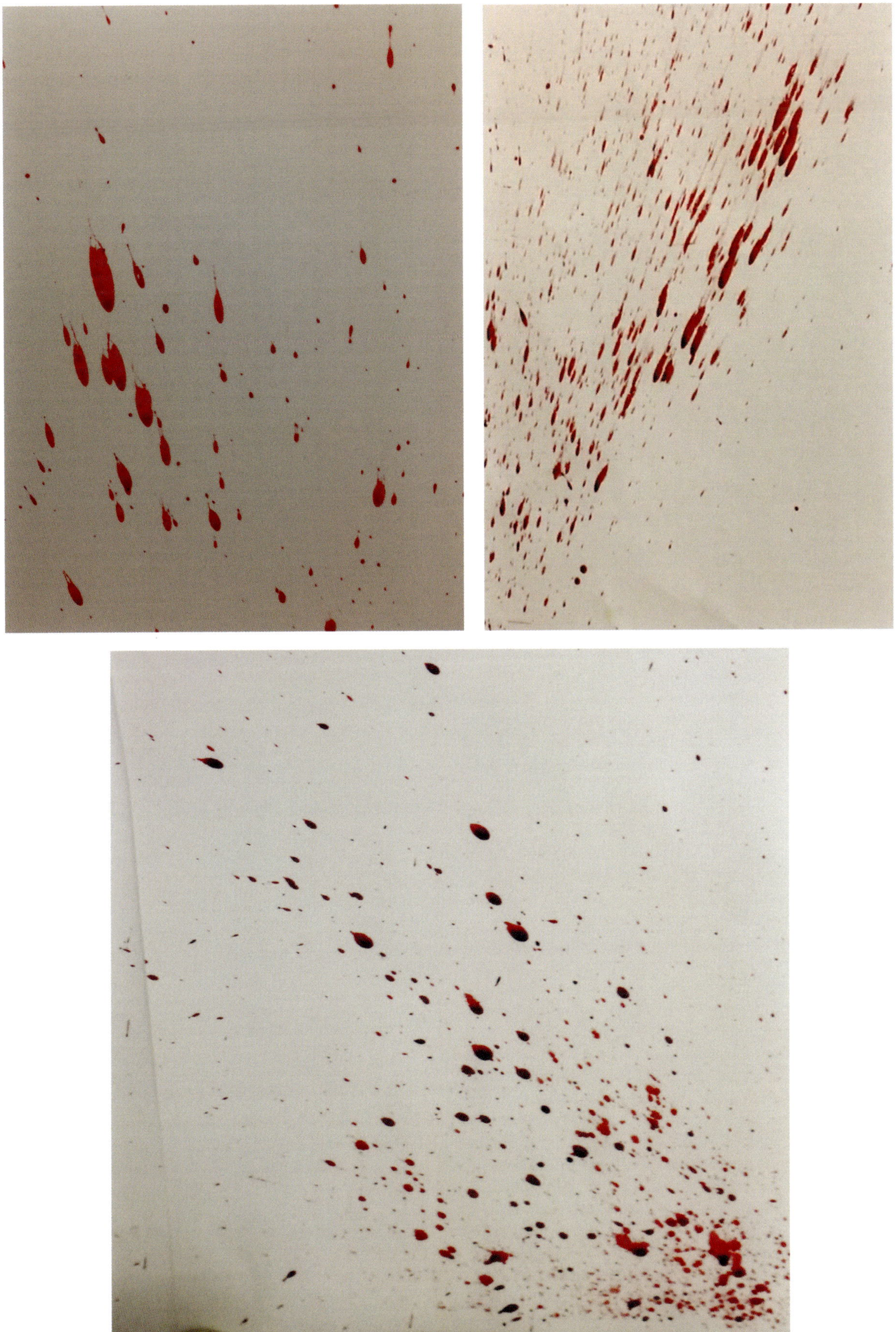

97.5 Impact spatter distributions, generated during BPA student training.

it may be possible to infer, from the numbers of individual linear patterns, an approximate number of swings of a putative weapon that might have caused the observed findings. It should be emphasized that this is not always straightforward, particularly when dealing with overlapping distributions. It should also be remembered that in inferring the number of blows struck in an assault scenario, the initial swing would cause no cast-off distribution since the weapon would likely be free of blood at that point.

Passive drip distributions are governed by the behavior of single drops as previously described. Frequently, these distributions are formed by blood dripping over a period of time, such that blood falls into blood. In this situation, a single blood spot becomes a stain of increasing size; blood dripping into a growing pool causing increasing numbers of splashes, manifest as satellite spatter extending further outward with increasing randomness of direction as more blood is added. The speed with which drips fall is also a factor in determining the spread of satellite spatter, a faster drip rate leading to a wider spread of satellite stains.

Drip trails may be formed by the movement of a person who is dripping wet blood. If the blood dripping is due to an actively bleeding injury, the blood will continue to drip as blood is replenished at the site of injury. Some of the spots within the drip trail may show directionality; indeed, these distributions are essentially cast off, and as such, fit the described criteria. These findings may indicate the extent of the person's movement throughout a scene.

Associated with cast off is **cessation cast off**, the blood flung from a moving object at the point at which it strikes. In training, this is often demonstrated by striking a bloodstained weapon on a solid object, such as a block of wood. The resultant cessation cast-off distribution is an area of fine, densely packed, localized spatter; some individual spatters being far smaller than 1 mm in diameter. In a casework scenario, particularly if there have been numerous blows and the injured party has bled extensively, the finer details of cessation cast off may not be distinguishable among the other bloodstains.

While not itself an airborne distribution, **percussive staining** should be considered. This is the blood pattern that may be observed on an object, such as a weapon, that has struck a surface with force. As a bloodstained weapon is swung, wet blood runs toward the tip, but the abrupt deceleration as the weapon strikes, causes wet blood to change direction, such that it begins to move in the direction of the blow. This rapid change of direction forms a characteristic feathered blood pattern on the weapon (Figure 97.7). Whether percussive staining is observed on weapons depends on them bearing sufficient wet blood to form the characteristic distribution, but not so much that the fine details of a percussive pattern are rendered invisible against a background of bloodstains. Items bearing percussive staining need not be weapons in the traditional sense at all. Indeed, percussive staining might be found on any object upon which wet blood is able to move, and which has been used to strike a surface with force. In casework practice, however, this distribution is relatively rare, but when it is observed, may provide significant evidence to suggest an object has been used to strike a surface with force. On occasion, percussive staining has been observed on clothing items in casework such as the lower leg of the trousers of an alleged kicker. In that case, this finding could not be explained by the accused's version of events that he had been present at, but played no active part in the kicking, and as such, this finding provided significant support for the Prosecution's case.

Projected stains are most often produced when an individual has an arterial injury. Blood is pumped out

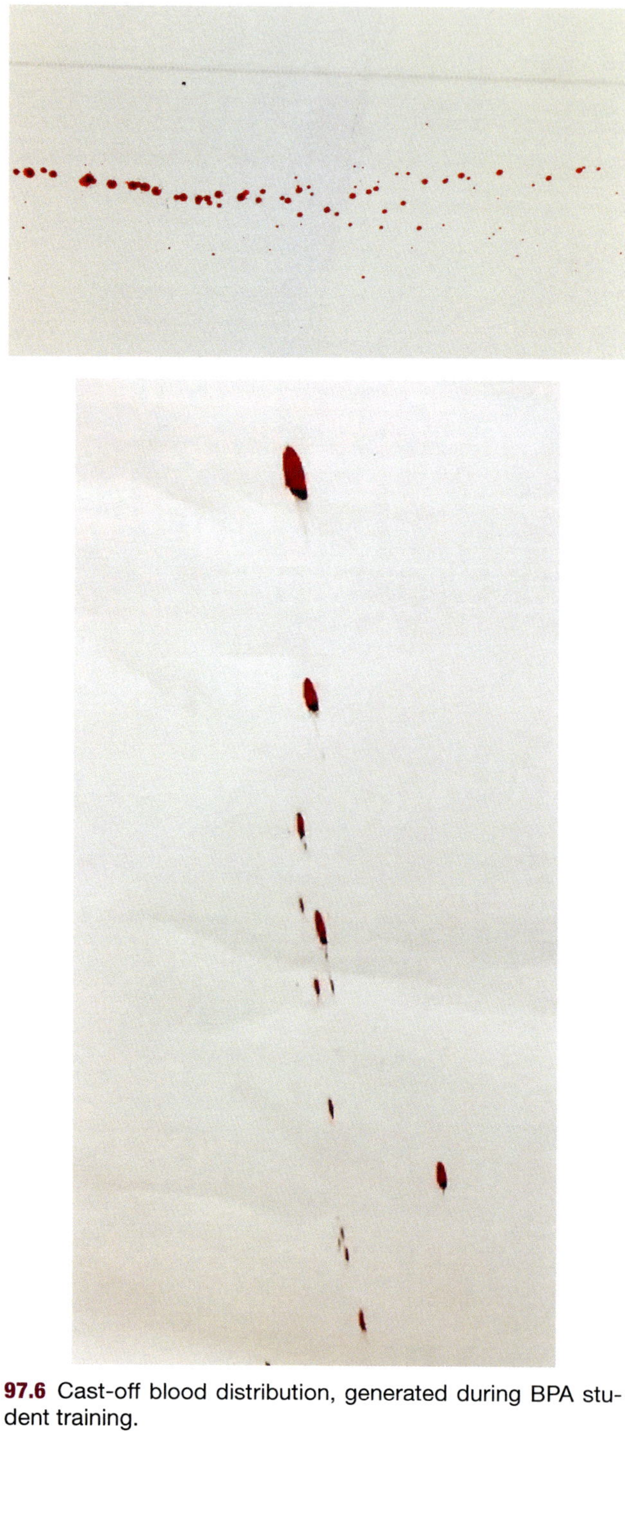

97.6 Cast-off blood distribution, generated during BPA student training.

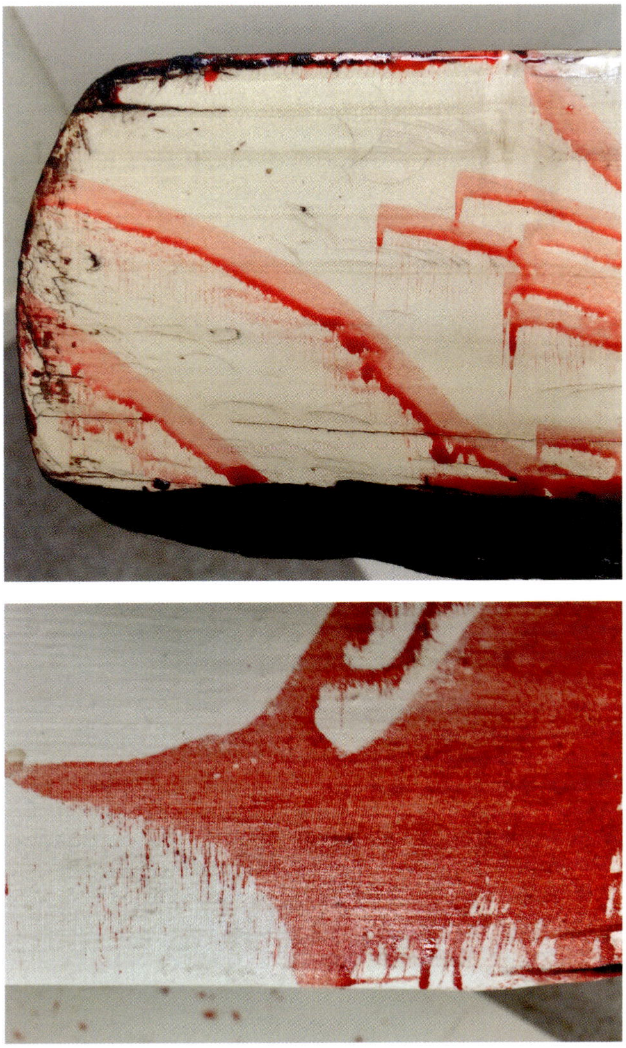

97.7 Percussive staining examples, generated during BPA student training.

97.8 Simulated blood spurt generated during BPA student training.

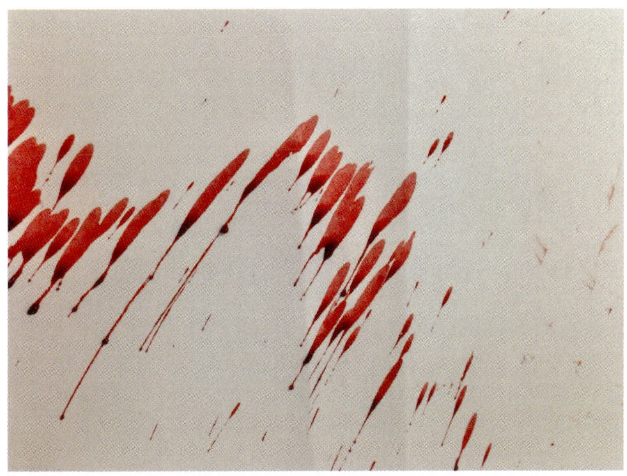

97.9 Simulated arterial projected stain, generated during BPA student training.

of the wound under pressure leading to various distributions, all of which comprise large volumes of blood leading to the vertical runs that characterize this type of distribution on vertical surfaces. These distributions might be made by a single blood spurt, resulting in one or more large starburst-shaped patterns, with heavy vertical runs of blood, and surrounded by extensive satellite spatters (Figure 97.8). More extensive projected staining may form distributions whose shapes show one or more peaks and troughs, the peaks corresponding to the pulse of the injured party as blood is projected. This effect was simulated by squeezing blood from a pipette pointed in an upwardly diagonal direction. The blood "fountain effect" caused the blood drops to land on the nearby wall in their downward trajectory (Figure 97.9). The high volume of blood in projected stains is manifest as large heavy circular blood spots on horizontal surfaces in the manner of those shown in Figure 97.2. Such blood spots may be densely arranged and overlapping, causing splashes and extensive satellite spatter as blood falls into blood. Some analysts describe these types of distributions as "arterial rain".

All distributions described here can be affected by numerous and complex conditions. Blood may begin to clot, stains may be affected by environmental conditions such as weather in outdoor locations, or there may be attempts to clean up a crime scene. Blood may become mixed with other substances: soil or vegetation in outdoor locations, or other body fluids depending on the types of injuries inflicted, or other activities that form part of an incident. Many of these types of distributions are frequently classified as **Physiologically Altered Blood Stains (PABS)**.

While the blood distributions created under controled laboratory conditions during training might be considered typical of some of the actions discussed later, it should be understood that such typical distributions are not guaranteed to be observed in casework. Assault scenarios are complex dynamic events. They often involve the movement and twisting of clothing, resulting in the finding of partial blood patterns and interrupted distributions. Such gaps in blood distributions are referred to as voids. If there have been multiple injury-causing actions during an incident, there are likely to be overlapping patterns at the scene, rendering interpretation a complex task. Critical checking and peer review are standard aspects of BPA, and seeking the agreement of colleagues in this way is built into most forensic science processes. Given this, practitioners should rarely be making BPA interpretations in isolation unless BPA questions are put to them for the first time in the witness box.

Consideration of expected bloodstains resulting from common injuries

These discussions are intended to consider a range of potential outcomes with respect to bloodstains, based on common variables surrounding specific injury types. These considerations are not intended to be exhaustive; indeed, a philosophy of continual learning in forensic science accepts that casework will repeatedly provide fresh circumstances and never-before-seen findings. Discussion will consider the types of blood distributions that might be found at the scene, on the clothing of the complainant and perpetrator and on any relevant objects involved in the incident.

SHARP FORCE TRAUMA: STABBING

The nature of blood loss due to stabbing is dependent on a variety of factors including the number of stab wounds, the nature of the stabbing implement, the location on the body of the wound, particularly whether major blood vessels are breached, and if so, which vessels, and the effects of clothing items worn by the injured person.

A single stab may not lead to the transfer of a significant amount of blood, particularly if the blade is left *in situ*, which may stem the flow of blood from the wound. As such, it is possible in these circumstances for no blood to be transferred to the scene or to the perpetrator. Conversely, multiple stab wounds in a sustained assault are likely to lead to extensive blood loss and therefore provide plenty of opportunity for blood transfer. As more wounds are created and the extent of bleeding increases, there is an increased chance of impact spatter being generated, particularly if subsequent stabbing actions are performed with force into a bloodstained area.

There is an increased chance that one or more arteries may be breached by multiple stabbing actions, leading to an increased chance of observing projected stain distributions. The extent and nature of these will depend on the number and location of stab wounds and the injured person's movements at the scene. It should not be assumed that all arterial injuries are caused by bladed instruments; blows to the scalp can lead to arterial injuries and the production of projected staining.

Stab wounds to the chest that pierce the lungs may lead to the mixing of blood with mucous-like lung surfactant. This, and the leaking of air from the lungs, may lead to the observation of bloodstains with frothy characteristics.

In multiple stabbings with extensive bloodshed, there is an increased expectation that blood will be cast off the blade and hands of the perpetrator as these become more heavily bloodstained. Indeed, it is not uncommon for bloodstained hands to slip on a knife, causing perpetrators to injure their own hand in the process of stabbing. If the perpetrator's blood can be identified at the scene from a passive drip or drip trail, this is likely to be a significant finding. Whether cast off from a stabbing action will produce a typical or complete cast-off distribution depends on factors such as the extent of bleeding, the length of the blade, and the motion of the stabbing actions, and it is possible that such cast-off blood may simply be manifest as randomly distributed blood spots around the general area of the incident.

Multiple stabbings are likely to result in extensive soaked-in stains on the clothing of the injured party, and areas of pooled blood, especially if the incident has had fatal consequences and there has been a delay before the body has been discovered. If the injured party has defensive wounds on their hands or arms, then these may also lead to the creation of drip patterns and contact stains on their clothing. Again, it should be remembered that clothing can be pulled and twisted during an assault scenario such that blood deposited when clothing is distorted may be found in unexpected locations not easily interpreted.

The presence of blood flows and large volume stains at a scene may increase the chance of a perpetrator walking through wet blood and creating footwear marks, which may provide evidence of an individual's presence at and movement within the scene at the time of the incident. If the footwear of suspects is to be examined for blood to address this issue, then the time between the incident and the seizure of the footwear is an important factor to consider when assessing one's expectations. If the footwear has been worn extensively after blood has been deposited on the sole, then most of the blood on the sole may have been lost during this time. However, if the sole has a deep tread, it is possible that traces of blood might remain in these recesses. The action of walking through wet blood can also cause blood to be splashed up onto the uppers, and this may not be as readily removed by wearing the footwear.

Blood may be transferred by the force of impact into wet blood or cast off the knife or hands of the perpetrator, and blood spots are likely to be found on the clothing of perpetrators of stabbing, but there is no typical blood distribution that one might expect to observe. Since the hands, or at least one hand of the perpetrator may be bloodstained, the production of contact stains on the perpetrator's clothing is also possible, and the fastenings and pockets of clothing should be thoroughly searched for signs of blood transferred from the hands.

It is not inevitable that blood will be found on a knife that has been used to stab an individual. Often, the removal of the blade from the wound through skin and layers of clothing causes blood to be wiped off. However, if there are multiple stab wounds and extensive bleeding, then there is more chance that traces of blood will remain on the knife, and, as well as the blade, these may be found on the handle and in the recesses around the hilt. Where blood has been deposited on a knife blade due to stabbing, it is often present in a striated pattern, oriented along the length of the blade, and often on both surfaces. In this distribution, blood is often observed mixed with greasy deposits, believed by some to be fat from the adipose layers of the skin. On serrated blades in particular, fragments of skin may be caught on the edge of the blade, between the teeth.

If a knife is set down at a scene or wiped on clothing, then a knife blade print in blood might be observed. Such marks found on clothing are often distorted by the wiping action, and interrupted by voids, which indicate an area where fabric has crumpled, folded or bunched together as it was held and wiped over the bloodstained surface. Knife marks in blood might be useful in addressing questions such as which knife, from a selection of putative knives, might have caused an injury. Such findings might be considered in conjunction with an examination of the stab cut damage to clothing items and wound morphology, and might be useful in eliminating candidate knives, but are unlikely to be definitive in identifying a particular knife.

Incidents of sharp force trauma with unusual implements (36–39) can occur in casework. The examples cited here suggest the range of unusual weapons that might be encountered, and these papers focus on the nature of the injuries rather than blood patterns formed as a result. However, they are cited to remind the reader that the value of experimentation to inform expectations in unusual casework scenarios should not be underestimated.

BLUNT FORCE TRAUMA

A wide variety of actions might result in blunt force trauma injuries. As discussed previously, assaults are dynamic situations involving movement, and may result in a series of blood distributions throughout a crime scene that tell a story of the sequence of actions that took place. Again, the greater the extent of bleeding, the more likely it is that recognizable blood distributions will be observed.

Punching most frequently results in head and facial bleeding injuries, with the potential for bleeding after the first blow. Subsequent punches to an area wet with blood will result in the generation of impact spatter, and this is likely to be deposited on surfaces at head height in the early stages of an assault. Impact spatter found at lower levels at the crime scene indicates that the injured person continued to be struck once they were on the ground, perhaps by punching, kicking or other means, and might indicate a location that they fell to the ground if this was not where the assault concluded.

The upper clothing of the injured party in a punching scenario is most likely to be bloodstained. Heavy, soaked-in bloodstains around the neck region and down the center front are common, as are drips to the front center from nosebleed and mouth injuries. The presence of passive drips on the uppers of the footwear, and potentially down the front of lower clothing, may be important in showing that the injured party was upright when bleeding started. Likewise, an absence of such might be equally important in showing that bleeding commenced only after the injured party was down. Depending on the case circumstances, an absence of blood on the lower clothing of the injured person might also indicate that the perpetrator sat astride the complainant while inflicting injury. This action would explain an observed void on the lower clothing of the complainant, and the suggestion might be supported by the finding of extensive impact spatter on the upper front of a suspect's clothing and the upper/inner thighs of their trousers or on the front of their skirt, potentially with multiple voids if skirt fabric had been bunched.

Contact bloodstains on the upper clothing of the injured party might also be present as a result of contact with the perpetrator during the assault. There may have been grappling and struggling between the protagonists, that might be indicated by contact stains on the complainant's clothing, such as finger marks in blood, for example.

The action of punching can cause a distinct distribution on the body and clothing of the perpetrator, which can be reproduced in experiment. Provided sufficient blood is present at the site of the punch, depending on the force involved, and the precise nature of the swing, a punch can result in transfer of contact bloodstaining and impact spatter to the fist of the assailant and their cuff, if long sleeves are worn. Contact stains and fine spatter may also be found on any watches or other wrist jewelery worn on the punching arm. Directional blood spatter may be found on any aspect of the sleeve of the punching arm; depending on the exact nature of the punch and the relative heights of the protagonists, this might be concentrated on the upper, lower or inner aspects of the sleeve. Indeed, during the examination of clothing and in describing the location of bloodstains, it is useful to remember that clothing, when worn, has three dimensions. As such, descriptions of front or back, based on flat, unworn items, may not effectively express where exactly on the wearer's body stains are located. In many punching distributions, directional spatter is often found across the upper chest of the perpetrator's clothing traveling away from the punching arm. Further, blood spots indicating a downward direction are sometimes found on the upper back below the shoulder of the punching arm. Some of these stains may be impact spatter from the site of the punch, or blood cast off the punching arm as it pulls back. A similar effect is seen in Figure 97.10 showing blood on the rear shoulder of a student who had struck into wet blood with a hammer. It should be emphasized here, that while these aspects of a punching distribution *can* be found, it does not follow that they are *always* found, based as they are on multiple complex variables, as previously explained.

The action of **kicking** is most frequently applied to complainants who are on the ground. Given the now familiar caveat that there must be sufficient bleeding to provide blood to transfer, then if there have been sufficient kicks to an area wet with blood, these are likely to generate impact spatter distributed at a low level at the crime scene. At indoor scenes, areas of concentrated impact blood spatter are likely to identify an obvious area or areas within the scene where injuries were inflicted. At outdoor scenes, the impact spatter might be dispersed on grass or vegetation, but the trained examiner with experience of outdoor scenes will be likely to find it. It may not be possible from these blood distributions to reliably specify whether injuries to the complainant while they were on the ground were caused by kicking or other means. The presence of cast off might indicate the use of a weapon, but its absence may not necessarily exclude one. However, contextual case information, and consideration of these findings alongside those from the clothing of suspected individuals, may ultimately allow the practitioner to provide an overall opinion of events for investigators.

Footwear and lower clothing of suspected individuals are the most important items to examine for blood in an alleged kicking scenario. A kicking action into wet blood can cause a distinct distribution on the footwear and lower clothing of the perpetrator, which can be reproduced in experiment. This blood distribution includes contact staining on the part of the footwear that made contact with wet blood during the kick – usually, but not always, the toe. Since this contact bloodstaining has been deposited with the force of the kick, it is expected to be found embedded in the welt and stitching or seams of the footwear. If trousers are worn by the perpetrator, then depending on their length and style, a contact stain may sometimes be found on the hem of the kicking leg. Contact stains are accompanied by directional, often fine spatter on the uppers of footwear pointing away from the site of the kick, and associated directional spatter on the trouser leg, which, depending on their style, may also be found on the lower portions of the *inner* surfaces of the kicking leg of the trousers, and may also be found on the inner aspect of the other leg. Again, based on complex variables, many of these aspects of a kicking distribution *may* be found, but are *not guaranteed* to be observed.

If a perpetrator's kicking action involves the upper of the foot making contact with the complainant, then blood may be transferred to the laces of the footwear, often with signs that the transfer was forceful. If the perpetrator carries out further kicks with the upper of the now bloodstained footwear, then this may transfer the pattern of laces in blood to some other location on the body of the injured person. This transfer mark, in conjunction with bloodstained laces on a suspect's footwear in a matching configuration, would be significant evidence of kicking, and unlikely to be explained by some other action. Marks made by footwear laces can also be found in bruising on the bodies of complainants in kickings and can provide valuable evidence if a matching item of footwear is identified, or even if one is not.

The action of **stamping** into wet blood will produce impact spatter at an extremely low level that may be projected further than that from a kick. This is due to the flat shape of the sole of footwear and the large surface area that makes contact during the stamping action, that has the effect of squeezing blood out from under the sole. The resulting impact spatter may comprise particularly elongated elliptical spatters if it is found on the ground, or on the clothing of the injured party, given that much of this blood would travel in a near horizontal trajectory.

The footwear of perpetrators of stamping may have bloodstains embedded in the tread of the sole. However, as with kicking, the time between the alleged stamping and seizure of the footwear should be borne in mind when considering the significance of findings, including an absence of blood, and wear could be responsible for removal of some or all of the blood transferred to the soles of footwear, for example, if the wearer has walked across wet grass.

Cases of **bludgeoning** may lead to the production of both impact spatter and cast-off blood distributions. In addition to the extent of bleeding, the appearance of these will also depend on the nature of the weapon and the force and location of the blows struck. Spatter patterns from bludgeonings to the head can contain tissue and bone fragments, depending on the extent of the injuries inflicted. Again, the positions of these blood distributions can provide information about the relative positions of complainant and perpetrator during the assault.

Like other blunt force injuries, if there has been extensive bleeding from the face and head, there is likely to be heavily soaked bloodstaining and spatter on the upper clothing of the injured party, with the possibility of downward drips on the lower clothing and footwear if bleeding had commenced when the person was upright, but not if by then they had fallen to the ground.

Multiple blows are also likely to result in the production of impact spatter patterns on the upper clothing of the perpetrator. These may be concentrated around the upper front and the striking arm. Some of the spatter transferred to perpetrator's clothing can be very fine. In the case of Rahan Arshad (40), convicted of bludgeoning his wife and children to death with a rounders bat in 2010, fine blood spatter with DNA profiles matching each of the children found on his clothing provided compelling evidence that he had struck the children and did not support his assertion that it was his wife who was responsible. There has been controversy in some cases, such as that of the murder of Billie-Jo Jenkins (41) who was struck with an iron tent peg, over whether fine spatter is the result of impact or expirated blood. In the Jenkins case, fine blood spatter on the clothing of the accused, Sion Jenkins, was reported by the Crown's expert as resulting from impact. Sion Jenkins was convicted, based in part on this evidence, but he was subsequently acquitted at a retrial in 2006, based on the evidence of a defense-instructed expert who opined that the spatter had been expirated onto his clothing as Billie-Jo lay dying in his arms. Expirated blood distributions may contain features not necessarily expected to be found in impact spatter distributions, such as string-like bloodstains or bubble rings due to the presence of mucous, but an absence of these features does not necessarily exclude the possibility that a spatter pattern was expirated.

Cast-off blood, depending on the dimensions of the weapon, might be transferred to the back of the perpetrator in bludgeoning cases, often to the rear of the striking arm shoulder (Figure 97.10).

Weapons in multiple bludgeonings are likely to become bloodstained. Heavy contact stains on the

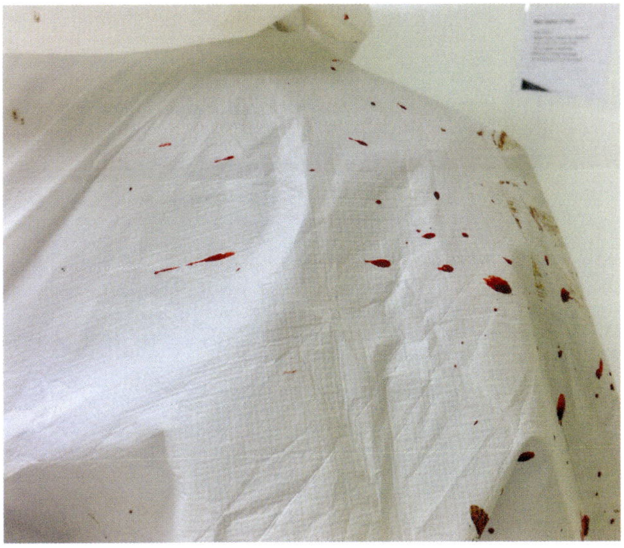

97.10 Blood on the rear of the right shoulder of a student after having created impact spatter using a hammer.

striking surfaces of weapons, surrounded by spatter, are not unusual features. When the head has been struck, bloody hair swipes might also be visible on weapons, and occasionally, hair, tissue or bone fragments may adhere in blood on the striking surfaces. Percussive stains are reliant on specific conditions – there being sufficient wet blood on the weapon when it strikes to allow a pattern to be formed by the moving blood, but not so much that the fine feathered detail of the percussive stain is obscured against a background of existing bloodstaining.

SHOOTING

The effects of gunshot injuries are dependent on the caliber of the firearm, the range of the shot and the location of the wound. Impact spatter distributions produced by gunshots are affected not only by the striking of the projectile, but also by the gases discharged by the weapon, which can cause the separation of blood droplets. Anita Wonder proposes that for these reasons, impact spatter distributions caused by gunshots are essentially composite patterns (16), comprising the overlapping impact distribution caused by the striking bullet, which may initially expose a source of wet blood, and a second impact spatter distribution, made by the interaction of rapidly expanding gases with the blood source, which can cause an atomized and explosive spatter pattern manifest as streaks and mists of blood. The similarity of such mists to expirated blood may be a common cause of misinterpretation, and again, the presence of mucous may cause string-like stains and bubble rings not necessarily expected in blood distributions from gunshots, depending on the location of the wound(s) on the body. However, blood distributions from some wounds may include fragments of tissue and bone. Gunshots can also involve secondary events, which contribute to the distribution of blood produced, such as blood being cast off the injured person as they fall, or the rapid dripping of blood into blood, resulting in extensive satellite spatter.

In some circumstances, blood droplets can be projected backward, against the direction of the shot, onto the firearm and the hand and arm of the shooter. Such distributions are most often seen in contact gunshot wounds to the head (42). For a while, the suggestion of "backspatter" was controversial and remained unrecognized by some experts, but it has since been demonstrated in experiments and recorded using high speed photography (43).

AREAS OF CURRENT RESEARCH IN BPA

The question of the age of bloodstains has long been the subject of discussion in casework, and there have been various investigations of blood drying times under specific casework circumstances or due to other variables (44). Various methods are currently being researched that might address the age of bloodstains over longer periods, beyond drying. These include methods for: measuring chemical and visual changes in stains (45), measuring the decreasing flexibility of the surface of dried stains (46), and measuring the degradation of mitochondrial DNA in stains (47). Such methods and others might be useful in BPA interpretation in addressing whether findings can be explained by competing versions of events, but only provided that methods can be validated as sufficiently discriminating, accurate and consistent, and can be made available as a test that can be conducted in a quick and cost-effective manner. None of these methods appears to have yet been developed to this stage.

An interesting method using RNA analysis to identify the source of wound cells found in bloodstains has been proposed (48). If successful, and made available in a usable format, such a test could be useful in crime scene reconstruction in determining which blood distributions corresponded to particular wounds. RNA methods are also being investigated for use in the identification of body fluids since current chemical methods are often limited by their presumptive nature.

It is encouraging that a number of investigations designed to address matters of quality and consistency in BPA interpretation have been conducted (29,49,50), some using software solutions (51). Further, models are being suggested to minimize the effects of bias in BPA interpretation by managing casework contextual data (52). Finally, a recent study proposes quantifying the outcomes of BPA interpretations from casework with the aim of building a knowledge base to inform future casework practice and interpretation (53). It is hoped that these quality-centered measures will be useful in countering arguments that BPA is limited by its subjectivity, and in so doing, will assist (in England & Wales) in satisfying Part 19.4 of the Criminal Procedure Rules and Practice Directions (54), which specifies the requirements of expert findings for admissibility – particularly CrimPD19A.4, that "*the court must be satisfied that there is a sufficiently reliable scientific basis for the evidence to be admitted.*"

CONCLUSION

The history of BPA is rooted in experimentation and observation. While the ethics of some of this early work were questionable, the science was robust, and successfully documented the behavior of blood drops under various forces, establishing the fundamental principles of BPA.

The discipline has developed by embracing technology, particularly by prompting development in such areas as imaging and software, yet the solutions to some questions, such as calculating the age of bloodstains, remain elusive in any practicable form, although research in these areas continues.

Modern BPA practice is reliant on training, competence and experience, all of which are immersive and hands-on. The effective interpretation of bloodstain patterns and the intelligible communication of these findings are reliant on a comprehensive and universal classification system, and the discipline has developed to include appropriate explanation of the basis of expert opinions, such that they appear less subjective than previous critics had perceived.

Interpretation of blood patterns is frequently dependent on context. Assaults are dynamic events affected by multiple and complex variables that may be impossible to anticipate. Given this, casework findings may vary significantly from the "typical" distributions created under controled laboratory conditions. An experienced practitioner is able to both manage this uncertainty and acknowledge the learning potential in each casework situation. Further, those using BPA evidence in the criminal justice system must understand that expert conclusions are not intended to be definitive. Investigative conclusions may provide potential explanations in a bid to adduce a sequence of events that led to the spilling of blood, while evaluative conclusions are balanced, considering at least two alternative propositions. Opinions most frequently provide levels of support that are rarely definitive yet have the potential to exclude a putative version of events if it can be said that the blood findings do not fit with the suggested actions.

Most encouragingly, much of current research and practice is highly quality-focused, seeking to establish standards of consistency in interpretation and inform future practice.

REFERENCES

1. Attinger D, Moore C, Donaldson A, et al. Fluid dynamics topics in bloodstain pattern analysis: Comparative review and research opportunities. *Forensic Sci Int* 2013; **231**: 375–96.
2. Laan N, de Bruin KG, Slenter D, et al. Bloodstain pattern analysis: Implementation of a fluid dynamic model for position determination of victims. *Sci Rep* 2015; **5**: 11461.
3. Attinger D. Charts based on millions of fluid dynamics simulations provide a simple tool to estimate how far from its source a specific blood stain can be found. *Forensic Sci Int* 2019; **298**: 97–105.
4. Arthur RM, Humburg PJ, Hoogenboom J, et al. An image-processing methodology for extracting bloodstain pattern features. *Forensic Sci Int* 2017; **277**: 122–32.
5. Dustin D, Liscio E. Accuracy and repeatability of the laser scanner and total station for crime and accident scene documentation. *J Assoc Crime Scene Reconstr* 2016; **20**: 57–67.
6. Home PH, Norman DG, Williams MA. Software for the trajectory analysis of blood-drops: A systematic review. *Forensic Sci Int* 2021; **328**: 110992.
7. Joris P, Develter W, Jenar E, et al. HemoVision: An automated and virtual approach to bloodstain pattern analysis. *Forensic Sci Int* 2015; **251**: 116–23.
8. Bettison A, Krosch MN, Chaseling J, Wright K. Bloodstain pattern analysis: Does experience equate to expertise? *J Forensic Sci* 2021; **66**(3): 866–78.
9. Committee on Identifying the Needs of the Forensic Sciences Community, National Research Council. Strengthening forensic science in the United States: A path forward. Available from: https://www.ojp.gov/pdffiles1/nij/grants/228091.pdf (Accessed 23 June 2023).
10. Millington J. The Barrister. BPA: Is it worth the paper it's spattered on? Available from: http://www.barristermagazine.com/blood-pattern-analysis-is-it-worth-the-paper-its-spattered-on/ (Accessed 23 June 2023).
11. James SH, Kish PE, Sutton TP. *Principles of Bloodstain Pattern Analysis: Theory and Practice*. Boca Raton: CRC Press; 2005.
12. Bevel T, Gardner RM. *Bloodstain Pattern Analysis with an Introduction to Crime Scene Reconstruction*, 3rd ed. Boca Raton: CRC Press/Taylor & Francis; 2008.
13. Balthazard V, Piedelievre R, Desoille H, Derobert L. Etude des gouttes de Sang prjete. *Med Soc Toxicol* 1939; **19**: 265–323.
14. Cleveland State University. Volume 04, 1966 trial transcript (retrial of Samuel H. Sheppard): Testimony; State rests; Motions for directed verdict and time, 1966. Available from: https://engagedscholarship.csuohio.edu/cgi/viewcontent.cgi?article=1003&context=sheppard_transcripts_1966 (Accessed 23 June 2023).
15. MacDonnell HL, Bialousz LF. *Flight Characteristics and Stain Patterns of Human Blood*. New York: Nile & CJ; 1971.
16. Wonder AY. *Blood Dynamics*. London: Academic Press; 2001.
17. Wonder AY. *Bloodstain Pattern Evidence: Objective Approaches and Case Applications*. Amsterdam/ London: Elsevier/ Academic Press; 2007.
18. Forensic Science Communications. Scientific working group on bloodstain pattern analysis: Recommended terminology, 2009. Available from: https://theiai.org/docs/SWGSTAIN_Terminology.pdf (Accessed 23 June 2023).
19. Arthur RM, Cockerton SL, de Bruin KG, Taylor MC. A novel, element-based approach for the objective classification of bloodstain patterns. *Forensic Sci Int* 2015; **257**: 220–8.
20. Wonder AY, Yezzo GM. *Bloodstain Patterns: Identification, Interpretation and Application*. Amsterdam: Elsevier; 2014.
21. Adam CD. Experimental and theoretical studies into the release of blood droplets from weapon tips. *Forensic Sci Int* 2019; **303**: 109934.
22. Kabaliuk N, Jermy MC, Morison K, et al. Blood drop size in passive dripping from weapons. *Forensic Sci Int* 2013; **228(1–3)**: 75–82.
23. Hulse-Smith L, Mehdizadeh NZ, Chandra S. Deducing drop size and impact velocity from circular bloodstains. *J Forensic Sci* 2005; **50(1)**: 1–10.
24. Gardner RM. Defining the diameter of the smallest parent stain produced by a drip. *J Forensic Identif* 2006; **56(2)**: 210.
25. Boos K, Orr A, Illes M, Stotesbury T. Characterizing drip patterns in bloodstain pattern analysis: An investigation of the influence of droplet impact velocity and number of droplets on static pattern features. *Forensic Sci Int* 2019; **301**: 55–66.
26. Miles HF, Morgan RM, Millington JE. The influence of fabric surface characteristics on satellite bloodstain morphology. *Sci Justice* 2014; **54(4)**: 262–66.
27. de Castro T, Nickson T, Carr D, Knock C. Interpreting the formation of

bloodstains on selected apparel fabrics. *Int J Legal Med* 2013; **127(1)**: 251–8.
28. Dicken L, Knock C, Carr DJ, Beckett S. The effect of reactive dyeing of fabric on the morphology of passive bloodstains. *Forensic Sci Int* 2022; **336**: 111317.
29. Taylor MC, Laber TL, Kish PE, et al. The reliability of pattern classification in bloodstain pattern analysis-PART 2: Bloodstain patterns on fabric surfaces. *J Forensic Sci* 2016; **61(6)**: 1461–6.
30. Carter AL. The directional analysis of bloodstain patterns theory and experimental validation. *J Can Soc Forensic Sci* 2001; **34(4)**: 173–89.
31. Knock C, Davison M. Predicting the position of the source of blood stains for angled impacts. *J Forensic Sci* 2007; **52(5)**: 1044–9.
32. Camana F. Determining the area of convergence in bloodstain pattern analysis: A probabilistic approach. *Forensic Sci Int* 2013; **231(1–3)**: 131–6.
33. Flight C, Jones M, Ballantyne KN. Determination of the maximum distance blood spatter travels from a vertical impact. *Forensic Sci Int* 2018; **293**: 27–36.
34. Williams EMP, Graham ES, Jermy MC, et al. The dynamics of blood drop release from swinging objects in the creation of cast-off bloodstain patterns. *J Forensic Sci* 2019; **64(2)**: 413–21.
35. Liscio E, Bozek P, Guryn H, Le Q. Observations and 3D analysis of controlled cast-off stains. *J Forensic Sci* 2020; **65(4)**: 1128–40.
36. Oki T, Asamura H, Hayashi T, Ota M. Unusual intracranial stab wounds inflicted with metal tent stakes for a case involving a family murder suicide. *Forensic Sci Int* 2010; **202(1–3)**: e19–21.
37. Krishna K, Behera C, Singh SR, Bhardwaj DN. Ice pick death: A case report and discussion of the injury pattern. *J Forensic Leg Med* 2013; **20(7)**: 803–5.
38. Muchuweti D, Muguti E. Penetrating thoracoabdominal injuries from multiple-spiked spear stabbing: Case report and literature review. *Clin Case Rep* 2020; **8(6)**: 1002–6.
39. Ihama Y, Nagai T, Ninomiya K, et al. A transnasal intracranial stab wound by a plastic-covered umbrella tip. *Forensic Sci Int* 2012; **214(1–3)**: e9–e11.
40. Manchester Evening News. Bloodstains evidence in Arshad case, 2010. Available from: https://www.manchestereveningnews.co.uk/news/greater-manchester-news/bloodstains-evidence-in-arshad-case-984801 (Accessed 23 June 2023).
41. Atkinson E. Billie-Jo Jenkins: Police review forensic material in major unsolved murder case, 2022. Available from: https://www.independent.co.uk/news/uk/crime/billiejo-jenkins-cold-case-murder-forensic-b2004380.html (Accessed 23 June 2023).
42. Stephens BG, Allen TB. Back spatter of blood from gunshot wounds - observations and experimental simulation. *J Forensic Sci* 1983; **28(2)**: 437–9.
43. Radford GE, Taylor MC, Kieser JA, et al. Simulating backspatter of blood from cranial gunshot wounds using pig models. *Int J Legal Med* 2016; **130(4)**: 985–94.
44. Ramsthaler F, Kroll AK, Verhoff M, et al. Effect of anticoagulation therapy on drying times in bloodstain pattern analysis. *Int J Legal Med* 2017; **131(4)**: 955–61.
45. Kumar R, Sharma K, Sharma V. Bloodstain age estimation through infrared spectroscopy and Chemometric models. *Sci Justice* 2020; **60(6)**: 538–46.
46. Smith FR, Nicloux C, Brutin D. A new forensic tool to date human blood pools. *Sci Rep* 2020; **10(1)**: 8598.
47. He H, Zhang Q, Niu Q, et al. Estimating bloodstain formation time by quantitative analysis of mtDNA degradation. *Forensic Sci Int* 2022; **339**: 111411.
48. Johnson DJ, Raymond DE, Chen C, et al. A molecular method to detect wound cells in bloodstains resultant of sharp force injuries for crime scene reconstruction. *J Forensic Sci* 2018; **63(3)**: 842–8.
49. Hicklin RA, Winer KR, Kish PE, et al. Accuracy and reproducibility of conclusions by forensic bloodstain pattern analysts. *Forensic Sci Int* 2021; **325**: 110856.
50. Taylor MC, Laber TL, Kish PE, et al. The reliability of pattern classification in bloodstain pattern analysis, Part 1: Bloodstain patterns on rigid non-absorbent surfaces. *J Forensic Sci* 2016; **61(4)**: 922–7.
51. Liscio E, Le Q. Inter observer errors of cast-off stains using FARO zone 3D. *Forensic Sci Int* 2022; **330**: 111098.
52. Osborne NKP, Taylor MC. Contextual information management: An example of independent-checking in the review of laboratory-based bloodstain pattern analysis. *Sci Justice* 2018; **58(3)**: 226–31.
53. Home PH, Norman DG, Palmer A, et al. Quantifying forensic investigations involving bloodstain pattern analysis within the UK. *Forensic Sci Int* 2022; **339**: 111424.
54. GOV.uk. Criminal procedure rules 2020 and criminal practice directions 2023, 2023. Available from: https://www.gov.uk/guidance/rules-and-practice-directions-2020 (Accessed 23 June 2023).

CHAPTER

98

Forensic Anthropology

Soren Blau

INTRODUCTION

Forensic anthropology is defined as the application of physical anthropology knowledge and techniques to matters of medicolegal significance, particularly those relating to the recovery, documentation and analysis of human remains. While forensic anthropology has its origins in biological (or physical) anthropology, it is now considered its own discipline (1). Over the last 40 years, the role of the forensic anthropologist has developed from focussing on the examination of "more or less skeletonized remains known to be, or suspected of being human" (2), to broader contributions that include the recovery of human remains employing archeological techniques the analysis of taphonomic processes and the examination and interpretation of peri-mortem bone trauma (3). This chapter provides a summary of contributions that a forensic anthropologist may make to a forensic investigation.

WHERE DO FORENSIC ANTHROPOLOGISTS WORK?

Depending on the context, forensic anthropologists may be employed by a range of organizations including institutes of forensic medicine (4), medical examiner offices (5), universities (6), or non-government organizations such as the International Committee of the Red Cross (ICRC) (7). As such, the forensic anthropologist may work on routine jurisdictional casework in domestic medicolegal contexts (8), disaster victim identifications (DVIs) (9,10), recovery and identification of servicemen and women missing in action (11,12), or cases (which are typically large scale) involving the recovery and identification of individuals missing (presumed deceased) as a result of political, ethnic and/or religious violence (13–15).

ROLE OF THE FORENSIC ANTHROPOLOGIST

The role of the forensic anthropologist will vary depending on the context and nature of the case and therefore, the questions that require answering. The extent to which a forensic anthropologist can address such questions will be determined primarily by the completeness (what percentage of the remains survive (16), and the preservation of the remains (Figure 98.1). Several variables influence decomposition including, but not exclusive to, the cause of death, method of body disposal, the environment in which the body was buried or dumped and the time between death and discovery (17). Consequently, a forensic anthropologist may examine remains that are in varying states of preservation, that is, complete (e.g. an intact body); complete but altered (e.g. decomposed, burnt, traumatized, scavenged, etc.); partial (i.e. a body part), or skeletonized (which could include a complete skeleton, multiple or single skeletal elements and/or bone fragments). The information provided by the forensic anthropologist may:

- Exclude a hypothesis, e.g. in the case of a missing person investigation where the missing person was an Asian male, the information provided by the forensic anthropologist indicated the unidentified human remains were those of a Caucasian female. This information allowed the initial identification hypothesis to be excluded.
- Be pivotal, e.g. in the case of a long-term missing person, 24 small bone fragments were all that survived. The results of the forensic anthropologic analysis not only contributed to the identification of the individual (i.e. provided initial information about the age of the individual), but also provided evidence of peri-mortem sharp force trauma which was important in understanding what happened to the person around the time of death.
- Be supportive (collaborative), e.g. evidence of patterned (long linear) blunt force trauma on an individual's cranium provided physical support to a confession provided to the investigator that the alleged offender struck the victim on the head with a shovel.

MEDICOLEGAL SIGNIFICANCE

The forensic anthropologist is responsible for the examination of material that, in the first instance, is believed

DOI: 10.1201/9781003138754-102

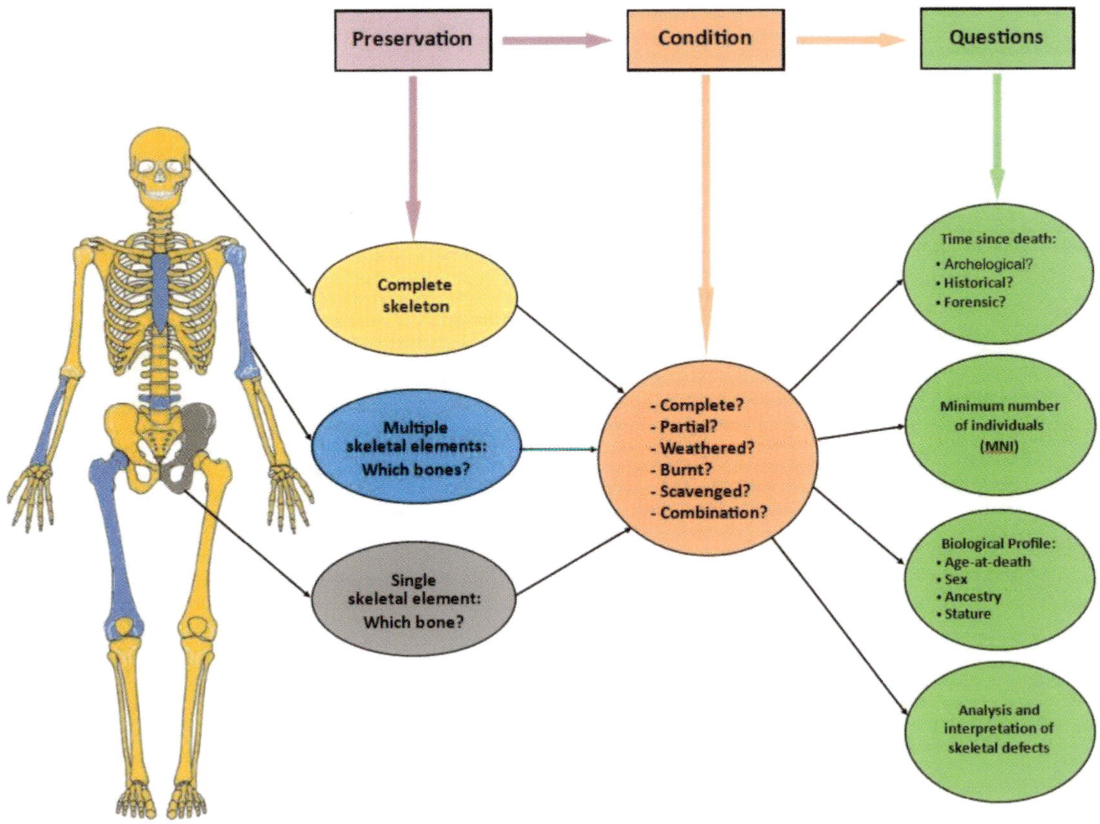

98.1 Factors that impact the extent to which specific questions can be answered by a forensic anthropologist.

to be recent human remains. The first part of a forensic anthropologic assessment is to determine whether the remains are of interest to the medicolegal death investigation. Typically, this involves confirming that the remains are in fact osseous (17) and if they are, drawing on expertise in comparative skeletal and dental anatomy to differentiate non-human from human remains (18,19). Although the question may be asked whether a bone or tooth is "human or animal," it should be remembered that humans are in fact animals. Therefore, it is more appropriate to refer to the remains being examined as either human or non-human. In routine casework, undertaken at an institute of forensic medicine or an office of a medical examiner, a large percentage of casework for forensic anthropologists involves differentiating human from non-human remains (20,21). The ability to differentiate human from non-human skeletal remains is also useful following small and large-scale disasters such as motor vehicle accidents or house fires where animals were also present in the car or house, bushfires where both animals and humans become victims of the fire (22) and bombings (e.g. in the September 11, 2001 terrorist attacks in New York both human and non-human remains were located because the World Trade Center housed offices and restaurants that served animal dishes). While non-human skeletal remains may be of forensic interest (e.g. in cases of illegal wildlife trade [23]), typically, they have no medicolegal significance.

TIME SINCE DEATH (POST-MORTEM INTERVAL)

In cases where the remains are clearly human in origin, the question may then be whether they are of medicolegal importance as opposed to archeological or historical interest. Depending on the context, legislation may define what constitutes medicolegally significant remains (24). Estimating the time since death (TSD) may also provide information about events that occured around the time of death (i.e. peri-mortem) or after death (post-mortem). Further, understanding the TSD may, narrow the number of potential missing persons thereby assist in the identification process and may clarify the circumstances that verify or refute an accused person's alibi.

While attempts have been made to create rules or models that correlate the stage of preservation with time and thus provide an accurate time since death, in reality, decomposition is a complex process (25). Consequently, based on a visual examination of the skeleton, TSD can only ever be an estimation. Decomposition is influenced by the interaction of numerous intrinsic and extrinsic variables (17) and consequently, may vary at different locations within the same body, even within the same bone element, or among multiple bodies in the same deposition context. While understanding all the variables that potentially influence decomposition is vital, and may allow the forensic anthropologist to provide an approximate time since death, alternative scientific techniques such as radiocarbon dating and bomb-pulse dating are often required (26).

NUMBER OF INDIVIDUALS

A death scene may involve multiple deceased, whether a motor vehicle incident or a natural or human-induced disaster, such as a bush fire or a terrorist bombing. Depending on the forces impacting on individuals, human remains may become commingled, fragmentary and/or burnt. In such cases, a forensic anthropologist may contribute to the investigation, both at the scene by being able to recognize differentially preserved human remains and therefore ensuring all fragments are appropriately collected (27), and in the mortuary by providing information about the number of individuals involved in the incident. A forensic anthropologic analysis only provides a minimum (as opposed to a maximum) number of individuals (MNI) (28,29).

BIOLOGICAL PROFILE

In cases of decomposed and/or skeletonized remains, the ability to visually identify a deceased individual is lost. In such cases, however, the forensic anthropologist may be able to provide information about the individual's age, sex, ancestry and stature, that is, a biological profile (30). While a summary of each component of the biological profile is provided below, it should be noted that the biological parameters are interrelated and potentially influence how each estimation is undertaken. For example, the relative age of an individual (i.e. child vs adult) will influence whether it is possible to estimate sex and ancestry, and the sex of a person may affect ancestry estimation (31).

Age estimation

Age estimation is an important component of the biological profile because even the broadest of age ranges can narrow down the parameters to assist in the identification process (32,33). Forensic anthropologists record changes in the skeleton and dentition that are indicative of physiological (i.e. biological) age as opposed to chronologic (calendrical) age. Estimating the age at death of an individual (as opposed to how long ago an individual died, i.e. time since death) involves analyses of specific anatomic regions known to alter in a particular sequence with age. These analyses are based on the premise that osseous and dental tissues undergo predictable and patterned changes throughout the life of the individual and that this change can be quantified and accurately correlated with calendar age (34).

Techniques available for age estimation can be separated into two categories: development traits used to assess juvenile remains (35) and the final stages of maturation (36), and degenerative traits which are used to

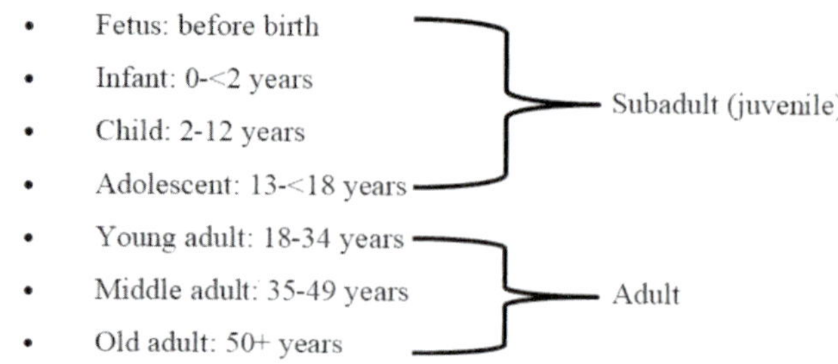

98.2 Age ranges used by forensic anthropologists.

assess age in older individuals (i.e. greater than 18 years) (37). In cases of fragmentary or incomplete skeletal remains, assessment of the histomorphometry of cortical bone samples from long bone shafts (e.g. femur, tibia, humerus, etc.) or other elements such as the mandible may be undertaken (38).

In general, age estimations of younger individuals (under about 30 years of age) are relatively more precise. The current methods tend to overage individuals in the 30–40 age group and underage those in the older group (39). In most cases, age categories are presented as a range (Figure 98.2), with each range having different precision. Older individuals are typically ascribed large age brackets with a significant degree of overlap (40).

While there are a variety of techniques used by forensic anthropologists to estimate age from the skeleton, all have their limitations and there is abundant research being undertaken to provide population-specific data (41) using the different techniques (42).

Sex estimation

The sex of an individual is a biologically determined variable and differs from the gender of a person, which is a social construct (43). In forensic cases, the estimation of biological sex is pivotal in contributing to the identification process as determining whether the individual was male or female halves the number of possibilities to search. The complexities of sex estimation techniques being rigidly binary are increasingly being acknowledged (44).

The relative age of the deceased person must also be assessed prior to estimating sex because sexual dimorphism does not develop until after puberty. The degree of sexual dimorphism in the juvenile skeleton is not distinct enough to allow an accurate evaluation of sex, particularly for forensic cases (45).

Depending on the nature of the investigation, there may be value in the forensic anthropologist attending the scene to view the remains *in situ*. For example, recognition of fetal bones in the pelvic region provides obvious evidence that the individual was female. In the mortuary, there are two main approaches to estimating the sex of an adult from the analysis of the skeleton: visual assessment of morphologic features of the skeleton, and/or the use of metric criteria in the form of indices (ratios of measurements) and/or discriminant functions (uni- or multivariate statistics) (46,47).

Morphologic assessments typically involve an analysis of the pelvis and the skull (48,49,50). Because of individual human variation, a scale to score the observed morphology is employed to record the results:

- 1 = female
- 2 = probably female
- 3 = ambiguous
- 4 = probably male
- 5 = male

Morphologic assessment of the skeleton is a subjective analysis and greatly depends on the experience of the practitioner. However, reliability tests of some of these methods have been undertaken. In cases involving the use of the skull to estimate sex, it was shown that clarity of definition, rather than number of character traits, was critical (51).

Several skeletal measurements can be taken that are then compared with measurements collected from individuals of known sex (52). Typically, measurements have focussed on post-cranial elements and include examining the diameters of the articular ends; the mid-shaft circumference of long bones, or the ischio-pubic index (53,54). In addition, functions (uni- or multivariate statistics) can be used in sex evaluation, for example, see (55) for an extensive list of cranial and post-cranial measurements used to estimate sex.

While metric assessments are seen as less subjective (and therefore more precise), the use of morphology is regarded as easier and has been demonstrated to provide equally reliable results (56). The decision about which method to use is influenced by the preservation of the skeletal remains (i.e. completeness and condition), the age of the individual and ultimately the experience of the practitioner (57).

Finally, the ability to extract DNA from skeletal remains of varying ages and preservations has meant that DNA analysis has also been used to determine the sex of both juvenile (58) as well as adult (59) skeletal remains. While extraction techniques become increasingly less invasive, molecular approaches to the determination of sex are nonetheless destructive and expensive. In addition, the success of DNA analysis is influenced by the relative preservation of the remains and therefore the ability to recover DNA.

Ancestry estimation

Ancestry as estimated from the analyses of skeletal remains in forensic contexts is defined as "the geographic region or ancestral origin of an individual" (60). Based on the principle that variation exists within and between populations from different geographic regions, practitioners are interested in skeletal evidence that may provide information about where a person's ancestors originated, that is, "before the mass voluntary and forced migrations of peoples that started around the world in the 15th Century BCE" (61).

It has been argued that "ancestry estimation is essential for biological profile estimation in forensic anthropology" (62). However, ancestry (previously referred to as "race") estimation is controversial (63,64) notably because of the complicated relationship between skeletal morphology and social constructs [65]. Consequently, there is discussion among some practitioners about whether ancestry estimations should be undertaken at all (66,67).

It is well accepted that physical attributes do not equate with social and/or cultural ability and that social identity may not correspond with physical skeletal features (e.g. in the case of some contemporary Australian Aboriginal people who identify as Aboriginal but have physical features that are more consistent with Caucasian ancestry). Nonetheless, it is possible to observe physical differences between populations that have been geographically and reproductively separated (68). Categories used to describe ancestry include (but are not limited to): African, Asian, Australoid and Caucasian (69).

Estimation of ancestry can be undertaken using three main techniques: morphologic assessment which typically focuses on the morphology of the skull, geographic origin and an individual's social race (70,71). While the use of non-metric traits is subjective and relies heavily on the experience of the observer, research is being undertaken to reduce the subjectivity using clear definitions and illustrations. This work showed that non-metric traits can be quantified and used successfully to estimate ancestry (72).

While morphologic traits are useful in estimating ancestry, it must be remembered that "no single trait is found exclusively in only one population" (73) but are found in higher or lower frequencies in different populations. Compared to the skull, post-cranial skeletal elements are used relatively little for metric assessment of ancestry.

Similar to methods that involve assessing cranial morphology to estimate ancestry, those that use measurements also focus on the skull and are based on the critical assumption that there is systematic geographic patterning of cranial variation (74). Metric analysis helps identify patterns in skull shape that may not be visually obvious (75). Depending on the preservation of the remains, a series of cranial measurements are taken using instruments such as sliding and spreading calipers (and more recently 3D geometric approaches [76]) and entered into a computer package that provides an ancestry assessment with related likelihood percentages. Two packages presently used are CRANID (77) and Fordisc 3.0 (78). Both packages use multivariate methods of discriminant analysis (based on algorithms developed in the 1930s). Fordisc has additional forensic samples from America, and CRANID has additional samples from parts of the world not covered by Howells, for example, the Indian subcontinent and Patagonia (61).

Stature estimation

A stature estimate may be a useful component of identification but relies on having access to stature recorded when the person was alive (e.g. on an individual's driving license, passport, or in military records) for comparison. Stature estimates are typically only undertaken on adult remains because subadults have not yet stopped growing and therefore reported statures for teenagers become quickly outdated (79). While stature can be estimated by measuring a series of bones, summing the measurements, and adding a soft-tissue component (80), the most common method involves measuring the maximum length of long bones such as the femur, tibia, humerus, radius and/or ulna. Combinations of these bones can also be used for estimates. Measurements are taken on an osteometric measuring board to the nearest millimeter. With the increasing use of computed tomography (CT) as part of the autopsy process, measurements can also be taken from CT images for stature estimation (81,82).

Depending on the skeletal elements and the ancestry of the remains, a specific regression equation is employed to determine stature (e.g. Caucasoid males and females [83]; Asian males and females [84]). However, if the ancestry of the person is unknown, there is also an approach to estimating stature that is not population or group-specific (85). More recently, software packages have been developed to automate the process of estimating stature (86). The practitioner enters the measurement into the database and selects the relevant population (e.g. "White male") to facilitate the appropriate regression formula calculation. With elderly individuals, corrections must be made to the estimate due to the reduction in stature associated with the aging and degeneration of the vertebral column that occurs around 45 years of age onward (87).

Analysis and interpretation of skeletal trauma

The forensic anthropologist is also responsible for describing and documenting alterations to the skeleton (88). The aim of a forensic anthropology assessment of skeletal defects is to provide an opinion about the timing of the changes relative to the death event and the trauma mechanism. The defect may show evidence of osteogenic reaction (i.e. the formation of new bone) and therefore be evidence of antemortem trauma, occurring before an individual's death (89). Other alterations may be indicative of post-mortem damage, that is, changes to the bone produced after death, and are un-associated with the death event (17). Post-mortem damage typically refers to taphonomic changes (90) including environmental (e.g. staining, cracking, etc), scavenging (17), or human-induced (91) alterations.

Typically, of most interest to an investigation is the identification of peri-mortem trauma, that is, trauma that occurred around the time of death (92). Unlike a forensic pathologist, who has soft and hard tissues available to examine and can usually provide a short time range in which the injuries occurred relative to the death, a forensic anthropologist is reliant solely on the hard tissue and is only able to provide an opinion on whether or not the skeletal injury occurred when the bone was in a biomechanically fresh state. Depending on the context and circumstances of death, bone can retain collagen (and therefore contain moisture) for weeks or months following death. Consequently, the peri-mortem period for a forensic anthropologist is typically relatively long compared to the time period provided by a forensic pathologist.

The anthropologist may also be able to provide information about the mechanism that resulted in the trauma, that is, the way force was applied to the bone (93). Trauma mechanism is typically classified as being the result of blunt (that is, relatively slow loading) force (94), high-velocity projectile force (that is, a very rapid application of force over a relatively small surface area, such as a gunshot wound) (95,96), low-velocity projectile force (97) (such as produced by an arrow), or sharp force (created by a tool with a point or beveled edge) (98), or a combination of different forces. Trauma analysis involves an examination of the morphology of the defect/s as well as a review of the pattern of alterations across the entire skeleton.

The effects of fire on the body, while not strictly trauma, are also of interest to the forensic anthropologist (99). With an understanding of the normal burn pattern (i.e. that observed in a body that is not covered or bound) (100), it may still be possible to distinguish peri-mortem trauma from post-mortem thermal alterations (101,102).

CONCLUSION

Working as part of a team which may include the forensic pathologist, odontologist and/or entomologist, the forensic anthropologist plays an important role in cases involving human skeletonized remains. Drawing on expertise in human skeletal and dental anatomy and experience working with a range of differentially preserved human remains, the forensic anthropologist may provide information about taphonomic changes, develop a biological profile and/or give an opinion regarding skeletal trauma. Forensic anthropology has proven itself to be an effective forensic science tool both in domestic and international investigations.

ACKNOWLEDGMENTS

I would like to thank Dr Melanie Archer for her comments on a draft of this chapter.

REFERENCES

1. Passalacqua NV, Pilloud MA, Congram D. Forensic anthropology as a discipline. *Biology* 2021; **10**(**8**): 691.
2. Stewart TD. *Essentials of Forensic Anthropology*. Springfield: Charles C. Thomas; 1979.
3. Fondebrider L. Forensic Anthropology: Definition. In: Smith C (ed), *Encyclopedia of Global Archaeology*. New York: Springer; 2014, pp. 2833–4.
4. Simpson E, Byard RW. A review of osteological remains submitted for forensic examination in south Australia over a 7-year period (2013–2019). *J Forensic Leg Med* 2020; **76**: 102074.
5. Crowder C, Wiersema J, Adams BJ, et al. The utility of forensic anthropology in the Medical Examiners Office. *Acad Forensic Pathol* 2016; **6**(**3**): 349–60.
6. Donlon D. The Development and Current State of Forensic Anthropology: An Australian Perspective. In: Blau S, Ubelaker DH (eds), *Handbook of Forensic Anthropology and Archaeology*. London: Routledge; 2016, pp. 126–39.
7. Drawdy SM, Katzmarzyk C. The Missing Files: The Experience of the International Committee of the Red Cross. In: Congram D (ed), *Missing Persons: Multidisciplinary Perspectives on the Disappeared*. Toronto: Canadian Scholar's Press; 2016, pp. 60–73.
8. Garvin HM, Langley NR, (eds). *Case Studies in Forensic Anthropology Bonified Skeletons*. Boca Raton: CRC Press; 2020.

9. De Boer HH, Blau S, Delabarde T, Hackman L. The role of forensic anthropology in disaster victim identification (DVI): Recent developments and future prospects. *Forensic Sci Res* 2018; **4**(**4**): 303–15.
10. Mundorff AZ. Integrating forensic anthropology into disaster victim identification. *Forensic Sci Med Pathol* 2012; **8**: 131–9.
11. Clegg L. The International Committee of the Red Cross and the protection of world war dead. *Forensic Sci Int* 2021; **319**: 110648.
12. Cox M, Loe L, Jones P. Fromelles: Forensic Archaeology and Anthropology in Identification. In: Blau S, Ubelaker DH (eds), *Handbook of Forensic Anthropology and Archaeology*, 2nd ed. London: Routledge; 2016, pp. 578–90.
13. Fondebrider L. Forensic Anthropology and the Investigation of Political Violence: Notes from the Field. In: Crossland Z, Joyce RA (eds), *Disturbing Bodies: Perspectives on Forensic Anthropology*. Sant Fe: School for Advanced Research; 2015, pp. 31–40.
14. Ubelaker DH, Shamlou A, Kunkle AE. Forensic anthropology in the global investigation of humanitarian and human rights abuse: Perspective from the published record. *Sci Justice* 2019; **59**(**2**): 203–9.
15. Puerto SM, Catelli L, Romanini C, et al. The Argentine Experience in Forensic Identification of Human Remains. In: Parra RC, Zapico SC, Ubelaker D (eds), *Forensic Science and Humanitarian Action: Interacting with the Dead and the Living*. Hoboken: John Wiley & Sons; 2020, pp. 549–58.
16. Rowbotham S, Blau S, Hislop-Jambrich J. Recording preservation for human skeletal remains: A new approach to documenting skeletal completeness. *Forensic Sci Int* 2017; **275**: 117–23.
17. Pokines J. Differential diagnosis of the taphonomic histories of common types of forensic osseous remains. *J Forensic Identif* 2018; **68**(**1**): 87–145.
18. France DL. *Human and Nonhuman Bone Identification: A Concise Field Guide*. Boca Raton: CRC Press; 2011.
19. Rissech C. The importance of human anatomy in forensic anthropology. *Eur J Anat* 2021; **25**: 1–18.
20. Klepinger LL. *Fundamentals of Forensic Anthropology*. Hoboken: John Wiley & Sons; 2006.
21. Donlon D, Croker S, Menzies J. Non-human bones in forensic casework: Not such a trivial problem. *Forensic Sci Med Pathol* 2020; **16**(**3**): 442–9.
22. Blau S, Briggs C. The 2009 Victorian Bushfires disaster: The role of forensic anthropology in Disaster Victim Identification (DVI). *Forensic Sci Int* 2010; **205**: 29–35.
23. Christensen A, Passalacqua NV, Bartelink EJ. *Forensic Anthropology: Current Methods and Practice*. London: Elsevier; 2019.
24. Medical Sciences Specialist Advisry Group. Guidelines for forensic anthropology practitioners, 2020. Available from: https://www.google.com/url?sa=t&rct=j&q=&esrc=s&source=web&cd=&cad=rja&uact=8&ved=2ahUKEwi_783O0tn_AhWQXsAKHZzDC0kQFnoECA0QAQ&url=https%3A%2F%2Fwww.anzpaa.org.au%2FArticleDocuments%2F2304%2FGuidelines%2520for%2520Forensic%2520Anthropology%2520%2520Practitioners%2520-%2520March%25202020.pdf.aspx&usg=AOvVaw11WxccQkVHAIPGzh-COdHQ&opi=89978449 (Accessed 23 June 2023).
25. Martin RE. *Taphonomy: A Process Issue. Cambridge Paleobiology Series 4*. Cambridge: Cambridge University Press; 1998.
26. Johnstone-Belford EC, Blau S. A review of bomb pulse dating and its use in the investigation of unidentified human remains. *J Forensic Sci* 2020; **65**(**3**): 676–85.
27. Porta D, Poppa P, Regazzola V, et al. The importance of an anthropological scene of crime investigation in the case of burnt remains in vehicles: 3 case studies. *Am J Forensic Med Pathol* 2013; **34**(**3**): 195–200.
28. Konigsberg LW, Adams BJ. Estimating the Number of Individuals Represented by Commingled Human Remains: A Critical Evaluation of Methods. In: Adams BJ, Byrd JE (eds), *Commingled Human Remains: Methods in Recovery, Analysis, and Identification*. Boston: Academic Press; 2014, pp. 193–220.
29. Lambacher N, Gerdau-Radonic K, Bonthorne E, Valle de Tarazaga Montero FJ. Evaluating three methods to estimate the number of individuals from a commingled context. *J Archaeol Sci Rep* 2016; **10**: 674–83.
30. Austin D, King RE. The biological profile of unidentified human remains in a forensic context. *Acad Forensic Pathol* 2016; **6**(**3**): 370–90.
31. Rowbotham SK. Anthropological Estimation of Sex. In: Blau S, Ubelaker DH (eds), *Handbook of Forensic Anthropology and Archaeology*, 2nd ed. London: Routledge; 2016, pp. 261–72.
32. Márquez-Grant N. An overview of age estimation in forensic anthropology: Perspectives and practical consideration. *Ann Hum Biol* 2015; **42**(**4**): 306–20.
33. Ubelaker DH, Khosrowshahi H. Estimation of age in forensic anthropology: Historical perspective and recent methodological advances. *Forensic Sci Res* 2019; **4**(**1**): 1–9.
34. Rogers T. Skeletal Age Estimation. In: Blau S, Ubelaker DH (eds), *Handbook of Forensic Anthropology and Archaeology*, 2nd ed. London: Routledge; 2016, pp. 273–92.
35. Scheuer L, Black, S. *Developmental Juvenile Osteology*. San Diego: Elsevier; 2000.
36. Garvin HM, Passalacqua NV. Current practices by forensic anthropologists in adult skeletal age estimation. *J Forensic Sci* 2012; **57**(**2**): 427–33.
37. Blau S. The Anthropology of Aging. In: Collins KA, Byard RW (eds), *Geriatric Forensic Medicine and Pathology*. Cambridge: Cambridge University Press; 2020, pp. 452–68.
38. Crowder SM, Heinrich JT, Dominguez VM. Histological Age Estimation. In: Blau S, Ubelaker DH, (eds), *Handbook of Forensic Anthropology and Archaeology*, 2nd ed. London: Routledge; 2016, pp. 293–307.
39. Cox M, Mays S. *Human Osteology: In Archaeology and Forensic Science*. London: Greenwich Medical Media; 2000.
40. Buckberry J. The (mis)use of adult age estimates in osteology. *Ann Hum Biol* 2015; **42**(**4**): 323–31.
41. Gocha TP, Ingvoldstad ME, Kolatorowicz A, et al. Testing the applicability of six macroscopic skeletal aging techniques on a modern Southeast Asian sample. *Forensic Sci Int* 2015; **249**: 318.
42. Merritt CE. Inaccuracy and bias in adult skeletal age estimation: Assessing the reliability of eight methods on individuals of varying body sizes. *Forensic Sci Int* 2017; **275**: 315.
43. Garofalo EM, Garvin HM. The Confusion Between Biological Sex and Gender and Potential Implications of Misinterpretations. In: Klales AR (ed), *Sex Estimation of the Human Skeleton: History, Methods and Emerging Techniques*. London: Academic Press; 2020, pp. 35–52.
44. Tallman SD, Kincer CD, Plemons ED. Centering transgender individuals in forensic anthropology and expanding binary sex estimation in casework and research. *Forensic Anthropol* 2022; **5**(**2**): 161–80.
45. Stull KE, Cirillo LE, Cole SJ, Hulse CN. Subadult Sex Estimation and KidStats. In: Klales AR (ed), *Sex Estimation of the Human Skeleton*. London: Academic Press; 2020, pp. 219–42.
46. Franklin D, Cardini A, Flavel A, Kuliukas A. The application of traditional and geometric morphometric analyses for forensic quantification of sexual dimorphism: Preliminary investigations in a Western Australian population. *Int J Leg Med* 2012; **126**(**4**): 549–58.
47. Moore MK. Sex Estimation and Assessment. In: DiGangi E, Moore M (eds), *Research Methods in Human Skeletal Biology*. London: Academic Press; 2013, pp. 91–116.
48. Spradley MK, Jantz RL. Sex estimation in forensic anthropology: Skull versus postcranial elements. *J Forensic Sci* 2011; **56**(**2**): 289–96.
49. Phenice TW. A newly developed visual method for sexing the os pubis. *Am J Phys Anthropol* 1969; **30**: 297–302.
50. Klales AR, Ousley SD, Vollner JM. A revised method of sexing the human innominate using Phenice's nonmetric traits and statistical methods. *Am J Phys Anthropol* 2012;149(1):104–14.
51. Walrath DE, Turner P, Bruzek J. Reliability test of the visual assessment of cranial traits for sex determination. *Am J Phys Anthropol* 2004;125(2):132–7.
52. Spradley MK. Metric methods for the biological profile in forensic anthropology: Sex, ancestry, and stature. *Acad Forensic Pathol* 2016; **6**(**3**): 391–9.
53. Işcan MY, Steyn M. *The Human Skeleton in Forensic Medicine*, 3rd ed. Springfield: Charles C. Thomas; 2013.
54. Robinson MS, Bidmos MA. An assessment of the accuracy of discriminant function equations of sex determination of the femur and tibia from a South African population. *Forensic Sci Int* 2011; **206**(**1–3**): e1–5.
55. Komar DA, Buikstra JE. *Forensic Anthropology. Contemporary Theory and Practice*. New York: Oxford University Press; 2008.
56. Klales AR. Practitioner Preferences for Sex Estimation from Human Skeletal Remains. In: Klales AR (ed), *Sex Estimation of the Human Skeleton: History,*

Methods and Emerging Techniques. London: Elsevier; 2020, pp. 11–23.
57. Duric M, Rakocevic Z, Donic D. The reliability of sex determination of skeletons from forensic context in the Balkans. *Forensic Sci Int* 2005; **147**: 159–64.
58. Tierney SN, Bird JM. Molecular sex identification of juvenile skeletal remains from an Irish medieval population using ancient DNA analysis. *J Archaeol Sci* 2015; **62**: 27–38.
59. Masuyama K, Shojo H, Nakanishi H, et al. Sex determination from fragmented and degenerated DNA by amplified product-length polymorphism bidirectional SNP analysis of amelogenin and SRY genes. *PloS one* 2017; **12(1)**: e0169348.
60. Dunn RR, Spiros MC, Kamnikar KR, et al. Ancestry estimation in forensic anthropology: A review. *WIREs Forensic Sci* 2020; **2(4)**: e1369.
61. Wright R. Ancestry Assessment. In: Smith C (ed), *Encyclopaedia of Global Archaeology*. New York: Springer; 2014, pp. 209–14.
62. Klales AR, Kenyhercz MW. Morphological assessment of ancestry using cranial macromorphoscopics. *J Forensic Sci* 2015; **60(1)**: 13–20.
63. Spradley MK, Weisensee K. Why Do Forensic Anthropologists Estimate Ancestry and Why is it So Controversial? In: Tersigni-Tarrant M, Shirley NR (eds), *Forensic Anthropology: An Introduction.* Boca Raton: CRC Press; 2013, pp. 231–44.
64. Plens CR, De Souza CD, Albanese J, et al. Reflections on methods to estimate race and ancestry on reference osteological samples in the Brazilian context. *Ethics Med Public Health* 2021; **18**: 100680.
65. Schultz JJ. Racialized osteology and athletic aptitude, or "black" bones as red herrings. *J Sport Hist* 2019; **46(3)**: 325–46.
66. Bethard JD, DiGangi E. Letter to the editor—Moving beyond a lost cause: Forensic anthropology and ancestry estimates in the United States. *J Forensic Sci* 2020; **65(5)**: 1791–2.
67. Ross AH, Williams SE. Ancestry studies in forensic anthropology: Back on the frontier of racism. *Biology* 2021; **10(7)**: 602.
68. Ousley S, Jantz R, Freid D. Understanding race and human variation: Why forensic anthropologists are good at identifying race. *Am J Phys Anthropol* 2009; **139(1)**: 68–76.
69. Berg GE, Ta'ala SC (eds). *Biological Affinity in Forensic Identification of Human Skeletal Remains: Beyond Black and White.* Boca Raton: Taylor and Francis; 2015.
70. Hefner JT. Cranial nonmetric variation and estimating ancestry. *J Forensic Sci* 2009; **54(5)**: 985–95.
71. Hefner JT, Ousley SD, Dirkmaat DC. Morphoscopic Traits and the Assessment of Ancestry. In: Dirkmaat D (ed), *A Companion to Forensic Anthropology.* Hoboken: Wiley-Blackwell; 2012, pp. 287–310.
72. Thomas RM, Parks CL, Richard AH. Accuracy rates of ancestry estimation by forensic anthropologists using identified forensic cases. *J Forensic Sci* 2017; **62(4)**: 971–4.
73. DiGangi EA, Hefner JT. Ancestry Estimation. In: DiGangi EA, Moore MK (eds), *Research Methods in Human Skeletal Biology*. Amsterdam: Academic Press; 2013, pp. 117–49.
74. Howells WW. *Skull Shapes and the Map.* Harvard: Harvard University; 1989.
75. Christensen AM, Passalacqua NV, Bartelink EJ. Ancestry Assessment. In: Christensen AM, Passalacqua NV, Bartelink EJ (eds), *Forensic Anthropology: Current Methods and Practice*, 2nd ed. Oxford: Academic Press; 2019, pp. 271–306.
76. Ross AH, Kimmerle EH. Contribution of Quantitative Methods in Forensic Anthropology: A New Era. In: Blau S, Ubelaker DH (eds), *Handbook of Forensic Anthropology and Archaeology.* London: Routledge; 2016, pp. 622–34.
77. Wright R. Detection of Likely Ancestry Using CRANID. In: Oxenham MF (ed), *Forensic Approaches to Death, Disaster and Abuse.* Queensland: Australian Academic Press; 2008, pp. 111–22.
78. Ousley S, Jantz R. Fordisc 3: Third generation of computer-aided forensic anthropology. *Rechtsmedizin* 2013; **23(2)**: 97–9.
79. Christensen A, Passalacqua NV, Bartelink EJ. Stature Estimation and Other Skeletal Metrics. In: Christensen A, Passalacqua NV, Bartelink EJ (eds), *Forensic Anthropology: Current Methods and Practice.* London: Elsevier; 2019, pp. 351–68.
80. Willey P. Stature Estimation. In: Blau S, Ubelaker DH (eds), *Handbook of Forensic Anthropology and Archaeology*, 2nd ed. London: Routledge; 2016, pp. 308–21.
81. Karakas HM, Celbis O, Harma A, Alicioglu B. Total body height estimation using sacrum height in Anatolian Caucasians: Multi-detector computed tomography-based virtual anthropometry. *Skeletal Radiol* 2011; **40**: 623–30.
82. Giurazza F, Del Vescovo R, Schena E, et al. Determination of stature from skeletal and skull measurements by CT scan evaluation. *Forensic Sci Int* 2012; **222(1–3)**: 398.
83. Ousley S. Should we estimate biological or forensic stature? *J Forensic Sci* 1995; **40(5)**: 768–73.
84. Trotter M, Gleser GC. A re-evaluation of estimation of stature based on measurements of stature taken during life and of long bones after death. *Am J Phys Anthropol* 1958; **16**: 79–123.
85. Albanese J, Tuck A, Gomes J, Cardoso HF. An alternative approach for estimating stature from long bones that is not population- or group-specific. *Forensic Sci Int* 2016; **259**: 59–68.
86. Manthey L, Jantz RL. Fordisc: Anthropological Software for Estimation of Ancestry, Sex, Time Period, and Stature. In: Obertová Z, Stewart A, Cattaneo C (eds), *Statistics and Probability in Forensic Anthropology*. London: Academic Press; 2020, pp. 275–87.
87. Galloway A. Estimating actual height in the older individual. *J Forensic Sci* 1988; **33**: 126–36.
88. Ubelaker DH. Recent advances in understanding hard tissue alterations related to trauma. *Forensic Sci Int* 2019; **299**: 235–7.
89. Cattaneo C, Cappella A, Cunha E. Post Mortem Anthropology and Trauma Analysis. In: Ferrara S (ed), *P5 Medicine and Justice: Innovation, Unitariness and Evidence.* Cham: Springer; 2017, pp. 166–79.
90. Beary M, Lyman R. The Use of Taphonomy in Forensic Anthropology: Past Trends and Future Prospects. In: Dirkmaat D (ed), *A Companion to Forensic Anthropology*. Chichester: Wiley; 2012, pp. 499–527.
91. Congram D. Deposition and Dispersal of Human Remains as a Result of Criminal Acts: Homo Sapiens Sapiens as a Taphonomic Agent. In: Pokines J, Symes S (ed), *Manual of Forensic Taphonomy*. Boca Raton: CRC Press; 2013, pp. 249–85.
92. Ubelaker DH. Perimortem and postmortem modification of human bone. Lessons from forensic anthropology. *Anthropologie* 1991; **29(3)**: 171–4.
93. Blau S, Ranson D, O'Donnell C. *An Atlas of Skeletal Trauma in Medico-Legal Contexts*. London: Elsevier; 2018.
94. Wedel VL, Galloway A (eds). *Broken Bones: Anthropological Analysis of Blunt Force Trauma*, 2nd ed. Springfield: Charles C. Thomas; 2014.
95. Viel G, Gehl A, Sperhake JP. Intersecting fractures of the skull and gunshot wounds. Case report and literature review. *Forensic Sci Med Pathol* 2009; **5(1)**: 22–7.
96. Langley NR. An anthropological analysis of gunshot wounds to the chest. *J Forensic Sci* 2007; **52(3)**: 532–7.
97. Humphrey C, Henneberg H. Anthropological analysis of projectile trauma to the bony regions of the trunk. *Anthropol Rev* 2017; **80(2)**: 207–18.
98. Love JC. Sharp force trauma analysis in bone and cartilage: A literature review. *Forensic Sci Int* 2019; **299**: 119–27.
99. Ellingham S, Adserias-Garriga J, Zapico SC, Ubelaker DH (eds). *Burnt Human Remains: Recovery Analysis and Interpretation.* Hoboken: Wiley; 2022.
100. Symes SA, Rainwater CW, Chapman EN, et al. Patterned Thermal Destruction of Human Remains in a Forensic Setting. In: Schmidt CW, Symes SA (eds), *The Analysis of Burned Human Remains*, 2nd ed. San Diego: Academic Press; 2015, pp. 17–59.
101. Blau S. Forensic anthropology and its contributions to police investigations. *Aust Police J* 2009; **63(1)**: 4–14.
102. de Gruchy S, Rogers TL. Identifying chop marks on cremated bone: A preliminary study. *J Forensic Sci* 2002; **47(5)**: 933–6.

CHAPTER 99

Veterinary Forensic Medicine

John E. Cooper and Margaret E. Cooper

> "Is there any point to which you would wish to draw my attention?"
> "To the curious incident of the dog in the night-time."
> "The dog did nothing in the night-time."
> "That was the curious incident," remarked Sherlock Holmes.
> (The Adventure of Silver Blaze. Sir Arthur Conan Doyle, 1892).

INTRODUCTION

Many medicolegal texts (1) portray "veterinary forensic medicine" as the domesticated animal version of human forensic investigation (2, 3).

Some years ago, however, the authors suggested that the definitions needed to be re-assessed. For instance, did the prefix "veterinary" imply work solely with domesticated animals (the word "veterinary" is derived from the Latin word for cattle) or, were other species included?

In a recent foreword (4,5), the authors suggested that, while veterinary forensic medicine can still be defined as "the application of veterinary knowledge to the purpose of the law", it increasingly embraces work with diverse mammals, birds, reptiles, amphibians, fish and invertebrates – a situation anticipated 20 years ago (6).

The authors also advocated that the label "veterinary forensic medicine" should include any forensic activity involving veterinary surgeons (veterinarians), not solely to criminal and civil legal proceedings and inquests but also to various situations outside the courts that require expert evidence of a forensic standard, such as insurance claims, tribunals, public inquiries, industrial disputes, checks on trading standards, environmental impact assessments, allegations of professional misconduct and the inspection of establishments such as zoological collections and pet shops.

Consequently, the authors now suggest that veterinary forensic medicine is metamorphosing into a more broadly based discipline that can best be described as "animal" or "comparative" forensic medicine.

The term "animal forensics" is increasingly gaining acceptance when describing scenarios in which members of the Kingdom Animalia play a substantial part. In 2021, this trend was given a boost as a result of the success of the "1st International Virtual Meeting of Forensic Animal Sciences (IVM-FAS)". Presentations covered topics of forensic significance ranging from animal welfare and wildlife conservation to terrorism and zoo-morphology. In a "Manifesto", the organizers proposed the adoption of the designation "Forensic Animal Science" for this broad-based discipline. It was argued that, although the modern veterinary profession encompasses specialists in fields ranging from anesthesia to zoological medicine and while veterinarians often play a leading part in animal forensic cases (as do medics in "human" forensic investigations), other specialists can be important contributors, among them zoologists, conservationists, ethologists, nutritionists and biomedical scientists (7).

Veterinary (and other) forensics are also framed by the law that forms the basis of a prosecution, civil claim or other judicial hearing. Together with the relevant procedural rules, it dictates the forensic evidence to be provided by a veterinary surgeon or other specialists in a court or other tribunal. It could be said that, in the absence of a law or legal right, there is no necessity for true forensic evidence – although of course forensic methods and standards are widely used in other situations.

Veterinary surgeons (veterinarians) have long played an important role as expert witnesses in court cases concerning domesticated species, such as horses, cattle, dogs and cats and continue to do so (8). Indeed, the widespread use of the term "to vet", meaning to make a careful and critical examination, is often considered testimony to the regard in which a veterinary surgeon's assessment is held.

The special "Focus Issue" of the *Journal of Veterinary Pathology* (9) was a major step forward in developing the scientific basis of veterinary forensic pathology as a discipline. There is, however, a need for close collaboration between the forensic pathologist and clinicians as discussed, in the context of the United Kingdom, by Newbery et al. (10).

ROLE OF ANIMALS IN FORENSIC SITUATIONS

Animals can be involved in criminal or other legal actions in various ways, such as an attack, other harm, or damage to property. They can be either:

- The victim of an incident, or
- The instigator of an incident

DOI: 10.1201/9781003138754-103

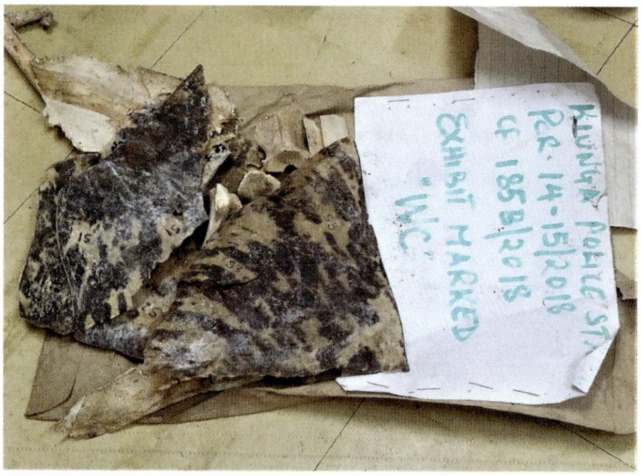

99.1 Material (evidence) seized by the authorities in Kenya and submitted for identification and forensic examination. A tortoise killed and collected unlawfully.

Alternatively, animals can:

- Serve as sentinels or witnesses
- Be a source of evidence

These categories are discussed in more detail below.

Animals as the victim

Injuries and other insults that may be inflicted by humans on animals, maliciously or accidentally, embrace a variety of attacks, perversions and mutilations (11–13). Examples include physical assault, injury due to trauma, heat, cold, immersion in water, neglect and abuse (14), sexual abuse (15), animal fighting (14), psychological ("emotional") stress due to neglect, deprivation of company or unsuitable social grouping, taunting, teasing or threatening.

Insults inflicted by humans on animals may cause death, injury, ill health, pain or distress but the extent of these and their implications differ widely, depending on the species of animal affected and the circumstances. A number of the examples mentioned above offer both links and parallels with human forensic work.

Insults caused to domesticated animals have been the subject of veterinary research for decades. Some attention has also been paid to injuries in free-living wildlife; these species are constantly at risk to spontaneous as well as to animal- or human-induced injuries (Figure 99.1) (16).

Non-accidental injuries (NAIs), those that are caused deliberately to an animal by a human, as a form of abuse, have attracted serious attention. The "battered pet" syndrome first described some years ago (17–20) led to the development of a new area of study, the "NAI" (2,12,13).

Intentional abuse of animals may range from isolated events (e.g., following an owner's loss of temper) to persistent, sadistic acts of cruelty. Research indicates that there may be an inter-relationship (21,22) between violence inflicted on animals, and the abuse of children and vulnerable adults.

Some years ago, it was recommended (11) that the terminology used by the medical profession for children (*see* Chapter 80 – "Findings After Sexual Assault – Adult") should be applied to animals.

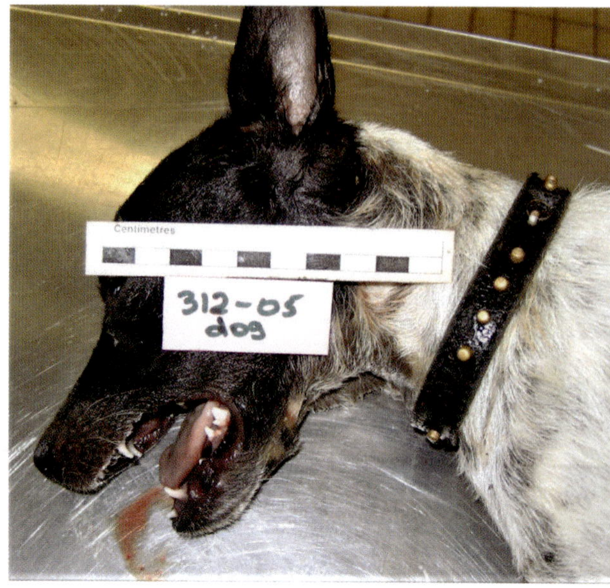

99.2 A dog submitted for a forensic post-mortem examination on account of multiple injuries, possibly non-accidental.

Whether or not there is a strong link between childhood animal cruelty and child maltreatment is challenged by some with study designs often being cited as a problem.

Veterinary surgeons who suspect the presence of NAIs have to balance their professional duty of confidentiality with reporting the NAIs in the interest of the welfare of the animal or person involved (23) in accordance with the Guidance provided by the Royal College of Veterinary Surgeons (RCVS) (24). There are varying legal and professional requirements in different countries regarding the reporting of animal abuse, notably in the USA where it is compulsory in some states (25).

It is important, especially in legal cases, that NAIs are distinguished from accidental and naturally or spontaneously induced lesions (Figure 99.2). McDonough and McEwen (26,27) discussed the role of the forensic necropsy in the investigation of cases of suspected animal abuse or neglect. McEwen (27) discussed this in more detail and drew attention to (for example) the importance of removing the entire skin of the animal because fur and feathers may mask the injuries.

In an additional category, various types of abuse or bizarre methods of slaughter are used in furtherance of ritual and superstitious beliefs, including occult and Satanic rituals such as African voodoo (2,28). Both animal and plant material may be among the samples that need to be investigated (Figure 99.3).

Advice is also sometimes sought over the identity and likely provenance of preserved (taxidermy) specimens and egg collections.

As far as wildlife is concerned, there has been extensive study of "human-induced" damage – for example, the effects of traps, snares and shooting on disparate species (see later) and injury or death in marine mammals (26,29–31). Some NAIs involving wildlife were listed by Cooper and Cooper (2).

The killing or infliction of injuries on free-living animals often amounts to an offense under wildlife conservation legislation (Figure 99.4) (31). Such laws provide

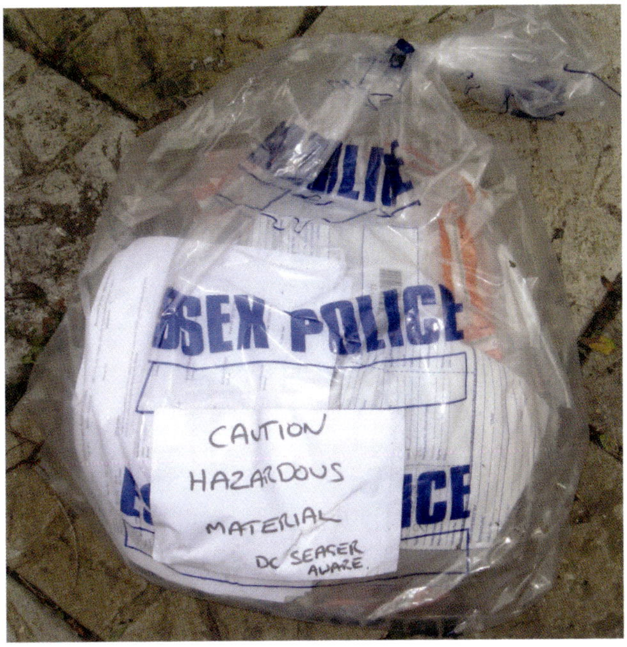

99.3 Part of a consignment of materials of animal, plant and mineral origin that was confiscated in Britain following its importation from West Africa. It was alleged that the items were intended for use in a "voodoo" ceremony.

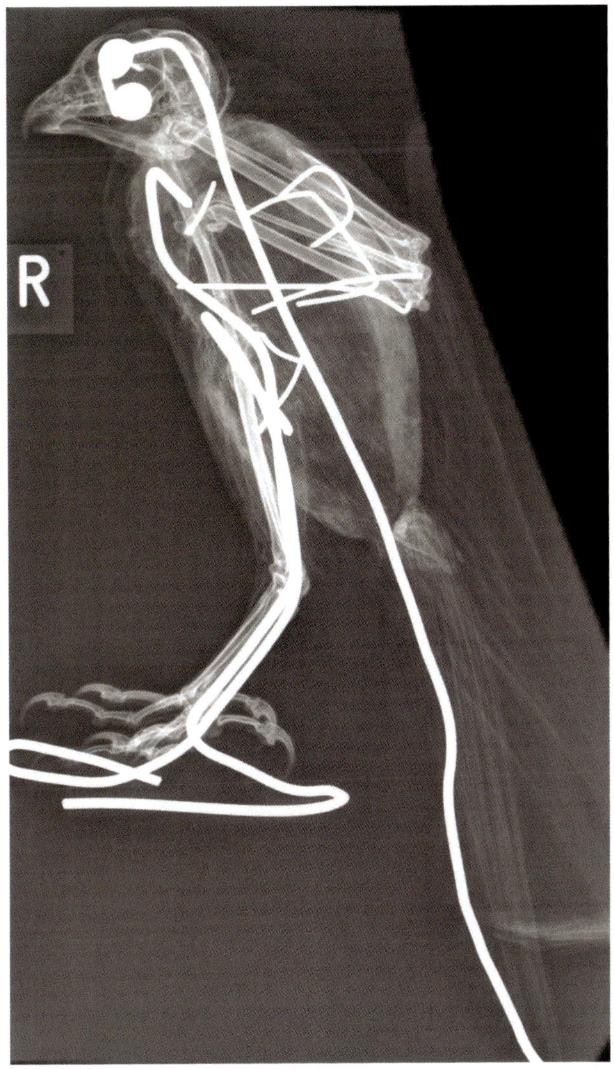

99.4 A lateral radiograph of a dead lanner falcon (*Falco biarmicus*) showing the materials used to preserve and mount it. Such forensic investigations can throw light on the provenance of specimens and help identify the taxidermist.

protection for listed species from killing, injuring, taking, possession, trade or the use of traps, snares, and firearms (Figure 99.5). "Wildlife crime" has grown exponentially and is often associated with other rural offenses or serious organized crime such as drug and human trafficking. As a consequence, so-called "wildlife forensics" has developed. Tackling wildlife crime, particularly the illegal trade in protected species, has an increasingly international orientation; for example, at the time of writing, plans are underway to establish a Wildlife Forensic Academy in Europe (32). Legal protection for wildlife often includes plants and locations since the habitat upon which free-living animals depend for survival can also be subject to illegal activities. Consequently, forensic investigations may necessitate an input by botanists and plant specialists. "Forestry forensics" is one of many newly-recognized forensic disciplines (33).

It is not just traumatic insults that impinge on animals. For instance, the illegal or irresponsible use of agricultural chemicals can have adverse effects on people as well as on both domestic and wild animals, plants and the environment. Environmental impacts can range from, for example, the hundreds of dead sea turtles washed ashore in 2021 when MV X-Press Pearl sank and liberated nitric acid into the sea – Sri Lanka's worst-ever marine disaster – to the more long-term, insidious, effects of climate change (*see* Chapter 29 – "Environmental Issues") and emerging zoonoses.

Animals as the instigator

Insults inflicted on humans by animals, domestic or wild, include bites, trauma (16,34,35), infection with pathogenic organisms (including zoonoses), electrocution (16), stings and hypersensitivity reactions. Animals can also cause harm or disturbance to humans by damaging property (36), by causing excessive noise or smell, by liberating allergens or by prompting irrational fears. Autoeroticism may also be associated with animals.

Bites, stings and other non-infectious insults may be caused by animals of many species, ranging from dogs, cats and wild (free-living) carnivores to venomous spiders and corals. Published accounts are often scattered but examples of resultant lesions are shown in Table 99.1.

Medical or dental investigation of bites and other animal-inflicted wounds can often benefit from input by veterinarians and zoologists (41,42).

Animal-inflicted injuries that occurred antemortem must be differentiated from those caused post mortem by scavengers, including domestic and wild carnivores and pigs or (in water) fish and crabs (43–45). Humans that die alone in their home may be scavenged by their own pet cat, dog or ferret.

Transmission of infectious agents

Pain is very often a feature of injuries inflicted by animals that can introduce pathogenic organisms, especially bacteria.

99.5 Examination of a wire snare that was placed in a tree in East Africa in order to catch a giraffe.

TABLE 99.1 Examples of bites, stings and other non-infectious insults caused by animals

Mammals	bites, bruising, skin wounds, irritation of mucous membranes, scratches, kicks, trampling, goring*
Birds	bites, stab, talon injuries, damage from wings, kicks
Reptiles	envenomation, bites, constriction leading to asphyxia, dislocation of limbs and drowning**
Amphibians	irritation of mucous membranes, envenomation (parotoid glands of certain species)
Invertebrates	envenomation, blood loss, local tissue damage, acute inflammation, pain, sometimes cardiac damage and systemic shock, irritation of mucous membranes/eyes, allergic reactions, anaphylaxis, including laryngeal edema

*Increasing numbers of publications throw light on the types of wound inflicted by different animals (37–40). ** There are various published accounts, with much on envenomation.

Pathogenic organisms may be transmitted by animals of any taxon. Zoonoses are defined here as "*those diseases and infections that are naturally transmitted between vertebrate animals and humans*" (based on World Health Organization [WHO] wording). They are of growing significance in forensic medicine. Zoonotic infections may be subclinical in some species under certain circumstances such as chlamydophilosis (ornithosis or psittacosis) in birds and this can engender debate in legal cases.

Infectious diseases are continually emerging and many of them are zoonotic (46,47). Among these is SARS-CoV-2 (COVID-19) which is generally assumed to have come from an animal host and the study of which would be facilitated by a better understanding of animal coronaviruses (48). Bowsher and colleagues (49) stressed that zoonotic diseases are leading threats to public health globally but "*repeated epidemics and pandemics from Ebola to COVID-19 have demonstrated the systematic disregard of zoonotic disease within what still remains a predominantly human-centric public health approach... The belief that medical and veterinarian communities should be synergistic collaborators in outbreak response has been largely neglected*".

Animals as sentinels or witnesses

Animals may serve as "sentinels" or "witnesses" in forensic investigations.

In a watershed case in Canada, a white domesticated cat called "Snowball" provided key evidence – genomic DNA from hair – that implicated a man in a murder (50). Since then, there have been many reported instances of forensic findings in animals that have led to convictions for the smuggling of cocaine on or in cats or dogs, for instance.

Animals can at times become "witnesses of fact". There have been reports of parrots and other "talking birds" repeating words that they had heard humans say and which proved to throw light on illegal activities.

Changes in the behavior of animals can provide forensic clues as noted by Sherlock Holmes regarding the dog that "did nothing in the night-time" quoted at the head of this chapter. The advancement of veterinary forensic behavioral medicine (VFBM) is likely to yield many examples (51).

Animals can act as indicators of the presence in the environment of noxious substances or infectious agents. Long ago miners carried caged canaries in coalmines to detect toxic gas dangerous to miners. Free-living birds, notably raptors being at the top of many food chains, can be important indicators of environmental poisons (52).

Cooper and Cooper (2) described an event in which large numbers of common starlings (*Sturnus vulgaris*) were killed in an explosion in a factory. Forensic examination of these birds provided valuable information about the incident and the chemicals thought to have caused it.

Fish are important indicators of pollution and thousands may die, over large stretches of waterway. Veterinarians and other experts are often involved in necropsies and toxicologic investigations in such incidents which can lead to criminal or civil litigation (30).

Animals as part of crime investigation

Animals of different species have been used for decades to assist in the prevention or investigation of crime. The techniques also have a place in conservation research (53). Cadaver dogs are trained to locate human bodies and "sniffer dogs" are used to detect drugs, explosives

99.6 A group of black vultures (*Coragyps atratus*) on the beach in an isolated bay on Trinidad. The presence of such scavenging birds can indicate the presence of tissue of animal or human origin.

and other substances (2). Animals help, actively or passively, in the detection of land mines; the former include species, vertebrate (and invertebrate, such as cockroaches) that are specifically trained to detect explosives (54); notable examples are dogs and African giant pouched rats (*Cricetomys* species) (55). Passive assistance/indication is unwittingly provided by cattle and other livestock that wander or are intentionally driven on to land containing land mines causing injury and suffering or death (2).

Animals such as birds of prey, hyaenas and a multitude of invertebrates help to reveal the presence of carcases (Figure 99.6). Vultures in Africa are often poisoned by poachers who want to prevent them from revealing the location where animals have been killed (56).

Animals have long been used in forensic research. Studies on live animals include areas such as drowning and gunshot wounds (2). In Britain and certain other countries, such work is regulated by strict legislation if the research is likely to cause pain or suffering.

Dead animals are subject to fewer legal constraints and less public concern; for example, studies on "blood spatter" based on pigs and cattle in slaughterhouses or the use of dead pigs rather than human cadavers to study post-mortem change (57). Much of relevance to *Homo sapiens* continues be learned from studies on naturally occurring phenomena in other species; for instance, recently Juniper et al. (58) described how the analysis of data on whale carcases found on the sea floor can aid the understanding of human body decomposition in the ocean.

Invertebrates (especially insects) have played a part in forensic investigations for centuries in China and many decades in Europe. The best-known example is the use of such creatures to estimate the minimum post-mortem interval but invertebrates can also supply information on poisons, detection of wound sites, duration of abuse or neglect and location (geographic trace evidence) (56,59).

Animals killed or injured in accidents ranging from landslides to terrorist attacks may provide information about the incident. Veterinarians often form part of the responding and investigating team.

Sometimes germane to legal cases are "service/assistance animals" that provide practical help to humans. Guide dogs for the blind were probably the earliest example. "Animal-assisted therapy" refers to treatment that involves animals ranging from horses and dogs to birds, fish and stick insects (60,61). The "human-companion animal bond" can be very strong and helps people with diverse health and social needs. This is not a new concept: the value of animals in hospitals and schools was being discussed three decades ago (62) and Florence Nightingale (1860) stated that "A small pet is often an excellent companion for the sick, for long chronic cases especially". Service animals need to be provided with veterinary healthcare to maintain their effectiveness and to minimize the risk of legal action if their welfare is compromised.

TYPES OF LEGAL CASE OR LEGISLATION (BASED ON UK LAWS) THAT INVOLVE ANIMALS

The highest-value legal cases that call for veterinary expert evidence involve animals as property and relate to claims for breach of contract, sale of goods or liability for personal injury or damage to property caused to, or by, animals. Ownership, pre-purchase examination and insurance disputes, theft and poaching also feature animals, litigation and veterinary forensic experts.

However, the legislation that most attracts public attention relates to animal welfare and wildlife conservation; law enforcement, led by both state authorities and charities, requires forensic evidence.

Modern animal welfare legislation has two key offenses that apply to the ill treatment of domesticated or captive non-domesticated vertebrate species.

- It is an offense to cause an animal unnecessary suffering. Many situations are described above relating to the role of animals in forensics.
- There is also a "duty of care" that requires the person responsible for an animal to provide what it needs to keep it in good welfare. While the intention is to prevent suffering, failure is an offense.
- There are specific welfare regulations and standards relating to livestock – on the farm, in the market, at slaughter and during transportation.

Local authorities enforce licensing and inspection requirements for a variety of commercial activities that involve animals, such as zoos, pet shops, entertainment, dog breeding, horse hire and the private keeping of dangerous species. Veterinary evidence may be needed in the event of enforcement litigation.

Animal health (disease control) laws regulate the movement of animals of most species both in-country and internationally and rely heavily on veterinary certification, inspection and evidence to support enforcement.

Veterinary professional negligence (malpractice) and professional disciplinary procedures may call for veterinary forensic evidence as do prosecutions under medicines legislation.

Wildlife conservation litigation includes species protection and the control of trade as mentioned above. Cooper (31) discussed the use of forensic evidence in wildlife conservation litigation.

Examples of law enforcement are reported in *Legal Eagle* (63) and in *TRAFFIC Bulletin Seizures and Prosecutions* (64). Cooper (65) summarized a wide range of UK legislation relating to wildlife.

BIOLOGICAL FEATURES OF ANIMALS RELEVANT TO FORENSIC WORK

The Animal Kingdom consists of millions of species. The majority are invertebrates, most of which do not play a large part in "animal forensics"; in addition, there are 6000 species of mammals, 10 000 species of birds and 35 000 species of fish.

Insofar as forensic work is concerned, many mammals closely resemble humans in terms of anatomy and physiology and in their responses to stimuli and insults. Nevertheless, Munro and Munro (66) cautioned that "*...much remains to be discovered about the development and resolution of lesions in different species; therein lie exciting possibilities for the expansion and refinement of the forensic veterinary pathology knowledge base*". McEwen (27) pointed out that although animals and people can be victims of the same types of injury, the different anatomy and physiology of species and breeds of animal are a challenge to veterinary pathologists.

Where species' differences exist, they usually relate to aspects of biology. Thus, physiologic and pathologic changes in organs and tissues of a bird and a reptile diverge because the former is a "warm-blooded" (endothermic) animal while the latter is "cold-blooded" (ectothemic). Changes are likely to take place more rapidly in the former, which can maintain its own body temperature than in the latter which can only thermoregulate by behavioral means. Some features of animals relevant to forensic investigation are given in Table 99.2.

The significance of these differences is twofold:

1. Forensic investigation of animal species must take into account their biological features and the veterinary (or other) expert must be prepared to explain the relevance of this in court.

TABLE 99.2 Biological features of animals of relevance to forensic investigation

Grouping (taxon)	Particular biological features	Relevance to forensic investigations
Mammals (Class Mammalia)	Vertebrate. Endothermic ('warm-blooded'). Haired. Lungs. Produce live young. Non-nucleated red blood cells. Predominant acute inflammatory cell is the neutrophil.	Predictable physiologic and pharmacologic responses. Hair usually available for analysis and identification. However, some features and characteristics may present challenges – for instance, the ability of some species to hibernate/aestivate and the unusual morphology and life style of marine mammals, especially cetaceans.
Birds (Class Aves)	Vertebrates. Endothermic. Feathered. Lungs. Lay eggs. Nucleated red blood cells. Predominant acute inflammatory cell is the heterophil.	Predictable physiologic and pharmacologic responses. Feathers and eggs available for forensic analysis and identification.
Reptiles (Class Reptilia)	Vertebrates. Ectothermic ("cold-blooded"). Ectodermal scales. Lungs. Lay eggs or produce live young. Nucleated red blood cells. Predominate acute inflammatory cell is the heterophil.	Physiologic and pharmacologic responses are temperature-dependent. Eggs, scales and shed skin available for analysis and identification.
Amphibians (Class Amphibia)	Vertebrates. Ectothermic. Mucous skin. Gills or lungs. Lay eggs or produce live young. Nucleated red blood cells. Acute inflammatory cell is the heterophil.	Physiologic and pharmacologic responses are temperature-dependent. Water samples often play a role in forensic investigations, especially relating to alleged chemical pollution.
Fish (Three classes)	Vertebrates. Ectothermic. Dependence on water. Mesodermal scales. Gills or (a few species) "lungs". Lay eggs or produce live young. Almost total dependence on water. Nucleated red blood cells. Acute inflammatory cell is the heterophil.	Physiologic and pharmacologic responses are temperature-dependent. Water samples can play a major role in investigations, especially relating to alleged chemical pollution.
Invertebrates (many phyla and classes)	No vertebral column. Ectothermic. Vary greatly. Some have tough exoskeletons. Gills or cutaneous diffusion of oxygen. Some species are terrestrial, some aquatic. Blood cells, when present, are usually amebocytes, which also have a phagocytic role.	Depends on the taxon. Much variation. Physiologic and pharmacologic responses are temperature-dependent. Knowledge of the species' biology is vital in forensic investigations. Eggs, scales and shed skin of some taxa available for analysis and identification. Millions of species exist, most still undescribed.

2. The forensic veterinarian should be willing to consult other disciplines. Thus, cases relating to whales or dolphins, such as allegations of boat or firearm damage, should involve veterinarians, cetologists and others with experience of marine mammals (67,68) (Figure 99.7). Investigations relating to reptiles and amphibians may need to include herpetologists (Figure 99.8) while bird of prey cases often require the input of raptor biologists.

It is not only when working with live animals that the forensic investigator needs to take into account taxonomic differences. For example, the estimation of post-mortem interval (PMI) in a dead reptile, amphibian or fish may, on account of their ectothermic nature, be more complex than it is in "warm-blooded" mammals or birds. Tissues may be resistant to hypoxia, especially since, in many such species, the animal's heart can continue to beat long after clinical death. Cooper (69) described studies on PMI in reptiles and amphibians, concluding that much remains to be learnt about this subject. Interestingly, more research has been carried out on the decomposition of fish than of reptiles and amphibians on account of food hygiene measures; a useful review is to be found on the Food and Agricultural Organization (FAO) website (70).

In fact, with the exception of some scholarly studies in domesticated livestock and laboratory rodents (2), there appears to be remarkably little focussed research on PMI in animals. Even in reference to studies on domesticated (beagle) dogs, Erlandsson and Munro (71) lamented that "*in the veterinary medical field there is a paucity of published data…*". The animal forensic investigator, therefore, always has to be circumspect, particularly when working with unfamiliar species.

PRACTICALITIES OF FORENSIC WORK WITH ANIMALS

Many aspects of forensic work with animals are similar to those encountered when dealing with humans. Differences usually relate to the disparate biological characteristics of some of the species involved (see earlier - Table 99.2) and, to a certain extent, the diversity and unpredictability of the locations of incidents, especially when free-living animals are part of the investigation.

The wide range of animal species means that no one technique is likely to be applicable to all, even if they are related taxa (72). For example, the standard necropsy technique for a lizard is totally inappropriate for a tortoise because the latter is effectively enclosed in a "bony box" (carapace and plastron). Forensic post-mortem protocols are available for only a few species (73–79).

Very large species, whether terrestrial or aquatic, often require a team effort. Small specimens such as embryos, eggs, fetuses and neonates present challenges because of both their size and their special features. They and small creatures such as certain amphibians, fish and invertebrates may require micro techniques – the so-called "mini-necropsy" and the use of special instruments, such as a magnifying loupe and ophthalmologic scissors. These small animals can be embedded and serially sectioned for histologic examination (40). Identification and investigation of skeletal material from different species may be facilitated by reference to texts on palaeopathology (80).

Forensic examination of live animals is influenced by the tractability or otherwise of the "patient"; thus investigation of presumed shotgun wounds in a free-living, still very active, red deer (*Cervus elaphus*) is likely to prove more challenging than the examination of comparable lesions in a pet dog (*Canis familiaris*). Assessment of pain is an important need in alleged cruelty cases; the veterinary clinician may find it helpful to work with an experienced ethologist (51) because different species of animals express pain in disparate ways.

99.7 Post-mortem examination of a 13-meter Bryde's whale (*Balaenoptera brydei*) in the West Indies. A team was needed in order to perform a necropsy before the tide came in and disposal (burying) of the carcase required an excavator.

99.8 One of a group of green iguanas (*Iguana iguana*) in the West Indies that had been stunned or killed, unlawfully, for sale as "wild (bush) meat".

As in human work, a wide range of investigative procedures can be performed on live animals, including CT scanning and MRI imaging (76).

Laboratory investigations on samples from live and dead animals are, broadly similar to those employed in human forensic medicine (*see* Chapter 78 – "Evidential Sampling"), with some important differences (2,81).

Investigation of wildlife crime can be difficult and sometimes dangerous because:

- The "crime scene" may range from the carcase (or parts) of a subsequently predated animal to terrain that encompasses topography as varied as forest, desert and inland or coastal waters.
- Often the location of the wildlife crime scene is isolated, with few facilities for proper investigation and a paucity or absence of police, enforcement officials or crime scene specialists (82).
- There may be no human witnesses or those who saw what happened are unwilling to testify for fear of recrimination – poachers in Africa and elsewhere are often willing to kill people who might divulge information.
- Evidence may be disturbed by wild animals, by wind, rain or snow. Scavengers will remove bodies or parts of them. Contamination is often a problem (*see* Chapter 79 – "Minimizing DNA Contamination").
- Many of the world's most threatened species live in poorer parts of the globe and/or in countries experiencing social unrest, necessitating special preparation and precautions and an ability to work internationally.

99.9 Forensic investigation of the last surviving mainland Javan rhinoceros (*Rhinoceros sondaicus*) in Vietnam. Examination confirmed that the animal had been shot, sustained a fracture of a forelimb and suffered a lingering death. Poachers then removed its "horn".

Equipment, investigative techniques and technology all need to be appropriate to, and the best available in, the circumstances. Effective investigation under field conditions is likely to call for a combination of portable and easy-to-use laboratory equipment, coupled with modern electronic methods of data collection and information transmission (83).

A synopsis of the challenges and vagaries of much wildlife crime scene work was presented by Cooper et al. (84) (Figure 99.9). Even in more "developed" countries forensic work with animals is not always straightforward. In Britain, for example, there is often an overlap between wildlife, rural and environmental and organized crime, calling for a wide range of expertise, investigative techniques and collaboration.

Criminal activity relating to rare and legally protected animals and plants is increasingly conducted online.

THE NEED FOR COMPARATIVE FORENSIC MEDICINE

In the "Introduction", the authors suggested that there has been a tendency when discussing types of forensic medicine to use the term "veterinary" in its classic sense – that is, relating to the health of domesticated animals (Latin "*veterinarius*"), a situation that is often reflected in legislation (6). However, the authors have pointed out that:

- The professional remit of the veterinary surgeon (veterinarian) has broadened enormously in recent years and nowadays s/he may be consulted on species ranging from stick insects to simian primates.
- Animals play a part in many aspects of forensic investigation, not just when they are the victims or instigators of an incident.
- There is therefore a need for human medical forensic clinicians and pathologists not only to be aware of the role played in crime investigation by animals, directly or indirectly, but to recognize the value at an early stage of consulting appropriate professionals in their deliberations. Forensic investigators do not hesitate to consult an entomologist when they find maggots. Why are some still so reluctant to involve a veterinarian or a zoologist when a vertebrate animal is involved?

At present, forensic veterinarians are most likely to be involved in cases where there are both animal and human elements such as dog bites, cattle trampling incidents and zoonotic infections. Less frequently, the forensic investigator may be presented with both the cadaver of a dead person and the carcase of a dead animal, for example, because an intruder has shot or poisoned both a householder and their pet dog or a human and an animal are killed in a traffic or drowning accident. In these circumstances, the veterinary clinician or pathologist is

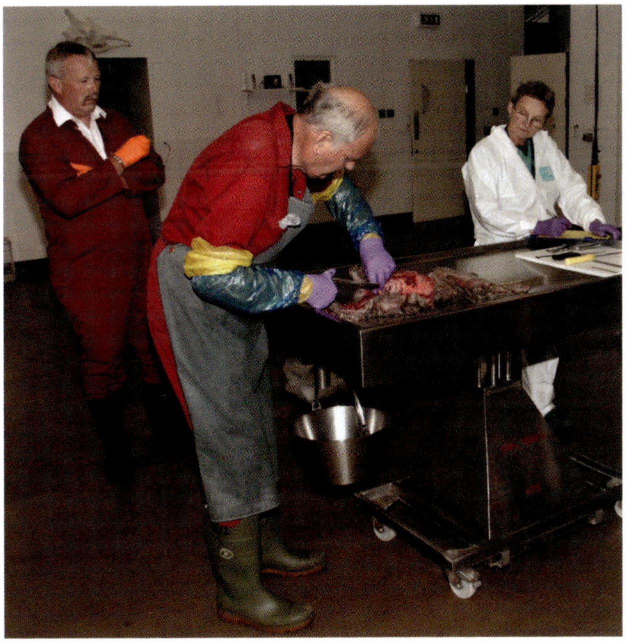

99.10 Post-mortem investigation of a dog that was found dead next to the body of its owner following a "break-in" in the United Kingdom. A detective observes the examination.

very likely to be working alongside, or in parallel, with medical counterparts (Figure 99.10).

The authors of this chapter have been involved over the years in various "human" cases which were satisfactorily resolved because the responsible medic thought "Perhaps a vet could help" – and asked for assistance. They have ranged from crocodile attacks in East Africa to undiagnosed chronic skin lesions attributed to a wild animal in a patient in Britain.

Dog bites inflicted on humans may call for medical and veterinary professional cooperation (85,86). The part played by each was illustrated by Cooper and Cooper (2) in the context of a potential legal case relating to severe injuries said to have been inflicted on a child by a Rottweiler dog.

The association between violence inflicted on animals and the abuse of humans clearly prescribes an interdisciplinary approach, as was so well illustrated at the ground-breaking "Symposium on the Pathology of Abuse in Animals and Humans" hosted by the Royal College of Pathologists in 2011. Participants included physicians, pediatricians, veterinary surgeons, pathologists, animal welfarists, social workers and police officers (23).

We therefore argue that there is a strong argument for fostering "comparative forensic medicine" as a discipline in its own right. It can rightly be considered part of the well-established field of comparative medicine – the bridge between studies on humans and other animals, epitomized in the words attributed to Virchow: "*Between animal and human medicine there is no dividing line – nor should there be. The object is different but the experience obtained contributes the basis of all medicine.*" In writing this, Virchow meant animals in general, not just domestic livestock and familiar household pets.

A comparative approach to animal forensic work implies learning from studies on different species and then applying the findings to taxa where specific information may be limited. The basic principles of forensic investigation, in relation to meticulous record-keeping, systematic examination and proper treatment of material are the same, regardless of whether the victim is human or animal. So also are many of the scientific techniques employed. This is exemplified when veterinary and medical clinicians or pathologists work together in order to capitalize on their different skills and knowledge, as described in the context of marine mammals by Byard et al. (87).

How, then, might "comparative forensic medicine" be defined? The authors have proposed (2) that it could be denoted as "the discipline concerned with forensic studies on different vertebrate and invertebrate species of animals, including humans, and the application of such work to the provision of scientific information to assist in judicial and other processes".

The need for such a comparative approach to investigation of diseases has assumed increased importance in recent years as global concern has burgeoned over the connections between emerging infections, climate change and reduction in biodiversity. This has led to the concept of "One Health" which recognizes the co-dependency of environmental factors and the health and welfare of all species, including humans (88). There is often a need when studying such relationships to employ forensic methods (89,90). This can be considered part of the growing field of "environmental forensics".

CONCLUSION

In closing, the authors suggest that in an increasingly blame-orientated and litigious world, the practice and reputation of forensic science and the quality of evidence are likely to be strengthened by a broader, more comparative approach. Medical, dental (*see* Chapter 92 – "Forensic Odontology") and other professionals who work in human forensic medicine stand to gain from the input of persons trained and experienced in the biology of animals, as will the courts, police, enforcement agencies and the judicial process. Comparative forensic medicine also provides a bridge between the work of the medical and veterinary professions and some of the many emerging areas of endeavor that constitute contemporary forensic science. The success of comparative forensic medicine will depend upon close interdisciplinary collaboration.

ACKNOWLEDGMENTS

We are grateful to the editors for inviting us to contribute this chapter and to friends and colleagues, especially in East Africa, who have worked with us in promoting and practicing veterinary, animal and comparative forensic medicine.

REFERENCES

1. Townley L, Ede R (eds). *Forensic Practice in Criminal Cases*. London: The Law Society; 2004.
2. Cooper JE, Cooper ME. *Introduction to Veterinary and Comparative Forensic Medicine*. Oxford: Blackwell; 2007.
3. Parry NMA, Stoll A. The rise of veterinary forensics. *Forensic Sci Int* 2020; **306**: 110069.
4. Cooper JE, Cooper ME. Foreword. In: Byrd JH, Norris P, Bradley-Siemens N (eds), *Veterinary Forensic Medicine and Forensic Sciences*. Boca Raton: CRC Press; 2020, pp. vii–ix.
5. Byrd JH, Norris P, Bradley-Siemens N (eds). *Veterinary Forensic Medicine and Forensic Sciences*. Boca Raton: CRC Press; 2020.
6. Cooper ME. Birds, exotic animals, and the law. *Semin Avian Exot Pet Med* 1998; 7(4): 166–75.
7. Gunn A. *Essential Forensic Biology*, 2nd ed. Oxford: Wiley-Blackwell; 2009.
8. Friedrich NO. Libro Medicina Veterinaria Aspectos legales y forenses MV, Ciudad de Córdoba, 2015. Available from: https://www.facebook.com/vlf.argentina/?locale=es_LA (Accessed 28 June 2023).
9. McDonough SP, McEwen BJ. Veterinary forensic pathology: The search for truth. *Vet Pathol* 2016; 53(5): 875–7.
10. Newbery SG, Cooke SW, Martineau HM. A perspective on veterinary forensic pathology and medicine in the United Kingdom. *Vet Pathol* 2016; 53(5): 894–7.
11. Arkow P, Munro H. The Veterinary Profession's Roles in Recognizing and Preventing Family Violence: The Experiences of the Human Medicine Field and the Development of Diagnostic Indicators of Non-Accidental Injury. In: Ascione FR (ed), *International Handbook of Animal Abuse and Cruelty: Theory, Research and Application*. West Lafayette: Purdue University Press; 2008, pp. 31–58.
12. Merck MD. *Veterinary Forensics: Animal Cruelty Investigations*. Oxford: Wiley-Blackwell; 2012.
13. Munro R, Munro HMC. *Animal Abuse and Unlawful Killing: Veterinary Forensic Pathology*. Edinburgh: Elsevier Saunders; 2008.
14. Bradley-Siemens N, Sheppard B. Animal Fighting and Hoarding. In: Byrd JH, Norris P, Bradley-Siemens N (eds), *Veterinary Forensic Medicine and Forensic Sciences*. Boca Raton: CRC Press; 2020, pp. 253–84.
15. Smith-Blackmore M, Bradley-Siemens N. Animal Sexual Abuse. In: Byrd, JH, Norris, P, Bradley-Siemens (eds), *Veterinary Forensic Medicine and Forensic Sciences*. Boca Raton: CRC Press; 2020, pp. 113–28.
16. Cooper JE. Physical Injury. In: Fairbrother A, Locke LN, Hoff GL (eds), *Non-infectious Diseases of Wildlife*, 2nd ed. Ames: Iowa State University Press; 1996, pp. 157–72.
17. Munro HMC, Thrusfield MV. 'Battered Pets': Features that raise suspicion of non-accidental injury. *J Small Anim Pract* 2001; **42**: 218–26.
18. Munro HMC, Thrusfield MV. 'Battered Pets': Non-accidental physical injuries found in dogs and cats. *J Small Anim Pract* 2001; **42**: 279–90.
19. Munro HMC, Thrusfield MV. 'Battered Pets': Sexual abuse. *J Small Anim Pract* 2001; **42**: 333–7.
20. Munro HMC, Thrusfield MV. 'Battered Pets': Munchausen syndrome by proxy (factitious illness by proxy). *J Small Anim Pract* 2001; **42**: 385–9.
21. Linsey A. *The Link Between Animal Abuse and Human Violence*. Eastbourne: Sussex Academic Press; 2009.
22. Tiplady C. *Animal Abuse: Helping Animals and People*. Wallingford: CABI Publishing; 2013.
23. Cooper ME. *Reporting of Abuse: The Professional Dilemma. Symposium on the Pathology of Abuse in Animals and Humans*. London: The Royal College of Pathologists; 2011.
24. Royal College of Veterinary Surgeons, London. Supporting Guidance to the Code of Professional Conduct for Veterinary Surgeons: 14 Client Confidentiality (2020). Available from: https://www.rcvs.org.uk/setting-standards/advice-and-guidance/code-of-professional-conduct-for-veterinary-surgeons/supporting-guidance/client-confidentiality/ (Accessed 30 June 2023).
25. National Link Coalition. Working together to stop violence against people and animals. Available from: https://nationallinkcoalition.org/ (Accessed 30 June 2023).
26. Campbell-Malone R, Bogomolni A. Marine Mammals; A Special Case. In: Cooper JE, Cooper ME (eds), *Wildlife Forensic Investigation: Principles and Practice*. Boca Raton: Taylor & Francis/CRC Press; 2013.
27. McEwen, B. Eternally vulnerable: The pathology of abuse in domestic animals. *Acad Forensic Pathol* 2017; 7(3): 353–69.
28. McDonough SP, Holoyda, B. Ritualistic Animal Killing. In: Brooks JW (ed), *Veterinary Forensic Pathology*, Vol 2. New York: Springer; 2021, pp. 129–38.
29. Cooper JE, Cooper ME. *Wildlife Forensic Investigation: Principles and Practice*. Boca Raton: Taylor & Francis/CRC Press; 2013.
30. Huffman JE, Wallace JR. *Wildlife Forensics: Methods and Applications*. Oxford: Wiley-Blackwell; 2012.
31. Cooper ME. Wildlife Conservation Law. In: Underkoffler SC, Adams HR (eds), *Wildlife Biodiversity Conservation: Multidisciplinary and Forensic Approaches*. New York: Springer; 2021, pp. 101–21.
32. Wildlife Forensic Academy. Available from: https://www.wildlifeforensicacademy.com/about-us (Accessed 30 June 2023.
33. Siregar IZ, Ramdhani MJ, Karlinasari L, et al. DNA isolation success rates from dried and fresh wood samples of selected tropical wood tree species for possible consideration in forensic forestry. *Sci Justice* 2021; **61**(5): 573–8.
34. Norris P. Blunt Force Trauma. In: Byrd JH, Norris P, Bradley-Siemens N (eds), *Veterinary Forensic Medicine and Forensic Sciences*. Boca Raton: CRC Press; 2020, pp. 129–44.
35. de Siqueira A, Norris P. Sharp Force Trauma. In: Byrd JH, Norris P, Bradley-Siemens N (eds), *Veterinary Forensic Medicine and Forensic Sciences*. Boca Raton: CRC Press; 2020, pp. 145–56.
36. Hone J. *Wildlife Damage Control: Principles for Managing Vertebrate Pests*. Wallingford: CSIRO; 2007.
37. Byard R. Causes and mechanisms of death in fatal water buffalo attacks. *J Forensic Sci* 2016; **62**(4): 934–6.
38. Byard R. Lethal recreational activities involving horses – a forensic study. *Leg Med* 2020; **46**: 101728.
39. Byard RW, Langlois NEI. Variable mechanisms of dog-related deaths. *Am J Forensic Med Pathol* 2020; **41**(4): 287–90.
40. Cooper JE. Wildlife Forensic Pathology. In: Underkoffler SC, Adams HR (eds), *Wildlife Biodiversity Conservation: Multidisciplinary and Forensic Approaches*. New York: Springer; 2021, pp. 211–86.
41. Berkovitz B, Shellis P. *The Teeth of Mammalian Vertebrates*. Amsterdam: Elsevier Academic Press; 2018.
42. Berkovitz B, Shellis P. *The Teeth of Non-Mammalian Vertebrates*. Amsterdam: Elsevier Academic Press; 2018.
43. Byard RW, James RA, Gilbert JD. Diagnostic problems associated with cadaveric trauma from animal activity. *Am J Forensic Med Pathol* 2002; **23**: 238–44.
44. Shepherd R, Simpson K. *Simpson's Forensic Medicine*. London: Arnold; 2003.
45. Williams DJ, Ansford AJ, Priday DS, et al. *Forensic Pathology*. Edinburgh/London: Churchill Livingstone; 1998.
46. Gibbs EPJ. Emerging zoonotic epidemics in the interconnected global community. *Vet Rec* 2005; **157**: 673–9.
47. Na Ayudhya SS, Kuiken T. Reverse zoonosis of COVID-19: Lessons from the 2009 influenza pandemic. *Vet Pathol* 2021; **58**(2): 234–42.
48. Brownlie J, Sibley D. What can animal coronaviruses tell us about emerging human coronaviruses? *Vet Rec* 2020; **186**(14): 446–8.
49. Bowsher G, McNamara T, Bernard R, et al. Veterinary intelligence: Integrating zoonotic threats into global health security. *J R Soc Med* 2021; **114**(2): 545–8.
50. Menotti-Raymond M, David VA, O'Brien SJ. Pet cat hair implicates murder suspect. *Nature* 1997; **386**: 774.
51. Shepherd K. What is veterinary forensic behavioural medicine, and when is it required? 2021. Available from: https://www.veterinary-practice.com/article/what-is-veterinary-forensic-behavioural-medicine-and-when-is-it-required (Accessed 28 June 2023).
52. Cooper JE. *Birds of Prey: Health & Disease*. Oxford: Blackwell Science; 2002.
53. Richards NL, Hartman J, Parker M, et al. The Role of Conservation Dog Detection and Ecological Monitoring in Supporting Environmental Forensics and Enforcement Initiatives. In: Underkoffler SC, Adam HR (eds), *Wildlife Biodiversity Conservation: Multidisciplinary and Forensic Approaches*. New York: Springer; 2021, pp. 287–322.

54. Cooper RG. *The African Giant/Pouched Rat (Cricetomys gambianus) – Its Physiology, Ecology, Care & Taming*. Raleigh: Lulu; 2014.
55. National Geographic. Meet the Giant Rats that are Sniffing out Landmines. Available from: https://www.nationalgeographic.com/animals/article/151006-giant-rats-landmines-cambodia-science-animals (Accessed 30 June 2023).
56. Odino M, Ogada D. The Intentional Use of Pesticides as Poison in Kenya. In: Underkoffler SC, Adam HR (eds), *Wildlife Biodiversity Conservation: Multidisciplinary and Forensic Approaches*. New York: Springer; 2021, pp. 421–38.
57. Barnes, KM. Forensic Entomology. In: Cooper JE, Cooper ME (eds), *Wildlife Forensic Investigation: Principles and Practice*. Boca Raton: Taylor & Francis/CRC Press; 2013, pp. 149–60.
58. Juniper F, Jameson BD, Juniper SK, et al. Can whale-fall studies inform human forensics? *Sci Justice* 2021; **61(5)**: 459–66.
59. Byrd JH, Brundage A. Forensic Entomology. In: Byrd JH, Norris P, Bradley-Siemens N (eds), *Veterinary Forensic Medicine and Forensic Sciences*. Boca Raton: CRC Press; 2020, pp. 67–112.
60. Edney ATB. Companion animals and human health: An overview. *J R Soc Med* 1995; **88**: 704P–8P.
61. Ben-Sefer E, Shields L. Animal Farm in healthcare: Definitions, policies, laws and implications for health professionals. *J R Soc Med* 2021; **114(4)**: 171–7.
62. Cooper JE. Pets in hospitals. *Br Med J* 1976; **1**: 698–700.
63. RSPB. *Legal Eagle* winter *2020–21, No 91*. Available from: https://www.rspb.org.uk/globalassets/downloads/documents/positions/wild-birds-and-the-law/legal-eagle-91.pdf (Accessed 30 June 2023).
64. TRAFFIC® The Wildlife Trade Monitoring Network. *TRAFFIC Bulletin Seizures and Prosecutions March 1977–October 2019*. Available from: https://www.traffic.org/site/assets/files/9287/traffic_bulletin_march_1997_-_october_2019.pdf (Accessed 30 June 2023).
65. Cooper ME. Law Affecting British Wildlife Casualties. In: Mullineaux E, Keeble E (eds), *BSAVA Manual of Wildlife Casualties*, 2nd ed. Quedgeley: British Small Animal Veterinary Association; 2016, pp. 7–16.
66. Munro R, Munro HMC. Some challenges in forensic veterinary pathology: A review. *J Comp Pathol* 2012; **149(1)**: 1–17.
67. Stolen M. Forensic Science in Marine Mammalogy: Applications and Limitations. In: Underkoffler SC, Adams HR, (eds), *Wildlife Biodiversity Conservation: Multidisciplinary and Forensic Approaches*. New York: Springer; 2021, pp. 383–400.
68. Byard RW, Gilbert JD, Kemper CM. Dolphin deaths: Forensic investigations. *Med J Aust* 2001; **175**: 623–4.
69. Cooper JE. The estimation of post-mortem interval (PMI) in reptiles and amphibians: Current knowledge and needs. *Herpetol J* 2012; **22**: 91–6.
70. Food and Agricultural Organization (FAO). Available from: http://www.fao.org/docrep/v7180e06.html (Accessed 30 June 2023).
71. Erlandsson M, Munro R. Estimation of the post-mortem interval in beagle dogs. *Sci Justice* 2008: **47(4)**: 150–4.
72. Wobeser G. Forensic (medico-legal) necropsy of wildlife. *J Wildl Dis* 1996; **32**: 240–9.
73. Brooks JW, (ed). *Veterinary Forensic Pathology*, Vol 1 and 2. New York: Springer; 2021.
74. Brownlie HB, Munro R. The veterinary forensic necropsy: A review of procedures and protocols. *Vet Pathol* 2016; **53(5)**: 919–28.
75. Cooper JE, Deacon AE, Nyariki T. Post-mortem examination and sampling of African flamingos (Phoenicopteridae) under field conditions. *Ostrich J Afr Ornithol* 2014; **85(1)**: 75–83.
76. Cooper JE, Hull G. *Gorilla Pathology and Health, with a Catalogue of Preserved Materials*. New York: Academic Press; 2017.
77. Cooper JE, Cunningham AA. Pathological investigation of captive invertebrates. *Int Zoo Yearb* 1991; **30**: 137–43.
78. Cooper JE, Cooper ME. Forensic Investigations in Avian Medicine. In: Samour J (ed), *Avian Medicine*. Amsterdam: Elsevier; 2016, pp. 582–5.
79. Cooper JE. Methods in herpetological forensic work—post-mortem techniques. *Appl Herpetol* 2008; **5**: 351–70.
80. Waldron T. *Palaeopathology (Cambridge Manuals in Archaeology)*. Cambridge: Cambridge University Press; 2008.
81. Rogers ER, Stern AW, (eds). *Veterinary Forensics Investigation, Evidence Collection, and Expert Testimony*. Boca Raton: CRC Press; 2018.
82. Cooper ME. Legal, ethical and practical considerations of working in the field. *J Exotic Pet Med* 2013; **22(1)**: 17–33.
83. Cooper JE. Field techniques in exotic animal medicine. *J Exotic Pet Med* 2013; **22(1)**: 4–6.
84. Cooper JE, Cooper ME, Budgen P. Wildlife crime scene investigation: Techniques, tools and technology. *Endanger Species Res* 2009; **9**: 229–38.
85. Cooper JE. Medico-veterinary collaboration. *Trop Dr* 1985; **15**: 187–92.
86. Dorion RBJ. *Bitemark Analysis*. Boca Raton: CRC Press; 2004.
87. Byard RW, Kemper CM, Bossley M, et al. Veterinary Forensic Pathology. The Assessment of Injuries to Dolphins at Postmortem. In: Tsokos M (ed), *Forensic Pathology Reviews*, Vol 4. Totowa: Humana Press; 2006.
88. Cooper JE. One health: Current and future challenges, 2020. Available from: https://www.pathologyinpractice.com/story/34331/one-health-current-and-future-challenges (Accessed 28 June 2023).
89. Haines AM, Webb SL, Wallace JR. Conservation Forensics: The Intersection of Wildlife Crime, Forensics, and Conservation. In: Underkoffler SC, Adams HR (eds), *Wildlife Biodiversity Conservation: Multidisciplinary and Forensic Approaches*. New York: Springer; 2021, pp. 125–146.
90. Underkoffler SC, Adams HR, (eds). *Wildlife Biodiversity Conservation: Multidisciplinary and Forensic Approaches*. New York: Springer; 2021.

CHAPTER 100

Media Engagement in Forensics

Xanthé Mallett

INTRODUCTION

There is no doubt that the media in all its many forms is highly influential in how the public see, and respond to, forensic evidence. Fictional true crime programs portray unrealistic timeframes for solving cases, based on technologies that often do not exist. They also encourage an exaggerated belief in forensic evidence being 100 percent accurate and reliable, especially established techniques such as DNA analysis and fingerprint comparison, with little discussion as to the importance of context.

The advent of true crime podcasts and explosion of social media has also led to a new issue – the rise of the armchair detective. Those with "an interest in" true crime are now content producers, and this content is readily digested by an undiscerning listener who cannot tell the difference between quality, validated research, and someone simply releasing their opinion into the world with little thought for the repercussions; on both those intimately involved in the case under discussion, as well as the legal process should anyone be brought to trial. There is also the issue with innocent people being wrongly accused, which leads to lives being ruined by speculation and inuendo. However, the ever-increasing public interest in true crime, and by extension forensic practice, is also a mechanism by which the public can be educated as to the realistic expectations of different techniques and technologies and dispel some of the widely held myths and misunderstandings.

This chapter reviews some of the positive and negative aspects of the media's engagement with forensic science and criminal cases more broadly. It will focus on three types of media influence, showcasing the good, the bad, and the ugly of true crime reporting. The first is the impact of online material on the criminal justice process, as discussed in relation to the English case of Adem Karakaya, whose conviction was overturned for the indecent assault and rape of his 17-year-old daughter in 2002, following a juror entering extraneous material into the jury room during deliberations that they had downloaded from the Internet, and the effect social media can have, discussed in relation to the murder of 29-year-old Jill Meagher by Adrian Bayley in Melbourne, Australia, in 2012. The second is the police use of the media to engage the public with ongoing investigations, as exemplified by the William Tyrrell case, and how lessons learned from the investigation can be seen to have positively influenced media strategy in later child abduction cases. Thirdly, the powerful effect the media can have when factual programs educate the public about problems with forensic evidence and how these can lead to wrongful convictions. This will be exemplified by the Western Australian case of Scott Austic, who was found guilty and later acquitted of the murder of Stacey Thorne, after it was found that he had suffered a miscarriage of justice, an outcome reached in no small way thanks to an investigation by Channel 7, a free-to-air network in Australia.

THE USE AND ABUSE OF ONLINE MATERIAL

The role of the jury is fundamental to the justice system in Australia and elsewhere, including the UK and the USA, and there are strict rules stating the jurors can only consider information provided to them as part of the trial process. Anything outside of that must be ignored. However, there is concern about the amount of information – much of it potentially prejudicial – that is available online and which jurors are routinely accessing, and that this is significantly affecting the integrity of the jury system. Judges direct juries not to search the Internet for either case-specific or more general information, but ultimately individuals will sometimes choose to ignore this direction and undertake their own Internet searches.

An example of the impact of extraneous information on the justice process can be seen in the English appeal case of *R v. Karakaya [2005] EWCA Crim 346* (1), which reviewed the conviction of Adem Karakaya for the indecent assault and rape of his 17-year-old daughter in 2002. A guilty verdict was originally handed down, however the conviction was overturned as unsafe at the court of appeal – the court found that the trial was conducted correctly, as was the summing up. The issue that made the conviction unsafe was that extraneous material was introduced during the jury's deliberations. This was discovered when a bailiff found Internet searches printed out in the jury room, some of which related to the problems associated with achieving convictions in cases of alleged sexual assault. No investigation was undertaken as to which juror (or jurors) had downloaded the

DOI: 10.1201/9781003138754-104

material and brought it to the jury room, nor was there an assessment of what impact the information may have had on one or more jury members' deliberations, and it is unknown how many jurors actually saw the material (1). Regardless, it is almost certain that the documents, and the information they contained, were introduced into the jury room following an overnight adjournment, part way through jury deliberations.

The material comprised two sets of documents. The first is described in the appeal documents as "the feminist position on rape", and the second looked at rape within the criminal justice process, as presented by a rape crisis organization. The QC for the appellant described the material as inaccurate, and further that the documents suggested that, in general, complaints in rape cases ought to be supported. Furthermore, handwritten notes on the back of the second document were suggestive that at least one juror had abdicated their responsibility to decide the case based solely on the evidence presented in court, as the material was clearly extraneous to evidence brought at trial.

This breaches a long-standing legal principle that no further evidence can be considered after the jury has retired to begin deliberations, and is based on two founding principles of the justice system: one that the defendant has a right to know what information the jury is using when reaching a decision, and two that both the defense and prosecution has the opportunity to address all of the material on which the jury is relying (1). If these principles are not upheld, as in this case, information that does not pass admissibility standards as reliable or being based on scientific or other merit can influence the jury and the outcome of their deliberations, threatening the defendant's constitutional right to a fair trial. On the basis that the conviction was then considered unsound, Karakaya was acquitted and granted a retrial.

This legal principle not only applies to websites, but also to social media content. In high profile cases there will often be intense and sustained discourse across all social media platforms, and the public often do not realise that comments made can affect the outcome of a trial. One case that garnered very significant public attention was the murder of Jill Meagher in 2012. Meagher had been walking home from an evening with friends in the inner-city suburb of Brunswick, Melbourne, Australia, in the early hours of the 22nd of September, when she was abducted. Meagher's body was found six days later around 50 km from where she was taken. She had been raped and murdered by Adrian Bayley, who was convicted in April 2013. Bayley was sentenced to life imprisonment, with a non-parole period of 35 years.

The case was high profile as Meagher worked for the ABC (the national broadcaster), mainly in an administrative capacity but with an occasional on-air presence. She was not engaging in risky behavior (e.g. drug taking), in addition to which she was young, female and Caucasian, all of which led to her being viewed as what criminologists would class as an "ideal victim", in that when they are the subject of a crime these individuals "*most readily are given the complete and legitimate status of being a victim*" (2). This type of victim often engenders more sympathy from the public, and therefore an increase in public and media interest.

Bayley was arrested and charged with Meagher's rape and murder, and on the 28th of September, the morning of his first court appearance, Meagher was being mentioned on social media (Twitter and Facebook) every 11 seconds. The Victoria Police immediately issued a message to the community via its Facebook page which read:

> "*To all our Facebook followers. PLEASE remember that it is inappropriate to post speculation or comments about matters before the courts. We ask you to refrain from posting anything on social media which could jeopardise or endanger the presumption of innocence, as this has the very high potential to interfere with the administration of justice.*" (3)

The police's concern was warranted – a Facebook hate page targeting Bayley was established, calling for him to be executed. The fear was that Bayley's identification as a suspect, and the widespread negative commentary spreading on social media, had the potential to jeopardize Bayley's right to a fair trial as the defense could argue any jury would also be relying on evidence obtained outside of the courtroom (4).

In Bayley's case, a ban was placed on the publication of damaging or potentially prejudicial material, with specific reference made to online material, following a defense submission to the court. While orders such as this are distributed to formal media outlets, and journalists understand the implications of breaching such orders, many social media users may either not be aware of the court order or may not understand that publishing material online is still classed as publication, and therefore still constitutes an infringement (3). Some social media users have very significant public reach, with tens of thousands of followers, and therefore the implications for prejudicing the legal process are significant and highly concerning.

This concern was raised again in the Cleo Smith case, the 3-year-old who was abducted from a campsite near Carnarvon, Western Australia (WA), in October 2021 and was held for 18 days before being found by police alive and physically unharmed in the home of a 36-year-old Terence Kelly in Carnarvon. As soon as an individual was arrested for her abduction, crime commentators stopped discussing the accused, and started asking the public to be aware of their obligations to not post potentially damaging material online, with a view to minimizing the potential for any criminal proceedings to be jeopardized. Through public engagement such as this, it is possible to inform the public of the rules around publication, and also the implications for the justice process when those directions are not followed.

POSITIVE POLICE MEDIA STRATEGY

From the outset, the disappearance of three-year-old William Tyrrell from a house in Kendall, New South Wales, Australia, on the12th September 2014 caused significant public interest. This is in part due to the strange nature of the case in that a little boy vanished without a trace with no witnesses, as well as the fact that pictures of William, which were released to the media shortly after his disappearance, resonated and stayed in people's minds. Everyone in Australia remembers the little boy in the Spider-Man suit (5).

This is an interesting case from a police media perspective, as there was clearly a public engagement agenda established that it was hoped would assist with finding out what had happened to William. Over nine years later, the case remains open, but lessons can still be learnt from the New South Wales Police Force's (NSWPF) media strategy, which can be seen to have influenced later investigations.

The case soon became one of NSWPF's largest investigations, with over 600 persons of interest, 15 000 pieces of information, and 1000 false sightings of William. The case remains the subject of much speculation as to what happened, but as things stand at the time of writing (September 2023), William was last seen playing in the garden of the house in Kendall, around 10 a.m. At 10:56 a.m. his foster mother called the police to report him missing. Despite an exhaustive initial search of the house, street, and surrounding bushland, no trace of William was found. A second search in 2018 also failed to find any trace of William, and a third search of three areas of bushland around 1 km from the home from which William disappeared occurred in November and December 2021, and a number of items were recovered during that search. No information has to date been released to the public as to the forensic significance of any of the exhibits, and no persons have been arrested in relation to William's disappearance.

Initially, the police were searching for a toddler who had wandered off. Later, it became clear that this was not the case, and an investigation was launched focussing on whether William had died as a result of misadventure or had been abducted. The impact of public appeals was diminished by the fact that William was in foster care, and the identity of his foster and biological parents suppressed. This meant that there was no one to advocate for William on a personal level, to appeal for information from the public, and to plea to the person who took him for his safe return.

Strike Force Rosann was established four days after William's disappearance, as the police now believed they were investigating a kidnapping. Within two weeks of William vanishing, the Homicide squad had taken carriage, initially under the command of Detective Chief Superintendent Hans Rupp, before (now-retired) Detective Chief Inspector Gary Jubelin took over the investigation in February 2015 when Rupp retired.

In the early stages, the police had decided to minimize and deflect from Homicide's involvement, which provided some breathing space for investigators. However, because of the high level of public interest, DCI Jubelin developed a targeted media strategy, which he saw as a key aspect of the policing strategy that should be used to investigative advantage. In addition, the approach to information dissemination needed to change following a number of search warrants being executed at the home and business of one person of interest, washing machine repair man, Bill Spedding, in January 2015. The media scrutiny of the investigation following the searches at Spedding's properties was intense, which was not necessarily helpful to the investigation. DCI Jubelin knew that a media strategy needed to be initiated that not only managed the optics of the investigation in relation to public perceptions, but that also worked with any other policing strategies in place.

A shift in focus then took place, and instead of minimizing Homicide's role, it was decided that they should become the public face of the investigation, showing that they were in control and giving confidence to the public regarding the direction of the investigation. This strategy also allowed the police to use the media to send specific messages to the public asking for assistance, when necessary, as well as giving the police a voice to speak directly to whomever may have taken William or those who knew what had happened to him – to leverage pressure.

DCI Jubelin also noted in his strategic plan (the purpose of which is to outline the circumstances of the crime, as well as direction moving forward) that, due to the very significant public and media interest following the execution of the Spedding warrants, the worst thing that the NSWPF, and Homicide as the lead command, could do would be nothing. DCI Jublelin then took lead in fronting the media in press conferences, providing a pivotal and authoritative voice to the investigative strategy. On the 12th of June 2018, DCI Jubelin announced a new, forensic search of around 3 km of bushland in close proximity to where William was last seen, and took the opportunity to speak, through the media, directly to those he strongly believed had information relating to what had happened to William and that he:

> "*wanted to make a point to those people, that if you do have information concerning what happened to William, you are at the risk of committing a criminal offence by concealing an offence if you don't come forward. I'd suggest you come to us before we come to you.*"(6)

This is an intelligent strategy, as there are many examples whereby criminals will follow the news as related to their crime – this occurs for a number of reasons. Firstly, because they may fear the police are closing in, and want a status update to evaluate their current risk level, or in some very violent serial offenders, because they get a thrill from seeing their crime in the media.

An example of the latter would be John Bunting, the primary offender in the series of violent homicides known as the "Snowtown murders". Twelve people died, eight of whom were found in barrels in a disused bank vault in Snowtown, South Australia. The crimes took place between August 1992 and May 1999, and were committed by Bunting and three main accomplices, Robert Wagner, James Vlassakis, and Mark Haydon. Vlassakis, who later turned Crown's evidence, reported that while watching "Australia's Most Wanted", Bunting allegedly boasted that the murder of Clinton Trezise (who had died as the result of blunt force trauma to the skull in 1994) was his "handiwork" (7).

Regardless of motivation for the interest, in a very high-profile case it is likely that the offender will monitor news around the event, and that this can lead to pressure on the accused to either confess to someone what they have done, or to make an error such as returning to a crime scene to check it has not been discovered or to dispose of incriminating evidence.

The media can also be used to distribute information that may appeal to accomplices or others who may have information relevant to a crime, and rewards can be utilized to incentivize people to report. In the Tyrrell matter, a $1 million was announced in 2016, marking the second anniversary of William's disappearance. This reward, which remains unclaimed, is unique in that it is offered for information that leads to the recovery of William and is not linked to the charging and successful prosecution of any person.

The Tyrrell case remains of very high public interest, and lessons learned during that investigation can be seen to have potentially influenced the investigative procedures initiated following later child abductions, including Cleo Smith in October 2021. From the outset, the police investigated all possible hypothesis simultaneously; that Cleo had wandered off, that she had been the victim of misadventure, or that she had been the target of criminal activity (kidnapping/murder). The WA police used the media to great effect, sharing information with the public to investigative benefit. Interestingly, six days after Cleo was abducted, a $1 million reward was offered – this was only the fourth time in WA history that a reward of this scale had been offered, and normally this occurs years or even decades after an event. In the Smith case, it was a matter of only a few days, and while the reward has not been claimed as she was located as a result of police intelligence, clearly the police and WA government were using every tool available in the early days in an attempt to find Cleo Smith.

POSITIVE IMPACT OF TRUE CRIME DOCUMENTARIES

The public often does not understand the difference between the functions of 24-hour news cycle reporting and long-format journalism. The news cycle lives and breathes current, fast-paced delivery. Details, interpretation, and nuance are not the focus. It's about getting to the story first, and is short, sharp and attention grabbing.

Longer format documentaries aim to delve more deeply into a story or issue, dedicating months of research to tracking down witnesses and interviewees, preparing detailed timelines and backgrounds, to take the viewer on a journey. In the forensic and true crime space, they have the opportunity to ask some of the hard questions, and address some important social justice issues, that are in the public interest to air.

One of those public interest areas is potential wrongful convictions. It is very difficult for incarcerated individuals who maintain their innocence to access the materials and evidence they need to demonstrate they should not have been convicted. With few resources and little influence, the balance of power is very much against them, and these people need a champion to take on their cause. This could take the form of a dedicated family member or friend, a lawyer, an innocence initiative, or, in the case of Scott Austic, a television network.

In 2007, pregnant woman Stacey Thorne was violently murdered in her own home in Boddington, Western Australia. In 2009, her casual boyfriend, Scott Austic, was found guilty of her murder and sentenced to life imprisonment with a minimum of 25 years non-parole. Over the proceeding years, a number of people in the legal and forensic community reviewed the evidence and recognized the significant problems with the case. A prolonged campaign for a review followed, and in 2020 the Court of Appeal ordered a retrial, on the basis that Austic was the subject of a miscarriage of justice, with a suggestion that evidence used to convict him had been planted – after the crime scenes had been secured by police. The Supreme Court heard the retrial in late 2020 (8), at which time, Austic was found not guilty and acquitted of all charges.

The context of the case was that on the 9th of December 2007, Austic attended the local pub in Boddington, where both the victim and Austic lived, only around 350 m apart. Austic was so drunk he was asked to leave the pub, at which point he walked first to the house of another woman who he was also in a casual sexual relationship with. When he discovered she was not home, he went to Thorne's home, arriving around 7:45 p.m., where he had sex with her. After which he walked home, arriving around 10 p.m., a time confirmed by Austic's housemates.

Thorne was stabbed multiple times in the kitchen of her home around 10:50 p.m. that evening, after which she staggered outside and died. The prosecution suggested Austic had returned to Thorne's house after his housemates had seen him at his home, thereby giving him opportunity to have murdered her.

At the original trial, the evidence against the accused appeared overwhelming, and it is easy to see why a jury reached a conclusion of guilt beyond reasonable doubt – the murder weapon was found covered in Thorne's blood in a paddock between Thorne and Austic's homes, he was placed at the scene by a beer can with his fingerprints on it outside of the victim's house, Thorne's blood was found on a cigarette packet at Austic's home, and there was evidence he had burned the clothes he had been wearing that night in the fire at his home. Austic had recently learnt that Thorne was carrying his baby, as a result also tendered in evidence was a text message that Austic sent to Thorne, asking her to reconsider having the baby. This was presented by the Crown as a motive for the murder, as Austic wanted Thorne to have an abortion.

In 2019, Channel 7 aired an episode of 7NEWS Spotlight entitled "*Framed: 'Proof that evidence was planted against Scott Austic in murder case'*." This investigative documentary represented over a year's work by the network to uncover the truth behind Austic's conviction. The documentary outlined a number of problems with the forensic evidence in this case. Firstly, there were two sets of digital images (still and video); one taken at the time the two crime scenes (Thorne's home and Austic's home) were secured by police, and the second 30 hours later, when the scene was still under police guard. The first set shows the outside of Thorne's home, the beer can is not present, but is visible in the images taken 30 hours later. The first set of images also show the table on the veranda at Austic's home where the bloody cigarette packet was found, it is not present in the original images but again can be seen in the second set. Only the second set of images was presented in court, so the jury were unaware of the inconsistencies between the two.

Secondly, Austic's housemates confirmed the fire had not been lit the night of the murder, nor was there evidence it had been lit when they got up in the morning; it was the height of an Australian summer, and it could reasonably be assumed they would have noted such an unusual event. Thirdly, it should also be highlighted that no bloody footprints or fingerprints were located inside Thorne's home that belonged to Austic, even though this was a frenzied and violent attack. Fourthly, a search had been conducted by the SES of the area between Thorne and Austic's homes, and the knife was not found. The knife was discovered later by the senior officers leading the investigation. Perhaps most damaging, later analysis determined that the knife presented at trial as the murder weapon could not have inflicted all of the wounds found on the victim as it was not long enough, and there was no suggestion that two knives had been used in the attack. The question was then raised as to how Thorne's blood could have been found on the knife, when it was clearly not the weapon used to kill her (8).

In short, all evidence that had led to Austic's conviction was unsafe. However, this would not have come to light if it were not for the investigation and advocacy of Channel 7, which shone such a public light on the flaws in the case that it was impossible for the court system in WA to ignore it. Therefore, it is possible, even likely, that Austic's case may not have been granted the later appeal without the intervention of Channel 7, which gave a public voice to his supporters and advocates.

At the time the WA Supreme Court overturned Austic's conviction on the grounds it was unsafe in 2020, he had spent 12 years and 6 months in prison. The WA police have reserved the right to retry Austic for Throne's murder, but this has not yet occurred. On the basis that the evidence presented in the original trial has been so publicly and summarily discredited, it would seem unlikely that Austic will be taken to court again.

In May 2023, Austic was awarded a $1.6 million Australia dollars *ex-gratia* payment as a result of his wrongful conviction.

This may seem like justice for Austic; however, a man has spent over 12 years in prison for a crime he did not commit, away from his family and friends. We should also not forget that the actual perpetrator of Thorne's murder remains unidentified. Both families still deserve answers as to what happened to Thorne.

This case highlights larger problems in the criminal justice system, that lead to wrongful convictions occurring. However, it also demonstrates the power of the media to draw attention to injustice, and to force a legal response against the odds; Austic was not a man of means or power, he had a strong case for appeal but did not know it, and it took the resources of a major television network to ensure he did not remain in prison.

CONCLUSION

The media has many faces and many functions, some very short-term and others with a longer tail. As this chapter has demonstrated, the influence the media can have for good and bad is significant. When engaging with forensics and true crime, consumers of content need to be aware of the implications of sharing potential damaging or prejudicial information or opinions online, and failure of people to understand their responsibilities is going to continue to be a problem going forward as the reach of social media continues to grow.

That is a negative side of our obsession with true crime. However, as we have seen, there are also positives – the police can use the media to share messages or request help from the public, to leverage pressure on potential perpetrators, and in general to benefit their investigative strategies. Further, media creators, such as television networks, can undertake well-resourced investigations into issues of social and criminal justice that require scrutiny such as potential wrongful convictions, holding our justice system publicly to account.

In summary, a balance must be found between responsible creation and consumption, and everybody has a part to play in ensuring the media is a force for good, and a source of information rather than misinformation. As individuals, we choose what we watch, what podcasts we choose to listen to, how we behave on social media, in essence what discourses we engage with and the nature of that engagement. I suggest we choose wisely, as the consequences on the justice process when we do not have implications for us all.

REFERENCES

1. England and Wales Court of Appeal (Criminal Division) Decisions. *R v. Karakaya*, EWCA Crim 346, 2005. Available from: http://www.bailii.org/ew/cases/EWCA/Crim/2005/346.html (Accessed 28 June 2023)
2. Christie N. The Ideal Victim. In: Fattah EA (ed), *From Crime Policy to Victim Policy*. Basingstoke: Macmillan; 1986, pp. 17–30.
3. Mezrani L. Fears of Trial by Social Media in Meagher Case, 2013. Available from: https://www.lawyersweekly.com.au/wig-chamber/11265-fears-of-trial-by-social-media-in-meagher-case (Accessed 28 June 2023).
4. Fitzpatrick L. Protecting the Right to a Fair Trial, 2013. Available from: http://classic.austlii.edu.au/au/journals/

PrecedentAULA/2013/50.pdf (Accessed 28 June 2023).
5. Mallett X. *Cold Case Investigations.* Sydney: Pan Macmillan; 2019.
6. FaceBook. Detective Chief Inspector Gary Jubelin said the New Forensic Search for William Tyrrell in Bushland at Kendall will Ensure Police have Covered all..., 2018. Available from: https://www.facebook.com/PortMacquarieNews/videos/1984141008286715 (Accessed 28 June 2023).
7. Pudney J. *Snowtown: The Bodies in the Barrels Murders.* Sydney: Harper Collins Publishers; 2005.
8. *Supreme Court of Western Australia. Austic v. the State of Western Australia*, 2020. Available from: http://www.austlii.edu.au/cgi-bin/viewdoc/au/cases/wa/WASCA/2020/75.html?context=1;query=austic;mask_path=au/cases/wa/WASC+au/cases/wa/WASCA+au/cases/wa/WALawRp+au/cases/wa/WADC+au/cases/wa/FCWA+au/cases/wa/FCWAM+au/cases/wa/WACIC+au/cases/wa/WAGAB+au/cases/wa/WAMB+au/cases/wa/WASAT+au/cases/wa/WASTR+au/cases/wa/WATPAT+au/cases/wa/WABDT+au/cases/wa/WAIRC+au/cases/wa/WAIRComm+au/cases/wa/WAICmr+au/cases/wa/WAWM+au/cases/wa/WASupC+au/legis/wa/consol_act+au/legis/wa/num_act+au/legis/wa/repealed_act+au/legis/wa/consol_reg+au/legis/wa/repealed_reg+au/legis/wa/bill+au/legis/wa/bill_em (Accessed 28 June 2023).

CHAPTER

101

Misinterpretation and Fallacies in Forensic Evidence

Linzi Wilson-Wilde

INTRODUCTION

Misinterpretations occur when there is an incorrect inference drawn from the forensic examination and fallacies refer to understandings attributed during the forensic examination that have later been shown to be false. Misinterpretations and fallacies in forensic evidence are more often the result of incorrectly understood or applied forensic science, rather than from nefarious actions. The USA Innocence Project has been successful in overturning 237 wrongful convictions cases in the USA as of the 1st May 2022 and list misused or misapplied forensic science as having contributed to 52 percent of the cases (1). In addition, since 1989, the USA National Registry of Exonerations (NRE) have recorded 3092 exonerations as of the 1st May 2022 and lists false or misleading forensic evidence as a contributing factor in 24 percent of all wrongful convictions in the USA (2,3). The NRE found that these wrongful conviction cases involved forensic evidence that was unreliable or invalid, or expert testimony that was misleading (through mistakes or misconduct) or the issues were attributed to advances in scientific understanding (4).

There have also been numerous international reports over the years examining forensic science disciplines. The 2009 USA National Research Council of the National Academy of Sciences Report "*Strengthening Forensic Science in the United States: A Path Forward*" (NAS Report) (5) identified several issues in forensic science service delivery including a lack of standardization, issues in validity and reliability, issues in independence of agencies, insufficient attention to addressing the impact of bias, insufficient training and competency, and deficiencies in quality certification and accreditation. Of particular interest, the report highlighted the need for research to investigate potential issues in accuracy, reliability and validity in forensic science (5).

The 2016 USA President's Council of Advisors on Science and Technology (PCAST) report "*Forensic Science in Criminal Courts: Ensuring Scientific Validity of Feature Comparison Methods*" (6) looked further into the issues identified in the NAS Report to determine what additional steps were needed to help ensure the validity of forensic evidence in the USA judicial system. Included in the PCAST recommendations were the need for the ongoing evaluation of the scientific validity of current and new forensic feature-matching technologies; a uniform language for testimony and reports; and the use of appropriate scientific criteria by the judiciary for assessing scientific validity when deciding on admissibility of expert testimony.

PCAST also detailed a requirement for all forensic methods to be foundationally valid, and for those methods to be applied in a correct and rigorous manner. While the report focuses on only six forensic disciplines, the principles detailed extend across all forensic methods, whether human (cognitive) or instrument (analytic) based. Many disciplines lack sufficient empirical data to show that the claims being made are valid, that the methods being employed are reliable and reproducible, and that practitioners have sufficient skill to apply the methods in a valid manner (6).

Wrongful convictions are not just a US issue. The Criminal Cases Review Commission (CCRC) operates in England, Wales and Northern Ireland and is responsible for "independently reviewing suspected and alleged miscarriages of criminal justice". As of the 31st March 2022, the CCRC has referred 788 cases to various courts of appeal and of these, 539 cases were successfully overturned (7). It should be noted that the basis for the appeals was extremely broad and included sentencing issues and therefore go well beyond forensic evidence issues, however, issues in the forensic evidence were involved in some cases.

The 2019 UK House of Lords Science and Technology Select Committee Report (8) discussed the forensic science environment in the UK and found a lack of high-level leadership, accountability and oversight. The forensic environment in the UK was found to be poorly regulated, with many service providers failing to meet appropriate quality standards. The Committee also found that research was underresourced and had serious concerns regarding the scientific validity of some disciplines.

In Australia, Dioso-Villa identified 71 wrongful convictions between 1922 and 2015 and in these cases,

DOI: 10.1201/9781003138754-105

they found many similar contributing factors to those found internationally. This included 22 percent (n = 31) of cases which found forensic error or misleading forensic evidence as a causal or contributing factor (9). The cases covered a range of offenses from serious offenses (murder, rape) to less serious offenses (theft, accessory after the fact). The forensic factors contributing to the wrongful convictions included exaggeration by experts, misinterpretation of the evidence during the investigation or at trial, or the use of untested or unreliable forensic techniques (9,10).

The Sydney Declaration (11) describes forensic science as "*a case-based (or multi case-based) research-oriented endeavour using the principles of science to study and understand traces – the remnants of past activities (such as an individual's presence and actions) – through their detection, recognition, examination and interpretation to understand anomalous events of public interest (e.g. crimes, litigations, security incidents)*". A key component of this definition is the requirement to use the principles of science in the study of traces. This requires the development of propositions to answer questions, coupled to the application of critical thinking and logical reasoning.

The forensic science definition is supported by seven principles (11) as follows:

1. Activity and presence produce traces that are fundamental vectors of information.
2. Scene investigation is a scientific and diagnostic endeavor requiring scientific expertise.
3. Forensic science is case-based and reliant on scientific knowledge, investigative methodology and logical reasoning.
4. Forensic science is an assessment of findings in context due to time asymmetry.
5. Forensic science deals with a continuum of uncertainties.
6. Forensic science has multi-dimensional purposes and contributions.
7. Forensic science findings acquire meaning in context.

The definition and principles in the Sydney Declaration are important as they recognize the importance and need for scientific foundational basis of forensic science, the importance and role of the trace and the need to frame the examiner's work in a structure that includes consideration of the context, time and uncertainties. It is also important for the delivery of forensic science services, that the examiner applies a broad scientific knowledge, ethical considerations, critical thinking and logical reasoning. These are vital elements in delivering a robust and reliable service, which should also be supported by efficient and effective training, research and practice (11).

In general, misinterpretation and fallacies in forensic evidence can be attributed to one of two main causes: insufficient application of scientific principles to the underpinning validity and reliability of forensic disciplines and a lack of understanding of the limitations and assumptions related to forensic evidence. The role of the expert is pivotal in addressing these issues and ensuring a robust and reliable service.

VALIDITY AND RELIABILITY IN FORENSICS

Without the proper application of scientific principles to forensic testing, any discipline could be subject to erroneous results and fallacies. Scientific principles should be applied to the development of forensic methods (foundational validity). Foundational validity includes the validation, based on empirical studies, of the forensic method, prior to implementation (12,13). These empirical studies are important to demonstrate that the forensic method is repeatable and reproducible and that the strength of evidence, including the false positive and false negative rates (error rates) are understood. Empirical studies should be performed in conditions similar to operational casework, so that the results of the studies can be more accurately applied to the questions relevant to the case (14).

Validation is also a requirement of accreditation to international standards such as ISO/IEC 17025, ISO/IEC 17020, ISO/IEC 15189 and ISO/IEC 21043 parts 1 and 2 and represents a component of a broader quality system that all forensic science service agencies should have. Quality systems are designed to ensure that the service or product produced performs as expected within a specified set of criteria (15).

Without foundational validity, erroneous forensic results can be presented to police or the judiciary. Hair microscopy comparison is a forensic discipline that was performed regularly in casework, comparing the microscopic features in hair between samples found at crime scenes and those collected from suspects. Verbal expressions of the strength of the match based on the expert's opinion, derived from training and experience, were provided. However, it has been shown that the methodology lacked meaningful empirical studies to support the conclusions. The 2009 NAS Report was critical of hair microscopy analysis stating that microscopic hair comparisons should not be used to match hair with a specific individual (5). However, it was not until 2015 that the USA Federal Bureau of Investigation (FBI) announced that they were ceasing hair microscopy comparison analysis following a review of 268 cases. The FBI found that hair microscopy experts had overstated the probability of a match between the hair evidence found at the crime scene and the reference hair sample from the defendant in 95 percent of cases (16).

Without appropriate and properly designed empirical studies, opinions can be developed from training and experience. These do not always correlate with correct results and can lead to the creation of "forensic urban myths". These myths occur when associations are made through experience and are not subsequently tested through a properly designed empirical study. The myths can then be passed on to other examiners through training. This is particularly evident in fire analysis, which has historically lacked sufficient foundational validity research to develop robust methodology, leading to misleading opinions provided by experts over a number of years (17).

In 1992, the USA National Fire Protection Association published the "Guide for Fire and Explosion Investigations" (18). The Guide updated the previous understanding of fire analysis, which included that alligatoring of wood (blistering patterns on wood), crazed glass and sagged furniture springs were indicators of deliberate fires. The revised understanding was that these features could also occur in accidental fires. This represented a major shift in understanding and the formulation of opinions regarding the cause of a fire. Previously, these feature patterns in fires had been used to develop expert opinions, leading to wrongful convictions (1,2).

Other forensic urban myths associated with fire analysis include that petrol burns hotter than wood, that V-burn patterns indicate a rapid hot fire and the greater the angle of the V-burn pattern the greater the speed of the fire, spalling patterns (breaking off small pieces of concrete or brick) indicate the use of an accelerant, crazed glass indicates the possible use of an accelerant and using the depth of the charring on burnt wood to determine the duration of the burning of the wood and also using this to determine the point of origin. These fire-burn pattern associations are no longer used in fire analysis (18,19).

If a forensic method is insufficiently validated, when applied it may not produce results that are repeatable and reproducible. This was seen in a 2007 study by the USA Bureau of Alcohol, Tobacco and Firearms who found issues in the interpretation of fire patterns by examiners, with reducing accuracy by experts the longer the fire burned past the flash-over point. At 30 seconds, 70 seconds and 180 seconds past the flash over point, the accuracy of expert's conclusions reduced from 89 percent, 69 percent and 25 percent respectively (20). In a 2012 study of fire analysis experts, of the 587 participants, only 77.7 percent were able to identify the correct point of origin of the fire (21). This was due to the complications in fire patterns caused by flash-over events, leading examiners to interpret the fire differently. This indicates issue in the reproducibility of the method.

Another relatively new forensic discipline associated with limited empirical studies is comparisons based on CCTV images. In many parts of the world, CCTV image capture is ubiquitous within police investigations. While guidelines exist for CCTV capture (22,23), much of the methodology remains untested. The UK Forensic Regulator has previously commented on her lack of confidence in opinions presented from comparisons of CCTV images (24). The issue centers on whether an examiner can reliably identify an individual or object from a CCTV image to the exclusion of all others. This has not been empirically tested and error rates are unknown.

Relying on any photographic information for identification purposes can be prone to misinterpretation, as was found in the inquest into the death of Romuald Todd Zak (25). In the disputed death (whether the death was suicide or murder), the forensic examiner provided a report and oral evidence to the coronial inquest on his interpretation of the scene, based solely on scene photographs taken. The examiner identified a red object as the back of a red chainsaw. This red object was later identified through the crime scene notes and photographs taken from other angles as a red Coca Cola can (25). This case highlights the dangers of making identifications based solely on photographs, which can lead to the misinterpretation of the evidence.

It should be noted that some disciplines cannot be tested, or it is extremely difficult to test. Properly designed validation studies require the use of ground truth known stimuli, which for some disciplines is extremely difficult or impossible. This particularly applies to forensic pathology and clinical forensic medicine, where recreating known events causing death or injury is not possible, such as cases involving gun shots or stabbings, although some attempts to address these issues have been conducted (26,27).

Validity, as applied, involves testing for human factors; the demonstration that a forensic examiner is capable of reliably applying the method to obtain the correct result. A forensic examiner's application of the method is often demonstrated using appropriate proficiency testing. However, proficiency tests are often simple and easily identifiable as a proficiency test. Even considering this, forensic examiners still make errors in the examination and interpretation of proficiency tests (28). Therefore, it must be conceivable that there are error rates in the forensic process used in casework. For many forensic disciplines, the error rates are unknown, but some work is being done to build this knowledge (29,30,31).

Due to the introduction of the human factor, given the same data, separate forensic examiners may formulate different opinions. This is less likely when the result of the analysis of the trace is clear, for example, a full DNA profile from a single individual, or a clear, un-smudged and complete fingerprint. However, when the trace is less clear, there can be differences in opinions between examiners. A 2011 study found that when 17 DNA examiners were presented with a DNA profile from a mixture source (more than one contributor), they reached different opinions as to whether a suspect was a contributor to the mixture. Opinions ranged from "cannot be excluded" to "inconclusive" to "excluded" (32).

A 2018 USA study found, of 108 crime laboratories that interpreted a complex mixture against three reference samples, 69 percent correctly included two reference samples as contributors but incorrectly included a third reference sample. A further 21 percent of the laboratories concluded the mixture profile as inconclusive, not including any of the three suspects and 4 percent of laboratories correctly included the two references samples and listed the third reference as inconclusive. Only 6 percent of laboratories correctly included the two reference samples and excluded the third (33).

Understanding the variation in a forensic examiner's capability to reliably apply the forensic method to obtain the correct result is an area where there has been limited research in all forensic disciplines. Significant further research is required.

LIMITATIONS AND ASSUMPTIONS OF FORENSIC EVIDENCE

In any forensic discipline, there are assumptions that underlie the analysis and interpretation processes and limitations to any opinions provided. These are not always well understood by the users of the forensic product. The limitations and assumptions begin when the evidence is collected at the crime scene and if this is done incorrectly or incompetently it can lead to the misinterpretation of the forensic evidence (34,35).

A common assumption is that the evidence or trace found is connected with the crime. In some instances, this connection can be ascertained from observations of the trace (e.g. a blood stained knife found next to a deceased body with stab wounds), however at other times, this is not as clear (e.g. a fingerprint found on the outside of a stolen motor vehicle). The dangers of making a connection without considering the alternative hypothesis as to the origin of the trace and connection to the crime is highlighted in a 2009 Victorian case. In this case, a conviction was later overturned due to the possibility of DNA contamination at the point of sample collection (36). Mr Farah Abdulkadir Jama was convicted of sexually assaulting a woman at a nightclub based solely on a DNA match. There was no evidence that Jama had attended the night club and there was no other circumstantial or forensic evidence in support of the case. No questions were asked, or any alternate hypothesis considered to explain how the DNA came to be on the swab (36).

After 15 months in jail, an investigation could not exclude the possibility of a contamination event at the time of sample collection (36). This case highlights the importance of considering alternate hypotheses and also the need for appropriate quality controls in sample collection, packaging, transport and storage as required in *ISO 21043.2 Forensic sciences–Part 2: Recognition, recording, collecting, transport and storage of items* (37).

Another case that highlights the impact of spurious contamination is the infamous Phantom of Heilbronn incidents, where over 40 cases across Europe were linked by DNA to the same female offender. The cases included burglary, theft, home invasion and various murders. The "offender" was ultimately traced to the contamination of sterile swabs during the manufacturing process by a female worker. This case highlights the need to consider alternate hypotheses in how the DNA was deposited. Ultimately, this consideration is how the spurious contamination was identified, when the DNA of the female "offender" was found on the fingerprints of a deceased male (38).

A link between a trace found at a crime scene and a person or object cannot always provide all the information in relation to an offense. This includes when and how the trace was deposited, whether the trace has been altered after depositing or after collection, the impact of the sampling technique, variations resulting from the analysis process and variation in the interpretation of the results. These factors should be considered when testing alternative hypotheses.

Other assumptions can be specific to the forensic discipline and are an integral part of the interpretation process. One such assumption is that, except for identical twins, a person's DNA is unique to them. This is logically sound, and we can be reasonably sure this is correct, but since we have not tested every person on the planet, we cannot be certain. Examiners also do not routinely test the entire DNA genome of a reference biological sample taken from a person involved in a crime. Instead, examiners analyze a set number of DNA markers comparing the DNA profiles of the samples. Examiners look at the genetic information (called alleles) at the markers between the DNA profiles of the samples. DNA experts use a statistical framework to provide a weighting to any DNA profile comparisons. The statistical weighting is calculated using a representative sample from the population and calculating the prevalence of the alleles in the subpopulation. The numerical prevalence of the alleles is then applied to the DNA profiles to determine the overall likelihood that two DNA profiles originate from the same source vs from a different source. It should be noted that the concept that the representative sample is actually representative of the entire population is another assumption.

Similar examples of assumptions can be seen in other disciplines, such as that a person's fingerprints are unique to them. Again, not every fingerprint in the world has been tested, however, police hold massive databases containing millions of fingerprints, which provides considerable support for at least an extreme rarity of coincidental features. In Gunshot Residue (GSR) analysis there were numerous assumptions, such as, that GSR can be deposited on items near the discharge of a firearm, or that GSR is rarely found as an environmental contaminant. Through empirical testing, these are now well understood and are no longer assumptions (39,40). Other assumptions such as the detection of large quantities of GSR on a person's hands and/or clothing supports the contention that the GSR was deposited recently have not been specifically tested but could be considered to have been empirically tested through studies on the rate of loss of GSR particles from objects (39,40).

For other disciplines, the assumptions that have been used to interpret the results have led to misinterpretations of the evidence. Comparative Bullet Lead Analysis (CBLA) was used to link bullets found at a crime scene to those found with a suspect. This was based on the assumption that the bullet lead composition was unique and shared only with the other bullets in the same manufacturing batch. This assumption was later found to be false (41).

In 1975, odontologists used bite mark analysis in a case to link an offender to the bite mark left on a murder victim. The odontologists used the principles of odonatologic identification used in disaster victim identification (DVI) to identify the offender as the marker of the partial bite mark. While the evidence was challenged, it was admitted, and the case later used as the basis for admitting bite mark evidence in other cases (42). The evidence is based on the assumption that each person's dentition is unique and that the features on the dentition can be used to accurately link individuals. The NAS Report was highly critical of this approach stating that "the uniqueness of the human dentition has not been scientifically established" and "the ability of the dentition, if unique, to transfer a unique pattern to human skin and the ability of the skin to maintain that uniqueness has not been scientifically established" (5). This was because "Unfortunately, bite marks on the skin will change over time and can be distorted by the elasticity of the skin, the unevenness of the bite surface, and swelling and healing. These features may severely limit the validity of forensic odontology" (5).

Another assumption is that forensic examiners can all accurately apply a validated method and interpret the results to obtain the correct opinion. This assumes that all forensic examiners using the same method on the same sample will interpret the results the same way to obtain the same opinion. However, when introducing human factors into any process, variations will occur. Therefore, the role of the expert is critical to the forensic process.

ROLE OF THE EXPERT

The role of the expert is critical in ensuring the forensic trace is collected, analyzed, interpreted and reported correctly, including that it is understood by the court and the appropriate weighting applied, consistent with the strength of the evidence. When accounting for the human factors in the forensic process, consideration should be given to maintaining independence and minimizing the impact of bias.

The concept of independence for forensic science is often discussed in terms of independence as an agency, being separate from police agencies and police governance. However, it is independence of thought that has the greatest impact, regardless of the broader governance. It is vital for examiners not to be influenced by what the client wants as an outcome, but instead focus on what the results of the analysis of the trace means. A lack of independence can result in the introduction of bias into the forensic process (43–45).

Dror identified eight sources of bias and error, which related to either human nature, environment, culture and experience, or were case-specific (46). Cognitive bias can have a significant impact on the forensic process and can take many forms, including contextual bias and confirmation bias.

Contextual bias can be introduced through overreliance on witness statements or provision of crime-/case-related information not relevant to the forensic examination, influencing the examination strategy and interpretation. Knowing a suspect's previous convictions, that the suspect had confessed to the crime, or the suspect had an alibi, or even some circumstances of the case, is not relevant to the forensic process (47). Examiners should also consider whether meta data about a victim or suspect such as their age, race, or occupation may also be domain-irrelevant for particular cases and examinations and whether the knowledge of which could influence the outcome of the examiners result or opinion (48).

The impact of contextual bias was seen in the examination of the fingerprints found during the investigation of the Madrid Train bombing in 2004. The FBI Latent Print Unit examined a fingerprint found during the investigation of the bombing and confirmed a match to another fingerprint from an individual on the database. Even though the match had been verified by other FBI experts, the match was later found to be incorrect (49). Dror et al. took this information and presented it to five fingerprint experts, however used two fingerprints unrelated to the Madrid Bombing, that the examiner had previously identified as a match during their normal casework years earlier. Having the contextual information prior to the analysis, only one examiner confirmed the match, one examiner now indicated there was insufficient information to confirm the match and three examiners changed their opinion to a non-match (50).

Contextual bias has been shown to impact numerous other disciplines including the analysis of DNA mixtures (51), fire investigation (52), odontology (53), anthropology in assessments of sex, ancestry and age at death (54). It is therefore important that the examiner maintains an objective application of the scientific method and disassociation of contextual or domain-irrelevant information.

Confirmation bias is a natural phenomenon for humans, stemming from a desire to seek out information that supports pre-existing beliefs (55). This can be influential in certain circumstances such as if a junior forensic examiner examines results produced by a more experienced senior examiner. Research indicates that a junior examiner is more likely to agree with the senior examiner (56). It is important for a forensic examiner to ensure the forensic process is such that it minimizes the impact of bias.

CONCLUSION

Forensic evidence can be a powerful tool for investigators and the triers of fact. However, if incorrectly used and applied, it can lead to misinterpretation and the creation of fallacies or forensic urban myths, resulting in opinions presented that cannot be supported by appropriately designed empirical studies. Over the last few years, considerable effort has been expended on this fundamental research, however, further research is required on the foundational validity and the application of the forensic method (validity as applied) to ensure a robust, reproducible and repeatable forensic process. Research should also continue to focus on understanding error rate and the impact of bias.

REFERENCES

1. Innocence Project. Wrongful convictions involving unvalidated or improper forensic science that were later overturned through DNA testing, 2022. Available from: https://www.innocenceproject.org/wp-content/uploads/2016/02/DNA_Exonerations_Forensic_Science.pdf (Accessed 29 June 2023).
2. The National Registry of Exonerations. Website, 2022. Available from: www.law.umich.edu/special/exoneration/Pages/about.aspx (Accessed 29 June 2023).
3. Gross SR, Shaffer M. Exonerations in the United States, 1989–2012. Available from: https://www.law.umich.edu/special/

exoneration/Documents/exonerations_us_1989_2012_full_report.pdf (Accessed 29 June 2023).
4. Laporte G. Wrongful convictions and DNA exonerations: Understanding the role of forensic science. *Natl Inst Justice J* 2018; **279**: 1–6.
5. Committee on Identifying the Needs of the Forensic Sciences Community, National Research Council. Strengthening forensic science in the United States: A path forward, 2009. Available from: https://www.ojp.gov/pdffiles1/nij/grants/228091.pdf (Accessed 29 June 2023).
6. President's Council of Advisors on Science and Technology. Forensic science in criminal courts: Ensuring scientific validity of feature-comparison methods, 2016. Available from: https://obamawhitehouse.archives.gov/sites/default/files/microsites/ostp/PCAST/pcast_forensic_science_report_final.pdf (Accessed 29 June 2023).
7. Criminal Cases Review Commission. CCRC marks 25 years of investigating miscarriages of justice, 2022. Available from: https://ccrc.gov.uk/news/ccrc-marks-25-years-of-investigating-miscarriages-of-justice/ (Accessed 29 June 2023).
8. Science and Technology Select Committee. Forensic science and the criminal justice system: A blueprint for change, 2019. Available from: https://publications.parliament.uk/pa/ld201719/ldselect/ldsctech/333/333.pdf (Accessed 29 June 2023).
9. Dioso-Villa R. A repository of wrongful convictions in Australia: First steps toward estimating prevalence and causal contributing factors. *Flind Law J* 2015; **17**(2): 163–202.
10. Dioso-Villa R, Julian R, Kebbell M, et al. Investigation to exoneration: A systemic review of wrongful conviction in Australia. *Curr Issues Crim Justice* 2016; **28**(2): 157–72.
11. Roux C, Bucht R, Crispino F, et al. The Sydney declaration–Revisiting the essence of forensic science through its fundamental principles. *Forensic Sci Int* 2022: **332**: 111182.
12. ANZPAA, NIFS. A guideline to forensic fundamentals: Identifying the underpinning science of human-based forensic science disciplines, 2016. Available from: https://www.google.com/url?sa=t&rct=j&q=&esrc=s&source=web&cd=&ved=2ahUKEwjK4Melouj_AhWXbcAKHTKOBPMQFnoECBIQAQ&url=https%3A%2F%2Fwww.anzpaa.org.au%2FArticleDocuments%2F2314%2FA%2520Guideline%2520to%2520Forensic%2520Fundamentals.pdf.aspx&usg=AOvVaw1qlG_98U3sq39R0vqk2lbC&opi=89978449 (Accessed 29 June 2023).
13. ANZPAA, NIFS. Empirical study design in forensic science, 2019. Available from: https://www.google.com/url?sa=t&rct=j&q=&esrc=s&source=web&cd=&ved=2ahUKEwiQgLT-quj_AhXYg1wKHfy4DYQQFnoECBQQAQ&url=https%3A%2F%2Fwww.anzpaa.org.au%2FArticleDocuments%2F2311%2FEmpirical%2520Study%2520Design%2520In%2520Forensic%2520Science%2520-%2520A%2520Guideline%2520to%2520Forensic%2520Fundamentals.pdf.aspx&usg=AOvVaw3AqDmo9FsPW839WtvX8zt9&opi=89978449 (Accessed 29 June 2023).
14. Ballantyne KN, Wilson-Wilde L. Assessing the reliability and validity of forensic science–an industry perspective. *Aust J Forensic Sci* 2020; **52**(3): 275–81.
15. Wilson-Wilde L. The international development of forensic science standards—a review. *Forensic Sci Int* 2018; **288**: 1–9.
16. Hsu SS. FBI admits flaws in hair analysis over decades, 2015. Available from https://www.washingtonpost.com/local/crime/fbi-overstated-forensic-hair-matches-in-nearly-all-criminal-trials-for-decades/2015/04/18/39c8d8c6-e515-11e4-b510-962fcfabc310_story.html?noredirect=on (Accessed 29 June 2023).
17. Dehghani-Tafti P, Bieber P. Folklore and forensics: The challenges of arson investigation and innocence claims. *W Va Law Rev* 2016; **119**: 549.
18. National Fire Protection Association. Guide for fire and explosion investigations, 1992. Available from: https://studylib.net/doc/18648668/national-fire-protection-association--nfpa-921--guide-for . . . (Accessed 29 June 2023).
19. Lentini JJ, CFEI F. The mythology of arson investigation, 2006. Available from: https://globalwrong.files.wordpress.com/2012/02/mythology_arson_investigation_07-copy.pdf (Accessed 29 June 2023).
20. Heenan, D. History of the post-flashover ventilation study, 2010. Available from: https://app.box.com/s/bqo78dcs2m-f93k9mqaicec1qoku8ldih (Accessed 29 June 2023).
21. Tinsley A, Gorbett G. Fire investigation origin determination survey, 2012. Available from: https://forensicfireinstitute.com/wp-content/uploads/2018/07/fire-investigation-origin-determination-survey-.pdf (Accessed 29 June 2023).
22. National Institute of Forensic Science. Australia and New Zealand police recommendations for CCTV systems, 2014. Available from: https://nla.gov.au/nla.obj-275378245/view (Accessed 29 June 2023).
23. UK Forensic Science Regulator. Video analysis: Codes of practice for forensic service providers, 2014. Available from: https://www.gov.uk/government/publications/video-analysis-codes-of-practice-for-forensic-service-providers (Accessed 29 June 2023).
24. Dodd V. Forensic science failures putting justice at risk, says regulator, 2020. Available from: https://www.theguardian.com/science/2020/feb/25/forensic-science-failures-putting-justice-at-risk-says-regulator (Accessed 29 June 2023).
25. Porter G. Zak coronial inquest and the interpretation of photographic evidence. *Curr Issues Crim Justice* 2012; **24**(1): 39–49.
26. Benson N, Dos Santos RO, Griffiths K, et al. The development of a stabbing machine for forensic textile damage analysis. *Forensic Sci Int* 2017; **273**: 132–9.
27. Sloan K, Robertson J, Fergusson M, Spratford W. Can a machine be used to replicate the biomechanics of human stabbing performance? *Sci Justice* 2022; **62**(2): 164–70.
28. Wilson-Wilde L, Romano H, Smith S. Error rates in proficiency testing in Australia. *Aust J Forensic Sci* 2019; **51**(**Suppl 1**): S268–71.
29. Spiegelman C, Tobin WA. Analysis of experiments in forensic firearms/toolmarks practice offered as support for low rates of practice error and claims of inferential certainty. *Law Probab Risk* 2013; **12**(2): 115–33.
30. Koehler JJ. Intuitive error rate estimates for the forensic sciences. *Jurimetrics* 2017: **57**: 153–68.
31. Du M. Analysis of errors in forensic science. *J Forensic Sci Med* 2017; **3**(3): 139.
32. Dror IE, Hampikian G. Subjectivity and bias in forensic DNA mixture interpretation. *Sci Justice* 2011; **51**(4): 204–8.
33. Butler JM, Kline MC, Coble MD. NIST interlaboratory studies involving DNA mixtures (MIX05 and MIX13): Variation observed and lessons learned. *Forensic Sci Int Genet* 2018; **37**: 81–94.
34. Julian RD, Kelty SF, Roux C, et al. What is the value of forensic science? An overview of the effectiveness of forensic science in the Australian criminal justice system project. *Aust J Forensic Sci* 2011; **43**(4): 217–29.
35. Julian R, Kelty SF. Forensic science as "risky business": Identifying key risk factors in the forensic process from crime scene to court. *J Criminol Res Policy Pract* 2015; 1(4): 195–206.
36. Vincent F. Vincent report: Inquiry into the circumstances that led to the conviction of Mr Farah Abdulkadir Jama, 2010. Available from: http://netk.net.au/DNA/Jama.pdf (Accessed 29 June 2023).
37. ISO/TC 272. Forensic sciences — Part 2: Recognition, recording, collecting, transport and storage of items. Available from: https://www.iso.org/standard/72041.html (Accessed 29 June 2023).
38. Neuhuber F, Dunkelmann B, Höckner G, et al. Female criminals—It's not always the offender! *Forensic Sci Int Genet Suppl Series* 2009; **2**(1): 145–6.
39. Brożek-Mucha Z. Distribution and properties of gunshot residue originating from a Luger 9 mm ammunition in the vicinity of the shooting gun. *Forensic Sci Int* 2009; **183**(1–3): 33–44.
40. Lucas N, Brown H, Cook M, et al. A study into the distribution of gunshot residue particles in the random population. *Forensic Sci Int* 2016; **262**: 150–5.
41. National Research Council Committee on Scientific Assessment of Bullet Lead Elemental Composition Comparison. *Forensic Analysis: Weighing Bullet Lead Evidence*. Washington DC: National Academies Press; 2004.
42. Saks MJ, Albright T, Bohan TL, et al. Forensic bitemark identification: Weak foundations, exaggerated claims. *J Law Biosci* 2016; **3**(3): 538–75.
43. Risinger DM, Saks MJ, Thompson WC, Rosenthal R. The Daubert/Kumho implications of observer effects in forensic science: Hidden problems of expectation and suggestion. *Cal Law Rev* 2002; **90**: 1.
44. Giannelli PC. Independent crime laboratories: The problem of motivational and cognitive bias. *Utah Law Rev* 2010: **247**.
45. Almazrouei MA. Comment on "Cognitive and human factors in expert decision making: Six fallacies and the eight sources of bias". *Anal Chem* 2020; **92**(18): 12725–6.
46. Dror IE. Cognitive and human factors in expert decision making: Six fallacies and the eight sources of bias. *Anal Chem* 2020; **92**(12): 7998–8004.

47. Hamnett HJ, Dror IE. The effect of contextual information on decision-making in forensic toxicology. *Forensic Sci Int Synerg* 2020; **2**: 339–48.
48. Dror I, Melinek J, Arden JL, et al. Cognitive bias in forensic pathology decisions. *J Forensic Sci* 2021; **66**(5): 1751–7.
49. Stacey RB, Unit T. Report on the erroneous fingerprint individualization in the Madrid train bombing case, 2005. Available from: https://www.ojp.gov/ncjrs/virtual-library/abstracts/report-erroneous-fingerprint-individualization-madrid-train-bombing (Accessed 29 June 2023).
50. Dror IE, Charlton D, Péron AE. Contextual information renders experts vulnerable to making erroneous identifications. *Forensic Sci Int* 2006; **156**(1): 74–8.
51. Dror IE, Hampikian G. Subjectivity and bias in forensic DNA mixture interpretation. *Sci Justice* 2011; **51**(4): 204–8.
52. Bieber P. Measuring the impact of cognitive bias in fire investigation, 2012. Available from: https://www.opd.ohio.gov/static/Law+Library/Training/Forensic+Training+Unit/Measuring+the+Impact+of+Cognitive+Bias+in+Fire+Investigation_Paul+Bieber.pdf (Accessed 29 June 2023).
53. Page M, Taylor J, Blenkin M. Expert interpretation of bitemark injuries - a contemporary qualitative study. *J Forensic Sci* 2013; **58**(3): 664–72.
54. Nakhaeizadeh S, Dror IE, Morgan RM. Cognitive bias in forensic anthropology: Visual assessment of skeletal remains is susceptible to confirmation bias. *Sci Justice* 2014; **54**(3): 208–14.
55. Kassin S, Dror I, Kukucka J. The forensic confirmation bias: Problems, perspectives, and proposed solutions. *J Appl Res Mem Cogn* 2013; **2**(1): 42–52.
56. Merlino M. Validity, reliability, accuracy, and bias in forensic signature identification, 2014. Available from: https://www.ojp.gov/ncjrs/virtual-library/abstracts/validity-reliability-accuracy-and-bias-forensic-signature (Accessed 29 June 2023).

CHAPTER 102

Forensic Entomology

Matt N. Krosch, Nikolas P. Johnston, Melanie Archer and James F. Wallman

INTRODUCTION

What is forensic entomology?

Entomology is the study of insects, which are six-legged animals without a backbone (animals without a backbone are collectively known as invertebrates). Examples of insects include ants, bees, flies, beetles and butterflies. Entomology includes many subspecialties, such as insect ecology, insect behavior and medical/veterinary entomology (i.e. studies on insects that cause disease in humans and other animals). Forensic entomology is another subspecialty that analyzes insect evidence in relation to civil or criminal legal matters and investigations (1,2). In this context, insects (and their residues) are considered "traces" in the forensic vernacular (3).

There are three branches of forensic entomology (2)

- **Stored products** addresses complaints about insect infestations in stored biological material and foodstuffs
- **Structural/urban** assists with legal problems involving insects such as termites, that damage human-made structures
- **Medicolegal** applies knowledge about insects in cases that involve the intersection between medicine and the law.

The remainder of this chapter will focus on medicolegal forensic entomology, which is mainly applied in human death investigations, but has wider applications, such as clinical forensic medicine. The techniques of medicolegal forensic entomology are also increasingly applied to cases involving the wrongful deaths of domestic and wild animals (e.g. by neglect or poaching), resulting in the emerging branch of wildlife and veterinary forensic entomology (4,5).

Who are forensic entomologists?

There are very few forensic entomologists worldwide, and even fewer are full-time practitioners (6–8). Most forensic entomologists work at universities, museums, police agencies, forensic medicine organizations or privately, where they may also conduct research, teaching or other entomology work. Many forensic entomologists have a background in another entomology subspecialty, most commonly medical or veterinary entomology, and sometimes agricultural entomology. This is because many of the most important species in medicolegal cases are also medically or agriculturally important. A Bachelor of Science with an emphasis on invertebrate zoology and a Masters degree or PhD in an entomological discipline are highly desirable. There are some universities that also offer postgraduate training specifically in forensic entomology (e.g. University of Florida).

Although there is no universally agreed training or accreditation pathway, nor formal standards, several strategies have been proposed for these and for research and discussed in the peer-reviewed literature (9–11). Many forensic entomologists conduct their work in accordance with international standards such as ISO17025, while others work in laboratories formally accredited by third-party certifiers against these standards. Accreditation by examination for American practitioners also exists through the American Board of Forensic Entomologists. In addition, membership of several professional societies dedicated to forensic entomology is available (e.g. European Association for Forensic Entomology, North American Forensic Entomology Association, Gruppo Italiano di Entomologia Forense).

APPLICATIONS

In medicolegal investigations, forensic entomological evidence is most often used to estimate the minimum time since death (also known as the minimum post-mortem interval, or mPMI) (12). However, such evidence can also be interpreted to provide a wealth of other intelligence, and we will explore some of these applications in more detail here.

Minimum post-mortem interval

When an animal dies, its body decomposes through a series of continuous stages until it is returned to its

DOI: 10.1201/9781003138754-106

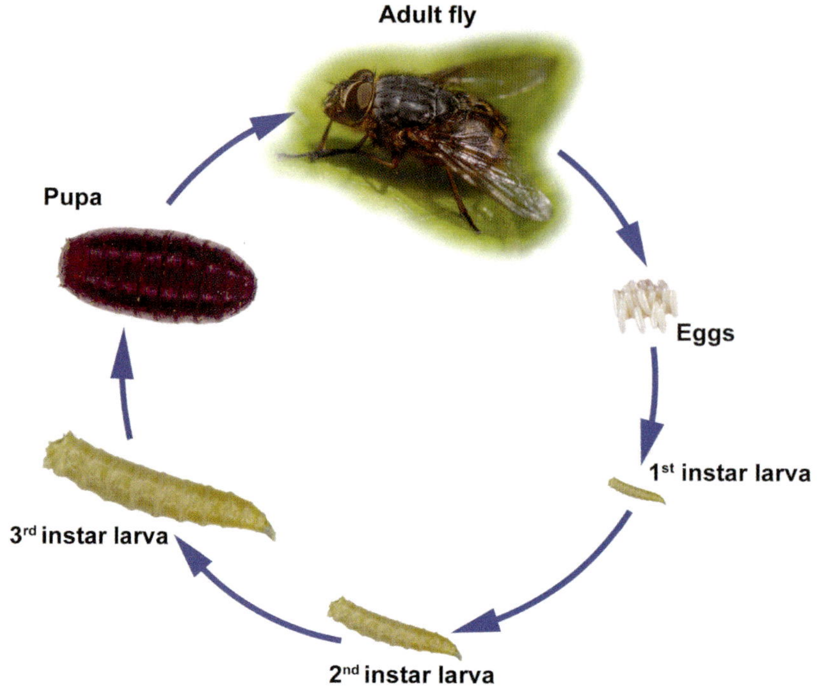

102.1 Illustration of the typical fly life cycle, highlighting the major developmental stages.

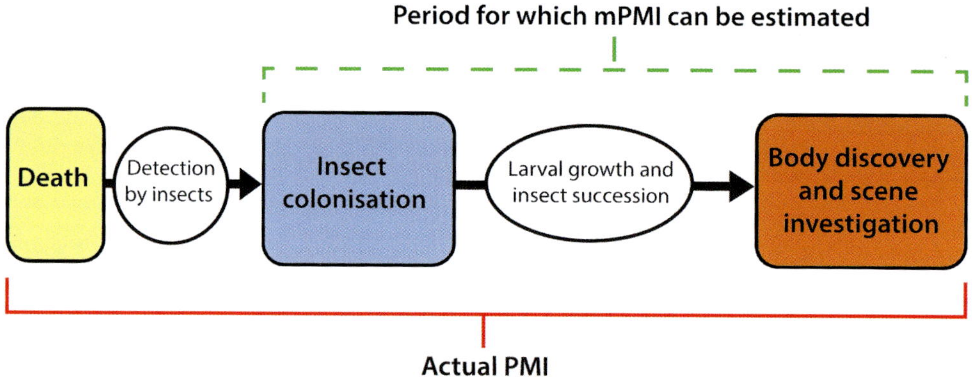

102.2 A diagram of the post-mortem interval (PMI) indicating the period of insect activity over which mPMI may be estimated.

component parts. In the case of larger animals, including humans, there are many species of invertebrate that will feed on the body as it decays, both on land and in water (13). Some of these species are specialized to breed in carrion (especially on land) and will occur with a semi-predictable order and timing. Blow flies (family: *Calliphoridae*) tend to arrive first and deposit their offspring, which grow through egg, larval (maggot) and pupal (transformative) stages before emerging as adults (Figure 102.1). Their growth rate is profoundly influenced by temperature (14). The first arriving flies are then followed by other fly and beetle species. This is known as ecologic succession, which is not limited to carrion, but applies to any new habitat resource that can be colonized by plants or animals (15).

The time since death is one of the most difficult forensic questions to answer, and there are no accurate methods to estimate this. However, entomologists can assist by using the principles of ecological succession and larval growth times. Insect evidence does not provide a time of death, but rather a mPMI, which is an estimate of the time elapsed since insects colonized the body (Figure 102.2). This is because the time to colonization can be unpredictable and substantially delayed by factors such as inclement weather, daylight availability or the body being inaccessible to insects (e.g. buried or in a car boot) (16,17). Conversely, insect colonization can precede death in very rare cases because some species of fly will breed in living tissues (e.g. open wounds), which is referred to as myiasis (18). It is therefore essential for an entomologist to recognize when this may have occurred, and the interpretation will be made especially in conjunction with a pathologist's opinion of whether a wound significantly predates death.

The mPMI is estimated using knowledge of insect succession (change in insect species composition present at the corpse over the course of decomposition) and insect development (correlating the age of insects on the corpse with laboratory-based developmental data to estimate insect colonization times) (1). A collection is made of the insects on the body, both at the death scene and the autopsy. The species present are then compared with field-generated data for the rate and composition of insect succession on carrion, which are collected either through human decomposition experiments (19) or by using animal carcasses as proxies for human bodies (most commonly pigs) (20). If the first colonizing generation of maggots is present, then the mPMI estimate may be made by estimating how long it took for the oldest life history stage on the body to develop.

Temperature at the death scene must be estimated in order to calculate the mPMI because the speed of larval growth and succession are temperature dependant. This may be done by measuring temperatures at the death scene and correlating them with the nearest weather station (21–23). Maggot masses can also produce heat independently if they are of sufficient size, which can accelerate body decomposition (24–27), and this may be difficult to account for in a mPMI estimate.

Many factors influence both succession and development (e.g. season, insect access to the corpse, presence of drugs, condition of the corpse). Insect species distributions and developmental rates also vary geographically and temporally (28,29). The accuracy of medicolegal forensic entomologic analyses therefore relies on robust fundamental data on carrion insect ecology, behavior, development, taxonomy and distributions in time and space (30), as well as relevant case-specific information being provided to the entomologist.

Season of death

When succession has concluded, the body will be skeletonized. It may no longer even be possible to determine in which year the death occurred. However, the insects that originally fed on the body may leave remnants, such as puparia (the puparium is the casing that surrounds the fly pupa while it transforms to an adult; see Figure 102.1), or dead insects. If these species have a defined activity time during the year, they can be used to determine the approximate season in which death was most likely to have occurred (31,32).

Insect-induced artefacts

Insects feeding on a body can produce lesions that may mimic injuries. An entomologist may assist the pathologist with differentiating insect-feeding damage from injuries in occasional cases. Insects that can produce such damage include ants and cockroaches, whose feeding artefacts may appear like chemical burns or abrasions (33–35). Lesions created by insect feeding can then subsequently act as oviposition sites for other necrophagous species. Although more common as a post-mortem event, insect feeding causing lesions can occur ante- or peri mortem (36). In addition to tissue damage, insect feeding may also cause alterations to hair (e.g. concave lesions that may mimic sharp force trauma (33,37) and clothing (38,39). Insects attending corpses may also alter bloodstains on the body, clothing or surrounding surfaces via their movement (e.g. larvae crawling through liquid blood) or by regurgitating/defecating fluids that can appear visually similar to bloodstains, thereby potentially causing confusion for bloodstain pattern analysis reconstructions (40,41).

Body history

The patterns of succession may be interrupted if the body undergoes any unusual treatment. If there is movement between geographic areas, insects characteristic from the original area may be transported somewhere they are not known to occur (28,42). This may be elucidated from the insects present on the body or recovered from vehicles used for transport (43). However, it is crucial to distinguish this from potential contaminating insect material that may be generated by an animal body also decomposing in the vicinity of a corpse at a death scene, or even contaminants accidentally collected in the mortuary that have come from other cases (44,45).

If a body decomposes in an environment that reduces insect access (e.g. wrapped in fabric or plastic, buried, indoors, inside vehicles or other sealed items) this can significantly alter the succession patterns (29,46–48). If colonization on the body is light, or even non-existent, this may indicate concealment of the body by wrappings or burial soon after death (49). Bodies may be burned in order to dispose of them, even after some decomposition has occurred. However, entomological evidence can survive fires, and burned carrion insects can therefore be a clue that there was a delay before burning the body (50). Burning can also create novel oviposition sites by exposing internal tissues, thereby accelerating colonization and decomposition (51). A period spent in water may also be reflected in the succession pattern, and a body may float after several days of decomposition underwater and be secondarily colonized by terrestrial species (52,53).

Entomotoxicology

Insects that feed on a dead body may ingest drugs that were in the deceased's system. Entomotoxicology is a subspecialty of forensic entomology that studies and applies the effects of this drug exposure on insects. Certain drugs can alter insect larval growth rates, and research is therefore conducted to measure the response of forensically important species to drugs that may affect them (54). Entomotoxicology also incorporates the use of insects as alternative toxicological specimens, which can be tested to recover drugs from their bodies (55) or their artefacts (56).

Parasite infestation and neglect

Entomologists may be of assistance when a deceased or living person, or other animal, presents with a parasite infestation, especially if that person or animal is in care, or is too young to look after themselves. Large numbers of parasites, such as human head lice, can indicate neglect, and an entomologist may provide expert commentary on this, including assessments of the duration of the neglect (57). Wounds or accumulated excrement can also be infested by maggots, which, as discussed above, is called myiasis when they are feeding on the flesh of the living. The entomologist can estimate the age of infesting fly larvae to help determine information such as time of last dressing or nappy change (58,59).

Veterinary and wildlife forensic entomology

This branch of the discipline applies forensic entomology techniques to legal problems affecting non-human animals (4,5). This may be done in the service of police or animal welfare agencies, or to aid investigations of offenses. Poaching cases can require an mPMI, and decomposing discarded body parts of hunted animals processed in the field may be used to make these estimates (5,60). Assessments of mPMI, myiasis or parasite infestations may be made as part of neglect/cruelty investigations involving domestic animals or livestock (61–63).

Cadaver discovery

Insect activity, and the heat it generates, can also be used as a novel means of detecting decomposing remains in the field. Traditional approaches for the detection of decomposing remains in outdoor environments include manual ground search, cadaver dogs and manned aerial reconnaissance during daylight. These methods are resource intense and may pose a risk to life for searchers, especially in rugged or densely forested terrain, and suboptimal weather conditions. An alternative may be to employ a helicopter or unmanned aerial vehicle (UAV)-mounted thermal imaging equipment to detect heat signatures emitted by insect activity on the decomposing remains. A growing body of research suggests that this method is operationally feasible (within its own set of limitations) for searches conducted during the early stages of death investigations into misadventure, homicide or mass casualties. The method is capable of successful detection of surface-deposited and buried/wrapped remains (64–68).

IDENTIFICATION OF FORENSICALLY IMPORTANT INSECTS

It is vital to be able to identify invertebrates present on a body in order to produce a forensic entomology-based opinion. Generally, this is achieved via examination of external morphology and comparison with identification keys (either dichotomous or matrix-based), and species descriptions. Morphological examination for most forensic species requires magnification to visualize minute features (e.g. hair arrangement, known as setation, as well as coloration of hairs and body plates called sclerites). This is particularly true for immature fly specimens, which may also necessitate slide-mounting of segments and sclerotized (hardened) mouthparts.

Indeed, accurate identification of eggs and early-instar fly larvae for many species is challenging even with high-magnification microscopy, though some keys exist (69,70). Adult insects generally possess more diagnostic morphological characters than immatures, and as such, species identification from adult specimens tends to be easier. It is for this reason that live samples of immature specimens are collected from infested remains and reared through to adulthood in forensic entomological investigations (9).

Many forensically relevant species are near-globally distributed – having been translocated outside their native range by human activity – and often are easily distinguished from local necrophagous species. However, some identification keys for forensic species only include those present in a specific geographic region, or do not include closely related species not known to feed on decomposing remains but which may be present in the local environment (71,72). This can limit their usefulness outside the stated range and lead to misidentification of species that are not included in the key. Additionally, some forensic species are distinguishable by only a few minute morphological characters in the adult (e.g. *Lucilia cuprina* and *Lucilia sericata*) [73]), which requires high-level technical skills and specialized taxonomic knowledge of character states and variability. Recent work also suggests that some forensically important fly species may be identified using geometric morphometrics of larvae (74) and adult wings (75–77), though this approach has not been broadly applied to date. Despite these challenges for forensic entomologists, species identification based on morphology remains the gold standard and is a critical component of forensic entomological analyses.

In situations where morphological species identification is equivocal, molecular methods are commonly employed to improve the accuracy of expert opinions (17,78,79). This approach relies on robust fundamental taxonomic research and the generation of data from genetic markers sufficiently variable at the species level – a technique referred to as DNA barcoding (80–82). The creation of databases of DNA barcode sequences attributed accurately to biological species names, such as the Barcode of Life Database (BOLD) (83), allows the rapid comparison and matching of queried sequences to facilitate DNA-based taxonomic identifications. This can be of particular importance in cases where only immature (eggs, larvae [84]) or partial specimens (including enclosed pupal casings (85) are available for analysis by the forensic entomologist. It can also be critical in resolving taxonomic ambiguities (e.g. specimens with morphology that do not fit available keys, or collected from outside the known geographic range of the species) or bridging a morphological expertise gap (i.e. the taxonomic impediment [86,87]).

The method is not perfect: it relies on the assumed accuracy and completeness of the DNA barcode database, and the output of comparisons still requires specific expertise for correct interpretation. Importantly, non-destructive methods have been developed that ensure retention, and hence 1:1 association, of morphological vouchers and DNA barcodes for individual specimens (88). In addition, the technologies used to obtain DNA barcode sequences are rapidly advancing, and it is now possible to sequence hundreds of samples at once (e.g. metabarcoding [89]) to enable rapid analysis of bulk samples of immature insects. Furthermore, the increasing sensitivity of such techniques means that smaller amounts of biological material are needed; for example, it is possible to identify insect species inhabiting an environment through trace amounts of DNA present in the air (90). Regardless of the specific approach taken, DNA barcoding to aid species identification will remain a crucial tool in the forensic entomologist's kit.

MOLECULAR GENETICS

A range of molecular genetic tools, largely adapted from the fields of evolutionary and ecological genetics, have been employed to complement and extend traditional forensic entomological analyses. Extracting case-relevant information from genetic material can thus be highly informative for reconstructing events, linking people and places, and improving the accuracy and precision of forensic entomological opinions (91,92).

Below the species level, insect population genetic data can be highly informative in forensic entomological analyses (91,92). As with DNA barcoding, this approach relies on robust fundamental research to understand existing genetic diversity and population genetic structure in forensically relevant species of interest across a target geographic region. This allows the forensic entomologist to compare genetic data from collected specimens and assign them to their original populations, thereby informing inferences about potential translocation of corpses (91–95). Additionally, there is a growing body of evidence that suggests many forensically relevant Diptera used to estimate mPMI may in fact exhibit distinct population-level variation in their developmental rates (e.g. *Lucilia sericata* [96]; *Cochliomyia macellaria* [97]). Therefore, genetic assignment of forensic samples to populations, alongside developmental data for those populations, will provide greater accuracy in mPMI estimations.

Molecular data can also be used to augment morphology-based estimates of the age of an insect specimen. Several studies have demonstrated that the expression of certain genes varies with age, most obviously those associated with growth and development (98–104). Although these techniques have not been widely implemented in casework settings, they may be especially useful for aging eggs and smaller larvae.

The isolation of human DNA from forensic insect samples can be achieved through two means: analysis of the gut contents of insects that have consumed human tissues/fluids (105–107), or of insect artefacts left behind at crime scenes (41). The former application is most often aimed at identifying a deceased person from feeding insects in situations where traditional identification may not be possible (e.g. level of decomposition, effect of burning) (108). It may also be implemented to identify a deceased where only insects remain (e.g. when a body has been moved and not recovered), to link body parts, or to link multiple locations where a deceased is suspected to have been decomposing (e.g. insects located in a vehicle used to transport the deceased between locations) (41). Analysis of insect gut contents can also be used to identify offenders; for example, where insects have consumed biological fluids deposited by the offender (e.g. seminal fluid [109]), or where insects have utilized the offender for a bloodmeal (e.g. ticks, bedbugs, lice, mosquitos [41,110–112]). The latter can be particularly useful for detecting the transfer of pubic lice in sexual assault cases (110).

As mentioned above, insect artefacts may be the result of their regurgitation or defecation of human biological fluids onto surfaces. This is most commonly done by adult flies and beetles, following feeding on human tissues or fluids (41,113). Such artefacts can be a rich source of human DNA, allowing generation of DNA profiles from victims (artefacts from insects that have fed on decomposing remains [114]) or offenders (from insects that have fed on deposited fluids, e.g. seminal fluid, blood [113]). A variety of morphological or contextual methods have been proposed for distinguishing between insect artefacts and human bloodstains, but these methods are best used in conjunction with molecular techniques to clarify the origin of a particular stain (40,41,115–118).

CONCLUSION

There is a growing awareness among forensic entomologists worldwide that we need to consolidate our knowledge and analyze our progress to date (119). Recent major literature reviews from various geographic regions across the USA encompass both fundamental research and casework records (120–122). These will assist forensic entomology practitioners and researchers by identifying knowledge gaps, inconsistencies and areas for improvement of practices while, at the same time, revealing aspects of the discipline where there is broad consensus in practice and opinion. For example, these reviews identified several regions that lacked sufficient data on common forensic insect species, including developmental and succession data, and for which very limited or even no casework data have been published. Similarly, for many other parts of the world, several knowledge gaps remain concerning succession, development and the taxonomy of species, particularly in the tropics and for certain carrion insect groups such as the beetles (123–127). Further, it is recognized that forensic entomology will benefit from critically reviewing casework data to explore which insect species are found on human remains and the factors that influence colonization, development and succession, and use this information to drive future research on those species in a process of reciprocal illumination (128).

REFERENCES

1. Anderson GS. The use of insects in death investigations: an analysis of cases in British Columbia over a five-year period. *Can Soc Forensic Sci J* 1995; **28**: 277–92.
2. Byrd JH, Castner JL. *Forensic Entomology: The Utility of Arthropods in Legal Investigations*, 3rd ed. Boca Raton: CRC Press; 2019, pp. xxiii–xxxiv.
3. Roux C, Ribaux O, Crispino F. Forensic science 2020 – the end of the crossroads? *Aust J Forensic Sci* 2018; **50**: 607–18.
4. Tomberlin JK, Sanford MR. Forensic Entomology and Wildlife. In: Huffman JE, Wallace JR (eds, *Wildlife Forensics: Methods and Applications*. Hoboken: John Wiley & Sons; 2011, pp. 81–107.
5. Anderson GS, Byrd JH. Wildlife Forensic Entomology. In: Byrd JH, Castner JL (eds), *Forensic Entomology: the Utility of Arthropods in Legal Investigations*, 3rd ed. Boca Raton: CRC Press; 2019, pp. 475–83.
6. Magni P, Guercini S, Leighton A, Dadour I. Forensic entomologists: An evaluation of their status. *J Insect Sci* 2013; **13**: 78.
7. Barnes KM, Long AS, Baker IS, Bulling MT. From crime scene to court: how should future research address the current limitations in forensic entomology. *J Forensic Entomol* 2022; **1**: 1–19.
8. Guimaraes SEF, Steindorff GS, Bicho CL, et al. Forensic entomology in research and practice: An overview of forensic experts' perceptions and scientific output in Brazil. *Int J Leg Med* 2022; **136**: 1149–61.
9. Amendt J, Campobasso CP, Gaudry E, et al. Best practice in forensic entomology – standards and guidelines. *Int J Leg Med* 2007; **121**: 90–104.
10. Goudry E, Dourel L. Forensic entomology: implementing quality assurance for expertise work. *Int J Legal Med* 2013; **127**: 1031–37.
11. Kotze Z, Aimar S, Amendt J, Anderson GS, Bourguignon L, Hall MJR, Tomberlin JK. Forensic entomology case report – a global perspective. *Insects* 2021; **12**: 283.
12. Wallman JF, Archer MS. The Application of Insects to the Time Since Death. In: Hayman J, Oxenham M (eds), *Estimation of the Time Since Death: Current Research and Future Trends*. Cambridge: Academic Press; 2020, pp. 57–74.
13. Amendt J. Forensic entomology. *Naturwissenschaften* 2004; **91**: 51–65.
14. Davidson J. On the relationship between temperature and rate of development of insects at constant temperatures. *J Animal Ecol* 1944; **13**: 26–38.
15. Michaud JP, Schoenly KG, Moreau G, Dykhuizen D. Rewriting ecological succession history: Did carrion ecologists get there first? *Q Rev Biol* 2015; **90**: 45–66.
16. Campobasso CP, Di Vella G, Introna F. Factors affecting decomposition and Diptera colonization. *Forensic Sci Int* 2001; **120**: 18–27.
17. Byrd J, Sutton L. Forensic entomology for the investigator. *WIREs Forensic Sci* 2020; **2**: e1370.
18. Hall M, Wall R. Myiasis of humans and domestic animals. *Adv Parasitol* 1995; **35**: 257–334.
19. Dawson BM, Barton PS, Wallman JF. Field succession studies and casework can help to identify forensically useful Diptera. *J Forensic Sci* 2021; **66**: 2319–28.
20. Matuszewski S, Hall MJR, Moreau G, et al. Pigs vs people: The use of pigs as analogues for humans in forensic entomology and taphonomy research. *Int J Leg Med* 2020; **134**: 793–210.
21. Johnson AP, Wallman JF, Archer MS. Experimental and casework validation of ambient temperature corrections in forensic entomology. *J Forensic Sci* 2012; **57**: 215–21.
22. Hofer IMJ, Hart AJ, Martin-Vega D, Hall MJR. Estimating crime scene temperatures from nearby meteorological station data. *Forensic Sci Int* 2020; **306**: 110028.
23. Lutz L, Amendt J. Stay cool or get hot? An applied primer for using temperature in forensic entomological case work. *Sci Justice* 2020; **60**: 415–22.
24. Slone, DH, Grunner, SV. Thermal regulation in larval aggregations of carrion-feeding blow flies (Diptera Calliphoridae). *J Med Entomol* 2007; **44**: 516–23.
25. Charabidze D, Bourel B, Gosset D. Larval-mass effect: Characterisation of heat emission by necrophagous blowflies (Diptera: Calliphoridae) larval aggregates. *Forensic Sci Int* 2011; **211**: 61–6.
26. Johnson AP, Mikac KM, Wallman JF. Thermogenesis in decomposing carcasses. *Forensic Sci Int* 2013; **231**: 271–7.
27. Heaton V, Moffatt C, Simmons T. Quantifying the temperature of maggot masses and its relationship to decomposition. *J Forensic Sci* 2014; **59**: 676–82.
28. Catts EP, Goff ML. Forensic entomology in criminal investigations. *Ann Rev Entomol* 1992; **37**: 253–72.
29. Amendt J, Richards CS, Campobasso CP, et al. Forensic entomology: Application and limitations. *Forensic Sci Med Pathol* 2011; **7**: 379–92.
30. Tomberlin JK, Mohr R, Benbow ME, et al. A roadmap for bridging basic and applied research in forensic entomology. *Ann Rev Entomol* 2011; **56**: 401–21.
31. Archer MS. Annual variation in arrival and departure times of carrion insects at carcasses: Implications for succession studies in forensic entomology. *Aust J Zool* 2003; **51**: 569–76.
32. Archer MS, Elgar MA. Yearly activity patterns in southern Victoria (Australia) of seasonally active carrion insects. *Forensic Sci Int* 2003; **132**: 173–6.
33. Viero A, Montisci M, Pelletti G, Vanin S. Crime scene and body alterations caused by arthropods: Implications in death investigation. *Int J Leg Med* 2019; **133**: 307–16.
34. de Souza AAF, de Rosa CTA, Arantes LC, Pujol-Luz JR. Artifacts caused by leaf-cutting ants of the genus *Atta* (Hymenoptera: Formicidae) postmortem bite injuries and the tearing of clothes. *J Forensic Sci* 2020; **65**: 1012–15.
35. Meyer F, Monroe MD, Williams HN, Goddard J. *Solenopsis invicta x richteri* (Hymenoptera: Formicidae) necrophagous behaviour causes post-mortem lesions in pigs which serve as oviposition sites for Diptera. *Forensic Sci Int Rep* 2020; **2**: 100067.
36. Shoemaker J. Cockroaches feeding on humans: Not only for the dead. *Am Entomol* 2022; **68**: 48–51.
37. Mazzarelli D, Vanin S, Gibelli D, et al. Splitting hairs: Differentiating between entomological activity, taphonomy, and sharp force trauma on hair. *Forensic Sci Med Pathol* 2014; **11**: 104–10.
38. Taupin JM, Cwiklik C. *Scientific Protocols for Forensic Examination of Clothing*. Boca Raton: CRC Press; 2011.
39. Ziogos SS, Pitts K, Dadour IR, Magni P. The effect of necrophagous entomofauna on textile damage during the summer in Western Australia, 2022. Available from: https://researchportal.murdoch.edu.au/esploro/outputs/conferencePresentation/The-effect-of-necrophagous-entomofauna-on/991005542115507891 (Accessed 2 July 2023).
40. Rivers DB, Geiman T. Insect artifacts are more than just altered bloodstains. *Insects* 2017; **8**: 37.
41. Durdle A. Insects as vectors of DNA in a forensic context. *WIREs Forensic Sci* 2020; **2**: e1355.
42. James R, Eitzen D, Hall R, et al. Autopsy and quarantine considerations in a case of illegal entry of a corpse into Australia. *J Law Med* 2000; **8**: 89–91.
43. Hall MJR, Whitaker A, Richards C. Forensic Entomology. In: Marquez-Grant N, Roberts J (eds), *Forensic Ecology Handbook: From Crime Scene to Court*. Hoboken: John Wiley & Sons; 2012, pp. 111–40.
44. Archer MS, Ranson DL. Potential contamination of forensic entomology samples collected in the mortuary: A case report. *Med Sci Law* 2005; **45**: 89–91.
45. Archer MS, Elgar MA, Briggs CA, Ranson CL. Fly pupae and puparia as potential contaminants of forensic entomology samples from sites of body discovery. *Int J Leg Med* 2006; **120**: 364–8.
46. Mann RW, Bass WM, Meadows L. Time since death and decomposition of the human body: Variables and observations in case and experimental field studies. *J Forensic Sci* 1990; **35**: 103–11.
47. Goff ML. Problems in estimation of postmortem interval resulting from wrapping of the corpse: A case study from Hawaii. *J Agric Entomol* 1992; **9**: 237–43.
48. Voss SC, Cook DF, Dadour IR. Decomposition and insect succession of clothed and unclothed carcasses in Western Australia. *Forensic Sci Int* 2011; **211**: 67–75.
49. Smith KGV. *A Manual of Forensic Entomology*. London: Trustees of the British Museum (Natural History); 1986.
50. Anderson GS. Effects of arson on forensic entomology evidence. *Can Soc Forensic Sci J* 2005; **38**: 49–67.
51. McIntosh CS, Dadour IR, Voss SC. A comparison of carcass decomposition and associated insect succession onto burnt and unburnt pig carcasses. *Int J Leg Med* 2017; **131**: 835–45.
52. Wallace JR, Merritt RW. The Role of Aquatic Organisms in Forensic Investigations. In: Byrd JH, Castner JL (eds), *Forensic Entomology: The Utility of Arthropods in Legal Investigations*, 3rd ed. Boca Raton: CRC Press; 2019, pp. 155–86.

53. Bray SK, Conlan XA, Harvey ML. A preliminary evaluation of the utility of insects and algae for PMI estimation in confined, still-water environments. *Aust J Forensic Sci* 2021; **55**: 1–12.
54. Goff ML, Lord WD. Entomotoxicology. A new area for forensic investigation. *Am J Forensic Med Pathol* 1994; **15**: 51–7.
55. Gagliano-Candela R, Aventaggiato, L. The detection of toxic substances in entomological specimens. *Int J Legal Med* 2001; **114**: 197–203.
56. Giorgetti A, Pelletti G, Fais P, et al. The use of fly artifacts in a crime scene: Is there any application for forensic toxicology. *J Forensic Sci* 2022; **67**: 749–55.
57. Lambiase S, Perotti MA. Using human head lice to unravel neglect and cause of death. *Parasitology* 2019; **146**: 678–84.
58. Benecke M, Lessig R. Child neglect and forensic entomology. *Forensic Sci Int* 2001; **120**: 155–159.
59. Benecke M, Josephi E, Zweihoff R. Neglect of the elderly: Forensic entomology cases and considerations. *Forensic Sci Int* 2004; **146S**: S195–S79.
60. Anderson GS. Wildlife forensic entomology: determining time of death in two illegally killed black bear cubs. *J Forensic Sci* 1999; **44**: 856–859.
61. Brundage A, Byrd JH. Forensic entomology in animal cruelty cases. *Vet Pathol* 2016; **53**: 898–909.
62. McGarry J, Ratsep E, Ressel L, et al. Introducing forensic entomology in cases of suspected animal neglect. *Vet Rec* 2018; **182**: 139.
63. Talley J, Machtinger E. Livestock Entomology. In: Byrd JH, Castner JL (eds), *Forensic Entomology: The Utility of Arthropods in Legal Investigations*, 3rd ed. Boca Raton: CRC Press; 2019, pp. 475–83.
64. DesMarais AM. Detection of cadaveric remains by thermal imaging cameras. *J Forensic Identif* 2014; **64**: 489–510.
65. Amendt J, Rodner S, Schuch C-P, et al. Helicopter thermal imaging for detecting insect infested cadavers. *Sci Justice* 2017; **57**: 366–72.
66. Lee MJ, Voss SC, Franklin D, Dadour IR. Preliminary investigation of aircraft mounted thermal imaging to locate decomposing remains via the heat produced by larval aggregations. *Forensic Sci Int* 2018; **289**: 175–85.
67. Bodnar SR, Ciotti J, Soroka J, et al. Drone-assisted thermal imaging to determine the location of unmarked graves. *J Forensic Identif* 2019; **69**: 378–92.
68. Butters O, Krosch MN, Roberts M, MacGregor D. Application of forward-looking infrared (FLIR) imaging from an unmanned aerial platform in the search for decomposing remains. *J Forensic Sci* 2020; **66**: 347–55.
69. O'Flynn MA, Moorhouse DE. Identification of early immature stages of some common Queensland carrion flies. *J Aus Entomol Soc* 1980; **19**: 53–61.
70. Szpila K, Wallman JF. Morphology and identification of first instar larvae of Australian blowflies of the genus *Chrysomya* of forensic importance. *Acta Trop* 2016; **162**: 146–54.
71. Wallman JF. Third-instar larvae of common carrion-breeding blowflies of the genus *Calliphora* (Diptera: Calliphoridae) in South Australia. *Invert Syst* 2001; **15**: 37–51.
72. Whitworth T. Keys to the genera and species of blow flies (Diptera: Calliphoridae) of America north of Mexico. *Proc Entomol Soc Wash* 2016; **108**: 689–725.
73. Holloway BA. Morphological characters to identify adult *Lucilia sericata* (Meigen, 1826) and *L. cuprina* (Wiedemann, 1830) (Diptera: Calliphoridae). *NZ J Zool* 1991; **18**: 413–20.
74. Nigoghosian G, Weidner LM, Stamper TI. A technique to mount Sarcophagidae and Calliphoridae (Diptera) larvae for forensic identification using geometric morphometrics. *Forensic Sci Int Syn* 2021; **3**: 100135.
75. Sontigun N, Sukontason KL, Zajac BK, et al. Wing morphometrics as a tool in species identification of forensically important blow flies of Thailand. *Parasites Vectors* 2017; **10**: 229.
76. Sontigun N, Samerjai C, Sukontason K, et al. Wing morphometric analysis of forensically important flesh flies (Diptera: Sarcophagidae) in Thailand. *Acta Trop* 2019; **190**: 312–19.
77. Szpila K, Johnston NP, Akbarzadeh K, et al. Wing measurements are a possible tool for the identification of European forensically important Sarcophagidae. *Forensic Sci Int* 2022; **340**: 111451.
78. Oliveira AR, Farinha A, Rebelo M, Dias D. Forensic entomology: Molecular identification of blowfly species (Diptera: Calliphoridae) in Portugal. *Forensic Sci Int Genet Suppl Ser* 2011; **3**: e439–40.
79. Park JH, Kim YH, Ham CS, et al. Molecular identification of forensically important calliphoridae and sarcophagidae species using ITS2 nucleotide sequences. *Forensic Sci Int* 2018; **284**: 1–4.
80. Hebert PDN, Cywinska A, Ball SL, deWaard JR. Biological identifications through DNA barcodes. *Proc R Soc B Biol Sci* 2003; **270**: 313–21.
81. Nelson LA, Wallman JF, Dowton M. Using DNA barcodes to identify forensically and medically important blowflies. *Med Vet Ent* 2007; **21**: 44–52.
82. Antil S, Abraham JS, Sripoorna S, et al. DNA barcoding, an effective tool for species identification: A review. *Mol Biol Rep* 2023; **50**: 761–75.
83. Barcode of Life Database. Available from www.boldsystems.org (Accessed 2 July 2023).
84. Meiklejohn KA, Wallman JF, Dowton M. DNA barcoding identifies all immature life stages of a forensically important flesh fly (*Diptera: Sarcophagidae*). *J Forensic Sci* 2013; **58**: 184–7.
85. Mazzanti M, Alessandrini F, Tagliabracci A, et al. DNA degradation and genetic analysis of empty puparia: Genetic identification limits in forensic entomology. *Forensic Sci Int* 2010; **195**: 99–102.
86. Hubert N, Hanner R. DNA barcoding, species delineation and taxonomy: A historical perspective. *DNA Barcodes* 2015; **3**: 44–58.
87. Engel MS, et al. The taxonomic impediment: a shortage of taxonomists, not the lack of technical approaches. *Zool J Linn Soc* 2021; **193**: 381–7.
88. Tuccia F, Giordani G, Vanin S. A combined protocol for identification of maggots of forensic interest. *Sci Justice* 2016; **56**: 264–8.
89. Chimeno C, Moriniere J, Podhorna J, et al. DNA barcoding in forensic entomology – establishing a DNA reference library of potentially forensic relevant arthropod species. *J Forensic Sci* 2019; **64**: 593–601.
90. Roger F, Ghanavi HR, Danielsson N, et al. Airborne environmental DNA metabarcoding for the monitoring of terrestrial insects - a proof of concept from the field. *Environ DNA* 2022; **4**: 790–807.
91. Wells JD, Stevens JR. Application of DNA-based methods in forensic entomology. *Annu Rev Entomol* 2008; **53**: 103–20.
92. Stevens JR, Picard CJ, Wells JD. Molecular Genetic Methods for Forensic Entomology. In: Byrd JH, Castner JL (eds), *Forensic Entomology: The Utility of arthropods in legal investigations*, 3rd ed. Boca Raton: CRC Press; 2019, pp. 253–68.
93. Picard CJ, Wells JD. A test for carrion fly full siblings: A tool for detecting postmortem relocation of a corpse. *J Forensic Sci* 2012; **57**: 535–8.
94. Picard CJ, Wells JD. The population genetic structure of North American *Lucilia sericata* (Diptera: Calliphoridae), and the utility of genetic assignment methods for reconstruction of postmortem corpse relocation. *Forensic Sci Int* 2010; **195**: 63–7.
95. Bao F, Wells JD. Population genetic structure of an invasive forensically important insect. *Electrophoresis* 2014; **35**: 3193–200.
96. Tarone AM, Picard CJ, Spiegelman C, Foran DR. Population and temperature effects on *Lucilia sericata* (Diptera: Calliphoridae) body size and minimum development time. *J Med Entomol* 2011; **48**: 1062–8.
97. Owings CG, Spiegelman C, Tarone AM, Tomberlin DK. Developmental variation among *Cochliomyia macellaria* Fabricius (Diptera: Calliphoridae) populations from three ecoregions of Texas, USA. *Int J Forensic Med* 2014; **128**: 709–17.
98. Tarone AM, Kimberley C, Jennings MS, David RF. Aging blowfly eggs using gene expression: A feasibility study. *J Forensic Sci* 2007; **52**: 1350–4.
99. Zehner R, Amendt J, Boehme P. Gene expression analysis as a tool for age estimation of blowfly pupae. *Forensic Sci Int Genet Suppl Ser* 2009; **2**: 292–3.
100. Tarone AM, Foran DR. Gene expression during blow fly development: Improving the precision of age estimates in forensic entomology. *J Forensic Sci* 2011; **56**: S112–S22.
101. Boehme P, Spahn P, Amendt J, Zehner R. Differential gene expression during metamorphosis a promising approach for age estimation of forensically important *Calliphora vicina* pupae (Diptera: Calliphoridae). *Int J Leg Med* 2013; **127**: 243–9.
102. Bala M, Sharma A. Review of some recent techniques of age determination of blow flies having forensic implications. *Egypt J Forensic Sci* 2016; **6**: 203–8.
103. Zajac BK, Amendt J, Horres R, et al. De novo transcriptome analysis and highly sensitive digital gene expression profiling of *Calliphora vicina* (Diptera: Calliphoridae) pupae using MACE (Massive Analysis of cDNA Ends). *Forensic Sci Int Genet* 2015; **15**: 137–46.

104. Alajmi R, Alotaibi F, Ahmed A, et al. Gene expression as age estimation marker in the larval stages of the blowfly, *Chrysomya albiceps*, at different temperatures. *J Forensic Leg Med* 2021; 77: 102096.
105. Campobasso CP, Linville JG, Wells JD, Introna F. Forensic genetic analysis of insect gut contents. *Am J Forensic Med Pathol* 2005; **26**: 161–5.
106. Powers J, van Oorschot RAH, Durdle A. Investigation into the presence of human DNA in the various life stages of forensically relevant Calliphorid species. *Aust J Forensic Sci* 2019; **51**: S234–S7.
107. Borland EM, Kading RC. Modernizing the toolkit for arthropod bloodmeal identification. *Insects* 2021; **12**: 37.
108. Lambiase S, Tarone AM. Forensic Entomology: The Utility of Insects at Court and in Human Identification. In: Pilli E, Berti A (eds), *Forensic DNA Analysis*. New York: Apple Academic Press; 2021, pp. 385–416.
109. Chamoun CA, Couri MS, Garrido RG, et al. Recovery and identification of human Y-STR DNA from immatures of *Chrysomya albiceps* (Diptera: Calliphoridae). Simulation of sexual crime investigation involving victim corpse in state of decay. *Forensic Sci Int* 2020; **310**: 110239.
110. Pilli E, Agostino A, Vergani D, et al. Human identification by lice: A next generation sequencing challenge. *Forensic Sci Int* 2016; **266**: e71–e8.
111. Schal C, Czado N, Gamble R, et al. Isolation, identification, and time course of human DNA typing from bed bugs, *Cimex lectularius*. *Forensic Sci Int* 2018; **293**: 1–6.
112. Gray SL, Tiedge TM, Butkus JM, et al. Determination of human identity from *Anopheles stephensi* mosquito blood meals using direct amplification and massively parallel sequencing. *Forensic Sci Int Genet* 2020; **48**: 102347.
113. Durdle A, Mitchell RJ, van Oorschot RAH. The human DNA content in artifacts deposited by the blowfly *Lucilia cuprina* fed human blood, semen and saliva. *Forensic Sci Int* 2013; **233**: 212–19.
114. Kulstein G, Amendt J, Zehner R. Blow fly artifacts from blood and putrefaction fluid on various surfaces: A source for forensic STR typing. *Entomol Exp Appl* 2015; **157**: 255–62.
115. Benecke M, Barksdale L. Distinction of bloodstain patterns from fly artifacts. *Forensic Sci Int* 2003; **137**: 152–9.
116. Durdle A, van Oorschot RAH, Mitchell RJ. The morphology of fecal and regurgitation artifacts deposited by the blow fly *Lucilia cuprina* fed a diet of human blood. *J Forensic Sci* 2013; **58**: 897–903.
117. Rivers DB, McGregor A. Morphological features of regurgitate and defecatory stains deposited by five species of necrophagous flies are influenced by adult diets and body size. *J Forensic Sci* 2017; **63**: 154–61.
118. Bini C, Giorgetti A, Iuvaro A, et al. A DNA-based method for distinction of fly artifacts from human bloodstains. *Int J Leg Med* 2021; **135**: 2155–61.
119. Tomberlin JK, Benbow ME. *Forensic Entomology. International Dimensions and Frontiers*. Boca Raton: CRC Press; 2020.
120. Sanford MR. Insects and associated arthropods analyzed during medicolegal death investigations in Harris County, Texas, USA: January 2013-April 2016. *PLOS One* 2017; **12**: e0179404.
121. Weidner LM, Nigoghosian G, Yoho KC, et al. An analysis of forensically important insects associated with human remains in Indiana, U.S.A. *J Forensic Sci* 2020; **65**: 2036–41.
122. Weidner LM, Byrd J, Sutton L, Hans KR. Forensic Entomology: An introduction to the literature of the United States. *WIREs Forensic Sci* 2021; **3**: e1435.
123. Wallman JF, Archer MS. Australia and New Zealand. In: Tomberlin JK, Benbow ME (eds), *Forensic Entomology: International Dimensions and Frontiers*. Boca Raton: CRC Press; 2015, pp. 53–72.
124. Archer MS, Wallman JF. The development of forensic entomology in Australia and New Zealand: An overview of casework practice, quality control and standards. *Aust J Forensic Sci* 2017; **49**: 125–33.
125. Griffiths K, Krosch MN, Wright KW. Variation in decomposition stages and carrion insect succession in a dry tropical climate and its effect on estimating postmortem interval. *Forensic Sci Res* 2020; **5**: 327–35.
126. Tembe D, Mukaratirwa S. Forensic entomology research and application in southern Africa: A scoping review (with corrigendum). *S Afr J Sci* 2020; **116**: 1–8.
127. Wang Y, Wang Y, Wang M, et al. Forensic entomology in China and its challenges. *Insects* 2021; **12**: 230.
128. Hall MJR. The relationship between research and casework in forensic entomology. *Insects* 2021; **12**: 174.

CHAPTER

103

Principles of Age Estimation in the Living

Jason Payne-James

INTRODUCTION

Age estimation in the living (also referred to age evaluation or age assessment) to determine unknown, or corroboration of stated, age of living individuals has assumed increasing importance in the last three decades particularly in the context of criminal culpability and legal or social categorization, and within the context of refugee and asylum claims. It has recently been stated that "*The relationship between chronological age (time elapsed since birth) and biological age (changes to body tissues with age), psychological age (maturation of the mind) or behavioral age is not, and likely never will be, a perfect correlation. The reasons for this are well documented and include general health, genetics, nutrition and life experiences. Therefore, it must be accepted that there is no infallible method for either biological or social-worker-led age assessment that will provide a perfect match to chronological age.*" The authors point out that "*it is arguably more relevant to ask the initial question of whether the claimed age is 'possible' rather than 'how old is the person?'*" (1).

Age is an important classifier in most judicial, societal and cultural settings, and in the absence of confirmatory legal documents (such as birth registration) bodies and organizations which seek to know age will often be wholly reliant upon clinical and scientific evidence. The utility and availability of such evidence, and whether or not it is utilized is dependent on local jurisdictional law, regulation and process (2). There may be conflict between professional bodies as to the accuracy and utility of age assessment techniques and whether they should or should not be used by some professional groups (1,3).

There are many areas in which the evaluation of age in the living has significant importance including aging of refugee and asylum seekers, perpetrators and complainants of crime and victims of modern slavery, human trafficking and child pornography (4–6). Age estimation may be required for children from those countries with poor birth registration records, (e.g. Sudan, Uganda) (7–11). Table 103.1 provides further examples.

Age therefore can confer certain rights of the child (*see* Chapter 68 – "Principles of Child Safeguarding") and can confer certain different penalties upon individuals when compared with adults which very generally means that being classified as a child is more likely to allow state support of that individual, more likely to result in lesser punishments in relation to criminal issues.

The UK Royal College of Paediatrics and Child Heath (11) notes that any young person judged to be under 18 years of age without an adult to care for them, is entitled to the same rights as other looked after children and young people and this will include accommodation, financial support, education and statutory health assessments, support and regular professional review meetings.

A day or two difference in age may therefore put someone in the category for that jurisdiction of being below the age of criminal responsibility, or for different care or management plans.

Geo-political instability is often accompanied by mass migration, loss of parents and loss of registration records and where there is movement from a country where date of birth is not regularly or formerly recorded to one where it is (and upon which a legal framework may be based). Age of unaccompanied asylum-seeking children (UASC) require a date of birth (and therefore a known, or assigned, age) to access services for minors (under the age of 18 years), including health, education and identity documents. However, most UASC are unable to provide documentary evidence of their date of birth on their arrival in the UK, and some may not know their exact chronological age (time elapsed since birth). Since January 2022, more than 500 children and young people have sought asylum in the UK, requesting access to, and protection within, the children's social care system and care standards require children to have age-appropriate provision in terms of their placement and education, and to meet their health needs. There is a duty to protect children in care and the wider community, particularly in schools, from individuals who claim to be younger than they really are. For example, where criminal acts are caused by those claiming to be children such as Aham Otak (12) and Lawangeen Abdulrahimzai (13). There is an equally important safeguarding issue when minors are incorrectly aged as adults and so inappropriately placed in adult facilities where they may be at risk. Therefore, it is essential that the methods used to assess the claimed age are as robust, repeatable and accurate as possible.

Tables 103.2A and 103.2B give examples of different ages of criminal responsibility and marriageable ages

DOI: 10.1201/9781003138754-107

TABLE 103.1 Examples of reasons for age estimation in the living when age unknown (does not apply to all jurisdictions)

Age of criminal responsibility	Employment recruitment
Age of individuals in pornographic material	Female genital mutilation
Age of marriage	Guardianship orders
Competency and legal capacity	Human trafficking
Complainant of sexual offense	Modern-day slavery
Consent for marriage	Pensions claims
Consent for medical treatment	Refugee and asylum seeker status
Consent for medical treatment or procedures	Stateless individuals
Differentiating between child and adult for care purposes	

TABLE 103.2A Examples of ages of criminal responsibility in different countries and states

Age (years)	Jurisdictions
6	North Carolina (USA)
7	Thailand, Singapore, India, Pakistan, South Africa
8	Scotland
10	England, Wales, Northern Ireland, Australia
11	Turkey
12	Canada, Netherlands
14	China, Austria, Germany, Japan, New Zealand
15	Sweden, Norway & Finland
16	Portugal
17	France
18	International Criminal Court, Belgium

which may be required for social and legal (criminal or civil) proceedings and illustrate the diversity of need for knowledge of chronological age in many communities.

Generally, the extent of migration in recent years has been a key international driver for recognition of the need for robust age estimation techniques (14), but advances have been slow. Ubelaker and Khosrowshahi (15) have credited the recent progress on the methodology of age estimation of the living to the work of the Study Group on Forensic Age Diagnostics (AGFAD) which was founded in Berlin, Germany in March 2000 (16). Recommended methodology focussed on the physical examination, radiography of the left hand and dental examination, including X-rays or related imagery (17). Following these recommendations, the relevance of the epiphyseal union of the clavicles was recognized and confirmed using CT scan (18). An updated summary of the methodological approaches and the related legal issues was published in 2016 (19). Other approaches to estimate age and to predict patterns of growth include the use of 3D facial prototypes (20), facial age estimation (21) and DNA methylation (22) but these are not yet used in routine practice although have some promise.

Estimation of age in the living remains challenging because of a mixture of practical and ethical issues including the limited visible interpretable data available and the professional ethical issues related to consent for radiographic and intrusive techniques, in addition to the background complexity introduced by population variation.

In the UK, governmental concerns about migration fears resulted in the establishment of an Age Estimation Science Advisory Committee which published an interim report, "Biological evaluation methods to assist in assessing the age of unaccompanied asylum-seeking children" (1). In part, this has been because in the UK age estimation has been primarily using the "Merton-compliant method" of age assessment. This age assessment is undertaken by two social workers, and typically involves a series of interviews with the young person. The responsible local authority can take into account the opinions of others such as foster carer, teacher, psychologist, police officer and pediatricians. There is no standardized approach to a "social-worker-led" age assessment, but current practice and guidance was substantially set out in *B v London Borough of Merton* [2003] EWHC 1689 (23), hence the term "Merton-compliant".

In the UK, the individual will be treated as a child (24) until the assessment has been undertaken. Following this assessment, the individual is informed of the findings and if accepted will be assigned a date of birth. The individual may challenge the findings but the route is slow and complex (1).

The UK is an outlier when compared with many countries when considering age assessment and many countries rely on scientific methods to assist with age estimation including dental radiography and clavicular and wrist radiology. The European Asylum Support Office (EASO) Practical Guide on Age Assessment (25) outlines practice in European and other countries which, in general, are more reliant on scientific methodology than the UK. Figure 103.1 provides a flowchart of the suggested EASO Age Assessment.

The volume of international migration in recent years has, in many respects, acted as an international driver for recognition of the need for robust age estimation techniques (14). It is also recognized that for many valid reasons (e.g. destruction of home, medical records, registration records, loss during escape) documentary evidence of identity and age may be absent. The emphasis must be that the age assessment takes into account as many factors as possible. Problems however may arise even when an age determination has been made. Internal conflicts within a country at administrative level may result in different bodies relying on different evidence of age and this can affect the outcome dependent on the setting relevant at the time.

TABLE 103.2B Examples of differences in marriage age in different countries and states

Age (yrs)	Gender	Jurisdiction
12	Traditional marriages for females	South Africa, Tanzania
14	Traditional marriages for males Female	South Africa Paraguay
14 (with judicial consent)	Male & Female	Canada, Mexico
14 (with parental consent)	Female	Venezuela
15 (with parental consent)	Male & Female	Estonia
16	Male & Female Male Female	Kenya, Scotland Paraguay Tanzania
16 (with parental consent)	Male & Female Male Female	Hong Kong, Belgium, Hungary, Netherlands, Portugal, Ireland, Canada, Mexico, US Venezuela, Argentina Pakistan, Japan
16 (with special license)	Female	Malaysia
17	Female	Armenia, Israel
17 (with parental consent)	Male & Female	Thailand, Turkey
18	Male & Female Male Female	South Africa, Belgium, Philippines, Turkey, France, UK, Canada, Mexico, US Tanzania, Armenia, Israel Algeria, India, Vietnam
18 (with parental consent)	Male & Female Male	Malaysia, South Korea Pakistan, Japan
20	Male & Female Male Female	Japan, South Korea Vietnam China
21	Male & Female Male	Hong Kong, Malaysia, Singapore, Argentina Algeria, India
22	Male	China

DOCUMENTATION OF AGE

Before consideration of biological methods of age assessment it is important to be aware of the multiple sources from which the required information may be sought. In many jurisdictions, documents and identity cards are issued which, if available, provide assistance and corroboration of age. However, the assessor will be aware of the easy access to false documents of age (paradoxically often used to exaggerate age). Occasionally, forensic document examiners may be required to determine authenticity. The legal weight or authority of the relevant document will be determined by the local jurisdiction. The most common form of legal documentation of age is the birth certificate.

The UN Convention on the Rights of the Child Article 7 states: "*1. The child shall be registered immediately after birth and shall have the right from birth to a name, the right to acquire a nationality and, as far as possible, the right to know and be cared for by his or her parents. 2. States Parties shall ensure the implementation of these rights in accordance with their national law and their obligations under the relevant international instruments in this field, in particular where the child would otherwise be stateless*". Unfortunately, not all states fulfill the rights of this Article and lack such registration documents. When such documentation is available, it is often useful and reliable and its authenticity can be checked.

Some countries require all citizens to have a government issued identity card. Such cards generally contain not only an image of the individual, but also date of birth, sex and a variety of other personal details that are kept. Biometric data may be incorporated. In general, data that can be retrieved from such identity cards may be conclusive in confirming identity, and thus age. For many countries, driving licenses fulfill a similar function and are often accepted as proof of identity. Not only do they identify an individual, they enable some estimation of age, as driving licenses are only issued to those who have reached a certain age. This, however, varies from 16 to 18 and also varies between whether the license is for a car or a motorcycle.

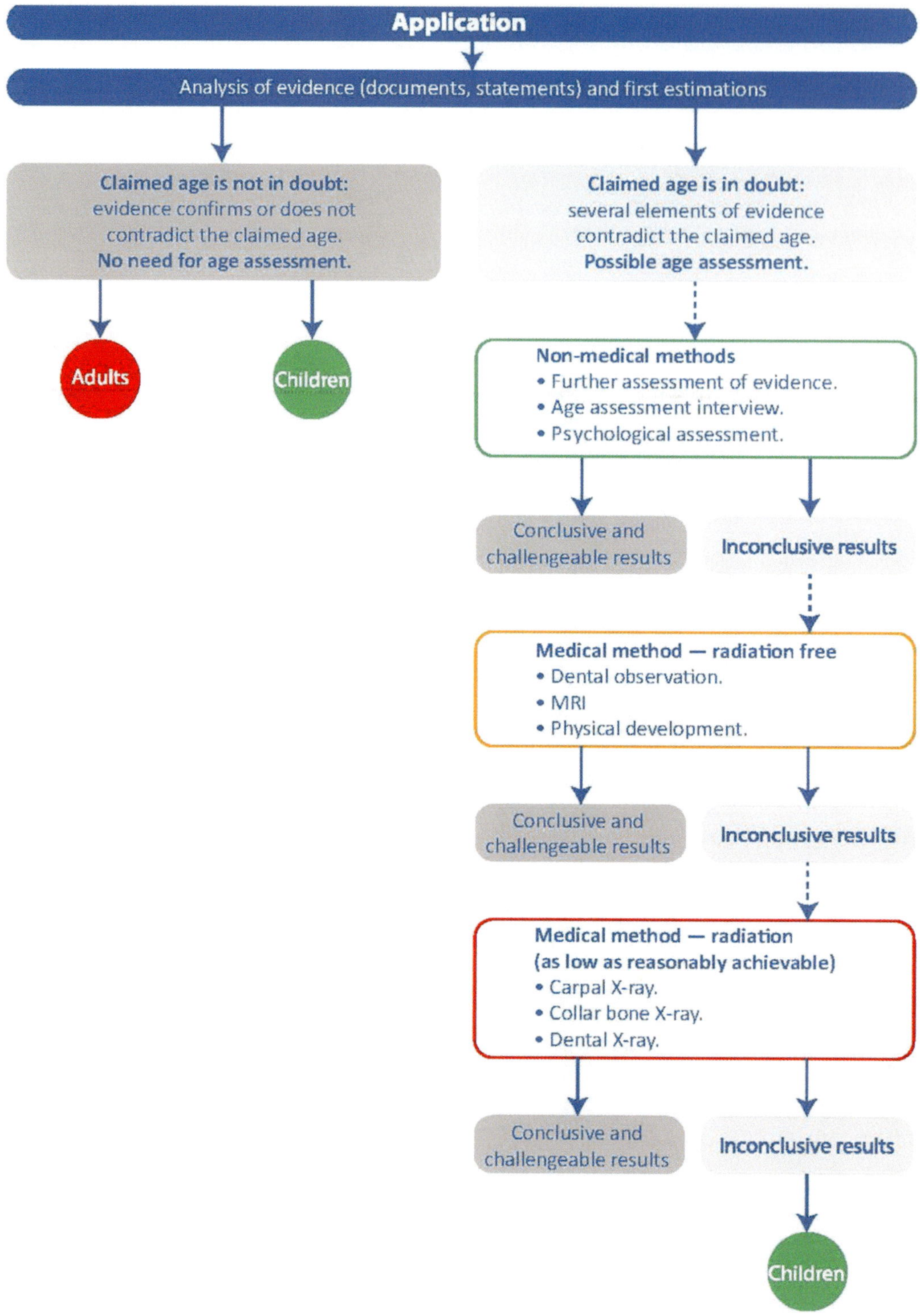

103.1 Flow chart of age assessment as suggested in EASO Age Assessment (25).

Passports are issued to nationals of a country which testify to the identity and details of an individual supported and verified by the issuing authority. For most governments, they confer some degree of assurance from the issuing authority on the authenticity of the details recorded on the document but for some governments or passport-issuing authorities these assurances are not in place. Passport forgery is common. Many individuals don't hold passports if they don't travel outside their own country. Biometric data are held on many passports and additionally electronic personal details and date of birth may be included.

There are many other documents which may provide some assistance in age determination or corroborate stated age including immunization cards, student cards and library cards. All can be considered when undertaking an age assessment.

TABLE 103.3 Questions to be *considered* before an age assessment is undertaken
Is the assessment appropriate?
Is the assessment lawful?
Have consents been sought and obtained from all relevant parties (e.g. the subject, legal or judicial bodies, health authorities, social workers, guardians)?
Is the age assessment being based on a biological or a legal boundary for age? (A question that asks the likely chronological age of the individual is different to the question that asks if the person is 21 years of age or younger)?
Do the assessors have the level of experience and training to undertake this investigation and to interpret the findings appropriately?
Are there other practitioners who should be involved in the assessment?
Is the appropriate reference data for comparison purposes available?
Are the assessors aware of the implications of the result of the assessment for matters outside the direct context of the assessment?

METHODS OF AGE ASSESSMENT

The three main methods of age assessment are clinical, dental and skeletal. The latter two are supported by a significant body or peer-reviewed published evidence. Clinical assessment is a broader, more general approach that may assist and corroborate dental and skeletal findings. The latter two will generally be undertaken by odontologists, radiologists and anthropologists. In many jurisdictions, forensic physicians and other forensic allied health professionals will be involved and undertake relevant examinations. Biological age is based on the analysis of maturational stages, each of which can be imaged and linked to a range of chronological ages rather than a single definitive age. Importantly for the final stage of maturation (representing the fully mature adult state) the lower limit for an individual's chronological age is set by the youngest age at which that stage has been observed. There is no upper limit for chronological age as the stage applies to all individuals who have reached maturity.

Any practitioner requested to undertake an age assessment should be aware of the reasons for, nature of and effects of the outcome of such an assessment. The questions in Table 103.3 should always be considered.

Clinical assessment

Clinical assessment by a forensic physician or other allied health professional examination may identify specific features (e.g. a name or date tattoo, a surgical scar) that itself may act as a clue, either to corroborate or disprove the claims of an individual. Clinical examination may also identify physical disease or deformity that may act as a unique identifier when taking all other aspects into account. Clinical examination may also identify clinical conditions (e.g. malnutrition) which impact bone maturity and skeletal development or tooth development which may themselves cause inappropriate interpretation of odontologic, radiologic or osteologic data if not considered. Similarly, retardation of puberty, or precocity or socioeconomic factors may be identified which need to be taken into account. Clinical examination is essential in determining the sexual maturity status by reviewing of development of secondary sexual characteristics. Tanner staging, also known as Sexual Maturity Rating (SMR), is an objective classification system that providers use to document and track the development and sequence of secondary sex characteristics of children during puberty. Anthropometric measurements may also be recorded which, although not able to directly contribute to age estimation, can assist in children in establishing whether development is following expected growth centile curves (26).

DENTAL MATURITY

Multiple studies of dental growth have focussed on tooth eruption which incorporates the development of the tooth from its formation in the alveolar crypts to full occlusion. Most studies relate to "emergence" which is restricted to the time when any part of the tooth finally clears the gingival margin and becomes visible in the mouth until the stage when the tooth finally comes into occlusion with its partner tooth from the opposing jaw (27,28).

Dental development is used as a means of age assessment throughout childhood but by the late teens focusses on the maturation of the third molars (wisdom teeth).

An age range can be assessed from third molar development in adolescence and young adults with a standard deviation of around two years for both males and females (29). Dental maturation appears to be less affected by environmental, social and health conditions than skeletal age and therefore both dental and skeletal age assessments can contribute to a final conclusion. Only one mandibular third molar is needed for assessment as development is generally comparable on the left and right sides. Once the third molar has reached maturity, age can no longer be assigned as it is the presence of active maturation that is an indicator of chronologic age. The earliest that maturity has been observed is approximately 14 years for both males and females, although the method is useful for assessing age up to 18 years. Third molar development is assessed by examination of radiographs taken either as intra-oral images or extra-oral images via an orthopantomogram (OPG).

Frequently used reference studies on the timeframe of third molars which are particularly relevant to age diagnostics in living individuals are widely accessible (30–35).

Skeletal maturation

The three relevant imaging modalities on which most research has been undertaken are radiography (X-ray), computed tomography (CT), and magnetic resonance imaging (MRI). Table 103.4 shows relevant radiation doses for different modalities and thus in order to minimize the risk of harm, the use of CT is not advocated. MRI is the preferred imaging method due to its safety through

TABLE 103.4 Comparative radiation doses (1)

Source of exposure	Average radiation dose (mSv)
Extremity X-ray (such as wrist or limb)[1]	Less than 0.001
Dental X-ray	0.005
Panoramic dental X-ray (full orthopantogram, OPG)[2]	0.018
Transatlantic flight	0.08
UK average annual background radiation dose	0.08
Computed tomography (CT) chest scan	6.6
Annual exposure limit for nuclear industry employees	20
Acute radiation effects, including nausea and reduced white cell blood count	1000

the absence of ionizing radiation particularly for assessment of age using the knee and clavicle.

There is a long history of age assessment using radiography of the hand/wrist. Most data on age assessment using teeth or the hand/wrist are based on radiographic images (X-rays). It can be argued that the low risk of harm from radiography of the teeth or hand/wrist is minimal when compared to advantages of swift and accurate age assessment.

Evaluation of skeletal maturation has proven a consistent means of chronologic age estimation and requires that at least one of the three phases of osseous development be assessed which are:

1. The age of appearance (i.e. ossification) of the different parts of the bone.
2. The morphologic appearance and/or size of the bone and its constituent parts
3. The timing of fusion of different parts of a bone (36).

The changes occur in well-documented patterns and with established timeframes. In addition to teeth, the clavicle, hand/wrist and knee have the most consistent available data while reducing proximity to radiosensitive organs (such as testes and ovaries).

Age assessment methods compare skeletal maturation markers in a young person to those recorded in reference datasets of children and adults of known age and ancestry. These datasets, in the form of atlases, were generally sourced from historic longitudinal studies of child growth based on radiographic images. The first hand/wrist atlas was published in 1898 (37). The atlas by Greulich and Pyle, the first edition of which was published in 1950, and the second improved edition in 1959, has been one of the most utilized approaches to skeletal evaluation of maturity (38). Recent datasets are created from images taken from individuals of known age and populations on a cross-sectional basis and may rely on existing medical images or be MRI sourced (39). Radiography of the hand/wrist to assess age is based primarily on maturation of the carpal, metacarpals, phalanges and radius and ulna (40).

Maturation is established by changes to the shape and relative size of the bones, and the degree of fusion between the epiphysis and the diaphysis. These generally fuse once maturity is reached and these changes occur over a well-established age range and can be correlated with chronologic age using a reference dataset which allows comparison between the appearance of the bones seen in the radiograph and the appearance that would be expected at known ages. The final hand/wrist bone to reach maturation is the distal radius where fusion is complete by around 16 years in females and 17 to 18 years in males.

The clavicle has the longest period of growth-related activity with the medial end of the clavicle often not completely maturing until the early to mid-20s. This is of use for those who claim to be minors but whose chronological age is over 18 years. The assessment utilizes appearance and fusion of the epiphysis to the remainder of the bone. The epiphysis appears and then fuses with the shaft of the bone throughout the late teenage period and into the early 20s. The earliest that full maturity has been observed is at age 21 years for both females and males but for most individuals, fusion remains incomplete until age 25. Substantial research supports MRI imaging of the clavicle (41–44).

Assessment of age using MRI of the knee is a more recent development than the use of radiography of the hand/wrist. The assessment of age using the knee relies on changes to shape and fusion between the epiphysis and the diaphysis at both the distal end of the femur and the proximal end of the tibia.

SEXUAL MATURITY

The process of maturation at puberty is a multidimensional set of events which can, and have been, utilized for age-related evaluation. Documentation of the progress of events during this process can be undertaken by pediatricians, to assess normal versus abnormal development and therefore the outcomes have not been specifically evaluated for the purposes of age determination. Puberty is a complex sequence of events that leads to sexual maturity and requires both gonadal and adrenal stimulation. Female maturation within this process is generally assessed on the age of onset of menses, degree of breast development and degree of axillary and pubic hair. Male maturation is generally assessed on the basis of testicular

TABLE 103.5 Tanner stages of development (47)

Tanner Stage 1 is the pre-pubertal form for all three sites of development with progression to Tanner Stage 5, the adult form	
Pubic hair scale (both males and females)	
Stage 1	No hair
Stage 2	Downy hair
Stage 3	Scant terminal hair
Stage 4	Terminal hair that fills the entire triangle overlying the pubic region
Stage 5	Terminal hair that extends beyond the inguinal crease onto the thigh
Female breast development scale	
Stage 1	No glandular breast tissue palpable
Stage 2	Breast bud palpable under the areola (1st pubertal sign in females)
Stage 3	Breast tissue palpable outside areola; no areolar development
Stage 4	Areola elevated above the contour of the breast, forming a "double scoop" appearance
Stage 5	Areolar mound recedes into single breast contour with areolar hyperpigmentation, papillae development, and nipple protrusion
Male external genitalia scale	
Stage 1	Testicular volume < 4 mL or long axis < 2.5 cm
Stage 2	4 ml–8 mL (or 2.5 to 3.3 cm long), 1st pubertal sign in males
Stage 3	9 ml–12 mL (or 3.4 to 4.0 cm long)
Stage 4	15–20 mL (or 4.1 to 4.5 cm long)
Stage 5	> 20 mL (or > 4.5 cm long)

and penile enlargement and also on the degree of hair development, mainly pubic, but also axillary and facial.

The development of the external genitalia lend themselves more readily to both visual and metric evaluation although the ethical and social issues that surround collecting this data are not insignificant. Tanner and Marshall produced longitudinal studies (as well as cross-sectional) which laid the groundwork for clinical evaluation of secondary sexual characteristics (45–47). The sexual maturity is generally described as "Tanner stages of secondary sexual development" and these are shown in Table 103.5.

Caution must be used when estimating age utilizing sexual maturation because of the wide range of scatter but the clinical examination in the course of age estimation is crucial to determine whether the physical development is congruent with the other age characteristics and whether there are indications of diseases that might affect the development.

EXAMPLES OF JURISDICTIONAL APPROACHES TO AGE ASSESSMENT

The international and interdisciplinary "Study Group on Forensic Age Diagnostics" (http://rechtsmedizin.klinikum.uni-muenster.de/agfad/index) was established in Berlin, Germany, on March 10, 2000 and pioneered recommendations for forensic age estimation in living individuals in a range of judicial, legal and tribunal proceedings (48–51). These recommendations have been widely accepted and as discussed above, are widely used in many jurisdictions.

However, the issues of consent, reliability and ethical concerns mean that some professional bodies or organizations do not support all these approaches. The United Kingdom Royal College of Paediatrics and Child Health (RCPCH) has raised concerns about age assessments of asylum-seeking young people because of the concerns regarding the evidence base for accurate age assessment and the ethical considerations relating to the impact on children. The RCPCH reasons are summarized in Table 103.6 (3,11).

Political imperatives within the UK resulted in the establishment of an Age Estimation Science Advisory Committee in 2021 with the following Terms of Reference: to provide the Home Office Chief Scientific Adviser (CSA) with independent advice with respect to the following: scientific and associated ethical advice and guidance on existing and emerging scientific approaches that could be utilized for the purpose of age assessment in the living; recommendations for best practice guidance on any existing and proposed scientific method(s); issues raised by key stakeholders relating to the implementation of scientific methods to assess chronological age in the living (52). Table 103.7 lists recent recommendations, the majority of which advise that further research is needed. The main conflict, it appears, is likely to be

TABLE 103.6 Key points of the UK Royal College of Paediatrics & Child Health rationale on why pediatricians should not be involved in age assessments (RCPCH 2023)

- Two main factors to consider regarding age assessment of young people – the accuracy of age assessments and the ethics of undertaking these assessments.
- It is difficult to determine a young person's age accurately. A child's physical, emotional and developmental presentation is influenced by myriad of factors including, but in no way limited to, their ethnicity, socio-economic environment and nutritional status. It is especially important to acknowledge the impact of adverse experiences, conflict, trauma, violence and forced migration on a child.
- Age assessment by examination and X-rays is imprecise and at best can determine what stage of puberty a child is at and with that an estimated range for their age.
- The British Society for Paediatric Endocrinology and Diabetes states that the timing of puberty is extremely variable and impacted by genetics as well as environmental and social factors. Completion of growth occurs at the end of puberty, so if a child starts puberty early, they will finish growing while still in their early teens. Conversely, if a child starts puberty late, they may not finish growing until well over the age of 18 years.
- Current methods for bone age X-ray assessments, such as the Greulich and Pyle method, use X-rays taken from "average" Caucasian children and again will vary enormously depending on what stage of puberty a child is at.
- The British Dental Association has vigorosly opposed the use of dental X-rays to determine whether asylum seekers have reached the age of 18, stressing they are not a reliable way establishing age and the use of dental X-rays can over- or underestimate the age of adolescents significantly.
- Exposing anyone to radiation from X-rays unnecessarily should be carefully considered and for non-clinical purposes the RCPCH considers it unethical.
- There have been a number of judgements in case law about who should hold the burden of proof about a child's age.
- Given the lack of evidence regarding the accuracy of age assessment the RCPCH believe that young people should be given the benefit of doubt with regards to their age.
- The RCPCH view is that age assessments require informed consent, which has to be freely given, and it is difficult to ensure this is taking place if vulnerable young people are assessed under duress. Consent is not valid if coerced.
- Young people in this situation may not have the capacity to consent to the age assessment process.
- The RCPCH believes there is a potentially harmful impact of enforced age assessment on a child's physical and emotional well-being.

TABLE 103.7 Recommendations of the Interim Committee on the use of biological methods to assist with the assessment of the age of unaccompanied asylum-seeking children (UASC) in the UK (Interim)

Recommendation
1. If biological age assessment is implemented, it should be used to assess whether the age claimed by UASC is possible.
2. Research into the accuracy and reliability of the Merton-compliant process should be undertaken as a piece of urgent baseline research.
3. **Any methodology used for the assessment of age must respect and prioritize the dignity of the individual being assessed and should minimize physical or psychological harm.**
4. **Biological age assessment can be carried out using an appropriate combination of dental and skeletal methods; assessment of development of the third molar using radiography, radiography of the hand/wrist or MRI of the knee, and MRI of the clavicle.**
5. **The use of ionizing radiation must be limited, with the ultimate aim of eradicating its use. Continuing research into the use of non-ionizing imaging, such as MRI, should be supported.**
6. **Where possible, the radiation dose should be limited through the use of recent pre-existing images, providing consent for the use of these images for age assessment had been freely obtained.**
7. Further research into the impact of socioeconomic factors and their effect on growth and maturational timing, particularly those factors likely to be experienced by UASC, should be supported.
8. **Dental and bone images should be acquired by those with the relevant training and expertise and reported by those with expertise in interpreting images for age estimation.**
9. A guide should be developed on how to deal with those situations where there is a discrepancy between the claimed/suspected age and the biological or social worker-led evaluation outputs which makes clear what weight should be placed on different sources of information.

TABLE 103.7 (Continued)

Recommendation
10. Consider adopting a likelihood ratio approach, using biological evidence of age, to compare the weight of evidence or "support" for the Merton assigned age versus the claimed age.
11. UASC should be provided with clear information explaining the risks and benefits of biological evaluation in a format that allows the person undergoing the process to give informed consent and no automatic assumptions or consequences should result from refusal to consent.
12. Further research to gauge the differential impact of the proposed age assessment processes on UASC with respect to the protected characteristics in the Equality Act 2010 should be undertaken.
13. Research into biological age assessment methods based on a wide range of ethnic or geographic sub-groups to confirm and improve accuracy and applicability of these methods should be supported.
14. A watching brief should be maintained over the development of emerging age estimation methods including, but not restricted to, facial images and DNA methylation.

Those highlighted in bold identify recommendations which may impact on forensic physicians and other relevant health professionals (e.g. pediatricians) who may be asked to contribute to assessments.

between the Committee recommendations and the views of professional bodies with regard to the ethics and validity of aspects of age assessments.

CONCLUSION

It is not possible to review such a subject as age estimation in the living without accepting that the need for such assessments puts a financial burden either on the state, or the individual themselves. The individual may not be eligible for or have access to legal advice, for many reasons (e.g. because of presumed age, lack of funds, language difficulties, fear of authorities) and thus no access to appropriate age assessments which may support their case. It is in most states' interest to minimize the possible burden of care for children or young people and the cynic might consider that it is most states' (financial and political) interest to err on the side of assuming individuals are adult. Whatever the case, it is right in any legal, clinical or medical setting where age may impact on care, treatment, autonomy or human rights that anyone should have access to an appropriate means of age assessment that can be robustly put forward in court. No healthcare or other professional should undertake the estimation of age in the living without adequate training and understanding of the available methods and their limitations and without the support of a multidisciplinary team of colleagues who can assist to make evaluations from a variety of means to produce the best age estimate that current knowledge will allow.

REFERENCES

1. Interim Age Estimation Science Advisory Committee. Biological evaluation methods to assist in assessing the age of unaccompanied asylum-seeking children, 2022. Available from: https://assets.publishing.service.gov.uk/government/uploads/system/uploads/attachment_data/file/1127181/14.169_HO_AESAC_report_V6_FINAL_WEB.pdf (Accessed 3 July 2023).
2. Black SM, Aggrawal A, Payne-James J. *Age Estimation in the Living: The Practitioner's Guide*. Oxford: Wiley-Blackwell; 2010.
3. Royal College of Paediatrics & Child Health. RCPCH responds to the age estimation scientific advisory committee's report on age assessment methods, 2023. Available from: https://www.rcpch.ac.uk/news-events/news/rcpch-responds-age-estimation-scientific-advisory-committees-report-age-assessment (Accessed 3 July 2023).
4. Lee SH, Lee JY, Park HK and Kim YK. Development of third molars in Korean juveniles and adolescents. *Forensic Sci Int* 2009; **188**: 107–11.
5. O'Donnell I, Milner C. *Child Pornography: Crime, Computers and Society*. Oregon: Willan Publishing, 2007.
6. Cattaneo C, Ritz-Timme S, Gabriel P, et al. The difficult issue of age assessment on pedo-pornographic material. *Forensic Sci Int* 2009; **183**: e21–e4.
7. UNICEF. The state of the world's children, 2021. Available from: https://www.unicef.org/reports/state-worlds-children-2021 (Accessed 3 July 2023).
8. Crossner CG, Mansfeld L. Determination of dental age in adopted non-European children. *Swed Dent J* 1983; **7**: 1–10
9. Melsen B, Wenzel A, Miletic T, et al. Dental and skeletal maturity in adoptive children: Assessments at arrival and after one year in the admitting country. *Ann Hum Biol* 1986; **13**: 153–9.
10. Fleischer-Peters A. Die Bedeutung der Zähne für die Altersschätzung von Findelkindern. *Dtsche Zahnärzt Z* 1987; **42**: 712–8.
11. Royal College of Paediatrics & Child Health. Refugee and asylum seeking children and young people - guidance for paediatricians, 2022. Available from: https://www.rcpch.ac.uk/resources/refugee-asylum-seeking-children-young-people-guidance-paediatricians safe guarding-and-child-protection-issues (Accessed 3 July 2023).
12. BBC News. Ahmad Otak jailed for 34 years for murdering two teenagers, 2012. Available from: https://www.bbc.co.uk/news/uk-england-leeds-20271840 (Accessed 3 July 2023).
13. The Telegraph. Murderer 'asked schoolgirls out' while posing as a 14-year-old to gain asylum, 2023. Available from: https://www.telegraph.co.uk/news/2023/01/25/aspiring-royal-marine-murdered-asylum-seeker-wanted-protect/ (Accessed 3 July 2023).
14. UNHCR. Global trends: Refugees, asylum-seekers, returnees, internally displaced and stateless persons, 2008. Available from: http://www.unhcr.org/cgi-bin/texis/vtx/search?page=search&docid=4a375c426&query=Global trends (Accessed 3 July 2023).
15. Ubelaker DH, Khosrowshahi H. Estimation of age in forensic anthropology:

Historical perspective and recent methodological advances. *Forensic Sci Res* 2019; **4**(1): 1–9.

16. Schmeling A, Geserick G, Reisinger W, et al. Age estimation. *Forensic Sci Int* 2007; **165**: 178–81.
17. Guo Y, Olze A, Ottow C, et al. Dental age estimation in living individuals using 3.0 T MRI of lower third molars. *Int J Leg Med* 2015; **129**: 1265–70.
18. Ufak F, Agladioglu K, Karabulut N. CT evaluation of medial clavicular epiphysis as a method of bone age determination in adolescents and young adults. *Diagn Interv Radiol* 2016; **22**(3): 241–6.
19. Schmeling A, Reisinger W, Geserick G, Olze A. The current state of forensic age estimation of live subjects for the purpose of criminal prosecution. *Forensic Sci Med Pathol* 2005; **1**(4): 239–46.
20. Mathews H, Penington A, Clement J, et al. Estimating age and synthesizing growth in children and adolescents using 3D facial prototypes. *Forensic Sci Int* 2018; **286**: 61–9.
21. Yoti. Yoti age estimation, 2022. Available from: https://www.yoti.com/wp-content/uploads/Yoti-Age-Estimation-White-Paper-May-2022.pdf (Accessed 3 July 2023).
22. Wu X, Chen W, Lin F, et al. DNA methylation profile is a quantitative measure of biological aging in children. *Aging* 2019; **11**(**22**): 10031–51.
23. European Database of Asylum Law. B (R on the application of) v Mayor and Burgesses of the London Borough of Merton [2003] EWHC 1689. Available from: https://www.asylumlawdatabase.eu/en/case-law/uk-court-appeal-14-july-2003-b-r-application-v-mayor-and-burgesses-london-borough-merton (Accessed 3 July 2023).
24. Home Office. Assessing age, 2023. Available from: https://assets.publishing.service.gov.uk/government/uploads/system/uploads/attachment_data/file/1119545/Assessing_age.pdf (Accessed 3 July 2023).
25. European Asylum Support Office. EASO practical guide on age assessment, 2018. Available from: https://euaa.europa.eu/sites/default/files/publications/2022-01/easo-practical-guide-on-age-assesment-v3–2018.pdf (Accessed 3 July 2023).
26. Martrille L, Baccino E. Age Estimation in the Living. In: Payne-James JJ, Byard R, Corey T, Henderson C (eds), *Encyclopedia of Forensic & Legal Medicine*. London: Elsevier Academic Press; 2005.
27. Demirjian A, Goldstein H, Tanner JM. A new system of dental age assessment. *Hum Biol* 1973; **45**(**2**): 211–27.
28. Scheuer L, Black S. *Developmental Juvenile Osteology*. London: Academic Press; 2000.
29. Liversidge HM, Marsden PH. Estimating age and the likelihood of having attained 18 years of age using mandibular third molars. *Br Dent J* 2010; **209**: E13.
30. Anderson DL, Thompson GW, Popovich F. Age of attainment of mineralization stages of the permanent dentition. *J Forensic Sci* 1976; **21**: 191–200.
31. Kahl B, Schwarze CW. Aktualisierung der Dentitionstabelle von I Schour und M Massler von 1941. *F Kieferorthop* 1988; **49**: 432–43.
32. Mincer HH, Harris EF, Berryman HE. The A.B.F.O. study of third molar development and its use as an estimator of chronological age. *J Forensic Sci* 1993; **38**: 379–90.
33. Köhler S, Schmelzle R, Loitz C, Püschel K. Die Entwicklung des Weisheitszahnes als Kriterium der Lebensalterbestimmung. *Ann Anat* 1994; **176**: 339–45.
34. Gunst K, Mesotten K, Carbonez A, Willems G. Third molar root development in relation to chronological age: A large sample sized retrospective study. *Forensic Sci Int* 2003; **136**: 52–7.
35. Olze A, Schmeling A, Taniguchi M, et al. Forensic age estimation in living subjects: The ethnic factor in wisdom tooth mineralization. *Int J Leg Med* 2004; **118**: 170–3.
36. Cunningham C, Scheuer L, Black S. *Developmental Juvenile Osteology*, 2nd ed. London: Academic Press; 2016.
37. Poland J. *Skiagraphic Atlas Showing the Development of the Bones of the Wrist and Hand*. London: Smith, Elder & Co; 1898.
38. Greulich WW, Pyle SI. *Radiographic Atlas of Skeletal Development of the Hand and Wrist*. Stanford: Stanford University Press; 1959.
39. Black S, Hackman L, Cole T, et al. Biological evaluation methods to assis in assessing the age of unaccompanied asylum-seeking children (accessible). 2023. Available from: https://www.gov.uk/government/publications/methods-to-assess-the-age-of-unaccompanied-asylum-seeking-children/biological-evaluation-methods-to-assist-in-assessing-the-age-of-unaccompanied-asylum-seeking-children-accessible#executive-summary (Accessed 21 September 2023).
40. Hackman L, Black S. Does mirror imaging a radiograph affect reliability of age assessment using the Greulich and Pyle Atlas? *J Forensic Sci* 2012; **57**(5): 1276–80.
41. Hillewig, E, Degroote, Van der Paelt, T, et al. Magnetic resonance imaging of the sternal extremity of the clavicle in forensic age estimation: Towards more sound age estimates. *Int J Leg Med* 2013; **127**(3): 677–89.
42. Schmidt S, Henke CA, Wittschieber D, et al. Optimising magnetic resonance imaging-based evaluation of the ossification of the medial clavicular epiphysis: A multi-centre study. *Int J Leg Med* 2016; **130**(**6**): 1615–21.
43. Schmidt S, Ottow C, Pfeiffer H, et al. Magnetic resonance imaging-based evaluation of ossification of the medial clavicular epiphysis in forensic age assessment. *Int J Leg Med* 2017; **131**(**6**): 1665–73.
44. De Tobel J, Bauwens J, Parmentier A, et al. Magnetic resonance imaging for forensic age estimation in living children and young adults: A systematic review. *Pediatr Radiol* 2020; **50**: 1691–708.
45. Marshall WA, Tanner JM. Variations in the pattern of pubertal changes in boys. *Arch Dis Child* 1970; **45**: 13–23.
46. Emmanuel M. *Tanner Stages*. Treasure Island: StatPearls Publishing; 2022.
47. Rivers E. Children: Stages of Growth and Development. In: Payne-James JJ, Byard RW (eds), *Encyclopedia of Forensic & Legal Medicine*, 2nd ed. Amsterdam: Academic Press; 2016.
48. Schmeling A, Olze A, Reisinger W, Geserick G. Age estimation of living people undergoing criminal proceedings. *Lancet* 2001; **358**: 89–90.
49. Schmeling A, Kaatsch H-J, Marré B, et al. Empfehlungen für die Altersdiagnostik bei Lebenden im Strafverfahren. *Rechtsmedizin* 2001; **11**: 1–3.
50. Schmeling A, Grundmann C, Fuhrmann A, et al. Criteria for age estimation in living individuals. *Int J Leg Med* 2008; **122**: 457–60.
51. Lockemann U, Fuhrmann A, Püschel K, et al. Empfehlungen für die Altersdiagnostik bei Jugendlichen und jungen Erwachsenen außerhalb des Strafverfahrens. *Rechtsmedizin* 2004; **14**: 123–5.
52. GOV.uk. Age estimation science advisory committee, 2021. Available from: https://www.gov.uk/government/groups/age-estimation-science-advisory-committee (Accessed 3 July 2023).

INDEX

Note: Page numbers in *italic* refer to tables, boxes or figures in the text